# LITERATURE

An Introduction to

## Fiction, Poetry, and Drama

Sixth Edition

X. J. Kennedy

Dana Gioia
Wesleyan University

HarperCollins*College*Publishers

An Instructor's Manual for *Literature: An Introduction to Fiction, Poetry, and Drama,* *Sixth Edition,* is available through your local HarperCollins representative or by writing to Literature Acquisitions Editor, HarperCollins College Division, 10 East 53rd Street, New York, NY 10022.

Acquisitions Editor: Lisa Moore
Developmental Editor: Katharine H. Glynn
Project Editor: Diane Williams
Art Director: Lucy Krikorian
Cover Design: PC&F
Cover Illustration: C. Michael Dudash
Photo Researcher: Scott, Foresman
Electronic Production Manager: Su Levine
Desktop Administrator: Laura Leever
Manufacturing Manager: Willie Lane
Electronic Page Makeup: Circa 86, Inc.
Printer and Binder: R. R. Donnelley & Sons
Cover Printer: Coral Graphic Services, Inc.

For permission to use copyrighted material, grateful acknowledgment is made to the copyright holders on pp. 1819–1830, which are hereby made part of this copyright page.

Literature: An Introduction to Fiction, Poetry, and Drama, Sixth Edition

Library of Congress Cataloging-in-Publication Data

Literature: an introduction to fiction, poetry, and drama / [compiled
    by] X. J. Kennedy, Dana Gioia.—6th ed.
        p.   cm.
    Includes bibliographical references and indexes.
    ISBN 0–673–52280–6 (student edition)—ISBN 0–673–52281–4 (free copy edition)
    1. Literature—Collections. I. Kennedy, X. J. II. Gioia, Dana.
PN6014.L58 1995
808—dc20                                                                94-9933
                                                                           CIP

94 95 96 97   9 8 7 6 5 4 3 2 1

# Topical Contents

# Supplement: Writing

# Contents

## 3 Character    67

## 4 Setting    110

# 11 Stories for Further Reading  392

*Point of View*
*Character — Irony*
*setting & style*
*Tone & theme*
*Symbol*

# 17 Imagery   660

## ABOUT HAIKU   668

## FOR REVIEW AND FURTHER STUDY   670

# 27 Alternatives    843

# 28 Evaluating a Poem    853

## 29 What Is Poetry?    881

## 30 Poems for Further Reading    885

# 31 Criticism: On Poetry    1023

# 32 Lives of the Poets    1035

# DRAMA    1061

# 33 Reading a Play    1063

## A PLAY IN ITS ELEMENTS    1065

# 40 Criticism: On Drama    1715

# SUPPLEMENT: WRITING    1733

# 1. Writing about Literature    1735

# 5. Critical Approaches to Literature   1790

# Preface

Literature, in the widest sense, is just about anything written. It is even what you receive in the mail if you send for free information about a weight-reducing plan or a motorcycle. In the sense that matters to us in this book, literature is a kind of art, usually written, which offers pleasure and illumination. We say it is *usually* written, for we have an oral literature, too. Few would deny the name of literature to "Bonny Barbara Allan" and other immortal folk ballads, though they were not set down in writing until centuries after they were originated.

*Literature*—the book in your hands—is really three books sharing one cover. Its opening third contains the whole of the text-anthology *An Introduction to Fiction, Sixth Edition;* its middle third, the whole of *An Introduction to Poetry, Eighth Edition;* and its closing third is composed of a text-anthology of drama that includes fifteen plays. All together, the book is an attempt to provide the college student with a reasonably compact introduction to the study and appreciation of stories, poems, and plays.

I assume that appreciation begins in loving attention to words on a page. Speed reading has its uses; but at times, as Robert Frost said, the reader who reads for speed "misses the best part of what a good writer puts into it." Close reading, then, is essential. Still, I do not believe that close reading tells us everything, that it is wrong to read a literary work by any light except that of the work itself. At times I suggest different approaches: referring to facts of an author's life; comparing an early draft with a finished version; looking for myth; seeing the conventions (or usual elements) of a kind of writing—seeing, for instance, that an old mansion, cobwebbed and creaking, is the setting for a Gothic horror story.

Although I cannot help having a few convictions about the meanings of stories, poems, and plays, I have tried to step back and give you room to make up your own mind. Here and there, in the wording of a question, a conviction may stick out. If you should notice any, please ignore them. Be assured that no one interpretation, laid down by authority, is the only right one, for any work of literature. Trust your own interpretation—provided that, in making it, you have looked clearly and carefully at the evidence.

Reading literature often will provide you with reason to write. At the back of the book, the large supplement has for the student writer some practical advice. It will guide you, step by step, in finding a topic, planning an essay, writing, revising, and putting your paper into finished form. Further, you will find there specific help in writing about fiction, poetry, and drama. (Even if you don't venture into creative writing, you will find these sections full of glimpses into the processes of literary composition.)

To help you express yourself easily and accurately, both in writing papers and in class discussion, this book supplies critical terms that may be of use to you. These words and phrases appear in **boldface** when they are first defined. If anywhere in this book you meet a critical term you don't know or don't recall—what is a *carpe diem* poem? a *dramatic question?*—just look it up in the Index of Terms on the inside back cover.

## A WORD ABOUT CAREERS

Most students agree that to read celebrated writers such as Faulkner and Tolstoi is probably good for the spirit, and most even take some pleasure in the experience. But many, not planning to teach English and impatient to begin some other career, wonder if the study of literature, however enjoyable, isn't a waste of time—or at least, an annoying obstacle.

This objection, reasonable though it may seem, rests on a shaky assumption. On the contrary, it can be argued, success in a career is not merely a matter of learning the information and skills required to join a profession. In most careers, according to one senior business executive, people often fail not because they don't understand their jobs, but because they don't understand the people they work with, or their clients or customers. They don't ever see the world from another person's point of view. Their problem is a failure of imagination.

To leap over the wall of self, to look through another's eyes—this is valuable experience, which literature offers. If you are lucky, you may never meet (or have to do business with) anyone *exactly* like Mrs. Turpin in the story "Revelation," and yet you will learn much about the kind of person she is from Flannery O'Connor's fictional portrait of her. In reading Tolstoi's *The Death of Ivan Ilych*, you will enter the mind and heart of another human being. He is someone unlike you: a Russian petty bureaucrat of the nineteenth century. Still, you may find him amazingly similar to many people now living in America.

What is it like to be black, a white may wonder? James Baldwin, Gwendolyn Brooks, Langston Hughes, Zora Neale Hurston, Dudley Randall, Alice Walker, August Wilson, and others have knowledge to impart. What is it like to be a woman? If a man would learn, let him read (for a start) Sandra Cisneros, Kate Chopin, Susan Glaspell, Beth Henley, Doris Lessing, Alice Munro, Sylvia Plath, Katherine Anne Porter, Flannery O'Connor, Tillie Olsen, Adrienne Rich, and Amy Tan, and perhaps, too, Henrik Ibsen's *A Doll's House* and John Steinbeck's "Chrysanthemums."

Plodding singlemindedly toward careers, some people are like horses wearing blinders. For many, the goals look fixed and predictable. Competent nurses, accountants, and dental technicians seem always in demand. Others may find that in our society some careers, like waves in the sea, will rise or fall unexpectedly. Think how many professions we now take for granted, which only a few years ago didn't even exist: computer programming, energy conservation, tofu manufacture, videotape rental. Others that once looked like lifetime meal tickets have been cut back and nearly ruined: shoe repairing, commercial fishing, railroading.

In a society perpetually in change, it may be risky to lock yourself on one track to a career, refusing to consider any other. "We are moving," writes John Naisbitt in *Megatrends*, a study of our changing society, "from the specialist, soon obsolete, to the generalist who can adapt." Perhaps the greatest opportunity in your whole life lies in a career that has yet to be invented. If you do change your career as you go along, you will be like most people. According to U.S. Department of Labor statistics, the average person in a working life changes occupations three times. When for some unforeseen reason you have to make such a change, basic skills may be your most valuable credentials—and a knowledge of humanity.

Literature has much practical knowledge to offer you. An art of words, it can help you become more sensitive to language, both your own and other people's. It can make you aware of the difference between the word that is exactly right and the word that is merely good enough—Mark Twain calls it "the difference between the lightning and the lightning-bug." Read a fine work of literature alertly, and some of its writer's sensitivity to words may grow on you. A Supreme Court justice, John Paul Stevens, gave his opinion (informally) that the best preparation for law school is to study poetry. Why? George D. Gopen, an English professor with a law degree, says it may be because "no other discipline so closely replicates the central question asked in the study of legal thinking: Here is a text; in how many ways can it have meaning?" (By the way, if a career you plan has anything to do with advertising, whether writing it or buying it or resisting it, be sure to read Chapter Sixteen, "Saying and Suggesting," on the hints inherent in words.)

Many careers today, besides law, call for close reading and for clear thinking expressed on paper. Lately, college placement directors have reported more demand for graduates who are good readers and writers. The reason is evident: employers need people who can handle words. In a recent survey conducted by Cornell University, business executives were asked to rank in importance the traits they look for when hiring. Leadership was first, but skill in writing and speaking came in fourth, ahead of managerial skill, ahead of skill in analysis. Times change, but to think cogently and to express yourself well are abilities the world still needs.

That is why most colleges, however thorough the career training they may provide, still insist on general training as well, including basic courses in the humanities. No one can promise that your study of literature will result in cash profit, but at least the kind of wealth that literature provides is immune to fluctuations of the Dow Jones average. A highly paid tool and die maker, asked by his community college English instructor why he had enrolled in an evening literature course, said, "Oh, I just decided there has to be more to life than work, a few beers, and the bowling alley." If you should discover in yourself a fondness for great reading, then in no season of your life are you likely to become incurably bored or feel totally alone—even after you make good in your career, even when there is nothing on television.

# TO THE INSTRUCTOR: CHANGES IN THIS EDITION

This new edition of *Literature* incorporates many changes. The most important help came from scores of instructors who use the book in their classrooms. Their suggestions helped confirm the stories, poems, and plays that worked best with students while identifying selections that seemed less valuable and could be retired to make room for new work.

The FICTION section now includes a great many new stories, bringing the total number of selections to fifty-six—an all-time high. Franz Kafka's unforgettable *The Metamorphosis* has been added—by popular demand—to Chapter Nine, "Reading Long Stories and Novels." Kafka's novella joins Leo Tolstoi's *The Death of Ivan Ilych*. The instructor now has the choice of teaching either or both works. Chapter Ten, "A Writer in Depth" currently focuses entirely on Flannery O'Connor. In addition to three of her most famous stories, two short critical selections by O'Connor have been added (including one that provides the author's own perspective on her story "A Good Man Is Hard to Find.") The current edition also contains two stories each by William Faulkner and Kate Chopin.

A great many new stories have been added. Chuang Tzu's famous short tale "Independence" now appears in the opening chapter, "Reading a Story," to provide a non-European perspective. The number of women and minority writers has been significantly expanded throughout the book. James Baldwin's "Sonny's Blues," Amy Tan's "A Pair of Tickets," Sandra Cisneros's "Barbie-Q," Charlotte Perkins Gilman's "The Yellow Wallpaper," Zora Neale Hurston's "Sweat," and Virginia Woolf's "A Haunted House" are among the twenty new stories. Alice Walker's "Everyday Use" and Doris Lessing's "A Woman on a Roof" have been returned to the anthology by popular demand.

Many renovations have been made in the POETRY section, while still retaining the best-liked material. A whole new chapter, "Poetry and Personal Identity," explores ways in which poets have defined themselves in personal, social, sexual, and ethnic terms. An opening section examines how a poet's cultural heritage can inform his or her work; and the chapter includes fifteen teachable new poems in praise of diversity. Please review this new chapter—its impact will be stronger than can be expressed in this brief summary.

In Chapter Thirteen, "Reading a Poem" a new section on dramatic poetry supplies information on a valuable kind of poetry that was previously ignored—instructors who missed Browning's "My Last Duchess" and wanted it restored will be glad to find it in the new Section. In Chapter Twenty-five, now called "Myth and Narrative," the section "Myth and Popular Culture" is brand new—and (unless I miss my guess) is provocative.

About a fifth of the poems in this edition are new. Presently there are considerably more women and minority poets, among them, Carole Satyamurti, Wendy Cope, Carolyn Forché, Alice Fulton, Julia Alvarez, Shirley Geok-lin Lim, Emma Lazarus, Louise Glück, Anne Stevenson, Emily Grosholz, N. Scott Momaday, Claude McKay, Alberto Ríos, Derek Walcott, José Emilio Pacheco,

Amy Uyematsu, Yusef Komunyakaa, and many more. Those interested in The Cowboy Poetry movement will now find a cowboy poem: Wallace McRae's "Reincarnation." A discussion of Rap has also been added to the chapter on Song. The Persian poet Omar Khayyam now occupies a central place in the section on translation in Chapter Twenty-seven. But veteran users of this book needn't fear that it has gone wildly trendy. It now has *two* of Keats's odes and more Donne, Frost, Millay, and Larkin than ever, and still clings to both "Elegy Written in a Country Churchyard" and "Lycidas."

The chapter "Poems for the Eye," little used, has disappeared to save space, but you will find its meat in Chapter Twenty-three under "Visual Poetry." Many of the questions and the *Suggestions for Writing* (useful topics that end practically every chapter) have been fine-tooled, and the popular section, "Lives of the Poets," has been updated.

The DRAMA section now includes Shakespeare's *Hamlet* as well as *Othello*. This addition will provide instructors the option of teaching either play as well as give students another play for research papers or further reading. A new chapter, "New Voices in American Drama," offers four diverse approaches to contemporary theater. It also highlights the increasing importance of women and minority playwrights to the American stage. Meanwhile we have heeded the request of many instructors to reinstate the classic Robert Fitzgerald/Dudley Fitts translations of *Oedipus the King* and *Antigonê*. The "Criticism: On Drama" section has been revamped and expanded to reflect contemporary concerns—not only about new plays but about the classics.

Finally, there is an entirely new supplement, "Critical Approaches to Literature," that many instructors and students wished to see included. Nine critical approaches—some immediately useful to students in writing papers—are explained. Each is followed by passages from prominent critics to illustrate how the method may be applied. Most of the critical selections refer to stories, poems, or plays found elsewhere in the book, so students will not find the approaches unnecessarily difficult or abstract. This substantial new feature reflects the increasing importance (and complexity) of theory and criticism to literary studies.

No doubt the most beneficent change, however, is the arrival of Dana Gioia as a collaborator. Why should the title page now claim two authors? Some explanation is due. For the book to stay alive, for it to keep responding to the newer and harder demands of students and instructors today, I realized, it was going to need the insights of someone younger and spryer, someone in the thick of current literary and intellectual life, someone actively engaged in the college classroom. Ideally, I hoped to enlist someone who would be both an outstanding writer and a courageous, broad-minded critic, someone with stamina, zeal, a sense of humor, with experience in both teaching and the rough-and-tumble workaday world that many students know—someone, I thought wistfully, exactly like Dana Gioia.

Born in Los Angeles, son of an Italian-American father and a Mexican-American mother, Dana Gioia (pronounced "Dane-a Joy-a") is used to working hard. On his way up, he garnered a B.A. and an M.B.A. from Stanford, and an M.A. in comparative literature from Harvard besides. Author of two admired collections of poetry, *Daily Horoscope* and *The Gods of Winter* (Graywolf Press, 1986 and 1991, respectively), he recently became the first American poet (as far as I know) to have a book selected by Britain's Poetry Book Society. "Can Poetry Matter?," the title essay in his 1992 collection of criticism from Graywolf Press, drew an unprecedented response from readers of *The Atlantic* when it first appeared in May of 1991. He has also translated Eugenio Montale's *Mottetti* (Graywolf, 1990) and co-edited two anthologies of Italian poetry. The perfect guy to tackle a literature textbook, I figured. But, as a busy and successful business executive, Dana was otherwise engaged.

Then, to my glee, a miracle happened. Dana Gioia gave up his business career to become a full-time writer and a teacher at Johns Hopkins, Sarah Lawrence, and (currently) Wesleyan University. Soon—I couldn't believe my luck!—we were sitting down together in my musty workspace, where old textbooks and textbook paraphernalia had gathered mold for over a quarter century, mulling the fresh new book that this sixth edition ought to be. I think we were both surprised by how easy it was to work together. This edition pleases me more than did any previous. It builds, I believe, a Golden Gate Bridge across a generation gap. The new chapter "Poetry and Personal Identity," the sections dealing with narrative poetry and with popular culture, and the supplement entitled "Critical Approaches to Literature" were all inspired by Dana. As it turned out, some thoughts from us both went into them, but mainly they embody his ideas, and indeed, his very words.

## USING THIS BOOK TO TEACH WRITING

The "Supplement: Writing," especially in "Writing about Literature," continues to derive from recent research. Until the last edition, this book's advice on writing had been traditional, quite uninformed by recent research in composition. In earlier editions, I used to see the writing of a paper as a lockstep trip through stages, with an always-foreseeable product at the end. This advice has since been recast, more accurately to describe real life. Strategies for discovering material are given priority. Students are still told they may find it helpful to state a thesis, but this advice is offered as only one possible way to write. Editing and mechanics, while given careful attention, take a back seat to more vital matters, such as the tendency of fresh ideas to arrive when it's time to revise. The directions for documenting sources now follow the latest *MLA Handbook for Writers of Research Papers*.

Many instructors use this book in teaching a combined literature-and-writing course. To serve their needs, effort has been made to improve the guidance offered to student writers—improve, but not greatly lengthen it, on the assumption that the editors's prose matters less to the study of fiction than William Faulkner's or Tillie Olsen's.

Several of the *Suggestions for Writing,* found at the end of every chapter in the body of the book, have had additions made to them or have been enlivened. Should instructors prefer to let students discover their own topics for papers, these suggestions may help them start thinking on their own. The well-received section "Criticism: On Fiction" is still here. While an instructor need not do anything about it, it can supply not only ideas for class discussion but further writing possibilities. So can the new feature, "Critical Approaches to Literature."

## TEXTS, DATES, AND A POSSIBLY PUZZLING ASTERISK

Every effort has been made to supply each selection in its most accurate text and (where necessary) in a lively, faithful translation. For the reader who wishes to know when a work was written, at the right of each title appears the date of its first publication in book form. Brackets around a date indicate the work's date of composition, given when it was composed much earlier than when it was first published.

In the poetry section, "Lives of the Poets" (Chapter Thirty-two) offers 76 brief biographies: one for most poets represented by two selections or more. For easy reference, they are tucked in one place (pages 1035–1060). Throughout the poetry pages, an asterisk (*) after a poet's byline indicates the subject of a biography.

## FICTION AND POETRY AVAILABLE SEPARATELY

Instructors who wish to use only the fiction section or only the poetry section of this book are assured that *An Introduction to Fiction, Sixth Edition*, and *An Introduction to Poetry, Eighth Edition*, contain the full and complete contents of these sections. Each book has a "Supplement: Writing" applicable to its subject, including "Writing about Literature." There is now also a compact edition in paperback of *Literature: An Introduction to Fiction, Poetry, and Drama* for instructors who find the full edition "too much book." Although this new compact version offers a slightly abridged Table of Contents, it still covers the complete range of topics presented in the full edition.

There is also a unique selection of support materials available free to instructors assigning either edition of *Literature*—in addition, of course, to the substantial *Instructor's Manual*, which provides commentary and teaching ideas for every selection in the book. First, there is David Peck's new book, *Issues in Teaching Multicultural Literature*, which has been specially designed to accompany the new edition of *Literature*. We were delighted to have David Peck, a professor at California State University in Long Beach, prepare this new supplementary volume since he is a widely acknowledged expert in the area of multicultural studies. *Issues in Teaching Multicultural Literature* should prove extremely useful to instructors in today's diverse classrooms. Second, there is another new volume, *Teaching Composition with Literature*, which has been put together to assist instructors who either use *Literature* in expository writing courses or have a special emphasis on writing in their literature courses. Edited by Dana Gioia, *Teaching Composition with Literature* collects proven writing assignments and classroom exercises from instructors around the nation. Each assignment or exercise uses one or more selections in *Literature* as its departure point. A great many instructors have enthusiastically shared their best writing assignments for *Teaching Composition with Literature*. They are acknowledged individually in the following section, "Thanks."

Finally, HarperCollins has a program to provide supplementary videos for *Literature*. To celebrate the addition of *Hamlet* to the new edition, a video of the excellent 1991 Franco Zefferelli version of Shakespeare's classic tragedy starring Mel Gibson, Glenn Close, Alan Bates, and Paul Scofield is available gratis to adopters of *Literature*. Other literary videos are also available to qualified adopters. Instructors should not be shy about getting the details of the program from their HarperCollins sales representatives.

For examination copies of any of these books or information on the video program, please contact your HarperCollins representative, or write to Humanities Marketing Manager, HarperCollins College Publishers Inc., 10 East 53rd Street, New York, NY 10022.

## THANKS

In the revision of this book and its manual, many instructors have contributed their advice and experience. (Some responded to the book in part, focusing their comments on the previous editions of *An Introduction to Poetry* and *An Introduction to Fiction*.) Among them, we deeply thank John Adair, Cumberland County College; William Adair, University of Maryland, Bangkok, Thailand; Jonathan Aldrich, Maine College of Art; Dick Allen, University of Bridgeport; David R. Anderson, Texas A & M University; Candace Andrews, San Joaquin Delta College; Herman Asarnow, University of Portland; Crystal V. Bacon, Gloucester County College; Raymond Bailey, Bishop State Community College; Carolyn Baker, San Antonio College; Bob Baron, Mesa Community College; Robert L. Barth, formerly of Xavier University; William W. Betts, Jr., Indiana University of Pennsylvania; Eric Birdsall, University of Akron; Adrienne Bond, Mercer University; Norman Bosley, Ocean County College; Mark Browning, University of Kansas and Johnson County Community College; Barbara M. Brumfield, Louisiana State University, Alexandria; Paul Buchanan, Biola University; John Campion, Austin Community College, Northridge Campus; Al Capovilla, Bella Vista High School; Eleanor Carducci, Sussex County Community College Commission; Gary L. Caret, Pima Community College; Thomas Carper, University of Southern Maine; Edward M. Cifelli, County College of Morris; Marcel Cornis-Pope, Virginia Commonwealth University; James Finn Cotter, Mount St. Mary College; Lynn Crabtree, Somerset Community College; Janis Crowe, Furman University; Allison Cummings, University of Wisconsin, Madison; Robert Darling, Keuka College; Allan Davis, Moorhead University; Phyllis Davis, J. Sargeant Reynolds Community College; Robert Dees, Orange Coast College; Kathleen R. DeGrave, Pittsburg State University; George Detrana, J. Sargeant Reynolds Community College; Mary R. Devine, Stephen F. Austin State University; Wilfred O. Dietrich, Blinn College; Esther DiMarzio, Kishwaukee Community College; Fred Dings, West Chester

University; Emanuel di Pasquale, Middlesex County College; Judith Doumas, Old Dominion University; Charles Clay Doyle, The University of Georgia; Kirby Duncan, Stephen F. Austin State University; Dixie Durham, Chapman University; Janet Eber, County College of Morris; Peggy Ellsberg, Barnard College; Ellen-Jo Emerson, Sussex County Community College; Lin Enger, Moorhead University; Craig Etchison, Glenville State College; Matthew A. Fike, Augustana College; Annie Finch, University of Northern Iowa; Robert Flanagan, Ohio Wesleyan University; Luellen Fletcher, Pima Community College; Deborah Ford, Carroll College; Peter Fortunato, Ithaca College; Bob Gassen, Hutchinson Community College; John Gery, University of New Orleans; Richard Gillin, Washington College; Michael J. Gilmartin, Corning Community College; Joseph Green, Lower Columbia College; Anne Greene, Wesleyan University; Nicole H. M. Greene, University of Southwestern Louisiana; John A. Gregg, San Diego Mesa College; Peter Griffin, Rhode Island School of Design; Huey S. Guagliardo, Louisiana State University, Eunice; R. S. Gwynn, Lamar University; Iris Rose Hart, Santa Fe Community College (Florida); Jim Hauser, William Paterson College; Marla J. Hefty, University of Kansas; James Heldman, Western Kentucky University; Michael A. Hendrick, The University of Georgia; Michel Hennessy, Southwest Texas State University; Barbara Hickey, Harper College; C. Hickman, University of Wisconsin, Platteville; Rose Higashi, Evergreen Valley Community College; Mary Piering Hiltbrand, University of Southern Colorado; Steven Hind, Hutchinson Community College; Bernard Alan Hirsch, University of Kansas; Jonathan Holden, Kansas State University; Lin T. Humphrey, Citrus College; Alan Jacobs, Wheaton College; David Johansson, Brevard Community College, Melbourne Campus; Ted E. Johnston, El Paso Community College; Lee Brewer Jones, De Kalb College, Gwinnett Center; Bill Kane, Wellesley College; Bob Klau, Austin Community College, Northridge Campus; Mary Klayder, University of Kansas; Jacob Korg, University of Washington; George H. Kugler, J. Sargeant Reynolds Community College; Chikako Kumamoto, College of Du Page; Paul Lake, Arkansas Technical University; Judy Lampert, San Antonio College; Dan Landau, Santa Monica College; Lynn A. Lee, University of Wisconsin, Platteville; M. K. Leighty, J. Sargeant Reynolds Community College; Steve Levinson, City College of San Francisco; Sarah J. Littlefield, Salve Regina University; Karen Locke, Lane Community College; F. J. Logan, University College, University of Maryland, Japan; David Lydic, Austin Community College, Northridge Campus; Samuel Maio, San Jose State University; Gene J. Mann, Queensborough Community College; Jane Marcellus, Pima Community College; David Mason, Moorhead State University; Thomas Mauch, Colorado College; David McCracken, Texas A & M University; MaryBeth McDuffee, Schenectady County Community College; Mark McLaughlin, Providence College; Leo F. McNamara, University of Michigan, Ann Arbor; Robert McPhillips, Iona College; Myra Mendible, University of Miami, Coral Gables; Mark S. Miller, Pikes Peak Community College; Gail Mooney, Middlesex Community College; David A. Moreland,

Louisiana State University at Eunice; Joseph P. Moriarty, Holyoke Community College; Dennis C. Morrill, Mount Wachusett Community College; Bernard E. Morris, Modesto Junior College; John G. Morris, Cameron University; Kevin Morris, Greenville Technical College; Kathleen Murray, Suffolk Community College; Edna H. Musso, Daytona Beach Community College; Madeline Mysko, Johns Hopkins University; Michele Noel, William Rainey Harper College; Jeannette Palmer, Motlow State Community College; Margaret R. Parish, University of North Carolina, Wilmington; Ruth Park, San Antonio College; Al Past, Bee County College; Lisa Pater-Faranda, Penn State University, Berks; Merry M. Pawlowski, California State University, Bakersfield; Dianne Peich, Delaware County Community College; Betty Jo Peters, Morehead State University; Norm Peterson, County College of Morris; Louis Phillips, School of Visual Arts; Robert Phillips, University of Houston; Fran Polek, Gonzaga University; Betty L. Porreca, Pima Community College; Verlene Potter, Pikes Peak Community College; Michael Ramirez, Hillsdale High School, San Mateo, California; Allen Ramsey, Central Missouri State University; Duke Rank, Governors State University; Ron Rash, Tri-County Technical College; William Rice, Harvard University; John M. Ridland, University of California, Santa Barbara; Fred W. Robbins, Southern Illinois University at Edwardsville; Noel Robinson, County College of Morris; Linda C. Rollins, Motlow State Community College; Deenie Roper, Del Mar College; David Rothman, Crested Butte Academy; Janis Rowell, North Shore Community College; Paul Ruffin, Sam Houston State University; Nikki Sahlin, Dean Junior College; Toni Saldivar, Mount St. Mary College; Mark Sanders, College of the Mainland; James Sanderson, Lamar University; Kay Satre, Carroll College; Roy Scheele, Doane College; Lissa Schneider, University of Miami; Beverly Schneller, Millersville University of Pennsylvania; Robin Schulze, University of Kansas; Linda S. Schwartz, Coastal Carolina College; Herbert Scott, Western Michigan University; William L. Scurrah, Pima Community College; Dee Seligman, Huston-Tillotson College; John N. Serio, Clarkson University; Neila C. Seshachari, Weber State University; Pamela K. Shaffer, Fort Hays State University; Michael Simms, Community College of Allegheny County; David L. Smith, Central Missouri State University; Stephen A. Smolen, Saddleback College; Edward V. Stackpoole, S.J., University of San Francisco; Paul H. Stacy, University of Hartford; Timothy Steele, California State University at Los Angeles; Joe Steinberg, Harper College; Dabney Stuart, Washington and Lee University; Stan Sulkes, Raymond Walters College, University of Cincinnati; Elaine L. Supowitz, Community College of Allegheny County; Debbie Sydow, Southwest Virginia Community College; Henry Taylor, American University; James G. Tipton, Chabot College; Khachig Toloyan, Wesleyan University; Lee Upton, Lafayette College; John Vacca, University of Wisconsin, Platteville; Nina Walker, Middlesex Community College; Sue B. Walker, University of South Alabama; Sheila D. Willard, Middlesex Community College; Terri Witek, Stetson University; William F. Woods, Wichita State University; G. Patton

Wright, University of Massachusetts, Boston; and Tom Zaniello, Northern Kentucky University. Many students sent helpful corrections and suggestions, and we thank them all, especially Mike DeVesta, Paul C. Ellis, and Joseph Grana.

On the publisher's staff, Lisa Moore, Katharine H. Glynn, Diane Williams, Tom Maeglin, William D. Young, and many others made contributions far beyond the call of duty. Once again Carolyn Woznick fought the battle of the permissions. Victor Peterson, Jennifer Goodrich, Amy Pollick, and Lauren Sarat helped with proofreading. Mary Gioia masterminded the complex logistics of the new edition. Past debts are outstanding to hundreds of instructors named in prefaces past, to Sylvan Barnet and Charles H. Christensen, and to Dorothy M. Kennedy, a co-author of the instructor's manual.

X. J. Kennedy

Publisher's Note: HarperCollins is pleased to announce the availability of an exclusive videotape interview with X. J. Kennedy and Dana Gioia. These poets read and discuss their own work, the writing process, and what it means to read literature in today's world. This interview is free to all adopters of the sixth edition of *Literature: An Introduction to Fiction, Poetry, and Drama*, as well as adopters of the paperback compact edition of *Literature*, the sixth eedition of *An Introduction to Fiction*, or the eighth edition of *An Introduction to Poetry*. For more information, please contact your HarperCollins representative or write to: English Literature Marketing Manger, HarperCollins College Publishers, 10 East 53rd Street, New York, NY 10022.

# FICTION

Here is a story, one of the shortest ever written and one of the most difficult to forget:

> A woman is sitting in her old, shuttered house. She knows that she is alone in the whole world; every other thing is dead.
>     The doorbell rings.

In a brief space this small tale of terror, credited to Thomas Bailey Aldrich, makes itself memorable. It sets a promising scene—is this a haunted house?—introduces a character, and places her in a strange and intriguing situation. Although in reading a story that is over so quickly we don't come to know the character well, for a moment we enter her thoughts and begin to share her feelings. Then something amazing happens. The story leaves us to wonder: who or what rang that bell?

Like many richer, longer, more complicated stories, this one, in its few words, engages the imagination. Evidently, how much a story contains and suggests doesn't depend on its size. In the opening chapter of this book, we will look first at other brief stories—examples of two ancient kinds of fiction, a fable and a tale—then at a contemporary short story. We will consider the elements of fiction one after another. By seeing a few short stories broken into their parts, you will come to a keener sense of how a story is put together. Not all stories are short, of course; later in the book, you will meet a chapter on reading long stories and novels.

All in all, here are fifty-six stories. Among them, may you find at least a few you'll enjoy and care to remember.

# 1 Reading a Story

After the shipwreck that marooned him on his desert island, Robinson Crusoe, in the story by Daniel Defoe, stood gazing over the water where pieces of cargo from his ship were floating by. Along came "two shoes, not mates." It is the qualification *not mates* that makes the detail memorable. We could well believe that a thing so striking and odd must have been seen, and not invented. But in truth Defoe, like other masters of the art of fiction, had the power to make us believe his imaginings. Borne along by the art of the storyteller, we trust what we are told, even though the story may be sheer fantasy.

**Fiction** (from the Latin *fictio*, "a shaping, a counterfeiting") is a name for stories not entirely factual, but at least partially shaped, made up, imagined. It is true that in some fiction, such as a historical novel, a writer draws upon factual information in presenting scenes, events, and characters. But the factual information in a historical novel, unlike that in a history book, is of secondary importance. Many firsthand accounts of the American Civil War were written by men who had fought in it, but few eyewitnesses give us so keen a sense of actual life on the battlefront as the author of *The Red Badge of Courage*, Stephen Crane, born after the war was over. In fiction, the "facts" may or may not be true, and a story is none the worse for their being entirely imaginary. We expect from fiction a sense of how people act, not an authentic chronicle of how, at some past time, a few people acted.

As children, we used to read (if we were lucky and formed the habit) to steep ourselves in romance, mystery, and adventure. As adults, we still do: at an airport, while waiting for a flight, we pass the time with some newsstand paperback full of fast action and brisk dialogue. Certain fiction, of course, calls for closer attention. To read a novel by the Russian master Dostoevsky instead of a thriller about secret agent James Bond is somewhat like playing chess instead of a game of tic-tac-toe. Not that a great novel does not provide entertainment. In fact, it may offer more deeply satisfying entertainment than a novel of violence and soft-core pornography, in which stick figures connive, go to bed, and kill one another in accord with some market-tested formula. Reading literary fiction (as distinguished from fiction as a commercial product—the formula kind of spy, detective, Western, romance or science fiction story), we are not necessarily led on by the promise of thrills; we do not keep reading mainly to find out what happens next. Indeed, a literary story might even disclose in its opening lines everything that happened, then spend the rest of its length revealing what that happening meant. Reading literary fiction is no merely passive activity, but one that demands both attention and insight-lending participation. In return, it offers rewards. In some works of literary fiction, in Stephen Crane's "The Open Boat" and Leo Tolstoi's "The Death of Ivan Ilych," we see more deeply into the minds and hearts of the characters than we ever see into those of our family, our close friends, our lovers—or even ourselves.

## FABLE AND TALE

Modern literary fiction in English has been dominated by two forms: the novel and the short story. The two have many elements in common (and in this book a further discussion of the novel as a special form will be given in Chapter Nine). Perhaps we will be able to define the short story more meaningfully—for it has traits more essential than just a particular length—if first, for comparison, we consider some related varieties of fiction: the fable and the tale. Ancient forms whose origins date back to the time of word-of-mouth storytelling, the fable and the tale are relatively simple in structure; in them we can plainly see elements also found in the short story (and in the novel). To begin, here is a **fable:** a brief story that sets forth some pointed statement of truth. The writer, W. Somerset Maugham, an English novelist and playwright (1874–1965), is retelling an Arabian folk story. (Samarra, by the way, is a city sixty miles from Bagdad.)

### W. Somerset Maugham
THE APPOINTMENT IN SAMARRA                                                 1933

*Death speaks:* There was a merchant in Bagdad who sent his servant to market to buy provisions and in a little while the servant came back, white and trembling, and said, Master, just now when I was in the marketplace I was jostled by a woman in the crowd and when I turned I saw it was Death that jostled me. She looked at me and made a threatening gesture; now, lend me your horse, and I will ride away from this city and avoid my fate. I will go to Samarra and there Death will not find me. The merchant lent him his horse, and the servant mounted it, and he dug his spurs in its flanks and as fast as the horse could gallop he went. Then the merchant went down to the marketplace and he saw me standing in the crowd and he came to me and said, Why did you make a threatening gesture to my servant when you saw him this morning? That was not a threatening gesture, I said, it was only a start of surprise. I was astonished to see him in Bagdad, for I had an appointment with him tonight in Samarra.

This brief story seems practically all skin and bones; that is, it contains little decoration. For in a fable everything leads directly to the **moral,** or message, sometimes stated at the end ("Moral: Haste makes waste"). In "The Appointment in Samarra" the moral isn't stated outright, it is merely implied. How would you state it in your own words?

You are probably acquainted with some of the fables credited to the Greek slave Aesop (about 620–560 B.C.), whose stories seem designed to teach lessons about human life. Such is the fable of "The Fox and the Grapes," in which a fox, unable to reach a bunch of grapes that hangs too high, decides that they were sour anyway (implied moral: "It is easy to spurn what we cannot attain"). Another is the fable of "The Tortoise and the Hare" (implied moral: "Slow, steady plodding wins the race"). The characters in a fable may be talking animals (as in many of Aesop's fables), inanimate objects, or people and supernatural beings (as in "The Appointment in Samarra"). Whoever they may be, these characters are merely sketched, not greatly developed. Evidently, it would not have helped Maugham's fable to put across its point if he had portrayed the merchant, the servant, and Death in fuller detail. A more elaborate description of the marketplace would not have improved the story. Probably, such a description would strike us as unnecessary and distracting. By its very bareness and simplicity, a fable fixes itself—and its message—in memory.

The name *tale* (from the Old English *talu,* "speech") is sometimes applied to any story, whether short or long, true or fictitious. *Tale* being a more evocative name than *story*, writers sometimes call their stories "tales" as if to imply something handed down from the past. But defined in a more limited sense, a **tale** is a story, usually short, that sets forth strange and wonderful events in more or less bare summary, without detailed character-drawing. "Tale" is pretty much synonymous with "yarn," for it implies a story in which the goal is revelation of the marvelous rather than revelation of character. In the English folk tale "Jack and the Beanstalk," we take away a more vivid impression of the miraculous beanstalk and the giant who dwells at its top than of Jack's mind or personality. Because such venerable stories were told aloud before someone set them down in writing, the storytellers had to limit themselves to brief descriptions. Probably spoken around a fire or hearth, such a tale tends to be less complicated and less closely detailed than a story written for the printed page, whose reader can linger over it. Still, such tales *can* be complicated. It is not merely greater length that makes a short story different from a tale or a fable: a mark of a short story is a fully delineated character.

Even modern tales favor supernatural or fantastic events: for instance, the **tall tale,** that variety of folk story which recounts the deeds of a superhero (Paul Bunyan, John Henry, Mike Fink) or of the storyteller. If the storyteller is telling about his own imaginary experience, his bragging yarn is usually told with a straight face to listeners who take pleasure in scoffing at it. Although the **fairy tale,** set in a world of magic and enchantment, is sometimes the work of a modern author (notably Hans Christian Andersen), well-known examples are those German folktales probably originated in the Middle Ages, collected by the brothers Grimm. The label *fairy tale* is something of an English misnomer, for in the Grimm stories, though witches and goblins abound, fairies are a minority.

## Jakob and Wilhelm Grimm

GODFATHER DEATH                                            1812 (FROM ORAL TRADITION)

*Translated by Lore Segal*

*Jakob Grimm (1785–1863) and Wilhelm Grimm (1786–1859), brothers and scholars, were born near Frankfurt-am-Main, Germany. For most of their lives they worked together—lived together, too, even when in 1825 Wilhelm married. In 1838, as librarians, they began toiling on their Deutsch Wörterbuch, or German dictionary, a vast project that was to outlive them by a century. (It was completed only in 1960.) In 1840 King Friedrich Wilhelm IV appointed both brothers to the Royal Academy of Sciences, and both taught at the University of Berlin for the rest of their*

Jakob and Wilhelm Grimm

*days. Although Jakob had a side-career as a diplomat, wrote a great Deutsche Grammatik, or German grammar (1819–37), and propounded Grimm's Law (an explanation of shifts in consonant sounds, of interest to students of linguistics), the name Grimm is best known to us for that splendid collection of ancient German folk stories we call Grimm's Fairy Tales—in German, Kinder- und Hausmärchen ("Childhood and Household Tales," 1812–15). This classic work spread German children's stories around the world. Many tales we hear early in life were collected by the Grimms: "Hansel and Gretel," "Snow White and the Seven Dwarfs," "Rapunzel," "Puss-in-Boots," "Little Red Riding Hood," "Rumpelstiltskin." Versions of some of these tales had been written down as early as the sixteenth century, but mainly the brothers relied on the memories of Hessian peasants who recited the stories aloud for them.*

A poor man had twelve children and worked night and day just to get enough bread for them to eat. Now when the thirteenth came into the world, he did not know what to do and in his misery ran out onto the great highway to ask the first person he met to be godfather. The first to come along was God, and he already knew what it was that weighed on the man's mind and said, "Poor man, I pity you. I will hold your child at the font and I will look after it and make it happy upon earth." "Who are you?" asked the man. "I am God." "Then I don't want you for a godfather," the man said. "You give to the rich and let the poor go hungry." That was how the man talked because he did not understand how wisely God shares out wealth and poverty, and thus he turned from the Lord and walked on. Next came the Devil and said, "What is it you want? If you let me be godfather to your child, I will give him gold as much as he can use, and all the pleasures of the world besides." "Who are you?" asked the man. "I am the Devil." "Then I don't want you for a godfather," said the man. "You deceive and mislead mankind." He walked on and along came spindle-legged Death striding toward him and said, "Take me as godfather." The man asked, "Who are you?" "I am Death who makes all men equal." Said the man, "Then you're the one for me; you take rich and poor without distinction. You shall be godfather." Answered Death: "I will make your child rich and famous, because the one who has me for a friend shall want for nothing." The man said, "Next Sunday is the baptism. Be there in good time." Death appeared as he had promised and made a perfectly fine godfather.

When the boy was of age, the godfather walked in one day, told him to come along, and led him out into the woods. He showed him an herb which grew there and said, "This is your christening gift. I shall make you into a famous doctor. When you are called to a patient's bedside I will appear and if I stand at the sick man's head you can boldly say that you will cure him and if you give him some of this herb he will recover. But if I stand at the sick man's feet, then he is mine, and you must say there is no help for him and no doctor on this earth could save him. But take care not to use the herb against my will or it could be the worse for you."

It wasn't long before the young man had become the most famous doctor in the whole world. "He looks at a patient and right away he knows how things stand, whether he will get better or if he's going to die." That is what they said about him, and from near and far the people came, took him to see the sick, and gave him so much money he became a rich man. Now it happened that the king fell ill. The doctor was summoned to say if he was going to get well. When he came to the bed, there stood Death at the feet of the sick man, so that no herb on earth could have done him any good. If I could only just this once outwit Death! thought the doctor. He'll be annoyed, I know, but I am his godchild and he's sure to turn a blind eye. I'll take my chance. And so he lifted the sick man and laid him the other way around so that Death was standing at his head. Then he gave him some of the herb and the king began to feel better and was soon in perfect health. But Death came toward the doctor, his face dark and angry, threatened him with raised forefinger, and said, "You have tricked me. This time I will let it pass because you are my godchild, but if you ever dare do such a thing again, you put your own head in the noose and it is you I shall carry away with me."

Soon after that, the king's daughter lapsed into a deep illness. She was his only child, he wept day and night until his eyes failed him and he let it be known that whoever saved the princess from death should become her husband and inherit the crown. When the doctor came to the sick girl's bed, he saw Death at her feet. He ought to have remembered his godfather's warning, but the great beauty of the princess and the happiness of becoming her husband so bedazzled him that he threw caution to the winds, nor did he see Death's angry glances and how he lifted his hand in the air and threatened him with his bony fist. He picked the sick girl up and laid her head where her feet had lain, then he gave her some of the herb and at once her cheeks reddened and life stirred anew.

When Death saw himself cheated of his property the second time, he strode toward the doctor on his long legs and said, "It is all up with you, and now it is your turn," grasped him harshly with his ice-cold hand so that the doctor could not resist, and led him to an underground cave, and here he saw thousands upon thousands of lights burning in rows without end, some big, some middle-sized, others small. Every moment some went out and others lit up so that the little flames seemed to be jumping here and there in perpetual exchange. "Look," said Death, "these are the life lights of mankind. The big ones belong to children, the middle-sized ones to married couples in their best years, the little ones belong to very old people. Yet children and the young often have only little lights." "Show me my life light," said the doctor, imagining that it must be one of the big ones. Death pointed to a little stub threatening to go out and said, "Here it is." "Ah, dear godfather," said the terrified doctor, "light me a new one, do it, for my sake, so that I may enjoy my life and become king and marry the beautiful princess." "I cannot," answered Death. "A light must go out before a new one lights up." "Then set the old on top of a new one so it can go on burning when the first is finished," begged the doctor. Death made as if to grant his wish, reached for a tall new taper, but because he wanted revenge he purposely fumbled and the little stub fell over and went out. Thereupon the doctor sank to the ground and had himself fallen into the hands of death.

## Chuang Tzu

INDEPENDENCE                                    CHOU DYNASTY (4TH CENTURY B.C.)

*Translated by Herbert Giles*

*Chuang Chou, usually known as Chuang Tzu (approximately 365–390 B.C.), was one of the great philosophers of the Chou period in China. He was born in the Sung feudal state and received an excellent education. Unlike most educated men, however, Chuang Tzu did not seek public office or political power. Influenced by Taoist philosophy, he believed that individuals should transcend their desire for success and wealth, as well as their fear of failure and poverty. True freedom, he maintained, came from escaping the distractions of worldly affairs. Chuang Tzu's writings have been particularly praised for their combination of humor and wisdom. His parables and stories are classics of Chinese literature.*

Chuang Tzu was one day fishing, when the Prince of Ch'u sent two high officials to interview him, saying that his Highness would be glad of Chuang Tzu's assistance in the administration of his government. The latter quietly fished on, and without looking round, replied, "I have heard that in the State of Ch'u there is a sacred tortoise, which has been dead three thousand years, and which the prince keeps packed up in a box on the altar in his ancestral shrine. Now do you think that tortoise would rather be dead and have its remains thus honoured, or be alive and wagging its tail in the mud?" The two officials answered that no doubt it would rather be alive and wagging its tail in the mud; whereupon Chuang Tzu cried out "Begone! I too elect to remain wagging my tail in the mud."

QUESTIONS

1. What part of this story is the exposition? How many sentences does Chuang Tzu use to set up the dramatic situation?
2. Why does the protagonist change the subject and mention the sacred tortoise? Why doesn't he answer the request directly and immediately? Does it serve any purpose that Chuang Tzu makes the officials answer a question to which he knows the answer?
3. What does this story tell us about the protagonist Chuang Tzu's personality?

# PLOT

Like a fable, the Grimm brothers' tale seems stark in its lack of detail and in the swiftness of its telling. Compared with the fully portrayed characters of many modern stories, the characters of father, son, king, princess, and even Death himself seem hardly more than stick figures. It may have been that to draw ample characters would not have contributed to the storytellers' design; that, indeed, to have done so would have been inartistic. Yet "Godfather Death" is a compelling story. By what methods does it arouse and sustain our interest?

From the opening sentence of the tale, we watch the unfolding of a **dramatic situation:** a person is involved in some conflict. First, this character is a poor man with children to feed, in conflict with the world; very soon, we find him in conflict with God and with the Devil besides. Drama in fiction occurs in any clash of wills, desires, or powers—whether it be a conflict of character against character, character against society, character against some natural force, or, as in "Godfather Death," character against some supernatural entity.

Like any shapely tale, "Godfather Death" has a beginning, a middle, and an end. In fact, it is unusual to find a story so clearly displaying the elements of structure that critics have found in many classic works of fiction and drama. The tale begins with an **exposition:** the opening portion that sets the scene (if any), introduces the main characters, tells us what happened before the story opened, and provides any other background information that we need in order to understand and care about the events to follow. In "Godfather Death," the exposition is brief—all in the opening paragraph. The middle section of the story begins with Death's giving the herb to the boy, and his warning not to defy him. This moment introduces a new conflict (a **complication**), and by this time it is clear that the son and not the father is to be the central human character of the story. Death's godson is the principal person who strives: the **protagonist** (a better term than **hero,** for it may apply equally well to a central character who is not especially brave or virtuous).

The **suspense,** the pleasurable anxiety we feel that heightens our attention to the story, inheres in our wondering how it will all turn out. Will the doctor triumph over Death? Even though we suspect, early in the story, that the doctor stands no chance against such a superhuman **antagonist,** we want to see for ourselves the outcome of his defiance. A storyteller can try to incite our anticipation by giving us some **foreshadowing** or indication of events to come. In "Godfather Death" the foreshadowings are apparent in Death's warnings ("but if you ever dare do such a thing again, you put your own head in the noose"). When the doctor defies his godfather for the first time—when he saves the king—we have a **crisis,** a moment of high tension. The tension is momentarily resolved when Death lets him off. Then an even greater crisis—the turning point in the action—occurs with the doctor's second defiance in restoring the princess to life. In the last section of the story, with the doctor in the underworld, events come to a **climax,** the moment of greatest tension at which the outcome is to be decided, when the terrified doctor begs for a new candle. Will Death grant him one? Will he live, become king, and marry the princess? The outcome or **conclusion**—also called the **resolution** or **dénouement** ("the untying of the knot")—quickly follows as Death allows the little candle to go out.

Such a structure of events arising out of a conflict may be called the plot of the story. Like many terms used in literary discussion, *plot* is blessed with several meanings. Sometimes it refers simply to the events in a story. In this book, **plot** will mean the artistic arrangement of those events. Different arrangements of the same material are possible. A writer might decide to tell of the events in chronological order, beginning with the earliest; or he might open his story with the last event, then tell what led up to it. Sometimes a writer chooses to skip rapidly over the exposition and begin **in medias res** (Latin, "in the midst of things"), first presenting some exciting or significant moment, then filling in what happened earlier. This method is by no means a modern invention: Homer begins the *Odyssey* with his hero mysteriously late in returning from war and his son searching for him; John Milton's *Paradise Lost* opens with Satan already defeated in his revolt against the Lord. A device useful to writers for filling in what happened earlier is the **flashback** (or **retrospect**), a scene relived in a character's memory.

To have a plot, a story does not need an intense, sustained conflict such as we find in "Godfather Death," a tale especially economical in its structure of crisis, climax, and conclusion. Although a highly dramatic story may tend to assume such a clearly recognizable structure, many contemporary writers avoid it, considering it too contrived and arbitrary. In commercial fiction, in which exciting conflict is everything and in which the writer has to manufacture all possible suspense, such a structure is often obvious. In popular detective, Western, and adventure novels; in juvenile fiction (the perennial Hardy Boys and Nancy Drew books); and in popular series on television (soap operas, police and hospital dramas, mysteries, and the three Star Trek series), it is often easy to recognize crisis, climax, and conclusion. The presence of these elements does not necessarily indicate inferior literature (as "Godfather Death" shows); yet when reduced to parts of a formula, the result may seem stale and contrived.[1] Such plots may be (as contemporary French novelist Alain Robbe-Grillet describes them) mere anecdotes, providing trumped-up surprises for "the panting reader."

## THE SHORT STORY

The teller of a tale relies heavily upon the method of **summary:** terse, general narration as in "Godfather Death" ("It wasn't long before the young man had become the most famous doctor in the whole world"). But in a **short story,** a form more realistic than the tale and of modern origin, the writer usually presents the main events in greater fullness. Fine writers of short stories, although they may use summary at times (often to give some portion of a story less emphasis), are skilled in rendering a **scene:** a vivid or dramatic moment described in enough detail to create the illusion that the reader is practically there. Avoiding long summary, they try to *show* rather than simply to *tell;* as if following Mark Twain's advice to authors: "Don't say, 'The old lady screamed.' Bring her on and let her scream."

A short story is more than just a sequence of happenings. A finely wrought short story has the richness and conciseness of an excellent lyric poem. Spontaneous and natural as the finished story may seem, the writer has written it so artfully that there is meaning in even seemingly casual speeches and apparently trivial details. If we skim it hastily, skipping the descriptive passages, we miss significant parts. Some literary short stories, unlike commercial fiction in which the main interest is in physical action or conflict, tell of an **epiphany:** some moment of insight, discovery, or revelation by which a character's life, or view of life, is greatly altered.[2] (For such moments in fiction, see the stories in this book by James Joyce, Leo Tolstoi, John Steinbeck, and Joyce Carol Oates.) Other short stories tell of a character initiated into experience or maturity: one such **story of initiation** is William Faulkner's "Barn Burning" (Chapter Five), in which a boy finds it necessary to defy his father and suddenly to grow into manhood. Less obviously dramatic, perhaps, than "Godfather Death," such a story may be no less powerful.

The fable and the tale are ancient forms; the short story is of more recent origin. In the nineteenth century, writers of fiction were encouraged by a large, literate audience of middle-class readers who wanted to see their lives reflected in faithful mirrors. Skillfully representing ordinary life, many writers perfected the art of the short story: in Russia, Anton Chekhov; in France, Honoré de Balzac, Gustave Flaubert, and Guy de Maupassant; and in America, Nathaniel

---

[1]In the heyday of the **pulp magazines** (so called for their cheap paper), some professional writers even relied on a mechanical device called Plotto: a tin arrow-spinner pointed to numbers and the writer looked them up in a book that listed necessary ingredients—type of hero, type of villain, sort of conflict, crisis, climax, conclusion.

[2]From the Greek *epiphainein*, "to show forth." In Christian tradition, the Feast of the Epiphany commemorates the revelation to the Magi of the birth of Christ. For James Joyce's description of epiphanies in everyday life, see page 574.

Hawthorne and Edgar Allan Poe (although the Americans seem less fond of everyday life than of dream and fantasy). It would be false to claim that, in passing from the fable and the tale to the short story, fiction has made a triumphant progress; or to claim that, because short stories are modern, they are superior to fables and tales. Fable, tale, and short story are distinct forms, each achieving its own effects. (Incidentally, fable and tale are far from being extinct today: you can find many recent examples.) Lately, in the hands of Jorge Luis Borges, Joyce Carol Oates, John Barth, and other innovative writers, the conventions of the short story have been changing; and at the moment, stories of epiphany and initiation have become scarcer.

But let us begin with a contemporary short story whose protagonist *does* undergo an initiation into maturity. To notice the difference between a short story and a tale, you may find it helpful to compare John Updike's "A & P" with "Godfather Death." Although Updike's short story is centuries distant from the Grimm tale in its method of telling and in its setting, you may be reminded of "Godfather Death" in the main character's dramatic situation. To defend a young woman, a young man has to defy his mentor—here, the boss of a supermarket! So doing, he places himself in jeopardy. Updike has the protagonist tell his own story, amply and with humor. How does it differ from a tale?

## John Updike

### A & P                                                                1961

John Updike, born in Shillingford, Pennsylvania, in 1932, received his B.A. from Harvard, then went to Oxford to study drawing and fine art. In the mid-1950s he worked on the staff of The New Yorker, at times doing errands for the aged James Thurber. Although he left the magazine to become a full-time writer, Updike has continued to supply it with memorable stories and searching reviews. His more than thirty books include essays, art criticism, light verse, and serious poetry. Updike is best known, however, as a hardworking,

John Updike

versatile, highly productive writer of fiction. For his novel The Centaur (1963) he received a National Book Award and for Rabbit Is Rich (1982), a Pulitzer prize and an American Book Award. The Witches of Eastwick (1984) was successfully adapted for a film starring Jack Nicholson. S. (1988), an interesting later novel, was partly inspired by Nathaniel Hawthorne's The Scarlet Letter. His recent novels include his fourth and final Rabbit Angstrom story, Rabbit at Rest (1990), and Memories of the Ford Administration (1992). His Collected Poems appeared in 1993.

In walks three girls in nothing but bathing suits. I'm in the third check-out slot, with my back to the door, so I don't see them until they're over by the bread. The one that caught my eye first was the one in the plaid green two-piece. She was a chunky kid, with a good tan and a sweet broad soft-looking can with those two crescents of white just under it, where the sun never seems to hit, at the top of the backs of her legs. I stood there with my hand on a box of HiHo crackers trying to remember if I rang it up or not. I ring it up again and the customer starts giving me hell. She's one of these cash-register-watchers, a witch about fifty with rouge on her cheekbones and no eyebrows, and I know it made her day to trip me up. She'd been watching cash registers for fifty years and probably never seen a mistake before.

By the time I got her feathers smoothed and her goodies into a bag—she gives me a little snort in passing, if she'd been born at the right time they would have burned her over in Salem—by the time I get her on her way the girls had circled around the bread and were coming back, without a pushcart, back my way along the counters, in the aisle between the check-outs and the Special bins. They didn't even have shoes on. There was this chunky one, with the two-piece—it was bright green and the seams on the bra were still sharp and her belly was still pretty pale so I guessed she just got it (the suit)—there was this one, with one of those chubby berry-faces, the lips all bunched together under her nose, this one, and a tall one, with black hair that hadn't quite frizzed right, and one of these sunburns right across under the eyes, and a chin that was too long—you know, the kind of girl other girls think is very "striking" and "attractive" but never quite makes it, as they very well know, which is why they like her so much—and then the third one, that wasn't quite so tall. She was the queen. She kind of led them, the other two peeking around and making their shoulders round. She didn't look around, not this queen, she just walked straight on slowly, on these long white prima-donna legs. She came down a little hard on her heels, as if she didn't walk in her bare feet that much, putting down her heels and then letting the weight move along to her toes as if she was testing the floor with every step, putting a little deliberate extra action into it. You never know for sure how girls' minds work (do you really think it's a mind in there or just a little buzz like a bee in a glass jar?) but you got the idea she had talked the other two into coming in here with her, and now she was showing them how to do it, walk slow and hold yourself straight.

She had on a kind of dirty-pink—beige maybe, I don't know—bathing suit with a little nubble all over it and, what got me, the straps were down. They were off her shoulders looped loose around the cool tops of her arms, and I guess as a result the suit had slipped a little on her, so all around the top of the cloth there was this shining rim. If it hadn't been there you wouldn't have known there could have been anything whiter than those shoulders. With the straps pushed off, there was nothing between the top of the suit and the top of her head except just *her*, this clean bare plane of the top of her chest down from the shoulder bones like a dented sheet of metal tilted in the light. I mean, it was more than pretty.

She had sort of oaky hair that the sun and salt had bleached, done up in a bun that was unraveling, and a kind of prim face. Walking into the A & P with your straps down, I suppose it's the only kind of face you *can* have. She held her head so high her neck, coming up out of those white shoulders, looked kind of stretched, but I didn't mind. The longer her neck was, the more of her there was.

She must have felt in the corner of her eye me and over my shoulder    5
Stokesie in the second slot watching, but she didn't tip. Not this queen. She kept her eyes moving across the racks, and stopped, and turned so slow it made my stomach rub the inside of my apron, and buzzed to the other two, who kind of huddled against her for relief, and they all three of them went up the cat-and-dog-food-breakfast-cereal-macaroni-rice-raisins-seasonings-spreads-spaghetti-soft-drinks-crackers-and-cookies aisle. From the third slot I look straight up this aisle to the meat counter, and I watched them all the way. The fat one with the tan sort of fumbled with the cookies, but on second thought she put the packages back. The sheep pushing their carts down the aisle—the girls were walking against the usual traffic (not that we have one-way signs or anything)—were pretty hilarious. You could see them, when Queenie's white shoulders dawned on them, kind of jerk, or hop, or hiccup, but their eyes snapped back to their own baskets and on they pushed. I bet you could set off dynamite in an A & P and the people would by and large keep reaching and checking oatmeal off their lists and muttering "Let me see, there was a third thing, began with A, asparagus, no, ah, yes, applesauce!" or whatever it is they do mutter. But there was no doubt, this jiggled them. A few houseslaves in pin curlers even looked around after pushing their carts past to make sure what they had seen was correct.

You know, it's one thing to have a girl in a bathing suit down on the beach, where what with the glare nobody can look at each other much anyway, and another thing in the cool of the A & P, under the fluorescent lights, against all those stacked packages, with her feet padding along naked over our checkerboard green-and-cream rubber-tile floor.

"Oh Daddy," Stokesie said beside me. "I feel so faint."

"Darling," I said. "Hold me tight." Stokesie's married, with two babies chalked up on his fuselage already, but as far as I can tell that's the only difference. He's twenty-two, and I was nineteen this April.

"Is it done?" he asks, the responsible married man finding his voice. I forgot to say he thinks he's going to be manager some sunny day, maybe in 1990 when it's called the Great Alexandrov and Petrooshki Tea Company or something.

What he meant was, our town is five miles from a beach, with a big summer    10
colony out on the Point, but we're right in the middle of town, and the women generally put on a shirt or shorts or something before they get out of the car into the street. And anyway these are usually women with six children and varicose veins mapping their legs and nobody, including them, could care less. As I say, we're right in the middle of town, and if you stand at our front doors you can see two banks and the Congregational church and the newspaper store and three real-estate offices and about twenty-seven old freeloaders tearing up Central Street because the sewer broke again. It's not as if we're on the Cape; we're north

of Boston and there's people in this town haven't seen the ocean for twenty years. The girls had reached the meat counter and were asking McMahon something. He pointed, they pointed, and they shuffled out of sight behind a pyramid of Diet Delight peaches. All that was left for us to see was old McMahon patting his mouth and looking after them sizing up their joints. Poor kids, I began to feel sorry for them, they couldn't help it.

Now here comes the sad part of the story, at least my family says it's sad but I don't think it's sad myself. The store's pretty empty, it being Thursday afternoon, so there was nothing much to do except lean on the register and wait for the girls to show up again. The whole store was like a pinball machine and I didn't know which tunnel they'd come out of. After a while they come around out of the far aisle, around the light bulbs, records at discount of the Caribbean Six or Tony Martin Sings or some such gunk you wonder they waste the wax on, six-packs of candy bars, and plastic toys done up in cellophane that fall apart when a kid looks at them anyway. Around they come, Queenie still leading the way, and holding a little gray jar in her hand. Slots Three through Seven are unmanned and I could see her wondering between Stokes and me, but Stokesie with his usual luck draws an old party in baggy gray pants who stumbles up with four giant cans of pineapple juice (what do these bums *do* with all that pineapple juice? I've often asked myself) so the girls come to me. Queenie puts down the jar and I take it into my fingers icy cold. Kingfish Fancy Herring Snacks in Pure Sour Cream: 49¢. Now her hands are empty, not a ring or a bracelet, bare as God made them, and I wonder where the money's coming from. Still with that prim look she lifts a folded dollar bill out of the hollow at the center of her nubbled pink top. The jar went heavy in my hand. Really, I thought that was so cute.

Then everybody's luck begins to run out. Lengel comes in from haggling with a truck full of cabbages on the lot and is about to scuttle into that door marked MANAGER behind which he hides all day when the girls touch his eye. Lengel's pretty dreary, teaches Sunday school and the rest, but he doesn't miss that much. He comes over and says, "Girls, this isn't the beach."

Queenie blushes, though maybe it's just a brush of sunburn I was noticing for the first time, now that she was so close. "My mother asked me to pick up a jar of herring snacks." Her voice kind of startled me, the way voices do when you see the people first, coming out so flat and dumb yet kind of tony, too, the way it ticked over "pick up" and "snacks." All of a sudden I slid right down her voice into her living room. Her father and the other men were standing around in ice-cream coats and bow ties and the women were in sandals picking up herring snacks on toothpicks off a big plate and they were all holding drinks the color of water with olives and sprigs of mint in them. When my parents have somebody over they get lemonade and if it's a real racy affair Schlitz in tall glasses with "They'll Do It Every Time" cartoons stencilled on.

"That's all right," Lengel said. "But this isn't the beach." His repeating this struck me as funny, as if it had just occurred to him, and he had been thinking all these years the A & P was a great big dune and he was the head lifeguard. He didn't like my smiling—as I say he doesn't miss much—but he concentrates on giving the girls that sad Sunday-school-superintendent stare.

Queenie's blush is no sunburn now, and the plump one in plaid, that I liked better from the back—a really sweet can—pipes up, "We weren't doing any shopping. We just came in for the one thing." 15

"That makes no difference," Lengel tells her, and I could see from the way his eyes went that he hadn't noticed she was wearing a two-piece before. "We want you decently dressed when you come in here."

"We *are* decent," Queenie says suddenly, her lower lip pushing, getting sore now that she remembers her place, a place from which the crowd that runs the A & P must look pretty crummy. Fancy Herring Snacks flashed in her very blue eyes.

"Girls, I don't want to argue with you. After this come in here with your shoulders covered. It's our policy." He turns his back. That's policy for you. Policy is what the kingpins want. What the others want is juvenile delinquency.

All this while, the customers had been showing up with their carts but, you know, sheep, seeing a scene, they had all bunched up on Stokesie, who shook open a paper bag as gently as peeling a peach, not wanting to miss a word. I could feel in the silence everybody getting nervous, most of all Lengel, who asks me, "Sammy, have you rung up this purchase?"

I thought and said "No" but it wasn't about that I was thinking. I go through 20 the punches, 4, 9, GROC, TOT—it's more complicated than you think, and after you do it often enough, it begins to make a little song, that you hear words to, in my case "Hello (*bing*) there, you (*gung*) hap-py *pee*-pul (*splat*)!"—the *splat* being the drawer flying out. I uncrease the bill, tenderly as you may imagine, it just having come from between the two smoothest scoops of vanilla I had ever known were there, and pass a half and a penny into her narrow pink palm, and nestle the herrings in a bag and twist its neck and hand it over, all the time thinking.

The girls, and who'd blame them, are in a hurry to get out, so I say "I quit" to Lengel quick enough for them to hear, hoping they'll stop and watch me, their unsuspected hero. They keep right on going, into the electric eye; the door flies open and they flicker across the lot to their car, Queenie and Plaid and Big Tall Goony-Goony (not that as raw material she was so bad), leaving me with Lengel and a kink in his eyebrow.

"Did you say something, Sammy?"

"I said I quit."

"I thought you did."

"You didn't have to embarrass them." 25

"It was they who were embarrassing us."

I started to say something that came out "Fiddle-de-doo." It's a saying of my grandmother's, and I know she would have been pleased.

"I don't think you know what you're saying," Lengel said.

"I know you don't," I said. "But I do." I pull the bow at the back of my apron and start shrugging it off my shoulders. A couple customers that had been heading for my slot begin to knock against each other, like scared pigs in a chute.

Lengel sighs and begins to look very patient and old and gray. He's been a <sup>30</sup> friend of my parents for years. "Sammy, you don't want to do this to your Mom and Dad," he tells me. It's true, I don't. But it seems to me that once you begin a gesture it's fatal not to go through with it. I fold the apron, "Sammy" stitched in red on the pocket, and put it on the counter, and drop the bow tie on top of it. The bow tie is theirs, if you've ever wondered. "You'll feel this for the rest of your life," Lengel says, and I know that's true, too, but remembering how he made that pretty girl blush makes me so scrunchy inside I punch the No Sale tab and the machine whirs "pee-pul" and the drawer splats out. One advantage to this scene taking place in summer, I can follow this up with a clean exit, there's no fumbling around getting your coat and galoshes, I just saunter into the electric eye in my white shirt that my mother ironed the night before, and the door heaves itself open, and outside the sunshine is skating around on the asphalt.

I look around for my girls, but they're gone, of course. There wasn't anybody but some young married screaming with her children about some candy they didn't get by the door of a powder-blue Falcon station wagon. Looking back in the big windows, over the bags of peat moss and aluminum lawn furniture stacked on the pavement, I could see Lengel in my place in the slot, checking the sheep through. His face was dark gray and his back stiff, as if he'd just had an injection of iron, and my stomach kind of fell as I felt how hard the world was going to be to me hereafter.

## QUESTIONS

1. Notice how artfully Updike arranges details to set the story in a perfectly ordinary supermarket. What details stand out for you as particularly true to life? What does this close attention to detail contribute to the story?

2. How fully does Updike draw the character of Sammy? What traits (admirable or otherwise) does Sammy show? Is he any less a hero for wanting the girls to notice his heroism? To what extent is he more thoroughly and fully portrayed than the doctor in "Godfather Death"?

3. What part of the story seems like the exposition? (See the definition of *exposition* on page 9.) Of what value to the story is the carefully detailed portrait of Queenie, the leader of the three girls?

4. As the story develops, do you detect any change in Sammy's feelings toward the girls?

5. Where in "A & P" does the dramatic conflict become apparent? What moment in the story brings the crisis? What is the climax of the story?

6. Why, exactly, does Sammy quit his job?

7. Does anything lead you to *expect* Sammy to make some gesture of sympathy for the three girls? What incident earlier in the story (before Sammy quits) seems a foreshadowing?

8. What do you understand from the conclusion of the story? What does Sammy mean when he acknowledges "how hard the world was going to be . . . hereafter"?

9. What comment does Updike—through Sammy—make on supermarket society?

## SUGGESTIONS FOR WRITING

1. In a paragraph or two, referring to John Updike's "A & P," consider this remark: "Sammy is a sexist pig who suddenly sees the light." What evidence supporting (or refuting) this comment do you find in the story?

2. Imagining you are Sammy, write a brief letter to a friend explaining why you quit your job.

3. Look up Anne Sexton's retelling of the Grimm tale "Godfather Death" in her book of poems *Transformations* (1971); also included in *The Complete Poems of Anne Sexton* (1981). In a short essay of three to five paragraphs, discuss the differences you find between the Grimm and Sexton versions. What is the effect of Sexton's retelling? What does she retain from the original? Which version of the story do you prefer? Why?

4. If you have had an experience in telling stories aloud (to children or to others), write a brief but detailed account of your experience, giving tips to adults who wish to become storytellers.

5. Write a brief fable of your own invention, perhaps illustrating some familiar proverb ("Too many cooks spoil the broth," "A rolling stone gathers no moss"). Your fable might be inspired by "The Appointment in Samarra" or a fable by Aesop. You can state a moral at the end, or, if you prefer, let the moral be unstated but obvious.

6. After you have written such a fable, write a short account of your writing process. Tell of the problems you encountered in thinking up your fable and in writing it, and how you surmounted them.

# 2 Point of View

In the opening lines of *The Adventures of Huckleberry Finn,* Mark Twain takes care to separate himself from the leading character, who is to tell his own story:

> You don't know about me, without you have read a book by the name of *The Adventures of Tom Sawyer,* but that ain't no matter. That book was made by Mr. Mark Twain, and he told the truth, mainly.

Twain wrote the novel, but the **narrator** or speaker is Huck Finn, the one from whose perspective the story is told. Obviously, in *Huckleberry Finn,* the narrator of a story is not the same person as the "real-life" author, the one given the byline. In employing Huck as his narrator, Twain selects a special angle of vision: not his own, exactly, but that of a resourceful boy moving through the thick of events, with a mind at times shrewd, at other times innocent. Through Huck's eyes, Twain takes in certain scenes, actions, and characters and—as only Huck's angle of vision could have enabled Twain to do so well—records them memorably.

Not every narrator in fiction is, like Huck Finn, a main character, one in the thick of events. Some narrators play only minor parts in the stories they tell; others take no active part at all. In the tale of "Godfather Death," we have a narrator who does not participate in the events he recounts. He is not a character in the story but is someone not even named, who stands at some distance from the action recording what the main characters say and do; recording also, at times, what they think, feel, or desire. He seems to have unlimited knowledge: he even knows the mind of Death, who "because he wanted revenge" let the doctor's candle go out. More humanly restricted in their knowledge, other narrators can see into the mind of only one character. They may be less willing to express opinions than the narrator of "Godfather Death" ("He ought to have remembered his godfather's warning"). A story may even be told by a narrator who seems so impartial and aloof that he limits himself to reporting only overheard conversation and to describing, without comment or opinion, the appearances of things. Evidently, narrators greatly differ in kind; however, because stories usually are told by someone, almost every story has some kind of narrator.[1] It is rare in modern fiction for the "real-life" author to try to step out from behind the typewriter and tell the story. Real persons can tell stories, but when such a story is *written*, the result is usually *non*fiction: a memoir, an account of travels, an autobiography.[2]

To identify the narrator of a story, describing any part he or she plays in the events and any limits placed upon his knowledge, is to identify the story's **point of view.** In a short story, it is usual for the writer to maintain one point of view from beginning to end, but there is nothing to stop him from introducing other points of view as well. In his long, panoramic novel *War and Peace*, encompassing the vast drama of Napoleon's invasion of Russia, Leo Tolstoi freely shifts the point of view in and out of the minds of many characters, among them Napoleon himself.

Theoretically, a great many points of view are possible. A narrator who says "I" might conceivably be involved in events to a much greater or a much lesser degree: as the protagonist, as some other major character, as some minor character, as a mere passive spectator, or even as a character who arrives late upon the scene and then tries to piece together what happened. Evidently, too, a narrator's knowledge might vary in gradations from total omniscience to almost total ignorance. But in reading fiction, again and again we encounter familiar and recognizable points of view. Here is a list of them—admittedly just a rough abstraction—that may provide a few terms with which to discuss the stories that you read and to describe their points of view:

*Narrator a Participant (Writing in the First Person):*

    1. a major character
    2. a minor character

*Narrator a Nonparticipant (Writing in the Third Person):*

    3. all-knowing (seeing into any of the characters)
    4. seeing into one major character
    5. seeing into one minor character
    6. objective (not seeing into any characters)

---

[1] Some theorists reserve the term *narrator* for a character who tells a story in the first person. We use it in a wider sense: to mean a recording consciousness that an author creates, who may or may not be a participant in the events of the story. In the view of Wayne C. Booth, the term *narrator* can be dispensed with in dealing with a rigorously impersonal "fly-on-the-wall" story, containing no editorializing and confined to the presentation of surfaces: "In Hemingway's 'The Killers,' for example, there is no narrator other than the implicit second self that Hemingway creates as he writes" (*The Rhetoric of Fiction* [Chicago: U of Chicago P, 1961] 151).

[2] Another relationship between the author and the story will be discussed in Chapter Five, "Tone and Style."

When the narrator is cast as a **participant** in the events of the story, he or she is a dramatized character who says "I." Such a narrator may be the protagonist (Huck Finn) or may be an **observer,** a minor character standing a little to one side, watching a story unfold that mainly involves someone else.

A narrator who remains a **nonparticipant** does not appear in the story as a character. Viewing the characters, perhaps seeing into the minds of one or more of them, such a narrator refers to them as "he," "she," or "they." When **all-knowing** (or **omniscient**), the narrator sees into the minds of all (or some) characters, moving when necessary from one to another. This is the point of view in "Godfather Death," whose narrator knows the feelings and motives of the father, of the doctor, and even of Death himself. In that he adds an occasional comment or opinion, this narrator may be said also to show **editorial omniscience** (as we can tell from his disapproving remark that the doctor "ought to have remembered" and his observation that the father did not understand "how wisely God shares out wealth and poverty"). A narrator who shows **impartial omniscience** presents the thoughts and actions of the characters, but does not judge them or comment on them.

When a nonparticipating narrator sees events through the eyes of a single character, whether a major character or a minor one, the resulting point of view is sometimes called **limited omniscience** or **selective omniscience.** The author, of course, selects which character to see through; the omniscience is his and not the narrator's. In William Faulkner's "Barn Burning" (Chapter Five), the narrator is almost entirely confined to knowing the thoughts and perceptions of a boy, the central character. Here is another example. Early in his novel *Madame Bovary*, Gustave Flaubert tells of the first time a young country doctor, Charles Bovary, meets Emma, the woman later to become his wife. The doctor has been summoned late at night to set the broken leg of a farmer, Emma's father.

A young woman wearing a blue merino dress with three flounces came to the door of the house to greet Monsieur Bovary, and she ushered him into the kitchen, where a big open fire was blazing. Around its edges the farm hands' breakfast was bubbling in small pots of assorted sizes. Damp clothes were drying inside the vast chimney-opening. The fire shovel, the tongs, and the nose of the bellows, all of colossal proportions, shone like polished steel; and along the walls hung a lavish array of kitchen utensils, glimmering in the bright light of the fire and in the first rays of the sun that were now beginning to come in through the window-panes.

Charles went upstairs to see the patient. He found him in bed, sweating under blankets, his nightcap lying where he had flung it. He was a stocky little man of fifty, fair-skinned, blue-eyed, bald in front and wearing earrings. On a chair beside him was a big decanter of brandy: he had been pouring himself drinks to keep up his courage. But as soon as he saw the doctor he dropped his bluster, and instead of cursing as he had been doing for the past twelve hours he began to groan weakly.

The fracture was a simple one, without complications of any kind. Charles couldn't have wished for anything easier. Then he recalled his teachers' bedside manner in accident cases, and proceeded to cheer up his patient with all kinds of facetious remarks—a truly surgical attention, like the oiling of a scalpel. For splints, they sent someone to bring a bundle of laths from the carriage shed. Charles selected one, cut it into lengths and smoothed it down with a piece of broken window glass, while the maidservant tore sheets for bandages and Mademoiselle Emma tried to sew some pads. She was a long time finding her workbox, and her father showed his impatience. She made no reply; but as she sewed she kept pricking her fingers and raising them to her mouth to suck.

Charles was surprised by the whiteness of her fingernails. They were almond-shaped, tapering, as polished and shining as Dieppe ivories. Her hands, however, were not pretty—not pale enough, perhaps, a little rough at the knuckles; and they were too long, without softness of line. The finest thing about her was her eyes. They were brown, but seemed black under the long eyelashes; and she had an open gaze that met yours with fearless candor.[3]

In this famous scene, Charles Bovary is beholding people and objects in a natural sequence. On first meeting Emma, he notices only her dress, as though less interested in the woman who opens the door than in passing through to the warm fire. Needing pads for his patient's splint, the doctor observes just the hands of the woman sewing them. Obliged to wait for the splints, he then has the leisure to notice her face, her remarkable eyes. (By the way, notice the effect of the word *yours* in the last sentence of the passage. It is as if the reader, seeing through the doctor's eyes, suddenly became one with him.) Who is the narrator? Not Charles Bovary, nor Gustave Flaubert, but someone able to enter the minds of others— here limited to knowing the thoughts and perceptions of one character.

In the **objective** point of view, the narrator does not enter the mind of any character but describes events from the outside. Telling us what people say and how their faces look, he leaves us to infer their thoughts and feelings. So inconspicuous is the narrator that this point of view has been called "the fly on the wall." This metaphor assumes the existence of a fly with a highly discriminating gaze, who knows which details to look for to communicate the deepest meaning. Some critics would say that in the objective point of view, the narrator disappears altogether. Consider this passage by a writer famous for remaining objective, Dashiell Hammett, in his mystery novel *The Maltese Falcon*, describing his private detective Sam Spade:

Spade's thick fingers made a cigarette with deliberate care, sifting a measured quantity of tan flakes down into curved paper, spreading the flakes so that they lay equal at the ends with a slight depression in the middle, thumbs rolling the paper's inner edge down and up under the outer edge as forefingers pressed it over, thumb and fingers sliding to the paper cylinder's ends to hold it even while tongue licked the flap, left forefinger and thumb pinching their ends while right forefinger and thumb smoothed the damp seam, right forefinger and thumb twisting their end and lifting the other to Spade's mouth.[4]

[3]*Madame Bovary*, translated by Francis Steegmuller (New York: Random House, 1957) 16–17.
[4]Chapter Two, "Death in the Fog," *The Maltese Falcon* (New York: Knopf, 1929).

In Hammett's novel, this sentence comes at a moment of crisis: just after Spade has been roused from bed in the middle of the night by a phone call telling him that his partner has been murdered. Even in time of stress (we infer) Spade is deliberate, cool, efficient, and painstaking. Hammett refrains from applying all those adjectives to Spade; to do so would be to exercise editorial omniscience and to destroy the objective point of view.

Besides the common points of view just listed, uncommon points of view are possible. In *Flush*, a fictional biography of Elizabeth Barrett Browning, Virginia Woolf employs an unusual observer as narrator: the poet's pet cocker spaniel. In "The Circular Valley," a short story by Paul Bowles, a man and a woman are watched by a sinister spirit trying to take possession of them, and we see the human characters through the spirit's vague consciousness. Possible also, but unusual, is a story written in the second person, *you*. This point of view results in an attention-getting directness, as in Jay McInerney's novel *Bright Lights, Big City* (1985), which begins:

> You are not the kind of guy who would be at a place like this at this time of the morning. But here you are, and you cannot say that the terrain is entirely unfamiliar, although the details are fuzzy. You are at a nightclub talking to a girl with a shaved head.

This arresting way to tell a story is effective, too, in a novel by Carlos Fuentes, *Aura* (1962), in some startling stories by Lorrie Moore in *Self-Help* (1985), and in a popular line of juvenile paperbound books, "The Adventures of You Series."[5]

The attitudes and opinions of a narrator aren't necessarily those of the author; in fact, we may notice a lively conflict between what we are told and what, apparently, we are meant to believe. A story may be told by an **innocent narrator** or a **naive narrator,** a character who fails to understand all the implications of the story. One such innocent narrator (despite his sometimes shrewd perceptions) is Huckleberry Finn. Because Huck accepts without question the morality and lawfulness of slavery, he feels guilty about helping Jim, a runaway slave. But, far from condemning Huck for his defiance of the law—"All right, then, I'll *go* to hell," Huck tells himself, deciding against returning Jim to captivity—the author, and the reader along with him, silently applaud. Naive in the extreme is the narrator of one part of William Faulkner's novel *The Sound and the Fury*, the idiot Benjy, a grown man with the intellect of a child. In a story told by an **unreliable narrator,** the point of view is that of a person who, we perceive, is deceptive, self-deceptive, deluded, or deranged. As though seeking ways to be faithful to uncertainty, contemporary writers have been particularly fond of unreliable narrators.

---

[5] Each book starts out with you, the main character, facing some challenge or danger. Then you are offered a choice: "Will you leap forward and struggle with the vampire? Turn to page 20. Will you flee? Turn to page 22." If you choose badly, you may be told, "Suddenly you feel the searing pain of a spear in your back. You sink to the ground—finished for good" (from Edward Packard, *Sugarcane Island* [New York: Pocket, 1978] 60).

Virginia Woolf compared life to "a luminous halo, a semi-transparent envelope surrounding us from the beginning of consciousness to the end."[6] To capture such a reality, modern writers of fiction have employed many strategies. One is the method of writing called **stream of consciousness,** from a phrase coined by psychologist William James to describe the procession of thoughts passing through the mind. In fiction, the stream of consciousness is a kind of selective omniscience: the presentation of thoughts and sense impressions in a lifelike fashion—not in a sequence arranged by logic, but mingled randomly. When in his novel *Ulysses* James Joyce takes us into the mind of Leopold Bloom, an ordinary Dublin mind well-stocked with trivia and fragments of odd learning, the reader may have an impression not of a smoothly flowing stream but of an ocean of miscellaneous things, all crowded and jostling.

> As he set foot on O'Connell bridge a puffball of smoke plumed up from the parapet. Brewery barge with export stout. England. Sea air sours it, I heard. Be interesting some day to get a pass through Hancock to see the brewery. Regular world in itself. Vats of porter, wonderful. Rats get in too. Drink themselves bloated as big as a collie floating.[7]

Perceptions—such as the smoke from the brewery barge—trigger Bloom's reflections. A moment later, as he casts a crumpled paper ball off the bridge, he recalls a bit of science he learned in school, the rate of speed of a falling body: "thirty-two feet per sec."

Stream-of-consciousness writing usually occurs in relatively short passages, but in *Ulysses* Joyce employs it extensively. Similar in method, an **interior monologue** is an extended presentation of a character's thoughts, not in the seemingly helter-skelter order of a stream of consciousness, but in an arrangement as if the character were speaking out loud to himself, for us to overhear. A famous interior monologue comes at the end of *Ulysses* when Joyce gives us the rambling memories and reflections of earth-mother Molly Bloom.

Every point of view has limitations. Even **total omniscience,** a knowledge of the minds of all the characters, has its disadvantages. Such a point of view requires high skill to manage, without the storyteller's losing his way in a multitude of perspectives. In fact, there are evident advantages in having a narrator not know everything. We are accustomed to seeing the world through one pair of eyes, to having truths gradually occur to us. Henry James, whose theory and practice of fiction have been influential, held that an excellent way to tell a story was through the fine but bewildered mind of an observer. "It seems probable," James wrote, "that if we were never bewildered there would never be a story to tell about us; we should partake of the superior nature of the all-knowing immortals whose annals are dreadfully dull so long as flurried humans are not, for the positive relief of bored Olympians, mixed up with them."[8]

---

[6]"Modern Fiction," in *Collected Essays* (New York: Harcourt, 1967).
[7]*Ulysses* (New York: Random, 1934) 150.
[8]Preface to *The Princess Casamassima,* reprinted in *The Art of the Novel,* ed. R. P. Blackmur (New York: Scribner's, 1934).

By using a particular point of view, an author may artfully withhold information, if need be, rather than immediately present it to us. If, for instance, the suspense in a story depends upon our not knowing until the end that the protagonist is a secret agent, the author would be ill advised to tell the story from the protagonist's point of view. If a character acts as the narrator, the author must make sure that the character possesses (or can obtain) enough information to tell the story adequately. Clearly, the author makes a fundamental decision in selecting, from many possibilities, a story's point of view. What we readers admire, if the story is effective, is not only skill in execution, but also judicious choice.

Here is a short story memorable for many reasons, among them its point of view.

## William Faulkner

A ROSE FOR EMILY                                                                                    1931

*William Faulkner (1897–1962) spent most of his days in Oxford, Mississippi, where he attended the University of Mississippi and where he served as postmaster until angry townspeople ejected him after they had long failed to receive mail. During World War I he served with the Royal Canadian Air Force and afterward worked as a feature writer for the New Orleans Times-Picayune. Faulkner's private life was a long struggle to stay solvent: even after fame came to him, he had to write Hollywood scripts and teach at the University of Virginia. The violent comic novel* Sanctuary *(1931) caused a stir and turned a profit, but critics tend most to admire* The

*William Faulkner*

Sound and the Fury *(1929), a tale partially told through the eyes of an idiot;* As I Lay Dying *(1930);* Light in August *(1932);* Absalom, Absalom *(1936); and* The Hamlet *(1940). Beginning with* Sartoris *(1929), Faulkner in his fiction imagines a Mississippi county named Yoknapatawpha and traces the fortunes of several of its families, including the aristocratic Compsons and Sartorises and the white-trash, dollar-grabbing Snopeses, from the Civil War to modern times. His influence on his fellow Southern writers (and others) has been profound. In 1950 he received the Nobel Prize for Literature with a stirring speech (quoted on pages 575–576). Although we think of Faulkner primarily as a novelist, he wrote nearly a hundred short stories. Forty-two of the best are available in his* Collected Stories *(1950).*

# I

When Miss Emily Grierson died, our whole town went to her funeral: the men through a sort of respectful affection for a fallen monument, the women mostly out of curiosity to see the inside of her house, which no one save an old manservant—a combined gardener and cook—had seen in at least ten years.

It was a big, squarish frame house that had once been white, decorated with cupolas and spires and scrolled balconies in the heavily lightsome style of the seventies, set on what had once been our most select street. But garages and cotton gins had encroached and obliterated even the august names of that neighborhood; only Miss Emily's house was left, lifting its stubborn and coquettish decay above the cotton wagons and the gasoline pumps—an eyesore among eyesores. And now Miss Emily had gone to join the representatives of those august names where they lay in the cedar-bemused cemetery among the ranked and anonymous graves of Union and Confederate soldiers who fell at the battle of Jefferson.

Alive, Miss Emily had been a tradition, a duty, and a care; a sort of hereditary obligation upon the town, dating from that day in 1894 when Colonel Sartoris, the mayor—he who fathered the edict that no Negro woman should appear on the streets without an apron—remitted her taxes, the dispensation dating from the death of her father on into perpetuity. Not that Miss Emily would have accepted charity. Colonel Sartoris invented an involved tale to the effect that Miss Emily's father had loaned money to the town, which the town, as a matter of business, preferred this way of repaying. Only a man of Colonel Sartoris' generation and thought could have invented it, and only a woman could have believed it.

When the next generation, with its more modern ideas, became mayors and aldermen, this arrangement created some little dissatisfaction. On the first of the year they mailed her a tax notice. February came, and there was no reply. They wrote her a formal letter, asking her to call at the sheriff's office at her convenience. A week later the mayor wrote her himself, offering to call or to send his car for her, and received in reply a note on paper of an archaic shape, in a thin, flowing calligraphy in faded ink, to the effect that she no longer went out at all. The tax notice was also enclosed, without comment.

They called a special meeting of the Board of Aldermen. A deputation waited upon her, knocked at the door through which no visitor had passed since she ceased giving china-painting lessons eight or ten years earlier. They were admitted by the old Negro into a dim hall from which a stairway mounted into still more shadow. It smelled of dust and disuse—a close, dank smell. The Negro led them into the parlor. It was furnished in heavy, leather-covered furniture. When the Negro opened the blinds of one window, they could see that the leather was cracked; and when they sat down, a faint dust rose sluggishly about their thighs, spinning with slow motes in the single sun-ray. On a tarnished gilt easel before the fireplace stood a crayon portrait of Miss Emily's father.

They rose when she entered—a small, fat woman in black, with a thin gold chain descending to her waist and vanishing into her belt, leaning on an ebony

5

cane with a tarnished gold head. Her skeleton was small and spare; perhaps that was why what would have been merely plumpness in another was obesity in her. She looked bloated, like a body long submerged in motionless water, and of that pallid hue. Her eyes, lost in the fatty ridges of her face, looked like two small pieces of coal pressed into a lump of dough as they moved from one face to another while the visitors stated their errand.

She did not ask them to sit. She just stood in the door and listened quietly until the spokesman came to a stumbling halt. Then they could hear the invisible watch ticking at the end of the gold chain.

Her voice was dry and cold. "I have no taxes in Jefferson. Colonel Sartoris explained it to me. Perhaps one of you can gain access to the city records and satisfy yourselves."

"But we have. We are the city authorities, Miss Emily. Didn't you get a notice from the sheriff, signed by him?"

"I received a paper, yes," Miss Emily said. "Perhaps he considers himself the     10
sheriff . . . I have no taxes in Jefferson."

"But there is nothing on the books to show that, you see. We must go by the—"

"See Colonel Sartoris. I have no taxes in Jefferson."

"But, Miss Emily—"

"See Colonel Sartoris." (Colonel Sartoris had been dead almost ten years.) "I have no taxes in Jefferson. Tobe!" The Negro appeared. "Show these gentlemen out."

## II

So she vanquished them, horse and foot, just as she had vanquished their     15
fathers thirty years before about the smell. That was two years after her father's death and a short time after her sweetheart—the one we believed would marry her—had deserted her. After her father's death she went out very little; after her sweetheart went away, people hardly saw her at all. A few of the ladies had the temerity to call, but were not received, and the only sign of life about the place was the Negro man—a young man then—going in and out with a market basket.

"Just as if a man—any man—could keep a kitchen properly," the ladies said; so they were not surprised when the smell developed. It was another link between the gross, teeming world and the high and mighty Griersons.

A neighbor, a woman, complained to the mayor, Judge Stevens, eighty years old.

"But what will you have me do about it, madam?" he said.

"Why, send her word to stop it," the woman said. "Isn't there a law?"

"I'm sure that won't be necessary," Judge Stevens said. "It's probably just a     20
snake or a rat that nigger of hers killed in the yard. I'll speak to him about it."

The next day he received two more complaints, one from a man who came in diffident deprecation. "We really must do something about it, Judge. I'd be the last one in the world to bother Miss Emily, but we've got to do something." That night the Board of Aldermen met—three graybeards and one younger man, a member of the rising generation.

"It's simple enough," he said. "Send her word to have her place cleaned up. Give her a certain time to do it in, and if she don't . . ."

"Dammit, sir," Judge Stevens said, "will you accuse a lady to her face of smelling bad?"

So the next night, after midnight, four men crossed Miss Emily's lawn and slunk about the house like burglars, sniffing along the base of the brickwork and at the cellar openings while one of them performed a regular sowing motion with his hand out of a sack slung from his shoulder. They broke open the cellar door and sprinkled lime there, and in all the outbuildings. As they recrossed the lawn, a window that had been dark was lighted and Miss Emily sat in it, the light behind her, and her upright torso motionless as that of an idol. They crept quietly across the lawn and into the shadow of the locusts that lined the street. After a week or two the smell went away.

That was when people had begun to feel really sorry for her. People in our town, remembering how old lady Wyatt, her great-aunt, had gone completely crazy at last, believed that the Griersons held themselves a little too high for what they really were. None of the young men were quite good enough for Miss Emily and such. We had long thought of them as a tableau, Miss Emily a slender figure in white in the background, her father a spraddled silhouette in the foreground, his back to her and clutching a horsewhip, the two of them framed by the back-flung front door. So when she got to be thirty and was still single, we were not pleased exactly, but vindicated; even with insanity in the family she wouldn't have turned down all of her chances if they had really materialized.

When her father died, it got about that the house was all that was left to her; and in a way, people were glad. At last they could pity Miss Emily. Being left alone, and a pauper, she had become humanized. Now she too would know the old thrill and the old despair of a penny more or less.

The day after his death all the ladies prepared to call at the house and offer condolence and aid, as is our custom. Miss Emily met them at the door, dressed as usual and with no trace of grief on her face. She told them that her father was not dead. She did that for three days, with the ministers calling on her, and the doctors, trying to persuade her to let them dispose of the body. Just as they were about to resort to law and force, she broke down, and they buried her father quickly.

We did not say she was crazy then. We believed she had to do that. We remembered all the young men her father had driven away, and we knew that with nothing left, she would have to cling to that which had robbed her, as people will.

### III

She was sick for a long time. When we saw her again, her hair was cut short, making her look like a girl, with a vague resemblance to those angels in colored church windows—sort of tragic and serene.

The town had just let the contracts for paving the sidewalks, and in the summer after her father's death they began the work. The construction company came with niggers and mules and machinery, and a foreman named Homer Barron, a Yankee—a big, dark, ready man, with a big voice and eyes lighter than his face. The little boys would follow in groups to hear him cuss the niggers, and the niggers singing in time to the rise and fall of picks. Pretty soon he knew everybody in town. Whenever you heard a lot of laughing anywhere about the square, Homer Barron would be in the center of the group. Presently we began to see him and Miss Emily on Sunday afternoons driving in the yellow-wheeled buggy and the matched team of bays from the livery stable.

At first we were glad that Miss Emily would have an interest, because the ladies all said, "Of course a Grierson would not think seriously of a Northerner, a day laborer." But there were still others, older people, who said that even grief could not cause a real lady to forget noblesse oblige°—without calling it noblesse oblige. They just said, "Poor Emily. Her kinsfolk should come to her." She had some kin in Alabama; but years ago her father had fallen out with them over the estate of old lady Wyatt, the crazy woman, and there was no communication between the two families. They had not even been represented at the funeral.

And as soon as the old people said, "Poor Emily," the whispering began. "Do you suppose it's really so?" they said to one another. "Of course it is. What else could . . . " This behind their hands; rustling of craned silk and satin behind jalousies closed upon the sun of Sunday afternoon as the thin, swift clop-clop-clop of the matched team passed: "Poor Emily."

She carried her head high enough—even when we believed that she was fallen. It was as if she demanded more than ever the recognition of her dignity as the last Grierson; as if it had wanted that touch of earthiness to reaffirm her imperviousness. Like when she bought the rat poison, the arsenic. That was over a year after they had begun to say "Poor Emily," and while the two female cousins were visiting her.

"I want some poison," she said to the druggist. She was over thirty then, still a slight woman, though thinner than usual, with cold, haughty black eyes in a face the flesh of which was strained across the temples and about the eye-sockets as you imagine a lighthouse-keeper's face ought to look. "I want some poison," she said.

"Yes, Miss Emily. What kind? For rats and such? I'd recom—"

"I want the best you have. I don't care what kind."

The druggist named several. "They'll kill anything up to an elephant. But what you want is—"

"Arsenic," Miss Emily said. "Is that a good one?"

"Is . . . arsenic? Yes, ma'am. But what you want—"

"I want arsenic."

The druggist looked down at her. She looked back at him, erect, her face like a strained flag. "Why, of course," the druggist said. "If that's what you want. But the law requires you to tell what you are going to use it for."

---

noblesse oblige: the obligation of a member of the nobility to behave with honor and dignity.

Miss Emily just stared at him, her head tilted back in order to look him eye for eye, until he looked away and went and got the arsenic and wrapped it up. The Negro delivery boy brought her the package; the druggist didn't come back. When she opened the package at home there was written on the box, under the skull and bones: "For rats."

## IV

So the next day we all said, "She will kill herself"; and we said it would be the best thing. When she had first begun to be seen with Homer Barron, we had said, "She will marry him." Then we said, "She will persuade him yet," because Homer himself had remarked—he liked men, and it was known that he drank with the younger men in the Elks' Club—that he was not a marrying man. Later we said, "Poor Emily," behind the jalousies as they passed on Sunday afternoon in the glittering buggy, Miss Emily with her head high and Homer Barron with his hat cocked and a cigar in his teeth, reins and whip in a yellow glove.

Then some of the ladies began to say that it was a disgrace to the town and a bad example to the young people. The men did not want to interfere, but at last the ladies forced the Baptist minister—Miss Emily's people were Episcopal—to call upon her. He would never divulge what happened during that interview, but he refused to go back again. The next Sunday they again drove about the streets, and the following day the minister's wife wrote to Miss Emily's relations in Alabama.

So she had blood-kin under her roof again and we sat back to watch developments. At first nothing happened. Then we were sure that they were to be married. We learned that Miss Emily had been to the jeweler's and ordered a man's toilet set in silver, with the letters H.B. on each piece. Two days later we learned that she had bought a complete outfit of men's clothing, including a nightshirt, and we said, "They are married." We were really glad. We were glad because the two female cousins were even more Grierson than Miss Emily had ever been.

So we were not surprised when Homer Barron—the streets had been finished some time since—was gone. We were a little disappointed that there was not a public blowing-off, but we believed that he had gone on to prepare for Miss Emily's coming, or to give her a chance to get rid of the cousins. (By that time it was a cabal, and we were all Miss Emily's allies to help circumvent the cousins.) Sure enough, after another week they departed. And, as we had expected all along, within three days Homer Barron was back in town. A neighbor saw the Negro man admit him at the kitchen door at dusk one evening.

And that was the last we saw of Homer Barron. And of Miss Emily for some time. The Negro man went in and out with the market basket, but the front door remained closed. Now and then we would see her at a window for a moment, as the men did that night when they sprinkled the lime, but for almost six months she did not appear on the streets. Then we knew that this was to be expected too;

as if that quality of her father which had thwarted her women's life so many times had been too virulent and too furious to die.

When we next saw Miss Emily, she had grown fat and her hair was turning gray. During the next few years it grew grayer and grayer until it attained an even pepper-and-salt iron-gray, when it ceased turning. Up to the day of her death at seventy-four it was still that vigorous iron-gray, like the hair of an active man.

From that time on her front door remained closed, save for a period of six or seven years, when she was about forty, during which she gave lessons in china-painting. She fitted up a studio in one of the downstairs rooms, where the daughters and granddaughters of Colonel Sartoris' contemporaries were sent to her with the same regularity and in the same spirit that they were sent to church on Sundays with a twenty-five-cent piece for the collection plate. Meanwhile her taxes had been remitted.

Then the newer generation became the backbone and the spirit of the town, and the painting pupils grew up and fell away and did not send their children to her with boxes of color and tedious brushes and pictures cut from the ladies' magazines. The front door closed upon the last one and remained closed for good. When the town got free postal delivery, Miss Emily alone refused to let them fasten the metal numbers above her door and attach a mailbox to it. She would not listen to them.

Daily, monthly, yearly we watched the Negro grow grayer and more stooped, going in and out with the market basket. Each December we sent her a tax notice, which would be returned by the post office a week later, unclaimed. Now and then we would see her in one of the downstairs windows—she had evidently shut up the top floor of the house—like the carven torso of an idol in a niche, looking or not looking at us, we could never tell which. Thus she passed from generation to generation—dear, inescapable, impervious, tranquil, and perverse.

And so she died. Fell ill in the house filled with dust and shadows, with only a doddering Negro man to wait on her. We did not even know she was sick; we had long since given up trying to get any information from the Negro. He talked to no one, probably not even to her, for his voice had grown harsh and rusty, as if from disuse.

She died in one of the downstairs rooms, in a heavy walnut bed with a curtain, her gray head propped on a pillow yellow and moldy with age and lack of sunlight.

V

The Negro met the first of the ladies at the front door and let them in, with their hushed, sibilant voices and their quick, curious glances, and then he disappeared. He walked right through the house and out the back and was not seen again.

The two female cousins came at once. They held the funeral on the second day, with the town coming to look at Miss Emily beneath a mass of bought flowers, with the crayon face of her father musing profoundly above the bier and the

50

55

ladies sibilant and macabre; and the very old men—some in their brushed Confederate uniforms—on the porch and the lawn, talking of Miss Emily as if she had been a contemporary of theirs, believing that they had danced with her and courted her perhaps, confusing time with its mathematical progression, as the old do, to whom all the past is not a diminishing road but, instead, a huge meadow which no winter ever quite touches, divided from them now by the narrow bottleneck of the most recent decade of years.

Already we knew that there was one room in that region above stairs which no one had seen in forty years, and which would have to be forced. They waited until Miss Emily was decently in the ground before they opened it.

The violence of breaking down the door seemed to fill this room with pervading dust. A thin, acrid pall as of the tomb seemed to lie everywhere upon this room decked and furnished as for a bridal: upon the valance curtains of faded rose color, upon the rose-shaded lights, upon the dressing table, upon the delicate array of crystal and the man's toilet things backed with tarnished silver, silver so tarnished that the monogram was obscured. Among them lay collar and tie, as if they had just been removed, which, lifted, left upon the surface a pale crescent in the dust. Upon a chair hung the suit, carefully folded; beneath it the two mute shoes and the discarded socks.

The man himself lay in the bed.

For a long while we just stood there, looking down at the profound and fleshless grin. The body had apparently once lain in the attitude of an embrace, but now the long sleep that outlasts love, that conquers even the grimace of love, had cuckolded him. What was left of him, rotted beneath what was left of the nightshirt, had become inextricable from the bed in which he lay; and upon him and upon the pillow beside him lay that even coating of the patient and biding dust.

Then we noticed that in the second pillow was the indentation of a head. 60 One of us lifted something from it, and leaning forward, that faint and invisible dust dry and acrid in the nostrils, we saw a long strand of iron-gray hair.

## Questions

1. What is meaningful in the final detail that the strand of hair on the second pillow is *iron-gray?*
2. Who is the unnamed narrator? For whom does he profess to be speaking?
3. Why does "A Rose for Emily" seem better told from his point of view than if it were told (like John Updike's "A & P") from the point of view of the main character?
4. What foreshadowings of the discovery of the body of Homer Barron are we given earlier in the story? Share your experience in reading "A Rose for Emily": did the foreshadowings give away the ending for you? Did they heighten your interest?
5. What contrasts does the narrator draw between changing reality and Emily's refusal or inability to recognize change?
6. How do the character and background of Emily Grierson differ from those of Homer Barron? What general observations about the society that Faulkner depicts can be made from his portraits of these two characters and from his account of life in this one Mississippi town?
7. Does the story seem to you totally grim, or do you find any humor in it?
8. What do you infer to be the author's attitude toward Emily Grierson? Is she simply a murderous madwoman? Why do you suppose Faulkner calls his story "A Rose. . . "?

## MISS BRILL 1922

*Katherine Mansfield Beauchamp (1888–1923), who shortened her byline, was born into a sedate Victorian family in New Zealand, daughter of a successful businessman. At fifteen she emigrated to England to attend school and did not ever permanently return Down Under. In 1918, after a time of wild-oat sowing in bohemian London, she married the journalist and critic John Middleton Murray. All at once, Mansfield found herself struggling to define her sexual identity, to earn a living by her pen, to endure World War I (in which her brother was killed in action), and to survive the ravages of tuberculosis. She died at thirty-four, in France, at a spiritualist com-*

*Katherine Mansfield*

*mune where she had sought to regain her health. Mansfield wrote no novels, but during her brief career concentrated on the short story, in which form of art she has few peers. Bliss (1920) and The Garden-Party and Other Stories (1922) were greeted with an acclaim that has continued; her Short Stories were collected in 1937. Some celebrate life, others wryly poke fun at it. Many reveal, in ordinary lives, small incidents that open like doorways into significances.*

Although it was so brilliantly fine—the blue sky powdered with gold and great spots of light like white wine splashed over the Jardins Publiques—Miss Brill was glad that she had decided on her fur. The air was motionless, but when you opened your mouth there was just a faint chill, like a chill from a glass of iced water before you sip, and now and again a leaf came drifting—from nowhere, from the sky. Miss Brill put up her hand and touched her fur. Dear little thing! It was nice to feel it again. She had taken it out of its box that afternoon, shaken out the moth-powder, given it a good brush, and rubbed the life back into the dim little eyes. "What has been happening to me?" said the sad little eyes. Oh, how sweet it was to see them snap at her again from the red eiderdown! . . . But the nose, which was of some black composition, wasn't at all firm. It must have had a knock, somehow. Never mind—a little dab of black sealing-wax when the time came—when it was absolutely necessary. . . . Little rogue! Yes, she really felt like that about it. Little rogue biting its tail just by her left ear. She could have taken it off and laid it on her lap and stroked it. She felt a tingling in her hands and arms, but that came from walking, she supposed. And when she breathed, something light and sad—no, not sad, exactly—something gentle seemed to move in her bosom.

There were a number of people out this afternoon, far more than last Sunday. And the band sounded louder and gayer. That was because the Season had begun. For although the band played all year round on Sundays, out of season it was never the same. It was like some one playing with only the family to listen; it didn't care how it played if there weren't any strangers present. Wasn't the conductor wearing a new coat, too? She was sure it was new. He scraped with his foot and flapped his arms like a rooster about to crow, and the bandsmen sitting in the green rotunda blew out their cheeks and glared at the music. Now there came a little "flutey" bit—very pretty!—a little chain of bright drops. She was sure it would be repeated. It was; she lifted her head and smiled.

Only two people shared her "special" seat: a fine old man in a velvet coat, his hands clasped over a huge carved walking-stick, and a big old woman, sitting upright, with a roll of knitting on her embroidered apron. They did not speak. This was disappointing, for Miss Brill always looked forward to the conversation. She had become really quite expert, she thought, at listening as though she didn't listen, at sitting in other people's lives just for a minute while they talked round her.

She glanced, sideways, at the old couple. Perhaps they would go soon. Last Sunday, too, hadn't been as interesting as usual. An Englishman and his wife, he wearing a dreadful Panama hat and she button boots. And she'd gone on the whole time about how she ought to wear spectacles; she knew she needed them; but that it was no good getting any; they'd be sure to break and they'd never keep on. And he'd been so patient. He'd suggested everything—gold rims, the kind that curved round your ears, little pads inside the bridge. No, nothing would please her. "They'll always be sliding down my nose!" Miss Brill wanted to shake her.

The old people sat on the bench, still as statues. Never mind, there was always the crowd to watch. To and fro, in front of the flower-beds and the band rotunda, the couples and groups paraded, stopped to talk, to greet, to buy a handful of flowers from the old beggar who had his tray fixed to the railings. Little children ran among them, swooping and laughing; little boys with big white silk bows under their chins, little girls, little French dolls, dressed up in velvet and lace. And sometimes a tiny staggerer came suddenly rocking into the open from under the trees, stopped, stared, as suddenly sat down "flop," until its small high-stepping mother, like a young hen, rushed scolding to its rescue. Other people sat on the benches and green chairs, but they were nearly always the same, Sunday after Sunday, and—Miss Brill had often noticed—there was something funny about nearly all of them. They were odd, silent, nearly all old, and from the way they stared they looked as though they'd just come from dark little rooms or even—even cupboards!

Behind the rotunda the slender trees with yellow leaves down drooping, and through them just a line of sea, and beyond the blue sky with gold-veined clouds.

Tum-tum-tum tiddle-um! tiddle-um! tum tiddley-um tum ta! blew the band.

Two young girls in red came by and two young soldiers in blue met them, and they laughed and paired and went off arm-in-arm. Two peasant women with funny straw hats passed, gravely, leading beautiful smoke-colored donkeys. A cold, pale nun hurried by. A beautiful woman came along and dropped her bunch of violets, and a little boy ran after to hand them to her, and she took them and threw them away as if they'd been poisoned. Dear me! Miss Brill didn't know whether to admire that or not! And now an ermine toque and a gentleman in grey met just in front of her. He was tall, stiff, dignified, and she was wearing the ermine toque she'd bought when her hair was yellow. Now everything, her hair, her face, even her eyes, was the same color as the shabby ermine, and her hand, in its cleaned glove, lifted to dab her lips, was a tiny yellowish paw. Oh, she was so pleased to see him—delighted! She rather thought they were going to meet that afternoon. She described where she'd been—everywhere, here, there, along by the sea. The day was so charming—didn't he agree? And wouldn't he, perhaps? . . . But he shook his head, lighted a cigarette, slowly breathed a great deep puff into her face, and, even while she was still talking and laughing, flicked the match away and walked on. The ermine toque was alone; she smiled more brightly than ever. But even the band seemed to know what she was feeling and played more softly, played tenderly, and the drum beat, "The Brute! The Brute!" over and over. What would she do? What was going to happen now? But as Miss Brill wondered, the ermine toque turned, raised her hand as though she'd seen some one else, much nicer, just over there, and pattered away. And the band changed again and played more quickly, more gaily than ever, and the old couple on Miss Brill's seat got up and marched away, and such a funny old man with long whiskers hobbled along in time to the music and was nearly knocked over by four girls walking abreast.

Oh, how fascinating it was! How she enjoyed it! How she loved sitting here, watching it all! It was like a play. It was exactly like a play. Who could believe the sky at the back wasn't painted? But it wasn't till a little brown dog trotted on solemn and then slowly trotted off, like a little "theatre" dog, a little dog that had been drugged, that Miss Brill discovered what it was that made it so exciting. They were all on the stage. They weren't only the audience, not only looking on; they were acting. Even she had a part and came every Sunday. No doubt somebody would have noticed if she hadn't been there; she was part of the performance after all. How strange she'd never thought of it like that before! And yet it explained why she made such a point of starting from home at just the same time each week—so as not to be late for the performance—and it also explained why she had quite a queer, shy feeling at telling her English pupils how she spent her Sunday afternoons. No wonder! Miss Brill nearly laughed out loud. She was on the stage. She thought of the old invalid gentleman to whom she read the newspaper four afternoons a week while he slept in the garden. She had got quite used to the frail head on the cotton pillow, the hollowed eyes, the open mouth and the high pinched nose. If he'd been dead she mightn't have noticed for weeks; she wouldn't have minded. But suddenly he knew he was having the paper read to him by an actress! "An actress!" The old head lifted; two points of light quivered in the old eyes. "An actress—are ye?" And Miss Brill smoothed the newspaper as though it were the manuscript of her part and said gently: "Yes, I have been an actress for a long time."

The band had been having a rest. Now they started again. And what they played was warm, sunny, yet there was just a faint chill—a something, what was it?—not sadness—no, not sadness—a something that made you want to sing. The tune lifted, lifted, the light shone; and it seemed to Miss Brill that in another moment all of them, all the whole company, would begin singing. The young ones, the laughing ones who were moving together, they would begin, and the men's voices, very resolute and brave, would join them. And then she too, she too, and the others on the benches—they would come in with a kind of accompaniment—something low, that scarcely rose or fell, something so beautiful—moving. . . . And Miss Brill's eyes filled with tears and she looked smiling at all the other members of the company. Yes, we understand, we understand, she thought—though what they understood she didn't know.

Just at that moment a boy and a girl came and sat down where the old couple had been. They were beautifully dressed; they were in love. The hero and heroine, of course, just arrived from his father's yacht. And still soundlessly singing, still with that trembling smile, Miss Brill prepared to listen.

"No, not now," said the girl. "Not here, I can't."

"But why? Because of that stupid old thing at the end there?" asked the boy. "Why does she come here at all—who wants her? Why doesn't she keep her silly old mug at home?"

"It's her fu-fur which is so funny," giggled the girl. "It's exactly like a fried whiting."

"Ah, be off with you!" said the boy in an angry whisper. Then: "Tell me, my petite chérie—"

"No, not here," said the girl. "Not yet."

On her way home she usually bought a slice of honeycake at the baker's. It was her Sunday treat. Sometimes there was an almond in her slice, sometimes not. It made a great difference. If there was an almond it was like carrying home a tiny present—a surprise—something that might very well not have been there. She hurried on the almond Sundays and struck the match for the kettle in quite a dashing way.

But to-day she passed the baker's boy, climbed the stairs, went into the little dark room—her room like a cupboard—and sat down on the red eiderdown. She sat there for a long time. The box that the fur came out of was on the bed. She unclasped the necklet quickly; quickly, without looking, laid it inside. But when she put the lid on she thought she heard something crying.

## QUESTIONS

1. What is the point of view in "Miss Brill"? Why is the story the better for this method of telling?
2. Where and in what season does Mansfield's story take place? How do we know? Would the effect be the same if the story were set, say, in a remote Alaskan village in the summertime?

3. What details provide revealing insights into Miss Brill's character and lifestyle?
4. What draws Miss Brill to the park every Sunday? What is the nature of the startling revelation that delights her on the day this story takes place?
5. Comment on the last line. What possible explanations might there be for Miss Brill's thinking that she "heard something crying"?
6. See Katherine Mansfield's comment on the writing of "Miss Brill" (page 575). Then indicate—and read aloud—any passage or passages in the story that, you believe, illustrate what she was striving for.

## James Baldwin

SONNY'S BLUES                                                                          1957

*James Baldwin (1924–1987) was born in Harlem, in New York City. His father was a Pentecostal minister, and the young Baldwin initially planned to become a clergyman. While still in high school, he preached sermons in a storefront church. At seventeen, however, Baldwin left home to live in Greenwich Village, where he worked at menial jobs and began publishing articles in* Commentary *and* The Nation. *Later he embarked on a series of travels that eventually brought him to France. Baldwin soon regarded France as a second home, a country in which he could avoid the racial discrimination he felt in America. Baldwin's first novel,* Go Tell It on the Mountain*

*James Baldwin*

(1953), which described a single day in the lives of the members of a Harlem church, immediately earned him a position as a leading African-American writer. His next two novels,* Giovanni's Room (1956) *and* Another Country (1962), *dealt with homosexual themes and drew criticism from some of his early champions. His collection of essays,* Notes of a Native Son (1955), *remains one of the key books of the civil rights movement. His short stories were not collected until* Going to Meet the Man *was published in 1965. Although he spent nearly forty years in France, Baldwin still considered himself an American. He was not an expatriate, he claimed, but a "commuter." He died in St. Paul de Vence, France, but was buried in Ardsley, New York.*

I read about it in the paper, in the subway, on my way to work. I read it, and I couldn't believe it, and I read it again. Then perhaps I just stared at it, at the newsprint spelling out his name, spelling out the story. I stared at it in the swinging lights of the subway car, and in the faces and bodies of the people, and in my own face, trapped in the darkness which roared outside.

It was not to be believed and I kept telling myself that, as I walked from the subway station to the high school. And at the same time I couldn't doubt it. I was scared, scared for Sonny. He became real to me again. A great block of ice got settled in my belly and kept melting there slowly all day long, while I taught my classes algebra. It was a special kind of ice. It kept melting, sending trickles of ice water all up and down my veins, but it never got less. Sometimes it hardened and seemed to expand until I felt my guts were going to come spilling out or that I was going to choke or scream. This would always be at a moment when I was remembering some specific thing Sonny had once said or done.

When he was about as old as the boys in my classes his face had been bright and open, there was a lot of copper in it; and he'd had wonderfully direct brown eyes, and great gentleness and privacy. I wondered what he looked like now. He had been picked up, the evening before, in a raid on an apartment downtown, for peddling and using heroin.

I couldn't believe it: but what I mean by that is that I couldn't find any room for it anywhere inside me. I had kept it outside me for a long time. I hadn't wanted to know. I had had suspicions, but I didn't name them, I kept putting them away. I told myself that Sonny was wild, but he wasn't crazy. And he'd always been a good boy, he hadn't ever turned hard or evil or disrespectful, the way kids can, so quick, so quick, especially in Harlem. I didn't want to believe that I'd ever see my brother going down, coming to nothing, all that light in his face gone out, in the condition I'd already seen so many others. Yet it had happened and here I was, talking about algebra to a lot of boys who might, every one of them for all I knew, be popping off needles every time they went to the head. Maybe it did more for them than algebra could.

I was sure that the first time Sonny had ever had horse,° he couldn't have     5
been much older than these boys were now. These boys, now, were living as we'd been living then, they were growing up with a rush and their heads bumped abruptly against the low ceiling of their actual possibilities. They were filled with rage. All they really knew were two darknesses, the darkness of their lives, which was now closing in on them, and the darkness of the movies, which had blinded them to that other darkness, and in which they now, vindictively, dreamed, at once more together than they were at any other time, and more alone.

When the last bell rang, the last class ended, I let out my breath. It seemed I'd been holding it for all that time. My clothes were wet—I may have looked as though I'd been sitting in a steam bath, all dressed up, all afternoon. I sat alone in the classroom a long time. I listened to the boys outside, downstairs, shouting and cursing and laughing. Their laughter struck me for perhaps the first time. It was not the joyous laughter which—God knows why—one associates with children. It was mocking and insular, its intent to denigrate. It was disenchanted, and in this, also, lay the authority of their curses. Perhaps I was listening to them because I was thinking about my brother and in them I heard my brother. And myself.

*horse:* heroin.

One boy was whistling a tune, at once very complicated and very simple, it seemed to be pouring out of him as though he were a bird, and it sounded very cool and moving through all that harsh, bright air, only just holding its own through all those other sounds.

I stood up and walked over to the window and looked down into the courtyard. It was the beginning of the spring and the sap was rising in the boys. A teacher passed through them every now and again, quickly, as though he or she couldn't wait to get out of that courtyard, to get those boys out of their sight and off their minds. I started collecting my stuff. I thought I'd better get home and talk to Isabel.

The courtyard was almost deserted by the time I got downstairs. I saw this boy standing in the shadow of a doorway, looking just like Sonny. I almost called his name. Then I saw that it wasn't Sonny, but somebody we used to know, a boy from around our block. He'd been Sonny's friend. He'd never been mine, having been too young for me, and, anyway, I'd never liked him. And now, even though he was a grown-up man, he still hung around that block, still spent hours on the street corners, was always high and raggy. I used to run into him from time to time and he'd often work around to asking me for a quarter or fifty cents. He always had some real good excuse, too, and I always gave it to him, I don't know why.

But now, abruptly, I hated him. I couldn't stand the way he looked at me,    10
partly like a dog, partly like a cunning child. I wanted to ask him what the hell he was doing in the school courtyard.

He sort of shuffled over to me, and he said, "I see you got the papers. So you already know about it."

"You mean about Sonny? Yes, I already know about it. How come they didn't get you?"

He grinned. It made him repulsive and it also brought to mind what he'd looked like as a kid. "I wasn't there. I stay away from them people."

"Good for you." I offered him a cigarette and I watched him through the smoke. "You come all the way down here just to tell me about Sonny?"

"That's right." He was sort of shaking his head and his eyes looked strange, as    15
though they were about to cross. The bright sun deadened his damp dark brown skin and it made his eyes look yellow and showed up the dirt in his kinked hair. He smelled funky. I moved a little away from him and I said, "Well, thanks. But I already know about it and I got to get home."

"I'll walk you a little ways," he said. We started walking. There were a couple of kids still loitering in the courtyard and one of them said goodnight to me and looked strangely at the boy beside me.

"What're you going to do?" he asked me. "I mean, about Sonny?"

"Look. I haven't seen Sonny for over a year. I'm not sure I'm going to do anything. Anyway, what the hell *can* I do?"

"That's right," he said quickly, "ain't nothing you can do. Can't much help old Sonny no more, I guess."

It was what I was thinking and so it seemed to me he had no right to say it.    20

"I'm surprised at Sonny, though," he went on—he had a funny way of talking, he looked straight ahead as though he were talking to himself—"I thought Sonny was a smart boy, I thought he was too smart to get hung."

"I guess he thought so too," I said sharply, "and that's how he got hung. And how about you? You're pretty goddamn smart, I bet."

Then he looked directly at me, just for a minute. "I ain't smart," he said. "If I was smart, I'd have reached for a pistol a long time ago."

"Look. Don't tell *me* your sad story, if it was up to me, I'd give you one." Then I felt guilty—guilty, probably, for never having supposed that the poor bastard *had* a story of his own, much less a sad one, and I asked, quickly, "What's going to happen to him now?"

He didn't answer this. He was off by himself some place. "Funny thing," he said, and from his tone we might have been discussing the quickest way to get to Brooklyn, "when I saw the papers this morning, the first thing I asked myself was if I had anything to do with it. I felt sort of responsible."

I began to listen more carefully. The subway station was on the corner, just before us, and I stopped. He stopped, too. We were in front of a bar and he ducked slightly, peering in, but whoever he was looking for didn't seem to be there. The juke box was blasting away with something black and bouncy and I half watched the barmaid as she danced her way from the juke box to her place behind the bar. And I watched her face as she laughingly responded to something someone said to her, still keeping time to the music. When she smiled one saw the little girl, one sensed the doomed, still-struggling woman beneath the battered face of the semiwhore.

"I never *give* Sonny nothing," the boy said finally, "but a long time ago I come to school high and Sonny asked me how it felt." He paused, I couldn't bear to watch him, I watched the barmaid, and I listened to the music which seemed to be causing the pavement to shake. "I told him it felt great." The music stopped, the barmaid paused and watched the juke box until the music began again. "It did."

All this was carrying me some place I didn't want to go. I certainly didn't want to know how it felt. It filled everything, the people, the houses, the music, the dark, quicksilver barmaid, with menace; and this menace was their reality.

"What's going to happen to him now?" I asked again.

"They'll send him away some place and they'll try to cure him." He shook his head. "Maybe he'll even think he's kicked the habit. Then they'll let him loose"—he gestured, throwing his cigarette into the gutter. "That's all."

"What do you mean, that's *all*?"

But I knew what he meant.

"I *mean*, that's *all*." He turned his head and looked at me, pulling down the corners of his mouth. "Don't you know what I mean?" he asked, softly.

"How the hell *would* I know what you mean?" I almost whispered it, I don't know why.

"That's right," he said to the air, "how would *he* know what I mean?" He turned toward me again, patient and calm, and yet I somehow felt him shaking, shaking as though he were going to fall apart. I felt that ice in my guts again, the dread I'd felt all afternoon; and again I watched the barmaid, moving about the bar, washing glasses, and singing. "Listen. They'll let him out and then it'll just start all over again. That's what I mean."

"You mean—they'll let him out. And then he'll just start working his way back in again. You mean he'll never kick the habit. Is that what you mean?"

"That's right," he said, cheerfully. "*You* see what I mean."

"Tell me," I said at last, "why does he want to die? He must want to die, he's killing himself, why does he want to die?"

He looked at me in surprise. He licked his lips. "He don't want to die. He wants to live. Don't nobody want to die, ever."

Then I wanted to ask him—too many things. He could not have answered, or if he had, I could not have borne the answers. I started walking. "Well, I guess it's none of my business."

"It's going to be rough on old Sonny," he said. We reached the subway station. "This is your station?" he asked. I nodded. I took one step down. "Damn!" he said, suddenly. I looked up at him. He grinned again. "Damn it if I didn't leave all my money home. You ain't got a dollar on you, have you? Just for a couple of days, is all."

All at once something inside gave and threatened to come pouring out of me. I didn't hate him any more. I felt that in another moment I'd start crying like a child.

"Sure," I said. "Don't sweat." I looked in my wallet and didn't have a dollar, I only had a five. "Here," I said. "That hold you?"

He didn't look at it—he didn't want to look at it. A terrible closed look came over his face, as though he were keeping the number on the bill a secret from him and me. "Thanks," he said, and now he was dying to see me go. "Don't worry about Sonny. Maybe I'll write him or something."

"Sure," I said. "You do that. So long."

"Be seeing you," he said. I went on down the steps.

And I didn't write Sonny or send him anything for a long time. When I finally did, it was just after my little girl died, he wrote me back a letter which made me feel like a bastard.

Here's what he said:

> Dear brother,
> You don't know how much I needed to hear from you. I wanted to write you many a time but I dug how much I must have hurt you and so I didn't write. But now I feel like a man who's been trying to climb up out of some deep, real deep and funky hole and just saw the sun up there, outside. I got to get outside.
> I can't tell you much about how I got here. I mean I don't know how to tell you. I guess I was afraid of something or I was trying to escape from something and you know I have never been very strong in the head (smile). I'm glad Mama and Daddy are dead and can't see what's happened to their son and I swear if I'd known what I was doing I would never have hurt you so, you and a lot of other fine people who were nice to me and who believed in me.

I don't want you to think it had anything to do with me being a musician. It's more than that. Or maybe less than that. I can't get anything straight
in my head down here and I try not to think about what's going to happen to
me when I get outside again. Sometime I think I'm going to flip and *never* get
outside and sometime I think I'll come straight back. I tell you one thing,
though, I'd rather blow my brains out than go through this again. But that's
what they all say, so they tell me. If I tell you when I'm coming to New York
and if you could meet me, I sure would appreciate it. Give my love to Isabel
and the kids and I was sure sorry to hear about little Gracie. I wish I could be
like Mama and say the Lord's will be done, but I don't know it seems to me
that trouble is the one thing that never does get stopped and I don't know
what good it does to blame it on the Lord. But maybe it does some good if you
believe it.

Your brother,<br>Sonny

Then I kept in constant touch with him and I sent him whatever I could and
I went to meet him when he came back to New York. When I saw him many
things I thought I had forgotten came flooding back to me. This was because I
had begun, finally, to wonder about Sonny, about the life that Sonny lived
inside. This life, whatever it was, had made him older and thinner and it had
deepened the distant stillness in which he had always moved. He looked very
unlike my baby brother. Yet, when he smiled, when we shook hands, the baby
brother I'd never known looked out from the depths of his private life, like an
animal waiting to be coaxed into the light.

"How you been keeping?" he asked me.                                          50

"All right. And you?"

"Just fine." He was smiling all over his face. "It's good to see you again."

"It's good to see you."

The seven years' difference in our ages lay between us like a chasm: I wondered if these years would ever operate between us as a bridge. I was remembering, and it made it hard to catch my breath, that I had been there when he was
born; and I had heard the first words he had ever spoken. When he started to
walk, he walked from our mother straight to me. I caught him just before he fell
when he took the first steps he ever took in this world.

"How's Isabel?"                                                              55

"Just fine. She's dying to see you."

"And the boys?"

"They're fine, too. They're anxious to see their uncle."

"Oh, come on. You know they don't remember me."

"Are you kidding? Of course they remember you."                             60

He grinned again. We got into a taxi. We had a lot to say to each other, far
too much to know how to begin.

As the taxi began to move, I asked, "You still want to go to India?"

He laughed. "You still remember that. Hell, no. This place is Indian enough
for me."

"It used to belong to them," I said.

And he laughed again. "They damn sure knew what they were doing when they got rid of it." 65

Years ago, when he was around fourteen, he'd been all hipped on the idea of going to India. He read books about people sitting on rocks, naked, in all kinds of weather, but mostly bad, naturally, and walking barefoot through hot coals and arriving at wisdom. I used to say that it sounded to me as though they were getting away from wisdom as fast as they could. I think he sort of looked down on me for that.

"Do you mind," he asked, "if we have the driver drive alongside the park? On the west side—I haven't seen the city in so long."

"Of course not," I said. I was afraid that I might sound as though I were humoring him, but I hoped he wouldn't take it that way.

So we drove along, between the green of the park and the stony, lifeless elegance of hotels and apartment buildings, toward the vivid, killing streets of our childhood. These streets hadn't changed, though housing projects jutted up out of them now like rocks in the middle of a boiling sea. Most of the houses in which we had grown up had vanished, as had the stores from which we had stolen, the basements in which we had first tried sex, the rooftops from which we had hurled tin cans and bricks. But houses exactly like the houses of our past yet dominated the landscape, boys exactly like the boys we once had been found themselves smothering in these houses, came down into the streets for light and air and found themselves encircled by disaster. Some escaped the trap, most didn't. Those who got out always left something of themselves behind, as some animals amputate a leg and leave it in the trap. It might be said, perhaps, that I had escaped, after all, I was a school teacher; or that Sonny had, he hadn't lived in Harlem for years. Yet, as the cab moved uptown through streets which seemed, with a rush, to darken with dark people, and as I covertly studied Sonny's face, it came to me that what we both were seeking through our separate cab windows was that part of ourselves which had been left behind. It's always at the hour of trouble and confrontation that the missing member aches.

We hit 110th Street and started rolling up Lenox Avenue. And I'd known 70 this avenue all my life, but it seemed to me again, as it had seemed on the day I'd first heard about Sonny's trouble, filled with a hidden menace which was its very breath of life.

"We almost there," said Sonny.

"Almost." We were both too nervous to say anything more.

We live in a housing project. It hasn't been up long. A few days after it was up it seemed uninhabitably new, now, of course, it's already rundown. It looks like a parody of the good, clean, faceless life—God knows the people who live in it do their best to make it a parody. The beat-looking grass lying around isn't enough to make their lives green, the hedges will never hold out the streets, and they know it. The big windows fool no one, they aren't big enough to make space out of no space. They don't bother with the windows, they watch the TV screen instead. The playground is most popular with the children who don't play at jacks, or skip rope, or roller skate, or swing, and they can be found in it after dark. We moved in partly because it's not too far from where I teach, and partly for the kids; but it's really just like the houses in which Sonny and I grew up. The same things happen, they'll have the same things to remember. The moment Sonny and I started into the house I had the feeling that I was simply bringing him back into the danger he had almost died trying to escape.

Sonny has never been talkative. So I don't know why I was sure he'd be dying to talk to me when supper was over the first night. Everything went fine, the oldest boy remembered him, and the youngest boy liked him, and Sonny had remembered to bring something for each of them; and Isabel, who is really much nicer than I am, more open and giving, had gone to a lot of trouble about dinner and was genuinely glad to see him. And she's always been able to tease Sonny in a way that I haven't. It was nice to see her face so vivid again and to hear her laugh and watch her make Sonny laugh. She wasn't, or, anyway, she didn't seem to be, at all uneasy or embarrassed. She chatted as though there were no subject which had to be avoided and she got Sonny past his first, faint stiffness. And thank God she was there, for I was filled with that icy dread again. Everything I did seemed awkward to me, and everything I said sounded freighted with hidden meaning. I was trying to remember everything I'd heard about dope addiction and I couldn't help watching Sonny for signs. I wasn't doing it out of malice. I was trying to find out something about my brother. I was dying to hear him tell me he was safe.

"Safe!" my father grunted, whenever Mama suggested trying to move to a neighborhood which might be safer for children. "Safe, hell! Ain't no place safe for kids, nor nobody."

He always went on like this, but he wasn't, ever, really as bad as he sounded, not even on weekends, when he got drunk. As a matter of fact, he was always on the lookout for "something a little better," but he died before he found it. He died suddenly, during a drunken weekend in the middle of the war, when Sonny was fifteen. He and Sonny hadn't ever got on too well. And this was partly because Sonny was the apple of his father's eye. It was because he loved Sonny so much and was frightened for him, that he was always fighting with him. It doesn't do any good to fight with Sonny. Sonny just moves back, inside himself, where he can't be reached. But the principal reason that they never hit it off is that they were so much alike. Daddy was big and rough and loud-talking, just the opposite of Sonny, but they both had—that same privacy.

Mama tried to tell me something about this, just after Daddy died. I was home on leave from the army.

This was the last time I ever saw my mother alive. Just the same, this picture gets all mixed up in my mind with pictures I had of her when she was younger. The way I always see her is the way she used to be on a Sunday afternoon, say, when the old folks were talking after the big Sunday dinner. I always see her wearing pale blue. She'd be sitting on the sofa. And my father would be sitting in the easy chair, not far from her. And the living room would be full of church folks and relatives. There they sit, in chairs all around the living room, and the night is creeping up outside, but nobody knows it yet. You can see the darkness growing against the windowpanes and you hear the street noises every now and again, or maybe the jangling beat of a tambourine from one of the churches close by, but it's real quiet in the room. For a moment nobody's talking, but every face looks darkening, like the sky outside. And my mother rocks a little from the waist, and my father's eyes are closed. Everyone is looking at something a child can't see. For a minute they've forgotten the children. Maybe a kid is lying on the rug, half asleep. Maybe somebody's got a kid in his lap and is absent-mindedly stroking the kid's head. Maybe there's a kid, quiet and big-eyed, curled up in a big chair in the corner. The silence, the darkness coming, and the darkness in the faces frightens the child obscurely. He hopes that the hand which strokes his forehead will never stop—will never die. He hopes that there will never come a time when the old folks won't be sitting around the living room, talking about where they've come from, and what they've seen, and what's happened to them and their kinfolk.

But something deep and watchful in the child knows that this is bound to end, is already ending. In a moment someone will get up and turn on the light. Then the old folks will remember the children and they won't talk any more that day. And when light fills the room, the child is filled with darkness. He knows that everytime this happens he's moved just a little closer to that darkness out- side. The darkness outside is what the old folks have been talking about. It's what they've come from. It's what they endure. The child knows that they won't talk any more because if he knows too much about what's happened to *them*, he'll know too much too soon, about what's going to happen to *him*.

The last time I talked to my mother, I remember I was restless. I wanted to get out and see Isabel. We weren't married then and we had a lot to straighten out between us.

There Mama sat, in black, by the window. She was humming an old church song, *Lord, you brought me from a long ways off*. Sonny was out somewhere. Mama kept watching the streets.

"I don't know," she said, "if I'll ever see you again, after you go off from here. But I hope you'll remember the things I tried to teach you."

"Don't talk like that," I said, and smiled. "You'll be here a long time yet."

She smiled, too, but she said nothing. She was quiet for a long time. And I said, "Mama, don't you worry about nothing. I'll be writing all the time, and you be getting the checks. . . ."

"I want to talk to you about your brother," she said, suddenly. "If anything happens to me he ain't going to have nobody to look out for him."

"Mama," I said, "ain't nothing going to happen to you *or* Sonny. Sonny's all right. He's a good boy and he's got good sense."

"It ain't a question of his being a good boy," Mama said, "nor of his having good sense. It ain't only the bad ones, nor yet the dumb ones that gets sucked under." She stopped, looking at me. "Your Daddy once had a brother," she said, and she smiled in a way that made me feel she was in pain. "You didn't never know that, did you?"

"No," I said, "I never knew that," and I watched her face.

"Oh, yes," she said, "your Daddy had a brother." She looked out of the window again. "I know you never saw your Daddy cry. But *I* did—many a time, through all these years."

I asked her, "What happened to his brother? How come nobody's ever talked about him?"

This was the first time I ever saw my mother look old.

"His brother got killed," she said, "when he was just a little younger than you are now. I knew him. He was a fine boy. He was maybe a little full of the devil, but he didn't mean nobody no harm."

Then she stopped and the room was silent, exactly as it had sometimes been on those Sunday afternoons. Mama kept looking out into the streets.

"He used to have a job in the mill," she said, "and, like all young folks, he just liked to perform on Saturday nights. Saturday nights, him and your father would drift around to different places, go to dances and things like that, or just sit around with people they knew, and your father's brother would sing, he had a fine voice, and play along with himself on his guitar. Well, this particular Saturday night, him and your father was coming home from some place, and they were both a little drunk and there was a moon that night, it was bright like day. Your father's brother was feeling kind of good, and he was whistling to himself, and he had his guitar slung over his shoulder. They was coming down a hill and beneath them was a road that turned off from the highway. Well, your father's brother, being always kind of frisky, decided to run down this hill, and he did, with that guitar banging and clanging behind him, and he ran across the road, and he was making water behind a tree. And your father was sort of amused at him and he was still coming down the hill, kind of slow. Then he heard a car motor and that same minute his brother stepped from behind the tree, into the road, in the moonlight. And he started to cross the road. And your father started to run down the hill, he says he don't know why. This car was full of white men. They was all drunk, and when they seen your father's brother they let out a great whoop and holler and they aimed the car straight at him. They was having fun, they just wanted to scare him, the way they do sometimes, you know. But they was drunk. And I guess the boy, being drunk, too, and scared, kind of lost his head. By the time he jumped it was too late. Your father says he heard his brother scream when the car rolled over him, and he heard the wood of that guitar when it give, and he heard them strings go flying, and he heard them white men shouting, and the car kept on a-going and it ain't stopped till this day. And, time your father got down the hill, his brother weren't nothing but blood and pulp."

Tears were gleaming on my mother's face. There wasn't anything I could say.

"He never mentioned it," she said, "because I never let him mention it before you children. Your Daddy was like a crazy man that night and for many a night thereafter. He says he never in his life seen anything as dark as that road after the lights of that car had gone away. Weren't nothing, weren't nobody on that road, just your Daddy and his brother and that busted guitar. Oh, yes. Your Daddy never did really get right again. Till the day he died he weren't sure but that every white man he saw was the man that killed his brother."

**46**    POINT OF VIEW

She stopped and took out her handkerchief and dried her eyes and looked at me.

"I ain't telling you all this," she said, "to make you scared or bitter or to make you hate nobody. I'm telling you this because you got a brother. And the world ain't changed."

I guess I didn't want to believe this. I guess she saw this in my face. She turned away from me, toward the window again, searching those streets.

"But I praise my Redeemer," she said at last, "that He called your Daddy 100 home before me. I ain't saying it to throw no flowers at myself, but, I declare, it keeps me from feeling too cast down to know I helped your father get safely through this world. Your father always acted like he was the roughest, strongest man on earth. And everybody took him to be like that. But if he hadn't had *me* there—to see his tears!"

She was crying again. Still, I couldn't move. I said, "Lord, Lord, Mama, I didn't know it was like that."

"Oh, honey," she said, "there's a lot that you don't know. But you are going to find it out." She stood up from the window and came over to me. "You got to hold on to your brother," she said, "and don't let him fall, no matter what it looks like is happening to him and no matter how evil you gets with him. You going to be evil with him many a time. But don't you forget what I told you, you hear?"

"I won't forget," I said. "Don't you worry, I won't forget. I won't let nothing happen to Sonny."

My mother smiled as though she were amused at something she saw in my face. Then, "You may not be able to stop nothing from happening. But you got to let him know you's *there*."

Two days later I was married, and then I was gone. And I had a lot of things 105 on my mind and I pretty well forgot my promise to Mama until I got shipped home on a special furlough for her funeral.

And, after the funeral, with just Sonny and me alone in the empty kitchen, I tried to find out something about him.

"What do you want to do?" I asked him.

"I'm going to be a musician," he said.

For he had graduated, in the time I had been away, from dancing to the juke box to finding out who was playing what, and what they were doing with it, and he had bought himself a set of drums.

"You mean, you want to be a drummer?" I somehow had the feeling that 110 being a drummer might be all right for other people but not for my brother Sonny.

"I don't think," he said, looking at me very gravely, "that I'll ever be a good drummer. But I think I can play a piano."

I frowned. I'd never played the role of the older brother quite so seriously before, had scarcely ever, in fact, *asked* Sonny a damn thing. I sensed myself in the presence of something I didn't really know how to handle, didn't understand. So I made my frown a little deeper as I asked: "What kind of musician do you want to be?"

He grinned. "How many kinds do you think there are?"

"Be *serious*," I said.

He laughed, throwing his head back, and then looked at me. "I *am* serious." 115

"Well, then, for Christ's sake, stop kidding around and answer a serious question. I mean, do you want to be a concert pianist, you want to play classical music and all that, or—or what?" Long before I finished he was laughing again. "For Christ's *sake*, Sonny!"

He sobered, but with difficulty. "I'm sorry. But you sound so—*scared!*" and he was off again.

"Well, you may think it's funny now, baby, but it's not going to be so funny when you have to make your living at it, let me tell you *that*." I was furious because I knew he was laughing at me and I didn't know why.

"No," he said, very sober now, and afraid, perhaps, that he'd hurt me, "I don't want to be a classical pianist. That isn't what interests me. I mean"—he paused, looking hard at me, as though his eyes would help me to understand, and then gestured helplessly, as though perhaps his hand would help—"I mean, I'll have a lot of studying to do, and I'll have to study *everything*, but, I mean, I want to play *with*—jazz musicians." He stopped. "I want to play jazz," he said.

Well, the word had never before sounded as heavy, as real, as it sounded 120 that afternoon in Sonny's mouth. I just looked at him and I was probably frowning a real frown by this time. I simply couldn't see why on earth he'd want to spend his time hanging around nightclubs, clowning around on bandstands, while people pushed each other around a dance floor. It seemed—beneath him, somehow. I had never thought about it before, had never been forced to, but I suppose I had always put jazz musicians in a class with what Daddy called "good-time people."

"Are you *serious*?"

"Hell, *yes*, I'm serious."

He looked more helpless than ever, and annoyed, and deeply hurt.

I suggested, helpfully: "You mean—like Louis Armstrong?"°

His face closed as though I'd struck him. "No. I'm not talking about none of 125 that old-time, down home crap."

"Well, look, Sonny, I'm sorry, don't get mad. I just don't altogether get it, that's all. Name somebody—you know, a jazz musician you admire."

"Bird."

"Who?"

"Bird! Charlie Parker!° Don't they teach you nothing in the goddamn army?"

I lit a cigarette. I was surprised and then a little amused to discover that I was 130 trembling. "I've been out of touch," I said. "You'll have to be patient with me. Now. Who's this Parker character?"

*Louis Armstrong:* jazz trumpeter and vocalist (1900–1971) born in New Orleans. In the 1950s his music would have been considered conservative by progressive jazz fans.     *Charlie Parker:* a jazz saxophonist (1920–1955) who helped create the progressive jazz style called bebop. Parker was a heroin addict who died at an early age.

"He's just one of the greatest jazz musicians alive," said Sonny, sullenly, his hands in his pockets, his back to me. "Maybe *the* greatest," he added, bitterly, "that's probably why *you* never heard of him."

"All right," I said, "I'm ignorant. I'm sorry. I'll go out and buy all the cat's records right away, all right?"

"It don't," said Sonny, with dignity, "make any difference to me. I don't care what you listen to. Don't do me no favors."

I was beginning to realize that I'd never seen him so upset before. With another part of my mind I was thinking that this would probably turn out to be one of those things kids go through and that I shouldn't make it seem important by pushing it too hard. Still, I didn't think it would do any harm to ask: "Doesn't all this take a lot of time? Can you make a living at it?"

He turned back to me and half leaned, half sat, on the kitchen table. 135 "Everything takes time," he said, "and—well, yes, sure, I can make a living at it. But what I don't seem to be able to make you understand is that it's the only thing I want to do."

"Well, Sonny," I said, gently, "you know people can't always do exactly what they *want* to do—"

"*No*, I don't know that," said Sonny, surprising me. "I think people *ought* to do what they want to do, what else are they alive for?"

"You getting to be a big boy," I said desperately, "it's time you started thinking about your future."

"I'm thinking about my future," said Sonny, grimly. "I think about it all the time."

I gave up. I decided, if he didn't change his mind, that we could always talk 140 about it later. "In the meantime," I said, "you got to finish school." We had already decided that he'd have to move in with Isabel and her folks. I knew this wasn't the ideal arrangement because Isabel's folks are inclined to be dicty and they hadn't especially wanted Isabel to marry me. But I didn't know what else to do. "And we have to get you fixed up at Isabel's."

There was a long silence. He moved from the kitchen table to the window. "That's a terrible idea. You know it yourself."

"Do you have a *better* idea?"

He just walked up and down the kitchen for a minute. He was as tall as I was. He had started to shave. I suddenly had the feeling that I didn't know him at all.

He stopped at the kitchen table and picked up my cigarettes. Looking at me with a kind of mocking, amused defiance, he put one between his lips. "You mind?"

"You smoking already?" 145

He lit the cigarette and nodded, watching me through the smoke. "I just wanted to see if I'd have the courage to smoke in front of you." He grinned and blew a great cloud of smoke to the ceiling. "It was easy." He looked at my face. "Come on, now. I bet you was smoking at my age, tell the truth."

I didn't say anything but the truth was on my face, and he laughed. But now there was something very strained in his laugh. "Sure. And I bet that ain't all you was doing."

He was frightening me a little. "Cut the crap," I said. "We already decided that you was going to go and live at Isabel's. Now what's got into you all of a sudden?"

"*You* decided it," he pointed out. "*I* didn't decide nothing." He stopped in front of me, leaning against the stove, arms loosely folded. "Look, brother. I don't want to stay in Harlem no more, I really don't." He was very earnest. He looked at me, then over toward the kitchen window. There was something in his eyes I'd never seen before, some thoughtfulness, some worry all his own. He rubbed the muscle of one arm. "It's time I was getting out of here."

"Where do you want to *go,* Sonny?" 150

"I want to join the army. Or the navy, I don't care. If I say I'm old enough, they'll believe me."

Then I got mad. It was because I was so scared. "You must be crazy. You god-damn fool, what the hell do you want to go and join the *army* for?"

"I just told you. To get out of Harlem."

"Sonny, you haven't even finished *school.* And if you really want to be a musician, how do you expect to study if you're in the *army?*"

He looked at me, trapped, and in anguish. "There's ways. I might be able to  155 work out some kind of deal. Anyway, I'll have the G.I. Bill when I come out."

"*If* you come out." We stared at each other. "Sonny, please. Be reasonable. I know the setup is far from perfect. But we got to do the best we can."

"I ain't learning nothing in school," he said. "Even when I go." He turned away from me and opened the window and threw his cigarette out into the narrow alley. I watched his back. "At least, I ain't learning nothing you'd want me to learn." He slammed the window so hard I thought the glass would fly out, and turned back to me. "And I'm sick of the stink of these garbage cans!"

"Sonny," I said, "I know how you feel. But if you don't finish school now, you're going to be sorry later that you didn't." I grabbed him by the shoulders. "And you only got another year. It ain't so bad. And I'll come back and I swear I'll help you do *whatever* you want to do. Just try to put up with it till I come back. Will you please do that? For me?"

He didn't answer and he wouldn't look at me.

"Sonny. You hear me?" 160

He pulled away. "I hear you. But you never hear anything *I* say."

I didn't know what to say to that. He looked out of the window and then back at me. "OK," he said, and sighed. "I'll try."

Then I said, trying to cheer him up a little, "They got a piano at Isabel's. You can practice on it."

And as a matter of fact, it did cheer him up for a minute. "That's right," he said to himself. "I forgot that." His face relaxed a little. But the worry, the thoughtfulness, played on it still, the way shadows play on a face which is staring into the fire.

But I thought I'd never hear the end of that piano. At first, Isabel would  165 write me, saying how nice it was that Sonny was so serious about his music and how, as soon as he came in from school, or wherever he had been when he was supposed to be at school, he went straight to that piano and stayed there until suppertime. And, after supper, he went back to that piano and stayed there until everybody went to bed. He was at the piano all day Saturday and all day Sunday. Then he bought a record player and started playing records. He'd play one record over and over again, all day long sometimes, and he'd improvise along with it on the piano. Or he'd play one section of the record, one chord, one change, one progression, then he'd do it on the piano. Then back to the record. Then back to the piano.

Well, I really don't know how they stood it. Isabel finally confessed that it wasn't like living with a person at all, it was like living with sound. And the sound didn't make any sense to her, didn't make any sense to any of them—naturally. They began, in a way, to be afflicted by this presence that was living in their home. It was as though Sonny were some sort of god, or monster. He moved in an atmosphere which wasn't like theirs at all. They fed him and he ate, he washed himself, he walked in and out of their door; he certainly wasn't nasty or unpleasant or rude, Sonny isn't any of those things; but it was as though he were all wrapped up in some cloud, some fire, some vision all his own; and there wasn't any way to reach him.

At the same time, he wasn't really a man yet, he was still a child, and they had to watch out for him in all kinds of ways. They certainly couldn't throw him out. Neither did they dare to make a great scene about that piano because even they dimly sensed, as I sensed, from so many thousands of miles away, that Sonny was at that piano playing for his life.

But he hadn't been going to school. One day a letter came from the school board and Isabel's mother got it—there had, apparently, been other letters but Sonny had torn them up. This day, when Sonny came in, Isabel's mother showed him the letter and asked where he'd been spending his time. And she finally got it out of him that he'd been down in Greenwich Village, with musicians and other characters, in a white girl's apartment. And this scared her and she started to scream at him and what came up, once she began—though she denies it to this day—was what sacrifices they were making to give Sonny a decent home and how little he appreciated it.

Sonny didn't play the piano that day. By evening, Isabel's mother had calmed down but then there was the old man to deal with, and Isabel herself. Isabel says she did her best to be calm but she broke down and started crying. She says she just watched Sonny's face. She could tell, by watching him, what was happening with him. And what was happening was that they penetrated his cloud, they had reached him. Even if their fingers had been a thousand times more gentle than human fingers ever are, he could hardly help feeling that they had stripped him naked and were spitting on that nakedness. For he also had to see that his presence, that music, which was life or death to him, had been torture for them and that they had endured it, not at all for his sake, but only for mine. And Sonny couldn't take that. He can take it a little better today than he could then but he's still not very good at it and, frankly, I don't know anybody who is.

The silence of the next few days must have been louder than the sound of all the music ever played since time began. One morning, before she went to work, Isabel was in his room for something and she suddenly realized that all of his records were gone. And she knew for certain that he was gone. And he was. He went as far as the navy would carry him. He finally sent me a postcard from some place in Greece and that was the first I knew that Sonny was still alive. I didn't see him any more until we were both back in New York and the war had long been over.

He was a man by then, of course, but I wasn't willing to see it. He came by the house from time to time, but we fought almost every time we met. I didn't like the way he carried himself, loose and dreamlike all the time, and I didn't like his friends, and his music seemed to be merely an excuse for the life he led. It sounded just that weird and disordered.

Then we had a fight, a pretty awful fight, and I didn't see him for months. By and by I looked him up, where he was living, in a furnished room in the Village, and I tried to make it up. But there were lots of people in the room and Sonny just lay on his bed, and he wouldn't come downstairs with me, and he treated these other people as though they were his family and I weren't. So I got mad and then he got mad, and then I told him that he might just as well be dead as live the way he was living. Then he stood up and he told me not to worry about him any more in life, that he *was* dead as far as I was concerned. Then he pushed me to the door and the other people looked on as though nothing were happening, and he slammed the door behind me. I stood in the hallway, staring at the door. I heard somebody laugh in the room and then the tears came to my eyes. I started down the steps, whistling to keep from crying, I kept whistling to myself, *You going to need me, baby, one of these cold, rainy days.*

I read about Sonny's trouble in the spring. Little Grace died in the fall. She was a beautiful little girl. But she only lived a little over two years. She died of polio and she suffered. She had a slight fever for a couple of days, but it didn't seem like anything and we just kept her in bed. And we would certainly have called the doctor, but the fever dropped, she seemed to be all right. So we thought it had just been a cold. Then, one day, she was up, playing, Isabel was in the kitchen fixing lunch for the two boys when they'd come in from school, and she heard Grace fall down in the living room. When you have a lot of children you don't always start running when one of them falls, unless they start screaming or something. And, this time, Grace was quiet. Yet, Isabel says that when she heard that *thump* and then that silence, something happened in her to make her afraid. And she ran to the living room and there was little Grace on the floor, all twisted up, and the reason she hadn't screamed was that she couldn't get her breath. And when she did scream, it was the worst sound, Isabel says, that she'd ever heard in all her life, and she still hears it sometimes in her dreams. Isabel will sometimes wake me up with a low, moaning, strangled sound and I have to be quick to awaken her and hold her to me and where Isabel is weeping against me seems a mortal wound.

I think I may have written Sonny the very day that little Grace was buried. I was sitting in the living room in the dark, by myself, and I suddenly thought of Sonny. My trouble made his real.

One Saturday afternoon, when Sonny had been living with us, or, anyway, been in our house, for nearly two weeks, I found myself wandering aimlessly about the living room, drinking from a can of beer, and trying to work up the courage to search Sonny's room. He was out, he was usually out whenever I was home, and Isabel had taken the children to see their grandparents. Suddenly I was standing still in front of the living room window, watching Seventh Avenue. The idea of searching Sonny's room made me still. I scarcely dared to admit to myself what I'd be searching for. I didn't know what I'd do if I found it. Or if I didn't.

On the sidewalk across from me, near the entrance to a barbecue joint, some people were holding an old-fashioned revival meeting. The barbecue cook, wearing a dirty white apron, his conked hair reddish and metallic in the pale sun, and a cigarette between his lips, stood in the doorway, watching them. Kids and older people paused in their errands and stood there, along with some older men and a couple of very tough-looking women who watched everything that happened on the avenue, as though they owned it, or were maybe owned by it. Well, they were watching this, too. The revival was being carried on by three sisters in black, and a brother. All they had were their voices and their Bibles and a tambourine. The brother was testifying and while he testified two of the sisters stood together, seeming to say, amen, and the third sister walked around with the tambourine outstretched and a couple of people dropped coins into it. Then the brother's testimony ended and the sister who had been taking up the collection dumped the coins into her palm and transferred them to the pocket of her long black robe. Then she raised both hands, striking the tambourine against the air, and then against one hand, and she started to sing. And the two other sisters and the brother joined in.

It was strange, suddenly, to watch, though I had been seeing these street meetings all my life. So, of course, had everybody else down there. Yet, they paused and watched and listened and I stood still at the window. *"Tis the old ship of Zion,"* they sang, and the sister with the tambourine kept a steady, jangling beat, *"it has rescued many a thousand!"* Not a soul under the sound of their voices was hearing this song for the first time, not one of them had been rescued. Nor had they seen much in the way of rescue work being done around them. Neither did they especially believe in the holiness of the three sisters and the brother, they knew too much about them, knew where they lived, and how. The woman with the tambourine, whose voice dominated the air, whose face was bright with joy, was divided by very little from the woman who stood watching her, a cigarette between her heavy, chapped lips, her hair a cuckoo's nest, her face scarred and swollen from many beatings, and her black eyes glittering like coal. Perhaps they both knew this, which was why, when, as rarely, they addressed each other, they addressed each other as Sister. As the singing filled the air the watching, listening faces underwent a change, the eyes focusing on something within; the music seemed to soothe a poison out of them; and time seemed, nearly, to fall away from the sullen, belligerent, battered faces, as though they were fleeing back to their first condition, while dreaming of their last. The barbecue cook half shook his head and smiled, and dropped his cigarette and disappeared into his joint. A man fumbled in his pockets for change and stood holding it in his hand impatiently, as though he had just remembered a pressing appointment further up the avenue. He looked furious. Then I saw Sonny, standing on the edge of the crowd. He was carrying a wide, flat notebook with a green cover, and it made him look, from where I was standing, almost like a schoolboy. The coppery sun brought out the copper in his skin, he was very faintly smiling, standing very still. Then the singing stopped, the tambourine turned into a collection plate again. The furious man dropped in his coins and vanished, so did a couple of the women, and Sonny dropped some change in the plate, looking directly at the woman with a little smile. He started across the avenue, toward the house. He has a slow, loping walk, something like the way Harlem hipsters walk, only he's imposed on this his own half-beat. I had never really noticed it before.

I stayed at the window, both relieved and apprehensive. As Sonny disappeared from my sight, they began singing again. And they were still singing when his key turned in the lock.

"Hey," he said.

"Hey, yourself. You want some beer?" 180

"No. Well, maybe." But he came up to the window and stood beside me, looking out. "What a warm voice," he said.

They were singing *If I could only hear my mother pray again!*

"Yes," I said, "and she can sure beat that tambourine."

"But what a terrible song," he said, and laughed. He dropped his notebook on the sofa and disappeared into the kitchen. "Where's Isabel and the kids?"

"I think they went to see their grandparents. You hungry?" 185

"No." He came back into the living room with his can of beer. "You want to come some place with me tonight?"

I sensed, I don't know how, that I couldn't possibly say no. "Sure. Where?"

He sat down on the sofa and picked up his notebook and started leafing through it. "I'm going to sit in with some fellows in a joint in the Village."

"You mean, you're going to play, tonight?"

"That's right." He took a swallow of his beer and moved back to the window. 190 He gave me a sidelong look. "If you can stand it."

"I'll try," I said.

He smiled to himself and we both watched as the meeting across the way broke up. The three sisters and the brother, heads bowed, were singing *God be with you till we meet again*. The faces around them were very quiet. Then the song ended. The small crowd dispersed. We watched the three women and the lone man walk slowly up the avenue.

"When she was singing before," said Sonny, abruptly, "her voice reminded me for a minute of what heroin feels like sometimes—when it's in your veins. It makes you feel sort of warm and cool at the same time. And distant. And—and sure." He sipped his beer, very deliberately not looking at me. I watched his face. "It makes you feel—in control. Sometimes you've got to have that feeling."

"Do you?" I sat down slowly in the easy chair.

"Sometimes." He went to the sofa and picked up his notebook again. "Some people do." 195

"In order," I asked, "to play?" And my voice was very ugly, full of contempt and anger.

"Well"—he looked at me with great, troubled eyes, as though, in fact, he hoped his eyes would tell me things he could never otherwise say—"they *think* so. And *if* they think so—!"

"And what do *you* think?" I asked.

He sat on the sofa and put his can of beer on the floor. "I don't know," he said, and I couldn't be sure if he were answering my question or pursuing his thoughts. His face didn't tell me. "It's not so much to *play*. It's to *stand* it, to be able to make it at all. On any level." He frowned and smiled: "In order to keep from shaking to pieces."

"But these friends of yours," I said, "they seem to shake themselves to pieces 200 pretty goddamn fast."

"Maybe." He played with the notebook. And something told me that I should curb my tongue, that Sonny was doing his best to talk, that I should listen. "But of course you only know the ones that've gone to pieces. Some don't—or at least they haven't *yet* and that's just about all *any* of us can say." He paused. "And then there are some who just live, really, in hell, and they know it and they see what's happening and they go right on. I don't know." He sighed, dropped the notebook, folded his arms. "Some guys, you can tell from the way they play, they on something *all* the time. And you can see that, well, it makes something real for them. But of course," he picked up his beer from the floor and sipped it and put the can down again, "they *want* to, too, you've got to see that. Even some of them that say they don't—*some*, not all."

"And what about you?" I asked—I couldn't help it. "What about you? Do *you* want to?"

He stood up and walked to the window and remained silent for a long time. Then he sighed. "Me," he said. Then: "While I was downstairs before, on my way here, listening to that woman sing, it struck me all of a sudden how much suffering she must have had to go through—to sing like that. It's *repulsive* to think you have to suffer that much."

I said: "But there's no way not to suffer—is there, Sonny?"

"I believe not," he said and smiled, "but that's never stopped anyone from 205 trying." He looked at me. "Has it?" I realized, with this mocking look, that there stood between us, forever, beyond the power of time or forgiveness, the fact that I had held silence—so long!—when he had needed human speech to help him. He turned back to the window. "No, there's no way not to suffer. But you try all kinds of ways to keep from drowning in it, to keep on top of it, and to make it seem—well, like *you*. Like you did something, all right, and now you're suffering for it. You know?" I said nothing. "Well you know," he said, impatiently, "why *do* people suffer? Maybe it's better to do something to give it a reason, *any* reason."

"But we just agreed," I said "that there's no way not to suffer. Isn't it better, then, just to—take it?"

"But nobody just takes it," Sonny cried, "that's what I'm telling you! *Everybody* tries not to. You're just hung up on the *way* some people try—it's not *your* way!"

The hair on my face began to itch, my face felt wet. "That's not true," I said, "that's not true. I don't give a damn what other people do, I don't even care how they suffer. I just care how *you* suffer." And he looked at me. "Please believe me," I said, "I don't want to see you—die—trying not to suffer."

"I won't," he said, flatly, "die trying not to suffer. At least, not any faster than anybody else."

"But there's no need," I said, trying to laugh, "is there? in killing yourself."    210

I wanted to say more, but I couldn't. I wanted to talk about will power and how life could be—well, beautiful. I wanted to say that it was all within; but was it? or, rather, wasn't that exactly the trouble? And I wanted to promise that I would never fail him again. But it would all have sounded—empty words and lies.

So I made the promise to myself and prayed that I would keep it.

"It's terrible sometimes, inside," he said, "that's what's the trouble. You walk these streets, black and funky and cold, and there's not really a living ass to talk to, and there's nothing shaking, and there's no way of getting it out—that storm inside. You can't talk it and you can't make love with it, and when you finally try to get with it and play it, you realize *nobody's* listening. So *you've* got to listen. You got to find a way to listen."

And then he walked away from the window and sat on the sofa again, as though all the wind had suddenly been knocked out of him. "Sometimes you'll do *anything* to play, even cut your mother's throat." He laughed and looked at me. "Or your brother's." Then he sobered. "Or your own." Then: "Don't worry. I'm all right now and I think I'll *be* all right. But I can't forget—where I've been. I don't mean just the physical place I've been, I mean where I've *been*. And *what* I've been."

"What have you been, Sonny?" I asked.    215

He smiled—but sat sideways on the sofa, his elbow resting on the back, his fingers playing with his mouth and chin, not looking at me. "I've been something I didn't recognize, didn't know I could be. Didn't know anybody could be." He stopped, looking inward, looking helplessly young, looking old. "I'm not talking about it now because I feel *guilty* or anything like that—maybe it would be better if I did, I don't know. Anyway, I can't really talk about it. Not to you, not to anybody," and now he turned and faced me. "Sometimes, you know, and it was actually when I was most *out* of the world, I felt that I was in it, that I was *with* it, really, and I could play or I didn't really have to *play*, it just came out of me, it was there. And I don't know how I played, thinking about it now, but I know I did awful things, those times, sometimes, to people. Or it wasn't that I *did* anything to them—it was that they weren't real." He picked up the beer can; it was empty; he rolled it between his palms: "And other times—well, I needed a fix, I needed to find a place to lean, I needed to clear a space to *listen*—and I couldn't find it, and I—went crazy, I did terrible things to *me*, I was terrible *for* me." He began pressing the beer can between his hands, I watched the metal begin to give. It glittered, as he played with it, like a knife, and I was afraid he would cut himself, but I said nothing. "Oh well. I can never tell you. I was all by myself at the bottom of something, stinking and sweating and crying and shaking, and I smelled it, you know? *my* stink, and I thought I'd die if I couldn't get away from it and yet, all the same, I knew that everything I was doing was just locking me in with it. And I didn't know," he paused, still flattening the beer can, "I didn't know, I still *don't* know, something kept telling me that maybe it was good to smell your own stink, but I didn't think that *that* was what I'd been trying to do—and—who can stand it?" and he abruptly dropped the ruined beer can, looking at me with a small, still smile, and then rose, walking to the window as though it were the lodestone rock. I watched his face, he watched the avenue. "I couldn't tell you when Mama died—but the reason I wanted to leave Harlem so bad was to get away from drugs. And then, when I ran away, that's what I was running from—really. When I came back, nothing had changed, *I* hadn't changed, I was just—older." And he stopped, drumming with his fingers on the windowpane. The sun had vanished, soon darkness would fall. I watched his face. "It can come again," he said, almost as though speaking to himself. Then he turned to me. "It can come again," he repeated. "I just want you to know that."

"All right," I said, at last. "So it can come again. All right."

He smiled, but the smile was sorrowful. "I had to try to tell you," he said.

"Yes," I said. "I understand that."

"You're my brother," he said, looking straight at me, and not smiling at all.     220

"Yes," I repeated, "yes. I understand that."

He turned back to the window, looking out. "All that hatred down there," he said, "all that hatred and misery and love. It's a wonder it doesn't blow the avenue apart."

We went to the only nightclub on a short, dark street, downtown. We squeezed through the narrow, chattering, jam-packed bar to the entrance of the big room, where the bandstand was. And we stood there for a moment, for the lights were very dim in this room and we couldn't see. Then, "Hello, boy," said a voice and an enormous black man, much older than Sonny or myself, erupted out of all that atmospheric lighting and put an arm around Sonny's shoulder. "I been sitting right here," he said, "waiting for you."

He had a big voice, too, and heads in the darkness turned toward us.

Sonny grinned and pulled a little away, and said, "Creole, this is my brother.     225
I told you about him."

Creole shook my hand. "I'm glad to meet you, son," he said, and it was clear that he was glad to meet me *there*, for Sonny's sake. And he smiled, "You got a real musician in *your* family," and he took his arm from Sonny's shoulder and slapped him, lightly, affectionately, with the back of his hand.

"Well. Now I've heard it all," said a voice behind us. This was another musician, and a friend of Sonny's, a coal-black, cheerful-looking man, built close to the ground. He immediately began confiding to me, at the top of his lungs, the most terrible things about Sonny, his teeth gleaming like a lighthouse and his laugh coming up out of him like the beginning of an earthquake. And it turned out that everyone at the bar knew Sonny, or almost everyone; some were musicians, working there, or nearby, or not working, some were simply hangers-on, and some were there to hear Sonny play. I was introduced to all of them and they were all very polite to me. Yet, it was clear that, for them, I was only Sonny's brother. Here, I was in Sonny's world. Or, rather: his kingdom. Here, it was not even a question that his veins bore royal blood.

They were going to play soon and Creole installed me, by myself, at a table in a dark corner. Then I watched them, Creole, and the little black man, and Sonny, and the others, while they horsed around, standing just below the bandstand. The light from the bandstand spilled just a little short of them and, watching them laughing and gesturing and moving about, I had the feeling that they, nevertheless, were being most careful not to step into that circle of light too suddenly: that if they moved into the light too suddenly, without thinking, they would perish in flame. Then, while I watched, one of them, the small, black man, moved into the light and crossed the bandstand and started fooling around with his drums. Then—being funny and being, also, extremely ceremonious—Creole took Sonny by the arm and led him to the piano. A woman's voice called Sonny's name and a few hands started clapping. And Sonny, also being funny and being ceremonious, and so touched, I think, that he could have cried, but neither hiding it nor showing it, riding it like a man, grinned, and put both hands to his heart and bowed from the waist.

Creole then went to the bass fiddle and a lean, very bright-skinned brown man jumped up on the bandstand and picked up his horn. So there they were, and the atmosphere on the bandstand and in the room began to change and tighten. Someone stepped up to the microphone and announced them. Then there were all kinds of murmurs. Some people at the bar shushed others. The waitress ran around, frantically getting in the last orders, guys and chicks got closer to each other, and the lights on the bandstand, on the quartet, turned to a kind of indigo. Then they all looked different there. Creole looked about him for the last time, as though he were making certain that all his chickens were in the coop, and then he—jumped and struck the fiddle. And there they were.

All I know about music is that not many people ever really hear it. And even 230 then, on the rare occasions when something opens within, and the music enters, what we mainly hear, or hear corroborated, are personal, private, vanishing evocations. But the man who creates the music is hearing something else, is dealing with the roar rising from the void and imposing order on it as it hits the air.

What is evoked in him, then, is of another order, more terrible because it has no words, and triumphant, too, for that same reason. And his triumph, when he triumphs, is ours. I just watched Sonny's face. His face was troubled, he was working hard, but he wasn't with it. And I had the feeling that, in a way, everyone on the bandstand was waiting for him, both waiting for him and pushing him along. But as I began to watch Creole, I realized that it was Creole who held them all back. He had them on a short rein. Up there, keeping the beat with his whole body, wailing on the fiddle, with his eyes half closed, he was listening to everything, but he was listening to Sonny. He was having a dialogue with Sonny. He wanted Sonny to leave the shoreline and strike out for the deep water. He was Sonny's witness that deep water and drowning were not the same thing—he had been there, and he knew. And he wanted Sonny to know. He was waiting for Sonny to do the things on the keys which would let Creole know that Sonny was in the water.

And, while Creole listened, Sonny moved, deep within, exactly like someone in torment. I had never before thought of how awful the relationship must be between the musician and his instrument. He has to fill it, this instrument, with the breath of life, his own. He has to make it do what he wants it to do. And a piano is just a piano. It's made out of so much wood and wires and little hammers and big ones, and ivory. While there's only so much you can do with it, the only way to find this out is to try; to try and make it do everything.

And Sonny hadn't been near a piano for over a year. And he wasn't on much better terms with his life, not the life that stretched before him now. He and the piano stammered, started one way, got scared, stopped; started another way, panicked, marked time, started again; then seemed to have found a direction, panicked again, got stuck. And the face I saw on Sonny I'd never seen before. Everything had been burned out of it, and, at the same time, things usually hidden were being burned in, by the fire and fury of the battle which was occurring in him up there.

Yet, watching Creole's face as they neared the end of the first set, I had the feeling that something had happened, something I hadn't heard. Then they finished, there was scattered applause, and then, without an instant's warning, Creole started into something else, it was almost sardonic, it was *Am I Blue*. And, as though he commanded, Sonny began to play. Something began to happen. And Creole let out the reins. The dry, low, black man said something awful on the drums, Creole answered, and the drums talked back. Then the horn insisted, sweet and high, slightly detached perhaps, and Creole listened, commenting now and then, dry, and driving, beautiful and calm and old. Then they all came together again, and Sonny was part of the family again. I could tell this from his face. He seemed to have found, right there beneath his fingers, a damn brand-new piano. It seemed that he couldn't get over it. Then, for awhile, just being happy with Sonny, they seemed to be agreeing with him that brand-new pianos certainly were a gas.

Then Creole stepped forward to remind them that what they were playing was the blues. He hit something in all of them, he hit something in me, myself, and the music tightened and deepened, apprehension began to beat the air. Creole began to tell us what the blues were all about. They were not about anything very new. He and his boys up there were keeping it new, at the risk of ruin, destruction, madness, and death, in order to find new ways to make us listen. For, while the tale of how we suffer, and how we are delighted, and how we may triumph is never new, it always must be heard. There isn't any other tale to tell, it's the only light we've got in all this darkness.

And this tale, according to that face, that body, those strong hands on those strings, has another aspect in every country, and a new depth in every generation. Listen, Creole seemed to be saying, listen. Now these are Sonny's blues. He made the little black man on the drums know it, and the bright, brown man on the horn. Creole wasn't trying any longer to get Sonny in the water. He was wishing him Godspeed.° Then he stepped back, very slowly, filling the air with the immense suggestion that Sonny speak for himself.

Then they all gathered around Sonny and Sonny played. Every now and again one of them seemed to say, amen. Sonny's fingers filled the air with life, his life. But that life contained so many others. And Sonny went all the way back, he really began with the spare, flat statement of the opening phrase of the song. Then he began to make it his. It was very beautiful because it wasn't hurried and it was no longer a lament. I seemed to hear with what burning he had made it his, with what burning we had yet to make it ours, how we could cease lamenting. Freedom lurked around us and I understood, at last, that he could help us to be free if we would listen, that he would never be free until we did. Yet, there was no battle in his face now. I heard what he had gone through, and would continue to go through until he came to rest in earth. He had made it his: that long line, of which we knew only Mama and Daddy. And he was giving it back, as everything must be given back, so that, passing through death, it can live forever. I saw my mother's face again, and felt, for the first time, how the stones of the road she had walked on must have bruised her feet. I saw the moonlit road where my father's brother died. And it brought something else back to me, and carried me past it. I saw my little girl again and felt Isabel's tears again, and I felt my own tears begin to rise. And I was yet aware that this was only a moment, that the world waited outside, as hungry as a tiger, and that trouble stretched above us, longer than the sky.

Then it was over. Creole and Sonny let out their breath, both soaking wet, and grinning. There was a lot of applause and some of it was real. In the dark, the girl came by and I asked her to take drinks to the bandstand. There was a long pause, while they talked up there in the indigo light and after awhile I saw the girl put a Scotch and milk on top of the piano for Sonny. He didn't seem to notice it, but just before they started playing again, he sipped from it and looked toward me, and nodded. Then he put it back on top of the piano. For me, then, as they began to play again, it glowed and shook above my brother's head like the very cup of trembling.

*wishing him Godspeed:* to wish success.

## QUESTIONS

1. From whose point of view is "Sonny's Blues" told? How do the narrator's values and experiences affect his view of the story?
2. What is the older brother's profession? Does it suggest anything about his personality?
3. How would this story change if it were told by Sonny?
4. What event prompts the narrator to write his brother?
5. What does the narrator's mother ask him to do for Sonny? Does the older brother keep his promise?
6. The major characters in this story are called Mama, Daddy, and Sonny (the older brother is never named or even nicknamed). How do these names affect our sense of the story?
7. Reread the last four paragraphs and explain the significance of the statement "Now these are Sonny's blues." How has Sonny made this music his own?

## *Edgar Allan Poe*

### THE TELL-TALE HEART
1850

*Edgar Allan Poe (1809–1849), orphaned child of traveling actors, was raised by well-off foster parents, John and Frances Allan, in Richmond, Virginia. At eighteen he published his first book of poems. When Poe ran up heavy gambling debts as a student at the University of Virginia, Allan called him home and eventually disowned him. After two years in the army and a brief stay at West Point, Poe became a successful editor in Richmond, Philadelphia, and New York and an industrious contributor to newspapers and magazines. Marriage in 1836 to his thirteen-year-old cousin Virginia Clemm increased his happiness but also his burdens; mercilessly, he drove his pen to support*

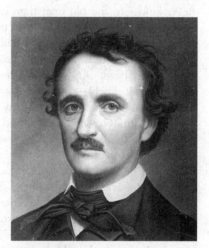

*Edgar Allan Poe*

*wife, self, and mother-in-law. Virginia, five years an invalid, died of tuberculosis in 1847. Poe, whose tolerance for alcohol was low, increased his drinking. He was found dead on a street in Baltimore. As a writer, Poe was a true innovator. His bizarre, macabre tales have held generations spellbound, as have some of his highly musical poems ("The Raven," "Annabel Lee"). His tales of private sleuth C. Auguste Dupin ("The Murders in the Rue Morgue," "The Purloined Letter") have earned him the title of father of the modern detective story. Other tales and his one novel,* The Narrative of Arthur Gordon Pym, *figure in the history of science fiction. A trail-blazing critic, Poe laid down laws for the short story (see page 570). His work has profoundly influenced not only American literature but European literature through French translations by Charles Baudelaire.*

True!—nervous—very, very dreadfully nervous I had been and am; but why *will* you say that I am mad? The disease had sharpened my senses—not destroyed—not dulled them. Above all was the sense of hearing acute. I heard all things in the heaven and in the earth. I heard many things in hell. How, then, am I mad? Hearken! and observe how healthily—how calmly I can tell you the whole story.

It is impossible to say how first the idea entered my brain; but once conceived, it haunted me day and night. Object there was none. Passion there was none. I loved the old man. He had never wronged me. He had never given me insult. For his gold I had no desire. I think it was his eye! yes, it was this! One of his eyes resembled that of a vulture—a pale blue eye, with a film over it. Whenever it fell upon me, my blood ran cold; and so by degrees—very gradually—I made up my mind to take the life of the old man, and thus rid myself of the eye for ever.

Now this is the point. You fancy me mad. Madmen know nothing. But you should have seen *me*. You should have seen how wisely I proceeded—with what caution—with what foresight—with what dissimulation I went to work! I was never kinder to the old man than during the whole week before I killed him. And every night, about midnight, I turned the latch of his door and opened it—oh, so gently! And then, when I had made an opening sufficient for my head, I put in a dark lantern, all closed, closed, so that no light shone out, and then I thrust in my head. Oh, you would have laughed to see how cunningly I thrust it in! I moved it slowly—very, very slowly, so that I might not disturb the old man's sleep. It took me an hour to place my whole head within the opening so far that I could see him as he lay upon his bed. Ha!—would a madman have been so wise as this? And then, when my head was well in the room, I undid the lantern cautiously—oh, so cautiously—cautiously (for the hinges creaked)—I undid it just so much that a single thin ray fell upon the vulture eye. And this I did for seven long nights—every night just at midnight—but I found the eye always closed; and so it was impossible to do the work; for it was not the old man who vexed me, but his Evil Eye. And every morning, when the day broke, I went boldly into the chamber, and spoke courageously to him, calling him by name in a hearty tone, and inquiring how he had passed the night. So you see he would have been a very profound old man, indeed, to suspect that every night, just at twelve, I looked in upon him while he slept.

Upon the eighth night I was more than usually cautious in opening the door. A watch's minute hand moves more quickly than did mine. Never before that night had I *felt* the extent of my own powers—of my sagacity. I could scarcely contain my feelings of triumph. To think that there I was, opening the door, little by little, and he not even to dream of my secret deeds or thoughts. I fairly chuckled at the idea; and perhaps he heard me; for he moved on the bed suddenly, as if startled. Now you may think that I drew back—but no. His room was as black as pitch with the thick darkness (for the shutters were close fastened, through fear of robbers), and so I knew that he could not see the opening of the door, and I kept pushing it on steadily, steadily.

I had my head in, and was about to open the lantern, when my thumb slipped upon the tin fastening, and the old man sprang up in the bed, crying out—"Who's there?"

I kept quite still and said nothing. For a whole hour I did not move a muscle, and in the meantime I did not hear him lie down. He was still sitting up in the bed listening;—just as I have done, night after night, hearkening to the death watches° in the wall.

Presently I heard a slight groan, and I knew it was the groan of mortal terror. It was not a groan of pain or of grief—oh, no!—it was the low stifled sound that arises from the bottom of the soul when overcharged with awe. I knew the sound very well. Many a night, just at midnight, when all the world slept, it has welled up from my own bosom, deepening, with its dreadful echo, the terrors that distracted me. I say I knew it well. I knew what the old man felt, and pitied him, although I chuckled at heart. I knew that he had been lying awake ever since the first slight noise, when he had turned in the bed. His fears had been ever since growing upon him. He had been trying to fancy them causeless, but could not. He had been saying to himself—"It is nothing but the wind in the chimney—it is only a mouse crossing the floor," or "it is merely a cricket which has made a single chirp." Yes, he had been trying to comfort himself with these suppositions; but he had found all in vain. *All in vain*; because Death, in approaching him, had stalked with his black shadow before him, and enveloped the victim. And it was the mournful influence of the unperceived shadow that caused him to feel—although he neither saw nor heard—to *feel* the presence of my head within the room.

When I had waited a long time, very patiently, without hearing him lie down, I resolved to open a little—a very, very little crevice in the lantern. So I opened it—you cannot imagine how stealthily, stealthily—until, at length, a single dim ray, like the thread of the spider, shot from out the crevice and full upon the vulture eye.

It was open—wide, wide open—and I grew furious as I gazed upon it. I saw it with perfect distinctness—all a dull blue, with a hideous veil over it that chilled the very marrow in my bones; but I could see nothing else of the old man's face or person: for I had directed the ray as if by instinct, precisely upon the damned spot.

And now have I not told you that what you mistake for madness is but over- acuteness of the senses?—now, I say, there came to my ears a low, dull, quick sound, such as a watch makes when enveloped in cotton. I knew *that* sound well too. It was the beating of the old man's heart. It increased my fury, as the beating of a drum stimulates the soldier into courage.

But even yet I refrained and kept still. I scarcely breathed. I held the lantern motionless. I tried how steadily I could maintain the ray upon the eye. Meantime the hellish tattoo of the heart increased. It grew quicker and quicker, and louder and louder every instant. The old man's terror *must* have been extreme! It grew louder, I say, louder every moment!—do you mark me well? I have told you that I

---

*death watches:* beetles that infest timbers. Their clicking sound was thought to be an omen of death.

am nervous: so I am. And now at the dead hour of the night, amid the dreadful silence of that old house, so strange a noise as this excited me to uncontrollable terror. Yet, for some minutes longer I refrained and stood still. But the beating grew louder, louder! I thought the heart must burst. And now a new anxiety seized me—the sound would be heard by a neighbor! The old man's hour had come! With a loud yell, I threw open the lantern and leaped into the room. He shrieked once—once only. In an instant I dragged him to the floor, and pulled the heavy bed over him. I then smiled gaily, to find the deed so far done. But, for many minutes, the heart beat on with a muffled sound. This, however, did not vex me; it would not be heard through the wall. At length it ceased. The old man was dead. I removed the bed and examined the corpse. Yes, he was stone, stone dead. I placed my hand upon the heart and held it there many minutes. There was no pulsation. He was stone dead. His eye would trouble me no more.

If still you think me mad, you will think so no longer when I describe the wise precautions I took for the concealment of the body. The night waned, and I worked hastily, but in silence. First of all I dismembered the corpse. I cut off the head and the arms and the legs.

I then took up three planks from the flooring of the chamber, and deposited all between the scantlings. I then replaced the boards so cleverly, so cunningly, that no human eye—not even *his*—could have detected anything wrong. There was nothing to wash out—no stain of any kind—no bloodspot whatever. I had been too wary for that. A tub had caught all—ha! ha!

When I had made an end of these labors, it was four o'clock—still dark as midnight. As the bell sounded the hour, there came a knocking at the street door. I went down to open it with a light heart,—for what had I *now* to fear? There entered three men, who introduced themselves, with perfect suavity, as officers of the police. A shriek had been heard by a neighbor during the night; suspicion of foul play had been aroused; information had been lodged at the police office, and they (the officers) had been deputed to search the premises.

I smiled,—for *what* had I to fear? I bade the gentlemen welcome. The shriek, I said, was my own in a dream. The old man, I mentioned, was absent in the country. I took my visitors all over the house. I bade them search—search *well*. I led them, at length, to *his* chamber. I showed them his treasures, secure, undisturbed. In the enthusiasm of my confidence, I brought chairs into the room, and desired them *here* to rest from their fatigues, while I myself, in the wild audacity of my perfect triumph, placed my own seat upon the very spot beneath which reposed the corpse of the victim.

The officers were satisfied. My *manner* had convinced them. I was singularly at ease. They sat, and while I answered cheerily, they chatted familiar things. But, ere long, I felt myself getting pale and wished them gone. My head ached, and I fancied a ringing in my ears: but still they sat and still they chatted. The ringing became more distinct:—it continued and became more distinct: I talked more freely to get rid of the feeling: but it continued and gained definitiveness—until, at length, I found that the noise was *not* within my ears.

No doubt I now grew *very* pale:—but I talked more fluently, and with a heightened voice. Yet the sound increased—and what could I do? It was *a low, dull, quick sound—much such a sound as a watch makes when enveloped in cotton.* I gasped for breath—and yet the officers heard it not. I talked more quickly—more vehemently; but the noise steadily increased. I arose and argued about trifles, in a high key and with violent gesticulations, but the noise steadily increased. Why *would* they not be gone? I paced the floor to and fro with heavy strides, as if excited to fury by the observation of the men—but the noise steadily increased. Oh God! what *could* I do? I foamed—I raved—I swore! I swung the chair upon which I had been sitting, and grated it upon the boards, but the noise arose over all and continually increased. It grew louder—louder—*louder!* And still the men chatted pleasantly, and smiled. Was it possible they heard not? Almighty God!—no, no! They heard!—they suspected!—they *knew!*—they were making a mockery of my horror!—this I thought, and this I think. But any thing was better than this agony! Any thing was more tolerable than this derision! I could bear those hypocritical smiles no longer! I felt that I must scream or die!—and now—again!—hark! louder! louder! louder! *louder!*—

"Villains!" I shrieked, "dissemble no more! I admit the deed!—tear up the planks!—here, here!—it is the beating of his hideous heart!"

## QUESTIONS

1. From what point of view is Poe's story told? Why is this point of view particularly effective for "The Tell-Tale Heart"?
2. Point to details in the story that identify its speaker as an unreliable narrator.
3. What do we know about the old man in the story? What motivates the narrator to kill him?
4. In spite of all his precautions, the narrator does not commit the perfect crime. What trips him up?
5. How do you account for the police officers' chatting calmly with the murderer instead of reacting to the sound that stirs the murderer into a frenzy?
6. See the students' comments on this story in "Writing about a Story" in the Supplement: Writing. What do they point out that enlarges your own appreciation of Poe's art?

## SUGGESTIONS FOR WRITING

1. Here is a writing exercise to help you sense what a difference a point of view makes. Write a short statement from the point of view of one of these characters: William Faulkner's Homer Barron (on "My Affair with Miss Emily"). Sonny from James Baldwin's "Sonny's Blues" (on how he managed to give up drugs). Edgar Allan Poe's old man (on "My Live-in Servant and His Little Peculiarities").
2. Write a brief narrative account of a decisive moment in your life—one that changed your outlook or your future—from two quite different, contrasting points of view. One instance: a memory of buying a first car, told in two ways: from the first-person point of view of the buyer and from the third-person point of view of a worried parent or a gloating car dealer. Another example: An account of meeting a person who profoundly affected your life, from (1) your point of view and then (2) from the point of view of that other person.

3. Topic for an essay of two or three paragraphs: How William Faulkner Sees North and South in "A Rose for Emily."
4. Taking examples from short stories in other chapters, point out some differences between male and female ways of looking at things. Some stories especially to consider: "A & P," "The Jilting of Granny Weatherall," "The Five-Forty-Eight," "First Confession," and "I Stand Here Ironing." (Note: Because a character holds a certain attitude in a specific situation doesn't oblige you to argue that such an attitude is universally held by women and men.)
5. Adopt the point of view of a naive, innocent commentator—either a younger, less-knowing version of yourself, or some imagined character. From this point of view, discuss the proposed ban on nuclear weapons, the case for legislation against the sale of pornography, or another issue in the news. Sound off like a true ignoramus. An effective paper will make clear to your reader that your speaker is full of malarkey. (This task means that you, the knowing writer, and not the uninformed speaker who is your mask, will need to know something about your subject.)
6. Choosing one of the "Stories for Further Reading" (in Chapter Eleven), briefly describe whatever point of view you find in it. Then, in a paragraph or two, explain why this angle of vision seems right and fitting to the telling of this story. If you like, you may argue that the story might be told more effectively from some other point of view.
7. Write a one-paragraph story in the first person. Some recent small event in your life is a possible subject. Then rewrite your story from the *objective*, or "fly-on-the-wall," point of view. (See the passage by Dashiell Hammett on page 22 for an illustration.) Following your two terse stories, make a comment summing up what this exercise told you about point of view.

# 3 Character

From popular fiction and drama, both classic and contemporary, we are acquainted with many stereotyped characters. Called **stock characters,** they are often known by some outstanding trait or traits: the *bragging* soldier of Greek and Roman comedy, the Prince *Charming* of fairy tales, the *mad* scientist of horror movies, the *loyal* sidekick of Westerns, the *greedy* explorer of Tarzan films, the *brilliant but alcoholic* brain surgeon of medical thrillers on television. Stock characters are especially convenient for writers of commercial fiction: they require little detailed portraiture, for we already know them well. Most writers of the literary story, however, attempt to create characters who strike us not as stereotypes but as unique individuals. Although stock characters tend to have single dominant virtues and vices, characters in the finest contemporary short stories tend to have many facets, like people we meet.

A **character,** then, is presumably an imagined person who inhabits a story—although that simple definition may admit to a few exceptions. In George Stewart's novel *Storm,* the protagonist is the wind; in Richard Adams's *Watership Down,* the main characters are rabbits. But usually we recognize, in the main characters of a story, human personalities that become familiar to us. If the story seems "true to life," we generally find that its characters act in a reasonably consistent manner, and that the author has provided them with **motivation:** sufficient reason to behave as they do. Should a character behave in a sudden and unexpected way, seeming to deny what we have been told about his nature or personality, we trust that he had a reason and that sooner or later we will discover it. This is not to claim that *all* authors insist that their characters behave with absolute consistency, for (as we shall see later in this chapter) some contemporary stories feature characters who sometimes act without apparent reason. Nor can we say that, in good fiction, characters never change or develop. In *A Christmas Carol,* Charles Dickens tells how Ebeneezer Scrooge, a tightfisted miser, reforms overnight, suddenly gives to the poor, and endeavors to assist his clerk's struggling family. But Dickens amply demonstrates why Scrooge had such a change of heart: four ghostly visitors, stirring kind memories the old miser had forgotten and also warning him of the probable consequences of his habits, provide the character (and hence the story) with adequate motivation.

To borrow the useful terms of the English novelist E. M. Forster, characters may seem **flat** or **round,** depending on whether a writer sketches or sculptures them. A flat character has only one outstanding trait or feature, or at most a few distinguishing marks: for example, the familiar stock character of the mad scientist, with his lust for absolute power and his crazily gleaming eyes. Flat characters, however, need not be stock characters: in all of literature there is probably only one Tiny Tim, though his functions in A *Christmas Carol* are mainly to invoke blessings and to remind others of their Christian duties. Some writers, notably Balzac, who peopled his many novels with hosts of characters, try to distinguish the flat ones by giving each a single odd physical feature or mannerism—a nervous twitch, a piercing gaze, an obsessive fondness for oysters. Round characters, however, present us with more facets—that is, their authors portray them in greater depth and in more generous detail. Such a round character may appear to us only as he appears to the other characters in the story. If their views of him differ, we will see him from more than one side. In other stories, we enter a character's mind and come to know him through his own thoughts, feelings, and perceptions. By the time we finish reading Katherine Mansfield's "Miss Brill" (in Chapter Two), we are well acquainted with the central character and find her amply three-dimensional.

Flat characters tend to stay the same throughout a story, but round characters often change—learn or become enlightened, grow or deteriorate. In William Faulkner's "Barn Burning" (Chapter Five), the boy Sarty Snopes, driven to defy his proud and violent father, becomes at the story's end more knowing and more mature. (Some critics call a fixed character **static;** a changing one, **dynamic.**) This is not to damn a flat character as an inferior work of art. In most fiction— even the greatest—minor characters tend to be flat instead of round. Why? Rounding them would cost time and space; and so enlarged, they might only distract us from the main characters.

"A character, first of all, is the noise of his name," according to novelist William Gass.[1] Names, chosen artfully, can indicate natures. A simple illustration is the completely virtuous Squire Allworthy, the foster father in *Tom Jones* by Henry Fielding. Subtler, perhaps, is the custom of giving a character a name that makes an **allusion:** a reference to some famous person, place, or thing in history, in other fiction, or in actuality. For his central characters in *Moby-Dick,* Herman Melville chose names from the Old Testament, calling his tragic and domineering Ahab after a Biblical tyrant who came to a bad end, and his wandering narrator Ishmael after a Biblical outcast. Whether or not it includes an allusion, a good name often reveals the character of the character. Charles Dickens, a vigorous and richly suggestive christener, named a charming confidence man Mr.

[1]"The Concept of Character in Fiction," in *Fiction and the Figures of Life* (New York: Knopf, 1970).

Jingle (suggesting something jingly, light, and superficially pleasant), named a couple of shyster lawyers Dodgson and Fogg (suggesting dodging evasiveness and foglike obfuscation), and named two heartless educators, who grimly drill their schoolchildren in "hard facts," Gradgind and M'Choakumchild. Henry James, who so loved names that he kept lists of them for characters he might someday conceive, chose for a sensitive, cultured gentleman the name of Lambert Strether; for a down-to-earth, benevolent individual, the name of Mrs. Bread. (But James may have wished to indicate that names cannot be identified with people absolutely, in giving the fragile, considerate heroine of *The Spoils of Poynton* the harsh sounding name of Fleda Vetch.)

Instead of a hero, many a recent novel has featured an **antihero:** a protagonist conspicuously lacking in one or more of the usual attributes of a traditional hero (bravery, skill, idealism, sense of purpose). The antihero is an ordinary, unglorious twentieth-century citizen, usually drawn (according to Sean O'Faolain) as someone "groping, puzzled, cross, mocking, frustrated, and isolated."[2] (Obviously, there are antiheroines, too.) If epic poets once drew their heroes as decisive leaders of their people, embodying their people's highest ideals, antiheroes tend to be loners, without perfections, just barely able to survive. Antiheroes lack "character," as defined by psychologist Anthony Quinton to mean a person's conduct or "persistence and consistency in seeking to realize his long-term aims."[3] A gulf separates Leopold Bloom, antihero of James Joyce's novel *Ulysses*, from the hero of the Greek *Odyssey*. In Homer's epic, Ulysses wanders the Mediterranean, battling monsters and overcoming enchantments. In Joyce's novel, Bloom wanders the littered streets of Dublin, peddling advertising space. Mersault, the title character of Albert Camus' novel *The Stranger*, is so alienated from his own life that he is unmoved at the news of his mother's death. In contemporary fiction, by the way, female antiheroes abound: Ellen, for instance, the aimlessly drifting central character of Edna O'Brien's novel *August Is a Wicked Month*.

Evidently, not only fashions in heroes but also attitudes toward human nature have undergone change. In the eighteenth century, Scottish philosopher David Hume argued that the nature of an individual is relatively fixed and unalterable. Hume mentioned, however, a few exceptions: "A person of an obliging disposition gives a peevish answer; but he has the toothache or has not dined. A stupid fellow discovers an obvious alacrity in his carriage; but he has met with a sudden piece of good fortune." For a long time after Hume, novelists and short-story writers seem to have assumed that characters behave nearly always in a predictable fashion and that their actions ought to be consistent with their personalities. Now and again, a writer differed: Jane Austen in *Pride and Prejudice* has her protagonist Elizabeth Bennet remark to the citified Mr. Darcy, who fears that life in the country cannot be amusing, "But people themselves alter so much, that there is something to be observed in them forever."

[2] *The Vanishing Hero* (Boston: Little, Brown & Co., 1957).
[3] "The Continuity of Persons," *Times Literary Supplement* on "The Nature of Character," 27 July 1973.

Many contemporary writers of fiction would deny even that people have definite selves to alter. Following Sigmund Freud and other modern psychologists, they assume that a large part of human behavior is shaped in the unconscious—that, for instance, a person might fear horses, not because of a basically timid nature, but because of unconscious memories of having been nearly trampled by a horse when a child. To some writers it now appears that what Hume called a "disposition" (now called a "personality") is more vulnerable to change from such causes as age, disease, neurosis, psychic shock, or brainwashing than was once believed. Hence, some characters in twentieth-century fiction appear to be shifting bundles of impulses. "You mustn't look in my novel for the old stable ego of character," wrote D. H. Lawrence to a friend about *The Rainbow*; and in that novel and other novels Lawrence demonstrated his view of individuals as bits of one vast Life Force, spurred to act by incomprehensible passions and urges—the "dark gods" in them. The idea of the **gratuitous act,** a deed without cause or motive, is explored in André Gide's novel *Lafcadio's Adventures*, in which an ordinary young man without homicidal tendencies abruptly and for no reason pushes a stranger from a speeding train. The usual limits of character are playfully violated by Virginia Woolf in *Orlando*, a novel whose protagonist, defying time, lives right on from Elizabethan days into the present, changing in midstory from a man into a woman. Characterization, as practiced by nineteenth-century novelists, almost entirely disappears in Franz Kafka's *The Castle*, whose protagonist has no home, no family, no definite appearance—not even a name, just the initial *K*. Characters are things of the past, insists the contemporary French novelist Alain Robbe-Grillet. Still, many writers of fiction go on portraying them.

## Katherine Anne Porter

THE JILTING OF GRANNY WEATHERALL                                        1930

*Katherine Anne Porter (1890–1980) was born in Indian Creek, Texas. Her mother died when she was two, and Porter was raised by a grandmother who surrounded the growing girl with books. At sixteen, apparently bored with her studies at an Ursuline convent, Porter ran away from home. Three years later, she began supporting herself as a news reporter in Chicago, Denver, and Fort Worth, and sometimes as an actress and ballad singer traveling through the South. Sojourns in Europe and in Mexico supplied her with matter for some of her finest stories. Her brilliant, sensitive short fiction, first collected in* Flowering

Katherine Anne Porter

Judas (1930), *won her a high reputation. Her one novel,* Ship of Fools *(1962), with which she had struggled for twenty years, received harsh critical notices, but proved a commercial success. Made into a movie, it ended Porter's lifelong struggle to earn a living. In 1965 her* Collected Stories *received a Pulitzer prize and a National Book Award.*

She flicked her wrist neatly out of Doctor Harry's pudgy careful fingers and pulled the sheet up to her chin. The brat ought to be in knee breeches. Doctoring around the country with spectacles on his nose! "Get along now, take your schoolbooks and go. There's nothing wrong with me."

Doctor Harry spread a warm paw like a cushion on her forehead where the forked green vein danced and made her eyelids twitch. "Now, now, be a good girl, and we'll have you up in no time."

"That's no way to speak to a woman nearly eighty years old just because she's down. I'd have you respect your elders, young man."

"Well, Missy, excuse me." Doctor Harry patted her cheek. "But I've got to warn you, haven't I? You're a marvel, but you must be careful or you're going to be good and sorry."

"Don't tell me what I'm going to be. I'm on my feet now, morally speaking.     5
It's Cornelia. I had to go to bed to get rid of her."

Her bones felt loose, and floated around in her skin, and Doctor Harry floated like a balloon around the foot of the bed. He floated and pulled down his waistcoat and swung his glasses on a cord. "Well, stay where you are, it certainly can't hurt you."

"Get along and doctor your sick," said Granny Weatherall. "Leave a well woman alone. I'll call for you when I want you. . . . Where were you forty years ago when I pulled through milk leg and double pneumonia? You weren't even born. Don't let Cornelia lead you on," she shouted, because Doctor Harry appeared to float up to the ceiling and out. "I pay my own bills, and I don't throw my money away on nonsense!"

She meant to wave good-by, but it was too much trouble. Her eyes closed of themselves, it was like a dark curtain drawn around the bed. The pillow rose and floated under her, pleasant as a hammock in a light wind. She listened to the leaves rustling outside the window. No, somebody was swishing newspapers: no, Cornelia and Doctor Harry were whispering together. She leaped broad awake, thinking they whispered in her ear.

"She was never like this, *never* like this!" "Well, what can we expect?" "Yes, eighty years old. . . ."

Well, and what if she was? She still had ears. It was like Cornelia to whisper     10
around doors. She always kept things secret in such a public way. She was always being tactful and kind. Cornelia was dutiful; that was the trouble with her. Dutiful and good: "So good and dutiful," said Granny, "that I'd like to spank her." She saw herself spanking Cornelia and making a fine job of it.

"What'd you say, Mother?"

Granny felt her face tying up in hard knots.

"Can't a body think, I'd like to know?"

"I thought you might want something."

"I do. I want a lot of things. First off, go away and don't whisper."                    15

She lay and drowsed, hoping in her sleep that the children would keep out and let her rest a minute. It had been a long day. Not that she was tired. It was always pleasant to snatch a minute now and then. There was always so much to be done, let me see: tomorrow.

Tomorrow was far away and there was nothing to trouble about. Things were finished somehow when the time came; thank God there was always a little margin over for peace: then a person could spread out the plan of life and tuck in the edges orderly. It was good to have everything clean and folded away, with the hair brushes and tonic bottles sitting straight on the white embroidered linen: the day started without fuss and the pantry shelves laid out with rows of jelly glasses and brown jugs and white stone-china jars with blue whirligigs and words painted on them: coffee, tea, sugar, ginger, cinnamon, allspice: and the bronze clock with the lion on top nicely dusted off. The dust that lion could collect in twenty-four hours! The box in the attic with all those letters tied up, well, she'd have to go through that tomorrow. All those letters—George's letters and John's letters and her letters to them both—lying around for the children to find afterwards made her uneasy. Yes, that would be tomorrow's business. No use to let them know how silly she had been once.

While she was rummaging around she found death in her mind and it felt clammy and unfamiliar. She had spent so much time preparing for death there was no need for bringing it up again. Let it take care of itself now. When she was sixty she had felt very old, finished, and went around making farewell trips to see her children and grandchildren, with a secret in her mind: This is the very last of your mother, children! Then she made her will and came down with a long fever. That was all just a notion like a lot of other things, but it was lucky too, for she had once for all got over the idea of dying for a long time. Now she couldn't be worried. She hoped she had better sense now. Her father had lived to be one hundred and two years old and had drunk a noggin of strong hot toddy on his last birthday. He told the reporters it was his daily habit, and he owed his long life to it. He had made quite a scandal and was very pleased about it. She believed she'd just plague Cornelia a little.

"Cornelia! Cornelia!" No footsteps, but a sudden hand on her cheek. "Bless you, where have you been?"

"Here, Mother."                    20

"Well, Cornelia, I want a noggin of hot toddy."

"Are you cold, darling?"

"I'm chilly, Cornelia. Lying in bed stops the circulation. I must have told you that a thousand times."

Well, she could just hear Cornelia telling her husband that Mother was getting a little childish and they'd have to humor her. The thing that most annoyed her was that Cornelia thought she was deaf, dumb, and blind. Little hasty glances and tiny gestures tossed around her and over her head saying, "Don't cross her, let her have her way, she's eighty years old," and she sitting there as if she lived in a thin glass cage. Sometimes Granny almost made up her mind to pack up and move back to her own house where nobody could remind her every minute that she was old. Wait, wait, Cornelia, till your own children whisper behind your back!

In her day she had kept a better house and had got more work done. She <sup>25</sup> wasn't too old yet for Lydia to be driving eighty miles for advice when one of the children jumped the track, and Jimmy still dropped in and talked things over: "Now, Mammy, you've a good business head, I want to know what you think of this? . . . " Old. Cornelia couldn't change the furniture around without asking. Little things, little things! They had been so sweet when they were little. Granny wished the old days were back again with the children young and everything to be done over. It had been a hard pull, but not too much for her. When she thought of all the food she had cooked, and all the clothes she had cut and sewed, and all the gardens she had made—well, the children showed it. There they were, made out of her, and they couldn't get away from that. Sometimes she wanted to see John again and point to them and say, Well, I didn't do so badly, did I? But that would have to wait. That was for tomorrow. She used to think of him as a man, but now all the children were older than their father, and he would be a child beside her if she saw him now. It seemed strange and there was something wrong in the idea. Why, he couldn't possibly recognize her. She had fenced in a hundred acres once, digging the post holes herself and clamping the wires with just a negro boy to help. That changed a woman. John would be looking for a young woman with the peaked Spanish comb in her hair and the painted fan. Digging post holes changed a woman. Riding country roads in the winter when women had their babies was another thing: sitting up nights with sick horses and sick negroes and sick children and hardly ever losing one. John, I hardly ever lost one of them! John would see that in a minute, that would be something he could understand, she wouldn't have to explain anything!

It made her feel like rolling up her sleeves and putting the whole place to rights again. No matter if Cornelia was determined to be everywhere at once, there were a great many things left undone on this place. She would start tomorrow and do them. It was good to be strong enough for everything, even if all you made melted and changed and slipped under your hands, so that by the time you finished you almost forgot what you were working for. What was it I set out to do? she asked herself intently, but she could not remember. A fog rose over the valley, she saw it marching across the creek swallowing the trees and moving up the hill like an army of ghosts. Soon it would be at the near edge of the orchard, and then it was time to go in and light the lamps. Come in, children, don't stay out in the night air.

Lighting the lamps had been beautiful. The children huddled up to her and breathed like little calves waiting at the bars in the twilight. Their eyes followed the match and watched the flame rise and settle in a blue curve, then they moved away from her. The lamp was lit, they didn't have to be scared and hang on to mother any more. Never, never, never more. God, for all my life I thank Thee. Without Thee, my God, I could never have done it. Hail, Mary, full of grace.

I want you to pick all the fruit this year and see that nothing is wasted. There's always someone who can use it. Don't let good things rot for want of using. You waste life when you waste good food. Don't let things get lost. It's bitter to lose things. Now, don't let me get to thinking, not when I am tired and taking a little nap before supper. . . .

The pillow rose about her shoulders and pressed against her heart and the memory was being squeezed out of it: oh, push down the pillow, somebody: it would smother her if she tried to hold it. Such a fresh breeze blowing and such a green day with no threats in it. But he had not come, just the same. What does a woman do when she has put on the white veil and set out the white cake for a man and he doesn't come? She tried to remember. No, I swear he never harmed me but in that. He never harmed me but in that . . . and what if he did? There was the day, the day, but a whirl of dark smoke rose and covered it, crept up and over into the bright field where everything was planted so carefully in orderly rows. That was hell, she knew hell when she saw it. For sixty years she had prayed against remembering him and against losing her soul in the deep pit of hell, and now the two things were mingled in one and the thought of him was a smoky cloud from hell that moved and crept in her head when she had just got rid of Doctor Harry and was trying to rest a minute. Wounded vanity, Ellen, said a sharp voice in the top of her mind. Don't let your wounded vanity get the upper hand of you. Plenty of girls get jilted. You were jilted, weren't you? Then stand up to it. Her eyelids wavered and let in streamers of blue-gray light like tissue paper over her eyes. She must get up and pull the shades down or she'd never sleep. She was in bed again and the shades were not down. How could that happen? Better turn over, hide from the light, sleeping in the light gave you nightmares. "Mother, how do you feel now?" and a stinging wetness on her forehead. But I don't like having my face washed in cold water!

Hapsy? George? Lydia? Jimmy? No, Cornelia, and her features were swollen    30 and full of little puddles. "They're coming, darling, they'll all be here soon." Go wash your face, child, you look funny.

Instead of obeying, Cornelia knelt down and put her head on the pillow. She seemed to be talking but there was no sound. "Well, are you tongue-tied? Whose birthday is it? Are you going to give a party?"

Cornelia's mouth moved urgently in strange shapes. "Don't do that, you bother me, daughter."

"Oh, no, Mother. Oh, no. . . ."

Nonsense. It was strange about children. They disputed your every word. "No what, Cornelia?"

"Here's Doctor Harry."    35

"I won't see that boy again. He just left three minutes ago."

"That was this morning, Mother. It's night now. Here's the nurse."

"This is Doctor Harry, Mrs. Weatherall. I never saw you look so young and happy!"

"Ah, I'll never be young again—but I'd be happy if they'd let me lie in peace and get rested."

She thought she spoke up loudly, but no one answered. A warm weight on her forehead, a warm bracelet on her wrist, and a breeze went on whispering, trying to tell her something. A shuffle of leaves in the everlasting hand of God. He blew on them and they danced and rattled. "Mother, don't mind, we're going to give you a little hypodermic." "Look here, daughter, how do ants get in this bed? I saw sugar ants yesterday." Did you send for Hapsy too?

It was Hapsy she really wanted. She had to go a long way back through a great many rooms to find Hapsy standing with a baby on her arm. She seemed to herself to be Hapsy also, and the baby on Hapsy's arm was Hapsy and himself and herself, all at once, and there was no surprise in the meeting. Then Hapsy melted from within and turned flimsy as gray gauze and the baby was a gauzy shadow, and Hapsy came up close and said, "I thought you'd never come," and looked at her very searchingly and said, "You haven't changed a bit!" They leaned forward to kiss, when Cornelia began whispering from a long way off, "Oh, is there anything you want to tell me? Is there anything I can do for you?"

Yes, she had changed her mind after sixty years and she would like to see George. I want you to find George. Find him and be sure to tell him I forgot him. I want him to know I had my husband just the same and my children and my house like any other woman. A good house too and a good husband that I loved and fine children out of him. Better than I hoped for even. Tell him I was given back everything he took away and more. Oh, no, oh, God, no, there was something else besides the house and the man and the children. Oh, surely they were not all? What was it? Something not given back . . . Her breath crowded down under her ribs and grew into a monstrous frightening shape with cutting edges; it bored up into her head, and the agony was unbelievable: Yes, John, get the Doctor now, no more talk, my time has come.

When this one was born it should be the last. The last. It should have been born first, for it was the one she had truly wanted. Everything came in good time. Nothing left out, left over. She was strong, in three days she would be as well as ever. Better. A woman needed milk in her to have her full health.

"Mother, do you hear me?"

"I've been telling you—"

"Mother, Father Connolly's here."

"I went to Holy Communion only last week. Tell him I'm not so sinful as all that."

"Father just wants to speak to you."

He could speak as much as he pleased. It was like him to drop in and inquire about her soul as if it were a teething baby, and then stay for a cup of tea and a round of cards and gossip. He always had a funny story of some sort, usually about an Irishman who made his little mistakes and confessed them, and the point lay in some absurd thing he would blurt out in the confessional showing his struggles between native piety and original sin. Granny felt easy about her soul. Cornelia, where are your manners? Give Father Connolly a chair. She had her secret comfortable understanding with a few favorite saints who cleared a straight road to God for her. All as surely signed and sealed as the papers for the new Forty Acres. Forever . . . heirs and assigns forever. Since the day the wedding cake was not cut, but thrown out and wasted. The whole bottom dropped out of the world, and there she was blind and sweating with nothing under her feet and walls falling away. His hand had caught her under the breast, she had not fallen, there was the freshly polished floor with the green rug on it, just as before. He had cursed like a sailor's parrot and said, "I'll kill him for you." Don't lay a hand on him, for my sake leave something to God. "Now, Ellen, you must believe what I tell you. . . ."

So there was nothing, nothing to worry about any more, except sometimes in the night one of the children screamed in a nightmare, and they both hustled out shaking and hunting for the matches and calling, "There, wait a minute, here we are!" John, get the doctor now, Hapsy's time has come. But there was Hapsy standing by the bed in a white cap. "Cornelia, tell Hapsy to take off her cap. I can't see her plain."

Her eyes opened very wide and the room stood out like a picture she had seen somewhere. Dark colors with the shadows rising towards the ceiling in long angles. The tall black dresser gleamed with nothing on it but John's picture, enlarged from a little one, with John's eyes very black when they should have been blue. You never saw him, so how do you know how he looked? But the man insisted the copy was perfect, it was very rich and handsome. For a picture, yes, but it's not my husband. The table by the bed had a linen cover and a candle and a crucifix. The light was blue from Cornelia's silk lampshades. No sort of light at all, just frippery. You had to live forty years with kerosene lamps to appreciate honest electricity. She felt very strong and she saw Doctor Harry with a rosy nimbus around him.

"You look like a saint, Doctor Harry, and I vow that's as near as you'll ever come to it."

"She's saying something."

"I heard you, Cornelia. What's all this carrying-on?"

"Father Connolly's saying—"

Cornelia's voice staggered and bumped like a cart in a bad road. It rounded corners and turned back again and arrived nowhere. Granny stepped up in the cart very lightly and reached for the reins, but a man sat beside her and she knew him by his hands, driving the cart. She did not look in his face, for she knew without seeing, but looked instead down the road where the trees leaned over and bowed to each other and a thousand birds were singing a Mass. She felt like singing too, but she put her hand in the bosom of her dress and pulled out a rosary, and Father Connolly murmured Latin in a very solemn voice and tickled her feet. My God, will you stop that nonsense? I'm a married woman. What if he did run away and leave me to face the priest by myself? I found another a whole world better. I wouldn't have exchanged my husband for anybody except St. Michael himself, and you may tell him that for me with a thank you in the bargain.

50

55

Light flashed on her closed eyelids, and a deep roaring shook her. Cornelia, is that lightning? I hear thunder. There's going to be a storm. Close all the windows. Call the children in. . . . "Mother, here we are, all of us." "Is that you, Hapsy?" "Oh, no, I'm Lydia. We drove as fast as we could." Their faces drifted above her, drifted away. The rosary fell out of her hands and Lydia put it back. Jimmy tried to help, their hands fumbled together, and Granny closed two fingers around Jimmy's thumb. Beads wouldn't do, it must be something alive. She was so amazed her thoughts ran round and round. So, my dear Lord, this is my death and I wasn't even thinking about it. My children have come to see me die. But I can't, it's not time. Oh, I always hated surprises. I wanted to give Cornelia the amethyst set—Cornelia, you're to have the amethyst set, but Hapsy's to wear it when she wants, and, Doctor Harry, do shut up. Nobody sent for you. Oh, my dear Lord, do wait a minute. I meant to do something about the Forty Acres, Jimmy doesn't need it and Lydia will later on, with that worthless husband of hers. I meant to finish the altar cloth and send six bottles of wine to Sister Borgia for her dyspepsia. I want to send six bottles of wine to Sister Borgia, Father Connolly, now don't let me forget.

Cornelia's voice made short turns and tilted over and crashed, "Oh, Mother, oh, Mother, oh, Mother. . . ."

"I'm not going, Cornelia. I'm taken by surprise. I can't go."

You'll see Hapsy again. What about her? "I thought you'd never come." 60 Granny made a long journey outward, looking for Hapsy. What if I don't find her? What then? Her heart sank down and down, there was no bottom to death, she couldn't come to the end of it. The blue light from Cornelia's lampshade drew into a tiny point in the center of her brain, it flickered and winked like an eye, quietly it fluttered and dwindled. Granny lay curled down within herself, amazed and watchful, staring at the point of light that was herself; her body was now only a deeper mass of shadow in an endless darkness and this darkness would curl around the light and swallow it up. God, give a sign!

For the second time there was no sign. Again no bridegroom and the priest in the house. She could not remember any other sorrow because this grief wiped them all away. Oh, no, there's nothing more cruel than this—I'll never forgive it. She stretched herself with a deep breath and blew out the light.

## QUESTIONS

1. In the very first paragraph, what does the writer tell us about Ellen (Granny) Weatherall?
2. What does the name of Weatherall have to do with Granny's nature (or her life story)? What other traits or qualities do you find in her?
3. "Her bones felt loose, and floated around in her skin, and Doctor Harry floated like a balloon" (paragraph 6). What do you understand from this statement? By what other remarks does the writer indicate Granny's condition? In paragraph 56, why does Father Connolly tickle Granny's feet? At what other moments in the story does she fail to understand what is happening, or confuse the present with the past?

4. Exactly what happened to Ellen Weatherall sixty years earlier? What effects did this event have on her?

5. In paragraph 49, who do you guess to be the man who "cursed like a sailor's parrot"? In paragraph 56, who do you assume to be the man driving the cart? Is the fact that these persons are not clearly labeled and identified a failure on the author's part?

6. What is stream of consciousness? (The term is discussed on page 24.) Would you call "The Jilting of Granny Weatherall" a stream of consciousness story? Refer to the story in your reply.

7. Sum up the character of the daughter Cornelia.

8. Why doesn't Granny's last child Hapsy come to her mother's deathbed?

9. Would you call the character of Doctor Harry "flat" or "round"? Why is his flatness (or roundness) appropriate to the story?

10. How is this the story of another "jilting"? What is similar between that fateful day of sixty years ago (described in paragraphs 29, 49, and 61) and the moment when Granny is dying? This time, who is the "bridegroom" not in the house?

11. "This is the story of an eighty-year-old woman lying in bed, getting groggy, and dying. I can't see why it should interest anybody." How would you answer this critic?

## John Cheever

### THE FIVE-FORTY-EIGHT                                                    1954

*John Cheever (1912–1982) was born in Quincy, Massachusetts. His parents had been modestly prosperous, but their liveli- hood declined substantially and was finally dashed by the 1929 stock market crash. Cheever was sent away to Thayer Academy, a prep school, where he was a poor student. When he was expelled at eigh- teen, he wrote a story about the incident that was published in* The New Republic *(1930). Cheever never finished high school or attended college, dedicating himself instead to writing. For years he lived in poverty in one tiny room, sustaining himself on "a bread and buttermilk diet." Gradually he became a celebrated writer.*

John Cheever

*Once famous, however, Cheever hid the financial problems of his parents and his youthful poverty with fanciful tales of an aristocratic background. Cheever's stories, most of which appeared in* The New Yorker, *often deal with the ordinary lives of mid- dle-class characters living in Manhattan or its suburbs.*

*Although his stories are realistic in plot and setting, they also often contain an underlying religious vision—exploring themes of guilt, grace, and redemption. Cheever's novels include* The Wapshot Chronicle *(1957), which won the National Book Award;*

Bullet Park (1969); and Falconer (1977). The Stories of John Cheever (1978), selected works from his five volumes of short fiction, not only won the Pulitzer Prize and National Book Critics Circle Award, it also became the first book of short stories in decades to make the best-seller list. After Cheever's death, his notebooks and letters revealed how tortured his life had been by sex and alcohol. While some early reviewers regarded Cheever's popular stories as "New Yorker fiction" (satiric views of middle-class life), critics now see the psychological and religious vision underlying his work. Cheever's central themes are sin, despair, and redemption. Once undervalued, Cheever is now generally regarded as one of the finest American short-story writers of the century.

When Blake stepped out of the elevator, he saw her. A few people, mostly men waiting for girls, stood in the lobby watching the elevator doors. She was among them. As he saw her, her face took on a look of such loathing and purpose that he realized she had been waiting for him. He did not approach her. She had no legitimate business with him. They had nothing to say. He turned and walked toward the glass doors at the end of the lobby, feeling that faint guilt and bewilderment we experience when we bypass some old friend or classmate who seems threadbare, or sick, or miserable in some other way. It was five-eighteen by the clock in the Western Union office. He could catch the express. As he waited his turn at the revolving doors, he saw that it was still raining. It had been raining all day, and he noticed now how much louder the rain made the noises of the street. Outside, he started walking briskly east toward Madison Avenue. Traffic was tied up, and horns were blowing urgently on a crosstown street in the distance. The sidewalk was crowded. He wondered what she had hoped to gain by a glimpse of him coming out of the office building at the end of the day. Then he wondered if she was following him.

Walking in the city, we seldom turn and look back. The habit restrained Blake. He listened for a minute—foolishly—as he walked, as if he could distinguish her footsteps from the worlds of sound in the city at the end of a rainy day. Then he noticed, ahead of him on the other side of the street, a break in the wall of buildings. Something had been torn down; something was being put up, but the steel structure had only just risen above the sidewalk fence and daylight poured through the gap. Blake stopped opposite here and looked into a store window. It was a decorator's or an auctioneer's. The window was arranged like a room in which people live and entertain their friends. There were cups on the coffee table, magazines to read, and flowers in the vases, but the flowers were dead and the cups were empty and the guests had not come. In the plate glass, Blake saw a clear reflection of himself and the crowds that were passing, like shadows, at his back. Then he saw her image—so close to him that it shocked him. She was standing only a foot or two behind him. He could have turned then and asked her what she wanted, but instead of recognizing her, he shied away abruptly from the reflection of her contorted face and went along the street. She might be meaning to do him harm—she might be meaning to kill him.

The suddenness with which he moved when he saw the reflection of her face tipped the water out of his hat brim in such a way that some of it ran down his neck. It felt unpleasantly like the sweat of fear. Then the cold water falling into his face and onto his bare hands, the rancid smell of the wet gutters and paving, the knowledge that his feet were beginning to get wet and that he might catch cold—all the common discomforts of walking in the rain—seemed to heighten the menace of his pursuer and to give him a morbid consciousness of his own physicalness and of the ease with which he could be hurt. He could see ahead of him the corner of Madison Avenue, where the lights were brighter. He felt that if he could get to Madison Avenue he would be all right. At the corner, there was a bakery shop with two entrances, and he went in by the door on the crosstown street, bought a coffee ring,° like any other commuter, and went out the Madison Avenue door. As he started down Madison Avenue, he saw her waiting for him by a hut where newspapers were sold.

She was not clever. She would be easy to shake. He could get into a taxi by one door and leave by the other. He could speak to a policeman. He could run— although he was afraid that if he did run, it might precipitate the violence he now felt sure she had planned. He was approaching a part of the city that he knew well and where the maze of street-level and underground passages, elevator banks, and crowded lobbies made it easy for a man to lose a pursuer. The thought of this, and a whiff of sugary warmth from the coffee ring, cheered him. It was absurd to imagine being harmed on a crowded street. She was foolish, misled, lonely perhaps—that was all it could amount to. He was an insignificant man, and there was no point in anyone's following him from his office to the station. He knew no secrets of any consequence. The reports in his briefcase had no bearing on war, peace, the dope traffic, the hydrogen bomb, or any of the other international skulduggeries that he associated with pursuers, men in trench coats, and wet sidewalks. Then he saw ahead of him the door of a men's bar. Oh, it was so simple!

He ordered a Gibson° and shouldered his way in between two other men at     5
the bar, so that if she should be watching from the window she would lose sight of him. The place was crowded with commuters putting down a drink before the ride home. They had brought in on their clothes—on their shoes and umbrellas—the rancid smell of the wet dusk outside, but Blake began to relax as soon as he tasted his Gibson and looked around at the common, mostly not-young faces that surrounded him and that were worried, if they were worried at all, about tax rates and who would be put in charge of merchandising. He tried to remember her name—Miss Dent, Miss Bent, Miss Lent—and he was surprised to find that he could not remember it, although he was proud of the retentiveness and reach of his memory and it had only been six months ago.

Personnel had sent her up one afternoon—he was looking for a secretary. He saw a dark woman—in her twenties, perhaps—who was slender and shy. Her

---

*coffee ring:* a sweet roll.    *Gibson:* a dry martini with a small pickled onion instead of an olive.

dress was simple, her figure was not much, one of her stockings was crooked, but her voice was soft and he had been willing to try her out. After she had been working for him a few days, she told him that she had been in the hospital for eight months and that it had been hard after this for her to find work, and she wanted to thank him for giving her a chance. Her hair was dark, her eyes were dark; she left with him a pleasant impression of darkness. As he got to know her better, he felt that she was oversensitive and, as a consequence, lonely. Once, when she was speaking to him of what she imagined his life to be—full of friend-ships, money, and a large and loving family—he had thought he recognized a peculiar feeling of deprivation. She seemed to imagine the lives of the rest of the world to be more brilliant than they were. Once, she had put a rose on his desk, and he had dropped it into the wastebasket. "I don't like roses," he told her.

She had been competent, punctual, and a good typist, and he had found only one thing in her that he could object to—her handwriting. He could not associ-ate the crudeness of her handwriting with her appearance. He would have expected her to write a rounded backhand, and in her writing there were inter-mittent traces of this, mixed with clumsy printing. Her writing gave him the feel-ing that she had been the victim of some inner—some emotional—conflict that had in its violence broken the continuity of the lines she was able to make on paper. When she had been working for him three weeks—no longer—they stayed late one night and he offered, after work, to buy her a drink. "If you really want a drink," she said. "I have some whiskey at my place."

She lived in a room that seemed to him like a closet. There were suit boxes and hatboxes piled in a corner, and although the room seemed hardly big enough to hold the bed, the dresser, and the chair he sat in, there was an upright piano against one wall, with a book of Beethoven sonatas on the rack. She gave him a drink and said that she was going to put on something more comfortable. He urged her to; that was, after all, what he had come for. If he had any qualms, they would have been practical. Her diffidence, the feeling of deprivation in her point of view, promised to protect him from any consequences. Most of the many women he had known had been picked for their lack of self-esteem.

When he put on his clothes again, an hour or so later, she was weeping. He felt too contented and warm and sleepy to worry much about her tears. As he was dressing, he noticed on the dresser a note she had written to a cleaning woman. The only light came from the bathroom—the door was ajar—and in this half light the hideously scrawled letters again seemed entirely wrong for her, and as if they must be the handwriting of some other and very gross woman. The next day, he did what he felt was the only sensible thing. When she was out for lunch, he called personnel and asked them to fire her. Then he took the afternoon off. A few days later, she came to the office, asking to see him. He told the switchboard girl not to let her in. He had not seen her again until this evening.

Blake drank a second Gibson and saw by the clock that he had missed the express. He would get the local—the five-forty-eight. When he left the bar the sky was still light; it was still raining. He looked carefully up and down the street and saw that the poor woman had gone. Once or twice, he looked over his shoulder, walking to the station, but he seemed to be safe. He was still not quite himself, he realized, because he had left his coffee ring at the bar, and he was not a man who forgot things. This lapse of memory pained him.

He bought a paper. The local was only half full when he boarded it, and he got a seat on the river side and took off his raincoat. He was a slender man with brown hair—undistinguished in every way, unless you could have divined in his pallor or his gray eyes his unpleasant tastes. He dressed—like the rest of us—as if he admitted the existence of sumptuary laws.° His raincoat was the pale buff color of a mushroom. His hat was dark brown; so was his suit. Except for the few bright threads in his necktie, there was a scrupulous lack of color in his clothing that seemed protective.

He looked around the car for neighbors. Mrs. Compton was several seats in front of him, to the right. She smiled, but her smile was fleeting. It died swiftly and horribly. Mr. Watkins was directly in front of Blake. Mr. Watkins needed a haircut, and he had broken the sumptuary laws; he was wearing a corduroy jacket. He and Blake had quarreled, so they did not speak.

The swift death of Mrs. Compton's smile did not affect Blake at all. The Comptons lived in the house next to the Blakes, and Mrs. Compton had never understood the importance of minding her own business. Louise Blake took her troubles to Mrs. Compton, Blake knew, and instead of discouraging her crying jags, Mrs. Compton had come to imagine herself a sort of confessor and had developed a lively curiosity about the Blakes' intimate affairs. She had probably been given an account of their most recent quarrel. Blake had come home one night, overworked and tired, and had found that Louise had done nothing about getting supper. He had gone into the kitchen, followed by Louise, and had pointed out to her that the date was the fifth. He had drawn a circle around the date on the kitchen calendar. "One week is the twelfth," he had said. "Two weeks will be the nineteenth." He drew a circle around the nineteenth. "I'm not going to speak to you for two weeks," he had said. "That will be the nineteenth." She had wept, she had protested, but it had been eight or ten years since she had been able to touch him with her entreaties. Louise had got old. Now the lines in her face were ineradicable, and when she clapped her glasses onto her nose to read the evening paper, she looked to him like an unpleasant stranger. The physical charms that had been her only attraction were gone. It had been nine years since Blake had built a bookshelf in the doorway that connected their rooms and had fitted into the bookshelf wooden doors that could be locked, since he did not want the children to see his books. But their prolonged estrangement didn't seem remarkable to Blake. He had quarreled with his wife, but so did every other man born of woman. It was human nature. In any place where you can hear their voices—a hotel courtyard, an air shaft, a street on a summer evening—you will hear harsh words.

The hard feeling between Blake and Mr. Watkins also had to do with Blake's family, but it was not as serious or as troublesome as what lay behind Mrs. Compton's fleeting smile. The Watkinses rented. Mr. Watkins broke the sumptuary laws day after day—he once went to the eight-fourteen in a pair of sandals—and he made his living as a commercial artist. Blake's oldest son—Charlie was fourteen—had made friends with the Watkins boy. He had spent a lot of time in the sloppy rented house where the Watkinses lived. The friendship had affected his manners and his neatness. Then he had begun to take some meals with the Watkinses, and to spend Saturday nights there. When he had moved most of his possessions over to the Watkinses' and had begun to spend more than half his nights there, Blake had been forced to act. He had spoken not to Charlie but to Mr. Watkins, and had, of necessity, said a number of things that must have sounded critical. Mr. Watkins' long and dirty hair and his corduroy jacket reassured Blake that he had been in the right.

But Mrs. Compton's dying smile and Mr. Watkins' dirty hair did not lessen    15
the pleasure Blake took in setting himself in an uncomfortable seat on the five-forty-eight deep underground. The coach was old and smelled oddly like a bomb shelter in which whole families had spent the night. The light that spread from the ceiling down onto their heads and shoulders was dim. The filth on the window glass was streaked with rain from some other journey, and clouds of rank pipe and cigarette smoke had begun to rise from behind each newspaper, but it was a scene that meant to Blake that he was on a safe path, and after his brush with danger he even felt a little warmth toward Mrs. Compton and Mr. Watkins.

The train traveled up from underground into the weak daylight, and the slums and the city reminded Blake vaguely of the woman who had followed him. To avoid speculation or remorse about her, he turned his attention to the evening paper. Out of the corner of his eye he could see the landscape. It was industrial and, at that hour, sad. There were machine sheds and warehouses, and above these he saw a break in the clouds—a piece of yellow light. "Mr. Blake," someone said. He looked up. It was she. She was standing there holding one hand on the back of the seat to steady herself in the swaying coach. He remembered her name then—Miss Dent. "Hello, Miss Dent," he said.

"Do you mind if I sit here?"

"I guess not."

"Thank you. It's very kind of you. I don't like to inconvenience you like this. I don't want to . . . ." He had been frightened when he looked up and saw her, but her timid voice rapidly reassured him. He shifted his hams—that futile and reflexive gesture of hospitality—and she sat down. She sighed. He smelled her wet clothing. She wore a formless black hat with a cheap crest stitched onto it. Her coat was thin cloth, he saw, and she wore gloves and carried a large pocketbook.

"Are you living out in this direction now, Miss Dent?"    20

"No."

She opened her purse and reached for her handkerchief. She had begun to cry. He turned his head to see if anyone in the car was looking, but no one was. He had sat beside a thousand passengers on the evening train. He had noticed their clothes, the holes in their gloves; and if they fell asleep and mumbled he had wondered what their worries were. He had classified almost all of them briefly before he buried his nose in the paper. He had marked them as rich, poor, brilliant or dull, neighbors or strangers, but no one of the thousand had ever wept. When she opened her purse, he remembered her perfume. It had clung to his skin the night he went to her place for a drink.

"I've been very sick," she said. "This is the first time I've been out of bed in two weeks. I've been terribly sick."

"I'm sorry that you've been sick, Miss Dent," he said in a voice loud enough to be heard by Mr. Watkins and Mrs. Compton. "Where are you working now?"

"What?" 25

"Where are you working now?"

"Oh, don't make me laugh," she said softly.

"I don't understand."

"You poisoned their minds."

He straightened his neck and braced his shoulders. These wrenching move- 30 ments expressed a brief—and hopeless—longing to be in some other place. She meant trouble. He took a breath. He looked with deep feeling at the half-filled, half-lighted coach to affirm his sense of actuality, of a world in which there was not very much bad trouble after all. He was conscious of her heavy breathing and the smell of her rain-soaked coat. The train stopped. A nun and a man in overalls got off. When it started again, Blake put on his hat and reached for his raincoat.

"Where are you going?" she said.

"I'm going to the next car."

"Oh, no," she said. "No, no, no." She put her white face so close to his ear that he could feel her warm breath on his cheek. "Don't do that," she whispered. "Don't try and escape me. I have a pistol and I'll have to kill you and I don't want to. All I want to do is to talk with you. Don't move or I'll kill you. Don't, don't, don't!"

Blake sat back abruptly in his seat. If he had wanted to stand and shout for help, he would not have been able to. His tongue had swelled to twice its size, and when he tried to move it, it stuck horribly to the roof of his mouth. His legs were limp. All he could think of to do then was to wait for his heart to stop its hysterical beating, so that he could judge the extent of his danger. She was sitting a little sidewise, and in her pocketbook was the pistol, aimed at his belly.

"You understand me now, don't you?" she said. "You understand that I'm 35 serious?" He tried to speak but he was still mute. He nodded his head. "Now we'll sit quietly for a little while," she said. "I got so excited that my thoughts are all confused. We'll sit quietly for a little while, until I can get my thoughts in order again."

Help would come, Blake thought. It was only a question of minutes. Someone, noticing the look on his face or her peculiar posture, would stop and interfere, and it would all be over. All he had to do was to wait until someone noticed his predicament. Out of the window he saw the river and the sky. The rain clouds were rolling down like a shutter, and while he watched, a streak of orange light on the horizon became brilliant. Its brilliance spread—he could see it move—across the waves until it raked the banks of the river with a dim firelight. Then it was put out. Help would come in a minute, he thought. Help would come before they stopped again; but the train stopped, there were some comings and goings, and Blake still lived on, at the mercy of the woman beside him. The possibility that help might not come was one that he could not face. The possibility that his predicament was not noticeable, that Mrs. Compton would guess that he was taking a poor relation out to dinner at Shady Hill, was something he would think about later. Then the saliva came back into his mouth and he was able to speak.

"Miss Dent?"

"Yes."

"What do you want?"

"I want to talk to you." 40

"You can come to my office."

"Oh, no. I went there every day for two weeks."

"You could make an appointment."

"No," she said. "I think we can talk here. I wrote you a letter but I've been too sick to go out and mail it. I've put down all my thoughts. I like to travel. I like trains. One of my troubles has always been that I could never afford to travel. I suppose you see this scenery every night and don't notice it any more, but it's nice for someone who's been in bed a long time. They say that He's not in the river and the hills but I think He is. 'Where shall wisdom be found?' it says. 'Where is the place of understanding? The depth saith it is not in me; the sea saith it is not with me. Destruction and death say we have heard the force with our ears.'°

"Oh, I know what you're thinking," she said. "You're thinking that I'm crazy, 45 and I have been very sick again but I'm going to be better. It's going to make me better to talk with you. I was in the hospital all the time before I came to work for you but they never tried to cure me, they only wanted to take away my self-respect. I haven't had any work now for three months. Even if I did have to kill you, they wouldn't be able to do anything to me except put me back in the hospital, so you see I'm not afraid. But let's sit quietly for a little while longer. I have to be calm."

*"Where shall wisdom be found?" it says . . . "the force with our ears."*: the *it* being the Bible. Miss Dent is remembering parts of the book of Job (28:12–22). In the Old Testament text, Job, who has suffered terribly, asks where he shall find understanding of God's ways, but he does not find it in the natural world.

The train continued its halting progress up the bank of the river, and Blake tried to force himself to make some plans for escape, but the immediate threat to his life made this difficult, and instead of planning sensibly, he thought of the many ways in which he could have avoided her in the first place. As soon as he had felt these regrets, he realized their futility. It was like regretting his lack of suspicion when she first mentioned her months in the hospital. It was like regretting his failure to have been warned by her shyness, her diffidence, and the handwriting that looked like the marks of a claw. There was no way of rectifying his mistakes, and he felt—for perhaps the first time in his mature life—the full force of regret. Out of the window, he saw some men fishing on the nearly dark river, and then a ramshackle boat club that seemed to have been nailed together out of scraps of wood that had been washed up on the shore.

Mr. Watkins had fallen asleep. He was snoring. Mrs. Compton read her paper. The train creaked, slowed, and halted infirmly at another station. Blake could see the southbound platform, where a few passengers were waiting to go into the city. There was a workman with a lunch pail, a dressed-up woman, and a woman with a suitcase. They stood apart from one another. Some advertisements were posted on the wall behind them. There was a picture of a couple drinking a toast in wine, a picture of a Cat's Paw rubber heel, and a picture of a Hawaiian dancer. Their cheerful intent seemed to go no farther than the puddles of water on the platform and to expire there. The platform and the people on it looked lonely. The train drew away from the station into the scattered lights of a slum and then into the darkness of the country and the river.

"I want you to read my letter before we get to Shady Hill," she said. "It's on the seat. Pick it up. I would have mailed it to you, but I've been too sick to go out. I haven't gone out for two weeks. I haven't had any work for three months. I haven't spoken to anybody but the landlady. Please read my letter."

He picked up the letter from the seat where she had put it. The cheap paper felt abhorrent and filthy to his fingers. It was folded and refolded. "Dear Husband," she had written, in that crazy, wandering hand, "they say that human love leads us to divine love, but is this true? I dream about you every night. I have such terrible desires. I have always had a gift for dreams. I dreamed on Tuesday of a volcano erupting with blood. When I was in the hospital they said they wanted to cure me but they only wanted to take away my self-respect. They only wanted me to dream about sewing and basketwork but I protected my gift for dreams. I'm clairvoyant.° I can tell when the telephone is going to ring. I've never had a true friend in my whole life . . . ."

The train stopped again. There was another platform, another picture of the   50
couple drinking a toast, the rubber heel, and the Hawaiian dancer. Suddenly she pressed her face close to Blake's again and whispered in his ear. "I know what you're thinking. I can see it in your face. You're thinking you can get away from me in Shady Hill, aren't you? Oh, I've been planning this for weeks. It's all I've had to think about. I won't harm you if you'll let me talk. I've been thinking

---

clairvoyant: a person who can see the future.

about devils. I mean, if there are devils in the world, if there are people in the world who represent evil, is it our duty to exterminate them? I know that you always prey on weak people. I can tell. Oh, sometimes I think I ought to kill you. Sometimes I think you're the only obstacle between me and my happiness. Sometimes . . ."

She touched Blake with the pistol. He felt the muzzle against his belly. The bullet, at that distance, would make a small hole where it entered, but it would rip out of his back a place as big as a soccer ball. He remembered the unburied dead he had seen in the war. The memory came in a rush; entrails, eyes, shattered bone, ordure, and other filth.

"All I've ever wanted in life is a little love," she said. She lightened the pressure of the gun. Mr. Watkins still slept. Mrs. Compton was sitting calmly with her hands folded in her lap. The coach rocked gently, and the coats and mushroom-colored raincoats that hung between the windows swayed a little as the car moved. Blake's elbow was on the window sill and his left shoe was on the guard above the steampipe. The car smelled like some dismal classroom. The passengers seemed asleep and apart, and Blake felt that he might never escape the smell of heat and wet clothing and the dimness of the light. He tried to summon the calculated self-deceptions with which he sometimes cheered himself, but he was left without any energy for hope of self-deception.

The conductor put his head in the door and said, "Shady Hill, next, Shady Hill."

"Now," she said. "Now you get out ahead of me."

Mr. Watkins waked suddenly, put on his coat and hat, and smiled at Mrs. Compton, who was gathering her parcels to her in a series of maternal gestures. They went to the door. Blake joined them, but neither of them spoke to him or seemed to notice the woman at his back. The conductor threw open the door, and Blake saw on the platform of the next car a few other neighbors who had missed the express, waiting patiently and tiredly in the wan light for their trip to end. He raised his head to see through the open door the abandoned mansion out of town, a NO TRESPASSING sign nailed to a tree, and then the oil tanks. The concrete abutments of the bridge passed, so close to the open door that he could have touched them. Then he saw the first of the lampposts on the northbound platform, the sign SHADY HILL in black and gold, and the little lawn and flower bed kept up by the Improvement Association, and then the cab stand and a corner of the old-fashioned depot. It was raining again; it was pouring. He could hear the splash of water and see the lights reflected in puddles and in the shining pavement, and the idle sound of splashing and dripping formed in his mind a conception of shelter, so light and strange that it seemed to belong to a time of his life that he could not remember.

He went down the steps with her at his back. A dozen or so cars were waiting by the station with their motors running. A few people got off from each of the other coaches; he recognized most of them, but none of them offered to give him a ride. They walked separately or in pairs—purposefully out of the rain to the shelter of the platform, where the car horns called to them. It was time to go

55

home, time for a drink, time for love, time for supper, and he could see the lights on the hill—lights by which children were being bathed, meat cooked, dishes washed—shining in the rain. One by one, the cars picked up the heads of families, until there were only four left. Two of the stranded passengers drove off in the only taxi the village had. "I'm sorry, darling," a woman said tenderly to her husband when she drove up a few minutes later. "All our clocks are slow." The last man looked at his watch, looked at the rain, and then walked off into it, and Blake saw him go as if they had some reason to say goodbye—not as we say goodbye to friends after a party but as we say goodbye when we are faced with an inexorable and unwanted parting of the spirit and the heart. The man's footsteps sounded as he crossed the parking lot to the sidewalk, and then they were lost. In the station, a telephone began to ring. The ringing was loud, evenly spaced, and unanswered. Someone wanted to know about the next train to Albany, but Mr. Flanagan, the stationmaster, had gone home an hour ago. He had turned on all his lights before he went away. They burned in the empty waiting room. They burned, tin-shaded, at intervals up and down the platform and with the peculiar sadness of dim and purposeless lights. They lighted the Hawaiian dancer, the couple drinking a toast, the rubber heel.

"I've never been here before," she said. "I thought it would look different. I didn't think it would look so shabby. Let's get out of the light. Go over there."

His legs felt sore. All his strength was gone. "Go on," she said.

North of the station there were a freight house and a coalyard and an inlet where the butcher and the baker and the man who ran the service station moored the dinghies, from which they fished on Sundays, sunk now to the gunwales with the rain. As he walked toward the freight house, he saw a movement on the ground and heard a scraping sound, and then he saw a rat take its head out of a paper bag and regard him. The rat seized the bag in its teeth and dragged it into a culvert.

"Stop," she said. "Turn around. Oh, I ought to feel sorry for you. Look at your poor face. But you don't know what I've been through. I'm afraid to go out in the daylight. I'm afraid the blue sky will fall down on me. I'm like poor Chicken-Licken. I only feel like myself when it begins to get dark. But still and all I'm better than you. I still have good dreams sometimes. I dream about picnics and heaven and the brotherhood of man, and about castles in the moonlight and a river with willow trees all along the edge of it and foreign cities, and after all I know more about love than you."

He heard from off the dark river the drone of an outboard motor, a sound that drew slowly behind it across the dark water such a burden of clear, sweet memories of gone summers and gone pleasures that it made his flesh crawl, and he thought of dark in the mountains and the children singing. "They never wanted to cure me," she said. "They . . . " The noise of a train coming down from the north drowned out her voice, but she went on talking. The noise filled his ears, and the windows where people ate, drank, slept, and read flew past. When the train had passed beyond the bridge, the noise grew distant, and he heard her screaming at him, "*Kneel down!* Kneel down! Do what I say. *Kneel down!*"

He got to his knees. He bent his head. "There," she said. "You see, if you do what I say, I won't harm you, because I really don't want to harm you, I want to help you, but when I see your face it sometimes seems to me that I can't help you. Sometimes it seems to me that if I were good and loving and sane—oh, much better than I am—sometimes it seems to me that if I were all these things and young and beautiful, too, and if I called to show you the right way, you wouldn't heed me. Oh, I'm better than you, I'm better than you, and I shouldn't waste my time or spoil my life like this. Put your face in the dirt. *Put your face in the dirt!* Do what I say. Put your face in the dirt."

He fell forward in the filth. The coal skinned his face. He stretched out on the ground, weeping. "Now I feel better," she said. "Now I can wash my hands of you, I can wash my hands of all this, because you see there is some kindness, some saneness in me that I can find and use. I can wash my hands." Then he heard her footsteps go away from him, over the rubble. He heard the clearer and more distant sound they made on the hard surface of the platform. He heard them diminish. He raised his head. He saw her climb the stairs of the wooden footbridge and cross it and go down to the other platform, where her figure in the dim light looked small, common, and harmless. He raised himself out of the dust—warily at first, until he saw by her attitude, her looks, that she had forgotten him; that she had completed what she had wanted to do, and that he was safe. He got to his feet and picked up his hat from the ground where it had fallen and walked home.

## Questions

1. Why doesn't Blake cry out for help on the train or try to run away? What does his inability to formulate an escape suggest about his character?
2. The narrator never gives us the full names of the characters. Why are they only Blake and Miss Dent?
3. What do we know about Miss Dent? What facts does the narrator tell us about her life?
4. Is Miss Dent's revenge an act of sanity or madness? Make a case for either theory.
5. When Miss Dent was Blake's secretary, what did he think of her? What did she think of him?
6. Once Miss Dent left a rose on Blake's desk. What does this gesture suggest about her character? What does his reaction suggest about his?
7. What does Miss Dent's room suggest about her character?
8. What does Blake's private room at home suggest about his character?
9. When Blake and Miss Dent get off the train, what does he notice happening at the Shady Hill station? How do his observations reflect on his life? How does Miss Dent view the same scene?
10. Why doesn't Miss Dent shoot Blake in the coalyard?
11. Is Blake changed by his ordeal? Is Miss Dent changed?

EVERYDAY USE                                                              1973

Alice Walker, a leading black writer and
social activist, was born in 1944 in
Eatonton, Georgia, the youngest of eight
children. Her father, a sharecropper and
dairy farmer, usually earned about $300 a
year; her mother helped by working as a
maid. Both entertained their children by
telling stories. When Alice Walker was
eight, she was accidentally struck by a pellet
from a brother's BB gun. She lost the sight
of one eye because the Walkers had no car
to rush her to the hospital. Later she attended Spelman College in Atlanta and finished
college at Sarah Lawrence College on a
scholarship. While working for the civil
rights movement in Mississippi, she met a

Alice Walker

young lawyer, Melvyn Leventhal. In 1967 they settled in Jackson, Mississippi, the first
legally married interracial couple in town. They returned to New York in 1974 and
were later divorced. First known as a poet, Walker has published four books of her
verse. She also has edited a collection of the work of neglected black woman author Zora
Neale Hurston, and has written a study of author Langston Hughes. She has collected
her essays in In Search of Our Mothers' Gardens: Womanist Prose (1983); in
which she recalls her mother and addresses her own daughter. (By womanist she means
"black feminist.") But the largest part of Walker's reading audience know her fiction:
two story collections, In Love and Trouble (1973), from which "Everyday Use" is
taken, and You Can't Keep a Good Woman Down (1981); and her novels, The
Third Life of Grange Copeland (1970); Meridian (1976), and best known, The
Color Purple (1982), which won a Pulitzer prize. In 1985 Steven Spielberg made the
last one into a film. Her recent novels include The Temple of My Familiar (1989)
and Possessing the Secret of Joy (1992). Walker now lives in northern California.

For your grandmama

    I will wait for her in the yard that Maggie and I made so clean and wavy yes-
terday afternoon. A yard like this is more comfortable than most people know. It
is not just a yard. It is like an extended living room. When the hard clay is swept
clean as a floor and the fine sand around the edges lined with tiny, irregular
grooves anyone can come and sit and look up into the elm tree and wait for the
breezes that never come inside the house.

Maggie will be nervous until after her sister goes: she will stand hopelessly in corners, homely and ashamed of the burn scars down her arms and legs, eyeing her sister with a mixture of envy and awe. She thinks her sister has held life always in the palm of one hand, that "no" is a word the world never learned to say to her.

You've no doubt seen those TV shows where the child who has "made it" is confronted, as a surprise, by her own mother and father, tottering in weakly from backstage. (A pleasant surprise, of course: What would they do if parent and child came on the show only to curse out and insult each other?) On TV mother and child embrace and smile into each other's faces. Sometimes the mother and father weep, the child wraps them in her arms and leans across the table to tell how she would not have made it without their help. I have seen these programs.°

Sometimes I dream a dream in which Dee and I are suddenly brought together on a TV program of this sort. Out of a dark and soft-seated limousine I am ushered into a bright room filled with many people. There I meet a smiling, gray, sporty man like Johnny Carson who shakes my hand and tells me what a fine girl I have. Then we are on the stage and Dee is embracing me with tears in her eyes. She pins on my dress a large orchid, even though she has told me once that she thinks orchids are tacky flowers.

In real life I am a large, big-boned woman with rough, man-working hands.    5 In the winter I wear flannel nightgowns to bed and overalls during the day. I can kill and clean a hog as mercilessly as a man. My fat keeps me hot in zero weather. I can work outside all day, breaking ice to get water for washing. I can eat pork liver cooked over the open fire minutes after it comes steaming from the hog. One winter I knocked a bull calf straight in the brain between the eyes with a sledge hammer and had the meat hung up to chill before nightfall. But of course all this does not show on television. I am the way my daughter would want me to be: a hundred pounds lighter, my skin like an uncooked barley pancake. My hair glistens in the hot bright lights. Johnny Carson has much to do to keep up with my quick and witty tongue.

But that is a mistake. I know even before I wake up. Who ever knew a Johnson with a quick tongue? Who can even imagine me looking a strange white man in the eye? It seems to me I have talked to them always with one foot raised in flight, with my head turned in whichever way is farthest from them. Dee, though. She would always look anyone in the eye. Hesitation was no part of her nature.

"How do I look, Mama?" Maggie says, showing just enough of her thin body enveloped in pink skirt and red blouse for me to know she's there, almost hidden by the door.

*these programs:* On the NBC television show "This Is Your Life," with Ralph Edwards as producer and master of ceremonies, people were publicly and often tearfully reunited with friends, relatives, and teachers they had not seen in years. It aired from 1952 to 1961 and 1970 to 1973.

"Come out into the yard," I say.

Have you ever seen a lame animal, perhaps a dog run over by some careless person rich enough to own a car, sidle up to someone who is ignorant enough to be kind to him? That is the way my Maggie walks. She has been like this, chin on chest, eyes on ground, feet in shuffle, ever since the fire that burned the other house to the ground.

Dee is lighter than Maggie, with nicer hair and a fuller figure. She's a woman now, though sometimes I forget. How long ago was it that the other house burned? Ten, twelve years? Sometimes I can still hear the flames and feel Maggie's arms sticking to me, her hair smoking and her dress falling off her in little black papery flakes. Her eyes seemed stretched open, blazed open by the flames reflected in them. And Dee. I see her standing off under the sweet gum tree she used to dig gum out of; a look of concentration on her face as she watched the last dingy gray board of the house fall in toward the red-hot brick chimney. Why don't you do a dance around the ashes? I'd wanted to ask her. She had hated the house that much.

I used to think she hated Maggie, too. But that was before we raised the money, the church and me, to send her to Augusta to school. She used to read to us without pity; forcing words, lies, other folks' habits, whole lives upon us two, sitting trapped and ignorant underneath her voice. She washed us in a river of make-believe, burned us with a lot of knowledge we didn't necessarily need to know. Pressed us to her with the serious way she read, to shove us away at just the moment, like dimwits, we seemed about to understand.

Dee wanted nice things. A yellow organdy dress to wear to her graduation from high school; black pumps to match a green suit she'd made from an old suit somebody gave me. She was determined to stare down any disaster in her efforts. Her eyelids would not flicker for minutes at a time. Often I fought off the temptation to shake her. At sixteen she had a style of her own: and knew what style was.

I never had an education myself. After second grade the school was closed down. Don't ask me why: in 1927 colored asked fewer questions than they do now. Sometimes Maggie reads to me. She stumbles along good-naturedly but can't see well. She knows she is not bright. Like good looks and money, quickness passed her by. She will marry John Thomas (who has mossy teeth in an earnest face) and then I'll be free to sit here and I guess just sing church songs to myself. Although I never was a good singer. Never could carry a tune. I was always better at a man's job. I used to love to milk till I was hoofed in the side in '49. Cows are soothing and slow and don't bother you, unless you try to milk them the wrong way.

I have deliberately turned my back on the house. It is three rooms, just like the one that burned, except the roof is tin; they don't make shingle roofs any more. There are no real windows, just some holes cut in the sides, like the portholes in a ship, but not round and not square, with rawhide holding the shutters up on the outside. This house is in a pasture, too, like the other one. No doubt when Dee sees it she will want to tear it down. She wrote me once that no matter where we "choose" to live, she will manage to come see us. But she will never bring her friends. Maggie and I thought about this and Maggie asked me, "Mama, when did Dee ever *have* any friends?"

She had a few. Furtive boys in pink shirts hanging about on washday after school. Nervous girls who never laughed. Impressed with her they worshiped the well-turned phrase, the cute shape, the scalding humor that erupted like bubbles in lye. She read to them.

When she was courting Jimmy T she didn't have much time to pay to us, but turned all her faultfinding power on him. He *flew* to marry a cheap gal from a family of ignorant flashy people. She hardly had time to recompose herself.

When she comes I will meet—but there they are!

Maggie attempts to make a dash for the house, in her shuffling way, but I stay her with my hand. "Come back here," I say. And she stops and tries to dig a well in the sand with her toe.

It is hard to see them clearly through the strong sun. But even the first glimpse of leg out of the car tells me it is Dee. Her feet were always neat-looking, as if God himself had shaped them with a certain style. From the other side of the car comes a short, stocky man. Hair is all over his head a foot long and hanging from his chin like a kinky mule tail. I hear Maggie suck in her breath. "Uhnnnh," is what it sounds like. Like when you see the wriggling end of a snake just in front of your foot on the road. "Uhnnnh."

Dee next. A dress down to the ground, in this hot weather. A dress so loud it hurts my eyes. There are yellows and oranges enough to throw back the light of the sun. I feel my whole face warming from the heat waves it throws out. Earrings, too, gold and hanging down to her shoulders. Bracelets dangling and making noises when she moves her arm up to shake the folds of the dress out of her armpits. The dress is loose and flows, and as she walks closer, I like it. I hear Maggie go "Uhnnnh" again. It is her sister's hair. It stands straight up like the wool on a sheep. It is black as night and around the edges are two long pigtails that rope about like small lizards disappearing behind her ears.

"Wa-su-zo-Tean-o!"° she says, coming on in that gliding way the dress makes her move. The short stocky fellow with the hair to his navel is all grinning and he follows up with "Asalamalakim,° my mother and sister!" He moves to hug Maggie but she falls back, right up against the back of my chair. I feel her trembling there and when I look up I see the perspiration falling off her chin.

"Don't get up," says Dee. Since I am stout it takes something of a push. You can see me trying to move a second or two before I make it. She turns, showing white heels through her sandals, and goes back to the car. Out she peeks next with a Polaroid. She stoops down quickly and lines up picture after picture of me

---

*Wa-su-zo-Tean-o!*: salutation in Swahili, an African language. Notice that Dee has to sound it out, syllable by syllable.    *Asalamalakim*: salutation in Arabic: "Peace be upon you."

15

20

sitting there in front of the house with Maggie cowering behind me. She never takes a shot without making sure the house is included. When a cow comes nibbling around the edge of the yard she snaps it and me and Maggie and the house. Then she puts the Polaroid in the back seat of the car, and comes up and kisses me on the forehead.

Meanwhile Asalamalakim is going through the motions with Maggie's hand. Maggie's hand is as limp as a fish, and probably as cold, despite the sweat, and she keeps trying to pull it back. It looks like Asalamalakim wants to shake hands but wants to do it fancy. Or maybe he don't know how people shake hands. Anyhow, he soon gives up on Maggie.

"Well," I say. "Dee."

"No, Mama," she says. "Not 'Dee,' Wangero Leewanika Kemanjo!'"                    25

"What happened to 'Dee'?" I wanted to know.

"She's dead," Wangero said. "I couldn't bear it any longer being named after the people who oppress me."

"You know as well as me you was named after your aunt Dicie," I said. Dicie is my sister. She named Dee. We called her "Big Dee" after Dee was born.

"But who was *she* named after?" asked Wangero.

"I guess after Grandma Dee," I said.                    30

"And who was she named after?" asked Wangero.

"Her mother," I said, and saw Wangero was getting tired. "That's about as far back as I can trace it," I said. Though, in fact, I probably could have carried it back beyond the Civil War through the branches.

"Well," said Asalamalakim, "there you are."

"Uhnnnh," I heard Maggie say.

"There I was not," I said, "before 'Dicie' cropped up in our family, so why    35
should I try to trace it that far back?"

He just stood there grinning, looking down on me like somebody inspecting a Model A car.° Every once in a while he and Wangero sent eye signals over my head.

"How do you pronounce this name?" I asked.

"You don't have to call me by it if you don't want to," said Wangero.

"Why shouldn't I?" I asked. "If that's what you want us to call you, we'll call you."

"I know it might sound awkward at first," said Wangero.                    40

"I'll get used to it," I said. "Ream it out again."

Well, soon we got the name out of the way. Asalamalakim had a name twice as long and three times as hard. After I tripped over it two or three times he told me to just call him Hakim-a-barber. I wanted to ask him was he a barber, but I didn't really think he was, so I didn't ask.

Model A car: popular low-priced automobile introduced by the Ford Motor Company in 1927.

"You must belong to those beef-cattle peoples down the road," I said. They said "Asalamalakim" when they met you, too, but they didn't shake hands. Always too busy: feeding the cattle, fixing the fences, putting up salt-lick shelters, throwing down hay. When the white folks poisoned some of the herd the men stayed up all night with rifles in their hands. I walked a mile and a half just to see the sight.

Hakim-a-barber said, "I accept some of their doctrines, but farming and raising cattle is not my style." (They didn't tell me, and I didn't ask, whether Wangero (Dee) had really gone and married him.)

We sat down to eat and right away he said he didn't eat collards and pork was unclean. Wangero, though, went on through the chitlins and corn bread, the greens and everything else. She talked a blue streak over the sweet potatoes. Everything delighted her. Even the fact that we still used the benches her daddy made for the table when we couldn't afford to buy chairs.

"Oh, Mama!" she cried. Then turned to Hakim-a-barber. "I never knew how lovely these benches are. You can feel the rump prints," she said, running her hands underneath her and along the bench. Then she gave a sigh and her hand closed over Grandma Dee's butter dish. "That's it!" she said. "I knew there was something I wanted to ask you if I could have." She jumped up from the table and went over in the corner where the churn stood, the milk in it clabber° by now. She looked at the churn and looked at it.

"This churn top is what I need," she said. "Didn't Uncle Buddy whittle it out of a tree you all used to have?"

"Yes," I said.

"Uh huh," she said happily. "And I want the dasher, too."

"Uncle Buddy whittle that, too?" asked the barber.

Dee (Wangero) looked up at me.

"Aunt Dee's first husband whittled the dash," said Maggie so low you almost couldn't hear her. "His name was Henry, but they called him Stash."

"Maggie's brain is like an elephant's," Wangero said, laughing. "I can use the churn top as a centerpiece for the alcove table," she said, sliding a plate over the churn, "and I'll think of something artistic to do with the dasher."

When she finished wrapping the dasher the handle stuck out. I took it for a moment in my hands. You didn't even have to look close to see where hands pushing the dasher up and down to make butter had left a kind of sink in the wood. In fact, there were a lot of small sinks; you could see where thumbs and fingers had sunk into the wood. It was beautiful light yellow wood, from a tree that grew in the yard where Big Dee and Stash had lived.

After dinner Dee (Wangero) went to the trunk at the foot of my bed and started rifling through it. Maggie hung back in the kitchen over the dishpan. Out

_clabber:_ sour milk or buttermilk.

came Wangero with two quilts. They had been pieced by Grandma Dee and then Big Dee and me had hung them on the quilt frames on the front porch and quilted them. One was in the Lone Star pattern. The other was Walk Around the Mountain. In both of them were scraps of dresses Grandma Dee had worn fifty and more years ago. Bits and pieces of Grandpa Jarrell's paisley shirts. And one teeny faded blue piece, about the piece of a penny matchbox, that was from Great Grandpa Ezra's uniform that he wore in the Civil War.

"Mama," Wangero said sweet as a bird. "Can I have these old quilts?"

I heard something fall in the kitchen, and a minute later the kitchen door slammed.

"Why don't you take one or two of the others?" I asked. "These old things was just done by me and Big Dee from some tops your grandma pieced before she died."

"No," said Wangero. "I don't want those. They are stitched around the borders by machine."

"That's make them last better," I said.                                             60

"That's not the point," said Wangero. "These are all pieces of dresses Grandma used to wear. She did all this stitching by hand. Imagine!" She held the quilts securely in her arms, stroking them.

"Some of the pieces, like those lavender ones, come from old clothes her mother handed down to her," I said, moving up to touch the quilts. Dee (Wangero) moved back just enough so that I couldn't reach the quilts. They already belonged to her.

"Imagine!" she breathed again, clutching them closely to her bosom.

"The truth is," I said, "I promised to give them quilts to Maggie, for when she marries John Thomas."

She gasped like a bee had stung her.                                               65

"Maggie can't appreciate these quilts!" she said. "She'd probably be backward enough to put them to everyday use."

"I reckon she would," I said. "God knows I been saving 'em for long enough with nobody using 'em. I hope she will!" I didn't want to bring up how I had offered Dee (Wangero) a quilt when she went away to college. Then she had told me they were old-fashioned, out of style.

"But they're *priceless!*" she was saying now, furiously; for she has a temper. "Maggie would put them on the bed and in five years they'd be in rags. Less than that!"

"She can always make some more," I said. "Maggie knows how to quilt."

Dee (Wangero) looked at me with hatred. "You just will not understand.     70 The point is these quilts, *these* quilts!"

"Well," I said, stumped. "What would *you* do with them?"

"Hang them," she said. As if that was the only thing you *could* do with quilts.

Maggie by now was standing in the door. I could almost hear the sound her feet made as they scraped over each other.

"She can have them, Mama," she said, like somebody used to never winning anything, or having anything reserved for her. "I can 'member Grandma Dee without the quilts."

I looked at her hard. She had filled her bottom lip with checkerberry snuff and it gave her face a kind of dopey, hangdog look. It was Grandma Dee and Big Dee who taught her how to quilt herself. She stood there with her scarred hands hidden in the folds of her skirt. She looked at her sister with something like fear but she wasn't mad at her. This was Maggie's portion. This was the way she knew God to work.

When I looked at her like that something hit me in the top of my head and ran down to the soles of my feet. Just like when I'm in church and the spirit of God touches me and I get happy and shout. I did something I never had done before: hugged Maggie to me, then dragged her on into the room, snatched the quilts out of Miss Wangero's hands and dumped them into Maggie's lap. Maggie just sat there on my bed with her mouth open.

"Take one or two of the others," I said to Dee.

But she turned without a word and went out to Hakim-a-barber.

"You just don't understand," she said, as Maggie and I came out to the car.

"What don't I understand?" I wanted to know.

"Your heritage," she said. And then she turned to Maggie, kissed her, and said, "You ought to try to make something of yourself, too, Maggie. It's really a new day for us. But from the way you and Mama still live you'd never know it."

She put on some sunglasses that hid everything above the tip of her nose and her chin.

Maggie smiled; maybe at the sunglasses. But a real smile, not scared. After we watched the car dust settle I asked Maggie to bring me a dip of snuff. And then the two of us sat there just enjoying, until it was time to go in the house and go to bed.

QUESTIONS

1. What is the basic conflict in "Everyday Use"?
2. What is the tone of Walker's story? By what means does the author communicate it?
3. From whose point of view is "Everyday Use" told? What does the story gain from this point of view—instead of, say, from the point of view of Dee (Wangero)?
4. What does the narrator of the story feel toward Dee? What seems to be Dee's present attitude toward her mother and sister?
5. What do you take to be the author's attitude toward each of her characters? How does she convey it?
6. What levels of meaning do you find in the story's title?
7. Contrast Dee's attitude toward her heritage with the attitudes of her mother and sister. How much truth is there in Dee's accusation that her mother and sister don't understand their heritage?
8. Does the knowledge that "Everyday Use" was written by a black writer in any way influence your reactions to it? Explain.

## Isaac Bashevis Singer

GIMPEL THE FOOL                                                      1953

*Translated by Saul Bellow*

*Isaac Bashevis Singer (1904–1991) was born in Poland, the son of a rabbi, and grew up in the Jewish ghetto in Warsaw in a family where money was scarce, but intellectual stimuli plentiful. "My father's house," he recalled, "was a study house, a court of justice, a house of prayer, of story-telling." For a time he pursued rabbinical studies. In 1935, when the Nazi invasion of Poland was imminent, he went to New York and became a journalist for the* Jewish Daily Forward, *a Yiddish-language newspaper for which he continued to write. For years he contributed a daily serial story to the* Forward *and for a time wrote scripts for a Yiddish soap opera on radio station*

*Isaac Bashevis Singer*

WEVD. *He became a naturalized United States citizen in 1943. Only in 1950 when* The Family Moskat, *a novel of three generations of Warsaw Jews, appeared in English translation, did a larger audience become aware of him. (Singer, whose command of English was excellent, always worked closely with his translators.) In 1978 he was awarded the Nobel prize for literature. Singer's work often (as in "Gimpel the Fool") recreates the vanished world of the shtetl, or Jewish village of Eastern Europe. Traditional Jewish legends inform many of his novels, including* Satan in Goray (1955), The Magician of Lublin (1960), *and* The Golem (1982). *Singer also wrote many volumes of short fiction (see* Collected Stories, 1982), *children's books, the play* Yentl (1975), *and three volumes of autobiography. He died in Surfside, Florida in 1991.*

### I

I am Gimpel the fool. I don't think myself a fool. On the contrary. But that's what folks call me. They gave me the name while I was still in school. I had seven names in all: imbecile, donkey, flax-head, dope, glump, ninny, and fool. The last name stuck. What did my foolishness consist of? I was easy to take in. They said, "Gimpel, you know the rabbi's wife has been brought to childbed?" So I skipped school. Well, it turned out to be a lie. How was I supposed to know? She hadn't had a big belly. But I never looked at her belly. Was that really so foolish? The gang laughed and hee-hawed, stomped and danced and chanted a good-night prayer. And instead of the raisins they give when a woman's lying in, they stuffed my hand full of goat turds. I was no weakling. If I slapped someone he'd see all the way to Cracow. But I'm really not a slugger by nature. I think to myself, Let it pass. So they take advantage of me.

I was coming home from school and heard a dog barking. I'm not afraid of dogs, but of course I never want to start up with them. One of them may be mad, and if he bites there's not a Tartar in the world who can help you. So I made tracks. Then I looked around and saw the whole marketplace wild with laughter. It was no dog at all but Wolf-Leib the thief. How was I supposed to know it was he? It sounded like a howling bitch.

When the pranksters and leg-pullers found that I was easy to fool, every one of them tried his luck with me. "Gimpel, the Czar is coming to Frampol; Gimpel, the moon fell down in Turbeen; Gimpel, little Hodel Furpiece found a treasure behind the bathhouse." And I like a _golem_° believed everyone. In the first place, everything is possible, as it is written in the Wisdom of the Fathers, I've forgotten just how. Second, I had to believe when the whole town came down on me! If I ever dared to say, "Ah, you're kidding!" there was trouble. People got angry. "What do you mean! You want to call everyone a liar?" What was I to do? I believed them, and I hope at least that did them some good.

I was an orphan. My grandfather who brought me up was already bent toward the grave. So they turned me over to a baker, and what a time they gave me there! Every woman or girl who came to bake a pan of cookies or dry a batch of noodles had to fool me at least once. "Gimpel, there's a fair in heaven; Gimpel, the rabbi gave birth to a calf in the seventh month; Gimpel, a cow flew over the roof and laid brass eggs." A student from the _yeshiva_° came once to buy a roll, and he said, "You, Gimpel, while you stand here scraping with your baker's shovel the Messiah has come. The dead have arisen." "What do you mean?" I said. "I heard no one blowing the ram's horn!" He said, "Are you deaf?" And all began to cry, "We heard it, we heard!" Then in came Reitze the candle-dipper and called out in her hoarse voice, "Gimpel, your father and mother have stood up from the grave. They're looking for you."

To tell the truth, I knew very well that nothing of the sort had happened, 5 but all the same, as folks were talking, I threw on my wool vest and went out. Maybe something had happened. What did I stand to lose by looking? Well, what a cat music went up! And then I took a vow to believe nothing more. But that was no go either. They confused me so that I didn't know the big end from the small.

I went to the rabbi to get some advice. He said, "It is written, better to be a fool all your days than for one hour to be evil. You are not a fool. They are the fools. For he who causes his neighbor to feel shame loses Paradise himself." Nevertheless the rabbi's daughter took me in. As I left the rabbinical court she said, "Have you kissed the wall yet?" I said, "No; what for?" She answered, "It's a law; you've got to do it after every visit." Well, there didn't seem to be any harm

_golem:_ simpleton. From the Hebrew: "a yet-unformed thing" (Psalms 139:16); a mere robot, a shape- less mass.    _yeshiva:_ school of theology.

in it. And she burst out laughing. It was a fine trick. She put one over on me, all right.

I wanted to go off to another town, but then everyone got busy matchmaking, and they were after me so they nearly tore my coat tails off. They talked at me and talked until I got water on the ear. She was no chaste maiden, but they told me she was virgin pure. She had a limp, and they said it was deliberate, from coyness. She had a bastard, and they told me the child was her little brother. I cried, "You're wasting your time. I'll never marry that whore." But they said indignantly, "What a way to talk! Aren't you ashamed of yourself? We can take you to the rabbi and have you fined for giving her a bad name." I saw then that I wouldn't escape them so easily and I thought, They're set on making me their butt. But when you're married the husband's the master, and if that's all right with her it's agreeable to me too. Besides, you can't pass through life unscathed, nor expect to.

I went to her clay house, which was built on the sand, and the whole gang, hollering and chorusing, came after me. They acted like bearbaiters. When we came to the well they stopped all the same. They were afraid to start anything with Elka. Her mouth would open as if it were on a hinge, and she had a fierce tongue. I entered the house. Lines were strung from wall to wall and clothes were drying. Barefoot she stood by the tub, doing the wash. She was dressed in a worn hand-me-down gown of plush. She had her hair put up in braids and pinned across her head. It took my breath away, almost, the reek of it all.

Evidently she knew who I was. She took a look at me and said, "Look who's here! He's come, the drip. Grab a seat."

I told her all; I denied nothing. "Tell me the truth," I said, "are you really a 10 virgin, and is that mischievous Yechiel actually your little brother? Don't be deceitful with me, for I'm an orphan."

"I'm an orphan myself," she answered, "and whoever tries to twist you up, may the end of his nose take a twist. But don't let them think they can take advantage of me. I want a dowry of fifty guilders, and let them take up a collection besides. Otherwise they can kiss my you-know-what." She was very plainspoken. I said, "Don't bargain with me. Either a flat 'yes' or a flat 'no'—go back where you came from."

I thought, No bread will ever be baked from *this* dough. But ours is not a poor town. They consented to everything and proceeded with the wedding. It so happened that there was a dysentery epidemic at the time. The ceremony was held at the cemetery gates, near the little corpse-washing hut. The fellows got drunk. While the marriage contract was being drawn up I heard the most pious high rabbi ask, "Is the bride a widow or a divorced woman?" And the sexton's wife answered for her, "Both a widow and divorced." It was a black moment for me. But what was I to do, run away from under the marriage canopy?

There was singing and dancing. An old granny danced opposite me, hugging a braided white *chalah*.° The master of revels made a "God 'a mercy" in memory

---

*chalah:* loaf of bread glazed with egg white, a Sabbath and holiday delicacy.

of the bride's parents. The schoolboys threw burrs, as on *Tishe b' Av* fast day.° There were a lot of gifts after the sermon: a noodle board, a kneading trough, a bucket, brooms, ladles, household articles galore. Then I took a look and saw two strapping young men carrying a crib. "What do we need this for?" I asked. So they said, "Don't rack your brains about it. It's all right, it'll come in handy." I realized I was going to be rooked. Take it another way though, what did I stand to lose? I reflected, I'll see what comes of it. A whole town can't go altogether crazy.

## II

At night I came where my wife lay, but she wouldn't let me in. "Say, look here, is this what they married us for?" I said. And she said, "My monthly has come." "But yesterday they took you to the ritual bath, and that's afterward, isn't it supposed to be?" "Today isn't yesterday," said she, "and yesterday's not today. You can beat it if you don't like it." In short, I waited.

Not four months later she was in childbed. The townsfolk hid their laughter    15 with their knuckles. But what could I do? She suffered intolerable pains and clawed at the walls. "Gimpel," she cried, "I'm going. Forgive me!" The house filled with women. They were boiling pans of water. The screams rose to the welkin.

The thing to do was to go to the House of Prayer to repeat Psalms, and that was what I did.

The townsfolk liked that, all right. I stood in a corner saying Psalms and prayers, and they shook their heads at me. "Pray, pray!" they told me. "Prayer never made any woman pregnant." One of the congregation put a straw to my mouth and said, "Hay for the cows." There was something to that too, by God!

She gave birth to a boy. Friday at the synagogue the sexton stood up before the Ark, pounded on the reading table, and announced, "The wealthy Reb Gimpel invites the congregation to a feast in honor of the birth of a son." The whole House of Prayer rang with laughter. My face was flaming. But there was nothing I could do. After all, I *was* the one responsible for the circumcision honors and rituals.

Half the town came running. You couldn't wedge another soul in. Women brought peppered chick-peas, and there was a keg of beer from the tavern. I ate and drank as much as anyone, and they all congratulated me. Then there was a circumcision, and I named the boy after my father, may he rest in peace. When all were gone and I was left with my wife alone, she thrust her head through the bed-curtain and called me to her.

"Gimpel," said she, "why are you silent? Has your ship gone and sunk?"    20

"What shall I say?" I answered. "A fine thing you've done to me! If my mother had known of it she'd have died a second time."

She said, "Are you crazy, or what?"

*Tishe b' Av*: day of mourning that commemorates disasters and persecutions.

"How can you make such a fool," I said, "of one who should be the lord and master?"

"What's the matter with you?" she said. "What have you taken it into your head to imagine?"

I saw that I must speak bluntly and openly. "Do you think this is the way to use an orphan?" I said. "You have borne a bastard." 25

She answered, "Drive this foolishness out of your head. The child is yours."

"How can he be mine?" I argued. "He was born seventeen weeks after the wedding."

She told me then that he was premature. I said, "Isn't he a little too premature?" She said she had had a grandmother who carried just as short a time and she resembled this grandmother of hers as one drop of water does another. She swore to it with such oaths that you would have believed a peasant at the fair if he had used them. To tell the plain truth, I didn't believe her; but when I talked it over the next day with the schoolmaster he told me that the very same thing had happened to Adam and Eve. Two they went up to bed, and four they descended.

"There isn't a woman in the world who is not the granddaughter of Eve," he said.

That was how it was—they argued me dumb. But then, who really knows how such things happen? 30

I began to forget my sorrow. I loved the child madly, and he loved me too. As soon as he saw me he'd wave his little hands and want me to pick him up, and when he was colicky I was the only one who could pacify him. I bought him a little bone teething ring and a little gilded cap. He was forever catching the evil eye from someone, and then I had to run to get one of those abracadabras for him that would get him out of it. I worked like an ox. You know how expenses go up when there's an infant in the house. I don't want to lie about it; I didn't dislike Elka either, for that matter. She swore at me and cursed, and I couldn't get enough of her. What strength she had! One of her looks could rob you of the power of speech. And her orations! Pitch and sulphur, that's what they were full of, and yet somehow also full of charm. I adored her every word. She gave me bloody wounds though.

In the evening I brought her a white loaf as well as a dark one, and also poppyseed rolls I baked myself. I thieved because of her and swiped everything I could lay hands on, macaroons, raisins, almonds, cakes. I hope I may be forgiven for stealing from the Saturday pots the women left to warm in the baker's oven. I would take out scraps of meat, a chunk of pudding, a chicken leg or head, a piece of tripe, whatever I could nip quickly. She ate and became fat and handsome.

I had to sleep away from home all during the week, at the bakery. On Friday nights when I got home she always made an excuse of some sort. Either she had heartburn, or a stitch in the side, or hiccups, or headaches. You know what women's excuses are. I had a bitter time of it. It was rough. To add to it, this little brother of hers, the bastard, was growing bigger. He'd put lumps on me, and when I wanted to hit back she'd open her mouth and curse so powerfully I saw a green haze floating before my eyes. Ten times a day she threatened to divorce me. Another man in my place would have taken French leave and disappeared. But I'm the type that bears it and says nothing. What's one to do? Shoulders are from God, and burdens too.

One night there was a calamity in the bakery; the oven burst, and we almost had a fire. There was nothing to do but go home, so I went home. Let me, I thought, also taste the joy of sleeping in bed in midweek. I didn't want to wake the sleeping mite and tiptoed into the house. Coming in, it seemed to me that I heard not the snoring of one but, as it were, a double snore, one a thin enough snore and the other like the snoring of a slaughtered ox. Oh, I didn't like that! I didn't like it at all. I went up to the bed, and things suddenly turned black. Next to Elka lay a man's form. Another in my place would have made an uproar, and enough noise to rouse the whole town, but the thought occurred to me that I might wake the child. A little thing like that—why frighten a little swallow like that, I thought. All right then, I went back to the bakery and stretched out on a sack of flour, and till morning I never shut an eye. I shivered as if I had had malaria. "Enough of being a donkey," I said to myself. "Gimpel isn't going to be a sucker all his life. There's a limit even to the foolishness of a fool like Gimpel."

In the morning I went to the rabbi to get advice, and it made a great commotion in the town. They sent the beadle for Elka right away. She came, carrying the child. And what do you think she did? She denied it, denied everything, bone and stone! "He's out of his head," she said. "I know nothing of dreams or divinations." They yelled at her, warned her, hammered on the table, but she stuck to her guns: it was a false accusation, she said.

The butchers and the horse-traders took her part. One of the lads from the slaughterhouse came by and said to me, "We've got our eye on you, you're a marked man." Meanwhile the child started to bear down and soiled itself. In the rabbinical court there was an Ark of the Covenant, and they couldn't allow that, so they sent Elka away.

I said to the rabbi, "What shall I do?"

"You must divorce her at once," said he.

"And what if she refuses?" I asked.

He said, "You must serve the divorce, that's all you'll have to do."

I said, "Well, all right, Rabbi. Let me think about it."

"There's nothing to think about," said he. "You mustn't remain under the same roof with her."

"And if I want to see the child?" I asked.

"Let her go, the harlot," said he, "and her brood of bastards with her."

The verdict he gave was that I mustn't even cross her threshold—never again, as long as I should live.

During the day it didn't bother me so much. I thought, it was bound to happen, the abscess had to burst. But at night when I stretched out upon the sacks I felt it all very bitterly. A longing took me, for her and for the child. I wanted to be angry, but that's my misfortune exactly, I don't have it in me to be really angry. In the first place—this was how my thoughts went—there's bound to be a slip sometimes. You can't live without errors. Probably that lad who was with her led her on and gave her presents and what not, and women are often long on hair and short on sense, and so he got around her. And then since she denies it so, maybe I was only seeing things? Hallucinations do happen. You see a figure or a mannikin or something, but when you come up closer it's nothing, there's not a thing there. And if that's so, I'm doing her an injustice. And when I got so far in my thoughts I started to weep. I sobbed so that I wet the flour where I lay. In the morning I went to the rabbi and told him that I had made a mistake. The rabbi wrote on with his quill, and he said that if that were so he would have to reconsider the whole case. Until he had finished I wasn't to go near my wife, but I might send her bread and money by messenger.

### III

Nine months passed before all the rabbis could come to an agreement. Letters went back and forth. I hadn't realized that there could be so much erudition about a matter like this.

Meantime Elka gave birth to still another child, a girl this time. On the Sabbath I went to the synagogue and invoked a blessing on her. They called me up to the Torah, and I named the child for my mother-in-law, may she rest in peace. The louts and loudmouths of the town who came into the bakery gave me a going over. All Frampol refreshed its spirits because of my trouble and grief. However, I resolved that I would always believe what I was told. What's the good of *not* believing? Today it's your wife you don't believe; tomorrow it's God Himself you won't take stock in.

By an apprentice who was her neighbor I sent her daily a corn or a wheat loaf, or a piece of pastry, rolls or bagels, or, when I got the chance, a slab of pudding, a slice of honeycake, or wedding strudel—whatever came my way. The apprentice was a goodhearted lad, and more than once he added something on his own. He had formerly annoyed me a lot, plucking my nose and digging me in the ribs, but when he started to be a visitor to my house he became kind and friendly. "Hey, you, Gimpel," he said to me, "you have a very decent little wife and two fine kids. You don't deserve them."

"But the things people say about her," I said.                                           50

"Well, they have long tongues," he said, "and nothing to do with them but babble. Ignore it as you ignore the cold of last winter."

One day the rabbi sent for me and said, "Are you certain, Gimpel, that you were wrong about your wife?"

I said, "I'm certain."

"Why, but look here! You yourself saw it."

"It must have been a shadow," I said.                                                   55

"The shadow of what?"

"Just of one of the beams, I think."

"You can go home then. You owe thanks to the Yanover rabbi. He found an obscure reference in Maimonides° that favored you."

I seized the rabbi's hand and kissed it.

I wanted to run home immediately. It's no small thing to be separated for so long a time from wife and child. Then I reflected, I'd better go back to work now, and go home in the evening. I said nothing to anyone, although as far as my heart was concerned it was like one of the Holy Days. The women teased and twitted me as they did every day, but my thought was, Go on, with your loose talk. The truth is out, like the oil upon the water. Maimonides says it's right, and therefore it is right!

At night, when I had covered the dough to let it rise, I took my share of bread and a little sack of flour and started homeward. The moon was full and the stars were glistening, something to terrify the soul. I hurried onward, and before me darted a long shadow. It was winter, and a fresh snow had fallen. I had a mind to sing, but it was growing late and I didn't want to wake the householders. Then I felt like whistling, but remembered that you don't whistle at night because it brings the demons out. So I was silent and walked as fast as I could.

Dogs in the Christian yards barked at me when I passed, but I thought, Bark your teeth out! What are you but mere dogs? Whereas I am a man, the husband of a fine wife, the father of promising children.

As I approached the house my heart started to pound as though it were the heart of a criminal. I felt no fear, but my heart went thump! thump! Well, no drawing back. I quietly lifted the latch and went in. Elka was asleep. I looked at the infant's cradle. The shutter was closed, but the moon forced its way through the cracks. I saw the newborn child's face and loved it as soon as I saw it—immediately—each tiny bone.

Then I came nearer to the bed. And what did I see but the apprentice lying there beside Elka. The moon went out all at once. It was utterly black, and I trembled. My teeth chattered. The bread fell from my hands and my wife waked and said, "Who is that, ah?"

I muttered, "It's me."

"Gimpel?" she asked. "How come you're here? I thought it was forbidden."

"The rabbi said," I answered and shook as with a fever.

"Listen to me, Gimpel," she said, "go out to the shed and see if the goat's all right. It seems she's been sick." I have forgotten to say that we had a goat. When I heard she was unwell I went into the yard. The nannygoat was a good little creature. I had a nearly human feeling for her.

With hesitant steps I went up to the shed and opened the door. The goat stood there on her four feet. I felt her everywhere, drew her by the arms, examined her udders, and found nothing wrong. She had probably eaten too much

*Maimonides:* Jewish philosopher (1135–1204) whose *Guide for the Perplexed* (1190) attempted to reconcile Judaism and the teachings of Aristotle.

bark. "Good night, little goat," I said. "Keep well." And the little beast answered with a "Maa" as though to thank me for the good will.

I went back. The apprentice had vanished. 70

"Where," I asked, "is the lad?"

"What lad?" my wife answered.

"What do you mean?" I said. "The apprentice. You were sleeping with him."

"The things I have dreamed this night and the night before," she said, "may they come true and lay you low, body and soul! An evil spirit has taken root in you and dazzles your sight." She screamed out, "You hateful creature! You moon calf! You spook! You uncouth man! Get out, or I'll scream all Frampol out of bed!"

Before I could move, her brother sprang out from behind the oven and struck 75 me a blow on the back of the head. I thought he had broken my neck. I felt that something about me was deeply wrong, and I said, "Don't make a scandal. All that's needed now is that people should accuse me of raising spooks and *dybbuks*°." For that was what she had meant. "No one will touch bread of my baking."

In short, I somehow calmed her.

"Well," she said, "that's enough. Lie down, and be shattered by wheels."

Next morning I called the apprentice aside. "Listen here, brother!" I said. And so on and so forth. "What do you say?" He stared at me as though I had dropped from the roof or something.

"I swear," he said, "you'd better go to an herb doctor or some healer. I'm afraid you have a screw loose, but I'll hush it up for you." And that's how the thing stood.

To make a long story short, I lived twenty years with my wife. She bore me 80 six children, four daughters and two sons. All kinds of things happened, but I neither saw nor heard. I believed, and that's all. The rabbi recently said to me, "Belief in itself is beneficial. It is written that a good man lives by his faith."

Suddenly my wife took sick. It began with a trifle, a little growth upon the breast. But she evidently was not destined to live long; she had no years. I spent a fortune on her. I have forgotten to say that by this time I had a bakery of my own and in Frampol was considered to be something of a rich man. Daily the healer came, and every witch doctor in the neighborhood was brought. They decided to use leeches, and after that to try cupping. They even called a doctor from Lublin, but it was too late. Before she died she called me to her bed and said, "Forgive me, Gimpel."

I said, "What is there to forgive? You have been a good and faithful wife."

"Woe, Gimpel!" she said. "It was ugly how I deceived you all these years. I want to go clean to my Maker, and so I have to tell you that the children are not yours."

If I had been clouted on the head with a piece of wood it couldn't have bewildered me more.

"Whose are they?" I asked. 85

---

*dybbuks:* demons, or souls of the dead, who take possession of people.

"I don't know," she said, "there were a lot. . . . But they're not yours." And as she spoke she tossed her head to the side, her eyes turned glassy, and it was all up with Elka. On her whitened lips there remained a smile.

I imagined that, dead as she was, she was saying, "I deceived Gimpel. That was the meaning of my brief life."

## IV

One night, when the period of mourning was done, as I lay dreaming on the flour sacks, there came the Spirit of Evil himself and said to me, "Gimpel, why do you sleep?"

I said, "What should I be doing? Eating *kreplach*°?"

"The whole world deceives you," he said, "and you ought to deceive the world in your turn."                                                                     90

"How can I deceive all the world?" I asked him.

He answered, "You might accumulate a bucket of urine every day and at night pour it into the dough. Let the sages of Frampol eat filth."

"What about judgment in the world to come?" I said.

"There is no world to come," he said. "They've sold you a bill of goods and talked you into believing you carried a cat in your belly. What nonsense!"

"Well then," I said, "and is there a God?"                                                               95

He answered, "There is no God either."

"What," I said, "*is* there, then?"

"A thick mire."

He stood before my eyes with a goatish beard and horns, longtoothed, and with a tail. Hearing such words, I wanted to snatch him by the tail, but I tumbled from the flour sacks and nearly broke a rib. Then it happened that I had to answer the call of nature, and, passing, I saw the risen bread, which seemed to say to me, "Do it!" In brief, I let myself be persuaded.

At dawn the apprentice came. We kneaded the dough, scattered caraway   100 seeds on it, and set it to bake. Then the apprentice went away, and I was left sitting in the little trench by the oven, on a pile of rags. Well, Gimpel, I thought, you've revenged yourself on them for all the shame they've put on you. Outside the frost glittered, but it was warm beside the oven. The flames heated my face. I bent my head and fell into a doze.

I saw in a dream, at once, Elka in her shroud. She called to me, "What have you done, Gimpel?"

I said to her, "It's all your fault," and started to cry.

"You fool!" she said. "You fool! Because I was false is everything false too? I never deceived anyone but myself. I'm paying for it all, Gimpel. They spare you nothing here."

I looked at her face. It was black. I was startled and waked, and remained sitting dumb. I sensed that everything hung in the balance. A false step now and I'd

---

*kreplach*: a kind of dumpling containing meat, cheese, or other filling.

lose Eternal Life. But God gave me His help. I seized the long shovel and took out the loaves, carried them into the yard, and started to dig a hole in the frozen earth.

My apprentice came back as I was doing it. "What are you doing, boss?" he said, and grew pale as a corpse. 105

"I know what I'm doing," I said, and I buried it all before his very eyes.

Then I went home, took my hoard from its hiding place, and divided it among the children. "I saw your mother tonight," I said. "She's turning black, poor thing."

They were so astounded they couldn't speak a word.

"Be well," I said, "and forget that such a one as Gimpel ever existed." I put on my short coat, a pair of boots, took the bag that held my prayer shawl in one hand, my stick in the other, and kissed the *mezzuzah.*° When people saw me in the street they were greatly surprised.

"Where are you going?" they said. 110

I answered, "Into the world." And so I departed from Frampol.

I wandered over the land, and good people did not neglect me. After many years I became old and white; I heard a great deal, many lies and falsehoods, but the longer I lived the more I understood that there were really no lies. Whatever doesn't really happen is dreamed at night. It happens to one if it doesn't happen to another, tomorrow if not today, or a century hence if not next year. What difference can it make? Often I heard tales of which I said, "Now this is a thing that cannot happen." But before a year had elapsed I heard that it actually had come to pass somewhere.

Going from place to place, eating at strange tables, it often happens that I spin yarns—improbable things that could never have happened—about devils, magicians, windmills, and the like. The children run after me, calling, "Grandfather, tell us a story." Sometimes they ask for particular stories, and I try to please them. A fat young boy once said to me, "Grandfather, it's the same story you told us before." The little rogue, he was right.

So it is with dreams too. It is many years since I left Frampol, but as soon as I shut my eyes I am there again. And whom do you think I see? Elka. She is standing by the washtub, as at our first encounter, but her face is shining and her eyes as radiant as the eyes of a saint, and she speaks outlandish words to me, strange things. When I wake I have forgotten it all. But while the dream lasts I am comforted. She answers all my queries, and what comes out is that all is right. I weep and implore, "Let me be with you." And she consoles me and tells me to be patient. The time is nearer than it is far. Sometimes she strokes and kisses me and weeps upon my face. When I awaken I feel her lips and taste the salt of her tears.

No doubt the world is entirely an imaginary world, but it is only once removed from the true world. At the door of the hovel where I lie, there stands the plank on which the dead are taken away. The gravedigger Jew has his spade ready. The grave waits and the worms are hungry; the shrouds are prepared—I 115

---

*mezzuzah:* a small oblong container, affixed near the front door of the house, which holds copies of Biblical verses (including a reminder to obey God's laws when traveling away from home).

carry them in my beggar's sack. Another *shnorrer*° is waiting to inherit my bed of straw. When the time comes I will go joyfully. Whatever may be there, it will be real, without complication, without ridicule, without deception. God be praised: there even Gimpel cannot be deceived.

## QUESTIONS

1. In what ways does Gimpel appear to deserve his nickname *the fool?* In what other ways is Gimpel not foolish at all?
2. What does Gimpel find to love in the character of Elka? Consider in particular the scene of her deathbed confession and her later appearance in Gimpel's dreams.
3. Why does Gimpel momentarily listen to the Devil? How is he delivered from temptation? For what reasons does he finally divide his wealth and become a poor wanderer? Would you call him a dynamic character, or a static character—one who grows and develops in the course of the story, or one who remains unchanged?
4. "No doubt the world is entirely an imaginary world, but it is only once removed from the true world." Comment on this statement in the closing paragraph. What do you think it means?
5. What elements of the supernatural do you find in "Gimpel the Fool"? What details of down-to-earth realism?
6. In what respects does the story resemble a fable? Is it possible to draw any moral from it?

## SUGGESTIONS FOR WRITING

1. Here is a topic for a lively essay if you are familiar with some variety of popular fiction—detective stories, science fiction, Gothic novels, romances, "adolescent agony" novels written for teenagers, or other kinds of paperback storytelling. Portray some of the stock characters you find prevalent in it. Suggestion: It might be simplistic to condemn stock characters as bad. They have long been valuable ingredients in much excellent literature. (For a discussion of stock characters, see page 67.)
2. Alternate topic: Portray a few stock characters we meet in current television programs. It might focus your essay to confine it to just one variety of stock character (for instance, the little man who peddles information to the police, the glamorous spy), or to just one kind of program (situation comedies, say, or soap operas, or police thrillers).
3. In a brief essay, study a dynamic character in a story, showing exactly how that character changed, or grew and developed. Possible subjects: Granny Weatherall, Gimpel, Sammy in John Updike's "A & P," the narrator in T. Coraghessan Boyle's "Greasy Lake," the boy Sarty Snopes in William Faulkner's "Barn Burning," the central character in Leo Tolstoi's "The Death of Ivan Ilych," Mrs. Turpin in Flannery O'Connor's "Revelation," and the narrator in Raymond Carver's "Cathedral." (For a discussion of dynamic characters, see page 68.)
4. Alternate topic: Have you ever in your life known anyone whose character, over months or years, has altered deeply? If so, try to explain what may have caused that person to be a "dynamic character."
5. Topics for brief papers:
   The motivation of Gimpel in leaving Frampol to wander the world.
   The motivation of Sammy in quitting his job (in "A & P").
   The motivation for the older brother writing to Sonny during his incarceration (in "Sonny's Blues").
   The motivation of someone (whether in your reading or in your experience) who made a similar gesture of throwing over everything.

*shnorrer:* a beggar, a traveling panhandler.

# 4  Setting

By the **setting** of a story, we mean its time and place. The word might remind you of the metal that holds a diamond in a ring, or of a *set* used in a play—perhaps a bare chair in front of a slab of painted canvas. But often, in an effective short story, setting may figure as more than mere background or underpinning. It can make things happen. It can prompt characters to act, bring them to realizations, or cause them to reveal their inmost natures.

To be sure, the idea of setting includes the physical environment of a story: a house, a street, a city, a landscape, a region. (*Where* a story takes place is sometimes called its **locale**.) Physical places mattered so greatly to French novelist Honoré de Balzac that sometimes, before writing a story set in a town, he would visit that town, select a few houses, and describe them in detail, down to their very smells. "The place in which an event occurred," Henry James admiringly said of him, "was in his view of equal moment with the event itself . . . it had a part to play; it needed to be made as definite as anything else."

But besides place, setting may crucially involve the *time* of the story—hour, year, or century. It might matter greatly that a story takes place at dawn, or on the day of the first moon landing. When we begin to read a historical novel, we are soon made aware that we aren't reading about life in the 1990s. In *The Scarlet Letter*, nineteenth-century author Nathaniel Hawthorne, by a long introduction and a vivid opening scene at a prison door, prepares us to witness events in the Puritan community of Boston in the earlier seventeenth century. This setting, together with scenes of Puritan times we recall from high school history, helps us understand what happens in the novel. We can appreciate the shocked agitation in town when a woman is accused of adultery: she has given illegitimate birth. Such an event might seem more nearly common today, but in the stern, God-fearing New England Puritan community, it was a flagrant defiance of church and state, which were all-powerful (and were all one). That reader will make no sense of *The Scarlet Letter* who ignores its setting—if to ignore the setting is possible, so much attention does Hawthorne pay to it.

That Hawthorne's novel takes place in a time remote from our own leads us to expect different customs, different attitudes. Some critics and teachers regard the setting of a story as its whole society, including the beliefs and assumptions of its characters. Still, we suggest that for now you keep your working definition of *setting* simple. Call it time and place. If later you should feel that your definition needs widening and deepening, you can always widen and deepen it.

Besides time and place, setting may also include the weather—which indeed, in some stories, may be crucial. Climate seems as substantial as any character in William Faulkner's "Dry September." After sixty-two rainless days, a long-unbroken spell of late-summer heat has frayed every nerve in a small town and caused the main character, a hotheaded white supremacist, to feel more and more irritation. The weather, someone remarks, is "enough to make a man do anything." When a false report circulates that a woman has been raped by a black man, the rumor, like a match flung into a dry field, ignites rage and provokes a lynching. Evidently, to understand the story we have to recognize its locale, a small town in Mississippi. The time (the 1930s) and that infernal heat wave matter, too. Fully to take in the meaning of Faulkner's story, we have to take in the setting in its entirety.

Physical place, by the way, is especially vital to a **regional writer,** who usually sets stories (or other work) in one geographic area. Such a writer, often a native of the place, tries to bring it alive to readers who live no matter where. William Faulkner, a distinguished regional writer, almost always sets his novels and stories in his native Mississippi. Though born in St. Louis, Kate Chopin became known as a regional writer for writing about Louisiana in many of her short stories and in her novel *The Awakening.* Willa Cather, for her novels of frontier Nebraska, often is regarded as another outstanding regionalist (though she also set fiction in Quebec, the Southwest, and in "Paul's Case," in Pittsburgh and New York). There is often something arbitrary, however, about calling an author a regional writer. The label often has a political tinge; it means the author describes an area outside the political and economic centers of a society. In a sense, we might think of James Joyce as a regional writer, in that all his fiction takes place in the city of Dublin, but instead we usually call him an Irish one.

As such writers show, a place can profoundly affect the character who grew up in it. Willa Cather is fond of portraying strong-minded, independent women, such as the heroine of her novel My *Antonía,* strengthened in part by years of coping with the hardships of life on the wind-lashed prairie. Not that every writer of stories in which a place matters greatly will draw the characters as helpless puppets of their environment. Few writers do so, although that may be what you find in novels of **naturalism**—fiction of grim realism, in which the writer observes human characters like a scientist observing ants, seeing them as the products and victims of environment and heredity.[1] Theodore Dreiser carries on

[1]The founder of naturalism in fiction was French novelist Émile Zola (1840–1902), who in a vast series of twenty novels about the family Rougon-Macquart traced a case of syphilis through several generations. In America, Stephen Crane wrote an early naturalist novel, *Maggie: A Girl of the Streets* (1893), and showed the way for later novelists such as Dreiser, Frank Norris, Upton Sinclair, and James T. Farrell.

the tradition of naturalism in such novels as *The Financier* (1912). It begins in a city setting. A young lad (who will grow up to be a ruthless industrialist) is watching a battle to death between a lobster and a squid in a fish-market tank. Dented for the rest of his life by this grim scene, he decides that's exactly the way to live in human society.

Setting may operate more subtly than that fish tank. Often, setting and character will reveal each other. Recall how Faulkner, at the start of "A Rose for Emily," depicts Emily Grierson's house, once handsome but now "an eyesore among eyesores" surrounded by gas stations. Still standing, refusing to yield its old-time horse-and-buggy splendor to the age of the automobile, the house in "its stubborn and coquettish decay" embodies the character of its owner. In some fiction, setting is closely bound with theme (what the story is saying)—as you will find in John Steinbeck's "The Chrysanthemums" (Chapter 7), a story beginning with a fog that has sealed off a valley from the rest of the world—a fog like the lid on a pot. In *The Scarlet Letter*, even small details contain powerful hints. At the beginning of his story, Hawthorne remarks of a colonial jailhouse:

> Before this ugly edifice, and between it and the wheel-track of the street, was a grass-plot, much overgrown with burdock, pigweed, apple-peru, and such unsightly vegetation, which evidently found something congenial in the soil that had so early borne the black flower of civilized society, a prison. But, on one side of the portal, and rooted almost at the threshold, was a wild rose-bush, covered, in this month of June, with its delicate gems, which might be imagined to offer their fragrance and fragile beauty to the prisoner as he went in, and to the condemned criminal as he came forth to his doom, in token that the deep heart of Nature could pity and be kind to him.

Apparently, Hawthorne wishes to show us that Puritan Boston, a town of rutted streets and an ugly jail with a tangled grass-plot, may be rough but has beauty in it. As the story unfolds, he will further suggest (among other things) that secret sin and a beautiful child may go together like pigweed and wild roses. In his artfully crafted novel, setting is one with—not separate from—characters, theme, and symbols.

In some stories, a writer will seem to draw a setting mainly to evoke atmosphere. In such a story, setting starts us feeling whatever the storyteller would have us feel. In "The Tell-Tale Heart," Poe's setting the action in an old, dark, lantern-lit house greatly contributes to our sense of unease—and so helps the story's effectiveness. (Old, dark mansions are favorite settings for the Gothic story, a long-popular kind of fiction mentioned again on page 261).

But be warned: you'll meet stories in which setting appears hardly to matter. In W. Somerset Maugham's fable, "The Appointment in Samarra," all we need be told about the setting is that it is a marketplace in Bagdad. In that brief fable, the inevitability of death is the point, not an exotic setting. In this chapter, though, you will meet four fine stories in which setting, for one reason or another, counts greatly. Without it, none of these stories could happen.

**Kate Chopin**

THE STORM                                                            1898

Kate Chopin (1851–1904) was born
Katherine O'Flaherty in St. Louis, daughter of an Irish immigrant grown wealthy in
retailing. On his death, young Kate was
raised by her mother's family: aristocratic
Creoles, descendants of the French and
Spaniards who had colonized Louisiana.
Young Kate received a convent schooling,
and at nineteen married Oscar Chopin, a
Creole cotton broker from New Orleans.
Later, the Chopins lived on a plantation
near Cloutierville, Louisiana, a region
whose varied people—Creoles, Cajuns,
blacks—Kate Chopin was later to write
about with loving care in Bayou Folk
(1894) and A Night in Arcadia (1897).

Kate Chopin

The shock of her husband's sudden death in 1883, which left her with the raising of six
children, seems to have plunged Kate Chopin into writing. She read and admired fine
woman writers of her day, such as the Maine realist Sarah Orne Jewett. She also read
Maupassant, Zola, and other new (and scandalous) French naturalist writers. She
began to bring into American fiction some of their hard-eyed observation and their passion for telling unpleasant truths. Determined, in defiance of her times, frankly to show
the sexual feelings of her characters, Chopin suffered from neglect and censorship. When
her major novel, The Awakening, appeared in 1899, critics were outraged by her candid portrait of a woman who seeks sexual and professional independence. After causing
such a literary scandal, Chopin was unable to get her later work published, and wrote
little more before she died. The Awakening and many of her stories had to wait seven
decades for a sympathetic audience.


*I*

The leaves were so still that even Bibi thought it was going to rain. Bobinôt,
who was accustomed to converse on terms of perfect equality with his little son,
called the child's attention to certain somber clouds that were rolling with sinister intention from the west, accompanied by a sullen, threatening roar. They
were at Friedheimer's store and decided to remain there till the storm had passed.
They sat within the door on two empty kegs. Bibi was four years old and looked
very wise.

"Mama'll be 'fraid, yes," he suggested with blinking eyes.

"She'll shut the house. Maybe she got Sylvie helpin' her this evenin',"
Bobinôt responded reassuringly.

"No; she ent got Sylvie. Sylvie was helpin' her yistiday," piped Bibi.

Bobinôt arose and going across to the counter purchased a can of shrimps, of  5
which Calixta was very fond. Then he returned to his perch on the keg and sat
stolidly holding the can of shrimps while the storm burst. It shook the wooden
store and seemed to be ripping great furrows in the distant field. Bibi laid his little
hand on his father's knee and was not afraid.

## II

Calixta, at home, felt no uneasiness for their safety. She sat at a side window
sewing furiously on a sewing machine. She was greatly occupied and did not
notice the approaching storm. But she felt very warm and often stopped to mop
her face on which the perspiration gathered in beads. She unfastened her white
sacque at the throat. It began to grow dark, and suddenly realizing the situation
she got up hurriedly and went about closing windows and doors.

Out on the small front gallery she had hung Bobinôt's Sunday clothes to air
and she hastened out to gather them before the rain fell. As she stepped outside,
Alcée Laballière rode in at the gate. She had not seen him very often since her
marriage, and never alone. She stood there with Bobinôt's coat in her hands, and
the big rain drops began to fall. Alcée rode his horse under the shelter of a side
projection where the chickens had huddled and there were plows and a harrow
piled up in the corner.

"May I come and wait on your gallery till the storm is over, Calixta?" he
asked.

"Come 'long in, M'sieur Alcée."

His voice and her own startled her as if from a trance, and she seized  10
Bobinôt's vest. Alcée, mounting to the porch, grabbed the trousers and snatched
Bibi's braided jacket that was about to be carried away by a sudden gust of wind.
He expressed an intention to remain outside, but it was soon apparent that he
might as well have been out in the open: the water beat in upon the boards in
driving sheets, and he went inside, closing the door after him. It was even necessary to put something beneath the door to keep the water out.

"My! what a rain! It's good two years sence it rain like that," exclaimed
Calixta as she rolled up a piece of bagging and Alcée helped her to thrust it
beneath the crack.

She was a little fuller of figure than five years before when she married; but
she had lost nothing of her vivacity. Her blue eyes still retained their melting
quality; and her yellow hair, dishevelled by the wind and rain, kinked more stubbornly than ever about her ears and temples.

The rain beat upon the low, shingled roof with a force and clatter that
threatened to break an entrance and deluge them there. They were in the dining
room—the sitting room—the general utility room. Adjoining was her bed room,
with Bibi's couch along side her own. The door stood open, and the room with its
white, monumental bed, its closed shutters, looked dim and mysterious.

Alcée flung himself into a rocker and Calixta nervously began to gather up
from the floor the lengths of a cotton sheet which she had been sewing.

"If this keeps up, *Dieu sait*° if the levees goin' to stan' it!" she exclaimed.

"What have you got to do with the levees?"

"I got enough to do! An' there's Bobinôt with Bibi out in that storm—if he only didn' left Friedheimer's!"

"Let us hope, Calixta, that Bobinôt's got sense enough to come in out of a cyclone."

She went and stood at the window with a greatly disturbed look on her face. She wiped the frame that was clouded with moisture. It was stiflingly hot. Alcée got up and joined her at the window, looking over her shoulder. The rain was coming down in sheets obscuring the view of far-off cabins and enveloping the distant wood in a gray mist. The playing of the lightning was incessant. A bolt struck a tall chinaberry tree at the edge of the field. It filled all visible space with a blinding glare and the crash seemed to invade the very boards they stood upon.

Calixta put her hands to her eyes, and with a cry, staggered backward.
Alcée's arm encircled her, and for an instant he drew her close and spasmodically to him.

"*Bonte!*°" she cried, releasing herself from his encircling arm and retreating from the window, "the house'll go next! If I only knew w'ere Bibi was!" She would not compose herself; she would not be seated. Alcée clasped her shoulders and looked into her face. The contact of her warm, palpitating body when he had unthinkingly drawn her into his arms, had aroused all the old-time infatuation and desire for her flesh.

"Calixta," he said, "don't be frightened. Nothing can happen. The house is too low to be struck, with so many tall trees standing about. There! aren't you going to be quiet? say, aren't you?" He pushed her hair back from her face that was warm and steaming. Her lips were as red and moist as pomegranate seed. Her white neck and a glimpse of her full, firm bosom disturbed him powerfully. As she glanced up at him the fear in her liquid blue eyes had given place to a drowsy gleam that unconsciously betrayed a sensuous desire. He looked down into her eyes and there was nothing for him to do but gather her lips in a kiss. It reminded him of Assumption.°

"Do you remember—in Assumption, Calixta?" he asked in a low voice broken by passion. Oh! she remembered; for in Assumption he had kissed her and kissed and kissed her; until his senses would well nigh fail, and to save her he would resort to a desperate flight. If she was not an immaculate dove in those days, she was still inviolate; a passionate creature whose very defenselessness had made her defense, against which his honor forbade him to prevail. Now—well, now—her lips seemed in a manner free to be tasted, as well as her round, white throat and her whiter breasts.

They did not heed the crashing torrents, and the roar of the elements made her laugh as she lay in his arms. She was a revelation in that dim, mysterious chamber; as white as the couch she lay upon. Her firm, elastic flesh that was knowing for the first time its birthright, was like a creamy lily that the sun invites to contribute its breath and perfume to the undying life of the world.

*Dieu sait:* God only knows.     *Bonte!:* Heavens!     *Assumption:* a parish west of New Orleans.

The generous abundance of her passion, without guile or trickery, was like a   25
white flame which penetrated and found response in depths of his own sensuous
nature that had never yet been reached.

When he touched her breasts they gave themselves up in quivering ecstasy,
inviting his lips. Her mouth was a fountain of delight. And when he possessed
her, they seemed to swoon together at the very borderland of life's mystery.

He stayed cushioned upon her, breathless, dazed, enervated, with his heart
beating like a hammer upon her. With one hand she clasped his head, her lips
lightly touching his forehead. The other hand stroked with a soothing rhythm his
muscular shoulders.

The growl of the thunder was distant and passing away. The rain beat softly
upon the shingles, inviting them to drowsiness and sleep. But they dared not yield.

The rain was over; and the sun was turning the glistening green world into a
palace of gems. Calixta, on the gallery, watched Alcée ride away. He turned and
smiled at her with a beaming face; and she lifted her pretty chin in the air and
laughed aloud.

### III

Bobinôt and Bibi, trudging home, stopped without at the cistern to make   30
themselves presentable.

"My! Bibi, w'at will yo' mama say! You ought to be ashame'. You oughtn' put
on those good pants. Look at 'em! An' that mud on yo' collar! How you got that
mud on yo' collar, Bibi? I never saw such a boy!" Bibi was the picture of pathetic
resignation. Bobinôt was the embodiment of serious solicitude as he strove to
remove from his own person and his son's the signs of their tramp over heavy
roads and through wet fields. He scraped the mud off Bibi's bare legs and feet
with a stick and carefully removed all traces from his heavy brogans. Then, prepared for the worst—the meeting with an overscrupulous housewife, they entered
cautiously at the back door.

Calixta was preparing supper. She had set the table and was dripping coffee
at the hearth. She sprang up as they came in.

"Oh, Bobinôt! You back! My! but I was uneasy. W'ere you been during the
rain? An' Bibi? he ain't wet? he ain't hurt?" She had clasped Bibi and was kissing
him effusively. Bobinôt's explanations and apologies which he had been composing all along the way, died on his lips as Calixta felt him to see if he were dry, and
seemed to express nothing but satisfaction at their safe return.

"I brought you some shrimps, Calixta," offered Bobinôt, hauling the can from
his ample side pocket and laying it on the table.

"Shrimps! Oh, Bobinôt! you too good fo' anything!" and she gave him a   35
smacking kiss on the cheek that resounded. "*J'vous reponds,*° we'll have feas' to
night! umph-umph!"

Bobinôt and Bibi began to relax and enjoy themselves, and when the three
seated themselves at table they laughed much and so loud that anyone might
have heard them as far away as Laballière's.

*J'vous reponds:* Let me tell you.

## IV

Alcée Laballière wrote to his wife, Clarisse, that night. It was a loving letter, full of tender solicitude. He told her not to hurry back, but if she and the babies liked it at Biloxi, to stay a month longer. He was getting on nicely; and though he missed them, he was willing to bear the separation a while longer—realizing that their health and pleasure were the first things to be considered.

## V

As for Clarisse, she was charmed upon receiving her husband's letter. She and the babies were doing well. The society was agreeable; many of her old friends and acquaintances were at the bay. And the first free breath since her marriage seemed to restore the pleasant liberty of her maiden days. Devoted as she was to her husband, their intimate conjugal life was something which she was more than willing to forego for a while.

So the storm passed and everyone was happy.

QUESTIONS

1. Exactly where does Chopin's story take place? How can you tell?
2. What circumstances introduced in Part I turn out to have a profound effect on events in the story?
3. What details in "The Storm" emphasize the fact that Bobinôt loves his wife? What details reveal how imperfectly he comprehends her nature?
4. What general attitudes toward sex, love, and marriage does Chopin imply? Cite evidence to support your answer.
5. What meanings do you find in the title "The Storm"?
6. In the story as a whole, how do setting and plot reinforce each other?

---

## Jack London

### TO BUILD A FIRE                                                               1910

*Jack London (1876–1916), born in San Francisco, won a large popular audience for his novels of the sea and the Yukon: The Call of the Wild (1903), The Sea-Wolf (1904), and White Fang (1906). Like Ernest Hemingway, he was a writer who lived a strenuous life. In 1893, he marched cross-country in Coxey's Army, an organized protest of the unemployed; in 1897, he took part in the Klondike gold rush; and later as a reporter he covered the Russo-Japanese war and the Mexican Revolution. Son of an unmarried mother and a father who denied his paternity, London grew up*

Jack London

*in poverty. At fourteen, he began holding hard jobs: working in a canning factory and a jute-mill, serving as a deck hand, pirating oysters in San Francisco Bay. These experiences persuaded him to join the Socialist Labor Party and crusade for workers' rights. In his political novel* The Iron Heel *(1908), London envisions a grim totalitarian America. Like himself, the hero of his novel* Martin Eden *(1909) is a man of brief schooling who gains fame as a writer, works for a cause, loses faith in it, and finds life without meaning. Though endowed with immense physical energy—he wrote 50 volumes—London drank hard, spent fast, and played out early. While his reputation as a novelist may have declined since his own day, some of his short stories have lasted triumphantly.*

Day had broken cold and gray, exceedingly cold and gray, when the man turned aside from the main Yukon trail and climbed the high earth-bank, where a dim and little-travelled trail led eastward through the fat spruce timberland. It was a steep bank, and he paused for breath at the top, excusing the act to himself by looking at his watch. It was nine o'clock. There was no sun nor hint of sun, though there was not a cloud in the sky. It was a clear day, and yet there seemed an intangible pall over the face of things, a subtle gloom that made the day dark, and that was due to the absence of sun. This fact did not worry the man. He was used to the lack of sun. It had been days since he had seen the sun, and he knew that a few more days must pass before that cheerful orb, due south, would just peep above the sky line and dip immediately from view.

The man flung a look back along the way he had come. The Yukon lay a mile wide and hidden under three feet of ice. On top of this ice were as many feet of snow. It was all pure white, rolling in gentle undulations where the ice jams of the freeze-up had formed. North and south, as far as the eye could see, it was unbroken white, save for a dark hairline that curved and twisted from around the spruce-covered island to the south, and that curved and twisted away into the north, where it disappeared behind another spruce-covered island. This dark hairline was the trail—the main trail—that led south five hundred miles to the Chilcoot Pass, Dyea, and salt water; and that led north seventy miles to Dawson, and still on to the north a thousand miles to Nulato, and finally to St. Michael, on Bering Sea, a thousand miles and half a thousand more.

But all this—the mysterious, far-reaching hairline trail, the absence of sun from the sky, the tremendous cold, and the strangeness and weirdness of it all— made no impression on the man. It was not because he was long used to it. He was a newcomer in the land, a *chechaquo*, and this was his first winter. The trouble with him was that he was without imagination. He was quick and alert in the things of life, but only in the things, and not in the significances. Fifty degrees below zero meant eighty-odd degrees of frost. Such fact impressed him as being cold and uncomfortable, and that was all. It did not lead him to meditate upon his frailty as a creature of temperature, and upon man's frailty in general, able only to live within certain narrow limits of heat and cold; and from there on it did not lead him to the conjectural field of immortality and man's place in the universe. Fifty degrees below zero stood for a bite of frost that hurt and that must be guarded against by the use of mittens, ear flaps, warm moccasins, and thick socks. Fifty degrees below zero was to him just precisely fifty degrees below zero. That there should be anything more to it than that was a thought that never entered his head.

As he turned to go on, he spat speculatively. There was a sharp, explosive crackle that startled him. He spat again. And again, in the air, before it could fall to the snow, the spittle crackled. He knew that at fifty below spittle crackled on the snow, but this spittle had crackled in the air. Undoubtedly it was colder than fifty below—how much colder he did not know. But the temperature did not matter. He was bound for the old claim on the left fork of Henderson Creek, where the boys were already. They had come over across the divide from the Indian Creek country, while he had come the roundabout way to take a look at the possibilities of getting out logs in the spring from the islands in the Yukon. He would be in to camp by six o'clock; a bit after dark, it was true, but the boys would be there, a fire would be going, and a hot supper would be ready. As for lunch, he pressed his hand against the protruding bundle under his jacket. It was also under his shirt, wrapped up in a handkerchief and lying against the naked skin. It was the only way to keep the biscuits from freezing. He smiled agreeably to himself as he thought of those biscuits, each cut open and sopped in bacon grease, and each enclosing a generous slice of fried bacon.

He plunged in among the big spruce trees. The trail was faint. A foot of snow had fallen since the last sled had passed over, and he was glad he was without a sled, travelling light. In fact, he carried nothing but the lunch wrapped in the handkerchief. He was surprised, however, at the cold. It certainly was cold, he concluded, as he rubbed his numb nose and cheekbones with his mittened hand. He was a warm-whiskered man, but the hair on his face did not protect the high cheekbones and the eager nose that thrust itself aggressively into the frosty air.

At the man's heels trotted a dog, a big native husky, the proper wolf dog, gray-coated and without any visible or temperamental difference from its brother, the wild wolf. The animal was depressed by the tremendous cold. It knew that it was no time for travelling. Its instinct told it a truer tale than was told to the man by the man's judgment. In reality, it was not merely colder than fifty below zero; it was colder than sixty below, than seventy below. It was seventy-five below zero. Since the freezing point is thirty-two above zero, it meant that one hundred and seven degrees of frost obtained. The dog did not know anything about thermometers. Possibly in its brain there was no sharp consciousness of a condition of very cold such as was in the man's brain. But the brute had its instinct. It experienced a vague but menacing apprehension that subdued it and made it slink along at the man's heels, and that made it question eagerly every unwonted movement of the man as if expecting him to go into camp or to seek shelter somewhere and build a fire. The dog had learned fire, and it wanted fire, or else to burrow under the snow and cuddle its warmth away from the air.

The frozen moisture of its breathing had settled on its fur in a fine powder of frost, and especially were its jowls, muzzle, and eyelashes whitened by its crystalled breath. The man's red beard and mustache were likewise frosted, but more solidly, the deposit taking the form of ice and increasing with every warm, moist breath he exhaled. Also, the man was chewing tobacco, and the muzzle of ice held his lips so rigidly that he was unable to clear his chin when he expelled the juice. The result was that a crystal beard of the color and solidity of amber was increasing its length on his chin. If he fell down it would shatter itself, like glass, into brittle fragments. But he did not mind the appendage. It was the penalty all tobacco chewers paid in that country, and he had been out before in two cold snaps. They had not been so cold as this, he knew, but by the spirit thermometer at Sixty Mile he knew they had been registered at fifty below and at fifty-five.

He held on through the level stretch of woods for several miles, crossed a wide flat, and dropped down a bank to the frozen bed of a small stream. This was Henderson Creek, and he knew he was ten miles from the forks. He looked at his watch. It was ten o'clock. He was making four miles an hour, and he calculated that he would arrive at the forks at half-past twelve. He decided to celebrate that event by eating his lunch there.

The dog dropped in again at his heels, with a tail drooping discouragement, as the man swung along the creek bed. The furrow of the old sled trail was plainly visible, but a dozen inches of snow covered the marks of the last runners. In a month no man had come up or down that silent creek. The man held steadily on. He was not much given to thinking, and just then particularly he had nothing to think about save that he would eat lunch at the forks and that at six o'clock he would be in camp with the boys. There was nobody to talk to; and, had there been, speech would have been impossible because of the ice muzzle on his mouth. So he continued monotonously to chew tobacco and to increase the length of his amber beard.

Once in a while the thought reiterated itself that it was very cold and that he had never experienced such cold. As he walked along he rubbed his cheekbones and nose with the back of his mittened hand. He did this automatically, now and again changing hands. But, rub as he would, the instant he stopped his cheekbones were numb, and the following instant the end of his nose went numb. He was sure to frost his cheeks; he knew that, and experienced a pang of regret that he had not devised a nose strap of the sort Bud wore in cold snaps. Such a strap passed across the cheeks, as well, and saved them. But it didn't matter much, after all. What were frosted cheeks? A bit painful, that was all; they were never serious.

Empty as the man's mind was of thoughts, he was keenly observant, and he noticed the changes in the creek, the curves and bends and timber jams, and always he sharply noted where he placed his feet. Once, coming around a bend, he shied abruptly, like a startled horse, curved away from the place where he had been walking, and retreated several paces back along the trail. The creek he knew was frozen clear to the bottom—no creek could contain water in that arctic winter—but he knew also that there were springs that bubbled out from the hillsides and ran along under the snow and on top the ice of the creek. He knew that the coldest snaps never froze these springs, and he knew likewise their danger. They were traps. They hid pools of water under the snow that might be three inches deep, or three feet. Sometimes a skin of ice half an inch thick covered

10

them, and in turn was covered by the snow. Sometimes there were alternate layers of water and ice skin, so that when one broke through he kept on breaking through for a while, sometimes wetting himself to the waist.

That was why he had shied in such panic. He had felt the give under his feet and heard the crackle of a snow-hidden ice skin. And to get his feet wet in such a temperature meant trouble and danger. At the very least it meant delay, for he would be forced to stop and build a fire, and under its protection to bare his feet while he dried his socks and moccasins. He stood and studied the creek bed and its banks, and decided that the flow of water came from the right. He reflected awhile, rubbing his nose and cheeks, then skirted to the left, stepping gingerly and testing the footing for each step. Once clear of the danger, he took a fresh chew of tobacco and swung along at his four-mile gait.

In the course of the next two hours he came upon several similar traps. Usually the snow above the hidden pools had a sunken, candied appearance that advertised the danger. Once again, however, he had a close call; and once, suspecting danger, he compelled the dog to go on in front. The dog did not want to go. It hung back until the man shoved it forward, and then it went quickly across the white, unbroken surface. Suddenly it broke through, floundered to one side, and got away to firmer footing. It had wet its forefeet and legs, and almost immediately the water that clung to it turned to ice. It made quick efforts to lick the ice off its legs, then dropped down in the snow and began to bite out the ice that had formed between the toes. This was a matter of instinct. To permit the ice to remain would mean sore feet. It did not know this. It merely obeyed the mysterious prompting that arose from the deep crypts of its being. But the man knew, having achieved a judgment on the subject, and he removed the mitten from his right hand and helped tear out the ice particles. He did not expose his fingers more than a minute, and was astonished at the swift numbness that smote them. It certainly was cold. He pulled on the mitten hastily, and beat the hand savagely across his chest.

At twelve o'clock the day was at its brightest. Yet the sun was too far south on its winter journey to clear the horizon. The bulge of the earth intervened between it and Henderson Creek, where the men walked under a clear sky at noon and cast no shadow. At half-past twelve, to the minute, he arrived at the forks of the creek. He was pleased at the speed he had made. If he kept it up, he would certainly be with the boys by six. He unbuttoned his jacket and shirt and drew forth his lunch. The action consumed no more than a quarter of a minute, yet in that brief moment the numbness laid hold of the exposed fingers. He did not put the mitten on, but, instead, struck the fingers a dozen sharp smashes against his leg. Then he sat down on a snow-covered log to eat. The sting that followed upon the striking of his fingers against his leg ceased so quickly that he was startled. He had had no chance to take a bite of biscuit. He struck the fingers repeatedly and returned them to the mitten, baring the other hand for the purpose of eating. He tried to take a mouthful, but the ice muzzle prevented. He had forgotten to build a fire and thaw out. He chuckled at his foolishness, and as he chuckled he noted the numbness creeping into the exposed fingers. Also, he noted that the stinging which had first come to his toes when he sat down was already passing away. He wondered whether the toes were warm or numb. He moved them inside the moccasins and decided that they were numb.

He pulled the mitten on hurriedly and stood up. He was a bit frightened. He 15 stamped up and down until the stinging returned into the feet. It certainly was cold, was his thought. That man from Sulphur Creek had spoken the truth when telling how cold it sometimes got in the country. And he had laughed at him at the time! That showed one must not be too sure of things. There was no mistake about it, it *was* cold. He strode up and down, stamping his feet and threshing his arms, until reassured by the returning warmth. Then he got out matches and proceeded to make a fire. From the undergrowth, where high water of the previous spring had lodged a supply of seasoned twigs, he got his firewood. Working carefully from a small beginning, he soon had a roaring fire, over which he thawed the ice from his face and in the protection of which he ate his biscuits. For the moment the cold of space was outwitted. The dog took satisfaction in the fire, stretching out close enough for warmth and far enough away to escape being singed.

When the man had finished, he filled his pipe and took his comfortable time over a smoke. Then he pulled on his mittens, settled the ear flaps of his cap firmly about his ears, and took the creek trail up the left fork. The dog was disappointed and yearned back toward the fire. This man did not know cold. Possibly all the generations of his ancestry had been ignorant of cold, of real cold, of cold one hundred and seven degrees below freezing point. But the dog knew; all its ancestry knew, and it had inherited the knowledge. And it knew that it was not good to walk abroad in such fearful cold. It was the time to lie snug in a hole in the snow and wait for a curtain of cloud to be drawn across the face of outer space whence this cold came. On the other hand, there was no keen intimacy between the dog and the man. The one was the toil slave of the other, and the only caresses it had ever received were the caresses of the whip lash and of harsh and menacing throat sounds that threatened the whip lash. So the dog made no effort to communicate its apprehension to the man. It was not concerned in the welfare of the man; it was for its own sake that it yearned back toward the fire. But the man whistled, and spoke to it with the sound of whip lashes, and the dog swung in at the man's heels and followed after.

The man took a chew of tobacco and proceeded to start a new amber beard. Also, his moist breath quickly powdered with white his mustache, eyebrows, and lashes. There did not seem to be so many springs on the left fork of the Henderson, and for half an hour the man saw no signs of any. And then it happened. At a place where there were no signs, where the soft, unbroken snow seemed to advertise solidity beneath, the man broke through. It was not deep. He wet himself halfway to the knees before he floundered out to the firm crust.

He was angry, and cursed his luck aloud. He had hoped to get into camp with the boys at six o'clock, and this would delay him an hour, for he would have to build a fire and dry out his footgear. This was imperative at that low temperature—he knew that much; and he turned aside to the bank, which he climbed.

On top, tangled in the underbrush about the trunks of several small spruce trees, was a high-water deposit of dry firewood—sticks and twigs, principally, but also larger portions of seasoned branches and fine, dry, last year's grasses. He threw down several large pieces on top of the snow. This served for a foundation and prevented the young flame from drowning itself in the snow it otherwise would melt. The flame he got by touching a match to a small shred of birch bark that he took from his pocket. This burned even more readily than paper. Placing it on the foundation, he fed the young flame with wisps of dry grass and with the tiniest dry twigs.

He worked slowly and carefully, keenly aware of his danger. Gradually, as the flame grew stronger, he increased the size of the twigs with which he fed it. He squatted in the snow, pulling the twigs out from their entanglement in the brush and feeding directly to the flame. He knew there must be no failure. When it is seventy-five below zero, a man must not fail in his first attempt to build a fire—that is, if his feet are wet. If his feet are dry, and he fails, he can run along the trail for half a mile and restore his circulation. But the circulation of wet and freezing feet cannot be restored by running when it is seventy-five below. No matter how fast he runs, the wet feet will freeze the harder.

All this the man knew. The old-timer on Sulphur Creek had told him about  20
it the previous fall, and now he was appreciating the advice. Already all sensation had gone out of his feet. To build the fire he had been forced to remove his mittens, and the fingers had quickly gone numb. His pace of four miles an hour had kept his heart pumping blood to the surface of his body and to all the extremities. But the instant he stopped, the action of the pump eased down. The cold of space smote the unprotected tip of the planet, and he, being on that unprotected tip, received the full force of the blow. The blood of his body recoiled before it. The blood was alive, like the dog, and like the dog it wanted to hide away and cover itself up from the fearful cold. So long as he walked four miles an hour, he pumped that blood, willy-nilly, to the surface; but now it ebbed away and sank down into the recesses of his body. The extremities were the first to feel its absence. His wet feet froze the faster, and his exposed fingers numbed the faster, though they had not yet begun to freeze. Nose and cheeks were already freezing, while the skin of all his body chilled as it lost its blood.

But he was safe. Toes and nose and cheeks would be only touched by the frost, for the fire was beginning to burn with strength. He was feeding it with twigs the size of his finger. In another minute he would be able to feed it with branches the size of his wrist, and then he could remove his wet footgear, and, while it dried, he could keep his naked feet warm by the fire, rubbing them at first, of course, with snow. The fire was a success. He was safe. He remembered the advice of the old-timer on Sulphur Creek, and smiled. The old-timer had been very serious in laying down the law that no man must travel alone in the Klondike after fifty below. Well, here he was; he had had the accident; he was alone; and he had saved himself. Those old-timers were rather womanish, some of them, he thought. All a man had to do was to keep his head, and he was all right. Any man who was a man could travel alone. But it was surprising, the rapidity with which his cheeks and nose were freezing. And he had not thought his fingers could go lifeless in so short a time. Lifeless they were, for he could scarcely make them move together to grip a twig, and they seemed remote from his body and from him. When he touched a twig, he had to look and see whether or not he had hold of it. The wires were pretty well down between him and his finger ends.

All of which counted for little. There was the fire, snapping and crackling and promising life with every dancing flame. He started to untie his moccasins. They were coated with ice; the thick German socks were like sheaths of iron halfway to the knees; and the moccasin strings were like rods of steel all twisted and knotted as by some conflagration. For a moment he tugged with his numb fingers, then, realizing the folly of it, he drew his sheath knife.

But before he could cut the strings, it happened. It was his own fault or, rather, his mistake. He should not have built the fire under the spruce tree. He should have built it in the open. But it had been easier to pull the twigs from the brush and drop them directly on the fire. Now the tree under which he had done this carried a weight of snow on its boughs. No wind had blown for weeks, and each bough was fully freighted. Each time he had pulled a twig he had communicated a slight agitation to the tree—an imperceptible agitation, so far as he was concerned, but an agitation sufficient to bring about the disaster. High up in the tree one bough capsized its load of snow. This fell on the boughs beneath, capsizing them. This process continued, spreading out and involving the whole tree. It grew like an avalanche, and it descended without warning upon the man and the fire, and the fire was blotted out! Where it had burned was a mantle of fresh and disordered snow.

The man was shocked. It was as though he had just heard his own sentence of death. For a moment he sat and stared at the spot where the fire had been. Then he grew very calm. Perhaps the old-timer on Sulphur Creek was right. If he had only had a trail mate he would have been in no danger now. The trail mate could have built the fire. Well, it was up to him to build the fire over again, and this second time there must be no failure. Even if he succeeded, he would most likely lose some toes. His feet must be badly frozen by now, and there would be some time before the second fire was ready.

Such were his thoughts, but he did not sit and think them. He was busy all 25 the time they were passing through his mind. He made a new foundation for a fire, this time in the open, where no treacherous tree could blot it out. Next he gathered dry grasses and tiny twigs from the high-water flotsam. He could not bring his fingers together to pull them out, but he was able to gather them by the handful. In this way he got many rotten twigs and bits of green moss that were undesirable, but it was the best he could do. He worked methodically, even collecting an armful of the larger branches to be used later when the fire gathered strength. And all the while the dog sat and watched him, a certain yearning wistfulness in its eye, for it looked upon him as the fire provider, and the fire was slow in coming.

When all was ready, the man reached in his pocket for a second piece of birch bark. He knew the bark was there, and, though he could not feel it with his fingers, he could hear its crisp rustling as he fumbled for it. Try as he would, he could not clutch hold of it. And all the time, in his consciousness, was the knowledge that each instant his feet were freezing. This thought tended to put him in a panic, but he fought against it and kept calm. He pulled on his mittens with his teeth, and threshed his arms back and forth, beating his hands with all his might against his sides. He did this sitting down, and he stood up to do it; and all the while the dog sat in the snow, its wolf brush of a tail curled around warmly over its forefeet, its sharp wolf ears pricked forward intently as it watched the man. And the man, as he beat and threshed with his arms and hands, felt a great surge of envy as he regarded the creature that was warm and secure in its natural covering.

After a time he was aware of the first faraway signals of sensation in his beaten fingers. The faint tingling grew stronger till it evolved into a stinging ache that was excruciating, but which the man hailed with satisfaction. He stripped the mitten from his right hand and fetched forth the birch bark. The exposed fingers were quickly going numb again. Next he brought out his bunch of sulphur matches. But the tremendous cold had already driven the life out of his fingers. In his effort to separate one match from the others, the whole bunch fell in the snow. He tried to pick it out of the snow, but failed. The dead fingers could neither touch nor clutch. He was very careful. He drove the thought of his freezing feet, and nose, and cheeks, out of his mind, devoting his whole soul to the matches. He watched, using the sense of vision in place of that of touch, and when he saw his fingers on each side the bunch, he closed them—that is, he willed to close them, for the wires were down, and the fingers did not obey. He pulled the mitten on the right hand, and beat it fiercely against his knee. Then, with both mittened hands, he scooped the bunch of matches, along with much snow, into his lap. Yet he was no better off.

After some manipulation he managed to get the bunch between the heels of his mittened hands. In this fashion he carried it to his mouth. The ice crackled and snapped when by a violent effort he opened his mouth. He drew the lower jaw in, curled the upper lip out of the way, and scraped the bunch with his upper teeth in order to separate a match. He succeeded in getting one, which he dropped on his lap. He was no better off. He could not pick it up. Then he devised a way. He picked it up in his teeth and scratched it on his leg. Twenty times he scratched before he succeeded in lighting it. As it flamed he held it with his teeth to the birch bark. But the burning brimstone went up his nostrils and into his lungs, causing him to cough spasmodically. The match fell into the snow and went out.

The old-timer on Sulphur Creek was right, he thought in the moment of controlled despair that ensued: after fifty below, a man should travel with a partner. He beat his hands, but failed in exciting any sensation. Suddenly he bared both hands, removing the mittens with his teeth. He caught the whole bunch between the heels of his hands. His arm muscles not being frozen enabled him to press the hand heels tightly against the matches. Then he scratched the bunch along his leg. It flared into flame, seventy sulphur matches at once! There was no wind to blow them out. He kept his head to one side to escape the strangling fumes, and held the blazing bunch to the birch bark. As he so held it, he became aware of sensation in his hand. His flesh was burning. He could smell it. Deep down below the surface he could feel it. The sensation developed into pain that grew acute. And still he endured it, holding the flame of the matches clumsily to the bark that would not light readily because his own burning hands were in the way, absorbing most of the flame.

At last, when he could endure no more, he jerked his hands apart. The blazing matches fell sizzling into the snow, but the birch bark was alight. He began laying dry grasses and the tiniest twigs on the flame. He could not pick and choose, for he had to lift the fuel between the heels of his hands. Small pieces of rotten wood and green moss clung to the twigs, and he bit them off as well as he could with his teeth. He cherished the flame carefully and awkwardly. It meant life, and it must not perish. The withdrawal of blood from the surface of his body now made him begin to shiver, and he grew more awkward. A large piece of green moss fell squarely on the little fire. He tried to poke it out with his fingers, but his shivering frame made him poke too far, and he disrupted the nucleus of the little fire, the burning grasses and tiny twigs separating and scattering. He tried to poke them together again, but in spite of the tenseness of the effort, his shivering got away from him, and the twigs were hopelessly scattered. Each twig gushed a puff of smoke and went out. The fire provider had failed. As he looked apathetically about him, his eyes chanced on the dog, sitting across the ruins of the fire from him, in the snow, making restless, hunching movements, slightly lifting one forefoot and then the other, shifting its weight back and forth on them with wistful eagerness.

The sight of the dog put a wild idea into his head. He remembered the tale of the man, caught in the blizzard, who killed a steer and crawled inside the carcass, and so was saved. He would kill the dog and bury his hands in the warm body until the numbness went out of them. Then he could build another fire. He spoke to the dog, calling it to him; but in his voice was a strange note of fear that frightened the animal, who had never known the man to speak in such a way before. Something was the matter, and its suspicious nature sensed danger—it knew not what danger, but somewhere, somehow, in its brain arose an apprehension of the man. It flattened its ears down at the sound of the man's voice, and its restless, hunching movements and the liftings and shiftings of its forefeet became more pronounced; but it would not come to the man. He got on his hands and knees and crawled toward the dog. This unusual posture again excited suspicion, and the animal sidled mincingly away.

The man sat up in the snow for a moment and struggled for calmness. Then he pulled on his mittens, by means of his teeth, and got upon his feet. He glanced down at first in order to assure himself that he was really standing up, for the absence of sensation in his feet left him unrelated to the earth. His erect position

30

in itself started to drive the webs of suspicion from the dog's mind; and when he spoke peremptorily, with the sound of whip lashes in his voice, the dog rendered its customary allegiance and came to him. As it came within reaching distance, the man lost his control. His arms flashed out to the dog, and he experienced genuine surprise when he discovered that his hands could not clutch, that there was neither bend nor feeling in the fingers. He had forgotten for the moment that they were frozen and that they were freezing more and more. All this happened quickly, and before the animal could get away, he encircled its body with his arms. He sat down in the snow, and in this fashion held the dog, while it snarled and whined and struggled.

But it was all he could do, hold its body encircled in his arms and sit there. He realized that he could not kill the dog. There was no way to do it. With his helpless hands he could neither draw nor hold his sheath knife nor throttle the animal. He released it, and it plunged wildly away, with tail between its legs, and still snarling. It halted forty feet away and surveyed him curiously, with ears sharply pricked forward.

The man looked down at his hands in order to locate them, and found them hanging on the ends of his arms. It struck him as curious that one should have to use his eyes in order to find out where his hands were. He began threshing his arms back and forth, beating the mittened hands against his sides. He did this for five minutes, violently, and his heart pumped enough blood up to the surface to put a stop to his shivering. But no sensation was aroused in the hands. He had an impression that they hung like weights on the ends of his arms, but when he tried to run the impression down, he could not find it.

A certain fear of death, dull and oppressive, came to him. This fear quickly 35 became poignant as he realized that it was no longer a mere matter of freezing his fingers and toes, or of losing his hands and feet, but that it was a matter of life and death with the chances against him. This threw him into a panic, and he turned and ran up the creek bed along the old, dim trail. The dog joined in behind and kept up with him. He ran blindly, without intention, in fear such as he had never known in his life. Slowly, as he plowed and floundered through the snow, he began to see things again—the banks of the creek, the old timber jams, the leafless aspens, and the sky. The running made him feel better. He did not shiver. Maybe, if he ran on, his feet would thaw out; and anyway, if he ran far enough, he would reach camp and the boys. Without doubt he would lose some fingers and toes and some of his face; but the boys would take care of him, and save the rest of him when he got there. And at the same time there was another thought in his mind that said he would never get to the camp and the boys; that it was too many miles away, that the freezing had too great a start on him, and that he would soon be stiff and dead. This thought he kept in the background and refused to consider. Sometimes it pushed itself forward and demanded to be heard, but he thrust it back and strove to think of other things.

It struck him as curious that he could run at all on feet so frozen that he could not feel them when they struck the earth and took the weight of his body. He seemed to himself to skim along above the surface, and to have no connection with the earth. Somewhere he had once seen a winged Mercury, and he wondered if Mercury felt as he felt when skimming over the earth.

His theory of running until he reached the camp and the boys had one flaw in it: he lacked the endurance. Several times he stumbled, and finally he tottered, crumpled up, and fell. When he tried to rise, he failed. He must sit and rest, he decided, and next time he would merely walk and keep on going. As he sat and regained his breath, he noted that he was feeling quite warm and comfortable. He was not shivering, and it even seemed that a warm glow had come to his chest and trunk. And yet, when he touched his nose and cheeks, there was no sensation. Running would not thaw them out. Nor would it thaw out his hands and feet. Then the thought came to him that the frozen portions of his body must be extending. He tried to keep this thought down, to forget it, to think of something else; he was aware of the panicky feeling that it caused, and he was afraid of the panic. But the thought asserted itself, and persisted, until it produced a vision of his body totally frozen. This was too much, and he made another wild run along the trail. Once he slowed down to a walk, but the thought of the freezing extending itself made him run again.

And all the time the dog ran with him, at his heels. When he fell down a second time, it curled its tail over its forefeet and sat in front of him, facing him, curiously eager and intent. The warmth and security of the animal angered him, and he cursed it till it flattened down its ears appeasingly. This time the shivering came more quickly upon the man. He was losing in his battle with the frost. It was creeping into his body from all sides. The thought of it drove him on, but he ran no more than a hundred feet, when he staggered and pitched headlong. It was his last panic. When he had recovered his breath and control, he sat up and entertained in his mind the conception of meeting death with dignity. However, the conception did not come to him in such terms. His idea of it was that he had been making a fool of himself, running around like a chicken with its head cut off—such was the simile that occurred to him. Well, he was bound to freeze anyway, and he might as well take it decently. With this new-found peace of mind came the first glimmerings of drowsiness. A good idea, he thought, to sleep off to death. It was like taking an anesthetic. Freezing was not so bad as people thought. There were lots worse ways to die.

He pictured the boys finding his body next day. Suddenly he found himself with them, coming along the trail and looking for himself. And, still with them, he came around a turn in the trail and found himself lying in the snow. He did not belong with himself any more, for even then he was out of himself, standing with the boys and looking at himself in the snow. It certainly was cold, was his thought. When he got back to the States he could tell the folks what real cold was. He drifted on from this to a vision of the old-timer on Sulphur Creek. He could see him quite clearly, warm and comfortable, and smoking a pipe.

"You were right, old hoss; you were right," the man mumbled to the old-timer of Sulphur Creek.                                                                          40

Then the man drowsed off into what seemed to him the most comfortable and satisfying sleep he had ever known. The dog sat facing him and waiting. The brief day drew to a close in a long, slow twilight. There were no signs of a fire to be made, and, besides, never in the dog's experience had it known a man to sit like that in the snow and make no fire. As the twilight drew on, its eager yearning for the fire mastered it, and with a great lifting and shifting of forefeet, it whined softly, then flattened its ears down in anticipation of being chidden by the man. But the man remained silent. Later the dog whined loudly. And still later it crept close to the man and caught the scent of death. This made the animal bristle and back away. A little longer it delayed, howling under the stars that leaped and danced and shone brightly in the cold sky. Then it turned and trotted up the trail in the direction of the camp it knew, where were the other food providers and fire providers.

## QUESTIONS

1. Roughly how much of London's story is devoted to describing the setting? What particular details make it memorable?
2. To what extent does setting determine what happens in this story?
3. From what point of view is London's story told?
4. In "To Build a Fire" the man is never given a name. What is the effect of his being called simply "the man" throughout the story?
5. From the evidence London gives us, what stages are involved in the process of freezing to death? What does the story gain from London's detailed account of the man's experience with each successive stage?
6. What are the most serious mistakes the man makes? To what factors do you attribute these errors?

## T. Coraghessan Boyle

GREASY LAKE                                                                        1985

*T. Coraghessan Boyle (the T. stands for Tom) was born in 1948 in Peekskill, New York, the son of Irish immigrants. He grew up, he recalls, "as a sort of pampered punk" who did not read a book until he was eighteen. After a brief period as a high school teacher, he studied in the University of Iowa Writers' Workshop, submitting a collection of stories for his Ph.D. He now teaches writing at the University of Southern California and sometimes plays saxophone in a rockabilly band. His stories in* Esquire, Paris Review, The Atlantic, *and other magazines quickly won him notice for their outrageous and macabre humor,*

T. Coraghessan Boyle

*verve, and inventiveness. Besides three story collections,* The Descent of Man *(1979),* Greasy Lake *(1985), and* If the River Was Whiskey *(1989), Boyle has written five novels:* Water Music *(1982),* about an eighteenth-century expedition to Africa; Budding Prospects *(1984),* a picaresque (or scoundrel-adventure) story of life among marijuana growers; World's End *(1987),* an account of three families that spans three centuries in his native Hudson River Valley; East is East *(1990),* a half-serious, half-comic story of a Japanese fugitive in an American writers' colony; and The Road to Wellville *(1993),* which takes place in 1907 in the sanitarium of Dr. John Harvey Kellogg of corn flakes fame, with cameo appearances by Henry Ford, Thomas Edison, and Harvey Firestone.

It's about a mile down on the dark side of Route 8.
—Bruce Springsteen

There was a time when courtesy and winning ways went out of style, when it was good to be bad, when you cultivated decadence like a taste. We were all dangerous characters then. We wore torn-up leather jackets, slouched around with toothpicks in our mouths, sniffed glue and ether and what somebody claimed was cocaine. When we wheeled our parents' whining station wagons out onto the street we left a patch of rubber half a block long. We drank gin and grape juice, Tango, Thunderbird, and Bali Hai. We were nineteen. We were bad. We read André Gide° and struck elaborate poses to show that we didn't give a shit about anything. At night, we went up to Greasy Lake.

Through the center of town, up the strip, past the housing developments and shopping malls, street lights giving way to the thin streaming illumination of the headlights, trees crowding the asphalt in a black unbroken wall: that was the way out to Greasy Lake. The Indians had called it Wakan, a reference to the clarity of its waters. Now it was fetid and murky, the mud banks glittering with broken glass and strewn with beer cans and the charred remains of bonfires. There was a single ravaged island a hundred yards from shore, so stripped of vegetation it looked as if the air force had strafed it. We went up to the lake because everyone went there, because we wanted to snuff the rich scent of possibility on the breeze, watch a girl take off her clothes and plunge into the festering murk, drink beer, smoke pot, howl at the stars, savor the incongruous full-throated roar of rock and roll against the primeval susurrus of frogs and crickets. This was nature.

I was there one night, late, in the company of two dangerous characters. Digby wore a gold star in his right ear and allowed his father to pay his tuition at Cornell; Jeff was thinking of quitting school to become a painter/musician/headshop proprietor. They were both expert in the social graces, quick with a sneer, able to manage a Ford with lousy shocks over a rutted and gutted blacktop road at eighty-five while rolling a joint as compact as a Tootsie Roll Pop stick. They could lounge against a bank of booming speakers and trade "man"s with the best of them or roll out across the dance floor as if their joints worked on bearings.

*André Gide:* controversial French writer (1869–1951) whose novels, including The Counterfeiters and Lafcadio's Adventures, often show individuals in conflict with accepted morality.

They were slick and quick and they wore their mirror shades at breakfast and dinner, in the shower, in closets and caves. In short, they were bad.

I drove. Digby pounded the dashboard and shouted along with Toots & the Maytals while Jeff hung his head out the window and streaked the side of my mother's Bel Air with vomit. It was early June, the air soft as a hand on your cheek, the third night of summer vacation. The first two nights we'd been out till dawn, looking for something we never found. On this, the third night, we'd cruised the strip sixty-seven times, been in and out of every bar and club we could think of in a twenty-mile radius, stopped twice for bucket chicken and forty-cent hamburgers, debated going to a party at the house of a girl Jeff's sister knew, and chucked two dozen raw eggs at mailboxes and hitchhikers. It was 2:00 A.M.; the bars were closing. There was nothing to do but take a bottle of lemon-flavored gin up to Greasy Lake.

The taillights of a single car winked at us as we swung into the dirt lot with    5
its tufts of weed and washboard corrugations; '57 Chevy, mint, metallic blue. On the far side of the lot, like the exoskeleton of some gaunt chrome insect, a chopper leaned against its kickstand. And that was it for excitement: some junkie halfwit biker and a car freak pumping his girlfriend. Whatever it was we were looking for, we weren't about to find it at Greasy Lake. Not that night.

But then all of a sudden Digby was fighting for the wheel. "Hey, that's Tony Lovett's car! Hey!" he shouted, while I stabbed at the brake pedal and the Bel Air nosed up to the gleaming bumper of the parked Chevy. Digby leaned on the horn, laughing, and instructed me to put my brights on. I flicked on the brights. This was hilarious. A joke. Tony would experience premature withdrawal and expect to be confronted by grim-looking state troopers with flashlights. We hit the horn, strobed the lights, and then jumped out of the car to press our witty faces to Tony's windows; for all we knew we might even catch a glimpse of some little fox's tit, and then we could slap backs with red-faced Tony, roughhouse a little, and go on to new heights of adventure and daring.

The first mistake, the one that opened the whole floodgate, was losing my grip on the keys. In the excitement, leaping from the car with the gin in one hand and a roach clip in the other, I spilled them in the grass—in the dark, rank, mysterious nighttime grass of Greasy Lake. This was a tactical error, as damaging and irreversible in its way as Westmoreland's decision to dig in at Khe Sanh°. I felt it like a jab of intuition, and I stopped there by the open door, peering vaguely into the night that puddled up round my feet.

The second mistake—and this was inextricably bound up with the first—was identifying the car as Tony Lovett's. Even before the very bad character in greasy jeans and engineer boots ripped out of the driver's door, I began to realize that this chrome blue was much lighter than the robin's-egg of Tony's car, and that

---

*Westmoreland's decision . . . Khe Sanh:* General William C. Westmoreland commanded United States troops in Vietnam (1964–68). In late 1967 the North Vietnamese and Viet Cong forces attacked Khe Sanh (or Khesanh) with a show of strength, causing Westmoreland to expend great effort to defend a plateau of relatively little tactical importance.

Tony's car didn't have rear-mounted speakers. Judging from their expressions, Digby and Jeff were privately groping toward the same inevitable and unsettling conclusion as I was.

In any case, there was no reasoning with this bad greasy character—clearly he was a man of action. The first lusty Rockette° kick of his steel-toed boot caught me under the chin, chipped my favorite tooth, and left me sprawled in the dirt. Like a fool, I'd gone down on one knee to comb the stiff hacked grass for the keys, my mind making connections in the most dragged-out, testudineous way, knowing that things had gone wrong, that I was in a lot of trouble, and that the lost ignition key was my grail and my salvation. The three or four succeeding blows were mainly absorbed by my right buttock and the tough piece of bone at the base of my spine.

Meanwhile, Digby vaulted the kissing bumpers and delivered a savage kung- 10 fu blow to the greasy character's collarbone. Digby had just finished a course in martial arts for phys-ed credit and had spent the better part of the past two nights telling us apocryphal tales of Bruce Lee types and of the raw power invested in lightning blows shot from coiled wrists, ankles, and elbows. The greasy character was unimpressed. He merely backed off a step, his face like a Toltec mask, and laid Digby out with a single whistling roundhouse blow . . . but by now Jeff had got into the act, and I was beginning to extricate myself from the dirt, a tinny compound of shock, rage, and impotence wadded in my throat.

Jeff was on the guy's back, biting at his ear. Digby was on the ground, curs- ing. I went for the tire iron I kept under the driver's seat. I kept it there because bad characters always keep tire irons under the driver's seat, for just such an occasion at this. Never mind that I hadn't been involved in a fight since sixth grade, when a kid with a sleepy eye and two streams of mucus depending from his nostrils hit me in the knee with a Louisville slugger°, never mind that I'd touched the tire iron exactly twice before, to change tires: it was there. And I went for it.

I was terrified. Blood was beating in my ears, my hands were shaking, my heart turning over like a dirtbike in the wrong gear. My antagonist was shirtless, and a single cord of muscle flashed across his chest as he bent forward to peel Jeff from his back like a wet overcoat. "Motherfucker," he spat, over and over, and I was aware in that instant that all four of us—Digby, Jeff, and myself included— were chanting "motherfucker, motherfucker," as if it were a battle cry. (What happened next? the detective asks the murderer from beneath the turned-down brim of his porkpie hat. I don't know, the murderer says, something came over me. Exactly.)

Digby poked the flat of his hand in the bad character's face and I came at him like a kamikaze, mindless, raging, stung with humiliation—the whole thing,

---

*Rockette:* member of a dancing troupe in the stage show at Radio City Music Hall, New York, famous for its ability to kick fast and high with wonderful coordination.    *Louisville slugger:* a brand of base- ball bat.

from the initial boot in the chin to this murderous primal instant involving no more than sixty hyperventilating, gland-flooding seconds—I came at him and brought the tire iron down across his ear. The effect was instantaneous, astonishing. He was a stunt man and this was Hollywood, he was a big grimacing toothy balloon and I was a man with a straight pin. He collapsed. Wet his pants. Went loose in his boots.

A single second, big as a zeppelin, floated by. We were standing over him in a circle, gritting our teeth, jerking our necks, our limbs and hands and feet twitching with glandular discharges. No one said anything. We just stared down at the guy, the car freak, the lover, the bad greasy character laid low. Digby looked at me; so did Jeff. I was still holding the tire iron, a tuft of hair clinging to the crook like dandelion fluff, like down. Rattled, I dropped it in the dirt, already envisioning the headlines, the pitted faces of the police inquisitors, the gleam of handcuffs, clank of bars, the big black shadows rising from the back of the cell . . . when suddenly a raw torn shriek cut through me like all the juice in all the electric chairs in the country.

It was the fox. She was short, barefoot, dressed in panties and a man's shirt. 15 "Animals!" she screamed, running at us with her fists clenched and wisps of blow-dried hair in her face. There was a silver chain round her ankle, and her toenails flashed in the glare of the headlights. I think it was the toenails that did it. Sure, the gin and the cannabis and even the Kentucky Fried may have had a hand in it, but it was the sight of those flaming toes that set us off—the toad emerging from the loaf in *Virgin Spring*°, lipstick smeared on a child; she was already tainted. We were on her like Bergman's deranged brothers—see no evil, hear none, speak none—panting, wheezing, tearing at her clothes, grabbing for flesh. We were bad characters, and we were scared and hot and three steps over the line—anything could have happened.

It didn't.

Before we could pin her to the hood of the car, our eyes masked with lust and greed and the purest primal badness, a pair of headlights swung into the lot. There we were, dirty, bloody, guilty, dissociated from humanity and civilization, the first of the Ur-crimes behind us, the second in progress, shreds of nylon panty and spandex brassiere dangling from our fingers, our flies open, lips licked—there we were, caught in the spotlight. Nailed.

We bolted. First for the car, and then, realizing we had no way of starting it, for the woods. I thought nothing. I thought escape. The headlights came at me like accusing fingers. I was gone.

Ram-bam-bam, across the parking lot, past the chopper and into the feculent undergrowth at the lake's edge, insects flying up in my face, weeds whipping, frogs and snakes and red-eyed turtles splashing off into the night: I was already ankle-deep in muck and tepid water and still going strong. Behind me, the girl's screams rose in intensity, disconsolate, incriminating, the screams of the Sabine

*Virgin Spring:* film by Swedish director Ingmar Bergman.

women°, the Christian martyrs, Anne Frank° dragged from the garret. I kept
going, pursued by those cries, imagining cops and bloodhounds. The water was up
to my knees when I realized what I was doing: I was going to swim for it. Swim
the breadth of Greasy Lake and hide myself in the thick clot of woods on the far
side. They'd never find me there.

I was breathing in sobs, in gasps. The water lapped at my waist as I looked    20
out over the moon-burnished ripples, the mats of algae that clung to the surface
like scabs. Digby and Jeff had vanished. I paused. Listened. The girl was quieter
now, screams tapering to sobs, but there were male voices, angry, excited, and the
high-pitched ticking of the second car's engine. I waded deeper, stealthy, hunted,
the ooze sucking at my sneakers. As I was about to take the plunge—at the very
instant I dropped my shoulder for the first slashing stroke—I blundered into
something. Something unspeakable, obscene, something soft, wet, moss-grown.
A patch of weed? A log? When I reached out to touch it, it gave like a rubber
duck, it gave like flesh.

In one of those nasty little epiphanies for which we are prepared by films and
TV and childhood visits to the funeral home to ponder the shrunken painted
forms of dead grandparents, I understood what it was that bobbed there so inad-
missibly in the dark. Understood, and stumbled back in horror and revulsion, my
mind yanked in six different directions (I was nineteen, a mere child, an infant,
and here in the space of five minutes I'd struck down one greasy character and
blundered into the waterlogged carcass of a second), thinking, The keys, the keys,
why did I have to go and lose the keys? I stumbled back, but the muck took hold
of my feet—a sneaker snagged, balance lost—and suddenly I was pitching face
forward into the buoyant black mass, throwing out my hands in desperation while
simultaneously conjuring the image of reeking frogs and muskrats revolving in
slicks of their own deliquescing juices. AAAAArrrgh! I shot from the water like
a torpedo, the dead man rotating to expose a mossy beard and eyes cold as the
moon. I must have shouted out, thrashing around in the weeds, because the voices behind me suddenly became animated.

"What was that?"

"It's them, it's them: they tried to, tried to . . . rape me!" Sobs.

A man's voice, flat Midwestern accent. "You sons a bitches, we'll kill you!"

Frogs, crickets.                                                               25

Then another voice, harsh, r-less, Lower East Side: "Motherfucker!" I recognized the verbal virtuosity of the bad greasy character in the engineer boots.
Tooth chipped, sneakers gone, coated in mud and slime and worse, crouching
breathless in the weeds waiting to have my ass thoroughly and definitively kicked
and fresh from the hideous stinking embrace of a three-days-dead-corpse, I sud-

---

*Sabine women:* members of an ancient tribe in Italy, according to legend, forcibly carried off by the
early Romans under Romulus to be their wives. The incident is depicted in a famous painting,
"The Rape of the Sabine Women," by seventeenth-century French artist Nicolas Poussin.
*Anne Frank:* German Jewish girl (1929–1945) whose diary written during the Nazi occupation of the
Netherlands later became world famous. She hid with her family in a secret attic in Amsterdam, but
was caught by storm troopers and sent to the concentration camp at Belsen, where she died.

denly felt a rush of joy and vindication: the son of a bitch was alive! Just as quickly, my bowels turned to ice. "Come on out of there, you pansy mothers!" the bad greasy character was screaming. He shouted curses till he was out of breath.

The crickets started up again, then the frogs. I held my breath. All at once was a sound in the reeds, a swishing, a splash: thunk-a-thunk. They were throwing rocks. The frogs fell silent. I cradled my head. Swish, swish, thunk-a-thunk. A wedge of feldspar the size of a cue ball glanced off my knee. I bit my finger.

It was then that they turned to the car. I heard a door slam, a curse, and then the sound of the headlights shattering—almost a good-natured sound, celebratory, like corks popping from the necks of bottles. This was succeeded by the dull booming of the fenders, metal on metal, and then the icy crash of the windshield. I inched forward, elbows and knees, my belly pressed to the muck, thinking of guerrillas and commandos and *The Naked and the Dead*°. I parted the weeds and squinted the length of the parking lot.

The second car—it was a Trans-Am—was still running, its high beams washing the scene in a lurid stagy light. Tire iron flailing, the greasy bad character was laying into the side of my mother's Bel Air like an avenging demon, his shadow riding up the trunks of the trees. Whomp. Whomp. Whomp-whomp. The other two guys—blond types, in fraternity jackets—were helping out with tree branches and skull-sized boulders. One of them was gathering up bottles, rocks, muck, candy wrappers, used condoms, poptops, and other refuse and pitching it through the window on the driver's side. I could see the fox, a white bulb behind the windshield of the '57 Chevy. "Bobbie," she whined over the thumping, "come on." The greasy character paused a moment, took one good swipe at the left taillight, and then heaved the tire iron halfway across the lake. Then he fired up the '57 and was gone.

Blond head nodded at blond head. One said something to the other, too low     30 for me to catch. They were no doubt thinking that in helping to annihilate my mother's car they'd committed a fairly rash act, and thinking too that there were three bad characters connected with that very car watching them from the woods. Perhaps other possibilities occurred to them as well—police, jail cells, justices of the peace, reparations, lawyers, irate parents, fraternal censure. Whatever they were thinking, they suddenly dropped branches, bottles, and rocks and sprang for their car in unison, as if they'd choreographed it. Five seconds. That's all it took. The engine shrieked, the tires squealed, a cloud of dust rose from the rutted lot and then settled back on darkness.

I don't know how long I lay there, the bad breath of decay all around me, my jacket heavy as a bear, the primordial ooze subtly reconstituting itself to accommodate my upper thighs and testicles. My jaws ached, my knee throbbed, my coccyx was on fire. I contemplated suicide, wondered if I'd need bridgework, scraped the recesses of my brain for some sort of excuse to give my parents—a tree had fallen on the car, I was blinded by a bread truck, hit and run, vandals had got to it while we were playing chess at Digby's. Then I thought of the dead man. He was

*The Naked and the Dead:* novel (1948) by Norman Mailer, of U.S. Army life in World War II.

probably the only person on the planet worse off than I was. I thought about him, fog on the lake, insects chirring eerily, and felt the tug of fear, felt the darkness opening up inside me like a set of jaws. Who was he, I wondered, this victim of time and circumstance bobbing sorrowfully in the lake at my back. The owner of the chopper, no doubt, a bad older character come to this. Shot during a murky drug deal, drowned while drunkenly frolicking in the lake. Another headline. My car was wrecked; he was dead.

When the eastern half of the sky went from black to cobalt and the trees began to separate themselves from the shadows, I pushed myself up from the mud and stepped out into the open. By now the birds had begun to take over for the crickets, and dew lay slick on the leaves. There was a smell in the air, raw and sweet at the same time, the smell of the sun firing buds and opening blossoms. I contemplated the car. It lay there like a wreck along the highway, like a steel sculpture left over from a vanished civilization. Everything was still. This was nature.

I was circling the car, as dazed and bedraggled as the sole survivor of an air blitz, when Digby and Jeff emerged from the trees behind me. Digby's face was crosshatched with smears of dirt; Jeff's jacket was gone and his shirt was torn across the shoulder. They slouched across the lot, looking sheepish, and silently came up beside me to gape at the ravaged automobile. No one said a word. After a while Jeff swung open the driver's door and began to scoop the broken glass and garbage off the seat. I looked at Digby. He shrugged. "At least they didn't slash the tires," he said.

It was true: the tires were intact. There was no windshield, the headlights were staved in, and the body looked as if it had been sledge-hammered for a quarter a shot at the county fair, but the tires were inflated to regulation pressure. The car was drivable. In silence, all three of us bent to scrape the mud and shattered glass from the interior. I said nothing about the biker. When we were finished, I reached in my pocket for the keys, experienced a nasty stab of recollection, cursed myself, and turned to search the grass. I spotted them almost immediately, no more than five feet from the open door, glinting like jewels in the first tapering shaft of sunlight. There was no reason to get philosophical about it: I eased into the seat and turned the engine over.

It was at that precise moment that the silver Mustang with the flame decals rumbled into the lot. All three of us froze; then Digby and Jeff slid into the car and slammed the door. We watched as the Mustang rocked and bobbed across the ruts and finally jerked to a halt beside the forlorn chopper at the far end of the lot. "Let's go," Digby said. I hesitated, the Bel Air wheezing beneath me.

Two girls emerged from the Mustang. Tight jeans, stiletto heels, hair like frozen fur. They bent over the motorcycle, paced back and forth aimlessly, glanced once or twice at us, and then ambled over to where the reeds sprang up in a green fence round the perimeter of the lake. One of them cupped her hands to her mouth. "Al," she called. "Hey, Al!"

"Come on," Digby hissed. "Let's get out of here."

But it was too late. The second girl was picking her way across the lot, unsteady on her heels, looking up at us and then away. She was older—twenty-five or -six—and as she came closer we could see there was something wrong with her: she was stoned or drunk, lurching now and waving her arms for balance. I gripped the steering wheel as if it were the ejection lever of a flaming jet, and Digby spat out my name, twice, terse and impatient.

"Hi," the girl said.

We looked at her like zombies, like war veterans, like deaf-and-dumb pencil 40 peddlers.

She smiled, her lips cracked and dry. "Listen," she said, bending from the waist to look in the window, "you guys seen Al?" Her pupils were pinpoints, her eyes glass. She jerked her neck. "That's his bike over there—Al's. You seen him?"

Al. I didn't know what to say. I wanted to get out of the car and retch, I wanted to go home to my parents' house and crawl into bed. Digby poked me in the ribs. "We haven't seen anybody," I said.

The girl seemed to consider this, reaching out a slim veiny arm to brace herself against the car. "No matter," she said, slurring the *t*'s, "he'll turn up." And then, as if she'd just taken stock of the whole scene—the ravaged car and our battered faces, the desolation of the place—she said: "Hey, you guys look like some pretty bad characters—been fightin', huh?" We stared straight ahead, rigid as catatonics. She was fumbling in her pocket and muttering something. Finally she held out a handful of tablets in glassine wrappers: "Hey, you want to party, you want to do some of these with me and Sarah?"

I just looked at her. I thought I was going to cry. Digby broke the silence. "No, thanks," he said, leaning over me. "Some other time."

I put the car in gear and it inched forward with a groan, shaking off pellets of 45 glass like an old dog shedding water after a bath, heaving over the ruts on its worn springs, creeping toward the highway. There was a sheen of sun on the lake. I looked back. The girl was still standing there, watching us, her shoulders slumped, hand outstretched.

## QUESTIONS

1. Around what year, would you say, was it that "courtesy and winning ways went out of style, when it was good to be bad, when you cultivated decadence like a taste"?
2. What is it about Digby and Jeff that inspires the narrator to call them "bad"?
3. Twice in "Greasy Lake"—in paragraphs 2 and 32—appear the words, "This was nature." What contrasts do you find between the "nature" of the narrator's earlier and later views?
4. What makes the narrator and his friends run off into the woods?
5. How does the heroes' encounter with the two girls at the end of the story differ from their earlier encounter with the girl from the blue Chevy? How do you account for the difference? When at the end of the story the girl offers to party with the three friends, what makes the narrator say, "I thought I was going to cry"?
6. How important to what happens in this story is Greasy Lake itself? What details about the lake and its shores strike you as particularly memorable (whether funny, disgusting, or both)?
7. The setting of Boyle's story is very different from that of James Joyce's "Araby." But in what ways do the two stories resemble each other?

## Amy Tan

### A PAIR OF TICKETS                                                    1989

Amy Tan was born in Oakland,
California, in 1952. Both of her parents
were recent Chinese immigrants. Her father
was an electrical engineer (as well as a
Baptist minister); her mother was a voca-
tional nurse. When her father and brother
both died of brain tumors, the fifteen-year-
old Tan and her mother moved to
Switzerland, where she attended high
school. On their return to the United States
Tan attended Linfield College, a Baptist
school in Oregon, but she eventually transferred to California State University at San
Jose. At this time Tan and her mother
argued about her future. The mother insisted her daughter take premedical studies in

Amy Tan

preparation for becoming a neurosurgeon. Tan wanted to do something else. For six
months the two did not speak to one another. Tan worked for IBM writing computer
manuals and also wrote free-lance business articles under a pseudonym. In 1987 Tan
and her mother visited China together. This experience, which is reflected in "A Pair of
Tickets," deepened Tan's sense of her Chinese-American identity. "As soon as my feet
touched China," she wrote, "I became Chinese." Soon after, Tan began writing her
first novel, The Joy Luck Club (1989), which consists of sixteen interrelated stories
about a group of Chinese-American mothers and their daughters. (The Joy Luck Club
of the title is a woman's social group.) The Joy Luck Club became both a critical success and a best-seller, and was made into a movie in 1993. In 1991 she published her
second novel, The Kitchen God's Wife. Her children's book, The Moon Lady,
appeared in 1992. Tan now lives in San Francisco with her husband. "A Pair of
Tickets" is the final story in Tan's first novel.

The minute our train leaves the Hong Kong border and enters Shenzhen,
China, I feel different. I can feel the skin on my forehead tingling, my blood rush-
ing through a new course, my bones aching with a familiar old pain. And I think,
My mother was right. I am becoming Chinese.

"Cannot be helped," my mother said when I was fifteen and had vigorously
denied that I had any Chinese whatsoever below my skin. I was a sophomore at
Galileo High in San Francisco, and all my Caucasian friends agreed: I was about
as Chinese as they were. But my mother had studied at a famous nursing school
in Shanghai, and she said she knew all about genetics. So there was no doubt in
her mind, whether I agreed or not: Once you are born Chinese, you cannot help
but feel and think Chinese.

"Someday you will see," said my mother. "It is in your blood, waiting to be let go."

And when she said this, I saw myself transforming like a werewolf, a mutant tag of DNA suddenly triggered, replicating itself insidiously into a *syndrome*°, a cluster of telltale Chinese behaviors, all those things my mother did to embarrass me—haggling with store owners, pecking her mouth with a toothpick in public, being color-blind to the fact that lemon yellow and pale pink are not good combinations for winter clothes.

But today I realize I've never really known what it means to be Chinese. I am thirty-six years old. My mother is dead and I am on a train, carrying with me her dreams of coming home. I am going to China.　　　　　　　　　　　　　　　　5

We are first going to Guangzhou, my seventy-two-year-old father, Canning Woo, and I, where we will visit his aunt, whom he has not seen since he was ten years old. And I don't know whether it's the prospect of seeing his aunt or if it's because he's back in China, but now he looks like he's a young boy, so innocent and happy I want to button his sweater and pat his head. We are sitting across from each other, separated by a little table with two cold cups of tea. For the first time I can ever remember, my father has tears in his eyes, and all he is seeing out the train window is a sectioned field of yellow, green, and brown, a narrow canal flanking the tracks, low rising hills, and three people in blue jackets riding an ox-driven cart on this early October morning. And I can't help myself. I also have misty eyes, as if I had seen this a long, long time ago, and had almost forgotten.

In less than three hours, we will be in Guangzhou, which my guidebook tells me is how one properly refers to Canton these days. It seems all the cities I have heard of, except Shanghai, have changed their spellings. I think they are saying China has changed in other ways as well. Chungking is Chongqing. And Kweilin is Guilin. I have looked these names up, because after we see my father's aunt in Guangzhou, we will catch a plane to Shanghai, where I will meet my two half-sisters for the first time.

They are my mother's twin daughters from her first marriage, little babies she was forced to abandon on a road as she was fleeing Kweilin for Chungking in 1944. That was all my mother had told me about these daughters, so they had remained babies in my mind, all these years, sitting on the side of a road, listening to bombs whistling in the distance while sucking their patient red thumbs.

And it was only this year that someone found them and wrote with this joyful news. A letter came from Shanghai, addressed to my mother. When I first heard about this, that they were alive, I imagined my identical sisters transforming from little babies into six-year-old girls. In my mind, they were seated next to each other at a table, taking turns with the fountain pen. One would write a neat row of characters: *Dearest Mama. We are alive.* She would brush back her wispy bangs and hand the other sister the pen, and she would write: *Come get us. Please hurry.*

---

*syndrome:* a group of symptoms that occur together as the sign of a particular disease or abnormality.

Of course they could not know that my mother had died three months 10
before, suddenly, when a blood vessel in her brain burst. One minute she was
talking to my father, complaining about the tenants upstairs, scheming how to
evict them under the pretense that relatives from China were moving in. The
next minute she was holding her head, her eyes squeezed shut, groping for the
sofa, and then crumpling softly to the floor with fluttering hands.

So my father had been the first one to open the letter, a long letter it turned
out. And they did call her Mama. They said they always revered her as their true
mother. They kept a framed picture of her. They told her about their life, from
the time my mother last saw them on the road leaving Kweilin to when they
were finally found.

And the letter had broken my father's heart so much—these daughters calling my mother from another life he never knew—that he gave the letter to my
mother's old friend Auntie Lindo and asked her to write back and tell my sisters,
in the gentlest way possible, that my mother was dead.

But instead Auntie Lindo took the letter to the Joy Luck Club and discussed
with Auntie Ying and Auntie An-mei what should be done, because they had
known for many years about my mother's search for her twin daughters, her endless hope. Auntie Lindo and the others cried over this double tragedy, of losing
my mother three months before, and now again. And so they couldn't help but
think of some miracle, some possible way of reviving her from the dead, so my
mother could fulfill her dream.

So this is what they wrote to my sisters in Shanghai: "Dearest Daughters, I
too have never forgotten you in my memory or in my heart. I never gave up hope
that we would see each other again in a joyous reunion. I am only sorry it has
been too long. I want to tell you everything about my life since I last saw you. I
want to tell you this when our family comes to see you in China. . . ." They
signed it with my mother's name.

It wasn't until all this had been done that they first told me about my sisters, 15
the letter they received, the one they wrote back.

"They'll think she's coming, then," I murmured. And I had imagined my sisters now being ten or eleven, jumping up and down, holding hands, their pigtails
bouncing, excited that their mother—*their* mother—was coming, whereas my
mother was dead.

"How can you say she is not coming in a letter?" said Auntie Lindo. "She is
their mother. She is your mother. You must be the one to tell them. All these
years, they have been dreaming of her." And I thought she was right.

But then I started dreaming, too, of my mother and my sisters and how it
would be if I arrived in Shanghai. All these years, while they waited to be found,
I had lived with my mother and then had lost her. I imagined seeing my sisters at
the airport. They would be standing on their tip-toes, looking anxiously, scanning from one dark head to another as we got off the plane. And I would recognize them instantly, their faces with the identical worried look.

"*Jyejye, Jyejye.* Sister, Sister. We are here," I saw myself saying in my poor
version of Chinese.

"Where is Mama?" they would say, and look around, still smiling, two 20 flushed and eager faces. "Is she hiding?" And this would have been like my mother, to stand behind just a bit, to tease a little and make people's patience pull a little on their hearts. I would shake my head and tell my sisters she was not hiding.

"Oh, that must be Mama, no?" one of my sisters would whisper excitedly, pointing to another small woman completely engulfed in a tower of presents. And that, too, would have been like my mother, to bring mountains of gifts, food, and toys for children—all bought on sale—shunning thanks, saying the gifts were nothing, and later turning the labels over to show my sisters, "Calvin Klein, 100% wool."

I imagined myself starting to say, "Sisters, I am sorry, I have come alone . . . " and before I could tell them—they could see it in my face—they were wailing, pulling their hair, their lips twisted in pain, as they ran away from me. And then I saw myself getting back on the plane and coming home.

After I had dreamed this scene many times—watching their despair turn from horror into anger—I begged Auntie Lindo to write another letter. And at first she refused.

"How can I say she is dead? I cannot write this," said Auntie Lindo with a stubborn look.

"But it's cruel to have them believe she's coming on the plane," I said. 25 "When they see it's just me, they'll hate me."

"Hate you? Cannot be." She was scowling. "You are their own sister, their only family."

"You don't understand," I protested.

"What I don't understand?" she said.

And I whispered, "They'll think I'm responsible, that she died because I didn't appreciate her."

And Auntie Lindo looked satisfied and sad at the same time, as if this were 30 true and I had finally realized it. She sat down for an hour, and when she stood up she handed me a two-page letter. She had tears in her eyes. I realized that the very thing I had feared, she had done. So even if she had written the news of my mother's death in English, I wouldn't have had the heart to read it.

"Thank you," I whispered.


The landscape has become gray, filled with low flat cement buildings, old factories, and then tracks and more tracks filled with trains like ours passing by in the opposite direction. I see platforms crowded with people wearing drab Western clothes, with spots of bright colors: little children wearing pink and yellow, red and peach. And there are soldiers in olive green and red, and old ladies in gray tops and pants that stop mid-calf. We are in Guangzhou.

Before the train even comes to a stop, people are bringing down their belongings from above their seats. For a moment there is a dangerous shower of heavy suitcases laden with gifts to relatives, half-broken boxes wrapped in miles of string to keep the contents from spilling out, plastic bags filled with yarn and vegetables and packages of dried mushrooms, and camera cases. And then we are caught in a stream of people rushing, shoving, pushing us along, until we find ourselves in one of a dozen lines waiting to go through customs. I feel as if I were getting on the number 30 Stockton bus in San Francisco. I am in China, I remind myself. And somehow the crowds don't bother me. It feels right. I start pushing too.

I take out the declaration forms and my passport. "Woo," it says at the top, and below that, "June May," who was born in "California, U.S.A.," in 1951. I wonder if the customs people will question whether I'm the same person in the passport photo. In this picture, my chin-length hair is swept back and artfully styled. I am wearing false eyelashes, eye shadow, and lip liner. My cheeks are hollowed out by bronze blusher. But I had not expected the heat in October. And now my hair hangs limp with the humidity. I wear no makeup; in Hong Kong my mascara had melted into dark circles and everything else had felt like layers of grease. So today my face is plain, unadorned except for a thin mist of shiny sweat on my forehead and nose.

Even without makeup, I could never pass for true Chinese. I stand five-foot- 35 six, and my head pokes above the crowd so that I am eye level only with other tourists. My mother once told me my height came from my grandfather, who was a northerner, and may have even had some Mongol blood. "This is what your grandmother once told me," explained my mother. "But now it is too late to ask her. They are all dead, your grandparents, your uncles, and their wives and children, all killed in the war, when a bomb fell on our house. So many generations in one instant."

She had said this so matter-of-factly that I thought she had long since gotten over any grief she had. And then I wondered how she knew they were all dead.

"Maybe they left the house before the bomb fell," I suggested.

"No," said my mother. "Our whole family is gone. It is just you and I."

"But how do you know? Some of them could have escaped."

"Cannot be," said my mother, this time almost angrily. And then her frown 40 was washed over by a puzzled blank look, and she began to talk as if she were trying to remember where she had misplaced something. "I went back to that house. I kept looking up to where the house used to be. And it wasn't a house, just the sky. And below, underneath my feet, were four stories of burnt bricks and wood, all the life of our house. Then off to the side I saw things blown into the yard, nothing valuable. There was a bed someone used to sleep in, really just a metal frame twisted up at one corner. And a book, I don't know what kind, because every page had turned black. And I saw a teacup which was unbroken but filled with ashes. And then I found my doll, with her hands and legs broken, her hair burned off. . . . When I was a little girl, I had cried for that doll, seeing it all alone in the store window, and my mother had bought it for me. It was an American doll with yellow hair. It could turn its legs and arms. The eyes moved up and down. And when I married and left my family home, I gave the doll to my youngest niece, because she was like me. She cried if that doll was not with her always. Do you see? If she was in the house with that doll, her parents were there, and so everybody was there, waiting together, because that's how our family was."

The woman in the customs booth stares at my documents, then glances at me briefly, and with two quick movements stamps everything and sternly nods me along. And soon my father and I find ourselves in a large area filled with thousands of people and suitcases. I feel lost and my father looks helpless.

"Excuse me," I say to a man who looks like an American. "Can you tell me where I can get a taxi?" He mumbles something that sounds Swedish or Dutch.

"Syau Yen! Syau Yen!" I hear a piercing voice shout from behind me. An old woman in a yellow knit beret is holding up a pink plastic bag filled with wrapped trinkets. I guess she is trying to sell us something. But my father is staring down at this tiny sparrow of a woman, squinting into her eyes. And then his eyes widen, his face opens up and he smiles like a pleased little boy.

"*Aiyi! Aiyi!*"—Auntie Auntie!—he says softly.

"Syau Yen!" coos my great-aunt. I think it's funny she has just called my   45 father "Little Wild Goose." It must be his baby milk name, the name used to discourage ghosts from stealing children.

They clasp each other's hands—they do not hug—and hold on like this, taking turns saying, "Look at you! You are so old. Look how old you've become!" They are both crying openly, laughing at the same time, and I bite my lip, trying not to cry. I'm afraid to feel their joy. Because I am thinking how different our arrival in Shanghai will be tomorrow, how awkward it will feel.

Now Aiyi beams and points to a Polaroid picture of my father. My father had wisely sent pictures when he wrote and said we were coming. See how smart she was, she seems to intone as she compares the picture to my father. In the letter, my father had said we would call her from the hotel once we arrived, so this is a surprise, that they've come to meet us. I wonder if my sisters will be at the airport.

It is only then that I remember the camera. I had meant to take a picture of my father and his aunt the moment they met. It's not too late.

"Here, stand together over here," I say, holding up the Polaroid. The camera flashes and I hand them the snapshot. Aiyi and my father still stand close together, each of them holding a corner of the picture, watching as their images begin to form. They are almost reverentially quiet. Aiyi is only five years older than my father, which makes her around seventy-seven. But she looks ancient, shrunken, a mummified relic. Her thin hair is pure white, her teeth are brown with decay. So much for stories of Chinese women looking young forever, I think to myself.

Now Aiyi is crooning to me: "*Jandale.*" So big already. She looks up at me, at   50 my full height, and then peers into her pink plastic bag—her gifts to us, I have figured out—as if she is wondering what she will give to me, now that I am so old and big. And then she grabs my elbow with her sharp pincerlike grasp and turns me around. A man and woman in their fifties are shaking hands with my father, everybody smiling and saying, "Ah! Ah!" They are Aiyi's oldest son and his wife, and standing next to them are four other people, around my age, and a little girl who's around ten. The introductions go by so fast, all I know is that one of them is Aiyi's grandson, with his wife, and the other is her granddaughter, with her husband. And the little girl is Lili, Aiyi's great-granddaughter.

Aiyi and my father speak the Mandarin dialect from their childhood, but the rest of the family speaks only the Cantonese of their village. I understand only Mandarin but can't speak it that well. So Aiyi and my father gossip unrestrained in Mandarin, exchanging news about people from their old village. And they stop only occasionally to talk to the rest of us, sometimes in Cantonese, sometimes in English.

"Oh, it is as I suspected," says my father, turning to me. "He died last summer." And I already understood this. I just don't know who this person, Li Gong, is. I feel as if I were in the United Nations and the translators had run amok.

"Hello," I say to the little girl. "My name is Jing-mei." But the little girl squirms to look away, causing her parents to laugh with embarrassment. I try to think of Cantonese words I can say to her, stuff I learned from friends in Chinatown, but all I can think of are swear words, terms for bodily functions, and short phrases like "tastes good," "tastes like garbage," and "she's really ugly." And then I have another plan: I hold up the Polaroid camera, beckoning Lili with my finger. She immediately jumps forward, places one hand on her hip in the manner of a fashion model, juts out her chest, and flashes me a toothy smile. As soon as I take the picture she is standing next to me, jumping and giggling every few seconds as she watches herself appear on the greenish film.

By the time we hail taxis for the ride to the hotel, Lili is holding tight on to my hand, pulling me along.

In the taxi, Aiyi talks nonstop, so I have no chance to ask her about the different sights we are passing by.                                                                                          55

"You wrote and said you would come only for one day," says Aiyi to my father in an agitated tone. "One day! How can you see your family in one day! Toishan is many hours' drive from Guangzhou. And this idea to call us when you arrive. This is nonsense. We have no telephone."

My heart races a little. I wonder if Auntie Lindo told my sisters we would call from the hotel in Shanghai?

Aiyi continues to scold my father. "I was so beside myself, ask my son, almost turned heaven and earth upside down trying to think of a way! So we decided the best was for us to take the bus from Toishan and come into Guangzhou—meet you right from the start."

And now I am holding my breath as the taxi driver dodges between trucks and buses, honking his horn constantly. We seem to be on some sort of long freeway overpass, like a bridge above the city. I can see row after row of apartments, each floor cluttered with laundry hanging out to dry on the balcony. We pass a public bus, with people jammed in so tight their faces are nearly wedged against the window. Then I see the skyline of what must be downtown Guangzhou. From a distance, it looks like a major American city, with high rises and construction going on everywhere. As we slow down in the more congested part of the city, I see scores of little shops, dark inside, lined with counters and shelves. And then there is a building, its front laced with scaffolding made of bamboo poles held together with plastic strips. Men and women are standing on narrow platforms, scraping the sides, working without safety straps or helmets. Oh, would OSHA° have a field day here, I think.

Aiyi's shrill voice rises up again: "So it is a shame you can't see our village, our house. My sons have been quite successful, selling our vegetables in the free market. We had enough these last few years to build a big house, three stories, all of new brick, big enough for our whole family and then some. And every year, the money is even better. You Americans aren't the only ones who know how to get rich!"

The taxi stops and I assume we've arrived, but then I peer out at what looks like a grander version of the Hyatt Regency. "This is communist China?" I wonder out loud. And then I shake my head toward my father. "This must be the wrong hotel." I quickly pull out our itinerary, travel tickets, and reservations. I had explicitly instructed my travel agent to choose something inexpensive, in the thirty-to-forty-dollar range. I'm sure of this. And there it says on our itinerary: Garden Hotel, Huanshi Dong Lu. Well, our travel agent had better be prepared to eat the extra, that's all I have to say.

The hotel is magnificent. A bellboy complete with uniform and sharp-creased cap jumps forward and begins to carry our bags into the lobby. Inside, the hotel looks like an orgy of shopping arcades and restaurants all encased in granite and glass. And rather than be impressed, I am worried about the expense, as well as the appearance it must give Aiyi, that we rich Americans cannot be without our luxuries even for one night.

But when I step up to the reservation desk, ready to haggle over this booking mistake, it is confirmed. Our rooms are prepaid, thirty-four dollars each. I feel sheepish, and Aiyi and the others seem delighted by our temporary surroundings. Lili is looking wide-eyed at an arcade filled with video games.

Our whole family crowds into one elevator, and the bellboy waves, saying he will meet us on the eighteenth floor. As soon as the elevator door shuts, every-body becomes very quiet, and when the door finally opens again, everybody talks at once in what sounds like relieved voices. I have the feeling Aiyi and the others have never been on such a long elevator ride.

Our rooms are next to each other and are identical. The rugs, drapes, bed-spreads are all in shades of taupe. There's a color television with remote-control panels built into the lamp table between the two twin beds. The bathroom has marble walls and floors. I find a built-in wet bar with a small refrigerator stocked with Heineken beer, Coke Classic, and Seven-Up, mini-bottles of Johnnie Walker Red, Bacardi rum, and Smirnoff vodka, and packets of M & M's, honey-roasted cashews, and Cadbury chocolate bars. And again I say out loud, "This is communist China?"

My father comes into my room. "They decided we should just stay here and visit," he says, shrugging his shoulders. "They say, Less trouble that way. More time to talk."

---

OSHA: Occupation, Safety, and Health Administration, a federal agency that regulates and moni-tors workplace safety conditions.

"What about dinner?" I ask. I have been envisioning my first real Chinese feast for many days already, a big banquet with one of those soups steaming out of a carved winter melon, chicken wrapped in clay, Peking duck, the works.

My father walks over and picks up a room service book next to a *Travel & Leisure* magazine. He flips through the pages quickly and then points to the menu. "This is what they want," says my father.

So it's decided. We are going to dine tonight in our rooms, with our family, sharing hamburgers, french fries, and apple pie à la mode.

Aiyi and her family are browsing the shops while we clean up. After a hot ride on the train, I'm eager for a shower and cooler clothes.

The hotel has provided little packets of shampoo which, upon opening, I discover is the consistency and color of hoisin sauce. This is more like it, I think. This is China. And I rub some in my damp hair.

Standing in the shower, I realize this is the first time I've been by myself in what seems like days. But instead of feeling relieved, I feel forlorn. I think about what my mother said, about activating my genes and becoming Chinese. And I wonder what she meant.

Right after my mother died, I asked myself a lot of things, things that couldn't be answered, to force myself to grieve more. It seemed as if I wanted to sustain my grief, to assure myself that I had cared deeply enough.

But now I ask the questions mostly because I want to know the answers. What was that pork stuff she used to make that had the texture of sawdust? What were the names of the uncles who died in Shanghai? What had she dreamt all these years about her other daughters? All the times when she got mad at me, was she really thinking about them? Did she wish I were they? Did she regret that I wasn't?

At one o'clock in the morning, I awake to tapping sounds on the window. I must have dozed off and now I feel my body uncramping itself. I'm sitting on the floor, leaning against one of the twin beds. Lili is lying next to me. The others are asleep, too, sprawled out on the beds and floor. Aiyi is seated at a little table, looking very sleepy. And my father is staring out the window, tapping his fingers on the glass. The last time I listened my father was telling Aiyi about his life since he last saw her. How he had gone to Yenching University, later got a post with a newspaper in Chungking, met my mother there, a young widow. How they later fled together to Shanghai to try to find my mother's family house, but there was nothing there. And then they traveled eventually to Canton and then to Hong Kong, then Haiphong and finally to San Francisco. . . .

"Suyuan didn't tell me she was trying all these years to find her daughters," he is now saying in a quiet voice. "Naturally, I did not discuss her daughters with her. I thought she was ashamed she had left them behind."

"Where did she leave them?" asks Aiyi. "How were they found?"

I am wide awake now. Although I have heard parts of this story from my mother's friends.

"It happened when the Japanese took over Kweilin," says my father.

"Japanese in Kweilin?" says Aiyi. "That was never the case. Couldn't be. The Japanese never came to Kweilin."

"Yes, that is what the newspapers reported. I know this because I was working for the news bureau at the time. The Kuomintang often told us what we could say and could not say. But we knew the Japanese had come into Kwangsi Province. We had sources who told us how they had captured the Wuchang-Canton railway. How they were coming overland, making very fast progress, marching toward the provincial capital."

Aiyi looks astonished. "If people did not know this, how could Suyuan know the Japanese were coming?"

"An officer of the Kuomintang secretly warned her," explains my father. "Suyuan's husband also was an officer and everybody knew that officers and their families would be the first to be killed. So she gathered a few possessions and, in the middle of the night, she picked up her daughters and fled on foot. The babies were not even one year old."

"How could she give up those babies!" sighs Aiyi. "Twin girls. We have never had such luck in our family." And then she yawns again.

"What were they named?" she asks. I listen carefully. I had been planning on using just the familiar "Sister" to address them both. But now I want to know how to pronounce their names.

"They have their father's surname, Wang," says my father. "And their given names are Chwun Yu and Chwun Hwa."

"What do the names mean?" I ask.

"Ah." My father draws imaginary characters on the window. "One means 'Spring Rain,' the other 'Spring Flower,'" he explains in English, "because they born in the spring, and of course rain come before flower, same order these girls are born. Your mother like a poet, don't you think?"

I nod my head. I see Aiyi nod her head forward, too. But it falls forward and stays there. She is breathing deeply, noisily. She is asleep.

"And what does Ma's name mean?" I whisper.

"'Suyuan,'" he says, writing more invisible characters on the glass. "The way she write it in Chinese, it mean 'Long-Cherished Wish.' Quite a fancy name, not so ordinary like flower name. See this first character, it mean something like 'Forever Never Forgotten.' But there is another way to write 'Suyuan.' Sound exactly the same, but the meaning is opposite." His finger creates the brushstrokes of another character. "The first part look the same: 'Never Forgotten.' But the last part add to first part make the whole word mean 'Long-Held Grudge.' Your mother get angry with me, I tell her her name should be Grudge."

My father is looking at me, moist-eyed. "See, I pretty clever, too, hah?"

I nod, wishing I could find some way to comfort him. "And what about my name," I ask, "what does 'Jing-mei' mean?"

"Your name also special," he says. I wonder if any name in Chinese is not something special. "'Jing' like excellent *jing*. Not just good, it's something pure, essential, the best quality. *Jing* is good leftover stuff when you take impurities out of something like gold, or rice, or salt. So what is left—just pure essence. And 'Mei,' this is common *mei*, as in *meimei*, 'younger sister.'"

I think about this. My mother's long-cherished wish. Me, the younger sister 95
who was supposed to be the essence of the others. I feed myself with the old grief,
wondering how disappointed my mother must have been. Tiny Aiyi stirs suddenly, her head rolls and then falls back, her mouth opens as if to answer my question. She grunts in her sleep, tucking her body more closely into the chair.

"So why did she abandon those babies on the road?" I need to know, because
now I feel abandoned too.

"Long time I wondered this myself," says my father. "But then I read that letter from her daughters in Shanghai now, and I talk to Auntie Lindo, all the others. And then I knew. No shame in what she done. None."

"What happened?"

"Your mother running away—" begins my father.

"No, tell me in Chinese," I interrupt. "Really, I can understand." 100

He begins to talk, still standing at the window, looking into the night.


After fleeing Kweilin, your mother walked for several days trying to find a
main road. Her thought was to catch a ride on a truck or wagon, to catch enough
rides until she reached Chungking, where her husband was stationed.

She had sewn money and jewelry into the lining of her dress, enough, she
thought, to barter rides all the way. If I am lucky, she thought, I will not have to
trade the heavy gold bracelet and jade ring. These were things from her mother,
your grandmother.

By the third day, she had traded nothing. The roads were filled with people,
everybody running and begging for rides from passing trucks. The trucks rushed
by, afraid to stop. So your mother found no rides, only the start of dysentery pains
in her stomach.

Her shoulders ached from the two babies swinging from scarf slings. Blisters 105
grew on her palms from holding two leather suitcases. And then the blisters burst
and began to bleed. After a while, she left the suitcases behind, keeping only the
food and a few clothes. And later she also dropped the bags of wheat flour and
rice and kept walking like this for many miles, singing songs to her little girls,
until she was delirious with pain and fever.

Finally, there was not one more step left in her body. She didn't have the
strength to carry those babies any farther. She slumped to the ground. She knew
she would die of her sickness, or perhaps from thirst, from starvation, or from the
Japanese, who she was sure were marching right behind her.

She took the babies out of the slings and sat them on the side of the road,
then lay down next to them. You babies are so good, she said, so quiet. They
smiled back, reaching their chubby hands for her, wanting to be picked up again.
And then she knew she could not bear to watch her babies die with her.

She saw a family with three young children in a cart going by. "Take my
babies, I beg you," she cried to them. But they stared back with empty eyes and
never stopped.

She saw another person pass and called out again. This time a man turned around, and he had such a terrible expression—your mother said it looked like death itself—she shivered and looked away.

When the road grew quiet, she tore open the lining of her dress, and stuffed jewelry under the shirt of one baby and money under the other. She reached into her pocket and drew out the photos of her family, the picture of her father and mother, the picture of herself and her husband on their wedding day. And she wrote on the back of each the names of the babies and this same message: "Please care for these babies with the money and valuables provided. When it is safe to come, if you bring them to Shanghai, 9 Weichang Lu, the Li family will be glad to give you a generous reward. Li Suyuan and Wang Fuchi."

And then she touched each baby's cheek and told her not to cry. She would go down the road to find them some food and would be back. And without looking back, she walked down the road, stumbling and crying, thinking only of this one last hope, that her daughters would be found by a kindhearted person who would care for them. She would not allow herself to imagine anything else.

She did not remember how far she walked, which direction she went, when she fainted, or how she was found. When she awoke, she was in the back of a bouncing truck with several other sick people, all moaning. And she began to scream, thinking she was now on a journey to Buddhist hell. But the face of an American missionary lady bent over her and smiled, talking to her in a soothing language she did not understand. And yet she could somehow understand. She had been saved for no good reason, and it was now too late to go back and save her babies.

When she arrived in Chungking, she learned her husband had died two weeks before. She told me later she laughed when the officers told her this news, she was so delirious with madness and disease. To come so far, to lose so much and to find nothing.

I met her in a hospital. She was lying on a cot, hardly able to move, her dysentery had drained her so thin. I had come in for my foot, my missing toe, which was cut off by a piece of falling rubble. She was talking to herself, mumbling.

"Look at these clothes," she said, and I saw she had on a rather unusual dress for wartime. It was silk satin, quite dirty, but there was no doubt it was a beautiful dress.

"Look at this face," she said, and I saw her dusty face and hollow cheeks, her eyes shining back. "Do you see my foolish hope?"

"I thought I had lost everything, except these two things," she murmured. "And I wondered which I would lose next. Clothes or hope? Hope or clothes?"

"But now, see here, look what is happening," she said, laughing, as if all her prayers had been answered. And she was pulling hair out of her head as easily as one lifts new wheat from wet soil.

It was an old peasant woman who found them. "How could I resist?" the peasant woman later told your sisters when they were older. They were still sitting obediently near where your mother had left them, looking like little fairy queens waiting for their sedan to arrive.

The woman, Mei Ching, and her husband, Mei Han, lived in a stone cave. 120 There were thousands of hidden caves like that in and around Kweilin so secret that the people remained hidden even after the war ended. The Meis would come out of their cave every few days and forage for food supplies left on the road, and sometimes they would see something that they both agreed was a tragedy to leave behind. So one day they took back to their cave a delicately painted set of rice bowls, another day a little footstool with a velvet cushion and two new wedding blankets. And once, it was your sisters.

They were pious people, Muslims, who believed the twin babies were a sign of double luck, and they were sure of this when, later in the evening, they discovered how valuable the babies were. She and her husband had never seen rings and bracelets like those. And while they admired the pictures, knowing the babies came from a good family, neither of them could read or write. It was not until many months later that Mei Ching found someone who could read the writing on the back. By then, she loved these baby girls like her own.

In 1952 Mei Han, the husband, died. The twins were already eight years old, and Mei Ching now decided it was time to find your sisters' true family.

She showed the girls the picture of their mother and told them they had been born into a great family and she would take them back to see their true mother and grandparents. Mei Ching told them about the reward, but she swore she would refuse it. She loved these girls so much, she only wanted them to have what they were entitled to—a better life, a fine house, educated ways. Maybe the family would let her stay on as the girls' amah. Yes, she was certain they would insist.

Of course, when she found the place at 9 Weichang Lu, in the old French Concession, it was something completely different. It was the site of a factory building, recently constructed, and none of the workers knew what had become of the family whose house had burned down on that spot.

Mei Ching could not have known, of course, that your mother and I, her 125 new husband, had already returned to that same place in 1945 in hopes of finding both her family and her daughters.

Your mother and I stayed in China until 1947. We went to many different cities—back to Kweilin, to Changsha, as far south as Kunming. She was always looking out of one corner of her eye for twin babies, then little girls. Later we went to Hong Kong, and when we finally left in 1949 for the United States, I think she was even looking for them on the boat. But when we arrived, she no longer talked about them. I thought, At last, they have died in her heart.

When letters could be openly exchanged between China and the United States, she wrote immediately to old friends in Shanghai and Kweilin. I did not know she did this. Auntie Lindo told me. But of course, by then, all the street names had changed. Some people had died, others had moved away. So it took many years to find a contact. And when she did find an old schoolmate's address and wrote asking her to look for her daughters, her friend wrote back and said this was impossible, like looking for a needle on the bottom of the ocean. How did she know her daughters were in Shanghai and not somewhere else in China? The friend, of course, did not ask, How do you know your daughters are still alive?

So her schoolmate did not look. Finding babies lost during the war was a matter of foolish imagination, and she had no time for that.

But every year, your mother wrote to different people. And this last year, I think she got a big idea in her head, to go to China and find them herself. I remember she told me, "Canning, we should go, before it is too late, before we are too old." And I told her we were already too old, it was already too late.

I just thought she wanted to be a tourist! I didn't know she wanted to go and 130 look for her daughters. So when I said it was too late, that must have put a terrible thought in her head that her daughters might be dead. And I think this possibility grew bigger and bigger in her head, until it killed her.

Maybe it was your mother's dead spirit who guided her Shanghai schoolmate to find her daughters. Because after your mother died, the schoolmate saw your sisters, by chance, while shopping for shoes at the Number One Department Store on Nanjing Dong Road. She said it was like a dream, seeing these two women who looked so much alike, moving down the stairs together. There was something about their facial expressions that reminded the schoolmate of your mother.

She quickly walked over to them and called their names, which of course, they did not recognize at first, because Mei Ching had changed their names. But your mother's friend was so sure, she persisted. "Are you not Wang Chwun Yu and Wang Chwun Hwa?" she asked them. And then these double-image women became very excited, because they remembered the names written on the back of an old photo, a photo of a young man and woman they still honored, as their much-loved first parents, who had died and become spirit ghosts still roaming the earth looking for them.


At the airport, I am exhausted. I could not sleep last night. Aiyi had followed me into my room at three in the morning, and she instantly fell asleep on one of the twin beds, snoring with the might of a lumberjack. I lay awake thinking about my mother's story, realizing how much I have never known about her, grieving that my sisters and I had both lost her.

And now at the airport, after shaking hands with everybody, waving good-bye, I think about all the different ways we leave people in this world. Cheerily waving good-bye to some at airports, knowing we'll never see each other again. Leaving others on the side of the road, hoping that we will. Finding my mother in my father's story and saying good-bye before I have a chance to know her better.

Aiyi smiles at me as we wait for our gate to be called. She is so old. I put one 135 arm around her and one around Lili. They are the same size, it seems. And then it's time. As we wave good-bye one more time and enter the waiting area, I get the sense I am going from one funeral to another. In my hand I'm clutching a pair of tickets to Shanghai. In two hours we'll be there.

The plane takes off. I close my eyes. How can I describe to them in my broken Chinese about our mother's life? Where should I begin?

"Wake up, we're here," says my father. And I awake with my heart pounding in my throat. I look out the window and we're already on the runway. It's gray outside.

And now I'm walking down the steps of the plane, onto the tarmac and toward the building. If only, I think, if only my mother had lived long enough to be the one walking toward them. I am so nervous I cannot even feel my feet. I am just moving somehow.

Somebody shouts, "She's arrived!" And then I see her. Her short hair. Her small body. And that same look on her face. She has the back of her hand pressed hard against her mouth. She is crying as though she had gone through a terrible ordeal and were happy it is over.

And I know it's not my mother, yet it is the same look she had when I was 140 five and had disappeared all afternoon, for such a long time, that she was convinced I was dead. And when I miraculously appeared, sleepy-eyed, crawling from underneath my bed, she wept and laughed, biting the back of her hand to make sure it was true.

And now I see her again, two of her, waving, and in one hand there is a photo, the Polaroid I sent them. As soon as I get beyond the gate, we run toward each other, all three of us embracing, all hesitations and expectations forgotten.

"Mama, Mama," we all murmur, as if she is among us.

My sisters look at me, proudly. "*Meimei jandale*," says one sister proudly to the other. "Little Sister has grown up." I look at their faces again and I see no trace of my mother in them. Yet they still look familiar. And now I also see what part of me is Chinese. It is so obvious. It is my family. It is in our blood. After all these years, it can finally be let go.

My sisters and I stand, arms around each other, laughing and wiping the tears from each other's eyes. The flash of the Polaroid goes off and my father hands me the snapshot. My sisters and I watch quietly together, eager to see what develops.

The gray-green surface changes to the bright colors of our three images, 145 sharpening and deepening all at once. And although we don't speak, I know we all see it: Together we look like our mother. Her same eyes, her same mouth, open in surprise to see, at last, her long-cherished wish.

QUESTIONS

1. How is the external setting of "A Pair of Tickets" essential to what happens internally to the narrator in the course of this story?
2. How does the narrator's view of her father change by seeing him in a different setting?

3. In what ways does the narrator feel at home in China? In what ways does she feel foreign?
4. What do the narrator and her half-sisters have in common? How does this factor relate to the theme of the story?
5. In what ways does the story explore specifically Chinese-American experiences? In what other ways is the story grounded in universal family issues?

## Suggestions for Writing

1. In a few paragraphs, not necessarily a complete essay or story, recreate a time and place you know intimately. Write about it like a fiction writer, giving reality to a setting in which a story is about to unfold. Imagine this setting in detail—or, if you can, go take a fresh look at it. Ensure that your reader can virtually see, hear, smell, and taste your chosen time and place.

   You might find it revealing to choose for your subject some nearby, present-day place that your audience will recognize, then read your paper aloud in class. If, without your dropping place names or giving them other obvious clues, your listeners can identify your subject, then you will have written well.

2. From a different chapter of this book, or from the Stories for Further Reading, choose a story that particularly interests you. Start out by defining for your reader its exact time and place. Then, in two or three more paragraphs, go on to show how this setting functions in the story. Does the setting supply atmosphere? Make things happen? Reveal the natures of certain people? Prompt a character to a realization? Suggested stories to work on (but your instructor may be saving some stories for other purposes and may wish to narrow or add to this list): "Gimpel the Fool," "A Clean, Well-Lighted Place," "Barn Burning," "Araby," "Young Goodman Brown," "The Chrysanthemums," "The Death of Ivan Ilych," "The Five-Forty-Eight," and "The Gospel According to Mark."

3. Rewrite the first page or two of a story you have read, picking up the characters and putting them down in an entirely different setting. This new time and place might be the setting of another story, or it might be some actual place your readers will recognize. As you write, you might find yourself deciding to seek laughs, or you might decide to make the rewrite serious. You might try, for instance, a satire in the vein of Monty Python, shifting Hawthorne's "Young Goodman Brown" to the setting of Updike's "A & P." Or, without trying to be funny, you might rewrite the opening of Joyce's "Araby," setting the story in the neighborhood where you grew up.

   End with a short comment in answer to the question: "What did this exercise prove to you?" If your attempt should seem to you a failure, try to explain why the original story proved so reluctant to give up its time and place. (The purpose of this exercise is not to produce a new masterpiece, but to experience at first hand how the setting of a story works.)

# 5 Tone and Style

In many Victorian novels it was customary for some commentator, presumably the author, to interrupt the story from time to time, remarking upon the action, offering philosophic asides, or explaining the procedures to be followed in telling the story.

> Two hours later, Dorothea was seated in an inner room or boudoir of a handsome apartment in the Via Sistina. I am sorry to add that she was sobbing bitterly . . .
>
> —George Eliot in *Middlemarch* (1873)

> But let the gentle-hearted reader be under no apprehension whatsoever. It is not destined that Eleanor shall marry Mr. Slope or Bertie Stanhope.
>
> —Anthony Trollope in *Barchester Towers* (1857)

> And, as we bring our characters forward, I will ask leave, as a man and a brother, not only to introduce, but occasionally step down from the platform, and talk about them: if they are good and kindly, to love them and shake them by the hand; if they are silly, to laugh at them confidentially in the reader's sleeve; if they are wicked and heartless, to abuse them in the strongest terms which politeness admits of.
>
> —William Makepeace Thackeray in *Vanity Fair* (1847–1848)

Of course, the voice of this commentator was not identical with that of the "real life" author—the one toiling over an inkpot, worrying about publication deadlines and whether the rent would be paid. At times the living author might have been far different in personality from that usually wise and cheerful intruder who kept addressing the reader of the book. Much of the time, to be sure, the author probably agreed with whatever attitudes his alter ego expressed. But, in effect, the author created the character of a commentator to speak for him and throughout the novel artfully sustained that character's voice.

Such intrusions, although sometimes useful to the "real" author and enjoyable to the reader, are today rare. Modern storytellers, carefully keeping out of sight, seldom comment on their plots and characters. Apparently they agree with Anton Chekhov that a writer should not judge the characters but should serve as their "impartial witness." And yet, no less definitely than Victorian novelists who introduced commentators, writers of effective stories no doubt have feelings toward their characters and events. The authors presumably care about these imaginary people and, in order for the story to grasp and sustain our interest, have to make us see these people in such a way that we, too, will care about them. When at the beginning of the short story "In Exile" Chekhov introduces us to a character, he does so with a description that arouses sympathy:

> The Tartar was worn out and ill, and wrapping himself in his rags, he talked about how good it was in the province of Simbirsk, and what a beautiful and clever wife he had left at home. He was not more than twenty-five, and in the firelight his pale, sickly face and woebegone expression made him seem like a boy.

Other than the comparison of the Tartar to a child, the details in this passage seem mostly factual: the young man's illness, ragged clothes, facial expression, and topics of conversation. But these details form a portrait that stirs pity. By his selection of these imaginary details out of countless others that he might have included, Chekhov firmly directs our feelings about the Tartar, so miserable and pathetic in his sickness and his homesickness. We cannot know, of course, exactly what the living Chekhov felt; but at least we can be sure that we are supposed to share the compassion and tenderness of the narrator—Chekhov's impartial (but human) witness.

Not only the author's choice of details may lead us to infer his or her attitude, but also choice of characters, events, and situations, and choice of words. When the narrator of Joseph Conrad's *Heart of Darkness* comes upon an African outpost littered with abandoned machines and notices "a boiler wallowing in the grass," the exact word *wallowing* conveys an attitude: that there is something swinish about this scene of careless waste. Whatever leads us to infer the author's attitude is commonly called **tone.** Like a tone of voice, the tone of a story may communicate amusement, anger, affection, sorrow, contempt. It implies the feelings of the author, so far as we can sense them. Those feelings may be similar to feelings expressed by the narrator of the story (or by any character), but sometimes they may be dissimilar, even sharply opposed. The characters in a story may regard an event as sad, but we sense that the author regards it as funny. To understand the tone of a story, then, is to understand some attitude more fundamental to the story than whatever attitude the characters explicitly declare.

The tone of a story, like a tone of voice, may convey not simply one attitude, but a medley. Reading "Gimpel the Fool" (Chapter Three), we have mingled feelings toward Gimpel and his "foolishness": amusement that Gimpel is so easily deceived; sympathy, perhaps, for his excessive innocence; admiration for his unwavering faith in God and fellow man. Often the tone of a literary story will be too rich and complicated to sum up in one or two words. But to try to describe the tone of such a story may be a useful way to penetrate to its center and to grasp the whole of it.

One of the clearest indications of the tone of a story is the **style** in which it is written. In general, style refers to the individual traits or characteristics of a piece of writing: to a writer's particular ways of managing words that we come to recognize as habitual or customary. A distinctive style marks the work of a fine writer: we can tell his or her work from that of anyone else. From one story to another, however, the writer may fittingly change style; and in some stories, style may be altered meaningfully as the story goes along. In his novel *As I Lay Dying,* William Faulkner changes narrators with every chapter, and he distinguishes the narrators one from another by giving each an individual style or manner of speaking. Though each narrator has his or her own style, the book as a whole demonstrates Faulkner's style as well. For instance, one chapter is written from the point of view of a small boy, Vardaman Bundren, member of a family of poor Mississippi tenant farmers, whose view of a horse in a barn reads like this:

> It is as though the dark were resolving him out of his integrity, into an unrelated scattering of components—snuffings and stampings; smells of cooling flesh and ammoniac hair; an illusion of a coordinated whole of splotched hide and strong bones within which, detached and secret and familiar, an *is* different from my is.[1]

How can a small boy unaccustomed to libraries use words like *integrity, components, illusion,* and *coordinated?* Elsewhere in the story, Vardaman says aloud, with no trace of literacy, "Hit was a-laying right there on the ground." Apparently, in the passage it is not the voice of the boy that we are hearing, but something resembling the voice of William Faulkner, elevated and passionate, expressing the boy's thoughts in a style that admits Faulknerian words.

Usually, *style* indicates a mode of expression: the language a writer uses. In this sense, the notion of style includes such traits as the length and complexity of sentences, and **diction,** or choice of words: abstract or concrete, bookish ("unrelated scattering of components") or close to speech ("Hit was a-laying right there on the ground"). Involved in the idea of style, too, is any habitual use of imagery, patterns of sound, figures of speech, or other devices.

Lately, several writers of realistic fiction, called **minimalists**—Ann Beattie, Raymond Carver, Mary Robison—have written with a flat, laid-back, unemotional tone, in an appropriately bare, unadorned style. Minimalists seem to give nothing but facts drawn from ordinary life, sometimes in picayune detail. Here is a sample passage, from Raymond Carver's story "A Small, Good Thing":

> She pulled into the driveway and cut the engine. She closed her eyes and leaned her head against the wheel for a minute. She listened to the ticking sounds the engine made as it began to cool. Then she got out of the car. She could hear the dog barking inside the house. She went to the front door,

[1]Modern Library edition (New York: Random House, 1930) 379.

which was unlocked. She went inside and turned on lights and put on a ket-tle of water for tea. She opened some dog food and fed Slug on the back porch. The dog ate in hungry little smacks. It kept running into the kitchen to see that she was going to stay.

Explicit feeling and showy language are kept at a minimum here. Taken out of context, this description may strike you as banal, as if the writer himself was bored; but it works effectively as a part of Carver's entire story. As in all good writing, the style here seems a faithful mirror of what is said in it. At its best, such writing achieves "a hard-won reduction, a painful stripping away of richness, a baring of bone."[2]

To see what style means, compare the stories in this chapter by William Faulkner ("Barn Burning") and by Ernest Hemingway ("A Clean, Well-Lighted Place"). Faulkner frequently falls into a style in which a statement, as soon as uttered, is followed by another statement expressing the idea in a more emphatic way. Sentences are interrupted with parenthetical elements (asides, like this) thrust into them unexpectedly. At times, Faulkner writes of seemingly ordinary matters as if giving a speech in a towering passion. Here, from "Barn Burning," is a description of how a boy's father delivers a rug:

> "Don't you want me to help?" he whispered. His father did not answer and now he heard again that stiff foot striking the hollow portico with that wooden and clocklike deliberation, that outrageous overstatement of the weight it carried. The rug, hunched, not flung (the boy could tell that even in the darkness) from his father's shoulder struck the angle of wall and floor with a sound unbelievably loud, thunderous, then the foot again, unhurried and enormous; a light came on in the house and the boy sat, tense, breathing steadily and quietly and just a little fast, though the foot itself did not increase its beat at all, descending the steps now; now the boy could see him.

Faulkner is not merely indulging in language for its own sake. As you will find when you read the whole story, this rug delivery is vital to the story, and so too is the father's profound defiance—indicated by his walk. By devices of style—by *metaphor* and *simile* ("wooden and clocklike"), by exact qualification ("not flung"), by emphatic adjectives ("loud, thunderous")—Faulkner is carefully plac-ing his emphases. By the words he selects to describe the father's stride, Faulkner directs how we feel toward the man and perhaps also indicates his own wonder-ing but skeptical attitude toward a character whose very footfall is "outrageous" and "enormous." (Fond of long sentences like the last one in the quoted passage, Faulkner remarked that there are sentences that need to be written in the way a circus acrobat pedals a bicycle on a high wire: rapidly, so as not to fall off.)

Hemingway's famous style includes both short sentences and long, but when the sentences are long they tend to be relatively simple in construction. Hemingway likes long compound sentences (clause plus clause plus clause), sometimes joined with "ands." He interrupts such a sentence with a dependent

[2]Letter in *The New York Times Book Review*, June 5, 1988.

clause or a parenthetical element much less frequently than Faulkner does. The effect is like listening to speech:

> In the day time the street was dusty, but at night the dew settled the dust and the old man liked to sit late because he was deaf and now at night it was quiet and he felt the difference.

Hemingway is a master of swift, terse dialogue, and often casts whole scenes in the form of conversation. As if he were a closemouthed speaker unwilling to let his feelings loose, the narrator of a Hemingway story often addresses us in understatement, implying greater depths of feeling than he puts into words. Read the following story and you will see that its style and tone cannot be separated.

### Ernest Hemingway

A CLEAN, WELL-LIGHTED PLACE                                                  1933

Ernest Hemingway

*Ernest Hemingway (1898–1961), born in Oak Park, Illinois, bypassed college to be a cub reporter. In World War I, as an eighteen-year-old volunteer ambulance driver in Italy, he was wounded in action. In 1922 he settled in Paris, then aswarm with writers; he later recalled that time in* A Moveable Feast *(1964). Hemingway won swift acclaim for his early stories,* In Our Time *(1925), and for his first, perhaps finest, novel,* The Sun Also Rises *(1926), portraying a "lost generation" of postwar American drifters in France and Spain.* For Whom the Bell Tolls *(1940) depicts life during the Spanish Civil War. Hemingway became a celebrity, often photographed as a marlin fisherman or a lion hunter. A fan of bullfighting, he wrote two nonfiction books on the subject:* Death in the Afternoon *(1932) and* The Dangerous Summer *(1985). After World War II, with his fourth wife, journalist Mary Welsh, he made his home in Cuba, where he wrote* The Old Man and the Sea *(1952). The Nobel prize for literature came to him in 1954. In 1961, mentally distressed and physically ailing, he shot himself. Hemingway brought a hard-bitten realism into American fiction. His heroes live dangerously, by personal codes of honor, courage, and endurance. Hemingway's distinctively crisp, unadorned style left American literature permanently changed.*

It was late and every one had left the café except an old man who sat in the shadow the leaves of the tree made against the electric light. In the day time the street was dusty, but at night the dew settled the dust and the old man liked to sit late because he was deaf and now at night it was quiet and he felt the difference. The two waiters inside the café knew that the old man was a little drunk, and while he was a good client they knew that if he became too drunk he would leave without paying, so they kept watch on him.

"Last week he tried to commit suicide," one waiter said.

"Why?"

"He was in despair."

"What about?"

"Nothing."

"How do you know it was nothing?"

"He has plenty of money."

They sat together at a table that was close against the wall near the door of the café and looked at the terrace where the tables were all empty except where the old man sat in the shadow of the leaves of the tree that moved slightly in the wind. A girl and a soldier went by in the street. The street light shone on the brass number on his collar. The girl wore no head covering and hurried beside him.

"The guard will pick him up," one waiter said.

"What does it matter if he gets what he's after?"

"He had better get off the street now. The guard will get him. They went by five minutes ago."

The old man sitting in the shadow rapped on his saucer with his glass. The younger waiter went over to him.

"What do you want?"

The old man looked at him. "Another brandy," he said.

"You'll be drunk," the waiter said. The old man looked at him. The waiter went away.

"He'll stay all night," he said to his colleague. "I'm sleepy now. I never get into bed before three o'clock. He should have killed himself last week."

The waiter took the brandy bottle and another saucer from the counter inside the café and marched out to the old man's table. He put down the saucer and poured the glass full of brandy.

"You should have killed yourself last week," he said to the deaf man. The old man motioned with his finger. "A little more," he said. The waiter poured on into the glass so that the brandy slopped over and ran down the stem into the top saucer of the pile. "Thank you," the old man said. The waiter took the bottle back inside the café. He sat down at the table with his colleague again.

"He's drunk now," he said.

"He's drunk every night."°

"What did he want to kill himself for?"

"How should I know?"

"How did he do it?"

---

*"He's drunk now," he said. "He's drunk every night"*: The younger waiter says both these lines. A device of Hemingway's style is sometimes to have a character pause, then speak again—as often happens in actual speech.

"He hung himself with a rope."                                                                    25
"Who cut him down?"
"His niece."
"Why did they do it?"
"Fear for his soul."
"How much money has he got?"                                                                      30
"He's got plenty."
"He must be eighty years old."
"Anyway I should say he was eighty."°
"I wish he would go home. I never get to bed before three o'clock. What kind of hour is that to go to bed?"
"He stays up because he likes it."                                                                35
"He's lonely. I'm not lonely. I have a wife waiting in bed for me."
"He had a wife once too."
"A wife would be no good to him now."
"You can't tell. He might be better with a wife."
"His niece looks after him."                                                                      40
"I know. You said she cut him down."
"I wouldn't want to be that old. An old man is a nasty thing."
"Not always. This old man is clean. He drinks without spilling. Even now, drunk. Look at him."
"I don't want to look at him. I wish he would go home. He has no regard for those who must work."
The old man looked from his glass across the square, then over at the wait-  45
ers.
"Another brandy," he said, pointing to his glass. The waiter who was in a hurry came over.
"Finished," he said, speaking with that omission of syntax stupid people employ when talking to drunken people or foreigners. "No more tonight. Close now."
"Another," said the old man.
"No. Finished." The waiter wiped the edge of the table with a towel and shook his head.
The old man stood up, slowly counted the saucers, took a leather coin purse  50
from his pocket and paid for the drinks, leaving half a peseta tip.
The waiter watched him go down the street, a very old man walking unsteadily but with dignity.
"Why didn't you let him stay and drink?" the unhurried waiter asked. They were putting up the shutters. "It is not half-past two."
"I want to go home to bed."
"What is an hour?"

*"He must be eighty years old." "Anyway I should say he was eighty"*: Is this another instance of the same character's speaking twice? Clearly, it is the younger waiter who says the next line, "I wish he would go home."

"More to me than to him."

"An hour is the same."

"You talk like an old man yourself. He can buy a bottle and drink at home."

"It's not the same."

"No, it is not," agreed the waiter with a wife. He did not wish to be unjust. He was only in a hurry.

"And you? You have no fear of going home before the usual hour?"

"Are you trying to insult me?"

"No, hombre, only to make a joke."

"No," the waiter who was in a hurry said, rising from pulling down the metal shutters. "I have confidence. I am all confidence."

"You have youth, confidence, and a job," the older waiter said. "You have everything."

"And what do you lack?"

"Everything but work."

"You have everything I have."

"No. I have never had confidence and I am not young."

"Come on. Stop talking nonsense and lock up."

"I am of those who like to stay late at the café," the older waiter said. "With all those who do not want to go to bed. With all those who need a light for the night."

"I want to go home and into bed."

"We are of two different kinds," the older waiter said. He was not dressed to go home. "It is not only a question of youth and confidence although those things are very beautiful. Each night I am reluctant to close up because there may be some one who needs the café."

"Hombre, there are bodegas° open all night long."

"You do not understand. This is a clean and pleasant café. It is well lighted. The light is very good and also, now, there are shadows of the leaves."

"Good night," said the younger waiter.

"Good night," the other said. Turning off the electric light he continued the conversation with himself. It is the light of course but it is necessary that the place be clean and pleasant. You do not want music. Certainly you do not want music. Nor can you stand before a bar with dignity although that is all that is provided for these hours. What did he fear? It was not fear or dread. It was a nothing that he knew too well. It was all a nothing and a man was nothing too. It was only that and light was all it needed and a certain cleanness and order. Some lived in it and never felt it but he knew it all was nada y pues nada y nada y pues nada°. Our nada who art in nada, nada be thy name thy kingdom nada thy will be nada in nada as it is in nada. Give us this nada our daily nada and nada us our nada as we nada our nadas and nada us not into nada but deliver us from nada;

---

bodegas: wineshops.    nada y pues . . . nada: nothing and then nothing and nothing and then nothing.

pues nada. Hail nothing full of nothing, nothing is with thee. He smiled and stood before a bar with a shining steam pressure coffee machine.

"What's yours?" asked the barman.

"Nada."

"Otro loco más°," said the barman and turned away.

"A little cup," said the waiter.

The barman poured it for him.

"The light is very bright and pleasant but the bar is unpolished," the waiter said.

The barman looked at him but did not answer. It was too late at night for conversation.

"You want another copita?°" the barman asked.

"No, thank you," said the waiter and went out. He disliked bars and bodegas. A clean, well-lighted café was a very different thing. Now, without thinking further, he would go home to his room. He would lie in the bed and finally, with daylight, he would go to sleep. After all, he said to himself, it is probably only insomnia. Many must have it.

## QUESTIONS

1. What besides insomnia makes the older waiter reluctant to go to bed? Comment especially on his meditation with its *nada* refrain. Why does he so well understand the old man's need for a café? What does the café represent for the two of them?
2. Compare the younger waiter and the older waiter in their attitudes toward the old man. Whose attitude do you take to be closer to that of the author? Even though Hemingway does not editorially state his own feelings, how does he make them clear to us?
3. Point to sentences that establish the style of the story. What is distinctive in them? What repetitions of words or phrases seem particularly effective? Does Hemingway seem to favor a simple or an erudite vocabulary?
4. What is the story's point of view? Discuss its appropriateness.

## William Faulkner

BARN BURNING                                                                           1939

*William Faulkner (1897–1962) receives a capsule biography on page 25, along with his story "A Rose for Emily." His "Barn Burning" is among his many contributions to the history of Yoknapatawpha, an imaginary Mississippi county in which the Sartorises and the de Spains are landed aristocrats living by a code of honor and the Snopeses—most of them—shiftless ne'er-do-wells.*

The store in which the Justice of the Peace's court was sitting smelled of cheese. The boy, crouched on his nail keg at the back of the crowded room, knew he smelled cheese, and more: from where he sat he could see the ranked shelves

*Otro loco más:* another lunatic.    *copita:* little cup.

close-packed with the solid, squat, dynamic shapes of tin cans whose labels his stomach read, not from the lettering which meant nothing to his mind but from the scarlet devils and the silver curve of fish—this, the cheese which he knew he smelled and the hermetic meat which his intestines believed he smelled coming in intermittent gusts momentary and brief between the other constant one, the smell and sense just a little of fear because mostly of despair and grief, the old fierce pull of blood. He could not see the table where the Justice sat and before which his father and his father's enemy (*our enemy* he thought in that despair: *ourn! mine and hisn both! He's my father!*) stood, but he could hear them, the two of them that is, because his father had said no word yet:

"But what proof have you, Mr. Harris?"

"I told you. The hog got into my corn. I caught it up and sent it back to him. He had no fence that would hold it. I told him so, warned him. The next time I put the hog in my pen. When he came to get it I gave him enough wire to patch up his pen. The next time I put the hog up and kept it. I rode down to his house and saw the wire I gave him still rolled on to the spool in his yard. I told him he could have the hog when he paid me a dollar pound fee. That evening a nigger came with the dollar and got the hog. He was a strange nigger. He said, 'He say to tell you wood and hay kin burn.' I said, 'What?' 'That whut he say to tell you,' the nigger said. 'Wood and hay kin burn.' That night my barn burned. I got the stock out but I lost the barn."

"Where's the nigger? Have you got him?"

"He was a strange nigger, I tell you. I don't know what became of him."  5

"But that's not proof. Don't you see that's not proof?"

"Get that boy up here. He knows." For a moment the boy thought too that the man meant his older brother until Harris said, "Not him. The little one. The boy," and, crouching, small for his age, small and wiry like his father, in patched and faded jeans even too small for him, with straight, uncombed, brown hair and eyes gray and wild as storm scud, he saw the men between himself and the table part and become a lane of grim faces, at the end of which he saw the Justice, a shabby, collarless, graying man in spectacles, beckoning him. He felt no floor under his bare feet; he seemed to walk beneath the palpable weight of the grim turning faces. His father, still in his black Sunday coat donned not for the trial but for the moving, did not even look at him. *He aims for me to lie,* he thought, again with that frantic grief and despair. *And I will have to do hit.*

"What's your name, boy?" the Justice said.

"Colonel Sartoris Snopes," the boy whispered.

"Hey?" the Justice said. "Talk louder. Colonel Sartoris? I reckon anybody  10 named for Colonel Sartoris in this country can't help but tell the truth, can they?" The boy said nothing. *Enemy! Enemy!* he thought; for a moment he could not even see, could not see that the Justice's face was kindly nor discern that his voice was troubled when he spoke to the man named Harris: "Do you want me to question this boy?" But he could hear, and during those subsequent long seconds while there was absolutely no sound in the crowded little room save that of quiet and intent breathing it was as if he had swung outward at the end of a grape vine, over a ravine, and at the top of the swing had been caught in a prolonged instant of mesmerized gravity, weightless in time.

"No!" Harris said violently, explosively. "Damnation! Send him out of here!" Now time, the fluid world, rushed beneath him again, the voices coming to him again through the smell of cheese and sealed meat, the fear and despair and the old grief of blood:

"This case is closed. I can't find against you, Snopes, but I can give you advice. Leave this country and don't come back to it."

His father spoke for the first time, his voice cold and harsh, level, without emphasis: "I aim to. I don't figure to stay in a country among people who . . . " he said something unprintable and vile, addressed to no one.

"That'll do," the Justice said. "Take your wagon and get out of this country before dark. Case dismissed."

His father turned, and he followed the stiff black coat, the wiry figure walk-       15
ing a little stiffly from where a Confederate provost's man's musket ball had taken him in the heel on a stolen horse thirty years ago, followed the two backs now, since his older brother had appeared from somewhere in the crowd, no taller than the father but thicker, chewing tobacco steadily, between the two lines of grim-faced men and out of the store and across the worn gallery and down the sagging steps and among the dogs and half-grown boys in the mild May dust, where as he passed a voice hissed:

"Barn burner!"

Again he could not see, whirling; there was a face in a red haze, moonlike, bigger than the full moon, the owner of it half again his size, he leaping in the red haze toward the face, feeling no blow, feeling no shock when his head struck the earth, scrabbling up and leaping again, feeling no blow this time either and tast-ing no blood, scrabbling up to see the other boy in full flight and himself already leaping into pursuit as his father's hand jerked him back, the harsh, cold voice speaking above him: "Go get in the wagon."

It stood in a grove of locusts and mulberries across the road. His two hulking sisters in their Sunday dresses and his mother and her sister in calico and sunbon-nets were already in it, sitting on and among the sorry residue of the dozen and more movings which even the boy could remember—the battered stove, the bro-ken beds and chairs, the clock inlaid with mother-of-pearl, which would not run, stopped at some fourteen minutes past two o'clock of a dead and forgotten day and time, which had been his mother's dowry. She was crying, though when she saw him she drew her sleeve across her face and began to descend from the wagon. "Get back," the father said.

"He's hurt. I got to get some water and wash his . . . "

"Get back in the wagon," his father said. He got in too, over the tail-gate.       20
His father mounted to the seat where the older brother already sat and struck the gaunt mules two savage blows with the peeled willow, but without heat. It was not even sadistic; it was exactly that same quality which in later years would cause his descendants to over-run the engine before putting a motor car into motion, striking and reining back in the same movement. The wagon went on,

the store with its quiet crowd of grimly watching men dropped behind; a curve in the road hid it. *Forever* he thought. *Maybe he's done satisfied now, now that he has . . .* stopping himself, not to say it aloud even to himself. His mother's hand touched his shoulder.

"Does hit hurt?" she said.

"Naw," he said. "Hit don't hurt. Lemme be."

"Can't you wipe some of the blood off before hit dries?"

"I'll wash to-night," he said. "Lemme be, I tell you."

The wagon went on. He did not know where they were going. None of them    25 ever did or ever asked, because it was always somewhere, always a house of sorts waiting for them a day or two days or even three days away. Likely his father had already arranged to make a crop on another farm before he . . . Again he had to stop himself. He (the father) always did. There was something about his wolflike independence and even courage when the advantage was at least neutral which impressed strangers, as if they got from his latent ravening ferocity not so much a sense of dependability as a feeling that his ferocious conviction in the rightness of his own actions would be of advantage to all whose interest lay with his.

That night they camped, in a grove of oaks and beeches where a spring ran. The nights were still cool and they had a fire against it, of a rail lifted from a nearby fence and cut into lengths—a small fire, neat, niggard almost, a shrewd fire; such fires were his father's habit and custom always, even in freezing weather. Older, the boy might have remarked this and wondered why not a big one; why should not a man who had not only seen the waste and extravagance of war, but who had in his blood an inherent voracious prodigality with material not his own, have burned everything in sight? Then he might have gone a step farther and thought that that was the reason: that niggard blaze was the living fruit of nights passed during those four years in the woods hiding from all men, blue and gray, with his strings of horses (captured horses, he called them). And older still, he might have divined the true reason: that the element of fire spoke to some deep mainspring of his father's being, as the element of steel or of powder spoke to other men, as the one weapon for the preservation of integrity, else breath were not worth the breathing, and hence to be regarded with respect and used with discretion.

But he did not think this now and he had seen those same niggard blazes all his life. He merely ate his supper beside it and was already half asleep over his iron plate when his father called him, and once more he followed the stiff back, the stiff and ruthless limp, up the slope and on to the starlit road where, turning, he could see his father against the stars but without face or depth—a shape black, flat, and bloodless as though cut from tin in the iron folds of the frockcoat which had not been made for him, the voice harsh like tin and without heat like tin:

"You were fixing to tell them. You would have told him."

He didn't answer. His father struck him with the flat of his hand on the side of the head, hard but without heat, exactly as he had struck the two mules at the store, exactly as he would strike either of them with any stick in order to kill a horse fly, his voice without heat or anger: "You're getting to be a man. You got to learn. You got to learn to stick to your own blood or you ain't going to have any blood to stick to you. Do you think either of them, any man there this morning, would? Don't you know all they wanted was a chance to get at me because they knew I had them beat? Eh?" Later, twenty years later, he was to tell himself, "If I had said they wanted only truth, justice, he would have hit me again." But now he said nothing. He was not crying. He just stood there. "Answer me," his father said.

"Yes," he whispered. His father turned. 30

"Get on to bed. We'll be there tomorrow."

Tomorrow they were there. In the early afternoon the wagon stopped before a paintless two-room house identical almost with the dozen others it had stopped before even in the boy's ten years, and again, as on the other dozen occasions, his mother and aunt got down and began to unload the wagon, although his two sisters and his father and brother had not moved.

"Likely hit ain't fitten for hawgs," one of the sisters said.

"Nevertheless, fit it will and you'll hog it and like it," his father said. "Get out of them chairs and help your Ma unload."

The two sisters got down, big, bovine, in a flutter of cheap ribbons; one of 35 them drew from the jumbled wagon bed a battered lantern, the other a worn broom. His father handed the reins to the older son and began to climb stiffly over the wheel. "When they get unloaded, take the team to the barn and feed them." Then he said, and at first the boy thought he was still speaking to his brother: "Come with me."

"Me?" he said.

"Yes," his father said. "You."

"Abner," his mother said. His father paused and looked back—the harsh level stare beneath the shaggy, graying, irascible brows.

"I reckon I'll have a word with the man that aims to begin tomorrow owning me body and soul for the next eight months."

They went back up the road. A week ago—or before last night, that is—he 40 would have asked where they were going, but not now. His father had struck him before last night but never before had he paused afterward to explain why; it was as if the blow and the following calm, outrageous voice still rang, repercussed, divulging nothing to him save the terrible handicap of being young, the light weight of his few years, just heavy enough to prevent his soaring free of the world as it seemed to be ordered but not heavy enough to keep him footed solid in it, to resist it and try to change the course of its events.

Presently he could see the grove of oaks and cedars and the other flowering trees and shrubs where the house would be, though not the house yet. They walked beside a fence massed with honeysuckle and Cherokee roses and came to a gate swinging open between two brick pillars, and now, beyond a sweep of drive, he saw the house for the first time and at that instant he forgot his father and the terror and despair both, and even when he remembered his father again (who had not stopped) the terror and despair did not return. Because, for all the twelve movings, they had sojourned until now in a poor country, a land of small farms and fields and houses, and he had never seen a house like this before. *Hit's big as a courthouse* he thought quietly, with a surge of peace and joy whose reason he could not have thought into words, being too young for that: *They are safe from him. People whose lives are a part of this peace and dignity are beyond his touch, he no more to them than a buzzing wasp: capable of stinging for a little moment but that's all; the spell of this peace and dignity rendering even the barns and stable and cribs which belong to it impervious to the puny flames he might contrive* . . . this, the peace and joy, ebbing for an instant as he looked again at the stiff black back, the stiff and implacable limp of the figure which was not dwarfed by the house, for the reason that it had never looked big anywhere and which now, against the serene columned backdrop, had more than ever that impervious quality of something cut ruthlessly from tin, depthless, as though, sidewise to the sun, it would cast no shadow. Watching him, the boy remarked the absolutely undeviating course which his father held and saw the stiff foot come squarely down in a pile of fresh droppings where a horse had stood in the drive and which his father could have avoided by a simple change of stride. But it ebbed only a moment, though he could not have thought this into words either, walking on in the spell of the house, which he could even want but without envy, without sorrow, certainly never with that ravening and jealous rage which unknown to him walked in the ironlike black coat before him: *Maybe he will feel it too. Maybe it will even change him now from what maybe he couldn't help but be.*

They crossed the portico. Now he could hear his father's stiff foot as it came down on the boards with clocklike finality, a sound out of all proportion to the displacement of the body it bore and which was not dwarfed either by the white door before it, as though it had attained to a sort of vicious and ravening minimum not to be dwarfed by anything—the flat, wide, black hat, the formal coat of broadcloth which had once been black but which had now that friction-glazed greenish cast of the bodies of old house flies, the lifted sleeve which was too large, the lifted hand like a curled claw. The door opened so promptly that the boy knew the Negro must have been watching them all the time, an old man with neat grizzled hair, in a linen jacket, who stood barring the door with his body, saying, "Wipe yo foots, white man, fo you come in here. Major ain't home nohow."

"Get out of my way, nigger," his father said, without heat too, flinging the door back and the Negro also and entering, his hat still on his head. And now the boy saw the prints of the stiff foot on the doorjamb and saw them appear on the pale rug behind the machinelike deliberation of the foot which seemed to bear (or transmit) twice the weight which the body compassed. The Negro was shouting "Miss Lula! Miss Lula!" somewhere behind them, then the boy, deluged as though by a warm wave by a suave turn of the carpeted stair and a pendant glitter of chandeliers and a mute gleam of gold frames, heard the swift feet and saw her too, a lady—perhaps he had never seen her like before either—in a gray, smooth gown with lace at the throat and an apron tied at the waist and the sleeves turned back, wiping cake or biscuit dough from her hands with a towel as she came up the hall, looking not at his father at all but at the tracks on the blond rug with an expression of incredulous amazement.

"I tried," the Negro cried. "I tole him to . . . "

"Will you please go away?" she said in a shaking voice. "Major de Spain is    45
not at home. Will you please go away?"

His father had not spoken again. He did not speak again. He did not even look at her. He just stood stiff in the center of the rug, in his hat, the shaggy iron-gray brows twitching slightly above the pebble-colored eyes as he appeared to examine the house with brief deliberation. Then with the same deliberation he turned; the boy watched him pivot on the good leg and saw the stiff foot drag around the arc of the turning, leaving a final long and fading smear. His father never looked at it, he never once looked down at the rug. The Negro held the door. It closed behind them, upon the hysteric and indistinguishable woman-wail. His father stopped at the top of the steps and scraped his boot clean on the edge of it. At the gate he stopped again. He stood for a moment, planted stiffly on the stiff foot, looking back at the house. "Pretty and white, ain't it?" he said. "That's sweat. Nigger sweat. Maybe it ain't white enough yet to suit him. Maybe he wants to mix some white sweat with it."

Two hours later the boy was chopping wood behind the house within which his mother and aunt and the two sisters (the mother and aunt, not the two girls, he knew that; even at this distance and muffled by walls the flat loud voices of the two girls emanated an incorrigible idle inertia) were setting up the stove to prepare a meal, when he heard the hooves and saw the linen-clad man on a fine sorrel mare, whom he recognized even before he saw the rolled rug in front of the Negro youth following on a fat bay carriage horse—a suffused, angry face vanishing, still at full gallop, beyond the corner of the house where his father and brother were sitting in the two tilted chairs; and a moment later, almost before he could have put the axe down, he heard the hooves again and watched the sorrel mare go back out of the yard, already galloping again. Then his father began to shout one of the sisters' names, who presently emerged backward from the kitchen door dragging the rolled rug along the ground by one end while the other sister walked behind it.

"If you ain't going to tote, go on and set up the wash pot," the first said.

"You, Sarty!" the second shouted. "Set up the wash pot!" His father appeared at the door, framed against that shabbiness, as he had been against that other bland perfection, impervious to either, the mother's anxious face at his shoulder.

"Go on," the father said. "Pick it up." The two sisters stooped, broad, lethar-    50
gic; stooping, they presented an incredible expanse of pale cloth and a flutter of tawdry ribbons.

"If I thought enough of a rug to have to git hit all the way from France I wouldn't keep hit where folks coming in would have to tromp on hit," the first said. They raised the rug.

"Abner," the mother said. "Let me do it."

"You go back and git dinner," his father said. "I'll tend to this."

From the woodpile through the rest of the afternoon the boy watched them, the rug spread flat in the dust beside the bubbling wash pot, the two sisters stooping over it with that profound and lethargic reluctance, while the father stood over them in turn, implacable and grim, driving them though never raising his voice again. He could smell the harsh homemade lye they were using; he saw his mother come to the door once and look toward them with an expression not anxious now but very like despair; he saw his father turn, and he fell to with the axe and saw from the corner of his eye his father raise from the ground a flattish fragment of field stone and examine it and return to the pot, and this time his mother actually spoke: "Abner. Abner. Please don't. Please, Abner."

Then he was done too. It was dusk; the whippoorwills had already begun. He   55 could smell coffee from the room where they would presently eat the cold food remaining from the mid-afternoon meal, though when he entered the house he realized they were having coffee again probably because there was a fire on the hearth, before which the rug now lay spread over the backs of the two chairs. The tracks of his father's foot were gone. Where they had been were now long, water-cloudy scoriations resembling the sporadic course of a lilliputian mowing machine.

It still hung there while they ate the cold food and then went to bed, scat-tered without order or claim up and down the two rooms, his mother in one bed, where his father would later lie, the older brother in the other, himself, the aunt, and the two sisters on pallets on the floor. But his father was not in bed yet. The last thing the boy remembered was the depthless, harsh silhouette of the hat and coat bending over the rug and it seemed to him that he had not even closed his eyes when the silhouette was standing over him, the fire almost dead behind it, the stiff foot prodding him awake. "Catch up the mule," his father said.

When he returned with the mule his father was standing in the back door, the rolled rug over his shoulder. "Ain't you going to ride?" he said.

"No. Give me your foot."

He bent his knee into his father's hand, the wiry, surprising power flowed smoothly, rising, he rising with it, on to the mule's bare back (they had owned a saddle once; the boy could remember it though not when or where) and with the same effortlessness his father swung the rug up in front of him. Now in the starlight they retraced the afternoon's path, up the dusty road rife with honey-suckle, through the gate and up the black tunnel of the drive to the lightless house, where he sat on the mule and felt the rough warp of the rug drag across his thighs and vanish.

"Don't you want me to help?" he whispered. His father did not answer and   60 now he heard again that stiff foot striking the hollow portico with that wooden and clocklike deliberation, that outrageous overstatement of the weight it car-ried. The rug, hunched, not flung (the boy could tell that even in the darkness) from his father's shoulder struck the angle of wall and floor with a sound unbe-lievably loud, thunderous, then the foot again, unhurried and enormous; a light came on in the house and the boy sat, tense, breathing steadily and quietly and just a little fast, though the foot itself did not increase its beat at all, descending the steps now; now the boy could see him.

"Don't you want to ride now?" he whispered. "We kin both ride now," the light within the house altering now, flaring up and sinking. *He's coming down the stairs now*, he thought. He had already ridden the mule up beside the horse block; presently his father was up behind him and he doubled the reins over and slashed the mule across the neck, but before the animal could begin to trot the hard, thin arm came around him, the hard, knotted hand jerking the mule back to a walk.

In the first red rays of the sun they were in the lot, putting plow gear on the mules. This time the sorrel mare was in the lot before he heard it at all, the rider collarless and even bareheaded, trembling, speaking in a shaking voice as the woman in the house had done, his father merely looking up once before stooping again to the hame he was buckling, so that the man on the mare spoke to his stooping back:

"You must realize you have ruined that rug. Wasn't there anybody here, any of your women . . . " he ceased, shaking, the boy watching him, the older brother leaning now in the stable door, chewing, blinking slowly and steadily at nothing apparently. "It cost a hundred dollars. But you never had a hundred dollars. You never will. So I'm going to charge you twenty bushels of corn against your crop. I'll add it in your contract and when you come to the commissary you can sign it. That won't keep Mrs. de Spain quiet but maybe it will teach you to wipe your feet off before you enter her house again."

Then he was gone. The boy looked at his father, who still had not spoken or even looked up again, who was now adjusting the logger-head in the hame.

"Pap," he said. His father looked at him—the inscrutable face, the shaggy 65 brows beneath where the gray eyes glinted coldly. Suddenly the boy went toward him, fast, stopping as suddenly. "You done the best you could!" he cried. "If he wanted hit done different why didn't he wait and tell you how? He won't git no twenty bushels! He won't git none! We'll gather hit and hide hit! I kin watch . . . "

"Did you put the cutter back in that straight stock like I told you?"

"No, sir," he said.

"Then go do it."

That was Wednesday. During the rest of that week he worked steadily, at what was within his scope and some which was beyond it, with an industry that did not need to be driven nor even commanded twice; he had this from his mother, with the difference that some at least of what he did he liked to do, such as splitting wood with the half-size axe which his mother and aunt had earned, or saved money somehow, to present him with at Christmas. In company with the two older women (and on one afternoon, even one of the sisters), he built pens for the shoat and the cow which were a part of his father's contract with the landlord, and one afternoon, his father being absent, gone somewhere on one of the mules, he went to the field.

They were running a middle buster now, his brother holding the plow 70 straight while he handled the reins, and walking beside the straining mule, the rich black soil shearing cool and damp against his bare ankles, he thought *Maybe this is the end of it. Maybe even that twenty bushels that seems hard to have to pay for just a rug will be a cheap price for him to stop forever and always from being what he used to be;* thinking, dreaming now, so that his brother had to speak sharply to him to mind the mule: *Maybe he even won't collect the twenty bushels. Maybe it will all add up and balance and vanish—corn, rug, fire; the terror and grief; the being pulled two ways like between two teams of horses—gone, done with for ever and ever.*

Then it was Saturday; he looked up from beneath the mule he was harnessing and saw his father in the black coat and hat. "Not that," his father said. "The wagon gear." And then, two hours later, sitting in the wagon bed behind his father and brother on the seat, the wagon accomplished a final curve, and he saw the weathered paintless store with its tattered tobacco- and patent-medicine posters and the tethered wagons and saddle animals below the gallery. He mounted the gnawed steps behind his father and brother, and there again was the lane of quiet, watching faces for the three of them to walk through. He saw the man in spectacles sitting at the plank table and he did not need to be told this was a Justice of the Peace; he sent one glare of fierce, exultant, partisan defiance at the man in collar and cravat now, whom he had seen but twice before in his life, and that on a galloping horse, who now wore on his face an expression not of rage but of amazed unbelief which the boy could not have known was at the incredible circumstance of being sued by one of his own tenants, and came and stood against his father and cried at the Justice: "He ain't done it! He ain't burnt ... "

"Go back to the wagon," his father said.

"Burnt?" the Justice said. "Do I understand this rug was burned too?"

"Does anybody here claim it was?" his father said. "Go back to the wagon." But he did not, he merely retreated to the rear of the room, crowded as that other had been, but not to sit down this time, instead, to stand pressing among the motionless bodies, listening to the voices:

"And you claim twenty bushels of corn is too high for the damage you did to    75
the rug?"

"He brought the rug to me and said he wanted the tracks washed out of it. I washed the tracks out and took the rug back to him."

"But you didn't carry the rug back to him in the same condition it was in before you made the tracks on it."

His father did not answer, and now for perhaps half a minute there was no sound at all save that of breathing, the faint, steady suspiration of complete and intent listening.

"You decline to answer that, Mr. Snopes?" Again his father did not answer. "I'm going to find against you, Mr. Snopes. I'm going to find that you were responsible for the injury to Major de Spain's rug and hold you liable for it. But twenty bushels of corn seems a little high for a man in your circumstances to have to pay. Major de Spain claims it cost a hundred dollars. October corn will be worth about fifty cents. I figure that if Major de Spain can stand a ninety-five dollar loss on something he paid cash for, you can stand a five-dollar loss you haven't earned yet. I hold you in damages to Major de Spain to the amount of ten bushels of corn over and above your contract with him, to be paid to him out of your crop at gathering time. Court adjourned."

It had taken no time hardly, the morning was but half begun. He thought    80
they would return home and perhaps back to the field, since they were late, far behind all other farmers. But instead his father passed on behind the wagon,

merely indicating with his hand for the older brother to follow with it, and crossed the road toward the blacksmith shop opposite, pressing on after his father, overtaking him, speaking, whispering up at the harsh, calm face beneath the weathered hat: "He won't git no ten bushels either. He won't git one. We'll . . . " until his father glanced for an instant down at him, the face absolutely calm, the grizzled eyebrows tangled above the cold eyes, the voice almost pleasant, almost gentle:

"You think so? Well, we'll wait till October anyway."

The matter of the wagon—the setting of a spoke or two and the tightening of the tires—did not take long either, the business of the tires accomplished by driving the wagon into the spring branch behind the shop and letting it stand there, the mules nuzzling into the water from time to time, and the boy on the seat with the idle reins, looking up the slope and through the sooty tunnel of the shed where the slow hammer rang and where his father sat on an upended cypress bolt, easily, either talking or listening, still sitting there when the boy brought the dripping wagon up out of the branch and halted it before the door.

"Take them on to the shade and hitch," his father said. He did so and returned. His father and the smith and a third man squatting on his heels inside the door were talking, about crops and animals; the boy, squatting too in the ammoniac dust and hoof-parings and scales of rust, heard his father tell a long and unhurried story out of the time before the birth of the older brother even when he had been a professional horsetrader. And then his father came up beside him where he stood before a tattered last year's circus poster on the other side of the store, gazing rapt and quiet at the scarlet horses, the incredible poisings and convulsions of tulle and tights and the painted leers of comedians, and said, "It's time to eat."

But not at home. Squatting beside his brother against the front wall, he watched his father emerge from the store and produce from a paper sack a segment of cheese and divide it carefully and deliberately into three with his pocket knife and produce crackers from the same sack. They all three squatted on the gallery and ate, slowly, without talking; then in the store again, they drank from a tin dipper tepid water smelling of the cedar bucket and of living beech trees. And still they did not go home. It was a horse lot this time, a tall rail fence upon and along which men stood and sat and out of which one by one horses were led, to be walked and trotted and then cantered back and forth along the road while the slow swapping and buying went on and the sun began to slant westward, they— the three of them—watching and listening, the older brother with his muddy eyes and his steady, inevitable tobacco, the father commenting now and then on certain of the animals, to no one in particular.

It was after sundown when they reached home. They ate supper by lamp-light, then, sitting on the doorstep, the boy watched the night fully accomplish, listening to the whippoorwills and the frogs, when he heard his mother's voice: "Abner! No! No! Oh, God. Oh, God. Abner!" and he rose, whirled, and saw the altered light through the door where a candle stub now burned in a bottle neck on the table and his father, still in the hat and coat, at once formal and burlesque as though dressed carefully for some shabby and ceremonial violence, emptying the reservoir of the lamp back into the five-gallon kerosene can from which it had been filled, while the mother tugged at his arm until he shifted the lamp to the other hand and flung her back, not savagely or viciously, just hard, into the wall, her hands flung out against the wall for balance, her mouth open and in her face the same quality of hopeless despair as had been in her voice. Then his father saw him standing in the door.

"Go to the barn and get that can of oil we were oiling the wagon with," he said. The boy did not move. Then he could speak.

"What . . . " he cried. "What are you . . . "

"Go get that oil," his father said. "Go."

Then he was moving, running, outside the house, toward the stable: this the old habit, the old blood which he had not been permitted to choose for himself, which had been bequeathed him willy nilly and which had run for so long (and who knew where, battening on what of outrage and savagery and lust) before it came to him. *I could keep on,* he thought. *I could run on and on and never look back, never need to see his face again. Only I can't. I can't,* the rusted can in his hand now, the liquid sploshing in it as he ran back to the house and into it, into the sound of his mother's weeping in the next room, and handed the can to his father.

"Ain't you going to even send a nigger?" he cried. "At least you sent a nigger 90 before!"

This time his father didn't strike him. The hand came even faster than the blow had, the same hand which had set the can on the table with almost excruciating care flashing from the can toward him too quick for him to follow it, gripping him by the back of his shirt and on to tiptoe before he had seen it quit the can, the face stooping at him in breathless and frozen ferocity, the cold, dead voice speaking over him to the older brother who leaned against the table, chewing with that steady, curious, sidewise motion of cows:

"Empty the can into the big one and go on. I'll catch up with you."

"Better tie him up to the bedpost," the brother said.

"Do like I told you," the father said. Then the boy was moving, his bunched shirt and the hard, bony hand between his shoulder-blades, his toes just touching the floor, across the room and into the other one, past the sisters sitting with spread heavy thighs in the two chairs over the cold hearth, and to where his mother and aunt sat side by side on the bed, the aunt's arm about his mother's shoulders.

"Hold him," the father said. The aunt made a startled movement. "Not you," 95 the father said. "Lennie. Take hold of him. I want to see you do it." His mother took him by the wrist. "You'll hold him better than that. If he gets loose don't you know what he is going to do? He will go up yonder." He jerked his head toward the road. "Maybe I'd better tie him."

"I'll hold him," his mother whispered.

"See you do then." Then his father was gone, the stiff foot heavy and measured upon the boards, ceasing at last.

Then he began to struggle. His mother caught him in both arms, he jerking and wrenching at them. He would be stronger in the end, he knew that. But he had no time to wait for it. "Lemme go!" he cried. "I don't want to have to hit you!"

"Let him go!" the aunt said. "If he don't go, before God, I am going up there myself!"

"Don't you see I can't?" his mother cried. "Sarty! Sarty! No! No! Help me, Lizzie!" 100

Then he was free. His aunt grasped at him but it was too late. He whirled, running, his mother stumbled forward on to her knees behind him, crying to the nearer sister: "Catch him, Net! Catch him!" But that was too late too, the sister (the sisters were twins, born at the same time, yet either of them now gave the impression of being, encompassing as much living meat and volume and weight as any other two of the family) not yet having begun to rise from the chair, her head, face, alone merely turned, presenting to him in the flying instant an astonishing expanse of young female features untroubled by any surprise even, wearing only an expression of bovine interest. Then he was out of the room, out of the house, in the mild dust of the starlit road and the heavy rifeness of honeysuckle, the pale ribbon unspooling with terrific slowness under his running feet, reaching the gate at last and turning in, running, his heart and lungs drumming, on up the drive toward the lighted house, the lighted door. He did not knock, he burst in, sobbing for breath, incapable for the moment of speech; he saw the astonished face of the Negro in the linen jacket without knowing when the Negro had appeared.

"De Spain!" he cried, panted. "Where's . . . " then he saw the white man too emerging from a white door down the hall. "Barn!" he cried. "Barn!"

"What?" the white man said. "Barn?"

"Yes!" the boy cried. "Barn!"

"Catch him!" the white man shouted. 105

But it was too late this time too. The Negro grasped his shirt, but the entire sleeve, rotten with washing, carried away, and he was out that door too and in the drive again, and had actually never ceased to run even while he was screaming into the white man's face.

Behind him the white man was shouting. "My horse! Fetch my horse!" and he thought for an instant of cutting across the park and climbing the fence into the road, but he did not know the park nor how the vine-massed fence might be and he dared not risk it. So he ran on down the drive, blood and breath roaring; presently he was in the road again though he could not see it. He could not hear either: the galloping mare was almost upon him before he heard her, and even then he held his course, as if the very urgency of his wild grief and need must in a moment more find him wings, waiting until the ultimate instant to hurl himself aside and into the weed-choked roadside ditch as the horse thundered past and on, for an instant in furious silhouette against the stars, the tranquil early summer night sky which, even before the shape of the horse and rider vanished, stained abruptly and violently upward: a long, swirling roar incredible and soundless, blotting the stars, and he springing up and into the road again, running again, knowing it was too late yet still running even after he heard the shot and an instant later, two shots, pausing now without knowing he had ceased to run, crying, "Pap! Pap!", running again before he knew he had begun to run, stumbling, tripping over something and scrabbling up again without ceasing to run, looking backward over his shoulder at the glare as he got up, running on among the invisible trees, panting, sobbing, "Father! Father!"

At midnight he was sitting on the crest of a hill. He did not know it was midnight and he did not know how far he had come. But there was no glare behind him now and he sat now, his back toward what he had called home for four days anyhow, his face toward the dark woods which he would enter when breath was strong again, small, shaking steadily in the chill darkness, hugging himself into the remainder of his thin, rotten shirt, the grief and despair now no longer terror and fear but just grief and despair. *Father. My father,* he thought. "He was brave!" he cried suddenly, aloud but not loud, no more than a whisper. "He was! He was in the war! He was in Colonel Sartoris' cav'ry!" not knowing that his father had gone to that war a private in the fine old European sense, wearing no uniform, admitting the authority of and giving fidelity to no man or army or flag, going to war as Malbrouck° himself did: for booty—it meant nothing and less than nothing to him if it were enemy booty or his own.

The slow constellations wheeled on. It would be dawn and then sun-up after a while and he would be hungry. But that would be tomorrow and now he was only cold, and walking would cure that. His breathing was easier now and he decided to get up and go on, and then he found that he had been asleep because he knew it was almost dawn, the night almost over. He could tell that from the whippoorwills. They were everywhere now among the dark trees below him, constant and inflectioned and ceaseless, so that, as the instant for giving over to the day birds drew nearer and nearer, there was no interval at all between them. He got up. He was a little stiff, but walking would cure that too as it would the cold, and soon there would be the sun. He went on down the hill, toward the dark woods within which the liquid silver voices of the birds called unceasing—the rapid and urgent beating of the urgent and quiring heart of the late spring night. He did not look back.

## QUESTIONS

1. After delivering his warning to Major de Spain, the boy Snopes does not actually witness what happens to his father and brother, nor what happens to the Major's barn. But what do you assume does happen? What evidence is given in the story?
2. What do you understand to be Faulkner's opinion of Abner Snopes? Make a guess, indicating details in the story that convey attitudes.
3. Which adjectives best describe the general tone of the story: calm, amused, disinterested, scornful, marveling, excited, impassioned? Point out passages that may be so described. What do you notice about the style in which these passages are written?

*Malbrouck:* John Churchill, Duke of Marlborough (1650–1722), English general victorious in the Battle of Blenheim (1704), which triumph drove the French army out of Germany. The French called him Malbrouck, a name they found easier to pronounce.

4. In tone and style, how does "Barn Burning" compare with Faulkner's story "A Rose for Emily" (Chapter Two)? To what do you attribute any differences?
5. Suppose that, instead of "Barn Burning," Faulkner had written another story told by Abner Snopes in the first person. Why would such a story need a style different from that of "Barn Burning"? (Suggestion: Notice Faulkner's descriptions of Abner Snopes's voice.)
6. Although "Barn Burning" takes place some thirty years after the Civil War, how does the war figure in it?

# IRONY

If a friend declares, "Oh, sure, I just *love* to have four papers fall due on the same day," you detect that the statement contains **irony.** This is **verbal irony,** the most familiar kind, in which we understand the speaker's meaning to be far from the usual meaning of the words—in this case, quite the opposite. (When the irony is found, as here, in a somewhat sour statement tinged with mockery, it is called **sarcasm.**)

Irony, of course, occurs in writing as well as in conversation. When in a comic moment in Isaac Bashevis Singer's "Gimpel the Fool" (Chapter Three) the sexton announces, "The wealthy Reb Gimpel invites the congregation to a feast in honor of the birth of a son," the people at the synagogue burst into laughter. They know that Gimpel, in contrast to the sexton's words, is not a wealthy man but a humble baker; that the son is not his own but his wife's lover's; and that the birth brings no honor to anybody. Verbal irony, then, implies a contrast or discrepancy between what is *said* and what is *meant*. But stories often contain other kinds of irony besides such verbal irony. A situation, for example, can be ironic if it contains some wry contrast or incongruity. In Jack London's "To Build a Fire" (Chapter Four), it is ironic that a freezing man, desperately trying to strike a match to light a fire and save himself, accidentally ignites all his remaining matches.

An entire story may be told from an **ironic point of view.** Whenever we sense a sharp distinction between the narrator of a story and the author, irony is likely to occur—especially when the narrator is telling us something that we are clearly expected to doubt or to interpret very differently. In "Gimpel the Fool," Gimpel (who tells his own story) keeps insisting on trusting people; but the author, a shrewder observer, makes it clear to us that the people Gimpel trusts are only tricking him. (This irony, by the way, does not prevent Gimpel from expressing a few things that Isaac Bashevis Singer believes, and perhaps expects us to believe.) And when we read Hemingway's "A Clean, Well-Lighted Place," surely we feel that most of the time the older waiter speaks for the author. Though the waiter gives us a respectful, compassionate view of a lonely old man, and we don't doubt that the view is Hemingway's, still, in the closing lines of the story we are reminded that author and waiter are not identical. Musing on the sleepless night ahead of him, the waiter tries to shrug off his problem—"After all, it is probably only insomnia"—but the reader, who recalls the waiter's bleak view of *nada*, nothingness, knows that it certainly isn't mere insomnia that keeps him awake but a dread of solitude and death. At that crucial moment, Hemingway and the older waiter part company, and we perceive an ironic point of view, and also a verbal irony, "After all, it is probably only insomnia."

Storytellers are sometimes fond of ironic twists of fate—developments that reveal a terrible distance between what people deserve and what they get, between what is and what ought to be. In the novels of Thomas Hardy, some hostile fate keeps playing tricks to thwart the main characters. In *Tess of the D'Urbervilles*, an all-important letter, thrust under a door, by chance slides beneath a carpet and is not received. An obvious prank of fate occurs in O. Henry's short story "The Gift of the Magi," in which a young wife sells her beautiful hair to buy her poor young husband a watch chain for Christmas, not knowing that, to buy combs for her hair, he has sold his watch. Such an irony is sometimes called an **irony of fate** or a **cosmic irony,** for it suggests that some malicious fate (or other spirit in the universe) is deliberately frustrating human efforts. (In O. Henry's story, however, the twist of fate leads to a happy ending; for the author suggests that, by their futile sacrifices, the lovers are drawn closer together.) Evidently, there is an irony of fate in the servant's futile attempt to escape Death in the fable "The Appointment in Samarra," and perhaps in the flaring up of the all-precious matches in "To Build a Fire" as well.

To notice an irony gives pleasure. It may move us to laughter, make us feel wonder, or arouse our sympathy. By so involving us, irony—whether in a statement, a situation, an unexpected event, or a point of view—can render a story more likely to strike us, to affect us, and to be remembered.

## James Joyce
ARABY                                                                                    1905

*James Joyce (1884–1941) quit Ireland at twenty to spend his mature life in voluntary exile on the continent, writing of nothing but Dublin, where he was born. In Trieste, Zurich, and Paris, he supported his family with difficulty, sometimes teaching in Berlitz language schools, until his writing won him fame and wealthy patrons. At first Joyce met difficulty in getting his work printed and circulated. Publication of* Dubliners *(1914), the collection of stories that includes "Araby," was delayed seven years because its prospective Irish publisher feared libel suits. (The book depicts local citizens, some of them recognizable, and views Dubliners mostly as a thwarted, self-*

James Joyce

*deceived lot.)* Portrait of the Artist as a Young Man *(1916), a novel of thinly veiled autobiography, recounts a young intellectual's breaking away from country, church, and home. Joyce's immense comic novel,* Ulysses *(1922), a parody of the* Odyssey, *spans eighteen hours in the life of a wandering Jew, a Dublin seller of advertising. Frank about sex but untitillating, the book was banned at one time by the U.S. Post Office. Joyce's later work stepped up its demands on readers. The challenging* Finnegans Wake *(1939), if read aloud, sounds as though a learned comic poet were sleep-talking, jumbling several languages. Joyce was an innovator whose bold experiments showed many other writers possibilities in fiction that had not earlier been imagined.*

North Richmond Street, being blind°, was a quiet street except at the hour when the Christian Brothers' School set the boys free. An uninhabited house of two stories stood at the blind end, detached from its neighbors in a square ground. The other houses of the street, conscious of decent lives within them, gazed at one another with brown imperturbable faces.

The former tenant of our house, a priest, had died in the back drawing-room. Air, musty from having long been enclosed, hung in all the rooms, and the waste room behind the kitchen was littered with old useless papers. Among these I found a few paper-covered books, the pages of which were curled and damp: *The Abbot,* by Walter Scott, *The Devout Communicant* and *The Memoirs of Vidocq°.* I liked the last best because its leaves were yellow. The wild garden behind the house contained a central apple-tree and a few straggling bushes under one of which I found the late tenant's rusty bicycle-pump. He had been a very charitable priest: in his will he had left all his money to institutions and the furniture of his house to his sister.

When the short days of winter came dusk fell before we had well eaten our dinners. When we met in the street the houses had grown somber. The space of sky above us was the color of ever-changing violet and towards it the lamps of the street lifted their feeble lanterns. The cold air stung us and we played till our bodies glowed. Our shouts echoed in the silent street. The career of our play brought us through the dark muddy lanes behind the houses where we ran the gantlet of the rough tribes from the cottages, to the back doors of the dark dripping gardens where odors arose from the ashpits, to the dark odorous stables where a coachman smoothed and combed the horse or shook music from the buckled harness. When we returned to the street light from the kitchen windows had filled the areas. If my uncle was seen turning the corner we hid in the shadow until we had seen him safely housed. Or if Mangan's sister° came out on the doorstep to call her brother in to his tea we watched her from our shadow peer up and down the street. We waited to see whether she would remain or go in and, if she remained, we left our shadow and walked up to Mangan's steps resignedly. She was waiting

---

*being blind:* being a dead-end street.     *The Abbot . . . Vidocq:* a popular historical romance (1820); a book of pious meditations by an eighteenth-century English Franciscan, Pacificus Baker; and the autobiography of François-Jules Vidocq (1775–1857), a criminal who later turned detective. *Mangan's sister:* an actual young woman in this story, but the phrase recalls Irish poet James Clarence Mangan (1803–1849) and his best-known poem, "Dark Rosaleen," which personifies Ireland as a beautiful woman for whom the poet yearns.

for us, her figure defined by the light from the half-opened door. Her brother always teased her before he obeyed and I stood by the railings looking at her. Her dress swung as she moved her body and the soft rope of her hair tossed from side to side.

Every morning I lay on the floor in the front parlor watching her door. The blind was pulled down within an inch of the sash so that I could not be seen. When she came out on the doorstep my heart leaped. I ran to the hall, seized my books and followed her. I kept her brown figure always in my eye and, when we came near the point at which our ways diverged, I quickened my pace and passed her. This happened morning after morning. I had never spoken to her, except for a few casual words, and yet her name was like a summons to all my foolish blood.

Her image accompanied me even in places the most hostile to romance. On Saturday evenings when my aunt went marketing I had to go to carry some of the parcels. We walked through the flaring streets, jostled by drunken men and bargaining women, amid the curses of laborers, the shrill litanies of shopboys who stood on guard by the barrels of pigs' cheeks, the nasal chanting of street singers, who sang a *come-all-you* about O'Donovan Rossa°, or a ballad about the troubles in our native land. These noises converged in a single sensation of life for me: I imagined that I bore my chalice safely through the throng of foes. Her name sprang to my lips at moments in strange prayers and praises which I myself did not understand. My eyes were often full of tears (I could not tell why) and at times a flood from my heart seemed to pour itself out into my bosom. I thought little of the future. I did not know whether I would ever speak to her or not or, if I spoke to her, how I could tell her of my confused adoration. But my body was like a harp and her words and gestures were like fingers running upon the wires.

One evening I went into the back drawing-room in which the priest had died. It was a dark rainy evening and there was no sound in the house. Through one of the broken panes I heard the rain impinge upon the earth, the fine incessant needles of water playing in the sodden beds. Some distant lamp or lighted window gleamed below me. I was thankful that I could see so little. All my senses seemed to desire to veil themselves and, feeling that I was about to slip from them, I pressed the palms of my hands together until they trembled, murmuring: *O love! O love!* many times.

At last she spoke to me. When she addressed the first words to me I was so confused that I did not know what to answer. She asked me was I going to *Araby*. I forget whether I answered yes or no. It would be a splendid bazaar, she said; she would love to go.

—And why can't you? I asked.

While she spoke she turned a silver bracelet round and round her wrist. She could not go, she said, because there would be a retreat that week in her

---

*come-all-you about O'Donovan Rossa:* the street singers earned their living by singing timely songs that usually began, "Come all you gallant Irishmen / And listen to my song." Their subject, also called Dynamite Rossa, was a popular hero jailed by the British for advocating violent rebellion.

convent°. Her brother and two other boys were fighting for their caps and I was alone at the railings. She held one of the spikes, bowing her head towards me. The light from the lamp opposite our door caught the white curve of her neck, lit up her hair that rested there and, falling, lit up the hand upon the railing. It fell over one side of her dress and caught the white border of a petticoat, just visible as she stood at ease.

—It's well for you, she said.                                                                                        10

—If I go, I said, I will bring you something.

What innumerable follies laid waste my waking and sleeping thoughts after that evening! I wished to annihilate the tedious intervening days. I chafed against the work of school. At night in my bedroom and by day in the classroom her image came between me and the page I strove to read. The syllables of the word *Araby* were called to me through the silence in which my soul luxuriated and cast an Eastern enchantment over me. I asked for leave to go to the bazaar on Saturday night. My aunt was surprised and hoped it was not some Freemason° affair. I answered few questions in class. I watched my master's face pass from amiability to sternness; he hoped I was not beginning to idle. I could not call my wandering thoughts together. I had hardly any patience with the serious work of life which, now that it stood between me and my desire, seemed to me child's play, ugly monotonous child's play.

On Saturday morning I reminded my uncle that I wished to go to the bazaar in the evening. He was fussing at the hall-stand, looking for the hatbrush, and answered me curtly:

—Yes, boy, I know.

As he was in the hall I could not go into the front parlor and lie at the win-    15 dow. I left the house in bad humor and walked slowly towards the school. The air was pitilessly raw and already my heart misgave me.

When I came home to dinner my uncle had not yet been home. Still it was early. I sat staring at the clock for some time and, when its ticking began to irritate me, I left the room. I mounted the staircase and gained the upper part of the house. The high cold empty gloomy rooms liberated me and I went from room to room singing. From the front window I saw my companions playing below in the street. Their cries reached me weakened and indistinct and, leaning my forehead against the cool glass, I looked over at the dark house where she lived. I may have stood there for an hour, seeing nothing but the brown-clad figure cast by my imagination, touched discreetly by the lamplight at the curved neck, at the hand upon the railings and at the border below the dress.

When I came downstairs again I found Mrs. Mercer sitting at the fire. She was an old garrulous woman, a pawnbroker's widow, who collected used stamps for some pious purpose. I had to endure the gossip of the tea-table. The meal was

---

*a retreat . . . in her convent:* a week devoted to religious observances more intense than usual, at the convent school Miss Mangan attends; probably she will have to listen to a number of hellfire sermons.    *Freemason:* Catholics in Ireland viewed the Masonic order as a Protestant conspiracy against them.

prolonged beyond an hour and still my uncle did not come. Mrs. Mercer stood up to go: she was sorry she couldn't wait any longer, but it was after eight o'clock and she did not like to be out late, as the night air was bad for her. When she had gone I began to walk up and down the room, clenching my fists. My aunt said:

—I'm afraid you may put off your bazaar for this night of Our Lord.

At nine o'clock I heard my uncle's latchkey in the halldoor. I heard him talking to himself and heard the hall-stand rocking when it had received the weight of his overcoat. I could interpret these signs. When he was midway through his dinner I asked him to give me the money to go to the bazaar. He had forgotten.

—The people are in bed and after their first sleep now, he said.          20

I did not smile. My aunt said to him energetically:

—Can't you give him the money and let him go? You've kept him late enough as it is.

My uncle said he was very sorry he had forgotten. He said he believed in the old saying: *All work and no play makes Jack a dull boy.* He asked me where I was going and, when I had told him a second time he asked me did I know *The Arab's Farewell to His Steed°.* When I left the kitchen he was about to recite the opening lines of the piece to my aunt.

I held a florin tightly in my hands as I strode down Buckingham Street towards the station. The sight of the streets thronged with buyers and glaring with gas recalled to me the purpose of my journey. I took my seat in a third-class carriage of a deserted train. After an intolerable delay the train moved out of the station slowly. It crept onward among ruinous houses and over the twinkling river. At Westland Row Station a crowd of people pressed to the carriage doors; but the porters moved them back, saying that it was a special train for the bazaar. I remained alone in the bare carriage. In a few minutes the train drew up beside an improvised wooden platform. I passed out on to the road and saw by the light-ed dial of a clock that it was ten minutes to ten. In front of me was a large build-ing which displayed the magical name.

I could not find any sixpenny entrance and, fearing that the bazaar would be          25
closed, I passed in quickly through a turnstile, handing a shilling to a weary-look-ing man. I found myself in a big hall girdled at half its height by a gallery. Nearly all the stalls were closed and the greater part of the hall was in darkness. I recog-nized a silence like that which pervades a church after a service. I walked into the center of the bazaar timidly. A few people were gathered about the stalls which were still open. Before a curtain, over which the words *Café Chantant°* were writ-ten in colored lamps, two men were counting money on a salver°. I listened to the fall of the coins.

---

*The Arab's Farewell to His Steed:* This sentimental ballad by a popular poet, Caroline Norton (1808–1877), tells the story of a nomad of the desert who, in a fit of greed, sells his beloved horse, then regrets the loss, flings away the gold he had received, and takes back his horse. Notice the echo of "Araby" in the song title.     *Café Chantant:* name for a Paris nightspot featuring topical songs. *salver:* a tray like that used in serving Holy Communion.

Remembering with difficulty why I had come I went over to one of the stalls and examined porcelain vases and flowered tea-sets. At the door of the stall a young lady was talking and laughing with two young gentlemen. I remarked their English accents and listened vaguely to their conversation.

—O, I never said such a thing!

—O, but you did!

—O, but I didn't!

—Didn't she say that? 30

—Yes. I heard her.

—O, there's a . . . fib!

Observing me the young lady came over and asked me did I wish to buy anything. The tone of her voice was not encouraging; she seemed to have spoken to me out of a sense of duty. I looked humbly at the great jars that stood like eastern guards at either side of the dark entrance to the stall and murmured:

—No, thank you.

The young lady changed the position of one of the vases and went back to 35 the two young men. They began to talk of the same subject. Once or twice the young lady glanced at me over her shoulder.

I lingered before her stall, though I knew my stay was useless, to make my interest in her wares seem the more real. Then I turned away slowly and walked down the middle of the bazaar. I allowed the two pennies to fall against the sixpence in my pocket. I heard a voice call from one end of the gallery that the light was out. The upper part of the hall was now completely dark.

Gazing up into the darkness I saw myself as a creature driven and derided by vanity; and my eyes burned with anguish and anger.

QUESTIONS

1. What images does the name of the bazaar conjure up for the boy? What ironic discrepancies appear between his dream of Araby and the reality?
2. How can it be claimed that "Araby" is told from an ironic point of view? Does the narrator of the story seem a boy—a naive or innocent narrator—or a mature man looking back through a boy's eyes?
3. Who besides the boy is the other central character in the story? How do we know that the boy's view of this character is not exactly the author's view? (It may help to look closely at the narrator's descriptions of the other major character, and of his own feelings.)
4. At what other moments in the story does the boy romanticize, or project an air of enchantment upon things?
5. In general, how would you describe the physical setting of "Araby" as Joyce details it in the first five paragraphs? Does he make Dublin seem a beautiful metropolis, a merry town, an ugly backwater, or what? And what do you make of the detail, in the opening sentence, that the boy's street has a dead end?
6. How does the time of day matter to this story? What is meaningful or suggestive, in the end, about the fall of night?

## Jorge Luis Borges

| THE GOSPEL ACCORDING TO MARK | 1970 |
|---|---|

*Translated by Norman Thomas di Giovanni in collaboration with the author*

*Jorge Luis Borges (1899–1986), an out-standing modern writer of Latin America, was born in Buenos Aires into a family prominent in Argentine history. Borges grew up bilingual, learning English from his English grandmother and receiving his early education from an English tutor. Caught in Europe by the outbreak of World War II, Borges lived in Switzerland and later Spain, where he joined the Ultraists, a group of experimental poets who renounced realism. On returning to Argentina, he edited a poetry magazine printed in the form of a poster and affixed to city walls. For his opposition to the regime of Colonel Juan*

Jorge Luis Borges

*Perón, Borges was forced to resign his post as a librarian and was mockingly offered a job as a chicken inspector. In 1955, after Perón was deposed, Borges became director of the national library and Professor of English Literature at the University of Buenos Aires. Since childhood a sufferer from poor eyesight, Borges eventually went blind. His eye problems may have encouraged him to work mainly in short, highly crafted forms: stories, essays, fables, and lyric poems full of elaborate music. His short stories, in* Ficciones *(1944),* El hacedor *(1960; translated as* Dreamtigers, *1964), and* Labyrinths *(1962), have been admired worldwide.*

These events took place at La Colorada ranch, in the southern part of the township of Junín, during the last days of March 1928. The protagonist was a medical student named Baltasar Espinosa. We may describe him, for now, as one of the common run of young men from Buenos Aires, with nothing more note-worthy about him than an almost unlimited kindness and a capacity for public speaking that had earned him several prizes at the English school° in Ramos Mejía. He did not like arguing, and preferred having his listener rather than him-self in the right. Although he was fascinated by the probabilities of chance in any game he played, he was a bad player because it gave him no pleasure to win. His wide intelligence was undirected; at the age of thirty-three, he still had not quali-fied for graduation in the subject to which he was most drawn. His father, who

English school: *a prep school that emphasized English (well-to-do Argentineans of this era wanted their children to learn English).*

was a freethinker° (like all the gentlemen of his day), had introduced him to the lessons of Herbert Spencer°, but his mother, before leaving on a trip for Montevideo, once asked him to say the Lord's Prayer and make the sign of the cross every night. Through the years, he had never gone back on that promise.

Espinosa was not lacking in spirit; one day, with more indifference than anger, he had exchanged two or three punches with a group of fellow-students who were trying to force him to take part in a university demonstration. Owing to an acquiescent nature, he was full of opinions, or habits of mind, that were questionable: Argentina mattered less to him than a fear that in other parts of the world people might think of us as Indians; he worshiped France but despised the French; he thought little of Americans but approved the fact that there were tall buildings, like theirs, in Buenos Aires; he believed the gauchos° of the plains to be better riders than those of hill or mountain country. When his cousin Daniel invited him to spend the summer months out at La Colorada, he said yes at once—not because he was really fond of the country, but more out of his natural complacency and also because it was easier to say yes than to dream up reasons for saying no.

The ranch's main house was big and slightly rundown; the quarters of the foreman, whose name was Gutre, were close by. The Gutres were three: the father, an unusually uncouth son, and a daughter of uncertain paternity. They were tall, strong, and bony, and had hair that was on the reddish side and faces that showed traces of Indian blood. They were barely articulate. The foreman's wife had died years before.

There in the country, Espinosa began learning things he never knew, or even suspected—for example, that you do not gallop a horse when approaching settlements, and that you never go out riding except for some special purpose. In time, he was to come to tell the birds apart by their calls.

After a few days, Daniel had to leave for Buenos Aires to close a deal on some cattle. At most, this bit of business might take him a week. Espinosa, who was already somewhat weary of hearing about his cousin's incessant luck with women and his tireless interest in the minute details of men's fashion, preferred staying on at the ranch with his textbooks. But the heat was unbearable, and even the night brought no relief. One morning at daybreak, thunder woke him. Outside, the wind was rocking the Australian pines. Listening to the first heavy drops of rain, Espinosa thanked God. All at once, cold air rolled in. That afternoon, the Salado overflowed its banks. 5

The next day, looking out over the flooded fields from the gallery of the main house, Baltasar Espinosa thought that the stock metaphor comparing the pampa to the sea was not altogether false—at least, not that morning—though W. H. Hudson° had remarked that the sea seems wider because we view it from a ship's deck and not from a horse or from eye level.

*freethinker:* person who rejects traditional beliefs, especially religious dogma, in favor of rational inquiry.   *Herbert Spencer:* a British philosopher (1870–1903) who championed the theory of evolution.   *gaucho:* a South American cowboy.   *W. H. Hudson:* an English naturalist and author (1841–1922) who wrote extensively about South America.

The rain did not let up. The Gutres, helped or hindered by Espinosa, the town dweller, rescued a good part of the livestock, but many animals were drowned. There were four roads leading to La Colorada; all of them were under water. On the third day, when a leak threatened the foreman's house, Espinosa gave the Gutres a room near the toolshed, at the back of the main house. This drew them all closer; they ate together in the big dining room. Conversation turned out to be difficult. The Gutres, who knew so much about country things, were hard put to it to explain them. One night, Espinosa asked them if people still remembered the Indian raids from back when the frontier command was located there in Junín. They told him yes, but they would have given the same answer to a question about the beheading of Charles I.° Espinosa recalled his father's saying that almost every case of longevity that was cited in the country was really a case of bad memory or of a dim notion of dates. Gauchos are apt to be ignorant of the year of their birth or of the name of the man who begot them.

In the whole house, there was apparently no other reading matter than a set of the *Farm Journal*, a handbook of veterinary medicine, a deluxe edition of the Uruguayan epic *Tabaré*, a history of shorthorn cattle in Argentina, a number of erotic or detective stories, and a recent novel called *Don Segundo Sombra*. Espinosa, trying in some way to bridge the inevitable after-dinner gap, read a couple of chapters of this novel to the Gutres, none of whom could read or write. Unfortunately, the foreman had been a cattle drover, and the doings of the hero, another cattle drover, failed to whet his interest. He said that the work was light, that drovers always traveled with a packhorse that carried everything they needed, and that, had he not been a drover, he would never have seen such far-flung places as the Laguna de Gómez, the town of Bragado, and the spread of the Núñez family in Chacabuco. There was a guitar in the kitchen; the ranch hands, before the time of the events I am describing, used to sit around in a circle. Someone would tune the instrument without ever getting around to playing it. This was known as a guitarfest.

Espinosa, who had grown a beard, began dallying in front of the mirror to study his new face, and he smiled to think how, back in Buenos Aires, he would bore his friends by telling them the story of the Salado flood. Strangely enough, he missed places he never frequented and never would: a corner of Cabrera Street on which there was a mailbox; one of the cement lions of a gateway on Jujuy Street, a few blocks from the Plaza del Once; an old barroom with a tiled floor, whose exact whereabouts he was unsure of. As for his brothers and his father, they would already have learned from Daniel that he was isolated—etymologically, the word was perfect—by the floodwaters.

Exploring the house, still hemmed in by the watery waste, Espinosa came 10 across an English Bible. Among the blank pages at the end, the Guthries—such was their original name—had left a handwritten record of their lineage. They were natives of Inverness;° had reached the New World, no doubt as common laborers, in the early part of the nineteenth century; and had intermarried with

---

*Charles I*: King of England, beheaded in 1649.    *Inverness*: a county in Scotland.

Indians. The chronicle broke off sometime during the 1870s, when they no longer knew how to write. After a few generations, they had forgotten English; their Spanish, at the time Espinosa knew them, gave them trouble. They lacked any religious faith, but there survived in their blood, like faint tracks, the rigid fanaticism of the Calvinist and the superstitions of the pampa Indian. Espinosa later told them of his find, but they barely took notice.

Leafing through the volume, his fingers opened it at the beginning of the Gospel according to Saint Mark. As an exercise in translation, and maybe to find out whether the Gutres understood any of it, Espinosa decided to begin reading them that text after their evening meal. It surprised him that they listened attentively, absorbed. Maybe the gold letters on the cover lent the book authority. It's still there in their blood, Espinosa thought. It also occurred to him that the generations of men, throughout recorded time, have always told and retold two stories—that of a lost ship which searches the Mediterranean seas for a dearly loved island, and that of a god who is crucified on Golgotha. Remembering his lessons in elocution from his schooldays in Ramos Mejía, Espinosa got to his feet when he came to the parables.

The Gutres took to bolting their barbecued meat and their sardines so as not to delay the Gospel. A pet lamb that the girl adorned with a small blue ribbon had injured itself on a strand of barbed wire. To stop the bleeding, the three had wanted to apply a cobweb to the wound, but Espinosa treated the animal with some pills. The gratitude that this treatment awakened in them took him aback. (Not trusting the Gutres at first, he'd hidden away in one of his books the 240 pesos he had brought with him.) Now, the owner of the place away, Espinosa took over and gave timid orders, which were immediately obeyed. The Gutres, as if lost without him, liked following him from room to room and along the gallery that ran around the house. While he read to them, he noticed that they were secretly stealing the crumbs he had dropped on the table. One evening, he caught them unawares, talking about him respectfully, in very few words.

Having finished the Gospel according to Saint Mark, he wanted to read another of the three Gospels that remained, but the father asked him to repeat the one he had just read, so that they could understand it better. Espinosa felt that they were like children, to whom repetition is more pleasing than variations or novelty. That night—this is not to be wondered at—he dreamed of the Flood; the hammer blows of the building of the Ark woke him up, and he thought that perhaps they were thunder. In fact, the rain, which had let up, started again. The cold was bitter. The Gutres had told him that the storm had damaged the roof of the toolshed, and that they would show it to him when the beams were fixed. No longer a stranger now, he was treated by them with special attention, almost to the point of spoiling him. None of them liked coffee, but for him there was always a small cup into which they heaped sugar.

The new storm had broken out on a Tuesday. Thursday night, Espinosa was awakened by a soft knock at his door, which, just in case, he always kept locked. He got out of bed and opened it; there was the girl. In the dark he could hardly make her out, but by her footsteps he could tell she was barefoot, and moments later, in bed, that she must have come all the way from the other end of the house naked. She did not embrace him or speak a single word; she lay beside him, trembling. It was the first time she had known a man. When she left, she did not kiss him; Espinosa realized that he didn't even know her name. For some reason that he did not want to pry into, he made up his mind that upon returning to Buenos Aires he would tell no one about what had taken place.

The next day began like the previous ones, except that the father spoke to    15
Espinosa and asked him if Christ had let Himself be killed so as to save all other men on earth. Espinosa, who was a freethinker but who felt committed to what he had read to the Gutres, answered, "Yes, to save everyone from Hell."

Gutre then asked, "What's Hell?"

"A place under the ground where souls burn and burn."

"And the Roman soldiers who hammered in the nails—were they saved, too?"

"Yes," said Espinosa, whose theology was rather dim.

All along, he was afraid that the foreman might ask him about what had    20
gone on the night before with his daughter. After lunch, they asked him to read the last chapters over again.

Espinosa slept a long nap that afternoon. It was a light sleep, disturbed by persistent hammering and by vague premonitions. Toward evening, he got up and went out onto the gallery. He said, as if thinking aloud, "The waters have dropped. It won't be long now."

"It won't be long now," Gutre repeated, like an echo.

The three had been following him. Bowing their knees to the stone pavement, they asked his blessing. Then they mocked at him, spat on him, and shoved him toward the back part of the house. The girl wept. Espinosa understood what awaited him on the other side of the door. When they opened it, he saw a patch of sky. A bird sang out. A goldfinch, he thought. The shed was without a roof; they had pulled down the beams to make the cross.

## QUESTIONS

1. What is about to happen to Baltasar Espinosa at the end of this story?
2. How old is Espinosa? What is ironic about his age?
3. What is the background of the Gutres family? How did they come to own an English Bible? Why is it ironic that they own this book?
4. The narrator claims that the protagonist, Espinosa, has only two noteworthy qualities: an almost unlimited kindness and a capacity for public speaking. How do these qualities become important in the story?
5. When Espinosa begins reading the Gospel of Saint Mark to the Gutres, what changes in their behavior does he notice?
6. What other action does Espinosa perform that earns the Gutres' gratitude?
7. Reread the last paragraph. Why is it ironic that the Gutres ask Espinosa's blessing and the daughter weeps?
8. Why do the Gutres kill Espinosa? What do they hope to gain?
9. Is the significance of Espinosa's death entirely ironic? Or does he resemble Christ in any important respect?

## Suggestions for Writing

1. Choose a subject you admire greatly: some person, place, film, sports team, work of fiction, or whatever. In a paragraph, describe it so that you make clear your admiration. Then rewrite the paragraph from the point of view of someone who detests the same subject. Try not to declare "I love this" or "I hate this," but select details and characteristics of your subject that will make the tone of each paragraph unmistakable.

2. Consider a short story in which the narrator is the central character: perhaps "A & P," "Greasy Lake," "Araby," "How I Met My Husband," "I Stand Here Ironing," or "The Use of Force." In a brief essay, show how the character of the narrator determines the style of the story. Examine language in particular—words or phrases, slang expressions, figures of speech, local or regional speech.

3. Take a short story or novel not included in this book—one by a writer of high reputation and distinctive style, such as William Faulkner, Ernest Hemingway, Raymond Carver, Flannery O'Connor, or another writer suggested by your instructor. Then write a passage of your own, in which you imitate the writer's style as closely as possible. Pay attention to tone, vocabulary, length and variety of sentences, amount of description. Find some place in the story to insert your original passage. Then type out two or three pages of the story, including your forgery, and make copies for the other members of the class. See if anyone can tell where the writer's prose stops and yours begins.

4. Freewrite for fifteen or twenty minutes, rapidly jotting down any thoughts you may have in answer to this question: From your daily contacts with people, what ironies do you at times become aware of? Consider ironies of language (in deliberately misleading or sarcastic remarks), ironies of situation (here you are, a trained computer programmer unable to convince a counterperson in a fast-food joint that you can correctly add up a check). Then, using any good perceptions you have generated, write and polish a short answer to the question, illustrating your remarks by reference to your own recalled experience and recent observations. Of course you might also find it useful to cite some ironies in any stories about everyday life.

5. Here are some other topics: "Irony in 'A Rose for Emily.'" "Irony in 'Greasy Lake.'" "Cosmic irony in Borges' 'The Gospel According to Mark.'" "Irony in 'The Jilting of Granny Weatherall.'" (Or what other story have you read that more keenly interests you?) What sorts of irony make the story more effective? In dealing with any of them, you may find the method of analysis a help to you. Before you write, read about this useful method in "Writing about a Story" in Supplement: Writing.

# 6 Theme

The **theme** of a story is whatever general idea or insight the entire story reveals. In some stories the theme is unmistakable. At the end of Aesop's fable about the council of the mice that can't decide who will bell the cat, the theme is stated in the moral: *It is easier to propose a thing than to carry it out.* In a work of commercial fiction, too, the theme (if any) is usually obvious. Consider a typical detective thriller in which, say, a rookie policeman trained in scientific methods of crime detection sets out to solve a mystery sooner than his rival, a veteran sleuth whose only laboratory is carried under his hat. Perhaps the veteran solves the case, leading to the conclusion (and the theme), "The old ways are the best ways after all." Another story by the same writer might dramatize the same rivalry but reverse the outcome, having the rookie win, thereby reversing the theme: "The times are changing! Let's shake loose from old-fashioned ways." In such commercial entertainments, a theme is like a length of rope with which the writer, patently and mechanically, trusses the story neatly (usually too neatly) into meaningful shape.

In literary fiction, a theme is seldom so obvious. That is, a theme need not be a moral or a message; it may be what the happenings add up to, what the story is about. When we come to the end of a finely wrought short story such as Ernest Hemingway's "A Clean, Well-Lighted Place" (Chapter Five), it may be easy to sum up the plot—to say what happens—but it is more difficult to sum up the story's main idea. Evidently, Hemingway relates events—how a younger waiter gets rid of an old man and how an older waiter then goes to a coffee bar—but in themselves these events seem relatively slight, though the story as a whole seems large (for its size) and full of meaning. For the meaning, we must look to other elements in the story besides what happens in it. And it is clear that Hemingway is most deeply interested in the thoughts and feelings of the older waiter, the character who has more and more to say as the story progresses, until at the end the story is entirely confined to his thoughts and perceptions. What is meaning-ful in these thoughts and perceptions? The older waiter understands the old man and sympathizes with his need for a clean, well-lighted place. If we say that, we are still talking about what happens in the story, though we have gone beyond merely recording its external events. But a theme is usually stated in *general* words. Another try: "Solitary people who cannot sleep need a cheerful, orderly place where they can drink with dignity." That's a little better. We have indicat-ed, at least, that Hemingway's story is about more than just an old man and a couple of waiters. But what about the older waiter's meditation on *nada*, nothing-ness? Coming near the end of the story, it takes great emphasis; and probably no good statement of Hemingway's theme can leave it out. Still another try at a statement: "Solitary people need a place of refuge from their terrible awareness that their lives (or perhaps, human lives) are essentially meaningless." Neither this nor any other statement of the story's theme is unarguably right, but at least the sentence helps the reader to bring into focus one primary idea that Hemingway seems to be driving at. When we finish reading "A Clean, Well-Lighted Place," we feel that there *is* such a theme, a unifying vision, even though we cannot reduce it absolutely to a tag. Like some freshwater lake alive with crea-tures, Hemingway's story is a broad expanse, reflecting in many directions. No wonder that many readers will view it differently.

Moral inferences may be drawn from the story, no doubt—for Hemingway is indirectly giving us advice for properly regarding and sympathizing with the lone-ly, the uncertain, and the old. But the story doesn't set forth a lesson that we are supposed to put into practice. One could argue that "A Clean, Well-Lighted Place" contains *several* themes—and other statements could be made to take in Hemingway's views of love, of communication between people, of dignity. Great short stories, like great symphonies, frequently have more than one theme.

In many a fine short story, theme is the center, the moving force, the princi-ple of unity. Clearly, such a theme is something other than the characters and events of its story. To say of James Joyce's "Araby" (page 177) that it is about a boy who goes to a bazaar to buy a gift for a young woman, only to arrive too late, is to summarize plot, not theme. (The theme *might* be put, "The illusions of a romantic child are vulnerable," or it might be put in any of a few hundred other ways.) Although the title of Isaac Bashevis Singer's "Gimpel the Fool" (Chapter Three) indicates the main character and suggests the subject (his "foolishness"), the theme—the larger realization that the story leaves us with—has to do not with foolishness, but with how to be wise.

Sometimes you will hear it said that the theme of a story (say, Faulkner's "Barn Burning") is "loss of innocence" or "initiation into maturity"; or that the theme of some other story (Thurber's "The Catbird Seat," for instance) is "the revolt of the downtrodden." This is to use *theme* in a larger and more abstract sense than we use it here. Although such general descriptions of theme can be useful—as in sorting a large number of stories into rough categories—we suggest that, in the beginning, you look for whatever truth or insight you think the writer of a story reveals. Try to sum it up *in a sentence*. By doing so, you will find yourself looking closely at the story, trying to define its principal meaning. You may find it helpful, in making your sentence-statement of theme, to consider these points:

1. Look back once more at the title of the story. From what you have read, what does it indicate?
2. Does the main character in any way change in the story? Does this character arrive at any eventual realization or understanding? Are you left with any realization or understanding you did not have before?
3. Does the author make any general observations about life or human nature? Do the characters make any? (Caution: Characters now and again will utter opinions with which the reader is not necessarily supposed to agree.)
4. Does the story contain any especially curious objects, mysterious flat characters, significant animals, repeated names, song titles, or whatever, that hint toward meanings larger than such things ordinarily have? In literary stories, such symbols may point to central themes. (For a short discussion of symbolism and a few illustrations, see Chapter Seven.)
5. When you have worded your statement of theme, have you cast your statement into general language, not just given a plot summary?
6. Does your statement hold true for the story as a whole, not for just part of it?

In distilling a statement of theme from a rich and complicated story, we have, of course, no more encompassed the whole story than a paleontologist taking a plaster mold of a petrified footprint has captured a living brontosaurus. A writer (other than a fabulist) does not usually set out with theme in hand, determined to make every detail in the story work to demonstrate it. Well then, the skeptical reader may ask, if only *some* stories have themes, if those themes may be hard to sum up, and if readers will probably disagree in their summations, why bother to state themes? Isn't it too much trouble? Surely it is, unless the effort to state a theme ends in pleasure and profit. Trying to sum up the point of a story in our own words is merely one way to make ourselves better aware of whatever we may have understood vaguely and tentatively. Attempted with loving care, such statements may bring into focus our scattered impressions of a rewarding story, may help to clarify and hold fast whatever wisdom the storyteller has offered us.

*Stephen Crane (1871–1900) was born in
Newark, New Jersey, a Methodist minister's last and fourteenth child. After flunk-
ing out of both Lafayette College and
Syracuse University, he became a journalist
in New York, specializing in grim life
among the down-and-out who people his
early self-published novel* Maggie: A Girl
of the Streets *(1893). Restlessly generat-
ing material for stories, Crane trekked to
the Southwest, New Orleans, and Mexico.
"The Open Boat" is based on experience.
En route to Havana to report the Cuban
revolution for the New York* Press, *Crane
was shipwrecked when the SS* Commodore
*sank in heavy seas east of New Smyrna,
Florida, on January 2, 1897. He escaped
in a ten-foot lifeboat with the captain and
two members of the crew. Later that year, Crane moved into a stately home in England
with Cora Taylor, former madam of a Florida brothel, hobnobbed with literary greats,
and lived beyond his means. Hounded by creditors, afflicted by tuberculosis, he died in
Germany at twenty-eight. Crane has been called the first writer of American realism.
His famed novel* The Red Badge of Courage *(1895) gives an imagined but convincing
account of a young Union soldier's initiation into battle. A handful of his short stories
appear immortal. He was an original poet, too, writing terse, sardonic poems in open
forms, at the time considered radical. In his short life, Crane greatly helped American
literature to come of age.*

Stephen Crane

> A Tale Intended to be after the Fact:
> Being the Experience of Four Men from the Sunk Steamer Commodore

### I

   None of them knew the color of the sky. Their eyes glanced level, and were
fastened upon the waves that swept toward them. These waves were of the hue of
slate, save for the tops, which were of foaming white, and all of the men knew
the colors of the sea. The horizon narrowed and widened, and dipped and rose,
and at all times its edge was jagged with waves that seemed thrust up in points
like rocks.

   Many a man ought to have a bathtub larger than the boat which here rode
upon the sea. These waves were most wrongfully and barbarously abrupt and tall,
and each frothtop was a problem in small-boat navigation.

The cook squatted in the bottom, and looked with both eyes at the six inches of gunwale which separated him from the ocean. His sleeves were rolled over his fat forearms, and the two flaps of his unbuttoned vest dangled as he bent to bail out the boat. Often he said, "Gawd! that was a narrow clip." As he remarked it he invariably gazed eastward over the broken sea.

The oiler, steering with one of the two oars in the boat, sometimes raised himself suddenly to keep clear of water that swirled in over the stern. It was a thin little oar, and it seemed often ready to snap.

The correspondent°, pulling at the other oar, watched the waves and wondered why he was there.

The injured captain, lying in the bow, was at this time buried in that profound dejection and indifference which comes, temporarily at least, to even the bravest and most enduring when, willy-nilly, the firm fails, the army loses, the ship goes down. The mind of the master of a vessel is rooted deep in the timbers of her, though he command for a day or a decade; and this captain had on him the stern impression of a scene in the grays of dawn of seven turned faces, and later a stump of a topmast with a white ball on it, that slashed to and fro at the waves, went low and lower, and down. Thereafter there was something strange in his voice. Although steady, it was deep with mourning, and of a quality beyond oration or tears.

"Keep 'er a little more south, Billie," said he.

"A little more south, sir," said the oiler in the stern.

A seat in this boat was not unlike a seat upon a bucking broncho, and by the same token a broncho is not much smaller. The craft pranced and reared and plunged like an animal. As each wave came, and she rose for it, she seemed like a horse making at a fence outrageously high. The manner of her scramble over these walls of water is a mystic thing, and, moreover, at the top of them were ordinarily these problems in white water, the foam racing down from the summit of each wave requiring a new leap, and a leap from the air. Then, after scornfully bumping a crest, she would slide and race and splash down a long incline, and arrive bobbing and nodding in front of the next menace.

A singular disadvantage of the sea lies in the fact that after successfully surmounting one wave you discover that there is another behind it just as important and just as nervously anxious to do something effective in the way of swamping boats. In a ten-foot dinghy one can get an idea of the resources of the sea in the line of waves that is not probable to the average experience which is never at sea in a dinghy. As each slaty wall of water approached, it shut all else from the view of the men in the boat, and it was not difficult to imagine that this particular wave was the final outburst of the ocean, the last effort of the grim water. There was a terrible grace in the move of the waves, and they came in silence, save for the snarling of the crests.

In the wan light the faces of the men must have been gray. Their eyes must have glinted in strange ways as they gazed steadily astern. Viewed from a balcony,

correspondent: foreign correspondent, newspaper reporter.

the whole thing would doubtless have been weirdly picturesque. But the men in the boat had no time to see it, and if they had had leisure, there were other things to occupy their minds. The sun swung steadily up the sky, and they knew it was broad day because the color of the sea changed from slate to emerald green streaked with amber lights, and the foam was like tumbling snow. The process of the breaking day was unknown to them. They were aware only of this effect upon the color of the waves that rolled toward them.

In disjointed sentences the cook and the correspondent argued as to the difference between a life-saving station and a house of refuge. The cook had said: "There's a house of refuge just north of the Mosquito Inlet Light, and as soon as they see us they'll come off in their boat and pick us up."

"As soon as who see us?" said the correspondent.

"The crew," said the cook.

"Houses of refuge don't have crews," said the correspondent. "As I under- 15 stand them, they are only places where clothes and grub are stored for the benefit of shipwrecked people. They don't carry crews."

"Oh, yes, they do," said the cook.

"No, they don't," said the correspondent.

"Well, we're not there yet, anyhow," said the oiler, in the stern.

"Well," said the cook, "perhaps it's not a house of refuge that I'm thinking of as being near Mosquito Inlet Light; perhaps it's a life-saving station."

"We're not there yet," said the oiler in the stern. 20


## II

As the boat bounced from the top of each wave the wind tore through the hair of the hatless men, and as the craft plopped her stern down again the spray slashed past them. The crest of each of these waves was a hill, from the top of which the men surveyed for a moment a broad tumultuous expanse, shining and wind-riven. It was probably splendid, it was probably glorious, this play of the free sea, wild with lights of emerald and white and amber.

"Bully good thing it's an on-shore wind," said the cook. "If not, where would we be? Wouldn't have a show."

"That's right," said the correspondent.

The busy oiler nodded his assent.

Then the captain, in the bow, chuckled in a way that expressed humor, con- 25 tempt, tragedy, all in one. "Do you think we've got much of a show now, boys?" said he.

Whereupon the three were silent, save for a trifle of hemming and hawing. To express any particular optimism at this time they felt to be childish and stupid, but they all doubtless possessed this sense of the situation in their minds. A young man thinks doggedly at such times. On the other hand, the ethics of their condition was decidedly against any open suggestion of hopelessness. So they were silent.

"Oh, well," said the captain, soothing his children, "we'll get ashore all right."

But there was that in his tone which made them think; so the oiler quoth, "Yes! if this wind holds."

The cook was bailing. "Yes! if we don't catch hell in the surf."

Canton-flannel gulls flew near and far. Sometimes they sat down on the sea, near patches of brown seaweed that rolled over the waves with a movement like carpets on a line in a gale. The birds sat comfortably in groups, and they were envied by some in the dinghy, for the wrath of the sea was no more to them than it was to a covey of prairie chickens a thousand miles inland. Often they came very close and stared at the men with black bead-like eyes. At these times they were uncanny and sinister in their unblinking scrutiny, and the men hooted angrily at them, telling them to be gone. One came, and evidently decided to alight on the top of the captain's head. The bird flew parallel to the boat and did not circle, but made short sidelong jumps in the air in chicken-fashion. His black eyes were wistfully fixed upon the captain's head. "Ugly brute," said the oiler to the bird. "You look as if you were made with a jacknife." The cook and the correspondent swore darkly at the creature. The captain naturally wished to knock it away with the end of the heavy painter, but he did not dare do it, because anything resembling an emphatic gesture would have capsized this freighted boat; and so, with his open hand, the captain gently and carefully waved the gull away. After it had been discouraged from the pursuit the captain breathed easier on account of his hair, and others breathed easier because the bird struck their minds at this time as being somehow gruesome and ominous.

In the meantime the oiler and the correspondent rowed. And also they rowed. They sat together in the same seat, and each rowed an oar. Then the oiler took both oars; then the correspondent took both oars; then the oiler; then the correspondent. They rowed and they rowed. The very ticklish part of the business was when the time came for the reclining one in the stern to take his turn at the oars. By the very last star of truth, it is easier to steal eggs from under a hen than it was to change seats in the dinghy. First the man in the stern slid his hand along the thwart and moved with care, as if he were of Sèvres.° Then the man in the rowing-seat slid his hand along the other thwart. It was all done with the most extraordinary care. As the two sidled past each other, the whole party kept watchful eyes on the coming wave, and the captain cried: "Look out, now! Steady, there!"

The brown mats of seaweed that appeared from time to time were like islands, bits of earth. They were travelling, apparently, neither one way nor the other. They were, to all intents, stationary. They informed the men in the boat that it was making progress slowly toward the land.

The captain, rearing cautiously in the bow after the dinghy soared on a great swell, said that he had seen the lighthouse at Mosquito Inlet. Presently the cook remarked that he had seen it. The correspondent was at the oars then, and for some reason he too wished to look at the lighthouse; but his back was toward the far shore, and the waves were important, and for some time he could not seize an

Sèvres: chinaware made in this French town.

opportunity to turn his head. But at last there came a wave more gentle than the others, and when at the crest of it he swiftly scoured the western horizon.

"See it?" said the captain.

"No," said the correspondent, slowly; "I didn't see anything." 35

"Look again," said the captain. He pointed. "It's exactly in that direction."

At the top of another wave the correspondent did as he was bid, and this time his eyes chanced on a small, still thing on the edge of the swaying horizon. It was precisely like the point of a pin. It took an anxious eye to find a lighthouse so tiny.

"Think we'll make it, Captain?"

"If this wind holds and the boat don't swamp, we can't do much else," said the captain.

The little boat, lifted by each towering sea and splashed viciously by the 40 crests, made progress that in the absence of seaweed was not apparent to those in her. She seemed just a wee thing wallowing, miraculously top up, at the mercy of five oceans. Occasionally a great spread of water, like white flames, swarmed into her.

"Bail her, cook," said the captain, serenely.

"All right, Captain," said the cheerful cook.

### III

It would be difficult to describe the subtle brotherhood of men that was here established on the seas. No one said that it was so. No one mentioned it. But it dwelt in the boat, and each man felt it warm him. They were a captain, an oiler, a cook, and a correspondent, and they were friends—friends in a more curiously iron-bound degree than may be common. The hurt captain, lying against the water-jar in the bow, spoke always in a low voice and calmly; but he could never command a more ready and swiftly obedient crew than the motley three of the dinghy. It was more than a mere recognition of what was best for the common safety. There was surely in it a quality that was personal and heart-felt. And after this devotion to the commander of the boat, there was this comradeship, that the correspondent, for instance, who had been taught to be cynical of men, knew even at the time was the best experience of his life. But no one said that it was so. No one mentioned it.

"I wish we had a sail," remarked the captain. "We might try my overcoat on the end of an oar, and give you two boys a chance to rest." So the cook and the correspondent held the mast and spread wide the overcoat; the oiler steered; and the little boat made good way with her new rig. Sometimes the oiler had to scull sharply to keep a sea from breaking into the boat, but otherwise sailing was a success.

Meanwhile the lighthouse had been growing slowly larger. It had now almost 45 assumed color, and appeared like a little gray shadow on the sky. The man at the oars could not be prevented from turning his head rather often to try for a glimpse of this little gray shadow.

At last, from the top of each wave, the men in the tossing boat could see land. Even as the lighthouse was an upright shadow on the sky, this land seemed but a long black shadow on the sea. It certainly was thinner than paper. "We must be about opposite New Smyrna," said the cook, who had coasted this shore often in schooners. "Captain, by the way, I believe they abandoned that life-saving station there about a year ago."

"Did they?" said the captain.

The wind slowly died away. The cook and the correspondent were not now obliged to slave in order to hold high the oar. But the waves continued their old impetuous swooping at the dinghy, and the little craft, no longer under way, struggled woundily over them. The oiler or the correspondent took the oars again.

Shipwrecks are apropos of nothing. If men could only train for them and have them occur when the men had reached pink condition, there would be less drowning at sea. Of the four in the dinghy none had slept any time worth mentioning for two days and two nights previous to embarking in the dinghy, and in the excitement of clambering about the deck of a foundering ship they had also forgotten to eat heartily.

For these reasons, and for others, neither the oiler nor the correspondent was    50
fond of rowing at this time. The correspondent wondered ingenuously how in the name of all that was sane could there be people who thought it amusing to row a boat. It was not an amusement; it was a diabolical punishment, and even a genius of mental aberrations could never conclude that it was anything but a horror to the muscles and crime against the back. He mentioned to the boat in general how the amusement of rowing struck him, and the weary-faced oiler smiled in full sympathy. Previously to the foundering, by the way, the oiler had worked double watch in the engine-room of the ship.

"Take her easy now, boys," said the captain. "Don't spend yourselves. If we have to run a surf you'll need all your strength, because we'll sure have to swim for it. Take your time."

Slowly the land arose from the sea. From a black line it became a line of black and a line of white—trees and sand. Finally the captain said that he could make out a house on the shore. "That's the house of refuge, sure," said the cook. "They'll see us before long, and come out after us."

The distant lighthouse reared high. "The keeper ought to be able to make us out now, if he's looking through a glass," said the captain. "He'll notify the life-saving people."

"None of those other boats could have got ashore to give word of the wreck," said the oiler, in a low voice, "else the life-boat would be out hunting us."

Slowly and beautifully the land loomed out of the sea. The wind came again.    55
It had veered from the north-east to the south-east. Finally a new sound struck the ears of the men in the boat. It was the low thunder of the surf on the shore. "We'll never be able to make the lighthouse now," said the captain. "Swing her head a little more north, Billie."

"A little more north, sir," said the oiler.

Whereupon the little boat turned her nose once more down the wind, and all but the oarsman watched the shore grow. Under the influence of this expansion doubt and direful apprehension were leaving the minds of the men. The management of the boat was still most absorbing, but it could not prevent a quiet cheerfulness. In an hour, perhaps, they would be ashore.

Their backbones had become thoroughly used to balancing in the boat, and they now rode this wild colt of a dinghy like circus men. The correspondent thought that he had been drenched to the skin, but happening to feel in the top pocket of his coat, he found therein eight cigars. Four of them were soaked with seawater; four were perfectly scatheless. After a search, somebody produced three dry matches; and thereupon the four waifs rode impudently in their little boat and, with an assurance of an impending rescue shining in their eyes, puffed at the big cigars, and judged well and ill of all men. Everybody took a drink of water.

## IV

"Cook," remarked the captain, "there don't seem to be any signs of life about your house of refuge."

"No," replied the cook. "Funny they don't see us!" 60

A broad stretch of lowly coast lay before the eyes of the men. It was of low dunes topped with dark vegetation. The roar of the surf was plain, and sometimes they could see the white lip of a wave as it spun up the beach. A tiny house was blocked out black upon the sky. Southward, the slim lighthouse lifted its little gray length.

Tide, wind, and waves were swinging the dinghy northward. "Funny they don't see us," said the men.

The surf's roar was here dulled, but its tone was nevertheless thunderous and mighty. As the boat swam over the great rollers the men sat listening to this roar. "We'll swamp sure," said everybody.

It is fair to say here that there was not a life-saving station within twenty miles in either direction; but the men did not know this fact, and in consequence they made dark and opprobrious remarks concerning the eyesight of the nation's life-savers. Four scowling men sat in the dinghy and surpassed records in the invention of epithets.

"Funny they don't see us." 65

The light-heartedness of a former time had completely faded. To their sharpened minds it was easy to conjure pictures of all kinds of incompetency and blindness and, indeed, cowardice. There was the shore of the populous land, and it was bitter and bitter to them that from it came no sign.

"Well," said the captain, ultimately, "I suppose we'll have to make a try for ourselves. If we stay out here too long, we'll none of us have strength left to swim after the boat swamps."

And so the oiler, who was at the oars, turned the boat straight for the shore. There was a sudden tightening of muscles. There was some thinking.

"If we don't all get ashore," said the captain—"if we don't all get ashore, I suppose you fellows know where to send news of my finish?"

They then briefly exchanged some addresses and admonitions. As for the 70 reflections of the men, there was a great deal of rage in them. Perchance they might be formulated thus: "If I am going to be drowned—if I am going to be drowned—if I am going to be drowned, why, in the name of the seven made gods who rule the sea, was I allowed to come thus far and contemplate sand and trees? Was I brought here merely to have my nose dragged away as I was about to nibble the sacred cheese of life? It is preposterous. If this old ninny-woman, Fate, cannot do better than this, she should be deprived of the management of men's fortunes. She is an old hen who knows not her intention. If she has decided to drown me, why did she not do it in the beginning and save me all this trouble? The whole affair is absurd.—But no; she cannot mean to drown me. She dare not drown me. She cannot drown me. Not after all this work." Afterward the man might have had an impulse to shake his fist at the clouds. "Just you drown me, now, and then hear what I call you!"

The billows that came at this time were more formidable. They seemed always just about to break and roll over the little boat in a turmoil of foam. There was a preparatory and long growl in the speech of them. No mind unused to the sea would have concluded that the dinghy could ascend these sheer heights in time. The shore was still afar. The oiler was a wily surfman. "Boys," he said swiftly, "she won't live three minutes more, and we're too far out to swim. Shall I take her to sea again, Captain?

"Yes; go ahead!" said the captain.

This oiler, by a series of quick miracles and fast and steady oarsmanship, turned the boat in the middle of the surf and took her safely to sea again.

There was a considerable silence as the boat bumped over the furrowed sea to deeper water. Then somebody in gloom spoke: "Well, anyhow, they must have seen us from the shore by now."

The gulls went in slanting flight up the wind toward the gray, desolate east. 75 A squall, marked by dinghy clouds and clouds brick-red like smoke from a burning building, appeared from the south-east.

"What do you think of those life-saving people? Ain't they peaches?"

"Funny they haven't seen us."

"Maybe they think we're out here for sport! Maybe they think we're fishin'. Maybe they think we're damned fools."

It was a long afternoon. A changed tide tried to force them southward, but wind and wave said northward. Far ahead, where coast-line, sea, and sky formed their mighty angle, there were little dots which seemed to indicate a city on the shore.

"St. Augustine?" 80

The captain shook his head. "Too near Mosquito Inlet."

And the oiler rowed, and then the correspondent rowed; then the oiler rowed. It was a weary business. The human back can become the seat of more aches and pains than are registered in books for the composite anatomy of a regiment. It is a limited area, but it can become the theatre of innumerable muscular conflicts, tangles, wrenches, knots, and other comforts.

"Did you ever like to row, Billie?" asked the correspondent.

"No," said the oiler; "hang it!"

When one exchanged the rowing-seat for a place in the bottom of the boat, he suffered a bodily depression that caused him to be careless of everything save an obligation to wiggle one finger. There was cold sea-water swashing to and fro in the boat, and he lay in it. His head, pillowed on a thwart, was within an inch of the swirl of a wave-crest, and sometimes a particularly obstreperous sea came inboard and drenched him once more. But these matters did not annoy him. It is almost certain that if the boat had capsized he would have tumbled comfortably upon the ocean as if he felt sure that it was a great soft mattress.

"Look! There's a man on the shore!"

"Where?"

"There! See 'im?"

"Yes, sure! He's walking along."

"Now he's stopped. Look! He's facing us!"

"He's waving at us!"

"So he is! By thunder!"

"Ah, now we're all right! Now we're all right! There'll be a boat out here for us in half an hour."

"He's going on. He's running. He's going up to that house there."

The remote beach seemed lower than the sea, and it required a searching glance to discern the little black figure. The captain saw a floating stick, and they rowed to it. A bath towel was by some weird chance in the boat, and, tying this on the stick, the captain waved it. The oarsman did not dare turn his head, so he was obliged to ask questions.

"What's he doing now?"

"He's standing still again. He's looking, I think.—There he goes again— toward the house.—Now he's stopped again."

"Is he waving at us?"

"No, not now; he was, though."

"Look! There comes another man!"

"He's running."

"Look at him go, would you!"

"Why, he's on a bicycle. Now he's met the other man. They're both waving at us. Look!"

"There comes something up the beach."

"What the devil is that thing?"

"Why, it looks like a boat."

"Why, certainly, it's a boat."

"No; it's on wheels."

"Yes, so it is. Well, that must be the life-boat. They drag them along shore on a wagon."

"That's the life-boat, sure."

"No, by God, it's—it's an omnibus."

"I tell you it's a life-boat."

"It is not! It's an omnibus. I can see it plain. See? One of the these big hotel omnibuses."

"By thunder, you're right. It's an omnibus, sure as fate. What do you suppose they are doing with an omnibus? Maybe they are going around collecting the life-crew, hey?"

"That's it, likely. Look! There's a fellow waving a little black flag. He's 115 standing on the steps of the omnibus. There come those other two fellows. Now they're all talking together. Look at the fellow with the flag. Maybe he ain't waving it!"

"That ain't a flag, is it? That's his coat. Why, certainly, that's his coat."

"So it is; it's his coat. He's taken it off and is waving it around his head. But would you look at him swing it!"

"Oh, say, there isn't any life-saving station there. That's just a winter-resort hotel omnibus that has brought over some of the boarders to see us drown."

"What's that idiot with the coat mean? What's he signalling, anyhow?"

"It looks as if he were trying to tell us to go north. There must be a life-sav- 120 ing station up there."

"No; he thinks we're fishing. Just giving us a merry hand. See? Ah, there, Willie!"

"Well, I wish I could make something out of those signals. What do you suppose he means?"

"He don't mean anything; he's just playing."

"Well, if he'd just signal us to try the surf again, or to go to sea and wait, or go north, or go south, or go to hell, there would be some reason in it. But look at him! He just stands there and keeps his coat revolving like a wheel. The ass!"

"There come more people." 125

"Now there's quite a mob. Look! Isn't that a boat?"

"Where? Oh, I see where you mean. No, that's no boat."

"That fellow is still waving his coat."

"He must think we like to see him do that. Why don't he quit it? It don't mean anything."

"I don't know. I think he is trying to make us go north. It must be that 130 there's a life-saving station there somewhere."

"Say, he ain't tired yet. Look at 'im wave!"

"Wonder how long he can keep that up. He's been revolving his coat ever since he caught sight of us. He's an idiot. Why aren't they getting men to bring a boat out? A fishing boat—one of those big yawls—could come out here all right. Why don't he do something?"

"Oh, it's all right now."

"They'll have a boat out here for us in less than no time, now that they've seen us."

A faint yellow tone came into the sky over the low land. The shadows on the 135 sea slowly deepened. The wind bore coldness with it, and the men began to shiver.

"Holy smoke!" said one, allowing his voice to express his impious mood, "If we keep on monkeying out here! If we've got to flounder out here all night!"

"Oh, we'll never have to stay here all night! Don't you worry. They've seen us now, and it won't be long before they'll come chasing out after us."

The shore grew dusky. The man waving a coat blended gradually into this gloom, and it swallowed in the same manner the omnibus and the group of people. The spray, when it dashed uproariously over the side, made the voyagers shrink and swear like men who were being branded.

"I'd like to catch the chump who waved the coat. I feel like socking him one, just for luck."

"Why? What did he do?"

"Oh, nothing, but then he seemed so damned cheerful."

In the meantime the oiler rowed, and then the correspondent rowed, and then the oiler rowed. Gray-faced and bowed forward, they mechanically, turn by turn, plied the leaden oars. The form of the lighthouse had vanished from the southern horizon, but finally a pale star appeared, just lifting from the sea. The streaked saffron in the west passed before the all-merging darkness, and the sea to the east was black. The land had vanished, and was expressed only by the low and drear thunder of the surf.

"If I am going to be drowned—if I am going to be drowned—if I am going to be drowned, why, in the name of the seven gods who rule the sea, was I allowed to come thus far and contemplate sand and trees? Was I brought here merely to have my nose dragged away as I was about to nibble the sacred cheese of life?"

The patient captain, drooped over the water-jar, was sometimes obliged to speak to the oarsman.

"Keep her head up! Keep her head up!"

"Keep her head, up, sir." The voices were weary and low.

This was surely a quiet evening. All save the oarsman lay heavily and listlessly in the boat's bottom. As for him, his eyes were just capable of noting the tall black waves that swept forward in a most sinister silence, save for an occasional subdued growl of a crest.

The cook's head was on a thwart, and he looked without interest at the water under this nose. He was deep in other scenes. Finally he spoke. "Billie," he murmured, dreamfully, "what kind of pie do you like best?"

## V

"Pie!" said the oiler and the correspondent, agitatedly. "Don't talk about those things, blast you!"

"Well," said the cook, "I was just thinking about ham sandwiches, and—"

A night on the sea in an open boat is a long night. As darkness settled finally, the shine of the light, lifting from the sea in the south, changed to full gold. On the northern horizon a new light appeared, a small bluish gleam on the edge of the waters. These two lights were the furniture of the world. Otherwise there was nothing but waves.

Two men huddled in the stern, and distances were so magnificent in the dinghy that the rower was enabled to keep his feet partly warm by thrusting them under his companions. Their legs indeed extended far under the rowingseat until they touched the feet of the captain forward. Sometimes, despite the efforts of the tired oarsman, a wave came piling into the boat, an icy wave of the night, and the chilling water soaked them anew. They would twist their bodies for a moment and groan, and sleep the dead sleep once more, while the water in the boat gurgled about them as the craft rocked.

The plan of the oiler and the correspondent was for one to row until he lost the ability, and then arouse the other from his sea-water couch in the bottom of the boat.

The oiler plied the oars until his head drooped forward and the overpowering sleep blinded him; and he rowed yet afterward. Then he touched a man in the bottom of the boat, and called his name. "Will you spell me for a little while?" he said meekly.

"Sure, Billie," said the correspondent, awaking and dragging himself to a sit- 155 ting position. They exchanged places carefully, and the oiler, cuddling down in the sea-water at the cook's side, seemed to go to sleep instantly.

The particular violence of the sea had ceased. The waves came without snarling. The obligation of the man at the oars was to keep the boat headed so that the tilt of the roller would not capsize her, and to preserve her from filling when the crests rushed past. The black waves were silent and hard to be seen in the darkness. Often one was almost upon the boat before the oarsman was aware.

In a low voice the correspondent addressed the captain. He was not sure that the captain was awake, although this iron man seemed to be always awake. "Captain, shall I keep her making for that light north, sir?"

The same steady voice answered him. "Yes. Keep it about two points off the port bow."

The cook had tied a life-belt around himself in order to get even the warmth which this clumsy cork contrivance could donate, and he seemed almost stove-like when a rower, whose teeth invariably chattered wildly as soon as he ceased his labor, dropped down to sleep.

The correspondent, as he rowed, looked down at the two men sleeping 160 underfoot. The cook's arm was around the oiler's shoulders, and, with their fragmentary clothing and haggard faces, they were the babes of the sea—a grotesque rendering of the old babes in the wood.

Later he must have grown stupid at his work, for suddenly there was a growling of water, and a crest came with a roar and a swash into the boat, and it was a wonder that it did not set the cook afloat in his life-belt. The cook continued to sleep, but the oiler sat up, blinking his eyes and shaking with the new cold.

"Oh, I'm awful sorry, Billie," said the correspondent, contritely.

"That's all right, old boy," said the oiler, and lay down again and was asleep.

Presently it seemed that even the captain dozed, and the correspondent thought that he was the one man afloat on all the oceans. The wind had a voice as it came over the waves, and it was sadder than the end.

There was a long, loud swishing astern of the boat, and a gleaming trail of 165 phosphorescence, like blue flame, was furrowed on the black waters. It might have been made by a monstrous knife.

Then there came a stillness, while the correspondent breathed with open mouth and looked at the sea.

Suddenly there was another swish and another long flash of bluish light, and this time it was alongside the boat, and might almost have been reached with an oar. The correspondent saw an enormous fin speed like a shadow through the water, hurling the crystalline spray and leaving the long glowing trail.

The correspondent looked over his shoulder at the captain. His face was hidden, and he seemed to be asleep. He looked at the babes of the sea. They certainly were asleep. So, being bereft of sympathy, he leaned a little way to one side and swore softly into the sea.

But the thing did not then leave the vicinity of the boat. Ahead or astern, on one side or the other, at intervals long or short, fled the long sparkling streak, and there was to be heard the *whirroo* of the dark fin. The speed and power of the thing was greatly to be admired. It cut the water like a gigantic and keen projectile.

The presence of this biding thing did not affect the man with the same hor- 170 ror that it would if he had been a picnicker. He simply looked at the sea dully and swore in an undertone.

Nevertheless, it is true that he did not wish to be alone with the thing. He wished one of his companions to awake by chance and keep him company with it. But the company hung motionless over the water-jar, and the oiler and the cook in the bottom of the boat were plunged in slumber.

## VI

"If I am going to be drowned—if I am going to be drowned—if I am going to be drowned, why, in the name of the seven mad gods who rule the sea, was I allowed to come thus far and contemplate sand and trees?"

During this dismal night, it may be remarked that a man would conclude that it was really the intention of the seven mad gods to drown him, despite the abominable injustice of it. For it was certainly an abominable injustice to drown a man who had worked so hard, so hard. The man felt it would be a crime most unnatural. Other people had drowned at sea since galleys swarmed with painted sails, but still—

When it occurs to a man that nature does not regard him as important, and that she feels she would not maim the universe by disposing of him, he at first wishes to throw bricks at the temple, and he hates deeply the fact that there are no bricks and no temples. Any visible expression of nature would surely be pelleted with his jeers.

Then, if there be no tangible thing to hoot, he feels, perhaps, the desire to 175 confront a personification and indulge in pleas, bowed to one knee, and with hands supplicant, saying, "Yes, but I love myself."

A high cold star on a winter's night is the word he feels that she says to him. Thereafter he knows the pathos of his situation.

The men in the dinghy had not discussed these matters, but each had, no doubt, reflected upon them in silence and according to his mind. There was seldom any expression upon their faces save the general one of complete weariness. Speech was devoted to the business of the boat.

To chime the notes of his emotion, a verse mysteriously entered the correspondent's head. He had even forgotten that he had forgotten this verse, but it suddenly was in his mind.

A soldier of the Legion lay dying in Algiers;
There was lack of woman's nursing, there was dearth of woman's tears;
But a comrade stood beside him, and he took that comrade's hand,
And he said, "I never more shall see my own, my native land."°

In his childhood the correspondent had been made acquainted with the fact that a soldier of the Legion lay dying in Algiers, but he had never regarded the fact as important. Myriads of his school-fellows had informed him of the soldier's plight, but the dinning had naturally ended by making him perfectly indifferent. He had never considered it his affair that a soldier of the Legion lay dying in Algiers, nor had it appeared to him as a matter for sorrow. It was less to him than the breaking of a pencil's point.

Now, however, it quaintly came to him as a human, living thing. It was no   180
longer merely a picture of a few throes in the breast of a poet, meanwhile drinking tea and warming his feet at the grate; it was an actuality—stern, mournful, and fine.

The correspondent plainly saw the soldier. He lay on the sand with his feet out straight and still. While his pale left hand was upon his chest in an attempt to thwart the going of his life, the blood came between his fingers. In the far Algerian distance, a city of low square forms was set against a sky that was faint with the last sunset hues. The correspondent, plying the oars and dreaming of the slow and slower movements of the lips of the soldier, was moved by a profound and perfectly impersonal comprehension. He was sorry for the soldier of the Legion who lay dying in Algiers.

The thing which had followed the boat and waited had evidently grown bored at the delay. There was no longer to be heard the slash of the cutwater, and there was no longer the flame of the long trail. The light in the north still glimmered, but it was apparently no nearer to the boat. Sometimes the boom of the surf rang in the correspondent's ears, and he turned the craft seaward then and rowed harder. Southward, some one had evidently built a watch-fire on the beach. It was too low and too far to be seen, but it made a shimmering, roseate reflection upon the bluff in back of it, and this could be discerned from the boat. The wind came stronger, and sometimes a wave suddenly raged out like a mountain cat, and there was to be seen the sheen and sparkle of a broken crest.

The captain, in the bow, moved on his water-jar and sat erect. "Pretty long night," he observed to the correspondent. He looked at the shore. "Those life-saving people take their time."

"Did you see that shark playing around?"

A *soldier of the Legion* . . . *native land:* The correspondent remembers a Victorian ballad about a German dying in the French Foreign Legion, "Bingen on the Rhine" by Caroline Norton.

"Yes, I saw him. He was a big fellow, all right."

"Wish I had known you were awake."

Later the correspondent spoke into the bottom of the boat.

"Billie!" There was a slow and gradual disentanglement.

"Billie, will you spell me?"

"Sure," said the oiler.

As soon as the correspondent touched the cold, comfortable sea-water in the bottom of the boat and had huddled close to the cook's life-belt he was deep in sleep, despite the fact that his teeth played all the popular airs. This sleep was so good to him that it was but a moment before he heard a voice call his name in a tone that demonstrated the last stages of exhaustion. "Will you spell me?"

"Sure, Billie."

The light in the north had mysteriously vanished, but the correspondent took his course from the wide-awake captain.

Later in the night they took the boat farther out to sea, and the captain directed the cook to take one oar at the stern and keep the boat facing the seas. He was to call out if he should hear the thunder of the surf. This plan enabled the oiler and the correspondent to get respite together. "We'll give those boys a chance to get into shape again," said the captain. They curled down and, after a few preliminary chatterings and trembles, slept once more the dead sleep. Neither knew they had bequeathed to the cook the company of another shark, or perhaps the same shark.

As the boat caroused on the waves, spray occasionally bumped over the side and gave them a fresh soaking, but this had no power to break their repose. The ominous slash of the wind and the water affected them as it would have affected mummies.

"Boys," said the cook, with the notes of every reluctance in his voice, "she's drifted in pretty close. I guess one of you had better take her to sea again." The correspondent, aroused, heard the crash of the toppled crests.

As he was rowing, the captain gave him some whisky-and-water, and this steadied the chills out of him. "If I ever get ashore and anybody shows me even a photograph of an oar—"

At last there was a short conversation.

"Billie!—Billie, will you spell me?"

"Sure," said the oiler.

## VII

When the correspondent again opened his eyes, the sea and sky were each of the gray hue of the dawning. Later, carmine and gold was painted upon the waters. The morning appeared finally, in its splendor, with a sky of pure blue, and the sunlight flamed on the tips of the waves.

On the distant dunes were set many little black cottages, and a tall white windmill reared above them. No man, nor dog, nor bicycle appeared on the beach. The cottages might have formed a deserted village.

The voyagers scanned the shore. A conference was held in the boat. "Well," said the captain, "if no help is coming, we might better try a run through the surf right away. If we stay out here much longer we will be too weak to do anything for ourselves at all." The others silently acquiesced in this reasoning. The boat was headed for the beach. The correspondent wondered if none ever ascended the tall wind-tower, and if they never looked seaward. This tower was a giant, standing with its back to the plight of the ants. It represented in a degree, to the correspondent, the serenity of nature amid the struggles of the individual—nature in the wind, and nature in the vision of men. She did not seem cruel to him then, nor beneficent, nor treacherous, nor wise. But she was indifferent, flatly indifferent. It is, perhaps, plausible that a man in this situation, impressed with the unconcern of the universe, should see the innumerable flaws of life, and have them taste wickedly in his mind, and wish for another chance. A distinction between right and wrong seems absurdly clear to him, then, in this new ignorance of the grave-edge, and he understands that if he were given another opportunity he would mend his conduct and his words, and be better and brighter during an introduction or at a tea.

"Now, boys," said the captain, "she is going to swamp sure. All we can do is to work her in as far as possible, and then when she swamps, pile out and scramble for the beach. Keep cool now, and don't jump until she swamps sure."

The oiler took the oars. Over his shoulders he scanned the surf. "Captain," he said, "I think I'd better bring her about and keep her head-on to the seas and back her in." 205

"All right, Billie," said the captain. "Back her in." The oiler swung the boat then, and, seated in the stern, the cook and the correspondent were obliged to look over their shoulders to contemplate the lonely and indifferent shore.

The monstrous inshore rollers heaved the boat high until the men were again enabled to see the white sheets of water scudding up the slanted beach. "We won't get in very close," said the captain. Each time a man could wrest his attention from the rollers, he turned his glance toward the shore, and in the expression of the eyes during this contemplation there was a singular quality. The correspondent, observing the others, knew that they were not afraid, but the full meaning of their glances was shrouded.

As for himself, he was too tired to grapple fundamentally with the fact. He tried to coerce his mind into thinking of it, but the mind was dominated at this time by the muscles, and the muscles said they did not care. It merely occurred to him that if he should drown it would be a shame.

There were no hurried words, no pallor, no plain agitation. The men simply looked at the shore. "Now, remember to get well clear of the boat when you jump," said the captain.

Seaward the crest of a roller suddenly fell with a thunderous crash, and the 210 long white comber came roaring down upon the boat.

"Steady now," said the captain. The men were silent. They turned their eyes from the shore to the comber and waited. The boat slid up the incline, leaped at the furious top, bounced over it, and swung down the long back of the wave. Some water had been shipped, and the cook bailed it out.

But the next crest crashed also. The tumbling, boiling flood of white water caught the boat and whirled it almost perpendicular. Water swarmed in from all sides. The correspondent had his hands on the gunwale at this time, and when the water entered at that place he swiftly withdrew his fingers, as if he objected to wetting them.

The little boat, drunken with this weight of water, reeled and snuggled deeper into the sea.

"Bail her out, cook! Bail her out!" said the captain.

"All right, Captain," said the cook. 215

"Now, boys, the next one will do for us sure," said the oiler. "Mind to jump clear of the boat."

The third wave moved forward, huge, furious, implacable. It fairly swallowed the dinghy, and almost simultaneously the men tumbled into the sea. A piece of life-belt had lain in the bottom of the boat, and as the correspondent went overboard he held this to his chest with his left hand.

The January water was icy, and he reflected immediately that it was colder than he had expected to find it off the coast of Florida. This appeared to his dazed mind as a fact important enough to be noted at the time. The coldness of the water was sad; it was tragic. This fact was somehow mixed and confused with his opinion of his own situation, so that it seemed almost a proper reason for tears. The water was cold.

When he came to the surface he was conscious of little but the noisy water. Afterward he saw his companions in the sea. The oiler was ahead in the race. He was swimming strongly and rapidly. Off to the correspondent's left, the cook's great white and corked back bulged out of the water; and in the rear the captain was hanging with his one good hand to the keel of the overturned dinghy.

There is a certain immovable quality to a shore, and the correspondent wondered at it amid the confusion of the sea. 220

It seemed also very attractive; but the correspondent knew that it was a long journey, and he paddled leisurely. The piece of life-preserver lay under him, and sometimes he whirled down the incline of a wave as if he were on a handsled.

But finally he arrived at a place in the sea where travel was beset with difficulty. He did not pause swimming to inquire what manner of current had caught him, but there his progress ceased. The shore was set before him like a bit of scenery on a stage, and he looked at it and understood with his eyes each detail of it.

As the cook passed, much farther to the left, the captain was calling to him, "Turn over on your back, cook! Turn over on your back and use the oar."

"All right, sir." The cook turned on his back, and, paddling with an oar, went ahead as if he were a canoe.

Presently the boat also passed to the left of the correspondent, with the 225 captain clinging with one hand to the keel. He would have appeared like a man raising himself to look over a board fence if it were not for the extraordinary gymnastics of the boat. The correspondent marvelled that the captain could still hold to it.

They passed on nearer to shore—the oiler, the cook, the captain—and following them went the water-jar, bouncing gaily over the seas.

The correspondent remained in the grip of this strange new enemy—a current. The shore, with its white slope of sand and its green bluff topped with little silent cottages, was spread like a picture before him. It was very near to him then, but he was impressed as one who, in a gallery, looks at a scene from Brittany or Algiers.

He thought: "I am going to drown? Can it be possible? Can it be possible? Can it be possible?" Perhaps an individual must consider his own death to be the final phenomenon of nature.

But later a wave perhaps whirled him out of this small deadly current, for he found suddenly that he could again make progress toward the shore. Later still he was aware that the captain, clinging with one hand to the keel of the dinghy, had his face turned away from the shore and toward him, and was calling his name. "Come to the boat! Come to the boat!"

In his struggle to reach the captain and the boat, he reflected that when one 230 gets properly wearied drowning must really be a comfortable arrangement—a cessation of hostilities accompanied by a large degree of relief; and he was glad of it, for the main thing in his mind for some moments had been horror of the temporary agony. He did not wish to be hurt.

Presently he saw a man running along the shore. He was undressing with most remarkable speed. Coat, trousers, shirt, everything flew magically off him.

"Come to the boat!" called the captain.

"All right, Captain." As the correspondent paddled, he saw the captain let himself down to bottom and leave the boat. Then the correspondent performed his one little marvel of the voyage. A large wave caught him and flung him with ease and supreme speed completely over the boat and far beyond it. It struck him even then as an event in gymnastics and a true miracle of the sea. An overturned boat in the surf is not a plaything to a swimming man.

The correspondent arrived in water that reached only to his waist, but his condition did not enable him to stand for more than a moment. Each wave knocked him into a heap, and the undertow pulled at him.

Then he saw the man who had been running and undressing, and undressing 235 and running, come bounding into the water. He dragged ashore the cook, and then waded toward the captain; but the captain waved him away and sent him to the correspondent. He was naked—naked as a tree in winter; but a halo was about his head, and he shone like a saint. He gave a strong pull, and a long drag, and a bully heave at the correspondent's hand. The correspondent, schooled in the minor formulae, said, "Thanks, old man." But suddenly the man cried, "What's that?" He pointed a swift finger. The correspondent said, "Go."

In the shallows, face downward, lay the oiler. His forehead touched sand that was periodically, between each wave, clear of the sea.

The correspondent did not know all that transpired afterward. When he achieved safe ground he fell, striking the sand with each particular part of his body. It was as if he had dropped from a roof, but the thud was grateful to him.

It seems that instantly the beach was populated with men with blankets, clothes, and flasks, and women with coffee-pots and all the remedies sacred to their minds. The welcome of the land to the men from the sea was warm and generous; but a still and dripping shape was carried slowly up the beach, and the land's welcome for it could only be the different and sinister hospitality of the grave.

When it came night, the white waves paced to and fro in the moonlight, and the wind brought the sound of the great sea's voice to the men on the shore, and they felt that they could then be interpreters.

QUESTIONS

1. In actuality, Crane, the captain of the *Commodore*, and the two crew members spent nearly thirty hours in the open boat. William Higgins, the oiler, was drowned as Crane describes. Does a knowledge of these facts in any way affect your response to the story? Would you admire the story less if you believed it to be pure fiction?

2. Sum up the personalities of each of the four men in the boat: captain, cook, oiler, and correspondent.

3. What is the point of view of the story?

4. In paragraph 9, we are told that as each wave came, the boat "seemed like a horse making at a fence outrageously high." Point to the other vivid similes or figures of speech. What do they contribute to the story's effectiveness?

5. Notice some of the ways in which Crane, as a storyteller conscious of plot, builds suspense. What enemies or obstacles do the men in the boat confront? What is the effect of the scene of the men who wave from the beach (paragraphs 86–141)? What is the climax of the story? (If you need to be refreshed on the meaning of *climax*, see page 10.)

6. In paragraph 70 (and again in paragraph 143), the men wonder, "Was I brought here merely to have my nose dragged away as I was about to nibble the sacred cheese of life?" What variety of irony do you find in this quotation?

7. Why does the scrap of verse about the soldier dying in Algiers (paragraph 178) suddenly come to mean so much to the correspondent?

8. What theme in "The Open Boat" seems most important to you? Where is it stated?

9. What secondary themes also enrich the story? See for instance paragraph 43 (the thoughts on comradeship).

10. How do you define *heroism*? Who is a hero in "The Open Boat"?

## Nathaniel Hawthorne

YOUNG GOODMAN BROWN                                        (1829–1835)

*Nathaniel Hawthorne (1804–1864) was*
*born in the clipper-ship seaport of Salem,*
*Massachusetts, son of a merchant captain*
*and grandson of a judge at the notorious*
*Salem witchcraft trials. Hawthorne takes a*
*keen interest in New England's sin-and-*
*brimstone Puritan past in this and many*
*other of his stories and in* The Scarlet
Letter *(1848), that enduring novel of a*
*woman taken in adultery. After college,*
*Hawthorne lived at home and trained to be*
*a writer. Only when his first collection,*
Twice-Told Tales *(1837), made money*
*did he feel secure enough to marry Sophia*
*Peabody and settle in the Old Manse in*
*Concord, Massachusetts. Three more nov-*
*els followed* The Scarlet Letter: The

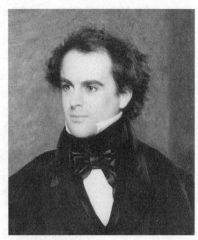

*Nathaniel Hawthorne*

House of the Seven Gables *(1851, a story tinged with nightmarish humor),* The
Blithedale Romance *(1852, drawn from his short, disgruntled stay at a Utopian com-*
*mune,* Brook Farm*), and* The Marble Faun *(1860, inspired by a stay in Italy).*
*Hawthorne wrote for children, too, retelling classic legends in* The Wonder Book
*(1852) and* Tanglewood Tales *(1853). At Bowdoin College, he had been a classmate*
*of Franklin Pierce; later, when Pierce ran for President of the United States,*
*Hawthorne wrote him a campaign biography. The victorious Pierce appointed his old*
*friend American consul at Liverpool, England. With his contemporary, Edgar Allan*
*Poe, Hawthorne sped the transformation of the American short story from popular mag-*
*azine filler into a form of art.*

Young Goodman° Brown came forth, at sunset, into the street of Salem vil-
lage°, but put his head back, after crossing the threshold, to exchange a parting
kiss with his young wife. And Faith, as the wife was aptly named, thrust her own
pretty head into the street, letting the wind play with the pink ribbons of her cap,
while she called to Goodman Brown.

"Dearest heart," whispered she, softly and rather sadly, when her lips were
close to his ear, "pray thee, put off your journey until sunrise, and sleep in your
own bed to-night. A lone woman is troubled with such dreams and such
thoughts, that she's afraid of herself, sometimes. Pray, tarry with me this night,
dear husband, of all nights in the year!"

---

*Goodman:* title given by Puritans to a male head of a household; a farmer or other ordinary citizen.
*Salem village:* in England's Massachusetts Bay Colony.

"My love and my Faith," replied young Goodman Brown, "of all nights in the year, this one night must I tarry away from thee. My journey, as thou callest it, forth and back again, must needs be done 'twixt now and sunrise. What, my sweet, pretty wife, dost thou doubt me already, and we but three months married!"

"Then, God bless you!" said Faith, with the pink ribbons, "and may you find all well, when you come back."

"Amen!" cried Goodman Brown. "Say thy prayers, dear Faith, and go to bed at dusk, and no harm will come to thee."                                                              5

So they parted; and the young man pursued his way, until, being about to turn the corner by the meeting-house, he looked back, and saw the head of Faith still peeping after him, with a melancholy air, in spite of her pink ribbons.

"Poor little Faith!" thought he, for his heart smote him. "What a wretch am I, to leave her on such an errand! She talks of dreams, too. Methought, as she spoke, there was trouble in her face, as if a dream had warned her what work is to be done to-night. But, no, no! 'twould kill her to think it. Well; she's a blessed angel on earth; and after this one night, I'll cling to her skirts and follow her to Heaven."

With this excellent resolve for the future, Goodman Brown felt himself justified in making more haste on his present evil purpose. He had taken a dreary road, darkened by all the gloomiest trees of the forest, which barely stood aside to let the narrow path creep through, and closed immediately behind. It was all as lonely as could be; and there is this peculiarity in such a solitude, that the traveller knows not who may be concealed by the innumerable trunks and the thick boughs overhead; so that, with lonely footsteps, he may yet be passing through an unseen multitude.

"There may be a devilish Indian behind every tree," said Goodman Brown, to himself; and he glanced fearfully behind him, as he added, "What if the devil himself should be at my very elbow!"

His head being turned back, he passed a crook of the road, and looking forward again, beheld the figure of a man, in grave and decent attire, seated at the foot of an old tree. He arose, at Goodman Brown's approach, and walked onward, side by side with him.                                                                    10

"You are late, Goodman Brown," said he. "The clock of the Old South was striking as I came through Boston; and that is full fifteen minutes agone°."

"Faith kept me back awhile," replied the young man, with a tremor in his voice, caused by the sudden appearance of his companion, though not wholly unexpected.

It was now deep dusk in the forest, and deepest in that part of it where these two were journeying. As nearly as could be discerned, the second traveller was about fifty years old, apparently in the same rank of life as Goodman Brown, and bearing a considerable resemblance to him, though perhaps more in expression than features. Still, they might have been taken for father and son. And yet, though the elder person was as simply clad as the younger, and as simple in manner too, he had an indescribable air of one who knew the world, and

---

*full fifteen minutes agone:* Apparently this mystery man has traveled in a flash from Boston's Old South Church all the way to the woods beyond Salem—as the crow flies, a good sixteen miles.

would not have felt abashed at the governor's dinner-table, or in King William's court,° were it possible that his affairs should call him thither. But the only thing about him, that could be fixed upon as remarkable, was his staff, which bore the likeness of a great black snake, so curiously wrought, that it might almost be seen to twist and wriggle itself, like a living serpent. This, of course, must have been an ocular deception, assisted by the uncertain light.

"Come, Goodman Brown!" cried his fellow-traveller, "this is dull pace for the beginning of a journey. Take my staff, if you are so soon weary."

"Friend," said the other, exchanging his slow pace for a full stop, "having kept covenant by meeting thee here, it is my purpose now to return whence I came. I have scruples, touching the matter thou wot'st° of." 15

"Sayest thou so?" replied he of the serpent, smiling apart. "Let us walk on, nevertheless, reasoning as we go, and if I convince thee not, thou shalt turn back. We are but a little way in the forest, yet."

"Too far, too far!" exclaimed the goodman, unconsciously resuming his walk. "My father never went into the woods on such an errand, nor his father before him. We have been a race of honest men and good Christians, since the days of the martyrs°. And shall I be the first of the name of Brown, that ever took this path, and kept—"

"Such company, thou wouldst say," observed the elder person, interpreting his pause. "Well said, Goodman Brown! I have been as well acquainted with your family as with ever a one among the Puritans; and that's no trifle to say. I helped your grandfather, the constable, when he lashed the Quaker woman so smartly through the streets of Salem. And it was I that brought your father a pitch-pine knot, kindled at my own hearth, to set fire to an Indian village, in King Philip's war°. They were my good friends, both; and many a pleasant walk have we had along this path, and returned merrily after midnight. I would fain be friends with you, for their sake."

"If it be as thou sayest," replied Goodman Brown, "I marvel they never spoke of these matters. Or, verily, I marvel not, seeing that the least rumor of the sort would have driven them from New-England. We are a people of prayer, and good works, to boot, and abide no such wickedness."

"Wickedness or not," said the traveller with the twisted staff, "I have a very general acquaintance here in New-England. The deacons of many a church have drunk the communion wine with me; the selectmen, of divers towns, make me their chairman; and a majority of the Great and General Court are firm supporters of my interest. The governor and I, too—but these are state-secrets." 20

---

King William's court: back in England, where William III reigned in 1689–1702.    wot'st: know. days of the martyrs: a time when many forebears of the New England Puritans had given their lives for their religious convictions—when Mary I (Mary Tudor, nicknamed "Bloody Mary"), queen of England from 1553 to 1558, briefly re-established the Roman Catholic Church in England and launched a campaign of persecution against Protestants.    King Philip's war: Metacomet, or King Philip (as the English called him), chief of the Wampanoag Indians, had led a bitter, widespread uprising of several New England tribes (1675–78). Metacomet died in the war, as did one out of every ten white male colonists.

"Can this be so!" cried Goodman Brown, with a stare of amazement at his undisturbed companion. "Howbeit, I have nothing to do with the governor and council; they have their own ways, and are no rule for a simple husbandman, like me. But, were I to go on with thee, how should I meet the eye of that good old man, our minister, at Salem village? Oh, his voice would make me tremble, both Sabbath-day and lecture-day°!"

Thus far, the elder traveller had listened with due gravity, but now burst into a fit of irrepressible mirth, shaking himself so violently, that his snake-life staff actually seemed to wriggle in sympathy.

"Ha! ha! ha!" shouted he, again and again; then composing himself, "Well, go on, Goodman Brown, go on; but pray thee, don't kill me with laughing!"

"Well, then, to end the matter at once," said Goodman Brown, considerably nettled, "there is my wife, Faith. It would break her dear little heart; and I'd rather break my own!"

"Nay, if that be the case," answered the other, "e'en go thy ways, Goodman 25 Brown. I would not, for twenty old women like the one hobbling before us, that Faith should come to any harm."

As he spoke, he pointed his staff at a female figure on the path, in whom Goodman Brown recognized a very pious and exemplary dame, who had taught him his catechism, in youth, and was still his moral and spiritual adviser, jointly with the minister and Deacon Gookin.

"A marvel, truly, that Goody° Cloyse should be so far in the wilderness, at night-fall!" said he. "But, with your leave, friend, I shall take a cut through the woods, until we have left this Christian woman behind. Being a stranger to you, she might ask whom I was consorting with, and whither I was going."

"Be it so," said his fellow-traveller. "Betake you to the woods, and let me keep the path."

Accordingly, the young man turned aside, but took care to watch his companion, who advanced softly along the road, until he had come within a staff's length of the old dame. She, meanwhile, was making the best of her way, with singular speed for so aged a woman, and mumbling some indistinct words, a prayer, doubtless, as she went. The traveller put forth his staff, and touched her withered neck with what seemed the serpent's tail.

"The devil!" screamed the pious old lady. 30

"Then Goody Cloyse knows her old friend?" observed the traveller, confronting her, and leaning on his writhing stick.

"Ah, forsooth, and is it your worship, indeed?" cried the good dame. "Yea, truly is it, and in the very image of my old gossip°, Goodman Brown, the grandfather of the silly fellow that now is. But—would your worship believe it?—my broomstick hath strangely disappeared, stolen, as I suspect, by that unhanged

---

*lecture-day:* a weekday when everyone had to go to church to hear a sermon or Bible-reading. *Goody:* short for Goodwife, title for a married woman of ordinary station. In his story, Hawthorne borrows from history the names of two "Goodys"—Goody Cloyse and Goody Cory—and one unmarried woman, Martha Carrier. In 1692 Hawthorne's great-grandfather, John Hawthorne, a judge in the Salem witchcraft trials, had condemned all three to be hanged. *gossip:* friend or kinsman.

witch, Goody Cory, and that, too, when I was all anointed with the juice of smallage and cinquefoil and wolf's bane—°"

"Mingled with fine wheat and the fat of a new-born babe," said the shape of old Goodman Brown.

"Ah, your worship knows the receipt," cried the old lady, cackling aloud. "So, as I was saying, being all ready for the meeting, and no horse to ride on, I made up my mind to foot it; for they tell me, there is a nice young man to be taken into communion to-night. But now your good worship will lend me your arm, and we shall be there in a twinkling."

"That can hardly be," answered her friend. "I may not spare you my arm, 35 Goody Cloyse, but here is my staff, if you will."

So saying, he threw it down at her feet, where, perhaps, it assumed life, being one of the rods which its owner had formerly lent to the Egyptian Magi°. Of this fact, however, Goodman Brown could not take cognizance. He had cast up his eyes in astonishment, and looking down again, beheld neither Goody Cloyse nor the serpentine staff, but his fellow-traveller alone, who waited for him as calmly as if nothing had happened.

"That old woman taught me my catechism!" said the young man; and there was a world of meaning in this simple comment.

They continued to walk onward, while the elder traveller exhorted his companion to make good speed and persevere in the path, discoursing so aptly, that his arguments seemed rather to spring up in the bosom of his auditor, than to be suggested by himself. As they went, he plucked a branch of maple, to serve for a walking-stick, and began to strip it of the twigs and little boughs, which were wet with evening dew. The moment his fingers touched them, they became strangely withered and dried up, as with a week's sunshine. Thus the pair proceeded, at a good free pace, until suddenly, in a gloomy hollow of the road, Goodman Brown sat himself down on the stump of a tree, and refused to go any farther.

"Friend," said he, stubbornly, "my mind is made up. Not another step will I budge on this errand. What if a wretched old woman do choose to go to the devil, when I thought she was going to Heaven! Is that any reason why I should quit my dear Faith, and go after her?"

"You will think better of this, by-and-by," said his acquaintance, composedly. 40 "Sit here and rest yourself awhile; and when you feel like moving again, there is my staff to help you along."

Without more words, he threw his companion the maple stick, and was as speedily out of sight, as if he had vanished into the deepening gloom. The young man sat a few moments, by the road-side, applauding himself greatly, and thinking with how clear a conscience he should meet the minister, in his morning-walk, nor shrink from the eye of good old Deacon Gookin. And what calm sleep would be his, that very night, which was to have been spent so wickedly, but

_smallage and cinquefoil and wolf's bane:_ wild plants—here, ingredients for a witch's brew.   _Egyptian Magi:_ In the Bible, Pharaoh's wise men and sorcerers who by their magical powers changed their rods into live serpents. (This incident, part of the story of Moses and Aaron, is related in Exodus 7:8–12.)

purely and sweetly now, in the arms of Faith! Amidst these pleasant and praise-worthy meditations, Goodman Brown heard the tramp of horses along the road, and deemed it advisable to conceal himself within the verge of the forest, conscious of the guilty purpose that had brought him thither, though now so happily turned from it.

On came the hoof-tramps and the voices of the riders, two grave old voices, conversing soberly as they drew near. These mingled sounds appeared to pass along the road, within a few yards of the young man's hiding-place; but owing, doubtless, to the depth of the gloom, at that particular spot, neither the travellers nor their steeds were visible. Though their figures brushed the small boughs by the way-side, it could not be seen that they intercepted, even for a moment, the faint gleam from the strip of bright sky, athwart which they must have passed. Goodman Brown alternately crouched and stood on tip-toe, pulling aside the branches, and thrusting forth his head as far as he durst, without discerning so much as a shadow. It vexed him the more, because he could have sworn, were such a thing possible, that he recognized the voices of the minister and Deacon Gookin, jogging along quietly, as they were wont to do, when bound to some ordination or ecclesiastical council. While yet within hearing, one of the riders stopped to pluck a switch.

"Of the two, reverend Sir," said the voice like the deacon's, "I had rather miss an ordination-dinner than to-night's meeting. They tell me that some of our community are to be here from Falmouth and beyond, and others from Connecticut and Rhode-Island; besides several of the Indian powows°, who, after their fashion, know almost as much deviltry as the best of us. Moreover, there is a goodly young woman to be taken into communion."

"Mighty well, Deacon Gookin!" replied the solemn old tones of the minister. "Spur up, or we shall be late. Nothing can be done, you know, until I get on the ground."

The hoofs clattered again, and the voices, talking so strangely in the empty air, passed on through the forest, where no church had ever been gathered, nor solitary Christian prayed. Whither, then, could these holy men be journeying, so deep into the heathen wilderness? Young Goodman Brown caught hold of a tree, for support, being ready to sink down on the ground, faint and overburdened with the heavy sickness of his heart. He looked up to the sky, doubting whether there really was a Heaven above him. Yet, there was the blue arch, and the stars brightening in it.

"With Heaven above, and Faith below, I will yet stand firm against the devil!" cried Goodman Brown.

While he still gazed upward, into the deep arch of the firmament, and had lifted his hands to pray, a cloud, though no wind was stirring, hurried across the zenith, and hid the brightening stars. The blue sky was still visible, except directly overhead, where this black mass of cloud was sweeping swiftly northward. Aloft in the air, as if from the depths of the cloud, came a confused and doubtful

45

---

powows: Indian priests or medicine men.

sound of voices. Once, the listener fancied that he could distinguish the accents of town's-people of his own, men and women, both pious and ungodly, many of whom he had met at the communion-table, and had seen others rioting at the tavern. The next moment, so indistinct were the sounds, he doubted whether he had heard aught but the murmur of the old forest, whispering without a wind. Then came a stronger swell of those familiar tones, heard daily in the sunshine, at Salem village, but never, until now, from a cloud of night. There was one voice, of a young woman, uttering lamentations, yet with an uncertain sorrow, and entreating for some favor, which, perhaps, it would grieve her to obtain. And all the unseen multitude, both saints and sinners, seemed to encourage her onward.

"Faith!" shouted Goodman Brown, in a voice of agony and desperation; and the echoes of the forest mocked him, crying—"Faith! Faith!" as if bewildered wretches were seeking her, all through the wilderness.

The cry of grief, rage, and terror, was yet piercing the night, when the unhappy husband held his breath for a response. There was a scream, drowned immediately in a louder murmur of voices, fading into far-off laughter, as the dark cloud swept away, leaving the clear and silent sky above Goodman Brown. But something fluttered lightly down through the air, and caught on the branch of a tree. The young man seized it, and beheld a pink ribbon.

"My Faith is gone!" cried he, after one stupefied moment. "There is no good 50 on earth; and sin is but a name. Come, devil! for to thee is this world given."

And maddened with despair, so that he laughed loud and long, did Goodman Brown grasp his staff and set forth again, at such a rate, that he seemed to fly along the forest-path, rather than to walk or run. The road grew wilder and drearier, and more faintly traced, and vanished at length, leaving him in the heart of the dark wilderness, still rushing onward, with the instinct that guides mortal man to evil. The whole forest was peopled with frightful sounds; the creaking of the trees, the howling of wild beasts, and the yell of Indians; while, sometimes, the wind tolled like a distant church-bell, and sometimes gave a broad roar around the traveller, as if all Nature were laughing him to scorn. But he was himself the chief horror of the scene, and shrank not from its other horrors.

"Ha! ha! ha!" roared Goodman Brown, when the wind laughed at him. "Let us hear which will laugh loudest! Think not to frighten me with your deviltry! Come witch, come wizard, come Indian powow, come devil himself! and here comes Goodman Brown. You may as well fear him as he fear you!"

In truth, all through the haunted forest, there could be nothing more frightful than the figure of Goodman Brown. On he flew, among the black pines, brandishing his staff with frenzied gestures, now giving vent to an inspiration of horrid blasphemy, and now shouting forth such laughter, as set all the echoes of the forest laughing like demons around him. The fiend in his own shape is less hideous, than when he rages in the breast of man. Thus sped the demoniac on his course, until, quivering among the trees, he saw a red light before him, as when the felled trunks and branches of a clearing have been set on fire, and throw up their lurid blaze against the sky, at the hour of midnight. He paused, in a lull of the tempest that had driven him onward, and heard the swell of what seemed a hymn, rolling solemnly from a distance, with the weight of many voices. He knew the tune; it was a familiar one in the choir of the village meeting-house. The verse died heavily away, and was lengthened by a chorus, not of human voices, but of all the sounds of the benighted wilderness, pealing in awful harmony together. Goodman Brown cried out; and his cry was lost to his own ear, by its unison with the cry of the desert.

In the interval of silence, he stole forward, until the light glared full upon his eyes. At one extremity of an open space, hemmed in by the dark wall of the forest, arose a rock, bearing some rude, natural resemblance either to an altar or a pulpit, and surrounded by four blazing pines, their tops aflame, their stems untouched, like candles at an evening meeting. The mass of foliage, that had overgrown the summit of the rock, was all on fire, blazing high into the night, and fitfully illuminating the whole field. Each pendent twig and leafy festoon was in a blaze. As the red light arose and fell, a numerous congregation alternately shone forth, then disappeared in shadow, and again grew, as it were, out of the darkness, peopling the heart of the solitary woods at once.

"A grave and dark-clad company!" quoth Goodman Brown.                          55

In truth, they were such. Among them, quivering to-and-fro, between gloom and splendor, appeared faces that would be seen, next day, at the council-board of the province, and others which, Sabbath after Sabbath, looked devoutly heavenward, and benignantly over the crowded pews, from the holiest pulpits in the land. Some affirm that the lady of the governor was there. At least, there were high dames well known to her, and wives of honored husbands, and widows, a great multitude, and ancient maidens, all of excellent repute, and fair young girls, who trembled, lest their mothers should espy them. Either the sudden gleams of light, flashing over the obscure field, bedazzled Goodman Brown, or he recognized a score of the church-members of Salem village, famous for their especial sanctity. Good old Deacon Gookin had arrived, and waited at the skirts of that venerable saint, his revered pastor. But, irreverently consorting with these grave, reputable, and pious people, these elders of the church, these chaste dames and dewy virgins, there were men of dissolute lives and women of spotted fame, wretches given over to all mean and filthy vice, and suspected even of horrid crimes. It was strange to see, that the good shrank not from the wicked, nor were the sinners abashed by the saints. Scattered, also, among their pale-faced enemies, were the Indian priests, or powows, who had often scared their native forest with more hideous incantations than any known to English witchcraft.

"But, where is Faith?" thought Goodman Brown; and, as hope came into his heart, he trembled.

Another verse of the hymn arose, a slow and mournful strain, such as the pious love, but joined to words which expressed all that our nature can conceive of sin, and darkly hinted at far more. Unfathomable to mere mortals is the lore of fiends. Verse after verse was sung, and still the chorus of the desert swelled between, like the deepest tone of a mighty organ. And, with the final peal of that dreadful anthem, there came a sound, as if the roaring wind, the rushing streams, the howling beasts, and every other voice of the unconverted wilderness, were mingling and according with the voice of guilty man, in homage to the prince of all. The four blazing pines threw up a loftier flame, and obscurely discovered shapes and visages of horror on the smoke-wreaths, above the impious assembly. At the same moment, the fire on the rock shot redly forth, and formed a glowing arch above its base, where now appeared a figure. With reverence be it spoken, the figure bore no slight similitude, both in garb and manner, to some grave divine of the New-England churches.

"Bring forth the converts!" cried a voice, that echoed through the field and rolled into the forest.

At the word, Goodman Brown stepped forth from the shadow of the trees, and approached the congregation, with whom he felt a loathful brotherhood, by the sympathy of all that was wicked in his heart. He could have well nigh sworn, that the shape of his own dead father beckoned him to advance, looking downward from a smoke-wreath, while a woman, with dim features of despair, threw out her hand to warn him back. Was it his mother? But he had no power to retreat one step, nor to resist, even in thought, when the minister and good old Deacon Gookin seized his arms, and led him to the blazing rock. Thither came also the slender form of a veiled female, led between Goody Cloyse, that pious teacher of the catechism, and Martha Carrier, who had received the devil's promise to be queen of hell. A rampant hag was she! And there stood the proselytes°, beneath the canopy of fire.

"Welcome, my children," said the dark figure, "to the communion of your race! Ye have found, thus young, your nature and your destiny. My children, look behind you!"

They turned; and flashing forth, as it were, in a sheet of flame, the fiend-worshippers were seen; the smile of welcome gleamed darkly on every visage.

"There," resumed the sable form, "are all whom ye have reverenced from youth. Ye deemed them holier than yourselves, and shrank from your own sin, contrasting it with their lives of righteousness, and prayerful aspirations heavenward. Yet, here are they all, in my worshipping assembly! This night it shall be granted you to know their secret deeds; how hoary-bearded elders of the church have whispered wanton words to the young maids of their households; how many a woman, eager for widow's weeds, has given her husband a drink at bed-time, and let him sleep his last sleep in her bosom; how beardless youths have made haste to inherit their fathers' wealth; and how fair damsels—blush not, sweet ones!—have dug little graves in the garden, and bidden me, the sole guest, to an infant's funeral. By the sympathy of your human hearts for sin, ye shall scent out all the places— whether in church, bed-chamber, street, field, or forest—where crime has been committed, and shall exult to behold the whole earth one stain of guilt, one mighty bloodspot. Far more than this! It shall be yours to penetrate, in every bosom, the deep mystery of sin, the fountain of all wicked arts, and which inexhaustibly supplies more evil impulses than human power—than my power, at its utmost!—can make manifest in deeds. And now, my children, look upon each other."

_proselytes:_ new converts.

They did so; and, by the blaze of the hell-kindled torches, the wretched man beheld his Faith, and the wife her husband, trembling before that unhallowed altar.

"Lo! there ye stand, my children," said the figure, in a deep and solemn tone, 65 almost sad, with its despairing awfulness, as if his once angelic nature could yet mourn for our miserable race. "Depending upon one another's hearts, ye had still hoped, that virtue were not all a dream. Now are ye undeceived! Evil is the nature of mankind. Evil must be your only happiness. Welcome, again, my children, to the communion of your race!"

"Welcome!" repeated the fiend-worshippers, in one cry of despair and triumph.

And there they stood, the only pair, as it seemed, who were yet hesitating on the verge of wickedness, in this dark world. A basin was hollowed, naturally, in the rock. Did it contain water, reddened by the lurid light? or was it blood? or, perchance, a liquid flame? Herein did the Shape of Evil dip his hand, and prepare to lay the mark of baptism upon their foreheads, that they might be partakers of the mystery of sin, more conscious of the secret guilt of others, both in deed and thought, than they could now be of their own. The husband cast one look at his pale wife, and Faith at him. What polluted wretches would the next glance show them to each other, shuddering alike at what they disclosed and what they saw!

"Faith! Faith!" cried the husband. "Look up to Heaven, and resist the Wicked one!"

Whether Faith obeyed, he knew not. Hardly had he spoken, when he found himself amid calm night and solitude, listening to a roar of the wind, which died heavily away through the forest. He staggered against the rock and felt it chill and damp, while a hanging twig, that had been all on fire, besprinkled his cheek with the coldest dew.

The next morning, young Goodman Brown came slowly into the street of 70 Salem village, staring around him like a bewildered man. The good old minister was taking a walk along the grave-yard, to get an appetite for breakfast and meditate his sermon, and bestowed a blessing, as he passed, on Goodman Brown. He shrank from the venerable saint, as if to avoid an anathema°. Old Deacon Goodkin was at domestic worship, and the holy words of his prayer were heard through the open window. "What God doth the wizard pray to?" quoth Goodman Brown. Goody Cloyse, that excellent old Christian, stood in the early sunshine, at her own lattice, catechizing a little girl, who had brought her a pint of morning's milk. Goodman Brown snatched away the child, as from the grasp of the fiend himself. Turning the corner by the meeting-house, he spied the head of Faith, with the pink ribbons, gazing anxiously forth, and bursting into such joy at sight of him, that she skipt along the street, and almost kissed her husband before the whole village. But, Goodman Brown looked sternly and sadly into her face, and passed on without a greeting.

---

*anathema:* an official curse, a decree that casts one out of a church and bans him from receiving the sacraments.

Had Goodman Brown fallen asleep in the forest, and only dreamed a wild dream of a witch-meeting?

Be it so, if you will. But, alas! it was a dream of evil omen for young Goodman Brown. A stern, a sad, a darkly meditative, a distrustful, if not a desperate man, did he become, from the night of that fearful dream. On the Sabbath-day, when the congregation were singing a holy psalm, he could not listen, because an anthem of sin rushed loudly upon his ear, and drowned all the blessed strain. When the minister spoke from the pulpit, with power and fervid eloquence, and, with his hand on the open Bible, of the sacred truths of our religion, and of saint-like lives and triumphant deaths, and of future bliss or misery unutterable, then did Goodman Brown turn pale, dreading, lest the roof should thunder down upon the gray blasphemer and his hearers. Often, awakening suddenly at midnight, he shrank from the bosom of Faith, and at morning or eventide, when the family knelt down at prayer, he scowled, and muttered to himself, and gazed sternly at his wife, and turned away. And when he had lived long, and was borne to his grave, a hoary corpse, followed by Faith, an aged woman, and children and grandchildren, a goodly procession, besides neighbors, not a few, they carved no hopeful verse upon his tombstone; for his dying hour was gloom.

QUESTIONS

1. When we learn (in the opening sentence) that this story begins in Salem village, what suggestions come to mind from our knowledge of American history? How does Salem make a more appropriate setting than some other colonial American village?
2. Why is Brown's wife Faith "aptly named" (as we are told in the opening paragraph)? Point to any passages in which the author seems to be punning on her name. What do you understand from them?
3. What do you make of the fact that the strange man in the woods closely resembles Brown himself (paragraphs 13, 32)?
4. As Brown and the stranger proceed deeper into the woods, what does Brown find out that troubles him? When the pink ribbon flutters to the ground, as though fallen from something airborne (paragraph 49), what does Brown assume? What effect does this event have upon his determination to resist the devil?
5. What is the purpose of the ceremony in the woods? Bring to your understanding of it anything you have heard or read about witchcraft, the witches' Sabbath, and the notion of making a pact with the devil.
6. What power does the devil promise to give his communicants (63)?
7. "Evil is the nature of mankind," declares the devil (65). Does Hawthorne agree with him? (Exactly what do we find in this story to suggest the author's view?)
8. Was Brown's experience in the woods all a dream, or wasn't it? Does Hawthorne favor one explanation, or the other?
9. Discuss this comment: "Even though Brown, at the last possible moment, refuses the "mark of baptism" and rejects the devil's gift, it turns out that he really did receive the gift after all. For the rest of his days, he definitely possesses the very same ability that the devil offered him."
10. How would you state the main theme of the story?

## Luke 15: 11–32

THE PARABLE OF THE PRODIGAL SON  *(Authorized or King James Version, 1611)*

And he said, A certain man had two sons: And the younger of them said to his father, Father, give me the portion of goods that falleth to me. And he divided unto them his living. And not many days after the younger son gathered all together, and took his journey into a far country, and there wasted his substance with riotous living. And when he had spent all, there arose a mighty famine in that land; and he began to be in want. And he went and joined himself to a citizen of that country; and he sent him into his fields to feed swine. And he would fain have filled his belly with the husks that the swine did eat: and no man gave unto him. And when he came to himself, he said, How many hired servants of my father's have bread enough and to spare, and I perish with hunger! I will arise and go to my father, and will say unto him, Father I have sinned against heaven, and before thee, And am no more worthy to be called thy son; make me as one of thy hired servants. And he arose, and came to his father. But when he was yet a great way off, his father saw him, and had compassion, and ran, and fell on his neck, and kissed him. And the son said unto him, Father I have sinned against heaven, and in thy sight, and am no more worthy to be called thy son. But the father said to his servants, Bring forth the best robe, and put it on him; and put a ring on his hand, and shoes on his feet: And bring hither the fatted calf, and kill it; and let us eat, and be merry: For this my son was dead, and is alive again; he was lost, and is found. And they began to be merry. Now his elder son was in the field: and he came and drew nigh to the house, he heard music and dancing. And he called one of the servants, and asked what these things meant. And he said unto him, Thy brother is come; and thy father hath killed the fatted calf, because he hath received him safe and sound. And he was angry, and would not go in: therefore came his father out, and entreated him. And he answering said to his father, Lo, these many years do I serve thee, neither transgressed I at any time thy commandment; and yet thou never gavest me a kid, that I might make merry with my friends: But as soon as this thy son was come, which hath devoured thy living with harlots, thou hast killed for him the fatted calf. And he said unto him, Son thou art ever with me, and all that I have is thine. It was meet that we should make merry, and be glad: for this thy brother was dead, and is alive again; and was lost, and is found.

### QUESTIONS

1. This story has traditionally been called "The Parable of the Prodigal Son." What does *prodigal* mean? Which of the two brothers is prodigal?
2. What position does the younger son expect when he returns to his father's house? What does the father give him?
3. When the older brother sees the celebration for his younger brother's return, he gets angry. He makes a very reasonable set of complaints to his father. He has indeed been a loyal and moral son, but what virtue does the older brother lack?
4. Is the father fair to the elder son? Explain your answer.
5. Theologians have discussed this parable's religious significance for two thousand years. What, in your own words, is the human theme of the story?

*Raymond Carver (1938–1988), whose
stories are mainly set in his native Pacific
Northwest, was born in Clatskanie, Oregon,
the son of a laborer. At nineteen, he found
himself married and the father of two children. After a series of low-paying jobs—
picking tulips, pumping gas, working as a
hospital janitor—he took a degree in 1963
from Humboldt State University (now
California State University, Humboldt). In
1966 he received an M.F.A. from the
University of Iowa. His first book, Near
Klamath (1968) was poetry; so was his
posthumous collection, A New Path to the
Waterfall (1989). Among his widely
praised story collections are Will You
Please Be Quiet, Please? (1977), What*

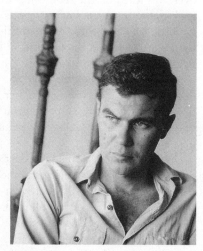

*Raymond Carver*

We Talk About When We Talk About Love *(1981),* Cathedral *(1984), and a
volume of new and selected stories,* Where I'm Calling From *(1988). Carver taught
creative writing at several schools: the University of California at Berkeley and Santa
Cruz, the University of Texas at El Paso, Goddard College, and Syracuse University.
In his last years, he lived in Port Angeles, Washington, with his second wife, the poet
and short story writer Tess Gallagher. He died of lung cancer in 1988. Recently,
Carver has received acclaim as a contemporary master of the short story, and his work
has been translated into more than twenty languages. Although his stories have been
much admired for, among other things, their knowledge of poor working people, Carver
once said that, until he read critics' reviews, he had not realized that his characters could
be pitied: "I never felt the people I was writing about were so bad off."*

This blind man, an old friend of my wife's, he was on his way to spend the
night. His wife had died. So he was visiting the dead wife's relatives in Connecticut. He called my wife from his in-laws'. Arrangements were made. He would
come by train, a five-hour trip, and my wife would meet him at the station. She
hadn't seen him since she worked for him one summer in Seattle ten years ago.
But she and the blind man had kept in touch. They made tapes and mailed
them back and forth. I wasn't enthusiastic about his visit. He was no one I knew.
And his being blind bothered me. My idea of blindness came from the movies.
In the movies, the blind moved slowly and never laughed. Sometimes they were
led by seeing-eye dogs. A blind man in my house was not something I looked
forward to.

That summer in Seattle she had needed a job. She didn't have any money.
The man she was going to marry at the end of the summer was in officers' training school. He didn't have any money, either. But she was in love with the guy,

and he was in love with her, etc. She'd seen something in the paper: HELP WANTED—*Reading to Blind Man*, and a telephone number. She phoned and went over, was hired on the spot. She'd worked with this blind man all summer. She read stuff to him, case studies, reports, that sort of thing. She helped him organize his little office in the county social-service department. They'd become good friends, my wife and the blind man. How do I know these things? She told me. And she told me something else. On her last day in the office, the blind man asked if he could touch her face. She agreed to this. She told me he touched his fingers to every part of her face, her nose—even her neck! She never forgot it. She even tried to write a poem about it. She was always trying to write a poem. She wrote a poem or two every year, usually after something really important had happened to her.

When we first started going out together, she showed me the poem. In the poem, she recalled his fingers and the way they had moved around over her face. In the poem, she talked about what she had felt at the time, about what went through her mind when the blind man touched her nose and lips. I can remember I didn't think much of the poem. Of course, I didn't tell her that. Maybe I just don't understand poetry. I admit it's not the first thing I reach for when I pick up something to read.

Anyway, this man who'd first enjoyed her favors, the officer-to-be, he'd been her childhood sweetheart. So okay. I'm saying that at the end of the summer she let the blind man run his hands over her face, said good-bye to him, married her childhood etc., who was now a commissioned officer, and she moved away from Seattle. But they'd kept in touch, she and the blind man. She made the first contact after a year or so. She called him up one night from an Air Force base in Alabama. She wanted to talk. They talked. He asked her to send a tape and tell him about her life. She did this. She sent the tape. On the tape, she told the blind man about her husband and about their life together in the military. She told the blind man she loved her husband but she didn't like it where they lived and she didn't like it that he was part of the military-industrial thing. She told the blind man she'd written a poem and he was in it. She told him that she was writing a poem about what it was like to be an Air Force officer's wife. The poem wasn't finished yet. She was still writing it. The blind man made a tape. He sent her the tape. She made a tape. This went on for years. My wife's officer was posted to one base and then another. She sent tapes from Moody AFB, McGuire, McConnell, and finally Travis, near Sacramento, where one night she got to feeling lonely and cut off from people she kept losing in that moving-around life. She got to feeling she couldn't go it another step. She went in and swallowed all the pills and capsules in the medicine chest and washed them down with a bottle of gin. Then she got into a hot bath and passed out.

But instead of dying, she got sick. She threw up. Her officer—why should he have a name? he was the childhood sweetheart, and what more does he want?—came home from somewhere, found her, and called the ambulance. In time, she put it all on a tape and sent the tape to the blind man. Over the years, she put all kinds of stuff on tapes and sent the tapes off lickety-split. Next to writing a poem

5

every year, I think it was her chief means of recreation. On one tape, she told the blind man she'd decided to live away from her officer for a time. On another tape, she told him about her divorce. She and I began going out, and of course she told her blind man about it. She told him everything, or so it seemed to me. Once she asked me if I'd like to hear the latest tape from the blind man. This was a year ago. I was on the tape, she said. So I said okay, I'd listen to it. I got us drinks and we settled down in the living room. We made ready to listen. First she inserted the tape into the player and adjusted a couple of dials. Then she pushed a lever. The tape squeaked and someone began to talk in this loud voice. She lowered the volume. After a few minutes of harmless chitchat, I heard my own name in the mouth of this stranger, this blind man I didn't even know! And then this: "From all you've said about him, I can only conclude—" But we were interrupted, a knock at the door, something, and we didn't ever get back to the tape. Maybe it was just as well. I'd heard all I wanted to.

Now this same blind man was coming to sleep in my house.

"Maybe I could take him bowling," I said to my wife. She was at the draining board doing scalloped potatoes. She put down the knife she was using and turned around.

"If you love me," she said, "you can do this for me. If you don't love me, okay. But if you had a friend, any friend, and the friend came to visit, I'd make him feel comfortable." She wiped her hands with the dish towel.

"I don't have any blind friends," I said.

"You don't have *any* friends," she said. "Period. Besides," she said, "goddamn it, his wife's just died! Don't you understand that? The man's lost his wife!"    10

I didn't answer. She'd told me a little about the blind man's wife. Her name was Beulah. Beulah! That's a name for a colored woman.

"Was his wife a Negro?" I asked.

"Are you crazy?" my wife said. "Have you just flipped or something?" She picked up a potato. I saw it hit the floor, then roll under the stove. "What's wrong with you?" she said. "Are you drunk?"

"I'm just asking," I said.

Right then my wife filled me in with more detail than I cared to know. I    15
made a drink and sat at the kitchen table to listen. Pieces of the story began to fall into place.

Beulah had gone to work for the blind man the summer after my wife had stopped working for him. Pretty soon Beulah and the blind man had themselves a church wedding. It was a little wedding—who'd want to go to such a wedding in the first place?—just the two of them, plus the minister and the minister's wife. But it was a church wedding just the same. It was what Beulah had wanted, he'd said. But even then Beulah must have been carrying the cancer in her glands. After they had been inseparable for eight years—my wife's word, *inseparable*—Beulah's health went into a rapid decline. She died in a Seattle hospital room, the blind man sitting beside the bed and holding on to her hand. They'd married, lived and worked together, slept together—had sex, sure—and then the blind man had to bury her. All this without his having ever seen what the goddamned woman looked like. It was beyond my understanding. Hearing this, I felt sorry for the blind man for a little bit. And then I found myself thinking what a pitiful life this woman must have led. Imagine a woman who could never see herself as she was seen in the eyes of her loved one. A woman who could go on day after day and never receive the smallest compliment from her beloved. A woman whose husband could never read the expression on her face, be it misery or something better. Someone who could wear makeup or not—what difference to him? She could, if she wanted, wear green eye-shadow around one eye, a straight pin in her nostril, yellow slacks, and purple shoes, no matter. And then to slip off into death, the blind man's hand on her hand, his blind eyes streaming tears—I'm imagining now—her last thought maybe this: that he never even knew what she looked like, and she on an express to the grave. Robert was left with a small insurance policy and a half of a twenty-peso Mexican coin. The other half of the coin went into the box with her. Pathetic.

So when the time rolled around, my wife went to the depot to pick him up. With nothing to do but wait—sure, I blamed him for that—I was having a drink and watching the TV when I heard the car pull into the drive. I got up from the sofa with my drink and went to the window to have a look.

I saw my wife laughing as she parked the car. I saw her get out of the car and shut the door. She was still wearing a smile. Just amazing. She went around to the other side of the car to where the blind man was already starting to get out. This blind man, feature this, he was wearing a full beard! A beard on a blind man! Too much, I say. The blind man reached into the backseat and dragged out a suitcase. My wife took his arm, shut the car door, and, talking all the way, moved him down the drive and then up the steps to the front porch. I turned off the TV. I finished my drink, rinsed the glass, dried my hands. Then I went to the door.

My wife said, "I want you to meet Robert. Robert, this is my husband. I've told you all about him." She was beaming. She had this blind man by his coat sleeve.

The blind man let go of his suitcase and up came his hand.    20

I took it. He squeezed hard, held my hand, and then he let it go.

"I feel like we've already met," he boomed.

"Likewise," I said. I didn't know what else to say. Then I said, "Welcome. I've heard a lot about you." We began to move then, a little group, from the porch into the living room, my wife guiding him by the arm. The blind man was carrying his suitcase in his other hand. My wife said things like, "To your left here, Robert. That's right. Now watch it, there's a chair. That's it. Sit down right here. This is the sofa. We just bought this sofa two weeks ago."

I started to say something about the old sofa. I'd liked that old sofa. But I didn't say anything. Then I wanted to say something else, small-talk, about the scenic ride along the Hudson. How going *to* New York, you should sit on the right-hand side of the train, and coming *from* New York, the left-hand side.

"Did you have a good train ride?" I said. "Which side of the train did you sit    25 on, by the way?"

"What a question, which side!" my wife said. "What's it matter which side?" she said.

"I just asked," I said.

"Right side," the blind man said. "I hadn't been on a train in nearly forty years. Not since I was a kid. With my folks. That's been a long time. I'd nearly forgotten the sensation. I have winter in my beard now," he said. "So I've been told, anyway. Do I look distinguished, my dear?" the blind man said to my wife.

"You look distinguished, Robert," she said. "Robert," she said. "Robert, it's just so good to see you."

My wife finally took her eyes off the blind man and looked at me. I had the feeling she didn't like what she saw. I shrugged. 30

I've never met, or personally known, anyone who was blind. This blind man was late forties, a heavy-set, balding man with stooped shoulders, as if he carried a great weight there. He wore brown slacks, brown shoes, a light-brown shirt, a tie, a sports coat. Spiffy. He also had this full beard. But he didn't use a cane and he didn't wear dark glasses. I'd always thought dark glasses were a must for the blind. Fact was, I wished he had a pair. At first glance, his eyes looked like anyone else's eyes. But if you looked close, there was something different about them. Too much white in the iris, for one thing, and the pupils seemed to move around in the sockets without his knowing it or being able to stop it. Creepy. As I stared at his face, I saw the left pupil turn in toward his nose while the other made an effort to keep in one place. But it was only an effort, for that eye was on the roam without his knowing it or wanting it to be.

I said, "Let me get you a drink. What's your pleasure? We have a little of everything. It's one of our pastimes."

"Bub, I'm a Scotch man myself," he said fast enough in this big voice.

"Right," I said. Bub! "Sure you are. I knew it."

He let his fingers touch his suitcase, which was sitting alongside the sofa. He was taking his bearings. I didn't blame him for that. 35

"I'll move that up to your room," my wife said.

"No, that's fine," the blind man said loudly. "It can go up when I go up."

"A little water with the Scotch?" I said.

"Very little," he said.

"I knew it," I said. 40

He said, "Just a tad. The Irish actor, Barry Fitzgerald? I'm like that fellow. When I drink water, Fitzgerald said, I drink water. When I drink whiskey, I drink whiskey." My wife laughed. The blind man brought his hand up under his beard. He lifted his beard slowly and let it drop.

I did the drinks, three big glasses of Scotch with a splash of water in each. Then we made ourselves comfortable and talked about Robert's travels. First the long flight from the West Coast to Connecticut, we covered that. Then from Connecticut up here by train. We had another drink concerning that leg of the trip.

I remembered having read somewhere that the blind didn't smoke because, as speculation had it, they couldn't see the smoke they exhaled. I thought I knew that much and that much only about blind people. But this blind man smoked his cigarette down to the nubbin and then lit another one. This blind man filled his ashtray and my wife emptied it.

When we sat down at the table for dinner, we had another drink. My wife heaped Robert's plate with cube steak, scalloped potatoes, green beans. I buttered him up two slices of bread. I said, "Here's bread and butter for you." I swallowed some of my drink. "Now let us pray," I said, and the blind man lowered his head. My wife looked at me, her mouth agape. "Pray the phone won't ring and the food doesn't get cold," I said.

We dug in. We ate everything there was to eat on the table. We ate like there was no tomorrow. We didn't talk. We ate. We scarfed. We grazed that table. We were into serious eating. The blind man had right away located his foods, he knew just where everything was on his plate. I watched with admiration as he used his knife and fork on the meat. He'd cut two pieces of meat, fork the meat into his mouth, and then go all out for the scalloped potatoes, the beans next, and then he'd tear off a hunk of buttered bread and eat that. He'd follow this up with a big drink of milk. It didn't seem to bother him to use his fingers once in a while, either.

We finished everything, including half a strawberry pie. For a few moments, we sat as if stunned. Sweat beaded on our faces. Finally, we got up from the table and left the dirty plates. We didn't look back. We took ourselves into the living room and sank into our places again. Robert and my wife sat on the sofa. I took the big chair. We had us two or three more drinks while they talked about the major things that had come to pass for them in the past ten years. For the most part, I just listened. Now and then I joined in. I didn't want him to think I'd left the room, and I didn't want her to think I was feeling left out. They talked of things that had happened to them—to them!—these past ten years. I waited in vain to hear my name on my wife's sweet lips: "And then my dear husband came into my life"—something like that. But I heard nothing of the sort. More talk of Robert. Robert had done a little of everything, it seemed, a regular blind jack-of-all-trades. But most recently he and his wife had had an Amway distributorship, from which, I gathered, they'd earned their living, such as it was. The blind man was also a ham radio operator. He talked in his loud voice about conversations he'd had with fellow operators in Guam, in the Philippines, in Alaska, and even in Tahiti. He said he'd have a lot of friends there if he ever wanted to go visit those places. From time to time, he'd turn his blind face toward me, put his hand under his beard, ask me something. How long had I been in my present position? (Three years.) Did I like my work? (I didn't.) Was I going to stay with it? (What were the options?) Finally, when I thought he was beginning to run down, I got up and turned on the TV.

My wife looked at me with irritation. She was heading toward a boil. Then she looked at the blind man and said, "Robert, do you have a TV?"

The blind man said, "My dear, I have two TVs. I have a color set and a black-and-white thing, an old relic. It's funny, but if I turn the TV on, and I'm always turning it on, I turn on the color set. It's funny, don't you think?"

I didn't know what to say to that. I had absolutely nothing to say to that. No opinion. So I watched the news program and tried to listen to what the announcer was saying.

"This is a color TV," the blind man said. "Don't ask me how, but I can tell."     50

"We traded up a while ago," I said.

The blind man had another taste of his drink. He lifted his beard, sniffed it, and let it fall. He leaned forward on the sofa. He positioned his ashtray on the coffee table, then put the lighter to his cigarette. He leaned back on the sofa and crossed his legs at the ankles.

My wife covered her mouth, and then she yawned. She stretched. She said, "I think I'll go upstairs and put on my robe. I think I'll change into something else. Robert, you make yourself comfortable," she said.

"I'm comfortable," the blind man said.

"I want you to feel comfortable in this house," she said.     55

"I am comfortable," the blind man said.

After she'd left the room, he and I listened to the weather report and then to the sports roundup. By that time, she'd been gone so long I didn't know if she was going to come back. I thought she might have gone to bed. I wished she'd come back downstairs. I didn't want to be left alone with a blind man. I asked him if he wanted another drink, and he said sure. Then I asked if he wanted to smoke some dope with me. I said I'd just rolled a number. I hadn't, but I planned to do so in about two shakes.

"I'll try some with you," he said.

"Damn right," I said. "That's the stuff."

I got our drinks and sat down on the sofa with him. Then I rolled us two fat     60 numbers. I lit one and passed it. I brought it to his fingers. He took it and inhaled.

"Hold it as long as you can," I said. I could tell he didn't know the first thing.

My wife came back downstairs wearing her pink robe and her pink slippers.

"What do I smell?" she said.

"We thought we'd have us some cannabis," I said.

My wife gave me a savage look. Then she looked at the blind man and said,     65 "Robert, I didn't know you smoked."

He said, "I do now, my dear. There's a first time for everything. But I don't feel anything yet."

"This stuff is pretty mellow," I said. "This stuff is mild. It's dope you can reason with," I said. "It doesn't mess you up."

"Not much it doesn't, bub," he said, and laughed.

My wife sat on the sofa between the blind man and me. I passed her the number. She took it and toked and then passed it back to me. "Which way is this going?" she said. Then she said, "I shouldn't be smoking this. I can hardly keep my eyes open as it is. That dinner did me in. I shouldn't have eaten so much."

"It was the strawberry pie," the blind man said. "That's what did it," he said, 70
and he laughed his big laugh. Then he shook his head.

"There's more strawberry pie," I said.

"Do you want some more, Robert?" my wife said.

"Maybe in a little while," he said.

We gave our attention to the TV. My wife yawned again. She said, "Your bed is made up when you feel like going to bed, Robert. I know you must have had a long day. When you're ready to go to bed, say so." She pulled his arm. "Robert?"

He came to and said, "I've had a real nice time. This beats tapes, doesn't it?" 75

I said, "Coming at you," and I put the number between his fingers. He inhaled, held the smoke, and then let it go. It was like he'd been doing it since he was nine years old.

"Thanks, bub," he said. "But I think this is all for me. I think I'm beginning to feel it," he said. He held the burning roach out for my wife.

"Same here," she said. "Ditto. Me, too." She took the roach and passed it to me. "I may just sit here for a while between you two guys with my eyes closed. But don't let me bother you, okay? Either one of you. If it bothers you, say so. Otherwise, I may just sit here with my eyes closed until you're ready to go to bed," she said. "Your bed's made up, Robert, when you're ready. It's right next to our room at the top of the stairs. We'll show you up when you're ready. You wake me up now, you guys, if I fall asleep." She said that and then she closed her eyes and went to sleep.

The news program ended. I got up and changed the channel. I sat back down on the sofa. I wished my wife hadn't pooped out. Her head lay across the back of the sofa, her mouth open. She'd turned so that her robe slipped away from her legs, exposing a juicy thigh. I reached to draw her robe back over her, and it was then that I glanced at the blind man. What the hell! I flipped the robe open again.

"You say when you want some strawberry pie," I said. 80

"I will," he said.

I said, "Are you tired? Do you want me to take you up to your bed? Are you ready to hit the hay?"

"Not yet," he said. "No, I'll stay up with you, bub. If that's all right. I'll stay up until you're ready to turn in. We haven't had a chance to talk. Know what I mean? I feel like me and her monopolized the evening." He lifted his beard and he let it fall. He picked up his cigarettes and his lighter.

"That's all right," I said. Then I said, "I'm glad for the company."

And I guess I was. Every night I smoked dope and stayed up as long as I could 85 before I fell asleep. My wife and I hardly ever went to bed at the same time. When I did go to sleep, I had these dreams. Sometimes I'd wake up from one of them, my heart going crazy.

Something about the church and the Middle Ages was on the TV. Not your run-of-the-mill TV fare. I wanted to watch something else. I turned to the other channels. But there was nothing on them, either. So I turned back to the first channel and apologized.

"Bub, it's all right," the blind man said. "It's fine with me. Whatever you want to watch is okay. I'm always learning something. Learning never ends. It won't hurt me to learn something tonight. I got ears," he said.

We didn't say anything for a time. He was leaning forward with his head turned at me, his right ear aimed in the direction of the set. Very disconcerting. Now and then his eyelids drooped and then they snapped open again. Now and then he put his fingers into his beard and tugged, like he was thinking about something he was hearing on the television.

On the screen, a group of men wearing cowls was being set upon and tormented by men dressed in skeleton costumes and men dressed as devils. The men dressed as devils wore devil masks, horns, and long tails. This pageant was part of a procession. The Englishman who was narrating the thing said it took place in Spain once a year. I tried to explain to the blind man what was happening.

"Skeletons," he said. "I know about skeletons," he said, and he nodded.        90

The TV showed this one cathedral. Then there was a long, slow look at another one. Finally, the picture switched to the famous one in Paris, with its flying buttresses and its spires reaching up to the clouds. The camera pulled away to show the whole of the cathedral rising above the skyline.

There were times when the Englishman who was telling the thing would shut up, would simply let the camera move around the cathedrals. Or else the camera would tour the countryside, men in fields walking behind oxen. I waited as long as I could. Then I felt I had to say something. I said, "They're showing the outside of this cathedral now. Gargoyles. Little statues carved to look like monsters. Now I guess they're in Italy. Yeah, they're in Italy. There's paintings on the walls of this one church."

"Are those fresco paintings, bub?" he asked, and he sipped from his drink.

I reached for my glass. But it was empty. I tried to remember what I could remember. "You're asking me are those frescoes?" I said. "That's a good question. I don't know."

The camera moved to a cathedral outside Lisbon. The differences in the        95 Portuguese cathedral compared with the French and Italian were not that great. But they were there. Mostly the interior stuff. Then something occurred to me, and I said, "Something has occurred to me. Do you have any idea what a cathedral is? What they look like, that is? Do you follow me? If somebody says cathedral to you, do you have any notion what they're talking about? Do you know the difference between that and a Baptist church, say?"

He let the smoke dribble from his mouth. "I know they took hundreds of workers fifty or a hundred years to build," he said. "I just heard the man say that, of course. I know generations of the same families worked on a cathedral. I heard him say that, too. The men who began their life's work on them, they never lived to see the completion of their work. In that wise, bub, they're no different from the rest of us, right?" He laughed. Then his eyelids drooped again. His head nodded. He seemed to be snoozing. Maybe he was imagining himself in Portugal. The TV was showing another cathedral now. This one was in Germany. The Englishman's voice droned on. "Cathedrals," the blind man said. He sat up and rolled his head back and forth. "If you want the truth, bub, that's about all I know. What I just said. What I heard him say. But maybe you could describe one to me? I wish you'd do it. I'd like that. If you want to know, I really don't have a good idea."

I stared hard at the shot of the cathedral on the TV. How could I even begin to describe it? But say my life depended on it. Say my life was being threatened by an insane guy who said I had to do it or else.

I stared some more at the cathedral before the picture flipped off into the countryside. There was no use. I turned to the blind man and said, "To begin with, they're very tall." I was looking around the room for clues. "They reach way up. Up and up. Toward the sky. They're so big, some of them, they have to have these supports. To help hold them up, so to speak. These supports are called buttresses. They remind me of viaducts, for some reason. But maybe you don't know viaducts, either? Sometimes the cathedrals have devils and such carved into the front. Sometimes lords and ladies. Don't ask me why this is," I said.

He was nodding. The whole upper part of his body seemed to be moving back and forth.

"I'm not doing so good, am I?" I said.                                                            100

He stopped nodding and leaned forward on the edge of the sofa. As he listened to me, he was running his fingers through his beard. I wasn't getting through to him, I could see that. But he waited for me to go on just the same. He nodded, like he was trying to encourage me. I tried to think what else to say. "They're really big," I said. "They're massive. They're built of stone. Marble, too, sometimes. In those olden days, when they built cathedrals, men wanted to be close to God. In those olden days, God was an important part of everyone's life. You could tell this from their cathedral-building. I'm sorry," I said, "but it looks like that's the best I can do for you. I'm just no good at it."

"That's all right, bub," the blind man said. "Hey, listen. I hope you don't mind my asking you. Can I ask you something? Let me ask you a simple question, yes or no. I'm just curious and there's no offense. You're my host. But let me ask if you are in any way religious? You don't mind my asking?"

I shook my head. He couldn't see that, though. A wink is the same as a nod to a blind man. "I guess I don't believe in it. In anything. Sometimes it's hard. You know what I'm saying?"

"Sure, I do," he said.

"Right," I said.                                                                                            105

The Englishman was still holding forth. My wife sighed in her sleep. She drew a long breath and went on with her sleeping.

"You'll have to forgive me," I said. "But I can't tell you what a cathedral looks like. It just isn't in me to do it. I can't do any more than I've done."

The blind man sat very still, his head down, as he listened to me.

I said, "The truth is, cathedrals don't mean anything special to me. Nothing. Cathedrals. They're something to look at on late-night TV. That's all they are."

It was then that the blind man cleared his throat. He brought something up. 110 He took a handkerchief from his back pocket. Then he said, "I get it, bub. It's okay. It happens. Don't worry about it," he said. "Hey, listen to me. Will you do me a favor? I got an idea. Why don't you find us some heavy paper? And a pen. We'll do something. We'll draw one together. Get us a pen and some heavy paper. Go on, bub, get the stuff," he said.

So I went upstairs. My legs felt like they didn't have any strength in them. They felt like they did after I'd done some running. In my wife's room, I looked around. I found some ballpoints in a little basket on her table. And then I tried to think where to look for the kind of paper he was talking about.

Downstairs, in the kitchen, I found a shopping bag with onion skins in the bottom of the bag. I emptied the bag and shook it. I brought it into the living room and sat down with it near his legs. I moved some things, smoothed the wrinkles from the bag, spread it out on the coffee table.

The blind man got down from the sofa and sat next to me on the carpet.

He ran his fingers over the paper. He went up and down the sides of the paper. The edges, even the edges. He fingered the corners.

"All right," he said. "All right, let's do her." 115

He found my hand, the hand with the pen. He closed his hand over my hand. "Go ahead, bub, draw," he said. "Draw. You'll see. I'll follow along with you. It'll be okay. Just begin now like I'm telling you. You'll see. Draw," the blind man said.

So I began. First I drew a box that looked like a house. It could have been the house I lived in. Then I put a roof on it. At either end of the roof, I drew spires. Crazy.

"Swell," he said. "Terrific. You're doing fine," he said. "Never thought anything like this could happen in your lifetime, did you, bub? Well, it's a strange life, we all know that. Go on now. Keep it up."

I put in windows with arches. I drew flying buttresses. I hung great doors. I couldn't stop. The TV station went off the air. I put down the pen and closed and opened my fingers. The blind man felt around over the paper. He moved the tips of his fingers over the paper, all over what I had drawn, and he nodded.

"Doing fine," the blind man said. 120

I took up the pen again, and he found my hand. I kept at it. I'm no artist. But I kept drawing just the same.

My wife opened up her eyes and gazed at us. She sat up on the sofa, her robe hanging open. She said, "What are you doing? Tell me, I want to know."

I didn't answer her.

The blind man said, "We're drawing a cathedral. Me and him are working on it. Press hard," he said to me. "That's right. That's good," he said. "Sure. You got it, bub, I can tell. You didn't think you could. But you can, can't you? You're cooking with gas now. You know what I'm saying? We're going to really have us something here in a minute. How's the old arm?" he said. "Put some people in there now. What's a cathedral without people?"

My wife said, "What's going on? Robert, what are you doing? What's going  125
on?"

"It's all right," he said to her. "Close your eyes now," the blind man said to
me.

I did it. I closed them just like he said.

"Are they closed?" he said. "Don't fudge."

"They're closed," I said.

"Keep them that way," he said. He said, "Don't stop now. Draw."  130

So we kept on with it. His fingers rode my fingers as my hand went over the
paper. It was like nothing else in my life up to now.

Then he said, "I think that's it. I think you got it," he said. "Take a look.
What do you think?"

But I had my eyes closed. I thought I'd keep them that way for a little longer.
I thought it was something I ought to do.

"Well?" he said. "Are you looking?"

My eyes were still closed. I was in my house. I knew that. But I didn't feel  135
like I was inside anything.

"It's really something," I said.

## QUESTIONS

1. What details in "Cathedral" make clear the narrator's initial attitude toward blind
   people? What hints does the author give about the reasons for this attitude? At what
   point in the story do the narrator's preconceptions about blind people start to change?
2. For what reason does the wife keep asking Robert if he'd like to go to bed (paragraphs
   74–78)? What motivates the narrator to make the same suggestion in paragraph 82?
   What effect does Robert's reply have on the narrator?
3. What makes the narrator start explaining what he's seeing on television?
4. How does the point of view contribute to the effectiveness of the story?
5. At the end, the narrator has an epiphany. How would you describe it?
6. How would you state the theme of "Cathedral" in your own words?

## SUGGESTIONS FOR WRITING

1. Have you, like the narrator of "The Open Boat," ever been in physical danger? Not
   that your life needs to be a television thriller, but think and see what you can recall.
   What have you learned from your experience? Tell of it, comparing your memory with
   what Crane observes of people in danger, with what Crane's correspondent reporter
   notices within himself.

   Note: In a sense, you are often in real danger from forces sometimes beyond your
   control (storms, rapists and other criminals, crazed souls who tamper with capsules in
   drugstores, disease carriers). In a way, passively to face such ordinary perils may seem
   less heroic than rowing an open boat in a heaving sea. In another way—well, if you're
   looking for a danger to recall, you might think about this comparison. Reading
   Crane's story, do you feel that, in any sense, you and the news correspondent are in
   the same boat?
2. In "The Open Boat," recall the poem that comes to matter greatly to the correspondent (paragraphs 178–181). Have you ever been in a situation when a story, an Aesop
   fable, a saying, a line of poetry, or a song lyric took on fresh and immediate meaning
   for you? If so, relate your experience. (If no such experience has befallen you, don't
   make one up.)

3. In 500 words or more, explain what you believe to be Hawthorne's opinion of the Puritans, as shown in "Young Goodman Brown."
4. Pick a story not included in this chapter and, in your own words, sum up its main theme. Then indicate what you find in the story that makes this theme clear. Among stories whose themes stand out are "Gimpel the Fool," "Barn Burning," "The Chrysanthemums," "The Death of Ivan Ilych," "I Stand Here Ironing," and "The Use of Force." Is the author making any statement you can agree or disagree with? Why do you feel the way you do?
5. Compare two stories similar in theme. Both Joyce in "Araby" and Singer in "Gimpel the Fool" set forth a conflict between illusion and reality. Flannery O'Connor's "A Good Man Is Hard To Find" and "Revelation" show how, by the grace of God, an ordinary individual can receive enlightenment. Browse in other chapters and in "Stories for Further Reading" and see what other pairs of stories go together in theme. Then set them side by side and point out their similarities and differences. This topic will lead you to compare and contrast, as discussed in "Writing about a Story" in Supplement: Writing.
6. Here is a topic for science fiction fans: Trace a general theme in two or more science fiction novels or stories you know. Choose works that express similar views. Suggestion: If you know two science fiction writers who distrust the benefits of technology, or who take a keen interest in the future of women, look closely at their work and you will probably find an intriguing theme.

# 7  Symbol

In F. Scott Fitzgerald's novel *The Great Gatsby*, a huge pair of bespectacled eyes stares across a wilderness of ash heaps, from a billboard advertising the services of an oculist. Repeatedly entering into the story, the advertisement comes to mean more than simply the availability of eye examinations. Fitzgerald has a character liken it to the eyes of God; he hints that some sad, compassionate spirit is brooding as it watches the passing procession of humanity. Such an object is a **symbol:** in literature, a thing that suggests more than its literal meaning. Symbols generally do not "stand for" any one meaning, nor for anything absolutely definite; they point, they hint, or, as Henry James put it, they cast long shadows. To take a large example: in Herman Melville's *Moby-Dick*, the great white whale of the book's title apparently means more than the literal dictionary-definition meaning of an aquatic mammal. He also suggests more than the devil, to whom some of the characters liken him. The great whale, as the story unfolds, comes to imply an amplitude of meanings: among them the forces of nature and the whole created universe.

This indefinite multiplicity of meanings is characteristic of a symbolic story and distinguishes it from an **allegory,** a story in which persons, places, and things form a system of clearly labeled equivalents. In a simple allegory, characters and other ingredients often stand for other definite meanings, which are often abstractions. You met such a character in the last chapter: Faith in Hawthorne's "Young Goodman Brown." Supreme allegories are found in some biblical parables ("The kingdom of Heaven is like a man who sowed good seed in his field . . . ," Matthew 13:24–30).[1] A classic allegory is the medieval play *Everyman*, whose hero represents us all, and who, deserted by false friends called Kindred and Goods, faces the judgment of God accompanied only by a faithful friend called Good Deeds. In John Bunyan's seventeenth-century *Pilgrim's*

---

[1]A **parable** is a brief story that teaches a lesson. Some (but not all) parables are allegories.

*Progress*, the protagonist, Christian, struggles along the difficult road toward salvation, meeting along the way persons such as Mr. Worldly Wiseman, who directs him into a more comfortable path (a wrong turn), and the residents of a town called Fair Speech, among them a hypocrite named Mr. Facing-both-ways. Not all allegories are simple: Dante's *Divine Comedy*, written in the Middle Ages, continues to reveal new meanings to careful readers. Allegory was much beloved in the Middle Ages, but in contemporary fiction it is rare. One modern instance is George Orwell's long fable *Animal Farm*, in which (among its double meanings) barnyard animals stand for human victims and totalitarian oppressors.

Symbols in fiction are not generally abstract terms like *love* or *truth*, but are likely to be perceptible objects (or worded descriptions that cause us to imagine them). In William Faulkner's "A Rose for Emily" (Chapter Two), Miss Emily's invisible watch ticking at the end of a golden chain not only indicates the passage of time, but suggests that time passes without even being noticed by the watch's owner, and the golden chain carries suggestions of wealth and authority. Often the symbols we meet in fiction are inanimate objects, but other things also may function symbolically. In James Joyce's "Araby" (Chapter Five), the very name of the bazaar, Araby—the poetic name for Arabia—suggests magic, romance, and *The Arabian Nights*; its syllables (the narrator tells us) "cast an Eastern enchantment over me." Even a locale, or a feature of physical topography, can provide rich suggestions. Recall Ernest Hemingway's "A Clean, Well-Lighted Place" (Chapter Five), in which the café is not merely a café, but an island of refuge from night, chaos, loneliness, old age, and impending death.

In some novels and stories, symbolic characters make brief cameo appearances. Such characters often are not well-rounded and fully known, but are seen fleetingly and remain slightly mysterious. In *Heart of Darkness*, a short novel by Joseph Conrad, a steamship company that hires men to work in the Congo maintains in its waiting room two women who knit black wool—like the classical Fates. Usually such a symbolic character is more a portrait than a person—or somewhat portraitlike, as Faulkner's Miss Emily, who twice appears at a window of her house "like the carven torso of an idol in a niche." Though Faulkner invests Miss Emily with life and vigor, he also clothes her in symbolic hints: she seems almost to personify the vanishing aristocracy of the antebellum South, still maintaining a black servant and being ruthlessly betrayed by a moneymaking Yankee. Sometimes a part of a character's body or an attribute may convey symbolic meaning: a baleful eye, as in Edgar Allan Poe's "The Tell-Tale Heart" (page 61).

Much as a symbolic whale holds more meaning than an ordinary whale, a **symbolic act** is a gesture with larger significance than usual. For the boy's father in Faulkner's "Barn Burning" (Chapter Five), the act of destroying a barn is no mere act of spite, but an expression of his profound hatred for anything not belonging to him. Faulkner adds that burning a barn reflects the father's memories of the "waste and extravagance of war"; and further adds that "the element of fire spoke to some deep mainspring" in his being. A symbolic act, however, doesn't have to be a gesture as large as starting a conflagration. Before setting out in pursuit of the great white whale, Melville's Captain Ahab in *Moby-Dick* deliberately snaps his tobacco pipe and throws it away, as if to suggest (among other things) that he will let no pleasure or pastime distract him from his vengeance.

Why do writers have to symbolize—why don't they tell us outright? One advantage of a symbol is that it is so compact, and yet so fully laden. Both starkly concrete and slightly mysterious, like Miss Emily's invisible ticking watch, it may impress us with all the force of something beheld in a dream or in a nightmare. The watch suggests, among other things, the slow and invisible passage of time. What this symbol says, it says more fully and more memorably than could be said, perhaps, in a long essay on the subject.

To some extent (it may be claimed), all stories are symbolic. Merely by holding up for our inspection these characters and their actions, the writer lends them *some* special significance. But this is to think of *symbol* in an extremely broad and inclusive way. For the usual purposes of reading a story and understanding it, there is probably little point in looking for symbolism in every word, in every stick or stone, in every striking of a match, in every minor character. Still, to be on the alert for symbols when reading fiction is perhaps wiser than to ignore them. Not to admit that symbolic meanings may be present, or to refuse to think about them, would be another way to misread a story—or to read no further than its outer edges.

How, then, do you recognize a symbol in fiction when you meet it? Fortunately, the storyteller often gives the symbol particular emphasis. It may be mentioned repeatedly throughout the story; it may even supply the story with a title ("Araby," "Barn Burning," "A Clean, Well-Lighted Place"). At times, a crucial symbol will open a story or end it. Unless an object, act, or character is given some such special emphasis and importance, we may generally feel safe in taking it at face value. Probably it isn't a symbol if it points clearly and unmistakably toward some one meaning, like a whistle in a factory, whose blast at noon means lunch. But an object, an act, or a character is surely symbolic (and almost as surely displays high literary art) if, when we finish the story, we realize that it was that item—those gigantic eyes; that clean, well-lighted café; that burning of a barn—which led us to the author's theme, the essential meaning.

## John Steinbeck
### THE CHRYSANTHEMUMS                                                      1938

*John Steinbeck (1902–1968), was born in
Salinas, California, in the fertile valley he
remembers in "The Chrysanthemums."
Off and on, he attended Stanford Uni-
versity, then sojourned in New York as a
reporter and a bricklayer. After years of
struggle to earn his living by fiction,
Steinbeck reached a large audience with*
Tortilla Flat *(1935), a loosely woven
novel portraying Mexican-Americans in
Monterey with fondness and sympathy.
Great acclaim greeted* The Grapes of
Wrath *(1939), the story of a family of
Oklahoma farmers who, ruined by dust
storms in the 1930s, join a mass migration
to California. Like Ernest Hemingway and
Stephen Crane, Steinbeck prided himself on
his journalism: in World War II, he filed
dispatches from battlefronts in Italy and
Africa, and in 1966 he wrote a column
from South Vietnam. Known widely behind
the Iron Curtain, Steinbeck accepted an invitation to visit the Soviet Union, and
reported his trip in* A Russian Journal *(1948). In 1962 he became the seventh
American to win the Nobel prize for literature, but critics have never placed Steinbeck
on the same high shelf with Faulkner and Hemingway. He wrote much, not all good,
and yet his best work adds to an impressive total. Besides* The Grapes of Wrath, *it
includes* In Dubious Battle *(1936), a novel of an apple-pickers' strike;* Of Mice and
Men, *a powerful short novel (also a play) of comradeship between a hobo and a
moron;* The Log from the Sea of Cortez, *a nonfiction account of a marine biological
expedition; and the short stories in* The Long Valley *(1938). Throughout the fiction
he wrote in his prime, Steinbeck maintains an appealing sympathy for the poor and
downtrodden, the lonely and dispossessed.*

*John Steinbeck*

     The high grey-flannel fog of winter closed off the Salinas Valley° from the
sky and from all the rest of the world. On every side it sat like a lid on the mountains and made of the great valley a closed pot. On the broad, level land floor the
gang plows bit deep and left the black earth shining like metal where the shares
had cut. On the foothill ranches across the Salinas River, the yellow stubble
fields seemed to be bathed in pale cold sunshine, but there was no sunshine in
the valley now in December. The thick willow scrub along the river flamed with
sharp and positive yellow leaves.

*Salinas Valley:* south of San Francisco in the Coast Ranges region of California.

It was a time of quiet and of waiting. The air was cold and tender. A light wind blew up from the southwest so that the farmers were mildly hopeful of a good rain before long; but fog and rain do not go together.

Across the river, on Henry Allen's foothill ranch there was little work to be done, for the hay was cut and stored and the orchards were plowed up to receive the rain deeply when it should come. The cattle on the higher slopes were becoming shaggy and rough-coated.

Elisa Allen, working in her flower garden, looked down across the yard and saw Henry, her husband, talking to two men in business suits. The three of them stood by the tractor shed, each man with one foot on the side of the little Fordson. They smoked cigarettes and studied the machine as they talked.

Elisa watched them for a moment and then went back to her work. She was    5
thirty-five. Her face was lean and strong and her eyes were as clear as water. Her figure looked blocked and heavy in her gardening costume, a man's black hat pulled low down over her eyes, clod-hopper shoes, a figured print dress almost completely covered by a big corduroy apron with four big pockets to hold the snips, the trowel and scratcher, the seeds and the knife she worked with. She wore heavy leather gloves to protect her hands while she worked.

She was cutting down the old year's chrysanthemum stalks with a pair of short and powerful scissors. She looked down toward the men by the tractor shed now and then. Her face was eager and mature and handsome; even her work with the scissors was over-eager, over-powerful. The chrysanthemum stems seemed too small and easy for her energy.

She brushed a cloud of hair out of her eyes with the back of her glove, and left a smudge of earth on her cheek in doing it. Behind her stood the neat white farm house with red geraniums close-banked around it as high as the windows. It was a hard-swept looking little house with hard-polished windows, and a clean mud-mat on the front steps.

Elisa cast another glance toward the tractor shed. The strangers were getting into their Ford coupe. She took off a glove and put her strong fingers down into the forest of new green chrysanthemum sprouts that were growing around the old roots. She spread the leaves and looked down among the close-growing stems. No aphids were there, no sowbugs or snails or cutworms. Her terrier fingers destroyed such pests before they could get started.

Elisa started at the sound of her husband's voice. He had come near quietly, and he leaned over the wire fence that protected her flower garden from cattle and dogs and chickens.

"At it again," he said. "You've got a strong new crop coming."    10

Elisa straightened her back and pulled on the gardening glove again. "Yes. They'll be strong this coming year." In her tone and on her face there was a little smugness.

"You've got a gift with things," Henry observed. "Some of those yellow chrysanthemums you had this year were ten inches across. I wish you'd work out in the orchard and raise some apples that big."

Her eyes sharpened. "Maybe I could do it, too. I've a gift with things, all right. My mother had it. She could stick anything in the ground and make it grow. She said it was having planters' hands that knew how to do it."

"Well, it sure works with flowers," he said.

"Henry, who were those men you were talking to?"                                    15

"Why, sure, that's what I came to tell you. They were from the Western Meat Company. I sold those thirty head of three-year-old steers. Got nearly my own price, too."

"Good," she said. "Good for you."

"And I thought," he continued, "I thought how it's Saturday afternoon, and we might go into Salinas for dinner at a restaurant, and then to a picture show— to celebrate, you see."

"Good," she repeated. "Oh, yes. That will be good."

Henry put on his joking tone. "There's fights tonight. How'd you like to go    20 to the fights?"

"Oh, no," she said breathlessly. "No, I wouldn't like fights."

"Just fooling, Elisa. We'll go to a movie. Let's see. It's two now. I'm going to take Scotty and bring down those steers from the hill. It'll take us maybe two hours. We'll go in town about five and have dinner at the Cominos Hotel. Like that?"

"Of course I'll like it. It's good to eat away from home."

"All right, then. I'll go get up a couple of horses."

She said, "I'll have plenty of time to transplant some of these sets, I guess."    25

She heard her husband calling Scotty down by the barn. And a little later she saw the two men ride up the pale yellow hillside in search of the steers.

There was a little square sandy bed kept for rooting the chrysanthemums. With her trowel she turned the soil over and over, and smoothed it and patted it firm. Then she dug ten parallel trenches to receive the sets. Back at the chrysanthemum bed she pulled out the little crisp shoots, trimmed off the leaves of each one with her scissors and laid it on a small orderly pile.

A squeak of wheels and plod of hoofs came from the road. Elisa looked up. The country road ran along the dense bank of willows and cottonwoods that bordered the river, and up this road came a curious vehicle, curiously drawn. It was an old spring-wagon, with a round canvas top on it like the cover of a prairie schooner. It was drawn by an old bay horse and a little grey-and-white burro. A big stubble-bearded man sat between the cover flaps and drove the crawling team. Underneath the wagon, between the hind wheels, a lean and rangy mongrel dog walked sedately. Words were painted on the canvas, in clumsy, crooked letters. "Pots, pans, knives, sisors, lawn mores, Fixed." Two rows of articles, and the triumphantly definitive "Fixed" below. The black paint had run down in little sharp points beneath each letter.

Elisa, squatting on the ground, watched to see the crazy, loose-jointed wagon pass by. But it didn't pass. It turned into the farm road in front of her house, crooked old wheels skirling and squeaking. The rangy dog darted from between the wheels and ran ahead. Instantly the two ranch shepherds flew out at him. Then all three stopped, and with stiff and quivering tails, with taut straight legs, with ambassadorial dignity, they slowly circled, sniffing daintily. The caravan pulled up to Elisa's wire fence and stopped. Now the newcomer dog, feeling outnumbered, lowered his tail and retired under the wagon with raised hackles and bared teeth.

The man on the wagon seat called out, "That's a bad dog in a fight when he 30 gets started."

Elisa laughed. "I see he is. How soon does he generally get started?"

The man caught up her laughter and echoed it heartily. "Sometimes not for weeks and weeks," he said. He climbed stiffly down, over the wheel. The horse and the donkey drooped like unwatered flowers.

Elisa saw that he was a very big man. Although his hair and beard were greying, he did not look old. His worn black suit was wrinkled and spotted with grease. The laughter had disappeared from his face and eyes the moment his laughing voice ceased. His eyes were dark, and they were full of the brooding that gets in the eyes of teamsters and of sailors. The calloused hands he rested on the wire fence were cracked, and every crack was a black line. He took off his battered hat.

"I'm off my general road, ma'am," he said. "Does this dirt road cut over across the river to the Los Angeles highway?"

Elisa stood up and shoved the thick scissors in her apron pocket. "Well, yes, 35 it does, but it winds around and then fords the river. I don't think your team could pull through the sand."

He replied with some asperity. "It might surprise you what them beasts can pull through."

"When they get started?" she asked.

He smiled for a second. "Yes. When they get started."

"Well," said Elisa, "I think you'll save time if you go back to the Salinas road and pick up the highway there."

He drew a big finger down the chicken wire and made it sing. "I ain't in any 40 hurry, ma'am. I go from Seattle to San Diego and back every year. Takes all my time. About six months each way. I aim to follow nice weather."

Elisa took off her gloves and stuffed them in the apron pocket with the scissors. She touched the under edge of her man's hat, searching for fugitive hairs. "That sounds like a nice kind of a way to live," she said.

He leaned confidentially over the fence. "Maybe you noticed the writing on my wagon. I mend pots and sharpen knives and scissors. You got any of them things to do?"

"Oh, no," she said quickly. "Nothing like that." Her eyes hardened with resistance.

"Scissors is the worst thing," he explained. "Most people just ruin scissors trying to sharpen 'em, but I know how. I got a special tool. It's a little bobbit kind of thing, and patented. But it sure does the trick."

"No. My scissors are all sharp." 45

"All right, then. Take a pot," he continued earnestly, "a bent pot, or a pot with a hole. I can make it like new so you don't have to buy no new ones. That's a saving for you."

"No," she said shortly. "I tell you I have nothing like that for you to do."

His face fell to an exaggerated sadness. His voice took on a whining undertone. "I ain't had a thing to do today. Maybe I won't have no supper tonight. You see I'm off my regular road. I know folks on the highway clear from Seattle to San Diego. They save their things for me to sharpen up because they know I do it so good and save them money."

"I'm sorry," Elisa said irritably. "I haven't anything for you to do."

His eyes left her face and fell to searching the ground. They roamed about 50 until they came to the chrysanthemum bed where she had been working. "What's them plants, ma'am?"

The irritation and resistance melted from Elisa's face. "Oh, those are chrysanthemums, giant whites and yellows. I raise them every year, bigger than anybody around here."

"Kind of a long-stemmed flower? Looks like a quick puff of colored smoke?" he asked.

"That's it. What a nice way to describe them."

"They smell kind of nasty till you get used to them," he said.

"It's a good bitter smell," she retorted, "not nasty at all." 55

He changed his tone quickly. "I like the smell myself."

"I had ten-inch blooms this year," she said.

The man leaned farther over the fence. "Look. I know a lady down the road a piece, has got the nicest garden you ever seen. Got nearly every kind of flower but no chrysanthemums. Last time I was mending a copper-bottom washtub for her (that's a hard job but I do it good), she said to me, 'If you ever run acrost some nice chrysanthemums I wish you'd try to get me a few seeds.' That's what she told me."

Elisa's eyes grew alert and eager. "She couldn't have known much about chrysanthemums. You *can* raise them from seed, but it's much easier to root the little sprouts you see there."

"Oh," he said. "I s'pose I can't take none to her, then." 60

"Why yes you can," Elisa cried. "I can put some in damp sand, and you can carry them right along with you. They'll take root in the pot if you keep them damp. And then she can transplant them."

"She'd sure like to have some, ma'am. You say they're nice ones?"

"Beautiful," she said. "Oh, beautiful." Her eyes shone. She tore off the battered hat and shook out her dark pretty hair. "I'll put them in a flower pot, and you can take them right with you. Come into the yard."

While the man came through the picket gate Elisa ran excitedly along the geranium-bordered path to the back of the house. And she returned carrying a big red flower pot. The gloves were forgotten now. She kneeled on the ground by the starting bed and dug up the sandy soil with her fingers and scooped it into the bright new flower pot. Then she picked up the little pile of shoots she had prepared. With her strong fingers she pressed them in the sand and tamped around them with her knuckles. The man stood over her. "I'll tell you what to do," she said. "You remember so you can tell the lady."

"Yes, I'll try to remember." 65

"Well, look. These will take root in about a month. Then she must set them out, about a foot apart in good rich earth like this, see?" She lifted a handful of dark soil for him to look at. "They'll grow fast and tall. Now remember this: In July tell her to cut them down, about eight inches from the ground."

"Before they bloom?" he asked.

"Yes, before they bloom." Her face was tight with eagerness. "They'll grow right up again. About the last of September the buds will start."

She stopped and seemed perplexed. "It's the budding that takes the most care," she said hesitantly. "I don't know how to tell you." She looked deep into his eyes, searchingly. Her mouth opened a little, and she seemed to be listening. "I'll try to tell you," she said. "Did you ever hear of planting hands?"

"Can't say I have, ma'am." 70

"Well, I can only tell you what it feels like. It's when you're picking off the buds you don't want. Everything goes right down into your fingertips. You watch your fingers work. They do it themselves. You can feel how it is. They pick and pick the buds. They never make a mistake. They're with the plant. Do you see? Your fingers and the plant. You can feel that, right up your arm. They know. They never make a mistake. You can feel it. When you're like that you can't do anything wrong. Do you see that? Can you understand that?"

She was kneeling on the ground looking up at him. Her breast swelled passionately.

The man's eyes narrowed. He looked away self-consciously. "Maybe I know," he said. "Sometimes in the night in the wagon there—"

Elisa's voice grew husky. She broke in on him, "I've never lived as you do, but I know what you mean. When the night is dark—why, the stars are sharp-pointed, and there's quiet. Why, you rise up and up! Every pointed star gets driven into your body. It's like that. Hot and sharp and—lovely."

Kneeling there, her hand went out toward his legs in the greasy black 75 trousers. Her hesitant fingers almost touched the cloth. Then her hand dropped to the ground. She crouched low like a fawning dog.

He said, "It's nice, just like you say. Only when you don't have no dinner, it ain't."

She stood up then, very straight, and her face was ashamed. She held the flower pot out to him and placed it gently in his arms. "Here. Put it in your wagon, on the seat, where you can watch it. Maybe I can find something for you to do."

At the back of the house she dug in the can pile and found two old and battered aluminum saucepans. She carried them back and gave them to him. "Here, maybe you can fix these."

His manner changed. He became professional. "Good as new I can fix them." At the back of his wagon he set a little anvil, and out of an oily tool box dug a small machine hammer. Elisa came through the gate to watch him while he pounded out the dents in the kettles. His mouth grew sure and knowing. At a difficult part of the work he sucked his under-lip.

"You sleep right in the wagon?" Elisa asked.

"Right in the wagon, ma'am. Rain or shine I'm dry as a cow in there."

"It must be nice," she said. "It must be very nice. I wish women could do such things."

"It ain't the right kind of a life for a woman."

Her upper lip raised a little, showing her teeth. "How do you know? How can you tell?" she said.

"I don't know, ma'am," he protested. "Of course I don't know. Now here's your kettles, done. You don't have to buy no new ones."

"How much?"

"Oh, fifty cents'll do. I keep my prices down and my work good. That's why I have all them satisfied customers up and down the highway."

Elisa brought him a fifty-cent piece from the house and dropped it in his hand. "You might be surprised to have a rival some time. I can sharpen scissors, too. And I can beat the dents out of little pots. I could show you what a woman might do."

He put his hammer back in the oily box and shoved the little anvil out of sight. "It would be a lonely life for a woman, ma'am, and a scarey life, too, with animals creeping under the wagon all night." He climbed over the single-tree, steadying himself with a hand on the burro's white rump. He settled himself in the seat, picked up the lines. "Thank you kindly, ma'am," he said. "I'll do like you told me; I'll go back and catch the Salinas road."

"Mind," she called, "if you're long in getting there, keep the sand damp."

"Sand, ma'am? . . . Sand? Oh, sure. You mean around the chrysanthemums. Sure I will." He clucked his tongue. The beasts leaned luxuriously into their collars. The mongrel dog took his place between the back wheels. The wagon turned and crawled out the entrance road and back the way it had come, along the river.

Elisa stood in front of her wire fence watching the slow progress of the caravan. Her shoulders were straight, her head thrown back, her eyes half-closed, so that the scene came vaguely into them. Her lips moved silently, forming the words "Good-bye—good-bye." Then she whispered, "That's a bright direction. There's a glowing there." The sound of her whisper startled her. She shook herself free and looked about to see whether anyone had been listening. Only the dogs had heard. They lifted their heads toward her from their sleeping in the dust, and then stretched out their chins and settled asleep again. Elisa turned and ran hurriedly into the house.

In the kitchen she reached behind the stove and felt the water tank. It was full of hot water from the noonday cooking. In the bathroom she tore off her soiled clothes and flung them into the corner. And then she scrubbed herself with a little block of pumice, legs and thighs, loins and chest and arms, until her skin was scratched and red. When she had dried herself she stood in front of a mirror in her bedroom and looked at her body. She tightened her stomach and threw out her chest. She turned and looked over her shoulder at her back.

After a while she began to dress, slowly. She put on her newest under-clothing and her nicest stockings and the dress which was the symbol of her prettiness. She worked carefully on her hair, penciled her eyebrows and rouged her lips.

Before she was finished she heard the little thunder of hoofs and the shouts of Henry and his helper as they drove the red steers into the corral. She heard the gate bang shut and set herself for Henry's arrival.

His step sounded on the porch. He entered the house calling, "Elisa, where are you?"

"In my room, dressing. I'm not ready. There's hot water for your bath. Hurry up. It's getting late."

When she heard him splashing in the tub, Elisa laid his dark suit on the bed, and shirt and socks and tie beside it. She stood his polished shoes on the floor beside the bed. Then she went to the porch and sat primly and stiffly down. She looked toward the river road where the willow-line was still yellow with frosted leaves so that under the high grey fog they seemed a thin band of sunshine. This was the only color in the grey afternoon. She sat unmoving for a long time. Her eyes blinked rarely.

Henry came banging out of the door, shoving his tie inside his vest as he came. Elisa stiffened and her face grew tight. Henry stopped short and looked at her. "Why—why, Elisa. You look so nice!"

"Nice? You think I look nice? What do you mean by 'nice'?"

Henry blundered on. "I don't know. I mean you look different, strong and happy."

"I am strong? Yes, strong. What do you mean 'strong'?"

He looked bewildered. "You're playing some kind of a game," he said helplessly. "It's a kind of a play. You look strong enough to break a calf over your knee, happy enough to eat it like a watermelon."

For a second she lost her rigidity. "Henry! Don't talk like that. You didn't know what you said." She grew complete again. "I'm strong," she boasted. "I never knew before how strong."

Henry looked down toward the tractor shed, and when he brought his eyes back to her, they were his own again. "I'll get out the car. You can put on your coat while I'm starting."

Elisa went into the house. She heard him drive to the gate and idle down his motor, and then she took a long time to put on her hat. She pulled it here and pressed it there. When Henry turned the motor off she slipped into her coat and went out.

The little roadster bounced along on the dirt road by the river, raising the birds and driving the rabbits into the brush. Two cranes flapped heavily over the willow-line and dropped into the river-bed.

Far ahead on the road Elisa saw a dark speck. She knew.

She tried not to look as they passed it, but her eyes would not obey. She whispered to herself sadly, "He might have thrown them off the road. That wouldn't have been much trouble, not very much. But he kept the pot," she explained. "He had to keep the pot. That's why he couldn't get them off the road."

The roadster turned a bend and she saw the caravan ahead. She swung full 110
around toward her husband so she could not see the little covered wagon and the
mismatched team as the car passed them.

In a moment it was over. The thing was done. She did not look back.

She said loudly, to be heard above the motor, "It will be good, tonight, a
good dinner."

"Now you're changed again," Henry complained. He took one hand from the
wheel and patted her knee. "I ought to take you in to dinner oftener. It would be
good for both of us. We get so heavy out on the ranch."

"Henry," she asked, "could we have wine at dinner?"

"Sure we could. Say! That will be fine." 115

She was silent for a while; then she said, "Henry, at those prize fights, do the
men hurt each other very much?"

"Sometimes a little, not often. Why?"

"Well, I've read how they break noses, and blood runs down their chests. I've
read how the fighting gloves get heavy and soggy with blood."

He looked around at her. "What's the matter, Elisa? I didn't know you read
things like that." He brought the car to a stop, then turned to the right over the
Salinas River bridge.

"Do any women ever go to the fights?" she asked. 120

"Oh, sure, some. What's the matter, Elisa? Do you want to go? I don't think
you'd like it, but I'll take you if you really want to go."

She relaxed limply in the seat. "Oh, no. No. I don't want to go. I'm sure I
don't." Her face was turned away from him. "It will be enough if we can have
wine. It will be plenty." She turned up her coat collar so he could not see that she
was crying weakly—like an old woman.

## QUESTIONS

1. When we first meet Elisa in her garden, with what details does Steinbeck delineate
   her character for us?
2. Elisa works inside a "wire fence that protected her flower garden from cattle and dogs
   and chickens" (paragraph 9). What does this wire fence suggest?
3. How would you describe Henry and Elisa's marriage? Cite details from the story to
   support your description.
4. For what motive does the traveling salesman take an interest in Elisa's chrysanthemums? What immediate effect does his interest have on Elisa?
5. For what possible purpose does Steinbeck give us such a detailed account of Elisa's
   preparations for her evening out? Notice her tearing off her soiled clothes, her scrubbing her body with pumice (paragraphs 93–94).
6. Of what significance to Elisa is the sight of the contents of the flower pot discarded in
   the road? Notice that, as her husband's car overtakes the covered wagon, Elisa averts
   her eyes; and then Steinbeck adds, "In a moment it was over. The thing was done.
   She did not look back" (paragraph 111). Explain this passage.
7. How do you interpret Elisa's asking for wine with dinner? How do you account for her
   new interest in prize fights?
8. In a sentence, try to state this short story's theme.
9. Why are Elisa Allen's chrysanthemums so important to this story? Sum up what you
   understand them to mean.

**Shirley Jackson**

THE LOTTERY                                                    1948

Shirley Jackson (1919–1965), a native of
San Francisco, moved in her teens to
Rochester, New York. She started college at
the University of Rochester, but had to drop
out, stricken by severe depression, a problem that was to recur at intervals throughout her life. Later she was graduated from
Syracuse University. With her husband
Stanley Edgar Hyman, a literary critic, she
settled in Bennington, Vermont, in a
sprawling house built in the nineteenth century. There Jackson conscientiously set herself to produce a fixed number of words
each day. She wrote novels: The Road
Through the Wall (1948), and three psychological thrillers—Hangsaman (1951),

Shirley Jackson

The Haunting of Hill House (1959), and We Have Always Lived in the Castle
(1962). She wrote light, witty articles for Good Housekeeping and other popular magazines about the horrors of housekeeping and rearing four children, collected in Life
among the Savages (1953) and Raising Demons (1957); but she claimed to have
written these only for money. When in 1948 "The Lottery" appeared in The New
Yorker, that issue of the magazine quickly sold out. Her purpose in writing the story,
Jackson declared, had been "to shock the story's readers with a graphic demonstration of
the pointless violence and general inhumanity in their own lives."

The morning of June 27th was clear and sunny, with the fresh warmth of a
full-summer day; the flowers were blossoming profusely and the grass was richly
green. The people of the village began to gather in the square, between the post
office and the bank, around ten o'clock; in some towns there were so many people that the lottery took two days and had to be started on June 26th, but in this
village, where there were only about three hundred people, the whole lottery
took less than two hours, so it could begin at ten o'clock in the morning and still
be through in time to allow the villagers to get home for noon dinner.

The children assembled first, of course. School was recently over for the
summer, and the feeling of liberty sat uneasily on most of them; they tended to
gather together quietly for a while before they broke into boisterous play, and
their talk was still of the classroom and the teacher, of books and reprimands.
Bobby Martin had already stuffed his pockets full of stones, and the other boys
soon followed his example, selecting the smoothest and roundest stones; Bobby
and Harry Jones and Dickie Delacroix—the villagers pronounced this name
"Dellacroy"—eventually made a great pile of stones in one corner of the square

and guarded it against the raids of the other boys. The girls stood aside, talking among themselves, looking over their shoulders at the boys, and the very small children rolled in the dust or clung to the hands of their older brothers or sisters.

Soon the men began to gather, surveying their own children, speaking of planting and rain, tractors and taxes. They stood together, away from the pile of stones in the corner, and their jokes were quiet and they smiled rather than laughed. The women, wearing faded house dresses and sweaters, came shortly after their menfolk. They greeted one another and exchanged bits of gossip as they went to join their husbands. Soon the women, standing by their husbands, began to call to their children, and the children came reluctantly, having to be called four or five times. Bobby Martin ducked under his mother's grasping hand and ran, laughing, back to the pile of stones. His father spoke up sharply, and Bobby came quickly and took his place between his father and his oldest brother.

The lottery was conducted—as were the square dances, the teenage club, the Halloween program—by Mr. Summers, who had time and energy to devote to civic activities. He was a roundfaced, jovial man and he ran the coal business, and people were sorry for him, because he had no children and his wife was a scold. When he arrived in the square, carrying the black wooden box, there was a murmur of conversation among the villagers and he waved and called, "Little late today, folks." The postmaster, Mr. Graves, followed him, carrying a three-legged stool, and the stool was put in the center of the square and Mr. Summers set the black box down on it. The villagers kept their distance, leaving a space between themselves and the stool, and when Mr. Summers said, "Some of you fellows want to give me a hand?" there was a hesitation before two men, Mr. Martin and his oldest son, Baxter, came forward to hold the box steady on the stool while Mr. Summers stirred up the papers inside it.

The original paraphernalia for the lottery had been lost long ago, and the black box now resting on the stool had been put into use even before Old Man Warner, the oldest man in town, was born. Mr. Summers spoke frequently to the villagers about making a new box, but no one liked to upset even as much tradition as was represented by the black box. There was a story that the present box had been made with some pieces of the box that had preceded it, the one that had been constructed when the first people settled down to make a village here. Every year, after the lottery, Mr. Summers began talking again about a new box, but every year the subject was allowed to fade off without anything's being done. The black box grew shabbier each year; by now it was no longer completely black but splintered badly along one side to show the original wood color, and in some places faded or stained.

Mr. Martin and his oldest son, Baxter, held the black box securely on the stool until Mr. Summers had stirred the papers thoroughly with his hand. Because so much of the ritual had been forgotten or discarded, Mr. Summers had been successful in having slips of paper substituted for the chips of wood that had been used for generations. Chips of wood, Mr. Summers had argued, had been all very well when the village was tiny, but now that the population was more than three hundred and likely to keep on growing, it was necessary to use something that

5

would fit more easily into the black box. The night before the lottery, Mr. Summers and Mr. Graves made up the slips of paper and put them in the box, and it was then taken to the safe of Mr. Summers's coal company and locked up until Mr. Summers was ready to take it to the square next morning. The rest of the year, the box was put away, sometimes one place, sometimes another; it had spent one year in Mr. Graves's barn and another year underfoot in the post office, and sometimes it was set on a shelf in the Martin grocery and left there.

There was a great deal of fussing to be done before Mr. Summers declared the lottery open. There were lists to make up—of heads of families, heads of households in each family, members of each household in each family. There was the proper swearing-in of Mr. Summers by the postmaster, as the official of the lottery; at one time, some people remembered, there had been a recital of some sort, performed by the official of the lottery, a perfunctory, tuneless chant that had been rattled off duly each year; some people believed that the official of the lottery used to stand just so when he said or sang it, others believed that he was supposed to walk among the people, but years and years ago this part of the ritual had been allowed to lapse. There had been, also, a ritual salute, which the official of the lottery had had to use in addressing each person who came up to draw from the box, but this also had changed with time, until now it was felt necessary only for the official to speak to each person approaching. Mr. Summers was very good at all this; in his clean white shirt and blue jeans, with one hand resting carelessly on the black box, he seemed very proper and important as he talked interminably to Mr. Graves and the Martins.

Just as Mr. Summers finally left off talking and turned to the assembled villagers, Mrs. Hutchinson came hurriedly along the path to the square, her sweater thrown over her shoulders, and slid into place in the back of the crowd. "Clean forgot what day it was," she said to Mrs. Delacroix, who stood next to her, and they both laughed softly. "Thought my old man was out back stacking wood," Mrs. Hutchinson went on, "and then I looked out the window and the kids were gone, and then I remembered it was the twenty-seventh and came a-running." She dried her hands on her apron, and Mrs. Delacroix said, "You're in time, though. They're still talking away up there."

Mrs. Hutchinson craned her neck to see through the crowd and found her husband and children standing near the front. She tapped Mrs. Delacroix on the arm as a farewell and began to make her way through the crowd. The people separated good-humoredly to let her through; two or three people said, in voices just loud enough to be heard across the crowd, "Here comes your Missus, Hutchinson," and "Bill, she made it after all." Mrs. Hutchinson reached her husband, and Mr. Summers, who had been waiting, said cheerfully, "Thought we were going to have to get on without you, Tessie." Mrs. Hutchinson said, grinning, "Wouldn't have me leave m'dishes in the sink, now would you, Joe?" and soft laughter ran through the crowd as the people stirred back into position after Mrs. Hutchinson's arrival.

"Well, now," Mr. Summers said soberly, "guess we better get started, get this over with, so's we can go back to work. Anybody ain't here?" 10

"Dunbar," several people said. "Dunbar, Dunbar."

Mr. Summers consulted his list. "Clyde Dunbar," he said. "That's right. He's broke his leg, hasn't he? Who's drawing for him?"

"Me, I guess," a woman said, and Mr. Summers turned to look at her. "Wife draws for her husband," Mr. Summers said. "Don't you have a grown boy to do it for you, Janey?" Although Mr. Summers and everyone else in the village knew the answer perfectly well, it was the business of the official of the lottery to ask such questions formally. Mr. Summers waited with an expression of polite interest while Mrs. Dunbar answered.

"Horace's not but sixteen yet," Mrs. Dunbar said regretfully. "Guess I gotta fill in for the old man this year."

"Right," Mr. Summers said. He made a note on the list he was holding. Then 15 he asked, "Watson boy drawing this year?"

A tall boy in the crowd raised his hand. "Here," he said. "I'm drawing for m'mother and me." He blinked his eyes nervously and ducked his head as several voices in the crowd said things like "Good fellow, Jack," and "Glad to see your mother's got a man to do it."

"Well," Mr. Summers said, "guess that's everyone. Old Man Warner make it?"

"Here," a voice said, and Mr. Summers nodded.

A sudden hush fell on the crowd as Mr. Summers cleared his throat and looked at the list. "All ready?" he called. "Now, I'll read the names—heads of families first—and the men come up and take a paper out of the box. Keep the paper folded in your hand without looking at it until everyone has had a turn. Everything clear?"

The people had done it so many times that they only half listened to the 20 directions; most of them were quiet, wetting their lips, not looking around. Then Mr. Summers raised one hand high and said, "Adams." A man disengaged himself from the crowd and came forward. "Hi, Steve," Mr. Summers said, and Mr. Adams said, "Hi, Joe." They grinned at one another humorlessly and nervously. Then Mr. Adams reached into the black box and took out a folded paper. He held it firmly by one corner as he turned and went hastily back to his place in the crowd, where he stood a little apart from his family, not looking down at his hand.

"Allen," Mr. Summers said. "Anderson. . . . Bentham."

"Seems like there's no time at all between lotteries any more," Mrs. Delacroix said to Mrs. Graves in the back row. "Seems like we got through with the last one only last week."

"Time sure goes fast," Mrs. Graves said.

"Clark. . . . Delacroix."

"There goes my old man," Mrs. Delacroix said. She held her breath while her 25 husband went forward.

"Dunbar," Mr. Summers said, and Mrs. Dunbar went steadily to the box while one of the women said, "Go on, Janey," and another said, "There she goes."

"We're next," Mrs. Graves said. She watched while Mr. Graves came around from the side of the box, greeted Mr. Summers gravely, and selected a slip of paper from the box. By now, all through the crowd there were men holding the small folded papers in their large hands, turning them over and over nervously. Mrs. Dunbar and her two sons stood together, Mrs. Dunbar holding the slip of paper.

"Harburt. . . . Hutchinson."

"Get up there, Bill," Mrs. Hutchinson said, and the people near her laughed.

"Jones." 30

"They do say," Mr. Adams said to Old Man Warner, who stood next to him, "that over in the north village they're talking of giving up the lottery."

Old Man Warner snorted. "Pack of crazy fools," he said. "Listening to the young folks, nothing's good enough for *them*. Next thing you know, they'll be wanting to go back to living in caves, nobody work any more, live *that* way for a while. Used to be a saying about 'Lottery in June, corn be heavy soon.' First thing you know, we'd all be eating stewed chickweed and acorns. There's *always* been a lottery," he added petulantly. "Bad enough to see young Joe Summers up there joking with everybody."

"Some places have already quit lotteries," Mrs. Adams said.

"Nothing but trouble in *that*," Old Man Warner said stoutly. "Pack of young fools."

"Martin." And Bobby Martin watched his father go forward. "Overdyke. . . . 35 Percy."

"I wish they'd hurry," Mrs. Dunbar said to her older son. "I wish they'd hurry."

"They're almost through," her son said.

"You get ready to run tell Dad," Mrs. Dunbar said.

Mr. Summers called his own name and then stepped forward precisely and selected a slip from the box. Then he called, "Warner."

"Seventy-seventh year I been in the lottery," Old Man Warner said as he 40 went through the crowd. "Seventy-seventh time."

"Watson." The tall boy came awkwardly through the crowd. Someone said, "Don't be nervous, Jack," and Mr. Summers said, "Take your time, son."

"Zanini."

After that, there was a long pause, a breathless pause, until Mr. Summers, holding his slip of paper in the air, said, "All right, fellows." For a minute, no one moved, and then all the slips of paper were opened. Suddenly, all women began to speak at once, saying, "Who is it?" "Who's got it?" "Is it the Dunbars?" "Is it the Watsons?" Then the voices began to say, "It's Hutchinson. It's Bill." "Bill Hutchinson's got it."

"Go tell your father," Mrs. Dunbar said to her older son.

People began to look around to see the Hutchinsons. Bill Hutchinson was 45 standing quiet, staring down at the paper in his hand. Suddenly, Tessie Hutchinson shouted to Mr. Summers, "You didn't give him time enough to take any paper he wanted. I saw you. It wasn't fair!"

"Be a good sport, Tessie," Mrs. Delacroix called, and Mrs. Graves said, "All of us took the same chance."

"Shut up, Tessie," Bill Hutchinson said.

"Well, everyone," Mr. Summers said, "that was done pretty fast, and now we've got to be hurrying a little more to get done in time." He consulted his next list. "Bill," he said, "you draw for the Hutchinson family. You got any other households in the Hutchinsons?"

"There's Don and Eva," Mrs. Hutchinson yelled. "Make *them* take their chance!"

"Daughters draw with their husbands' families, Tessie," Mr. Summers said    50
gently. "You know that as well as anyone else."

"It wasn't fair," Tessie said.

"I guess not, Joe," Bill Hutchinson said regretfully. "My daughter draws with her husband's family, that's only fair. And I've got no other family except the kids."

"Then, as far as drawing for families is concerned, it's you," Mr. Summers said in explanation, "and as far as drawing for households is concerned, that's you, too. Right?"

"Right," Bill Hutchinson said.

"How many kids, Bill?" Mr. Summers asked formally.    55

"Three," Bill Hutchinson said. "There's Bill, Jr., and Nancy, and little Dave. And Tessie and me."

"All right, then," Mr. Summers said. "Harry, you got their tickets back?"

Mr. Graves nodded and held up the slips of paper. "Put them in the box, then," Mr. Summers directed. "Take Bill's and put it in."

"I think we ought to start over," Mrs. Hutchinson said, as quietly as she could. "I tell you it wasn't *fair*. You didn't give him time enough to choose. *Everybody* saw that."

Mr. Graves had selected the five slips and put them in the box, and he    60
dropped all the papers but those onto the ground, where the breeze caught them and lifted them off.

"Listen, everybody," Mrs. Hutchinson was saying to the people around her.

"Ready, Bill?" Mr. Summers asked, and Bill Hutchinson, with one quick glance around at his wife and children, nodded.

"Remember," Mr. Summers said, "take the slips and keep them folded until each person has taken one. Harry, you help little Dave." Mr. Graves took the hand of the little boy, who came willingly with him up to the box. "Take a paper out of the box, Davy," Mr. Summers said. Davy put his hand into the box and laughed. "Take just *one* paper," Mr. Summers said. "Harry, you hold it for him." Mr. Graves took the child's hand and removed the folded paper from the tight fist and held it while little Dave stood next to him and looked up at him wonderingly.

"Nancy next," Mr. Summers said. Nancy was twelve, and her school friends breathed heavily as she went forward, switching her skirt, and took a slip daintily from the box. "Bill, Jr.," Mr. Summers said, and Billy, his face red and his feet over-large, nearly knocked the box over as he got a paper out. "Tessie," Mr. Summers said. She hesitated for a minute, looking around defiantly, and then set her lips and went up to the box. She snatched a paper out and held it behind her.

"Bill," Mr. Summers said, and Bill Hutchinson reached into the box and felt 65
around, bringing his hand out at last with the slip of paper in it.

The crowd was quiet. A girl whispered, "I hope it's not Nancy," and the
sound of the whisper reached the edges of the crowd.

"It's not the way it used to be," Old Man Warner said clearly. "People ain't
the way they used to be."

"All right," Mr. Summers said. "Open the papers. Harry, you open little
Dave's."

Mr. Graves opened the slip of paper and there was a general sigh through the
crowd as he held it up and everyone could see that it was blank. Nancy and Bill,
Jr., opened theirs at the same time, and both beamed and laughed, turning
around to the crowd and holding their slips of paper above their heads.

"Tessie," Mr. Summers said. There was a pause, and then Mr. Summers 70
looked at Bill Hutchinson, and Bill unfolded his paper and showed it. It was blank.

"It's Tessie," Mr. Summers said, and his voice was hushed. "Show us her
paper, Bill."

Bill Hutchinson went over to his wife and forced the slip of paper out of her
hand. It had a black spot on it, the black spot Mr. Summers had made the night
before with the heavy pencil in the coal-company office. Bill Hutchinson held it
up, and there was a stir in the crowd.

"All right, folks," Mr. Summers said, "let's finish quickly."

Although the villagers had forgotten the ritual and lost the original black
box, they still remembered to use stones. The pile of stones the boys had made
earlier was ready; there were stones on the ground with the blowing scraps of
paper that had come out of the box. Mrs. Delacroix selected a stone so large she
had to pick it up with both hands and turned to Mrs. Dunbar. "Come on," she
said. "Hurry up."

Mrs. Dunbar had small stones in both hands, and she said, gasping for 75
breath, "I can't run at all. You'll have to go ahead and I'll catch up with you."

The children had stones already, and someone gave little Davy Hutchinson
a few pebbles.

Tessie Hutchinson was in the center of a cleared space by now, and she held
her hands out desperately as the villagers moved in on her. "It isn't fair," she said.
A stone hit her on the side of the head.

Old Man Warner was saying, "Come on, come on, everyone." Steve Adams
was in the front of the crowd of villagers, with Mrs. Graves beside him.

"It isn't fair, it isn't right," Mrs. Hutchinson screamed, and then they were
upon her.

QUESTIONS

1. Where do you think "The Lottery" takes place? What purpose do you suppose the
   writer has in making this setting appear so familiar and ordinary?
2. In paragraphs 2 and 3, what details foreshadow the ending of the story?
3. Take a close look at Jackson's description of the black wooden box (paragraph 5) and
   of the black spot on the fatal slip of paper (paragraph 72). What do these objects suggest to you? Are there any other symbols in the story?

4. What do you understand to be the writer's own attitude toward the lottery and the stoning? Exactly what in the story makes her attitude clear to us?
5. What do you make of Old Man Warner's saying, "Lottery in June, corn be heavy soon"?
6. What do you think Shirley Jackson is driving at? Consider each of the following interpretations and, looking at the story, see if you can find any evidence for it.

> Jackson takes a primitive fertility rite and playfully transfers it to a small town in North America.

> Jackson, writing her story soon after World War II, indirectly expresses her horror at the Holocaust. She assumes that the massacre of the Jews was carried out by unwitting, obedient people, like these villagers.

> Jackson is satirizing our own society, in which men are selected for the army by lottery.

> Jackson is just writing a memorable story that signifies nothing at all.


## Ursula K. Le Guin
THE ONES WHO WALK AWAY FROM OMELAS                                    1973

*Ursula K. Le Guin was born in 1929 in Berkeley, California, the daughter of Theodora Kroeber, a folklorist, and Alfred L. Kroeber, a renowned anthropologist. After graduating from Radcliffe, she took an M.A. degree at Columbia. Le Guin, who launched a successful career as a writer while rearing three children and holding an outside job, first won a devoted following for her stories in science fiction magazines.* Roncannon's World *(1966) was her first book. Her fifth novel,* The Left Hand of Darkness *(1969), won both the Hugo and Nebula awards, the two major science fiction prizes, as did her later book* The Dispossessed *(1974)—an unprecedented feat in the history of the genre. Like the*

Ursula K. Le Guin

*novels of Kurt Vonnegut, Jr. and J. G. Ballard, Le Guin's work has appealed to a wider audience than science fiction fans. Bringing a social scientist's eye and a feminist's sensibility to science fiction, she has employed this speculative genre to criticize contemporary civilization. Many of her stories—like "The Ones Who Walk Away from Omelas"—create complex imaginary civilizations, envisioned with anthropological authority. Le Guin has also written poetry and juvenile fiction, including the Earthsea trilogy,* Wizard of Earthsea *(1968),* The Tombs of Atuan *(1971), and* The Farthest Shore *(1972), which rank among the classics of modern children's literature. She lives in Portland, Oregon.*

With a clamor of bells that set the swallows soaring, the Festival of Summer came to the city. Omelas, bright-towered by the sea. The rigging of the boats in harbor sparkled with flags. In the streets between houses with red roofs and painted walls, between old moss-grown gardens and under avenues of trees, past great parks and public buildings, processions moved. Some were decorous: old people in long stiff robes of mauve and grey, grave master workmen, quiet, merry women carrying their babies and chatting as they walked. In other streets the music beat faster, a shimmering of gong and tambourine, and the people went dancing, the procession was a dance. Children dodged in and out, their high calls rising like the swallows' crossing flights over the music and the singing. All the processions wound towards the north side of the city, where on the great water-meadow called the Green Fields boys and girls, naked in the bright air, with mud-stained feet and ankles and long, lithe arms, exercised their restive horses before the race. The horses wore no gear at all but a halter without bit. Their manes were braided with streamers of silver, gold, and green. They flared their nostrils and pranced and boasted to one another; they were vastly excited, the horse being the only animal who has adopted our ceremonies as his own. Far off to the north and west the mountains stood up half encircling Omelas on her bay. The air of morning was so clear that the snow still crowning the Eighteen Peaks burned with white-gold fire across the miles of sunlit air, under the dark blue of the sky. There was just enough wind to make the banners that marked the racecourse snap and flutter now and then. In the silence of the broad green meadows one could hear the music winding through the city streets, farther and nearer and ever approaching, a cheerful faint sweetness of the air that from time to time trembled and gathered together and broke out into the great joyous clanging of the bells.

Joyous! How is one to tell about joy? How describe the citizens of Omelas?

They were not simple folk, you see, though they were happy. But we do not say the words of cheer much any more. All smiles have become archaic. Given a description such as this one tends to make certain assumptions. Given a description such as this one tends to look next for the King, mounted on a splendid stallion and surrounded by his noble knights, or perhaps in a golden litter borne by great-muscled slaves. But there was no king. They did not use swords, or keep slaves. They were not barbarians. I do not know the rules and laws of their society, but I suspect that they were singularly few. As they did without monarchy and slavery, so they also got on without the stock exchange, the advertisement, the secret police, and the bomb. Yet I repeat that these were not simple folk, not dulcet shepherds, noble savages, bland utopians. They were not less complex than us. The trouble is that we have a bad habit, encouraged by pedants and sophisticates, of considering happiness as something rather stupid. Only pain is intellectual, only evil interesting. This is the treason of the artist: a refusal to admit the banality of evil and the terrible boredom of pain. If you can't lick 'em, join 'em. If it hurts, repeat it. But to praise despair is to condemn delight, to embrace violence is to lose hold of everything else. We have almost lost hold; we can no longer describe a happy man, nor make any celebration of joy. How can I tell you about the people of Omelas? They were not naïve and happy children—

though their children were, in fact, happy. They were mature, intelligent, passionate adults whose lives were not wretched. O miracle! but I wish I could describe it better. I wish I could convince you. Omelas sounds in my words like a city in a fairy tale, long ago and far away, once upon a time. Perhaps it would be best if you imagined it as your own fancy bids, assuming it will rise to the occasion, for certainly I cannot suit you all. For instance, how about technology? I think that there would be no cars or helicopters in and above the streets; this follows from the fact that the people of Omelas are happy people. Happiness is based on a just discrimination of what is necessary, what is neither necessary nor destructive, and what is destructive. In the middle category, however—that of the unnecessary but undestructive, that of comfort, luxury, exuberance, etc.— they could perfectly well have central heating, subway trains, washing machines, and all kinds of marvelous devices not yet invented here, floating light-sources, fuelless power, a cure for the common cold. Or they could have none of that: it doesn't matter. As you like it. I incline to think that people from towns up and down the coast have been coming in to Omelas during the last days before the Festival on very fast little trains and double-decked trams and that the train station of Omelas is actually the handsomest building in town, though plainer than the magnificent Farmers' Market. But even granted trains, I fear that Omelas so far strikes some of you as goody-goody. Smiles, bells, parades, horses, bleh. If so, please add an orgy. If an orgy would help, don't hesitate. Let us not, however, have temples from which issue beautiful nude priests and priestesses already half in ecstasy and ready to copulate with any man or woman, lover or stranger, who desires union with the deep godhead of the blood, although that was my first idea. But really it would be better not to have any temples in Omelas—at least, not manned temples. Religion yes, clergy no. Surely the beautiful nudes can just wander about, offering themselves like divine soufflés to the hunger of the needy and the rapture of the flesh. Let them join the processions. Let tambourines be struck above the copulations, and the glory of desire be proclaimed upon the gongs, and (a not unimportant point) let the offspring of these delightful rituals be beloved and looked after by all. One thing I know there is none of in Omelas is guilt. But what else should there be? I thought at first there were no drugs, but that is puritanical. For those who like it, the faint insistent sweetness of *drooz* may perfume the ways of the city, *drooz* which first brings a great lightness and brilliance to the mind and limbs, and then after some hours a dreamy languor, and wonderful visions at last of the very arcana and inmost secrets of the Universe, as well as exciting the pleasure of sex beyond all belief; and it is not habit-forming. For more modest tastes I think there ought to be beer. What else, what else belongs in the joyous city? The sense of victory, surely, the celebration of courage. But as we did without clergy, let us do without soldiers. The joy built upon successful slaughter is not the right kind of joy; it will not do; it is fearful and it is trivial. A boundless and generous contentment, a magnanimous triumph felt not against some outer enemy but in communion with the finest and fairest in the souls of all men everywhere and the splendor of the world's summer: this is what swells the hearts of the people of Omelas, and the victory they celebrate is that of life. I really don't think many of them need to take *drooz*.

Most of the processions have reached the Green Fields by now. A marvelous smell of cooking goes forth from the red and blue tents of the provisioners. The faces of small children are amiably sticky; in the benign grey beard of a man a couple of crumbs of rich pastry are entangled. The youths and girls have mounted their horses and are beginning to group around the starting line of the course. An old woman, small, fat, and laughing, is passing out flowers from a basket, and tall young men wear her flowers in their shining hair. A child of nine or ten sits at the edge of the crowd, alone, playing on a wooden flute. People pause to listen, and they smile, but they do not speak to him, for he never ceases playing and never sees them, his dark eyes wholly rapt in the sweet, thin magic of the tune.

He finishes, and slowly lowers his hands holding the wooden flute. 5

As if that little private silence were the signal, all at once a trumpet sounds from the pavillion near the starting line: imperious, melancholy, piercing. The horses rear on their slender legs, and some of them neigh in answer. Sober-faced, the young riders stroke the horses' necks and soothe them, whispering, "Quiet, quiet, there my beauty, my hope. . . ." They begin to form in rank along the starting line. The crowds along the racecourse are like a field of grass and flowers in the wind. The Festival of Summer has begun.

Do you believe? Do you accept the festival, the city, the joy? No? Then let me describe one more thing.

In a basement under one of the beautiful public buildings of Omelas, or perhaps in the cellar of one of its spacious private homes, there is a room. It has one locked door, and no window. A little light seeps in dustily between cracks in the boards, secondhand from a cobwebbed window somewhere across the cellar. In one corner of the little room a couple of mops, with stiff, clotted, foul-smelling heads, stand near a rusty bucket. The floor is dirt, a little damp to the touch, as cellar dirt usually is. The room is about three paces long and two wide: a mere broom closet or disused tool room. In the room a child is sitting. It could be a boy or a girl. It looks about six, but actually is nearly ten. It is feeble-minded. Perhaps it born defective, or perhaps it has become imbecile through fear, malnutrition, and neglect. It picks its nose and occasionally fumbles vaguely with its toes or genitals, as it sits hunched in the corner farthest from the bucket and the two mops. It is afraid of the mops. It finds them horrible. It shuts its eyes, but it knows the mops are still standing there; and the door is locked; and nobody will come. The door is always locked; and nobody ever comes, except that sometimes—the child has no understanding of time or interval—sometimes the door rattles terribly and opens, and a person, or several people, are there. One of them may come in and kick the child to make it stand up. The others never come close, but peer in at it with frightened, disgusted eyes. The food bowl and the water jug are hastily filled, the door is locked, the eyes disappear. The people at the door never say anything, but the child, who has not always lived in the tool room, and can remember sunlight and its mother's voice, sometimes speaks. "I will be good," it says. "Please let me out. I will be good!" They never answer. The child used to scream for help at night, and cry a good deal, but now it only makes a kind of whining, "eh-haa, eh-haa," and it speaks less and less often. It is so thin there are no calves to its legs; its belly protrudes; it lives on a half-bowl of corn meal and grease a day. It is naked. Its buttocks and thighs are a mass of festered sores, as it sits in its own excrement continually.

They all know it is there, all the people of Omelas. Some of them have come to see it, others are content merely to know it is there. They all know that it has to be there. Some of them understand why, and some do not, but they all understand that their happiness, the beauty of their city, the tenderness of their friendships, the health of their children, the wisdom of their scholars, the skill of their makers, even the abundance of their harvest and the kindly weathers of their skies, depend wholly on this child's abominable misery.

This is usually explained to children when they are between eight and twelve, whenever they seem capable of understanding; and most of those who come to see the child are young people, though often enough an adult comes, or comes back, to see the child. No matter how well the matter has been explained to them, these young spectators are always shocked and sickened at the sight. They feel disgust, which they had thought themselves superior to. They feel anger, outrage, impotence, despite all the explanations. They would like to do something for the child. But there is nothing they can do. If the child were brought up into the sunlight out of that vile place, if it were cleaned and fed and comforted, that would be a good thing, indeed; but if it were done, in that day and hour all the prosperity and beauty and delight of Omelas would wither and be destroyed. Those are the terms. To exchange all the goodness and grace of every life in Omelas for that single, small improvement: to throw away the happiness of thousands for the chance of the happiness of one: that would be to let guilt within the walls indeed.

The terms are strict and absolute; there may not even be a kind word spoken to the child.

Often the young people go home in tears, or in a tearless rage, when they have seen the child and faced this terrible paradox. They may brood over it for weeks or years. But as time goes on they begin to realize that even if the child could be released, it would not get much good of its freedom: a little vague pleasure of warmth and food, no doubt, but little more. It is too degraded and imbecile to know any real joy. It has been afraid too long ever to be free of fear. Its habits are too uncouth for it to respond to humane treatment. Indeed, after so long it would probably be wretched without walls about it to protect it, and darkness for its eyes, and its own excrement to sit in. Their tears at the bitter injustice dry when they begin to perceive the terrible justice of reality and to accept it. Yet it is their tears and anger, the trying of their generosity and the acceptance of their helplessness, which are perhaps the true source of the splendor of their lives. Theirs is no vapid, irresponsible happiness. They know that they, like the child, are not free. They know compassion. It is the existence of the child, and their knowledge of its existence, that makes possible the nobility of their architecture, the poignancy of their music, the profundity of their science. It is because of the child that they are so gentle with children. They know that if the wretched one were not there snivelling in the dark, the other one, the flute-player, could make no joyful music as the young riders line up in their beauty for the race in the sunlight of the first morning of summer.

Now do you believe in them? Are they not more credible? But there is one more thing to tell, and this is quite incredible.

At times one of the adolescent girls or boys who go to see the child does not go home to weep or rage, does not, in fact, go home at all. Sometimes also a man or woman much older falls silent for a day or two, and then leaves home. These people go out into the street, and walk down the street alone. They keep walking, and walk straight out of the city of Omelas, through the beautiful gates. They keep walking across the farmlands of Omelas. Each one goes alone, youth or girl, man or woman. Night falls; the traveler must pass down village streets, between the houses with yellow-lit windows, and on out into the darkness of the fields. Each alone, they go west or north, towards the mountains. They go on. They leave Omelas, they walk ahead into the darkness, and they do not come back. The place they go towards is a place even less imaginable to most of us than the city of happiness. I cannot describe it at all. It is possible that it does not exist. But they seem to know where they are going, the ones who walk away from Omelas.

QUESTIONS

1. Does the narrator live in Omelas? What do we know about the narrator's society?
2. What is the narrator's opinion of Omelas? Does the author seem to share that opinion?
3. What is the narrator's attitude toward "the ones who walk away from Omelas?" Would the narrator have been one of those who walked away?
4. How do you account for the narrator's willingness to let us readers add to the story anything we like?—"If an orgy would help, don't hesitate" (page 257). Doesn't Ursula Le Guin care what her story includes?
5. What does the locked, dark cellar in which the child sits suggest? What other details in the story are suggestive enough to be called symbolic?
6. Do you find in the story any implied criticism of our own society?

SUGGESTIONS FOR WRITING

1. Reexamine one of these stories you have already read: "A Rose for Emily," "The Tell-Tale Heart," "Greasy Lake," "Barn Burning," "A Clean, Well-Lighted Place," "The Storm," "Araby," "The Open Boat," "Young Goodman Brown." In writing, indicate what actions and objects now seem to you symbolic in their suggestions. Do these actions or objects point toward any central theme in the story?
2. For an alternate topic, look for symbols in a story you have not read before. In the Stories for Further Reading, you might take a look at D.H. Lawrence's "The Rocking Horse Winner," Virginia Woolf's "A Haunted House," and Joyce Carol Oates' "Where Are You Going, Where Have You Been?"
3. Write a short comment inspired by the title "Absolutely Nothing Is Symbolic" or "There Isn't a Thing You Can't Make a Symbol of." Draw upon your experiences in reading the stories in this chapter, or any other literature. Give concrete examples.
4. Pick a tangible *thing* that intrigues you—an animal, a plant, or another part of nature; a house or another man-made object. Recall it, observe it, meditate on it. Then write an opening paragraph for a story that will make a symbol of that object, doing your best to fill the passage with hints. For inspiration, look back over John Steinbeck's "The Chrysanthemums."

# 8  Evaluating a Story

When we **evaluate** a story, we consider it and place a value on it. Perhaps we decide that it is a masterpiece, or a bit of trash, or (like most fiction we read) a work of some value in between. No cut-and-dried method of judgment will work on every story, and so in this chapter I have none to propose. Still, there are things we can look for in a story—usually clear indications of its author's competence.

In judging the quality of a baseball glove, we first have to be aware that a catcher's mitt differs—for good reasons—from a first baseman's glove. It is no less true that, before evaluating a story, we need to recognize its nature. To see, for instance, that a story is a fable (or perhaps a tale) may save us from condemning it as a failed short story.

Good critics of literature have at least a working knowledge of some of its conventions. By **conventions** we mean usual devices and features of a literary work, by which we can recognize its kind. When in movies or on television we watch a yarn about a sinister old mansion full of horrors, we recognize the conventions of that long-lived species of fiction, the **Gothic story.** *The Castle of Otranto, A Gothic Story* (1764), by English author Horace Walpole, started the genre, supplied its name, and established its favorite trappings. In Walpole's short novel, Otranto is a cobwebbed ruin full of underground passages and massive doors that slam unexpectedly. There are awful objects: a statue that bleeds, a portrait that steps from its frame, a giant helmet that falls and leaves its victim "dashed to pieces." Atmosphere is essential to a Gothic story: dusty halls, shadowy landscapes, whispering servants "seen at a distance imperfectly through the dusk" (I quote from Anne Radcliffe's novel *The Mysteries of Udolpho,* 1794). In Charlotte Brontë's *Jane Eyre* (1847), we find the model for a legion of heroines in the Gothic fiction of our own day. In the best-selling Gothic romances of Victoria Holt, Phyllis A. Whitney, and others, young women similarly find love while working as governesses in ominous mansions. Lacking English castles,

American authors of Gothic fiction have had to make do with dark old houses—like those in Nathaniel Hawthorne's novel *The House of the Seven Gables*, in Charlotte Perkins Gilman's "The Yellow Wallpaper," and in the short stories of Edgar Allan Poe, such as "The Tell-Tale Heart." William Faulkner, who brought the tradition to Mississippi, gives "A Rose for Emily" some familiar conventions: a rundown mansion, a mysterious servant, a madwoman, a hideous secret. But Faulkner's story, in its portrait of an aristocrat who refuses to admit that her world has vanished, goes far beyond Gothic conventions. Evidently, when you set up court as a judge of stories, to recognize such conventions will be an advantage. Knowing a Gothic story for what it is, you won't condemn it for lacking "realism." And to be aware of the Gothic elements in "A Rose for Emily" may help you see how original Faulkner manages to be, though employing some handed-down conventions.

Is the story a piece of commercial fiction tailored to a formula, or is it unique in its design? You can't demand the subtlety of a Katherine Anne Porter of a writer of hard-boiled detective stories. Neither can you put down "The Jilting of Granny Weatherall" for lacking slam-bang action. Some stories are no more than light, entertaining bits of fluff—no point in damning them, unless you dislike fluff or find them written badly. Of course, you are within your rights to prefer solidity to fluff, or to prefer a Porter story to a typical paperback romance by a hack writer. James Thurber's "The Catbird Seat," though a simpler and briefer story than Leo Tolstoi's "The Death of Ivan Ilych," is no less finished, complete, and satisfactory a work of art. Yet, considered in another light, Tolstoi's short novel may well seem a greater work than Thurber's. It reveals greater meaning and enfolds more life.

Masterpieces often have flaws; and so, whenever we can, we need to consider a story in its entirety. Some novels by Thomas Hardy and by Theodore Dreiser impress (on the whole), despite passages of stilted dialogue and other clumsy writing. If a story totally fails to enlist our sympathies, probably it suffers from some basic ineptitude: choice of an inappropriate point of view, a style ill suited to its theme, or possibly insufficient knowledge of human beings. In some ineffectual stories, things important to the writer (and to the story) remain private and unmentioned. In other stories, the writer's interests may be perfectly clear but they may not interest the reader, for they are not presented with sufficient art.

Some stories fail from **sentimentality,** a defect in a work whose writer seems to feel tremendous emotion and implies that we too should feel it, but does not provide us enough reason to share such feelings. Sentimentality is rampant in televised weekday afternoon soap operas, whose characters usually palpitate with passion for reasons not quite known, and who speak in melodramatic tones as if heralding the end of the world. In some fiction, conventional objects (locks of baby hair, posthumously awarded medals, pressed roses) frequently signal, "Let's have a good cry!" Revisiting home after her marriage, the character Amelia in William Makepeace Thackeray's *Vanity Fair* effuses about the bed she slept in when a virgin: "Dear little bed! how many a long night had she wept on its pillow."[1] Teary sentimentality is more common in nineteenth-century fiction than in ours. We have gone to the other extreme, some critics think, into a sentimentality of the violent and the hard-boiled. But in a grossly sentimental work of any kind, failure inheres in our refusal to go along with the author's implied attitudes. We laugh when we are expected to cry, feel delight when we are supposed to be horrified.

In evaluating a story, we may usefully ask a few questions:

1. What is the tone of the story? By what means and how effectively is it communicated?
2. What is the point of view? Does it seem appropriate and effective in this story? Imagine the story told from a different point of view; would such a change be for the worse or for the better?
3. Does the story show us unique and individual scenes, events, and characters—or weary stereotypes?
4. Are any symbols evident? If so, do they direct us to the story's central theme, or do they distract us from it?
5. How appropriate to the theme of the story, and to its subject matter, are its tone and style? Is it ever difficult or impossible to sympathize with the attitudes of the author (insofar as we can tell what they are)?
6. Does our interest in the story mainly depend on following its plot, on finding out what will happen next? Or does the author go beyond the events to show us what they mean? Are the events (however fantastic) credible, or are they incredibly melodramatic? Does the plot greatly depend upon farfetched coincidence?
7. Has the writer caused characters, events, and settings to come alive? Are they full of breath and motion, or simply told about in the abstract ("She was a lovable girl whose life had been highly exciting")? Unless the story is a fable or a tale, which need no detailed description or deep portrayal of character, then we may well expect the story to contain enough vividly imagined detail to make us believe in it.

## Suggestions for Writing

1. In a short essay, take two stories that you find differing markedly in quality and evaluate them, giving evidence to support your judgments. Stories similar enough to compare might include two character studies of women, as in "The Jilting of Granny Weatherall" and "The Chrysanthemums."
2. Write a blast against a story in this book that you dislike intensely. Stick to the text of the story in making your criticisms and support your charges with plenty of evidence.
3. Find two stories that strike you as similar in some important way (e.g., "Greasy Lake" and "Barn Burning" are both stories about hard-won maturity). Write a comparison of the two stories that serves to evaluate them.

---

[1]Sentimentality in fiction is older than the Victorians. Popular in eighteenth-century England, the **sentimental novel** (or **novel of sensibility**) specialized in characters whose ability to shed quick and copious tears signified their virtuous hearts. Oliver Goldsmith's *The Vicar of Wakefield* (1766) and Henry Mackenzie's *The Man of Feeling* (1771) are classics of the genre. An abundance of tears does not prevent such novels from having merit.

# 9  Reading Long Stories and Novels

Among the forms of imaginative literature in our language, the novel has been the favorite of both writers and readers for more than two hundred years. Broadly defined, a **novel** is a book-length story in prose, whose author tries to create the sense that while we read, we experience actual life.

This sense of actuality, also found in artful short stories, may be the quality that sets the novel apart from other long prose narratives. Why do we not apply the name *novel* to, for instance, *Gulliver's Travels?* In his marvel-filled account of Lemuel Gulliver's voyages among pygmies, giants, civilized horses, and noxious humanoid swine, Jonathan Swift does not seem primarily to care if we find his story credible. Though he arrays the adventures of Gulliver in painstaking detail (and, ironically, has Gulliver swear to the truth of them), Swift neither attempts nor achieves a convincing illusion of life. For his book is a fantastic satire that finds resemblances between noble horses and man's reasoning faculties, between debased apes and man's kinship with the beasts.

Unlike other major literary forms—drama, lyric, ballad, and epic—the novel is a relative newcomer. Originally, the drama in ancient Greece came alive only when actors performed it; the epic or heroic poem (from the classic *Iliad* through the Old English *Beowulf*), only when a bard sang or chanted it. But the English novel came to maturity in literate times, in the eighteenth century, and by its nature was something different: a story to be communicated silently, at whatever moment and at whatever pace (whether quickly or slowly and meditatively) the reader desired.

Some definitions of the novel would more strictly limit its province. "The Novel is a picture of real life and manners, and of the time in which it was written," declared Clara Reeve in 1785, thus distinguishing the novel from the romance, which "describes what never happened nor is likely to happen." By so specifying that the novel depicts life in the present day, the critic was probably observing the derivation of the word *novel*. Akin to the French word for "news" (*nouvelles*), it comes from the Italian *novella* ("something new and small"), a term applied to a newly made story taking place in recent times, and not a traditional story taking place long ago.

Also drawing a line between novel and romance, Nathaniel Hawthorne, in his preface to *The House of the Seven Gables* (1851), restricted the novel "not merely to the possible, but to the probable and ordinary course of man's experience." A **romance** had no such limitations. Such a definition would deny the name of *novel* to any fantastic or speculative story—to, say, the Gothic novel and the science fiction novel. Carefully bestowed, the labels *novel* and *romance* may be useful to distinguish between the true-to-life story of usual people in ordinary places (such as George Eliot's *Silas Marner* or John Updike's *Couples*) and the larger-than-life story of daring deeds and high adventure, set in the past or future or in some timeless land (such as Walter Scott's *Ivanhoe* or J. R. R. Tolkien's *Lord of the Rings*). But the labels are difficult to apply to much modern fiction, in which ordinary life is sometimes mingled with outlandishness. Who can say that James Joyce's *Ulysses* is not a novel, though it contains moments of dream and drunken hallucination? And yet the total effect, as in any successful novel, is a sense of the actual.

This sense of the actual is, perhaps, the hallmark of a novel, whether or not the events it relates are literally possible. To achieve this sense, novelists have employed many devices, and frequently have tried to pass off their storytelling as reporting. Nathaniel Hawthorne, in his introduction to *The Scarlet Letter*, gives a minute account of his finding documents on which he claims to base his novel, tied with a faded red ribbon and gathering dust in a customshouse. More recently, Vladimir Nabokov's *Pale Fire* (1962) tells its story in the form of a scholarly edition of a 999-line poem, complete with a biographical commentary by a friend of the late poet. Samuel Richardson's casting *Pamela* (1740) into the form of personal letters helped lend the story an appearance of being not invented, but discovered. Alice Walker's *The Color Purple* (1982) is also an **epistolary novel,** though some of the letters that tell the story are addressed to God. Another method favored by novelists is to write as though setting down a memoir or an autobiography. Daniel Defoe, whose skill in feigning such memoirs was phenomenal, even succeeded in writing the supposedly true confessions of a woman retired from a life of crime, *Moll Flanders* (1722), and in maintaining a vivid truthfulness:

> Going through Aldersgate Street, there was a pretty little child who had been at a dancing-school, and was going home all alone: and my prompter, like a true devil, set me upon this innocent creature. I talked to it, and it prattled to me again, and I took it by the hand and led it along till I came to a paved alley that goes into Bartholomew Close, and I led it in there. The child said that was not its way home. I said, "Yes, my dear, it is; I'll show you the way home." The child had a little necklace on of gold beads, and I had my eye upon that, and in the dark of the alley I stooped, pretending to mend the child's clog that was loose, and took off her necklace, and the child never felt it, and so led the child on again. Here, I say, the devil put me upon killing

the child in the dark alley, that it might not cry, but the very thought frightened me so that I was ready to drop down; but I turned the child about and bade it go back again. . . . The last affair left no great concern upon me, for as I did the poor child no harm, I only said to myself, I had given the parents a just reproof for their negligence in leaving the poor little lamb to come home by itself, and it would teach them to take more care of it another time.

What could sound more like the voice of an experienced child-robber than this manner of excusing her crime, and even justifying it?

Informed that a student had given up the study of mathematics to become a novelist, the logician David Hilbert drily remarked, "It was just as well: he did not have enough imagination to become a first-rate mathematician."[1] It is true that some novelists place great emphasis on research and notetaking. James A. Michener, the internationally best-selling author of novels like *Centennnial* (which tracks life in Colorado from prehistory through modern times) and *Chesapeake* (which describes 400 years of events on Maryland's Eastern Shore), starts work on a book by studying everything available about his chosen subject. He also travels to locations that might appear in the book, interviews local people, and compiles immense amounts of scientific, historical, and cultural data. Research alone, however, is not enough to finish a novel. A novel grows to completion only through the slow mental process of creation, selection, and arrangement. But raw facts can sometimes provide a beginning. Many novels started when the author read some arresting episode in a newspaper or magazine. Theodore Dreiser's impressive study of a murder, *An American Tragedy* (1925), for example, was inspired by a journalist's account of a real-life case.

In "The Open Boat," Stephen Crane brings high literary art to bear upon his own experience. The result is a short story based on fact. More recently, we have heard much about the **nonfiction novel,** in which the author presents actual people and events in story form. Norman Mailer, in *The Executioner's Song* (1979), chronicles the life and death of Gary Gilmore, the Utah murderer who demanded his own execution. Truman Capote's *In Cold Blood* (1966) sets forth an account of crime and punishment in Kansas, based on interviews with the accused and other principals. Perhaps the name "nonfiction novel" (Capote's name for it) or "true life novel" (as Mailer calls his Gilmore story) is newer than the form. In the past, writers of autobiography have cast their memoirs into what looks like novel form: Richard Wright in *Black Boy* (1945), William Burroughs in *Junkie* (1953). Derived not from the author's memory but from his reporting, John Hersey's *Hiroshima* (1946) reconstructs the lives of six survivors of the atom bomb as if they were fictional. In reading such works we may nearly forget we are reading literal truth, so well do the techniques of the novel lend remembered facts an air of immediacy.

A familiar kind of fiction that claims a basis in fact is the **historical novel,** a detailed reconstruction of life in another time, perhaps in another place. In some

---

[1]Quoted by William H. Gass, *Fiction and the Figures of Life* (New York: Knopf, 1970).

historical novels the author attempts a faithful picture of daily life in another era, as does Robert Graves in *I, Claudius* (1934), a novel of patrician Rome. More often, history is a backdrop for an exciting story of love and heroic adventure. Nathaniel Hawthorne's *The Scarlet Letter* (set in Puritan Boston), Herman Melville's *Moby-Dick* (set in the heyday of Yankee whalers), and Stephen Crane's *The Red Badge of Courage* (set in the battlefields of the Civil War) are historical novels in that their authors lived considerably later than the scenes and events that they depicted—and strove for truthfulness, by imaginative means.

Other varieties of novel will be familiar to anyone who scans the racks of paperback books in any drugstore: the mystery or detective novel, the Western novel, the science fiction novel, and other enduring types. Classified according to less well-known species, novels are sometimes said to belong to a category if they contain some recognizable kind of structure or theme. Such a category is the **bildungsroman** (German for a "novel of growth or development"), sometimes called the **apprenticeship novel** after its classic example, *Wilhelm Meister's Apprenticeship* (1796) by Johann Wolfgang von Goethe. This is the kind of novel in which a youth struggles toward maturity, seeking, perhaps, some consistent world view or philosophy of life. Sometimes the apprenticeship novel is evidently the author's recollection of his own early life: James Joyce's *Portrait of the Artist as a Young Man* and Mark Twain's *Tom Sawyer*.

In a **picaresque novel** (another famous category), a likable scoundrel wanders through adventures, living by his wits, duping the straight citizenry. The name comes from Spanish: *Pícaro*, "rascal" or "rogue." The classic picaresque novel is the anonymous Spanish *Life of Lazarillo de Tormes* (1554), imitated by many English writers, among them Henry Fielding in his story of a London thief and racketeer, *Jonathan Wild* (1743). Mark Twain's *Huckleberry Finn* owes something to the tradition; like early picaresque novels, it is told in episodes rather than in one all-unifying plot and is narrated in the first person by a hero at odds with respectable society ("dismal regular and decent," Huck Finn calls it). In Twain's novel, however, the traveling swindlers who claim to be a duke and a dauphin are much more typical rogues of picaresque fiction than Huck himself, an honest innocent. Modern novels worthy of the name include J. P. Donleavy's *The Ginger Man* (1965), Saul Bellow's *The Adventures of Augie March* (1953), Erica Jong's *Fanny* (1981), and Seth Morgan's *Homeboy* (1990).

The term **short novel** (or **novella**) mainly describes the size of a narrative; it refers to a narrative midway in length between a short story and a novel. (E. M. Forster once said that a novel should be at least 50,000 words in length, and most editors and publishers would agree with that definition.) Generally a short novel, like a short story, focuses on just one or two characters; but, unlike a short story, it has room to examine them in greater depth and detail. A short novel also often explores them over a greater period of time. Many writers like Thomas Mann, Henry James, Joseph Conrad, and Willa Cather favored the novella (called **nouvelle** in France) as a perfect medium between the necessary compression of the short story and the potential sprawl of the novel. Two famous short novels are included in this book—Leo Tolstoi's *The Death of Ivan Ilych* and Franz Kafka's

*The Metamorphosis*. When the term **novelette** is used, it usually refers (often disapprovingly) to a short novel written for a popular magazine, especially in fields like science fiction, Westerns, and horror.

Trying to perceive a novel as a whole, we may find it helpful to look for the same elements that we have noticed in reading short stories. By asking ourselves leading questions, we may be drawn more deeply into the novel's world, and may come to recognize and appreciate the techniques of the novelist. Does the novel have themes, or an overall theme? Who is its main character? What is the author's kind of narrative voice? What do we know about the tone, style, and use of irony? Why is this novel written from one point of view rather than from another? If the novel in question is large and thickly populated, it may help to read it with a pencil, taking brief notes. Forced to put the novel aside and later return to it, the reader may find that the notes refresh the memory. Notetaking habits differ, but perhaps these might be no more than, say, "Theme introduced, p. 27," or, "Old clothes dealer, p. 109—walking symbol?" Some readers find it useful to list briefly whatever each chapter accomplishes. Others make lists of a novel's characters, especially when reading classic Russian novels in which the reader has to recall that Alexey Karamazov is also identified by his pet name Aloysha, or that, in Leo Tolstoi's *Anna Karenina*, Princess Catherine Alexándrovna Shcherbátskaya and "Kitty" are one and the same.

Once our reading of a novel is finished and we prepare to discuss it or write about it, it may be a good idea to browse through it again, rereading brief portions. This method of overall browsing may also help when first approaching a bulky and difficult novel. Just as an explorer mapping unfamiliar territory may find it best to begin by taking an aerial view of it, so too the reader approaching an exceptionally thick and demanding novel may wish, at the start, to look for its general shape. This is the method of some professional book reviewers, who size up a novel (even an easy-to-read spy story, because they are not reading for pleasure) by skimming the first chapter, a middle chapter or two, and the last chapter; then going back and browsing at top speed through the rest. Reading a novel in this grim fashion, of course, the reviewer does not really know it thoroughly, any more than a tourist knows the mind and heart of foreign people after just strolling in a capital city and riding a tour bus to a few monuments. The reviewer's method will, however, provide a general notion of what the author is doing, and at the very least will tell something of her tone, style, point of view, and competence. We suggest this method only as a way to *approach* a book that, otherwise, the reader might not want to approach at all. It may be a comfort in studying some obdurate-looking or highly experimental novel, such as James Joyce's *Ulysses* or Henry James's *The Sacred Fount*. But the reader will find it necessary to return to the book, in order to know it, and to read it honestly, in detail. There is, of course, no short cut to novel reading, and probably the best method is to settle in comfort and read the book through: with your own eyes, not with the borrowed glasses of literary criticism.

The death of the novel has been frequently announced. Competition from television, VCRs, and video games, critics claim, will overwhelm the habit of reading; the public is lazy and will follow the easiest route available for entertainment. But in England and America television and films have been sending people back in vast numbers to the books they dramatize. Films like *Howard's End, A Passage to India*, and *Where Angels Fear to Tread* have made E. M. Forster into a best-selling novelist. Stylish adaptations of Philip K. Dick's off-beat science fiction like *Blade Runner* and *Total Recall* have created a cult for his once neglected work. Even experimental novels like Virginia Woolf's *Orlando* and William Burroughs' *Naked Lunch* have become successful films that have in turn sent a new generation of readers back to the novels. Sometimes Hollywood even helps bring a good book into print. No one would publish Thomas Disch's sophisticated children's novella, *The Brave Little Toaster*, until Walt Disney turned it into a cartoon movie. A major publisher not only rushed it into print, but commissioned a sequel, as well.

Meanwhile, each year new novels by the hundreds continue to appear, their authors wistfully looking for a public. A chosen few reach tens of thousands of readers through book clubs, and, through paperback reprint editions, occasionally millions more. To forecast the end of the novel seems risky. For the novel exercises the imagination of the beholder. At any hour, at a touch of the hand, it opens and (with no warm-up) begins to speak. Once printed, it consumes no further energy. Often so small it may be carried in a pocket, it may yet survive by its ability to contain multitudes (a "capacious vessel," Henry James called it): a thing both a work of art and an amazingly compact system for the storage and retrieval of imagined life.

## Leo Tolstoi

THE DEATH OF IVAN ILYCH                                                 1886

*Translated by Louise and Aylmer Maude*

*Leo Tolstoi (1828–1910), who inherited the title of Count, was born into a family who owned vast lands in Tula province, Russia. As a young man disgruntled with self and schooling, he left Kazan University without taking a degree. After a period of fast living in Moscow and St. Petersburg, he became an army officer and took part in the siege of Sevastopol in the Crimean War. Returning to his estate, Tolstoi opened a school for the children of serfs, based on the ideas (then radical) that learning should be a joy and that individuals should be taught according to their needs. In 1862 he mar-*

Leo Tolstoi

ried young, well-educated Sophia Bers. Thirteen children followed, as did Tolstoi's years of tremendous achievement as a novelist. About 1876, after a religious illumination, Tolstoi became convinced that one should do good, eschew alcohol, tobacco, meat, and violence, and stop owning things. These tenets brought him into conflict with his wife and family, the Russian Orthodox Church, and the Czarist government. Tolstoi renounced his lands and his book royalties. He dressed like a peasant, made his own boots, and dug potatoes. From his driven pen poured books, tracts, and articles expounding his radically Christian moral and social ideas. In What Is Art? (1898) he held that artists have a God-given duty to produce only what most people can understand and appreciate. In his seventh decade Tolstoi returned to the novel, seeing in fiction a means to preach. Yet, impressive though they are, The Kreutzer Sonata (1891) and Resurrection (1899) have never won readers' love as have his earlier masterpieces War and Peace (1863–69), that immense saga of Russian society before, during, and after Napoleon's invasion, and Anna Karenina (1875–77), a compassionate history of the decline and fall of a woman who defies convention.

## I

During an interval in the Melvinski trial in the large building of the Law Courts, the members and public prosecutor met in Ivan Egorovich Shebek's private room, where the conversation turned on the celebrated Krasovski case. Fëdor Vasilievich warmly maintained that it was not subject to their jurisdiction, Ivan Egorovich maintained the contrary, while Peter Ivanovich, not having entered into the discussion at the start, took no part in it but looked through the *Gazette* which had just been handed in.

"Gentlemen," he said, "Ivan Ilych has died!"

"You don't say so!"

"Here, read it yourself," replied Peter Ivanovich, handing Fëdor Vasilievich the paper still damp from the press. Surrounded by a black border were the words: "Praskovya Fëdorovna Goloviná, with profound sorrow, informs relatives and friends of the demise of her beloved husband Ivan Ilych Golovin, Member of the Court of Justice, which occurred on February the 4th of this year 1882. The funeral will take place on Friday at one o'clock in the afternoon."

Ivan Ilych had been a colleague of the gentlemen present and was liked by 5 them all. He had been ill for some weeks with an illness said to be incurable. His post had been kept open for him, but there had been conjectures that in case of his death Alexeev might receive his appointment, and that either Vinnikov or Shtabel would succeed Alexeev. So on receiving the news of Ivan Ilych's death the first thought of each of the gentlemen in that private room was of the changes and promotions it might occasion among themselves or their acquaintances.

"I shall be sure to get Shtabel's place or Vinnikov's," thought Fëdor Vasilievich. "I was promised that long ago, and the promotion means an extra eight hundred rubles a year for me besides the allowance."

"Now I must apply for my brother-in-law's transfer from Kaluga," thought Peter Ivanovich. "My wife will be very glad, and then she won't be able to say that I never do anything for her relations."

"I thought he would never leave his bed again," said Peter Ivanovich aloud. "It's very sad."

"But what really was the matter with him?"

"The doctors couldn't say—at least they could, but each of them said something different. When last I saw him I thought he was getting better." 10

"And I haven't been to see him since the holidays. I always meant to go."

"Had he any property?"

"I think his wife had a little—but something quite trifling."

"We shall have to go to see her, but they live so terribly far away."

"Far away from you, you mean. Everything's far away from your place." 15

"You see, he never can forgive my living on the other side of the river," said Peter Ivanovich, smiling at Shebek. Then, still talking of the distances between different parts of the city, they returned to the Court.

Besides considerations as to the possible transfers and promotions likely to result from Ivan Ilych's death, the mere fact of the death of a near acquaintance aroused, as usual, in all who heard of it the complacent feeling that "it is he who is dead and not I."

Each one thought or felt, "Well, he's dead but I'm alive!" But the more intimate of Ivan Ilych's acquaintances, his so-called friends, could not help thinking also that they would now have to fulfil the very tiresome demands of propriety by attending the funeral service and paying a visit of condolence to the widow.

Fëdor Vasilievich and Peter Ivanovich had been his nearest acquaintances. Peter Ivanovich had studied law with Ivan Ilych and had considered himself to be under obligations to him.

Having told his wife at dinner-time of Ivan Ilych's death and of his conjecture that it might be possible to get her brother transferred to their circuit, Peter Ivanovich sacrificed his usual nap, put on his evening clothes, and drove to Ivan Ilych's house. 20

At the entrance stood a carriage and two cabs. Leaning against the wall in the hall downstairs near the cloak-stand was a coffin-lid covered with cloth of gold, ornamented with gold cord and tassels, that had been polished up with metal powder. Two ladies in black were taking off their fur cloaks. Peter Ivanovich recognized one of them as Ivan Ilych's sister, but the other was a stranger to him. His colleague Schwartz was just coming downstairs, but on seeing Peter Ivanovich enter he stopped and winked at him, as if to say: "Ivan Ilych has made a mess of things—not like you and me."

Schwartz's face with his Piccadilly whiskers and his slim figure in evening dress had as usual an air of elegant solemnity which contrasted with the playfulness of his character and had a special piquancy here, or so it seemed to Peter Ivanovich.

Peter Ivanovich allowed the ladies to precede him and slowly followed them upstairs. Schwartz did not come down but remained where he was, and Peter Ivanovich understood that he wanted to arrange where they should play bridge that evening. The ladies went upstairs to the widow's room, and Schwartz with seriously compressed lips but a playful look in his eyes, indicated by a twist of his eyebrows the room to the right where the body lay.

Peter Ivanovich, like everyone else on such occasions, entered feeling uncertain what he would have to do. All he knew was that at such times it is always safe to cross oneself. But he was not quite sure whether one should make obeisances while doing so. He therefore adopted a middle course. On entering the room he began crossing himself and made a slight movement resembling a bow. At the same time, as far as the motion of his head and arm allowed, he surveyed the room. Two young men—apparently nephews, one of whom was a high-school pupil—were leaving the room, crossing themselves as they did so. An old woman was standing motionless, and a lady with strangely arched eyebrows was saying something to her in a whisper. A vigorous, resolute Church Reader, in a frock-coat, was reading something in a loud voice with an expression that precluded any contradiction. The butler's assistant, Gerasim, stepping lightly in front of Peter Ivanovich, was strewing something on the floor. Noticing this, Peter Ivanovich was immediately aware of a faint odor of a decomposing body.

The last time he had called on Ivan Ilych, Peter Ivanovich had seen Gerasim 25 in the study. Ivan Ilych had been particularly fond of him and he was performing the duty of a sick nurse.

Peter Ivanovich continued to make the sign of the cross, slightly inclining his head in an intermediate direction between the coffin, the Reader, and the icons on the table in a corner of the room. Afterwards, when it seemed to him that this movement of his arm in crossing himself had gone on too long, he stopped and began to look at the corpse.

The dead man lay, as dead men always lie, in a specially heavy way, his rigid limbs sunk in the soft cushions of the coffin, with the head forever bowed on the pillow. His yellow waxen brow with bald patches over his sunken temples was thrust up in the way peculiar to the dead, the protruding nose seeming to press on the upper lip. He was much changed and had grown even thinner since Peter Ivanovich had last seen him, but, as is always the case with the dead, his face was handsomer and above all more dignified than when he was alive. The expression on the face said that what was necessary had been accomplished, and accomplished rightly. Besides this there was in that expression a reproach and a warning to the living. This warning seemed to Peter Ivanovich out of place, or at least not applicable to him. He felt a certain discomfort and so he hurriedly crossed himself once more and turned and went out of the door—too hurriedly and too regardless of propriety, as he himself was aware.

Schwartz was waiting for him in the adjoining room with legs spread wide apart and both hands toying with his top-hat behind his back. The mere sight of that playful, well-groomed, and elegant figure refreshed Peter Ivanovich. He felt that Schwartz was above all these happenings and would not surrender to any depressing influences. His very look said that this incident of a church service for Ivan Ilych could not be a sufficient reason for infringing the order of the session—in other words, that it would certainly not prevent his unwrapping a new pack of cards and shuffling them that evening while a footman placed four fresh candles on the table: in fact, that there was no reason for supposing that this incident would hinder their spending the evening agreeably. Indeed he said this in a whisper as Peter Ivanovich passed him, proposing that they should meet for a game at Fëdor Vasilievich's. But apparently Peter Ivanovich was not destined to play bridge that evening. Praskovya Fëdorovna (a short, fat woman who despite all efforts to the contrary had continued to broaden steadily from her shoulders downwards and who had the same extraordinarily arched eyebrows as the lady who had been standing by the coffin), dressed all in black, her head covered with lace, came out of her own room with some other ladies, conducted them to the room where the dead body lay, and said: "The service will begin immediately. Please go in."

Schwartz, making an indefinite bow, stood still, evidently neither accepting nor declining this invitation. Praskovya Fëdorovna, recognizing Peter Ivanovich, sighed, went close up to him, took his hand, and said: "I know you were a true friend of Ivan Ilych . . . " and looked at him awaiting some suitable response. And Peter Ivanovich knew that, just as it had been the right thing to cross himself in that room, so what he had to do here was to press her hand, sigh, and say, "Believe me. . . ." So he did all this and as he did it felt that the desired result had been achieved: that both he and she were touched.

"Come with me. I want to speak to you before it begins," said the widow.     30
"Give me your arm."

Peter Ivanovich gave her his arm and they went to the inner rooms, passing Schwartz, who winked at Peter Ivanovich compassionately.

"That does for our bridge! Don't object if we find another player. Perhaps you can cut in when you do escape," said his playful look.

Peter Ivanovich sighed still more deeply and despondently, and Praskovya Fëdorovna pressed his arm gratefully. When they reached the drawing-room, upholstered in pink cretonne and lighted by a dim lamp, they sat down at the table—she on a sofa and Peter Ivanovich on a low pouffe, the springs of which yielded spasmodically under his weight. Praskovya Fëdorovna had been on the point of warning him to take another seat, but felt that such a warning was out of keeping with her present condition and so changed her mind. As he sat down on the pouffe Peter Ivanovich recalled how Ivan Ilych had arranged this room and had consulted him regarding this pink cretonne with green leaves. The whole room was full of furniture and knick-knacks, and on her way to the sofa the lace of the widow's black shawl caught on the carved edge of the table. Peter Ivanovich rose to detach it, and the springs of the pouffe, relieved of his weight, rose also and gave him a push. The widow began detaching her shawl herself, and Peter Ivanovich again sat down, suppressing the rebellious springs of the pouffe under him. But the widow had not quite freed herself and Peter Ivanovich got up again, and again the pouffe rebelled and even creaked. When this was all over she took out a clean cambric handkerchief and began to weep. The episode with the shawl and the struggle with the pouffe had cooled Peter Ivanovich's emotions and he sat there with a sullen look on his face. This awkward situation was inter-rupted by Sokolov, Ivan Ilych's butler, who came to report that the plot in the cemetery that Praskovya Fëdorovna had chosen would cost two hundred rubles. She stopped weeping and, looking at Peter Ivanovich with the air of a victim, remarked in French that it was very hard for her. Peter Ivanovich made a silent gesture signifying his full conviction that it must indeed be so.

"Please smoke," she said in a magnanimous yet crushed voice, and turned to discuss with Sokolov the price of the plot for the grave.

Peter Ivanovich while lighting his cigarette heard her inquiring very circum- 35
stantially into the prices of different plots in the cemetery and finally decide which she would take. When that was done she gave instructions about engaging the choir. Sokolov then left the room.

"I look after everything myself," she told Peter Ivanovich, shifting the albums that lay on the table; and noticing that the table was endangered by his cigarette-ash, she immediately passed him an ashtray, saying as she did so: "I consider it an affectation to say that my grief prevents my attending to practical affairs. On the contrary, if anything can—I won't say console me, but—distract me, it is seeing to everything concerning him." She again took out her handkerchief as if preparing to cry, but suddenly, as if mastering her feeling, she shook herself and began to speak calmly. "But there is something I want to talk to you about."

Peter Ivanovich bowed, keeping control of the springs of the pouffe, which immediately began quivering under him.

"He suffered terribly the last few days."

"Did he?" said Peter Ivanovich.

"Oh, terribly! He screamed unceasingly, not for minutes but for hours. For 40
the last three days he screamed incessantly. It was unendurable. I cannot understand how I bore it; you could hear him three rooms off. Oh, what I have suffered!"

"Is it possible that he was conscious all that time?" asked Peter Ivanovich.

"Yes," she whispered. "To the last moment. He took leave of us a quarter of an hour before he died, and asked us to take Volodya away."

The thought of the sufferings of this man he had known so intimately, first as a merry little boy, then as a school-mate, and later as a grown-up colleague, suddenly struck Peter Ivanovich with horror, despite an unpleasant consciousness of his own and this woman's dissimulation. He again saw that brow, and that nose pressing down on the lip, and felt afraid for himself.

"Three days of frightful suffering and then death! Why, that might suddenly, at any time, happen to me," he thought, and for a moment felt terrified. But—he did not himself know how—the customary reflection at once occurred to him that this had happened to Ivan Ilych and not to him, and that it should not and could not happen to him, and that to think that it could would be yielding to depression which he ought not to do, as Schwartz's expression plainly showed. After which reflection Peter Ivanovich felt reassured, and began to ask with interest about the details of Ivan Ilych's death, as though death was an accident natural to Ivan Ilych but certainly not to himself.

After many details of the really dreadful physical sufferings Ivan Ilych had 45
endured (which details he learnt only from the effect those sufferings had pro-

duced on Praskovya Fëdorovna's nerves) the widow apparently found it necessary to get to business.

"Oh, Peter Ivanovich, how hard it is! How terribly, terribly hard!" and she again began to weep.

Peter Ivanovich sighed and waited for her to finish blowing her nose. When she had done so he said, "Believe me . . . " and she again began talking and brought out what was evidently her chief concern with him—namely, to question him as to how she could obtain a grant of money from the government on the occasion of her husband's death. She made it appear that she was asking Peter Ivanovich's advice about her pension, but he soon saw that she already knew about that to the minutest detail, more even than he did himself. She knew how much could be got out of the government in consequence of her husband's death, but wanted to find out whether she could not possibly extract something more. Peter Ivanovich tried to think of some means of doing so, but after reflecting for a while and, out of propriety, condemning the government for its niggardliness, he said he thought that nothing more could be got. Then she sighed and evidently began to devise means of getting rid of her visitor. Noticing this, he put out his cigarette, rose, pressed her hand, and went out into the anteroom.

In the dining-room where the clock stood that Ivan Ilych had liked so much and had bought at an antique shop, Peter Ivanovich met a priest and a few acquaintances who had come to attend the service, and he recognized Ivan Ilych's daughter, a handsome young woman. She was in black and her slim figure appeared slimmer than ever. She had a gloomy, determined, almost angry expression, and bowed to Peter Ivanovich as though he were in some way to blame. Behind her, with the same offended look, stood a wealthy young man, an examining magistrate, whom Peter Ivanovich also knew and who was her fiancé, as he had heard. He bowed mournfully to them and was about to pass into the death-chamber, when from under the stairs appeared the figure of Ivan Ilych's schoolboy son, who was extremely like his father. He seemed a little Ivan Ilych, such as Peter Ivanovich remembered when they studied law together. His tear-stained eyes had in them the look that is seen in the eyes of boys of thirteen of fourteen who are not pureminded. When he saw Peter Ivanovich he scowled morosely and shamefacedly. Peter Ivanovich nodded to him and entered the death-chamber. The service began: candles, groans, incense, tears, and sobs. Peter Ivanovich stood looking gloomily down at his feet. He did not look once at the dead man, did not yield to any depressing influence, and was one of the first to leave the room. There was no one in the anteroom, but Gerasim darted out of the dead man's room, rummaged with his strong hands among the fur coats to find Peter Ivanovich's, and helped him on with it.

"Well, friend Gerasim," said Peter Ivanovich, so as to say something. "It's a sad affair, isn't it?"

"It's God's will. We shall all come to it some day," said Gerasim, displaying his teeth—the even, white teeth of a healthy peasant—and, like a man in the thick of urgent work, he briskly opened the front door, called the coachman,

50

helped Peter Ivanovich into the sledge, and sprang back to the porch as if in readiness for what he had to do next.

Peter Ivanovich found the fresh air particularly pleasant after the smell of incense, the dead body, and carbolic acid.

"Where to, sir?" asked the coachman.

"It's not too late even now . . . I'll call round on Fëdor Vasilievich."

He accordingly drove there and found them just finishing the first rubber, so that it was quite convenient for him to cut in.

## II

Ivan Ilych's life had been most simple and most ordinary and therefore most terrible.

He had been a member of the Court of Justice, and died at the age of forty-five. His father had been an official who after serving in various ministries and departments in Petersburg had made the sort of career which brings men to positions from which by reason of their long service they cannot be dismissed, though they are obviously unfit to hold any responsible position, and for whom therefore posts are specially created, which though fictitious carry salaries of from six to ten thousand rubles that are not fictitious, and in receipt of which they live on to a great age.

Such was the Privy Councillor and superfluous member of various superfluous institutions, Ilya Epimovich Golovin.

He had three sons, of whom Ivan Ilych was the second. The eldest son was following in his father's footsteps only in another department, and was already approaching that stage in the service at which a similar sinecure would be reached. The third son was a failure. He had ruined his prospects in a number of positions and was now serving in the railway department. His father and brothers, and still more their wives, not merely disliked meeting him, but avoided remembering his existence unless compelled to do so. His sister had married Baron Greff, a Petersburg official of her father's type. Ivan Ilych was *le phénix de la famille*° as people said. He was neither as cold and formal as his elder brother nor as wild as the younger, but was a happy mean between them—an intelligent, polished, lively, and agreeable man. He had studied with his younger brother at the School of Law, but the latter had failed to complete the course and was expelled when he was in the fifth class. Ivan Ilych finished the course well. Even when he was at the School of Law he was just what he remained for the rest of his life: a capable, cheerful, good-natured, and sociable man, though strict in the fulfillment of what he considered to be his duty: and he considered his duty to be what was so considered by those in authority. Neither as a boy nor as a man was he a toady, but from early youth was by nature attracted to people of high station as a fly is drawn to the light, assimilating their ways and views of life and establishing friendly relations with them. All the enthusiasms of childhood and youth passed without leaving much trace on him; he succumbed to sensuality, to vanity, and

*le phénix de la famille:* "the prize of the family."

latterly among the highest classes to liberalism, but always within limits which his instinct unfailingly indicated to him as correct.

At school he had done things which had formerly seemed to him very horrid and made him feel disgusted with himself when he did them; but when later on he saw that such actions were done by people of good position and that they did not regard them as wrong, he was able not exactly to regard them as right, but to forget about them entirely or not be at all troubled at remembering them.

Having graduated from the School of Law and qualified for the tenth rank of the civil service, and having received money from his father for his equipment, Ivan Ilych ordered himself clothes at Scharmer's, the fashionable tailor, hung a medallion inscribed *respice finem*° on his watch-chain, took leave of his professor and the prince who was patron of the school, had a farewell dinner with his comrades at Donon's first-class restaurant, and with his new and fashionable portmanteau, linen, clothes, shaving and other toilet appliances, and a travelling rug all purchased at the best shops, he set off for one of the provinces where through his father's influence, he had been attached to the Governor as an official for special service.

In the province Ivan Ilych soon arranged as easy and agreeable a position for himself as he had had at the School of Law. He performed his official tasks, made his career, and at the same time amused himself pleasantly and decorously. Occasionally he paid official visits to country districts, where he behaved with dignity both to his superiors and inferiors, and performed the duties entrusted to him, which related chiefly to the sectarians°, with an exactness and incorruptible honesty of which he could not but feel proud.

In official matters, despite his youth and taste for frivolous gaiety, he was exceedingly reserved, punctilious, and even severe; but in society he was often amusing and witty, and always good-natured, correct in his manner, and *bon enfant*°, as the Governor and his wife—with whom he was like one of the family—used to say of him.

In the province he had an affair with a lady who made advances to the elegant young lawyer, and there was also a milliner; and there were carousals with aides-de-camp who visited the district, and after-supper visits to a certain outlying street of doubtful reputation; and there was too some obsequiousness to his chief and even to his chief's wife, but all this was done with such a tone of good breeding that no hard names could be applied to it. It all came under the heading of the French saying: "*Il faut que jeunesse se passe.*"° It was all done with clean hands, in clean linen, with French phrases, and above all among people of the best society and consequently with the approval of people of rank.

So Ivan Ilych served for five years and then came a change in his official life. The new and reformed judicial institutions were introduced, and new men were needed. Ivan Ilych became such a new man. He was offered the post of examining magistrate, and he accepted it though the post was in another province and

---

*respice finem:* "Think of the end (of your life)."     *sectarians:* dissenters from the Orthodox Church.
*bon enfant:* like a well-behaved child.     "*Il faut que jeunesse se passe*": "Youth doesn't last."

obliged him to give up the connections he had formed and to make new ones. His friends met to give him a send-off; they had a group-photograph taken and presented him with a silver cigarette-case, and he set off to his new post.

As examining magistrate Ivan Ilych was just as *comme il faut*° and decorous a man, inspiring general respect and capable of separating his official duties from his private life, as he had been when acting as an official on special service. His duties now as examining magistrate were far more interesting and attractive than before. In his former position it had been pleasant to wear an undress uniform made by Scharmer, and to pass through the crowd of petitioners and officials who were timorously awaiting an audience with the Governor, and who envied him as with free and easy gait he went straight into his chief's private room to have a cup of tea and a cigarette with him. But not many people had been directly dependent on him—only police officials and the sectarians when he went on special missions—and he liked to treat them politely, almost as comrades, as if he were letting them feel that he who had the power to crush them was treating them in this simple, friendly way. There were then but few such people. But now, as an examining magistrate, Ivan Ilych felt that everyone without exception, even the most important and self-satisfied, was in his power, and that he need only write a few words on a sheet of paper with a certain heading, and this or that important, self-satisfied person would be brought before him in the role of an accused person or a witness, and if he did not choose to allow him to sit down, would have to stand before him and answer his questions. Ivan Ilych never abused his power; he tried on the contrary to soften its expression, but the consciousness of it and of the possibility of softening its effect, supplied the chief interest and attraction of his office. In his work itself, especially in his examinations, he very soon acquired a method of eliminating all considerations irrelevant to the legal aspect of the case, and reducing even the most complicated case to a form in which it would be presented on paper only in its externals, completely excluding his personal opinion of the matter, while above all observing every prescribed formality. The work was new and Ivan Ilych was one of the first men to apply the new Code of 1864°.

On taking up the post of examining magistrate in a new town, he made new acquaintances and connections, placed himself on a new footing, and assumed a somewhat different tone. He took up an attitude of rather dignified aloofness towards the provincial authorities, but picked out the best circle of legal gentlemen and wealthy gentry living in the town and assumed a tone of slight dissatisfaction with the government, of moderate liberalism, and of enlightened citizenship. At the same time, without at all altering the elegance of his toilet, he ceased shaving his chin and allowed his beard to grow as it pleased.

Ivan Ilych settled down very pleasantly in this new town. The society there, which inclined towards opposition to the Governor, was friendly, his salary was

---

*comme il faut:* "as required," rule-abiding.     *Code of 1864:* The emancipation of the serfs in 1861 was followed by a thorough all-round reform of judicial proceedings. [Translators' note.]

larger, and he began to play *vint*°, which he found added not a little to the pleasure of life, for he had a capacity for cards, played good-humoredly, and calculated rapidly and astutely, so that he usually won.

After living there for two years he met his future wife, Praskovya Fëdorovna Mikhel, who was the most attractive, clever, and brilliant girl of the set in which he moved, and among other amusements and relaxations from his labors as examining magistrate, Ivan Ilych established light and playful relations with her.

While he had been an official on special service he had been accustomed to dance, but now as an examining magistrate it was exceptional for him to do so. If he danced now, he did it as if to show that though he served under the reformed order of things, and had reached the fifth official rank, yet when it came to dancing he could do it better than most people. So at the end of an evening he sometimes danced with Praskovya Fëdorovna, and it was chiefly during these dances that he captivated her. She fell in love with him. Ivan Ilych had at first no definite intention of marrying, but when the girl fell in love with him he said to himself: "Really, why shouldn't I marry?"

Praskovya Fëdorovna came of a good family, was not bad-looking, and had some little property. Ivan Ilych might have aspired to a more brilliant match, but even this was good. He had his salary, and she, he hoped, would have an equal income. She was well connected, and was a sweet, pretty, and thoroughly correct young woman. To say that Ivan Ilych married because he fell in love with Praskovya Fëdorovna and found that she sympathized with his views of life would be as incorrect as to say that he married because his social circle approved of the match. He was swayed by both these considerations: the marriage gave him personal satisfaction, and at the same time it was considered the right thing by the most highly placed of his associates.

So Ivan Ilych got married.

The preparations for marriage and the beginning of married life, with its conjugal caresses, the new furniture, new crockery, and new linen, were very pleasant until his wife became pregnant—so that Ivan Ilych had begun to think that marriage would not impair the easy, agreeable, gay, and always decorous character of his life, approved of by society and regarded by himself as natural, but would even improve it. But from the first months of his wife's pregnancy, something new, unpleasant, depressing, and unseemly, and from which there was no way of escape, unexpectedly showed itself.

His wife, without any reason—*de gaieté de coeur*° as Ivan Ilych expressed it to himself—began to disturb the pleasure and propriety of their life. She began to be jealous without any cause, expected him to devote his whole attention to her, found fault with everything, and made coarse and ill-mannered scenes.

At first Ivan Ilych hoped to escape from the unpleasantness of this state of affairs by the same easy and decorous relation to life that had served him heretofore: he tried to ignore his wife's disagreeable moods, continued to live in his

70

---

*vint:* a form of bridge. [Translators' note.]     *de gaieté de coeur:* "from pure whim."

usual easy and pleasant way, invited friends to his house for a game of cards, and also tried going out to his club or spending his evenings with friends. But one day his wife began upbraiding him so vigorously, using such coarse words, and continued to abuse him every time he did not fulfil her demands, so resolutely and with such evident determination not to give way till he submitted—that is, till he stayed at home and was bored just as she was—that he became alarmed. He now realized that matrimony—at any rate with Praskovya Fëdorovna—was not always conducive to the pleasures and amenities of life, but on the contrary often infringed both comfort and propriety, and that he must therefore entrench himself against such infringement. And Ivan Ilych began to seek for means of doing so. His official duties were the one thing that imposed upon Praskovya Fëdorovna, and by means of his official work and the duties attached to it he began struggling with his wife to secure his own independence.

With the birth of their child, the attempts to feed it and the various failures in doing so, and with the real and imaginary illnesses of mother and child, in which Ivan Ilych's sympathy was demanded but about which he understood nothing, the need of securing for himself an existence outside his family life became still more imperative. 75

As his wife grew more irritable and exacting and Ivan Ilych transferred the center of gravity of his life more and more to his official work, so did he grow to like his work better and become more ambitious than before.

Very soon, within a year of his wedding, Ivan Ilych had realized that marriage, though it may add some comforts to life, is in fact a very intricate and difficult affair towards which in order to perform one's duty, that is, to lead a decorous life approved of by society, one must adopt a definite attitude just as towards one's official duties.

And Ivan Ilych evolved such an attitude towards married life. He only required of it those conveniences—dinner at home, housewife, and bed—which it could give him, and above all that propriety of external forms required by public opinion. For the rest he looked for light-hearted pleasure and propriety, and was very thankful when he found them, but if he met with antagonism and querulousness he at once retired into his separate fenced-off world of official duties, where he found satisfaction.

Ivan Ilych was esteemed a good official, and after three years was made Assistant Public Prosecutor. His new duties, their importance, the possibility of indicting and imprisoning anyone he chose, the publicity his speeches received, and the success he had in all these things, made his work still more attractive.

More children came. His wife became more and more querulous and ill-tempered, but the attitude Ivan Ilych had adopted towards his home life rendered him almost impervious to her grumbling. 80

After seven years' service in that town he was transferred to another province as Public Prosecutor. They moved, but were short of money and his wife did not like the place they moved to. Though the salary was higher the cost of living was greater, besides which two of their children died and family life became still more unpleasant for him.

Praskovya Fëdorovna blamed her husband for every inconvenience they encountered in their new home. Most of the conversations between husband and wife, especially as to the children's education, led to topics which recalled former disputes, and those disputes were apt to flare up again at any moment. There remained only those rare periods of amorousness which still came to them at times but did not last long. These were islets at which they anchored for a while and then again set out upon that ocean of veiled hostility which showed itself in their aloofness from one another. This aloofness might have grieved Ivan Ilych had he considered that it ought not to exist, but he now regarded the position as normal, and even made it the goal at which he aimed in family life. His aim was to free himself more and more from those unpleasantnesses and to give them a semblance of harmlessness and propriety. He attained this by spending less and less time with his family, and when obliged to be at home he tried to safeguard his position by the presence of outsiders. The chief thing, however, was that he had his official duties. The whole interest of his life now centered in the official world and that interest absorbed him. The consciousness of his power, being able to ruin anybody he wished to ruin, the importance, even the external dignity of his entry into court, or meetings with his subordinates, his success with superiors and inferiors, and above all his masterly handling of cases, of which he was conscious—all this gave him pleasure and filled his life, together with chats with his colleagues, dinners, and bridge. So that on the whole Ivan Ilych's life continued to flow as he considered it should do—pleasantly and properly.

So things continued for another seven years. His eldest daughter was already sixteen, another child had died, and only one son was left, a schoolboy and a subject of dissension. Ivan Ilych wanted to put him in the School of Law, but to spite him Praskovya Fëdorovna entered him at the High School. The daughter had been educated at home and had turned out well; the boy did not learn badly either.

### III

So Ivan Ilych lived for seventeen years after his marriage. He was already a Public Prosecutor of long standing, and had declined several proposed transfers while awaiting a more desirable post, when an unanticipated and unpleasant occurrence quite upset the peaceful course of his life. He was expecting to be offered the post of presiding judge in a University town, but Happe somehow came to the front and obtained the appointment instead. Ivan Ilych became irritable, reproached Happe, and quarrelled both with him and with his immediate superiors—who became colder to him and again passed him over when other appointments were made.

This was in 1880, the hardest year of Ivan Ilych's life. It was then that it 85 became evident on the one hand that his salary was insufficient for them to live on, and on the other that he had been forgotten, and not only this, but that what was for him the greatest and most cruel injustice appeared to others a quite ordinary occurrence. Even his father did not consider it his duty to help him. Ivan

Ilych felt himself abandoned by everyone, and that they regarded his position with a salary of 3,500 rubles as quite normal and even fortunate. He alone knew that with the consciousness of the injustices done him, with his wife's incessant nagging, and with the debts he had contracted by living beyond his means, his position was far from normal.

In order to save money that summer he obtained leave of absence and went with his wife to live in the country at her brother's place.

In the country, without his work, he experienced *ennui* for the first time in his life, and not only *ennui* but intolerable depression, and he decided that it was impossible to go on living like that, and that it was necessary to take energetic measures.

Having passed a sleepless night pacing up and down the veranda, he decided to go to Petersburg and bestir himself, in order to punish those who had failed to appreciate him and to get transferred to another ministry.

Next day, despite many protests from his wife and her brother, he started for Petersburg with the sole object of obtaining a post with a salary of five thousand rubles a year. He was no longer bent on any particular department, or tendency, or kind of activity. All he now wanted was an appointment to another post with a salary of five thousand rubles, either in the administration, in the banks, with the railways, in one of the Empress Marya's Institutions°, or even in the customs—but it had to carry with it a salary of five thousand rubles and be in a ministry other than that in which they had failed to appreciate him.

And this quest of Ivan Ilych's was crowned with remarkable and unexpected  90
success. At Kursk an acquaintance of his, F. I. Ilyin, got into the first-class carriage, sat down beside Ivan Ilych, and told him of a telegram just received by the Governor of Kursk announcing that a change was about to take place in the ministry: Peter Ivanovich was to be superseded by Ivan Semënovich.

The proposed change, apart from its significance for Russia, had a special significance for Ivan Ilych, because by bringing forward a new man, Peter Petrovich, and consequently his friend Zachar Ivanovich, it was highly favorable for Ivan Ilych, since Zachar Ivanovich was a friend and colleague of his.

In Moscow this news was confirmed, and on reaching Petersburg Ivan Ilych found Zachar Ivanovich and received a definite promise of an appointment in his former department of Justice.

A week later he telegraphed to his wife: "Zachar in Miller's place. I shall receive appointment on presentation of report."

Thanks to this change of personnel, Ivan Ilych had unexpectedly obtained an appointment in his former ministry which placed him two stages above his former colleagues besides giving him five thousand rubles salary and three thousand five hundred rubles for expenses connected with his removal. All his ill humor towards his former enemies and the whole department vanished, and Ivan Ilych was completely happy.

*Empress Marya's Institutions:* orphanages.

He returned to the country more cheerful and contented than he had been for a long time. Praskovya Fëdorovna also cheered up and a truce was arranged between them. Ivan Ilych told of how he had been fêted by everybody in Petersburg, how all those who had been his enemies were put to shame and now fawned on him, how envious they were of his appointment, and how much everybody in Petersburg had liked him.

Praskovya Fëdorovna listened to all this and appeared to believe it. She did not contradict anything, but only made plans for their life in the town to which they were going. Ivan Ilych saw with delight that these plans were his plans, that he and his wife agreed, and that, after a stumble, his life was regaining its due and natural character of pleasant lightheartedness and decorum.

Ivan Ilych had come back for a short time only, for he had to take up his new duties on the 10th of September. Moreover, he needed time to settle into the new place, to move all his belongings from the province, and to buy and order many additional things: in a word, to make such arrangements as he had resolved on, which were almost exactly what Praskovya Fëdorovna too had decided on.

Now that everything had happened so fortunately, and that he and his wife were at one in their aims and moreover saw so little of one another, they got on together better than they had done since the first years of marriage. Ivan Ilych had thought of taking his family away with him at once, but the insistence of his wife's brother and her sister-in-law, who had suddenly become particularly amiable and friendly to him and his family, induced him to depart alone.

So he departed, and the cheerful state of mind induced by his success and by the harmony between his wife and himself, the one intensifying the other, did not leave him. He found a delightful house, just the thing both he and his wife had dreamt of. Spacious, lofty reception rooms in the old style, a convenient and dignified study, rooms for his wife and daughter, a study for his son—it might have been specially built for them. Ivan Ilych himself superintended the arrangements, chose the wallpapers, supplemented the furniture (preferably with antiques which he considered particularly *comme il faut*), and supervised the upholstering. Everything progressed and progressed and approached the ideal he had set himself: even when things were only half completed they exceeded his expectations. He saw what a refined and elegant character, free from vulgarity, it would all have when it was ready. On falling asleep he pictured to himself how the reception-room would look. Looking at the yet unfinished drawing-room he could see the fireplace, the screen, the what-not, the little chairs dotted here and there, the dishes and plates on the walls, and the bronzes, as they would be when everything was in place. He was pleased by the thought of how his wife and daughter, who shared his taste in this matter, would be impressed by it. They were certainly not expecting as much. He had been particularly successful in finding, and buying cheaply, antiques which gave a particularly aristocratic character to the whole place. But in his letters he intentionally understated everything in order to be able to surprise them. All this so absorbed him that his new duties—though he liked his official work—interested him less than he had expected. Sometimes he even had moments of absentmindedness during the

Court Sessions, and would consider whether he should have straight or curved cornices for his curtains. He was so interested in it all that he often did things himself, rearranging the furniture, or rehanging the curtains. Once when mounting a stepladder to show the upholsterer, who did not understand, how he wanted the hangings draped, he made a false step and slipped, but being a strong and agile man he clung on and only knocked his side against the knob of the window frame. The bruised place was painful but the pain soon passed, and he felt particularly bright and well just then. He wrote: "I feel fifteen years younger." He thought he would have everything ready by September, but it dragged on till mid-October. But the result was charming not only in his eyes but to everyone who saw it.

In reality it was just what is usually seen in the houses of people of moderate 100 means who want to appear rich, and therefore succeed only in resembling others like themselves: there were damasks, dark wood, plants, rugs, and dull and polished bronzes—all the things people of a certain class have in order to resemble other people of that class. His house was so like the others that it would never have been noticed, but to him it all seemed to be quite exceptional. He was very happy when he met his family at the station and brought them to the newly furnished house all lit up, where a footman in a white tie opened the door into the hall decorated with plants, and when they went on into the drawing-room and the study uttering exclamations of delight. He conducted them everywhere, drank in their praises eagerly, and beamed with pleasure. At tea that evening, when Praskovya Fëdorovna among other things asked him about his fall, he laughed and showed them how he had gone flying and had frightened the upholsterer.

"It's a good thing I'm a bit of an athlete. Another man might have been killed, but I merely knocked myself, just there; it hurts when it's touched, but it's passing off already—it's only a bruise."

So they began living in their new home—in which, as always happens, when they got thoroughly settled in they found they were just one room short—and with the increased income, which as always was just a little (some five hundred rubles) too little, but it was all very nice.

Things went particularly well at first, before everything was finally arranged and while something had still to be done: this thing bought, that thing ordered, another thing moved, and something else adjusted. Though there were some disputes between husband and wife, they were both so well satisfied and had so much to do that it all passed off without any serious quarrels. When nothing was left to arrange it became rather dull and something seemed to be lacking, but they were then making acquaintances, forming habits, and life was growing fuller.

Ivan Ilych spent his mornings at the law courts and came home to dinner, and at first he was generally in good humor, though he occasionally became irritable just on account of his house. (Every spot on the tablecloth or the upholstery, and every broken window-blind string, irritated him. He had devoted so much trouble to arranging it all that every disturbance of it distressed him.) But on the whole his life ran its course as he believed life should do: easily, pleasantly, and decorously.

He got up at nine, drank his coffee, read the paper, and then put on his
undress uniform and went to the law courts. There the harness in which he
worked had already been stretched to fit him and he donned it without a hitch:
petitioners, inquiries at the chancery, the chancery itself, and the sittings public
and administrative. In all this the thing was to exclude everything fresh and vital,
which always disturbs the regular course of official business, and to admit only
official relations with people, and then only on official grounds. A man would
come, for instance, wanting some information. Ivan Ilych, as one in whose sphere
the matter did not lie, would have nothing to do with him: but if the man had
some business with him in his official capacity, something that could be
expressed on officially stamped paper, he would do everything, positively everything he could within the limits of such relations, and in doing so would maintain the semblance of friendly human relations, that is, would observe the courte-
sies of life. As soon as the official relations ended, so did everything else. Ivan
Ilych possessed this capacity to separate his real life from the official side of affairs
and not mix the two, in the highest degree, and by long practice and natural aptitude had brought it to such a pitch that sometimes, in the manner of a virtuoso,
he would even allow himself to let the human and official relations mingle. He
let himself do this just because he felt that he could at any time he chose resume
the strictly official attitude again and drop the human relation. And he did it all
easily, pleasantly, correctly, and even artistically. In the intervals between the
sessions he smoked, drank tea, chatted a little about politics, a little about general
topics, a little about cards, but most of all about official appointments. Tired, but
with the feelings of a virtuoso—one of the first violins who has played his part in
an orchestra with precision—he would return home to find that his wife and
daughter had been out paying calls, or had a visitor, and that his son had been to
school, had done his homework with his tutor, and was duly learning what is
taught at High Schools. Everything was as it should be. After dinner, if they had
no visitors, Ivan Ilych sometimes read a book that was being much discussed at
the time, and in the evening settled down to work, that is, read official papers,
compared the depositions of witnesses, and noted paragraphs of the Code applying to them. This was neither dull nor amusing. It was dull when he might have
been playing bridge, but if no bridge was available it was at any rate better than
doing nothing or sitting with his wife. Ivan Ilych's chief pleasure was giving little
dinners to which he invited men and women of good social position, and just as
his drawing-room resembled all other drawing-rooms so did his enjoyable little
parties resemble all other such parties.

Once they even gave a dance. Ivan Ilych enjoyed it and everything went off
well, except that it led to a violent quarrel with his wife about the cakes and
sweets. Praskovya Fëdorovna had made her own plans, but Ivan Ilych insisted on
getting everything from an expensive confectioner and ordered too many cakes,
and the quarrel occurred because some of those cakes were left over and the confectioner's bill came to forty-five rubles. It was a great and disagreeable quarrel.
Praskovya Fëdorovna called him "a fool and an imbecile," and he clutched at his
head and made angry allusions to divorce.

But the dance itself had been enjoyable. The best people were there, and Ivan Ilych had danced with Princess Trufonova, a sister of the distinguished founder of the Society "Bear My Burden."

The pleasures connected with his work were pleasures of ambition; his social pleasures were those of vanity; but Ivan Ilych's greatest pleasure was playing bridge. He acknowledged that whatever disagreeable incident happened in his life, the pleasure that beamed like a ray of light above everything else was to sit down to bridge with good players, not noisy partners, and of course to four-handed bridge (with five players it was annoying to have to stand out, though one pretended not to mind), to play a clever and serious game (when the cards allowed it), and then to have supper and drink a glass of wine. After a game of bridge, especially if he had won a little (to win a large sum was unpleasant), Ivan Ilych went to bed in specially good humor.

So they lived. They formed a circle of acquaintances among the best people and were visited by people of importance and by young folk. In their views as to their acquaintances, husband, wife, and daughter were entirely agreed, and tacitly and unanimously kept at arm's length and shook off the various shabby friends and relations who, with much show of affection, gushed into the drawing-room with its Japanese plates on the walls. Soon these shabby friends ceased to obtrude themselves and only the best people remained in the Golovins' set.

Young men made up to Lisa, and Petrishchev, an examining magistrate and 110 Dmitri Ivanovich Petrischev's son and sole heir, began to be so attentive to her that Ivan Ilych had already spoken to Praskovya Fëdorovna about it, and considered whether they should not arrange a party for them, or get up some private theatricals.

So they lived, and all went well, without change, and life followed pleasantly.

## IV

They were all in good health. It could not be called ill health if Ivan Ilych sometimes said that he had a queer taste in his mouth and felt some discomfort in his left side.

But this discomfort increased and, though not exactly painful, grew into a sense of pressure in his side accompanied by ill humor. And his irritability became worse and worse and began to mar the agreeable, easy, and correct life that had established itself in the Golovin family. Quarrels between husband and wife became more and more frequent, and soon the ease and amenity disappeared and even the decorum was barely maintained. Scenes again became frequent, and very few of those islets remained on which husband and wife could meet without an explosion. Praskovya Fëdorovna now had good reason to say that her husband's temper was trying. With characteristic exaggeration she said he had always had a dreadful temper, and that it had needed all her good nature to put up with it for twenty years. It was true that now the quarrels were started by him. His bursts of temper always came just before dinner, often just as he began to eat his soup. Sometimes he noticed that a plate or dish was chipped, or the food was not right, or his son put his elbow on the table, or his daughter's hair was not done as he liked it, and for all this he blamed Praskovya Fëdorovna. At first she retorted and said disagreeable things to him, but once or twice he fell into such a rage at the beginning of dinner that she realized it was due to some physical derangement brought on by taking food, and so she restrained herself and did not answer, but only hurried to get the dinner over. She regarded this self-restraint as highly praiseworthy. Having come to the conclusion that her husband had a dreadful temper and made her life miserable, she began to feel sorry for herself, and the more she pitied herself the more she hated her husband. She began to wish he would die; yet she did not want him to die because then his salary would cease. And this irritated her against him still more. She considered herself dreadfully unhappy just because not even his death could save her, and though she concealed her exasperation, that hidden exasperation of hers increased his irritation also.

After one scene in which Ivan Ilych had been particularly unfair and after which he had said in explanation that he certainly was irritable but that it was due to his not being well, she said that if he was ill it should be attended to, and insisted on his going to see a celebrated doctor.

He went. Everything took place as he had expected and as it always does. 115 There was the usual waiting and the important air assumed by the doctor, with which he was so familiar (resembling that which he himself assumed in court), and the sounding and listening, and the questions which called for answers that were foregone conclusions and were evidently unnecessary, and the look of importance which implied that "if only you put yourself in our hands we will arrange everything—we know indubitably how it has to be done, always in the same way for everybody alike." It was all just as it was in the law courts. The doctor put on just the same air towards him as he himself put on towards an accused person.

The doctor said that so-and-so indicated that there was so-and-so inside the patient, but if the investigation of so-and-so did not confirm this, then he must assume that and that. If he assumed that and that, then . . . and so on. To Ivan Ilych only one question was important: was his case serious or not? But the doctor ignored that inappropriate question. From his point of view it was not the one under consideration, the real question was to decide between a floating kidney, chronic catarrh, or appendicitis. It was not a question of Ivan Ilych's life or death, but one between a floating kidney and appendicitis. And that question the doctor solved brilliantly, as it seemed to Ivan Ilych, in favor of the appendix, with the reservation that should an examination of the urine give fresh indications the matter would be reconsidered. All this was just what Ivan Ilych had himself brilliantly accomplished a thousand times in dealing with men on trial. The doctor summed up just as brilliantly, looking over his spectacles triumphantly and even gaily at the accused. From the doctor's summing up Ivan Ilych concluded that things were bad, but that for the doctor, and perhaps for everybody else, it was a matter of indifference, though for him it was bad. And this conclusion struck him painfully, arousing in him a great feeling of pity for himself and of bitterness towards the doctor's indifference to a matter of such importance.

He said nothing of this, but rose, placed the doctor's fee on the table, and remarked with a sigh: "We sick people probably often put inappropriate questions. But tell me, in general, is this complaint dangerous, or not? . . . "

The doctor looked at him sternly over his spectacles with one eye, as if to say: "Prisoner, if you will not keep to the questions put to you, I shall be obliged to have you removed from the court."

"I have already told you what I consider necessary and proper. The analysis may show something more." And the doctor bowed.

Ivan Ilych went out slowly, seated himself disconsolately in his sledge, and    120
drove home. All the way home he was going over what the doctor had said, trying to translate those complicated, obscure, scientific phrases into plain language and find in them an answer to the question: "Is my condition bad? Is it very bad? Or is there as yet nothing much wrong?" And it seemed to him that the meaning of what the doctor had said was that it was very bad. Everything in the streets seemed depressing. The cabmen, the houses, the passers-by, and the shops, were dismal. His ache, this dull gnawing ache that never ceased for a moment, seemed to have acquired a new and more serious significance from the doctor's dubious remarks. Ivan Ilych now watched it with a new and oppressive feeling.

He reached home and began to tell his wife about it. She listened, but in the middle of his account his daughter came in with her hat on, ready to go out with her mother. She sat down reluctantly to listen to this tedious story, but could not stand it long, and her mother too did not hear him to the end.

"Well, I am very glad," she said. "Mind now to take your medicine regularly. Give me the prescription and I'll send Gerasim to the chemist's." And she went to get ready to go out.

While she was in the room Ivan Ilych had hardly taken time to breathe, but he sighed deeply when she left it.

"Well," he thought, "perhaps it isn't so bad after all."

He began taking his medicine and following the doctor's directions, which    125
had been altered after the examination of the urine. But then it happened that there was a contradiction between the indications drawn from the examination of the urine and the symptoms that showed themselves. It turned out that what was happening differed from what the doctor had told him, and that he had either forgotten, or blundered, or hidden something from him. He could not, however, be blamed for that, and Ivan Ilych still obeyed his orders implicitly and at first derived some comfort from doing so.

From the time of his visit to the doctor, Ivan Ilych's chief occupation was the exact fulfilment of the doctor's instructions regarding hygiene and the taking of medicine, and the observation of his pain and his excretions. His chief interests came to be people's ailments and people's health. When sickness, deaths, or recoveries were mentioned in his presence, especially when the illness resembled his own, he listened with agitation which he tried to hide, asked questions, and applied what he heard to his own case.

The pain did not grow less, but Ivan Ilych made efforts to force himself to think that he was better. And he could do this so long as nothing agitated him.

But as soon as he had any unpleasantness with his wife, any lack of success in his official work, or held bad cards at bridge, he was at once acutely sensible of his disease. He had formerly borne such mischances, hoping soon to adjust what was wrong, to master it and attain success, or make a grand slam. But now every mischance upset him and plunged him into despair. He would say to himself: "There now, just as I was beginning to get better and the medicine had begun to take effect, comes this accursed misfortune, or unpleasantness. . . ." And he was furious with the mishap, or with the people who were causing the unpleasantness and killing him, for he felt that this fury was killing him but could not restrain it. One would have thought that it should have been clear to him that this exasperation with circumstances and people aggravated his illness, and that he ought therefore to ignore unpleasant occurrences. But he drew the very opposite conclusion: he said that he needed peace, and he watched for everything that might disturb it and became irritable at the slightest infringement of it. His condition was rendered worse by the fact that he read medical books and consulted doctors. The progress of his disease was so gradual that he could deceive himself when comparing one day with another—the difference was so slight. But when he consulted the doctors it seemed to him that he was getting worse, and even very rapidly. Yet despite this he was continually consulting them.

That month he went to see another celebrity, who told him almost the same as the first had done but put his questions rather differently, and the interview with this celebrity only increased Ivan Ilych's doubts and fears. A friend of a friend of his, a very good doctor, diagnosed his illness again quite differently from the others, and though he predicted recovery, his questions and suppositions bewildered Ivan Ilych still more and increased his doubts. A homeopathist diagnosed the disease in yet another way, and prescribed medicine which Ivan Ilych took secretly for a week. But after a week, not feeling any improvement and having lost confidence both in the former doctor's treatment and in this one's, he became still more despondent. One day a lady acquaintance mentioned a cure effected by a wonder-working icon. Ivan Ilych caught himself listening attentively and beginning to believe that it had occurred. This incident alarmed him. "Has my mind really weakened to such an extent?" he asked himself. "Nonsense! It's all rubbish. I mustn't give way to nervous fears but having chosen a doctor must keep strictly to his treatment. That is what I will do. Now it's all settled. I won't think about it, but will follow the treatment seriously till summer, and then we shall see. From now there must be no more of this wavering!" This was easy to say but impossible to carry out. The pain in his side oppressed him and seemed to grow worse and more incessant, while the taste in his mouth grew stranger and stranger. It seemed to him that his breath had a disgusting smell, and he was conscious of a loss of appetite and strength. There was no deceiving himself: something terrible, new, and more important than anything before in his life, was taking place within him of which he alone was aware. Those about him did not understand or would not understand it, but thought everything in the world was going on as usual. That tormented Ivan Ilych more than anything. He saw that his household, especially his wife and daughter who were in a perfect whirl of visiting, did not understand anything of it and were annoyed that he was so depressed and so exacting, as if he were to blame for it. Though they tried to disguise it he saw that he was an obstacle in their path, and that his wife had adopted a definite line in regard to his illness and kept to it regardless of anything he said or did. Her attitude was this: "You know," she would say to her friends, "Ivan Ilych can't do as other people do, and keep to the treatment prescribed for him. One day he'll take his drops and keep strictly to his diet and go to bed in good time, but the next day unless I watch him he'll suddenly forget his medicine, eat sturgeon—which is forbidden—and sit up playing cards till one o'clock in the morning."

"Oh, come, when was that?" Ivan Ilych would ask in vexation. "Only once at Peter Ivanovich's."

"And yesterday with Shebek."                                                                                                      130

"Well, even if I hadn't stayed up, this pain would have kept me awake."

"Be that as it may you'll never get well like that, but will always make us wretched."

Praskovya Fëdorovna's attitude to Ivan Ilych's illness, as she expressed it both to others and to him, was that it was his own fault and was another of the annoyances he caused her. Ivan Ilych felt that this opinion escaped her involuntarily—but that did not make it easier for him.

At the law courts too, Ivan Ilych noticed, or thought he noticed, a strange attitude towards himself. It sometimes seemed to him that people were watching him inquisitively as a man whose place might soon be vacant. Then again, his friends would suddenly begin to chaff him in a friendly way about his low spirits, as if the awful, horrible, and unheard-of thing that was going on within him, incessantly gnawing at him and irresistibly drawing him away, was a very agreeable subject for jests. Schwartz in particular irritated him by his jocularity, vivacity, and *savoir-faire*, which reminded him of what he himself had been ten years ago.

Friends came to make up a set and they sat down to cards. They dealt, bend-  135 ing the new cards to soften them, and he sorted the diamonds in his hand and found he had seven. His partner said "No trumps" and supported him with two diamonds. What more could be wished for? It ought to be jolly and lively. They would make a grand slam. But suddenly Ivan Ilych was conscious of that gnawing pain, that taste in his mouth, and it seemed ridiculous that in such circumstances he should be pleased to make a grand slam.

He looked at his partner Mikhail Mikhaylovich, who rapped the table with his strong hand and instead of snatching up the tricks pushed the cards courteously and indulgently towards Ivan Ilych that he might have the pleasure of gathering them up without the trouble of stretching out his hand for them. "Does he think I am too weak to stretch out my arm?" thought Ivan Ilych, and forgetting what he was doing he over-trumped his partner, missing the grand slam by three tricks. And what was most awful of all was that he saw how upset Mikhail Mikhaylovich was about it but did not himself care. And it was dreadful to realize why he did not care.

They all saw that he was suffering, and said: "We can stop if you are tired. Take a rest." Lie down? No, he was not at all tired, and he finished the rubber. All were gloomy and silent. Ivan Ilych felt that he had diffused this gloom over them and could not dispel it. They had supper and went away, and Ivan Ilych was left alone with the consciousness that his life was poisoned and was poisoning the lives of others, and that this poison did not weaken but penetrated more and more deeply into his whole being.

With this consciousness, and with physical pain besides the terror, he must go to bed, often to lie awake the greater part of the night. Next morning he had to get up again, dress, go to the law courts, speak, and write; or if he did not go out, spend at home those twenty-four hours a day each of which was a torture. And he had to live thus all alone on the brink of an abyss, with no one who understood or pitied him.

## V

So one month passed and then another. Just before the New Year his brother-in-law came to town and stayed at their house. Ivan Ilych was at the law courts and Praskovya Fëdorovna had gone shopping. When Ivan Ilych came home and entered his study he found his brother-in-law there—a healthy, florid man—unpacking his portmanteau himself. He raised his head on hearing Ivan Ilych's footsteps and looked up at him for a moment without a word. That stare told Ivan Ilych everything. His brother-in-law opened his mouth to utter an exclamation of surprise but checked himself, and that action confirmed it all.

"I have changed, eh?"                                                                          140

"Yes, there is a change."

And after that, try as he would to get his brother-in-law to return to the subject of his looks, the latter would say nothing about it. Praskovya Fëdorovna came home and her brother went out to her. Ivan Ilych locked the door and began to examine himself in the glass, first full face, then in profile. He took up a portrait of himself taken with his wife, and compared it with what he saw in the glass. The change in him was immense. Then he bared his arms to the elbow, looked at them, drew the sleeves down again, sat down on an ottoman, and grew blacker than night.

"No, no, this won't do!" he said to himself, and jumped up, went to the table, took up some law papers, and began to read them, but could not continue. He unlocked the door and went into the reception-room. The door leading to the drawing-room was shut. He approached it on tiptoe and listened.

"No, you are exaggerating!" Praskovya Fëdorovna was saying.

"Exaggerating! Don't you see it? Why, he's a dead man! Look at his eyes—  145 there's no light in them. But what is it that is wrong with him?"

"No one knows. Nikolaevich said something, but I don't know what. And Leshchetitsky° said quite the contrary . . . "

---

*Nikolaevich, Leshchetitsky:* two doctors, the latter a celebrated specialist. [Translators' note.]

Ivan Ilych walked away, went to his own room, lay down, and began musing: "The kidney, a floating kidney." He recalled all the doctors had told him of how it detached itself and swayed about. And by an effort of imagination he tried to catch that kidney and arrest it and support it. So little was needed for this, it seemed to him. "No, I'll go to see Peter Ivanovich° again." He rang, ordered the carriage, and got ready to go.

"Where are you going, Jean?" asked his wife, with a specially sad and exceptionally kind look.

This exceptionally kind look irritated him. He looked morosely at her.

"I must go to see Peter Ivanovich." 150

He went to see Peter Ivanovich, and together they went to see his friend, the doctor. He was in, and Ivan Ilych had a long talk with him.

Reviewing the anatomical and physiological details of what in the doctor's opinion was going on inside him, he understood it all.

There was something, a small thing, in the vermiform appendix. It might all come right. Only stimulate the energy of one organ and check the activity of another, then absorption would take place and everything would come right. He got home rather late for dinner, ate his dinner, and conversed cheerfully, but could not for a long time bring himself to go back to work in his room. At last, however, he went to his study and did what was necessary, but the consciousness that he had put something aside—an important, intimate matter which he would revert to when his work was done—never left him. When he finished his work he remembered that this intimate matter was the thought of his vermiform appendix. But he did not give himself up to it, and went to the drawing-room for tea. There were callers there, including the examining magistrate who was a desirable match for his daughter, and they were conversing, playing the piano, and singing. Ivan Ilych, as Praskovya Fëdorovna remarked, spent that evening more cheerfully than usual, but he never for a moment forgot that he had postponed the important matter of the appendix. At eleven o'clock he said good-night and went to his bedroom. Since his illness he had slept alone in a small room next to his study. He undressed and took up a novel by Zola, but instead of reading it he fell into thought, and in his imagination that desired improvement in the vermiform appendix occurred. There was the absorption and evacuation and the re-establishment of normal activity. "Yes, that's it!" he said to himself. "One need only assist nature, that's all." He remembered his medicine, rose, took it, and lay down on his back watching for the beneficent action of the medicine and for it to lessen the pain. "I need only take it regularly and avoid all injurious influences. I am already feeling better, much better." He began touching his side: it was not painful to the touch. "There, I really don't feel it. It's much better already." He put out the light and turned on his side . . . "The appendix is getting better, absorption is occurring." Suddenly he felt the old, familiar, dull, gnawing pain, stubborn and serious. There was the same familiar loathsome taste in this mouth. His heart sank and he felt dazed. "My God! My God!" he muttered. "Again,

Peter Ivanovich: That was the friend whose friend was a doctor. [Translators' note.]

again! and it will never cease." And suddenly the matter presented itself in a quite different aspect. "Vermiform appendix! Kidney!" he said to himself. "It's not a question of appendix or kidney, but of life and . . . death. Yes, life was there and now it is going, going and I cannot stop it. Yes. Why deceive myself? Isn't it obvious to everyone but me that I'm dying, and that it's only a question of weeks, days . . . it may happen this moment. There was light and now there is darkness. I was here and now I'm going there! Where?" A chill came over him, his breathing ceased, and he felt only the throbbing of his heart.

"When I am not, what will there be? There will be nothing. Then where shall I be when I am no more? Can this be dying? No, I don't want to!" He jumped up and tried to light the candle, felt for it with trembling hands, dropped candle and candlestick on the floor, and fell back on his pillow.

"What's the use? It makes no difference," he said to himself, staring with 155 wide-open eyes into the darkness. "Death. Yes, death. And none of them know or wish to know it, and they have no pity for me. Now they are playing." (He heard through the door the distant sound of a song and its accompaniment.) "It's all the same to them, but they will die too! Fools! I first, and they later, but it will be the same for them. And now they are merry . . . the beasts!"

Anger choked him and he was agonizingly, unbearably miserable. "It is impossible that all men have been doomed to suffer this awful horror!" He raised himself.

"Something must be wrong. I must calm myself—must think it all over from the beginning." And he again began thinking. "Yes, the beginning of my illness: I knocked my side, but I was still quite well that day and the next. It hurt a little, then rather more. I saw the doctors, then followed despondency and anguish, more doctors, and I drew nearer to the abyss. My strength grew less and I kept coming nearer and nearer, and now I have wasted away and there is no light in my eyes. I think of the appendix—but this is death! I think of mending the appendix, and all the while here is death! Can it really be death?" Again terror seized him and he gasped for breath. He leant down and began feeling for the matches, pressing with his elbow on the stand beside the bed. It was in his way and hurt him, he grew furious with it, pressed on it still harder, and upset it. Breathless and in despair he fell on his back, expecting death to come immediately.

Meanwhile the visitors were leaving. Praskovya Fëdorovna was seeing them off. She heard something fall and came in.

"What has happened?"

"Nothing. I knocked it over accidentally." 160

She went out and returned with a candle. He lay there panting heavily, like a man who has run a thousand yards, and stared upwards at her with a fixed look.

"What is it, Jean?"

"No . . . o . . . thing. I upset it." ("Why speak of it? She won't understand," he thought.)

And in truth she did not understand. She picked up the stand, lit his candle, and hurried away to see another visitor off. When she came back he still lay on his back, looking upwards.

"What is it? Do you feel worse?"

"Yes."

She shook her head and sat down.

"Do you know, Jean, I think we must ask Leshchetitsky to come and see you here."

This meant calling in the famous specialist, regardless of expense. He smiled malignantly and said "No." She remained a little longer and then went up to him and kissed his forehead.

While she was kissing him he hated her from the bottom of his soul and with difficulty refrained from pushing her away.

"Good-night. Please God you'll sleep."

"Yes."

## VI

Ivan Ilych saw that he was dying, and he was in continual despair.

In the depth of his heart he knew he was dying, but not only was he not accustomed to the thought, he simply did not and could not grasp it.

The syllogism he had learnt from Kiezewetter's Logic: "Caius is a man, men are mortal, therefore Caius is mortal," had always seemed to him correct as applied to Caius, but certainly not as applied to himself. That Caius—man in the abstract—was mortal, was perfectly correct, but he was not Caius, not an abstract man, but a creature quite, quite separate from all others. He had been little Vanya, with a mamma and a papa, with Mitya and Volodya, with the toys, a coachman and a nurse, afterwards with Katenka and with all the joys, griefs, and delights of childhood, boyhood, and youth. What did Caius know of the smell of that striped leather ball Vanya had been so fond of? Had Caius kissed his mother's hand like that, and did the silk of her dress rustle so for Caius? Had he rioted like that at school when the pastry was bad? Had Caius been in love like that? Could Caius preside at a session as he did? "Caius really was mortal, and it was right for him to die; but for me, little Vanya, Ivan Ilych, with all my thoughts and emotions, it's altogether a different matter. It cannot be thought I ought to die. That would be too terrible."

Such was his feeling.

"If I had to die like Caius I should have known it was so. An inner voice would have told me so, but there was nothing of the sort in me and I and all my friends felt that our case was quite different from that of Caius. And now here it is!" he said to himself. "It can't be. It's impossible! But here it is. How is this? How is one to understand it?"

He could not understand it, and tried to drive this false, incorrect, morbid thought away and to replace it by other proper and healthy thoughts. But that thought, and not the thought only but the reality itself, seemed to come and confront him.

And to replace that thought he called up a succession of others, hoping to find in them some support. He tried to get back into the former current of thoughts that had once screened the thought of death from him. But strange to say, all that had formerly shut off, hidden, and destroyed his consciousness of death, no longer had that effect. Ivan Ilych now spent most of his time in attempting to re-establish that old current. He would say to himself: "I will take up my duties again—after all I used to live by them." And banishing all doubts he would go to the law courts, enter into conversation with his colleagues, and sit carelessly as was his wont, scanning the crowd with a thoughtful look and leaning both his emaciated arms on the arms of his oak chair; bending over as usual to a colleague and drawing his papers nearer he would interchange whispers with him, and then suddenly raising his eyes and sitting erect would pronounce certain words and open the proceedings. But suddenly in the midst of those proceedings the pain in his side, regardless of the stage the proceedings had reached, would begin its own gnawing work. Ivan Ilych would turn his attention to it and try to drive the thought of it away, but without success. *It* would come and stand before him and look at him, and he would be petrified and the light would die out of his eyes, and he would again begin asking himself whether *It* alone was true. And his colleagues and subordinates would see with surprise and distress that he, the brilliant and subtle judge, was becoming confused and making mistakes. He would shake himself, try to pull himself together, manage somehow to bring the sitting to a close, and return home with the sorrowful consciousness that his judicial labors could not as formerly hide from him what he wanted them to hide, and could not deliver him from *It*. And what was worst of all was that *It* drew his attention to itself not in order to make him take some action but only that he should look at *It*, look it straight in the face: look at it and, without doing anything, suffer inexpressibly.

And to save himself from this condition Ivan Ilych looked for consolation— 180 new screens—and new screens were found and for a while seemed to save him, but then they immediately fell to pieces or rather became transparent, as if *It* penetrated them and nothing could veil *It*.

In these latter days he would go into the drawing-room he had arranged— that drawing-room where he had fallen and for the sake of which (how bitterly ridiculous it seemed) he had sacrificed his life—for he knew that his illness originated with that knock. He would enter and see that something had scratched the polished table. He would look for the cause of this and find that it was the bronze ornamentation of an album, that had got bent. He would take up the expensive album which he had lovingly arranged, and feel vexed with his daughter and her friends for their untidiness—for the album was torn here and there and some of the photographs turned upside down. He would put it carefully in order and bend the ornamentation back into position. Then it would occur to him to place all those things in another corner of the room, near the plants. He could call the footman, but his daughter or wife would come to help him. They would not agree, and his wife would contradict him, and he would dispute and grow angry. But that was all right, for then he did not think about *It*. *It* was invisible.

But then, when he was moving something himself, his wife would say: "Let the servants do it. You will hurt yourself again." And suddenly *It* would flash through the screen and he would see it. It was just a flash, and he hoped it would disappear, but he would involuntarily pay attention to his side. "It sits there as before, gnawing just the same!" And he could no longer forget It, but could distinctly see it looking at him from behind the flowers. "What is it all for?"

"It really is so! I lost my life over that curtain as I might have done when storming a fort. Is that possible? How terrible and how stupid. It can't be true! It can't, but it is."

He would go to his study, lie down, and again be alone with It: face to face with It. And nothing could be done with It except to look at it and shudder.

## VII

How it happened it is impossible to say because it came about step by step, 185 unnoticed, but in the third month of Ivan Ilych's illness, his wife, his daughter, his son, his acquaintances, the doctors, the servants, and above all he himself, were aware that the whole interest he had for the other people was whether he would soon vacate his place, and at last release the living from the discomfort caused by his presence and be himself released from his sufferings.

He slept less and less. He was given opium and hypodermic injections of morphine, but this did not relieve him. The dull depression he experienced in a somnolent condition at first gave him a little relief, but only as something new, afterwards it became as distressing as the pain itself or even more so.

Special foods were prepared for him by the doctor's orders, but all those foods became increasingly distasteful and disgusting to him.

For his excretions also special arrangements had to be made, and this was a torment to him every time—a torment from the uncleanliness, the unseemliness, and the smell, and from knowing that another person had to take part in it.

But just through this most unpleasant matter, Ivan Ilych obtained comfort. Gerasim, the butler's young assistant, always came in to carry the things out. Gerasim was a clean, fresh peasant lad, grown stout on town food and always cheerful and bright. At first the sight of him, in his clean Russian peasant costume, engaged on that disgusting task embarrassed Ivan Ilych.

Once when he got up from the commode too weak to draw up his trousers, 190 he dropped into a soft armchair and looked with horror at his bare, enfeebled thighs with the muscles so sharply marked on them.

Gerasim with a firm light tread, his heavy boots emitting a pleasant smell of tar and fresh winter air, came in wearing a clean Hessian apron, the sleeves of his print shirt tucked up over his strong, bare young arms; and refraining from looking at his sick master out of consideration for his feelings, and restraining the joy of life that beamed from his face, he went up to the commode.

"Gerasim!" said Ivan Ilych in a weak voice.

Gerasim started, evidently afraid he might have committed some blunder, and with a rapid movement turned his fresh, kind, simple young face which just showed the first downy signs of a beard.

"Yes, sir?"

"That must be very unpleasant for you. You must forgive me. I am helpless." 195

"Oh, why, sir," and Gerasim's eyes beamed and he showed his glistening white teeth, "what's a little trouble? It's a case of illness with you, sir."

And his deft strong hands did their accustomed task, and he went out of the room stepping lightly. Five minutes later he as lightly returned.

Ivan Ilych was still sitting in the same position in the armchair.

"Gerasim," he said when the latter had replaced the freshly washed utensil. "Please come here and help me." Gerasim went up to him. "Lift me up. It is hard for me to get up, and I have sent Dmitri away."

Gerasim went up to him, grasped his master with his strong arms deftly but 200 gently, in the same way that he stepped—lifted him, supported him with one hand, and with the other drew up his trousers and would have set him down again, but Ivan Ilych asked to be led to the sofa. Gerasim, without an effort and without apparent pressure, led him, almost lifting him, to the sofa and placed him on it.

"Thank you. How easily and well you do it all!"

Gerasim smiled again and turned to leave the room. But Ivan Ilych felt his presence such a comfort that he did not want to let him go.

"One thing more, please move up that chair. No, the other one—under my feet. It is easier for me when my feet are raised."

Gerasim brought the chair, set it down gently in place, and raised Ivan Ilych's legs on to it. It seemed to Ivan Ilych that he felt better while Gerasim was holding up his legs.

"It's better when my legs are higher," he said. "Place that cushion under 205 them."

Gerasim did so. He again lifted the legs and placed them, and again Ivan Ilych felt better while Gerasim held his legs. When he set them down Ivan Ilych fancied he felt worse.

"Gerasim," he said. "Are you busy now?"

"Not at all, sir," said Gerasim, who had learnt from the townsfolk how to speak to gentlefolk.

"What have you still to do?"

"What have I to do? I've done everything except chopping the logs for 210 tomorrow."

"Then hold my legs up a bit higher, can you?"

"Of course I can. Why not?" And Gerasim raised his master's legs higher and Ivan Ilych thought that in that position he did not feel any pain at all.

"And how about the logs?"

"Don't trouble about that, sir. There's plenty of time."

Ivan Ilych told Gerasim to sit down and hold his legs, and began to talk to 215 him. And strange to say it seemed to him that he felt better while Gerasim held his legs up.

After that Ivan Ilych would sometimes call Gerasim and get him to hold his legs on his shoulders, and he liked talking to him. Gerasim did it all easily, willingly, simply, and with a good nature that touched Ivan Ilych. Health, strength, and vitality in other people were offensive to him, but Gerasim's strength and vitality did not mortify but soothed him.

What tormented Ivan Ilych most was the deception, the lie, which for some reason they all accepted, that he was not dying but was simply ill, and that he only need keep quiet and undergo a treatment and then something very good would result. He, however, knew that do what they would nothing would come of it, only still more agonizing suffering and death. This deception tortured him— their not wishing to admit what they all knew and what he knew, but wanting to lie to him concerning his terrible condition, and wishing and forcing him to participate in that lie. Those lies—lies enacted over him on the eve of his death and destined to degrade this awful, solemn act to the level of their visitings, their curtains, their sturgeon for dinner—were a terrible agony for Ivan Ilych. And strangely enough, many times when they were going through their antics over him he had been within a hairbreadth of calling out to them: "Stop lying! You know and I know that I am dying. Then at least stop lying about it!" But he had never had the spirit to do it. The awful, terrible act of his dying was, he could see, reduced by those about him to the level of a casual, unpleasant, and almost indecorous incident (as if someone entered a drawing-room diffusing an unpleasant odor) and this was done by that very decorum which he had served all his life long. He saw that no one felt for him, because no one even wished to grasp his position. Only Gerasim recognized it and pitied him. And so Ivan Ilych felt at ease only with him. He felt comforted when Gerasim supported his legs (sometimes all night long) and refused to go to bed, saying: "Don't you worry, Ivan Ilych. I'll get sleep enough later on," or when he suddenly became familiar and exclaimed: "If you weren't sick it would be another matter, but as it is, why should I grudge a little trouble?" Gerasim alone did not lie; everything showed that he alone understood the facts of the case and did not consider it necessary to disguise them, but simply felt sorry for his emaciated and enfeebled master. Once when Ivan Ilych was sending him away he even said straight out: "We shall all of us die, so why should I grudge a little trouble?"—expressing the fact that he did not think his work burdensome, because he was doing it for a dying man and hoped someone would do the same for him when his time came.

Apart from this lying, or because of it, what most tormented Ivan Ilych was that no one pitied him as he wished to be pitied. At certain moments after prolonged suffering he wished most of all (though he would have been ashamed to confess it) for someone to pity him as a sick child is pitied. He longed to be petted and comforted. He knew he was an important functionary, that he had a beard turning grey, and that therefore what he longed for was impossible, but still he longed for it. And in Gerasim's attitude towards him there was something akin to what he wished for, and so that attitude comforted him. Ivan Ilych wanted to weep, wanted to be petted and cried over, and then his colleague Shebek would come, and instead of weeping and being petted, Ivan Ilych would assume a serious, severe, and profound air, and by force of habit would express his opinion on a decision of the Court of Cassation and would stubbornly insist on that view. This falsity around him and within him did more than anything else to poison his last days.

## VIII

It was morning. He knew it was morning because Gerasim had gone, and Peter the footman had come and put out the candles, drawn back one of the curtains, and begun quietly to tidy up. Whether it was morning or evening, Friday or Sunday, made no difference, it was all just the same: the gnawing, unmitigated, agonizing pain, never ceasing for an instant, the consciousness of life inexorably waning but not yet extinguished, the approach of that ever dreaded and hateful Death which was the only reality, and always the same falsity. What were days, weeks, hours, in such a case?

"Will you have some tea, sir?"                                                                    220

"He wants things to be regular, and wishes the gentlefolk to drink tea in the morning," thought Ivan Ilych, and only said "No."

"Wouldn't you like to move onto the sofa, sir?"

"He wants to tidy up the room, and I'm in the way. I am uncleanliness and disorder," he thought, and said only:

"No, leave me alone."

The man went on bustling about. Ivan Ilych stretched out his hand. Peter   225
came up, ready to help.

"What is it, sir?"

"My watch."

Peter took the watch which was close at hand and gave it to his master.

"Half-past eight. Are they up?"

"No, sir, except Vladimir Ivanovich" (the son) "who has gone to school.   230
Praskovya Fëdorovna ordered me to wake her if you asked for her. Shall I do so?"

"No, there's no need to." "Perhaps I'd better have some tea," he thought, and added aloud: "Yes, bring me some tea."

Peter went to the door, but Ivan Ilych dreaded being left alone. "How can I keep him here? Oh yes, my medicine." "Peter, give me my medicine." "Why not? Perhaps it may still do me some good." He took a spoonful and swallowed it. "No, it won't help. It's all tomfoolery, all deception," he decided as soon as he became aware of the familiar, sickly, hopeless taste. "No, I can't believe in it any longer. But the pain, why this pain? If it would only cease just for a moment!" And he moaned. Peter turned towards him. "It's all right. Go and fetch me some tea."

Peter went out. Left alone Ivan Ilych groaned not so much with pain, terrible though that was, as from mental anguish. Always and forever the same, always these endless days and nights. If only it would come quicker! If only *what* would come quicker? Death, darkness? . . . No, no! Anything rather than death!

When Peter returned with the tea on a tray, Ivan Ilych stared at him for a time in perplexity, not realizing who and what he was. Peter was disconcerted by that look and his embarrassment brought Ivan Ilych to himself.

"Oh, tea! All right, put it down. Only help me to wash and put on a clean shirt."   235

And Ivan Ilych began to wash. With pauses for rest, he washed his hands and then his face, cleaned his teeth, brushed his hair, and looked in the glass. He was terrified by what he saw, especially by the limp way in which his hair clung to his pallid forehead.

While his shirt was being changed he knew that he would be still more frightened at the sight of his body, so he avoided looking at it. Finally he was ready. He drew on a dressing-gown, wrapped himself in a plaid, and sat down in the armchair to take his tea. For a moment he felt refreshed, but soon as he began to drink the tea he was again aware of the same taste, and the pain also returned. He finished it with an effort, and then lay down stretching out his legs, and dismissed Peter.

Always the same. Now a spark of hope flashes up, then a sea of despair rages, and always pain; always pain, always despair, and always the same. When alone he had a dreadful and distressing desire to call someone, but he knew beforehand that with others present it would be still worse. "Another dose of morphine—to lose consciousness. I will tell him, the doctor, that he must think of something else. It's impossible, impossible, to go on like this."

An hour and another pass like that. But now there is a ring at the door bell. Perhaps it's the doctor? It is. He comes in fresh, hearty, plump, and cheerful, with that look on his face that seems to say: "There now, you're in a panic about something, but we'll arrange it all for you directly!" The doctor knows this expression is out of place here, but he has put it on once for all and can't take it off—like a man who has put on a frock-coat in the morning to pay a round of calls.

The doctor rubs his hands vigorously and reassuringly. 240

"Brr! How cold it is! There's such a sharp frost; just let me warm myself!" he says, as if it were only a matter of waiting till he was warm, and then he would put everything right.

"Well now, how are you?"

Ivan Ilych feels that the doctor would like to say: "Well, how are our affairs?" but that even he feels that this would not do, and says instead: "What sort of a night have you had?"

Ivan Ilych looks at him as much as to say: "Are you really never ashamed of lying?" But the doctor does not wish to understand this question, and Ivan Ilych says: "Just as terrible as ever. The pain never leaves me and never subsides. If only something. . . ."

"Yes, you sick people are always like that. . . . There, now I think I am warm 245 enough. Even Praskovya Fëdorovna, who is so particular, could find no fault with my temperature. Well, now I can say good-morning," and the doctor presses his patient's hand.

Then, dropping his former playfulness, he begins with a most serious face to examine the patient, feeling his pulse and taking his temperature, and then begins the sounding and auscultation.

Ivan Ilych knows quite well and definitely that all this is nonsense and pure deception, but when the doctor, getting down on his knee, leans over him, putting his ear first higher then lower, and performs various gymnastic movements over him with a significant expression on his face, Ivan Ilych submits to it all as he used to submit to the speeches of the lawyers, though he knew very well that they were all lying and why they were lying.

The doctor, kneeling on the sofa, is still sounding him when Praskovya Fëdorovna's silk dress rustles at the door and she is heard scolding Peter for not having let her know of the doctor's arrival.

She comes in, kisses her husband, and at once proceeds to prove that she has been up a long time already, and only owing to a misunderstanding failed to be there when the doctor arrived.

Ivan Ilych looks at her, scans her all over, sets against her the whiteness and plumpness and cleanness of her hands and neck, the gloss of her hair, and the sparkle of her vivacious eyes. He hates her with his whole soul. And the thrill of hatred he feels for her makes him suffer from her touch.

Her attitude towards him and his disease is still the same. Just as the doctor had adopted a certain relation to his patient which he could not abandon, so had she formed one towards him—that he was not doing something he ought to do and was himself to blame, and that she reproached him lovingly for this—and she could not now change that attitude.

"You see he doesn't listen to me and doesn't take his medicine at the proper time. And above all he lies in a position that is no doubt bad for him—with his legs up."

She described how he made Gerasim hold his legs up.

The doctor smiled with a contemptuous affability that said: "What's to be done? These sick people do have foolish fancies of that kind, but we must forgive them."

When the examination was over the doctor looked at his watch, and then Praskovya Fëdorovna announced to Ivan Ilych that it was of course as he pleased, but she had sent today for a celebrated specialist who would examine him and have a consultation with Michael Danilovich (their regular doctor).

"Please don't raise any objections. I am doing this for my own sake," she said ironically, letting it be felt that she was doing it all for his sake and only said this to leave him no right to refuse. He remained silent, knitting his brows. He felt that he was so surrounded and involved in a mesh of falsity that it was hard to unravel anything.

Everything she did for him was entirely for her own sake, and she told him she was doing for herself what she actually was doing for herself, as if that was so incredible that he must understand the opposite.

At half-past eleven the celebrated specialist arrived. Again the sounding began and the significant conversations in his presence and in another room, about the kidneys and the appendix, and the questions and answers, with such an air of importance that again, instead of the real question of life and death which now alone confronted him, the question arose of the kidney and appendix which were not behaving as they ought to and would now be attacked by Michael Danilovich and the specialist and forced to amend their ways.

The celebrated specialist took leave of him with a serious though not hopeless look, and in reply to the timid question Ivan Ilych, with eyes glistening with fear and hope, put to him as to whether there was a chance of recovery, said that he could not vouch for it but there was a possibility. The look of hope with which Ivan Ilych watched the doctor out was so pathetic that Praskovya Fëdorovna, seeing it, even wept as she left the room to hand the doctor his fee.

The gleam of hope kindled by the doctor's encouragement did not last long. The same room, the same pictures, curtains, wallpaper, medicine bottles, were all there, and the same aching suffering body, and Ivan Ilych began to moan. They gave him a subcutaneous injection and he sank into oblivion.

It was twilight when he came to. They brought him his dinner and he swallowed some beef tea with difficulty, and then everything was the same again and night was coming on.

After dinner, at seven o'clock, Praskovya Fëdorovna came into the room in evening dress, her full bosom pushed up by her corset, and with traces of powder on her face. She had reminded him in the morning that they were going to the theatre. Sarah Bernhardt was visiting the town and they had a box, which he had insisted on their taking. Now he had forgotten about it and her toilet offended him, but he concealed his vexation when he remembered that he had himself insisted on their securing a box and going because it would be an instructive and aesthetic pleasure for the children.

Praskovya Fëdorovna came in, self-satisfied but yet with a rather guilty air. She sat down and asked how he was, but, as he saw, only for the sake of asking and not in order to learn about it, knowing that there was nothing to learn—and then went on to what she really wanted to say: that she would not on any account have gone but that the box had been taken and Helen and their daughter were going, as well as Petrishchev (the examining magistrate, their daughter's fiancé), and that it was out of the question to let them go alone; but that she would have much preferred to sit with him for a while; and he must be sure to follow the doctor's orders while she was away.

"Oh, and Fëdor Petrovich" (the fiancé) "would like to come in. May he? And Lisa?"

"All right."                                                                                                    265

Their daughter came in in full evening dress, her fresh young flesh exposed (making a show of that very flesh which in his own case caused so much suffering), strong, healthy, evidently in love, and impatient with illness, suffering, and death, because they interfered with her happiness.

Fëdor Petrovich came in too, in evening dress, his hair curled à la Capoul°, a tight stiff collar round his long sinewy neck, an enormous white shirtfront, and narrow black trousers tightly stretched over his strong thighs. He had one white glove tightly drawn on, and was holding his opera hat in his hand.

Following him the schoolboy crept in unnoticed, in a uniform, poor little fellow, and wearing gloves. Terribly dark shadows showed under his eyes, the meaning of which Ivan Ilych knew well.

His son had always seemed pathetic to him, and now it was dreadful to see the boy's frightened look of pity. It seemed to Ivan Ilych that Vasya was the only one besides Gerasim who understood and pitied him.

They all sat down and again asked how he was. A silence followed. Lisa   270 asked her mother about the opera-glasses, and there was an altercation between mother and daughter as to who had taken them and where they had been put. This occasioned some unpleasantness.

à la Capoul: imitating the hair-do of Victor Capoul, a contemporary French singer.

Fëdor Petrovich inquired of Ivan Ilych whether he had ever seen Sarah Bernhardt. Ivan Ilych did not at first catch the question, but then replied: "No, have you seen her before?"

"Yes, in *Adrienne Lecouvreur*."

Praskovya Fëdorovna mentioned some rôles in which Sarah Bernhardt was particularly good. Her daughter disagreed. Conversation sprang up as to the elegance and realism of her acting—the sort of conversation that is always repeated and is always the same.

In the midst of the conversation Fëdor Petrovich glanced at Ivan Ilych and became silent. The others also looked at him and grew silent. Ivan Ilych was staring with glittering eyes straight before him, evidently indignant with them. This had to be rectified, but it was impossible to do so. The silence had to be broken, but for a time no one dared to break it and they all became afraid that the conventional deception would suddenly become obvious and the truth become plain to all. Lisa was the first to pluck up courage and break that silence, but by trying to hide what everybody was feeling, she betrayed it.

"Well, if we are going it's time to start," she said, looking at her watch, a present from her father, and with a faint and significant smile at Fëdor Petrovich relating to something known only to them. She got up with a rustle of her dress. 275

They all rose, said good-night, and went away.

When they had gone it seemed to Ivan Ilych that he felt better: the falsity had gone with them. But the pain remained—that same pain and that same fear that made everything monotonously alike, nothing harder and nothing easier. Everything was worse.

Again minute followed minute and hour followed hour. Everything remained the same and there was no cessation. And the inevitable end of it all became more and more terrible.

"Yes, send Gerasim here," he replied to a question Peter asked.

## IX

His wife returned late at night. She came in on tiptoe, but he heard her, opened his eyes, and made haste to close them again. She wished to send Gerasim away and to sit with him herself, but he opened his eyes and said: "No, go away." 280

"Are you in great pain?"

"Always the same."

"Take some opium."

He agreed and took some. She went away.

Till about three in the morning he was in a state of stupefied misery. It seemed to him that he and his pain were being thrust into a narrow, deep black sack, but though they were pushed further and further in they could not be pushed to the bottom. And this, terrible enough in itself, was accompanied by suffering. He was frightened yet wanted to fall through the sack, he struggled but yet cooperated. And suddenly he broke through, fell, and regained consciousness. 285

Gerasim was sitting at the foot of the bed dozing quietly and patiently, while he himself lay with his emaciated stockinged legs resting on Gerasim's shoulders; the same shaded candle was there and the same unceasing pain.

"Go away, Gerasim," he whispered.

"It's all right, sir. I'll stay a while."

"No. Go away."

He removed his legs from Gerasim's shoulders, turned sideways onto his arm, and felt sorry for himself. He only waited till Gerasim had gone into the next room and then restrained himself no longer but wept like a child. He wept on account of his helplessness, his terrible loneliness, the cruelty of man, the cruelty of God, and the absence of God.

"Why hast Thou done all this? Why hast Thou brought me here? Why, why  290 dost Thou torment me so terribly?"

He did not expect an answer and yet wept because there was no answer and could be none. The pain grew more acute, but he did not stir and did not call. He said to himself: "Go on! Strike me! But what is it for? What have I done to Thee? What is it for?"

Then he grew quiet and not only ceased weeping but even held his breath and became all attention. It was as though he was listening not to an audible voice but to the voice of his soul, to the current of thoughts arising within him.

"What is it you want?" was the first clear conception capable of expression in words, that he heard.

"What do you want? What do you want?" he repeated to himself.

"What do I want? To live and not to suffer," he answered.  295

And again he listened with such concentrated attention that even his pain did not distract him.

"To live? How?" asked his inner voice.

"Why, to live as I used to—well and pleasantly."

"As you lived before, well and pleasantly?" the voice repeated.

And in imagination he began to recall the best moments of his pleasant life.  300 But strange to say none of those best moments of his pleasant life now seemed at all what they had then seemed—none of them except the first recollections of childhood. There, in childhood, there had been something really pleasant with which it would be possible to live if it could return. But the child who had experienced that happiness existed no longer, it was like a reminiscence of somebody else.

As soon as the period began which had produced the present Ivan Ilych, all that had then seemed joys now melted before his sight and turned into something trivial and often nasty.

And the further he departed from childhood and the nearer he came to the present the more worthless and doubtful were the joys. This began with the School of Law. A little that was really good was still found there—there was lightheartedness, friendship, and hope. But in the upper classes there had already been fewer of such good moments. Then during the first years of his official career, when he was in the service of the Governor, some pleasant moments again occurred; they were the memories of love for a woman. Then all became confused and there was still less of what was good; later on again there was still less that was good, and the further he went the less there was. His marriage, a mere accident, then the disenchantment that followed it, his wife's bad breath and the sensuality and hypocrisy; then that deadly official life and those preoccupations about money, a year of it, and two, and ten, and twenty, and always the same thing. And the longer it lasted the more deadly it became. "It is as if I had been going downhill while I imagined I was going up. And that is really what it was. I was going up in public opinion, but to the same extent life was ebbing away from me. And now it is all done and there is only death."

"Then what does it mean? Why? It can't be that life is so senseless and horrible. But if it really has been so horrible and senseless, why must I die and die in agony? There is something wrong!"

"Maybe I did not live as I ought to have done," it suddenly occurred to him. "But how could that be, when I did everything properly?" he replied, and immediately dismissed from his mind this, the sole solution of all the riddles of life and death, as something quite impossible.

"Then what do you want now? To live? Live how? Live as you lived in the 305 law courts when the usher proclaimed 'The judge is coming!' The judge is coming, the judge!" he repeated to himself. "Here he is, the judge. But I am not guilty!" he exclaimed angrily. "What is it for?" And he ceased crying, but turning his face to the wall continued to ponder on the same question: Why, and for what purpose, is there all this horror? But however much he pondered he found no answer. And whenever the thought occurred to him, as it often did, that it all resulted from his not having lived as he ought to have done, he at once recalled the correctness of his whole life and dismissed so strange an idea.

## X

Another fortnight passed. Ivan Ilych now no longer left his sofa. He would not lie in bed but lay on the sofa, facing the wall nearly all the time. He suffered ever the same unceasing agonies and in his loneliness pondered always on the same insoluble question: "What is this? Can it be that it is Death?" And the inner voice answered: "Yes, it is Death."

"Why these sufferings?" And the voice answered, "For no reason—they just are so." Beyond and besides this there was nothing.

From the very beginning of his illness, ever since he had first been to see the doctor, Ivan Ilych's life had been divided between two contrary and alternating moods: now it was despair and the expectation of this uncomprehended and terrible death, and now hope and an intently interested observation of the functioning of his organs. Now before his eyes there was only a kidney or an intestine that temporarily evaded its duty, and now only that incomprehensible and dreadful death from which it was impossible to escape.

These two states of mind had alternated from the very beginning of his illness, but the further it progressed the more doubtful and fantastic became the conception of the kidney, and the more real the sense of impending death.

He had but to call to mind what he had been three months before and what he was now, to call to mind with what regularity he had been going downhill, for every possibility of hope to be shattered.

Latterly during that loneliness in which he found himself as he lay facing the back of the sofa, a loneliness in the midst of a populous town and surrounded by numerous acquaintances and relations but that yet could not have been more complete anywhere—either at the bottom of the sea or under the earth—during that terrible loneliness Ivan Ilych had lived only in memories of the past. Pictures of his past rose before him one after another. They always began with what was nearest in time and then went back to what was most remote—to his childhood—and rested there. If he thought of the stewed prunes that had been offered him that day, his mind went back to the raw shrivelled French plums of his childhood, their peculiar flavor and the flow of saliva when he sucked their stones, and along with the memory of that taste came a whole series of memories of those days: his nurse, his brother, and their toys. "No, I mustn't think of that. . . . It is too painful," Ivan Ilych said to himself, and brought himself back to the present—to the button on the back of the sofa and the creases in its morocco. "Morocco is expensive, but it does not wear well: there had been a quarrel about it. It was a different kind of quarrel and a different kind of morocco that time when we tore father's portfolio and were punished, and mamma brought us some tarts. . . ." And again his thoughts dwelt on his childhood, and again it was painful and he tried to banish them and fix his mind on something else.

Then again together with that chain of memories another series passed through his mind—of how his illness had progressed and grown worse. There also the further back he looked the more life there had been. There had been more of what was good in life and more of life itself. The two merged together. "Just as the pain went on getting worse and worse, so my life grew worse and worse," he thought. "There is one bright spot there at the back, at the beginning of life, and afterwards all becomes blacker and blacker and proceeds more and more rapidly—in inverse ratio to the square of the distance from death," thought Ivan Ilych. And the example of a stone falling downwards with increasing velocity entered his mind. Life, a series of increasing sufferings, flies further and further towards its end—the most terrible suffering. "I am flying. . . ." He shuddered, shifted himself, and tried to resist, but was already aware that resistance was impossible, and again, with eyes weary of gazing but unable to cease seeing what was before them, he stared at the back of the sofa and waited—awaiting that dreadful fall and shock and destruction.

"Resistance is impossible!" he said to himself. "If I could only understand what it is all for! But that too is impossible. An explanation would be possible if it could be said that I have not lived as I ought to. But it is impossible to say that," and he remembered all the legality, correctitude, and propriety of his life. "That at any rate can certainly not be admitted," he thought, and his lips smiled ironically as if someone could see that smile and be taken in by it. "There is no explanation! Agony, death. . . . What for?"

# XI

Another two weeks went by in this way and during that fortnight an event occurred that Ivan Ilych and his wife had desired. Petrishchev formally proposed. It happened in the evening. The next day Praskovya Fëdorovna came into her husband's room considering how best to inform him of it, but that very night there had been a fresh change for the worse in his condition. She found him still lying on the sofa but in a different position. He lay on his back, groaning and staring fixedly straight in front of him.

She began to remind him of his medicines, but he turned his eyes towards 315 her with such a look that she did not finish what she was saying; so great an animosity, to her in particular, did that look express.

"For Christ's sake let me die in peace!" he said.

She would have gone away, but just then their daughter came in and went up to say good morning. He looked at her as he had done at his wife, and in reply to her inquiry about his health said dryly that he would soon free them all of himself. They were both silent and after sitting with him for a while went away.

"Is it our fault?" Lisa said to her mother. "It's as if we were to blame! I am sorry for papa, but why should we be tortured?"

The doctor came at his usual time. Ivan Ilych answered "Yes" and "No," never taking his angry eyes from him, and at last said: "You know you can do nothing for me, so leave me alone."

"We can ease your sufferings." 320

"You can't even do that. Let me be."

The doctor went into the drawing-room and told Praskovya Fëdorovna that the case was very serious and that the only resource left was opium to allay her husband's sufferings, which must be terrible.

It was true, as the doctor said, that Ivan Ilych's physical sufferings were terrible, but worse than the physical sufferings were his mental sufferings, which were his chief torture.

His mental sufferings were due to the fact that one night, as he looked at Gerasim's sleepy, good-natured face with its prominent cheekbones, the question suddenly occurred to him: "What if my whole life has really been wrong?"

It occurred to him that what had appeared perfectly impossible before, name- 325 ly that he had not spent his life as he should have done, might after all be true. It occurred to him that his scarcely perceptible attempts to struggle against what was considered good by the most highly placed people, those scarcely noticeable impulses which he had immediately suppressed, might have been the real thing, and all the rest false. And his professional duties and the whole arrangement of his life and of his family, and all his social and official interests, might all have been false. He tried to defend all those things to himself and suddenly felt the weakness of what he was defending. There was nothing to defend.

"But if that is so," he said to himself, "and I am leaving this life with the consciousness that I have lost all that was given me and it is impossible to rectify it— what then?"

He lay on his back and began to pass his life in review in quite a new way. In the morning when he saw first his footman, then his wife, then his daughter, and then the doctor, their every word and movement confirmed to him the awful truth that had been revealed to him during the night. In them he saw himself—all that for which he had lived—and saw clearly that it was not real at all, but a terrible and huge deception which had hidden both life and death. This consciousness intensified his physical suffering tenfold. He groaned and tossed about, and pulled at his clothing which choked and stifled him. And he hated them on that account.

He was given a large dose of opium and became unconscious, but at noon his sufferings began again. He drove everybody away and tossed from side to side.

His wife came to him and said:

"Jean, my dear, do this for me. It can't do any harm and often helps. Healthy 330 people often do it."

He opened his eyes wide.

"What? Take communion? Why? It's unnecessary! However . . . "

She began to cry.

"Yes, do, my dear. I'll send for our priest. He is such a nice man."

"All right. Very well," he muttered. 335

When the priest came and heard his confession, Ivan Ilych was softened and seemed to feel a relief from his doubts and consequently from his sufferings, and for a moment there came a ray of hope. He again began to think of the vermiform appendix and the possibility of correcting it. He received the sacrament with tears in his eyes.

When they laid him down again afterwards he felt a moment's ease, and the hope that he might live awoke in him again. He began to think of the operation that had been suggested to him. "To live! I want to live!" he said to himself.

His wife came in to congratulate him after his communion, and when uttering the usual conventional words she added:

"You feel better, don't you?"

Without looking at her he said "Yes." 340

Her dress, her figure, the expression of her face, the tone of her voice, all revealed the same thing. "This is wrong, it is not as it should be. All you have lived for and still live for is falsehood and deception, hiding life and death from you." And as soon as he admitted that thought, his hatred and his agonizing physical suffering again sprang up, and with that suffering a consciousness of the unavoidable, approaching end. And to this was added a new sensation of grinding shooting pain and a feeling of suffocation.

The expression of his face when he uttered that "yes" was dreadful. Having uttered it, he looked her straight in the eyes, turned on his face with a rapidity extraordinary in his weak state and shouted:

"Go away! Go away and leave me alone!"

## XII

From that moment the screaming began that continued for three days, and was so terrible that one could not hear it through two closed doors without horror. At the moment he answered his wife he realized that he was lost, that there was no return, that the end had come, the very end, and his doubts were still unsolved and remained doubts.

"Oh! Oh! Oh!" he cried in various intonations. He had begun by screaming 345 "I won't!" and continued screaming on the letter O.

For three whole days, during which time did not exist for him, he struggled in that black sack into which he was being thrust by an invisible, resistless force. He struggled as a man condemned to death struggles in the hands of the executioner, knowing that he cannot save himself. And every moment he felt that despite all his efforts he was drawing nearer and nearer to what terrified him. He felt that his agony was due to his being thrust into that black hole and still more to his not being able to get right into it. He was hindered from getting into it by his conviction that his life had been a good one. That very justification of his life held him fast and prevented his moving forward, and it caused him most torment of all.

Suddenly some force struck him in the chest and side, making it still harder to breathe, and he fell through the hole and there at the bottom was a light. What had happened to him was like the sensation one sometimes experiences in a railway carriage when one thinks one is going backwards while one is really going forwards and suddenly becomes aware of the real direction.

"Yes, it was all not the right thing," he said to himself, "but that's no matter. It can be done. But what *is* the right thing?" he asked himself, and suddenly grew quiet.

This occurred at the end of the third day, two hours before his death. Just then his schoolboy son had crept softly in and gone up to the bedside. The dying man was still screaming desperately and waving his arms. His hand fell on the boy's head, and the boy caught it, pressed it to his lips, and began to cry.

At that very moment Ivan Ilych fell through and caught sight of the light, 350 and it was revealed to him that though his life had not been what it should have been, this could still be rectified. He asked himself, "What *is* the right thing?" and grew still, listening. Then he felt that someone was kissing his hand. He opened his eyes, looked at his son, and felt sorry for him. His wife came up to him and he glanced at her. She was gazing at him open-mouthed, with undried tears on her nose and cheek and a despairing look on her face. He felt sorry for her too.

"Yes, I am making them wretched," he thought. "They are sorry, but it will be better for them when I die." He wished to say this but had not the strength to utter it. "Besides, why speak? I must act," he thought. With a look at his wife he indicated his son and said: "Take him away . . . sorry for him . . . sorry for you too. . . ." He tried to add, "Forgive me," but said "forgo" and waved his hand, knowing that He whose understanding mattered would understand.

And suddenly it grew clear to him that what had been oppressing him and would not leave him was all dropping away at once from two sides, from ten sides, and from all sides. He was sorry for them, he must act so as not to hurt them: release them and free himself from these sufferings. "How good and how simple!" he thought. "And the pain?" he asked himself. "What has become of it? Where are you, pain?"

He turned his attention to it.

"Yes, here it is. Well, what of it? Let the pain be."

"And death . . . where is it?"                                                                  355

He sought his former accustomed fear of death and did not find it. "Where is it? What death?" There was no fear because there was no death.

In place of death there was light.

"So that's what it is!" he suddenly exclaimed aloud. "What joy!"

To him all this happened in a single instant, and the meaning of that instant did not change. For those present his agony continued for another two hours. Something rattled in his throat, his emaciated body twitched, then the gasping and rattle became less and less frequent.

"It is finished!" said someone near him.                                                        360

He heard these words and repeated them in his soul.

"Death is finished," he said to himself. "It is no more!"

He drew in a breath, stopped in the midst of a sigh, stretched out, and died.

QUESTIONS

1. Sum up the reactions of Ivan's colleagues to the news of his death. What is implied in Tolstoi's calling them not friends but "nearest acquaintances"?

2. What comic elements do you find in the account of the wake that Peter Ivanovich attends?

3. In Tolstoi's description of the corpse and its expression (paragraph 27), what details seem especially revealing and meaningful?

4. Do you think Tolstoi would have improved the story had he placed the events in chronological order? What if the opening scene of Ivan's colleagues at the Law Courts and the wake scene were to be given last? What would be lost?

5. Would you call Ivan, when we first meet him, a religious man? Sum up his goals in life, his values, his attitudes.

6. By what "virtues" and abilities does Ivan rise through the ranks? While he continues to succeed in his career, what happens to his marriage?

7. "Every spot on the tablecloth or the upholstery, and every broken window-blind string, irritated him. He had devoted so much trouble to arranging it all that every disturbance of it distressed him" (paragraph 104). What do you make of this passage? What is its tone? Does the narrator sympathize with Ivan's attachment to his possessions?

8. Consider the account of Ivan's routine ("He got up at nine. . . .," paragraph 105). What elements of a full life, what higher satisfactions, does this routine omit?

9. What caused Ivan's illness? How would it probably be diagnosed today? What is the narrator's attitude toward Ivan's doctors?

10. In what successive stages does Tolstoi depict Ivan's growing isolation as his progressive illness sets him more and more apart?

11. What are we apparently supposed to admire in the character and conduct of the servant Gerasim?

12. What do you understand from the statement that Ivan's justification of his life "prevented his moving forward, and it caused him most torment of all" (paragraph 346)?

13. What is memorable in the character of Ivan's schoolboy son? Why is he crucial to the story? (Suggestion: Look closely at paragraphs 349–350.)

14. What realization allows Ivan to triumph over pain? Why does he die gladly?

15. Henri Troyat has said that through the story of Ivan Ilych we imagine what our own deaths will be. Is it possible to identify with an aging, selfish, worldly, nineteenth-century Russian judge?

# Franz Kafka

## THE METAMORPHOSIS                          1915

*Translated by Willa and Edwin Muir*

*Franz Kafka*

*Franz Kafka (1883–1924) was born into a German-speaking Jewish family in Prague, Czechoslovakia (then part of the Austro-Hungarian empire). He was the only surviving son of a domineering, successful father. After earning a law degree, Kafka worked as a claims investigator for the state accident insurance company. He worked on his stories at night, especially during his frequent bouts of insomnia. He never married, and lived mostly with his parents. Kafka was such a careful and self-conscious writer that he found it difficult to finish his work and send it out for publication. During his lifetime he published only a few thin volumes of short fiction, most notably* The Metamorphosis *(1915) and* In the Penal Colony *(1919). He never finished to his own satisfaction any of his three novels (all published posthumously):* Amerika *(1927),* The Trial *(1925), and* The Castle *(1926). As Kafka was dying of tuberculosis, he begged his friend and literary executor, Max Brod, to burn his uncompleted manuscripts. Brod pondered this request but didn't obey. Kafka's two major novels,* The Trial *and* The Castle, *both depict huge, remote, bumbling, irresponsible bureaucracies in whose power the individual feels helpless and blind. Kafka's works appear startlingly prophetic to readers looking back on them in the later light of Stalinism, World War II, and the Holocaust. His haunting vision of an alienated modern world led the poet W. H. Auden to remark at mid-century, "Had one to name the author who comes nearest to bearing the same kind of relation to our age as Dante, Shakespeare, and Goethe bore to theirs, Kafka is the first one would think of." The long story, "The Metamorphosis," which arguably has the most famous opening sentence in twentieth-century literature, shows Kafka's dreamlike fiction at its most brilliant and most disturbing.*

## I

As Gregor Samsa awoke one morning from uneasy dreams he found himself transformed in his bed into a gigantic insect. He was lying on his hard, as it were armor-plated, back and when he lifted his head a little he could see his dome-like brown belly divided into stiff arched segments on top of which the bed quilt could hardly keep in position and was about to slide off completely. His numerous legs, which were pitifully thin compared to the rest of his bulk, waved helplessly before his eyes.

What has happened to me? he thought. It was no dream. His room, a regular human bedroom, only rather too small, lay quiet between the four familiar walls. Above the table on which a collection of cloth samples was unpacked and spread out—Samsa was a commercial traveler°—hung the picture which he had recently cut out of an illustrated magazine and put into a pretty gilt frame. It showed a lady, with a fur cap on and a fur stole, sitting upright and holding out to the spectator a huge fur muff into which the whole of her forearm had vanished!

Gregor's eyes turned next to the window, and the overcast sky—one could hear rain drops beating on the window gutter—made him quite melancholy. What about sleeping a little longer and forgetting all this nonsense, he thought, but it could not be done, for he was accustomed to sleep on his right side and in his present condition he could not turn himself over. However violently he forced himself towards his right side he always rolled on to his back again. He tried it at least a hundred times, shutting his eyes to keep from seeing his struggling legs, and only desisted when he began to feel in his side a faint dull ache he had never experienced before.

Oh God, he thought, what an exhausting job I've picked on! Traveling about day in, day out. It's much more irritating work than doing the actual business in the office, and on top of that there's the trouble of constant traveling, of worrying about train connections, the bed and irregular meals, casual acquaintances that are always new and never become intimate friends. The devil take it all! He felt a slight itching up on his belly; slowly pushed himself on his back nearer to the top of the bed so that he could lift his head more easily; identified the itching place which was surrounded by many small white spots the nature of which he could not understand and made to touch it with a leg, but drew the leg back immediately, for the contact made a cold shiver run through him.

He slid down again into his former position. This getting up early he     5
thought, makes one quite stupid. A man needs his sleep. Other commercials live like harem women. For instance, when I come back to the hotel of a morning to write up the orders I've got, these others are only sitting down to breakfast. Let me just try that with my chief; I'd be sacked on the spot. Anyhow, that might be quite a good thing for me, who can tell? If I didn't have to hold my hand because of my parents I'd have given notice long ago, I'd have gone to the chief and told him exactly what I think of him. That would knock him endways from his desk! It's a queer way of doing, too, this sitting on high at a desk and talking down to employees, especially when they have to come quite near because the chief is hard of hearing. Well, there's still hope; once I've saved enough money to pay back my parents' debts to him—that should take another five or six years—I'll do it without fail. I'll cut myself completely loose then. For the moment, though, I'd better get up, since my train goes at five.

He looked at the alarm clock ticking on the chest. Heavenly Father! he thought. It was half-past six o'clock and the hands were quietly moving on, it was even past the half-hour, it was getting on toward a quarter to seven. Had the

_commercial traveler:_ a traveling salesman.

alarm clock not gone off? From the bed one could see that it had been properly set for four o'clock; of course it must have gone off. Yes, but was it possible to sleep quietly through that ear-splitting noise? Well, he had not slept quietly, yet apparently all the more soundly for that. But what was he to do now? The next train went at seven o'clock; to catch that he would need to hurry like mad and his samples weren't even packed up, and he himself wasn't feeling particularly fresh and active. And even if he did catch the train he wouldn't avoid a row with the chief, since the firm's porter would have been waiting for the five o'clock train and would have long since reported his failure to turn up. The porter was a creature of the chief's, spineless and stupid. Well, supposing he were to say he was sick? But that would be most unpleasant and would look suspicious, since during his five years' employment he had not been ill once. The chief himself would be sure to come with the sick-insurance doctor, would reproach his parents with their son's laziness and would cut all excuses short by referring to the insurance doctor, who of course regarded all mankind as perfectly healthy malingerers. And would he be so far wrong on this occasion? Gregor really felt quite well, apart from a drowsiness that was utterly superfluous after such a long sleep, and he was even unusually hungry.

As all this was running through his mind at top speed without his being able to decide to leave his bed—the alarm clock had just struck a quarter to seven—there came a cautious tap at the door behind the head of his bed. "Gregor," said a voice—it was his mother's—"it's a quarter to seven. Hadn't you a train to catch?" That gentle voice! Gregor had a shock as he heard his own voice answering hers, unmistakably his own voice, it was true, but with a persistent horrible twittering squeak behind it like an undertone, that left the words in their clear shape only for the first moment and then rose up reverberating round them to destroy their sense, so that one could not be sure one had heard them rightly. Gregor wanted to answer at length and explain everything, but in the circumstances he confined himself to saying: "Yes, yes, thank you, Mother, I'm getting up now." The wooden door between them must have kept the change in his voice from being noticeable outside, for his mother contented herself with this statement and shuffled away. Yet this brief exchange of words had made the other members of the family aware that Gregor was still in the house, as they had not expected, and at one of the side doors his father was already knocking, gently, yet with his fist. "Gregor, Gregor," he called, "what's the matter with you?" And after a little while he called again in a deeper voice: "Gregor! Gregor!" At the other side door his sister was saying in a low, plaintive tone: "Gregor? Aren't you well? Are you needing anything?" He answered them both at once: "I'm just ready," and did his best to make his voice sound as normal as possible by enunciating the words very clearly and leaving long pauses between them. So his father went back to his breakfast, but his sister whispered: "Gregor, open the door, do." However, he was not thinking of opening the door, and felt thankful for the prudent habit he had acquired in traveling of locking all doors during the night, even at home.

His immediate intention was to get up quietly without being disturbed, to put on his clothes and above all eat his breakfast, and only then to consider what else was to be done, since in bed, he was well aware, his meditations would come to no sensible conclusion. He remembered that often enough in bed he had felt small aches and pains, probably caused by awkward postures, which had proved purely imaginary once he got up, and he looked forward eagerly to seeing this morning's delusions gradually fall away. That the change in his voice was nothing but the precursor of a severe chill, a standing ailment of commercial travelers, he had not the least possible doubt.

To get rid of the quilt was quite easy; he had only to inflate himself a little and it fell off by itself. But the next move was difficult, especially because he was so uncommonly broad. He would have needed arms and hands to hoist himself up; instead he had only the numerous little legs which never stopped waving in all directions and which he could not control in the least. When he tried to bend one of them it was the first to stretch itself straight; and did he succeed at last in making it do what he wanted, all the other legs meanwhile waved the more wildly in a high degree of unpleasant agitation. "But what's the use of lying idle in bed," said Gregor to himself.

He thought that he might get out of bed with the lower part of his body first, 10 but this lower part, which he had not yet seen and of which he could form no clear conception, proved too difficult to move; it shifted so slowly; and when finally, almost wild with annoyance, he gathered his forces together and thrust out recklessly, he had miscalculated the direction and bumped heavily against the lower end of the bed, and the stinging pain he felt informed him that precisely this lower part of his body was at the moment probably the most sensitive.

So he tried to get the top part of himself out first, and cautiously moved his head towards the edge of the bed. That proved easy enough, and despite its breadth and mass the bulk of his body at last slowly followed the movement of his head. Still, when he finally got his head free over the edge of the bed he felt too scared to go on advancing, for after all if he let himself fall in this way it would take a miracle to keep his head from being injured. And at all costs he must not lose consciousness now, precisely now; he would rather stay in bed.

But when after a repetition of the same efforts he lay in his former position again, sighing, and watched his little legs struggling against each other more wildly than ever, if that were possible, and saw no way of bringing any order into this arbitrary confusion, he told himself again that it was impossible to stay in bed and that the most sensible course was to risk everything for the smallest hope of getting away from it. At the same time he did not forget meanwhile to remind himself that cool reflection, the coolest possible, was much better than desperate resolves. In such moments he focused his eyes as sharply as possible on the window, but, unfortunately, the prospect of the morning fog, which muffled even the other side of the narrow street, brought him little encouragement and comfort. "Seven o'clock already," he said to himself when the alarm clock chimed again, "seven o'clock already and still such a thick fog." And for a little while he lay quiet, breathing lightly, as if perhaps expecting such complete repose to restore all things to their real and normal condition.

But then he said to himself: "Before it strikes a quarter past seven I must be quite out of this bed, without fail. Anyhow, by that time someone will have come from the office to ask for me, since it opens before seven." And he set himself to rocking his whole body at once in a regular rhythm, with the idea of swinging it out of the bed. If he tipped himself out in that way he could keep his head from injury by lifting it at an acute angle when he fell. His back seemed to be hard and was not likely to suffer from a fall on the carpet. His biggest worry was the loud crash he would not be able to help making, which would probably cause anxiety, if not terror, behind all the doors. Still, he must take the risk.

When he was already half out of the bed—the new method was more a game than an effort, for he needed only to hitch himself across by rocking to and fro—it struck him how simple it would be if he could get help. Two strong people—he thought of his father and the servant girl—would be amply sufficient; they would only have to thrust their arms under his convex back, lever him out of the bed, bend down with their burden and then be patient enough to let him turn himself right over on to the floor, where it was to be hoped his legs would then find their proper function. Well, ignoring the fact that the doors were all locked, ought he really to call for help? In spite of his misery he could not suppress a smile at the very idea of it.

He had got so far that he could barely keep his equilibrium when he rocked   15
himself strongly, and he would have to nerve himself very soon for the final deci-sion since in five minutes' time it would be a quarter past seven—when the front doorbell rang. "That's someone from the office," he said to himself, and grew almost rigid, while his little legs only jigged about all the faster. For a moment everything stayed quiet. "They're not going to open the door," said Gregor to himself, catching at some kind of irrational hope. But then of course the servant girl went as usual to the door with her heavy tread and opened it. Gregor needed only to hear the first good morning of the visitor to know immediately who it was—the chief clerk himself. What a fate, to be condemned to work for a firm where the smallest omission at once gave rise to the gravest suspicion! Were all employees in a body nothing but scoundrels, was there not among them one sin-gle loyal devoted man who, had he wasted only an hour or so of the firm's time in a morning, was so tormented by conscience as to be driven out of his mind and actually incapable of leaving his bed? Wouldn't it really have been sufficient to send an apprentice to inquire—if any inquiry were necessary at all—did the chief clerk himself have to come and thus indicate to the entire family, an innocent family, that this suspicious circumstance could be investigated by no one less versed in affairs than himself? And more through the agitation caused by these reflections than through any act of will Gregor swung himself out of bed with all his strength. There was a loud thump, but it was not really a crash. His fall was broken to some extent by the carpet, his back, too, was less stiff than he thought, and so there was merely a dull thud, not so very startling. Only he had not lifted his head carefully enough and had hit it; he turned it and rubbed it on the carpet in pain and irritation.

"That was something falling down in there," said the chief clerk in the next room to the left. Gregor tried to suppose to himself that something like what had happened to him today might some day happen to the chief clerk; one really could not deny that it was possible. But as if in brusque reply to this supposition the chief clerk took a couple of firm steps in the next-door room and his patent leather boots creaked. From the right-hand room his sister was whispering to inform him of the situation: "Gregor, the chief clerk's here." "I know," muttered Gregor to himself; but he didn't dare to make his voice loud enough for his sister to hear it.

"Gregor," said his father now from the left-hand room, "the chief clerk has come and wants to know why you didn't catch the early train. We don't know what to say to him. Besides, he wants to talk to you in person. So open the door, please. He will be good enough to excuse the untidiness of your room." "Good morning, Mr. Samsa," the chief clerk was calling amiably meanwhile. "He's not well," said his mother to the visitor, while his father was still speaking through the door, "he's not well, sir, believe me. What else would make him miss a train! The boy thinks about nothing but his work. It makes me almost cross the way he never goes out in the evenings; he's been here the last eight days and has stayed at home every single evening. He just sits there quietly at the table reading a newspaper or looking through railway timetables. The only amusement he gets is doing fretwork. For instance, he spent two or three evenings cutting out a little picture frame; you would be surprised to see how pretty it is; it's hanging in his room; you'll see it in a minute when Gregor opens the door. I must say I'm glad you've come, sir; we should never have got him to unlock the door by ourselves; he's so obstinate; and I'm sure he's unwell, though he wouldn't have it to be so this morning." "I'm just coming," said Gregor slowly and carefully, not moving an inch for fear of losing one word of the conversation. "I can't think of any other explanation, madam," said the chief clerk, "I hope it's nothing serious. Although on the other hand I must say that we men of business—fortunately or unfortunately— very often simply have to ignore any slight indisposition, since business must be attended to." "Well, can the chief clerk come in now?" asked Gregor's father impatiently, again knocking on the door. "No," said Gregor. In the left-hand room a painful silence followed this refusal, in the right-hand room his sister began to sob.

Why didn't his sister join the others? She was probably newly out of bed and hadn't even begun to put on her clothes yet. Well, why was she crying? Because he wouldn't get up and let the chief clerk in, because he was in danger of losing his job, and because the chief would begin dunning his parents again for the old debts? Surely these were things one didn't need to worry about for the present. Gregor was still at home and not in the least thinking of deserting the family. At the moment, true, he was lying on the carpet and no one who knew the condition he was in could seriously expect him to admit the chief clerk. But for such a small discourtesy, which could plausibly be explained away somehow later on, Gregor could hardly be dismissed on the spot. And it seemed to Gregor that it would be much more sensible to leave him in peace for the present than to trouble him with tears and entreaties. Still, of course, their uncertainty bewildered them all and excused their behavior.

"Mr. Samsa," the chief clerk called now in a louder voice, "what's the matter with you? Here you are, barricading yourself in your room, giving only 'yes' and 'no' for answers, causing your parents a lot of unnecessary trouble and neglecting—I mention this only in passing—neglecting your business duties in an incredible fashion. I am speaking here in the name of your parents and of your chief, and I beg you quite seriously to give me an immediate and precise explanation. You amaze me, you amaze me. I thought you were a quiet, dependable person, and now all at once you seem bent on making a disgraceful exhibition of yourself. The chief did hint to me early this morning a possible explanation for your disappearance—with reference to the cash payments that were entrusted to you recently—but I almost pledged my solemn word of honor that this could not be so. But now that I see how incredibly obstinate you are, I no longer have the slightest desire to take your part at all. And your position in the firm is not so unassailable. I came with the intention of telling you all this in private, but since you are wasting my time so needlessly I don't see why your parents shouldn't hear it too. For some time past your work has been most unsatisfactory; this is not the season of the year for a business boom, of course, we admit that, but a season of the year for doing no business at all, that does not exist, Mr. Samsa, must not exist."

"But, sir," cried Gregor, beside himself and in his agitation forgetting everything else, "I'm just going to open the door this very minute. A slight illness, an attack of giddiness, has kept me from getting up. I'm still lying in bed. But I feel all right again. I'm getting out of bed now. Just give me a moment or two longer! I'm not quite so well as I thought. But I'm all right, really. How a thing like that can suddenly strike one down! Only last night I was quite well, my parents can tell you, or rather I did have a slight presentiment. I must have showed some sign of it. Why didn't I report it at the office! But one always thinks that an indisposition can be got over without staying in the house. Oh sir, do spare my parents! All that you're reproaching me with now has no foundation; no one has ever said a word to me about it. Perhaps you haven't looked at the last orders I sent in. Anyhow, I can still catch the eight o'clock train, I'm much the better for my few hours' rest. Don't let me detain you here, sir; I'll be attending to business very soon, and do be good enough to tell the chief so and to make my excuses to him!"

And while all this was tumbling out pell-mell and Gregor hardly knew what he was saying, he had reached the chest quite easily, perhaps because of the practice he had had in bed, and was now trying to lever himself upright by means of it. He meant actually to open the door, actually to show himself and speak to the chief clerk; he was eager to find out what the others, after all their insistence, would say at the sight of him. If they were horrified then the responsibility was no longer his and he could stay quiet. But if they took it calmly, then he had no reason either to be upset, and could really get to the station for the eight o'clock train if he hurried. At first he slipped down a few times from the polished surface of the chest, but at length with a last heave he stood upright; he paid no more attention to the pains in the lower part of his body, however they smarted. Then he let himself fall against the back of a near-by chair, and clung with his little legs to the edges of it. That brought him into control of himself again and he stopped speaking, for now he could listen to what the chief clerk was saying.

"Did you understand a word of it?" the chief clerk was asking; "surely he can't be trying to make fools of us?" "Oh dear," cried his mother, in tears, "perhaps he's terribly ill and we're tormenting him. Grete! Grete!" she called out then. "Yes, Mother?" called his sister from the other side. They were calling to each other across Gregor's room. "You must go this minute for the doctor. Gregor is ill. Go for the doctor, quick. Did you hear how he was speaking?" "That was no human voice," said the chief clerk in a voice noticeably low beside the shrillness of the mother's. "Anna! Anna!" his father was calling through the hall to the kitchen, clapping his hands, "get a locksmith at once!" And the two girls were already running through the hall with a swish of skirts—how could his sister have got dressed so quickly?—and were tearing the front door open. There was no sound of its closing again; they had evidently left it open, as one does in houses where some great misfortune has happened.

But Gregor was now much calmer. The words he uttered were no longer understandable, apparently, although they seemed clear enough to him, even clearer than before, perhaps because his ear had grown accustomed to the sound of them. Yet at any rate people now believed that something was wrong with him, and were ready to help him. The positive certainty with which these first measures had been taken comforted him. He felt himself drawn once more into the human circle and hoped for great and remarkable results from both the doctor and the locksmith, without really distinguishing precisely between them. To make his voice as clear as possible for the decisive conversation that was now imminent he coughed a little, as quietly as he could, of course, since this noise too might not sound like a human cough for all he was able to judge. In the next room meanwhile there was complete silence. Perhaps his parents were sitting at the table with the chief clerk, whispering, perhaps they were all leaning against the door and listening.

Slowly Gregor pushed the chair towards the door, then let go of it, caught hold of the door for support—the soles at the end of his little legs were somewhat sticky—and rested against it for a moment after his efforts. Then he set himself to turning the key in the lock with his mouth. It seemed, unhappily, that he hadn't really any teeth—what could he grip the key with?—but on the other hand his jaws were certainly very strong; with their help he did manage to set the key in motion, heedless of the fact that he was undoubtedly damaging them somewhere, since a brown fluid issued from his mouth, flowed over the key and dripped on the floor. "Just listen to that," said the chief clerk next door; "he's turning the key." That was a great encouragement to Gregor; but they should all have shouted encouragement to him, his father and mother too: "Go on, Gregor," they should have called out, "keep going, hold on to that key!" And in the belief that they were all following his efforts intently, he clenched his jaws recklessly on the key with all the force at his command. As the turning of the key progressed he circled round the lock, holding on now only with his mouth, pushing on the key, as required, or pulling it down again with all the weight of his body. The louder click of the finally yielding lock literally quickened Gregor. With a deep breath of relief he said to himself: "So I didn't need the locksmith," and laid his head on the handle to open the door wide.

Since he had to pull the door towards him, he was still invisible when it was really wide open. He had to edge himself slowly round the near half of the double door, and to do it very carefully if he was not to fall plump upon his back just on the threshold. He was still carrying out this difficult manoeuvre, with no time to observe anything else, when he heard the chief clerk utter a loud "Oh!"—it sounded like a gust of wind—and now he could see the man, standing as he was nearest to the door, clapping one hand before his open mouth and slowly backing away as if driven by some invisible steady pressure. His mother—in spite of the chief clerk's being there her hair was still undone and sticking up in all directions—first clasped her hands and looked at his father, then took two steps towards Gregor and fell on the floor among her outspread skirts, her face hidden on her breast. His father knotted his fist with a fierce expression on his face as if he meant to knock Gregor back into his room, then looked uncertainly round the living room, covered his eyes with his hands and wept till his great chest heaved.

Gregor did not go now into the living room, but leaned against the inside of the firmly shut wing of the door, so that only half his body was visible and his head above it bending sideways to look at the others. The light had meanwhile strengthened; on the other side of the street one could see clearly a section of the endlessly long, dark gray building opposite—it was a hospital—abruptly punctuated by its row of regular windows; the rain was still falling, but only in large singly discernible and literally singly splashing drops. The breakfast dishes were set out on the table lavishly, for breakfast was the most important meal of the day to Gregor's father, who lingered it out for hours over various newspapers. Right opposite Gregor on the wall hung a photograph of himself on military service, as a lieutenant, hand on sword, a carefree smile on his face, inviting one to respect his uniform and military bearing. The door leading to the hall was open, and one could see that the front door stood open too, showing the landing beyond and the beginning of the stairs going down.

"Well," said Gregor, knowing perfectly that he was the only one who had retained any composure, "I'll put my clothes on at once, pack up my samples and start off. Will you only let me go? You see, sir, I'm not obstinate, and I'm willing to work; traveling is a hard life, but I couldn't live without it. Where are you going, sir? To the office? Yes? Will you give a true account of all this? One can be temporarily incapacitated, but that's just the moment for remembering former services and bearing in mind that later on, when the incapacity has been got over, one will certainly work with all the more industry and concentration. I'm loyally bound to serve the chief, you know that very well. Besides, I have to provide for my parents and my sister. I'm in great difficulties, but I'll get out of them again. Don't make things any worse for me than they are. Stand up for me in the firm. Travelers are not popular there, I know. People think they earn sacks of money and just have a good time. A prejudice there's no particular reason for revising. But you, sir, have a more comprehensive view of affairs than the rest of the staff, yes, let me tell you in confidence, a more comprehensive view than the chief himself, who, being the owner, lets his judgment easily be swayed against one of his employees. And you know very well that the traveler, who is never seen in the office almost the whole year round, can so easily fall a victim to gossip and ill luck and unfounded complaints, which he mostly knows nothing about, except when he comes back exhausted from his rounds, and only then suffers in person from their evil consequences, which he can no longer trace back to the original causes. Sir, sir, don't go away without a word to me to show that you think me in the right at least to some extent!"

But at Gregor's very first words the chief clerk had already backed away and only stared at him with parted lips over one twitching shoulder. And while Gregor was speaking he did not stand still one moment but stole away towards the door, without taking his eyes off Gregor, yet only an inch at a time, as if obeying some secret injunction to leave the room. He was already at the hall, and the suddenness with which he took his last step out of the living room would have made one believe he had burned the sole of his foot. Once in the hall he stretched his right arm before him towards the staircase, as if some supernatural power were waiting there to deliver him.

Gregor perceived that the chief clerk must on no account be allowed to go away in this frame of mind if his position in the firm were not to be endangered to the utmost. His parents did not understand this so well; they had convinced themselves in the course of years that Gregor was settled for life in this firm, and besides they were so occupied with their immediate troubles that all foresight had forsaken them. Yet Gregor had this foresight. The chief clerk must be detained, soothed, persuaded and finally won over; the whole future of Gregor and his family depended on it! If only his sister had been there! She was intelligent; she had begun to cry while Gregor was still lying quietly on his back. And no doubt the chief clerk, so partial to ladies, would have been guided by her; she would have shut the door of the flat and in the hall talked him out of his horror. But she was not there, and Gregor would have to handle the situation himself. And without remembering that he was still unaware what powers of movement he possessed, without even remembering that his words in all possibility, indeed in all likelihood, would again be unintelligible, he let go the wing of the door, pushed himself through the opening, started to walk towards the chief clerk, who was already ridiculously clinging with both hands to the railing on the landing; but immediately, as he was feeling for a support, he fell down with a little cry upon all his numerous legs. Hardly was he down when he experienced for the first time this morning a sense of physical comfort; his legs had firm ground under them; they were completely obedient, as he noted with joy; they even strove to carry him forward in whatever direction he chose; and he was inclined to believe that a final relief from all his sufferings was at hand. But in the same moment as he found himself on the floor, rocking with suppressed eagerness to move, not far from his mother, indeed just in front of her, she, who had seemed so completely crushed, sprang all at once to her feet, her arms and fingers outspread, cried: "Help, for God's sake, help!" bent her head down as if to see Gregor better, yet on the contrary kept backing senselessly away; had quite forgotten that the laden table stood behind her; sat upon it hastily, as if in absence of mind, when she bumped into it; and seemed altogether unaware that the big coffee pot beside her was upset and pouring coffee in a flood over the carpet.

"Mother, Mother," said Gregor in a low voice, and looked up at her. The 30 chief clerk, for the moment, had quite slipped from his mind; instead, he could not resist snapping his jaws together at the sight of the streaming coffee. That made his mother scream again, she fled from the table and fell into the arms of his father, who hastened to catch her. But Gregor had now no time to spare for his parents; the chief clerk was already on the stairs; with his chin on the banisters he was taking one last backward look. Gregor made a spring, to be as sure as possible of overtaking him; the chief clerk must have divined his intention, for he leaped down several steps and vanished; he was still yelling "Ugh!" and it echoed through the whole staircase.

Unfortunately, the flight of the chief clerk seemed completely to upset Gregor's father, who had remained relatively calm until now, for instead of running after the man himself, or at least not hindering Gregor in his pursuit, he seized in his right hand the walking stick which the chief clerk had left behind on a chair, together with a hat and greatcoat, snatched in his left hand a large newspaper from the table and began stamping his feet and flourishing the stick and the newspaper to drive Gregor back into his room. No entreaty of Gregor's availed, indeed no entreaty was even understood, however humbly he bent his head his father only stamped on the floor the more loudly. Behind his father his mother had torn open a window, despite the cold weather, and was leaning far out of it with her face in her hands. A strong draught set in from the street to the staircase, the window curtains blew in, the newspapers on the table fluttered, stray pages whisked over the floor. Pitilessly Gregor's father drove him back, hissing and crying "Shoo!" like a savage. But Gregor was quite unpracticed in walking backwards, it really was a slow business. If he only had a chance to turn round he could get back to his room at once, but he was afraid of exasperating his father by the slowness of such a rotation and at any moment the stick in his father's hand might hit him a fatal blow on the back or on the head. In the end, however, nothing else was left for him to do since to his horror he observed that in moving backwards he could not even control the direction he took; and so, keeping an anxious eye on his father all the time over his shoulder, he began to turn round as quickly as he could, which was in reality very slowly. Perhaps his father noted his good intentions, for he did not interfere except every now and then to help him in the manoeuvre from a distance with the point of the stick. If only he would have stopped making that unbearable hissing noise! It made Gregor quite lose his head. He had turned almost completely round when the hissing noise so distracted him that he even turned a little the wrong way again. But when at last his head was fortunately right in front of the doorway, it appeared that his body was too broad simply to get through the opening. His father, of course, in his present mood was far from thinking of such a thing as opening the other half of the door, to let Gregor have enough space. He had merely the fixed idea of driving Gregor back into his room as quickly as possible. He would never have suffered Gregor to make the circumstantial preparations for standing up on end and perhaps slipping his way through the door. Maybe he was now making more noise than ever to urge Gregor forward, as if no obstacle impeded him; to Gregor, anyhow, the noise in his rear sounded no longer like the voice of one single father; this was really no joke, and Gregor thrust himself—come what might—into the doorway. One side of his body rose up, he was tilted at an angle in the doorway, his flank was quite bruised, horrid blotches stained the white door, soon he was stuck fast and, left to himself, could not have moved at all, his legs on one side fluttered trembling to the air, those on the other were crushed painfully to the floor—when from behind his father gave him a strong push which was literally a deliverance and he flew far into the room, bleeding freely. The door was slammed behind him with the stick, and then at last there was silence.

## II

Not until it was twilight did Gregor awake out of a deep sleep, more like a swoon than a sleep. He would certainly have waked up of his own accord not much later, for he felt himself sufficiently rested and well-slept, but it seemed to him as if a fleeting step and a cautious shutting of the door leading into the hall had aroused him. The electric lights in the street cast a pale sheen here and there on the ceiling and the upper surfaces of the furniture, but down below, where he lay, it was dark. Slowly, awkwardly trying out his feelers, which he now first learned to appreciate, he pushed his way to the door to see what had been happening there. His left side felt like one single long, unpleasant tense scar, and he had actually to limp on his two rows of legs. One little leg, moreover, had been severely damaged in the course of that morning's events—it was almost a miracle that only one had been damaged—and trailed uselessly behind him.

He had reached the door before he discovered what had really drawn him to it: the smell of food. For there stood a basin filled with fresh milk in which floated little sops of white bread. He could almost have laughed with joy, since he was now still hungrier than in the morning, and he dipped his head almost over the eyes straight into the milk. But soon in disappointment he withdrew it again; not only did he find it difficult to feed because of his tender left side—and he could only feed with the palpitating collaboration of his whole body—he did not like the milk either, although milk had been his favorite drink and that was certainly why his sister had set it there for him, indeed it was almost with repulsion that he turned away from the basin and crawled back to the middle of the room.

He could see through the crack of the door that the gas was turned on in the living room, but while usually at this time his father made a habit of reading the afternoon newspaper in a loud voice to his mother and occasionally to his sister as well, not a sound was now to be heard. Well, perhaps his father had recently given up this habit of reading aloud, which his sister had mentioned so often in conversation and in her letters. But there was the same silence all around, although the flat was certainly not empty of occupants. "What a quiet life our family has been leading," said Gregor to himself, and as he sat there motionless staring into the darkness he felt great pride in the fact that he had been able to provide such a life for his parents and sister in such a fine flat. But what if all the quiet, the comfort, the contentment were now to end in horror? To keep himself from being lost in such thoughts Gregor took refuge in movement and crawled up and down the room.

Once during the long evening one of the side doors was opened a little and quickly shut again, later the other side door too; someone had apparently wanted to come in and then thought better of it. Gregor now stationed himself immediately before the living room door, determined to persuade any hesitating visitor to come in or at least to discover who it might be; but the door was not opened again and he waited in vain. In the early morning, when the doors were locked, they had all wanted to come in, now that he had opened one door and the other had apparently been opened during the day, no one came in and even the keys were on the other side of the doors.

It was late at night before the gas went out in the living room, and Gregor could easily tell that his parents and his sister had all stayed awake until then, for he could clearly hear the three of them stealing away on tiptoe. No one was likely to visit him, not until the morning, that was certain; so he had plenty of time to meditate at his leisure on how he was to arrange his life afresh. But the lofty, empty room in which he had to lie flat on the floor filled him with an apprehension he could not account for, since it had been his very own room for the past five years—and with a half-unconscious action, not without a slight feeling of shame, he scuttled under the sofa, where he felt comfortable at once, although his back was a little cramped and he could not lift his head up, and his only regret was that his body was too broad to get the whole of it under the sofa.

He stayed there all night, spending the time partly in a light slumber, from which his hunger kept waking him up with a start, and partly in worrying and sketching vague hopes, which all led to the same conclusion, that he must lie low for the present and, by exercising patience, and the utmost consideration, help the family to bear the inconvenience he was bound to cause them in his present condition.

Very early in the morning, it was still almost night, Gregor had the chance to test the strength of his new resolutions, for his sister, nearly fully dressed, opened the door from the hall and peered in. She did not see him at once, yet when she caught sight of him under the sofa—well, he had to be somewhere, he couldn't have flown away, could he?—she was so startled that without being able to help it she slammed the door shut again. But as if regretting her behavior she opened the door again immediately and came in on tiptoe, as if she were visiting an invalid or even a stranger. Gregor had pushed his head forward to the very edge of the sofa and watched her. Would she notice that he had left the milk standing, and not for lack of hunger, and would she bring in some other kind of food more to his taste? If she did not do it of her own accord, he would rather starve than draw her attention to the fact, although he felt a wild impulse to dart out from under the sofa, throw himself at her feet and beg her for something to eat. But his sister at once noticed, with surprise, that the basin was still full, except for a little milk that had been spilt all around it, she lifted it immediately, not with her bare hands, true, but with a cloth and carried it away. Gregor was wildly curious to know what she would bring instead, and made various speculations about it. Yet what she actually did next, in the goodness of her heart, he could never have guessed at. To find out what he liked she brought him a whole selection of food, all set out on an old newspaper. There were old, half-decayed vegetables, bones from last night's supper covered with a white sauce that had thickened; some raisins and almonds; a piece of cheese that Gregor would have called uneatable two days ago; a dry roll of bread, a buttered roll, and a roll both buttered and salted. Besides all that, she set down again the same basin, into which she had poured some water, and which was apparently to be reserved for his exclusive use. And with fine tact, knowing that Gregor would not eat in her presence, she withdrew quickly and even turned the key, to let him understand that he could take his ease as much as he liked. Gregor's legs all whizzed towards the food. His wounds must have healed completely, moreover, for he felt no disability, which amazed him and made him reflect how more than a month ago he had cut one finger a little with a knife and had still suffered pain from the wound only the day before yesterday. Am I less sensitive now? he thought, and sucked greedily at the cheese, which above all the other edibles attracted him at once and strongly. One after another and with tears of satisfaction in his eyes he quickly devoured the cheese, the vegetables and the sauce; the fresh food, on the other hand, had no charms for him, he could not even stand the smell of it and actually dragged away to some little distance the things he could eat. He had long finished his meal and was only lying lazily on the same spot when his sister turned the key slowly as a sign for him to retreat. That roused him at once, although he was nearly asleep, and he hurried under the sofa again. But it took considerable self-control for him to stay under the sofa, even for the short time his sister was in the room, since the large meal had swollen his body somewhat and he was so cramped he could hardly breathe. Slight attacks of breathlessness afflicted him and his eyes were starting a little out of his head as he watched his unsuspecting sister sweeping together with a broom not only the remains of what he had eaten but even the things he had not touched, as if these were now of no use to anyone, and hastily shoveling it all into a bucket, which she covered with a wooden lid and carried away. Hardly had she turned her back when Gregor came from under the sofa and stretched and puffed himself out.

In this manner Gregor was fed, once in the early morning while his parents and the servant girl were still asleep, and a second time after they had all had their midday dinner, for then his parents took a short nap and the servant girl could be sent out on some errand or other by his sister. Not that they would have wanted him to starve, of course, but perhaps they could not have borne to know more about his feeding than from hearsay, perhaps too his sister wanted to spare them such little anxieties wherever possible, since they had quite enough to bear as it was.

Under what pretext the doctor and the locksmith had been got rid of on that first morning Gregor could not discover, for since what he had said was not understood by the others it never struck any of them, not even his sister, that he could understand what they said, and so whenever his sister came into his room he had to content himself with hearing her utter only a sigh now and then and an occasional appeal to the saints. Later on, when she had got a little used to the situation—of course she could never get completely used to it—she sometimes threw out a remark which was kindly meant or could be so interpreted. "Well, he liked his dinner today," she would say when Gregor had made a good clearance of his food; and when he had not eaten, which gradually happened more and more often, she would say almost sadly: "Everything's been left standing again."

But although Gregor could get no news directly, he overheard a lot from the neighboring rooms, and as soon as voices were audible, he would run to the door of the room concerned and press his whole body against it. In the first few days especially there was no conversation that did not refer to him somehow, even if only indirectly. For two whole days there were family consultations at every mealtime about what should be done; but also between meals the same subject was discussed, for there were always at least two members of the family at home, since no one wanted to be alone in the flat and to leave it quite empty was unthinkable. And on the very first of these days the household cook—it was not quite clear what and how much she knew of the situation—went down on her knees to his mother and begged leave to go, and when she departed, a quarter of an hour later, gave thanks for her dismissal with tears in her eyes as if for the greatest benefit that could have been conferred on her, and without any prompting swore a solemn oath that she would never say a single word to anyone about what had happened.

Now Gregor's sister had to cook too, helping her mother; true, the cooking did not amount to much, for they ate scarcely anything. Gregor was always hearing one of the family vainly urging another to eat and getting no answer but: "Thanks, I've had all I want," or something similar. Perhaps they drank nothing either. Time and again his sister kept asking his father if he wouldn't like some beer and offered kindly to go and fetch it herself, and when he made no answer suggested that she could ask the concierge° to fetch it, so that he need feel no sense of obligation, but then a round "No" came from his father and no more was said about it.

In the course of that very first day Gregor's father explained the family's financial position and prospects to both his mother and his sister. Now and then he rose from the table to get some voucher or memorandum out of the small safe he had rescued from the collapse of his business five years earlier. One could hear him opening the complicated lock and rustling papers out and shutting it again.

concierge: the attendant at the entrance of a building who often provides services for the residents; the doorman.

This statement made by his father was the first cheerful information Gregor had heard since his imprisonment. He had been of the opinion that nothing at all was left over from his father's business, at least his father had never said anything to the contrary, and of course he had not asked him directly. At the time Gregor's sole desire was to do his utmost to help the family to forget as soon as possible the catastrophe which had overwhelmed the business and thrown them all into a state of complete despair. And so he had set to work with unusual ardor and almost overnight had become a commercial traveler instead of a little clerk, with of course much greater chances of earning money, and his success was immediately translated into good round coin which he could lay on the table for his amazed and happy family. These had been fine times, and they had never recurred, at least not with the same sense of glory, although later on Gregor had earned so much money that he was able to meet the expenses of the whole household and did so. They had simply got used to it, both the family and Gregor; the money was gratefully accepted and gladly given, but there was no special uprush of warm feeling. With his sister alone had he remained intimate, and it was a secret plan of his that she, who loved music, unlike himself, and could play movingly on the violin, should be sent next year to study at the Conservatorium°, despite the great expense that would entail, which must be made up in some other way. During his brief visits home the Conservatorium was often mentioned in the talks he had with his sister, but always merely as a beautiful dream which could never come true, and his parents discouraged even these innocent references to it; yet Gregor had made up his mind firmly about it and meant to announce the fact with due solemnity on Christmas Day.

Such were the thoughts, completely futile in his present condition, that went through his head as he stood clinging upright to the door and listening. Sometimes out of sheer weariness he had to give up listening and let his head fall negligently against the door, but he always had to pull himself together again at once, for even the slight sound his head made was audible next door and brought all conversation to a stop. "What can he be doing now?" his father would say after a while, obviously turning towards the door, and only then would the interrupted conversation gradually be set going again.

Gregor was now informed as amply as he could wish—for his father tended to repeat himself in his explanations, partly because it was a long time since he had handled such matters and partly because his mother could not always grasp things at once—that a certain amount of investments, a very small amount it was true, had survived the wreck of their fortunes and had even increased a little because the dividends had not been touched meanwhile. And besides that, the money Gregor brought home every month—he had kept only a few dollars for himself—had never been quite used up and now amounted to a small capital sum. Behind the door Gregor nodded his head eagerly, rejoiced at this evidence of unexpected thrift and foresight. True, he could really have paid off some more of his father's debts to the chief with his extra money, and so brought much near-

_Conservatorium:_ a music school for advanced students.

er the day on which he could quit his job, but doubtless it was better the way his father had arranged it.

Yet this capital was by no means sufficient to let the family live on the interest of it; for one year, perhaps, or at the most two, they could live on the principal, that was all. It was simply a sum that ought not to be touched and should be kept for a rainy day; money for living expenses would have to be earned. Now his father was still hale enough but an old man, and he had done no work for the past five years and could not be expected to do much; during these five years, the first years of leisure in his laborious though unsuccessful life, he had grown rather fat and become sluggish. And Gregor's old mother, how was she to earn a living with her asthma, which troubled her even when she walked through the flat and kept her lying on a sofa every other day panting for breath beside an open window? And was his sister to earn her bread, she who was still a child of seventeen and whose life hitherto had been so pleasant, consisting as it did in dressing herself nicely, sleeping long, helping in the housekeeping, going out to a few modest entertainments and above all playing the violin? At first whenever the need for earning money was mentioned Gregor let go his hold on the door and threw himself down on the cool leather sofa beside it, he felt so hot with shame and grief.

Often he just lay there the long nights through without sleeping at all, scrabbling for hours on the leather. Or he nerved himself to the great effort of pushing an armchair to the window, then crawled up over the window sill and, braced against the chair, leaned against the windowpanes, obviously in some recollection of the sense of freedom that looking out of a window always used to give him. For in reality day by day things that were even a little way off were growing dimmer to his sight; the hospital across the street, which he used to execrate for being all too often before his eyes, was now quite beyond his range of vision, and if he had not known that he lived in Charlotte Street, a quiet street but still a city street, he might have believed that his window gave on a desert waste where gray sky and gray land blended indistinguishably into each other. His quick-witted sister only needed to observe twice that the armchair stood by the window; after that whenever she had tidied the room she always pushed the chair back to the same place at the window and even left the inner casements open.

If he could have spoken to her and thanked her for all she had to do for him, he could have borne her ministrations better; as it was, they oppressed him. She certainly tried to make as light as possible of whatever was disagreeable in her task, and as time went on she succeeded, of course, more and more, but time brought more enlightenment to Gregor too. The very way she came in distressed him. Hardly was she in the room when she rushed to the window, without even taking time to shut the door, careful as she was usually to shield the sight of Gregor's room from the others, and as if she were almost suffocating tore the casements open with hasty fingers, standing then in the open draught for a while even in the bitterest cold and drawing deep breaths. This noisy scurry of hers upset Gregor twice a day; he would crouch trembling under the sofa all the time, knowing quite well that she would certainly have spared him such a disturbance had she found it at all possible to stay in his presence without opening a window.

On one occasion, about a month after Gregor's metamorphosis, when there was surely no reason for her to be still startled at his appearance, she came a little earlier than usual and found him gazing out of the window, quite motionless, and thus well placed to look like a bogey°. Gregor would not have been surprised had she not come in at all, for she could not immediately open the window while he was there, but not only did she retreat, she jumped back as if in alarm and banged the door shut; a stranger might well have thought that he had been lying in wait for her there meaning to bite her. Of course he hid himself under the sofa at once, but he had to wait until midday before she came again, and she seemed more ill at ease than usual. This made him realize how repulsive the sight of him still was to her, and that it was bound to go on being repulsive, and what an effort it must cost her not to run away even from the sight of the small portion of his body that stuck out from under the sofa. In order to spare her that, therefore, one day he carried a sheet on his back to the sofa—it cost him four hours' labor—and arranged it there in such a way as to hide him completely, so that even if she were to bend down she could not see him. Had she considered the sheet unnecessary, she would certainly have stripped it off the sofa again, for it was clear enough that this curtaining and confining of himself was not likely to conduce Gregor's comfort, but she left it where it was, and Gregor even fancied that he caught a thankful glance from her eye when he lifted the sheet carefully a very little with his head to see how she was taking the new arrangement.

For the first fortnight his parents could not bring themselves to the point of 50 entering his room, and he often heard them expressing their appreciation of his sister's activities, whereas formerly they had frequently scolded her for being as they thought a somewhat useless daughter. But now, both of them often waited outside the door, his father and his mother, while his sister tidied his room, and as soon as she came out she had to tell them exactly how things were in the room, what Gregor had eaten, how he had conducted himself this time and whether there was not perhaps some slight improvement in his condition. His mother, moreover, began relatively soon to want to visit him, but his father and sister dissuaded her at first with arguments which Gregor listened to very attentively and altogether approved. Later, however, she had to be held back by main force, and when she cried out: "Do let me in to Gregor, he is my unfortunate son! Can't you understand that I must go to him?" Gregor thought that it might be well to have her come in, not every day, of course, but perhaps once a week; she understood things, after all, much better than his sister, who was only a child despite the efforts she was making and had perhaps taken on so difficult a task merely out of childish thoughtlessness.

Gregor's desire to see his mother was soon fulfilled. During the daytime he did not want to show himself at the window, out of consideration for his parents, but he could not crawl very far around the few square yards of floor space he had, nor could he bear lying quietly at rest all during the night, while he was fast losing

bogey: goblin or phantom.

any interest he had ever taken in food, so that for mere recreation he had formed the habit of crawling crisscross over the walls and ceiling. He especially enjoyed hanging suspended from the ceiling; it was much better than lying on the floor; one could breathe more freely; one's body swung and rocked lightly; and in the almost blissful absorption induced by this suspension it could happen to his own surprise that he let go and fell plump on the floor. Yet he now had his body much better under control than formerly, and even such a big fall did him no harm. His sister at once remarked the new distraction Gregor had found for himself—he left traces behind him of the sticky stuff on his soles wherever he crawled—and she got the idea in her head of giving him as wide a field as possible to crawl in and of removing the pieces of furniture that hindered him, above all the chest of drawers and the writing desk. But that was more than she could manage all by herself; she did not dare ask her father to help her; and as for the servant girl, a young creature of sixteen who had had the courage to stay on after the cook's departure, she could not be asked to help, for she had begged as an especial favor that she might keep the kitchen door locked and open it only on a definite summons; so there was nothing left but to apply to her mother at an hour when her father was out. And the old lady did come, with exclamations of joyful eagerness, which, however, died away at the door of Gregor's room. Gregor's sister, of course, went in first, to see that everything was in order before letting his mother enter. In great haste Gregor pulled the sheet lower and rucked it more in folds so that it really looked as if it had been thrown accidentally over the sofa. And this time he did not peer out from under it; he renounced the pleasure of seeing his mother on this occasion and was only glad that she had come at all. "Come in, he's out of sight," said his sister, obviously leading her mother in by the hand. Gregor could now hear the two women struggling to shift the heavy old chest from its place, and his sister claiming the greater part of the labor for herself, without listening to the admonitions of her mother who feared she might overstrain herself. It took a long time. After at least a quarter of an hour's tugging his mother objected that the chest had better be left where it was, for in the first place it was too heavy and could never be got out before his father came home, and standing in the middle of the room like that it would only hamper Gregor's movements, while in the second place it was not at all certain that removing the furniture would be doing a service to Gregor. She was inclined to think to the contrary; the sight of the naked walls made her own heart heavy, and why shouldn't Gregor have the same feeling, considering that he had been used to his furniture for so long and might feel forlorn without it. "And doesn't it look," she concluded in a low voice—in fact she had been almost whispering all the time as if to avoid letting Gregor, whose exact whereabouts she did not know, hear even the tones of her voice, for she was convinced that he could not understand her words—"doesn't it look as if we were showing him, by taking away his furniture, that we have given up hope of his ever getting better and are just leaving him coldly to himself? I think it would be best to keep his room exactly as it has always been, so that when he comes back to us he will find everything unchanged and be able all the more easily to forget what has happened in between."

On hearing these words from his mother Gregor realized that the lack of all direct human speech for the past two months together with the monotony of family life must have confused his mind, otherwise he could not account for the fact that he had quite earnestly looked forward to having his room emptied of furnishing. Did he really want his warm room, so comfortably fitted with old family furniture, to be turned into a naked den in which he would certainly be able to crawl unhampered in all directions but at the price of shedding simultaneously all recollection of his human background? He had indeed been so near the brink of forgetfulness that only the voice of his mother, which he had not heard for so long, had drawn him back from it. Nothing should be taken out of his room; everything must stay as it was; he could not dispense with the good influence of the furniture on his state of mind; and even if the furniture did hamper him in his senseless crawling round and round, that was no drawback but a great advantage.

Unfortunately his sister was of the contrary opinion; she had grown accustomed, and not without reason, to consider herself an expert in Gregor's affairs as against her parents, and so her mother's advice was now enough to make her determined on the removal not only of the chest and the writing desk, which had been her first intention, but of all the furniture except the indispensable sofa. This determination was not, of course, merely the outcome of childish recalcitrance and of the self-confidence she had recently developed so unexpectedly and at such cost; she had in fact perceived that Gregor needed a lot of space to crawl about in, while on the other hand he never used the furniture at all, so far as could be seen. Another factor might have been also the enthusiastic temperament of an adolescent girl, which seeks to indulge itself on every opportunity and which now tempted Grete to exaggerate the horror of her brother's circumstances in order that she might do all the more for him. In a room where Gregor lorded it all alone over empty walls no one save herself was likely ever to set foot.

And so she was not to be moved from her resolve by her mother who seemed moreover to be ill at ease in Gregor's room and therefore unsure of herself, was soon reduced to silence and helped her daughter as best she could to push the chest outside. Now, Gregor could do without the chest, if need be, but the writing desk he must retain. As soon as the two women had got the chest out of his room, groaning as they pushed it, Gregor stuck his head out from under the sofa to see how he might intervene as kindly and cautiously as possible. But as bad luck would have it, his mother was the first to return, leaving Grete clasping the chest in the room next door where she was trying to shift it all by herself, without of course moving it from the spot. His mother however was not accustomed to the sight of him, it might sicken her and so in alarm Gregor backed quickly to the other end of the sofa, yet could not prevent the sheet from swaying a little in front. That was enough to put her on the alert. She paused, stood still for a moment and then went back to Grete.

Although Gregor kept reassuring himself that nothing out of the way was 55 happening, but only a few bits of furniture were being changed round, he soon had to admit that all this trotting to and fro of the two women, their little ejaculations and the scraping of furniture along the floor affected him like a vast disturbance coming from all sides at once, and however much he tucked in his head and legs and cowered to the very floor he was bound to confess that he would not be able to stand it for long. They were clearing his room out; taking away everything he loved; the chest in which he kept his fret saw and other tools was already dragged off; they were now loosening the writing desk which had almost sunk into the floor, the desk at which he had done all his homework when he was at the commercial academy, at the grammar school before that, and, yes, even at the primary school—he had no more time to waste in weighing the good intentions of the two women, whose existence he had by now almost forgotten, for they were so exhausted that they were laboring in silence and nothing could be heard but the heavy scuffling of their feet.

And so he rushed out—the women were just leaning against the writing desk in the next room to give themselves a breather—and four times changed his direction, since he really did not know what to rescue first, then on the wall opposite, which was already otherwise cleared, he was struck by the picture of the lady muffled in so much fur and quickly crawled up to it and pressed himself to the glass, which was a good surface to hold on to and comforted his hot belly. This picture at least, which was entirely hidden beneath him, was going to be removed by nobody. He turned his head towards the door of the living room so as to observe the women when they came back.

They had not allowed themselves much of a rest and were already coming; Grete had twined her arm round her mother and was almost supporting her. "Well, what shall we take now?" said Grete, looking round. Her eyes met Gregor's from the wall. She kept her composure, presumably because of her mother, bent her head down to her mother, to keep her from looking up, and said, although in a fluttering, unpremeditated voice: "Come, hadn't we better go back to the living room for a moment?" Her intentions were clear enough to Gregor, she wanted to bestow her mother in safety and then chase him down from the wall. Well, just let her try it! He clung to his picture and would not give it up. He would rather fly in Grete's face.

But Grete's words had succeeded in disquieting her mother, who took a step to one side, caught sight of the huge brown mass on the flowered wallpaper, and before she was really conscious that what she saw was Gregor screamed in a loud, hoarse voice: "Oh God, oh God!" fell with outspread arms over the sofa as if giving up and did not move. "Gregor!" cried his sister, shaking her fist and glaring at him. This was the first time she had directly addressed him since his metamorphosis. She ran into the next room for some aromatic essence° with which to rouse her mother from her fainting fit. Gregor wanted to help too—there was still time to rescue the picture—but he was stuck fast to the glass and had to tear himself loose; he then ran after his sister into the next room as if he could advise her, as he used to do; but then had to stand helplessly behind her; she meanwhile searched among various small bottles and when she turned round started in alarm at the sight of him; one bottle fell on the floor and broke; a splinter of glass cut Gregor's face and some kind of corrosive medicine splashed him; without pausing a moment longer Grete gathered up all the bottles she could carry and ran to her

aromatic essence: an aromatic medicine like smelling salts.

mother with them; she banged the door shut with her foot. Gregor was now cut off from his mother, who was perhaps nearly dying because of him; he dared not open the door for fear of frightening away his sister, who had to stay with her mother; there was nothing he could do but wait; and harassed by self-reproach and worry he began now to crawl to and fro, over everything, wall, furniture and ceiling, and finally in his despair, when the whole room seemed to be reeling round him, fell down on to the middle of the big table.

A little while elapsed, Gregor was still lying there feebly and all around was quiet, perhaps that was a good omen. Then the doorbell rang. The servant girl was of course locked in her kitchen, and Grete would have to open the door. It was his father. "What's been happening?" were his first words; Grete's face must have told him everything. Grete answered in a muffled voice, apparently hiding her head on his breast: "Mother has been fainting, but she's better now. Gregor's broken loose." "Just what I expected," said his father, "just what I've been telling you, but you women would never listen." It was clear to Gregor that his father had taken the worst interpretation of Grete's all too brief statement and was assuming that Gregor had been guilty of some violent act. Therefore Gregor must now try to propitiate his father, since he had neither time nor means for an explanation. And so he fled to the door of his own room and crouched against it, to let his father see as soon as he came in from the hall that his son had the good intention of getting back into his room immediately and that it was not necessary to drive him there, but that if only the door were opened he would disappear at once.

Yet his father was not in the mood to perceive such fine distinctions. "Ah!"  60
he cried as soon as he appeared, in a tone which sounded at once angry and exultant. Gregor drew his head back from the door and lifted it to look at his father. Truly, this was not the father he had imagined to himself; admittedly he had been too absorbed of late in his new recreation of crawling over the ceiling to take the same interest as before in what was happening elsewhere in the flat, and he ought really to be prepared for some changes. And yet, and yet, could that be his father? The man who used to lie wearily sunk in bed whenever Gregor set out on a business journey; who welcomed him back of an evening lying in a long chair in a dressing gown; who could not really rise to his feet but only lifted his arms in greeting, and on the rare occasions when he did go out with his family, on one or two Sundays a year and on high holidays, walked between Gregor and his mother, who were slow walkers anyhow, even more slowly than they did, muffled in his old greatcoat, shuffling laboriously forward with the help of his crook-handled stick which he set down most cautiously at every step and, whenever he wanted to say anything, nearly always came to a full stop and gathered his escort around him? Now he was standing there in fine shape; dressed in a smart blue uniform with gold buttons, such as bank messengers wear; his strong double chin bulged over the stiff high collar of his jacket; from under his bushy eyebrows his black eyes darted fresh and penetrating glances; his onetime tangled white hair had been combed flat on either side of a shining and carefully exact parting. He pitched his cap, which bore a gold monogram, probably the badge of some

bank, in a wide sweep across the whole room on to a sofa and with the tail-ends of his jacket thrown back, his hands in his trouser pockets, advanced with a grim visage towards Gregor. Likely enough he did not himself know what he meant to do; at any rate he lifted his feet uncommonly high, and Gregor was dumbfounded at the enormous size of his shoe soles. But Gregor could not risk standing up to him, aware as he had been from the very first day of his new life that his father believed only the severest measures suitable for dealing with him. And so he ran before his father, stopping when he stopped and scuttling forward again when his father made any kind of move. In this way they circled the room several times without anything decisive happening; indeed the whole operation did not even look like a pursuit because it was carried out so slowly. And so Gregor did not leave the floor, for he feared that his father might take as a piece of peculiar wickedness any excursion of his over the walls or the ceiling. All the same, he could not stay this course much longer, for while his father took one step he had to carry out a whole series of movements. He was already beginning to feel breathless, just as in his former life his lungs had not been very dependable. As he was staggering along, trying to concentrate his energy on running, hardly keeping his eyes open; in his dazed state never even thinking of any other escape than simply going forward; and having almost forgotten that the walls were free to him, which in this room were well provided with finely carved pieces of furniture full of knobs and crevices—suddenly something lightly flung landed close behind him and rolled before him. It was an apple; a second apple followed immediately; Gregor came to a stop in alarm; there was no point in running on, for his father was determined to bombard him. He had filled his pockets with fruit from the dish on the sideboard and was now shying apple after apple, without taking particularly good aim for the moment. The small red apples rolled about the floor as if magnetized and cannoned into each other. An apple thrown without much force grazed Gregor's back and glanced off harmlessly. But another following immediately landed right on his back and sank in; Gregor wanted to drag himself forward, as if this startling, incredible pain could be left behind him: but he felt as if nailed to the spot and flattened himself out in a complete derangement of all his senses. With his last conscious look he saw the door of his room being torn open and his mother rushing out ahead of his screaming sister, in her underbodice, for her daughter had loosened her clothing to let her breathe more freely and recover from her swoon, he saw his mother rushing towards his father, leaving one after another behind her on the floor her loosened petticoats, stumbling over her petticoats straight to his father and embracing him, in complete union with him—but here Gregor's sight began to fail—with her hands clasped round his father's neck as she begged for her son's life.

### III

The serious injury done to Gregor, which disabled him for more than a month—the apple went on sticking in his body as a visible reminder, since no one ventured to remove it—seemed to have made even his father recollect that

Gregor was a member of the family, despite his present unfortunate and repulsive shape, and ought not to be treated as an enemy, that, on the contrary, family duty required the suppression of disgust and the exercise of patience, nothing but patience.

And although his injury had impaired, probably forever, his power of movement, and for the time being it took him long, long minutes to creep across his room like an old invalid—there was no question now of crawling up the wall—yet in his own opinion he was sufficiently compensated for this worsening of his condition by the fact that towards evening the living-room door, which he used to watch intently for an hour or two beforehand, was always thrown open, so that lying in the darkness of his room, invisible to the family, he could see them all at the lamp-lit table and listen to their talk, by general consent as it were, very different from his earlier eavesdropping.

True, their intercourse lacked the lively character of former times, which he had always called to mind with a certain wistfulness in the small hotel bedrooms where he had been wont to throw himself down, tired out, on damp bedding. They were now mostly very silent. Soon after supper his father would fall asleep in his armchair; his mother and sister would admonish each other to be silent; his mother, bending low over the lamp, stitched at fine sewing for an underwear firm; his sister, who had taken a job as a salesgirl, was learning shorthand and French in the evenings on the chance of bettering herself. Sometimes his father woke up, and as if quite unaware that he had been sleeping said to his mother: "What a lot of sewing you're doing today!" and at once fell asleep again, while the two women exchanged a tired smile.

With a kind of mulishness his father persisted in keeping his uniform on even in the house; his dressing gown hung uselessly on its peg and he slept fully dressed where he sat, as if he were ready for service at any moment and even here only at the beck and call of his superior. As a result, his uniform, which was not brand-new to start with, began to look dirty, despite all the loving care of the mother and sister to keep it clean, and Gregor often spent whole evenings gazing at the many greasy spots on the garment, gleaming with gold buttons always in a high state of polish, in which the old man sat sleeping in extreme discomfort and yet quite peacefully.

As soon as the clock struck ten his mother tried to rouse his father with gentle words and to persuade him after that to get into bed, for sitting there he could not have a proper sleep and that was what he needed most, since he had to go to duty at six. But with the mulishness that had obsessed him since he became a bank messenger he always insisted on staying longer at the table, although he regularly fell asleep again and in the end only with the greatest trouble could be got out of his armchair and into his bed. However insistently Gregor's mother and sister kept urging him with gentle reminders, he would go on slowly shaking his head for a quarter of an hour, keeping his eyes shut, and refuse to get to his feet. The mother plucked at his sleeve, whispering endearments in his ear, the sister left her lessons to come to her mother's help, but Gregor's father was not to be caught. He would only sink down deeper in his chair. Not until the two women hoisted him up by the armpits did he open his eyes and look at them both, one after the other, usually with the remark: "This is a life. This is the peace and quiet of my old age." And leaning on the two of them he would heave himself up, with difficulty, as if he were a great burden to himself, suffer them to lead him as far as the door and then wave them off and go on alone, while the mother abandoned her needlework and the sister her pen in order to run after him and help him farther.

Who could find time, in this overworked and tired-out family, to bother about Gregor more than was absolutely needful? The household was reduced more and more; the servant girl was turned off; a gigantic bony charwoman with white hair flying round her head came in morning and evening to do the rough work; everything else was done by Gregor's mother, as well as great piles of sewing. Even various family ornaments, which his mother and sister used to wear with pride at parties and celebrations, had to be sold, as Gregor discovered of an evening from hearing them all discuss the prices obtained. But what they lamented most was the fact that they could not leave the flat which was much too big for their present circumstances, because they could not think of any way to shift Gregor. Yet Gregor saw well enough that consideration for him was not the main difficulty preventing the removal, for they could have easily shifted him in some suitable box with a few air holes in it; what really kept them from moving into another flat was rather their own complete hopelessness and the belief that they had been singled out for a misfortune such as had never happened to any of their relations or acquaintances. They fulfilled to the uttermost all that the world demands of poor people, the father fetched breakfast for the small clerks in the bank, the mother devoted her energy to making underwear for strangers, the sister trotted to and fro behind the counter at the behest of customers, but more than this they had not the strength to do. And the wound in Gregor's back began to nag at him afresh when his mother and sister, after getting his father into bed, came back again, left their work lying, drew close to each other and sat cheek by cheek; when his mother, pointing towards his room, said: "Shut that door now, Grete," and he was left again in darkness, while next door the women mingled their tears or perhaps sat dry-eyed staring at the table.

Gregor hardly slept at all by night or by day. He was often haunted by the idea that next time the door opened he would take the family's affairs in hand again just as he used to do; once more, after this long interval, there appeared in his thoughts the figures of the chief and the chief clerk, the commercial travelers and the apprentices, the porter who was so dull-witted, two or three friends in other firms, a chambermaid in one of the rural hotels, a sweet and fleeting memory, a cashier in a milliner's shop, whom he had wooed earnestly but too slowly— they all appeared, together with strangers or people he had quite forgotten, but instead of helping him and his family they were one and all unapproachable and he was glad when they vanished. At other times he would not be in the mood to bother about his family, he was only filled with rage at the way they were neglecting him, and although he had no clear idea of what he might care to eat he would make plans for getting into the larder to take the food that was after all his due, even if he were not hungry. His sister no longer took thought to bring him what might especially please him, but in the morning and at noon before she went to business hurriedly pushed into his room with her foot any food that was available, and in the evening cleared it out again with one sweep of the broom, heedless of whether it had been merely tasted, or—as most frequently happened—left untouched. The cleaning of his room, which she now did always in the evenings, could not have been more hastily done. Streaks of dirt stretched along the walls, here and there lay balls of dust and filth. At first Gregor used to station himself in some particularly filthy corner when his sister arrived, in order to reproach her with it, so to speak. But he could have sat there for weeks without getting her to make any improvements; she could see the dirt as well as he did, but she had simply made up her mind to leave it alone. And yet, with a touchiness that was new to her, which seemed anyhow to have infected the whole family, she jealously guarded her claim to be the sole caretaker of Gregor's room. His mother once subjected his room to a thorough cleaning, which was achieved only by means of several buckets of water—all this dampness of course upset Gregor too and he lay widespread, sulky and motionless on the sofa—but she was well punished for it. Hardly had his sister noticed the changed aspect of his room than she rushed in high dudgeon into the living room and, despite the imploringly raised hands of her mother, burst into a storm of weeping, while her parents—her father had of course been startled out of his chair—looked on at first in helpless amazement; then they too began to go into action; the father reproached the mother on his right for not having left the cleaning of Gregor's room to his sister; shrieked at the sister on his left that never again was she to be allowed to clean Gregor's room; while the mother tried to pull the father into his bedroom, since he was beyond himself with agitation; the sister, shaken with sobs, then beat upon the table with her small fists; and Gregor hissed loudly with rage because not one of them thought of shutting the door to spare him such a spectacle and so much noise.

Still, even if the sister, exhausted by her daily work, had grown tired of looking after Gregor as she did formerly, there was no need for his mother's intervention or for Gregor's being neglected at all. The charwoman was there. This old widow, whose strong bony frame had enabled her to survive the worst a long life could offer, by no means recoiled from Gregor. Without being in the least curious she had once by chance opened the door of his room and at the sight of Gregor, who, taken by surprise, began to rush to and fro although no one was chasing him, merely stood there with her arms folded. From that time she never failed to open his door a little for a moment, morning and evening, to have a look at him. At first she even used to call him to her, with words which apparently she took to be friendly, such as: "Come along, then, you old dung beetle!" or "Look at the old dung beetle, then!" To such allocutions Gregor made no answer, but stayed motionless where he was, as if the door had never been opened. Instead of being allowed to disturb him so senselessly whenever the whim took her, she should rather have been ordered to clean out his room daily, that charwoman! Once, early in the morning—heavy rain was lashing on the windowpanes, perhaps a sign that spring was on the way—Gregor was so exasperated when she began addressing him again that he ran at her, as if to attack her, although slowly and feebly enough. But the charwoman instead of showing fright merely lifted high a chair that happened to be beside the door, and as she stood there with her mouth wide open it was clear that she meant to shut it only when she brought the chair down on Gregor's back. "So you're not coming any nearer?" she asked, as Gregor turned away again, and quietly put the chair back into the corner.

Gregor was now eating hardly anything. Only when he happened to pass the food laid out for him did he take a bit of something in his mouth as a pastime, kept it there for an hour at a time and usually spat it out again. At first he thought it was chagrin over the state of his room that prevented him from eating, yet he soon got used to the various changes in his room. It had become a habit in the family to push into his room things there was no room for elsewhere, and there were plenty of these now, since one of the rooms had been let to three lodgers. These serious gentlemen—all three of them with full beards, as Gregor once observed through a crack in the door—had a passion for order, not only in their own room but, since they were now members of the household, in all its arrangements, especially in the kitchen. Superfluous, not to say dirty, objects they could not bear. Besides, they had brought with them most of the furnishings they needed. For this reason many things could be dispensed with that it was no use trying to sell but that should not be thrown away either. All of them found their way into Gregor's room. The ash can likewise and the kitchen garbage can. Anything that was not needed for the moment was simply flung into Gregor's room by the charwoman, who did everything in a hurry; fortunately Gregor usually saw only the object, whatever it was, and the hand that held it. Perhaps she intended to take the things away again as time and opportunity offered, or to collect them until she could throw them all out in a heap, but in fact they just lay wherever she happened to throw them, except when Gregor pushed his way through the junk heap and shifted it somewhat, at first out of necessity, because he had not room enough to crawl, but later with increasing enjoyment, although after such excursions, being sad and weary to death, he would lie motionless for hours. And since the lodgers often ate their supper at home in the common living room, the living room door stayed shut many an evening, yet Gregor reconciled himself quite easily to the shutting of the door, for often enough on evenings when it was opened he had disregarded it entirely and lain in the darkest corner of his room, quite unnoticed by the family. But on one occasion the charwoman left the door open a little and it stayed ajar even when the lodgers came in for supper and the lamp was lit. They set themselves at the top end of the table where formerly Gregor and his father and mother had eaten their meals, unfolded their napkins and took knife and fork in hand. At once his mother appeared in the other doorway with a dish of meat and close behind her his sister with a dish of potatoes piled high. The food steamed with a thick vapor. The lodgers bent over the food set before them as if to scrutinize it before eating, in fact the man in the middle, who seemed to pass for an authority with the other two, cut a piece of meat as it lay on the dish, obviously to discover if it were tender or should be sent back to the kitchen. He showed satisfaction, and Gregor's mother and sister, who had been watching anxiously, breathed freely and began to smile.

The family itself took its meals in the kitchen. Nonetheless, Gregor's father came into the living room before going in to the kitchen and with one prolonged bow, cap in hand, made a round of the table. The lodgers all stood up and murmured something in their beards. When they were alone again they ate their food in almost complete silence. It seemed remarkable to Gregor that among the various noises coming from the table he could always distinguish the sound of their masticating teeth, as if this were a sign to Gregor that one needed teeth in order to eat, and that with toothless jaws even of the finest make one could do nothing. "I'm hungry enough," said Gregor sadly to himself, "but not for that kind of food. How these lodgers are stuffing themselves, and here am I dying of starvation!"

On that very evening—during the whole of his time there Gregor could not remember ever having heard the violin—the sound of violin-playing came from the kitchen. The lodgers had already finished their supper, the one in the middle had brought out a newspaper and given the other two a page apiece, and now they were leaning back at ease reading and smoking. When the violin began to play they pricked up their ears, got to their feet, and went on tiptoe to the hall door where they stood huddled together. Their movements must have been heard in the kitchen, for Gregor's father called out: "Is the violin-playing disturbing you, gentlemen? It can be stopped at once." "On the contrary," said the middle lodger, "could not Fräulein Samsa come and play in this room, beside us, where it is much more convenient and comfortable?" "Oh certainly," cried Gregor's father, as if he were the violin-player. The lodgers came back into the living room and waited. Presently Gregor's father arrived with the music stand, his mother carrying the music and his sister with the violin. His sister quietly made everything ready to start playing; his parents, who had never let rooms before and so had an exaggerated idea of the courtesy due to lodgers, did not venture to sit down on their own chairs; his father leaned against the door, the right hand thrust between two buttons of his livery coat, which was formally buttoned up; but his mother was offered a chair by one of the lodgers and, since she left the chair just where he had happened to put it, sat down in a corner to one side.

Gregor's sister began to play; the father and mother, from either side, intently watched the movements of her hands. Gregor, attracted by the playing, ventured to move forward a little until his head was actually inside the living room. He felt hardly any surprise at his growing lack of consideration for the others; there had been a time when he prided himself on being considerate. And yet just on this occasion he had more reason than ever to hide himself, since owing to the amount of dust which lay thick in his room and rose into the air at the slightest movement, he too was covered with dust; fluff and hair and remnants of food trailed with him, caught on his back and along his sides; his indifference to everything was much too great for him to turn on his back and scrape himself clean on the carpet, as once he had done several times a day. And in spite of his condition, no shame deterred him from advancing a little over the spotless floor of the living room.

To be sure, no one was aware of him. The family was entirely absorbed in the violin-playing; the lodgers, however, who first of all had stationed themselves, hands in pockets, much too close behind the music stand so that they could all have read the music, which must have bothered his sister, had soon retreated to the window, half-whispering with downbent heads, and stayed there while his father turned an anxious eye on them. Indeed, they were making it more than obvious that they had been disappointed in their expectation of hearing good or enjoyable violin-playing, that they had more than enough of the performance and only out of courtesy suffered a continued disturbance of their peace. From the way they all kept blowing the smoke of their cigars high in the air through nose and mouth one could divine their irritation. And yet Gregor's sister was playing so beautifully. Her face leaned sideways, intently and sadly her eyes followed the notes of music. Gregor crawled a little farther forward and lowered his head to the ground so that it might be possible for his eyes to meet hers. Was he an animal, that music had such an effect upon him? He felt as if the way were opening before him to the unknown nourishment he craved. He was determined to push forward till he reached his sister, to pull at her skirt and so let her know that she was to come into his room with her violin, for no one here appreciated her playing as he would appreciate it. He would never let her out of his room, at least, not so long as he lived; his frightful appearance would become, for the first time, useful to him; he would watch all the doors of his room at once and spit at intruders; but his sister should need no constraint, she should stay with him of her own free will; she should sit beside him on the sofa, bend down her ear to him and hear him confide that he had had the firm intention of sending her to the Conservatorium, and that, but for his mishap, last Christmas—surely Christmas was long past?—he would have announced it to everybody without allowing a single objection. After this confession his sister would be so touched that she would burst into tears, and Gregor would then raise himself to her shoulder and kiss her on the neck, which, now that she went to business, she kept free of any ribbon or collar.

"Mr. Samsa!" cried the middle lodger, to Gregor's father, and pointed, without wasting any more words, at Gregor, now working himself slowly forwards. The violin fell silent, the middle lodger first smiled to his friends with a shake of the head and then looked at Gregor again. Instead of driving Gregor out, his father seemed to think it more needful to begin by soothing down the lodgers, although they were not at all agitated and apparently found Gregor more entertaining than the violin-playing. He hurried toward them and spreading out his arms, tried to urge them back into their own room and at the same time to block their view of Gregor. They now began to be really a little angry, one could not tell whether because of the old man's behavior or because it had just dawned on them that all unwittingly they had such a neighbor as Gregor next door. They demanded explanations of his father, they waved their arms like him, tugged uneasily at their beards, and only with reluctance backed towards their room. Meanwhile Gregor's sister, who stood there as if lost when her playing was so abruptly broken off, came to life again, pulled herself together all at once after standing for a while holding violin and bow in nervelessly hanging hands and staring at her music, pushed her violin into the lap of her mother, who was still sitting in her chair fighting asthmatically for breath, and ran into the lodgers' room to which they were now being shepherded by her father rather more quickly than before. One could see the pillows and blankets on the beds flying under her accustomed fingers and being laid in order. Before the lodgers had actually reached their room she had finished making the beds and slipped out.

The old man seemed once more to be so possessed by his mulish self-assertiveness that he was forgetting all the respect he should show to his lodgers. He kept driving them on and driving them on until in the very door of the bedroom the middle lodger stamped his foot loudly on the floor and so brought him to a halt. "I beg to announce," said the lodger, lifting one hand and looking also at Gregor's mother and sister, "that because of the disgusting conditions prevailing in this household and family"—here he spat on the floor with emphatic brevity—"I give you notice on the spot. Naturally I won't pay you a penny for the days I have lived here, on the contrary I shall consider bringing an action for damages against you, based on claims—believe me—that will be easily susceptible of proof." He ceased and stared straight in front of him, as if he expected something. In fact his two friends at once rushed into the breach with these words: "And we too give notice on the spot." On that he seized the door-handle and shut the door with a slam.

Gregor's father, groping with his hands, staggered forward and fell into his chair; it looked as if he were stretching himself there for his ordinary evening nap, but the marked jerkings of his head, which was as if uncontrollable, showed that he was far from asleep. Gregor had simply stayed quietly all the time on the spot where the lodgers had espied him. Disappointment at the failure of his plan, perhaps also the weakness arising from extreme hunger, made it impossible for him to move. He feared, with a fair degree of certainty, that at any moment the general tension would discharge itself in a combined attack upon him, and he lay waiting. He did not react even to the noise made by the violin as it fell off his mother's lap from under her trembling fingers and gave out a resonant note.

"My dear parents," said his sister, slapping her hand on the table by way of introduction, "things can't go on like this. Perhaps you don't realize that, but I do. I won't utter my brother's name in the presence of this creature, and so all I say is: we must try to get rid of it. We've tried to look after it and to put up with it as far as is humanly possible, and I don't think anyone could reproach us in the slightest."

"She is more than right," said Gregor's father to himself. His mother, who was still choking for lack of breath, began to cough hollowly into her hand with a wild look in her eyes.

His sister rushed over to her and held her forehead. His father's thoughts seemed to have lost their vagueness at Grete's words, he sat more upright, fingering his service cap that lay among the plates still lying on the table from the lodgers' supper, and from time to time looked at the still form of Gregor.

"We must try to get rid of it," his sister now said explicitly to her father, since    80
her mother was coughing too much to hear a word, "it will be the death of both
of you, I can see that coming. When one has to work as hard as we do, all of us,
one can't stand this continual torment at home on top of it. At least I can't stand
it any longer." And she burst into such a passion of sobbing that her tears
dropped on her mother's face, where she wiped them off mechanically.

"My dear," said the old man sympathetically, and with evident understanding, "but what can we do?"

Gregor's sister merely shrugged her shoulders to indicate the feeling of helplessness that had now overmastered her during her weeping fit, in contrast to her
former confidence.

"If he could understand us," said her father, half questioningly; Grete, still
sobbing, vehemently waved a hand to show how unthinkable that was.

"If he could understand us," repeated the old man, shutting his eyes to consider his daughter's conviction that understanding was impossible, "then perhaps
we might come to some agreement with him. But as it is—"

"He must go," cried Gregor's sister. "That's the only solution, Father. You    85
must just try to get rid of the idea that this is Gregor. The fact that we've believed
it for so long is the root of all our trouble. But how can it be Gregor? If this were
Gregor, he would have realized long ago that human beings can't live with such a
creature, and he'd have gone away on his own accord. Then we wouldn't have
any brother, but we'd be able to go on living and keep his memory in honor. As it
is, this creature persecutes us, drives away our lodgers, obviously wants the whole
apartment to himself and would have us all sleep in the gutter. Just look, Father,"
she shrieked all at once, "he's at it again!" And in an access of panic that was
quite incomprehensible to Gregor she even quitted her mother, literally thrusting
the chair from her as if she would rather sacrifice her mother than stay so near to
Gregor, and rushed behind her father, who also rose up, being simply upset by her
agitation, and half-spread his arms out as if to protect her.

Yet Gregor had not the slightest intention of frightening anyone, far less his
sister. He had only begun to turn round in order to crawl back to his room, but it
was certainly a startling operation to watch, since because of his disabled condition he could not execute the difficult turning movements except by lifting his
head and then bracing it against the floor over and over again. He paused and
looked round. His good intentions seemed to have been recognized; the alarm
had only been momentary. Now they were all watching him in melancholy
silence. His mother lay in her chair, her legs stiffly outstretched and pressed
together, her eyes almost closing for sheer weariness; his father and his sister were
sitting beside each other, his sister's arm around the old man's neck.

Perhaps I can go on turning round now, thought Gregor, and began his
labors again. He could not stop himself from panting with the effort, and had to
pause now and then to take breath. Nor did anyone harass him, he was left
entirely to himself. When he had completed the turn-round he began at once to
crawl straight back. He was amazed at the distance separating him from his room
and could not understand how in his weak state he had managed to accomplish

the same journey so recently, almost without remarking it. Intent on crawling as fast as possible, he barely noticed that not a single word, not an ejaculation from his family, interfered with his progress. Only when he was already in the doorway did he turn his head round, not completely, for his neck muscles were getting stiff, but enough to see that nothing had changed behind him except that his sister had risen to her feet. His last glance fell on his mother, who was not quite overcome by sleep.

Hardly was he well inside his room when the door was hastily pushed shut, bolted, and locked. The sudden noise in his rear startled him so much that his little legs gave beneath him. It was his sister who had shown such haste. She had been standing ready waiting and had made a light spring forward. Gregor had not even heard her coming, and she cried "At last!" to her parents as she turned the key in the lock.

"And what now?" said Gregor to himself, looking round in the darkness. Soon he made the discovery that he was now unable to stir a limb. This did not surprise him, rather it seemed unnatural that he should ever actually have been able to move on these feeble little legs. Otherwise he felt relatively comfortable. True, his whole body was aching, but it seemed that the pain was gradually growing less and would finally pass away. The rotting apple in his back and the inflamed area around it, all covered with soft dust, already hardly troubled him. He thought of his family with tenderness and love. The decision that he must disappear was one that he held to even more strongly than his sister, if that were possible. In this state of vacant and peaceful meditation he remained until the tower clock struck three in the morning. The first broadening of light in the world outside the window entered his consciousness once more. Then his head sank to the floor of its own accord and from his nostrils came the last faint flicker of his breath.

When the charwoman arrived early in the morning—what between her strength and her impatience she slammed all the doors so loudly, never mind how often she had been begged not to do so, that no one in the whole apartment could enjoy any quiet sleep after her arrival—she noticed nothing unusual as she took her customary peep into Gregor's room. She thought he was lying motionless on purpose, pretending to be in the sulks; she credited him with every kind of intelligence. Since she happened to have the long-handed broom in her hand she tried to tickle him up with it from the doorway. When that too produced no reaction she felt provoked and poked at him a little harder, and only when she had pushed him along the floor without meeting any resistance was her attention aroused. It did not take her long to establish the truth of the matter, and her eyes widened, she let out a whistle, yet did not waste much time over it but tore open the door of the Samsas' bedroom and yelled into the darkness at the top of her voice: "Just look at this, it's dead; it's lying here dead and done for!"

Mr. and Mrs. Samsa started up in their double bed and before they realized the nature of the charwoman's announcement had some difficulty in overcoming the shock of it. But then they got out of bed quickly, one on either side, Mr. Samsa throwing a blanket over his shoulders, Mrs. Samsa in nothing but her

90

nightgown; in this array they entered Gregor's room. Meanwhile the door of the living room opened, too, where Grete had been sleeping since the advent of the lodgers; she was completely dressed as if she had not been to bed, which seemed to be confirmed also by the paleness of her face. "Dead?" said Mrs. Samsa, looking questioningly at the charwoman, although she could have investigated for herself, and the fact was obvious enough without investigation. "I should say so," said the charwoman, proving her words by pushing Gregor's corpse a long way to one side with her broomstick. Mrs. Samsa made a movement as if to stop her, but checked it. "Well," said Mr. Samsa, "now thanks be to God." He crossed himself, and the three women followed his example. Grete, whose eyes never left the corpse, said: "Just see how thin he was. It's such a long time since he's eaten anything. The food came out again just as it went in." Indeed, Gregor's body was completely flat and dry, as could only now be seen when it was no longer supported by the legs and nothing prevented one from looking closely at it.

"Come in beside us, Grete, for a little while," said Mrs. Samsa with a tremulous smile, and Grete, not without looking back at the corpse, followed her parents into their bedroom. The charwoman shut the door and opened the window wide. Although it was so early in the morning a certain softness was perceptible in the fresh air. After all, it was already the end of March.

The three lodgers emerged from their room and were surprised to see no breakfast; they had been forgotten. "Where's our breakfast?" said the middle lodger peevishly to the charwoman. But she put her finger to her lips and hastily, without a word, indicated by gestures that they should go into Gregor's room. They did so and stood, their hands in the pockets of their somewhat shabby coats, around Gregor's corpse in the room where it was now fully light.

At that the door of the Samsas' bedroom opened and Mr. Samsa appeared in his uniform, his wife on one arm, his daughter on the other. They all looked a little as if they had been crying; from time to time Grete hid her face on her father's arm.

"Leave my house at once!" said Mr. Samsa, and pointed to the door without disengaging himself from the women. "What do you mean by that?" said the middle lodger, taken somewhat aback, with a feeble smile. The two others put their hands behind them and kept rubbing them together, as if in gleeful expectation of a fine set-to in which they were bound to come off the winners. "I mean just what I say," answered Mr. Samsa, and advanced in a straight line with his two companions towards the lodger. He stood his ground at first quietly, looking at the floor as if his thoughts were taking a new pattern in his head. "Then let us go, by all means," he said, and looked up at Mr. Samsa as if in a sudden access of humility he were expecting some renewed sanction for this decision. Mr. Samsa merely nodded briefly once or twice with meaning eyes. Upon that the lodger really did go with long strides into the hall, his two friends had been listening and had quite stopped rubbing their hands for some moments and now went scuttling after him as if afraid that Mr. Samsa might get into the hall before them and cut them off from their leader. In the hall they all three took their hats from the rack, their sticks from the umbrella stand, bowed in silence and quitted the apartment.

With a suspiciousness which proved quite unfounded Mr. Samsa and the two women followed them out to the landing; leaning over the banister they watched the three figures slowly but surely going down the long stairs, vanishing from sight at a certain turn of the staircase on every floor and coming into view again after a moment or so; the more they dwindled, the more the Samsa family's interest in them dwindled, and when a butcher's boy met them and passed them on the stairs coming up proudly with a tray on his head, Mr. Samsa and the two women soon left the landing and as if a burden had been lifted from them went back into their apartment.

They decided to spend this day in resting and going for a stroll; they had not only deserved such a respite from work but absolutely needed it. And so they sat down at the table and wrote three notes of excuse, Mr. Samsa to his board of management, Mrs. Samsa to her employer, and Grete to the head of her firm. While they were writing, the charwoman came in to say that she was going now, since her morning's work was finished. At first they only nodded without looking up, but as she kept hovering there they eyed her irritably. "Well?" said Mr. Samsa. The charwoman stood grinning in the doorway as if she had good news to impart to the family but meant not to say a word unless properly questioned. The small ostrich feather standing upright on her hat, which had annoyed Mr. Samsa ever since she was engaged, was waving gaily in all directions. "Well, what is it then?" asked Mrs. Samsa, who obtained more respect from the charwoman than the others. "Oh," said the charwoman, giggling so amiably that she could not at once continue, "just this, you don't need to bother about how to get rid of the thing next door. It's been seen to already." Mrs. Samsa and Grete bent over their letters again, as if preoccupied; Mr. Samsa, who perceived that she was eager to begin describing it all in detail, stopped her with a decisive hand. But since she was not allowed to tell her story, she remembered the great hurry she was in, being obviously deeply huffed: "Bye, everybody," she said, whirling off violently, and departed with a frightful slamming of doors.

"She'll be given notice tonight," said Mr. Samsa, but neither from his wife nor his daughter did he get any answer, for the charwoman seemed to have shattered again the composure they had barely achieved. They rose, went to the window and stayed there, clasping each other tight. Mr. Samsa turned in his chair to look at them and quietly observed them for a little. Then he called out: "Come along, now, do. Let bygones be bygones. And you might have some consideration for me." The two of them complied at once, hastened to him, caressed him and quickly finished their letters.

Then they all three left the apartment together, which was more than they had done for months, and went by tram into the open country outside the town. The tram, in which they were the only passengers, was filled with warm sunshine. Leaning comfortably back in their seats they canvassed their prospects for the future, and it appeared on closer inspection that these were not at all bad, for the jobs they had got, which so far they had never really discussed with each other, were all three admirable and likely to lead to better things later on. The greatest immediate improvement in their condition would of course arise from moving to another house; they wanted to take a smaller and cheaper but also better situated and more easily run apartment than the one they had, which Gregor had selected. While they were thus conversing, it struck both Mr. and Mrs. Samsa, almost at the same moment, as they became aware of their daughter's increasing vivacity, that in spite of all the sorrow of recent times, which had made her cheeks pale, she had bloomed into a pretty girl with a good figure. They grew quieter and half unconsciously exchanged glances of complete agreement, having come to the conclusion that it would soon be time to find a good husband for her. And it was like a confirmation of their new dreams and excellent intentions that at the end of their journey their daughter sprang to her feet first and stretched her young body.

## QUESTIONS

1. What was Gregor's occupation before his transformation? How did he come to his particular job? What keeps him working for his firm?
2. When Gregor wakes to discover he has become a gigantic insect, he is mostly intent on the practical implications of his metamorphosis—how to get out of bed, how to get to his job, and so on. He never wonders why or how he has been changed. What does this odd reaction suggest about Gregor?
3. When Gregor's parents first see the gigantic insect (paragraph 25), do they recognize it as their son? What do their initial reactions suggest about their attitude about their son?
4. How does each family member react to Gregor after his transformation? What is different about each reaction? What is similar?
5. What things about Gregor have been changed? What seems to have remained the same? List specific qualities.
6. "The Metamorphosis" takes place entirely in the Samsa family apartment. How does the story's setting shape its themes?
7. What family member first decides that they must "get rid of" the insect? What rationale is given? In what specific ways does the family's decision affect Gregor?
8. How does the family react to Gregor's death?
9. Does Grete change in the course of the story? If so, how does she change?
10. In what ways is Gregor's metamorphosis symbolic?

## SUGGESTIONS FOR WRITING

1. In a single, carefully thought-out paragraph, try to sum up what you believe Tolstoi is saying in *The Death of Ivan Ilych*.
2. Compare Tolstoi's short novel with another story of spiritual awakening: Flannery O'Connor's "Revelation" or "A Good Man Is Hard To Find," or perhaps Isaac Bashevis Singer's "Gimpel the Fool." In each, what brings about the enlightenment of the central character?
3. Compare the last thoughts of Ivan Ilych with the last thoughts of Katherine Anne Porter's Granny Weatherall, or Franz Kafka's Gregor Samsa.
4. Topic for a long term paper: Read either *War and Peace* or *Anna Karenina* and show how some theme present in *Ivan Ilych* is essential to it as well.
5. Explore how Gregor Samsa's metamorphosis into a giant insect is symbolic of his earlier life and relations with his family. (For a discussion of literary symbols, see Chapter 7, "Symbol.")

6. Topic for a medium-length paper (600–1,000 words): Discuss the mixture of comic and tragic elements in Kafka's *The Metamorphosis*. Is everything in the story sad and horrifying, or are there grotesquely funny moments as well?

7. Compare the story of *The Metamorphosis* to the plot of a famous horror film in which the protagonist is accidentally transformed into a monster. Some possible films include David Cronenberg's version of *The Fly* (1986), Neil Jordan's *The Company of Wolves* (1984), Val Lewton's *The Curse of the Cat People* (1944), Brian de Palma's *Carrie* (1976), George Waggner's original *The Wolf Man* (1940), and Jack Arnold's *The Incredible Shrinking Man* (1957). Discuss in which ways the two works are similar, and in which ways they differ. Does Kafka's work compel the reader to explore psychological questions untouched by the film?

8. Read a novel chosen from a list provided by your instructor, or chosen with your instructor's approval. Selecting some element in it that interests you, write an essay in which you demonstrate the importance to the book of that one element. You might write, for instance, on "The Character of the Monster in Mary Shelley's *Frankenstein*"; for an essay on theme, "A Plea for Paganism in D. H. Lawrence's *The Plumed Serpent*"; "Setting as a Force in Thomas Pynchon's *Vineland*"; "Symbolism in *The Scarlet Letter*" (or in *The Great Gatsby*). (Suggestion: You might find it helpful to read the discussion of analysis in "Writing about a Story" in Supplement: Writing.)

# 10 A Writer in Depth

## Flannery O'Connor

### EVERYTHING THAT RISES MUST CONVERGE — 1965

Mary Flannery O'Connor (she dropped the first name from her byline) spent most of her life (1925–1964) in Milledgeville, Georgia. While she was a student at Georgia State College for Women, in her home town, her fledgling stories won her local fame. She went on to study at the Writers Workshop of the University of Iowa, from which in 1946 she obtained her M.F.A. degree. On discovering that she was afflicted with lupus erythematosus, the progressive and incurable blood disease that had killed her father, O'Connor returned to Milledgeville to live with her mother, undergo treatment, raise peacocks, and write. The bulk of her work consists of two novels, Wise Blood (1952) and The Violent Bear It Away (1960); Complete Stories of Flannery O'Connor (1971); a

Flannery O'Connor

book of essays and talks, Mystery and Manners (1961); her brilliant, modest, cheerful letters, collected in The Habit of Being (1979); and terse book reviews written for Catholic newspapers in Georgia, collected in The Presence of Grace (1983). Since O'Connor's early death, her fiction, once decried as gratuitously violent and jarringly grotesque, has enjoyed a steady and triumphant rise in critical favor. Its themes derive from her devoutly Christian faith, but its dark and often hilarious humor derives from her own view—perhaps also from a native Georgian tradition of tall-tale telling.

Her doctor had told Julian's mother that she must lose twenty pounds on account of her blood pressure, so on Wednesday nights Julian had to take her downtown on the bus for a reducing class at the Y. The reducing class was designed for working girls over fifty, who weighed from 165 to 200 pounds. His mother was one of the slimmer ones, but she said ladies did not tell their age or weight. She would not ride the buses by herself at night since they had been integrated, and because the reducing class was one of her few pleasures, necessary for her health, and *free*, she said Julian could at least put himself out to take her, considering all she did for him. Julian did not like to consider all she did for him, but every Wednesday night he braced himself and took her.

She was almost ready to go, standing before the hall mirror, putting on her hat, while he, his hands behind him, appeared pinned to the door frame, waiting like Saint Sebastian for the arrows to begin piercing him°. The hat was new and had cost her seven dollars and a half. She kept saying, "Maybe I shouldn't have paid that for it. No, I shouldn't have. I'll take it off and return it tomorrow. I shouldn't have bought it."

Julian raised his eyes to heaven. "Yes, you should have bought it," he said. "Put it on and let's go." It was a hideous hat. A purple velvet flap came down on one side of it and stood up on the other; the rest of it was green and looked like a cushion with the stuffing out. He decided it was less comical than jaunty and pathetic. Everything that gave her pleasure was small and depressed him.

She lifted the hat one more time and set it down slowly on top of her head. Two wings of gray hair protruded on either side of her florid face, but her eyes, sky-blue, were as innocent and untouched by experience as they must have been when she was ten. Were it not that she was a widow who had struggled fiercely to feed and clothe and put him through school and who was supporting him still, "until he got on his feet," she might have been a little girl that he had to take to town.

"It's all right, it's all right," he said. "Let's go." He opened the door himself 5 and started down the walk to get her going. The sky was a dying violet and the houses stood out darkly against it, bulbous liver-colored monstrosities of a uniform ugliness though no two were alike. Since this had been a fashionable neighborhood forty years ago, his mother persisted in thinking they did well to have an apartment in it. Each house had a narrow collar of dirt around it in which sat, usually, a grubby child. Julian walked with his hands in his pockets, his head down and thrust forward and his eyes glazed with the determination to make himself completely numb during the time he would be sacrificed to her pleasure.

The door closed and he turned to find the dumpy figure, surmounted by the atrocious hat, coming toward him. "Well," she said, "you only live once and paying a little more for it, I at least won't meet myself coming and going."

"Some day I'll start making money," Julian said gloomily—he knew he never would—"and you can have one of those jokes whenever you take the fit." But

---

*Saint Sebastian . . . piercing him:* During the reign of the Roman emperor Diocletian (284–305 A.D.), Sebastian was sentenced to be shot to death by archers. Painters of the Italian Renaissance portrayed him riddled with arrows.

first they would move. He visualized a place where the nearest neighbors would be three miles away on either side.

"I think you're doing fine," she said, drawing on her gloves. "You've only been out of school a year. Rome wasn't built in a day."

She was one of the few members of the Y reducing class who arrived in hat and gloves and who had a son who had been to college: "It takes time," she said, "and the world is in such a mess. This hat looked better on me than any of the others, though when she brought it out I said, 'Take that thing back. I wouldn't have it on my head,' and she said, 'Now wait till you see it on,' and when she put it on me, I said, 'We-ull,' and she said, 'If you ask me, that hat does something for you and you do something for the hat, and besides,' she said, 'with that hat, you won't meet yourself coming and going.'"

Julian thought he could have stood his lot better if she had been selfish, if 10 she had been an old hag who drank and screamed at him. He walked along, saturated in depression, as if in the midst of his martyrdom he had lost his faith. Catching sight of his long, hopeless, irritated face, she stopped suddenly with a grief-stricken look, and pulled back on his arm. "Wait on me," she said. "I'm going back to the house and take this thing off and tomorrow I'm going to return it. I was out of my head. I can pay the gas bill with that seven-fifty."

He caught her arm in a vicious grip. "You are not going to take it back," he said. "I like it."

"Well," she said, "I don't think I ought . . . "

"Shut up and enjoy it," he muttered, more depressed than ever.

"With the world in the mess it's in," she said, "it's a wonder we can enjoy anything. I tell you, the bottom rail is on the top."

Julian sighed. 15

"Of course," she said, "if you know who you are, you can go anywhere." She said this every time he took her to the reducing class. "Most of them in it are not our kind of people," she said, "but I can be gracious to anybody. I know who I am."

"They don't give a damn for your graciousness," Julian said savagely. "Knowing who you are is good for one generation only. You haven't the foggiest idea where you stand now or who you are."

She stopped and allowed her eyes to flash at him. "I most certainly do know who I am," she said, "and if you don't know who you are, I'm ashamed of you."

"Oh hell," Julian said.

"Your great-grandfather was a former governor of this state," she said. "Your 20 grandfather was a prosperous landowner. Your grandmother was a Godhigh."

"Will you look around you," he said tensely, "and see where you are now?" and he swept his arm jerkily out to indicate the neighborhood, which the growing darkness at least made less dingy.

"You remain what you are," she said. "Your great-grandfather had a plantation and two hundred slaves."

"There are no more slaves," he said irritably.

"They were better off when they were," she said. He groaned to see that she was off on that topic. She rolled onto it every few days like a train on an open track. He knew every stop, every junction, every swamp along the way, and knew the exact point at which her conclusion would roll majestically into the station: "It's ridiculous. It's simply not realistic. They should rise, yes, but on their own side of the fence."

"Let's skip it," Julian said.

"The ones I feel sorry for," she said, "are the ones that are half white. They're tragic."

"Will you skip it?"

"Suppose we were half white. We would certainly have mixed feelings."

"I have mixed feelings now," he groaned.

"Well let's talk about something pleasant," she said. "I remember going to Grandpa's when I was a little girl. Then the house had double stairways that went up to what was really the second floor—all the cooking was done on the first. I used to like to stay down in the kitchen on account of the way the walls smelled. I would sit with my nose pressed against the plaster and take deep breaths. Actually the place belonged to the Godhighs but your grandfather Chestny paid the mortgage and saved it for them. They were in reduced circumstances," she said, "but reduced or not, they never forgot who they were."

"Doubtless that decayed mansion reminded them," Julian muttered. He never spoke of it without contempt or thought of it without longing. He had seen it once when he was a child before it had been sold. The double stairways had rotted and been torn down. Negroes were living in it. But it remained in his mind as his mother had known it. It appeared in his dreams regularly. He would stand on the wide porch, listening to the rustle of oak leaves, then wander through the high-ceilinged hall into the parlor that opened onto it and gaze at the worn rugs and faded draperies. It occurred to him that it was he, not she, who could have appreciated it. He preferred its threadbare elegance to anything he could name and it was because of it that all the neighborhoods they had lived in had been a torment to him—whereas she had hardly known the difference. She called her insensitivity "being adjustable."

"And I remember the old darky who was my nurse, Caroline. There was no better person in the world. I've always had a great respect for my colored friends," she said. "I'd do anything in the world for them and they'd . . . "

"Will you for God's sake get off that subject?" Julian said. When he got on a bus by himself, he made it a point to sit down beside a Negro, in reparation as it were for his mother's sins.

"You're mighty touchy tonight," she said. "Do you feel all right?"

"Yes I feel all right," he said. "Now lay off."

She pursed her lips. "Well, you certainly are in a vile humor," she observed. "I just won't speak to you at all."

They had reached the bus stop. There was no bus in sight and Julian, his hands still jammed in his pockets and his head thrust forward, scowled down the empty street. The frustration of having to wait on the bus as well as ride on it began to creep up his neck like a hot hand. The presence of his mother was borne in upon him as she gave a pained sigh. He looked at her bleakly. She was holding herself very erect under the preposterous hat, wearing it like a banner of her imaginary dignity. There was in him an evil urge to break her spirit. He suddenly unloosened his tie and pulled it off and put it in his pocket.

She stiffened. "Why must you look like *that* when you take me to town?" she said. "Why must you deliberately embarrass me?"

"If you'll never learn where you are," he said, "you can at least learn where I am."

"You look like a—thug," she said. 40

"Then I must be one," he murmured.

"I'll just go home," she said. "I will not bother you. If you can't do a little thing like that for me . . . "

Rolling his eyes upward, he put his tie back on. "Restored to my class," he muttered. He thrust his face toward her and hissed, "True culture is in the mind, the *mind*," he said, and tapped his head, "the mind."

"It's in the heart," she said, "and in how you do things and how you do things is because of who you *are*."

"Nobody in the damn bus cares who you are." 45

"I care who I am," she said icily.

The lighted bus appeared on top of the next hill and as it approached, they moved out into the street to meet it. He put his hand under her elbow and hoisted her up on the creaking step. She entered with a little smile, as if she were going into a drawing room where everyone had been waiting for her. While he put in the tokens, she sat down on one of the broad front seats for three which faced the aisle. A thin woman with protruding teeth and long yellow hair was sitting on the end of it. His mother moved up beside her and left room for Julian beside herself. He sat down and looked at the floor across the aisle where a pair of thin feet in red and white canvas sandals were planted.

His mother immediately began a general conversation meant to attract anyone who felt like talking. "Can it get any hotter?" she said and removed from her purse a folding fan, black with a Japanese scene on it, which she began to flutter before her.

"I reckon it might could," the woman with the protruding teeth said, "but I know for a fact my apartment couldn't get no hotter."

"It must get the afternoon sun," his mother said. She sat forward and looked 50 up and down the bus. It was half filled. Everybody was white. "I see we have the bus to ourselves," she said. Julian cringed.

"For a change," said the woman across the aisle, the owner of the red and white canvas sandals. "I come on one the other day and they were thick as fleas—up front and all through."

"The world is in a mess everywhere," his mother said. "I don't know how we've let it get in this fix."

"What gets my goat is all those boys from good families stealing automobile tires," the woman with the protruding teeth said. "I told my boy, I said you may not be rich but you been raised right and if I ever catch you in any such mess, they can send you on to the reformatory. Be exactly where you belong."

"Training tells," his mother said. "Is your boy in high school?"

"Ninth grade," the woman said.

"My son just finished college last year. He wants to write but he's selling typewriters until he gets started," his mother said.

The woman leaned forward and peered at Julian. He threw her such a malevolent look that she subsided against the seat. On the floor across the aisle there was an abandoned newspaper. He got up and got it and opened it out in front of him. His mother discreetly continued the conversation in a lower tone but the woman across the aisle said in a loud voice, "Well that's nice. Selling typewriters is close to writing. He can go right from one to the other."

"I tell him," his mother said, "that Rome wasn't built in a day."

Behind the newspaper Julian was withdrawing into the inner compartment of his mind where he spent most of his time. This was a kind of mental bubble in which he established himself when he could not bear to be a part of what was going on around him. From it he could see out and judge but in it he was safe from any kind of penetration from without. It was the only place where he felt free of the general idiocy of his fellows. His mother had never entered it but from it he could see her with absolute clarity.

The old lady was clever enough and he thought that if she had started from any of the right premises, more might have been expected of her. She lived according to the laws of her own fantasy world, outside of which he had never seen her set foot. The law of it was to sacrifice herself for him after she had first created the necessity to do so by making a mess of things. If he had permitted her sacrifices, it was only because her lack of foresight had made them necessary. All of her life had been a struggle to act like a Chestny without the Chestny goods, and to give him everything she thought a Chestny ought to have; but since, said she, it was fun to struggle, why complain? And when you had won, as she had won, what fun to look back on the hard times! He could not forgive her that she had enjoyed the struggle and that she thought *she* had won.

What she meant when she said she had won was that she had brought him up successfully and had sent him to college and that he had turned out so well— good looking (her teeth had gone unfilled so that his could be straightened), intelligent (he realized he was too intelligent to be a success), and with a future ahead of him (there was of course no future ahead of him). She excused his gloominess on the grounds that he was still growing up and his radical ideas on his lack of practical experience. She said he didn't yet know a thing about "life," that he hadn't even entered the real world—when already he was as disenchanted with it as a man of fifty.

The further irony of all this was that in spite of her, he had turned out so well. In spite of going to only a third-rate college, he had, on his own initiative, come out with a first-rate education; in spite of growing up dominated by a small mind, he had ended up with a large one; in spite of all her foolish views, he was free of prejudice and unafraid to face facts. Most miraculous of all, instead of being blinded by love for her as she was for him, he had cut himself emotionally free of her and could see her with complete objectivity. He was not dominated by his mother.

The bus stopped with a sudden jerk and shook him from his meditation. A woman from the back lurched forward with little steps and barely escaped falling in his newspaper as she righted herself. She got off and a large Negro got on. Julian kept his paper lowered to watch. It gave him a certain satisfaction to see injustice in daily operation. It confirmed his view that with a few exceptions there was no one worth knowing within a radius of three hundred miles. The Negro was well dressed and carried a briefcase. He looked around and then sat down on the other end of the seat where the woman with the red and white canvas sandals was sitting. He immediately unfolded a newspaper and obscured himself behind it. Julian's mother's elbow at once prodded insistently into his ribs. "Now you see why I won't ride on these buses by myself," she whispered.

The woman with the red and white canvas sandals had risen at the same time the Negro sat down and had gone further back in the bus and taken the seat of the woman who had got off. His mother leaned forward and cast her an approving look.

Julian rose, crossed the aisle, and sat down in the place of the woman with    65
the canvas sandals. From this position, he looked serenely across at his mother. Her face had turned an angry red. He stared at her, making his eyes the eyes of a stranger. He felt his tension suddenly lift as if he had openly declared war on her.

He would have liked to get in conversation with the Negro and to talk with him about art or politics or any subject that would be above the comprehension of those around them, but the man remained entrenched behind his paper. He was either ignoring the change of seating or had never noticed it. There was no way for Julian to convey his sympathy.

His mother kept her eyes fixed reproachfully on his face. The woman with the protruding teeth was looking at him avidly as if he were a type of monster new to her.

"Do you have a light?" he asked the Negro.

Without looking away from his paper, the man reached in his pocket and handed him a packet of matches.

"Thanks," Julian said. For a moment he held the matches foolishly. A NO    70
SMOKING sign looked down upon him from over the door. This alone would not have deterred him; he had no cigarettes. He had quit smoking some months before because he could not afford it. "Sorry," he muttered and handed back the matches. The Negro lowered the paper and gave him an annoyed look. He took the matches and raised the paper again.

His mother continued to gaze at him but she did not take advantage of his momentary discomfort. Her eyes retained their battered look. Her face seemed to be unnaturally red, as if her blood pressure had risen. Julian allowed no glimmer of sympathy to show on his face. Having got the advantage, he wanted desperately to keep it and carry it through. He would have liked to teach her a lesson that would last her a while, but there seemed no way to continue the point. The Negro refused to come out from behind his paper.

Julian folded his arms and looked stolidly before him, facing her but as if he did not see her, as if he had ceased to recognize her existence. He visualized a scene in which, the bus having reached their stop, he would remain in his seat and when she said, "Aren't you going to get off?" he would look at her as at a stranger who had rashly addressed him. The corner they got off on was usually deserted, but it was well lighted and it would not hurt her to walk by herself the four blocks to the Y. He decided to wait until the time came and then decide whether or not he would let her get off by herself. He would have to be at the Y at ten to bring her back, but he could leave her wondering if he was going to show up. There was no reason for her to think she could always depend on him.

He retired again into the high-ceilinged room sparsely settled with large pieces of antique furniture. His soul expanded momentarily but then he became aware of his mother across from him and the vision shriveled. He studied her coldly. Her feet in little pumps dangled like a child's and did not quite reach the floor. She was training on him an exaggerated look of reproach. He felt completely detached from her. At that moment he could with pleasure have slapped her as he would have slapped a particularly obnoxious child in his charge.

He began to imagine various unlikely ways by which he could teach her a lesson. He might make friends with some distinguished Negro professor or lawyer and bring him home to spend the evening. He would be entirely justified but her blood pressure would rise to 300. He could not push her to the extent of making her have a stroke, and moreover, he had never been successful at making any Negro friends. He had tried to strike up an acquaintance on the bus with some of the better types, with ones that looked like professors or ministers or lawyers. One morning he had sat down next to a distinguished-looking dark brown man who had answered his questions with a sonorous solemnity but who had turned out to be an undertaker. Another day he had sat down beside a cigar-smoking Negro with a diamond ring on his finger, but after a few stilted pleasantries, the Negro had rung the buzzer and risen, slipping two lottery tickets into Julian's hand as he climbed over him to leave.

He imagined his mother lying desperately ill and his being able to secure 75 only a Negro doctor for her. He toyed with that idea for a few minutes and then dropped it for a momentary vision of himself participating as a sympathizer in a sit-in demonstration. This was possible but he did not linger with it. Instead, he approached the ultimate horror. He brought home a beautiful suspiciously Negroid woman. Prepare yourself, he said. There is nothing you can do about it. This is the woman I've chosen. She's intelligent, dignified, even good, and she's suffered and she hasn't thought it *fun*. Now persecute us, go ahead and persecute us. Drive her out of here, but remember, you're driving me too. His eyes were narrowed and through the indignation he had generated, he saw his mother across the aisle, purple-faced, shrunken to the dwarf-like proportions of her moral nature, sitting like a mummy beneath the ridiculous banner of her hat.

He was tilted out of his fantasy again as the bus stopped. The door opened with a sucking hiss and out of the dark a large, gaily dressed, sullen-looking colored woman got on with a little boy. The child, who might have been four, had on a short plaid suit and a Tyrolean hat with a blue feather in it. Julian hoped that he would sit down beside him and that the woman would push in beside his mother. He could think of no better arrangement.

As she waited for her tokens, the woman was surveying the seating possibilities—he hoped with the idea of sitting where she was least wanted. There was something familiar-looking about her but Julian could not place what it was. She was a giant of a woman. Her face was set not only to meet opposition but to seek it out. The downward tilt of her large lower lip was like a warning sign: DON'T TAMPER WITH ME. Her bulging figure was encased in a green crepe dress and her feet overflowed in red shoes. She had on a hideous hat. A purple velvet flap came down on one side of it and stood up on the other; the rest of it was green and looked like a cushion with the stuffing out. She carried a mammoth red pocketbook that bulged throughout as if it were stuffed with rocks.

To Julian's disappointment, the little boy climbed up on the empty seat beside his mother. His mother lumped all children, black and white, into the common category, "cute," and she thought little Negroes were on the whole cuter than little white children. She smiled at the little boy as he climbed on the seat.

Meanwhile the woman was bearing down upon the empty seat beside Julian. To his annoyance, she squeezed herself into it. He saw his mother's face change as the woman settled herself next to him and he realized with satisfaction that this was more objectionable to her than it was to him. Her face seemed almost gray and there was a look of dull recognition in her eyes, as if suddenly she had sickened at some awful confrontation. Julian saw that it was because she and the woman had, in a sense, swapped sons. Though his mother would not realize the symbolic significance of this, she would feel it. His amusement showed plainly on his face.

The woman next to him muttered something unintelligible to herself. He was conscious of a kind of bristling next to him, a muted growling like that of an angry cat. He could not see anything but the red pocketbook upright on the bulging green thighs. He visualized the woman as she had stood waiting for her tokens—the ponderous figure, rising from the red shoes upward over the solid hips, the mammoth bosom, the haughty face, to the green and purple hat.

His eyes widened.

The vision of the two hats, identical, broke upon him with the radiance of a brilliant sunrise. His face was suddenly lit with joy. He could not believe that Fate had thrust upon his mother such a lesson. He gave a loud chuckle so that she would look at him and see that he saw. She turned her eyes on him slowly. The blue in them seemed to have turned a bruised purple. For a moment he had an uncomfortable sense of her innocence, but it lasted only a second before principle rescued him. Justice entitled him to laugh. His grin hardened until it said to her as plainly as if he were saying aloud: Your punishment exactly fits your pettiness. This should teach you a permanent lesson.

Her eyes shifted to the woman. She seemed unable to bear looking at him and to find the woman preferable. He became conscious again of the bristling presence at his side. The woman was rumbling like a volcano about to become active. His mother's mouth began to twitch slightly at one corner. With a sinking heart, he saw incipient signs of recovery on her face and realized that this was going to strike her suddenly as funny and was going to be no lesson at all. She

80

kept her eyes on the woman and an amused smile came over her face as if the woman were a monkey that had stolen her hat. The little Negro was looking up at her with large fascinated eyes. He had been trying to attract her attention for some time.

"Carver!" the woman said suddenly. "Come heah!"

When he saw that the spotlight was on him at last, Carver drew his feet up and turned himself toward Julian's mother and giggled.

"Carver!" the woman. "You heah me? Come heah!"

Carver slid down from the seat but remained squatting with his back against the base of it, his head turned slyly around toward Julian's mother, who was smiling at him. The woman reached a hand across the aisle and snatched him to her. He righted himself and hung backwards on her knees, grinning at Julian's mother. "Isn't he cute?" Julian's mother said to the woman with the protruding teeth.

"I reckon he is," the woman said without conviction.

The Negress yanked him upright but he eased out of her grip and shot across the aisle and scrambled, giggling wildly, onto the seat beside his love.

"I think he likes me," Julian's mother said, and smiled at the woman. It was the smile she used when she was being particularly gracious to an inferior. Julian saw everything lost. The lesson had rolled off her like rain on a roof.

The woman stood up and yanked the little boy off the seat as if she were snatching him from contagion. Julian could feel the rage in her at having no weapon like his mother's smile. She gave the child a sharp slap across his leg. He howled once and then thrust his head into her stomach and kicked his feet against her shins. "Be-have," she said vehemently.

The bus stopped and the Negro who had been reading the newspaper got off. The woman moved over and set the little boy down with a thump between herself and Julian. She held him firmly by the knee. In a moment he put his hands in front of his face and peeped at Julian's mother through his fingers.

"I see yoooooooo!" she said and put her hand in front of her face and peeped at him.

The woman slapped his hand down. "Quit yo' foolishness," she said, "before I knock the living Jesus out of you!"

Julian was thankful that the next stop was theirs. He reached up and pulled the cord. The woman reached up and pulled it at the same time. Oh my God, he thought. He had the terrible intuition that when they got off the bus together, his mother would open her purse and give the little boy a nickel. The gesture would be as natural to her as breathing. The bus stopped and the woman got up and lunged to the front, dragging the child, who wished to stay on, after her. Julian and his mother got up and followed. As they neared the door, Julian tried to relieve her of her pocketbook.

"No," she murmured. "I want to give the little boy a nickel."

"No!" Julian hissed. "No!"

She smiled down at the child and opened her bag. The bus door opened and the woman picked him up by the arm and descended with him, hanging at her hip. Once in the street she set him down and shook him.

Julian's mother had to close her purse while she got down the bus step but as soon as her feet were on the ground, she opened it again and began to rummage inside. "I can't find but a penny," she whispered, "but it looks like a new one."

"Don't do it!" Julian said fiercely between his teeth. There was a streetlight 100 on the corner and she hurried to get under it so that she could better see into her pocketbook. The woman was heading off rapidly down the street with the child still hanging backward on her hand.

"Oh little boy!" Julian's mother called and took a few quick steps and caught up with them just beyond the lamppost. "Here's a bright new penny for you," and she held out the coin, which shone bronze in the dim light.

The huge woman turned and for a moment stood, her shoulders lifted and her face frozen with frustrated rage, and stared at Julian's mother. Then all at once she seemed to explode like a piece of machinery that had been given one ounce of pressure too much. Julian saw the black fist swing out with the red pocketbook. He shut his eyes and cringed as he heard the woman shout, "He don't take nobody's pennies!" When he opened his eyes, the woman was disappearing down the street with the little boy staring wide-eyed over her shoulder. Julian's mother was sitting on the sidewalk.

"I told you not to do that," Julian said angrily. "I told you not to do that!"

He stood over her for a minute, gritting his teeth. Her legs were stretched out in front of her and her hat was on her lap. He squatted down and looked her in the face. It was totally expressionless. "You got exactly what you deserved," he said. "Now get up."

He picked up her pocketbook and put what had fallen out back in it. He 105 picked the hat up off her lap. The penny caught his eye on the sidewalk and he picked that up and let it drop before her eyes into the purse. Then he stood up and leaned over and held his hands out to pull her up. She remained immobile. He sighed. Rising above them on either side were black apartment buildings, marked with irregular rectangles of light. At the end of the block a man came out of a door and walked off in the opposite direction. "All right," he said, "suppose somebody happens by and wants to know why you're sitting on the sidewalk?"

She took the hand and, breathing hard, pulled heavily up on it and then stood for a moment, swaying slightly as if the spots of light in the darkness were circling around her. Her eyes, shadowed and confused, finally settled on his face. He did not try to conceal his irritation. "I hope this teaches you a lesson," he said. She leaned forward and her eyes raked his face. She seemed trying to determine his identity. Then, as if she found nothing familiar about him, she started off with a headlong movement in the wrong direction.

"Aren't you going on to the Y?" he asked.

"Home," she muttered.

"Well, are we walking?"

For answer she kept going. Julian followed along, his hands behind him. He 110 saw no reason to let the lesson she had had go without backing it up with an explanation of its meaning. She might as well be made to understand what had happened to her. "Don't think that was just an uppity Negro woman," he said.

"That was the whole colored race which will no longer take your condescending pennies. That was your black double. She can wear the same hat as you, and to be sure," he added gratuitously (because he thought it was funny), "it looked better on her than it did on you. What all this means," he said, "is that the old world is gone. The old manners are obsolete and your graciousness is not worth a damn." He thought bitterly of the house that had been lost for him. "You aren't who you think you are," he said.

She continued to plow ahead, paying no attention to him. Her hair had come undone on one side. She dropped her pocketbook and took no notice. He stooped and picked it up and handed it to her but she did not take it.

"You needn't act as if the world had come to an end," he said, "because it hasn't. From now on you've got to live in a new world and face a few realities for a change. Buck up," he said, "it won't kill you."

She was breathing fast.

"Let's wait on the bus," he said.

"Home," she said thickly. 115

"I hate to see you behave like this," he said. "Just like a child. I should be able to expect more of you." He decided to stop where he was and make her stop and wait for a bus. "I'm not going any farther," he said, stopping. "We're going on the bus."

She continued to go on as if she had not heard him. He took a few steps and caught her arm and stopped her. He looked into her face and caught his breath. He was looking into a face he had never seen before. "Tell Grandpa to come get me," she said.

He stared, stricken.

"Tell Caroline to come get me," she said.

Stunned, he let her go and she lurched forward again, walking as if one leg 120 were shorter than the other. A tide of darkness seemed to be sweeping her from him. "Mother!" he cried. "Darling, sweetheart, wait!" Crumpling, she fell to the pavement. He dashed forward and fell at her side, crying, "Mamma, Mamma!" He turned her over. Her face was fiercely distorted. One eye, large and staring, moved slightly to the left as if it had become unmoored. The other remained fixed on him, raked his face again, found nothing and closed.

"Wait here, wait here!" he cried and jumped up and began to run for help toward a cluster of lights he saw in the distance ahead of him. "Help, help!" he shouted, but his voice was thin, scarcely a thread of sound. The lights drifted farther away the faster he ran and his feet moved numbly as if they carried him nowhere. The tide of darkness seemed to sweep him back to her, postponing from moment to moment his entry into the world of guilt and sorrow.

## QUESTIONS

1. In what ways is Julian's mother, in her attitudes and assumptions, typical of an earlier generation of privileged people? What is her family history?
2. How would you describe Julian's attitude toward his mother? His attitude toward himself? The author's view of him? (How can you tell? Look for evidence.)

3. Julian thinks his mother lives in "her own fantasy world" (paragraph 60). How might it be charged that, ironically, he lives in a fantasy world of his own?
4. Think about the mother's offering Carver a penny—and the consequences of this small act. What are we to think of it? Do you take it, as perhaps Carver's mother does, to be a gesture of contempt and bigotry?
5. What does O'Connor make of the fact that Julian's and Carver's mothers happen to wear identical hats? How does Julian interpret this fact, and what does it tell us about him?
6. What do you make of the title, "Everything That Rises Must Converge"?
7. Try stating the theme of the story.

## Flannery O'Connor

A GOOD MAN IS HARD TO FIND                                                1955

The grandmother didn't want to go to Florida. She wanted to visit some of her connections in east Tennessee and she was seizing at every chance to change Bailey's mind. Bailey was the son she lived with, her only boy. He was sitting on the edge of his chair at the table, bent over the orange sports section of the *Journal*. "Now look here, Bailey," she said, "see here, read this," and she stood with one hand on her thin hip and the other rattling the newspaper at his bald head. "Here this fellow that calls himself The Misfit is aloose from the Federal Pen and headed toward Florida and you read here what it says he did to these people. Just you read it. I wouldn't take my children in any direction with a criminal like that aloose in it. I couldn't answer to my conscience if I did."

Bailey didn't look up from his reading so she wheeled around then and faced the children's mother, a young woman in slacks, whose face was as broad and innocent as a cabbage and was tied around with a green head-kerchief that had two points on the top like rabbit's ears. She was sitting on the sofa, feeding the baby his apricots out of a jar. "The children have been to Florida before," the old lady said. "You all ought to take them somewhere else for a change so they would see different parts of the world and be broad. They never have been to east Tennessee."

The children's mother didn't seem to hear her but the eight-year-old boy, John Wesley, a stocky child with glasses, said, "If you don't want to go to Florida, why dontcha stay at home?" He and the little girl, June Star, were reading the funny papers on the floor.

"She wouldn't stay at home to be queen for a day," June Star said without raising her yellow head.

"Yes and what would you do if this fellow, The Misfit, caught you?" the     5
grandmother said.

"I'd smack his face," John Wesley said.

"She wouldn't stay at home for a million bucks," June Star said. "Afraid she'd miss something. She has to go everywhere we go."

"All right, Miss," the grandmother said. "Just remember that the next time you want me to curl your hair."

June Star said her hair was naturally curly.

The next morning the grandmother was the first one in the car, ready to go.
She had her big black valise that looked like the head of a hippopotamus in one
corner, and underneath it she was hiding a basket with Pitty Sing, the cat, in it.
She didn't intend for the cat to be left alone in the house for three days because
he would miss her too much and she was afraid he might brush against one of the
gas burners and accidentally asphyxiate himself. Her son, Bailey, didn't like to
arrive at a motel with a cat.

She sat in the middle of the back seat with John Wesley and June Star on
either side of her. Bailey and the children's mother and the baby sat in front and
they left Atlanta at eight forty-five with the mileage on the car at 55890. The
grandmother wrote this down because she thought it would be interesting to say
how many miles they had been when they got back. It took them twenty minutes
to reach the outskirts of the city.

The old lady settled herself comfortably, removing her white cotton gloves
and putting them up with her purse on the shelf in front of the back window.
The children's mother still had on slacks and still had her hair tied up in a green
kerchief, but the grandmother had on a navy blue straw sailor hat with a bunch
of white violets on the brim and a navy blue dress with a small white dot in the
print. Her collars and cuffs were white organdy trimmed with lace and at her
neckline she had pinned a purple spray of cloth violets containing a sachet. In
case of an accident, anyone seeing her dead on the highway would know at once
that she was a lady.

She said she thought it was going to be a good day for driving, neither too
hot nor too cold, and she cautioned Bailey that the speed limit was fifty-five
miles an hour and that the patrolmen hid themselves behind billboards and small
clumps of trees and sped out after you before you had a chance to slow down. She
pointed out interesting details of the scenery: Stone Mountain; the blue granite
that in some places came up to both sides of the highway; the brilliant red clay
banks slightly streaked with purple; and the various crops that made rows of green
lace-work on the ground. The trees were full of silver-white sunlight and the
meanest of them sparkled. The children were reading comic magazines and their
mother had gone back to sleep.

"Let's go through Georgia fast so we won't have to look at it much," John
Wesley said.

"If I were a little boy," said the grandmother, "I wouldn't talk about my
native state that way. Tennessee has the mountains and Georgia has the hills."

"Tennessee is just a hillbilly dumping ground," John Wesley said, "and
Georgia is a lousy state too."

"You said it," June Star said.

"In my time," said the grandmother, folding her thin veined fingers, "children were more respectful of their native states and their parents and everything
else. People did right then. Oh look at the cute little pickaninny!" she said and
pointed to a Negro child standing in the door of a shack. "Wouldn't that make a
picture, now?" she asked and they all turned and looked at the little Negro out of
the back window. He waved.

"He didn't have any britches on," June Star said.

"He probably didn't have any," the grandmother explained. "Little niggers in the country don't have things like we do. If I could paint, I'd paint that picture," she said.

The children exchanged comic books.

The grandmother offered to hold the baby and the children's mother passed him over the front seat to her. She set him on her knee and bounced him and told him about the things they were passing. She rolled her eyes and screwed up her mouth and stuck her leathery thin face into his smooth bland one. Occasionally he gave her a faraway smile. They passed a large cotton field with five or six graves fenced in the middle of it, like a small island. "Look at the graveyard!" the grandmother said, pointing it out. "That was the old family burying ground. That belonged to the plantation."

"Where's the plantation?" John Wesley asked.

"Gone With the Wind," said the grandmother. "Ha. Ha."

When the children finished all the comic books they had brought, they opened the lunch and ate it. The grandmother ate a peanut butter sandwich and an olive and would not let the children throw the box and the paper napkins out the window. When there was nothing else to do they played a game by choosing a cloud and making the other two guess what shape it suggested. John Wesley took one the shape of a cow and June Star guessed a cow and John Wesley said, no, an automobile, and June Star said he didn't play fair, and they began to slap each other over the grandmother.

The grandmother said she would tell them a story if they would keep quiet. When she told a story, she rolled her eyes and waved her head and was very dramatic. She said once when she was a maiden lady she had been courted by a Mr. Edgar Atkins Teagarden from Jasper, Georgia. She said he was a very good-looking man and a gentleman and that he brought her a watermelon every Saturday afternoon with his initials cut in it, E. A. T. Well, one Saturday, she said, Mr. Teagarden brought the watermelon and there was nobody at home and he left it on the front porch and returned in his buggy to Jasper, but she never got the watermelon, she said, because a nigger boy ate it when he saw the initials, E. A. T.!

This story tickled John Wesley's funny bone and he giggled and giggled but June Star didn't think it was any good. She said she wouldn't marry a man that just brought her a watermelon on Saturday. The grandmother said she would have done well to marry Mr. Teagarden because he was a gentleman and had bought Coca-Cola stock when it first came out and that he had died only a few years ago, a very wealthy man.

They stopped at The Tower for barbecued sandwiches. The Tower was a part stucco and part wood filling station and dance hall set in a clearing outside of Timothy. A fat man named Red Sammy Butts ran it and there were signs stuck here and there on the building and for miles up and down the highway saying, TRY RED SAMMY'S FAMOUS BARBECUE. NONE LIKE FAMOUS RED SAMMY'S! RED SAM! THE FAT BOY WITH THE HAPPY LAUGH. A VETERAN! RED SAMMY'S YOUR MAN!

Red Sammy was lying on the bare ground outside The Tower with his head under a truck while a gray monkey about a foot high, chained to a small chinaberry tree, chattered nearby. The monkey sprang back into the tree and got on the highest limb as soon as he saw the children jump out of the car and run toward him.

Inside, The Tower was a long dark room with a counter at one end and tables at the other and dancing space in the middle. They all sat down at a board table next to the nickelodeon and Red Sam's wife, a tall burnt-brown woman with hair and eyes lighter than her skin, came and took their order. The children's mother put a dime in the machine and played "The Tennessee Waltz," and the grandmother said that tune always made her want to dance. She asked Bailey if he would like to dance but he only glared at her. He didn't have a naturally sunny disposition like she did and trips made him nervous. The grandmother's brown eyes were very bright. She swayed her head from side to side and pretended she was dancing in her chair. June Star said play something she could tap to so the children's mother put in another dime and played a fast number and June Star stepped out onto the dance floor and did her tap routine.

"Ain't she cute?" Red Sam's wife said, leaning over the counter. "Would you like to come be my little girl?"

"No I certainly wouldn't," June Star said. "I wouldn't live in a broken-down place like this for a million bucks!" and she ran back to the table.

"Ain't she cute?" the woman repeated, stretching her mouth politely.

"Ain't you ashamed?" hissed the grandmother.

Red Sam came in and told his wife to quit lounging on the counter and hurry up with these people's order. His khaki trousers reached just to his hip bones and his stomach hung over them like a sack of meal swaying under his shirt. He came over and sat down at a table nearby and let out a combination sigh and yodel. "You can't win," he said. "You can't win," and he wiped his sweating red face off with a gray handkerchief. "These days you don't know who to trust," he said. "Ain't that the truth?"

"People are certainly not nice like they used to be," said the grandmother.

"Two fellers come in here last week," Red Sammy said, "driving a Chrysler. It was a old beat-up car but it was a good one and these boys looked all right to me. Said they worked at the mill and you know I let them fellers charge the gas they bought? Now why did I do that?"

"Because you're a good man!" the grandmother said at once.

"Yes'm, I suppose so," Red Sam said as if he were struck with this answer.

His wife brought the orders, carrying the five plates all at once without a tray, two in each hand and one balanced on her arm. "It isn't a soul in this green world of God's that you can trust," she said. "And I don't count nobody out of that, not nobody," she repeated, looking at Red Sammy.

"Did you read about that criminal, The Misfit, that's escaped?" asked the grandmother.

"I wouldn't be a bit surprised if he didn't attact this place right here," said the woman. "If he hears about it being here, I wouldn't be none surprised to see him. If he hears it's two cent in the cash register, I wouldn't be a-tall surprised if he . . . "

"That'll do," Red Sam said. "Go bring these people their Co'-Colas," and the woman went off to get the rest of the order.

"A good man is hard to find," Red Sammy said. "Everything is getting terrible. I remember the day you could go off and leave your screen door unlatched. Not no more."

He and the grandmother discussed better times. The old lady said that in her opinion Europe was entirely to blame for the way things were now. She said the way Europe acted you would think we were made of money and Red Sam said it was no use talking about it, she was exactly right. The children ran outside into the white sunlight and looked at the monkey in the lacy chinaberry tree. He was busy catching fleas on himself and biting each one carefully between his teeth as if it were a delicacy.

They drove off again into the hot afternoon. The grandmother took cat naps and woke up every five minutes with her own snoring. Outside of Toombsboro she woke up and recalled an old plantation that she had visited in this neighborhood once when she was a young lady. She said the house had six white columns across the front and that there was an avenue of oaks leading up to it and two little wooden trellis arbors on either side in front where you sat down with your suitor after a stroll in the garden. She recalled exactly which road to turn off to get to it. She knew that Bailey would not be willing to lose any time looking at an old house, but the more she talked about it, the more she wanted to see it once again and find out if the little twin arbors were still standing. "There was a secret panel in this house," she said craftily, not telling the truth but wishing that she were, "and the story went that all the family silver was hidden in it when Sherman° came through but it was never found . . . "

"Hey!" John Wesley said. "Let's go see it! We'll find it! We'll poke all the woodwork and find it! Who lives there? Where do you turn off at? Hey, Pop, can't we turn off there?"

"We never have seen a house with a secret panel!" June Star shrieked. "Let's go to the house with the secret panel! Hey Pop, can't we go see the house with the secret panel!"

"It's not far from here, I know," the grandmother said. "It wouldn't take over twenty minutes."

Bailey was looking straight ahead. His jaw was as rigid as a horseshoe. "No," he said.

The children began to yell and scream that they wanted to see the house with the secret panel. John Wesley kicked the back of the front seat and June Star hung over her mother's shoulder and whined desperately into her ear that they never had any fun even on their vacation, that they could never do what THEY wanted to do. The baby began to scream and John Wesley kicked the back of the seat so hard that his father could feel the blows in his kidney.

---

*Sherman:* General William Tecumseh Sherman, Union commander, whose troops burned Atlanta in 1864, then made a devastating march to the sea.

"All right!" he shouted and drew the car to a stop at the side of the road. "Will you all shut up? Will you all just shut up for one second? If you don't shut up, we won't go anywhere."

"It would be very educational for them," the grandmother murmured.

"All right," Bailey said, "but get this: this is the only time we're going to stop for anything like this. This is the one and only time."

"The dirt road that you have to turn down is about a mile back," the grand- 55
mother directed. "I marked it when we passed."

"A dirt road," Bailey groaned.

After they had turned around and were headed toward the dirt road, the grandmother recalled other points about the house, the beautiful glass over the front doorway and the candle-lamp in the hall. John Wesley said that the secret panel was probably in the fireplace.

"You can't go inside this house," Bailey said. "You don't know who lives there."

"While you all talk to the people in front, I'll run around behind and get in a window," John Wesley suggested.

"We'll all stay in the car," his mother said. 60

They turned onto the dirt road and the car raced roughly along in a swirl of pink dust. The grandmother recalled the times when there were no paved roads and thirty miles was a day's journey. The dirt road was hilly and there were sudden washes in it and sharp curves on dangerous embankments. All at once they would be on a hill, looking down over the blue tops of trees for miles around, then the next minute, they would be in a red depression with the dust-coated trees looking down on them.

"This place had better turn up in a minute," Bailey said, "or I'm going to turn around."

The road looked as if no one had traveled on it for months.

"It's not much farther," the grandmother said and just as she said it, a horrible thought came to her. The thought was so embarrassing that she turned red in the face and her eyes dilated and her feet jumped up, upsetting her valise in the corner. The instant the valise moved, the newspaper top she had over the basket under it rose with a snarl and Pitty Sing, the cat, sprang onto Bailey's shoulder.

The children were thrown to the floor and their mother, clutching the baby, 65
was thrown out the door onto the ground; the old lady was thrown into the front seat. The car turned over once and landed right-side-up in a gulch off the side of the road. Bailey remained in the driver's seat with the cat—gray-striped with a broad white face and an orange nose—clinging to his neck like a caterpillar.

As soon as the children saw they could move their arms and legs, they scrambled out of the car, shouting, "We've had an ACCIDENT!" The grandmother was curled up under the dashboard, hoping she was injured so that Bailey's wrath would not come down on her all at once. The horrible thought she had had before the accident was that the house she had remembered so vividly was not in Georgia but in Tennessee.

Bailey removed the cat from his neck with both hands and flung it out the window against the side of a pine tree. Then he got out of the car and started looking for the children's mother. She was sitting against the side of the red gutted ditch, holding the screaming baby, but she only had a cut down her face and a broken shoulder. "We've had an ACCIDENT!" the children screamed in a frenzy of delight.

"But nobody's killed," June Star said with disappointment as the grandmother limped out of the car, her hat still pinned to her head but the broken front brim standing up at a jaunty angle and the violet spray hanging off the side. They all sat down in the ditch, except the children, to recover from the shock. They were all shaking.

"Maybe a car will come along," said the children's mother hoarsely.

"I believe I have injured an organ," said the grandmother, pressing her side, 70 but no one answered her. Bailey's teeth were clattering. He had on a yellow sport shirt with bright blue parrots designed in it and his face was as yellow as the shirt. The grandmother decided that she would not mention that the house was in Tennessee.

The road was about ten feet above and they could see only the tops of the trees on the other side of it. Behind the ditch they were sitting in there were more woods, tall and dark and deep. In a few minutes they saw a car some distance away on top of a hill, coming slowly as if the occupants were watching them. The grandmother stood up and waved both her arms dramatically to attract their attention. The car continued to come on slowly, disappeared around a bend and appeared again, moving even slower, on top of the hill they had gone over. It was a big black battered hearse-like automobile. There were three men in it.

It came to a stop just over them and for some minutes, the driver looked down with a steady expressionless gaze to where they were sitting, and didn't speak. Then he turned his head and muttered something to the other two and they got out. One was a fat boy in black trousers and a red sweat shirt with a silver stallion embossed on the front of it. He moved around on the right side of them and stood staring, his mouth partly open in a kind of loose grin. The other had on khaki pants and a blue striped coat and a gray hat pulled down very low, hiding most of his face. He came around slowly on the left side. Neither spoke.

The driver got out of the car and stood by the side of it, looking down at them. He was an older man than the other two. His hair was just beginning to gray and he wore silver-rimmed spectacles that gave him a scholarly look. He had a long creased face and didn't have on any shirt or undershirt. He had on blue jeans that were too tight for him and was holding a black hat and a gun. The two boys also had guns.

"We've had an ACCIDENT!" the children screamed.

The grandmother had the peculiar feeling that the bespectacled man was 75 someone she knew. His face was as familiar to her as if she had known him all her life but she could not recall who he was. He moved away from the car and began to come down the embankment, placing his feet carefully so that he wouldn't slip. He had on tan and white shoes and no socks, and his ankles were red and thin. "Good afternoon," he said. "I see you all had you a little spill."

"We turned over twice!" said the grandmother.

"Oncet," he corrected. "We seen it happen. Try their car and see will it run, Hiram," he said quietly to the boy with the gray hat.

"What you got that gun for?" John Wesley asked. "Whatcha gonna do with that gun?"

"Lady," the man said to the children's mother, "would you mind calling them children to sit down by you? Children make me nervous. I want all you all to sit down right together there where you're at."

"What are you telling US what to do for?" June Star asked.

Behind them the line of woods gaped like a dark open mouth. "Come here," said their mother.

"Look here now," Bailey began suddenly, "we're in a predicament! We're in . . ."

The grandmother shrieked. She scrambled to her feet and stood staring. "You're The Misfit!" she said. "I recognized you at once!"

"Yes'm," the man said, smiling slightly as if he were pleased in spite of himself to be known, "but it would have been better for all of you, lady, if you hadn't of reckernized me."

Bailey turned his head sharply and said something to his mother that shocked even the children. The old lady began to cry and The Misfit reddened.

"Lady," he said, "don't you get upset. Sometimes a man says things he don't mean. I don't reckon he meant to talk to you thataway."

"You wouldn't shoot a lady, would you?" the grandmother said and removed a clean handkerchief from her cuff and began to slap at her eyes with it.

The Misfit pointed the toe of his shoe into the ground and made a little hole and then covered it up again. "I would hate to have to," he said.

"Listen," the grandmother almost screamed, "I know you're a good man. You don't look a bit like you have common blood. I know you must come from nice people!"

"Yes ma'am," he said, "finest people in the world." When he smiled he showed a row of strong white teeth. "God never made a finer woman than my mother and my daddy's heart was pure gold," he said. The boy with the red sweat shirt had come around behind them and was standing with his gun at his hip. The Misfit squatted down on the ground. "Watch them children, Bobby Lee," he said. "You know they make me nervous." He looked at the six of them huddled together in front of him and he seemed to be embarrassed as if he couldn't think of anything to say. "Ain't a cloud in the sky," he remarked, looking up at it. "Don't see no sun but don't see no cloud neither."

"Yes, it's a beautiful day," said the grandmother. "Listen," she said, "you shouldn't call yourself The Misfit because I know you're a good man at heart. I can just look at you and tell."

"Hush!" Bailey yelled. "Hush! Everybody shut up and let me handle this!" He was squatting in the position of a runner about to sprint forward but he didn't move.

"I pre-chate that, lady," The Misfit said and drew a little circle in the ground with the butt of his gun.

"It'll take a half a hour to fix this here car," Hiram called, looking over the raised hood of it.

"Well, first you and Bobby Lee get him and that little boy to step over yon- <sup>95</sup> der with you," The Misfit said, pointing to Bailey and John Wesley. "The boys want to ast you something," he said to Bailey. "Would you mind stepping back in them woods there with them?"

"Listen," Bailey began, "we're in a terrible predicament! Nobody realizes what this is," and his voice cracked. His eyes were as blue and intense as the parrots in his shirt and he remained perfectly still.

The grandmother reached up to adjust her hat brim as if she were going to the woods with him but it came off in her hand. She stood staring at it and after a second she let it fall on the ground. Hiram pulled Bailey up by the arm as if he were assisting an old man. John Wesley caught hold of his father's hand and Bobby Lee followed. They went off toward the woods and just as they reached the dark edge, Bailey turned and supporting himself against a gray naked pine trunk, he shouted, "I'll be back in a minute, Mamma, wait on me!"

"Come back this instant!" his mother shrilled but they all disappeared into the woods.

"Bailey Boy!" the grandmother called in a tragic voice but she found she was looking at The Misfit squatting on the ground in front of her. "I just know you're a good man," she said desperately. "You're not a bit common!"

"Nome, I ain't a good man," The Misfit said after a second as if he had con- <sup>100</sup> sidered her statement carefully, "but I ain't the worst in the world neither. My daddy said I was a different breed of dog from my brothers and sisters. 'You know,' Daddy said, 'it's some that can live their whole life out without asking about it and it's others has to know why it is, and this boy is one of the latters. He's going to be into everything!'" He put on his black hat and looked up suddenly and then away deep into the woods as if he were embarrassed again. "I'm sorry I don't have on a shirt before you ladies," he said, hunching his shoulders slightly. "We buried our clothes that we had on when we escaped and we're just making do until we can get better. We borrowed these from some folks we met," he explained.

"That's perfectly all right," the grandmother said. "Maybe Bailey has an extra shirt in his suitcase."

"I'll look and see terrectly," The Misfit said.

"Where are they taking him?" the children's mother screamed.

"Daddy was a card himself," The Misfit said. "You couldn't put anything over on him. He never got in trouble with the Authorities though. Just had the knack of handling them."

"You could be honest too if you'd only try," said the grandmother. "Think <sup>105</sup> how wonderful it would be to settle down and live a comfortable life and not have to think about somebody chasing you all the time."

The Misfit kept scratching in the ground with the butt of his gun as if he were thinking about it. "Yes'm, somebody is always after you," he murmured.

The grandmother noticed how thin his shoulder blades were just behind his hat because she was standing up looking down on him. "Do you ever pray?" she asked.

He shook his head. All she saw was the black hat wiggle between his shoulder blades. "Nome," he said.

There was a pistol shot from the woods, followed closely by another. Then silence. The old lady's head jerked around. She could hear the wind move through the tree tops like a long satisfied insuck of breath. "Bailey Boy!" she called.

"I was a gospel singer for a while," The Misfit said. "I been most everything.  110
Been in the arm service, both land and sea, at home and abroad, been twict married, been an undertaker, been with the railroads, plowed Mother Earth, been in a tornado, seen a man burnt alive oncet," and he looked up at the children's mother and the little girl who were sitting close together, their faces white and their eyes glassy; "I even seen a woman flogged," he said.

"Pray, pray," the grandmother began, "pray, pray . . ."

"I never was a bad boy that I remember of," The Misfit said in an almost dreamy voice, "but somewheres along the line I done something wrong and got sent to the penitentiary. I was buried alive," and he looked up and held her attention to him by a steady stare.

"That's when you should have started to pray," she said. "What did you do to get sent up to the penitentiary that first time?"

"Turn to the right, it was a wall," The Misfit said, looking up again at the cloudless sky. "Turn to the left, it was a wall. Look up it was a ceiling, look down it was a floor. I forget what I done, lady. I set there and set there, trying to remember what it was I done and I ain't recalled it to this day. Oncet in a while, I would think it was coming to me, but it never come."

"Maybe they put you in by mistake," the old lady said vaguely.  115

"Nome," he said. "It wasn't no mistake. They had the papers on me."

"You must have stolen something," she said.

The Misfit sneered slightly. "Nobody had nothing I wanted," he said. "It was a head-doctor at the penitentiary said what I had done was kill my daddy but I known that for a lie. My daddy died in nineteen ought nineteen of the epidemic flu and I never had a thing to do with it. He was buried in the Mount Hopewell Baptist churchyard and you can go there and see for yourself."

"If you would pray," the old lady said, "Jesus would help you."

"That's right," The Misfit said.  120

"Well then, why don't you pray?" she asked trembling with delight suddenly.

"I don't want no hep," he said. "I'm doing all right by myself."

Bobby Lee and Hiram came ambling back from the woods. Bobby Lee was dragging a yellow shirt with bright blue parrots in it.

"Thow me that shirt, Bobby Lee," The Misfit said. The shirt came flying at him and landed on his shoulder and he put it on. The grandmother couldn't name what the shirt reminded her of. "No, lady," The Misfit said while he was buttoning it up, "I found out the crime don't matter. You can do one thing or you can do another, kill a man or take a tire off his car, because sooner or later you're going to forget what it was you done and just be punished for it."

The children's mother had begun to make heaving noises as if she couldn't 125 get her breath. "Lady," he asked, "would you and that little girl like to step off yonder with Bobby Lee and Hiram and join your husband?"

"Yes, thank you," the mother said faintly. Her left arm dangled helplessly and she was holding the baby, who had gone to sleep, in the other. "Hep that lady up, Hiram," The Misfit said as she struggled to climb out of the ditch, "and Bobby Lee, you hold onto that little girl's hand."

"I don't want to hold hands with him," June Star said. "He reminds me of a pig."

The fat boy blushed and laughed and caught her by the arm and pulled her off into the woods after Hiram and her mother.

Alone with The Misfit, the grandmother found that she had lost her voice. There was not a cloud in the sky nor any sun. There was nothing around her but woods. She wanted to tell him that he must pray. She opened and closed her mouth several times before anything came out. Finally she found herself saying, "Jesus. Jesus," meaning, Jesus will help you, but the way she was saying it, it sounded as if she might be cursing.

"Yes'm," The Misfit said as if he agreed. "Jesus thown everything off balance. 130 It was the same case with Him as with me except He hadn't committed any crime and they could prove I had committed one because they had the papers on me. Of course," he said, "they never shown me my papers. That's why I sign myself now. I said long ago, you get you a signature and sign everything you do and keep a copy of it. Then you'll know what you done and you can hold up the crime to the punishment and see do they match and in the end you'll have something to prove you ain't been treated right. I call myself The Misfit," he said, "because I can't make what all I done wrong fit what all I gone through in punishment."

There was a piercing scream from the woods, followed closely by a pistol report. "Does it seem right to you, lady, that one is punished a heap and another ain't punished at all?"

"Jesus!" the old lady cried. "You've got good blood! I know you wouldn't shoot a lady! I know you come from nice people! Pray! Jesus, you ought not to shoot a lady. I'll give you all the money I've got!"

"Lady," The Misfit said, looking beyond her far into the woods, "there never was a body that give the undertaker a tip."

There were two more pistol reports and the grandmother raised her head like a parched old turkey hen crying for water and called, "Bailey Boy, Bailey Boy!" as if her heart would break.

"Jesus was the only One that ever raised the dead," The Misfit continued, 135 "and He shouldn't have done it. He thown everything off balance. If He did what He said, then it's nothing for you to do but thow away everything and follow Him, and if He didn't, then it's nothing for you to do but enjoy the few minutes you got left the best way you can—by killing somebody or burning down his house or doing some other meanness to him. No pleasure but meanness," he said and his voice had become almost a snarl.

"Maybe He didn't raise the dead," the old lady mumbled, not knowing what she was saying and feeling so dizzy that she sank down in the ditch with her legs twisted under her.

"I wasn't there so I can't say He didn't," The Misfit said. "I wisht I had of been there," he said, hitting the ground with his fist. "It ain't right I wasn't there because if I had of been there I would of known. Listen lady," he said in a high voice, "if I had of been there I would of known and I wouldn't be like I am now." His voice seemed about to crack and the grandmother's head cleared for an instant. She saw the man's face twisted close to her own as if he were going to cry and she murmured, "Why you're one of my babies. You're one of my own children!" She reached out and touched him on the shoulder. The Misfit sprang back as if a snake had bitten him and shot her three times through the chest. Then he put his gun down on the ground and took off his glasses and began to clean them.

Hiram and Bobby Lee returned from the woods and stood over the ditch, looking down at the grandmother who half sat and half lay in a puddle of blood with her legs crossed under her like a child's and her face smiling up at the cloudless sky.

Without his glasses, The Misfit's eyes were red-rimmed and pale and defenseless-looking. "Take her off and thow her where you thown the others," he said, picking up the cat that was rubbing itself against his leg.

"She was a talker, wasn't she?" Bobby Lee said, sliding down the ditch with a yodel. 140

"She would of been a good woman," The Misfit said, "if it had been somebody there to shoot her every minute of her life."

"Some fun!" Bobby Lee said.

"Shut up, Bobby Lee," The Misfit said. "It's no real pleasure in life."

## QUESTIONS

1. How early in the story does O'Connor foreshadow what will happen in the end? What further hints does she give us along the way? How does the scene at Red Sammy's Barbecue advance the story toward its conclusion?
2. When we first meet the grandmother, what kind of person is she? What do her various remarks reveal about her? Does she remain a static character, or does she in any way change as the story goes on?
3. When the grandmother's head clears for an instant (paragraph 137), what does she suddenly understand? Reread this passage carefully and prepare to discuss what it means.
4. What do we learn from the conversation between The Misfit and the grandmother while the others go out to the woods? How would you describe The Misfit's outlook on the world? Compare it with the author's, from whatever you know about Flannery O'Connor and from the story itself.
5. How would you respond to a reader who complained, "The title of this story is just an obvious platitude"?

The doctor's waiting room, which was very small, was almost full when the Turpins entered and Mrs. Turpin, who was very large, made it look even smaller by her presence. She stood looming at the head of the magazine table set in the center of it, a living demonstration that the room was inadequate and ridiculous. Her little bright black eyes took in all the patients as she sized up the seating situation. There was one vacant chair and a place on a sofa occupied by a blond child in a dirty blue romper who should have been told to move over and make room for the lady. He was five or six, but Mrs. Turpin saw at once that no one was going to tell him to move over. He was slumped down in the seat, his arms idle at his sides and his eyes idle in his head; his nose ran unchecked.

Mrs. Turpin put a firm hand on Claud's shoulder and said in a voice that included anyone who wanted to listen, "Claud, you sit in that chair there," and gave him a push down into the vacant one. Claud was florid and bald and sturdy, somewhat shorter than Mrs. Turpin, but he sat down as if he were accustomed to doing what she told him to.

Mrs. Turpin remained standing. The only man in the room besides Claud was a lean stringy old fellow with a rusty hand spread out on each knee, whose eyes were closed as if he were asleep or dead or pretending to be so as not to get up and offer her his seat. Her gaze settled agreeably on a well-dressed grey-haired lady whose eyes met hers and whose expression said: if that child belonged to me, he would have some manners and move over—there's plenty of room there for you and him too.

Claud looked up with a sigh and made as if to rise.

"Sit down," Mrs. Turpin said. "You know you're not supposed to stand on          5
that leg. He has an ulcer on his leg," she explained.

Claud lifted his foot onto the magazine table and rolled his trouser leg up to reveal a purple swelling on a plump marble-white calf.

"My!" the pleasant lady said. "How did you do that?"

"A cow kicked him," Mrs. Turpin said.

"Goodness!" said the lady.

Claud rolled his trouser leg down.                                              10

"Maybe the little boy would move over," the lady suggested, but the child did not stir.

"Somebody will be leaving in a minute," Mrs. Turpin said. She could not understand why a doctor—with as much money as they made charging five dollars a day to just stick their head in the hospital door and look at you—couldn't afford a decent-sized waiting room. This one was hardly bigger than a garage. The table was cluttered with limp-looking magazines and at one end of it there was a big green glass ash tray full of cigaret butts and cotton wads with little blood spots on them. If she had had anything to do with the running of the place, that would have been emptied every so often. There were no chairs against the wall at the head of the room. It had a rectangular-shaped panel in it that permitted a view of the office where the nurse came and went and the secretary listened to the radio. A plastic fern in a gold pot sat in the opening and trailed its fronds down almost to the floor. The radio was softly playing gospel music.

Just then the inner door opened and a nurse with the highest stack of yellow hair Mrs. Turpin had ever seen put her face in the crack and called for the next patient. The woman sitting beside Claud grasped the two arms of her chair and hoisted herself up; she pulled her dress free from her legs and lumbered through the door where the nurse had disappeared.

Mrs. Turpin eased into the vacant chair, which held her tight as a corset. "I wish I could reduce," she said, and rolled her eyes and gave a comic sigh.

"Oh, *you* aren't fat," the stylish lady said.                                                                    15

"Ooooo I am too," Mrs. Turpin said. "Claud he eats all he wants to and never weighs over one hundred and seventy-five pounds, but me I just look at something good to eat and I gain some weight," and her stomach and shoulders shook with laughter. "You can eat all you want to, can't you, Claud?" she asked, turning to him.

Claud only grinned.

"Well, as long as you have such a good disposition," the stylish lady said, "I don't think it makes a bit of difference what size you are. You just can't beat a good disposition."

Next to her was a fat girl of eighteen or nineteen, scowling into a thick blue book which Mrs. Turpin saw was entitled *Human Development*. The girl raised her head and directed her scowl at Mrs. Turpin as if she did not like her looks. She appeared annoyed that anyone should speak while she tried to read. The poor girl's face was blue with acne and Mrs. Turpin thought how pitiful it was to have a face like that at that age. She gave the girl a friendly smile but the girl only scowled the harder. Mrs. Turpin herself was fat but she had always had good skin, and, though she was forty-seven years old, there was not a wrinkle in her face except around her eyes from laughing too much.

Next to the ugly girl was the child, still in exactly the same position, and    20
next to him was a thin leathery old woman in a cotton print dress. She and Claud had three sacks of chicken feed in their pump house that was in the same print. She had seen from the first that the child belonged with the old woman. She could tell by the way they sat—kind of vacant and white-trashy, as if they would sit there until Doomsday if nobody called and told them to get up. And at right angles but next to the well-dressed pleasant lady was a lank-faced woman who was certainly the child's mother. She had on a yellow sweat shirt and wine-colored slacks, both gritty-looking, and the rims of her lips were stained with snuff. Her dirty yellow hair was tied behind with a little piece of red paper ribbon. Worse than niggers any day, Mrs. Turpin thought.

The gospel hymn playing was, "When I looked up and He looked down," and Mrs. Turpin, who knew it, supplied the last line mentally, "And wona these days I know I'll we-eara crown."

Without appearing to, Mrs. Turpin always noticed people's feet. The well-dressed lady had on red and grey suede shoes to match her dress. Mrs. Turpin had on her good black patent leather pumps. The ugly girl had on Girl Scout shoes and heavy socks. The old woman had on tennis shoes and the white-trashy mother had on what appeared to be bedroom slippers, black straw with gold braid threaded through them—exactly what you would have expected her to have on.

Sometimes at night when she couldn't go to sleep, Mrs. Turpin would occupy herself with the question of who she would have chosen to be if she couldn't have been herself. If Jesus had said to her before he made her, "There's only two places available for you. You can either be a nigger or white-trash," what would she have said? "Please, Jesus, please," she would have said, "just let me wait until there's another place available," and he would have said, "No, you have to go right now and I have only those two places so make up your mind." She would have wiggled and squirmed and begged and pleaded but it would have been no use and finally she would have said, "All right, make me a nigger then—but that don't mean a trashy one." And he would have made her a neat clean respectable Negro-woman, herself but black.

Next to the child's mother was a red-headed youngish woman, reading one of the magazines and working a piece of chewing gum, hell for leather, as Claud would say. Mrs. Turpin could not see the woman's feet. She was not white-trash, just common. Sometimes Mrs. Turpin occupied herself at night naming the classes of people. On the bottom of the heap were most colored people, not the kind she would have been if she had been one, but most of them; then next to them— not above, just away from—were the white-trash; then above them were the home-owners, and above them the home-and-land owners, to which she and Claud belonged. Above she and Claud° were people with a lot of money and much bigger houses and much more land. But here the complexity of it would begin to bear in on her, for some of the people with a lot of money were common and ought to be below she and Claud and some of the people who had good blood had lost their money and had to rent and then there were colored people who owned their homes and land as well. There was a colored dentist in town who had two red Lincolns and a swimming pool and a farm with registered white-face cattle on it. Usually by the time she had fallen asleep all the classes of people were moiling and roiling around in her head, and she would dream they were all crammed in together in a box car, being ridden off to be put in a gas oven.

"That's a beautiful clock," she said and nodded to her right. It was a big wall 25 clock, the face encased in a brass sunburst.

"Yes, it's very pretty," the stylish lady said agreeably. "And right on the dot too," she added, glancing at her watch.

The ugly girl beside her cast an eye upward at the clock, smirked, then looked directly at Mrs. Turpin and smirked again. Then she returned her eyes to her book. She was obviously the lady's daughter because, although they didn't look anything alike as to disposition, they both had the same shape of face and

---

*Above she and Claud:* ungrammatical construction. Putting herself first, Mrs. Turpin presumably would say (if she were speaking aloud), "Above I and Claud . . . "

the same blue eyes. On the lady they sparkled pleasantly but in the girl's seared face they appeared alternately to smolder and to blaze.

What if Jesus had said, "All right, you can be white-trash or a nigger or ugly"!

Mrs. Turpin felt an awful pity for the girl, though she thought it was one thing to be ugly and another to act ugly.

The woman with the snuff-stained lips turned around in her chair and 30 looked up at the clock. Then she turned back and appeared to look a little to the side of Mrs. Turpin. There was a cast in one of her eyes. "You want to know wher you can get one of them ther clocks?" she asked in a loud voice.

"No, I already have a nice clock," Mrs. Turpin said. Once somebody like her got a leg in the conversation, she would be all over it.

"You can get you one with green stamps," the woman said. "That's most likely wher he got hisn. Save you up enough, you can get you most anythang. I got me some joo'ry."

Ought to have got you a wash rag and some soap, Mrs. Turpin thought.

"I get contour sheets with mine," the pleasant lady said.

The daughter slammed her book shut. She looked straight in front of her, 35 directly through Mrs. Turpin and on through the yellow curtain and the plate glass window which made the wall behind her. The girl's eyes seemed lit all of a sudden with a peculiar light, an unnatural light like night road signs give. Mrs. Turpin turned her head to see if there was anything going on outside that she should see, but she could not see anything. Figures passing cast only a pale shadow through the curtain. There was no reason the girl should single her out for her ugly looks.

"Miss Finley," the nurse said, cracking the door. The gum chewing woman got up and passed in front of her and Claud and went into the office. She had on red high-heeled shoes.

Directly across the table, the ugly girl's eyes were fixed on Mrs. Turpin as if she had some very special reason for disliking her.

"This is wonderful weather, isn't it?" the girl's mother said.

"It's good weather for cotton if you can get the niggers to pick it," Mrs. Turpin said, "but niggers don't want to pick cotton any more. You can't get the white folks to pick it and now you can't get the niggers—because they got to be right up there with the white folks."

"They gonna *try* anyways," the white-trash woman said, leaning forward. 40

"Do you have one of those cotton-picking machines?" the pleasant lady asked.

"No," Mrs. Turpin said, "they leave half the cotton in the field. We don't have much cotton anyway. If you want to make it farming now, you have to have a little of everything. We got a couple of acres of cotton and a few hogs and chickens and just enough white-face that Claud can look after them himself."

"One thang I don't want," the white-trash woman said, wiping her mouth with the back of her hands. "Hogs. Nasty stinking things, a-gruntin and a-rootin all over the place."

Mrs. Turpin gave her the merest edge of her attention. "Our hogs are not dirty and they don't stink," she said. "They're cleaner than some children I've seen. Their feet never touch the ground. We have a pig-parlor—that's where you raise them on concrete," she explained to the pleasant lady, "and Claud scoots them down with the hose every afternoon and washes off the floor." Cleaner by far than that child right there, she thought. Poor nasty little thing. He had not moved except to put the thumb of his dirty hand into his mouth.

The woman turned her face away from Mrs. Turpin. "I know I wouldn't scoot down no hog with no hose," she said to the wall.    45

You wouldn't have no hog to scoot down, Mrs. Turpin said to herself.

"A-gruntin and a-rootin and a-groanin," the woman muttered.

"We got a little of everything," Mrs. Turpin said to the pleasant lady. "It's no use in having more than you can handle yourself with help like it is. We found enough niggers to pick our cotton this year but Claud he has to go after them and take them home again in the evening. They can't walk that half a mile. No they can't. I tell you," she said and laughed merrily, "I sure am tired of buttering up niggers, but you got to love em if you want em to work for you. When they come in the morning, I run out and I say, 'Hi yawl this morning?' and when Claud drives them off to the field I just wave to beat the band and they just wave back." And she waved her hand rapidly to illustrate.

"Like you read out of the same book," the lady said, showing she understood perfectly.

"Child, yes," Mrs. Turpin said. "And when they come in from the field, I run    50 out with a bucket of icewater. That's the way it's going to be from now on," she said. "You may as well face it."

"One thang I know," the white-trash woman said. "Two thangs I ain't going to do: love no niggers or scoot down no hog with no hose." And she let out a bark of contempt.

The look that Mrs. Turpin and the pleasant lady exchanged indicated they both understood that you had to *have* certain things before you could *know* certain things. But every time Mrs. Turpin exchanged a look with the lady, she was aware that the ugly girl's peculiar eyes were still on her, and she had trouble bringing her attention back to the conversation.

"When you got something," she said, "you got to look after it." And when you ain't got a thing but breath and britches, she added to herself, you can afford to come to town every morning and just sit on the Court House coping and spit.

A grotesque revolving shadow passed across the curtain behind her and was thrown palely on the opposite wall. Then a bicycle clattered down against the outside of the building. The door opened and a colored boy glided in with a tray from the drug store. It had two large red and white paper cups on it with tops on them. He was a tall, very black boy in discolored white pants and a green nylon shirt. He was chewing gum slowly, as if to music. He set the tray down in the office opening next to the fern and stuck his head through to look for the secretary. She was not in there. He rested his arms on the ledge and waited, his narrow bottom stuck out, swaying slowly to the left and right. He raised a hand over his head and scratched the base of his skull.

"You see that button there, boy?" Mrs. Turpin said. "You can punch that and 55 she'll come. She's probably in the back somewhere."

"Is thas right?" the boy said agreeably, as if he had never seen the button before. He leaned to the right and put his finger on it. "She sometime out," he said and twisted around to face his audience, his elbows behind him on the counter. The nurse appeared and he twisted back again. She handed him a dollar and he rooted in his pocket and made the change and counted it out to her. She gave him fifteen cents for a tip and he went out with the empty tray. The heavy door swung to slowly and closed at length with the sound of suction. For a moment no one spoke.

"They ought to send all them niggers back to Africa," the white-trash woman said. "That's wher they come from in the first place."

"Oh, I couldn't do without my good colored friends," the pleasant lady said.

"There's a heap of things worse than a nigger," Mrs. Turpin agreed. "It's all kinds of them just like it's all kinds of us."

"Yes, and it takes all kinds to make the world go round," the lady said in her 60 musical voice.

As she said it, the raw-complexioned girl snapped her teeth together. Her lower lip turned downwards and inside out, revealing the pale pink inside of her mouth. After a second it rolled back up. It was the ugliest face Mrs. Turpin had ever seen anyone make and for a moment she was certain that the girl had made it at her. She was looking at her as if she had known and disliked her all her life—all of Mrs. Turpin's life, it seemed too, not just all the girl's life. Why, girl, I don't even know you, Mrs. Turpin said silently.

She forced her attention back to the discussion. "It wouldn't be practical to send them back to Africa," she said. "They wouldn't want to go. They got it too good here."

"Wouldn't be what they wanted—if I had anythang to do with it," the woman said.

"It wouldn't be a way in the world you could get all the niggers back over there," Mrs. Turpin said. "They'd be hiding out and lying down and turning sick on you and wailing and hollering and raring and pitching. It wouldn't be a way in the world to get them over there."

"They got over here," the trashy woman said. "Get back like they got over." 65

"It wasn't so many of them then," Mrs. Turpin explained.

The woman looked at Mrs. Turpin as if here was an idiot indeed but Mrs. Turpin was not bothered by the look, considering where it came from.

"Nooo," she said, "they're going to stay here where they can go to New York and marry white folks and improve their color. That's what they all want to do, every one of them, improve their color."

"You know what comes of that, don't you?" Claud asked.

"No, Claud, what?" Mrs. Turpin said. 70

Claud's eyes twinkled. "White-faced niggers," he said with never a smile.

Everybody in the office laughed except the white-trash and the ugly girl. The girl gripped the book in her lap with white fingers. The trashy woman looked around her from face to face as if she thought they were all idiots. The old woman in the feed sack dress continued to gaze expressionless across the floor at the hightop shoes of the man opposite her, the one who had been pretending to be asleep when the Turpins came in. He was laughing heartily, his hands still spread out on his knees. The child had fallen to the side and was lying now almost face down in the old woman's lap.

While they recovered from their laughter, the nasal chorus on the radio kept the room from silence.

> "You go to blank blank
> And I'll go to mine
> But we'll all blank along
> To-geth-ther,
> And all along the blank
> We'll hep each other out
> Smile-ling in any kind of
> Weath-ther!"

Mrs. Turpin didn't catch every word but she caught enough to agree with the spirit of the song and it turned her thoughts sober. To help anybody out that needed it was her philosophy of life. She never spared herself when she found somebody in need, whether they were white or black, trash or decent. And of all she had to be thankful for, she was most thankful that this was so. If Jesus had said, "You can be high society and have all the money you want and be thin and svelte-like, but you can't be a good woman with it," she would have had to say, "Well don't make me that then. Make me a good woman and it don't matter what else, how fat or how ugly or how poor!" Her heart rose. He had not made her a nigger or white-trash or ugly! He had made her herself and given her a little of everything. Jesus, thank you! she said. Thank you thank you thank you! Whenever she counted her blessings she felt as buoyant as if she weighed one hundred and twenty-five pounds instead of one hundred and eighty.

"What's wrong with your little boy?" the pleasant lady asked the white-trashy woman.

"He has a ulcer," the woman said proudly. "He ain't give me a minute's peace since he was born. Him and her are just alike," she said, nodding at the old woman, who was running her leathery fingers through the child's pale hair. "Look like I can't get nothing down them two but Co' Cola and candy."

That's all you try to get down em, Mrs. Turpin said to herself. Too lazy to light the fire. There was nothing you could tell her about people like them that she didn't know already. And it was not just that they didn't have anything. Because if you gave them everything, in two weeks it would all be broken or filthy or they would have chopped it up for lightwood. She knew all this from her own experience. Help them you must, but help them you couldn't.

All at once the ugly girl turned her lips inside out again. Her eyes were fixed like two drills on Mrs. Turpin. This time there was no mistaking that there was something urgent behind them.

Girl, Mrs. Turpin exclaimed silently, I haven't done a thing to you! The girl might be confusing her with somebody else. There was no need to sit by and let herself be intimidated. "You must be in college," she said boldly, looking directly at the girl. "I see you reading a book there."

The girl continued to stare and pointedly did not answer.

Her mother blushed at this rudeness. "The lady asked you a question, Mary Grace," she said under her breath.

"I have ears," Mary Grace said.

The poor mother blushed again. "Mary Grace goes to Wellesley College," she explained. She twisted one of the buttons on her dress. "In Massachusetts," she added with a grimace. "And in the summer she just keeps right on studying. Just reads all the time, a real book worm. She's done real well at Wellesley; she's taking English and Math and History and Psychology and Social Studies," she rattled on, "and I think it's too much. I think she ought to get out and have fun."

The girl looked as if she would like to hurl them all through the plate glass window.

"Way up north," Mrs. Turpin murmured and thought, well, it hasn't done much for her manners.

"I'd almost rather to have him sick," the white-trash woman said, wrenching the attention back to herself. "He's so mean when he ain't. Look like some children just take natural to meanness. It's some gets bad when they get sick but he was the opposite. Took sick and turned good. He don't give me no trouble now. It's me waitin to see the doctor," she said.

If I was going to send anybody back to Africa, Mrs. Turpin thought, it would be your kind, woman. "Yes, indeed," she said aloud, but looking up at the ceiling, "it's a heap of things worse than a nigger." And dirtier than a hog, she added to herself.

"I think people with bad dispositions are more to be pitied than anyone on earth," the pleasant lady said in a voice that was decidedly thin.

"I thank the Lord he has blessed me with a good one," Mrs. Turpin said. "The day has never dawned that I couldn't find something to laugh at."

"Not since she married me anyways," Claud said with a comical straight face.

Everybody laughed except the girl and the white-trash.

Mrs. Turpin's stomach shook. "He's such a caution," she said, "that I can't help but laugh at him."

The girl made a loud ugly noise through her teeth.

Her mother's mouth grew thin and straight. "I think the worst thing in the world," she said, "is an ungrateful person. To have everything and not appreciate it. I know a girl," she said, "who has parents who would give her anything, a little brother who loves her dearly, who is getting a good education, who wears the best clothes, but who can never say a kind word to anyone, who never smiles, who just criticizes and complains all day long."

"Is she too old to paddle?" Claud asked.

The girl's face was almost purple.

"Yes," the lady said, "I'm afraid there's nothing to do but leave her to her folly. Some day she'll wake up and it'll be too late."

"It never hurt anyone to smile," Mrs. Turpin said. "It just makes you feel better all over."

"Of course," the lady said sadly, "but there are just some people you can't tell 100 anything to. They can't take criticism."

"If it's one thing I am," Mrs. Turpin said with feeling, "it's grateful. When I think who all I could have been besides myself and what all I got, a little of everything, and a good disposition besides, I just feel like shouting, 'Thank you, Jesus, for making everything the way it is!' It could have been different!" For one thing, somebody else could have got Claud. At the thought of this, she was flooded with gratitude and a terrible pang of joy ran through her. "Oh thank you, Jesus, Jesus, thank you!" she cried aloud.

The book struck her directly over her left eye. It struck almost at the same instant that she realized the girl was about to hurl it. Before she could utter a sound, the raw face came crashing across the table toward her, howling. The girl's fingers sank like clamps into the soft flesh of her neck. She heard the mother cry out and Claud shout, "Whoa!" There was an instant when she was certain that she was about to be in an earthquake.

All at once her vision narrowed and she saw everything as if it were happening in a small room far away, or as if she were looking at it through the wrong end of a telescope. Claud's face crumpled and fell out of sight. The nurse ran in, then out, then in again. Then the gangling figure of the doctor rushed out of the inner door. Magazines flew this way and that as the table turned over. The girl fell with a thud and Mrs. Turpin's vision suddenly reversed itself and she saw everything large instead of small. The eyes of the white-trashy woman were staring hugely at the floor. There the girl, held down on one side by the nurse and on the other by her mother, was wrenching and turning in their grasp. The doctor was kneeling astride her, trying to hold her arm down. He managed after a second to sink a long needle into it.

Mrs. Turpin felt entirely hollow except for her heart which swung from side to side as if it were agitated in a great empty drum of flesh.

"Somebody that's not busy call for the ambulance," the doctor said in the 105 off-hand voice young doctors adopt for terrible occasions.

Mrs. Turpin could not have moved a finger. The old man who had been sitting next to her skipped nimbly into the office and made the call, for the secretary still seemed to be gone.

"Claud!" Mrs. Turpin called.

He was not in his chair. She knew she must jump up and find him but she felt like some one trying to catch a train in a dream, when everything moves in slow motion and the faster you try to run the slower you go.

"Here I am," a suffocated voice, very unlike Claud's, said.

He was doubled up in the corner on the floor, pale as paper, holding his leg. 110 She wanted to get up and go to him but she could not move. Instead, her gaze was drawn slowly downward to the churning face on the floor, which she could see over the doctor's shoulder.

The girl's eyes stopped rolling and focused on her. They seemed a much lighter blue than before, as if a door that had been tightly closed behind them was now open to admit light and air.

Mrs. Turpin's head cleared and her power of motion returned. She leaned forward until she was looking directly into the fierce brilliant eyes. There was no doubt in her mind that the girl did know her, knew her in some intense and personal way, beyond time and place and condition. "What you got to say to me?" she asked hoarsely and held her breath, waiting, as for a revelation.

The girl raised her head. Her gaze locked with Mrs. Turpin's. "Go back to hell where you came from, you old wart hog," she whispered. Her voice was low but clear. Her eyes burned for a moment as if she saw with pleasure that her message had struck its target.

Mrs. Turpin sank back in her chair.

After a moment the girl's eyes closed and she turned her head wearily to the side.    115

The doctor rose and handed the nurse the empty syringe. He leaned over and put both hands for a moment on the mother's shoulders, which were shaking. She was sitting on the floor, her lips pressed together, holding Mary Grace's hand in her lap. The girl's fingers were gripped like a baby's around her thumb. "Go on to the hospital," he said. "I'll call and make the arrangements."

"Now let's see that neck," he said in a jovial voice to Mrs. Turpin. He began to inspect her neck with his first two fingers. Two little moon-shaped lines like pink fish bones were indented over her windpipe. There was the beginning of an angry red swelling above her eye. His fingers passed over this also.

"Lea'me be," she said thickly and shook him off. "See about Claud. She kicked him."

"I'll see about him in a minute," he said and felt her pulse. He was a thin gray-haired man, given to pleasantries. "Go home and have yourself a vacation the rest of the day," he said and patted her on the shoulder.

Quit your pattin me, Mrs. Turpin growled to herself.    120

"And put an ice pack over that eye," he said. Then he went and squatted down beside Claud and looked at his leg. After a moment he pulled him up and Claud limped after him into the office.

Until the ambulance came, the only sounds in the room were the tremulous moans of the girl's mother, who continued to sit on the floor. The white-trash woman did not take her eyes off the girl. Mrs. Turpin looked straight ahead at nothing. Presently the ambulance drew up, a long dark shadow, behind the curtain. The attendants came in and set the stretcher down beside the girl and lifted her expertly onto it and carried her out. The nurse helped the mother gather up her things. The shadow of the ambulance moved silently away and the nurse came back in the office.

"That ther girl is going to be a lunatic, ain't she?" the white-trash woman asked the nurse, but the nurse kept on to the back and never answered her.

"Yes, she's going to be a lunatic," the white-trash woman said to the rest of them.

"Po' critter," the old woman murmured. The child's face was still in her lap. His eyes looked idly out over her knees. He had not moved during the disturbance except to draw one leg up under him.

"I thank Gawd," the white-trash woman said fervently, "I ain't a lunatic."

Claud came limping out and the Turpins went home.

As their pick-up truck turned into their own dirt road and made the crest of the hill, Mrs. Turpin gripped the window ledge and looked out suspiciously. The land sloped gracefully down through a field dotted with lavender weeds and at the start of the rise their small yellow frame house, with its little flower beds spread out around it like a fancy apron, sat primly in its accustomed place between two giant hickory trees. She would not have been startled to see a burnt wound between two blackened chimneys.

Neither of them felt like eating so they put on their house clothes and lowered the shade in the bedroom and lay down, Claud with his leg on a pillow and herself with a damp washcloth over her eye. The instant she was flat on her back, the image of a razor-backed hog with warts on its face and horns coming out behind its ears snorted into her head. She moaned, a low quiet moan.

"I am not," she said tearfully, "a wart hog. From hell." But the denial had no force. The girl's eyes and her words, even the tone of her voice, low but clear, directed only to her, brooked no repudiation. She had been singled out for the message, though there was trash in the room to whom it might justly have been applied. The full force of this fact struck her only now. There was a woman there who was neglecting her own child but she had been overlooked. The message had been given to Ruby Turpin, a respectable, hard-working, church-going woman. The tears dried. Her eyes began to burn instead with wrath.

She rose on her elbow and the washcloth fell into her hand. Claud was lying on his back, snoring. She wanted to tell him what the girl had said. At the same time, she did not wish to put the image of herself as a wart hog from hell into his mind.

"Hey, Claud," she muttered and pushed his shoulder.

Claud opened one pale baby blue eye.

She looked into it warily. He did not think about anything. He just went his way.

"Wha, whasit?" he said and closed the eye again.

"Nothing," she said. "Does your leg pain you?"

"Hurts like hell," Claud said.

"It'll quit terreckly," she said and lay back down. In a moment Claud was snoring again. For the rest of the afternoon they lay there. Claud slept. She scowled at the ceiling. Occasionally she raised her fist and made a small stabbing motion over her chest as if she was defending her innocence to invisible guests who were like the comforters of Job, reasonable-seeming but wrong.

About five-thirty Claud stirred. "Got to go after those niggers," he sighed, not moving.

She was looking straight up as if there were unintelligible handwriting on 140
the ceiling. The protuberance over her eye had turned a greenish-blue. "Listen
here," she said.

"What?"

"Kiss me."

Claud leaned over and kissed her loudly on the mouth. He pinched her side
and their hands interlocked. Her expression of ferocious concentration did not
change. Claud got up, groaning and growling, and limped off. She continued to
study the ceiling.

She did not get up until she heard the pick-up truck coming back with the
Negroes. Then she rose and thrust her feet in her brown oxfords, which she did
not bother to lace, and stumped out onto the back porch and got her red plastic
bucket. She emptied a tray of ice cubes into it and filled it half full of water and
went out into the back yard. Every afternoon after Claud brought the hands in,
one of the boys helped him put out hay and the rest waited in the back of the
truck until he was ready to take them home. The truck was parked in the shade
under one of the hickory trees.

"Hi yawl this evening?" Mrs. Turpin asked grimly, appearing with the bucket 145
and the dipper. There were three women and a boy in the truck.

"Us doin nicely," the oldest woman said. "Hi you doin?" and her gaze stuck
immediately on the dark lump on Mrs. Turpin's forehead. "You done fell down,
ain't you?" she asked in a solicitous voice. The old woman was dark and almost
toothless. She had on an old felt hat of Claud's set back on her head. The other
two women were younger and lighter and they both had new bright green sun
hats. One of them had hers on her head; the other had taken hers off and the boy
was grinning beneath it.

Mrs. Turpin set the bucket down on the floor of the truck. "Yawl hep yourselves," she said. She looked around to make sure Claud had gone. "No. I didn't
fall down," she said, folding her arms. "It was something worse than that."

"Ain't nothing bad happen to you!" the old woman said. She said it as if they
all knew Mrs. Turpin was protected in some special way by Divine Providence.
"You just had you a little fall."

"We were in town at the doctor's office for where the cow kicked Mr.
Turpin," Mrs. Turpin said in a flat tone that indicated they could leave off their
foolishness. "And there was this girl there. A big fat girl with her face all broke
out. I could look at that girl and tell she was peculiar but I couldn't tell how. And
me and her mama were just talking and going along and all of a sudden WHAM!
She throws this big book she reading at me and . . . "

"Naw!" the old woman cried out. 150

"And then she jumps over the table and commences to choke me."

"Naw!" they all exclaimed, "naw!"

"Hi come she do that?" the old woman asked. "What ail her?"

Mrs. Turpin only glared in front of her.

"Something ail her," the old woman said. 155

"They carried her off in an ambulance," Mrs. Turpin continued, "but before she went she was rolling on the floor and they were trying to hold her down to give her a shot and she said something to me." She paused. "You know what she said to me?"

"What she say?" they asked.

"She said," Mrs. Turpin began, and stopped, her face very dark and heavy. The sun was getting whiter and whiter, blanching the sky overhead so that the leaves of the hickory tree were black in the face of it. She could not bring forth the words. "Something real ugly," she muttered.

"She sho shouldn't said nothin ugly to you," the old woman said. "You so sweet. You the sweetest lady I know."

"She pretty too," the one with the hat on said.                                         160

"And stout," the other one said. "I never knowed no sweeter white lady."

"That's the truth befo' Jesus," the old woman said. "Amen! You des as sweet and pretty as you can be."

Mrs. Turpin knew just exactly how much Negro flattery was worth and it added to her rage. "She said," she began again and finished this time with a fierce rush of breath, "that I was an old wart hog from hell."

There was an astounded silence.

"Where she at?" the youngest woman cried in a piercing voice.                            165
"Lemme see her. I'll kill her!"

"I'll kill her with you!" the other one cried.

"She b'long in the sylum," the old woman said emphatically. "You the sweetest white lady I know."

"She pretty too," the other two said. "Stout as she can be and sweet. Jesus satisfied with her!"

"Deed he is," the old woman declared.                                                     170

Idiots! Mrs. Turpin growled to herself. You could never say anything intelligent to a nigger. You could talk at them but not with them. "Yawl ain't drunk your water," she said shortly. "Leave the bucket in the truck when you're finished with it. I got more to do than just stand around and pass the time of day," and she moved off and into the house.

She stood for a moment in the middle of the kitchen. The dark protuberance over her eye looked like a miniature tornado cloud which might any moment sweep across the horizon of her brow. Her lower lip protruded dangerously. She squared her massive shoulders. Then she marched into the front of the house and out the side door and started down the road to the pig parlor. She had the look of a woman going single-handed, weaponless, into battle.

The sun was a deep yellow now like a harvest moon and was riding westward very fast over the far tree line as if it meant to reach the hogs before she did. The road was rutted and she kicked several good-sized stones out of her path as she strode along. The pig parlor was on a little knoll at the end of a lane that ran off from the side of the barn. It was a square of concrete as large as a small room, with a board fence about four feet high around it. The concrete floor sloped slightly so that the hog wash could drain off into a trench where it was carried to the field for fertilizer. Claud was standing on the outside, on the edge of the concrete, hanging onto the top board, hosing down the floor inside. The hose was connected to the faucet of a water trough nearby.

Mrs. Turpin climbed up beside him and glowered down at the hogs inside. There were seven long-snouted bristly shoats in it—tan with liver-colored spots—and an old sow a few weeks off from farrowing. She was lying on her side grunting. The shoats were running about shaking themselves like idiot children, their little slit pig eyes searching the floor for anything left. She had read that pigs were the most intelligent animal. She doubted it. They were supposed to be smarter than dogs. There had even been a pig astronaut. He had performed his assignment perfectly but died of a heart attack afterwards because they left him in his electric suit, sitting upright throughout his examination when naturally a hog should be on all fours.

A-gruntin and a-rootin and a-groanin.                                                      175

"Gimme that hose," she said, yanking it away from Claud. "Go on and carry them niggers home and then get off that leg."

"You look like you might have swallowed a mad dog," Claud observed, but he got down and limped off. He paid no attention to her humors.

Until he was out of earshot, Mrs. Turpin stood on the side of the pen, holding the hose and pointing the stream of water at the hind quarters of any shoat that looked as if it might try to lie down. When he had had time to get over the hill, she turned her head slightly and her wrathful eyes scanned the path. He was nowhere in sight. She turned back again and seemed to gather herself up. Her shoulders rose and she drew in her breath.

"What do you send me a message like that for?" she said in a low fierce voice, barely above a whisper but with the force of a shout in its concentrated fury. "How am I a hog and me both? How am I saved and from hell too?" Her free fist was knotted and with the other she gripped the hose, blindly pointing the stream of water in and out of the eye of the old sow whose outraged squeal she did not hear.

The pig parlor commanded a view of the back pasture where their twenty      180 beef cows were gathered around the hay-bales Claud and the boy had put out. The freshly cut pasture sloped down to the highway. Across it was their cotton field and beyond that a dark green dusty wood which they owned as well. The sun was behind the wood, very red, looking over the paling of trees like a farmer inspecting his own hogs.

"Why me?" she rumbled. "It's no trash around here, black or white, that I haven't given to. And break my back to the bone every day working. And do for the church."

She appeared to be the right size woman to command the arena before her. "How am I a hog?" she demanded. "Exactly how am I like them?" and she jabbed the stream of water at the shoats. "There was plenty of trash there. It didn't have to be me."

"If you like trash better, go get yourself some trash then," she railed. "You could have made me trash. Or a nigger. If trash is what you wanted why didn't you make me trash?" She shook her fist with the hose in it and a watery snake appeared momentarily in the air. "I could quit working and take it easy and be filthy," she growled. "Lounge about the sidewalks all day drinking root beer. Dip snuff and spit in every puddle and have it all over my face. I could be nasty.

"Or you could have made me a nigger. It's too late for me to be a nigger," she said with deep sarcasm, "but I could act like one. Lay down in the middle of the road and stop traffic. Roll on the ground."

In the deepening light everything was taking on a mysterious hue. The pasture was growing a peculiar glassy green and the streak of highway had turned lavender. She braced herself for a final assault and this time her voice rolled out over the pasture. "Go on," she yelled, "call me a hog! Call me a hog again. From hell. Call me a wart hog from hell. Put that bottom rail on top. There'll still be a top and bottom!"

A garbled echo returned to her.

A final surge of fury shook her and she roared, "Who do you think you are?"

The color of everything, field and crimson sky, burned for a moment with a transparent intensity. The question carried over the pasture and across the highway and the cotton field and returned to her clearly like an answer from beyond the wood.

She opened her mouth but no sound came out of it.

A tiny truck, Claud's, appeared on the highway, heading rapidly out of sight. Its gears scraped thinly. It looked like a child's toy. At any moment a bigger truck might smash into it and scatter Claud's and the niggers' brains all over the road.

Mrs. Turpin stood there, her gaze fixed on the highway, all her muscles rigid, until in five or six minutes the truck reappeared, returning. She waited until it had had time to turn into their own road. Then like a monumental statue coming to life, she bent her head slowly and gazed, as if through the very heart of mystery, down into the pig parlor at the hogs. They had settled all in one corner around the old sow who was grunting softly. A red glow suffused them. They appeared to pant with a secret life.

Until the sun slipped finally behind the tree line, Mrs. Turpin remained there with her gaze bent to them as if she were absorbing some abysmal life-giving knowledge. At last she lifted her head. There was only a purple streak in the sky, cutting through a field of crimson and leading, like an extension of the highway, into the descending dusk. She raised her hands from the side of the pen in a gesture hieratic and profound. A visionary light settled in her eyes. She saw the streak as a vast swinging bridge extending upward from the earth through a field of living fire. Upon it a vast horde of souls were rumbling toward heaven. There were whole companies of white-trash, clean for the first time in their lives, and bands of black niggers in white robes, and battalions of freaks and lunatics shouting and clapping and leaping like frogs. And bringing up the end of the procession was a tribe of people whom she recognized at once as those who, like herself and Claud, had always had a little of everything and the God-given wit to use it right. She leaned forward to observe them closer. They were marching behind the others with great dignity, accountable as they had always been for good order and common sense and respectable behavior. They alone were on key. Yet she could see by their shocked and altered faces that even their virtues were being burned away. She lowered her hands and gripped the rail of the hog pen, her eyes small but fixed unblinkingly on what lay ahead. In a moment the vision faded but she remained where she was, immobile.

At length she got down and turned off the faucet and made her slow way on the darkening path to the house. In the woods around her the invisible cricket choruses had struck up, but what she heard were the voices of the souls climbing upward into the starry field and shouting hallelujah.

QUESTIONS

1. How does Mrs. Turpin see herself before Mary Grace calls her a wart hog?
2. What is the narrator's attitude toward Mrs. Turpin in the beginning of the story? How can you tell? Does this attitude change, or stay the same, at the end?
3. Describe the relationship between Mary Grace and her mother. What annoying platitudes does the mother mouth? Which of Mrs. Turpin's opinions seem especially to anger Mary Grace?
4. Sketch the plot of the story. What moment or event do you take to be the crisis, or turning point? What is the climax? What is the conclusion?
5. What do you infer from Mrs. Turpin's conversation with the black farm workers? Is she their friend? Why does she now find their flattery unacceptable ("Jesus satisfied with her")?
6. When, near the end of the story, Mrs. Turpin roars, "Who do you think you are?" an echo "returned to her clearly like an answer from beyond the wood" (paragraph 188). Explain.
7. What is the final revelation given to Mrs. Turpin? (To state it is to state the theme of the story.) What new attitude does the revelation impart? (How is Mrs. Turpin left with a new vision of humanity?)
8. Other stories in this book contain revelations: "Gimpel the Fool," "The Death of Ivan Ilych," "Young Goodman Brown," "On the Road." If you have read them, try to sum up the supernatural revelation made to the central character in each story. In each, is the revelation the same as a statement of the story's main theme?

## *Flannery O'Connor*

THE ELEMENT OF SUSPENSE IN "A GOOD MAN IS HARD TO FIND"    1963

A story really isn't any good unless it successfully resists paraphrase, unless it hangs on and expands in the mind. Properly, you analyze to enjoy, but it's equally true that to analyze with any discrimination, you have to have enjoyed already, and I think that the best reason to hear a story read is that it should stimulate that primary enjoyment.

I don't have any pretensions to being an Aeschylus or Sophocles and providing you in this story with a cathartic experience out of your mythic background, though this story I'm going to read certainly calls up a good deal of the South's mythic background, and it should elicit from you a degree of pity and terror, even though its way of being serious is a comic one. I do think, though, that like the Greeks you should know what is going to happen in this story so that any element of suspense in it will be transferred from its surface to its interior.

I would be most happy if you had already read it, happier still if you knew it well, but since experience has taught me to keep my expectations along these lines modest, I'll tell you that this is the story of a family of six which, on its way driving to Florida, gets wiped out by an escaped convict who calls himself the Misfit. The family is made up of the Grandmother and her son, Bailey, and his children, John Wesley and June Star and the baby, and there is also the cat and the children's mother. The cat is named Pitty Sing, and the Grandmother is taking him with them, hidden in a basket.

Now I think it behooves me to try to establish with you the basis on which reason operates in this story. Much of my fiction takes its character from a reasonable use of the unreasonable, though the reasonableness of my use of it may not always be apparent. The assumptions that underlie this use of it, however, are those of the central Christian mysteries. These are assumptions to which a large part of the modern audience takes exception. About this I can only say that there are perhaps other ways than my own in which this story could be read, but none other by which it could have been written. Belief, in my own case anyway, is the engine that makes perception operate.

The heroine of this story, the Grandmother, is in the most significant position life offers the Christian. She is facing death. And to all appearances she, like the rest of us, is not too well prepared for it. She would like to see the event postponed. Indefinitely.

I've talked to a number of teachers who use this story in class and who tell their students that the Grandmother is evil, that in fact, she's a witch, even down to the cat. One of these teachers told me that his students, and particularly his southern students, resisted this interpretation with a certain bemused vigor, and he didn't understand why. I had to tell him that they resisted it because they all had grandmothers or great-aunts just like her at home, and they knew, from personal experience, that the old lady lacked comprehension, but that she had a good heart. The southerner is usually tolerant of those weaknesses that proceed from innocence, and he knows that a taste for self-preservation can be readily combined with the missionary spirit.

This same teacher was telling his students that morally the Misfit was several cuts above the Grandmother. He had a really sentimental attachment to the Misfit. But then a prophet gone wrong is almost always more interesting than your grandmother, and you have to let people take their pleasures where they find them.

It is true that the old lady is a hypocritical old soul; her wits are no match for the Misfit's, nor is her capacity for grace equal to his; yet I think the unprejudiced reader will feel that the Grandmother has a special kind of triumph in this story which instinctively we do not allow to someone altogether bad.

I often ask myself what makes a story work, and what makes it hold up as a story, and I have decided that it is probably some action, some gesture of a character that is unlike any other in the story, one which indicates where the real heart of the story lies. This would have to be an action or a gesture which was both totally right and totally unexpected; it would have to be one that was both in character and beyond character; it would have to suggest both the world and eternity. The action or gesture I'm talking about would have to be on the anagogical level, that is, the level which has to do with the Divine life and our participation in it. It would be a gesture that transcended any neat allegory that might have been intended or any pat moral categories a reader could make. It would be a gesture which somehow made contact with mystery.

There is a point in this story where such a gesture occurs. The Grandmother 10 is at last alone, facing the Misfit. Her head clears for an instant and she realizes, even in her limited way, that she is responsible for the man before her and joined to him by ties of kinship which have their roots deep in the mystery she has been merely prattling about so far. And at this point, she does the right thing, she makes the right gesture.

I find that students are often puzzled by what she says and does here, but I think myself that if I took out this gesture and what she says with it, I would have no story. What was left would not be worth your attention. Our age not only does not have a very sharp eye for the almost imperceptible intrusions of grace, it no longer has much feeling for the nature of the violences which precede and follow them. The devil's greatest wile, Baudelaire has said, is to convince us that he does not exist.

I suppose the reasons for the use of so much violence in modern fiction will differ with each writer who uses it, but in my own stories I have found that violence is strangely capable of returning my characters to reality and preparing them to accept their moment of grace. Their heads are so hard that almost nothing else will do the work. This idea, that reality is something to which we must be returned at considerable cost, is one which is seldom understood by the casual reader, but it is one which is implicit in the Christian view of the world.

I don't want to equate the Misfit with the devil. I prefer to think that, however unlikely this may seem, the old lady's gesture, like the mustard-seed, will grow to be a great crow-filled tree in the Misfit's heart, and will be enough of a pain to him there to turn him into the prophet he was meant to become. But that's another story.

This story has been called grotesque, but I prefer to call it literal. A good story is literal in the same sense that a child's drawing is literal. When a child draws, he doesn't intend to distort but to set down exactly what he sees, and as his gaze is direct, he sees the lines that create motion. Now the lines of motion that interest the writer are usually invisible. They are lines of spiritual motion. And in this story you should be on the lookout for such things as the action of grace in the Grandmother's soul, and not for the dead bodies.

We hear many complaints about the prevalence of violence in modern fic- 15 tion, and it is always assumed that this violence is a bad thing and meant to be an end in itself. With the serious writer, violence is never an end in itself. It is the extreme situation that best reveals what we are essentially, and I believe these are times when writers are more interested in what we are essentially than in the tenor of our daily lives. Violence is a force which can be used for good or evil, and among other things taken by it is the kingdom of heaven. But regardless of what can be taken by it, the man in the violent situation reveals those qualities least dispensable in his personality, those qualities which are all he will have to take into eternity with him; and since the characters in this story are all on the verge of eternity, it is appropriate to think of what they take with them. In any case, I hope that if you consider these points in connection with the story, you will come to see it as something more than an account of a family murdered on the way to Florida.

—"On Her Own Work"

## Flannery O'Connor

### THE SERIOUS WRITER AND THE TIRED READER                    1960

Those writers who speak for and with their age are able to do so with a great deal more ease and grace than those who speak counter to prevailing attitudes. I once received a letter from an old lady in California who informed me that when the tired reader comes home at night, he wishes to read something that will lift up his heart. And it seems her heart had not been lifted up by anything of mine she had read. I think that if her heart had been in the right place, it would have been lifted up.

You may say that the serious writer doesn't have to bother about the tired reader, but he does, because they are all tired. One old lady who wants her heart lifted up wouldn't be so bad, but you multiply her two hundred and fifty thousand times and what you get is a book club. I used to think it should be possible to write for some supposed elite, for the people who attend the universities and sometimes know how to read, but I have since found that though you may publish your stories in Botteghe Oscure°, if they are any good at all, you are eventually going to get a letter from some old lady in California, or some inmate of the Federal Penitentiary or the state insane asylum or the local poorhouse, telling you where you have failed to meet his needs.

And his need, of course, is to be lifted up. There is something in us, as storytellers and as listeners to stories, that demands the redemptive act, that demands that what falls at least be offered the chance to be restored. The reader of today looks for this motion, and rightly so, but what he has forgotten is the cost of it. His sense of evil is diluted or lacking altogether and so he has forgotten the price of restoration. When he reads a novel, he wants either his senses tormented or his spirits raised. He wants to be transported, instantly, either to a mock damnation or a mock innocence.

Botteghe Oscure: distinguished (and high-priced) literary magazine of the time, published in Rome for a small international audience.

I am often told that the model of balance for the novelist should be Dante, who divided his territory up pretty evenly between hell, purgatory, and paradise. There can be no objection to this, but also there can be no reason to assume that the result of doing it in these times will give us the balanced picture that it gave in Dante's. Dante lived in the 13th century when that balance was achieved in the faith of his age. We live now in an age which doubts both fact and value, which is swept this way and that by momentary convictions. Instead of reflecting a balance from the world around him, the novelist now has to achieve one from a felt balance inside himself. There are ages when it is possible to woo the reader; there are others when something more drastic is necessary.

There is no literary orthodoxy that can be prescribed as settled for the fiction writer, not even that of Henry James who balanced the elements of traditional realism and romance so admirably within each of his novels. But this much can be said. The great novels we get in the future are not going to be those that the public thinks it wants, or those that critics demand. They are going to be the kind of novels that interest the novelist. And the novels that interest the novelist are those that have not already been written. They are those that put the greatest demands on him, that require him to operate at the maximum of his intelligence and his talents, and to be true to the particularities of his own vocation. The direction of many of us will be toward concentration and the distortion that is necessary to get our vision across; it will be more toward poetry than toward the traditional novel.

The problem for such a novelist will be to know how far he can distort without destroying, and in order not to destroy, he will have to descend far enough into himself to reach those underground springs that give life to his work. This descent into himself will, at the same time, be a descent into his region. It will be a descent through the darkness of the familiar into a world where, like the blind man cured in the gospels, he sees men as if they were trees, but walking. This is the beginning of vision, and I feel it is a vision which we in the South must at least try to understand if we want to participate in the continuance of a vital Southern literature. I hate to think that in twenty years Southern writers too may be writing about men in grey flannel suits and may have lost their ability to see that these gentlemen are even greater freaks than what we are writing about now. I hate to think of the day when the Southern writer will satisfy the tired reader.

—"The Grotesque in Southern Fiction."

SUGGESTIONS FOR WRITING:

1. How do the stories of Flannery O'Connor make manifest the principles she states in her remarks entitled "The Serious Writer and the Tired Reader"?
2. Compare Mrs. Turpin's defiance of God in "Revelation" ("Who do you think you are?" paragraph 187) with the urge of a shipwrecked man in "The Open Boat" to shake his fist at the clouds ("Just you drown me, now, and then hear what I call you!," paragraph 70). Do Flannery O'Connor and Stephen Crane express similar or different concepts of Whoever runs the universe?

3. "In most good stories it is the character's personality that creates the action of the story," O'Connor declares in her essay "Writing Short Stories." "If you start with a real personality, a real character, then something is bound to happen." Discuss this statement as it applies to one or more of the O'Connor stories you have read. Do O'Connor's characters seem to you to be real people, or do you see them as mere vessels for the author's religious views?

4. Compare the woman protagonists in these three stories of Flannery O'Connor: Julian's mother, the grandmother who confronts The Misfit, and Mrs. Turpin.

5. In 750–1,000 words, comment on O'Connor's use of humor. How does comedy help her say what she has to say?

# 11  Stories for Further Reading

For human intercourse, as soon as we look at it for its own sake and not as a social adjunct, is seen to be haunted by a specter. We cannot understand each other, except in a rough-and-ready way; we cannot reveal ourselves, even when we want to; what we call intimacy is only a makeshift; perfect knowledge is an illusion. But in the novel we can know people perfectly, and, apart from the general pleasure of reading, we can find here a compensation for their dimness in life. In this direction fiction is truer than history, because it goes beyond the evidence, and each of us knows from his own experience that there is something beyond the evidence, and even if the novelist has not got it correctly, well—he has tried.

—E. M. Forster, *Aspects of the Novel*

## Ambrose Bierce

AN OCCURRENCE AT OWL CREEK BRIDGE                                          1891

*Ambrose Bierce (1842–1914?) was born in Horse Cave Creek, Ohio, the youngest child of nine in an impoverished farm family. A year at Kentucky Military Academy was his only formal schooling. Enlisting as a drummer boy in the Union Army, Bierce saw action at Shiloh and Chickamauga, took part in Sherman's march to the sea, and came out of the army a brevet major. Then he became a writer, later an editor, for San Francisco newspapers. For a while Bierce thrived. He and his wife, on her ample dowry, lived five years in London, where Bierce wrote for London papers, honed his style, and cultivated his wit. But his wife left*

Ambrose Bierce

him, his two sons died (one of gunfire and the other of alcoholism), and in late life Bierce came to deserve his nickname "Bitter Bierce." In 1913, at seventy-one, he trekked off to Mexico and vanished without a trace, although one report had him riding with the forces of revolutionist Pancho Villa. (A recent movie, Old Gringo, imagines Bierce's last days.) Bierce, who regarded the novel as "a short story padded," favored shorter lengths: short story, fable, newspaper column, aphorism. Sardonically, in The Devil's Dictionary (1911), he defines diplomacy as "the patriotic art of lying for one's country," and saint as "a dead sinner revised and edited." Master of both realism and of the ghost story, he collected his best Civil War fiction, including "An Occurrence at Owl Creek Bridge," in Tales of Soldiers and Civilians (1891), later retitled In the Midst of Life.

## I

A man stood upon a railroad bridge in northern Alabama, looking down into the swift water twenty feet below. The man's hands were behind his back, the wrists bound with a cord. A rope closely encircled his neck. It was attached to a stout cross-timber above his head and the slack fell to the level of his knees. Some loose boards laid upon the sleepers supporting the metals of the railway supplied a footing for him and his executioners—two private soldiers of the Federal army, directed by a sergeant who in civil life may have been a deputy sheriff. At a short remove upon the same temporary platform was an officer in the uniform of his rank, armed. He was a captain. A sentinel at each end of the bridge stood with his rifle in the position known as "support," that is to say, vertical in front of the left shoulder, the hammer resting on the forearm thrown straight across the chest—a formal and unnatural position, enforcing an erect carriage of the body. It did not appear to be the duty of these two men to know what was occurring at the center of the bridge; they merely blockaded the two ends of the foot planking that traversed it.

Beyond one of the sentinels nobody was in sight; the railroad ran straight away into a forest for a hundred yards, then, curving, was lost to view. Doubtless there was an outpost farther along. The other bank of the stream was open ground—a gentle acclivity topped with a stockade of vertical tree trunks, loop-holed for rifles, with a single embrasure through which protruded the muzzle of a brass cannon commanding the bridge. Midway of the slope between bridge and fort were the spectators—a single company of infantry in line, at "parade rest," the butts of the rifles on the ground, the barrels inclining slightly backward against the right shoulder, the hands crossed upon the stock. A lieutenant stood at the right of the line, the point of his sword upon the ground, his left hand resting upon his right. Excepting the group of four at the center of the bridge, not a man moved. The company faced the bridge, staring stonily, motionless. The sentinels, facing the banks of the stream, might have been statues to adorn the bridge. The captain stood with folded arms, silent, observing the work of his subordinates, but making no sign. Death is a dignitary who when he comes announced is to be received with formal manifestations of respect, even by those most familiar with him. In the code of military etiquette silence and fixity are forms of deference.

The man who was engaged in being hanged was apparently about thirty-five years of age. He was a civilian, if one might judge from his habit, which was that of a planter. His features were good—a straight nose, firm mouth, broad forehead, from which his long, dark hair was combed straight back, falling behind his ears to the collar of his well-fitting frock-coat. He wore a mustache and pointed beard, but no whiskers; his eyes were large and dark gray, and had a kindly expression which one would hardly have expected in one whose neck was in the hemp. Evidently this was no vulgar assassin. The liberal military code makes provision for hanging many kinds of persons, and gentlemen are not excluded.

The preparations being complete, the two private soldiers stepped aside and each drew away the plank upon which he had been standing. The sergeant turned to the captain, saluted and placed himself immediately behind that officer, who in turn moved apart one pace. These movements left the condemned man and the sergeant standing on the two ends of the same plank, which spanned three of the cross-ties of the bridge. The end upon which the civilian stood almost, but not quite, reached a fourth. This plank had been held in place by the weight of the captain; it was now held by that of the sergeant. At a signal from the former the latter would step aside, the plank would tilt and the condemned man go down between two ties. The arrangement commended itself to his judgment as simple and effective. His face had not been covered nor his eyes bandaged. He looked a moment at his "unsteadfast footing," then let his gaze wander to the swirling water of the stream racing madly beneath his feet. A piece of dancing driftwood caught his attention and his eyes followed it down the current. How slowly it appeared to move! What a sluggish stream!

He closed his eyes in order to fix his last thoughts upon his wife and children. The water, touched to gold by the early sun, the brooding mists under the banks at some distance down the stream, the fort, the soldiers, the piece of drift— all had distracted him. And now he became conscious of a new disturbance. Striking through the thought of his dear ones was a sound which he could neither ignore nor understand, a sharp, distinct, metallic percussion like the stroke of a blacksmith's hammer upon the anvil; it had the same ringing quality. He wondered what it was, and whether immeasurably distant or near by—it seemed both. Its recurrence was regular, but as slow as the tolling of a death knell. He awaited each stroke with impatience and—he knew not why—apprehension. The intervals of silence grew progressively longer; the delays became maddening. With their greater infrequency the sounds increased in strength and sharpness. They hurt his ear like the thrust of a knife; he feared he would shriek. What he heard was the ticking of his watch.

He unclosed his eyes and saw again the water below him. "If I could free my hands," he thought, "I might throw off the noose and spring into the stream. By diving I could evade the bullets and, swimming vigorously, reach the bank, take to the woods and get away home. My home, thank God, is as yet outside their lines; my wife and little ones are still beyond the invader's farthest advance."

As these thoughts, which have here to be set down in words, were flashed into the doomed man's brain rather than evolved from it the captain nodded to the sergeant. The sergeant stepped aside.

## II

Peyton Farquhar was a well-to-do planter, of an old and highly respected Alabama family. Being a slave owner and like other slave owners a politician he was naturally an original secessionist and ardently devoted to the Southern cause. Circumstances of an imperious nature, which it is unnecessary to relate here, had prevented him from taking service with the gallant army that had fought the disastrous campaigns ending with the fall of Corinth, and he chafed under the inglorious restraint, longing for the release of his energies, the larger life of the soldier, the opportunity for distinction. That opportunity, he felt, would come, as it comes to all in war time. Meanwhile he did what he could. No service was too humble to him to perform in aid of the South, no adventure too perilous for him to undertake if consistent with the character of a civilian who was at heart a soldier, and who in good faith and without too much qualification assented to at least a part of the frankly villainous dictum that all is fair in love and war.

One evening while Farquhar and his wife were sitting on a rustic bench near the entrance to his grounds, a gray-clad soldier rode up to the gate and asked for a drink of water. Mrs. Farquhar was only too happy to serve him with her own white hands. While she was fetching the water her husband approached the dusty horseman and inquired eagerly for news from the front.

"The Yanks are repairing the railroads," said the man, "and are getting ready 10 for another advance. They have reached the Owl Creek bridge, put it in order and built a stockade on the north bank. The commandant has issued an order, which is posted everywhere, declaring that any civilian caught interfering with the railroad, its bridges, tunnels or trains will be summarily hanged. I saw the order."

"How far is it to the Owl Creek bridge?" Farquhar asked.

"About thirty miles."

"Is there no force on this side the creek?"

"Only a picket post half a mile out, on the railroad, and a single sentinel at this end of the bridge."

"Suppose a man—a civilian and student of hanging—should elude the pick- 15 et post and perhaps get the better of the sentinel," said Farquhar, smiling, "what could he accomplish?"

The soldier reflected. "I was there a month ago," he replied. "I observed that the flood of last winter had lodged a great quantity of driftwood against the wooden pier at this end of the bridge. It is now dry and would burn like tow."

The lady had now brought the water, which the soldier drank. He thanked her ceremoniously, bowed to her husband and rode away. An hour later, after nightfall, he repassed the plantation, going northward in the direction from which he had come. He was a Federal scout.

*III*

As Peyton Farquhar fell straight downward through the bridge he lost consciousness and was as one already dead. From this state he was awakened—ages later, it seemed to him—by the pain of a sharp pressure upon his throat, followed by a sense of suffocation. Keen, poignant agonies seemed to shoot from his neck downward through every fiber of his body and limbs. These pains appeared to flash along well-defined lines of ramification and to beat with an inconceivably rapid periodicity. They seemed like streams of pulsating fire heating him to an intolerable temperature. As to his head, he was conscious of nothing but a feeling of fulness—of congestion. These sensations were unaccompanied by thought. The intellectual part of his nature was already effaced; he had power only to feel, and feeling was torment. He was conscious of motion. Encompassed in a luminous cloud, of which he was now merely the fiery heart, without material substance, he swung through unthinkable arcs of oscillation, like a vast pendulum. Then all at once, with terrible suddenness, the light about him shot upward with the noise of a loud plash; a frightful roaring was in his ears, and all was cold and dark. The power of thought was restored; he knew that the rope had broken and he had fallen into the stream. There was no additional strangulation; the noose about his neck was already suffocating him and kept the water from his lungs. To die of hanging at the bottom of a river!—the idea seemed to him ludicrous. He opened his eyes in the darkness and saw above him a gleam of light, but how distant, how inaccessible! He was still sinking, for the light became fainter and fainter until it was a mere glimmer. Then it began to grow and brighten, and he knew that he was rising toward the surface—knew it with reluctance, for he was now very comfortable. "To be hanged and drowned," he thought, "that is not so bad; but I do not wish to be shot. No; I will not be shot; that is not fair."

He was not conscious of an effort, but a sharp pain in his wrist apprised him that he was trying to free his hands. He gave the struggle his attention, as an idler might observe the feat of a juggler, without interest in the outcome. What splendid effort!—what magnificent, what superhuman strength! Ah, that was a fine endeavor! Bravo! The cord fell away; his arms parted and floated upward, the hands dimly seen on each side in the growing light. He watched them with a new interest as first one and then the other pounced upon the noose at his neck. They tore it away and thrust it fiercely aside, its undulations resembling those of a water-snake. "Put it back, put it back!" He thought he shouted these words to his hands, for the undoing of the noose had been succeeded by the direst pang that he had yet experienced. His neck ached horribly; his brain was on fire; his heart, which had been fluttering faintly, gave a great leap, trying to force itself out at his mouth. His whole body was racked and wrenched with an insupportable anguish! But his disobedient hands gave no heed to the command. They beat the water vigorously with quick, downward strokes, forcing him to the surface. He felt his head emerge; his eyes were blinded by the sunlight; his chest expanded convulsively, and with a supreme and crowning agony his lungs engulfed a great draught of air, which instantly he expelled in a shriek!

He was now in full possession of his physical senses. They were, indeed, preternaturally keen and alert. Something in the awful disturbance of his organic system had so exalted and refined them that they made record of things never before perceived. He felt the ripples upon his face and heard their separate sounds as they struck. He looked at the forest on the bank of the stream, saw the individual trees, the leaves and the veining of each leaf—saw the very insects upon them: the locusts, the brilliant-bodied flies, the gray spiders stretching their webs from twig to twig. He noted the prismatic colors in all the dewdrops upon a million blades of grass. The humming of the gnats that danced above the eddies of the stream, the beating of the dragon-flies' wings, the strokes of the water-spiders' legs, like oars which had lifted their boat—all these made audible music. A fish slid along beneath his eyes and he heard the rush of its body parting the water.

He had come to the surface facing down the stream; in a moment the visible world seemed to wheel slowly round, himself the pivotal point, and he saw the bridge, the fort, the soldiers upon the bridge, the captain, the sergeant, the two privates, his executioners. They were in silhouette against the blue sky. They shouted and gesticulated, pointing at him. The captain had drawn his pistol, but did not fire; the others were unarmed. Their movements were grotesque and horrible, their forms gigantic.

Suddenly he heard a sharp report and something struck the water smartly within a few inches of his head, spattering his face with spray. He heard a second report, and saw one of the sentinels with his rifle at his shoulder, a light cloud of blue smoke rising from the muzzle. The man in the water saw the eye of the man on the bridge gazing into his own through the sights of the rifle. He observed that it was a gray eye and remembered having read that gray eyes were keenest, and that all famous markmen had them. Nevertheless, this one had missed.

A counter-swirl had caught Farquhar and turned him half round; he was again looking into the forest on the bank opposite the fort. The sound of a clear, high voice in a monotonous singsong now rang out behind him and came across the water with a distinctness that pierced and subdued all other sounds, even the beating of the ripples in his ears. Although no soldier, he had frequented camps enough to know the dread significance of that deliberate, drawling, aspirated chant; the lieutenant on shore was taking a part in the morning's work. How coldly and pitilessly—with what an even, calm intonation, presaging, and enforcing tranquility in the men—with what accurately measured intervals fell those cruel words:

"Attention, company! . . . Shoulder arms! . . . Ready! . . . Aim! . . . Fire!"

Farquhar dived—dived as deeply as he could. The water roared in his ears like the voice of Niagara, yet he heard the dulled thunder of the volley and, rising again toward the surface, met shining bits of metal, singularly flattened, oscillating slowly downward. Some of them touched him on the face and hands, then fell away, continuing their descent. One lodged between his collar and neck; it was uncomfortably warm and he snatched it out.

As he rose to the surface, gasping for breath, he saw that he had been a long time under water; he was perceptibly farther down stream—nearer to safety. The soldiers had almost finished reloading; the metal ramrods flashed all at once in the sunshine as they were drawn from the barrels, turned in the air, and thrust into their sockets. The two sentinels fired again, independently and ineffectually.

The hunted man saw all this over his shoulder; he was now swimming vigorously with the current. His brain was as energetic as his arms and legs; he thought with the rapidity of lightning.

"The officer," he reasoned, "will not make that martinet's error a second time. It is as easy to dodge a volley as a single shot. He has probably already given the command to fire at will. God help me, I cannot dodge them all!"

An appalling plash within two yards of him was followed by a loud, rushing sound, *diminuendo*°, which seemed to travel back through the air to the fort and died in an explosion which stirred the very river to its deeps! A rising sheet of water curved over him, fell down upon him, blinded him, strangled him! The cannon had taken a hand in the game. As he shook his head free from the commotion of the smitten water he heard the deflected shot humming through the air ahead, and in an instant it was cracking and smashing the branches in the forest beyond.

"They will not do that again," he thought; "the next time they will use a charge of grape. I must keep my eye upon the gun; the smoke will apprise me— the report arrives too late; it lags behind the missile. That is a good gun."  30

Suddenly he felt himself whirled round and round—spinning like a top. The water, the banks, the forests, the now distant bridge, fort and men—all were commingled and blurred. Objects were represented by their colors only; circular horizontal streaks of color—that was all he saw. He had been caught in a vortex and was being whirled on with a velocity of advance and gyration that made him giddy and sick. In a few moments he was flung upon the gravel at the foot of the left bank of the stream—the southern bank—and behind a projecting point which concealed him from his enemies. The sudden arrest of his motion, the abrasion of one of his hands on the gravel, restored him, and he wept with delight. He dug his fingers into the sand, threw it over himself in handfuls and audibly blessed it. It looked like diamonds, rubies, emeralds; he could think of nothing beautiful which it did not resemble. The trees upon the bank were giant garden plants; he noted a definite order in their arrangement, inhaled the fragrance of their blooms. A strange, roseate light shone through the spaces among their trunks and the wind made in their branches the music of aeolian harps. He had no wish to perfect his escape—was content to remain in that enchanting spot until retaken.

A whiz and rattle of grapeshot among the branches high above his head roused him from his dream. The baffled cannoneer had fired him a random farewell. He sprang to his feet, rushed up the sloping bank, and plunged into the forest.

All that day he traveled, laying his course by the rounding sun. The forest seemed interminable; nowhere did he discover a break in it, not even a woodman's

---

*diminuendo*: diminishing (Italian); a term from music indicating a gradual decrease in loudness or force.

road. He had not known that he lived in so wild a region. There was something uncanny in the revelation.

By nightfall he was fatigued, footsore, famishing. The thought of his wife and children urged him on. At last he found a road which led him in what he knew to be the right direction. It was as wide and straight as a city street, yet it seemed untraveled. No fields bordered it, no dwelling anywhere. Not so much as the barking of a dog suggested human habitation. The black bodies of the trees formed a straight wall on both sides, terminating on the horizon in a point, like a diagram in a lesson in perspective. Overhead, as he looked up through this rift in the wood, shone great golden stars looking unfamiliar and grouped in strange constellations. He was sure they were arranged in some order which had a secret and malign significance. The wood on either side was full of singular noises, among which—once, twice, and again—he distinctly heard whispers in an unknown tongue.

His neck was in pain and lifting his hand to it he found it horribly swollen. 35 He knew that it had a circle of black where the rope had bruised it. His eyes felt congested; he could no longer close them. His tongue was swollen with thirst; he relieved its fever by thrusting it forward from between his teeth into the cold air. How softly the turf had carpeted the untraveled avenue—he could no longer feel the roadway beneath his feet!

Doubtless, despite his suffering, he had fallen asleep while walking, for now he sees another scene—perhaps he has merely recovered from a delirium. He stands at the gate of his own home. All is as he left it, and all bright and beautiful in the morning sunshine. He must have traveled the entire night. As he pushes open the gate and passes up the wide white walk, he sees a flutter of female garments; his wife, looking fresh and cool and sweet, steps down from the veranda to meet him. At the bottom of the steps she stands waiting, with a smile of ineffable joy, an attitude of matchless grace and dignity. Ah, how beautiful she is! He springs forward with extended arms. As he is about to clasp her he feels a stunning blow upon the back of the neck; a blinding white light blazes all about him with a sound like the shock of a cannon—then all is darkness and silence!

Peyton Farquhar was dead; his body, with a broken neck, swung gently from side to side beneath the timbers of the Owl Creek bridge.

# Willa Cather

*Willa Cather (1876–1947) was born in Gore, Virginia, but at nine moved to Webster County, Nebraska, where pioneer sod houses still clung to the windswept plains. There, mainly in the town of Red Cloud, she grew up among Scandinavians, Czechs, Bohemians, and other immigrant settlers, for whom she felt a quick kinship: they too had been displaced from their childhood homes. After graduation from the University of Nebraska, Cather went east to spend ten years in Pittsburgh, where the story "Paul's Case" opens. (When she wrote the story, she was a high school teacher of Latin and English and music critic for a newspaper.) Then, because her early stories had attracted notice, New York beckoned. A*

Willa Cather

*job on the staff of* McClure's *led to her becoming managing editor of the popular magazine. Her early novels of Nebraska won immense popularity:* O Pioneers! *(1913),* My Ántonia *(1918), and* A Lost Lady *(1923). In her later novels Cather explores other regions of the North American past: in* Death Comes to the Archbishop *(1927), frontier New Mexico; in* Shadows on the Rock *(1931), seventeenth-century Quebec. She does not romanticize the rugged lives of farm people on the plains, or glamorize village life. Often, as in* The Song of the Lark *(1915), the story of a Colorado girl who becomes an opera singer, she depicts a small town as stifling. With remarkable skill, she may tell a story from a man's point of view, but her favorite characters are likely to be women of strong will who triumph over obstacles.*

It was Paul's afternoon to appear before the faculty of the Pittsburgh High School to account for his various misdemeanors. He had been suspended a week ago, and his father had called at the Principal's office and confessed his perplexity about his son. Paul entered the faculty room suave and smiling. His clothes were a trifle outgrown and the tan velvet on the collar of his open overcoat was frayed and worn; but for all that there was something of the dandy about him, and he wore an opal pin in his neatly knotted black four-in-hand, and a red carnation in his buttonhole. This latter adornment the faculty somehow felt was not properly significant of the contrite spirit befitting a boy under the ban of suspension.

Paul was tall for his age and very thin, with high, cramped shoulders and a narrow chest. His eyes were remarkable for a certain hysterical brilliancy and he continually used them in a conscious, theatrical sort of way, peculiarly offensive in a boy. The pupils were abnormally large, as though he were addicted to belladonna, but there was a glassy glitter about them which that drug does not produce.

When questioned by the Principal as to why he was there, Paul stated, politely enough, that he wanted to come back to school. This was a lie, but Paul was quite accustomed to lying; found it, indeed, indispensable for overcoming friction. His teachers were asked to state their respective charges against him, which they did with such a rancor and aggrievedness as evinced that this was not a usual case. Disorder and impertinence were among the offenses named, yet each of his instructors felt that it was scarcely possible to put into words the real cause of the trouble, which lay in a sort of hysterically defiant manner of the boy's; in the contempt which they all knew he felt for them, and which he seemingly made not the least effort to conceal. Once, when he had been making a synopsis of a paragraph at the blackboard, his English teacher had stepped to his side and attempted to guide his hand. Paul had started back with a shudder and thrust his hands violently behind him. The astonished woman could scarcely have been more hurt and embarrassed had he struck at her. The insult was so involuntary and definitely personal as to be unforgettable. In one way and another, he had made all his teachers, men and women alike, conscious of the same feeling of physical aversion. In one class he habitually sat with his hand shading his eyes; in another he always looked out of the window during the recitation; in another he made a running commentary on the lecture, with humorous intention.

His teachers felt this afternoon that his whole attitude was symbolized by his shrug and his flippantly red carnation flower, and they fell upon him without mercy, his English teacher leading the pack. He stood through it smiling, his pale lips parted over his white teeth. (His lips were continually twitching, and he had a habit of raising his eyebrows that was contemptuous and irritating to the last degree.) Older boys than Paul had broken down and shed tears under that baptism of fire, but his set smile did not once desert him, and his only sign of discomfort was the nervous trembling of the fingers that toyed with the buttons of his overcoat, and an occasional jerking of the other hand that held his hat. Paul was always smiling, always glancing about him, seeming to feel that people might be watching him and trying to detect something. This conscious expression, since it was as far as possible from boyish mirthfulness, was usually attributed to insolence or "smartness."

As the inquisition proceeded, one of his instructors repeated an impertinent remark of the boy's, and the Principal asked him whether he thought that a courteous speech to have made a woman. Paul shrugged his shoulders slightly and his eyebrows twitched.

"I don't know," he replied. "I didn't mean to be polite or impolite, either. I guess it's a sort of way I have of saying things regardless."

The Principal, who was a sympathetic man, asked him whether he didn't think that a way it would be well to get rid of. Paul grinned and said he guessed so. When he was told that he could go, he bowed gracefully and went out. His bow was but a repetition of the scandalous red carnation.

His teachers were in despair, and his drawing master voiced the feeling of them all when he declared there was something about the boy which none of them understood. He added: "I don't really believe that smile of his comes altogether from insolence; there's something sort of haunted about it. The boy is not strong, for one thing. I happen to know that he was born in Colorado, only a few months before his mother died out there of a long illness. There is something wrong about the fellow."

The drawing master had come to realize that, in looking at Paul, one saw only his white teeth and the forced animation of his eyes. One warm afternoon the boy had gone to sleep at his drawing-board, and his master had noted with amazement what a white, blue-veined face it was; drawn and wrinkled like an old man's about the eyes, the lips twitching even in his sleep, and stiff with a nervous tension that drew them back from his teeth.

His teachers left the building dissatisfied and unhappy; humiliated to have    10
felt so vindictive toward a mere boy, to have uttered this feeling in cutting terms, and to have set each other on, as it were, in the gruesome game of intemperate reproach. Some of them remembered having seen a miserable street cat set at bay by a ring of tormentors.

As for Paul, he ran down the hill whistling the Soldiers' Chorus from *Faust*°, looking wildly behind him now and then to see whether some of his teachers were not there to writhe under his light-heartedness. As it was now late in the afternoon and Paul was on duty that evening as usher at Carnegie Hall°, he decided that he would not go home to supper. When he reached the concert hall the doors were not yet open and, as it was chilly outside, he decided to go up into the picture gallery—always deserted at this hour—where there were some of Raffaelli's° gay studies of Paris streets and an airy blue Venetian scene or two that always exhilarated him. He was delighted to find no one in the gallery but the old guard, who sat in one corner, a newspaper on his knee, a black patch over one eye and the other closed. Paul possessed himself of the place and walked confidently up and down, whistling under his breath. After a while he sat down before a blue Rico° and lost himself. When he bethought him to look at his watch, it was after seven o'clock, and he rose with a start and ran downstairs, making a face at Augustus, peering out from the cast-room°, and an evil gesture at the Venus of Milo as he passed her on the stairway.

When Paul reached the ushers' dressing-room half-a-dozen boys were there already, and he began excitedly to tumble into his uniform. It was one of the few that at all approached fitting, and Paul thought it very becoming—though he knew that the tight, straight coat accentuated his narrow chest, about which he was exceedingly sensitive. He was always considerably excited while he dressed, twanging all over to the tuning of the strings and the preliminary flourishes of the horns in the music-room; but tonight he seemed quite beside himself, and he

*Faust:* tragic grand opera (1859) by French composer Charles Gounod.    *Carnegie Hall:* concert hall endowed by Pittsburgh steel manufacturer Andrew Carnegie, not to be confused with the better-known Carnegie Hall in New York City.    *Raffaelli:* Jean-Francois Raffaelli (1850–1921), painter and graphic artist, native and lifelong resident of Paris, attained great popularity for his paintings and drawings of that city.    *Rico:* (flourished 1500–1550), painter of the Byzantine school, a native of Crete.    *Augustus . . . cast-room:* Paul mocks a plaster cast of the Vatican Museum's famous statue of the first Roman emperor (63 B.C.-A.D. 14), whom an unknown sculptor posed sternly pointing an index finger at his beholders.

teased and plagued the boys until, telling him that he was crazy, they put him down on the floor and sat on him.

Somewhat calmed by his suppression, Paul dashed out to the front of the house to seat the early comers. He was a model usher; gracious and smiling he ran up and down the aisles; nothing was too much trouble for him; he carried messages and brought programmes as though it were his greatest pleasure in life, and all the people in his section thought him a charming boy, feeling that he remembered and admired them. As the house filled, he grew more and more vivacious and animated, and the color came to his cheeks and lips. It was very much as though this were a great reception and Paul were the host. Just as the musicians came out to take their places, his English teacher arrived with checks for the seats which a prominent manufacturer had taken for the season. She betrayed some embarrassment when she handed Paul the tickets, and a hauteur° which subsequently made her feel very foolish. Paul was startled for a moment, and had the feeling of wanting to put her out; what business had she here among all these fine people and gay colors? He looked her over and decided that she was not appropriately dressed and must be a fool to sit downstairs in such togs. The tickets had probably been sent her out of kindness, he reflected as he put down a seat for her, and she had about as much right to sit there as he had.

When the symphony began Paul sank into one of the rear seats with a long sigh of relief, and lost himself as he had done before the Rico. It was not that symphonies, as such, meant anything in particular to Paul, but the first sigh of the instruments seemed to free some hilarious and potent spirit within him; something that struggled there like the Genius° in the bottle found by the Arab fisherman. He felt a sudden zest of life; the lights danced before his eyes and the concert hall blazed into unimaginable splendor. When the soprano soloist came on, Paul forgot even the nastiness of his teacher's being there and gave himself up to the peculiar stimulus such personages always had for him. The soloist chanced to be a German woman, by no means in her first youth, and the mother of many children; but she wore an elaborate gown and a tiara, and above all she had that indefinable air of achievement, that world-shine upon her, which, in Paul's eyes, made her a veritable queen of Romance.

After a concert was over Paul was always irritable and wretched until he got to sleep, and tonight he was even more than usually restless. He had the feeling of not being able to let down, of its being impossible to give up this delicious excitement which was the only thing that could be called living at all. During the last number he withdrew and, after hastily changing his clothes in the dressing-room, slipped out to the side door where the soprano's carriage stood. Here he began pacing rapidly up and down the walk, waiting to see her come out.

Over yonder the Schenley, in its vacant stretch, loomed big and square through the fine rain, the windows of its twelve stories glowing like those of a

---

*hauteur:* haughtiness.    *Genius:* genie in a tale from *The Arabian Nights.*

lighted cardboard house under a Christmas tree. All the actors and singers of the better class stayed there when they were in the city, and a number of the big manufacturers of the place lived there in the winter. Paul had often hung about the hotel, watching the people go in and out, longing to enter and leave school-masters and dull care behind him forever.

At last the singer came out, accompanied by the conductor, who helped her into her carriage and closed the door with a cordial *auf wiedersehen°* which set Paul to wondering whether she were not an old sweetheart of his. Paul followed the carriage over to the hotel, walking so rapidly as not to be far from the entrance when the singer alighted and disappeared behind the swinging glass doors that were opened by a negro in a tall hat and a long coat. In the moment that the door was ajar it seemed to Paul that he, too, entered. He seemed to feel himself go after her up the steps, into the warm, lighted building, into an exotic, a tropical world of shiny, glistening surfaces and basking ease. He reflected upon the mysterious dishes that were brought into the dining-room, the green bottles in buckets of ice, as he had seen them in the supper party pictures of the *Sunday World* supplement. A quick gust of wind brought the rain down with sudden vehemence, and Paul was startled to find that he was still outside in the slush of the gravel driveway; that his boots were letting in the water and his scanty over-coat was clinging wet about him; that the lights in front of the concert hall were out, and that the rain was driving in sheets between him and the orange glow of the windows above him. There it was, what he wanted—tangibly before him, like the fairy world of a Christmas pantomime, but mocking spirits stood guard at the doors, and, as the rain beat in his face, Paul wondered whether he were destined always to shiver in the black night outside, looking up at it.

He turned and walked reluctantly toward the car tracks. The end had to come sometime; his father in his night-clothes at the top of the stairs, explana-tions that did not explain, hastily improvised fictions that were forever tripping him up, his upstairs room and its horrible yellow wall-paper, the creaking bureau with the greasy plush collar-box, and over his painted wooden bed the pictures of George Washington and John Calvin°, and the framed motto, "Feed my Lambs," which had been worked in red worsted by his mother.

Half an hour later, Paul alighted from his car and went slowly down one of the side streets off the main thoroughfare. It was a highly respectable street, where all the houses were exactly alike, and where businessmen of moderate means begot and reared large families of children, all of whom went to Sabbath-school and learned the shorter catechism, and were interested in arithmetic; all of whom were as exactly alike as their homes, and of a piece with the monotony in which they lived. Paul never went up Cordelia Street without a shudder of loathing. His home was next to the house of the Cumberland° minister. He

*auf wiedersehen:* German equivalent of *au revoir*, or "here's to seeing you again." *John Calvin:* French Protestant theologian of the Reformation (1509–1564) whose teachings are the basis of Presbyterianism. *Cumberland:* The minister, a Cumberland Presbyterian, belongs to a frontier denomination that had splintered away from the Presbyterian Church and whose ministers were ordained after a briefer training.

approached it tonight with the nerveless sense of defeat, the hopeless feeling of sinking back forever into ugliness and commonness that he had always had when he came home. The moment he turned into Cordelia Street he felt the waters close above his head. After each of these orgies of living, he experienced all the physical depression which follows a debauch; the loathing of respectable beds, of common food, of a house penetrated by kitchen odors; a shuddering repulsion for the flavorless, colorless mass of every-day existence; a morbid desire for cool things and soft lights and fresh flowers.

The nearer he approached the house, the more absolutely unequal Paul felt 20 to the sight of it all; his ugly sleeping chamber; the cold bathroom with the grimy zinc tub, the cracked mirror, the dripping spigots; his father, at the top of the stairs, his hairy legs sticking out from his night-shirt, his feet thrust into carpet slippers. He was so much later than usual that there would certainly be inquiries and reproaches. Paul stopped short before the door. He felt that he could not be accosted by his father tonight; that he could not toss again on that miserable bed. He would not go in. He would tell his father that he had no car fare, and it was raining so hard he had gone home with one of the boys and stayed all night.

Meanwhile, he was wet and cold. He went around to the back of the house and tried one of the basement windows, found it open, raised it cautiously, and scrambled down the cellar wall to the floor. There he stood, holding his breath, terrified by the noise he had made, but the floor above him was silent, and there was no creak on the stairs. He found a soap-box, and carried it over to the soft ring of light that streamed from the furnace door, and sat down. He was horribly afraid of rats, so he did not try to sleep, but sat looking distrustfully at the dark, still terrified lest he might have awakened his father. In such reactions, after one of the experiences which made days and nights out of the dreary blanks of the calendar, when his senses were deadened, Paul's head was always singularly clear. Suppose his father had heard him getting in at the window and had come down and shot him for a burglar? Then, again, suppose his father had come down, pistol in hand, and he had cried out in time to save himself, and his father had been horrified to think how nearly he had killed him? Then, again, suppose a day should come when his father would remember that night, and wish there had been no warning cry to stay his hand? With this last supposition Paul entertained himself until daybreak.

The following Sunday was fine; the sodden November chill was broken by the last flash of autumnal summer. In the morning Paul had to go to church and Sabbath-school, as always. On seasonable Sunday afternoons the burghers of Cordelia Street always sat out on their front "stoops," and talked to their neighbors on the next stoop, or called to those across the street in neighborly fashion. The men usually sat on gay cushions placed upon the steps that led down to the sidewalk, while the women, in their Sunday "waists," sat in rockers on the cramped porches, pretending to be greatly at their ease. The children played in the streets; there was so many of them that the place resembled the recreation grounds of a kindergarten. The men on the steps—all in their shirt sleeves, their vests unbuttoned—sat with their legs well apart, their stomachs comfortably protruding, and talked of the prices of things, or told anecdotes of the sagacity of their various chiefs and overlords. They occasionally looked over the multitude of squabbling children, listened affectionately to their high-pitched, nasal voices, smiling to see their own proclivities reproduced in their offspring, and interspersed their legends of the iron kings with remarks about their sons' progress at school, their grades in arithmetic, and the amounts they had saved in their toy banks.

On this last Sunday of November, Paul sat all the afternoon on the lowest step of his "stoop," staring into the street, while his sisters, in their rockers, were talking to the minister's daughters next door about how many shirt-waists they had made in the last week, and how many waffles some one had eaten at the last church supper. When the weather was warm, and his father was in a particularly jovial frame of mind, the girls made lemonade, which was always brought out in a red-glass pitcher, ornamented with forget-me-nots in blue enamel. This the girls thought very fine, and the neighbors always joked about the suspicious color of the pitcher.

Today Paul's father sat on the top step, talking to a young man who shifted a restless baby from knee to knee. He happened to be the young man who was daily held up to Paul as a model, and after whom it was his father's dearest hope that he would pattern. This young man was of a ruddy complexion, with a compressed, red mouth, and faded, near-sighted eyes, over which he wore thick spectacles, with gold bows that curved about his ears. He was clerk to one of the magnates of a great steel corporation, and was looked upon in Cordelia Street as a young man with a future. There was a story that, some five years ago—he was now barely twenty-six—he had been a trifle dissipated but in order to curb his appetites and save the loss of time and strength that a sowing of wild oats might have entailed, he had taken his chief's advice oft reiterated to his employees, and at twenty-one had married the first woman whom he could persuade to share his fortunes. She happened to be an angular school-mistress, much older than he, who also wore thick glasses, and who had now borne him four children, all near-sighted, like herself.

The young man was relating how his chief, now cruising in the Mediterranean, 25 kept in touch with all the details of the business, arranging his office hours on his yacht just as though he were at home, and "knocking off work enough to keep two stenographers busy." His father told, in turn, the plan his corporation was considering, of putting in an electric railway plant at Cairo. Paul snapped his teeth; he had an awful apprehension that they might spoil it all before he got there. Yet he rather liked to hear these legends of the iron kings, that were told and retold on Sundays and holidays; these stories of palaces in Venice, yachts on the Mediterranean, and high play at Monte Carlo appealed to his fancy, and he was interested in the triumphs of these cash boys who had become famous, though he had no mind for the cash-boy stage.

After supper was over, and he had helped to dry the dishes, Paul nervously asked his father whether he could go to George's to get some help in his geometry, and still more nervously asked for car fare. This latter request he had to repeat, as his father, on principle, did not like to hear requests for money, whether much or little. He asked Paul whether he could not go to some boy who lived nearer, and told him that he ought not to leave his school work until Sunday; but he gave him the dime. He was not a poor man, but he had a worthy ambition to come up in the world. His only reason for allowing Paul to usher was, that he thought a boy ought to be earning a little.

Paul bounded upstairs, scrubbed the greasy odor of the dish-water from his hands with the ill-smelling soap he hated, and then shook over his fingers a few drops of violet water from the bottle he kept hidden in his drawer. He left the house with his geometry conspicuously under his arm, and the moment he got out of Cordelia Street and boarded a downtown car, he shook off the lethargy of two deadening days, and began to live again.

The leading juvenile of the permanent stock company which played at one of the downtown theatres was an acquaintance of Paul's, and the boy had been invited to drop in at the Sunday-night rehearsals whenever he could. For more than a year Paul had spent every available moment loitering about Charley Edwards's dressing-room. He had won a place among Edward's following not only because the young actor, who could not afford to employ a dresser, often found him useful, but because he recognized in Paul something akin to what churchmen term "vocation."

It was at the theatre and at Carnegie Hall that Paul really lived; the rest was but a sleep and a forgetting. This was Paul's fairy tale, and it had for him all the allurement of a secret love. The moment he inhaled the gassy, painty, dusty odor behind the scenes, he breathed like a prisoner set free, and felt within him the possibility of doing or saying splendid, brilliant, poetic things. The moment the cracked orchestra beat out the overture from *Martha*°, or jerked at the serenade from *Rigoletto*°, all stupid and ugly things slid from him, and his senses were deliciously, yet delicately fired.

Perhaps it was because, in Paul's world, the natural nearly always wore the guise of ugliness, that a certain element of artificiality seemed to him necessary in beauty. Perhaps it was because his experience of life elsewhere was so full of Sabbath-school picnics, petty economies, wholesome advice as to how to succeed in life, and the unescapable odors of cooking, that he found this existence so alluring, these smartly-clad men and women so attractive, that he was so moved by these starry apple orchards that bloomed perennially under the limelight. 30

It would be difficult to put it strongly enough how convincingly the stage entrance of that theatre was for Paul the actual portal of Romance. Certainly none of the company ever suspected it, least of all Charley Edwards. It was very like the old stories that used to float about London of fabulously rich Jews, who had subterranean halls there, with palms, and fountains, and soft lamps and richly apparelled women who never saw the disenchanting light of London day. So, in the midst of that smoke-palled city, enamored of figures and grimy toil, Paul

---

*Martha:* grand opera about romance among English aristocrats (1847) by German composer Friedrich von Flotow.     *Rigoletto:* tragic grand opera (1851) by Italian composer Giuseppe Verdi.

had his secret temple, his wishing carpet, his bit of blue-and-white Mediterranean shore bathed in perpetual sunshine.

Several of Paul's teachers had a theory that his imagination had been perverted by garish fiction, but the truth was that he scarcely ever read at all. The books at home were not such as would either tempt or corrupt a youthful mind, and as for reading the novels that some of his friends urged upon him—well, he got what he wanted much more quickly from music; any sort of music, from an orchestra to a barrel organ. He needed only the spark, the indescribable thrill that made his imagination master of his senses, and he could make plots and pictures enough of his own. It was equally true that he was not stage struck—not, at any rate, in the usual acceptation of that expression. He had no desire to become an actor, any more than he had to become a musician. He felt no necessity to do any of these things; what he wanted was to see, to be in the atmosphere, float on the wave of it, to be carried out, blue league after blue league, away from everything.

After a night behind the scenes, Paul found the school-room more than ever repulsive; the bare floors and naked walls; the prosy men who never wore frock coats, or violets in their buttonholes; the women with their dull gowns, shrill voices, and pitiful seriousness about prepositions that govern the dative. He could not bear to have the other pupils think, for a moment, that he took these people seriously; he must convey to them that he considered it all trivial, and was there only by way of a jest, anyway. He had autographed pictures of all the members of the stock company which he showed his classmates, telling them the most incredible stories of his familiarity with these people, of his acquaintance with the soloists who came to Carnegie Hall, his suppers with them and the flowers he sent them. When these stories lost their effect, and his audience grew listless, he became desperate and would bid all the boys good-bye, announcing that he was going to travel for a while; going to Naples, to Venice, to Egypt. Then, next Monday, he would slip back, conscious and nervously smiling; his sister was ill, and he should have to defer his voyage until spring.

Matters went steadily worse with Paul at school. In the itch to let his instructors know how heartily he despised them and their homilies, and how thoroughly he was appreciated elsewhere, he mentioned once or twice that he had no time to fool with theorems; adding—with a twitch of the eyebrows and a touch of that nervous bravado which so perplexed them—that he was helping the people down at the stock company; they were old friends of his.

The upshot of the matter was that the Principal went to Paul's father, and Paul was taken out of school and put to work. The manager at Carnegie Hall was told to get another usher in his stead; the door-keeper at the theatre was warned not to admit him to the house; and Charley Edwards remorsefully promised the boy's father not to see him again. 35

The members of the stock company were vastly amused when some of Paul's stories reached them—especially the women. They were hardworking women, most of them supporting indigent husbands or brothers, and they laughed rather bitterly at having stirred the boy to such fervid and florid inventions. They agreed with the faculty and with his father that Paul's was a bad case.

The east-bound train was ploughing through a January snow-storm; the dull dawn was beginning to show grey when the engine whistled a mile out of Newark. Paul started up from the seat where he had lain curled in uneasy slumber, rubbed the breath-misted window glass with his hand, and peered out. The snow was whirling in curling eddies above the white bottom lands, and the drifts lay already deep in the fields and along the fences, while here and there the long dead grass and dried weed stalks protruded black above it. Lights shone from the scattered houses, and a gang of laborers who stood beside the track waved their lanterns.

Paul had slept very little, and he felt grimy and uncomfortable. He had made the all-night journey in a day coach, partly because he was ashamed, dressed as he was, to go into a Pullman, and partly because he was afraid of being seen there by some Pittsburgh businessmen, who might have noticed him in Denny & Carson's office. When the whistle awoke him, he clutched quickly at his breast pocket, glancing about him with an uncertain smile. But the little, clay-bespattered Italians were still sleeping, the slatternly women across the aisle were in open-mouthed oblivion, and even the crumby, crying babies were for the nonce stilled. Paul settled back to struggle with his impatience as best as he could.

When he arrived at the Jersey City station, he hurried through his breakfast, manifestly ill at ease and keeping a sharp eye about him. After he reached the Twenty-third Street station°, he consulted a cabman, and had himself driven to a men's furnishing establishment that was just opening for the day. He spent upward of two hours there, buying with endless reconsidering and great care. His new street suit he put on in the fitting-room; the frock coat and dress clothes he had bundled into the cab with his linen. Then he drove to a hatter's and a shoe house. His next errand was at Tiffany's, where he selected his silver and a new scarf-pin. He would not wait to have his silver marked, he said. Lastly, he stopped at a trunk shop on Broadway, and had his purchases packed into various travelling bags.

It was a little after one-o'clock when he drove up to the Waldorf, and after 40 settling with the cabman, went into the office. He registered from Washington; said his mother and father had been abroad, and that he had come down to await the arrival of their steamer. He told his story plausibly and had no trouble, since he volunteered to pay for them in advance, in engaging his rooms; a sleeping-room, sitting-room and bath.

Not once, but a hundred times Paul had planned this entry into New York. He had gone over every detail of it with Charley Edwards, and in his scrap book at home there were pages of description about New York hotels, cut from the Sunday papers. When he was shown to his sitting-room on the eighth floor, he saw at a glance that everything was as it should be; there was but one detail in his mental picture that the place did not realize, so he rang for the bell boy and sent him down for flowers. He moved about nervously until the boy returned, putting away his new linen and fingering it delightfully as he did so. When the flowers

Twenty-third Street station: The scene is now New York City.

came, he put them hastily into water, and then tumbled into a hot bath. Presently he came out of his white bath-room, resplendent in his new silk underwear, and playing with the tassels of his red robe. The snow was whirling so fiercely outside his windows that he could scarcely see across the street, but within the air was deliciously soft and fragrant. He put the violets and jonquils on the taboret beside the couch, and threw himself down, with a long sigh, covering himself with a Roman blanket. He was thoroughly tired; he had been in such haste, he had stood up to such a strain, covered so much ground in the last twenty-four hours, that he wanted to think how it had all come about. Lulled by the sound of the wind, the warm air, and the cool fragrance of the flowers, he sank into deep, drowsy retrospection.

It had been wonderfully simple; when they had shut him out of the theatre and concert hall, when they had taken away his bone, the whole thing was virtually determined. The rest was a mere matter of opportunity. The only thing that at all surprised him was his own courage—for he realized well enough that he had always been tormented by fear, a sort of apprehensive dread that, of late years, as the meshes of the lies he had told closed about him, had been pulling the muscles of his body tighter and tighter. Until now, he could not remember the time when he had not been dreading something. Even when he was a little boy, it was always there—behind him, or before, or on either side. There had always been the shadowed corner, the dark place into which he dared not look, but from which something seemed always to be watching him—and Paul had done things that were not pretty to watch, he knew.

But now he had a curious sense of relief, as though he had at last thrown down the gauntlet to the thing in the corner.

Yet it was but a day since he had been sulking in the traces; but yesterday afternoon that he had been sent to the bank with Denny & Carson's deposit, as usual—but this time he was instructed to leave the book to be balanced. There was above two thousand dollars in checks, and nearly a thousand in the bank notes which he had taken from the book and quietly transferred to his pocket. At the bank he had made out a new deposit slip. His nerves had been steady enough to permit of his returning to the office, where he had finished his work and asked for a full day's holiday tomorrow, Saturday, giving a perfectly reasonable pretext. The bank book, he knew, would not be returned before Monday or Tuesday, and his father would be out of town for the next week. From the time he slipped the bank notes into his pocket until he boarded the night train for New York, he had not known a moment's hesitation. It was not the first time Paul had steered through treacherous waters.

How astonishingly easy it had all been; here he was, the thing done; and this time there would be no awakening, no figure at the top of the stairs. He watched the snow flakes whirling by his window until he fell asleep.

When he awoke, it was three o'clock in the afternoon. He bounded up with a start; half of one of his precious days gone already! He spent more than an hour in dressing, watching every stage of his toilet carefully in the mirror. Everything was quite perfect; he was exactly the kind of boy he had always wanted to be.

When he went downstairs, Paul took a carriage and drove up Fifth Avenue toward the Park. The snow had somewhat abated; carriages and tradesmen's wagons were hurrying soundlessly to and fro in the winter twilight; boys in woollen mufflers were shovelling off the doorsteps; the avenue stages made fine spots of color against the white street. Here and there on the corners were stands, with whole flower gardens blooming under glass cases, against the sides of which the snow flakes stuck and melted; violets, roses, carnations, lilies of the valley— somewhat vastly more lovely and alluring that they blossomed thus unnaturally in the snow. The Park itself was a wonderful stage winterpiece.

When he returned, the pause of the twilight had ceased, and the tune of the streets had changed. The snow was falling faster, lights streamed from the hotels that reared their dozen stories fearlessly up into the storm, defying the raging Atlantic winds. A long, black stream of carriages poured down the avenue, intersected here and there by other streams, tending horizontally. There were a score of cabs about the entrance of his hotel, and his driver had to wait. Boys in livery were running in and out of the awning stretched across the sidewalk, up and down the red velvet carpet laid from the door to the street. Above, about, within it all was the rumble and roar, the hurry and toss of thousands of human beings as hot for pleasure as himself, and on every side of him towered the glaring affirmation of the omnipotence of wealth.

The boy set his teeth and drew his shoulders together in a spasm of realization: the plot of all dramas, the text of all romances, the nerve-stuff of all sensations was whirling about him like the snow flakes. He burnt like a faggot in a tempest.

When Paul went down to dinner, the music of the orchestra came floating up the elevator shaft to greet him. His head whirled as he stepped into the thronged corridor, and he sank back into one of the chairs against the wall to get his breath. The lights, the chatter, the perfumes, the bewildering medley of color—he had, for a moment, the feeling of not being able to stand it. But only for a moment; these were his own people, he told himself. He went slowly about the corridors, through the writing-rooms, smoking-rooms, reception-rooms, as though he were exploring the chambers of an enchanted palace, built and peopled for him alone.

When he reached the dining-room he sat down at a table near a window. The flowers, the white linen, the many-colored wine glasses, the gay toilettes of the women, the low popping of corks, the undulating repetitions of the *Blue Danube* from the orchestra, all flooded Paul's dream with bewildering radiance. When the roseate tinge of his champagne was added—that cold, precious, bubbling stuff that creamed and foamed in his glass—Paul wondered that there were honest men in the world at all. This was what all the world was fighting for, he reflected; this was what all the struggle was about. He doubted the reality of his past. Had he ever known a place called Cordelia Street, a place where fagged-looking businessmen got on the early car; mere rivets in a machine they seemed to Paul—sickening men, with combings of children's hair always hanging to their coats, and the smell of cooking in their clothes. Cordelia Street—Ah! that belonged to another time and country; had he not always been thus, had he not sat here night after night, from as far back as he could remember, looking pensively over just such shimmering textures, and slowly twirling the stem of a glass like this one between his thumb and middle finger? He rather thought he had.

He was not in the least abashed or lonely. He had no especial desire to meet or to know any of these people; all he demanded was the right to look on and conjecture, to watch the pageant. The mere stage properties were all he contended for. Nor was he lonely later in the evening, in his loge at the Metropolitan. He was now entirely rid of his nervous misgivings, of his forced aggressiveness, of the imperative desire to show himself different from his surroundings. He felt now that his surroundings explained him. Nobody questioned the purple; he had only to wear it passively. He had only to glance down at his attire to reassure himself that here it would be impossible for anyone to humiliate him.

He found it hard to leave his beautiful sitting-room to go to bed that night, and sat long watching the raging storm from his turret window. When he went to sleep it was with the lights turned on in his bedroom; partly because of his old timidity, and partly so that, if he should wake in the night, there would be no wretched moment of doubt, no horrible suspicion of yellow wall-paper, or of Washington and Calvin above his bed.

Sunday morning the city was practically snow-bound. Paul breakfasted late, and in the afternoon he fell in with a wild San Francisco boy, a freshman at Yale, who said he had run down for a "little flyer" over Sunday. The young man offered to show Paul the night side of the town, and the two boys went out together after dinner, not returning to the hotel until seven o'clock the next morning. They had started out in the confiding warmth of a champagne friendship, but their parting in the elevator was singularly cool. The freshman pulled himself together to make his train, and Paul went to bed. He awoke at two o'clock in the afternoon, very thirsty and dizzy, and rang for ice-water, coffee, and the Pittsburgh papers.

On the part of the hotel management, Paul excited no suspicion. There was this to be said for him, that he wore his spoils with dignity and in no way made himself conspicuous. Even under the glow of his wine he was never boisterous, though he found the stuff like a magician's wand for wonder-building. His chief greediness lay in his ears and eyes, and his excesses were not offensive ones. His dearest pleasures were the grey winter twilights in his sitting-room; his quiet enjoyment of his flowers, his clothes, his wide divan, his cigarette, and his sense of power. He could not remember a time when he had felt so at peace with himself. The mere release from the necessity of petty lying, lying every day and every day, restored his self-respect. He had never lied for pleasure, even at school; but to be noticed and admired, to assert his difference from other Cordelia Street boys; and he felt a good deal more manly, more honest, even, now that he had no need for boastful pretensions, now that he could, as his actor friends used to say, "dress the part." It was characteristic that remorse did not occur to him. His golden days went by without a shadow, and he made each as perfect as he could.

On the eighth day after his arrival in New York, he found the whole affair exploited in the Pittsburgh papers, exploited with a wealth of detail which indicated that local news of a sensational nature was at a low ebb. The firm of Denny & Carson announced that the boy's father had refunded the full amount of the theft, and that they had no intention of prosecuting. The Cumberland minister had been interviewed, and expressed his hope of yet reclaiming the motherless lad, and his Sabbath-school teacher declared that she would spare no effort to that end. The rumor had reached Pittsburgh that the boy had been seen in a New York hotel, and his father had gone East to find him and bring him home.

Paul had just come in to dress for dinner; he sank into a chair, weak to the knees, and clasped his head in his hands. It was to be worse than jail, even; the tepid waters of Cordelia Street were to close over him finally and forever. The gray monotony stretched before him in hopeless, unrelieved years; Sabbath-school, Young People's Meeting, the yellow-papered room, the damp dish-towels; it all rushed back upon him with a sickening vividness. He had the old feeling that the orchestra had suddenly stopped, the sinking sensation that the play was over. The sweat broke out on his face, and he sprang to his feet, looked about him with his white, conscious smile, and winked at himself in the mirror. With something of the old childish belief in miracles with which he had so often gone to class, all his lessons unlearned, Paul dressed and dashed whistling down the corridor to the elevator.

He had no sooner entered the dining-room and caught the measure of the music than his remembrance was lightened by his old elastic power of claiming the moment, mounting with it, and finding it all sufficient. The glare and glitter about him, the mere scenic accessories had again, and for the last time, their old potency. He would show himself that he was game, he would finish the thing splendidly. He doubted, more than ever, the existence of Cordelia Street, and for the first time he drank his wine recklessly. Was he not, after all, one of those fortunate beings born to the purple, was he not still himself and in his own place? He drummed a nervous accompaniment to the Pagliacci music and looked about him, telling himself over and over that it had paid.

He reflected drowsily, to the swell of the music and the chill sweetness of his wine, that he might have done it more wisely. He might have caught an outbound steamer and been well out of their clutches before now. But the other side of the world had seemed too far away and too uncertain then; he could not have waited for it; his need had been too sharp. If he had to choose over again, he would do the same thing tomorrow. He looked affectionately about the dining-room, now gilded with a soft mist. Ah, it had paid indeed!

Paul was awakened next morning by a painful throbbing in his head and feet. He had thrown himself across the bed without undressing, and had slept with his shoes on. His limbs and hands were lead heavy, and his tongue and throat were parched and burnt. There came upon him one of those fateful attacks of clear-headedness that never occurred except when he was physically exhausted and his nerves hung loose. He lay still and closed his eyes and let the tide of things wash over him.

His father was in New York; "stopping at some joint or other," he told himself. The memory of successive summers on the front stoop fell upon him like a weight of black water. He had not a hundred dollars left; and he knew now, more than ever, that money was everything, the wall that stood between all he loathed and all he wanted. The thing was winding itself up; he had thought of that on his first glorious day in New York, and had even provided a way to snap the thread. It lay on his dressing-table now; he had got it out last night when he came blindly up from dinner, but the shiny metal hurt his eyes, and he disliked the looks of it.

He rose and moved about with a painful effort, succumbing now and again to attacks of nausea. It was the old depression exaggerated; all the world had become Cordelia Street. Yet somehow he was not afraid of anything, was absolutely calm; perhaps because he had looked into the dark corner at last and knew. It was bad enough, what he saw there, but somehow not so bad as his long fear of it had been. He saw everything clearly now. He had a feeling that he had made the best of it, that he had lived the sort of life he was meant to live, and for half an hour he sat staring at the revolver. But he told himself that was not the way, so he went downstairs and took a cab to the ferry.

When Paul arrived at Newark, he got off the train and took another cab, directing the driver to follow the Pennsylvania tracks out of the town. The snow lay heavy on the roadways and had drifted deep in the open fields. Only here and there the dead grass or dried weed stalks projected, singularly black, above it. Once well into the country, Paul dismissed the carriage and walked, floundering along the tracks, his mind a medley of irrelevant things. He seemed to hold in his brain an actual picture of everything he had seen that morning. He remembered every feature of both his drivers, of the toothless old woman from whom he had bought the red flowers in his coat, the agent from whom he had got his ticket, and all of his fellow-passengers on the ferry. His mind, unable to cope with vital matters near at hand, worked feverishly and deftly at sorting and grouping these images. They made for him a part of the ugliness of the world, of the ache in his head, and the bitter burning on his tongue. He stooped and put a handful of snow into his mouth as he walked, but that, too, seemed hot. When he reached a little hillside, where the tracks ran through a cut some twenty feet below him, he stopped and sat down.

The carnations in his coat were drooping with the cold, he noticed; their red glory all over. It occurred to him that all the flowers he had seen in the glass cases that first night must have gone the same way, long before this. It was only one splendid breath they had, in spite of their brave mockery at the winter outside the glass; and it was a losing game in the end, it seemed, this revolt against the homilies by which the world is run. Paul took one of the blossoms carefully from his coat and scooped a little hole in the snow, where he covered it up. Then he dozed a while, from his weak condition, seemingly insensible to the cold.

The sound of an approaching train awoke him, and he started to his feet, remembering only his resolution, and afraid lest he should be too late. He stood watching the approaching locomotive, his teeth chattering, his lips drawn away from them in a frightened smile; once or twice he glanced nervously sidewise, as though he were being watched. When the right moment came, he jumped. As he fell, the folly of his haste occurred to him with merciless clearness, the vastness of

65

what he had left undone. There flashed through his brain, clearer than ever before, the blue of Adriatic water, the yellow of Algerian sands.

He felt something strike his chest, and that his body was being thrown swiftly through the air, on and on, immeasurably far and fast, while his limbs were gently relaxed. Then, because the picture making mechanism was crushed, the disturbing visions flashed into black, and Paul dropped back into the immense design of things.

## Anton Chekov

### MISERY                                                                 1886

*Translated by Constance Garnett*

*Anton Chekov*

*Anton Chekhov (1860–1904), one of the Russian writers who helped shape modern fiction, is remembered especially for his plays and short stories. Born in the provincial town of Taganrog, the grandson of a serf who had bought his own freedom, Chekhov as a boy worked in his father's general store, a hangout for vodka-drinking storytellers. As a young man, he studied at Moscow University and became a doctor of medicine. To earn money while a medical student, he wrote his first stories for magazines. By 1886, his work had become so celebrated that he gave up medicine for writing, though continuing to treat sick peasants at his home without fee and to work in clinics during times of famine and epidemic. From 1896 to 1904, Chekhov wrote his great plays for the Moscow Art Theater, where they were directed by the influential director Konstantin Stanislavsky: The Seagull, The Cherry Orchard, Uncle Vanya, and The Three Sisters. Chekhov's last years were brightened by his marriage to Olga Knipper, a star of the theater company. He died at 44, after a long struggle against tuberculosis.*

"To Whom Shall I Tell My Grief?"°

The twilight of evening. Big flakes of wet snow are whirling lazily about the street lamps, which have just been lighted, and lying in a thin soft layer on roofs, horses' backs, shoulders, caps. Iona Potapov, the sledge-driver, is all white like a ghost. He sits on the box without stirring, bent as double as the living body can

---

"*To whom shall . . . grief?*": a line from a Russian folk lament.

be bent. If a regular snowdrift fell on him it seems as though even then he would not think it necessary to shake it off. . . . His little mare is white and motionless too. Her stillness, the angularity of her lines, and the stick-like straightness of her legs make her look like a halfpenny gingerbread horse. She is probably lost in thought. Anyone who has been torn away from the plough, from the familiar gray landscapes, and cast into this slough, full of monstrous lights, of unceasing uproar and hurrying people, is bound to think.

It is a long time since Iona and his nag have budged. They came out of the yard before dinner-time and not a single fare yet. But now the shades of evening are falling on the town. The pale light of the street lamps changes to a vivid color, and the bustle of the street grows noisier.

"Sledge to Vyborgskaya!" Iona hears. "Sledge!"

Iona starts, and through his snow-plastered eyelashes sees an officer in a military overcoat with a hood over his head.

"To Vyborgskaya," repeats the officer. "Are you asleep? To Vyborgskaya!"    5

In token of assent Iona gives a tug at the reins which sends cakes of snow flying from the horse's back and shoulders. The officer gets into the sledge. The sledge-driver clicks to the horse, cranes his neck like a swan, rises in his seat, and more from habit than necessity brandishes his whip. The mare cranes her neck, too, crooks her stick-like legs, and hesitatingly sets off. . . .

"Where are you shoving, you devil?" Iona immediately hears shouts from the dark mass shifting to and fro before him. "Where the devil are you going? Keep to the r-right!"

"You don't know how to drive! Keep to the right," says the officer angrily.

A coachman driving a carriage swears at him; a pedestrian crossing the road and brushing the horse's nose with his shoulder looks at him angrily and shakes the snow off his sleeve. Iona fidgets on the box as though he were sitting on thorns, jerks his elbows, and turns his eyes about like one possessed, as though he did not know where he was or why he was there.

"What rascals they all are!" says the officer jocosely. "They are simply doing    10
their best to run up against you or fall under the horse's feet. They must be doing it on purpose."

Iona looks at his fare and moves his lips. . . . Apparently he means to say something, but nothing comes out but a sniff.

"What?" inquires the officer.

Iona gives a wry smile, and straining his throat, brings out huskily: "My son . . . , er . . . my son died this week, sir."

"H'm! What did he die of?"

Iona turns his whole body round to his fare, and says:    15

"Who can tell! It must have been from fever. . . . He lay three days in the hospital and then he died. . . . God's will."

"Turn round, you devil!" comes out of the darkness. "Have you gone cracked, you old dog? Look where you are going!"

"Drive on! drive on! . . . " says the officer. "We shan't get there till tomorrow going on like this. Hurry up!"

The sledge-driver cranes his neck again, rises in his seat, and with heavy grace swings his whip. Several times he looks round at the officer, but the latter keeps his eyes shut and is apparently disinclined to listen. Putting his fare down at Vyborgskaya, Iona stops by a restaurant, and again sits huddled up on the box. . . . Again the wet snow paints him and his horse white. One hour passes, and then another. . . .

Three young men, two tall and thin, one short and hunchbacked, come up, 20 railing at each other and loudly stamping on the pavement with their galoshes.

"Cabby, to the Police Bridge!" the hunchback cries in a cracked voice. "The three of us, . . . twenty kopecks!"

Iona tugs at the reins and clicks to his horse. Twenty kopecks is not a fair price, but he has no thoughts for that. Whether it is a rouble or whether it is five kopecks does not matter to him now so long as he has a fare. . . . The three young men, shoving each other and using bad language, go up to the sledge, and all three try to sit down at once. The question remains to be settled: Which are to sit down and which one is to stand? After a long altercation, ill-temper, and abuse, they come to the conclusion that the hunchback must stand because he is the shortest.

"Well, drive on," says the hunchback in his cracked voice, settling himself and breathing down Iona's neck. "Cut along! What a cap you've got, my friend! You wouldn't find a worse one in all Petersburg. . . ."

"He-he! . . . he-he! . . . " laughs Iona. "It's nothing to boast of!"

"Well, then, nothing to boast of, drive on! Are you going to drive like this 25 all the way? Eh? Shall I give you one in the neck?"

"My head aches," says one of the tall ones. "At the Dukmasovs' yesterday Vaska and I drank four bottles of brandy between us."

"I can't make out why you talk such stuff," says the other tall one angrily. "You lie like a brute."

"Strike me dead, it's the truth! . . . "

"It's about as true as that a louse coughs."

"He-he!" grins Iona. "Me-er-ry gentlemen!" 30

"Tfoo! the devil take you!" cries the hunchback indignantly. "Will you get on, you old plague, or won't you? Is that the way to drive? Give her one with the whip. Hang it all, give it her well."

Iona feels behind his back the jolting person and quivering voice of the hunchback. He hears abuse addressed to him, he sees people, and the feeling of loneliness begins little by little to be less heavy on his heart. The hunchback swears at him, till he chokes over some elaborately whimsical string of epithets and is overpowered by his cough. His tall companions begin talking of a certain Nadyezhda Petrovna. Iona looks round at them. Waiting till there is a brief pause, he looks round once more and says:

"This week . . . er . . . my . . . er . . . son died!"

"We shall all die, . . . " says the hunchback with a sigh, wiping his lips after coughing. "Come, drive on! drive on! My friends, I simply cannot stand crawling like this! When will he get us there?"

"Well, you give him a little encouragement . . . one in the neck!" 35

"Do you hear, you old plague? I'll make you smart. If one stands on ceremony with fellows like you one may as well walk. Do you hear, you old dragon? Or don't you care a hang what we say?"

And Iona hears rather than feels a slap on the back of his neck.

"He-he! . . ." he laughs. "Merry gentlemen . . . God give you health!"

"Cabman, are you married?" asks one of the tall ones.

"I? He-he! Me-er-ry gentlemen. The only wife for me now is the damp earth. . . .  40
He-ho-ho! . . . The grave that is! . . . Here my son's dead and I am alive. . . . It's a strange thing, death has come in at the wrong door. . . . Instead of coming for me it went for my son. . . ."

And Iona turns round to tell them how his son died, but at that point the hunchback gives a faint sigh and announces that, thank God! they have arrived at last. After taking his twenty kopecks, Iona gazes for a long while after the revelers, who disappear into a dark entry. Again he is alone and again there is silence for him. . . . The misery which has been for a brief space eased comes back again and tears his heart more cruelly than ever. With a look of anxiety and suffering Iona's eyes stray restlessly among the crowds moving to and fro on both sides of the street: can he not find among those thousands someone who will listen to him? But the crowds flit by heedless of him and his misery. . . . His misery is immense, beyond all bounds. If Iona's heart were to burst and his misery to flow out, it would flood the whole world, it seems, but yet it is not seen. It has found a hiding-place in such an insignificant shell that one would not have found it with a candle by daylight. . . .

Iona sees a house-porter with a parcel and makes up his mind to address him.

"What time will it be, friend?" he asks.

"Going on for ten. . . . Why have you stopped here? Drive on!"

Iona drives a few paces away, bends himself double, and gives himself up to  45
his misery. He feels it is no good to appeal to people. But before five minutes have passed he draws himself up, shakes his head as though he feels a sharp pain, and tugs at the reins. . . . He can bear it no longer.

"Back to the yard!" he thinks. "To the yard!"

And his little mare, as though she knew his thoughts, falls to trotting. An hour and a half later Iona is sitting by a big dirty stove. On the stove, on the floor, and on the benches are people snoring. The air is full of smells and stuffiness. Iona looks at the sleeping figures, scratches himself, and regrets that he has come home so early. . . .

"I have not earned enough to pay for the oats, even," he thinks. "That's why I am so miserable. A man who knows how to do his work, . . . who has had enough to eat, and whose horse has had enough to eat, is always at ease. . . ."

In one of the corners a young cabman gets up, clears his throat sleepily, and makes for the waterbucket.

"Want a drink?" Iona asks him.  50

"Seems so."

"May it do you good. . . . But my son is dead, mate. . . . Do you hear? This week in the hospital. . . . It's queer business. . . ."

Iona looks to see the effect produced by his words, but he sees nothing. The young man has covered his head over and is already asleep. The old man sighs and scratches himself. . . . Just as the young man had been thirsty for water, he thirsts for speech. His son will soon have been dead a week, and he has not really talked to anybody yet. . . . He wants to talk of it properly, with deliberation. . . . He wants to tell how his son was taken ill, how he suffered, what he said before he died, how he died. . . . He wants to describe the funeral, and how he went to the hospital to get his son's clothes. He still has his daughter Anisya in the country. . . . And he wants to talk about her too. . . . Yes, he has plenty to talk about now. His listener ought to sigh and exclaim and lament. . . . It would be even better to talk to women. Though they are silly creatures, they blubber at the first word.

"Let's go out and have a look at the mare," Iona thinks. "There is always time for sleep. . . . You'll have sleep enough, no fear. . . ."

He puts on his coat and goes into the stables where his mare is standing. He     55
thinks about oats, about hay, about the weather. . . . He cannot think about his son when he is alone. . . . To talk about him with someone is possible, but to think of him and picture him is insufferable anguish. . . .

"Are you munching?" Iona asks his mare, seeing her shining eyes. "There, munch away, munch away. . . . Since we have not earned enough for oats, we will eat hay. . . . Yes, . . . I have grown too old to drive. . . . My son ought to be driving, not I. . . . He was a real coachman. . . . He ought to have lived. . . ."

Iona is silent for a while, and then he goes on:

"That's how it is, old girl. . . . Kuzma Ionitch is gone. . . . He said good-by to me. . . . He went and died for no reason. . . . Now, suppose you had a little colt, and you were that little colt's own mother. . . . And all at once that same little colt went and died. . . . You'd be sorry, wouldn't you? . . . "

The little mare munches, listens, and breathes on her master's hands. Iona is carried away and tells her all about it.

## Kate Chopin

THE STORY OF AN HOUR                                                     1894

*Kate Chopin (1851–1904) demonstrates again, as in "The Storm" in Chapter Four, her ability to write short stories of compressed intensity. For a brief biography and a portrait see page 113.*

Knowing that Mrs. Mallard was afflicted with a heart trouble, great care was taken to break to her as gently as possible the news of her husband's death.

It was her sister Josephine who told her, in broken sentences, veiled hints that revealed in half concealing. Her husband's friend Richards was there, too, near her. It was he who had been in the newspaper office when intelligence of the railroad disaster was received, with Brently Mallard's name leading the list of "killed." He had only taken the time to assure himself of its truth by a second telegram, and had hastened to forestall any less careful, less tender friend in bearing the sad message.

She did not hear the story as many women have heard the same, with a paralyzed inability to accept its significance. She wept at once, with sudden, wild abandonment, in her sister's arms. When the storm of grief had spent itself she went away to her room alone. She would have no one follow her.

There stood, facing the open window, a comfortable, roomy armchair. Into this she sank, pressed down by a physical exhaustion that haunted her body and seemed to reach into her soul.

She could see in the open square before her house the tops of trees that were all aquiver with the new spring life. The delicious breath of rain was in the air. In the street below a peddler was crying his wares. The notes of a distant song which some one was singing reached her faintly, and countless sparrows were twittering in the eaves.

There were patches of blue sky showing here and there through the clouds that had met and piled one above the other in the west facing her window.

She sat with her head thrown back upon the cushion of the chair, quite motionless, except when a sob came up into her throat and shook her, as a child who has cried itself to sleep continues to sob in its dreams.

She was young, with a fair, calm face, whose lines bespoke repression and even a certain strength. But now there was a dull stare in her eyes, whose gaze was fixed away off yonder on one of those patches of blue sky. It was not a glance of reflection, but rather indicated a suspension of intelligent thought.

There was something coming to her and she was waiting for it, fearfully. What was it? She did not know; it was too subtle and elusive to name. But she felt it, creeping out of the sky, reaching toward her through the sounds, the scents, the color that filled the air.

Now her bosom rose and fell tumultuously. She was beginning to recognize this thing that was approaching to possess her, and she was striving to beat it back with her will—as powerless as her two white slender hands would have been.

When she abandoned herself a little whispered word escaped her slightly parted lips. She said it over and over under her breath: "Free, free, free!" The vacant stare and the look of terror that had followed it went from her eyes. They stayed keen and bright. Her pulses beat fast, and the coursing blood warmed and relaxed every inch of her body.

She did not stop to ask if it were not a monstrous joy that held her. A clear and exalted perception enabled her to dismiss the suggestion as trivial.

She knew that she would weep again when she saw the kind, tender hands folded in death; the face that had never looked save with love upon her, fixed and gray and dead. But she saw beyond that bitter moment a long procession of years to come that would belong to her absolutely. And she opened and spread her arms out to them in welcome.

There would be no one to live for during those coming years; she would live for herself. There would be no powerful will bending her in that blind persistence with which men and women believe they have a right to impose a private will upon a fellow creature. A kind intention or a cruel intention made the act seem no less a crime as she looked upon it in that brief moment of illumination.

And yet she had loved him—sometimes. Often she had not. What did it 15 matter! What could love, the unsolved mystery, count for in face of this possession of self-assertion which she suddenly recognized as the strongest impulse of her being.

"Free! Body and soul free!" she kept whispering.

Josephine was kneeling before the closed door with her lips to the keyhole, imploring for admission. "Louise, open the door! I beg; open the door—you will make yourself ill. What are you doing, Louise? For heaven's sake open the door."

"Go away. I am not making myself ill." No; she was drinking in a very elixir of life through that open window.

Her fancy was running riot along those days ahead of her. Spring days, and summer days, and all sorts of days that would be her own. She breathed a quick prayer that life might be long. It was only yesterday she had thought with a shudder that life might be long.

She arose at length and opened the door to her sister's importunities. There 20 was a feverish triumph in her eyes, and she carried herself unwittingly like a goddess of Victory. She clasped her sister's waist, and together they descended the stairs. Richards stood waiting for them at the bottom.

Some one was opening the front door with a latchkey. It was Brently Mallard who entered, a little travel-stained, composedly carrying his gripsack and umbrella. He had been far from the scene of the accident, and did not even know there had been one. He stood amazed at Josephine's piercing cry; at Richards' quick motion to screen him from the view of his wife.

But Richards was too late.

When the doctors came they said she had died of heart disease—of joy that kills.

## Sandra Cisneros

### BARBIE-Q

*Sandra Cisneros was born in Chicago in 1954. The daughter of a Mexican father and a Mexican-American mother, she was the only daughter in a family that also had six sons. She attended Loyola University of Chicago and then received a master's degree from the University of Iowa Writers Workshop. She has instructed high-school dropouts, but more recently she has taught as a visiting writer at numerous universities, including the University of California at Irvine and at Berkeley, and the University of Michigan. Her first published works were poetry: Bad Boys (1980) and My Wicked Ways (1987). Her fiction collections, The House on Mango Street (1984) and Women Hollering Creek (1991), however, earned her a broader audience. Her fiction style, as in "Barbie-Q," often resembles a prose poem, with its overt delight in colorful images and the music of words. Cisneros currently lives in San Antonio, Texas.*

*Sandra Cisneros*

for Licha

Yours is the one with mean eyes and a ponytail. Striped swimsuit, stilettos, sunglasses, and gold hoop earrings. Mine is the one with bubble hair. Red swimsuit, stilettos, pearl earrings, and a wire stand. But that's all we can afford, besides one extra outfit apiece. Yours, "Red Flair," sophisticated A-line coatdress with a Jackie Kennedy pillbox hat, white gloves, handbag, and heels included. Mine, "Solo in the Spotlight," evening elegance in black glitter strapless gown with a puffy skirt at the bottom like a mermaid tail, formal-length gloves, pink chiffon scarf, and mike included. From so much dressing and undressing, the black glitter wears off where her titties stick out. This and a dress invented from an old sock when we cut holes here and here and here, the cuff rolled over for the glamorous, fancy-free, off-the-shoulder look.

Every time the same story. Your Barbie is roommates with my Barbie, and my Barbie's boyfriend comes over and your Barbie steals him, okay? Kiss kiss kiss. Then the two Barbies fight. You dumbbell! He's mine. Oh no he's not, you stinky! Only Ken's invisible, right? Because we don't have money for a stupid-looking boy doll when we'd both rather ask for a new Barbie outfit next

Christmas. We have to make do with your mean-eyed Barbie and my bubblehead Barbie and our one outfit apiece not including the sock dress.

Until next Sunday when we are walking through the flea market on Maxwell Street and *there!* Lying on the street next to some tool bits, and platform shoes with the heels all squashed, and a fluorescent green wicker wastebasket, and aluminum foil, and hubcaps, and a pink shag rug, and windshield wiper blades, and dusty mason jars, and a coffee can full of rusty nails. *There!* Where? Two Mattel boxes. One with the "Career Gal" ensemble, snappy black-and-white business suit, three-quarter-length sleeve jacket with kick-pleat skirt, red sleeveless shell, gloves, pumps, and matching hat included. The other, "Sweet Dreams," dreamy pink-and-white plaid nightgown and matching robe, lace-trimmed slippers, hairbrush and hand mirror included. How much? Please, please, please, please, please, please, please, until they say okay.

On the outside you and me skipping and humming but inside we are doing loopity-loops and pirouetting. Until at the next vendor's stand, next to boxed pies, and bright orange toilet brushes, and rubber gloves, and wrench sets, and bouquets of feather flowers, and glass towel racks, and steel wool, and Alvin and the Chipmunks records, *there!* And *there!* And *there!* And *there!* and *there!* and *there!* and *there!* Bendable Legs Barbie with her new page-boy hairdo. Midge, Barbie's best friend. Ken, Barbie's boyfriend. Skipper, Barbie's little sister. Tutti and Todd, Barbie and Skipper's tiny twin sister and brother. Skipper's friends, Scooter and Ricky. Alan, Ken's buddy. And Francie, Barbie's MOD'ern cousin.

Everybody today selling toys, all of them damaged with water and smelling of 5 smoke. Because a big toy warehouse on Halsted Street burned down yesterday— see there?—the smoke still rising and drifting across the Dan Ryan expressway. And now there is a big fire sale at Maxwell Street, today only.

So what if we didn't get our new Bendable Legs Barbie and Midge and Ken and Skipper and Tutti and Todd and Scooter and Ricky and Alan and Francie in nice clean boxes and had to buy them on Maxwell Street, all water-soaked and sooty. So what if our Barbies smell like smoke when you hold them up to your nose even after you wash and wash and wash them. And if the prettiest doll, Barbie's MOD'ern cousin Francie with real eyelashes, eyelash brush included, has a left foot that's melted a little—so? If you dress her in her new "Prom Pinks" outfit, satin splendor with matching coat, gold belt, clutch, and hair bow included, so long as you don't lift her dress, right?—who's to know.

*Charlotte Perkins Gilman (1860–1935)
was born in Hartford, Connecticut. Her
father was the writer Frederick Beecher
Perkins (a nephew of reformer-novelist
Harriet Beecher Stowe, author of* Uncle
Tom's Cabin, *and abolitionist minister
Henry Ward Beecher), but he abandoned
the family shortly after his daughter's birth.
Raised in meager surroundings, the young
Gilman adopted her intellectual Beecher
aunts as role models. Because she and her
mother moved from one relation to another,
Gilman's early education was neglected—
at fifteen she had had only four years of
schooling. In 1878 she studied commercial
art at the Rhode Island School of Design. In
1884 she married Walter Stetson, an artist.*

Charlotte Perkins Gilman

*After the birth of her one daughter, she experienced a severe depression. The rest cure
her doctor prescribed became the basis of her most famous story, "The Yellow
Wallpaper." This tale combines standard elements of Gothic fiction (the isolated country mansion, the brooding atmosphere of the room, the aloof but dominating husband)
with the fresh clarity of Gilman's feminist perspective. Gilman's first marriage ended in
an amicable divorce. A celebrated essayist and public speaker, Gilman became an
important early figure in American feminism. Her study,* Women and Economics
*(1898), stressed the importance of both sexes having a place in the working world. Her
feminist-Utopian novel,* Herland *(1915), describes a thriving nation of women without
men. In 1900 Gilman married a second time—this time, more happily—to her cousin
George Houghton Gilman. After his sudden death in 1934, Gilman discovered she had
inoperable breast cancer. After finishing her autobiography, she killed herself with chlo-
roform in Pasadena, California.*

It is very seldom that mere ordinary people like John and myself secure
ancestral halls for the summer.

A colonial mansion, a hereditary estate, I would say a haunted house and
reach the height of romantic felicity—but that would be asking too much of fate!

Still I will proudly declare that there is something queer about it.

Else, why should it be let so cheaply? And why have stood so long untenanted?

John laughs at me, of course, but one expects that.                               5

John is practical in the extreme. He has no patience with faith, an intense
horror of superstition, and he scoffs openly at any talk of things not to be felt and
seen and put down in figures.

John is a physician, and *perhaps*—(I would not say it to a living soul, of course, but this is dead paper and a great relief to my mind)—*perhaps* that is one reason I do not get well faster.

You see, he does not believe I am sick! And what can one do?

If a physician of high standing, and one's own husband, assures friends and relatives that there is really nothing the matter with one but temporary nervous depression—a slight hysterical tendency—what is one to do?

My brother is also a physician, and also of high standing, and he says the same thing.

So I take phosphates or phosphites—whichever it is—and tonics, and air and exercise, and journeys, and am absolutely forbidden to "work" until I am well again.

Personally, I disagree with their ideas.

Personally, I believe that congenial work, with excitement and change, would do me good.

But what is one to do?

I did write for a while in spite of them; but it *does* exhaust me a good deal—having to be so sly about it, or else meet with heavy opposition.

I sometimes fancy that in my condition, if I had less opposition and more society and stimulus—but John says the very worst thing I can do is to think about my condition, and I confess it always makes me feel bad.

So I will let it alone and talk about the house.

The most beautiful place! It is quite alone, standing well back from the road, quite three miles from the village. It makes me think of English places that you read about, for there are hedges and walls and gates that lock, and lots of separate little houses for the gardeners and people.

There is a *delicious* garden! I never saw such a garden—large and shady, full of box-bordered paths, and lined with long grape-covered arbors with seats under them.

There were greenhouses, but they are all broken now.

There was some legal trouble, I believe, something about the heirs and co-heirs; anyhow, the place has been empty for years.

That spoils my ghostliness, I am afraid, but I don't care—there is something strange about the house—I can feel it.

I even said so to John one moonlight evening, but he said what I felt was a draught, and shut the window.

I get unreasonably angry with John sometimes. I'm sure I never used to be so sensitive. I think it is due to this nervous condition.

But John says if I feel so I shall neglect proper self-control; so I take pains to control myself—before him, at least, and that makes me very tired.

I don't like our room a bit. I wanted one downstairs that opened onto the piazza and had roses all over the window, and such pretty old-fashioned chintz hangings! But John would not hear of it.

He said there was only one window and not room for two beds, and no near room for him if he took another.

He is very careful and loving, and hardly lets me stir without special direction.

I have a schedule prescription for each hour in the day; he takes all care from me, and so I feel basely ungrateful not to value it more.

He said he came here solely on my account, that I was to have perfect rest 30 and all the air I could get. "Your exercise depends on your strength, my dear," said he, "and your food somewhat on your appetite; but air you can absorb all the time." So we took the nursery at the top of the house.

It is a big, airy room, the whole floor nearly, with windows that look all ways, and air and sunshine galore. It was a nursery first, and then playroom and gymnasium, I should judge, for the windows are barred for little children, and there are rings and things in the walls.

The paint and paper look as if a boys' school had used it. It is stripped off— the paper—in great patches all around the head of my bed, about as far as I can reach, and in a great place on the other side of the room low down. I never saw a worse paper in my life. One of those sprawling, flamboyant patterns committing every artistic sin.

It is dull enough to confuse the eye in following, pronounced enough constantly to irritate and provoke study, and when you follow the lame uncertain curves for a little distance they suddenly commit suicide—plunge off at outrageous angles, destroy themselves in unheard-of contradictions.

The color is repellent, almost revolting: a smouldering unclean yellow, strangely faded by the slow-turning sunlight. It is a dull yet lurid orange in some places, a sickly sulphur tint in others.

No wonder the children hated it! I should hate it myself if I had to live in 35 this room long.

There comes John, and I must put this away—he hates to have me write a word.

We have been here two weeks, and I haven't felt like writing before, since that first day.

I am sitting by the window now, up in this atrocious nursery, and there is nothing to hinder my writing as much as I please, save lack of strength.

John is away all day, and even some nights when his cases are serious.

I am glad my case is not serious!                                                           40

But these nervous troubles are dreadfully depressing.

John does not know how much I really suffer. He knows there is no reason to suffer, and that satisfies him.

Of course it is only nervousness. It does weigh on me so not to do my duty in any way!

I meant to be such a help to John, such a real rest and comfort, and here I am a comparative burden already!

Nobody would believe what an effort it is to do what little I am able—to 45 dress and entertain, and order things.

It is fortunate Mary is so good with the baby. Such a dear baby!

And yet I *cannot* be with him, it makes me so nervous.

I suppose John never was nervous in his life. He laughs at me so about this wallpaper!

At first he meant to repaper the room, but afterward he said that I was letting it get the better of me, and that nothing was worse for a nervous patient than to give way to such fancies.

He said that after the wallpaper was changed it would be the heavy bedstead, and then the barred windows, and then that gate at the head of the stairs, and so on.

"You know the place is doing you good," he said, "and really, dear, I don't care to renovate the house just for a three months' rental."

"Then do let us go downstairs," I said. "There are such pretty rooms there."

Then he took me in his arms and called me a blessed little goose, and said he would go down to the cellar, if I wished, and have it whitewashed into the bargain.

But he is right enough about the beds and windows and things.

It is as airy and comfortable a room as anyone need wish, and, of course, I would not be so silly as to make him uncomfortable just for a whim.

I'm really getting quite fond of the big room, all but that horrid paper.

Out of one window I can see the garden—those mysterious deep-shaded arbors, the riotous old-fashioned flowers, and bushes and gnarly trees.

Out of another I get a lovely view of the bay and a little private wharf belonging to the estate. There is a beautiful shaded lane that runs down there from the house. I always fancy I see people walking in these numerous paths and arbors, but John has cautioned me not to give way to fancy in the least. He says that with my imaginative power and habit of storymaking, a nervous weakness like mine is sure to lead to all manner of excited fancies, and that I ought to use my will and good sense to check the tendency. So I try.

I think sometimes that if I were only well enough to write a little it would relieve the press of ideas and rest me.

But I find I get pretty tired when I try.

It is so discouraging not to have any advice and companionship about my work. When I get really well, John says we will ask Cousin Henry and Julia down for a long visit; but he says he would as soon put fireworks in my pillow-case as to let me have those stimulating people about now.

I wish I could get well faster.

But I must not think about that. This paper looks to me as if it *knew* what a vicious influence it had!

There is a recurrent spot where the pattern lolls like a broken neck and two bulbous eyes stare at you upside down.

I get positively angry with the impertinence of it and the everlastingness. Up and down and sideways they crawl, and those absurd unblinking eyes are everywhere. There is one place where two breadths didn't match, and the eyes go all up and down the line, one a little higher than the other.

I never saw so much expression in an inanimate thing before, and we all know how much expression they have! I used to lie awake as a child and get more entertainment and terror out of blank walls and plain furniture than most children could find in a toy-store.

I remember what a kindly wink the knobs of our big old bureau used to have, and there was one chair that always seemed like a strong friend.

I used to feel that if any of the other things looked too fierce I could always hop into that chair and be safe.

The furniture in this room is no worse than inharmonious, however, for we had to bring it all from downstairs. I suppose when this was used as a playroom they had to take the nursery things out, and no wonder! I never saw such ravages as the children have made here.

The wallpaper, as I said before, is torn off in spots, and it sticketh closer than a brother—they must have had perseverance as well as hatred.

Then the floor is scratched and gouged and splintered, the plaster itself is dug out here and there, and this great heavy bed, which is all we found in the room, looks as if it had been through the wars.

But I don't mind it a bit—only the paper.

There comes John's sister. Such a dear girl as she is, and so careful of me! I must not let her find me writing.

She is a perfect and enthusiastic housekeeper, and hopes for no better profession. I verily believe she thinks it is the writing which made me sick!

But I can write when she is out, and see her a long way off from these windows.

There is one that commands the road, a lovely shaded winding road, and one that just looks off over the country. A lovely country, too, full of great elms and velvet meadows.

This wallpaper has a kind of subpattern in a different shade, a particularly irritating one, for you can only see it in certain lights, and not clearly then.

But in the places where it isn't faded and where the sun is just so—I can see a strange, provoking, formless sort of figure that seems to skulk about behind that silly and conspicuous front design.

There's sister on the stairs!

Well, the Fourth of July is over! The people are all gone, and I am tired out. John thought it might do me good to see a little company, so we just had Mother and Nellie and the children down for a week.

Of course I didn't do a thing. Jennie sees to everything now.

But it tired me all the same.

John says if I don't pick up faster he shall send me to Weir Mitchell° in the fall.

But I don't want to go there at all. I had a friend who was in his hands once, and she says he is just like John and my brother, only more so!

Weir Mitchell (1829–1914): famed nerve specialist who actually treated the author, Charlotte Perkins Gilman, for nervous prostration with his well-known "rest cure." (The cure was not successful.) Also the author of *Diseases of the Nervous System, Especially of Women* (1881).

Besides, it is such an undertaking to go so far.                                             85

I don't feel as if it was worthwhile to turn my hand over for anything, and I'm getting dreadfully fretful and querulous.

I cry at nothing, and cry most of the time.

Of course I don't when John is here, or anybody else, but when I am alone.

And I am alone a good deal just now. John is kept in town very often by serious cases, and Jennie is good and lets me alone when I want her to.

So I walk a little in the garden or down that lovely lane, sit on the porch   90
under the roses, and lie down up here a good deal.

I'm getting really fond of the room in spite of the wallpaper. Perhaps *because* of the wallpaper.

It dwells in my mind so!

I lie here on this great immovable bed—it is nailed down, I believe—and follow that pattern about by the hour. It is as good as gymnastics, I assure you. I start, we'll say, at the bottom, down in the corner over there where it has not been touched, and I determine for the thousandth time that I *will* follow that pointless pattern to some sort of a conclusion.

I know a little of the principle of design, and I know this thing was not arranged on any laws of radiation°, or alternation, or repetition, or symmetry, or anything else that I ever heard of.

It is repeated, of course, by the breadths, but not otherwise.                              95

Looked at in one way, each breadth stands alone; the bloated curves and flourishes—a kind of "debased Romanesque" with delirium tremens go waddling up and down in isolated columns of fatuity.

But, on the other hand, they connect diagonally, and the sprawling outlines run off in great slanting waves of optic horror, like a lot of wallowing sea-weeds in full chase.

The whole thing goes horizontally, too, at least it seems so, and I exhaust myself trying to distinguish the order of its going in that direction.

They have used a horizontal breadth for a frieze, and that adds wonderfully to the confusion.

There is one end of the room where it is almost intact, and there, when the   100
crosslights fade and the low sun shines directly upon it, I can almost fancy radiation after all—the interminable grotesque seems to form around a common center and rush off in headlong plunges of equal distraction.

It makes me tired to follow it. I will take a nap, I guess.

I don't know why I should write this.

I don't want to.

I don't feel able.

And I know John would think it absurd. But I *must* say what I feel and think   105
in some way—it is such a relief!

But the effort is getting to be greater than the relief.

*laws of radiation:* a principle of design in which all elements are arranged in some circular pattern around a center.

Half the time now I am awfully lazy, and lie down ever so much. John says I mustn't lose my strength, and has me take cod liver oil and lots of tonics and things, to say nothing of ale and wines and rare meat.

Dear John! He loves me very dearly, and hates to have me sick. I tried to have a real earnest reasonable talk with him the other day, and tell him how I wish he would let me go and make a visit to Cousin Henry and Julia.

But he said I wasn't able to go, nor able to stand it after I got there; and I did not make out a very good case for myself, for I was crying before I had finished.

It is getting to be a great effort for me to think straight. Just this nervous    110
weakness, I suppose.

And dear John gathered me up in his arms, and just carried me upstairs and laid me on the bed, and sat by me and read to me till it tired my head.

He said I was his darling and his comfort and all he had, and that I must take care of myself for his sake, and keep well.

He says no one but myself can help me out of it, that I must use my will and self-control and not let any silly fancies run away with me.

There's one comfort—the baby is well and happy, and does not have to occupy this nursery with the horrid wallpaper.

If we had not used it, that blessed child would have! What a fortunate    115
escape! Why, I wouldn't have a child of mine, an impressionable little thing, live in such a room for worlds.

I never thought of it before, but it is lucky that John kept me here after all; I can stand it so much easier than a baby, you see.

Of course I never mention it to them any more—I am too wise—but I keep watch for it all the same.

There are things in the wallpaper that nobody knows about but me, or ever will.

Behind that outside pattern the dim shapes get clearer every day.

It is always the same shape, only very numerous.    120

And it is like a woman stooping down and creeping about behind that pattern. I don't like it a bit. I wonder—I begin to think—I wish John would take me away from here!

It is so hard to talk with John about my case, because he is so wise, and because he loves me so.

But I tried it last night.

It was moonlight. The moon shines in all around just as the sun does.

I hate to see it sometimes, it creeps so slowly, and always comes in by one    125
window or another.

John was asleep and I hated to waken him, so I kept still and watched the moonlight on that undulating wallpaper till I felt creepy.

The faint figure behind seemed to shake the pattern, just as if she wanted to get out.

I got up softly and went to feel and see if the paper *did* move, and when I came back John was awake.

"What is it, little girl?" he said. "Don't go walking about like that—you'll get cold."

I thought it was a good time to talk, so I told him that I really was not gain- 130
ing here, and that I wished he would take me away.

"Why, darling!" said he. "Our lease will be up in three weeks, and I can't see
how to leave before.

"The repairs are not done at home, and I cannot possibly leave town just
now. Of course, if you were in any danger, I could and would, but you really are
better, dear, whether you can see it or not. I am a doctor, dear, and I know. You
are gaining flesh and color, your appetite is better, I feel really much easier about
you."

"I don't weigh a bit more," said I, "nor as much; and my appetite may be better in the evening when you are here but it is worse in the morning when you are
away!"

"Bless her little heart!" said he with a big hug. "She shall be as sick as she
pleases! But now let's improve the shining hours by going to sleep, and talk about
it in the morning!"

"And you won't go away?" I asked gloomily. 135

"Why, how can I, dear? It is only three weeks more and then we will take a
nice little trip for a few days while Jennie is getting the house ready. Really, dear,
you are better!"

"Better in body perhaps—" I began, and stopped short, for he sat up straight
and looked at me with such a stern, reproachful look that I could not say another
word.

"My darling," said he, "I beg you, for my sake and for our child's sake, as well
as for your own, that you will never for one instant let that idea enter your mind!
There is nothing so dangerous, so fascinating, to a temperament like yours. It is a
false and foolish fancy. Can you trust me as a physician when I tell you so?"

So of course I said no more on that score, and we went to sleep before long.
He thought I was asleep first, but I wasn't, and lay there for hours trying to decide
whether that front pattern and the back pattern really did move together or separately.

On a pattern like this, by daylight, there is a lack of sequence, a defiance of 140
law, that is a constant irritant to a normal mind.

The color is hideous enough, and unreliable enough, and infuriating enough,
but the pattern is torturing.

You think you have mastered it, but just as you get well under way in following, it turns a back-somersault and there you are. It slaps you in the face, knocks
you down, and tramples upon you. It is like a bad dream.

The outside pattern is a florid arabesque°, reminding one of a fungus. If you
can imagine a toadstool in joints, an interminable string of toadstools, budding
and sprouting in endless convolutions—why, that is something like it.

That is, sometimes!

There is one marked peculiarity about this paper, a thing nobody seems to 145
notice but myself, and that is that it changes as the light changes.

---

*arabesque:* a type of ornamental style (Arabic in origin) that uses flowers, foliage, fruit, or other figures to create an intricate pattern of interlocking shapes and lines.

When the sun shoots in through the east window—I always watch for that first long, straight ray—it changes so quickly that I never can quite believe it.

That is why I watch it always.

By moonlight—the moon shines in all night when there is a moon—I wouldn't know it was the same paper.

At night in any kind of light, in twilight, candlelight, lamplight, and worst of all by moonlight, it becomes bars! The outside pattern, I mean, and the woman behind it is as plain as can be.

I didn't realize for a long time what the thing was that showed behind, that dim subpattern, but now I am quite sure it is a woman.

By daylight she is subdued, quiet. I fancy it is the pattern that keeps her so still. It is so puzzling. It keeps me quiet by the hour.

I lie down ever so much now. John says it is good for me, and to sleep all I can.

Indeed he started the habit by making me lie down for an hour after each meal.

It is a very bad habit, I am convinced, for you see, I don't sleep.

And that cultivates deceit, for I don't tell them I'm awake—oh, no!

The fact is I am getting a little afraid of John.

He seems very queer sometimes, and even Jennie has an inexplicable look.

It strikes me occasionally, just as a scientific hypothesis, that perhaps it is the paper!

I have watched John when he did not know I was looking, and come into the room suddenly on the most innocent excuses, and I've caught him several times *looking at the paper!* And Jennie too. I caught Jennie with her hand on it once.

She didn't know I was in the room, and when I asked her in a quiet, a very quiet voice, with the most restrained manner possible, what she was doing with the paper, she turned around as if she had been caught stealing, and looked quite angry—asked me why I should frighten her so!

Then she said that the paper stained everything it touched, that she had found yellow smooches° on all my clothes and John's and she wished we would be more careful!

Did not that sound innocent? But I know she was studying that pattern, and I am determined that nobody shall find it out but myself!

Life is very much more exciting now than it used to be. You see, I have something more to expect, to look forward to, to watch. I really do eat better, and am more quiet than I was.

John is so pleased to see me improve! He laughed a little the other day, and said I seemed to be flourishing in spite of my wallpaper.

I turned it off with a laugh. I had no intention of telling him it was *because* of the wallpaper—he would make fun of me. He might even want to take me away.

*smooches:* smudges or smears.

I don't want to leave now until I have found it out. There is a week more, and I think that will be enough.

I'm feeling so much better!

I don't sleep much at night, for it is so interesting to watch developments; but I sleep a good deal during the daytime.

In the daytime it is tiresome and perplexing.

There are always new shoots on the fungus, and new shades of yellow all over it. I cannot keep count of them, though I have tried conscientiously.

It is the strangest yellow, that wallpaper! It makes me think of all the yellow things I ever saw—not beautiful ones like buttercups, but old, foul, bad yellow things.

But there is something else about that paper—the smell! I noticed it the moment we came into the room, but with so much air and sun it was not bad. Now we have had a week of fog and rain, and whether the windows are open or not, the smell is here.

It creeps all over the house.

I find it hovering in the dining-room, skulking in the parlor, hiding in the hall, lying in wait for me on the stairs.

It gets into my hair.

Even when I go to ride, if I turn my head suddenly and surprise it—there is that smell!

Such a peculiar odor, too! I have spent hours in trying to analyze it, to find what it smelled like.

It is not bad—at first—and very gentle, but quite the subtlest, most enduring odor I ever met.

In this damp weather it is awful. I wake up in the night and find it hanging over me.

It used to disturb me at first. I thought seriously of burning the house—to reach the smell.

But now I am used to it. The only thing I can think of that it is like is the *color* of the paper! A yellow smell.

There is a very funny mark on this wall, low down, near the mopboard. A streak that runs round the room. It goes behind every piece of furniture, except the bed, a long, straight, even *smooch*, as if it had been rubbed over and over.

I wonder how it was done and who did it, and what they did it for. Round and round and round—round and round and round—it makes me dizzy!

I really have discovered something at last.

Through watching so much at night, when it changes so, I have finally found out.

The front pattern *does* move—and no wonder! The woman behind shakes it!

Sometimes I think there are a great many women behind, and sometimes only one, and she crawls around fast, and her crawling shakes it all over.

Then in the very bright spots she keeps still, and in the very shady spots she just takes hold of the bars and shakes them hard.

And she is all the time trying to climb through. But nobody could climb through that pattern—it strangles so; I think that is why it has so many heads.

They get through and then the pattern strangles them off and turns them 190 upside down, and makes their eyes white!

If those heads were covered or taken off it would not be half so bad.

I think that woman gets out in the daytime!

And I'll tell you why—privately—I've seen her!

I can see her out of every one of my windows!

It is the same woman, I know, for she is always creeping, and most women do 195 not creep by daylight.

I see her in that long shaded lane, creeping up and down. I see her in those dark grape arbors, creeping all round the garden.

I see her on that long road under the trees, creeping along, and when a carriage comes she hides under the blackberry vines.

I don't blame her a bit. It must be very humiliating to be caught creeping by daylight!

I always lock the door when I creep by daylight. I can't do it at night, for I know John would suspect something at once.

And John is so queer now that I don't want to irritate him. I wish he would 200 take another room! Besides, I don't want anybody to get that woman out at night but myself.

I often wonder if I could see her out of all the windows at once.

But, turn as fast as I can, I can only see out of one at one time.

And though I always see her, she *may* be able to creep faster than I can turn! I have watched her sometimes away off in the open country, creeping as fast as a cloud shadow in a wind.

If only that top pattern could be gotten off from the under one! I mean to try it, little by little.

I have found out another funny thing, but I shan't tell it this time! It does 205 not do to trust people too much.

There are only two more days to get this paper off, and I believe John is beginning to notice. I don't like the look in his eyes.

And I heard him ask Jennie a lot of professional questions about me. She had a very good report to give.

She said I slept a good deal in the daytime.

John knows I don't sleep very well at night, for all I'm so quiet!

He asked me all sorts of questions too, and pretended to be very loving and 210 kind.

As if I couldn't see through him!

Still, I don't wonder he acts so, sleeping under this paper for three months.

It only interests me, but I feel sure John and Jennie are affected by it.


Hurrah! This is the last day, but it is enough. John is to stay in town over night, and won't be out until this evening.

Jennie wanted to sleep with me—the sly thing; but I told her I should undoubtedly rest better for a night all alone.

That was clever, for really I wasn't alone a bit! As soon as it was moonlight and that poor thing began to crawl and shake the pattern, I got up and ran to help her.

I pulled and she shook. I shook and she pulled, and before morning we had peeled off yards of that paper.

A strip about as high as my head and half around the room.

And then when the sun came and that awful pattern began to laugh at me, I declared I would finish it today!

We go away tomorrow, and they are moving all my furniture down again to leave things as they were before.

Jennie looked at the wall in amazement, but I told her merrily that I did it out of pure spite at the vicious thing.

She laughed and said she wouldn't mind doing it herself, but I must not get tired.

How she betrayed herself that time!

But I am here, and no person touches this paper but Me—not *alive!*

She tried to get me out of the room—it was too patent! But I said it was so quiet and empty and clean now that I believed I would lie down again and sleep all I could, and not to wake me even for dinner—I would call when I woke.

So now she is gone, and the servants are gone, and the things are gone, and there is nothing left but that great bedstead nailed down, with the canvas mattress we found on it.

We shall sleep downstairs tonight, and take the boat home tomorrow.

I quite enjoy the room, now it is bare again.

How those children did tear about here!

This bedstead is fairly gnawed!

But I must get to work.

I have locked the door and thrown the key down into the front path.

I don't want to go out, and I don't want to have anybody come in, till John comes.

I want to astonish him.

I've got a rope up here that even Jennie did not find. If that woman does get out, and tries to get away, I can tie her!

But I forgot I could not reach far without anything to stand on!

This bed will *not* move!

I tried to lift and push it until I was lame, and then I got so angry I bit off a little piece at one corner—but it hurt my teeth.

Then I peeled off all the paper I could reach standing on the floor. It sticks horribly and the pattern just enjoys it! All those strangled heads and bulbous eyes and waddling fungus growths just shriek with derision!

I am getting angry enough to do something desperate. To jump out of the window would be admirable exercise, but the bars are too strong even to try.

Besides I wouldn't do it. Of course not. I know well enough that a step like that is improper and might be misconstrued.

I don't like to *look* out of the windows even—there are so many of those creeping women, and they creep so fast.

I wonder if they all come out of that wallpaper as I did!

But I am securely fastened now by my well-hidden rope—you don't get *me* out in the road there!

I suppose I shall have to get back behind the pattern when it comes night, 245 and that is hard!

It is so pleasant to be out in this great room and creep around as I please!

I don't want to go outside. I won't, even if Jennie asks me to.

For outside you have to creep on the ground, and everything is green instead of yellow.

But here I can creep smoothly on the floor, and my shoulder just fits in that long smooch around the wall, so I cannot lose my way.

Why, there's John at the door! 250

It is no use, young man, you can't open it!

How he does call and pound!

Now he's crying to Jennie for an axe.

It would be a shame to break down that beautiful door!

"John, dear!" said I in the gentlest voice. "The key is down by the front steps, 255 under a plantain leaf!"

That silenced him for a few moments.

Then he said, very quietly indeed, "Open the door, my darling!"

"I can't," said I. "The key is down by the front door under a plantain leaf!" And then I said it again, several times, very gently and slowly, and said it so often that he had to go and see, and he got it of course, and came in. He stopped short by the door.

"What is the matter?" he cried. "For God's sake, what are you doing!"

I kept on creeping just the same, but I looked at him over my shoulder. 260

"I've got out at last," said I, "in spite of you and Jane. And I've pulled off most of the paper, so you can't put me back!"

Now why should that man have fainted? But he did, and right across my path by the wall, so that I had to creep over him every time!

## Nadine Gordimer

Nadine Gordimer was born in 1923 in Springs, a small gold-mining town near Johannesburg, South Africa. Her father was a Lithuanian Jewish immigrant, her mother an idealistic Englishwoman who founded a day care center in the local black township. After attending convent school, Gordimer entered the University of Witwatersrand. Having started publishing stories locally at fifteen, Gordimer began her short fiction writing with Face to Face (1949) and The Soft Voice of the Serpent (1952). Her first novel, The Lying Days, appeared in 1953. Gordimer was quickly recognized as a writer of international stature. A firm critic of South Africa's apartheid policy, she saw several of her novels banned in her native land. Meanwhile, her careful literary style and her exploration of the common humanity of all her characters—black, white, and Asian— struck many leftist critics as irrelevant to their revolutionary politics. Her novels include A Guest of Honor (1970), The Burger's Daughter (1979), A Sport of Nature (1987), and My Son's Story (1990). In 1986 she won The Hudson Review's Bennett Award for lifetime achievement. In 1991 she received the Nobel Prize in literature. Gordimer currently lives in Johannesburg.

Nadine Gordimer

My mother did not want me to go near the Concession stores° because they smelled, and were dirty, and the natives spat tuberculosis germs into the dust. She said it was no place for little girls.

But I used to go down there sometimes, in the afternoon, when static four o'clock held the houses of our Mine, and the sun washed over them like the waves of the sea over sand castles. I felt that life was going on down there at the Concession stores: noise, and movement and—yes, bad smells, even—and so I would wander down the naked road, with the hot sun uncomfortably drying the membrane inside my nose, seeing the irregular line of narrow white shops lying away ahead like a jumble of shoe boxes.

The signs of life that I craved were very soon evident: rich and careless of its vitality, it overflowed from the crowded pavement of the stores, and the surrounding veld° was littered with sucked-out oranges and tatters of dirty paper,

---

Concession stores: stores authorized by the mining company or local government.      veld: a South African word for sparsely wooded grassland.

and worn into the shabby barrenness peculiar to earth much trampled upon by the feet of men. A fat, one-legged native, with the patient detachment of the businessman who knows himself indispensable, sat on the bald veld beside the path that led from the Compound, his stock of walking sticks, standing up, handles tied together, points splayed out fanwise, his pyramids of bright, thin-skinned oranges waiting. Sometimes he had mealies° as well—those big, hard, full-grown ears with rows of yellowish tombstones instead of little pearly teeth—and a brazier° made from a paraffin tin to roast them by. Propped against the chipped pillars of the pavement, there were always other vendors, making their small way in lucky beans, herbs, bracelets beaten from copper wire, knitted caps in wonderful colors—blooming like great hairy petunias, or bursting suns, from the needles of old, old native women—and, of course, oranges. Everywhere there were oranges; the pushing, ambling crowds filling the pavement ate them as they stared at the windows, the gossips, sitting with their blankets drawn close and their feet in the gutter, sucked at them, the Concession store cats sniffed at the skins where they lay, hollow-cheeked, discarded in every doorway.

Quite often I had to flick the white pith from where it had landed, on my shoe or even my dress, spat negligently by some absorbed orange-eater contemplating a shirt through breath-smudged plate glass. The wild, wondering dirty men came up from the darkness of the mine and they lay themselves out to the sun on the veld, and to their mouths they put the round fruit of the sun; and it was the expression of their need.

I would saunter along the shopwindows amongst them, and for me there was    5 a quickening of glamour about the place: the air was thicker with their incense-like body smell, and the sudden rank shock of their strongest sweat, as a bare armpit lifted over my head. The clamor of their voices—always shouting, but so merry, so angry!—and the size of their laughter, and the open-mouthed startle with which they greeted every fresh sight: I felt vaguely the spell of the books I had read, returning; markets in Persia, bazaars in Cairo. . . . Nevertheless, I was careful not to let them brush too closely past me, lest some unnamable *something* crawl from their dusty blankets or torn cotton trousers onto my clean self, and I did not like the way they spat, with that terrible gurgle in the throat, into the gutter, or, worse still, blew their noses loudly between finger and thumb, and flung the excrement horribly to the air.

And neither did I like the heavy, sickening, greasy carrion-breath that poured from the mouth of the Hotela la Bantu, where the natives hunched intent at zinc-topped forms, eating steaming no-color chunks of horror that bore no relation to meat as I knew it. The down on my arms prickled in revulsion from the pulpy entrails hanging in dreadful enticement at the window, and the blood-embroidered sawdust spilling out of the doorway.

I know that I wondered how the storekeepers' wives, who sat on soap boxes outside the doorways of the shops on either side of the eating house, could stand the breath of that maw.° How they could sit, like lizards in the sun; and all the

---

*mealies:* a South African term for Indian corn.    *brazier:* metal pan for holding burning coals.
*maw:* the throat of jaws of an animal, especially of a carnivore.

time they breathed in the breath of the eating house: took it deep into the recesses of their being, whilst my throat closed against it in disgust.

It was down there one burning afternoon that I met Mrs. Saiyetovitz. She was one of the storekeepers' wives, and I had seen her many times before, sitting before the deep, blanket-hung cave of her husband's store, where a pile of tinsel-covered wooden trunks shimmered and flashed a pink or green eye out of the gloom into the outside—wearing her creased alpaca apron, her fat insteps leaning over her down-at-heel shoes. Sometimes she knitted, and sometimes she just sat. On this day there was a small girl hanging about her, drawing on the shopwindow with a sticky forefinger. When the child turned to look at me, I recognized her as one of the girls from "our school"; a girl from my class, as a matter of fact, called Miriam Saiyetovitz. Yes, that was her name: I remembered it because it was ugly—I was always sorry for girls with ugly names.

Miriam was a tousled, black-haired little girl, who wore a red bow in her hair. Now she recognized me, and we stood looking at one another; all at once the spare line of the name "Miriam Saiyetovitz," that was like the scrolled pattern of an iron gate with only the sky behind it, shifted its perspective in my mind, so that now between the cold curly M's and the implacable A's of that gate's framework, I saw a house, a complication of buildings and flowers and figures walking, where before there was nothing but the sky. Miriam Saiyetovitz—and this: behind her name and her school self, the hot and buzzing world of the stores. And I smiled at her, very friendly.

So she knew we had decided to recognize one another and she sauntered 10 over to talk to me. I stood with her in the doorway of her father's store, and I, too, wrote my name and drew cats composed of two capital O's and a sausage tail, with the point of my hot and sticky finger on the window. Of course, she did not exactly introduce me to her mother—children never do introduce their mothers; they merely let it be known, by referring to the woman in question offhand, in the course of play, or going up to speak to her in such a way that the relationship becomes obvious. Miriam went up to her mother and said diffidently: "Ma, I know this girl from school—she's in class with me, can we have some red lemonade?"

And the woman lifted her head from where she sat, widelegged, so that you couldn't help seeing the knee-elastic of her striped pink silk bloomers holding over the cotton tops of her stockings and said, peering, "Take it! Take it! Go, have it!"

Because I did not then know her, I thought that she was angry, she spoke with such impatience; but soon I knew that it was only her eager generosity that made her fling permission almost fiercely at Miriam whenever the child made some request. Mrs. Saiyetovitz's glance wavered over to me, but she did not seem to be seeing me very clearly: indeed, she could not, for her small, pale, pale eyes narrowed into her big, simple, heavy face were half-blind, and she had always to peer at everything, and never quite see.

I saw that she was very ugly.

Ugly, with the blunt ugliness of a toad; the ugliness of seeming not entirely at home in any element—as if the earth were the wrong place, too heavy and magnetic for a creature already so blunt; and the water would be no better: too subtle and contour-swayed for a creature so graceless. And yet her ugliness was without repellence. When I grew older I often wondered why; she should have been repellent, one should have turned from her, but one did not. She was only ugly. She had the short, stunted yet heavy bones of generations of oppression in the Ghettos of Europe; breasts, stomach, hips crowded sadly, no height, wide strong shoulders and a round back. Her head settled right down between her shoulders without even the grace of a neck, and her dun flat hair was cut at the level of her ears. Her features were not essentially Semitic; there was nothing so *definite* as that about her: she had no distinction whatever.

Miriam reappeared from the shades of the store, carrying two bottles of red    15
lemonade. A Shangaan emerged at the same time, clutching a newspaper parcel and puzzling over his handful of change, not looking where he was going. Miriam swept past him, the dusty African with his odd, troglodyte unsureness, and his hair plastered into savage whorls with red clay. With one swift movement she knocked the tin caps off the bottles against the scratched frame of the shopwindow, and handed my lemonade to me. "Where did you get it so quickly?" I asked, surprised. She jerked her head back towards the store: "In the kitchen," she said—and applied herself to the bottle.

And so I knew that the Saiyetovitzes lived there, behind the Concession store.

Saturday afternoons were the busiest. Mrs. Saiyetovitz's box stood vacant outside and she helped her husband in the shop. Saturday afternoon was usually my afternoon for going down there, too; my mother and father went out to golf, and I was left with the tick of the clock, the purring monologue of our cat, and the doves gurgling in the empty garden.

On Saturdays every doorway was crowded; a continual shifting stream snaked up and down the pavements; flies tangled overhead, the air smelled hotter, and from the doorway of every store the high, wailing blare and repetition of native songs, played on the gramophone, swung out upon the air and met in discord with the tune of the record being played next door.

Miriam's mother's brother was the proprietor of the Hotela la Bantu, and another uncle had the bicycle shop two doors down. Sometimes she had a message to deliver at the bicycle shop, and I would go in with her. Spare wheels hung across the ceiling, there was a battered wooden counter with a pile of puncture repair outfits, a sewing machine or two for sale, and, in the window, bells and pumps and mascots cut out of tin, painted yellow and red for the adornment of handle bars. We were invariably offered a lemonade by the uncle, and we invariably accepted. At home I was not allowed to drink lemonades unlimited; they might "spoil my dinner"; but Miriam drank them whenever she pleased.

Wriggling in and out amongst the gray-dusty bodies of the natives—their    20
silky brown skin dies in the damp fug° under-ground: after a few months down

---

*fug*: a bad smell, especially from a poorly ventilated area.

the mine, it reflects only weariness—Miriam looked with her own calm, quick self-possession upon the setting in which she found herself. Like someone sitting in a swarm of ants; and letting them swarm, letting them crawl all over and about her. Not lifting a hand to flick them off. Not crying out against them in disgust; nor explaining, saying, well, I *like* ants. Just sitting there and letting them swarm, and looking out of herself as if to say: What ants? What ants are you talking about? I giggled and shuddered in excitement at the sight of the dried bats and cobwebby snakeskins rotting in the bleary little window of the medicine shop, but Miriam tugged at my dress and said, "Oh, come on—" I exclaimed at the purple and red shirts lying amongst the dead flies in the wonderful confusion of Saiyetovitz's store window, but Miriam was telling me about her music exam in September, and only frowned at the interruption. I was approaching the confusion of adolescence, and sometimes an uncomfortable, terrible, fascinating curiosity—like a headless worm which lay shamefully hidden in the earth of my soul—crawled out into my consciousness at the sight of the animal obviousness of the natives' male bodies in their scanty covering; but the flash of my guilt at these moments met no answer in Miriam, although she was the same age as I.

If the sight of a boy interrupting his conversation to step out a yard or two onto the veld to relieve himself filled me with embarrassment and real disgust, so that I wanted to go and look at flowers—it seemed that Miriam did not see.

It was quite a long time before she took me into her father's store.

For months it remained a vague, dark, dust-moted world beyond the blanket-hung doorway, into which she was swallowed up and appeared again, whilst I waited outside, with the boys who looked and looked and looked at the windows. Then one day, as she was entering, she paused, and said suddenly and calmly: "Aren't you coming. . . ?" Without a word, I followed her in.

It was cool in the store, and the coolness was a surprise. Out of the sun-baked pavement—and into the store that was cool, like a cellar! Light danced only furtively along the folds of the blankets that hung from the ceiling: crackling silent and secret little fires in the curly woolen furze. The blankets were dark somber hangings, in proud colors, bold and primal. They hung like dark stalactites in the cave, still and heavy, communing only their own colors back to themselves. They brooded over the shop; and over Mr. Saiyetovitz there beneath, treading the worn cement with his disgruntled, dispossessed air of doing his best, but . . . I had glimpsed him before. He lurked within the depths of his store like a beast in its lair, and now and then I had seen the glimmer of his pale, pasty face with the wide upper lip under which the lower closed glumly and puffily.

John Saiyetovitz (his name wasn't John at all, really—it was Yanka, but when he arrived at Cape Town, long ago, the Immigration authorities were tired of attempting to understand and spell the unfamiliar names of the immigrants pouring off the boat, and by the time they'd got the "Saiyetovitz" spelt right, they couldn't be bothered puzzling over the "Yanka," so they scrawled "John" on his papers, and John he was)—John Saiyetovitz was a gentle man, with an almost hangdog gentleness, but when he was trading with the natives, strange blasts of power seemed to blow up in his soul. Africans are the slowest buyers in the world;

to them, buying is a ritual, a slow and solemn undertaking. They must go carefully; they nervously scent pitfalls on every side. And confronted with a selection of different kinds of the one thing they want, they are as confused as a child before a plate of pastries; fingering, hesitating, this or that . . . ? On a busy Saturday they must be allowed to stand about the shop endlessly, looking up and about, pausing to shake their heads and give a profound "OW!"; sauntering off; going to press their noses against the window again; coming back. And Mr. Saiyetovitz—always the same, unshaven and collarless—lugging a blanket down from the shelves, flinging it upon the counter—and another, and then another, and standing, arms hanging, sullen and smoldering before the blank-faced purchaser. The boy with his helpless stance, and his eyes rolling up in the agony of decision, filling the shop with the sickly odor of his anxious sweat, and clutching his precious guitar.

Waiting, waiting.

And then Mr. Saiyetovitz swooping away in a gesture of rage and denial; don't care, sick-to-death. And the boy anxious, edging forward to feel the cloth again, and the whole business starting up all over again; more blankets, different colors, down from the shelf and hooked from the ceiling—stalactites crumpled to woolen heaps to wonder over. Mr. Saiyetovitz throwing them down, moving in jerks of rage now, and then roughly bullying the boy into a decision. Shouting at him, bundling his purchase into his arms, snatching the money, gesturing him cowed out of the store.

Mr. Saiyetovitz treated the natives honestly, but with bad grace. He forced them to feel their ignorance, their inadequacy, and their submission to the white man's world of money. He spiritually maltreated them, and bitterly drove his nail into the coffin of their confidence.

With me, he was shy, he smiled widely and his hand went to the stud swinging loose at the neck of his half-buttoned shirt, and drew as if in apology over the stubbled landscape of his jaw. He always called me "little girl" and he liked to talk to me in the way that he thought children like to be talked to, but I found it very difficult to make a show of reply, because his English was so broken and fragmentary. So I used to stand there, and say yes, Mr. Saiyetovitz, and smile back and say thank you! to anything that sounded like a question, because the question usually was did I want a lemonade?, and of course, I usually did.

The first time Miriam ever came to my home was the day of my birthday 30 party.

Our relationship at school had continued unchanged, just as before; she had her friends and I had mine, but outside of school there was the curious plane of intimacy on which we had, as it were, surprised one another wandering, and so which was shared peculiarly by us.

I had put Miriam's name down on my guest list; she was invited; and she came. She wore a blue taffeta dress which Mrs. Saiyetovitz had made for her (on the old Singer on the counter in the shop, I guessed) and it was quite nice if a bit too frilly. My home was pretty and well-furnished and full of flowers and personal touches of my mother's hands; there was space, and everything shone. Miriam did not open her eyes at it; I saw her finger a bowl of baby-skinned pink roses in the passing, but all afternoon she looked out indifferently as she did at home.

The following Saturday at the store we were discussing the party. Miriam was telling Mrs. Saiyetovitz about my presents, and I was standing by in a pleasurable embarrassment at my own importance.

"Well, please God, Miri," said Mrs. Saiyetovitz at the finish, "you'll also have a party for your birday in April. . . . Ve'll be in d'house, and everyting'll be nice, just like you want."—They were leaving the rooms behind the shop—the mournful green plush curtains glooming the archway between the bedroom and the living room; the tarnished samovar; the black beetles in the little kitchen; Miriam's old black piano with the candlesticks, wheezing in the drafty passage; the damp puddly yard piled with empty packing cases and eggshells and banana skins; the hovering smell of fish frying. They were going to live in a little house in the township nearby.

But when April came, Miriam took ten of her friends to the Saturday afternoon bioscope in celebration of her birthday. "And to Costas Café afterwards for ice cream," she stated to her mother, looking out over her head. I think Mrs. Saiyetovitz was disappointed about the party, but she reasoned then, as always, that as her daughter went to school and was educated and could speak English, whilst she herself knew nothing, wasn't clever at all, the little daughter must know best what was right and what was *nice*.

I know now what of course I did not know then: that Miriam Saiyetovitz and I were intelligent little girls into whose brains there never had, and never would, come the freak and wonderful flash that is brilliance. Ours were alabaster intellects: clear, perfect, light; no streaks of dark, unknown granite splitting to reveal secret veins of brightness, like thin gold, between stratum and stratum. We were fitted to be good schoolteachers, secretaries, organizers; we did everything well, nothing badly, and nothing remarkably. But to the Saiyetovitzes, Miriam's brain blazed like the sun, warming their humbleness.

In the year-by-year passage through school, our classmates thinned out one by one; the way seedlings come up in a bunch to a certain stage in their development, and then by some inexplicable process of natural selection, one or two continue to grow and branch up into the air, whilst the others wither or remain small and weedy. The other girls left to go and learn shorthand-and-typewriting: weeded out by the necessity of earning a living. Or moved, and went to other schools: transplanted to some ground of their own. Miriam and I remained, growing straight and steadily. . . .

During our matriculation year a sense of wonder and impending change came upon us both; the excitement of coming to an end that is also a beginning. We felt this in one another, and so were drawn together in new earnestness. Miriam came to study with me in the garden at my house, and oftener than ever, I slipped down to the Concession stores to exchange a book or discuss work with her. For although they now had a house, the Saiyetovitzes crept about, very quiet, talking to one another only in hoarse, respectful whispers.

It was during this year, when the wonder of our own capacity to learn was reaching out and catching into light like a veld fire within us, that we began to talk of the University. And, all at once, we talked of nothing else. I spoke to my father of it, and he was agreeable, although my mother thought a girl could do better with her time. But so long as my father was willing to send me, I knew I should go. Ah yes, said Miriam. She liked my father very much; I knew that. In fact she said to me once—it was a strange thing to say, and almost emotionally, she said it, and at a strange time, because we were on the bus going into the town to buy a new winter coat which she had wanted very badly and talked about longingly for days, and her father had just given her the money to get it—she said to me: You know, I think your father's just right.—I mean, if you had to choose somebody, a certain kind of person for a father, well, your father'd be just the kind you'd want.

When she broached the subject of University to her parents, they were   40 agreeable for her to go, too. Indeed, they wanted her to go almost more than she herself did. But they worried a great deal about the money side of it; every time I went down to the store there'd be a discussion of ways and means, Saiyetovitz slowly munching his bread and garlic polony lunch, and worrying. Miriam didn't worry about it; they'll find the money, she said. She was a tall girl, now, with beautiful breasts, and a large, dark-featured face that had a certain capable elegance, although her father's glum mouth was unmistakable and on her upper lip faint dark down foreshadowed a heavy middle-age. Her parents were peasants; but she was the powerful young Jewess. Beside her, I felt pale in my Scotch gingery-fairness: lightly drawn upon the mind's eye, whilst she was painted in oils.

We both matriculated; not so well as we thought we should, but well enough; and we went to the University. And there too, we did well enough. We had both decided upon the same course: teaching. In the end, it had seemed the only thing to do. Neither of us had any particular bent.

It must have been a hard struggle for the Saiyetovitzes to keep Miriam at the University, buy her clothes, and pay for her board and lodging in Johannesburg. There is a great deal of money to be made out of native trade concessions purchased from the government; and it doesn't require education or trained commercial astuteness to make it—in fact, trading of this sort seems to flourish in response to something very different: what is needed is instinctive peasant craftiness such as can only be found in the uneducated, in those who have scratched up their own resources. Storekeepers with this quality of peasant craft made money all about Mr. Saiyetovitz, bought houses and motorcars and banded their wives' retired hands with diamonds in mark of their new idleness. But Mr. Saiyetovitz was a peasant without the peasant's craft; without that flaw in his simplicity that might have given him checks and deeds of transfer to sign, even if he were unable to read the print on the documents. . . . Without this craft, the peasant has only one thing left to him: hard work, dirty work, with the sweet, sickly body-smell of the black men about him all day. Saiyetovitz made no money: only worked hard and long, standing in his damp shirt amidst the clamor of the stores and the death-smell from the eating house always in his nose.

Meanwhile, Miriam fined down into a lady. She developed a half-bored, half-intolerant shrug of the shoulders in place of the childish sharpness that had been filed jagged by the rub-rub of rough life and harsh contrasts. She became soft-voiced, where she had been loud and gay. She watched and conformed; and soon took on the attitude of liberal-mindedness that sets the doors of the mind slackly open, so that any idea may walk in and out again, leaving very little impression: she could appreciate Bach and Stravinsky, and spend a long evening listening to swing music in the dark of somebody's flat.

Race and creed had never meant very much to Miriam and me, but at the University she sifted naturally towards the young Jews who were passing easily and enthusiastically, with their people's extraordinary aptitude for creative and scientific work, through Medical School. They liked her; she was invited to their homes for tennis parties, swimming on Sundays, and dances, and she seemed as unimpressed by the luxury of their ten-thousand-pound houses as she had been by the contrast of our clean, pleasant little home, long ago, when she herself was living behind the Concession store.

She usually spent part of the vacations with friends in Johannesburg; I missed her—wandering about the Mine on my own, out of touch, now, with the girls I had left behind in the backwater of the small town. During the second half of one July vacation—she had spent the first two weeks in Johannesburg—she asked me if she could come and spend Sunday at my home, and in the afternoon, one of the Medical students arrived at our house in his small car. He had come from Johannesburg; Miriam had evidently told him she would be with us. I gathered her parents did not know of the young man's visit, and I did not speak of it before them.

So the four years of our training passed. Miriam Saiyetovitz and I had dropped like two leaves, side by side into the same current, and been carried downstream together: now the current met a swirl of dead logs, reeds, and the force of other waters, and broke up, divided its drive and its one direction. The leaves floated clear; divergent from one another. Miriam got a teaching post in Johannesburg, but I was sent to a small school in the Northern Transvaal°. We met seldom during the first six months of our adult life: Miriam went to Capetown during the vacation, and I flew to Rhodesia with the first profits of my independence. Then came the war, and I, glad to escape so soon the profession I had once anticipated with such enthusiasm, joined the nursing service and went away for the long, strange interlude of four years. Whilst I was with a field hospital in Italy, I heard that Miriam had married—a Doctor Somebody-or-other: my informant wasn't sure of the name. I guessed it must be one of the boys whom she had known as students, I sent a cable of congratulation, to the Saiyetovitzes' address.

Northern Transvaal: the northeastern region of South Africa.

45

NADINE GORDIMER    445

And then, one day, I came back to the small mining town and found it there, the same; like a face that has been waiting a long time. My mother, and my Dad, the big wheels of the shaft turning, the trees folding their wings about the Mine houses; and our house, with the green, square lawn and the cat watching the doves. For the first few weeks I faltered about the old life, feeling my way in a dream so like the old reality that it hurt.

There was a feel about an afternoon that made my limbs tingle with familiarity. . . . What . . . ? And then, lying on our lawn under the hot sky, I knew: just the sort of glaring summer afternoon that used to send me down to the Concession stores, feeling isolated in the heat. Instantly, I thought of the Saiyetovitzes, and I wanted to go and see them, see if they were still there; what Miriam was doing; where she was, now.

Down at the stores it was the same as ever, only dirtier, smaller, more chipped and smeared—the way reality often is in contrast with the image carried long in the mind. As I stepped so strangely on that old pocked pavement, with the skeleton cats and the orange peel and the gobs of spit, my heart tightened with the thought of the Saiyetovitzes. I was in a kind of excitement to see the store again. And there it was; and excitement sank out at the evidence of the monotony of "things." Blankets swung a little in the doorway. Flies crawled amongst the shirts and shoes posed in the window, the hot, wet, sickening fatty smell came over from the eating house. I met it with the old revulsion: it was like breathing inside someone's stomach. And in the store, amongst the wicked glitter of the tin trunks, beneath the secret whispering of the blankets, the old Saiyetovitzes sat glumly, with patience, waiting. . . . As animals wait in a cage; for nothing.

In their delight at seeing me again, I saw that they were older, sadder; that     50 they had somehow given themselves into the weight of their own humbleness, they were without a pinnacle on which to fix their eyes. Whatever place it was that they looked upon now, it was flat.

Mr. Saiyetovitz's mouth had creased in further to the dead folds of his chin; his hair straggled to the rims of his ears. As he spoke to me, I noticed that his hands lay, with a curious helpless indifference, curled on the counter. Mrs. Saiyetovitz shuffled off at once to the back of the shop to make a cup of tea for me, and carried it in, slopping over into the saucer. She was uglier than ever, now, her back hunched up to meet her head, her old thick legs spiraled in crêpe bandages because of varicose veins. And blinder too, I could see: that enquiring look of the blind or deaf smiling unsure at you from her face.

The talk turned almost at once to Miriam, and as they answered my questions about her, I saw them go inert. Yes, she was married; had married a doctor— a flicker of pride in the old man at this. She lived in Johannesburg. Her husband was doing very well. There was a photograph of her home, in one of the more expensive suburbs; a large, white modern house, with flower borders and a fishpond. And there was Miri's little boy, sitting on his swing; and a studio portrait of him, taken with his mother.

There was the face of Miriam Saiyetovitz, confident, carefully made-up and framed in a good hairdresser's version of her dark hair, smiling queenly over the face of her child. One hand lay on the child's shoulder, a smooth hand, wearing large, plain, expensive diamond rings. Her bosom was proud and rounded now—a little too heavy, a little overripe in the climate of ease.

I could see in her face that she had forgotten a lot of things.

When his wife had gone into the back of the shop to refill my teacup, old Saiyetovitz went silent, looking at the hand that lay before him on the counter, the fingers twitching a little under the gaze.

It doesn't come out like you think, he said, it doesn't come out like you think.

He looked up at me with a comforting smile.

And then he told me that they had seen Miriam's little boy only three times since he was born. Miriam they saw hardly at all; her husband never. Once or twice a year she came out from Johannesburg to visit them, staying an hour on a Sunday afternoon, and then driving herself back to Town again. She had not invited her parents to her home at any time; they had been there only once, on the occasion of the birth of their grandson.

Mrs. Saiyetovitz came back into the store: she seemed to know of what we had been speaking. She sat down on a shot-purple tin trunk, and folded her arms over her breast. Ah yes, she breathed, ah yes. . . .

I stood there in Miriam's guilt before the Saiyetovitzes, and they were silent, in the accusation of the humble.


But in a little while a Swazi° in a tobacco-colored blanket sauntered dreamily into the shop, and Mr. Saiyetovitz rose heavy with defeat.

Through the eddy of dust in the lonely interior and the wavering fear round the head of the native and the bright hot dance of the jazz blankets and the dreadful submission of Mrs. Saiyetovitz's conquered voice in my ear, I heard his voice strike like a snake at my faith: angry and browbeating, sullen and final, lashing weakness at the weak.

Mr. Saiyetovitz and the native.

Defeated, and without understanding in their defeat.

*Swazi:* one of the largest Bantu tribes of southeastern Africa.

**Langston Hughes**

*Langston Hughes (1902–1967), who dropped his first name, James, was born in Joplin, Missouri. As a high school senior in Cleveland, he wrote a poem still often reprinted, "The Negro Speaks of Rivers." When a young man, he worked as a merchant seaman, visited Africa, and lived for a time in Paris and Rome. The Weary Blues (1926) earned him an immediate reputation as a poet; his interest in fiction developed later. In his autobiography I Wonder As I Wander (1956), he credits D. H. Lawrence's stories, particularly "The Rocking-Horse Winner," with inspiring him to write short fiction himself. Hughes's writing won him a scholarship to Lincoln University, from which he was graduated in 1929. He became a major fig-*

Langston Hughes

*ure in the Harlem Renaissance of the 1920s and early 1930s, a period when that section of New York City proved a lively center for African-American writers, artists, and musicians. Tireless in his efforts to win new respect for African-American culture, Hughes compiled twenty-eight anthologies of African-American folklore and poetry. He was a prolific and protean writer: among his original works are plays, song lyrics, children's books, memoirs, newspaper columns, translations, and essays reporting his imaginary conversations with a Harlem citizen called Simple, a streetwise philosopher. A Langston Hughes Reader (1958) gives some idea of the scope of his writing, its richness and variety.*

He was not interested in snow. When he got off the freight, one early evening during the depression, Sargeant never even noticed the snow. But he must have felt it seeping down his neck, cold, wet, sopping in his shoes. But if you had asked him, he wouldn't have known it was snowing. Sargeant didn't see the snow, not even under the bright lights of the main street, falling white and flaky against the night. He was too hungry, too sleepy, too tired.

The Reverend Mr. Dorset, however, saw the snow when he switched on his porch light, opened the front door of his parsonage, and found standing there before him a big black man with snow on his face, a human piece of night with snow on his face—obviously unemployed.

Said the Reverend Mr. Dorset before Sargeant even realized he'd opened his mouth: "I'm sorry. No! Go right on down this street four blocks and turn to your left, walk up seven and you'll see the Relief Shelter. I'm sorry. No!" He shut the door. Sargeant wanted to tell the holy man that he had already been to the Relief Shelter, been to hundreds of relief shelters during the depression years, the beds were always gone and supper was over, the place was full, and they drew the color line anyhow. But the minister said, "No," and shut the door. Evidently he didn't want to hear about it. And he *had* a door to shut.

The big black man turned away. And even yet he didn't see the snow, walking right into it. Maybe he sensed it, cold, wet, sticking to his jaws, wet on his black hands, sopping in his shoes. He stopped and stood on the sidewalk hunched over—hungry, sleepy, cold—looking up and down. Then he looked right where he was—in front of a church! Of course! A church! Sure, right next to a parsonage, certainly a church.

It had *two* doors. 5

Broad white steps in the night all snowy white. Two high arched doors with slender stone pillars on either side. And way up, a round lacy window with a stone crucifix in the middle and Christ on the crucifix in stone. All this was pale in the street lights, solid and stony pale in the snow.

Sargeant blinked. When he looked up, the snow fell into his eyes. For the first time that night he *saw* the snow. He shook his head. He shook the snow from his coat sleeves, felt hungry, felt lost, felt not lost, felt cold. He walked up the steps of the church. He knocked at the door. No answer. He tried the handle. Locked. He put his shoulder against the door and his long black body slanted like a ramrod. He pushed. With loud rhythmic grunts, like the grunts in a chain-gang song, he pushed against the door.

"I'm tired . . . Huh! . . . Hongry . . . Uh! . . . I'm sleepy . . . Huh! I'm cold . . . I got to sleep somewheres," Sargeant said. "This here is a church, ain't it? Well, uh!"

He pushed against the door.

Suddenly, with an undue cracking and screaking, the door began to give way 10 to the tall black Negro who pushed ferociously against it.

By now two or three white people had stopped in the street, and Sargeant was vaguely aware of some of them yelling at him concerning the door. Three or four more came running, yelling at him.

"Hey!" they said. "Hey!"

"Uh-huh," answered the big tall Negro, "I know it's a white folks' church, but I got to sleep somewhere." He gave another lunge at the door. "Huh!"

And the door broke open.

But just when the door gave way, two white cops arrived in a car, ran up the 15 steps with their clubs, and grabbed Sargeant. But Sargeant for once had no intention of being pulled or pushed away from the door.

Sargeant grabbed, but not for anything so weak as a broken door. He grabbed for one of the tall stone pillars beside the door, grabbed at it and caught it. And held it. The cops pulled. Sargeant pulled. Most of the people in the street got behind the cops and helped them pull.

"A big black unemployed Negro holding onto our church!" thought the people. "The idea!"

The cops began to beat Sargeant over the head, and nobody protested. But he held on.

And then the church fell down.

Gradually, the big stone front of the church fell down, the walls and the rafters, the crucifix and the Christ. Then the whole thing fell down, covering the cops and the people with bricks and stones and debris. The whole church fell down in the snow.

Sargeant got out from under the church and went walking on up the street with the stone pillar on his shoulder. He was under the impression that he had buried the parsonage and the Reverend Mr. Dorset who said, "No!" So he laughed, and threw the pillar six blocks up the street and went on.

Sargeant thought he was alone, but listening to the *crunch, crunch, crunch* on the snow of his own footsteps, he heard other footsteps, too, doubling his own. He looked around, and there was Christ walking along beside him, the same Christ that had been on the cross on the church—still stone with a rough stone surface, walking along beside him just like he was broken off the cross when the church fell down.

"Well, I'll be dogged," said Sargeant. "This here's the first time I ever seed you off the cross."

"Yes," said Christ, crunching his feet in the snow. "You had to pull the church down to get me off the cross."

"You glad?" said Sargeant.

"I sure am," said Christ.

They both laughed.

"I'm a hell of a fellow, ain't I?" said Sargeant. "Done pulled the church down!"

"You did a good job," said Christ. "They have kept me nailed on a cross for nearly two thousand years."

'Whee-ee-e!" said Sargeant. "I know you are glad to get off."

"I sure am," said Christ.

They walked on in the snow. Sargeant looked at the man of stone.

"And you have been up there two thousand years?"

"I sure have," Christ said.

"Well, if I had a little cash," said Sargeant, "I'd show you around a bit."

"I been around," said Christ.

"Yeah, but that was a long time ago."

"All the same," said Christ, "I've been around."

They walked on in the snow until they came to the railroad yards. Sargeant was tired, sweating and tired.

"Where you goin'?" Sargeant said, stopping by the tracks. He looked at Christ. Sargeant said, "I'm just a bum on the road. How about you? Where you goin'?"

"God knows," Christ said, "but I'm leavin' here."

They saw the red and green lights of the railroad yard half veiled by the snow that fell out of the night. Away down the track they saw a fire in a hobo jungle.

"I can go there and sleep," Sargeant said.

"You can?"

"Sure," said Sargeant. "That place ain't got no doors."

Outside the town, along the tracks, there were barren trees and bushes below the embankment, snow-gray in the dark. And down among the trees and bushes there were makeshift houses made out of boxes and tin and old pieces of wood and canvas. You couldn't see them in the dark, but you knew they were there if you'd ever been on the road, if you had ever lived with the homeless and hungry in a depression.

"I'm side-tracking," Sargeant said. "I'm tired."

"I'm gonna make it on to Kansas City," said Christ.

"O.K.," Sargeant said. "So long!"

He went down into the hobo jungle and found himself a place to sleep. He 50 never did see Christ no more. About 6:00 A.M. a freight came by. Sargeant scrambled out of the jungle with a dozen or so more hobos and ran along the track, grabbing at the freight. It was dawn, early dawn, cold and gray.

"Wonder where Christ is by now?" Sargeant thought. "He musta gone on way on down the road. He didn't sleep in this jungle."

Sargeant grabbed the train and started to pull himself up into a moving coal car, over the edge of a wheeling coal car. But strangely enough, the car was full of cops. The nearest cop rapped Sargeant soundly across the knuckles with his night stick. Wham! Rapped his big black hands for clinging to the top of the car. Wham! But Sargeant did not turn loose. He clung on and tried to pull himself into the car. He hollered at the top of his voice, "Damn it, lemme in this car!"

"Shut up," barked the cop. "You crazy coon!" He rapped Sargeant across the knuckles and punched him in the stomach. "You ain't out in no jungle now. This ain't no train. You in jail."

Wham! across his bare black fingers clinging to the bars of his cell. Wham! between the steel bars low down against his shins.

Suddenly Sargeant realized that he really was in jail. He wasn't on no train. 55 The blood of the night before had dried on his face, his head hurt terribly, and a cop outside in the corridor was hitting him across the knuckles for holding onto the door, yelling and shaking the cell door.

"They musta took me to jail for breaking down the door last night," Sargeant thought, "that church door."

Sargeant went over and sat on a wooden bench against the cold stone wall. He was emptier than ever. His clothes were wet, clammy cold wet, and shoes sloppy with snow water. It was just about dawn. There he was, locked up behind a cell door, nursing his bruised fingers.

The bruised fingers were his, but not the *door*.

Not the *club* but the fingers.

"You wait," mumbled Sargeant, black against the jail wall. "I'm gonna break 60 down this door, too."

"Shut up—or I'll paste you one," said the cop.

"I'm gonna break down this door," yelled Sargeant as he stood up in his cell.

Then he must have been talking to himself because he said, "I wonder where Christ's gone? I wonder if he's gone to Kansas City?"

## Zora Neale Hurston

SWEAT                                                                    1926

*Zora Neale Hurston (1901?–1960) was
born in Eatonsville, Florida, but no record
of her actual date of birth exists (best guesses range from 1900 to 1903). Hurston was
one of eight children. Her father, a carpenter and Baptist preacher, was also the three-
term mayor of Eatonsville, the first all-black
town incorporated in the United States.
When Hurston's mother died in 1912, the
father moved the children from one relative
to another. Consequently, Hurston never
finished grammar school, although in 1918
she began taking classes at Howard University, paying her way through by working as
a manicurist and maid. While at Howard
she published her first story. In early 1925
she moved to New York, arriving with
"$1.50, no job, no friends, and a lot of
hope." She soon became an important
member of the "Harlem Renaissance," a*

Zora Neale Hurston

*group of young black artists (including Langston Hughes, Countee Cullen, Jean
Toomer, and Claude McKay) who sought "spiritual emancipation" for African-
Americans by exploring black heritage and identity in the arts. Hurston eventually
became, according to critic Laura Zaidman, "the most prolific black American woman
writer of her time." In 1925 she became the first black student at Barnard College,
where she completed a B.A. in anthropology. Hurston's most famous story, "Sweat,"
appeared in the only issue of* Fire!!, *a 1926 avant-garde Harlem Renaissance magazine
edited by Hurston, Hughes, and Wallace Thurman. This powerful story of an unhappy
marriage turned murderous was particularly noteworthy for having the characters speak
in the black country dialect of Hurston's native Florida. Hurston achieved only modest
success during her lifetime, despite the publication of her memorable novel,* Their Eyes
Were Watching God *(1937), and her many contributions to the study of African-
American folklore. She died, poor and neglected, in a Florida welfare home and was
buried in an unmarked grave. In 1973 novelist Alice Walker erected a gravestone for
her carved with the words:*

Zora Neale Hurston
"A Genius of the South"
1901 – 1960
Novelist, Folklorist
Anthropologist

*I*

It was eleven o'clock of a Spring night in Florida. It was Sunday. Any other night, Delia Jones would have been in bed for two hours by this time. But she was a washwoman, and Monday morning meant a great deal to her. So she collected the soiled clothes on Saturday when she returned the clean things. Sunday night after church, she sorted and put the white things to soak. It saved her almost a half-day's start. A great hamper in the bedroom held the clothes that she brought home. It was so much neater than a number of bundles lying around.

She squatted on the kitchen floor beside the great pile of clothes, sorting them into small heaps according to color, and humming a song in a mournful key, but wondering through it all where Sykes, her husband, had gone with her horse and buckboard.°

Just then something long, round, limp, and black fell upon her shoulders and slithered to the floor beside her. A great terror took hold of her. It softened her knees and dried her mouth so that it was a full minute before she could cry out or move. Then she saw that it was the big bull whip her husband liked to carry when he drove.

She lifted her eyes to the door and saw him standing there bent over with laughter at her fright. She screamed at him.

"Sykes, what you throw dat whip on me like dat? You know it would skeer me—looks just like a snake, an' you knows how skeered Ah is of snakes."

"Course Ah knowed it! That's how come Ah done it." He slapped his leg with his hand and almost rolled on the ground in his mirth. "If you such a big fool dat you got to have a fit over a earth worm or a string, Ah don't keer how bad Ah skeer you."

"You ain't got no business doing it. Gawd knows it's a sin. Some day Ah'm gointuh drop dead from some of yo' foolishness. 'Nother thing, where you been wid mah rig? Ah feeds dat pony. He ain't fuh you to be drivin' wid no bull whip."

"You sho' is one aggravatin' nigger woman!" he declared and stepped into the room. She resumed her work and did not answer him at once. "Ah done tole you time and again to keep them white folks' clothes outa dis house."

He picked up the whip and glared at her. Delia went on with her work. She went out into the yard and returned with a galvanized tub and set it on the washbench. She saw that Sykes had kicked all of the clothes together again, and now stood in her way truculently, his whole manner hoping, *praying*, for an argument. But she walked calmly around him and commenced to re-sort the things.

"Next time, Ah'm gointer kick 'em outdoors," he threatened as he struck a match along the leg of his corduroy breeches.

Delia never looked up from her work, and her thin, stooped shoulders sagged further.

---

*buckboard:* a four-wheeled open carriage with the seat resting on a spring platform.

"Ah ain't for no fuss t'night Sykes. Ah just come from taking sacrament at the church house."

He snorted scornfully. "Yeah, you just come from de church house on a Sunday night, but heah you is gone to work on them clothes. You ain't nothing but a hypocrite. One of them amen-corner Christians—sing, whoop, and shout, then come home and wash white folks' clothes on the Sabbath."

He stepped roughly upon the whitest pile of things, kicking them helter-skelter as he crossed the room. His wife gave a little scream of dismay, and quickly gathered them together again.

"Sykes, you quit grindin' dirt into these clothes! How can Ah git through by  15
Sat'day if Ah don't start on Sunday?"

"Ah don't keer if you never git through. Anyhow, Ah done promised Gawd and a couple of other men, Ah ain't gointer have it in mah house. Don't gimme no lip neither, else Ah'll throw 'em out and put mah fist up side yo' head to boot."

Delia's habitual meekness seemed to slip from her shoulders like a blown scarf. She was on her feet; her poor little body, her bare knuckly hands bravely defying the strapping hulk before her.

"Looka heah, Sykes, you done gone too fur. Ah been married to you fur fifteen years, and Ah been takin' in washin' fur fifteen years. Sweat, sweat, sweat! Work and sweat, cry and sweat, pray and sweat!"

"What's that got to do with me?" he asked brutally.

"What's it got to do with you, Sykes? Mah tub of suds is filled yo' belly with  20
vittles more times than yo' hands is filled it. Mah sweat is done paid for this house and Ah reckon Ah kin keep on sweatin' in it."

She seized the iron skillet from the stove and struck a defensive pose, which act surprised him greatly, coming from her. It cowed him and he did not strike her as he usually did.

"Naw you won't," she panted, "that ole snaggle-toothed black woman you runnin' with ain't comin' heah to pile up on *mah* sweat and blood. You ain't paid for nothin' on this place, and Ah'm gointer stay right heah till Ah'm toted out foot foremost."

"Well, you better quit gittin' me riled up, else they'll be totin' you out sooner than you expect. Ah'm so tired of you Ah don't know whut to do. Gawd! How Ah hates skinny wimmen!"

A little awed by this new Delia, he sidled out of the door and slammed the back gate after him. He did not say where he had gone, but she knew too well. She knew very well that he would not return until nearly daybreak also. Her work over, she went on to bed but not to sleep at once. Things had come to a pretty pass!

She lay awake, gazing upon the debris that cluttered their matrimonial trail.  25
Not an image left standing along the way. Anything like flowers had long ago been drowned in the salty stream that had been pressed from her heart. Her tears, her sweat, her blood. She had brought love to the union and he had brought a longing after the flesh. Two months after the wedding, he had given her the first

brutal beating. She had the memory of his numerous trips to Orlando with all of his wages when he had returned to her penniless, even before the first year had passed. She was young and soft then, but now she thought of her knotty, muscled limbs, her harsh knuckly hands, and drew herself up into an unhappy little ball in the middle of the big feather bed. Too late now to hope for love, even if it were not Bertha it would be someone else. This case differed from the others only in that she was bolder than the others. Too late for everything except her little home. She had built it for her old days, and planted one by one the trees and flowers there. It was lovely to her, lovely.

Somehow, before sleep came, she found herself saying aloud: "Oh well, whatever goes over the Devil's back, is got to come under his belly. Sometime or ruther, Sykes, like everybody else, is gointer reap his sowing." After that she was able to build a spiritual earthworks° against her husband. His shells could no longer reach her. AMEN. She went to sleep and slept until he announced his presence in bed by kicking her feet and rudely snatching the covers away.

"Gimme some kivah heah, an' git yo' damn foots over on yo' own side! Ah oughter mash you in yo' mouf fuh drawing dat skillet on me."

Delia went clear to the rail without answering him. A triumphant indifference to all that he was or did.

## II

The week was full of work for Delia as all other weeks, and Saturday found her behind her little pony, collecting and delivering clothes.

It was a hot, hot day near the end of July. The village men on Joe Clarke's porch even chewed cane listlessly. They did not hurl the cane-knots as usual. They let them dribble over the edge of the porch. Even conversation had collapsed under the heat.

"Heah come Delia Jones," Jim Merchant said, as the shaggy pony came 'round the bend of the road toward them. The rusty buckboard was heaped with baskets of crisp, clean laundry.

"Yep," Joe Lindsay agreed. "Hot or col', rain or shine, jes'ez reg'lar ez de weeks rool roun' Delia carries 'em an' fetches 'em on Sat'day."

"She better if she wanter eat," said Moss. "Syke Jones ain't wuth de shot an' powder hit would tek tuh kill 'em. Not to *huh* he ain't."

"He sho' ain't," Walter Thomas chimed in. "It's too bad, too, cause she wuz a right pretty li'l trick when he got huh. Ah'd uh mah'ied huh mahself if he hadnter beat me to it."

Delia nodded briefly at the men as she drove past.

"Too much knockin' will ruin *any* 'oman. He done beat huh 'nough tuh kill three women, let 'lone change they looks," said Elijah Moseley. "How Syke kin stommuck dat big black greasy Mogul he's layin' roun' wid, gits me. Ah swear dat

---

*spiritual earthworks:* earthworks are military fortifications made of earth; here Hurston uses it metaphorically to mean Delia's emotional *defenses*.

30

35

eight-rock couldn't kiss a sardine can Ah done thowed out de back do' 'way las' yeah."

"Aw, she's fat, thass how come. He's allus been crazy 'bout fat women," put in Merchant. "He'd a' been tied up wid one long time ago if he could a' found one tuh have him. Did Ah tell yuh 'bout him come sidlin' roun' *mah* wife—bringin' her a basket uh peecans outa his yard fuh a present? Yessir, mah wife! She tol' him tuh take 'em right straight back home, 'cause Delia works so hard ovah dat washtub she reckon everything on de place taste lak sweat an' soapsuds. Ah jus' wisht Ah'd a' caught 'im 'roun' dere! Ah'd a' made his hips ketch on fiah down dat shell road."

"Ah know he done it, too. Ah sees 'im grinnin' at every 'oman dat passes," Walter Thomas said. "But even so, he useter eat some mighty big hunks uh humble pie tuh git dat li'l 'oman he got. She wuz ez pritty ez a speckled pup! Dat wuz fifteen years ago. He useter be so skeered uh losin' huh, she could make him do some parts of a husband's duty. Dey never wuz de same in de mind."

"There oughter be a law about him," said Lindsay. "He ain't fit tuh carry guts tuh a bear."

Clarke spoke for the first time. "Tain't no law on earth dat kin make a man    40
be decent if it ain't in 'im. There's plenty men dat takes a wife lak dey do a joint uh sugar-cane. It's round, juicy, an' sweet when dey gits it. But dey squeeze an' grind, squeeze an' grind an' wring tell dey wring every drop uh pleasure dat's in 'em out. When dey's satisfied dat dey is wrung dry, dey treats 'em jes' lak dey do a cane-chew. Dey thows 'em away. Dey knows whut dey is doin' while dey is at it, an' hates theirselves fuh it but they keeps on hangin' after huh tell she's empty. Den dey hates huh fuh bein' a cane-chew an' in de way."

"We oughter take Syke an' dat stray 'oman uh his'n down in Lake Howell swamp an' lay on de rawhide till they cain't say Lawd a' mussy. He allus wuz uh ovahbearin niggah, but since dat white 'oman from up north done teached 'im how to run a automobile, he done got too beggety to live—an' we oughter kill 'im," Old Man Anderson advised.

A grunt of approval went around the porch. But the heat was melting their civic virtue and Elijah Moseley began to bait Joe Clarke.

"Come on, Joe, git a melon outa dere an' slice it up for yo' customers. We'se all sufferin' wid de heat. De bear's done got *me!*"

"Thass right, Joe, a watermelon is jes' whut Ah needs tuh cure de eppizu-dicks," Walter Thomas joined forces with Moseley. "Come on dere, Joe. We all is steady customers an' you ain't set us up in a long time. Ah chooses dat long, bow-legged Floridy favorite."

"A god, an' be dough. You all gimme twenty cents and slice away," Clarke    45
retorted. "Ah needs a col' slice m'self. Heah, everybody chip in. Ah'll lend y'all mah meat knife."

The money was all quickly subscribed and the huge melon brought forth. At that moment, Sykes and Bertha arrived. A determined silence fell on the porch and the melon was put away again.

Merchant snapped down the blade of his jackknife and moved toward the store door.

"Come on in, Joe, an' gimme a slab uh sow belly an' uh pound uh coffee— almost fuhgot 'twas Sat'day. Got to git on home." Most of the men left also.

Just then Delia drove past on her way home, as Sykes was ordering magnificently for Bertha. It pleased him for Delia to see.

"Git whutsoever yo' heart desires, Honey. Wait a minute, Joe. Give huh two bottles uh strawberry soda-water, uh quart parched ground-peas, an' a block uh chewin' gum." 50

With all this they left the store, with Sykes reminding Bertha that this was his town and she could have it if she wanted it.

The men returned soon after they left, and held their watermelon feast.

"Where did Syke Jones git da 'oman from nohow?" Lindsay asked.

"Ovah Apopka. Guess dey musta been cleanin' out de town when she lef'. She don't look lak a thing but a hunk uh liver wid hair on it."

"Well, she sho' kin squall," Dave Carter contributed. "When she gits ready tuh laff, she jes' opens huh mouf an' latches it back tuh de las' notch. No ole granpa alligator down in Lake Bell ain't got nothin' on huh." 55

### III

Bertha had been in town three months now. Sykes was still paying her room-rent at Della Lewis'—the only house in town that would have taken her in. Sykes took her frequently to Winter Park to "stomps." He still assured her that he was the swellest man in the state.

"Sho' you kin have dat li'l ole house soon's Ah git dat 'oman outadere. Everything b'longs tuh me an' you sho' kin have it. Ah sho' 'bominates uh skinny 'oman. Lawdy, you sho' is got one portly shape on you! You kin git *anything* you wants. Dis is *mah* town an' you sho' kin have it."

Delia's work-worn knees crawled over the earth in Gethsemane° and up the rocks of Calvary° many, many times during these months. She avoided the villagers and meeting places in her efforts to be blind and deaf. But Bertha nullified this to a degree, by coming to Delia's house to call Sykes out to her at the gate.

Delia and Sykes fought all the time now with no peaceful interludes. They slept and ate in silence. Two or three times Delia had attempted a timid friendliness, but she was repulsed each time. It was plain that the breaches must remain agape.

The sun had burned July to August. The heat streamed down like a million hot arrows, smiting all things living upon the earth. Grass withered, leaves browned, snakes went blind in shedding, and men and dogs went mad. Dog days! 60

Delia came home one day and found Sykes there before her. She wondered, but started to go on into the house without speaking, even though he was standing in the kitchen door and she must either stoop under his arm or ask him to move. He made no room for her. She noticed a soap box beside the steps, but paid no particular attention to it, knowing that he must have brought it there. As

---

*Gethsemane:* the garden outside Jerusalem that was the scene of Jesus's agony and arrest (see Matthew 26:36–57); hence, a scene of great suffering.   *Calvary:* the hill outside Jerusalem where Jesus was crucified.

she was stooping to pass under his outstretched arm, he suddenly pushed her backward, laughingly.

"Look in de box dere Delia, Ah done brung yuh somethin'!"

She nearly fell upon the box in her stumbling, and when she saw what it held, she all but fainted outright.

"Syke! Syke, mah Gawd! You take dat rattlesnake 'way from heah! You *got-tuh*. Oh, Jesus, have mussy!"

"Ah ain't got tuh do nuthin' uh de kin'—fact is Ah ain't got tuh do nothin' but die. Tain't no use uh you puttin' on airs makin' out lak you skeered uh dat snake—he's gointer stay right heah tell he die. He wouldn't bite me cause Ah knows how tuh handle 'im. Nohow he wouldn't risk breakin' out his fangs 'gin yo skinny laigs." 65

"Naw, now Syke, don't keep dat thing 'round tryin' tuh skeer me tuh death. You knows Ah'm even feared uh earth worms. Thass de biggest snake Ah evah did see. Kill 'im Syke, please."

"Doan ast me tuh do nothin' fuh yuh. Goin' 'round tryin' tuh be so damn asterperious.° Naw, Ah ain't gonna kill it. Ah think uh damn sight mo' uh him dan you! Dat's a nice snake an' anybody doan lak 'im kin jes' hit de grit."

The village soon heard that Sykes had the snake, and came to see and ask questions.

"How de hen-fire did you ketch dat six-foot rattler, Syke?" Thomas asked.

"He's full uh frogs so he cain't hardly move, thass how Ah eased up on 'm. But Ah'm a snake charmer an' knows how tuh handle 'em. Shux, dat ain't nothin'. Ah could ketch one eve'y day if Ah so wanted tuh." 70

"Whut he needs is a heavy hick'ry club leaned real heavy on his head. Dat's de bes' way tuh charm a rattlesnake."

"Naw, Walt, y'all jes' don't understand dese diamon' backs lak Ah do," said Sykes in a superior tone of voice.

The village agreed with Walter, but the snake stayed on. His box remained by the kitchen door with its screen wire covering. Two or three days later it had digested its meal of frogs and literally came to life. It rattled at every movement in the kitchen or the yard. One day as Delia came down the kitchen steps she saw his chalky-white fangs curved like scimitars hung in the wire meshes. This time she did not run away with averted eyes as usual. She stood for a long time in the doorway in a red fury that grew bloodier for every second that she regarded the creature that was her torment.

That night she broached the subject as soon as Sykes sat down to the table.

"Syke, Ah wants you tuh take dat snake 'way fum heah. You done starved me an' Ah put up widcher, you done beat me an Ah took dat, but you done kilt all mah insides bringin' dat varmint heah." 75

Sykes poured out a saucer full of coffee and drank it deliberately before he answered her.

"A whole lot Ah keer 'bout how you feels inside uh out. Dat snake ain't goin' no damn wheah till Ah gits ready fuh 'im tuh go. So fur as beatin' is concerned, yuh ain't took near all dat you gointer take ef yuh stay 'round *me*."

*asterperious:* haughty.

Delia pushed back her plate and got up from the table. "Ah hates you, Sykes," she said calmly. "Ah hates you tuh de same degree dat Ah useter love yuh. Ah done took an' took till mah belly is full up tuh mah neck. Dat's de reason Ah got mah letter fum de church an' moved mah membership tuh Woodbridge—so Ah don't haftuh take no sacrament wid yuh. Ah don't wantuh see yuh 'round me atall. Lay 'round wid dat 'oman all yuh wants tuh, but gwan 'way fum me an' mah house. Ah hates yuh lak uh suck-egg dog."

Sykes almost let the huge wad of corn bread and collard greens he was chewing fall out of his mouth in amazement. He had a hard time whipping himself up to the proper fury to try to answer Delia.

"Well, Ah'm glad you does hate me. Ah'm sho' tiahed uh you hangin' ontuh  80
me. Ah don't want yuh. Look at yuh stringey ole neck! Yo' rawbony laigs an' arms is enough tuh cut uh man tuh death. You looks jes' lak de devvul's doll-baby tuh *me*. You cain't hate me no worse dan Ah hates you. Ah been hatin' *you* fuh years."

"Yo' ole black hide don't look lak nothin' tuh me, but uh passle uh wrinkled up rubber, wid yo' big ole yeahs flappin' on each side lak uh paih uh buzzard wings. Don't think Ah'm gointuh be run 'way fum mah house neither. Ah'm goin' tuh de white folks 'bout *you*, mah young man, de very nex' time you lay yo' han's on me. Mah cup is done run ovah." Delia said this with no signs of fear and Sykes departed from the house, threatening her, but made not the slightest move to carry out any of them.

That night he did not return at all, and the next day being Sunday, Delia was glad she did not have to quarrel before she hitched up her pony and drove the four miles to Woodbridge.

She stayed to the night service—"love feast"—which was very warm and full of spirit. In the emotional winds her domestic trials were borne far and wide so that she sang as she drove homeward,

> Jurden water,° black an' col
> Chills de body, not de soul
> An' Ah wantah cross Jurden in uh calm time.

She came from the barn to the kitchen door and stopped.

"Whut's de mattah, ol' Satan, you ain't kickin' up yo' racket?" She addressed the snake's box. Complete silence. She went on into the house with a new hope in its birth struggles. Perhaps her threat to go to the white folks had frightened Sykes! Perhaps he was sorry! Fifteen years of misery and suppression had brought Delia to the place where she would hope *anything* that looked towards a way over or through her wall of inhibitions.

She felt in the match-safe behind the stove at once for a match. There was  85
only one there.

---

Jurden water: black Southern dialect for the River Jordan, which represents the last boundary before entering heaven. It comes from the Old Testament, when the Jews had to cross the River Jordan to reach the Promised Land.

"Dat niggah wouldn't fetch nothin' heah tuh save his rotten neck, but he kin run thew whut Ah brings quick enough. Now he done toted off nigh on tuh haff uh box uh matches. He done had dat 'oman heah in mah house, too."

Nobody but a woman could tell how she knew this even before she struck the match. But she did and it put her into a new fury.

Presently she brought in the tubs to put the white things to soak. This time she decided she need not bring the hamper out of the bedroom; she would go in there and do the sorting. She picked up the pot-bellied lamp and went in. The room was small and the hamper stood hard by the foot of the white iron bed. She could sit and reach through the bedposts—resting as she worked.

"*Ah wantah cross Jurden in uh calm time.*" She was singing again. The mood of the "love feast" had returned. She threw back the lid of the basket almost gaily. Then, moved by both horror and terror, she sprang back toward the door. *There lay the snake in the basket!* He moved sluggishly at first, but even as she turned round and round, jumped up and down in an insanity of fear, he began to stir vigorously. She saw him pouring his awful beauty from the basket upon the bed, then she seized the lamp and ran as fast as she could to the kitchen. The wind from the open door blew out the light and the darkness added to her terror. She sped to the darkness of the yard, slamming the door after her before she thought to set down the lamp. She did not feel safe even on the ground, so she climbed up in the hay barn.

There for an hour or more she lay sprawled upon the hay a gibbering wreck. 90

Finally she grew quiet, and after that came coherent thought. With this stalked through her a cold, bloody rage. Hours of this. A period of introspection, a space of retrospection, then a mixture of both. Out of this an awful calm.

"Well, Ah done de bes' Ah could. If things ain't right, Gawd knows tain't mah fault."

She went to sleep—a twitch sleep—and woke up to a faint gray sky. There was a loud hollow sound below. She peered out. Sykes was at the wood-pile, demolishing a wire-covered box.

He hurried to the kitchen door, but hung outside there some minutes before he entered, and stood some minutes more inside before he closed it after him.

The gray in the sky was spreading. Delia descended without fear now, and 95 crouched beneath the low bedroom window. The drawn shade shut out the dawn, shut in the night. But the thin walls held back no sound.

"Dat ol' scratch° is woke up now!" She mused at the tremendous whirr inside, which every woodsman knows, is one of the sound illusions. The rattler is a ventriloquist. His whirr sounds to the right, to the left, straight ahead, behind, close under foot—everywhere but where it is. Woe to him who guesses wrong unless he is prepared to hold up his end of the argument! Sometimes he strikes without rattling at all.

Inside, Sykes heard nothing until he knocked a pot lid off the stove while trying to reach the match-safe in the dark. He had emptied his pockets at Bertha's.

*scratch:* a folk expression for the devil.

The snake seemed to wake up under the stove and Sykes made a quick leap into the bedroom. In spite of the gin he had had, his head was clearing now.

"Mah Gawd!" he chattered, "ef Ah could on'y strack uh light!"

The rattling ceased for a moment as he stood paralyzed. He waited. It seemed 100 that the snake waited also.

"Oh, fuh de light! Ah thought he'd be too sick"—Sykes was muttering to himself when the whirr began again, closer, right underfoot this time. Long before this, Sykes' ability to think had been flattened down to primitive instinct and he leaped—onto the bed.

Outside Delia heard a cry that might have come from a maddened chimpanzee, a stricken gorilla. All the terror, all the horror, all the rage that man possibly could express, without a recognizable human sound.

A tremendous stir inside there, another series of animal screams, the intermittent whirr of the reptile. The shade torn violently down from the window, letting in the red dawn, a huge brown hand seizing the window stick, great dull blows upon the wooden floor punctuating the gibberish of sound long after the rattle of the snake had abruptly subsided. All this Delia could see and hear from her place beneath the window, and it made her ill. She crept over to the four o'clocks and stretched herself on the cool earth to recover.

She lay there. "Delia, Delia!" She could hear Sykes calling in a most despairing tone as one who expected no answer. The sun crept on up, and he called. Delia could not move—her legs had gone flabby. She never moved, he called, and the sun kept rising.

"Mah Gawd!" She heard him moan, "Mah Gawd fum Heben!" She heard 105 him stumbling about and got up from her flower-bed. The sun was growing warm. As she approached the door she heard him call out hopefully, "Delia, is dat you Ah heah?"

She saw him on his hands and knees as soon as she reached the door. He crept an inch or two toward her—all that he was able, and she saw his horribly swollen neck and his one open eye shining with hope. A surge of pity too strong to support bore her away from that eye that must, could not, fail to see the tubs. He would see the lamp. Orlando with its doctors was too far. She could scarcely reach the chinaberry tree, where she waited in the growing heat while inside she knew the cold river was creeping up and up to extinguish that eye which must know by now that she knew.

# D. H. Lawrence

D. H. Lawrence

*David Herbert Lawrence (1885–1930) was born in Nottinghamshire, England, child of a coalminer and a schoolteacher who hated her husband's toil and vowed that her son should escape it. He took up fiction writing, attaining early success. During World War I, Lawrence and his wife were unjustly suspected of treason (he because of his pacifism, she because of her aristocratic German birth). After the armistice they left England and, seeking a climate healthier for Lawrence, who suffered from tuberculosis, wandered in Italy, France, Australia, Mexico, and the American Southwest. Lawrence is an impassioned spokesman for our unconscious, instinctive natures, which we moderns (he argues) have neglected in favor of our overweening intellects. In* Lady Chatterley's Lover *(1928), he strove to restore explicit sexuality to English fiction. The book, which today seems tame and repetitious, was long banned in Britain and the United States. Deeper Lawrence novels include* Sons and Lovers *(1913), a veiled account of his breaking away from his fiercely possessive mother;* The Rainbow *(1915);* Women in Love *(1921); and* The Plumed Serpent *(1926), about a revival of pagan religion in Mexico. Besides fiction, Lawrence left a rich legacy of poetry, essays, criticism (*Studies in Classic American Literature, *1923, is especially shrewd and funny), and travel writing. Lawrence exerted deep influence on others, both by the message in his work and by his personal magnetism.*

There was a woman who was beautiful, who started with all the advantages, yet she had no luck. She married for love, and the love turned to dust. She had bonny children, yet she felt they had been thrust upon her, and she could not love them. They looked at her coldly, as if they were finding fault with her. And hurriedly she felt she must cover up some fault in herself. Yet what it was that she must cover up she never knew. Nevertheless, when her children were present, she always felt the center of her heart go hard. This troubled her, and in her manner she was all the more gentle and anxious for her children, as if she loved them very much. Only she herself knew that at the center of her heart was a hard little place that could not feel love, no, not for anybody. Everybody else said of her: "She is such a good mother. She adores her children." Only she herself, and her children themselves, knew it was not so. They read it in each other's eyes.

There were a boy and two little girls. They lived in a pleasant house, with a garden, and they had discreet servants, and felt themselves superior to anyone in the neighborhood.

Although they lived in style, they felt always an anxiety in the house. There was never enough money. The mother had a small income, and the father had a small income, but not nearly enough for the social position which they had to keep up. The father went in to town to some office. But though he had good prospects, these prospects never materialized. There was always the grinding sense of the shortage of money, though the style was always kept up.

At last the mother said: "I will see if I can't make something." But she did not know where to begin. She racked her brains, and tried this thing and the other, but could not find anything successful. The failure made deep lines come into her face. Her children were growing up, they would have to go to school. There must be more money, there must be more money. The father, who was always very handsome and expensive in his tastes, seemed as if he never *would* be able to do anything worth doing. And the mother, who had a great belief in herself, did not succeed any better, and her tastes were just as expensive.

And so the house came to be haunted by the unspoken phrase: *There must be more money! There must be more money!* The children could hear it all the time, though nobody said it aloud. They heard it at Christmas, when the expensive and splendid toys filled the nursery. Behind the shining modern rocking-horse, behind the smart doll's house, a voice would start whispering: "There *must* be more money! There *must* be more money!" And the children would stop playing, to listen for a moment. They would look into each other's eyes, to see if they had all heard. And each one saw in the eyes of the other two that they too had heard. "There *must* be more money! There *must* be more money!"

It came whispering from the springs of the still-swaying rocking-horse, and even the horse, bending his wooden, champing head, heard it. The big doll, sitting so pink and smirking in her new pram, could hear it quite plainly, and seemed to be smirking all the more self-consciously because of it. The foolish puppy, too, that took the place of the teddy-bear, he was looking so extraordinarily foolish for no other reason but that he heard the secret whisper all over the house: "There *must* be more money!"

Yet nobody ever said it aloud. The whisper was everywhere, and therefore no one spoke it. Just as no one ever says: "We are breathing!" in spite of the fact that breath is coming and going all the time.

"Mother," said the boy Paul one day, "why don't we keep a car of our own? Why do we always use uncle's, or else a taxi?"

"Because we're the poor members of the family," said the mother.

"But why *are* we, mother?"

"Well—I suppose," she said slowly and bitterly, "it's because your father has no luck."

The boy was silent for some time.

"Is luck money, mother?" he asked rather timidly.

"No, Paul. Not quite. It's what causes you to have money."

"Oh!" said Paul vaguely. "I thought when Uncle Oscar said *filthy lucker*, it   15
meant money."

"*Filthy lucre* does mean money," said the mother. "But it's lucre, not luck."

"Oh!" said the boy. "Then what *is* luck, mother?"

"It's what causes you to have money. If you're lucky you have money. That's
why it's better to be born lucky than rich. If you're rich, you may lose your
money. But if you're lucky, you will always get more money."

"Oh! Will you? And is father not lucky?"

"Very unlucky, I should say," she said bitterly.   20

The boy watched her with unsure eyes.

"Why?" he asked.

"I don't know. Nobody ever knows why one person is lucky and another
unlucky."

"Don't they? Nobody at all? Does *nobody* know?"

"Perhaps God. But He never tells."   25

"He ought to, then. And aren't you lucky either, mother?"

"I can't be, if I married an unlucky husband."

"But by yourself, aren't you?"

"I used to think I was, before I married. Now I think I am very unlucky
indeed."

"Why?"   30

"Well—never mind! Perhaps I'm not really," she said.

The child looked at her, to see if she meant it. But he saw, by the lines of her
mouth, that she was only trying to hide something from him.

"Well, anyhow," he said stoutly, "I'm a lucky person."

"Why?" said his mother, with a sudden laugh.

He stared at her. He didn't even know why he had said it.   35

"God told me," he asserted, brazening it out.

"I hope He did, dear!" she said, again with a laugh, but rather bitter.

"He did, mother!"

"Excellent!" said the mother, using one of her husband's exclamations.

The boy saw she did not believe him; or, rather, that she paid no attention   40
to his assertion. This angered him somewhat, and made him want to compel her
attention.

He went off by himself, vaguely, in a childish way, seeking for the clue to
"luck." Absorbed, taking no heed of other people, he went about with a sort of
stealth, seeking inwardly for luck. He wanted luck, he wanted it, he wanted it.
When the two girls were playing dolls in the nursery, he would sit on his big rocking-horse, charging madly into space, with a frenzy that made the little girls peer
at him uneasily. Wildly the horse careered, the waving dark hair of the boy tossed,
his eyes had a strange glare in them. The little girls dared not speak to him.

When he had ridden to the end of his mad little journey, he climbed down
and stood in front of his rocking-horse, staring fixedly into its lowered face. Its
red mouth was slightly open, its big eye was wide and glassy-bright.

"Now!" he would silently command the snorting steed. "Now, take me to where there is luck! Now take me!"

And he would slash the horse on the neck with the little whip he had asked Uncle Oscar for. He *knew* the horse could take him to where there was luck, if only he forced it. So he would mount again, and start on his furious ride, hoping at last to get there. He knew he could get there.

"You'll break your horse, Paul!" said the nurse.

"He's always riding like that! I wish he'd leave off!" said his elder sister Joan.

But he only glared down on them in silence. Nurse gave him up. She could make nothing of him. Anyhow he was growing beyond her.

One day his mother and his Uncle Oscar came in when he was on one of his furious rides. He did not speak to them.

"Hallo, you young jockey! Riding a winner?" said his uncle.

"Aren't you growing too big for a rocking-horse? You're not a very little boy any longer, you know," said his mother.

But Paul only gave a blue glare from his big, rather close-set eyes. He would speak to nobody when he was in full tilt. His mother watched him with an anxious expression on her face.

At last he suddenly stopped forcing his horse into the mechanical gallop, and slid down.

"Well, I got there!" he announced fiercely, his blue eyes still flaring, and his sturdy long legs straddling apart.

"Where did you get to?" asked his mother.

"Where I wanted to go," he flared back at her.

"That's right, son!" said Uncle Oscar. "Don't you stop till you get there. What's the horse's name?"

"He doesn't have a name," said the boy.

"Gets on without all right?" asked the uncle.

"Well, he has different names. He was called Sansovino last week."

"Sansovino, eh? Won the Ascot. How did you know his name?"

"He always talks about horse-races with Bassett," said Joan.

The uncle was delighted to find that his small nephew was posted with all the racing news. Bassett, the young gardener, who had been wounded in the left foot in the war and had got his present job through Oscar Cresswell, whose batman° he had been, was a perfect blade of the "turf." He lived in the racing events, and the small boy lived with him.

Oscar Cresswell got it all from Bassett.

"Master Paul comes and asks me, so I can't do more than tell him, sir," said Bassett, his face terribly serious, as if he were speaking of religious matters.

"And does he ever put anything on a horse he fancies?"

"Well—I don't want to give him away—he's a young sport, a fine sport, sir. Would you mind asking him himself? He sort of takes a pleasure in it, and perhaps he'd feel I was giving him away, sir, if you don't mind."

---

*batman:* an enlisted man who serves as valet to a cavalry officer.

Bassett was serious as a church.

The uncle went back to his nephew and took him off for a ride in the car.

"Say, Paul, old man, do you ever put anything on a horse?" the uncle asked.

The boy watched the handsome man closely.

"Why, do you think I oughtn't to?" he parried.

"Not a bit of it. I thought perhaps you might give me a tip for the Lincoln."

The car sped on into the country, going down to Uncle Oscar's place in Hampshire.

"Honor bright?" said the nephew.

"Honor bright, son!" said the uncle.

"Well, then, Daffodil."

"Daffodil! I doubt it, sonny. What about Mirza?"

"I only know the winner," said the boy. "That's Daffodil."

"Daffodil, eh?"

There was a pause. Daffodil was an obscure horse comparatively.

"Uncle!"

"Yes, son?"

"You won't let it go any further, will you? I promised Bassett."

"Bassett be damned, old man! What's he got to do with it?"

"We're partners. We've been partners from the first. Uncle, he lent me my first five shillings, which I lost. I promised him, honor bright, it was only between me and him; only you gave me that ten-shilling note I started winning with, so I thought you were lucky. You won't let it go any further, will you?"

The boy gazed at his uncle from those big, hot, blue eyes, set rather close together. The uncle stirred and laughed uneasily.

"Right you are, son! I'll keep your tip private. Daffodil, eh? How much are you putting on him?"

"All except twenty pounds," said the boy. "I keep that in reserve."

The uncle thought it a good joke.

"You keep twenty pounds in reserve, do you, you young romancer? What are you betting, then?"

"I'm betting three hundred," said the boy gravely. "But it's between you and me, Uncle Oscar! Honor bright?"

The uncle burst into a roar of laughter.

"It's between you and me all right, you young Nat Gould°," he said, laughing. "But where's your three hundred?"

"Bassett keeps it for me. We're partners."

"You are, are you! And what is Bassett putting on Daffodil?"

"He won't go quite as high as I do, I expect. Perhaps he'll go a hundred and fifty."

"What, pennies?" laughed the uncle.

"Pounds," said the child, with a surprised look at his uncle. "Bassett keeps a bigger reserve than I do."

*Nat Gould:* celebrated English gambler of the 1920s.

Between wonder and amusement Uncle Oscar was silent. He pursued the matter no further, but he determined to take his nephew with him to the Lincoln races.

"Now, son," he said, "I'm putting twenty on Mirza, and I'll put five for you on any horse you fancy. What's your pick?"

"Daffodil, uncle."

"No, not the fiver on Daffodil!"

"I should if it was my own fiver," said the child.

"Good! Good! Right you are! A fiver for me and a fiver for you on Daffodil."

The child had never been to a race-meeting before, and his eyes were blue fire. He pursed his mouth tight, and watched. A Frenchman just in front had put his money on Lancelot. Wild with excitement, he flayed his arms up and down, yelling, "*Lancelot! Lancelot!*" in his French accent.

Daffodil came in first, Lancelot second, Mirza third. The child, flushed and with eyes blazing, was curiously serene. His uncle brought him four five-pound notes, four to one.

"What am I to do with these?" he cried, waving them before the boy's eyes.

"I suppose we'll talk to Bassett," said the boy. "I expect I have fifteen hundred now; and twenty in reserve; and this twenty."

His uncle studied him for some moments.

"Look here, son!" he said. "You're not serious about Bassett and that fifteen hundred, are you?"

"Yes, I am. But it's between you and me, uncle. Honor bright!"

"Honor bright all right, son! But I must talk to Bassett."

"If you'd like to be a partner, uncle, with Bassett and me, we could all be partners. Only, you'd have to promise, honor bright, uncle, not to let it go beyond us three. Bassett and I are lucky, and you must be lucky, because it was your ten shillings I started winning with. . . ."

Uncle Oscar took both Bassett and Paul into Richmond Park for an afternoon, and there they talked.

"It's like this, you see, sir," Bassett said. "Master Paul would get me talking about racing events, spinning yarns, you know, sir. And he was always keen on knowing if I'd made or if I'd lost. It's about a year since, now, that I put five shillings on Blush of Dawn for him—and we lost. Then the luck turned, and with that ten shillings he had from you, that we put on Singhalese. And since that time, it's been pretty steady, all things considering. What do you say, Master Paul?"

"We're all right when we're sure," said Paul. "It's when we're not quite sure that we go down."

"Oh, but we're careful then," said Bassett.

"But when are you *sure?*" smiled Uncle Oscar.

"It's Master Paul, sir," said Bassett, in a secret, religious voice. "It's as if he had it from heaven. Like Daffodil, now, for the Lincoln. That was as sure as eggs."

"Did you put anything on Daffodil?" asked Oscar Cresswell.

"Yes, sir. I made my bit."

"And my nephew?"

Bassett was obstinately silent, looking at Paul.

"I made twelve hundred, didn't I, Bassett? I told uncle I was putting three hundred on Daffodil."

"That's right," said Bassett, nodding.

"But where's the money?" asked the uncle.

"I keep it safe locked up, sir. Master Paul he can have it any minute he likes to ask for it."

"What, fifteen hundred pounds?"

"And twenty! And *forty*, that is, with the twenty he made on the course."

"It's amazing!" said the uncle.

"If Master Paul offers you to be partners, sir, I would, if I were you; if you'll excuse me," said Bassett.

Oscar Cresswell thought about it.

"I'll see the money," he said.

They drove home again, and sure enough, Bassett came round to the garden-house with fifteen hundred pounds in notes. The twenty pounds reserve was left with Joe Glee, in the Turf Commission deposit.

"You see, it's all right, uncle, when I'm *sure!* Then we go strong, for all we're worth. Don't we, Bassett!"

"We do that, Master Paul."

"And when are you sure?" said the uncle, laughing.

"Oh, well, sometimes I'm *absolutely* sure, like about Daffodil," said the boy; "and sometimes I have an idea; and sometimes I haven't even an idea, have I, Bassett? Then we're careful, because we mostly go down."

"You do, do you! And when you're sure, like about Daffodil, what makes you sure, sonny?"

"Oh, well, I don't know," said the boy uneasily. "I'm sure, you know, uncle; that's all."

"It's as if he had it from heaven, sir," Bassett reiterated.

"I should say so!" said the uncle.

But he became a partner. And when the Leger was coming on, Paul was "sure" about Lively Spark, which was a quite inconsiderable horse. The boy insisted on putting a thousand on the horse, Bassett went for five hundred, and Oscar Cresswell two hundred. Lively Spark came in first, and the betting had been ten to one against him. Paul had made ten thousand.

"You see," he said, "I was absolutely sure of him."

Even Oscar Cresswell had cleared two thousand.

"Look here, son," he said, "this sort of thing makes me nervous."

"It needn't, uncle! Perhaps I shan't be sure again for a long time."

"But what are you going to do with your money?" asked the uncle.

"Of course," said the boy, "I started it for mother. She said she had no luck, because father is unlucky, so I thought if *I* was lucky, it might stop whispering."

"What might stop whispering?"

"Our house. I *hate* our house for whispering."

"What does it whisper?"

"Why—why"—the boy fidgeted—"why, I don't know. But it's always short of money, you know, uncle."

"I know it, son, I know it."

"You know people send mother writs, don't you, uncle?"                  155

"I'm afraid I do," said the uncle.

"And then the house whispers, like people laughing at you behind your back. It's awful, that is! I thought if I was lucky . . . "

"You might stop it," added the uncle.

The boy watched him with big blue eyes, that had an uncanny cold fire in them, and he said never a word.

"Well, then!" said the uncle. "What are we doing?"                  160

"I shouldn't like mother to know I was lucky," said the boy.

"Why not, son?"

"She'd stop me."

"I don't think she would."

"Oh!"—and the boy writhed in an odd way—"I *don't* want her to know,  165 uncle."

"All right, son! We'll manage it without her knowing."

They managed it very easily. Paul, at the other's suggestion, handed over five thousand pounds to his uncle, who deposited it with the family lawyer, who was then to inform Paul's mother that a relative had put five thousand pounds into his hands, which sum was to be paid out a thousand pounds at a time, on the mother's birthday, for the next five years.

"So she'll have a birthday present of a thousand pounds for five successive years," said Uncle Oscar. "I hope it won't make it all the harder for her later."

Paul's mother had her birthday in November. The house had been "whispering" worse than ever lately, and, even in spite of his luck, Paul could not bear up against it. He was very anxious to see the effect of the birthday letter, telling his mother about the thousand pounds.

When there were no visitors, Paul now took his meals with his parents, as he  170 was beyond the nursery control. His mother went into town nearly every day. She had discovered that she had an odd knack of sketching furs and dress materials, so she worked secretly in the studio of a friend who was the chief "artist" for the leading drapers. She drew the figures of ladies in furs and ladies in silk and sequins for the newspaper advertisements. This young woman artist earned several thousand pounds a year, but Paul's mother only made several hundreds, and she was again dissatisfied. She so wanted to be first in something, and she did not succeed, even in making sketches for drapery advertisements.

She was down to breakfast on the morning of her birthday. Paul watched her face as she read the letters. He knew the lawyer's letter. As his mother read it, her face hardened and became more expressionless. Then a cold, determined look came on her mouth. She hid the letter under the pile of others, and said not a word about it.

"Didn't you have anything nice in the post for your birthday, mother?" said Paul.

"Quite moderately nice," she said, her voice cold and absent.

She went away to town without saying more.

But in the afternoon Uncle Oscar appeared. He said Paul's mother had had a long interview with the lawyer, asking if the whole five thousand could not be advanced at once, as she was in debt. 175

"What do you think, uncle?" said the boy.

"I leave it to you, son."

"Oh, let her have it, then! We can get some more with the other," said the boy.

"A bird in the hand is worth two in the bush, laddie!" said Uncle Oscar.

"But I'm sure to *know* for the Grand National; or the Lincolnshire; or else the Derby. I'm sure to know for *one* of them," said Paul. 180

So Uncle Oscar signed the agreement, and Paul's mother touched the whole five thousand. Then something very curious happened. The voices in the house suddenly went mad, like a chorus of frogs on a spring evening. There were certain new furnishings, and Paul had a tutor. He was *really* going to Eton, his father's school, in the following autumn. There were flowers in the winter, and a blossoming of the luxury Paul's mother had been used to. And yet the voices in the house, behind the sprays of mimosa and almond blossom, and from under the piles of iridescent cushions, simply trilled and screamed in a sort of ecstasy: "There *must* be more money! Oh-h-h; there *must* be more money. Oh, now, now-w! Now-w-w— there *must* be more money—more than ever! More than ever!"

It frightened Paul terribly. He studied away at his Latin and Greek with his tutors. But his intense hours were spent with Bassett. The Grand National had gone by: he had not "known," and had lost a hundred pounds. Summer was at hand. He was in agony for the Lincoln. But even for the Lincoln he didn't "know," and he lost fifty pounds. He became wild-eyed and strange, as if something were going to explode in him.

"Let it alone, son! Don't you bother about it!" urged Uncle Oscar. But it was as if the boy couldn't really hear what his uncle was saying.

"I've got to know for the Derby! I've got to know for the Derby!" the child reiterated, his big blue eyes blazing with a sort of madness.

His mother noticed how overwrought he was. 185

"You'd better go to the seaside. Wouldn't you like to go now to the seaside, instead of waiting? I think you'd better," she said, looking down at him anxiously, her heart curiously heavy because of him.

But the child lifted his uncanny blue eyes.

"I couldn't possibly go before the Derby, mother!" he said. "I couldn't possibly!"

"Why not?" she said, her voice becoming heavy when she was opposed. "Why not? You can still go from the seaside to see the Derby with your Uncle Oscar, if that's what you wish. No need for you to wait here. Besides, I think you care too much about these races. It's a bad sign. My family has been a gambling family, and you won't know till you grow up how much damage it has done. But it has done damage. I shall have to send Bassett away, and ask Uncle Oscar not to talk racing to you, unless you promise to be reasonable about it; go away to the seaside and forget it. You're all nerves!"

"I'll do what you like, mother, so long as you don't send me away till after the Derby," the boy said.

"Send you away from where? Just from this house?"

"Yes," he said, gazing at her.

"Why, you curious child, what makes you care about this house so much, suddenly? I never knew you loved it."

He gazed at her without speaking. He had a secret within a secret, something he had not divulged, even to Bassett or to his Uncle Oscar.

But his mother, after standing undecided and a little bit sullen for some moments, said:

"Very well, then! Don't go to the seaside till after the Derby, if you don't wish it. But promise me you won't let your nerves go to pieces. Promise you won't think so much about horse-racing and *events,* as you call them!"

"Oh, no," said the boy casually. "I won't think much about them, mother. You needn't worry. I wouldn't worry, mother, if I were you."

"If you were me and I were you," said his mother, "I wonder what we *should* do!"

"But you know you needn't worry, mother, don't you?" the boy repeated.

"I should be awfully glad to know it," she said wearily.

"Oh, well, you *can,* you know. I mean, you *ought* to know you needn't worry," he insisted.

"Ought I? Then I'll see about it," she said.

Paul's secret of secrets was his wooden horse, that which had no name. Since he was emancipated from a nurse and a nursery-governess, he had had his rockinghorse removed to his own bedroom at the top of the house.

"Surely, you're too big for a rocking-horse!" his mother had remonstrated.

"Well, you see, mother, till I can have a *real* horse, I like to have *some* sort of animal about," had been his quaint answer.

"Do you feel he keeps you company?" she laughed.

"Oh, yes! He's very good, he always keeps me company, when I'm there," said Paul.

So the horse, rather shabby, stood in an arrested prance in the boy's bedroom.

The Derby was drawing near, and the boy grew more and more tense. He hardly heard what was spoken to him, he was very frail, and his eyes were really uncanny. His mother had sudden strange seizures of uneasiness about him. Sometimes, for half-an-hour, she would feel a sudden anxiety about him that was almost anguish. She wanted to rush to him at once, and know he was safe.

Two nights before the Derby, she was at a big party in town, when one of her rushes of anxiety about her boy, her first-born, gripped her heart till she could hardly speak. She fought with the feeling, might and main, for she believed in common-sense. But it was too strong. She had to leave the dance and go downstairs to telephone to the country. The children's nursery-governess was terribly surprised and startled at being rung up in the night.

"Are the children all right, Miss Wilmot?"

"Oh, yes, they are quite all right."

"Master Paul? Is he all right?"

"He went to bed as right as a trivet. Shall I run up and look at him?"

"No," said Paul's mother reluctantly. "No! Don't trouble. It's all right. Don't 215
sit up. We shall be home fairly soon." She did not want her son's privacy intruded
upon.

"Very good," said the governess.

It was about one-o'clock when Paul's mother and father drove up to their
house. All was still. Paul's mother went to her room and slipped off her white fur
cloak. She had told her maid not to wait up for her. She heard her husband
downstairs, mixing a whisky-and-soda.

And then, because of the strange anxiety at her heart, she stole upstairs to
her son's room. Noiselessly she went along the upper corridor. Was there a faint
noise? What was it?

She stood, with arrested muscles, outside his door, listening. There was a
strange, heavy, and yet not loud noise. Her heart stood still. It was a soundless
noise, yet rushing and powerful. Something huge, in violent, hushed motion.
What was it? What in God's name was it? She ought to know. She felt that she
knew the noise. She knew what it was.

Yet she could not place it. She couldn't say what it was. And on and on it 220
went, like a madness.

Softly, frozen with anxiety and fear, she turned the door-handle.

The room was dark. Yet in the space near the window, she heard and saw
something plunging to and fro. She gazed in fear and amazement.

Then suddenly she switched on the light, and saw her son, in his green pajamas, madly surging on the rocking-horse. The blaze of light suddenly lit him up,
as he urged the wooden horse, and lit her up, as she stood, blonde, in her dress of
pale green and crystal, in the doorway.

"Paul!" she cried. "Whatever are you doing?"

"It's Malabar!" he screamed, in a powerful, strange voice. "It's Malabar!" 225

His eyes blazed at her for one strange and senseless second, as he ceased urging his wooden horse. Then he fell with a crash to the ground, and she, all her
tormented motherhood flooding upon her, rushed to gather him up.

But he was unconscious, and unconscious he remained, with some brain-
fever. He talked and tossed, and his mother sat stonily by his side.

"Malabar! It's Malabar! Bassett, Bassett I know! It's Malabar!"

So the child cried, trying to get up and urge the rocking-horse that gave him
his inspiration.

"What does he mean by Malabar?" asked the heart-frozen mother. 230

"I don't know," said the father stonily.

"What does he mean by Malabar?" she asked her brother Oscar.

"It's one of the horses running for the Derby," was the answer.

And, in spite of himself, Oscar Cresswell spoke to Bassett, and himself put a
thousand on Malabar: at fourteen to one.

The third day of the illness was critical: they were waiting for a change. The boy, with his rather long, curly hair, was tossing ceaselessly on the pillow. He neither slept nor regained consciousness, and his eyes were like blue stones. His mother sat, feeling her heart had gone, turned actually into a stone.

In the evening, Oscar Cresswell did not come, but Bassett sent a message, saying could he come up for one moment, just one moment? Paul's mother was very angry at the intrusion, but on second thought she agreed. The boy was the same. Perhaps Bassett might bring him to consciousness.

The gardener, a shortish fellow with a little brown moustache, and sharp little brown eyes, tiptoed into the room, touched his imaginary cap to Paul's mother, and stole to the bedside, staring with glittering, smallish eyes, at the tossing, dying child.

"Master Paul!" he whispered. "Master Paul! Malabar came in first all right, a clean win. I did as you told me. You've made over seventy thousand pounds, you have; you've got over eighty thousand. Malabar came in all right, Master Paul."

"Malabar! Malabar! Did I say Malabar, mother? Did I say Malabar? Do you think I'm lucky, mother? I knew Malabar, didn't I? Over eighty thousand pounds! I call that lucky, don't you, mother? Over eighty thousand pounds! I knew, didn't I know I knew? Malabar came in all right. If I ride my horse till I'm sure, then I tell you, Bassett, you can go as high as you like. Did you go for all you were worth, Bassett?"

"I went a thousand on it, Master Paul."

"I never told you, mother, that if I can ride my horse, and *get there*, then I'm absolutely sure—oh, absolutely! Mother, did I ever tell you? I *am* lucky!"

"No, you never did," said the mother.

But the boy died in the night.

And even as he lay dead, his mother heard her brother's voice saying to her: "My God, Hester, you're eighty-odd thousand to the good, and a poor devil of a son to the bad. But, poor devil, poor devil, he's best gone out of a life where he rides his rocking-horse to find a winner."

235

240

## Doris Lessing

A WOMAN ON THE ROOF                                                        1963

*Doris Lessing was born Doris Taylor in
Iran in 1919. At five she moved with her
family to a remote farm in the white-con-
trolled British colony of Rhodesia (today
Zimbabwe). She attended a convent school
in Salisbury, the capital city. Like Isak
Dinesen and Muriel Sparks, Lessing found
that her African experience nurtured her
early writing. Her years in Africa led to her
first novel,* The Grass Is Singing *(1950),
and two collections of short stories. In her
teens she quit school, an act of defiance
against her mother's plans to give her a
proper, ladylike British education. In 1949,
with her third child, she settled in London to
earn her living as a writer. For a short time
she belonged to the British Communist*

Doris Lessing

*party, working as an organizer. Soon Lessing attracted a following in Britain and
America for her five-novel series,* Children of Violence *(1950–69), based on her own
varied experiences, and* The Golden Notebook *(1962), exploring the lives of intelligent women who struggle for independence. Though Lessing became a heroine to feminists, she has declared herself mainly interested in larger social and cultural issues.
Lately these questions have led her to write a five-volume series of science-fiction novels,*
Canopus in Argus: Archives *(1979–83). With* The Good Terrorist *(1985) and*
The Fifth Child *(1988), Lessing returned to the realistic vein of fiction that made her
famous. However, she has never hesitated to try something new. She recently published
two novels under a pseudonym to escape reviewers' preconceptions of her work. In
1993 she wrote* Playing the Game, *a graphic novel (a novel told in a comic book format). Lessing currently lives in London.*

It was during the week of hot sun, that June.

Three men were at work on the roof, where the leads got so hot they had the
idea of throwing water on to cool them. But the water steamed, then sizzled; and
they made jokes about getting an egg from some woman in the flats under them,
to poach it for their dinner. By two it was not possible to touch the guttering they
were replacing, and they speculated about what workmen did in regularly hot
countries. Perhaps they should borrow kitchen gloves with the egg? They were all
a bit dizzy, not used to the heat; and they shed their coats and stood side by side
squeezing themselves into a foot-wide patch of shade against a chimney, careful
to keep their feet in the thick socks and boots out of the sun. There was a fine
view across several acres of roofs. Not far off a man sat in a deck chair reading the
newspapers. Then they saw her, between chimneys, about fifty yards away. She

lay face down on a brown blanket. They could see the top part of her: black hair, a flushed solid back, arms spread out.

"She's stark naked," said Stanley, sounding annoyed.

Harry, the oldest, a man of about forty-five, said: "Looks like it."

Young Tom, seventeen, said nothing, but he was excited and grinning.

Stanley said: "Someone'll report her if she doesn't watch out."

"She thinks no one can see," said Tom, craning his head all ways to see more.

At this point the woman, still lying prone, brought her two hands up behind her shoulders with the ends of a scarf in them, tied it behind her back, and sat up. She wore a red scarf tied around her breasts and brief red bikini pants. This being the first day of the sun she was white, flushing red. She sat smoking, and did not look up when Stanley let out a wolf whistle. Harry said: "Small things amuse small minds," leading the way back to their part of the roof, but it was scorching. Harry said: "Wait, I'm going to rig up some shade," and disappeared down the skylight into the building. Now that he'd gone, Stanley and Tom went to the farthest point they could to peer at the woman. She had moved, and all they could see were two pink legs stretched on the blanket. They whistled and shouted but the legs did not move. Harry came back with a blanket and shouted: "Come on, then." He sounded irritated with them. They clambered back to him and he said to Stanley: "What about your missus?" Stanley was newly married, about three months. Stanley said, jeering: "What about my missus?"—preserving his independence. Tom said nothing, but his mind was full of the nearly naked woman. Harry slung the blanket, which he had borrowed from a friendly woman downstairs, from the stem of a television aerial to a row of chimney-pots.° This shade fell across the piece of gutter they had to replace. But the shade kept moving, they had to adjust the blanket, and not much progress was made. At last some of the heat left the roof, and they worked fast, making up for lost time. First Stanley, then Tom, made a trip to the end of the roof to see the woman. "She's on her back," Stanley said, adding a jest which made Tom snicker, and the older man smile tolerantly. Tom's report was that she hadn't moved, but it was a lie. He wanted to keep what he had seen to himself: he had caught her in the act of rolling down the little red pants over her hips, till they were no more than a small triangle. She was on her back, fully visible, glistening with oil.

Next morning, as soon as they came up, they went to look. She was already there, face down, arms spread out, naked except for the little red pants. She had turned brown in the night. Yesterday she was a scarlet-and-white woman, today she was a brown woman. Stanley let out a whistle. She lifted her head, startled, as if she'd been asleep, and looked straight over at him. The sun was in her eyes, she blinked and stared, then she dropped her head again. At this gesture of indifference, they all three, Stanley, Tom and old Harry, let out whistles and yells. Harry was doing it in parody of the younger men, making fun of them, but he was also angry. They were all angry because of her utter indifference to the three men watching her.

---

*chimney-pots:* the pipe, usually of earthenware or metal, fitted on a roof to the top of a chimney.

"Bitch," said Stanley.

"She should ask us over," said Tom, snickering.

Harry recovered himself and reminded Stanley: "If she's married, her old man wouldn't like that."

"Christ," said Stanley virtuously, "if my wife lay about like that, for everyone to see, I'd soon stop her."

Harry said, smiling: "How do you know, perhaps she's sunning herself at this very moment?"

"Not a chance, not on our roof." The safety of his wife put Stanley into a good humor, and they went to work. But today it was hotter than yesterday; and several times one or the other suggested they should tell Matthew, the foreman, and ask to leave the roof until the heat wave was over. But they didn't. There was work to be done in the basement of the big block of flats, but up here they felt free, on a different level from ordinary humanity shut in the streets or the build-ings. A lot more people came out on to the roofs that day, for an hour at midday. Some married couples sat side by side in deck chairs, the women's legs stocking-less and scarlet, the men in vests with reddening shoulders.

The woman stayed on her blanket, turning herself over and over. She ignored them, no matter what they did. When Harry went off to fetch more screws, Stanley said: "Come on." Her roof belonged to a different system of roofs, separated from theirs at one point by about twenty feet. It meant a scrambling climb from one level to another, edging along parapets,° clinging to chimneys, while their big boots slipped and slithered, but at last they stood on a small square projecting roof looking straight down at her, close. She sat smoking, reading a book. Tom thought she looked like a poster, or a magazine cover, with the blue sky behind her and her legs stretched out. Behind her a great crane at work on a new building in Oxford Street° swung its black arm across roofs in a great arc. Tom imagined himself at work on the crane, adjusting the arm to swing over and pick her up and swing her back across the sky to drop her near him.

They whistled. She looked up at them, cool and remote, then went on read-ing. Again, they were furious. Or, rather, Stanley was. His sun-heated face was screwed into a rage as he whistled again and again, trying to make her look up. Young Tom stopped whistling. He stood beside Stanley, excited, grinning; but he felt as if he were saying to the woman: Don't associate me with *him*, for his grin was apologetic. Last night he had thought of the unknown woman before he slept, and she had been tender with him. This tenderness he was remembering as he shifted his feet by the jeering, whistling Stanley, and watched the indifferent, healthy brown woman a few feet off, with the gap that plunged to the street between them. Tom thought it was romantic, it was like being high on two hill-tops. But there was a shout from Harry, and they clambered back. Stanley's face was hard, really angry. The boy kept looking at him and wondered why he hated the woman so much, for by now he loved her.

---

parapets: generally a rampart, in this case, the low railing around the edge of a roof.     Oxford Street: busy shopping street in central London.

They played their little games with the blanket, trying to trap shade to work under; but again it was not until nearly four that they could work seriously, and they were exhausted, all three of them. They were grumbling about the weather by now. Stanley was in a thoroughly bad humor. When they made their routine trip to see the woman before they packed up for the day, she was apparently asleep, face down, her back all naked save for the scarlet triangle on her buttocks. "I've got a good mind to report her to the police," said Stanley, and Harry said: "What's eating you? What harm's she doing?"

"I tell you, if she was my wife!"

"But she isn't, is she?" Tom knew that Harry, like himself, was uneasy at   20
Stanley's reaction. He was normally a sharp young man, quick at his work, making a lot of jokes, good company.

"Perhaps it will be cooler tomorrow," said Harry.

But it wasn't; it was hotter, if anything, and the weather forecast said the good weather would last. As soon as they were on the roof, Harry went over to see if the woman was there, and Tom knew it was to prevent Stanley going, to put off his bad humor. Harry had grownup children, a boy the same age as Tom, and the youth trusted and looked up to him.

Harry came back and said: "She's not there."

"I bet her old man has put his foot down," said Stanley, and Harry and Tom caught each other's eyes and smiled behind the young married man's back.

Harry suggested they should get permission to work in the basement, and   25
they did, that day. But before packing up Stanley said: "Let's have a breath of fresh air." Again Harry and Tom smiled at each other as they followed Stanley up to the roof, Tom in the devout conviction that he was there to protect the woman from Stanley. It was about five-thirty, and a calm, full sunlight lay over the roofs. The great crane still swung its black arm from Oxford Street to above their heads. She was not there. Then there was a flutter of white from behind a parapet, and she stood up, in a belted, white dressing gown. She had been there all day, probably, but on a different patch of roof, to hide from them. Stanley did not whistle; he said nothing, but watched the woman bend to collect papers, books, cigarettes, then fold the blanket over her arm. Tom was thinking: If they weren't here, I'd go over and say . . . what? But he knew from his nightly dreams of her that she was kind and friendly. Perhaps she would ask him down to her flat? Perhaps . . . He stood watching her disappear down the skylight. As she went, Stanley let out a shrill derisive yell; she started, and it seemed as if she nearly fell. She clutched to save herself, they could hear things falling. She looked straight at them, angry. Harry said, facetiously: "Better be careful on those slippery ladders, love." Tom knew he said it to save her from Stanley, but she could not know it. She vanished, frowning. Tom was full of a secret delight, because he knew her anger was for the others, not for him.

"Roll on some rain," said Stanley, bitter, looking at the blue evening sky.

Next day was cloudless, and they decided to finish the work in the basement. They felt excluded, shut in the grey cement basement fitting pipes, from the holiday atmosphere in London in a heat wave. At lunchtime they came up for some air, but while the married couples, and the men in shirt-sleeves or vests, were there, she was not there, either on her usual patch of roof or where she had been yesterday. They all, even Harry, clambered about, between chimney-pots, over parapets, the hot leads stinging their fingers. There was not a sign of her. They took off their shirts and vests and exposed their chests, feeling their feet sweaty and hot. They did not mention the woman. But Tom felt alone again. Last night she had him into her flat: it was big and had fitted white carpets and a bed with a padded white leather headboard. She wore a black filmy negligée and her kindness to Tom thickened his throat as he remembered it. He felt she had betrayed him by not being there.

And again after work they climbed up, but still there was nothing to be seen of her. Stanley kept repeating that if it was as hot as this tomorrow he wasn't going to work and that's all there was to it. But they were all there next day. By ten the temperature was in the middle seventies, and it was eighty long before noon. Harry went to the foreman to say it was impossible to work on the leads in that heat; but the foreman said there was nothing else he could put them on, and they'd have to. At midday they stood, silent, watching the skylight on her roof open, and then she slowly emerged in her white gown, holding a bundle of blanket. She looked at them, gravely, then went to the part of the roof where she was hidden from them. Tom was pleased. He felt she was more his when the other men couldn't see her. They had taken off their shirts and vests, but now they put them back again, for they felt the sun bruising their flesh. "She must have the hide of a rhino," said Stanley, tugging at guttering and swearing. They stopped work, and sat in the shade, moving around behind chimney stacks. A woman came to water a yellow window box opposite them. She was middleaged, wearing a flowered summer dress. Stanley said to her: "We need a drink more than them." She smiled and said: "Better drop down to the pub quick, it'll be closing in a minute." They exchanged pleasantries, and she left them with a smile and a wave.

"Not like Lady Godiva,"° said Stanley. "She can give us a bit of a chat and a smile."

"You didn't whistle at *her*," said Tom, reproving. 30

"Listen to him," said Stanley, "you didn't whistle, then?"

But the boy felt as if he hadn't whistled, as if only Harry and Stanley had. He was making plans, when it was time to knock off work, to get left behind and somehow make his way over to the woman. The weather report said the hot spell was due to break, so he had to move quickly. But there was no chance of being left.

The other two decided to knock off work at four, because they were exhausted. As they went down, Tom quickly climbed a parapet and hoisted himself higher by pulling his weight up a chimney. He caught a glimpse of her lying on her

---

*Lady Godiva:* the 11th-century noblewoman who rode naked through the streets of Coventry, England, to save the common people from crippling taxes. Out of respect the townspeople did not look at her, except for one young man named Tom, who legend claims was struck blind. Posterity remembers him as "Peeping Tom."

back, her knees up, eyes closed, a brown woman lolling in the sun. He slipped and clattered down, as Stanley looked for information: "She's gone down," he said. He felt as if he had protected her from Stanley, and that she must be grateful to him. He could feel the bond between the woman and himself.

Next day, they stood around on the landing below the roof, reluctant to climb up into the heat. The woman who had lent Harry the blanket came out and offered them a cup of tea. They accepted gratefully, and sat around Mrs. Pritchett's kitchen an hour or so, chatting. She was married to an airline pilot. A smart blonde, of about thirty, she had an eye for the handsome sharp-eyed Stanley; and the two teased each other while Harry sat in a corner, watching, indulgent, though his expression reminded Stanley that he was married. And young Tom felt envious of Stanley's ease in badinage;° felt, too, that Stanley's getting off with Mrs. Pritchett left his romance with the woman on the roof safe and intact.

"I thought they said the heat wave'd break," said Stanley, sullen, as the time   35
approached when they really would have to climb up into the sunlight.

"You don't like it, then?" asked Mrs. Pritchett.

"All right for some," said Stanley. "Nothing to do but lie about as if it was a beach up there. Do you ever go up?"

"Went up once," said Mrs. Pritchett. "But it's a dirty place up there, and it's too hot."

"Quite right too," said Stanley.

Then they went up, leaving the cool neat little flat and the friendly Mrs.   40
Pritchett.

As soon as they were up they saw her. The three men looked at her, resentful at her ease in this punishing sun. Then Harry said, because of the expression on Stanley's face: "Come on, we've got to pretend to work, at least."

They had to wrench another length of guttering that ran beside a parapet out of its bed, so that they could replace it. Stanley took it in his two hands, tugged, swore, stood up. "Fuck it," he said, and sat down under a chimney. He lit a cigarette. "Fuck them," he said. "What do they think we are, lizards? I've got blisters all over my hands." Then he jumped up and climbed over the roofs and stood with his back to them. He put his fingers either side of his mouth and let out a shrill whistle. Tom and Harry squatted, not looking at each other, watching him. They could just see the woman's head, the beginnings of her brown shoulders. Stanley whistled again. Then he began stamping with his feet, and whistled and yelled and screamed at the woman, his face getting scarlet. He seemed quite mad, as he stamped and whistled, while the woman did not move, she did not move a muscle.

"Barmy," said Tom.

"Yes," said Harry, disapproving.

Suddenly the older man came to a decision. It was, Tom knew, to save some   45
sort of scandal or real trouble over the woman. Harry stood up and began packing

*badinage:* (French), teasing, playful conversation.

tools into a length of oily cloth. "Stanley," he said, commanding. At first Stanley took no notice, but Harry said: "Stanley, we're packing it in, I'll tell Matthew."

Stanley came back, cheeks mottled, eyes glaring.

"Can't go on like this," said Harry. "It'll break in a day or so. I'm going to tell Matthew we've got sunstroke, and if he doesn't like it, it's too bad." Even Harry sounded aggrieved, Tom noted. The small, competent man, the family man with his grey hair, who was never at a loss, sounded really off balance. "Come on," he said, angry. He fitted himself into the open square in the roof, and went down, watching his feet on the ladder. Then Stanley went, with not a glance at the woman. Then Tom, who, his throat beating with excitement, silently promised her on a backward glance: Wait for me, wait, I'm coming.

On the pavement Stanley said: "I'm going home." He looked white now, so perhaps he really did have sunstroke. Harry went off to find the foreman who was at work on the plumbing of some flats down the street. Tom slipped back, not into the building they had been working on, but the building on whose roof the woman lay. He went straight up, no one stopping him. The skylight stood open, with an iron ladder leading up. He emerged on to the roof a couple of yards from her. She sat up, pushing back her black hair with both hands. The scarf across her breasts bound them tight, and brown flesh bulged around it. Her legs were brown and smooth. She stared at him in silence. The boy stood grinning, foolish, claiming the tenderness he expected from her.

"What do you want?" she asked.

"I . . . I came to . . . make your acquaintance," he stammered, grinning,    50
pleading with her.

They looked at each other, the slight, scarlet-faced excited boy, and the serious, nearly naked woman. Then, without a word, she lay down on her brown blanket, ignoring him.

"You like the sun, do you?" he enquired of her glistening back.

Not a word. He felt panic, thinking of how she had held him in her arms, stroked his hair, brought him where he sat, lordly, in her bed, a glass of some exhilarating liquor he had never tasted in life. He felt that if he knelt down, stroked her shoulders, her hair, she would turn and clasp him in her arms.

He said: "The sun's all right for you, isn't it?"

She raised her head, set her chin on two small fists: "Go away," she said. He    55
did not move. "Listen," she said, in a slow reasonable voice, where anger was kept in check, though with difficulty; looking at him, her face weary with anger, "if you get a kick out of seeing women in bikinis, why don't you take a sixpenny bus ride to the Lido?° You'd see dozens of them, without all this mountaineering."

She hadn't understood him. He felt her unfairness pale him. He stammered: "But I like you, I've been watching you and . . . "

"Thanks," she said, and dropped her face again, turned away from him.

She lay there. He stood there. She said nothing. She had simply shut him out. He stood, saying nothing at all, for some minutes. He thought: She'll have to

Lido: an outdoor swimming spot with sunbathing facilities in London's Hyde Park.

say something if I stay. But the minutes went past, with no sign of them in her, except in the tension of her back, her thighs, her arms—the tension of waiting for him to go.

He looked up at the sky, where the sun seemed to spin in heat; and over the roofs where he and his mates had been earlier. He could see the heat quivering where they had worked. And they expect us to work in these conditions! he thought, filled with righteous indignation. The woman hadn't moved. A bit of hot wind blew her black hair softly; it shone, and was iridescent. He remembered how he had stroked it last night.

Resentment of her at last moved him off and away down the ladder, through the building, into the street. He got drunk then, in hatred of her. 60

Next day when he woke the sky was grey. He looked at the wet grey and thought, vicious: Well, that's fixed you, hasn't it now? That's fixed you good and proper.

The three men were at work early on the cool leads, surrounded by damp drizzling roofs where no one came to sun themselves, black roofs, slimy with rain. Because it was cool now, they would finish the job that day, if they hurried.

## Gabriel García Márquez

The Woman Who Came at Six O'Clock                                    1950

*Translated by Gregory Rabassa*

*Gabriel García Márquez*

*Gabriel García Márquez, among the most eminent of living Latin American writers, was born in 1929 in Aracataca, a Caribbean port in Colombia, one of sixteen children of an impoverished telegraph operator. For a time he studied law in Bogotá, then became a newspaper reporter. Although he never joined the Communist party, García Márquez outspokenly advocated many left-wing proposals for reform. In 1954, despairing of any prospect for political change, he left Colombia to live in Mexico City. Though at nineteen he had already completed a book of short stories, La hojo-rasca (Leafstorm), he waited until 1955 to publish it. Soon he began to build a tow-ering reputation among readers of Spanish. His celebrated novel, Cien años de soledad (1967), published in English as One Hundred Years of Solitude (1969), traces the history of a Colombian family through six generations. Called by Chilean poet Pablo*

Neruda *"the greatest revelation in the Spanish language since* Don Quixote," *the book has sold more than twelve million copies in thirty languages. In 1982 García Márquez was awarded the Nobel prize for literature. His fiction, rich in myth and invention, has reminded American readers of the work of William Faulkner, another explorer of his native turf; indeed, García Márquez has called Faulkner "my master." His recent novels have included* Love in the Time of Cholera *(1988) and* The General in His Labyrinth *(1990). He also wrote the screenplay for* Eréndira *(1984), a film based on the title story from* Innocent Eréndira *(1978). "The Woman Who Came at Six O'Clock" comes from the same collection.*

The swinging door opened. At that hour there was nobody in José's restaurant. It had just struck six and the man knew that the regular customers wouldn't begin to arrive until six-thirty. His clientele was so conservative and regular that the clock hadn't finished striking six when a woman entered, as on every day at that hour, and sat down on the stool without saying anything. She had an unlighted cigarette tight between her lips.

"Hello, queen," José said when he saw her sit down. Then he went to the other end of the counter, wiping the streaked surface with a dry rag. Whenever anyone came into the restaurant José did the same thing. Even with the woman, with whom he'd almost come to acquire a degree of intimacy, the fat and ruddy restaurant owner put on his daily comedy of a hard-working man. He spoke from the other end of the counter.

"What do you want today?" he said.

"First of all I want to teach you how to be a gentleman," the woman said. She was sitting at the end of the stools, her elbows on the counter, the extinguished cigarette between her lips. When she spoke, she tightened her mouth so that José would notice the unlighted cigarette.

"I didn't notice," José said.                                                                                          5

"You still haven't learned to notice anything," said the woman.

The man left the cloth on the counter, walked to the dark cupboards which smelled of tar and dusty wood, and came back immediately with the matches. The woman leaned over to get the light that was burning in the man's rustic, hairy hands. José saw the woman's lush hair, all greased with cheap, thick Vaseline. He saw her uncovered shoulder above the flowered brassiere. He saw the beginning of her twilight breast when the woman raised her head, the lighted butt between her lips now.

"You're beautiful tonight, queen," José said.

"Stop your nonsense," the woman said. "Don't think that's going to help me pay you."

"That's not what I meant, queen," José said. "I'll bet your lunch didn't agree     10
with you today."

The woman sucked in the first drag of thick smoke, crossed her arms, her elbows still on the counter, and remained looking at the street through the wide restaurant window. She had a melancholy expression. A bored and vulgar melancholy.

"I'll fix you a good steak," José said.

"I still haven't got any money," the woman said.

"You haven't had any money for three months and I always fix you something good," José said.

"Today's different," said the woman somberly, still looking out at the street.

"Every day's the same," José said. "Every day the clock says six, then you come in and say you're hungry as a dog and then I fix you something good. The only difference is this: today you didn't say you were as hungry as a dog but that today is different."

"And it's true," the woman said. She turned to look at the man, who was at the other end of the counter checking the refrigerator. She examined him for two or three seconds. Then she looked at the clock over the cupboard. It was three minutes after six. "It's true, José. Today is different," she said. She let the smoke out and kept on talking with crisp, impassioned words. "I didn't come at six today, that's why it's different, José."

The man looked at the clock.

"I'll cut off my arm if that clock is one minute slow," he said.

"That's not it, José. I didn't come at six o'clock today," the woman said.

"It just struck six, queen," José said. "When you came in it was just finishing."

"I've got a quarter of an hour that says I've been here," the woman said.

José went over to where she was. He put his great puffy face up to the woman while he tugged on one of his eyelids with his index finger.

"Blow on me here," he said.

The woman threw her head back. She was serious, annoyed, softened, beautified by a cloud of sadness and fatigue.

"Stop your foolishness, José. You know I haven't had a drink for six months."

"Tell it to somebody else," he said, "not to me. I'll bet you've had a pint or two at least."

"I had a couple of drinks with a friend," she said.

"Oh, now I understand," José said.

"There's nothing to understand," the woman said. "I've been here for a quarter of an hour."

The man shrugged his shoulders.

"Well, if that's the way you want it, you've got a quarter of an hour that says you've been here," he said. "After all, what difference does it make, ten minutes this way, ten minutes that way?"

"It makes a difference, José," the woman said. And she stretched her arms over the glass counter with an air of careless abandon. She said: "And it isn't that I wanted it that way; it's just that I've been here for a quarter of an hour." She looked at the clock again and corrected herself: "What am I saying—it's been twenty minutes."

"O.K., queen," the man said. "I'd give you a whole day and the night that goes with it just to see you happy."

During all this time José had been moving about behind the counter, changing things, taking something from one place and putting it in another. He was playing his role.

"I want to see you happy," he repeated. He stopped suddenly, turning to where the woman was. "Do you know that I love you very much?"

The woman looked at him coldly.

"Ye-e-es . . . ? What a discovery, José. Do you think I'd go with you even for a million pesos?"

"I didn't mean that, queen," José said. "I repeat, I bet your lunch didn't agree with you."

"That's not why I said it," the woman said. And her voice became less indo- 40 lent. "No woman could stand a weight like yours, even for a million pesos."

José blushed. He turned his back to the woman and began to dust the bottles on the shelves. He spoke without turning his head.

"You're unbearable today, queen. I think the best thing is for you to eat your steak and go home to bed."

"I'm not hungry," the woman said. She stayed looking out at the street again, watching the passers-by of the dusking city. For an instant there was a murky silence in the restaurant. A peacefulness broken only by José's fiddling about in the cupboard. Suddenly the woman stopped looking out into the street and spoke with a tender, soft, different voice.

"Do you really love me, Pepillo?"

"I do," José said dryly, not looking at her. 45

"In spite of what I've said to you?" the woman asked.

"What did you say to me?" José asked, still without any inflection in his voice, still without looking at her.

"That business about a million pesos," the woman said.

"I'd already forgotten," José said.

"So do you love me?" the woman asked. 50

"Yes," said José.

There was a pause. José kept moving about, his face turned toward the cabinets, still not looking at the woman. She blew out another mouthful of smoke, rested her bust on the counter, and then, cautiously and roguishly, biting her tongue before saying it, as if speaking on tiptoe:

"Even if you didn't go to bed with me?" she asked.

And only then did José turn to look at her.

"I love you so much that I wouldn't go to bed with you," he said. Then he 55 walked over to where she was. He stood looking into her face, his powerful arms leaning on the counter in front of her, looking into her eyes. He said: "I love you so much that every night I'd kill the man who goes with you."

At the first instant the woman seemed perplexed. Then she looked at the man attentively, with a wavering expression of compassion and mockery. Then she had a moment of brief disconcerted silence. And then she laughed noisily.

"You're jealous, José. That's wild, you're jealous!"

José blushed again with frank, almost shameful timidity, as might have happened to a child who'd revealed all his secrets all of a sudden. He said:

"This afternoon you don't seem to understand anything, queen." And he wiped himself with the rag. He said:

"This bad life is brutalizing you."

But now the woman had changed her expression.

"So, then," she said. And she looked into his eyes again, with a strange glow in her look, confused and challenging at the same time.

"So you're not jealous."

"In a way I am," José said. "But it's not the way you think."

He loosened his collar and continued wiping himself, drying his throat with the cloth.

"So?" the woman asked.

"The fact is I love you so much that I don't like your doing it," José said.

"What?" the woman asked.

"This business of going with a different man every day," José said.

"Would you really kill him to stop him from going with me?" the woman asked.

"Not to stop him from going with you, no," José said. "I'd kill him because he *went* with you."

"It's the same thing," the woman said.

The conversation had reached an exciting density. The woman was speaking in a soft, low, fascinated voice. Her face was almost stuck up against the man's healthy, peaceful face, as he stood motionless, as if bewitched by the vapor of the words.

"That's true," José said.

"So," the woman said, and reached out her hand to stroke the man's rough arm. With the other she tossed away her butt. "So you're capable of killing a man?"

"For what I told you, yes," José said. And his voice took on an almost dramatic stress.

The woman broke into convulsive laughter, with an obvious mocking intent.

"How awful, José. How awful," she said, still laughing. "José killing a man. Who would have known that behind the fat and sanctimonious man who never makes me pay, who cooks me a steak every day and has fun talking to me until I find a man, there lurks a murderer. How awful, José! You scare me!"

José was confused. Maybe he felt a little indignation. Maybe, when the woman started laughing, he felt defrauded.

"You're drunk, silly," he said. "Go get some sleep. You don't even feel like eating anything."

But the woman had stopped laughing now and was serious again, pensive, leaning on the counter. She watched the man go away. She saw him open the refrigerator and close it again without taking anything out. Then she saw him move to the other end of the counter. She watched him polish the shining glass, the same as in the beginning. Then the woman spoke again with the tender and soft tone of when she said: "Do you really love me, Pepillo?"

"José," she said.

The man didn't look at her.

"José!"

"Go home and sleep," José said. "And take a bath before you go to bed so you can sleep it off." 85

"Seriously, José," the woman said. "I'm not drunk."

"Then you've turned stupid," José said.

"Come here, I've got to talk to you," the woman said.

The man came over stumbling, halfway between pleasure and mistrust.

"Come closer!" 90

He stood in front of the woman again. She leaned forward, grabbed him by the hair, but with a gesture of obvious tenderness.

"Tell me again what you said at the start," she said.

"What do you mean?" José asked. He was trying to look at her with his head turned away, held by the hair.

"That you'd kill a man who went to bed with me," the woman said.

"I'd kill a man who went to bed with you, queen. That's right," José said. 95

The woman let him go.

"In that case you'd defend me if I killed him, right?" she asked affirmatively, pushing José's enormous pig head with a movement of brutal coquettishness. The man didn't answer anything. He smiled.

"Answer me, José," the woman said. "Would you defend me if I killed him?"

"That depends," José said. "You know it's not as easy as you say."

"The police wouldn't believe anyone more than you," the woman said. 100

José smiled, honored, satisfied. The woman leaned over toward him again, over the counter.

"It's true, José. I'm willing to bet that you've never told a lie in your life," she said.

"You won't get anywhere this way," José said.

"Just the same," the woman said. "The police know you and they'll believe anything without asking you twice."

José began pounding on the counter opposite her, not knowing what to say. 105 The woman looked out at the street again. Then she looked at the clock and modified the tone of her voice, as if she were interested in finishing the conversation before the first customers arrived.

"Would you tell a lie for me, José?" she asked. "Seriously."

And then José looked at her again, sharply, deeply, as if a tremendous idea had come pounding up in his head. An idea that had entered through one ear, spun about for a moment, vague, confused, and gone out through the other, leaving behind only a warm vestige of terror.

"What have you got yourself into, queen?" José asked. He leaned forward, his arms folded over the counter again. The woman caught the strong and ammonia-smelling vapor of his breathing, which had become difficult because of the pressure that the counter was exercising on the man's stomach.

"This is really serious, queen. What have you got yourself into?" he asked.

The woman made her head spin in the opposite direction. 110

"Nothing," she said. "I was just talking to amuse myself."

Then she looked at him again.

"Do you know you may not have to kill anybody?"

"I never thought about killing anybody," José said, distressed.

"No, man," the woman said. "I mean nobody goes to bed with me." 115

"Oh!" José said. "Now you're talking straight out. I always thought you had no need to prowl around. I'll make a bet that if you drop all this I'll give you the biggest steak I've got every day, free."

"Thank you, José," the woman said. "But that's not why. It's because I *can't* go to bed with anyone any more."

"You're getting things all confused again," José said. He was becoming impatient.

"I'm not getting anything confused," the woman said. She stretched out on the seat and José saw her flat, sad breasts underneath her brassiere.

"Tomorrow I'm going away and I promise you I won't come back and bother 120 you ever again. I promise you I'll never go to bed with anyone."

"Where'd you pick up that fever?" José asked.

"I decided just a minute ago," the woman said. "Just a minute ago I realized it's a dirty business."

José grabbed the cloth again and started to clean the glass in front of her. He spoke without looking at her.

He said:

"Of course, the way you do it it's a dirty business. You should have known 125 that a long time ago."

"I was getting to know it a long time ago," the woman said, "but I was only convinced of it just a little while ago. Men disgust me."

José smiled. He raised his head to look at her, still smiling, but he saw her concentrated, perplexed, talking with her shoulders raised, twirling on the stool with a taciturn expression, her face gilded by premature autumnal grain.

"Don't you think they ought to lay off a woman who kills a man because after she's been with him she feels disgust with him and everyone who's been with her?"

"There's no reason to go that far," José said, moved, a thread of pity in his voice.

"What if the woman tells the man he disgusts her while she watches him get 130 dressed because she remembers that she's been rolling around with him all afternoon and feels that neither soap nor sponge can get his smell off her?"

"That all goes away, queen," José said, a little indifferent now, polishing the counter. "There's no reason to kill him. Just let him go."

But the woman kept on talking, and her voice was a uniform, flowing, passionate current.

"But what if the woman tells him he disgusts her and the man stops getting dressed and runs over to her again, kisses her again, does . . . ?"

"No decent man would ever do that," José says.

"What if he does?" the woman asks, with exasperating anxiety. "What if the 135 man isn't decent and does it and then the woman feels that he disgusts her so much that she could die, and she knows that the only way to end it all is to stick a knife in under him?"

"That's terrible," José said. "Luckily there's no man who would do what you say."

"Well," the woman said, completely exasperated now. "What if he did? Suppose he did."

"In any case it's not that bad," José said. He kept on cleaning the counter without changing position, less intent on the conversation now.

The woman pounded the counter with her knuckles. She became affirmative, emphatic.

"You're a savage, José," she said. "You don't understand anything." She grabbed him firmly by the sleeve. "Come on, tell me that the woman should kill him."

"O.K.," José said with a conciliatory bias. "It's all probably just the way you say it is."

"Isn't that self-defense?" the woman asked, grabbing him by the sleeve.

Then José gave her a lukewarm and pleasant look.

"Almost, almost," he said. And he winked at her, with an expression that was at the same time a cordial comprehension and a fearful compromise of complicity. But the woman was serious. She let go of him.

"Would you tell a lie to defend a woman who does that?" she asked.        145

"That depends," said José.

"Depends on what?" the woman asked.

"Depends on the woman," said José.

"Suppose it's a woman you love a lot," the woman said. "Not to be with her, but like you say, you love her a lot."

"O.K., anything you say, queen," José said, relaxed, bored.        150

He'd gone off again. He'd looked at the clock. He'd seen that it was going on half-past six. He'd thought that in a few minutes the restaurant would be filling up with people and maybe that was why he began to polish the glass with greater effort, looking at the street through the window. The woman stayed on her stool, silent, concentrating, watching the man's movements with an air of declining sadness. Watching him as a lamp about to go out might have looked at a man. Suddenly, without reacting, she spoke again with the unctuous voice of servitude.

"José!"

The man looked at her with a thick, sad tenderness, like a maternal ox. He didn't look at her to hear her, just to look at her, to know that she was there, waiting for a look that had no reason to be one of protection or solidarity. Just the look of a plaything.

"I told you I was leaving tomorrow and you didn't say anything," the woman said.

"Yes," José said. "You didn't tell me where."        155

"Out there," the woman said. "Where there aren't any men who want to sleep with somebody."

José smiled again.

"Are you really going away?" he asked, as if becoming aware of life, quickly changing the expression on his face.

"That depends on you," the woman said. "If you know enough to say what time I got here, I'll go away tomorrow and I'll never get mixed up in this again. Would you like that?"

José gave an affirmative nod, smiling and concrete. The woman leaned over 160 to where he was.

"If I come back here someday I'll get jealous when I find another woman talking to you, at this time and on this same stool."

"If you come back here you'll have to bring me something," José said.

"I promise you that I'll look everywhere for the tame bear, bring him to you," the woman said.

José smiled and waved the cloth through the air that separated him from the woman, as if he were cleaning an invisible pane of glass. The woman smiled too, with an expression of cordiality and coquetry now. Then the man went away, polishing the glass to the other end of the counter.

"What, then?" José said without looking at her. 165

"Will you really tell anyone who asks you that I got here at a quarter to six?" the woman said.

"What for?" José said, still without looking at her now, as if he had barely heard her.

"That doesn't matter," the woman said. "The thing is that you do it."

José then saw the first customer come in through the swinging door and walk over to a corner table. He looked at the clock. It was six-thirty on the dot.

"O.K., queen," he said distractedly. "Anything you say. I always do whatever 170 you want."

"Well," the woman said. "Start cooking my steak, then."

The man went to the refrigerator, took out a plate with a piece of meat on it, and left it on the table. Then he lighted the stove.

"I'm going to cook you a good farewell steak, queen," he said.

"Thank you, Pepillo," the woman said.

She remained thoughtful as if suddenly she had become sunken in a strange 175 subworld peopled with muddy, unknown forms. Across the counter she couldn't hear the noise that the raw meat made when it fell into the burning grease. Afterward she didn't hear the dry and bubbling crackle as José turned the flank over in the frying pan and the succulent smell of the marinated meat by measured moments saturated the air of the restaurant. She remained like that, concentrated, reconcentrated, until she raised her head again, blinking as if she were coming back out of a momentary death. Then she saw the man beside the stove, lighted up by the happy, rising fire.

"Pepillo."

"What!"

"What are you thinking about?" the woman asked.

"I was wondering whether you could find the little wind-up bear someplace," José said.

"Of course I can," the woman said. "But what I want is for you to give me      180
everything I asked for as a going-away present."

José looked at her from the stove.

"How often have I got to tell you?" he said. "Do you want something besides
the best steak I've got?"

"Yes," the woman said.

"What is it?" José asked.

"I want another quarter of an hour."      185

José drew back and looked at the clock. Then he looked at the customer,
who was still silent, waiting in the corner, and finally at the meat roasting in the
pan. Only then did he speak.

"I really don't understand, queen," he said.

"Don't be foolish, José," the woman said. "Just remember that I've been here
since five-thirty."

---

### *Bobbie Ann Mason*

SHILOH                                                                              1982

*Bobbie Ann Mason, one of the leading
voices in the new Southern fiction, was
born in 1940 in Mayfield, Kentucky, growing up on a dairy farm in a region of western Kentucky whose people often appear in
her stories. After her graduation from the
University of Kentucky, she wrote for popular magazines including* Movie Life *and*
TV Star Parade, *then began a now-sus-
pended career in college teaching, taking her
Ph.D. at the University of Connecticut and
writing the critical studies* Nabokov's
Garden *(1974) and* The Girl Sleuth: A
Feminist Guide to the Bobbsey Twins,
Nancy Drew, and Their Sisters *(1975).
Her first collection,* Shiloh and Other
Stories *(1982), received wide attention,*

Bobbie Ann Mason

*and with the novels* In Country *(1985) and* Spence & Lila *(1988), her audience has
continued to grow. Anonymously, Mason has also written many contributions to the
feature "Talk of the Town" in* The New Yorker. *Her second collection of stories,* Love
Life, *appeared in 1989. Mason now lives in rural Pennsylvania.*

Leroy Moffitt's wife, Norma Jean, is working on her pectorals. She lifts three-
pound dumbbells to warm up, then progresses to a twenty-pound barbell.
Standing with her legs apart, she reminds Leroy of Wonder Woman.

"I'd give anything if I could just get these muscles to where they're real hard," says Norma Jean. "Feel this arm. It's not as hard as the other one."

"That's 'cause you're right-handed," says Leroy, dodging as she swings the barbell in an arc.

"Do you think so?"

"Sure."

Leroy is a truckdriver. He injured his leg in a highway accident four months ago, and his physical therapy which involves weights and a pulley, prompted Norma Jean to try building herself up. Now she is attending a body-building class. Leroy has been collecting temporary disability since his tractor-trailer jackknifed in Missouri, badly twisting his left leg in its socket. He has a steel pin in his hip. He will probably not be able to drive his rig again. It sits in the backyard, like a gigantic bird that has flown home to roost. Leroy has been home in Kentucky for three months, and his leg is almost healed, but the accident frightened him and he does not want to drive any more long hauls. He is not sure what to do next. In the meantime, he makes things from craft kits. He started by building a miniature log cabin from notched Popsicle sticks. He varnished it and placed it on the TV set, where it remains. It reminds him of a rustic Nativity scene. Then he tried string art (sailing ships on black velvet), a macramé owl kit, a snap-together B-17 Flying Fortress, and a lamp made out of a model truck, with a light fixture screwed in the top of the cab. At first the kits were diversions, something to kill time, but now he is thinking about building a full-scale log house from a kit. It would be considerably cheaper than building a regular house, and besides, Leroy has grown to appreciate how things are put together. He has begun to realize that in all the years he was on the road he never took time to examine anything. He was always flying past scenery.

"They won't let you build a log cabin in any of the new subdivisions," Norma Jean tells him.

"They will if I tell them it's for you," he says, teasing her. Ever since they were married, he has promised Norma Jean he would build her a new home one day. They have always rented, and the house they live in is small and nondescript. It does not even feel like a home, Leroy realizes now.

Norma Jean works at the Rexall drugstore, and she has acquired an amazing amount of information about cosmetics. When she explains to Leroy the three stages of complexion care, involving creams, toners, and moisturizers, he thinks happily of other petroleum products—axle grease, diesel fuel. This is a connection between him and Norma Jean. Since he has been home, he has felt unusually tender about his wife and guilty over his long absences. But he can't tell what she feels about him. Norma Jean has never complained about his traveling; she has never made hurt remarks, like calling his truck a "widow-maker." He is reasonably certain she has been faithful to him, but he wishes she would celebrate his permanent home-coming more happily. Norma Jean is often startled to find Leroy at home, and he thinks she seems a little disappointed about it. Perhaps he reminds her too much of the early days of their marriage, before he went on the road. They had a child who died as an infant, years ago. They never speak about their memories of Randy, which have almost faded, but now that Leroy is home all the time, they sometimes feel awkward around each other, and Leroy wonders if one of them should mention the child. He has the feeling that they are waking up out of a dream together—that they must create a new marriage, start afresh. They are lucky they are still married. Leroy has read that for most people losing a child destroys the marriage—or else he heard this on *Donahue*. He can't always remember where he learns things anymore.

At Christmas, Leroy bought an electric organ for Norma Jean. She used to 10 play the piano when she was in high school. "It don't leave you," she told him once. "It's like riding a bicycle."

The new instrument had so many keys and buttons that she was bewildered by it at first. She touched the keys tentatively, pushed some buttons, then pecked out "Chopsticks." It came out in an amplified fox-trot rhythm, with marimba sounds.

"It's an orchestra!" she cried.

The organ had a pecan-look finish and eighteen preset chords, with optional flute, violin, trumpet, clarinet, and banjo accompaniments. Norma Jean mastered the organ almost immediately. At first she played Christmas songs. Then she bought *The Sixties Songbook* and learned every tune in it, adding variations to each with the rows of brightly colored buttons.

"I didn't like these old songs back then," she said. "But I have this crazy feeling I missed something."

"You didn't miss a thing," said Leroy. 15

Leroy likes to lie on the couch and smoke a joint and listen to Norma Jean play "Can't Take My Eyes Off You" and "I'll Be Back." He is back again. After fifteen years on the road, he is finally settling down with the woman he loves. She is still pretty. Her skin is flawless. Her frosted curls resemble pencil trimmings.

Now that Leroy has come home to stay, he notices how much the town has changed. Subdivisions are spreading across western Kentucky like an oil slick. The sign at the edge of town says "Pop: 11,500"—only seven hundred more than it said twenty years before. Leroy can't figure out who is living in all the new houses. The farmers who used to gather around the courthouse square on Saturday afternoons to play checkers and spit tobacco juice have gone. It has been years since Leroy has thought about the farmers, and they have disappeared without his noticing.

Leroy meets a kid named Stevie Hamilton in the parking lot at the new shopping center. While they pretend to be strangers meeting over a stalled car, Stevie tosses an ounce of marijuana under the front seat of Leroy's car. Stevie is wearing orange jogging shoes and a T-shirt that says CHATTAHOOCHEE SUPER RAT. His father is a prominent doctor who lives in one of the expensive subdivisions in a new white-columned brick house that looks like a funeral parlor. In the phone book under his name there is a separate number, with the listing "Teenagers."

"Where do you get this stuff?" asks Leroy. "From your pappy?"

"That's for me to know and you to find out," Stevie says. He is slit-eyed and  20
skinny.

"What else you got?"

"What you interested in?"

"Nothing special. Just wondered."

Leroy used to take speed on the road. Now he has to go slowly. He needs to be mellow. He leans back against the car and says, "I'm aiming to build me a log house, soon as I get time. My wife, though, I don't think she likes the idea."

"Well, let me know when you want me again," Stevie says. He has a ciga-  25
rette in his cupped palm, as though sheltering it from the wind. He takes a long drag, then stomps it on the asphalt and slouches away.

Stevie's father was two years ahead of Leroy in high school. Leroy is thirty-four. He married Norma Jean when they were both eighteen, and their child Randy was born a few months later, but he died at the age of four months and three days. He would be about Stevie's age now. Norma Jean and Leroy were at the drive-in, watching a double feature (*Dr. Strangelove* and *Lover Come Back*), and the baby was sleeping in the back seat. When the first movie ended, the baby was dead. It was the sudden infant death syndrome. Leroy remembers handing Randy to a nurse at the emergency room, as though he were offering her a large doll as a present. A dead baby feels like a sack of flour. "It just happens some-times," said the doctor, in what Leroy always recalls as a nonchalant tone. Leroy can hardly remember the child anymore, but he still sees vividly a scene from *Dr. Strangelove*° in which the President of the United States was talking in a folksy voice on the hot line to the Soviet premier about the bomber accidentally head-ed toward Russia. He was in the War Room, and the world map was lit up. Leroy remembers Norma Jean standing catatonically beside him in the hospital and himself thinking: Who is this strange girl? He had forgotten who she was. Now scientists are saying that crib death is caused by a virus. Nobody knows anything, Leroy thinks. The answers are always changing.

When Leroy gets home from the shopping center, Norma Jean's mother, Mabel Beasley, is there. Until this year, Leroy has not realized how much time she spends with Norma Jean. When she visits, she inspects the closets and then the plants, informing Norma Jean when a plant is droopy or yellow. Mabel calls the plants "flowers," although there are never any blooms. She also notices if Norma Jean's laundry is piling up. Mabel is a short, overweight woman whose tight, brown-dyed curls look more like a wig than the actual wig she sometimes wears. Today she has brought Norma Jean an off-white dust ruffle she made for the bed; Mabel works in a custom upholstery shop.

"This is the tenth one I made this year," Mabel says. "I got started and couldn't stop."

"It's real pretty," says Norma Jean.

---

*Dr. Strangelove:* Stanley Kubrick's classic 1963 suspense comedy film about a mad U.S. general who launches an unauthorized nuclear attack on Russia.

"Now we can hide things under the bed," says Leroy, who gets along with his <sup>30</sup> mother-in-law primarily by joking with her. Mabel has never really forgiven him for disgracing her by getting Norma Jean pregnant. When the baby died, she said that fate was mocking her.

"What's that thing?" Mabel says to Leroy in a loud voice, pointing to a tangle of yarn on a piece of canvas.

Leroy holds it up for Mabel to see. "It's my needlepoint," he explains. "This is a *Star Trek* pillow cover."

"That's what a woman would do," says Mabel. "Great day in the morning!"

"All the big football players on TV do it," he says.

"Why, Leroy, you're always trying to fool me. I don't believe you for one <sup>35</sup> minute. You don't know what to do with yourself—that's the whole trouble. Sewing!"

"I'm aiming to build us a log house," says Leroy. "Soon as my plans come."

"Like *heck* you are," says Norma Jean. She takes Leroy's needlepoint and shoves it into a drawer. "You have to find a job first. Nobody can afford to build now anyway."

Mabel straightens her girdle and says, "I still think before you get tied down y'all ought to take a little run to Shiloh."

"One of these days, Mama," Norma Jean says impatiently.

Mabel is talking about Shiloh, Tennessee. For the past few years, she has <sup>40</sup> been urging Leroy and Norma Jean to visit the Civil War battleground there. Mabel went there on her honeymoon—the only real trip she ever took. Her husband died of a perforated ulcer when Norma Jean was ten, but Mabel, who was accepted into the United Daughters of the Confederacy in 1975, is still preoccupied with going back to Shiloh.

"I've been to kingdom come and back in that truck out yonder," Leroy says to Mabel, "but we never set foot in that battleground. Ain't that something? How did I miss it?"

"It's not even that far," Mabel says.

After Mabel leaves, Norma Jean reads to Leroy from a list she has made. "Things you could do," she announces. "You could get a job as a guard at Union Carbide, where they'd let you set on a stool. You could get on at the lumberyard. You could do a little carpenter work, if you want to build so bad. You could—"

"I can't do something where I'd have to stand up all day."

"You ought to try standing up all day behind a cosmetics counter. It's amaz- <sup>45</sup> ing that I have strong feet, coming from two parents that never had strong feet at all." At the moment Norma Jean is holding on to the kitchen counter, raising her knees one at a time as she talks. She is wearing two-pound ankle weights.

"Don't worry," says Leroy. "I'll do something."

"You could truck calves to slaughter for somebody. You wouldn't have to drive any big old truck for that."

"I'm going to build you this house," says Leroy. "I want to make you a real home."

"I don't want to live in any log cabin."

"It's not a cabin. It's a house."                                              50
"I don't care. It looks like a cabin."
"You and me together could lift those logs. It's just like lifting weights."
Norma Jean doesn't answer. Under her breath, she is counting. Now she is marching through the kitchen. She is doing goose steps.°

Before his accident, when Leroy came home he used to stay in the house with Norma Jean, watching TV in bed and playing cards. She would cook fried chicken, picnic ham, chocolate pie—all his favorites. Now he is home alone much of the time. In the mornings, Norma Jean disappears, leaving a cooling place in the bed. She eats a cereal called Body Buddies, and she leaves the bowl on the table, with the soggy tan balls floating in a milk puddle. He sees things about Norma Jean that he never realized before. When she chops onions, she stares off into a corner, as if she can't bear to look. She puts on her house slippers almost precisely at nine o'clock every evening and nudges her jogging shoes under the couch. She saves bread heels for the birds. Leroy watches the birds at the feeder. He notices the peculiar way goldfinches fly past the window. They close their wings, then fall, then spread their wings to catch and lift themselves. He wonders if they close their eyes when they fall. Norma Jean closes her eyes when they are in bed. She wants the lights turned out. Even then, he is sure she closes her eyes.

He goes for long drives around town. He tends to drive a car rather careless-   55
ly. Power steering and an automatic shift make a car feel so small and inconsequential that his body is hardly involved in the driving process. His injured leg stretches out comfortably. Once or twice he has almost hit something, but even the prospect of an accident seems minor in a car. He cruises the new subdivisions, feeling like a criminal rehearsing for a robbery. Norma Jean is probably right about a log house being inappropriate here in the new subdivision. All the houses look grand and complicated. They depress him.

One day when Leroy comes home from a drive he finds Norma Jean in tears. She is in the kitchen making a potato and mushroom-soup casserole, with grated cheese topping. She is crying because her mother caught her smoking.

"I didn't hear her coming. I was standing here puffing away pretty as you please," Norma Jean says, wiping her eyes.

"I knew it would happen sooner or later," says Leroy, putting his arm around her.

"She don't know the meaning of the word 'knock,'" says Norma Jean. "It's a wonder she hadn't caught me years ago."

"Think of it this way," Leroy says. "What if she caught me with a joint?"       60

"You better not let her!" Norma Jean shrieks. "I'm warning you, Leroy Moffitt!"

---

*goose steps:* a stiff-kneed, straight-legged marching step used in military parades. Used here as an exercise routine.

"I'm just kidding. Here, play me a tune. That'll help you relax."

Norma Jean puts the casserole in the oven and sets the timer. Then she plays a ragtime tune, with horns and banjo, as Leroy lights up a joint and lies on the couch, laughing to himself about Mabel's catching him at it. He thinks of Stevie Hamilton—a doctor's son pushing grass. Everything is funny. The whole town seems crazy and small. He is reminded of Virgil Mathis, a boastful policeman Leroy used to shoot pool with. Virgil recently led a drug bust in a back room at a bowling alley, where he seized ten thousand dollars' worth of marijuana. The newspaper had a picture of him holding up the bags of grass and grinning widely. Right now, Leroy can imagine Virgil breaking down the door and arresting him with a lungful of smoke. Virgil would probably have been alerted to the scene because of all the racket Norma Jean is making. Now she sounds like a hard-rock band. Norma Jean is terrific. When she switches to a Latin-rhythm version of "Sunshine Superman," Leroy hums along. Norma Jean's foot goes up and down, up and down.

"Well, what do you think?" Leroy says, when Norma Jean pauses to search through her music.

"What do I think about what?" 65

His mind has gone blank. Then he says, "I'll sell my rig and build us a house." That wasn't what he wanted to say. He wanted to know what she thought—what she *really* thought—about them.

"Don't start in on that again," says Norma Jean. She begins playing "Who'll Be the Next in Line?"

Leroy used to tell hitchhikers his whole life story—about his travels, his hometown, the baby. He would end with a question: "Well, what do you think?" It was just a rhetorical question. In time, he had the feeling that he'd been telling the same story over and over to the same hitchhikers. He quit talking to hitchhikers when he realized how his voice sounded—whining and self-pitying, like some teenage-tragedy song. Now Leroy has the sudden impulse to tell Norma Jean about himself, as if he had just met her. They have known each other so long they have forgotten a lot about each other. They could become reacquainted. But when the oven timer goes off and she runs to the kitchen, he forgets why he wants to do this.

The next day, Mabel drops by. It is Saturday and Norma Jean is cleaning. Leroy is studying the plans of his log house, which have finally come in the mail. He has them spread out on the table—big sheets of stiff blue paper, with diagrams and numbers printed in white. While Norma Jean runs the vacuum, Mabel drinks coffee. She sets her coffee cup on a blueprint.

"I'm just waiting for time to pass," she says to Leroy, drumming her fingers on 70 the table.

As soon as Norma Jean switches off the vacuum, Mabel says in a loud voice, "Did you hear about the datsun dog that killed the baby?"

Norma Jean says, "The word is 'dachshund.'"

"They put the dog on trial. It chewed the baby's legs off. The mother was in the next room all the time." She raises her voice. "They thought it was neglect."

Norma Jean is holding her ears. Leroy manages to open the refrigerator and get some Diet Pepsi to offer Mabel. Mabel still has some coffee and she waves away the Pepsi.

"Datsuns are like that," Mabel says. "They're jealous dogs. They'll tear a place to pieces if you don't keep an eye on them."

"You better watch out what you're saying, Mabel," says Leroy.

"Well, facts is facts."

Leroy looks out the window at his rig. It is like a huge piece of furniture gathering dust in the backyard. Pretty soon it will be an antique. He hears the vacuum cleaner. Norma Jean seems to be cleaning the living room rug again.

Later, she says to Leroy, "She just said that about the baby because she caught me smoking. She's trying to pay me back."

"What are you talking about?" Leroy says, nervously shuffling blueprints.

"You know good and well," Norma Jean says. She is sitting in a kitchen chair with her feet up and her arms wrapped around her knees. She looks small and helpless. She says, "The very idea, her bringing up a subject like that! Saying it was neglect."

"She didn't mean that," Leroy says.

"She might not have *thought* she meant it. She always says things like that. You don't know how she goes on."

"But she didn't really mean it. She was just talking."

Leroy opens a king-sized bottle of beer and pours it into two glasses, dividing it carefully. He hands a glass to Norma Jean and she takes it from him mechanically. For a long time, they sit by the kitchen window watching the birds at the feeder.

Something is happening. Norma Jean is going to night school. She has graduated from her six-week body-building course and now she is taking an adult-education course in composition at Paducah Community College. She spends her evenings outlining paragraphs.

"First, you have a topic sentence," she explains to Leroy. "Then you divide it up. Your secondary topic has to be connected to your primary topic."

To Leroy, this sounds intimidating. "I never was any good in English," he says.

"It makes a lot of sense."

"What are you doing this for, anyhow?"

She shrugs. "It's something to do." She stands up and lifts her dumbbells a few times.

"Driving a rig, nobody cared about my English."

"I'm not criticizing your English."

Norma Jean used to say, "If I lose ten minutes' sleep, I just drag all day." Now she stays up late, writing compositions. She got a B on her first paper—a how-to theme on soup-based casseroles. Recently Norma Jean has been cooking unusual foods—tacos, lasagna, Bombay chicken. She doesn't play the organ anymore, though her second paper was called "Why Music Is Important to Me." She sits at the kitchen table, concentrating on her outlines, while Leroy plays with his log house plans, practicing with a set of Lincoln Logs. The thought of getting a truckload of notched, numbered logs scares him, and he wants to be prepared. As he and Norma Jean work together at the kitchen table, Leroy has the hopeful thought that they are sharing something, but he knows he is a fool to think this. Norma Jean is miles away. He knows he is going to lose her. Like Mabel, he is just waiting for time to pass.

One day, Mabel is there before Norma Jean gets home from work, and Leroy   95 finds himself confiding in her. Mabel, he realizes, must know Norma Jean better than he does.

"I don't know what's got into that girl," Mabel says. "She used to go to bed with the chickens. Now you say she's up all hours. Plus her a-smoking. I like to died."

"I want to make her this beautiful home," Leroy says, indicating the Lincoln Logs. "I don't think she even wants it. Maybe she was happier with me gone."

"She don't know what to make of you, coming home like this."

"Is that it?"

Mabel takes the roof off his Lincoln Log cabin. "You couldn't get me in a log   100 cabin," she says. "I was raised in one. It's no picnic, let me tell you."

"They're different now," says Leroy.

"I tell you what," Mabel says, smiling oddly at Leroy.

"What?"

"Take her on down to Shiloh. Y'all need to get out together, stir a little. Her brain's all balled up over them books."

Leroy can see traces of Norma Jean's features in her mother's face. Mabel's   105 worn face has the texture of crinkled cotton, but suddenly she looks pretty. It occurs to Leroy that Mabel has been hinting all along that she wants them to take her with them to Shiloh.

"Let's all go to Shiloh," he says. "You and me and her. Come Sunday."

Mabel throws up her hand in protest. "Oh, no, not me. Young folks want to be by theirselves."

When Norma Jean comes in with groceries, Leroy says excitedly, "Your mama here's been dying to go to Shiloh for thirty-five years. It's about time we went, don't you think?"

"I'm not going to butt in on anybody's second honeymoon," Mabel says.

"Who's going on a honeymoon, for Christ's sake?" Norma Jean says loudly.   110

"I never raised no daughter of mine to talk that-a-way," Mabel says.

"You ain't seen nothing yet," says Norma Jean. She starts putting away boxes and cans, slamming cabinet doors.

"There's a log cabin at Shiloh," Mabel says. "It was there during the battle. There's bullet holes in it."

"When are you going to *shut up* about Shiloh, Mama?" asks Norma Jean.

"I always thought Shiloh was the prettiest place, so full of history," Mabel 115
goes on. "I just hoped y'all could see it once before I die, so you could tell me
about it." Later, she whispers to Leroy, "You do what I said. A little change is
what she needs."

"Your name means 'the king,'" Norma Jean says to Leroy that evening. He is
trying to get her to go to Shiloh, and she is reading a book about another century.
"Well, I reckon I ought to be right proud."
"I guess so."
"Am I still king around here?"
Norma Jean flexes her biceps and feels them for hardness. "I'm not fooling 120
around with anybody, if that's what you mean," she says.
"Would you tell me if you were?"
"I don't know."
"What does *your* name mean?"
"It was Marilyn Monroe's real name."
"No kidding!"                                                                                     125
"Norma comes from the Normans. They were invaders," she says. She closes
her book and looks hard at Leroy. "I'll go to Shiloh with you if you'll stop staring
at me."

On Sunday, Norma Jean packs a picnic and they go to Shiloh. To Leroy's
relief Mabel says she does not want to come with them. Norma Jean drives, and
Leroy, sitting beside her, feels like some boring hitchhiker she has picked up. He
tries some conversation, but she answers him in monosyllables. At Shiloh, she
drives aimlessly through the park, past bluffs and trails and steep ravines. Shiloh
is an immense place, and Leroy cannot see it as a battleground. It is not what he
expected. He thought it would look like a golf course. Monuments are everywhere, showing through the thick clusters of trees. Norma Jean passes the log
cabin Mabel mentioned. It is surrounded by tourists looking for bullet holes.
"That's not the kind of log house I've got in mind," says Leroy apologetically.
"I know *that*."
"This is a pretty place. Your mama was right."                                                   130
"It's O.K.," says Norma Jean. "Well, we've seen it. I hope she's satisfied."
They burst out laughing together.
At the park museum, a movie on Shiloh is shown every half hour, but they
decide that they don't want to see it. They buy a souvenir Confederate flag for
Mabel, and then they find a picnic spot near the cemetery. Norma Jean has
brought a picnic cooler, with pimiento sandwiches, soft drinks, and Yodels. Leroy
eats a sandwich and then smokes a joint, hiding it behind the picnic cooler.
Norma Jean has quit smoking altogether. She is picking cake crumbs from the
cellophane wrapper, like a fussy bird.
Leroy says, "So the boys in gray ended up in Corinth. The Union soldiers
zapped 'em finally. April 7, 1862."

They both know that he doesn't know any history. He is just talking about 135
some of the historical plaques they have read. He feels awkward, like a boy on a
date with an older girl. They are still just making conversation.

"Corinth is where Mama eloped to," says Norma Jean.

They sit in silence and stare at the cemetery for the Union dead and,
beyond, at a tall cluster of trees. Campers are parked nearby, bumper to bumper,
and small children in bright clothing are cavorting and squealing. Norma Jean
wads up the cake wrapper and squeezes it tightly in her hand. Without looking at
Leroy, she says, "I want to leave you."

Leroy takes a bottle of Coke out of the cooler and flips off the cap. He holds
the bottle poised near his mouth but cannot remember to take a drink. Finally he
says, "No, you don't."

"Yes, I do."

"I won't let you." 140

"You can't stop me."

"Don't do me that way."

Leroy knows Norma Jean will have her own way. "Didn't I promise to be
home from now on?" he says.

"In some ways, a woman prefers a man who wanders," says Norma Jean.
"That sounds crazy, I know."

"You're not crazy." Leroy remembers to drink from his Coke. Then he says, 145
"Yes, you *are* crazy. You and me could start all over again. Right back at the
beginning."

"We *have* started all over again," says Norma Jean. "And this is how it turned
out."

"What did I do wrong?"

"Nothing."

"Is this one of those women's lib things?" Leroy asks.

"Don't be funny." 150

The cemetery, a green slope dotted with white markers, looks like a subdivision site. Leroy is trying to comprehend that his marriage is breaking up, but for
some reason he is wondering about white slabs in a graveyard.

"Everything was fine till Mama caught me smoking," says Norma Jean,
standing up. "That set something off."

"What are you talking about?"

"She won't leave me alone—*you* won't leave me alone." Norma Jean seems
to be crying, but she is looking away from him. "I feel eighteen again. I can't face
that all over again." She starts walking away. "No, it *wasn't* fine. I don't know
what I'm saying. Forget it."

Leroy takes a lungful of smoke and closes his eyes as Norma Jean's words sink 155
in. He tries to focus on the fact that thirty-five hundred soldiers died on the
grounds around him. He can only think of that war as a board game with plastic
soldiers. Leroy almost smiles, as he compares the Confederates' daring attack on
the Union camps and Virgil Mathis's raid on the bowling alley. General Grant,
drunk and furious, shoved the Southerners back to Corinth, where Mabel and Jet

Beasley were married years later, when Mabel was still thin and good-looking. The next day, Mabel and Jet visited the battleground, and then Norma Jean was born, and then she married Leroy and they had a baby, which they lost, and now Leroy and Norma Jean are here at the same battleground. Leroy knows he is leaving out a lot. He is leaving out the insides of history. History was always just names and dates to him. It occurs to him that building a house of logs is similarly empty—too simple. And the real inner workings of a marriage, like most of history, have escaped him. Now he sees that building a log house is the dumbest idea he could have had. It was clumsy of him to think Norma Jean would want a log house. It was a crazy idea. He'll have to think of something else, quickly. He will wad the blueprints into tight balls and fling them into the lake. Then he'll get moving again. He opens his eyes. Norma Jean has moved away and is walking through the cemetery, following a serpentine brick path.

Leroy gets up to follow his wife, but his good leg is asleep and his bad leg still hurts him. Norma Jean is far away, walking rapidly toward the bluff by the river, and he tries to hobble toward her. Some children run past him, screaming noisily. Norma Jean has reached the bluff, and she is looking out over the Tennessee River. Now she turns toward Leroy and waves her arms. Is she beckoning to him? She seems to be doing an exercise for her chest muscles. The sky is unusually pale—the color of the dust ruffle Mabel made for their bed.

## Alice Munro

### HOW I MET MY HUSBAND                                          1974

*Alice Munro, one of the most widely admired contemporary writers in Canada, was born of farm parents in 1931 in Wingham, in southwestern Ontario, an area in which she has spent most of her life. Its small-town people figure in many of her stories. For two years, she attended the University of Western Ontario, but dropped out at twenty, after her first marriage. The mother of three daughters, Munro is a particularly sensitive explorer of the relations between parents and children, yet she ranges widely in choosing her themes. She has written seven remarkable collections of short fiction:* Dance of the Happy Shades *(1968),* Lives of Girls and Women *(1971),* Something I've Been Meaning to Tell You *(1974),* The

*Alice Munro*

Beggar Maid *(1982),* The Moons of Jupiter *(1983),* The Progress of Love *(1986), and* Friend of My Youth *(1990). Three of her books have won Canada's prestigious*

*Governor General's Literary Award. Although* Lives of Girls and Women *has been called a novel, Munro regards it as a book of "interrelated stories." Clearly the short story is her medium, and she has declared her preference for "the story that will zero in and give you intense, but not connected, moments of experience."*

We heard the plane come over at noon, roaring through the radio news, and we were sure it was going to hit the house, so we all ran out into the yard. We saw it come in over the treetops, all red and silver, the first close-up plane I ever saw. Mrs. Peebles screamed.

"Crash landing," their little boy said. Joey was his name.

"It's okay," said Dr. Peebles. "He knows what he's doing." Dr. Peebles was only an animal doctor, but had a calming way of talking, like any doctor.

This was my first job—working for Dr. and Mrs. Peebles, who had bought an old house out on the Fifth Line, about five miles out of town. It was just when the trend was starting of town people buying up old farms, not to work them but to live on them.

We watched the plane land across the road, where the fairgrounds used to be. It did make a good landing field, nice and level for the old race track, and the barns and display sheds torn down now for scrap lumber so there was nothing in the way. Even the old grandstand bays had burned. 5

"All right," said Mrs. Peebles, snappy as she always was when she got over her nerves. "Let's go back in the house. Let's not stand here gawking like a set of farmers."

She didn't say that to hurt my feelings. It never occurred to her.

I was just setting the dessert down when Loretta Bird arrived, out of breath, at the screen door.

"I thought it was going to crash into the house and kill youse all!"

She lived on the next place and the Peebleses thought she was a country-woman, they didn't know the difference. She and her husband didn't farm, he worked on the roads and had a bad name for drinking. They had seven children and couldn't get credit at the HiWay Grocery. The Peebleses made her welcome, not knowing any better, as I say, and offered her dessert. 10

Dessert was never anything to write home about, at their place. A dish of Jell-O or sliced bananas or fruit out of a tin. "Have a house without a pie, be ashamed until you die," my mother used to say, but Mrs. Peebles operated differently.

Loretta Bird saw me getting the can of peaches.

"Oh, never mind," she said. "I haven't got the right kind of a stomach to trust what comes out of those tins, I can only eat home canning."

I could have slapped her. I bet she never put down fruit in her life.

"I know what he's landed here for," she said. "He's got permission to use the fairgrounds and take people up for rides. It costs a dollar. It's the same fellow who was over at Palmerston° last week and was up the lakeshore before that. I wouldn't go up, if you paid me." 15

*Palmerston:* a town in southern Ontario, Canada.

"I'd jump at the chance," Dr. Peebles said. "I'd like to see this neighborhood from the air."

Mrs. Peebles said she would just as soon see it from the ground. Joey said he wanted to go and Heather did, too. Joey was nine and Heather was seven.

"Would you, Edie?" Heather said.

I said I didn't know. I was scared, but I never admitted that, especially in front of children I was taking care of.

"People are going to be coming out here in their cars raising dust and tram-  20
pling your property, if I was you I would complain." Loretta said. She hooked her legs around the chair rung and I knew we were in for a lengthy visit. After Dr. Peebles went back to his office or out on his next call and Mrs. Peebles went for her nap, she would hang around me while I was trying to do the dishes. She would pass remarks about the Peebleses in their own house.

"She wouldn't find time to lay down in the middle of the day, if she had seven kids like I got."

She asked me did they fight and did they keep things in the dresser drawer not to have babies with. She said it was a sin if they did. I pretended I didn't know what she was talking about.

I was fifteen and away from home for the first time. My parents had made the effort and sent me to high school for a year, but I didn't like it. I was shy of strangers and the work was hard, they didn't make it nice for you or explain the way they do now. At the end of the year the averages were published in the paper, and mine came out at the very bottom, 37 percent. My father said that's enough and I didn't blame him. The last thing I wanted, anyway, was to go on and end up teaching school. It happened the very day the paper came out with my disgrace in it, Dr. Peebles was staying at our place for dinner, having just helped one of the cows have twins, and he said I looked smart to him and his wife was looking for a girl to help. He said she felt tied down, with the two children, out in the country. I guess she would, my mother said, being polite, though I could tell from her face she was wondering what on earth it would be like to have only two children and no barn work, and then to be complaining.

When I went home I would describe to them the work I had to do, and it made everybody laugh. Mrs. Peebles had an automatic washer and dryer, the first I ever saw. I have had those in my own home for such a long time now it's hard to remember how much of a miracle it was to me, not having to struggle with the wringer and hang up and haul down. Let alone not having to heat water. Then there was practically no baking. Mrs. Peebles said she couldn't make pie crust, the most amazing thing I ever heard a woman admit. I could, of course, and I could make light biscuits and a white cake and dark cake, but they didn't want it, she said they watched their figures. The only thing I didn't like about working there, in fact, was feeling half hungry a lot of the time. I used to bring back a box of doughnuts made out at home, and hide them under my bed. The children found out, and I didn't mind sharing, but I thought I better bind them to secrecy.

The day after the plane landed Mrs. Peebles put both children in the car and  25
drove over to Chesley, to get their hair cut. There was a good woman then at

Chesley for doing hair. She got hers done at the same place, Mrs. Peebles did, and that meant they would be gone a good while. She had to pick a day Dr. Peebles wasn't going out into the country, she didn't have her own car. Cars were still in short supply then, after the war.

I loved being left in the house alone, to do my work at leisure. The kitchen was all white and bright yellow, with fluorescent lights. That was before they ever thought of making the appliances all different colors and doing the cupboards like dark old wood and hiding the lighting. I loved light. I loved the double sink. So would anybody new-come from washing dishes in a dishpan with a rag-plugged hole on an oilcloth-covered table by light of a coal-oil lamp. I kept everything shining.

The bathroom too. I had a bath in there once a week. They wouldn't have minded if I took one oftener, but to me it seemed like asking too much, or maybe risking making it less wonderful. The basin and the tub and the toilet were all pink, and there were glass doors with flamingoes painted on them, to shut off the tub. The light had a rosy cast and the mat sank under your feet like snow, except that it was warm. The mirror was three-way. With the mirror all steamed up and the air like a perfume cloud, from things I was allowed to use, I stood up on the side of the tub and admired myself naked, from three directions. Sometimes I thought about the way we lived out at home and the way we lived here and how one way was so hard to imagine when you were living the other way. But I thought it was still a lot easier, living the way we lived at home, to picture something like this, the painted flamingoes and the warmth and the soft mat, than it was anybody knowing only things like this to picture how it was the other way. And why was that?

I was through my jobs in no time, and had the vegetables peeled for supper and sitting in cold water besides. Then I went into Mrs. Peebles' bedroom. I had been in there plenty of times, cleaning, and I always took a good look in her closet, at the clothes she had hanging there. I wouldn't have looked in her drawers, but a closet is open to anybody. That's a lie. I would have looked in drawers, but I would have felt worse doing it and been more scared she could tell.

Some clothes in her closet she wore all the time, I was quite familiar with them. Others she never put on, they were pushed to the back. I was disappointed to see no wedding dress. But there was one long dress I could just see the skirt of, and I was hungering to see the rest. Now I took note of where it hung and lifted it out. It was satin, a lovely weight on my arm, light bluish-green in color, almost silvery. It had a fitted, pointed waist and a full skirt and an off-the-shoulder fold hiding the little sleeves.

Next thing was easy. I got out of my own things and slipped it on. I was slim- 30 mer at fifteen than anybody would believe who knows me now and the fit was beautiful. I didn't, of course, have a strapless bra on, which was what it needed, I just had to slide my straps down my arms under the material. Then I tried pinning up my hair, to get the effect. One thing led to another. I put on rouge and lipstick and eyebrow pencil from her dresser. The heat of the day and the weight of the satin and all the excitement made me thirsty, and I went out to the kitchen, got-up as I was, to get a glass of ginger ale with ice cubes from the refrigerator. The Peebleses drank ginger ale, or fruit drinks, all day, like water, and I was getting so I did too. Also there was no limit on ice cubes, which I was so fond of I would even put them in a glass of milk.

I turned from putting the ice tray back and saw a man watching me through the screen. It was the luckiest thing in the world I didn't spill the ginger ale down the front of me then and there.

"I never meant to scare you. I knocked but you were getting the ice out, you didn't hear me."

I couldn't see what he looked like, he was dark the way somebody is pressed up against a screen door with the bright daylight behind them. I only knew he wasn't from around here.

"I'm from the plane over there. My name is Chris Watters and what I was wondering was if I could use that pump."

There was a pump in the yard. That was the way the people used to get their water. Now I noticed he was carrying a pail.                                                                                    35

"You're welcome," I said. "I can get it from the tap and save you pumping." I guess I wanted him to know we had piped water, didn't pump ourselves.

"I don't mind the exercise." He didn't move, though, and finally he said, "Were you going to a dance?"

Seeing a stranger there had made me entirely forget how I was dressed.

"Or is that the way ladies around here generally get dressed up in the afternoon?"

I didn't know how to joke back then. I was too embarrassed.                                        40

"You live here? Are you the lady of the house?"

"I'm the hired girl."

Some people change when they find that out, their whole way of looking at you and speaking to you changes, but his didn't.

"Well, I just wanted to tell you you look very nice. I was so surprised when I looked in the door and saw you. Just because you looked so nice and beautiful."

I wasn't even old enough then to realize how out of the common it is, for a        45
man to say something like that to a woman, or somebody he is treating like a woman. For a man to say a word like *beautiful*. I wasn't old enough to realize or to say anything back, or in fact to do anything but wish he would go away. Not that I didn't like him, but just that it upset me so, having him look at me, and me trying to think of something to say.

He must have understood. He said good-bye, and thanked me, and went and started filling his pail from the pump. I stood behind the Venetian blinds in the dining room, watching him. When he had gone, I went into the bedroom and took the dress off and put it back in the same place. I dressed in my own clothes and took my hair down and washed my face, wiping it on Kleenex, which I threw in the wastebasket.


The Peebleses asked me what kind of man he was. Young, middle-aged, short, tall? I couldn't say.

"Good-looking?" Dr. Peebles teased me.

I couldn't think a thing but that he would be coming to get his water again, he would be talking to Dr. or Mrs. Peebles, making friends with them, and he would mention seeing me that first afternoon, dressed up. Why not mention it? He would think it was funny. And no idea of the trouble it would get me into.

After supper the Peebleses drove into town to go to a movie. She wanted to  50
go somewhere with her hair fresh done. I sat in my bright kitchen wondering what to do, knowing I would never sleep. Mrs. Peebles might not fire me, when she found out, but it would give her a different feeling about me altogether. This was the first place I ever worked but I already had picked up things about the way people feel when you are working for them. They like to think you aren't curious. Not just that you aren't dishonest, that isn't enough. They like to feel you don't notice things, that you don't think or wonder about anything but what they liked to eat and how they liked things ironed, and so on. I don't mean they weren't kind to me, because they were. They had me eat my meals with them (to tell the truth I expected to, I didn't know there were families who don't) and sometimes they took me along in the car. But all the same.

I went up and checked on the children being asleep and then I went out. I had to do it. I crossed the road and went in the old fairgrounds gate. The plane looked unnatural sitting there, and shining with the moon. Off at the far side of the fairgrounds where the bush was taking over, I saw his tent.

He was sitting outside it smoking a cigarette. He saw me coming.

"Hello, were you looking for a plane ride? I don't start taking people up till tomorrow." Then he looked again and said, "Oh, it's you. I didn't know you without your long dress on."

My heart was knocking away, my tongue was dried up. I had to say something. But I couldn't. My throat was closed and I was like a deaf-and-dumb.

"Did you want a ride? Sit down. Have a cigarette."  55

I couldn't even shake my head to say no, so he gave me one.

"Put it in your mouth or I can't light it. It's a good thing I'm used to shy ladies."

I did. It wasn't the first time I had smoked a cigarette, actually. My girlfriend out home, Muriel Lowe, used to steal them from her brother.

"Look at your hand shaking. Did you just want to have a chat, or what?"

In one burst I said, "I wisht you wouldn't say anything about that dress."  60

"What dress? Oh, the long dress."

"It's Mrs. Peebles'."

"Whose? Oh, the lady you work for? She wasn't home so you got dressed up in her dress, eh? You got dressed up and played queen. I don't blame you. You're not smoking the cigarette right. Don't just puff. Draw it in. Did anybody ever show you how to inhale? Are you scared I'll tell on you? Is that it?"

I was so ashamed at having to ask him to connive this way I couldn't nod. I just looked at him and he saw *yes*.

"Well I won't. I won't in the slightest way mention it or embarrass you. I give  65
you my word of honor."

Then he changed the subject, to help me out, seeing I couldn't even thank him.

"What do you think of this sign?"

It was a board sign lying practically at my feet.

SEE THE WORLD FROM THE SKY. ADULTS $1.00, CHILDREN 50¢. QUALIFIED PILOT.

"My old sign was getting pretty beat up, I thought I'd make a new one. 70 That's what I've been doing with my time today."

The lettering wasn't all that handsome, I thought. I could have done a better one in half an hour.

"I'm not an expert at sign making."

"It's very good," I said.

"I don't need it for publicity, word of mouth is usually enough. I turned away two carloads tonight. I felt like taking it easy. I didn't tell them ladies were dropping in to visit me."

Now I remembered the children and I was scared again, in case one of them 75 had waked up and called me and I wasn't there.

"Do you have to go so soon?"

I remembered some manners. "Thank you for the cigarette."

"Don't forget. You have my word of honor."

I tore off across the fairgrounds, scared I'd see the car heading home from town. My sense of time was mixed up, I didn't know how long I'd been out of the house. But it was all right, it wasn't late, the children were asleep. I got in my bed myself and lay thinking what a lucky end to the day, after all, and among things to be grateful for I could be grateful Loretta Bird hadn't been the one who caught me.

The yard and borders didn't get trampled, it wasn't as bad as that. All the 80 same it seemed very public, around the house. The sign was on the fairgrounds gate. People came mostly after supper but a good many in the afternoon, too. The Bird children all came without fifty cents between them and hung on the gate. We got used to the excitement of the plane coming in and taking off, it wasn't excitement anymore. I never went over, after that one time, but would see him when he came to get his water. I would be out on the steps doing sitting-down work, like preparing vegetables, if I could.

"Why don't you come over? I'll take you up in my plane."

"I'm saving my money," I said, because I couldn't think of anything else.

"For what? For getting married?"

I shook my head.

"I'll take you up for free if you come sometime when it's slack. I thought you 85 would come, and have another cigarette."

I made a face to hush him, because you never could tell when the children would be sneaking around the porch, or Mrs. Peebles herself listening in the house. Sometimes she came out and had a conversation with him. He told her things he hadn't bothered to tell me. But then I hadn't thought to ask. He told her he had been in the war, that was where he learned to fly a plane, and how he couldn't settle down to ordinary life, this was what he liked. She said she couldn't imagine anybody liking such a thing. Though sometimes, she said, she was almost bored enough to try anything herself, she wasn't brought up to living in the country. It's all my husband's idea, she said. This was news to me.

"Maybe you ought to give flying lessons," she said.

"Would you take them?"

She just laughed.

Sunday was a busy flying day in spite of it being preached against from two pulpits. We were all sitting out watching. Joey and Heather were over on the fence with the Bird kids. Their father had said they could go, after their mother saying all week they couldn't.

A car came down the road past the parked cars and pulled up right in the drive. It was Loretta Bird who got out, all importance, and on the driver's side another woman got out, more sedately. She was wearing sunglasses.

"This is a lady looking for the man that flies the plane," Loretta Bird said. "I heard her inquire in the hotel coffee shop where I was having a Coke and I brought her out."

"I'm sorry to bother you," the lady said. "I'm Alice Kelling, Mr. Watters' fiancée."

This Alice Kelling had on a pair of brown and white checked slacks and a yellow top. Her bust looked to me rather low and bumpy. She had a worried face. Her hair had had a permanent, but had grown out, and she wore a yellow band to keep it off her face. Nothing in the least pretty or even young-looking about her. But you could tell from how she talked she was from the city, or educated, or both.

Dr. Peebles stood up and introduced himself and his wife and me and asked her to be seated.

"He's up in the air right now, but you're welcome to sit and wait. He gets his water here and he hasn't been yet. He'll probably take his break about five."

"That is him, then?" said Alice Kelling, wrinkling and straining at the sky.

"He's not in the habit of running out on you, taking a different name?" Dr. Peebles laughed. He was the one, not his wife, to offer iced tea. Then she sent me into the kitchen to fix it. She smiled. She was wearing sunglasses too.

"He never mentioned his fiancée," she said.

I loved fixing iced tea with lots of ice and slices of lemon in tall glasses. I ought to have mentioned before, Dr. Peebles was an abstainer, at least around the house, or I wouldn't have been allowed to take the place. I had to fix a glass for Loretta Bird too, though it galled me, and when I went out she had settled in my lawn chair, leaving me the steps.

"I knew you was a nurse when I first heard you in that coffee shop."

"How would you know a thing like that?"

"I get my hunches about people. Was that how you met him, nursing?"

"Chris? Well yes. Yes, it was."

"Oh, were you overseas?" said Mrs. Peebles.

"No, it was before he went overseas. I nursed him when he was stationed at Centralia and had a ruptured appendix. We got engaged and then he went overseas. My, this is refreshing, after a long drive."

"He'll be glad to see you," Dr. Peebles said. "It's a rackety kind of life, isn't it, not staying one place long enough to really make friends."

"Youse've had a long engagement," Loretta Bird said.

Alice Kelling passed that over. "I was going to get a room at the hotel, but when I was offered directions I came on out. Do you think I could phone them?"

"No need," Dr. Peebles said. "You're five miles away from him if you stay at the hotel. Here, you're right across the road. Stay with us. We've got rooms on rooms, look at this big house." 110

Asking people to stay, just like that, is certainly a country thing, and maybe seemed natural to him now, but not to Mrs. Peebles, from the way she said, oh yes, we have plenty of room. Or to Alice Kelling, who kept protesting, but let herself be worn down. I got the feeling it was a temptation to her, to be that close. I was trying for a look at her ring. Her nails were painted red, her fingers were freckled and wrinkled. It was a tiny stone. Muriel Lowe's cousin had one twice as big.

Chris came to get his water, late in the afternoon just as Dr. Peebles had predicted. He must have recognized the car from a way off. He came smiling.

"Here I am chasing after you to see what you're up to," called Alice Kelling. She got up and went to meet him and they kissed, just touched, in front of us.

"You're going to spend a lot on gas that way," Chris said.

Dr. Peebles invited Chris to stay for supper, since he had already put up the sign that said: NO MORE RIDES TILL 7 P.M. Mrs. Peebles wanted it served in the yard, in spite of the bugs. One thing strange to anybody from the country is this eating outside. I had made a potato salad earlier and she had made a jellied salad, that was one thing she could do, so it was just a matter of getting those out, and some sliced meat and cucumbers and fresh leaf lettuce. Loretta Bird hung around for some time saying, "Oh, well, I guess I better get home to those yappers," and, "It's so nice just sitting here, I sure hate to get up," but nobody invited her, I was relieved to see, and finally she had to go. 115

That night after rides were finished Alice Kelling and Chris went off somewhere in her car. I lay awake till they got back. When I saw the car lights sweep my ceiling I got up to look down on them through the slats of my blind. I don't know what I thought I was going to see. Muriel Lowe and I used to sleep on her front veranda and watch her sister and her sister's boy friend saying good night. Afterward we couldn't get to sleep, for longing for somebody to kiss us and rub against us and we would talk about suppose you were out in a boat with a boy and he wouldn't bring you in to shore unless you did it, or what if somebody got you trapped in a barn, you would have to, wouldn't you, it wouldn't be your fault. Muriel said her two girl cousins used to try with a toilet paper roll that one of them was a boy. We wouldn't do anything like that; just lay and wondered.

All that happened was that Chris got out of the car on one side and she got out on the other and they walked off separately—him toward the fairgrounds and her toward the house. I got back in bed and imagined about me coming home with him, not like that.

Next morning Alice Kelling got up late and I fixed a grapefruit for her the way I had learned and Mrs. Peebles sat down with her to visit and have another cup of coffee. Mrs. Peebles seemed pleased enough now, having company. Alice Kelling said she guessed she better get used to putting in a day just watching Chris take off and come down, and Mrs. Peebles said she didn't know if she should suggest it because Alice Kelling was the one with the car, but the lake was only twenty-five miles away and what a good day for a picnic.

Alice Kelling took her up on the idea and by eleven o'clock they were in the car, with Joey and Heather and a sandwich lunch I had made. The only thing was that Chris hadn't come down, and she wanted to tell him where they were going.

"Edie'll go over and tell him," Mrs. Peebles said. "There's no problem." 120

Alice Kelling wrinkled her face and agreed.

"Be sure and tell him we'll be back by five!"

I didn't see that he would be concerned about knowing this right away, and I thought of him eating whatever he ate over there, alone, cooking on his camp stove, so I got to work and mixed up a crumb cake and baked it, in between the other work I had to do; then, when it was a bit cooled, wrapped it in a tea towel. I didn't do anything to myself but take off my apron and comb my hair. I would like to have put some makeup on, but I was too afraid it would remind him of the way he first saw me, and that would humiliate me all over again.

He had come and put another sign on the gate: NO RIDES THIS P.M. APOLOGIES. I worried that he wasn't feeling well. No sign of him outside and the tent flap was down. I knocked on the pole.

"Come in," he said, in a voice that would just as soon have said *Stay out.* 125

I lifted the flap.

"Oh, it's you. I'm sorry. I didn't know it was you."

He had been just sitting on the side of the bed, smoking. Why not at least sit and smoke in the fresh air?

"I brought a cake and hope you're not sick," I said.

"Why would I be sick? Oh—that sign. That's all right. I'm just tired of talk- 130 ing to people. I don't mean you. Have a seat." He pinned back the tent flap. "Get some fresh air in here."

I sat on the edge of the bed, there was no place else. It was one of those foldup cots, really: I remembered and gave him his fiancée's message.

He ate some of the cake. "Good."

"Put the rest away for when you're hungry later."

"I'll tell you a secret. I won't be around here much longer."

"Are you getting married?" 135

"Ha ha. What time did you say they'd be back?"

"Five o'clock."

"Well, by that time this place will have seen the last of me. A plane can get further than a car." He unwrapped the cake and ate another piece of it, absentmindedly.

"Now you'll be thirsty."

"There's some water in the pail."

"It won't be very cold. I could bring some fresh. I could bring some ice from the refrigerator."

"No," he said. "I don't want you to go. I want a nice long time of saying good-bye to you."

He put the cake away carefully and sat beside me and started those little kisses, so soft, I can't ever let myself think about them, such kindness in his face and lovely kisses, all over my eyelids and neck and ears, all over, then me kissing back as well as I could (I had only kissed a boy on a dare before, and kissed my own arms for practice) and we lay back on the cot and pressed together, just gently, and he did some other things, not bad things or not in a bad way. It was lovely in the tent, that smell of grass and hot tent cloth with the sun beating down on it, and he said, "I wouldn't do you any harm for the world." Once, when he had rolled on top of me and we were sort of rocking together on the cot, he said softly, "Oh, no," and freed himself and jumped up and got the water pail. He splashed some of it on his neck and face, and the little bit left, on me lying there.

"That's to cool us off, miss."

When we said good-bye I wasn't at all sad, because he held my face and said, "I'm going to write you a letter. I'll tell you where I am and maybe you can come and see me. Would you like that? Okay then. You wait." I was really glad I think to get away from him, it was like he was piling presents on me I couldn't get the pleasure of till I considered them alone.

No consternation at first about the plane being gone. They thought he had taken somebody up, and I didn't enlighten them. Dr. Peebles had phoned he had to go to the country, so there was just us having supper, and then Loretta Bird thrusting her head in the door and saying, "I see he's took off."

"What?" said Alice Kelling, and pushed back her chair.

"The kids come and told me this afternoon he was taking down his tent. Did he think he'd run through all the business there was around here? He didn't take off without letting you know, did he?"

"He'll send me word," Alice Kelling said. "He'll probably phone tonight. He's terribly restless, since the war."

"Edie, he didn't mention to you, did he?" Mrs. Peebles said. "When you took over the message?"

"Yes," I said. So far so true.

"Well why didn't you say?" All of them were looking at me. "Did he say where he was going?"

"He said he might try Bayfield," I said. What made me tell such a lie? I didn't intend it.

"Bayfield, how far is that?" said Alice Kelling.

Mrs. Peebles said, "Thirty, thirty-five miles."

"That's not far. Oh, well, that's really not far at all. It's on the lake, isn't it?"

You'd think I'd be ashamed of myself, setting her on the wrong track. I did it to give him more time, whatever time he needed. I lied for him, and also, I have to admit, for me. Women should stick together and not do things like that. I see that now, but didn't then. I never thought of myself as being in any way like her, or coming to the same troubles, ever.

She hadn't taken her eyes off me. I thought she suspected my lie.

"When did he mention this to you?"

"Earlier." 160

"When you were over at the plane?"

"Yes."

"You must've stayed and had a chat." She smiled at me, not a nice smile. "You must've stayed and had a little visit with him."

"I took a cake," I said, thinking that telling some truth would spare me telling the rest.

"We didn't have a cake," said Mrs. Peebles rather sharply. 165

"I baked one."

Alice Kelling said, "That was very friendly of you."

"Did you get permission," said Loretta Bird. "You never know what these girls'll do next," she said. "It's not they mean harm so much, as they're ignorant."

"The cake is neither here nor there," Mrs. Peebles broke in. "Edie, I wasn't aware you knew Chris that well."

I didn't know what to say. 170

"I'm not surprised," Alice Kelling said in a high voice. "I knew by the look of her as soon as I saw her. We get them at the hospital all the time." She looked hard at me with her stretched smile. "Having their babies. We have to put them in a special ward because of their diseases. Little country tramps. Fourteen and fifteen years old. You should see the babies they have, too."

"There was a bad woman here in town had a baby that pus was running out of its eyes," Loretta Bird put in.

"Wait a minute," said Mrs. Peebles. "What is this talk? Edie. What about you and Mr. Watters? Were you intimate with him?"

"Yes," I said. I was thinking of us lying on the cot and kissing, wasn't that intimate? And I would never deny it.

They were all one minute quiet, even Loretta Bird. 175

"Well," said Mrs. Peebles. "I am surprised. I think I need a cigarette. This is the first of any such tendencies I've seen in her," she said, speaking to Alice Kelling, but Alice Kelling was looking at me.

"Loose little bitch." Tears ran down her face. "Loose little bitch, aren't you? I knew as soon as I saw you. Men despise girls like you. He just made use of you and went off, you know that, don't you? Girls like you are just nothing, they're just public conveniences, just filthy little rags!"

"Oh, now," said Mrs. Peebles.

"Filthy," Alice Kelling sobbed. "Filthy little rags!"

"Don't get yourself upset," Loretta Bird said. She was swollen up with plea- 180 sure at being in on this scene. "Men are all the same."

"Edie, I'm very surprised," Mrs. Pebbles said. "I thought your parents were so strict. You don't want to have a baby, do you?"

I'm still ashamed of what happened next. I lost control, just like a six-year-old, I started howling. "You don't get a baby from just doing that!"

"You see. Some of them are that ignorant," Loretta Bird said.

But Mrs. Peebles jumped up and caught my arms and shook me.

"Calm down. Don't get hysterical. Calm down. Stop crying. Listen to me. 185
Listen I'm wondering, if you know what being intimate means. Now tell me. What did you think it meant?"

"Kissing," I howled.

She let go. "Oh, Edie. Stop it. Don't be silly. It's all right. It's all a misunderstanding. Being intimate means a lot more than that. Oh, I *wondered*."

"She's trying to cover up, now," said Alice Kelling. "Yes. She's not so stupid. She sees she got herself in trouble."

"I believe her," Mrs. Peebles said. "This is an awful scene."

"Well there is one way to find out," said Alice Kelling, getting up. "After all, 190
I am a nurse."

Mrs. Peebles drew a breath and said, "No. No. Go to your room, Edie. And stop that noise. This is too disgusting."

I heard the car start in a little while. I tried to stop crying, pulling back each wave as it started over me. Finally I succeeded, and lay heaving on the bed.

Mrs. Peebles came and stood in the doorway.

"She's gone," she said. "That Bird woman too. Of course, you know you should never have gone near that man and that is the cause of all this trouble. I have a headache. As soon as you can, go and wash your face in cold water and get at the dishes and we will not say any more about this."

Nor we didn't. I didn't figure out till years later the extent of what I had been 195
saved from. Mrs. Peebles was not very friendly to me afterward, but she was fair. Not very friendly is the wrong way of describing what she was. She had never been very friendly. It was just that now she had to see me all the time and it got on her nerves, a little.

As for me, I put it all out of my mind like a bad dream and concentrated on waiting for my letter. The mail came every day except Sunday, between one-thirty and two in the afternoon, a good time for me because Mrs. Peebles was always having her nap. I would get the kitchen all cleaned and then go up to the mailbox and sit in the grass, waiting. I was perfectly happy, waiting. I forgot all about Alice Kelling and her misery and awful talk and Mrs. Peebles and her chilliness and the embarrassment of whether she told Dr. Peebles and the face of Loretta Bird, getting her fill of other people's troubles. I was always smiling when the mailman got there, and continued smiling even after he gave me the mail and I saw today wasn't the day. The mailman was a Carmichael. I knew by his face because there are a lot of Carmichaels living out by us and so many of them have a sort of sticking-out top lip. So I asked his name (he was a young man, shy, but good-humored, anybody could ask him anything) and then I said, "I knew by your face!" He was pleased by that and always glad to see me and got a little less shy. "You've got the smile I've been waiting for all day!" he used to holler out the car window.

It never crossed my mind for a long time a letter might not come. I believed in it coming just like I believed the sun would rise in the morning. I just put off my hope from day to day, and there was the goldenrod out around the mailbox and the children gone back to school, and the leaves turning, and I was wearing a sweater when I went to wait. One day walking back with the hydro bill stuck in my hand, that was all, looking across at the fairgrounds with the full-blown milkweed and dark teasels, so much like fall, it just struck me: *No letter was ever going to come*. It was an impossible idea to get used to. No, not impossible. If I thought about Chris's face when he said he was going to write me, it was impossible, but if I forgot that and thought about the actual tin mailbox, empty, it was plain and true. I kept on going to meet the mail, but my heart was heavy now like a lump of lead. I only smiled because I thought of the mailman counting on it, and he didn't have an easy life, with the winter driving ahead.

Till it came to me one day there were women doing this with their lives, all over. There were women just waiting and waiting by mailboxes for one letter or another. I imagined me making this journey day after day and year after year, and my hair starting to get gray, and I thought, I was never made to go on like that. So I stopped meeting the mail. If there were women all through life waiting, and women busy and not waiting, I knew which I had to be. Even though there might be things the second kind of women have to pass up and never know about, it still is better.

I was surprised when the mailman phoned the Peebleses' place in the evening and asked for me. He said he missed me. He asked if I would like to go to Goderich, where some well-known movie was on, I forget now what. So I said yes, and I went out with him for two years and he asked me to marry him, and we were engaged a year more while I got my things together, and then we did marry. He always tells the children the story of how I went after him by sitting by the mailbox every day, and naturally I laugh and let him, because I like for people to think what pleases them and makes them happy.

## Joyce Carol Oates

# WHERE ARE YOU GOING, WHERE HAVE YOU BEEN? 1970

*Joyce Carol Oates was born in 1938 into a blue-collar, Catholic family in Lockport, New York. As an undergraduate at Syracuse University, she won a Mademoiselle magazine award for fiction. After graduation with top honors, she took a master's degree in English at the University of Wisconsin and went on to teach at universities: Detroit, Windsor, and Princeton. She now lives in Princeton, New Jersey, where together with her husband, Raymond Smith, she directs the Ontario Review Press, a small literary publisher. A remarkably prolific writer, Oates so far has produced nearly half a hundred collections of stories; more than twenty novels including* Them, *winner of a National Book Award in*

Joyce Carol Oates

*1970, and* Because It Is Bitter, and Because It Is My Heart *(1990); and poetry, plays, and literary criticism.* Woman Writer: Occasions & Opportunities *(1988) is a book of varied essays;* On Boxing *(1987) is a nonfiction memoir and study of fighters and fighting.* Foxfire *(1993), her twenty-second novel, is the story of a girl gang in upstate New York. Violence and the macabre may inhabit her best stories, but Oates has insisted that these elements in her work are never gratuitous. The film,* Smooth Talk, *directed by Joyce Chopra, was based on "Where Are You Going, Where Have You Been?"*

For Bob Dylan

Her name was Connie. She was fifteen and she had a quick nervous giggling habit of craning her neck to glance into mirrors, or checking other people's faces to make sure her own was all right. Her mother, who noticed everything and knew everything and who hadn't much reason any longer to look at her own face, always scolded Connie about it. "Stop gawking at yourself, who are you? You think you're so pretty?" she would say. Connie would raise her eyebrows at these familiar complaints and look right through her mother, into a shadowy vision of herself as she was right at that moment: she knew she was pretty and that was everything. Her mother had been pretty once too, if you could believe those old snapshots in the album, but now her looks were gone and that was why she was always after Connie.

"Why don't you keep your room clean like your sister? How've you got your hair fixed—what the hell stinks? Hair spray? You don't see your sister using that junk."

Her sister June was twenty-four and still lived at home. She was a secretary in the high school Connie attended, and if that wasn't bad enough—with her in the same building—she was so plain and chunky and steady that Connie had to hear her praised all the time by her mother and her mother's sisters. June did this, June did that, she saved money and helped clean the house and cooked and Connie couldn't do a thing, her mind was all filled with trashy daydreams. Their father was away at work most of the time and when he came home he wanted supper and he read the newspaper at supper and after supper he went to bed. He didn't bother talking much to them, but around his bent head Connie's mother kept picking at her until Connie wished her mother was dead and she herself was dead and it was all over. "She makes me want to throw up sometimes," she complained to her friends. She had a high, breathless, amused voice which made everything she said sound a little forced, whether it was sincere or not.

There was one good thing: June went places with girl friends of hers, girls who were just as plain and steady as she, and so when Connie wanted to do that her mother had no objections. The father of Connie's best girl friend drove the girls the three miles to town and left them off at a shopping plaza, so that they could walk through the stores or go to a movie, and when he came to pick them up again at eleven he never bothered to ask what they had done.

They must have been familiar sights, walking around that shopping plaza in their shorts and flat ballerina slippers that always scuffed the sidewalk, with charm bracelets jingling on their thin wrists; they would lean together to whisper and laugh secretly if someone passed by who amused or interested them. Connie had long dark blond hair that drew anyone's eye to it, and she wore part of it pulled up on her head and puffed out and the rest of it she let fall down her back. She wore a pull-over jersey blouse that looked one way when she was at home and another way when she was away from home. Everything about her had two sides to it, one for home and one for anywhere that was not home: her walk that could be childlike and bobbing, or languid enough to make anyone think she was hearing music in her head, her mouth which was pale and smirking most of the time, but bright and pink on these evenings out, her laugh which was cynical and drawling at home—"Ha, ha, very funny"—but high-pitched and nervous anywhere else, like the jingling of the charms on her bracelet.

Sometimes they did go shopping or to a movie, but sometimes they went across the highway, ducking fast across the busy road, to a drive-in restaurant where older kids hung out. The restaurant was shaped like a big bottle, though squatter than a real bottle, and on its cap was a revolving figure of a grinning boy who held a hamburger aloft. One night in mid-summer they ran across, breathless with daring, and right away someone leaned out a car window and invited them over, but it was just a boy from high school they didn't like. It made them feel good to be able to ignore him. They went up through the maze of parked and cruising cars to the bright-lit, fly-infested restaurant, their faces pleased and expectant as if they were entering a sacred building that loomed out of the night to give them what haven and what blessing they yearned for. They sat at the counter and crossed their legs at the ankles, their thin shoulders rigid with excitement, and listened to the music that made everything so good: the music was always in the background like music at a church service, it was something to depend upon.

A boy named Eddie came in to talk with them. He sat backwards on his stool, turning himself jerkily around in semi-circles and then stopping and turning again, and after a while he asked Connie if she would like something to eat. She said she did and so she tapped her friend's arm on her way out—her friend pulled her face up into a brave droll look—and Connie said she would meet her at eleven, across the way. "I just hate to leave her like that," Connie said earnestly, but the boy said that she wouldn't be alone for long. So they went out to his car and on the way Connie couldn't help but let her eyes wander over the windshields and faces all around her, her face gleaming with a joy that had nothing to do with Eddie or even this place; it might have been the music. She drew her shoulders up and sucked in her breath with the pure pleasure of being alive, and just at that moment she happened to glance at a face just a few feet from hers. It was a boy with shaggy black hair, in a convertible jalopy painted gold. He stared at her and then his lips widened into a grin. Connie slit her eyes at him and turned away, but she couldn't help glancing back and there he was still watching her. He wagged a finger and laughed and said, "Gonna get you, baby," and Connie turned away again without Eddie noticing anything.

She spent three hours with him, at the restaurant where they ate hamburgers and drank Cokes in wax cups that were always sweating, and then down an alley a mile or so away, and when he left her off at five to eleven only the movie house was still open at the plaza. Her girl friend was there, talking with a boy. When Connie came up the two girls smiled at each other and Connie said, "How was the movie?" and the girl said, "*You* should know." They rode off with the girl's father, sleepy and pleased, and Connie couldn't help but look at the darkened shopping plaza with its big empty parking lot and its signs that were faded and ghostly now, and over at the drive-in restaurant where cars were still circling tirelessly. She couldn't hear the music at this distance.

Next morning June asked her how the movie was and Connie said, "So-so."

She and that girl and occasionally another girl went out several times a week that way, and the rest of the time Connie spent around the house—it was summer vacation—getting in her mother's way and thinking, dreaming, about the boys she met. But all the boys fell back and dissolved into a single face that was not even a face, but an idea, a feeling, mixed up with the urgent insistent pounding of the music and the humid night air of July. Connie's mother kept dragging her back to the daylight by finding things for her to do or saying, suddenly, "What's this about the Pettinger girl?"

And Connie would say nervously, "Oh, her. That dope." She always drew thick clear lines between herself and such girls, and her mother was simple and kindly enough to believe her. Her mother was so simple, Connie thought, that it was maybe cruel to fool her so much. Her mother went scuffling around the house in old bedroom slippers and complained over the telephone to one sister about the other, then the other called up and the two of them complained about the third one. If June's name was mentioned her mother's tone was approving, and if Connie's name was mentioned it was disapproving. This did not really mean she disliked Connie and actually Connie thought that her mother preferred her to June because she was prettier, but the two of them kept up a pretense of exasperation, a sense that they were tugging and struggling over something of little value to either of them. Sometimes, over coffee, they were almost friends, but something would come up—some vexation that was like a fly buzzing suddenly around their heads—and their faces went hard with contempt.

One Sunday Connie got up at eleven—none of them bothered with church—and washed her hair so that it could dry all day long, in the sun. Her parents and sister were going to a barbecue at an aunt's house and Connie said no, she wasn't interested, rolling her eyes to let her mother know just what she thought of it. "Stay home alone then," her mother said sharply. Connie sat out back in a lawn chair and watched them drive away, her father quiet and bald, hunched around so that he could back the car out, her mother with a look that was still angry and not at all softened through the windshield, and in the back seat poor old June all dressed up as if she didn't know what a barbecue was, with all the running yelling kids and the flies. Connie sat with her eyes closed in the sun, dreaming and dazed with the warmth about her as if this were a kind of love, the caresses of love, and her mind slipped over onto thoughts of the boy she had been with the night before and how nice he had been, how sweet it always was, not the way someone like June would suppose but sweet, gentle, the way it was in movies and promised in songs; and when she opened her eyes she hardly knew where she was, the back yard ran off into weeds and a fence-line of trees and behind it the sky was perfectly blue and still. The asbestos "ranch house" that was now three years old startled her—it looked small. She shook her head as if to get awake.

It was too hot. She went inside the house and turned on the radio to drown out the quiet. She sat on the edge of her bed, barefoot, and listened for an hour and a half to a program called XYZ Sunday Jamboree, record after record of hard, fast, shrieking songs she sang along with, interspersed by exclamations from "Bobby King": "An' look here you girls at Napoleon's—Son and Charley want you to pay real close attention to this song coming up!"

And Connie paid close attention herself, bathed in a glow of slow-pulsed joy that seemed to rise mysteriously out of the music itself and lay languidly about the airless little room, breathed in and breathed out with each gentle rise and fall of her chest.

After a while she heard a car coming up the drive. She sat up at once, startled, because it couldn't be her father so soon. The gravel kept crunching all the way in from the road—the driveway was long—and Connie ran to the window. It was a car she didn't know. It was an open jalopy, painted a bright gold that caught the sunlight opaquely. Her heart began to pound and her fingers snatched at her hair, checking it, and she whispered "Christ, Christ," wondering how bad she looked. The car came to a stop at the side door and the horn sounded four short taps as if this were a signal Connie knew.

She went into the kitchen and approached the door slowly, then hung out the screen door, her bare toes curling down off the step. There were two boys in the car and now she recognized the driver: he had shaggy, shabby black hair that looked crazy as a wig and he was grinning at her.

"I ain't late, am I?" he said.

"Who the hell do you think you are?" Connie said.

"Toldja I'd be out, didn't I?"

"I don't even know who you are."                                                                    20

She spoke sullenly, careful to show no interest or pleasure, and he spoke in a fast bright monotone. Connie looked past him to the other boy, taking her time. He had fair brown hair, with a lock that fell onto his forehead. His sideburns gave him a fierce, embarrassed look, but so far he hadn't even bothered to glance at her. Both boys wore sunglasses. The driver's glasses were metallic and mirrored everything in miniature.

"You wanta come for a ride?" he said.

Connie smirked and let her hair fall loose over one shoulder.

"Don'tcha like my car? New paint job," he said. "Hey."

"What?"                                                                                             25

"You're cute."

She pretended to fidget, chasing flies away from the door.

"Don'tcha believe me, or what?" he said.

"Look, I don't even know who you are," Connie said in disgust.

"Hey, Ellie's got a radio, see. Mine's broke down." He lifted his friend's arm       30
and showed her the little transistor the boy was holding, and now Connie began to hear the music. It was the same program that was playing inside the house.

"Bobby King?" she said.

"I listen to him all the time. I think he's great."

"He's kind of great," Connie said reluctantly.

"Listen, that guy's *great*. He knows where the action is."

Connie blushed a little, because the glasses made it impossible for her to see       35
just what this boy was looking at. She couldn't decide if she liked him or if he was just a jerk, and so she dawdled in the doorway and wouldn't come down or go back inside. She said, "What's all that stuff painted on your car?"

"Can'tcha read it?" He opened the door very carefully, as if he was afraid it might fall off. He slid out just as carefully, planting his feet firmly on the ground, the tiny metallic world in his glasses slowing down like gelatine hardening and in the midst of it Connie's bright green blouse. "This here is my name, to begin with," he said. ARNOLD FRIEND was written in tarlike black letters on the side, with a drawing of a round grinning face that reminded Connie of a pumpkin, except it wore sunglasses. "I wanta introduce myself, I'm Arnold Friend and that's my real name and I'm gonna be your friend, honey, and inside the car's Ellie Oscar, he's kinda shy." Ellie brought his transistor radio up to his shoulder and balanced it there. "Now these numbers are a secret code, honey," Arnold Friend explained. He read off the numbers 33, 19, 17 and raised his eyebrows at her to see what she thought of that, but she didn't think much of it. The left rear fender had been smashed and around it was written, on the gleaming gold background: DONE BY CRAZY WOMAN DRIVER. Connie had to laugh at that. Arnold Friend was pleased at her laughter and looked up at her. "Around the other side's a lot more—you wanta come and see them?"

"No."

"Why not?"

"Why should I?"

"Don'tcha wanta see what's on the car? Don'tcha wanta go for a ride?"     40

"I don't know."

"Why not?"

"I got things to do."

"Like what?"

"Things."     45

He laughed as if she had said something funny. He slapped his thighs. He was standing in a strange way, leaning back against the car as if he were balancing himself. He wasn't tall, only an inch or so taller than she would be if she came down to him. Connie liked the way he was dressed, which was the way all of them dressed: tight faded jeans stuffed into black, scuffed boots, a belt that pulled his waist in and showed how lean he was, and a white pull-over shirt that was a little soiled and showed the hard small muscles of his arms and shoulders. He looked as if he probably did hard work, lifting and carrying things. Even his neck looked muscular. And his face was a familiar face, somehow: the jaw and chin and cheeks slightly darkened, because he hadn't shaved for a day or two, and the nose long and hawk-like, sniffing as if she were a treat he was going to gobble up and it was all a joke.

"Connie, you ain't telling the truth. This is your day set aside for a ride with me and you know it," he said, still laughing. The way he straightened and recovered from his fit of laughing showed that it had been all fake.

"How do you know what my name is?" she said suspiciously.

"It's Connie."

"Maybe and maybe not."     50

"I know my Connie," he said, wagging his finger. Now she remembered him even better, back at the restaurant, and her cheeks warmed at the thought of how she sucked in her breath just at the moment she passed him—how she must have looked to him. And he had remembered her. "Ellie and I come out here especially for you," he said. "Ellie can sit in back. How about it?"

"Where?"

"Where what?"

"Where're we going?"

He looked at her. He took off the sunglasses and she saw how pale the skin     55 around his eyes was, like holes that were not in shadow but instead in light. His eyes were chips of broken glass that catch the light in an amiable way. He smiled.

It was as if the idea of going for a ride somewhere, to some place, was a new idea to him.

"Just for a ride, Connie sweetheart."

"I never said my name was Connie," she said.

"But I know what it is. I know your name and all about you, lots of things," Arnold Friend said. He had not moved yet but stood still leaning back against the side of his jalopy. "I took a special interest in you, such a pretty girl, and found out all about you like I know your parents and sister are gone somewheres and I know where and how long they're going to be gone, and I know who you were with last night, and your best girl friend's name is Betty. Right?"

He spoke in a simple lilting voice, exactly as if he were reciting the words to a song. His smile assured her that everything was fine. In the car Ellie turned up the volume on his radio and did not bother to look around at them.

"Ellie can sit in the back seat," Arnold Friend said. He indicated his friend   60
with a casual jerk of his chin, as if Ellie did not count and she should not bother
with him.

"How'd you find out all that stuff?" Connie said.

"Listen: Betty Schultz and Tony Fitch and Jimmy Pettinger and Nancy
Pettinger," he said, in a chant. "Raymond Stanley and Bob Hutter—"

"Do you know all those kids?"

"I know everybody."

"Look, you're kidding. You're not from around here."   65

"Sure."

"But—how come we never saw you before?"

"Sure you saw me before," he said. He looked down at his boots, as if he were
a little offended. "You just don't remember."

"I guess I'd remember you," Connie said.

"Yeah?" He looked up at this, beaming. He was pleased. He began to mark   70
time with the music from Ellie's radio, tapping his fists lightly together. Connie
looked away from his smile to the car, which was painted so bright it almost hurt
her eyes to look at it. She looked at that name, ARNOLD FRIEND. And up at
the front fender was an expression that was familiar—MAN THE FLYING
SAUCERS. It was an expression kids had used the year before, but didn't use this
year. She looked at it for a while as if the words meant something to her that she
did not yet know.

"What're you thinking about? Huh?" Arnold Friend demanded. "Not worried
about your hair blowing around in the car, are you?"

"No."

"Think I maybe can't drive good?"

"How do I know?"

"You're a hard girl to handle. How come?" he said. "Don't you know I'm your   75
friend? Didn't you see me put my sign in the air when you walked by?"

"What sign?"

"My sign." And he drew an X in the air, leaning out toward her. They were
maybe ten feet apart. After his hand fell back to his side the X was still in the air,

almost visible. Connie let the screen door close and stood perfectly still inside it, listening to the music from her radio and the boy's blend together. She stared at Arnold Friend. He stood there so stiffly relaxed, pretending to be relaxed, with one hand idly on the door handle as if he were keeping himself up that way and had no intention of ever moving again. She recognized most things about him, the tight jeans that showed his thighs and buttocks and the greasy leather boots and the tight shirt, and even that slippery friendly smile of his, that sleepy dreamy smile that all the boys used to get across ideas they didn't want to put into words. She recognized all this and also the singsong way he talked, slightly mocking, kidding, but serious and a little melancholy, and she recognized the way he tapped one fist against the other in homage to the perpetual music behind him. But all these things did not come together.

She said suddenly, "Hey, how old are you?"

His smile faded. She could see then that he wasn't a kid, he was much older—thirty, maybe more. At this knowledge her heart began to pound faster.

"That's a crazy thing to ask. Can'tcha see I'm your own age?"                    80

"Like hell you are."

"Or maybe a coupla years older, I'm eighteen."

"Eighteen?" she said doubtfully.

He grinned to reassure her and lines appeared at the corners of his mouth. His teeth were big and white. He grinned so broadly his eyes became slits and she saw how thick the lashes were, thick and black as if painted with a black tarlike material. Then he seemed to become embarrassed, abruptly, and looked over his shoulder at Ellie. "*Him,* he's crazy," he said. "Ain't he a riot, he's a nut, a real character." Ellie was still listening to the music. His sunglasses told nothing about what he was thinking. He wore a bright orange shirt unbuttoned halfway to show his chest, which was a pale, bluish chest and not muscular like Arnold Friend's. His shirt collar was turned up all around and the very tips of the collar pointed out past his chin as if they were protecting him. He was pressing the transistor radio up against his ear and sat there in a kind of daze, right in the sun.

"He's kinda strange," Connie said.                                                 85

"Hey, she says you're kinda strange! Kinda strange!" Arnold Friend cried. He pounded on the car to get Ellie's attention. Ellie turned for the first time and Connie saw with shock that he wasn't a kid either—he had a fair, hairless face, cheeks reddened slightly as if the veins grew too close to the surface of his skin, the face of a forty-year-old baby. Connie felt a wave of dizziness rise in her at this sight and she stared at him as if waiting for something to change the shock of the moment, make it all right again. Ellie's lips kept shaping words, mumbling along, with the words blasting in his ear.

"Maybe you two better go away," Connie said faintly.

"What? How come?" Arnold Friend cried. "We come out here to take you for a ride. It's Sunday." He had the voice of the man on the radio now. It was the same voice, Connie thought. "Don'tcha know it's Sunday all day and honey, no matter who you were with last night today you're with Arnold Friend and don't you forget it!—Maybe you better step out here," he said, and this last was in a different voice. It was a little flatter, as if the heat was finally getting to him.

"No. I got things to do."

"Hey." 90

"You two better leave."

"We ain't leaving until you come with us."

"Like hell I am—"

"Connie, don't fool around with me. I mean, I mean, don't fool *around*," he said, shaking his head. He laughed incredulously. He placed his sunglasses on top of his head, carefully, as if he were indeed wearing a wig, and brought the stems down behind his ears. Connie stared at him, another wave of dizziness and fear rising in her so that for a moment he wasn't even in focus but was just a blur, standing there against his gold car, and she had the idea that he had driven up the driveway all right but had come from nowhere before that and belonged nowhere and that everything about him and even about the music that was so familiar to her was only half real.

"If my father comes and sees you—" 95

"He ain't coming. He's at the barbecue."

"How do you know that?"

"Aunt Tillie's. Right now they're—uh—they're drinking. Sitting around," he said vaguely, squinting as if he were staring all the way to town and over to Aunt Tillie's backyard. Then the vision seemed to get clear and he nodded energetically. "Yeah. Sitting around. There's your sister in a blue dress, huh? And high heels, the poor sad bitch—nothing like you, sweetheart! And your mother's helping some fat woman with the corn, they're cleaning the corn—husking the corn—"

"What fat woman?" Connie cried.

"How do I know what fat woman. I don't know every goddam fat woman in the world!" Arnold Friend laughed. 100

"Oh, that's Mrs. Hornby. . . . Who invited her?" Connie said. She felt a little light-headed. Her breath was coming quickly.

"She's too fat. I don't like them fat. I like them the way you are, honey," he said, smiling sleepily at her. They stared at each other for a while, through the screen door. He said softly, "Now what you're going to do is this: you're going to come out that door. You're going to sit up front with me and Ellie's going to sit in the back, the hell with Ellie, right? This isn't Ellie's date. You're my date. I'm your lover, honey."

"What? You're crazy—"

"Yes, I'm your lover. You don't know what that is but you will," he said. "I know that too. I know all about you. But look: it's real nice and you couldn't ask for nobody better than me, or more polite. I always keep my word. I'll tell you how it is, I'm always nice at first, the first time. I'll hold you so tight you won't think you have to try to get away or pretend anything because you'll know you can't. And I'll come inside you where it's all secret and you'll give in to me and you'll love me—"

"Shut up! You're crazy!" Connie said. She backed away from the door. She 105 put her hands against her ears as if she'd heard something terrible, something not meant for her. "People don't talk like that, you're crazy," she muttered. Her heart was almost too big now for her chest and its pumping made sweat break out all over her. She looked out to see Arnold Friend pause and then take a step toward the porch lurching. He almost fell. But, like a clever drunken man, he managed to catch his balance. He wobbled in his high boots and grabbed hold of one of the porch posts.

"Honey?" he said. "You still listening?"

"Get the hell out of here!"

"Be nice, honey. Listen."

"I'm going to call the police—"

He wobbled again and out of the side of his mouth came a fast spat curse, an 110 aside not meant for her to hear. But even this "Christ!" sounded forced. Then he began to smile again. She watched this smile come, awkward as if he were smiling from inside a mask. His whole face was a mask, she thought wildly, tanned down onto his throat but then running out as if he had plastered make-up on his face but had forgotten about his throat.

"Honey—? Listen, here's how it is. I always tell the truth and I promise you this: I ain't coming in that house after you."

"You better not! I'm going to call the police if you—if you don't—"

"Honey," he said, talking right through her voice, "honey, I'm not coming in there but you are coming out here. You know why?"

She was panting. The kitchen looked like a place she had never seen before, some room she had run inside but which wasn't good enough, wasn't going to help her. The kitchen window had never had a curtain, after three years, and there were dishes in the sink for her to do—probably—and if you ran your hand across the table you'd probably feel something sticky there.

"You listening, honey? Hey?" 115

"—going to call the police—"

"Soon as you touch the phone I don't need to keep my promise and can come inside. You won't want that."

She rushed forward and tried to lock the door. Her fingers were shaking. "But why lock it," Arnold Friend said gently, talking right into her face. "It's just a screen door. It's just nothing." One of his boots was at a strange angle, as if his foot wasn't in it. It pointed out to the left, bent at the ankle. "I mean, anybody can break through a screen door and glass and wood and iron or anything else if he needs to, anybody at all and specially Arnold Friend. If the place got lit up with a fire honey you'd come running out into my arms, right into my arms and safe at home—like you knew I was your lover and'd stopped fooling around. I don't mind a nice shy girl but I don't like no fooling around." Part of those words were spoken with a slight rhythmic lilt, and Connie somehow recognized them—the echo of a song from last year, about a girl rushing into her boyfriend's arms and coming home again—

Connie stood barefoot on the linoleum floor, staring at him. "What do you want?" she whispered.

"I want you," he said. 120

"What?"

"Seen you that night and thought, that's the one, yes sir. I never needed to look any more."

"But my father's coming back. He's coming to get me. I had to wash my hair first—" She spoke in a dry, rapid voice, hardly raising it for him to hear.

"No, your daddy is not coming and yes, you had to wash your hair and you washed it for me. It's nice and shining and all for me, I thank you, sweetheart," he said, with a mock bow, but again he almost lost his balance. He had to bend and adjust his boots. Evidently his feet did not go all the way down; the boots must have been stuffed with something so that he would seem taller. Connie stared out at him and behind him Ellie in the car, who seemed to be looking off toward Connie's right, into nothing. This Ellie said, pulling the words out of the air one after another as if he were just discovering them, "You want me to pull out the phone?"

"Shut your mouth and keep it shut," Arnold Friend said, his face red from 125 bending over or maybe from embarrassment because Connie had seen his boots. "This ain't none of your business."

"What—what are you doing? What do you want?" Connie said. "If I call the police they'll get you, they'll arrest you—"

"Promise was not to come in unless you touch that phone, and I'll keep that promise," he said. He resumed his erect position and tried to force his shoulders back. He sounded like a hero in a movie, declaring something important. He spoke too loudly and it was as if he were speaking to someone behind Connie. "I ain't made plans for coming in that house where I don't belong but just for you to come out to me, the way you should. Don't you know who I am?"

"You're crazy," she whispered. She backed away from the door but did not want to go into another part of the house, as if this would give him permission to come through the door. "What do you . . . You're crazy, you . . . "

"Huh? What're you saying, honey?"

Her eyes darted everywhere in the kitchen. She could not remember what it 130 was, this room.

"This is how it is, honey: you come out and we'll drive away, have a nice ride. But if you don't come out we're gonna wait till your people come home and then they're all going to get it."

"You want that telephone pulled out?" Ellie said. He held the radio away from his ear and grimaced, as if without the radio the air was too much for him.

"I toldja shut up, Ellie," Arnold Friend said, "you're deaf, get a hearing aid, right? Fix yourself up. This little girl's no trouble and's gonna be nice to me, so Ellie keep to yourself, this ain't your date—right? Don't hem in on me. Don't hog. Don't crush. Don't bird dog. Don't trail me," he said in a rapid meaningless voice, as if he were running through all the expressions he'd learned but was no longer sure which one of them was in style, then rushing on to new ones, making them up with his eyes closed, "Don't crawl under my fence, don't squeeze in my chipmunk hole, don't sniff my glue, suck my popsicle, keep your own greasy fingers on yourself!" He shaded his eyes and peered in at Connie, who was backed against the kitchen table. "Don't mind him honey he's just a creep. He's a dope. Right? I'm the boy for you and like I said you come out here nice like a lady and give me your hand, and nobody else gets hurt, I mean, your nice old bald-headed daddy and your mummy and your sister in her high heels. Because listen: why bring them in this?"

"Leave me alone," Connie whispered.

"Hey, you know that old woman down the road, the one with the chickens and stuff—you know her?"

"She's dead!"

"Dead? What? You know her?" Arnold Friend said.

"She's dead—"

"Don't you like her?"

"She's dead—she's—she isn't here any more—"

"But don't you like her, I mean, you got something against her? Some grudge or something?" Then his voice dipped as if he were conscious of a rudeness. He touched the sunglasses perched on top of his head as if to make sure they were still there. "Now you be a good girl."

"What are you going to do?"

"Just two things, or maybe three," Arnold Friend said. "But I promise it won't last long and you'll like me that way you get to like people you're close to. You will. It's all over for you here, so come on out. You don't want your people in any trouble, do you?"

She turned and bumped against a chair or something, hurting her leg, but she ran into the back room and picked up the telephone. Something roared in her ear, a tiny roaring, and she was so sick with fear that she could do nothing but listen to it—the telephone was clammy and very heavy and her fingers groped down to the dial but were too weak to touch it. She began to scream into the phone, into the roaring. She cried out, she cried for her mother, she felt her breath start jerking back and forth in her lungs as if it were something Arnold Friend were stabbing her with again and again with no tenderness. A noisy sorrowful wailing rose all about her and she was locked inside it the way she was locked inside the house.

After a while she could hear again. She was sitting on the floor with her wet back against the wall.

Arnold Friend was saying from the door, "That's a good girl. Put the phone back."

She kicked the phone away from her.

"No, honey. Pick it up. Put it back right."

She picked it up and put it back. The dial tone stopped.

"That's a good girl. Now come outside."

She was hollow with what had been fear, but what was now just an emptiness. All that screaming had blasted it out of her. She sat, one leg cramped under her, and deep inside her brain was something like a pinpoint of light that kept going and would not let her relax. She thought, I'm not going to see my mother again. She thought, I'm not going to sleep in my bed again. Her bright green blouse was all wet.

Arnold Friend said, in a gentle-loud voice that was like a stage voice, "The place where you came from ain't there any more, and where you had in mind to go is cancelled out. This place you are now—inside your daddy's house—is nothing but a cardboard box I can knock down any time. You know that and always did know it. You hear me?"

She thought, I have got to think. I have to know what to do.

"We'll go out to a nice field, out in the country here where it smells so nice and it's sunny," Arnold Friend said. "I'll have my arms around you so you won't need to try to get away and I'll show you what love is like, what it does. The hell with this house! It looks solid all right," he said. He ran a fingernail down the screen and the noise did not make Connie shiver, as it would have the day before. "Now put your hand on your heart, honey. Feel that? That feels solid too but we know better, be nice to me, be sweet like you can because what else is there for a girl like you but to be sweet and pretty and give in?—and get away before her people come back?"

She felt her pounding heart. Her hand seemed to enclose it. She thought for   155
the first time in her life that it was nothing that was hers, that belonged to her, but just a pounding, living thing inside this body that wasn't really hers either.

"You don't want them to get hurt," Arnold Friend went on. "Now get up, honey. Get up all by yourself."

She stood up.

"Now turn this way. That's right. Come over here to me—Ellie, put that away, didn't I tell you? You dope. You miserable creepy dope," Arnold Friend said. His words were not angry but only part of an incantation. The incantation was kindly. "Now come out through the kitchen to me honey and let's see a smile, try it, you're a brave sweet little girl and now they're eating corn and hot-dogs cooked to bursting over an outdoor fire, and they don't know one thing about you and never did and honey you're better than them because not a one of them would have done this for you."

Connie felt the linoleum under her feet; it was cool. She brushed her hair back out of her eyes. Arnold Friend let go of the post tentatively and opened his arms for her, his elbows pointing in toward each other and his wrists limp, to show that this was an embarrassed embrace and a little mocking, he didn't want to make her self-conscious.

She put out her hand against the screen. She watched herself push the door   160
slowly open as if she were safe back somewhere in the other doorway, watching this body and this head of long hair moving out into the sunlight where Arnold Friend waited.

"My sweet little blue-eyed girl," he said, in a half-sung sigh that had nothing to do with her brown eyes but was taken up just the same by the vast sunlit reaches of the land behind him and on all sides of him, so much land that Connie had never seen before and did not recognize except to know that she was going to it.

# Frank O'Connor

## FIRST CONFESSION
1952

Frank O'Connor was the pen name that
Michael O'Donovan (1903–1966) adopted
when he feared that to be known as a writer
would hurt his career in civil service. He
was born in Cork, Ireland's second city.
Desperate poverty forced his parents to take
him out of school after he had completed
only fourth grade. During the troubles of
1918–21 that led to the new Irish Free
State, he served in the Republican Army.
After peace came, he worked as a librarian
and for several years served as a director of
Dublin's influential Abbey Theatre. America offered O'Connor-O'Donovan early
hospitality: in 1931 The Atlantic printed
his first story. In the 1950s he lived in
America, teaching at Northwestern and

Frank O'Connor

Harvard. For a time he regularly appeared on CBS television on Sunday mornings, just
sitting and telling stories. A fine literary critic, besides, he wrote The Mirror in the
Roadway (1956), a study of the novel, and The Lonely Voice (1963), a study of the
short story. In Kings, Lords & Commons (1959), he proved himself a master translator of Gaelic poetry. O'Connor toiled hard over his stories, trying to polish each to the
perfection of a good lyric. "First Confession" appeared in print in three versions because
he kept rewriting it. The story is based upon his boyhood memories.

All the trouble began when my grandfather died and my grandmother—my
father's mother—came to live with us. Relations in the one house are a strain at
the best of times, but, to make matters worse, my grandmother was a real old
countrywoman and quite unsuited to the life in town. She had a fat, wrinkled old
face, and, to Mother's great indignation, went round the house in bare feet—the
boots had her crippled, she said. For dinner she had a jug of porter and a pot of
potatoes with—sometimes—a bit of salt fish, and she poured out the potatoes on
the table and ate them slowly, with great relish, using her fingers by way of a fork.

Now, girls are supposed to be fastidious, but I was the one who suffered most
from this. Nora, my sister, just sucked up to the old woman for the penny she got
every Friday out of the old-age pension, a thing I could not do. I was too honest,
that was my trouble; and when I was playing with Bill Connell, the sergeant-
major's son, and saw my grandmother steering up the path with the jug of porter
sticking out from beneath her shawl I was mortified. I made excuses not to let
him come into the house, because I could never be sure what she would be up to
when we went in.

When Mother was at work and my grandmother made the dinner I wouldn't touch it. Nora once tried to make me, but I hid under the table from her and took the bread-knife with me for protection. Nora let on to be very indignant (she wasn't, of course, but she knew Mother saw through her, so she sided with Gran) and came after me. I lashed out at her with the bread-knife, and after that she left me alone. I stayed there till Mother came in from work and made my dinner, but when Father came in later Nora said in a shocked voice: "Oh, Dadda, do you know what Jackie did at dinnertime?" Then, of course, it all came out; Father gave me a flaking; Mother interfered, and for days after that he didn't speak to me and Mother barely spoke to Nora. And all because of that old woman! God knows, I was heart-scalded.

Then, to crown my misfortunes, I had to make my first confession and communion. It was an old woman called Ryan who prepared us for these. She was about the one age with Gran; she was well-to-do, lived in a big house on Montenotte, wore a black cloak and bonnet, and came every day to school at three o'clock when we should have been going home, and talked to us of hell. She may have mentioned the other place as well, but that could only have been by accident, for hell had the first place in her heart.

She lit a candle, took out a new half-crown, and offered it to the first boy    5
who would hold one finger—only one finger!—in the flame for five minutes by the school clock. Being always very ambitious I was tempted to volunteer, but I thought it might look greedy. Then she asked were we afraid of holding one finger—only one finger!—in a little candle flame for five minutes and not afraid of burning all over in roasting hot furnaces for all eternity. "All eternity! Just think of that! A whole lifetime goes by and it's nothing, not even a drop in the ocean of your sufferings." The woman was really interesting about hell, but my attention was all fixed on the half-crown. At the end of the lesson she put it back in her purse. It was a great disappointment; a religious woman like that, you wouldn't think she'd bother about a thing like a half-crown.

Another day she said she knew a priest who woke one night to find a fellow he didn't recognize leaning over the end of his bed. The priest was a bit frightened—naturally enough—but he asked the fellow what he wanted, and the fellow said in a deep, husky voice that he wanted to go to confession. The priest said it was an awkward time and wouldn't it do in the morning, but the fellow said that last time he went to confession, there was one sin he kept back, being ashamed to mention it, and now it was always on his mind. Then the priest knew it was a bad case, because the fellow was after making a bad confession and committing a mortal sin. He got up to dress, and just then the cock crew in the yard outside, and—lo and behold!—when the priest looked round there was no sign of the fellow, only a smell of burning timber, and when the priest looked at his bed didn't he see the print of two hands burned in it? That was because the fellow had made a bad confession. This story made a shocking impression on me.

But the worst of all was when she showed us how to examine our conscience. Did we take the name of the Lord, our God, in vain? Did we honor our father and our mother? (I asked her did this include grandmothers and she said it did.) Did we love our neighbors as ourselves? Did we covet our neighbor's goods? (I thought of the way I felt about the penny that Nora got every Friday.) I decided that, between one thing and another, I must have broken the whole ten commandments, all on account of that old woman, and so far as I could see, so long as she remained in the house I had no hope of ever doing anything else.

I was scared to death of confession. The day the whole class went I let on to have a toothache, hoping my absence wouldn't be noticed; but at three o'clock, just as I was feeling safe, along comes a chap with a message from Mrs. Ryan that I was to go to confession myself on Saturday and be at the chapel for communion with the rest. To make it worse, Mother couldn't come with me and sent Nora instead.

Now, that girl had ways of tormenting me that Mother never knew of. She held my hand as we went down the hill, smiling sadly and saying how sorry she was for me, as if she were bringing me to the hospital for an operation.

"Oh, God help us!" she moaned. "Isn't it a terrible pity you weren't a good 10 boy? Oh, Jackie, my heart bleeds for you! How will you ever think of all your sins? Don't forget you have to tell him about the time you kicked Gran on the shin."

"Lemme go!" I said, trying to drag myself free of her. "I don't want to go to confession at all."

"But sure, you'll have to go to confession, Jackie," she replied in the same regretful tone. "Sure, if you didn't, the parish priest would be up to the house, looking for you. 'Tisn't, God knows, that I'm not sorry for you. Do you remember the time you tried to kill me with the bread-knife under the table? And the language you used to me? I don't know what he'll do with you at all, Jackie. He might have to send you up to the bishop."

I remember thinking bitterly that she didn't know the half of what I had to tell—if I told it. I knew I couldn't tell it, and understood perfectly why the fellow in Mrs. Ryan's story made a bad confession; it seemed to me a great shame that people wouldn't stop criticizing him. I remember that steep hill down to the church, and the sunlit hillsides beyond the valley of the river, which I saw in the gaps between the houses like Adam's last glimpse of Paradise.

Then, when she had maneuvered me down the long flight of steps to the chapel yard, Nora suddenly changed her tone. She became the raging malicious devil she really was.

"There you are!" she said with a yelp of triumph, hurling me through the 15 church door. "And I hope he'll give you the penitential psalms, you dirty little caffler."°

I knew then I was lost, given up to eternal justice. The door with the colored glass panels swung shut behind me, the sunlight went out and gave place to deep shadow, and the wind whistled outside so that the silence within seemed to crackle like ice under my feet. Nora sat in front of me by the confession box. There were a couple of old women ahead of her, and then a miserable-looking poor devil came and wedged me in at the other side, so that I couldn't escape

*caffler:* scamp, rascal.

even if I had the courage. He joined his hands and rolled his eyes in the direction of the roof, muttering aspirations in an anguished tone, and I wondered had he a grandmother too. Only a grandmother could account for a fellow behaving in that heartbroken way, but he was better off than I, for he at least could go and confess his sins; while I would make a bad confession and then die in the night and be continually coming back and burning people's furniture.

Nora's turn came, and I heard the sound of something slamming, and then her voice as if butter wouldn't melt in her mouth, and then another slam, and out she came. God, the hypocrisy of women! Her eyes were lowered, her head was bowed, and her hands were joined very low down on her stomach, and she walked up the aisle to the side altar looking like a saint. You never saw such an exhibition of devotion; and I remembered the devilish malice with which she had tormented me all the way from our door, and wondered were all religious people like that, really. It was my turn now. With the fear of damnation in my soul I went in, and the confessional door closed of itself behind me.

It was pitch-dark and I couldn't see priest or anything else. Then I really began to be frightened. In the darkness it was a matter between God and me, and He had all the odds. He knew what my intentions were before I even started; I had no chance. All I had ever been told about confession got mixed up in my mind, and I knelt to one wall and said: "Bless me, father, for I have sinned; this is my first confession." I waited for a few minutes, but nothing happened, so I tried it on the other wall. Nothing happened there either. He had me spotted all right.

It must have been then that I noticed the shelf at about one height with my head. It was really a place for grown-up people to rest their elbows, but in my distracted state I thought it was probably the place you were supposed to kneel. Of course, it was on the high side and not very deep, but I was always good at climbing and managed to get up all right. Staying up was the trouble. There was room only for my knees, and nothing you could get a grip on but a sort of wooden moulding a bit above it. I held on to the moulding and repeated the words a little louder, and this time something happened all right. A slide was slammed back; a little light entered the box, and a man's voice said: "Who's there?"

"'Tis me, father," I said for fear he mightn't see me and go away again. I couldn't see him at all. The place the voice came from was under the moulding, about level with my knees, so I took a good grip of the moulding and swung myself down till I saw the astonished face of a young priest looking up at me. He had to put his head on one side to see me, and I had to put mine on one side to see him, so we were more or less talking to one another upside-down. It struck me as a queer way of hearing confessions, but I didn't feel it my place to criticize.

"Bless me, father, for I have sinned; this is my first confession," I rattled off all in one breath, and swung myself down the least shade more to make it easier for him.

"What are you doing up there?" he shouted in an angry voice, and the strain the politeness was putting on my hold of the moulding, and the shock of being addressed in such an uncivil tone, were too much for me. I lost my grip, tumbled, and hit the door an unmerciful wallop before I found myself flat on my back in

20

the middle of the aisle. The people who had been waiting stood up with their mouths open. The priest opened the door of the middle box and came out, pushing his biretta back from his forehead; he looked something terrible. Then Nora came scampering down the aisle.

"Oh, you dirty little caffler!" she said. "I might have known you'd do it. I might have known you'd disgrace me. I can't leave you out of my sight for one minute."

Before I could even get to my feet to defend myself she bent down and gave me a clip across the ear. This reminded me that I was so stunned I had even forgotten to cry, so that people might think I wasn't hurt at all, when in fact I was probably maimed for life. I gave a roar out of me.

"What's all this about?" the priest hissed, getting angrier than ever and push-  25
ing Nora off me. "How dare you hit the child like that, you little vixen?"

"But I can't do my penance with him, father," Nora cried, cocking an outraged eye up at him.

"Well, go and do it, or I'll give you some more to do," he said, giving me a hand up. "Was it coming to confession you were, my poor man?" he asked me.

"'Twas, father," said I with a sob.

"Oh," he said respectfully, "a big hefty fellow like you must have terrible sins. Is this your first?"

"'Tis, father," said I.  30

"Worse and worse," he said gloomily. "The crimes of a life-time. I don't know will I get rid of you at all today. You'd better wait now till I'm finished with these old ones. You can see by the looks of them they haven't much to tell."

"I will, father," I said with something approaching joy.

The relief of it was really enormous. Nora stuck out her tongue at me from behind his back, but I couldn't even be bothered retorting. I knew from the very moment that man opened his mouth that he was intelligent above the ordinary. When I had time to think, I saw how right I was. It only stood to reason that a fellow confessing after seven years would have more to tell than people that went every week. The crimes of a lifetime, exactly as he said. It was only what he expected, and the rest was the cackle of old women and girls with their talk of hell, the bishop, and the penitential psalms. That was all they knew. I started to make my examination of conscience, and barring the one bad business of my grandmother it didn't seem so bad.

The next time, the priest steered me into the confession box himself and left the shutter back the way I could see him get in and sit down at the further side of the grille from me.

"Well, now," he said, "what do they call you?"  35

"Jackie, father," said I.

"And what's a-trouble to you, Jackie?"

"Father," I said, feeling I might as well get it over while I had him in good humor, "I had it all arranged to kill my grandmother."

He seemed a bit shaken by that, all right, because he said nothing for quite a while.

"My goodness," he said at last, "that'd be a shocking thing to do. What put  40
that into your head?"

"Father," I said, feeling very sorry for myself, "she's an awful woman."

"Is she?" he asked, "What way is she awful?"

"She takes porter, father," I said, knowing well from the way Mother talked
of it that this was a mortal sin, and hoping it would make the priest take a more
favorable view of my case.

"Oh my!" he said, and I could see he was impressed.

"And snuff, father," said I.  45

"That's a bad case, sure enough, Jackie," he said.

"And she goes round in her bare feet, father," I went on in a rush of self-pity,
"and she knows I don't like her, and she gives pennies to Nora and none to me,
and my da sides with her and flakes me, and one night I was so heart-scalded I
made up my mind I'd have to kill her."

"And what would you do with the body?" he asked with great interest.

"I was thinking I could chop that up and carry it away in a barrow I have," I
said.

"Begor, Jackie," he said, "do you know you're a terrible child?"  50

"I know, father," I said, for I was just thinking the same thing myself. "I tried
to kill Nora too with a bread-knife under the table, only I missed her."

"Is that the little girl that was beating you just now?" he asked.

"'Tis, father."

"Someone will go for her with a bread-knife one day, and he won't miss her,"
he said rather cryptically. "You must have great courage. Between ourselves,
there's a lot of people I'd like to do the same to but I'd never have the nerve.
Hanging is an awful death."

"Is it, father?" I asked with the deepest interest—I was always very keen on  55
hanging. "Did you ever see a fellow hanged?"

"Dozens of them," he said solemnly. "And they all died roaring."

"Jay!" I said.

"Oh, a horrible death!" he said with great satisfaction. "Lots of the fellows I
saw killed their grandmothers too, but they all said 'twas never worth it."

He had me there for a full ten minutes talking, and then walked out the
chapel yard with me. I was genuinely sorry to part with him, because he was the
most entertaining character I'd ever met in the religious line. Outside, after the
shadow of the church, the sunlight was like the roaring of waves on a beach; it
dazzled me; and when the frozen silence melted and I heard the screech of trams
on the road my heart soared. I knew now I wouldn't die in the night and come
back, leaving marks on my mother's furniture. It would be a great worry to her,
and the poor soul had enough.

Nora was sitting on the railing, waiting for me, and she put on a very sour  60
puss when she saw the priest with me. She was mad jealous because a priest had
never come out of the church with her.

"Well," she asked coldly, after he left me, "what did he give you?"

"Three Hail Marys," I said.

"Three Hail Marys," she repeatedly incredulously. "You mustn't have told him anything."

"I told him everything," I said confidently.

"About Gran and all?" 65

"About Gran and all."

(All she wanted was to be able to go home and say I'd made a bad confession.)

"Did you tell him you went for me with the bread-knife?" she asked with a frown.

"I did to be sure."

"And he only gave you three Hail Marys?" 70

"That's all."

She slowly got down from the railing with a baffled air. Clearly, this was beyond her. As we mounted the steps back to the main road she looked at me suspiciously.

"What are you sucking?" she asked.

"Bullseyes."

"Was it the priest gave them to you?" 75

"'Twas."

"Lord God," she wailed bitterly, "some people have all the luck! 'Tis no advantage to anybody trying to be good. I might just as well be a sinner like you."

## Tillie Olsen

I STAND HERE IRONING                                    1961

*Tillie Olsen*

*Tillie Olsen was born in Omaha in 1912, into a family of blue-collar workers who had fled Czarist Russia to escape persecution. Olsen grew up in poverty and quit school in eleventh grade to work. She later declared, "Public libraries were my college." As a member of the Young Communist League, she strove to organize Kansas City meat-packers, and was once thrown into jail. After her first husband deserted her, leaving her with one child, she married a printer and labor activist, Jack Olsen, by whom she had three more children. Although in the 1930s she published fiction in a distinguished little magazine, Partisan Review, the demands of motherhood, political activity, and factory and office jobs left her scant time to write until 1955. Then her youngest daughter began school and Olsen was awarded a creative-writing fellowship at Stanford University. Long a crusader for causes, she has been active in the recent feminist movement. "I Stand Here Ironing," from her first book,* Tell Me a Riddle *(1961), reads like autobiography. Olsen has since published* Yonnondio *(1974), an unfinished novel begun at age nineteen, and* Silences *(1978), a study of why writers—especially women writers—dry up. She holds several honorary degrees. In 1981 the city of San Francisco, where she has long resided, designated a Tillie Olsen day.*

I stand here ironing, and what you asked me moves tormented back and forth with the iron.

"I wish you would manage the time to come in and talk with me about your daughter. I'm sure you can help me understand her. She's a youngster who needs help and whom I'm deeply interested in helping."

"Who needs help." . . . Even if I came, what good would it do? You think because I am her mother I have a key, or that in some way you could use me as a key? She has lived for nineteen years. There is all that life that has happened outside of me, beyond me.

And when is there time to remember, to sift, to weigh, to estimate, to total? I will start and there will be an interruption and I will have to gather it all together again. Or I will become engulfed with all I did or did not do, with what should have been and what cannot be helped.

She was a beautiful baby. The first and only one of our five that was beautiful 5 at birth. You do not guess how new and uneasy her tenancy in her now-loveliness. You did not know her all those years she was thought homely, or see her poring over her baby pictures, making me tell her over and over how beautiful she had been—and would be, I would tell her—and was now, to the seeing eye. But the seeing eyes were few or nonexistent. Including mine.

I nursed her. They feel that's important nowadays. I nursed all the children, but with her, with all the fierce rigidity of first motherhood, I did like the books then said. Though her cries battered me to trembling and my breasts ached with swollenness, I waited till the clock decreed.

Why do I put that first? I do not even know if it matters, or if it explains anything.

She was a beautiful baby. She blew shining bubbles of sound. She loved motion, loved light, loved color and music and textures. She would lie on the floor in her blue overalls patting the surface so hard in ecstasy her hands and feet would blur. She was a miracle to me, but when she was eight months old I had to leave her daytimes with the woman downstairs to whom she was no miracle at all, for I worked or looked for work and for Emily's father, who "could no longer endure" (he wrote in his good-bye note) "sharing want with us."

I was nineteen. It was the pre-relief, pre-WPA world of the depression. I would start running as soon as I got off the streetcar, running up the stairs, the place smelling sour, and awake or asleep to startle awake, when she saw me she would break into a clogged weeping that could not be comforted, a weeping I can hear yet.

After a while I found a job hashing at night so I could be with her days, and 10 it was better. But it came to where I had to bring her to his family and leave her.

It took a long time to raise the money for her fare back. Then she got chicken pox and I had to wait longer. When she finally came, I hardly knew her, walking quick and nervous like her father, looking like her father, thin, and dressed in a shoddy red that yellowed her skin and glared at the pockmarks. All the baby loveliness gone.

She was two. Old enough for nursery school they said, and I did not know then what I know now—the fatigue of the long day, and the lacerations of group life in the kinds of nurseries that are only parking places for children.

Except that it would have made no difference if I had known. It was the only place there was. It was the only way we could be together, the only way I could hold a job.

And even without knowing, I knew. I knew the teacher that was evil because all these years it has curdled into my memory, the little boy hunched in the corner, her rasp, "why aren't you outside, because Alvin hits you? that's no reason, go out, scaredy." I knew Emily hated it even if she did not clutch and implore "don't go Mommy" like the other children, mornings.

She always had a reason why we should stay home. Momma, you look sick.  15
Momma, I feel sick. Momma, the teachers aren't there today, they're sick. Momma, we can't go, there was a fire there last night. Momma, it's a holiday today, no school, they told me.

But never a direct protest, never rebellion. I think of our others in their three-four-year-oldness—the explosions, the tempers, the denunciations, the demands—and I feel suddenly ill. I put the iron down. What in me demanded that goodness in her? And what was the cost, the cost to her of such goodness?

The old man living in the back once said in his gentle way: "You should smile at Emily more when you look at her." What *was* in my face when I looked at her? I loved her. There were all the acts of love.

It was only with the others I remembered what he said, and it was the face of joy, and not of care or tightness or worry I turned to them—too late for Emily. She does not smile easily, let alone almost always as her brothers and sisters do. Her face is closed and somber, but when she wants, how fluid. You must have seen it in her pantomimes, you spoke of her rare gift for comedy on the stage that rouses laughter out of the audience so dear they applaud and applaud and do not want to let her go.

Where does it come from, that comedy? There was none of it in her when she came back to me that second time, after I had had to send her away again. She had a new daddy now to learn to love, and I think perhaps it was a better time.

Except when we left her alone nights, telling ourselves she was old enough.  20

"Can't you go some other time, Mommy, like tomorrow?" she would ask. "Will it be just a little while you'll be gone? Do you promise?"

The time we came back, the front door open, the clock on the floor in the hall. She rigid awake. "It wasn't just a little while. I didn't cry. Three times I called you, just three times, and then I ran downstairs to open the door so you could come faster. The clock talked loud. I threw it away, it scared me what it talked."

She said the clock talked loud again that night I went to the hospital to have Susan. She was delirious with the fever that comes from red measles, but she was fully conscious all the week I was gone and the week after we were home when she could not come near the new baby or me.

She did not get well. She stayed skeleton thin, not wanting to eat, and night after night she had nightmares. She would call for me, and I would rouse from exhaustion to sleepily call back: "You're all right, darling, go to sleep, it's just a dream," and if she still called, in a sterner voice, "now go to sleep, Emily, there's nothing to hurt you." Twice, only twice, when I had to get up for Susan anyhow, I went in to sit with her.

Now when it is too late (as if she would let me hold and comfort her like I do the others) I get up and go to her at once at her moan or restless stirring. "Are you awake, Emily? Can I get you something?" And the answer is always the same: "No, I'm all right, go back to sleep, Mother."

They persuaded me at the clinic to send her away to a convalescent home in the country where "she can have the kind of food and care you can't manage for her, and you'll be free to concentrate on the new baby." They still send children to that place. I see pictures on the society page of sleek young women planning affairs to raise money for it, or dancing at the affairs, or decorating Easter eggs or filling Christmas stockings for the children.

They never have a picture of the children so I do not know if the girls still wear those gigantic red bows and the ravaged looks on the every other Sunday when parents can come to visit "unless otherwise notified"—as we were notified the first six weeks.

Oh it is a handsome place, green lawns and tall trees and fluted flower beds. High up on the balconies of each cottage the children stand, the girls in their red bows and white dresses, the boys in white suits and giant red ties. The parents stand below shrieking up to be heard and the children shriek down to be heard, and between them the invisible wall: "Not to Be Contaminated by Parental Germs or Physical Affection."

There was a tiny girl who always stood hand in hand with Emily. Her parents never came. One visit she was gone. "They moved her to Rose Cottage," Emily shouted in explanation. "They don't like you to love anybody here."

She wrote once a week, the labored writing of a seven-year-old. "I am fine. How is the baby. If I write my leter nicly I will have a star. Love." There never was a star. We wrote every other day, letters she could never hold or keep but only hear read—once. "We simply do not have room for children to keep any personal possessions," they patiently explained when we pieced one Sunday's shrieking together to plead how much it would mean to Emily, who loved so to keep things, to be allowed to keep her letters and cards.

Each visit she looked frailer. "She isn't eating," they told us.

(They had runny eggs for breakfast or mush with lumps, Emily said later, I'd hold it in my mouth and not swallow. Nothing ever tasted good, just when they had chicken.)

It took us eight months to get her released home, and only the fact that she gained back so little of her seven lost pounds convinced the social worker.

I used to try to hold and love her after she came back, but her body would stay stiff, and after a while she'd push away. She ate little. Food sickened her, and I think much of life too. Oh she had physical lightness and brightness, twinkling by on skates, bouncing like a ball up and down up and down over the jump rope, skimming over the hill: but these were momentary.

She fretted about her appearance, thin and dark and foreign-looking at a 35 time when every little girl was supposed to look or thought she should look a chubby blonde replica of Shirley Temple. The doorbell sometimes rang for her, but no one seemed to come and play in the house or be a best friend. Maybe because we moved so much.

There was a boy she loved painfully through two school semesters. Months later she told me how she had taken pennies from my purse to buy him candy. "Licorice was his favorite and I brought him some every day, but he still liked Jennifer better'n me. Why, Mommy?" The kind of question for which there is no answer.

School was a worry to her. She was not glib or quick in a world where glibness and quickness were easily confused with ability to learn. To her overworked and exasperated teachers she was an overconscientious "slow learner" who kept trying to catch up and was absent entirely too often.

I let her be absent, though sometimes the illness was imaginary. How different from my now-strictness about attendance with the others. I wasn't working. We had a new baby, I was home anyhow. Sometimes, after Susan grew old enough, I would keep her home from school, too, to have them all together.

Mostly Emily had asthma, and her breathing, harsh and labored, would fill the house with a curiously tranquil sound. I would bring the two old dresser mirrors and her boxes of collections to her bed. She would select beads and single earrings, bottle tops and shells, dried flowers and pebbles, old postcards and scraps, all sorts of oddments; then she and Susan would play Kingdom, setting up landscapes and furniture, peopling them with action.

Those were the only times of peaceful companionship between her and 40 Susan. I have edged away from it, that poisonous feeling between them, that terrible balancing of hurts and needs I had to do between the two, and did so badly, those earlier years.

Oh there are conflicts between the others too, each one human, needing, demanding, hurting, taking—but only between Emily and Susan, no, Emily toward Susan that corroding resentment. It seems so obvious on the surface, yet it is not obvious. Susan, the second child, Susan, golden- and curly-haired and chubby, quick and articulate and assured, everything in appearance and manner Emily was not; Susan, not able to resist Emily's precious things, losing or sometimes clumsily breaking them; Susan telling jokes and riddles to company for applause while Emily sat silent (to say to me later: that was *my* riddle, Mother, I told it to Susan); Susan, who for all the five years' difference in age was just a year behind Emily in developing physically.

I am glad for that slow physical development that widened the difference between her and her contemporaries, though she suffered over it. She was too vulnerable for that terrible world of youthful competition, of preening and parading, of constant measuring of yourself against every other, of envy, "If I had the copper hair," "If I had that skin. . . ." She tormented herself enough about not looking like the others, there was enough of the unsureness, the having to be conscious of words before you speak, the constant caring—what are they thinking of me? without having it all magnified by the merciless physical drives.

Ronnie is calling. He is wet and I change him. It is rare there is such a cry now. That time of motherhood is almost behind me when the ear is not one's own but must always be racked and listening for the child cry, the child call. We sit for a while and I hold him, looking out over the city spread in charcoal with its soft aisles of light. "Shoogily," he breathes and curls closer. I carry him back to bed, asleep. Shoogily. A funny word, a family word, inherited from Emily, invented by her to say: comfort.

In this and other ways she leaves her seal, I say aloud. And startle at my saying it. What do I mean? What did I start to gather together, to try and make coherent? I was at the terrible, growing years. War years. I do not remember them well. I was working, there were four smaller ones now, there was not time for her. She had to help be a mother, and housekeeper, and shopper. She had to set her seal. Mornings of crisis and near hysteria trying to get lunches packed, hair combed, coats and shoes found, everyone to school or Child Care on time, the baby ready for transportation. And always the paper scribbled on by a smaller one, the book looked at by Susan then mislaid, the homework not done. Running out to that huge school where she was one, she was lost, she was a drop; suffering over the unpreparedness, stammering and unsure in her classes.

There was so little time left at night after the kids were bedded down. She    45
would struggle over books, always eating (it was in those years she developed her enormous appetite that is legendary in our family) and I would be ironing, or preparing food for the next day, or writing V-mail to Bill, or tending the baby. Sometimes, to make me laugh, or out of her despair, she would imitate happenings or types at school.

I think I said once: "Why don't you do something like this in the school amateur show?" One morning she phoned me at work, hardly understandable through the weeping: "Mother, I did it. I won, I won; they gave me first prize; they clapped and clapped and wouldn't let me go."

Now suddenly she was Somebody, and as imprisoned in her difference as she had been in anonymity.

She began to be asked to perform at other high schools, even in colleges, then at city and statewide affairs. The first one we went to, I only recognized her that first moment when thin, shy, she almost drowned herself into the curtains. Then: Was this Emily? The control, the command, the convulsing and deadly clowning, the spell, then the roaring, stamping audience, unwilling to let this rare and precious laughter out of their lives.

Afterwards: You ought to do something about her with a gift like that—but without money or knowing how, what does one do? We have left it all to her, and the gift has as often eddied inside, clogged and clotted, as been used and growing.

She is coming. She runs up the stairs two at a time with her light graceful 50
step, and I know she is happy tonight. Whatever it was that occasioned your call
did not happen today.

"Aren't you ever going to finish the ironing, Mother? Whistler painted his
mother in a rocker. I'd have to paint mine standing over an ironing board." This
is one of her communicative nights and she tells me everything and nothing as
she fixes herself a plate of food out of the icebox.

She is so lovely. Why did you want me to come in at all? Why were you concerned? She will find her way.

She starts up the stairs to bed. "Don't get me up with the rest in the morning." "But I thought you were having midterms." "Oh, those," she comes back in,
kisses me, and says quite lightly, "in a couple of years when we'll all be atom-dead
they won't matter a bit."

She has said it before. She *believes* it. But because I have been dredging the
past, and all that compounds a human being is so heavy and meaningful in me, I
cannot endure it tonight.

I will never total it all. I will never come in to say: She was a child seldom 55
smiled at. Her father left me before she was a year old. I had to work her first six
years when there was work, or I sent her home and to his relatives. There were
years she had care she hated. She was dark and thin and foreign-looking in a
world where the prestige went to blondeness and curly hair and dimples, she was
slow where glibness was prized. She was a child of anxious, not proud, love. We
were poor and could not afford for her the soil of easy growth. I was a young
mother, I was a distracted mother. There were other children pushing up,
demanding. Her younger sister seemed all that she was not. There were years she
did not want me to touch her. She kept too much in herself, her life was such she
had to keep too much in herself. My wisdom came too late. She has much to her
and probably little will come of it. She is a child of her age, of depression, of war,
of fear.

Let her be. So all that is in her will not bloom—but in how many does it?
There is still enough left to live by. Only help her to know—help make it so
there is cause for her to know—that she is more than this dress on the ironing
board, helpless before the iron.

THE CONVERSION OF THE JEWS                                           1959

*Philip Roth, called "the inventor of the Jewish novel of manners," was born in 1933 in Newark, New Jersey. He first attended college on the local campus of Rutgers University, later transferred to Bucknell, completed his M.A. degree at the University of Chicago, and served a year in the Army. He has taught fiction writing at three universities: Iowa, Pennsylvania, and Princeton. Roth's first book, the collection of stories* Goodbye, Columbus *(1955), from which we take "The Conversion of the Jews," won him immediate fame.* Portnoy's Complaint, *a sardonically comic novel of a man's sexual obsession, topped the best-seller list in 1969. Three novels about a writer named Zuckerman have been collected as* Zuckerman Bound *(1985); Zuckerman's saga is amplified in* The Counterlife

Philip Roth

*(1988) and* Deception *(1990). Roth has also written plays and literary criticism, notably* Reading Myself and Others *(1975), and* The Facts: A Novelist's Autobiography *(1988).*

"You're a real one for opening your mouth in the first place," Itzie said. "What do you open your mouth all the time for?"

"I didn't bring it up, Itz, I didn't," Ozzie said.

"What do you care about Jesus Christ for anyway?"

"I didn't bring up Jesus Christ. He did. I didn't even know what he was talking about. Jesus is historical, he kept saying. Jesus is historical." Ozzie mimicked the monumental voice of Rabbi Binder.

"Jesus was a person that lived like you and me," Ozzie continued. "That's        5 what Binder said—"

"Yeah?... So what! What do I give two cents whether he lived or not. And what do you gotta open your mouth!" Itzie Lieberman favored closed-mouthedness, especially when it came to Ozzie Freedman's questions. Mrs. Freedman had to see Rabbi Binder twice before about Ozzie's questions and this Wednesday at four-thirty would be the third time. Itzie preferred to keep *his* mother in the kitchen; he settled for behind-the-back subtleties such as gestures, faces, snarls and other less delicate barnyard noises.

"He was a real person, Jesus, but he wasn't like God, and we don't believe he is God." Slowly, Ozzie was explaining Rabbi Binder's position to Itzie, who had been absent from Hebrew School the previous afternoon.

"The Catholics," Itzie said helpfully, "they believe in Jesus Christ, that he's God." Itzie Lieberman used "the Catholics" in its broadest sense—to include the Protestants.

Ozzie received Itzie's remark with a tiny head bob, as though it were a footnote, and went on. "His mother was Mary, and his father probably was Joseph," Ozzie said. "But the New Testament says his real father was God."

"His *real* father?"

"Yeah," Ozzie said, "that's the big thing, his father's supposed to be God." 10

"Bull."

"That's what Rabbi Binder says, that it's impossible—"

"Sure it's impossible. That stuff's all bull. To have a baby you gotta get laid," Itzie theologized. "Mary hadda get laid."

"That's what Binder says: 'The only way a woman can have a baby is to have 15 intercourse with a man.'"

"He said *that*, Ozz?" For a moment it appeared that Itzie had put the theological question aside. "He said that, intercourse?" A little curled smile shaped itself in the lower half of Itzie's face like a pink mustache. "What you guys do, Ozz, you laugh or something?"

"I raised my hand."

"Yeah? Whatja say?"

"That's when I asked the question."

Itzie's face lit up. "Whatja ask about—intercourse?" 20

"No, I asked the question about God, how if He could create the heaven and earth in six days, and make all the animals and the fish and the light in six days—the light especially, that's what always gets me, that He could make the light. Making fish and animals, that's pretty good—"

"That's damn good." Itzie's appreciation was honest but unimaginative: it was as though God had just pitched a one-hitter.

"But making light . . . I mean when you think about it, it's really something," Ozzie said. "Anyway, I asked Binder if He could make all that in six days, and He could *pick* the six days He wanted right out of nowhere, why couldn't He let a woman have a baby without having intercourse?"

"You said intercourse, Ozz, to Binder?"

"Yeah."

"Right in class?" 25

"Yeah."

Itzie smacked the side of his head.

"I mean, no kidding around," Ozzie said, "that'd really be nothing. After all that other stuff, that'd practically be nothing."

Itzie considered a moment. "What'd Binder say?" 30

"He started all over again explaining how Jesus was historical and how he lived like you and me but he wasn't God. So I said I understood that. What I wanted to know was different."

What Ozzie wanted to know was always different. The first time he had wanted to know how Rabbi Binder could call the Jews "The Chosen People" if the Declaration of Independence claimed all men to be created equal. Rabbi Binder tried to distinguish for him between political equality and spiritual legitimacy, but what Ozzie wanted to know, he insisted vehemently, was different. That was the first time his mother had to come.

Then there was the plane crash. Fifty-eight people had been killed in a plane crash at La Guardia°. In studying a casualty list in the newspaper his mother had discovered among the list of those dead eight Jewish names (his grandmother had nine but she counted Miller as a Jewish name); because of the eight she said the plane crash was "a tragedy." During free-discussion time on Wednesday Ozzie had brought to Rabbi Binder's attention this matter of "some of his relations" always picking out the Jewish names. Rabbi Binder had begun to explain cultural unity and some other things when Ozzie stood up at his seat and said that what he wanted to know was different. Rabbi Binder insisted that he sit down and it was then that Ozzie shouted that he wished all fifty-eight were Jews. That was the second time his mother came.

"And he kept explaining about Jesus being historical, and so I kept asking him. No kidding, Itz, he was trying to make me look stupid."

"So what he finally do?"                                                35

"Finally he starts screaming that I was deliberately simple-minded and a wise guy, and that my mother had to come, and this was the last time. And that I'd never get bar-mitzvahed if he could help it. Then, Itz, then he starts talking in that voice like a statue, real slow and deep, and he says that I better think over what I said about the Lord. He told me to go to his office and think it over." Ozzie leaned his body towards Itzie. "Itz, I thought it over for a solid hour, and now I'm convinced God could do it."

Ozzie had planned to confess his latest transgression to his mother as soon as she came home from work. But it was a Friday night in November and already dark, and when Mrs. Freedman came through the door she tossed off her coat, kissed Ozzie quickly on the face, and went to the kitchen table to light the three yellow candles, two for the Sabbath and one for Ozzie's father.

When his mother lit the candles she would move her two arms slowly towards her, dragging them through the air, as though persuading people whose minds were half made up. And her eyes would get glassy with tears. Even when his father was alive Ozzie remembered that her eyes had gotten glassy, so it didn't have anything to do with his dying. It had something to do with lighting the candles.

As she touched the flaming match to the unlit wick of a Sabbath candle, the phone rang, and Ozzie, standing only a foot from it, plucked it off the receiver and held it muffled to his chest. When his mother lit candles Ozzie felt there should be no noise; even breathing, if you could manage it, should be softened. Ozzie pressed the phone to his breast and watched his mother dragging whatever she was dragging, and he felt his own eyes get glassy. His mother was a round,

La Guardia: a New York City airport.

tired, gray-haired penguin of a woman whose gray skin had begun to feel the tug of gravity and the weight of her own history. Even when she was dressed up she didn't look like a chosen person. But when she lit candles she looked like something better; like a woman who knew momentarily that God could do anything.

After a few mysterious minutes she was finished. Ozzie hung up the phone 40 and walked to the kitchen table where she was beginning to lay the two places for the four-course Sabbath meal. He told her that she would have to see Rabbi Binder next Wednesday at four-thirty, and then he told her why. For the first time in their life together she hit Ozzie across the face with her hand.

All through the chopped liver and chicken soup part of the dinner Ozzie cried; he didn't have any appetite for the rest.

On Wednesday, in the largest of the three basement classrooms of the synagogue, Rabbi Marvin Binder, a tall, handsome, broad-shouldered man of thirty with thick strong-fibered black hair, removed his watch from his pocket and saw that it was four o'clock. At the rear of the room Yakov Blotnik, the seventy-one-year-old custodian, slowly polished the large window, mumbling to himself, unaware that it was four o'clock or six o'clock, Monday or Wednesday. To most of the students Yakov Blotnik's mumbling, along with his brown curly beard, scythe nose, and two heel-trailing black cats, made of him an object of wonder, a foreigner, a relic, towards whom they were alternately fearful and disrespectful. To Ozzie the mumbling had always seemed a monotonous, curious prayer; what made it curious was that old Blotnik had been mumbling so steadily for so many years, Ozzie suspected he had memorized the prayers and forgotten all about God.

"It is now free-discussion time," Rabbi Binder said. "Feel free to talk about any Jewish matter at all—religion, family, politics, sports—"

There was silence. It was a gusty, clouded November afternoon and it did not seem as though there ever was or could be a thing called baseball. So nobody this week said a word about that hero from the past, Hank Greenberg—which limited free discussion considerably.

And the soul-battering Ozzie Freedman had just received from Rabbi Binder 45 had imposed its limitation. When it was Ozzie's turn to read aloud from the Hebrew book the rabbi had asked him petulantly why he didn't read more rapidly. He was showing no progress. Ozzie said he could read faster but that if he did he was sure not to understand what he was reading. Nevertheless, at the rabbi's repeated suggestion Ozzie tried, and showed a great talent, but in the midst of a long passage he stopped short and said he didn't understand a word he was reading, and started in again at a drag-footed pace. Then came the soul-battering.

Consequently when free-discussion time rolled around none of the students felt too free. The rabbi's invitation was answered only by the mumbling of feeble old Blotnik.

"Isn't there anything at all you would like to discuss?" Rabbi Binder asked again, looking at his watch. "No questions or comments?"

There was a small grumble from the third row. The rabbi requested that Ozzie rise and give the rest of the class the advantage of his thought.

Ozzie rose. "I forget it now," he said, and sat down in his place.

Rabbi Binder advanced a seat towards Ozzie and poised himself on the edge 50
of the desk. It was Itzie's desk and the rabbi's frame only a dagger's-length away
from his face snapped him to sitting attention.

"Stand up again, Oscar," Rabbi Binder said calmly, "and try to assemble your
thoughts."

Ozzie stood up. All his classmates turned in their seats and watched as he
gave an unconvincing scratch to his forehead.

"I can't assemble any," he announced, and plunked himself down.

"Stand up!" Rabbi Binder advanced from Itzie's desk to the one directly in
front of Ozzie; when the rabbinical back was turned Ozzie gave it five-fingers off
the tip of his nose, causing a small titter in the room. Rabbi Binder was too
absorbed in squelching Ozzie's nonsense once and for all to bother with titters.
"Stand up, Oscar. What's your question about?"

Ozzie pulled a word out of the air. It was the handiest word. "Religion." 55

"Oh, now you remember?"

"Yes."

"What is it?"

Trapped, Ozzie blurted the first thing that came to him. "Why can't He
make anything He wants to make!"

As Rabbi Binder prepared an answer, a final answer, Itzie, ten feet behind 60
him, raised one finger on his left hand, gestured it meaningfully towards the
rabbi's back, and brought the house down.

Binder twisted quickly to see what had happened and in the midst of the
commotion Ozzie shouted into the rabbi's back what he couldn't have shouted to
his face. It was a loud, toneless sound that had the timbre of something stored
inside for about six days.

"You don't know! You don't know anything about God!"

The rabbi spun back towards Ozzie. "What?"

"You don't know—you don't—"

"Apologize, Oscar, apologize!" It was a threat. 65

"You don't—"

Rabbi Binder's hand flicked out at Ozzie's cheek. Perhaps it had only been
meant to clamp the boy's mouth shut, but Ozzie ducked and the palm caught him
squarely on the nose.

The blood came in a short, red spurt on to Ozzie's shirt front.

The next moment was all confusion. Ozzie screamed, "You bastard, you bastard!" and broke for the classroom door. Rabbi Binder lurched a step backwards,
as though his own blood had started flowing violently in the opposite direction,
then gave a clumsy lurch forward and bolted out the door after Ozzie. The class
followed after the rabbi's huge blue-suited back, and before old Blotnik could turn
from his window, the room was empty and everyone was headed full speed up the
three flights leading to the roof.

If one should compare the light of the day to the life of man: sunrise to birth; 70
sunset—the dropping down over the edge—to death; then as Ozzie Freedman

wiggled through the trapdoor of the synagogue roof, his feet kicking backwards bronco-style at Rabbi Binder's outstretched arms—at that moment the day was fifty years old. As a rule, fifty or fifty-five reflects accurately the age of late afternoons in November, for it is in that month, during those hours, that one's awareness of light seems no longer a matter of seeing, but of hearing: light begins clicking away. In fact, as Ozzie locked shut the trapdoor in the rabbi's face, the sharp click of the bolt into the lock might momentarily have been mistaken for the sound of the heavier gray that had just throbbed through the sky.

With all his weight Ozzie kneeled on the locked door; any instant he was certain that Rabbi Binder's shoulder would fling it open, splintering the wood into shrapnel and catapulting his body into the sky. But the door did not move and below him he heard only the rumble of feet, first loud and then dim, like thunder rolling away.

A question shot through his brain. "Can this be *me?*" For a thirteen-year-old who had just labeled his religious leader a bastard, twice, it was not an improper question. Louder and louder the question came to him—"Is it me? Is it me?"—until he discovered himself no longer kneeling, but racing crazily towards the edge of the roof, his eyes crying, his throat screaming, and his arms flying everywhichway as though not his own.

"Is it me? Is it me ME ME ME ME! It has to be me—but is it!"

It is the question a thief must ask himself the night he jimmies open his first window, and it is said to be the question with which bridegrooms quiz themselves before the altar.

In the few wild seconds it took Ozzie's body to propel him to the edge of the  75
roof, his self-examination began to grow fuzzy. Gazing down at the street, he became confused as to the problem beneath the question: was it, is-it-me-who-called-Binder-a-bastard? or, is-it-me-prancing-around-on-the-roof? However, the scene below settled all, for there is an instant in any action when whether it is you or somebody else is academic. The thief crams the money in his pockets and scoots out the window. The bridegroom signs the hotel register for two. And the boy on the roof finds a streetful of people gaping at him, necks stretched backwards, faces up, as though he were the ceiling of the Hayden Planetarium. Suddenly you know it's you.

"Oscar! Oscar Freedman!" A voice rose from the center of the crowd, a voice that, could it have been seen, would have looked like the writing on a scroll. "Oscar Freedman, get down from there. Immediately!" Rabbi Binder was pointing one arm stiffly up at him; and at the end of that arm, one finger aimed menacingly. It was the attitude of a dictator, but one—the eyes confessed all—whose personal valet had spit neatly in his face.

Ozzie didn't answer. Only for a blink's length did he look towards Rabbi Binder. Instead his eyes began to fit together the world beneath him, to sort out people from places, friends from enemies, participants from spectators. In little jagged starlike clusters his friends stood around Rabbi Binder, who was still pointing. The topmost point on a star compounded not of angels but of five adolescent boys was Itzie. What a world it was, with those stars below, Rabbi Binder below . . .

Ozzie, who a moment earlier hadn't been able to control his own body, started to feel the meaning of the word control: he felt Peace and he felt Power.

"Oscar Freedman, I'll give you three to come down."

Few dictators give their subjects three to do anything; but, as always, Rabbi Binder only looked dictatorial.

"Are you ready, Oscar?"

Ozzie nodded his head yes, although he had no intention in the world—the lower one or the celestial one he'd just entered—of coming down even if Rabbi Binder should give him a million.

"All right then," said Rabbi Binder. He ran a hand through his black Samson hair as though it were the gesture prescribed for uttering the first digit. Then, with his other hand cutting a circle out of the small piece of sky around him, he spoke. "One!"

There was no thunder. On the contrary, at that moment, as though "one" was the cue for which he had been waiting, the world's least thunderous person appeared on the synagogue steps. He did not so much come out the synagogue door as lean out, onto the darkening air. He clutched at the doorknob with one hand and looked up at the roof.

"Oy!"

Yakov Blotnik's old mind hobbled slowly, as if on crutches, and though he couldn't decide precisely what the boy was doing on the roof, he knew it wasn't good—that is, it wasn't-good-for-the-Jews. For Yakov Blotnik life had fractionated itself simply: things were either good-for-the-Jews or no-good-for-the-Jews.

He smacked his free hand to his in-sucked cheek, gently. "Oy, Gut!" And then quickly as he was able, he jacked down his head and surveyed the street. There was Rabbi Binder (like a man at an auction with only three dollars in his pocket, he had just delivered a shaky "Two!"); there were the students, and that was all. So far it-wasn't-so-bad-for-the-Jews. But the boy had to come down immediately, before anybody saw. The problem: how to get the boy off the roof?

Anybody who has ever had a cat on the roof knows how to get him down. You call the fire department. Or first you call the operator and you ask her for the fire department. And the next thing there is great jamming of brakes and clanging of bells and shouting of instructions. And then the cat is off the roof. You do the same thing to get a boy off the roof.

That is, you do the same thing if you are Yakov Blotnik and you once had a cat on the roof.

When the engines, all four of them, arrived, Rabbi Binder had four times given Ozzie the count of three. The big hook-and-ladder swung around the corner and one of the firemen leaped from it, plunging headlong towards the yellow fire hydrant in front of the synagogue. With a huge wrench he began to unscrew the top nozzle. Rabbi Binder raced over to him and pulled at his shoulder.

"There's no fire . . . ."

The fireman mumbled back over his shoulder and, heatedly, continued working at the nozzle.

"But there's no fire, there's no fire ..." Binder shouted. When the fireman mumbled again, the rabbi grasped his face with both his hands and pointed it up at the roof.

To Ozzie it looked as though Rabbi Binder was trying to tug the fireman's head out of his body, like a cork from a bottle. He had to giggle at the picture they made: it was a family portrait—rabbi in black skullcap, fireman in red hat, and the little yellow hydrant squatting beside like a kid brother, bareheaded. From the edge of the roof Ozzie waved at the portrait, a one-handed, flapping, mocking wave; in doing it his right foot slipped from under him. Rabbi Binder covered his eyes with his hands.

Firemen work fast. Before Ozzie had even regained his balance, a big, round, yellowed net was being held on the synagogue lawn. The firemen who held it looked up at Ozzie with stern, feelingless faces.

One of the firemen turned his head towards Rabbi Binder. "What, is the kid nuts or something?"  95

Rabbi Binder unpeeled his hands from his eyes, slowly, painfully, as if they were tape. Then he checked: nothing on the sidewalk, no dents in the net.

"Is he gonna jump, or what?" the fireman shouted.

In a voice not at all like a statue, Rabbi Binder finally answered. "Yes, yes, I think so ... He's been threatening to ..."

Threatening to? Why, the reason he was on the roof, Ozzie remembered, was to get away; he hadn't even thought about jumping. He had just run to get away, and the truth was that he hadn't really headed for the roof as much as he'd been chased there.

"What's his name, the kid?"  100

"Freedman," Rabbi Binder answered. "Oscar Freedman."

The fireman looked up at Ozzie. "What is it with you, Oscar? You gonna jump, or what?"

Ozzie did not answer. Frankly, the question had just arisen.

"Look, Oscar, if you're gonna jump, jump—and if you're not gonna jump, don't jump. But don't waste our time, willya?"

Ozzie looked at the fireman and then at Rabbi Binder. He wanted to see  105
Rabbi Binder cover his eyes one more time.

"I'm going to jump."

And then he scampered around the edge of the roof to the corner, where there was no net below, and he flapped his arms at his sides, swishing the air and smacking his palms to his trousers on the downbeat. He began screaming like some kind of engine, "Wheeeee ... wheeeeee," and leaning way out over the edge with the upper half of his body. The firemen whipped around to cover the ground with the net. Rabbi Binder mumbled a few words to Somebody and covered his eyes. Everything happened quickly, jerkily, as in a silent movie. The crowd, which had arrived with the fire engines, gave out a long, Fourth-of-July fireworks oooh-aahhh. In the excitement no one had paid the crowd much heed, except, of course, Yakov Blotnik, who swung from the doorknob counting heads.

"Fier und tsvantsik . . . finf und tsvantsik . . . Oy, Gut!"° It wasn't like this with the cat.

Rabbi Binder peeked through his fingers, checked the sidewalk and net. Empty. But there was Ozzie racing to the other corner. The firemen raced with him but were unable to keep up. Whenever Ozzie wanted to he might jump and splatter himself upon the sidewalk, and by the time the firemen scooted to the spot all they could do with their net would be to cover the mess.

"Wheeeee . . . wheeeee . . . "

"Hey, Oscar," the winded fireman yelled, "What the hell is this, a game or 110 something?"

"Wheeeee . . . wheeeee . . . "

"Hey, Oscar—"

But he was off now to the other corner, flapping his wings fiercely. Rabbi Binder couldn't take it any longer—the fire engines from nowhere, the screaming suicidal boy, the net. He fell to his knees, exhausted, and with his hands curled together in front of his chest like a little dome, he pleaded, "Oscar, stop it, Oscar. Don't jump, Oscar. Please come down . . . Please don't jump."

And further back in the crowd a single voice, a single young voice, shouted a lone word to the boy on the roof.

"Jump!"                                                                                                           115

It was Itzie. Ozzie momentarily stopped flapping.

"Go ahead, Ozz—jump!" Itzie broke off his point of the star and courageously, with the inspiration not of a wise-guy but of a disciple, stood alone. "Jump, Ozz, jump!"

Still on his knees, his hands still curled, Rabbi Binder twisted his body back. He looked at Itzie, then, agonizingly, back to Ozzie.

"Oscar, Don't Jump! Please, Don't Jump . . . please please . . . "

"Jump!" This time it wasn't Itzie but another point of the star. By the time 120 Mrs. Freedman arrived to keep her four-thirty appointment with Rabbi Binder, the whole little upside down heaven was shouting and pleading for Ozzie to jump, and Rabbi Binder no longer was pleading with him not to jump, but was crying into the dome of his hands.


Understandably Mrs. Freedman couldn't figure out what her son was doing on the roof. So she asked.

"Ozzie, my Ozzie, what are you doing? My Ozzie, what is it?"

Ozzie stopped wheeeeeing and slowed his arms down to a cruising flap, the kind birds use in soft winds, but he did not answer. He stood against the low, clouded, darkening sky—light clicked down swiftly now, as on a small gear—flapping softly and gazing down at the small bundle of a woman who was his mother.

"What are you doing, Ozzie?" She turned towards the kneeling Rabbi Binder and rushed so close that only a paper-thickness of dusk lay between her stomach and his shoulders.

*Fier . . . Gut!:* "Twenty-four . . . twenty-five . . . Oh, God!"

"What is my baby doing?"

Rabbi Binder gaped up at her but he too was mute. All that moved was the dome of his hands; it shook back and forth like a weak pulse.

"Rabbi, get him down! He'll kill himself. Get him down, my only baby . . . "

"I can't," Rabbi Binder said, "I can't . . . " and he turned his handsome head towards the crowd of boys behind him. "It's them. Listen to them."

And for the first time Mrs. Freedman saw the crowd of boys, and she heard what they were yelling.

"He's doing it for them. He won't listen to me. It's them." Rabbi Binder spoke like one in a trance.

"For them?"

"Yes."

"Why for them?"

"They want him to . . . "

Mrs. Freedman raised her two arms upward as though she were conducting the sky. "For them he's doing it!" And then in a gesture older than pyramids, older than prophets and floods, her arms came slapping down to her sides. "A martyr I have. Look!" She tilted her head to the roof. Ozzie was still flapping softly. "My martyr."

"Oscar, come down, *please*," Rabbi Binder groaned.

In a startlingly even voice Mrs. Freedman called to the boy on the roof. "Ozzie, come down, Ozzie. Don't be a martyr, my baby."

As though it were a litany, Rabbi Binder repeated her words. "Don't be a martyr, my baby. Don't be a martyr."

"Gawhead, Ozz—*be* a Martin!" It was Itzie. "Be a Martin, be a Martin," and all the voices joined in singing for Martindom, whatever *it* was. "Be a Martin, be a Martin . . . "

Somehow when you're on a roof the darker it gets the less you can hear. All Ozzie knew was that two groups wanted two new things; his friends were spirited and musical about what they wanted; his mother and the rabbi were even-toned, chanting, about what they didn't want. The rabbi's voice was without tears now and so was his mother's.

The big net stared up at Ozzie like a sightless eye. The big, clouded sky pushed down. From beneath it looked like a gray corrugated board. Suddenly, looking up into that unsympathetic sky, Ozzie realized all the strangeness of what these people, his friends, were asking: they wanted him to jump, to kill himself; they were singing about it now—it made them that happy. And there was an even greater strangeness: Rabbi Binder was on his knees, trembling. If there was a question to be asked now it was not "Is it me?" but rather "Is it us? . . . Is it us?"

Being on the roof, it turned out, was a serious thing. If he jumped would the singing become dancing? Would it? What would jumping stop? Yearningly, Ozzie wished he could rip open the sky, plunge his hands through, and pull out the sun; and on the sun, like a coin, would be stamped JUMP or DON'T JUMP.

Ozzie's knees rocked and sagged a little under him as though they were set-ting him for a dive. His arms tightened, stiffened, froze, from shoulders to finger-nails. He felt as if each part of his body were going to vote as to whether he should kill himself or not—and each part as though it were independent of *him*.

The light took an unexpected click down and the new darkness, like a gag, hushed the friends singing for this and the mother and rabbi chanting for that.

Ozzie stopped counting votes, and in a curiously high voice, like one who 145 wasn't prepared for speech, he spoke.

"Mamma?"

"Yes, Oscar."

"Mamma, get down on your knees, like Rabbi Binder."

"Oscar—"

"Get down on your knees," he said, "or I'll jump." 150

Ozzie heard a whimper, then a quick rustling, and when he looked down where his mother had stood he saw the top of a head and beneath that a circle of dress. She was kneeling beside Rabbi Binder.

He spoke again. "Everybody kneel." There was the sound of everybody kneeling.

Ozzie looked around. With one hand he pointed towards the synagogue entrance. "Make *him* kneel."

There was a noise, not of kneeling, but of body-and-cloth stretching. Ozzie could hear Rabbi Binder saying in a gruff whisper, ". . . or he'll *kill* himself," and when next he looked there was Yakov Blotnik off the doorknob and for the first time in his life upon his knees in the Gentile posture of prayer.

As for the firemen—it is not as difficult as one might imagine to hold a net 155 taut while you are kneeling.

Ozzie looked around again; and then he called to Rabbi Binder.

"Rabbi?"

"Yes, Oscar."

"Rabbi Binder, do you believe in God?"

"Yes." 160

"Do you believe God can do Anything?" Ozzie leaned his head out into the darkness. "Anything?"

"Oscar, I think—"

"Tell me you believe God can do Anything."

There was a second's hesitation. Then: "God can do Anything."

"Tell me you believe God can make a child without intercourse." 165

"He can."

"Tell me!"

"God," Rabbi Binder admitted, "can make a child without intercourse."

"Mamma, you tell me."

"God can make a child without intercourse," his mother said. 170

"Make *him* tell me." There was no doubt who *him* was.

In a few moments Ozzie heard an old comical voice say something to the increasing darkness about God.

Next, Ozzie made everybody say it. And then he made them all say they believed in Jesus Christ—first one at a time, then all together.

When the catechizing was through it was the beginning of evening. From the street it sounded as if the boy on the roof might have sighed.

"Ozzie?" A woman's voice dared to speak. "You'll come down now?" 175

There was no answer, but the woman waited, and when a voice finally did speak it was thin and crying, and exhausted as that of an old man who has just finished pulling the bells.

"Mamma, don't you see—you shouldn't hit me. He shouldn't hit me. You shouldn't hit me about God, Mamma. You should never hit anybody about God—"

"Ozzie, please come down now."

"Promise me, promise me you'll never hit anybody about God."

He had asked only his mother, but for some reason everyone kneeling in the 180 street promised he would never hit anybody about God.

Once again there was silence.

"I can come down now, Mamma," the boy on the roof finally said. He turned his head both ways as though checking the traffic lights. "Now I can come down . . ."

And he did, right into the center of the yellow net that glowed in the evening's edge like an overgrown halo.

## James Thurber

THE CATBIRD SEAT                                                           1945

*James Thurber (1894–1961), a humorist sometimes mentioned in the same breath with Mark Twain, was born in Columbus, Ohio, and took a degree from Ohio State University. As a young man he gravitated to New York, where he became a prolific contributor to* The New Yorker *along with E. B. White, his collaborator on a book-length spoof of popular psychology,* Is Sex Necessary? *(1929). Despite weak eyesight, Thurber gained fame as a cartoonist known for his childlike drawings of timid little men and hound dogs with floppy ears. As blindness descended in his last years, Thurber drew less and less, wrote more and more. Besides essays and stories, his works include a fable for children,* The Thirteen Clocks *(1950); a memoir of working on* The New Yorker, The Years with Ross *(1959); and with Elliott Nugent, a comedy,* The Male Animal, *produced on Broadway in 1940.*

James Thurber

Mr. Martin bought the pack of Camels on Monday night in the most crowded cigar store on Broadway. It was theater time and seven or eight men were buying cigarettes. The clerk didn't even glance at Mr. Martin, who put the pack in his overcoat pocket and went out. If any of the staff at F & S had seen him buy the cigarettes, they would have been astonished, for it was generally known that Mr. Martin did not smoke, and never had. No one saw him.

It was just a week to the day since Mr. Martin had decided to rub out Mrs. Ulgine Barrows. The term "rub out" pleased him because it suggested nothing more than the correction of an error—in this case an error of Mr. Fitweiler. Mr. Martin had spent each night of the past week working out his plan and examining it. As he walked home now he went over it again. For the hundredth time he resented the element of imprecision, the margin of guesswork that entered into the business. The project as he had worked it out was casual and bold, the risks were considerable. Something might go wrong anywhere along the line. And therein lay the cunning of his scheme. No one would ever see in it the cautious, painstaking hand of Erwin Martin, head of the filing department at F & S, of whom Mr. Fitweiler had once said, "Man is fallible but Martin isn't." No one would see his hand, that is, unless it were caught in the act.

Sitting in his apartment, drinking a glass of milk, Mr. Martin reviewed his case against Mrs. Ulgine Barrows, as he had every night for seven nights. He began at the beginning. Her quacking voice and braying laugh had first profaned the halls of F & S on March 7, 1941 (Mr. Martin had a head for dates). Old Roberts, the personnel chief, had introduced her as the newly appointed special adviser to the president of the firm, Mr. Fitweiler. The woman had appalled Mr. Martin instantly, but he hadn't shown it. He had given her his dry hand, a look of studious concentration, and a faint smile. "Well," she had said, looking at the papers on his desk, "are you lifting the oxcart out of the ditch?" As Mr. Martin recalled that moment, over his milk, he squirmed slightly. He must keep his mind on her crimes as a special adviser, not on her peccadillos as a personality. This he found difficult to do, in spite of entering an objection and sustaining it. The faults of the woman as a woman kept chattering on in his mind like an unruly witness. She had, for almost two years now, baited him. In the halls, in the elevator, even in his own office, into which she romped now and then like a circus horse, she was constantly shouting out these silly questions at him. "Are you lifting the oxcart out of the ditch? Are you tearing up the pea patch? Are you hollering down the rain barrel? Are you scraping around the bottom of the pickle barrel? Are you sitting in the catbird seat?"

It was Joey Hart, one of Mr. Martin's two assistants, who had explained what the gibberish meant. "She must be a Dodger fan°," he had said. "Red Barber announces the Dodger games over the radio and he uses those expressions—picked 'em up down South." Joey had gone on to explain one or two. "Tearing up the pea patch" meant going on a rampage; "sitting in the catbird seat" meant sitting pretty, like a batter with three balls and no strikes on him. Mr. Martin

Dodger fan: At the time of this story, the Dodgers were the Brooklyn Dodgers.

dismissed all this with an effort. It had been annoying, it had driven him near to distraction, but he was too solid a man to be moved to murder by anything so childish. It was fortunate, he reflected as he passed on to the important charges against Mrs. Barrows, that he had stood up under it so well. He had maintained always an outward appearance of polite tolerance. "Why, I even believe you like the woman," Miss Paird, his other assistant, had once said to him. He had simply smiled.

A gavel rapped in Mr. Martin's mind and the case proper was resumed. Mrs. 5 Ulgine Barrows stood charged with willful, blatant, and persistent attempts to destroy the efficiency and system of F & S. It was competent, material, and relevant to review her advent and rise to power. Mr. Martin had got the story from Miss Paird, who seemed always able to find things out. According to her, Mrs. Barrows had met Mr. Fitweiler at a party, where she had rescued him from the embraces of a powerfully built drunken man who had mistaken the president of F & S for a famous retired Middle Western football coach. She had led him to a sofa and somehow worked upon him a monstrous magic. The aging gentleman had jumped to the conclusion there and then that this was a woman of singular attainments, equipped to bring out the best in him and in the firm. A week later he had introduced her into F & S as his special adviser. On that day confusion got its foot in the door. After Miss Tyson, Mr. Brundage, and Mr. Bartlett had been fired and Mr. Munson had taken his hat and stalked out, mailing in his resignation later, old Roberts had been emboldened to speak to Mr. Fitweiler. He mentioned that Mr. Munson's department had been "a little disrupted" and hadn't they perhaps better resume the old system there? Mr. Fitweiler had said certainly not. He had the greatest faith in Mrs. Barrows' ideas. "They require a little seasoning, a little seasoning is all," he had added. Mr. Roberts had given it up. Mr. Martin reviewed in detail all the changes wrought by Mrs. Barrows. She had begun chipping at the cornices of the firm's edifice and now she was swinging at the foundation stones with a pickaxe.

Mr. Martin came now, in his summing up, to the afternoon of Monday, November 2, 1942—just one week ago. On that day, at 3 P.M., Mrs. Barrows had bounced into his office. "Boo!" she had yelled. "Are you scraping around the bottom of the pickle barrel?" Mr. Martin had looked at her from under his green eyeshade, saying nothing. She had begun to wander about the office, taking it in with her great, popping eyes. "Do you really need *all* these filing cabinets?" she had demanded suddenly. Mr. Martin's heart had jumped. "Each of these files," he had said, keeping his voice even, "plays an indispensable part in the system of F & S." She had brayed at him, "Well, don't tear up the pea patch!" and gone to the door. From there she had bawled, "But you sure have got a lot of fine scrap in here!" Mr. Martin could no longer doubt that the finger was on his beloved department. Her pickaxe was on the upswing, poised for the first blow. It had not come yet; he had received no blue memo from the enchanted Mr. Fitweiler bearing nonsensical instructions deriving from the obscene woman. But there was no doubt in Mr. Martin's mind that one would be forthcoming. He must act quickly. Already a precious week had gone by. Mr. Martin stood up in his living room, still holding his milk glass. "Gentlemen of the jury," he said to himself, "I demand the death penalty for this horrible person."

The next day Mr. Martin followed his routine, as usual. He polished his glasses more often and once sharpened an already sharp pencil, but not even Miss Paird noticed. Only once did he catch sight of his victim; she swept past him in the hall with a patronizing "Hi!" At five-thirty he walked home, as usual, and had a glass of milk, as usual. He had never drunk anything stronger in his life—unless you could count ginger ale. The late Sam Schlosser, the S of F & S, had praised Mr. Martin at a staff meeting several years before for his temperate habits. "Our most efficient worker neither drinks nor smokes," he had said. "The results speak for themselves." Mr. Fitweiler had sat by, nodding approval.

Mr. Martin was still thinking about that red-letter day as he walked over to the Schrafft's on Fifth Avenue near Forty-sixth Street. He got there, as he always did, at eight o'clock. He finished his dinner and the financial page of the *Sun* at a quarter to nine, as he always did. It was his custom after dinner to take a walk. This time he walked down Fifth Avenue at a casual pace. His gloved hands felt moist and warm, his forehead cold. He transferred the Camels from his overcoat to a jacket pocket. He wondered, as he did so, if they did not represent an unnecessary note of strain. Mrs. Barrows smoked only Luckies. It was his idea to puff a few puffs on a Camel (after the rubbing-out), stub it out in the ashtray holding her lipstick-stained Luckies, and thus drag a small red herring across the trail. Perhaps it was not a good idea. It would take time. He might even choke, too loudly.

Mr. Martin had never seen the house on West Twelfth Street where Mrs. Barrows lived, but he had a clear enough picture of it. Fortunately, she had bragged to everybody about her ducky first-floor apartment in the perfectly darling three-story redbrick. There would be no doorman or other attendants; just the tenants of the second and third floors. As he walked along, Mr. Martin realized that he would get there before nine-thirty. He had considered walking north on Fifth Avenue from Schrafft's to a point from which it would take him until ten o'clock to reach the house. At that hour people were less likely to be coming in or going out. But the procedure would have made an awkward loop in the straight thread of his casualness, and he had abandoned it. It was impossible to figure when people would be entering or leaving the house, anyway. There was a great risk at any hour. If he ran into anybody, he would simply have to place the rubbing-out of Ulgine Barrows in the inactive file forever. The same thing would hold true if there were someone in her apartment. In that case he would just say that he had been passing by, recognized her charming house and thought to drop in.

It was eighteen minutes after nine when Mr. Martin turned into Twelfth Street. A man passed him, and a man and a woman talking. There was no one within fifty paces when he came to the house, halfway down the block. He was up the steps and in the small vestibule in no time, pressing the bell under the card that said "Mrs. Ulgine Barrows." When the clicking in the lock started, he jumped forward against the door. He got inside fast, closing the door behind him. A bulb in a lantern hung from the hall ceiling on a chain seemed to give a monstrously bright light. There was nobody on the stair, which went up ahead of him along the left wall. A door opened down the hall in the wall on the right. He went toward it swiftly, on tiptoe.

"Well, for God's sake, look who's here!" bawled Mrs. Barrows, and her braying laugh rang out like the report of a shotgun. He rushed past her like a football tackle, bumping her. "Hey, quit shoving!" she said, closing the door behind them. They were in her living room, which seemed to Mr. Martin to be lighted by a hundred lamps. "What's after you?" she said. "You're as jumpy as a goat." He found he was unable to speak. His heart was wheezing in his throat. "I—yes," he finally brought out. She was jabbering and laughing as she started to help him off with his coat. "No, no," he said. "I'll put it there." He took it off and put it on a chair near the door. "Your hat and gloves, too," she said. "You're in a lady's house." He put his hat on top of the coat. Mrs. Barrows seemed larger than he had thought. He kept his gloves on. "I was passing by," he said. "I recognized—is there anyone here?" She laughed louder than ever. "No," she said, "we're all alone. You're as white as a sheet, you funny man. Whatever *has* come over you? I'll mix you a toddy." She started toward a door across the room. "Scotch-and-soda be all right? But say, you don't drink, do you?" She turned and gave him her amused look. Mr. Martin pulled himself together. "Scotch-and-soda will be all right," he heard himself say. He could hear her laughing in the kitchen.

Mr. Martin looked quickly around the living room for the weapon. He had counted on finding one there. There were andirons and a poker and something in a corner that looked like an Indian club. None of them would do. It couldn't be that way. He began to pace around. He came to a desk. On it lay a metal knife with an ornate handle. Would it be sharp enough? He reached for it and knocked over a small brass jar. Stamps spilled out of it and it fell to the floor with a clatter. "Hey," Mrs. Barrows yelled from the kitchen, "are you tearing up the pea patch?" Mr. Martin gave a strange laugh. Picking up the knife, he tried its point against his left wrist. It was blunt. It wouldn't do.

When Mrs. Barrows reappeared, carrying two highballs, Mr. Martin, standing there with his gloves on, became acutely conscious of the fantasy he had wrought. Cigarettes in his pocket, a drink prepared for him—it was all too grossly improbable. It was more than that; it was impossible. Somewhere in the back of his mind a vague idea stirred, sprouted. "For heaven's sake, take off those gloves," said Mrs. Barrows. "I always wear them in the house," said Mr. Martin. The idea began to bloom, strange and wonderful. She put the glasses on a coffee table in front of a sofa and sat on the sofa. "Come over here, you odd little man," she said. Mr. Martin went over and sat beside her. It was difficult getting a cigarette out of the pack of Camels, but he managed it. She held a match for him, laughing. "Well," she said, handing him his drink, "this is perfectly marvelous. You with a drink and cigarette."

Mr. Martin puffed, not too awkwardly, and took a gulp of the highball. "I drink and smoke all the time," he said. He clinked his glass against hers. "Here's nuts to that old windbag, Fitweiler," he said, and gulped again. The stuff tasted awful, but he made no grimace. "Really, Mr. Martin," she said, her voice and posture changing, "you are insulting our employer." Mrs. Barrows was now all special adviser to the president. "I am preparing a bomb," said Mr. Martin, "which will blow the old goat higher than hell." He had only had a little of the drink, which was not strong. It couldn't be that. "Do you take dope or something?" Mrs. Barrows asked coldly. "Heroin," said Mr. Martin. "I'll be coked to the gills when I bump that old buzzard off." "Mr. Martin!" she shouted, getting to her feet. "That will be all of that. You must go at once." Mr. Martin took another swallow of his drink. He tapped his cigarette out in the ashtray and put the pack of Camels on the coffee table. Then he got up. She stood glaring at him. He walked over and put on his hat and coat. "Not a word about this," he said, and laid an index finger against his lips. All Mrs. Barrows could bring out was "Really!" Mr. Martin put his hand on the doorknob. "I'm sitting in the catbird seat," he said. He stuck his tongue out at her and left. Nobody saw him go.

Mr. Martin got to his apartment, walking, well before eleven. No one saw him go in. He had two glasses of milk after brushing his teeth, and he felt elated. It wasn't tipsiness, because he hadn't been tipsy. Anyway, the walk had worn off all effects of the whiskey. He got in bed and read a magazine for a while. He was asleep before midnight.

Mr. Martin got to the office at eight-thirty the next morning, as usual. At a quarter to nine, Ulgine Barrows, who had never before arrived at work before ten, swept into his office. "I'm reporting to Mr. Fitweiler now!" she shouted. "If he turns you over to the police, it's no more than you deserve!" Mr. Martin gave her a look of shocked surprise. "I beg your pardon?" he said. Mrs. Barrows snorted and bounced out of the room, leaving Miss Paird and Joey Hart staring after her. "What's the matter with that old devil now?" asked Miss Paird. "I have no idea," said Mr. Martin, resuming his work. The other two looked at him and then at each other. Miss Paird got up and went out. She walked slowly past the closed door of Mr. Fitweiler's office. Mrs. Barrows was yelling inside, but she was not braying. Miss Paird could not hear what the woman was saying. She went back to her desk.

Forty-five minutes later, Mrs. Barrows left the president's office and went into her own, shutting the door. It wasn't until half an hour later that Mr. Fitweiler sent for Mr. Martin. The head of the filing department, neat, quiet, attentive, stood in front of the old man's desk. Mr. Fitweiler was pale and nervous. He took his glasses off and twiddled them. He made a small, bruffing sound in his throat. "Martin," he said, "you have been with us more than twenty years." "Twenty-two, sir," said Mr. Martin. "In that time," pursued the president, "your work and your—uh—manner have been exemplary." "I trust so, sir," said Mr. Martin. "I have understood, Martin," said Mr. Fitweiler, "that you have never taken a drink or smoked." "That is correct, sir," said Mr. Martin. "Ah, yes." Mr. Fitweiler polished his glasses. "You may describe what you did after leaving the office yesterday, Martin," he said. Mr. Martin allowed less than a second for his bewildered pause. "Certainly, sir," he said. "I walked home. Then I went to Schrafft's for dinner. Afterward I walked home again. I went to bed early, sir, and read a magazine for a while. I was asleep before eleven." "Ah, yes," said Mr. Fitweiler again. He was silent for a moment, searching for the proper words to say to the head of the filing department. "Mrs. Barrows," he said finally, "Mrs. Barrows has worked hard, Martin, very hard. It grieves me to report that she has suffered a severe breakdown. It has taken the form of a persecution complex accompanied by distressing hallucinations." "I am very sorry, sir," said Mr. Martin. "Mrs. Barrows is under the delusion," continued Mr. Fitweiler, "that you visited her last evening and behaved yourself in an—uh—unseemly manner." He raised his hand to silence Mr. Martin's little pained outcry. "It is the nature of these psychological diseases," Mr. Fitweiler said, "to fix upon the least likely and most innocent party as the—uh—source of persecution. These matters are not for the lay mind to grasp, Martin. I've just had my psychiatrist, Dr. Fitch, on the phone. He would not, of course, commit himself, but he made enough generalizations to substantiate my suspicions. I suggested to Mrs. Barrows when she had completed her—uh—story to me this morning, that she visit Dr. Fitch, for I suspected a condition at once. She flew, I regret to say, into a rage, and demanded—uh—requested that I call you on the carpet. You may not know, Martin, but Mrs. Barrows had planned a reorganization of your department—subject to my approval, of course, subject to my approval. This brought you, rather than anyone else, to her mind—but again that is a phenomenon for Dr. Fitch and not for us. So, Martin, I am afraid Mrs. Barrows' usefulness here is at an end." "I am dreadfully sorry, sir," said Mr. Martin.

It was at this point that the door to the office blew open with the suddenness of a gas-main explosion and Mrs. Barrows catapulted through it. "Is the little rat denying it?" she screamed. "He can't get away with that!" Mr. Martin got up and moved discreetly to a point beside Mr. Fitweiler's chair. "You drank and smoked at my apartment," she bawled at Mr. Martin, "and you know it! You called Mr. Fitweiler an old windbag and said you were going to blow him up when you got coked to the gills on your heroin!" She stopped yelling to catch her breath and a new glint came into her popping eyes. "If you weren't such a drab, ordinary little man," she said, "I'd think you'd planned it all. Sticking your tongue out, saying you were sitting in the catbird seat, because you thought no one would believe me when I told it! My God, it's really too perfect!" She brayed loudly and hysterically, and the fury was on her again. She glared at Mr. Fitweiler. "Can't you see how he has tricked us, you old fool? Can't you see his little game?" But Mr. Fitweiler had been surreptitiously pressing all the buttons under the top of his desk and employees of F & S began pouring into the room. "Stockton," said Mr. Fitweiler, "you and Fishbein will take Mrs. Barrows to her home. Mrs. Powell, you will go with them." Stockton, who had played a little football in high school, blocked Mrs. Barrows as she made for Mr. Martin. It took him and Fishbein together to force her out of the door into the hall, crowded with stenographers and office boys. She was still screaming imprecations at Mr. Martin, tangled and contradictory imprecations. The hubbub finally died out down the corridor.

"I regret that this has happened," said Mr. Fitweiler. "I shall ask you to dismiss it from your mind, Martin." "Yes, sir," said Mr. Martin, anticipating his chief's "That will be all," by moving to the door. "I will dismiss it." He went out and shut the door, and his step was light and quick in the hall. When he entered his department he had slowed down to his customary gait, and he walked quietly across the room to the W20 file, wearing a look of studious concentration.

## Eudora Welty

A VISIT OF CHARITY                                                    1941

*Eudora Welty was born in 1909 in Jackson, Mississippi, daughter of an insurance company president. She grew up within a stone's throw of the state capitol and still lives in her childhood home. Like William Faulkner, another Mississippi writer, she has stayed close to her roots for practically all her life, except for short sojourns at the University of Wisconsin, where she took her B.A., and in New York City, where she studied advertising. Although she is a novelist distinguished for* The Robber Bridegroom *(1942),* Delta Wedding *(1946),* The Ponder Heart *(1954), and* Losing Battles *(1970), many critics think her finest work is in the short-story form.* The Collected Stories

Eudora Welty

of Eudora Welty *(1980) gathers the work of more than forty years. Welty's other books include memoirs,* The Optimist's Daughter *(1972) and* One Writer's Beginnings *(1984), and* The Eye of the Story *(1977), a book of sympathetic criticism on the fiction of other writers, including Willa Cather, Virginia Woolf, Katherine Anne Porter, and Isak Dinesen.*

It was mid-morning—a very cold, bright day. Holding a potted plant before her, a girl of fourteen jumped off the bus in front of the Old Ladies' Home, on the outskirts of town. She wore a red coat, and her straight yellow hair was hanging down loose from the pointed white cap all the little girls were wearing that year. She stopped for a moment beside one of the prickly dark shrubs with which the city had beautified the Home, and then proceeded slowly toward the building, which was of whitewashed brick and reflected the winter sunlight like a block of ice. As she walked vaguely up the steps she shifted the small pot from hand to hand; then she had to set it down and remove her mittens before she could open the heavy door.

"I'm a Campfire Girl. . . . I have to pay a visit to some old lady," she told the nurse at the desk. This was a woman in a white uniform who looked as if she were cold; she had close-cut hair which stood up on the very top of her head exactly like a sea wave. Marian, the little girl, did not tell her that this visit would give her a minimum of only three points in her score.

"Acquainted with any of our residents?" asked the nurse. She lifted one eyebrow and spoke like a man.

"With any old ladies? No—but—that is, any of them will do," Marian stammered. With her free hand she pushed her hair behind her ears, as she did when it was time to study Science.

The nurse shrugged and rose. "You have a nice *multiflora cineraria*° there," she   5
remarked as she walked ahead down the hall of closed doors to pick out an old lady.

There was loose, bulging linoleum on the floor. Marian felt as if she were walking on the waves, but the nurse paid no attention to it. There was a smell in the hall like the interior of a clock. Everything was silent until, behind one of the doors, an old lady of some kind cleared her throat like a sheep bleating. This decided the nurse. Stopping in her tracks, she first extended her arm, bent her elbow, and leaned forward from the hips—all to examine the watch strapped to her wrist; then she gave a loud double-rap on the door.

"There are two in each room," the nurse remarked over her shoulder.

"Two what?" asked Marian without thinking. The sound like a sheep's bleating almost made her turn around and run back.

One old woman was pulling the door open in short, gradual jerks, and when she saw the nurse a strange smile forced her old face dangerously awry. Marian, suddenly propelled by the strong, impatient arm of the nurse, saw next the side-face of another old woman, even older, who was lying flat in bed with a cap on and a counterpane° drawn up to her chin.

"Visitor," said the nurse, and after one more shove she was off up the hall.   10

Marian stood tongue-tied; both hands held the potted plant. The old woman, still with that terrible, square smile (which was a smile of welcome) stamped on her bony face, was waiting. . . . Perhaps she said something. The old woman in bed said nothing at all, and she did not look around.

Suddenly Marian saw a hand, quick as a bird claw, reach up in the air and pluck the white cap off her head. At the same time, another claw to match drew her all the way into the room, and the next moment the door closed behind her.

"My, my, my," said the old lady at her side.

Marian stood enclosed by a bed, a washstand and a chair; the tiny room had altogether too much furniture. Everything smelled wet—even the bare floor. She held on to the back of the chair, which was wicker and felt soft and damp. Her heart beat more and more slowly, her hands got colder and colder, and she could not hear whether the old women were saying anything or not. She could not see them very clearly. How dark it was! The window shade was down, and the only

---

*multiflora cineraria*: a popular house plant with heart-shaped leaves and clusters of bright flowers.
*counterpane*: bedspread.

door was shut. Marian looked at the ceiling. . . . It was like being caught in a robbers' cave, just before one was murdered.

"Did you come to be our little girl for a while?" the first robber asked.

Then something was snatched from Marian's hand—the little potted plant.

"Flowers!" screamed the old woman. She stood holding the pot in an undecided way. "Pretty flowers," she added.

Then the old woman in bed cleared her throat and spoke. "They are not pretty," she said, still without looking around, but very distinctly.

Marian suddenly pitched against the chair and sat down in it.

"Pretty flowers," the first old woman insisted. "Pretty—pretty . . . "

Marian wished she had the little pot back for just a moment—she had forgotten to look at the plant herself before giving it away. What did it look like?

"Stinkweeds," said the other old woman sharply. She had a bunchy white forehead and red eyes like a sheep. Now she turned them toward Marian. The fogginess seemed to rise in her throat again, and she bleated, "Who—are—you?"

To her surprise, Marian could not remember her name. "I'm a Campfire Girl," she said finally.

"Watch out for the germs," said the old woman like a sheep, not addressing anyone.

"One came out last month to see us," said the first old woman.

A sheep or a germ? wondered Marian dreamily, holding on to the chair.

"Did not!" cried the other old woman.

"Did so! Read to us out of the Bible, and we enjoyed it!" screamed the first.

"Who enjoyed it!" said the woman in bed. Her mouth was unexpectedly small and sorrowful, like a pet's.

"We enjoyed it," insisted the other. "You enjoyed it—I enjoyed it."

"We all enjoyed it," said Marian, without realizing that she had said a word.

The first old woman had just finished putting the potted plant high, high on the top of the wardrobe, where it could hardly be seen from below. Marian wondered how she had ever succeeded in placing it there, how she could ever have reached so high.

"You mustn't pay any attention to old Addie," she now said to the little girl. "She's ailing today."

"Will you shut your mouth?" said the woman in bed. "I am not."

"You're a story."

"I can't stay but a minute—really, I can't," said Marian suddenly. She looked down at the wet floor and thought that if she were sick in here they would have to let her go.

With much to-do the first old woman sat down in a rocking chair—still another piece of furniture!—and began to rock. With the fingers of one hand she touched a very dirty cameo pin on her chest. "What do you do at school?" she asked.

"I don't know . . . " said Marian. She tried to think but she could not.

"Oh, but the flowers are beautiful," the old woman whispered. She seemed to rock faster and faster; Marian did not see how anyone could rock so fast.

"Ugly," said the woman in bed.                                                     40

"If we bring flowers—" Marian began, and then fell silent. She had almost said that if Campfire Girls brought flowers to the Old Ladies' Home, the visit would count one extra point, and if they took a Bible with them on the bus and read it to the old ladies, it counted double. But the old woman had not listened, anyway; she was rocking and watching the other one, who watched back from the bed.

"Poor Addie is ailing. She has to take medicine—see?" she said, pointing a horny finger at a row of bottles on the table, and rocking so high that her black comfort shoes lifted off the floor like a little child's.

"I am no more sick than you are," said the woman in bed.

"Oh, yes you are!"

"I just got more sense than you have, that's all," said the other old woman,   45
nodding her head.

"That's only the contrary way she talks when *you all* come," said the first old lady with sudden intimacy. She stopped the rocker with a neat pat of her feet and leaned toward Marian. Her hand reached over—it felt like a petunia leaf, clinging and just a little sticky.

"Will you hush! Will you hush!" cried the other one.

Marian leaned back rigidly in her chair.

"When I was a little girl like you, I went to school and all," said the old woman in the same intimate, menacing voice. "Not here—another town . . . "

"Hush!" said the sick woman. "You never went to school. You never came   50
and you never went. You never were anything—only here. You never were born! You don't know anything. Your head is empty, your heart and hands and your old black purse are all empty, even that little old box that you brought with you you brought empty—you showed it to me. And yet you talk, talk, talk, talk, talk all the time until I think I'm losing my mind! Who are you? You're a stranger—a perfect stranger! Don't you know you're a stranger? Is it possible that they have actually done a thing like this to anyone—sent them in a stranger to talk, and rock, and tell away her whole long rigmarole? Do they seriously suppose that I'll be able to keep it up, day in, day out, night in, night out, living in the same room with a terrible old woman—forever?"

Marian saw the old woman's eyes grow bright and turn toward her. This old woman was looking at her with despair and calculation in her face. Her small lips suddenly dropped apart, and exposed a half circle of false teeth with tan gums.

"Come here, I want to tell you something," she whispered. "Come here!"

Marian was trembling, and her heart nearly stopped beating altogether for a moment.

"Now, now, Addie," said the first old woman. "That's not polite. Do you know what's really the matter with old Addie today?" She, too, looked at Marian; one of her eyelids dropped low.

"The matter?" the child repeated stupidly. "What's the matter with her?"   55

"Why, she's mad because it's her birthday!" said the first old woman, beginning to rock again and giving a little crow as though she had answered her own riddle.

"It is not, it is not!" screamed the old woman in bed. "It is not my birthday, no one knows when that is but myself, and will you please be quiet and say nothing more, or I'll go straight out of my mind!" She turned her eyes toward Marian again, and presently she said in the soft, foggy voice, "When the worst comes to the worst, I ring this bell, and the nurse comes." One of her hands was drawn out from under the patched counterpane—a thin little hand with enormous black freckles. With a finger which would not hold still she pointed to a little bell on the table among the bottles.

"How old are you?" Marian breathed. Now she could see the old woman in bed very closely and plainly, and very abruptly, from all sides, as in dreams. She wondered about her—she wondered for a moment as though there was nothing else in the world to wonder about. It was the first time such a thing had happened to Marian.

"I won't tell!"

The old face on the pillow, where Marian was bending over it, slowly gathered and collapsed. Soft whimpers came out of the small open mouth. It was a sheep that she sounded like—a little lamb. Marian's face drew very close, the yellow hair hung forward. 60

"She's crying!" She turned a bright, burning face up to the first old woman.

"That's Addie for you," the old woman said spitefully.

Marian jumped up and moved toward the door. For the second time, the claw almost touched her hair, but it was not quick enough. The little girl put her cap on.

"Well, it was a real visit," said the old woman, following Marian through the doorway and all the way out into the hall. Then from behind she suddenly clutched the child with her sharp little fingers. In an affected, high-pitched whine she cried, "Oh, little girl, have you a penny to spare for a poor old woman that's not got anything of her own? We don't have a thing in the world—not a penny for candy—not a thing! Little girl, just a nickel—a penny—"

Marian pulled violently against the old hands for a moment before she was free. Then she ran down the hall, without looking behind her and without looking at the nurse, who was reading *Field & Stream* at her desk. The nurse, after another triple motion to consult her wrist watch, asked automatically the question put to visitors in all institutions: "Won't you stay and have dinner with us?" 65

Marian never replied. She pushed the heavy door open into the cold air and ran down the steps.

Under the prickly shrub she stooped and quickly, without being seen, retrieved a red apple she had hidden there.

Her yellow hair under the white cap, her scarlet coat, her bare knees all flashed in the sunlight as she ran to meet the big bus rocketing through the street.

"Wait for me!" she shouted. As though at an imperial command, the bus ground to a stop.

She jumped on and took a big bite out of the apple. 70

## William Carlos Williams

THE USE OF FORCE                                            1938

*William Carlos Williams (1883–1963) was born in Rutherford, New Jersey, studied at the universities of Pennsylvania and Leipzig, then practiced medicine as a pediatrician in his home town for forty-one years. His mother, who was Puerto Rican, gave him his Spanish middle name. Amazingly prolific for a busy doctor, Williams even wrote during office hours: between patients, he would haul out his typewriter and devote every spare minute to literary work. His encouragement of younger writers, among them Allen Ginsberg (whose baby-doctor he was), and the influential example of his formally open poetry made him a father figure to a generation of poets that included Gary Snyder, Denise Levertov, Robert Creeley,*

William Carlos Williams

*and Robert Lowell. Williams believed in truth-telling and in the worth of ordinary life. Some of his stories, like "The Use of Force," read like tales drawn from his working experience. In all his writing, Williams championed plain speech "out of the mouths of Polish mothers." His fiction included four novels, among them* White Mule *(1937) and its sequel* In the Money *(1940), and stories collected in* The Farmer's Daughter *(1961). Combining poetry with prose (including documents and statistics), his five-part poem* Paterson *(1946–58) explores the past, present, and future of the New Jersey industrial city near which he lived. For the shorter poems see* Collected Poems *in two volumes (1986 and 1988). Williams also wrote plays, criticism, history (*In the American Grain, *1925), and an Autobiography (1951).*

They were new patients to me, all I had was the name, Olson. Please come down as soon as you can, my daughter is very sick.

When I arrived I was met by the mother, a big startled looking woman, very clean and apologetic who merely said, Is this the doctor? and let me in. In the back, she added. You must excuse us, doctor, we have her in the kitchen where it is warm. It is very damp here sometimes.

The child was fully dressed and sitting on her father's lap near the kitchen table. He tried to get up, but I motioned for him not to bother, took off my overcoat and started to look things over. I could see that they were all very nervous, eyeing me up and down distrustfully. As often, in such cases, they weren't telling me more than they had to, it was up to me to tell them; that's why they were spending three dollars on me.

The child was fairly eating me up with her cold, steady eyes, and no expression to her face whatever. She did not move and seemed, inwardly, quiet; an unusually attractive little thing, and as strong as a heifer in appearance. But her face was flushed, she was breathing rapidly, and I realized that she had a high fever. She had magnificent blonde hair, in profusion. One of those picture children often reproduced in advertising leaflets and the photogravure sections of the Sunday papers.

She's had a fever for three days, began the father and we don't know what it comes from. My wife has given her things, you know, like people do, but it don't do no good. And there's been a lot of sickness around. So we tho't you'd better look her over and tell us what is the matter.

As doctors often do I took a trial shot at it as a point of departure. Has she had a sore throat?

Both parents answered me together, No . . . No, she says her throat don't hurt her.

Does your throat hurt you? added the mother to the child. But the little girl's expression didn't change nor did she move her eyes from my face.

Have you looked?

I tried to, said the mother, but I couldn't see.

As it happens we had been having a number of cases of diphtheria in the school to which this child went during that month and we were all, quite apparently, thinking of that, though no one had as yet spoken of the thing.

Well, I said, suppose we take a look at the throat first. I smiled in my best professional manner and asking for the child's first name I said, come on, Mathilda, open your mouth and let's take a look at your throat.

Nothing doing.

Aw, come on, I coaxed, just open your mouth wide and let me take a look. Look, I said opening both hands wide, I haven't anything in my hands. Just open up and let me see.

Such a nice man, put in the mother. Look how kind he is to you. Come on, do what he tells you to. He won't hurt you.

At that I ground my teeth in disgust. If only they wouldn't use the word "hurt" I might be able to get somewhere. But I did not allow myself to be hurried or disturbed but speaking quietly and slowly I approached the child again.

As I moved my chair a little nearer suddenly with one cat-like movement both her hands clawed instinctively for my eyes and she almost reached them too. In fact she knocked my glasses flying and they fell, though unbroken, several feet away from me on the kitchen floor.

Both the mother and father almost turned themselves inside out in embarrassment and apology. You bad girl, said the mother, taking her and shaking her by one arm. Look what you've done. The nice man . . .

For heaven's sake, I broke in. Don't call me a nice man to her. I'm here to look at her throat on the chance that she might have diphtheria and possibly die of it. But that's nothing to her. Look here, I said to the child, we're going to look at your throat. You're old enough to understand what I'm saying. Will you open it now by yourself or shall we have to open it for you?

Not a move. Even her expression hadn't changed. Her breaths however were coming faster and faster. Then the battle began. I had to do it. I had to have a throat culture for her own protection. But first I told the parents that it was entirely up to them. I explained the danger but said that I would not insist on a throat examination so long as they would take the responsibility.

If you don't do what the doctor says you'll have to go to the hospital, the mother admonished her severely.

Oh yeah? I had to smile to myself. After all, I had already fallen in love with the savage brat, the parents were contemptible to me. In the ensuing struggle they grew more and more abject, crushed, exhausted while she surely rose to magnificent heights of insane fury of effort bred of her terror of me.

The father tried his best, and he was a big man but the fact that she was his daughter, his shame at her behavior and his dread of hurting her made him release her just at the critical moment several times when I had almost achieved success, till I wanted to kill him. But his dread also that she might have diphtheria made him tell me to go on, go on though he himself was almost fainting, while the mother moved back and forth behind us raising and lowering her hands in an agony of apprehension.

Put her in front of you on your lap, I ordered, and hold both her wrists.

But as soon as he did the child let out a scream. Don't, you're hurting me. 25 Let go of my hands. Let them go I tell you. Then she shrieked terrifyingly, hysterically. Stop it! Stop it! You're killing me!

Do you think she can stand it, doctor! said the mother.

You get out, said the husband to his wife. Do you want her to die of diphtheria?

Come on now, hold her, I said.

Then I grasped the child's head with my left hand and tried to get the wooden tongue depressor between her teeth. She fought, with clenched teeth, desperately! But now I also had grown furious—at a child. I tried to hold myself down but I couldn't. I know how to expose a throat for inspection. And I did my best. When finally I got the wooden spatula behind the last teeth and just the point of it into the mouth cavity, she opened up for an instant but before I could see anything she came down again and gripping the wooden blade between her molars she reduced it to splinters before I could get it out again.

Aren't you ashamed, the mother yelled at her. Aren't you ashamed to act 30 like that in front of the doctor?

Get me a smooth-handled spoon of some sort, I told the mother. We're going through with this. The child's mouth was already bleeding. Her tongue was cut and she was screaming in wild hysterical shrieks. Perhaps I should have desisted and come back in an hour or more. No doubt it would have been better. But I have seen at least two children lying dead in bed of neglect in such cases, and feeling that I must get a diagnosis now or never I went at it again. But the worst of it was that I too had got beyond reason. I could have torn the child apart in my own fury and enjoyed it. It was a pleasure to attack her. My face was burning with it.

The damned little brat must be protected against her own idiocy, one says to one's self at such times. Others must be protected against her. It is social necessity.

And all these things are true. But a blind fury, a feeling of adult shame, bred of a longing for muscular release are the operatives. One goes on to the end.

In a final unreasoning assault I overpowered the child's neck and jaws. I forced the heavy silver spoon back of her teeth and down her throat till she gagged. And there it was—both tonsils covered with membrane. She had fought valiantly to keep me from knowing her secret. She had been hiding that sore throat for three days at least and lying to her parents in order to escape just such an outcome as this.

Now truly she *was* furious. She had been on the defensive before but now she attacked. Tried to get off her father's lap and fly at me while tears of defeat blinded her eyes.

## Virginia Woolf

A HAUNTED HOUSE                                                1921

*Virginia (Stephen) Woolf (1882–1941) was born in London, the daughter of Sir Leslie Stephen, an influential critic and editor of the voluminous* Dictionary of National Biography. *Virginia and her sister Vanessa (who later married Clive Bell, English critic) were largely self-educated by means of their father's extensive library. They were both aware that had they been male they would have gone to college like their brothers. After their father's death, Virginia and Vanessa moved to Bloomsbury, a bohemian neighborhood of London near the British Museum, where they became the center of the "Bloomsbury Group," a collection of progressive British artists and intellectuals. In 1912 Virginia*

Virginia Woolf

*married Leonard Woolf, a journalist and novelist. Always in frail health, she experienced episodes of mental disturbance. In 1917, as therapy, she and Leonard set up a handpress in their home and started the Hogarth Press, one of the most celebrated small presses of the century. In addition to Woolf's own books, it issued books and pamphlets by T. S. Eliot, Katherine Mansfield, Robinson Jeffers, and E. A. Robinson. Woolf's first novel,* The Voyage Out, *appeared in 1915 and, though quite realistic, it already foreshadowed the psychological depth and poetic force of her late work. In her innovative novels like* Mrs. Dalloway *(1925),* To the Lighthouse *(1927),* Orlando *(1928), and* The Waves *(1931), Woolf became one of the central modernist fiction writers in English. She pioneered "stream of consciousness" narration, a style which tries to portray the seemingly random way in which thoughts and feelings flow through a character's mind (see page 24 for a fuller discussion of this technique). Woolf's critical essays, col-lected in her two volumes,* The Common Reader *(1925, 1932), remain influential and her long essay,* A Room of One's Own *(1929), is a classic of the feminist move-ment. After several nervous breakdowns, Woolf, fearing for her sanity, drowned herself in 1941.*

Whatever hour you woke there was a door shutting. From room to room they went, hand in hand, lifting here, opening there, making sure—a ghostly couple.

"Here we left it," she said. And he added, "Oh, but here too!" "It's upstairs," she murmured. "And in the garden," he whispered. "Quietly," they said, "or we shall wake them."

But it wasn't that you woke us. Oh, no. "They're looking for it; they're draw-ing the curtain," one might say, and so read on a page or two. "Now they've found it," one would be certain, stopping the pencil on the margin. And then, tired of reading, one might rise and see for oneself, the house all empty, the doors standing open, only the wood pigeons bubbling with content and the hum of the threshing machine sounding from the farm. "What did I come in here for? What did I want to find?" My hands are empty. "Perhaps it's upstairs then?" The apples were in the loft. And so down again, the garden still as ever, only the book had slipped into the grass.

But they had found it in the drawing-room. Not that one could ever see them. The window panes reflected apples, reflected roses; all the leaves were green in the glass. If they moved in the drawing-room, the apple only turned its yellow side. Yet, the moment after, if the door was opened, spread about the floor, hung upon the walls, pendant from the ceiling—what? My hands were empty. The shadow of a thrush crossed the carpet; from the deepest wells of silence the wood pigeon drew its bubble of sound. "Safe, safe, safe," the pulse of the house beat softly. "The treasure buried; the room . . . " the pulse stopped short. Oh, was that the buried treasure?

A moment later the light had faded. Out in the garden then? But the trees spun darkness for a wandering beam of sun. So fine, so rare, coolly sunk beneath the surface the beam I sought always burnt behind the glass. Death was the glass; death was between us; coming to the woman first, hundreds of years ago, leaving the house, sealing all the windows; the rooms were darkened. He left it, left her, went North, went East, saw the stars turned in the Southern sky; sought the house, found it dropped beneath the Downs. "Safe, safe, safe," the pulse of the house beat gladly. "The Treasure yours."

The wind roars up the avenue. Trees stoop and bend this way and that. Moonbeams splash and spill wildly in the rain. But the beam of the lamp falls straight from the window. The candle burns stiff and still. Wandering through the house, opening the windows, whispering not to wake us, the ghostly couple seek their joy.

"Here we slept," she says. And he adds, "Kisses without number." "Waking in the morning—" "Silver between the trees—" "Upstairs—" "In the garden—"

5

"When summer came—" "In winter snowtime—" The doors go shutting far in the distance, gently knocking like the pulse of a heart.

Nearer they come; cease at the doorway. The wind falls, the rain slides silver down the glass. Our eyes darken; we hear no steps beside us; we see no lady spread her ghostly cloak. His hands shield the lantern. "Look," he breathes. "Sound asleep. Love upon their lips."

Stooping, holding their silver lamp above us, long they look and deeply. Long they pause. The wind drives straightly; the flame stoops slightly. Wild beams of moonlight cross both floor and wall, and, meeting, stain the faces bent; the faces pondering; the faces that search the sleepers and seek their hidden joy.

"Safe, safe, safe," the heart of the house beats proudly. "Long years—" he sighs. "Again you found me." "Here," she murmurs, "sleeping; in the garden reading; laughing, rolling apples in the loft. Here we left our treasure—" Stooping, their light lifts the lids upon my eyes. "Safe! safe! safe!" the pulse of the house beats wildly. Waking, I cry "Oh, is this *your* buried treasure? The light in the heart."

# 12 Criticism: On Fiction

The critical power is of lower rank than the creative. True, but in assenting to this proposition, one or two things are to be kept in mind. It is undeniable that the exercise of a creative power, that of a free creative activity, is the true function of man; it is proved to be so by man's finding in it his true happiness. But it is undeniable, also, that men may have the sense of exercising this free creative activity in other ways than in producing great works of literature or art; if it were not so, all but a very few men would be shut out from the true happiness of all men; they may have it in well-doing, they may have it in learning, they may have it even in criticizing.

—Matthew Arnold, "The Function of Criticism"

## Edgar Allan Poe (1809–1849)

THE TALE AND ITS EFFECT                                                    1842

Were we called upon, however, to designate that class of composition which, next to [a short lyric poem], should best fulfill the demands of high genius—should offer it the most advantageous field of exertion—we should unhesitatingly speak of the prose tale, as Mr. Hawthorne has here exemplified it. We allude to the short prose narrative, requiring from a half-hour to one or two hours in its perusal. The ordinary novel is objectionable, from its length, for reasons already stated in substance. As it cannot be read at one sitting, it deprives itself, of course, of the immense force derivable from *totality*. Worldly interests intervening during the pauses of perusal, modify, annul, or counteract, in a greater or less degree, the impressions of the book. But simple cessation in reading would, of itself, be sufficient to destroy the true unity. In the brief tale, however, the author is enabled to carry out the fullness of his intention, be it what it may. During the hour of perusal the soul of the reader is at the writer's control. There are no external or extrinsic influences—resulting from weariness or interruption.

A skillful literary artist has constructed a tale. If wise, he has not fashioned his thoughts to accommodate his incidents; but having conceived, with deliberate care, a certain unique or single *effect* to be wrought out, he then invents such incidents—he then combines such events as may best aid him in establishing this preconceived effect. If his very initial sentence tend not to the outbringing of this effect, then he has failed in his first step. In the whole composition there should be no word written, of which the tendency, direct or indirect, is not to the one pre-established design. And by such means, with such care and skill, a picture is at length painted which leaves in the mind of him who contemplates it with a kindred art, a sense of the fullest satisfaction. The idea of the tale has been presented unblemished, because undisturbed; and this is an end unattainable by the novel. Undue brevity is just as exceptionable here as in the poem; but undue length is yet more to be avoided.

> —*Twice-Told Tales*, by Nathaniel Hawthorne: A Review

## Charlotte Brontë (1816–1855)

THE WRITER'S PASSIVE WORK                                              1850

Whether it is right or advisable to create beings like Heathcliff°, I do not know: I scarcely think it is. But this I know: the writer who possesses the creative gift owns something of which he is not always master—something that, at times, strangely wills and works for itself. He may lay down rules and devise principles, and to rules and principles it will perhaps for years lie in subjection; and then, haply without any warning of revolt, there comes a time when it will no longer consent to "harrow the valleys, or be bound with a band in the furrow"—when it "laughs at the multitude of the city, and regards not the crying of the driver"— when, refusing absolutely to make ropes out of sea-sand any longer, it sets to work on statue-hewing, and you have a Pluto or Jove, a Tisiphone or a Psyche, a Mermaid or a Madonna, as Fate or Inspiration direct. Be the work grim or glorious, dread or divine, you have little choice left but quiescent adoption. As for you—the nominal artist—your share in it has been to work passively under dictates you neither delivered nor could question—that would not be uttered at your prayer, nor suppressed nor changed at your caprice. If the result be attractive, the World will praise you, who little deserve praise; if it be repulsive, the same World will blame you, who almost as little deserve blame.

> —Preface to the Second Edition of *Wuthering Heights* (by Emily Brontë)

---

Heathcliff: Central character of the novel *Wuthering Heights:* "a man's shape animated by demon life" (in Charlotte Brontë's view).

## Gustave Flaubert (1821–1880)

### THE LABOR OF STYLE                                                    1854

*Translated by Francis Steegmuller*

I have just made a fresh copy of what I have written since New Year, or rather since the middle of February, for on my return from Paris I burned all my January work. It amounts to thirteen pages, no more, no less, thirteen pages in seven weeks. However, they are in shape, I think, and as perfect as I can make them. There are only two or three repetitions of the same word which must be removed, and two turns of phrase that are still too much alike. At last something is completed. It was a difficult transition: the reader had to be led gradually and imperceptibly from psychology to action. Now I am about to begin the dramatic, eventful part. Two or three more big pushes and the end will be in sight. By July or August I hope to tackle the denouement. What a struggle it has been! My God, what a struggle! Such drudgery! Such discouragement! I spent all last evening frantically poring over surgical texts. I am studying the theory of clubfeet. In three hours I devoured an entire volume on this interesting subject and took notes. I came upon some really fine sentences. "The maternal breast is an impenetrable and mysterious sanctuary, where . . . etc." An excellent treatise, incidentally. Why am I not young? How I should work! One ought to know everything, to write. All of us scribblers are monstrously ignorant. If only we weren't so lacking in stamina, what a rich field of ideas and similes we could tap! Books that have been the source of entire literatures, like Homer and Rabelais, contain the sum of all the knowledge of their times. They knew everything, those fellows, and we know nothing. Ronsard's poetics contain a curious precept: he advises the poet to become well versed in the arts and crafts—to frequent blacksmiths, goldsmiths, locksmiths, etc.—in order to enrich his stock of metaphors. And indeed that is the sort of thing that makes for rich and varied language. The sentences in a book must quiver like the leaves in a forest, all dissimilar in their similarity.

—Letter to Louise Colet, April 7, 1854, during the writing of *Madame Bovary*

## Henry James (1843–1916)

### THE MIRROR OF A CONSCIOUSNESS                                         1908

This in fact I have ever found rather terribly the point—that the figures in any picture, the agents in any drama, are interesting only in proportion as they feel their respective situations; since the consciousness, on their part, of the complication exhibited forms for us their link of connection with it. But there are degrees of feeling—the muffled, the faint, the just sufficient, the barely intelligent, as we may say; and the acute, the intense, the complete, in a word—the power to be finely aware and richly responsible. It is those moved in this latter fashion who "get most" out of all that happens to them and who in so doing enable us, as readers of their record, as participators by a fond attention, also to get most. Their being finely aware—as Hamlet and Lear, say, are finely aware—*makes* absolutely the intensity of their adventure, gives the maximum of sense to what befalls them. We care, our curiosity and our sympathy care, comparatively little for what happens to the stupid, the coarse and the blind; care for it, and for the effects of it, at the most as helping to precipitate what happens to the more deeply wondering, to the really sentient. Hamlet and Lear are surrounded, amid their complications, by the stupid and the blind, who minister in all sorts of ways to their recorded fate. . . .

Verily even, I think, no "story" is possible without its fools—as most of the fine painters of life, Shakespeare, Cervantes and Balzac, Fielding, Scott, Thackeray, Dickens, George Meredith, George Eliot, Jane Austen, have abundantly felt. At the same time I confess I never see the *leading* interest of any human hazard but in a consciousness (on the part of the moved and moving creature) subject to fine intensification and wide enlargement. It is as mirrored in that consciousness that the gross fools, the headlong fools, the fatal fools play their part for us—they have much less to show us in themselves. The troubled life mostly at the center of our subject—whatever our subject, for the artistic hour, happens to be—embraces them and deals with them for its amusement and its anguish: they are apt largely indeed, on a near view, to be all the cause of its trouble. This means, exactly, that the person capable of feeling in the given case more than another of what is to be felt for it, and so serving in the highest degree to *record* it dramatically and objectively, is the only sort of person on whom we can count not to betray, to cheapen or, as we say, give away, the value and beauty of the thing. By so much as the affair matters *for* some such individual, by so much do we get the best there is of it, and by so much as it falls within the scope of a denser and duller, a more vulgar and more shallow capacity, do we get a picture dim and meager.

The great chroniclers have clearly always been aware of this; they have at least always either placed a mind of some sort—in the sense of a reflecting and coloring medium—in possession of the general adventure . . . or else paid signally, as to the interest created for their failure to do so.

—Preface to *The Princess Casamassima*

## Anton Chekhov (1860–1904)

NATURAL DESCRIPTION AND "THE CENTER OF GRAVITY"          1886

*Translated by Irina Prishvin*

A fine description of nature, I think, has to be brief and to the point. Banalities—"the setting sun, drowning in the darkening waves of the sea," and all that, or, "the swallows, skimming over the crest of the ocean, tweeted happily"—such banalities have to be left out. When describing nature, a writer should seize upon small details, arranging them so that the reader will see an image in his mind after he closes his eyes. For instance: you will capture the truth of a moonlit night if you'll write that a gleam like starlight shone from the pieces of a broken bottle, and then the dark, plump shadow of a dog or wolf appeared. You will bring life to nature only if you don't shrink from similes that liken its activities to those of humankind.

In displaying the psychology of your characters, minute particulars are essential. God save us from vague generalizations! Be sure *not* to discuss your hero's state of mind. Make it clear from his actions. Nor is it necessary to portray many main characters. Let two people be the center of gravity in your story: he and she.

—Letter to his brother Alexander Chekhov, May 10, 1886.

## James Joyce (1882–1941)

EPIPHANIES                                              1904–1906

He° was passing through Eccles Street one evening, one misty evening, with all these thoughts dancing the dance of unrest in his brain when a trivial incident set him composing some ardent verses which he entitled a 'Villanelle of the Temptress.' A young lady was standing on the steps of one of those brown brick houses which seem the very incarnation of Irish paralysis. A young gentleman was leaning on the rusty railings of the area. Stephen as he passed on his quest heard the following fragment of colloquy out of which he received an impression keen enough to afflict his sensitiveness very severely.

THE YOUNG LADY—(drawling discreetly) . . . O, yes . . . I was . . . at the . . . cha . . . pel. . . .

THE YOUNG GENTLEMAN—(inaudibly) . . . I . . . (again inaudibly) . . . I . . .

THE YOUNG LADY—(softly) . . . O . . . but you're . . . ve . . . ry . . . wick . . . ed. . . .

This triviality made him think of collecting many such moments together in a book of epiphanies. By an epiphany he meant a sudden spiritual manifestation, whether in the vulgarity of speech or of gesture or in a memorable phase of the mind itself. He believed that it was for the man of letters to record these epiphanies with extreme care, seeing that they themselves are the most delicate and evanescent of moments. He told Cranly° that the clock of the Ballast Office was capable of an epiphany. Cranly questioned the inscrutable dial of the Ballast Office with his no less inscrutable countenance.

—Yes, said Stephen. I will pass it time after time, allude to it, refer to it, catch a glimpse of it. It is only an item in the catalogue of Dublin's street furniture. Then all at once I see it and I know at once what it is: epiphany. . . .

—*Stephen Hero*

He: Stephen Dedalus, protagonist of Joyce's novel (an early version of *Portrait of the Artist as a Young Man*), a young Dublin intellectual resembling Joyce himself.     Cranly: a fellow student.

## Katherine Mansfield (1888–1923)

### WRITING "MISS BRILL" 1921

In "Miss Brill," I choose not only the length of every sentence, but even the sound of every sentence. I choose the rise and fall of every paragraph to fit her, and to fit her on that day at that very moment. After I'd written it I read it aloud—numbers of times—just as one would *play over* a musical composition—trying to get it nearer and nearer to the expression of Miss Brill—until it fitted her.

Don't think I'm vain about the little sketch. It's only the method I wanted to explain. I often wonder whether other writers do the same—if a thing has really come off it seems to me there mustn't be one single word out of place, or one word that could be taken out. That's how I *aim* at writing. It will take some time to get anywhere near there.

—Letter to Richard Murry

## William Faulkner (1897–1962)

### "THE HUMAN HEART IN CONFLICT WITH ITSELF" 1950

Our tragedy today is a general and universal physical fear so long sustained by now that we can even bear it. There are no longer problems of the spirit. There is only the question: When will I be blown up? Because of this, the young man or woman writing today has forgotten the problems of the human heart in conflict with itself which alone can make good writing because only that is worth writing about, worth the agony and the sweat.

He must learn them again. He must teach himself that the basest of all things is to be afraid; and, teaching himself that, forget it forever, leaving no room in his workshop for anything but the verities and truths of the heart, the old universal truths lacking which any story is ephemeral and doomed—love and honor and pity and pride and compassion and sacrifice. Until he does so, he labors under a curse. He writes not of love but of lust, of defeats in which nobody loses anything of value, of victories without hope and, worst of all, without pity or compassion. His griefs grieve on no universal bones, leaving no scars. He writes not of the heart but of the glands.

Until he relearns these things, he will write as though he stood among and watched the end of man. I decline to accept the end of man. It is easy enough to say that man is immortal simply because he will endure; that when the last ding-dong of doom has clanged and faded from the last worthless rock hanging tideless in the last red and dying evening, that even then there will still be one more sound: that of his puny inexhaustible voice, still talking. I refuse to accept this. I believe that man will not merely endure: he will prevail. He is immortal, not because he alone among creatures has an inexhaustible voice, but because he has a soul, a spirit capable of compassion and sacrifice and endurance. The poet's, the writer's, duty is to write about these things. It is his privilege to help man endure by lifting his heart, by reminding him of the courage and honor and hope and pride and compassion and pity and sacrifice which have been the glory of his past. The poet's voice need not merely be the record of man, it can be one of the props, the pillars to help him endure and prevail.

—Speech of Acceptance for the award of the Nobel Prize for Literature

## Nadine Gordimer

HOW THE SHORT STORY DIFFERS FROM THE NOVEL                    1968

It would seen unnecessary for us to go over the old definitions of where and how the short story differs from the novel, but the answer to the question must lie somewhere here. Both novel and story use the same material: human experience. Both have the same aim: to communicate it. Both use the same medium: the written word. There is a general and recurrent dissatisfaction with the novel as a means of netting ultimate reality—another term for the quality of human life— and inevitably there is even a tendency to blame the tools: words have become hopelessly blunted by overuse, dinned to death by admen, and, above all, debased by political creeds that have twisted and changed their meaning. Various ways out have been sought. In England, a return to classicism in technique and a turning to the exoticism of sexual aberration and physical and mental abnormality as an extension of human experience and therefore of subject matter; in Germany and America, a splendid abandon in making a virtue of the vice of the novel's inherent clumsiness by stuffing it not with nineteenth-century horsehair narrative but twentieth-century anecdotal-analytical plastic foam; in France, the "laboratory novel" struggling to get away from the anthropocentric curse of the form and the illusion of depth of the psychological novel, and landing up very much where Virginia Woolf was, years ago, staring at the mark on the wall. Burroughs° has invented the reader-participation novel. For the diseased word, George Steiner has even suggested silence.

If the short story is alive while the novel is dead, the reason must lie in approach and method. The short story, as a form and as a *kind of creative vision*, must be better equipped to attempt the capture of ultimate reality at a time when (whichever way you choose to see it) we are drawing nearer to the mystery of life or are losing ourselves in a bellowing wilderness of mirrors, as the nature of that reality becomes more fully understood or more bewilderingly concealed by the discoveries of science and the proliferation of communication media outside the printed word.

Certainly the short story always has been more flexible and open to experiment than the novel. Short-story writers always have been subject at the same time to both a stricter technical discipline and a wider freedom than the novelist.

*William Burroughs* (b. 1914): author of *Naked Lunch, Junkie,* and other experimental novels. His fiction uses surrealistic techniques.

Short-story writers have known—and solved by nature of their choice of form—what novelists seem to have discovered in despair only now: the strongest convention of the novel, prolonged coherence of tone, to which even the most experimental of novels must conform unless it is to fall apart, is false to the nature of whatever can be grasped of human reality. How shall I put it? Each of us has a thousand lives and a novel gives a character only one. *For the sake of the form.* The novelist may juggle about with chronology and throw narrative overboard; all the time his characters have the reader by the hand, there is a consistency of relationship throughout the experience that cannot and does not convey the quality of human life, where contact is more like the flash of fireflies, in and out, now here, now there, in darkness. Short-story writers see by the light of the flash; theirs is the art of the only thing one can be sure of—the present moment. Ideally, they have learned to do without explanation of what went before, and what happens beyond this point. How the characters will appear, think, behave, comprehend, tomorrow or at any other time in their lives, is irrelevant. A discrete moment of truth is aimed at—not *the* moment of truth, because the short story does not deal in cumulatives.

—"The Flash of Fireflies"

## Raymond Carver (1938-1988)

"Commonplace but Precise Language"                                    1983

It's possible, in a poem or a short story, to write about commonplace things and objects using commonplace but precise language, and to endow those things—a chair, a window curtain, a fork, a stone, a woman's earring—with immense, even startling power. It is possible to write a line of seemingly innocuous dialogue and have it send a chill along the reader's spine—the source of artistic delight, as Nabokov would have it. That's the kind of writing that most interests me. I hate sloppy or haphazard writing whether it flies under the banner of experimentation or else is just clumsily rendered realism. In Isaac Babel's wonderful short story "Guy de Maupassant," the narrator has this to say about the writing of fiction: "No iron can pierce the heart with such force as a period put just at the right place." This too ought to go on a three-by-five.

Evan Connell said once that he knew he was finished with a short story when he found himself going through it and taking out commas and then going through the story again and putting commas back in the same places. I like that way of working on something. I respect that kind of care for what is being done. That's all we have, finally, the words, and they had better be the right ones, with the punctuation in the right places so that they can best say what they are meant to say. If the words are heavy with the writer's own unbridled emotions, or if they are imprecise and inaccurate for some other reason—if the words are in any way blurred—the reader's eyes will slide right over them and nothing will be achieved. The reader's own artistic sense will simply not be engaged. Henry James called this sort of hapless writing "weak specification."

I have friends who've told me they had to hurry a book because they needed the money, their editor or their wife was leaning on them or leaving them—something, some apology for the writing not being very good. "It would have been better if I'd taken the time." I was dumbfounded when I heard a novelist friend say this. I still am, if I think about it, which I don't. It's none of my business. But if the writing can't be made as good as it is within us to make it, then why do it? In the end, the satisfaction of having done our best, and the proof of that labor, is the one thing we can take into the grave.

—"On Writing," *Fires*

# POETRY

## TO THE MUSE

Give me leave, Muse, in plain view to array
Your shift and bodice by the light of day.
I would have brought an epic. Be not vexed
Instead to grace a niggling schoolroom text;
Let down your sanction, help me to oblige
Him who would lead fresh devots to your liege,
And at your altar, grant that in a flash
They, he and I know incense from dead ash.
—X.J.K.

What is poetry? Pressed for an answer, Robert Frost made a classic reply: "Poetry is the kind of thing poets write." In all likelihood, Frost was not trying merely to evade the question but to chide his questioner into thinking for himself. A trouble with definitions is that they may stop thought. If Frost had said, "Poetry is a rhythmical composition of words expressing an attitude, designed to surprise and delight, and to arouse an emotional response," the questioner might have settled back in his chair, content to have learned the truth about poetry. He would have learned nothing, or not so much as he might learn by continuing to wonder.

The nature of poetry eludes simple definitions. (In this respect it is rather like jazz. Asked after one of his concerts, "What is jazz?" Louis Armstrong replied, "Man, if you gotta ask, you'll never know.") Definitions will be of little help at first, if we are to know poetry and respond to it. We have to go to it willing to see and hear. For this reason, you are asked in reading this book not to be in any hurry to decide what poetry is, but instead to study poems and to let them grow in your mind. At the end of our discussions of poetry, the problem of definition will be taken up again (for those who may wish to pursue it).

Confronted with a formal introduction to poetry, you may be wondering, "Who needs it?" and you may well be right. It's unlikely that you have avoided meeting poetry before; and perhaps you already have a friendship, or at least a fair acquaintance, with some of the great English-speaking poets of all time. What this book provides is an introduction to the *study* of poetry. It tries to help you look at a poem closely, to offer you a wider and more accurate vocabulary with which to express what poems say to you. It will suggest ways to judge for yourself the poems you read. It may set forth some poems new to you.

A frequent objection is that poetry ought not to be studied at all. In this view, a poem is either a series of gorgeous noises to be funneled through one ear and out the other without being allowed to trouble the mind, or an experience so holy that to analyze it in a classroom is as cruel and mechanical as dissecting a hummingbird. To the first view, it might be countered that a good poem has something to say that is well worth listening to. To the second view, it might be argued that poems are much less perishable than hummingbirds, and luckily, we can study them in flight. The risk of a poem's dying from observation is not nearly so great as the risk of not really seeing it at all. It is doubtful that any excellent poem has ever vanished from human memory because people have read it too closely. More likely, poems that vanish are poems that no one reads closely, for no one cares.

That poetry matters to the people who write it has been shown unmistakably by the ordeal of Soviet poet Irina Ratushinskaya, now living in the West. Sentenced to prison for three and a half years, she was given paper and pencil only twice a month to write letters to her husband and her parents and was not allowed to write anything else. Nevertheless, Ratushinskaya composed more than two hundred poems in her cell, engraving them with a burnt match in a bar of soap, then memorizing the lines. "I would read the poem and read it," she said, "until it was committed to memory—then with one washing of my hands, it would be gone."

Good poetry is something that readers and listeners, too, can care about. In fact, an ancient persuasion of humankind is that the hearing of a poem, as well as the making of a poem, can be a religious act. Poetry, in speech and song, was part of classic Greek drama, which for playwright, actor, and spectator alike was a holy-day ceremony. The Greeks' belief that a poet writes a poem only by supernatural assistance is clear from the invocations to the Muse that begin the *Iliad* and the *Odyssey* and from the opinion of Socrates (in Plato's *Ion*) that a poet has no powers of invention until divinely inspired. Among the ancient Celts, poets were regarded as magicians and priests, and whoever insulted one of them might expect to receive a curse in rime potent enough to afflict him with boils and to curdle the milk of his cows. Such identifications between the poet and the magician are less common these days, although we know that poetry is involved in the primitive white-magic of children, who bring themselves good luck in a game with the charm "Roll, roll, Tootsie-roll! / Roll the marble in the hole!" and who warn against a hex while jumping along a sidewalk: "Step on a crack, / Break your mother's back." But in this age when we pride ourselves that a computer may solve the riddle of all creation as soon as it is programmed, magic seems to some people of small importance and so too does poetry. It is dangerous, however, to dismiss what we do not logically understand. To read a poem at all, we have to be willing to offer it responses *besides* a logical understanding. Whether we attribute the effect of a poem to a divine spirit or to the reactions of our glands and cortexes, we have to take the reading of poetry seriously (not solemnly), if only because—as some of the poems in this book may demonstrate—few other efforts can repay us so generously, both in wisdom and in joy.

If, as I hope you will do, you sometimes browse in the book for fun, you may be annoyed to see so many questions following the poems. Should you feel this way, try reading with a slip of paper to cover up the questions. You will then—if the Muse should inspire you—have paper in hand to write a poem.

# 13  Reading a Poem

How do you read a poem? The literal-minded might say, "Just let your eye light on it"; but there is more to poetry than meets the eye. What Shakespeare called "the mind's eye" also plays a part. Many a reader who has no trouble understanding and enjoying prose finds poetry difficult. This is to be expected. At first glance, a poem usually will make some sense and give some pleasure, but it may not yield everything at once. Sometimes it only hints at meaning still to come if we will keep after it. Poetry is not to be galloped over like the daily news: a poem differs from most prose in that it is to be read slowly, carefully, and attentively. Not all poems are difficult, of course, and some can be understood and enjoyed on first seeing. But good poems yield more if read twice; and the best poems—after ten, twenty, or a hundred readings—still go on yielding.

Approaching a thing written in lines and surrounded with white space, we need not expect it to be a poem just because it is **verse.** (Any composition in lines of more or less regular rhythm, usually ending in rimes, is verse.) Here, for instance, is a specimen of verse that few will call poetry:

> Thirty days hath September,
> April, June, and November;
> All the rest have thirty-one
> Excepting February alone,
> To which we twenty-eight assign
> Till leap year makes it twenty-nine.

To a higher degree than that classic memory-tickler, poetry appeals to the mind and arouses feelings. Poetry may state facts, but, more important, it makes imaginative statements that we may value even if its facts are incorrect. Coleridge's error in placing a star within the horns of the crescent moon in "The Rime of the Ancient Mariner" does not stop the passage from being good poetry, though it is faulty astronomy. According to one poet, Gerard Manley Hopkins, poetry is "to be heard for its own sake and interest even over and above its interest of meaning." There are other elements in a poem besides plain prose sense: sounds, images, rhythms, figures of speech. These may strike us and please us even before we ask, "But what does it all mean?"

This is a truth not readily grasped by anyone who regards a poem as a kind of puzzle written in secret code with a message slyly concealed. The effect of a poem (one's whole mental and emotional response to it) consists in much more than simply a message. By its musical qualities, by its suggestions, it can work on the reader's unconscious. T. S. Eliot put it well when he said in *The Use of Poetry and the Use of Criticism* that the prose sense of a poem is chiefly useful in keeping the reader's mind "diverted and quiet, while the poem does its work upon him." Eliot went on to liken the meaning of a poem to the bit of meat a burglar brings along to throw to the family dog. What is the work of a poem? To touch us, to stir us, to make us glad, and possibly even to tell us something.

How to set about reading a poem? Here are a few suggestions.

To begin with, read the poem once straight through, with no particular expectations; read open-mindedly. Let yourself experience whatever you find, without worrying just yet about the large general and important ideas the poem contains (if indeed it contains any). Don't dwell on a troublesome word or difficult passage—just push on. Some of the difficulties may seem smaller when you read the poem for a second time; at least, they will have become parts of a whole for you.

On second reading, read for the exact sense of all the words; if there are words you don't understand, look them up in a dictionary. Dwell on any difficult parts as long as you need to.

If you read the poem silently to yourself, sound its words in your mind. (This is a technique that will get you nowhere in a speed-reading course, but it may help the poem to do its work on you.) Better still, read the poem aloud, or hear someone else read it. You may discover meanings you didn't perceive in it before. Even if you are no actor, to decide how to speak a poem can be an excellent method of getting to understand it. Some poems, like bells, seem heavy till heard. Listen while reading the following lines from Alexander Pope's *Dunciad*. Attacking the minor poet James Ralph, who had sung the praises of a mistress named Cynthia, Pope makes the goddess of Dullness exclaim:

> "Silence, ye wolves! while Ralph to Cynthia howls,
> And makes night hideous—answer him, ye owls!"

When *ye owls* slide together and become *yowls*, poor Ralph's serenade is turned into the nightly outcry of a cat.

Try to **paraphrase** the poem as a whole, or perhaps just the more difficult lines. In paraphrasing, we put into our own words what we understand the poem to say, restating ideas that seem essential, coming out and stating what the poem may only suggest. This may sound like a heartless thing to do to a poem, but good poems can stand it. In fact, to compare a poem to its paraphrase is a good way to see the distance between poetry and prose. In making a paraphrase, we generally work through a poem or a passage line by line. The statement that results may take as many words as the original, if not more. A paraphrase, then, is ampler than a **summary,** a brief condensation of gist, main idea, or story. (Summary of a horror film in *TV Guide:* "Demented biologist, coveting power over New York, swells sewer rats to hippopotamus-size.") Here is a poem worth considering line by line. The poet writes of an island in a lake in the west of Ireland, in a region where he spent many summers as a boy.

---

## *William Butler Yeats* (1865–1939)*

### The Lake Isle of Innisfree                                              1892

I will arise and go now, and go to Innisfree,
And a small cabin build there, of clay and wattles made:
Nine bean-rows will I have there, a hive for the honey-bee,
And live alone in the bee-loud glade.

And I shall have some peace there, for peace comes dropping slow,      5
Dropping from the veils of the morning to where the cricket sings;
There midnight's all a glimmer, and noon a purple glow,
And evening full of the linnet's wings.

I will arise and go now, for always night and day
I hear lake water lapping with low sounds by the shore;                     10
While I stand on the roadway, or on the pavements gray,
I hear it in the deep heart's core.

Though relatively simple, this poem is far from simple-minded. We need to absorb it slowly and thoughtfully. At the start, for most of us, it raises problems: what are *wattles,* from which the speaker's dream-cabin is to be made? We might guess, but in this case it will help to consult a dictionary: they are "poles interwoven with sticks or branches, formerly used in building as frameworks to support walls or roofs." Evidently, this getaway house will be built in an old-fashioned way: it won't be a prefabricated log cabin or A-frame house, nothing modern or citified. The phrase *bee-loud glade* certainly isn't commonplace language of the sort we find on a cornflake package, but right away, we can understand it, at least partially: it's a place loud with bees. What is a *glade*? Experience might tell us that it is an open space in woods, but if that word stops us, we can look it up. Although the *linnet* doesn't live in North America, it is a creature with wings—a songbird of the finch family, adds the dictionary. But even if we don't make a special trip to the dictionary to find *linnet*, we probably recognize that the word means "bird," and the line makes sense to us.

A paraphrase of the whole poem might go something like this (in language easier to forget than that of the original): "I'm going to get up now, go to Innisfree, build a cabin, plant beans, keep bees, and live peacefully by myself amid nature and beautiful light. I want to, because I can't forget the sound of that lake water. When I'm in the city, a gray and dingy place, I seem to hear it deep inside me."

These dull remarks, roughly faithful to what Yeats is saying, seem a long way from poetry. Nevertheless, they make certain things clear. For one, they spell out what the poet merely hints at in his choice of the word *gray*: that he finds the city dull and depressing. He stresses the word; instead of saying *gray pavements*, in the usual word-order, he turns the phrase around and makes *gray* stand at the end of the line, where it rimes with *day* and so takes extra emphasis. The grayness of the city therefore seems important to the poem, and the paraphrase tries to make its meaning obvious.

Whenever you paraphrase, you stick your neck out. You affirm what the poem gives you to understand. And making a paraphrase can help you see the central thought of the poem, its **theme.** Theme isn't the same as **subject,** the main topic, whatever the poem is "about." In Yeats's poem, the subject is the lake isle of Innisfree, or a wish to retreat to it. But the theme is, "I yearn for an ideal place where I will find perfect peace and happiness." Themes can be stated variously, depending on what you believe most matters in the poem. Taking a different view of the poem, placing more weight on the speaker's wish to escape the city, you might instead state the theme: "This city is getting me down—I want to get back to nature." But after taking a second look at that statement, you might want to sharpen it. After all, this Innisfree seems a special, particular place, where the natural world means more to the poet than just any old trees and birds he might see in a park. Perhaps a stronger statement of theme, one closer to what matters most in the poem, might be: "I want to quit the city for my heaven on earth." That, of course, is saying in an obvious way what Yeats says more subtly, more memorably.

Not all poems clearly assert a proposition, but many do; some even declare their themes in their opening lines: "Gather ye rose-buds while ye may!"—that is, enjoy love before it's too late. This theme, stated in that famous first line of Robert Herrick's "To the Virgins, to Make Much of Time" (page 937), is so familiar that we give it a name: **carpe diem,** Latin for "seize the day." (For the original *carpe diem* poem, see the Latin poet Horace's ode on page 845.) Seizing the joys of the present moment is a favorite argument of poets. You will meet it in more than these two poems in this book.

A paraphrase, of course, never tells *all* that a poem contains; nor will every reader agree that a particular paraphrase is accurate. We all make our own interpretations; and sometimes the total meaning of a poem evades even the poet who wrote it. Asked to explain his difficult *Sordello*, Robert Browning replied that when he had written the poem only God and he knew what it meant; but "Now, only God knows." Still, to analyze a poem *as if* we could be certain of its meaning is, in general, more fruitful than to proceed as if no certainty could ever be had. The latter approach is likely to end in complete subjectivity: the attitude of the reader who says, "Yeats's 'Lake Isle of Innisfree' is really about the lost island of Atlantis. It is, because I think it is. How can you prove me wrong?" Interpretations can't be proven "wrong." A more fruitful question might be, "What can we understand from the poem's very words?"

All of us bring personal associations to the poems we read. "The Lake Isle of Innisfree" might give you special pleasure if you have ever vacationed on a small island or on the shore of a lake. Such associations are inevitable, even to be welcomed, as long as they don't interfere with our reading the words on the page. We need to distinguish irrelevant responses from those the poem calls for. The reader who can't stand "The Lake Isle of Innisfree" because she is afraid of bees isn't reading a poem by Yeats, but one of her own invention.

Now and again we meet a poem—perhaps startling and memorable— into which the method of paraphrase won't take us far. Some portion of any deep poem resists explanation, but certain poems resist it almost entirely. Many poems of religious mystics seem closer to dream than waking. So do poems that purport to record drug experiences, such as Coleridge's "Kubla Khan" (page 906), as well as poems that embody some private system of beliefs, such as Blake's "The Sick Rose" (page 899), or the same poet's lines from *Jerusalem*,

> For a Tear is an Intellectual thing,
> And a Sigh is the Sword of an Angel King.

So do nonsense poems, translations of primitive folk songs, and surreal poems.[1] Such poetry may move us and give pleasure (although not, perhaps, the pleasure of mental understanding). We do it no harm by trying to paraphrase it, though we may fail. Whether logically clear or strangely opaque, good poems appeal to the intelligence and do not shrink from it.

So far, we have taken for granted that poetry differs from prose; yet all our strategies for reading poetry—plowing straight on through and then going back, isolating difficulties, trying to paraphrase, reading aloud, using a dictionary—are no different from those we might employ in unraveling a complicated piece of prose. Poetry, after all, is similar to prose in most respects. At the very least, it is written in the same language. Like prose,

---

[1]The French poet André Breton, founder of **surrealism,** a movement in art and writing, declared that a higher reality exists, which to mortal eyes looks absurd. To mirror that reality, surrealist poets are fond of bizarre and dreamlike objects such as soluble fish and white-haired revolvers.

poetry shares knowledge with us. It tells us, for instance, of a beautiful island in Lake Gill, County Sligo, Ireland, of how one man feels toward it. Maybe the poet knows no more about Innisfree than a writer of a travel guidebook knows. And yet Yeats's poem indicates a kind of knowledge that tourist guidebooks do not ordinarily reveal: that the human heart can yearn for peace and happiness, that the lake isle of Innisfree with its "low sounds by the shore" can echo and reecho in memory forever.

## Lyric Poetry

Originally, as its Greek name suggests, a *lyric* was a poem sung to the music of a lyre. This earlier meaning—a poem made for singing—is still current today, when we use *lyrics* to mean the words of a popular song. But the kind of printed poem we now call a *lyric* is usually something else, for over the past five hundred years, the nature of lyric poetry has changed greatly. Ever since the rise of the printing press in the fifteenth century, poets have written less often for singers, more often for readers. In general, this tendency has made lyric poems contain less word-music and (since they can be pondered on a page) more thought—and perhaps more complicated feelings.

Here is a rough definition of a **lyric** as it is written today: a short poem expressing the thoughts and feelings of a single speaker. Often a poet will write a lyric in the first person ("I will arise and go now, and go to Innisfree"), but not always. Instead, a lyric might describe an object or recall an experience without the speaker's ever bringing himself or herself into it. (For an example of such a lyric, one in which the poet refrains from saying "I," see William Carlos Williams's "The Red Wheelbarrow" on page 609, Theodore Roethke's "Root Cellar" on page 662, or Gerard Manley Hopkins's "Pied Beauty" on page 667.)

Perhaps because, rightly or wrongly, some people still think of lyrics as lyre-strummings, they expect a lyric to be an outburst of feeling, somewhat resembling a song, at least containing musical elements such as rime, rhythm, or sound effects. Such expectations are fulfilled in "The Lake Isle of Innisfree," that impassioned lyric full of language rich in sound (as you will hear if you'll read it aloud). In practice, though, many contemporary poets write short poems in which they voice opinions or complicated feelings—poems that no reader would dream of trying to sing. Most people would call such poems lyrics, too; one recent commentator has argued that a lyric may contain an argument.[2]

But in the sense in which we use it, *lyric* will usually apply to a kind of poem you can easily recognize. Here, for instance, are two lyrics. They differ sharply in subject and theme, but they have traits in common: both are short, and (as you will find) both set forth one speaker's definite, unmistakable feelings.

[2]Jeffrey Walker, "Aristotle's Lyric," *College English* 51 (January, 1989) 5–26.

## D. H. Lawrence (1885–1930)*

PIANO                                                        1918

Softly, in the dusk, a woman is singing to me;
Taking me back down the vista of years, till I see
A child sitting under the piano, in the boom of the tingling strings
And pressing the small, poised feet of a mother who smiles as she
      sings.

In spite of myself, the insidious mastery of song                    5
Betrays me back, till the heart of me weeps to belong
To the old Sunday evenings at home, with winter outside
And hymns in the cozy parlor, the tinkling piano our guide.

So now it is vain for the singer to burst into clamor
With the great black piano appassionato. The glamor              10
Of childish days is upon me, my manhood is cast
Down in the flood of remembrance, I weep like a child for the past.

QUESTIONS

1. Jot down a brief paraphrase of this poem. In your paraphrase, clearly show what
   the speaker says is happening at present and also what he finds himself remembering. Make clear which seems the more powerful in its effect on him.
2. What are the speaker's various feelings? What do you understand from the words
   *insidious* and *betrays?*
3. With what specific details does the poem make the past seem real?
4. What is the subject of Lawrence's poem? How would you state its theme?

## May Swenson (1913–1989)

FOUR-WORD LINES        1967

Your eyes are just
like bees, and I
feel like a flower.
Their brown power makes
a breeze go over                                                     5
my skin. When your
lashes ride down and
rise like brown bees'
legs, your pronged gaze
makes my eyes gauze.                                                10
I wish we were
in some shade and
no swarm of other
eyes to know that
I'm a flower breathing                                               15

bare, laid open to
your bees' warm stare.
I'd let you wade
in me and seize
with your eager brown                                                    20
bees' power a sweet
glistening at my core.

## QUESTIONS:

1. The language of "Four-Word Lines" is relatively simple and straightforward. In
   what ways, however, does it differ from the prose you might read in a newspaper
   or magazine?
2. The poem grows out of two comparisons made at the beginning (lines 1–3). What
   are the comparisons and where do they lead?
3. A swarm of bees could easily be a threatening image. Why doesn't the speaker find
   them scary?
4. The poem's title explains its unusual form, but Swenson occasionally sneaks in
   some other poetic devices. How many rhymes can you find hidden in the poem?
   (Hint: not all the rhymes are at the end of lines.)

## NARRATIVE POETRY

Although a lyric sometimes relates an incident, or like "Piano" draws a
scene, it does not usually relate a series of events. That happens in a **narrative
poem,** one whose main purpose is to tell a story.

In Western literature, narrative poetry dates back to the Babylonian epic
of Gilgamesh (composed before 2000 B.C.) and Homer's epic *Iliad* and *Odyssey* (composed before 700 B.C.). It may well have originated much earlier. In
England and Scotland, storytelling poems have long been popular; in the late
Middle Ages, ballads—or storytelling songs—circulated widely. Some, like
"Sir Patrick Spence" and "Bonny Barbara Allan," survive in our day, and
folksingers sometimes perform them.

Evidently the art of narrative poetry invites the skills of a writer of
fiction: the ability to draw characters and settings briefly, to engage attention,
to shape a plot. Needless to say, it calls for all the skills of a poet besides.
Here are two narrative poems: one medieval, one modern. How would you
paraphrase the stories they tell? How do they hold your attention to their
stories?

### ***Anonymous*** (traditional Scottish ballad)

### SIR PATRICK SPENCE

The king sits in Dumferling toune,
    Drinking the blude-reid wine:
"O whar will I get guid sailor
    To sail this schip of mine?"

Up and spak an eldern knicht,                                        5
  Sat at the kings richt kne:
"Sir Patrick Spence is the best sailor
  That sails upon the se."

The king has written a braid letter,
  And signed it wi' his hand,                                        10
And sent it to Sir Patrick Spence,
  Was walking on the sand.

The first line that Sir Patrick red,
  A loud lauch lauchèd he;
The next line that Sir Patrick red,                                  15
  The teir blinded his ee.

"O wha° is this has don this deid,                                    *who*
  This ill deid don to me,
To send me out this time o' the yeir,
  To sail upon the se!                                               20

"Mak haste, mak haste, my mirry men all,
  Our guid schip sails the morne."
"O say na sae°, my master deir,                                       *so*
  For I feir a deadlie storme.

"Late late yestreen I saw the new moone,                             25
  Wi' the auld moone in hir arme,
And I feir, I feir, my deir master,
  That we will cum to harme."

O our Scots nobles wer richt laith°                                   *loath*
  To weet° their cork-heild schoone°,                   *wet; shoes*   30
Bot lang owre° a' the play wer playd,                               *before*
  Their hats they swam aboone°.                     *above (their heads)*

O lang, lang may their ladies sit,
  Wi' their fans into their hand,
Or ere° they se Sir Patrick Spence                           *long before*   35
  Cum sailing to the land.

O lang, lang may the ladies stand,
  Wi' their gold kems° in their hair,                              *combs*
Waiting for their ain° deir lords,                                   *own*
  For they'll se thame na mair.                                     40

Haf owre°, haf owre to Aberdour,                            *halfway over*
  It's fiftie fadom deip,
And thair lies guid Sir Patrick Spence,
  Wi' the Scots lords at his feit.

SIR PATRICK SPENCE. 9 *braid:* Broad, but broad in what sense? Among guesses are *plain-spoken,*
*official,* and *on wide paper.*

1. That the king drinks "blood-red wine" (line 2)—what meaning do you find in that detail? What does it hint, or foreshadow?
2. What do you make of this king and his motives for sending Spence and the Scots lords out into an impending storm? Is he a fool, is he cruel and inconsiderate, is he deliberately trying to drown Sir Patrick and his crew, or can't we possibly know? Let your answer depend on the poem alone, not on anything you read into it.
3. Comment on this ballad's methods of storytelling. Is the story told too briefly for us to care what happens to Spence and his men, or does the poet by any means make us feel compassion for them? Do you resent the lack of a detailed account of the shipwreck?
4. Lines 25–28—the new moon with the old moon in her arm—has been much admired as poetry. What does this stanza contribute to the story as well?

---

**Robert Frost** (1874–1963)*

"OUT, OUT—" 1916

The buzz-saw snarled and rattled in the yard
And made dust and dropped stove-length sticks of wood,
Sweet-scented stuff when the breeze drew across it.
And from there those that lifted eyes could count
Five mountain ranges one behind the other 5
Under the sunset far into Vermont.
And the saw snarled and rattled, snarled and rattled,
As it ran light, or had to bear a load.
And nothing happened: day was all but done.
Call it a day, I wish they might have said 10
To please the boy by giving him the half hour
That a boy counts so much when saved from work.
His sister stood beside them in her apron
To tell them "Supper." At the word, the saw,
As if to prove saws knew what supper meant, 15
Leaped out at the boy's hand, or seemed to leap—
He must have given the hand. However it was,
Neither refused the meeting. But the hand!
The boy's first outcry was a rueful laugh,
As he swung toward them holding up the hand 20
Half in appeal, but half as if to keep
The life from spilling. Then the boy saw all—
Since he was old enough to know, big boy
Doing a man's work, though a child at heart—
He saw all spoiled. "Don't let him cut my hand off— 25
The doctor, when he comes. Don't let him, sister!"
So. But the hand was gone already.

The doctor put him in the dark of ether.
He lay and puffed his lips out with his breath.
And then—the watcher at his pulse took fright.     30
No one believed. They listened at his heart.
Little—less—nothing!—and that ended it.
No more to build on there. And they, since they
Were not the one dead, turned to their affairs.

"Out, Out—" The title of this poem echoes the words of Shakespeare's Macbeth on receiving news that his queen is dead: "Out, out, brief candle! / Life's but a walking shadow, a poor player / That struts and frets his hour upon the stage / And then is heard no more. It is a tale / Told by an idiot, full of sound and fury, / Signifying nothing" (*Macbeth* V, v, 23–28).

## Questions

1. How does Frost make the buzz-saw appear sinister? How does he make it seem, in another way, like a friend?
2. What do you make of the people who surround the boy—the "they" of the poem? Who might they be? Do they seem to you concerned and compassionate, cruel, indifferent, or what?
3. What does Frost's reference to *Macbeth* contribute to your understanding of "Out, Out—"? How would you state the theme of Frost's poem?
4. Set this poem side by side with "Sir Patrick Spence." How does "Out, Out—" resemble that medieval folk ballad in subject, or differ from it? How is Frost's poem similar or different in its way of telling a story?

# Dramatic Poetry

A third kind of poetry is **dramatic poetry** that presents the voice of an imaginary character (or characters) speaking directly, without any additional narration by the author. A dramatic poem, according to T. S. Eliot, does not consist of "what the poet would say in his own person, but only what he can say within the limits of one imaginary character addressing another imaginary character." Strictly speaking, the term *dramatic poetry* describes any verse written for the stage (and until a few centuries ago most playwrights, like Shakespeare and Molière, wrote their plays mainly in verse). But the term most often refers to the **dramatic monologue,** a poem written as a speech made by a character (other than the author) at some decisive moment. A dramatic monologue is usually addressed by the speaker to some other character who remains silent. If the listener replies, the poem becomes a dialogue (like the traditional ballad "Edward" on page 886) in which the story unfolds in the conversation between two speakers.

The Victorian poet Robert Browning, who developed the form of the dramatic monologue, liked to put words in the mouths of characters who were conspicuously nasty, weak, reckless, or crazy: see, for instance, Browning's "Soliloquy of the Spanish Cloister" (page 902) in which the speaker is an obsessively proud and jealous monk. The dramatic monologue has been a popular form among American poets, including Edwin Arlington

Robinson, Robert Frost, Ezra Pound, Randall Jarrell, and Sylvia Plath. The most famous dramatic monologue ever written is probably Browning's "My Last Duchess" in which the poet creates a Renaissance Italian Duke whose words reveal more about himself than the aristocratic speaker intends.

### *Robert Browning* (1812–1889)*

MY LAST DUCHESS                                                          1842

*Ferrara*

That's my last Duchess painted on the wall,
Looking as if she were alive. I call
That piece a wonder, now; Frà Pandolf's hands
Worked busily a day, and there she stands.
Will't please you sit and look at her? I said                              5
"Frà Pandolf" by design, for never read
Strangers like you that pictured countenance,
The depth and passion of its earnest glance,
But to myself they turned (since none puts by
The curtain I have drawn for you, but I)                                   10
And seemed as they would ask me, if they durst,
How such a glance came there; so, not the first
Are you to turn and ask thus. Sir, 'twas not
Her husband's presence only, called that spot
Of joy into the Duchess' cheek; perhaps                                    15
Frà Pandolf chanced to say, "Her mantle laps
Over my lady's wrist too much," or "Paint
Must never hope to reproduce the faint
Half-flush that dies along her throat." Such stuff
Was courtesy, she thought, and cause enough                                20
For calling up that spot of joy. She had
A heart—how shall I say?—too soon made glad,
Too easily impressed; she liked whate'er
She looked on, and her looks went everywhere.
Sir, 'twas all one! My favor at her breast,                                25
The dropping of the daylight in the West,
The bough of cherries some officious fool
Broke in the orchard for her, the white mule
She rode with round the terrace—all and each
Would draw from her alike the approving speech,                           30
Or blush, at least. She thanked men,—good! but thanked
Somehow—I know not how—as if she ranked
My gift of a nine-hundred-years-old name
With anybody's gift. Who'd stoop to blame

This sort of trifling? Even had you skill           35
In speech—which I have not—to make your will
Quite clear to such an one, and say "Just this
Or that in you disgusts me; here you miss,
Or there exceed the mark"—and if she let
Herself be lessoned so, nor plainly set           40
Her wits to yours, forsooth, and made excuse—
E'en then would be some stooping; and I choose
Never to stoop. Oh, sir, she smiled, no doubt,
Whene'er I passed her; but who passed without
Much the same smile? This grew; I gave commands;    45
Then all smiles stopped together. There she stands
As if alive. Will't please you rise? We'll meet
The company below, then. I repeat,
The Count your master's known munificence
Is ample warrant that no just pretense          50
Of mine for dowry will be disallowed;
Though his fair daughter's self, as I avowed
At starting, is my object. Nay, we'll go
Together down, sir. Notice Neptune, though,
Taming a sea-horse, thought a rarity,          55
Which Claus of Innsbruck cast in bronze for me!

My Last Duchess. Ferrara, a city in northern Italy, is the scene. Browning may have modeled his speaker after Alonzo, Duke of Ferrara (1533–1598). 3. *Frà Pandolf* and 56. *Claus of Innsbruck*: fictitious names of artists.

## Questions

1. Who is the Duke addressing? What is this person's business in Ferrara?
2. What is the Duke's opinion of his last Duchess's personality? Do we see her character differently?
3. If the Duke was unhappy with the Duchess's behavior, why didn't he make his displeasure known? Cite a specific passage to explain his reticence.
4. How much do we know about the fate of the last Duchess? Would it help our understanding of the poem to know more?
5. Does Browning imply any connection between the Duke's art collection and his attitude toward his wife?

    Today, lyrics in the English language seem more plentiful than other kinds of poetry. Although there has recently been a revival of interest in writing narrative poems, they have a far smaller audience today than long verse narratives, like Henry Wadsworth Longfellow's *Evangeline* and Alfred, Lord Tennyson's *Idylls of the King,* enjoyed in the nineteenth century.

    Also more fashionable in former times was a fourth variety of poetry, **didactic poetry:** that apparently written to state a message or teach a body of knowledge. In a lyric, a speaker may express sadness; in a didactic poem, he or she may explain that sadness is inherent in life. Poems that impart a body of knowledge, like Ovid's *Art of Love* and Lucretius's *On the Nature of*

*Things,* are didactic. Such instructive poetry was favored especially by classical Latin poets and by English poets of the eighteenth century. In *The Fleece* (1757), John Dyer celebrated the British woolen industry and included practical advice on raising sheep:

> In cold stiff soils the bleaters oft complain
> Of gouty ails, by shepherds termed the halt:
> Those let the neighboring fold or ready crook
> Detain, and pour into their cloven feet
> Corrosive drugs, deep-searching arsenic,
> Dry alum, verdegris, or vitriol keen.

One might agree with Dr. Johnson's comment on Dyer's effort: "The subject, Sir, cannot be made poetical." But it may be argued that the subject of didactic poetry does not make it any less poetical. Good poems, it seems, can be written about anything under the sun. Like Dyer, John Milton also described sick sheep in "Lycidas," a poem few readers have thought unpoetic:

> The hungry sheep look up, and are not fed,
> But, swoll'n with wind and the rank mist they draw,
> Rot inwardly, and foul contagion spread . . .

What makes Milton's lines better poetry than Dyer's is, among other things, a difference in attitude. Sick sheep to Dyer mean the loss of a few shillings and pence; to Milton, whose sheep stand for English Christendom, they mean a moral catastrophe.

## Suggestion for Writing

Write a concise, accurate paraphrase of a poem from the Poems for Further Reading (pages 885–1022). Your instructor may wish to suggest a poem or poems. Although your paraphrase should take in the entire poem, it need not mention everything. Just try to include the points that seem most vital and try to state the poem's main thought, or *theme.* Be ready to share your paraphrase with the rest of the class and to compare it with other paraphrases of the same poem. You may then be able to test yourself as a reader of poetry. What in the poem whizzed by you that other students noticed? What did you discover that others ignored?

# 14 *Listening to a Voice*

## TONE

In late-show Westerns, when one hombre taunts another, it is customary for the second to drawl, "Smile when you say that, pardner" or "Mister, I don't like your tone of voice." Sometimes in reading a poem, although we can neither see a face nor hear a voice, we can infer the poet's attitude from other evidence.

Like tone of voice, **tone** in literature often conveys an attitude toward the person addressed. Like the manner of a person, the manner of a poem may be friendly or belligerent toward its reader, condescending or respectful. Again like tone of voice, the tone of a poem may tell us how the speaker feels about himself or herself: cocksure or humble, sad or glad. But usually when we ask, "What is the tone of a poem?" we mean, "What attitude does the poet take toward a theme or a subject?" Is the poet being affectionate, hostile, earnest, playful, sarcastic, or what? We may never be able to know, of course, the poet's personal feelings. All we need know is how to feel when we read the poem.

Strictly speaking, tone isn't an attitude; it is whatever in the poem makes an attitude clear to us: the choice of certain words instead of others, the picking out of certain details. In A. E. Housman's "Loveliest of trees," for example, the poet communicates his admiration for a cherry tree's beauty by singling out for attention its white blossoms; had he wanted to show his dislike for the tree, he might have concentrated on its broken branches, birdlime, or snails. Rightly to perceive the tone of a poem, we need to read the poem carefully, paying attention to whatever suggestions we find in it.

My Papa's Waltz        1948

The whiskey on your breath
Could make a small boy dizzy;
But I hung on like death:
Such waltzing was not easy.

We romped until the pans                                    5
Slid from the kitchen shelf;
My mother's countenance
Could not unfrown itself.

The hand that held my wrist
Was battered on one knuckle;                                10
At every step you missed
My right ear scraped a buckle.

You beat time on my head
With a palm caked hard by dirt,
Then waltzed me off to bed                                  15
Still clinging to your shirt.

What is the tone of this poem? Most readers find the speaker's attitude toward his father affectionate and take this recollection of childhood to be a happy one. But at least one reader, concentrating on certain details, once wrote: "Roethke expresses his resentment for his father, a drunken brute with dirty hands and a whiskey breath who carelessly hurt the child's ear and manhandled him." Although this reader accurately noticed some of the events in the poem and perceived that in the son's hanging on to the father "like death" there is something desperate, he missed the tone of the poem and so misunderstood it altogether. Among other things, this reader didn't notice the rollicking rhythms of the poem; the playfulness of a rime like *dizzy* and *easy*; the joyful suggestions of the words *waltz*, *waltzing*, and *romped*. Probably the reader didn't stop to visualize this scene in all its comedy, with kitchen pans falling and the father happily using his son's head for a drum. Nor did he stop to feel the suggestions in the last line, with the boy *still clinging* with persistent love.

Such a poem, though it includes lifelike details that aren't pretty, has a tone relatively easy to recognize. So does **satiric poetry,** a kind of comic poetry that generally conveys a message. Usually its tone is one of detached amusement, withering contempt, and implied superiority. In a satiric poem, the poet ridicules some person or persons (or perhaps some kind of human behavior), examining the victim by the light of certain principles and implying that the reader, too, ought to feel contempt for the victim.

## Countee Cullen (1903–1946)

### FOR A LADY I KNOW                1925

She even thinks that up in heaven
   Her class lies late and snores,
While poor black cherubs rise at seven
   To do celestial chores.

### QUESTIONS

1. What is Cullen's message?
2. How would you characterize the tone of this poem? Wrathful? Amused?

    In some poems the poet's attitude may be plain enough; while in other poems attitudes may be so mingled that it is hard to describe them tersely without doing injustice to the poem. Does Andrew Marvell in "To His Coy Mistress" (page 957) take a serious or playful attitude toward the fact that he and his lady are destined to be food for worms? No one-word answer will suffice. And what of T. S. Eliot's "Love Song of J. Alfred Prufrock" (page 916)? In his attitude toward his redemption-seeking hero who wades with trousers rolled, Eliot is seriously funny. Such a mingled tone may be seen in the following poem by the wife of a governor of the Massachusetts Bay Colony and the earliest American poet of note. Anne Bradstreet's first book, *The Tenth Muse Lately Sprung Up in America* (1650), had been published in England without her consent. She wrote these lines to preface a second edition:

## Anne Bradstreet (1612?–1672)

### THE AUTHOR TO HER BOOK                1678

Thou ill-formed offspring of my feeble brain,
Who after birth did'st by my side remain,
Till snatched from thence by friends, less wise than true,
Who thee abroad exposed to public view;
Made thee in rags, halting, to the press to trudge,     5
Where errors were not lessened, all may judge.
At thy return my blushing was not small,
My rambling brat (in print) should mother call;
I cast thee by as one unfit for light,
Thy visage was so irksome in my sight;     10
Yet being mine own, at length affection would
Thy blemishes amend, if so I could:
I washed thy face, but more defects I saw,

And rubbing off a spot, still made a flaw.
I stretched thy joints to make thee even feet,                          15
Yet still thou run'st more hobbling than is meet;
In better dress to trim thee was my mind,
But nought save homespun cloth in the house I find.
In this array, 'mongst vulgars may'st thou roam;
In critics' hands beware thou dost not come;                            20
And take thy way where yet thou are not known.
If for thy Father asked, say thou had'st none;
And for thy Mother, she alas is poor,
Which caused her thus to send thee out of door.

In the author's comparison of her book to an illegitimate ragamuffin, we may
be struck by the details of scrubbing and dressing a child: details that might
well occur to a mother who had scrubbed and dressed many. As she might
feel toward such a child, so she feels toward her book. She starts by deplor-
ing it but, as the poem goes on, cannot deny it her affection. Humor enters
(as in the pun in line 15). She must dress the creature in *homespun cloth*,
something both crude and serviceable. By the end of her poem, Bradstreet
seems to regard her book-child with tenderness, amusement, and a certain
indulgent awareness of its faults. To read this poem is to sense its mingling
of several attitudes. Simultaneously, a poet can be merry and in earnest.

## *Walt Whitman* (1819–1892)*

## TO A LOCOMOTIVE IN WINTER                                            1881

Thee for my recitative,
Thee in the driving storm even as now, the snow, the winter-day
    declining,
Thee in thy panoply°, thy measur'd dual throbbing and thy             *suit of*
    beat convulsive,                                                   *armor*
Thy black cylindric body, golden brass and silvery steel,
Thy ponderous side-bars, parallel and connecting rods, gyrating,
    shuttling at thy sides,                                              5
Thy metrical, now swelling pant and roar, now tapering in the
    distance,
Thy great protruding head-light fix'd in front,
Thy long, pale, floating vapor-pennants, tinged with delicate purple,
The dense and murky clouds out-belching from thy smoke-stack,
Thy knitted frame, thy springs and valves, the tremulous twinkle of
    thy wheels,                                                        10
Thy train of cars behind, obedient, merrily following,
Through gale or calm, now swift, now slack, yet steadily careering;
Type of the modern—emblem of motion and power—pulse of the
    continent,

For once come serve the Muse and merge in verse, even as here I
    see thee,
With storm and buffeting gusts of wind and falling snow,                    15
By day thy warning ringing bell to sound its notes,
By night thy silent signal lamps to swing.
Fierce-throated beauty!
Roll through my chant with all thy lawless music, thy swinging
    lamps at night,
Thy madly-whistled laughter, echoing, rumbling like an earthquake,
    rousing all,                                                            20
Law of thyself complete, thine own track firmly holding,
(No sweetness debonair of tearful harp or glib piano thine,)
Thy trills of shrieks by rocks and hills return'd,
Launch'd o'er the prairies wide, across the lakes,
To the free skies unpent and glad and strong.                              25

---

## Emily Dickinson (1830–1886)*

### I LIKE TO SEE IT LAP THE MILES          (about 1862)

I like to see it lap the Miles–
And lick the Valleys up–
And stop to feed itself at Tanks–
And then–prodigious step

Around a Pile of Mountains–                                                  5
And supercilious peer
In Shanties–by the sides of Roads–
And then a Quarry pare

To fit its Ribs
And crawl between                                                          10
Complaining all the while
In horrid–hooting stanza–
Then chase itself down Hill–

And neigh like Boanerges–
Then–punctual as a Star                                                    15
Stop–docile and omnipotent
At its own stable door–

## QUESTIONS

1. What differences in tone do you find between Whitman's and Dickinson's poems?
   Point out in each poem whatever contributes to these differences.
2. *Boanerges* in Dickinson's last stanza means "sons of thunder," a name given by
   Jesus to the disciples John and James (see Mark 3:17). How far should the reader
   work out the particulars of this comparison? Does it make the tone of the poem
   serious?

3. In Whitman's opening line, what is a *recitative?* What other specialized terms from the vocabulary of music and poetry does each poem contain? How do they help underscore Whitman's theme?
4. Poets and song-writers probably have regarded the locomotive with more affection than they have shown most other machines. Why do you suppose this to be? Can you think of any other poems or songs for example?
5. What do these two poems tell you about locomotives that you would not be likely to find in a technical book on railroading?
6. Are the subjects of the two poems identical? Discuss.

## *Langston Hughes* (1902–1967)*

### HOMECOMING                    1959

I went back in the alley
And I opened up my door.
All her clothes was gone:
She wasn't home no more.

I pulled back the covers,                                        5
I made down the bed.
A *whole* lot of room
Was the only thing I had.

### QUESTIONS

1. How does the speaker feel about this sudden disappearance? Exactly what in the poem makes his feelings clear?
2. Suppose the speaker had ranted, cried, felt sorry for himself, and discussed his anger, frustration, and grief at great length. Do you suppose a better poem might have resulted? What do you find to admire in the poem as it is?

## *Weldon Kees* (1914–1955)

### FOR MY DAUGHTER                    1940

Looking into my daughter's eyes I read
Beneath the innocence of morning flesh
Concealed, hintings of death she does not heed.
Coldest of winds have blown this hair, and mesh
Of seaweed snarled these miniatures of hands;                   5
The night's slow poison, tolerant and bland,
Has moved her blood. Parched years that I have seen
That may be hers appear: foul, lingering
Death in certain war, the slim legs green.
Or, fed on hate, she relishes the sting                         10
Of others' agony; perhaps the cruel

Bride of a syphilitic or a fool.
These speculations sour in the sun.
I have no daughter. I desire none.

## QUESTIONS

1. How does the last line of this sonnet affect the meaning of the poem?
2. "For My Daughter" was first published in 1940. What considerations might a potential American parent have felt at that time? Are these historical concerns mirrored in the poem?
3. Donald Justice has said that "Kees is one of the bitterest poets in history." Is bitterness the only attitude the speaker reveals in this poem?

# THE PERSON IN THE POEM

The tone of a poem, we said, is like tone of voice in that both communicate feelings. Still, this comparison raises a question: When we read a poem, whose "voice" speaks to us?

"The poet's" is one possible answer; and in the case of many a poem, that answer may be right. Reading Anne Bradstreet's "The Author to Her Book," we can be reasonably sure that the poet speaks of her very own book, and of her own experiences. In order to read a poem, we seldom need to read a poet's biography; but in truth there are certain poems whose full effect depends upon our knowing at least a fact or two of the poet's life. In this poem, surely the poet refers to himself:

## *Trumbull Stickney* (1874–1904)

SIR, SAY NO MORE         1905

Sir, say no more,
Within me 'tis as if
The green and climbing eyesight of a cat
Crawled near my mind's poor birds.

The subject of Stickney's poem is not some nightmare or hallucination. The poem may mean more to you if you know that Stickney, who wrote it shortly before his death, had been afflicted by cancer of the brain. But the poem is not a prosaic entry in the diary of a dying man, nor is it a good poem because a dying man wrote it. Not only does it tell truth from experience, it speaks in memorable words.

Most of us can tell the difference between a person we meet in life and a person we meet in a work of art—unlike the moviegoer in the Philippines who, watching a villain in an exciting film, pulled out a revolver and peppered the screen. And yet, in reading poems, we are liable to temptation.

When the poet says "I," we may want to assume that he or she, like Trumbull Stickney, is making a personal statement. But reflect: do all poems have to be personal? Here is a brief poem inscribed on the tombstone of an infant in Burial Hill cemetery, Plymouth, Massachusetts:

> Since I have been so quickly done for,
> I wonder what I was begun for.

We do not know who wrote those lines, but it is clear that the poet was not a short-lived infant writing from personal experience. In other poems, the speaker is obviously a **persona** or fictitious character: not the poet, but the poet's creation. As a grown man, William Blake, a skilled professional engraver, wrote a poem in the voice of a boy, an illiterate chimney sweeper. (The poem appears on page 621.) No law decrees that the speaker in a poem even has to be human: good poems have been uttered by clouds, pebbles, and cats.

Let's consider a poem spoken not by a poet, but by a persona—in this case not even a human persona, but a tree. The poem is a monologue, but not a dramatic monologue. It gives us the spoken thoughts of a single persona, but the moment isn't particularly dramatic, nor does there seem to be a specific listener implied in the poem. (For a definition of a dramatic monologue, see page 593).

## *Howard Moss* (1922–1987)*

## THE PRUNED TREE                    1965

As a torn paper might seal up its side,
Or a streak of water stitch itself to silk
And disappear, my wound has been my healing,
And I am made more beautiful by losses.
See the flat water in the distance nodding                    5
Approval, the light that fell in love with statues,
Seeing me alive, turn its motion toward me.
Shorn, I rejoice in what was taken from me.

What can the moonlight do with my new shape
But trace and retrace its miracle of order?                    10
I stand, waiting for the strange reaction
Of insects who knew me in my larger self,
Unkempt, in a naturalness I did not love.
Even the dog's voice rings with a new echo,
And all the little leaves I shed are singing,                    15
Singing to the moon of shapely newness.

Somewhere what I lost I hope is springing
To life again. The roofs, astonished by me,

Are taking new bearings in the night, the owl
Is crying for a further wisdom, the lilac                                    20
Putting forth its strongest scent to find me.
Butterflies, like sails in grooves, are winging
Out of the water to wash me, wash me.
Now, I am stirring like a seed in China.

QUESTIONS

1. The literal subject of "The Pruned Tree" is how a tree can grow stronger and more
   beautiful by having its branches pruned. Is the poem about anything else less
   obvious?
2. What is the tree's attitude toward its "wound"?
3. Why would a poet want to write a poem in the voice of a tree? Is anything gained
   by using a non-human voice?

In a famous definition, William Wordsworth calls poetry "the spontaneous overflow of powerful feelings . . . recollected in tranquillity."[1] But
in the case of the following poem, Wordsworth's feelings weren't all his;
they didn't just overflow spontaneously; and the process of tranquil recollection had to go on for years.

---

### William Wordsworth (1770–1850)*

### I WANDERED LONELY AS A CLOUD          1807

I wandered lonely as a cloud
   That floats on high o'er vales and hills,
When all at once I saw a crowd,
   A host, of golden daffodils,
Beside the lake, beneath the trees,                                          5
Fluttering and dancing in the breeze.

Continuous as the stars that shine
   And twinkle on the milky way,
They stretched in never-ending line
   Along the margin of a bay:                                                10
Ten thousand saw I at a glance,
Tossing their heads in sprightly dance.

The waves beside them danced; but they
   Out-did the sparkling waves in glee;
A poet could not but be gay,                                                 15
   In such a jocund company;
I gazed—and gazed—but little thought
What wealth the show to me had brought:

[1]For a fuller text of Wordsworth's statement, see page 1027.

For oft, when on my couch I lie
  In vacant or in pensive mood,
They flash upon that inward eye
  Which is the bliss of solitude;
And then my heart with pleasure fills,
And dances with the daffodils.

20

Between the first printing of the poem in 1807 and the version of 1815 given here, Wordsworth made several deliberate improvements. He changed *dancing* to *golden* in line 4, *Along* to *Beside* in line 5, *Ten thousand* to *Fluttering and* in line 6, *laughing* to *jocund* in line 16, and he added a whole stanza (the second). In fact, the writing of the poem was unspontaneous enough for Wordsworth, at a loss for lines 21–22, to take them from his wife Mary. It is likely that the experience of daffodil-watching was not entirely his to begin with but was derived in part from the recollections his sister Dorothy Wordsworth had set down in her journal of April 15, 1802, two years before he first drafted his poem:

> When we were in the woods beyond Gowbarrow Park we saw a few daffodils close to the water-side. We fancied that the lake had floated the seeds ashore, and that the little colony had so sprung up. But as we went along there were more and yet more; and at last, under the boughs of the trees, we saw that there was a long belt of them along the shore, about the breadth of a country turnpike road. I never saw daffodils so beautiful. They grew among the mossy stones about and about them; some rested their heads upon these stones as on a pillow for weariness; and the rest tossed and reeled and danced, and seemed as if they verily laughed with the wind, that flew upon them over the Lake; they looked so gay, ever glancing, ever changing. This wind blew directly over the Lake to them. There was here and there a little knot, and a few stragglers a few yards higher up; but they were so few as not to disturb the simplicity, unity, and life of that one busy highway.

Notice that Wordsworth's poem echoes a few of his sister's observations. Weaving poetry out of their mutual memories, Wordsworth has offered the experience as if altogether his own, made himself lonely, and left Dorothy out. The point is not that Wordsworth is a liar or a plagiarist but that, like any other good poet, he has transformed ordinary life into art. A process of interpreting, shaping, and ordering had to intervene between the experience of looking at daffodils and the finished poem.

We need not deny that a poet's experience can contribute to a poem nor that the emotion in the poem can indeed be the poet's. Still, to write a good poem one has to do more than live and feel. It seems a pity that, as Randall Jarrell has said, a cardinal may write verses worse than his youngest choirboy's. But writing poetry takes skill and imagination—qualities that extensive travel and wide experience do not necessarily give. For much of her life, Emily Dickinson seldom strayed from her family's house and grounds in

Amherst, Massachusetts; yet her rimed lifestudies of a snake, a bee, and a hummingbird contain more poetry than we find in any firsthand description (so far) of the surface of the moon.

## James Stephens (1882–1950)*

### A Glass of Beer                                          1918

The lanky hank of a she in the inn over there
Nearly killed me for asking the loan of a glass of beer;
May the devil grip the whey-faced slut by the hair,
And beat bad manners out of her skin for a year.

That parboiled ape, with the toughest jaw you will see          5
On virtue's path, and a voice that would rasp the dead,
Came roaring and raging the minute she looked at me,
And threw me out of the house on the back of my head!

If I asked her master he'd give me a cask a day;
But she, with the beer at hand, not a gill° would arrange!     *quarter-pint*   10
May she marry a ghost and bear him a kitten, and may
The High King of Glory permit her to get the mange.

### Questions

1. Who do you take to be the speaker? Is it the poet? The speaker may be angry, but what is the tone of this poem?
2. Would you agree with a commentator who said, "To berate anyone in truly memorable language is practically a lost art in America"? How well does the speaker (an Irishman) succeed? Which of his epithets and curses strike you as particularly imaginative?

## Anne Sexton (1928–1974)

### Her Kind                                                 1960

I have gone out, a possessed witch,
haunting the black air, braver at night;
dreaming evil, I have done my hitch
over the plain houses, light by light:
lonely thing, twelve-fingered, out of mind.                    5
A woman like that is not a woman, quite.
I have been her kind.

I have found the warm caves in the woods,
filled them with skillets, carvings, shelves,
closets, silks, innumerable goods;                            10
fixed the suppers for the worms and the elves:

whining, rearranging the disaligned.
A woman like that is misunderstood.
I have been her kind.

I have ridden in your cart, driver,                                    15
waved my nude arms at villages going by,
learning the last bright routes, survivor
where your flames still bite my thigh
and my ribs crack where your wheels wind.
A woman like that is not ashamed to die.                               20
I have been her kind.


QUESTIONS

1. Who is the speaker of this poem? What do we know about her?
2. What does the speaker mean by ending each stanza with the statement, "I have
   been her kind?"
3. Who are the figures with whom the speaker identifies? What do these figures tell
   us about the speaker's state of mind?


## Paul Zimmer (b. 1934)

## THE DAY ZIMMER LOST RELIGION          1976


The first Sunday I missed Mass on purpose
I waited all day for Christ to climb down
Like a wiry flyweight from the cross and
Club me on my irreverent teeth, to wade into
My blasphemous gut and drop me like a                                  5
Red hot thurible°, the devil roaring in              *vessel for incense*
Reserved seats until he got the hiccups.

It was a long cold way from the old days
When cassocked and surpliced I mumbled Latin
At the old priest and rang his obscure bell.                           10
A long way from the dirty wind that blew
The soot like venial sins across the school yard
Where God reigned as a threatening,
One-eyed triangle high in the fleecy sky.

The first Sunday I missed Mass on purpose                              15
I waited all day for Christ to climb down
Like the playground bully, the cuts and mice
Upon his face agleam, and pound me
Till my irreligious tongue hung out.
But of course He never came, knowing that                              20
I was grown up and ready for Him now.

1. Who is the person in this poem? The mature poet? The poet as a child? Some fictitious character?
2. What do you understand to be the speaker's attitude toward religion at the present moment?

## EXPERIMENT: *Reading with and without Biography*

Read the following poem and state what you understand from it. Then consider the circumstances in which it probably came to be written. (Some information is offered in a note on page 622.) Does the meaning of the poem change? To what extent does an appreciation of the poem need the support of biography?

*William Carlos Williams* (1883–1963)*

## THE RED WHEELBARROW          1923

so much depends
upon

a red wheel
barrow

glazed with rain                                                    5
water

beside the white
chickens.

## IRONY

To see a distinction between the poet and the words of a fictitious character—between Robert Browning and "My Last Duchess"—is to be aware of **irony:** a manner of speaking that implies a discrepancy. If the mask says one thing and we sense that the writer is in fact saying something else, the writer has adopted an **ironic point of view.** No finer illustration exists in English than Jonathan Swift's "A Modest Proposal," an essay in which Swift speaks as an earnest, humorless citizen who sets forth his reasonable plan to aid the Irish poor. The plan is so monstrous no sane reader can assent to it: the poor are to sell their children as meat for the tables of their landlords. From behind his falseface, Swift is actually recommending not cannibalism but love and Christian charity.

A poem is often made complicated and more interesting by another kind of irony. **Verbal irony** occurs whenever words say one thing but mean something else, usually the opposite. The word *love* means *hate* here: "I just *love* to stay home and do my hair on a Saturday night!" If the verbal irony is conspicuously bitter, heavy-handed, and mocking, it is **sarcasm:** "Oh, he's the biggest spender in the world, all right!" (The sarcasm, if that statement were spoken, would be underscored by the speaker's tone of voice.) A famous instance of sarcasm is Mark Antony's line in his oration over the body of slain Julius Caesar: "Brutus is an honorable man." Antony repeats this line until the enraged populace begins shouting exactly what he means to call Brutus and the other conspirators: traitors, villains, murderers. We had best be alert for irony on the printed page, for if we miss it, our interpretations of a poem may go wild.

### *Robert Creeley* (b. 1926)

Oh No                                    1959

If you wander far enough
you will come to it
and when you get there
they will give you a place to sit

for yourself only, in a nice chair,                          5
and all your friends will be there
with smiles on their faces
and they will likewise all have places.

This poem is rich in verbal irony. The title helps point out that between the speaker's words and attitude lie deep differences. In line 2, what is *it?* Old age? The wandering suggests a conventional metaphor: the journey of life. Is *it* literally a rest home for "senior citizens," or perhaps some naïve popular concept of heaven (such as we meet in comic strips: harps, angels with hoops for halos) in which the saved all sit around in a ring, smugly congratulating one another? We can't be sure, but the speaker's attitude toward this final sitting-place is definite. It is a place for the selfish, as we infer from the phrase *for yourself only.* And *smiles on their faces* may hint that the smiles are unchanging and forced. There is a difference between saying "They had smiles on their faces" and "They smiled": the latter suggests that the smiles came from within. The word *nice* is to be regarded with distrust. If we see through this speaker, as Creeley implies we can do, we realize that, while pretending to be sweet-talking us into a seat, actually he is revealing the horror of a little hell. And the title is the poet's reaction to it (or the speaker's unironic, straightforward one): "Oh no! Not *that!*"

   **Dramatic irony,** like verbal irony, contains an element of contrast, but it usually refers to a situation in a play wherein a character, whose knowledge is limited, says, does, or encounters something of greater significance than he or she knows. We, the spectators, realize the meaning of this speech or action, for the playwright has afforded us superior knowledge. In Sophocles' *King Oedipus*, when Oedipus vows to punish whoever has brought down a plague upon the city of Thebes, we know—as he does not—that the man he would punish is himself. (Referring to such a situation that precedes the downfall of a hero in a tragedy, some critics speak of **tragic irony** instead of dramatic irony.) Superior knowledge can be enjoyed not only by spectators in a theater but by readers of poetry as well. In *Paradise Lost*, we know in advance that Adam will fall into temptation, and we recognize his overconfidence when he neglects a warning. The situation of Oedipus contains also **cosmic irony,** or **irony of fate:** some Fate with a grim sense of humor seems cruelly to trick a human being. Cosmic irony clearly exists in poems in which fate or the Fates are personified and seen as hostile, as in Thomas Hardy's "The Convergence of the Twain" (page 927); and it may be said to occur too in Robinson's "Richard Cory" (page 703). Evidently it is a twist of fate for the most envied man in town to kill himself.

To sum up: the effect of irony depends upon the reader's noticing some incongruity or discrepancy between two things. In *verbal irony*, there is a contrast between the speaker's words and meaning; in an *ironic point of view*, between the writer's attitude and what is spoken by a fictitious character; in *dramatic irony*, between the limited knowledge of a character and the fuller knowledge of the reader or spectator; in *cosmic irony*, between a character's aspiration and the treatment he or she receives at the hands of Fate. Although in the work of an inept poet irony can be crude and obvious sarcasm, it is invaluable to a poet of more complicated mind, who imagines more than one perspective.

### W. H. Auden (1907–1973)*

THE UNKNOWN CITIZEN                                          1940

*(To JS/07/M/378
This Marble Monument
Is Erected by the State)*

He was found by the Bureau of Statistics to be
One against whom there was no official complaint,
And all the reports on his conduct agree
That, in the modern sense of an old-fashioned word, he was a saint,
For in everything he did he served the Greater Community.          5
Except for the War till the day he retired
He worked in a factory and never got fired,
But satisfied his employers, Fudge Motors Inc.
Yet he wasn't a scab or odd in his views,

For his Union reports that he paid his dues, 10
(Our report on his Union shows it was sound)
And our Social Psychology workers found
That he was popular with his mates and liked a drink.
The Press are convinced that he bought a paper every day
And that his reactions to advertisements were normal in every way. 15
Policies taken out in his name prove that he was fully insured,
And his Health-card shows he was once in hospital but left it cured.
Both Producers Research and High-Grade Living declare
He was fully sensible to the advantages of the Installment Plan
And had everything necessary to the Modern Man, 20
A phonograph, a radio, a car and a frigidaire.
Our researchers into Public Opinion are content
That he held the proper opinions for the time of year;
When there was peace, he was for peace; when there was war, he
    went.
He was married and added five children to the population, 25
Which our Eugenist says was the right number for a parent of his
    generation,
And our teachers report that he never interfered with their
    education.
Was he free? Was he happy? The question is absurd:
Had anything been wrong, we should certainly have heard.

### QUESTIONS

1. Read the three-line epitaph at the beginning of the poem as carefully as you read
   what follows. How does the epitaph help establish the voice by which the rest of
   the poem is spoken?
2. Who is speaking?
3. What ironic discrepancies do you find between the speaker's attitude toward the
   subject and that of the poet himself? By what is the poet's attitude made clear?
4. In the phrase "The Unknown Soldier" (of which "The Unknown Citizen" reminds us), what does the word *unknown* mean? What does it mean in the title of
   Auden's poem?
5. What tendencies in our civilization does Auden satirize?
6. How would you expect the speaker to define a Modern Man, if a CD player, a
   radio, a car, and a refrigerator are "everything" a Modern Man needs?

### *Sharon Olds* (b. 1942)*

RITES OF PASSAGE      1983

As the guests arrive at my son's party
they gather in the living room—

short men, men in first grade
with smooth jaws and chins.
Hands in pockets, they stand around                                    5
jostling, jockeying for place, small fights
breaking out and calming. One says to another
*How old are you? Six. I'm seven. So?*
They eye each other, seeing themselves
tiny in the other's pupils. They clear their                          10
throats a lot, a room of small bankers,
they fold their arms and frown. *I could beat you
up*, a seven says to a six,
the dark cake, round and heavy as a
turret, behind them on the table. My son,                             15
freckles like specks of nutmeg on his cheeks,
chest narrow as the balsa keel of a
model boat, long hands
cool and thin as the day they guided him
out of me, speaks up as a host                                        20
for the sake of the group.
*We could easily kill a two-year-old,*
he says in his clear voice. The other
men agree, they clear their throats
like Generals, they relax and get down to                             25
playing war, celebrating my son's life.

## QUESTIONS

1. What is ironic about the way the speaker describes the first grade boys at her son's birthday party?
2. What other irony does the author underscore in the last two lines?
3. Does this mother sentimentalize her own son by seeing him as better than the other little boys?

---

*John Betjeman* (1906–1984)

## IN WESTMINSTER ABBEY   1940

Let me take this other glove off
    As the *vox humana* swells,
And the beauteous fields of Eden
    Bask beneath the Abbey bells.
Here, where England's statesmen lie,                                   5
Listen to a lady's cry.

Gracious Lord, oh bomb the Germans.
   Spare their women for Thy Sake,
And if that is not too easy
   We will pardon Thy Mistake.                     10
But, gracious Lord, whate'er shall be,
Don't let anyone bomb me.

Keep our Empire undismembered,
   Guide our Forces by Thy Hand,
Gallant blacks from far Jamaica,                      15
   Honduras and Togoland;
Protect them Lord in all their fights,
And, even more, protect the whites.

Think of what our Nation stands for:
   Books from Boots' and country lanes,       20
Free speech, free passes, class distinction,
   Democracy and proper drains.
Lord, put beneath Thy special care
One-eighty-nine Cadogan Square.

Although dear Lord I am a sinner,                25
   I have done no major crime;
Now I'll come to Evening Service
   Whensoever I have the time.
So, Lord, reserve for me a crown,
And do not let my shares° go down.            *stocks*  30

I will labor for Thy Kingdom,
   Help our lads to win the war,
Send white feathers to the cowards,
   Join the Women's Army Corps,
Then wash the Steps around Thy Throne      35
In the Eternal Safety Zone.

Now I feel a little better,
   What a treat to hear Thy Word,
Where the bones of leading statesmen
   Have so often been interred.               40
And now, dear Lord, I cannot wait
Because I have a luncheon date.

In Westminster Abbey. First printed during World War II. 2 *vox humana:* an organ stop that makes tones similar to those of the human voice. 20 *Boots':* a chain of pharmacies whose branches had lending libraries.

## Questions

1. Who is the speaker? What do we know about her life style? About her prejudices?
2. Point out some of the places in which she contradicts herself.

3. How would you describe the speaker's attitude toward religion?
4. Through the medium of irony, what positive points do you believe Betjeman makes?

## Sarah N. Cleghorn (1876–1959)

### THE GOLF LINKS                1917

The golf links lie so near the mill
   That almost every day
The laboring children can look out
   And see the men at play.

### QUESTIONS

1. Is this brief poem satiric? Does it contain any verbal irony? Is the poet making a matter-of-fact statement in words that mean just what they say?
2. What other kind of irony is present in the poem?
3. Sarah N. Cleghorn's poem dates from before the enactment of legislation against child labor. Is it still a good poem, or is it hopelessly dated?
4. How would you state its theme?
5. Would you call this poem lyric, narrative, or didactic?

## Louise Glück (b. 1943)

### GRATITUDE                1975

Do not think I am not grateful for your small
kindness to me.
I like small kindnesses.
In fact I actually prefer them to the more
substantial kindness, that is always eying you,        5
like a large animal on a rug,
until your whole life reduces
to nothing but waking up morning after morning
cramped, and the bright sun shining on its tusks.

### QUESTIONS

1. What is the speaker's attitude toward the person she addresses? Is she being ironic or sincere in the first two lines?
2. Why does she claim to prefer small kindnesses to larger ones? What does she compare large kindness to?
3. How should we interpret the title of this poem? Is the author using it sarcastically?

Point out the kinds of irony that occur in the following poem.

## Thomas Hardy (1840–1928)*

### THE WORKBOX                     1914

"See, here's the workbox, little wife,
   That I made of polished oak."
He was a joiner°, of village life;                    *carpenter*
   She came of borough folk.

He holds the present up to her                                              5
   As with a smile she nears
And answers to the profferer,
   " 'Twill last all my sewing years!"

"I warrant it will. And longer too.
   'Tis a scantling that I got                                   10
Off poor John Wayward's coffin, who
   Died of they knew not what.

"The shingled pattern that seems to cease
   Against your box's rim
Continues right on in the piece                                            15
   That's underground with him.

"And while I worked it made me think
   Of timber's varied doom:
One inch where people eat and drink,
   The next inch in a tomb.                                       20

"But why do you look so white, my dear,
   And turn aside your face?
You knew not that good lad, I fear,
   Though he came from your native place?"

"How could I know that good young man,                                     25
   Though he came from my native town,
When he must have left far earlier than
   I was a woman grown?"

"Ah, no. I should have understood!
   It shocked you that I gave                                    30
To you one end of a piece of wood
   Whose other is in a grave?"

"Don't, dear, despise my intellect,
   Mere accidental things

Of that sort never have effect                                    35
    On my imaginings."

Yet still her lips were limp and wan,
    Her face still held aside,
As if she had known not only John,
    But known of what he died.                                    40

## For Review and Further Study

### Exercise: *Telling Tone*

Here are two radically different poems on a similar subject. Try stating the theme of
each poem in your own words. How is tone (the speaker's attitude) different in the
two poems?

---

### *Richard Lovelace* (1618–1658)

## To Lucasta                            1649

*On Going to the Wars*

Tell me not, Sweet, I am unkind
    That from the nunnery
Of thy chaste breast and quiet mind,
    To war and arms I fly.

True, a new mistress now I chase,                                5
    The first foe in the field;
And with a stronger faith embrace
    A sword, a horse, a shield.

Yet this inconstancy is such
    As you too shall adore;                                       10
I could not love thee, Dear, so much,
    Loved I not Honor more.

---

### *Wilfred Owen* (1893–1918)*

## Dulce et Decorum Est                        1920

Bent double, like old beggars under sacks,
Knock-kneed, coughing like hags, we cursed through sludge,
Till on the haunting flares we turned our backs
And towards our distant rest began to trudge.
Men marched asleep. Many had lost their boots                    5

But limped on, blood-shod. All went lame; all blind;
Drunk with fatigue; deaf even to the hoots
Of tired, outstripped Five-Nines° that dropped behind.          *gas-shells*

Gas! Gas! Quick, boys!—An ecstasy of fumbling,
Fitting the clumsy helmets just in time;                                        10
But someone still was yelling out and stumbling
And flound'ring like a man in fire or lime . . .
Dim, through the misty panes and thick green light,
As under a green sea, I saw him drowning.
In all my dreams, before my helpless sight,                                  15
He plunges at me, guttering, choking, drowning.

If in some smothering dreams you too could pace
Behind the wagon that we flung him in,
And watch the white eyes writhing in his face,
His hanging face, like a devil's sick of sin;                                   20
If you could hear, at every jolt, the blood
Come gargling from the froth-corrupted lungs,
Obscene as cancer, bitter as the cud
Of vile, incurable sores on innocent tongues,—
My friend, you would not tell with such high zest                          25
To children ardent for some desperate glory,
The old Lie: Dulce et decorum est
Pro patria mori.

DULCE ET DECORUM EST. Owen was a British infantry officer in World War I. 17 *you too*: Some
manuscript versions of this poem carry the dedication "To Jessie Pope" (a writer of patriotic
verse) or "To a certain Poetess." 27–28 *Dulce et . . . mori*: a quotation from the Latin poet
Horace, "It is sweet and fitting to die for one's country."

---

**Bettie Sellers** (b. 1926)

IN THE COUNSELOR'S WAITING ROOM          1981

The terra cotta girl
with the big flat farm feet
traces furrows in the rug
with her toes,
reads an existentialist paperback                                               5
from psychology class,
finds no ease there
from the guilt of loving
the quiet girl down the hall.
Their home soil has seen to this visit,                                        10

their Baptist mothers,
who weep for the waste of sturdy hips
ripe for grandchildren.

IN THE COUNSELOR'S WAITING ROOM. The poet is a teacher and administrator at a small college in Georgia. 1 *terra cotta:* fired clay, light brownish orange in hue. 5 *existentialist:* of the twentieth-century school of philosophy that holds (among other tenets) that an individual is alone and isolated, free and yet responsible, and ordinarily subject to guilt, anxiety, and dread.

## QUESTIONS

1. For what sort of counseling is this girl waiting?
2. Point out all the words that refer to plowing, to clay and earth. Why are the mothers called "home soil"? How do these references to earth relate to the idea in the last line?
3. What irony inheres in this situation?
4. Does the poet appear to sympathize with the girls? With their weeping mothers? In what details does this poem hint at any of the poet's own attitude or attitudes?

---

### *Jonathan Swift* (1667–1745)*

ON STELLA'S BIRTHDAY          (1718–1719)

Stella this day is thirty-four
(We shan't dispute a year or more)—
However, Stella, be not troubled,
Although thy size and years are doubled,
Since first I saw thee at sixteen,                                    5
The brightest virgin on the green,
So little is thy form declined,
Made up so largely in thy mind.
Oh, would it please the gods, to split
Thy beauty, size, and years, and wit,                                10
No age could furnish out a pair
Of nymphs so graceful, wise, and fair,
With half the luster of your eyes,
With half your wit, your years, and size.
And then, before it grew too late,                                   15
How should I beg of gentle Fate
(That either nymph might have her swain)
To split my worship too in twain.

ON STELLA'S BIRTHDAY. For many years Swift made an annual birthday gift of a poem to his close friend Mrs. Esther Johnson, the degree of whose nearness to the proud and lonely Swift remains an enigma to biographers. 18 *my worship:* as Dean of St. Patrick's in Dublin, Swift was addressed as "Your Worship."

1. If you were Stella, would you be amused or insulted by the poet's references to your *size*?
2. According to Swift in lines 7–8, what has compensated Stella for what the years have taken away?
3. Comment on the last four lines. Does Swift exempt himself from growing old?
4. How would you describe the tone of this poem? Offensive (like the speaker's complaints in "A Glass of Beer," page 607)? Playfully tender? Sad over Stella's growing fat and old?

---

## *José Emilio Pacheco* (b. 1939)

### HIGH TREASON             1969

I do not love my country. Its abstract lustre
is beyond my grasp.
But (although it sounds bad) I would give my life
for ten places in it, for certain people,
seaports, pinewoods, fortresses,                 5
a run-down city, gray, grotesque,
various figures from its history,
mountains
(and three or four rivers).

                    —Translated from Spanish
                       by Alastair Reid

HIGH TREASON. José Emilio Pacheco, one of Mexico's leading poets, was born in Mexico City in 1939. He currently teaches at the University of Maryland.

### QUESTION

Does this speaker truly not love his country? Explain what he means by his opening remark.

---

## *John Ciardi* (1916–1986)

### IN PLACE OF A CURSE           1959

At the next vacancy for God, if I am elected,
I shall forgive last the delicately wounded
who, having been slugged no harder than anyone else,
never got up again, neither to fight back,
nor to finger their jaws in painful admiration.         5

They who are wholly broken, and they in whom
mercy is understanding, I shall embrace at once

and lead to pillows in heaven. But they who are
the meek by trade, baiting the best of their betters
with the extortions of a mock-helplessness                    10

I shall take last to love, and never wholly.
Let them all into Heaven—I abolish Hell—
but let it be read over them as they enter:
"Beware the calculations of the meek, who gambled nothing,
gave nothing, and could never receive enough."                15

QUESTIONS

1. What kinds of people does the speaker dislike? Whom does he feel compassion
   for?
2. How would you describe the tone of this poem? How can you tell it isn't entirely
   serious?


**William Stafford** (1914–1993)*

AT THE UN-NATIONAL MONUMENT
ALONG THE CANADIAN BORDER          1977

This is the field where the battle did not happen,
where the unknown soldier did not die.
This is the field where grass joined hands,
where no monument stands,
and the only heroic thing is the sky.                          5

Birds fly here without any sound,
unfolding their wings across the open.
No people killed—or were killed—on this ground
hallowed by neglect and an air so tame
that people celebrate it by forgetting its name.               10

QUESTIONS

1. What non-event does this poem celebrate? What is the speaker's attitude toward
   it?
2. The speaker describes an empty field. What is odd about the way in which he
   describes it?
3. What words does the speaker appear to use ironically?


**William Blake** (1757–1827)*

THE CHIMNEY SWEEPER          1789

When my mother died I was very young,
And my father sold me while yet my tongue

Could scarcely cry " 'weep! 'weep! 'weep! 'weep!"
So your chimneys I sweep, and in soot I sleep.

There's little Tom Dacre, who cried when his head,                    5
That curled like a lamb's back, was shaved: so I said
"Hush, Tom! never mind it, for when your head's bare
You know that the soot cannot spoil your white hair."

And so he was quiet, and that very night,
As Tom was a-sleeping, he had such a sight!                          10
That thousands of sweepers, Dick, Joe, Ned, and Jack,
Were all of them locked up in coffins of black.

And by came an Angel who had a bright key,
And he opened the coffins and set them all free;
Then down a green plain leaping, laughing, they run,                 15
And wash in a river, and shine in the sun.

Then naked and white, all their bags left behind,
They rise upon clouds and sport in the wind;
And the Angel told Tom, if he'd be a good boy,
He'd have God for his father, and never want joy.                   20

And so Tom awoke; and we rose in the dark,
And got with our bags and our brushes to work.
Though the morning was cold, Tom was happy and warm;
So if all do their duty they need not fear harm.

QUESTIONS

1. What does Blake's poem reveal about conditions of life in the London of his day?
2. What does this poem have in common with "The Golf Links" (page 615)?
3. Sum up your impressions of the speaker's character. What does he say and do that displays it to us?
4. What pun do you find in line 3? Is its effect comic or serious?
5. In Tom Dacre's dream (lines 11–20), what wishes come true? Do you understand them to be the wishes of the chimney sweepers, of the poet, or of both?
6. In the last line, what is ironic in the speaker's assurance that the dutiful *need not fear harm?* What irony is there in his urging all to *do their duty?* (Who have failed in their duty to *him?*)
7. What is the tone of Blake's poem? Angry? Hopeful? Sorrowful? Compassionate? (Don't feel obliged to sum it up in a single word.)

INFORMATION FOR EXPERIMENT: *Reading with and without Biography*

THE RED WHEELBARROW (p. 609). Dr. Williams's poem reportedly contains a personal experience: he was gazing from the window of the house where one of his patients, a small girl, lay suspended between life and death. (This account, from the director of the public library in Williams's native Rutherford, N.J., is given by Geri M. Rhodes in "The Paterson Metaphor in William Carlos Williams' *Paterson*," master's essay, Tufts University, June 1965.)

## Suggestions for Writing

1. In a paragraph, sum up your initial reactions to "The Red Wheelbarrow." Then, taking another look at the poem in light of information noted above, write a second paragraph summing up your further reactions.
2. Write a short essay titled "What Thomas Hardy Leaves Unsaid in 'The Work-box'."
3. Write a verbal profile or short character sketch of the speaker of John Betjeman's "In Westminster Abbey."
4. In a brief essay, consider the tone of two poems on a similar subject. Compare and contrast Walt Whitman and Emily Dickinson as locomotive-fanciers; or, in the poems by Richard Lovelace and Wilfred Owen, compare and contrast attitudes toward war. (For advice on writing about poetry by the method of comparison and contrast, see page 1770.)

# 15 Words

## Literal Meaning: What A Poem Says First

Although successful as a painter, Edgar Degas struggled to produce sonnets, and found poetry discouragingly hard to write. To his friend, the poet Stéphane Mallarmé, he complained, "What a business! My whole day gone on a blasted sonnet, without getting an inch further . . . and it isn't ideas I'm short of . . . I'm full of them, I've got too many . . ."

"But Degas," said Mallarmé, "you can't make a poem with ideas—you make it with *words*!"[1]

Like the celebrated painter, some people assume that all it takes to make a poem is a bright idea. Poems state ideas, to be sure, and sometimes the ideas are invaluable; and yet the most impressive idea in the world will not make a poem unless its words are selected and arranged with loving art. Some poets take great pains to find the right word. Unable to fill a two-syllable gap in an unfinished line that went, "The seal's wide—gaze toward Paradise," Hart Crane paged through an unabridged dictionary. When he reached S, he found the object of his quest in *spindrift*: "spray skimmed from the sea by a strong wind." The word is exact and memorable. Any word can be the right word, however, if artfully chosen and placed. It may be a word as ordinary as *from*. Consider the difference between "The sedge is withered *on* the lake" (a misquotation of a line by Keats) and "The sedge is withered *from* the lake" (what Keats in fact wrote). Keats's original line suggests, as the altered line doesn't, that because the sedge (a growth of grasslike plants) has withered *from* the lake, it has withdrawn mysteriously.

In reading a poem, some people assume that its words can be skipped

---

[1] Paul Valéry, *Degas . . . Manet . . . Morisot*, translated by David Paul (New York: Pantheon, 1960) 62.

over rapidly, and they try to leap at once to the poem's general theme. It is as if they fear being thought clods unless they can find huge ideas in the poem (whether or not there are any). Such readers often ignore the literal meanings of words: the ordinary, matter-of-fact sense to be found in a dictionary. (As you will see in Chapter Sixteen, "Saying and Suggesting," words possess not only dictionary meanings—**denotations**—but also many associations and suggestions—**connotations**.) Consider the following poem and see what you make of it.

## *William Carlos Williams* (1883–1963)*

THIS IS JUST TO SAY        1934

I have eaten
the plums
that were in
the icebox
and which        5
you were probably
saving
for breakfast

Forgive me
they were delicious        10
so sweet
and so cold

Some readers distrust a poem so simple and candid. They think, "What's wrong with me? There has to be more to it than this!" But poems seldom are puzzles in need of solutions. We can begin by accepting the poet's statements, without suspecting the poet of trying to hoodwink us. On later reflection, of course, we might possibly decide that the poet is playfully teasing or being ironic; but Williams gives us no reason to think that. There seems no need to look beyond the literal sense of his words, no profit in speculating that the plums symbolize worldly joys and that the icebox stands for the universe. Clearly, a reader who held such a grand theory would have overlooked (in eagerness to find a significant idea) the plain truth that the poet makes clear to us: that ice-cold plums are a joy to taste.

To be sure, Williams's small poem is simpler than most poems are; and yet in reading any poem, no matter how complicated, you will do well to reach slowly and reluctantly for a theory to explain it by. To find the general theme of a poem, you first need to pay attention to its words. Recall Yeats's "The Lake Isle of Innisfree" (page 585), a poem that makes a statement—crudely summed up, "I yearn to leave the city and retreat to a place of ideal peace and happiness." And yet before we can realize this theme, we have to notice details: nine bean rows, a glade loud with bees, "lake water lapping with low sounds by the shore," the gray of a pavement. These details and not some abstract remark make clear what the poem is saying: that the city is drab, while the island hideaway is sublimely beautiful.

Poets often strive for words that point to physical details and solid objects. They may do so even when speaking of an abstract idea:

Beauty is but a flower
Which wrinkles will devour;
Brightness falls from the air,
Queens have died young and fair,
Dust hath closed Helen's eye.
I am sick, I must die:
  Lord, have mercy on us!

In these lines by Thomas Nashe, the abstraction *beauty* has grown petals that shrivel. Brightness may be a general name for light, but Nashe succeeds in giving it the weight of a falling body.

If a poem reads *daffodils* instead of *plant life*, *diaper years* instead of *infancy*, we call its **diction**, or choice of words, **concrete** rather than **abstract.** Concrete words refer to what we can immediately perceive with our senses: *dog, actor, chemical*, or particular individuals who belong to those general classes: *Bonzo the fox terrier, Clint Eastwood, hydrogen sulfate*. Abstract words express ideas or concepts: *love, time, truth*. In abstracting, we leave out some characteristics found in each individual, and instead observe a quality common to many. The word *beauty*, for instance, denotes what may be observed in numerous persons, places, and things.

Most poets favor concrete diction, at least part of the time. In an apt criticism, William Butler Yeats once took to task the poems of W. E. Henley for being "abstract, as even an actor's movement can be when the thought of doing is plainer to his mind than the doing itself: the straight line from cup to lip, let us say, more plain than the hand's own sensation weighed down by that heavy spillable cup."[2] To convey the sense of that heavy spillable cup was to Yeats a goal, one that surely he attained in "Among School Children" by describing a woman's stark face: "Hollow of cheek as though it drank the wind / And took a mess of shadows for its meat." A more abstract-minded poet might have written "Her hollow cheek and wasted, hungry look."

Ezra Pound gave a famous piece of advice to his fellow poets: "Go in fear of abstractions." This is not to say that a poet cannot employ abstract words, nor that all poems have to be about physical things. Much of T. S. Eliot's *Four Quartets* is concerned with time, eternity, history, language, reality, and other things that cannot be handled. But Eliot, however high he may soar for a larger view, keeps returning to earth. He makes us aware of *things*.

[2]*The Trembling of the Veil* (1922), reprinted in *The Autobiography of William Butler Yeats* (New York: Macmillan, 1953) 177.

## Marianne Moore (1887–1972)*

### SILENCE                                                                1924

My father used to say,
"Superior people never make long visits,
have to be shown Longfellow's grave
or the glass flowers at Harvard.
Self-reliant like the cat—                                                   5
that takes its prey to privacy,
the mouse's limp tail hanging like a shoelace from its mouth—
they sometimes enjoy solitude,
and can be robbed of speech
by speech which has delighted them.                                          10
The deepest feeling always shows itself in silence;
not in silence, but restraint."
Nor was he insincere in saying, "Make my house your inn."
Inns are not residences.

### QUESTIONS

1. Almost all of "Silence" consists of quotation. What are some possible reasons
   why the speaker prefers using another person's words?
2. What are the words the father uses to describe people he admires?
3. The poem makes an important distinction between two similar words (lines
   13–14). Explain the distinction Moore implies.
4. Why is "Silence" an appropriate title for this poem?

## Henry Taylor (b. 1942)

### RIDING A ONE-EYED HORSE                    1975

One side of his world is always missing.
You may give it a casual wave of the hand
or rub it with your shoulder as you pass,
but nothing on his blind side ever happens.

Hundreds of trees slip past him into darkness,                               5
drifting into a hollow hemisphere
whose sounds you will have to try to explain.
Your legs will tell him not to be afraid

if you learn never to lie. Do not forget
to turn his head and let what comes come seen:                               10
he will jump the fences he has to if you swing
toward them from the side that he can see

and hold his good eye straight. The heavy dark
will stay beside you always; let him learn

to lean against it. It will steady him                                                    15
and see you safely through diminished fields.

QUESTION

Do you read this poem as a fable in which the horse stands for something, or as a set
of instructions for riding a one-eyed horse?

### *Robert Graves* (1895–1985)

## DOWN, WANTON, DOWN!          1933

Down, wanton, down! Have you no shame
That at the whisper of Love's name,
Or Beauty's, presto! up you raise
Your angry head and stand at gaze?

Poor bombard-captain, sworn to reach                                                      5
The ravelin and effect a breach—
Indifferent what you storm or why,
So be that in the breach you die!

Love may be blind, but Love at least
Knows what is man and what mere beast;                                                    10
Or Beauty wayward, but requires
More delicacy from her squires.

Tell me, my witless, whose one boast
Could be your staunchness at the post,
When were you made a man of parts                                                         15
To think fine and profess the arts?

Will many-gifted Beauty come
Bowing to your bald rule of thumb,
Or Love swear loyalty to your crown?
Be gone, have done! Down, wanton, down!                                                   20

DOWN, WANTON, DOWN! 5 *bombard-captain*: officer in charge of a bombard, an early type of
cannon that hurled stones. 6 *ravelin*: fortification with two faces that meet in a protruding angle.
*effect a breach*: break an opening through (a fortification). 15 *man of parts*: man of talent or ability.

### QUESTIONS

1. How do you define a wanton?
2. What wanton does the poet address?
3. Explain the comparison drawn in the second stanza.
4. In line 14, how many meanings do you find in *staunchness at the post*?
5. Explain any other puns you find in lines 15–19.
6. Do you take this to be a cynical poem making fun of Love and Beauty, or is Graves
   making fun of stupid, animal lust?

**Peter Davison** (b. 1928)

## THE LAST WORD 1970

When I saw your head bow, I knew I had beaten you.
You shed no tears—not near me—but held your neck
Bare for the blow I had been too frightened
Ever to deliver, even in words. And now,
In spite of me, plummeting it came.                    5
Frozen we both waited for its fall.

Most of what you gave me I have forgotten
With my mind but taken into my body,
But this I remember well: the bones of your neck
And the strain in my shoulders as I heaved up that huge    10
Double blade and snapped my wrists to swing
The handle down and hear the axe's edge
Nick through your flesh and creak into the block.

### QUESTIONS

1. "The Last Word" stands fourth in a series titled "Four Love Poems." Sum up
   what happens in this poem. Do you take this to be *merely* a literal account of an
   execution? Explain the comparison.
2. Which words embody concrete things and show us physical actions? Which
   words have sounds that especially contribute to the poem's effectiveness?

**John Donne** (1572–1631)*

## BATTER MY HEART,
## THREE-PERSONED GOD, FOR YOU        (about 1610)

Batter my heart, three-personed God, for You
As yet but knock, breathe, shine, and seek to mend.
That I may rise and stand, o'erthrow me, and bend
Your force to break, blow, burn, and make me new.
I, like an usurped town to another due,                5
Labor to admit You, but Oh! to no end.
Reason, Your viceroy in me, me should defend,
But is captived, and proves weak or untrue.
Yet dearly I love You, and would be lovèd fain,
But am betrothed unto Your enemy;                      10
Divorce me, untie or break that knot again;
Take me to You, imprison me, for I,
Except You enthrall me, never shall be free,
Nor ever chaste, except You ravish me.

1. In the last line of this sonnet, to what does Donne compare the onslaught of God's love? Do you think the poem weakened by the poet's comparing a spiritual experience to something so grossly carnal? Discuss.
2. Explain the seeming contradiction in the last line: in what sense can a ravished person be *chaste?* Explain the seeming contradictions in lines 3–4 and 12–13: how can a person thrown down and destroyed be enabled to *rise and stand;* an imprisoned person be *free?*
3. In lines 5–6 the speaker compares himself to a *usurped town* trying to throw off its conqueror by admitting an army of liberation. Who is the "usurper" in this comparison?
4. Explain the comparison of *Reason* to a *viceroy* (lines 7–8).
5. Sum up in your own words the message of Donne's poem. In stating its theme, did you have to read the poem for literal meanings, figurative comparisons, or both?

# THE VALUE OF A DICTIONARY

If a poet troubles to seek out the best words available, the least we can do is to find out what the words mean. The dictionary is a firm ally in reading poems; if the poems are more than a century old, it is indispensable. Meanings change. When the Elizabethan poet George Gascoigne wrote, "O Abraham's brats, O brood of blessed seed," the word *brats* implied neither irritation nor contempt. When in the seventeenth century Andrew Marvell imagined two lovers' "vegetable love," he referred to a vegetative or growing love, not one resembling a lettuce. And when King George III called a building an "awful artificial spectacle," he was not condemning it but praising it as an awe-inspiring work of art.

In reading poetry, there is nothing to be done about this inevitable tendency of language except to watch out for it. If you suspect that a word has shifted in meaning over the years, most standard desk dictionaries will be helpful, an unabridged dictionary more helpful yet, and most helpful of all the *Oxford English Dictionary (OED)*, which gives, for each definition, successive examples of the word's written use through the past thousand years. You need not feel a grim obligation to keep interrupting a poem in order to rummage the dictionary; but if the poem is worth reading very closely, you may wish any aid you can find.

One of the valuable services of poetry is to recall for us the concrete, physical sense that certain words once had, but since have lost. As the English critic H. Coombes has remarked in *Literature and Criticism,*

> We use a word like *powerful* without feeling that it is really "power-full." We do not seem today to taste the full flavor of words as we feel that Falstaff (and Shakespeare, and probably his audience) tasted them when he was applauding the virtues of "good sherris-sack," which makes the brain "apprehensive, quick, forgetive, full of nimble, fiery, and delectable shapes." And being less aware of the life and substantial-

ity of words, we are probably less aware of the things . . . that these words stand for.

"Every word which is used to express a moral or intellectual fact," said Emerson in his study *Nature*, "if traced to its root, is found to be borrowed from some material appearance. *Right* means straight; *wrong* means twisted. *Spirit* primarily means wind; *transgression*, the crossing of a line; *supercilious*, the raising of an eyebrow." Browse in a dictionary and you will discover such original concretenesses. These are revealed in your dictionary's etymologies, or brief notes on the derivation of words, given in most dictionaries near the beginning of an entry on a word; in some dictionaries, at the end of the entry. Look up *squirrel*, for instance, and you will find it comes from two Greek words meaning "shadow-tail." For another example of a common word that originally contained a poetic metaphor, look up the origin of *daisy*.

## EXPERIMENT: *Seeing Words' Origins*

Much of the effect of the following poem depends upon our awareness of the precision with which the poet has selected his words. We can better see this by knowing their derivations. For instance, *potpourri* comes from French: *pot* plus *pourri*. What do these words mean? (If you do not know French, look up the etymology of the word in a dictionary.) Look up the definitions and etymologies of *revenance*, *circumstance*, *inspiration*, *conceptual*, *commotion*, *cordial*, and *azure*; and try to state the meanings these words have in Wilbur's poem.

---

### *Richard Wilbur* (b. 1921)*

IN THE ELEGY SEASON                    1950

Haze, char, and the weather of All Souls':
A giant absence mopes upon the trees:
Leaves cast in casual potpourris
Whisper their scents from pits and cellar-holes.

Or brewed in gulleys, steeped in wells, they spend          5
In chilly steam their last aromas, yield
From shallow hells a revenance of field
And orchard air. And now the envious mind

Which could not hold the summer in my head
While bounded by that blazing circumstance          10
Parades these barrens in a golden trance,
Remembering the wealthy season dead,

And by an autumn inspiration makes
A summer all its own. Green boughs arise
Through all the boundless backward of the eyes,          15
And the soul bathes in warm conceptual lakes.

Less proud than this, my body leans an ear
Past cold and colder weather after wings'
Soft commotion, the sudden race of springs,
The goddess' tread heard on the dayward stair,                    20

Longs for the brush of the freighted air, for smells
Of grass and cordial lilac, for the sight
Of green leaves building into the light
And azure water hoisting out of wells.

An **allusion** is an indirect reference to any person, place, or thing—
fictitious, historical, or actual. Sometimes, to understand an allusion in a
poem, we have to find out something we didn't know before. But usually the
poet asks of us only common knowledge. When, in his poem "To Helen"
(page 978), Edgar Allan Poe refers to "the glory that was Greece / And the
grandeur that was Rome," he assumes that we have heard of those places. He
also expects that we will understand his allusion to the cultural achievements
of those ancient nations and perhaps even catch the subtle contrast between
those two similar words *glory* and *grandeur,* with its suggestion that, for all
its merits, Roman civilization was also more pompous than Greek.

Allusions not only enrich the meaning of a poem, they also save space.
In "The Love Song of J. Alfred Prufrock" (page 916), T. S. Eliot, by giving
a brief introductory quotation from the speech of a damned soul in Dante's
*Inferno,* is able to suggest that his poem will be the confession of a soul in
torment, who sees no chance of escape.

Often in reading a poem you will meet a name you don't recognize, on
which the meaning of a line (or perhaps a whole poem) seems to depend. In
this book, most such unfamiliar references and allusions are glossed or
footnoted, but when you venture out on your own in reading poems, you
may find yourself needlessly perplexed unless you look up such names, the
way you look up any other words. Unless the name is one that the poet made
up, you will probably find it in one of the larger desk dictionaries, such as
*Webster's New Collegiate Dictionary, The American Heritage Dictionary,* or
*Webster's II.* If you don't solve your problem there, try an encyclopedia, a
world atlas, or *The New Century Cyclopedia of Names.*

Some allusions are quotations from other poems. In L. E. Sissman's "In
and Out: A Home Away from Home," the narrator, a male college student,
describes his sleeping love,

This Sally now does like a garment wear
The beauty of the evening; silent, bare,
Hips, shoulders, arms, tresses, and temples lie.

(For the source of these lines, see Wordsworth's "Composed upon Westminster Bridge," page 1016.)

EXERCISE: *Catching Allusions*

From your knowledge, supplemented by a dictionary or other reference work if need be, explain the allusions in the following poems.

## *J. V. Cunningham* (1911–1985)*

### FRIEND, ON THIS SCAFFOLD
### THOMAS MORE LIES DEAD       1960

Friend, on this scaffold Thomas More lies dead
Who would not cut the Body from the Head.

## *Nina Cassian* (b. 1924)

### LIKE GULLIVER       1990

Like Gulliver who towed a hundred ships,
I drag you to the shore, my motley lovers,
so artful, all with rapiers at your hips,
and bent on war, so many silly rovers.

Like Gulliver I spare you all, although       5
you hit my forehead, hoping it will crack;
I laugh at you through streaks of blood,—oh, you,
my savage lovers, avid to attack.

—Translated from Romanian
by Petre Solomon

LIKE GULLIVER. Nina Cassian was born in Romania, but in 1985 she sought political asylum in the United States. She now lives in New York City.

## *Henry Wadsworth Longfellow* (1807–1882)

### AFTERMATH       1873

When the summer fields are mown,
When the birds are fledged and flown,
   And the dry leaves strew the path;
With the falling of the snow,
With the cawing of the crow,
Once again the fields we mow       5
   And gather in the aftermath.

Not the sweet, new grass with flowers
In this harvesting of ours;
   Not the upland clover bloom;          10
But the rowen mixed with weeds,
Tangled tufts from marsh and meads,
Where the poppy drops its seeds
   In the silence and the gloom.

### QUESTIONS

1. How does the etymology and meaning of *aftermath* help explain this poem? (Look the word up in your dictionary.)
2. What is the meaning of *fledged* (line 2) and *rowen* (line 11)?
3. Once you understand the literal meaning of the poem, do you think that Longfellow intended any further significance to the poem?

---

## James Wright (1927–1980)*

SAINT JUDAS                           1959

When I went out to kill myself, I caught
A pack of hoodlums beating up a man.
Running to spare his suffering, I forgot
My name, my number, how my day began,
How soldiers milled around the garden stone       5
And sang amusing songs; how all that day
Their javelins measured crowds; how I alone
Bargained the proper coins, and slipped away.

Banished from heaven, I found this victim beaten,
Stripped, kneed, and left to cry. Dropping my rope     10
Aside, I ran, ignored the uniforms:
Then I remembered bread my flesh had eaten,
The kiss that ate my flesh. Flayed without hope,
I held the man for nothing in my arms.

---

## John Clare (1793–1864)

MOUSE'S NEST                  (about 1835)

I found a ball of grass among the hay
And progged it as I passed and went away;
And when I looked I fancied something stirred,
And turned again and hoped to catch the bird—
When out an old mouse bolted in the wheats       5
With all her young ones hanging at her teats;

She looked so odd and so grotesque to me,
I ran and wondered what the thing could be,
And pushed the knapweed bunches where I stood;
Then the mouse hurried from the craking° brood.            *crying*    10
The young ones squeaked, and as I went away
She found her nest again among the hay.
The water o'er the pebbles scarce could run
And broad old cesspools glittered in the sun.

## QUESTIONS

1. "To prog" (line 2) means "to poke about for food, to forage." In what ways does this word fit more exactly here than *prodded, touched,* or *searched?*
2. Is *craking* (line 10) better than *crying?* Which word better fits the poem? Why?
3. What connections do you find between the last two lines and the rest of the poem? To what are water that *scarce could run* and *broad old cesspools* (lines 13 and 14) likened?

# WORD CHOICE AND WORD ORDER

Even if Samuel Johnson's famous *Dictionary* of 1755 had been as thick as Webster's unabridged, an eighteenth-century poet searching through it for words to use would have had a narrower choice. For in English literature of the **neoclassical period** or **Augustan age**—that period from about 1660 into the late eighteenth century—many poets subscribed to a belief in **poetic diction**: "A system of words," said Dr. Johnson, "refined from the grossness of domestic use." The system admitted into a serious poem only certain words and subjects, excluding others as violations of **decorum** (propriety). Accordingly such common words as *rat, cheese, big, sneeze,* and *elbow,* although admissible to satire, were thought inconsistent with the loftiness of tragedy, epic, ode, and elegy. Dr. Johnson's biographer, James Boswell, tells how a poet writing an epic reconsidered the word "rats" and instead wrote "the whiskered vermin race." Johnson himself objected to Lady Macbeth's allusion to her "keen knife," saying that "we do not immediately conceive that any crime of importance is to be committed with a knife; or who does not, at last, from the long habit of connecting a knife with sordid offices, feel aversion rather than terror?" Probably Johnson was here the victim of his age, and Shakespeare was right, but Johnson in one of his assumptions was right too: there are inappropriate words as well as appropriate ones.

Neoclassical poets chose their classical models more often from Roman writers than from Greek, as their diction suggests by the frequency of Latin derivatives. For example, a *net,* according to Dr. Johnson's dictionary, is "any thing reticulated or decussated, at equal distances, with interstices between the intersections." In company with Latinate words often appeared fixed combinations of adjective and noun ("finny prey" for "fish"), poetic names (a song to a lady named Molly might rechristen her Parthenia), and allusions to classical mythology. Neoclassical poetic diction was evidently being abused when, instead of saying "uncork the bottle," a poet could write,

> Apply thine engine to the spongy door,
> Set *Bacchus* from his glassy prison free,

in some bad lines ridiculed by Alexander Pope in *Peri Bathous, or, Of the Art of Sinking in Poetry.*

Not all poetic diction is excess baggage. To a reader who knew at first hand both living sheep and the pastoral poems of Virgil—as most readers nowadays do not—such a fixed phrase as "the fleecy care," which seems stilted to us, conveyed pleasurable associations. But "fleecy care" was more than a highfalutin way of saying "sheep"; as one scholar has pointed out, "when they wished, our poets could say 'sheep' as clearly and as often as anybody else. In the first place, 'fleecy' drew attention to wool, and demanded the appropriate visual image of sheep; for aural imagery the poets would refer to 'the bleating kind'; it all depended upon what was happening in the poem."[3]

Other poets have found some special kind of poetic language valuable: Old English poets, with their standard figures of speech ("whale-road" for the sea, "ring-giver" for a ruler); makers of folk ballads who, no less than neoclassicists, love fixed epithet-noun combinations ("milk-white steed," "blood-red wine," "steel-driving man"); and Edmund Spenser, whose example made popular the adjective ending in *-y* (*fleecy, grassy, milky*).

When Wordsworth, in his Preface to *Lyrical Ballads*, asserted that "the language really spoken by men," especially by humble rustics, is plainer, more emphatic, and conveys "elementary feelings . . . in a state of greater simplicity," he was, in effect, advocating a new poetic diction. Wordsworth's ideas invited freshness into English poetry and, by admitting words that neoclassical poets would have called "low" ("His poor old *ankles* swell"), helped rid poets of the fear of being thought foolish for mentioning a commonplace.

This theory of the superiority of rural diction was, as Coleridge pointed out, hard to adhere to, and, in practice, Wordsworth was occasionally to write a language as Latinate and citified as these lines on yew trees:

> Huge trunks!—and each particular trunk a growth
> Of intertwisted fibers serpentine
> Up-coiling, and inveterately convolved . . .

Language so Latinate sounds pedantic to us, especially the phrase *inveterately convolved*. In fact, some poets, notably Gerard Manley Hopkins, have subscribed to the view that English words derived from Anglo-Saxon (Old English) have more force and flavor than their Latin equivalents. *Kingly*, one may feel, has more power than *regal*. One argument for this view is that so

[3]Bonamy Dobrée, *English Literature in the Early Eighteenth Century, 1700–1740* (New York: Oxford UP, 1959) 161.

many words of Old English origin—*man, wife, child, house, eat, drink, sleep*—are basic to our living speech. It may be true that a language closer to Old English is particularly fit for rendering abstract notions concretely—as does the memorable title of a medieval work of piety, the *Ayenbite of Inwit* ("again-bite of inner wisdom" or "remorse of conscience"). And yet this view, if accepted at all, must be accepted with reservations. Some words of Latin origin carry meanings both precise and physical. In the King James Bible is the admonition, "See then that ye walk circumspectly, not as fools, but as wise" (Ephesians 5:15). To be *circumspect* (a word from two Latin roots meaning "to look" and "around") is to be watchful on all sides—a meaning altogether lost in a modernized wording of the passage once printed on a subway poster for a Bible society: "Be careful how you live, not thoughtlessly but thoughtfully."

When E. E. Cummings begins a poem, "mr youse needn't be so spry / concernin questions arty," we recognize another kind of diction available to poetry: **vulgate** (speech not much affected by schooling). Handbooks of grammar sometimes distinguish various **levels of usage.** A sort of ladder is imagined, on whose rungs words, phrases, and sentences may be ranked in an ascending order of formality, from the curses of an illiterate thug to the commencement-day address of a doctor of divinity. These levels range from vulgate through **colloquial** (the casual conversation or informal writing of literate people) and **general English** (most literate speech and writing, more studied than colloquial but not pretentious), up to **formal English** (the impersonal language of educated persons, usually only written, possibly spoken on dignified occasions). Recently, however, lexicographers have been shunning such labels. The designation *colloquial* has been expelled (*bounced* would be colloquial; *trun out,* vulgate) from *Webster's Third New International Dictionary* on the grounds that "it is impossible to know whether a word out of context is colloquial or not" and that the diction of Americans nowadays is more fluid than the labels suggest. Aware that we are being unscientific, we may find the labels useful. They may help roughly to describe what happens when, as in the following poem, a poet shifts from one level of usage to another. This poem employs, incidentally, a colloquial device throughout: omitting the subjects of sentences. In keeping the characters straight, it may be helpful to fill in the speaker for each *said* and for the verbs *saw* and *ducked* (lines 9 and 10).

---

*Josephine Miles* (1911–1985)

REASON                                                                    1955

Said, Pull her up a bit will you, Mac, I want to unload there.
Said, Pull her up my rear end, first come first serve.
Said, Give her the gun, Bud, he needs a taste of his own bumper.
Then the usher came out and got into the act:

Said, Pull her up, pull her up a bit, we need this space, sir.  5
Said, For God's sake, is this still a free country or what?
You go back and take care of Gary Cooper's horse
And leave me handle my own car.

Saw them unloading the lame old lady,
Ducked out under the wheel and gave her an elbow,  10
Said, All you needed to do was just explain;
*Reason, Reason* is my middle name.

Language on more than one level enlivens this miniature comedy; the vulgate of the resentful driver ("Pull her up my rear end," "leave me handle my own car") and the colloquial of the bystander ("Give her the gun"). There is also a contrast in formality between the old lady's driver, who says "Mac," and the usher, who says "sir." These varied levels of language distinguish the speakers in the poem from one another.

The diction of "Reason" is that of speech. At present, most poetry in English appears to be shunning expressions such as "fleecy care" in favor of general English and the colloquial. In Scotland, there has been an interesting development: for instance, the formation of an active group of poets who write in Scots, a **dialect** (variety of language spoken by a social group or spoken in a certain locality). Perhaps, whether poets write in language close to speech or in language of greater formality, their poems will ring true if they choose appropriate words.

### EXPERIMENT: *Making Sense of Synes*

Below are the first two stanzas of a song in Scots many Americans know by heart, though few of them understand every word they sing each New Year's Eve. The first stanza was copied down by Robert Burns from an old man's singing. They come from the tradition of Scottish folk song. The second stanza Burns added. Translate this song into standard modern English. Then try to assess what the lyrics have gained or lost.

Should auld° acquaintance be forgot,                          *old*
And never brought to mind?
Should auld acquaintance be forgot
And days of auld lang syne°?                                *long since*
And days of auld lang syne, my dear,
And days of auld lang syne,
Should auld acquaintance be forgot,
And days of auld lang syne?

We twa° ha'e run aboot the braes°        *two/hillsides, banks*
And pu'd the gowans° fine,                          *daisies*
We've wander'd mony a weary foot,
Sin' auld lang syne:
Sin' auld lang syne, my dear,

Sin' auld lang syne,
We've wander'd mony a weary foot,
Sin' auld lang syne.

Not only the poet's choice of words makes a poem seem more formal, or less, but also the way the words are arranged into sentences. Compare these lines,

Jack and Jill went up the hill
To fetch a pail of water.
Jack fell down and broke his crown
And Jill came tumbling after.

with Milton's account of a more significant downfall:

Earth trembled from her entrails, as again
In pangs, and Nature gave a second groan;
Sky loured, and, muttering thunder, some sad drops
Wept at completing of the mortal sin
Original; while Adam took no thought
Eating his fill, nor Eve to iterate
Her former trespass feared, the more to soothe
Him with her loved society, that now
As with new wine intoxicated both
They swim in mirth, and fancy that they feel
Divinity within them breeding wings
Wherewith to scorn the Earth.

Not all the words in Milton's lines are bookish: indeed, many of them can be found in nursery rimes. What helps, besides diction, to distinguish this account of the Biblical fall from "Jack and Jill" is that Milton's nonstop sentence seems further removed from usual speech in its length (83 words), in its complexity (subordinate clauses), and in its word order ("with new wine intoxicated both" rather than "both intoxicated with new wine"). Should we think less (or more highly) of Milton for choosing a style so elaborate and formal? No judgment need be passed: both Mother Goose and the author of *Paradise Lost* use language appropriate to their purposes.

Among languages, English is by no means the most flexible. English words must be used in fairly definite and inviolable patterns, and whoever departs too far from them will not be understood. In the sentence "Cain slew Abel," if you change the word order, you change the meaning: "Abel slew Cain." Such inflexibility was not true of Latin, in which a poet could lay down words in almost any sequence and, because their endings (inflections) showed what parts of speech they were, could trust that no reader would mistake a subject for an object or a noun for an adjective. (E. E. Cummings has striven, in certain of his poems, for the freedom of Latin. One such poem, "anyone lived in a pretty how town," appears on page 646.)

The rigidity of English word order invites the poet to defy it and to achieve unusual effects by inverting it. It is customary in English to place adjective in front of noun *(a blue mantle, new pastures)*. But an unusual emphasis is achieved when Milton ends "Lycidas" by reversing the pattern:

> At last he rose, and twitched his mantle blue:
> Tomorrow to fresh woods, and pastures new.

Perhaps the inversion in *mantle blue* gives more prominence to the color associated with heaven (and in "Lycidas," heaven is of prime importance). Perhaps the inversion in *pastures new*, stressing the *new*, heightens the sense of a rebirth.

Coleridge offered two "homely definitions of prose and poetry; that is, *prose*: words in their best order; *poetry*: the best words in the best order." If all goes well, a poet may fasten the right word into the right place, and the result may be—as T. S. Eliot said in "Little Gidding"—a "complete consort dancing together."

---

## Emma Lee Warrior (b. 1941)

### How I Came to Have a Man's Name          1988

It's a good thing Dad deserted Mom
and all us kids for a cousin's wiles,
cause then we learned from Grampa
how to pray to the Sun, the Moon and Stars.

Before a January dawn, under a moondog sky,                                5
Yellow Dust hitched up a team to a strawfilled sleigh.
Snow squeaked against the runners
in reply to the crisp crackling cottonwoods.
They bundled up bravely in buffalo robes,
their figures pronounced by the white of night;                           10
the still distance of the Wolf Trail° greeted them,           *Milky Way*
and Ipisowahs,° the boy child of Natosi,°          *morning star/the sun*
and Kokomiikiisom° watched their hurry.                           *the moon*
My momma's body was bent with pain.
Otohkostskaksin° sensed the Morning Star's              *Yellow Dust*  15
presence and so he beseeched him:

"Aayo, Ipisowahs, you see us now,
pitiful creatures.
We are thankful there is no wind.
We are thankful for your light.                                           20
Guide us safely to our destination.

May my daughter give birth in a warm place.
May her baby be a boy; may he have your name.
May he be fortunate because of your name.
May he live long and be happy.                                    25
Bestow your name upon him, Ipisowahs.
His name will be Ipisowahs.
Aayo, help us, we are pitiful."

And Ipisowahs led them that icy night
through the Old Man River Valley                                  30
and out onto the frozen prairie.
They rushed to the hospital
where my mother pushed me into this world
and nobody bothered to change my name.

How I Came to Have a Man's Name. The words glossed in the margin of the poem are the
poet's translations from the Blackfoot language.

## QUESTIONS

1. What do the words from the Blackfoot language contribute to this poem? (Suggestion: Try reading them aloud as best you can.)
2. If the unborn child was to be named Ipisowahs, "morning star," then why do you
   suppose the poet signs herself Emma Lee Warrior?

---

## *Thomas Hardy* (1840–1928)*

### THE RUINED MAID                                               1901

"O 'Melia, my dear, this does everything crown!
Who could have supposed I should meet you in Town?
And whence such fair garments, such prosperi-ty?"—
"O didn't you know I'd been ruined?" said she.

—"You left us in tatters, without shoes or socks,             5
Tired of digging potatoes, and spudding up docks°;        *spading up dockweed*
And now you've gay bracelets and bright feathers three!"—
"Yes: that's how we dress when we're ruined," said she.

—"At home in the barton° you said 'thee' and 'thou,'            *farmyard*
And 'thik oon,' and 'theäs oon,' and 't'other'; but now         10
Your talking quite fits 'ee for high compa-ny!"—
"Some polish is gained with one's ruin," said she.

—"Your hands were like paws then, your face blue and bleak
But now I'm bewitched by your delicate cheek,
And your little gloves fit as on any la-dy!"—                    15
"We never do work when we're ruined," said she.

—"You used to call home-life a hag-ridden dream,
And you'd sigh, and you'd sock°; but at present you seem          *groan*
To know not of megrims° or melancho-ly!"—                        *blues*
"True. One's pretty lively when ruined," said she.                20

—"I wish I had feathers, a fine sweeping gown,
And a delicate face, and could strut about Town!"—
"My dear—a raw country girl, such as you be,
Cannot quite expect that. You ain't ruined," said she.

## QUESTIONS

1. Where does this dialogue take place? Who are the two speakers?
2. Comment on Hardy's use of the word *ruined*. What is the conventional meaning of the word when applied to a woman? As 'Melia applies it to herself what is its meaning?
3. Sum up the attitude of each speaker toward the other. What details of the new 'Melia does the first speaker most dwell upon? Would you expect Hardy to be so impressed by all these details, or is there, between his view of the characters and their view of themselves, any hint of an ironic discrepancy?
4. In losing her country dialect (*thik oon* and *theäs oon* for *this one* and *that one*), 'Melia is presumed to have gained in sophistication. What does Hardy suggest by her *ain't* in the last line?

## *Richard Eberhart* (b. 1904)

### THE FURY OF AERIAL BOMBARDMENT          1947

You would think the fury of aerial bombardment
Would rouse God to relent; the infinite spaces
Are still silent. He looks on shock-pried faces.
History, even, does not know what is meant.

You would feel that after so many centuries                        5
God would give man to repent; yet he can kill
As Cain could, but with multitudinous will,
No farther advanced than in his ancient furies.

Was man made stupid to see his own stupidity?
Is God by definition indifferent, beyond us all?                   10
Is the eternal truth man's fighting soul
Wherein the Beast ravens in its own avidity?

Of Van Wettering I speak, and Averill,
Names on a list, whose faces I do not recall
But they are gone to early death, who late in school               15
Distinguished the belt feed lever from the belt holding pawl.

## QUESTIONS

1. As a naval officer during World War II, Richard Eberhart was assigned for a time as an instructor in a gunnery school. How has this experience apparently contributed to the diction of his poem?
2. In his *Life of John Dryden*, complaining about a description of a sea fight Dryden had filled with nautical language, Samuel Johnson argued that technical terms should be excluded from poetry. Is this criticism applicable to Eberhart's last line? Can a word succeed for us in a poem, even though we may not be able to define it? (For more evidence, see also the technical terms in Henry Reed's "Naming of Parts," p. 982.)
3. Some readers have found a contrast in tone between the first three stanzas of this poem and the last stanza. How would you describe this contrast? What does diction contribute to it?

---

### *Wendy Cope* (1945)*

LONELY HEARTS                                           1986

Can someone make my simple wish come true?
Male biker seeks female for touring fun.
Do you live in North London? Is it you?

Gay vegetarian whose friends are few,
I'm into music, Shakespeare and the sun,                          5
Can someone make my simple wish come true?

Executive in search of something new—
Perhaps bisexual woman, arty, young.
Do you live in North London? Is it you?

Successful, straight and solvent? I am too—                        10
Attractive Jewish lady with a son.
Can someone make my simple wish come true?

I'm Libran, inexperienced and blue—
Need slim non-smoker, under twenty-one.
Do you live in North London? Is it you?                            15

Please write (with photo) to Box 152.
Who knows where it may lead once we've begun?
Can someone make my simple wish come true?
Do you live in North London? Is it you?

LONELY HEARTS. The form of this poem is a *villanelle*, a fixed form developed by French courtly poets in imitation of Italian folk song. Villanelles use only two rime sounds, as the first and third lines are repeated in a set pattern throughout the poem. For other villanelles, see Elizabeth Bishop's "One Art" (page 897) and Dylan Thomas's "Do not go gentle into that good night" (page 771).

QUESTIONS

1. What sort of language does Wendy Cope borrow for this poem?
2. The form of the villanelle requires that the poet end each stanza with one of two repeating lines. What special use does the author make of these mandatory repetitions?
3. How many speakers are there in the poem? Does the author's voice ever enter or is the entire poem spoken by individuals in personal ads?
4. The poem seems to begin satirically. Does the poem ever move beyond the critical, mocking tone typical of satire?

## FOR REVIEW AND FURTHER STUDY

*David B. Axelrod* (b. 1943)

ONCE IN A WHILE A PROTEST POEM          1976

Over and over again the papers print
the dried-out tit of an African woman
holding her starving child. Over
and over, cropping it each time to one
prominent, withered tit, the feeble                        5
infant face. Over and over to toughen
us, teach us to ignore the foam turned
dusty powder on the infant's lips,
the mother's sunken face (is cropped)
and filthy dress. The tit remains;                         10
the tit held out for everyone to see,
reminding us only that we are not so hungry
ogling the tit, admiring it and in our
living rooms, making it a symbol of starving
millions; our sympathy as real as silicone.               15

QUESTIONS

1. Why is the last word in this poem especially meaningful?
2. What does the poet protest?

*Lewis Carroll*
*[Charles Lutwidge Dodgson]* (1832–1898)

JABBERWOCKY                                1871

'Twas brillig, and the slithy toves
    Did gyre and gimble in the wabe:
All mimsy were the borogoves,
    And the mome raths outgrabe.

"Beware the Jabberwock, my son!                            5
    The jaws that bite, the claws that catch!

Beware the Jubjub bird, and shun
  The frumious Bandersnatch!"

He took his vorpal sword in hand;
  Long time the manxome foe he sought—                    10
So rested he by the Tumtum tree
  And stood awhile in thought.

And, as in uffish thought he stood,
  The Jabberwock, with eyes of flame,
Came whiffling through the tulgey wood,                   15
  And burbled as it came!

One, two! One, two! And through and through
  The vorpal blade went snicker-snack!
He left it dead, and with its head
  He went galumphing back.                                20

"And hast thou slain the Jabberwock?
  Come to my arms, my beamish boy!
O frabjous day! Callooh, Callay!"
  He chortled in his joy.

'Twas brillig, and the slithy toves                       25
  Did gyre and gimble in the wabe:
All mimsy were the borogoves,
  And the mome raths outgrabe.

JABBERWOCKY. Fussy about pronunciation, Carroll in his preface to *The Hunting of the Snark*
declares: "The first 'o' in 'borogoves' is pronounced like the 'o' in 'borrow.' I have heard people
try to give it the sound of the 'o' in 'worry.' Such is Human Perversity." *Toves*, he adds, rimes
with *groves*.

## QUESTIONS

1. Look up *chortled* (line 24) in your dictionary and find out its definition and origin.
2. In *Through the Looking-Glass*, Alice seeks the aid of Humpty Dumpty to decipher
   the meaning of this nonsense poem. *"Brillig,"* he explains, "means four o'clock in
   the afternoon—the time when you begin *broiling* things for dinner." Does *brillig*
   sound like any other familiar word?
3. *"Slithy,"* the explanation goes on, "means 'lithe and slimy.' 'Lithe' is the same as
   'active.' You see it's like a portmanteau—there are two meanings packed up into
   one word." *Mimsy* is supposed to pack together both "flimsy" and "miserable."
   In the rest of the poem, what other portmanteau—or packed suitcase—words can
   you find?

---

### Jonathan Holden (b. 1941)

THE NAMES OF THE RAPIDS                    1985

Snaggle-Tooth, Maytag, Taylor Falls—
long before we measured with our eyes
the true size of each monstrosity

its name, downriver, was famous to us.
It lay in wait, something to be slain                          5
while our raft, errant, eddied
among glancing pinpricks of sun
and every bend giving way to bend
seemed a last reprieve.
But common terror has a raw taste.                           10
It's all banality, as when
you stare straight into a bad cut—
this sense of being slightly more
awake than you might like.
When the raft pitches sideways off                           15
a ledge, what you land on is less
than its name. It's a mechanism. None
of the demented expressions
that the fleshly water forms
over that stone profile                                      20
is more than another collision,
a fleeting logic lost and
forming, now lost in the melee.
When the world is most serious
we approach it with wholly open eyes                         25
even as we start the plunge
and the stone explanation.

QUESTION

From the names of the three rapids mentioned in line 1, describe what you think each
one would probably be like.

---

## *E. E. Cummings* (1894–1962)*

### ANYONE LIVED IN A PRETTY HOW TOWN         1940

anyone lived in a pretty how town
(with up so floating many bells down)
spring summer autumn winter
he sang his didn't he danced his did.

Women and men (both little and small)            5
cared for anyone not at all
they sowed their isn't they reaped their same
sun moon stars rain

children guessed (but only a few
and down they forgot as up they grew            10
autumn winter spring summer)
that noone loved him more by more

when by now and tree by leaf
she laughed his joy she cried his grief
bird by snow and stir by still                    15
anyone's any was all to her

someones married their everyones
laughed their cryings and did their dance
(sleep wake hope and then) they
said their nevers they slept their dream           20

stars rain sun moon
(and only the snow can begin to explain
how children are apt to forget to remember
with up so floating many bells down)

one day anyone died i guess                        25
(and noone stooped to kiss his face)
busy folk buried them side by side
little by little and was by was

all by all and deep by deep
and more by more they dream their sleep            30
noone and anyone earth by april
wish by spirit and if by yes.

Women and men (both dong and ding)
summer autumn winter spring
reaped their sowing and went their came            35
sun moon stars rain

## QUESTIONS

1. Summarize the story told in this poem. Who are the characters?
2. Rearrange the words in the two opening lines into the order you would expect them usually to follow. What effect does Cummings obtain by his unconventional word order?
3. Another of Cummings's strategies is to use one part of speech as if it were another; for instance, in line 4, *didn't* and *did* ordinarily are verbs, but here they are used as nouns. What other words in the poem perform functions other than their expected ones?

## EXERCISE: *Different Kinds of English*

Read the following poems and see what kinds of diction and word order you find in them. Which poems are least formal in their language and which most formal? Is there any use of vulgate English? Any dialect? What does each poem achieve that its own kind of English makes possible?

### *Anonymous* (American oral verse)

### CARNATION MILK     (about 1900?)

Carnation Milk is the best in the land;
Here I sit with a can in my hand—

No tits to pull, no hay to pitch,
You just punch a hole in the son of a bitch.

CARNATION MILK. "This quatrain is imagined as the caption under a picture of a rugged-looking cowboy seated upon a bale of hay," notes William Harmon in his *Oxford Book of American Light Verse* (New York: Oxford UP, 1979). Possibly the first to print this work was David Ogilvy (b. 1911), who quotes it in his *Confessions of an Advertising Man* (New York: Atheneum, 1963).

## William Wordsworth (1770–1850)*

MY HEART LEAPS UP WHEN I BEHOLD          1807

My heart leaps up when I behold
    A rainbow in the sky:
So was it when my life began;
So is it now I am a man;
So be it when I shall grow old,                                                5
    Or let me die!
The Child is father of the Man;
And I could wish my days to be
Bound each to each by natural piety.

## William Wordsworth (1770–1850)*

MUTABILITY                                     1822

From low to high doth dissolution climb,
And sink from high to low, along a scale
Of awful notes, whose concord shall not fail;
A musical but melancholy chime,
Which they can hear who meddle not with crime,                  5
Nor avarice, nor over-anxious care.
Truth fails not; but her outward forms that bear
The longest date do melt like frosty rime°,              *frozen dew*
That in the morning whitened hill and plain
And is no more; drop like the tower sublime                       10
Of yesterday, which royally did wear
His crown of weeds, but could not even sustain
Some casual shout that broke the silent air,
Or the unimaginable touch of Time.

## Anonymous

SCOTTSBORO                                    1936

Paper come out—done strewed de news
Seven po' chillun moan deat' house blues,

Seven po' chillun moanin' deat' house blues.
Seven nappy° heads wit' big shiny eye                                    *frizzy*
All boun' in jail and framed to die,                                          5
All boun' in jail and framed to die.

Messin' white woman—snake lyin' tale
Hang and burn and jail wit' no bail.
Dat hang and burn and jail wit' no bail.
Worse ol' crime in white folks' lan'                                         10
Black skin coverin' po' workin' man,
Black skin coverin' po' workin' man.

Judge and jury—all in de stan'
Lawd, biggety name for same lynchin' ban',
Lawd, biggety name for same lynchin' ban'.                                  15
White folks and nigger in great co't house
Like cat down cellar wit' nohole mouse.
Like cat down cellar wit' nohole mouse.

SCOTTSBORO. This folk blues, collected by Lawrence Gellert in *Negro Songs of Protest* (New York: Carl Fischer, Inc., 1936), is a comment on the Scottsboro case. In 1931 nine black youths of Scottsboro, Alabama, were arrested and charged with the rape of two white women. Though eventually, after several trials, they were found not guilty, some of them at the time this song was composed had been convicted and sentenced to death.

## SUGGESTIONS FOR WRITING

1. Choosing a poem that strikes you as particularly inventive or unusual in its language, such as E. E. Cummings's "anyone lived in a pretty how town" (page 646), or Gerard Manley Hopkins's "The Windhover" (page 941), or Wendy Cope's "Lonely Hearts" (page 643), write a brief analysis of it. Concentrate on the diction of the poem and word order. For what possible purposes does the poet depart from standard English or incorporate unusual vocabulary? (For pointers on writing about poetry by the method of analysis, see page 1767.)
2. In a short essay, set forth the pleasures of browsing in a dictionary. As you browse, see if you can discover any "found poems."
3. "Printing poetry in dialect, such as 'Scottsboro,' insults the literacy of a people." Think about this critical charge and comment on it.

# 16 *Saying and Suggesting*

To write so clearly that they might bring "all things as near the mathematical plainness" as possible—that was the goal of scientists according to Bishop Thomas Sprat, who lived in the seventeenth century. Such an effort would seem bound to fail, because words, unlike numbers, are ambiguous indicators. Although it may have troubled Bishop Sprat, the tendency of a word to have multiplicity of meaning rather than mathematical plainness opens broad avenues to poetry.

Every word has at least one **denotation:** a meaning as defined in a dictionary. But the English language has many a common word with so many denotations that a reader may need to think twice to see what it means in a specific context. The noun *field*, for instance, can denote a piece of ground, a sports arena, the scene of a battle, part of a flag, a profession, and a number system in mathematics. Further, the word can be used as a verb ("he fielded a grounder") or an adjective ("field trip," "field glasses").

A word also has **connotations:** overtones or suggestions of additional meaning that it gains from all the contexts in which we have met it in the past. The word *skeleton*, according to a dictionary, denotes "the bony framework of a human being or other vertebrate animal, which supports the flesh and protects the organs." But by its associations, the word can rouse thoughts of war, of disease and death, or (possibly) of one's plans to go to medical school. Think, too, of the difference between "Old Doc Jones" and "Abner P. Jones, M.D." In the mind's eye, the former appears in his shirtsleeves; the latter has a gold nameplate on his door. That some words denote the same thing but have sharply different connotations is pointed out in this anonymous Victorian jingle:

> Here's a little ditty that you really ought to know:
> Horses "sweat" and men "perspire," but ladies only "glow."

The terms *druggist, pharmacist,* and *apothecary* all denote the same occupation, but apothecaries lay claim to special distinction.

Poets aren't the only people who care about the connotations of language. Advertisers know that connotations make money. Nowadays many automobile dealers advertise their secondhand cars not as "used" but as "pre-owned," as if fearing that "used car" would connote an old heap with soiled upholstery and mysterious engine troubles that somebody couldn't put up with. "Pre-owned," however, suggests that the previous owner has taken the trouble of breaking in the car for you. Not long ago prune-packers, alarmed by a slump in sales, sponsored a survey to determine the connotations of prunes in the public consciousness. Asked, "What do you think of when you hear the word *prunes?*" most people replied, "dried up," "wrinkled," or "constipated." Dismayed, the packers hired an advertising agency to create a new image for prunes, in hopes of inducing new connotations. Soon, advertisements began to show prunes in brightly colored settings, in the company of bikinied bathing beauties.

In imaginative writing, connotations are as crucial as they are in advertising. Consider this sentence: "A new brand of journalism is being born, or spawned" (Dwight Macdonald writing in *The New York Review of Books*). The last word, by its associations with fish and crustaceans, suggests that this new journalism is scarcely the product of human beings. And what do we make of Romeo's assertion that Juliet "is the sun"? Surely even a lovesick boy cannot mean that his sweetheart is "the incandescent body of gases about which the earth and other planets revolve" (a dictionary definition). He means, of course, that he thrives in her sight, that he feels warm in her presence or even at the thought of her, that she illumines his world and is the center of his universe. Because in the mind of the hearer these and other suggestions are brought into play, Romeo's statement, literally absurd, makes excellent sense.

Here is a famous poem that groups together things with similar connotations: certain ships and their cargoes. (A *quinquireme,* by the way, was an ancient Assyrian vessel propelled by sails and oars.)

---

**John Masefield** (1878–1967)

CARGOES                                                              1902

Quinquireme of Nineveh from distant Ophir,
Rowing home to haven in sunny Palestine,
With a cargo of ivory,
And apes and peacocks,
Sandalwood, cedarwood, and sweet white wine.                         5

Stately Spanish galleon coming from the Isthmus,
Dipping through the Tropics by the palm-green shores,

With a cargo of diamonds,
Emeralds, amethysts,
Topazes, and cinnamon, and gold moidores°.                    *Portuguese coins*   10

Dirty British coaster with a salt-caked smoke stack,
Butting through the Channel in the mad March days,
With a cargo of Tyne coal,
Road-rails, pig-lead,
Firewood, iron-ware, and cheap tin trays.                                        15

To us, as well as to the poet's original readers, the place-names in the first
two stanzas suggest the exotic and faraway. Ophir, a vanished place, may
have been in Arabia; according to the Bible, King Solomon sent there for its
celebrated pure gold, also for ivory, apes, peacocks, and other luxury items.
(See I Kings 9–10.) In his final stanza, Masefield groups commonplace things
(mostly heavy and metallic), whose suggestions of crudeness, cheapness, and
ugliness he deliberately contrasts with those of the precious stuffs he has
listed earlier. For British readers, the Tyne is a stodgy and familiar river; the
English Channel in March, choppy and likely to upset a stomach. The
quinquireme is *rowing*, the galleon is *dipping*, but the dirty British freighter
is *butting*, aggressively pushing. Conceivably, the poet could have described
firewood and even coal as beautiful, but evidently he wants them to convey
sharply different suggestions here, to go along with the rest of the coaster's
cargo. In drawing such a sharp contrast between past and present, Masefield
does more than merely draw up bills-of-lading. Perhaps he even implies a wry
and unfavorable comment upon life in the present day. His meaning lies not
so much in the dictionary definitions of his words ("*moidores:* Portuguese
gold coins formerly worth approximately five pounds sterling") as in their
rich and vivid connotations.

### William Blake (1757–1827)*

LONDON                                             1794

I wander through each chartered street,
Near where the chartered Thames does flow,
And mark in every face I meet
Marks of weakness, marks of woe.

In every cry of every man,                                                       5
In every infant's cry of fear,
In every voice, in every ban,
The mind-forged manacles I hear.

How the chimney-sweeper's cry
Every black'ning church appalls                                                  10

And the hapless soldier's sigh
Runs in blood down palace walls.

But most through midnight streets I hear
How the youthful harlot's curse
Blasts the new born infant's tear                                        15
And blights with plagues the marriage hearse.

Here are only a few of the possible meanings of three of Blake's words:

*chartered* (lines 1, 2)

DENOTATIONS: Established by a charter (a written grant or a certificate of
incorporation); leased or hired.

CONNOTATIONS: Defined, limited, restricted, channeled, mapped, bound
by law; bought and sold (like a slave or an inanimate object); Magna
Carta; charters given crown colonies by the King.

OTHER WORDS IN THE POEM WITH SIMILAR CONNOTATIONS: *Ban*, which
can denote (1) a legal prohibition; (2) a churchman's curse or malediction; (3) in medieval times, an order summoning a king's vassals to
fight for him. *Manacles*, or shackles, restrain movement. *Chimney-
sweeper*, *soldier*, and *harlot* are all hirelings.

INTERPRETATION OF THE LINES: The street has had mapped out for it the
direction in which it must go; the Thames has had laid down to it the
course it must follow. Street and river are channeled, imprisoned,
enslaved (like every inhabitant of London).

*black'ning* (line 10)

DENOTATION: Becoming black.

CONNOTATIONS: The darkening of something once light, the defilement
of something once clean, the deepening of guilt, the gathering of
darkness at the approach of night.

OTHER WORDS IN THE POEM WITH SIMILAR CONNOTATIONS: Objects
becoming marked or smudged (*marks of weakness, marks of woe* in the
faces of passers-by; bloodied walls of a palace; marriage blighted with
plagues); the word *appalls* (denoting not only "to overcome with
horror" but "to make pale" and also "to cast a pall or shroud over");
*midnight streets*.

INTERPRETATION OF THE LINE: Literally, every London church grows
black from soot and hires a chimney-sweeper (a small boy) to help
clean it. But Blake suggests too that by profiting from the suffering of
the child laborer, the church is soiling its original purity.

*Blasts, blights* (lines 15–16)

DENOTATIONS: Both *blast* and *blight* mean "to cause to wither" or "to
ruin and destroy." Both are terms from horticulture. Frost *blasts* a bud
and kills it; disease *blights* a growing plant.

CONNOTATIONS: Sickness and death; gardens shriveled and dying; gusts of wind and the ravages of insects; things blown to pieces or rotted and warped.

OTHER WORDS IN THE POEM WITH SIMILAR CONNOTATIONS: Faces marked with weakness and woe; the child become a chimney-sweep; the soldier killed by war; blackening church and bloodied palace; young girl turned harlot; wedding carriage transformed into a hearse.

INTERPRETATION OF THE LINES: Literally, the harlot spreads the plague of syphilis, which, carried into marriage, can cause a baby to be born blind. In a larger and more meaningful sense, Blake sees the prostitution of even one young girl corrupting the entire institution of matrimony and endangering every child.

Some of these connotations are more to the point than others; the reader of a poem nearly always has the problem of distinguishing relevant associations from irrelevant ones. We need to read a poem in its entirety and, when a word leaves us in doubt, look for other things in the poem to corroborate or refute what we think it means. Relatively simple and direct in its statement, Blake's account of his stroll through the city at night becomes an indictment of a whole social and religious order. The indictment could hardly be this effective if it were "mathematically plain," its every word restricted to one denotation clearly spelled out.

---

**_Wallace Stevens_** (1879–1955)*

DISILLUSIONMENT OF TEN O'CLOCK          1923

The houses are haunted
By white night-gowns.
None are green,
Or purple with green rings,
Or green with yellow rings,                              5
Or yellow with blue rings.
None of them are strange,
With socks of lace
And beaded ceintures.
People are not going                                     10
To dream of baboons and periwinkles.
Only, here and there, an old sailor,
Drunk and asleep in his boots,
Catches tigers
In red weather.                                          15

1. What are *beaded ceintures*? What does the phrase suggest?
2. What contrast does Stevens draw between the people who live in these houses and the old sailor? What do the connotations of *white night-gowns* and *sailor* add to this contrast?
3. What is lacking in these people who wear white night-gowns? Why should the poet's view of them be a "disillusionment"?

---

*Gwendolyn Brooks* (b. 1917)*

## THE BEAN EATERS                                                    1960

They eat beans mostly, this old yellow pair.
Dinner is a casual affair.
Plain chipware on a plain and creaking wood,
Tin flatware.

Two who are Mostly Good.                                              5
Two who have lived their day,
But keep on putting on their clothes
And putting things away.

And remembering . . .
Remembering, with tinklings and twinges,                             10
As they lean over the beans in their rented back room that is full of
     beads and receipts and dolls and cloths, tobacco crumbs, vases
     and fringes.

QUESTIONS
1. What do we infer about this old couple and their life style from the details in lines 1–4 about their diet, dishes, dinner table, and cutlery?
2. In that long last line, what is suggested by the things they have saved and stored?

---

*Richard Snyder* (1925–1986)

## A MONGOLOID CHILD HANDLING
## SHELLS ON THE BEACH                    1971

She turns them over in her slow hands,
as did the sea sending them to her;
broken bits from the mazarine maze,
they are the calmest things on this sand.

The unbroken children splash and shout,                              5
rough as surf, gay as their nesting towels.

But she plays soberly with the sea's
small change and hums back to it its slow vowels.

## QUESTIONS

1. In what ways is the phrase *the mazarine maze* more valuable to this poem than if
   the poet had said "the deep blue sea"?
2. What is suggested by calling the other children *unbroken?* By saying that their
   towels are *nesting?*
3. How is the child like the sea? How are the other children like the surf? What do
   the differences between sea and surf contribute to Richard Snyder's poem?
4. What is the poet's attitude toward the child? How can you tell?
5. Since 1971, when this poem first appeared, the congenital condition once commonly named *mongolism* has come to be called *Down's syndrome,* after the physician
   who first identified its characteristics. The denotations of *mongolism* and *Down's
   syndrome* are identical. What connotations of the word *mongoloid* seem responsible
   for the word's fall from favor?

---

## Timothy Steele (b. 1948)*

EPITAPH                                                    1979

Here lies Sir Tact, a diplomatic fellow
Whose silence was not golden, but just yellow.

### QUESTIONS

1. To what famous saying does the poet allude?
2. What are the connotations of *golden?* Of *yellow?*

---

## Geoffrey Hill (b. 1932)

MERLIN                                                     1959

I will consider the outnumbering dead:
For they are the husks of what was rich seed.
Now, should they come together to be fed,
They would outstrip the locusts' covering tide.

Arthur, Elaine, Mordred; they are all gone                         5
Among the raftered galleries of bone.
By the long barrows of Logres they are made one,
And over their city stands the pinnacled corn.

MERLIN. In medieval legend, Merlin was a powerful magician and a seer, an aide of King Arthur.
5 *Elaine:* in Arthurian romance, the beloved of Sir Launcelot. *Mordred:* Arthur's treacherous
nephew by whose hand the king died. 7 *barrows:* earthworks for burial of the dead. *Logres:* name
of an ancient British kingdom, according to the twelfth-century historian Geoffrey of Mon-
mouth, who gathered legends of King Arthur.

1. What does the title "Merlin" contribute to this poem? Do you prefer to read the poem as though it is Merlin who speaks to us—or the poet?
2. Line 4 alludes to the plague of locusts that God sent upon Egypt (Exodus 10): "For they covered the face of the whole earth, so that the land was darkened . . ." With this allusion in mind, explain the comparison of the dead to locusts.
3. Why are the suggestions inherent in the names of *Arthur, Elaine,* and *Mordred* more valuable to this poem than those we might find in the names of other dead persons called, say, Gus, Tessie, and Butch?
4. Explain the phrase in line 6: *the raftered galleries of bone.*
5. In the last line, what *city* does the poet refer to? Does he mean some particular city, or is he making a comparison?
6. What is interesting in the adjective *pinnacled?* How can it be applied to corn?

---

*Walter de la Mare* (1873–1956)

THE LISTENERS                                        1912

"Is there anybody there?" said the Traveller,
    Knocking on the moonlit door;
And his horse in the silence champed the grasses
    Of the forest's ferny floor:
And a bird flew up out of the turret,                            5
    Above the Traveller's head:
And he smote upon the door again a second time;
    "Is there anybody there?" he said.
But no one descended to the Traveller;
    No head from the leaf-fringed sill                           10
Leaned over and looked into his gray eyes,
    Where he stood perplexed and still.
But only a host of phantom listeners
    That dwelt in the lone house then
Stood listening in the quiet of the moonlight                    15
    To that voice from the world of men:
Stood thronging the faint moonbeams on the dark stair
    That goes down to the empty hall,
Hearkening in an air stirred and shaken
    By the lonely Traveller's call.                              20
And he felt in his heart their strangeness,
    Their stillness answering his cry,
While his horse moved, cropping the dark turf,
    'Neath the starred and leafy sky;
For he suddenly smote on the door, even                          25
    Louder, and lifted his head:—
"Tell them I came, and no one answered,
    That I kept my word," he said.

Never the least stir made the listeners,
   Though every word he spake                       30
Fell echoing through the shadowiness of the still house
   From the one man left awake:
Ay, they heard his foot upon the stirrup,
   And the sound of iron on stone,
And how the silence surged softly backward,          35
   When the plunging hoofs were gone.

## QUESTIONS

1. Before you had read this poem, what suggestions did its title bring to mind?
2. Now that you have read the poem, what do you make of these "listeners"? Who or what do you imagine them to be?
3. Why is *the moonlit door* (in line 2) a phrase more valuable to this poem than if the poet had written simply "the door"?
4. What does *turret* (in line 5) suggest?
5. Reconstruct some earlier events that might have preceded the Traveller's visit. Who might this Traveller be? Who are the unnamed persons—"them" (line 27)—for whom the Traveller leaves a message? What promise has he kept? (The poet doesn't tell us; we can only guess.)
6. Do you think this poem any the worse for the fact that its setting, characters, and action are so mysterious? What does "The Listeners" gain from not telling us all?

### *Robert Frost* (1874–1963)*

FIRE AND ICE          1923

Some say the world will end in fire,
Some say in ice.
From what I've tasted of desire
I hold with those who favor fire.
But if it had to perish twice,         5
I think I know enough of hate
To say that for destruction ice
Is also great
And would suffice.

## QUESTIONS

1. To whom does Frost refer in line 1? In line 2?
2. What connotations of *fire* and *ice* contribute to the richness of Frost's comparison?

## SUGGESTIONS FOR WRITING

1. In a short essay, analyze a poem full of words that radiate suggestions. Looking into the Poems for Further Reading that begins on page 885, you might consider T. S. Eliot's "The Love Song of J. Alfred Prufrock," John Keats's "To Autumn,"

Sylvia Plath's "Daddy," or many others. Focus on particular words: explain their connotations and show how these suggestions are part of the poem's meaning. (For guidelines on writing about poetry by the method of analysis, see page 1767.)

2. In a current newspaper or magazine, select an advertisement that tries to surround a product with an aura. A new car, for instance, might be described in terms of some powerful jungle cat ("purring power, ready to spring"). Likely hunting-grounds for such ads are magazines that cater to the affluent (*New Yorker, Vogue,* and others). Clip or photocopy the ad and circle words in it that seem especially suggestive. Then, in an accompanying paper, unfold the suggestions in these words and try to explain the ad's appeal. How is the purpose of connotative language used in advertising copy different from that of such language when used in poetry?

# 17  Imagery

**Ezra Pound** (1885–1972)*

IN A STATION OF THE METRO          1916

The apparition of these faces in the crowd;
Petals on a wet, black bough.

Pound said he wrote this poem to convey an experience: emerging one
day from a train in the Paris subway *(Métro)*, he beheld "suddenly a beautiful
face, and then another and another." Originally he had described his impression in a poem thirty lines long. In this final version, each line contains an
**image,** which, like a picture, may take the place of a thousand words.

Though the term *image* suggests a thing seen, when speaking of images
in poetry we generally mean *a word or sequence of words that refers to any sensory
experience.* Often this experience is a sight (**visual imagery,** as in Pound's
poem), but it may be a sound (**auditory imagery**) or a touch (**tactile imagery,**
as a perception of roughness or smoothness). It may be an odor or a taste or
perhaps a bodily sensation such as pain, the prickling of gooseflesh, the
quenching of thirst, or—as in the following brief poem—the perception of
something cold.

**Taniguchi Buson** (1716–1783)

THE PIERCING CHILL I FEEL                    (about 1760)

The piercing chill I feel:
      my dead wife's comb, in our bedroom,
            under my heel . . .
                        —Translated by Harold G. Henderson

As in this **haiku** (in Japanese, a poem of about seventeen syllables) an image can convey a flash of understanding. Had he wished, the poet might have spoken of the dead woman, of the contrast between her death and his memory of her, of his feelings toward death in general. But such a discussion would be quite different from the poem he actually wrote. Striking his bare foot against the comb, now cold and motionless but associated with the living wife (perhaps worn in her hair), the widower feels a shock as if he had touched the woman's corpse. A literal, physical sense of death is conveyed; the abstraction "death" is understood through the senses. To render the abstract in concrete terms is what poets often try to do; in this attempt, an image can be valuable.

An image may occur in a single word, a phrase, a sentence, or, as in this case, an entire short poem. To speak of the **imagery** of a poem—all its images taken together—is often more useful than to speak of separate images. To divide Buson's haiku into five images—*chill, wife, comb, bedroom, heel*—is possible, for any noun that refers to a visible object or a sensation is an image, but this is to draw distinctions that in themselves mean little and to disassemble a single experience.

Does an image cause a reader to experience a sense impression? Not quite. Reading the word *petals,* no one literally sees petals; but the occasion is given for imagining them. The image asks to be seen with the mind's eye. And although "In a Station of the Metro" records what Ezra Pound saw, it is of course not necessary for a poet actually to have lived through a sensory experience in order to write of it. Keats may never have seen a newly discovered planet through a telescope, despite the image in his sonnet on Chapman's Homer (p. 948).

It is tempting to think of imagery as mere decoration, particularly when we read Keats, who fills his poems with an abundance of sights, sounds, odors, and tastes. But a successful image is not just a dab of paint or a flashy bauble. When Keats opens "The Eve of St. Agnes" with what have been called the coldest lines in literature, he evokes by a series of images a setting and a mood:

> St. Agnes' eve—Ah, bitter chill it was!
> The owl, for all his feathers, was a-cold;
> The hare limped trembling through the frozen grass,
> And silent was the flock in woolly fold:
> Numb were the Beadsman's fingers, while he told
> His rosary, and while his frosted breath,
> Like pious incense from a censer old,
> Seemed taking flight for heaven, without a death, . . .

Indeed, some literary critics look for much of the meaning of a poem in its imagery, wherein they expect to see the mind of the poet more truly revealed than in whatever the poet explicitly claims to believe. In his investigation of Wordsworth's "Ode: Intimations of Immortality," the critic Cleanth

Brooks devotes his attention to the imagery of light and darkness, which he finds carries on and develops Wordsworth's thought.[1]

Though Shakespeare's Theseus (in *A Midsummer Night's Dream*) accuses poets of being concerned with "airy nothings," poets are usually very much concerned with what is in front of them. This concern is of use to us. Perhaps, as Alan Watts has remarked, Americans are not the materialists they are sometimes accused of being. How could anyone taking a look at an American city think that its inhabitants deeply cherish material things? Involved in our personal hopes and apprehensions, anticipating the future so hard that much of the time we see the present through a film of thought across our eyes, perhaps we need a poet occasionally to remind us that even the coffee we absentmindedly sip comes in (as Yeats put it) a "heavy spillable cup."

## T. S. Eliot (1888–1965)*

### THE WINTER EVENING SETTLES DOWN          1917

The winter evening settles down
With smell of steaks in passageways.
Six o'clock.
The burnt-out ends of smoky days.
And now a gusty shower wraps                                  5
The grimy scraps
Of withered leaves about your feet
And newspapers from vacant lots;
The showers beat
On broken blinds and chimney-pots,                           10
And at the corner of the street
A lonely cab-horse steams and stamps.

And then the lighting of the lamps.

#### QUESTIONS

1. What mood is evoked by the images in Eliot's poem?
2. What kind of city neighborhood has the poet chosen to describe? How can you tell?

## Theodore Roethke (1908–1963)*

### ROOT CELLAR                                               1948

Nothing would sleep in that cellar, dank as a ditch,
Bulbs broke out of boxes hunting for chinks in the dark,

[1]"Wordsworth and the Paradox of the Imagination," in *The Well Wrought Urn* (New York: Harcourt, 1956).

Shoots dangled and drooped,
Lolling obscenely from mildewed crates,
Hung down long yellow evil necks, like tropical snakes.                5
And what a congress of stinks!—
Roots ripe as old bait,
Pulpy stems, rank, silo-rich,
Leaf-mold, manure, lime, piled against slippery planks.
Nothing would give up life:                                            10
Even the dirt kept breathing a small breath.

## QUESTIONS

1. As a boy growing up in Saginaw, Michigan, Theodore Roethke spent much of his
   time in a large commercial greenhouse run by his family. What details in his poem
   show more than a passing acquaintance with growing things?
2. What varieties of image does "Root Cellar" contain? Point out examples.
3. What do you understand to be Roethke's attitude toward the root cellar? Does he
   view it as a disgusting chamber of horrors? Pay special attention to the last two
   lines.

## *Elizabeth Bishop* (1911–1979)*

THE FISH                    1946

I caught a tremendous fish
and held him beside the boat
half out of water, with my hook
fast in a corner of his mouth.
He didn't fight.                                                       5
He hadn't fought at all.
He hung a grunting weight,
battered and venerable
and homely. Here and there
his brown skin hung in strips                                          10
like ancient wall-paper,
and its pattern of darker brown
was like wall-paper:
shapes like full-blown roses
stained and lost through age.                                          15
He was speckled with barnacles,
fine rosettes of lime,
and infested
with tiny white sea-lice,
and underneath two or three                                            20
rags of green weed hung down.
While his gills were breathing in
the terrible oxygen
—the frightening gills,

fresh and crisp with blood,                               25
that can cut so badly—
I thought of the coarse white flesh
packed in like feathers,
the big bones and the little bones,
the dramatic reds and blacks                              30
of his shiny entrails,
and the pink swim-bladder
like a big peony.
I looked into his eyes
which were far larger than mine                           35
but shallower, and yellowed,
the irises backed and packed
with tarnished tinfoil
seen through the lenses
of old scratched isinglass.                               40
They shifted a little, but not
to return my stare.
—It was more like the tipping
of an object toward the light.
I admired his sullen face,                                45
the mechanism of his jaw,
and then I saw
that from his lower lip
—if you could call it a lip—
grim, wet, and weapon-like,                               50
hung five old pieces of fish-line,
or four and a wire leader
with the swivel still attached,
with all their five big hooks
grown firmly in his mouth.                                55
A green line, frayed at the end
where he broke it, two heavier lines,
and a fine black thread
still crimped from the strain and snap
when it broke and he got away.                            60
Like medals with their ribbons
frayed and wavering,
a five-haired beard of wisdom
trailing from his aching jaw.
I stared and stared                                       65
and victory filled up
the little rented boat,
from the pool of bilge
where oil had spread a rainbow
around the rusted engine                                  70
to the bailer rusted orange,

the sun-cracked thwarts,
the oarlocks on their strings,
the gunnels—until everything
was rainbow, rainbow, rainbow!                              75
And I let the fish go.

## QUESTIONS

1. How many abstract words does this poem contain? What proportion of the poem
   is imagery?
2. What is the speaker's attitude toward the fish? Comment in particular on lines
   61–64.
3. What attitude do the images of the rainbow of oil (line 69), the orange bailer
   (bailing bucket, line 71), the *sun-cracked thwarts* (line 72) convey? Does the poet
   expect us to feel mournful because the boat is in such sorry condition?
4. What is meant by *rainbow, rainbow, rainbow?*
5. How do these images prepare us for the conclusion? Why does the speaker let the
   fish go?

---

### *Anne Stevenson* (b. 1933)*

## THE VICTORY                    1974

I thought you were my victory
though you cut me like a knife
when I brought you out of my body
into your life.

Tiny antagonist, gory,                                       5
blue as a bruise. The stains
of your cloud of glory
bled from my veins.

How can you dare, blind thing,
blank insect eyes?                                          10
You barb the air. You sting
with bladed cries.

Snail! Scary knot of desires!
Hungry snarl! Small son.
Why do I have to love you?                                  15
How have you won?

## QUESTIONS

1. Newborn babies are often described as "little angels" or "bundles of joy." How
   does the speaker of "The Victory" describe her son?
2. Why does the speaker describe the child as an "antagonist" (line 5)?
3. Why is the poem titled "The Victory"?
4. Why is the infant compared to a knife in both lines 2 and 12?

## John Haines (b. 1924)

### Winter News        1966

They say the wells
are freezing
at Northway where
the cold begins.

Oil tins bang                                    5
as evening comes on,
and clouds of
steaming breath drift
in the street.

Men go out to feed                               10
the stiffening dogs,

the voice of the snowman
calls the white-
haired children home.

### Questions

1. Which of the images in this poem strike you as the most vivid? To which senses
   do Haines's images appeal?
2. Why are the children described as "white-haired"?

## Emily Dickinson (1830–1886)*

### A Route of Evanescence        (1879)

A Route of Evanescence
With a revolving Wheel–
A Resonance of Emerald–
A Rush of Cochineal°–                            *red dye*
And every Blossom on the Bush                    5
Adjusts its tumbled Head–
The mail from Tunis, probably,
An easy Morning's Ride–

A Route of Evanescence. 1 *Evanescence*; ornithologist's term for the luminous sheen of certain
birds' feathers. 7 *Tunis*: capital city of Tunisia, North Africa.

### Question

What is the subject of this poem? How can you tell?

## Jean Toomer (1894–1967)

### REAPERS                                                      1923

Black reapers with the sound of steel on stones
Are sharpening scythes. I see them place the hones
In their hip-pockets as a thing that's done,
And start their silent swinging, one by one.
Black horses drive a mower through the weeds,                    5
And there, a field rat, startled, squealing bleeds,
His belly close to ground. I see the blade,
Blood-stained, continue cutting weeds and shade.

### QUESTIONS

1. Imagine the scene Jean Toomer describes. Which particulars most vividly strike
   the mind's eye?
2. What kind of image is *silent swinging?*
3. Read the poem aloud. Notice especially the effect of the words *sound of steel on
   stones* and *field rat, startled, squealing bleeds.* What interesting sounds are present
   in the very words that contain these images?
4. What feelings do you get from this poem as a whole? Would you agree with
   someone who said, "This poem gives us a sense of happy, carefree life down on
   the farm, close to nature"? Exactly what in "Reapers" makes you feel the way you
   do? Besides appealing to our auditory and visual imagination, what do the images
   contribute?

## Gerard Manley Hopkins (1844–1889)*

### PIED BEAUTY                                                  (1877)

Glory be to God for dappled things—
    For skies of couple-color as a brinded° cow;                 *streaked*
      For rose-moles all in stipple upon trout that swim;
Fresh-firecoal chestnut-falls; finches' wings;
    Landscape plotted and pieced—fold, fallow, and plow;         5
      And áll trádes, their gear and tackle and trim°.             *equipment*

All things counter, original, spare, strange;
    Whatever is fickle, freckled (who knows how?)
      With swift, slow; sweet, sour; adazzle, dim;
He fathers-forth whose beauty is past change:                   10
        Praise him.

### QUESTIONS

1. What does the word *pied* mean? (Hint: what does a Pied Piper look like?)
2. According to Hopkins, what do *skies, cow, trout, ripe chestnuts, finches' wings,* and
   *landscapes* all have in common? What landscapes can the poet have in mind? (Have

you ever seen any *dappled* landscape while looking down from an airplane, or from a mountain or high hill?)
3. What do you make of line 6: what can carpenters' saws and ditch-diggers' spades possibly have in common with the dappled things in lines 2–4?
4. Does Hopkins refer only to contrasts that meet the eye? What other kinds of variation interest him?
5. Try to state in your own words the theme of this poem. How essential to our understanding of this theme are Hopkins's images?

# ABOUT HAIKU

### *Taniguchi Buson* (1716–1783)

## ON THE ONE-TON TEMPLE BELL          (about 1770)

On the one-ton temple bell
a moonmoth, folded into sleep,
sits still.
          —English version by X. J. Kennedy

The name *haiku* means "beginning-verse" in Japanese—perhaps because the form may have originated in a game. Players, given a haiku, were supposed to extend its three lines into a longer poem. Haiku (the word can also be plural) tend to consist mainly of imagery, but as we saw in Buson's lines on the cold comb, their imagery is not always only pictorial. In the following haiku by Basho, the senses of sight and sound are strikingly intermingled.

### *Matsuo Basho* (1644–1694)

## HEAT-LIGHTNING STREAK          (1694)

Heat-lightning streak—
through darkness pierces
the heron's shriek.
          —English version by X. J. Kennedy

Note that a haiku has little room for abstract thoughts or general observations. The following attempt, though in seventeen syllables, is far from haiku in spirit:

Now that our love is gone
I feel within my soul
a nagging distress.

Unlike the author of those lines, haiku poets look out upon a literal world, seldom looking inward to *discuss* their feelings. Japanese haiku tend to be seasonal in subject, but because they are so highly compressed, they usually just *imply* a season: a blossom indicates spring; a crow on a branch, autumn; snow, winter. Not just pretty little sketches of nature (as some Westerners think), haiku assume a view of the universe in which observer and nature are not separated.

A haiku in Japanese is rimeless, its seventeen syllables usually arranged in three lines, often following a pattern of five, seven, and five syllables. Haiku written in English frequently ignore such a pattern; they may be rimed (like the English versions of Buson and Basho), or unrimed as the poet prefers. What English haiku try hardest to preserve is the powerful way their Japanese models capture the intensity of a particular moment, usually by linking two concrete images.

If you care to try your hand at haiku-writing, here are a few suggestions. Make every word matter. Include few adjectives, shun needless conjunctions. Set your poem in the present—"Haiku," said Basho, "is simply what is happening in this place at this moment." Confine your poem to what can be seen, heard, smelled, tasted, or touched. Mere sensory reports, however, will be meaningless unless they make the reader feel something—as a contemporary American writer points out in this spoof.

---

**Richard Brautigan** (1935–1985)

Haiku Ambulance        1968

A piece of green pepper fell
off the wooden salad bowl:
so what?

Here, freely translated, are two more Japanese haiku to inspire you. The first is the most famous poem by Basho, sometimes called the Shakespeare of the haiku.

In the old stone pool
a frogjump:
*splishhhhh.*

The second (in a translation by Cid Corman) is by Issa (1763–1827), a poet noted for wit.

only one guy and
only one fly trying to
make the guest room do

Finally, here are eight more recent haiku written in English. (Don't expect them all to observe a strict arrangement of seventeen syllables.) Haiku, in any language, is an art of few words, many suggestions. A haiku starts us thinking and feeling. "So the reader," Raymond Roseliep wrote, "keeps getting on where the poet got off."

After weeks of watching the roof leak
     I fixed it tonight
by moving a single board
     —Gary Snyder

Lying in the field
by night making new
     constellations from old stars
     —Michael B. Stillman

broken bowl
the pieces
still rocking
     —Penny Harter

on the cardboard box
holding the frozen wino
Fragile: Do not crush.
     —Nicholas A. Virgilio

The green cockleburs
Caught in the thick woolly hair
Of the black boy's head.
     —Richard Wright

Let my snow-tracks lead
on, on. Let them, where they stop
stop. There, in mid-field.
     —Hayden Carruth

SLEEPLESS AT CROWN POINT

All night, this headland
Lunges into the rumpling
Capework of the wind.
     —Richard Wilbur

THE LAZY MAN'S HAIKU

out in the night
a wheelbarrowful
of moonlight
     —John Ridland

## FOR REVIEW AND FURTHER STUDY

### John Keats (1795–1821)*

#### BRIGHT STAR! WOULD I WERE STEADFAST AS THOU ART     (1819)

Bright star! would I were steadfast as thou art—
    Not in lone splendor hung aloft the night,
And watching, with eternal lids apart,
    Like nature's patient, sleepless Eremite°          *hermit*
The moving waters at their priest-like task          5
    Of pure ablution round earth's human shores,
Or gazing on the new soft-fallen mask
    Of snow upon the mountains and the moors—
No—yet still steadfast, still unchangeable,
    Pillowed upon my fair love's ripening breast,      10
To feel for ever its soft fall and swell,
    Awake for ever in a sweet unrest,
Still, still to hear her tender-taken breath,
And so live ever—or else swoon to death.

## QUESTIONS

1. Stars are conventional symbols for love and a loved one. (Love, Shakespeare tells us in a sonnet, "is the star to every wandering bark.") In this sonnet, why is it not possible for the star to have this meaning? How does Keats use it?
2. What seems concrete and particular in the speaker's observations?
3. Suppose Keats had said *slow and easy* instead of *tender-taken* in line 13. What would have been lost?

---

**Timothy Steele** (b. 1948)*

## SUMMER                                                                          1986

Voluptuous in plenty, summer is
Neglectful of the earnest ones who've sought her.
She best resides with what she images:
Lakes windless with profound sun-shafted water;
Dense orchards in which high-grassed heat grows thick;                      5
The one-lane country road where, on his knees,
A boy initials soft tar with a stick;
Slow creeks which bear flecked light through depths of trees.

And he alone is summer's who relents
In his poor enterprisings; who can sense,                                   10
In alleys petal-blown, the wealth of chance;
Or can, supine in a deep meadow, pass
Warm hours beneath a moving sky's expanse,
Chewing the sweetness from long stalks of grass.

## QUESTIONS

1. Define *voluptuous*. How does this word prepare us for the images to follow?
2. How many of the senses does this poem evoke?
3. What would be lost in the impact of line 5 if *dense* were omitted?
4. What images does the poem use to evoke the slow, heavy feeling of summer?
5. What is the form of this poem?

## EXPERIMENT: *Writing with Images*

Taking the following poems as examples from which to start rather than as models to be slavishly copied, try to compose a brief poem that consists largely of imagery.

---

**Walt Whitman** (1819–1892)*

## THE RUNNER                                                     1867

On a flat road runs the well-train'd runner;
He is lean and sinewy, with muscular legs;

He is thinly clothed—he leans forward as he runs,
With lightly closed fists, and arms partially rais'd.

## T. E. Hulme (1883–1917)

IMAGE                                    (about 1910)

Old houses were scaffolding once
                and workmen whistling.

## William Carlos Williams (1883–1963)*

THE GREAT FIGURE                         1921

Among the rain
and lights
I saw the figure 5
in gold
on a red                                                    5
firetruck
moving
tense
unheeded
to gong clangs                                              10
siren howls
and wheels rumbling
through the dark city.

## Robert Bly (b. 1926)*

DRIVING TO TOWN LATE TO MAIL A LETTER         1962

It is a cold and snowy night. The main street is deserted.
The only things moving are swirls of snow.
As I lift the mailbox door, I feel its cold iron.
There is a privacy I love in this snowy night.
Driving around, I will waste more time.

## Gary Snyder (b. 1930)

### MID-AUGUST AT SOURDOUGH
### MOUNTAIN LOOKOUT      1959

Down valley a smoke haze
Three days heat, after five days rain
Pitch glows on the fir-cones
Across rocks and meadows
Swarms of new flies.        5

I cannot remember things I once read
A few friends, but they are in cities.
Drinking cold snow-water from a tin cup
Looking down for miles
Through high still air.        10

MID-AUGUST AT SOURDOUGH MOUNTAIN LOOKOUT. *Sourdough Mountain:* in the state of Washington, where the poet's job at the time was to watch for forest fires.

## H. D. [Hilda Doolittle] (1886–1961)*

### HEAT      1916

O wind, rend open the heat,
cut apart the heat,
rend it to tatters.

Fruit cannot drop
through this thick air—        5
fruit cannot fall into heat
that presses up and blunts
the points of pears
and rounds the grapes.

Cut the heat—        10
plough through it,
turning it on either side
of your path.

## Philip Larkin (1922–1985)*

### TOADS      1955

Why should I let the toad *work*
    Squat on my life?

Can't I use my wit as a pitchfork
　　And drive the brute off?

Six days of the week it soils
　　With its sickening poison—　　　　　　　　　　　　　　　　5
Just for paying a few bills!
　　That's out of proportion.

Lots of folk live on their wits:
　　Lecturers, lispers,　　　　　　　　　　　　　　　　　　　10
Losels°, loblolly-men°, louts—　　　　　　　　*worthless persons; boors*
　　They don't end as paupers;

Lots of folk live up lanes
　　With fires in a bucket,
Eat windfalls and tinned sardines—　　　　　　　　　　　　　15
　　They seem to like it.

Their nippers have got bare feet,
　　Their unspeakable wives
Are skinny as whippets°—and yet　　　　　　　　　*small, thin dogs*
　　No one actually *starves*.　　　　　　　　　　　　　　　20

Ah, were I courageous enough
　　To shout *Stuff your pension!*
But I know, all too well, that's the stuff
　　That dreams are made on:

For something sufficiently toad-like　　　　　　　　　　　　25
　　Squats in me, too;
Its hunkers are heavy as hard luck,
　　And cold as snow,

And will never allow me to blarney
　　My way to getting　　　　　　　　　　　　　　　　　　30
The fame and the girl and the money
　　All at one sitting.

I don't say, one bodies the other
　　One's spiritual truth;
But I do say it's hard to lose either,　　　　　　　　　　　35
　　When you have both.


**_Emily Grosholz_** (b. 1950)

LETTER FROM GERMANY　　　　1984

Though it is only February, turned
less than a week ago,

and though the latitude is upward here
of Newfoundland's north shore,
Mother, spring is out. It's almost hot,                                    5
simmering above and underground,
and in my veins! where your blood also runs.
The hazels dangle down
green flowery catkins, and the alders too,
those bushy, water-loving trees,                                          10
have a like ornament, in purple-red.
Spring is so forward here.
Snowbells swing in garden beds;
the pussy willows that you liked to bring
inside, to force their silver fur,                                        15
are open in the air;
witch hazel in the formal park,
still leafless, wears a ribbon-petaled bloom
of yellow and pale orange.
Once or twice I've walked through clouds                                  20
of insects by the river to the east
of town; the ducks are back on the canal
now that the ice is gone, loud and in love.
I wish that I could bring you here
to see this fast, unseasonable spring;                                    25
I wish that I could write a letter home.
But since a year you are not anywhere,
not even underground,
so that the words I might have written down
I say aloud into the atmosphere                                           30
of pollen and fresh clouds.
I say the litany of my desires,
and wonder, knowing better, if you hear
through some light-rooted organ of the air.


**Stevie Smith** (1902–1971)*

NOT WAVING BUT DROWNING                          1959

Nobody heard him, the dead man,
But still he lay moaning:
I was much further out than you thought
And not waving but drowning.

Poor chap, he always loved larking                                        5
And now he's dead
It must have been too cold for him his heart gave way,
They said.

Oh, no no no, it was too cold always                                    10
(Still the dead one lay moaning)
I was much too far out all my life
And not waving but drowning.

## SUGGESTIONS FOR WRITING

1. Choose, from Poems for Further Reading which begins on page 885, a poem that appeals to you. Then write a brief account of your experience in reading it, paying special notice to its imagery. What images strike you, and why? What do they contribute to the poem as a whole? Poems rich in imagery include Samuel Taylor Coleridge's "Kubla Khan," Robert Frost's "Birches," John Keats's "Ode on Melancholy," Charlotte Mew's "The Farmer's Bride," William Carlos Williams's "Spring and All (By the road to the contagious hospital)" and many more.

2. After you have read the haiku and the discussion of haiku-writing in this chapter, write three or four haiku of your own. Then write a brief prose account of your experience in writing them. What, if anything, did you find out?

3. Reflect on Samuel Johnson's famous remarks on "the business of the poet" (page 1027). Try applying Johnson's view to some recent poem—say, Elizabeth Bishop's "The Fish" (in this chapter). Would Johnson find Bishop a seer of "general and transcendental truths" or a counter of tulip-streaks? Then, in a short critical statement of your own, support or attack Johnson's view.

# 18 *Figures of Speech*

## WHY SPEAK FIGURATIVELY?

"I will speak daggers to her, but use none," says Hamlet, preparing to confront his mother. His statement makes sense only because we realize that *daggers* is to be taken two ways: literally (denoting sharp, pointed weapons) and nonliterally (referring to something that can be used *like* weapons—namely, words). Reading poetry, we often meet comparisons between two things whose similarity we have never noticed before. When Marianne Moore observes that a fir tree has "an emerald turkey-foot at the top," the result is a pleasure that poetry richly affords: the sudden recognition of likenesses.

A treetop like a turkey-foot, words like daggers—such comparisons are called **figures of speech.** In its broadest definition, a figure of speech may be said to occur whenever a speaker or writer, for the sake of freshness or emphasis, departs from the usual denotations of words. Certainly, when Hamlet says he will speak daggers, no one expects him to release pointed weapons from his lips, for *daggers* is not to be read solely for its denotation. Its connotations—sharp, stabbing, piercing, wounding—also come to mind, and we see ways in which words and daggers work alike. (Words too can hurt: by striking through pretenses, possibly, or by wounding their hearer's self-esteem.) In the statement "A razor is sharper than an ax," there is no departure from the usual denotations of *razor* and *ax*, and no figure of speech results. Both objects are of the same class; the comparison is not offensive to logic. But in "How sharper than a serpent's tooth it is to have a thankless child," the objects—snake's tooth (fang) and ungrateful offspring—are so unlike that no reasonable comparison may be made between them. To find similarity, we attend to the connotations of *serpent's tooth*—biting, piercing, venom, pain—rather than to its denotations. If we are aware of the connotations of *red rose* (beauty, softness, freshness, and so forth), then the line "My love is like a red, red rose" need not call to mind a woman with a scarlet face and a thorny neck.

Figures of speech are not devices to state what is demonstrably untrue. Indeed they often state truths that more literal language cannot communicate; they call attention to such truths; they lend them emphasis.

## Alfred, Lord Tennyson (1809–1892)*

### THE EAGLE                    1851

He clasps the crag with crooked hands;
Close to the sun in lonely lands,
Ringed with the azure world, he stands.

The wrinkled sea beneath him crawls;
He watches from his mountain walls,
And like a thunderbolt he falls.

This brief poem is rich in figurative language. In the first line, the phrase *crooked hands* may surprise us. An eagle does not have hands, we might protest; but the objection would be a quibble, for evidently Tennyson is indicating exactly how an eagle clasps a crag, in the way that human fingers clasp a thing. By implication, too, the eagle is a person. *Close to the sun,* if taken literally, is an absurd exaggeration, the sun being a mean distance of 93,000,000 miles from the earth. For the eagle to be closer to it by the altitude of a mountain is an approach so small as to be insignificant. But figuratively, Tennyson conveys that the eagle stands above the clouds, perhaps silhouetted against the sun, and for the moment belongs to the heavens rather than to the land and sea. The word *ringed* makes a circle of the whole world's horizons and suggests that we see the world from the eagle's height; the sea becomes an aged, sluggish animal; *mountain walls,* possibly literal, also suggests a fort or castle; and finally the eagle itself is likened to a thunderbolt in speed and in power, perhaps also in that its beak is—like our abstract conception of a lightning bolt—pointed. How much of the poem can be taken literally? Only *he clasps the crag, he stands, he watches, he falls.* The rest is made of figures of speech. The result is that, reading Tennyson's poem, we gain a bird's-eye view of sun, sea, and land—and even of bird. Like imagery, figurative language refers us to the physical world.

## William Shakespeare (1564–1616)*

### SHALL I COMPARE THEE TO A SUMMER'S DAY?        1609

Shall I compare thee to a summer's day?
Thou art more lovely and more temperate.

Rough winds do shake the darling buds of May,
And summer's lease hath all too short a date.
Sometime too hot the eye of heaven shines,                                    5
And often is his gold complexion dimmed;
And every fair° from fair sometimes declines,                     *fair one*
By chance, or nature's changing course, untrimmed.
But thy eternal summer shall not fade,
Nor lose possession of that fair thou ow'st°;          *ownest, have*   10
Nor shall death brag thou wand'rest in his shade,
When in eternal lines to time thou grow'st.
　　So long as men can breathe or eyes can see,
　　So long lives this, and this gives life to thee.


### *Howard Moss* (1922–1987)*

## SHALL I COMPARE THEE TO A SUMMER'S DAY?　　　1976

Who says you're like one of the dog days?
You're nicer. And better.
Even in May, the weather can be gray,
And a summer sub-let doesn't last forever.
Sometimes the sun's too hot;                                                   5
Sometimes it is not.
Who can stay young forever?
People break their necks or just drop dead!
But you? Never!
If there's just one condensed reader left                                     10
Who can figure out the abridged alphabet,
　　After you're dead and gone,
　　In this poem you'll live on!

SHALL I COMPARE THEE TO A SUMMER'S DAY (MOSS). *Dog days:* the hottest days of summer. The ancient Romans believed that the Dog-star, Sirius, added heat to summer months.

## QUESTIONS

1. In Howard Moss's streamlined version of Shakespeare, from a series called "Modified Sonnets (Dedicated to adapters, abridgers, digesters, and condensers everywhere)," to what extent does the poet use figurative language? In Shakespeare's original sonnet, how high a proportion of Shakespeare's language is figurative?
2. Compare some of Moss's lines to the corresponding lines in Shakespeare's sonnet. Why is *Even in May, the weather can be gray* less interesting than the original? In the lines on the sun (5–6 in both versions), what has Moss's modification deliberately left out? Why is Shakespeare's seeing death as a braggart memorable? Why aren't you greatly impressed by Moss's last two lines?
3. Can you explain Shakespeare's play on the word *untrimmed* (line 8)? Evidently the word can mean "divested of trimmings," but what other suggestions do you find in it?

4. How would you answer someone who argued, "Maybe Moss's language isn't as good as Shakespeare's, but the meaning is still there. What's wrong with putting Shakespeare into up-to-date words that can be understood by everybody?"

## Jon Stallworthy (b. 1935)

### SINDHI WOMAN                      1963

Barefoot through the bazaar,
and with the same undulant grace
as the cloth blown back from her face,
she glides with a stone jar
high on her head                                                    5
and not a ripple in her tread.

Watching her cross erect
stones, garbage, excrement, and crumbs
of glass in the Karachi slums,
I, with my stoop, reflect                                          10
they stand most straight
who learn to walk beneath a weight.

SINDHI WOMAN. The Sindhi are the predominantly Moslem people of Sind, a former province of India now in Pakistan. 9 Karachi: located on the Arabian Sea, from 1948 to 1959 the capital of Pakistan.

### QUESTION

Where in the poem does the most striking figurative language occur? What other figurative language does the poet use?

## METAPHOR AND SIMILE

> Life, like a dome of many-colored glass,
> Stains the white radiance of Eternity.

The first of these lines (from Shelley's "Adonais") is a **simile:** a comparison of two things, indicated by some connective, usually *like, as, than,* or a verb such as *resembles.* A simile expresses a similarity. Still, for a simile to exist, the things compared have to be dissimilar in kind. It is no simile to say, "Your fingers are like mine," it is a literal observation. But to say, "Your fingers are like sausages" is to use a simile. Omit the connective—say, "Your fingers are sausages"—and the result is a **metaphor,** a statement that one thing *is* something else, which, in a literal sense, it is not. In the second of Shelley's lines, it is *assumed* that Eternity is light or radiance, and we have an **implied metaphor,** one that uses neither a connective nor the verb *to be.* Here are examples:

| | |
|---|---|
| Oh, my love is like a red, red rose. | *Simile* |
| Oh, my love resembles a red, red rose. | *Simile* |
| Oh, my love is redder than a rose. | *Simile* |
| Oh, my love is a red, red rose. | *Metaphor* |
| Oh, my love has red petals and sharp thorns. | *Implied metaphor* |
| Oh, I placed my love into a long-stem vase | |
| And I bandaged my bleeding thumb. | *Implied metaphor* |

Often you can tell a metaphor from a simile by much more than just the presence or absence of a connective. In general, a simile refers to only one characteristic that two things have in common, while a metaphor is not plainly limited in the number of resemblances it may indicate. To use the simile "He eats like a pig" is to compare man and animal in one respect: eating habits. But to say "He's a pig" is to use a metaphor that might involve comparisons of appearance and morality as well.

For scientists as well as poets, the making of metaphors is customary. In 1933 George Lemaitre, the Belgian priest and physicist credited with the Big Bang theory of the origin of the universe, conceived of a primal atom that existed before anything else, which expanded and produced everything. And so, he remarked, making a wonderful metaphor, the evolution of the cosmos as it is today "can be compared to a display of fireworks that has just ended." As astrophysicist and poet Alan Lightman has noted, we can't help envisioning scientific discoveries in terms of things we know from daily life—spinning balls, waves in water, pendulums, weights on springs. "We have no other choice," Lightman reasons. "We cannot avoid forming mental pictures when we try to grasp the meaning of our equations, and how can we picture what we have not seen?"[1] In science as well as in poetry, it would seem, metaphors are necessary instruments of understanding.

In everyday speech, simile and metaphor occur frequently. We use metaphors ("She's a doll") and similes ("The tickets are selling like hotcakes") without being fully conscious of them. If, however, we are aware that words possess literal meanings as well as figurative ones, we do not write *died in the wool* for *dyed in the wool* or *tow the line* for *toe the line*, nor do we use **mixed metaphors** as did the writer who advised, "Water the spark of knowledge and it will bear fruit," or the speaker who urged, "To get ahead, keep your nose to the grindstone, your shoulder to the wheel, your ear to the ground, and your eye on the ball." Perhaps the unintended humor of these statements comes from our seeing that the writer, busy stringing together stale metaphors, was not aware that they had any physical reference.

Unlike a writer who thoughtlessly mixes metaphors, a good poet can join together incongruous things and still keep the reader's respect. In his ballad "Thirty Bob a Week," John Davidson has a British workingman tell how it feels to try to support a large family on small wages:

[1]"Physicists' Use of Metaphor," *The American Scholar* (Winter 1989) 99.

It's a naked child against a hungry wolf;
   It's playing bowls upon a splitting wreck;
It's walking on a string across a gulf
   With millstones fore-and-aft about your neck;
But the thing is daily done by many and many a one;
   And we fall, face forward, fighting, on the deck.

Like the man with his nose to the grindstone, Davidson's wage-earner is in an absurd fix; but his balancing act seems far from merely nonsensical. For every one of the poet's comparisons—of workingman to child, to bowler, to tight-rope walker, and to seaman—offer suggestions of a similar kind. All help us see (and imagine) the workingman's hard life: a brave and unyielding struggle against impossible odds.

A poem may make a series of comparisons, like Davidson's, or the whole poem may be one extended comparison:

### Richard Wilbur (b. 1921)*

## A Simile for Her Smile       1950

Your smiling, or the hope, the thought of it,
Makes in my mind such pause and abrupt ease
As when the highway bridgegates fall,
Balking the hasty traffic, which must sit
On each side massed and staring, while     5
Deliberately the drawbridge starts to rise:

Then horns are hushed, the oilsmoke rarifies,
Above the idling motors one can tell
The packet's smooth approach, the slip,
Slip of the silken river past the sides,     10
The ringing of clear bells, the dip
And slow cascading of the paddle wheel.

How much life metaphors bring to poetry may be seen by comparing two poems by Tennyson and Blake.

### Alfred, Lord Tennyson (1809–1892)*

## Flower in the Crannied Wall       1869

Flower in the crannied wall,
I pluck you out of the crannies,
I hold you here, root and all, in my hand,

Little flower—but *if* I could understand
What you are, root and all, and all in all,
I should know what God and man is.

How many metaphors does this poem contain? None. Compare it with a
briefer poem on a similar theme: the quatrain that begins Blake's "Auguries
of Innocence." (We follow here the opinion of W. B. Yeats, who, in editing
Blake's poems, thought the lines ought to be printed separately.)

## *William Blake* (1757–1827)*

TO SEE A WORLD IN A GRAIN OF SAND         (about 1803)

To see a world in a grain of sand
And a heaven in a wild flower,
Hold infinity in the palm of your hand
And eternity in an hour.

Set beside Blake's poem, Tennyson's—short though it is—seems lengthy.
What contributes to the richness of "To see a world in a grain of sand" is
Blake's use of a metaphor in every line. And every metaphor is loaded with
suggestion. Our world does indeed resemble a grain of sand: in being round,
in being stony, in being one of a myriad (the suggestions go on and on). Like
Blake's grain of sand, a metaphor holds much, within a small circumference.

## *Sylvia Plath* (1932–1963)*

METAPHORS                 1960

I'm a riddle in nine syllables,
An elephant, a ponderous house,
A melon strolling on two tendrils.
O red fruit, ivory, fine timbers!
This loaf's big with its yeasty rising.                                    5
Money's new-minted in this fat purse.
I'm a means, a stage, a cow in calf.
I've eaten a bag of green apples,
Boarded the train there's no getting off.

QUESTIONS

1. To what central fact do all the metaphors in this poem refer?
2. In the first line, what has the speaker in common with a riddle? Why does she say
   she has *nine* syllables?

3. How would you describe the tone of this poem? (Perhaps the poet expresses more than one attitude.) What attitude is conveyed in the metaphors of an elephant, "a ponderous house," "a melon strolling on two tendrils"? By the metaphors of red fruit, ivory, fine timbers, new-minted money? By the metaphor in the last line?

### Emily Dickinson (1830–1886)*

## IT DROPPED SO LOW—IN MY REGARD          (about 1863)

It dropped so low—in my Regard—
I heard it hit the Ground—
And go to pieces on the Stones
At bottom of my Mind—

Yet blamed the Fate that flung it—*less*                     5
Than I denounced Myself,
For entertaining Plated Wares
Upon My Silver Shelf—

### QUESTIONS

1. What is *it*? What two things are compared?
2. How much of the poem develops and amplifies this comparison?

### N. Scott Momaday (b. 1934)

## SIMILE                              1974

What did we say to each other
that now we are as the deer
who walk in single file
with heads high
with ears forward                                      5
with eyes watchful
with hooves always placed on firm ground
in whose limbs there is latent flight

### QUESTIONS

1. Momaday never tells us what was said. Does this omission keep us from understanding the comparison?
2. The comparison is extended with each detail adding some new twist. Explain the implications of the last line.

EXPERIMENT: *Likening*

Write a poem that follows the method of N. Scott Momaday's "Simile," consisting of one long comparison between two objects. Possible subjects might include: Talking to a loved one long distance. What you feel like going to a weekend job. Being on a diet. Not being noticed by someone you love. Winning a lottery.

## *Ruth Whitman* (b. 1922)

CASTOFF SKIN                    1973

She lay in her girlish sleep at ninety-six,
small as a twig.
*Pretty good figure*

*for an old lady*, she said to me once.
Then she crawled away, leaving                    5
a tiny stretched transparence

behind her. When I kissed her paper cheek
I thought of the snake,
of his quick motion.

QUESTIONS

1. Explain the central metaphor in "Castoff Skin."
2. What other figures of speech does the poem contain?

EXERCISE: *What Is Similar?*

Each of these quotations contains a simile or a metaphor. In each of these figures of speech, what two things is the poet comparing? Try to state exactly what you understand the two things to have in common: the most striking similarity or similarities that the poet sees.

1.        All the world's a stage,
    And all the men and women merely players:
    They have their exits and their entrances,
    And one man in his time plays many parts,
    His acts being seven ages.
                —William Shakespeare, *As You Like It*
2. When the hounds of spring are on winter's traces . . .
                —Algernon Charles Swinburne, "Atalanta in Calydon"
3. . . . the sun gnaws the night's bone
    down through the meat and gristle.
                —John Ridland, "Elegy for My Aunt"
4. The scarlet of the maples can shake me like a cry
    Of bugles going by.
                —Bliss Carman, "A Vagabond Song"
5. "Hope" is the thing with feathers—
    That perches in the soul—

And sings the tune without the words—
And never stops—at all—
                    —Emily Dickinson, an untitled poem

6. Work without Hope draws nectar in a sieve . . .
                    —Samuel Taylor Coleridge, "Work Without Hope"

7. A new electric fence,
   Its five barbed wires tight
   As a steel-stringed banjo.
                    —Van K. Brock, "Driving at Dawn"

8. Spring stirs Gossamer Beynon schoolmistress like a spoon.
                    —Dylan Thomas, *Under Milk Wood*

9. Our headlights caught, as in a flashbulb's flare,
   A pair of hitchhikers.
                    —Paul Lake, "Two Hitchhikers"

10. The skin prickles, outraged as a cactus
    at this cold.
                    —Alice Fulton, "Snow-Kiln"

## OTHER FIGURES

When Shakespeare asks, in a sonnet,

> O! how shall summer's honey breath hold out
> Against the wrackful siege of batt'ring days,

it might seem at first that he mixes metaphors. How can a *breath* confront the battering ram of an invading army? But it is summer's breath and, by giving it to summer, Shakespeare makes the season a man or woman. It is as if the fragrance of summer were the breath within a person's body, and winter were the onslaught of old age.

Such is one instance of **personification:** a figure of speech in which a thing, an animal, or an abstract term (*truth, nature*) is made human. A personification extends throughout this whole short poem:

*James Stephens* (1882–1950)*

THE WIND                                          1915

The wind stood up and gave a shout.
He whistled on his fingers and

Kicked the withered leaves about
And thumped the branches with his hand

And said he'd kill and kill and kill,
And so he will and so he will.

The wind is a wild man, and evidently it is not just any autumn breeze but a hurricane or at least a stiff gale. In poems that do not work as well as this one, personification may be employed mechanically. Hollow-eyed personifications walk the works of lesser English poets of the eighteenth century: Coleridge has quoted the beginning of one such neoclassical ode, "Inoculation! heavenly Maid, descend!" It is hard for the contemporary reader to be excited by William Collins's "The Passions, An Ode for Music" (1747), which personifies, stanza by stanza, Fear, Anger, Despair, Hope, Revenge, Pity, Jealousy, Love, Hate, Melancholy, and Cheerfulness, and has them listen to Music, until even "Brown Exercise rejoiced to hear, / And Sport leapt up, and seized his beechen spear." Still, the portraits of the Seven Deadly Sins in the fourteenth-century *Vision of Piers Plowman* remain memorable: "Thanne come Slothe al bislabered, with two slimy eiyen. . . ." In "Two Sonnets on Fame" John Keats makes an abstraction come alive in seeing Fame as "a wayward girl."

Hand in hand with personification often goes **apostrophe:** a way of addressing someone or something invisible or not ordinarily spoken to. In an apostrophe, a poet (in these examples Wordsworth) may address an inanimate object ("Spade! with which Wilkinson hath tilled his lands"), some dead or absent person ("Milton! thou shouldst be living at this hour"), an abstract thing ("Return, Delights!"), or a spirit ("Thou Soul that art the eternity of thought"). More often than not, the poet uses apostrophe to announce a lofty and serious tone. An "O" may even be put in front of it ("O moon!") since, according to W. D. Snodgrass, every poet has a right to do so at least once in a lifetime. But apostrophe doesn't have to be highfalutin. It is a means of giving life to the inanimate. It is a way of giving body to the intangible, a way of speaking to it person to person, as in the words of a moving American spiritual: "Death, ain't you got no shame?"

Most of us, from time to time, emphasize a point with a statement containing exaggeration: "Faster than greased lightning," "I've told him a thousand times." We speak, then, not literal truth but use a figure of speech called **overstatement** (or **hyperbole**). Poets too, being fond of emphasis, often exaggerate for effect. Instances are Marvell's profession of a love that should grow "Vaster than empires, and more slow" and John Burgon's description of Petra: "A rose-red city, half as old as Time." Overstatement can be used also for humorous purposes, as in a fat woman's boast (from a blues song): "Every time I shake, some skinny gal loses her home."[2] The opposite is **understatement,** implying more than is said. Mark Twain in *Life on the Mississippi* recalls how, as an apprentice steamboat-pilot asleep when supposed to be on watch, he was roused by the pilot and sent clambering to the pilot house: "Mr. Bixby was close behind, commenting." Another example is Robert Frost's line "One could do worse than be a swinger of birches"—the conclusion of a poem that has suggested that to swing on a birch tree is one of the most deeply satisfying activities in the world.

In **metonymy,** the name of a thing is substituted for that of another

[2]Quoted by Amiri Baraka [LeRoi Jones] in *Blues People* (New York: Morrow, 1963).

closely associated with it. For instance, we say "The White House decided," and mean the president did. When John Dyer writes in "Grongar Hill,"

> A little rule, a little sway,
> A sun beam on a winter's day,
> Is all the proud and mighty have
> Between the cradle and the grave,

we recognize that *cradle* and *grave* signify birth and death. A kind of metonymy, **synecdoche** is the use of a part of a thing to stand for the whole of it or vice versa. We say "She lent a hand," and mean that she lent her entire presence. Similarly, Milton in "Lycidas" refers to greedy clergymen as "blind mouths." Another kind of metonymy is the **transferred epithet**: a device of emphasis in which the poet attributes some characteristic of a thing to another thing closely associated with it. When Thomas Gray observes that, in the evening pastures, "drowsy tinklings lull the distant folds," he well knows that sheep's bells do not drowse, but sheep do. When Hart Crane, describing the earth as seen from an airplane, speaks of "nimble blue plateaus," he attributes the airplane's motion to the earth.

**Paradox** occurs in a statement that at first strikes us as self-contradictory but that on reflection makes some sense. "The peasant," said G. K. Chesterton, "lives in a larger world than the globe-trotter." Here, two different meanings of *larger* are contrasted: "greater in spiritual values" versus "greater in miles." Some paradoxical statements, however, are much more than plays on words. In a moving sonnet, the blind John Milton tells how one night he dreamed he could see his dead wife. The poem ends in a paradox:

> But oh, as to embrace me she inclined,
> I waked, she fled, and day brought back my night.

Exercise: *Paradox*

What paradoxes do you find in the following poem? For each, explain the sense that underlies the statement.

---

### *Chidiock Tichborne* (1568?–1586)

### Elegy, Written with His Own Hand
### in the Tower Before His Execution        1586

My prime of youth is but a frost of cares,
   My feast of joy is but a dish of pain,
My crop of corn is but a field of tares°,                                         *weeds*
   And all my good is but vain hope of gain:
The day is past, and yet I saw no sun,                                              5
And now I live, and now my life is done.

My tale was heard, and yet it was not told,
  My fruit is fall'n, and yet my leaves are green,
My youth is spent, and yet I am not old,
  I saw the world, and yet I was not seen:                    10
My thread is cut, and yet it is not spun,
And now I live, and now my life is done.

I sought my death, and found it in my womb,
  I looked for life, and saw it was a shade,
I trod the earth, and knew it was my tomb,                    15
  And now I die, and now I was but made:
My glass is full, and now my glass is run,
And now I live, and now my life is done.

ELEGY, WRITTEN WITH HIS OWN HAND. Accused of taking part in the Babington Conspiracy, a plot by Roman Catholics against the life of Queen Elizabeth I, eighteen-year-old Chidiock Tichborne was hanged, drawn, and quartered at the Tower of London. That is virtually all we know about him.

Asked to tell the difference between men and women, Samuel Johnson replied, "I can't conceive, madam, can you?" The great dictionary-maker was using a figure of speech known to classical rhetoricians as *paronomasia*, better known to us as a **pun** or play on words. How does a pun operate? It reminds us of another word (or other words) of similar or identical sound but of very different denotation. Although puns at their worst can be mere piddling quibbles, at best they can sharply point to surprising but genuine resemblances. The name of a dentist's country estate, Tooth Acres, is accurate: aching teeth paid for the property. In his novel *Moby-Dick*, Herman Melville takes up questions about whales that had puzzled scientists: for instance, are the whale's spoutings water or gaseous vapor? And when Melville speaks pointedly of the great whale "sprinkling and mistifying the gardens of the deep," we catch his pun, and conclude that the creature both mistifies and mystifies at once.

In poetry, a pun may be facetious, as in Thomas Hood's ballad of "Faithless Nelly Gray":

Ben Battle was a soldier bold,
  And used to war's alarms;
But a cannon-ball took off his legs,
  So he laid down his arms!

Or it may be serious, as in these lines on war by E. E. Cummings:

the bigness of cannon
is skillful,

(*is skillful* becoming *is kill-ful* when read aloud), or perhaps, as in Shakespeare's song in *Cymbeline*, "Fear no more the heat o' th' sun," both facetious and serious at once:

Golden lads and girls all must,
As chimney-sweepers, come to dust.

## George Herbert (1593–1633)*

THE PULLEY                                    1633

When God at first made man,
Having a glass of blessings standing by—
Let us (said he) pour on him all we can;
Let the world's riches, which dispersèd lie,
    Contract into a span.                              5

So strength first made a way,
Then beauty flowed, then wisdom, honor, pleasure:
When almost all was out, God made a stay,
Perceiving that, alone of all His treasure,
    Rest in the bottom lay.                           10

For if I should (said he)
Bestow this jewel also on My creature,
He would adore My gifts instead of Me,
And rest in Nature, not the God of Nature:
    So both should losers be.                         15

Yet let him keep the rest,
But keep them with repining restlessness;
Let him be rich and weary, that at least,
If goodness lead him not, yet weariness
    May toss him to My breast.                        20

QUESTIONS

1. What different senses of the word *rest* does Herbert bring into this poem?
2. How do God's words in line 16, *Yet let him keep the rest*, seem paradoxical?
3. What do you feel to be the tone of Herbert's poem? Does the punning make the poem seem comic?
4. Why is the poem called "The Pulley"? What is its implied metaphor?

To sum up: even though figures of speech are not to be taken *only* literally, they refer us to a tangible world. By *personifying* an eagle, Tennyson reminds us that the bird and humankind have certain characteristics in common. Through *metonymy*, a poet can focus our attention on a particular detail in a larger object; through *hyperbole* and *understatement*, make us see the physical actuality in back of words. *Pun* and *paradox* cause us to realize this actuality, too, and probably surprise us enjoyably at the same time. Through *apostrophe*, the poet animates the inanimate and asks it to listen—speaks directly to an immediate god or to the revivified dead. Put to such uses, figures of speech have power. They are more than just ways of playing with words.

## Edmund Waller (1606–1687)*

ON A GIRDLE                                1645

That which her slender waist confined,
Shall now my joyful temples bind;
No monarch but would give his crown,
His arms might do what this has done.

It was my heaven's extremest sphere,                          5
The pale° which held that lovely deer;              *enclosure*
My joy, my grief, my hope, my love,
Did all within this circle move!

A narrow compass! and yet there
Dwelt all that's good, and all that's fair!                    10
Give me but what this riband bound,
Take all the rest the sun goes round!

ON A GIRDLE. This girdle is a waistband or sash—not, of course, a modern "foundation garment." 1–2 *That which . . . temples bind:* A courtly lover might bind his brow with a lady's ribbon, to signify he was hers. 5 *extremest sphere:* In Ptolemaic astronomy, the outermost of the concentric spheres that surround the earth. In its wall the farthest stars are set.

### QUESTIONS

1. To what things is the girdle compared?
2. Explain the pun in line 4. What effect does it have upon the tone of the poem?
3. Why is the effect of this pun different from that of Thomas Hood's play on the same word in "Faithless Nelly Gray" (quoted on p. 689)?
4. What does *compass* denote in line 9?
5. What paradox occurs in lines 9–10?
6. How many of the poem's statements are hyperbolic? Is the compliment the speaker pays his lady too grandiose to be believed? Explain.

## Theodore Roethke (1908–1963)*

I KNEW A WOMAN                             1958

I knew a woman, lovely in her bones,
When small birds sighed, she would sigh back at them;
Ah, when she moved, she moved more ways than one:
The shapes a bright container can contain!
Of her choice virtues only gods should speak,                 5
Or English poets who grew up on Greek
(I'd have them sing in chorus, cheek to cheek).

How well her wishes went! She stroked my chin,
She taught me Turn, and Counter-turn, and Stand;
She taught me Touch, that undulant white skin;                10

I nibbled meekly from her proffered hand;
She was the sickle; I, poor I, the rake,
Coming behind her for her pretty sake
(But what prodigious mowing we did make).

Love likes a gander, and adores a goose:                                 15
Her full lips pursed, the errant note to seize;
She played it quick, she played it light and loose;
My eyes, they dazzled at her flowing knees;
Her several parts could keep a pure repose,
Or one hip quiver with a mobile nose                                     20
(She moved in circles, and those circles moved).

Let seed be grass, and grass turn into hay:
I'm martyr to a motion not my own;
What's freedom for? To know eternity.
I swear she cast a shadow white as stone.                                25
But who would count eternity in days?
These old bones live to learn her wanton ways:
(I measure time by how a body sways).

## QUESTIONS

1. What outrageous puns do you find in Roethke's poem? Describe the effect of
   them.
2. What kind of figure of speech occurs in all three lines: *Of her choice virtues only gods
   should speak*; *My eyes, they dazzled at her flowing knees*; and *I swear she cast a shadow
   white as stone?*
3. What sort of figure is the poet's reference to himself as *old bones?*
4. Do you take *Let seed be grass, and grass turn into hay* as figurative language, or literal
   statement?
5. If you agree that the tone of this poem is witty and playful, do you think the poet
   is making fun of the woman? What is his attitude toward her? What part do figures
   of speech play in communicating it?

# FOR REVIEW AND FURTHER STUDY

### *Robert Frost* (1874–1963)*

THE SILKEN TENT                              1942

She is as in a field a silken tent
At midday when a sunny summer breeze
Has dried the dew and all its ropes relent,
So that in guys° it gently sways at ease,              *attachments that steady it*
And its supporting central cedar pole,                                   5
That is its pinnacle to heavenward
And signifies the sureness of the soul,
Seems to owe naught to any single cord,

But strictly held by none, is loosely bound
By countless silken ties of love and thought                    10
To everything on earth the compass round,
And only by one's going slightly taut
In the capriciousness of summer air
Is of the slightest bondage made aware.

QUESTIONS

1. Is Frost's comparison of woman and tent a simile or a metaphor?
2. What are the ropes or cords?
3. Does the poet convey any sense of this woman's character? What sort of person
   do you believe her to be?
4. Paraphrase the poem, trying to state its implied meaning. (If you need to be
   refreshed about paraphrase, turn back to page 584.) Be sure to include the implications of the last three lines.

### Denise Levertov (b. 1923)*

## LEAVING FOREVER                     1964

He says the waves in the ship's wake
are like stones rolling away.
I don't see it that way.
But I see the mountain turning,
turning away its face as the ship
takes us away.

QUESTIONS

1. What do you understand to be the man's feelings about leaving forever? How does
   the speaker feel? With what two figures of speech does the poet express these
   conflicting views?
2. Suppose that this poem had ended in another simile (instead of its three last lines):

   I see the mountain as a suitcase
   left behind on the shore
   as the ship takes us away.

   How is Denise Levertov's choice of a figure of speech a much stronger one?

### Jane Kenyon (b. 1947)

## THE SUITOR                          1978

We lie back to back. Curtains
lift and fall,
like the chest of someone sleeping.
Wind moves the leaves of the box elder;
they show their light undersides,                               5

turning all at once
like a school of fish.
Suddenly I understand that I am happy.
For months this feeling
has been coming closer, stopping                 10
for short visits, like a timid suitor.

QUESTION
In each simile you find in this poem, exactly what is the similarity?


## Robert Frost (1874–1963)*

### THE SECRET SITS           1936

We dance round in a ring and suppose,
But the Secret sits in the middle and knows.


## Margaret Atwood (b. 1939)*

### YOU FIT INTO ME     1971

you fit into me
like a hook into an eye

a fish hook
an open eye


## W. S. Merwin (b. 1927)

### SONG OF MAN CHIPPING AN ARROWHEAD    1973

Little children you will all go
but the one you are hiding
will fly


## John Ashbery (b. 1927)*

### THE CATHEDRAL IS     1979

Slated for demolition

QUESTION
Where is the pun in this poem?

## Robinson Jeffers (1887–1962)*

### HANDS                                                          1929

Inside a cave in a narrow canyon near Tassajara
The vault of rock is painted with hands,
A multitude of hands in the twilight, a cloud of men's palms,
    no more,
No other picture. There's no one to say
Whether the brown shy quiet people who are dead intended          5
Religion or magic, or made their tracings
In the idleness of art; but over the division of years these
    careful
Signs-manual are now like a sealed message
Saying: "Look: we also were human; we had hands, not paws.
    All hail
You people with the cleverer hands, our supplanters              10
In the beautiful country; enjoy her a season, her beauty, and
    come down
And be supplanted; for you also are human."

### QUESTION
Identify examples of personification and apostrophe in "Hands."

## Robert Burns (1759–1796)*

### OH, MY LOVE IS LIKE A RED, RED ROSE          (about 1788)

Oh, my love is like a red, red rose
    That's newly sprung in June;
My love is like the melody
    That's sweetly played in tune.

So fair art thou, my bonny lass,                                 5
    So deep in love am I;
And I will love thee still, my dear,
    Till a' the seas gang° dry.                                  *go*

Till a' the seas gang dry, my dear,
    And the rocks melt wi' the sun;                              10
And I will love thee still, my dear,
    While the sands o' life shall run.

And fare thee weel, my only love!
    And fare thee weel awhile!
And I will come again, my love                                   15
    Though it were ten thousand mile.

1. Freely using your imagination, write a paragraph in which you make as many hyperbolic statements as possible. Then write another version, changing all your exaggeration to understatement. Then, in a concluding paragraph, sum up what this experiment shows you about figurative language. Some possible topics are "The Most Gratifying (or Terrifying) Moment of My Life," "The Job I Almost Landed," "The Person I Most Admire."
2. Choose a short poem rich in figurative language: Sylvia Plath's "Metaphors," say, or Burns's "Oh, my love is like a red, red rose." Rewrite the poem, taking for your model Howard Moss's deliberately bepiddling version of "Shall I compare thee to a summer's day?" Eliminate every figure of speech. Turn the poem into language as flat and unsuggestive as possible. (Just ignore any rime or rhythm in the original.) Then, in a paragraph, indicate lines in your revised version that seem glaringly worsened. In conclusion, sum up what your barbaric rewrite tells you about the nature of poetry.

# 19  Song

## SINGING AND SAYING

Most poems are more memorable than most ordinary speech, and when music is combined with poetry the result can be more memorable still. The differences between speech, poetry, and song may appear if we consider, first of all, this fragment of an imaginary conversation between two lovers:

> Let's not drink; let's just sit here and look at each other. Or put a kiss inside my goblet and I won't want anything to drink.

Forgettable language, we might think; but let's try to make it a little more interesting:

> Drink to me only with your eyes, and I'll pledge my love to you with
> my eyes;
> Or leave a kiss within the goblet, that's all I'll want to drink.

The passage is closer to poetry, but still has a distance to go. At least we now have a figure of speech—the metaphor that love is wine, implied in the statement that one lover may salute another by lifting an eye as well as by lifting a goblet. But the sound of the words is not yet especially interesting. Here is another try, by Ben Jonson:

> Drink to me only with thine eyes,
>   And I will pledge with mine;
> Or leave a kiss but in the cup,
>   And I'll not ask for wine.

In these opening lines from Jonson's poem "To Celia," the improvement is noticeable. These lines are poetry; their language has become special. For one thing, the lines rime (with an additional rime sound on *thine*). There is interest, too, in the proximity of the words *kiss* and *cup*: the repetition (or alliteration) of the *k* sound. The rhythm of the lines has become regular; generally every other word (or syllable) is stressed:

> DRINK to me ON-ly WITH thine EYES,
>     And I will PLEDGE with MINE;
> OR LEAVE a KISS but IN the CUP,
>     And I'LL not ASK for WINE.

All these devices of sound and rhythm, together with metaphor, produce a pleasing effect—more pleasing than the effect of "Let's not drink; let's look at each other." But the words became more pleasing still when later set to music:

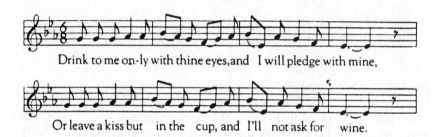

Drink to me on-ly with thine eyes, and I will pledge with mine,

Or leave a kiss but in the cup, and I'll not ask for wine.

In this memorable form, the poem is still alive today.

---

**Ben Jonson** (1573?–1637)*

TO CELIA                                    1616

Drink to me only with thine eyes,
    And I will pledge with mine;
Or leave a kiss but in the cup,
    And I'll not ask for wine.
The thirst that from the soul doth rise                    5
    Doth ask a drink divine;
But might I of Jove's nectar sup,
    I would not change for thine.

I sent thee late a rosy wreath,
    Not so much honoring thee                              10
As giving it a hope that there
    It could not withered be.
But thou thereon didst only breathe,
    And sent'st it back to me;
Since when it grows, and smells, I swear,                  15
    Not of itself but thee.

A compliment to a lady has rarely been put in language more graceful, more wealthy with interesting sounds. Other figures of speech besides metaphor make them unforgettable: for example, the hyperbolic tributes to the power of the lady's sweet breath, which can start picked roses growing again, and her kisses, which even surpass the nectar of the gods.

This song falls into stanzas—as many poems that resemble songs also do. A **stanza** (Italian for "station," "stopping-place," or "room") is a group of lines whose pattern is repeated throughout the poem. Most songs have more than one stanza. When printed, the stanzas of songs and poems usually are set off from one another by space. When sung, stanzas of songs are indicated by a pause or by the introduction of a refrain, or chorus (a line or lines repeated). The word **verse,** which strictly refers to one line of a poem, is sometimes loosely used to mean a whole stanza: "All join in and sing the second verse!" In speaking of a stanza, whether sung or read, it is customary to indicate by a convenient algebra its **rime scheme,** the order in which rimed words recur. For instance, the rime scheme of this stanza by Herrick is *a b a b*; the first and third lines rime and so do the second and fourth:

> Round, round, the roof doth run;
> And being ravished thus,
> Come, I will drink a tun
> To my Propertius.

**Refrains** are words, phrases, or lines repeated at intervals in a song or songlike poem. A refrain usually follows immediately after a stanza, and when it does, it is called **terminal refrain.** A refrain whose words change slightly with each recurrence is called an **incremental refrain.** Sometimes we also hear an **internal refrain:** one that appears within a stanza, generally in a position that stays fixed throughout a poem. Both internal refrains and terminal refrains are used to great effect in the traditional song "The Cruel Mother":

---

***Anonymous*** (traditional Scottish ballad)

## THE CRUEL MOTHER

She sat down below a thorn,
  *Fine flowers in the valley,*
And there she has her sweet babe born
  *And the green leaves they grow rarely.*

"Smile na sae° sweet, my bonny babe,"                    *so*    5
  *Fine flowers in the valley,*
"And° ye smile sae sweet, ye'll smile me dead."          *if*
  *And the green leaves they grow rarely.*

She's taen out her little pen-knife,
   *Fine flowers in the valley,*                                  10
And twinned° the sweet babe o' its life,               *severed*
   *And the green leaves they grow rarely.*

She's howket° a grave by the light of the moon,      *dug*
   *Fine flowers in the valley,*
And there she's buried her sweet babe in              15
   *And the green leaves they grow rarely.*

As she was going to the church,
   *Fine flowers in the valley,*
She saw a sweet babe in the porch
   *And the green leaves they grow rarely.*             20

"O sweet babe, and thou were mine,"
   *Fine flowers in the valley,*
"I wad cleed° thee in the silk so fine."              *dress*
   *And the green leaves they grow rarely.*

"O mother dear, when I was thine,"              25
   *Fine flowers in the valley,*
"You did na prove to me sae kind."
   *And the green leaves they grow rarely.*

Taken by themselves, the refrain lines might seem mere pretty nonsense. But interwoven with the story of the murdered child, they form a terrible counterpoint. What do they come to mean? Possibly that Nature keeps going about her chores, unmindful of sin and suffering. The effect is an ironic contrast. Besides, by hearing the refrain over and over and over, we find it hard to forget.

We usually meet poems as words on a page, but songs we generally first encounter as sounds in the air. Consequently, songs tend to be written in language simple enough to be understood on first hearing. But some contemporary songwriters have created songs that require listeners to pay close and repeated attention to their words. Beginning in the 1960s with performers like Bob Dylan, Leonard Cohen, Joni Mitchell, and Frank Zappa, some pop songwriters crafted deliberately challenging songs. More recently, Sting, Robert Smith, Bono, and Suzanne Vega have written complex lyrics, often full of strange, dreamlike imagery. To unravel them, a listener may have to play the recording many times, with the treble turned up all the way. Anyone who feels that literary criticism is solely an academic enterprise should listen to high school and college students discuss the lyrics of their favorite songs.

One of the most interesting musical and literary developments of the 1980s was the emergence of **rap,** a form of popular music in which words are recited to a driving rhythmic beat. It differs from mainstream popular music in several ways, but, most interesting in literary terms, rap lyrics are *spoken* rather than sung. In that sense, rap is a form of popular poetry as well as popular music. In Black English, *rap* means "to talk" ("Let's rap about it"), and in most current rap songs, the lead performer or "M.C." talks or recites, usually at top speed, long, rhythmic, four-stress lines that end in rimes. Although today most rap singers and groups use electronic or sampled backgrounds, rap began on city streets in the game of "signifying," in which two poets aim rimed insults at each other, sometimes accompanying their tirades with a beat made by clapping or finger-snapping. This game also included boasts made by the players on both sides about their own abilities. Anyone interested in the form will enjoy listening to Run DMC, Public Enemy, N.W.A., L. L. Cool J, Hammer, and other performers currently popular. Here, for instance, is a transcription of a rap lyric by Run DMC that shows a sophisticated understanding of the traditions of English popular poetry.

## Run D.M.C. (J. Simmons/D. McDaniels/R. Rubin)

*from* PETER PIPER                                          1986

Now Dr. Seuss and Mother Goose both did their thing
But Jam Master's getting loose and D.M.C.'s the king
'Cuz he's the adult entertainer, child educator
Jam Master Jay king of the cross-fader
He's the better of the best, best believe he's the baddest        5
Perfect timing when I'm climbing I'm the rhyming acrobatist
Lotta guts, when he cuts girls move their butts
His name is Jay, here to play, he must be nuts
And on the mix real quick, and I'd like to say
He's not Flash but he's fast and his name is Jay.                10

It goes a one, two, three and . . .
Jay's like King Midas, as I was told,
Everything that he touched turned to gold
He's the greatest of the great get it straight he's great
Claim fame 'cuz his name is known in every state              15
His name is Jay to see him play will make you say
God damn that D.J. made my day
Like the butcher, the baker, the candlestick maker
He's a maker, a breaker, and a title taker
Like the little old lady who lived in a shoe                    20
If cuts were kids he would be through
Not lying y'all he's the best I know
And if I lie my nose will grow
Like a little wooden boy named Pinnochio
And you all know how the story go                               25

Trix are for kids he plays much gigs
He's the big bad wolf and you're the 3 pigs
He's the big bad wolf in your neighborhood
Not bad meaning bad but bad meaning good . . . There it is!
We're Run D.M.C. got a beef to settle                                30
Dee's not Hansel, he's not Gretel
Jay's a winner, not a beginner
His pocket gets fat, others' get thinner
Jump on Jay like cow jumped moon
People chase Jay like dish and spoon                                 35
And like all fairy tales end
You'll see Jay again my friend, hough!

PETER PIPER. (These lyrics were transcribed from the Run D.M.C. hit.) 2 *Jam Master Jay:* the
DJ who provides beats and scratching in the rap group. 4 *Cross-fader:* scratching device. 10 *Flash:*
allusion either to Grandmaster Flash, another DJ, or the comic book superhero Flash; rap critics
debate this point.

Many familiar poems began life as songs, but today, their tunes forgotten, they survive only in poetry anthologies. Shakespeare studded his plays
with songs, and many of his contemporaries wrote verses to fit existing
tunes. Some poets were themselves musicians (like Thomas Campion), and
composed both words and music. In Shakespeare's day, **madrigals,** short
secular songs for three or more voices arranged in counterpoint, enjoyed
great popularity. A madrigal by Chidiock Tichborne is given on page 688 and
another by an unknown poet, "The Silver Swan," on page 711. A madrigal
is always short, usually just one stanza, and rarely exceeded twelve or thirteen lines. Elizabethans loved to sing, and a person was considered a dolt if
he or she could not join in a three-part song. Here is a madrigal from one of
Shakespeare's comedies:

## *William Shakespeare* (1564–1616)*

### TAKE, O, TAKE THOSE LIPS AWAY          (1604)

Take, O, take those lips away
  That so sweetly were forsworn,
And those eyes, the break of day,
  Lights that do mislead the morn;
But my kisses bring again, bring again,                              5
Seals of love, but seal'd in vain, seal'd in vain.

TAKE, O, TAKE THOSE LIPS AWAY. This short song appears in *Measure for Measure.* It is sung
by a boy in Act IV, just as we see Mariana, a deserted lover, for the first time.

Some poets who were not composers printed their work in madrigal
books for others to set to music. In the seventeenth century, however,
poetry and song seem to have fallen away from each other. By the end of the
century, much new poetry, other than songs for plays, was written to be

printed and to be silently read. Poets who wrote popular songs—like Thomas D'Urfey, compiler of the collection *Pills to Purge Melancholy*—were considered somewhat disreputable. With the notable exceptions of John Gay, who took existing popular tunes for *The Beggar's Opera*, and Robert Burns, who rewrote folk songs or made completely new words for them, few important English poets since Campion have been first-rate song-writers.

Occasionally, a poet has learned a thing or two from music. "But for the opera I could never have written *Leaves of Grass*," said Walt Whitman, who loved the Italian art form for its expansiveness. Coleridge, Hardy, Auden, and many others have learned from folk ballads, and T. S. Eliot patterned his thematically repetitive *Four Quartets* after the structure of a quartet in classical music. "Poetry," said Ezra Pound, "begins to atrophy when it gets too far from music." Still, even in the twentieth century, the poet has been more often a corrector of printer's proofs than a tunesmith or performer.

Some people think that to make a poem and to travel about singing it, as many rock singer-composers now do, is a return to the venerable tradition of the **troubadours,** minstrels of the late Middle Ages. But there are differences. No doubt the troubadours had to please their patrons, but for better or worse their songs were not affected by a stopwatch in a producer's hand or by the technical resources of a sound studio. Bob Dylan has denied that he is a poet, and Paul Simon once told an interviewer, "If you want poetry read Wallace Stevens." Nevertheless, much has been made lately of current song lyrics as poetry. Are rock songs poems? Clearly some, but not all, are. That the lyrics of a song cannot stand the scrutiny of a reader does not necessarily invalidate them, though; song-writers do not usually write in order to be read. Pete Seeger has quoted a saying of his father: "A printed folk song is like a photograph of a bird in flight." Still there is no reason not to photograph birds, or to read song lyrics. If the words seem rich and interesting, we may possibly increase our enjoyment of them and perhaps be able to sing them more accurately. Like most poems and songs of the past, most current songs may end in the trash can of time. And yet, certain memorable rimed and rhythmic lines may live on, especially if music has served them for a base and if singers have given them wide exposure.

### EXERCISE: *Comparing Poem and Song*

Compare the following poem by Edwin Arlington Robinson and a popular song lyric based on it. Notice what Paul Simon had to do to Robinson's original in order to make it into a song, and how Simon altered Robinson's conception.

---

### *Edwin Arlington Robinson* (1869–1935)*

RICHARD CORY                                        1897

Whenever Richard Cory went down town,
We people on the pavement looked at him:

He was a gentleman from sole to crown,
Clean favored, and imperially slim.

And he was always quietly arrayed,                                      5
And he was always human when he talked;
But still he fluttered pulses when he said,
"Good-morning," and he glittered when he walked.

And he was rich—yes, richer than a king—
And admirably schooled in every grace:                                 10
In fine°, we thought that he was everything          *in short*
To make us wish that we were in his place.

So on we worked, and waited for the light,
And went without the meat, and cursed the bread;
And Richard Cory, one calm summer night,                               15
Went home and put a bullet through his head.

---

**Paul Simon** (b. 1942)

RICHARD CORY                              1966

*With Apologies to E. A. Robinson*

They say that Richard Cory owns
One half of this old town,
With elliptical connections
To spread his wealth around.
Born into Society,                                                      5
A banker's only child,
He had everything a man could want:
Power, grace and style.

*Refrain:*

*But I, I work in his factory*
*And I curse the life I'm livin'*                                      10
*And I curse my poverty*
*And I wish that I could be*
*Oh I wish that I could be*
*Oh I wish that I could be*
*Richard Cory.*                                                        15

The papers print his picture
Almost everywhere he goes:
Richard Cory at the opera,
Richard Cory at a show
And the rumor of his party                                             20

And the orgies on his yacht—
Oh he surely must be happy
With everything he's got.     *(Refrain.)*

He freely gave to charity,
He had the common touch,                                                  25
And they were grateful for his patronage
And they thanked him very much,
So my mind was filled with wonder
When the evening headlines read:
    "Richard Cory went home last night                                    30
    And put a bullet through his head."     *(Refrain.)*

RICHARD CORY by Paul Simon. If possible, listen to the ballad sung by Simon and Garfunkel on *Sounds of Silence* (Columbia recording CL 2469, stereo CS 9269), © 1966 by Paul Simon. Used by permission.

# BALLADS

Any narrative song, like Paul Simon's "Richard Cory," may be called a **ballad.** In English, some of the most famous ballads are **folk ballads,** loosely defined as anonymous story-songs transmitted orally before they were ever written down. Sir Walter Scott, a pioneer collector of Scottish folk ballads, drew the ire of an old woman whose songs he had transcribed: "They were made for singing and no' for reading, but ye ha'e broken the charm now and they'll never be sung mair." The old singer had a point. Print freezes songs and tends to hold them fast to a single version. If Scott and others had not written them down, however, many would have been lost.

In his monumental work *The English and Scottish Popular Ballads* (1882–1898), the American scholar Francis J. Child winnowed out 305 folk ballads he considered authentic—that is, creations of illiterate or semiliterate people who had preserved them orally. Child, who worked by insight as well as by learning, did such a good job of telling the difference between folk ballads and other kinds that later scholars have added only about a dozen ballads to his count. Often called **Child ballads,** his texts include "The Three Ravens," "Sir Patrick Spence," "The Twa Corbies," "Edward," "The Cruel Mother," and many others still on the lips of singers. Here is one of the best-known Child ballads.

### *Anonymous* (traditional Scottish ballad)

BONNY BARBARA ALLAN

It was in and about the Martinmas time,
    When the green leaves were afalling,

That Sir John Graeme, in the West Country,
    Fell in love with Barbara Allan.

He sent his men down through the town,                 5
    To the place where she was dwelling;
"O haste and come to my master dear,
    Gin° ye be Barbara Allan."                         *if*

O hooly°, hooly rose she up,                      *slowly*
    To the place where he was lying,             10
And when she drew the curtain by:
    "Young man, I think you're dying."

"O it's I'm sick, and very, very sick,
    And 'tis a' for Barbara Allan."—
"O the better for me ye's never be,            15
    Tho your heart's blood were aspilling.

"O dinna ye mind°, young man," said she,     *don't you remember*
    "When ye was in the tavern adrinking,
That ye made the health° gae round and round,     *toasts*
    And slighted Barbara Allan?"             20

He turned his face unto the wall,
    And death was with him dealing:
"Adieu, adieu, my dear friends all,
    And be kind to Barbara Allan."

And slowly, slowly raise she up,                25
    And slowly, slowly left him,
And sighing said she could not stay,
    Since death of life had reft him.

She had not gane a mile but twa,
    When she heard the dead-bell ringing,        30
And every jow° that the dead-bell geid,         *stroke*
    It cried, "Woe to Barbara Allan!"

"O mother, mother, make my bed!
    O make it saft and narrow!
Since my love died for me today,             35
    I'll die for him tomorrow."

BONNY BARBARA ALLAN. 1 *Martinmas:* Saint Martin's day, November 11.

## QUESTIONS

1. In any line does the Scottish dialect cause difficulty? If so, try reading the line aloud.
2. Without ever coming out and explicitly calling Barbara hard-hearted, this ballad reveals that she is. In which stanza and by what means is her cruelty demonstrated?
3. At what point does Barbara evidently have a change of heart? Again, how does the poem dramatize this change without explicitly talking about it?

4. In many American versions of this ballad, noble knight John Graeme becomes an ordinary citizen. The gist of the story is the same, but at the end are these further stanzas, incorporated from a different ballad:

They buried Willie in the old churchyard
  And Barbara in the choir;
And out of his grave grew a red, red rose,
  And out of hers a briar.

They grew and grew to the steeple top
  Till they could grow no higher;
And there they locked in a true love's knot,
  The red rose round the briar.

Do you think this appendage heightens or weakens the final impact of the story? Can the American ending be defended as an integral part of a new song? Explain.
5. Paraphrase lines 9, 15–16, 22, 25–28. By putting these lines into prose, what has been lost?

As you can see from "Bonny Barbara Allan," in a traditional English or Scottish folk ballad the storyteller speaks of the lives and feelings of others. Even if the pronoun "I" occurs, it rarely has much personality. Characters often exchange dialogue, but no one character speaks all the way through. Events move rapidly, perhaps because some of the dull transitional stanzas have been forgotten. The events themselves, as ballad scholar Albert B. Friedman has said, are frequently "the stuff of tabloid journalism—sensational tales of lust, revenge and domestic crime. Unwed mothers slay their newborn babes; lovers unwilling to marry their pregnant mistresses brutally murder the poor women, for which, without fail, they are justly punished."[1] There are also many ballads of the supernatural ("The Twa Corbies") and of gallant knights ("Sir Patrick Spence"), and there are a few humorous ballads, usually about unhappy marriages.

The ballad-spinner has at hand a fund of ready-made epithets: steeds are usually "milk-white" or "berry-brown," lips "rosy" or "ruby-red," corpses and graves "clay-cold," beds (like Barbara Allan's) "soft and narrow." At the least, these conventional phrases are terse and understandable. Sometimes they add meaning: the king who sends Sir Patrick Spence to his doom drinks "blood-red wine." The clothing, steeds, and palaces of ladies and lords are always luxurious: a queen may wear "grass-green silk" or "Spanish leather" and ride a horse with "fifty silver bells and nine." Such descriptions are naive, for as Friedman points out, ballad-singers were probably peasants imagining what they had seen only from afar: the life of the nobility. This may be why the skin of ladies in folk ballads is ordinarily "milk-white," "lily-white," or "snow-white." In an agrarian society, where most people worked in the fields, not to be suntanned was a sign of gentility.

A favorite pattern of ballad-makers is the so-called **ballad stanza,** four lines rimed *a b c b*, tending to fall into 8, 6, 8, and 6 syllables:

[1]Introduction to *The Viking Book of Folk Ballads of the English-Speaking World*, edited by Albert B. Friedman (New York: Viking, 1956).

> Clerk Saunders and Maid Margaret
> Walked owre yon garden green,
> And deep and heavy was the love
> That fell thir twa between°.                    *between those two*

Though not the only possible stanza for a ballad, this easily singable quatrain has continued to attract poets since the Middle Ages. Close kin to the ballad stanza is **common meter,** a stanza found in hymns such as "Amazing Grace," by the eighteenth-century English hymnist John Newton:

> Amazing grace! how sweet the sound
> That saved a wretch like me!
> I once was lost, but now am found,
> Was blind, but now I see.

Notice that its pattern is that of the ballad stanza except for its *two* pairs of rimes. That all its lines rime is probably a sign of more literate artistry than we usually hear in folk ballads. Another sign of schoolteachers' influence is that Newton's rimes are exact. (Rimes in folk ballads are often rough-and-ready, as if made by ear, rather than polished and exact, as if the riming words had been matched for their similar spellings. In "Barbara Allan," for instance, the hard-hearted lover's name rimes with *afalling, dwelling, aspilling, dealing,* and even with *ringing* and *adrinking.*) That so many hymns were written in common meter may have been due to convenience. If a congregation didn't know the tune to a hymn in common meter, they readily could sing its words to the tune of another such hymn they knew. Besides hymnists, many poets have favored common meter, among them A. E. Housman and Emily Dickinson.

Related to traditional folk ballads but displaying characteristics of their own, **broadside ballads** (so called because they were printed on one sheet of paper) often were set to traditional tunes. Most broadside ballads were an early form of journalism made possible by the development of cheap printing and by the growth of audiences who could read, just barely. Sometimes merely humorous or tear-jerking, often they were rimed accounts of sensational news events. That they were widespread and often scorned in Shakespeare's day is attested by the character of Autolycus in *A Winter's Tale,* an itinerant hawker of ballads about sea monsters and strange pregnancies ("a usurer's wife was brought to bed of twenty money-bags"). Although many broadsides tend to be **doggerel** (verse full of irregularities due not to skill but to incompetence), many excellent poets had their work taken up and peddled in the streets—among them Marvell, Swift, and Byron.[2]

**Literary ballads,** not meant for singing, are written by sophisticated

[2]A generous collection of broadsides has been assembled by Vivian de Sola Pinto and A. E. Rodway in *The Common Muse: An Anthology of Popular British Ballad Poetry, XVth–XXth Century* (St. Clair Shores, Mich.: Scholarly Press, 1957). See also *Irish Street Ballads,* edited by Colm O. Lochlainn (New York: Corinth Books, 1960), and Olive Woolley Burt, *American Murder Ballads and Their Stories* (New York: Oxford UP, 1958).

poets for book-educated readers who enjoy being reminded of folk ballads. Literary ballads imitate certain features of folk ballads: they may tell of dramatic conflicts or of mortals who encounter the supernatural; they may use conventional figures of speech or ballad stanzas. Well-known poems of this kind include Keats's "La Belle Dame Sans Merci," Coleridge's "Rime of the Ancient Mariner," and (in our time) Dudley Randall's "Ballad of Birmingham."

## Dudley Randall (b. 1914)*

### BALLAD OF BIRMINGHAM                                    1966

(On the Bombing of a Church in
Birmingham, Alabama, 1963)

"Mother dear, may I go downtown
Instead of out to play,
And march the streets of Birmingham
In a Freedom March today?"

"No, baby, no, you may not go,                                    5
For the dogs are fierce and wild,
And clubs and hoses, guns and jail
Aren't good for a little child."

"But, mother, I won't be alone.
Other children will go with me,                                   10
And march the streets of Birmingham
To make our country free."

"No, baby, no, you may not go,
For I fear those guns will fire.
But you may go to church instead                                  15
And sing in the children's choir."

She has combed and brushed her night-dark hair,
And bathed rose petal sweet,
And drawn white gloves on her small brown hands,
And white shoes on her feet.                                      20

The mother smiled to know her child
Was in the sacred place,
But that smile was the last smile
To come upon her face.

For when she heard the explosion,                                 25
Her eyes grew wet and wild.
She raced through the streets of Birmingham
Calling for her child.

She clawed through bits of glass and brick,
Then lifted out a shoe.                                              30
"O here's the shoe my baby wore,
But, baby, where are you?"

## QUESTIONS

1. This poem, about a dynamite blast set off in a black people's church by a racial
   terrorist (later convicted), delivers a message without preaching. How would you
   sum up this message, its implied theme?
2. What is ironic in the mother's denying her child permission to take part in a
   protest march?
3. How does this modern poem resemble a traditional ballad?

## EXPERIMENT: *Seeing the Traits of Ballads*

In the section Poems for Further Reading, read the Child ballads "Edward," "The
Three Ravens," and "The Twa Corbies" (pages 886–888). With these ballads in
mind, consider one or more of these modern poems:

W. H. Auden, "As I Walked Out One Evening" (page 893)
William Jay Smith, "American Primitive" (page 997)
William Butler Yeats, "Crazy Jane Talks with the Bishop" (page 1019).

What characteristics of folk ballads do you find in them? In what ways do these
modern poets depart from the traditions of folk ballads of the Middle Ages?

# FOR REVIEW AND FURTHER STUDY

## *John Lennon* (1940–1980)
## *Paul McCartney* (b. 1942)

### ELEANOR RIGBY                                               1966

Ah, look at all the lonely people!
Ah, look at all the lonely people!

Eleanor Rigby
Picks up the rice in the church where a wedding has been,
Lives in a dream,                                                    5
Waits at the window
Wearing the face that she keeps in a jar by the door.
Who is it for?

All the lonely people,
Where do they all come from?                                         10
All the lonely people,
Where do they all belong?

Father McKenzie,
Writing the words of a sermon that no one will hear,
No one comes near                                                          15
Look at him working,
Darning his socks in the night when there's nobody there.
What does he care?

All the lonely people
Where do they all come from?                                               20
All the lonely people
Where do they all belong?

Eleanor Rigby
Died in the church and was buried along with her name.
Nobody came.                                                               25
Father McKenzie,
Wiping the dirt from his hands as he walks from the grave,
No one was saved.

All the lonely people,
Where do they all come from?                                               30
All the lonely people,
Where do they all belong?

Ah, look at all the lonely people!
Ah, look at all the lonely people!

## QUESTION

Is there any reason to call this famous song lyric a ballad? Compare it with a traditional ballad, such as "Bonny Barbara Allan." Do you notice any similarity? What are the differences?

---

***Anonymous*** (English madrigal)

## THE SILVER SWAN, WHO LIVING HAD NO NOTE          1612

The silver swan, who living had no note,
When death approached unlocked her silent throat;
Leaning her breast against the reedy shore,
Thus sung her first and last, and sung no more.
Farewell, all joys; O death, come close mine eyes;
More geese than swans now live, more fools than wise.

This anonymous madrigal was first published in the composer Orlando Gibbons's songbook, *The First Set of Madrigals and Mottets* in 1612. If we did not know the poem's origin, however, what features in it would suggest to us that it was a madrigal?

## William Blake (1757–1827)*

JERUSALEM (from *MILTON*)          1804–1810

And did those feet in ancient time
Walk upon England's mountains green?
And was the holy Lamb of God
On England's pleasant pastures seen?

And did the Countenance Divine                          5
Shine forth upon our clouded hills?
And was Jerusalem builded here
Among these dark Satanic Mills?

Bring me my Bow of burning gold:
Bring me my Arrows of desire:                           10
Bring me my Spear: O clouds unfold!
Bring me my Chariot of fire.

I will not cease from Mental Fight,
Nor shall my Sword sleep in my hand
Till we have built Jerusalem                            15
In England's green & pleasant Land.

JERUSALEM. In Blake's book *Milton*, this hymn-like poem is untitled. When the composer Hubert Parry set it to music, at the suggestion of Robert Bridges, in 1916, he titled it "Jerusalem" after its central, visionary image. Originally performed at a "Votes for Women" concert, Parry's hymn has become a famous anthem for progressive causes.

### QUESTIONS

1. Who is the unnamed figure Blake presents in lines 1 and 2? What evidence does the poem give elsewhere to help us determine the figure's identity?
2. Does Blake suggest that the historical city of Jerusalem was once actually located in England? What does that city's name suggest about Blake's vision of ancient England?
3. What are the "dark Satanic Mills"? What is their relation to the city of Jerusalem? (Does the date of the poem's publication suggest any additional historical meaning to the phrase?)
4. Why does the speaker want weapons? What sort of warfare does the speaker plan to fight?
5. Most hymns are simple and direct expressions of faith. Blake's hymn is a complex and mysterious poem, and yet it has become immensely popular in England. Do you have any ideas on what attracts so many people to this poem?

## Suggestions for Writing

1. Write a short study of a lyric (or lyrics) by a recent popular song-writer. Show why you believe the song-writer's work deserves the name of poetry.
2. Compare and contrast the English folk ballad "The Three Ravens" with the Scottish folk ballad "The Twa Corbies" (both in Poems for Further Reading).
3. Compare the versions of "Richard Cory" by Edwin Arlington Robinson and by Paul Simon. Point out changes Simon apparently made in the poem to render it singable. What other changes did he make? How did he alter Robinson's story and its characters?
4. After listening to some recent examples of rap (see page 700), compose a short rap lyric of your own, one that tells a story.

# 20  Sound

## Sound as Meaning

Isak Dinesen, in a memoir of her life on a plantation in East Africa, tells how some Kikuyu tribesmen reacted to their first hearing of rimed verse:

> The Natives, who have a strong sense of rhythm, know nothing of verse, or at least did not know anything before the times of the schools, where they were taught hymns. One evening out in the maize-field, where we had been harvesting maize, breaking off the cobs and throwing them on to the ox-carts, to amuse myself, I spoke to the field laborers, who were mostly quite young, in Swahili verse. There was no sense in the verses, they were made for the sake of rime—"Ngumbe na-penda chumbe, Malaya mbaya. Wakamba na-kula mamba." The oxen like salt—whores are bad—The Wakamba eat snakes. It caught the interest of the boys, they formed a ring round me. They were quick to understand that meaning in poetry is of no consequence, and they did not question the thesis of the verse, but waited eagerly for the rime, and laughed at it when it came. I tried to make them themselves find the rime and finish the poem when I had begun it, but they could not, or would not, do that, and turned away their heads. As they had become used to the idea of poetry, they begged: "Speak again. Speak like rain." Why they should feel verse to be like rain I do not know. It must have been, however, an expression of applause, since in Africa rain is always longed for and welcomed.[1]

What the tribesmen had discovered is that poetry, like music, appeals to the ear. However limited it may be in comparison with the sound of an orchestra—or a tribal drummer—the sound of words in itself gives pleasure. However, we might doubt Isak Dinesen's assumption that "meaning in

[1]Isak Dinesen, *Out of Africa* (New York: Random, 1972).

poetry is of no consequence." "Hey nonny-nonny" and such nonsense has a place in song lyrics and other poems, and we might take pleasure in hearing rimes in Swahili; but most good poetry has meaningful sound as well as musical sound. Certainly the words of a song have an effect different from that of wordless music: they go along with their music and, by making statements, add more meaning. The French poet Isidore Isou, founder of a literary movement called *lettrisme*, maintained that poems can be written not only in words but in letters (sample lines: *xyl, xyl, | prprali dryl | znglo trpylo pwi*). But the sound of letters alone, without denotation and connotation, has not been enough to make Letterist poems memorable. In the response of the Kikuyu tribesmen, there may have been not only the pleasure of hearing sounds but also the agreeable surprise of finding that things not usually associated had been brought together.

More powerful when in the company of meaning, not apart from it, the sounds of consonants and vowels can contribute greatly to a poem's effect. The sound of *s*, which can suggest the swishing of water, has rarely been used more accurately than in Surrey's line "Calm is the sea, the waves work less and less." When, in a poem, the sound of words working together with meaning pleases mind and ear, the effect is **euphony,** as in the following lines from Tennyson's "Come down, O maid":

> Myriads of rivulets hurrying through the lawn,
> The moan of doves in immemorial elms,
> And murmuring of innumerable bees.

Its opposite is **cacophony:** a harsh, discordant effect. It too is chosen for the sake of meaning. We hear it in Milton's scornful reference in "Lycidas" to corrupt clergymen whose songs "Grate on their scrannel pipes of wretched straw." (Read that line and one of Tennyson's aloud and see which requires lips, teeth, and tongue to do more work.) But note that although Milton's line is harsh in sound, the line (when we meet it in his poem) is pleasing because it is artful. In a famous passage from his *Essay on Criticism*, Pope has illustrated both euphony and cacophony. (Given here as Pope printed it, the passage relies heavily on italics and capital letters, for particular emphasis. If you will read these lines aloud, dwelling a little longer or harder on the words italicized, you will find that Pope has given you very good directions for a meaningful reading.)

### *Alexander Pope* (1688–1744)*

#### TRUE EASE IN WRITING COMES FROM ART, NOT CHANCE                            1711

True Ease in Writing comes from Art, not Chance,
As those move easiest who have learned to dance.
'Tis not enough no Harshness gives Offence,

The *Sound* must seem an *Echo* to the *Sense.*
Soft is the strain when *Zephyr*° gently blows,           *the west wind*   5
And the *smooth Stream* in *smoother Numbers*° flows;      *metrical rhythm*
But when loud Surges lash the sounding Shore,
The *hoarse, rough Verse* should like the *Torrent* roar.
When *Ajax* strives, some Rock's vast Weight to throw,
The Line too *labors,* and the Words move *slow;*                    10
Not so, when swift *Camilla* scours the Plain,
Flies o'er th' unbending Corn, and skims along the Main°.   *expanse (of sea)*
Hear how *Timotheus'* varied Lays surprise,
And bid Alternate Passions fall and rise!
While, at each Change, the Son of *Lybian Jove*                  15
Now *burns* with Glory, and then *melts* with Love;
Now his *fierce Eyes* with *sparkling Fury* glow;
Now *Sighs* steal out, and *Tears begin to flow:*
Persians and Greeks like *Turns of Nature* found,
And the *World's Victor* stood subdued by *Sound!*                20
*The Pow'rs of Music* all our Hearts allow;
And what *Timotheus* was, is *Dryden* now.

TRUE EASE IN WRITING COMES FROM ART, NOT CHANCE (*An Essay on Criticism,* lines 362–383).
9 *Ajax:* Greek hero, almost a superman, who in Homer's account of the siege of Troy hurls an
enormous rock that momentarily flattens Hector, the Trojan prince (*Iliad* VII, 268–272). 11
*Camilla:* a kind of Amazon or warrior woman of the Volcians, whose speed and lightness of step
are praised by the Roman poet Virgil: "She could have skimmed across an unmown grainfield
/ Without so much as bruising one tender blade; / She could have sped across an ocean's surge
/ Without so much as wetting her quicksilver soles" (*Aeneid* VII, 808–811). 13 *Timotheus:*
favorite musician of Alexander the Great. In "Alexander's Feast, or The Power of Music," John
Dryden imagines him: "Timotheus, placed on high / Amid the tuneful choir, / With flying
fingers touched the lyre: / The trembling notes ascend the sky, / And heavenly joys inspire."
15 *Lybian Jove:* name for Alexander. A Libyan oracle had declared the king to be the son of the
god Zeus Ammon.

Notice the pleasing effect of all the *s* sounds in the lines about the west
wind and the stream, and in another meaningful place, the effect of the
consonants in *Ajax strives,* a phrase that makes our lips work almost as hard
as Ajax throwing the rock.

Is sound identical with meaning in lines such as these? Not quite. In the
passage from Tennyson, for instance, the cooing of doves is not *exactly* a
moan. As John Crowe Ransom pointed out, the sound would be almost the
same but the meaning entirely different in "The murdering of innumerable
beeves." While it is true that the consonant sound *sl-* will often begin a word
that conveys ideas of wetness and smoothness—*slick, slimy, slippery, slush*—
we are so used to hearing it in words that convey nothing of the kind—*slave,
slow, sledgehammer*—that it is doubtful whether, all by itself, the sound
communicates anything definite. The most beautiful phrase in the English
language, according to Dorothy Parker, is *cellar door.* Another wit once
nominated, as our most euphonious word, not *sunrise* or *silvery* but *syphilis.*

Relating sound more closely to meaning, the device called **onomatopoeia** is an attempt to represent a thing or action by a word that imitates

the sound associated with it: *zoom, whiz, crash, bang, ding-dong, pitter-patter, yakety-yak*. Onomatopoeia is often effective in poetry, as in Emily Dickinson's line about the fly with its "uncertain stumbling Buzz," in which the nasal sounds *n, m, ng* and the sibilants *c, s* help make a droning buzz, and in Robert Lowell's transcription of a bird call, "yuck-a, yuck-a, yuck-a" (in "Falling Asleep over the Aeneid").

Like the Kikuyu tribesmen, others who care for poetry have discovered in the sound of words something of the refreshment of cool rain. Dylan Thomas, telling how he began to write poetry, said that from early childhood words were to him "as the notes of bells, the sounds of musical instruments, the noises of wind, sea, and rain, the rattle of milkcarts, the clopping of hooves on cobbles, the fingering of branches on the window pane, might be to someone, deaf from birth, who has miraculously found his hearing."[2] For readers, too, the sound of words can have a magical spell, most powerful when it points to meaning. James Weldon Johnson in *God's Trombones* has told of an old-time preacher who began his sermon, "Brothers and sisters, this morning I intend to explain the unexplainable—find out the indefinable—ponder over the imponderable—and unscrew the inscrutable!" The repetition of sound in *unscrew* and *inscrutable* has appeal, but the magic of the words is all the greater if they lead us to imagine the mystery of all Creation as an enormous screw that the preacher's mind, like a screw-driver, will loosen. Though the sound of a word or the meaning of a word may have value all by itself, both become more memorable when taken together.

## *William Butler Yeats* (1865–1939)*

### WHO GOES WITH FERGUS?      1892

Who will go drive with Fergus now,
And pierce the deep wood's woven shade,
And dance upon the level shore?
Young man, lift up your russet brow,
And lift your tender eyelids, maid,      5
And brood on hopes and fear no more.

And no more turn aside and brood
Upon love's bitter mystery;
For Fergus rules the brazen cars°,                    *chariots*
And rules the shadows of the wood,                    10
And the white breast of the dim sea
And all dishevelled wandering stars.

WHO GOES WITH FERGUS? *Fergus*: Irish king who gave up his throne to be a wandering poet.

[2]"Notes on the Art of Poetry," *Modern Poetics*, ed. James Scully (New York: McGraw-Hill, 1965).

QUESTIONS

1. In what lines do you find euphony?
2. In what line do you find cacophony?
3. How do the sounds of these lines stress what is said in them?

EXERCISE: *Listening to Meaning*

Read aloud the following brief poems. In the sounds of which particular words are meanings well captured? In which of the poems below do you find onomatopoeia?

## *John Updike* (b. 1932)*

### RECITAL                    1963

ROGER BOBO GIVES
  RECITAL ON TUBA
  *Headline in the Times*

Eskimos in Manitoba,
  Barracuda off Aruba,
Cock an ear when Roger Bobo
  Starts to solo on the tuba.

Men of every station—Pooh-Bah,                    5
  Nabob, bozo, toff, and hobo—
Cry in unison, "Indubi-
  Tably, there is simply nobo-

Dy who oompahs on the tubo,
Solo, quite like Roger Bubo!"                    10


## *Frances Cornford* (1886–1960)*

### THE WATCH                    1923

I wakened on my hot, hard bed,
Upon the pillow lay my head;
Beneath the pillow I could hear
My little watch was ticking clear.
I thought the throbbing of it went                    5
Like my continual discontent.
I thought it said in every tick:
I am so sick, so sick, so sick.
O death, come quick, come quick, come quick,
Come quick, come quick, come quick, come quick!                    10

## William Wordsworth (1770–1850)*

## A Slumber Did My Spirit Seal                    1800

A slumber did my spirit seal;
  I had no human fears—
She seemed a thing that could not feel
  The touch of earthly years

No motion has she now, no force;                                   5
  She neither hears nor sees;
Rolled round in earth's diurnal course,
  With rocks, and stones, and trees.

## Emanuel di Pasquale (b. 1943)

## Rain                    1971

Like a drummer's brush,
the rain hushes the surface of tin porches.

## Aphra Behn (1640?–1689)

## When maidens are young                    1687

When maidens are young, and in their spring,
Of pleasure, of pleasure let 'em take their full swing,
  Full swing, full swing,
And love, and dance, and play, and sing,
For Silvia, believe it, when youth is done,                       5
There's nought but hum-drum, hum-drum, hum-drum,
There's nought but hum-drum, hum-drum, hum-drum.

## ALLITERATION AND ASSONANCE

Listening to a symphony in which themes are repeated throughout each movement, we enjoy both their recurrence and their variation. We take similar pleasure in the repetition of a phrase or a single chord. Something like this pleasure is afforded us frequently in poetry.

Analogies between poetry and wordless music, it is true, tend to break down when carried far, since poetry—to mention a single difference—has denotation. But like musical compositions, poems have patterns of sounds. Among such patterns long popular in English poetry is **alliteration**, which has been defined as a succession of similar sounds. Alliteration occurs in the repetition of the same consonant sound at the beginning of successive words—"round and round the rugged rocks the ragged rascal ran"—or inside the words, as in Milton's description of the gates of Hell:

> On a sudden open fly
> With impetuous recoil and jarring sound
> The infernal doors, and on their hinges grate
> Harsh thunder, that the lowest bottom shook
> Of Erebus.

The former kind is called **initial alliteration**, the latter **internal alliteration** or **hidden alliteration**. We recognize alliteration by sound, not by spelling: *know* and *nail* alliterate, *know* and *key* do not. In a line by E. E. Cummings, "colossal hoax of clocks and calendars," the sound of *x* within *hoax* alliterates with the *cks* in *clocks*. Incidentally, the letter *r* does not *always* lend itself to cacophony: elsewhere in *Paradise Lost* Milton said that

> Heaven opened wide
> Her ever-during gates, harmonious sound
> On golden hinges moving . . .

By itself, a letter-sound has no particular meaning. This is a truth forgotten by people who would attribute the effectiveness of Milton's lines on the Heavenly Gates to, say, "the mellow *o*'s and liquid *l* of *harmonious* and *golden*." Mellow *o*'s and liquid *l*'s occur also in the phrase *moldy cold oatmeal*, which may have a quite different effect. Meaning depends on larger units of language than letters of the alphabet.

Today good prose writers usually avoid alliteration; in the past, some cultivated it. "There is nothing more swifter than time, nothing more sweeter," wrote John Lyly in *Euphues* (1579), and he went on—playing especially with the sounds of *v, n, t, s, l,* and *b*—"we have not, as Seneca saith, little time to live, but we lose much; neither have we a short life by nature, but we make it shorter by naughtiness." Poetry, too, formerly contained more alliteration than it usually contains today. In Old English verse, each line was held together by alliteration, a basic pattern still evident in the fourteenth century, as in the following description of the world as a "fair field" in *Piers Plowman*:

> A *f*eir *f*eld *f*ul of *f*olk *f*ond I ther bi-twene,
> Of alle *m*aner of *m*en, the *m*ene and the riche . . .

Most poets nowadays save alliteration for special occasions. They may use it to give emphasis, as Edward Lear does: "Far and *f*ew, far and *f*ew, / Are the *l*ands where the Jumblies *l*ive." With its aid they can point out the relationship between two things placed side by side, as in Pope's line on things of little worth: "The courtier's *p*romises, and sick man's *p*rayers." Alliteration, too, can be a powerful aid to memory. It is hard to forget such tongue twisters as "Peter Piper picked a peck of pickled peppers," or common expressions like "green as grass," "tried and true," and "from stem to stern." In fact, because alliteration directs our attention to something, it had best be used neither thoughtlessly nor merely for decoration, lest it call attention to emptiness. A case in point may be a line by Philip James Bailey, a reaction to a lady's weeping: "I saw, but *spared* to *speak*." If the poet chose the word *spared* for any meaningful reason other than that it alliterates with *speak*, the reason is not clear.

As we have seen, to repeat the sound of a consonant is to produce alliteration, but to repeat the sound of a *vowel* is to produce **assonance.** Like alliteration, assonance may occur either initially—"*all* the *awful auguries*"[3] —or internally—Edmund Spenser's "Her goodly *eyes* like sapphires shining bright, / Her forehead *ivory* white . . ." and it can help make common phrases unforgettable: "eager beaver," "holy smoke." Like alliteration, it slows the reader down and focuses attention.


## A. E. Housman (1859–1936)*

### EIGHT O'CLOCK                          1922

He stood, and heard the steeple
   Sprinkle the quarters on the morning town.
One, two, three, four, to market-place and people
   It tossed them down.

Strapped, noosed, nighing his hour,                          5
   He stood and counted them and cursed his luck;
And then the clock collected in the tower
   Its strength, and struck.


### QUESTIONS

1. Why does the protagonist in this brief drama curse his luck? What is his situation?
2. For so short a poem, "Eight O'Clock" carries a great weight of alliteration. What patterns of initial alliteration do you find? What patterns of internal alliteration? What effect is created by all this heavy emphasis?


## Robert Herrick (1591–1674)*

### UPON JULIA'S VOICE                          1648

So smooth, so sweet, so silv'ry is thy voice,
As, could they hear, the damned would make no noise,
But listen to thee (walking in thy chamber)
Melting melodious words, to lutes of amber.

[3]Some prefer to call the repetition of an initial vowel-sound by the name of alliteration: "apt alliteration's artful aid."

4 *amber*: either the fossilized resin from which pipestems are sometimes made today, and which might have inlaid the body of a lute; or an alloy of four parts silver and one part gold.

## QUESTIONS

1. Is Julia speaking or singing? How do we know for sure?
2. In what moments in this brief poem does the sound of words especially help convey meaning?
3. Does Herrick's reference to *the damned* (presumably howling from Hell's torments) seem out of place?

## *Janet Lewis* (b. 1899)

### GIRL HELP          1927

Mild and slow and young,
She moves about the room,
And stirs the summer dust
With her wide broom.

In the warm, lofted air,                                          5
Soft lips together pressed,
Soft wispy hair,
She stops to rest,

And stops to breathe,
Amid the summer hum,                                             10
The great white lilac bloom
Scented with days to come.

## QUESTIONS

1. What assonance and alliteration do you find in this poem? (Suggestion: It may help to read the poem aloud.)
2. In this particular poem, how are these repetitions (or echoes) of sound valuable?

## EXERCISE: *Hearing How Sound Helps*

Which of these translations of the same passage from Petrarch do you think is better poetry? Why? What do assonance and alliteration have to do with your preference?

1. Love that liveth and reigneth in my thought,
   That built his seat within my captive breast,
   Clad in the arms wherein with me he fought,
   Oft in my face he doth his banner rest.
                    —Henry Howard, Earl of Surrey (1517?–1547)

2. The long love that in my thought doth harbor,
   And in mine heart doth keep his residence,
   Into my face presseth with bold pretense
   And therein campeth, spreading his banner.
                    —Sir Thomas Wyatt (1503?–1542)

Try reading aloud as rapidly as possible the following poem by Tennyson. From the difficulties you encounter, you may be able to sense the slowing effect of assonance. Then read the poem aloud a second time, with consideration.

## Alfred, Lord Tennyson (1809–1892)*

THE SPLENDOR FALLS ON CASTLE WALLS                1850

The splendor falls on castle walls
    And snowy summits old in story;
The long light shakes across the lakes,
    And the wild cataract leaps in glory.
Blow, bugle, blow, set the wild echoes flying,           5
Blow, bugle; answer, echoes, dying, dying, dying.

    O hark, O hear! how thin and clear,
        And thinner, clearer, farther going!
    O sweet and far from cliff and scar°         *jutting rock*
        The horns of Elfland faintly blowing!       10
Blow, let us hear the purple glens replying:
Blow, bugle; answer, echoes, dying, dying, dying.

    O love, they die in yon rich sky,
        They faint on hill or field or river;
    Our echoes roll from soul to soul,         15
        And grow for ever and for ever.
Blow, bugle, blow, set the wild echoes flying,
And answer, echoes, answer, dying, dying, dying.

## RIME

Isak Dinesen's tribesmen, to whom rime was a new phenomenon, recognized at once that rimed language is special language. So do we, for, although much English poetry is unrimed, rime is one means to set poetry apart from ordinary conversation and bring it closer to music. A **rime** (or rhyme), defined most narrowly, occurs when two or more words or phrases contain an identical or similar vowel-sound, usually accented, and the consonant-sounds (if any) that follow the vowel-sound are identical: *hay* and *sleigh*, *prairie schooner* and *piano tuner*.[4] From these examples it will be seen that rime depends not on spelling but on sound.

    Excellent rimes surprise. It is all very well that a reader may anticipate which vowel-sound is coming next, for patterns of rime give pleasure by satisfying expectations; but riming becomes dull clunking if, at the end of

---

[4]Some definitions of *rime* would apply the term to the repetition of any identical or similar sound, not only a vowel-sound. In this sense, assonance is a kind of rime; so is alliteration (called **initial rime**).

each line, the reader can predict the word that will end the next. Hearing many a jukebox song for the first time, a listener can do so: *charms* lead to *arms, skies above* to *love*. As Alexander Pope observes of the habits of dull rimesters,

> Where'er you find "the cooling western breeze,"
> In the next line it "whispers through the trees";
> If crystal streams "with pleasing murmurs creep,"
> The reader's threatened (not in vain) with "sleep" . . .

But who—given the opening line of this comic poem—could predict the lines that follow?

### William Cole (b. 1919)

#### ON MY BOAT ON LAKE CAYUGA      1985

> On my boat on Lake Cayuga
> I have a horn that goes "Ay-oogah!"
> I'm not the modern kind of creep
> Who has a horn that goes "beep beep."

Robert Herrick, in a more subtle poem, made good use of rime to indicate a startling contrast:

> Then while time serves, and we are but decaying,
> Come, my Corinna, come, let's go a-Maying.

Though good rimes seem fresh, not all will startle, and probably few will call to mind things so unlike as *May* and *decay, Cayuga* and *Ay-oogah.* Some masters of rime often link words that, taken out of text, might seem common and unevocative. Here, for instance, is Alexander Pope's comment on a trifling courtier:

> Yet let me flap this bug with gilded wings,
> This painted child of dirt, that stinks and stings;
> Whose buzz the witty and the fair annoys,
> Yet wit ne'er tastes, and beauty ne'er enjoys:
> So well-bred spaniels civilly delight
> In mumbling of the game they dare not bite.
> Eternal smiles his emptiness betray,
> As shallow streams run dimpling all the way.

Pope's rime-words are not especially memorable—and yet these lines are, because (among other reasons) they rime. Wit may be driven home without rime, but it is rime that rings the doorbell. Admittedly, some rimes wear thin from too much use. More difficult to use freshly than before the establishment of Tin Pan Alley, rimes such as *moon, June, croon* seem leaden and to ring true would need an extremely powerful context. *Death* and *breath* are a rime that poets have used with wearisome frequency; another is *birth, earth, mirth.* And yet we cannot exclude these from the diction of poetry, for they might be the very words a poet would need in order to say something new and original. The following brief poem seems fresher than its rimes (if taken out of context) would lead us to expect.

---

**William Blake** (1757–1827)*

THE ANGEL THAT PRESIDED O'ER MY BIRTH          (1808–1811)

The Angel that presided o'er my birth
Said, "Little creature, formed of Joy and Mirth,
Go love without the help of any thing on earth."

What matters to rime is freshness—not of a word but of the poet's way of seeing.

Good poets, said John Dryden, learn to make their rime "so properly a part of the verse, that it should never mislead the sense, but itself be led and governed by it." The comment may remind us that skillful rime—unlike poor rime—is never a distracting ornament. "Rime the rudder is of verses, / With which, like ships, they steer their courses," wrote the seventeenth-century poet Samuel Butler. Like other patterns of sound, rime can help a poet to group ideas, emphasize particular words, and weave a poem together. It can start reverberations between words and can point to connections of meaning.

To have an **exact rime,** sounds following the vowel sound have to be the same: *red* and *bread, wealthily* and *stealthily, walk to her* and *talk to her.* If final consonant sounds are the same but the vowel sounds are different, the result is **slant rime,** also called **near rime, off rime,** or **imperfect rime:** *sun* riming with *bone, moon, rain, green, gone, thin.* By not satisfying the reader's expectation of an exact chime, but instead giving a clunk, a slant rime can help a poet say some things in a particular way. It works especially well for disappointed let-downs, negations, and denials, as in Blake's couplet:

He who the ox to wrath has moved
Shall never be by woman loved.

Many poets have admired the unexpected and arresting effects of slant rime. One of the first poets to explore the possibilities of rhyming conso-nants in a consistent way was Wilfred Owen, an English soldier in World War I, who wrote his best poems in the thirteen months before being killed in action in 1918 at the age of twenty-five. Seeking a poetic language strong enough to describe the harsh reality of modern war, Owen experimented with matching consonant sounds in striking ways:

Now men will go content with what we spoiled
Or, discontent, boil bloody, and be spilled,
They will be swift with the swiftness of the tigress.
None will break ranks, though nations trek from progress.

Courage was mine, and I had mystery,
Wisdom was mine, and I had mastery:
To miss the march of this retreating world
Into vain citadels that are not walled.

**Consonance,** a kind of slant rime, occurs when the rimed words or phrases have the same beginning and ending consonant sounds but a different vowel, as in *chitter* and *chatter*. Owen rimes *spoiled* and *spilled* in this way. Consonance is used in a traditional nonsense poem, "The Cutty Wren": " 'O where are you going?' says *Milder* to *Malder*." (W. H. Auden wrote a variation on it that begins, " 'O where are you going?' said *reader* to *rider*," thus keeping the consonance.)

**End rime,** as its name indicates, comes at the ends of lines, **internal rime** within them. Most rime tends to be end rime. Few recent poets have used internal rime so heavily as Wallace Stevens in the beginning of "Bantams in Pine-Woods": "Chieftain Iffucan of Azcan in caftan / Of tan with henna hackles, halt!" (lines also heavy on alliteration). A poet may employ both end rime and internal rime in the same poem, as in Robert Burns's satiric ballad "The Kirk's Alarm":

Orthodox, Orthodox, wha believe in John Knox,
    Let me sound an alarm to your conscience:
There's a heretic blast has been blawn i' the wast°,           *west*
    "That what is not sense must be nonsense."

**Masculine rime** is a rime of one-syllable words *(jail, bail)* or (in words of more than one syllable) stressed final syllables: *di-VORCE, re-MORSE,* or *horse, re-MORSE.* **Feminine rime** is a rime of two or more syllables, with stress on a syllable other than the last: *TUR-tle, FER-tile,* or (to take an example from Byron) *in-tel-LECT-u-al, hen-PECKED you all.* Often it lends itself to comic verse, but can occasionally be valuable to serious poems, as in Wordsworth's "Resolution and Independence":

We poets in our youth begin in gladness,
But thereof come in the end despondency and madness.

or as in Anne Sexton's seriously witty "Eighteen Days Without You":

and of course we're not married, we are a pair of scissors
who come together to cut, without towels saying His. Hers.

Serious poems containing feminine rimes of three syllables have been attempted, notably by Thomas Hood in "The Bridge of Sighs":

Take her up tenderly,
Lift her with care;
Fashioned so slenderly,
Young, and so fair!

But the pattern is hard to sustain without lapsing into unintended comedy, as in the same poem:

Still, for all slips of hers,
One of Eve's family—
Wipe those poor lips of hers,
Oozing so clammily.

It works better when comedy is wanted:

## *Hilaire Belloc* (1870–1953)

### THE HIPPOPOTAMUS      1896

I shoot the Hippopotamus
  with bullets made of platinum,
Because if I use leaden ones
  his hide is sure to flatten 'em.

In **eye rime,** spellings look alike but pronunciations differ—*rough* and
*dough, idea* and *flea, Venus* and *menus.* Strictly speaking, eye rime is not rime
at all.

In the early 1960s in American poetry, rime suffered a significant fall
from favor. A new generation of poets took for models the open forms of
Whitman, Pound, and William Carlos Williams. Recently, however, young
poets have begun skillfully using rime again in their work. Often called the
"New Formalists," these poets include Julia Alvarez, R. L. Barth, R. S.
Gwynn, Paul Lake, Charles Martin, Molly Peacock, Gjertrud Schnackenberg, and Timothy Steele. Their poems often use rime to present unusual
subjects, as in this unsentimental sonnet about childhood.

## *R. S. Gwynn* (b. 1948)

### SCENES FROM THE PLAYROOM      1986

Now Lucy with her family of dolls
Disfigures Mother with an emery board,
While Charles, with match and rubbing alcohol,
Readies the struggling cat, for Chuck is bored.

The young ones pour more ink into the water          5
Through which the latest goldfish gamely swims,
Laughing, pointing at naked, neutered Father.
The toy chest is a Buchenwald of limbs.

Mother is so lovely; Father, so late.
The cook is off, yet dinner must go on.          10
With onions as her only cause for tears
She hacks the red meat from the slippery bone,
Setting the table, where the children wait,
Her grinning babies, clean behind the ears.

1. Explain the allusion to Buchenwald in line 8.
2. What do we know about this family and their life-style? What is revealed by the word *latest* (line 6)?
3. What do you think of these children and their parents? What does the poet think of them? By what details is his attitude made clear?

Still, most American poets don't write in rime; some even consider it exhausted. Such a view may be a reaction against the wearing-thin of rimes by overuse or the mechanical and meaningless application of a rime scheme. Yet anyone who listens to children skipping rope in the street, making up rimes to delight themselves as they go along, may doubt that the pleasures of rime are ended; and certainly the practice of Yeats and Emily Dickinson, to name only two, suggests that the possibilities of slant rime may be nearly infinite. If successfully employed, as it has been at times by a majority of English-speaking poets whose work we care to save, rime runs through its poem like a spine: the creature moves by means of it.

## William Butler Yeats (1865–1939)*

### LEDA AND THE SWAN                    1924

A sudden blow: the great wings beating still
Above the staggering girl, her thighs caressed
By the dark webs, her nape caught in his bill,
He holds her helpless breast upon his breast.

How can those terrified vague fingers push          5
The feathered glory from her loosening thighs?
And how can body, laid in that white rush,
But feel the strange heart beating where it lies?

A shudder in the loins engenders there
The broken wall, the burning roof and tower          10
And Agamemnon dead.
             Being so caught up,
So mastered by the brute blood of the air,
Did she put on his knowledge with his power
Before the indifferent beak could let her drop?

QUESTIONS

1. According to Greek mythology, the god Zeus in the form of a swan descended upon Leda, a Spartan queen. Among Leda's children were Clytemnestra, Agamemnon's unfaithful wife who conspired in his murder, and Helen, on whose account the Trojan war was fought. What does a knowledge of these allusions contribute to our understanding of the poem's last two lines?
2. The slant rime *up* / *drop* (lines 11, 14) may seem accidental or inept. Is it? Would this poem have ended nearly so well if Yeats had made an exact rime like *up* / *cup* or like *stop* / *drop*?

## Gerard Manley Hopkins (1844–1889)*

### GOD'S GRANDEUR                                                    (1877)

The world is charged with the grandeur of God.
   It will flame out, like shining from shook foil;
   It gathers to a greatness, like the ooze of oil
Crushed. Why do men then now not reck his rod?
Generations have trod, have trod, have trod;           5
   And all is seared with trade; bleared, smeared with toil;
   And wears man's smudge and shares man's smell: the soil
Is bare now, nor can foot feel, being shod.

And for all this, nature is never spent;
   There lives the dearest freshness deep down things;     10
And though the last lights off the black West went
   Oh, morning, at the brown brink eastward, springs—
Because the Holy Ghost over the bent
   World broods with warm breast and with ah! bright wings.

GOD'S GRANDEUR. 1 *charged:* as though with electricity. 3–4 *It gathers . . . Crushed:* The grandeur of God will rise and be manifest, as oil rises and collects from crushed olives or grain. 4 *reck his rod:* heed His law. 10 *deep down things:* Tightly packing the poem, Hopkins omits the preposition *in* or *within* before *things.* 11 *last lights . . . went:* When in 1534 Henry VIII broke ties with the Roman Catholic Church and created the Church of England?

### QUESTIONS

1. In a letter Hopkins explained *shook foil* (line 2): "I mean foil in its sense of leaf or tinsel. . . . Shaken goldfoil gives off broad glares like sheet lightning and also, and this is true of nothing else, owing to its zigzag dints and creasings and network of small many cornered facets, a sort of fork lightning too." What do you think he meant by the phrase *ooze of oil* (line 3)? Would you call this phrase an example of alliteration?
2. What instances of internal rime does the poem contain? How would you describe their effects?
3. Point out some of the poet's uses of alliteration and assonance. Do you believe that Hopkins perhaps goes too far in his heavy use of devices of sound, or would you defend his practice?
4. Why do you suppose Hopkins, in the last two lines, says *over the bent / World* instead of (as we might expect) *bent over the world?* How can the world be bent? Can you make any sense out of this wording, or is Hopkins just trying to get his rime scheme to work out?

## Fred Chappell (b. 1936)

### NARCISSUS AND ECHO                          1985

Shall the water not remember    *Ember*
my hand's slow gesture, tracing above   *of*
its mirror my half-imaginary    *airy*

portrait? My only belonging    *longing;*
is my beauty, which I take    *ache*                                        5
away and then return, as love    *of*
teasing playfully the one being    *unbeing.*
whose gratitude I treasure    *Is your*
moves me. I live apart    *heart*
from myself, yet cannot    *not*                                          10
live apart. In the water's tone,    *stone?*
that brilliant silence, a flower    *Hour,*
whispers my name with such slight    *light:*
moment, it seems filament of air,    *fare*
the world become cloudswell.    *well.*                                   15

NARCISSUS AND ECHO. This poem is an example of Echo Verse, a form (which dates back to late classical Greek poetry) in which the final syllables of the lines are repeated back as a reply or commentary, often a punning one. *Narcissus:* a beautiful young man, in Greek mythology, who fell in love with his own reflection in the water of a well. He gradually pined away because he could not reach his love; upon dying, he changed into the flower that bears his name. *Echo:* a nymph who, according to Roman tradition, loved Narcissus. When her love was not returned, she pined away until only her voice was left.

## QUESTIONS

1. This poem is a dialogue. What is the relation between the two voices? Does the first voice hear the second?
2. How does the meaning of the poem change if we read the speech of each voice separately?
3. Is the echo technique used in this poem a gimmick? Or does it allow the poet to express something he might not be able to in any other way?

---

### *Robert Frost* (1874–1963)*

DESERT PLACES                                          1936

Snow falling and night falling fast, oh, fast
In a field I looked into going past,
And the ground almost covered smooth in snow,
But a few weeds and stubble showing last.

The woods around it have it—it is theirs.                                 5
All animals are smothered in their lairs,
I am too absent-spirited to count;
The loneliness includes me unawares.

And lonely as it is, that loneliness
Will be more lonely ere it will be less—                                  10
A blanker whiteness of benighted snow
With no expression, nothing to express.

They cannot scare me with their empty spaces
Between stars—on stars where no human race is.

I have it in me so much nearer home                                    15
To scare myself with my own desert places.

## Questions

1. What are these desert places that the speaker finds in himself? (More than one theory is possible. What is yours?)
2. Notice how many times, within the short space of lines 8–10, Frost says *lonely* (or *loneliness*). What other words in the poem contain similar sounds that reinforce these words?
3. In the closing stanza, the feminine rimes *spaces*, *race is*, and *places* might well occur in light or comic verse. Does "Desert Places" leave you laughing? If not, what does it make you feel?


# Reading and Hearing Poems Aloud

Thomas Moore's "The light that lies in women's eyes"—a line rich in internal rime, alliteration, and assonance—is harder to forget than "The light burning in the gaze of a woman." Because of sound, it is possible to remember the obscure line Christopher Smart wrote while in an insane asylum: "Let Ross, house of Ross rejoice with the Great Flabber Dabber Flat Clapping Fish with hands." Such lines, striking as they are even when read silently, become still more effective when said out loud. Reading poems aloud is a way to understand them. For this reason, practice the art of lending poetry your voice.

Before trying to read a poem aloud to other people, understand its meaning as thoroughly as possible. If you know what the poet is saying and the poet's attitude toward it, you will be able to find an appropriate tone of voice and to give each part of the poem a proper emphasis.

Except in the most informal situations and in some class exercises, read a poem to yourself before trying it on an audience. No actor goes before the footlights without first having studied the script, and the language of poems usually demands even more consideration than the language of most contemporary plays. Prepare your reading in advance. Check pronunciations you are not sure of. Underline things to be emphasized.

Read deliberately, more slowly than you would read aloud from a newspaper. Keep in mind that you are saying something to somebody. Don't race through the poem as if you are eager to get it over with.

Don't lapse into singsong. A poem may have a definite swing, but swing should never be exaggerated at the cost of sense. If you understand what the poem is saying and utter the poem as if you do, the temptation to fall into such a mechanical intonation should not occur. Observe the punctuation, making slight pauses for commas, longer pauses for full stops (periods, question marks, exclamation points).

If the poem is rimed, don't raise your voice and make the rimes stand out unnaturally. They should receive no more volume than other words in the poem, though a faint pause at the end of each line will call the listener's attention to them. This advice is contrary to a school that holds that, if a line does not end in any punctuation, one should not pause but run it together with the line following. The trouble is that, from such a reading, a listener may not be able to identify the rimes; besides, the line, that valuable unit of rhythm, is destroyed.

In some older poems rimes that look like slant rimes may have been exact rimes in their day:

> Still so perverse and opposite,
> As if they worshiped God for spite.
> —Samuel Butler, *Hudibras* (1663)

> Soft yielding minds to water glide away,
> And sip, with nymphs, their elemental tea.
> —Alexander Pope, "The Rape of the Lock" (1714)

> Tyger! Tyger! burning bright
> In the forests of the night,
> What immortal hand or eye
> Could frame thy fearful symmetry?
> —William Blake, "The Tyger" (1794)

You may wish to establish a consistent policy toward such shifting usage: is it worthwhile to distort current pronunciation for the sake of the rime?

Listening to a poem, especially if it is unfamiliar, calls for concentration. Merciful people seldom read poetry uninterruptedly to anyone for more than a few minutes at a time. Robert Frost, always kind to his audiences, used to intersperse poems with many silences and seemingly casual remarks—shrewdly giving his hearers a chance to rest from their labors and giving his poems a chance to settle in.

If, in first listening to a poem, you don't take in all its meaning, don't be discouraged. With more practice in listening, your attention span and your ability to understand poems read aloud will increase. Incidentally, following the text of poems in a book while hearing them read aloud may increase your comprehension, but it may not necessarily help you to *listen*. At least some of the time, close your book and let your ears make the poems welcome. That way, their sounds may better work for you.

Hearing recordings of poets reading their work can help both your ability to read aloud and your ability to listen. Not all poets read their poems well, but there is much to be relished in both the highly dramatic reading style of a Dylan Thomas and the quiet underplay of a Robert Frost. You need feel no obligation, of course, to imitate the poet's reading of a poem. You have to feel about the poem in your own way, in order to read it with conviction and naturalness.

Even if you don't have an audience, the act of speaking poetry can have its own rewards. Perhaps that is what Yvor Winters meant when he said that, even though poetry was written for "the mind's ear" as well as the physical ear, "yet the mind's ear can be trained only by way of the other, and the matter, practically considered, comes inescapably back to the reading of poetry aloud."[5]

### EXERCISE: *Reading for Sound and Meaning*

Read these brief poems aloud. What devices of sound do you find in each of them? Try to explain what sound contributes to the total effect of the poem and how it reinforces what the poet is saying.

## *Michael Stillman* (b. 1940)

### IN MEMORIAM JOHN COLTRANE     1972

Listen to the coal
rolling, rolling through the cold
    steady rain, wheel on

wheel, listen to the
turning of the wheels this night                                    5
    black as coal dust, steel

on steel, listen to
these cars carry coal, listen
    to the coal train roll.

IN MEMORIAM JOHN COLTRANE. John Coltrane (1926–1967) was a saxophonist whose original-ity, passion, and technical wizardry have had a deep influence on the history of modern jazz.

## *William Shakespeare* (1564–1616)*

### FULL FATHOM FIVE THY FATHER LIES        (about 1611)

Full fathom five thy father lies;
    Of his bones are coral made;
Those are pearls that were his eyes:
    Nothing of him that doth fade,
But doth suffer a sea change                                       5
Into something rich and strange.
Sea nymphs hourly ring his knell:
    *Ding-dong.*
Hark! now I hear them—*Ding-dong, bell.*

FULL FATHOM FIVE THY FATHER LIES. The spirit Ariel sings this song in *The Tempest* to Ferdinand, prince of Naples, who mistakenly thinks his father is drowned.

[5]"The Audible Reading of Poetry" (1951), reprinted in *The Function of Criticism* (Denver, Alan Swallow, 1957) 81.

## A. E. Housman (1859–1936)*

### WITH RUE MY HEART IS LADEN      1896

With rue my heart is laden
   For golden friends I had,
For many a rose-lipt maiden
   And many a lightfoot lad.

By brooks too broad for leaping           5
   The lightfoot boys are laid;
The rose-lipt girls are sleeping
   In fields where roses fade.

## T. S. Eliot (1888–1965)*

### VIRGINIA      1934

Red river, red river,
Slow flow heat is silence
No will is still as a river
Still. Will heat move
Only through the mocking-bird           5
Heard once? Still hills
Wait. Gates wait. Purple trees,
White trees, wait, wait,
Delay, decay. Living, living,
Never moving. Ever moving           10
Iron thoughts came with me
And go with me:
Red river, river, river.

VIRGINIA. This poem is one of a series entitled "Landscapes."

### SUGGESTIONS FOR WRITING

1. Write about a personal experience with reading poems aloud.
2. Explain why contemporary poets are right (or wrong) to junk rime.
3. Consider the verbal music in W. H. Auden's "As I Walked Out One Evening" (or another selection from Poems for Further Reading). Analyze the poem for language with ear-appeal and show how the poem's sound is of a piece with its meaning.

# 21  Rhythm

## STRESSES AND PAUSES

Rhythms affect us powerfully. We are lulled by a hammock's sway, awakened by an alarm clock's repeated yammer. Long after we come home from a beach, the rising and falling of waves and tides continue in memory. How powerfully the rhythms of poetry also move us may be felt in folk songs of railroad workers and chain gangs whose words were chanted in time to the lifting and dropping of a sledgehammer, and in verse that marching soldiers shout, putting a stress on every word that coincides with a footfall:

> Your LEFT! TWO! THREE! FOUR!
> Your LEFT! TWO! THREE! FOUR!
> You LEFT your WIFE and TWEN-ty-one KIDS
> And you LEFT! TWO! THREE! FOUR!
> You'll NEV-er get HOME to-NIGHT!

A rhythm is produced by a series of recurrences: the returns and departures of the seasons, the repetitions of an engine's stroke, the beats of the heart. A rhythm may be produced by the recurrence of a sound (the throb of a drum, a telephone's busy-signal), but rhythm and sound are not identical. A totally deaf person at a parade can sense rhythm from the motions of the marchers' arms and feet, from the shaking of the pavement as they tramp. Rhythms inhere in the motions of the moon and stars, even though when they move we hear no sound.

In poetry, several kinds of recurrent *sound* are possible, including (as we saw in the last chapter) rime, alliteration, and assonance. But most often when we speak of the **rhythm** of a poem we mean the recurrence of stresses and pauses in it. When we hear a poem read aloud, stresses and pauses are, of course, part of its sound. It is possible to be aware of rhythms in poems read silently, too.

A **stress** (or **accent**) is a greater amount of force given to one syllable in speaking than is given to another. We favor a stressed syllable with a little more breath and emphasis, with the result that it comes out slightly louder, higher in pitch, or longer in duration than other syllables. In this manner we place a stress on the first syllable of words such as *eagle, impact, open,* and *statue,* and on the second syllable in *cigar, mystique, precise,* and *until.* Each word in English carries at least one stress, except (usually) for the articles *a, an,* and *the,* and one-syllable prepositions: *at, by, for, from, of, to, with.* Even these, however, take a stress once in a while: "Get WITH it!" "You're not THE Dolly Parton?" One word by itself is seldom long enough for us to notice a rhythm in it. Usually a sequence of at least a few words is needed for stresses to establish their pattern: a line, a passage, a whole poem. Strong rhythms may be seen in most Mother Goose rimes, to which children have been responding for hundreds of years. This rime is for an adult to chant while jogging a child up and down on a knee:

> Here goes my lord
> A trot, a trot, a trot, a trot!
> Here goes my lady
> A canter, a canter, a canter, a canter!
> Here goes my young master
> Jockey-hitch, jockey-hitch, jockey-hitch, jockey-hitch!
> Here goes my young miss
> An amble, an amble, an amble, an amble!
> The footman lags behind to tipple ale and wine
> And goes gallop, a gallop, a gallop, to make up his time.

More than one rhythm occurs in these lines, as the make-believe horse changes pace. How do these rhythms differ? From one line to the next, the interval between stresses lengthens or grows shorter. In "a TROT a TROT a TROT a TROT," the stress falls on every other syllable. But in the middle of the line "A CAN-ter a CAN-ter a CAN-ter a CAN-ter," the stress falls on every third syllable. When stresses recur at fixed intervals as in these lines, the result is called a **meter.** The line "A trot a trot a trot a trot" is in **iambic** meter, a succession of alternate unstressed and stressed syllables.[1] Of all rhythms in the English language, this one is most familiar; most of our traditional poetry is written in it and ordinary speech tends to resemble it. Most poems, less obvious in rhythm than nursery rimes are, rarely stick to their meters with such jog-trot regularity. The following lines also contain a

---

[1]Another kind of meter is possible, in which the intervals between stresses vary. This is **accentual** meter, not often found in contemporary poetry. It is discussed in the second part of this chapter.

horseback-riding rhythm. (The poet, Gerard Manley Hopkins, is comparing the pell-mell plunging of a burn—Scottish word for a brook—to the motion of a wild horse.)

> This darksome burn, horseback brown,
> His rollrock highroad roaring down,
> In coop and in comb the fleece of his foam
> Flutes and low to the lake falls home.

In the third line, when the brook courses through coop and comb ("hollow" and "ravine"), the passage breaks into a gallop; then, with the two-beat *falls home*, almost seems reined to a sudden halt.

Stresses embody meanings. Whenever two or more fall side by side, words gain in emphasis. Consider these hard-hitting lines from John Donne, in which accent marks have been placed, dictionary-fashion, to indicate the stressed syllables:

> Bat'ter my heart', three'-per'soned God', for You'
> As yet' but knock', breathe', shine', and seek' to mend';
> That I may rise' and stand', o'er'throw' me, and bend'
> Your force' to break', blow', burn', and make' me new'.

Unstressed (or **slack**) syllables also can direct our attention to what the poet means. In a line containing few stresses and a great many unstressed syllables, there can be an effect not of power and force but of hesitation and uncertainty. Yeats asks in "Among School Children" what young mother, if she could see her baby grown to be an old man, would think him

> A com'pen·sa'tion for the pang' of his birth'
> Or the un·cer'tain·ty of his set'ting forth'?

When unstressed syllables recur in pairs, the result is a rhythm that trips and bounces, as in Robert Service's rollicking line:

> A bunch' of the boys' were whoop'ing it up' in the Mal'a·mute sa·loon'
> . . .

or in Poe's lines—also light but probably supposed to be serious:

> For the moon' nev·er beams' with·out bring'ing me dreams'
> Of the beau'ti·ful An'na·bel Lee'.

Apart from the words that convey it, the rhythm of a poem has no meaning. There are no essentially sad rhythms, nor any essentially happy ones. But some rhythms enforce certain meanings better than others do. The bouncing rhythm of Service's line seems fitting for an account of a merry night in a Klondike saloon; but it may be distracting when encountered in Poe's wistful elegy.

EXERCISE: *Appropriate and Inappropriate Rhythms*

In each of the following passages decide whether rhythm enforces meaning and tone or works against these elements and consequently against the poem's effectiveness.

1. Alfred, Lord Tennyson, "Break, break, break":

    Break, break, break,
    On thy cold gray stones, O Sea!

2. Edgar Allan Poe, "Ulalume":

    Then my heart it grew ashen and sober
        As the leaves that were crispèd and sere—
        As the leaves that were withering and sere,
    And I cried: "It was surely October
        On *this* very night of last year
        That I journey—I journeyed down here—
        That I brought a dread burden down here—
        On this night of all nights in the year,
        Ah, what demon has tempted me here?"

3. Greg Keeler, "There Ain't No Such Thing as a Montana Cowboy" (a song lyric):

    I couldn't be cooler, I come from Missoula,
    And I rope and I chew and I ride.
    But I'm a heroin dealer, and I drive a four-wheeler
    With stereo speakers inside.
    My ol' lady Phoebe's out rippin' off C.B.'s
    From the rigs at the Wagon Wheel Bar,
    Near a Montana truck stop and a shit-outta-luck stop
    For a trucker who's driven too far.

4. Annie Finch, "Dickinson":

    Of all the lives I cannot live,
    I have elected one

    to haunt me till the margins give
    and I am left alone.

    One life has sounded in my voice
    and made me like a stone—

    one that the falling leaves can sink
    not over, but upon.

5. Eliza Cook, "Song of the Sea-Weed":

    Many a lip is gaping for drink,
        And madly calling for rain;
    And some hot brains are beginning to think
        Of a messmate's opened vein.

6. William Shakespeare, song from *The Tempest*:

    The master, the swabber, the boatswain, and I,
    The gunner and his mate

Loved Moll, Meg, and Marian, and Margery,
But none of us cared for Kate;
For she had a tongue with a tang
Would cry to a sailor "Go hang!"—
She loved not the savor of tar nor of pitch
Yet a tailor might scratch her where'er she did itch;
Then to sea, boys, and let her go hang!

Rhythms in poetry are due not only to stresses but also to pauses. "Every nice ear," observed Alexander Pope (*nice* meaning "finely tuned"), "must, I believe, have observed that in any smooth English verse of ten syllables, there is naturally a pause either at the fourth, fifth, or sixth syllable." Such a light but definite pause within a line is called a **cesura** (or caesura), "a cutting." More liberally than Pope, we apply the name to any pause in a line of any length, after any word in the line. In studying a poem, we often indicate a cesura by double lines(‖). Usually, a cesura will occur at a mark of punctuation, but there can be a cesura even if no punctuation is present. Sometimes you will find it at the end of a phrase or clause or, as in these lines by William Blake, after an internal rime:

And priests in black gowns‖were walking their rounds
And binding with briars‖my joys and desires.

Lines of ten or twelve syllables (as Pope knew) tend to have just one cesura, though sometimes there are more:

Cover her face:‖mine eyes dazzle:‖she died young.

Pauses also tend to recur at more prominent places—namely, after each line. At the end of a verse (from *versus*, "a turning"), the reader's eye, before turning to go on to the next line, makes a pause, however brief. If a line ends in a full pause—usually indicated by some mark of punctuation—we call it **end-stopped.** All the lines in this passage from Christopher Marlowe's *Doctor Faustus* (in which Faustus addresses the apparition of Helen of Troy) are end-stopped:

Was this the face that launch'd a thousand ships,
And burnt the topless towers of Ilium?
Sweet Helen, make me immortal with a kiss.
Her lips suck forth my soul: see, where it flies!
Come, Helen, come, give me my soul again.
Here will I dwell, for heaven is in these lips,
And all is dross that is not Helena.

A line that does not end in punctuation and that therefore is read with only a slight pause after it is called a **run-on line.** Because a run-on line gives us only part of a phrase, clause, or sentence, we have to read on to the line or lines following, in order to complete a thought. All these lines from Robert Browning's "My Last Duchess" are run-on lines:

> . . . Sir, 'twas not
> Her husband's presence only, called that spot
> Of joy into the Duchess' cheek: perhaps
> Frà Pandolf chanced to say "Her mantle laps
> Over my lady's wrist too much," or "Paint
> Must never hope to reproduce the faint
> Half-flush that dies along her throat." Such stuff
> Was courtesy, she thought . . .[2]

A passage in run-on lines has a rhythm different from that of a passage like Marlowe's in end-stopped lines. When emphatic pauses occur in the quotation from Browning, they fall within a line rather than at the end of one. The passage by Marlowe and that by Browning are in lines of the same meter (iambic) and the same length (ten syllables). What makes the big difference in their rhythms is the running on, or lack of it.

To sum up: rhythm is recurrence. In poems, it is made of stresses and pauses. The poet can produce it by doing any of several things: making the intervals between stresses fixed or varied, long or short; indicating pauses (cesuras) within lines; end-stopping lines or running them over; writing in short or long lines. Rhythm in itself cannot convey meaning. And yet if a poet's words have meaning, their rhythm must be one with it.

---

### *Gwendolyn Brooks* (b. 1917)*

### WE REAL COOL          1960

*The Pool Players.*
*Seven at the Golden Shovel.*

We real cool. We
Left school. We

Lurk late. We
Strike straight. We

Sing sin. We                                                                    5
Thin gin. We

Jazz June. We
Die soon.

#### QUESTION

Describe the rhythms of this poem. By what techniques are they produced?

[2]The complete poem, "My Last Duchess" appears on page 594.

## Robert Frost (1874–1963)*

### Never Again Would Birds' Song Be the Same          1942

He would declare and could himself believe
That the birds there in all the garden round
From having heard the daylong voice of Eve
Had added to their own an oversound,
Her tone of meaning but without the words.                          5
Admittedly an eloquence so soft
Could only have had an influence on birds
When call or laughter carried it aloft.
Be that as may be, she was in their song.
Moreover her voice upon their voices crossed                        10
Had now persisted in the woods so long
That probably it never would be lost.
Never again would birds' song be the same.
And to do that to birds was why she came.

### Questions

1. Who is *he?*
2. In reading aloud line 9, do you stress *may?* (Do you say "as MAY be" or "as may BE"?) What guide do we have to the poet's wishes here?
3. Which lines does Frost cast mostly or entirely into monosyllables? How would you describe the impact of these lines?
4. In his *Essay on Criticism,* Alexander Pope made fun of poets who wrote mechanically, without wit: "And ten low words oft creep in one dull line." Do you think this criticism applicable to Frost's lines of monosyllables? Explain.

## Ben Jonson (1573?–1637)*

### Slow, slow, fresh fount, keep time
### with my salt tears                                    1600

Slow, slow, fresh fount, keep time with my salt tears;
 Yet slower yet, oh faintly, gentle springs;
List to the heavy part the music bears,
 Woe weeps out her division° when she sings.          *a part in a song*
  Droop herbs and flowers,                              5
  Fall grief in showers;
  Our beauties are not ours;
   Oh, I could still,
Like melting snow upon some craggy hill,
 Drop, drop, drop, drop,                                      10
Since nature's pride is now a withered daffodil.

SLOW, SLOW, FRESH FOUNT. The nymph Echo sings this lament over the youth Narcissus in Jonson's play *Cynthia's Revels*. In mythology, Nemesis, goddess of vengeance, to punish Narcissus for loving his own beauty, caused him to pine away and then transformed him into a narcissus (another name for a *daffodil*, line 11).

## QUESTIONS

1. Read the first line aloud rapidly. Why is it difficult to do so?
2. Which lines rely most heavily on stressed syllables?
3. In general, how would you describe the rhythm of this poem? How is it appropriate to what is said?

## *Alexander Pope* (1688–1744)*

ATTICUS                                                           1735

How did they fume, and stamp, and roar, and chafe!
And swear, not Addison himself was safe.
    Peace to all such! but were there one whose fires
True genius kindles, and fair fame inspires;
Blest with each talent, and each art to please,                            5
And born to write, converse, and live with ease,
Should such a man, too fond to rule alone,
Bear, like the Turk, no brother near the throne,
View him with scornful, yet with jealous eyes,
And hate for arts that caused himself to rise;                             10
Damn with faint praise, assent with civil leer,
And, without sneering, teach the rest to sneer;
Willing to wound, and yet afraid to strike,
Just hint a fault, and hesitate dislike;
Alike reserved to blame, or to commend,                                    15
A timorous foe, and a suspicious friend;
Dreading e'en fools, by flatterers besieged,
And so obliging, that he ne'er obliged;
Like Cato, give his little Senate laws,
And sit attentive to his own applause:                                     20
While wits and Templars every sentence raise,
And wonder with a foolish face of praise—
Who but must laugh, if such a man there be?
Who would not weep, if Atticus were he?

ATTICUS. In this selection from "An Epistle to Dr. Arbuthnot," Pope has been referring to dull versifiers and their angry reception of his satiric thrusts at them. With *Peace to all such!* (line 3) he turns to his celebrated portrait of a rival man of letters, Joseph Addison. 19 *Cato*: Roman senator about whom Addison had written a tragedy. 21 *Templars*: London lawyers who dabbled in literature.

1. In these lines—one of the most famous damnations in English poetry—what positive virtues, in Pope's view, does Addison lack?
2. Which lines are end-stopped? What is the effect of these lines upon the rhythm of this passage? (Suggestion: Read "Atticus" aloud.)

### EXERCISE: *Two Kinds of Rhythm*

The following compositions in verse have lines of similar length, yet they differ greatly in rhythm. Explain how they differ and why.

---

### *Sir Thomas Wyatt* (1503?–1542)*

WITH SERVING STILL            (1528–1536)

With serving still°                                                    *continually*
  This have I won,
For my goodwill
  To be undone;

And for redress                                                              5
  Of all my pain,
Disdainfulness
  I have again°;                                              *in return*

And for reward
  Of all my smart                                                  10
Lo, thus unheard,
  I must depart!

Wherefore all ye
  That after shall
By fortune be,                                                              15
  As I am, thrall,

Example take
  What I have won,
Thus for her sake
  To be undone!                                                     20

---

### *Dorothy Parker* (1893–1967)

RÉSUMÉ            1926

Razors pain you;
Rivers are damp;

Acids stain you;
And drugs cause cramp.
Guns aren't lawful;                                                    5
Nooses give;
Gas smells awful;
You might as well live.


# METER

To enjoy the rhythms of a poem, no special knowledge of meter is necessary. All you need do is pay attention to stresses and where they fall, and you will perceive the basic pattern, if there is any. However, there is nothing occult about the study of meter. Most people find they can master its essentials in no more time than it takes to learn a complicated game such as chess. If you take the time, you will then have the pleasure of knowing what is happening in the rhythms of many a fine poem, and pleasurable knowledge may even deepen your insight into poetry. The following discussion, then, will be of interest only to those who care to go deeper into **prosody,** the study of metrical structures in poetry.

Far from being artificial constructions found only in the minds of poets, meters occur in everyday speech and prose. As the following example will show, they may need only a poet to recognize them. The English satirist Max Beerbohm, after contemplating the title page of his first book, took his pen and added two more lines.


## *Max Beerbohm* (1872–1956)

ON THE IMPRINT OF THE FIRST ENGLISH EDITION OF
THE WORKS OF MAX BEERBOHM             (1896)

"London: JOHN LANE, *The Bodley Head*
   New York: Charles Scribner's Sons."
This plain announcement, nicely read,
   Iambically runs.

In everyday life, nobody speaks or writes in perfect iambic rhythm, except at moments: "a HAM on RYE and HIT the MUStard HARD!" (As we have seen, iambic rhythm consists of a series of syllables alternately unstressed and stressed.) Poets rarely speak in it for long, either—at least, not with absolute consistency. If you read aloud Max Beerbohm's lines, you'll hear an iambic rhythm, but not an unvarying one. And yet all of us speak with a rising and falling of stress *somewhat like* iambic meter. Perhaps, as the poet and scholar John Thompson has maintained, "The iambic metrical pattern has dominated English verse because it provides the best symbolic model of our language."[3]

To make ourselves aware of a meter, we need only listen to a poem, or sound its words to ourselves. If we care to work out exactly what a poet is doing, we *scan* a line or a poem by indicating the stresses in it. **Scansion**, the art of so doing, is not just a matter of pointing to syllables; it is also a matter of listening to a poem and making sense of it. To scan a poem is one way to indicate how to read it aloud; in order to see where stresses fall, you have to see the places where the poet wishes to put emphasis. That is why, when scanning a poem, you may find yourself suddenly understanding it.

An objection might be raised against scanning: isn't it too simple to pretend that all language (and poetry) can be divided neatly into stressed syllables and unstressed syllables? Indeed it is. As the linguist Otto Jespersen has said, "In reality there are infinite gradations of stress, from the most penetrating scream to the faintest whisper."[4] However, the idea in scanning a poem is not to reproduce the sound of a human voice. For that we would do better to buy a tape recorder. To scan a poem, rather, is to make a diagram of the stresses (and absences of stress) we find in it. Various marks are used in scansion; in this book we use ´ for a stressed syllable and ˘ for an unstressed syllable. Some scanners, wishing a little more precision, also use the **half-stress** ( ˋ ); this device can be helpful in many instances when a syllable usually not stressed comes at a place where it takes some emphasis, as in the last syllable in a line:

Bound each to each with nat·u·ral pi·e·ty.

Here, with examples, are some of the principal meters we find in English poetry. Each is named for its basic **foot,** or molecule (usually one stressed and one or two unstressed syllables).

1. **Iambic** (foot: the **iamb,** ˘ ´):
   The fall·ing out of faith·ful friends, re·new·ing is of love

2. **Anapestic** (foot: the **anapest,** ˘ ˘ ´):
   I am mon·arch of all I sur·vey

3. **Trochaic** (foot: the **trochee,** ´ ˘):
   Dou·ble, dou·ble, toil and trou·ble

4. **Dactylic** (foot: the **dactyl,** ´ ˘ ˘):
   Take her up ten·der·ly

Iambic and anapestic meters are called **rising** meters because their movement rises from unstressed syllable (or syllables) to stress; trochaic and dactylic

[3]*The Founding of English Metre* (New York: Columbia UP, 1966) 12.
[4]"Notes on Metre," (1933), reprinted in *The Structure of Verse: Modern Essays on Prosody,* ed. Harvey Gross, 2nd ed. (New York: Echo Press, 1978).

meters are called **falling.** In the twentieth century, the bouncing meters—anapestic and dactylic—have been used more often for comic verse than for serious poetry. Called feet, though they contain no unaccented syllables, are the **monosyllabic foot** (′) and the **spondee** (″). Meters are not ordinarily made up of them; if one were, it would be like the steady impact of nails being hammered into a board—no pleasure to hear or to dance to. But inserted now and then, they can lend emphasis and variety to a meter, as Yeats well knew when he broke up the predominantly iambic rhythm of "Who Goes with Fergus?" (page 717) with the line,

> And the white breast of the dim sea,

in which occur two spondees. Meters are classified also by line lengths: *trochaic monometer*, for instance, is a line one trochee long, as in this anonymous brief comment on microbes:

> Adam
> Had 'em.

A frequently heard metrical description is **iambic pentameter:** a line of five iambs, a meter especially familiar because it occurs in all blank verse (such as Shakespeare's plays and Milton's *Paradise Lost*), heroic couplets, and sonnets. The commonly used names for line lengths follow:

| | | | |
|---|---|---|---|
| **monometer** | one foot | **pentameter** | five feet |
| **dimeter** | two feet | **hexameter** | six feet |
| **trimeter** | three feet | **heptameter** | seven feet |
| **tetrameter** | four feet | **octameter** | eight feet |

Lines of more than eight feet are possible but are rare. They tend to break up into shorter lengths in the listening ear.

When Yeats chose the spondees *white breast* and *dim sea*, he was doing what poets who write in meter do frequently for variety—using a foot other than the expected one. Often such a substitution will be made at the very beginning of a line, as in the third line of this passage from Christopher Marlowe's *Tragical History of Doctor Faustus*:

> Was this the face that launched a thou·sand ships
>
> And burnt the top·less tow'rs of Il·i·um?
>
> Sweet Hel·en, make me im·mor·tal with a kiss.

How, we might wonder, can that last line be called iambic at all? But it is, just as a waltz that includes an extra step or two, or leaves a few steps out, remains a waltz. In the preceding lines the basic iambic pentameter is established, and though in the third line the regularity is varied from, it does not altogether disappear. It continues for a while to run on in the reader's mind, where (if the poet does not stay away from it for too long) the meter will be when the poem comes back to it.

Like a basic dance step, a meter is not to be slavishly adhered to. The fun in reading a metrical poem often comes from watching the poet continually departing from perfect regularity, giving a few heel-kicks to display a bit of joy or ingenuity, then easing back into the basic step again. Because meter is orderly and the rhythms of living speech are unruly, poets can play one against the other, in a sort of counterpoint. Robert Frost, a master at pitting a line of iambs against a very natural-sounding and irregular sentence, declared, "I am never more pleased than when I can get these into strained relation. I like to drag and break the intonation across the meter as waves first comb and then break stumbling on a shingle."[5]

Evidently Frost's skilled effects would be lost to a reader who, scanning a Frost poem or reading it aloud, distorted its rhythms to fit the words exactly to the meter. With rare exceptions, a good poem can be read and scanned the way we would speak its sentences if they were ours. This, for example, is an unreal scansion:

That's my̆ lást Dŭch·ĕss paı̆nt·ĕd ŏn thĕ wáll.

—because no speaker of English would say that sentence in that way. We are likely to stress *That's* and *last*.

Variety in rhythm is not merely desirable in poetry, it is a necessity, and the poem that fails to depart often enough from absolute regularity is in trouble. If the beat of its words slips into a mechanical pattern, the poem marches robot-like right into its grave. Luckily, few poets, except writers of greeting cards, favor rhythms that go "a TROT a TROT a TROT a TROT" for very long. Robert Frost told an audience one time that if when writing a poem he found its rhythm becoming monotonous, he knew that the poem was going wrong and that he himself didn't believe what it was saying.

Although in good poetry we seldom meet a very long passage of absolute metrical regularity, we sometimes find (in a line or so) a monotonous rhythm that is effective. Words fall meaningfully in Macbeth's famous statement of world-weariness: "Tomorrow and tomorrow and tomorrow . . ." and in the opening lines of Thomas Gray's "Elegy":

Thĕ cúr·fĕw tólls thĕ knéll ŏf párt·ı̆ng dáy,

Thĕ lów·ı̆ng hérd wı̆nd slów·ly̆ ó'er thĕ léa,

Thĕ plów·măn hóme·wărd plóds hı̆s wéar·y̆ wáy,

Ănd léaves thĕ wórld tŏ dárk·nĕss ănd tŏ mé.[6]

Although certain unstressed syllables in these lines seem to call for more emphasis than others—you might, for instance, care to throw a little more weight on the second syllable of *curfew* in the opening line—we can still say

[5]Letter to John Cournos in 1914, in *Selected Letters of Robert Frost*, ed. Lawrance Thompson (New York: Holt, 1964) 128.
[6]The complete poem, "Elegy Written in a Country Churchyard," appears on page 873.

the lines are notably iambic. Their almost unvarying rhythm seems just right to convey the tolling of a bell and the weary setting down of one foot after the other.

Besides the two rising meters (iambic, anapestic) and the two falling meters (trochaic, dactylic), English poets have another valuable meter. It is **accentual meter,** in which the poet does not write in feet (as in the other meters) but instead counts accents (stresses). The idea is to have the same number of stresses in every line. The poet may place them anywhere in the line and may include practically any number of unstressed syllables, which do not count. In "Christabel," for instance, Coleridge keeps four stresses to a line, though the first line has only eight syllables and the last line has eleven:

> There is not wind e·nough to twirl
> The one red leaf, the last of its clan,
> That dan·ces as of·ten as dance it can,
> Hang·ing so light, and hang·ing so high,
> On the top-most twig that looks up at the sky.

The history of accentual meter is long and honorable. Old English poetry was written in a kind of accentual meter, but its line was more rule-bound than Coleridge's: four stresses arranged two on either side of a cesura, plus alliteration of three of the stressed syllables. In "Junk," Richard Wilbur revives the pattern:

> An axe an·gles ‖ from my neigh·bor's ash·can . . .

Many poets, from the authors of Mother Goose rimes to Gerard Manley Hopkins, have sometimes found accentual meters congenial.

It has been charged that the importation of Greek names for meters and of the classical notion of feet was an unsuccessful attempt to make a Parthenon out of English wattles. The charge is open to debate, but at least it is certain that Greek names for feet cannot mean to us what they meant to Aristotle. Greek and Latin poetry is measured not by stressed and unstressed syllables but by long and short vowel sounds. An iamb in classical verse is one short syllable followed by a long syllable. Such a meter constructed on the principle of vowel length is called a **quantitative meter.** Campion's "Rose-cheeked Laura" was an attempt to demonstrate it in English, but probably we enjoy the rhythm of the poem's well-placed stresses whether or not we notice its vowel sounds.

*Thomas Campion* (1567–1620)*

ROSE-CHEEKED LAURA, COME        1602

Rose-cheeked Laura, come,
Sing thou smoothly with thy beauty's

Silent music, either other
     Sweetly gracing.

Lovely forms do flow                                                        5
From concent° divinely framèd;                             *harmony*
Heav'n is music, and thy beauty's
     Birth is heavenly.

These dull notes we sing
Discords need for helps to grace them;                     10
Only beauty purely loving
     Knows no discord,

But still moves delight,
Like clear springs renewed by flowing,
Ever perfect, ever in them-                                       15
     Selves eternal.

Although less popular among poets today than formerly, meter endures. Major poets from Shakespeare through Yeats have fashioned their work by it, and if we are to read their poems with full enjoyment, we need to be aware of it. To enjoy metrical poetry—even to write it—you do not have to slice lines into feet; you do need to recognize when a meter is present in a line, and when the line departs from it. An argument in favor of meter is that it reminds us of body rhythms such as breathing, walking, the beating of the heart. In an effective metrical poem, these rhythms cannot be separated from what the poet is saying—or, in the words of an old jazz song, "It don't mean a thing if you ain't got that swing." As critic Paul Fussell has put it: "No element of a poem is more basic—and I mean physical—in its effect upon the reader than the metrical element, and perhaps no technical triumphs reveal more readily than the metrical the poet's sympathy with that universal human nature . . . which exists outside his own."[7]

## Walter Savage Landor (1775–1864)

### ON SEEING A HAIR OF LUCRETIA BORGIA        (1825)

Borgia, thou once wert almost too august
And high for adoration; now thou'rt dust.
All that remains of thee these plaits unfold,
Calm hair, meandering in pellucid gold.

### QUESTIONS

1. Who was Lucretia Borgia and when did she live? Because of her reputation, what connotations does her name add to Landor's poem?
2. What does *meander* mean? How can a hair meander?

[7]*Poetic Meter and Poetic Form* (New York: Random, 1965) 110.

3. Scan the poem, indicating stressed syllables. What is the basic meter of most of the poem? What happens to this meter in the last line? Note especially *meandering in pel-*. How many light, unstressed syllables are there in a row? Does rhythm in any way reinforce what Landor is saying?

## EXERCISE: *Meaningful Variation*

At what place or places in each of these passages does the poet depart from basic iambic meter? How does each departure help underscore the meaning?

1. John Dryden, "Mac Flecknoe" (speech of Flecknoe, prince of Nonsense, referring to Thomas Shadwell, poet and playwright):

   Shadwell alone of all my sons is he
   Who stands confirmed in full stupidity.
   The rest to some faint meaning make pretense,
   But Shadwell never deviates into sense.

2. Alexander Pope, *An Essay on Criticism*:

   A needless Alexandrine ends the song
   That, like a wounded snake, drags its slow length along.

3. George Gordon, Lord Byron, *Childe Harold's Pilgrimage*:

   Roll on, thou deep and dark blue Ocean—roll!
   Ten thousand fleets sweep over thee in vain;
   Man marks the earth with ruin—his control
   Stops with the shore; upon the watery plain
   The wrecks are all thy deed, nor doth remain
   A shadow of man's ravage, save his own,
   When, for a moment, like a drop of rain,
   He sinks into thy depths with bubbling groan,
   Without a grave, unknell'd, uncoffin'd, and unknown.

4. Henry Wadsworth Longfellow, "Mezzo Cammin":

   Half-way up the hill, I see the Past
       Lying beneath me with its sounds and sights,—
   A city in the twilight dim and vast,
       With smoking roofs, soft bells, and gleaming lights,—
   And hear above me on the autumnal blast
       The cataract of Death far thundering from the heights.

5. Wallace Stevens, "Sunday Morning":

   Deer walk upon our mountains, and the quail
   Whistle about us their spontaneous cries;
   Sweet berries ripen in the wilderness;
   And, in the isolation of the sky,
   At evening, casual flocks of pigeons make
   Ambiguous undulations as they sink,
   Downward to darkness, on extended wings.

Which of the following poems contain predominant meters? Which poems are not wholly metrical, but are metrical in certain lines? Point out any such lines. What reasons do you see, in such places, for the poet's seeking a metrical effect?

---

### Edna St. Vincent Millay (1892–1950)*

COUNTING-OUT RHYME          1928

Silver bark of beech, and sallow
Bark of yellow birch and yellow
    Twig of willow.

Stripe of green in moosewood maple,
Color seen in leaf of apple,                                    5
    Bark of popple.

Wood of popple pale as moonbeam,
Wood of oak for yoke and barn-beam,
    Wood of hornbeam.

Silver bark of beech, and hollow                               10
Stem of elder, tall and yellow
    Twig of willow.

---

### A. E. Housman (1859–1936)*

WHEN I WAS ONE-AND-TWENTY          1896

When I was one-and-twenty
    I heard a wise man say,
"Give crowns and pounds and guineas
    But not your heart away;
Give pearls away and rubies                                    5
    But keep your fancy free."
But I was one-and-twenty,
    No use to talk to me.

When I was one-and-twenty
    I heard him say again,                                     10
"The heart out of the bosom
    Was never given in vain;
'Tis paid with sighs a plenty
    And sold for endless rue."
And I am two-and-twenty,                                       15
    And oh, 'tis true, 'tis true.

**William Carlos Williams** (1883–1963)*

## THE DESCENT OF WINTER (SECTION 10/30)      1934

To freight cars in the air

all the slow
   clank, clank
   clank, clank
moving about the treetops            5

the
   wha, wha
of the hoarse whistle

   pah, pah, pah
   pah, pah, pah, pah, pah          10
   piece and piece
   piece and piece
moving still trippingly
through the morningmist

   long after the engine          15
has fought by
         and disappeared
in silence
         to the left

**Walt Whitman** (1819–1892)*

## BEAT! BEAT! DRUMS!               (1861)

Beat! beat! drums!—blow! bugles! blow!
Through the windows—through doors—burst like a ruthless force,
Into the solemn church, and scatter the congregation,
Into the school where the scholar is studying;
Leave not the bridegroom quiet—no happiness must he have now
   with his bride,            5
Nor the peaceful farmer any peace, ploughing his field or gathering
   his grain,
So fierce you whirr and pound you drums—so shrill you bugles
   blow.

Beat! beat! drums!—blow! bugles! blow!
Over the traffic of cities—over the rumble of wheels in the streets;
Are beds prepared for sleepers at night in the houses? no sleepers
   must sleep in those beds,          10

No bargainer's bargains by day—no brokers or speculators—would
    they continue?
Would the talkers be talking? would the singer attempt to sing?
Would the lawyer rise in the court to state his case before the
    judge?
Then rattle quicker, heavier drums—you bugles wilder blow.

Beat! beat! drums!—blow! bugles! blow!                       15
Make no parley—stop for no expostulation,
Mind not the timid—mind not the weeper or prayer,
Mind not the old man beseeching the young man,
Let not the child's voice be heard, nor the mother's entreaties,
Make even the trestles to shake the dead where they lie awaiting the
    hearses.                                            20
So strong you thump O terrible drums—so loud you bugles blow.


### Langston Hughes (1902–1967)*

## DREAM BOOGIE         1951

Good morning, daddy!
Ain't you heard
The boogie-woogie rumble
Of a dream deferred?

Listen closely:                                      5
You'll hear their feet
Beating out and beating out a—

    *You think*
    *It's a happy beat?*

Listen to it closely:                              10
Ain't you heard
something underneath
like a—

    *What did I say?*

Sure,                                          15
I'm happy!
Take it away!

    *Hey, pop!*
    *Re-bop!*
    *Mop!*                                     20

      *Y-e-a-h!*

## Suggestions for Writing

1. When has a rhythm of any kind (whether or not in poetry) stirred you, picked you up, and carried you along with it? Write an account of your experience.
2. The fact that most contemporary poets have given up meter, in the view of Stanley Kunitz, has made poetry "easier to write, but harder to remember." Why so? Comment on Kunitz's remark, or quarrel with it, in two or three paragraphs.
3. Ponder Robert Frost's idea of "the sound of sense" (page 1030). Then, in a paragraph or two, try to show what light this idea sheds upon Frost's "Never Again Would Birds' Song Be the Same" (or any other Frost poem in this book).

# 22  Closed Form

Form, as a general idea, is the design of a thing as a whole, the configuration of all its parts. No poem can escape having some kind of form, whether its lines are as various in length as broomstraws, or all in hexameter. To put this point in another way: if you were to listen to a poem read aloud in a language unknown to you, or if you saw the poem printed in that foreign language, whatever in the poem you could see or hear would be the form of it.[1]

Writing in **closed form,** a poet follows (or finds) some sort of pattern, such as that of a sonnet with its rime scheme and its fourteen lines of iambic pentameter. On a page, poems in closed form tend to look regular and symmetrical, often falling into stanzas that indicate groups of rimes. Along with William Butler Yeats, who held that a successful poem will "come shut with a click, like a closing box," the poet who writes in closed form apparently strives for a kind of perfection—seeking, perhaps, to lodge words so securely in place that no word can be budged without a worsening. For the sake of meaning, though, a competent poet often will depart from a symmetrical pattern. As Robert Frost observed, there is satisfaction to be found in things not mechanically regular: "We enjoy the straight crookedness of a good walking stick."

The poet who writes in **open form** usually seeks no final click. Often, such a poet views the writing of a poem as a process, rather than a quest for an absolute. Free to use white space for emphasis, able to shorten or lengthen lines as the sense seems to require, the poet lets the poem discover its shape as it goes along, moving as water flows downhill, adjusting to its terrain, engulfing obstacles. (Open form will provide the focus of the next chapter.)

Most poetry of the past is in closed form, exhibiting at least a pattern of rime or meter, but since the early 1960s most American poets have preferred

---

[1]For a good summary of the uses of the term **form** in criticism of poetry, see the article "Form" by G. N. G. Orsini in *Princeton Encyclopedia of Poetry and Poetics,* 2nd ed., eds. Preminger, Warnke, and Hardison (Princeton: Princeton UP, 1975).

forms that stay open. Lately, the situation has been changing yet again, with closed form reappearing in much recent poetry. Whatever the fashion of the moment, the reader who seeks a wide understanding of poetry of both the present and the past will need to know both the closed and open varieties.

Closed form gives some poems a valuable advantage: it makes them more easily memorable. The **epic** poems of nations—long narratives tracing the adventures of popular heroes: the Greek *Iliad* and *Odyssey*, the French *Song of Roland*, the Spanish *Cid*—tend to occur in patterns of fairly consistent line length or number of stresses because these works were sometimes transmitted orally. Sung to the music of a lyre or chanted to a drumbeat, they may have been easier to memorize because of their patterns. If a singer forgot something, the song would have a noticeable hole in it, so rime or fixed meter probably helped prevent an epic from deteriorating when passed along from one singer to another. It is no coincidence that so many English playwrights of Shakespeare's day favored iambic pentameter. Companies of actors, often called upon to perform a different play daily, could count on a fixed line length to aid their burdened memories.

Some poets complain that closed form is a straitjacket, a limit to free expression. Other poets, however, feel that, like fires held fast in a narrow space, thoughts stated in a tightly binding form may take on a heightened intensity. "Limitation makes for power," according to one contemporary practitioner of closed form, Richard Wilbur; "the strength of the genie comes of his being confined in a bottle." Compelled by some strict pattern to arrange and rearrange words, delete, and exchange them, poets must focus on them the keenest attention. Often they stand a chance of discovering words more meaningful than the ones they started out with. And at times, in obedience to a rime scheme, the poet may be surprised by saying something quite unexpected. Composing a poem is like walking blindfolded down a dark road, with one's hand in the hand of an inexorable guide. With the conscious portion of the mind, the poet may wish to express what seems to be a good idea. But a line ending in *year* must be followed by another ending in *atmosphere, beer, bier, bombardier, cashier, deer, friction-gear, frontier*, or some other rime word that otherwise might not have entered the poem. That is why rime schemes and stanza patterns can be mighty allies and valuable disturbers of the unconscious. As Rolfe Humphries has said about strict form: "It makes you think of better things than you would all by yourself."

## FORMAL PATTERNS

The best-known one-line pattern for a poem in English is **blank verse:** unrimed iambic pentameter. (This pattern is not a stanza: stanzas have more than one line.) Most portions of Shakespeare's plays are in blank verse, and so are Milton's *Paradise Lost*, Tennyson's "Ulysses," certain dramatic monologues of Browning and Frost, and thousands of other poems. Here is a poem in blank verse that startles us by dropping out of its pattern in the final line. Keats appears to have written it late in his life to his fiancée Fanny Brawne.

## THIS LIVING HAND, NOW WARM AND CAPABLE (1819?)

This living hand, now warm and capable
Of earnest grasping, would, if it were cold
And in the icy silence of the tomb,
So haunt thy days and chill thy dreaming nights
That thou wouldst wish thine own heart dry of blood                    5
So in my veins red life might stream again,
And thou be conscience-calmed—see here it is—
I hold it towards you.

The **couplet** is a two-line stanza, usually rimed. Its lines often tend to be equal in length, whether short or long. Here are two examples:

Blow,
Snow!

As I in hoary winter's night stood shivering in the snow,
Surprised I was with sudden heat which made my heart to glow.

Actually, any pair of rimed lines that contains a complete thought is called a couplet, even if it is not a stanza, such as the couplet that ends a sonnet by Shakespeare. Unlike other stanzas, couplets are often printed solid, one couplet not separated from the next by white space. This practice is usual in printing the **heroic couplet**—or **closed couplet**—two rimed lines of iambic pentameter, the first ending in a light pause, the second more heavily end-stopped. George Crabbe, in *The Parish Register*, described a shotgun wedding:

Next at our altar stood a luckless pair,
Brought by strong passions and a warrant there:
By long rent cloak, hung loosely, strove the bride,
From every eye, what all perceived, to hide;
While the boy bridegroom, shuffling in his place,
Now hid awhile and then exposed his face.
As shame alternately with anger strove
The brain confused with muddy ale to move,
In haste and stammering he performed his part,
And looked the rage that rankled in his heart.

Though employed by Chaucer, the heroic couplet was named from its later use by Dryden and others in poems, translations of classical epics, and verse plays of epic heroes. It continued in favor through most of the eighteenth century. Much of our pleasure in reading good heroic couplets comes from the seemingly easy precision with which a skilled poet unites statements and strict pattern. In doing so, the poet may place a pair of words, phrases, clauses, or sentences side by side in agreement or similarity, forming a

**parallel,** or in contrast and opposition, forming an **antithesis.** The effect is neat. For such skill in manipulating parallels and antitheses, John Denham's lines on the river Thames were much admired:

> O could I flow like thee, and make thy stream
> My great example, as it is my theme!
> Though deep, yet clear; though gentle, yet not dull;
> Strong without rage, without o'erflowing full.

These lines were echoed by Pope, ridiculing a poetaster, in two heroic couplets in *The Dunciad*:

> Flow, Welsted, flow! like thine inspirer, Beer:
> Though stale, not ripe; though thin, yet never clear;
> So sweetly mawkish, and so smoothly dull;
> Heady, not strong; o'erflowing, though not full.

Reading long poems in so exact a form, one may feel like a spectator at a ping-pong match unless the poet skillfully keeps varying rhythms. One way of escaping such metronome-like monotony is to keep the cesura (see page 739) shifting about from place to place—now happening early in a line, now happening late—and at times unexpectedly to hurl in a second or third cesura. This skill, among other things, distinguishes the work of Dryden and Pope. If you care to see it in action, try working through Dryden's elegy for Oldham (page 914) or Pope's acid portrait of Atticus (page 742), noticing where the cesuras fall. You'll find that the pauses skip around with lively variety.

A **tercet** is a group of three lines. If rimed, they usually keep to one rime sound, as in this anonymous English children's jingle:

> Julius Caesar,
> The Roman geezer,
> Squashed his wife with a lemon-squeezer.

(That, by the way, is a great demonstration of surprising and unpredictable rimes.) **Terza rima,** the form Dante employs in *The Divine Comedy*, is made of tercets linked together by the rime scheme *a b a, b c b, c d c, d e d, e f e,* and so on. Harder to do in English than in Italian—with its greater resources of riming words—the form nevertheless has been managed by Shelley in "Ode to the West Wind" (with the aid of some slant rimes):

> Make me thy lyre, even as the forest is:
> What if my leaves are falling like its own!
> The tumult of thy mighty harmonies
>
> Will take from both a deep, autumnal tone,
> Sweet though in sadness. Be thou, spirit fierce,
> My spirit! Be thou me, impetuous one!

The workhorse of English poetry is the **quatrain,** a stanza consisting of four lines. Quatrains are used in more rimed poems than any other form.

They come in many line lengths, and sometimes contain lines of varying length, as in the ballad stanza (see page 707). Most often, poets rime the second and fourth lines of quatrains, as in the ballad, but the rimes can occur in any combination the poet chooses. Here are two quatrains from Tennyson's long, elegiac poem, *In Memoriam*. Tennyson's unusual rime scheme, *a b b a*, became so celebrated that this pattern is now called the *"In Memoriam"* stanza:

> Be near me when my light is low,
> > When the blood creeps, and the nerves prick
> > And tingle; and the heart is sick,
> And all the wheels of being slow.
>
> Be near me when the sensuous frame
> > Is rack'd with pangs that conquer trust;
> > And Time, a maniac scattering dust,
> And Life, a Fury slinging flame.

Longer and more complicated stanzas are, of course, possible, but couplet, tercet, and quatrain have been called the building blocks of our poetry because most longer stanzas are made up of them. What short stanzas does John Donne mortar together to make the longer stanza of his "Song"?

### John Donne (1572–1631)*

SONG                                        1633

Go and catch a falling star,
  Get with child a mandrake root,
Tell me where all past years are,
  Or who cleft the Devil's foot,
Teach me to hear mermaids singing,                      5
  Or to keep off envy's stinging,
      And find
      What wind
Serves to advance an honest mind.

If thou be'st borne to strange sights,                  10
  Things invisible to see,
Ride ten thousand days and nights,
  Till age snow white hairs on thee,
Thou, when thou return'st, wilt tell me
  All strange wonders that befell thee,                 15
      And swear
      Nowhere
Lives a woman true, and fair.

If thou findst one, let me know,
  Such a pilgrimage were sweet—                          20

Yet do not, I would not go,
    Though at next door we might meet;
Though she were true, when you met her,
    And last, till you write your letter,
        Yet she                                                    25
        Will be
False, ere I come, to two, or three.

Recently in vogue is a form known as **syllabic verse**, in which the poet establishes a pattern of a certain number of syllables to a line. Either rimed or rimeless but usually stanzaic, syllabic verse has been hailed as a way for poets to escape "the tyranny of the iamb" and discover less conventional rhythms, since, if they take as their line length an *odd* number of syllables, then iambs, being feet of *two* syllables, cannot fit perfectly into it. Offbeat victories have been scored in syllabics by such poets as W. H. Auden, W. D. Snodgrass, Donald Hall, Thom Gunn, and Marianne Moore. A well-known syllabic poem is Dylan Thomas's "Fern Hill" (page 1005). Notice its shape on the page, count the syllables in its lines, and you'll perceive its perfect symmetry. Although like playing a game, the writing of such a poem is apparently more than finger exercise: the discipline can help a poet to sing well, though (with Thomas) singing "in . . . chains like the sea."

Poets who write in demanding forms seem to enjoy taking on an arbitrary task for the fun of it, as ballet dancers do, or weightlifters. Much of our pleasure in reading such poems comes from watching words fall into a shape. It is the pleasure of seeing any hard thing done skillfully—a leap executed in a dance, a basketball swished through a basket. Still, to be excellent, a poem needs more than skill; and to enjoy a poem it isn't always necessary for the reader to be aware of the skill that went into it. Unknowingly, the editors of *The New Yorker* once printed an **acrostic**—a poem in which the initial letter of each line, read downward, spells out a word or words—that named (and insulted) a well-known anthologist. Evidently, besides being ingenious, the acrostic was a printable poem. In the Old Testament book of Lamentations, profoundly moving songs tell of the sufferings of the Jews after the destruction of Jerusalem. Four of the songs are written as an alphabetical acrostic, every stanza beginning with a letter of the Hebrew alphabet. However ingenious, such sublime poetry cannot be dismissed as merely witty; nor can it be charged that a poet who writes in such a form does not express deep feeling.

Patterns of sound and rhythm can, however, be striven after in a dull mechanical way, for which reason many poets today think them dangerous. Swinburne, who loved alliterations and tripping meters, had enough detachment to poke fun at his own excessive patterning:

From the depth of the dreamy decline of the dawn through a notable
    nimbus of nebulous noonshine,
    Pallid and pink as the palm of the flag-flower that flickers with fear
    of the flies as they float,

Are the looks of our lovers that lustrously lean from a marvel of mystic
    miraculous moonshine,
      These that we feel in the blood of our blushes that thicken and
    threaten with throbs through the throat?

This is bad, but bad deliberately. Viewed mechanically, as so many empty
boxes somehow to be filled up, stanzas can impose the most hollow sort of
discipline. If any good at all, a poem in a fixed pattern, such as a sonnet, is
created not only by the craftsman's chipping away at it but by the explosion
of a sonnet-shaped *idea*.

---

## *Ronald Gross* (b. 1935)

YIELD           1967

Yield.
No Parking.
Unlawful to Pass.
Wait for Green Light.
Yield.            5

Stop.
Narrow Bridge.
Merging Traffic Ahead
Yield.

Yield.            10

QUESTIONS

1. This poem by Ronald Gross is a "found poem." After reading it, how would you
   define **found poetry**?
2. Does "Yield" have a theme? If so, how would you state it?
3. What makes "Yield" mean more than traffic signs ordinarily mean to us?

Ronald Gross, who produces his "found poetry" by arranging prose from
such unlikely places as traffic signs and news stories into poem-like lines, has
told of making a discovery:

> As I worked with labels, tax forms, commercials, contracts, pin-up
> captions, obituaries, and the like, I soon found myself rediscovering all
> the traditional verse forms in found materials: ode, sonnet, epigram,
> haiku, free verse. Such finds made me realize that these forms are not
> mere artifices, but shapes that language naturally takes when carrying
> powerful thoughts or feelings.[2]

[2]"Speaking of Books: Found Poetry," *The New York Times Book Review*, June 11, 1967. See also
Gross's *Pop Poems* (New York: Simon, 1967).

Though Gross is a playful experimenter, his remark is true of serious poetry. Traditional verse forms like sonnets and haiku aren't a lot of hollow pillowcases for a poet to stuff with verbiage. At best, in the hands of a skilled poet, they can be shapes into which living language seems to fall naturally.

It is fun to see words tumble gracefully into such a shape. Consider, for instance, one famous "found poem," a sentence discovered in a physics textbook: "And so no force, however great, can stretch a cord, however fine, into a horizontal line which shall be absolutely straight."[3] What a good clear sentence containing effective parallels ("however great . . . however fine"), you might say, taking pleasure in it. Yet this plain statement gives extra pleasure if arranged like this:

> And so no force, however great,
>> Can stretch a cord, however fine,
>> Into a horizontal line
> Which shall be absolutely straight.

So spaced, in lines that reveal its built-in rimes and rhythms, the sentence would seem one of those "shapes that language naturally takes" that Ronald Gross finds everywhere. (It is possible, of course, that the textbook writer was gleefully planting a quatrain for someone to find; but perhaps it is more likely that he knew much rimed, metrical poetry by heart and couldn't help writing it unconsciously.) Inspired by pop artists who reveal fresh vistas in Brillo boxes and comic strips, found poetry has had a recent flurry of activity. Earlier practitioners include William Carlos Williams, whose long poem *Paterson* quotes historical documents and statistics. Prose, wrote Williams, can be a "laboratory" for poetry: "It throws up jewels which may be cleaned and grouped."

### EXPERIMENT: *Finding a Poem*

In a newspaper, magazine, catalogue, textbook, or advertising throwaway, find a sentence or passage that (with a little artistic manipulation on your part) shows promise of becoming a poem. Copy it into lines like poetry, being careful to place what seem to be the most interesting words at the ends of lines to give them greatest emphasis. According to the rules of found poetry, you may excerpt, delete, repeat, and rearrange elements but not add anything. What does this experiment tell you about poetic form? About ordinary prose?

## THE SONNET

When we speak, with Ronald Gross, of "traditional verse forms," we usually mean **fixed forms.** If written in a fixed form a poem inherits from other poems certain familiar elements of structure: an unvarying number of lines, say, or a stanza pattern. In addition, it may display certain **conven-**

[3]William Whewell, *Elementary Treatise on Mechanics* (Cambridge, England, 1819).

tions: expected features such as themes, subjects, attitudes, or figures of speech. In medieval folk ballads a "milk-white steed" is a conventional figure of speech; and if its rider be a cruel and beautiful witch who kidnaps mortals, she is a conventional character. (*Conventional* doesn't necessarily mean uninteresting.)

In the poetry of western Europe and America, the **sonnet** is the fixed form that has attracted for the longest time the largest number of noteworthy practitioners. Originally an Italian form (*sonnetto:* "little song"), the sonnet owes much of its prestige to Petrarch (1304–1374), who wrote in it of his love for the unattainable Laura. So great was the vogue for sonnets in England at the end of the sixteenth century that a gentleman might have been thought a boor if he couldn't turn out a decent one. Not content to adopt merely the sonnet's fourteen-line pattern, English poets also tried on its conventional mask of the tormented lover. They borrowed some of Petrarch's similes (a lover's heart, for instance, is like a storm-tossed boat) and invented others. (If you would like more illustrations of Petrarchan conventions, see Shakespeare's sonnet on page 869.)

Soon after English poets imported the sonnet in the middle of the sixteenth century, they worked out their own rime scheme—one easier for them to follow than Petrarch's, which calls for a greater number of riming words than English can readily provide. (In Italian, according to an exaggerated report, practically everything rimes.) In the following **English sonnet,** sometimes called a **Shakespearean sonnet,** the rimes cohere in four clusters: *a b a b, c d c d, e f e f, g g.* Because a rime scheme tends to shape the poet's statements to it, the English sonnet has three places where the procession of thought is likely to turn in another direction. Within its form, a poet may pursue one idea throughout the three quatrains and then in the couplet end with a surprise.

---

### *Michael Drayton* (1563–1631)

## Since there's no help, come let us kiss and part        1619

Since there's no help, come let us kiss and part;
Nay, I have done, you get no more of me,
And I am glad, yea, glad with all my heart
That thus so cleanly I myself can free;
Shake hands for ever, cancel all our vows,                    5
And when we meet at any time again,
Be it not seen in either of our brows
That we one jot of former love retain.
Now at the last gasp of Love's latest breath,
When, his pulse failing, Passion speechless lies,            10

When Faith is kneeling by his bed of death,
And Innocence is closing up his eyes,
  Now if thou wouldst, when all have given him over,
  From death to life thou mightst him yet recover.

Less frequently met in English poetry, the **Italian sonnet,** or **Petrarchan sonnet,** follows the rime scheme *a b b a, a b b a* in its first eight lines, the **octave,** and then adds new rime sounds in the last six lines, the **sestet.** The sestet may rime *c d c d c d, c d e c d e, c d c c d c,* or in almost any other variation that doesn't end in a couplet. This organization into two parts sometimes helps arrange the poet's thoughts. In the octave, the poet may state a problem, and then, in the sestet, may offer a resolution. A lover, for example, may lament all octave long that a loved one is neglectful, then in line 9 begin to foresee some outcome: the speaker will die, or accept unhappiness, or trust that the beloved will have a change of heart.

### *Elizabeth Barrett Browning* (1806–1861)*

GRIEF                                                              1844

I tell you, hopeless grief is passionless;
  That only men incredulous of despair,
  Half-taught in anguish, through the midnight air
Beat upward to God's throne in loud access
Of shrieking and reproach. Full desertness                        5
  In souls, as countries, lieth silent-bare
  Under the blanching, vertical eye-glare
Of the absolute Heavens. Deep-hearted man, express
Grief for the Dead in silence like to death:
  Most like a monumental statue set                               10
In everlasting watch and moveless woe
Till itself crumble to the dust beneath.
  Touch it: the marble eyelids are not wet—
If it could weep, it could arise and go.

In this Italian sonnet, the division in thought comes a bit early—in the middle of line 8. Few English-speaking poets who have used the form seem to feel strictly bound by it.

"The sonnet," in the view of Robert Bly, a modern critic, "is where old professors go to die." And yet the use of the form by such twentieth-century poets as Yeats, Frost, Auden, Thomas, Pound, Cummings, Berryman, and Lowell suggests that it may be far from exhausted. Like the hero of the popular ballad "Finnegan's Wake," literary forms (though not professors) declared dead have a habit of springing up again. No law compels sonnets to adopt an exalted tone, or confines them to an Elizabethan vocabulary, as this sonnet by a contemporary poet makes clear.

## Thomas Carper (b. 1936)

FACTS                                                                    1991

It is important that a son should know
His role, and should be told the woman's role,
And know it is effeminate to show
Emotion, or the least lapse of control
That might mean caring for another man—                                    5
Even a father. "Never say, 'I love
You,' " I was told. If ever tears began
After an argument, he would reprove
Me mockingly: "Only fags cry." The first
Time that he said this to me, I misheard                                   10
The slangy phrase, but knew my tears were worst
Of possible betrayals. Yet that word
Stays with me, and when my father shall die,
No man will weep because only facts cry.

FACTS. The author, who teaches at the University of Southern Maine, reports that this poem
is based on the experience of a student.

### QUESTIONS

1. What does the father's language reveal about his attitudes on masculinity?
2. How does the son reveal his attitudes? Does he ever state them directly?
3. This sonnet incorporates an abusive slang term. Would the poem be stronger
   without the use of this term? Or does the term add something that more acceptable
   language could not?
4. If this poem discusses differing views of masculinity, what purpose does the title
   "Facts" serve? Does the title add meaning to the poem or merely distract attention
   from its real subject?

When we hear the terms, closed form or fixed form, we imagine traditional poetic forms as a series of immutable rules. But, in the hands of the
best poets, metrical forms are fluid concepts that change to suit the occasion.
Here, for example, is a haunting poem by Robert Frost that simultaneously
fulfills the rules of two traditional forms. Is it an innovative sonnet or a poem
in terza rima? (See page 758 for a discussion of terza rima.) Frost combined
the features of both forms to create a compressed and powerfully lyric poem.

## Robert Frost (1874–1963)*

ACQUAINTED WITH THE NIGHT    1928

I have been one acquainted with the night.
I have walked out in rain—and back in rain.
I have outwalked the furthest city light.

I have looked down the saddest city lane.
I have passed by the watchman on his beat          5
And dropped my eyes, unwilling to explain.

I have stood still and stopped the sound of feet
When far away an interrupted cry
Came over houses from another street,

But not to call me back or say good-bye;          10
And further still at an unearthly height,
One luminary clock against the sky

Proclaimed the time was neither wrong nor right
I have been one acquainted with the night.

EXERCISE: *Knowing Two Kinds of Sonnets*

Find other sonnets in this book. Which are English in form? Which are Italian? Some
poems you might wish to consider are Weldon Kees's "For My Daughter" (page
602), William Wordsworth's "Mutability" (page 648), R. S. Gwynn's "Scenes from
the Playroom" (page 727), and Emma Lazarus's "The New Colossus" (page 878). You
may also wish to try your hand at writing both kinds of sonnet and experience the
difference for yourself.


# EPIGRAMS

Oscar Wilde said that a cynic is "a man who knows the price of everything
and the value of nothing." Such a terse, pointed statement is called an
epigram. In poetry, however, an **epigram** is a form: "A short poem ending
in a witty or ingenious turn of thought, to which the rest of the composition
is intended to lead up" (according to the *Oxford English Dictionary*). Often it
is a malicious gibe with an unexpected stinger in the final line—perhaps in
the very last word:


*Alexander Pope* (1688–1744)*

EPIGRAM ENGRAVED ON THE COLLAR OF A DOG
WHICH I GAVE TO HIS ROYAL HIGHNESS          1738

I am his Highness' dog at Kew;
Pray tell me, sir, whose dog are you?

Cultivated by the Roman poet Martial—for whom the epigram was a
short poem, sometimes satiric but not always—this form has been especially
favored by English poets who love Latin. Few characteristics of the English
epigram seem fixed. Its pattern tends to be brief and rimed, its tone playfully
merciless.

## Martial (A.D. 40?–102?)

### READERS AND LISTENERS PRAISE MY BOOKS          A.D. 90

Readers and listeners praise my books;
You swear they're worse than a beginner's.
Who cares? I always plan my dinners
To please the diners, not the cooks.
                              —Translated by R. L. Barth


## Sir John Harrington (1561?–1612)

### OF TREASON                              1618

Treason doth never prosper; what's the reason?
For if it prosper, none dare call it treason.


## William Blake (1757–1827)*

### HER WHOLE LIFE IS AN EPIGRAM          (1793)

Her whole life is an epigram: smack smooth°, and          *perfectly smooth*
          neatly penned,
Platted° quite neat to catch applause, with a sliding          *plaited, woven*
          noose at the end.


## E. E. Cummings (1894–1962)*

### A POLITICIAN                      1944

a politician is an arse upon
which everyone has sat except a man


## Langston Hughes (1902–1967)*

### GREEN MEMORY                1951

A wonderful time—the War:
when money rolled in
and blood rolled out.

But blood
was far away
from here—

Money was near.

## *J. V. Cunningham* (1911–1985)*

THIS *HUMANIST* WHOM NO BELIEFS CONSTRAINED          1947

This *Humanist* whom no beliefs constrained
Grew so broad-minded he was scatter-brained.

## *John Frederick Nims* (b. 1913)*

CONTEMPLATION                                        1967

"I'm Mark's alone!" you swore. Given cause to doubt you,
I think less of you, dear. But more about you.

## *Stevie Smith* (1902–1971)*

THIS ENGLISHWOMAN          1937

This Englishwoman is so refined
She has no bosom and no behind.

## *Thom Gunn* (b. 1929)

JAMESIAN          1992

Their relationship consisted
In discussing if it existed.

## *Bruce Bennett* (b. 1940)

IRONIST                    1987

I mean the opposite of what I say.
You've got it now? No, it's the other way.

## Hilaire Belloc (1870–1956)

### FATIGUE                                            1923

I'm tired of Love: I'm still more tired of Rhyme.
But Money gives me pleasure all the time.

## Wendy Cope (b. 1945)*

### VARIATION ON BELLOC'S "FATIGUE"          1992

I hardly ever tire of love or rhyme—
That's why I'm poor and have a rotten time.

### EXPERIMENT: *Expanding an Epigram*

Rewrite any of the preceding epigrams, taking them out of rime (if they are in rime)
and adding a few more words to them. See if your revisions have nearly the same
effect as the originals.

### EXERCISE: *Reading for Couplets*

Read all the sonnets by Shakespeare in this book. How do the final couplets of some
of them resemble epigrams? Does this similarity diminish their effect of "seriousness"?

In English the only other fixed form to rival the sonnet and the epigram
in favor is the **limerick:** five anapestic lines usually riming *a a b b a*. Here is
a sample, attributed to W. R. Inge (1860–1954):

> There was an old man of Khartoum
> Who kept a tame sheep in his room,
>     "To remind me," he said,
>     "Of someone who's dead,
> But I never can recollect whom."

The limerick was made popular by Edward Lear (1812–1888), English
painter and author of nonsense, whose own custom was to make the last line
hark back to the first: "That oppressive old man of Khartoum."

### EXPERIMENT: *Contriving a Clerihew*

The **clerihew,** a fixed form named for its inventor, Edmund Clerihew Bentley (1875–
1956), has straggled behind the limerick in popularity. Here are three examples: how
would you define the form and what are its rules? Who or what is its conventional
subject matter? Try writing your own example.

James Watt
Was the hard-boiled kind of Scot:

He thought any dream
Sheer waste of steam.
—W. H. Auden

Sir Christopher Wren
Said, "I am going to dine with some men.
If anybody calls
Say I am designing St. Paul's."
—Edmund Clerihew Bentley

Etienne de Silhouette
(It's a good bet)
Has the shadiest claim
To fame.
—Cornelius J. Ter Maat

## *Keith Waldrop* (b. 1932)*

PROPOSITION II                          1975

Each grain of sand has an architecture, but
a desert displays the structure of the wind.

QUESTIONS
1. How is this poem like an epigram?
2. How is it dissimilar?

## OTHER FORMS

There are many other verse forms used in English. Some forms, like the villanelle and sestina (discussed below), come from other European literatures. But English has borrowed fixed forms from an astonishing variety of sources. The rubaiyat stanza (see page 847), for instance, comes from Persian poetry; the haiku (see page 668) and tanka originated in Japan. Other borrowed forms include the ghazal (Arabic), pantoum (Malay), and sapphics (Greek). Even blank verse (see page 756), which seems as English as the Royal Family, began as an attempt by Elizabethan poets to copy an Italian eleven syllable line. To conclude this chapter, here are poems in four widely used closed forms—the villanelle, rondeau, triolet, and sestina. Their patterns, which are sometimes called "French forms," have been particularly fascinating to English-language poets because they do not merely require the repetition of rime sounds; instead, they demand more elaborate echoing, involving the repetition of either full words or whole lines of verse. Sometimes difficult to master, these forms can create a powerful musical effect unlike ordinary riming.

## Dylan Thomas (1914–1953)*

DO NOT GO GENTLE INTO THAT GOOD NIGHT          1952

Do not go gentle into that good night,
Old age should burn and rave at close of day;
Rage, rage against the dying of the light.

Though wise men at their end know dark is right,
Because their words had forked no lightning they          5
Do not go gentle into that good night.

Good men, the last wave by, crying how bright
Their frail deeds might have danced in a green bay,
Rage, rage against the dying of the light.

Wild men who caught and sang the sun in flight,          10
And learn, too late, they grieved it on its way,
Do not go gentle into that good night.

Grave men, near death, who see with blinding sight
Blind eyes could blaze like meteors and be gay,
Rage, rage against the dying of the light.          15

And you, my father, there on the sad height,
Curse, bless, me now with your fierce tears, I pray,
Do not go gentle into that good night.
Rage, rage against the dying of the light.

### QUESTIONS

1. "Do not go gentle into that good night" is a **villanelle:** a fixed form originated by French courtly poets of the Middle Ages. What are its rules?
2. Whom does the poem address? What is the speaker saying?
3. Villanelles are sometimes criticized as elaborate exercises in trivial wordplay. How would you defend Thomas's poem against this charge?

## Leigh Hunt (1784–1859)

RONDEAU          1838

Jenny kissed me when we met,
    Jumping from the chair she sat in;
Time, you thief, who love to get
    Sweets into your list, put that in:
Say I'm weary, say I'm sad,          5
    Say that health and wealth have missed me,
Say I'm growing old, but add,
    Jenny kissed me.

Here is a fresh contemporary version of Hunt's "Rondeau" that yanks open the form of the rimed original:

Jenny kissed me when we met,
jumping from her chair;
Time, you thief, who love to add
sweets into your list, put that in:
say I'm weary, say I'm sad,
say I'm poor and in ill health,
say I'm growing old—but note, too,
Jenny kissed me.

That revised version says approximately the same thing as Hunt's original, doesn't it? Why is it less effective?

## *Robert Bridges* (1844–1930)

### TRIOLET                                            1879

When first we met we did not guess
That Love would prove so hard a master;
Of more than common friendliness
When first we met we did not guess.
Who could foretell this sore distress,                    5
This irretrievable disaster
When first we met—We did not guess
That Love would prove so hard a master.

TRIOLET. The triolet is a short lyric form borrowed from the French; its two opening lines are repeated according to a set pattern, as Bridges's poem illustrates. The triolet is often used for light verse, but Bridges's poem demonstrates how it can carry heavier emotional loads, if used with sufficient skill.

QUESTION

How do the first two lines change in meaning when they reappear at the end of the poem?

## *Elizabeth Bishop* (1911–1979)*

### SESTINA                                            1965

September rain falls on the house.
In the failing light, the old grandmother
sits in the kitchen with the child
beside the Little Marvel Stove,
reading the jokes from the almanac,                    5
laughing and talking to hide her tears.

She thinks that her equinoctial tears
and the rain that beats on the roof of the house
were both foretold by the almanac,
but only known to a grandmother.                                    10
The iron kettle sings on the stove.
She cuts some bread and says to the child,

*It's time for tea now*; but the child
is watching the teakettle's small hard tears
dance like mad on the hot black stove,                              15
the way the rain must dance on the house.
Tidying up, the old grandmother
hangs up the clever almanac

on its string. Birdlike, the almanac
hovers half open above the child,                                   20
hovers above the old grandmother
and her teacup full of dark brown tears.
She shivers and says she thinks the house
feels chilly, and puts more wood in the stove.

*It was to be*, says the Marvel Stove.                              25
*I know what I know*, says the almanac.
With crayons the child draws a rigid house
and a winding pathway. Then the child
puts in a man with buttons like tears
and shows it proudly to the grandmother.                            30

But secretly, while the grandmother
busies herself about the stove,
the little moons fall down like tears
from between the pages of the almanac
into the flower bed the child                                       35
has carefully placed in the front of the house.

*Time to plant tears*, says the almanac.
The grandmother sings to the marvellous stove
and the child draws another inscrutable house.

SESTINA. As its title indicates, this poem is written in the trickiest of medieval fixed forms, that
of the **sestina** (or "song of sixes"), said to have been invented in Provence in the thirteenth
century by the troubadour poet Arnaut Daniel. In six six-line stanzas, the poet repeats six
end-words (in a prescribed order), then reintroduces the six repeated words (in any order) in a
closing **envoy** of three lines. Elizabeth Bishop strictly follows the troubadour rules for the order
in which the end-words recur. (If you care, you can figure out the formula: in the first stanza,
the six words are arranged A B C D E F; in the second, F A E B D C; and so on.) Notable
sestinas in English have been written also by Sir Philip Sidney, Algernon Charles Swinburne,
and Rudyard Kipling, more recently by Ezra Pound ("Sestina: Altaforte"), by W. H. Auden
("Hearing of Harvests Rotting in the Valleys" and others), and by contemporary poets, among
them John Ashbery, Tom Disch, Marilyn Hacker, Michael Heffernan, Donald Justice, Peter
Klappert, William Meredith, Howard Nemerov, John Frederick Nims, Robert Pack, Henry
Taylor, and Mona Van Duyn.

## QUESTIONS

1. A perceptive comment from a student: "Something seems to be going on here that the child doesn't understand. Maybe some terrible loss has happened." Test this guess by reading the poem closely.
2. Then consider this possibility. We don't know that "Sestina" is autobiographical; still, does any information about the poet's early life contribute to your reading of the poem? (See "Lives of the Poets," page 1038).
3. In the "little moons" that fall from the almanac (line 33), does the poem introduce dream or fantasy, or do you take these to be small round pieces of paper?
4. What is the tone of this poem—the speaker's apparent attitude toward the scene described?
5. In an essay, "The Sestina," in *A Local Habitation* (U of Michigan P, 1985), John Frederick Nims defends the form against an obvious complaint against it:

   A shallow view of the sestina might suggest that the poet writes a stanza, and then is stuck with six words which he has to juggle into the required positions through five more stanzas and an envoy—to the great detriment of what passion and sincerity would have him say. But in a good sestina the poet has six words, six images, six ideas so urgently in his mind that he cannot get away from them; he wants to test them in all possible combinations and come to a conclusion about their relationship.

   How well does this description of a good sestina fit "Sestina"?

## EXPERIMENT: *Urgent Repetition*

Write a sestina and see what you find out by doing so. (Even if you fail in the attempt, you just might learn something interesting.) To start, pick six words you think worth repeating six times. This elaborate pattern gives you much help: as John Ashbery has pointed out, writing a sestina is "like riding downhill on a bicycle and having the pedals push your feet." Here is some encouragement from a poet and critic, John Heath-Stubbs: "I have never read a sestina that seemed to me a total failure."

## SUGGESTIONS FOR WRITING

1. William Carlos Williams, in an interview, delivered this blast:

   Forcing twentieth-century America into a sonnet—gosh, how I hate sonnets—is like putting a crab into a square box. You've got to cut his legs off to make him fit. When you get through, you don't have a crab any more.

   In a two-page essay, defend the modern American sonnet against Williams's charge. Or instead, open fire on it, using Williams's view for ammunition. Some sonnets to consider: R. S. Gwynn's "Scenes from the Playroom" (page 727), Gwendolyn Brooks's "The Rites for Cousin Vit" (page 901), and Archibald MacLeish's "The End of the World" (page 956).
2. Write an unserious argument for or against the abolition of limericks. Give illustrations of limericks you think worthy of abolition (or preservation).
3. Compare Dylan Thomas's "Do not go gentle into that good night" with Wendy Cope's "Lonely Hearts" (page 643). Discuss how it is possible for the same form to be used to create such different kinds of poem.

# 23 Open Form

Writing in **open form**, a poet seeks to discover a fresh and individual arrangement for words in every poem. Such a poem, generally speaking, has neither a rime scheme nor a basic meter informing the whole of it. Doing without those powerful (some would say hypnotic) elements, the poet who writes in open form relies on other means to engage and to sustain the reader's attention. Novice poets often think that open form looks easy, not nearly so hard as riming everything; but in truth, formally open poems are easy to write only if written carelessly. To compose lines with keen awareness of open form's demands, and of its infinite possibilities, calls for skill: at least as much as that needed to write in meter and rime, if not more. Should the poet succeed, then the discovered arrangement will seem exactly right for what the poem is saying. Words will seem at home in their positions, as naturally as the words of a decent sonnet.

## *Denise Levertov* (b. 1923)*

### Six Variations (part iii)          1961

Shlup, shlup, the dog
as it laps up
water
makes intelligent
music, resting                                                 5
now and then to take breath in irregular
measure.

Open form, in this brief poem, affords Denise Levertov certain advantages. Able to break off a line at whatever point she likes (a privilege not available to the poet writing, say, a conventional sonnet, who has to break off each line after its tenth syllable), she selects her pauses artfully. Line-breaks lend emphasis: a word or phrase at the end of a line takes a little more stress (and receives a little more attention), because the ending of the line compels the reader to make a slight pause, if only for the brief moment it takes to sling back one's eyes (like a typewriter carriage) and fix them on the line following. Slight pauses, then, follow the words and phrases *the dog | laps up | water | intelligent | resting | irregular | measure*—all of these being elements that apparently the poet wishes to call our attention to. (The pause after a line-break also casts a little more weight upon the *first* word or phrase of each succeeding line.) Levertov makes the most of white space—another means of calling attention to things, as any good picture-framer knows. By setting a word all alone on a line *(water | measure)*, she makes it stand out more than it would do in a line of pentameter. She feels free to include a bit of rime *(Shlup, shlup | up)*. She creates rhythms: if you will read aloud the phrases *intelligent | music* and *irregular | measure*, you will sense that in each phrase the arrangement of pauses and stresses is identical. Like the dog's halts to take breath, the lengths of the lines seem naturally irregular. The result is a fusion of meaning and form: indeed, an "intelligent music."

Poetry in open form used to be called **free verse** (from the French ***vers libre***), suggesting a kind of verse liberated from the shackles of rime and meter. "Writing free verse," said Robert Frost, who wasn't interested in it, "is like playing tennis with the net down." And yet, as Denise Levertov and many other poets demonstrate, high scores can be made in such an unconventional game, provided it doesn't straggle all over the court. For a successful poem in open form, the term *free verse* seems inaccurate. "Being an art form," said William Carlos Williams, "verse cannot be 'free' in the sense of having *no* limitations or guiding principles."[1] Various substitute names have been suggested: organic poetry, composition by field, raw (as against cooked) poetry, open form poetry. "But what does it matter what you call it?" remark the editors of an anthology called *Naked Poetry*. The best poems of the last twenty years "don't rhyme (usually) and don't move on feet of more or less equal duration (usually). That nondescription moves toward the only technical principle they all have in common."[2]

And yet many poems in open form have much more in common than absences and lacks. One positive principle has been Ezra Pound's famous suggestion that poets "compose in the sequence of the musical phrase, not in the sequence of the metronome"—good advice, perhaps, even for poets who write inside fixed forms. In Charles Olson's influential theory of **projec-**

[1] "Free Verse," article in *Princeton Encyclopedia of Poetry and Poetics*.
[2] Stephen Berg and Robert Mezey, eds., foreword to *Naked Poetry: Recent American Poetry in Open Forms* (Indianapolis: Bobbs, 1969).

**tive verse**, poets compose by listening to their own breathing. On paper, they indicate the rhythms of a poem by using a little white space or a lot, a slight indentation or a deep one, depending on whether a short pause or a long one is intended. Words can be grouped in clusters on the page (usually no more words than a lungful of air can accommodate). Heavy cesuras are sometimes shown by breaking a line in two and lowering the second part of it.[3] (An Olson poem appears on page 795.)

To the poet working in open form, no less than to the poet writing a sonnet, line length can be valuable. Walt Whitman, who loved to expand vast sentences for line after line, knew well that an impressive rhythm can accumulate if the poet will keep long lines approximately the same length, causing a pause to recur at about the same interval after every line. Sometimes, too, Whitman repeats the same words at each line's opening. An instance is the masterly sixth section of "When Lilacs Last in the Dooryard Bloom'd," an elegy for Abraham Lincoln:

> Coffin that passes through lanes and streets,
> Through day and night with the great cloud darkening the land,
> With the pomp of the inloop'd flags with the cities draped in black,
> With the show of the States themselves as of crape-veil'd women
>     standing,
> With processions long and winding and the flambeaus of the night,
> With the countless torches lit, with the silent sea of faces and the
>     unbared heads,
> With the waiting depot, the arriving coffin, and the somber faces,
> With dirges through the night, with the thousand voices rising strong
>     and solemn,
> With all the mournful voices of the dirges pour'd around the coffin,
> The dim-lit churches and the shuddering organs—where amid these
>     you journey,
> With the tolling tolling bells' perpetual clang,
> Here, coffin that slowly passes,
> I give you my sprig of lilac.

There is music in such solemn, operatic arias. Whitman's lines echo another model: the Hebrew **psalms**, or sacred songs, as translated in the King James Version of the Bible. In Psalm 150, repetition also occurs inside of lines:

> Praise ye the Lord. Praise God in his sanctuary: praise him in the
> firmament of his power.
>     Praise him for his mighty acts: praise him according to his excellent
> greatness.

[3]See Olson's essays "Projective Verse" and "Letter to Elaine Feinstein" in *Selected Writings*, edited by Robert Creeley (New York: New Directions, 1966). Olson's letters to Cid Corman are fascinating: *Letters for Origin, 1950–1955*, edited by Albert Glover (New York: Grossman, 1970).

Praise him with the sound of the trumpet: praise him with the psaltery and harp.

Praise him with the timbrel and dance: praise him with stringed instruments and organs.

Praise him upon the loud cymbals: praise him upon the high sounding cymbals.

Let every thing that hath breath praise the Lord. Praise ye the Lord.

In Biblical Psalms, we are in the presence of (as Robert Lowell has said) "supreme poems, written when their translators merely intended prose and were forced by the structure of their originals to write poetry."[4]

Whitman was a more deliberate craftsman than he let his readers think, and to anyone interested in writing in open form, his work will repay close study. He knew that repetitions of any kind often make memorable rhythms, as in this passage from "Song of Myself," with every line ending on an *-ing* word (a stressed syllable followed by an unstressed syllable):

> Here and there with dimes on the eyes walking,
> To feed the greed of the belly the brains liberally spooning,
> Tickets buying, taking, selling, but in to the feast never once going,
> Many sweating, ploughing, thrashing, and then the chaff for payment
>     receiving,
> A few idly owning, and they the wheat continually claiming.

Much more than simply repetition, of course, went into the music of those lines—the internal rime *feed, greed,* the use of assonance, the trochees that begin the third and fourth lines, whether or not they were calculated.

In such classics of open form poetry, sound and rhythm are positive forces. When speaking a poem in open form, you often may find that it makes a difference for the better if you pause at the end of each line. Try pausing there, however briefly; but don't allow your voice to drop. Read just as you would normally read a sentence in prose (except for the pauses, of course). Why do the pauses matter? Open form poetry usually has no meter to lend it rhythm. *Some* lines in an open form poem, as we have seen in Whitman's "dimes on the eyes" passage, do fall into metrical feet; sometimes the whole poem does. Usually lacking meter's aid, however, open form, in order to have more and more noticeable rhythms, has need of all the recurring pauses it can get. When reading their own work aloud, open form poets like Robert Creeley and Allen Ginsberg often pause very definitely at each line break. Such a habit makes sense only in reading artful poems.

Some poems, to be sure, seem more widely open in form than others. A poet, for instance, may employ rime, but have the rimes recur at various

---

[4]"On Freedom in Poetry," in Berg and Mezey, *Naked Poetry.*

intervals; or perhaps rime lines of various lengths. (See T. S. Eliot's famous "Love Song of J. Alfred Prufrock" on page 916. Is it a closed poem left ajar or an open poem trying to slam itself?) No law requires a poet to split thoughts into verse lines at all. Charles Baudelaire, Rainer Maria Rilke, Jorge Luis Borges, Alexander Solzhenitsyn, T. S. Eliot, and many others have written **prose poems**, in which, without caring that eye appeal and some of the rhythm of a line structure may be lost, the poet prints words in a block like a prose paragraph. For an example see Karl Shapiro's "The Dirty Word" (page 993).[5]

"Farewell, stale pale skunky pentameters (the only honest English meter, gloop! gloop!)," Kenneth Koch has exulted, suggesting that it was high time to junk such stale conventions. Many poets who agree with him believe that it is wrong to fit words into any pattern that already exists, and instead believe in letting a poem seek its own shape as it goes along. (Traditionalists might say that that is what all good poems do anyway: sonnets rarely know they are going to be sonnets until the third line has been written. However, there is no doubt that the sonnet form already exists, at least in the back of the head of any poet who has ever read sonnets.) Some open form poets offer a historical motive: they want to reflect the nervous, staccato, disconnected pace of our bumper-to-bumper society. Others see open form as an attempt to suit thoughts and words to a more spontaneous order than the traditional verse forms allow. "Better," says Gary Snyder, quoting from Zen, "the perfect, easy discipline of the swallow's dip and swoop, 'without east or west.' "[6]

At the moment, much exciting new poetry is being written in both open form and closed. Today, many younger poets (labeled New Formalists) have taken up rime and meter and have been writing sonnets, epigrams, and poems in rimed stanzas, giving "pale skunky pentameters" a fresh lease on life.[7]

---

### E. E. Cummings (1894–1962)*

BUFFALO BILL 'S      1923

Buffalo Bill 's
defunct

[5]For more examples see *The Prose Poem, An International Anthology*, edited by Michael Benedikt (New York: Dell, 1976).
[6]"Some Yips & Barks in the Dark," in Berg and Mezey, *Naked Poetry*.
[7]For more samples of recent formal poetry than this book provides, see *The Direction of Poetry* ed. Robert Richman (Boston: Houghton, 1988), *Ecstatic Occasions, Expedient Forms* ed. David Lehman (New York: Collier, 1987), and *Strong Measures: Contemporary American Poetry in Traditional Forms* ed. Philip Dacey and David Jauss (New York: Harper, 1986).

who used to
ride a watersmooth-silver
                                        stallion                              5
and break onetwothreefourfive pigeonsjustlikethat
                                                    Jesus
he was a handsome man
                        and what i want to know is
how do you like your blueeyed boy                                            10
Mister Death

## QUESTION

Cummings's poem would look like this if given conventional punctuation and set in a solid block like prose:

Buffalo Bill's defunct, who used to ride a water-smooth silver stallion and break one, two, three, four, five pigeons just like that. Jesus, he was a handsome man. And what I want to know is: "How do you like your blue-eyed boy, Mister Death?"

If this were done, by what characteristics would it still be recognizable as poetry? But what would be lost?

## *Emily Dickinson* (1830–1886)*

### VICTORY COMES LATE                    (1861)

Victory comes late—
And is held low to freezing lips—
Too rapt with frost
To take it—
How sweet it would have tasted—                                5
Just a Drop—
Was God so economical?
His Table's spread too high for Us—
Unless We dine on tiptoe—
Crumbs—fit such little mouths—                                10
Cherries—suit Robins—
The Eagle's Golden Breakfast strangles—Them—
God keep His Oath to Sparrows—
Who of little Love—know how to starve—

## QUESTIONS

1. In this specimen of poetry in open form, can you see any other places at which the poet might have broken off any of her lines? To place a word last in a line gives it a greater emphasis; she might, for instance, have ended line 12 with *Breakfast* and begun a new line with the word *strangles*. Do you think she

knows what she is doing here or does the pattern of this poem seem decided by whim? Discuss.

2. Read the poem aloud. Try pausing for a fraction of a second at every dash. Is there any justification for the poet's unorthodox punctuation?

DETAIL, "THE KERMESS" OR "PEASANT DANCE" by Pieter Breughel (1520?–1569)

## *William Carlos Williams* (1883–1963)*

### THE DANCE                                    1944

In Breughel's great picture, The Kermess,
the dancers go round, they go round and
around, the squeal and the blare and the
tweedle of bagpipes, a bugle and fiddles
tipping their bellies (round as the thick-                5
sided glasses whose wash they impound)
their hips and their bellies off balance
to turn them. Kicking and rolling about
the Fair Grounds, swinging their butts, those
shanks must be sound to bear up under such       10
rollicking measures, prance as they dance
in Breughel's great picture, The Kermess.

THE DANCE. Breughel, a Flemish painter known for his scenes of peasant activities, represented in "The Kermess" a celebration on the feast day of a local patron saint.

1. Scan this poem and try to describe the effect of its rhythms.
2. Williams, widely admired for his free verse, insisted for many years that what he sought was a form not in the least bit free. What effect does he achieve by ending lines on such weak words as the articles *and* and *the?* By splitting *thick- / sided?* By splitting a prepositional phrase with the break at the end of line 8? By using line breaks to split *those* and *such* from what they modify? What do you think he is trying to convey?
3. Is there any point in his making line 12 a repetition of the opening line?
4. Look at the reproduction of Breughel's painting "The Kermess" (also called "Peasants Dancing"). Aware that the rhythms of dancers, the rhythms of a painting, and the rhythms of a poem are not all the same, can you put in your own words what Breughel's dancing figures have in common with Williams's descriptions of them?
5. Compare with "The Dance" another poem that refers to a Breughel painting: W. H. Auden's "Musée des Beaux Arts" on page 895. What seems to be each poet's main concern: to convey in words a sense of the painting, or to visualize the painting in order to state some theme?

## *Stephen Crane* (1871–1900)

THE HEART                    1895

In the desert
I saw a creature, naked, bestial,
Who, squatting upon the ground,
Held his heart in his hands,
And ate of it.                                                                5

I said, "Is it good, friend?"
"It is bitter—bitter," he answered;
"But I like it
Because it is bitter,
And because it is my heart."                                            10

## *Walt Whitman* (1819–1892)*

CAVALRY CROSSING A FORD                                            (1865)

A line in long array where they wind betwixt green islands,
They take a serpentine course, their arms flash in the sun—hark to
    the musical clank,
Behold the silvery river, in it the splashing horses loitering stop to
    drink,
Behold the brown-faced men, each group, each person a picture, the
    negligent rest on the saddles,

Some emerge on the opposite bank, others are just entering
    the ford—while,                                            5
Scarlet and blue and snowy white,
The guidon flags flutter gayly in the wind.

## QUESTIONS

The following nit-picking questions are intended to help you see exactly what makes
these two open form poems by Crane and Whitman so different in their music.

1. What devices of sound occur in Whitman's phrase *silvery river* (line 3)? Where else
   in his poem do you find these devices?
2. Does Crane use any such devices?
3. In number of syllables, Whitman's poem is almost twice as long as Crane's.
   Which poem has more pauses in it? (Count pauses at the ends of lines, at marks
   of punctuation.)
4. Read the two poems aloud. In general, how would you describe the effect of their
   sounds and rhythms? Is Crane's poem necessarily an inferior poem for having less
   music?

## *Wallace Stevens* (1879–1955)*

## THIRTEEN WAYS OF LOOKING AT A BLACKBIRD      1923

*I*

Among twenty snowy mountains,
The only moving thing
Was the eye of the blackbird.

*II*

I was of three minds,
Like a tree                                           5
In which there are three blackbirds.

*III*

The blackbird whirled in the autumn winds.
It was a small part of the pantomime.

*IV*

A man and a woman
Are one.                                              10
A man and a woman and a blackbird
Are one.

V

I do not know which to prefer,
The beauty of inflections
Or the beauty of innuendoes,                                    15
The blackbird whistling
Or just after.


VI

Icicles filled the long window
With barbaric glass.
The shadow of the blackbird                                     20
Crossed it, to and fro.
The mood
Traced in the shadow
An indecipherable cause.


VII

O thin men of Haddam,                                          25
Why do you imagine golden birds?
Do you not see how the blackbird
Walks around the feet
Of the women about you?


VIII

I know noble accents                                           30
And lucid, inescapable rhythms;
But I know, too,
That the blackbird is involved
In what I know.


IX

When the blackbird flew out of sight,                          35
It marked the edge
Of one of many circles.


X

At the sight of blackbirds
Flying in a green light,
Even the bawds of euphony                                      40
Would cry out sharply.

## XI

He rode over Connecticut
In a glass coach.
Once, a fear pierced him,
In that he mistook                                                              45
The shadow of his equipage
For blackbirds.

## XII

The river is moving.
The blackbird must be flying.

## XIII

It was evening all afternoon.                                                   50
It was snowing
And it was going to snow.
The blackbird sat
In the cedar-limbs.

THIRTEEN WAYS OF LOOKING AT A BLACKBIRD. 25 *Haddam:* This Biblical-sounding name is that
of a town in Connecticut.

## QUESTIONS

1. What is the speaker's attitude toward the men of Haddam? What attitude toward
   this world does he suggest they lack? What is implied by calling them *thin* (line 25)?
2. What do the landscapes of winter contribute to the poem's effectiveness? If
   Stevens had chosen images of summer lawns, what would have been lost?
3. In which sections of the poem does Stevens suggest that a unity exists between
   human being and blackbird, between blackbird and the entire natural world? Can
   we say that Stevens "philosophizes"? What role does imagery play in Stevens's
   statement of his ideas?
4. What sense can you make of Part X? Make an enlightened guess.
5. Consider any one of the thirteen parts. What patterns of sound and rhythm do
   you find in it? What kind of structure does it have?
6. If the thirteen parts were arranged in some different order, would the poem be just
   as good? Or can we find a justification for its beginning with Part I and ending with
   Part XIII?
7. Does the poem seem an arbitrary combination of thirteen separate poems? Or is
   there any reason to call it a whole?

### *Gary Gildner* (b. 1938)

## FIRST PRACTICE                    1969

After the doctor checked to see
we weren't ruptured,

the man with the short cigar took us
under the grade school,
where we went in case of attack                                    5
or storm, and said
he was Clifford Hill, he was
a man who believed dogs
ate dogs, he had once killed
for his country, and if                                            10
there were any girls present
for them to leave now.
                         No one
left. OK, he said, he said I take
that to mean you are hungry
men who hate to lose as much                                       15
as I do. OK. Then
he made two lines of us
facing each other,
and across the way, he said,
is the man you hate most                                           20
in the world,
and if we are to win
that title I want to see how.
But I don't want to see
any marks when you're dressed,                                     25
he said. He said, *Now.*

## Questions

1. What do you make of Hill and his world-view?
2. How does the speaker reveal his own view? Why, instead of quoting Hill directly
   ("This is a dog-eat-dog world"), does he call him *a man who believed dogs ate dogs*
   (lines 8–9)?
3. What effect is made by breaking off and lowering *No one* at the end of line 12?
4. What is gained by having a rime on the poem's last word?
5. For the sake of understanding how right the form of Gildner's poem is for it,
   imagine the poem in meter and a rime scheme, and condensed into two stanzas:

   Then he made two facing lines of us
   And he said, Across the way,
   Of all the men there are in the world
   Is the man you most want to slay,

   And if we are to win that title, he said,
   I want you to show me how.
   But I don't want to see any marks when you're dressed,
   He said. Go get him. *Now.*

   Why would that rewrite be so unfaithful to what Gildner is saying?
6. How would you answer someone who argued, "This can't be a poem—its subject
   is ugly and its language isn't beautiful"?

*Carolyn Forché* (b. 1950)

THE COLONEL                                                    1982

What you have heard is true. I was in his house. His wife carried a tray
of coffee and sugar. His daughter filed her nails, his son went out for
the night. There were daily papers, pet dogs, a pistol on the cushion
beside him. The moon swung bare on its black cord over the house. On
the television was a cop show. It was in English. Broken bottles were
embedded in the walls around the house to scoop the kneecaps from
a man's legs or cut his hands to lace. On the windows there were
gratings like those in liquor stores. We had dinner, rack of lamb, good
wine, a gold bell was on the table for calling the maid. The maid
brought green mangoes, salt, a type of bread. I was asked how I enjoyed
the country. There was a brief commercial in Spanish. His wife took
everything away. There was some talk then of how difficult it had
become to govern. The parrot said hello on the terrace. The colonel
told it to shut up, and pushed himself from the table. My friend said
to me with his eyes: say nothing. The colonel returned with a sack used
to bring groceries home. He spilled many human ears on the table.
They were like dried peach halves. There is no other way to say this.
He took one of them in his hands, shook it in our faces, dropped it into
a water glass. It came alive there. I am tired of fooling around he said.
As for the rights of anyone, tell your people they can go fuck themselves. He swept the ears to the floor with his arm and held the last of
his wine in the air. Something for your poetry, no? he said. Some of the
ears on the floor caught this scrap of his voice. Some of the ears on the
floor were pressed to the ground.

                                                          *May 1978*


QUESTIONS

1. Should we consider "The Colonel" a prose poem or a very short piece of prose?
   If it is poetry, what features distinguish it from prose? If it should be considered
   prose, what essential features of poetry does it lack?
2. Forché begins "The Colonel" by saying "What you have heard is true." Who is
   the *you*? Does she assume a specific person?
3. Should we believe that this story is true? If so, what leads us to believe its veracity?
4. Why does the author end "The Colonel" by giving a date?


VISUAL POETRY

Let's look at a famous poem with a distinctive visible shape. In the seventeenth century, ingenious poets trimmed their lines into the silhouettes of
altars and crosses, pillars and pyramids. Here is one. Is it anything more than
a demonstration of ingenuity?

## George Herbert (1593–1633)*

### EASTER WINGS                                           1633

Lord, who createdst man in wealth and store,
  Though foolishly he lost the same,
    Decaying more and more
      Till he became
        Most poor;
        With thee
      Oh, let me rise
    As larks, harmoniously,
  And sing this day thy victories;
Then shall the fall further the flight in me.

My tender age in sorrow did begin;
  And still with sicknesses and shame
    Thou didst so punish sin,
      That I became
        Most thin.
        With thee
      Let me combine,
    And feel this day thy victory;
  For if I imp my wing on thine,
Affliction shall advance the flight in me.

In the next-to-last line, *imp* is a term from falconry meaning to repair the wing of an injured bird by grafting feathers into it.

If we see it merely as a picture, we will have to admit that Herbert's word design does not go far. It renders with difficulty shapes that a sketcher's pencil could set down in a flash, in more detail, more accurately. Was Herbert's effort wasted? It might have been, were there not more to his poem than meets the eye. The mind, too, is engaged by the visual pattern, by the realization that the words *most thin* are given emphasis by their narrow form. Here, visual pattern points out meaning. Heard aloud, too, "Easter Wings" gives further pleasure. Its rimes, its rhythm are perceptible.

Ever since George Herbert's day, poets have continued to experiment with the looks of printed poetry. Notable efforts to entertain the eye are Lewis Carroll's rimed mouse's tail in *Alice in Wonderland*; and the *Calligrammes* of Guillaume Apollinaire, who arranged words in the shapes of a necktie, of the Eiffel Tower, of spears of falling rain. Here is a bird-shaped poem of more recent inspiration than Herbert's. What does its visual form have to do with what the poet is saying?

*John Hollander* (b. 1929)

Swan and Shadow                                                                 1969

<pre>
                              Dusk
                           Above the
                       water hang the
                               loud
                               flies
                               Here
                               O so
                               gray
                               then
                     What              A pale signal will appear
                     When            Soon before its shadow fades
                     Where          Here in this pool of opened eye
                     In us       No Upon us As at the very edges
                        of where we take shape in the dark air
                           this object bares its image awakening
                              ripples of recognition that will
                                 brush darkness up into light
           even after this bird this hour both drift by atop the perfect sad instant now
                                 already passing out of sight
                              toward yet-untroubled reflection
                           this image bears its object darkening
                        into memorial shades Scattered bits of
                     light          No of water Or something across
                     water            Breaking up No Being regathered
                     soon                Yet by then a swan will have
                     gone                 Yet out of mind into what
                               vast
                               pale
                               hush
                               of a
                               place
                               past
                        sudden dark as
                           if a swan
                               sang
</pre>

A whole poem doesn't need to be such a verbal silhouette, of course, for its appearance on the page to seem meaningful. In some lines of a longer poem, William Carlos Williams has conveyed the way an energetic bellhop (or hotel porter) runs downstairs:

```
ta tuck a
        ta tuck a
                ta tuck a
                        ta tuck a
                                ta tuck a
```

This is not only good onomatopoeia and an accurate description of a rhythm; the steplike appearance of the lines goes together with their meaning.

At least some of our pleasure in silently reading a poem derives from the way it looks upon its page. A poem in an open form can engage the eye with snowfields of white space and thickets of close-set words. A poem in stanzas can please us by its visual symmetry. And, far from being merely decorative, the visual devices of a poem can be meaningful, too. White space—as poets demonstrate who work in open forms—can indicate pauses. If white space entirely surrounds a word or phrase or line, then that portion of the poem obviously takes special emphasis. Typographical devices such as capital letters and italics also can lay stress upon words. In most traditional poems, a capital letter at the beginning of each new line helps indicate the importance the poet places upon line-divisions, whose regular intervals make a rhythm out of pauses. And the poet may be trying to show us that certain lines rime by indenting them.

Though too much importance can be given to the visual element of poetry and though many poets seem hardly to care about it, it can be another dimension that sets apart poetry from prose. It is at least arguable that some of Walt Whitman's long-line, page-filling descriptions of the wide ocean, open landscapes, and broad streets of his America, which meet the eye as wide expanses of words, would lose something—besides rhythm—if couched in lines only three or four syllables long.

In recent years, a movement called **concrete poetry** has traveled far and wide. Though practitioners of the art disagree over its definition, what most concretists seem to do is make designs out of letters and words. Other concrete poets wield typography like a brush dipped in paint, using such techniques as blow-up, montage, and superimposed elements (the same words printed many times on top of the same impression, so that the result is blurriness). They may even keep words in a usual order, perhaps employing white space as freely as any writer of open form verse. (More freely sometimes—Aram Saroyan has a concrete poem that consists of a page blank except for the word *oxygen*.) Poet Richard Kostelanetz has suggested that a more accurate name for concrete poetry might be "word-imagery." He sees it occupying an area somewhere between conventional poetry and visual art.

Admittedly, some concrete poems mean less than meets the eye. That many pretentious doodlers have taken up concretism may have caused a *Time* writer to sneer: did Joyce Kilmer miss all that much by never having seen a poem lovely as a

t

ttt

rrrrr

rrrrrrr

eeeeeeeee

???

Like other structures of language, however, concrete poems evidently can have the effect of poetry, if written by poets. Whether or not it ought to be dubbed "poetry," this art can do what poems traditionally have done: use language in delightful ways that reveal meanings to us.

---

*Dorthi Charles* (b. 1963)

CONCRETE CAT                                                    1971

## QUESTIONS

1. What does this writer indicate by capitalizing the *a* in *ear?* The *y* in *eye?* The *u* in mouth? By using spaces between the letters in the word *tail?*
2. Why is the word *mouse* upside down?
3. What possible pun might be seen in the cat's middle stripe?
4. What is the tone of "Concrete Cat"? How is it made evident?
5. Do these words seem chosen for their connotations or only for their denotations? Would you call this work of art a poem?

## Experiment: *Do It Yourself*

Make a concrete poem of your own. If you need inspiration, pick some familiar object or animal and try to find words that look like it. For more ideas, study the typography of a magazine or newspaper; cut out interesting letters and numerals and try pasting them into arrangements. What (if anything) do your experiments tell you about familiar letters and words?

## Suggestions for Writing

1. Consider whether concrete poetry is a vital new art form or merely visual trivia.
2. Should a poem be illustrated, or is it better left to the mind's eye? Discuss this question in a brief essay. You might care to consider William Blake's illustration for "A Poison Tree" or the illustrations in a collection of poems for children.

## Exercise: *Seeing the Logic of Open Form Verse*

Read the following poems in open form silently to yourself, noticing what each poet does with white space, repetitions, line breaks, and indentations. Then read the poems aloud, trying to indicate by slight pauses where lines end and also pausing slightly at any space inside a line. Can you see any reasons for the poet's placing his words in this arrangement rather than in a prose paragraph? Do any of these poets seem to care also about visual effect? (As with other kinds of poetry, there may not be any obvious logical reason for everything that happens in these poems.)

### *E. E. Cummings* (1894–1962)*

IN JUST-  1923

in Just-
spring      when the world is mud-
luscious the little
lame balloonman

whistles      far      and wee      5

and eddieandbill come
running from marbles and
piracies and it's
spring

when the world is puddle-wonderful      10

the queer
old balloonman whistles
far      and      wee
and bettyandisbel come dancing

from hop-scotch and jump-rope and      15

it's
spring

and
   the
      goat-footed                                                    20
balloonMan        whistles
far
and
wee


## Linda Pastan (b. 1932)*

### JUMP CABLING                          1984

| | |
|---|---|
| When our cars | touched |
| When you lifted the hood | of mine |
| To see the intimate workings | underneath, |
| When we were bound | together |
| By a pulse of pure | energy, |
| When my car like the | princess |
| In the tale woke with a | start, |

I thought why not ride the rest of the way together?


## A. R. Ammons (b. 1926)

### THE CITY LIMITS                       1971

When you consider the radiance, that it does not withhold
itself but pours its abundance without selection into every
nook and cranny not overhung or hidden; when you consider

that birds' bones make no awful noise against the light but
lie low in the light as in a high testimony; when you consider          5
the radiance, that it will look into the guiltiest

swervings of the weaving heart and bear itself upon them,
not flinching into disguise or darkening; when you consider
the abundance of such resource as illuminates the glow-blue

bodies and gold-skeined wings of flies swarming the dumped              10
guts of a natural slaughter or the coil of shit and in no
way winces from its storms of generosity; when you consider

that air or vacuum, snow or shale, squid or wolf, rose or lichen,
each is accepted into as much light as it will take, then
the heart moves roomier, the man stands and looks about, the           15

leaf does not increase itself above the grass, and the dark
work of the deepest cells is of a tune with May bushes
and fear lit by the breadth of such calmly turns to praise.


### Carole Satyamurti (b. 1939)

I SHALL PAINT MY NAILS RED          1990

Because a bit of colour is a public service.

Because I am proud of my hands.

Because it will remind me I'm a woman.

Because I will look like a survivor.

Because I can admire them in traffic jams.          5

Because my daughter will say ugh.

Because my lover will be surprised.

Because it is quicker than dyeing my hair.

Because it is a ten-minute moratorium.

Because it is reversible.          10

QUESTION

"I Shall Paint My Nails Red" is written in free verse, but the poem has several organizing principles. How many can you discover?


### Alice Fulton (b. 1952)

WHAT I LIKE          1983

Friend—the face I wallow toward
through a scrimmage of shut faces.
Arms like towropes to haul me home, aide-
memoire, my lost childhood docks, a bottled ark
in harbor. *Friend*—I can't forget          5
how even the word contains an *end*.
We circle each other in a scared bolero,
imagining stratagems: postures and imposters.
Cold convictions keep us solo. I ahem
and hedge my affections. Who'll blow the first kiss,          10
land it like the lifeforces we feel
tickling at each wrist? It should be easy

easy to take your hand, whisper down this distance
labeled hers or his: what I like about you is

Does this poem have an ending? Does it need to have an ending to be a successful
poem?

## *Charles Olson* (1910–1970)

LA CHUTE                                                                    1967

my drum, hollowed out thru the thin slit,
carved from the cedar wood, the base I took
when the tree was felled

o my lute, wrought from the tree's crown

my drum, whose lustiness                                                        5
was not to be resisted
                    my lute,

from whose pulsations
not one could turn away

                                        They                              10
are where the dead are, my drum fell
where the dead are, who
will bring it up, my lute
who will bring it up where it fell in the face of them
where they are, where my lute and drum have fallen?              15

LA CHUTE. The French title means "The Fall."

## SUGGESTIONS FOR WRITING

1. Take any poem in open form from this chapter or the Anthology (which begins
   on page 885) and demonstrate how its language and organization differ from prose.
   Some poems in the section Poems for Further Reading you might consider include
   John Ashbery's "At North Farm," Rita Dove's "Daystar," H. D.'s "Helen,"
   Robinson Jeffers's "To the Stone-cutters," and William Carlos Williams' "To
   Waken an Old Lady."
2. Is "free verse" totally free? Argue this question in a short essay, drawing evidence
   from open-form poems that interest you.

# 24  Symbol

The national flag is supposed to bestir our patriotic feelings. When a black cat crosses his path, a superstitious man shivers, foreseeing bad luck. To each of these, by custom, our society expects a standard response. A flag, a black cat's crossing one's path—each is a **symbol:** a visible object or action that suggests some further meaning in addition to itself. In literature, a symbol might be the word *flag* or the words *a black cat crossed his path* or every description of flag or cat in an entire novel, story, play, or poem.

A flag and the crossing of a black cat may be called **conventional symbols,** since they can have a conventional or customary effect on us. Conventional symbols are also part of the language of poetry, as we know when we meet the red rose, emblem of love, in a lyric, or the Christian cross in the devotional poems of George Herbert. More often, however, symbols in literature have no conventional, long-established meaning, but particular meanings of their own. In Melville's novel *Moby-Dick*, to take a rich example, whatever we associate with the great white whale is *not* attached unmistakably to white whales by custom. Though Melville tells us that men have long regarded whales with awe and relates Moby Dick to the celebrated fish that swallowed Jonah, the reader's response is to one particular whale, the creature of Herman Melville. Only the experience of reading the novel in its entirety can give Moby Dick his particular meaning.

We should say *meanings*, for as Eudora Welty has observed, it is a good thing Melville made Moby Dick a whale, a creature large enough to contain all that critics have found in him. A symbol in literature, if not conventional, has more than just one meaning. In "The Raven," by Edgar Allan Poe, the appearance of a strange black bird in the narrator's study is sinister; and indeed, if we take the poem seriously, we may even respond with a sympathetic shiver of dread. Does the bird mean death, fate, melancholy, the loss of a loved one, knowledge in the service of evil? All these, perhaps. Like any well-chosen symbol, Poe's raven sets going within the reader an unending train of feelings and associations.

We miss the value of a symbol, however, if we think it can mean absolutely anything we wish. If a poet has any control over our reactions, the poem will guide our responses in a certain direction.

## T. S. Eliot (1888–1965)*

### THE BOSTON EVENING TRANSCRIPT                    1917

The readers of the Boston Evening Transcript
Sway in the wind like a field of ripe corn.

When evening quickens faintly in the street,
Wakening the appetites of life in some
And to others bringing the Boston Evening Transcript,                    5
I mount the steps and ring the bell, turning
Wearily, as one would turn to nod good-bye to La Rochefoucauld,
If the street were time and he at the end of the street,
And I say, "Cousin Harriet, here is the Boston Evening Transcript."

The newspaper, whose name Eliot purposely repeats so monotonously, indicates what this poem is about. Now defunct, the Transcript covered in detail the slightest activity of Boston's leading families and was noted for the great length of its obituaries. Eliot, then, uses the newspaper as a symbol for an existence of boredom, fatigue (Wearily), petty and unvarying routine (since an evening newspaper, like night, arrives on schedule). The Transcript evokes a way of life without zest or passion, for, opposed to people who read it, Eliot sets people who do not: those whose desires revive, not expire, when the working day is through. Suggestions abound in the ironic comparison of the Transcript's readers to a cornfield late in summer. To mention only a few: the readers sway because they are sleepy; they vegetate; they are drying up; each makes a rattling sound when turning a page. It is not necessary that we know the remote and similarly disillusioned friend to whom the speaker might nod: La Rochefoucauld, whose cynical Maxims entertained Parisian society under Louis XIV (sample: "All of us have enough strength to endure the misfortunes of others"). We understand that the nod is symbolic of an immense weariness of spirit. We know nothing about Cousin Harriet, whom the speaker addresses, but imagine from the greeting she inspires that she is probably a bore.

If Eliot wishes to say that certain Bostonians lead lives of sterile boredom, why does he couch his meaning in symbols? Why doesn't he tell us directly what he means? These questions imply two assumptions not necessarily true: first, that Eliot has a message to impart; second, that he is concealing it. We have reason to think that Eliot did not usually have a message in mind when beginning a poem, for as he once told a critic: "The conscious problems with which one is concerned in the actual writing are more those of a quasi musical nature . . . than of a conscious exposition of ideas." Poets sometimes discover what they have to say while in the act of saying it. And it may be that in his *Transcript* poem, Eliot is saying exactly what he means. By communicating his meaning through symbols instead of statements, he may be choosing the only kind of language appropriate to an idea of great subtlety and complexity. (The paraphrase "Certain Bostonians are bored" hardly begins to describe the poem in all its possible meaning.) And by his use of symbolism, Eliot affords us the pleasure of finding our own entrances to his poem.

This power of suggestion that a symbol contains is, perhaps, its greatest advantage. Sometimes, as in the following poem by Emily Dickinson, a symbol will lead us from a visible object to something too vast to be perceived.

### Emily Dickinson (1830–1886)*

THE LIGHTNING IS A YELLOW FORK          (about 1870)

The Lightning is a yellow Fork
From Tables in the sky
By inadvertent fingers dropt
The awful Cutlery

Of mansions never quite disclosed                              5
And never quite concealed
The Apparatus of the Dark
To ignorance revealed.

If the lightning is a fork, then whose are the fingers that drop it, the table from which it slips, the household to which it belongs? The poem implies this question without giving an answer. An obvious answer is "God," but can we be sure? We wonder, too, about these partially lighted mansions: if our vision were clearer, what would we behold?[1]

---

[1]In its suggestion of an infinite realm that mortal eyes cannot quite see, but whose nature can be perceived fleetingly through things visible, Emily Dickinson's poem, by coincidence, resembles the work of late-nineteenth-century French poets called **symbolists.** To a symbolist the shirt-tail of Truth is continually seen disappearing around a corner. With their Neoplatonic view of ideal realities existing in a great beyond, whose corresponding symbols are the perceptible cats that bite us and tangible stones we stumble over, French poets such as Charles Baudelaire, Jules Laforgue, and Stéphane Mallarmé were profoundly to affect poets writing in English, notably Yeats (who said a poem "entangles . . . a part of the Divine essence") and Eliot. But we consider in this chapter symbolism as an element in certain poems, not Symbolism, the literary movement.

"But how am I supposed to know a symbol when I see one?" The best approach is to read poems closely, taking comfort in the likelihood that it is better not to notice symbols at all than to find significance in every literal stone and huge meanings in every thing. In looking for the symbols in a poem, pick out all the references to concrete objects—newspapers, black cats, twisted pins. Consider these with special care. Notice any that the poet emphasizes by detailed description, by repetition, or by placing at the very beginning or end of the poem. Ask: What is the poem about, what does it add up to? If, when the poem is paraphrased, the paraphrase depends primarily upon the meaning of certain concrete objects, these richly suggestive objects may be the symbols.

There are some things a literary symbol usually is *not*. A symbol is not an abstraction. Such terms as *truth, death, love,* and *justice* cannot work as symbols (unless personified, as in the traditional figure of Justice holding a scale). Most often, a symbol is something we can see in the mind's eye: a newspaper, a lightning bolt, a gesture of nodding good-bye.

In narratives, a well-developed character who speaks much dialogue and is not the least bit mysterious is usually not a symbol. But watch out for an executioner in a black hood; a character, named for a Biblical prophet, who does little but utter a prophecy; a trio of old women who resemble the Three Fates. (It has been argued, with good reason, that Milton's fully rounded character of Satan in *Paradise Lost* is a symbol embodying evil and human pride, but a narrower definition of symbol is more frequently useful.) A symbol *may* be a part of a person's body (the baleful eye of the murder victim in Poe's story "The Tell-Tale Heart") or a look, a voice, a mannerism.

A symbol usually is not the second term of a metaphor. In the line "The lightning is a yellow fork," the symbol is the lightning, not the fork.

Sometimes a symbol addresses a sense other than sight: the sound of a mysterious harp at the end of Chekhov's play *The Cherry Orchard*; or, in William Faulkner's tale "A Rose for Emily," the odor of decay that surrounds the house of the last survivor of a town's leading family—suggesting not only physical dissolution but also the decay of a social order. A symbol is a special kind of image, for it exceeds the usual image in the richness of its connotations. The dead wife's cold comb in the haiku of Buson (discussed on page 661) works symbolically, suggesting among other things the chill of the grave, the contrast between the living and the dead.

Holding a narrower definition than that used in this book, some readers of poetry prefer to say that a symbol is always a concrete object, never an act. They would deny the label "symbol" to Ahab's breaking his tobacco pipe before setting out to pursue Moby Dick (suggesting, perhaps, his determination to allow no pleasure to distract him from the chase) or to any large motion (as Ahab's whole quest). This distinction, while confining, does have the merit of sparing one from seeing all motion to be possibly symbolic. Some would call Ahab's gesture not a symbol but a **symbolic act.**

To sum up: a symbol radiates hints or casts long shadows (to use Henry James's metaphor). We are unable to say it "stands for" or "represents" a meaning. It evokes, it suggests, it manifests. It demands no single necessary interpretation, such as the interpretation a driver gives to a red traffic light. Rather, like Emily Dickinson's lightning bolt, it points toward an indefinite meaning, which may lie in part beyond the reach of words. In a symbol, as Thomas Carlyle said in *Sartor Resartus*, "the Infinite is made to blend with the Finite, to stand visible, and as it were, attainable there."

---

### *Thomas Hardy* (1840–1928)*

NEUTRAL TONES                                         1898

We stood by a pond that winter day,
And the sun was white, as though chidden of God,
And a few leaves lay on the starving sod;
   —They had fallen from an ash, and were gray.

Your eyes on me were as eyes that rove                            5
Over tedious riddles of years ago;
And some words played between us to and fro
   On which lost the more by our love.

The smile on your mouth was the deadest thing
Alive enough to have strength to die;                            10
And a grin of bitterness swept thereby
   Like an ominous bird a-wing. . . .

Since then, keen lessons that love deceives,
And wrings with wrong, have shaped to me
Your face, and the God-curst sun, and a tree,                    15
   And a pond edged with grayish leaves.

QUESTIONS

1. Sum up the story told in this poem. In lines 1–12, what is the dramatic situation? What has happened in the interval between the experience related in these lines and the reflection in the last stanza?
2. What meanings do you find in the title?
3. Explain in your own words the metaphor in line 2.
4. What connotations appropriate to this poem does the *ash* (line 4) have, that *oak* or *maple* would lack?
5. What visible objects in the poem function symbolically? What actions or gestures?

If we read of a ship, its captain, its sailors, and the rough seas, and we realize we are reading about a commonwealth and how its rulers and workers keep it going even in difficult times, then we are reading an **allegory.** Closely akin to symbolism, allegory is a description—usually narrative—in which persons, places, and things are employed in a continuous system of equivalents.

   Although more strictly limited in its suggestions than symbolism, allegory need not be thought inferior. Few poems continue to interest readers more than Dante's allegorical *Divine Comedy*. Sublime evidence of the appeal of allegory may be found in Christ's use of the **parable:** a brief narrative— usually allegorical but sometimes not—that teaches a moral.

### Matthew 13:24–30
### (Authorized or King James Version, 1611)

## THE PARABLE OF THE GOOD SEED

The kingdom of heaven is likened unto a man which sowed good seed in his field:

But while men slept, his enemy came and sowed tares among the wheat, and went his way.

But when the blade was sprung up, and brought forth fruit, then appeared the tares also.

So the servants of the householder came and said unto him, Sir, didst not thou sow good seed in thy field? From whence then hath it tares?

He said unto them, An enemy hath done this. The servants said unto him, Wilt thou then that we go and gather them up?                                    5

But he said, Nay; lest while ye gather up the tares, ye root up also the wheat with them.

Let both grow together until the harvest: and in the time of harvest I will say to the reapers, Gather ye together first the tares, and bind them in bundles to burn them: but gather the wheat into my barn.

The sower is the Son of man, the field is the world, the good seed are the children of the Kingdom, the tares are the children of the wicked one, the enemy is the devil, the harvest is the end of the world, the reapers are angels. "As therefore the tares are gathered and burned in the fire; so shall it be in the end of this world" (Matthew 13:36–42).

Usually, as in this parable, the meanings of an allegory are plainly labeled or thinly disguised. In John Bunyan's allegorical narrative *The Pilgrim's Progress*, it is clear that the hero Christian, on his journey through places with such pointed names as Vanity Fair, the Valley of the Shadow of Death, and Doubting Castle, is the soul, traveling the road of life on the way toward Heaven. An allegory, when carefully built, is systematic. It makes one principal comparison, the working out of whose details may lead to further comparisons, then still further comparisons: Christian, thrown by Giant Despair into the dungeon of Doubting Castle, escapes by means of a key called Promise. Such a complicated design may take great length to unfold, as in Spenser's *Faerie Queene*; but the method may be seen in a short poem:

## George Herbert (1593–1633)*

### REDEMPTION                                              1633

Having been tenant long to a rich Lord,
  Not thriving, I resolvèd to be bold,
And make a suit unto him to afford
A new small-rented lease and cancel th' old.
In Heaven at his manor I him sought.                        5
  They told me there that he was lately gone
About some land which he had dearly bought
  Long since on earth, to take possessiòn.
I straight returned, and knowing his great birth,
  Sought him accordingly in great resorts,                  10
In cities, theaters, gardens, parks, and courts.
At length I heard a ragged noise and mirth
  Of thieves and murderers; there I him espied,
  Who straight "Your suit is granted," said, and died.

### QUESTIONS

1. In this allegory, what equivalents does Herbert give each of these terms: *tenant, Lord, not thriving, suit, new lease, old lease, manor, land, dearly bought, take possession, his great birth?*
2. What scene is depicted in the last three lines?

An object in allegory is like a bird whose cage is clearly lettered with its identity—"RAVEN, *Corvus corax*; habitat of specimen, Maine." A symbol, by contrast, is a bird with piercing eyes that mysteriously appears one evening in your library. It is there; you can touch it. But what does it mean? You look at it. It continues to look at you.

Whether an object in literature is a symbol, part of an allegory, or no such thing at all, it has at least one sure meaning. Moby Dick is first a whale, the *Boston Evening Transcript* a newspaper. Besides deriving a multitude of intangible suggestions from the title symbol in Eliot's long poem *The Waste Land,* its readers cannot fail to carry away a sense of the land's physical appearance: a river choked with sandwich papers and cigarette ends, London Bridge "under the brown fog of a winter dawn." A virtue of *The Pilgrim's Progress* is that its walking abstractions are no mere abstractions but are also human: Giant Despair is a henpecked husband. The most vital element of a literary work may pass us by, unless before seeking further depths in a thing, we look to the thing itself.

## Emily Dickinson (1830–1886)*

### I HEARD A FLY BUZZ—WHEN I DIED          (about 1862)

I heard a Fly buzz—when I died—
The Stillness in the Room

Was like the Stillness in the Air—
Between the Heaves of Storm—

The Eyes around—had wrung them dry—                              5
And Breaths were gathering firm
For that last Onset—when the King
Be witnessed—in the Room—

I willed my Keepsakes—Signed away
What portion of me be                                           10
Assignable—and then it was
There interposed a Fly—

With Blue—uncertain stumbling Buzz—
Between the light—and me—
And then the Windows failed—and then                            15
I could not see to see—

## QUESTIONS

1. Why is the poem written in the past tense? Where is the speaker at present?
2. What do you understand from the repetition of the word *see* in the last line?
3. What does the poet mean by *Eyes around* (line 5), *that last Onset* (line 7), *the King* (line 7), and *What portion of me be | Assignable* (lines 10–11)?
4. In line 13, how can a sound be called *Blue* and *stumbling*?
5. What further meaning might *the Windows* (line 15) suggest, in addition to denoting the windows of the room?
6. What connotations of the word *fly* seem relevant to an account of a death?
7. Summarize your interpretation of the poem. What does the fly mean?

---

### *Robert Frost* (1874–1963)*

## THE ROAD NOT TAKEN          1916

Two roads diverged in a yellow wood,
And sorry I could not travel both
And be one traveler, long I stood
And looked down one as far as I could
To where it bent in the undergrowth;                            5

Then took the other, as just as fair,
And having perhaps the better claim,
Because it was grassy and wanted wear;
Though as for that the passing there
Had worn them really about the same,                            10

And both that morning equally lay
In leaves no step had trodden black.
Oh, I kept the first for another day!

Yet knowing how way leads on to way,
I doubted if I should ever come back.                                    15

I shall be telling this with a sigh
Somewhere ages and ages hence:
Two roads diverged in a wood, and I—
I took the one less traveled by,
And that has made all the difference.                                    20

## QUESTION

What symbolism do you find in this poem, if any? Back up your claim with evidence.

### *Christina Rossetti* (1830–1894)

UPHILL                                                        1862

Does the road wind uphill all the way?
    Yes, to the very end.
Will the day's journey take the whole long day?
    From morn to night, my friend.

But is there for the night a resting-place?                               5
    A roof for when the slow dark hours begin.
May not the darkness hide it from my face?
    You cannot miss that inn.

Shall I meet other wayfarers at night?
    Those who have gone before.                                          10
Then must I knock, or call when just in sight?
    They will not keep you standing at that door.

Shall I find comfort, travel-sore and weak?
    Of labor you shall find the sum.
Will there be beds for me and all who seek?                               15
    Yea, beds for all who come.

## QUESTIONS

1. At what line in reading this poem did you tumble to the fact that the poet is
   building an allegory?
2. For what does each thing stand?
3. What does the title of the poem suggest to you?
4. Recast the meaning of line 14, a knotty line, in your own words.
5. Discuss the possible identities of the two speakers—the apprehensive traveler and
   the character with all the answers. Are they specific individuals? Allegorical figures?
6. Compare "Uphill" with Robert Creeley's "Oh No" (page 610). What striking
   similarities do you find in these two dissimilar poems?

## Gjertrud Schnackenberg (b. 1953)

SIGNS                                                        1974

Threading the palm, a web of little lines
Spells out the lost money, the heart, the head,
The wagging tongues, the sudden deaths, in signs
We would smooth out, like imprints on a bed,

In signs that can't be helped, geese heading south,            5
In signs read anxiously, like breath that clouds
A mirror held to a barely open mouth,
Like telegrams, the gathering of crowds—

The plane's X in the sky, spelling disaster:
Before the whistle and hit, a tracer flare;                    10
Before rubble, a hairline crack in plaster
And a housefly's panicked scribbling on the air.

QUESTIONS

1. What are "signs" in this poet's sense of the word?
2. The poem gives a list of signs. What unmistakable meaning does each indicate?
3. Compare Schnackenberg's fly and Emily Dickinson's (page 802). Which insect
   seems loaded with more suggestions?
4. Can you think of any familiar signs that *aren't* ominous?
5. This poem was written when the poet was a student at Mount Holyoke College.
   Knowing this fact, do you like it any less, or any more?

EXERCISE: *Symbol Hunting*

After you have read each of these poems, decide which description best suits it:
1. The poem has a central symbol.
2. The poem contains no symbolism, but is to be taken literally.

## Hugo Williams (b. 1942)

KITES                                                        1979

Our lives fly well—white specks with faces
Running out against blue. While far below
We stand staring after them,
Trying to remember what they were like,
These prize possessions of ours,                               5
Unraveling so cheerfully before our eyes.

By now we are winding in the runaway spools
For all we are worth. Whatever was there
Has begun to recede, like the dead stars,

Faster than the speed of their light          10
Can reach back to us here,
Where we hang on these empty strings.


## William Carlos Williams (1883–1963)*

POEM                              1934

As the cat
climbed over
the top of

the jamcloset                                5
first the right
forefoot

carefully
then the hind
stepped down
into the pit of                              10
the empty
flowerpot


## Lorine Niedecker (1903–1970)*

POPCORN-CAN COVER          (c. 1959)

Popcorn-can cover
screwed to the wall
over a hole
        so the cold
can't mouse in                               5


## Wallace Stevens (1879–1955)*

ANECDOTE OF THE JAR          1923

I placed a jar in Tennessee,
And round it was, upon a hill.
It made the slovenly wilderness
Surround that hill.

The wilderness rose up to it,                 5
And sprawled around, no longer wild.

The jar was round upon the ground
And tall and of a port in air.

It took dominion everywhere.
The jar was gray and bare. 10
It did not give of bird or bush,
Like nothing else in Tennessee.

## Suggestions for Writing

1. Write a paraphrase of Emily Dickinson's "I heard a Fly buzz—when I died."
   Make clear whatever meanings you find in the fly (and other concrete objects).
2. Discuss the symbolism in a poem in the section Poems for Further Reading
   beginning on page 885. Likely poems to study (among many) are Louise Bogan's
   "The Dream," T. S. Eliot's "The Love Song of J. Alfred Prufrock," Robert
   Lowell's "Skunk Hour," Howard Nemerov's "The Snow Globe," and Adrienne
   Rich's "Aunt Jennifer's Tigers."
3. Take some relatively simple, straightforward poem, such as William Carlos Williams's "This Is Just to Say" (page 625), and write a burlesque critical interpretation of it. Claim to discover symbols in the poem that it doesn't contain. While
   letting your ability to "read into" a poem run wild, don't invent anything that you
   can't somehow support from the text of the poem itself. At the end of your
   burlesque, add a paragraph summing up what this exercise indicates about how to
   read poems, or how not to.

# 25 Myth and Narrative

Poets have long been fond of retelling **myths,** narrowly defined as traditional stories about the exploits of immortal beings. Such stories taken collectively may also be called **myth** or **mythology.** In one of the most celebrated collections of myth ever assembled, the *Metamorphoses,* the Roman poet Ovid told—to take one example from many—how Phaeton, child of the sun god, rashly tried to drive his father's fiery chariot on its daily round, lost control of the horses, and caused disaster both to himself and to the world. Our use of the term *myth* in discussing poetry, then, differs from its use in expressions such as "the myth of communism" and "the myth of democracy." In these examples, myth is used broadly to represent any idea people believe in, whether true or false. Nor do we mean—to take another familiar use of the word—a cock-and-bull story: "Judge Rapp doesn't roast speeders alive; that's just a *myth.*" In the following discussion, *myth* will mean a kind of story—either from ancient or modern sources—whose actions implicitly symbolize some profound truth about human or natural existence. Myths are stories that operate, in the words of the critic Northrop Frye, "near or at the conceivable limits of desire."

Traditional myths tell us stories of gods or heroes—their battles, their lives, their loves, and often their suffering—all on a scale of magnificence larger than our life. These exciting stories usually reveal part of a culture's worldview. Myths often try to explain universal natural phenomena, like the phases of the moon or the turning of the seasons. But some myths tell the story of purely local phenomena; one Greek legend, for example, recounts how grief-stricken King Aegeus threw himself into the sea when he mistakenly believed his son, Theseus, had been killed; consequently, the body of water between Greece and Turkey was called the Aegean Sea.

Modern psychologists, like Sigmund Freud and Carl Jung, have been fascinated by myth and legend, since they believe these stories symbolically enact deep truths about human nature. Our myths, psychologists believe, express our wishes, dreams, and nightmares. Whether or not we believe myths, we recognize their psychological power. Even in the first century B.C., Ovid did not believe in the literal truth of the legends he so suavely retold; he confessed, "I prate of ancient poets' monstrous lies."

And yet it is characteristic of a myth that it *can* be believed. Throughout history, myths have accompanied religious doctrines and rituals. They have helped sanction or recall the reasons for religious observances. A sublime instance is the New Testament account of the Last Supper. Because of its record of the words of Jesus, "Do this in remembrance of Me," Christians have continued to re-enact the offering and partaking of the body and blood of their Lord, under the appearances of bread and wine. It is essential to recall that, just because a myth narrates the acts of a god, we do not necessarily mean by the term a false or fictitious narrative. When we speak of the "myth of Islam" or "the Christian myth," we do so without implying either belief or disbelief.

Myths can also help sanction customs and institutions other than religious ones. At the same time as the baking of bread was introduced to ancient Greece—one theory goes—the myth of Demeter, goddess of grain, appeared. Demeter was a kindly deity who sent her emissary to teach humankind the valuable art of baking—thus helping to persuade the distrustful that bread was a good thing. Some myths seem designed to divert and regale, not to sanction anything. Such may be the story of the sculptor Pygmalion, who fell in love with the statue he had carved of a beautiful woman; so exquisite was his work, so deep was his feeling, that Aphrodite, the goddess of Love, brought the statue to life. And yet perhaps the story goes deeper than mere diversion: perhaps it is a way of saying that works of art achieve a reality of their own, that love can transform or animate its object.

How does a myth begin? Several theories have been proposed, none universally accepted. One is that a myth is a way to explain some natural phenomenon. Winter comes and the vegetation perishes because Persephone, child of Demeter, must return to the underworld for four months every year. This theory, as classical scholar Edith Hamilton has pointed out, may lead us to think incorrectly that Greek mythology was the creation of a primitive people. Tales of the gods of Mount Olympus may reflect an earlier inheritance, but the Greek myths known to us were transcribed in an era of high civilization. Anthropologists have questioned whether primitive people generally find beauty in the mysteries of nature. "From my own study of living myths among savages," wrote Bronislaw Malinowski, "I should say that primitive man has to a very limited extent the purely artistic or scientific interest in nature; there is but little room for symbolism in his ideas and tales; and myth, in fact, is not an idle rhapsody . . . but a hard-working, extremely important cultural force."[1] Such a practical function was seen by Sir James Frazer in *The Golden Bough*: myths were originally expressions of human hope that nature would be fertile. Still another theory is that, once upon a time, heroes of myth were human prototypes. The Greek philosopher Euhemerus declared myths to be tales of real persons, which poets had

[1]Bronislaw Malinowski, *Myth in Primitive Psychology* (1926); reprinted in *Magic, Science and Religion* (New York: Doubleday, 1954) 97.

exaggerated. Most present-day historians of myth would seek no general explanation but would say that different myths probably have different origins.

Poets have many coherent mythologies on which to draw; perhaps those most frequently consulted by British and American poets are the classical, the Christian, the Norse, the Native American, and the folk tales of the American frontier (embodying the deeds of superhuman characters such as Paul Bunyan). Some poets have taken inspiration from other myths as well: T. S. Eliot's *The Waste Land*, for example, is enriched by allusions to Buddhism and to pagan vegetation-cults. Robert Bly borrowed the terrifying Death Goddess of Aztec, Hindu, and Balinese mythology to make her the climactic figure of his long poem, "The Teeth Mother Naked at Last."

A tour through any good art museum will demonstrate how thoroughly myth pervades the painting and sculpture of nearly every civilization. In literature, one evidence of its continuing value to recent poets and storytellers is how frequently ancient myths are retold. Even in modern society, writers often turn to myth when they try to tell stories of deep significance. Mythic structures still touch a powerful and primal part of the human imagination. William Faulkner's story "The Bear" recalls tales of Indian totem animals; John Updike's novel *The Centaur* presents the horse-man Chiron as a modern high school teacher; James Joyce's *Ulysses* retells *The Odyssey* in modern Dublin; T. S. Eliot's plays bring into the drawing room the myths of Alcestis (*The Cocktail Party*) and the Eumenides (*The Family Reunion*); Bernard Shaw retells the Pygmalion story in his popular Edwardian social comedy, *Pygmalion*, later the basis of the hit musical *My Fair Lady*; Jean Cocteau's film *Orphée* shows us Eurydice riding to the underworld with an escort of motorcycles. Popular interest in such works may testify to the profound appeal myths continue to hold for us. Like other varieties of poetry, myth is a kind of knowledge, not at odds with scientific knowledge but existing in addition to it.

### *Robert Frost* (1874–1963)*

NOTHING GOLD CAN STAY          1923

Nature's first green is gold,
Her hardest hue to hold.
Her early leaf's a flower;
But only so an hour.
Then leaf subsides to leaf.          5
So Eden sank to grief,
So dawn goes down to day.
Nothing gold can stay.

1. To what myth does this poem allude? Does Frost sound as though he believes in the myth or as though he rejects it?
2. When Frost says, "Nature's first green is gold," he is describing how many leaves first appear as tiny yellow buds and blossoms. But what else does this line imply?
3. What would happen to the poem's meaning if line 6 were omitted?

## D. H. Lawrence (1885–1930)*

BAVARIAN GENTIANS                                                1932

Not every man has gentians in his house
in soft September, at slow, sad Michaelmas.

Bavarian gentians, big and dark, only dark
darkening the daytime, torch-like with the smoking blueness of
    Pluto's gloom,
ribbed and torch-like, with their blaze of darkness spread blue          5
down flattening into points, flattened under the sweep of white day
torch-flower of the blue-smoking darkness, Pluto's dark-blue daze,
black lamps from the halls of Dis, burning dark blue,
giving off darkness, blue darkness, as Demeter's pale lamps give off
    light,
lead me then, lead the way.                                             10

Reach me a gentian, give me a torch!
let me guide myself with the blue, forked torch of this flower
down the darker and darker stairs, where blue is darkened on
    blueness
even where Persephone goes, just now, from the frosted September
to the sightless realm where darkness is awake upon the dark          15
and Persephone herself is but a voice
or a darkness invisible enfolded in the deeper dark
of the arms Plutonic, and pierced with the passion of dense gloom,
among the splendor of torches of darkness, shedding darkness on
    the lost bride and her groom.

BAVARIAN GENTIANS. 2 *Michaelmas:* The feast of St. Michael (September 29). 4 *Pluto:* Roman name for Hades, in Greek mythology the ruler of the underworld, who abducted Persephone to be his bride. Each spring Persephone returns to earth and is welcomed by her mother Demeter, goddess of fruitfulness; each winter she departs again, to dwell with her husband below. 8 *Dis:* Pluto's realm.

## QUESTIONS

1. Read this poem aloud. What devices of sound do you hear in it?
2. What characteristics of gentians appear to remind Lawrence of the story of Persephone? What significance do you attach to the poem's being set in September? How does the fact of autumn matter to the gentians and to Persephone?

## Thomas Hardy (1840–1928)*

### THE OXEN                                                     1915

Christmas Eve, and twelve of the clock.
   "Now they are all on their knees,"
An elder said as we sat in a flock
   By the embers in hearthside ease.

We pictured the meek mild creatures where                         5
   They dwelt in their strawy pen,
Nor did it occur to one of us there
   To doubt they were kneeling then.

So fair a fancy few would weave
   In these years! Yet, I feel,                              10
If someone said on Christmas Eve,
   "Come; see the oxen kneel

"In the lonely barton° by yonder coomb°         *farmyard; a hollow*
   Our childhood used to know,"
I should go with him in the gloom,                                15
   Hoping it might be so.

THE OXEN. This ancient belief has had wide currency among peasants and farmers of Western Europe. Some also say that on Christmas Eve the beasts can speak.

### QUESTIONS

1. What body of myth is Hardy's subject and what are his speaker's attitudes toward it? Perhaps, in Hardy's view, the pious report about oxen is only part of it.
2. Read this poem aloud and notice its sound and imagery. What contrast do you find between the sounds of the first stanza and the sounds of the last stanza? Which words make the difference? What images enforce a contrast in tone between the beginning of the poem and its ending?
3. G. K. Chesterton, writing as a defender of Christian faith, called Hardy's writings "the mutterings of the village atheist." See other poems by Hardy in the section Poems for Further Reading. What do you think Chesterton might have meant? Can "The Oxen" be called a hostile mutter?

## William Wordsworth (1770–1850)*

### THE WORLD IS TOO MUCH WITH US            1807

The world is too much with us; late and soon,
Getting and spending, we lay waste our powers;
Little we see in Nature that is ours;
We have given our hearts away, a sordid boon!
This Sea that bares her bosom to the moon;                         5

The winds that will be howling at all hours,
And are up-gathered now like sleeping flowers;
For this, for everything, we are out of tune;
It moves us not. Great God! I'd rather be
A Pagan suckled in a creed outworn;                                    10
So might I, standing on this pleasant lea,
Have glimpses that would make me less forlorn;
Have sight of Proteus rising from the sea;
Or hear old Triton blow his wreathèd horn.

QUESTIONS

1. In this sonnet by Wordsworth what condition does the poet complain about? To
   what does he attribute this condition?
2. How does it affect him as an individual?

## PERSONAL MYTH

Sometimes poets have been inspired to make up myths of their own, to
embody their own visions of life. "I must create a system or be enslaved by
another man's," said William Blake, who in his "prophetic books" peopled
the cosmos with supernatural beings having names like Los, Urizen, and
Vala (side by side with recognizable figures from the Old Testament and New
Testament). This kind of system-making probably has advantages and draw-
backs. T. S. Eliot, in his essay on Blake, wishes that the author of *The Four
Zoas* had accepted traditional myths, and he compares Blake's thinking to a
piece of homemade furniture whose construction diverted valuable energy
from the writing of poems. Others have found Blake's untraditional cosmos
an achievement—notably William Butler Yeats, himself the author of an
elaborate personal mythology. Although we need not know all of Yeats's
mythology to enjoy his poems, to know of its existence can make a few great
poems deeper for us and less difficult.

### *William Butler Yeats* (1865–1939)*

### THE SECOND COMING                                    1921

Turning and turning in the widening gyre°                            *spiral*
The falcon cannot hear the falconer;
Things fall apart; the center cannot hold;
Mere anarchy is loosed upon the world,
The blood-dimmed tide is loosed, and everywhere                       5
The ceremony of innocence is drowned;
The best lack all conviction, while the worst
Are full of passionate intensity.

Surely some revelation is at hand;
Surely the Second Coming is at hand;                                    10
The Second Coming! Hardly are those words out
When a vast image out of *Spiritus Mundi*
Troubles my sight: somewhere in sands of the desert
A shape with lion body and the head of a man,
A gaze blank and pitiless as the sun,                                   15
Is moving its slow thighs, while all about it
Reel shadows of the indignant desert birds.
The darkness drops again; but now I know
That twenty centuries of stony sleep
Were vexed to nightmare by a rocking cradle,                            20
And what rough beast, its hour come round at last,
Slouches towards Bethlehem to be born?


What kind of Second Coming does Yeats expect? Evidently it is not to
be a Christian one. Yeats saw human history as governed by the turning of
a Great Wheel, whose phases influence events and determine human personalities—rather like the signs of the Zodiac in astrology. Every two thousand
years comes a horrendous moment: the Wheel completes a turn; one civilization ends and another begins. Strangely, a new age is always announced by
birds and by acts of violence. Thus the Greek-Roman world arrives with the
descent of Zeus in swan's form and the burning of Troy, the Christian era
with the descent of the Holy Spirit—traditionally depicted as a dove—and
the Crucifixion. In 1919 when Yeats wrote "The Second Coming," his
Ireland was in the midst of turmoil and bloodshed; the Western Hemisphere
had been severely shaken by World War I. A new millennium seemed
imminent. What sphinxlike, savage deity would next appear on earth, with
birds proclaiming it angrily? Yeats imagines it emerging from *Spiritus Mundi,*
Soul of the World, a collective unconscious from which a human being
(since the individual soul touches it) receives dreams, nightmares, and racial
memories.[2]

It is hard to say whether a poet who discovers a personal myth does so
to have something to live by or to have something to write about. Robert
Graves, who professed his belief in a White Goddess ("Mother of All Living,
the ancient power of love and terror"), declared that he wrote his poetry in
a trance, inspired by his Goddess-Muse.[3] Luckily, we do not have to know
a poet's religious affiliation before we can read the poems. Perhaps most
personal myths that enter poems are not acts of faith but works of art: stories
that resemble traditional mythology.


[2]Yeats fully explains his system in *A Vision* (1938; reprinted New York: Macmillan, 1956).
[3]See Graves's *The White Goddess,* rev. ed. (New York: Farrar, 1966), or for a terser statement
of his position, see his lecture "The Personal Muse" in *On Poetry: Collected Talks and Essays*
(New York: Doubleday, 1969).

## Dick Allen (b. 1939)

### NIGHT DRIVING                    1987

Cold hands on the cold wheel of his car,
Driving from Bridgeport, he watches
The long line of red taillights
Curving before him, remembers
How his father used to say they were cats' eyes          5
Staring back at them, a long line of cats
Watching from the distance—never Fords,
Buicks, Chevrolets, filled with the heads
Of children, lovers, lonely businessmen,
But cats in the darkness. Half asleep,                   10
He can believe, or make himself believe
The truth of his father—all the lies
Not really lies: images which make
The world come closer, cats' eyes up ahead.

### QUESTIONS

1. How does personal myth function in this poem?
2. What suggestions can you find in the poem's title?


## Frances Cornford (1886–1950)*

### ALL SOULS' NIGHT          1948

My love came back to me
Under the November tree
Shelterless and dim.
He put his hand upon my shoulder,
He did not think me strange or older,                    5
Nor I, him.

ALL SOULS' NIGHT. The Feast of All Souls (November 2) is dedicated to praying for the souls
of the departed, especially those suffering in Purgatory.

### QUESTION

"Frances Cornford's 'All Souls' Night' is not a Christian poem. The author has
mixed in all sorts of her own superstitions into the poem." How would you respond
to this opinion?

## MYTH AND POPULAR CULTURE

If one can find myths in an art museum, one can also find them abundantly
in popular culture. Movies and comic books, for example, are full of myths

in modern guise. What is Superman, if not a mythic hero who has adapted himself to modern urban life? Marvel Comics even made the Norse thunder god, Thor, into a super hero, although they obliged him, like Clark Kent, to get a job. We also see myths retold on the technicolor screen. Sometimes Hollywood presents the traditional story directly, as in Walt Disney's *Cinderella*; more often the ancient tales acquire contemporary settings, as in the latest celluloid Cinderella story, *Pretty Woman*. (See how Anne Sexton has retold the Cinderella story from a feminist perspective, later in this chapter or find a recording of Dana Dane's Brooklyn housing project version of the fairy tale done from a masculine perspective in his underground rap hit "Cinderfella.") George Lucas' *Star Wars* trilogy borrowed the structure of medieval quest legends. In quest stories, young knights pursued their destiny, often by seeking the Holy Grail, the cup Christ used at the Last Supper; in *Star Wars*, Luke Skywalker searched for his own parentage and identity, but his interstellar quest brought him to a surprisingly similar cast of knights, monsters, princesses, and wizards. Medieval Grail romances, which influenced Eliot's *The Waste Land*, also shaped recent films like *The Fisher King* and *Brazil*. Science fiction also commonly uses myth to novel effect. Extraterrestrial visitors usually appear as either munificent mythic gods or nightmarish demons. Steven Spielberg's *E.T.*, for example, revealed a gentle, Christ-like alien recognized by innocent children, but persecuted by adults. E.T. even healed the sick, fell into a death-like coma, and was resurrected.

It hardly matters whether the popular audience recognizes the literal source of a myth; the viewers intuitively understand the structure of the story and feel its deep imaginative resonance. That is why poets retell these myths; they are powerful sources of collective psychic energy, waiting to be tapped. Just as Hollywood screenwriters have learned that often the most potent way to use a myth is to disguise it, poets sometimes borrow the forms of popular culture to retell their myths. Here are two contemporary narrative poems that borrow imagery from motion pictures to re-enact stories that not only predate cinema but, most probably, stretch back before the invention of writing itself.

---

### *Charles Martin* (b. 1942)

TAKEN UP                                                    1978

Tired of earth, they dwindled on their hill,
Watching and waiting in the moonlight until
The aspens' leaves quite suddenly grew still,

No longer quaking as the disc descended,
That glowing wheel of lights whose coming ended          5
All waiting and watching. When it landed

The ones within it one by one came forth,
Stalking out awkwardly upon the earth,
And those who watched them were confirmed in faith:

Mysterious voyagers from outer space,                                    10
Attenuated, golden—shreds of lace
Spun into seeds of the sunflower's spinning face—

Light was their speech, spanning mind to mind:
*We come here not believing what we find—*
*Can it be your desire to leave behind*                                   15

*The earth, which those called angels bless,*
*Exchanging amplitude for emptiness?*
And in a single voice they answered *Yes,*

Discord of human melodies all blent
To the unearthly strain of their assent.                                  20
*Come then,* the Strangers said, and those that were taken, went.

QUESTIONS

1. What myths does this poem recall?
2. This poem was written about the same time that Steven Spielberg's film *Close Encounters of the Third Kind* (1977) appeared. If you recall the movie, compare its ending with the ending of the poem. Martin had not seen the film before writing "Taken Up." How can we account for the similarity?

*Edward Field* (b. 1924)

CURSE OF THE CAT WOMAN                                    1967

It sometimes happens
that the woman you meet and fall in love with
is of that strange Transylvanian people
with an affinity for cats.

You take her to a restaurant, say, or a show,                             5
on an ordinary date, being attracted
by the glitter in her slitty eyes and her catlike walk,
and afterwards of course you take her in your arms
and she turns into a black panther
and bites you to death.                                                   10

Or perhaps you are saved in the nick of time
and she is tormented by the knowledge of her tendency:
That she daren't hug a man
unless she wants to risk clawing him up.

This puts you both in a difficult position—                                    15
panting lovers who are prevented from touching
not by bars but by circumstance:
You have terrible fights and say cruel things
for having the hots does not give you a sweet temper.

One night you are walking down a dark street                                    20
And hear the pad-pad of a panther following you,
but when you turn around there are only shadows,
or perhaps one shadow too many.

You approach, calling, "Who's there?"
and it leaps on you.                                                            25
Luckily you have brought along your sword
and you stab it to death.

And before your eyes it turns into the woman you love,
her breast impaled on your sword,
her mouth dribbling blood saying she loved you                                  30
but couldn't help her tendency.

So death released her from the curse at last,
and you knew from the angelic smile on her dead face
that in spite of a life the devil owned,
love had won, and heaven pardoned her.                                         35

CURSE OF THE CAT WOMAN. Edward Field's poem borrows much of its story from Val Lewton's classic B movie, *Cat People* (1942). The film was remade in 1982, starring Natassia Kinski.

## QUESTIONS

1. This poem parodies a sentimental Hollywood horror film, but it also falls under the film's emotional spell. What details does Field introduce for comic effect? When does he give in to the romantic nature of the story?
2. Is the last stanza just a parody of a slick Hollywood ending or does Field invite us to take his finale seriously, too?

Why do poets retell myths? Why don't they just make up their own stories? First, using myth allows poets to be concise. By alluding to stories that their audiences know, they can draw on powerful associations with just a few words. If someone describes an acquaintance, "He thinks he's James Bond," that one allusion speaks volumes. Likewise, when Robert Frost inserts the single line, "So Eden sank to grief," in "Nothing Gold Can Stay," those five words summon up a wealth of associations. They tie the perishable quality of spring's beauty to the equally transient nature of human youth. They also suggest that everything in the human world is subject to time's ravages, that perfection is impossible for us to maintain just as it was for Adam and Eve.

Second, poets know that many stories fall into familiar mythic patterns, and that the most powerful stories of human existence tend to be the same, generation after generation. Sometimes using an old story allows a writer to

describe a new situation in a fresh and surprising way. Novels often try to
capture the exact texture of a social situation; they need to present the
everyday details to evoke the world in which their characters live. Myths
tend to tell their stories more quickly and in more general terms. They give
just the essential actions and leave out everything else. Narrative poems also
work best when they focus on just the essential elements. The Italian philosopher Giambattista Vico felt that primitive myths were essentially poetic. We
might say the opposite is equally true: poets often view the world in mythic
terms. Especially when poets tell stories, they tend to give human action a
mythic structure. Here are two contemporary narrative poems that retell
traditional myths to make contemporary interpretations.

## A. D. Hope (b. 1907)

IMPERIAL ADAM                                              1952

Imperial Adam, naked in the dew,
Felt his brown flanks and found the rib was gone.
Puzzled he turned and saw where, two and two,
The mighty spoor of Jahweh marked the lawn.

Then he remembered through mysterious sleep                    5
The surgeon fingers probing at the bone,
The voice so far away, so rich and deep:
"It is not good for him to live alone."

Turning once more he found Man's counterpart
In tender parody breathing at his side.                      10
He knew her at first sight, he knew by heart
Her allegory of sense unsatisfied.

The pawpaw drooped its golden breasts above
Less generous than the honey of her flesh;
The innocent sunlight showed the place of love;             15
The dew on its dark hairs winked crisp and fresh.

This plump gourd severed from his virile root,
She promised on the turf of Paradise
Delicious pulp of the forbidden fruit;
Sly as the snake she loosed her sinuous thighs,             20

And waking, smiled up at him from the grass;
Her breasts rose softly and he heard her sigh—
From all the beasts whose pleasant task it was
In Eden to increase and multiply

Adam had learned the jolly deed of kind:                    25
He took her in his arms and there and then,

Like the clean beasts, embracing from behind,
Began in joy to found the breed of men.

Then from the spurt of seed within her broke
Her terrible and triumphant female cry,                                          30
Split upward by the sexual lightning stroke.
It was the beasts now who stood watching by:

The gravid elephant, the calving hind,
The breeding bitch, the she-ape big with young
Were the first gentle midwives of mankind;                                       35
The teeming lioness rasped her with her tongue;

The proud vicuña nuzzled her as she slept
Lax on the grass; and Adam watching too
Saw how her dumb breasts at their ripening wept,
The great pod of her belly swelled and grew,                                     40

And saw its water break, and saw, in fear,
Its quaking muscles in the act of birth,
Between her legs a pigmy face appear,
And the first murderer lay upon the earth.

IMPERIAL ADAM. Hope's poem retells the story of Adam and Eve. For the Biblical version, see
*Genesis* 2:18–4:1. 4: *Jahweh*: the Lord of the Old Testament. The Hebrew name of God was
written as JHVH, but it was considered too sacred to say aloud. Yahweh and Jehovah are the
other most common versions of the voweless Hebrew name. 25: *deed of kind*: the act of
procreation. This particular expression is usually used to describe the mating of animals. 44: *the
first murderer*: Cain, Adam and Eve's first child, who murdered his brother, Abel. See *Genesis*
4:1–16.

## QUESTIONS

1. Why is Adam called "imperial?" What empire does he command?
2. What does Hope imply in lines 18–20, when he describes Eve's sexuality?
3. There is no serpent in Hope's version of the Adam and Eve story. And yet by the
   end of the poem, evil has entered Paradise. What has introduced it?
4. How does the last line of "Imperial Adam" affect the meaning of the poem?

## *Anne Sexton* (1928–1974)

CINDERELLA                        1971

You always read about it:
the plumber with twelve children
who wins the Irish Sweepstakes.
From toilets to riches.
That story.                                                                       5

Or the nursemaid,
some luscious sweet from Denmark

who captures the oldest son's heart.
From diapers to Dior.
That story.                                                      10

Or a milkman who serves the wealthy,
eggs, cream, butter, yogurt, milk,
the white truck like an ambulance
who goes into real estate
and makes a pile.                                                15
From homogenized to martinis at lunch.

Or the charwoman
who is on the bus when it cracks up
and collects enough from the insurance.
From mops to Bonwit Teller.                                      20
That story.

Once
the wife of a rich man was on her deathbed
and she said to her daughter Cinderella:
Be devout. Be good. Then I will smile                            25
down from heaven in the seam of a cloud.
The man took another wife who had
two daughters, pretty enough
but with hearts like blackjacks.
Cinderella was their maid.                                       30
She slept on the sooty hearth each night
and walked around looking like Al Jolson.
Her father brought presents home from town,
jewels and gowns for the other women
but the twig of a tree for Cinderella.                           35
She planted that twig on her mother's grave
and it grew to a tree where a white dove sat.
Whenever she wished for anything the dove
would drop it like an egg upon the ground.
The bird is important, my dears, so heed him.                    40

Next came the ball, as you all know.
It was a marriage market.
The prince was looking for a wife.
All but Cinderella were preparing
and gussying up for the big event.                               45
Cinderella begged to go too.
Her stepmother threw a dish of lentils
into the cinders and said: Pick them
up in an hour and you shall go.
The white dove brought all his friends;                          50
all the warm wings of the fatherland came,
and picked up the lentils in a jiffy.

No, Cinderella, said the stepmother,
you have no clothes and cannot dance.
That's the way with stepmothers.                              55

Cinderella went to the tree at the grave
and cried forth like a gospel singer:
Mama! Mama! My turtledove,
send me to the prince's ball!
The bird dropped down a golden dress                          60
and delicate little gold slippers.
Rather a large package for a simple bird.
So she went. Which is no surprise.
Her stepmother and sisters didn't
recognize her without her cinder face                         65
and the prince took her hand on the spot
and danced with no other the whole day.

As nightfall came she thought she'd better
get home. The prince walked her home
and she disappeared into the pigeon house                     70
and although the prince took an axe and broke
it open she was gone. Back to her cinders.
These events repeated themselves for three days.
However on the third day the prince
covered the palace steps with cobbler's wax                   75
and Cinderella's gold shoe stuck upon it.
Now he would find whom the shoe fit
and find his strange dancing girl for keeps.
He went to their house and the two sisters
were delighted because they had lovely feet.                  80
The eldest went into a room to try the slipper on
but her big toe got in the way so she simply
sliced it off and put on the slipper.
The prince rode away with her until the white dove
told him to look at the blood pouring forth.                  85
That is the way with amputations.
They don't just heal up like a wish.
The other sister cut off her heel
but the blood told as blood will.
The prince was getting tired.                                 90
He began to feel like a shoe salesman.
But he gave it one last try.
This time Cinderella fit into the shoe
like a love letter into its envelope.

At the wedding ceremony                                       95
the two sisters came to curry favor
and the white dove pecked their eyes out.

Two hollow spots were left
like soup spoons.

Cinderella and the prince                                              100
lived, they say, happily ever after,
like two dolls in a museum case
never bothered by diapers or dust,
never arguing over the timing of an egg,
never telling the same story twice,                                    105
never getting a middle-aged spread,
their darling smiles pasted on for eternity.
Regular Bobbsey Twins.
That story.

## QUESTIONS

1. Most of Sexton's "Cinderella" straightforwardly retells a version of the famous
   fairy tale. But in the beginning and ending of the poem, how does Sexton change
   the story?
2. How does Sexton's refrain of "That story" alter the meaning of the episodes it
   describes? What is the tone of this poem (the poet's attitude toward her material)?
3. What does Sexton's final stanza suggest about the way fairy tales usually end?

## SUGGESTIONS FOR WRITING

1. Read the original version of either the story of Adam and Eve (the first four
   chapters of *Genesis*) or "Cinderella" (in Charles Perrault's *Mother Goose Tales*) and
   compare it to the corresponding poem in this chapter. Which elements in the
   myth does the poet change and which does he or she retain?
2. Write an explication of D. H. Lawrence's "Bavarian Gentians" or Thomas
   Hardy's "The Oxen." (For hints on writing about poetry by the method of
   explication, see page 1762.)
3. Take any famous myth or fairy tale and retell it to reflect your personal philosophy.

# 26 *Poetry and Personal Identity*

Only a naive reader assumes that all poems directly reflect the personal experience of their authors. That would be like believing that a TV sitcom actually describes the real family life of its cast. As you will recall if you read "The Person in the Poem" (page 603), poets often speak in voices other than their own. These voices may be borrowed or imaginary. Stevie Smith appropriates the voice of a dead swimmer in her poem, "Not Waving but Drowning," (page 675), and Howard Moss imagines a non-human voice in "The Pruned Tree" (page 604). Some poets also try to give their personal poems a universal feeling. Edna St. Vincent Millay's emotion-charged sonnet, "Well, I Have Lost You; and I Lost You Fairly," (page 840) describes the end of a difficult love affair with a younger man, but she dramatizes the situation in such a way that it seems deliberately independent of any particular time and place. Even her lover remains shadowy and nameless. No one has ever been able to identify the characters in Shakespeare's sonnets with actual people, but that fact does not diminish our pleasure in them as poems.

And yet there are times when poets try to speak openly in their own voices. What could be a more natural subject for a poet than examining his or her own life? The autobiographical elements in a poem may be indirect, as in Chidiock Tichborne's elegy, written before his execution for treason in 1586 (page 688), or it may form the central subject, as in Sylvia Plath's "Lady Lazarus," which discusses her suicide attempts. In either case, the poem's autobiographical stance affects a reader's response. Although we respond to a poem's formal elements, we cannot also help reacting to what we know about its human origins. To learn that the elegant elegy we have just read was written by an eighteen-year-old boy, who would soon be horribly executed, adds a special poignancy to the poem's content. Likewise, to read Plath's chilling exploration of her death wish, while knowing that within a few months the poet would kill herself, we receive an extra jolt of emotion. In a good autobiographical poem, that shock of veracity adds to the poem's power. In an unsuccessful poem, the autobiographical facts become a substitute for emotions not credibly conveyed by the words themselves.

One literary movement, *Confessional Poetry*, has made such frank self-definition its main purpose. As the name implies, Confessional poetry renders personal experience as candidly as possible, even sharing confidences that may violate social conventions or propriety. Confessional poets sometimes shock their readers with admissions of experiences so intimate and painful—adultery, family violence, suicide attempts—that most people would try to suppress them, or at least not proclaim them to the world.

Some Confessional poets, such as Anne Sexton, W. D. Snodgrass, and Robert Lowell, underwent psychoanalysis, and at times their poems sound like patients telling their analysts every detail of their personal lives. For this reason, Confessional poems run the danger of being more interesting to their authors than their readers. But when a poet successfully frames his or her personal experience so that the reader can feel an extreme emotion from the inside, the result can be extraordinarily powerful. Here is a chilling poem that takes us within the troubled psyche of a poet who contemplates suicide.

---

### *Sylvia Plath* (1932–1963)*

LADY LAZARUS                               1965

I have done it again.
One year in every ten
I manage it—

A sort of walking miracle, my skin
Bright as a Nazi lampshade,                              5
My right foot

A paperweight,
My face a featureless, fine
Jew linen.

Peel off the napkin                                     10
O my enemy.
Do I terrify?—

The nose, the eye pits, the full set of teeth?
The sour breath
Will vanish in a day.                                   15

Soon, soon the flesh
The grave cave ate will be
At home on me

And I a smiling woman.
I am only thirty.
And like the cat I have nine times to die.

This is Number Three.
What a trash
To annihilate each decade.

What a million filaments.
The peanut-crunching crowd
Shoves in to see

Them unwrap me hand and foot—
The big strip tease.
Gentleman, ladies,

These are my hands,
My knees.
I may be skin and bone,

Nevertheless, I am the same, identical woman.
The first time it happened I was ten.
It was an accident.

The second time I meant
To last it out and not come back at all.
I rocked shut

As a seashell.
They had to call and call
And pick the worms off me like sticky pearls.

Dying
Is an art, like everything else.
I do it exceptionally well.

I do it so it feels like hell.
I do it so it feels real.
I guess you could say I've a call.

It's easy enough to do it in a cell.
It's easy enough to do it and stay put.
It's the theatrical

Comeback in broad day
To the same place, the same face, the same brute
Amused shout:

"A miracle!"
That knocks me out.
There is a charge

For the eyeing of my scars, there is a charge
For the hearing of my heart—
It really goes.                                              60

And there is a charge, a very large charge,
For the word or a touch
Or a bit of blood

Or a piece of my hair or my clothes.
So, so, Herr Doktor.                                        65
So, Herr Enemy.

I am your opus,
I am your valuable,
The pure gold baby

That melts to a shriek.                                      70
I turn and burn.
Do not think I underestimate your great concern.

Ash, ash—
You poke and stir.
Flesh, bone, there is nothing there—                         75

A cake of soap,
A wedding ring,
A gold filling,

Herr God, Herr Lucifer,
Beware                                                       80
Beware.

Out of the ash
I rise with my red hair.
And I eat men like air.

## QUESTIONS

1. Although the poem is openly autobiographical, Plath uses certain symbols to represent herself (Lady Lazarus, a Jew murdered in a concentration camp, a cat with nine lives, etc.). What do these symbols tell us about Plath's attitude toward herself and the world around her?
2. In her biography of Plath, *Bitter Fame*, the poet Anne Stevenson says that this poem penetrates "the furthest reaches of disdain and rage . . . bereft of all 'normal' human feelings." What do you think Stevenson means? Does anything in the poem strike you as particularly chilling?
3. The speaker in "Lady Lazarus" says "Dying/Is an art, like everything else" (lines 43–44). What sense do you make of this metaphor?
4. Does the ending of "Lady Lazarus" imply that the speaker assumes that she will outlive her suicide attempts? Set forth your final understanding of the poem.

Not all autobiographical poetry needs to shock the reader, as Plath overtly does in "Lady Lazarus." Poets can also try to share the special moments that illuminate their day-to-day lives, as Elizabeth Bishop does in "Filling Station" (page 896), when she describes a roadside gas station whose shabby bric-a-brac she saw as symbols of love. But when poets attempt to place their own lives under scrutiny, they face certain difficulties. Honest, thorough self-examination isn't as easy as it might seem. It is one thing to examine oneself in the mirror; it is quite another to sketch what one sees there accurately. Even if we have the skill to describe ourselves in words (or in paint) so that a stranger would recognize the self-portrait, there is the challenge of honesty. Drawing or writing our own self-portrait, most of us yield—often unconsciously—to the temptation of making ourselves a little nobler or better-looking than we really are. The best self-portraits, like Rembrandt's unflattering self-examinations, are usually critical. No one enjoys watching someone else preen in front of a dressing mirror, unless the intention is satiric.

Autobiographical poetry requires a hunger for honest self-examination. Many poets find that, in order to understand themselves and who they are, they must scrutinize more than the self in isolation. Other forces may shape their identities: their ethnic background, their families, their race, their gender, their religion, their economic status, and their age. Aware of these elements, many recent poets have written memorable, personal poems. The Dominican-American poet Julia Alvarez wrote an autobiographical sequence of thirty-three sonnets, as she turned thirty-three. These poems frankly explore her conflicting identities as daughter, sister, divorcee, lover, writer, Dominican, and American. They earn the reader's trust by being open and self-critical. The subject of one sonnet is Alvarez's admission that she is not as beautiful as either her mother or her sister. Reading that admission, we instinctively sympathize with the author.

---

## Julia Alvarez (b.1950)

### THE WOMEN ON MY MOTHER'S SIDE WERE KNOWN (from "33")　　　1984

The women on my mother's side were known
for beauty and were given lovely names
passed down for generations. I knew them
as my pretty aunts: Laura, who could turn
any head once, and Anna, whose husband　　　　　　　5
was so devoted he would lay his handkerchief
on seats for her and when she rose thanked

her; there was Rosa, who got divorced twice,
her dark eyes and thick hair were to blame;
and my mother Julia, who was a catch                                    10
and looks it in her wedding photographs.
My sister got her looks, I got her name,
and it suits me that between resemblance
and words, I got the right inheritance.


## RACE AND ETHNICITY

One of the personal issues Julia Alvarez faces in "33" is her dual identity as Dominican and American. The daughter of immigrants, she was born in New York but spent her childhood in the Dominican Republic. Consequently, self-definition for her has meant resolving the claims of two potentially contradictory cultures. In this sonnet, Alvarez talks about inheriting two kinds of beauty from her mother's side of the family. First, there is the beauty of the flesh, which has been passed onto Alvarez's sister. Second, there is a poetic impulse to create beauty with words, fulfilled by the family names, which Alvarez herself has inherited. Here Alvarez touches on the central issue facing the autobiographical poet—using *words* to embody experience. For a writer, the gift of words is "the right inheritance," even if those words are, for an immigrant poet, sometimes in a different language from that of one's parents. American poetry is rich in immigrant cultures, written both by first-generation writers like Alvarez or John Ciardi, and foreign-born authors like Joseph Brodsky (Russia), Nina Cassian (Romania), Claude McKay (Jamaica), Eamon Grennan (Ireland), Thom Gunn (England), Shirley Geok-lin Lim (Malaysia), Emanuel di Pasquale (Italy), José Emilio Pacheco (Mexico), Herberto Padilla (Cuba), and Derek Walcott (St. Lucia). Some literary immigrants, like the late Russian novelist and poet Vladimir Nabokov, make the difficult transition to writing in English. Others like Cassian or Pacheco continue to write in their native languages. A few like Brodsky write bilingually. Such poetry often reminds us of the multicultural nature of American poetry. Here is a poem by one literary immigrant that raises some important issues of personal identity.


### *Claude McKay* (1890–1948)

AMERICA                                                    1922

Although she feeds me bread of bitterness,
And sinks into my throat her tiger's tooth,

Stealing my breath of life, I will confess
I love this cultured hell that tests my youth.
Her vigor flows like tides into my blood,                                     5
Giving me strength erect against her hate,
Her bigness sweeps my being like a flood.
Yet, as a rebel fronts a king in state,
I stand within her walls with not a shred
Of terror, malice, not a word of jeer.                                        10
Darkly I gaze into the days ahead,
And see her might and granite wonders there,
Beneath the touch of Time's unerring hand,
Like priceless treasures sinking in the sand.

## Questions

1. Is "America" written in a personal or public voice? What specific elements seem
   personal? What elements seem public?
2. McKay was a black immigrant from Jamaica, but he does not mention either his
   race or national origin in the poem. Is his personal background important to
   understanding "America"?
3. "America" is written in a traditional form. How does the poem's form contribute
   to its impact?

Claude McKay's "America" raises the question of how an author's race and
ethnic identity influence the poetry he or she writes. (*Race* usually refers to
human traits based on biological descent whereas *ethnic* background assumes
the more complex influence of racial, national, cultural, linguistic, and religious characteristics.) In the 1920's, for instance, there was an ongoing discussion among black poets as to whether their poetry should deal specifically
with the African-American experience. Did black poetry exist apart from the
rest of American poetry or was it, in the words of Robert Hayden, "shaped
over some three centuries by social, moral, and literary forces essentially
American?" Should black authors primarily address a black audience or
should they try to engage a broader literary public? Should black poetry
focus on specifically black subjects, forms, and idioms or should it rely
mainly on the traditions of English literature? Black poets divided into two
camps. Claude McKay and Countee Cullen were among the writers who
favored universal themes. (Cullen, for example, insisted he be called a
"poet," not a "Negro poet.") Langston Hughes and Jean Toomer were
among the "new" poets who believed black poetry must reflect racial
themes. They believed, as James Weldon Johnson had once said, that race
was "perforce the thing that the American Negro Poet knows best." Writers
on both sides of the debate produced excellent poems, but their work has a
very different character. Compare McKay's "America" to the "new" poet

Langston Hughes' "Theme for English B." Hughes' poem is not strictly autobiographical, but it unmistakably reflects a lifetime of specifically black American experience.

## Langston Hughes (1902–1967)*

THEME FOR ENGLISH B                                                  1951

The instructor said,

> Go home and write
> a page tonight.
> And let that page come out of you—
> Then, it will be true.                                              5

I wonder if it's that simple?
I am twenty-two, colored, born in Winston-Salem.
I went to school there, then Durham, then here
to this college on the hill above Harlem.
I am the only colored student in my class.                           10
The steps from the hill lead down into Harlem,
through a park, then I cross St. Nicholas,
Eighth Avenue, Seventh, and I come to the Y,
the Harlem Branch Y, where I take the elevator
up to my room, sit down, and write this page:                        15

It's not easy to know what is true for you and me
at twenty-two, my age. But I guess I'm what
I feel and see and hear, Harlem, I hear you:
hear you, hear me—we two—you, me, talk on this page.
(I hear New York, too.) Me—who?                                      20
Well, I like to eat, sleep, drink, and be in love.
I like to work, read, learn, and understand life.
I like a pipe for a Christmas present,
or records—Bessie, bop, or Bach.
I guess being colored doesn't make me not like                       25
the same things other folks like who are other races.
So will my page be colored that I write?
Being me, it will not be white.

But it will be
a part of you, instructor.                                           30
You are white—
yet a part of me, as I am a part of you.
That's American.

Sometimes perhaps you don't want to be a part of me.
Nor do I often want to be a part of you.                                35
But we are, that's true!
As I learn from you,
I guess you learn from me—
although you're older—and white—
and somewhat more free.                                                  40

This is my page for English B.

THEME FOR ENGLISH B. 24 *Bessie:* Bessie Smith (1898?–1937) was a popular blues singer often
called the "Empress of the Blues."

QUESTIONS

1. Both "America" and "Theme for English B" are written in the first person. How
   does the use of the first person differ from McKay to Hughes?
2. What do you learn about the narrator of Hughes' poem that you don't learn about
   the speaker of "America"? Are these details important or trivial?
3. McKay's poem is overtly political. What parts of Hughes' poem make subtle
   political statements?

   The debate between ethnicity and universality has echoed among American writers of every racial and religious minority. Today, we find the same issues being discussed by Arab, Asian, Hispanic, Italian, Jewish, and Native-American authors. There is, ultimately, no one correct answer to the questions of identity, for individual artists need the freedom to pursue their own imaginative vision. But considering the issues of race and ethnicity does help a poet think through the artist's sometimes conflicting responsibilities between group and personal identity. Even in poets who have pursued their individual vision, we often see how unmistakably they write from their racial, social, cultural background. There may seem to be little overtly Hispanic content in Julia Alvarez's sonnet, but her poem implicitly reflects the close extended family structure of Latin cultures. Alvarez's poem also points out that we inherit our bodies as well as our cultures. Our body represents our genetic inheritance that goes back to the beginning of time. Sometimes a poet's ethnic background becomes part of his or her private mythology. In the following poem, Samuel Menashe talks about how his physical appearance reveals his ethnic identity.

*Samuel Menashe* (b. 1925)

THE SHRINE WHOSE SHAPE I AM                         1961

The shrine whose shape I am
Has a fringe of fire
Flames skirt my skin

There is no Jerusalem but this
Breathed in flesh by shameless love                                          5
Built high upon the tides of blood
I believe the Prophets and Blake
And like David I bless myself
With all my might

I know many hills were holy once                                            10
But now in the level lands to live
Zion ground down must become marrow
Thus in my bones I'm the King's son
And through death's domain I go
Making my own procession                                                     15

QUESTIONS

1. What does the poem tell you about the race and religion of the author? How is
   this information conveyed? Point to specific lines.
2. The ancient Jews located the center of Judaism at the Temple of Jerusalem,
   destroyed by the Romans in 70 A.D. When Menashe declares "There is no Jerusalem but this," what does he mean? What is he specifically referring to?
3. What does this poem imply about the nature of ethnic identity?

## *Francisco X. Alarcón* (b. 1948)

### THE X IN MY NAME          1993

the poor
signature
of my illiterate
and peasant
self                                                                          5
giving away
all rights
in a deceiving
contract for life

QUESTION

What does the speaker imply the X in his name signifies?

## GENDER

In her celebrated study, *You Just Don't Understand: Women and Men in
Conversation* (1990), Georgetown University linguist Deborah Tannen explored how men and women use language differently. Tannen compared
many everyday conversations between husbands and wives to "cross-cul-
tural communications," as if people from separate worlds lived under the
same roof. (Denise Levertov's "Leaving Forever," on p. 693, describes the

same situation quite vividly.) While analyzing the divergent ways in which women and men converse, Tannen carefully emphasizes that neither linguistic style was superior, only different.

While it would be simplistic to assume that all poems reveal the gender of their authors, many poems do become both richer and clearer when we examine their sexual assumptions. Philip Larkin's "Toads" (p. 673) is hardly a macho poem, but it does reflect the burdens of a middle-class man of an older generation who has been taught that he must shoulder the responsibility of being the family breadwinner. By contrast, Sylvia Plath's "Metaphors" (p. 683), which describes her own pregnancy through a series of images, deals with an experience that, by biological definition, only a woman can know first-hand. *Feminist criticism* has shown us how gender influences literary texts in subtler ways. (See p. 1802 for a discussion of feminist theory.) The central insight of feminist criticism seems inarguable—our gender does often influence how we speak, write, and interpret language. But that insight need not be intimidating. It can also invite us to bring our whole life experience, as women or men, to reading a poem. It reminds us that poetry, the act of using language with the greatest clarity and specificity, is a means to see the world through the eyes of the opposite sex. Sometimes the messages we get from this exchange aren't pleasant, but at least they may shock us into better understanding.

### *Anne Stevenson* (1933)*

Sous-Entendu          1969

Don't think

that I don't know
that as you talk to me
the hand of your mind
is inconspicuously                                                   5
taking off my stocking,
moving in resourceful blindness
up along my thigh.
Don't think
that I don't know                                                   10
that you know
everything I say
is a garment.

Sous-Entendu. The title is a French expression for "hidden meaning" or "implication." It describes something left unsaid but assumed to be understood.

1. What is left unsaid but assumed to be understood between the two people in this poem?
2. Could this poem have been written by a man? If so, under what circumstances? If not, why not?

### *Song of Songs* 2:3–13
### (Authorized or King James Version, 1611)

## AS THE APPLE TREE AMONG THE
## TREES OF THE WOOD          (about 500 B.C.)

As the apple tree among the trees of the wood,
So is my beloved among the sons.
I sat down under his shadow with great delight,
And his fruit was sweet to my taste.

He brought me to the banqueting house,                                    5
And his banner over me was love.

Stay me with flagons, comfort me with apples:
For I am sick of love.

His left hand is under my head,
And his right hand doth embrace me.                                        10

I charge you, O ye daughters of Jerusalem,
By the roes, and by the hinds of the field,
That ye stir not up, nor awake my love,
Till he please.

The voice of my beloved! behold, he cometh                                 15
Leaping upon the mountains, skipping upon the hills.

My beloved is like a roe or a young hart:
Behold, he standeth behind our wall,
He looketh forth at the windows,
Showing himself through the lattice.                                       20

My beloved spake, and said unto me,
Rise up, my love, my fair one, and come away.

For, lo, the winter is past,
The rain is over and gone;

The flowers appear on the earth;                                           25
The time of the singing of birds is come,
And the voice of the turtle is heard in our land;

The fig tree putteth forth her green figs,
And the vines with the tender grape give a good smell.
Arise, my love, my fair one, and come away. 30

SONG OF SONGS. The *Song of Songs* is the only book of love poetry in the Bible. For centuries, both Christian and Jewish scholars have considered these love songs as an allegory of human love for God; more recently, scholars have explored the book's literal meaning, a celebration of sexual love within marriage.

QUESTION

Many modern Biblical scholars speculate that the *Song of Songs* was written by a woman. Are there any elements in this passage that would support or rebut this position?

For society to exist, people have to try to understand one another, but, as society grows larger and more complex, the task of comprehending others becomes more daunting. An Italian farmer of one hundred years ago proba-bly understood his neighbors, who shared language, race, religion, class, and occupation with him, better than his great-granddaughter, a heavy-metal rock singer living in Brooklyn, understands her neighbors from a dozen different countries. Poetry isn't a scientific instrument, but it can build imaginative bridges from one mind to another—across gaps of culture, race, gender, age, and religion. It can even let us talk to the dead, by reading poems of another age. For an example of a personal poem that builds a bridge of imaginative sympathy across a chasm of pain and confusion, there can be few better recent examples than Yusef Komunyakaa's description of visiting the Vietnam Veteran's Memorial in Washington, D.C.

### *Yusef Komunyakaa* (b. 1947)

FACING IT                    1988

My black face fades,
hiding inside the black granite.
I said I wouldn't,
dammit: No tears.
I'm stone. I'm flesh. 5
My clouded reflection eyes me
like a bird of prey, the profile of night
slanted against morning. I turn
this way—the stone lets me go.
I turn that way—I'm inside 10
the Vietnam Veterans Memorial
again, depending on the light
to make a difference.
I go down the 58,022 names,

half-expecting to find                                                        15
my own in letters like smoke.
I touch the name Andrew Johnson;
I see the booby trap's white flash.
Names shimmer on a woman's blouse
but when she walks away                                                       20
the names stay on the wall.
Brushstrokes flash, a red bird's
wings cutting across my stare.
The sky. A plane in the sky.
A white vet's image floats                                                    25
closer to me, then his pale eyes
look through mine. I'm a window.
He's lost his right arm
inside the stone. In the black mirror
a woman's trying to erase names:                                              30
No, she's brushing a boy's hair.

## QUESTIONS

1. How does the title of "Facing It" relate to the poem? Does it have more than one meaning?
2. The narrator describes the people around him by their reflections on the polished granite rather than by looking at them directly. What does this indirect way of scrutinizing contribute to the poem?
3. This poem comes out of the life experience of a black Vietnam veteran. Is Komunyakaa writing closer to McKay's "universal" method or closer to Hughes' "ethnic" style?

## EXERCISE

Rewrite either of the following poems from the perspective of another gender. Then evaluate in what ways the new poem has changed the original's meaning, and in which ways the original poem comes through more or less unaltered.

---

### *Donald Justice* (b. 1925)

MEN AT FORTY                                            1967

Men at forty
Learn to close softly
The doors to rooms they will not be
Coming back to.

At rest on a stair landing,                                                    5
They feel it
Moving beneath them now like the deck of a ship,
Though the swell is gentle.

And deep in mirrors
They rediscover
The face of the boy as he practices tying
His father's tie there in secret

And the face of that father,
Still warm with the mystery of lather.
They are more fathers than sons themselves now.
Something is filling them, something

That is like the twilight sound
Of the crickets, immense,
Filling the woods at the foot of the slope
Behind their mortgaged houses.

10

15

20

---

## Adrienne Rich (b. 1929)*

### WOMEN                                                        1968

My three sisters are sitting
on rocks of black obsidian.
For the first time, in this light, I can see who they are.

My first sister is sewing her costume for the procession.
She is going as the Transparent Lady
and all her nerves will be visible.

My second sister is also sewing,
at the seam over her heart which has never healed entirely,
At last, she hopes, this tightness in her chest will ease.

My third sister is gazing
at a dark-red crust spreading westward far out on the sea.
Her stockings are torn but she is beautiful.

5

10

### FOR REVIEW AND FURTHER STUDY

---

## Shirley Geok-lin Lim (b. 1944)

### TO LI PO                                                      1980

I read you in a stranger's tongue,
Brother whose eyes were slanted also.
But you never left to live among
Foreign devils. Seeing the rice you ate grow

In your own backyard, you stayed on narrow                    5
Village paths. Only your mind travelled
Easily: east, north, south, and west
Compassed in observation of field
And family. All men were guests
To one who knew traditions, the best                          10
Of race. Country man, you believed to be Chinese
No more than a condition of human history.
Yet I cannot speak your tongue with ease,
No longer from China. Your stories
Stir griefs of dispersion and find                            15
Me in simplicity of kin.

Li Po. Li Po, also known as Li T'ai-po (701–62), was one of the great Chinese poets of the T'ang
dynasty.

## QUESTION

This poem is about a Chinese poet of the T'ang dynasty, but what does it tell us about
the speaker?

### *Alberto Ríos* (b. 1952)

## SPRING IN THE ONLY PLACE SPRING WAS          1982

At twelve I remember jumping
in and out of several open graves
onto the cool lawn here that was green
and shaved, like nothing else in Arizona,
ten, fifty, a hundred of us                                   5
crazy like canes
old men lift dresses with,
the two of us running
so fast we'd never get caught,
running through a hundred lives                               10
with our feet
and only our feet have grown old
so that now we look down
and wonder whose they are.

## QUESTION

We often think of spring as a universal experience. What does this poem from the
Southwest suggest about how our geographical background shapes our notion of the
seasons?

## Andrew Hudgins (b. 1951)

# Elegy for My Father, Who Is Not Dead    1991

One day I'll lift the telephone
and be told my father's dead. He's ready.
In the sureness of his faith, he talks
about the world beyond this world
as though his reservations have                           5
been made. I think he wants to go,
a little bit—a new desire
to travel building up, an itch
to see fresh worlds. Or older ones.
He thinks that when I follow him                          10
he'll wrap me in his arms and laugh,
the way he did when I arrived
on earth. I do not think he's right.
He's ready. I am not. I can't
just say good-bye as cheerfully                           15
as if he were embarking on a trip
to make my later trip go well.
I see myself on deck, convinced
his ship's gone down, while he's convinced
I'll see him standing on the dock                         20
and waving, shouting, Welcome back.

## QUESTIONS

1. The speaker describes his father's view of the afterlife in this poem. What image
   does he use to describe his father's vision of life after death?
2. What metaphor does the poet use to describe his own religious uncertainty?

## Edna St. Vincent Millay (1892–1950)*

# WELL, I HAVE LOST YOU;
# AND I LOST YOU FAIRLY    1931

Well, I have lost you; and I lost you fairly;
In my own way, and with my full consent.
Say what you will, kings in a tumbrel rarely
Went to their deaths more proud than this one went.
Some nights of apprehension and hot weeping                5
I will confess; but that's permitted me;
Day dried my eyes; I was not one for keeping
Rubbed in a cage a wing that would be free.
If I had loved you less or played you slyly
I might have held you for a summer more,                   10

But at the cost of words I value highly,
And no such summer as the one before.
Should I outlive this anguish—and men do—
I shall have only good to say of you.

Well, I Have Lost You. *Tumbrels:* Farmer's carts that were used during the French Revolution to transport condemned aristocrats to the guillotine.

## QUESTIONS

1. We feel we know a great deal about this love affair from Millay's sonnet, but what facts does she not share?
2. Would anything in the text of this sonnet be different if it had been written by a man?

## *Philip Larkin* (1922–1985)*

AUBADE                                                                              1977

I work all day, and get half-drunk at night.
Waking at four to soundless dark, I stare.
In time the curtain-edges will grow light.
Till then I see what's really always there:
Unresting death, a whole day nearer now,                                          5
Making all thought impossible but how
And where and when I shall myself die.
Arid interrogation: yet the dread
Of dying, and being dead,
Flashes afresh to hold and horrify.                                               10

The mind blanks at the glare. Not in remorse
—The good not done, the love not given, time
Torn off unused—nor wretchedly because
An only life can take so long to climb
Clear of its wrong beginnings, and may never;                                      15
But at the total emptiness for ever,
The sure extinction that we travel to
And shall be lost in always. Not to be here,
Not to be anywhere,
And soon; nothing more terrible, nothing more true.                                20

This is a special way of being afraid.
No trick dispels. Religion used to try,
That vast moth-eaten musical brocade
Created to pretend we never die,
And specious stuff that says *No rational being*                                   25
*Can fear a thing it will not feel*, not seeing
That this is what we fear—no sight, no sound,

No touch or taste or smell, nothing to think with,
Nothing to love or link with,
The anaesthetic from which none come round. 30

And so it stays just on the edge of vision,
A small unfocused blur, a standing chill
That slows each impulse down to indecision.
Most things may never happen: this one will,
And realisation of it rages out 35
In furnace-fear when we are caught without
People or drink. Courage is no good:
It means not scaring others. Being brave
Lets no one off the grave.
Death is no different whined at than withstood. 40

Slowly light strengthens, and the room takes shape.
It stands plain as a wardrobe, what we know,
Have always known, known that we can't escape,
Yet can't accept. One side will have to go.
Meanwhile telephones crouch, getting ready to ring 45
In locked-up offices, and all the uncaring
Intricate rented world begins to rouse.
The sky is white as clay, with no sun.
Work has to be done.
Postmen like doctors go from house to house. 50

## Questions

1. Is "Aubade" a confessional poem? If so, what social taboo does it violate?
2. What embarrassing facts about the narrator does the poem reveal? Do these confessions lead us to trust or distrust him?
3. The narrator says that "Courage is no good" (stanza 4). How might he defend this statement?
4. Would a twenty-year-old reader respond differently to this poem from a seventy-year-old reader? Would a devout Christian respond differently to the poem from an atheist?

## Suggestions For Writing

1. Find another poem in the Poems for Further Reading section (which begins on page 885) in which the poet, like Julia Alvarez, considers his or her own family. Tell in a paragraph or two, what the poem reveals about the author.
2. Compare Larkin's "Aubade" with another poem about old age and death, such as William Butler Yeats' "Sailing to Byzantium" (page 866), Frances Cornford's "The Watch" (page 718) and "All Souls' Night" (page 815), William Shakespeare's "That time of year thou mayst in me behold" (page 991), or Ruth Whitman's "Castoff Skin" (page 685).

# 27 Alternatives

## TRANSLATIONS

Poetry, said Robert Frost, is what gets lost in translation. If absolutely true, the comment is bad news for most of us, who have to depend on translations for our only knowledge of great poems in many other languages. However, some translators seem able to save a part of their originals and bring it across the language gap. At times they may even add more poetry of their own, as if to try to compensate for what is lost.

Unlike the writer of an original poem, the translator begins with a meaning that already exists. To convey it, the translator may decide to stick closely to the denotations of the original words or else to depart from them, more or less freely, after something he or she values more. The latter aim is evident in the *Imitations* of Robert Lowell, who said he had been "reckless with literal meaning" and instead had "labored hard to get the tone." Particularly defiant of translation are poems in dialect, uneducated speech, and slang: what can be used for English equivalents? Ezra Pound, in a bold move, translates the song of a Chinese peasant in *The Classic Anthology Defined by Confucius*:

> Yaller bird, let my corn alone,
> Yaller bird, let my crawps alone,
> These folks here won't let me eat,
> I wanna go back whaar I can meet
> the folks I used to know at home,
> > I got a home an' I wanna' git goin'.

Here, it is our purpose to judge a translation not by its fidelity to its original, but by the same standards we apply to any other poem written in

English. To do so may be another way to see the difference between appropriate and inappropriate words.

## Federico García Lorca (1899–1936)

| LA GUITARRA | 1921 | GUITAR | 1967 |
|---|---|---|---|

| | |
|---|---|
| Empieza el llanto | Begins the crying |
| de la guitarra. | of the guitar. |
| Se rompen las copas | From earliest dawn |
| de la madrugada. | the strokes are breaking. |
| Empieza el llanto | Begins the crying 5 |
| de la guitarra. | of the guitar. |
| Es inútil | It is futile |
| callarla. | to stop its sound. |
| Es imposible | It is impossible |
| callarla. | to stop its sound. 10 |
| Llora monótona | It is crying a monotone |
| como llora el agua, | like the crying of water, |
| como llora el viento | like the crying of wind |
| sobre la nevada. | over fallen snow. |
| Es imposible | It is impossible 15 |
| callarla. | to stop its sound. |
| Llora por cosas | It is crying over things |
| lejanas. | far off. |
| Arena del Sur caliente | Burning sand of the South |
| que pide camelias blancas. | which covets white camelias. 20 |
| Llora flecha sin blanco, | It is crying the arrow without aim, |
| la tarde sin mañana, | the evening without tomorrow, |
| y el primer pájaro muerto | and the first dead bird on the branch. |
| sobre la rama. | O guitar! |
| ¡Oh, guitarra! | Heart heavily wounded 25 |
| Corazón malherido | by five sharp swords. |
| por cinco espadas. | |

—Translated by Keith Waldrop

## QUESTIONS

1. Someone who knows Spanish should read aloud the original and the translation. Although it is impossible for any translation fully to capture the resonance of García Lorca's poem, in what places is the English version most nearly able to approximate it?
2. Another translation renders line 21: "It mourns for the targetless arrow." What is the difference between mourning for something and being the cry of it?
3. Throughout his translation, Waldrop closely follows the line divisions of the original, but in line 23 he combines García Lorca's lines 23 and 24. Can you see any point in his doing so? Would "on the branch" by itself be a strong line of English poetry?

Which English translation of each of the following poems is the best poetry? The originals may be of interest to some. For those who do not know the foreign language, the editor's line-by-line prose paraphrases may help indicate what the translator had to work with and how much of the translation is the translator's own idea. In which do you find the diction most felicitous? In which do pattern and structure best move as one? What differences in tone are apparent? It is doubtful that any one translation will surpass the others in every detail.

Our verb *translate* is derived from the Latin word *translatus*, the past participle of "to transfer" or "to carry across." The first set of translations try to carry across into English one of the most influential short poems ever written—Horace's ode, which ends with the advice, *carpe diem* ("seize the day"), has left its mark on countless poems. One even sees its imprint on contemporary novels (like Saul Bellow's *Seize the Day*) and films (like *Dead Poets Society*) that echo Horace's command to live in the present moment because no one knows what the future will bring.

## *Horace* (65–8 B.C.)

## ODES I (11)                    (About 20 B.C.)

Tu ne quaesieris—scire nefas—quem mihi, quem tibi
finem di dederint, Leuconoe, nec Babylonios
temptaris numeros. Ut melius, quicquid erit, pati!
seu plures hiemes, seu tribuit Iuppiter ultimam,
quae nunc oppositis debilitat pumicibus mare          5
Tyrrhenum. Sapias, vina liques, et spatio brevi
spem longam reseces. Dum loquimur, fugerit invida
aetas: carpe diem, quam minimum credula postero.

ODES I (11). Prose translation: (1 & 2) Do not ask, Leuconoe—to know is not permitted—what end the gods have given to you and me, do not (3) consult Babylonian horoscopes. It will be better to endure whatever comes, (4) whether Jupiter grants us more winters or whether this is the last one, (5) which now against the opposite cliffs wears out (6) the Tuscan sea. Be wise, decant the wine, and since our space is brief, (7) cut back your far-reaching hope. Even while we talk, envious time has fled away: (8) seize the day, put little trust in what is to come.

1. Edwin Arlington Robinson, *Horace to Leuconoe*                    1891

I pray you not, Leuconoe, to pore
With unpermitted eyes on what may be
Appointed by the gods for you and me,
Nor on Chaldean figures any more.
'T were infinitely better to implore          5
The present only:—whether Jove decree
More winters yet to come, or whether he

Make even this, whose hard, wave-eaten shore
Shatters the Tuscan seas to-day, the last—
Be wise withal, and rack your wine, nor fill

Your bosom with large hopes; for while I sing,
The envious close of time is narrowing;—
So seize the day, or ever it be past,
And let the morrow come for what it will.

2. James Michie                                               1963

Don't ask (we may not know), Leuconoe,
    What the gods plan for you or me.
        Leave the Chaldees to parse
        The sentence of the stars.

Better to bear the outcome, good or bad,
    Whether Jove purposes to add
        Fresh winters to the past
        Or to make this the last

Which now tires out the Tuscan sea and mocks
    Its strength with barricades of rocks.
        Be wise, strain clear the wine
        And prune the rambling vine

Of expectation. Life's short. Even while
    We talk Time, hateful, runs a mile.
        Don't trust tomorrow's bough
        For fruit. Pluck this, here, now.

3. John Frederick Nims,* Horace Coping                        1990

Don't ask—knowing's taboo—what's in the cards,
        darling, for you, for me,
what end heaven intends. Meddle with palm, planet,
        séance, tea leaves?
—rubbish! Shun the occult. Better by far take in
        your stride what comes.
Long life?—possible. Or—? Maybe the gods mean it
        your last, this grim
winter shaking the shore, booming the surf, wearying
        wave and rock.
Well then! Learn to be wise; out with the wine.
        Knowing the time so short,
no grand hopes, do you hear? Now, as we talk,
        huffishly time goes by.
So take hold of the day. Hugging it close. Nothing
        beyond is yours.

1. Which translation seems closest to the literal meaning of the Latin? Does that fidelity help or hinder its impact as a new poem in English?
2. The Nims translation tries to recreate Horace's original meter (Asclepiadean), a measure rarely found in English. Does Nims make this unusual classical meter work naturally in English?
3. If Nims copied a classical meter for his translation, E. A. Robinson used a more familiar English form. What is it?

The second set of translations try to recreate a short lyric by the classical Persian poet Omar Khayyam, the master of the *rubai*, a four-line stanza rimed *a a b a*. This Persian form was introduced in English by Edward FitzGerald (1809–1883) in his hugely popular translation, *The Rubaiyat of Omar Khayyam* (rubaiyat is the plural of rubai). In FitzGerald's Victorian version, Omar Khayyam became one of the most frequently quoted poets in English. Eugene O'Neill borrowed the title of his play *Ah, Wilderness!* from the *Rubaiyat* and expected his audience to catch the allusion. More recently, T.V. buffs may have heard Khayyam's poetry quoted habitually by the SWAT-team commander Howard Hunt on *Hill Street Blues*. Here are three poetic translations of a famous rubai. Which qualities of the original does each translation seem to capture?

## *Omar Khayyam* (1048–1131)

RUBAI                                    (about 1100)

Tongi-ye may-e la'l kh'aham o divani
    Sadd-e ramaghi bayad o nesf-e nani
Vangah man o to neshasteh dar virani
    Khoshtar bovad as mamlekat-e soltani.

RUBAI. Prose translation: (1) I want a jug of ruby wine and a book of poems. (2) There must be something to stop my breath from departing, and a half loaf of bread. (3) Then you and I sitting in some deserted ruin (4) Would be sweeter than the realm of a sultan.

1. Edward FitzGerald                                    1879

A Book of Verses underneath the Bough,
A Jug of Wine, a Loaf of Bread—and Thou
    Beside me singing in the Wilderness—
Oh, Wilderness were Paradise enow°!                    *enough*

2. Robert Graves and Omar Ali-Shah                    1968

Should our day's portion be one mancel loaf,
A haunch of mutton and a gourd of wine

Set for us two alone on the wide plain,
No Sultan's bounty could evoke such joy.


3. Dick Davis                                                          1992

I need a bare sufficiency—red wine,
    Some poems, half a loaf on which to dine
With you beside me in some ruined shrine:
    A king's state then is not as sweet as mine!


EXERCISE: PERSIAN VERSIONS

Write a rubai of your own on any topic. Some possible subjects include: what you
plan to do next weekend to relax; advice to a friend to stop worrying; an invitation
to a loved one; a four-line *carpe diem* ode. For your inspiration, here are a few more
rubaiyat from Edward FitzGerald's celebrated translation.


Wake! For the Sun who scattered into flight
The Stars before him from the Field of Night,
    Drives Night along with them from Heaven, and strikes
The Sultan's Turret with a Shaft of Light.

                    *       *       *       *

Come, fill the Cup, and in the Fire of Spring
Your Winter-garment of Repentence fling:
    The Bird of Time has but a little way
To flutter—and the Bird is on the Wing.

                    *       *       *       *

Some for the Glories of this World; and some
Sigh for the Prophet's Paradise to come;
    Ah, take the Cash, and let the Credit go,
Nor heed the rumble of a Distant Drum!

                    *       *       *       *

The Moving Finger writes; and, having writ,
Moves on: nor all your Piety nor Wit
    Shall lure it back to cancel half a Line
Nor all your Tears wash out a Word of it.

                    *       *       *       *

Ah Love! could you and I with Him conspire
To grasp this sorry Scheme of Things entire,
    Would we not shatter it to bits—and then
Remould it nearer to the Heart's desire.

# Parody

In a **parody**, one writer imitates another writer or another work, for the purpose of poking fun. Parody is a favorite medium for child poets, as shown in this jingle made up by children on the streets of Edinburgh.

## Anonymous

### We four lads from Liverpool are (about 1963)

We four lads from Liverpool are—
Paul in a taxi, John in a car,
George on a scooter, tootin' his hooter,
Following Ringo Starr.

Skillfully written, parody can be a devastating form of literary criticism. Rather than merely flinging abuse, the wise parodist imitates with understanding, even with sympathy. The many crude parodies of T. S. Eliot's difficult poem *The Waste Land* show parodists mocking what they cannot fathom, with the result that, instead of illuminating the original, they belittle it (and themselves). Good parodists have an ear for the sounds and rhythms of their originals, as does James Camp, who echoes Walt Whitman's stately "Out of the Cradle Endlessly Rocking" in his line "Out of the crock endlessly ladling" (what a weary teacher feels he is doing). Parody can be aimed at poems good or bad; yet there are poems of such splendor and dignity that no parodist seems able to touch them without looking like a small dog defiling a cathedral, and others so illiterate that good parody would be squandered on them. Sometimes parodies are even an odd form of flattery; poets poke fun at poems they simply can't get out of their head any other way except by rewriting, as in these three parodies of the *Rubaiyat of Omar Khayyam* by Wendy Cope. For devastating comic effect, Cope sets her contemporary versions of Khayyam in down-at-the-heels contemporary London.

## Wendy Cope (b. 1945)*

### from "From Strugnell's Rubaiyat" 1986

(11)

Here with a Bag of Crisps beneath the Bough,
A Can of Beer, a Radio—and Thou

Beside me half-asleep in Brockwell Park
And Brockwell Park is Paradise enow.

(12)

Some Men to everlasting Bliss aspire,
Their Lives, Auditions for the heavenly Choir;
Oh, use your Credit Card and waive the Rest—
Brave Music of a distant Amplifier!

(51)

The Moving Telex writes and having writ
Moves on; nor all thy Therapy nor Wit
Shall lure it back to cancel half a line
Nor Daz nor Bold wash out a Word of it.


## Hugh Kingsmill
### [Hugh Kingsmill Lunn] (1889–1949)

WHAT, STILL ALIVE AT TWENTY-TWO?                (about 1920)

What, still alive at twenty-two,
A clean, upstanding chap like you?
Sure, if your throat 'tis hard to slit,
Slit your girl's, and swing for it.

Like enough, you won't be glad                                    5
When they come to hang you, lad:
But bacon's not the only thing
That's cured by hanging from a string.

So, when the spilt ink of the night
Spreads o'er the blotting-pad of light,                           10
Lads whose job is still to do
Shall whet their knives, and think of you.

QUESTIONS

1. A. E. Housman considered this the best of many parodies of his poetry. Read his
   poems in this book, particularly "Eight O'Clock" (page 721), "When I was
   one-and-twenty" (page 751), and "To an Athlete Dying Young" (page 942). What
   characteristics of theme, form, and language does Hugh Kingsmill's parody convey?
2. What does Kingsmill exaggerate?

## Bruce Bennett (b. 1940)

### THE LADY SPEAKS AGAIN                    1992

"I lift my lamp beside the golden door."
More golden now than ever; don't ask why.
Just list your assets, where you can get more,
and who you know. No others need apply.

#### QUESTIONS
1. Who is the "lady" speaking? What poem is echoed in Bennett's parody?
2. Is Bennett making fun of the original poem? Or is there another object for his satire?

#### EXERCISE: *Spotting the Originals*

In the following parody, what poem or poet is being kidded? Does the parodist seem only to be having fun, or is he making any critical point?

## George Starbuck (b. 1931)

### MARGARET ARE YOU DRUG                    1966

Cool it Mag.
Sure it's a drag
With all that green flaked out.
Next thing you know they'll be changing the color of bread.

But look, Chick,                                                           5
Why panic?
Sevennyeighty years, we'll *all* be dead.

Roll with it, Kid.
I did.
Give it the old benefit of the doubt.                                     10

I mean leaves
Schmeaves.
You sure you aint just feeling sorry for yourself?

MARGARET ARE YOU DRUG. This is one of a series of "Translations from the English."

#### SUGGESTION FOR WRITING
1. Write a poem in the manner of Emily Dickinson, William Carlos Williams, E. E. Cummings, or any other modern poet whose work interests you and which you feel able to imitate. Decide, before you start, whether to write a serious imitation

(that could be slipped into the poet's *Collected Poems* without anyone being the wiser), or a humorous parody. Read all the poet's poems included in this book; perhaps you will find it helpful also to consult a larger selection or collection of the poet's work. It might be simplest to choose a particular poem as your model; but, if you like, you may echo any number of poems. Choose a model within the range of your own skill: to imitate a sonnet, for instance, you need to be able to rime and to write in meter. Probably, if your imitation is serious, and not a parody, it is a good idea to pick a subject or theme characteristic of the poet. This is a difficult project, but if you can do it even fairly well, you will know a great deal more about poetry and your poet.

# 28  *Evaluating a Poem*

## TELLING GOOD FROM BAD

Why do we call some poems "bad"? We are talking not about their moral implications. Rather, we mean that, for one or more of many possible reasons, the poem has failed to move us or to engage our sympathies. Instead, it has made us doubt that the poet is in control of language and vision; perhaps it has aroused our antipathies or unwittingly appealed to our sense of the comic, though the poet is serious. Some poems can be said to succeed despite burdensome faults. But in general such faults are symptoms of deeper malady: some weakness in a poem's basic conception or in the poet's competence.

Nearly always, a bad poem reveals only a dim and distorted awareness of its probable effect on its audience. Perhaps the sound of words may clash with what a poem is saying, as in the jarring last word of this opening line of a tender lyric (author unknown, quoted by Richard Wilbur): "Come into the tent, my love, and close the flap." A bad poem usually overshoots or falls short of its mark by the poet's thinking too little or too much. Thinking too much, a poet contrives an excess of ingenuity like that quoted by Alexander Pope in *Peri Bathous, or Of the Art of Sinking in Poetry*: a hounded stag who "Hears his own feet, and thinks they sound like more; / And fears the hind feet will o'ertake the fore." Thinking too little, a poet writes redundantly, as Wordsworth in "The Thorn": "And they had fixed the wedding-day, / The morning that must wed them both."

In a poem that has a rime scheme or a set line length, when all is well, pattern and structure move inseparably with the rest of their poem, the way a tiger's skin and bones move with their tiger. But sometimes, in a poem that fails, the poet evidently has had difficulty in fitting the statements into a formal pattern. English poets have long felt free to invert word order for a special effect (Milton: "ye myrtles brown"), but the poet having trouble keeping to a rime scheme may invert words for no apparent reason but convenience. Needing a rime for *barge* may lead to ending a line with a *policedog large* instead of *a large policedog*. Another sign of trouble is a profusion of adjectives. If a line of iambic pentameter reads, "Her lovely skin, like dear sweet white old silk," we suspect the poet of stuffing the line to make it long enough. (But no one suspects Matthew Arnold of padding the last line of "To Marguerite": "The unplumbed, salt, estranging sea.")

Even great poets write awful poems, and after their deaths, their worst efforts are collected with their masterpieces with no consumer warning labels to inform the reader. Some lines in the canon of celebrated bards make us wonder, "How could they have written this?" Wordsworth, Shelley, Whitman, and Browning are among the great whose failures can be painful, and sometimes an excellent poem will have a bad spot in it. To be unwilling to read them, though, would be as ill advised as to refuse to see Venice just because the Grand Canal is said to contain impurities. The seasoned reader of poetry thinks no less of Tennyson for having written, "Form, Form, Riflemen Form! . . . Look to your butts, and take good aims!" The collected works of a duller poet may contain no such lines of unconscious double meaning, but neither do they contain any poem as good as "Ulysses." If the duller poet never had a spectacular failure, it may be because of failure to take risks. "In poetry," said Ronsard, "the greatest vice is mediocrity."

Often, inept poems fall into familiar categories. At one extreme is the poem written entirely in conventional diction, dimly echoing Shakespeare, Wordsworth, and the Bible, but garbling them. Couched in a rhythm that ticks along like a metronome, this kind of poem shows no sign that its author has ever taken a hard look at anything that can be tasted, handled, and felt. It employs loosely and thoughtlessly the most abstract of words: *love, beauty, life, death, time, eternity.* Littered with old-fashioned contractions (*'tis, o'er, where'er*), it may end in a simple preachment or platitude. George Orwell's complaint against much contemporary writing (not only poetry) is applicable: "As soon as certain topics are raised"—and one thinks of such standard topics for poetry as spring, a first kiss, and stars—"the concrete melts into the abstract and no one seems able to think of turns of speech that are not hackneyed." Writers, Orwell charged, too often make their sentences out of tacked-together phrases "like the sections of a prefabricated hen-house."[1] Versifiers often do likewise.

At the opposite extreme is the poem that displays no acquaintance with

---

[1] George Orwell, "Politics and the English Language," from *Shooting an Elephant and Other Essays* (New York: Harcourt, 1945).

poetry of the past but manages, instead, to fabricate its own clichés. Slightly paraphrased, a manuscript once submitted to *The Paris Review* began:

Vile
    rottenflush
        o                —*screaming*—
      f CORPSEBLOOD!!        ooze
STRANGLE my
        *eyes* . . .
                  HELL's
           O, ghastly       stench**!!!

At most, such a work has only a private value. The writer has vented personal frustrations upon words, instead of kicking stray dogs. In its way, "Vile Rottenflush" is as self-indulgent as the oldfangled "first kiss in spring" kind of poem. "I dislike," said John Livingston Lowes, "poems that black your eyes, or put up their mouths to be kissed."

As jewelers tell which of two diamonds is fine by seeing which scratches the other, two poems may be tested by comparing them. This method works only on poems similar in length and kind: an epigram cannot be held up to test an epic. Most poems we meet are neither sheer trash nor obvious masterpieces. Because good diamonds to be proven need softer ones to scratch, in this chapter you will find a few clear-cut gems and a few clinkers.

---

**Anonymous** (English)

## O MOON, WHEN I GAZE ON THY
BEAUTIFUL FACE           (about 1900)

O Moon, when I gaze on thy beautiful face,
Careering along through the boundaries of space,
The thought has often come into my mind
If I ever shall see thy glorious behind.

O MOON. Sir Edmund Gosse, the English critic (1849–1928), offered this quatrain as the work of his maidservant, but there is reason to suspect him of having written it.

QUESTIONS

1. To what fact of astronomy does the last line refer?
2. Which words seem chosen with too little awareness of their denotations and connotations?
3. Even if you did not know that these lines probably were deliberately bad, how would you argue with someone who maintained that the opening *O* in the poem was admirable as a bit of concrete poetry?

## Grace Treasone

LIFE                    (about 1963)

Life is like a jagged tooth
that cuts into your heart;
fix the tooth and save the root,
and laughs, not tears, will start.

QUESTIONS

1. Try to paraphrase this poem. What is the poet saying?
2. How consistent is the working out of the comparison of life to a tooth?

## Stephen Tropp (b. 1930)

MY WIFE IS MY SHIRT          1960

My wife is my shirt
I put my hands through her armpits
slide my head through her mouth
& finally button her blood around my hands

QUESTIONS

1. How consistently is the metaphor elaborated?
2. Why can this metaphor be said to work in exactly the opposite way from a personification?
3. A paraphrase might discover this simile: "My wife is as intimate, familiar, and close to me as the shirt on my back." If this is the idea and the poem is supposed to be a love poem, how precisely is its attitude expressed?

## Emily Dickinson (1830–1886)*

A DYING TIGER—MOANED FOR DRINK          (ABOUT 1862)

A Dying Tiger—moaned for Drink—
I hunted all the Sand—
I caught the Dripping of a Rock
And bore it in my Hand—

His Mighty Balls—in death were thick—                    5
But searching—I could see
A Vision on the Retina
Of Water—and of me—

'Twas not my blame—who sped too slow—
'Twas not his blame—who died                              10

While I was reaching him—
But 'twas—the fact that He was dead—

## QUESTION

How does this poem compare in success with other poems of Emily Dickinson that you know? Justify your opinion by pointing to some of this poem's particulars.

## EXERCISE: *Ten Terrible Moments in Poetry*

Here is a small anthology of bad moments in poetry. For what reasons does each selection fail? In which passages do you attribute the failure to inappropriate sound or diction? To awkward word order? To inaccurate metaphor? To excessive overstatement? To forced rime? To monotonous rhythm? To redundancy? To simple-mindedness or excessive ingenuity?

1. Last lines of *Enoch Arden* by Alfred, Lord Tennyson:

   So passed the strong heroic soul away.
   And when they buried him, the little port
   Had seldom seen a costlier funeral.

2. From *Purely Original Verse* (1891) by J. Gordon Coogler (1865–1901), of Columbia, South Carolina:

   Alas for the South, her books have grown fewer—
   She never was much given to literature.

3. From "Lines Written to a Friend on the Death of His Brother, Caused by a Railway Train Running Over Him Whilst He Was in a State of Inebriation" by James Henry Powell:

   Thy mangled corpse upon the rails in frightful shape was found.
   The ponderous train had killed thee as its heavy wheels went round,
   And thus in dreadful form thou met'st a drunkard's awful death
   And I, thy brother, mourn thy fate, and breathe a purer breath.

4. From *Dolce Far Niente* by the American poet Francis Saltus Saltus, who flourished in the 1890s:

   Her laugh is like sunshine, full of glee,
   And her sweet breath smells like fresh-made tea.

5. From another gem by Francis Saltus Saltus, "The Spider":

   Then all thy feculent majesty recalls
       The nauseous mustiness of forsaken bowers,
   The leprous nudity of deserted halls—
       The positive nastiness of sullied flowers.

   And I mark the colours yellow and black
       That fresco thy lithe, dictatorial thighs,
   I dream and wonder on my drunken back
       How God could possibly have created flies!

6. From "Song to the Suliotes" by George Gordon, Lord Byron:

   Up to battle! Sons of Suli
   Up, and do your duty duly!
   There the wall—and there the moat is:

Bouwah! Bouwah! Suliotes,
There is booty—there is beauty!
Up my boys and do your duty!

7. From a juvenile poem of John Dryden, "Upon the Death of the Lord Hastings" (a victim of smallpox):

Each little pimple had a tear in it,
To wail the fault its rising did commit . . .

8. From "The Abbey Mason" by Thomas Hardy:

When longer yet dank death had wormed
The brain wherein the style had germed

From Gloucester church it flew afar—
The style called Perpendicular.—

To Winton and to Westminster
It ranged, and grew still beautifuller . . .

9. A metaphor from "The Crucible of Life" by the once-popular American newspaper poet Edgar A. Guest:

Sacred and sweet is the joy that must come
From the furnace of life when you've poured off the scum.

10. From an elegy for Queen Victoria by one of her subjects:

Dust to dust, and ashes to ashes,
Into the tomb the Great Queen dashes.

**Sentimentality** is a failure of writers who seem to feel a great emotion but who fail to give us sufficient grounds for sharing it. The emotion may be an anger greater than its object seems to call for, as in these lines to a girl who caused scandal (the exact nature of her act never being specified): "The gossip in each hall / Will curse your name . . . / Go! better cast yourself right down the falls!"[2] Or it may be an enthusiasm quite unwarranted by its subject: in *The Fleece* John Dyer temptingly describes the pleasures of life in a workhouse for the poor. The sentimental poet is especially prone to tenderness. Great tears fill his eyes at a glimpse of an aged grandmother sitting by a hearth. For all the poet knows, she may be the manager of a casino in Las Vegas who would be startled to find herself an object of pity, but the sentimentalist doesn't care to know about the woman herself. She is a general excuse for feeling maudlin. Any other conventional object will serve as well: a faded valentine, the strains of an old song, a baby's cast-off pacifier. An instance of such emotional self-indulgence is "The Old Oaken Bucket," by Samuel Woodworth, a stanza of which goes:

How sweet from the green, mossy brim to receive it,
    As, poised on the curb, it inclined to my lips!
Not a full-flushing goblet could tempt me to leave it,
    Tho' filled with the nectar that Jupiter sips.

[2]Ali. S. Hilmi, "The Preacher's Sermon," in *Verse at Random* (Larnaca, Cyprus: Ohanian Press, 1953).

> And now, far removed from the loved habitation,
>    The tear of regret will intrusively swell,
> As fancy reverts to my father's plantation,
>    And sighs for the bucket that hung in the well.

The staleness of the phrasing and imagery (Jove's nectar, *tear of regret*) suggests that the speaker is not even seeing the actual physical bucket, and the tripping meter of the lines is inappropriate to an expression of tearful regret. Perhaps the poet's nostalgia is genuine. Indeed, as Keith Waldrop has put it, "a bad poem is always sincere." However sincere in their feelings, sentimental poets are insincere in their art—otherwise, wouldn't they trouble to write better poems? Wet-eyed and sighing for a bucket, Woodworth achieves not pathos but **bathos:** a description that can move us to laughter instead of tears.[3] Tears, of course, can be shed for good reason. A piece of sentimentality is not to be confused with a well-wrought poem whose tone is tenderness.

## Rod McKuen (b. 1933)

### THOUGHTS ON CAPITAL PUNISHMENT           1954

There ought to be capital punishment for cars
that run over rabbits and drive into dogs
and commit the unspeakable, unpardonable crime
of killing a kitty cat still in his prime.

Purgatory, at the very least                                                    5
                    should await the driver
    driving over a beast.

Those hurrying headlights coming out of the dark
that scatter the scampering squirrels in the park
should await the best jury that one might compose          10
of fatherless chipmunks and husbandless does.

And then found guilty, after too fair a trial
should be caged in a cage with a hyena's smile
or maybe an elephant with an elephant gun
should shoot out his eyes when the verdict is done.          15

There ought to be something, something that's fair
to avenge Mrs. Badger as she waits in her lair

---

[3]*Bathos* in poetry can also mean an abrupt fall from the sublime to the trivial or incongruous. A sample, from Nicholas Rowe's play *The Fair Penitent:* "Is it the voice of thunder, or my father?" Another, from John Close, a minor Victorian: "Around their heads a dazzling halo shone, / No need of mortal robes, or any hat." When, however, such a letdown is used for a *desirable* effect of humor or contrast, it is usually called an **anticlimax:** as in Alexander Pope's lines on the queen's palace, "Here thou, great Anna! whom three realms obey, / Dost sometimes counsel take—and sometimes tea."

for her husband who lies with his guts spilling out
cause he didn't know what automobiles are about.

Hell on the highway, at the very least                                    20
               should await the driver
   driving over a beast.

Who kills a man kills a bit of himself
But a cat too is an extension of God.

---

**William Stafford** (1914–1993)*

TRAVELING THROUGH THE DARK                          1962

Traveling through the dark I found a deer
dead on the edge of the Wilson River road.
It is usually best to roll them into the canyon:
that road is narrow; to swerve might make more dead.

By glow of the tail-light I stumbled back of the car          5
and stood by the heap, a doe, a recent killing;
she had stiffened already, almost cold.
I dragged her off; she was large in the belly.

My fingers touching her side brought me the reason—
her side was warm; her fawn lay there waiting,                10
alive, still, never to be born.
Beside that mountain road I hesitated.

The car aimed ahead its lowered parking lights;
under the hood purred the steady engine.
I stood in the glare of the warm exhaust turning red;        15
around our group I could hear the wilderness listen.

I thought hard for us all—my only swerving—
then pushed her over the edge into the river.

## QUESTIONS

1. Compare these poems by Rod McKuen and William Stafford. How are they similar?
2. Explain Stafford's title. Who are all those traveling through the dark?
3. Comment on McKuen's use of language. Consider especially: *unspeakable, unpardonable crime* (line 3), *kitty cat* (4), *scatter the scampering squirrels* (9), and *cause he didn't know* (19).
4. Compare the meaning of Stafford's last two lines and McKuen's last two. Does either poem have a moral? Can either poem be said to moralize?
5. Which poem might be open to the charge of sentimentality? Why?

Which of the following five poems do you find sentimental? Which would you defend? At least one kind of evidence to look for is minute, detailed observation of physical objects. In a successful poem, the poet is likely at least occasionally to notice the world beyond his or her own skin; in a sentimental poem, this world is likely to be ignored.

## *Julia A. Moore* (1847–1920)

### LITTLE LIBBY                    1876

One more little spirit to Heaven has flown,
    To dwell in that mansion above,
Where dear little angels, together roam,
    In God's everlasting love.

One little flower has withered and died,           5
    A bud nearly ready to bloom,
Its life on earth is marked with pride;
    Oh, sad it should die so soon.

Sweet little Libby, that precious flower
    Was a pride in her parents' home,          10
They miss their little girl *every* hour,
    Those friends that are left to mourn.

Her sweet silvery voice no more is heard
    In the home where she once roamed;
Her place is *vacant* around the hearth,          15
    Where her friends are mourning lone.

They are mourning the loss of a little girl,
    With black eyes and auburn hair,
She was a treasure to them in this world,
    This beautiful child so fair.          20

One morning in April, a short time ago,
    Libby was active and gay;
Her Saviour called her, she had to go,
    E're the close of that pleasant day.

While eating dinner, this dear little child          25
    Was choked on a piece of beef.
Doctors came, tried their skill awhile,
    But none could give relief.

She was ten years of age, I am told,
    And in school stood very high.          30

Her little form now the earth enfolds,
  In her embrace it must ever lie.

Her friends and schoolmates will not forget
  Little Libby that is no more;
She is waiting on the shining step,                                    35
  To welcome home friends once more.

## *Bill Knott* (b. 1940)

### POEM                                          1968

The only response
to a child's grave is
to lie down before it and play dead

## *Dabney Stuart* (b. 1937)

### CRIB DEATH                                    1987

Kisses are for the living.
Even if the terrible breath of the dead
Never rose from the earth's mouth,
Dread of it would turn our heads aside
As relatives at a funeral meet and kiss.                               5
Living in such air is what the living have,
Less choice than a stone what's cut into its face.

## *Michael Harper* (b. 1938)

### REUBEN, REUBEN                                1970

I reach from pain
to music great enough
to bring me back,
swollenhead, madness,
lovefruit, a pickle of hate                                            5
so sour my mouth twicked
up and would not sing;
there's nothing in the beat
to hold it in
melody and turn human skin;                                           10
a brown berry gone
to rot just two days on the branch;

we've lost a son,
the music, *jazz*, comes in.

## Ted Kooser (b. 1939)

### A CHILD'S GRAVE MARKER   1985

A small block of granite
engraved with her name and the dates
just wasn't quite pretty enough
for this lost little girl
or her parents, who added a lamb                          5
cast in plaster of paris,
using the same kind of cake mold
my grandmother had—iron,
heavy and black as a skillet.
The lamb came out coconut-white,                          10
and seventy years have proven it
soft in the rain. On this hill,
overlooking a river in Iowa,
it melts in its own sweet time.

In recent years, the belief that poetry cannot be popular has been shaken
by practitioners of **cowboy poetry,** verse about life on the range, written by
people who know that life at first hand. Usually realistic, riming and metrical, cowboy poetry is designed to be read aloud or recited to audiences such
as the large throng that assembles each January at the Cowboy Poetry Gathering in Elko, Nevada. This kind of folk poetry "has its own criteria of good
and bad," insists Gibbs Smith, publisher of two best-selling cowboy poetry
anthologies; "it has its own rules; its own tradition, and we should respect
that."[4] Devotees of cowboy poetry regard the following poem as a classic.
Read it and see if you agree.

## Wallace McRae (b. 1936)

### REINCARNATION        1980

"What does reincarnation mean?"
A cowpoke ast his friend.
His pal replied, "It happens when

[4]Quoted by Sara Terry, "Poem on the Range," *Boston Globe Magazine*, Jan. 19, 1992. The
anthologies, edited by Hal Cannon, are *Cowboy Poetry: A Gathering* and *New Cowboy Poetry* (Salt
Lake City: Gibbs M. Smith, 1985 and 1990).

Yer life has reached its end.
They comb yer hair, and warsh yer neck,          5
And clean yer fingernails,
And lay you in a padded box
Away from life's travails.

"The box and you goes in a hole,
That's been dug into the ground.               10
Reincarnation starts in when
Yore planted 'neath a mound.
Them clods melt down, just like yer box,
And you who is inside.
And then yore just beginnin' on                15
Yer transformation ride.

"In a while the grass'll grow
Upon yer rendered mound.
Till some day on yer moldered grave
A lonely flower is found.                       20
And say a hoss should wander by
And graze upon this flower
That once wuz you, but now's become
Yer vegetative bower.

"The posey that the hoss done ate              25
Up, with his other feed,
Makes bone, and fat, and muscle
Essential to the steed.
But some is left that he can't use
And so it passes through,                       30
And finally lays upon the ground.
This thing, that once wuz you.

"Then say, by chance, I wanders by
And sees this upon the ground,
And I ponders, and I wonders at,               35
This object that I found.
I thinks of reincarnation,
Of life, and death, and such,
And come away concludin': Slim,
You ain't changed, all that much."             40

## Questions

1. If you were Slim, how would you react to that last line?
2. Discuss this harsh judgment: "This isn't much of a poem. The poet is only playing an elaborate joke on Slim and on the rest of us."

3. In general, do you believe that a poem is any the worse for a lack of total seriousness?
4. Take a close look at the poem's language. Which words or phrases seem un-schooled cowboy speech? Which might be criticized as stilted or bookish? How do you account for this discrepancy?
5. Compare the poem's central idea with a similar notion advanced by Shakespeare's *Hamlet, Prince of Denmark*:

> *Hamlet:* A man may fish with the worm that hath eat of a king, and eat of the fish that hath fed of that worm.
> *King:* What dost thou mean by this?
> *Hamlet:* Nothing but to show you how a king may go to progress through the guts of a beggar.
>
> (Hamlet IV, iii, 27–32)

Notice that Hamlet, like Slim's friend, also puts his listener on the receiving end of an insult. But how might it be claimed that Shakespeare makes a simple idea rich and complicated?
6. Do you agree with Gibbs Smith that we should judge cowboy poetry only by its own rules (not oblige it to live up to standards we might apply to a passage of Shakespeare or a poem by Robert Frost)?

## KNOWING EXCELLENCE

How can we tell an excellent poem from any other? To give reasons for excellence in poetry is harder than to give reasons for failure in poetry (so often due to familiar kinds of imprecision and sentimentality). A bad poem tends to be stereotyped, an excellent poem unique. In judging either, we can have no absolute specifications. A poem is not like an electric toaster that an inspector can test by a check-off list. It has to be judged on the basis of what it is trying to be and how well it succeeds in the effort.

To judge a poem, we first have to understand it. At least, we need to understand it *almost* all the way; there is, to be sure, a poem such as Hop-kins's "The Windhover" (page 941), which most readers probably would call excellent even though its meaning is still being debated. Although it is a good idea to give a poem at least a couple of considerate readings before judging it, sometimes our first encounter starts turning into an act of evalua-tion. Moving along into the poem, becoming more deeply involved in it, we may begin forming an opinion. In general, the more a poem contains for us to understand, the more rewarding we are likely to find it. Of course, an obscure and highly demanding poem is not always to be preferred to a relatively simple one. Difficult poems can be pretentious and incoherent; still, there is something to be said for the poem complicated enough to leave us something to discover on our fifteenth reading (unlike most limericks, which yield their all at a look). Here is such a poem, one not readily fath-omed and exhausted.

## William Butler Yeats (1865–1939)*

### SAILING TO BYZANTIUM         1927

That is no country for old men. The young
In one another's arms, birds in the trees
—Those dying generations—at their song,
The salmon-falls, the mackerel-crowded seas,
Fish, flesh, or fowl, commend all summer long         5
Whatever is begotten, born, and dies.
Caught in that sensual music all neglect
Monuments of unaging intellect.

An aged man is but a paltry thing,
A tattered coat upon a stick, unless         10
Soul clap its hands and sing, and louder sing
For every tatter in its mortal dress,
Nor is there singing school but studying
Monuments of its own magnificence;
And therefore I have sailed the seas and come         15
To the holy city of Byzantium.

O sages standing in God's holy fire
As in the gold mosaic of a wall,
Come from the holy fire, perne in a gyre°,         *spin down a spiral*
And be the singing-masters of my soul.         20
Consume my heart away; sick with desire
And fastened to a dying animal
It knows not what it is; and gather me
Into the artifice of eternity.

Once out of nature I shall never take         25
My bodily form from any natural thing,
But such a form as Grecian goldsmiths make
Of hammered gold and gold enameling
To keep a drowsy Emperor awake;
Or set upon a golden bough to sing         30
To lords and ladies of Byzantium
Of what is past, or passing, or to come.

SAILING TO BYZANTIUM. Byzantium was the capital of the Byzantine Empire, the city now called Istanbul. Yeats means, though, not merely the physical city. Byzantium is also a name for his conception of paradise.

Though *salmon-falls* (line 4) suggests Yeats's native Ireland, the poem, as we find out in line 25, is about escaping from the entire natural world. If the poet desires this escape, then probably the *country* mentioned in the opening line is no political nation but the cycle of birth and death in which human beings are trapped; and, indeed, the poet says his heart is "fastened to a dying animal." Imaginary landscapes, it would seem, are merging with the historical Byzantium. Lines 17–18 refer to mosaic images, adornments of the Byzantine cathedral of St. Sophia, in which the figures of saints are inlaid against backgrounds of gold. The clockwork bird of the last stanza is also a reference to something actual. Yeats noted: "I have read somewhere that in the Emperor's palace at Byzantium was a tree made of gold and silver, and artificial birds that sang." This description of the role the poet would seek—that of a changeless, immortal singer—directs us back to the earlier references to music and singing. Taken all together, they point toward the central metaphor of the poem: the craft of poetry can be a kind of singing. One kind of everlasting monument is a great poem. To study masterpieces of poetry is the only "singing school"—the only way to learn to write a poem.

We have no more than skimmed through a few of this poem's suggestions, enough to show that, out of allusion and imagery, Yeats has woven at least one elaborate metaphor. Surely one thing the poem achieves is that, far from merely puzzling us, it makes us aware of relationships between what a person can imagine and the physical world. There is the statement that a human heart is bound to the body that perishes, and yet it is possible to see consciousness for a moment independent of flesh, to sing with joy at the very fact that the body is crumbling away. Expressing a similar view of mortality, the Japanese artist Hokusai has shown a withered tree letting go of its few remaining leaves, while under it two graybeards shake with laughter. Like Hokusai's view, that of Yeats is by no means simple. Much of the power of Yeats's poem comes from the physical terms with which he states the ancient quarrel between body and spirit, body being a "tattered coat upon a stick." There is all the difference in the world between the work of the poet like Yeats whose eye is on the living thing and whose mind is awake and passionate, and that of the slovenly poet whose dull eye and sleepy mind focus on nothing more than some book read hastily long ago. The former writes a poem out of compelling need, the latter as if it seems a nice idea to write something.

Yeats's poem has the three qualities essential to beauty, according to the definition of Thomas Aquinas: wholeness, harmony, and radiance. The poem is all one; its parts move in peace with one another; it shines with emotional intensity. There is an orderly progression going on in it: from the speaker's statement of his discontent with the world of "sensual music," to his statement that he is quitting this world, to his prayer that the sages will take him in, and his vision of future immortality. And the images of the poem relate to one another—*dying generations* (line 3), *dying animal* (line 22), and the undying golden bird (lines 27–32)—to mention just one series of related things. "Sailing to Byzantium" is not the kind of poem that has, in Pope's words, "One simile, that solitary shines / In the dry desert of a thousand lines." Rich in figurative language, Yeats's whole poem develops a metaphor, with further metaphors as its tributaries.

"Sailing to Byzantium" has a theme that matters to us. What human being does not long, at times, to shed timid, imperfect flesh, to live in a state of absolute joy, unperishing? Being human, perhaps we too are stirred by Yeats's prayer: "Consume my heart away, sick with desire / And fastened to a dying animal. . . ." If it is true that in poetry (as Ezra Pound declared) "only emotion endures," then Yeats's poem ought to endure. (No reasons to be moved by a poem, however, can be of much use. If you happen not to feel moved by this poem, try another—but come back to "Sailing to Byzantium" after a while.)

Most excellent poems, it might be argued, contain significant themes, as does "Sailing to Byzantium." But the presence of such a theme is not enough to render a poem excellent. Not theme alone makes an excellent poem, but how well a theme is stated.

Yeats's poem, some would say, is the match for any lyric in our language. Some might call it inferior to an epic (to Milton's *Paradise Lost*, say, or to the *Iliad*), but this claim is to lead us into a different argument: whether certain genres are innately better than others. Such an argument usually leads to a dead end. Evidently, *Paradise Lost* has greater range, variety, matter, length, and ambitiousness. But any poem—whether an epic or an epigram— may be judged by how well it fulfills the design it undertakes. God, who created both fleas and whales, pronounced all good. Fleas, like epigrams, have no reason to feel inferior.

### EXERCISE: *Two Poems to Compare*

Here are two poems with a similar theme. Which contains more qualities of excellent poetry? Decide whether the other is bad or whether it may be praised for achieving something different.

### *Arthur Guiterman* (1871–1943)

ON THE VANITY OF EARTHLY GREATNESS   1936

The tusks that clashed in mighty brawls
Of mastodons, are billiard balls.

The sword of Charlemagne the Just
Is ferric oxide, known as rust.

The grizzly bear whose potent hug       5
Was feared by all, is now a rug.

Great Caesar's bust is on the shelf,
And I don't feel so well myself.

### Percy Bysshe Shelley (1792–1822)*

OZYMANDIAS                                    1818

I met a traveler from an antique land
Who said: Two vast and trunkless legs of stone
Stand in the desert. Near them, on the sand,
Half sunk, a shattered visage lies, whose frown,
And wrinkled lip, and sneer of cold command,                    5
Tell that its sculptor well those passions read
Which yet survive, stamped on these lifeless things,
The hand that mocked° them and the heart that fed;          imitated
And on the pedestal these words appear:
"My name is Ozymandias, king of kings:                          10
Look on my works, ye Mighty, and despair!"
Nothing beside remains. Round the decay
Of that colossal wreck, boundless and bare
The lone and level sands stretch far away.

Some excellent poems of the past will remain sealed to us unless we are willing to sympathize with their conventions. Pastoral poetry, for instance —Marlowe's "Passionate Shepherd" and Milton's "Lycidas"—asks us to accept certain conventions and situations that may seem old-fashioned: idle swains, oaten flutes. We are under no grim duty, of course, to admire poems whose conventions do not appeal to us. But there is no point in blaming a poet for playing a particular game or for observing its rules.

Bad poems, of course, can be woven together out of conventions, like patchwork quilts made of old unwanted words. In Shakespeare's England, poets were busily imitating the sonnets of Petrarch, the Italian poet whose praise of his beloved Laura had become well known. The result of their industry was a surplus of Petrarchan **conceits,** or elaborate comparisons (from the Italian *concetto:* concept, bright idea). In the following sonnet, Shakespeare, who at times helped himself generously from the Petrarchan stockpile, pokes fun at poets who thoughtlessly use such handed-down figures of speech.

### William Shakespeare (1564–1616)*

MY MISTRESS' EYES ARE NOTHING LIKE THE SUN          1609

My mistress' eyes are nothing like the sun;
Coral is far more red than her lips' red;
If snow be white, why then her breasts are dun;
If hairs be wires, black wires grow on her head.
I have seen roses damasked red and white,                       5

But no such roses see I in her cheeks;
And in some perfumes is there more delight
Than in the breath that from my mistress reeks.
I love to hear her speak, yet well I know
That music hath a far more pleasing sound;                    10
I grant I never saw a goddess go:
My mistress, when she walks, treads on the ground.
   And yet, by heaven, I think my love as rare
   As any she°, belied with false compare.                 *woman*

Contrary to what you might expect, for years after Shakespeare's time, poets
continued to write fine poems with Petrarchan conventions.

### *Thomas Campion* (1567–1620)*

THERE IS A GARDEN IN HER FACE     1617

   There is a garden in her face
Where roses and white lilies grow;
   A heav'nly paradise is that place
Wherein all pleasant fruits do flow.
   There cherries grow which none may buy          5
   Till "Cherry-ripe" themselves do cry.

   Those cherries fairly do enclose
Of orient pearl a double row,
   Which when her lovely laughter shows,
They look like rose-buds filled with snow;              10
   Yet them nor° peer nor prince can buy,           *neither*
   Till "Cherry-ripe" themselves do cry.

   Her eyes like angels watch them still;
Her brows like bended bows do stand,
   Threat'ning with piercing frowns to kill          15
All that attempt, with eye or hand
   Those sacred cherries to come nigh
   Till "Cherry-ripe" themselves do cry.

THERE IS A GARDEN IN HER FACE. 6 *"Cherry-ripe"*: cry of fruit-peddlers in London streets.

### QUESTIONS

1. What does Campion's song owe to Petrarchan tradition?
2. What in it strikes you as fresh observation of actual life?
3. Comment in particular on the last stanza. Does the comparison of eyebrows to threatening bowmen seem too silly or far-fetched? What sense do you find in it?
4. Try to describe the tone of this poem. What do you understand, from this portrait of a young girl, to be the poet's feelings?

Excellent poetry might be easier to recognize if each poet had a fixed position on the slopes of Mount Parnassus, but from one century to the next, the reputations of some poets have taken humiliating slides, or made impressive clambers. We decide for ourselves which poems to call excellent, but readers of the future may reverse our opinions. Most of us no longer would share this popular view of Walt Whitman by one of his contemporaries:

> Walt Whitman (1819–1892), by some regarded as a great poet; by others, as no poet at all. Most of his so-called poems are mere catalogues of things, without meter or rime, but in a few more regular poems and in lines here and there he is grandly poetical, as in "O Captain! My Captain!"[5]

---

### Walt Whitman (1819–1892)*

## O Captain! My Captain!                                    1865

O Captain! my Captain! our fearful trip is done,
The ship has weather'd every rack, the prize we sought is won,
The port is near, the bells I hear, the people all exulting,
While follow eyes the steady keel, the vessel grim and daring;
    But O heart! heart! heart!                                   5
      O the bleeding drops of red,
        Where on the deck my Captain lies,
        Fallen cold and dead.

O Captain! my Captain! rise up and hear the bells;
Rise up—for you the flag is flung—for you the bugle trills,        10
For you bouquets and ribbon'd wreaths—for you the shores
    a-crowding,
For you they call, the swaying mass, their eager faces turning;
    Here Captain! dear father!
      This arm beneath your head!
        It is some dream that on the deck,                           15
        You've fallen cold and dead.

My Captain does not answer, his lips are pale and still,
My father does not feel my arm, he has no pulse nor will,
The ship is anchor'd safe and sound, its voyage closed and done,
From fearful trip the victor ship comes in with object won;        20
    Exult O shores, and ring O bells!
    But I with mournful tread,

[5]J. Willis Westlake, A.M., in *Common-school Literature, English and American, with Several Hundred Extracts to be Memorized* (Philadelphia, 1898).

Walk the deck my Captain lies,
    Fallen cold and dead.

O Captain! My Captain! Written soon after the death of Abraham Lincoln, this was, in Whitman's lifetime, by far the most popular of his poems.

## Questions

1. Compare this with other Whitman poems. (See another elegy for Lincoln, "When Lilacs Last in the Dooryard Bloom'd.") In what ways is "O Captain! My Captain!" uncharacteristic of his works? Do you agree with J. Willis Westlake that this is one of the few occasions on which Whitman is "grandly poetical?"
2. Comment on the appropriateness to its subject of the poem's rhythms.
3. Do you find any evidence in this poem that an excellent poet wrote it?

There is nothing to do but commit ourselves and praise or blame and, if need be, let time erase our error. In a sense, all readers of poetry are constantly reexamining the judgments of the past by choosing those poems they care to go on reading. In the end, we have to admit that the critical principles set forth in this chapter are all very well for admiring excellent poetry we already know, but they cannot be carried like a yardstick in the hand, to go out looking for it. As Ezra Pound said in his *ABC of Reading*, "A classic is classic not because it conforms to certain structural rules, or fits certain definitions (of which its author had quite probably never heard). It is classic because of a certain eternal and irrepressible freshness."

The best poems, like "Sailing to Byzantium," may offer a kind of religious experience. In the last decade of the twentieth century, some of us rarely set foot outside an artificial environment. Whizzing down four-lane superhighways, we observe lakes and trees in the distance. In a way our cities are to us as anthills are to ants: no less than anthills, they are "natural" structures. But the "unnatural" world of school or business is, as Wordsworth says, too much with us. Locked in the shells of our ambitions, our self-esteem, we forget our kinship to earth and sea. We fabricate self-justifications. But a great poem shocks us into another order of perception. It points beyond language to something still more essential. It ushers us into an experience so moving and true that we feel (to quote King Lear) "cut to the brain." In bad or indifferent poetry, words are all there is.

## *Carl Sandburg* (1878–1967)

Fog                    1916

The fog comes
on little cat feet.
It sits looking
over harbor and city

on silent haunches
and then moves on.

## QUESTION

In lines 15–22 of "The Love Song of J. Alfred Prufrock" (page 916), T. S. Eliot also likens fog to a cat. Compare Sandburg's lines and Eliot's. Which passage tells us more about fogs and cats?

## Thomas Gray (1716–1771)*

### ELEGY WRITTEN IN A COUNTRY CHURCHYARD      1753

The curfew tolls the knell of parting day,
  The lowing herd wind slowly o'er the lea,
The plowman homeward plods his weary way,
  And leaves the world to darkness and to me.

Now fades the glimmering landscape on the sight,       5
  And all the air a solemn stillness holds,
Save where the beetle wheels his droning flight,
  And drowsy tinklings lull the distant folds;

Save that from yonder ivy-mantled tower
  The moping owl does to the moon complain       10
Of such, as wand'ring near her secret bower,
  Molest her ancient solitary reign.

Beneath those rugged elms, that yew tree's shade,
  Where heaves the turf in many a mold'ring heap,
Each in his narrow cell forever laid,       15
  The rude° forefathers of the hamlet sleep.       *simple, ignorant*

The breezy call of incense-breathing morn,
  The swallow twitt'ring from the straw-built shed,
The cock's shrill clarion, or the echoing horn°,       *fox-hunters' horn*
  No more shall rouse them from their lowly bed.       20

For them no more the blazing hearth shall burn,
  Or busy housewife ply her evening care;
No children run to lisp their sire's return,
  Or climb his knees the envied kiss to share.

Oft did the harvest to their sickle yield,       25
  Their furrow oft the stubborn glebe° has broke;       *turf*

ELEGY WRITTEN IN A COUNTRY CHURCHYARD. In English poetry, an **elegy** has come to mean a lament or a sadly meditative poem, sometimes written on the occasion of a death. Other elegies in this book include Chidiock Tichborne's "Elegy," Milton's "Lycidas," A. E. Housman's "To an Athlete Dying Young," and in more recent poetry, "The Rites for Cousin Vit" by Gwendolyn Brooks and "Elegy for Jane" by Theodore Roethke.

How jocund did they drive their team afield!
   How bowed the woods beneath their sturdy stroke!

Let not Ambition mock their useful toil,
   Their homely joys, and destiny obscure;           30
Nor Grandeur hear with a disdainful smile
   The short and simple annals of the poor.

The boast of heraldry°, the pomp of pow'r,          *noble birth*
   And all that beauty, all that wealth e'er gave,
Awaits alike th' inevitable hour.           35
   The paths of glory lead but to the grave.

Nor you, ye proud, impute to these the fault,
   If Mem'ry o'er their tomb no trophies raise,
Where through the long-drawn aisle and fretted° vault   *inlaid with designs*
   The pealing anthem swells the note of praise.      40

Can storied urn or animated bust
   Back to its mansion call the fleeting breath?
Can Honor's voice provoke the silent dust,
   Or Flatt'ry soothe the dull cold ear of Death?

Perhaps in this neglected spot is laid          45
   Some heart once pregnant with celestial fire;
Hands that the rod of empire might have swayed,
   Or waked to ecstasy the living lyre.

But knowledge to their eyes her ample page
   Rich with the spoils of time did ne'er unroll;      50
Chill Penury° repressed their noble rage,          *Poverty*
   And froze the genial current of the soul.

Full many a gem of purest ray serene,
   The dark unfathomed caves of ocean bear:
Full many a flower is born to blush unseen,      55
   And waste its sweetness on the desert air.

Some village Hampden, that with dauntless breast
   The little tyrant of his field withstood;
Some mute inglorious Milton here may rest,
   Some Cromwell, guiltless of his country's blood.      60

---

41 *storied urn:* vessel holding the ashes of the dead after cremation. *Storied* can mean (1) decorated with scenes; (2) inscribed with a life's story; or (3) celebrated in story or history. The *animated bust* is a lifelike sculpture of the dead, placed on a tomb. 57 *Hampden:* John Hampden (1594–1643), member of Parliament, had resisted illegal taxes on his lands imposed by Charles I. 60 *Cromwell . . . his country's blood:* Gray blames Oliver Cromwell (1599–1658) for strife and tyranny. As general of the armies of Parliament, Cromwell had won the Civil War against Charles I and had signed the king's death warrant. As Lord Protector of England (1653–1658), he had ruled with an iron hand.

Th' applause of list'ning senates to command,
    The threats of pain and ruin to despise,
To scatter plenty o'er a smiling land,
    And read their hist'ry in a nation's eyes,

Their lot forbade; nor circumscribed alone                                    65
    Their growing virtues, but their crimes confined;
Forbade to wade through slaughter to a throne,
    And shut the gates of mercy on mankind,

The struggling pangs of conscious truth to hide,
    To quench the blushes of ingenuous° shame,                *innocent*   70
Or heap the shrine of Luxury and Pride
    With incense kindled at the Muse's flame.

Far from the madding° crowd's ignoble strife,                     *frenzied*
    Their sober wishes never learned to stray;
Along the cool sequestered vale of life                                        75
    They kept the noiseless tenor° of their way.         *ongoing motion*

Yet ev'n these bones from insult to protect
    Some frail memorial still erected nigh,
With uncouth rhymes and shapeless sculpture decked,
    Implores the passing tribute of a sigh.                                    80

Their name, their years, spelt by th' unlettered Muse,
    The place of fame and elegy supply:
And many a holy text around she strews,
    That teach the rustic moralist to die.

For who to dumb Forgetfulness a prey,                                          85
    This pleasing anxious being e'er resigned,
Left the warm precincts of the cheerful day,
    Nor cast one longing ling'ring look behind?

On some fond breast the parting soul relies,
    Some pious drops the closing eye requires;                                 90
Ev'n from the tomb the voice of Nature cries,
    Ev'n in our ashes live their wonted° fires.                    *customary*

For thee, who mindful of th' unhonored dead
    Dost in these lines their artless tale relate;
If chance°, by lonely contemplation led,                        *if by chance*   95
    Some kindred spirit shall inquire thy fate,

Haply° some hoary-headed swain° may say,           *perhaps; gray-haired shepherd*
    "Oft have we seen him at the peep of dawn
Brushing with hasty steps the dews away
    To meet the sun upon the upland lawn.                                      100

71–72 *heap the shrine . . . Muse's flame:* Gray chides mercenary poets who write poems to please
their rich, high-living patrons.

"There at the foot of yonder nodding beech
    That wreathes its old fantastic roots so high,
His listless length at noontide would he stretch,
    And pore upon the brook that babbles by.

"Hard by yon wood, now smiling as in scorn,                                    105
    Mutt'ring his wayward fancies he would rove,
Now drooping, woeful wan, like one forlorn,
    Or crazed with care, or crossed in hopeless love.

"One morn I missed him, on the customed hill,
    Along the heath and near his fav'rite tree;                                110
Another came; nor yet beside the rill°,                              *brook*
    Nor up the lawn, nor at the wood was he;

"The next with dirges due in sad array
    Slow through the churchway path we saw him borne.
Approach and read (for thou canst read) the lay°,        *song or poem* 115
    Graved on the stone beneath yon aged thorn."

*The Epitaph*

*Here rests his head upon the lap of Earth*
    *A youth to Fortune and to Fame unknown.*
*Fair Science° frowned not on his humble birth,*                    *Knowledge*
    *And Melancholy marked him for her own.*                                  120

*Large was his bounty, and his soul sincere,*
    *Heav'n did a recompense as largely send:*
*He gave to Mis'ry all he had, a tear,*
    *He gained from Heav'n ('twas all he wished) a friend.*

*No farther seek his merits to disclose,*                                     125
    *Or draw his frailties from their dread abode,*
*(There they alike in trembling hope repose),*
    *The bosom of His Father and his God.*

QUESTIONS

1. In contrasting the unknown poor buried in this village churchyard and famous
   men buried in cathedrals (in *fretted vault*, line 39), what is Gray's theme? What
   do you understand from the line, *The paths of glory lead but to the grave?*
2. Carl J. Weber thinks that Gray's compassion for the village poor anticipates the
   democratic sympathies of the American Revolution: "Thomas Gray is the pioneer literary spokesman for the Ordinary Man." But another critic, Lyle Glazier,
   argues that the "Elegy" isn't political at all: that we misread if we think the poet
   meant "to persuade the poor and obscure that their barren lives are meaningful";
   and also misread if we think he meant to assure the privileged classes "in whose
   ranks Gray was proud to consider himself" that they need not worry about the
   poor, "who have already all essential riches." How much truth do you find in
   either of these views?

3. Cite lines and phrases that show Gray's concern for the musical qualities of words.

4. Who is the *youth* of the closing Epitaph? By *thee* (line 93) does Gray mean himself? Does he mean some fictitious poet supposedly writing the "Elegy"—the first-person speaker (line 4)? Does he mean some village stonecutter, a crude poet whose illiterate Muse (line 81) inspired him to compose tombstone epitaphs? Or could the Epitaph possibly refer to Gray's close friend of school and undergraduate days, the promising poet Richard West, who had died in 1742? Which interpretation seems to you the most reasonable? (Does our lack of absolute certainty negate the value of the poem?)

5. Walter Savage Landor called the Epitaph a tin kettle tied to the tail of a noble dog. Do you agree that the Epitaph is inferior to what has gone before it? What is its function in Gray's poem?

6. Many sources for Gray's phrases and motifs have been found in earlier poets: Virgil, Horace, Dante, Milton, and many more. Even if it could be demonstrated that Gray's poem has not one original line in it, would it be possible to dismiss the "Elegy" as a mere rag-bag of borrowings?

7. Gray's poem, a pastoral elegy, is in the same genre as another famous English poem: John Milton's "Lycidas." What conventions are common to both?

8. In the earliest surviving manuscript of Gray's poem, lines 73–76 read:

No more with Reason and thyself at strife;
Give anxious cares and endless wishes room
But through the cool sequester'd vale of Life
Pursue the silent tenor of thy doom.

In what ways does the final version of those lines seem superior?

9. Perhaps the best-known poem in English, Gray's "Elegy" has inspired hundreds of imitations, countless parodies, and translations into eighteen or more languages. (Some of these languages contain dozens of attempts to translate it.) To what do you attribute the poem's fame? What do you suppose has proved so universally appealing in it?

10. Compare Gray's "Elegy" with Shelley's "Ozymandias" and Arthur Guiterman's "On the Vanity of Earthly Greatness." What do the three poems have in common? How would you rank them in order of excellence?

## EXERCISE: *Reevaluating Popular Classics*

In this exercise you will read two of the most popular American poems of the nineteenth century. In their time, these poems were not only considered classics by serious critics, but thousands of ordinary readers knew them by heart. Recently, however, these two poems have fallen out of critical favor. They no longer appear in most academic anthologies.

Your assignment is to read these poems carefully and make your own personal, tentative evaluation of each poem's merit. Here are some questions you might ask yourself, as you consider each poem:

Do these poems engage your sympathies? Do they stir you and touch your feelings?

What, if anything, might make them memorable? Do they have any vivid images? Any metaphors, understatement, overstatement, or other figures of speech? Do these poems appeal to the ear?

What are the poets saying? Do they tell you anything?

Do the poems exhibit any wild incompetence? Do you find any forced rimes, inappropriate words, or other unintentionally comic features? Can the poems be accused of bathos or sentimentality, or do you trust the poet to report honest feelings?

How well does the poet seem in control of language? Does the poet's language reflect in any detail the physical world we know?

Do these poems seem entirely drawn from other poetry of the past, or do you have a sense that the poet is thinking and feeling on her (or his) own? Does the poet show any evidence of having read other poets' poetry?

What is the poet trying to do in each poem? How successful, in your opinion, is the attempt?

Try setting these poems next to similar poems you know and admire. (You might try comparing Emma Lazarus's "The New Colossus" to Percy Bysshe Shelley's "Ozymandias," found in this chapter; both are sonnets, and their subjects have interesting similarities and contrasts. Or compare Edgar Allan Poe's "Annabel Lee" to John Crowe Ransom's "Bells for John Whiteside's Daughter" or A. E. Housman's "To an Athlete Dying Young," both found in the Poems for Further Reading).

Are these poems sufficiently rich and interesting to repay more than one reading?

Do you think that these poems still deserve to be considered classics? Or do they no longer speak powerfully to a contemporary audience?

---

## *Emma Lazarus* (1849–1887)

## THE NEW COLOSSUS                           1883

Not like the brazen giant of Greek fame,
With conquering limbs astride from land to land;
Here at our sea-washed, sunset gates shall stand
A mighty woman with a torch, whose flame
Is the imprisoned lightning, and her name                          5
Mother of Exiles. From her beacon-hand
Glows world-wide welcome; her mild eyes command
The air-bridged harbor that twin cities frame.
"Keep, ancient lands, your storied pomp!" cries she
With silent lips. "Give me your tired, your poor,                    10
Your huddled masses yearning to breathe free,
The wretched refuse of your teeming shore.
Send these, the homeless, tempest-tost to me,
I lift my lamp beside the golden door!"

THE NEW COLOSSUS. In 1883, a committee formed to raise funds to build a pedestal for what would be the largest statue in the world, "Liberty Enlightening the World" by Fréderic-Auguste Bartholdi, which was a gift from the French people to celebrate America's first bicentennial. American authors were asked to donate manuscripts for a fund-raising auction. The young poet Emma Lazarus, whose parents had come to America as immigrants, sent in this sonnet composed for the occasion. When President Grover Cleveland unveiled the Statue of Liberty in October, 1886, Lazarus's sonnet was read at the ceremony. In 1903, the poem was carved on the statue's pedestal. The reference in the opening line to "the brazen giant of Greek fame" refers to the famous Colossus of Rhodes, a huge bronze statue that once stood in the harbor on the Aegean island of Rhodes. Built to commemorate a military victory, the statue was considered one of the so-called Seven Wonders of the World.

## Edgar Allan Poe (1809–1849)

ANNABEL LEE                                                    1849

It was many and many a year ago,
    In a kingdom by the sea,
That a maiden there lived whom you may know
    By the name of Annabel Lee;
And this maiden she lived with no other thought          5
    Than to love and be loved by me.

I was a child and *she* was a child,
    In this kingdom by the sea,
But we loved with a love that was more than love—
    I and my Annabel Lee—                                10
With a love that the wingéd seraphs of Heaven
    Coveted her and me.

And this was the reason that, long ago,
    In this kingdom by the sea,
A wind blew out of a cloud, chilling                     15
    My beautiful Annabel Lee;
So that her highborn kinsmen came
    And bore her away from me,
To shut her up in a sepulchre
    In this kingdom by the sea.                          20

The angels, not half so happy in Heaven,
    Went envying her and me:—
Yes!—that was the reason (as all men know,
    In this kingdom by the sea)
That the wind came out of the cloud by night,           25
    Chilling and killing my Annabel Lee.

But our love it was stronger by far than the love
    Of those who were older than we—
    Of many far wiser than we—
And neither the angels in Heaven above,                 30
    Nor the demons down under the sea,
Can ever dissever my soul from the soul
    Of the beautiful Annabel Lee:—

For the moon never beams, without bringing me dreams
    Of the beautiful Annabel Lee;                        35
And the stars never rise, but I feel the bright eyes
    Of the beautiful Annabel Lee:
And so, all the night-tide, I lie down by the side
Of my darling—my darling—my life and my bride,
    In the sepulchre there by the sea—                  40
    In her tomb by the sounding sea.

## Suggestions for Writing

1. Write a brief evaluation of either "The New Colossus" by Emma Lazarus or "Annabel Lee" by Edgar Allan Poe.

2. Concoct the worst poem you can possibly write and, in a brief accompanying essay, recount the difficulties you met and overcame in writing it. Quote, for example, any lines you wrote but had to discard for not being bad enough.

3. In the Poems for Further Reading section that begins on page 885, find a poem you particularly admire or dislike. In a brief essay (300–500 words), evaluate it. Refer to particulars in the poem to support your opinion of it.

# 29  *What Is Poetry?*

---

***Robert Francis*** (1901–1987)

CATCH                                                        1950

Two boys uncoached are tossing a poem together,
Overhand, underhand, backhand, sleight of hand, every hand,
Teasing with attitudes, latitudes, interludes, altitudes,
High, make him fly off the ground for it, low, make him stoop,
Make him scoop it up, make him as-almost-as-possible miss it,         5
Fast, let him sting from it, now, now fool him slowly,
Anything, everything tricky, risky, nonchalant,
Anything under the sun to outwit the prosy,
Over the tree and the long sweet cadence down,
Over his head, make him scramble to pick up
     the meaning,
                                                                     10
And now, like a posy, a pretty one plump in his hands.

As Robert Francis hints in this playful poem, the pitching poet keeps the
catching reader alert by creating little difficulties. Reading some of the poems
in this book, you have probably felt like the boy or girl on the receiving end:
sometimes having to work to make the catch, once in a while encountering
a poem that lands with an easy *plump* right in the middle of your understanding.

What, then, is poetry? By now, perhaps, you have formed your own
idea, whether or not you can define it. Robert Frost made a try at a definition: "A poem is an idea caught in the act of dawning." Just in case further
efforts at definition can be useful, here are a few memorable ones (including,
for a second look, some given earlier):

things that are true expressed in words that are beautiful.
                        —Dante

the art of uniting pleasure with truth by calling imagination to the help of reason.
                        —Samuel Johnson

the best words in the best order.
                        —Samuel Taylor Coleridge

the spontaneous overflow of powerful feelings.
                        —William Wordsworth

musical thought.
                        —Thomas Carlyle

emotion put into measure.
                        —Thomas Hardy

If I read a book and it makes my whole body so cold no fire can ever warm me, I know that it is poetry. If I feel physically as if the top of my head were taken off, I know that it is poetry. These are the only ways I know it. Is there any other way?
                        —Emily Dickinson

speech framed . . . to be heard for its own sake and interest even over and above its interest of meaning.
                        —Gerard Manley Hopkins

a way of remembering what it would impoverish us to forget.
                        —Robert Frost

a revelation in words by means of the words.
                        —Wallace Stevens

not the assertion that something is true, but the making of that truth more fully real to us.
                        —T. S. Eliot

the body of linguistic constructions that men usually refer to as poems.
                        —J. V. Cunningham

hundreds of things coming together at the right moment.
                        —Elizabeth Bishop

anything said in such a way, or put on the page in such a way, as to invite from the hearer or the reader a certain kind of attention.
                        —William Stafford

the clear expression of mixed feelings.
                        —W. H. Auden

A poem differs from most prose in several ways. For one, both writer and reader tend to regard it differently. The poet's attitude is something like this: I offer this piece of writing to be read not as prose but as a poem—that is, more perceptively, thoughtfully, and considerately, with more attention to sounds and connotations. This is a great deal to expect, but in return, the reader, too, has a right to certain expectations. Approaching the poem in the anticipation of out-of-the-ordinary knowledge and pleasure, the reader assumes that the poem may use certain enjoyable devices not available to prose: rime, alliteration, meter, and rhythms—definite, various, or emphatic. (The poet may not *always* decide to use these things.) The reader expects the poet to make greater use, perhaps, of resources of meaning such as figurative language, allusion, symbol, and imagery. As readers of prose we might seek no more than meaning: no more than what could be paraphrased without serious loss. Meeting any figurative language or graceful turns of word order, we think them pleasant extras. But in poetry all these "extras" matter as much as the paraphraseable content, if not more. For, when we finish reading a good poem, we cannot explain precisely to ourselves what we have experienced—without repeating, word for word, the language of the poem itself. Archibald MacLeish makes this point memorably in his "Ars Poetica":

A poem should not mean
But be.

"Poetry is to prose as dancing is to walking," remarked Paul Valéry. It is doubtful, however, that anyone can draw an immovable boundary between poetry and prose. Certain prose needs only to be arranged in lines to be seen as poetry—especially prose that conveys strong emotion in vivid, physical imagery and in terse, figurative, rhythmical language. Even in translation the words of Chief Joseph of the Nez Percé tribe, at the moment of his surrender to the U.S. Army in 1877, still move us and are memorable:

Hear me, my warriors, my heart is sick and sad:
Our chiefs are killed,
The old men all are dead,
It is cold and we have no blankets.

The little children freeze to death.

Hear me, my warriors, my heart is sick and sad:
From where the sun now stands I will fight no more forever.

It may be that a poem can point beyond words to something still more essential. Language has its limits, and probably Edgar Allan Poe was the only poet ever to claim he could always find words for whatever he wished to express. For, of all a human being can experience and imagine, words say only part. "Human speech," said Flaubert, who strove after the best of it, "is like a cracked kettle on which we hammer out tunes to make bears dance, when what we long for is the compassion of the stars."

Like Yeats's chestnut-tree in "Among School Children" (which when asked whether it is leaf, blossom, or bole, has no answer), a poem is to be seen not as a confederation of form, rime, image, metaphor, tone, and theme, but as a whole. We study a poem one element at a time because the intellect best comprehends what it can separate. But only our total attention, involving the participation of our blood and marrow, can see all elements in a poem fused, all dancing together. Yeats knew how to make poems and how to read them:

> God guard me from those thoughts men think
> In the mind alone;
> He that sings a lasting song
> Thinks in a marrow-bone.

Throughout this book, we have been working on the assumption that the patient and conscious explication of poems will sharpen unconscious perceptions. We can only hope that it will; the final test lies in whether you care to go on by yourself, reading other poems, finding in them pleasure and enlightenment. Pedagogy must have a stop; so too must the viewing of poems as if their elements fell into chapters. For the total experience of reading a poem surpasses the mind's categories. The wind in the grass, says a proverb, cannot be taken into the house.

# **30** *Poems for Further Reading*

Sit a while dear son,
Here are biscuits to eat and here is milk to drink,
But as soon as you sleep and renew yourself in sweet clothes,
I kiss you with a good-by kiss and open the gates for your egress
    hence.

Long enough have you dream'd contemptible dreams,
Now I wash the gum from your eyes,
You must habit yourself to the dazzle of the light and of every
    moment of your life.

Long have you timidly waded holding a plank by the shore,
Now I will you to be a bold swimmer,
To jump off in the midst of the sea, rise again, nod to me, shout,
    and laughingly dash with your hair.
            —Walt Whitman, "Song of Myself"

**Anonymous** (traditional Scottish ballad)

## EDWARD

"Why dois your brand° sae° drap wi' bluid,      *sword; so*
    Edward, Edward?
Why dois your brand sae drap wi' bluid?
  And why sae sad gang° yee, O?"         *go*
"O, I hae killed my hauke sae guid,         5
    Mither, mither,
O, I hae killed my hauke sae guid,
  And I had nae mair bot° hee, O."       *but*

"Your haukis bluid was nevir sae reid,
    Edward, Edward,          10
Your haukis bluid was nevir sae reid,
  My deir son I tell thee, O."
"O, I hae killed my reid-roan steid,
    Mither, mither,
O, I hae killed my reid-roan steid,      15
  That erst° was sa fair and frie°, O."   *once; free*

"Your steid was auld, and ye hae gat mair,
    Edward, Edward,
Your steid was auld, and ye hae gat mair,
  Sum other dule° ye drie°, O."    *sorrow; suffer* 20
"O, I hae killed my fadir deir,
    Mither, mither,
O, I hae killed my fadir deir,
  Alas, and wae° is mee, O!"         *woe*

"And whatten penance wul ye drie for that,   25
    Edward, Edward?
And whatten penance will ye drie for that?
  My deir son, now tell me, O."
"Ile set my feit in yonder boat,
    Mither, mither,          30
Ile set my feit in yonder boat,
  And Ile fare ovir the sea, O."

"And what wul ye doe wi' your towirs and your ha'°,  *hall*
    Edward, Edward,
And what wul ye doe wi' your towirs and your ha',   35
  That were sae fair to see, O?"
"Ile let thame stand tul they doun fa',
    Mither, mither,
Ile let thame stand tul they doun fa',
  For here nevir mair maun° I bee, O."    *must* 40

"And what wul ye leive to your bairns° and your wife,       *children*
     Edward, Edward?
And what wul ye leive to your bairns and your wife,
    When ye gang ovir the sea, O?"
"The warldis° room, late° them beg thrae° life,    *world's; let; through*  45
     Mither, mither
The warldis room, late them beg thrae life,
    For thame nevir mair wul I see, O."

"And what wul ye leive to your ain° mither deir,      *own*
     Edward, Edward?                             50
And what wul ye leive to your ain mither deir?
    My deir son, now tell me, O."
"The curse of hell frae me sall ye beir,
     Mither, mither,
The curse of hell frae me sall ye beir,                 55
    Sic° counseils° ye gave to me, O."        *such; counsel*

COMPARE:

"Edward" with a modern ballad such as "Ballad of Birmingham" by Dudley Randall (page 709).

---

***Anonymous*** (traditional English ballad)

# THE THREE RAVENS

There were three ravens sat on a tree,
   *Down a down, hay down, hay down,*
There were three ravens sat on a tree,
   *With a down,*
There were three ravens sat on a tree,            5
They were as black as they might be.
   *With a down derry, derry, derry, down, down.*

The one of them said to his mate,
"Where shall we our breakfast take?"

"Down in yonder greene field,              10
There lies a knight slain under his shield.

"His hounds they lie down at his feet,
So well they can their master keep.

"His hawks they fly so eagerly,
There's no fowl dare him come nigh."          15

Down there comes a fallow doe,
As great with young as she might go.

She lift up his bloody head,
And kist his wounds that were so red.

She got him up upon her back,                                              20
And carried him to earthen lake°.                              *the grave*

She buried him before the prime,
She was dead herself ere evensong time.

God send every gentleman
Such hawks, such hounds, and such a leman°.              *lover*   25

THE THREE RAVENS. The lines of refrain are repeated in each stanza. "Perhaps in the folk mind
the doe is the form the soul of a human mistress, now dead, has taken," Albert B. Friedman
has suggested (in *The Viking Book of Folk Ballads*). "Most probably the knight's beloved was
understood to be an enchanted woman who was metamorphosed at certain times into an
animal." 22–23 *prime, evensong*: two of the canonical hours set aside for prayer and worship.
Prime is at dawn, evensong at dusk.


**Anonymous** (traditional Scottish ballad)

## THE TWA CORBIES

As I was walking all alane,
I heard twa corbies° making a mane°;              *ravens; moan*
The tane° unto the t'other say,                              *one*
"Where sall we gang° and dine today?"                         *go*

"In behint yon auld fail dyke°,                        *turf wall*   5
I wot° there lies a new slain knight;                       *know*
And naebody kens° that he lies there,                     *knows*
But his hawk, his hound, and lady fair.

"His hound is to the hunting gane,
His hawk to fetch the wild-fowl hame,                          10
His lady's ta'en another mate,
So we may mak our dinner sweet.

"Ye'll sit on his white hause-bane°,                 *neck bone*
And I'll pike out his bonny blue een;
Wi' ae° lock o' his gowden hair                            *one*   15
We'll theek° our nest when it grows bare.              *thatch*

"Mony a one for him makes mane,
But nane sall ken where he is gane;
O'er his white banes, when they are bare,
The wind sall blaw for evermair."                             20

THE TWA CORBIES. Sir Walter Scott, the first to print this ballad in his *Minstrelsy of the Scottish
Border* (1802–1803), calls it "rather a counterpart than a copy" of "The Three Ravens." M. J.
C. Hodgart and other scholars think he may have written most of it himself.

## Anonymous (English lyric)

### SUMER IS ICUMEN IN          (thirteenth century)

| | |
|---|---|
| Sumer is icumen in | Summer is acoming in— |
| Lhude sing cuccu | Loudly sing, cuckoo! |
| Groweþ sed and bloweþ med | Groweth seed and bloweth mead |
| and springþ þe wde nu | And springeth the wood new. |
| Sing cuccu | Sing, cuckoo! |

| | |
|---|---|
| Awe bleteþ after lomb | Ewe bleateth after lamb, |
| lhouþ after calue cu | Loweth after calf cow, |
| Bulluc sterteþ bucke uerteþ | Bullock starteth, buck farteth— |
| Murie sing cuccu | Merrily sing, cuckoo! |
| Cuccu cuccu | Cuckoo, cuckoo, |
| Wel singes þu cuccu | Well singest thou, cuckoo! |
| ne swik þu nauer nu | Cease thou never now. |

| | |
|---|---|
| Sing cuccu nu Sing cuccu | Sing, cuckoo now! Sing, cuckoo! |
| Sing cuccu Sing cuccu nu | Sing, cuckoo! Sing, cuckoo, now! |

SUMER IS ICUMEN IN. On the left, this famous song is printed as it appears in a thirteenth-century manuscript: a commonplace book, or book of songs and obituaries set down by various monks at Reading Abbey (Harley manuscript 978, now in the British Museum). On the right, words and spellings have been modernized and punctuation added, but word-order kept unaltered. In the opening line, *acoming* is not quite a faithful translation: *is icumen* means "has come." Summer is already here. The character þ is called a *thorn*, and is pronounced like the spelling *th*. 8 *starteth*: starts, jumps up and runs.

## Anonymous (English lyric)

### WESTERN WIND          (about 1500)

Western wind, when wilt thou blow,
The° small rain down can rain?                          *(so that) the*
Christ, if my love were in my arms,
And I in my bed again!

COMPARE:

"Western Wind" with "Disclosure" by David Mason (page 958).

## Anonymous

### LAST WORDS OF THE PROPHET          (NAVAJO MOUNTAIN CHANT)

Farewell, my younger brother!
From the holy places the gods come for me.

You will never see me again; but when the showers pass and the
    thunders peal,
"There," you will say, "is the voice of my elder brother."
And when the harvest comes, of the beautiful birds and
    grasshoppers you will say,          5
"There is the ordering of my elder brother!"

             —Translated by Washington Matthews

## Matthew Arnold (1822–1888)

### DOVER BEACH                       1867

The sea is calm tonight.
The tide is full, the moon lies fair
Upon the straits;—on the French coast the light
Gleams and is gone; the cliffs of England stand,
Glimmering and vast, out in the tranquil bay.      5
Come to the window, sweet is the night-air!
Only, from the long line of spray
Where the sea meets the moon-blanched land,
Listen! you hear the grating roar
Of pebbles which the waves draw back, and fling,      10
At their return, up the high strand,
Begin, and cease, and then again begin,
With tremulous cadence slow, and bring
The eternal note of sadness in.

Sophocles long ago      15
Heard it on the Aegean, and it brought
Into his mind the turbid ebb and flow
Of human misery; we
Find also in the sound a thought,
Hearing it by this distant northern sea.      20

The Sea of Faith
Was once, too, at the full, and round earth's shore
Lay like the folds of a bright girdle furled.
But now I only hear
Its melancholy, long, withdrawing roar,      25
Retreating, to the breath
Of the night-wind, down the vast edges drear
And naked shingles° of the world.      *gravel beaches*

Ah, love, let us be true
To one another! for the world, which seems      30
To lie before us like a land of dreams,
So various, so beautiful, so new,

Hath really neither joy, nor love, nor light,
Nor certitude, nor peace, nor help for pain;
And we are here as on a darkling° plain          *darkened or darkening*   35
Swept with confused alarms of struggle and flight,
Where ignorant armies clash by night.


## John Ashbery (b. 1927)*

### AT NORTH FARM                                              1984

Somewhere someone is traveling furiously toward you,
At incredible speed, traveling day and night,
Through blizzards and desert heat, across torrents, through narrow
        passes.
But will he know where to find you,
Recognize you when he sees you,                                   5
Give you the thing he has for you?

Hardly anything grows here,
Yet the granaries are bursting with meal,
The sacks of meal piled to the rafters.
The streams run with sweetness, fattening fish;                 10
Birds darken the sky. Is it enough
That the dish of milk is set out at night,
That we think of him sometimes,
Sometimes and always, with mixed feelings?


## Margaret Atwood (b. 1939)*

### SIREN SONG                    1976

This is the one song everyone
would like to learn: the song
that is irresistible:

the song that forces men
to leap overboard in squadrons                                   5
even though they see the beached skulls

the song nobody knows
because anyone who has heard it
is dead, and the others can't remember.

Shall I tell you the secret                                    10
and if I do, will you get me
out of this bird suit?

I don't enjoy it here
squatting on this island
looking picturesque and mythical                               15

with these two feathery maniacs,
I don't enjoy singing
this trio, fatal and valuable.

I will tell the secret to you,
to you, only to you.                                           20
Come closer. This song

is a cry for help: Help me!
Only you, only you can,
you are unique

at last. Alas                                                  25
it is a boring song
but it works every time.

SIREN SONG. In Greek mythology, sirens were half-woman, half-bird nymphs who lured sailors
to their deaths by singing hypnotically beautiful songs.

*Margaret Atwood*

W. H. Auden

## W. H. Auden (1907–1973)*

As I Walked Out One Evening          1940

As I walked out one evening,
   Walking down Bristol Street,
The crowds upon the pavement
   Were fields of harvest wheat.

And down by the brimming river         5
   I heard a lover sing
Under an arch of the railway:
   "Love has no ending.

"I'll love you, dear, I'll love you
   Till China and Africa meet,         10
And the river jumps over the mountain
   And the salmon sing in the street,

"I'll love you till the ocean
   Is folded and hung up to dry
And the seven stars go squawking         15
   Like geese about the sky.

"The years shall run like rabbits,
   For in my arms I hold
The Flower of the Ages,
   And the first love of the world."         20

But all the clocks in the city
    Began to whirr and chime:
"O let not Time deceive you,
    You cannot conquer Time.

"In the burrows of the Nightmare
    Where Justice naked is,
Time watches from the shadow
    And coughs when you would kiss.

"In headaches and in worry
    Vaguely life leaks away,
And Time will have his fancy
    Tomorrow or today.

"Into many a green valley
    Drifts the appalling snow;
Time breaks the threaded dances
    And the diver's brilliant bow.

"O plunge your hands in water,
    Plunge them in up to the wrist;
Stare, stare in the basin
    And wonder what you've missed.

"The glacier knocks in the cupboard,
    The desert sighs in the bed,
And the crack in the teacup opens
    A lane to the land of the dead.

"Where the beggars raffle the banknotes
    And the Giant is enchanting to Jack,
And the Lily-white Boy is a Roarer,
    And Jill goes down on her back.

"O look, look in the mirror,
    O look in your distress;
Life remains a blessing
    Although you cannot bless.

"O stand, stand at the window
    As the tears scald and start;
You shall love your crooked neighbor
    With your crooked heart."

It was late, late in the evening,
    The lovers they were gone;
The clocks had ceased their chiming,
    And the deep river ran on.

"THE FALL OF ICARUS" by Pieter Breughel (1520?–1569)

## W. H. Auden (1907–1973)*

### MUSÉE DES BEAUX ARTS                                1940

About suffering they were never wrong,
The Old Masters: how well they understood
Its human position; how it takes place
While someone else is eating or opening a window or just walking
    dully along;
How, when the aged are reverently, passionately waiting          5
For the miraculous birth, there always must be
Children who did not specially want it to happen, skating
On a pond at the edge of the wood:
They never forgot
That even the dreadful martyrdom must run its course          10
Anyhow in a corner, some untidy spot
Where the dogs go on with their doggy life and the torturer's
    horse
Scratches its innocent behind on a tree.
In Brueghel's *Icarus*, for instance: how everything turns away
Quite leisurely from the disaster; the ploughman may          15

Have heard the splash, the forsaken cry,
But for him it was not an important failure; the sun shone
As it had to on the white legs disappearing into the green
Water; and the expensive delicate ship that must have seen
Something amazing, a boy falling out of the sky,                              20
Had somewhere to get to and sailed calmly on.

COMPARE:

"Musée des Beaux Arts" with "The Dance" by William Carlos Williams (page 781)
and the painting by Pieter Breughel to which each poem refers.

## *R. L. Barth* (b. 1947)*

### THE INSERT                                                               1981

Our view of sky, jungle, and fields constricts
Into a sink hole covered with sawgrass

Undulating, soon whipped slant as the chopper
Hovers at four feet. Rapt, boot-deep in slime,

We deploy ourselves in a loose perimeter,                                      5
Listening for incoming rockets above

The thump of rotor blades; edgy for contact,
Junkies of terror impatient to shoot up.

Nothing moves, nothing sounds: then, single file,
We move across a streambed toward high ground.                                10

The terror of the insert's quickly over.
Too quickly . . . and more quickly every time . . .

THE INSERT. R. L. Barth, a U.S. Marine in 1966–69, served as a long-range reconnaissance leader
in Vietnam. An *insert* is the dropping of troops into an area by helicopter.

COMPARE:

"The Insert" with the poems of Wilfred Owen: "Dulce et Decorum Est" (page 617)
and "Anthem for Doomed Youth" (page 972).

## *Elizabeth Bishop* (1911–1979)*

### FILLING STATION                  1965

Oh, but it is dirty!
—this little filling station,
oil-soaked, oil-permeated
to a disturbing, over-all

black translucency.                                                    5
Be careful with that match!

Father wears a dirty,
oil-soaked monkey suit
that cuts him under the arms,
and several quick and saucy                                           10
and greasy sons assist him
(it's a family filling station),
all quite thoroughly dirty.

Do they live in the station?
It has a cement porch                                                 15
behind the pumps, and on it
a set of crushed and grease-
impregnated wickerwork;
on the wicker sofa
a dirty dog, quite comfy.                                             20

Some comic books provide
the only note of color—
of certain color. They lie
upon a big dim doily
draping a taboret                                                     25
(part of the set), beside
a big hirsute begonia.

Why the extraneous plant?
Why the taboret?
Why, oh why, the doily?                                               30
(Embroidered in daisy stitch
with marguerites, I think,
and heavy with gray crochet.)

Somebody embroidered the doily.
Somebody waters the plant,                                            35
or oils it, maybe. Somebody
arranges the rows of cans
so that they softly say:
ESSO—SO—SO—SO
to high-strung automobiles.                                           40
Somebody loves us all.

---

**_Elizabeth Bishop_** (1911–1979)*

ONE ART                          1976

The art of losing isn't hard to master;
so many things seem filled with the intent
to be lost that their loss is no disaster.

Lose something every day. Accept the fluster
of lost door keys, the hour badly spent.                                    5
The art of losing isn't hard to master.

Then practice losing farther, losing faster:
places, and names, and where it was you meant
to travel. None of these will bring disaster.

I lost my mother's watch. And look! my last, or                            10
next-to-last, of three loved houses went.
The art of losing isn't hard to master.

I lost two cities, lovely ones. And, vaster,
some realms I owned, two rivers, a continent.
I miss them, but it wasn't a disaster.                                      15

—Even losing you (the joking voice, a gesture
I love) I shan't have lied. It's evident
the art of losing's not too hard to master
though it may look like (*Write* it!) like disaster.

Compare:

"One Art" with "Do not go gentle into that good night" by Dylan Thomas (page 771)
and "Lonely Hearts" by Wendy Cope (page 643).

*Elizabeth Bishop*

### William Blake (1757–1827)*

#### THE SICK ROSE      1794

O Rose, thou art sick!
The invisible worm
That flies in the night,
In the howling storm,

Has found out thy bed                     5
Of crimson joy,
And his dark secret love
Does thy life destroy.

William Blake

### William Blake (1757–1827)*

#### THE TYGER      1794

Tyger! Tyger! burning bright
In the forests of the night,
What immortal hand or eye
Could frame thy fearful symmetry?

In what distant deeps or skies                   5
Burnt the fire of thine eyes?
On what wings dare he aspire?
What the hand dare seize the fire?

And what shoulder, and what art,
Could twist the sinews of thy heart?
And when thy heart began to beat,
What dread hand? and what dread feet?

What the hammer? what the chain?
In what furnace was thy brain?
What the anvil? what dread grasp
Dare its deadly terrors clasp?

When the stars threw down their spears,
And watered heaven with their tears,
Did he smile his work to see?
Did he who made the Lamb make thee?

Tyger! Tyger! burning bright
In the forests of the night,
What immortal hand or eye
Dare frame thy fearful symmetry?

## *Louise Bogan* (1897–1970)

### THE DREAM                                         1941

O God, in the dream the terrible horse began
To paw at the air, and make for me with his blows.
Fear kept for thirty-five years poured through his mane,
And retribution equally old, or nearly, breathed through his nose.

Coward complete, I lay and wept on the ground
When some strong creature appeared, and leapt for the rein.
Another woman, as I lay half in a swound,
Leapt in the air, and clutched at the leather and chain.

Give him, she said, something of yours as a charm.
Throw him, she said, some poor thing you alone claim.
No, no, I cried, he hates me; he's out for harm,
And whether I yield or not, it is all the same.

But, like a lion in a legend, when I flung the glove
Pulled from my sweating, my cold right hand,
The terrible beast, that no one may understand,
Came to my side, and put down his head in love.

## *Emily Brontë* (1818–1848)

### LOVE AND FRIENDSHIP          (1839)

Love is like the wild rose-briar,
Friendship like the holly-tree—

The holly is dark when the rose-briar blooms
But which will bloom most constantly?

The wild rose-briar is sweet in spring,                                    5
Its summer blossoms scent the air;
Yet wait till winter comes again
And who will call the wild-briar fair?


## *Gwendolyn Brooks* (b. 1917)*

### THE RITES FOR COUSIN VIT                    1949

Carried her unprotesting out the door.
Kicked back the casket-stand. But it can't hold her,
That stuff and satin aiming to enfold her,
The lid's contrition nor the bolts before.
Oh oh. Too much. Too much. Even now, surmise,          5
She rises in the sunshine. There she goes,
Back to the bars she knew and the repose
In love-rooms and the things in people's eyes.
Too vital and too squeaking. Must emerge.
Even now she does the snake-hips with a hiss,          10
Slops the bad wine across her shantung, talks
Of pregnancy, guitars and bridgework, walks
In parks or alleys, comes haply on the verge
Of happiness, haply hysterics. Is.

Gwendolyn Brooks

## Gwendolyn Brooks (b. 1917)*

### A Street in Bronzeville: Southeast Corner          1945

The School of Beauty's a tavern now.
The Madam is underground.
Out at Lincoln, among the graves
Her own is early found.
Where the thickest, tallest monument                                    5
Cuts grandly into the air
The Madam lies, contentedly.
Her fortune, too, lies there,
Converted into cool hard steel
And right red velvet lining;                                           10
While over her tan impassivity
Shot silk is shining.


## Elizabeth Barrett Browning (1806–1861)*

### How Do I Love Thee?
### Let Me Count the Ways          1850

How do I love thee? Let me count the ways.
I love thee to the depth and breadth and height
My soul can reach, when feeling out of sight
For the ends of being and ideal grace.
I love thee to the level of every day's                                5
Most quiet need, by sun and candle-light.
I love thee freely, as men strive for right.
I love thee purely, as they turn from praise.
I love thee with the passion put to use
In my old griefs, and with my childhood's faith.                      10
I love thee with a love I seemed to lose
With my lost saints. I love thee with the breath,
Smiles, tears, of all my life; and, if God choose,
I shall but love thee better after death.


## Robert Browning (1812–1889)*

### Soliloquy of the Spanish Cloister          1842

Gr-r-r—there go, my heart's abhorrence!
    Water your damned flower-pots, do!
If hate killed men, Brother Lawrence,
    God's blood, would not mine kill you!

What? your myrtle-bush wants trimming?                                              5
    Oh, that rose has prior claims—
Needs its leaden vase filled brimming?
    Hell dry you up with its flames!

At the meal we sit together;
    *Salve tibi!*° I must hear                                    *Hail to thee!*   10
Wise talk of the kind of weather,
    Sort of season, time of year:
*Not a plenteous cork-crop: scarcely*
    *Dare we hope oak-galls, I doubt;*
*What's the Latin name for "parsley"?*                                             15
    What's the Greek name for "swine's snout"?

Whew! We'll have our platter burnished,
    Laid with care on our own shelf!
With a fire-new spoon we're furnished,
    And a goblet for ourself,                                                      20
Rinsed like something sacrificial
    Ere 'tis fit to touch our chaps—
Marked with L. for our initial!
    (He-he! There his lily snaps!)

*Saint*, forsooth! While Brown Dolores                                            25
    Squats outside the Convent bank
With Sanchicha, telling stories,
    Steeping tresses in the tank,
Blue-black, lustrous, thick like horsehairs,
    —Can't I see his dead eye glow,                                               30
Bright as 'twere a Barbary corsair's?
    (That is, if he'd let it show!)

When he finishes refection,
    Knife and fork he never lays
Cross-wise, to my recollection,                                                   35
    As I do, in Jesu's praise.
I the Trinity illustrate,
    Drinking watered orange-pulp—
In three sips the Arian frustrate;
    While he drains his at one gulp!                                              40

Oh, those melons! if he's able
    We're to have a feast; so nice!
One goes to the Abbot's table,
    All of us get each a slice.

SOLILOQUY OF THE SPANISH CLOISTER. 3 *Brother Lawrence:* one of the speaker's fellow monks. 31
*Barbary corsair:* a pirate operating off the Barbary coast of Africa. 39 *Arian:* a follower of Arius,
heretic who denied the doctrine of the Trinity.

How go on your flowers? None double? 45
    Not one fruit-sort can you spy?
Strange!—And I, too, at such trouble,
    Keep them close-nipped on the sly!

There's a great text in Galatians,
    Once you trip on it, entails 50
Twenty-nine distinct damnations,
    One sure, if another fails;
If I trip him just a-dying,
    Sure of heaven as sure can be,
Spin him round and send him flying 55
    Off to hell, a Manichee?

Or, my scrofulous French novel
    On grey paper with blunt type!
Simply glance at it, you grovel
    Hand and foot in Belial's gripe; 60
If I double down its pages
    At the woeful sixteenth print,
When he gathers his greengages,
    Ope a sieve and slip it in't?

Or, there's Satan!—one might venture 65
    Pledge one's soul to him, yet leave
Such a flaw in the indenture
    As he'd miss till, past retrieve,
Blasted lay that rose-acacia
    We're so proud of! *Hy, Zy, Hine.* . . . 70
'St, there's Vespers! *Plena gratia
    Ave, Virgo!°* Gr-r-r—you swine!          *Hail, Virgin, full of grace!*

49 *a great text in Galatians:* a difficult verse in this book of the Bible. Brother Lawrence will be
damned as a heretic if he wrongly interprets it. 56 *Manichee:* another kind of heretic, one who
(after the Persian philosopher Mani) sees in the world a constant struggle between good and evil,
neither able to win. 60 *Belial:* Here, not specifically Satan but (as used in the Old Testament)
a name for wickedness. 70 *Hy, Zy, Hine:* Possibly the sound of a bell to announce evening
devotions.

### *Thomas Carew* (1594?–1640)

ASK ME NO MORE WHERE JOVE BESTOWS          1640

Ask me no more where Jove bestows,
When June is past, the fading rose;
For in your beauty's orient deep
These flowers, as in their causes, sleep.

Ask me no more whither do stray 5
The golden atoms of the day;

For in pure love heaven did prepare
Those powders to enrich your hair.

Ask me no more whither doth haste
The nightingale when May is past,                                          10
For in your sweet dividing throat
She winters, and keeps warm her note.

Ask me no more where those stars light
That downwards fall in dead of night,
For in your eyes they sit, and there                                       15
Fixèd become, as in their sphere.

Ask me no more if east or west
The phoenix builds her spicy nest,
For unto you at last she flies
And in your fragrant bosom dies.                                           20

ASK ME NO MORE WHERE JOVE BESTOWS. 3 *orient:* radiant, glowing. (In our time, this sense of the
word is obsolete.) 4 *These flowers . . . sleep:* as they slept before they came into existence. (A *cause,*
that which gives being, is a term from Aristotle and the Scholastic philosophers.) 11 *dividing:*
singing, uttering a "division" or melodic phrase added to a basic tune. 18 *phoenix:* In legend, an
Arabian bird believed to subsist on incense and perfumes. It was supposed to reproduce by
going up in flames, to rise again out of its ashes.

---

*Geoffrey Chaucer* (1340?–1400)

### YOUR ŸEN TWO WOL SLEE ME SODENLY

(late fourteenth century)

Your ÿen° two wol slee° me sodenly;                                *eyes; slay*
I may the beautee of hem° not sustene°,                          *them; resist*
So woundeth hit thourghout my herte kene.

And but° your word wol helen° hastily                            *unless, heal*
My hertes wounde, while that hit is grene°,                         *new*    5
    Your ÿen two wol slee me sodenly;
    I may the beautee of hem not sustene.

Upon my trouthe° I sey you feithfully                               *word*
That ye ben of my lyf and deeth the quene;
For with my deeth the trouthe° shal be sene.                        *truth*  10
    Your ÿen two wol slee me sodenly;
    I may the beautee of hem not sustene,
    So woundeth it thourghout my herte kene.

YOUR ŸEN TWO WOL SLEE ME SODENLY. This poem is one of a group of three roundels, collectively titled "Merciles Beaute." A *roundel* (or *rondel*) is an English form consisting of 11 lines
with 3 stanzas rimed with a refrain. 3 *so woundeth . . . kene:* "So deeply does it wound me through
the heart."

## G. K. Chesterton (1874–1936)

### THE DONKEY                    1900

When fishes flew and forests walked
   And figs grew upon thorn,
Some moment when the moon was blood
   Then surely I was born;

With monstrous head and sickening cry                    5
   And ears like errant wings,
The devil's walking parody
   On all four-footed things.

The tattered outlaw of the earth,
   Of ancient crooked will;                    10
Starve, scourge, deride me: I am dumb,
   I keep my secret still.

Fools! For I also had my hour;
   One far fierce hour and sweet:
There was a shout about my ears,                    15
   And palms before my feet.

THE DONKEY. For more details of the donkey's hour of triumph see Matthew 21:1–8.


## Samuel Taylor Coleridge (1772–1834)*

### KUBLA KHAN                    (1797–1798)

*Or, a Vision in a Dream. A Fragment.*

In Xanadu did Kubla Khan
A stately pleasure-dome decree:
Where Alph, the sacred river, ran
Through caverns measureless to man
   Down to a sunless sea.                    5
So twice five miles of fertile ground
With walls and towers were girdled round;
And there were gardens bright with sinuous rills,
Where blossomed many an incense-bearing tree;
And here were forests ancient as the hills,                    10
Enfolding sunny spots of greenery.

But oh! that deep romantic chasm which slanted
Down the green hill athwart a cedarn cover!
A savage place! as holy and enchanted

As e'er beneath a waning moon was haunted                                                 15
By woman wailing for her demon-lover!
And from this chasm, with ceaseless turmoil seething,
As if this earth in fast thick pants were breathing,
A mighty fountain momently was forced:
Amid whose swift half-intermitted burst                                                   20
Huge fragments vaulted like rebounding hail,
Or chaffy grain beneath the thresher's flail:
And 'mid these dancing rocks at once and ever
It flung up momently the sacred river.
Five miles meandering with a mazy motion                                                  25
Through wood and dale the sacred river ran,
Then reached the caverns measureless to man,
And sank in tumult to a lifeless ocean:
And 'mid this tumult Kubla heard from far
Ancestral voices prophesying war!                                                         30

    The shadow of the dome of pleasure
    Floated midway on the waves;
    Where was heard the mingled measure
    From the fountain and the caves.
It was a miracle of rare device,                                                          35
A sunny pleasure-dome with caves of ice!

    A damsel with a dulcimer
    In a vision once I saw:
    It was an Abyssinian maid,
    And on her dulcimer she played,                                              40
    Singing of Mount Abora.
    Could I revive within me
    Her symphony and song,
    To such a deep delight 'twould win me,
That with music loud and long,                                                            45
I would build that dome in air,
That sunny dome! those caves of ice!
And all who heard should see them there,
And all should cry, Beware! Beware!
His flashing eyes, his floating hair!                                                     50
Weave a circle round him thrice,
And close your eyes with holy dread,
For he on honey-dew hath fed,
And drunk the milk of Paradise.

KUBLA KHAN. There was an actual Kublai Khan, a thirteenth-century Mongol emperor, and a
Chinese city of Xamdu; but Coleridge's dream vision also borrows from travelers' descriptions
of such other exotic places as Abyssinia and America. 51 *circle*: a magic circle drawn to keep
away evil spirits.

*Emily Dickinson*

---

## *Emily Dickinson* (1830–1886)*

### BECAUSE I COULD NOT STOP FOR DEATH       (1863)

Because I could not stop for Death–
He kindly stopped for me–
The Carriage held but just Ourselves–
And Immortality.

We slowly drove–He knew no haste            5
And I had put away
My labor and my leisure too,
For His Civility–

We passed the School, where Children strove
At Recess–in the Ring–                        10
We passed the Fields of Gazing Grain–
We passed the Setting Sun–

Or rather–He passed Us–
The Dews drew quivering and chill–
For only Gossamer, my Gown–              15
My Tippet°–only Tulle–                   *cape*

We paused before a House that seemed
A Swelling of the Ground–

BECAUSE I COULD NOT STOP FOR DEATH. In the version of this poem printed by Emily Dickinson's first editors in 1890, stanza four was left out. In line 9 *strove* was replaced by *played*; line 10 was made to read "Their lessons scarcely done."

The Roof was scarcely visible—
The Cornice—in the Ground—                                                    20

Since then—'tis Centuries—and yet
Feels shorter than the Day
I first surmised the Horses' Heads
Were toward Eternity—

20, "The cornice but a mound"; 21, "Since then 'tis centuries, but each"; and capitalization and
punctuation were made conventional.


## Emily Dickinson (1830–1886)*

### I STARTED EARLY—TOOK MY DOG          (1862)

I started Early—Took my Dog—
And visited the Sea—
The Mermaids in the Basement
Came out to look at me—

And Frigates—in the Upper Floor                                               5
Extended Hempen Hands—
Presuming Me to be a Mouse—
Aground—upon the Sands—

But no Man moved Me—till the Tide
Went past my simple Shoe—                                                     10
And past my Apron—and my Belt
And past my Bodice—too—

And made as He would eat me up—
As wholly as a Dew
Upon a Dandelion's Sleeve—                                                    15
And then—I started—too—

And He—He followed—close behind—
I felt His Silver Heel
Upon my Ankle—Then my Shoes
Would overflow with Pearl—                                                    20

Until We met the Solid Town—
No One He seemed to know—
And bowing—with a Mighty look—
At me—The Sea withdrew—

*Emily Dickinson* (1830–1886)*

## MY LIFE HAD STOOD—A LOADED GUN          (about 1863)

My Life had stood—a Loaded Gun—
In Corners—till a Day
The Owner passed—identified—
And carried Me away—

And now We roam in Sovreign Woods—                                    5
And now We hunt the Doe—
And every time I speak for Him—
The Mountains straight reply—

And do I smile, such cordial light
Upon the Valley glow—                                                 10
It is as a Vesuvian face
Had let its pleasure through—

And when at Night—Our good Day done—
I guard My Master's Head—
'Tis better than the Eider-Duck's                                     15
Deep Pillow—to have shared—

To foe of His—I'm deadly foe—
None stir the second time—
On whom I lay a Yellow Eye—
Or an emphatic Thumb—                                                 20

Though I than He—may longer live
He longer must—than I—
For I have but the power to kill,
Without—the power to die—


*John Donne* (1572–1631)*

## DEATH BE NOT PROUD          (about 1610)

Death be not proud, though some have callèd thee
Mighty and dreadful, for thou art not so;
For those whom thou think'st thou dost overthrow
Die not, poor death, nor yet canst thou kill me.
From rest and sleep, which but thy pictures be,                       5
Much pleasure, then from thee much more must flow,
And soonest our best men with thee do go,
Rest of their bones, and soul's delivery.
Thou art slave to fate, chance, kings, and desperate men,
And dost with poison, war, and sickness dwell,                        10
And poppy, or charms can make us sleep as well,

And better than thy stroke; why swell'st thou then?
One short sleep past, we wake eternally,
And death shall be no more; death, thou shalt die.

John Donne

## *John Donne* (1572–1631)*

THE FLEA                                                    1633

Mark but this flea, and mark in this
How little that which thou deny'st me is;
It sucked me first, and now sucks thee,
And in this flea our two bloods mingled be;
Thou know'st that this cannot be said                      5
A sin, nor shame, nor loss of maidenhead,
    Yet this enjoys before it woo,
    And pampered swells with one blood made of two,
    And this, alas, is more than we would do.

Oh stay, three lives in one flea spare,                    10
Where we almost, yea more than married are.
This flea is you and I, and this
Our marriage bed, and marriage temple is;
Though parents grudge, and you, we're met
And cloistered in these living walls of jet.               15
    Though use° make you apt to kill me,         *custom*
    Let not to that, self-murder added be,
    And sacrilege, three sins in killing three.

Cruel and sudden, hast thou since
Purpled thy nail in blood of innocence?                    20
Wherein could this flea guilty be,

Except in that drop it sucked from thee?
Yet thou triumph'st, and say'st that thou
Find'st not thyself, nor me, the weaker now;
    'Tis true; then learn how false, fears be;          25
    Just so much honor, when thou yield'st to me,
    Will waste, as this flea's death took life from thee.


## *John Donne* (1572–1631)*

### A Valediction: Forbidding Mourning    (1611)

As virtuous men pass mildly away,
    And whisper to their souls to go,
Whilst some of their sad friends do say
    The breath goes now, and some say no:

So let us melt, and make no noise,          5
    No tear-floods, nor sigh-tempests move;
'Twere profanation of our joys
    To tell the laity° our love.          *common people*

Moving of th' earth° brings harms and fears;      *earthquake*
    Men reckon what it did and meant;          10
But trepidation of the spheres,
    Though greater far, is innocent°.          *harmless*

Dull sublunary lovers' love
    (Whose soul is sense) cannot admit
Absence, because it doth remove          15
    Those things which elemented° it.          *constituted*

But we, by a love so much refined
    That ourselves know not what it is,
Inter-assurèd of the mind,
    Care less, eyes, lips, and hands to miss.          20

Our two souls, therefore, which are one,
    Though I must go, endure not yet
A breach, but an expansiòn,
    Like gold to airy thinness beat.

If they be two, they are two so          25
    As stiff twin compasses are two:
Thy soul, the fixed foot, makes no show
    To move, but doth, if th' other do.

And though it in the center sit,
    Yet when the other far doth roam,                                   30
It leans and harkens after it,
    And grows erect as that comes home.

Such wilt thou be to me, who must,
    Like th' other foot, obliquely run;
Thy firmness makes my circle just°,                          *perfect*  35
    And makes me end where I begun.

A Valediction: Forbidding Mourning. According to Donne's biographer Izaak Walton, Donne's wife received this poem as a gift before the poet departed on a journey to France. 11 *spheres:* In Ptolemaic astronomy, the concentric spheres surrounding the earth. The trepidation or motion of the ninth sphere was thought to change the date of the equinox. 19 *Inter-assurèd of the mind:* Each sure in mind that the other is faithful. 24 *gold to airy thinness:* Gold is so malleable that, if beaten to the thickness of gold leaf (1/250,000 of one inch), one ounce of gold would cover 250 square feet.


## *Rita Dove* (b. 1952)

### Daystar                                    1986

She wanted a little room for thinking:
but she saw diapers steaming on the line,
a doll slumped behind the door.

So she lugged a chair behind the garage
to sit out the children's naps.                                5

Sometimes there were things to watch—
the pinched armor of a vanished cricket,
a floating maple leaf. Other days
she stared until she was assured
when she closed her eyes                                10
she'd see only her own vivid blood.

She had an hour, at best, before Liza appeared
pouting from the top of the stairs.
And just *what* was mother doing
out back with the field mice? Why,                      15

building a palace. Later
that night when Thomas rolled over and
lurched into her, she would open her eyes
and think of the place that was hers
for an hour—where                                  20
she was nothing,
pure nothing, in the middle of the day.

## John Dryden (1631–1700)*

### To the Memory of Mr. Oldham          1684

Farewell, too little and too lately known,
Whom I began to think and call my own;
For sure our souls were near allied, and thine
Cast in the same poetic mold with mine.
One common note on either lyre did strike,                    5
And knaves and fools we both abhorred alike.
To the same goal did both our studies drive:
The last set out the soonest did arrive.
Thus Nissus fell upon the slippery place,
While his young friend performed and won the race.            10
O early ripe! to thy abundant store
What could advancing age have added more?
It might (what Nature never gives the young)
Have taught the numbers° of thy native tongue.      *meters*
But satire needs not those, and wit will shine               15
Through the harsh cadence of a rugged line.
A noble error, and but seldom made,
When poets are by too much force betrayed.
Thy gen'rous fruits, though gathered ere their prime,
Still showed a quickness; and maturing time                  20
But mellows what we write to the dull sweets of rhyme.
Once more, hail, and farewell! farewell, thou young
But ah! too short, Marcellus of our tongue!
Thy brows with ivy and with laurels bound;
But fate and gloomy night encompass thee around.             25

To the Memory of Mr. Oldham. John Oldham, poet best remembered for his *Satires upon the Jesuits*, had died at thirty. 9–10 *Nissus; his young friend:* These two close friends, as Virgil tells us in the *Aeneid*, ran a race for the prize of an olive crown. 23 *Marcellus:* Had he not died in his twentieth year, he would have succeeded the Roman emperor Augustus. 25 This line echoes the *Aeneid* (VI, 886), in which Marcellus is seen walking under the black cloud of his impending doom.

Compare:

"To the Memory of Mr. Oldham" with "Lycidas" by John Milton (page 962).

## T. S. Eliot (1888–1965)*

### Journey of the Magi          1927

"A cold coming we had of it,
Just the worst time of the year
For a journey, and such a long journey:
The ways deep and the weather sharp,
The very dead of winter."                                     5

And the camels galled, sore-footed, refractory,
Lying down in the melting snow.
There were times we regretted
The summer palaces on slopes, the terraces,
And the silken girls bringing sherbet.                                              10
Then the camel men cursing and grumbling
And running away, and wanting their liquor and women,
And the night-fires going out, and the lack of shelters,
And the cities hostile and the towns unfriendly
And the villages dirty and charging high prices:                                    15
A hard time we had of it.
At the end we preferred to travel all night,
Sleeping in snatches,
With the voices singing in our ears, saying
That this was all folly.                                                            20

Then at dawn we came down to a temperate valley,
Wet, below the snow line, smelling of vegetation;
With a running stream and a water-mill beating the darkness,
And three trees on the low sky,
And an old white horse galloped away in the meadow.                                 25
Then we came to a tavern with vine-leaves over the lintel,
Six hands at an open door dicing for pieces of silver,
And feet kicking the empty wine-skins.
But there was no information, and so we continued
And arrived at evening, not a moment too soon                                       30
Finding the place; it was (you may say) satisfactory.
All this was a long time ago, I remember,
And I would do it again, but set down
This set down
This: were we led all that way for                                                  35
Birth or Death? There was a Birth, certainly,
We had evidence and no doubt. I had seen birth and death,
But had thought they were different; this Birth was
Hard and bitter agony for us, like Death, our death.
We returned to our places, these Kingdoms,                                          40
But no longer at ease here, in the old dispensation,
With an alien people clutching their gods.
I should be glad of another death.

JOURNEY OF THE MAGI. The story of the Magi, the three wise men who traveled to Bethlehem
to behold the baby Jesus, is told in Matthew 2:1–12. That the three were kings is a later
tradition. 1–5 *A cold coming . . . winter:* Eliot quotes with slight changes from a sermon preached
on Christmas day, 1622, by Bishop Lancelot Andrewes. 24 *three trees:* foreshadowing the three
crosses on Calvary (see Luke 23:32–33). 25 *white horse:* perhaps the steed that carried the
conquering Christ in the vision of St. John the Divine (Revelation 19:11–16). 41 *old dispensation:*
older, pagan religion about to be displaced by Christianity.

## COMPARE:

"Journey of the Magi" with "The Magi" by William Butler Yeats (page 1021).

*T. S. Eliot*

**T. S. Eliot** (1888–1965)*

## THE LOVE SONG OF J. ALFRED PRUFROCK                 1917

*S'io credessi che mia risposta fosse
A persona che mai tornasse al mondo,
Questa fiamma staria senza piu scosse.
Ma perciocche giammai di questo fondo
Non torno vivo alcun, s'i'odo il vero,
Senza tema d'infamia ti rispondo.*

Let us go then, you and I,
When the evening is spread out against the sky
Like a patient etherized upon a table;
Let us go, through certain half-deserted streets,
The muttering retreats                                      5
Of restless nights in one-night cheap hotels
And sawdust restaurants with oyster-shells:
Streets that follow like a tedious argument
Of insidious intent
To lead you to an overwhelming question . . .              10
Oh, do not ask, "What is it?"
Let us go and make our visit.

In the room the women come and go
Talking of Michelangelo.

The yellow fog that rubs its back upon the window-panes,    15
The yellow smoke that rubs its muzzle on the window-panes
Licked its tongue into the corners of the evening,

Lingered upon the pools that stand in drains,
Let fall upon its back the soot that falls from chimneys,
Slipped by the terrace, made a sudden leap, 20
And seeing that it was a soft October night,
Curled once about the house, and fell asleep.

And indeed there will be time
For the yellow smoke that slides along the street,
Rubbing its back upon the window-panes; 25
There will be time, there will be time
To prepare a face to meet the faces that you meet;
There will be time to murder and create,
And time for all the works and days of hands
That lift and drop a question on your plate; 30
Time for you and time for me,
And time yet for a hundred indecisions,
And for a hundred visions and revisions,
Before the taking of a toast and tea.

In the room the women come and go 35
Talking of Michelangelo.

And indeed there will be time
To wonder, "Do I dare?" and, "Do I dare?"
Time to turn back and descend the stair,
With a bald spot in the middle of my hair— 40
(They will say: "How his hair is growing thin!")
My morning coat, my collar mounting firmly to the chin,
My necktie rich and modest, but asserted by a simple pin—
(They will say: "But how his arms and legs are thin!")
Do I dare 45
Disturb the universe?
In a minute there is time
For decisions and revisions which a minute will reverse.

For I have known them all already, known them all:—
Have known the evenings, mornings, afternoons, 50
I have measured out my life with coffee spoons;
I know the voices dying with a dying fall
Beneath the music from a farther room.
    So how should I presume?

And I have known the eyes already, known them all— 55
The eyes that fix you in a formulated phrase,
And when I am formulated, sprawling on a pin,
When I am pinned and wriggling on the wall,
Then how should I begin
To spit out all the butt-ends of my days and ways? 60
    And how should I presume?

And I have known the arms already, known them all—
Arms that are braceleted and white and bare
(But in the lamplight, downed with light brown hair!)
Is it perfume from a dress                                              65
That makes me so digress?
Arms that lie along a table, or wrap about a shawl.
    And should I then presume?
    And how should I begin?

· · · · · ·

Shall I say, I have gone at dusk through narrow streets               70
And watched the smoke that rises from the pipes
Of lonely men in shirt-sleeves, leaning out of windows? . . .

I should have been a pair of ragged claws
Scuttling across the floors of silent seas.

And the afternoon, the evening, sleeps so peacefully!                 75
Smoothed by long fingers,
Asleep . . . tired . . . or it malingers,
Stretched on the floor, here beside you and me.
Should I, after tea and cakes and ices,
Have the strength to force the moment to its crisis?                  80
But though I have wept and fasted, wept and prayed,
Though I have seen my head (grown slightly bald) brought in upon
    a platter,
I am no prophet—and here's no great matter;
I have seen the moment of my greatness flicker,
And I have seen the eternal Footman hold my coat, and snicker,       85
And in short, I was afraid.

And would it have been worth it, after all,
After the cups, the marmalade, the tea,
Among the porcelain, among some talk of you and me,
Would it have been worth while,                                      90
To have bitten off the matter with a smile,
To have squeezed the universe into a ball
To roll it toward some overwhelming question,
To say: "I am Lazarus, come from the dead,
Come back to tell you all, I shall tell you all"—                    95
If one, settling a pillow by her head,
    Should say: "That is not what I meant at all.
    That is not it, at all."

And would it have been worth it, after all,
Would it have been worth while,                                      100
After the sunsets and the dooryards and the sprinkled streets,
After the novels, after the teacups, after the skirts that trail along
    the floor—

And this, and so much more?—
It is impossible to say just what I mean!
But as if a magic lantern threw the nerves in patterns on a screen:          105
Would it have been worth while
If one, settling a pillow or throwing off a shawl,
And turning toward the window, should say:
    "That is not it at all,
    That is not what I meant, at all."          110

. . . . . .

No! I am not Prince Hamlet, nor was meant to be;
Am an attendant lord, one that will do
To swell a progress, start a scene or two,
Advise the prince; no doubt, an easy tool,
Deferential, glad to be of use,          115
Politic, cautious, and meticulous;
Full of high sentence, but a bit obtuse;
At times, indeed, almost ridiculous—
Almost, at times, the Fool.

I grow old . . . I grow old . . .          120
I shall wear the bottoms of my trousers rolled.

Shall I part my hair behind? Do I dare to eat a peach?
I shall wear white flannel trousers, and walk upon the beach.
I have heard the mermaids singing, each to each.

I do not think that they will sing to me.          125

I have seen them riding seaward on the waves
Combing the white hair of the waves blown back
When the wind blows the water white and black.

We have lingered in the chambers of the sea
By sea-girls wreathed with seaweed red and brown          130
Till human voices wake us, and we drown.

THE LOVE SONG OF J. ALFRED PRUFROCK. The epigraph, from Dante's *Inferno*, is the speech of
one dead and damned, who thinks that his hearer also is going to remain in Hell. Count Guido
da Montefeltro, whose sin has been to give false counsel after a corrupt prelate had offered him
prior absolution and whose punishment is to be wrapped in a constantly burning flame, offers
to tell Dante his story: "If I thought my reply were to someone who could ever return to the
world, this flame would waver no more. But since, I'm told, nobody ever escapes from this pit,
I'll tell you without fear of ill fame." 29 *works and days*: title of a poem by Hesiod (eighth century
B.C.), depicting his life as a hard-working Greek farmer and exhorting his brother to be like him.
82 *head . . . platter*: like that of John the Baptist, prophet and praiser of chastity, whom King
Herod beheaded at the demand of Herodias, his unlawfully wedded wife (see Mark 6:17–28).
92–93 *squeezed . . . To roll it*: an echo from Marvell's "To His Coy Mistress," lines 41–42 (see
p. 350). 94 *Lazarus*: Probably the Lazarus whom Jesus called forth from the tomb (John
11:1–44), but possibly the beggar seen in Heaven by the rich man in Hell (Luke 16:19–25).

## Louise Erdrich (b. 1954)

### INDIAN BOARDING SCHOOL: THE RUNAWAYS          1984

Home's the place we head for in our sleep.
Boxcars stumbling north in dreams
don't wait for us. We catch them on the run.
The rails, old lacerations that we love,
shoot parallel across the face and break                                                5
just under Turtle Mountains. Riding scars
you can't get lost. Home is the place they cross.

The lame guard strikes a match and makes the dark
less tolerant. We watch through cracks in boards
as the land starts rolling, rolling till it hurts                                          10
to be here, cold in regulation clothes.
We know the sheriff's waiting at midrun
to take us back. His car is dumb and warm.
The highway doesn't rock, it only hums
like a wing of long insults. The worn-down welts                                    15
of ancient punishments lead back and forth.

All runaways wear dresses, long green ones,
the color you would think shame was. We scrub
the sidewalks down because it's shameful work.
Our brushes cut the stone in watered arcs                                             20
and in the soak frail outlines shiver clear
a moment, things us kids pressed on the dark
face before it hardened, pale, remembering
delicate old injuries, the spines of names and leaves.

INDIAN BOARDING SCHOOL: THE RUNAWAYS. 6. *Turtle Mountains:* in North Dakota and Manitoba. The poet, of German and Native American descent, belongs to the Turtle Mountain Band of the Chippewa.

## Robert Frost (1874–1963)*

### BIRCHES          1916

When I see birches bend to left and right
Across the lines of straighter darker trees,
I like to think some boy's been swinging them.
But swinging doesn't bend them down to stay
As ice storms do. Often you must have seen them                                   5
Loaded with ice a sunny winter morning
After a rain. They click upon themselves
As the breeze rises, and turn many-colored

As the stir cracks and crazes their enamel.
Soon the sun's warmth makes them shed crystal shells 10
Shattering and avalanching on the snow crust—
Such heaps of broken glass to sweep away
You'd think the inner dome of heaven had fallen.
They are dragged to the withered bracken by the load,
And they seem not to break; though once they are bowed 15
So low for long, they never right themselves:
You may see their trunks arching in the woods
Years afterwards, trailing their leaves on the ground
Like girls on hands and knees that throw their hair
Before them over their heads to dry in the sun. 20
But I was going to say when Truth broke in
With all her matter of fact about the ice storm,
I should prefer to have some boy bend them
As he went out and in to fetch the cows—
Some boy too far from town to learn baseball, 25
Whose only play was what he found himself,
Summer or winter, and could play alone.
One by one he subdued his father's trees
By riding them down over and over again
Until he took the stiffness out of them, 30
And not one but hung limp, not one was left
For him to conquer. He learned all there was
To learn about not launching out too soon
And so not carrying the tree away
Clear to the ground. He always kept his poise 35
To the top branches, climbing carefully
With the same pains you use to fill a cup
Up to the brim, and even above the brim.
Then he flung outward, feet first, with a swish,
Kicking his way down through the air to the ground. 40
So was I once myself a swinger of birches.
And so I dream of going back to be.
It's when I'm weary of considerations,
And life is too much like a pathless wood
Where your face burns and tickles with the cobwebs 45
Broken across it, and one eye is weeping
From a twig's having lashed across it open.
I'd like to get away from earth awhile
And then come back to it and begin over.
May no fate willfully misunderstand me 50
And half grant what I wish and snatch me away
Not to return. Earth's the right place for love:
I don't know where it's likely to go better.
I'd like to go by climbing a birch tree,

And climb black branches up a snow-white trunk                    55
*Toward* heaven, till the tree could bear no more,
But dipped its top and set me down again.
That would be good both going and coming back.
One could do worse than be a swinger of birches.


## Robert Frost (1874–1963)*

### MENDING WALL                                              1914

Something there is that doesn't love a wall,
That sends the frozen-ground-swell under it,
And spills the upper boulders in the sun;
And makes gaps even two can pass abreast.
The work of hunters is another thing:                             5
I have come after them and made repair
Where they have left not one stone on a stone,
But they would have the rabbit out of hiding,
To please the yelping dogs. The gaps I mean,
No one has seen them made or heard them made,                    10
But at spring mending-time we find them there.
I let my neighbour know beyond the hill;
And on a day we meet to walk the line
And set the wall between us once again.
We keep the wall between us as we go.                             15
To each the boulders that have fallen to each.
And some are loaves and some so nearly balls
We have to use a spell to make them balance:
"Stay where you are until our backs are turned!"
We wear our fingers rough with handling them.                    20
Oh, just another kind of out-door game,
One on a side. It comes to little more:
There where it is we do not need the wall:
He is all pine and I am apple orchard.
My apple trees will never get across                             25
And eat the cones under his pines, I tell him.
He only says, "Good fences make good neighbours."
Spring is the mischief in me, and I wonder
If I could put a notion in his head:
"*Why* do they make good neighbours? Isn't it                    30
Where there are cows? But here there are no cows.
Before I built a wall I'd ask to know
What I was walling in or walling out,
And to whom I was like to give offence.
Something there is that doesn't love a wall,                     35

That wants it down." I could say "Elves" to him,
But it's not elves exactly, and I'd rather
He said it for himself. I see him there
Bringing a stone grasped firmly by the top
In each hand, like an old-stone savage armed.                    40
He moves in darkness as it seems to me,
Not of woods only and the shade of trees.
He will not go behind his father's saying,
And he likes having thought of it so well
He says again, "Good fences make good neighbours."              45


**_Robert Frost_** (1874–1963)*

STOPPING BY WOODS ON A SNOWY EVENING          1923

Whose woods these are I think I know.
His house is in the village though;
He will not see me stopping here
To watch his woods fill up with snow.

My little horse must think it queer                             5
To stop without a farmhouse near
Between the woods and frozen lake
The darkest evening of the year.

He gives his harness bells a shake
To ask if there is some mistake.                                10
The only other sound's the sweep
Of easy wind and downy flake.

The woods are lovely, dark and deep,
But I have promises to keep,
And miles to go before I sleep,                                 15
And miles to go before I sleep.

COMPARE:

"Stopping by Woods on a Snowy Evening" with "Desert Places" by Robert Frost
(page 730).


**_Allen Ginsberg_** (b. 1926)

A SUPERMARKET IN CALIFORNIA                    1956

    What thoughts I have of you tonight, Walt Whitman, for I walked
down the sidestreets under the trees with a headache self-conscious
looking at the full moon.

In my hungry fatigue, and shopping for images, I went into the neon fruit supermarket, dreaming of your enumerations!

What peaches and what penumbras! Whole families shopping at night! Aisles full of husbands! Wives in the avocados, babies in the tomatoes!—and you, Garcia Lorca, what were you doing down by the watermelons?

I saw you, Walt Whitman, childless, lonely old grubber, poking among the meats in the refrigerator and eyeing the grocery boys.

I heard you asking questions of each: Who killed the pork chops? What price bananas? Are you my Angel?                                                                 5

I wandered in and out of the brilliant stacks of cans following you, and followed in my imagination by the store detective.

We strode down the open corridors together in our solitary fancy tasting artichokes, possessing every frozen delicacy, and never passing the cashier.

Where are we going, Walt Whitman? The doors close in an hour. Which way does your beard point tonight?

(I touch your book and dream of our odyssey in the supermarket and feel absurd.)

Will we walk all night through solitary streets? The trees add shade to shade, lights out in the houses, we'll both be lonely.                               10

Will we stroll dreaming of the lost America of love past blue automobiles in driveways, home to our silent cottage?

Ah, dear father, graybeard, lonely old courage-teacher, what America did you have when Charon quit poling his ferry and you got out on a smoking bank and stood watching the boat disappear on the black waters of Lethe?

A SUPERMARKET IN CALIFORNIA. *2 enumerations:* Many of Whitman's poems contain lists of observed details. *3 Garcia Lorca:* modern Spanish poet who wrote an "Ode to Walt Whitman" in his booklength sequence *Poet in New York.* (A poem by Lorca appears on page 844.) *12 Charon . . . Lethe:* Is the poet confusing two underworld rivers? Charon, in Greek and Roman mythology, is the boatman who ferries the souls of the dead across the River Styx. The River Lethe also flows through Hades, and a drink of its waters makes the dead lose their painful memories of loved ones thay have left behind.

COMPARE:

"A Supermarket in California" with Walt Whitman's "To a Locomotive in Winter" (page 600) and "I Saw in Louisiana a Live-Oak Growing" (page 1010).

---

*Dana Gioia* (b. 1950)

CALIFORNIA HILLS IN AUGUST                    1982

I can imagine someone who found
these fields unbearable, who climbed
the hillside in the heat, cursing the dust,

cracking the brittle weeds underfoot,
wishing a few more trees for shade.                                    5

An Easterner especially, who would scorn
the meagreness of summer, the dry
twisted shapes of black elm,
scrub oak, and chaparral—a landscape
August has already drained of green.                                   10

One who would hurry over the clinging
thistle, foxtail, golden poppy,
knowing everything was just a weed,
unable to conceive that these trees
and sparse brown bushes were alive.                                    15

And hate the bright stillness of the noon,
without wind, without motion,
the only other living thing
a hawk, hungry for prey, suspended
in the blinding, sunlit blue.                                          20

And yet how gentle it seems to someone
raised in a landscape short of rain—
the skyline of a hill broken by no more
trees than one can count, the grass,
the empty sky, the wish for water.                                     25


## H. D. [Hilda Doolittle] (1886–1961)*

HELEN                                    1924

All Greece hates
the still eyes in the white face,
the lustre as of olives
where she stands,
and the white hands.                                                   5

All Greece reviles
the wan face when she smiles,
hating it deeper still
when it grows wan and white,
remembering past enchantments                                          10
and past ills.

Greece sees unmoved,
God's daughter, born of love,
the beauty of cool feet
and slenderest knees,                                                  15
could love indeed the maid,

only if she were laid,
white ash amid funereal cypresses.

HELEN. In Greek mythology, Helen, most beautiful of all women, was the daughter of a mortal, Leda, by the god Zeus. Her kidnapping set off the long and devastating Trojan War. While married to Menelaus, king of the Greek city-state of Sparta, Helen was carried off by Paris, prince of Troy. Menelaus and his brother Agammemnon raised an army, besieged Troy for ten years, and eventually recaptured her. One episode of the Trojan War is related in the *Iliad*, Homer's epic poem, composed before 700 B.C.

COMPARE:

"Helen" with "Long-legged Fly" by William Butler Yeats (page 1020) and "To Helen" by Edgar Allan Poe (page 978).

*H. D.*

## *Donald Hall* (b. 1928)

NAMES OF HORSES                                                    1978

All winter your brute shoulders strained against collars, padding
and steerhide over the ash hames, to haul
sledges of cordwood for drying through spring and summer,
for the Glenwood stove next winter, and for the simmering range.

In April you pulled cartloads of manure to spread on the fields,          5
dark manure of Holsteins, and knobs of your own clustered with
    oats.
All summer you mowed the grass in meadow and hayfield, the
    mowing machine
clacketing beside you, while the sun walked high in the morning;

and after noon's heat, you pulled a clawed rake through the same
    acres,

gathering stacks, and dragged the wagon from stack to stack,               10
and the built hayrack back, uphill to the chaffy barn,
three loads of hay a day from standing grass in the morning.

Sundays you trotted the two miles to church with the light load
of a leather quartertop buggy, and grazed in the sound of hymns.
Generation on generation, your neck rubbed the windowsill                  15
of the stall, smoothing the wood as the sea smooths glass.

When you were old and lame, when your shoulders hurt bending to
    graze,
one October the man, who fed you and kept you, and harnessed
    you every morning,
led you through corn stubble to sandy ground above Eagle Pond,
and dug a hole beside you where you stood shuddering in your
    skin,                                                                  20

and lay the shotgun's muzzle in the boneless hollow behind your
    ear,
and fired the slug into your brain, and felled you into your grave,
shoveling sand to cover you, setting goldenrod upright above you,
where by next summer a dent in the ground made your monument.

For a hundred and fifty years, in the pasture of dead horses,             25
roots of pine trees pushed through the pale curves of your ribs,
yellow blossoms flourished above you in autumn, and in winter
frost heaved your bones in the ground—old toilers, soil makers:

O Roger, Mackerel, Riley, Ned, Nellie, Chester, Lady Ghost.

COMPARE:

"Names of Horses" with "The Bull Calf" by Irving Layton (page 953).

---

### *Thomas Hardy* (1840–1928)*

## THE CONVERGENCE OF THE TWAIN                    1912

*Lines on the Loss of the "Titanic"*

I

          In a solitude of the sea
          Deep from human vanity,
And the Pride of Life that planned her, stilly couches she.

II

          Steel chambers, late the pyres
          Of her salamandrine fires,                                       5
Cold currents thrid°, and turn to rhythmic tidal lyres.        *thread*

### III

Over the mirrors meant
To glass the opulent
The sea-worm crawls—grotesque, slimed, dumb, indifferent.

### IV

Jewels in joy designed                                        10
To ravish the sensuous mind
Lie lightless, all their sparkles bleared and black and blind.

### V

Dim moon-eyed fishes near
Gaze at the gilded gear
And query: "What does this vaingloriousness down here?"        15

### VI

Well: while was fashioning
This creature of cleaving wing,
The Immanent Will that stirs and urges everything

### VII

Prepared a sinister mate
For her—so gaily great—                                       20
A Shape of Ice, for the time far and dissociate.

### VIII

And as the smart ship grew
In stature, grace, and hue,
In shadowy silent distance grew the Iceberg too.

### IX

Alien they seemed to be:                                      25
No mortal eye could see
The intimate welding of their later history,

### X

Or sign that they were bent
By paths coincident
On being anon twin halves of one august event.                30

### XI

Till the Spinner of the Years
Said "Now!" And each one hears,
And consummation comes, and jars two hemispheres.

THE CONVERGENCE OF THE TWAIN. The luxury liner *Titanic*, supposedly unsinkable, went down
in 1912 after striking an iceberg, on its first Atlantic voyage. 5 *salamandrine*: like the salamander,
a lizard that supposedly thrives in fires, or like a spirit of the same name that inhabits fire
(according to alchemists).

### COMPARE:

"The Convergence of the Twain" with "Titanic" by David R. Slavitt (page 994).

*Thomas Hardy*

---

**Thomas Hardy** (1840–1928)*

DURING WIND AND RAIN          1917

They sing their dearest songs—
He, she, all of them—yea,
Treble and tenor and bass,
   And one to play;
With the candles mooning each face. . . .          5
   Ah, no; the years O!
How the sick leaves reel down in throngs!

They clear the creeping moss—
Elders and juniors—aye,
Making the pathways neat          10
   And the garden gay;
And they build a shady seat. . . .
   Ah, no; the years, the years;
See, the white storm-birds wing across!

They are blithely breakfasting all—          15
Men and maidens—yea,
Under the summer tree,
   With a glimpse of the bay,
While pet fowl come to the knee. . . .
   Ah, no! the years O!          20
And the rotten rose is ripped from the wall.

They change to a high new house,
He, she, all of them—aye,

Clocks and carpets and chairs
    On the lawn all day,                                                25
And brightest things that are theirs. . . .
    Ah, no; the years, the years;
Down their carved names the rain-drop plows.


COMPARE:

"During Wind and Rain" with "anyone lived in a pretty how town" by E. E.
Cummings (page 646).


### *Thomas Hardy* (1840–1928)*

HAP                                                               1866


If but some vengeful god would call to me
From up the sky, and laugh: "Thou suffering thing,
Know that thy sorrow is my ecstasy,
That thy love's loss is my hate's profiting!"

Then would I bear it, clench myself, and die,                      5
Steeled by the sense of ire unmerited;
Half-eased in that a Powerfuller than I
Had willed and meted me the tears I shed.

But not so. How arrives it joy lies slain,
And why unblooms the best hope ever sown?                          10
—Crass Casualty obstructs the sun and rain,
And dicing Time for gladness casts a moan . . .
These purblind Doomsters had as readily strown
Blisses about my pilgrimage as pain.


### *Thomas Hardy* (1840–1928)*

IN CHURCH                                                         1914


"And now to God the Father," he ends,
And his voice thrills up to the topmost tiles:
Each listener chokes as he bows and bends,
And emotion pervades the crowded aisles.
Then the preacher glides to the vestry-door,                      5
And shuts it, and thinks he is seen no more.

The door swings softly ajar meanwhile,
And a pupil of his in the Bible class,
Who adores him as one without gloss or guile
Sees her idol stand with a satisfied smile                        10
And re-enact at the vestry-glass

Each pulpit gesture in deft dumb-show
That had moved the congregation so.

Robert Hayden

## Robert Hayden (1913–1980)*

### THE WHIPPING                    1970

The old woman across the way
  is whipping the boy again
and shouting to the neighborhood
  her goodness and his wrongs.

Wildly he crashes through elephant ears,     5
  pleads in dusty zinnias,
while she in spite of crippling fat
  pursues and corners him.

She strikes and strikes the shrilly circling
  boy till the stick breaks     10
in her hand. His tears are rainy weather
  to woundlike memories:

My head gripped in bony vise
  of knees, the writhing struggle
to wrench free, the blows, the fear     15
  worse than blows that hateful

Words could bring, the face that I
  no longer knew or loved. . . .
Well, it is over now, it is over
  and the boy sobs in his room,     20

And the woman leans muttering against
    a tree, exhausted, purged—
avenged in part for lifelong hidings
    she has had to bear.


## Robert Hayden (1913–1980)*

### THOSE WINTER SUNDAYS                    1962

Sundays too my father got up early
and put his clothes on in the blueblack cold,
then with cracked hands that ached
from labor in the weekday weather made
banked fires blaze. No one ever thanked him.                    5

I'd wake and hear the cold splintering, breaking.
When the rooms were warm, he'd call,
and slowly I would rise and dress,
fearing the chronic angers of that house,

Speaking indifferently to him,                                  10
who had driven out the cold
and polished my good shoes as well.
What did I know, what did I know
of love's austere and lonely offices?

COMPARE:

"Those Winter Sundays" with "My Father's Martial Art" by Stephen Shu-ning Liu
(page 954) and "Daddy" by Sylvia Plath (page 975).


## James Hayford (1913–1993)

### DRY NOON                    1983

Their low house nooning in the maple shade,
The pair inside remember having hayed.

The day today is dry and very fine—
Good haying weather, he has said, yes sir—
He who will hay no more, come rain or shine.                    5

In all the valley, not a breeze to stir
The old man's breeches drying on the line.

DIGGING                                                    1966

Between my finger and my thumb
The squat pen rests; snug as a gun.

Under my window, a clean rasping sound
When the spade sinks into gravelly ground.
My father, digging. I look down                                        5

Till his straining rump among the flowerbeds
Bends low, comes up twenty years away
Stooping in rhythm through potato drills
Where he was digging.

The coarse boot nestled on the lug, the shaft              10
Against the inside knee was levered firmly.
He rooted out tall tops, buried the bright edge deep
To scatter new potatoes that we picked
Loving their cool hardness in our hands.

By God, the old man could handle a spade.                 15
Just like his old man.

My grandfather cut more turf in a day
Than any other man on Toner's bog.
Once I carried him milk in a bottle
Corked sloppily with paper. He straightened up            20
To drink it, then fell to right away

Nicking and slicing neatly, heaving sods
Over his shoulder, going down and down
For the good turf. Digging.

The cold smell of potato mould, the squelch and slap      25
Of soggy peat, the curt cuts of an edge
Through living roots awaken in my head.
But I've no spade to follow men like them.

Between my finger and my thumb
The squat pen rests.                                      30
I'll dig with it.

**Seamus Heaney** (b. 1939)*

MOTHER OF THE GROOM            1972

What she remembers
Is his glistening back

In the bath, his small boots
In the ring of boots at her feet.

Hands in her voided lap,                                                    5
She hears a daughter welcomed.
It's as if he kicked when lifted
And slipped her soapy hold.

Once soap would ease off
The wedding ring                                                          10
That's bedded forever now
In her clapping hand.

---

### Anthony Hecht (b. 1923)

ADAM                                                                  1967

*Hath the rain a father? or who hath begotten the drops of dew?*

"Adam, my child, my son,
These very words you hear
Compose the fish and starlight
Of your untroubled dream.
When you awake, my child,                                                  5
It shall all come true.
Know that it was for you
That all things were begun."

Adam, my child, my son,
Thus spoke Our Father in heaven                                            10
To his first, fabled child,
The father of us all.
And I, your father, tell
The words over again
As innumerable men                                                        15
From ancient times have done.

Tell them again in pain,
And to the empty air.
Where you are men speak
A different mother tongue.                                                 20
Will you forget our games,
Our hide-and-seek and song?
Child, it will be long
Before I see you again.

Adam, there will be                                                       25
Many hard hours,

As an old poem says,
Hours of loneliness.
I cannot ease them for you;
They are our common lot.                                    30
During them, like as not,
You will dream of me.

When you are crouched away
In a strange clothes closet
Hiding from one who's "It"                                  35
And the dark crowds in,
Do not be afraid—
O, if you can, believe
In a father's love
That you shall know some day.                               40

Think of the summer rain
Or seedpearls of the mist;
Seeing the beaded leaf,
Try to remember me.
From far away                                               45
I send my blessing out
To circle the great globe.
It shall reach you yet.

ADAM. According to Genesis 2:6–7, God created Adam, the first man, from the dust of
the earth; Adam is also the name of Anthony Hecht's first son. *Epigraph: "Hath the rain a
father . . . ?"*: These words are spoken to Job by the voice of God in Job 38:28.

## COMPARE

Compare Anthony Hecht's "Adam" to A. D. Hope's "Imperial Adam" (page 819).

---

## *George Herbert* (1593–1633)*

### LOVE                                                   1633

Love bade me welcome; yet my soul drew back,
      Guilty of dust and sin.
But quick-eyed Love, observing me grow slack
      From my first entrance in,
Drew nearer to me, sweetly questioning                      5
      If I lacked anything.

"A guest," I answered, "worthy to be here";
      Love said, "You shall be he."
"I, the unkind, ungrateful? Ah, my dear,
      I cannot look on Thee."                        10

Love took my hand, and smiling did reply,
    "Who made the eyes but I?"

"Truth, Lord, but I have marred them; let my shame
    Go where it doth deserve."
"And know you not," says Love, "who bore the blame?"        15
    "My dear, then I will serve."
"You must sit down," says Love, "and taste My meat."
    So I did sit and eat.

COMPARE

"Love" with "Batter my heart, three-personed God" by John Donne (page 629).

*George Herbert*

### Robert Herrick (1591–1674)*

## THE BAD SEASON MAKES THE POET SAD     1648

Dull to myself and almost dead to these
My many fresh and fragrant mistresses,
Lost to all music now, since everything
Puts on the semblance here of sorrowing.
Sick is the land to th' heart, and doth endure        5
More dangerous faintings by her desp'rate cure.
But if that golden age would come again
And Charles here rule, as he before did reign,
If smooth and unperplexed the seasons were
As when the sweet Maria livèd here,        10

I should delight to have my curls half drowned
In Tyrian dews, and head with roses crowned,
And once more yet, ere I am laid out dead,
Knock at a star with my exalted head.

THE BAD SEASON MAKES THE POET SAD. *1–2 these . . . mistresses:* This line may appear to suggest
that Herrick was a Don Juan, but see his brief biography in *Lives of the Poets* (page 1045). To what
"mistresses" might he refer? *5 Sick is the land:* Civil War had erupted in England in 1642. *6
desp'rate cure:* Herrick probably means rule by Parliament, which had brought an uneasy peace.
In 1645 the forces of Parliament, led by Oliver Cromwell, had defeated the armies of Charles
I, and the king had fled the country. *10 Maria:* Henrietta Maria, wife of Charles. *12 Tyrian dews:*
perfumes from Tyre, in ancient Phoenicia.

## *Robert Herrick* (1591–1674)*

### TO THE VIRGINS, TO MAKE MUCH OF TIME          1648

Gather ye rose-buds while ye may,
   Old Time is still a-flying;
And this same flower that smiles today,
   Tomorrow will be dying.

The glorious lamp of heaven, the sun,                                  5
   The higher he's a-getting,
The sooner will his race be run,
   And nearer he's to setting.

That age is best which is the first,
   When youth and blood are warmer;                          10
But being spent, the worse, and worst
   Times still succeed the former.

Then be not coy, but use your time,
   And while ye may, go marry;
For having lost but once your prime,                                    15
   You may for ever tarry.

COMPARE:

"To the Virgins, to Make Much of Time" with "To His Coy Mistress" by Andrew
Marvell (page 957) and "Go, Lovely Rose" by Edmund Waller (page 1009).

## *Garrett Hongo* (b. 1951)

### THE CADENCE OF SILK          1988

When I lived in Seattle, I loved watching
the Sonics play basketball; something

about that array of trained and energetic
bodies set in motion to attack a more
sluggish, less physically intelligent opponent                    5
appealed to me, taught me about cadence
and play, the offguard breaking free
before the rebound, "releasing," as is said
in the parlance of the game, getting to
the center's downcourt pass and streaking                         10
to the basket for a scoopshot layup
off the glass, all in rhythm, all in
perfect declensions of action, smooth
and strenuous as Gorgiasian rhetoric.
I was hooked on the undulant ballet                               15
of the pattern offense, on the set play
back-door under the basket, and, at times,
even on the auctioneer's pace and elocution
of the play-by-play man. Now I watch
the Lakers, having returned to Los Angeles                        20
some years ago, love them even more than
the Seattle team, long since broken up and aging.
The Lakers are incomparable, numerous
options for any situation, their players
the league's quickest, most intelligent,                          25
and, it is my opinion, frankly, the most *cool*.
Few bruisers, they are sleek as arctic seals,
especially the small forward
as he dodges through the key, away from
the ball, rubbing off his man on the screen,                      30
setting for his shot. Then, slick as spit,
comes the ball from the point guard,
and my man goes up, cradling the ball
in his right hand like a waiter balancing
a tray piled with champagne in stemmed glasses,                   35
cocking his arm and bringing the ball
back behind his ear, pumping, letting fly then
as he jumps, popcorn-like, in the corner,
while the ball, launched, slung dextrously
with a slight backspin, slashes through                           40
the basket's silk net with a small,
sonorous splash of completion.

---

THE CADENCE OF SILK. 14 *Gorgiasian rhetoric*: art of persuasive speaking as practiced by Gorgias
(485?–380? B.C.), Greek Sophist philosopher, who argued that nothing exists.


COMPARE:

"The Cadence of Silk" with "Ex-Basketball Player" by John Updike (page 1006).

*Garrett Hongo*

## Gerard Manley Hopkins (1844–1889)*

### Spring and Fall         (1880)

*To a young child*

Márgarét, áre you grieving
Over Goldengrove unleaving°?          *shedding its leaves*
Leáves, líke the things of man, you
With your fresh thoughts care for, can you?
Áh! ás the heart grows older                              5
It will come to such sights colder
By and by, nor spare a sigh
Though worlds of wanwood leafmeal lie;
And yet you *will* weep and know why.
Now no matter, child, the name:                          10
Sórrow's spríngs áre the same.
Nor mouth had, no nor mind, expressed
What heart heard of, ghost° guessed:              *spirit*
It ís the blight man was born for,
It is Margaret you mourn for.                       15

### Compare:

"Spring and Fall" with "Margaret Are You Drug" by George Starbuck (page 851).

*Gerard Manley Hopkins*

## Gerard Manley Hopkins (1844–1889)*

### THOU ART INDEED JUST, LORD, IF I CONTEND (1889)

*Justus quidem tu es, Domine, si disputem tecum: verumtamen justa loquar
ad te: Quare via impiorum prosperatur? &c.*

Thou art indeed just, Lord, if I contend
With thee; but, sir, so what I plead is just.
Why do sinners' ways prosper? and why must
Disappointment all I endeavor end?
Wert thou my enemy, O thou my friend,                               5
How wouldst thou worse, I wonder than thou dost
Defeat, thwart me? Oh, the sots and thralls of lust
Do in spare hours more thrive than I that spend,

Sir, life upon thy cause. See, banks and brakes°           *ferny marshes*
Now, leavèd how thick! lacèd they are again                            10
With fretty chervil°, look, and fresh wind shakes            *wild herb*

Them; birds build—but not I build; no, but strain,
Time's eunuch, and not breed one work that wakes.
Mine, O thou lord of life, send my roots rain.

THOU ART INDEED JUST, LORD, IF I CONTEND. In the first two sentences of this poem, Hopkins
translates the Latin quotation from the Vulgate Bible (Jeremiah 12:1).

### COMPARE:

"Thou art indeed just, Lord . . ." with "When I consider how my light is spent" by
John Milton (page 968) or with "Hap" by Thomas Hardy (page 930).

## Gerard Manley Hopkins (1844–1889)*

### THE WINDHOVER (1877)

*To Christ Our Lord*

I caught this morning morning's minion, king-
    dom of daylight's dauphin, dapple-dawn-drawn Falcon, in
      his riding
Of the rolling level underneath him steady air, and striding
High there, how he rung upon the rein of a wimpling wing
In his ecstasy! then off, off forth on swing,             5
    As a skate's heel sweeps smooth on a bow-bend: the hurl and
      gliding
Rebuffed the big wind. My heart in hiding
Stirred for a bird,—the achieve of, the mastery of the thing!

Brute beauty and valor and act, oh, air, pride, plume, here
    Buckle! AND the fire that breaks from thee then, a billion    10
Times told lovelier, more dangerous, O my chevalier!

No wonder of it: shéer plód makes plow down sillion°      *furrow*
Shine, and blue-bleak embers, ah my dear,
    Fall, gall themselves, and gash gold-vermilion.

THE WINDHOVER. A windhover is a kestrel, or small falcon, so called because it can hover upon the wind. 4 *rung . . . wing*: A horse is "rung upon the rein" when its trainer holds the end of a long rein and has the horse circle him. The possible meanings of *wimpling* include (1) curving; (2) pleated, arranged in many little folds one on top of another; (3) rippling or undulating like the surface of a flowing stream.

## A. E. Housman (1859–1936)*

### LOVELIEST OF TREES, THE CHERRY NOW 1896

Loveliest of trees, the cherry now
Is hung with bloom along the bough,
And stands about the woodland ride°      *path*
Wearing white for Eastertide.

Now, of my threescore years and ten,      5
Twenty will not come again,
And take from seventy springs a score,
It only leaves me fifty more.

And since to look at things in bloom
Fifty springs are little room,      10
About the woodlands I will go
To see the cherry hung with snow.

COMPARE:

"Loveliest of trees, the cherry now" with "To the Virgins, to Make Much of Time" by Robert Herrick (page 937) and "Spring and Fall" by Gerard Manley Hopkins (page 939).

A. E. Housman

## A. E. Housman (1859–1936)*

### To an Athlete Dying Young          1896

The time you won your town the race
We chaired you through the market-place;
Man and boy stood cheering by,
And home we brought you shoulder-high.

Today, the road all runners come,                                    5
Shoulder-high we bring you home,
And set you at your threshold down,
Townsman of a stiller town.

Smart lad, to slip betimes away
From fields where glory does not stay,                               10
And early though the laurel grows
It withers quicker than the rose.

Eyes the shady night has shut
Cannot see the record cut,
And silence sounds no worse than cheers                              15
After earth has stopped the ears.

Now you will not swell the rout
Of lads that wore their honors out,

Runners whom renown outran
And the name died before the man.                                    20

So set, before its echoes fade,
The fleet foot on the sill of shade,
And hold to the low lintel up
The still-defended challenge-cup.

And round that early-laureled head                                   25
Will flock to gaze the strengthless dead,
And find unwithered on its curls
The garland briefer than a girl's.

COMPARE:

"To an Athlete Dying Young" with "Ex-Basketball Player" by John Updike (page
1006).

---

### *Langston Hughes* (1902–1967)*

DREAM DEFERRED                   1951

What happens to a dream deferred?

　Does it dry up
　like a raisin in the sun?
　Or fester like a sore—
　And then run?                                                      5
　Does it stink like rotten meat?
　Or crust and sugar over—
　like a syrupy sweet?

　Maybe it just sags
　like a heavy load.                                                 10

　*Or does it explode?*

COMPARE:

"Dream Deferred" with Langston Hughes's "Dream Boogie" (page 753) and "Ballad
of Birmingham" by Dudley Randall (page 709).

---

### *Langston Hughes* (1902–1967)*

THE NEGRO SPEAKS OF RIVERS                                1926

I've known rivers:
I've known rivers ancient as the world and older than the flow of
　human blood in human veins.

My soul has grown deep like the rivers.

I bathed in the Euphrates when dawns were young.
I built my hut near the Congo and it lulled me to sleep.                 5
I looked upon the Nile and raised the pyramids above it.
I heard the singing of the Mississippi when Abe Lincoln went down
    to New Orleans, and I've seen its muddy bosom turn all golden
    in the sunset.

I've known rivers:
Ancient, dusky rivers.

My soul has grown deep like the rivers.                                  10

Langston Hughes

### Randall Jarrell (1914–1965)*

## THE DEATH OF THE BALL TURRET GUNNER       1945

From my mother's sleep I fell into the State
And I hunched in its belly till my wet fur froze.
Six miles from earth, loosed from its dream of life,
I woke to black flak and the nightmare fighters.
When I died they washed me out of the turret with a hose.

THE DEATH OF THE BALL TURRET GUNNER. Jarrell has written: "A ball turret was a plexiglass sphere set into the belly of a B-17 or B-24, and inhabited by two .50 caliber machine-guns and one man, a short small man. When this gunner tracked with his machine-guns a fighter attacking his bomber from below, he revolved with the turret; hunched in his little sphere, he looked like the fetus in the womb. The fighters which attacked him were armed with cannon firing explosive shells. The hose was a steam hose."

COMPARE:

"The Death of the Ball Turret Gunner" with "Dulce et Decorum Est" by Wilfred
Owen (page 617) and "The Insert" by R. L. Barth (page 896).

*Randall Jarrell*

## Robinson Jeffers (1887–1962)

### To the Stone-cutters                                      1925

Stone-cutters fighting time with marble, you foredefeated
Challengers of oblivion
Eat cynical earnings, knowing rock splits, records fall down,
The square-limbed Roman letters
Scale in the thaws, wear in the rain. The poet as well          5
Builds his monument mockingly;
For man will be blotted out, the blithe earth die, the brave
    sun
Die blind, his heart blackening:
Yet stones have stood for a thousand years, and pained
    thoughts found
The honey peace in old poems.                                   10

COMPARE:

"To the Stone-cutters" with "Not marble nor the gilded monuments" by William
Shakespeare (page 990).

## Elizabeth Jennings (b. 1926)

### I FEEL                                    1975

I feel I could be turned to ice
If this goes on, if this goes on.
I feel I could be buried twice
And still the death not yet be done.

I feel I could be turned to fire                                    5
If there can be no end to this.
I know within me such desire
No kiss could satisfy, no kiss.

I feel I could be turned to stone,
A solid block not carved at all,                                    10
Because I feel so much alone.
I could be grave-stone or a wall.

But better to be turned to earth
Where other things at least can grow.
I could be then a part of birth,                                    15
Passive, not knowing how to know.


## Ben Jonson (1573?–1637)*

### ON MY FIRST SON                          (1603)

Farewell, thou child of my right hand, and joy.
My sin was too much hope of thee, loved boy;
Seven years thou wert lent to me, and I thee pay,
Exacted by thy fate, on the just day.
Oh, could I lose all father° now. For why              *fatherhood*   5
Will man lament the state he should envy?—
To have so soon 'scaped world's and flesh's rage,
And, if no other misery, yet age.
Rest in soft peace, and asked, say, "Here doth lie
Ben Jonson his best piece of poetry,"                                10
For whose sake henceforth all his vows be such
As what he loves may never like° too much.                   *thrive*

ON MY FIRST SON. 1 *child of my right hand:* Jonson's son was named Benjamin; this phrase translates the Hebrew name. 4 *the just day:* the very day. The boy had died on his seventh birthday. 10 *poetry:* Jonson uses the word *poetry* here reflecting its Greek root *poiesis*, which means *creation.*

### COMPARE:

"On My First Son" with the five poems on the deaths of children on pages 861–863.

## Donald Justice (b. 1925)

### On the Death of Friends in Childhood     1960

We shall not ever meet them bearded in heaven,
Nor sunning themselves among the bald of hell;
If anywhere, in the deserted schoolyard at twilight,
Forming a ring, perhaps, or joining hands
In games whose very names we have forgotten.     5
Come, memory, let us seek them there in the shadows.

#### Compare:

"On the Death of Friends in Childhood" and "With rue my heart is laden" by
A. E. Housman (page 734).

## John Keats (1795–1821)*

### Ode on a Grecian Urn     1820

Thou still unravished bride of quietness,
    Thou foster-child of silence and slow time,
Sylvan historian, who canst thus express
    A flowery tale more sweetly than our rhyme:
What leaf-fringed legend haunts about thy shape     5
    Of deities or mortals, or of both,
        In Tempe or the dales of Arcady?
    What men or gods are these? What maidens loth?
What mad pursuit? What struggle to escape?
        What pipes and timbrels? What wild ecstasy?     10

Heard melodies are sweet, but those unheard
    Are sweeter; therefore, ye soft pipes, play on;
Not to the sensual° ear, but, more endeared,     *physical*
    Pipe to the spirit ditties of no tone:
Fair youth, beneath the trees, thou canst not leave     15
    Thy song, nor ever can those trees be bare;
        Bold Lover, never, never canst thou kiss,
Though winning near the goal—yet, do not grieve;
        She cannot fade, though thou hast not thy bliss,
    For ever wilt thou love, and she be fair!     20

Ah, happy, happy boughs! that cannot shed
    Your leaves, nor ever bid the Spring adieu;
And, happy melodist, unwearièd,
    For ever piping songs for ever new;
More happy love! more happy, happy love!     25

For ever warm and still to be enjoyed,
　　For ever panting, and for ever young;
All breathing human passion far above,
　　That leaves a heart high-sorrowful and cloyed,
　　　A burning forehead, and a parching tongue.　　　　　　　30

Who are these coming to the sacrifice?
　　To what green altar, O mysterious priest,
Lead'st thou that heifer lowing at the skies,
　　And all her silken flanks with garlands drest?
What little town by river or sea shore,　　　　　　　　　　35
　　Or mountain-built with peaceful citadel,
　　　Is emptied of this folk, this pious morn?
And, little town, thy streets for evermore
　　Will silent be; and not a soul to tell
　　　Why thou art desolate, can e'er return.　　　　　　　40

O Attic shape! Fair attitude! with brede°　　　　　　　　*design*
　　Of marble men and maidens overwrought,
With forest branches and the trodden weed;
　　Thou, silent form, dost tease us out of thought
As doth Eternity: Cold Pastoral!　　　　　　　　　　　　45
　　When old age shall this generation waste,
　　　Thou shalt remain, in midst of other woe
Than ours, a friend to man, to whom thou say'st,
Beauty is truth, truth beauty,—that is all
　　Ye know on earth, and all ye need to know.　　　　　　50

ODE ON A GRECIAN URN. 7. *Tempe, dales of Arcady:* valleys in Greece. 41. *Attic:* Athenian,
possessing a classical simplicity and grace. 49–50: If Keats had put the urn's words in quotation
marks, critics might have been spared much ink. Does the urn say just "beauty is truth, truth
beauty," or does its statement take in the whole of the last two lines?

---

*John Keats* (1795–1821)*

ON FIRST LOOKING INTO CHAPMAN'S HOMER　　　　　1816

Much have I traveled in the realms of gold,
　　And many goodly states and kingdoms seen;
　　Round many western islands have I been
Which bards in fealty to Apollo hold.
Oft of one wide expanse had I been told　　　　　　　　5
　　That deep-browed Homer ruled as his demesne°,　　　*domain*
　　　Yet did I never breathe its pure serene
Till I heard Chapman speak out loud and bold.
Then felt I like some watcher of the skies
　　When a new planet swims into his ken;　　　　　　　10

Or like stout Cortez when with eagle eyes
   He stared at the Pacific—and all his men
Looked at each other with a wild surmise—
   Silent, upon a peak in Darien.

ON FIRST LOOKING INTO CHAPMAN'S HOMER. When one evening in October 1816 Keats's friend and former teacher Cowden Clarke introduced the young poet to George Chapman's vigorous Elizabethan translations of the *Iliad* and the *Odyssey*, Keats stayed up all night reading and discussing them in high excitement; then went home at dawn to compose this sonnet, which Clarke received at his breakfast table. 4 *fealty*: in feudalism, the loyalty of a vassal to his lord; *Apollo*: classical god of poetic inspiration. 11 *stout Cortez*: the best-known boner in English poetry. (What Spanish explorer *was* the first European to view the Pacific?) 14 *Darien*: old name for the Isthmus of Panama.

John Keats

## *John Keats* (1795–1821)*

### WHEN I HAVE FEARS THAT I MAY CEASE TO BE          (1818)

When I have fears that I may cease to be
   Before my pen has gleaned my teeming brain,
Before high-pilèd books, in charact'ry°,                              *written language*
   Hold like rich garners° the full-ripened grain;                   *storehouses*
When I behold, upon the night's starred face,                        5
   Huge cloudy symbols of a high romance,
And think that I may never live to trace
   Their shadows with the magic hand of chance;
And when I feel, fair creature of an hour,
   That I shall never look upon thee more,                           10
Never have relish in the fairy° power                                *supernatural*
   Of unreflecting love—then on the shore

Of the wide world I stand alone, and think
　　Till love and fame to nothingness do sink.

WHEN I HAVE FEARS THAT I MAY CEASE TO BE. 12 *unreflecting*: thoughtless and spontaneous, rather than deliberate.

---

### *John Keats* (1795–1821)*

## TO AUTUMN　　　　　　　　　　　　　　　　1820

*I*

Season of mists and mellow fruitfulness,
　　Close bosom-friend of the maturing sun;
Conspiring with him how to load and bless
　　With fruit the vines that round the thatch-eaves run;
To bend with apples the mossed cottage-trees,　　　　　　　5
　　And fill all fruit with ripeness to the core;
　　　　To swell the gourd, and plump the hazel shells
With a sweet kernel; to set budding more,
And still more, later flowers for the bees,
Until they think warm days will never cease,　　　　　　　10
　　　　For Summer has o'er-brimmed their clammy cells.

*II*

Who hath not seen thee oft amid thy store?
　　Sometimes whoever seeks abroad may find
Thee sitting careless on a granary floor,
　　Thy hair soft-lifted by the winnowing wind;　　　　　　15
Or on a half-reaped furrow sound asleep,
　　Drowsed with the fume of poppies, while thy hook°　　　*sickle*
　　　　Spares the next swath and all its twinèd flowers:
And sometimes like a gleaner thou dost keep
　　Steady thy laden head across a brook;　　　　　　　　20
　　Or by a cider-press, with patient look,
　　　　Thou watchest the last oozings hours by hours.

*III*

Where are the songs of Spring? Ay, where are they?
　　Think not of them, thou hast thy music too,—
While barrèd clouds bloom the soft-dying day,　　　　　　25
　　And touch the stubble-plains with rosy hue;
Then in a wailful choir the small gnats mourn
　　Among the river sallows°, borne aloft　　　　　　　*willows*
　　　　Or sinking as the light wind lives or dies;
And full-grown lambs loud bleat from hilly bourn;　　　　30

Hedge-crickets sing; and now with treble soft
The red-breast whistles from a garden-croft°          *garden plot*
    And gathering swallows twitter in the skies.

ODE TO AUTUMN. *12 thee:* Autumn personified. *14 Thy hair . . . winnowing wind:* Autumn's hair
is a billowing cloud of straw. In winnowing, whole blades of grain were laid on a granary floor
and beaten with wooden flails, then the beaten mass was tossed in a blanket until the yellow
straw (or *chaff*) drifted away on the air, leaving kernels of grain. *30 bourn:* perhaps meaning a
brook. In current English, the word is a cousin of *burn*, as in the first line of Gerard Manley
Hopkins's "Inversnaid"; but in archaic English, which Keats sometimes liked, a *bourn* can also
be a boundary, or a destination. What possible meaning makes most sense to you?

COMPARE:

"To Autumn" with "In the Elegy Season" by Richard Wilbur (page 631).

Philip Larkin

## *Philip Larkin* (1922–1985)*

### HOME IS SO SAD                    1964

Home is so sad. It stays as it was left,
Shaped to the comfort of the last to go
As if to win them back. Instead, bereft
Of anyone to please, it withers so,
Having no heart to put aside the theft                               5

And turn again to what it started as,
A joyous shot at how things ought to be,
Long fallen wide. You can see how it was:
Look at the pictures and the cutlery.
The music in the piano stool. That vase. 10

*Philip Larkin* (1922–1985)*

## POETRY OF DEPARTURES 1955

Sometimes you hear, fifth-hand,
As epitaph:
*He chucked up everything*
*And just cleared off,*
And always the voice will sound 5
Certain you approve
This audacious, purifying,
Elemental move.

And they are right, I think.
We all hate home 10
And having to be there:
I detest my room,
Its specially-chosen junk,
The good books, the good bed,
And my life, in perfect order: 15
So to hear it said

*He walked out on the whole crowd*
Leaves me flushed and stirred,
Like *Then she undid her dress*
Or *Take that you bastard;* 20
Surely I can, if he did?
And that helps me stay
Sober and industrious.
But I'd go today,

Yes, swagger the nut-strewn roads, 25
Crouch in the fo'c'sle
Stubbly with goodness, if
It weren't so artificial,
Such a deliberate step backwards
To create an object: 30
Books; china; a life
Reprehensibly perfect.

*Irving Layton* (b. 1912)

# THE BULL CALF                                          1959

The thing could barely stand. Yet taken
from his mother and the barn smells
he still impressed with his pride,
with the promise of sovereignty in the way
his head moved to take us in.                                        5
The fierce sunlight tugging the maize from the ground
licked at his shapely flanks.
He was too young for all that pride.
I thought of the deposed Richard II.

"No money in bull calves," Freeman had said.                         10
The visiting clergyman rubbed the nostrils
now snuffing pathetically at the windless day.
"A pity," he sighed.
My gaze slipped off his hat toward the empty sky
that circled over the black knot of men,                             15
over us and the calf waiting for the first blow.

Struck,
the bull calf drew in his thin forelegs
as if gathering strength for a mad rush . . .
tottered . . . raised his darkening eyes to us,                      20
and I saw we were at the far end
of his frightened look, growing smaller and smaller
till we were only the ponderous mallet
that flicked his bleeding ear
and pushed him over on his side, stiffly,                            25
like a block of wood.

Below the hill's crest
the river snuffled on the improvised beach.
We dug a deep pit and threw the dead calf into it.
It made a wet sound, a sepulchral gurgle,                            30
as the warm sides bulged and flattened.
Settled, the bull calf lay as if asleep,
one foreleg over the other,
bereft of pride and so beautiful now,
without movement, perfectly still in the cool pit,                   35
I turned away and wept.

COMPARE:

"The Bull Calf" with "Names of Horses" by Donald Hall (page 926).

## Philip Levine (b. 1928)

### Animals Are Passing from Our Lives    1968

It's wonderful how I jog
on four honed-down ivory toes
my massive buttocks slipping
like oiled parts with each light step.

I'm to market. I can smell         5
the sour, grooved block, I can smell
the blade that opens the hole
and the pudgy white fingers

that shake out the intestines
like a hankie. In my dreams         10
the snouts drool on the marble,
suffering children, suffering flies,

suffering the consumers
who won't meet their steady eyes
for fear they could see. The boy         15
who drives me along believes

that any moment I'll fall
on my side and drum my toes
like a typewriter or squeal
and shit like a new housewife         20

discovering television,
or that I'll turn like a beast
cleverly to hook his teeth
with my teeth. No. Not this pig.

Compare:

"Animals Are Passing from Our Lives" with "Butcher Shop" by Charles Simic (page 993).

## Stephen Shu-ning Liu (b. 1930)

### My Father's Martial Art    1982

When he came home Mother said he looked
like a monk and stank of green fungus.
At the fireside he told us about life
at the monastery: his rock pillow,
his cold bath, his steel-bar lifting         5
and his wood-chopping. He didn't see
a woman for three winters, on Mountain O Mei.

"My Master was both light and heavy.
He skipped over treetops like a squirrel.
Once he stood on a chair, one foot tied                     10
to a rope. We four pulled; we couldn't
move him a bit. His kicks could split
a cedar's trunk."

I saw Father break into a pumpkin
with his fingers. I saw him drop a hawk                     15
with bamboo arrows. He rose before dawn, filled
our backyard with a harsh sound *hah, hah, hah*:
there was his Black Dragon Sweep, his Crane Stand,
his Mantis Walk, his Tiger Leap, his Cobra Coil . . .
Infrequently he taught me tricks and made me              20
fight the best of all the village boys.

From a busy street I brood over high cliffs
on O Mei, where my father and his Master sit:
shadows spread across their faces as the smog
between us deepens into a funeral pyre.                     25

But don't retreat into night, my father.
Come down from the cliffs. Come
with a single Black Dragon Sweep and hush
this oncoming traffic with your *hah, hah, hah.*


## Robert Lowell (1917–1977)*

### SKUNK HOUR                                             1959

*For Elizabeth Bishop*

Nautilus Island's hermit
heiress still lives through winters in her Spartan cottage;
her sheep still graze above the sea.
Her son's a bishop. Her farmer
is first selectman in our village;                          5
she's in her dotage.

Thirsting for
the hierarchic privacy
of Queen Victoria's century,
she buys up all                                            10
the eyesores facing her shore,
and lets them fall.

The season's ill—
we've lost our summer millionaire,
who seemed to leap from an L. L. Bean                       15
catalogue. His nine-knot yawl

was auctioned off to lobstermen.
A red fox stain covers Blue Hill.

And now our fairy
decorator brightens his shop for fall;                              20
his fishnet's filled with orange cork,
orange, his cobbler's bench and awl;
there is no money in his work,
he'd rather marry.

One dark night,                                                    25
my Tudor Ford climbed the hill's skull;
I watched for love-cars. Lights turned down,
they lay together, hull to hull,
where the graveyard shelves on the town. . . .
My mind's not right.                                               30

A car radio bleats,
"Love, O careless Love. . . ." I hear
my ill-spirit sob in each blood cell,
as if my hand were at its throat. . . .
I myself am hell;                                                  35
nobody's here—

only skunks, that search
in the moonlight for a bite to eat.
They march on their soles up Main Street:
white stripes, moonstruck eyes' red fire                           40
under the chalk-dry and spar spire
of the Trinitarian Church.

I stand on top
of our back steps and breathe the rich air—
a mother skunk with her column of kittens swills the garbage pail.  45
She jabs her wedge-head in a cup
of sour cream, drops her ostrich tail,
and will not scare.


## Archibald MacLeish (1892–1982)

### THE END OF THE WORLD                1926

Quite unexpectedly as Vasserot
The armless ambidextrian was lighting
A match between his great and second toe,
And Ralph the lion was engaged in biting
The neck of Madame Sossman while the drum            5
Pointed, and Teeny was about to cough

In waltz-time swinging Jocko by the thumb—
Quite unexpectedly the top blew off:

And there, there overhead, there, there hung over
Those thousands of white faces, those dazed eyes,                    10
There in the starless dark the poise, the hover,
There with vast wings across the canceled skies,
There in the sudden blackness the black pall
Of nothing, nothing, nothing—nothing at all.

## *Andrew Marvell* (1621–1678)

### TO HIS COY MISTRESS          1681

| | |
|---|---|
| Had we but world enough and time, | |
| This coyness°, lady, were no crime. | *modesty, reluctance* |
| We would sit down and think which way | |
| To walk, and pass our long love's day. | |
| Thou by the Indian Ganges' side | 5 |
| Should'st rubies find; I by the tide | |
| Of Humber would complain°. I would | *sing sad songs* |
| Love you ten years before the Flood, | |
| And you should, if you please, refuse | |
| Till the conversion of the Jews. | 10 |
| My vegetable° love should grow | *vegetative, flourishing* |
| Vaster than empires, and more slow. | |
| An hundred years should go to praise | |
| Thine eyes, and on thy forehead gaze, | |
| Two hundred to adore each breast, | 15 |
| But thirty thousand to the rest. | |
| An age at least to every part, | |
| And the last age should show your heart. | |
| For, lady, you deserve this state°, | *pomp, ceremony* |
| Nor would I love at lower rate. | 20 |
|    But at my back I always hear | |
| Time's wingèd chariot hurrying near, | |
| And yonder all before us lie | |
| Deserts of vast eternity. | |
| Thy beauty shall no more be found, | 25 |
| Nor in thy marble vault shall sound | |
| My echoing song; then worms shall try | |
| That long preserved virginity, | |
| And your quaint honor turn to dust, | |
| And into ashes all my lust. | 30 |
| The grave's a fine and private place, | |

But none, I think, do there embrace.
   Now therefore, while the youthful hue
Sits on thy skin like morning glew°                                      *glow*
And while thy willing soul transpires                             35
At every pore with instant° fires,                                *eager*
Now let us sport us while we may;
And now, like amorous birds of prey,
Rather at once our time devour
Than languish in his slow-chapped° power.             *slow-jawed*  40
Let us roll all our strength and all
Our sweetness up into one ball
And tear our pleasures with rough strife
Thorough° the iron gates of life.                            *through*
Thus, though we cannot make our sun                          45
Stand still, yet we will make him run.

To His Coy Mistress. 7 *Humber:* a river that flows by Marvell's town of Hull (on the side of the world opposite from the Ganges). 10 *conversion of the Jews:* an event that, according to St. John the Divine, is to take place just before the end of the world. 35 *transpires:* exudes, as a membrane lets fluid or vapor pass through it.

Compare:

"To His Coy Mistress" with "To the Virgins, to Make Much of Time" by Robert Herrick (page 937).

---

## *David Mason* (b. 1954)

Disclosure                              1991

With blue official flap and legalese
the state acknowledges an end to what
began in privacy, in passing glances.
What I remember of your voice is not
an issue lawyers willingly address,                               5
and I've avoided their neat document.
There was a time when the word "wife" warmed me,
but as you say I think too much of words.

Many nights I raised my head from the pillow,
watched you sleeping, wife in a girl's flannel,                   10
there by the bed your window open.
Long-stemmed, unnamable flower in whom
I was lost and saved for ten brief years,
my rancor can't contain these images:
your hair lightened to its roots by Greek sun,                   15
my maps of married pleasure on your skin.

It's strange what we can make ourselves believe.
Memory saves; recrimination uses
every twisted syllable of the past.
Still, with all the errors I acknowledge                    20
added to those I fail or refuse to see,
I say our marriage was a gentle thing,
a secret bargain children sometimes make
and then forget when the weather's changed.

Lawyers put it another way; they don't know               25
how small exchanges still take place, of gifts
collected long ago, drawings of a house
we lived in, letters from friends we haven't told.
How separately we stumble on some object,
a book I signed, a scarf you knitted,                     30
and call to tell the other it is there,
wondering if it will be wanted back.

COMPARE:

"Disclosure" to Denise Levertov's "Leaving Forever" (page 693).

## George Meredith (1828–1909)

### LUCIFER IN STARLIGHT                          1883

On a starred night Prince Lucifer uprose,
   Tired of his dark dominion, swung the fiend
   Above the rolling ball in cloud part screened,
Where sinners hugged their specter of repose.
Poor prey to his hot fit of pride were those.           5
   And now upon his western wing he leaned,
   Now his huge bulk o'er Afric's sands careened,
Now the black planet shadowed Arctic snows.
Soaring through wider zones that pricked his scars
   With memory of the old revolt from Awe,              10
He reached a middle height, and at the stars,
Which are the brain of heaven, he looked, and sank.
Around the ancient track marched, rank on rank,
   The army of unalterable law.

## James Merrill (b. 1926)

### CHARLES ON FIRE                               1966

Another evening we sprawled about discussing
Appearances. And it was the consensus

That while uncommon physical good looks
Continued to launch one, as before, in life
(Among its vaporous eddies and false calms),                    5
Still, as one of us said into his beard,
"Without your intellectual and spiritual
Values, man, you are sunk." No one but squared
The shoulders of his own unloveliness.
Long-suffering Charles, having cooked and served the meal,      10
Now brought out little tumblers finely etched
He filled with amber liquor and then passed.
"Say," said the same young man, "in Paris, France,
They do it this way"—bounding to his feet
And touching a lit match to our host's full glass.             15
A blue flame, gentle, beautiful, came, went
Above the surface. In a hush that fell
We heard the vessel crack. The contents drained
As who should step down from a crystal coach.
Steward of spirits, Charles's glistening hand                   20
All at once gloved itself in eeriness.
The moment passed. He made two quick sweeps and
Was flesh again. "It couldn't matter less,"
He said, but with a shocked, unconscious glance
Into the mirror. Finding nothing changed,                       25
He filled a fresh glass and sank down among us.


## *Charlotte Mew* (1869–1928)

### THE FARMER'S BRIDE                    1916

Three Summers since I chose a maid,
Too young maybe—but more's to do
At harvest-time than bide and woo.
 When us was wed she turned afraid
Of love and me and all things human;                            5
Like the shut of a winter's day.
Her smile went out, and 'twasn't a woman—
 More like a little frightened fay.°                   *elf*
  One night, in the Fall, she runned away.

"Out 'mong the sheep, her be," they said,                       10
'Should properly have been abed;
But sure enough she wasn't there
Lying awake with her wide brown stare.
So over seven-acre field and up-along across the down
We chased her, flying like a hare                               15
Before our lanterns. To Church-Town
 All in a shiver and a scare

We caught her, fetched her home at last
   And turned the key upon her, fast.

She does the work about the house                 20
As well as most, but like a mouse:
   Happy enough to chat and play
   With birds and rabbits and such as they,
   So long as men-folk keep away.
"Not near, not near!" her eyes beseech              25
When one of us comes within reach.
   The women say that beasts in stall
   Look round like children at her call.
   *I've* hardly heard her speak at all.
Shy as a leveret°, swift as he,                 *hare* 30
Straight and slight as a young larch tree,
Sweet as the first wild violets, she,
To her wild self. But what to me?

The short days shorten and the oaks are brown,
   The blue smoke rises to the low gray sky,       35
One leaf in the still air falls slowly down,
   A magpie's spotted feathers lie
On the black earth spread white with rime,°       *frost*
The berries redden up to Christmas-time.
   What's Christmas-time without there be     40
   Some other in the house than we!

   She sleeps up in the attic there
   Alone, poor maid. 'Tis but a stair
Betwixt us. Oh! my God! the down,
The soft young down of her, the brown,         45
The brown of her—her eyes, her hair, her hair!

---

**Edna St. Vincent Millay** (1892–1950)*

RECUERDO                      1920

We were very tired, we were very merry—
We had gone back and forth all night on the ferry.
It was bare and bright, and smelled like a stable—
But we looked into a fire, we leaned across a table,
We lay on a hill-top underneath the moon;           5
And the whistles kept blowing, and the dawn came soon.

We were very tired, we were very merry—
We had gone back and forth all night on the ferry;
And you ate an apple, and I ate a pear,

From a dozen of each we had bought somewhere;                    10
And the sky went wan, and the wind came cold,
And the sun rose dripping, a bucketful of gold.

We were very tired, we were very merry,
We had gone back and forth all night on the ferry.
We hailed, "Good morrow, mother!" to a shawl-covered head,        15
And bought a morning paper, which neither of us read;
And she wept, "God bless you!" for the apples and pears,
And we gave her all our money but our subway fares.

RECUERDO. The Spanish title means "a recollection" or "a memory."

---

## *John Milton* (1608–1674)*

LYCIDAS                                                          1637

*In this monody the author bewails a learned friend, unfortunately
drowned in his passage from Chester on the Irish Seas, 1637.
And by occasion foretells the ruin of our corrupted clergy then in
their height.*

Yet once more, O ye laurels, and once more,
Ye myrtles brown°, with ivy never sere,                                    *dark*
I come to pluck your berries harsh and crude°,                          *immature*
And with forced fingers rude
Shatter your leaves before the mellowing year.                               5
Bitter constraint and sad occasion dear
Compels me to disturb your season due;
For Lycidas is dead, dead ere his prime,
Young Lycidas, and hath not left his peer.
Who would not sing for Lycidas? he knew                                      10
Himself to sing, and build the lofty rhyme.
He must not float upon his wat'ry bier
Unwept, and welter° to the parching wind,                                *toss about*

LYCIDAS. A *monody* is a song for a single voice, generally a lament. Milton's *learned friend* was
Edward King, a young scholar and poet, a fellow student at Cambridge University where Milton
was studying for the ministry. "Lycidas" is a *pastoral poem* that uses the rural setting of the
shepherd's world often to contrast the simple virtues of country life with the weary sophistication of big cities. In English pastoral poetry, convention required that the characters and even
places be given classical names. In calling the late Edward King Lycidas, a common shepherd's
name, Milton signals to his readers that he will employ the conventions of the pastoral and give
all of his English characters classical names. Pastoral poems often used their simple but honest
characters to question the moral corruption of the powerful, as Milton does in "Lycidas" by
criticizing the presumed dishonesty of Roman Catholic clergy. 1–2: *laurels, myrtles:* Evergreens
in the crowns traditionally bestowed upon poets.

Without the meed° of some melodious tear.                    tribute
   Begin, then, Sisters of the Sacred Well                        15
That from beneath the seat of Jove doth spring,
Begin, and somewhat loudly sweep the string.
Hence with denial vain and coy excuse:
So may some gentle Muse°                                          poet
With lucky words favor my destined urn,                          20
And, as he passes, turn,
And bid fair peace be to my sable shroud!
For we were nursed upon the self-same hill,
Fed the same flocks, by fountain, shade, and rill;
   Together both, ere the high lawns appeared          25
Under the opening eyelids of the Morn,
We drove a-field, and both together heard
What time the gray-fly winds° her sultry horn,                  sounds
Batt'ning° our flocks with the fresh dews of night,            feeding
Oft till the star that rose at evening bright                   30
Toward Heav'n's descent had sloped his westering wheel.
Meanwhile the rural ditties were not mute,
Tempered to the oaten° flute,                          made of an oat stalk
Rough satyrs danced, and fauns with cloven heel
From the glad sound would not be absent long;                  35
And old Damoetas loved to hear our song.
   But, O the heavy change, now thou art gone,
Now thou art gone, and never must return!
Thee, Shepherd, thee the woods and desert caves,
With wild thyme and the gadding° vine o'ergrown,        wandering  40
And all their echoes mourn.
The willows, and the hazel copses green,
Shall now no more be seen
Fanning their joyous leaves to thy soft lays.
As killing as the canker to the rose,                          45
Or taint-worm to the weanling herds that graze,
Or frost to flowers, that their gay wardrobe wear
When first the white thorn blows°;                            blossoms
Such, Lycidas, thy loss to shepherd's ear.
   Where were ye, Nymphs, when the remorseless deep      50
Closed o'er the head of your loved Lycidas?
For neither were ye playing on the steep
Where your old bards, the famous Druids, lie,
Nor on the shaggy top of Mona high,

15 *Sisters of the Sacred Well:* the nine Muses, the divine patronesses of the arts and learning. 16 *seat of Jove:* Mount Olympus, the home of the Greek and Roman gods. 36 *Damoetas:* the name of a shepherd in a poem by Virgil; Milton is probably using it to refer to a tutor at Cambridge who taught both him and Edward King. 53 *Druids:* priests and poets of the Celts in pre-Christian Britain. 54 *Mona:* Roman name for the Isle of Man, near which King was drowned.

Nor yet where Deva spreads her wizard stream.　　　　　　　55
Ay me! I fondly° dream!　　　　　　　　　　　　　　　*foolishly*
"Had ye been there"—for what could that have done?
What could the Muse herself that Orpheus bore,
The Muse herself, for her enchanting son,
Whom universal Nature did lament,　　　　　　　　　　60
When, by the rout° that made the hideous roar,　　　　*mob*
His gory visage down the stream was sent,
Down the swift Hebrus to the Lesbian shore?
　　Alas! What boots it° with uncessant care　　*what good does it do*
To tend the homely, slighted shepherd's trade,　　　　65
And strictly meditate the thankless Muse?
Were it not better done, as others use°,　　　　　　　　*do*
To sport with Amaryllis in the shade,
Or with the tangles of Neaera's hair?
Fame is the spur that the clear spirit doth raise　　　70
(That last infirmity of noble mind)
To scorn delights and live laborious days;
But the fair guerdon when we hope to find,
And think to burst out into sudden blaze
Comes the blind Fury with th' abhorrèd shears,　　　75
And slits the thin-spun life. "But not the praise,"
Phoebus replied, and touched my trembling ears:
"Fame is no plant that grows on mortal soil,
Nor in the glistering° foil,　　　　　　　　　　　　*glittering*
Set off to the world, nor in broad rumor° lies,　　*reputation* 80
But lives and spreads aloft by those pure eyes
And perfect witness of all-judging Jove;
As he pronounces lastly on each deed,
Of so much fame in Heav'n expect thy meed°."　　　　*reward*
　　O fountain Arethuse, and thou honored flood,　　85
Smooth-sliding Mincius, crowned with vocal reeds,
That strain I heard was of a higher mood:

55 *Deva*: the River Dee, flowing between England and Wales. Its shifts of course were said to augur good luck for one country or the other. 58 *the Muse herself that Orpheus bore*: the great poet-singer Orpheus was the son of Calliope, the Muse of epic poetry. 61–63 *the rout . . . sent*: Orpheus was torn to pieces by his female admirers because he was indifferent to all other women after the death of his beloved Eurydice: his head was thrown into the River Hebrus and carried to the sea, eventually reaching the shores of Lesbos, an island in the Aegean, famed for poetry. 68–69 *Amaryllis, Neaera*: conventional names for shepherdesses. 70 *the clear spirit doth raise*: does raise the clear spirit. 75 *the blind Fury*: Atropos, the Fate who cuts the thread of a person's life, which her other sisters have spun. 77 *touched . . . ears*: gesture signifying "Remember!" 79 *foil*: a gold or silver leaf setting, used to make a gem appear more brilliant. 85–86 *Arethuse, Mincius*: a fountain and a river near the birthplaces of Theocritus and Virgil, respectively; Milton uses these famous place names to recall the most celebrated pastoral poets of Greece (Theocritus) and Rome (Virgil).

But now my oat proceeds,
And listens to the Herald of the Sea,
That came in Neptune's plea. 90
He asked the waves, and asked the felon winds,
What hard mishap hath doomed this gentle swain?
And questioned every gust of rugged wings
That blows from off each beakèd promontory:
They knew not of his story; 95
And sage Hippotades their answer brings,
That not a blast was from his dungeon strayed:
The air was calm, and on the level brine
Sleek Panope with all her sisters played.
It was that fatal and perfidious bark, 100
Built in th' eclipse, and rigged with curses dark,
That sunk so low that sacred head of thine.
   Next, Camus, reverend sire, went footing slow,
His mantle hairy, and his bonnet sedge,
Inwrought with figures dim, and on the edge 105
Like to that sanguine flower inscribed with woe.
"Ah! who hath reft," quoth he, "my dearest pledge?"
Last came, and last did go,
The pilot of the Galilean lake;
Two massy keys he bore of metals twain 110
(The golden opes, the iron shuts amain°).    *with force*
He shook his mitered locks, and stern bespake:—
"How well could I have spared for thee, young swain,
Enow° of such as for their bellies' sake,    *enough*
Creep, and intrude, and climb into the fold! 115
Of other care they little reck'ning make
Than how to scramble at the shearers' feast,
And shove away the worthy bidden guest.
Blind mouths! that scarce themselves know how to hold
A sheep-hook, or have learned aught else the least 120
That to the faithful herdsman's art belongs!

88 *oat*: a shepherd's pipe carved out of an oat straw. 89 *Herald of the Sea*: Triton, the son of Neptune (the God of the sea) whose trumpet could command the waves. 90 *Neptune's plea*: Triton delivers his father's plea that he is "not guilty" of King's death. 96 *Hippotades*: Aeolus, son of Hippotas, who commanded the winds; he, too, claims he is not guilty of King's death by shipwreck. 99 *Panope*: a sea nymph; her name means "one who sees all." 101 *eclipse*: thought to be an omen of evil fortune. 103 *Camus*: the spirit of the river Cam that runs through Cambridge, therefore a personification of Cambridge University. 106 *that sanguine flower*: the hyacinth, a flower thought to have been created from the blood of Hyacinthus, whom Apollo accidentally killed. 109–112 *pilot*: Saint Peter, once a fisherman in Galilee, to whom Jesus gave the keys of Heaven (Matthew 16:19). As first Bishop of Rome, he wears the miter, a bishop's emblematic head-covering. 115 *fold*: the Church of England. 120 *sheep-hook*: a bishop's staff or crozier, which resembles a shepherd's crook.

What recks it them? What need they? they are sped°;                    *prosperous*
And, when they list°, their lean and flashy songs                      *so incline*
Grate on their scrannel° pipes of wretched straw;                     *feeble, harsh*
The hungry sheep look up, and are not fed,                                    125
But, swoll'n with wind and the rank mist they draw,
Rot inwardly, and foul contagion spread;
Besides what the grim wolf with privy° paw                              *stealthy*
Daily devours apace, and nothing said;
But that two-handed engine at the door                                        130
Stands ready to smite once, and smite no more."
    Return, Alpheus; the dread voice is past
That shrunk thy streams; return, Sicilian Muse,
And call the vales, and bid them hither cast
Their bells and flow'rets of a thousand hues.                                 135
Ye valleys low, where the mild whispers use°                             *resort*
Of shades, and wanton winds, and gushing brooks,
On whose fresh lap the swart star sparely looks,
Throw hither all your quaint enameled eyes,
That on the green turf suck the honied showers,                              140
And purple all the ground with vernal flowers.
Bring the rathe° primrose that forsaken dies,                            *early*
The tufted crow-toe, and pale jessamine,
The white pink, and the pansy freaked° with jet,                        *streaked*
The glowing violet,                                                            145
The musk-rose, and the well-attired woodbine,
With cowslips wan that hang the pensive head,
And every flower that sad embroidery wears;
Bid amaranthus all his beauty shed,
And daffadillies fill their cups with tears,                                   150
To strew the laureate hearse where Lycid lies.
For so, to interpose a little ease,
Let our frail thoughts dally with false surmise,
Ay me! whilst thee the shores and sounding seas
Wash far away, where'er thy bones are hurled;                                 155
Whether beyond the stormy Hebrides,
Where thou, perhaps, under the whelming tide

128 *wolf*: probably the Church of Rome. Jesuits in England at the time were winning converts.
130 *two-handed engine*: This disputed phrase may refer (among other possibilities) to the punishing sword of The Word of God (Revelation 19:13–15 and Hebrews 4:12). Perhaps Milton sees
it as a lightning bolt, as does Spenser, to whom Jove's wrath is a "three-forked engine" (*Faerie
Queene*, VIII, 9). 131 *smite once . . . no more*: Because, in the proverb, lightning never strikes twice
in the same place? 132 *Alpheus*: a river god who loved the nymph Arethusa. She tried to escape
him by fleeing to Sicily, but he took his river under the sea and came up in Sicily. She then
turned into the fountain mentioned in line 85, and their waters commingled. 133 *Sicilian Muse*:
who inspired Theocritus, a native of Sicily. 138 *swart star*: Sirius, at its zenith in summer, was
thought to turn vegetation black. 153 *false surmise*: futile hope that the body of Lycidas could
be recovered.

Visit'st the bottom of the monstrous° world;              *full of sea monsters*
Or whether thou, to our moist vows° denied,                          *prayers*
Sleep'st by the fable of Bellerus old,                                160
Where the great Vision of the guarded mount
Looks toward Namancos and Bayona's hold°:                        *stronghold*
Look homeward, angel, now, and melt with ruth°;                       *pity*
And, O ye dolphins, waft the hapless youth.
        Weep no more, woeful shepherds, weep no more,                  165
For Lycidas, your sorrow, is not dead,
Sunk though he be beneath the wat'ry floor:
So sinks the day-star in the ocean bed
And yet anon repairs his drooping head,
And tricks° his beams, and with new-spangled ore°       *arrays; gold*  170
Flames in the forehead of the morning sky:
So Lycidas sunk low, but mounted high,
Through the dear might of Him that walked the waves,
Where, other groves and other streams along,
With nectar pure his oozy locks he laves,                            175
And hears the unexpressive nuptial song,
In the blest kingdoms meek of Joy and Love.
There entertain him all the Saints above,
In solemn troops, and sweet societies,
That sing, and singing in their glory move,                          180
And wipe the tears forever from his eyes.
Now, Lycidas, the shepherds weep no more;
Henceforth thou art the Genius° of the shore,              *guardian spirit*
In thy large recompense, and shalt be good
To all that wander in that perilous flood.                          185

    Thus sang the uncouth° swain to th' oaks and rills,   *rustic (or little-known)*
While the still Morn went out with sandals gray;
He touched the tender stops of various quills°,     *reeds of a shepherd's pipe*
With eager thought warbling his Doric lay:
And now the sun had stretched out all the hills,                    190
And now was dropped into the western bay.
At last he rose, and twitched° his mantle blue:                     *donned*
Tomorrow to fresh woods and pastures new.

160 *Bellerus:* legendary giant of Land's End, the far tip of Cornwall. 161 *guarded mount:* Saint
Michael's Mount, off Land's End, said to be under the protection of the archangel. 162
*Namancos, Bayona:* on the coast of Spain. 164 *dolphins:* In Greek legend, these kindly mammals
carried the spirits of the dead to the Blessed Isles. 166 *is not dead:* like mythological figures
previously mentioned in the poem (Hyacinthus and Arethusa), King has been given immortality
by metamorphosis—he has been changed into the genius (or protecting deity) of the Irish sea.
173 *Him that walked the waves:* Christ, whom the disciples saw walk on the Sea of Galilee (Mark
6:45–49). 176 *unexpressive nuptial song:* inexpressibly beautiful song for the marriage feast of the
Lamb (Revelation 19:9). 189 *Doric lay:* pastoral poem. Doric is the dialect of Greek employed
by Theocritus.

### John Milton (1608–1674)*

## WHEN I CONSIDER HOW MY LIGHT IS SPENT          (1655?)

When I consider how my light is spent,
  Ere half my days in this dark world and wide,
  And that one talent which is death to hide
Lodged with me useless, though my soul more bent
To serve therewith my Maker, and present          5
  My true account, lest He returning chide;
  "Doth God exact day-labor, light denied?"
I fondly° ask. But Patience, to prevent          *foolishly*
That murmur, soon replies, "God doth not need
  Either man's work or His own gifts. Who best          10
  Bear His mild yoke, they serve Him best. His state
Is kingly: thousands at His bidding speed,
  And post o'er land and ocean without rest;
  They also serve who only stand and wait."

WHEN I CONSIDER HOW MY LIGHT IS SPENT. 1 *my light is spent:* Milton had become blind. 3 *that one talent:* For Jesus's parable of the talents (measures of money), see Matthew 25:14–30.

### COMPARE:

"When I consider how my light is spent" with "Thou art indeed just, Lord, if I contend" by Gerard Manley Hopkins (page 940).

### Marianne Moore (1887–1972)*

## THE MIND IS AN ENCHANTING THING          1944

is an enchanted thing
  like the glaze on a
katydid-wing
    subdivided by sun
    till the nettings are legion.          5
Like Gieseking playing Scarlatti;

like the apteryx-awl
  as a beak, or the
kiwi's rain-shawl
    of haired feathers, the mind          10
    feeling its way as though blind,
walks along with its eyes on the ground.

It has memory's ear
  that can hear without
having to hear.          15

Like the gyroscope's fall,
 truly unequivocal
because trued by regnant certainty,

it is a power of
 strong enchantment. It                                        20
is like the dove-
 neck animated by
 sun; it is memory's eye;
it's conscientious inconsistency.

It tears off the veil; tears                                   25
 the temptation, the
mist the heart wears,
 from its eyes,—if the heart
 has a face; it takes apart
dejection. It's fire in the dove-neck's                        30

iridescence; in the
 inconsistencies
of Scarlatti.
 Unconfusion submits
 its confusion to proof; it's                                  35
not a Herod's oath that cannot change.

THE MIND IS AN ENCHANTING THING. 6 *Gieseking . . . Scarlatti:* Walter Gieseking (1895–1956), German pianist, was a celebrated performer of the difficult sonatas of Italian composer Domenico Scarlatti (1685–1757). 7 *apteryx-awl:* awl-shaped beak of the apteryx, one of the kiwi family. (An awl is a pointed tool for piercing wood or leather.) 36 *Herod's oath:* King Herod's order condemning to death all infants in Bethlehem (Matthew 2:1–16). In one medieval English version of the Herod story, a pageant play, the king causes the death of his own child by refusing to withdraw his command.

*Marianne Moore*

## Frederick Morgan (b. 1922)

### THE MASTER                                          1982

When Han Kan was summoned
to the imperial capital
it was suggested he sit at the feet of
the illustrious senior court painter
to learn from him the refinements of the art.                5

"No, thank you," he replied,
"I shall apprentice myself to the stables."

And he installed himself and his brushes amid the dung and the
    flies,
and studied the horses—their bodies' keen alertness—
eye-sparkle of one, another's sensitive stance,             10
the way a third moved graceful in his bulk—
and painted at last the emperor's favorite,
the charger named "Nightshining White,"

whose likeness after centuries still dazzles.


## Howard Nemerov (b. 1920)

### THE SNOW GLOBE                                      1955

A long time ago, when I was a child,
They left my light on while I went to sleep,
As though they would have wanted me beguiled
By brightness if at all; dark was too deep.

And they left me one toy, a village white            5
With the fresh snow and silently in glass
Frozen forever. But if you shook it,
The snow would rise up in the rounded space

And from the limits of the universe
Snow itself down again. O world of white,             10
First home of dreams! Now that I have my dead,
I want so cold an emblem to rehearse
How many of them have gone from the world's light,
As I have gone, too, from my snowy bed.

*Lorine Niedecker*

---

## **Lorine Niedecker** (1903–1970)*

### SORROW MOVES IN WIDE WAVES      (c. 1950)

Sorrow moves in wide waves,
   it passes, lets us be.
It uses us, we use it,
   it's blind while we see.

Consciousness is illimitable,              5
   too good to forsake
tho what we feel be misery
   and we know will break.

Old Mother turns blue and from us,
   "Don't let my head drop to the earth.        10
I'm blind and deaf." Death from the heart,
   a thimble in her purse.

"It's a long day since last night.
   Give me space. I need
floors. Wash the floors, Lorine!            15
   Wash clothes! Weed!"

## Sharon Olds (b. 1942)*

### THE ONE GIRL AT THE BOYS PARTY     1983

When I take my girl to the swimming party
I set her down among the boys. They tower and
bristle, she stands there smooth and sleek,
her math scores unfolding in the air around her.
They will strip to their suits, her body hard and     5
indivisible as a prime number,
they'll plunge in the deep end, she'll subtract
her height from ten feet, divide it into
hundreds of gallons of water, the numbers
bouncing in her mind like molecules of chlorine     10
in the bright blue pool. When they climb out,
her ponytail will hang its pencil lead
down her back, her narrow silk suit
with hamburgers and french fries printed on it
will glisten in the brilliant air, and they will     15
see her sweet face, solemn and
sealed, a factor of one, and she will
see their eyes, two each,
their legs, two each, and the curves of their sexes,
one each, and in her head she'll be doing her     20
wild multiplying, as the drops
sparkle and fall to the power of a thousand from her body.

## Wilfred Owen (1893–1918)*

### ANTHEM FOR DOOMED YOUTH     (1917?)

What passing-bells for these who die as cattle?
     Only the monstrous anger of the guns.
Only the stuttering rifles' rapid rattle
Can patter out their hasty orisons.
No mockeries now for them; no prayers nor bells,     5
     Nor any voice of mourning save the choirs,—
The shrill, demented choirs of wailing shells;
     And bugles calling for them from sad shires°.     *counties*

What candles may be held to speed them all?
     Not in the hands of boys, but in their eyes     10
     Shall shine the holy glimmers of good-byes.
The pallor of girls' brows shall be their pall;
Their flowers the tenderness of patient minds,
And each slow dusk a drawing-down of blinds.

Linda Pastan

## Linda Pastan (b. 1932)*

ETHICS                                                    1980

In ethics class so many years ago
our teacher asked this question every fall:
if there were a fire in a museum
which would you save, a Rembrandt painting
or an old woman who hadn't many                           5
years left anyhow? Restless on hard chairs
caring little for pictures or old age
we'd opt one year for life, the next for art
and always half-heartedly. Sometimes
the woman borrowed my grandmother's face                  10
leaving her usual kitchen to wander
some drafty, half imagined museum.
One year, feeling clever, I replied
why not let the woman decide herself?
Linda, the teacher would report, eschews                  15
the burdens of responsibility.
This fall in a real museum I stand
before a real Rembrandt, old woman,
or nearly so, myself. The colors
within this frame are darker than autumn,                 20
darker even than winter—the browns of earth,
though earth's most radiant elements burn
through the canvas. I know now that woman
and painting and season are almost one
and all beyond saving by children.                        25

## Octavio Paz (b. 1914)

| Con Los Ojos Cerrados | With Our Eyes Shut | 1968 |
|---|---|---|

| | | |
|---|---|---|
| Con los ojos cerrados | With your eyes shut | |
| Te iluminas por dentro | You light up from within | |
| Eres la piedra ciega | You are blind stone | |
| | | |
| Noche a noche te labro | Night by night I carve you | |
| Con los ojos cerrados | With my eyes shut | 5 |
| Eres la piedra franca | You are clear stone | |
| | | |
| Nos volvemos inmensos | We become immense | |
| Solo por conocernos | Just knowing each other | |
| Con los ojos cerrados | With our eyes shut | |

—Translated by John Felstiner

## Robert Phillips (b. 1938)

| Running on Empty | 1981 |
|---|---|

As a teenager I would drive Father's
Chevrolet cross-county, given me

reluctantly: "Always keep the tank
half full, boy, half full, ya hear?"

The fuel gauge dipping, dipping      5
toward Empty, hitting Empty, then

—thrilling!—'way below Empty,
myself driving cross-county

mile after mile, faster and faster,
all night long, this crazy kid driving      10

the earth's rolling surface,
against all laws, defying chemistry,

rules, and time, riding on nothing
but fumes, pushing luck harder

than anyone pushed before, the wind      15
screaming past like the Furies . . .

I stranded myself only once, a white
night with no gas station open, ninety miles

from nowhere. Panicked for a while,
at standstill, myself stalled.                                    20

At dawn the car and I both refilled. But,
Father, I am running on empty still.

RUNNING ON EMPTY. 16 *Furies:* In Greek mythology, deities who pursue and torment evildoers.

*Sylvia Plath*

### *Sylvia Plath* (1932–1963)*

DADDY                                                   1965

You do not do, you do not do
Any more, black shoe
In which I have lived like a foot
For thirty years, poor and white,
Barely daring to breathe or Achoo.                                5

Daddy, I have had to kill you.
You died before I had time—
Marble-heavy, a bag full of God,
Ghastly statue with one grey toe
Big as a Frisco seal                                              10

And a head in the freakish Atlantic
Where it pours bean green over blue
In the waters off beautiful Nauset.
I used to pray to recover you.
Ach, du.                                                    15

In the German tongue, in the Polish town
Scraped flat by the roller
Of wars, wars, wars.
But the name of the town is common.
My Polack friend                                           20

Says there are a dozen or two.
So I never could tell where you
Put your foot, your root,
I never could talk to you.
The tongue stuck in my jaw.                                25

It stuck in a barb wire snare.
Ich, ich, ich, ich,
I could hardly speak.
I thought every German was you.
And the language obscene                                   30

An engine, an engine
Chuffing me off like a Jew.
A Jew to Dachau, Auschwitz, Belsen.
I began to talk like a Jew.
I think I may well be a Jew.                               35

The snows of the Tyrol, the clear beer of Vienna
Are not very pure or true.
With my gypsy ancestress and my weird luck
And my Taroc pack and my Taroc pack
I may be a bit of a Jew.                                   40

I have always been scared of *you*,
With your Luftwaffe, your gobbledygoo.
And your neat moustache
And your Aryan eye, bright blue.
Panzer-man, panzer-man, O You—                             45

Not God but a swastika
So black no sky could squeak through.
Every woman adores a Fascist,
The boot in the face, the brute
Brute heart of a brute like you.                           50

15 *Ach, du:* Oh, you. 27 *Ich, ich, ich, ich:* I, I, I, I.

You stand at the blackboard, daddy,
In the picture I have of you,
A cleft in your chin instead of your foot
But no less a devil for that, no not
Any less the black man who                                    55

Bit my pretty red heart in two.
I was ten when they buried you.
At twenty I tried to die
And get back, back, back to you.
I thought even the bones will do.                             60

But they pulled me out of the sack,
And they stuck me together with glue.
And then I knew what to do.
I made a model of you,
A man in black with a Meinkampf look                          65

And a love of the rack and the screw.
And I said I do, I do.
So daddy, I'm finally through.
The black telephone's off at the root,
The voices just can't worm through.                           70

If I've killed one man, I've killed two—
The vampire who said he was you
And drank my blood for a year,
Seven years, if you want to know.
Daddy, you can lie back now.                                  75

There's a stake in your fat black heart
And the villagers never liked you.
They are dancing and stamping on you.
They always *knew* it was you.
Daddy, daddy, you bastard, I'm through.                       80

DADDY. Introducing this poem in a reading, Sylvia Plath remarked:

The poem is spoken by a girl with an Electra complex. Her father died while she thought he was
God. Her case is complicated by the fact that her father was also a Nazi and her mother very
possibly part Jewish. In the daughter the two strains marry and paralyze each other—she has
to act out the awful little allegory before she is free of it.

(Quoted by A. Alvarez, *Beyond All This Fiddle*, New York, 1971.) In some details "Daddy" is
autobiography: the poet's father, Otto Plath, a German, had come to the United States from
Grabow, Poland. He had died following amputation of a gangrened foot and leg, when Sylvia
was eight years old. Politically, Otto Plath was a Republican, not a Nazi; but was apparently a
somewhat domineering head of the household. (See the recollections of the poet's mother,
Aurelia Schober Plath, in her edition of *Letters Home* by Sylvia Plath, New York, 1975.)

51 *blackboard*: Otto Plath had been a professor of biology at Boston University. 65 *Meinkampf*:
Adolf Hitler entitled his autobiography *Mein Kampf* ("My Struggle").

COMPARE:

"Daddy" with "American Primitive" by William Jay Smith (page 997).

Edgar Allan Poe

---

### Edgar Allan Poe (1809–1849)

## To Helen                            1831

Helen, thy beauty is to me
   Like those Nicean barks of yore,
That gently, o'er a perfumed sea,
   The weary, way-worn wanderer bore
   To his own native shore.               5

On desperate seas long wont to roam,
   Thy hyacinth hair, thy classic face,
Thy Naiad airs have brought me home
   To the glory that was Greece
And the grandeur that was Rome.      10

Lo! in yon brilliant window-niche
   How statue-like I see thee stand!
   The agate lamp within thy hand,
Ah! Psyche, from the regions which
   Are Holy Land!                15

---

### Alexander Pope (1688–1744)*

## A Little Learning Is A Dang'rous Thing
## (from An Essay on Criticism)        1711

   A *little Learning* is a dang'rous Thing;
Drink deep, or taste not the *Pierian* Spring:
There *shallow Draughts* intoxicate the Brain,
And drinking *largely* sobers us again.

Fir'd at first Sight with what the *Muse* imparts,                    5
In *fearless Youth* we tempt the Heights of Arts,
While from the bounded *Level* of our Mind,
*Short Views* we take, nor see the *Lengths behind,*
But *more advanc'd,* behold with strange Surprize
New, distant Scenes of *endless* Science rise!                        10
So pleas'd at first, the towring *Alps* we try,
Mount o'er the Vales, and seem to tread the Sky;
Th' Eternal Snows appear already past,
And the first *Clouds* and *Mountains* seem the last:
But *those attain'd,* we tremble to survey                           15
The growing Labours of the lengthen'd Way,
Th' *increasing* Prospect *tires* our wandring Eyes,
Hills peep o'er Hills, and *Alps* on *Alps* arise!

A Little Learning Is A Dang'rous Thing. 2 *Pierian Spring:* the spring of the Muses.

*Ezra Pound*

## *Ezra Pound* (1885–1972)*

## The Garret                                                1915

Come, let us pity those who are better off than we are.
Come, my friend, and remember
        that the rich have butlers and no friends,
And we have friends and no butlers.
Come, let us pity the married and the unmarried.             5

Dawn enters with little feet
    like a gilded Pavlova,
And I am near my desire.
Nor has life in it aught better
Than this hour of clear coolness,                         10
    the hour of waking together.

THE GARRETT. 7 *Pavlova:* Anna Pavlova (1885–1931) was a celebrated Russian ballerina.

## *Ezra Pound* (1885–1972)*

### THE RIVER-MERCHANT'S WIFE: A LETTER         1915

While my hair was still cut straight across my forehead
I played about the front gate, pulling flowers.
You came by on bamboo stilts, playing horse,
You walked about my seat, playing with blue plums.
And we went on living in the village of Chokan:                5
Two small people, without dislike or suspicion.
At fourteen I married My Lord you.
I never laughed, being bashful.
Lowering my head, I looked at the wall.
Called to, a thousand times, I never looked back.            10

At fifteen I stopped scowling,
I desired my dust to be mingled with yours
Forever and forever and forever.
Why should I climb the lookout?

At sixteen you departed,                                   15
You went into far Ku-to-yen, by the river of swirling eddies,
And you have been gone five months.
The monkeys make sorrowful noise overhead.

You dragged your feet when you went out.
By the gate now, the moss is grown, the different mosses,      20
Too deep to clear them away!
The leaves fall early this autumn, in wind.
The paired butterflies are already yellow with August
Over the grass in the West garden;
They hurt me. I grow older.                                25
If you are coming down through the narrows of the river Kiang,
Please let me know before hand,
And I will come out to meet you
    As far as Cho-fu-sa.

THE RIVER-MERCHANT'S WIFE: A LETTER. A free translation from the Chinese poet Li Po (eighth century).

*Dudley Randall*

## *Dudley Randall* (b. 1914)*

OLD WITHERINGTON                                          1966

Old Witherington had drunk too much again.
The children changed their play and packed around him
To jeer his latest brawl. Their parents followed.

Prune-black, with bloodshot eyes and one white tooth,
He tottered in the night with legs spread wide         5
Waving a hatchet. "Come on, come on," he piped,
"And I'll baptize these bricks with bloody kindling.
I may be old and drunk, but not afraid
To die. I've died before. A million times
I've died and gone to hell. I live in hell.         10
If I die now I die, and put an end
To all this loneliness. Nobody cares
Enough to even fight me now, except
This crazy bastard here."

                  And with these words
He cursed the little children, cursed his neighbors,     15
Cursed his father, mother, and his wife,
Himself, and God, and all the rest of the world,

All but his grinning adversary, who, crouched,
Danced tenderly around him with a jag-toothed bottle,
As if the world compressed to one old man                    20
Who was the sun, and he sole faithful planet.


## John Crowe Ransom (1888–1974)

### BELLS FOR JOHN WHITESIDE'S DAUGHTER          1924

There was such speed in her little body,
And such lightness in her footfall,
It is no wonder her brown study
Astonishes us all.

Her wars were bruited in our high window.                    5
We looked among orchard trees and beyond,
Where she took arms against her shadow,
Or harried unto the pond

The lazy geese, like a snow cloud
Dripping their snow on the green grass,                       10
Tricking and stopping, sleepy and proud,
Who cried in goose, Alas,

For the tireless heart within the little
Lady with rod that made them rise
From their noon apple-dreams, and scuttle                    15
Goose-fashion under the skies!

But now go the bells, and we are ready;
In one house we are sternly stopped
To say we are vexed at her brown study,
Lying so primly propped.                                     20

COMPARE:

"Bells for John Whiteside's Daughter" with "Elegy for Jane" by Theodore Roethke
(page 987).


## Henry Reed (1914–1986)

### NAMING OF PARTS          1946

Today we have naming of parts. Yesterday,
We had daily cleaning. And tomorrow morning,
We shall have what to do after firing. But today,
Today we have naming of parts. Japonica

Glistens like coral in all of the neighboring gardens,                    5
    And today we have naming of parts.

This is the lower sling swivel. And this
Is the upper sling swivel, whose use you will see,
When you are given your slings. And this is the piling swivel,
Which in your case you have not got. The branches           10
Hold in the gardens their silent, eloquent gestures,
    Which in our case we have not got.

This is the safety-catch, which is always released
With an easy flick of the thumb. And please do not let me
See anyone using his finger. You can do it quite easy       15
If you have any strength in your thumb. The blossoms
Are fragile and motionless, never letting anyone see
    Any of them using their finger.

And this you can see is the bolt. The purpose of this
Is to open the breech, as you see. We can slide it          20
Rapidly backwards and forwards: we call this
Easing the spring. And rapidly backwards and forwards
The early bees are assaulting and fumbling the flowers:
    They call it easing the Spring.

They call it easing the Spring: it is perfectly easy        25
If you have any strength in your thumb: like the bolt,
And the breech, and the cocking-piece, and the point of balance,
Which in our case we have not got; and the almond-blossom
Silent in all of the gardens and the bees going backwards and
    forwards,
    For today we have naming of parts.                      30

Compare:

"Naming of Parts" with "The Fury of Aerial Bombardment" by Richard Eberhart
(page 642).

---

### *Alastair Reid* (b. 1926)

## Speaking A Foreign Language          1963

How clumsy on the tongue, these acquired idioms,
after the innuendos of our own. How far
we are from foreigners, what faith
we rest in one sentence, hoping a smile will follow
on the appropriate face, always wallowing               5
between what we long to say and what we can,
trusting the phrase is suitable to the occasion,

the accent passable, the smile real,
always asking the traveller's fearful question—
what is being lost in translation?                                          10

Something, to be sure. And yet, to hear
the stumbling of foreign friends, how little we care
for the wreckage of word or tense. How endearing they are,
and how our speech reaches out, like a helping hand,
or limps in sympathy. Easy to understand,                                   15
through the tangle of language, the heart behind
groping toward us, to make the translation of
syntax into love.

*Adrienne Rich*

## *Adrienne Rich* (b. 1929)*

### AUNT JENNIFER'S TIGERS                              1951

Aunt Jennifer's tigers prance across a screen,
Bright topaz denizens of a world of green.
They do not fear the men beneath the tree;
They pace in sleek chivalric certainty.

Aunt Jennifer's fingers fluttering through her wool          5
Find even the ivory needle hard to pull.
The massive weight of Uncle's wedding band
Sits heavily upon Aunt Jennifer's hand.

When Aunt is dead, her terrified hands will lie
Still ringed with ordeals she was mastered by.                10

The tigers in the panel that she made
Will go on prancing, proud and unafraid.


**Adrienne Rich** (b. 1929)*

PEELING ONIONS                                    1963

Only to have a grief
equal to all these tears!

There's not a sob in my chest.
Dry-hearted as Peer Gynt
I pare away, no hero,                                                          5
merely a cook.

Crying was labor, once
when I'd good cause.
Walking, I felt my eyes like wounds
raw in my head,                                                               10
so postal-clerks, I thought, must stare.
A dog's look, a cat's, burnt to my brain—
yet all that stayed
stuffed in my lungs like smog.

These old tears in the chopping-bowl.                                          15

PEELING ONIONS. 4 *Peer Gynt:* Peer Gynt is the title character of Henrik Ibsen's 1867 play. In the
play's last act, Gynt has returned to Norway as an old man. Peeling away the layers of an onion,
he imagines that each one represents a stage of his life. He then discovers there is nothing at the
core of the onion—only separate layers.


**Adrienne Rich** (b. 1929)*

POWER                                                        1978

Living   in the earth-deposits   of our history

Today a backhoe divulged   out of a crumbling flank of earth
one bottle   amber   perfect   a hundred-year-old
cure for fever   or melancholy   a tonic
for living on this earth   in the winters of this climate                      5

Today I was reading about Marie Curie:
she must have known she suffered   from radiation sickness
her body bombarded for years   by the element
she had purified
It seems she denied to the end                                                10

the source of the cataracts on her eyes
the cracked and suppurating skin   of her finger-ends
till she could no longer hold   a test-tube or a pencil

She died   a famous woman   denying
her wounds                                                                                              15
denying
her wounds   came   from the same source as her power

POWER. 6 *Marie Curie:* the Polish scientist (1867–1934) who helped discover polonium and
radium. She was the first person to win two Nobel Prizes.

### *Edwin Arlington Robinson* (1869–1935)*

## MINIVER CHEEVY                                                   1910

Miniver Cheevy, child of scorn,
    Grew lean while he assailed the seasons;
He wept that he was ever born,
    And he had reasons.

Miniver loved the days of old                                                        5
    When swords were bright and steeds were prancing;
The vision of a warrior bold
    Would set him dancing.

Miniver sighed for what was not,
    And dreamed, and rested from his labors;                             10
He dreamed of Thebes and Camelot,
    And Priam's neighbors.

Miniver mourned the ripe renown
    That made so many a name so fragrant;
He mourned Romance, now on the town,                                15
    And Art, a vagrant.

Miniver loved the Medici,
    Albeit he had never seen one;
He would have sinned incessantly
    Could he have been one.                                                            20

Miniver cursed the commonplace
    And eyed a khaki suit with loathing;
He missed the medieval grace
    Of iron clothing.

Miniver scorned the gold he sought,                                          25
    But sore annoyed was he without it;
Miniver thought, and thought, and thought,
    And thought about it.

Miniver Cheevy, born too late,
    Scratched his head and kept on thinking;                                    30
Miniver coughed, and called it fate,
    And kept on drinking.

MINIVER CHEEVY. 11 *Thebes*: a city in ancient Greece and the setting of many famous Greek
myths; *Camelot*: the legendary site of King Arthur's Court. 12 *Priam*: the last king of Troy, his
"neighbors" would have included Helen of Troy, Aeneas, and other famous figures. 17 *the
Medici*: the ruling family of Florence during the high Renaissance, the Medici were renowned
patrons of the arts.

*Theodore Roethke*

## *Theodore Roethke* (1908–1963)*

ELEGY FOR JANE                                                                 1953

*My Student, Thrown by a Horse*

I remember the neckcurls, limp and damp as tendrils;
And her quick look, a sidelong pickerel smile;
And how, once startled into talk, the light syllables leaped for her,
And she balanced in the delight of her thought,
A wren, happy, tail into the wind,                                              5
Her song trembling the twigs and small branches.
The shade sang with her;
The leaves, their whispers turned to kissing;
And the mold sang in the bleached valleys under the rose.

Oh, when she was sad, she cast herself down into such a pure
        depth,                                                                 10

Even a father could not find her:
Scraping her cheek against straw;
Stirring the clearest water.

My sparrow, you are not here,
Waiting like a fern, making a spiny shadow.          15
The sides of wet stones cannot console me,
Nor the moss, wound with the last light.

If only I could nudge you from this sleep,
My maimed darling, my skittery pigeon.
Over this damp grave I speak the words of my love:    20
I, with no rights in this matter,
Neither father nor lover.

COMPARE:

"Elegy for Jane" with "Bells for John Whiteside's Daughter" by John Crowe Ransom
(page 982).

Mary Jo Salter

## *Mary Jo Salter* (b. 1954)

## WELCOME TO HIROSHIMA          1984

is what you first see, stepping off the train:
a billboard brought to you in living English

by Toshiba Electric. While a channel
silent in the TV of the brain

projects those flickering re-runs of a cloud                                  5
that brims its risen columnful like beer
and, spilling over, hangs its foamy head,
you feel a thirst for history: what year

it started to be safe to breathe the air,
and when to drink the blood and scum afloat                                  10
on the Ohta River. But no, the water's clear,
they pour it for your morning cup of tea

in one of the countless sunny coffee shops
whose plastic dioramas advertise
mutations of cuisine behind the glass:                                       15
a pancake sandwich; a pizza someone tops

with a maraschino cherry. Passing by
the Peace Park's floral hypocenter (where
how bravely, or with what mistaken cheer,
humanity erased its own erasure),                                            20

you enter the memorial museum
and through more glass are served, as on a dish
of blistered grass, three mannequins. Like gloves
a mother clips to coatsleeves, strings of flesh

hang from their fingertips; or as if tied                                    25
to recall a duty for us, *Reverence*
*the dead whose mourners too shall soon be dead,*
but all commemoration's swallowed up

in questions of bad taste, how re-created
horror mocks the grim original,                                              30
and thinking at last *They should have left it all*
you stop. This is the wristwatch of a child.

Jammed on the moment's impact, resolute
to communicate some message, although mute,
it gestures with its hands at eight-fifteen                                  35
and eight-fifteen and eight-fifteen again

while tables of statistics on the wall
update the news by calling on a roll
of tape, death gummed on death, and in the case
adjacent, an exhibit under glass                                             40

is glass itself: a shard the bomb slammed in
a woman's arm at eight-fifteen, but some
three decades on—as if to make it plain
hope's only as renewable as pain,

and as if all the unsung                                                        45
debasements of the past may one day come
rising to the surface once again—
worked its filthy way out like a tongue.

## *William Shakespeare* (1564–1616)*

### NOT MARBLE NOR THE GILDED MONUMENTS          1609

Not marble, nor the gilded monuments
Of princes, shall outlive this powerful rhyme;
But you shall shine more bright in these contents
Than unswept stone, besmeared with sluttish time.
When wasteful war shall statues overturn,                                       5
And broils root out the work of masonry,
Nor Mars his sword nor war's quick fire shall burn
The living record of your memory.
'Gainst death and all-oblivious enmity
Shall you pace forth; your praise shall still find room                        10
Even in the eyes of all posterity
That wear this world out to the ending doom.
   So, till the judgment that yourself arise,
   You live in this, and dwell in lovers' eyes.

COMPARE:

"Not marble nor the gilded monuments" with "To the Stone-cutters" by Robinson
Jeffers (page 945).

William Shakespeare

## William Shakespeare (1564–1616)*

### THAT TIME OF YEAR THOU MAYST IN ME BEHOLD      1609

That time of year thou mayst in me behold  
When yellow leaves, or none, or few, do hang  
Upon those boughs which shake against the cold,  
Bare ruined choirs where late the sweet birds sang.  
In me thou see'st the twilight of such day      5  
As after sunset fadeth in the west,  
Which by-and-by black night doth take away,  
Death's second self that seals up all in rest.  
In me thou see'st the glowing of such fire  
That on the ashes of his youth doth lie,      10  
As the deathbed whereon it must expire,  
Consumed with that which it was nourished by.  
   This thou perceiv'st, which makes thy love more strong,  
   To love that well which thou must leave ere long.

## William Shakespeare (1564–1616)*

### WHEN, IN DISGRACE WITH FORTUNE AND MEN'S EYES      1609

When, in disgrace with Fortune and men's eyes,  
I all alone beweep my outcast state,  
And trouble deaf heaven with my bootless° cries,      *futile*  
And look upon myself and curse my fate,  
Wishing me like to one more rich in hope,      5  
Featured like him, like him with friends possessed,  
Desiring this man's art, and that man's scope,  
With what I most enjoy contented least,  
Yet in these thoughts myself almost despising,  
Haply° I think on thee, and then my state,      *luckily*    10  
Like to the lark at break of day arising  
From sullen earth, sings hymns at heaven's gate;  
   For thy sweet love rememb'red such wealth brings  
   That then I scorn to change my state with kings.

## William Shakespeare (1564–1616)*

### WHEN DAISIES PIED AND VIOLETS BLUE      1598

When daisies pied and violets blue  
   And lady-smocks all silver-white

And cuckoo-buds° of yellow hue                                          *buttercups*
    Do paint the meadows with delight,
The cuckoo then, on every tree,                                                    5
Mocks married men; for thus sings he,
                    "Cuckoo,
Cuckoo, cuckoo!"—O word of fear,
Unpleasing to a married ear!

When shepherds pipe on oaten straws,                                      10
    And merry larks are ploughmen's clocks,
When turtles tread°, and rooks, and daws,                    *turtledoves mate*
    And maidens bleach their summer smocks,
The cuckoo then, on every tree,
Mocks married men; for thus sings he,                                        15
                    "Cuckoo,
Cuckoo, cuckoo!"—O word of fear,
Unpleasing to a married ear!

WHEN DAISIES PIED. This song and "When icicles hang by the wall" conclude the play *Love's Labor's Lost*. 2 *lady-smocks:* also named cuckoo-flowers. 8 *O word of fear:* because it sounds like *cuckold,* a man whose wife has deceived him.

## *William Shakespeare* (1564–1616)*

WHEN ICICLES HANG BY THE WALL          1598

When icicles hang by the wall,
    And Dick the shepherd blows his nail,
And Tom bears logs into the hall,
    And milk comes frozen home in pail,
When blood is nipped and ways° be foul,                          *roads*   5
    Then nightly sings the staring owl:
                "Tu-whit, to-who!"
            A merry note,
While greasy Joan doth keel° the pot.        *cool (as by skimming or stirring)*

When all aloud the wind doth blow,                                         10
    And coughing drowns the parson's saw°,            *old saw, platitude*
And birds sit brooding in the snow,
    And Marian's nose looks red and raw,
When roasted crabs° hiss in the bowl,                            *crab apples*
    Then nightly sings the staring owl:                                     15
                "Tu-whit, to-who!"
            A merry note,
While greasy Joan doth keel the pot.

## Karl Shapiro (b. 1913)

THE DIRTY WORD                                                                                   1947

The dirty word hops in the cage of the mind like the Pondicherry vulture, stomping with its heavy left claw on the sweet meat of the brain and tearing it with its vicious beak, ripping and chopping the flesh. Terrified, the small boy bears the big bird of the dirty word into the house, and grunting, puffing, carries it up the stairs to his own        5
room in the skull. Bits of black feather cling to his clothes and his hair as he locks the staring creature in the dark closet.

All day the small boy returns to the closet to examine and feed the bird, to caress and kick the bird, that now snaps and flaps its wings savagely whenever the door is opened. How the boy trembles and        10
delights at the sight of the white excrement of the bird! How the bird leaps and rushes against the walls of the skull, trying to escape from the zoo of the vocabulary! How wildly snaps the sweet meat of the brain in its rage.

And the bird outlives the man, being freed at the man's death-        15
funeral by a word from the rabbi.

(But I one morning went upstairs and opened the door and entered the closet and found in the cage of my mind the great bird dead. Softly I wept it and softly removed it and softly buried the body of the bird in the hollyhock garden of the house I lived in twenty years before.        20
And out of the worn black feathers of the wing have I made these pens to write these elegies, for I have outlived the bird, and I have murdered it in my early manhood.)

## Charles Simic (b. 1938)

BUTCHER SHOP                                                        1971

Sometimes walking late at night
I stop before a closed butcher shop.
There is a single light in the store
Like the light in which the convict digs his tunnel.

An apron hangs on the hook:                                                                5
The blood on it smeared into a map
Of the great continents of blood,
The great rivers and oceans of blood.

There are knives that glitter like altars
In a dark church                                                                          10

Where they bring the cripple and the imbecile
To be healed.

There's a wooden block where bones are broken,
Scraped clean—a river dried to its bed
Where I am fed,                                                           15
Where deep in the night I hear a voice.

<small>COMPARE:</small>

"Butcher Shop" with "Animals Are Passing from Our Lives" by Philip Levine (page 954).

---

## *David R. Slavitt* (b. 1935)

### TITANIC                                                               1983

Who does not love the *Titanic?*
If they sold passage tomorrow for that same crossing,
who would not buy?

To go down . . . We all go down, mostly
alone. But with crowds of people, friends, servants,                      5
well fed, with music, with lights! Ah!

And the world, shocked, mourns, as it ought to do
and almost never does. There will be the books and movies
to remind our grandchildren who we were
and how we died, and give them a good cry.                                10

Not so bad, after all. The cold
water is anaesthetic and very quick.
The cries on all sides must be a comfort.

We all go: only a few, first-class.

<small>COMPARE:</small>

"Titanic" with "The Convergence of the Twain" by Thomas Hardy (page 927).

---

## *Christopher Smart* (1722–1771)

### FOR I WILL CONSIDER MY CAT JEOFFRY                    (1759–1763)

For I will consider my Cat Jeoffry.
For he is the servant of the Living God, duly and daily serving him.
For at the first glance of the glory of God in the East he worships in
   his way.

For is this done by wreathing his body seven times round with
    elegant quickness.
For then he leaps up to catch the musk°, which is the          *catnip*
    blessing of God upon his prayer.                                      5
For he rolls upon prank to work it in.
For having done duty and received blessing he begins to consider
    himself.
For this he performs in ten degrees.
For first he looks upon his fore-paws to see if they are clean.
For secondly he kicks up behind to clear away there.             10
For thirdly he works it upon stretch° with the fore-paws    *he works his*
    extended.                                   *muscles, stretching*
For fourthly he sharpens his paws by wood.
For fifthly he washes himself.
For sixthly he rolls upon wash.
For seventhly he fleas himself, that he may not be interrupted upon
    the beat°.                                  *his patrol*  15
For eighthly he rubs himself against a post.
For ninthly he looks up for his instructions.
For tenthly he goes in quest of food.
For having considered God and himself he will consider his
    neighbor.
For if he meets another cat he will kiss her in kindness.         20
For when he takes his prey he plays with it to give it a chance.
For one mouse in seven escapes by his dallying.
For when his day's work is done his business more properly begins.
For he keeps the Lord's watch in the night against the Adversary.
For he counteracts the powers of darkness by his electrical skin and
    glaring eyes.                                     25
For he counteracts the Devil, who is death, by brisking about the
    life.
For in his morning orisons he loves the sun and the sun loves him.
For he is of the tribe of Tiger.
For the Cherub Cat is a term of the Angel Tiger.
For he has the subtlety and hissing of a serpent, which in goodness
    he suppresses.                                     30
For he will not do destruction if he is well-fed, neither will he spit
    without provocation.
For he purrs in thankfulness when God tells him he's a good Cat.
For he is an instrument for the children to learn benevolence upon.
For every house is incomplete without him, and a blessing is lacking
    in the spirit.
For the Lord commanded Moses concerning the cats at the
    departure of the Children of Israel from Egypt.         35
For every family had one cat at least in the bag.
For the English cats are the best in Europe.

For he is the cleanest in the use of his fore-paws of any quadruped.
For the dexterity of his defense is an instance of the love of God to
    him exceedingly.
For he is the quickest to his mark of any creature. 40
For he is tenacious of his point.
For he is a mixture of gravity and waggery.
For he knows that God is his Savior.
For there is nothing sweeter than his peace when at rest.
For there is nothing brisker than his life when in motion. 45
For he is of the Lord's poor, and so indeed is he called by
    benevolence perpetually—Poor Jeoffry! poor Jeoffry! the rat has
    bit thy throat.
For I bless the name of the Lord Jesus that Jeoffry is better.
For the divine spirit comes about his body to sustain it in complete
    cat.
For his tongue is exceeding pure so that it has in purity what it
    wants in music. 50
For he is docile and can learn certain things.
For he can sit up with gravity which is patience upon approbation.
For he can fetch and carry, which is patience in employment.
For he can jump over a stick which is patience upon proof positive.
For he can spraggle upon waggle at the word of command. 55
For he can jump from an eminence into his master's bosom.
For he can catch the cork and toss it again.
For he is hated by the hypocrite and miser.
For the former is afraid of detection.
For the latter refuses the charge. 60
For he camels his back to bear the first notion of business.
For he is good to think on, if a man would express himself neatly.
For he made a great figure in Egypt for his signal services.
For he killed the Icneumon-rat, very pernicious by land.
For his ears are so acute that they sting again. 65
For from this proceeds the passing quickness of his attention.
For by stroking of him I have found out electricity.
For I perceived God's light about him both wax and fire.
For the electrical fire is the spiritual substance which God sends
    from heaven to sustain the bodies both of man and beast.
For God has blessed him in the variety of his movements. 70
For, though he cannot fly, he is an excellent clamberer.
For his motions upon the face of the earth are more than any other
    quadruped.
For he can tread to all the measures upon the music.
For he can swim for life.
For he can creep. 75

FOR I WILL CONSIDER MY CAT JEOFFRY. This is a self-contained extract from Smart's long poem *Jubilate Agno* ("Rejoice in the Lamb"), written during his confinement for insanity. 35 *For the*

*Lord commanded Moses concerning the cats:* No such command is mentioned in Scripture. 54
*spraggle upon waggle:* W. F. Stead, in his edition of Smart's poem, suggests that this means
Jeoffry will sprawl when his master waggles a finger or a stick. 59 *the charge:* perhaps the cost
of feeding a cat.

## William Jay Smith (b. 1918)

### AMERICAN PRIMITIVE                              1953

Look at him there in his stovepipe hat,
His high-top shoes, and his handsome collar;
Only my Daddy could look like that,
And I love my Daddy like he loves his Dollar.

The screen door bangs, and it sounds so funny—                          5
There he is in a shower of gold;
His pockets are stuffed with folding money,
His lips are blue, and his hands feel cold.

He hangs in the hall by his black cravat,
The ladies faint, and the children holler:                              10
Only my Daddy could look like that,
And I love my Daddy like he loves his Dollar.

### COMPARE:

"American Primitive" with "Daddy" by Sylvia Plath (page 975).

## W. D. Snodgrass (b. 1926)

### DISPOSAL                                        1970

The unworn long gown, meant for dances
She would have scarcely dared attend,
Is fobbed off on a friend—
Who can't help wondering if it's spoiled
But thinks, well, she can take her chances.                             5

We roll her spoons up like old plans
Or failed securities, seal their case,
Then lay them back. One lace
Nightthing lies in the chest, unsoiled
By wear, untouched by human hands.                                      10

We don't dare burn those canceled patterns
And markdowns that she actually wore,
Yet who do we know so poor

They'd take them? Spared all need, all passion,
Saved from loss, she lies boxed in satins. 15

Like a pair of party shoes
That seemed to never find a taker;
We send back to its maker
A life somehow gone out of fashion
But still too good to use. 20

## William Stafford (1914–1993)*

### AT THE KLAMATH BERRY FESTIVAL 1966

The war chief danced the old way—
the eagle wing he held before his mouth—
and when he turned the boom-boom
stopped. He took two steps. A sociologist
was there; the Scout troop danced. 5
I envied him the places where he had not been.

The boom began again. Outside he heard
the stick game, and the Blackfoot gamblers
arguing at poker under lanterns.
Still-moccasined and bashful, holding 10
the eagle wing before his mouth,
listening and listening, he danced after others stopped.

He took two steps, the boom caught up,
the mountains rose, the still deep river
slid but never broke its quiet. 15
I looked back when I left:
he took two steps, he took two steps,
past the sociologist.

AT THE KLAMATH BERRY FESTIVAL. The Klamath Indians have a reservation at the base of the
Cascade Range in southern Oregon.

## Wallace Stevens (1879–1955)*

### PETER QUINCE AT THE CLAVIER 1923

*I*

Just as my fingers on these keys
Make music, so the selfsame sounds
On my spirit make a music, too.

Music is feeling, then, not sound;
And thus it is that what I feel,
Here in this room, desiring you,                                    5

Thinking of your blue-shadowed silk,
Is music. It is like the strain
Waked in the elders by Susanna.

Of a green evening, clear and warm,                                10
She bathed in her still garden, while
The red-eyed elders watching, felt

The basses of their beings throb
In witching chords, and their thin blood
Pulse pizzicati of Hosanna.                                        15

II

In the green water, clear and warm,
Susanna lay.
She searched
The touch of springs,

And found                                                          20
Concealed imaginings.
She sighed,
For so much melody.

Upon the bank, she stood
In the cool                                                        25
Of spent emotions.
She felt, among the leaves,
The dew
Of old devotions.

She walked upon the grass,                                         30
Still quavering.
The winds were like her maids,
On timid feet,
Fetching her woven scarves,
Yet wavering.                                                      35

A breath upon her hand
Muted the night.
She turned—
A cymbal crashed,
And roaring horns.                                                 40

III

Soon, with a noise like tambourines,
Came her attendant Byzantines.

They wondered why Susanna cried
Against the elders by her side;

And as they whispered, the refrain
Was like a willow swept by rain.

Anon, their lamps' uplifted flame
Revealed Susanna and her shame.

And then, the simpering Byzantines
Fled, with a noise like tambourines.

*IV*

Beauty is momentary in the mind—
The fitful tracing of a portal;
But in the flesh it is immortal.

The body dies; the body's beauty lives.
So evenings die, in their green going,
A wave, interminably flowing.
So gardens die, their meek breath scenting
The cowl of winter, done repenting.
So maidens die, to the auroral
Celebration of a maiden's choral.

Susanna's music touched the bawdy strings
Of those white elders; but, escaping,
Left only Death's ironic scraping.
Now, in its immortality, it plays
On the clear viol of her memory,
And makes a constant sacrament of praise.

PETER QUINCE AT THE CLAVIER. In Shakespeare's *Midsummer Night's Dream*, Peter Quince is a clownish carpenter who stages a mock-tragic play. In The Book of Susanna in the Apocrypha, two lustful elders who covet Susanna, a virtuous married woman, hide in her garden, spy on her as she bathes, then threaten to make false accusations against her unless she submits to them. When she refuses, they cry out, and her servants come running. All ends well when the prophet Daniel cross-examines the elders and proves them liars. 15 *pizzicati*: thin notes made by plucking a stringed instrument. 42 *Byzantines*: Susanna's maidservants.

## *Wallace Stevens* (1879–1955)*

### THE EMPEROR OF ICE-CREAM    1923

Call the roller of big cigars,
The muscular one, and bid him whip
In kitchen cups concupiscent curds.
Let the wenches dawdle in such dress
As they are used to wear, and let the boys

Bring flowers in last month's newspapers.
Let be be finale of seem.
The only emperor is the emperor of ice-cream.

Take from the dresser of deal,
Lacking the three glass knobs, that sheet                    10
On which she embroidered fantails once
And spread it so as to cover her face.
If her horny feet protrude, they come
To show how cold she is, and dumb.
Let the lamp affix its beam.                                 15
The only emperor is the emperor of ice-cream.

THE EMPEROR OF ICE-CREAM. 9 *deal*: fir or pine wood used to make cheap furniture.

*Wallace Stevens*

## *Ruth Stone* (b. 1915)

### SECOND HAND COAT                           1982

I feel
in her pockets; she wore nice cotton gloves,
kept a handkerchief box, washed her undies,
ate at the Holiday Inn, had a basement freezer,
belonged to a bridge club.                                   5
I think when I wake in the morning
that I have turned into her.
She hangs in the hall downstairs,

a shadow with pulled threads.
I slip her over my arms, skin of a matron.                                    10
Where are you? I say to myself, to the orphaned body,
and her coat says,
Get your purse, have you got your keys?


**Jonathan Swift** (1667–1745)*

A Description of the Morning                               1711

Now hardly here and there an hackney-coach°,                    *horse-drawn cab*
Appearing, showed the ruddy morn's approach.
Now Betty from her master's bed had flown
And softly stole to discompose her own.
The slipshod 'prentice from his master's door                              5
Had pared the dirt, and sprinkled round the floor.
Now Moll had whirled her mop with dextrous airs,
Prepared to scrub the entry and the stairs.
The youth with broomy stumps began to trace
The kennel°-edge, where wheels had worn the place.              *gutter*   10
The small-coal man was heard with cadence deep
Till drowned in shriller notes of chimneysweep,
Duns° at his lordship's gate began to meet,                       *bill-collectors*
And Brickdust Moll had screamed through half the street.
The turnkey° now his flock returning sees,                        *jailkeeper*  15
Duly let out a-nights to steal for fees;
The watchful bailiffs° take their silent stands;                  *constables*
And schoolboys lag with satchels in their hands.

A Description of the Morning. 9 *youth with broomy stumps*: a young man sweeping the gutter's edge with worn-out brooms, looking for old nails fallen from wagonwheels, which were valuable. 14 *Brickdust Moll*: woman selling brickdust to be used for scouring.


**Alfred, Lord Tennyson** (1809–1892)*

Dark House, by Which Once More I Stand               1850

Dark house, by which once more I stand
  Here in the long unlovely street,
  Doors, where my heart was used to beat
So quickly, waiting for a hand,

A hand that can be clasped no more—                    5
    Behold me, for I cannot sleep,
    And like a guilty thing I creep
At earliest morning to the door.

He is not here; but far away
    The noise of life begins again,                    10
    And ghastly through the drizzling rain
On the bald street breaks the blank day.

DARK HOUSE. This poem is one part of the series *In Memoriam*, an elegy for Tennyson's friend
Arthur Henry Hallam.

*Alfred, Lord Tennyson*

## Alfred, Lord Tennyson (1809–1892)*

### ULYSSES                                        (1833)

It little profits that an idle king,
By this still hearth, among these barren crags,
Matched with an agèd wife, I mete and dole
Unequal laws unto a savage race
That hoard, and sleep, and feed, and know not me.        5
I cannot rest from travel; I will drink
Life to the lees. All times I have enjoyed
Greatly, have suffered greatly, both with those
That loved me, and alone; on shore, and when
Through scudding drifts the rainy Hyades                 10
Vexed the dim sea. I am become a name;

For always roaming with a hungry heart
Much have I seen and known—cities of men
And manners, climates, councils, governments,
Myself not least, but honored of them all—                    15
And drunk delight of battle with my peers,
Far on the ringing plains of windy Troy.
I am a part of all that I have met;
Yet all experience is an arch wherethrough
Gleams that untraveled world whose margin fades              20
Forever and forever when I move.
How dull it is to pause, to make an end,
To rust unburnished, not to shine in use!
As though to breathe were life! Life piled on life
Were all too little, and of one to me                        25
Little remains; but every hour is saved
From that eternal silence, something more,
A bringer of new things; and vile it were
For some three suns to store and hoard myself,
And this grey spirit yearning in desire                      30
To follow knowledge like a sinking star,
Beyond the utmost bound of human thought.

    This is my son, mine own Telemachus,
To whom I leave the scepter and the isle—
Well-loved of me, discerning to fulfill                      35
This labor, by slow prudence to make mild
A rugged people, and through soft degrees
Subdue them to the useful and the good.
Most blameless is he, centered in the sphere
Of common duties, decent not to fail                         40
In offices of tenderness, and pay
Meet adoration to my household gods,
When I am gone. He works his work, I mine.

    There lies the port; the vessel puffs her sail;
There gloom the dark, broad seas. My mariners,              45
Souls that have toiled, and wrought, and thought with me—
That ever with a frolic welcome took
The thunder and the sunshine, and opposed
Free hearts, free foreheads—you and I are old;
Old age hath yet his honor and his toil.                     50
Death closes all; but something ere the end,
Some work of noble note, may yet be done,
Not unbecoming men that strove with Gods.
The lights begin to twinkle from the rocks;
The long day wanes; the low moon climbs; the deep           55
Moans round with many voices. Come, my friends,
'Tis not too late to seek a newer world.

Push off, and sitting well in order smite
The sounding furrows; for my purpose holds
To sail beyond the sunset, and the baths                                60
Of all the western stars, until I die.
It may be that the gulfs will wash us down;
It may be we shall touch the Happy Isles,
And see the great Achilles, whom we knew.
Though much is taken, much abides; and though                           65
We are not now that strength which in old days
Moved earth and heaven, that which we are, we are—
One equal temper of heroic hearts,
Made weak by time and fate, but strong in will
To strive, to seek, to find, and not to yield.                         70

ULYSSES. 10 *Hyades:* daughters of Atlas, who were transformed into a group of stars. Their rising with the sun was thought to be a sign of rain. 63 *Happy Isles:* Elysium, a paradise believed to be attainable by sailing west.

COMPARE:

"Ulysses" with "Sir Patrick Spence" (page 590).


## *Dylan Thomas* (1914–1953)*

FERN HILL                                                              1946

Now as I was young and easy under the apple boughs
About the lilting house and happy as the grass was green,
        The night above the dingle° starry,                    *wooded valley*
            Time let me hail and climb
            Golden in the heydays of his eyes,                           5
And honored among wagons I was prince of the apple towns
And once below a time I lordly had the trees and leaves
            Trail with daisies and barley
            Down the rivers of the windfall light.

And as I was green and carefree, famous among the barns               10
About the happy yard and singing as the farm was home,
            In the sun that is young once only,
            Time let me play and be
            Golden in the mercy of his means,
And green and golden I was huntsman and herdsman, the calves          15
Sang to my horn, the foxes on the hills barked clear and cold,
            And the sabbath rang slowly
            In the pebbles of the holy streams.

All the sun long it was running, it was lovely, the hay
Fields high as the house, the tunes from the chimneys, it was air     20

And playing, lovely and watery
          And fire green as grass.
     And nightly under the simple stars
As I rode to sleep the owls were bearing the farm away,
All the moon long I heard, blessed among stables, the nightjars          25
          Flying with the ricks, and the horses
               Flashing into the dark.

And then to awake, and the farm, like a wanderer white
With the dew, come back, the cock on his shoulder: it was all
          Shining, it was Adam and maiden,                     30
               The sky gathered again
          And the sun grew round that very day.
So it must have been after the birth of the simple light
In the first, spinning place, the spellbound horses walking warm
          Out of the whinnying green stable                    35
               On to the fields of praise.

And honored among foxes and pheasants by the gay house
Under the new made clouds and happy as the heart was long,
          In the sun born over and over,
               I ran my heedless ways,                         40
          My wishes raced through the house high hay
And nothing I cared, at my sky blue trades, that time allows
In all his tuneful turning so few and such morning songs
          Before the children green and golden
               Follow him out of grace,                        45

Nothing I cared, in the lamb white days, that time would take me
Up to the swallow thronged loft by the shadow of my hand,
          In the moon that is always rising,
               Nor that riding to sleep
          I should hear him fly with the high fields           50
And wake to the farm forever fled from the childless land.
Oh as I was young and easy in the mercy of his means,
          Time held me green and dying
          Though I sang in my chains like the sea.

---

### *John Updike* (b. 1932)*

## Ex-Basketball Player                               1958

Pearl Avenue runs past the high-school lot,
Bends with the trolley tracks, and stops, cut off
Before it has a chance to go two blocks,
At Colonel McComsky Plaza. Berth's Garage
Is on the corner facing west, and there,                       5
Most days, you'll find Flick Webb, who helps Berth out.

Flick stands tall among the idiot pumps—
Five on a side, the old bubble-head style,
Their rubber elbows hanging loose and low.
One's nostrils are two S's, and his eyes                                      10
An E and O. And one is squat, without
A head at all—more of a football type.

Once Flick played for the high-school team, the Wizards.
He was good: in fact, the best. In '46
He bucketed three hundred ninety points,                                      15
A county record still. The ball loved Flick.
I saw him rack up thirty-eight or forty
In one home game. His hands were like wild birds.

He never learned a trade, he just sells gas,
Checks oil, and changes flats. Once in a while,                               20
As a gag, he dribbles an inner tube,
But most of us remember anyway.
His hands are fine and nervous on the lug wrench.
It makes no difference to the lug wrench, though.

Off work, he hangs around Mae's luncheonette.                                 25
Grease-gray and kind of coiled, he plays pinball,
Smokes those thin cigars, nurses lemon phosphates.
Flick seldom says a word to Mae, just nods
Beyond her face toward bright applauding tiers
Of Necco Wafers, Nibs, and Juju Beads.                                        30

COMPARE:

"Ex-Basketball Player" with "The Cadence of Silk" by Garrett Hongo (page 937) and
"To an Athlete Dying Young" by A. E. Housman (page 942).


*Amy Uyematsu* (b. 1956)

RED ROOSTER, YELLOW SKY          1992

The grandmother who never spoke
brought me this card from Japan
drawn in a child's hand:
just rooster, sun, and sky.
Under a red sun                                                                5
the rooster's red body
splits in two uneven parts,
each sturdy black foot
holding its own weight.
It was the year of the rooster                                                10
when I was still ten,

learning to stand myself upright—
my own sky rising yellow
like new, uncut lemons.

*Amy Uyematsu*

## *Mona Van Duyn* (b. 1921)

### EARTH TREMORS FELT IN MISSOURI          1964

The quake last night was nothing personal,
you told me this morning. I think one always wonders,
unless, of course, something is visible: tremors
that take us, private and willy-nilly, are usual.

But the earth said last night that what I feel,                    5
you feel; what secretly moves you, moves me.
One small, sensuous catastrophe
makes inklings letters, spelled in a worldly tremble.

The earth, with others on it, turns in its course
as we turn toward each other, less than ourselves, gross,      10
mindless, more than we were. Pebbles, we swell
to planets, nearing the universal roll,
in our conceit even comprehending the sun,
whose bright ordeal leaves cool men woebegone.

## *Derek Walcott* (b. 1930)

### THE VIRGINS          1976

Down the dead streets of sun-stoned Frederiksted,
the first free port to die for tourism,
strolling at funeral pace, I am reminded

of life not lost to the American dream;
but my small-islander's simplicities                                      5
can't better our new empire's civilized
exchange of cameras, watches, perfumes, brandies
for the good life, so cheaply underpriced
that only the crime rate is on the rise
in streets blighted with sun, stone arches                               10
and plazas blown dry by the hysteria
of rumour. A condominium drowns
in vacancy; its bargains are dusted,
but only a jewelled housefly drones
over the bargains. The roulettes spin                                    15
rustily to the wind—the vigorous trade
that every morning would begin afresh
by revving up green water round the pierhead
heading for where the banks of silver thresh.

THE VIRGINS. The title of this poem refers to the Virgin Islands, a group of 100 small islands
in the Caribbean. 1 *Frederiksted:* the biggest seaport in St. Croix, the largest of the American
Virgin Islands. 2 *free port:* a port city where goods can be bought and sold without paying
customs taxes. 5 *small-islander's:* Walcott was born on St. Lucia, another island in the West
Indies. 16 *trade:* trade winds.

*Derek Walcott*

## Edmund Waller (1606–1687)*

### GO, LOVELY ROSE          1645

   Go, lovely rose,
Tell her that wastes her time and me
   That now she knows,

When I resemble° her to thee,                                    *compare*
How sweet and fair she seems to be.                                        5

   Tell her that's young
And shuns to have her graces spied,
   That hadst thou sprung
In deserts where no men abide,
Thou must have uncommended died.                                          10

   Small is the worth
Of beauty from the light retired:
   Bid her come forth,
Suffer herself to be desired,
And not blush so to be admired.                                          15

   Then die, that she
The common fate of all things rare
   May read in thee,
How small a part of time they share
That are so wondrous sweet and fair.                                      20

COMPARE:

"Go, Lovely Rose" with "To the Virgins, to Make Much of Time" by Robert
Herrick (page 937) and "To His Coy Mistress" by Andrew Marvell (page 957).

## *Walt Whitman* (1819–1892)*

### A NOISELESS PATIENT SPIDER                                        (1876)

A noiseless patient spider,
I mark'd where on a little promontory it stood isolated,
Mark'd how to explore the vacant vast surrounding,
It launch'd forth filament, filament, filament, out of itself,
Ever unreeling them, ever tirelessly speeding them.                        5
And you O my soul where you stand,
Surrounded, detached, in measureless oceans of space,
Ceaselessly musing, venturing, throwing, seeking the spheres to
    connect them,
Till the bridge you will need be form'd, till the ductile anchor hold,
Till the gossamer thread you fling catch somewhere, O my soul.            10

## *Walt Whitman* (1819–1892)*

### I SAW IN LOUISIANA A LIVE-OAK GROWING                1867

I saw in Louisiana a live-oak growing,
All alone stood it and the moss hung down from the branches,

Without any companion it grew there uttering joyous leaves of dark
    green,
And its look, rude, unbending, lusty, made me think of myself,
But I wonder'd how it could utter joyous leaves standing alone
    there without its friend near, for I knew I could not,        5
And I broke off a twig with a certain number of leaves upon it, and
    twined around it a little moss,
And brought it away, and I have placed it in sight in my room,
It is not needed to remind me as of my own dear friends,
(For I believe lately I think of little else than of them,)
Yet it remains to me a curious token, it makes me think of manly
    love;        10
For all that, and though the live-oak glistens there in Louisiana
    solitary in a wide flat space,
Uttering joyous leaves all its life without a friend a lover near,
I know very well I could not.

COMPARE:

"I Saw in Louisiana a Live-Oak Growing" with "A Supermarket in California" by
Allen Ginsberg (page 923).

*Walt Whitman*

---

### *Richard Wilbur* (b. 1921)*

TRANSIT        1988

A woman I have never seen before
Steps from the darkness of her town-house door
At just that crux of time when she is made
So beautiful that she or time must fade.

What use to claim that as she tugs her gloves                    5
A phantom heraldry of all the loves
Blares from the lintel? That the staggered sun
Forgets, in his confusion, how to run?

Still, nothing changes as her perfect feet
Click down the walk that issues in the street.                   10
Leaving the stations of her body there
As a whip maps the countries of the air.

*Richard Wilbur*

## *Richard Wilbur* (b. 1921)*

THE WRITER                                                      1976

In her room at the prow of the house
Where light breaks, and the windows are tossed with linden,
My daughter is writing a story.

I pause in the stairwell, hearing
From her shut door a commotion of typewriter-keys               5
Like a chain hauled over a gunwale.

Young as she is, the stuff
Of her life is a great cargo, and some of it heavy:
I wish her a lucky passage.

But now it is she who pauses,
As if to reject my thought and its easy figure.               10
A stillness greatens, in which

The whole house seems to be thinking,
And then she is at it again with a bunched clamor
Of strokes, and again is silent.                              15

I remember the dazed starling
Which was trapped in that very room, two years ago;
How we stole in, lifted a sash

And retreated, not to affright it;
And how for a helpless hour, through the crack of the door,   20
We watched the sleek, wild, dark

And iridescent creature
Batter against the brilliance, drop like a glove
To the hard floor, or the desk-top.

And wait then, humped and bloody,                             25
For the wits to try it again; and how our spirits
Rose when, suddenly sure,

It lifted off from a chair-back,
Beating a smooth course for the right window
And clearing the sill of the world.                           30

It is always a matter, my darling,
Of life or death, as I had forgotten. I wish
What I wished you before, but harder.


---

**Miller Williams** (b. 1930)

## Thinking About Bill, Dead of AIDS          1989

We did not know the first thing about
how blood surrenders to even the smallest threat
when old allergies turn inside out,

the body rescinding all its normal orders
to all defenders of flesh, betraying the head,            5
pulling its guards back from all its borders.

Thinking of friends afraid to shake your hand,
we think of your hand shaking, your mouth set,
your eyes drained of any reprimand.

Loving, we kissed you, partly to persuade          10
both you and us, seeing what eyes had said,
that we were loving and were not afraid.

If we had had more, we would have given more.
As it was we stood next to your bed,
stopping, though, to set our smiles at the door.          15

Not because we were less sure at the last.
Only because, not knowing anything yet,
we didn't know what look would hurt you least.

---

## *William Carlos Williams* (1883–1963)*

SPRING AND ALL          1923

By the road to the contagious hospital
under the surge of the blue
mottled clouds driven from the
northeast—a cold wind. Beyond, the
waste of broad, muddy fields          5
brown with dried weeds, standing and fallen

patches of standing water
the scattering of tall trees

All along the road the reddish
purplish, forked, upstanding, twiggy          10
stuff of bushes and small trees
with dead, brown leaves under them
leafless vines—

Lifeless in appearance, sluggish
dazed spring approaches—          15

They enter the new world naked,
cold, uncertain of all
save that they enter. All about them
the cold, familiar wind—

Now the grass, tomorrow          20
the stiff curl of wildcarrot leaf
One by one objects are defined—
It quickens: clarity, outline of leaf

But now the stark dignity of
entrance—Still, the profound change          25
has come upon them: rooted, they
grip down and begin to awaken

COMPARE:

"Spring and All" with "in Just-" by E. E. Cummings (page 792) and "Root Cellar" by Theodore Roethke (page 662).

*William Carlos Williams*

---

### *William Carlos Williams* (1883–1963)*

## To Waken an Old Lady     1921

Old age is
a flight of small
cheeping birds
skimming
bare trees                                            5
above a snow glaze.
Gaining and failing
they are buffeted
by a dark wind—
But what?                                             10
On harsh weedstalks
the flock has rested,
the snow
is covered with broken
seedhusks                                             15
and the wind tempered
by a shrill
piping of plenty.

COMPARE:

"To Waken an Old Lady" with "Castoff Skin" by Ruth Whitman (page 685).

## Yvor Winters (1900–1968)

### AT THE SAN FRANCISCO AIRPORT                1960

*To My Daughter, 1954*

This is the terminal: the light
Gives perfect vision, false and hard;
The metal glitters, deep and bright.
Great planes are waiting in the yard—
They are already in the night.                5

And you are here beside me, small,
Contained and fragile, and intent
On things that I but half recall—
Yet going whither you are bent.
I am the past, and that is all.               10

But you and I in part are one:
The frightened brain, the nervous will,
The knowledge of what must be done,
The passion to acquire the skill
To face that which you dare not shun.         15

The rain of matter upon sense
Destroys me momently. The score:
There comes what will come. The expense
Is what one thought, and something more—
One's being and intelligence.                 20

This is the terminal, the break.
Beyond this point, on lines of air,
You take the way that you must take;
And I remain in light and stare—
In light, and nothing else, awake.            25

## William Wordsworth (1770–1850)*

### COMPOSED UPON WESTMINSTER BRIDGE        1807

Earth has not anything to show more fair:
Dull would he be of soul who could pass by
A sight so touching in its majesty:

This City now doth, like a garment, wear
The beauty of the morning; silent, bare,                                   5
Ships, towers, domes, theatres, and temples lie
Open unto the fields, and to the sky;
All bright and glittering in the smokeless air.
Never did sun more beautifully steep
In his first splendor, valley, rock, or hill;                               10
Ne'er saw I, never felt, a calm so deep!
The river glideth at his own sweet will:
Dear God! the very houses seem asleep;
And all that mighty heart is lying still!

*William Wordsworth*

## James Wright (1927–1980)*

A BLESSING                                                                1961

Just off the highway to Rochester, Minnesota,
Twilight bounds softly forth on the grass.
And the eyes of those two Indian ponies
Darken with kindness.
They have come gladly out of the willows                                     5
To welcome my friend and me.
We step over the barbed wire into the pasture
Where they have been grazing all day, alone.
They ripple tensely, they can hardly contain their happiness
That we have come.                                                        10
They bow shyly as wet swans. They love each other.
There is no loneliness like theirs.

At home once more,
They begin munching the young tufts of spring in the darkness.
I would like to hold the slenderer one in my arms, 15
For she has walked over to me
And nuzzled my left hand.
She is black and white,
Her mane falls wild on her forehead,
And the light breeze moves me to caress her long ear 20
That is delicate as the skin over a girl's wrist.
Suddenly I realize
That if I stepped out of my body I would break
Into blossom.

James Wright

*James Wright* (1927–1980)*

## AUTUMN BEGINS IN MARTINS FERRY, OHIO      1963

In the Shreve High football stadium,
I think of Polacks nursing long beers in Tiltonsville,
And gray faces of Negroes in the blast furnace at Benwood,
And the ruptured night watchman of Wheeling Steel,
Dreaming of heroes. 5

All the proud fathers are ashamed to go home.
Their women cluck like starved pullets,
Dying for love.

Therefore,
Their sons grow suicidally beautiful                                    10
At the beginning of October,
And gallop terribly against each other's bodies.


## Sir Thomas Wyatt (1503?–1542)*

### THEY FLEE FROM ME THAT SOMETIME DID ME SEKË     (ABOUT 1535)

They flee from me that sometime did me sekë
  With naked fotë° stalking in my chamber.                        *foot*
I have seen them gentle, tame and mekë
  That now are wild, and do not remember
  That sometime they put themself in danger                         5
To take bread at my hand; and now they range
Busily seeking with a continual change.

Thankèd be fortune, it hath been otherwise
  Twenty times better; but once in speciàll,
In thin array, after a pleasant guise,                                  10
  When her loose gown from her shoulders did fall,
  And she me caught in her armës long and small,
Therëwith all sweetly did me kiss,
And softly said, *Dear heart, how like you this?*

It was no dremë: I lay broadë waking.                                   15
  But all is turned thorough° my gentleness                         *through*
Into a strangë fashion of forsaking;
  And I have leave to go of her goodness,
  And she also to use newfangleness°.                        *to seek novelty*
But since that I so kindëly am served                                   20
I would fain knowë what she hath deserved.

THEY FLEE FROM ME THAT SOMETIME DID ME SEKË. Some latter-day critics have called Sir Thomas
Wyatt a careless poet because some of his lines appear faltering and metrically inconsistent;
others have thought he knew what he was doing. It is uncertain whether the final *e*'s in English
spelling were still pronounced in Wyatt's day as they were in Chaucer's, but if they were,
perhaps Wyatt has been unjustly blamed. In this text, spellings have been modernized except
in words where the final *e* would make a difference in rhythm. To sense how it matters, try
reading the poem aloud leaving out the *e*'s and then putting them in wherever indicated. Sound
them like the *a* in *sofa*. 20 *kindëly:* according to my kind (or hers); that is, as befits the nature
of man (or woman). Perhaps there is also irony here, and the word means "unkindly."


## William Butler Yeats (1865–1939)*

### CRAZY JANE TALKS WITH THE BISHOP     1933

I met the Bishop on the road
And much said he and I.
"Those breasts are flat and fallen now,

Those veins must soon be dry;
Live in a heavenly mansion,                              5
Not in some foul sty."

"Fair and foul are near of kin,
And fair needs foul," I cried.
"My friends are gone, but that's a truth
Nor° grave nor bed denied,                   *neither*   10
Learned in bodily lowliness
And in the heart's pride.

"A woman can be proud and stiff
When on love intent;
But Love has pitched his mansion in          15
The place of excrement;
For nothing can be sole or whole
That has not been rent."

William Butler Yeats

## *William Butler Yeats* (1865–1939)*

### LONG-LEGGED FLY                    1940

That civilization may not sink,
Its great battle lost,
Quiet the dog, tether the pony
To a distant post;
Our master Caesar is in the tent          5

Where the maps are spread,
His eyes fixed upon nothing,
A hand under his head.

Like a long-legged fly upon the stream
His mind moves upon silence.                                    10

That the topless towers be burnt
And men recall that face,
Move most gently if move you must
In this lonely place.
She thinks, part woman, three parts a child,                   15
That nobody looks; her feet
Practice a tinker shuffle
Picked up on the street.

Like a long-legged fly upon the stream
Her mind moves upon silence.                                    20

That girls at puberty may find
The first Adam in their thought,
Shut the door of the Pope's chapel,
Keep those children out.
There on that scaffolding reclines                             25
Michael Angelo.
With no more sound than the mice make
His hand moves to and fro.

Like a long-legged fly upon the stream
His mind moves upon silence.                                    30

LONG-LEGGED FLY. This "fly" is the fresh-water insect also known as the water strider. 11 *topless towers:* of Troy, burned by the Greeks. Yeats echoes the description of Helen of Troy (whose abduction started the war) given in Christopher Marlowe's play *The Tragical History of Doctor Faustus:* "Was this the face that launched a thousand ships, / And burnt the topless towers of Ilium?" 23 *the Pope's Chapel:* Michelangelo had to lie on his back to paint upon the ceiling of the Sistine Chapel his celebrated frescoes depicting the creation, fall, and final judgment of humankind.

COMPARE:

"Long-legged Fly" with "Helen" by H. D. (page 925).

---

*William Butler Yeats* (1865–1939)*

THE MAGI                                                        1914

Now as at all times I can see in the mind's eye,
In their stiff, painted clothes, the pale unsatisfied ones
Appear and disappear in the blue depth of the sky

With all their ancient faces like rain-beaten stones,
And all their helms of silver hovering side by side,                     5
And all their eyes still fixed, hoping to find once more,
Being by Calvary's turbulence unsatisfied,
The uncontrollable mystery on the bestial floor.

COMPARE:

"The Magi" with "Journey of the Magi" by T. S. Eliot (page 914).

## William Butler Yeats (1865–1939)*

WHEN YOU ARE OLD                                    1893

When you are old and grey and full of sleep,
And nodding by the fire, take down this book,
And slowly read, and dream of the soft look
Your eyes had once, and of their shadows deep;

How many loved your moments of glad grace,                               5
And loved your beauty with love false or true,
But one man loved the pilgrim soul in you,
And loved the sorrows of your changing face;

And bending down beside the glowing bars,
Murmur, a little sadly, how Love fled                                     10
And paced upon the mountains overhead
And hid his face amid a crowd of stars.

# 31 Criticism: On Poetry

What is a modern Poet's fate?
To write his thoughts upon a slate—
The Critic spits on what is done,
Gives it a wipe—and all is gone.
          —Thomas Hood, "To the Reviewers"

"A poem is a pheasant," said Wallace Stevens. Studying poetry, you may find it useful at times to have the exact words of critics who have tried to describe that elusive, easily startled bird. Here then are fifteen critical statements about the nature of poetry made by poets and philosophers. This short selection includes some of the best-known, most stimulating remarks about poetry ever made. May it widen your own thinking about the art and give you something tough to argue with. After each passage, its source is indicated. Should one of these ideas capture your interest, why settle for the excerpt given here?

## Plato (427?–347? B.C.)

INSPIRATION[1]                            (ABOUT 390 B.C.)

For all good poets, epic as well as lyric, compose their beautiful poems not by art, but because they are inspired and possessed. And as the Corybantian revelers when they dance are not in their right mind, so the lyric poets are not in their right mind when they are composing their beautiful strains: but when falling under the power of music and meter they are inspired and possessed; like Bacchic maidens who draw milk and honey from the rivers when they are under the influence of Dionysus but not when they are in their right mind. And the soul of the lyric poet does the same, as they themselves say; for they tell us that they bring songs from honeyed fountains, culling them out of the gardens and dells of the Muses; they, like the bees, winging

[1]Translated by Benjamin Jowett.

their way from flower to flower. And this is true. For the poet is a light and winged and holy thing, and there is no invention in him until he has been inspired and is out of his senses, and the mind is no longer in him: when he has not attained to this state, he is powerless and is unable to utter his oracles. . . . They are simply inspired to utter that to which the Muse impels them, and that only; and when inspired, one of them will make dithyrambs, another hymns of praise, another choral strains, another epic or iambic verses—and he who is good at one is not good at any other kind of verse: for not by art does the poet sing, but by power divine. Had he learned by rules of art, he would have known how to speak not of one theme only, but of all; and therefore God takes away the minds of poets, and uses them as his ministers, as he also uses diviners and holy prophets, in order that we who hear them may know them to be speaking not of themselves who utter these priceless words in a state of unconsciousness, but that God himself is the speaker, and that through them he is conversing with us.

Ion

INSPIRATION. Plato records a dialogue between his master, the philosopher Socrates (469 B.C.– 399 B.C.) and Ion, a young man of Athens. *Corybantian revellers:* The Corybants, priests or attendants of the nature goddess Cybele, deity of the ancient peoples of Asia Minor, were given to orgiastic rites and frenzied dances. *Bacchic maidens:* attendants of the god of wine and fertility, called Dionysus by the Greeks, Bacchus by the Romans. *Muses:* In Greek mythology, nine sister goddesses who presided over poetry and song, the arts and sciences.

---

## *Aristotle* (384–322 B.C.)

## TWO CAUSES OF POETRY[2]                                    (ABOUT 330 B.C.)

Poetry in general seems to have sprung from two causes, each of them lying deep in our nature. First, the instinct of imitation is implanted in man from childhood, one difference between him and other animals being that he is the most imitative of living creatures; and through imitation he learns his earliest lessons; and no less universal is the pleasure felt in things imitated. We have evidence of this in the facts of experience. Objects which in themselves we view with pain, we delight to contemplate when reproduced with minute fidelity: such as the forms of the most ignoble animals and of dead bodies. The cause of this again is, that to learn gives the liveliest pleasure, not only to philosophers but to men in general; whose capacity, however, of learning is more limited. Thus the reason why men enjoy seeing a likeness is, that in contemplating it they find themselves learning or inferring, and saying perhaps, "Ah, that is he." For if you happen not to have seen the original, the pleasure will be due not to the imitation as such, but to the execution, the coloring, or some such other cause.

[2]Translated by S. H. Butcher.

Imitation, then, is one instinct of our nature. Next, there is the instinct for "harmony" and rhythm, meters being manifestly sections of rhythm. Persons, therefore, starting with this natural gift developed by degrees their special aptitudes, till their rude improvisations gave birth to Poetry.

*Poetics,* IV

## Samuel Johnson (1709–1784)

### THE BUSINESS OF A POET                                               1759

The business of a poet is to examine, not the individual, but the species; to remark general properties and large appearances; he does not number the streaks of the tulip, or describe the different shades in the verdure of the forest. He is to exhibit in his portraits of nature such prominent and striking features as recall the original to every mind, and must neglect the minuter discriminations, which one may have remarked and another have neglected, for those characteristics which are alike obvious to vigilance and carelessness.

But the knowledge of nature is only half the task of a poet; he must be acquainted likewise with all the modes of life. His character requires that he estimate the happiness and misery of every condition, observe the power of all the passions in all their combinations, and trace the changes of the human mind as they are modified by various institutions and accidental influences of climate or custom, from the sprightliness of infancy to the despondency of decrepitude. He must divest himself of the prejudices of his age or country; he must consider right and wrong in their abstracted and variable state; he must disregard present laws and opinions, and rise to general and transcendental truths, which will always be the same.

*The History of Rasselas,*
*Prince of Abyssinia*

## William Wordsworth (1770–1850)

### EMOTION RECOLLECTED IN TRANQUILLITY                                  1800

I have said that poetry is the spontaneous overflow of powerful feelings: it takes its origin from emotion recollected in tranquillity: the emotion is contemplated till, by a species of reaction, the tranquillity gradually disappears, and an emotion, kindred to that which was before the subject of contemplation, is gradually produced, and does itself actually exist in the mind. In this mood successful composition generally begins, and in a mood similar to this it is carried on; but the emotion, of whatever kind, and in whatever degree, from various causes, is qualified by various pleasures, so that in describing any passions whatsoever, which are voluntarily described, the mind will, upon the whole, be in a state of enjoyment. If Nature be thus cautious to preserve in a state of enjoyment a being so employed, the Poet ought to profit by the lesson held forth to him, and ought especially to take care, that, whatever passions he communicates to his Reader, those passions, if his Reader's mind be sound and vigorous, should always be accompanied with an overbalance of pleasure. Now the music of harmonious metrical language, the sense of difficulty overcome, and the blind association of pleasure which has been previously received from works of rhyme or meter of the same or similar construction, an indistinct perception perpetually renewed of language closely resembling that of real life, and yet, in the circumstance of meter, differing from it so widely—all these imperceptibly make up a complex feeling of delight, which is of the most important use in tempering the painful feeling always found intermingled with powerful descriptions of the deeper passions. This effect is always produced in pathetic and impassioned poetry; while, in lighter compositions, the ease and gracefulness with which the Poet manages his numbers are themselves confessedly a principal source of the gratification of the Reader. All that it is *necessary* to say, however, upon this subject, may be effected by affirming, what few persons will deny, that, of two descriptions, either of passions, manners, or characters, each of them equally well executed, the one in prose and the other in verse, the verse will be read a hundred times where the prose is read once.

Preface to *Lyrical Ballads,*
second edition

EMOTION RECOLLECTED IN TRANQUILLITY. For information on Wordsworth's methods of composition in his poem "I Wandered Lonely as a Cloud," see page 605.

---

## *Samuel Taylor Coleridge* (1772–1834)

IMAGINATION                                                                       1817

What is poetry?—is so nearly the same question with, what is a poet?—that the answer to the one is involved in the solution of the other. For it is a distinction resulting from the poetic genius itself, which sustains and modifies the images, thoughts, and emotions of the poet's own mind.

    The poet, described in ideal perfection, brings the whole soul of man into activity, with the subordination of its faculties to each other according to their relative worth and dignity. He diffuses a tone and spirit of unity, that blends, and (as it were) *fuses*, each into each, by that synthetic and magical power, to which I would exclusively appropriate the name of Imagination. This power, first put in action by the will and understanding, and retained under their irremissive, though gentle and unnoticed, control, *laxis effertur habenis°*, reveals itself in the balance or reconcilement of opposite or discordant qualities; of sameness, with difference; of the general with the concrete;

the idea with the image; the individual with the representative; the sense of novelty and freshness with old and familiar objects; a more than usual state of emotion with more than usual order; judgment ever awake and steady self-possession, with enthusiasm and feeling profound and vehement; and while it blends and harmonizes the natural and the artificial, still subordinates art to nature; the manner to the matter; and our admiration of the poet to our sympathy with the poetry.

> Biographia Literaria: or, Biographical Sketches
> of My Literary Life and Opinions, Chapter XIV

IMAGINATION. The Latin phrase *laxis effertur habenis* means "is driven with reins relaxed."

## Percy Bysshe Shelley (1792–1822)

### UNACKNOWLEDGED LEGISLATORS (1821)

The most unfailing herald, companion, and follower of the awakening of a great people to work a beneficial change in opinion or institution, is poetry. At such periods there is an accumulation of the power of communicating and receiving intense and impassioned conceptions respecting man and nature. The persons in whom this power resides, may often, as far as regards many portions of their nature, have little apparent correspondence with that spirit of good of which they are the ministers. But even whilst they deny and abjure, they are yet compelled to serve, the power which is seated on the throne of their own soul. It is impossible to read the compositions of the most celebrated writers of the present day without being startled with the electric life which burns within their words. They measure the circumference and sound the depths of human nature with a comprehensive and all-penetrating spirit, and they are themselves perhaps the most sincerely astonished at its manifestations; for it is less their spirit than the spirit of the age. Poets are the hierophants of an unapprehended inspiration; the mirrors of the gigantic shadows which futurity casts upon the present; the words which express what they understand not; the trumpets which sing to battle, and feel not what they inspire; the influence which is moved not, but moves. Poets are the unacknowledged legislators of the world.

> A Defense of Poetry

## Ralph Waldo Emerson (1803–1882)

### METER-MAKING ARGUMENT 1844

For it is not meters, but a meter-making argument that makes a poem,—a thought so passionate and alive that like the spirit of a plant or an animal it has an architecture of its own, and adorns nature with a new thing. The thought and the form are equal in the order of time, but in the order of genesis the thought is prior to the form. The poet has a new thought; he has a whole new experience to unfold; he will tell us how it was with him, and all men will be the richer in his fortune. For the experience of each new age requires a new confession, and the world seems always waiting for its poet.

The Poet

## *Edgar Allan Poe* (1809–1849)

### A LONG POEM DOES NOT EXIST                                         1848

I hold that a long poem does not exist. I maintain that the phrase, "a long poem," is simply a flat contradiction in terms.

 I need scarcely observe that a poem deserves its title only inasmuch as it excites, by elevating the soul. The value of the poem is in the ratio of its elevative excitement. But all excitements are, through a psychal necessity, transient. That degree of excitement which would entitle a poem to be so called at all cannot be sustained throughout a composition of any great length. After the lapse of half an hour, at the very utmost, it flags—fails—a revulsion ensues—and then the poem is in effect, and in fact, no longer such.

The Poetic Principle

## *Emily Dickinson* (1830–1886)

### RECOGNIZING POETRY                                                 1870

If I read a book and it makes my whole body so cold no fire can ever warm me, I know that is poetry. If I feel physically as if the top of my head were taken off, I know that is poetry. These are the only ways I know it. Is there any other way?

in conversation to Thomas Wentworth Higginson

## *Robert Frost* (1874–1963)

### THE SOUND OF SENSE                                                 (1913)

I alone of English writers have consciously set myself to make music out of what I may call the sound of sense. Now it is possible to have sense without the sound of sense (as in much prose that is supposed to pass muster but makes very dull reading) and the sound of sense without sense (as in Alice in Wonderland which makes anything but dull reading). The best place to get the abstract sound of sense is from voices behind a door that cuts off the words. Ask yourself how these sentences would sound without the words in which they are embodied:

> You mean to tell me you can't read?
> I said no such thing.
> Well read then.
> You're not my teacher.
>
> .   .   .
>
> He says it's too late.
> Oh, say!
> Damn an Ingersoll watch anyway.
>
> .   .   .
>
> One-two-three—go!
> No good! Come back—come back.
> Haslam go down there and make those kids get out of the track.
>
> .   .   .

Those sounds are summoned by the [audial] imagination and they must be positive, strong, and definitely and unmistakably indicated by the context. The reader must be at no loss to give his voice the posture proper to the sentence. The simple declarative sentence used in making a plain statement is one sound. But Lord love ye it mustn't be worked to death. It is against the law of nature that whole poems should be written in it. If they are written they won't be read. The sound of sense, then. You get that. It is the abstract vitality of our speech. It is pure sound—pure form. One who concerns himself with it more than the subject is an artist. But remember we are still talking merely of the raw material of poetry. An ear and an appetite for these sounds of sense is the first qualification of a writer, be it of prose or verse. But if one is to be a poet he must learn to get cadences by skillfully breaking the sounds of sense with all their irregularity of accent across the regular beat of the meter. Verse in which there is nothing but the beat of the meter furnished by the accents of the polysyllabic words we call doggerel. Verse is not that. Neither is it the sound of sense alone. It is a resultant from those two. There are only two or three meters that are worth anything. We depend for variety on the infinite play of accents in the sound of sense. The high possibility of emotional expression all lets in this mingling of sense-sound and word-accent. A curious thing. And all this has its bearing on your prose, me boy. Never if you can help it write down a sentence in which the voice will not know how to posture *specially*.

Letter to John T. Bartlett, from *Selected Letters
of Robert Frost*, ed. Lawrance Thompson
(New York: Holt, 1964)

## William Carlos Williams (1883–1963)

### THE RHYTHM PERSISTS (1913?)

No action, no creative action is complete but a period from a greater action going in rhythmic course. . . . Imagination creates an image, point by point, piece by piece, segment by segment—into a whole, living. But each part as it plays into its neighbor, each segment into its neighbor segment and every part into every other, causing the whole—exists naturally in rhythm, and as there are waves there are tides and as there are ridges in the sand there are bars after bars. . . .

I do not believe in *vers libre*, this contradiction in terms. Either the motion continues or it does not continue, either there is rhythm or no rhythm. *Vers libre* is prose. In the hands of Whitman it was a good tool, a kind of synthetic chisel—the best he had. In his bag of chunks even lie some of the pieces of rhythmic life of which we must build. This is honor enough. *Vers libre* is finished—Whitman did all that was necessary with it. Verse has nothing to gain here and all to lose. . . .

Each piece of work, rhythmic in whole, is then in essence an assembly of tides, waves, ripples—in short, of greater and lesser rhythmic particles regularly repeated or destroyed.

Essay "Speech Rhythm" quoted by Mike Weaver,
*William Carlos Williams, The American Background*
(New York: Cambridge University Press, 1971)

## Ezra Pound (1885–1972)

### POETRY AND MUSIC 1934

The great lyric age lasted while Campion made his own music, while Lawes set Waller's verses, while verses, if not actually sung or set to music, were at least made with the intention of going to music.

Music rots when it gets *too far* from the dance. Poetry atrophies when it gets too far from music.

*ABC of Reading*

## T. S. Eliot (1888–1965)

### EMOTION AND PERSONALITY 1920

It is not in his personal emotions, the emotions provoked by particular events in his life, that the poet is in any way remarkable or interesting. His particular emotions may be simple, or crude, or flat. The emotion in his poetry will be a very complex thing, but not with the complexity of the emotions of people who have very complex or unusual emotions in life. One error, in fact, of eccentricity in poetry is to seek for new human emotions to express; and in this search for novelty in the wrong place it discovers the perverse. The business of the poet is not to find new emotions, but to use the ordinary ones and, in working them up into poetry, to express feelings which are not in actual emotions at all. And emotions which he has never experienced will serve his turn as well as those familiar to him. Consequently, we must believe that "emotion recollected in tranquillity" is an inexact formula. For it is neither emotion, nor recollection, nor, without distortion of meaning, tranquillity. It is a concentration, and a new thing resulting from the concentration, of a very great number of experiences which to the practical and active person would not seem to be experiences at all; it is a concentration which does not happen consciously or of deliberation. These experiences are not "recollected," and they finally unite in an atmosphere which is "tranquil" only in that it is a passive attending upon the event. Of course this is not quite the whole story. There is a great deal, in the writing of poetry, which must be conscious and deliberate. In fact, the bad poet is usually unconscious where he ought to be conscious, and conscious where he ought to be unconscious. Both errors tend to make him "personal." Poetry is not a turning loose of emotion, but an escape from emotion; it is not the expression of personality, but an escape from personality. But, of course, only those who have personality and emotions know what it means to want to escape from these things.

Tradition and the Individual Talent

## *Adrienne Rich* (b. 1929)

### FEMINIST RE-VISION 1971

Re-vision—the act of looking back, of seeing with fresh eyes, of entering an old text from a new critical direction—is for women more than a chapter in cultural history: it is an act of survival. Until we can understand the assumptions in which we are drenched we cannot know ourselves. And this drive to self-knowledge, for women, is more than a search for identity: it is part of our refusal of the self-destructiveness of male-dominated society. A radical critique of literature, feminist in its impulse, would take the work first of all as a clue to how we live, how we have been living, how we have been led to imagine ourselves, how our language has trapped as well as liberated us, how the very act of naming has been till now a male prerogative, and how we can begin to see and name—and therefore live—afresh. A change in the concept of sexual identity is essential if we are not going to see the old political order reassert itself in every new revolution. We need to know the writing of the past, and know it differently than we have ever known it; not to pass on a tradition but to break its hold over us.

For writers, and at this moment for women writers in particular, there is the challenge and promise of a whole new psychic geography to be explored. But there is also a difficult and dangerous walking on the ice, as we try to find language and images for a consciousness we are just coming into, and with little in the past to support us.

When We Dead Awaken: Writing as Re-Vision
*On Lies, Secrets, and Silence: Selected Prose 1966–1978*

---

## *Octavio Paz* (b. 1914)

### EUROPEAN LANGUAGES AND THE
### LITERATURE OF THE AMERICAS                                    1990

Languages are vast realities that transcend those political and historical entities we call nations. The European languages we speak in the Americas illustrate this. The special position of our literatures, when compared to those of England, Spain, Portugal, and France, derives precisely from this fundamental fact: they are literatures written in transplanted tongues. Languages are born and grow in the native soil, nourished by a common history. The European languages were uprooted and taken to an unknown and unnamed world: in the new soil of the societies of America, they grew and were transformed. The same plant, yet a different plant. Our literatures did not passively accept the changing fortunes of their transplanted languages: they participated in the process and even accelerated it. Soon they ceased to be mere transatlantic reflections. At times they have been the negation of the literatures of Europe; more often, they have been a reply.

In spite of these oscillations, the link has never been broken. My classics are those of my language, and I consider myself to be a descendant of Lope and Quevedo, as any Spanish writer would . . . yet I am not a Spaniard. I think that most writers of Spanish America as well as those from the United States, Brazil, and Canada would say the same as regards the English, Portuguese, and French traditions. To understand more clearly the special position of writers in the Americas, we should compare it to the dialogue maintained by Japanese, Chinese, or Arabic writers with the different literatures of Europe: a dialogue that cuts across multiple languages and civilizations. Our dialogue, on the other hand, takes place within the same language. We are Europeans, yet we are not Europeans. What are we, then? It is difficult to define what we are, but our works speak for us.

1990 Nobel Prize Lecture

EUROPEAN LANGUAGES AND THE LITERATURE OF THE AMERICAS. *Lope and Quevedo:* Lope de Vega (1562–1635) was a celebrated Spanish dramatist and poet; Francisco Gomez de Quevedo (1580–1645) was a major Spanish novelist and poet. The Spanish refer to their literary era as The Golden Age.

# 32 Lives of the Poets

Here you will find a brief biographical note for most poets represented in the book by more than one selection. There is also a note for Thomas Gray, author of the long poem "Elegy in a Country Churchyard." A note for Edgar Allan Poe appears on page 61.

## John Ashbery

John Ashbery, born in Rochester, New York, in 1927, was educated at Deerfield Academy, Harvard, and Columbia. In 1960 he became an art critic in Paris for the *New York Herald Tribune*, and from 1966 to 1972 served as executive editor of the magazine *Art News* in New York. His first full collection of poetry, *Some Trees* (1956), was chosen by W. H. Auden for publication in the Yale Series of Younger Poets; his *Self-Portrait in a Convex Mirror* (1976) garnered praise and three leading literary prizes, and sold well for a book of serious poetry. Ashbery has written plays and a novel (with James Schuyler), *A Nest of Ninnies* (1969). He now lives in New York and teaches part time in the writing program at Brooklyn College. Some critics have speculated that Ashbery's experience as an art critic has tinged his poetry: that he performs in words what an abstract expressionist performs on canvas in oils. His work can annoy readers who expect poems to make clear statements to be taken in only one way; others think him the foremost living American poet and major heir to the tradition of Wallace Stevens—that is, to the art of suggesting rather than depicting, of arranging words primarily for their own sake.

## Margaret Atwood

Margaret Atwood, born in Ottawa in 1939, is a staunchly Canadian poet, short story writer, and novelist whose literary reputation has extended well beyond the borders of her native country. She published her first book of poems, *Double Persephone*, in 1962, the same year she was graduated from the University of Toronto. She went on to earn a master's degree at Radcliffe and to study Victorian fantasy at Harvard. She has advanced her country's cultural identity by publishing *Survival* (1972), a book about Canadian literature, and has edited *The Oxford Book of Canadian Verse* (1982). Her fiction and poetry, at once comic and grim, often deal with alienation and the destructive nature of human relationships. Her recent novel, *Cat's Eye* (1989), won attention on both sides of the Canadian border. The cream of her poetry has been skimmed in *Selected Poems* (1976) and *Selected Poems II* (1987).

## W. H. Auden

W. H. Auden (1907–1973), born in York, England, as a young man in the 1930s became the acknowledged spokesman for a generation of English poets that included Stephen Spender, C. Day-Lewis, Christopher Isherwood, and Louis MacNeice. His early work was characterized by blithe wit, a Marxist outlook, and a knowledge of Freudian psychology; in later life, he professed Christianity and (in his views of poetry) increasing conservatism. In 1939 Auden emigrated to America, and in 1946 became a United States citizen. A prolific editor, anthologist, and translator of poetry, he collaborated on verse plays, travel memoirs, and (with his longtime friend Chester Kallman) librettos for operas, including Igor Stravinsky's *The Rake's Progress* (1951). He wrote influential criticism, notably that collected in *The Dyer's Hand* (1962). Auden divided his last years among England, Italy, Austria, and New York.

## R. L. Barth

R. L. Barth was born in 1947 in Covington, Kentucky. From 1966 until 1969 he served as a patrol leader with the First Reconnaissance Battalion of the U.S.

Marines in Vietnam. Later he held a Wallace Stegner fellowship in creative writing at Stanford. He now teaches English at Xavier University in Cincinnati. As Robert L. Barth, he operates a small publishing house in Florence, Kentucky, issuing chapbooks of poetry by contemporary formalists Edgar Bowers, Turner Cassity, Dick Davis, Timothy Dekin, Thom Gunn, Paul Lake, Janet Lewis, John Ridland, Don Stanford, Timothy Steele, William Wilborn, and others. His own classically taut poems of the Vietnam War have been gathered in *A Soldier's Time* (1987).

## Elizabeth Bishop

Elizabeth Bishop (1911–1979) was born in Worcester, Massachusetts. After her father died (in her first year) and her mother was stricken with mental illness, she lived until age six with her grandmother in a coastal village in Nova Scotia. A sufferer from asthma, she received scant elementary schooling, but she read widely and deeply at home. At sixteen she entered Walnut Hill, a boarding school, and later graduated from Vassar. Her undergraduate poems won her the friendship of the poet Marianne Moore, who persuaded her not to go on to medical school, but instead to write. Fond of travel and flower-filled climates, Bishop lived for nine years in Key West, Florida, then for fifteen years in Brazil, dividing her time between the mountains and Rio de Janeiro. In 1966 she returned to the United States to teach: first at the University of Washington, then at Harvard from 1969 until 1977, when she retired. Most of her sparely disciplined work is contained in two volumes: *Complete Poems 1927–1979* (1983) and *Collected Prose* (1984). Her sharp-eyed poems, full of vivid images and apt metaphors, have affected the work of other poets, among them her friends Randall Jarrell and Robert Lowell.

## William Blake

William Blake (1757–1827), poet, painter, and visionary, was born in the Soho district of London and early in life was apprenticed to an engraver. Becoming a skilled craftsman, he earned his living illustrating books, among them Dante's *Divine Comedy*, Milton's poems, and the Book of Job. A remarkable and original graphic artist whose only formal training came from a few months at the Royal Academy, Blake published his own poems, engraving them in a careful script embellished with hand-colored illustrations and decorations. His wife Catherine Boucher, whom he taught to read and write, shared his visions and helped him do the coloring. *Songs of Innocence* (1789) and *Songs of Experience* (1794), brief lyrics written from a child's point of view, are easy to enjoy; but anyone deeply interested in Blake copes also with the longer, more demanding "Prophetic Books," among them *The Book of Thel* (1789), *The Marriage of Heaven and Hell* (1790), and *Jerusalem* (1804–20). In these later works, out of his readings in alchemy, the Bible, and the works of Plato and Swedenborg, Blake derived support for his lifelong hatred of scientific rationalism and created his own mythology, complete with devils and deities. A sympathizer with both American and French revolutions, Blake was once accused of sedition, but the charges were dismissed. In his lifetime, Wordsworth and Coleridge were among the few admirers of his short lyrics; his "Prophetic Books" have had to wait until our century for compassionate readers.

## Robert Bly

Robert Bly was born on a farm in Madison, Minnesota, in 1926, and continued to live there for most of his life. He was graduated from Harvard, where he began studies in mathematics before deciding to devote his life to poetry. Rather than teaching, Bly has preferred to support himself and his family by giving poetry readings and by translating books and poems from Scandinavian and other languages. In 1958 he launched a poetry magazine, *The Fifties* (later renamed, as decades went by, *The Sixties* and *The Seventies*). In it he spoofed academic critics, urged American poets to open their work to dream and surrealism, and introduced in translation the work of important poets of Europe and Latin America. Bly has vitally influenced the work of James Wright, Donald Hall, and many younger poets. His readings, in which he sometimes chants and dons primitive masks, have drawn throngs. In the 1960s he organized (with David Ray) American Writers Against the Vietnam War, and over the years has championed many causes, usually pacifist and antinuclear. Lately he has been leading retreats for men, trying to help them understand their male natures.

## Gwendolyn Brooks

Gwendolyn Brooks, born in 1917 in Topeka, Kansas, moved early in life to Chicago's South Side, whose people she has commemorated in her poetry and in a novel, *Maud Martha* (1953). Recipient of the Pulitzer prize for poetry in 1950, for *Annie Allen*, Brooks has long been recognized as a leading voice in modern American letters. She has combined several teaching positions with raising two children. Since 1967, when she took part in a conference for black writers at Fisk University and was impressed with young black poets' views, she has increasingly been an activist, teaching teenage black writers in Chicago and addressing her work especially to black audiences. Instead of continuing to publish with a mainstream New York publishing house, she switched her work to Broadside, a small literary press in De-

troit founded by black poet Dudley Randall. Her memoir *Report from Part One* (1972) discusses her altered outlook. In 1985 she was named Consultant in Poetry to the Library of Congress. Her goals in life, she has declared, are "to be clean of heart, clear of mind, and claiming of what is right and just."

## Elizabeth Barrett Browning

Elizabeth Barrett (1806–1861) was born in a large country house outside Durham, England. The eldest of twelve children, she was raised in a close, affectionate family ruled by her possessive father. Ill health kept her at home as an adult, but she nonetheless achieved literary fame and corresponded with many famous writers. The day after she met one correspondent, Robert Browning, in 1845, he sent her a declaration of love, which she insisted he withdraw if he ever wanted to visit again. Gradually, however, she fell in love with her devoted visitor, but the affair was conducted in secret, since her father had forbidden his children to marry. In 1846 she and Browning eloped to Italy where the couple lived happily until her death in 1861. When William Wordsworth died in 1850, Mrs. Browning was considered for the office of poet laureate (which eventually went to Tennyson). She was the most highly regarded woman poet of the nineteenth century, and her work was immensely popular with both critics and general readers.

## Robert Browning

Robert Browning (1812–1889), born in a suburb of London, was educated mainly in his father's six-thousand-volume library. With *Pauline* (1833), he began to print his poetry. After the death of his wife Elizabeth Barrett Browning, with whom he had lived in Italy, he returned to England to become (Henry James wrote) an "accomplished, saturated, sane, sound man of the London world." There, as he neared sixty, he enjoyed late but loud applause and the adulation of the Browning Society: faithful readers whose local groups met over their teacups to explicate him. Readers have most greatly favored Browning's story-poems in a form he perfected, the dramatic monologue—such as "My Last Duchess" and "Soliloquy of the Spanish Cloister"—in which he brings to life persons from the past (some of them famous), has them speak their inmost thoughts and reveal their characters. His masterpiece, *The Ring and the Book* (1868 –69), is a long narrative poem in twelve monologues, based on a seventeenth-century Roman murder trial. Browning also wrote several plays, among them *A Blot in the 'Scutcheon* (1842). Through the praise and emulation of his later admirers Ezra Pound and T. S. Eliot, Browning has profoundly affected modern poetry. A formal experimenter, he speaks to us in energetic, punchy words—and like many later poets he introduces learning into his poems without apology. More important, Browning is among the great yea-sayers in English poetry: an affirmer and celebrant of life.

### Robert Burns

Robert Burns (1759–1796), the preeminent poet of Scotland, was born in a two-room farm cottage in Alloway, a hamlet on the River Doon, the son of a farmer who worked himself to death. For most of his days Burns too struggled to farm poor soil. Though his schooling lasted only three years, he eagerly read Shakespeare and Pope as a boy and let poetry pour from his own pen. Only in 1786, when he felt he needed money to emigrate to Jamaica, did he publish his *Poems, Chiefly in the Scottish Dialect*, depicting Scottish rural life with warm humor, tender compassion, and rugged exuberance. The book scored an immediate hit and Burns remained in Scotland for the rest of his days. After Edin-

burgh's stylish society, which had lionized him for a time, let him drop, he returned to his plough, married Jean Armour (who earlier had borne him two sets of twins), and continued to farm until 1791, when he retired to the easier life of a tax official. But worn from toil, hardship, and poverty, Burns died at thirty-seven. Among his legacies are songs, such as "Flow Gently, Sweet Afton," "Comin' Through the Rye," and a song still heard in this country each New Year's eve, "Auld Lang Syne." Like Hugh MacDiarmid, Burns wrote poetry in both standard English and Scots dialect—in the latter whenever, as in "The Jolly Beggars" and "Address to the Unco Guid," he expressed defiantly unconventional views.

### Thomas Campion

Thomas Campion (1567–1620), Elizabethan courtier, physician, musician, and poet, was the author of several books of solo songs with lute accompaniment, much admired for their masterly unity of words and music. In 1602 Campion wrote a tract, *Observations in the Art of English Poesy*, in which he argued in favor of writing quantitative verse in English, after the example of the ancient Greek and Latin poets. "Rose-cheeked Laura" was apparently written to illustrate his theories. In the same tract, he opposed the writing of any more poetry in rime and traditional English meters—in which, however, he excelled.

### Samuel Taylor Coleridge

Samuel Taylor Coleridge (1772–1834) was born in Devonshire, England, a clergyman's thirteenth child. With poet Robert Southey, a fellow student at Cambridge University, he once planned to go to the United States and found a utopian community, but the scheme was never fulfilled. A brilliant talker and sometime professional lecturer, Coleridge wrote ably on philosophy and religion as well as on literature. As a young man, he collaborated with William Wordsworth on the influential *Lyrical Ballads* (1798), a milestone of English Romantic poetry. Among Coleridge's best-known poems are "The Rime of the Ancient Mariner," "Cristabel," and "Kubla Khan"—ornate poems of the exotic and supernatural. His *Biographia Literaria* (1817) combines literary criticism with autobiography, and sets forth views of poetry and the imagination (see page 1028) heavily indebted to German idealist philosophy. Long troubled by an addiction to opium, Coleridge went to London in 1816 to live in the household of Dr. James Gilman, under whose care he passed the rest of his days.

## Wendy Cope

Wendy Cope was born in Kent, England in 1945. Her father, who was nearly sixty when she was born, was a poetry enthusiast of Victorian sensibilities, who often recited Tennyson and Fitzgerald's *Rubaiyat* to the family. After leaving school, she became a primary school music teacher. Cope claims she "forgot about poetry for more than ten years." Her father's death in 1971, however, triggered a depression that eventually led her to seek psychological help. As she regained her self-esteem, Cope began reading poetry again and soon started writing. She first gained notice for her brilliant parodies of famous poems (which include a retelling of T. S. Eliot's *The Waste Land* in five limericks), but gradually her bittersweet and incisive love poems have become equally prized. Her two collections, *Making Cocoa for Kingsley Amis* (1986) and *Serious Concerns* (1992), have become bestsellers in England.

## Frances Cornford

Frances Darwin Cornford (1886–1960) was born and died in Cambridge, England. The grandaughter of Charles Darwin, Cornford grew up in a rich milieu of artists and intellectuals. In 1908, she married a classical scholar, Francis Cornford. Their son John, a talented young poet, was killed in the Spanish Civil War. Frances Cornford's poetry is easy to undervalue. Modest, concise, and deceptively simple, it discloses its full wealth of meaning only after careful rereading. Recent feminist critics, in particular, have revealed how often Cornford's quiet elegiac poems reflect pain and isolation.

## E. E. Cummings

E[dward] E[stlin] Cummings (1894 – 1962) was born in Cambridge, Massachusetts, the son of a minister. As a young man at Harvard, he studied Greek and Latin. In World War I, while serving as an ambulance driver, he was mistakenly arrested and confined to a French prison—an experience that gave rise to a novel filled with vivid portraits of his fellow prisoners, *The Enormous Room* (1922). Off and on throughout the 1920s, Cummings lived in Paris. In *Eimi* (1933) he scathingly and satirically reported on a trip to the Soviet Union. Although many of his lyric poems revel in typographical experiment, in theme and sentiment they are often more conventional than they appear. Besides poetry Cummings wrote essays, plays including *Him* (1927) and *Santa Claus* (1946), and the ballet *Tom* (1935), and produced substantial work as a painter and a graphic artist. Throughout his career, he upheld simple themes: love is good, pomp is silly, one individual is worth a thousand faceless societies.

## J. V. Cunningham

J[ames] V[incent] Cunningham (1911–1985) was born in Maryland, but spent his early life in Montana. A Shakespeare scholar with a Stanford Ph.D., Cunningham taught English at Brandeis for many years (1953–80) and for eight years served as chairman of the department. A reader of Latin and Greek, he became the modern master of the terse, pithy English verse epigram in the classical manner. All his poems have a similar brevity, firm control, and a cold, hardboiled manner. "Poetry is what looks like poetry, what sounds like poetry," he stated. "It is metrical composition." His relatively slim *Collected Poems and Epigrams* (1971) gathers most of his work in verse; his *Collected Essays* (1976), most of his work in prose, including an earlier study, *Woe and Wonder: The Emotional Effect of Shakespearean Tragedy*. In a late critical work, *Dickinson: Lyric and Legend* (1980), Cunningham took a withering look at the bard of Amherst.

## Emily Dickinson

Emily Dickinson (1830–1886) passed nearly all her life in her family home in Amherst, Massachusetts. Her father was a prominent lawyer and for a time a United States congressman. One trip to Washington, D.C. and a short, unhappy period as a college student at New England Female Seminary (later Mount Holyoke) were the extent of her distant travels, and as the years passed Dickinson withdrew from town activities and retired into deeper seclusion. Though she wrote more than a thousand poems, she published only seven. The extent of her work was known only after her death, when her manuscripts were discovered in a trunk in the homestead attic, stitched into little booklets and peppered with an idiosyncratic system of punctuation. From 1890 until midcentury, nine posthumous collections of her poems were assembled by friends and relatives, some of whom rewrote her work to make it more conventional. Thomas H. Johnson's three-volume edition of the *Poems* (1955) established a better text. In relatively few and simple forms clearly indebted to the hymns she heard in church, Dickinson succeeded in being a true visionary and a poet of colossal originality.

## John Donne

John Donne (1572–1631), English poet and divine, wrote his subtle, worldly love lyrics as a young man in the court of Queen Elizabeth I. At the time, he came to be known in London as (wrote his contemporary, Richard Baker) "a great visitor of ladies, a great frequenter of plays, a great writer of conceited verses." The poems of his *Songs and Sonnets* were first circulated in manuscript, for in his lifetime Donne printed little. When in 1601 he married without the consent of his bride's father, he was dismissed from his secretarial post at court. For several years he endured poverty. His longer poems, *The First Anniversary* and *The Second Anniversary* (1611, 1612), suffused with gloom, see the order of the universe shaken by science and doubt. In 1615 Donne—apparently with some reluctance, for he had been raised a Catholic —became a priest of the Anglican church. From 1621 until he died he was dean of St. Paul's Cathedral in London, where he preached sermons known for their eloquence. His "Holy Sonnets" date from later life. Almost forgotten for two centuries, Donne's work has had much influence in our time. H. J. C. Grierson brought out a great scholarly edition of it in 1912; shortly thereafter it was championed by T. S. Eliot.

## T. S. Eliot

T[homas] S[tearns] Eliot (1888–1965) was born of a New England family who had moved to St. Louis. After study at Harvard, Eliot emigrated to London, became a bank clerk and later an influential editor for the publishing house of Faber. In 1927 he became a British citizen and joined the Church of England. During the fire bombings of London in World War II, he served as an air raid warden. Although Eliot strove to keep his private life private, a recent biographer, Peter Ackroyd in *T. S. Eliot* (1984), throws light upon his troubled early marriage.

Early poems such as "The Love Song of J. Alfred Prufrock" (1917) and *The Waste Land* (1922), an allusive and seemingly disconnected complaint about the sterility of contemporary city life, enormously influenced young poets. Eliot was mainly responsible for bringing French Symbolism into English poetry, and as a critic he helped revive interest in John Donne and other Metaphysical poets. In an early essay, "Tradition and the Individual Talent" (1919), he finds a necessary continuity in Western civilization. *Four Quartets*, completed in 1943, was Eliot's last major work of poetry: an attempt to structure a long thematic poem like a work of music. In later years he devoted himself to writing verse plays for the London stage; the best received was *The Cocktail Party* (1950), in which Alec Guinness played a psychiatrist. In 1948 Eliot received the Nobel Prize for Literature.

## Robert Frost

Robert Frost (1874–1963), though born in San Francisco, came to be popularly known as a spokesman of rural New England. In periods of farming, teaching school, and raising chickens and writing for poultry journals, Frost struggled until his late thirties to support his family and to publish his poems, with little success. Moving to England to write and farm in 1912–15, he had his first book published in London: *A Boy's Will* (1913). Returning to America, he settled in New Hampshire, later teaching for many years (in a casual way) at Amherst College in Massachusetts. Audiences responded warmly to the poet's public readings; he was awarded four Pulitzer prizes. In late years the white-haired Frost became a sort of elder statesman and poet laureate of the John F. Kennedy administration: invited to read a poem at President Kennedy's inauguration, dispatched to Russia as a cultural emissary. Frost is sometimes admired for putting colloquial Yankee speech into poetry

—and he did, but more essentially he mastered the art of laying conversational American speech along a metrical line. In a three-volume biography (1966–76), Lawrance Thompson made Frost out to be an overweening egotist who tormented his family, and we are only now coming around again to seeing him as more than that.

## Thomas Gray

Thomas Gray (1716–1771), author of the most often quoted poem in English, was born in London into a middle-class home (his father was a scrivener, his mother kept a hat shop). He was the only one of twelve children to survive infancy. He attended Eton and later Cambridge University, where he studied for four years but did not take a degree. After a tour of Europe with his schoolmate Horace Walpole (the first Gothic novelist) and a short sojourn with his mother in the village of Stoke Poges, Gray returned to Cambridge to spend the rest of his life in seclusion as a sort of perpetual graduate student. He stayed around the university so long and became so widely learned in architecture, heraldry, botany, Greek, Old Norse, and other matters that in 1768, at fifty-two, he was appointed Regius Professor of History. So retiring was Gray that he first published his "Elegy in a Country Churchyard" anonymously—and only when friends browbeat him into printing it. He seems to have suffered from a constitutional lack of energy. He dreaded being known, and when the post of poet laureate was offered him, he rejected it. A dilettante, Gray considered himself an amateur in whatever he did. Poetry was only one of his interests, but in his "Elegy" and his Pindaric odes "The Bard" and "The Progress of Poesy," he spurred English poetry to break away from neoclassicism and move toward plainer speech, more various forms, infatuation with the colorful, primitive Old English past, and love of nature and countryside. Gray is buried in Stoke Poges, in the churchyard for which we remember him.

## H. D. (Hilda Doolittle)

Hilda Doolittle (1886–1961), daughter of a Moravian mother and a professor of mathematics and astronomy, spent her first eight years in Bethlehem, Pennsylvania. At Bryn Mawr, she failed English and suffered a nervous collapse. By 1911, she had become a confirmed expatriate, living in London. At one time she was engaged to Ezra Pound, who submitted her early poems to Harriet Monroe's magazine *Poetry* and signed them "H. D. Imagiste." In 1913, she married poet and translator Richard Aldington, and in 1916 published *Sea Change*, her first book of poems. During World War I, H. D. went through a marital breakup and a number of misfortunes recalled in her novel *Palimpsest* (1926). Alone and in poor health, she was rescued by Winifred Ellerman, a writer signing herself Bryher, who adopted the poet's daughter by Cecil Gray and befriended H. D. for life. During 1933 and 1934, H. D. was a patient of Sigmund Freud, an experience she recalls in *Tribute to Freud* (1956). After World War II, the poet moved to Switzerland. Her last works of poetry were epic-long: *Trilogy* (1944–46) and the dramatic monologue *Helen in Egypt* (1961). Her earlier poems are available in *Collected Poems 1912–1944* (1983), edited by Louis L. Martz. In 1960, back in the United States for the last time, H. D. was given the American Academy of Arts and Letters Award of Merit for Poetry.

## Thomas Hardy

Thomas Hardy (1840–1928) was both a major Victorian novelist and a great poet of the twentieth century. After his novel *Jude the Obscure* (1896) was trounced by critics who objected to its dismal morbidity, Hardy, who by then had made a modest fortune from his fiction, switched exclusively to his first love, po-etry. Hardy was born in the English county of Dorsetshire ("Wessex" in his fiction and poetry), and as a young man worked as an architect. Determined to be a novelist, he first won success with *Far from the Madding Crowd* (1874), followed by *The Return of the Native* (1878), *The Mayor of Casterbridge* (1886), and his masterpiece *Tess of the D'Urbervilles* (1891). After the death of his first wife Emma, with whom he appears to have had a rather cold and troubled relationship, Hardy was inspired to write a great spate of love poems in her memory. In old age he wrote a two-volume autobiography and charged his second wife, Florence, to publish it after his death under her own name. In both fiction and poetry, Hardy's view of the universe is somber: God appears to have forgotten us, and happiness usually arrives too late. *The Dynasts* (1903–08), a long epic poem, makes amused gods sneer down on the Napoleonic wars. Many modern poets have credited Hardy with teaching them a good deal, probably about irony and the use of spoken language, among them W. H. Auden, Philip Larkin, Dylan Thomas, and W. D. Snodgrass.

## Robert Hayden

Robert Hayden (1913–1980) was born in Detroit, Michigan. He attended Detroit City College (now called Wayne State University) and the University of Michigan where he studied with W. H. Auden. In 1946, he began teaching at Fisk University in pre-Civil Rights era Nashville, where Hayden, an African-American, experienced racial segregation for the first time. Although he lived in Nashville until 1968, he eventually sent his wife and daughter to New York where schools were integrated. In 1941, Hayden became a convert to the Baha'i faith, a universalist religion that emphasizes charity, tolerance, and equality; his poetry reflects the compassionate moral courage of that creed. Hayden edited the influential 1967 anthology, *Kaleidoscope:*

Poems by American Negro Poets. In 1976, he was appointed the Consultant in Poetry at the Library of Congress, the first African-American to hold that influential office.

## Seamus Heaney

Seamus Heaney, the best-known living Irish poet, was born on a farm in County Derry, Northern Ireland, in 1939. He taught at Queens University, Belfast, before leaving Northern Ireland in 1972 to make his home in Dublin. A guest lecturer at the University of California in Berkeley during the 1971–1972 academic year, he now divides his time between Dublin and America, where he teaches at Harvard. Among his recent books of verse are *Station Island* (1985) and *The Haw Lantern* (1987). Rich with images of love and loss, Heaney's poetry draws inventively on the history of Ireland and the Irish from ancient times to the violent present.

## George Herbert

George Herbert (1593–1633), English devotional poet, the son of an aristocratic family, began writing poems as an undergraduate at Cambridge University. After dabbling for a time in worldly affairs, he entered the priesthood of the Church of England, to live out his days in a country parish. Herbert's poems have many references to music; according to his contemporary John Aubrey, he "had a very good hand on the lute, and set [to music] his own lyrics and sacred poems." Herbert did not publish his poems in his lifetime, but after his death friends collected them in *The Temple* (1633). The book is said to have stimulated Henry Vaughan to follow in Herbert's footsteps as a poet. Herbert makes the religious experience personal, definite, and familiar. For his use of startling "metaphysical" figures of speech, he has been compared with John Donne; but a rare sweetness and plain-spokenness make him unique among poets in English.

## Robert Herrick

Robert Herrick (1591–1674), after serving as a goldsmith's apprentice, entered Cambridge University at twenty-two, then a late age. For nine years he seems to have lived in London, consorting with a group of poets and wits whose chief was Ben Jonson. In 1629 he became parish priest in Dean Prior, in rural Devonshire, where he lived out his days, sometimes chafing about the boorishness of his parishioners. When in 1647 the Puritans temporarily ousted him from his pulpit, Herrick returned to London. There at fifty-six he brought out his first book, *Noble Numbers* (1647), pious poems; then reprinted them together with five times as many sportive, secular poems in *Hesperides* (1648). Unluckily, the books came too late to cause a stir, Herrick's early fame as a poet having withered and the vogue for chiseled classical lyrics having gone by. Like his master Jonson, Herrick writes songlike poems inspired by Greek and Latin pastoral (or shepherd-and-shepherdess) poetry. We go to him not for profound ideas, but for fresh, tough speech and resonant music. Herrick, who remained a bachelor clergyman, probably imagined the mistresses he praised. He declared in *Hesperides*, "To his book's end this last line he'd have placed: / Jocund his Muse was, but his life was chaste."

## Gerard Manley Hopkins

Gerard Manley Hopkins (1844–1889), born in Essex, England, was, like Emily Dickinson, a major poet not known until our century. At twenty, a student at Oxford, he was converted to Roman Catholicism and received into that church by Cardinal Newman. Ordained a Jesuit, Hopkins at first served as parish priest and teacher in working-class sections of large cities (London, Glasgow, Liverpool, Manchester), where poverty and suffering distressed him. But his sermons were reportedly so strange (in one, he likened the church to a cow we milk and whose moo we follow) that his superiors removed him from public view, making him Professor of Greek at University College, Dublin. He died of typhoid fever at forty-four. Nearly thirty years after Hopkins's death, his friend Robert Bridges published his *Poems* (1918), having thought them too demanding for earlier readers. That much of Hopkins's work sounds odd to us may be due to the poet's admiration for Old English, with its gutsy monosyllables, and for Welsh poetry, rich in patterns of sound. Hopkins developed his own theory of versification: "sprung rhythm"—in brief, a kind of accentual verse. Though on entering the priesthood he had renounced poetry, he welcomed the suggestion of a superior that he contribute to a Jesuit magazine a poem on the drowning of five Franciscan nuns. The result, "The Wreck of the *Deutschland*," received a rejection slip. This challenging poem has been called "the dragon guarding the door to Hopkins's poetry," but most readers have gone in by the back door of his more quickly accessible nature poems. In these, the sensuous world bursts forth in irrepressible testimony to its Maker's glory.

## A. E. Housman

A. E. Housman (1859–1936), English poet and professor of Latin, was born in a village in rural Shropshire, England. Although as a student at Oxford he distinguished himself as a promising scholar of the classics, he failed his exams, apparently because of some inner crisis precipitated by his love for a fellow male student. Determined to overcome this setback, Housman, while working as a clerk in the British Patent Office, at night wrote scholarly articles. Within ten

years these academic writings, bristling with cold sarcasms and scathing putdowns of rival scholars, had won him such high repute that he was invited to be Professor of Latin at the University of London. Later he stepped up to Cambridge University, to spend the rest of his days living a retiring academic life befitting his shy temperament. Though Housman published only two slim collections of poems—the instantly and enormously popular *A Shropshire Lad* (1898) and the conclusively titled *Last Poems* (1922)—his place as a minor master of the English lyric seems unshakable. Like many Latin poets he admired, he insists in well-turned lines that life is short and comes to a bad end.

## Langston Hughes

Langston Hughes (1902–1967), who dropped his first name, James, was born in Joplin, Missouri. As a high school senior in Cleveland, he wrote a poem still often reprinted, "The Negro Speaks of Rivers." When a young man, Hughes worked as a merchant seaman, visited Africa, and lived for a time in Rome and Paris. While working as a busboy at a Washington, D.C., hotel, he showed his poems to hotel guest Vachel Lindsay, a poet then celebrated, and Lindsay urged them on a publisher. *The Weary Blues* (1926) earned him a considerable reputation. Hughes's work in poetry won him a scholarship to Lincoln University, from which he was graduated in 1929. He became a major figure in the Harlem Renaissance of the 1920s and early 1930s —a period when that district of New York City became a lively center for black writers, artists, and musicians. A versatile writer and teacher, Hughes, one of the first practicing poets to teach poetry writing in elementary schools, was also among the few poets to earn a living by giving readings and lecturing. Among his other works are novels, stories, plays, song lyrics, children's books, memoirs, translations, and essays reporting conversations with a Harlem dweller called Simple, a streetwise philosopher. A *Langston Hughes Reader* (1958) gives some idea of his richness and variety.

## Randall Jarrell

Randall Jarrell (1914–1965) was born in Nashville, Tennessee, and served as a private in the army air force in World War II, an experience that gave rise to several of his best early poems. Much of his life was spent in academe. At Vanderbilt, a psychology major, he studied literature with poet-critic John Crowe Ransom, who changed the direction of Jarrell's career. When Ransom moved to Kenyon College, Jarrell followed as an English instructor. At Kenyon, he formed another lifelong friendship: with a student who was to become a distinguished poet, Robert Lowell. Later Jarrell taught at the University of Texas, Sarah Lawrence, Princeton, Illinois, and for many years (1947–65) at the Woman's College of the University of North Carolina (now the U.N.C., Greensboro). His one novel, *Pictures from an Institution* (1954), is a satire set on a campus. As poetry editor for *The Nation* in the mid-1940s, Jarrell drew attention for his witty, astute, outspoken reviews of poetry. *Poetry and the Age* (1953) includes especially brilliant essays on Robert Frost and Wallace Stevens. Jarrell, who loved the German language, translated Goethe's *Faust* (Part I) and some of the Grimm fairy tales. In later years he wrote four books for children (with beautiful drawings by Maurice Sendak) including *The Bat Poet* (1964) and the posthumous *Fly by Night* (1976).

## Robinson Jeffers

John Robinson Jeffers (1887–1962) was born in Pittsburgh, but had part of his early education in European boarding schools. In 1903, Jeffers's family moved to Southern California where Jeffers entered Occidental College. Graduating at 19, Jeffers studied medicine, forestry, and literature on a graduate level before devoting his life to poetry. In 1906, he met Una Kuster, who was married to an attorney. Their tempestuous love affair eventually led—in 1913—to their marriage. In 1914 the couple visited Carmel, California and Jeffers knew that it was his "inevitable place"—he would spend his remaining fifty-eight years there. With the help of a local stonemason, Jeffers built his own house on the edge of the Pacific, quarrying stone from the beach. Jeffers's poetry reflects the closeness to nature that made up his daily life. His philosophy of "inhumanism" refused to put mankind above the rest of nature; he demanded that humanity see itself as part of the vast interdependent reality of nature—a message that has made his poetry esteemed by environmentalists. Jeffers's Tor House in Carmel is now a national historic monument.

## Ben Jonson

Ben Jonson (1573?–1637), posthumous son of a Scottish minister, was a native Londoner. As a boy he received a firm grounding in Latin and Greek at Westminster School, but instead of enrolling in a university, took up bricklaying, then served as a soldier in Flanders. Home from the wars, he married and became an actor and playwright in London. Although a coolly rational classicist by persuasion, Jonson seems to have been an outspoken hothead, given to quarrels and brawls. In 1598 he killed a fellow actor in a duel and escaped the gallows only by claiming an ancient law that forbade hanging anyone who could read. From about 1606, Jonson frequented the Mermaid Tavern in London's Fleet Street, a favorite hangout of writers and actors. There, on the first Friday of each month, he presided over famed literary discussions; according to one report, his friend Shakespeare would take part at times and match wits with him. Later changing pubs (to the Devil and St. Dunstan), Jonson and his circle became known as the "Tribe of Ben"; Thomas Carew and Robert Herrick were younger members. Later Jonson became the leading writer of masks, elaborate plays with music and dancing produced at court. As a poet Jonson, in his precise Latinate lyrics, odes, and epigrams, helped get rid of worn-out Petrarchan conventions (those Shakespeare mocks in "My mistress' eyes are nothing like the sun"). As a playwright, he excelled; his comedies, especially *Volpone, or The Fox* (1606) and *The Alchemist* (1610), are among the crown jewels of the English stage.

## John Keats

John Keats (1795–1821), son of a London stable keeper, studied to become a physician and served as a surgeon's apprentice before deciding on poetry as a career. In 1817 he published his first book, *Poems,* including "On First Looking into Chapman's Homer." Despite critics' hostility to his narrative poem *Endymion* (1818), Keats persisted. In 1818 he fell in love with sixteen-year-old Fanny Brawne, but, stricken with tuberculosis, postponed plans for marriage. In 1820, shortly after publication of his third and last book, Keats went to Italy in hopes of regaining his health, but his poetry soon slowed to a stop. In the following year, at twenty-five, he died in Rome and was buried there beneath the epitaph he wrote for himself: "Here lies one whose name was writ in water." His name, however, has continued to endure. No English poet wrote poems richer in sensuous imagery (as in his great odes, among them "Ode on Melancholy" and "To Autumn"), nor quite so beautifully reimagined the Middle Ages (in poems such as "La Belle Dame sans Merci" and "The Eve of St. Agnes"). He

wrote several of the finest sonnets in the language, an unfinished epic of great interest, *Hyperion,* hilarious light verse, and scores of superb letters.

## Philip Larkin

Philip Larkin (1922–1985), born in Coventry, England, has been called the most influential British poet since World War II. After studies at Oxford, he drifted into being a librarian, and for many years was head librarian for the University of Hull. Early in his career Larkin wrote two novels, *Jill* (1946) and *A Girl in Winter* (1947). He also reviewed jazz recordings for a London newspaper. A self-declared foe of modernism in music, art, and literature, he published only four slim volumes of poems, traditional in form. The earliest collection was heavily indebted to Yeats: *The North Ship* (1945, reissued in 1966 with a preface making fun of it). With *The Less Deceived* (1955), Larkin hit his characteristic stride, writing most of the poems in the voice of a tough-minded, disillusioned, self-deprecating man facing a dreary urban landscape of quiet frustration. This voice drew an immediate response from readers in postwar England.

## D. H. Lawrence

David Herbert Lawrence (1885–1930) was born in Nottinghamshire, England, child of a coalminer and a schoolteacher who hated her husband's toil and vowed that her son should escape it. He took up fiction writing, attaining early success. During World War I, Lawrence and his wife were unjustly suspected of treason (he because of his pacifism, she because of her aristocratic German birth). After the armistice they left England and, seeking a climate healthier for Lawrence, who suffered from tuberculosis, wandered in Italy, France, Australia, Mexico, and the American Southwest. Lawrence is an impassioned spokesman for our unconscious, instinctive natures, which we moderns (he argues) have neglected in favor of our overweening intellects. In *Lady Chatterley's Lover* (1928), he strove to restore explicit sexuality to English fiction. The book, which today seems tame and repetitious, was long banned in Britain and the United States. Deeper Lawrence novels include *Sons and Lovers* (1913), a veiled account of his breaking away from his fiercely possessive mother; *The Rainbow* (1915); *Women in Love* (1921); and *The Plumed Serpent* (1926), about a revival of pagan religion in Mexico. Besides fiction, Lawrence left a rich legacy of poetry, essays, criticism (*Studies in Classic American Literature*, 1923, is especially shrewd and funny), and travel writing. Lawrence exerted deep influence on others, both by the message in his work and by his personal magnetism.

## Denise Levertov

Denise Levertov was born in 1923 in Essex, England, daughter of a Welsh mother and a Russian Jewish-born priest of the Anglican church. She was educated at home, reading in her father's library. She served as a nurse in World War II. In 1947 she married an American novelist, Mitchell Goodman, and in the following year came to the United States. Her first book, published in England, had observed traditional poetic conventions (including rime and meter), but in America she discovered the work of William Carlos Williams and other open-form poets, and began to write in a different, freer mode. With Robert Creeley and others of the Black Mountain group, she has exerted much influence among younger poets. Her critical essays have been collected in *The Poet in the World* (1973) and *Light up the Cave* (1981). Levertov has been a tireless political activist, prominent in peace movements of the 1960s, 1970s, and 1980s. She now makes her home in Somerville, Massachusetts, and recently has been teaching poetry writing at Stanford on one coast and at Brandeis on the other.

## Robert Lowell

Robert Lowell (1917–1977), born in Boston, came from a famous New England family that included three distinguished poets: James Russell, Maria, and Amy. He attended Harvard, then on the advice of his psychiatrist transferred to Kenyon, where he studied with poet-critics John Crowe Ransom and Randall Jarrell. During World War II he served time in a federal prison for resisting the draft. Lowell's early poems in *Lord Weary's Castle* (1946) were violent in imagery and tightly traditional in form. With the deliberately looser *Life Studies* (1959), he showed that he had learned from William Carlos Williams and the Beat poets, and his work became more open in form, more colloquial in speech, and more direct in its use of his own experience. Some of these poems were labeled "confessional poetry." As "Skunk Hour" tells us, Lowell's mind was sometimes "not right"; he suffered from recurrent manic depression that required him to spend periods in a hospital. Besides poetry, he wrote plays based on stories by Hawthorne and Melville: *The Old Glory* (1964, enlarged edition 1968) —as well as English versions of the *Phaedra* of Racine (1961) and the *Prometheus Bound* of Aeschylus (1969). Lowell was also a remarkable critic of poetry.

## Edna St. Vincent Millay

Edna St. Vincent Millay (1892–1950), born in Rockland, Maine, was the eldest of three daughters. When she was twelve, her father deserted the family. At twenty, she had already published "Renascence," one of her most celebrated poems. In 1917, she was graduated from Vassar College and settled in Greenwich Village, where she became as famous for her vivacious personality, her bohemian life-style, her acting and playwriting, and her feminism, as for her verse. Even as she wrote *The Harp Weaver*, a serious volume of verse that won her a Pulitzer Prize in 1923, Millay did hack writing to pay her bills. Among other work for which she is known are verse dramas such as *Aria da Capo* (1920) and the sonnet cycle *Fatal Interview* (1931). In 1923, she married Eugen Jan Boissevain, Dutch businessman and widower of feminist Inez Milholland. In 1927, Millay's political activism expressed itself in poems about Sacco and Vanzetti, two anarchists accused of murder, and involved her in an unsuccessful campaign to prevent their execution. Though she kept writing poetry well into the 1940s and received several honorary degrees, her reputation waned. Darkened by a nervous breakdown in 1944 and the poet's growing sense that the public had deserted her, Millay's life ended with a heart attack.

## John Milton

John Milton (1608–1674), author of *Paradise Lost*, the greatest English epic, was born in London, the son of a scrivener who composed music. His mother early began schooling him to be a minister. He studied zealously. As he later recalled: "From my twelfth year I scarcely ever went to bed before midnight, which was the first cause of injury to my eyes." After he received his B.A. from Cambridge University in 1629, his father supported him through eight years of further study. "Lycidas" (1638), a poem of this period, shows his deepening seriousness about religion and his growing resentment of corruptions in the church, which were to lead him to the Puritan cause. Milton wrote much prose in the service of causes. In *Areopagitica* (1644), he argues for freedom of the press and opposes the strict censorship that had been imposed by Parliament. His unhappy marriage to Mary Powell led him to write tracts in favor of divorce. When Oliver Cromwell and the Puritans ousted King Charles and declared England a commonwealth, Milton's writings were remembered, and earned him a post as Cromwell's foreign secretary. His eyesight strained by years of hard study, Milton went blind and had to dictate his correspondence (in Latin) to clerks, one of whom was fellow poet Andrew Marvell. With the Restoration of Charles II in 1660, Milton's world came crashing down. In retirement, at last he turned to a project he had planned as a young man: his major heroic poem, *Paradise Lost* (1667), about Satan's rebellion and the Fall of Adam and Eve. This epic was followed by *Paradise Regained* (1671) and a verse drama modeled on a Greek tragedy, *Samson Agonistes* (1671).

## Marianne Moore

Marianne Moore (1887–1972), whose poems earned praise from fellow poets as dissimilar as William Carlos Williams and T. S. Eliot, was born in Kirkwood, Missouri, a suburb of St. Louis. Her father abandoned the family in 1894, and Moore moved to Pennsylvania. In 1909, she was graduated from Bryn Mawr, where a classmate was the poet H. D. For a time, Moore taught business courses at the U.S. Indian School in Carlisle, Pennsylvania, where the athlete Jim Thorpe was among her students. By 1915, her poems—witty, satirical, intellectual, disruptive, and innovative—had begun to appear in *Poetry* magazine. Until her mother died in 1947, Moore, a dutiful daughter, lived with her in Brooklyn, supporting herself by a series of conventional jobs. From 1925 to 1929 she edited *The Dial*, a literary magazine in whose pages she published many of the best poets of her day. Besides poems, Moore wrote essays, reviews, and translations including *The Fables of La Fontaine* (1945). For her *Collected Poems* (1951), she won a Pulitzer Prize, the Bollingen Prize, and a National Book Award; her *Complete Poems* appeared in 1967. Late in life, Moore became a media figure for her fondness for the Brooklyn

Dodgers and her penchant for three-cornered hats. She stayed in Brooklyn, writing and rewriting, through an active and vigorous old age.

## Howard Moss

Howard Moss (1922–1987) was born in New York City and, except for his undergraduate years in Michigan and Wisconsin, he lived there all his life. Moss was, as the critic J. D. McClatchy has observed, the quintessential New York poet—"sophisticated, skeptical, witty." In 1948, he joined the staff of *The New Yorker* and, two years later, became its first poetry editor, a position he held until his death nearly four decades later. Moss's influence as an editor has often obscured his considerable accomplishments as a poet, but his best work has a charm, musicality, and compassion that is distinctive and original.

## Lorine Niedecker

Lorine Niedecker (1903–1970) spent nearly all her life on Blackhawk Island near Fort Atkinson, Wisconsin, where her father worked as a carp fisherman. After two years at Beloit College, she returned home to care for her ailing mother. Following a brief marriage in 1928, Niedecker held jobs as proofreader, librarian's helper, and cleaning worker in a hospital. After her marriage in 1963 she lived in Milwaukee, but on her husband's retirement the couple moved into a house they had built by the Rock River, and the poet returned to her native grounds. Although she lived an outwardly quiet life remote from publishing centers, Niedecker read widely and maintained a vigorous life of the mind. In the early 1930s she struck up a correspondence with poet and teacher Louis Zukofsky, who encouraged her poetry. In the 1950s poet Cid Corman printed her work in his avant garde little magazine *Origin*. During her lifetime she

published sparingly, but *From This Condensery: The Complete Writing of Lorine Niedecker* (1985) contains a large body of poems, as well as critical essays, experimental prose, and five radio plays. Her life and work are the subject of Kristine Thatcher's play *Niedecker*, given an off-Broadway production in 1989.

## John Frederick Nims

John Frederick Nims, born in 1913 in Muskegon, Michigan, has had a distinguished career as poet and translator, teacher and editor. He has taught at Florida, Illinois (Urbana and Chicago), Missouri, Notre Dame, Toronto, and other universities, and has held visiting professorships at Harvard and in Florence, Milan, and Madrid. The poems in his first book *The Iron Pastoral* (1947) deal wittily with jukeboxes, penny arcades, poolrooms, and other features of the contemporary scene. In *Of Flesh and Bone* (1967) Nims shows his mastery of the epigram. His *Selected Poems* appeared in 1982. A translator of poetry from languages as varied as classical Greek, Catalan, and Galacian, Nims has splendidly rendered into English *The Poems of St. John of the Cross* (1959, revised edition 1968). For several years (1978–85) he was editor of *Poetry* magazine. He is the author of an introduction to poetry, *Western Wind*, and editor of *The Harper Anthology of Poetry* (1981).

## Sharon Olds

Sharon Olds was born in San Francisco in 1942 and attended Stanford University. After graduation in 1964, she came East and eventually took a Ph.D. from Columbia University in 1972. Her first collection of poems, *Satan Says* (1980), was well received, but her second volume, *The Dead and the Living* (1984), scored a major critical success by winning both the Lamont prize and National Book Critics Circle. Olds's work often graphically depicts the passions, joys, and pain of family life. She currently teaches at New York University.

## Wilfred Owen

Wilfred Owen (1893–1918) was, like A. E. Housman, a native of Shropshire, England. He attended London University and for a time served as lay assistant to a minister, helping the sick and poor. In 1916, during World War I, he enlisted in the British army, became a company commander, and in less than two years wrote all his famous antiwar poems of life in the trenches. The army seems suddenly to have changed Owen from a competent minor poet with little to say into a powerful voice of pacifism. At age twenty-five, while trying to get his men across a canal under enemy fire on the French front, he was killed in action only a week before the war ended. Though Owen published only four poems, after his death a collection of his work was edited by another front-line war poet, Siegfried Sassoon (1920). Owen is preeminent among English poets who wrote of that conflict, and the reputation of his work has continued to grow.

## Linda Pastan

Linda Pastan was born Linda Olenik in New York in 1932. After her graduation from Radcliffe, she took two master's degrees at Simmons (M.L.S.) and Brandeis (M.A.). She married in 1953 and has a daughter and two sons. Her first book, *A Perfect Circle of the Sun* (1971), established her as an up-and-comer; *Selected Poems* appeared in 1979, confirming her accomplishment. Her subtle, often powerful poems are exceptionally clear and accessible.

## Sylvia Plath

Sylvia Plath (1932–1963), one of the most remarkable poets in English of the past half-century, was born in Boston, the daughter of German immigrants who both taught at Boston University. The death of her father when the poet was eight came as a trauma from which she seems never quite to have recovered. As a scholarship-winning student at Smith College, Plath revealed early promise, and her work received early publication. Like Esther Greenwood, protagonist of her one novel *The Bell Jar* (1963), Plath won a student contest that sent her to work in New York for a national magazine, and struggled with a year-long siege of mental illness for which she underwent shock treatments. Returning to Smith, she was graduated with top honors. Later she studied at Cambridge University in England, where she met and in 1956 married the poet Ted Hughes. Estranged from her husband, she died a suicide in London, leaving two children and, in manuscript, the intense, powerful poems that went into her posthumous, highly acclaimed collection, *Ariel* (1965).

## Alexander Pope

Alexander Pope (1688–1744), the leading English poet of the early eighteenth century, was born in London, son of a Roman Catholic linen merchant. A sickly, stunted, pockmarked child, he suffered from weak health and continual exhaustion throughout his life, and was said to have worn padded clothes to disguise his misshapen frame. Pope early excelled as a poet, composing his *Pastorals* (1709) at age sixteen. His rimed translations of the *Iliad* (1720) and the *Odyssey* (1725–26) and his edition of Shakespeare (1725), bestsellers in their day, made him independently wealthy, and he was able to buy an estate at Twickenham and live in style. Pope did not write an epic, but instead translated epics and wrote great mock epics: *The Rape of the Lock* (1714), in which he voices compassion for women transformed into wives, and *The Dunciad* (1728–43), in which he mocks his many literary enemies. He was a master satirist and splendid craftsman of the heroic couplet. Romantic critics generally think him no poet at all, but G. K. Chesterton remarked, "If Pope be not a poet, then who is?"

## Ezra Pound

Ezra Pound (1885–1972), among the most influential (and still controversial) poets of our century, was born in Hailey, Idaho. He readied himself for a teaching career, but when in 1907 he lost his job at Wabash College for sheltering a penniless prostitute, he left America. Settling in England and later in Paris, he wielded influence on the work of T. S. Eliot, whose long poem *The Waste Land* he edited; W. B. Yeats, whom he served as secretary and critic; and James Joyce. Pound was perpetually championing writers then unknown, like Robert Frost. In 1924 Pound settled permanently in Italy, where he came to admire Mussolini's economic policies. During World War II he made broadcasts to America by Italian radio, deemed treasonous. When American armed forces arrested him in 1944, Pound spent three weeks in a cage in an army camp in Pisa. Flown to the United States to stand trial, he was declared incompetent and for twelve years was confined in St. Elizabeth's in Washington, a hospital for the criminally insane. In 1958, at the intervention of Robert Frost, Archibald MacLeish, and other old friends, he was pronounced incurable and allowed to return to Italy to spend his last, increasingly silent years. In his prime, Pound is a swaggeringly confident critic, a berater of smugness and mediocrity, a delectable humorist. Among his lasting books are *Personae* (enlarged edition, 1949), short poems; his *ABC of Reading* (1934), an introduction to poetry; and *Literary Es-*

*says* (1954). His *Cantos*, a vast poem woven of historical themes published in instalments over forty years, Pound never finished. He is a great translator of poetry from Italian, Provençal, Chinese, and other languages. Pare away his delusions, and a remarkable human being and splendid poet remains.

## Dudley Randall

Dudley Randall was born in 1914 in Washington, D.C. He was graduated from Wayne State University and the University of Michigan, and has worked as librarian and poet-in-residence at the University of Detroit. A pioneer in the modern movement to publish the work of black writers, Randall founded what has been called the most influential small publishing house in America, Broadside Press. He also edited an important anthology, *The Black Poets* (1971). Randall's *A Litany of Friends: New and Selected Poems* was published in 1981.

## Adrienne Rich

Adrienne Rich was born in Baltimore in 1929, into a father-dominated Jewish family of comfortable means. While still an undergraduate at Radcliffe, she published her first book of poems, *A Change of World* (1951), with an introduction by W. H. Auden. Later she studied at Oxford. In 1953 she married an economist and soon bore three sons—an experience she said had been "radicalizing." During the Vietnam War, she took an active part in the peace movement. In 1970 after the suicide of her estranged husband, perhaps obliquely referred to in the poem "Diving into the Wreck," Rich turned increasingly to feminist matters, expressed not only in poetry but in prose: in *Of Woman Born* (1976), a study of the institution of motherhood. With Michelle Cliff, she has coedited *Sinister Wisdom*, a lesbian little magazine. Rich has taught at City College of New York, Columbia, Brandeis, Smith, Douglass, and elsewhere. Few woman poets in recent years have commanded a more devoted audience.

## Edwin Arlington Robinson

Edwin Arlington Robinson (1869–1935) was raised in Gardiner, Maine, the model for Tilbury Town, the setting for many of his poems. After a stint at Harvard, Robinson moved to New York City. Initially, he published three books, but slowly sank into poverty and alcoholism. In 1902 President Theodore Roosevelt discovered Robinson's work and obtained for him a government position with virtually no duties. Robinson used this fortunate intercession to embark on a series of literary projects, and he gradually became the most widely esteemed American poet of the early twentieth century. He won the Pulitzer Prize three times in seven years, and his long poem *Tristram* (1927) became a bestseller. Although Robinson's work has suffered from critical neglect in recent years, he remains an important American poet. His austere style, penetrating psychology, and bitter realism represent a turning point in American poetry from nineteenth century romanticism to the threshold of modernism. His work decisively influenced the poetry of Robert Frost.

## Theodore Roethke

Theodore Roethke (1908–1963) was born in Saginaw, Michigan, where his family ran a large greenhouse. (No poet seems wealthier in his knowledge of vegetation.) He went to the University of Michigan and (for a year) to Harvard. As a young poet teaching college at a time when creative writing teachers without Ph.D.s were suspect, Roethke held impermanent jobs before coming to rest at the University of Washington in Seattle. There, from 1947 until his death, he was

an influential teacher of poetry and poetry writing; among his students were Carolyn Kizer, David Wagoner, and James Wright. Roethke was a large, heavyset man light on his feet (he once coached varsity tennis at Lafayette), and would sometimes prepare for a poetry reading by pacing the stage like an athlete warming up. His poetry developed from rather conventional and imitative lyrics through a phase of disconnected stream of consciousness into (at the end) a meditative poetry reminiscent in its open lines of Walt Whitman's.

## William Shakespeare

William Shakespeare (1564–1616), the supreme writer of English, was born, baptized, and buried in the market town of Stratford-on-Avon, eighty miles from London. Son of a glovemaker and merchant who was high bailiff (or mayor) of the town, he probably attended grammar school and learned to read Latin authors in the original. At eighteen he married Anne Hathaway, twenty-six, by whom he had three children, including twins. By 1592 he had become well known and envied as an actor and playwright in London. From 1594 until he retired, he belonged to the same theatrical company, the Lord Chamberlain's Men (later renamed the King's Men in honor of their patron, James I), for whom he wrote thirty-six plays—some of them, such as *Hamlet* and *King Lear*, profound reworkings of old plays. As an actor, Shakespeare is believed to have played supporting roles, such as Hamlet's father's ghost. The company prospered, moved into the Globe in 1599, and in 1608 bought the fashionable Blackfriars as well; Shakespeare owned an interest in both theaters. When plagues shut down the theaters from 1592 to 1594, Shakespeare turned to poetry; his great Sonnets (published only in 1609) probably date from the 1590s. Plays were regarded as entertainments of little literary merit, like comic books today, and Shakespeare did not bother to supervise their publication. He did, however, carefully see through press his sonnets and the narrative poems *Venus and Adonis* (1593) and *The Rape of Lucrece* (1594).

## Percy Bysshe Shelley

Percy Bysshe Shelley (1792–1822) married his first wife, sixteen-year-old Harriet Westbrook, in 1811, the same year he was expelled from Oxford for coauthoring a pamphlet defending atheism. His first major poem, *Queen Mab*, which advocated the abolishment of a number of established institutions, was privately printed in 1813. In 1814 Shelley went to France with Mary Wollstonecraft, later famous as the author of *Frankenstein* (1818). They were married after Harriet's suicide in 1816. In 1818 they settled in Italy, where Shelley wrote some of his best lyrics, including "Ode to the West Wind," "To a Skylark," and "Ozymandias"; poetic dramas; and *Adonais*, an elegy to his friend John Keats. "A Defense of Poetry," the poet's most important prose work, was written in 1821. While sailing during a storm, Shelley was drowned. He is remembered as a staunch believer in the eighteenth-century ideals of reason and the perfectibility of the human race.

## Stevie Smith

Stevie Smith (1902–1971), was born in Hull, Yorkshire, christened Florence Margaret Smith. Being wiry and short, she acquired her nickname from a popular jockey, Stevie Donahue. For more than sixty years, beginning at age three, Smith lived with her aunt in Palmers Green, a suburb of London, and worked for thirty years as a publisher's secretary. Of her three novels, *Novel on Yellow Paper* (1936) is the best known. Her poetry readings, in public and on BBC radio, widened her audience. *Collected Poems* (1976) is illustrated with her own witty, slapdash, and rakishly charming

drawings. *Me Again: Uncollected Writings* (1982) contains poems, stories, essays, and a play for radio. In a film, *Stevie* (1978), based on a stage play by Hugh Whitemore, Glenda Jackson plays the poet with keen empathy.

## William Stafford

William Stafford (1914–1993) was born in Hutchinson, Kansas. He graduated from the University of Kansas and later took a doctorate at the University of Iowa. During World War II he was interned as a conscientious objector, an experience he recalled in his prose memoir *Down in My Heart* (1947). For many years he taught at Lewis and Clark College in Portland, Oregon, and in 1970–71 he served as Consultant in Poetry for the Library of Congress. *Traveling Through the Dark* (1962) won the National Book Award, and in 1977 Stafford published a large volume of his collected poems, *Stories That Could Be True*. In much of his work he traced the landscapes of the Midwest and of the Pacific Northwest, where for many years he lived. He described his poetry as "much like talk, with some enhancement."

## Timothy Steele

Timothy Steele, born in Burlington, Vermont, in 1948, took his doctorate in English at Brandeis, where he studied literature with J. V. Cunningham. A Californian by adoption, he has taught and held a Wallace Stegner fellowship in creative writing at Stanford, and currently teaches at California State University, Los Angeles. His first collection, *Uncertainties and Rest*, appeared in 1979, and his most recent, *Sapphics Against Anger and Other Poems*, in 1986. *Missing Measures: Modern Poetry and the Revolt against Meter* (1990) is a critical study in literary history. His poems wear a Yankee reticence and a tendency toward precise understatement, holding much power within their strict limits. Steele writes exclusively in traditional forms, in which he demonstrates mastery.

## James Stephens

James Stephens (1882–1950), born in Dublin, Ireland, was a famous member of the Irish Literary Renaissance, a movement early in the century that included William Butler Yeats and the playwrights Lady Gregory, J. M. Synge, and Sean O'Casey. As a young man Stephens took a job as a typist in a lawyer's office, where access to a typewriter started him writing fantastic fiction, some of it based on Irish folklore, such as his most popular novel, The Crock of Gold (1912). Other imaginative novels followed, including The Demi-Gods (1914) and Deirdre (1923). Irish Fairy Tales (1920) retells classic legends for young readers. Although best remembered for such books, Stephens was a considerable poet as well. His first collection appeared in 1909, and in 1926 he published his Collected Poems. Some of his poems are actually free translations from the Irish: "A Glass of Beer," for instance, is a version of a poem by Dáibhí Ó Bruadair (about 1625–98).

## Wallace Stevens

Wallace Stevens (1879–1955) was born in Reading, Pennsylvania; his father was a successful lawyer; his mother, a former schoolteacher. As a special student at Harvard, he became president of the student literary magazine, the Harvard Advocate, but he did not want a liberal arts degree. Instead, he became a lawyer in New York City, and in 1916 joined the legal staff of the Hartford Accident and Indemnity Company. In 1936 he was elected a vice-president. Stevens, who would write poems in his head while walking to work and then dictate them to his secretary, was a leading expert on surety claims. Once asked how he was able to combine poetry and insurance, he replied that the two occupations had an element in common: "calculated risk." As a young man in New York, Stevens made lasting friendships with poets Marianne Moore and William Carlos Williams, but he did not seek literary society. Though his poems are full of references to Europe and remote places, his only travels were annual vacation trips to Key West. He printed his early poems in Poetry magazine, but did not publish a book until Harmonium appeared in 1923, when he was forty-four. Living quietly in Hartford, Connecticut, Stevens sought to discover order in a chaotic world with his subtle and exotic imagination. His critical essays, collected in The Necessary Angel (1951), and his Letters (1966), edited by his daughter Holly Stevens, reveal a penetrating, philosophic mind. His Collected Poems (1954), published on his seventy-fifth birthday, garnered major prizes and belated recognition for Stevens as a major American poet.

## Anne Stevenson

Anne Stevenson is the quintessential trans-Atlantic poet. Born in England in 1933 of American poets, she was educated in the U.S. After graduating from the University of Michigan, she returned to England. She has taught in both countries and now lives in Durham. Combining two cultures in her background, Stevenson has also combined the careers of scholar and poet. In 1966, she published the first full-length study of Elizabeth Bishop, and, in 1989, she released Bitter Fame: A Life of Sylvia Plath, a controversial but authoritative biography. Her Selected Poems, which surveyed the work of seven individual volumes, appeared in 1987.

## Jonathan Swift

Jonathan Swift (1667–1745), Anglo-Irish poet, satirist, journalist, and clergyman, was born in Dublin, said to have been sired by an English steward. Uncles helped him attend Trinity College, Dublin, from which he was graduated "by special grace," having shone only in his studies of the classics. In 1694 Swift entered the Church of England and held parish appointments in Ireland, finally becoming Dean of St. Patrick's Cathedral, Dublin—to his disappointment, for he loved London and had hoped for a position there. His cousin John Dryden is reported to have told him, "Cousin Swift, you will never be a poet," a prophecy that time has proved inaccurate. In a life crowded with church duties, political agitation, literary society, and long and perhaps sexless love affairs, especially with his former pupil Esther Johnson (whom he called Stella), Swift found occasion to write much excellent verse. Still, he is best remembered for *Gulliver's Travels* (1726), an affectionate tribute to the reasoning part of "that animal called man," a scathing and scatological rebuke to the rest of him.

## Alfred, Lord Tennyson

Alfred, Lord Tennyson (1809–1892), was born Alfred Tennyson in Lincolnshire, England, the son of an alcoholic rural minister. When Queen Victoria made him a baron in 1883 (at seventy-five), he added the "Lord" to his byline. A precocious poet, Tennyson began writing verse at five, and when still in his teens collaborated with his brother Charles on *Poems by Two Brothers* (1827). As a student at Cambridge, he was unusual: he kept a snake for a pet, won a medal for poetry, and went home without taking a degree. But in college he made influential friendships, especially that of Arthur Hallam, whose death in 1833 inspired Tennyson's *In Memoriam* (1850), the elegiac sequence that contains "Dark house by which once more I stand." The year 1850 was a banner one for Tennyson in other ways: he at last felt prosperous enough to marry Emily Sellwood, who had remained engaged to him for fourteen years, and Queen Victoria

named him poet laureate, in which capacity he served for four decades, writing poems for state occasions. Between 1859 and 1888 Tennyson completed *Idylls of the King*, a twelve-part narrative poem of Arthur and his Round Table. In his mid-sixties he wrote several plays. A spokesman for the Victorian age and its militant colonialism, Tennyson is still respected as a poet of varied assets, including an excellent ear.

## Dylan Thomas

Dylan Thomas (1914–1953) was born in the coastal town of Swansea, Wales, the son of a teacher of English. Much of Thomas's life was a bitter struggle to support his wife and children, a struggle intensified by fondness for spending freely. Lacking a university education, Thomas found most paying literary work barred to him in Britain, although late in life he received many assignments to write film and radio scripts. A resonant reader-aloud of poetry, he made broadcasts for BBC radio and undertook several immensely popular reading tours of America, preceded by a reputation for heavy drinking and gustatorial lovemaking. He died in a hospital in New York City after drinking a procession of straight whiskeys, apparently courting the end. Thomas wrote not only poems (in the early ones he brought surrealism into English poetry), he also wrote remarkable stories and a "play for voices," *Under Milk Wood* (1954), based on memories of his home town in Wales.

## John Updike

John Updike, born in Shillingford, Pennsylvania, in 1932, is primarily regarded as a novelist. But his first book was verse, *The Carpentered Hen* (1954), from which we take "Ex-Basketball Player"; and ever since, he has continued to produce verse both light and serious. He received his B.A. from Harvard, then went to Oxford to study drawing and fine art. From 1955 to 1957 he worked on the staff of *The New Yorker*. Though he left the magazine to write full-time, he has continued to supply it with bright stories and searching book reviews. Hardly a fall goes by without a new Updike novel. *The Witches of Eastwick* (1984) was made into a successful motion picture.

## Keith Waldrop

Keith Waldrop, born in 1932 in Emporia, Kansas, grew up in a family divided by his father's militant atheism and his mother's pious Christian fundamentalism. He took his doctorate at the University of Michigan with a thesis on obscenity in literature, and has since taught at Wesleyan University and at Brown. Waldrop has directed and acted in films and plays. His first book of poems, *A Windmill near Calvary* (1968), was nominated for the National Book Award. He lives in Providence, Rhode Island, with his wife, the poet and translator Rosmarie Waldrop, thousands of books and recordings, and a basement printing press that produces more books under the imprint Burning Deck.

## Edmund Waller

Edmund Waller (1606–1687), born into a rich country family, is remembered in England not only as a poet but also as a member of Parliament. In 1643 he hatched "Waller's Plot," an attempt to turn London over to the exiled Charles I; it failed, but Parliament later pardoned him. His smooth, elegant poems included tributes to important public figures as well as courtly love lyrics. Written chiefly in iambic pentameter couplets, these later helped establish the heroic couplet as a favorite poetic form among English poets of the eighteenth century.

## Walt Whitman

Walt Whitman (1819–1892) was born on Long Island, son of an impoverished farmer. He spent his early years as a school teacher, a temperance propagandist, a carpenter, a printer, and a newspaper editor on the Brooklyn *Eagle*. He began writing poetry in youth, sometimes declaiming his lines above the crash of waves on New York beaches. Apparently he was also inspired to write wide, spacious, confident lines by attending performances of Italian opera. His self-published *Leaves of Grass* (1855) won praise from Ralph Waldo Emerson and gained Whitman readers in England. For the rest of his life, he kept revising and enlarging it, ceasing with a ninth or "deathbed edition" in 1891–92. Americans at first were slow to accept Whitman's unconventionally open verse forms, his sexual frankness, and his gregarious egoism. The poet of boundless faith in American democracy, Whitman tempered his vision by his experiences as a volunteer hospital nurse during the Civil War (described in his poems *Drum-Taps* and his wartime letters). After the war, he held secretarial jobs to support himself, and lost one such job when his employer's scandalized eye fell upon the *Leaves*. In old age, a semi-invalid after a stroke, Whitman made his home in Camden, New Jersey. Before he died he saw his work finally winning respect and worldwide acceptance. Whitman's influence on later American poetry has been profound, both by the example of his open forms and by his bold encompassing of subject matter that had formerly been considered unpoetic. (In "Song of the Exposition," read aloud at an industrial show in New York, the poet exclaims of his Muse: "She's here, install'd amid the kitchen ware!")

## Richard Wilbur

Richard Wilbur, born in 1921 in New York City, was graduated from Amherst College, then served in the army in World War II. He has taught English at Harvard, Wellesley, Wesleyan, and Smith. With his first two collections,

*The Beautiful Changes* (1947) and *Ceremony* (1950), Wilbur acquired a high reputation for a poetry of sensitivity, wit, grace, and command of traditional forms. Besides writing poetry, for which he has received many prizes, including two Pulitzer Prizes and a National Book Award, Wilbur has edited the poetry of Shakespeare and Poe. He has written song lyrics for *Candide*, a Broadway musical by Lillian Hellman and Leonard Bernstein (1956); *Loudmouse*, a story for children (1963); and *Responses*, literary criticism (1976); and he has translated plays of Molière and Racine into wonderfully skillful English verse. He divides his time between Cummington, Massachusetts, where he has a home adjacent to an apple orchard, and Key West, Florida. In 1987 he was named United States Poet Laureate by the Library of Congress. His *New and Collected Poems* (1988) gathers most of his original work in poetry.

## William Carlos Williams

William Carlos Williams (1883–1963) was born in Rutherford, New Jersey, where he remained in later life as a practicing pediatrician. While taking his M.D. degree at the University of Pennsylvania, he made friends with the poets Ezra Pound and H. D. (Hilda Doolittle). Surprisingly prolific for a busy doctor, Williams wrote (besides poetry) novels and short stories, plays, criticism, and essays in history (*In the American Grain*, 1939). He kept a fliptop desk in his office and between patients would haul out his typewriter and dash off poems. His encouragement of younger poets, among them Allen Ginsberg (whose doctor he was when Ginsberg was a baby), and the long-sustained example of his formally open poetry made him an appealing father figure to the generation of the Beat poets and the Black Mountain poets —Ginsberg, Gary Snyder, and Robert Creeley. But he also had great influence on Robert Lowell, and on a whole

younger generation of American poets in our day. Williams believed in truthtelling about ordinary life, championed plain speech "out of the mouths of Polish mothers," and insisted that there can be "no ideas but in things." Combining poetry with prose (including documents and statistics), his long poem in five parts, *Paterson* (1946–58) explores the past, present, and future of the New Jersey industrial city near which Williams lived for most of his days.

## William Wordsworth

William Wordsworth (1770–1850) was born in England's Lake District, whose landscapes and people were to inform many of his poems. As a young man he visited France, sympathized with the Revolution, and met a young Frenchwoman who bore him a child. The Reign of Terror prevented him from returning to France, and he and Annette Vallon never married. With his sister Dorothy (1771–1855), his lifelong intellectual companion and the author of remarkable journals, he settled in Dorsetshire. Later they moved to Grasmere, in the Lake District, where Wordsworth lived the rest of his life. In 1798 his friendship with Samuel Taylor Coleridge resulted in their joint publication of *Lyrical Ballads*, a book credited with introducing Romanticism to English poetry. (Wordsworth contributed "Tintern Abbey" and other poems.) To the second edition of 1800, Wordsworth supplied a preface calling for a poetry written "in the real language of men." Time brought him a small official job, a marriage, a swing from left to right in his political sentiments, and appointment as poet laureate. Although he kept on writing, readers have generally preferred his earlier poems. *The Prelude*, a long poem-memoir completed in 1805, did not appear till after the poet's death. One of the most original of writers, Wordsworth— especially for his poems of nature and simple rustics—occupies a popular place in English poetry, much like that of Robert Frost in America.

## James Wright

James Wright (1927–1980) was born in Martins Ferry, Ohio. After taking his doctorate at the University of Washington, where he studied with Theodore Roethke, he taught at the University of Minnesota, Macalester College, and Hunter College in New York. His first book, A Green Wall (1957), in the Yale Series of Younger Poets, established him as a traditional formalist of great skill. With Robert Bly, by whom he was persuaded to branch out of traditional forms, he translated the poems of Cesar Valejo, Pablo Neruda, and George Trakl. In 1972 he received the Pulitzer Prize for his Collected Poems. Wright was a memorable teacher, a great quoter of poetry from memory, and a fine critic. "I try and say how I love my country and how I despise the way it is treated," he declared. "I try and speak of the beauty and again of the ugliness in the lives of the poor and neglected."

## Sir Thomas Wyatt

Sir Thomas Wyatt (1503?–1542) was both poet and man of action: diplomat, soldier, and courtier. He was born in his father's castle in Kent, England, and as a boy he was sent to court. In 1516 he entered St. John's College, Cambridge. Wyatt twice saw the inside of prison when he slipped from the favor of King Henry VIII. He is thought to have been a lover of Anne Boleyn, later the King's wife, a fact that perhaps affects some of his remarkable love lyrics. A prominent man in Tudor England, Wyatt carried out diplomatic missions, served as ambassador to Spain, was a member of Parliament and the king's privy council, and was Commander of the Fleet. Wyatt's

mission to Italy in 1527 had great consequence for English poetry, for he brought back knowledge of the works of Petrarch and other Italian love poets. In imitation of them, Wyatt wrote some of the first sonnets in our language— also lyrics, rondels, satires, and psalms.

## William Butler Yeats

William Butler Yeats (1865–1939), poet and playwright, an Irishman of English ancestry, was born in Dublin, the son of painter John Butler Yeats. For a time he studied art himself and was irregularly schooled in Dublin and in London. Early in life Yeats sought to transform Irish folklore and legend into mellifluous poems. He overcame shyness to take an active part in cataclysmic events: he became involved in the movement for an Irish nation (partly drawn into it by his unrequited love for Maud Gonne, a crusading nationalist) and in founding the Irish Literary Theatre (1898) and the Irish National Theatre, which in 1904 moved to the renowned Abbey Theatre in Dublin. Dublin audiences were difficult: in 1899 they jeered Yeats's first play, The Countess Cathleen, for portraying a woman who, defying the church, sells her soul to the devil to buy bread for starving peasants. Eventually Yeats retired from the fray, to write plays given in drawing rooms, like Purgatory. After the establishment of the Irish Free State, Yeats served as a senator (1922–28). His lifelong interest in the occult culminated in his writing of A Vision (1937), a view of history as governed by the phases of the moon; Yeats believed the book inspired by spirit masters who dictated communications to his wife, Georgie Hyde-Lees. Had Yeats stopped writing in 1900, he would be remembered as an outstanding minor Victorian. Instead, he went on to become one of the most influential poets of the twentieth century.

# DRAMA

*In all ages the drama, through its portrayal of the acting and suffering spirit of man, has been more closely allied than any other art to his deeper thoughts concerning his nature and his destiny.*

—Ludwig Lewisohn, The Modern Drama, 1915

Unlike a short story or a novel, a **play** is a work of storytelling in which actors represent the characters. In another essential, a play differs from a work of fiction: it is addressed not to readers but to spectators.

To be part of an audience in a theater is an experience far different from reading a story in solitude. Expectant as the house lights dim and the curtain rises, we become members of a community. The responses of people around us affect our own responses. We, too, contribute to the community's response whenever we laugh, sigh, applaud, murmur in surprise, or catch our breath in excitement. In contrast, when all alone we watch a movie by means of a videocassette recorder—say, a slapstick comedy—we probably laugh less often than if we were watching the same film in a theater, surrounded by a roaring crowd. Of course, no one is spilling popcorn down the back of our necks. Each kind of theatrical experience, to be sure, has its advantages.

A theater of live actors has another advantage: a sensitive give-and-take between actors and audience. Such rapport, of course, depends on the actors being skilled and the audience being perceptive. Although professional actors may try to give a top-class performance on all occasions, it is natural for them to feel more keenly inspired by a lively, appreciative audience than by a dull, lethargic one. No doubt a large turnout of spectators also helps draw the best from performers on stage: the *Othello* you get may be somewhat less inspired if you are part of an audience that may be counted on the fingers of one hand. But at any rate, as veteran playgoers well know, something unique and wonderful can happen when good actors and a good audience respond to each other.

In another sense, a play is more than actors and audience: like a short story or a poem, a play is a work of art made of words. The playwright devoted thought and care and skill to the selection and arrangement of language. Watching a play, of course, we do not notice the playwright standing between us and the characters.[1] If the play is absorbing, it flows before our eyes. In a silent reading, the usual play consists mainly of **dialogue,** exchanges of speech, punctuated by stage directions.[2] In performance, though, stage directions vanish. And although the thoughtful efforts of perhaps a hundred people—actors, director, producer, stage designer, costumer, makeup artist, technicians—may have gone into a production, a successful play makes us forget its artifice. We may even forget that the play is literature, for its gestures, facial expressions, bodily stances, lighting, and special effects are as much a part of it as the playwright's written words. Even though words are not all there is to a living play, they are its bones. And the whole play, the finished production, is the total of whatever transpires on stage.

The sense of immediacy we derive from **drama** is suggested by the root of the word. *Drama* means "action" or "deed" (from the Greek *dran*, "to do"). We use *drama* as a synonym for *plays*, but the word has several meanings. Sometimes it refers to one play ("a stirring drama"); or to the work of a playwright, or **dramatist** ("Ibsen's drama"); or perhaps to a body of plays written in a particular time or place ("Elizabethan drama," "French drama of the seventeenth century"). In yet another familiar sense, *drama* often means events that elicit high excitement: "A real-life drama," a news story might begin, "was enacted today before lunchtime crowds in downtown Manhattan as firemen battled to free two children trapped on the sixteenth floor of a burning building." In this sense, whatever is "dramatic" implies suspense, tension, or conflict. Plays, as we shall see, frequently contain such "dramatic" chains of events; and yet, if we expect all plays to be crackling with suspense or conflict, we may be disappointed. "Good drama," said critic George Jean Nathan, "is anything that interests an intelligently emotional group of persons assembled together in an illuminated hall."

In partaking of the nature of ritual—something to be repeated in front of an audience on a special occasion—drama is akin to a festival (whether a religious festival or a rock festival) or a church service. Twice in the history of Europe, drama has sprung forth as a part of worship: when in ancient Greece, plays were performed on feast days; and when in the Christian church of the Middle Ages, a play was introduced as an adjunct to the Easter mass with the enactment of the meeting between the three Marys and the angel at Jesus's empty tomb. Evidently something in drama remains constant over the years—something as old, perhaps, as the deepest desires and highest aspirations of humanity.

---

[1]The word *playwright*, by the way, invites misspelling. Notice that it is not *playwrite*. The suffix-*wright* (from Old English) means "one who makes"—like a *boatwright*, a worker in a trade.

[2]Not all plays employ dialogue. There is also **pantomime**—generally, a play without words (sometimes also called a **dumb show**). Originally, in ancient Rome, a pantomime meant an actor who singlehandedly played all the parts. An eminent modern pantomime (or **mime**) is French stage and screen actor Marcel Marceau.

# 33   Reading a Play

Most plays are written not to be read in books but to be performed. Finding plays in a literature anthology, the student may well ask, Isn't there something wrong with the idea of reading plays on the printed page? To do so—to treat them as literature—isn't that a perversion of their nature?

True, plays are meant to be seen on stage, but equally true, reading a play may afford advantages. One is that it is better to know some masterpieces by reading them than never to know them at all. Even if you live in a large city with many theaters, even if you attend a college with many theatrical productions, to succeed in your lifetime in witnessing, say, all the plays of Shakespeare might well be impossible. In print, they are as near-to-hand as a book on a shelf, ready to be enacted (if you like) on the stage of the mind.

After all, a play is literature before it comes alive in a theater; and it might be argued that when we read an unfamiliar play, we meet it in the same form in which it first appears to its actors and its director. If a play is rich and complex, or if it dates from the remote past and contains difficulties of language and allusion, to read it on the page enables us to study it at our leisure, to return to the parts that demand greater scrutiny.

Let us admit, by the way, that some plays, whatever the intentions of their authors, are destined to be read more often than they are acted. Such a play is sometimes called a **closet drama**—"closet" meaning a small, private room. Percy Bysshe Shelley's neo-Shakespearean tragedy *The Cenci* (1819) has seldom escaped from its closet, even though Shelley tried without luck to have it performed on the London stage. Perhaps too rich in talk to please an audience or too sparse in opportunities for actors to use their bodies, such works nevertheless may lead long, respectable lives on their own, solely as literature.

But even if a play may be seen in a theater, sometimes to read it in print may be our way of knowing it as the author wrote it in its entirety. Far from regarding Shakespeare's words as holy writ, producers of *Hamlet, King Lear, Othello,* and other masterpieces often leave out whole speeches and scenes, or shorten them. Besides, the nature of the play, as far as you can tell from a stage production, may depend upon decisions of the director. Shall Othello dress as a Renaissance Moor, or as a jet-set contemporary? Every actor who plays Iago in *Othello* makes his own interpretation of this knotty character. Some see Iago as a figure of pure evil; others, as a madman; still others, as a suffering human being consumed by hatred, jealousy, and pride. What do you think Shakespeare meant? You can always read the play and decide for yourself. If every stage production of a play is a fresh interpretation, so, too, is every reader's reading of it.

Some readers, when silently reading a play to themselves, try to visualize a stage, imagining the characters in costume and under lights. If such a reader is an actor or a director and is reading the play with an eye to staging it, then that reader may try to imagine every detail of a possible production, even shades of makeup and loudness of sound effects. But the nonprofessional reader, who regards the play as literature, need not attempt such exhaustive imagining. Although some readers find it enjoyable to imagine the play taking place upon a stage, others prefer to imagine the people and events that the play brings vividly to mind. Sympathetically following the tangled life of Nora in *A Doll's House* by Henrik Ibsen, we forget that we are reading printed stage directions and instead find ourselves in the presence of human conflict. Thus regarded, a play becomes a form of storytelling, and the playwright's instructions to the actors and the director become a conventional mode of narrative that we accept much as we accept the methods of a novel or short story. If we read *A Doll's House* caring more about Nora's fate than the imagined appearance of an actress portraying her, we speed through an ordinary passage such as this (from a scene in which Nora's husband hears the approach of an unwanted caller, Dr. Rank):

> Helmer (*with quiet irritation*): Oh, what does he want now? (*Aloud.*) Hold on. (*Goes and opens the door.*) Oh, how nice that you didn't just pass us by!

We read the passage, if the story absorbs us, as though we were reading a novel whose author, employing the conventional devices for recording speech in fiction, might have written:

> "Oh, what does he want now?" said Helmer under his breath, in annoyance. Aloud, he called, "Hold on," then walked to the door and opened it and greeted Rank with all the cheer he could muster—"Oh, how nice that you didn't pass us by!"

Such is the power of an excellent play to make us ignore the playwright's artistry that it becomes a window through which the reader's gaze, given focus, encompasses more than language and typography and beholds a scene of imagined life.

Most plays, whether seen in a theater or in print, employ *some* **conventions:** customary methods of presenting an action, usual and recognizable devices that an audience is willing to accept. In reading a great play from the past, such as *Oedipus the King* or *Othello,* it will help if we know some of the conventions of the classical Greek theater or the Elizabethan theater. When in *Oedipus the King* we encounter a character called the Chorus, it may be useful to be aware that this is a group of citizens who stand to one side of the action, conversing with the principal character and commenting. In *Othello*, when the sinister Iago, left on stage alone, begins to speak (at the end of Act II, Scene I), we recognize the conventional device of a **soliloquy,** a dramatic monologue in which we seem to overhear the character's inmost thoughts uttered aloud. Like conventions in poetry, such familiar methods of staging a story afford us a happy shock of recognition. Often, as in these examples, they are ways of making clear to us exactly what the playwright would have us know.

## A PLAY IN ITS ELEMENTS

When we read a play on the printed page and find ourselves swept forward by the motion of its story, we need not wonder how—and of what ingredients—the playwright put it together. Still, to analyze the structure of a play is one way to understand and appreciate a playwright's art. Analysis is complicated, however, because in an excellent play the elements (including plot, theme, and characters) do not stand in isolation. Often, deeds clearly follow from the kinds of people the characters are, and from those deeds it is left to the reader to infer the **theme** of the play—the general point or truth about human beings that may be drawn from it. Perhaps the most meaningful way to study the elements of a play (and certainly the most enjoyable) is to consider a play in its entirety.

Here is a short, famous one-act play worth reading for the boldness of its elements—and for its own sake. *Trifles* tells the story of a murder. As you will discover, the "trifles" mentioned in its title are not of trifling stature. In reading the play, you will probably find yourself imagining what you might see on stage if you were in a theater. You may also care to imagine what took place in the lives of the characters before the curtain rose. All this imagining may sound like a tall order, but don't worry. Just read the play for enjoyment the first time through, and then we will consider whatever makes it effective.

## Susan Glaspell

TRIFLES                                                                      1916

Susan Glaspell (1882–1948), grew up in
her native Davenport, Iowa, daughter of a
grain dealer. After four years at Drake
University and a reporting job in Des
Moines, she settled in New York's
Greenwich Village. In 1915, with her husband George Cram Cook, a theatrical
director, she founded the Provincetown
Players, the first influential noncommercial
theater troupe in America. Summers, in a
makeshift playhouse on a Cape Cod pier,
the Players staged the earliest plays of
Eugene O'Neill and work by John Reed,
Edna St. Vincent Millay, and Glaspell herself. (Later transplanting the company to
New York, Glaspell and Cook renamed it

Susan Glaspell

the Playwrights' Theater.) Glaspell wrote several still-remembered plays, among them a
pioneering work of feminist drama, The Verge (1921), and the Pulitzer Prize-winning
Alison's House (1930), about the family of a reclusive poet like Emily Dickinson who,
after her death, squabble over the right to publish her poems. First widely known for her
fiction with an Iowa background, Glaspell wrote ten novels, including Fidelity (1915)
and The Morning Is Near Us (1939). Shortly after writing the play Trifles, she
rewrote it as a short story, "A Jury of Her Peers."


Characters

George Henderson, county attorney
Henry Peters, sheriff
Lewis Hale, a neighboring farmer
Mrs. Peters
Mrs. Hale


Scene. The kitchen in the now abandoned farmhouse of John Wright, a gloomy kitchen,
and left without having been put in order—unwashed pans under the sink, a loaf of
bread outside the breadbox, a dish towel on the table—other signs of incompleted work.
At the rear the outer door opens and the Sheriff comes in followed by the County
Attorney and Hale. The Sheriff and Hale are men in middle life, the County Attorney
is a young man; all are much bundled up and go at once to the stove. They are followed
by two women—the Sheriff's wife first; she is a slight wiry woman, a thin nervous face.
Mrs. Hale is larger and would ordinarily be called more comfortable looking, but she is
disturbed now and looks fearfully about as she enters. The women have come in slowly,
and stand close together near the door.

County Attorney: [Rubbing his hands.] This feels good. Come up to the fire, ladies.

Mrs. Peters: [After taking a step forward.] I'm not—cold.

Sheriff: [Unbuttoning his overcoat and stepping away from the stove as if to mark the beginning of official business.] Now, Mr. Hale, before we move things about, you explain to Mr. Henderson just what you saw when you came here yesterday morning.

County Attorney: By the way, has anything been moved? Are things just as you left them yesterday?

Sheriff: [Looking about.] It's just the same. When it dropped below zero last night I thought I'd better send Frank out this morning to make a fire for us—no use getting pneumonia with a big case on, but I told him not to touch anything except the stove—and you know Frank.

County Attorney: Somebody should have been left here yesterday.

Sheriff: Oh—yesterday. When I had to send Frank to Morris Center for that man who went crazy—I want you to know I had my hands full yesterday, I knew you could get back from Omaha by today and as long as I went over everything here myself—

County Attorney: Well, Mr. Hale, tell just what happened when you came here yesterday morning.

Hale: Harry and I had started to town with a load of potatoes. We came along the road from my place and as I got here I said, "I'm going to see if I can't get John Wright to go in with me on a party telephone." I spoke to Wright about it once before and he put me off, saying folks talked too much anyway, and all he asked was peace and quiet—I guess you know about how much he talked himself; but I thought maybe if I went to the house and talked about it before his wife, though I said to Harry that I didn't know as what his wife wanted made much difference to John—

County Attorney: Let's talk about that later, Mr. Hale. I do want to talk about that, but tell now just what happened when you got to the house.

Hale: I didn't hear or see anything; I knocked at the door, and still it was all quiet inside. I knew they must be up, it was past eight o'clock. So I knocked again, and I thought I heard somebody say, "Come in." I wasn't sure, I'm not sure yet, but I opened the door—this door [Indicating the door by which the two women are still standing] and there in that rocker—[Pointing to it] sat Mrs. Wright.

[They all look at the rocker.]

County Attorney: What—was she doing?

Hale: She was rockin' back and forth. She had her apron in her hand and was kind of—pleating it.

County Attorney: And how did she—look?

Hale: Well, she looked queer.

County Attorney: How do you mean—queer?

Hale: Well, as if she didn't know what she was going to do next. And kind of done up.

*County Attorney:* How did she seem to feel about your coming?

*Hale:* Why, I don't think she minded—one way or other. She didn't pay much attention. I said, "How do, Mrs. Wright, it's cold, ain't it?" And she said, "Is it?"—and went on kind of pleating at her apron. Well, I was surprised; she didn't ask me to come up to the stove, or to set down, but just sat there, not even looking at me, so I said, "I want to see John." And then she—laughed. I guess you would call it a laugh. I thought of Harry and the team outside, so I said a little sharp: "Can't I see John?" "No," she says, kind o' dull like. "Ain't he home?" says I. "Yes," says she, "he's home." "Then why can't I see him?" I asked her, out of patience. "'Cause he's dead," says she. "*Dead?*" says I. She just nodded her head, not getting a bit excited, but rockin' back and forth. "Why—where is he?" says I, not knowing what to say. She just pointed upstairs—like that *[Himself pointing to the room above.]* I got up, with the idea of going up there. I walked from there to here—then I says, "Why, what did he die of?" "He died of a rope round his neck," says she, and just went on pleatin' at her apron. Well, I went out and called Harry. I thought I might— need help. We went upstairs and there he was lyin'—

*County Attorney:* I think I'd rather have you go into that upstairs, where you can point it all out. Just go on now with the rest of the story.

*Hale:* Well, my first thought was to get that rope off. It looked . . . *[Stops, his face twitches]* . . . but Harry, he went up to him, and he said, "No, he's dead all right, and we'd better not touch anything." So we went back down stairs. She was still sitting that same way. "Has anybody been notified?" I asked. "No," says she, unconcerned. "Who did this, Mrs. Wright?" said Harry. He said it businesslike—and she stopped pleatin' of her apron. "I don't know," she says. "You don't *know?*" says Harry. "No," says she. "Weren't you sleepin' in the bed with him?" says Harry. "Yes," says she, "but I was on the inside." "Somebody slipped a rope round his neck and strangled him and you didn't wake up?" says Harry. "I didn't wake up," she said after him. We must 'a looked as if we didn't see how that could be, for after a minute she said, "I sleep sound." Harry was going to ask her more questions but I said maybe we ought to let her tell her story first to the coroner, or the sheriff, so Harry went fast as he could to Rivers' place, where there's a telephone.

*County Attorney:* And what did Mrs. Wright do when she knew that you had gone for the coroner?

*Hale:* She moved from that chair to this one over here *[Pointing to a small chair in the corner]* and just sat there with her hands held together and looking down. I got a feeling that I ought to make some conversation, so I said I had come in to see if John wanted to put in a telephone, and at that she started to laugh, and then she stopped and looked at me—scared. *[The County Attorney, who has had his notebook out, makes a note.]* I dunno, maybe it wasn't scared. I wouldn't like to say it was. Soon Harry got back, and then Dr. Lloyd came, and you, Mr. Peters, and so I guess that's all I know that you don't.

*County Attorney:* *[Looking around.]* I guess we'll go upstairs first—and then out to the barn and around there. *[To the Sheriff]* You're convinced that there was nothing important here—nothing that would point to any motive.

*Sheriff*: Nothing here but kitchen things.

[*The County Attorney, after again looking around the kitchen, opens the door of a cupboard closet. He gets up on a chair and looks on a shelf. Pulls his hand away, sticky.*]

*County Attorney*: Here's a nice mess.

[*The women draw nearer.*]

*Mrs. Peters*: [*To the other woman.*] Oh, her fruit; it did freeze. [*To the County Attorney*] She worried about that when it turned so cold. She said the fire'd go out and her jars would break.

*Sheriff*: Well, can you beat the women! Held for murder and worryin' about her preserves.

*County Attorney*: I guess before we're through she may have something more serious than preserves to worry about.

*Hale*: Well, women are used to worrying over trifles.

[*The two women move a little closer together.*]

*County Attorney*: [*With the gallantry of a young politician.*] And yet, for all their worries, what would we do without the ladies? [*The women do not unbend. He goes to the sink, takes a dipperful of water from the pail and pouring it into a basin, washes his hands. Starts to wipe them on the roller towel, turns it for a cleaner place.*] Dirty towels! [*Kicks his foot against the pans under the sink.*] Not much of a housekeeper, would you say, ladies?

*Mrs. Hale*: [*Stiffly.*] There's a great deal of work to be done on a farm.

*County Attorney*: To be sure. And yet [*With a little bow to her*] I know there are some Dickson county farmhouses which do not have such roller towels.

[*He gives it a pull to expose its full length again.*]

*Mrs. Hale*: Those towels get dirty awful quick. Men's hands aren't always as clean as they might be.

*County Attorney*: Ah, loyal to your sex, I see. But you and Mrs. Wright were neighbors. I suppose you were friends, too.

*Mrs. Hale*: [*Shaking her head.*] I've not seen much of her of late years. I've not been in this house—it's more than a year.

*County Attorney*: And why was that? You didn't like her?

*Mrs. Hale*: I liked her all well enough. Farmers' wives have their hands full, Mr. Henderson. And then—

*County Attorney*: Yes—?

*Mrs. Hale*: [*Looking about.*] It never seemed a very cheerful place.

*County Attorney*: No—it's not cheerful. I shouldn't say she had the homemaking instinct.

*Mrs. Hale*: Well, I don't know as Wright had, either.

*County Attorney*: You mean that they didn't get on very well?

*Mrs. Hale*: No, I don't mean anything. But I don't think a place'd be any cheerfuller for John Wright's being in it.

County Attorney: I'd like to talk more of that a little later. I want to get the lay of things upstairs now.

[He goes to the left, where three steps lead to a stair door.]

Sheriff: I suppose anything Mrs. Peters does'll be all right. She was to take in some clothes for her, you know, and a few little things. We left in such a hurry yesterday.

County Attorney: Yes, but I would like to see what you take, Mrs. Peters, and keep an eye out for anything that might be of use to us.

Mrs. Peters: Yes, Mr. Henderson.

[The women listen to the men's steps on the stairs, then look about the kitchen.]

Mrs. Hale: I'd hate to have men coming into my kitchen, snooping around and criticizing.

[She arranges the pans under sink which the County Attorney had shoved out of place.]

Mrs. Peters: Of course it's no more than their duty.

Mrs. Hale: Duty's all right, but I guess that deputy sheriff that came out to make the fire might have got a little of this on. [Gives the roller towel a pull.] Wish I'd thought of that sooner. Seems mean to talk about her for not having things slicked up when she had to come away in such a hurry.

Mrs. Peters: [Who has gone to a small table in the left rear corner of the room, and lifted one end of a towel that covers a pan.] She had bread set.

[Stands still.]

Mrs. Hale: [Eyes fixed on a loaf of bread beside the breadbox, which is on a low shelf at the other side of the room. Moves slowly toward it.] She was going to put this in there. [Picks up loaf, then abruptly drops it. In a manner of returning to familiar things.] It's a shame about her fruit. I wonder if it's all gone. [Gets up on the chair and looks.] I think there's some here that's all right, Mrs. Peters. Yes—here; [Holding it toward the window] this is cherries, too. [Looking again.] I declare I believe that's the only one. [Gets down, bottle in her hand. Goes to the sink and wipes it off on the outside.] She'll feel awful bad after all her hard work in the hot weather. I remember the afternoon I put up my cherries last summer.

[She puts the bottle on the big kitchen table, center of the room. With a sigh, is about to sit down in the rocking-chair. Before she is seated realizes what chair it is; with a slow look at it, steps back. The chair which she has touched rocks back and forth.]

Mrs. Peters: Well, I must get those things from the front room closet. [She goes to the door at the right, but after looking into the other room, steps back.] You coming with me, Mrs. Hale? You could help me carry them.

[They go in the other room; reappear, Mrs. Peters carrying a dress and skirt, Mrs. Hale following with a pair of shoes.]

**Mrs. Peters:** My, it's cold in there.

[She puts the clothes on the big table, and hurries to the stove.]

**Mrs. Hale:** [Examining her skirt.] Wright was close. I think maybe that's why she kept so much to herself. She didn't even belong to the Ladies Aid. I suppose she felt she couldn't do her part, and then you don't enjoy things when you feel shabby. She used to wear pretty clothes and be lively, when she was Minnie Foster, one of the town girls singing in the choir. But that—oh, that was thirty years ago. This all you was to take in?

**Mrs. Peters:** She said she wanted an apron. Funny thing to want, for there isn't much to get you dirty in jail, goodness knows. But I suppose just to make her feel more natural. She said they was in the top drawer in this cupboard. Yes, here. And then her little shawl that always hung behind the door. [Opens stair door and looks.] Yes, here it is.

[Quickly shuts door leading upstairs.]

**Mrs. Hale:** [Abruptly moving toward her.] Mrs. Peters?

**Mrs. Peters:** Yes, Mrs. Hale?

**Mrs. Hale:** Do you think she did it?

**Mrs. Peters:** [In a frightened voice.] Oh, I don't know.

**Mrs. Hale:** Well, I don't think she did. Asking for an apron and her little shawl. Worrying about her fruit.

**Mrs. Peters:** [Starts to speak, glances up, where footsteps are heard in the room above. In a low voice.] Mr. Peters says it looks bad for her. Mr. Henderson is awful sarcastic in a speech and he'll make fun of her sayin' she didn't wake up.

**Mrs. Hale:** Well, I guess John Wright didn't wake when they was slipping that rope under his neck.

**Mrs. Peters:** No, it's strange. It must have been done awful crafty and still. They say it was such a—funny way to kill a man, rigging it all up like that.

**Mrs. Hale:** That's just what Mr. Hale said. There was a gun in the house. He says that's what he can't understand.

**Mrs. Peters:** Mr. Henderson said coming out that what was needed for the case was a motive; something to show anger, or—sudden feeling.

**Mrs. Hale:** [Who is standing by the table.] Well, I don't see any signs of anger around here. [She puts her hand on the dish towel which lies on the table, stands looking down at table, one half of which is clean, the other half messy.] It's wiped to here. [Makes a move as if to finish work, then turns and looks at loaf of bread outside the breadbox. Drops towel. In that voice of coming back to familiar things.] Wonder how they are finding things upstairs. I hope she had it a little more red-up° up there. You know, it seems kind of sneaking. Locking her up in town and then coming out here and trying to get her own house to turn against her!

**Mrs. Peters:** But Mrs. Hale, the law is the law.

red-up: (slang) readied up, ready to be seen.

Mrs. Hale: I s'pose 'tis. [Unbuttoning her coat.] Better loosen up your things, Mrs. Peters. You won't feel them when you go out.

[Mrs. Peters takes off her fur tippet, goes to hang it on hook at back of room, stands looking at the under part of the small corner table.]

Mrs. Peters: She was piecing a quilt.

[She brings the large sewing basket and they look at the bright pieces.]

Mrs. Hale: It's a log cabin pattern. Pretty, isn't it? I wonder if she was goin' to quilt it or just knot it?

[Footsteps have been heard coming down the stairs. The Sheriff enters followed by Hale and the County Attorney.]

Sheriff: They wonder if she was going to quilt it or just knot it!

[The men laugh; the women look abashed.]

County Attorney: [Rubbing his hands over the stove.] Frank's fire didn't do much up there, did it? Well, let's go out to the barn and get that cleared up.

[The men go outside.]

Mrs. Hale: [Resentfully.] I don't know as there's anything so strange, our takin' up our time with little things while we're waiting for them to get the evidence. [She sits down at the big table smoothing out a block with decision.] I don't see as it's anything to laugh about.

Mrs. Peters: [Apologetically.] Of course they've got awful important things on their minds.

[Pulls up a chair and joins Mrs. Hale at the table.]

Mrs. Hale: [Examining another block.] Mrs. Peters, look at this one. Here, this is the one she was working on, and look at the sewing! All the rest of it has been so nice and even. And look at this! It's all over the place! Why, it looks as if she didn't know what she was about!

[After she has said this they look at each, then start to glance back at the door. After an instant Mrs. Hale has pulled at a knot and ripped the sewing.]

Mrs. Peters: Oh, what are you doing, Mrs. Hale?

Mrs. Hale: [Mildly.] Just pulling out a stitch or two that's not sewed very good. [Threading a needle.] Bad sewing always made me fidgety.

Mrs. Peters: [Nervously.] I don't think we ought to touch things.

Mrs. Hale: I'll just finish up this end. [Suddenly stopping and leaning forward.] Mrs. Peters?

Mrs. Peters: Yes, Mrs. Hale?

Mrs. Hale: What do you suppose she was so nervous about?

Mrs. Peters: Oh—I don't know. I don't know as she was nervous. I sometimes sew awful queer when I'm just tired. [Mrs. Hale starts to say something, looks at

*Mrs. Peters, then goes on sewing.]* Well, I must get these things wrapped up. They may be through sooner than we think. *[Putting apron and other things together.]* I wonder where I can find a piece of paper, and string.

Mrs. Hale: In that cupboard, maybe.

Mrs. Peters: *[Looking in cupboard.]* Why, here's a birdcage. *[Holds it up.]* Did she have a bird, Mrs. Hale?

Mrs. Hale: Why, I don't know whether she did or not—I've not been here for so long. There was a man around last year selling canaries cheap, but I don't know as she took one; maybe she did. She used to sing real pretty herself.

Mrs. Peters: *[Glancing around.]* Seems funny to think of a bird here. But she must have had one, or why would she have a cage? I wonder what happened to it.

Mrs. Hale: I s'pose maybe the cat got it.

Mrs. Peters: No, she didn't have a cat. She's got that feeling some people have about cats—being afraid of them. My cat got in her room and she was real upset and asked me to take it out.

Mrs. Hale: My sister Bessie was like that. Queer, ain't it?

Mrs. Peters: *[Examining the cage.]* Why, look at this door. It's broke. One hinge is pulled apart.

Mrs. Hale: *[Looking too.]* Looks as if someone must have been rough with it.

Mrs. Peters: Why, yes.

*[She brings the cage forward and puts it on the table.]*

Mrs. Hale: I wish if they're going to find any evidence they'd be about it. I don't like this place.

Mrs. Peters: But I'm awful glad you came with me, Mrs. Hale. It would be lonesome for me sitting here alone.

Mrs. Hale: It would, wouldn't it? *[Dropping her sewing.]* But I tell you what I do wish, Mrs. Peters. I wish I had come over sometimes when *she* was here. I— *[Looking around the room.]*—wish I had.

Mrs. Peters: But of course you were awful busy, Mrs. Hale—your house and your children.

Mrs. Hale: I could've come. I stayed away because it weren't cheerful—and that's why I ought to have come. I—I've never liked this place. Maybe because it's down in a hollow and you don't see the road. I dunno what it is but it's a lonesome place and always was. I wish I had come over to see Minnie Foster sometimes. I can see now—

*[Shakes her head.]*

Mrs. Peters: Well, you mustn't reproach yourself, Mrs. Hale. Somehow we just don't see how it is with other folks until—something comes up.

Mrs. Hale: Not having children makes less work—but it makes a quiet house, and Wright out to work all day, and no company when he did come in. Did you know John Wright, Mrs. Peters?

Mrs. Peters: Not to know him; I've seen him in town. They say he was a good man.

Mrs. Hale: Yes—good; he didn't drink, and kept his word as well as most, I guess, and paid his debts. But he was a hard man, Mrs. Peters. Just to pass the time of day with him—[Shivers.] Like a raw wind that gets to the bone. [Pauses, her eye falling on the cage.] I should think she would'a wanted a bird. But what do you suppose went with it?

Mrs. Peters: I don't know, unless it got sick and died.

[She reaches over and swings the broken door, swings it again. Both women watch it.]

Mrs. Hale: You weren't raised round here, were you? [Mrs. Peters shakes her head.] You didn't know—her?

Mrs. Peters: Not till they brought her yesterday.

Mrs. Hale: She—come to think of it, she was kind of a like a bird herself—real sweet and pretty, but kind of timid and—fluttery. How—she—did—change. [Silence; then as if struck by a happy thought and relieved to get back to everyday things.] Tell you what, Mrs. Peters, why don't you take the quilt in with you? It might take up her mind.

Mrs. Peters: Why, I think that's a real nice idea, Mrs. Hale. There couldn't possibly be any objection to it, could there? Now, just what would I take? I wonder if her patches are in here—and her things.

[They look in the sewing basket.]

Mrs. Hale: Here's some red. I expect this has got sewing things in it. [Brings out a fancy box.] What a pretty box. Looks like something somebody would give you. Maybe her scissors are in here. [Opens box. Suddenly puts her hand to her nose.] Why—[Mrs. Peters bends nearer, then turns her face away.] There's something wrapped up in this piece of silk.

Mrs. Peters: Why, this isn't her scissors.

Mrs. Hale: [Lifting the silk.] Oh, Mrs. Peters—it's—

[Mrs. Peters bends closer.]

Mrs. Peters: It's the bird.

Mrs. Hale: [Jumping up.] But, Mrs. Peters—look at it! Its neck! Look at its neck! It's all—other side too.

Mrs. Peters: Somebody—wrung—its—neck.

[Their eyes meet. A look of growing comprehension, of horror. Steps are heard outside. Mrs. Hale slips box under quilt pieces, and sinks into her chair. Enter Sheriff and County Attorney. Mrs. Peters rises.]

County Attorney: [As one turning from serious things to little pleasantries.] Well, ladies, have you decided whether she was going to quilt it or knot it?

Mrs. Peters: We think she was going to—knot it.

County Attorney: Well, that's interesting, I'm sure. [Seeing the birdcage.] Has the bird flown?

Mrs. Hale: [Putting more quilt pieces over the box.] We think the—cat got it.

County Attorney: [Preoccupied.] Is there a cat?

[Mrs. Hale glances in a quick covert way at Mrs. Peters.]

Mrs. Peters: Well, not now. They're superstitious, you know. They leave.

County Attorney: [To Sheriff Peters, continuing an interrupted conversation.] No sign at all of anyone having come from the outside. Their own rope. Now let's go up again and go over it piece by piece. [They start upstairs.] It would have to have been someone who knew just the—

[Mrs. Peters sits down. The two women sit there not looking at one another, but as if peering into something and at the same time holding back. When they talk now it is in the manner of feeling their way over strange ground, as if afraid of what they are saying, but as if they cannot help saying it.]

Mrs. Hale: She liked the bird. She was going to bury it in that pretty box.

Mrs. Peters: [In a whisper.] When I was a girl—my kitten—there was a boy took a hatchet, and before my eyes—and before I could get there—[Covers her face an instant.] If they hadn't held me back I would have—[Catches herself, looks upstairs where steps are heard, falters weakly]—hurt him.

Mrs. Hale: [With a slow look around her.] I wonder how it would seem never to have had any children around. [Pause.] No, Wright wouldn't like the bird—a thing that sang. She used to sing. He killed that, too.

Mrs. Peters: [Moving uneasily.] We don't know who killed the bird.

Mrs. Hale: I knew John Wright.

Mrs. Peters: It was an awful thing was done in this house that night, Mrs. Hale. Killing a man while he slept, slipping a rope around his neck that choked the life out of him.

Mrs. Hale: His neck. Choked the life out of him.

[Her hand goes out and rests on the birdcage.]

Mrs. Peters: [With rising voice.] We don't know who killed him. We don't know.

Mrs. Hale: [Her own feeling not interrupted.] If there'd been years and years of nothing, then a bird to sing to you, it would be awful—still, after the bird was still.

Mrs. Peters: [Something within her speaking.] I know what stillness is. When we homesteaded in Dakota, and my first baby died—after he was two years old, and me with no other then—

Mrs. Hale: [Moving.] How soon do you suppose they'll be through looking for the evidence?

Mrs. Peters: I know what stillness is. [Pulling herself back.] The law has got to punish crime, Mrs. Hale.

Mrs. Hale: [Not as if answering that.] I wish you'd seen Minnie Foster when she wore a white dress with blue ribbons and stood up there in the choir and sang. [A look around the room.] Oh, I wish I'd come over here once in a while! That was a crime! That was a crime! Who's going to punish that?

Mrs. Peters: [Looking upstairs.] We mustn't—take on.

*Mrs. Hale:* I might have known she needed help! I know how things can be—for women. I tell you, it's queer, Mrs. Peters. We live close together and we live far apart. We all go through the same things—it's all just a different kind of the same thing. *[Brushes her eyes; noticing the bottle of fruit, reaches out for it.]* If I was you I wouldn't tell her her fruit was gone. Tell her it *ain't*. Tell her it's all right. Take this in to prove it to her. She—she may never know whether it was broke or not.

*Mrs. Peters:* *[Takes the bottle, looks about for something to wrap it in; takes petticoat from the clothes brought from the other room, very nervously begins winding this around the bottle. In a false voice.]* My, it's a good thing the men couldn't hear us. Wouldn't they just laugh! Getting all stirred up over a little thing like a—dead canary. As if that could have anything to do with—with—wouldn't they *laugh!*

*[The men are heard coming down stairs.]*

*Mrs. Hale:* *[Under her breath.]* Maybe they would—maybe they wouldn't.

*County Attorney:* No, Peters, it's all perfectly clear except a reason for doing it. But you know juries when it comes to women. If there was some definite thing. Something to show—something to make a story about—a thing that would connect up with this strange way of doing it—

*[The women's eyes meet for an instant. Enter Hale from outer door.]*

*Hale:* Well, I've got the team around. Pretty cold out there.

*County Attorney:* I'm going to stay here a while by myself. *[To the Sheriff.]* You can send Frank out for me, can't you? I want to go over everything. I'm not satisfied that we can't do better.

*Sheriff:* Do you want to see what Mrs. Peters is going to take in?

*[The County Attorney goes to the table, picks up the apron, laughs.]*

*County Attorney:* Oh, I guess they're not very dangerous things the ladies have picked out. *[Moves a few things about, disturbing the quilt pieces which cover the box. Steps back.]* No, Mrs. Peters doesn't need supervising. For that matter, a sheriff's wife is married to the law. Ever think of it that way, Mrs. Peters?

*Mrs. Peters:* Not—just that way.

*Sheriff:* *[Chuckling.]* Married to the law. *[Moves toward the other room.]* I just want you to come in here a minute, George. We ought to take a look at these windows.

*County Attorney:* *[Scoffingly.]* Oh, windows!

*Sheriff:* We'll be right out, Mr. Hale.

*[Hale goes outside. The Sheriff follows the County Attorney into the other room. Then Mrs. Hale rises, hands tight together, looking intensely at Mrs. Peters, whose eyes make a slow turn, finally meeting Mrs. Hale's. A moment Mrs. Hale holds her, then her own eyes point the way to where the box is concealed. Suddenly Mrs. Peters throws back quilt pieces and tries to put the box in the bag she is wearing. It*

*is too big. She opens box, starts to take bird out, cannot touch it, goes to pieces, stands there helpless. Sound of a knob turning in the other room. Mrs. Hale snatches the box and puts it in the pocket of her big coat. Enter County Attorney and Sheriff.]*

County Attorney: *[Facetiously.]* Well, Henry, at least we found out that she was not going to quilt it. She was going to—what is it you call it, ladies?

Mrs. Hale: *[Her hand against her pocket.]* We call it—knot it, Mr. Henderson.

CURTAIN

## QUESTIONS

1. What attitudes toward women do the Sheriff and the County Attorney express? How do Mrs. Hale and Mrs. Peters react to these sentiments?
2. Why does the County Attorney care so much about discovering a motive for the killing?
3. What does Glaspell show us about the position of women in this early twentieth-century community?
4. What do we learn about the married life of the Wrights? By what means is this knowledge revealed to us?
5. What is the setting of this play, and how does it help us to understand Mrs. Wright's deed?
6. What do you infer from the wildly stitched block in Minnie's quilt? Why does Mrs. Hale rip out the crazy stitches?
7. What is so suggestive in the ruined birdcage and the dead canary wrapped in silk? What do these objects have to do with Minnie Foster Wright? What similarity do you notice between the way the canary died and John Wright's own death?
8. What thoughts and memories confirm Mrs. Peters and Mrs. Hale in their decision to help Minnie beat the murder rap?
9. In what places does Mrs. Peters show that she is trying to be a loyal, law-abiding sheriff's wife? How do she and Mrs. Hale differ in background and temperament?
10. What ironies does the play contain? Comment on Mrs. Hale's closing speech: "We call it—knot it, Mr. Henderson." Why is that little hesitation before "knot it" such a meaningful pause?
11. Point out some moments in the play when the playwright gives us to understand much without needing a spoken word.
12. How would you sum up the play's major theme?
13. How does this play, first produced in 1916, show its age? In what ways does it seem still remarkably new?
14. "*Trifles* is a lousy mystery. All the action took place before the curtain went up. Almost in the beginning, on the third page, we find out 'who done it.' So there isn't really much reason for us to sit through the rest of the play." Discuss this view.

Some plays endure, perhaps because (among other reasons) actors take pleasure in performing them. *Trifles* is such a play: a showcase for the skills of its two principals. While the men importantly bumble about, trying to discover a motive, Mrs. Peters and Mrs. Hale solve the case right under their dull noses. The two players in these leading roles face a challenging task: to show both characters growing onstage before us. Discovering a secret that binds them, the two must realize painful truths in their own lives, become aware of all they have in common with Minnie Wright, and gradually resolve to side with the accused against the men. That *Trifles* has lately enjoyed a revival of attention may reflect its evident feminist views, its convincing portrait of two women forced reluctantly to make a moral judgment and to make a defiant move.

Some critics say that the essence of drama is conflict. Evidently, Glaspell's play is rich in this essential, even though its most violent conflict—the war between John and Minnie Wright—takes place earlier, off scene. Right away, when the menfolk barge through the door into the warm room, letting the women trail in after them; right away, when the sheriff makes fun of Minnie for worrying about "trifles" and the county attorney (that slick politician) starts crudely trying to flatter the "ladies," we sense a conflict between officious, self-important men and the women they expect to wait on them. What is the play's *theme?* Surely the title points to it: Women, who men say worry over trifles, can find in those little things large meanings.

Like a carefully constructed traditional short story, *Trifles* has a **plot,** a term sometimes taken to mean whatever happens in a story, but more exactly referring to the unique arrangement of events that the author has made. (For more about plot in a story, see Chapter One.) If Glaspell had elected to tell the story of John and Minnie Wright in chronological order, the sequence in which events took place in time, she might have written a much longer play, opening perhaps with a scene of Minnie's buying her canary and John's cold complaint, "That damned bird keeps twittering all day long!" She might have included scenes showing John strangling the canary and swearing when it beaks him; the Wrights in their loveless bed while Minnie knots her noose; and farmer Hale's entrance after the murder, with Minnie rocking. Only at the end would she have shown us what happened after the crime. That arrangement of events would have made for a quite different play than the short, tight one Glaspell wrote. By telling of events in retrospect, by having the women detectives piece together what happened, Glaspell leads us to focus not only on the murder but, more importantly, on the developing bond between the two women and their growing compassion for the accused.

If *Trifles* may be said to have a **protagonist,** a leading character—a word we usually save for the primary figure of a larger and more eventful play such as *Othello* or *Death of a Salesman*—then you would call the two women dual protagonists. Both act in unison to make the plot unfold. Or you could argue that Mrs. Hale, because she destroys the wild stitching in the quilt; because she finds the dead canary; because she invents a cat to catch the bird (thus deceiving the county attorney); and because in the end when Mrs. Peters helplessly "goes to pieces" it is she who takes the initiative and seizes the evidence, deserves to be called the protagonist. More than anyone else in the play, you could claim, the more decisive Mrs. Hale makes things happen.

A vital part in most plays is an **exposition,** the part in which we first meet the characters, learn what happened before the curtain rose, and find out what is happening now. For a one-act play, *Trifles* has a fairly long exposition, extending from the opening of the kitchen door through the end of farmer Hale's story. Clearly, this substantial exposition is necessary to set the situation and to fill in the facts of the crime. By comparison, Shakespeare's far longer *Tragedy of Richard III* begins almost abruptly, with its protagonist, a duke who yearns to be king, summing up history in an opening speech and revealing his evil character: "And therefore, since I cannot prove a lover . . . I am determined to prove a villain." But Glaspell, too, knows her craft. In the exposition, we are given a **foreshadowing** (or hint of what is to come) in Hale's dry remark, "I didn't know as what his wife wanted made much difference to John." The remark announces the play's theme that men often ignore women's feelings, and it hints at Minnie Wright's motive, later to be revealed. The county attorney, failing to pick up a valuable clue, tables the discussion. (Still another foreshadowing occurs in Mrs. Hale's ripping out the wild, panicky stitches in Minnie's quilt. In the end, Mrs. Hale will make a similar final move to conceal the evidence.)

With the county attorney's speech to the sheriff, "You're convinced that there was nothing important here—nothing that would point to any motive," we begin to understand what he seeks. As he will make even clearer later, the attorney needs a motive in order to convict the accused wife of murder in the first degree. Will Minnie's motive in killing her husband be discovered? Through the first two-thirds of *Trifles*, this is the play's **dramatic question.** Whether or not we state such a question in our minds, and it is doubtful that we do, our interest quickens as we sense that here is a problem to be solved, an uncertainty to be dissipated. When Mrs. Hale and Mrs. Peters find the dead canary with the twisted neck, the question is answered. We know that Minnie killed John to repay him for his act of gross cruelty. But the playwright now raises a *new* dramatic question. Having discovered Minnie's motive, will the women reveal it to the lawmen? Or (if you care to phrase the new question differently), what will they do with the incriminating evidence? We keep reading, or stay clamped to our theater seats, because we want that question answered. We share the women's secret now, and we want to see what they will do with it.

Tightly packed, the one-act *Trifles* contains but one plot: the story of how two women discover evidence that might hang another woman and then hide it. But some plays, usually longer ones, may be more complicated. They may contain a **double plot** (or **subplot**), a secondary arrangement of incidents, involving not the protagonist but someone less important. In Henrik Ibsen's *A Doll's House*, the main plot involves a woman and her husband. But they are joined by a second couple, whose fortunes we also follow with interest and whose futures pose another dramatic question.

Step by step, *Trifles* builds to a **climax:** a moment, usually coming late in a play, when tension reaches its greatest height. At such a moment, we sense that the play's dramatic question (or its final dramatic question, if the writer has posed two or more) is about to be answered. In *Trifles*, this climax occurs when Mrs. Peters finds herself torn between her desire to save Minnie and her duty to the law. "It was an awful thing that was done in this house that night," she reminds herself in one speech, suggesting that Minnie deserves to be punished; then in the next speech she insists, "We don't know who killed him. We don't *know*." Shortly after that, in one speech she voices two warring attitudes. Remembering the loss of her first child, she sympathizes with Minnie: "I know what stillness is." But in her next breath she recalls once more her duty to be a loyal sheriff's wife: "The law has got to punish crime, Mrs. Hale." For a moment, she is placed in conflict with Mrs. Hale, who knew Minnie personally. The two now stand on the edge of a fateful brink. Which way will they decide?[1]

From this moment of climax, the play, like its protagonist (or if you like, protagonists), will make a final move. Mrs. Peters takes her stand. Mrs. Hale, too, decides. She owes Minnie something to make up for her own "crime"—her failure to visit the desperate woman. The plot now charges ahead to its outcome or **resolution,** also called the **conclusion** or **dénouement** (French: untying of a knot). The two women act: they scoop up the damaging evidence. Seconds before the very end, Glaspell heightens the **suspense,** our enjoyable anxiety, by making Mrs. Peters fumble with the incriminating box as the sheriff and the county attorney draw near. Mrs. Hale's swift grab for the evidence saves the day and presumably saves Minnie's life. The sound of the doorknob turning in the next room, as the lawmen return, is a small but effective bit of **stage business**— any nonverbal action that engages the attention of an audience. When Mrs. Hale almost sits down in Minnie's place, the empty chair that ominously starts rocking is another brilliant piece of stage business. Not only does it give us something interesting to watch, but it also gives us something to think about.

Some critics maintain that events in a plot can be arranged in the outline of a pyramid.[2] In this view, a play begins with a **rising action,** that part of the story (including the exposition) in which events start moving toward a climax. After the climax, the story tapers off in a **falling action:** the subsequent events, including a resolution. In a tragedy, this falling action usually is recognizable: the protagonist's fortunes proceed downhill to an inexorable end.

Some plays indeed have demonstrable pyramids. In *Trifles,* we might claim that in the first two-thirds of the play a rising action builds up in intensity. It proceeds through each main incident: the finding of the crazily stitched quilt, Mrs. Hale's ripping out the evidence, the discovery of the bird cage, then the bird itself, and Mrs. Hale's concealing it. At the climax, the peak of the pyramid, the two women seem about to clash as Mrs. Peters wavers uncertainly. The action then falls to a swift resolution. But if you outlined that pyramid on paper, it would look lopsided—a long rise and a short, steep fall. The pyramid metaphor seems more meaningfully to fit longer plays, among them some classic tragedies. Try it on *Oedipus the King* or, for an even neater fit, on Shakespeare's *Julius*

---

[1]You will sometimes hear *climax* used in a different sense: to mean any **crisis**—that is, a moment of tension when one or another outcome is possible. What *crisis* means will be easy to remember if you think of a crisis in medicine: the turning point in a disease when it becomes clear that a patient will either die or recover. In talking about plays, you will probably find both *crisis* and *climax* useful. You can say that a play has more than one crisis, perhaps several. In such a play, the last and most decisive crisis is the climax. A play has only one climax.

[2]The metaphor of a play as a pyramid was invented by German critic Gustav Freytag in his *Techniques of the Drama,* 1904; reprint ed., New York: Arno (1968).

*Caesar*—an unusual play in that its climax, the assassination of Caesar, occurs exactly in the middle (III, 1), right where a good pyramid's point ought to be. But in most other plays, it is hard to find a symmetrical pyramid. (For a demonstration of another, quite different way to outline *Trifles*, see "Writing a Card Report" on pages 1782–1785.)

Because its action occurs all at one time and in one place, *Trifles* happens to observe the **unities,** certain principles of good drama laid down by Italian literary critics in the sixteenth century. Interpreting the theories of Aristotle as binding laws, these critics set down three basic principles: a good play, they maintained, should display unity of *action*, unity of *time*, and unity of *place*. In practical terms, this theory maintained that a play must represent a single series of interrelated actions that take place within twenty-four hours in a single location. Further, they insisted, to have true unity of action, a play had to be entirely serious or entirely funny. Mixing tragic and comic elements was not allowed. That Glaspell consciously strove to obey those critics is doubtful and certainly many great plays, like Shakespeare's *Othello*, defy such arbitrary rules. Still, it is at least arguable that some of the power of *Trifles* (or Sophocles's *Oedipus the King*) comes from the intensity of the playwright's concentration on what happens in one place, in one short expanse of time.

Brief though it is, *Trifles* has main elements you will find in much longer, more complicated plays. It even has **symbols,** things that hint at large meanings: the broken bird cage and the dead canary, both suggesting the music and the joy that John Wright stifled in Minnie and the terrible stillness that followed his killing the one thing she loved. Perhaps the lone remaining jar of cherries, too, radiates suggestions: it is the one bright, cheerful thing poor Minnie has to show for a whole summer of toil. Symbols in drama may be as big as a house—the home in Ibsen's *A Doll's House*, for instance—or they may appear to be trifles. In Glaspell's rich art, such trifles aren't trifling at all.[3]

## TRAGEDY AND COMEDY

By **tragedy,** generally speaking, we mean a play that portrays a conflict between human beings and some superior, overwhelming force. It ends sorrowfully and disastrously, and this outcome seems inevitable. Few spectators of *Oedipus the King* wonder how the play will turn out or wish for a happy ending. "In a tragedy," French playwright Jean Anouilh has remarked, "nothing is in doubt and everyone's destiny is known. . . . Tragedy is restful, and the reason is that hope, that foul, deceitful thing, has no part in it. There isn't any hope. You're trapped. The whole sky has fallen on you, and all you can do about it is shout."[4]

---

[3]Plays can also contain symbolic characters (generally flat ones like a prophet who croaks, "Beware the ides of March"), symbolic settings, and symbolic gestures. For more about symbolism, see Chapters Seven and Twenty-four.

[4]Preface to *Antigonê*, translated by Louis Galantière (New York: Random, 1946).

Many of our ideas of tragedy go back to ancient Athens; the plays of the Greek dramatists Sophocles, Aeschylus, and Euripides exemplify the art of tragedy. In the fourth century B.C., the philosopher Aristotle described Sophocles's *Oedipus the King* and other tragedies he had seen, analyzing their elements and trying to account for their power over our emotions. Aristotle's observations will make more sense after you read *Oedipus the King*, so let us save discussion of them for the next chapter. For now, to understand something of the nature of tragedy, we suggest you begin by reading not a classic Greek tragedy but a gripping modern tragedy by the Irish poet and playwright John Millington Synge.

The people of Synge's play are simple fisherfolk who live in the Aran Islands, outposts of barren rock washed by the stormy North Atlantic. They are speakers of Gaelic, the old Irish language. Living in their midst, Synge studied their plain, colorful speech and tried to convey a sense of it in the English of this play. Notice how slowly and quietly the tragedy begins. Gradually, disturbing facts fit into place until we know the whole story of a family that has long struggled with the sea, a dangerous and demanding friend, a relentless enemy.

## John Millington Synge

John Millington Synge

*John Millington Synge (pronounced "Sing," 1871–1909), a leading figure in the Irish literary revival at the turn of this century, was born near Dublin, where he died. After graduation from Dublin's Trinity College, he studied music in Germany, Italy, and France. In 1899 he struck up a friendship with poet and playwright William Butler Yeats, who advised him to go to the Aran Islands off Ireland's west coast, listen to the spoken language, and observe the life of the islanders. For Synge, this advice bore fruit: in his plays* The Shadow of the Glen *(1903) and* Riders to the Sea *(1904), and in a book of impressions,* The Aran Islands *(1907). When first performed at the Abbey Theater in Dublin in 1907, Synge's dark comedy* The Playboy of the Western World *caused a riot, some in the audience objecting to its unflattering, satiric view of rural Irishmen. Later, its Irish-American audiences rioted in Boston, Philadelphia, and New York. A considerable poet as well as a playwright, Synge struggled for years against lymphatic sarcoma, a disease which curtailed his life. His unfinished tragedy,* Deirdre of the Sorrows, *was produced after his death.*

Characters

Maurya, an old woman
Bartley, her son
Cathleen, her daughter
Nora, a younger daughter
Men and Women

Scene. *An Island off the West of Ireland.*
*Cottage kitchen, with nets, oil-skins, spinning-wheel, some new boards standing by the wall, etc. Cathleen, a girl of about twenty, finishes kneading cake, and puts it down in the pot-oven by the fire; then wipes her hands, and begins to spin at the wheel. Nora, a young girl, puts her head in at the door.*

---

Riders to the Sea: The title alludes to a well-known Bible story. After Moses opens a corridor in the sea for the children of Israel to pass through, he obeys the Lord and lets the waters "come again upon the Egyptians, upon their chariots, and upon their horsemen." Then he and the Israelites "sing unto the Lord, for he has triumphed gloriously: the horse and his rider hath he thrown into the sea" (*Exodus* 14:21–31, 15:1–5).

*Nora (in a low voice):* Where is she?

*Cathleen:* She's lying down, God help her, and may be sleeping, if she's able.

> *Nora comes in softly, and takes a bundle from under her shawl.*

*Cathleen (spinning the wheel rapidly):* What is it you have?

*Nora:* The young priest is after bringing them.° It's a shirt and a plain stocking were got off a drowned man in Donegal.

> *Cathleen stops her wheel with a sudden movement, and leans out to listen.*

*Nora:* We're to find out if it's Michael's they are, some time herself will be down looking by the sea.

*Cathleen:* How would they be Michael's, Nora? How would he go the length of that way to the far north?

*Nora:* The young priest says he's known the like of it. "If it's Michael's they are," says he, "you can tell yourself he's got a clean burial by the grace of God, and if they're not his, let no one say a word about them, for she'll be getting her death," says he, "with crying and lamenting."

> *The door which Nora half-closed is blown open by a gust of wind.*

*Cathleen (looking out anxiously):* Did you ask him would he stop Bartley going this day with the horses to the Galway fair?

*Nora:* "I won't stop him," says he, "but let you not be afraid. Herself does be saying prayers half through the night, and the Almighty God won't leave her destitute," says he, "with no son living."

*Cathleen:* Is the sea bad by the white rocks, Nora?

*Nora:* Middling bad, God help us. There's a great roaring in the west, and it's worse it'll be getting when the tide's turned to the wind.

> *She goes over to the table with the bundle.*

Shall I open it now?

*Cathleen:* Maybe she'd wake up on us, and come in before we'd done. (*Coming to the table.*) It's a long time we'll be, and the two of us crying.

*Nora (goes to the inner door and listens):* She's moving about on the bed. She'll be coming in a minute.

*Cathleen:* Give me the ladder, and I'll put them up in the turf-loft, the way she won't know of them at all, and maybe when the tide turns she'll be going down to see would he be floating from the east.

> *They put the ladder against the gable of the chimney; Cathleen goes up a few steps and hides the bundle in the turf-loft. Maurya comes from the inner room.*

*Maurya (looking up at Cathleen and speaking querulously):* Isn't it turf enough you have for this day and evening?

---

*is after bringing them:* has just brought them.

*Cathleen*: There's a cake baking at the fire for a short space (*throwing down the turf*) and Bartley will want it when the tide turns if he goes to Connemara.

*Nora picks up the turf and puts it round the pot-oven.*

*Maurya* (*sitting down on a stool at the fire*): He won't go this day with the wind rising from the south and west. He won't go this day, for the young priest will stop him surely.

*Nora*: He'll not stop him, mother, and I heard Eamon Simon and Stephen Pheety and Colum Shawn saying he would go.

*Maurya*: Where is he itself?

*Nora*: He went down to see would there be another boat sailing in the week, and I'm thinking it won't be long till he's here now, for the tide's turning at the green head, and the hooker's° tacking from the east.

*Cathleen*: I hear some one passing the big stones.

*Nora* (*looking out*): He's coming now, and he in a hurry.

*Bartley* (*comes in and looks round the room. Speaking sadly and quietly*): Where is the bit of new rope, Cathleen, was bought in Connemara?

*Cathleen* (*coming down*): Give it to him, Nora; it's on a nail by the white boards. I hung it up this morning, for the pig with the black feet was eating it.

*Nora* (*giving him a rope*): Is that it, Bartley?

*Maurya*: You'd do right to leave that rope, Bartley, hanging by the boards. (*Bartley takes the rope.*) It will be wanting in this place. I'm telling you, if Michael is washed up to-morrow morning, or the next morning, or any morning in the week, for it's a deep grave we'll make him by the grace of God.

*Bartley* (*beginning to work with the rope*): I've no halter the way I can ride down on the mare, and I must go now quickly. This is the one boat going for two weeks or beyond it, and the fair will be a good fair for horses I heard them saying below.

*Maurya*: It's a hard thing they'll be saying below if the body is washed up and there's no man in it to make the coffin, and I after giving a big price for the finest white boards you'd find in Connemara.

*She looks round at the boards.*

*Bartley*: How would it be washed up, and we after looking each day for nine days, and a strong wind blowing a while back from the west and south?

*Maurya*: If it wasn't found itself, that wind is raising the sea, and there was a star up against the moon, and it rising in the night. If it was a hundred horses, or a thousand horses you had itself, what is the price of a thousand horses against a son where there is one son only?

*Bartley* (*working at the halter, to Cathleen*): Let you go down each day, and see the sheep aren't jumping in on the rye, and if the jobber comes you can sell the pig with the black feet if there is a good price going.

---

*hooker:* a one-masted fishing boat.

*Maurya:* How would the like of her get a good price for a pig?

*Bartley (to Cathleen):* If the west wind holds with the last bit of the moon let you and Nora get up weed enough for another cock for the kelp.° It's hard set we'll be from this day with no one in it but one man to work.

*Maurya:* It's hard set we'll be surely the day you're drownd'd with the rest. What way will I live and the girls with me, and I an old woman looking for the grave?

*Bartley lays down the halter, takes off his old coat, and puts on a newer one of the same flannel.*

*Bartley (to Nora):* Is she coming to the pier?

*Nora (looking out):* She's passing the green head and letting fall her sails.

*Bartley (getting his purse and tobacco):* I'll have half an hour to go down, and you'll see me coming again in two days, or in three days, or maybe in four days if the wind is bad.

*Maurya (turning round to the fire, and putting her shawl over her head):* Isn't it a hard and cruel man won't hear a word from an old woman, and she holding him from the sea?

*Cathleen:* It's the life of a young man to be going on the sea, and who would listen to an old woman with one thing and she saying it over?

*Bartley (taking the halter):* I must go now quickly. I'll ride down on the red mare, and the gray pony'll run behind me. . . . The blessing of God on you.

*He goes out.*

*Maurya (crying out as he is in the door):* He's gone now, God spare us, and we'll not see him again. He's gone now, and when the black night is falling I'll have no son left me in the world.

*Cathleen:* Why wouldn't you give him your blessing and he looking round in the door? Isn't it sorrow enough is on every one in this house without your sending him out with an unlucky word behind him, and a hard word in his ear?

*Maurya takes up the tongs and begins raking the fire aimlessly without looking round.*

*Nora (turning towards her):* You're taking away the turf from the cake.

*Cathleen (crying out):* The Son of God forgive us, Nora, we're after forgetting his bit of bread.

*She comes over to the fire.*

*Nora:* And it's destroyed he'll be going till dark night, and he after eating nothing since the sun went up.

---

*another cock for the kelp:* another pile of seaweed. The islanders harvest the weed to fertilize their sparse, rocky soil.

*Cathleen (turning the cake out of the oven):* It's destroyed he'll be, surely. There's no sense left on any person in a house where an old woman will be talking for ever.

*Maurya sways herself on her stool.*

*Cathleen (cutting off some of the bread and rolling it in a cloth; to Maurya):* Let you go down now to the spring well and give him this and he passing. You'll see him then and the dark word will be broken, and you can say "God speed you," the way he'll be easy in his mind.

*Maurya (taking the bread):* Will I be in it as soon as himself?

*Cathleen:* If you go now quickly.

*Maurya (standing up unsteadily):* It's hard set I am to walk.

*Cathleen (looking at her anxiously):* Give her the stick, Nora, or maybe she'll slip on the big stones.

*Nora:* What stick?

*Cathleen:* The stick Michael brought from Connemara.

*Maurya (taking a stick Nora gives her):* In the big world the old people do be leaving things after them for their sons and children, but in this place it is the young men do be leaving things behind for them that do be old.

*She goes out slowly. Nora goes over to the ladder.*

*Cathleen:* Wait, Nora, maybe she'd turn back quickly. She's that sorry, God help her, you wouldn't know the thing she'd do.

*Nora:* Is she gone around by the bush?

*Cathleen (looking out):* She's gone now. Throw it down quickly, for the Lord knows when she'll be out of it again.

*Nora (getting the bundle from the loft):* The young priest said he'd be passing tomorrow, and we might go down and speak to him below if it's Michael's they are surely.

*Cathleen (taking the bundle):* Did he say what way they were found?

*Nora (coming down):* "There were two men," says he, "and they rowing round with poteen before the cocks crowed,° and the oar of one of them caught the body, and they passing the black cliffs of the north."

*Cathleen (trying to open the bundle):* Give me a knife, Nora, the strings perished with the salt water, and there's a black knot on it you wouldn't loosen in a week.

*Nora (giving her a knife):* I've heard tell it was a long way to Donegal.

*Cathleen (cutting the string):* It is surely. There was a man in here a while ago—the man sold us that knife—and he said if you set off walking from the rock beyond, it would be seven days you'd be in Donegal.

*Nora:* And what time would a man take, and he floating?

---

*rowing round with poteen . . . crowed:* transporting moonshine whiskey under cover of darkness.

*Cathleen opens the bundle and takes out a bit of a stocking. They look at them eagerly.*

Cathleen *(in a low voice)*: The Lord spare us, Nora! isn't it a queer hard thing to say if it's his they are surely?

Nora: I'll get his shirt off the hook the way we can put the one flannel on the other. *(She looks through some clothes hanging in the corner.)* It's not with them, Cathleen, and where will it be?

Cathleen: I'm thinking Bartley put it on him in the morning, for his own shirt was heavy with the salt in it. *(Pointing to the corner.)* There's a bit of a sleeve was of the same stuff. Give me that and it will do.

*Nora brings it to her and they compare the flannel.*

Cathleen: It's the same stuff, Nora; but if it is itself aren't there great rolls of it in the shops of Galway, and isn't it many another man may have a shirt of it as well as Michael himself?

Nora *(who has taken up the stocking and counted the stitches, crying out)*: It's Michael, Cathleen, it's Michael; God spare his soul, and what will herself say when she hears this story, and Bartley on the sea?

Cathleen *(taking the stocking)*: It's a plain stocking.

Nora: It's the second one of the third pair I knitted, and I put up three score stitches, and I dropped four of them.

Cathleen *(counts the stitches)*: It's that number is in it. *(Crying out.)* Ah, Nora, isn't it a bitter thing to think of him floating that way to the far north, and no one to keen° him but the black hags that do be flying on the sea?

Nora *(swinging herself round, and throwing out her arms on the clothes)*: And isn't it a pitiful thing when there is nothing left of a man who was a great rower and fisher, but a bit of an old shirt and a plain stocking?

Cathleen *(after an instant)*: Tell me is herself coming, Nora? I hear a little sound on the path.

Nora *(looking out)*: She is, Cathleen. She's coming up to the door.

Cathleen: Put these things away before she'll come in. Maybe it's easier she'll be after giving her blessing to Bartley, and we won't let on we've heard anything the time he's on the sea.

Nora *(helping Cathleen to close the bundle)*: We'll put them here in the corner.

*They put them into a hole in the chimney corner. Cathleen goes back to the spinning-wheel.*

Nora: Will she see it was crying I was?

Cathleen: Keep your back to the door the way the light'll not be on you.

*Nora sits down at the chimney corner, with her back to the door. Maurya comes in very slowly, without looking at the girls, and goes over to her stool at the other side*

---

keen: weep and wail.

*of the fire. The cloth with the bread is still in her hand. The girls look at each other, and Nora points to the bundle of bread.*

Cathleen *(after spinning for a moment)*: You didn't give him his bit of bread?

*Maurya begins to keen softly, without turning round.*

Cathleen: Did you see him riding down?

*Maurya goes on keening.*

Cathleen *(a little impatiently)*: God forgive you; isn't it a better thing to raise your voice and tell what you seen, than to be making lamentation for a thing that's done? Did you see Bartley, I'm saying to you.
Maurya *(with a weak voice)*: My heart's broken from this day.
Cathleen *(as before)*: Did you see Bartley?
Maurya: I seen the fearfulest thing.
Cathleen *(leaves her wheel and looks out)*: God forgive you; he's riding the mare now over the green head, and the gray pony behind him.
Maurya *(starts, so that her shawl falls back from her head and shows her white tossed hair. With a frightened voice)*: The gray pony behind him.
Cathleen *(coming to the fire)*: What is it ails you, at all?
Maurya *(speaking very slowly)*: I've seen the fearfulest thing any person has seen, since the day Bride Dara seen the dead man with the child in his arms.
Cathleen and Nora: Uah.°

*They crouch down in front of the old woman at the fire.*

Nora: Tell us what it is you seen.
Maurya: I went down to the spring well, and I stood there saying a prayer to myself. Then Bartley came along, and he riding on the red mare with the gray pony behind him. *(She puts up her hands, as if to hide something from her eyes.)* The Son of God spare us, Nora!
Cathleen: What is it you seen?
Maurya: I seen Michael himself.
Cathleen *(speaking softly)*: You did not Mother; it wasn't Michael you seen, for his body is after being found in the far north, and he's got a clean burial by the grace of God.
Maurya *(a little defiantly)*: I'm after seeing him this day, and he riding and galloping. Bartley came first on the red mare; and I tried to say "God speed you," but something choked the words in my throat. He went by quickly; and "the blessing of God on you," says he, and I could say nothing. I looked up then, and I crying, at the gray pony, and there was Michael upon it—with fine clothes on him, and new shoes on his feet.
Cathleen *(begins to keen)*: It's destroyed we are from this day. It's destroyed, surely.

___

*Uah:* exclamation of horror and surprise.

*Nora:* Didn't the young priest say the Almighty God wouldn't leave her destitute with no son living?

*Maurya (in a low voice, but clearly):* It's little the like of him knows of the sea. . . . Bartley will be lost now, and let you call in Eamon and make me a good coffin out of the white boards, for I won't live after them. I've had a husband, and a husband's father, and six sons in this house—six fine men, though it was a hard birth I had with every one of them and they coming to the world—and some of them were found and some of them were not found, but they're gone now the lot of them. . . . There were Stephen, and Shawn, were lost in the great wind, and found after in the Bay of Gregory of the Golden Mouth, and carried up the two of them on the one plank, and in by that door.

*She pauses for a moment, the girls start as if they heard something through the door that is half open behind them.*

*Nora (in a whisper):* Did you hear that, Cathleen? Did you hear a noise in the north-east?

*Cathleen (in a whisper):* There's some one after crying out by the seashore.

*Maurya (continues without hearing anything):* There was Sheamus and his father, and his own father again, were lost in a dark night, and not a stick or sign was seen of them when the sun went up. There was Patch after was drowned out of a curagh° that turned over. I was sitting here with Bartley, and he a baby, lying on my two knees, and I seen two women, and three women, and four women coming in, and they crossing themselves, and not saying a word. I looked out then, and there were men coming after them, and they holding a thing in the half of a red sail, and water dripping out of it—it was a dry day, Nora—and leaving a track to the door.

*She pauses again with her hand stretched out towards the door. It opens softly and old women begin to come in, crossing themselves on the threshold, and kneeling down in front of the stage with red petticoats over their heads.*

*Maurya (half in a dream, to Cathleen):* Is it Patch, or Michael, or what is it at all?

*Cathleen:* Michael is after being found in the far north, and when he is found there how could he be here in this place?

*Maurya:* There does be a power of young men floating round in the sea, and what way would they know if it was Michael they had, or another man like him, for when a man is nine days in the sea, and the wind blowing, it's hard set his own mother would be to say what man was it.

*Cathleen:* It's Michael, God spare him, for they're after sending us a bit of his clothes from the far north.

*She reaches out and hands Maurya the clothes that belonged to Michael. Maurya stands up slowly and takes them in her hand. Nora looks out.*

---

*curagh:* a canvas-bottomed boat.

*Nora*: They're carrying a thing among them and there's water dripping out of it and leaving a track by the big stones.

*Cathleen (in a whisper to the women who have come in)*: Is it Bartley it is?

*One of the Women*: It is surely, God rest his soul.

*Two younger women come in and pull out the table. Then men carry in the body of Bartley, laid on a plank, with a bit of sail over it, and lay it on the table.*

*Cathleen (to the women, as they are doing so)*: What way was he drowned?

*One of the Women*: The gray pony knocked him into the sea, and he was washed out where there is a great surf on the white rocks.

*Maurya has gone over and knelt down at the head of the table. The women are keening softly and swaying themselves with a slow movement. Cathleen and Nora kneel at the other end of the table. The men kneel near the door.*

*Maurya (raising her head and speaking as if she did not see the people around her)*: They're all gone now, and there isn't anything more the sea can do to me. . . . I'll have no call now to be up crying and praying when the wind breaks from the south and you can hear the surf is in the east, and the surf is in the west, making a great stir with the two noises, and they hitting one on the other. I'll have no call now to be going down and getting Holy Water in the dark nights after Samhain,° and I won't care what way the sea is when the other women will be keening. *(To Nora.)* Give me the Holy Water, Nora, there's a small cup still on the dresser.

*Nora gives it to her.*

*Maurya (drops Michael's clothes across Bartley's feet, and sprinkles the Holy Water over him.)*: It isn't that I haven't prayed for you, Bartley, to the Almighty God. It isn't that I haven't said prayers in the dark night till you wouldn't know what I'ld be saying; but it's a great rest I'll have now, and it's time surely. It's a great rest I'll have now, and great sleeping in the long nights after Samhain, if it's only a bit of wet flour we do have to eat, and maybe a fish that would be stinking.

*She kneels down again, crossing herself, and saying prayers under her breath.*

*Cathleen (to an old man)*: Maybe yourself and Eamon would make a coffin when the sun rises. We have fine white boards herself bought, God help her, thinking Michael would be found, and I have a new cake you can eat while you'll be working.

*The Old Man (looking at the boards)*: Are there nails with them?

*Cathleen*: There are not, Colum; we didn't think of the nails.

*Another Man*: It's a great wonder she wouldn't think of the nails, and all the coffins she's been made already.

---

*Samhain*: All Saints' Day.

*Cathleen*: It's getting old she is, and broken.

> *Maurya stands up again very slowly and spreads out the pieces of Michael's clothes beside the body, sprinkling them with the last of the Holy Water.*

*Nora (in a whisper to Cathleen)*: She's quiet now and easy; but the day Michael was drowned you could hear her crying out from this to the spring well. It's fonder she was of Michael, and would any one have thought that?

*Cathleen (slowly and clearly)*: An old woman will be soon tired with anything she will do, and isn't it nine days herself is after crying and keening, and making great sorrow in the house?

*Maurya (puts the empty cup mouth downwards on the table, and lays her hands together on Bartley's feet)*: They're all together this time, and the end is come. May the Almighty God have mercy on Bartley's soul, and on Michael's soul, and on the souls of Sheamus and Patch, and Stephen and Shawn *(bending her head)*; and may He have mercy on my soul, Nora, and on the soul of every one is left living in the world.

> *She pauses, and the keen rises a little more loudly from the women, then sinks away.*

*Maurya (continuing)*: Michael has a clean burial in the far north, by the grace of the Almighty God. Bartley will have a fine coffin out of the white boards, and a deep grave surely. What more can we want than that? No man at all can be living for ever, and we must be satisfied.

> *She kneels down again and the curtain falls slowly.*

## QUESTIONS

1. What is the situation at the start of *Riders to the Sea*? What motivates Cathleen and Nora to hide Michael's clothes from their mother?
2. What suggestions of deeper meaning do you find in the abruptness with which Cathleen stops her spinning wheel at Nora's mention of the clothes that have been found? in the gust of wind that opens the half-closed door?
3. What motivates the priest not to interfere with Bartley's plan to take the horses to the Galway fair? Why does his mother want him to stay home? How do Cathleen, Nora, and Bartley react to their mother's request?
4. What does Maurya see when she goes to the spring well to give Bartley his bread? What is there about her account of it that makes Cathleen say, "It's destroyed we are from this day. It's destroyed, surely"?
5. How does Bartley die? At what moment is his death foreshadowed?
6. Do you agree with Cathleen's observation at the end of the play that Maurya is "broken"? Explain.
7. Does *Riders to the Sea* have any protagonist? If so, what character has this central role?

**Comedy,** from the Greek *komos*, "a revel," is thought to have originated in festivities to celebrate spring: ritual performances in praise of Dionysus, god of fertility and wine. In drama, comedy may be broadly defined as whatever makes us laugh. A comedy may be a name for one entire play, or we may say that there is comedy in only part of a play—as in a comic character or a comic situation.

The best-known traditional emblem of drama—a pair of masks, one sorrowful (representing tragedy) and one smiling (representing comedy)—suggests that tragedy and comedy, although opposites, are close relatives. Often, comedy shows people getting into trouble through error or weakness; in this respect it is akin to tragedy. But an important difference between comedy and tragedy lies in the attitude toward human failing that is expected of us. When a main character in a comedy suffers from overweening pride, as does Oedipus, or if he fails to recognize that his bride-to-be is actually his mother, we laugh—something we would never do in watching a competent performance of *Oedipus the King.*

Many theories have been propounded to explain why we laugh; most of these notions fall into a few familiar types. One school, exemplified by French philosopher Henri Bergson, sees laughter as a form of ridicule, implying a feeling of disinterested superiority: all jokes are *on* somebody. Bergson suggests that laughter springs from situations in which we sense a conflict between some mechanical or rigid pattern of behavior and our sense of a more natural or "organic" kind of behavior that is possible.[1] An example occurs in Buster Keaton's comic film *The Boat*: having launched a little boat that springs a leak, Keaton rigidly goes down with it, with frozen face. (The more natural and organic thing to do would be to swim for shore.) Other thinkers view laughter as our response to expectations fulfilled, or to expectations set up but then suddenly frustrated. Some hold it to be the expression of our delight in seeing our suppressed urges acted out (as when a comedian hurls an egg at a pompous stuffed shirt); some, to be our defensive reaction to a painful and disturbing truth.

Derisive humor is basic to **satiric comedy,** in which human weakness or folly is ridiculed from a vantage point of supposedly enlightened superiority. Satiric comedy may be coolly malicious and gently biting, but it tends to be critical of people, their manners, and their morals. It is at least as old as the comedies of Aristophanes, who thrived in the fifth century B.C. In *Lysistrata*, the satirist shows how the women of two warring cities speedily halt a war by agreeing to deny themselves to their husbands. (The satirist's target is men so proud that they go to war rather than make the slightest concession.)

Comedy is often divided into two varieties—"high" and "low." **High comedy** relies more on wit and wordplay than on physical action for its humor. It tries to address the audience's intelligence by pointing out the pretension and hypocrisy of human behavior. High comedy also generally avoids derisive humor—jokes about physical appearances would, for example, be avoided. One technique it employs to appeal to a sophisticated, verbal audience is use of the **epigram,** a brief and witty statement that memorably expresses some truth, large or small. Oscar Wilde's plays like *The Importance of Being Earnest* (1895) and *Lady Windermere's Fan* (1892) sparkle with such brilliant epigrams as: "I can resist everything except temptation"; "Experience is the name everyone gives to their mistakes"; "There is only one thing worse than being talked about, and that is not being talked about." A type of high comedy is the **comedy of manners,** a

---

[1]See Bergson's essay "Le Rire" (1900), translated as "Laughter" in *Comedy*, ed. Wylie Sypher (New York: Anchor, 1956).

witty satire set in elite or fashionable society. The comedy of manners was especially popular in the **Restoration period** (the period after 1660 when Charles II, restored to the English throne, reopened the London playhouse, which had been closed by the Puritans who considered theater immoral). The great Restoration playwrights like William Congreve and George Farquhar especially excelled at comedies of manners. In the twentieth century splendid comedies of manners continue to be written. Bernard Shaw's *Pygmalion* (1913), which eventually became the musical *My Fair Lady*, contrasts life in the streets of London with that in aristocratic drawing rooms. Contemporary playwrights like Tom Stoppard, Michael Frayn, Tina Howe, and the late Joe Orton have all created memorable comedies of manners.

**Low comedy** explores the opposite extreme of humor. It places greater emphasis on physical action and visual gags, and its verbal jokes do not require much intellect to appreciate (as in Groucho Marx's pithy put-down to his brother Chico, "You have the brain of a five-year-old, and I bet he was glad to get rid of it!"). Low comedy does not avoid derisive humor; rather it revels in making fun of whatever will get a good laugh. Drunkenness, stupidity, lust, senility, trickery, insult, and clumsiness are inexhaustible staples for this style of comedy. Although it is all too easy for critics to dismiss low comedy, like high comedy it also serves a valuable purpose in satirizing human failings. Shakespeare indulged in coarse humor in some of his noblest plays. Low comedy is usually the preferred style of popular culture, and it has inspired many incisive satires on modern life—from the classic films of Laurel and Hardy and the Marx Brothers to the weekly TV antics of *Monty Python's Flying Circus* and Matt Groening's *The Simpsons*.

Low comedy includes several distinct types. One is the **burlesque,** a broadly humorous parody or travesty of another play or kind of play. (In the United States, *burlesque* is something else: a once-popular form of show business featuring stripteases interspersed with bits of ribald low comedy.) Another valuable type of low comedy is the **farce,** a broadly humorous play whose action is usually fast-moving and improbable. The farce is a descendant of the Italian **commedia dell' arte** ("artistic comedy") of the late Renaissance, a kind of theater developed by comedians who traveled from town to town, regaling crowds at country fairs and in marketplaces. This popular art featured familiar stock characters in masks or whiteface: Harlequin, a clown; Columbine, his peppery sweetheart; and Pantaloon, a doddering duffer. Lately making a comeback, the more modern farces of French playwright Georges Feydeau (1862–1891) are practically all plot, with only the flattest of characters: mindless ninnies who play frantic games of hide-and-seek in order to deceive their spouses. **Slapstick comedy** (such as that of the Three Stooges) is a kind of farce. Featuring pratfalls, pie-throwing, fisticuffs, and other violent action, it takes its name from a circus clown's device: a bat with two boards that loudly clap together when one clown swats another.

Still another traditional sort of comedy, **romantic comedy,** is subtler. Its main characters are generally lovers, and its plot unfolds their ultimately successful strivings to be united. Unlike satiric comedy, romantic comedy portrays its characters not with withering contempt but with kindly indulgence. It may take place in the everyday world, or perhaps in some never-never land, such as the forest of Arden in Shakespeare's *As You Like It*.

Here is a contemporary comedy by one of America's master humorists, Garrison Keillor. Retelling an ancient story in a thoroughly up-to-the-minute manner, Keillor mixes old and new with amusing results. Before beginning this comic sketch, you might want to read (or, for most students, reread) "The Parable of the Prodigal Son" found on page 222. One can appreciate Keillor's humor without having read the original, but, like any parody, it is funniest to those who know the original.

## Garrison Keillor

PRODIGAL SON
1991

Garrison Keillor

*Garrison Keillor (b. 1942) was born in Anoka, Minnesota. His parents were members of the Plymouth Brethren, a strict fundamentalist sect that forbade many types of entertainment. But their members, Keillor recalls, were "wonderful storytellers, and the purpose of their stories was to imbue us with compassion." While at the University of Minnesota he worked at the campus radio station. Later Keillor worked for Minnesota Public Radio, where in 1974 he created, and was host of "A Prairie Home Companion," a weekly live radio variety show that featured music, comedy, and storytelling. The centerpiece of each show was Keillor's weekly monologue, "News from Lake Wobegon," a fictional account of the happenings of a small Minnesota town "that time forgot and the decades cannot improve." Keillor populated his imaginary hometown with a cast of memorable individuals and local businesses (like Bob's Bank whose motto is "Neither a borrower or lender be"). Keillor's gentle satire poked fun at the absurdities and pathos of small-town life. As "A Prairie Home Companion" grew in popularity (it was eventually broadcast by two hundred stations), Keillor began publishing his monologues and stories. His first collection of stories and comic pieces, Happy to Be Here, appeared in 1982, followed by the best-selling novel Lake Wobegon Days in 1985. Keillor shut down "A Prairie Home Companion" in 1987 and moved to New York where two years later he created a new radio variety show, "The American Radio Company." He has produced a steady stream of novels and short stories, including We Are Still Married (1989) and WLT: A Radio Romance (1991). Now a celebrated fiction writer, Keillor remains best known for his ingenious use of live radio, including the comic sketch. "Prodigal Son" is an example of Keillor's radio drama, which tells its story entirely through voices and sound effects.*

Characters

Narrator
Dad
Dwight
Wally
Wise and foolish virgins
Loose companions
Bimbo
Publican
Farmer
Samaritan

Sunny piano

Narrator: A happy day, a sunny street, you're young and in love and life is good and you're on your way to lunch, when suddenly a cold shadow falls and (*Loathsome laugh.*) you feel a cold slimy hand touch your face. (*Worse laugh.*) And it's your own hand. (*Worst laugh.*) That's evil. Where does evil come from? Whose fault is it? The American Council of Remorse—a nonprofit organization working for greater contrition on the part of people who do terrible things—brings you: The Prodigal Son.

(*Theme.*)

Dad: I run a feed-lot operation here in Judea, fattening feeder calves for the Jerusalem market, in partnership with my two sons: my prodigal son, Wally, and my older son, Dwight. One morning about two years ago, I came down to breakfast and—no Wally. Morning, Dwight.
Dwight: (*Sitting at table, reading newspaper.*) Morning.
Dad: You see your brother this morning?
Dwight: In bed.
Dad: I promised Harry Shepherd I'd be over to his place by seven-thirty. He's got a lost sheep out on the mountain wild and steep.
Dwight: Says here that fatted calves are down one and three-quarter shekels on the Damascus market, Dad. Makes me wonder if maybe *lean* calves wouldn't have a higher profit margin, and then we could spend more time in the vineyard—Dad, are you listening to me?
Dad: I'm worried about your brother.
Dwight: We can't afford to stand still, Dad. Look at the Stewarts—they're buying up land left and right! You've got to move ahead or you lose ground. . . .
Wally: (*Thickly.*) Morning, Dad. Morning, Dwight. (*He sits down, groans, puts his head in his hands.*)
Dad: You look a little peaked, son.
Wally: I donno—it's some kind of morning sickness, Dad. I feel real good at night and then I wake up and hurt all over.

*Dwight:* I noticed a couple empty wineskins behind the fig tree this morning.

*Wally:* I dropped them and they spilled! Honest!

*Dad:* Where were you taking them?

*Wally:* I was putting them outside! Wine's got to breathe, you know. And so do I, Dad. I've got a real breathing problem here. I'm worried about my health, Dad. I read an article the other day in *Assyrian Digest* that says bad feelings may be environmental. I donno. Maybe I need to get away for a while, Dad. Get my head straight. Work out some things.

*Dad:* Well, if that's how you feel, I guess I . . .

*Wally:* I was thinking I'd sort of take my share of the farm and head for a far country for a while until I get back on my feet, headwise, and then come back a brand-new guy.

*Dwight:* Dad, could we discuss this?

(*Theme.*)

*Narrator:* And not many days after, the younger son gathered his inheritance together, and took his journey into a far country. . . .

*Wally:* (*Walking.*)

I'm walkin' . . . to a far-out land.

I'm talkin' . . . got cash in hand.

I'm hot now . . . don't you understand. (*Yokel voices offstage.*)

You're lookin' at a brand-new man.

(*Foolish virgins° enter, harnessed together, led by a wise virgin.*)

Hey! Who's this?

Hey. What's shakin', babes?

*Wise:* I'm taking these five foolish virgins home, mister. We were supposed to be at a wedding an hour ago, but they're low on oil. You see an oil station that way?

*Wally:* Hey, they don't look foolish to me. They look like kinda fun people. Tell you what, they can come with me. I'll buy them oil. My treat.

*Wise:* Sorry, mister. I've got to look after these virgins myself. They take a lot of supervision. You gotta watch 'em pretty close so they don't bunch up and walk up each other's backs.

(*Crash.*)

*Wally:* Whoops—dropped your lamp, huh? Good thing it *didn't* have oil in it. Well, 'bye! Don't do anything I wouldn't do.

We're movin' . . . down the ole highway.

We're improvin' . . . every day.

We're groovin' . . . and we're okay.

---

*Foolish virgins:* in Matthew 25:2–12, Jesus tells a parable of five foolish maidens who forgot to bring oil for their lamps at a wedding and five wise maidens who brought oil. The five foolish virgins must go out to buy oil and miss the bridegroom's arrival.

*Narrator*: And he took his journey into a far country, and there wasted his substance in riotous living. . . . (*Enter Loose Companions, dancing, drinking, feasting, whooping. Bimbo on Wally's arm.*)

*Wally*: Take it off! Take it all off! Go for it! Put it on and take it off again!

(*To audience.*) Hey, you Pharisees, loosen up—

(*To pianist.*) Hey, you know "Hey, Judea"?

*Bimbo*: You're such a wonderful, vital person.

*Wally*: (*To "Hey Jude."*)

Hey, Judea—you're a real great place.

You're the best spot in the Bi-i-i-ible. . . .

You're right there by Canaan and Galilee,

You're family, you're tribal.

Hey, publican! Another round of wine for my pals! Put it on my tab!

Phhhh! Blaaaaghhhhh! What is this??? Lite wine?

*Publican*: You don't like it?

*Wally*: Give it to some virgins—and bring me your best.

*Publican*: I'll give you a jar to take with you—it's closing time. Time to lock up,
Mr. Wally.

*Wally*: Hey! I'll pay. Let's party!

*Bimbo*: Oh, Wally! You're so joyful! So many persons with a farm background,
they don't know how to let go and have a good time.

*Wally*: Not me, Wanda! Life is a feast if you know where to find it.

*Publican*: Here's your bill, Mr. Wally.

*Bimbo*: That's so beautiful: "Life is a feast." So many people—they place such
restrictions on themselves. (*He reads bill, page after page, then searches his
pockets and brings out a few coins.*) You have a better sense of who you are.
You have that rare quality of trusting yourself. Believing in festivity, not neg-
ativity. In a smile, not denial. Sure, rules are good for people who need 'em.
But you prefer freedom. You have this tremendous—this great—It's not a
structured thing. You know? Your energy is so focused. Like a locust.

*Wally*: That's the last of my money. That's all I have left. Amazing.

*Publican*: You all right? You need a ride home?

*Wally*: No.

*Bimbo*: Wally—listen. It's been great. Three of the best weeks of my life. Bye.

(*The Bimbo, the Publican, and the Loose Companions leave, one by one.*)

*Narrator*: And when he had spent all, there arose across a mighty famine in that
land, and he began to be in want. And he went and lived with a farmer who
sent him into his fields to feed swine.

*Farmer*: You ever feed swine before?

*Wally*: No, but I fed calves. You just dump the husks and swill down in front of
them, right?

*Farmer*: Lot more to it than that. Usually we require swine feeders to have at least
four years of professional experience. But tell you what—I'll put you in my
internship program.

*Wally*: What does it pay?

*Farmer*: Pay! I'm offering you a chance to learn the swine business from the mud up.

*Wally*: So, you mean I'll sleep out here and eat with the pigs?

*Farmer*: You want it or not?

*Wally*: Fine. Just want to get it clear in my own mind, that's all. C'mon, hogs. Sooo-eyyy! C'mon, piggy, piggy, piggy.

*Narrator*: And when he came to himself, he said:

*Wally*: How many hired servants of my father's have bread enough and to spare, and I perish with hunger! I will arise and go to my father, and will say unto him: "Father, I have sinned against heaven and before thee, and am no more worthy to be called thy son: make me as one of thy hired servants."

No, that doesn't sound good.

I will arise and go to my father and will say unto him, "Father, it was a great learning experience, and now I'm back, looking for an entry-level position— No. I will arise and go to my father and will say unto him, "Hi, Dad, how you been? Oh, I'm fine. Had a good trip. Say, you got anything to eat around here?"

*Narrator*: And he arose and came to his father.

*Wally*: I'm ruined . . . I lost my goods.

So I'm goin' back to my roots.

*Samaritan*: °(*Enters and latches on to him.*) Here, let me help you!

*Wally*: Hey! Let go!

*Samaritan*: Easy. Everything's going to be all right. I'll bind up your wounds here—

*Wally*: I don't have any wounds! Let go!

*Samaritan*: Easy.

*Wally*: Let go!

*Samaritan*: You sure I can't help?

*Wally*: Yes! Let go!

*Samaritan*: Sure you're okay?

*Wally*: Yes! Let go.

*Samaritan*: Okay. 'Bye. (*He leaves, reluctantly.*)

*Wally*: Boy, sometimes those Samaritans won't take no for an answer.

*Narrator*: And when he was yet a great way off, his father saw him, and had compassion on him, and ran, and fell on his neck, and kissed him. . . .

*Dad*: Wally! Son! Oh, Wally! (*He shouts offstage.*) Bring some clothes! And a ring! And some shoes! And not those running shoes! The dress shoes! And make that two rings!

(*Offstage clamor.*)

---

*Samaritan:* in the parable of the Good Samaritan (Luke 10: 30–37) a compassionate Samaritan comes across a man beaten up by thieves, binds his wounds, and takes him to an inn to recover.

*Wally*: I spent all the money, Dad.

*Dad*: And bring the fatted calf—let's eat and be merry! My son who was dead is alive again; he was lost and now he is found. Amazing!

*Wally*: Mind if I invite some friends too?

(*The Foolish Virgins enter, roped together.*)

I met them on the road. They're okay people once you get to know them.

*Dad*: More rings! More shoes! Another fatted calf! You look good. You look like you've lost weight.

*Wally*: I've been on a high-husk diet.

*Dad*: Dwight! Look who's here! It's Wally!

*Dwight*: (*Enters reluctantly.*) Hi. Nice to see you. (*His Dad turns to Wally, and Dwight shakes both his fists and sticks out his tongue and makes a vulgar gesture.*)

*Dad*: We're having veal tonight, Dwight! Wally's home.

*Wally*: I'm going to go get some of that calf, Dad. Be right back.

*Dwight*: Dad, I don't want this to sound negative in any way, but—how many years have I been working here?

*Dad*: All your life.

*Dwight*: Have I ever disobeyed you, Dad?

*Dad*: Never.

*Dwight*: And have you ever given *me* a fatted calf and thrown a big party for me and *my* friends?

*Dad*: No, but, son—

*Dwight*: But the minute this *bozo* comes hoofing it home—this leaker—

*Dad*: But your brother was dead and he's alive again! He was lost and now he's found!

*Dwight*: I don't think you're hearing what I'm saying, Dad. You never ran up to me and hugged me—I'd just like to point that out.

*Dad*: I'm not a hugger, I guess.

*Wally*: (*Enters, mouth full.*) Have some calf, you guys. That fat won't keep, you know. Sure is good fatted calf, Dad. Sure beats husks. (*Off.*) Care for another piece, you virgins?

*Dwight*: Ever stop to think who *fatted* that calf, Wally? That was our best calf, Dad. The *best* one. (*The others slowly leave, talking among themselves.*) Try to think how I feel. I'm hoeing corn all day, come in bone-tired, there's my brother smelling of pig manure, and they got the beer on ice and *my calf* on the barbecue! And MY RING on his hand! *My ring!* You promised it to me, but oh no—can't give it to the son who's worked his tail off for thirty years, oh no, gotta give it to the weasel who comes dragging his butt in the door— Oh great—Wonderful, Dad. Terrific.

Maybe I'll go sleep with the pigs, seeing as you go for that. See ya later, Wally. Help yourself to the rest of my stuff—clothes, jewels, shekels, just take what you want. Take my room. Don't worry about me. I'll be in the pigpen.

(*He leaves. Offstage sounds: A stove being kicked, muttered curses, pots and pans being thrown, dishes broken.*)

## QUESTIONS

1. Divide this play into elements. How much of the play is *exposition?* Who is the *protagonist?* What is the *climax* of the play, the moment when the tension is at its height?
2. Comedy usually portrays human failings. What weaknesses does Wally have? Do Dad and Dwight also have weaknesses?
3. Does Keillor change any important elements of the plot from the original parable? ("The Parable of the Prodigal Son" is found on page 222.) If so, what part or parts of the plot does he alter?
4. How does Keillor turn this famous parable into a comedy? What elements of setting, characterization, or tone does he shift to get his comic effects?
5. Is Keillor's parody disrespectful of the original parable? Or does he explore the same theme in a different way? Is it possible for a comedy to pursue the same themes as a more earnest work?
6. How can this play be considered a comedy if Dwight is so unhappy at the end?

## SUGGESTIONS FOR WRITING

1. Write an account of the *Trifles* case—the discovery of the murder and the arrest of Mrs. Wright—as a newspaper might have reported it. Then, in a separate paragraph or two, sum up the important facts that a reporter couldn't know, but that Susan Glaspell makes clear to us.
2. Write an essay in praise of the language spoken by the characters in *Riders to the Sea.* Arrive at some generalizations about it. (One suggestion: Turn back to Chapter Eighteen and refresh your acquaintance with metaphors and other figures of speech.)
3. Write an essay titled "Comedy on Campus" or "Comedy in Everyday Life." This essay might depend on what you have lately observed, heard reported in conversation, or noticed in current news media. Give an array of examples.
4. Write an analysis of Keillor's *The Prodigal Son* in relation to its source in the Gospel of Luke. (The original parable is printed on page 222, and the sources for two other parables are cited in footnotes to Keillor's text.) Examine how Keillor uses comedy to dramatize the same themes as the original parables. You should also note any moments that you think Keillor departs from the moral spirit of the original parables.
5. What particular human follies does Keillor satirize in *The Prodigal Son?* Write a short essay in which you note and discuss the particular shortcomings of at least three characters.

# 34  The Theater of Sophocles

For a citizen of Athens in the fifth century B.C. when the surviving classical Greek tragedies originated, a play was a religious occasion. Plays were given at the Lenaea, or feast of the winepress, in January; or during the Great Dionysia, the feast of Dionysus, god of wine and crops, in the spring. So well did the Athenians love contests that at the spring festival each playwright was to present—in competition—three tragedies on successive days, the last tragedy to be followed by a short comedy of a special sort. The comedy was a **satyr play,** a parody of a mythic story, with a chorus of actors playing *satyrs*, creatures half goat or horse, half man.

Seated in the open air, in a hillside amphitheater, as many as fourteen thousand spectators could watch a performance that must have somewhat resembled an opera or a modern musical. The audience, arranged in rows, looked out across a rounded **orchestra**, or dancing-place, where the chorus of fifteen (the number was fixed by Sophocles) sang passages of lyric poetry and executed dance movements. (It is also possible that actors and chorus sometimes shared the orchestra.) The modern custom of dividing a play into acts and scenes may have originated in these song and dance interludes. Besides providing stage business, the chorus had a function in telling the story: in the plays of Sophocles, they converse with the main character and sometimes comment on the action, offering words of warning and other unwanted advice. As they *physically* stand between the audience and principal actors, the members of the chorus serve as middlemen who seem to voice the spectators' reactions.

Behind the orchestra stood the actors, in front of a stage house, or **skene** (the source of our word *scene*). Originally, the *skene* was a dressing room; later it is believed to have borne a painted backdrop. Directly behind the *skene*, a **colonnade** or row of pillars provided (according to one scholarly guess) a ready-made set for a palace. (This is a rough description of the Athenian theater of Dionysus; several other Greek cities had theaters, each unique in details.)

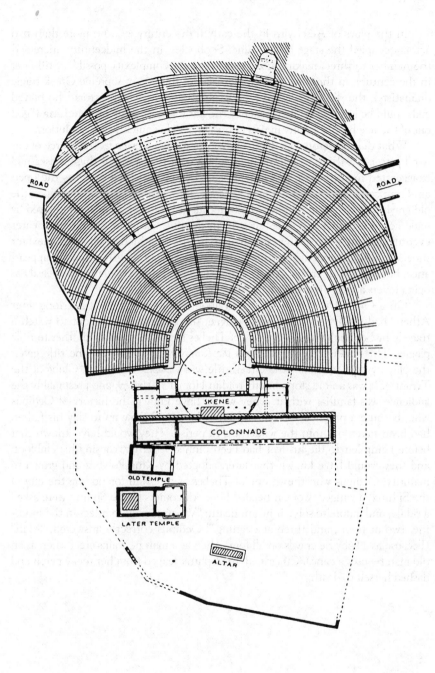

ROAD

ROAD

SKENE

COLONNADE

OLD TEMPLE

LATER TEMPLE

ALTAR

*The theater of Dionysus at Athens in the time of Sophocles; a modern drawing based on scholarly guesswork.*
*From R. C. Flickinger,* The Greek Theater and Its Drama *(1918).*

In the plays of Aeschylus in the early fifth century B.C., no more than two actors occupied the stage at any time. Sophocles, in the midcentury, increased the number to three, making situations of greater complexity possible. Still later in the century, in the time of Euripides (last of the trio of supreme Greek tragic dramatists), the *skene* supported a hook and pulley by which actors who played gods could be lowered or lifted—hence the Latin phrase **deus ex machina** ("god out of the machine") for any means of bringing a play quickly to a resolution.

What did the actors look like? They wore **masks** (*personae*, the source of our word *person:* "a thing through which sound comes"); some of these masks had exaggerated mouthpieces, probably designed to project speech across the open air. From certain conventional masks the spectators recognized familiar types: the old graybeard, the young soldier, the beautiful girl (women's parts were played by male actors). Perhaps in order to gain in dignity, actors in the Greek theater eventually came to wear the **cothurnus**, or buskin, a high, thick-soled elevator shoe. All this equipment must have given the actors a slightly inhuman appearance, but we may infer that the spectators accepted such conventions as easily as opera lovers accept an opera's natural artifice.

On a Great Dionysia feast day in about the year 430 B.C., not long after Athens had survived a devastating plague, the audience turned out to watch a tragedy by Sophocles, set in the city of Thebes at the moment of another terrible plague. This timely play was *Oedipus the King* ("King Clubfoot," the title given the play by later scholars—the Greek title was *Oedipus Tyrannos*, "Clubfoot the Tyrant"). It was an old story, briefly told in Homer's *Odyssey*, and presumably the audience was familiar with it. They would have known the history of Oedipus who, because a prophecy had foretold that he would grow up to slay his father, had been taken out into the wilderness to perish. They would have known that before being left to die his feet had been pinned together, causing his clubfoot; and they would have known that later, adopted by King Polybus and grown to maturity, Oedipus won the throne of Thebes as a reward for ridding the city of the Sphinx, a winged, woman-headed lion. All comers to the Sphinx were asked a riddle, and failure to solve it meant death: "What goes on four legs in the morning, two at noon, and three at evening?" Oedipus correctly answered, "Man" (because as a baby he crawls on all fours, then as a man he walks erect, then as an old man he uses a cane). Chagrined, the Sphinx leaped from her rocky perch and dashed herself to death.

# Sophocles

## OEDIPUS THE KING

Translated by Dudley Fitts and Robert
Fitzgerald

Sophocles (496?–406 B.C.), tragic dramatist, priest, for a time one of ten Athenian
generals, was among three great ancient
Greek writers of tragedy. (The other two
were his contemporaries: Aeschylus, his
senior, and Euripides, his junior.) Sophocles
won his first victory in the Athenian spring
drama competition in 468 B.C., when a
tragedy he had written defeated a tragedy by
Aeschylus. He went on to win many prizes,
writing more than 120 plays, of which only
seven have survived in their entirety--Ajax,
Antigonê, Oedipus the King, Electra,
Philoctetes, The Trachinian Women,
and Oedipus at Colonus. (Of the lost

Sophocles

plays, about a thousand fragments remain.) In his long life, Sophocles saw Greece rise to
supremacy over the Persian Empire. He enjoyed the favor of the statesman Pericles, who,
making peace with enemy Sparta, ruled Athens during a Golden Age (461–429 B.C.),
during which the Parthenon was built and music, art, drama, and philosophy flourished.
The playwright lived on to see his native city-state in decline, its strength drained by the
disastrous Peloponnesian War. His last play, Oedipus at Colonus, set twenty years
after the events of Oedipus the King, shows the former king in old age, ragged and blind,
cast into exile by his sons, but still accompanied by his faithful daughter Antigonê. It was
written when Sophocles was nearly ninety. Oedipus the King is believed to have been
first produced in 425 B.C., five years after plague had broken out in Athens.

Characters°

Oedipus
A Priest
Creon
Teiresias
Iocastê
Messenger
Shepherd of Laïos
Second Messenger
Chorus of Theban Elders

Characters: Some of these names are usually Anglicized: Jocasta, Laius. In this version, the translators
prefer spelling names more nearly like the Greek.

Scene: *Before the palace of Oedipus, King of Thebes. A central door and two lateral doors open onto a platform which runs the length of the façade. On the platform, right and left, are altars; and three steps lead down into the "orchestra," or chorus-ground. At the beginning of the action these steps are crowded by suppliants° who have brought branches and chaplets of olive leaves and who lie in various attitudes of despair. Oedipus enters.*

## PROLOGUE°

*Oedipus:* My children, generations of the living
    In the line of Kadmos,° nursed at his ancient hearth:
    Why have you strewn yourself before these altars
    In supplication, with your boughs and garlands?
    The breath of incense rises from the city           5
    With a sound of prayer and lamentation.
                       Children,
    I would not have you speak through messengers,
    And therefore I have come myself to hear you—
    I, Oedipus, who bear the famous name.
    *(To a Priest.)* You, there, since you are eldest in the company,
    Speak for them all, tell me what preys upon you,           10
    Whether you come in dread, or crave some blessing:
    Tell me, and never doubt that I will help you
    In every way I can; I should be heartless
    Were I not moved to find you suppliant here.
*Priest:* Great Oedipus, O powerful King of Thebes!           15
    You see how all the ages of our people
    Cling to your altar steps: here are boys
    Who can barely stand alone, and here are priests
    By weight of age, as I am a priest of God,
    And young men chosen from those yet unmarried;          20
    As for the others, all that multitude,
    They wait with olive chaplets in the squares,
    At the two shrines of Pallas,° and where Apollo°
    Speaks in the glowing embers.
                   Your own eyes
    Must tell you: Thebes is tossed on a murdering sea        25
    And can not lift her head from the death surge.

---

*suppliants:* persons come to ask some favor of the king.     *Prologue:* portion of the play containing the exposition.     2 *line of Kadmos:* according to legend the city of Thebes, where the play takes place, had been founded by the hero Cadmus.     23 *Pallas:* title for Athena, goddess of wisdom. 23 *Apollo:* god of music, poetry, and prophecy. At his shrine near Thebes, the ashes of fires were used to divine the future.

A rust consumes the buds and fruits of the earth;
The herds are sick; children die unborn,
And labor is vain. The god of plague and pyre
Raids like detestable lightning through the city,                                30
And all the house of Kadmos is laid waste,
All emptied, and all darkened: Death alone
Battens upon the misery of Thebes.

You are not one of the immortal gods, we know;
Yet we have come to you to make our prayer                                       35
As to the man surest in mortal ways
And wisest in the ways of God. You saved us
From the Sphinx, that flinty singer, and the tribute
We paid to her so long; yet you were never
Better informed than we, nor could we teach you:                                 40
It was some god breathed in you to set us free.

Therefore, O mighty King, we turn to you:
Find us our safety, find us a remedy,
Whether by counsel of the gods or men.
A king of wisdom tested in the past                                              45
Can act in a time of troubles, and act well.
Noblest of men, restore
Life to your city! Think how all men call you
Liberator for your triumph long ago;
Ah, when your years of kingship are remembered,                                  50
Let them not say *We rose, but later fell*—
Keep the State from going down in the storm!
Once, years ago, with happy augury,
You brought us fortune; be the same again!
No man questions your power to rule the land:                                     55
But rule over men, not over a dead city!
Ships are only hulls, citadels are nothing,
When no life moves in the empty passageways.
*Oedipus:* Poor children! You may be sure I know
    All that you longed for in your coming here.                                 60
    I know that you are deathly sick; and yet,
    Sick as you are, not one is as sick as I.
    Each of you suffers in himself alone
    His anguish, not another's; but my spirit
    Groans for the city, for myself, for you.                                    65

    I was not sleeping, you are not waking me.
    No, I have been in tears for a long while
    And in my restless thought walked many ways.
    In all my search, I found one helpful course,

And that I have taken: I have sent Creon,                          70
Son of Menoikeus, brother of the Queen,
To Delphi, Apollo's place of revelation,°
To learn there, if he can,
What act or pledge of mine may save the city.
I have counted the days, and now, this very day,                   75
I am troubled, for he has overstayed his time.
What is he doing? He has been gone too long.
Yet whenever he comes back, I should do ill
To scant whatever duty God reveals.

*Priest:* It is a timely promise. At this instant                  80
    They tell me Creon is here.

*Oedipus:*                          O Lord Apollo!
    May his news be fair as his face is radiant!

*Priest:* It could not be otherwise: he is crowned with bay,
    The chaplet is thick with berries.

*Oedipus:*                          We shall soon know;
    He is near enough to hear us now.

    *Enter Creon.*

                                    O Prince:                      85
    Brother: son of Menoikeus:
    What answer do you bring us from the god?

*Creon:* A strong one. I can tell you, great afflictions
    Will turn out well, if they are taken well.

*Oedipus:* What was the oracle? These vague words                  90
    Leave me still hanging between hope and fear.

*Creon:* Is it your pleasure to hear me with all these
    Gathered around us? I am prepared to speak,
    But should we not go in?

*Oedipus:*                          Let them all hear it
    It is for them I suffer, more than for myself.                 95

*Creon:* Then I will tell you what I heard at Delphi.

    In plain words
    The god commands us to expel from the land of Thebes
    An old defilement we are sheltering.
    It is a deathly thing, beyond cure.                            100
    We must not let it feed upon us longer.

*Oedipus:* What defilement? How shall we rid ourselves of it?

*Creon:* By exile or death, blood for blood. It was

---

72 *Delphi . . . revelation:* In the temple of Delphi at the foot of Mount Parnassus, a priestess of
Dionysos, while in an ecstatic trance, would speak the wine god's words. Such a priestess was called
an *oracle;* the word can also mean a message from the god.

Murder that brought the plague-wind on the city.

*Oedipus:* Murder of whom? Surely the god has named him?

*Creon:* My lord: long ago Laïos was our king,
Before you came to govern us.

*Oedipus:*                                   I know;
I learned of him from others; I never saw him.

*Creon:* He was murdered; and Apollo commands us now
To take revenge upon whoever killed him.

*Oedipus:* Upon whom? Where are they? Where shall we find a clue
To solve that crime, after so many years?

*Creon:* Here in this land, he said.
                                   If we make enquiry,
We may touch things that otherwise escape us.

*Oedipus:* Tell me: Was Laïos murdered in his house,
Or in the fields, or in some foreign country?

*Creon:* He said he planned to make a pilgrimage.
He did not come home again.

*Oedipus:*                                   And was there no one,
No witness, no companion, to tell what happened?

*Creon:* They were all killed but one, and he got away
So frightened that he could remember one thing only.

*Oedipus:* What was that one thing? One may be the key
To everything, if we resolve to use it.

*Creon:* He said that a band of highwaymen attacked them,
Outnumbered them, and overwhelmed the King.

*Oedipus:* Strange, that a highwayman should be so daring—
Unless some faction here bribed him to do it.

*Creon:* We thought of that. But after Laïos' death
New troubles arose and we had no avenger.

*Oedipus:* What troubles could prevent your hunting down the killers?

*Creon:* The riddling Sphinx's song
Made us deaf to all mysteries but her own.

*Oedipus:* Then once more I must bring what is dark to light.
It is most fitting that Apollo shows,
As you do, this compunction for the dead.
You shall see how I stand by you, as I should,
To avenge the city and the city's god,
And not as though it were for some distant friend,
But for my own sake, to be rid of evil.
Whoever killed King Laïos might—who knows?—
Decide at any moment to kill me as well.
By avenging the murdered king I protect myself.

Come, then, my children: leave the altar steps,
Lift up your olive boughs!

                    One of you go
And summon the people of Kadmos to gather here.                                        145
I will do all that I can; you may tell them that.

*Exit a Page.*

So, with the help of God,
We shall be saved—or else indeed we are lost.
*Priest:* Let us rise, children. It was for this we came,
And now the King has promised it himself.                                              150
Phoibos° has sent us an oracle; may he descend
Himself to save us and drive out the plague.

*Exeunt Oedipus and Creon into the palace by the central door. The Priest and the*
*Suppliants disperse right and left. After a short pause the Chorus enters the orchestra.*

# PÁRODOS°

*Strophe° 1*

*Chorus:* What is God singing in his profound
          Delphi of gold and shadow?
          What oracle for Thebes, the sunwhipped city?

Fear unjoints me, the roots of my heart tremble.

Now I remember, O Healer, your power, and wonder:                                       5
Will you send doom like a sudden cloud, or weave it
Like nightfall of the past?

Speak, speak to us, issue of holy sound:
Dearest to our expectancy: be tender!

*Antistrophe° 1*

Let me pray to Athenê, the immortal daughter of Zeus,                                   10
And to Artemis her sister
Who keeps her famous throne in the market ring,
And to Apollo, bowman at the far butts of heaven—

O gods, descend! Like three streams leap against
The fires of our grief, the fires of darkness;                                          15
Be swift to bring us rest!

As in the old time from the brilliant house
Of air you stepped to save us, come again!

---

151 *Phoibos:* the sun god Phoebus Apollo.      *Párodos:* part to be sung by the chorus on first entering. A *strophe* (according to theory) was sung while the chorus danced from stage right to stage left;
an *antistrophe,* while they danced back again.

Now our afflictions have no end,
Now all our stricken host lies down                    20
And no man fights off death with his mind;

The noble plowland bears no grain,
And groaning mothers can not bear—

See, how our lives like birds take wing,
Like sparks that fly when a fire soars,                25
To the shore of the god of evening.

The plague burns on, it is pitiless,
Though pallid children laden with death
Lie unwept in the stony ways,

And old gray women by every path                       30
Flock to the strand about the altars

There to strike their breasts and cry
Worship of Phoibos in wailing prayers:
Be kind, God's golden child!

There are no swords in this attack by fire,            35
No shields, but we are ringed with cries.

Send the besieger plunging from our homes
Into the vast sea-room of the Atlantic
Or into the waves that foam eastward of Thrace—

For the day ravages what the night spares—             40

Destroy our enemy, lord of the thunder!
Let him be riven by lightning from heaven!

Phoibos Apollo, stretch the sun's bowstring,
That golden cord, until it sing for us,
Flashing arrows in heaven!
                          Artemis, Huntress,            45
Race with flaring lights upon our mountains!

O scarlet god, O golden-banded brow,
O Theban Bacchos in a storm of Maenads,°

---

48 *Bacchos . . . Maenads:* god of wine with his attendant girl revelers.

*Enter Oedipus, center.*

Whirl upon Death, that all the Undying hate!
Come with blinding torches, come in joy!                                    50

## SCENE I

*Oedipus:* Is this your prayer? It may be answered. Come,
　　Listen to me, act as the crisis demands,
　　And you shall have relief from all these evils.

　　Until now I was a stranger to this tale,
　　As I had been a stranger to the crime.                                    5
　　Could I track down the murderer without a clue?
　　But now, friends,
　　As one who became a citizen after the murder,
　　I make this proclamation to all Thebans:

　　If any man knows by whose hand Laïos, son of Labdakos,                    10
　　Met his death, I direct that man to tell me everything,
　　No matter what he fears for having so long withheld it.
　　Let it stand as promised that no further trouble
　　Will come to him, but he may leave the land in safety.

　　Moreover: If anyone knows the murderer to be foreign,                    15
　　Let him not keep silent: he shall have his reward from me.
　　However, if he does conceal it; if any man
　　Fearing for his friend or for himself disobeys this edict,
　　Hear what I propose to do:

　　I solemnly forbid the people of this country,                            20
　　Where power and throne are mine, ever to receive that man
　　Or speak to him, no matter who he is, or let him
　　Join in sacrifice, lustration, or in prayer.
　　I decree that he be driven from every house,
　　Being, as he is, corruption itself to us: the Delphic                    25
　　Voice of Zeus has pronounced this revelation.
　　Thus I associate myself with the oracle
　　And take the side of the murdered king.

　　As for the criminal, I pray to God—
　　Whether it be a lurking thief, or one of a number—                       30
　　I pray that that man's life be consumed in evil and wretchedness.
　　And as for me, this curse applies no less
　　If it should turn out that the culprit is my guest here,
　　Sharing my hearth.
　　　　　　　　You have heard the penalty.

I lay it on you now to attend to this                35
For my sake, for Apollo's, for the sick
Sterile city that heaven has abandoned.
Suppose the oracle had given you no command:
Should this defilement go uncleansed for ever?
You should have found the murderer: your king,      40
A noble king, had been destroyed!
                        Now I,
Having the power that he held before me,
Having his bed, begetting children there
Upon his wife, as he would have, had he lived—
Their son would have been my children's brother,     45
If Laïos had had luck in fatherhood!
(But surely ill luck rushed upon his reign)—
I say I take the son's part, just as though
I were his son, to press the fight for him
And see it won! I'll find the hand that brought     50
Death to Labdakos' and Polydoros' child,
Heir of Kadmos' and Agenor's line.
And as for those who fail me,
May the gods deny them the fruit of the earth,
Fruit of the womb, and may they rot utterly!     55
Let them be wretched as we are wretched, and worse!

For you, for loyal Thebans, and for all
Who find my actions right, I pray the favor
Of justice, and of all the immortal gods.
*Choragos°:* Since I am under oath, my lord, I swear     60
    I did not do the murder, I can not name
    The murderer. Might not the oracle
    That has ordained the search tell where to find him?
*Oedipus:* An honest question. But no man in the world
    Can make the gods do more than the gods will.     65
*Choragos:* There is one last expedient—
*Oedipus:*                      Tell me what it is.
    Though it seem slight, you must not hold it back.
*Choragos:* A lord clairvoyant to the lord Apollo,
    As we all know, is the skilled Teiresias.
    One might learn much about this from him, Oedipus.     70
*Oedipus:* I am not wasting time:
    Creon spoke of this, and I have sent for him—
    Twice, in fact; it is strange that he is not here.
*Choragos:* The other matter—that old report—seems useless.

60 *Choragos:* spokesman for the chorus.

*Oedipus:* Tell me. I am interested in all reports. 75
*Choragos:* The King was said to have been killed by highwaymen.
*Oedipus:* I know. But we have no witnesses to that.
*Choragos:* If the killer can feel a particle of dread,
    Your curse will bring him out of hiding!
*Oedipus:* No.
    The man who dared that act will fear no curse. 80

    *Enter the blind seer Teiresias, led by a Page.*

*Choragos:* But there is one man who may detect the criminal.
    This is Teiresias, this is the holy prophet
    In whom, alone of all men, truth was born.
*Oedipus:* Teiresias: seer: student of mysteries,
    Of all that's taught and all that no man tells, 85
    Secrets of Heaven and secrets of the earth:
    Blind though you are, you know the city lies
    Sick with plague; and from this plague, my lord,
    We find that you alone can guard or save us.

    Possibly you did not hear the messengers? 90
    Apollo, when we sent to him,
    Sent us back word that this great pestilence
    Would lift, but only if we established clearly
    The identity of those who murdered Laïos.
    They must be killed or exiled.
                Can you use 95
    Birdflight or any art of divination
    To purify yourself, and Thebes, and me
    From this contagion? We are in your hands.
    There is no fairer duty
    Than that of helping others in distress. 100
*Teiresias:* How dreadful knowledge of the truth can be
    When there's no help in truth! I knew this well,
    But made myself forget. I should not have come.
*Oedipus:* What is troubling you? Why are your eyes so cold?
*Teiresias:* Let me go home. Bear your own fate, and I'll 105
    Bear mine. It is better so: trust what I say.
*Oedipus:* What you say is ungracious and unhelpful
    To your native country. Do not refuse to speak.
*Teiresias:* When it comes to speech, your own is neither temperate
    Nor opportune. I wish to be more prudent. 110
*Oedipus:* In God's name, we all beg you—
*Teiresias:* You are all ignorant.
    No; I will never tell you what I know.

Now it is my misery; then, it would be yours.
*Oedipus:* What! You do know something, and will not tell us?
    You would betray us all and wreck the State? 115
*Teiresias:* I do not intend to torture myself, or you.
    Why persist in asking? You will not persuade me.
*Oedipus:* What a wicked old man you are! You'd try a stone's
    Patience! Out with it! Have you no feeling at all?
*Teiresias:* You call me unfeeling. If you could only see 120
    The nature of your own feelings . . .
*Oedipus:*                    Why,
    Who would not feel as I do? Who could endure
    Your arrogance toward the city?
*Teiresias:*               What does it matter!
    Whether I speak or not; it is bound to come.
*Oedipus:* Then, if "it" is bound to come, you are bound to tell me. 125
*Teiresias:* No, I will not go on. Rage as you please.
*Oedipus:* Rage? Why not!
                And I'll tell you what I think:
    You planned it, you had it done, you all but
    Killed him with your own hands: if you had eyes,
    I'd say the crime was yours, and yours alone. 130
*Teiresias:* So? I charge you, then,
    Abide by the proclamation you have made:
    From this day forth
    Never speak again to these men or to me;
    You yourself are the pollution of this country. 135
*Oedipus:* You dare say that! Can you possibly think you have
    Some way of going free, after such insolence?
*Teiresias:* I have gone free. It is the truth sustains me.
*Oedipus:* Who taught you shamelessness? It was not your craft.
*Teiresias:* You did. You made me speak. I did not want to. 140
*Oedipus:* Speak what? Let me hear it again more clearly.
*Teiresias:* Was it not clear before? Are you tempting me?
*Oedipus:* I did not understand it. Say it again.
*Teiresias:* I say that you are the murderer whom you seek.
*Oedipus:* Now twice you have spat out infamy. You'll pay for it! 145
*Teiresias:* Would you care for more? Do you wish to be really angry?
*Oedipus:* Say what you will. Whatever you say is worthless.
*Teiresias:* I say you live in hideous shame with those
    Most dear to you. You can not see the evil.
*Oedipus:* It seems you can go on mouthing like this for ever. 150
*Teiresias:* I can, if there is power in truth.
*Oedipus:*                   There is:
    But not for you, not for you,

You sightless, witless, senseless, mad old man!
*Teiresias:* You are the madman. There is no one here
    Who will not curse you soon, as you curse me.          155
*Oedipus:* You child of endless night! You can not hurt me
    Or any other man who sees the sun.
*Teiresias:* True: it is not from me your fate will come.
    That lies within Apollo's competence,
    As it is his concern.
*Oedipus:*              Tell me:          160
    Are you speaking for Creon, or for yourself?
*Teiresias:* Creon is no threat. You weave your own doom.
*Oedipus:* Wealth, power, craft of statesmanship!
    Kingly position, everywhere admired!
    What savage envy is stored up against these,          165
    If Creon, whom I trusted, Creon my friend,
    For this great office which the city once
    Put in my hands unsought—if for this power
    Creon desires in secret to destroy me!

    He has brought this decrepit fortune-teller, this          170
    Collector of dirty pennies, this prophet fraud—
    Why, he is no more clairvoyant than I am!
                         Tell us:
    Has your mystic mummery ever approached the truth?
    When that hellcat the Sphinx was performing here,
    What help were you to these people?          175
    Her magic was not for the first man who came along:
    It demanded a real exorcist. Your birds—
    What good were they? or the gods, for the matter of that?
    But I came by,
    Oedipus, the simple man, who knows nothing—          180
    I thought it out for myself, no birds helped me!
    And this is the man you think you can destroy,
    That you may be close to Creon when he's king!
    Well, you and your friend Creon, it seems to me,
    Will suffer most. If you were not an old man,          185
    You would have paid already for your plot.
*Choragos:* We can not see that his words or yours
    Have been spoken except in anger, Oedipus,
    And of anger we have no need. How can God's will
    Be accomplished best? That is what most concerns us.          190
*Teiresias:* You are a king. But where argument's concerned
    I am your man, as much a king as you.
    I am not your servant, but Apollo's.
    I have no need of Creon to speak for me.

Listen to me. You mock my blindness, do you? 195
But I say that you, with both your eyes, are blind:
You can not see the wretchedness of your life,
Nor in whose house you live, no, nor with whom.
Who are your father and mother? Can you tell me?
You do not even know the blind wrongs 200
That you have done them, on earth and in the world below.
But the double lash of your parents' curse will whip you
Out of this land some day, with only night
Upon your precious eyes.
Your cries then—where will they not be heard? 205
What fastness of Kithairon will not echo them?
And that bridal-descant of yours—you'll know it then,
The song they sang when you came here to Thebes
And found your misguided berthing.
All this, and more, that you can not guess at now, 210
Will bring you to yourself among your children.

Be angry, then. Curse Creon. Curse my words.
I tell you, no man that walks upon the earth
Shall be rooted out more horribly than you.
*Oedipus:* Am I to bear this from him?—Damnation 215
   Take you! Out of this place! Out of my sight!
*Teiresias:* I would not have come at all if you had not asked me.
*Oedipus:* Could I have told that you'd talk nonsense, that
   You'd come here to make a fool of yourself, and of me?
*Teiresias:* A fool? Your parents thought me sane enough. 220
*Oedipus:* My parents again!—Wait: who were my parents?
*Teiresias:* This day will give you a father, and break your heart.
*Oedipus:* Your infantile riddles! Your damned abracadabra!
*Teiresias:* You were a great man once at solving riddles.
*Oedipus:* Mock me with that if you like; you will find it true. 225
*Teiresias:* It was true enough. It brought about your ruin.
*Oedipus:* But if it saved this town?
*Teiresias (to the Page):*          Boy, give me your hand.
*Oedipus:* Yes, boy; lead him away.
                              —While you are here
   We can do nothing. Go; leave us in peace.
*Teiresias:* I will go when I have said what I have to say. 230
   How can you hurt me? And I tell you again:
   The man you have been looking for all this time,
   The damned man, the murderer of Laïos,
   That man is in Thebes. To your mind he is foreignborn,
   But it will soon be shown that he is a Theban, 235
   A revelation that will fail to please.

A blind man,
Who has his eyes now; a penniless man, who is rich now;
And he will go tapping the strange earth with his staff;
To the children with whom he lives now he will be
Brother and father—the very same; to her                                    240
Who bore him, son and husband—the very same
Who came to his father's bed, wet with his father's blood.

Enough. Go think that over.
If later you find error in what I have said,
You may say that I have no skill in prophecy.                                245

*Exit Teiresias, led by his Page. Oedipus goes into the palace.*

## ODE I°

*Strophe 1*

Chorus: The Delphic stone of prophecies
    Remembers ancient regicide
    And a still bloody hand.
    That killer's hour of flight has come.
    He must be stronger than riderless                                       5
    Coursers of untiring wind,
    For the son of Zeus° armed with his father's thunder
    Leaps in lightning after him;
    And the Furies° follow him, the sad Furies.

*Antistrophe 1*

    Holy Parnassos' peak of snow                                             10
    Flashes and blinds that secret man,
    That all shall hunt him down:
    Though he may roam the forest shade
    Like a bull gone wild from pasture
    To rage through glooms of stone.                                         15
    Doom comes down on him; flight will not avail him;
    For the world's heart calls him desolate,
    And the immortal Furies follow, for ever follow.

*Strophe 2*

    But now a wilder thing is heard

Ode: a choral song. Here again (as in the *párodos*) *strophe* and *antistrophe* probably indicate the movements of a dance.      7 *son of Zeus:* Apollo.      9 *Furies:* three horrific female spirits whose task was
to seek out and punish evildoers.

From the old man skilled at hearing Fate in the wingbeat of a bird.  20
Bewildered as a blown bird, my soul hovers and can not find
Foothold in this debate, or any reason or rest of mind.
But no man ever brought—none can bring
Proof of strife between Thebes' royal house,
Labdakos' line,° and the son of Polybos;°  25
And never until now has any man brought word
Of Laïos' dark death staining Oedipus the King.

*Antistrophe 2*

Divine Zeus and Apollo hold
Perfect intelligence alone of all tales ever told;
And well though this diviner works, he works in his own night;  30
No man can judge that rough unknown or trust in second sight,
For wisdom changes hands among the wise.
Shall I believe my great lord criminal
At a raging word that a blind old man let fall?
I saw him, when the carrion woman faced him of old,  35
Prove his heroic mind! These evil words are lies.

# SCENE II

*Creon:* Men of Thebes:
  I am told that heavy accusations
  Have been brought against me by King Oedipus.

  I am not the kind of man to bear this tamely.

  If in these present difficulties  5
  He holds me accountable for any harm to him
  Through anything I have said or done—why, then,
  I do not value life in this dishonor.

  It is not as though this rumor touched upon
  Some private indiscretion. The matter is grave.  10
  The fact is that I am being called disloyal
  To the State, to my fellow citizens, to my friends.
*Choragos:* He may have spoken in anger, not from his mind.
*Creon:* But did you not hear him say I was the one
  Who seduced the old prophet into lying?  15
*Choragos:* The thing was said; I do not know how seriously.
*Creon:* But you were watching him! Were his eyes steady?

25 *Labdakos' line:* descendants of Laïos (true father of Oedipus, although the chorus does not know it).    25 *Polybos:* king who adopted the child Oedipus.

Did he look like a man in his right mind?

Choragos:                                        I do not know.
I can not judge the behavior of great men.
But here is the King himself.

*Enter Oedipus.*

Oedipus:                              So you dared come back.                                    20
Why? How brazen of you to come to my house,
You murderer!
                              Do you think I do not know
That you plotted to kill me, plotted to steal my throne?
Tell me, in God's name: am I coward, a fool,
That you should dream you could accomplish this?                      25
A fool who could not see your slippery game?
A coward, not to fight back when I saw it?
You are the fool, Creon, are you not? hoping
Without support or friends to get a throne?
Thrones may be won or bought: you could do neither.                  30
Creon: Now listen to me. You have talked; let me talk, too.
You can not judge unless you know the facts.
Oedipus: You speak well: there is one fact; but I find it hard
To learn from the deadliest enemy I have.
Creon:    That above all I must dispute with you.                        35
Oedipus: That above all I will not hear you deny.
Creon: If you think there is anything good in being stubborn
Against all reason, then I say you are wrong.
Oedipus: If you think a man can sin against his own kind
And not be punished for it, I say you are mad.                            40
Creon: I agree. But tell me: what have I done to you?
Oedipus: You advised me to send for that wizard, did you not?
Creon: I did. I should do it again.
Oedipus:                              Very well. Now tell me:
How long has it been since Laïos—
Creon:                                        What of Laïos?
Oedipus: Since he vanished in that onset by the road?                   45
Creon: It was long ago, a long time.
Oedipus:                              And this prophet,
Was he practicing here then?
Creon:                                        He was; and with honor, as now.
Oedipus: Did he speak of me at that time?
Creon:                                        He never did;
At least, not when I was present.
Oedipus:                              But . . . the enquiry?
I suppose you held one?
Creon:                              We did, but we learned nothing.        50

*Oedipus:* Why did the prophet not speak against me then?
*Creon:* I do not know; and I am the kind of man
    Who holds his tongue when he has no facts to go on.
*Oedipus:* There's one fact that you know, and you could tell it.
*Creon:* What fact is that? If I know it, you shall have it. 55
*Oedipus:* If he were not involved with you, he could not say
    That it was I who murdered Laïos.
*Creon:* If he says that, you are the one that knows it!—
    But now it is my turn to question you.
*Oedipus:* Put your questions. I am no murderer. 60
*Creon:* First then: You married my sister?
*Oedipus:*                                 I married your sister.
*Creon:* And you rule the kingdom equally with her?
*Oedipus:* Everything that she wants she has from me.
*Creon:* And I am the third, equal to both of you?
*Oedipus:* That is why I call you a bad friend. 65
*Creon:* No. Reason it out, as I have done.
    Think of this first: Would any sane man prefer
    Power, with all a king's anxieties,
    To that same power and the grace of sleep?
    Certainly not I. 70
    I have never longed for the king's power—only his rights.
    Would any wise man differ from me in this?
    As matters stand, I have my way in everything
    With your consent, and no responsibilities.
    If I were king, I should be a slave to policy. 75

    How could I desire a scepter more
    Than what is now mine—untroubled influence?
    No, I have not gone mad; I need no honors,
    Except those with the perquisites I have now.
    I am welcome everywhere; every man salutes me, 80
    And those who want your favor seek my ear,
    Since I know how to manage what they ask.
    Should I exchange this ease for that anxiety?
    Besides, no sober mind is treasonable.
    I hate anarchy 85
    And never would deal with any man who likes it.

    Test what I have said. Go to the priestess
    At Delphi, ask if I quoted her correctly.
    And as for this other thing: if I am found
    Guilty of treason with Teiresias, 90
    Then sentence me to death! You have my word
    It is a sentence I should cast my vote for—

But not without evidence!
                              You do wrong
When you take good men for bad, bad men for good.
A true friend thrown aside—why, life itself                                    95
Is not more precious!
                              In time you will know this well:
For time, and time alone, will show the just man,
Though scoundrels are discovered in a day.
*Choragos:* This is well said, and a prudent man would ponder it.
    Judgments too quickly formed are dangerous.                                100
*Oedipus:* But is he not quick in his duplicity?
    And shall I not be quick to parry him?
    Would you have me stand still, hold my peace, and let
    This man win everything, through my inaction?
*Creon:* And you want—what is it, then? To banish me?                         105
*Oedipus:* No, not exile. It is your death I want,
    So that all the world may see what treason means.
*Creon:* You will persist, then? You will not believe me?
*Oedipus:* How can I believe you?
*Creon:*                              Then you are a fool.
*Oedipus:* To save myself?
*Creon:*                    In justice, think of me.                          110
*Oedipus:* You are evil incarnate.
*Creon:*                              But suppose that you are wrong?
*Oedipus:* Still I must rule.
*Creon:*                    But not if you rule badly.
*Oedipus:* O city, city!
*Creon:*              It is my city, too!
*Choragos:* Now, my lords, be still. I see the Queen,
    Iocastê, coming from her palace chambers;                                115
    And it is time she came, for the sake of you both.
    This dreadful quarrel can be resolved through her.

    *Enter Iocastê.*

*Iocastê:* Poor foolish men, what wicked din is this?
    With Thebes sick to death, is it not shameful
    That you should rake some private quarrel up?                            120
    *(To Oedipus.)* Come into the house.
                              —And you, Creon, go now:
    Let us have no more of this tumult over nothing.
*Creon:* Nothing? No, sister: what your husband plans for me
    Is one of two great evils: exile or death.
*Oedipus:* He is right.
                              Why, woman, I have caught him squarely          125
    Plotting against my life.
*Creon:*                    No! Let me die

Accurst if ever I have wished you harm!
Iocastê: Ah, believe it, Oedipus!
   In the name of the gods, respect this oath of his
   For my sake, for the sake of these people here!                    130

*Strophe 1*

Choragos: Open your mind to her, my lord. Be ruled by her, I beg you!
Oedipus: What would you have me do?
Choragos: Respect Creon's word. He has never spoken like a fool,
   And now he has sworn an oath.
Oedipus:                              You know what you ask?
Choragos:                                               I do.
Oedipus:                                          Speak on, then.
Choragos: A friend so sworn should not be baited so,                  135
   In blind malice, and without final proof.
Oedipus: You are aware, I hope, that what you say
   Means death for me, or exile at the least.

*Strophe 2*

Choragos: No, I swear by Helios, first in Heaven!
   May I die friendless and accurst,                                  140
   The worst of deaths, if ever I meant that!
      It is the withering fields
         That hurt my sick heart:
      Must we bear all these ills,
         And now your bad blood as well?                              145
Oedipus: Then let him go. And let me die, if I must,
   Or be driven by him in shame from the land of Thebes.
   It is your unhappiness, and not his talk,
   That touches me.
                  As for him—
   Wherever he goes, hatred will follow him.                          150
Creon: Ugly in yielding, as you were ugly in rage!
   Natures like yours chiefly torment themselves.
Oedipus: Can you not go? Can you not leave me?
Creon:                                          I can.
   You do not know me; but the city knows me,
   And in its eyes I am just, if not in yours.                        155

*Exit Creon.*

*Antistrophe 1*

Choragos: Lady Iocastê, did you not ask the King to go to his chambers?
Iocastê: First tell me what has happened.
Choragos: There was suspicion without evidence; yet it rankled
   As even false charges will.
Iocastê:                        On both sides?

| *Choragos:* | On both. |
|---|---|
| *Iocastê:* | But what was said? |

*Choragos:*

 Oh let it rest, let it be done with!        160
 Have we not suffered enough?

*Oedipus:* You see to what your decency has brought you:
 You have made difficulties where my heart saw none.

Antistrophe 2

*Choragos:* Oedipus, it is not once only I have told you—
 You must know I should count myself unwise     165
 To the point of madness, should I now forsake you—
  You, under whose hand,
   In the storm of another time,
  Our dear land sailed out free.
   But now stand fast at the helm!       170

*Iocastê:* In God's name, Oedipus, inform your wife as well:
 Why are you so set in this hard anger?

*Oedipus:* I will tell you, for none of these men deserves
 My confidence as you do. It is Creon's work,
 His treachery, his plotting against me.       175

*Iocastê:* Go on, if you can make this clear to me.

*Oedipus:* He charges me with the murder of Laïos.

*Iocastê:* Has he some knowledge? Or does he speak from hearsay?

*Oedipus:* He would not commit himself to such a charge,
 But he has brought in that damnable soothsayer    180
 To tell his story.

*Iocastê:*     Set your mind at rest.
 If it is a question of soothsayers, I tell you
 That you will find no man whose craft gives knowledge
 Of the unknowable.
      Here is my proof:

 An oracle was reported to Laïos once       185
 (I will not say from Phoibos himself, but from
 His appointed ministers, at any rate)
 That his doom would be death at the hands of his own son—
 His son, born of his flesh and of mine!

 Now, you remember the story: Laïos was killed    190
 By marauding strangers where three highways meet;
 But his child had not been three days in this world
 Before the King had pierced the baby's ankles
 And left him to die on a lonely mountainside.

Thus, Apollo never caused that child                                    195
To kill his father, and it was not Laïos' fate
To die at the hands of his son, as he had feared.
This is what prophets and prophecies are worth!
Have no dread of them.
      It is God himself
Who can show us what he wills, in his own way.                           200
*Oedipus:* How strange a shadowy memory crossed my mind,
 Just now while you were speaking; it chilled my heart.
*Iocastê:* What do you mean? What memory do you speak of?
*Oedipus:* If I understand you, Laïos was killed
 At a place where three roads meet.
*Iocastê:*       So it was said;                205
 We have no later story.
*Oedipus:*     Where did it happen?
*Iocastê:* Phokis, it is called: at a place where the Theban Way
 Divides into the roads toward Delphi and Daulia.
*Oedipus:* When?
*Iocastê:*    We had the news not long before you came
 And proved the right to your succession here.                         210
*Oedipus:* Ah, what net has God been weaving for me?
*Iocastê:* Oedipus! Why does this trouble you?
*Oedipus:*       Do not ask me yet.
 First, tell me how Laïos looked, and tell me
 How old he was.
*Iocastê:*    He was tall, his hair just touched
 With white; his form was not unlike your own.                         215
*Oedipus:* I think that I myself may be accurst
 By my own ignorant edict.
*Iocastê:*      You speak strangely.
 It makes me tremble to look at you, my King.
*Oedipus:* I am not sure that the blind man can not see.
 But I should know better if you were to tell me—                      220
*Iocastê:* Anything—though I dread to hear you ask it.
*Oedipus:* Was the King lightly escorted, or did he ride
 With a large company, as a ruler should?
*Iocastê:* There were five men with him in all: one was a herald,
 And a single chariot, which he was driving.                           225
*Oedipus:* Alas, that makes it plain enough!
        But who—
 Who told you how it happened?
*Iocastê:*      A household servant,
 The only one to escape.
*Oedipus:*    And is he still
 A servant of ours?

Iocastê:                    No; for when he came back at last
     And found you enthroned in the place of the dead king,                    230
     He came to me, touched my hand with his, and begged
     That I would send him away to the frontier district
     Where only the shepherds go—
     As far away from the city as I could send him.
     I granted his prayer; for although the man was a slave,                    235
     He had earned more than this favor at my hands.
Oedipus: Can he be called back quickly?
Iocastê:                              Easily.
     But why?
Oedipus:     I have taken too much upon myself
     Without enquiry; therefore I wish to consult him.
Iocastê: Then he shall come.
                         But am I not one also                    240
     To whom you might confide these fears of yours?
Oedipus: That is your right; it will not be denied you,
     Now least of all; for I have reached a pitch
     Of wild foreboding. Is there anyone
     To whom I should sooner speak?                    245

     Polybos of Corinth is my father.
     My mother is a Dorian: Meropê.
     I grew up chief among the men of Corinth
     Until a strange thing happened—
     Not worth my passion, it may be, but strange.                    250

     At a feast, a drunken man maundering in his cups
     Cries out that I am not my father's son!

     I contained myself that night, though I felt anger
     And a sinking heart. The next day I visited
     My father and mother, and questioned them. They stormed,                    255
     Calling it all the slanderous rant of a fool;
     And this relieved me. Yet the suspicion
     Remained always aching in my mind;
     I knew there was talk; I could not rest;
     And finally, saying nothing to my parents,                    260
     I went to the shrine at Delphi.
     The god dismissed my question without reply;
     He spoke of other things.
                         Some were clear,
     Full of wretchedness, dreadful, unbearable:
     As, that I should lie with my own mother, breed                    265
     Children from whom all men would turn their eyes;
     And that I should be my father's murderer.

I heard all this, and fled. And from that day
Corinth to me was only in the stars
Descending in that quarter of the sky,                                   270
As I wandered farther and farther on my way
To a land where I should never see the evil
Sung by the oracle. And I came to this country
Where, so you say, King Laïos was killed.

I will tell you all that happened there, my lady.                        275

There were three highways
Coming together at a place I passed;
And there a herald came towards me, and a chariot
Drawn by horses, with a man such as you describe
Seated in it. The groom leading the horses                               280
Forced me off the road at his lord's command;
But as this charioteer lurched over towards me
I struck him in my rage. The old man saw me
And brought his double goad down upon my head
As I came abreast.
                        He was paid back, and more!                       285
Swinging my club in this right hand I knocked him
Out of his car, and he rolled on the ground.
                                        I killed him.

I killed them all.
Now if that stranger and Laïos were—kin,
Where is a man more miserable than I?                                    290
More hated by the gods? Citizen and alien alike
Must never shelter me or speak to me—
I must be shunned by all.
                        And I myself
Pronounced this malediction upon myself!

Think of it: I have touched you with these hands,                        295
These hands that killed your husband. What defilement!

Am I all evil, then? It must be so,
Since I must flee from Thebes, yet never again
See my own countrymen, my own country,
For fear of joining my mother in marriage                                300
And killing Polybos, my father.
                        Ah,
If I was created so, born to this fate,
Who could deny the savagery of God?

O holy majesty of heavenly powers!

May I never see that day! Never! 305
Rather let me vanish from the race of men
Than know the abomination destined me!
*Choragos:* We too, my lord, have felt dismay at this.
But there is hope: you have yet to hear the shepherd.
*Oedipus:* Indeed, I fear no other hope is left me. 310
*Iocastê:* What do you hope from him when he comes?
*Oedipus:*                                   This much:
If his account of the murder tallies with yours,
Then I am cleared.
*Iocastê:*                   What was it that I said
Of such importance?
*Oedipus:*                       Why, "marauders," you said,
Killed the King, according to this man's story. 315
If he maintains that still, if there were several,
Clearly the guilt is not mine: I was alone.
But if he says one man, singlehanded, did it,
Then the evidence all points to me.
*Iocastê:* You may be sure that he said there were several; 320
And can he call back that story now? He can not.
The whole city heard it as plainly as I.
But suppose he alters some detail of it:
He can not ever show that Laïos' death
Fulfilled the oracle: for Apollo said 325
My child was doomed to kill him; and my child—
Poor baby!—it was my child that died first.

No. From now on, where oracles are concerned,
I would not waste a second thought on any.
*Oedipus:* You may be right.
                              But come: let someone go 330
For the shepherd at once. This matter must be settled.
*Iocastê:* I will send for him.
I would not wish to cross you in anything,
And surely not in this.—Let us go in.

*Exeunt into the palace.*

# ODE II

*Strophe 1*

*Chorus:* Let me be reverent in the ways of right,
Lowly the paths I journey on;
Let all my words and actions keep
The laws of the pure universe
From highest Heaven handed down. 5
For Heaven is their bright nurse,

Those generations of the realms of light;
Ah, never of mortal kind were they begot,
Nor are they slaves of memory, lost in sleep:
Their Father is greater than Time, and ages not.                    10

The tyrant is a child of Pride
Who drinks from his great sickening cup
Recklessness and vanity,
Until from his high crest headlong
He plummets to the dust of hope.                                    15
That strong man is not strong.
But let no fair ambition be denied;
May God protect the wrestler for the State
In government, in comely policy,
Who will fear God, and on His ordinance wait.                       20

Haughtiness and the high hand of disdain
Tempt and outrage God's holy law;
And any mortal who dares hold
No immortal Power in awe
Will be caught up in a net of pain:                                 25
The price for which his levity is sold.
Let each man take due earnings, then,
And keep his hands from holy things,
And from blasphemy stand apart—
Else the crackling blast of heaven                                  30
Blows on his head, and on his desperate heart;
Though fools will honor impious men,
In their cities no tragic poet sings.

Shall we lose faith in Delphi's obscurities,
We who have heard the world's core                                  35
Discredited, and the sacred wood
Of Zeus at Elis praised no more?
The deeds and the strange prophecies
Must make a pattern yet to be understood.
Zeus, if indeed you are lord of all,                                40
Throned in light over night and day,
Mirror this in your endless mind:
Our masters call the oracle
Words on the wind, and the Delphic vision blind!
Their hearts no longer know Apollo,                                 45
And reverence for the gods has died away.

# SCENE III

*Enter Iocastê.*

*Iocastê:* Princes of Thebes, it has occurred to me
    To visit the altars of the gods, bearing
    These branches as a suppliant, and this incense.
    Our King is not himself: his noble soul
    Is overwrought with fantasies of dread, 5
    Else he would consider
    The new prophecies in the light of the old.
    He will listen to any voice that speaks disaster,
    And my advice goes for nothing.

*She approaches the altar, right.*

                               To you, then, Apollo,
    Lycean lord, since you are nearest, I turn in prayer. 10
    Receive these offerings, and grant us deliverance
    From defilement. Our hearts are heavy with fear
    When we see our leader distracted, as helpless sailors
    Are terrified by the confusion of their helmsman.

*Enter Messenger.*

*Messenger:* Friends, no doubt you can direct me: 15
    Where shall I find the house of Oedipus,
    Or, better still, where is the King himself?
*Choragos:* It is this very place, stranger; he is inside.
    This is his wife and mother of his children.
*Messenger:* I wish her happiness in a happy house, 20
    Blest in all the fulfillment of her marriage.
*Iocastê:* I wish as much for you: your courtesy
    Deserves a like good fortune. But now, tell me:
    Why have you come? What have you to say to us?
*Messenger:* Good news, my lady, for your house and your husband. 25
*Iocastê:* What news? Who sent you here?
*Messenger:*                         I am from Corinth.
    The news I bring ought to mean joy for you,
    Though it may be you will find some grief in it.
*Iocastê:* What is it? How can it touch us in both ways?
*Messenger:* The word is that the people of the Isthmus 30
    Intend to call Oedipus to be their king.
*Iocastê:* But old King Polybos—is he not reigning still?
*Messenger:* No. Death holds him in his sepulchre.
*Iocastê:* What are you saying? Polybos is dead?
*Messenger:* If I am not telling the truth, may I die myself. 35

*Iocastê* (*to a Maidservant*): Go in, go quickly; tell this to your master.

O riddlers of God's will, where are you now!
This was the man whom Oedipus, long ago,
Feared so, fled so, in dread of destroying him—
But it was another fate by which he died.                    40

*Enter Oedipus, center.*

*Oedipus:* Dearest Iocastê, why have you sent for me?
*Iocastê:* Listen to what this man says, and then tell me
   What has become of the solemn prophecies.
*Oedipus:* Who is this man? What is his news for me?
*Iocastê:* He has come from Corinth to announce your father's death!   45
*Oedipus:* Is it true, stranger? Tell me in your own words.
*Messenger:* I can not say it more clearly: the King is dead.
*Oedipus:* Was it by treason? Or by an attack of illness?
*Messenger:* A little thing brings old men to their rest.
*Oedipus:* It was sickness, then?
*Messenger:*                          Yes, and his many years.         50
*Oedipus:* Ah!
   Why should a man respect the Pythian hearth,° or
   Give heed to the birds that jangle above his head?
   They prophesied that I should kill Polybos,
   Kill my own father; but he is dead and buried,               55
   And I am here—I never touched him, never,
   Unless he died of grief for my departure,
   And thus, in a sense, through me. No. Polybos
   Has packed the oracles off with him underground.
   They are empty words.
*Iocastê:*                   Had I not told you so?                    60
*Oedipus:* You had; it was my faint heart that betrayed me.
*Iocastê:* From now on never think of those things again.
*Oedipus:* And yet—must I not fear my mother's bed?
*Iocastê:* Why should anyone in this world be afraid,
   Since Fate rules us and nothing can be foreseen?            65
   A man should live only for the present day.

   Have no more fear of sleeping with your mother:
   How many men, in dreams, have lain with their mothers!
   No reasonable man is troubled by such things.
*Oedipus:* That is true; only—                                        70
   If only my mother were not still alive!
   But she is alive. I can not help my dread.

---

52 *Pythian hearth:* the shrine at Delphi, whose priestess was famous for her prophecies.

*Iocastê:* Yet this news of your father's death is wonderful.

*Oedipus:* Wonderful. But I fear the living woman.

*Messenger:* Tell me, who is this woman that you fear?                    75

*Oedipus:* It is Meropê, man; the wife of King Polybos.

*Messenger:* Meropê? Why should you be afraid of her?

*Oedipus:* An oracle of the gods, a dreadful saying.

*Messenger:* Can you tell me about it or are you sworn to silence?

*Oedipus:* I can tell you, and I will.                    80

  Apollo said through his prophet that I was the man
  Who should marry his own mother, shed his father's blood
  With his own hands. And so, for all these years
  I have kept clear of Corinth, and no harm has come—
  Though it would have been sweet to see my parents again.                    85

*Messenger:* And is this the fear that drove you out of Corinth?

*Oedipus:* Would you have me kill my father?

*Messenger:*        As for that
  You must be reassured by the news I gave you.

*Oedipus:* If you could reassure me, I would reward you.

*Messenger:* I had that in mind, I will confess: I thought                    90
  I could count on you when you returned to Corinth.

*Oedipus:* No: I will never go near my parents again.

*Messenger:* Ah, son, you still do not know what you are doing—

*Oedipus:* What do you mean? In the name of God tell me!

*Messenger:* —If these are your reasons for not going home.                    95

*Oedipus:* I tell you, I fear the oracle may come true.

*Messenger:* And guilt may come upon you through your parents?

*Oedipus:* That is the dread that is always in my heart.

*Messenger:* Can you not see that all your fears are groundless?

*Oedipus:* How can you say that? They are my parents, surely?                    100

*Messenger:* Polybos was not your father.

*Oedipus:*        Not my father?

*Messenger:* No more your father than the man speaking to you.

*Oedipus:* But you are nothing to me!

*Messenger:*        Neither was he.

*Oedipus:* Then why did he call me son?

*Messenger:*        I will tell you:
  Long ago he had you from my hands, as a gift.                    105

*Oedipus:* Then how could he love me so, if I was not his?

*Messenger:* He had no children, and his heart turned to you.

*Oedipus:* What of you? Did you buy me? Did you find me by chance?

*Messenger:* I came upon you in the crooked pass of Kithairon.

*Oedipus:* And what were you doing there?

*Messenger:*        Tending my flocks.                    110

*Oedipus:* A wandering shepherd?

*Messenger:*      But your savior, son, that day.

*Oedipus:* From what did you save me?

*Messenger:*                                    Your ankles should tell you that.

*Oedipus:* Ah, stranger, why do you speak of that childhood pain?

*Messenger:* I cut the bonds that tied your ankles together.

*Oedipus:* I have had the mark as long as I can remember.                    115

*Messenger:* That was why you were given the name you bear.

*Oedipus:* God! Was it my father or my mother who did it?
   Tell me!

*Messenger:*    I do not know. The man who gave you to me
   Can tell you better than I.                                              120

*Oedipus:* It was not you that found me, but another?

*Messenger:* It was another shepherd gave you to me.

*Oedipus:* Who was he? Can you tell me who he was?

*Messenger:* I think he was said to be one of Laïos' people.

*Oedipus:* You mean the Laïos who was king here years ago?                    125

*Messenger:* Yes; King Laïos; and the man was one of his herdsmen.

*Oedipus:* Is he still alive? Can I see him?

*Messenger:*                                    These men here
   Know best about such things.

*Oedipus:*                                    Does anyone here
   Know this shepherd that he is talking about?
   Have you seen him in the fields, or in the town?                          130
   If you have, tell me. It is time things were made plain.

*Choragos:* I think the man he means is that same shepherd
   You have already asked to see. Iocastê perhaps
   Could tell you something.

*Oedipus:*                                    Do you know anything
   About him, Lady? Is he the man we have summoned?                         135
   Is that the man this shepherd means?

*Iocastê:*                                    Why think of him?
   Forget this herdsman. Forget it all.
   This talk is a waste of time.

*Oedipus:*                                    How can you say that,
   When the clues to my true birth are in my hands?

*Iocastê:* For God's love, let us have no more questioning!                    140
   Is your life nothing to you?
   My own is pain enough for me to bear.

*Oedipus:* You need not worry. Suppose my mother a slave,
   And born of slaves: no baseness can touch you.

*Iocastê:* Listen to me, I beg you: do not do this thing!                      145

*Oedipus:* I will not listen; the truth must be made known.

*Iocastê:* Everything that I say is for your own good!

*Oedipus:*                                    My own good
   Snaps my patience, then; I want none of it.

*Iocastê:* You are fatally wrong! May you never learn who you are!

*Oedipus:* Go, one of you, and bring the shepherd here.                    150
        Let us leave this woman to brag of her royal name.
*Iocastê:* Ah, miserable!
        That is the only word I have for you now.
        That is the only word I can ever have.

        *Exit into the palace.*

*Choragos:*
        Why has she left us, Oedipus? Why has she gone                    155
        In such a passion of sorrow? I fear this silence:
        Something dreadful may come of it.
*Oedipus:*                              Let it come!
        However base my birth, I must know about it.
        The Queen, like a woman, is perhaps ashamed
        To think of my low origin. But I                                  160
        Am a child of Luck; I can not be dishonored.
        Luck is my mother; the passing months, my brothers,
        Have seen me rich and poor.
                              If this is so,
        How could I wish that I were someone else?
        How could I not be glad to know my birth?                         165

# ODE III

*Chorus:* If ever the coming time were known
        To my heart's pondering,
        Kithairon, now by Heaven I see the torches
        At the festival of the next full moon,
        And see the dance, and hear the choir sing                         5
        A grace to your gentle shade:
        Mountain where Oedipus was found,
        O mountain guard of a noble race!
        May the god who heals us lend his aid,
        And let that glory come to pass                                   10
        For our king's cradling-ground.

        Of the nymphs that flower beyond the years,
        Who bore you, royal child,
        To Pan of the hills or the timberline Apollo,
        Cold in delight where the upland clears,                          15
        Or Hermês for whom Kyllenê's° heights are piled?

16 *Kyllenê:* a sacred mountain, birthplace of Hermês, the deities's messenger. The chorus assumes
that the mountain was created in order to afford him birth.

Or flushed as evening cloud,
Great Dionysos, roamer of mountains,
He—was it he who found you there,
And caught you up in his own proud                                    20
Arms from the sweet god-ravisher
Who laughed by the Muses' fountains?

# SCENE IV

*Oedipus:* Sirs: though I do not know the man,
  I think I see him coming, this shepherd we want:
  He is old, like our friend here, and the men
  Bringing him seem to be servants of my house.
  But you can tell, if you have ever seen him.                         5

  *Enter Shepherd escorted by servants.*

*Choragos:* I know him, he was Laïos' man. You can trust him.
*Oedipus:* Tell me first, you from Corinth: is this the shepherd
    We were discussing?
*Messenger:*                      This is the very man.
*Oedipus (to Shepherd):* Come here. No, look at me. You must answer
    Everything I ask.—You belonged to Laïos?                          10
*Shepherd:* Yes: born his slave, brought up in his house.
*Oedipus:* Tell me: what kind of work did you do for him?
*Shepherd:* I was a shepherd of his, most of my life.
*Oedipus:* Where mainly did you go for pasturage?
*Shepherd:* Sometimes Kithairon, sometimes the hills near-by.         15
*Oedipus:* Do you remember ever seeing this man out there?
*Shepherd:* What would he be doing there? This man?
*Oedipus:* This man standing here. Have you ever seen him before?
*Shepherd:* No. At least, not to my recollection.
*Messenger:* And that is not strange, my lord. But I'll refresh        20
    His memory: he must remember when we two
    Spent three whole seasons together, March to September,
    On Kithairon or thereabouts. He had two flocks;
    I had one. Each autumn I'd drive mine home
    And he would go back with his to Laïos' sheepfold.—               25
    Is this not true, just as I have described it?
*Shepherd:* True, yes; but it was all so long ago.
*Messenger:* Well, then: do you remember, back in those days
    That you gave me a baby boy to bring up as my own?
*Shepherd:* What if I did? What are you trying to say?                 30
*Messenger:* King Oedipus was once that little child.
*Shepherd:* Damn you, hold your tongue!
*Oedipus:*                                  No more of that!
    It is your tongue needs watching, not this man's.

*Shepherd:* My King, my Master, what is it I have done wrong?
*Oedipus:* You have not answered his question about the boy. 35
*Shepherd:* He does not know . . . He is only making trouble . . .
*Oedipus:* Come, speak plainly, or it will go hard with you.
*Shepherd:* In God's name, do not torture an old man!
*Oedipus:* Come here, one of you; bind his arms behind him.
*Shepherd:* Unhappy king! What more do you wish to learn? 40
*Oedipus:* Did you give this man the child he speaks of?
*Shepherd:*                                                     I did.
     And I would to God I had died that very day.
*Oedipus:* You will die now unless you speak the truth.
*Shepherd:* Yet if I speak the truth, I am worse than dead.
*Oedipus:* Very well; since you insist upon delaying— 45
*Shepherd:* No! I have told you already that I gave him the boy.
*Oedipus:* Where did you get him? From your house? From somewhere else?
*Shepherd:* Not from mine, no. A man gave him to me.
*Oedipus:* Is that man here? Do you know whose slave he was?
*Shepherd:* For God's love, my King, do not ask me any more! 50
*Oedipus:* You are a dead man if I have to ask you again.
*Shepherd:* Then . . . Then the child was from the palace of Laïos.
*Oedipus:* A slave child? or a child of his own line?
*Shepherd:* Ah, I am on the brink of dreadful speech!
*Oedipus:* And I of dreadful hearing. Yet I must hear. 55
*Shepherd:* If you must be told, then . . .
                              They said it was Laïos' child;
     But it is your wife who can tell you about that.
*Oedipus:* My wife!—Did she give it to you?
*Shepherd:*                                           My lord, she did.
*Oedipus:* Do you know why?
*Shepherd:*                          I was told to get rid of it.
*Oedipus:* An unspeakable mother!
*Shepherd:*                                There had been prophecies . . . 60
*Oedipus:* Tell me.
*Shepherd:* It was said that the boy would kill his own father.
*Oedipus:* Then why did you give him over to this old man?
*Shepherd:* I pitied the baby, my King,
     And I thought that this man would take him far away
     To his own country.
                              He saved him—but for what a fate! 65
     For if you are what this man says you are,
     No man living is more wretched than Oedipus.
*Oedipus:* Ah God!
     It was true!
              All the prophecies!
                         —Now,

O Light, may I look on you for the last time!                                  70
I, Oedipus,
Oedipus, damned in his birth, in his marriage damned,
Damned in the blood he shed with his own hand!

*He rushes into the palace.*

# ODE IV

*Strophe 1*

*Chorus:* Alas for the seed of men.

What measure shall I give these generations
That breathe on the void and are void
And exist and do not exist?

Who bears more weight of joy                                                    5
Than mass of sunlight shifting in images,
Or who shall make his thought stay on
That down time drifts away?

Your splendor is all fallen.

O naked brow of wrath and tears,                                               10
O change of Oedipus!
I who saw your days call no man blest—
Your great days like ghosts gone.

*Antistrophe 1*

That mind was a strong bow.

Deep, how deep you drew it then, hard archer,                                  15
At a dim fearful range,
And brought dear glory down!

You overcame the stranger—
The virgin with her hooking lion claws—
And though death sang, stood like a tower                                      20
To make pale Thebes take heart.

Fortress against our sorrow!

Divine king, giver of laws,
Majestic Oedipus!
No prince in Thebes had ever such renown,                                      25
No prince won such grace of power.

*Strophe 2*

And now of all men ever known
Most pitiful is this man's story:

His fortunes are most changed, his state
Fallen to a low slave's                                              30
Ground under bitter fate.

O Oedipus, most royal one!
The great door that expelled you to the light
Gave at night—ah, gave night to your glory:
As to the father, to the fathering son.                              35

All understood too late.

How could that queen whom Laïos won,
The garden that he harrowed at his height,
Be silent when that act was done?

But all eyes fail before time's eye,                                 40
All actions come to justice there.
Though never willed, though far down the deep past,
Your bed, your dread sirings,
Are brought to book at last.
Child by Laïos doomed to die,                                        45
Then doomed to lose that fortunate little death,
Would God you never took breath in this air
That with my wailing lips I take to cry:

For I weep the world's outcast.

I was blind, and now I can tell why:                                 50
Asleep, for you had given ease of breath
To Thebes, while the false years went by.

# ÉXODOS°

*Enter, from the palace, Second Messenger.*

*Second Messenger:* Elders of Thebes, most honored in this land,
    What horrors are yours to see and hear, what weight
    Of sorrow to be endured, if, true to your birth,
    You venerate the line of Labdakos!
    I think neither Istros nor Phasis, those great rivers,           5
    Could purify this place of the corruption
    It shelters now, or soon must bring to light—

---

*Éxodos:* final scene, containing the resolution.

Evil not done unconsciously, but willed.

The greatest griefs are those we cause ourselves.
*Choragos:* Surely, friend, we have grief enough already;                    10
    What new sorrow do you mean?
*Second Messenger:*                          The Queen is dead.
*Choragos:* Iocastê? Dead? But at whose hand?
*Second Messenger:*                              Her own.
    The full horror of what happened, you can not know,
    For you did not see it; but I, who did, will tell you
    As clearly as I can how she met her death.                              15

    When she had left us,
    In passionate silence, passing through the court,
    She ran to her apartment in the house,
    Her hair clutched by the fingers of both hands.
    She closed the doors behind her; then, by that bed                       20
    Where long ago the fatal son was conceived—
    That son who should bring about his father's death—
    We heard her call upon Laïos, dead so many years,
    And heard her wail for the double fruit of her marriage,
    A husband by her husband, children by her child.                         25

    Exactly how she died I do not know:
    For Oedipus burst in moaning and would not let us
    Keep vigil to the end: it was by him
    As he stormed about the room that our eyes were caught.
    From one to another of us he went, begging a sword,                      30
    Cursing the wife who was not his wife, the mother
    Whose womb had carried his own children and himself.
    I do not know: it was none of us aided him,
    But surely one of the gods was in control!
    For with a dreadful cry                                                   35
    He hurled his weight, as though wrenched out of himself,
    At the twin doors: the bolts gave, and he rushed in.
    And there we saw her hanging, her body swaying
    From the cruel cord she had noosed about her neck.
    A great sob broke from him, heartbreaking to hear,                       40
    As he loosed the rope and lowered her to the ground.

    I would blot out from my mind what happened next!
    For the King ripped from her gown the golden brooches
    That were her ornament, and raised them, and plunged them down
    Straight into his own eyeballs, crying, "No more,                        45
    No more shall you look on the misery about me,
    The horrors of my own doing! Too long you have known

The faces of those whom I should never have seen,
Too long been blind to those for whom I was searching!
From this hour, go in darkness!" And as he spoke, 50
He struck at his eyes—not once, but many times;
And the blood spattered his beard,
Bursting from his ruined sockets like red hail.

So from the unhappiness of two this evil has sprung,
A curse on the man and woman alike. The old 55
Happiness of the house of Labdakos
Was happiness enough: where is it today?
It is all wailing and ruin, disgrace, death—all
The misery of mankind that has a name—
And it is wholly and for ever theirs. 60
Choragos: Is he in agony still? Is there no rest for him?
Second Messenger: He is calling for someone to lead him to the gates
So that all the children of Kadmos may look upon
His father's murderer, his mother's—no,
I can not say it!
                      And then he will leave Thebes, 65
Self-exiled, in order that the curse
Which he himself pronounced may depart from the house.
He is weak, and there is none to lead him,
So terrible is his suffering.
                      But you will see:
Look, the doors are opening; in a moment 70
You will see a thing that would crush a heart of stone.

*The central door is opened; Oedipus, blinded, is led in.*

Choragos: Dreadful indeed for men to see.
    Never have my own eyes
    Looked on a sight so full of fear.

    Oedipus! 75
    What madness came upon you, what daemon
    Leaped on your life with heavier
    Punishment than a mortal man can bear?
    No: I can not even
    Look at you, poor ruined one. 80
    And I would speak, question, ponder,
    If I were able. No.
    You make me shudder.
Oedipus: God.  God.
    Is there a sorrow greater? 85
    Where shall I find harbor in this world?

My voice is hurled far on a dark wind.
What has God done to me?
*Choragos:* Too terrible to think of, or to see.

*Strophe 1*

*Oedipus:* O cloud of night,                                                        90
    Never to be turned away: night coming on,
    I can not tell how: night like a shroud!

    My fair winds brought me here.
                       Oh God. Again
    The pain of the spikes where I had sight,
    The flooding pain                                                        95
    Of memory, never to be gouged out.
*Choragos:* This is not strange.
    You suffer it all twice over, remorse in pain,
    Pain in remorse.

*Antistrophe 1*

*Oedipus:* Ah dear friend                                                        100
    Are you faithful even yet, you alone?
    Are you still standing near me, will you stay here,
    Patient, to care for the blind?
                        The blind man!
    Yet even blind I know who it is attends me,
    By the voice's tone—                                                        105
    Though my new darkness hide the comforter.
*Choragos:* Oh fearful act!
    What god was it drove you to rake black
    Night across your eyes?

*Strophe 2*

*Oedipus:* Apollo. Apollo. Dear                                                        110
    Children, the god was Apollo.
    He brought my sick, sick fate upon me.
    But the blinding hand was my own!
    How could I bear to see
    When all my sight was horror everywhere?                                                        115
*Choragos:* Everywhere; that is true.
*Oedipus:* And now what is left?
    Images? Love? A greeting even,
    Sweet to the senses? Is there anything?
    Ah, no, friends: lead me away.                                                        120
    Lead me away from Thebes.
                    Lead the great wreck
    And hell of Oedipus, whom the gods hate.
*Choragos:* Your fate is clear, you are not blind to that.
    Would God you had never found it out!

*Oedipus:* Death take the man who unbound
    My feet on that hillside
    And delivered me from death to life! What life?
    If only I had died,
    This weight of monstrous doom
    Could not have dragged me and my darlings down.                    130
*Choragos:* I would have wished the same.
*Oedipus:* Oh never to have come here
    With my father's blood upon me! Never
    To have been the man they call his mother's husband!
    Oh accurst! Oh child of evil,                                       135
    To have entered that wretched bed—
                  the selfsame one!
    More primal than sin itself, this fell to me.
*Choragos:* I do not know how I can answer you.
    You were better dead than alive and blind.
*Oedipus:* Do not counsel me any more. This punishment                      140
    That I have laid upon myself is just.
    If I had eyes,
    I do not know how I could bear the sight
    Of my father, when I came to the house of Death,
    Or my mother: for I have sinned against them both                   145
    So vilely that I could not make my peace
    By strangling my own life.
                Or do you think my children,
    Born as they were born, would be sweet to my eyes?
    Ah never, never! Nor this town with its high walls,
    Nor the holy images of the gods.
              For I,                                        150
    Thrice miserable!—Oedipus, noblest of all the line
    Of Kadmos, have condemned myself to enjoy
    These things no more, by my own malediction
    Expelling that man whom the gods declared
    To be a defilement in the house of Laïos.                           155
    After exposing the rankness of my own guilt,
    How could I look men frankly in the eyes?
    No, I swear it,
    If I could have stifled my hearing at its source,
    I would have done it and made all this body                         160
    A tight cell of misery, blank to light and sound:
    So I should have been safe in a dark agony
    Beyond all recollection.
               Ah Kithairon!
    Why did you shelter me? When I was cast upon you,

Why did I not die? Then I should never                                           165
Have shown the world my execrable birth.

Ah Polybos! Corinth, city that I believed
The ancient seat of my ancestors: how fair
I seemed, your child! And all the while this evil
Was cancerous within me!
                              For I am sick                                       170
In my daily life, sick in my origin.

O three roads, dark ravine, woodland and way
Where three roads met: you, drinking my father's blood,
My own blood, spilled by my own hand: can you remember
The unspeakable things I did there, and the things                               175
I went on from there to do?
                              O marriage, marriage!
The act that engendered me, and again the act
Performed by the son in the same bed—
                              Ah, the net
Of incest, mingling fathers, brothers, sons,
With brides, wives, mothers: the last evil                                       180
That can be known by men: no tongue can say
How evil!
              No. For the love of God, conceal me
Somewhere far from Thebes; or kill me; or hurl me
Into the sea, away from men's eyes for ever.

Come, lead me. You need not fear to touch me.                                    185
Of all men, I alone can bear this guilt.

*Enter Creon.*

*Choragos:* We are not the ones to decide; but Creon here
    May fitly judge of what you ask. He only
    Is left to protect the city in your place.
*Oedipus:* Alas, how can I speak to him? What right have I                       190
    To beg his courtesy whom I have deeply wronged?
*Creon:* I have not come to mock you, Oedipus,
    Or to reproach you, either.
    *(To Attendants.)*          —You, standing there:
    If you have lost all respect for man's dignity,
    At least respect the flame of Lord Helios:                                   195
    Do not allow this pollution to show itself
    Openly here, an affront to the earth
    And Heaven's rain and the light of day. No, take him
    Into the house as quickly as you can.
    For it is proper                                                             200

That only the close kindred see his grief.

*Oedipus:* I pray you in God's name, since your courtesy
Ignores my dark expectation, visiting
With mercy this man of all men most execrable:
Give me what I ask—for your good, not for mine.                205

*Creon:* And what is it that you would have me do?

*Oedipus:* Drive me out of this country as quickly as may be
To a place where no human voice can ever greet me.

*Creon:* I should have done that before now—only,
God's will had not been wholly revealed to me.                210

*Oedipus:* But his command is plain: the parricide
Must be destroyed. I am that evil man.

*Creon:* That is the sense of it, yes; but as things are,
We had best discover clearly what is to be done.

*Oedipus:* You would learn more about a man like me?                215

*Creon:* You are ready now to listen to the god.

*Oedipus:* I will listen. But it is to you
That I must turn for help. I beg you, hear me.

The woman in there—
Give her whatever funeral you think proper:                220
She is your sister.
                    —But let me go, Creon!
Let me purge my father's Thebes of the pollution
Of my living here, and go out to the wild hills,
To Kithairon, that has won such fame with me,
The tomb my mother and father appointed for me,                225
And let me die there, as they willed I should.
And yet I know
Death will not ever come to me through sickness
Or in any natural way: I have been preserved
For some unthinkable fate. But let that be.                230

As for my sons, you need not care for them.
They are men, they will find some way to live.
But my poor daughters, who have shared my table,
Who never before have been parted from their father—
Take care of them, Creon; do this for me.                235
And will you let me touch them with my hands
A last time, and let us weep together?
Be kind, my lord,
Great prince, be kind!
                    Could I but touch them,
They would be mine again, as when I had my eyes.                240

*Enter Antigonê and Ismene, attended.*

Ah, God!
Is it my dearest children I hear weeping?
Has Creon pitied me and sent my daughters?
Creon: Yes, Oedipus: I knew that they were dear to you
    In the old days, and know you must love them still.             245
Oedipus: May God bless you for this—and be a friendlier
    Guardian to you than he has been to me!

Children, where are you?
Come quickly to my hands: they are your brother's—
Hands that have brought your father's once clear eyes         250
To this way of seeing—
                  Ah dearest ones,
I had neither sight nor knowledge then, your father
By the woman who was the source of his own life!
And I weep for you—having no strength to see you—,
I weep for you when I think of the bitterness           255
That men will visit upon you all your lives.
What homes, what festivals can you attend
Without being forced to depart again in tears?
And when you come to marriageable age,
Where is the man, my daughters, who would dare        260
Risk the bane that lies on all my children?
Is there any evil wanting? Your father killed
His father; sowed the womb of her who bore him;
Engendered you at the fount of his own existence!
That is what they will say of you.
                      Then, whom        265
Can you ever marry? There are no bridegrooms for you,
And your lives must wither away in sterile dreaming.

O Creon, son of Menoikeus!
You are the only father my daughters have,
Since we, their parents, are both of us gone for ever.        270
They are your own blood: you will not let them
Fall into beggary and loneliness;
You will keep them from the miseries that are mine!
Take pity on them; see, they are only children,
Friendless except for you. Promise me this,        275
Great Prince, and give me your hand in token of it.

*Creon clasps his right hand.*

Children:
I could say much, if you could understand me,
But as it is, I have only this prayer for you:

Live where you can, be as happy as you can—                                         280
Happier, please God, than God has made your father!
*Creon:* Enough. You have wept enough. Now go within.
*Oedipus:* I must; but it is hard.
*Creon:*                                      Time eases all things.
*Oedipus:* But you must promise—
*Creon:*                                          Say what you desire.
*Oedipus:* Send me from Thebes!
*Creon:*                                      God grant that I may!                   285
*Oedipus:* But since God hates me . . .
*Creon:*                                              No, he will grant your wish.
*Oedipus:* You promise?
*Creon:*                      I can not speak beyond my knowledge.
*Oedipus:* Then lead me in.
*Creon:*                              Come now, and leave your children.
*Oedipus:* No! Do not take them from me!
*Creon:*                                              Think no longer
That you are in command here, but rather think                                        290
How, when you were, you served your own destruction.

*Exeunt into the house all but the Chorus; the Choragos chants directly to the audience.*

*Choragos:* Men of Thebes: look upon Oedipus.

This is the king who solved the famous riddle
And towered up, most powerful of men.
No mortal eyes but looked on him with envy,                                           295
Yet in the end ruin swept over him.

Let every man in mankind's frailty
Consider his last day; and let none
Presume on his good fortune until he find
Life, at his death, a memory without pain.                                            300

## QUESTIONS

1. How explicitly does the prophet Teiresias reveal the guilt of Oedipus? Does it seem to you stupidity on the part of Oedipus, or a defect in Sophocles's play, that the king takes so long to recognize his guilt and to admit to it?
2. How does Oedipus exhibit weakness of character? Point to lines that reveal him as imperfectly noble in his words, deeds, or treatment of others.
3. "Oedipus is punished not for any fault in himself, but for his ignorance. Not knowing his family history, unable to recognize his parents on sight, he is blameless; and in slaying his father and marrying his mother, he behaves as any sensible person might behave in the same circumstances." Do you agree with this interpretation?
4. Besides the predictions of Teiresias, what other foreshadowings of the shepherd's revelation does the play contain?

5. Consider the character of Iocastê. Is she a "flat" character—a generalized queen figure—or an individual with distinctive traits of personality? Point to speeches or details in the play to back up your opinion.

6. Do the choral interludes merely interrupt the play with wordy poetry? Other than providing song, dance, and variety, do they have any value to the telling of the story?

7. What is dramatic irony? Besides the example given on page 610, what other instances of dramatic irony do you find in *Oedipus the King*? What do they contribute to the effectiveness of the play?

8. In the drama of Sophocles, violence and bloodshed take place offstage; thus, the suicide of Iocastê is only reported to us. Nor do we witness Oedipus's removal of his eyes; this horror is only given in the report by the second messenger. Of what advantage or disadvantage to the play is this limitation?

9. For what reason does Oedipus blind himself? What meaning, if any, do you find in his choice of a surgical instrument?

10. What are your feelings toward him as the play ends?

11. Read the famous interpretation of this play offered by Sigmund Freud (page 1805). How well does Freud explain why the play moves you?

12. With what attitude toward the gods does the play leave you? By inflicting a plague upon Thebes, by causing barrenness, by cursing both the people and their king, do the gods seem cruel, unjust, or tyrannical? Does the play show any reverence toward them?

13. Does this play end in total gloom?

## ARISTOTLE'S CONCEPT OF TRAGEDY

> A tragedy, then, is an imitation of an action that is serious, complete in itself, and of a certain magnitude; in a language embellished with each kind of artistry . . . cast in the form of drama, not narrative; accomplishing through incidents that arouse pity and fear the purgation of these emotions.
>
> —Aristotle, *Poetics*, Chapter VI

Aristotle's famous definition of tragedy, constructed in the fourth century B.C., is the testimony of one who probably saw many classical tragedies performed. In making his observations, Aristotle does not seem to be laying down laws for what a tragedy ought to be. More likely, he is drawing—from tragedies he has seen or read—a general description of them.

Aristotle observes that the protagonist, the hero or chief character of a tragedy, is a person of "high estate," apparently a king or queen or other member of a royal family. In thus being as keenly interested as contemporary dramatists in the private lives of the powerful, Greek dramatists need not be accused of snobbery. It is the nature of tragedy that the protagonist must fall from power and from happiness; his high estate gives him a place of dignity to fall from and perhaps makes his fall seem all the more a calamity in that it involves an entire nation or people. Nor is the protagonist extraordinary merely in his position in society. Oedipus is not only a king but also a noble soul who suffers profoundly and who employs splendid speech to express his suffering.

But the tragic hero is not a superman; he is fallible. The hero's downfall is the result, as Aristotle said, of his **hamartia:** his error or transgression or (as some translators would have it) his flaw or weakness of character. The notion that a tragic hero has such a **tragic flaw** has often been attributed to Aristotle, but it is by no means clear that Aristotle meant just that. According to this interpretation, every tragic hero has some fatal weakness, some moral Achilles's heel, that brings him to a bad end. In some classical tragedies, his transgression is a weakness the Greeks called **hubris:** extreme pride, leading to overconfidence.

Whatever Aristotle had in mind, however, many later critics find value in the idea of the tragic flaw. In this view, the downfall of a hero follows from his very nature. But whatever view we take—whether we find the hero's sufferings due to a flaw of character or to an error of judgment—we will probably find that his downfall results from acts for which he himself is responsible. In a Greek tragedy, the hero is a character amply capable of making choices—capable, too, of accepting the consequences.

It may be useful to take another look at Aristotle's definition of tragedy, with which we began. By **purgation** (or **katharsis**), did the ancient theorist mean that after witnessing a tragedy we feel relief, having released our pent-up emotions? Or did he mean that our feeling are purified, refined into something more ennobling? Scholars continue to argue. Whatever his exact meaning, clearly Aristotle implies that after witnessing a tragedy we feel better, not worse—not depressed but somehow elated. We take a kind of pleasure in the spectacle of a noble man being abased, but surely this pleasure is a legitimate one. For tragedy, Edith Hamilton wrote, affects us as "pain transmuted into exaltation by the alchemy of poetry."[1]

Aristotle, in describing the workings of this inexorable force in *Oedipus the King*, uses terms that later critics have found valuable. One is **recognition**, or discovery (*anagnorisis*): the revelation of some fact not known before or some person's true identity. Oedipus makes such a discovery: he recognizes that he himself was the child whom his mother had given over to be destroyed. Such a recognition also occurs in Shakespeare's *Macbeth* when Macduff reveals himself to have been "from his mother's womb/ Untimely ripped," thus disclosing a double meaning in the witches's prophecy that Macbeth could be harmed by "none of woman born," and sweeping aside Macbeth's last shred of belief that he is infallible. Modern critics have taken the term to mean also the terrible enlightenment that accompanies such a recognition. "To see things plain—that is *anagnorisis*," Clifford Leech observes, "and it is the ultimate experience we shall have if we have leisure at the point of death. . . . It is what tragedy ultimately is about: the realization of the unthinkable."[2]

Having made his discovery, Oedipus suffers a reversal in his fortunes: he goes off into exile, blinded and dethroned. Such a fall from happiness seems intrinsic to tragedy, but we should know that Aristotle has a more particular meaning for

[1]"The Idea of Tragedy" in *The Greek Way to Western Civilization* (New York: Norton, 1942).
[2]*Tragedy* (London: Methuen, 1969) 65.

his term **reversal** (*peripeteia*, Anglicized as **peripety**). He means an action that turns out to have the opposite effect from the one its doer had intended. One of his illustrations of such an ironic reversal is from *Oedipus the King:* the first messenger intends to cheer Oedipus with the partially good news that, contrary to the prophecy that Oedipus would kill his father, his father has died of old age. The reversal is in the fact that, when the messenger further reveals that old Polybos was Oedipus's father only by adoption, the king, instead of having his fears allayed, is stirred to new dread.

We are not altogether sorry, perhaps, to see an arrogant man such as Oedipus humbled, and yet it is difficult not to feel that the punishment of Oedipus is greater than he deserves. Possibly this feeling is what Aristotle meant in his observation that a tragedy arouses our pity and our fear: our compassion for Oedipus and our terror as we sense the remorselessness of a universe in which a man is doomed. Notice, however, that at the end of the play Oedipus does not curse God and die. Although such a complex play is open to many interpretations, it is probably safe to say that the play is not a bitter complaint against the universe. At last, Oedipus accepts the divine will, prays for blessings upon his children, and prepares to endure his exile—fallen from high estate, but uplifted in moral dignity.

## SUGGESTIONS FOR WRITING

1. Suppose you face the task of directing and producing a new stage production of *Oedipus the King*. Decide how you would go about it. Would you use masks? How would you render the chorus? Would you set the play in contemporary North America? Justify your decisions by referring to the play itself.
2. Write a brief comment on the play, under the title: "Does Sophocles's Oedipus Have an Oedipus Complex?" Consider psychiatrist Sigmund Freud's famous observations (quoted on page 1805). Your comment can be either serious or light.
3. Compare the version of *Oedipus the King* given in this book with a different English translation of the play. You might see, for instance, any of the versions by Gilbert Murray, J. T. Sheppard, and H. D. F. Kitto; by Paul Roche (in a Signet paperback); by William Butler Yeats (in his *Collected Plays*); by David Grene (University of Chicago Press, 1942); or by Stephen Berg and Diskin Clay (Oxford UP, 1978). Point to significant differences between the two texts. What decisions did the translators have to make? Which version do you prefer? Why?
4. Read *Antigonê* (in "Plays for Further Reading"), and in a brief essay demonstrate its relationship to *Oedipus the King*.
5. John Millington Synge's *Riders to the Sea* (in Chapter Thirty-three) has been called the closest approximation to a Greek tragedy in English. Does Synge's play resemble a tragedy of Sophocles in any ways? How does it noticeably differ?

# 35 The Theater of Shakespeare

Compared with the technical resources of a theater of today, those of a London public theater in the time of Queen Elizabeth I seem hopelessly limited. Plays had to be performed by daylight, and scenery had to be kept simple: a table, a chair, a throne, perhaps an artificial tree or two to suggest a forest. But these limitations were in a sense advantages. What the theater of today can spell out for us realistically, with massive scenery and electric lighting, Elizabethan playgoers had to imagine and the playwright had to make vivid for them by means of language. Not having a lighting technician to work a panel, Shakespeare had to indicate the dawn by having Horatio, in *Hamlet*, say in a speech rich in metaphor and descriptive detail:

> But look, the morn in russet mantle clad
> Walks o'er the dew of yon high eastward hill.

And yet the theater of Shakespeare was not bare, for the playwright did have *some* valuable technical resources. Costumes could be elaborate, and apparently some costumes conveyed recognized meanings: one theater manager's inventory included "a robe for to go invisible in." There could be musical accompaniment and sound effects such as gunpowder explosions and the beating of a pan to simulate thunder.

The stage itself was remarkably versatile. At its back were doors for exits and entrances and a curtained booth or alcove useful for hiding inside. Above the stage was a higher acting area—perhaps a porch or balcony—useful for a Juliet to stand upon and for a Romeo to raise his eyes to. And in the stage floor was a trapdoor leading to a "hell" or cellar, especially useful for ghosts or devils who had to appear or disappear. The stage itself was a rectangular platform that projected into a yard enclosed by three-storied galleries.

The building was round or octagonal: in *Henry V*, Shakespeare calls it a "wooden O." The audience sat in these galleries or else stood in the yard in front of the stage and at its sides. A roof or awning protected the stage and the high-priced gallery seats, but in a sudden rain, the *groundlings*, who paid a penny to stand in the yard, must have been dampened.

Built by the theatrical company to which Shakespeare belonged, the Globe, most celebrated of Elizabethan theaters, was not in the city of London itself but on the south bank of the Thames River. This location had been chosen because earlier, in 1574, public plays had been banished from the city by an ordinance

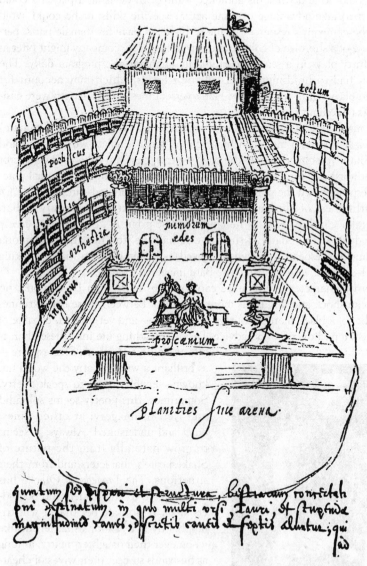

*Johannes de Witt, a continental visitor to London, made a drawing of the Swan Theater about 1596. The original drawing is lost; this is Arend van Buchel's copy of it.*

that blamed them for "corruptions of youth and other enormities" (such as providing opportunities for prostitutes and purse-cutters).

A playwright had to please all members of the audience, not only the mannered and educated. This obligation may help to explain the wide range of matter and tone in an Elizabethan play: passages of subtle poetry, of deep philosophy, of coarse bawdry; scenes of sensational violence and of quiet psychological conflict (not that most members of the audience did not enjoy all these elements). Because he was an actor as well as a playwright, Shakespeare well knew what his company could do and what his audience wanted. In devising a play, he could write a part to take advantage of some actor's specific skills; or he could avoid straining the company's resources (some of his plays have few female parts, perhaps because of a shortage of competent boy actors). The company might offer as many as thirty plays in a season, customarily changing the program daily. The actors thus had to hold many parts in their heads, which may account for Elizabethan playwrights' fondness for blank verse. Lines of fixed length were easier for actors to commit to memory.

*The Tragedy of Othello,* here offered for study, may be (if you are fortunate) new to you. It is seldom taught in high school, for it is ablaze with passion and violence. But if you already know the play, we trust that you (like your instructor and your editors) still have much more to learn from it. Following his usual practice, Shakespeare based the play on a story he had appropriated—from a tale, "Of the Unfaithfulness of Husbands and Wives," by a sixteenth-century Italian writer, Giraldi Cinthio. And as he could not help but do, Shakespeare freely transformed his source material. In the original tale, the heroine Disdemona (whose name Shakespeare so hugely improved) is beaten to death with a stocking full of sand—a shoddier death than the Bard imagined for her.

Surely no character in literature can touch us more than Desdemona; no character can shock and disgust us more than Iago. Between these two extremes stands Othello, a black man of courage and dignity—and yet human, capable of being fooled, a pushover for bad advice. Besides breathing life into these characters and a host of others, Shakespeare—as brilliant a writer as any the world has known—enables them to speak poetry. Sometimes, this poetry seems splendid and rich in imagery; at other times, quiet and understated. Always, it seems to grow naturally from the nature of Shakespeare's characters and from their situations. *The Tragedy of Othello* has never ceased to grip readers and beholders alike. It is a safe bet that it will triumphantly live as long as fathers dislike whomever their daughters marry, as long as husbands suspect their wives of cheating, as long as blacks remember slavery, and as long as the ambitious court favor

*James Earl Jones as Othello*

and the jealous work deceit. The play may well make sense as long as public officials connive behind smiling faces, and it may even endure as long as the world
makes room for the kind, the true, the beautiful—the blessed pure in heart.

## William Shakespeare

THE TRAGEDY OF OTHELLO, THE MOOR OF VENICE                    1604?

*Edited by David Bevington°*

*William Shakespeare (1564–1616), the
supreme writer of English, was born, baptized, and buried in the market town of
Stratford-on-Avon, eighty miles from London. Son of a glove maker and merchant
who was high bailiff (or mayor) of the
town, he probably attended grammar
school and learned to read Latin authors in
the original. At eighteen he married Anne
Hathaway, twenty-six, by whom he had
three children, including twins. By 1592 he
had become well known and envied as an
actor and playwright in London. From 1594
until he retired, he belonged to the same theatrical company, the Lord Chamberlain's*

William Shakespeare

*Men (later renamed the King's Men in honor of their patron, James I), for whom he
wrote thirty-six plays—some of them, such as* Hamlet *and* King Lear, *profound reworkings of old plays. As an actor, Shakespeare is believed to have played supporting roles,
such as Hamlet's father's ghost. The company prospered, moved into the Globe in 1599,
and in 1608 bought the fashionable Blackfriars as well; Shakespeare owned an interest in
both theaters. When plagues shut down the theaters from 1592 to 1594, Shakespeare
turned to story poems; his great Sonnets (published only in 1609) probably also date
from the 1590s. Plays were regarded as entertainments of little literary merit, like comic
books today, and Shakespeare did not bother to supervise their publication. After* The
Tempest *(1611), the last play entirely from his hand, he retired to Stratford, where since
1597 he had owned the second largest house in town. Most critics agree that when he
wrote* Othello, *about 1604, Shakespeare was at the height of his powers.*

---

*Edited by David Bevington:* This text of *Othello* is based on that of the First Folio, or large collection, of
Shakespeare's plays (1623). But there are many differences between the Folio text and that of the
play's first printing in the Quarto, or small volume, of 1621 (eighteen or nineteen years after the
play's first performance). Some readings from the Quarto are included. For the reader's convenience,
some material has been added by the editor (some indications of scene, some stage directions). Such
additions are enclosed in brackets. Mr. Bevington's text and notes were prepared for his book, *The
Complete Works of Shakespeare,* 4th edition (New York: HarperCollins, 1992).

Characters

*Othello*, the Moor
*Brabantio*, [a senator] father to Desdemona
*Cassio*, an honorable lieutenant [to Othello]
*Iago*, [Othello's ancient,] a villain
*Roderigo*, a gulled gentleman
*Duke of Venice*
*Senators* [of Venice]
*Montano*, governor of Cyprus
*Gentlemen of Cyprus*
*Lodovico and Gratiano*, [kinsmen to Brabantio,] two noble Venetians
*Sailors*
*Clown*
*Desdemona*, [daughter to Brabantio and] wife to Othello
*Emilia*, wife to Iago
*Bianca*, a courtesan [and mistress to Cassio]
[*A Messenger*
*A Herald*
*A Musician*
*Servants, Attendants, Officers, Senators, Musicians, Gentlemen*
*Scene: Venice; a seaport in Cyprus*]

# ACT I

### Scene I [*Venice. A Street.*]

 *Enter Roderigo and Iago.*

*Roderigo:* Tush, never tell me! I take it much unkindly
 That thou, Iago, who hast had my purse
 As if the strings were thine, shouldst know of this.
*Iago:* 'Sblood, but you'll not hear me.
 If ever I did dream of such a matter,         5
 Abhor me.
*Roderigo:* Thou toldst me thou didst hold him in thy hate.
*Iago:* Despise me
 If I do not. Three great ones of the city,
 In personal suit to make me his lieutenant,       10
 Off-capped to him; and by the faith of man,
 I know my price, I am worth no worse a place.

---

1 *never tell me* (An expression of incredulity, like "tell me another one.")  3 *this* i.e., Desdemona's
elopement  4 *'Sblood* by His (Christ's) blood  11 *him* i.e., Othello

But he, as loving his own pride and purposes,
Evades them with a bombast circumstance
Horribly stuffed with epithets of war,                                    15
And, in conclusion,
Nonsuits my mediators. For, "Certes," says he,
"I have already chose my officer."
And what was he?
Forsooth, a great arithmetician,                                          20
One Michael Cassio, a Florentine,
A fellow almost damned in a fair wife,
That never set a squadron in the field
Nor the division of a battle knows
More than a spinster—unless the bookish theoric,                          25
Wherein the togaed consuls can propose
As masterly as he. Mere prattle without practice
Is all his soldiership. But he, sir, had th' election;
And I, of whom his eyes had seen the proof
At Rhodes, at Cyprus, and on other grounds                                30
Christened and heathen, must be beeled and calmed
By debitor and creditor. This countercaster,
He, in good time, must his lieutenant be,
And I—God bless the mark!—his Moorship's ancient.
Roderigo: By heaven, I rather would have been his hangman.                35
Iago: Why, there's no remedy. 'Tis the curse of service;
Preferment goes by letter and affection,
And not by old gradation, where each second
Stood heir to th' first. Now, sir, be judge yourself
Whether I in any just term am affined                                     40
To love the Moor.
Roderigo: I would not follow him then.
Iago: O sir, content you.

---

14 *bombast circumstance* wordy evasion. (*Bombast* is cotton padding.)    15 *epithets of war* military
expressions    17 *Nonsuits* rejects the petition of.    *Certes* certainly    20 *arithmetician* i.e., a
man whose military knowledge is merely theoretical, based on books of tactics    22 *A . . . wife*
(Cassio does not seem to be married, but his counterpart in Shakespeare's source does have a woman
in his house. See also Act IV, Scene I, line 127.)    24 *division of a battle* disposition of a military
unit    25 *a spinster* i.e., a housewife, one whose regular occupation is spinning. *theoric* theory
26 *togaed* wearing the toga.    *consuls* counselors, senators.    *propose* discuss    29 *his* i.e.,
Othello's    31 *Christened* Christian.    *beeled and calmed* left to leeward without wind, becalmed.
(A sailing metaphor.)    32 *debitor and creditor* (A name for a system of bookkeeping, here used as a
contemptuous nickname for Cassio.)    *countercaster* i.e., bookkeeper, one who tallies with *counters*,
or "metal disks." (Said contemptuously.)    33 *in good time* opportunely, i.e., forsooth    34 *God
bless the mark* (Perhaps originally a formula to ward off evil; here an expression of impatience.)
*ancient* standard-bearer, ensign    35 *his hangman* the executioner of him    37 *Preferment* promotion.    *letter and affection* personal influence and favoritism    38 *old gradation* step-by-step senior-
ity, the traditional way    40 *term* respect    *affined* bound    43 *content you* don't you worry
about that

I follow him to serve my turn upon him.
We cannot all be masters, nor all masters                               45
Cannot be truly followed. You shall mark
Many a duteous and knee-crooking knave
That, doting on his own obsequious bondage,
Wears out his time, much like his master's ass,
For naught but provender, and when he's old, cashiered.                  50
Whip me such honest knaves. Others there are
Who, trimmed in forms and visages of duty,
Keep yet their hearts attending on themselves,
And, throwing but shows of service on their lords,
Do well thrive by them, and when they have lined their coats,            55
Do themselves homage. These fellows have some soul,
And such a one do I profess myself. For, sir,
It is as sure as you are Roderigo,
Were I the Moor I would not be Iago.
In following him, I follow but myself—                                   60
Heaven is my judge, not I for love and duty,
But seeming so for my peculiar end.
For when my outward action doth demonstrate
The native act and figure of my heart
In compliment extern, 'tis not long after                               65
But I will wear my heart upon my sleeve
For daws to peck at. I am not what I am.
*Roderigo:* What a full fortune does the thick-lips owe
        If he can carry 't thus!
*Iago:*                       Call up her father.
        Rouse him, make after him, poison his delight,                  70
        Proclaim him in the streets; incense her kinsmen,
        And, though he in a fertile climate dwell,
        Plague him with flies. Though that his joy be joy,
        Yet throw such changes of vexation on 't
        As it may lose some color.                                      75
*Roderigo:* Here is her father's house. I'll call aloud.

<hr>

46 *truly* faithfully     50 *cashiered* dismissed from service     51 *Whip me* whip, as far as I'm concerned     52 *trimmed . . . duty* dressed up in the mere form and show of dutifulness     55 *lined their
coats* i.e., stuffed their purses     56 *Do themselves homage* i.e., attend to self-interest solely     59
*Were . . . Iago* i.e., if I were able to assume command, I certainly would not choose to remain a subordinate, or, I would keep a suspicious eye on a flattering subordinate     62 *peculiar* particular, personal     64 *native* innate.     *figure* shape, intent     65 *compliment extern* outward show (conforming
in this case to the inner workings and intention of the heart)     67 *daws* small crowlike birds,
proverbially stupid and avaricious.     *I am not what I am* i.e., I am not one who wears his heart on
his sleeve     68 *full* swelling.     *thick-lips* (Elizabethans often applied the term "Moor" to Negroes.)
*owe* own     69 *carry 't thus* carry this off     72–73 *though . . . flies* though he seems prosperous and
happy now, vex him with misery     73 *Though . . . be joy* although he seems fortunate and happy.
(Repeats the idea of line 72.)     74 *changes of vexation* vexing changes     75 *As it may* that may
cause it to.     *some color* some of its fresh gloss

*Iago:* Do, with like timorous accent and dire yell
    As when, by night and negligence, the fire
    Is spied in populous cities.
*Roderigo:* What ho, Brabantio! Signor Brabantio, ho!
*Iago:* Awake! What ho, Brabantio! Thieves, thieves, thieves!     80
    Look to your house, your daughter, and your bags!
    Thieves, thieves!

    *Brabantio [enters] above [at a window].*

*Brabantio:* What is the reason of this terrible summons?
    What is the matter there?     85
*Roderigo:* Signor, is all your family within?
*Iago:* Are your doors locked?
*Brabantio:*                  Why, wherefore ask you this?
*Iago:* Zounds, sir, you're robbed. For shame, put on your gown!
    Your heart is burst; you have lost half your soul.
    Even now, now, very now, an old black ram     90
    Is tupping your white ewe. Arise, arise!
    Awake the snorting citizens with the bell,
    Or else the devil will make a grandsire of you.
    Arise, I say!
*Brabantio:*         What, have you lost your wits?
*Roderigo:* Most reverend signor, do you know my voice?     95
*Brabantio:* Not I. What are you?
*Roderigo:* My name is Roderigo.
*Brabantio:* The worser welcome.
    I have charged thee not to haunt about my doors.
    In honest plainness thou hast heard me say     100
    My daughter is not for thee; and now, in madness,
    Being full of supper and distempering drafts,
    Upon malicious bravery dost thou come
    To start my quiet.
*Roderigo:* Sir, sir, sir—
*Brabantio:*         But thou must needs be sure     105
    My spirits and my place have in their power
    To make this bitter to thee.
*Roderigo:*              Patience, good sir.

---

77 *timorous* frightening    78 *and negligence* i.e., by negligence    82 s.d. *at a window* (This stage direction, from the Quarto, probably calls for an appearance on the gallery above and rearstage.) 85 *the matter* your business    88 *Zounds* by His (Christ's) wounds    91 *tupping* covering, copulating with. (Said of sheep.)    92 *snorting* snoring    93 *the devil* (The devil was conventionally pictured as black.)    102 *distempering* intoxicating    103 *Upon malicious bravery* with hostile intent to defy me    104 *start* startle, disrupt    106 *My spirits and my place* my temperament and my authority of office.    *have in* have it in

*Brabantio*: What tell'st thou me of robbing? This is Venice;
　　My house is not a grange.
*Roderigo*:　　　　　　　　　Most grave Brabantio,
　　In simple and pure soul I come to you. 110
*Iago*: Zounds, sir, you are one of those that will not serve God if the devil bid you.
　　Because we come to do you service and you think we are ruffians, you'll have
　　your daughter covered with a Barbary horse; you'll have your nephews neigh
　　to you; you'll have coursers for cousins and jennets for germans.
*Brabantio*: What profane wretch art thou? 115
*Iago*: I am one, sir, that comes to tell you your daughter and the Moor are now
　　making the beast with two backs.
*Brabantio*: Thou art a villain.
*Iago*:　　　　　　　　　You are—a senator.
*Brabantio*: This thou shalt answer. I know thee, Roderigo.
*Roderigo*: Sir, I will answer anything. But I beseech you, 120
　　If 't be your pleasure and most wise consent—
　　As partly I find it is—that your fair daughter,
　　At this odd-even and dull watch o' the night,
　　Transported with no worse nor better guard
　　But with a knave of common hire, a gondolier, 125
　　To the gross clasps of a lascivious Moor—
　　If this be known to you and your allowance
　　We then have done you bold and saucy wrongs.
　　But if you know not this, my manners tell me
　　We have your wrong rebuke. Do not believe 130
　　That, from the sense of all civility,
　　I thus would play and trifle with your reverence.
　　Your daughter, if you have not given her leave,
　　I say again, hath made a gross revolt,
　　Tying her duty, beauty, wit, and fortunes 135
　　In an extravagant and wheeling stranger
　　Of here and everywhere. Straight satisfy yourself.
　　If she be in her chamber or your house,
　　Let loose on me the justice of the state
　　For thus deluding you. 140

---

109 *grange* isolated country house　　110 *simple* sincere　　113 *Barbary* from northern Africa (and hence associated with Othello)　　*nephews* i.e., grandsons.　　114 *coursers* powerful horses *cousins* kinsmen.　　*jennets* small Spanish horses.　　*germans* near relatives　　118 *a senator* (Said with mock politeness, as though the word itself were an insult.)　　119 *answer* be held accountable for　　121 *wise* well-informed　　123 *odd-even* between one day and the next, i.e., about midnight 124 *with* by　　125 *But with a knave* than by a low fellow, a servant　　127 *allowance* permission 128 *saucy* insolent　　131 *from* contrary to.　　*civility* good manners, decency　　132 *your reverence* the respect due to you　　135 *wit* intelligence　　136 *extravagant* expatriate, wandering far from home.　　*wheeling* roving about, vagabond.　　*stranger* foreigner　　137 *Straight* straightway

*Brabantio*: Strike on the tinder, ho!
    Give me a taper! Call up all my people!
    This accident is not unlike my dream.
    Belief of it oppresses me already.
    Light, I say, light!                        *Exit [above].*
*Iago*:                 Farewell, for I must leave you.       145
    It seems not meet nor wholesome to my place
    To be producted—as, if I stay, I shall—
    Against the Moor. For I do know the state,
    However this may gall him with some check,
    Cannot with safety cast him, for he's embarked      150
    With such loud reason to the Cyprus wars,
    Which even now stands in act, that, for their souls,
    Another of his fathom they have none
    To lead their business; in which regard,
    Though I do hate him as I do hell pains,      155
    Yet for necessity of present life
    I must show out a flag and sign of love,
    Which is indeed but sign. That you shall surely find him,
    Lead to the Sagittary the raisèd search,
    And there will I be with him. So farewell.      *Exit.*  160

    *Enter [below] Brabantio [in his nightgown] with servants and torches.*

*Brabantio*: It is too true an evil. Gone she is;
    And what's to come of my despisèd time
    Is naught but bitterness. Now, Roderigo,
    Where didst thou see her?—O unhappy girl!—
    With the Moor, sayst thou?—Who would be a father!—    165
    How didst thou know 'twas she?—O, she deceives me
    Past thought!—What said she to you?—Get more tapers.
    Raise all my kindred.—Are they married, think you?
*Roderigo*: Truly, I think they are.
*Brabantio*: O heaven! How got she out? O treason of the blood!    170
    Fathers, from hence trust not your daughters' minds
    By what you see them act. Is there not charms

---

141 *tinder* charred linen ignited by a spark from flint and steel, used to light torches or *tapers* (lines 142, 167)    143 *accident* occurrence, event    146 *meet* fitting.    *place* position (as ensign) 147 *producted* produced (as a witness)    149 *gall* rub; oppress.    *check* rebuke    150 *cast* dismiss. *embarked* engaged    151 *loud reason* unanimous shout of confirmation (in the Senate)    152 *stands in act* are going on.    *for their souls* to save themselves    153 *fathom* i.e., ability, depth of experience    154 *in which regard* out of regard for which    156 *life* livelihood    159 *Sagittary* (An inn or house where Othello and Desdemona are staying, named for its sign of Sagittarius, or Centaur.)    *raisèd search* search party roused out of sleep    160 s.d. *nightgown* dressing gown. (This costuming is specified in the Quarto text.)    162 *time* i.e., remainder of life    172 *charms* spells

By which the property of youth and maidhood
May be abused? Have you not read, Roderigo,
Of some such thing?
*Roderigo:*                    Yes, sir, I have indeed.                    175
*Brabantio:* Call up my brother.—O, would you had had her!—
Some one way, some another.—Do you know
Where we may apprehend her and the Moor?
*Roderigo:* I think I can discover him, if you please
To get good guard and go along with me.                    180
*Brabantio:* Pray you, lead on. At every house I'll call;
I may command at most.—Get weapons, ho!
And raise some special officers of night.—
On, good Roderigo. I will deserve your pains.

*Exeunt.*


### Scene II [Venice. Another Street, Before Othello's Lodgings.]

*Enter Othello, Iago, attendants with torches.*

*Iago:* Though in the trade of war I have slain men,
Yet do I hold it very stuff o' the conscience
To do no contrived murder. I lack iniquity
Sometimes to do me service. Nine or ten times
I had thought t' have yerked him here under the ribs.                    5
*Othello:* 'Tis better as it is.
*Iago:*                    Nay, but he prated,
And spoke such scurvy and provoking terms
Against your honor
That, with the little godliness I have,
I did full hard forbear him. But, I pray you, sir,                    10
Are you fast married? Be assured of this,
That the magnifico is much beloved,
And hath in his effect a voice potential
As double as the Duke's. He will divorce you,
Or put upon you what restraint or grievance                    15
The law, with all his might to enforce it on,
Will give him cable.

---

173 *property* special quality, nature    174 *abused* deceived    179 *discover* reveal, uncover    182
*command* demand assistance    184 *deserve* show gratitude for    2 *very stuff* essence, basic material
(continuing the metaphor of *trade* from line 1)    3 *contrived* premeditated    5 *yerked* stabbed.
*him* i.e., Roderigo    10 *I . . . him* I restrained myself with great difficulty from assaulting him    12
*magnifico* Venetian grandee, i.e., Brabantio    13 *in his effect* at his command.    *potential* powerful
17 *cable* i.e., scope

*Othello:* Let him do his spite.
My services which I have done the seigniory
Shall out-tongue his complaints. 'Tis yet to know—
Which, when I know that boasting is an honor, 20
I shall promulgate—I fetch my life and being
From men of royal siege, and my demerits
May speak unbonneted to as proud a fortune
As this that I have reached. For know, Iago,
But that I love the gentle Desdemona, 25
I would not my unhousèd free condition
Put into circumscription and confine
For the sea's worth. But look, what lights come yond?

*Enter Cassio [and certain officers] with torches.*

*Iago:* Those are the raisèd father and his friends.
You were best go in.
*Othello:* Not I. I must be found. 30
My parts, my title, and my perfect soul
Shall manifest me rightly. Is it they?
*Iago:* By Janus, I think no.
*Othello:* The servants of the Duke? And my lieutenant?
The goodness of the night upon you, friends! 35
What is the news?
*Cassio:* The Duke does greet you, General,
And he requires your haste-post-haste appearance
Even on the instant.
*Othello:* What is the matter, think you?
*Cassio:* Something from Cyprus, as I may divine.
It is a business of some heat. The galleys 40
Have sent a dozen sequent messengers
This very night at one another's heels,
And many of the consuls, raised and met,
Are at the Duke's already. You have been hotly called for;
When, being not at your lodging to be found, 45
The Senate hath sent about three several quests
To search you out.

---

18 *seigniory* Venetian government      19 *yet to know* not yet widely known      22 *siege* i.e., rank. (Literally, a seat used by a person of distinction.)      *demerits* deserts      23 *unbonneted* without removing the hat, i.e., on equal terms (? Or "with hat off," "in all due modesty.")      26 *unhousèd* unconfined, undomesticated      27 *circumscription and confine* restriction and confinement      28 *the sea's worth* all the riches at the bottom of the sea.      *s.d. officers* (The Quarto text calls for "Cassio with lights, officers with torches.")      31 *My . . . soul* my natural gifts, my position or reputation, and my unflawed conscience      33 *Janus* Roman two-faced god of beginnings      38 *matter* business      39 *divine* guess      40 *heat* urgency      41 *sequent* successive      43 *consuls* senators      46 *about* all over the city.      *several* separate

*Othello:*               'Tis well I am found by you.

     I will but spend a word here in the house

     And go with you.                            [*Exit.*]

*Cassio:*            Ancient, what makes he here?

*Iago:* Faith, he tonight hath boarded a land carrack.        50

     If it prove lawful prize, he's made forever.

*Cassio:* I do not understand.

*Iago:*              He's married.

*Cassio:*                   To who?

     [*Enter Othello.*]

*Iago:* Marry, to—Come, Captain, will you go?

*Othello:* Have with you.

*Cassio:* Here comes another troop to seek for you.        55

     *Enter Brabantio, Roderigo, with officers and torches.*

*Iago:* It is Brabantio. General, be advised.

     He comes to bad intent.

*Othello:*               Holla! Stand there!

*Roderigo:* Signor, it is the Moor.

*Brabantio:*              Down with him, thief!

     [*They draw on both sides.*]

*Iago:* You, Roderigo! Come, sir, I am for you.

*Othello:* Keep up your bright swords, for the dew will rust them.    60

     Good signor, you shall more command with years

     Than with your weapons.

*Brabantio:* O thou foul thief, where hast thou stowed my daughter?

     Damned as thou art, thou hast enchanted her!

     For I'll refer me to all things of sense,                  65

     If she in chains of magic were not bound

     Whether a maid so tender, fair, and happy,

     So opposite to marriage that she shunned

     The wealthy curlèd darlings of our nation,

     Would ever have, t' incur a general mock,             70

---

49 *makes* does     50 *boarded* gone aboard and seized as an act of piracy (with sexual suggestion). *carrack* large merchant ship     51 *prize* booty     53 *Marry* (An oath, originally "by the Virgin Mary"; here used with wordplay on *married.*)     54 *Have with you* i.e., let's go     55 s.d. *officers and torches* (The Quarto text calls for "others with lights and weapons.")     56 *be advised* be on your guard     60 *Keep up* keep in the sheath     65 *refer me* submit my case.     *things of sense* common-sense understandings, or, creatures possessing common sense

Run from her guardage to the sooty bosom
Of such a thing as thou—to fear, not to delight.
Judge me the world if 'tis not gross in sense
That thou hast practiced on her with foul charms,
Abused her delicate youth with drugs or minerals          75
That weakens motion. I'll have 't disputed on;
'Tis probable and palpable to thinking.
I therefore apprehend and do attach thee
For an abuser of the world, a practicer
Of arts inhibited and out of warrant.—                    80
Lay hold upon him! If he do resist,
Subdue him at his peril.
*Othello:*                    Hold your hands,
Both you of my inclining and the rest.
Were it my cue to fight, I should have known it
Without a prompter.—Whither will you that I go           85
To answer this your charge?
*Brabantio:* To prison, till fit time
Of law and course of direct session
Call thee to answer.
*Othello:*                    What if I do obey?
How may the Duke be therewith satisfied,                  90
Whose messengers are here about my side
Upon some present business of the state
To bring me to him?
*Officer:*                    'Tis true, most worthy signor.
The Duke's in council, and your noble self,
I am sure, is sent for.
*Brabantio:*                    How? The Duke in council?      95
In this time of the night? Bring him away.
Mine's not an idle cause. The Duke himself,
Or any of my brothers of the state,
Cannot but feel this wrong as 'twere their own;
For if such actions may have passage free,                100
Bondslaves and pagans shall our statesmen be.

*Exeunt.*

---

71 *her guardage* my guardianship of her     73 *gross in sense* obvious     75 *minerals* i.e., poisons
76 *weakens motion* impair the vital faculties.     *disputed on* argued in court by professional counsel,
debated by experts     78 *attach* arrest     80 *arts inhibited* prohibited arts, black magic.     *out of*
*warrant* illegal     83 *inclining* following, party     88 *course of direct session* regular or specially con-
vened legal proceedings     96 *away* right along     97 *idle* trifling     100 *have passage free* are
allowed to go unchecked

**Scene III** *[Venice. A Council Chamber.]*

*Enter Duke [and] Senators [and sit at a table, with lights], and Officers. [The Duke and Senators are reading dispatches.]*

*Duke:* There is no composition in these news
    That gives them credit.
*First Senator:* Indeed, they are disproportioned.
    My letters say a hundred and seven galleys.
*Duke:* And mine, a hundred forty.
*Second Senator:*               And mine, two hundred.       5
    But though they jump not on a just account—
    As in these cases, where the aim reports
    'Tis oft with difference—yet do they all confirm
    A Turkish fleet, and bearing up to Cyprus.
*Duke:* Nay, it is possible enough to judgment.       10
    I do not so secure me in the error
    But the main article I do approve
    In fearful sense.
*Sailor (within):*     What ho, what ho, what ho!

*Enter Sailor.*

*Officer:* A messenger from the galleys.
*Duke:* Now, what's the business?       15
*Sailor:* The Turkish preparation makes for Rhodes.
    So was I bid report here to the state
    By Signor Angelo.
*Duke:* How say you by this change?
*First Senator:*               This cannot be
    By no assay of reason. 'Tis a pageant       20
    To keep us in false gaze. When we consider
    Th' importancy of Cyprus to the Turk,
    And let ourselves again but understand
    That, as it more concerns the Turk than Rhodes,
    So may he with more facile question bear it,       25
    For that it stands not in such warlike brace,
    But altogether lacks th' abilities
    That Rhodes is dressed in—if we make thought of this,

---

s.d. *Enter . . . Officers* (The Quarto text calls for the Duke and senators to "sit at a table with lights and attendants.")   1 *composition* consistency    3 *disproportioned* inconsistent    6 *jump* agree. *just* exact    7 *the aim* conjecture    11–12 *I do not . . . approve* I do not take such (false) comfort in the discrepancies that I fail to perceive the main point, i.e., that the Turkish fleet is threatening   16 *preparation* fleet prepared for battle    19 *by* about    20 *assay* test.    *pageant* mere show   21 *in false gaze* looking the wrong way    25 *So may . . . it* so also he (the Turk) can more easily capture it (Cyprus)    26 *For that* since.    *brace* state of defense    27 *abilities* means of self-defense 28 *dressed in* equipped with

We must not think the Turk is so unskillful
To leave that latest which concerns him first,                    30
Neglecting an attempt of ease and gain
To wake and wage a danger profitless.
*Duke:* Nay, in all confidence, he's not for Rhodes.
*Officer:* Here is more news.

    *Enter a Messenger.*

*Messenger:* The Ottomites, reverend and gracious,                35
    Steering with due course toward the isle of Rhodes,
    Have there injointed them with an after fleet.
*First Senator:* Ay, so I thought. How many, as you guess?
*Messenger:* Of thirty sail; and now they do restem
    Their backward course, bearing with frank appearance    40
    Their purposes toward Cyprus. Signor Montano,
    Your trusty and most valiant servitor,
    With his free duty recommends you thus,
    And prays you to believe him.
*Duke:* 'Tis certain then for Cyprus.                            45
    Marcus Luccicos, is not he in town?
*First Senator:* He's now in Florence.
*Duke:* Write from us to him, post-post-haste. Dispatch.
*First Senator:* Here comes Brabantio and the valiant Moor.

    *Enter Brabantio, Othello, Cassio, Iago, Roderigo, and officers.*

*Duke:* Valiant Othello, we must straight employ you             50
    Against the general enemy Ottoman.
    *[To Brabantio.]* I did not see you; welcome, gentle signor.
    We lacked your counsel and your help tonight.
*Brabantio:* So did I yours. Good Your Grace, pardon me;
    Neither my place nor aught I heard of business          55
    Hath raised me from my bed, nor doth the general care
    Take hold on me, for my particular grief
    Is of so floodgate and o'erbearing nature
    That it engluts and swallows other sorrows
    And it is still itself.
*Duke:*           Why, what's the matter?    60

---

29 *unskillful* deficient in judgment    30 *latest* last    32 *wake* stir up.    *wage* risk    37 *injointed them* joined themselves.    *after* second, following    39–40 *restem . . . course* retrace their original course    40 *frank appearance* undisguised intent    42 *servitor* officer under your command    43 *free duty* freely given and loyal service.    *recommends* commends himself and reports to    50 *straight* straightway    51 *general enemy* universal enemy to all Christendom    52 *gentle* noble    55 *place* official position    57 *particular* personal    58 *floodgate* i.e., overwhelming (as when floodgates are opened)    59 *engluts* engulfs    60 *is still itself* remains undiminished

*Brabantio:* My daughter! O, my daughter!

*Duke and Senators:*                    Dead?

*Brabantio:*                                        Ay, to me.
    She is abused, stol'n from me, and corrupted
    By spells and medicines bought of mountebanks;
    For nature so preposterously to err,
    Being not deficient, blind, or lame of sense,        65
    Sans witchcraft could not.

*Duke:* Whoe'er he be that in this foul proceeding
    Hath thus beguiled your daughter of herself,
    And you of her, the bloody book of law
    You shall yourself read in the bitter letter        70
    After your own sense—yea, though our proper son
    Stood in your action.

*Brabantio:*                    Humbly I thank Your Grace.
    Here is the man, this Moor, whom now it seems
    Your special mandate for the state affairs
    Hath hither brought.

*All:*                    We are very sorry for 't.        75

*Duke [to Othello]:* What, in your own part, can you say to this?

*Brabantio:* Nothing, but this is so.

*Othello:* Most potent, grave, and reverend signors,
    My very noble and approved good masters:
    That I have ta'en away this old man's daughter,        80
    It is most true; true, I have married her.
    The very head and front of my offending
    Hath this extent, no more. Rude am I in my speech,
    And little blessed with the soft phrase of peace;
    For since these arms of mine had seven years' pith,        85
    Till now some nine moons wasted, they have used
    Their dearest action in the tented field;
    And little of this great world can I speak
    More than pertains to feats of broils and battle,
    And therefore little shall I grace my cause        90
    In speaking for myself. Yet, by your gracious patience,
    I will a round unvarnished tale deliver
    Of my whole course of love—what drugs, what charms,

---

62 *abused* deceived    65 *deficient* defective.    *lame of sense* deficient in sensory perception    66
*Sans* without    71 *After . . . sense* according to your own interpretation.    *our proper* my own
72 *Stood . . . action* were under your accusation    79 *approved* proved, esteemed    82 *head and front* height and breadth, entire extent    83 *Rude* unpolished    85 *since . . . pith* i.e., since I was seven.    *pith* strength, vigor    86 *Till . . . wasted* until some nine months ago (since when Othello has evidently not been on active duty, but in Venice)    87 *dearest* most valuable    92 *round* plain

What conjuration, and what mighty magic,
For such proceeding I am charged withal,                                95
I won his daughter.
*Brabantio:*                   A maiden never bold;
Of spirit so still and quiet that her motion
Blushed at herself; and she, in spite of nature,
Of years, of country, credit, everything,
To fall in love with what she feared to look on!                        100
It is a judgment maimed and most imperfect
That will confess perfection so could err
Against all rules of nature, and must be driven
To find out practices of cunning hell
Why this should be. I therefore vouch again                             105
That with some mixtures powerful o'er the blood,
Or with some dram conjured to this effect,
He wrought upon her.
*Duke:*                        To vouch this is no proof,
Without more wider and more overt test
Than these thin habits and poor likelihoods                             110
Of modern seeming do prefer against him.
*First Senator:* But Othello, speak.
Did you by indirect and forcèd courses
Subdue and poison this young maid's affections?
Or came it by request and such fair question                            115
As soul to soul affordeth?
*Othello:*                        I do beseech you,
Send for the lady to the Sagittary
And let her speak of me before her father.
If you do find me foul in her report,
The trust, the office I do hold of you                                   120
Not only take away, but let your sentence
Even fall upon my life.
*Duke:*                        Fetch Desdemona hither.
*Othello:* Ancient, conduct them. You best know the place.

*[Exeunt Iago and attendants.]*

---

95 *withal* with    97–98 *her . . . herself* i.e., she blushed easily at herself. (*Motion* can suggest the
impulse of the soul or of the emotions, or physical movement.)    99 *years* i.e., difference in age.
*credit* virtuous reputation    102 *confess* concede (that)    104 *practices* plots    105 *vouch* assert
106 *blood* passions    107 *dram . . . effect* dose made by magical spells to have this effect    109
*more wider* fuller.    *test* testimony    110 *habits* garments, i.e., appearances.    *poor likelihoods*
weak inferences    111 *modern seeming* commonplace assumption.    *prefer* bring forth    113
*forcèd courses* means used against her will    115 *question* conversation

And, till she come, as truly as to heaven
I do confess the vices of my blood,                                    125
So justly to your grave ears I'll present
How I did thrive in this fair lady's love,
And she in mine.
*Duke*: Say it, Othello.
*Othello*: Her father loved me, oft invited me,                        130
Still questioned me the story of my life
From year to year—the battles, sieges, fortunes
That I have passed.
I ran it through, even from my boyish days
To th' very moment that he bade me tell it,                            135
Wherein I spoke of most disastrous chances,
Of moving accidents by flood and field,
Of hairbreadth scapes i' th' imminent deadly breach,
Of being taken by the insolent foe
And sold to slavery, of my redemption thence,                         140
And portance in my travels' history,
Wherein of antres vast and deserts idle,
Rough quarries, rocks, and hills whose heads touch heaven,
It was my hint to speak—such was my process—
And of the Cannibals that each other eat,                             145
The Anthropophagi, and men whose heads
Do grow beneath their shoulders. These things to hear
Would Desdemona seriously incline;
But still the house affairs would draw her thence,
Which ever as she could with haste dispatch                           150
She'd come again, and with a greedy ear
Devour up my discourse. Which I, observing,
Took once a pliant hour, and found good means
To draw from her a prayer of earnest heart
That I would all my pilgrimage dilate,                                155
Whereof by parcels she had something heard,
But not intentively. I did consent,
And often did beguile her of her tears,
When I did speak of some distressful stroke
That my youth suffered. My story being done,                          160
She gave me for my pains a world of sighs.

125 *blood* passions, human nature    126 *justly* truthfully, accurately    131 *Still* continually
137 *moving accidents* stirring happenings    138 *imminent . . . breach* death-threatening gaps made in
a fortification    141 *portance* conduct    142 *antres* caverns.    *idle* barren, desolate    143
*Rough quarries* rugged rock formations    144 *hint* occasion, opportunity    146 *Anthropophagi*
man-eaters. (A term from Pliny's *Natural History*.)    153 *pliant* well-suiting    155 *dilate* relate in
detail    156 *by parcels* piecemeal    157 *intentively* with full attention, continuously

She swore, in faith, 'twas strange, 'twas passing strange,
'Twas pitiful, 'twas wondrous pitiful.
She wished she had not heard it, yet she wished
That heaven had made her such a man. She thanked me,                    165
And bade me, if I had a friend that loved her,
I should but teach him how to tell my story,
And that would woo her. Upon this hint I spake.
She loved me for the dangers I had passed,
And I loved her that she did pity them.                                 170
This only is the witchcraft I have used.
Here comes the lady. Let her witness it.

*Enter Desdemona, Iago, [and] attendants.*

*Duke:* I think this tale would win my daughter too.
    Good Brabantio,
    Take up this mangled matter at the best.                    175
    Men do their broken weapons rather use
    Than their bare hands.
*Brabantio:*               I pray you, hear her speak.
    If she confess that she was half the wooer,
    Destruction on my head if my bad blame
    Light on the man!—Come hither, gentle mistress.             180
    Do you perceive in all this noble company
    Where most you owe obedience?
*Desdemona:*             My noble Father,
    I do perceive here a divided duty.
    To you I am bound for life and education;
    My life and education both do learn me                       185
    How to respect you. You are the lord of duty;
    I am hitherto your daughter. But here's my husband,
    And so much duty as my mother showed
    To you, preferring you before her father,
    So much I challenge that I may profess                       190
    Due to the Moor my lord.
*Brabantio:* God be with you! I have done.
    Please it Your Grace, on to the state affairs.
    I had rather to adopt a child than get it.
    Come hither, Moor.        *[He joins the hands of Othello and Desdemona.]*  195
    I here do give thee that with all my heart

---

162 *passing* exceedingly    165 *made her* created her to be    168 *hint* opportunity. (Othello does
not mean that she was dropping hints.)    175 *Take . . . best* make the best of a bad bargain
184 *education* upbringing    185 *learn* teach    186 *of duty* to whom duty is due    190 *challenge*
claim    194 *get* beget    196 *with all my heart* wherein my whole affection has been engaged

Which, but thou hast already, with all my heart
I would keep from thee.—For your sake, jewel,
I am glad at soul I have no other child,
For thy escape would teach me tyranny,                                200
To hang clogs on them.—I have done, my lord.

*Duke:* Let me speak like yourself, and lay a sentence
Which, as a grece or step, may help these lovers
Into your favor.
When remedies are past, the griefs are ended                          205
By seeing the worst, which late on hopes depended.
To mourn a mischief that is past and gone
Is the next way to draw new mischief on.
What cannot be preserved when fortune takes,
Patience her injury a mockery makes.                                   210
The robbed that smiles steals something from the thief;
He robs himself that spends a bootless grief.

*Brabantio:* So let the Turk of Cyprus us beguile,
We lose it not, so long as we can smile.
He bears the sentence well that nothing bears                          215
But the free comfort which from thence he hears,
But he bears both the sentence and the sorrow
That, to pay grief, must of poor patience borrow.
These sentences, to sugar or to gall,
Being strong on both sides, are equivocal.                            220
But words are words. I never yet did hear
That the bruisèd heart was piercèd through the ear.
I humbly beseech you, proceed to th' affairs of state.

*Duke:* The Turk with a most mighty preparation makes for Cyprus. Othello, the
fortitude of the place is best known to you; and though we have there a sub-      225
stitute of most allowed sufficiency, yet opinion, a sovereign mistress of
effects, throws a more safer voice on you. You must therefore be content to
slubber the gloss of your new fortunes with this more stubborn and boisterous
expedition.

---

197 *with all my heart* willingly, gladly    198 *For your sake* on your account    200 *escape* elopement    201 *clogs* (Literally, blocks of wood fastened to the legs of criminals or convicts to inhibit
escape.)    202 *like yourself* i.e., as you would, in your proper temper.    *lay a sentence* apply a
maxim    203 *grece* step    205 *remedies* hopes of remedy    206 *which . . . depended* which griefs
were sustained until recently by hopeful anticipation    207 *mischief* misfortune, injury    208 *next*
nearest    209 *What* whatever    210 *Patience . . . makes* patience laughs at the injury inflicted by
fortune (and thus eases the pain)    212 *spends a bootless grief* indulges in unavailing grief
215–218 *He bears . . . borrow* a person well bears out your maxim who can enjoy its platitudinous
comfort, free of all genuine sorrow, but anyone whose grief bankrupts his poor patience is left with
your saying and his sorrow, too. (*Bears the sentence* also plays on the meaning, "receives judicial sentence.")    219–220 *These . . . equivocal* these fine maxims are equivocal, either sweet or bitter in
their application    222 *piercèd . . . ear* i.e., surgically lanced and cured by mere words of advice
225 *fortitude* strength    226 *substitute* deputy.    *allowed* acknowledged    226–227 *opinion . . .
on you* general opinion, an important determiner of affairs, chooses you as the best man    228 *slubber* soil, sully.    *stubborn* harsh, rough

*Othello:* The tyrant custom, most grave senators,                              230
    Hath made the flinty and steel couch of war
    My thrice-driven bed of down. I do agnize
    A natural and prompt alacrity
    I find in hardness, and do undertake
    These present wars against the Ottomites.                                   235
    Most humbly therefore bending to your state,
    I crave fit disposition for my wife,
    Due reference of place and exhibition,
    With such accommodation and besort
    As levels with her breeding.                                                240
*Duke:* Why, at her father's.
*Brabantio:*                   I will not have it so.
*Othello:* Nor I.
*Desdemona:*   Nor I. I would not there reside,
    To put my father in impatient thoughts
    By being in his eye. Most gracious Duke,
    To my unfolding lend your prosperous ear,                                   245
    And let me find a charter in your voice,
    T' assist my simpleness.
*Duke:* What would you, Desdemona?
*Desdemona:* That I did love the Moor to live with him,
    My downright violence and storm of fortunes                                 250
    May trumpet to the world. My heart's subdued
    Even to the very quality of my lord.
    I saw Othello's visage in his mind,
    And to his honors and his valiant parts
    Did I my soul and fortunes consecrate.                                      255
    So that, dear lords, if I be left behind
    A moth of peace, and he go to the war,
    The rites for why I love him are bereft me,
    And I a heavy interim shall support
    By his dear absence. Let me go with him.                                    260

232 *thrice-driven* thrice sifted, winnowed.     *agnize* know in myself, acknowledge     234 *hardness* hardship     236 *bending . . . state* bowing or kneeling to your authority     238 *reference . . . exhibition* provision of appropriate place to live and allowance of money     239 *accommodation* suitable provision.     *besort* attendance     240 *levels* equals, suits.     *breeding* social position, upbringing     245 *unfolding* explanation, proposal.     *prosperous* propitious     246 *charter* privilege, authorization     250 *My . . . fortunes* my plain and total breach of social custom, taking my future by storm and disrupting my whole life     251–252 *My heart's . . . lord* my heart is brought wholly into accord with Othello's virtues; I love him for his virtues     254 *parts* qualities     257 *moth* i.e., one who consumes merely     258 *rites* rites of love (with a suggestion, too, of "rights," sharing)     260 *dear* (1) heartfelt (2) costly

*Othello*: Let her have your voice.

    Vouch with me, heaven, I therefor beg it not

    To please the palate of my appetite,

    Nor to comply with heat—the young affects

    In me defunct—and proper satisfaction,          265

    But to be free and bounteous to her mind.

    And heaven defend your good souls that you think

    I will your serious and great business scant

    When she is with me. No, when light-winged toys

    Of feathered Cupid seel with wanton dullness       270

    My speculative and officed instruments,

    That my disports corrupt and taint my business,

    Let huswives make a skillet of my helm,

    And all indign and base adversities

    Make head against my estimation!          275

*Duke*: Be it as you shall privately determine,

    Either for her stay or going. Th' affair cries haste,

    And speed must answer it.

*A Senator:*                You must away tonight.

*Desdemona*: Tonight, my lord?

*Duke*:             This night.

*Othello*:                  With all my heart.

*Duke*: At nine i' the morning here we'll meet again.       280

    Othello, leave some officer behind,

    And he shall our commission bring to you,

    With such things else of quality and respect

    As doth import you.

*Othello*:             So please Your Grace, my ancient;

    A man he is of honesty and trust.          285

    To his conveyance I assign my wife,

    With what else needful Your Good Grace shall think

    To be sent after me.

*Duke*:             Let it be so.

    Good night to everyone. *[To Brabantio.]* And, noble signor,

    If virtue no delighted beauty lack,

    Your son-in-law is far more fair than black.      290

*First Senator*: Adieu, brave Moor. Use Desdemona well.

---

261 *voice* consent    264 *heat* sexual passion.    *young affects* passions of youth, desires    265 *proper* personal    266 *free* generous    267 *defend* forbid.    *think* should think    270 *seel* i.e., make blind (as in falconry, by sewing up the eyes of the hawk during training)    271 *speculative . . . instruments* eyes and other faculties used in the performance of duty    272 *That* so that.    *disports* sexual pastimes.    *taint* impair    274 *indign* unworthy, shameful    275 *Make head* raise an army.    *estimation* reputation    283 *of quality and respect* of importance and relevance    284 *import* concern    290 *delighted* capable of delighting

*Brabantio*: Look to her, Moor, if thou hast eyes to see.
     She has deceived her father, and may thee.

                    *Exeunt [Duke, Brabantio, Cassio, Senators, and officers].*

*Othello*: My life upon her faith! Honest Iago,                          295
     My Desdemona must I leave to thee.
     I prithee, let thy wife attend on her,
     And bring them after in the best advantage.
     Come, Desdemona. I have but an hour
     Of love, of worldly matters and direction,                         300
     To spend with thee. We must obey the time.

                                        *Exit [with Desdemona].*

*Roderigo*: Iago—
*Iago*: What sayst thou, noble heart?
*Roderigo*: What will I do, think'st thou?
*Iago*: Why, go to bed and sleep.                                       305
*Roderigo*: I will incontinently drown myself.
*Iago*: If thou dost, I shall never love thee after. Why, thou silly gentleman?
*Roderigo*: It is silliness to live when to live is torment; and then have we a pre-
     scription to die when death is our physician.
*Iago*: O villainous! I have looked upon the world for four times seven years, and,   310
     since I could distinguish betwixt a benefit and an injury, I never found man
     that knew how to love himself. Ere I would say I would drown myself for the
     love of a guinea hen, I would change my humanity with a baboon.
*Roderigo*: What should I do? I confess it is my shame to be so fond, but it is not in
     my virtue to amend it.                                             315
*Iago*: Virtue? A fig! 'Tis in ourselves that we are thus or thus. Our bodies are our
     gardens, to the which our wills are gardeners; so that if we will plant nettles
     or sow lettuce, set hyssop and weed up thyme, supply it with one gender of
     herbs or distract it with many, either to have it sterile with idleness or
     manured with industry—why, the power and corrigible authority of this lies   320
     in our wills. If the beam of our lives had not one scale of reason to poise
     another of sensuality, the blood and baseness of our natures would conduct
     us to most preposterous conclusions. But we have reason to cool our raging
     motions, our carnal stings, our unbitted lusts, whereof I take this that you
     call love to be a sect or scion.                                   325

---

298 *in . . . advantage* at the most favorable opportunity     300 *direction* instructions     301 *the time*
the urgency of the present crisis     306 *incontinently* immediately, without self-restraint
308–309 *prescription* (1) right based on long-established custom (2) doctor's prescription     310 *villainous* i.e., what perfect nonsense     313 *guinea hen* (A slang term for a prostitute.)     314 *fond*
infatuated.     315 *virtue* strength, nature     316 *fig* (To give a fig is to thrust the thumb between
the first and second fingers in a vulgar and insulting gesture.)     318 *hyssop* a herb of the mint family     *gender* kind.     319 *distract it with* divide it among     *idleness* want of cultivation     320
*corrigible authority* power to correct     321 *beam* balance     *poise* counterbalance     322 *blood* natural passions     324 *motions* appetites     *unbitted* unbridled, uncontrolled     325 *sect or scion* cutting or offshoot

*Roderigo:* It cannot be.

*Iago:* It is merely a lust of the blood and a permission of the will. Come, be a man. Drown thyself? Drown cats and blind puppies. I have professed me thy friend, and I confess me knit to thy deserving with cables of perdurable toughness. I could never better stead thee than now. Put money in thy purse. Follow thou 330 the wars; defeat thy favor with an usurped beard. I say, put money in thy purse. It cannot be long that Desdemona should continue her love to the Moor—put money in thy purse—nor he his to her. It was a violent commencement in her, and thou shalt see an answerable sequestration—put but money in thy purse. These Moors are changeable in their wills—fill thy 335 purse with money. The food that to him now is as luscious as locusts shall be to him shortly as bitter as coloquintida. She must change for youth; when she is sated with his body, she will find the error of her choice. She must have change, she must. Therefore put money in thy purse. If thou wilt needs damn thyself, do it a more delicate way than drowning. Make all the money 340 thou canst. If sanctimony and a frail vow betwixt an erring barbarian and a supersubtle Venetian be not too hard for my wits and all the tribe of hell, thou shalt enjoy her. Therefore make money. A pox of drowning thyself! It is clean out of the way. Seek thou rather to be hanged in compassing thy joy than to be drowned and go without her. 345

*Roderigo:* Wilt thou be fast to my hopes if I depend on the issue?

*Iago:* Thou art sure of me. Go, make money. I have told thee often, and I retell thee again and again, I hate the Moor. My cause is hearted; thine hath no less reason. Let us be conjunctive in our revenge against him. If thou canst cuckold him, thou dost thyself a pleasure, me a sport. There are many events 350 in the womb of time which will be delivered. Traverse, go, provide thy money. We will have more of this tomorrow. Adieu.

*Roderigo:* Where shall we meet i' the morning?

*Iago:* At my lodging.

*Roderigo:* I'll be with thee betimes. *[He starts to leave.]* 355

*Iago:* Go to, farewell.—Do you hear, Roderigo?

*Roderigo:* What say you?

*Iago:* No more of drowning, do you hear?

*Roderigo:* I am changed.

---

329 *perdurable* very durable.     330 *stead* assist     331 *defeat thy favor* disguise your face. *usurped* (The suggestion is that Roderigo is not man enough to have a beard of his own.)     334 *an answerable sequestration* a corresponding separation or estrangement     335 *wills* carnal appetites 336 *locusts* fruit of the carob tree (see Matthew 3:4), or perhaps honeysuckle     337 *coloquintida* colocynth or bitter apple, a purgative     340 *Make* raise, collect     341 *sanctimony* sacred ceremony     *erring* wandering, vagabond, unsteady     344 *clean . . . way* entirely unsuitable as a course of action     *compassing* encompassing, embracing     346 *fast* true     *issue* (successful) outcome 348 *hearted* fixed in the heart, heartfelt     349 *conjunctive* united     351 *Traverse* (A military marching term.)     355 *betimes* early

*Iago:* Go to, farewell. Put money enough in your purse.                  360
*Roderigo:* I'll sell all my land.                                    *Exit.*
*Iago:* Thus do I ever make my fool my purse;
    For I mine own gained knowledge should profane
    If I would time expend with such a snipe
    But for my sport and profit. I hate the Moor;              365
    And it is thought abroad that twixt my sheets
    He's done my office. I know not if 't be true;
    But I, for mere suspicion in that kind,
    Will do as if for surety. He holds me well;
    The better shall my purpose work on him.                  370
    Cassio's a proper man. Let me see now:
    To get his place and to plume up my will
    In double knavery—How, how?—Let's see:
    After some time, to abuse Othello's ear
    That he is too familiar with his wife.                    375
    He hath a person and a smooth dispose
    To be suspected, framed to make women false.
    The Moor is of a free and open nature,
    That thinks men honest that but seem to be so,
    And will as tenderly be led by the nose                   380
    As asses are.
    I have 't. It is engendered. Hell and night
    Must bring this monstrous birth to the world's light.

    *[Exit.]*

# ACT II

### Scene I [*A Seaport in Cyprus. An Open Place Near the Quay.*]

    *Enter Montano and two Gentlemen.*

*Montano:* What from the cape can you discern at sea?
*First Gentleman:* Nothing at all. It is a high-wrought flood.
    I cannot, twixt the heaven and the main,
    Descry a sail.
*Montano:* Methinks the wind hath spoke aloud at land;              5
    A fuller blast ne'er shook our battlements.

---

364 *snipe* woodcock, i.e., fool   366 *it is thought abroad* it is rumored   367 *my office* i.e., my sexual function as husband   369 *do . . . surety* act as if on certain knowledge.   *holds me well* regards me favorably   371 *proper* handsome   372 *plume up* put a feather in the cap of, i.e., glorify, gratify   374 *abuse* deceive   375 *he* i.e., Cassio   376 *dispose* disposition   378 *free* frank, generous.   *open* unsuspicious   380 *tenderly* readily   2 *high-wrought flood* very agitated sea
3 *main* ocean (also at line 41)

If it hath ruffianed so upon the sea,
What ribs of oak, when mountains melt on them,
Can hold the mortise? What shall we hear of this?
*Second Gentleman:* A segregation of the Turkish fleet.          10
For do but stand upon the foaming shore,
The chidden billow seems to pelt the clouds;
The wind-shaked surge, with high and monstrous mane,
Seems to cast water on the burning Bear
And quench the guards of th' ever-fixèd pole.          15
I never did like molestation view
On the enchafèd flood.
*Montano:* If that the Turkish fleet
Be not ensheltered and embayed, they are drowned;
It is impossible to bear it out.          20

*Enter a [Third] Gentleman.*

*Third Gentleman:* News, lads! Our wars are done.
The desperate tempest hath so banged the Turks
That their designment halts. A noble ship of Venice
Hath seen a grievous wreck and sufferance
On most part of their fleet.          25
*Montano:* How? Is this true?
*Third Gentleman:* The ship is here put in,
A Veronesa; Michael Cassio,
Lieutenant to the warlike Moor Othello,
Is come on shore; the Moor himself at sea,          30
And is in full commission here for Cyprus.
*Montano:* I am glad on 't. 'Tis a worthy governor.
*Third Gentleman:* But this same Cassio, though he speak of comfort
Touching the Turkish loss, yet he looks sadly
And prays the Moor be safe, for they were parted          35
With foul and violent tempest.
*Montano:*                              Pray heaven he be,
For I have served him, and the man commands

---

7 *ruffianed* raged     8 *mountains* i.e., of water     9 *hold the mortise* hold their joints together. (A *mortise* is the socket hollowed out in fitting timbers.)     10 *segregation* dispersal     12 *chidden* i.e., rebuked, repelled (by the shore), and thus shot into the air     13 *monstrous mane* (The surf is like the mane of a wild beast.)     14 *the burning Bear* i.e., the constellation Ursa Minor or the Little Bear, which includes the polestar (and hence regarded as the *guards of th' ever-fixèd pole* in the next line; sometimes the term *guards* is applied to the two "pointers" of the Big Bear or Dipper, which may be intended here.)     16 *like molestation* comparable disturbance     17 *enchafèd* angry     18 *If that* if     19 *embayed* sheltered by a bay     20 *bear it out* survive, weather the storm     23 *designment* design, enterprise.     *halts* is lame     24 *wreck* shipwreck.     *sufferance* damage, disaster     28 *Veronesa* i.e., fitted out in Verona for Venetian service, or possibly *Verennessa* (the Folio spelling), i.e., *verrinessa*, a cutter (from *verrinare*, "to cut through")     34 *sadly* gravely

Like a full soldier. Let's to the seaside, ho!
As well to see the vessel that's come in
As to throw out our eyes for brave Othello,                                40
Even till we make the main and th' aerial blue
An indistinct regard.
*Third Gentleman:*          Come, let's do so,
For every minute is expectancy
Of more arrivance.

    *Enter Cassio.*

*Cassio:* Thanks, you the valiant of this warlike isle,                     45
That so approve the Moor! O, let the heavens
Give him defense against the elements,
For I have lost him on a dangerous sea.
*Montano:* Is he well shipped?
*Cassio:* His bark is stoutly timbered, and his pilot                       50
Of very expert and approved allowance;
Therefore my hopes, not surfeited to death,
Stand in bold cure.
*[A cry] within:*          "A sail, a sail, a sail!"
*Cassio:* What noise?
*A Gentleman:* The town is empty. On the brow o' the sea                    55
Stand ranks of people, and they cry "A sail!"
*Cassio:* My hopes do shape him for the governor.

    *[A shot within.]*

*Second Gentleman:* They do discharge their shot of courtesy;
Our friends at least.
*Cassio:*                I pray you, sir, go forth,
And give us truth who 'tis that is arrived.                                 60
*Second Gentleman:* I shall.                                    *Exit.*
*Montano:* But, good Lieutenant, is your general wived?
*Cassio:* Most fortunately. He hath achieved a maid
That paragons description and wild fame,
One that excels the quirks of blazoning pens,                              65
And in th' essential vesture of creation

---

38 *full* perfect   41 *the main . . . blue* the sea and the sky   42 *An indistinct regard* indistinguishable in our view   43 *is expectancy* gives expectation   44 *arrivance* arrival   46 *approve* admire,
honor   51 *approved allowance* tested reputation   52 *surfeited to death* i.e., overextended, worn
thin through repeated application or delayed fulfillment   53 *in bold cure* in strong hopes of fulfillment   55 *brow o' the sea* cliff-edge   57 *My . . . for* I hope it is   58 *discharge . . . courtesy* fire
a salute in token of respect and courtesy   64 *paragons* surpasses.   *wild fame* extravagant report
65 *quirks* witty conceits.   *blazoning* setting forth as though in heraldic language

Does tire the enginer.

*Enter [Second] Gentleman.*

　　　　　　　　　How now? Who has put in?
*Second Gentleman:* 'Tis one Iago, ancient to the General.
*Cassio:* He's had most favorable and happy speed.
　　Tempests themselves, high seas, and howling winds,　　　　　　70
　　The guttered rocks and congregated sands—
　　Traitors ensteeped to clog the guiltless keel—
　　As having sense of beauty, do omit
　　Their mortal natures, letting go safely by
　　The divine Desdemona.
*Montano:*　　　　　　　　What is she?　　　　　　　　　　　　75
*Cassio:* She that I spake of, our great captain's captain,
　　Left in the conduct of the bold Iago,
　　Whose footing here anticipates our thoughts
　　A sennight's speed. Great Jove, Othello guard,
　　And swell his sail with thine own powerful breath,　　　　　80
　　That he may bless this bay with his tall ship,
　　Make love's quick pants in Desdemona's arms,
　　Give renewed fire to our extincted spirits,
　　And bring all Cyprus comfort!

*Enter Desdemona, Iago, Roderigo, and Emilia.*

　　　　　　　　　　　O, behold,
　　The riches of the ship is come on shore!　　　　　　　　　85
　　You men of Cyprus, let her have your knees.

*[The gentlemen make curtsy to Desdemona.]*

　　Hail to thee, lady! And the grace of heaven
　　Before, behind thee, and on every hand
　　Enwheel thee round!
*Desdemona:*　　　　　　I thank you, valiant Cassio.
　　What tidings can you tell me of my lord?　　　　　　　　90
*Cassio:* He is not yet arrived, nor know I aught
　　But that he's well and will be shortly here.
*Desdemona:* O, but I fear—How lost you company?
*Cassio:* The great contention of the sea and skies
　　Parted our fellowship.

　　　*(Within)* "A sail, a sail!" *[A shot.]*

*Second Gentleman:* They give their greeting to the citadel.

    This likewise is a friend.

*Cassio:*               See for the news.

    *[Exit Second Gentleman.]*

    Good Ancient, you are welcome. *[Kissing Emilia.]* Welcome, mistress.

    Let it not gall your patience, good Iago,

    That I extend my manners; 'tis my breeding        100

    That gives me this bold show of courtesy.

*Iago:* Sir, would she give you so much of her lips

    As of her tongue she oft bestows on me,

    You would have enough.

*Desdemona:* Alas, she has no speech!        105

*Iago:* In faith, too much.

    I find it still, when I have list to sleep.

    Marry, before your ladyship, I grant,

    She puts her tongue a little in her heart

    And chides with thinking.

*Emilia:*            You have little cause to say so.    110

*Iago:* Come on, come on. You are pictures out of doors,

    Bells in your parlors, wildcats in your kitchens,

    Saints in your injuries, devils being offended,

    Players in your huswifery, and huswives in your beds.

*Desdemona:* O, fie upon thee, slanderer!    115

*Iago:* Nay, it is true, or else I am a Turk.

    You rise to play, and go to bed to work.

*Emilia:* You shall not write my praise.

*Iago:*               No, let me not.

*Desdemona:* What wouldst write of me, if thou shouldst praise me?

*Iago:* O gentle lady, do not put me to 't,    120

    For I am nothing if not critical.

*Desdemona:* Come on, essay.—There's one gone to the harbor?

*Iago:* Ay, madam.

*Desdemona:* I am not merry, but I do beguile

    The thing I am by seeming otherwise.    125

    Come, how wouldst thou praise me?

---

100 *extend* give scope to.    *breeding* training in the niceties of etiquette    105 *she has no speech* i.e., she's not a chatterbox, as you allege    107 *still* always.    *list* desire    110 *with thinking* i.e., in her thoughts only    111 *pictures out of doors* i.e., silent and well-behaved in public    112 *Bells* i.e., jangling, noisy, and brazen.    *in your kitchens* i.e., in domestic affairs. (Ladies would not do the cooking.)    113 *Saints* martyrs    114 *Players* idlers, triflers, or deceivers.    *huswifery* house-keeping.    *huswives* hussies (i.e., women are "busy" in bed, or unduly thrifty in dispensing sexual favors)    116 *a Turk* an infidel, not to be believed    121 *critical* censorious    122 *essay* try    125 *The thing I am* i.e., my anxious self

*Iago:* I am about it, but indeed my invention
    Comes from my pate as birdlime does from frieze—
    It plucks out brains and all. But my Muse labors,
    And thus she is delivered:                          130
    If she be fair and wise, fairness and wit,
    The one's for use, the other useth it.
*Desdemona:* Well praised! How if she be black and witty?
*Iago:* If she be black, and thereto have a wit,
    She'll find a white that shall her blackness fit.         135
*Desdemona:* Worse and worse.
*Emilia:*                    How if fair and foolish?
*Iago:* She never yet was foolish that was fair,
    For even her folly helped her to an heir.
*Desdemona:* These are old fond paradoxes to make fools laugh i' th' alehouse.
    What miserable praise hast thou for her that's foul and foolish?    140
*Iago:* There's none so foul and foolish thereunto,
    But does foul pranks which fair and wise ones do.
*Desdemona:* O heavy ignorance! Thou praisest the worst best. But what praise
    couldst thou bestow on a deserving woman indeed, one that, in the authority
    of her merit, did justly put on the vouch of very malice itself?    145
*Iago:* She that was ever fair, and never proud,
    Had tongue at will, and yet was never loud,
    Never lacked gold and yet went never gay,
    Fled from her wish, and yet said, "Now I may,"
    She that being angered, her revenge being nigh,    150
    Bade her wrong stay and her displeasure fly,
    She that in wisdom never was so frail
    To change the cod's head for the salmon's tail,
    She that could think and ne'er disclose her mind,
    See suitors following and not look behind,    155
    She was a wight, if ever such wight were—
*Desdemona:* To do what?
*Iago:* To suckle fools and chronicle small beer.

---

128 *birdlime* sticky substance used to catch small birds.     *frieze* coarse woolen cloth     129 *labors*
(1) exerts herself (2) prepares to deliver a child (with a following pun on *delivered* in line 130)
132 *The one's . . . it* i.e., her cleverness will make use of her beauty     133 *black* dark-complexioned,
brunette     135 *a white* a fair person (with word-play on "wight," a person).     *fit* (with sexual suggestion of mating)     138 *folly* (with added meaning of "lechery, wantonness").     *to an heir* i.e., to
bear a child     139 *fond* foolish     141 *foul* ugly     141 *thereunto* in addition     142 *foul* sluttish
145 *put . . . vouch* compel the approval     148 *gay* extravagantly clothed     149 *Fled . . . may*
avoided temptation where the choice was hers     151 *Bade . . . stay* i.e., resolved to put up with her
injury patiently     153 *To . . . tail* i.e., to exchange a lackluster husband for a sexy lover (?) (*Cod's
head* is slang for "penis," and *tail,* for "pudendum.")     158 *suckle fools* breastfeed babies.     *chronicle small beer* i.e., keep petty household accounts, keep track of trivial matters

*Desdemona:* O most lame and impotent conclusion! Do not learn of him, Emilia, though he be thy husband. How say you, Cassio? Is he not a most profane 160 and liberal counselor?

*Cassio:* He speaks home, madam. You may relish him more in the soldier than in the scholar.

*[Cassio and Desdemona stand together, conversing intimately.]*

*Iago [aside]:* He takes her by the palm. Ay, well said, whisper. With as little a web as this will I ensnare as great a fly as Cassio. Ay, smile upon her, do; I will 165 gyve thee in thine own courtship. You say true; 'tis so, indeed. If such tricks as these strip you out of your lieutenantry, it had been better you had not kissed your three fingers so oft, which now again you are most apt to play the sir in. Very good; well kissed! An excellent courtesy! 'Tis so, indeed. Yet again your fingers to your lips? Would they were clyster pipes for your sake! 170 *[Trumpet within.]* The Moor! I know his trumpet.

*Cassio:* 'Tis truly so.

*Desdemona:* Let's meet him and receive him.

*Cassio:* Lo, where he comes!

*Enter Othello and attendants.*

*Othello:* O my fair warrior!

*Desdemona:*               My dear Othello! 175

*Othello:* It gives me wonder great as my content
    To see you here before me. O my soul's joy,
    If after every tempest come such calms,
    May the winds blow till they have wakened death,
    And let the laboring bark climb hills of seas 180
    Olympus-high, and duck again as low
    As hell's from heaven! If it were now to die,
    'Twere now to be most happy, for I fear
    My soul hath her content so absolute
    That not another comfort like to this 185
    Succeeds in unknown fate.

*Desdemona:*               The heavens forbid
    But that our loves and comforts should increase
    Even as our days do grow!

*Othello:* Amen to that, sweet powers!
    I cannot speak enough of this content. 190

---

160 *profane* irreverent, ribald    161 *liberal* licentious, free-spoken    162 *home* right to the target. (A term from fencing.)    *relish* appreciate    *in* in the character of    164 *well said* well done 166 *gyve* fetter, shackle.    *courtship* courtesy, show of courtly manners.    *You say true* i.e., that's right, go ahead    169 *the sir* i.e., the fine gentleman    *clyster pipes* tubes used for enemas and douches    186 *Succeeds . . . fate* i.e., can follow in the unknown future

It stops me here; it is too much of joy.
And this, and this, the greatest discords be

*[They kiss]*

That e'er our hearts shall make!
*Iago [aside]:* O, you are well tuned now!
But I'll set down the pegs that make this music,                    195
As honest as I am.
*Othello:* Come, let us to the castle.
    News, friends! Our wars are done, the Turks are drowned.
    How does my old acquaintance of this isle?—
    Honey, you shall be well desired in Cyprus;                      200
    I have found great love amongst them. O my sweet,
    I prattle out of fashion, and I dote
    In mine own comforts.—I prithee, good Iago,
    Go to the bay and disembark my coffers.
    Bring thou the master to the citadel;                           205
    He is a good one, and his worthiness
    Does challenge much respect.—Come, Desdemona.—
    Once more, well met at Cyprus!

*Exeunt Othello and Desdemona [and all but Iago and Roderigo].*

*Iago [to an attendant]:* Do thou meet me presently at the harbor. *[To Roderigo.]*
    Come hither. If thou be'st valiant—as, they say, base men being in love have   210
    then a nobility in their natures more than is native to them—list me. The
    Lieutenant tonight watches on the court of guard. First, I must tell thee this:
    Desdemona is directly in love with him.
*Roderigo:* With him? Why, 'tis not possible.
*Iago:* Lay thy finger thus, and let thy soul be instructed. Mark me with what vio-   215
    lence she first loved the Moor, but for bragging and telling her fantastical lies.
    To love him still for prating? Let not thy discreet heart think it. Her eye must
    be fed; and what delight shall she have to look on the devil? When the blood
    is made dull with the act of sport, there should be, again to inflame it and to
    give satiety a fresh appetite, loveliness in favor, sympathy in years, manners,   220
    and beauties—all which the Moor is defective in. Now, for want of these
    required conveniences, her delicate tenderness will find itself abused, begin
    to heave the gorge, disrelish and abhor the Moor. Very nature will instruct
    her in it and compel her to some second choice. Now, sir, this granted—as it

192 s.d. *They kiss* (The direction is from the Quarto.)     195 *set down* loosen (and hence untune the
instrument)     196 *As . . . I am* for all my supposed honesty     200 *desired* welcomed     202 *out
of fashion* irrelevantly, incoherently (?)     204 *coffers* chests, baggage     205 *master* ship's captain
207 *challenge* lay claim to, deserve     210 *base men* even lowly born men     211 *list* listen to
212 *court of guard* guardhouse. (Cassio is in charge of the watch.)     215 *thus* i.e., on your lips
216 *but* only     219 *the act of sport* sex     220 *favor* appearance     *sympathy* correspondence, similarity     222 *required conveniences* things conducive to sexual compatibility     *abused* cheated,
revolted.     223 *heave the gorge* experience nausea     *Very nature* her very instincts

is a most pregnant and unforced position—who stands so eminent in the 225
degree of this fortune as Cassio does? A knave very voluble, no further conscionable than in putting on the mere form of civil and humane seeming for
the better compassing of his salt and most hidden loose affection. Why, none,
why, none. A slipper and subtle knave, a finder out of occasions, that has an
eye can stamp and counterfeit advantages, though true advantage never pre- 230
sent itself; a devilish knave. Besides, the knave is handsome, young, and hath
all those requisites in him that folly and green minds look after. A pestilent
complete knave, and the woman hath found him already.

*Roderigo:* I cannot believe that in her. She's full of most blessed condition.

*Iago:* Blessed fig's end! The wine she drinks is made of grapes. If she had been 235
blessed, she would never have loved the Moor. Blessed pudding! Didst thou
not see her paddle with the palm of his hand? Didst not mark that?

*Roderigo:* Yes, that I did; but that was but courtesy.

*Iago:* Lechery, by this hand. An index and obscure prologue to the history of lust
and foul thoughts. They met so near with their lips that their breaths 240
embraced together. Villainous thoughts, Roderigo! When these mutualities
so marshal the way, hard at hand comes the master and main exercise, th'
incorporate conclusion. Pish! But, sir, be you ruled by me. I have brought
you from Venice. Watch you tonight; for the command, I'll lay 't upon you.
Cassio knows you not. I'll not be far from you. Do you find some occasion to 245
anger Cassio, either by speaking too loud, or tainting his discipline, or from
what other course you please, which the time shall more favorably minister.

*Roderigo:* Well.

*Iago:* Sir, he's rash and very sudden in choler, and haply may strike at you. Provoke
him that he may, for even out of that will I cause these of Cyprus to mutiny, 250
whose qualification shall come into no true taste again but by the displanting
of Cassio. So shall you have a shorter journey to your desires by the means I
shall then have to prefer them, and the impediment most profitably removed,
without the which there were no expectation of our prosperity.

*Roderigo:* I will do this, if you can bring it to any opportunity. 255

*Iago:* I warrant thee. Meet me by and by at the citadel. I must fetch his necessaries ashore. Farewell.

*Roderigo:* Adieu.                                                                                            *Exit.*

---

225 *pregnant* evident, cogent    225–226 *in . . . of* as next in line for    226 *voluble* facile, glib
227 *conscionable* conscientious, conscience-bound    *humane* polite, courteous    228 *salt* licentious.    *affection* passion    229 *slipper* slippery    229–230 *an eye can stamp* an eye that can
coin, create    230 *advantages* favorable opportunities    232 *folly* wantonness.    *green* immature
233 *found him* sized him up, perceived his intent    234 *condition* disposition    235 *fig's end* (See
Act I, Scene III, line 316 for the vulgar gesture of the fig.)    236 *pudding* sausage    239 *index*
table of contents.    *obscure* (i.e., the *lust and foul thoughts,* are secret, hidden from view)    241
*mutualities* exchanges, intimacies.    242 *hard at hand* closely following    243 *incorporate* carnal
244 *Watch you* stand watch    *for the command . . . you* I'll arrange for you to be appointed, given
orders    246 *tainting* disparaging    247 *minister* provide    249 *choler* wrath    *haply* perhaps
250 *mutiny* riot    251 *qualification* appeasement.    *true taste* i.e., acceptable state    253 *prefer*
advance    256 *warrant* assure.    *by and by* immediately

*Iago:* That Cassio loves her, I do well believe 't;
That she loves him, 'tis apt and of great credit. 260
The Moor, howbeit that I endure him not,
Is of a constant, loving, noble nature,
And I dare think he'll prove to Desdemona
A most dear husband. Now, I do love her too,
Not out of absolute lust—though peradventure 265
I stand accountant for as great a sin—
But partly led to diet my revenge
For that I do suspect the lusty Moor
Hath leaped into my seat, the thought whereof
Doth, like a poisonous mineral, gnaw my innards; 270
And nothing can or shall content my soul
Till I am evened with him, wife for wife,
Or failing so, yet that I put the Moor
At least into a jealousy so strong
That judgment cannot cure. Which thing to do, 275
If this poor trash of Venice, whom I trace
For his quick hunting, stand the putting on,
I'll have our Michael Cassio on the hip,
Abuse him to the Moor in the rank garb—
For I fear Cassio with my nightcap too— 280
Make the Moor thank me, love me, and reward me
For making him egregiously an ass
And practicing upon his peace and quiet
Even to madness. 'Tis here, but yet confused.
Knavery's plain face is never seen till used. *Exit.* 285

## Scene II [*Cyprus. A Street.*]

*Enter Othello's Herald with a proclamation.*

*Herald:* It is Othello's pleasure, our noble and valiant general, that, upon certain
tidings now arrived, importing the mere perdition of the Turkish fleet, every
man put himself into triumph: some to dance, some to make bonfires, each
man to what sport and revels his addiction leads him. For, besides these beneficial news, it is the celebration of his nuptial. So much was his pleasure 5
should be proclaimed. All offices are open, and there is full liberty of feasting

---

260 *apt* probable.    *credit* credibility    266 *accountant* accountable    267 *diet* feed    276 *trace*
i.e., train, or follow (?), or perhaps *trash*, a hunting term, meaning to put weights on a hunting dog in
order to slow him down    277 *For* to make more eager.    *stand . . . on* respond properly when I
incite him to quarrel    278 *on the hip* at my mercy, where I can throw him. (A wrestling term.)
279 *Abuse* slander.    *rank garb* coarse manner, gross fashion    280 *with my nightcap* i.e., as a rival
in my bed, as one who gives me cuckold's horns    283 *practicing upon* plotting against    2 *mere*
*perdition* complete destruction    3 *triumph* public celebration    4 *addiction* inclination    6
*offices* rooms where food and drink are kept

from this present hour of five till the bell have told eleven. Heaven bless the isle of Cyprus and our noble general Othello!

*Exit*

## Scene III [*Cyprus. The Citadel.*]

*Enter Othello, Desdemona, Cassio, and attendants.*

*Othello:* Good Michael, look you to the guard tonight.
   Let's teach ourselves that honorable stop
   Not to outsport discretion.
*Cassio:* Iago hath direction what to do,
   But notwithstanding, with my personal eye                         5
   Will I look to 't.
*Othello:*                    Iago is most honest.
   Michael, good night. Tomorrow with your earliest
   Let me have speech with you. [*To Desdemona.*]
                       Come, my dear love,
   The purchase made, the fruits are to ensue;
   That profit's yet to come 'tween me and you.—                     10
   Good night.

*Exit [Othello, with Desdemona and attendants].*

*Enter Iago.*

*Cassio:* Welcome, Iago. We must to the watch.
*Iago:* Not this hour, Lieutenant; 'tis not yet ten o' the clock. Our general cast us thus early for the love of his Desdemona; who let us not therefore blame. He hath not yet made wanton the night with her, and she is sport for Jove.      15
*Cassio:* She's a most exquisite lady.
*Iago:* And, I'll warrant her, full of game.
*Cassio:* Indeed, she's a most fresh and delicate creature.
*Iago:* What an eye she has! Methinks it sounds a parley to provocation.
*Cassio:* An inviting eye, and yet methinks right modest.              20
*Iago:* And when she speaks, is it not an alarum to love?
*Cassio:* She is indeed perfection.
*Iago:* Well, happiness to their sheets! Come, Lieutenant, I have a stoup of wine, and here without are a brace of Cyprus gallants that would fain have a measure to the health of black Othello.                                          25

---

2 *stop* restraint    3 *outsport* celebrate beyond the bounds of    7 *with your earliest* at your earliest convenience    9–10 *The purchase . . . you* i.e., though married, we haven't yet consummated our love    13 *Not this hour* not for an hour yet    *cast* dismissed    14 *who* i.e., Othello    19 *sounds a parley* calls for a conference, issues an invitation    21 *alarum* signal calling men to arms (continuing the military metaphor of *parley*, line 19)    23 *stoup* measure of liquor, two quarts. 24 *without* outside.    *brace* pair    *fain have a measure* gladly drink a toast

*Cassio:* Not tonight, good Iago. I have very poor and unhappy brains for drinking. I could well wish courtesy would invent some other custom of entertainment.

*Iago:* O, they are our friends. But one cup! I'll drink for you.

*Cassio:* I have drunk but one cup tonight, and that was craftily qualified too, and behold what innovation it makes here. I am unfortunate in the infirmity and dare not task my weakness with any more. 30

*Iago:* What, man? 'Tis a night of revels. The gallants desire it.

*Cassio:* Where are they?

*Iago:* Here at the door. I pray you, call them in.

*Cassio:* I'll do 't, but it dislikes me.                                                          *Exit.* 35

*Iago:* If I can fasten but one cup upon him,
With that which he hath drunk tonight already,
He'll be as full of quarrel and offense
As my young mistress' dog. Now, my sick fool Roderigo,
Whom love hath turned almost the wrong side out, 40
To Desdemona hath tonight caroused
Potations pottle-deep; and he's to watch.
Three lads of Cyprus—noble swelling spirits,
That hold their honors in a wary distance,
The very elements of this warlike isle— 45
Have I tonight flustered with flowing cups,
And they watch too. Now, 'mongst this flock of drunkards
Am I to put our Cassio in some action
That may offend the isle.—But here they come.

*Enter Cassio, Montano, and gentlemen; [servants following with wine].*

If consequence do but approve my dream, 50
My boat sails freely both with wind and stream.

*Cassio:* 'Fore God, they have given me a rouse already.

*Montano:* Good faith, a little one; not past a pint, as I am a soldier.

*Iago:* Some wine, ho! [*He sings.*]
                    "And let me the cannikin clink, clink, 55
                    And let me the cannikin clink.
                    A soldier's a man,
                    O, man's life's but a span;
                    Why, then, let a soldier drink."

       Some wine, boys! 60

28 *for you* in your place. (Iago will do the steady drinking to keep the gallants company while Cassio has only one cup.)   29 *qualified* diluted.        30 *innovation* disturbance, insurrection        30 *here* i.e., in my head        35 *it dislikes me* i.e., I'm reluctant        38 *offense* readiness to take offense        41 *caroused* drunk off        42 *pottle-deep* to the bottom of the tankard.        *watch* stand watch        43 *swelling* proud        44 *hold . . . distance* i.e., are extremely sensitive of their honor        45 *very elements* typical sort        47 *watch* are members of the guard        50 *If . . . dream* if subsequent events will only substantiate my scheme        51 *stream* current        52 *rouse* full draft of liquor        55 *cannikin* small drinking vessel        58 *span* brief span of time. (Compare Psalm 39:5 as rendered in the Book of Common Prayer: "Thou hast made my days as it were a span long.")

*Cassio:* 'Fore God, an excellent song.

*Iago:* I learned it in England, where indeed they are most potent in potting. Your Dane, your German, and your swag-bellied Hollander—drink, ho!—are nothing to your English.

*Cassio:* Is your Englishman so exquisite in his drinking? 65

*Iago:* Why, he drinks you, with facility, your Dane dead drunk; he sweats not to overthrow your Almain; he gives your Hollander a vomit ere the next pottle can be filled.

*Cassio:* To the health of our general!

*Montano:* I am for it, Lieutenant, and I'll do you justice. 70

*Iago:* O sweet England! *[He sings.]*

> "King Stephen was and-a worthy peer,
> His breeches cost him but a crown;
> He held them sixpence all too dear,
> With that he called the tailor lown. 75
>
> He was a wight of high renown,
> And thou art but of low degree.
> 'Tis pride that pulls the country down;
> Then take thy auld cloak about thee."

Some wine, ho! 80

*Cassio:* 'Fore God, this is a more exquisite song than the other.

*Iago:* Will you hear 't again?

*Cassio:* No, for I hold him to be unworthy of his place that does those things. Well, God's above all; and there be souls must be saved, and there be souls must not be saved. 85

*Iago:* It's true, good Lieutenant.

*Cassio:* For mine own part—no offense to the General, nor any man of quality—I hope to be saved.

*Iago:* And so do I too, Lieutenant.

*Cassio:* Ay, but, by your leave, not before me; the lieutenant is to be saved before 90 the ancient. Let's have no more of this; let's to our affairs.—God forgive us our sins!—Gentlemen, let's look to our business. Do not think, gentlemen, I am drunk. This is my ancient; this is my right hand, and this is my left. I am not drunk now. I can stand well enough, and speak well enough.

*Gentlemen:* Excellent well. 95

*Cassio:* Why, very well then; you must not think then that I am drunk. *Exit.*

*Montano:* To th' platform, masters. Come, let's set the watch.

*[Exeunt Gentlemen.]*

---

62 *potting* drinking    66 *drinks you* drinks.    *your Dane* your typical Dane    *sweats not* i.e., need not exert himself.    67 *Almain* German    70 *I'll . . . justice* i.e., I'll drink as much as you    75 *lown* lout, rascal    78 *pride* i.e., extravagance in dress    79 *auld* old    87 *quality* rank    97 *set the watch* mount the guard

*Iago:* You see this fellow that is gone before.
  He's a soldier fit to stand by Caesar
  And give direction; and do but see his vice.                         100
  'Tis to his virtue a just equinox,
  The one as long as th' other. 'Tis pity of him.
  I fear the trust Othello puts him in,
  On some odd time of his infirmity,
  Will shake this island.
*Montano:*                    But is he often thus?                     105
*Iago:* 'Tis evermore the prologue to his sleep.
  He'll watch the horologe a double set,
  If drink rock not his cradle.
*Montano:*                    It were well
  The General were put in mind of it.
  Perhaps he sees it not, or his good nature                           110
  Prizes the virtue that appears in Cassio
  And looks not on his evils. Is not this true?

    *Enter Roderigo.*

*Iago [aside to him]:* How now, Roderigo?
  I pray you, after the Lieutenant; go.               *[Exit Roderigo.]*
*Montano:* And 'tis great pity that the noble Moor                     115
  Should hazard such a place as his own second
  With one of an engraffed infirmity.
  It were an honest action to say so
  To the Moor.
*Iago:*           Not I, for this fair island.
  I do love Cassio well and would do much                             120
  To cure him of this evil.            *[Cry within: "Help! Help!"]*
            But, hark! What noise?

    *Enter Cassio, pursuing Roderigo.*

*Cassio:* Zounds, you rogue! You rascal!
*Montano:* What's the matter, Lieutenant?
*Cassio:* A knave teach me my duty? I'll beat the knave into a twiggen bottle.
*Roderigo:* Beat me?                                                   125
*Cassio:* Dost thou prate, rogue?              *[He strikes Roderigo.]*
*Montano:* Nay, good Lieutenant. *[Restraining him.]* I pray you, sir, hold your hand.
*Cassio:* Let me go, sir, or I'll knock you o'er the mazard.

---

101 *just equinox* exact counterpart. (*Equinox* is an equal length of days and nights.)    107 *watch . . .
set* stay awake twice around the clock or *horologe*    116–117 *hazard . . . With* risk giving such an
important position as his second in command to    117 *engraffed* engrafted, inveterate    121 s.d.
*pursuing* (The Quarto text reads, "driving in.")    124 *twiggen* wicker-covered. (Cassio vows to assail
Roderigo until his skin resembles wickerwork or until he has driven Roderigo through the holes in a
wickerwork.)    128 *mazard* i.e., head. (Literally, a drinking vessel.)

*Montano*: Come, come, you're drunk.
*Cassio*: Drunk? [*They fight.*] 130
*Iago [aside to Roderigo]*: Away, I say. Go out and cry a mutiny.

[*Exit Roderigo.*]

Nay, good Lieutenant—God's will, gentlemen—
Help, ho!—Lieutenant—sir—Montano—sir—
Help, masters!—Here's a goodly watch indeed!

[*A bell rings.*]

Who's that which rings the bell?—Diablo, ho! 135
The town will rise. God's will, Lieutenant, hold!
You'll be ashamed forever.

*Enter Othello and attendants [with weapons].*

*Othello*: What is the matter here?
*Montano*: Zounds, I bleed still.
I am hurt to th' death. He dies! [*He thrusts at Cassio.*]
*Othello*: Hold, for your lives!
*Iago*: Hold, ho! Lieutenant—sir—Montano—gentlemen— 140
Have you forgot all sense of place and duty?
Hold! The General speaks to you. Hold, for shame!
*Othello*: Why, how now, ho! From whence ariseth this?
Are we turned Turks, and to ourselves do that
Which heaven hath forbid the Ottomites? 145
For Christian shame, put by this barbarous brawl!
He that stirs next to carve for his own rage
Holds his soul light; he dies upon his motion.
Silence that dreadful bell. It frights the isle
From her propriety. What is the matter, masters? 150
Honest Iago, that looks dead with grieving,
Speak. Who began this? On thy love, I charge thee.
*Iago*: I do not know. Friends all but now, even now,
In quarter and in terms like bride and groom
Devesting them for bed; and then, but now— 155
As if some planet had unwitted men—
Swords out, and tilting one at others' breasts
In opposition bloody. I cannot speak

131 *mutiny* riot    134 *masters* sirs.    s.d. *A bell rings* (This direction is from the Quarto, as are *Exit Roderigo* at line 114, *They fight* at line 130, and *with weapons* at line 137.)    135 *Diablo* the devil    136 *rise* grow riotous    144–145 *to ourselves . . . Ottomites* inflict on ourselves the harm that heaven has prevented the Turks from doing (by destroying their fleet)    147 *carve for* i.e., indulge, satisfy with his sword    148 *Holds . . . light* i.e., places little value on his life.    *upon his motion* if he moves    150 *propriety* proper state or condition    154 *In quarter* in friendly conduct, within bounds.    *in terms* on good terms    155 *Devesting them* undressing themselves    158 *speak* explain

Any beginning to this peevish odds;
And would in action glorious I had lost 160
Those legs that brought me to a part of it!

*Othello:* How comes it, Michael, you are thus forgot?

*Cassio:* I pray you, pardon me. I cannot speak.

*Othello:* Worthy Montano, you were wont be civil;
The gravity and stillness of your youth 165
The world hath noted, and your name is great
In mouths of wisest censure. What's the matter
That you unlace your reputation thus
And spend your rich opinion for the name
Of a night-brawler? Give me answer to it. 170

*Montano:* Worthy Othello, I am hurt to danger.
Your officer, Iago, can inform you—
While I spare speech, which something now offends me—
Of all that I do know; nor know I aught
By me that's said or done amiss this night, 175
Unless self-charity be sometimes a vice,
And to defend ourselves it be a sin
When violence assails us.

*Othello:*                          Now, by heaven,
My blood begins my safer guides to rule,
And passion, having my best judgment collied, 180
Essays to lead the way. Zounds, if I stir,
Or do but lift this arm, the best of you
Shall sink in my rebuke. Give me to know
How this foul rout began, who set it on;
And he that is approved in this offense, 185
Though he had twinned with me, both at a birth,
Shall lose me. What? In a town of war
Yet wild, the people's hearts brim full of fear,
To manage private and domestic quarrel?
In night, and on the court and guard of safety? 190
'Tis monstrous. Iago, who began 't?

*Montano [to Iago]:* If partially affined, or leagued in office,
Thou dost deliver more or less than truth,
Thou art no soldier.

---

159 *peevish odds* childish quarrel     162 *are thus forgot* have forgotten yourself thus     164 *wont be* accustomed to be     165 *stillness* sobriety     167 *censure* judgment     168 *unlace* undo, lay open (as one might loose the strings of a purse containing reputation)     169 *opinion* reputation     173 *something* somewhat.     *offends* pains     179 *blood* passion (of anger).     *guides* i.e., reason 180 *collied* darkened     181 *Essays* undertakes     184 *rout* riot     185 *approved in* found guilty of 187 *town of* town garrisoned for     189 *manage* undertake     190 *on . . . safety* at the main guardhouse or headquarters and on watch     192 *partially affined* made partial by some personal relationship.     *leagued in office* in league as fellow officers

Iago:                    Touch me not so near.
I had rather have this tongue cut from my mouth                    195
Than it should do offense to Michael Cassio;
Yet, I persuade myself, to speak the truth
Shall nothing wrong him. Thus it is, General.
Montano and myself being in speech,
There comes a fellow crying out for help,                    200
And Cassio following him with determined sword
To execute upon him. Sir, this gentleman

*[indicating Montano]*

Steps in to Cassio and entreats his pause.
Myself the crying fellow did pursue,
Lest by his clamor—as it so fell out—                    205
The town might fall in fright. He, swift of foot,
Outran my purpose, and I returned, the rather
For that I heard the clink and fall of swords
And Cassio high in oath, which till tonight
I ne'er might say before. When I came back—                    210
For this was brief—I found them close together
At blow and thrust, even as again they were
When you yourself did part them.
More of this matter cannot I report.
But men are men; the best sometimes forget.                    215
Though Cassio did some little wrong to him,
As men in rage strike those that wish them best,
Yet surely Cassio, I believe, received
From him that fled some strange indignity,
Which patience could not pass.
Othello:                    I know, Iago,                    220
Thy honesty and love doth mince this matter,
Making it light to Cassio. Cassio, I love thee,
But nevermore be officer of mine.

*Enter Desdemona, attended.*

Look if my gentle love be not raised up.
I'll make thee an example.                    225
Desdemona: What is the matter, dear?
Othello:                    All's well now, sweeting;
Come away to bed. [*To Montano.*] Sir, for your hurts,
Myself will be your surgeon.—Lead him off.

*[Montano is led off.]*

---

202 *execute* give effect to (his anger)    203 *his pause* him to stop    207 *rather* sooner    215 *forget* forget themselves    217 *those . . . best* i.e., even those who are well disposed    220 *pass* pass over, overlook    228 *be your surgeon* i.e., make sure you receive medical attention

Iago, look with care about the town
And silence those whom this vile brawl distracted.                                                    230
Come, Desdemona. 'Tis the soldiers' life
To have their balmy slumbers waked with strife.

*Exit [with all but Iago and Cassio].*

*Iago:* What, are you hurt, Lieutenant?
*Cassio:* Ay, past all surgery.
*Iago:* Marry, God forbid!                                                                           235
*Cassio:* Reputation, reputation, reputation! O, I have lost my reputation! I have
    lost the immortal part of myself, and what remains is bestial. My reputation,
    Iago, my reputation!
*Iago:* As I am an honest man, I thought you had received some bodily wound;
    there is more sense in that than in reputation. Reputation is an idle and        240
    most false imposition, oft got without merit and lost without deserving. You
    have lost no reputation at all, unless you repute yourself such a loser. What,
    man, there are more ways to recover the General again. You are but now cast
    in his mood—a punishment more in policy than in malice, even so as one
    would beat his offenseless dog to affright an imperious lion. Sue to him again   245
    and he's yours.
*Cassio:* I will rather sue to be despised than to deceive so good a commander with
    so slight, so drunken, and so indiscreet an officer. Drunk? And speak parrot?
    And squabble? Swagger? Swear? And discourse fustian with one's own shad-
    ow? O thou invisible spirit of wine, if thou hast no name to be known by, let    250
    us call thee devil!
*Iago:* What was he that you followed with your sword? What had he done to you?
*Cassio:* I know not.
*Iago:* Is 't possible?
*Cassio:* I remember a mass of things, but nothing distinctly; a quarrel, but nothing    255
    wherefore. O God, that men should put an enemy in their mouths to steal
    away their brains! That we should, with joy, pleasance, revel, and applause
    transform ourselves into beasts!
*Iago:* Why, but you are now well enough. How came you thus recovered?
*Cassio:* It hath pleased the devil drunkenness to give place to the devil wrath.       260
    One unperfectness shows me another, to make me frankly despise myself.
*Iago:* Come, you are too severe a moraler. As the time, the place, and the condi-
    tion of this country stands, I could heartily wish this had not befallen; but
    since it is as it is, mend it for your own good.

---

241 *false imposition* thing artificially imposed and of no real value      243 *recover* regain favor with
243–244 *cast in his mood* dismissed in a moment of anger      244 *in policy* done for expediency's sake
and as a public gesture      245 *would . . . lion* i.e., would make an example of a minor offender in
order to deter more important and dangerous offenders      *Sue* petition      248 *slight* worthless.
*speak parrot* talk nonsense, rant.      256 *wherefore* why      257 *applause* desire for applause      263
*moraler* moralizer

*Cassio:* I will ask him for my place again; he shall tell me I am a drunkard. Had I   265
as many mouths as Hydra, such an answer would stop them all. To be now a
sensible man, by and by a fool, and presently a beast! O, strange! Every inor-
dinate cup is unblessed, and the ingredient is a devil.

*Iago:* Come, come, good wine is a good familiar creature, if it be well used.
Exclaim no more against it. And, good Lieutenant, I think you think I love   270
you.

*Cassio:* I have well approved it, sir. I drunk!

*Iago:* You or any man living may be drunk at a time, man. I'll tell you what you
shall do. Our general's wife is now the general—I may say so in this respect,
for that he hath devoted and given up himself to the contemplation, mark,   275
and denotement of her parts and graces. Confess yourself freely to her;
importune her help to put you in your place again. She is of so free, so kind,
so apt, so blessed a disposition, she holds it a vice in her goodness not to do
more than she is requested. This broken joint between you and her husband
entreat her to splinter; and, my fortunes against any lay worth naming, this   280
crack of your love shall grow stronger than it was before.

*Cassio:* You advise me well.

*Iago:* I protest, in the sincerity of love and honest kindness.

*Cassio:* I think it freely; and betimes in the morning I will beseech the virtuous
Desdemona to undertake for me. I am desperate of my fortunes if they check   285
me here.

*Iago:* You are in the right. Good night, Lieutenant. I must to the watch.

*Cassio:* Good night, honest Iago.                              *Exit Cassio.*

*Iago:* And what's he then that says I play the villain,
When this advice is free I give, and honest,                              290
Probal to thinking, and indeed the course
To win the Moor again? For 'tis most easy
Th' inclining Desdemona to subdue
In any honest suit; she's framed as fruitful
As the free elements. And then for her                              295
To win the Moor—were 't to renounce his baptism,
All seals and symbols of redeemèd sin—
His soul is so enfettered to her love
That she may make, unmake, do what she list,

---

266 *Hydra* the Lernaean Hydra, a monster with many heads and the ability to grow two heads when one was cut off, slain by Hercules as the second of his twelve labors    272 *approved* proved    273 *at a time* at one time or another    274–275 *in . . . that* in view of this fact, that    275–276 *mark, and denotement* (Both words mean "observation.")    276 *parts* qualities    277 *free* generous    280 *splinter* bind with splints    *lay* stake, wager    283 *protest* insist, declare    284 *freely* unreservedly    285 *check* repulse    290 *free* (1) free from guile (2) freely given    291 *Probal* probable, reasonable    293 *inclining* favorably disposed.    *subdue* persuade    294 *framed as fruitful* created as generous    295 *free elements* i.e., earth, air, fire, and water, unrestrained and spontaneous

Even as her appetite shall play the god                                        300
With his weak function. How am I then a villain,
To counsel Cassio to this parallel course
Directly to his good? Divinity of hell!
When devils will the blackest sins put on,
They do suggest at first with heavenly shows,                                   305
As I do now. For whiles this honest fool
Plies Desdemona to repair his fortune,
And she for him pleads strongly to the Moor,
I'll pour this pestilence into his ear,
That she repeals him for her body's lust;                                       310
And by how much she strives to do him good,
She shall undo her credit with the Moor.
So will I turn her virtue into pitch,
And out of her own goodness make the net
That shall enmesh them all.

*Enter Roderigo.*

                      How now, Roderigo?                                  315

*Roderigo:* I do follow here in the chase, not like a hound that hunts, but one that
fills up the cry. My money is almost spent; I have been tonight exceedingly
well cudgeled; and I think the issue will be I shall have so much experience
for my pains, and so, with no money at all and a little more wit, return again
to Venice.                                                                      320

*Iago:* How poor are they that have not patience!
What wound did ever heal but by degrees?
Thou know'st we work by wit, and not by witchcraft,
And wit depends on dilatory time.
Does 't not go well? Cassio hath beaten thee,                                   325
And thou, by that small hurt, hast cashiered Cassio.
Though other things grow fair against the sun,
Yet fruits that blossom first will first be ripe.
Content thyself awhile. By the Mass, 'tis morning!
Pleasure and action make the hours seem short.                                 330
Retire thee; go where thou art billeted.
Away, I say! Thou shalt know more hereafter.
Nay, get thee gone.                                           *Exit Roderigo.*
            Two things are to be done.

---

300 *her appetite* her desire, or, perhaps, his desire for her      301 *function* exercise of faculties (weakened by his fondness for her)      302 *parallel* corresponding to these facts and to his best interests
303 *Divinity of hell* inverted theology of hell (which seduces the soul to its damnation)      304 *put on*
further, instigate      305 *suggest* tempt      310 *repeals him* attempts to get him restored      313 *pitch*
i.e., (1) foul blackness (2) a snaring substance      317 *fills up the cry* merely takes part as one of the
pack      318 *so much* just so much and no more      326 *cashiered* dismissed from service
327–328 *Though . . . ripe* i.e., plans that are well prepared and set expeditiously in motion will soonest ripen into success

My wife must move for Cassio to her mistress;
I'll set her on;                                                                        335
Myself the while to draw the Moor apart
And bring him jump when he may Cassio find
Soliciting his wife. Ay, that's the way.
Dull not device by coldness and delay.                               *Exit.*

# ACT III

### Scene I *[Before the Chamber of Othello and Desdemona.]*

*Enter Cassio [and] Musicians.*

Cassio: Masters, play here—I will content your pains—
    Something that's brief, and bid "Good morrow,
    General."                                                                          *[They play.]*

*[Enter] Clown.*

Clown: Why, masters, have your instruments been in Naples, that they speak i'
    the nose thus?
A Musician: How, sir, how?                                                        5
Clown: Are these, I pray you, wind instruments?
A Musician: Ay, marry, are they, sir.
Clown: O, thereby hangs a tail.
A Musician: Whereby hangs a tale, sir?
Clown: Marry, sir, by many a wind instrument that I know. But, masters, here's   10
    money for you. *[He gives money.]* And the General so likes your music that
    he desires you, for love's sake, to make no more noise with it.
A Musician: Well, sir, we will not.
Clown: If you have any music that may not be heard, to 't again; but, as they say,
    to hear music the General does not greatly care.                    15
A Musician: We have none such, sir.
Clown: Then put up your pipes in your bag, for I'll away. Go, vanish into air,
    away!                                                                              *Exeunt Musicians.*
Cassio: Dost thou hear, mine honest friend?
Clown: No, I hear not your honest friend; I hear you.                     20
Cassio: Prithee, keep up thy quillets. There's a poor piece of gold for thee. *[He gives*
    *money.]* If the gentle-woman that attends the General's wife be stirring, tell
    her there's one Cassio entreats her a little favor of speech. Wilt thou do this?

---

334 *move* plead     337 *jump* precisely     339 *device* plot.     *coldness* lack of zeal     1 *content your*
*pains* reward your efforts     4 *speak i' the nose* (1) sound nasal (2) sound like one whose nose has
been attacked by syphilis. (Naples was popularly supposed to have a high incidence of venereal disease.)     10 *wind instrument* (With a joke on flatulence. The *tail*, line 8, that hangs nearby the *wind*
*instrument* suggests the penis.)     13 *for love's sake* (1) out of friendship and affection (2) for the sake
of lovemaking in Othello's marriage     14 *may not* cannot     17 *I'll away* (Possibly a misprint, or a
snatch of song?)     21 *keep up* do not bring out, do not use.     *quillets* quibbles, puns     23 *a little*
*. . . speech* the favor of a brief talk

*Clown:* She is stirring, sir. If she will stir hither, I shall seem to notify unto her.    25
*Cassio:* Do, good my friend.                                    *Exit Clown.*

    *Enter Iago.*

                   In happy time, Iago.
*Iago:* You have not been abed, then?
*Cassio:* Why, no. The day had broke
    Before we parted. I have made bold, Iago,
    To send in to your wife. My suit to her    30
    Is that she will to virtuous Desdemona
    Procure me some access.
*Iago:* I'll send her to you presently;
    And I'll devise a means to draw the Moor
    Out of the way, that your converse and business    35
    May be more free.
*Cassio:* I humbly thank you for 't.                        *Exit [Iago].*
                I never knew
    A Florentine more kind and honest.

    *Enter Emilia.*

*Emilia:* Good morrow, good Lieutenant. I am sorry
    For your displeasure; but all will sure be well.    40
    The General and his wife are talking of it,
    And she speaks for you stoutly. The Moor replies
    That he you hurt is of great fame in Cyprus
    And great affinity, and that in wholesome wisdom
    He might not but refuse you; but he protests he loves you    45
    And needs no other suitor but his likings
    To take the safest occasion by the front
    To bring you in again.
*Cassio:*               Yet I beseech you,
    If you think fit, or that it may be done,
    Give me advantage of some brief discourse    50
    With Desdemon alone.
*Emilia:* Pray you, come in.
               I will bestow you where you shall have time
    To speak your bosom freely.
*Cassio:* I am much bound to you.                        *[Exeunt.]*

---

25 *stir* bestir herself (with a play on *stirring,* "rousing herself from rest")    *seem* deem it good, think
fit    27 *In happy time* i.e., well met    38 *Florentine* i.e., even a fellow Florentine. (Iago is a
Venetian; Cassio is a Florentine.)    40 *displeasure* fall from favor    42 *stoutly* spiritedly    43
*fame* reputation, importance    44 *affinity* kindred, family connection    45 *protests* insists    47
*occasion . . . front* opportunity by the forelock    53 *bosom* inmost thoughts

## Scene II [The Citadel.]

*Enter Othello, Iago, and Gentlemen.*

*Othello [giving letters]:* These letters give, Iago, to the pilot,
    And by him do my duties to the Senate.
    That done, I will be walking on the works;
    Repair there to me.
*Iago:*               Well, my good lord, I'll do 't.
*Othello:* This fortification, gentlemen, shall we see 't?         5
*Gentlemen:* We'll wait upon your lordship.          *Exeunt.*

## Scene III [The Garden of the Citadel.]

*Enter Desdemona, Cassio, and Emilia.*

*Desdemona:* Be thou assured, good Cassio, I will do
    All my abilities in thy behalf.
*Emilia:* Good madam, do. I warrant it grieves my husband
    As if the cause were his.
*Desdemona:* O, that's an honest fellow. Do not doubt, Cassio,    5
    But I will have my lord and you again
    As friendly as you were.
*Cassio:*              Bounteous madam,
    Whatever shall become of Michael Cassio,
    He's never anything but your true servant.
*Desdemona:* I know 't. I thank you. You do love my lord;     10
    You have known him long, and be you well assured
    He shall in strangeness stand no farther off
    Than in a politic distance.
*Cassio:*              Ay, but, lady,
    That policy may either last so long,
    Or feed upon such nice and waterish diet,         15
    Or breed itself so out of circumstance,
    That, I being absent and my place supplied,
    My general will forget my love and service.
*Desdemona:* Do not doubt that. Before Emilia here
    I give thee warrant of thy place. Assure thee,     20
    If I do vow a friendship I'll perform it
    To the last article. My lord shall never rest.

---

2 *do my duties* convey my respects    3 *works* breastworks, fortifications    4 *Repair* return, come
6 *wait upon* attend    12 *strangeness* aloofness    13 *politic* required by wise policy    15 *Or . . .
diet* or sustain itself at length upon such trivial and meager technicalities    16 *breed . . . circumstance* continually renew itself so out of chance events, or yield so few chances for my being pardoned
17 *supplied* filled by another person    19 *doubt* fear    20 *warrant* guarantee

I'll watch him tame and talk him out of patience;
His bed shall seem a school, his board a shrift;
I'll intermingle everything he does                                    25
With Cassio's suit. Therefore be merry, Cassio,
For thy solicitor shall rather die
Than give thy cause away.

*Enter Othello and Iago [at a distance].*

*Emilia:* Madam, here comes my lord.
*Cassio:* Madam, I'll take my leave.                                    30
*Desdemona:* Why, stay, and hear me speak.
*Cassio:* Madam, not now. I am very ill at ease,
    Unfit for mine own purposes.
*Desdemona:* Well, do your discretion.                    *Exit Cassio.*
*Iago:* Ha? I like not that.                                           35
*Othello:* What dost thou say?
*Iago:* Nothing, my lord; or if—I know not what.
*Othello:* Was not that Cassio parted from my wife?
*Iago:* Cassio, my lord? No, sure, I cannot think it,
    That he would steal away so guiltylike,                             40
    Seeing you coming.
*Othello:* I do believe 'twas he.
*Desdemona:* How now, my lord?
    I have been talking with a suitor here,
    A man that languishes in your displeasure.                         45
*Othello:* Who is 't you mean?
*Desdemona:* Why, your lieutenant, Cassio. Good my lord,
    If I have any grace or power to move you,
    His present reconciliation take;
    For if he be not one that truly loves you,                         50
    That errs in ignorance and not in cunning,
    I have no judgment in an honest face.
    I prithee, call him back.
*Othello:* Went he hence now?
*Desdemona:* Yes, faith, so humbled                                    55
    That he hath left part of his grief with me
    To suffer with him. Good love, call him back.
*Othello:* Not now, sweet Desdemon. Some other time.
*Desdemona:* But shall 't be shortly?

23 *watch him tame* tame him by keeping him from sleeping. (A term from falconry.)     *out of patience* past his endurance     24 *board* dining table.     *shrift* confessional     27 *solicitor* advocate     28 *away* up     34 *do your discretion* act according to your own discretion     49 *His . . . take* let him be reconciled to you right away     51 *in cunning* wittingly

*Othello:* The sooner, sweet, for you.                                               60
*Desdemona:* Shall 't be tonight at supper?
*Othello:* No, not tonight.
*Desdemona:* Tomorrow dinner, then?
*Othello:* I shall not dine at home.
    I meet the captains at the citadel.                              65
*Desdemona:* Why, then, tomorrow night, or Tuesday morn,
    On Tuesday noon, or night, on Wednesday morn.
    I prithee, name the time, but let it not
    Exceed three days. In faith, he's penitent;
    And yet his trespass, in our common reason—                        70
    Save that, they say, the wars must make example
    Out of her best—is not almost a fault
    T' incur a private check. When shall he come?
    Tell me, Othello. I wonder in my soul
    What you would ask me that I should deny,                          75
    Or stand so mammering on. What? Michael Cassio,
    That came a-wooing with you, and so many a time,
    When I have spoke of you dispraisingly,
    Hath ta'en your part—to have so much to do
    To bring him in! By 'r Lady, I could do much—                      80
*Othello:* Prithee, no more. Let him come when he will;
    I will deny thee nothing.
*Desdemona:* Why, this is not a boon.
    'Tis as I should entreat you wear your gloves,
    Or feed on nourishing dishes, or keep you warm,                    85
    Or sue to you to do a peculiar profit
    To your own person. Nay, when I have a suit
    Wherein I mean to touch your love indeed,
    It shall be full of poise and difficult weight,
    And fearful to be granted.                                         90
*Othello:* I will deny thee nothing.
    Whereon, I do beseech thee, grant me this,
    To leave me but a little to myself.
*Desdemona:* Shall I deny you? No. Farewell, my lord.
*Othello:* Farewell, my Desdemona. I'll come to thee straight.                        95
Desdemona: Emilia, come.—Be as your fancies teach you;
    Whate'er you be, I am obedient.                    *Exit [with Emilia].*

---

63 *dinner* (The noontime meal.)     70 *common reason* everyday judgments     71–72 *Save . . . best*
were it not that, as the saying goes, military discipline requires making an example of the very best
men. (*Her* refers to *wars* as a singular concept.)     72 *not almost* scarcely     73 *a private check* even
a private reprimand     76 *mammering on* wavering about     80 *bring him in* restore him to favor
86 *peculiar* particular, personal     88 *touch* test     89 *poise* weight, heaviness; or equipoise, delicate
balance involving hard choice     92 *Whereon* in return for which     95 *straight* straightway     96
*fancies* inclinations

*Othello:* Excellent wretch! Perdition catch my soul
    But I do love thee! And when I love thee not,
    Chaos is come again.                                       100
*Iago:* My noble lord—
*Othello:* What dost thou say, Iago?
*Iago:* Did Michael Cassio, when you wooed my lady,
    Know of your love?
*Othello:* He did, from first to last. Why dost thou ask?          105
*Iago:* But for a satisfaction of my thought;
    No further harm.
*Othello:*                  Why of thy thought, Iago?
*Iago:* I did not think he had been acquainted with her.
*Othello:* O, yes, and went between us very oft.
*Iago:* Indeed?                                              110
*Othello:* Indeed? Ay, indeed. Discern'st thou aught in that?
    Is he not honest?
*Iago:* Honest, my lord?
*Othello:* Honest. Ay, honest.
*Iago:* My lord, for aught I know.                        115
*Othello:* What dost thou think?
*Iago:* Think, my lord?
*Othello:* "Think, my lord?" By heaven, thou echo'st me,
    As if there were some monster in thy thought
    Too hideous to be shown. Thou dost mean something.     120
    I heard thee say even now, thou lik'st not that,
    When Cassio left my wife. What didst not like?
    And when I told thee he was of my counsel
    In my whole course of wooing, thou criedst "Indeed?"
    And didst contract and purse thy brow together       125
    As if thou then hadst shut up in thy brain
    Some horrible conceit. If thou dost love me,
    Show me thy thought.
*Iago:* My lord, you know I love you.
*Othello:* I think thou dost;                                  130
    And, for I know thou'rt full of love and honesty,
    And weigh'st thy words before thou giv'st them breath,
    Therefore these stops of thine fright me the more;
    For such things in a false disloyal knave

---

98 *wretch* (A term of affectionate endearment.)     99–100 *And . . . again* i.e., my love for you will
last forever, until the end of time when chaos will return. (But with an unconscious, ironic suggestion
that, if anything should induce Othello to cease loving Desdemona, the result would be chaos.)
123 *of my counsel* in my confidence     125 *purse* knit     127 *conceit* fancy     131 *for* because
133 *stops* pauses

Are tricks of custom, but in a man that's just                    135
They're close dilations, working from the heart
That passion cannot rule.
*Iago:*                         For Michael Cassio,
I dare be sworn I think that he is honest.
*Othello:* I think so too.
*Iago:*                    Men should be what they seem;
Or those that be not, would they might seem none!           140
*Othello:* Certain, men should be what they seem.
*Iago:* Why, then, I think Cassio's an honest man.
*Othello:* Nay, yet there's more in this.
I prithee, speak to me as to thy thinkings,
As thou dost ruminate, and give thy worst of thoughts         145
The worst of words.
*Iago:*                    Good my lord, pardon me.
Though I am bound to every act of duty,
I am not bound to that all slaves are free to.
Utter my thoughts? Why, say they are vile and false,
As where's the palace whereinto foul things                   150
Sometimes intrude not? Who has that breast so pure
But some uncleanly apprehensions
Keep leets and law days, and in sessions sit
With meditations lawful?
*Othello:* Thou dost conspire against thy friend, Iago,        155
If thou but think'st him wronged and mak'st his ear
A stranger to thy thoughts.
*Iago:*                         I do beseech you,
Though I perchance am vicious in my guess—
As I confess it is my nature's plague
To spy into abuses, and oft my jealousy                       160
Shapes faults that are not—that your wisdom then,
From one that so imperfectly conceits,
Would take no notice, nor build yourself a trouble
Out of his scattering and unsure observance.
It were not for your quiet nor your good,                     165
Nor for my manhood, honesty, and wisdom,
To let you know my thoughts.

135 *of custom* customary    136 *close dilations* secret or involuntary expressions or delays    137
*That passion cannot rule* i.e., that are too passionately strong to be restrained (referring to the workings), or, that cannot rule its own passions (referring to the heart).    *For* as for    140 *none* i.e.,
not to be men, or not seem to be honest    148 *that* that which.    *free to* free with respect to
153 *Keep leets and law days* i.e., hold court, set up their authority in one's heart. (*Leets* are a kind of
manor court; *law days* are the days courts sit in session, or those sessions.)    154 *With* along with.
*lawful* innocent    155 *thy friend* i.e., Othello    158 *vicious* wrong    160 *jealousy* suspicious
nature    161 *then* on that account    162 *one* i.e., myself, Iago.    *conceits* judges, conjectures
164 *scattering* random

*Othello:* What dost thou mean?

*Iago:* Good name in man and woman, dear my lord,
  Is the immediate jewel of their souls.
  Who steals my purse steals trash; 'tis something, nothing;           170
  'Twas mine, 'tis his, and has been slave to thousands;
  But he that filches from me my good name
  Robs me of that which not enriches him
  And makes me poor indeed.

*Othello:* By heaven, I'll know thy thoughts.                          175

*Iago:* You cannot, if my heart were in your hand,
  Nor shall not, whilst 'tis in my custody.

*Othello:* Ha?

*Iago:* O, beware, my lord, of jealousy.
  It is the green-eyed monster which doth mock
  The meat it feeds on. That cuckold lives in bliss                    180
  Who, certain of his fate, loves not his wronger;
  But O, what damnèd minutes tells he o'er
  Who dotes, yet doubts, suspects, yet fondly loves!

*Othello:* O misery!

*Iago:* Poor and content is rich, and rich enough,                    185
  But riches fineless is as poor as winter
  To him that ever fears he shall be poor.
  Good God, the souls of all my tribe defend
  From jealousy!

*Othello:* Why, why is this?                                          190
  Think'st thou I'd make a life of jealousy,
  To follow still the changes of the moon
  With fresh suspicions? No! To be once in doubt
  Is once to be resolved. Exchange me for a goat
  When I shall turn the business of my soul                           195
  To such exsufflicate and blown surmises
  Matching thy inference. 'Tis not to make me jealous
  To say my wife is fair, feeds well, loves company,
  Is free of speech, sings, plays, and dances well;
  Where virtue is, these are more virtuous.                           200
  Nor from mine own weak merits will I draw
  The smallest fear or doubt of her revolt,

169 *immediate* essential, most precious    176 *if* even if    179–180 *doth mock . . . on* mocks and torments the heart of its victim, the man who suffers jealousy    181 *his wronger* i.e., his faithless wife. (The unsuspecting cuckold is spared the misery of loving his wife only to discover she is cheating on him.)    182 *tells* counts    185 *Poor . . . enough* to be content with what little one has is the greatest wealth of all. (Proverbial.)    186 *fineless* boundless    192–193 *To follow . . . suspicions* to be constantly imagining new causes for suspicion, changing incessantly like the moon    194 *once* once and for all.    *resolved* free of doubt, having settled the matter    196 *exsufflicate and blown* inflated and blown up, rumored about, or, spat out and flyblown, hence, loathsome, disgusting    197 *inference* description or allegation    202 *doubt . . . revolt* fear of her unfaithfulness

For she had eyes, and chose me. No, Iago,
I'll see before I doubt; when I doubt, prove;
And on the proof, there is no more but this— 205
Away at once with love or jealousy.

*Iago:* I am glad of this, for now I shall have reason
To show the love and duty that I bear you
With franker spirit. Therefore, as I am bound,
Receive it from me. I speak not yet of proof. 210
Look to your wife; observe her well with Cassio.
Wear your eyes thus, not jealous nor secure.
I would not have your free and noble nature,
Out of self-bounty, be abused. Look to 't.
I know our country disposition well; 215
In Venice they do let God see the pranks
They dare not show their husbands; their best conscience
Is not to leave 't undone, but keep 't unknown.

*Othello:* Dost thou say so?

*Iago:* She did deceive her father, marrying you; 220
And when she seemed to shake and fear your looks,
She loved them most.

*Othello:*                            And so she did.

*Iago:*                                      Why, go to, then!
She that, so young, could give out such a seeming,
To seel her father's eyes up close as oak,
He thought 'twas witchcraft! But I am much to blame. 225
I humbly do beseech you of your pardon
For too much loving you.

*Othello:* I am bound to thee forever.

*Iago:* I see this hath a little dashed your spirits.

*Othello:* Not a jot, not a jot.

*Iago:*                            I' faith, I fear it has. 230
I hope you will consider what is spoke
Comes from my love. But I do see you're moved.
I am to pray you not to strain my speech
To grosser issues nor to larger reach
Than to suspicion. 235

*Othello:* I will not.

*Iago:* Should you do so, my lord,
My speech should fall into such vile success

---

212 *not* neither.      *secure* free from uncertainty      214 *self-bounty* inherent or natural goodness
and generosity.      *abused* deceived      222 *go to* (An expression of impatience.)      223 *seeming*
false appearance      224 *seel* blind. (A term from falconry.)      *oak* (A close-grained wood.)
228 *bound* indebted (but perhaps with ironic sense of "tied")      234 *issues* significances.      *reach*
meaning, scope      238 *success* effect, result

Which my thoughts aimed not. Cassio's my worthy friend.
My lord, I see you're moved.
*Othello:*                                   No, not much moved.                              240
I do not think but Desdemona's honest.
*Iago:* Long live she so! And long live you to think so!
*Othello:* And yet, how nature erring from itself—
*Iago:* Ay, there's the point! As—to be bold with you—
Not to affect many proposèd matches                                                          245
Of her own clime, complexion, and degree,
Whereto we see in all things nature tends—
Foh! One may smell in such a will most rank,
Foul disproportion, thoughts unnatural.
But pardon me. I do not in position                                                          250
Distinctly speak of her, though I may fear
Her will, recoiling to her better judgment,
May fall to match you with her country forms
And happily repent.
*Othello:*                       Farewell, farewell!
If more thou dost perceive, let me know more.                                                255
Set on thy wife to observe. Leave me, Iago.
*Iago [going]:* My lord, I take my leave.
*Othello:* Why did I marry? This honest creature doubtless
Sees and knows more, much more, than he unfolds.
*Iago [returning]:* My Lord, I would I might entreat your honor                              260
To scan this thing no farther. Leave it to time.
Although 'tis fit that Cassio have his place—
For, sure, he fills it up with great ability—
Yet, if you please to hold him off awhile,
You shall by that perceive him and his means.                                               265
Note if your lady strain his entertainment
With any strong or vehement importunity;
Much will be seen in that. In the meantime,
Let me be thought too busy in my fears—
As worthy cause I have to fear I am—                                                         270
And hold her free, I do beseech your honor.
*Othello:* Fear not my government.
*Iago:* I once more take my leave.                                    *Exit.*

---

241 *honest* chaste   245 *affect* prefer, desire   246 *clime . . . degree* country, color, and social position   248 *will* sensuality, appetite   249 *disproportion* abnormality   250 *position* argument,
proposition   252 *recoiling* reverting   *better* i.e., more natural and reconsidered   253 *fall . . .
forms* undertake to compare you with Venetian norms of handsomeness   254 *happily repent* haply
repent her marriage   261 *scan* scrutinize   265 *his means* the method he uses (to regain his post)
266 *strain his entertainment* urge his reinstatement   269 *busy* interfering   271 *hold her free* regard
her as innocent   272 *government* self-control, conduct

*Othello*: This fellow's of exceeding honesty,
    And knows all qualities, with a learnèd spirit,        275
    Of human dealings. If I do prove her haggard,
    Though that her jesses were my dear heartstrings,
    I'd whistle her off and let her down the wind
    To prey at fortune. Haply, for I am black
    And have not those soft parts of conversation        280
    That chamberers have, or for I am declined
    Into the vale of years—yet that's not much—
    She's gone. I am abused, and my relief
    Must be to loathe her. O curse of marriage,
    That we can call these delicate creatures ours        285
    And not their appetites! I had rather be a toad
    And live upon the vapor of a dungeon
    Than keep a corner in the thing I love
    For others' uses. Yet, 'tis the plague of great ones;
    Prerogatived are they less than the base.        290
    'Tis destiny unshunnable, like death.
    Even then this forkèd plague is fated to us
    When we do quicken. Look where she comes.

*Enter Desdemona and Emilia.*

    If she be false, O, then heaven mocks itself!
    I'll not believe 't.
*Desdemona*:          How now, my dear Othello?        295
    Your dinner, and the generous islanders
    By you invited, do attend your presence.
*Othello*: I am to blame.
*Desdemona*:          Why do you speak so faintly?
    Are you not well?
*Othello*: I have a pain upon my forehead here.        300
*Desdemona*: Faith, that's with watching. 'Twill away again.

    *[She offers her handkerchief.]*

---

275 *qualities* natures, types    276 *haggard* wild (like a wild female hawk)    277 *jesses* straps fastened around the legs of a trained hawk    278 *I'd . . . wind* i.e., I'd let her go forever. (To release a hawk downwind was to invite it not to return.)    279 *prey at fortune* fend for herself in the wild. *Haply, for* perhaps because    280 *soft . . . conversation* pleasing graces of social behavior    281 *chamberers* gallants    283 *abused* deceived    290 *Prerogatived* privileged (to have honest wives). *the base* ordinary citizens. (Socially prominent men are especially prone to the unavoidable destiny of being cuckolded and to the public shame that goes with it.)    292 *forkèd* (An allusion to the horns of the cuckold.)    293 *quicken* receive life. (*Quicken* may also mean to swarm with maggots as the body festers, as in Act IV, Scene II, line 69, in which case lines 292–293 suggest that *even then*, in death, we are cuckolded by *forkèd* worms.)    296 *generous* noble    297 *attend* await    301 *watching* too little sleep

Let me but bind it hard, within this hour
It will be well.
*Othello:*           Your napkin is too little.
Let it alone. Come, I'll go in with you.

*[He puts the handkerchief from him, and it drops.]*

*Desdemona:* I am very sorry that you are not well.          305

    *Exit [with Othello].*

*Emilia [picking up the handkerchief]:* I am glad I have found this napkin.
This was her first remembrance from the Moor.
My wayward husband hath a hundred times
Wooed me to steal it, but she so loves the token—
For he conjured her she should ever keep it—          310
That she reserves it evermore about her
To kiss and talk to. I'll have the work ta'en out,
And give 't Iago. What he will do with it
Heaven knows, not I;
I nothing but to please his fantasy.          315

    *Enter Iago.*

*Iago:* How now? What do you here alone?
*Emilia:* Do not you chide. I have a thing for you.
*Iago:* You have a thing for me? It is a common thing—
*Emilia:* Ha?
*Iago:* To have a foolish wife.          320
*Emilia:* O, is that all? What will you give me now
    For that same handkerchief?
*Iago:* What handkerchief?
*Emilia:* What handkerchief?
    Why, that the Moor first gave to Desdemona;         325
    That which so often you did bid me steal.
*Iago:* Hast stolen it from her?
*Emilia:* No, faith. She let it drop by negligence,
    And to th' advantage I, being here, took 't up.
    Look, here 'tis.
*Iago:*          A good wench! Give it me.         330
*Emilia:* What will you do with 't, that you have been so earnest
    To have me filch it?
*Iago [snatching it]:*         Why, what is that to you?

303 *napkin* handkerchief    304 *Let it alone* i.e., never mind    308 *wayward* capricious    312 *work ta'en out* design of the embroidery copied    315 *fantasy* whim    318 *common thing* (With bawdy suggestion; *common* suggests coarseness and availability to all comers, and *thing* is a slang term for the pudendum.)    329 *to th' advantage* taking the opportunity

*Emilia:* If it be not for some purpose of import,
   Give 't me again. Poor lady, she'll run mad
   When she shall lack it.
*Iago:*                             Be not acknown on 't.     335
   I have use for it. Go, leave me.                    *Exit Emilia.*
   I will in Cassio's lodging lose this napkin
   And let him find it. Trifles light as air
   Are to the jealous confirmations strong
   As proofs of Holy Writ. This may do something.       340
   The Moor already changes with my poison.
   Dangerous conceits are in their natures poisons,
   Which at the first are scarce found to distaste,
   But with a little act upon the blood
   Burn like the mines of sulfur.

   *Enter Othello.*

                             I did say so.               345
   Look where he comes! Not poppy nor mandragora
   Nor all the drowsy syrups of the world
   Shall ever medicine thee to that sweet sleep
   Which thou owedst yesterday.
*Othello:*                        Ha, ha, false to me?
*Iago:* Why, how now, General? No more of that.          350
*Othello:* Avaunt! Begone! Thou hast set me on the rack.
   I swear 'tis better to be much abused
   Than but to know 't a little.
*Iago:*                        How now, my lord?
*Othello:* What sense had I of her stolen hours of lust?
   I saw 't not, thought it not, it harmed not me.       355
   I slept the next night well, fed well, was free and merry;
   I found not Cassio's kisses on her lips.
   He that is robbed, not wanting what is stolen,
   Let him not know 't and he's not robbed at all.
*Iago:* I am sorry to hear this.                          360
*Othello:* I had been happy if the general camp,
   Pioners and all, had tasted her sweet body,
   So I had nothing known. O, now, forever
   Farewell the tranquil mind! Farewell content!
   Farewell the plumèd troops and the big wars           365
   That makes ambition virtue! O, farewell!

---

335 *lack* miss.    *Be . . . on't* do not confess knowledge of it    337 *lose* (The Folio spelling, *loose*,
is a normal spelling for "lose," but it may also contain the idea of "let go," "release.")    342 *conceits*
fancies, ideas    343 *distaste* be distasteful    344 *act* action, working    346 *mandragora* an opiate
made of the mandrake root    349 *thou owedst* you did own    356 *free* carefree    358 *wanting*
missing    362 *Pioners* diggers of mines, the lowest grade of soldiers    363 *So* provided    365 *big*
stately

Farewell the neighing steed and the shrill trump,
The spirit-stirring drum, th' ear-piercing fife,
The royal banner, and all quality,
Pride, pomp, and circumstance of glorious war!                                  370
And O, you mortal engines, whose rude throats
Th' immortal Jove's dread clamors counterfeit,
Farewell! Othello's occupation's gone.

*Iago:* Is 't possible, my lord?

*Othello:* Villain, be sure thou prove my love a whore!                         375
    Be sure of it. Give me the ocular proof,
    Or, by the worth of mine eternal soul,
    Thou hadst been better have been born a dog
    Than answer my waked wrath!

*Iago:*                                   Is 't come to this?

*Othello:* Make me to see 't, or at the least so prove it                       380
    That the probation bear no hinge nor loop
    To hang a doubt on, or woe upon thy life!

*Iago:* My noble lord—

*Othello:* If thou dost slander her and torture me,
    Never pray more; abandon all remorse;                                       385
    On horror's head horrors accumulate;
    Do deeds to make heaven weep, all earth amazed;
    For nothing canst thou to damnation add
    Greater than that.

*Iago:*                         O grace! O heaven forgive me!
    Are you a man? Have you a soul or sense?                                     390
    God b' wi' you; take mine office. O wretched fool,
    That lov'st to make thine honesty a vice!
    O monstrous world! Take note, take note, O world,
    To be direct and honest is not safe.
    I thank you for this profit, and from hence                                 395
    I'll love no friend, sith love breeds such offense.

*Othello:* Nay, stay. Thou shouldst be honest.

*Iago:* I should be wise, for honesty's a fool
    And loses that it works for.

*Othello:*                            By the world,

---

369 *quality* character, essential nature    370 *Pride* rich display.    *circumstance* pageantry    371
*mortal engines* i.e., cannon. (*Mortal* means "deadly.")    372 *Jove's dread clamors* i.e., thunder
381 *probation* proof    385 *remorse* pity, penitent hope for salvation    386 *horrors accumulate* add
still more horrors    387 *amazed* confounded with horror    391 *O wretched fool* (Iago addresses himself as a fool for having carried honesty too far.)    392 *vice* failing, something overdone    395
*profit* profitable instruction.    *hence* henceforth    396 *sith* since.    *offense* i.e., harm to the one
who offers help and friendship    397 *Thou shouldst be* it appears that you are. (But Iago replies in
the sense of "ought to be.")    399 *that* what

I think my wife be honest and think she is not;                            400
I think that thou art just and think thou art not.
I'll have some proof. My name, that was as fresh
As Dian's visage, is now begrimed and black
As mine own face. If there be cords, or knives,
Poison, or fire, or suffocating streams,                                    405
I'll not endure it. Would I were satisfied!
*Iago:* I see, sir, you are eaten up with passion.
I do repent me that I put it to you.
You would be satisfied?
*Othello:*                     Would? Nay, and I will.
*Iago:* And may; but how? How satisfied, my lord?                          410
Would you, the supervisor, grossly gape on?
Behold her topped?
*Othello:*                     Death and damnation! O!
*Iago:* It were a tedious difficulty, I think,
To bring them to that prospect. Damn them then,
If ever mortal eyes do see them bolster                                     415
More than their own. What then? How then?
What shall I say? Where's satisfaction?
It is impossible you should see this,
Were they as prime as goats, as hot as monkeys,
As salt as wolves in pride, and fools as gross                             420
As ignorance made drunk. But yet I say,
If imputation and strong circumstances
Which lead directly to the door of truth
Will give you satisfaction, you might have 't.
*Othello:* Give me a living reason she's disloyal.                          425
*Iago:* I do not like the office.
But sith I am entered in this cause so far,
Pricked to 't by foolish honesty and love,
I will go on. I lay with Cassio lately,
And being troubled with a raging tooth                                     430
I could not sleep. There are a kind of men
So loose of soul that in their sleeps will mutter
Their affairs. One of this kind is Cassio.
In sleep I heard him say, "Sweet Desdemona,

---

403 *Dian* Diana, goddess of the moon and of chastity    411 *supervisor* onlooker    414 *Damn them then* i.e., they would have to be really incorrigible    415 *bolster* go to bed together, share a bolster
416 *More* other.    *own* own eyes    419 *prime* lustful    420 *salt* wanton, sensual.    *pride* heat
422 *imputation . . . circumstances* strong circumstantial evidence    427 *sith* since    428 *Pricked* spurred

Let us be wary, let us hide our loves!"  435
And then, sir, would he grip and wring my hand,
Cry "O sweet creature!", then kiss me hard,
As if he plucked up kisses by the roots
That grew upon my lips; then laid his leg
Over my thigh, and sighed, and kissed, and then  440
Cried, "Cursèd fate that gave thee to the Moor!"
*Othello:* O monstrous! Monstrous!
*Iago:*                                    Nay, this was but his dream.
*Othello:* But this denoted a foregone conclusion.
'Tis a shrewd doubt, though it be but a dream.
*Iago:* And this may help to thicken other proofs  445
That do demonstrate thinly.
*Othello:*                            I'll tear her all to pieces.
*Iago:* Nay, but be wise. Yet we see nothing done;
She may be honest yet. Tell me but this:
Have you not sometimes seen a handkerchief
Spotted with strawberries in your wife's hand?  450
*Othello:* I gave her such a one. 'Twas my first gift.
*Iago:* I know not that; but such a handkerchief—
I am sure it was your wife's—did I today
See Cassio wipe his beard with.
*Othello:*                                If it be that—
*Iago:* If it be that, or any that was hers,  455
It speaks against her with the other proofs.
*Othello:* O, that the slave had forty thousand lives!
One is too poor, too weak for my revenge.
Now do I see 'tis true. Look here, Iago,
All my fond love thus do I blow to heaven.  460
'Tis gone.
Arise, black vengeance, from the hollow hell!
Yield up, O love, thy crown and hearted throne
To tyrannous hate! Swell, bosom, with thy freight,
For 'tis of aspics' tongues!  465
*Iago:* Yet be content.
*Othello:* O, blood, blood, blood!
*Iago:* Patience, I say. Your mind perhaps may change.
*Othello:* Never, Iago. Like to the Pontic Sea,
Whose icy current and compulsive course  470
Ne'er feels retiring ebb, but keeps due on

---

443 *foregone conclusion* concluded experience or action      444 *shrewd doubt* suspicious circumstance
450 *Spotted with strawberries* embroidered with a strawberry pattern      457 *the slave* i.e., Cassio
460 *fond* foolish (but also suggesting "affectionate")      463 *hearted* fixed in the heart      464 *freight*
burden      465 *aspics'* venomous serpents'      466 *content* calm      469 *Pontic Sea* Black Sea

To the Propontic and the Hellespont,
Even so my bloody thoughts with violent pace
Shall ne'er look back, ne'er ebb to humble love,
Till that a capable and wide revenge                                    475
Swallow them up. Now, by yond marble heaven,
[*Kneeling*] In the due reverence of a sacred vow
I here engage my words.
*Iago:*                          Do not rise yet.
[*He kneels.*] Witness, you ever-burning lights above,
You elements that clip us round about,                                 480
Witness that here Iago doth give up
The execution of his wit, hands, heart,
To wronged Othello's service. Let him command,
And to obey shall be in me remorse,
What bloody business ever.                           [*They rise.*]
*Othello:*                          I greet thy love,                   485
Not with vain thanks, but with acceptance bounteous,
And will upon the instant put thee to 't.
Within these three days let me hear thee say
That Cassio's not alive.
*Iago:*                          My friend is dead;
'Tis done at your request. But let her live.                           490
*Othello:* Damn her, lewd minx! O, damn her, damn her!
Come, go with me apart. I will withdraw
To furnish me with some swift means of death
For the fair devil. Now art thou my lieutenant.
*Iago:* I am your own forever.                           *Exeunt.*  495

### Scene IV [*Before the Citadel.*]

*Enter Desdemona, Emilia, and Clown.*

*Desdemona:* Do you know, sirrah, where Lieutenant Cassio lies?
*Clown:* I dare not say he lies anywhere.
*Desdemona:* Why, man?
*Clown:* He's a soldier, and for me to say a soldier lies, 'tis stabbing.
*Desdemona:* Go to. Where lodges he?                                   5
*Clown:* To tell you where he lodges is to tell you where I lie.

472 *Propontic* Sea of Marmora, between the Black Sea and the Aegean.      *Helllespont* Dardanelles,
straits where the Sea of Marmora joins with the Aegean      475 *capable* ample, comprehensive
476 *marble* i.e., gleaming like marble and unrelenting      479 s.d. *He kneels* (In the Quarto text, Iago
kneels here after Othello has knelt at line 477.)      480 *clip* encompass      482 *execution* exercise,
action.      *wit* mind      484 *remorse* pity (for Othello's wrongs)      485 *ever* soever      487 *to 't* to
the proof      491 *minx* wanton      1 *sirrah* (A form of address to an inferior.)      1 *lies* lodges. (But
the Clown makes the obvious pun.)

*Desdemona:* Can anything be made of this?

*Clown:* I know not where he lodges, and for me to devise a lodging and say he lies here, or he lies there, were to lie in mine own throat.

*Desdemona:* Can you inquire him out, and be edified by report? 10

*Clown:* I will catechize the world for him; that is, make questions, and by them answer.

*Desdemona:* Seek him, bid him come hither. Tell him I have moved my lord on his behalf and hope all will be well.

*Clown:* To do this is within the compass of man's wit, and therefore I will attempt 15
the doing it. *Exit Clown.*

*Desdemona:* Where should I lose that handkerchief, Emilia?

*Emilia:* I know not, madam.

*Desdemona:* Believe me, I had rather have lost my purse
    Full of crusadoes; and but my noble Moor 20
    Is true of mind and made of no such baseness
    As jealous creatures are, it were enough
    To put him to ill thinking.

*Emilia:*                Is he not jealous?

*Desdemona:* Who, he? I think the sun where he was born
    Drew all such humors from him.

*Emilia:*                   Look where he comes. 25

    *Enter Othello.*

*Desdemona:* I will not leave him now till Cassio
    Be called to him.—How is 't with you, my lord?

*Othello:* Well, my good lady. [*Aside.*] O, hardness to dissemble!—
    How do you, Desdemona?

*Desdemona:*               Well, my good lord.

*Othello:* Give me your hand. [*She gives her hand.*] This hand is moist, my lady. 30

*Desdemona:* It yet hath felt no age nor known no sorrow.

*Othello:* This argues fruitfulness and liberal heart.
    Hot, hot, and moist. This hand of yours requires
    A sequester from liberty, fasting and prayer,
    Much castigation, exercise devout; 35
    For here's a young and sweating devil here
    That commonly rebels. 'Tis a good hand,
    A frank one.

*Desdemona:*     You may indeed say so,
    For 'twas that hand that gave away my heart.

---

9 *lie . . . throat* (1) lie egregiously and deliberately (2) use the windpipe to speak a lie    13 *moved* petitioned    20 *crusadoes* Portuguese gold coins    25 *humors* (Refers to the four bodily fluids thought to determine temperament.)    32 *argues* gives evidence of.    *fruitfulness* generosity, amorousness, and fecundity.    *liberal* generous and sexually free    34 *sequester* separation, sequestration    35 *castigation* corrective discipline.    *exercise devout* i.e., prayer, religious meditation, etc. 38 *frank* generous, open (with sexual suggestion)

*Othello:* A liberal hand. The hearts of old gave hands,                    40
    But our new heraldry is hands, not hearts.
*Desdemona:* I cannot speak of this. Come now, your promise.
*Othello:* What promise, chuck?
*Desdemona:* I have sent to bid Cassio come speak with you.
*Othello:* I have a salt and sorry rheum offends me;                         45
    Lend me thy handkerchief.
*Desdemona:* Here, my lord.                    *[She offers a handkerchief.]*
*Othello:* That which I gave you.
*Desdemona:*                    I have it not about me.
*Othello:* Not?
*Desdemona:* No, faith, my lord.                                            50
*Othello:* That's a fault. That handkerchief
    Did an Egyptian to my mother give.
    She was a charmer, and could almost read
    The thoughts of people. She told her, while she kept it
    'Twould make her amiable and subdue my father              55
    Entirely to her love, but if she lost it
    Or made a gift of it, my father's eye
    Should hold her loathèd and his spirits should hunt
    After new fancies. She, dying, gave it me,
    And bid me, when my fate would have me wived,              60
    To give it her. I did so; and take heed on 't;
    Make it a darling like your precious eye.
    To lose 't or give 't away were such perdition
    As nothing else could match.
*Desdemona:*                    Is 't possible?
*Othello:* 'Tis true. There's magic in the web of it.                       65
    A sibyl, that had numbered in the world
    The sun to course two hundred compasses,
    In her prophetic fury sewed the work;
    The worms were hallowed that did breed the silk,
    And it was dyed in mummy which the skillful                 70
    Conserved of maidens' hearts.
*Desdemona:*                    I' faith! Is 't true?
*Othello:* Most veritable. Therefore look to 't well.
*Desdemona:* Then would to God that I had never seen 't!

---

40 *The hearts . . . hands* i.e., in former times, people would give their hearts when they gave their
hands to something    41 *But . . . hearts* i.e., in our decadent times, the joining of hands is no longer
a badge to signify the giving of hearts    43 *chuck* (A term of endearment.)    45 *salt . . . rheum*
distressful head cold or watering of the eyes    53 *charmer* sorceress    55 *amiable* desirable    59
*fancies* loves    61 *her* i.e., to my wife    63 *perdition* loss    65 *web* fabric, weaving    67 *com-
passes* annual circlings. (The *sibyl*, or prophetess, was two hundred years old.)    68 *prophetic fury*
frenzy of prophetic inspiration.    *work* embroidered pattern    70 *mummy* medicinal or magical
preparation drained from mummified bodies    71 *Conserved of* prepared or preserved out of

*Othello:* Ha? Wherefore?

*Desdemona:* Why do you speak so startingly and rash? 75

*Othello:* Is 't lost? Is 't gone? Speak, is 't out o' the way?

*Desdemona:* Heaven bless us!

*Othello:* Say you?

*Desdemona:* It is not lost; but what an if it were?

*Othello:* How? 80

*Desdemona:* I say it is not lost.

*Othello:*                                    Fetch 't, let me see 't.

*Desdemona:* Why, so I can, sir, but I will not now.

This is a trick to put me from my suit.

Pray you, let Cassio be received again.

*Othello:* Fetch me the handkerchief! My mind misgives. 85

*Desdemona:* Come, come,

You'll never meet a more sufficient man.

*Othello:* The handkerchief!

*Desdemona:*                         I pray, talk me of Cassio.

*Othello:* The handkerchief!

*Desdemona:*                         A man that all his time

Hath founded his good fortunes on your love, 90

Shared dangers with you—

*Othello:* The handkerchief!

*Desdemona:* I' faith, you are to blame.

*Othello:* Zounds!                                    *Exit Othello.*

*Emilia:* Is not this man jealous? 95

*Desdemona:* I ne'er saw this before.

Sure, there's some wonder in this handkerchief.

I am most unhappy in the loss of it.

*Emilia:* 'Tis not a year or two shows us a man.

They are all but stomachs, and we all but food; 100

They eat us hungerly, and when they are full

They belch us.

*Enter Iago and Cassio.*

Look you, Cassio and my husband.

*Iago [to Cassio]:* There is no other way; 'tis she must do 't.

And, lo, the happiness! Go and importune her.

*Desdemona:* How now, good Cassio? What's the news with you? 105

*Cassio:* Madam, my former suit. I do beseech you

---

75 *startingly and rash* disjointedly and impetuously, excitedly    76 *out o' the way* lost, misplaced
79 *an if* if    87 *sufficient* able, complete    88 *talk* talk to    89 *all his time* throughout his career
99 *'Tis . . . man* i.e., you can't really know a man even in a year or two of experience (?), or, real men
come along seldom (?)    100 *but* nothing but    101 *hungerly* hungrily    104 *the happiness* in
happy time, fortunately met

That by your virtuous means I may again
Exist and be a member of his love
Whom I, with all the office of my heart,
Entirely honor. I would not be delayed.                                    110
If my offense be of such mortal kind
That nor my service past, nor present sorrows,
Nor purposed merit in futurity
Can ransom me into his love again,
But to know so must be my benefit;                                         115
So shall I clothe me in a forced content,
And shut myself up in some other course,
To fortune's alms.
Desdemona:              Alas, thrice-gentle Cassio,
My advocation is not now in tune.
My lord is not my lord; nor should I know him,                            120
Were he in favor as in humor altered.
So help me every spirit sanctified
As I have spoken for you all my best
And stood within the blank of his displeasure
For my free speech! You must awhile be patient.                          125
What I can do I will, and more I will
Than for myself I dare. Let that suffice you.
Iago: Is my lord angry?
Emilia:              He went hence but now,
And certainly in strange unquietness.
Iago: Can he be angry? I have seen the cannon                             130
When it hath blown his ranks into the air,
And like the devil from his very arm
Puffed his own brother—and is he angry?
Something of moment then. I will go meet him.
There's matter in 't indeed, if he be angry.                             135
Desdemona: I prithee, do so.                                    Exit [Iago].
                    Something, sure, of state,
Either from Venice, or some unhatched practice
Made demonstrable here in Cyprus to him,
Hath puddled his clear spirit; and in such cases
Men's natures wrangle with inferior things,                              140
Though great ones are their object. 'Tis even so;

107 *virtuous* efficacious      109 *office* loyal service      111 *mortal* fatal      112 *nor . . . nor* neither . . .
nor      115 *But . . . benefit* merely to know that my case is hopeless will have to content me (and
will be better than uncertainty)      117 *shut . . . in* confine myself to      118 *To fortune's alms*
throwing myself on the mercy of fortune      119 *advocation* advocacy      121 *favor* appearance.
*humor* mood      124 *within the blank* within point-blank range. (The *blank* is the center of the target.)      134 *of moment* of immediate importance, momentous      136 *of state* concerning state
affairs      137 *unhatched practice* as yet unexecuted or undiscovered plot      139 *puddled* muddied

For let our finger ache, and it indues
Our other, healthful members even to a sense
Of pain. Nay, we must think men are not gods,
Nor of them look for such observancy                                    145
As fits the bridal. Beshrew me much, Emilia,
I was, unhandsome warrior as I am,
Arraigning his unkindness with my soul;
But now I find I had suborned the witness,
And he's indicted falsely.
Emilia:                          Pray heaven it be                        150
    State matters, as you think, and no conception
    Nor no jealous toy concerning you.
Desdemona: Alas the day! I never gave him cause.
Emilia: But jealous souls will not be answered so;
    They are not ever jealous for the cause,                           155
    But jealous for they're jealous. It is a monster
    Begot upon itself, born on itself.
Desdemona: Heaven keep that monster from Othello's mind!
Emilia: Lady, amen.
Desdemona: I will go seek him. Cassio, walk hereabout.                    160
    If I do find him fit, I'll move your suit
    And seek to effect it to my uttermost.
Cassio: I humbly thank your ladyship.

    *Exit [Desdemona with Emilia].*

    *Enter Bianca.*

Bianca: Save you, friend Cassio!
Cassio:                          What make you from home?
    How is 't with you, my most fair Bianca?                           165
    I' faith, sweet love, I was coming to your house.
Bianca: And I was going to your lodging, Cassio.
    What, keep a week away? Seven days and nights?
    Eightscore-eight hours? And lovers' absent hours
    More tedious than the dial eightscore times?                       170
    O weary reckoning!
Cassio:                          Pardon me, Bianca.
    I have this while with leaden thoughts been pressed;
    But I shall, in a more continuate time,

---

142 *indues* brings to the same condition    145 *observancy* attentiveness    146 *bridal* wedding (when a bridegroom is newly attentive to his bride).    *Beshrew me* (A mild oath.)    147 *unhandsome* insufficient, unskillful    148 *with* before the bar of    149 *suborned the witness* induced the witness to give false testimony    152 *toy* fancy    156 *for* because    157 *Begot upon itself* generated solely from itself    164 *Save* God save.    *make* do    169 *Eightscore-eight* one hundred sixty-eight, the number of hours in a week    170 *the dial* a complete revolution of the clock    173 *continuate* uninterrupted

Strike off this score of absence. Sweet Bianca,

*[giving her Desdemona's handkerchief]*

Take me this work out.

Bianca:                               O Cassio, whence came this?          175
This is some token from a newer friend.
To the felt absence now I feel a cause.
Is 't come to this? Well, well.

Cassio:                               Go to, woman!
Throw your vile guesses in the devil's teeth,
From whence you have them. You are jealous now          180
That this is from some mistress, some remembrance.
No, by my faith, Bianca.

Bianca:                               Why, whose is it?

Cassio: I know not, neither. I found it in my chamber.
I like the work well. Ere it be demanded—
As like enough it will—I would have it copied.          185
Take it and do 't, and leave me for this time.

Bianca: Leave you? Wherefore?

Cassio: I do attend here on the General,
And think it no addition, nor my wish,
To have him see me womaned.          190

Bianca: Why, I pray you?

Cassio: Not that I love you not.

Bianca: But that you do not love me.
I pray you, bring me on the way a little,
And say if I shall see you soon at night.          195

Cassio: 'Tis but a little way that I can bring you,
For I attend here; but I'll see you soon.

Bianca: 'Tis very good. I must be circumstanced.

*Exeunt omnes.*

# Act IV

### Scene I [Before the Citadel.]

*Enter Othello and Iago.*

Iago: Will you think so?

Othello:                               Think so, Iago?

Iago:                                              What,
To kiss in private?

---

174 *Strike . . . score* settle this account      175 *Take . . . out* copy this embroidery for me      176
*friend* mistress      184 *demanded* inquired for      185 *like* likely      189 *addition* i.e., addition to my
reputation      194 *bring* accompany      198 *be circumstanced* be governed by circumstance, yield to
your conditions

*Othello:*                    An unauthorized kiss!

*Iago:* Or to be naked with her friend in bed
    An hour or more, not meaning any harm?

*Othello:* Naked in bed, Iago, and not mean harm?                    5
    It is hypocrisy against the devil.
    They that mean virtuously and yet do so,
    The devil their virtue tempts, and they tempt heaven.

*Iago:* If they do nothing, 'tis a venial slip.
    But if I give my wife a handkerchief—                    10

*Othello:* What then?

*Iago:* Why then, 'tis hers, my lord, and being hers,
    She may, I think, bestow 't on any man.

*Othello:* She is protectress of her honor too.
    May she give that?                    15

*Iago:* Her honor is an essence that's not seen;
    They have it very oft that have it not.
    But, for the handkerchief—

*Othello:* By heaven, I would most gladly have forgot it.
    Thou saidst—O, it comes o'er my memory                    20
    As doth the raven o'er the infectious house,
    Boding to all—he had my handkerchief.

*Iago:* Ay, what of that?

*Othello:*                    That's not so good now.

*Iago:*                                        What
    If I had said I had seen him do you wrong?
    Or heard him say—as knaves be such abroad,                    25
    Who having, by their own importunate suit,
    Or voluntary dotage of some mistress,
    Convincèd or supplied them, cannot choose
    But they must blab—

*Othello:*                    Hath he said anything?

*Iago:* He hath, my lord; but, be you well assured,                    30
    No more than he'll unswear.

*Othello:*                    What hath he said?

*Iago:* Faith, that he did—I know not what he did.

*Othello:* What? What?

*Iago:* Lie—

*Othello:*    With her?

*Iago:*                    With her, on her; what you will.

---

9 *venial* pardonable    17 *They have it* i.e., they enjoy a reputation for it    21 *raven . . . house*
(Allusion to the belief that the raven hovered over a house of sickness or infection, such as one visit-
ed by the plague.)    25 *abroad* around about    27 *voluntary dotage* willing infatuation    28
*Convincèd or supplied* seduced or sexually gratified

*Othello:* Lie with her? Lie on her? We say "lie on her" when they belie her. Lie   35
    with her? Zounds, that's fulsome.—Handkerchief—confessions—handker-
    chief!—To confess and be hanged for his labor—first to be hanged and then
    to confess.—I tremble at it. Nature would not invest herself in such shadow-
    ing passion without some instruction. It is not words that shakes me thus.
    Pish! Noses, ears, and lips.—Is 't possible?—Confess—handkerchief!—O   40
    devil!

    *Falls in a trance.*

*Iago:* Work on,
    My medicine, work! Thus credulous fools are caught,
    And many worthy and chaste dames even thus,
    All guiltless, meet reproach.—What, ho! My lord!   45
    My lord, I say! Othello!

    *Enter Cassio.*

                    How now, Cassio?
*Cassio:* What's the matter?
*Iago:* My lord is fall'n into an epilepsy.
    This is his second fit. He had one yesterday.
*Cassio:* Rub him about the temples.
*Iago:*                    No, forbear.   50
    The lethargy must have his quiet course.
    If not, he foams at mouth, and by and by
    Breaks out to savage madness. Look, he stirs.
    Do you withdraw yourself a little while.
    He will recover straight. When he is gone,   55
    I would on great occasion speak with you.

    *[Exit Cassio.]*

    How is it, General? Have you not hurt your head?
*Othello:* Dost thou mock me?
*Iago:*                  I mock you not, by heaven.
    Would you would bear your fortune like a man!
*Othello:* A hornèd man's a monster and a beast.   60
*Iago:* There's many a beast then in a populous city,
    And many a civil monster.

---

35 *belie* slander    36 *fulsome* foul    37–38 *first . . . to confess* (Othello reverses the proverbial *confess and be hanged*; Cassio is to be given no time to confess before he dies.)    38–39 *Nature . . .
instruction* i.e., without some foundation in fact, nature would not have dressed herself in such an
overwhelming passion that comes over me now and fills my mind with images, or in such a lifelike
fantasy as Cassio had in his dream of lying with Desdemona    39 *words* mere words    51 *lethargy*
coma.  *his* its    56 *on great occasion* on a matter of great importance    58 *mock me* (Othello
takes Iago's question about hurting his head to be a mocking reference to the cuckold's horns.)
62 *civil* i.e., dwelling in a city

*Othello:* Did he confess it?

*Iago:* Good sir, be a man.
> Think every bearded fellow that's but yoked                65
> May draw with you. There's millions now alive
> That nightly lie in those unproper beds
> Which they dare swear peculiar. Your case is better.
> O, 'tis the spite of hell, the fiend's arch-mock,
> To lip a wanton in a secure couch                          70
> And to suppose her chaste! No, let me know,
> And knowing what I am, I know what she shall be.

*Othello:* O, thou art wise. 'Tis certain.

*Iago:* Stand you awhile apart;
> Confine yourself but in a patient list.                    75
> Whilst you were here o'erwhelmèd with your grief—
> A passion most unsuiting such a man—
> Cassio came hither. I shifted him away,
> And laid good 'scuse upon your ecstasy,
> Bade him anon return and here speak with me,               80
> The which he promised. Do but encave yourself
> And mark the fleers, the gibes, and notable scorns
> That dwell in every region of his face;
> For I will make him tell the tale anew,
> Where, how, how oft, how long ago, and when                85
> He hath and is again to cope your wife.
> I say, but mark his gesture. Marry, patience!
> Or I shall say you're all-in-all in spleen,
> And nothing of a man.

*Othello:*                         Dost thou hear, Iago?
> I will be found most cunning in my patience;               90
> But—dost thou hear?—most bloody.

*Iago:*                                  That's not amiss;
> But yet keep time in all. Will you withdraw?

*[Othello stands apart.]*

> Now will I question Cassio of Bianca,
> A huswife that by selling her desires

---

65 *yoked* (1) married (2) put into the yoke of infamy and cuckoldry     66 *draw with you* pull as you do, like oxen who are yoked, i.e., share your fate as cuckold     67 *unproper* not exclusively their own     68 *peculiar* private, their own.     *better* i.e., because you know the truth     70 *lip* kiss. *secure* free from suspicion     72 *what I am* i.e., a cuckold.     *she shall be* will happen to her     75 *in . . . list* within the bounds of patience     78 *shifted him away* used a dodge to get rid of him     79 *ecstasy* trance     81 *encave* conceal     82 *fleers* sneers.     *notable* obvious     86 *cope* encounter with, have sex with     88 *all-in-all in spleen* utterly governed by passionate impulses     92 *keep time* keep yourself steady (as in music)     94 *huswife* hussy

Buys herself bread and clothes. It is a creature                                    95
That dotes on Cassio—as 'tis the strumpet's plague
To beguile many and be beguiled by one.
He, when he hears of her, cannot restrain
From the excess of laughter. Here he comes.

*Enter Cassio.*

As he shall smile, Othello shall go mad;                                            100
And his unbookish jealousy must conster
Poor Cassio's smiles, gestures, and light behaviors
Quite in the wrong.—How do you now, Lieutenant?
*Cassio:* The worser that you give me the addition
   Whose want even kills me.                                                        105
*Iago:* Ply Desdemona well and you are sure on 't.
   [*Speaking lower.*] Now, if this suit lay in Bianca's power,
   How quickly should you speed!
*Cassio [laughing]:* Alas, poor caitiff!
*Othello [aside]:* Look how he laughs already!                                       110
*Iago:* I never knew a woman love man so.
*Cassio:* Alas, poor rogue! I think, i' faith, she loves me.
*Othello:* Now he denies it faintly, and laughs it out.
*Iago:* Do you hear, Cassio?
*Othello:*                        Now he importunes him
   To tell it o'er. Go to! Well said, well said.                                     115
*Iago:* She gives it out that you shall marry her.
   Do you intend it?
*Cassio:* Ha, ha, ha!
*Othello:* Do you triumph, Roman? Do you triumph?
*Cassio:* I marry her? What? A customer? Prithee, bear some charity to my wit; do     120
   not think it so unwholesome. Ha, ha, ha!
*Othello:* So, so, so, so! They laugh that win.
*Iago:* Faith, the cry goes that you shall marry her.
*Cassio:* Prithee, say true.
*Iago:* I am a very villain else.                                                    125
*Othello:* Have you scored me? Well.
*Cassio:* This is the monkey's own giving out. She is persuaded I will marry her out
   of her own love and flattery, not out of my promise.

98 *restrain* refrain    101 *unbookish* uninstructed.    *conster* construe    104 *addition* title    105
*Whose want* the lack of which    109 *caitiff* wretch    115 *Go to* (An expression of remonstrance.)
*Well said* well done    119 *Roman* (The Romans were noted for their *triumphs* or triumphal processions.)    120 *customer* i.e., prostitute    *bear . . . wit* be more charitable to my judgment    122
*They . . . win* i.e., they that laugh last laugh best    123 *cry* rumor    125 *I . . . else* call me a complete rogue if I'm not telling the truth    126 *scored me* scored off me, beaten me, made up my reckoning, branded me    128 *flattery* self-flattery, self-deception

*Othello:* Iago beckons me. Now he begins the story.

*Cassio:* She was here even now; she haunts me in every place. I was the other day  130
talking on the seabank with certain Venetians, and thither comes the
bauble, and, by this hand, she falls me thus about my neck—

*[He embraces Iago.]*

*Othello:* Crying, "O dear Cassio!" as it were; his gesture imports it.

*Cassio:* So hangs and lolls and weep upon me, so shakes and pulls me. Ha, ha, ha!

*Othello:* Now he tells how she plucked him to my chamber. O, I see that nose of  135
yours, but not that dog I shall throw it to.

*Cassio:* Well, I must leave her company.

*Iago:* Before me, look where she comes.

*Enter Bianca [with Othello's handkerchief].*

*Cassio:* 'Tis such another fitchew! Marry, a perfumed one.—What do you mean
by this haunting of me?  140

*Bianca:* Let the devil and his dam haunt you! What did you mean by that same
handkerchief you gave me even now? I was a fine fool to take it. I must take
out the work? A likely piece of work, that you should find it in your chamber
and know not who left it there! This is some minx's token, and I must take
out the work? There; give it your hobbyhorse. *[She gives him the handkerchief.]*  145
Wheresoever you had it, I'll take out no work on 't.

*Cassio:* How now, my sweet Bianca? How now? How now?

*Othello:* By heaven, that should be my handkerchief!

*Bianca:* If you'll come to supper tonight, you may; if you will not, come when you
are next prepared for.  150

*Exit.*

*Iago:* After her, after her.

*Cassio:* Faith, I must. She'll rail in the streets else.

*Iago:* Will you sup there?

*Cassio:* Faith, I intend so.

*Iago:* Well, I may chance to see you, for I would very fain speak with you.  155

*Cassio:* Prithee, come. Will you?

*Iago:* Go to. Say no more.  *[Exit Cassio.]*

*Othello [advancing]:* How shall I murder him, Iago?

*Iago:* Did you perceive how he laughed at his vice?

---

129 *beckons* signals  131 *seabank* seashore  132 *bauble* plaything  *by this hand* I make my vow
136 *not . . . to* (Othello imagines himself cutting off Cassio's nose and throwing it to a dog.)  138
*Before me* i.e., on my soul  139 *'Tis . . . fitchew* what a polecat she is! Just like all the others.
(Polecats were often compared with prostitutes because of their rank smell and presumed lechery.)
141 *dam* mother  143 *A likely . . . work* a fine story  145 *hobbyhorse* harlot  148 *should be*
must be  149–150 *when . . . for* when I'm ready for you (i.e., never)  157 *Go to* (An expression
of remonstrance.)

*Othello:* O, Iago! 160

*Iago:* And did you see the handkerchief?

*Othello:* Was that mine?

*Iago:* Yours, by this hand. And to see how he prizes the foolish woman your wife! She gave it him, and he hath given it his whore.

*Othello:* I would have him nine years a-killing. A fine woman! A fair woman! A 165 sweet woman!

*Iago:* Nay, you must forget that.

*Othello:* Ay, let her rot and perish, and be damned tonight, for she shall not live. No, my heart is turned to stone; I strike it, and it hurts my hand. O, the world hath not a sweeter creature! She might lie by an emperor's side and 170 command him tasks.

*Iago:* Nay, that's not your way.

*Othello:* Hang her! I do but say what she is. So delicate with her needle! An admirable musician! O, she will sing the savageness out of a bear. Of so high and plenteous wit and invention! 175

*Iago:* She's the worse for all this.

*Othello:* O, a thousand, a thousand times! And then, of so gentle a condition!

*Iago:* Ay, too gentle.

*Othello:* Nay, that's certain. But yet the pity of it, Iago! O, Iago, the pity of it, Iago! 180

*Iago:* If you are so fond over her iniquity, give her patent to offend, for if it touch not you it comes near nobody.

*Othello:* I will chop her into messes. Cuckold me?

*Iago:* O, 'tis foul in her.

*Othello:* With mine officer? 185

*Iago:* That's fouler.

*Othello:* Get me some poison, Iago, this night. I'll not expostulate with her, lest her body and beauty unprovide my mind again. This night, Iago.

*Iago:* Do it not with poison. Strangle her in her bed, even the bed she hath contaminated. 190

*Othello:* Good, good! The justice of it pleases. Very good.

*Iago:* And for Cassio, let me be his undertaker. You shall hear more by midnight.

*Othello:* Excellent good. [*A trumpet within.*] What trumpet is that same?

*Iago:* I warrant, something from Venice.

*Enter Lodovico, Desdemona, and attendants.*

'Tis Lodovico. This comes from the Duke. 195
See, your wife's with him.

---

172 *your way* i.e., the way you should think of her    175 *invention* imagination    177 *gentle a condition* wellborn and well-bred    178 *gentle* generous, yielding (to other men)    181 *fond* foolish. *patent* license    183 *messes* portions of meat, i.e., bits    188 *unprovide* weaken, render unfit    192 *be his undertaker* undertake to dispatch him

*Lodovico:* God save you, worthy General!

*Othello:*                             With all my heart, sir.

*Lodovico [giving him a letter]:* The Duke and the senators of Venice greet you.

*Othello:* I kiss the instrument of their pleasures.

    *[He opens the letter, and reads.]*

*Desdemona:* And what's the news, good cousin Lodovico?         200

*Iago:* I am very glad to see you, signor.

    Welcome to Cyprus.

*Lodovico:* I thank you. How does Lieutenant Cassio?

*Iago:* Lives, sir.

*Desdemona:* Cousin, there's fall'n between him and my lord         205

    An unkind breach; but you shall make all well.

*Othello:* Are you sure of that?

*Desdemona:* My lord?

*Othello [reads]:* "This fail you not to do, as you will—"

*Lodovico:* He did not call; he's busy in the paper.         210

    Is there division twixt my lord and Cassio?

*Desdemona:* A most unhappy one. I would do much

    T' atone them, for the love I bear to Cassio.

*Othello:* Fire and brimstone!

*Desdemona:* My lord?         215

*Othello:* Are you wise?

*Desdemona:* What, is he angry?

*Lodovico:*                     Maybe the letter moved him;

    For, as I think, they do command him home,

    Deputing Cassio in his government.

*Desdemona:* By my troth, I am glad on 't.         220

*Othello:* Indeed?

*Desdemona:* My lord?

*Othello:* I am glad to see you mad.

*Desdemona:* Why, sweet Othello—

*Othello [striking her]:* Devil!         225

*Desdemona:* I have not deserved this.

*Lodovico:* My lord, this would not be believed in Venice,

    Though I should swear I saw 't. 'Tis very much.

    Make her amends; she weeps.

*Othello:*                    O devil, devil!

    If that the earth could teem with woman's tears,         230

---

197 *With all my heart* i.e., I thank you most heartily    206 *unkind* unnatural, contrary to their natures; hurtful    213 *atone* reconcile    219 *government* office    220 *on 't* of it    223 *I am . . . mad* i.e., I am glad to see that you are insane enough to rejoice in Cassio's promotion (? Othello bitterly plays on Desdemona's *I am glad.*)    228 *very much* too much, outrageous    230 *teem* breed, be impregnated

Each drop she falls would prove a crocodile.
Out of my sight!
*Desdemona:*         I will not stay to offend you. *[Going.]*
*Lodovico:* Truly, an obedient lady.
    I do beseech your lordship, call her back.
*Othello:* Mistress!                                   235
*Desdemona [returning]:* My lord?
*Othello:* What would you with her, sir?
*Lodovico:* Who, I, my lord?
*Othello:* Ay, you did wish that I would make her turn.
    Sir, she can turn, and turn, and yet go on          240
    And turn again; and she can weep, sir, weep;
    And she's obedient, as you say, obedient,
    Very obedient.—Proceed you in your tears.—
    Concerning this, sir—O well-painted passion!—
    I am commanded home.—Get you away;         245
    I'll send for you anon.—Sir, I obey the mandate
    And will return to Venice.—Hence, avaunt!

    *[Exit Desdemona.]*

    Cassio shall have my place. And, sir, tonight
    I do entreat that we may sup together.
    You are welcome, sir, to Cyprus.—Goats and monkeys!    *Exit.*  250
*Lodovico:* Is this the noble Moor whom our full Senate
    Call all in all sufficient? Is this the nature
    Whom passion could not shake? Whose solid virtue
    The shot of accident nor dart of chance
    Could neither graze nor pierce?
*Iago:*                      He is much changed.         255
*Lodovico:* Are his wits safe? Is he not light of brain?
*Iago:* He's that he is. I may not breathe my censure
    What he might be. If what he might he is not,
    I would to heaven he were!
*Lodovico:*               What, strike his wife?
*Iago:* Faith, that was not so well; yet would I knew        260
    That stroke would prove the worst!

---

231 *falls* lets fall.    *crocodile* (Crocodiles were supposed to weep hypocritical tears for their victims.)
237 *What . . . sir* (Othello implies that Desdemona is pliant and will do a *turn*, lines 239–241, for any
man.)    242 *obedient* (With much the same sexual connotation as *turn* in lines 239–241.)    244
*passion* i.e., grief    250 *Goats and monkeys* (See Act III, Scene III, line 419.)    257–259 *I may
. . . were* i.e., I dare not venture an opinion as to whether he's of unsound mind, as you suggest, but, if
he isn't, then it might be better to wish he were in fact insane, since only that could excuse his wild
behavior

Lodovico:                          Is it his use?
   Or did the letters work upon his blood
   And new-create his fault?
Iago:                               Alas, alas!
   It is not honesty in me to speak
   What I have seen and known. You shall observe him,                    265
   And his own courses will denote him so
   That I may save my speech. Do but go after,
   And mark how he continues.
Lodovico: I am sorry that I am deceived in him.                    *Exeunt.*

### Scene II [The Citadel.]

   *Enter Othello and Emilia.*

Othello: You have seen nothing then?
Emilia: Nor ever heard, nor ever did suspect.
Othello: Yes, you have seen Cassio and she together.
Emilia: But then I saw no harm, and then I heard
   Each syllable that breath made up between them.                    5
Othello: What, did they never whisper?
Emilia: Never, my lord.
Othello: Nor send you out o' the way?
Emilia: Never.
Othello: To fetch her fan, her gloves, her mask, nor nothing?                    10
Emilia: Never, my lord.
Othello: That's strange.
Emilia: I durst, my lord, to wager she is honest,
   Lay down my soul at stake. If you think other,
   Remove your thought; it doth abuse your bosom.                    15
   If any wretch have put this in your head,
   Let heaven requite it with the serpent's curse!
   For if she be not honest, chaste, and true,
   There's no man happy; the purest of their wives
   Is foul as slander.
Othello:                          Bid her come hither. Go.                    20

   *Exit Emilia.*

261 *use* custom     262 *blood* passions     266 *courses will denote* actions will reveal     14 *at stake* as
the wager     15 *abuse your bosom* deceive you     17 *the serpent's curse* the curse pronounced by
God on the serpent for deceiving Eve, just as some man has done to Othello and Desdemona. (See
Genesis 3:14.)

She says enough; yet she's a simple bawd
That cannot say as much. This is a subtle whore,
A closet lock and key of villainous secrets.
And yet she'll kneel and pray; I have seen her do 't.

*Enter Desdemona and Emilia.*

*Desdemona:* My lord, what is your will?                                    25
*Othello:* Pray you, chuck, come hither.
*Desdemona:* What is your pleasure?
*Othello:*                     Let me see your eyes.
      Look in my face.
*Desdemona:*            What horrible fancy's this?
*Othello [to Emilia]:* Some of your function, mistress.
      Leave procreants alone and shut the door;                            30
      Cough or cry "hem" if anybody come.
      Your mystery, your mystery! Nay, dispatch.

*Exit Emilia.*

*Desdemona [kneeling]:* Upon my knees, what doth your speech import?
      I understand a fury in your words,
      But not the words.                                                   35
*Othello:* Why, what art thou?
*Desdemona:*                   Your wife, my lord, your true
      And loyal wife.
*Othello:*             Come, swear it, damn thyself,
      Lest, being like one of heaven, the devils themselves
      Should fear to seize thee. Therefore be double damned:
      Swear thou art honest.
*Desdemona:*                  Heaven doth truly know it.                    40
*Othello:* Heaven truly knows that thou art false as hell.
*Desdemona:* To whom, my lord? With whom? How am I false?
*Othello [weeping]:* Ah, Desdemon! Away, away, away!
*Desdemona:* Alas the heavy day! Why do you weep?
      Am I the motive of these tears, my lord?                             45
      If haply you my father do suspect
      An instrument of this your calling back,
      Lay not your blame on me. If you have lost him,
      I have lost him too.

---

21–22 *she's . . . much* i.e., any procuress or go-between who couldn't make up as plausible a story as
Emilia's would have to be pretty stupid       22 *This* i.e., Desdemona       23 *closet lock and key* i.e.,
concealer       29 *Some . . . function* i.e., practice your chosen profession, that of bawd (by guarding
the door)       30 *procreants* mating couples       32 *mystery* trade, occupation       38 *being . . . heaven*
looking like an angel       45 *motive* cause

*Othello:*                    Had it pleased heaven
   To try me with affliction, had they rained                                50
   All kinds of sores and shames on my bare head,
   Steeped me in poverty to the very lips,
   Given to captivity me and my utmost hopes,
   I should have found in some place of my soul
   A drop of patience. But, alas, to make me                                 55
   A fixèd figure for the time of scorn
   To point his slow and moving finger at!
   Yet could I bear that too, well, very well.
   But there where I have garnered up my heart,
   Where either I must live or bear no life,                                 60
   The fountain from the which my current runs
   Or else dries up—to be discarded thence!
   Or keep it as a cistern for foul toads
   To knot and gender in! Turn thy complexion there,
   Patience, thou young and rose-lipped cherubin—                           65
   Ay, there look grim as hell!
*Desdemona:* I hope my noble lord esteems me honest.
*Othello:* O, ay, as summer flies are in the shambles,
   That quicken even with blowing. O thou weed,
   Who art so lovely fair and smell'st so sweet                             70
   That the sense aches at thee, would thou hadst ne'er been born!
*Desdemona:* Alas, what ignorant sin have I committed?
*Othello:* Was this fair paper, this most goodly book,
   Made to write "whore" upon? What committed?
   Committed? O thou public commoner!                                       75
   I should make very forges of my cheeks,
   That would to cinders burn up modesty,
   Did I but speak thy deeds. What committed?
   Heaven stops the nose at it and the moon winks;
   The bawdy wind, that kisses all it meets,                                80
   Is hushed within the hollow mine of earth
   And will not hear 't. What committed?
   Impudent strumpet!

---

50 *they* i.e., heavenly powers    56 *time of scorn* i.e., scornful world    57 *his* its.    *slow and moving finger* i.e., hour hand of the clock, moving so slowly it seems hardly to move at all. (Othello envisages himself as being eternally pointed at by the scornful world as the numbers on a clock are pointed at by the hour hand.)    59 *garnered* stored    61 *fountain* spring    63 *cistern* cesspool    64 *knot* couple.    *gender* engender.    *Turn . . . there* change your color, grow pale, at such a sight    65–66 *Patience . . . hell* (Even Patience, that rose-lipped cherub, will look grim and pale at this spectacle.)    67 *honest* chaste    68 *shambles* slaughterhouse    69 *quicken* come to life.    *with blowing* i.e., with the puffing up of something rotten in which maggots are breeding    72 *ignorant sin* sin in ignorance    75 *commoner* prostitute    79 *winks* closes her eyes. (The moon symbolizes chastity.)    80 *bawdy* kissing one and all    81 *mine* cave (where the winds were thought to dwell)

*Desdemona:*              By heaven, you do me wrong.

*Othello:* Are not you a strumpet?

*Desdemona:* No, as I am a Christian.                                                 85
    If to preserve this vessel for my lord
    From any other foul unlawful touch
    Be not to be a strumpet, I am none.

*Othello:* What, not a whore?

*Desdemona:* No, as I shall be saved.                                                 90

*Othello:* Is 't possible?

*Desdemona:* O, heaven forgive us!

*Othello:*                         I cry you mercy, then.
    I took you for that cunning whore of Venice
    That married with Othello. *[Calling out.]* You, mistress,
    That have the office opposite to Saint Peter                               95
    And keep the gate of hell!

    *Enter Emilia.*

                You, you, ay, you!
    We have done our course. There's money for your pains.     *[He gives money.]*
    I pray you, turn the key and keep our counsel.                    *Exit.*

*Emilia:* Alas, what does this gentleman conceive?
    How do you, madam? How do you, my good lady?                            100

*Desdemona:* Faith, half asleep.

*Emilia:* Good madam, what's the matter with my lord?

*Desdemona:* With who?

*Emilia:* Why, with my lord, madam.

*Desdemona:* Who is thy lord?

*Emilia:*                         He that is yours, sweet lady.                        105

*Desdemona:* I have none. Do not talk to me, Emilia.
    I cannot weep, nor answers have I none
    But what should go by water. Prithee, tonight
    Lay on my bed my wedding sheets, remember;
    And call thy husband hither.                                             110

*Emilia:* Here's a change indeed!                                        *Exit.*

*Desdemona:* 'Tis meet I should be used so, very meet.
    How have I been behaved, that he might stick
    The small'st opinion on my least misuse?

    *Enter Iago and Emilia.*

---

86 *vessel* body     92 *cry you mercy* beg your pardon     97 *course* business (with an indecent suggestion of "trick," turn at sex)     99 *conceive* suppose, think     101 *half asleep* i.e., dazed     108 *go by*
*water* be expressed by tears     112 *meet* fitting     113 *stick* attach     114 *opinion* censure.     *least*
*misuse* slightest misconduct

*Iago:* What is your pleasure, madam? How is 't with you?                          115
*Desdemona:* I cannot tell. Those that do teach young babes
  Do it with gentle means and easy tasks.
  He might have chid me so, for, in good faith,
  I am a child to chiding.
*Iago:* What is the matter, lady?                                                 120
*Emilia:* Alas, Iago, my lord hath so bewhored her,
  Thrown such despite and heavy terms upon her,
  That true hearts cannot bear it.
*Desdemona:* Am I that name, Iago?
*Iago:* What name, fair lady?                                                     125
*Desdemona:* Such as she said my lord did say I was.
*Emilia:* He called her whore. A beggar in his drink
  Could not have laid such terms upon his callet.
*Iago:* Why did he so?
*Desdemona [weeping]:* I do not know. I am sure I am none such.                   130
*Iago:* Do not weep, do not weep. Alas the day!
*Emilia:* Hath she forsook so many noble matches,
  Her father and her country and her friends,
  To be called whore? Would it not make one weep?
*Desdemona:* It is my wretched fortune.
*Iago:*                            Beshrew him for 't!                            135
  How comes this trick upon him?
*Desdemona:*                       Nay, heaven doth know.
*Emilia:* I will be hanged if some eternal villain,
  Some busy and insinuating rogue,
  Some cogging, cozening slave, to get some office,
  Have not devised this slander. I will be hanged else.                          140
*Iago:* Fie, there is no such man. It is impossible.
*Desdemona:* If any such there be, heaven pardon him!
*Emilia:* A halter pardon him! And hell gnaw his bones!
  Why should he call her whore? Who keeps her company?
  What place? What time? What form? What likelihood?                             145
  The Moor's abused by some most villainous knave,
  Some base notorious knave, some scurvy fellow.
  O heaven, that such companions thou'dst unfold,
  And put in every honest hand a whip
  To lash the rascals naked through the world                                   150
  Even from the east to th' west!

---

128 *callet* whore     135 *Beshrew* curse     136 *trick* strange behavior, delusion     137 *eternal* inveterate     138 *insinuating* ingratiating, fawning, wheedling     139 *cogging* cheating.     *cozening*
defrauding     143 *halter* hangman's noose     145 *form* appearance, circumstance     148 *that*
would that.     *companions* fellows.     *unfold* expose

*Iago:*                                    Speak within door.

*Emilia:* O, fie upon them! Some such squire he was

That turned your wit the seamy side without

And made you to suspect me with the Moor.

*Iago:* You are a fool. Go to.

*Desdemona:*                    Alas, Iago,                                                      155

What shall I do to win my lord again?

Good friend, go to him; for, by this light of heaven,

I know not how I lost him. Here I kneel. *[She kneels.]*

If e'er my will did trespass 'gainst his love,

Either in discourse of thought or actual deed,                           160

Or that mine eyes, mine ears, or any sense

Delighted them in any other form;

Or that I do not yet, and ever did,

And ever will—though he do shake me off

To beggarly divorcement—love him dearly,                              165

Comfort forswear me! Unkindness may do much,

And his unkindness may defeat my life,

But never taint my love. I cannot say "whore."

It does abhor me now I speak the word;

To do the act that might the addition earn                                170

Not the world's mass of vanity could make me.

*[She rises.]*

*Iago:* I pray you, be content. 'Tis but his humor.

The business of the state does him offense,

And he does chide with you.

*Desdemona:* If 'twere no other—                                                    175

*Iago:* It is but so, I warrant.                                          *[Trumpets within.]*

Hark, how these instruments summon you to supper!

The messengers of Venice stays the meat.

Go in, and weep not. All things shall be well.

*Exeunt Desdemona and Emilia.*

*Enter Roderigo.*

How now, Roderigo?                                                                    180

*Roderigo:* I do not find that thou deal'st justly with me.

---

151 *within door* i.e., not so loud    152 *squire* fellow    153 *seamy side without* wrong side out
155 *Go to* i.e., that's enough    160 *discourse of thought* process of thinking    161 *that* if. (Also in
line 163.)    162 *Delighted them* took delight    163 *yet* still    166 *Comfort forswear* may heavenly comfort forsake    167 *defeat* destroy    169 *abhor* (1) fill me with abhorrence (2) make me
whorelike    170 *addition* title    171 *vanity* showy splendor    172 *humor* mood    178 *stays the
meat* are waiting to dine

*Iago:* What in the contrary?

*Roderigo:* Every day thou daff'st me with some device, Iago, and rather, as it seems to me now, keep'st from me all conveniency than suppliest me with the least advantage of hope. I will indeed no longer endure it, nor am I yet persuaded 185 to put up in peace what already I have foolishly suffered.

*Iago:* Will you hear me, Roderigo?

*Roderigo:* Faith, I have heard too much, for your words and performances are no kin together.

*Iago:* You charge me most unjustly. 190

*Roderigo:* With naught but truth. I have wasted myself out of my means. The jewels you have had from me to deliver Desdemona would half have corrupted a votarist. You have told me she hath received them and returned me expectations and comforts of sudden respect and acquaintance, but I find none.

*Iago:* Well, go to, very well. 195

*Roderigo:* "Very well"! "Go to"! I cannot go to, man, nor 'tis not very well. By this hand, I think it is scurvy, and begin to find myself fopped in it.

*Iago:* Very well.

*Roderigo:* I tell you 'tis not very well. I will make myself known to Desdemona. If she will return me my jewels, I will give over my suit and repent my unlawful 200 solicitation; if not, assure yourself I will seek satisfaction of you.

*Iago:* You have said now?

*Roderigo:* Ay, and said nothing but what I protest intendment of doing.

*Iago:* Why, now I see there's mettle in thee, and even from this instant do build on thee a better opinion than ever before. Give me thy hand, Roderigo. 205 Thou hast taken against me a most just exception; but yet I protest I have dealt most directly in thy affair.

*Roderigo:* It hath not appeared.

*Iago:* I grant indeed it hath not appeared, and your suspicion is not without wit and judgment. But, Roderigo, if thou hast that in thee indeed which I have 210 greater reason to believe now than ever—I mean purpose, courage, and valor—this night show it. If thou the next night following enjoy not Desdemona, take me from this world with treachery and devise engines for my life.

*Roderigo:* Well, what is it? Is it within reason and compass? 215

*Iago:* Sir, there is especial commission come from Venice to depute Cassio in Othello's place.

---

183 *thou daff'st me* you put me off.    *device* excuse, trick    184 *conveniency* advantage, opportunity    185 *advantage* increase    186 *put up* submit to, tolerate    192 *deliver* deliver to    193 *votarist* nun    194 *sudden respect* immediate consideration    196 *I cannot go to* (Roderigo changes Iago's *go to*, an expression urging patience, to *I cannot go to*, "I have no opportunity for success in wooing.")    197 *fopped* fooled, duped    199 *not very well* (Roderigo changes Iago's *very well*, "all right, then," to *not very well*, "not at all good.")    201 *satisfaction* repayment. (The term normally means settling of accounts in a duel.)    202 *You . . . now* have you finished?    203 *intendment* intention    213 *engines for* plots against

*Roderigo:* Is that true? Why, then Othello and Desdemona return again to
Venice.

*Iago:* O, no; he goes into Mauritania and takes away with him the fair Desdemona,   220
unless his abode be lingered here by some accident; wherein none can be so
determinate as the removing of Cassio.

*Roderigo:* How do you mean, removing of him?

*Iago:* Why, by making him uncapable of Othello's place—knocking out his
brains.   225

*Roderigo:* And that you would have me to do?

*Iago:* Ay, if you dare do yourself a profit and a right. He sups tonight with a harlotry, and thither will I go to him. He knows not yet of his honorable fortune. If you will watch his going thence, which I will fashion to fall out
between twelve and one, you may take him at your pleasure. I will be near to   230
second your attempt, and he shall fall between us. Come, stand not amazed
at it, but go along with me. I will show you such a necessity in his death that
you shall think yourself bound to put it on him. It is now high suppertime,
and the night grows to waste. About it.

*Roderigo:* I will hear further reason for this.   235

*Iago:* And you shall be satisfied.                             *Exeunt.*

## Scene III [The Citadel.]

*Enter Othello, Lodovico, Desdemona, Emilia, and attendants.*

*Lodovico:* I do beseech you, sir, trouble yourself no further.

*Othello:* O, pardon me; 'twill do me good to walk.

*Lodovico:* Madam, good night. I humbly thank your ladyship.

*Desdemona:* Your honor is most welcome.

*Othello:*                           Will you walk, sir?
O, Desdemona!   5

*Desdemona:* My lord?

*Othello:* Get you to bed on th' instant. I will be returned forthwith. Dismiss your
attendant there. Look 't be done.

*Desdemona:* I will, my lord.   10

*Exit [Othello, with Lodovico and attendants].*

*Emilia:* How goes it now? He looks gentler than he did.

*Desdemona:* He says he will return incontinent,
And hath commanded me to go to bed,
And bid me to dismiss you.

*Emilia:* Dismiss me?   15

---

222 *determinate* conclusive    227–228 *harlotry* slut    229 *fall out* occur    233 *high* fully    234
*grows to waste* wastes away    12 *incontinent* immediately

*Desdemona:* It was his bidding. Therefore, good Emilia,
  Give me my nightly wearing, and adieu.
  We must not now displease him.
*Emilia:* I would you had never seen him!
*Desdemona:* So would not I. My love doth so approve him          20
  That even his stubbornness, his checks, his frowns—
  Prithee, unpin me—have grace and favor in them.

  *[Emilia prepares Desdemona for bed.]*

*Emilia:* I have laid those sheets you bade me on the bed.
*Desdemona:* All's one. Good faith, how foolish are our minds!     25
  If I do die before thee, prithee shroud me
  In one of these same sheets.
*Emilia:*                    Come, come, you talk.
*Desdemona:* My mother had a maid called Barbary.
  She was in love, and he she loved proved mad
  And did forsake her. She had a song of "Willow."                 30
  An old thing 'twas, but it expressed her fortune,
  And she died singing it. That song tonight
  Will not go from my mind; I have much to do
  But to go hang my head all at one side
  And sing it like poor Barbary. Prithee, dispatch.                35
*Emilia:* Shall I go fetch your nightgown?
*Desdemona:* No, unpin me here.
  This Lodovico is a proper man.
*Emilia:* A very handsome man.
*Desdemona:* He speaks well.                                       40
*Emilia:* I know a lady in Venice would have walked barefoot to a
  touch of his nether lip.
*Desdemona [singing]:*
          "The poor soul sat sighing by a sycamore tree,
          Sing all a green willow;
          Her hand on her bosom, her head on her knee,             45
          Sing willow, willow, willow.
          The fresh streams ran by her and murmured her moans;
          Sing willow, willow, willow;
          Her salt tears fell from her, and softened the stones—"
  Lay by these.                                                    50
          *[Singing.]* "Sing willow, willow, willow—"
  Prithee, hie thee. He'll come anon.

---

21 *stubbornness* roughness.  *checks* rebukes   25 *All's one* all right. It doesn't really matter   27 *talk* i.e., prattle   29 *mad* wild, i.e., faithless   33–34 *I . . . hang* I can scarcely keep myself from hanging   36 *nightgown* dressing gown   38 *proper* handsome   44 *willow* (A conventional emblem of disappointed love.)   52 *hie thee* hurry.   *anon* right away

*[Singing.]* "Sing all a green willow must be my garland.
          Let nobody blame him; his scorn I approve—"
Nay, that's not next.—Hark! Who is 't that knocks?                          55
*Emilia:* It's the wind.
*Desdemona [singing]:* "I called my love false love; but what said he then?
          Sing willow, willow, willow;
          If I court more women, you'll couch with more men."
So, get thee gone. Good night. Mine eyes do itch;                           60
Doth that bode weeping?
*Emilia:*                              'Tis neither here nor there.
*Desdemona:* I have heard it said so. O, these men, these men!
Dost thou in conscience think—tell me, Emilia—
That there be women do abuse their husbands
In such gross kind?
*Emilia:*                    There be some such, no question.                65
*Desdemona:* Wouldst thou do such a deed for all the world?
*Emilia:* Why, would not you?
*Desdemona:*                        No, by this heavenly light!
*Emilia:* Nor I neither by this heavenly light;
I might do 't as well i' the dark.
*Desdemona:* Wouldst thou do such a deed for all the world?                 70
*Emilia:* The world's a huge thing. It is a great price
For a small vice.
*Desdemona:* Good troth, I think thou wouldst not.
*Emilia:* By my troth, I think I should, and undo 't when I had done. Marry, I
would not do such a thing for a joint ring, nor for measures of lawn, nor for   75
gowns, petticoats, nor caps, nor any petty exhibition. But for all the whole
world! Uds pity, who would not make her husband a cuckold to make him a
monarch? I should venture purgatory for 't.
*Desdemona:* Beshrew me if I would do such a wrong
For the whole world.                                                        80
*Emilia:* Why, the wrong is but a wrong i' the world, and having the world for your
labor, 'tis a wrong in your own world, and you might quickly make it right.
*Desdemona:* I do not think there is any such woman.
*Emilia:* Yes, a dozen, and as many
To th' vantage as would store the world they played for.                    85
But I do think it is their husbands' faults
If wives do fall. Say that they slack their duties
And pour our treasures into foreign laps,
Or else break out in peevish jealousies,

---

64 *abuse* deceive    75 *joint ring* a ring made in separate halves.    *lawn* fine linen    76 *exhibition* gift    77 *Uds* God's    85 *To th' vantage* in addition, to boot.    *store* populate.    *played* (1) gambled (2) sported sexually    87 *duties* marital duties    88 *pour . . . laps* i.e., are unfaithful, give what is rightfully ours (semen) to other women

Throwing restraint upon us? Or say they strike us, 90
Or scant our former having in despite?
Why, we have galls, and though we have some grace,
Yet have we some revenge. Let husbands know
Their wives have sense like them. They see, and smell,
And have their palates both for sweet and sour, 95
As husbands have. What is it that they do
When they change us for others? Is it sport?
I think it is. And doth affection breed it?
I think it doth. Is 't frailty that thus errs?
It is so, too. And have not we affections, 100
Desires for sport, and frailty, as men have?
Then let them use us well; else let them know,
The ills we do, their ills instruct us so.
*Desdemona*: Good night, good night. God me such uses send
Not to pick bad from bad, but by bad mend! 105

*Exeunt.*

# ACT V

### Scene I [*A Street in Cyprus.*]

*Enter Iago and Roderigo.*

*Iago*: Here stand behind this bulk. Straight will he come.
Wear thy good rapier bare, and put it home.
Quick, quick! Fear nothing. I'll be at thy elbow.
It makes us or it mars us. Think on that,
And fix most firm thy resolution. 5
*Roderigo*: Be near at hand. I may miscarry in 't.
*Iago*: Here, at thy hand. Be bold, and take thy stand.

[*Iago stands aside. Roderigo conceals himself.*]

*Roderigo*: I have no great devotion to the deed;
And yet he hath given me satisfying reasons.
'Tis but a man gone. Forth, my sword! He dies. 10

[*He draws.*]

---

90 *Throwing . . . us* i.e., jealously restricting our freedom to see other men    91 *scant . . . despite* reduce our allowance to spite us    92 *have galls* i.e., are capable of resenting injury and insult    94 *sense* physical sense    97 *sport* sexual pastime    98 *affection* passion    104 *uses* habit, practice    105 *Not . . . mend* i.e., not to learn bad conduct from others' badness (as Emilia has suggested women learn from men), but to mend my ways by perceiving what badness is, making spiritual benefit out of evil and adversity    1 *bulk* framework projecting from the front of a shop    2 *bare* unsheathed

*Iago*: I have rubbed this young quat almost to the sense,
　　And he grows angry. Now, whether he kill Cassio
　　Or Cassio him, or each do kill the other,
　　Every way makes my gain. Live Roderigo,
　　He calls me to a restitution large　　　　　　　　　　　　　　　15
　　Of gold and jewels that I bobbed from him
　　As gifts to Desdemona.
　　It must not be. If Cassio do remain,
　　He hath a daily beauty in his life
　　That makes me ugly; and besides, the Moor　　　　　　　　20
　　May unfold me to him; there stand I in much peril.
　　No, he must die. Be 't so. I hear him coming.

　　*Enter Cassio.*

*Roderigo [coming forth]:* I know his gait, 'tis he.—Villain, thou diest!

　　*[He attacks Cassio.]*

*Cassio*: That thrust had been mine enemy indeed,
　　But that my coat is better than thou know'st.　　　　　　　25
　　I will make proof of thine.

　　*[He draws, and wounds Roderigo.]*

*Roderigo*:　　　　　　　　　　　O, I am slain!　　　　　　　　　　*[He falls.]*

　　*[Iago, from behind, wounds Cassio in the leg, and exit.]*

*Cassio*: I am maimed forever. Help, ho! Murder! Murder!

　　*Enter Othello.*

*Othello*: The voice of Cassio! Iago keeps his word.
*Roderigo*: O, villain that I am!
*Othello*: It is even so.　　　　　　　　　　　　　　　　　　　　　30
*Cassio*: O, help, ho! Light! A surgeon!
*Othello*: 'Tis he. O brave Iago, honest and just,
　　That hast such noble sense of thy friend's wrong!
　　Thou teachest me. Minion, your dear lies dead,
　　And your unblest fate hies. Strumpet, I come.　　　　　　35
　　Forth of my heart those charms, thine eyes, are blotted;
　　Thy bed, lust-stained, shall with lust's blood be spotted.　　*Exit Othello.*

　　*Enter Lodovico and Gratiano.*

---

11 *quat* pimple, pustule.　　*to the sense* to the quick　　14 *Live Roderigo* if Roderigo lives　　16 *bobbed* swindled　　21 *unfold* expose　　25 *coat* (Possibly a garment of mail under the outer clothing, or simply a tougher coat than Roderigo expected.)　　26 *proof* a test　　34 *Minion* hussy (i.e., Desdemona)　　35 *hies* hastens on　　36 *Forth of* from out

*Cassio:* What ho! No watch? No passage? Murder! Murder!
*Gratiano:* 'Tis some mischance. The voice is very direful.
*Cassio:* O, help!      40
*Lodovico:* Hark!
*Roderigo:* O wretched villain!
*Lodovico:* Two or three groan. 'Tis heavy night;
      These may be counterfeits. Let's think 't unsafe
      To come in to the cry without more help.      45

      *[They remain near the entrance.]*

*Roderigo:* Nobody come? Then shall I bleed to death.

      *Enter Iago [in his shirtsleeves, with a light].*

*Lodovico:* Hark!
*Gratiano:* Here's one comes in his shirt, with light and weapons.
*Iago:* Who's there? Whose noise is this that cries on murder?
*Lodovico:* We do not know.
*Iago:*                 Did not you hear a cry?      50
*Cassio:* Here, here! For heaven's sake, help me!
*Iago:*                           What's the matter?

      *[He moves toward Cassio.]*

*Gratiano [to Lodovico]:* This is Othello's ancient, as I take it.
*Lodovico [to Gratiano]:* The same indeed, a very valiant fellow.
*Iago [to Cassio]:* What are you here that cry so grievously?
*Cassio:* Iago? O, I am spoiled, undone by villains!      55
      Give me some help.
*Iago:* O me, Lieutenant! What villains have done this?
*Cassio:* I think that one of them is hereabout,
      And cannot make away.
*Iago:*                 O treacherous villains!
      *[To Lodovico and Gratiano.]*
      What are you there? Come in, and give some help.      *[They advance.]*   60
*Roderigo:* O, help me there!
*Cassio:* That's one of them.
*Iago:*                 O murderous slave! O villain!

      *[He stabs Roderigo.]*

*Roderigo:* O damned Iago! O inhuman dog!
*Iago:* Kill men i' the dark?—Where be these bloody thieves?—
      How silent is this town!—Ho! Murder, murder!—      65
      *[To Lodovico and Gratiano.]* What may you be? Are you of good or evil?

---

38 *passage* people passing by     43 *heavy* thick, dark     45 *come in to* approach     49 *cries on* cries
out     54 *What* who (also at lines 60 and 66)     55 *spoiled* ruined, done for     59 *make* get

*Lodovico:* As you shall prove us, praise us.

*Iago:* Signor Lodovico?

*Lodovico:* He, sir.

*Iago:* I cry you mercy. Here's Cassio hurt by villains.                    70

*Gratiano:* Cassio?

*Iago:* How is 't, brother?

*Cassio:* My leg is cut in two.

*Iago:* Marry, heaven forbid!

Light, gentlemen! I'll bind it with my shirt.                    75

*[He hands them the light, and tends to Cassio's wound.]*

*Enter Bianca.*

*Bianca:* What is the matter, ho? Who is 't that cried?

*Iago:* Who is 't that cried?

*Bianca:*                    O my dear Cassio!

My sweet Cassio! O Cassio, Cassio, Cassio!

*Iago:* O notable strumpet! Cassio, may you suspect

Who they should be that have thus mangled you?                    80

*Cassio:* No.

*Gratiano:* I am sorry to find you thus. I have been to seek you.

*Iago:* Lend me a garter. *[He applies a tourniquet.]* So.—O, for a chair,

To bear him easily hence!

*Bianca:* Alas, he faints! O Cassio, Cassio, Cassio!                    85

*Iago:* Gentlemen all, I do suspect this trash

To be a party in this injury.—

Patience awhile, good Cassio.—Come, come;

Lend me a light. *[He shines the light on Roderigo.]*

Know we this face or no?

Alas, my friend and my dear countryman                    90

Roderigo! No.—Yes, sure.—O heaven! Roderigo!

*Gratiano:* What, of Venice?

*Iago:* Even he, sir. Did you know him?

*Gratiano:* Know him? Ay.

*Iago:* Signor Gratiano? I cry your gentle pardon.                    95

These bloody accidents must excuse my manners

That so neglected you.

*Gratiano:*                    I am glad to see you.

*Iago:* How do you, Cassio? O, a chair, a chair!

*Gratiano:* Roderigo!

---

67 *praise* appraise    70 *I cry you mercy* I beg your pardon    83 *chair* litter    95 *gentle* noble
96 *accidents* sudden events

_Iago:_ He, he, 'tis he. *[A litter is brought in.]* O, that's well said; the chair.                     100
　　Some good man bear him carefully from hence;
　　I'll fetch the General's surgeon. *[To Bianca.]* For you, mistress,
　　Save you your labor.—He that lies slain here, Cassio,
　　Was my dear friend. What malice was between you?
_Cassio:_ None in the world, nor do I know the man.                     105
_Iago [to Bianca]:_ What, look you pale?—O, bear him out o' th' air.

　　*[Cassio and Roderigo are borne off.]*

　　Stay you, good gentlemen.—Look you pale, mistress?—
　　Do you perceive the gastness of her eye?—
　　Nay, if you stare, we shall hear more anon.—
　　Behold her well; I pray you, look upon her.                     110
　　Do you see, gentlemen? Nay, guiltiness
　　Will speak, though tongues were out of use.

　　*[Enter Emilia.]*

_Emilia:_ 'Las, what's the matter? What's the matter, husband?
_Iago:_ Cassio hath here been set on in the dark
　　By Roderigo and fellows that are scaped.                     115
　　He's almost slain, and Roderigo dead.
_Emilia:_ Alas, good gentleman! Alas, good Cassio!
_Iago:_ This is the fruits of whoring. Prithee, Emilia,
　　Go know of Cassio where he supped tonight.
　　*[To Bianca.]* What, do you shake at that?                     120
_Bianca:_ He supped at my house, but I therefore shake not.
_Iago:_ O, did he so? I charge you go with me.
_Emilia:_ O, fie upon thee, strumpet!
_Bianca:_ I am no strumpet, but of life as honest
　　As you that thus abuse me.                     125
_Emilia:_ As I? Faugh! Fie upon thee!
_Iago:_ Kind gentlemen, let's go see poor Cassio dressed.—
　　Come, mistress, you must tell's another tale.
　　Emilia, run you to the citadel
　　And tell my lord and lady what hath happed.—                     130
　　Will you go on afore? *[Aside.]* This is the night
　　That either makes me or fordoes me quite.                     *Exeunt.*

---

100 _well said_ well done      103 _Save . . . labor_ i.e., never you mind tending Cassio      104 _malice_
enmity      106 _bear . . . air_ (Fresh air was thought to be dangerous for a wound.)      107 _Stay you_
(Lodovico and Gratiano are evidently about to leave.)      108 _gastness_ terror      109 _stare_ (Iago pretends to interpret Bianca's wild looks as an involuntary confession of guilt.)      119 _know_ learn
124 _honest_ chaste      127 _Cassio dressed_ Cassio's wounds dressed      132 _fordoes_ undoes, ruins

**Scene II [A Bedchamber in the Citadel.]**

*Enter Othello [with a light], and Desdemona in her bed.*

*Othello:* It is the cause, it is the cause, my soul.
    Let me not name it to you, you chaste stars!
    It is the cause. Yet I'll not shed her blood,
    Nor scar that whiter skin of hers than snow,
    And smooth as monumental alabaster.         5
    Yet she must die, else she'll betray more men.
    Put out the light, and then put out the light.
    If I quench thee, thou flaming minister,
    I can again thy former light restore,
    Should I repent me; but once put out thy light,     10
    Thou cunning'st pattern of excelling nature,
    I know not where is that Promethean heat
    That can thy light relume. When I have plucked thy rose,
    I cannot give it vital growth again;
    It needs must wither. I'll smell thee on the tree.     15

*[He kisses her.]*

    O balmy breath, that dost almost persuade
    Justice to break her sword! One more, one more.
    Be thus when thou art dead, and I will kill thee,
    And love thee after. One more, and that's the last.

*[He kisses her.]*

    So sweet was ne'er so fatal. I must weep,     20
    But they are cruel tears. This sorrow's heavenly;
    It strikes where it doth love. She wakes.
*Desdemona:* Who's there? Othello?
*Othello:* Ay, Desdemona.
*Desdemona:* Will you come to bed, my lord?     25
*Othello:* Have you prayed tonight, Desdemon?
*Desdemona:* Ay, my lord.
*Othello:* If you bethink yourself of any crime
    Unreconciled as yet to heaven and grace,
    Solicit for it straight.     30

---

s.d. *in her bed* (Either the curtains are drawn back to reveal the bed in a recessed area backstage, or the bed is "thrust out" onstage as the scene begins.)    1 *cause* i.e., cause of justice, the offense itself, which Othello must correct as an agent of justice    5 *monumental* i.e., used in making tombs and funeral monuments    7 *the light . . . light* the torch or lamp . . . Desdemona's life    8 *flaming minister* torch or lamp that serves me    10 *repent me* change my mind    11 *Thou . . . pattern* you skillfully wrought perfect example    12 *Promethean heat* divine fire. (Alluding to the theft of fire from heaven by Prometheus.)    13 *relume* rekindle    21 *cruel* unrelenting    22 *It . . . love* (Compare Hebrews 12:6: "For whom the Lord loveth he chasteneth.")    28 *crime* sin    30 *Solicit* petition, pray.    *straight* immediately

*Desdemona:* Alack, my lord, what may you mean by that?

*Othello:* Well, do it, and be brief. I will walk by.
    I would not kill thy unpreparèd spirit.
    No, heaven forfend! I would not kill thy soul.

*Desdemona:* Talk you of killing?

*Othello:*                  Ay, I do.

*Desdemona:*                     Then heaven           35
    Have mercy on me!

*Othello:*             Amen, with all my heart!

*Desdemona:* If you say so, I hope you will not kill me.

*Othello:* Humh!

*Desdemona:* And yet I fear you; for you're fatal then
    When your eyes roll so. Why I should fear I know not,      40
    Since guiltiness I know not; but yet I feel I fear.

*Othello:* Think on thy sins.

*Desdemona:*               They are loves I bear to you.

*Othello:* Ay, and for that thou diest.

*Desdemona:* That death's unnatural that kills for loving.
    Alas, why gnaw you so your nether lip?         45
    Some bloody passion shakes your very frame.
    These are portents; but yet I hope, I hope,
    They do not point on me.

*Othello:* Peace, and be still!

*Desdemona:* I will so. What's the matter?         50

*Othello:* That handkerchief which I so loved and gave thee
    Thou gav'st to Cassio.

*Desdemona:*             No, by my life and soul!
    Send for the man and ask him.

*Othello:* Sweet soul, take heed, take heed of perjury.
    Thou art on thy deathbed.         55

*Desdemona:* Ay, but not yet to die.

*Othello:*                 Yes, presently.
    Therefore confess thee freely of thy sin;
    For to deny each article with oath
    Cannot remove nor choke the strong conception
    That I do groan withal. Thou art to die.         60

*Desdemona:* Then Lord have mercy on me!

*Othello:*                 I say, amen.

*Desdemona:* And have you mercy too! I never did
    Offend you in my life; never loved Cassio

---

34 *forfend* forbid     42 *They are . . . you* i.e., if I sinned, it was in loving you more than my father or more than God     48 *point on* point at, predict what is to happen to     56 *presently* immediately 59 *conception* (1) belief in your guilt (2) plan in my mind     60 *groan withal* (1) groan at in sorrow (2) as in giving birth     63 *Offend* wrong

But with such general warranty of heaven
As I might love. I never gave him token. 65
Othello: By heaven, I saw my handkerchief in 's hand.
O perjured woman! Thou dost stone my heart,
And makes me call what I intend to do
A murder, which I thought a sacrifice.
I saw the handkerchief.
Desdemona: He found it, then. 70
I never gave it him. Send for him hither;
Let him confess a truth.
Othello: He hath confessed.
Desdemona: What, my lord?
Othello: That he hath used thee.
Desdemona: How? Unlawfully?
Othello: Ay.
Desdemona: He will not say so.
Othello: No, his mouth is stopped; 75
Honest Iago hath ta'en order for 't.
Desdemona: O, my fear interprets. What, is he dead?
Othello: Had all his hairs been lives, my great revenge
Had stomach for them all.
Desdemona: Alas, he is betrayed and I undone! *[She weeps.]* 80
Othello: Out, strumpet! Weep'st thou for him to my face?
Desdemona: O, banish me, my lord, but kill me not!
Othello: Down, strumpet!
Desdemona: Kill me tomorrow; let me live tonight!
Othello: Nay, if you strive— 85
Desdemona: But half an hour!
Othello: Being done, there is no pause.
Desdemona: But while I say one prayer!
Othello: It is too late.

*Smothers her.*

Emilia *[at the door]*: My lord, my lord! What, ho! My lord, my lord!
Othello: What noise is this? Not dead? Not yet quite dead?
I that am cruel am yet merciful; 90
I would not have thee linger in thy pain.

*[He dispatches her.]*

So, so.
Emilia *[within]*: What, ho! My lord, my lord!

---

64 *warranty* sanction    67 *stone* turn to stone, harden    76 *ta'en order* taken measures    86
*Being done* i.e., since justice has begun its relentless course

Othello: Who's there?

Emilia [within]: O, good my lord, I would speak a word with you!

Othello: Yes, 'tis Emilia.—By and by.—She's dead.
    'Tis like she comes to speak of Cassio's death.—       95
    The noise was here. Ha! No more moving?
    Still as the grave. Shall she come in? Were 't good?—
    I think she stirs again. No. What's best to do?
    If she come in, she'll sure speak to my wife.
    My wife! My wife! What wife? I have no wife.       100
    O, insupportable! O heavy hour!
    Methinks it should be now a huge eclipse
    Of sun and moon, and that th' affrighted globe
    Should yawn at alteration.

Emilia [within]:         I do beseech you
    That I may speak with you, O, good my lord!       105

Othello: I had forgot thee. O, come in, Emilia.—
    Soft, by and by. Let me the curtains draw.—

*[He closes the bed-curtains and opens the door.]*

    Where art thou?

*Enter Emilia.*

           What's the matter with thee now?

Emilia: O, my good lord, yonder's foul murders done!

Othello: What, now?       110

Emilia: But now, my lord.

Othello: It is the very error of the moon;
    She comes more nearer earth than she was wont,
    And makes men mad.

Emilia: Cassio, my lord, hath killed a young Venetian       115
    Called Roderigo.

Othello:         Roderigo killed?
    And Cassio killed?

Emilia:         No, Cassio is not killed.

Othello: Not Cassio killed? Then murder's out of tune,
    And sweet revenge grows harsh.

Desdemona: O, falsely, falsely murdered!       120

Emilia: O Lord, what cry is that?

Othello: That? What?

---

95 *like* likely that    96 *here* (The Folio's *high* is possible, suggesting that the commotion of the attack on Cassio was loud.)    104 *yawn* gape in amazement, i.e., move in an earthquake. (According to Pliny, earthquakes often happen during eclipses.)    *at alteration* at these cataclysmic events in nature, well suited to express the horror of Desdemona's death    107 *Soft* wait a minute 112 *error* aberration, irregularity

*Emilia:* Out and alas, that was my lady's voice.

[*She opens the bed-curtains.*]

    Help, help, ho, help! O lady, speak again!
    Sweet Desdemona! O sweet mistress, speak! 125
*Desdemona:* A guiltless death I die.
*Emilia:* O, who hath done this deed?
*Desdemona:* Nobody; I myself. Farewell.
    Commend me to my kind lord. O, farewell!        [*She dies.*]
*Othello:* Why, how should she be murdered?
*Emilia:*                       Alas, who knows? 130
*Othello:* You heard her say herself it was not I.
*Emilia:* She said so. I must needs report the truth.
*Othello:* She's like a liar gone to burning hell!
    'Twas I that killed her.
*Emilia:*                 O, the more angel she,
    And you the blacker devil! 135
*Othello:* She turned to folly, and she was a whore.
*Emilia:* Thou dost belie her, and thou art a devil.
*Othello:* She was false as water.
*Emilia:*            Thou art rash as fire to say
    That she was false. O, she was heavenly true! 140
*Othello:* Cassio did top her. Ask thy husband else.
    O, I were damned beneath all depth in hell
    But that I did proceed upon just grounds
    To this extremity. Thy husband knew it all.
*Emilia:* My husband? 145
*Othello:* Thy husband.
*Emilia:* That she was false to wedlock?
*Othello:* Ay, with Cassio. Nay, had she been true,
    If heaven would make me such another world
    Of one entire and perfect chrysolite, 150
    I'd not have sold her for it.
*Emilia:* My husband?
*Othello:* Ay, 'twas he that told me on her first.
    An honest man he is, and hates the slime
    That sticks on filthy deeds. 155
*Emilia:* My husband?
*Othello:* What needs this iterance, woman? I say thy husband.
*Emilia:* O mistress, villainy hath made mocks with love!
    My husband say she was false?

---

123 *Out* (A cry of dismay, intensifying *alas.*)     136 *folly* i.e., wantonness, fleshly sin     137 *belie* slander     141 *else* i.e., if you don't believe me     150 *chrysolite* precious topaz     157 *iterance* iteration, repetition     158 *made mocks with* derided, made sport of

*Othello:*                                        He, woman;
     I say thy husband. Dost understand the word?                                    160
     My friend, thy husband, honest, honest Iago.
*Emilia:* If he say so, may his pernicious soul
     Rot half a grain a day! He lies to th' heart.
     She was too fond of her most filthy bargain.
*Othello:* Ha?                                                          [*He draws.*]   165
*Emilia:* Do thy worst!
     This deed of thine is no more worthy heaven
     Than thou wast worthy her.
*Othello:*                                        Peace, you were best.
*Emilia:* Thou hast not half that power to do me harm
     As I have to be hurt. O gull! O dolt!                                           170
     As ignorant as dirt! Thou hast done a deed—
     I care not for thy sword; I'll make thee known,
     Though I lost twenty lives.—Help! Help, ho, help!
     The Moor hath killed my mistress! Murder, murder!

     *Enter Montano, Gratiano, and Iago.*

*Montano:* What is the matter? How now, General?                                   175
*Emilia:* O, are you come, Iago? You have done well,
     That men must lay their murders on your neck.
*Gratiano:* What is the matter?
*Emilia [to Iago]:* Disprove this villain, if thou be'st a man.
     He says thou toldst him that his wife was false.                               180
     I know thou didst not; thou'rt not such a villain.
     Speak, for my heart is full.
*Iago:* I told him what I thought, and told no more
     Than what he found himself was apt and true.
*Emilia:* But did you ever tell him she was false?                                 185
*Iago:* I did.
*Emilia:* You told a lie, an odious, damnèd lie!
     Upon my soul, a lie, a wicked lie.
     She false with Cassio? Did you say with Cassio?
*Iago:* With Cassio, mistress. Go to, charm your tongue.                           190
*Emilia:* I will not charm my tongue; I am bound to speak.
     My mistress here lies murdered in her bed—
*All:* O heavens forfend!
*Emilia:* And your reports have set the murder on.
*Othello:* Nay, stare not, masters. It is true indeed.                             195
*Gratiano:* 'Tis a strange truth.

---

168 *you were best* it would be best for you     170 *to be hurt* i.e., to endure hurt.        *gull* dupe     184
*apt* plausible     190 *charm* keep silent (as though by a magic spell)

*Montano:* O monstrous act!

*Emilia:*                              Villainy, villainy, villainy!
  I think upon 't—I think I smell 't! O villainy!
  I thought so then—I'll kill myself for grief—
  O villainy, villainy!                                                           200
*Iago:* What, are you mad? I charge you, get you home.
*Emilia:* Good gentlemen, let me have leave to speak.
  'Tis proper I obey him, but not now.
  Perchance, Iago, I will ne'er go home.
*Othello:* O! O! O!                              *[Othello falls on the bed.]*
*Emilia:*                    Nay, lay thee down and roar,                          205
  For thou hast killed the sweetest innocent
  That e'er did lift up eye.
*Othello [rising]:*                    O, she was foul!
  I scarce did know you, uncle. There lies your niece,
  Whose breath indeed these hands have newly stopped.
  I know this act shows horrible and grim.                                        210
*Gratiano:* Poor Desdemon! I am glad thy father's dead.
  Thy match was mortal to him, and pure grief
  Shore his old thread in twain. Did he live now,
  This sight would make him do a desperate turn,
  Yea, curse his better angel from his side,                                     215
  And fall to reprobance.
*Othello:* 'Tis pitiful. But yet Iago knows
  That she with Cassio hath the act of shame
  A thousand times committed. Cassio confessed it;
  And she did gratify his amorous works                                          220
  With that recognizance and pledge of love
  Which I first gave her. I saw it in his hand;
  It was a handkerchief, an antique token
  My father gave my mother.
*Emilia:* O God! O heavenly God!                                                 225
*Iago:* Zounds, hold your peace.
*Emilia:*                    'Twill out, 'twill out! I peace?
  No, I will speak as liberal as the north.
  Let heaven and men and devils, let them all,
  All, all, cry shame against me, yet I'll speak.

---

199 *then* (Perhaps at Act III, Scene III, lines 331–332 and Act IV, Scene II, lines 137–154.)     205
s.d. *Othello . . . bed* (This direction is from the Quarto, as also *He kisses her* at line 19 and *She dies* at
line 129.)     207 *lift up eye* i.e., lift her eyes to heaven     210 *shows* looks     213 *Shore . . . thread*
sheared the thread of his old age (as Atropos, one of the three Fates, was thought to do)     214 *turn*
deed     216 *reprobance* damnation, i.e., suicide     220 *gratify* reward     221 *recognizance* token
227 *liberal as the north* freely as the north wind (blows)

*Iago*: Be wise, and get you home.
*Emilia*:                                    I will not.

   *[Iago threatens Emilia.]*

*Gratiano*:                                    Fie                                                    230
   Your sword upon a woman?
*Emilia*: O thou dull Moor! That handkerchief thou speak'st of
   I found by fortune and did give my husband;
   For often, with a solemn earnestness,
   More than indeed belonged to such a trifle,                          235
   He begged of me to steal 't.
*Iago*:                                    Villainous whore!
*Emilia*: She give it Cassio? No, alas! I found it,
   And I did give 't my husband.
*Iago*:                                    Filth, thou liest!
*Emilia*: By heaven, I do not, I do not, gentlemen.
   O murderous coxcomb! What should such a fool                240
   Do with so good a wife?
*Othello*: Are there no stones in heaven
   But what serves for the thunder?—Precious villain!

   *[He runs at Iago; Montano disarms Othello. Iago, from behind, stabs Emilia.]*

*Gratiano*: The woman falls! Sure he hath killed his wife.
*Emilia*: Ay, ay. O, lay me by my mistress' side.                    245

   *Exit [Iago.]*

*Gratiano*: He's gone, but his wife's killed.
*Montano*: 'Tis a notorious villain. Take you this weapon,
   Which I have here recovered from the Moor.
   Come, guard the door without. Let him not pass,
   But kill him rather. I'll after that same villain,                    250
   For 'tis a damnèd slave.

   *Exit [with all but Othello and Emilia, who has been laid by Desdemona's side].*

*Othello*: I am not valiant neither,
   But every puny whipster gets my sword.
   But why should honor outlive honesty?
   Let it go all.

---

235 *belonged* was appropriate     240 *coxcomb* fool. (Addressed to Othello.)     242 *stones* bolts,
such as those used for thunderbolts     243 *Precious* i.e., arrant, utter.     s.d. *He . . . Emilia* (The
Quarto text reads, "The Moor runs at Iago. Iago kills his wife." The Quarto also specifies the exit of
Iago at line 245 and the death of Emilia at line 260.)     253 *whipster* contemptible fellow (one who
is always ready to whip out his sword)     254 *honor* i.e., the bravery for which one enjoys a soldier's
reputation.     *honesty* true integrity

Emilia:        What did thy song bode, lady?                                     255
    Hark, canst thou hear me? I will play the swan,
    And die in music. [She sings.] "Willow, willow, willow."
    Moor, she was chaste. She loved thee, cruel Moor.
    So come my soul to bliss as I speak true.
    So speaking as I think, alas, I die.                        [She dies.]  260
Othello: I have another weapon in this chamber;
    It was a sword of Spain, the ice-brook's temper—
    O, here it is. [He finds a sword.] Uncle, I must come forth.
Gratiano [within]: If thou attempt it, it will cost thee dear.
    Thou hast no weapon, and perforce must suffer.                            265
Othello: Look in upon me then and speak with me,
    Or, naked as I am, I will assault thee.

    [Enter Gratiano.]

Gratiano: What is the matter?
Othello:                        Behold, I have a weapon;
    A better never did itself sustain
    Upon a soldier's thigh. I have seen the day                               270
    That, with this little arm and this good sword,
    I have made my way through more impediments
    Than twenty times your stop. But O, vain boast!
    Who can control his fate? 'Tis not so now.
    Be not afraid, though you do see me weaponed;                             275
    Here is my journey's end, here is my butt
    And very seamark of my utmost sail.

    [Gratiano steps back.]

    Do you go back dismayed? 'Tis a lost fear;
    Man but a rush against Othello's breast
    And he retires. Where should Othello go?                                  280

    [He turns to Desdemona.]

    Now, how dost thou look now? O ill-starred wench!
    Pale as thy smock! When we shall meet at compt,
    This look of thine will hurl my soul from heaven,
    And fiends will snatch at it. Cold, cold, my girl?
    Even like thy chastity. O cursèd, cursèd slave!                           285
    Whip me, ye devils,
    From the possession of this heavenly sight!

---

262 the icebrook's temper tempered in ice-cold water    267 naked unarmed    273 stop power (to
stop)    276 butt goal, limit. (An archery term.)    277 seamark beacon (marking his destination
or limit)    278 lost wasted, unneeded    279 Man . . . rush wield no more than a reed    282
compt account, judgment day    285 slave i.e., Othello himself

Blow me about in winds! Roast me in sulfur!
Wash me in steep-down gulfs of liquid fire!
O Desdemon! Dead, Desdemon! Dead! O! O!                                    290

*Enter Lodovico, Cassio [carried in a litter], Montano, and Iago [prisoner], with officers.*

Lodovico: Where is this rash and most unfortunate man?
Othello: That's he that was Othello. Here I am.
Lodovico: Where is that viper? Bring the villain forth.

*[Iago is led forward.]*

Othello: I look down towards his feet; but that's a fable.
If that thou be'st a devil, I cannot kill thee.                            295

*[He wounds Iago.]*

Lodovico: Wrench his sword from him.                    *[Othello is disarmed.]*
Iago:                                   I bleed, sir, but not killed.
Othello: I am not sorry neither. I'd have thee live,
For in my sense 'tis happiness to die.
Lodovico: O thou Othello, that was once so good,
Fall'n in the practice of a cursèd slave,                                  300
What shall be said to thee?
Othello:                                 Why, anything.
An honorable murderer, if you will,
For naught I did in hate, but all in honor.
Lodovico: This wretch hath part confessed his villainy.
Did you and he consent in Cassio's death?                                  305
Othello: Ay.
Cassio: Dear General, I never gave you cause.
Othello: I do believe it, and I ask your pardon.
Will you, I pray, demand that demi-devil
Why he hath thus ensnared my soul and body?                               310
Iago: Demand me nothing. What you know, you know.
From this time forth I never will speak word.
Lodovico: What, not to pray?
Gratiano: Torments will ope your lips.
Othello: Well, thou dost best.                                             315
Lodovico: Sir, you shall understand what hath befall'n,
Which, as I think, you know not. Here is a letter
Found in the pocket of the slain Roderigo;

---

290 s.d. *in a litter* (The Quarto specifies that Cassio is "in a chair.")    294 *towards his feet* i.e., to see
if they are cloven, as the devil's are fabled to be    298 *in my sense* to one who feels as I do    300
*in the practice* through the plotting, into the snare.    *slave* villain    305 *consent* agree    314
*Torments* torture

And here another. *[He produces letters.]* The one of them imports
    The death of Cassio, to be undertook                     320
    By Roderigo.
*Othello:* O villain!
*Cassio:*         Most heathenish and most gross!
*Lodovico [showing another paper]:* Now here's another discontented paper
    Found in his pocket too. And this, it seems,
    Roderigo meant t' have sent this damnèd villain;          325
    But that belike Iago in the interim
    Came in and satisfied him.
*Othello:* O thou pernicious caitiff!—
    How came you, Cassio, by that handkerchief
    That was my wife's?
*Cassio:*             I found it in my chamber;        330
    And he himself confessed but even now
    That there he dropped it for a special purpose
    Which wrought to his desire.
*Othello:*                O fool, fool, fool!
*Cassio:* There is besides in Roderigo's letter
    How he upbraids Iago, that he made him          335
    Brave me upon the watch, whereon it came
    That I was cast; and even but now he spake,
    After long seeming dead, Iago hurt him,
    Iago set him on.
*Lodovico [to Othello]:* You must forsake this room and go with us.    340
    Your power and your command is taken off,
    And Cassio rules in Cyprus. For this slave,
    If there be any cunning cruelty
    That can torment him much and hold him long,
    It shall be his. You shall close prisoner rest        345
    Till that the nature of your fault be known
    To the Venetian state.—Come, bring away.
*Othello:* Soft you; a word or two before you go.
    I have done the state some service, and they know 't.
    No more of that. I pray you, in your letters,        350
    When you shall these unlucky deeds relate,
    Speak of me as I am; nothing extenuate,
    Nor set down aught in malice. Then must you speak
    Of one that loved not wisely but too well;

322 *gross* monstrous    323 *discontented* full of discontent    326 *belike* most likely    327 *Came . . . him* interposed and gave him satisfactory explanation    333 *wrought . . . desire* worked out as he wished, fitted in with his plan    336 *Brave* defy.    *whereon it came* whereof it came about    337 *cast* dismissed    341 *taken off* taken away    344 *hold him long* keep him alive a long time (during his torture)    345 *rest* remain    348 *Soft you* one moment    351 *unlucky* unfortunate

Of one not easily jealous but, being wrought,                    355
Perplexed in the extreme; of one whose hand,
Like the base Indian, threw a pearl away
Richer than all his tribe; of one whose subdued eyes,
Albeit unusèd to the melting mood,
Drops tears as fast as the Arabian trees                          360
Their medicinable gum. Set you down this;
And say besides that in Aleppo once,
Where a malignant and a turbaned Turk
Beat a Venetian and traduced the state,
I took by th' throat the circumcisèd dog                          365
And smote him, thus.                                    *[He stabs himself.]*
Lodovico: O bloody period!
Gratiano: All that is spoke is marred.
Othello: I kissed thee ere I killed thee. No way but this,
    Killing myself, to die upon a kiss.                           370

    *[He kisses Desdemona and] dies.*

Cassio: This did I fear, but thought he had no weapon;
    For he was great of heart.
Lodovico [to Iago]:        O Spartan dog,
    More fell than anguish, hunger, or the sea!
    Look on the tragic loading of this bed.
    This is thy work. The object poisons sight;                   375
    Let it be hid. Gratiano, keep the house,

    *[The bed curtains are drawn]*

    And seize upon the fortunes of the Moor,
    For they succeed on you. *[To Cassio.]* To you, Lord Governor,
    Remains the censure of this hellish villain,
    The time, the place, the torture. O, enforce it!               380
    Myself will straight aboard, and to the state
    This heavy act with heavy heart relate.                 *Exeunt.*

---

355 *wrought* worked upon, worked into a frenzy    356 *Perplexed* distraught    357 *Indian* (This reading from the Quarto pictures an ignorant savage who cannot recognize the value of a precious jewel. The Folio reading, *Iudean* or *Judean*, i.e., infidel or disbeliever, may refer to Herod, who slew Miriamne in a fit of jealousy, or to Judas Iscariot, the betrayer of Christ.)    358 *subdued* i.e., overcome by grief    361 *gum* i.e., myrrh    366 s.d. *He stabs himself* (This direction is in the Quarto text.)    367 *period* termination, conclusion    372 *Spartan dog* (Spartan dogs were noted for their savagery and silence.)    373 *fell* cruel    376 *Let it be hid* i.e., draw the bed curtains. (No stage direction specifies that the dead are to be carried offstage at the end of the play.)    *keep* remain in    377 *seize upon* take legal possession of    378 *succeed on* pass as though by inheritance to    379 *censure* sentencing

## ACT 1

1. What is Othello's position in society? How is he regarded by those who know him? By his own words, when we first meet him in Scene II, what traits of character does he manifest?
2. How do you account for Brabantio's dismay on learning of his daughter's marriage, despite the fact that Desdemona has married a man so generally honored and admired?
3. What is Iago's view of human nature? In his fondness for likening men to animals (as in I, i, 49–50; I, i, 90–91; and I, iii, 381–382), what does he tell us about himself?
4. What reasons does Iago give for his hatred of Othello?
5. In Othello's defense before the senators (Scene III), how does he explain Desdemona's gradual falling in love with him?
6. Is Brabantio's warning to Othello (I, iii, 293–294) an accurate or an inaccurate prophecy?
7. By what strategy does Iago enlist Roderigo in his plot against the Moor? In what lines do we learn Iago's true feelings toward Roderigo?

## ACT II

1. What do the Cypriots think of Othello? Do their words (in Scene I) make him seem to us a lesser man or a larger one?
2. What cruelty does Iago display toward Emilia? How well founded is his distrust of his wife's fidelity?
3. In II, iii, 221, Othello speaks of Iago's "honesty and love." How do you account for Othello's being so totally deceived?
4. For what major events does the merrymaking (proclaimed in Scene II) give opportunity?

## ACT III

1. Trace the steps by which Iago rouses Othello to suspicion. Is there anything in Othello's character or circumstances that renders him particularly susceptible to Iago's wiles?
2. In III, iv, 49–98, Emilia knows of Desdemona's distress over the lost handkerchief. At this moment, how do you explain her failure to relieve Desdemona's mind? Is Emilia aware of her husband's villainy?

## ACT IV

1. In this act, what circumstantial evidence is added to Othello's case against Desdemona?
2. How plausible do you find Bianca's flinging the handkerchief at Cassio just when Othello is looking on? How important is the handkerchief in this play? What does it represent? What suggestions or hints do you find in it?
3. What prevents Othello from being moved by Desdemona's appeal (IV, ii, 35–91)?
4. When Roderigo grows impatient with Iago (IV, ii, 181–203), how does Iago make use of his fellow plotter's discontent?
5. What does the conversation between Emilia and Desdemona (Scene III) tell us about the nature of each?
6. In this act, what scenes (or speeches) contain memorable dramatic irony?

## ACT V

1. Summarize the events that lead to Iago's unmasking.

2. How does Othello's mistaken belief that Cassio is slain (V, i, 27–34) affect the outcome of the play?
3. What is Iago's motive in stabbing Roderigo?
4. In your interpretation of the play, exactly what impels Othello to kill Desdemona? Jealousy? Desire for revenge? Excess idealism? A wish to be a public avenger who punishes, "else she'll betray more men"?
5. What do you understand by Othello's calling himself "one that loved not wisely but too well" (V, ii, 354)?
6. In your view, does Othello's long speech in V, ii, 348–366 succeed in restoring his original dignity and nobility? Do you agree with Cassio (V, ii, 372) that Othello was "great of heart"?

## GENERAL QUESTIONS

1. What motivates Iago to carry out his schemes? Do you find him a devil incarnate, a madman, or a rational human being?
2. Whom besides Othello does Iago deceive? What is Desdemona's opinion of him? Emilia's? Cassio's (before Iago is found out)? To what do you attribute Iago's success as a deceiver?
3. How essential to the play is the fact that Othello is a black man, a Moor, and not a native of Venice?
4. In the introduction to his edition of the play in *The Complete Signet Classic Shakespeare*, Alvin Kernan remarks:

   *Othello* is probably the most neatly, the most formally constructed of Shakespeare's plays. Every character is, for example, balanced by another similar or contrasting character. Desdemona is balanced by her opposite, Iago; love and concern for others at one end of the scale, hatred and concern for self at the other.

   Besides Desdemona and Iago, what other pairs of characters strike balances?
5. Consider any passage of the play in which there is a shift from verse to prose, or from prose to verse. What is the effect of this shift?
6. Indicate a passage that you consider memorable for its poetry. Does the passage seem introduced for its own sake? Does it in any way advance the action of the play, express theme, or demonstrate character?
7. Does the play contain any tragic *recognition*—as discussed on page 1148, a moment of terrible enlightenment, a "realization of the unthinkable"?
8. Does the downfall of Othello proceed from any flaw in his nature, or is his downfall entirely the work of Iago?

## SUGGESTIONS FOR WRITING

1. Write a defense of Iago.
2. "Never was any play fraught, like this of Othello, with improbabilities," wrote Thomas Rymer in a famous attack (*A Short View of Tragedy*, 1692). Consider Rymer's objections to the play (see page 1717), either answering them or finding evidence to back up Rymer.
3. Suppose yourself a casting director assigned to a film version of *Othello*. What well-known stars would you cast in the principal roles? Write a report justifying your choices. Don't merely discuss the stars and their qualifications; discuss (with specific reference to the play) what Shakespeare appears to call for.
4. Emilia's long speech at the end of Act IV (iii, 84–103) has been called a Renaissance plea for women's liberation. Do you agree? Write a brief close analysis of this speech. How timely is it?
5. "The downfall of Oedipus is the work of the gods; the downfall of Othello is self-inflicted." Test this comment with reference to the two plays, and report your findings.

# 36  The Modern Theater

As the twentieth century began, realism in the theaters of Western Europe, England, and America appeared to have won a resounding victory. (**Realism** in drama, like realism in fiction, may be broadly defined as an attempt to reproduce faithfully the surface appearance of life, especially that of ordinary people in everyday situations.) The theater had been slow to admit controversial or unpleasant themes, and slow to shed its traditional conventions. From Italian playhouses of the sixteenth century, it had inherited the **picture-frame stage:** one that holds the action within a **proscenium arch,** a gateway standing (as the word *proscenium* indicates) "in front of the scenery." This manner of constructing a playhouse in effect divided the actors from their audience; most commercial theaters even today are so constructed. But as the new century began, actors less often declaimed their passions in oratorical style in front of backdrops painted with waterfalls and volcanoes, while stationed exactly at the center of the stage as if to sing "duets meant to bring forth applause" (as Swedish playwright August Strindberg complained). By 1891 even Victorian London had witnessed a production of a play that frankly portrayed a man dying of venereal disease—Henrik Ibsen's *Ghosts*.

In the theater of realism, a room was represented by a **box set**—three walls that joined in two corners and a ceiling that tilted as if seen in perspective—replacing drapery walls that had billowed and doors that had flapped, not slammed. Instead of posing at stage-center to deliver key speeches, actors were instructed to speak from wherever the dramatic situation placed them and now and then turn their backs upon the audience. They were to behave as if they lived in a room with the fourth wall sliced away, unaware that they had an audience.

This realistic convention is familiar to us today, not only from realistic plays but from the typical television soap opera or situation comedy that takes place in such a three-walled room, with every cup and spoon revealed by the camera. But such realism went against a long tradition. Watching a play by Sophocles, the spectators, we may safely assume, had to exert their imagination. We do not expect an ancient Greek tragedy literally to represent the lives of ordinary people in everyday situations. On the contrary a tragedy, according to Aristotle, its leading ancient theorist, represents an "action of supreme importance," an extraordinary moment in the life of a king or queen or other person of high estate. An open-air stage, though Sophocles adorned it with painted scenery, could hardly change day into night as lighting technicians commonly do today, nor aspire to reproduce in detail a whole palace. Such limitations prevail upon the theater of Shakespeare as well, encouraging the Bard to flesh out his scene with vivid language, making the spectator willing to imagine that the simple stage—the "wooden O"—is a forest, a storm-swept landscape, or a battlefield. In the classic Nō theater of Japan, spectators recognize conventional props: a simple framework is a boat, four posts and a roof are a palace, an actor's fan may be any useful object—a paintbrush, say, or a knife. In such a nonrealistic theater, the playwright, unhampered by stage sets, can shift scenes as rapidly as the audience can imagine.

In the realistic three-walled room, actors could hardly rant (or, Hamlet said, "tear a passion to tatters") without seeming foolish. Another effect of more lifelike direction was to discourage use of such devices as the soliloquy and the **aside** (villain to audience: "Heh! heh! Now she's in my power!"). To encourage actors even further in imitating reality, the influential director Constantin Stanislavsky of the Moscow Art Theater developed his famous system to help actors feel at home inside a playwright's characters. One of Stanislavsky's exercises was to have actors search their memories for personal experiences like those of the characters in the play; another was to have the actors act out things a character did *not* do in the play but might do in life. The system enabled Stanislavsky to bring authenticity to his productions of Chekhov's plays and of Maxim Gorky's *The Lower Depths* (1902), a play that showed the tenants in a sordid lodging house drinking themselves to death (and hanging themselves) in surroundings of realistic squalor.

Gorky's play is a masterpiece of **naturalism,** a kind of realism in fiction and drama dealing with the more brutal or unpleasant aspects of reality. As codified by French novelist and playwright Émile Zola, who influenced Ibsen, naturalism viewed a person as a creature whose acts are determined by heredity and environment; Zola urged writers to study their characters' behavior with the detachment of zoologists studying animals.

No sooner had realism and naturalism won the day than a reaction arose. One opposing force was the **Symbolist movement** in the French theater, most influentially expressed by Belgian playwright Maurice Maeterlinck. Like French Symbolist poets Charles Baudelaire and Stéphane Mallarmé, Maeterlinck assumes that the visible world reflects a spirit world we cannot directly perceive. Accordingly, his plays are filled with hints and portents: suggestive objects (jeweled rings, veils, distant candles), mysterious locales (crumbling castles, dim grottoes), vague sounds from afar, dialogue rich in silences and unfinished sentences.

In *The Intruder* (1890), a blind man sees the approach of Death. In *Pelléas and Mélisande* (1892) occurs a typical bit of Symbolist stage business: a small boy stands on his grandfather's shoulders to peer through a high window and speak of wonders invisible to an audience. (For more about symbolism and Symbolists, see Chapters Seven and Twenty-four.)

Elsewhere, others were working along similar lines. In Russia, Anton Chekhov, whose plays on the surface appeared realistic, built some of his best around a symbol (*The Seagull, The Cherry Orchard*). In Ireland, poet William Butler Yeats, who in 1899 had helped found the Irish Dramatic Movement, was himself of a different mind from the realistic playwrights whose work he had helped produce in Dublin's Abbey Theater. Drawing on Irish lore and legend, Yeats wrote (among other plays) "plays for dancers" to be performed in drawing rooms, often in friends's homes, with simple costumes and props, a few masked actors, and a very few musicians. In Sweden, August Strindberg, who earlier had won fame as a naturalist, reversed direction and in *The Dream Play* (1902) and *The Ghost Sonata* (1907) introduced characters who change their identities and, ignoring space and time, move across dreamlike landscapes. In these plays Strindberg anticipated the movement called **expressionism** in German theater after World War I. Delighting in bizarre sets and exaggerated makeup and costuming, expressionist playwrights and producers sought to reflect intense states of emotion and, sometimes, to depict the world through lunatic eyes. A classic example (on film) is *The Cabinet of Dr. Caligari*, made in Berlin in 1919–1920, in which a hypnotist sends forth a subject to murder people. Garbed in jet black, the killer sleepwalks through a town of lopsided houses, twisted streets, and railings that tilt at gravity-defying angles. In expressionist movies and plays, madness is objectified and dreams become realities.

In 1893 Strindberg had complained of producers who represented a kitchen by a drapery painted with pictures of kettles; but by 1900, realistic play production had gone to opposite extremes. In the 1920s the curtain rose upon a Broadway play with a detailed replica of a Schrafft's restaurant, complete to the last fork and folded napkin. (Still, critic George Jean Nathan remarked, no matter how elaborate a stage dinner, the table never seemed to have any butter.) Theaters housed increasingly complicated machines, making it all the easier to present scenes full of realistic detail. Elevators lifted heavy sets swiftly and quietly into place; other sets, at the touch of a button, revolved on giant turntables. Theaters became warehouses for huge ready-made scenery.

Some playwrights fought domination by the painstakingly realistic set. Bertolt Brecht in Germany and Luigi Pirandello in Italy conceived plays to be performed on bare stages—gas pipes and plaster in full view—to remind spectators that they beheld events in a theater, not in the world. In reaction against the traditional picture-frame stage, new kinds of theaters were designed, such as the **arena theater** or **theater in the round,** in which the audience sits on all four sides of the performing area; and the **flexible theater,** in which the seats are movable. Such theaters usually are not commercial (most of which maintain their traditional picture-frame stages, built decades ago). Rather, the alternative theaters are found in college and civic playhouses, in large cities, in storefronts, and in converted lofts. Proponents of arena staging claim that it brings actors and audience into greater intimacy; opponents, that it keeps the actors artificially circulating like goldfish in a bowl. Perhaps it is safe to say only that some plays lend themselves to being seen head-on in a picture frame; others, to being surrounded.

## Henrik Ibsen

A DOLL'S HOUSE                                                                        1879

*Translated by James McFarlane*

*Henrik Ibsen (1828–1906) was born in Skien, a seaport in Norway. When he was six, his father's business losses suddenly reduced his wealthy family to poverty. After a brief attempt to study medicine, young Ibsen worked as a stage manager in provincial Bergen; then, becoming known as a playwright, moved to Oslo as artistic director of the National Theater—practical experiences that gained him firm grounding in his craft. Discouraged when his theater failed and the king turned down his plea for a grant to enable him to write, Ibsen left Norway and for twenty-seven years lived in Italy and Germany. There, in his middle years (1879–91), he wrote most of his famed plays about small-town life, among them A Doll's House, Ghosts, An Enemy of the People, The Wild Duck, and Hedda Gabler. Introducing social problems to the stage, these plays aroused storms of controversy. Although best known as a realist, Ibsen early in his career wrote poetic dramas based on Norwegian history and folklore: the tragedy Brand (1866) and the powerful, wildly fantastic Peer Gynt (1867). He ended as a Symbolist in John Gabriel Borkman (1896) and When We Dead Awaken (1899), both encompassing huge mountains that heaven-assaulting heroes try to climb. Late in life Ibsen returned to Oslo, honored at last both at home and abroad.*

Henrik Ibsen

Characters

*Torvald Helmer*, a lawyer
*Nora*, his wife
*Dr. Rank*
*Mrs. Kristine Linde*
*Nils Krogstad*
*Anne Marie*, the nursemaid
*Helene*, the maid

The Helmers' three children
A Porter
The action takes place in the Helmers' flat.

## ACT I

A pleasant room, tastefully but not expensively furnished. On the back wall, one door on the right leads to the entrance hall, a second door on the left leads to Helmer's study. Between these two doors, a piano. In the middle of the left wall, a door; and downstage from it, a window. Near the window a round table with armchairs and a small sofa. In the right wall, upstage, a door; and on the same wall downstage, a porcelain stove with a couple of armchairs and a rocking chair. Between the stove and the door a small table. Etchings on the walls. A whatnot with china and other small objets d'art; a small bookcase with books in handsome bindings. Carpet on the floor; a fire burns in the stove. A winter's day.

The front door-bell rings in the hall; a moment later, there is the sound of the front door being opened. Nora comes into the room, happily humming to herself. She is dressed in her outdoor things, and is carrying lots of parcels which she then puts down on the table, right. She leaves the door into the hall standing open; a Porter can be seen outside holding a Christmas tree and a basket; he hands them to the Maid who has opened the door for them.

Nora: Hide the Christmas tree away carefully, Helene. The children mustn't see it till this evening when it's decorated. [To the Porter, taking out her purse.] How much?
Porter: Fifty öre.
Nora: There's a crown. Keep the change.

[The Porter thanks her and goes. Nora shuts the door. She continues to laugh quietly and happily to herself as she takes off her things. She takes a bag of macaroons out of her pocket and eats one or two; then she walks stealthily across and listens at her husband's door.]

Nora: Yes, he's in.

[She begins humming again as she walks over to the table, right.]

Helmer [in his study]: Is that my little sky-lark chirruping out there?
Nora [busy opening some of the parcels]: Yes, it is.
Helmer: Is that my little squirrel frisking about?
Nora: Yes!
Helmer: When did my little squirrel get home?
Nora: Just this minute. [She stuffs the bag of macaroons in her pocket and wipes her mouth.] Come on out, Torvald, and see what I've bought.
Helmer: I don't want to be disturbed! [A moment later, he opens the door and looks out, his pen in his hand.] 'Bought', did you say? All that? Has my little spendthrift been out squandering money again?

*Nora*: But, Torvald, surely this year we can spread ourselves just a little. This is the first Christmas we haven't had to go carefully.

*Helmer*: Ah, but that doesn't mean we can afford to be extravagant, you know.

*Nora*: Oh yes, Torvald, surely we can afford to be just a little bit extravagant now, can't we? Just a teeny-weeny bit. You are getting quite a good salary now, and you are going to earn lots and lots of money.

*Helmer*: Yes, after the New Year. But it's going to be three whole months before the first pay cheque comes in.

*Nora*: Pooh! We can always borrow in the meantime.

*Helmer*: Nora! *[Crosses to her and takes her playfully by the ear.]* Here we go again, you and your frivolous ideas! Suppose I went and borrowed a thousand crowns today, and you went and spent it all over Christmas, then on New Year's Eve a slate fell and hit me on the head and there I was. . . .

*Nora [putting her hand over his mouth]*: Sh! Don't say such horrid things.

*Helmer*: Yes, but supposing something like that did happen . . . what then?

*Nora*: If anything as awful as that did happen, I wouldn't care if I owed anybody anything or not.

*Helmer*: Yes, but what about the people I'd borrowed from?

*Nora*: Them? Who cares about them! They are only strangers!

*Helmer*: Nora, Nora! Just like a woman! Seriously though, Nora, you know what I think about these things. No debts! Never borrow! There's always something inhibited, something unpleasant, about a home built on credit and borrowed money. We two have managed to stick it out so far, and that's the way we'll go on for the little time that remains.

*Nora [walks over to the stove]*: Very well, just as you say, Torvald.

*Helmer [following her]*: There, there! My little singing bird mustn't go drooping her wings, eh? Has it got the sulks, that little squirrel of mine? *[Takes out his wallet.]* Nora, what do you think I've got here?

*Nora [quickly turning round]*: Money!

*Helmer*: There! *[He hands her some notes.]* Good heavens, I know only too well how Christmas runs away with the housekeeping.

*Nora [counts]*: Ten, twenty, thirty, forty. Oh, thank you, thank you, Torvald! This will see me quite a long way.

*Helmer*: Yes, it'll have to.

*Nora*: Yes, yes, I'll see that it does. But come over here, I want to show you all the things I've bought. And so cheap! Look, some new clothes for Ivar . . . and a little sword. There's a horse and a trumpet for Bob. And a doll and a doll's cot for Emmy. They are not very grand but she'll have them all broken before long anyway. And I've got some dress material and some handkerchiefs for the maids. Though, really, dear old Anne Marie should have had something better.

*Helmer*: And what's in this parcel here?

*Nora [shrieking]*: No, Torvald! You mustn't see that till tonight!

*Helmer*: All right. But tell me now, what did my little spendthrift fancy for herself?

*Nora:* For me? Puh, I don't really want anything.

*Helmer:* Of course you do. Anything reasonable that you think you might like, just tell me.

*Nora:* Well, I don't really know. As a matter of fact, though, Torvald . . .

*Helmer:* Well?

*Nora [toying with his coat buttons, and without looking at him]:* If you did want to give me something, you could . . . you could always . . .

*Helmer:* Well, well, out with it!

*Nora [quickly]:* You could always give me money, Torvald. Only what you think you could spare. And then I could buy myself something with it later on.

*Helmer:* But Nora. . . .

*Nora:* Oh, please, Torvald dear! Please! I beg you. Then I'd wrap the money up in some pretty gilt paper and hang it on the Christmas tree. Wouldn't that be fun?

*Helmer:* What do we call my pretty little pet when it runs away with all the money?

*Nora:* I know, I know, we call it a spendthrift. But please let's do what I said, Torvald. Then I'll have a bit of time to think about what I need most. Isn't that awfully sensible, now, eh?

*Helmer [smiling]:* Yes, it is indeed—that is, if only you really could hold on to the money I gave you, and really did buy something for yourself with it. But it just gets mixed up with the housekeeping and frittered away on all sorts of useless things, and then I have to dig into my pocket all over again.

*Nora:* Oh but, Torvald. . . .

*Helmer:* You can't deny it, Nora dear. *[Puts his arm round her waist.]* My pretty little pet is very sweet, but it runs away with an awful lot of money. It's incredible how expensive it is for a man to keep such a pet.

*Nora:* For shame! How can you say such a thing? As a matter of fact I save everything I can.

*Helmer [laughs]:* Yes, you are right there. Everything you *can*. But you simply can't.

*Nora [hums and smiles quietly and happily]:* Ah, if you only knew how many expenses the likes of us sky-larks and squirrels have, Torvald!

*Helmer:* What a funny little one you are! Just like your father. Always on the look-out for money, wherever you can lay your hands on it; but as soon as you've got it, it just seems to slip through your fingers. You never seem to know what you've done with it. Well, one must accept you as you are. It's in the blood. Oh yes, it is, Nora. That sort of thing is hereditary.

*Nora:* Oh, I only wish I'd inherited a few more of Daddy's qualities.

*Helmer:* And I wouldn't want my pretty little song-bird to be the least bit different from what she is now. But come to think of it, you look rather . . . rather . . . how shall I put it? . . . rather guilty today. . . .

*Nora:* Do I?

*Helmer:* Yes, you do indeed. Look me straight in the eye.

*Nora [looks at him]:* Well?

*Helmer [wagging his finger at her]:* My little sweet-tooth surely didn't forget herself in town today?

*Nora:* No, whatever makes you think that?

*Helmer:* She didn't just pop into the confectioner's for a moment?

*Nora:* No, I assure you, Torvald. . . !

*Helmer:* Didn't try sampling the preserves?

*Nora:* No, really I didn't.

*Helmer:* Didn't go nibbling a macaroon or two?

*Nora:* No, Torvald, honestly, you must believe me. . . !

*Helmer:* All right then! It's really just my little joke. . . .

*Nora [crosses to the table]:* I would never dream of doing anything you didn't want me to.

*Helmer:* Of course not, I know that. And then you've given me your word. . . . *[Crosses to her.]* Well then, Nora dearest, you shall keep your little Christmas secrets. They'll all come out tonight, I dare say, when we light the tree.

*Nora:* Did you remember to invite Dr. Rank?

*Helmer:* No. But there's really no need. Of course he'll come and have dinner with us. Anyway, I can ask him when he looks in this morning. I've ordered some good wine. Nora, you can't imagine how I am looking forward to this evening.

*Nora:* So am I. And won't the children enjoy it, Torvald!

*Helmer:* Oh, what a glorious feeling it is, knowing you've got a nice, safe job, and a good fat income. Don't you agree? Isn't it wonderful, just thinking about it?

*Nora:* Oh, it's marvellous!

*Helmer:* Do you remember last Christmas? Three whole weeks beforehand you shut yourself up every evening till after midnight making flowers for the Christmas tree and all the other splendid things you wanted to surprise us with. Ugh, I never felt so bored in all my life.

*Nora:* I wasn't the least bit bored.

*Helmer [smiling]:* But it turned out a bit of an anticlimax, Nora.

*Nora:* Oh, you are not going to tease me about that again! How was I to know the cat would get in and pull everything to bits?

*Helmer:* No, of course you weren't. Poor little Nora! All you wanted was for us to have a nice time—and it's the thought behind it that counts, after all. All the same, it's a good thing we've seen the back of those lean times.

*Nora:* Yes, really it's marvellous.

*Helmer:* Now there's no need for me to sit here all on my own, bored to tears. And you don't have to strain your dear little eyes, and work those dainty little fingers to the bone. . . .

*Nora [clapping her hands]:* No, Torvald, I don't, do I? Not any more. Oh, how marvellous it is to hear that! *[Takes his arm.]* Now I want to tell you how I've been thinking we might arrange things, Torvald. As soon as Christmas is over. . . . *[The door-bell rings in the hall.]* Oh, there's the bell. *[Tidies one or two things in the room.]* It's probably a visitor. What a nuisance!

*Helmer:* Remember I'm not at home to callers.

*Maid [in the doorway]:* There's a lady to see you, ma'am.

*Nora:* Show her in, please.

*Maid [to Helmer]:* And the doctor's just arrived, too, sir.

*Helmer:* Did he go straight into my room?
*Maid:* Yes, he did, sir.

[*Helmer goes into his study. The Maid shows in Mrs. Linde, who is in travelling clothes, and closes the door after her.*]

*Mrs. Linde [subdued and rather hesitantly]:* How do you do, Nora?
*Nora [uncertainly]:* How do you do?
*Mrs. Linde:* I'm afraid you don't recognize me.
*Nora:* No, I don't think I . . . And yet I seem to. . . . [*Bursts out suddenly.*] Why! Kristine! Is it really you?
*Mrs. Linde:* Yes, it's me.
*Nora:* Kristine! Fancy not recognizing you again! But how was I to, when . . . [*Gently.*] How you've changed, Kristine!
*Mrs. Linde:* I dare say I have. In nine . . . ten years. . . .
*Nora:* Is it so long since we last saw each other? Yes, it must be. Oh, believe me these last eight years have been such a happy time. And now you've come up to town, too? All that long journey in wintertime. That took courage.
*Mrs. Linde:* I just arrived this morning on the steamer.
*Nora:* To enjoy yourself over Christmas, of course. How lovely! Oh, we'll have such fun, you'll see. Do take off your things. You are not cold, are you? [*Helps her.*] There now! Now let's sit down here in comfort beside the stove. No, here, you take the armchair, I'll sit here on the rocking chair. [*Takes her hands.*] Ah, now you look a bit more like your old self again. It was just that when I first saw you. . . . But you are a little paler, Kristine . . . and perhaps even a bit thinner!
*Mrs. Linde:* And much, much older, Nora.
*Nora:* Yes, perhaps a little older . . . very, very little, not really very much. [*Stops suddenly and looks serious.*] Oh, what a thoughtless creature I am, sitting here chattering on like this! Dear, sweet Kristine, can you forgive me?
*Mrs. Linde:* What do you mean, Nora?
*Nora [gently]:* Poor Kristine, of course you're a widow now.
*Mrs. Linde:* Yes, my husband died three years ago.
*Nora:* Oh, I remember now. I read about it in the papers. Oh, Kristine, believe me I often thought at the time of writing to you. But I kept putting it off, something always seemed to crop up.
*Mrs. Linde:* My dear Nora, I understand so well.
*Nora:* No, it wasn't very nice of me, Kristine. Oh, you poor thing, what you must have gone through. And didn't he leave you anything?
*Mrs. Linde:* No.
*Nora:* And no children?
*Mrs. Linde:* No.
*Nora:* Absolutely nothing?
*Mrs. Linde:* Nothing at all . . . not even a broken heart to grieve over.
*Nora [looks at her incredulously]:* But, Kristine, is that possible?
*Mrs. Linde [smiles sadly and strokes Nora's hair]:* Oh, it sometimes happens, Nora.

*Nora:* So utterly alone. How terribly sad that must be for you. I have three lovely children. You can't see them for the moment, because they're out with their nanny. But now you must tell me all about yourself. . . .

*Mrs. Linde:* No, no, I want to hear about you.

*Nora:* No, you start. I won't be selfish today. I must think only about your affairs today. But there's just one thing I really must tell you. Have you heard about the great stroke of luck we've had in the last few days?

*Mrs. Linde:* No. What is it?

*Nora:* What do you think? My husband has just been made Bank Manager!

*Mrs. Linde:* Your husband? How splendid!

*Nora:* Isn't it tremendous! It's not a very steady way of making a living, you know, being a lawyer, especially if he refuses to take on anything that's the least bit shady—which of course is what Torvald does, and I think he's quite right. You can imagine how pleased we are! He starts at the Bank straight after New Year, and he's getting a big salary and lots of commission. From now on we'll be able to live quite differently . . . we'll do just what we want. Oh, Kristine, I'm so happy and relieved. I must say it's lovely to have plenty of money and not have to worry. Isn't it?

*Mrs. Linde:* Yes. It must be nice to have enough, at any rate.

*Nora:* No, not just enough, but pots and pots of money.

*Mrs. Linde [smiles]:* Nora, Nora, haven't you learned any sense yet? At school you used to be an awful spendthrift.

*Nora:* Yes, Torvald still says I am. *[Wags her finger.]* But little Nora isn't as stupid as everybody thinks. Oh, we haven't really been in a position where I could afford to spend a lot of money. We've both had to work.

*Mrs. Linde:* You too?

*Nora:* Yes, odd jobs—sewing, crochet-work, embroidery and things like that. *[Casually.]* And one or two other things, besides. I suppose you know that Torvald left the Ministry when we got married. There weren't any prospects of promotion in his department, and of course he needed to earn more money than he had before. But the first year he wore himself out completely. He had to take on all kinds of extra jobs, you know, and he found himself working all hours of the day and night. But he couldn't go on like that; and he became seriously ill. The doctors said it was essential for him to go South.

*Mrs. Linde:* Yes, I believe you spent a whole year in Italy, didn't you?

*Nora:* That's right. It wasn't easy to get away, I can tell you. It was just after I'd had Ivar. But of course we had to go. Oh, it was an absolutely marvellous trip. And it saved Torvald's life. But it cost an awful lot of money, Kristine.

*Mrs. Linde:* That I can well imagine.

*Nora:* Twelve hundred dollars. Four thousand eight hundred crowns. That's a lot of money, Kristine.

*Mrs. Linde:* Yes, but in such circumstances, one is very lucky if one has it.

*Nora:* Well, we got it from Daddy, you see.

*Mrs. Linde:* Ah, that was it. It was just about then your father died, I believe, wasn't it?

*Nora:* Yes, Kristine, just about then. And do you know, I couldn't even go and look after him. Here was I expecting Ivar any day. And I also had poor Torvald, gravely ill, on my hands. Dear, kind Daddy! I never saw him again, Kristine. Oh, that's the saddest thing that has happened to me in all my married life.

*Mrs. Linde:* I know you were very fond of him. But after that you left for Italy?

*Nora:* Yes, we had the money then, and the doctors said it was urgent. We left a month later.

*Mrs. Linde:* And your husband came back completely cured?

*Nora:* Fit as a fiddle!

*Mrs. Linde:* But . . . what about the doctor?

*Nora:* How do you mean?

*Mrs. Linde:* I thought the maid said something about the gentleman who came at the same time as me being a doctor.

*Nora:* Yes, that was Dr. Rank. But this isn't a professional visit. He's our best friend and he always looks in at least once a day. No, Torvald has never had a day's illness since. And the children are fit and healthy, and so am I. [*Jumps up and claps her hands.*] Oh God, oh God, isn't it marvellous to be alive, and to be happy, Kristine! . . . Oh, but I ought to be ashamed of myself . . . Here I go on talking about nothing but myself. [*She sits on a low stool near Mrs. Linde and lays her arms on her lap.*] Oh, please, you mustn't be angry with me! Tell me, is it really true that you didn't love your husband? What made you marry him, then?

*Mrs. Linde:* My mother was still alive; she was bedridden and helpless. And then I had my two young brothers to look after as well. I didn't think I would be justified in refusing him.

*Nora:* No, I dare say you are right. I suppose he was fairly wealthy then?

*Mrs. Linde:* He was quite well off, I believe. But the business was shaky. When he died, it went all to pieces, and there just wasn't anything left.

*Nora:* What then?

*Mrs. Linde:* Well, I had to fend for myself, opening a little shop, running a little school, anything I could turn my hand to. These last three years have been one long relentless drudge. But now it's finished, Nora. My poor dear mother doesn't need me any more, she's passed away. Nor the boys either; they're at work now, they can look after themselves.

*Nora:* What a relief you must find it. . . .

*Mrs. Linde:* No, Nora! Just unutterably empty. Nobody to live for any more. [*Stands up restlessly.*] That's why I couldn't stand it any longer being cut off up there. Surely it must be a bit easier here to find something to occupy your mind. If only I could manage to find a steady job of some kind, in an office perhaps. . . .

*Nora:* But, Kristine, that's terribly exhausting; and you look so worn out even before you start. The best thing for you would be a little holiday at some quiet little resort.

*Mrs. Linde* [*crosses to the window*]: I haven't any father I can fall back on for the money, Nora.

*Nora [rises]:* Oh, please, you mustn't be angry with me!

*Mrs. Linde [goes to her]:* My dear Nora, you mustn't be angry with me either. That's the worst thing about people in my position, they become so bitter. One has nobody to work for, yet one has to be on the look-out all the time. Life has to go on, and one starts thinking only of oneself. Believe it or not, when you told me the good news about your step up, I was pleased not so much for your sake as for mine.

*Nora:* How do you mean? Ah, I see. You think Torvald might be able to do something for you.

*Mrs. Linde:* Yes, that's exactly what I thought.

*Nora:* And so he shall, Kristine. Just leave things to me. I'll bring it up so cleverly . . . I'll think up something to put him in a good mood. Oh, I do so much want to help you.

*Mrs. Linde:* It is awfully kind of you, Nora, offering to do all this for me, particularly in your case, where you haven't known much trouble or hardship in your own life.

*Nora:* When I . . . ? I haven't known much . . . ?

*Mrs. Linde [smiling]:* Well, good heavens, a little bit of sewing to do and a few things like that. What a child you are, Nora!

*Nora [tosses her head and walks across the room]:* I wouldn't be too sure of that, if I were you.

*Mrs. Linde:* Oh?

*Nora:* You're just like the rest of them. You all think I'm useless when it comes to anything really serious. . . .

*Mrs. Linde:* Come, come. . . .

*Nora:* You think I've never had anything much to contend with in this hard world.

*Mrs. Linde:* Nora dear, you've only just been telling me all the things you've had to put up with.

*Nora:* Pooh! They were just trivialities! *[Softly.]* I haven't told you about the really big thing.

*Mrs. Linde:* What big thing? What do you mean?

*Nora:* I know you rather tend to look down on me, Kristine. But you shouldn't, you know. You are proud of having worked so hard and so long for your mother.

*Mrs. Linde:* I'm sure I don't look down on anybody. But it's true what you say: I am both proud and happy when I think of how I was able to make Mother's life a little easier towards the end.

*Nora:* And you are proud when you think of what you have done for your brothers, too.

*Mrs. Linde:* I think I have every right to be.

*Nora:* I think so too. But now I'm going to tell you something, Kristine. I too have something to be proud and happy about.

*Mrs. Linde:* I don't doubt that. But what is it you mean?

*Nora:* Not so loud. Imagine if Torvald were to hear! He must never on any account . . . nobody must know about it, Kristine, nobody but you.

*Mrs. Linde:* But what is it?

*Nora:* Come over here. *[She pulls her down on the sofa beside her.]* Yes, Kristine, I too have something to be proud and happy about. I was the one who saved Torvald's life.

*Mrs. Linde:* Saved . . . ? How . . . ?

*Nora:* I told you about our trip to Italy. Torvald would never have recovered but for that. . . .

*Mrs. Linde:* Well? Your father gave you what money was necessary. . . .

*Nora [smiles]:* That's what Torvald thinks, and everybody else. But . . .

*Mrs. Linde:* But . . . ?

*Nora:* Daddy never gave us a penny. I was the one who raised the money.

*Mrs. Linde:* You? All that money?

*Nora:* Twelve hundred dollars. Four thousand eight hundred crowns. What do you say to that!

*Mrs. Linde:* But, Nora, how was it possible? Had you won a sweepstake or something?

*Nora [contemptuously]:* A sweepstake? Pooh! There would have been nothing to it then.

*Mrs. Linde:* Where did you get it from, then?

*Nora [hums and smiles secretively]:* H'm, tra-la-la!

*Mrs. Linde:* Because what you couldn't do was borrow it.

*Nora:* Oh? Why not?

*Mrs. Linde:* Well, a wife can't borrow without her husband's consent.

*Nora [tossing her head]:* Ah, but when it happens to be a wife with a bit of a sense for business . . . a wife who knows her way about things, then. . . .

*Mrs. Linde:* But, Nora, I just don't understand. . . .

*Nora:* You don't have to. I haven't said I did borrow the money. I might have got it some other way. *[Throws herself back on the sofa.]* I might even have got it from some admirer. Anyone as reasonably attractive as I am. . . .

*Mrs. Linde:* Don't be so silly!

*Nora:* Now you must be dying of curiosity, Kristine.

*Mrs. Linde:* Listen to me now, Nora dear—you haven't done anything rash, have you?

*Nora [sitting up again]:* Is it rash to save your husband's life?

*Mrs. Linde:* I think it was rash to do anything without telling him. . . .

*Nora:* But the whole point was that he mustn't know anything. Good heavens, can't you see! He wasn't even supposed to know how desperately ill he was. It was me the doctors came and told his life was in danger, that the only way to save him was to go South for a while. Do you think I didn't try talking him into it first? I began dropping hints about how nice it would be if I could be taken on a little trip abroad, like other young wives. I wept, I pleaded. I told him he ought to show some consideration for my condition, and let me have a bit of my own way. And then I suggested he might take out a loan. But at that he nearly lost his temper, Kristine. He said I was being frivolous, that it was his duty as a husband not to give in to all these whims and fancies of mine—as I do believe he called them. All right, I thought, somehow you've got to be saved. And it was then I found a way. . . .

Mrs. *Linde*: Did your husband never find out from your father that the money hadn't come from him?

*Nora*: No, never. It was just about the time Daddy died. I'd intended letting him into the secret and asking him not to give me away. But when he was so ill . . . I'm sorry to say it never became necessary.

Mrs. *Linde*: And you never confided in your husband?

*Nora*: Good heavens, how could you ever imagine such a thing! When he's so strict about such matters! Besides, Torvald is a man with a good deal of pride—it would be terribly embarrassing and humiliating for him if he thought he owed anything to me. It would spoil everything between us; this happy home of ours would never be the same again.

Mrs. *Linde*: Are you never going to tell him?

*Nora [reflectively, half-smiling]*: Oh yes, some day perhaps . . . in many years time, when I'm no longer as pretty as I am now. You mustn't laugh! What I mean of course is when Torvald isn't quite so much in love with me as he is now, when he's lost interest in watching me dance, or get dressed up, or recite. Then it might be a good thing to have something in reserve. . . . *[Breaks off.]* What nonsense! That day will never come. Well, what have you got to say to my big secret, Kristine? Still think I'm not much good for anything? One thing, though, it's meant a lot of worry for me, I can tell you. It hasn't always been easy to meet my obligations when the time came. You know in business there is something called quarterly interest, and other things called instalments, and these are always terribly difficult things to cope with. So what I've had to do is save a little here and there, you see, wherever I could. I couldn't really save anything out of the housekeeping, because Torvald has to live in decent style. I couldn't let the children go about badly dressed either—I felt any money I got for them had to go on them alone. Such sweet little things!

Mrs. *Linde*: Poor Nora! So it had to come out of your own allowance?

*Nora*: Of course. After all, I was the one it concerned most. Whenever Torvald gave me money for new clothes and such-like, I never spent more than half. And always I bought the simplest and cheapest things. It's a blessing most things look well on me, so Torvald never noticed anything. But sometimes I did feel it was a bit hard, Kristine, because it is nice to be well dressed, isn't it?

Mrs. *Linde*: Yes, I suppose it is.

*Nora*: I have had some other sources of income, of course. Last winter I was lucky enough to get quite a bit of copying to do. So I shut myself up every night and sat and wrote through to the small hours of the morning. Oh, sometimes I was so tired, so tired. But it was tremendous fun all the same, sitting there working and earning money like that. It was almost like being a man.

Mrs. *Linde*: And how much have you been able to pay off like this?

*Nora*: Well, I can't tell exactly. It's not easy to know where you are with transactions of this kind, you understand. All I know is I've paid off just as much as I could scrape together. Many's the time I was at my wit's end. *[Smiles.]* Then I used to sit here and pretend that some rich old gentleman had fallen in love with me. . . .

*Mrs. Linde:* What! What gentleman?

*Nora:* Oh, rubbish! . . . and that now he had died, and when they opened his will, there in big letters were the words: 'My entire fortune is to be paid over, immediately and in cash, to charming Mrs. Nora Helmer.'

*Mrs. Linde:* But my dear Nora—who *is* this man?

*Nora:* Good heavens, don't you understand? There never was any old gentleman; it was just something I used to sit here pretending, time and time again, when I didn't know where to turn next for money. But it doesn't make very much difference; as far as I'm concerned, the old boy can do what he likes, I'm tired of him; I can't be bothered any more with him or his will. Because now all my worries are over. [*Jumping up.*] Oh God, what a glorious thought, Kristine! No more worries! Just think of being without a care in the world . . . being able to romp with the children, and making the house nice and attractive, and having things just as Torvald likes to have them! And then spring will soon be here, and blue skies. And maybe we can go away somewhere. I might even see something of the sea again. Oh yes! When you're happy, life is a wonderful thing!

[*The door-bell is heard in the hall.*]

*Mrs. Linde [gets up]:* There's the bell. Perhaps I'd better go.

*Nora:* No, do stay, please. I don't suppose it's for me; it's probably somebody for Torvald. . . .

*Maid [in the doorway]:* Excuse me, ma'am, but there's a gentleman here wants to see Mr. Helmer, and I didn't quite know . . . because the Doctor is in there. . . .

*Nora:* Who is the gentleman?

*Krogstad [in the doorway]:* It's me, Mrs. Helmer.

[*Mrs. Linde starts, then turns away to the window.*]

*Nora [tense, takes a step towards him and speaks in a low voice]:* You? What is it? What do you want to talk to my husband about?

*Krogstad:* Bank matters . . . in a manner of speaking. I work at the bank, and I hear your husband is to be the new manager. . . .

*Nora:* So it's . . .

*Krogstad:* Just routine business matters, Mrs. Helmer. Absolutely nothing else.

*Nora:* Well then, please go into his study.

[*She nods impassively and shuts the hall door behind him; then she walks across and sees to the stove.*]

*Mrs. Linde:* Nora . . . who was that man?

*Nora:* His name is Krogstad.

*Mrs. Linde:* So it really was him.

*Nora:* Do you know the man?

*Mrs. Linde:* I used to know him . . . a good many years ago. He was a solicitor's clerk in our district for a while.

*Nora:* Yes, so he was.

*Mrs. Linde:* How he's changed!

*Nora:* His marriage wasn't a very happy one, I believe.

*Mrs. Linde:* He's a widower now, isn't he?

*Nora:* With a lot of children. There, it'll burn better now.

[*She closes the stove door and moves the rocking chair a little to one side.*]

*Mrs. Linde:* He does a certain amount of business on the side, they say?

*Nora:* Oh? Yes, it's always possible. I just don't know. . . . But let's not think about business . . . it's all so dull.

[*Dr. Rank comes in from Helmer's study.*]

*Dr. Rank [still in the doorway]:* No, no, Torvald, I won't intrude. I'll just look in on your wife for a moment. [*Shuts the door and notices Mrs. Linde.*] Oh, I beg your pardon. I'm afraid I'm intruding here as well.

*Nora:* No, not at all! [*Introduces them.*] Dr. Rank . . . Mrs. Linde.

*Rank:* Ah! A name I've often heard mentioned in this house. I believe I came past you on the stairs as I came in.

*Mrs. Linde:* I have to take things slowly going upstairs. I find it rather a trial.

*Rank:* Ah, some little disability somewhere, eh?

*Mrs. Linde:* Just a bit run down, I think, actually.

*Rank:* Is that all? Then I suppose you've come to town for a good rest—doing the rounds of the parties?

*Mrs. Linde:* I have come to look for work.

*Rank:* Is that supposed to be some kind of sovereign remedy for being run down?

*Mrs. Linde:* One must live, Doctor.

*Rank:* Yes, it's generally thought to be necessary.

*Nora:* Come, come, Dr. Rank. You are quite as keen to live as anybody.

*Rank:* Quite keen, yes. Miserable as I am, I'm quite ready to let things drag on as long as possible. All my patients are the same. Even those with a moral affliction are no different. As a matter of fact, there's a bad case of that kind in talking with Helmer at this very moment. . . .

*Mrs. Linde [softly]:* Ah!

*Nora:* Whom do you mean?

*Rank:* A person called Krogstad—nobody you would know. He's rotten to the core. But even he began talking about having to *live,* as though it were something terribly important.

*Nora:* Oh? And what did he want to talk to Torvald about?

*Rank:* I honestly don't know. All I heard was something about the Bank.

*Nora:* I didn't know that Krog . . . that this Mr. Krogstad had anything to do with the Bank.

*Rank:* Oh yes, he's got some kind of job down there. [*To Mrs. Linde.*] I wonder if you've got people in your part of the country too who go rushing round sniffing out cases of moral corruption, and then installing the individuals concerned in nice, well-paid jobs where they can keep them under observation. Sound, decent people have to be content to stay out in the cold.

Mrs. Linde: Yet surely it's the sick who most need to be brought in.

Rank [shrugs his shoulders]: Well, there we have it. It's that attitude that's turning society into a clinic.

[Nora, lost in her own thoughts, breaks into smothered laughter and claps her hands.]

Rank: Why are you laughing at that? Do you know in fact what society is?

Nora: What do I care about your silly old society? I was laughing about something quite different . . . something frightfully funny. Tell me, Dr. Rank, are all the people who work at the Bank dependent on Torvald now?

Rank: Is that what you find so frightfully funny?

Nora [smiles and hums]: Never you mind! Never you mind! [Walks about the room.] Yes, it really is terribly amusing to think that we . . . that Torvald now has power over so many people. [She takes the bag out of her pocket.] Dr. Rank, what about a little macaroon?

Rank: Look at this, eh? Macaroons. I thought they were forbidden here.

Nora: Yes, but these are some Kristine gave me.

Mrs. Linde: What? I . . . ?

Nora: Now, now, you needn't be alarmed. You weren't to know that Torvald had forbidden them. He's worried in case they ruin my teeth, you know. Still . . . what's it matter once in a while! Don't you think so, Dr. Rank? Here! [She pops a macaroon into his mouth.] And you too, Kristine. And I shall have one as well; just a little one . . . or two at the most. [She walks about the room again.] Really I am so happy. There's just one little thing I'd love to do now.

Rank: What's that?

Nora: Something I'd love to say in front of Torvald.

Rank: Then why can't you?

Nora: No, I daren't. It's not very nice.

Mrs. Linde: Not very nice?

Rank: Well, in that case it might not be wise. But to us, I don't see why. . . . What is this you would love to say in front of Helmer?

Nora: I would simply love to say: 'Damn'.

Rank: Are you mad!

Mrs. Linde: Good gracious, Nora . . . !

Rank: Say it! Here he is!

Nora [hiding the bag of macaroons]: Sh! Sh!

[Helmer comes out of his room, his overcoat over his arm and his hat in his hand.]

Nora [going over to him]: Well, Torvald dear, did you get rid of him?

Helmer: Yes, he's just gone.

Nora: Let me introduce you. This is Kristine, who has just arrived in town. . . .

Helmer: Kristine . . . ? You must forgive me, but I don't think I know . . .

Nora: Mrs. Linde, Torvald dear. Kristine Linde.

Helmer: Ah, indeed. A school-friend of my wife's, presumably.

*Mrs. Linde:* Yes, we were girls together.

*Nora:* Fancy, Torvald, she's come all this long way just to have a word with you.

*Helmer:* How is that?

*Mrs. Linde:* Well, it wasn't really. . . .

*Nora:* The thing is, Kristine is terribly clever at office work, and she's frightfully keen on finding a job with some efficient man, so that she can learn even more. . . .

*Helmer:* Very sensible, Mrs. Linde.

*Nora:* And then when she heard you'd been made Bank Manager—there was a bit in the paper about it—she set off at once. Torvald please! You *will* try and do something for Kristine, won't you? For my sake?

*Helmer:* Well, that's not altogether impossible. You are a widow, I presume?

*Mrs. Linde:* Yes.

*Helmer:* And you've had some experience in business?

*Mrs. Linde:* A fair amount.

*Helmer:* Well, it's quite probable I can find you a job, I think. . . .

*Nora [clapping her hands]:* There, you see!

*Helmer:* You have come at a fortunate moment, Mrs. Linde. . . .

*Mrs. Linde:* Oh, how can I ever thank you . . . ?

*Helmer:* Not a bit. *[He puts on his overcoat.]* But for the present I must ask you to excuse me. . . .

*Rank:* Wait. I'm coming with you.

*[He fetches his fur coat from the hall and warms it at the stove.]*

*Nora:* Don't be long, Torvald dear.

*Helmer:* Not more than an hour, that's all.

*Nora:* Are you leaving too, Kristine?

*Mrs. Linde [putting on her things]:* Yes, I must go and see if I can't find myself a room.

*Helmer:* Perhaps we can all walk down the road together.

*Nora [helping her]:* What a nuisance we are so limited for space here. I'm afraid it just isn't possible. . . .

*Mrs. Linde:* Oh, you mustn't dream of it! Goodbye, Nora dear, and thanks for everything.

*Nora:* Goodbye for the present. But . . . you'll be coming back this evening, of course. And you too, Dr. Rank? What's that? If you are up to it? Of course you'll be up to it. Just wrap yourself up well.

*[They go out, talking, into the hall; children's voices can be heard on the stairs.]*

*Nora:* Here they are! Here they are! *[She runs to the front door and opens it. Anne Marie, the nursemaid, enters with the children.]* Come in! Come in! *[She bends down and kisses them.]* Ah! my sweet little darlings. . . . You see them, Kristine? Aren't they lovely!

*Rank:* Don't stand here chattering in this draught!

*Helmer:* Come along, Mrs. Linde. The place now becomes unbearable for any-body except mothers.

*[Dr. Rank, Helmer and Mrs. Linde go down the stairs: the Nursemaid comes into the room with the children, then Nora, shutting the door behind her.]*

*Nora:* How fresh and bright you look! My, what red cheeks you've got! Like apples and roses. *[During the following, the children keep chattering away to her.]* Have you had a nice time? That's splendid. And you gave Emmy and Bob a ride on your sledge? Did you now! Both together! Fancy that! There's a clever boy, Ivar. Oh, let me take her a little while, Anne Marie. There's my sweet little baby-doll! *[She takes the youngest of the children from the nursemaid and dances with her.]* All right, Mummy will dance with Bobby too. What? You've been throwing snowballs? Oh, I wish I'd been there. No, don't bother, Anne Marie, I'll help them off with their things. No, please, let me—I like doing it. You go on in, you look frozen. You'll find some hot coffee on the stove. *[The nurse-maid goes into the room, left. Nora takes off the children's coats and hats and throws them down anywhere, while the children all talk at once.]* Really! A great big dog came running after you? But he didn't bite. No, the doggies wouldn't bite my pretty little dollies. You mustn't touch the parcels, Ivar! What are they? Wouldn't you like to know! No, no, that's nasty. Now? Shall we play some-thing? What shall we play? Hide and seek? Yes, let's play hide and seek. Bob can hide first. Me first? All right, let me hide first.

*[She and the children play, laughing and shrieking, in this room and in the adjacent room on the right. Finally Nora hides under the table; the children come rushing in to look for her but cannot find her; they hear her stifled laughter, rush to the table, lift up the tablecloth and find her. Tremendous shouts of delight. She creeps out and pretends to frighten them. More shouts. Meanwhile there has been a knock at the front door, which nobody has heard. The door half opens, and Krogstad can be seen. He waits a little; the game continues.]*

*Krogstad:* I beg your pardon, Mrs. Helmer. . . .

*Nora [turns with a stifled cry and half jumps up]:* Ah! What do you want?

*Krogstad:* Excuse me. The front door was standing open. Somebody must have forgotten to shut it. . . .

*Nora [standing up]:* My husband isn't at home, Mr. Krogstad.

*Krogstad:* I know.

*Nora:* Well . . . what are you doing here?

*Krogstad:* I want a word with you.

*Nora:* With . . . ? *[Quietly, to the children.]* Go to Anne Marie. What? No, the strange man won't do anything to Mummy. When he's gone we'll have another game. *[She leads the children into the room, left, and shuts the door after them; tense and uneasy.]* You want to speak to me?

*Krogstad:* Yes, I do.

*Nora:* Today? But it isn't the first of the month yet. . . .

*Krogstad:* No, it's Christmas Eve. It depends entirely on you what sort of Christmas you have.

*Nora:* What do you want? Today I can't possibly . . .

*Krogstad:* Let's not talk about that for the moment. It's something else. You've got a moment to spare?

*Nora:* Yes, I suppose so, though . . .

*Krogstad:* Good. I was sitting in Olsen's café, and I saw your husband go down the road . . .

*Nora:* Did you?

*Krogstad:* . . . with a lady.

*Nora:* Well?

*Krogstad:* May I be so bold as to ask whether that lady was a Mrs. Linde?

*Nora:* Yes.

*Krogstad:* Just arrived in town?

*Nora:* Yes, today.

*Krogstad:* And she's a good friend of yours?

*Nora:* Yes, she is. But I can't see . . .

*Krogstad:* I also knew her once.

*Nora:* I know.

*Krogstad:* Oh? So you know all about it. I thought as much. Well, I want to ask you straight: is Mrs. Linde getting a job in the Bank?

*Nora:* How dare you cross-examine me like this, Mr. Krogstad? You, one of my husband's subordinates? But since you've asked me, I'll tell you. Yes, Mrs. Linde *has* got a job. And I'm the one who got it for her, Mr. Krogstad. Now you know.

*Krogstad:* So my guess was right.

*Nora [walking up and down]:* Oh, I think I can say that some of us have a little influence now and again. Just because one happens to be a woman, that doesn't mean. . . . People in subordinate positions, ought to take care they don't offend anybody . . . who . . . hm . . .

*Krogstad:* . . . has influence?

*Nora:* Exactly.

*Krogstad [changing his tone]:* Mrs. Helmer, will you have the goodness to use your influence on my behalf?

*Nora:* What? What do you mean?

*Krogstad:* Will you be so good as to see that I keep my modest little job at the Bank?

*Nora:* What do you mean? Who wants to take it away from you?

*Krogstad:* Oh, you needn't try and pretend to me you don't know. I can quite see that this friend of yours isn't particularly anxious to bump up against me. And I can also see now whom I can thank for being given the sack.

*Nora:* But I assure you. . . .

*Krogstad:* All right, all right. But to come to the point: there's still time. And I advise you to use your influence to stop it.

*Nora:* But, Mr. Krogstad, I *have* no influence.

*Krogstad:* Haven't you? I thought just now you said yourself. . .

*Nora:* I didn't mean it that way, of course. Me? What makes you think I've got any influence of that kind over my husband?

*Krogstad:* I know your husband from our student days. I don't suppose he is any more steadfast than other married men.

*Nora:* You speak disrespectfully of my husband like that and I'll show you the door.

*Krogstad:* So the lady's got courage.

*Nora:* I'm not frightened of you any more. After New Year I'll soon be finished with the whole business.

*Krogstad [controlling himself]:* Listen to me, Mrs. Helmer. If necessary I shall fight for my little job in the Bank as if I were fighting for my life.

*Nora:* So it seems.

*Krogstad:* It's not just for the money, that's the last thing I care about. There's something else . . . well, I might as well out with it. You see it's like this. You know as well as anybody that some years ago I got myself mixed up in a bit of trouble.

*Nora:* I believe I've heard something of the sort.

*Krogstad:* It never got as far as the courts; but immediately it was as if all paths were barred to me. So I started going in for the sort of business you know about. I had to do something, and I think I can say I haven't been one of the worst. But now I have to get out of it. My sons are growing up; for their sake I must try and win back what respectability I can. That job in the Bank was like the first step on the ladder for me. And now your husband wants to kick me off the ladder again, back into the mud.

*Nora:* But in God's name, Mr. Krogstad, it's quite beyond my power to help you.

*Krogstad:* That's because you haven't the will to help me. But I have ways of making you.

*Nora:* You wouldn't go and tell my husband I owe you money?

*Krogstad:* Suppose I did tell him?

*Nora:* It would be a rotten shame. [*Half choking with tears.*] That secret is all my pride and joy—why should he have to hear about it in this nasty, horrid way . . . hear about it from *you*. You would make things horribly unpleasant for me. . . .

*Krogstad:* Merely unpleasant?

*Nora [vehemently]:* Go on, do it then! It'll be all the worse for you. Because then my husband will see for himself what a bad man you are, and then you certainly won't be able to keep your job.

*Krogstad:* I asked whether it was only a bit of domestic unpleasantness you were afraid of?

*Nora:* If my husband gets to know about it, he'll pay off what's owing at once. And then we'd have nothing more to do with you.

*Krogstad [taking a pace towards her]:* Listen, Mrs. Helmer, either you haven't a very good memory, or else you don't understand much about business. I'd better make the position a little bit clearer for you.

*Nora:* How do you mean?

*Krogstad:* When your husband was ill, you came to me for the loan of twelve hundred dollars.

*Nora:* I didn't know of anybody else.

*Krogstad:* I promised to find you the money. . . .

*Nora:* And you did find it.

*Krogstad:* I promised to find you the money on certain conditions. At the time you were so concerned about your husband's illness, and so anxious to get the money for going away with, that I don't think you paid very much attention to all the incidentals. So there is perhaps some point in reminding you of them. Well, I promised to find you the money against an IOU which I drew up for you.

*Nora:* Yes, and which I signed.

*Krogstad:* Very good. But below that I added a few lines, by which your father was to stand security. This your father was to sign.

*Nora:* Was to . . . ? He did sign it.

*Krogstad:* I had left the date blank. The idea was that your father was to add the date himself when he signed it. Remember?

*Nora:* Yes, I think. . . .

*Krogstad:* I then gave you the IOU to post to your father. Wasn't that so?

*Nora:* Yes.

*Krogstad:* Which of course you did at once. Because only about five or six days later you brought it back to me with your father's signature. I then paid out the money.

*Nora:* Well? Haven't I paid the instalments regularly?

*Krogstad:* Yes, fairly. But . . . coming back to what we were talking about . . . that was a pretty bad period you were going through then, Mrs. Helmer.

*Nora:* Yes, it was.

*Krogstad:* Your father was seriously ill, I believe.

*Nora:* He was very near the end.

*Krogstad:* And died shortly afterwards?

*Nora:* Yes.

*Krogstad:* Tell me, Mrs. Helmer, do you happen to remember which day your father died? The exact date, I mean.

*Nora:* Daddy died on 29 September.

*Krogstad:* Quite correct. I made some inquiries. Which brings up a rather curious point [*takes out a paper*] which I simply cannot explain.

*Nora:* Curious . . . ? I don't know . . .

*Krogstad:* The curious thing is, Mrs. Helmer, that your father signed this document three days after his death.

*Nora:* What? I don't understand. . . .

*Krogstad:* Your father died on 29 September. But look here. Your father has dated his signature 2 October. Isn't that rather curious, Mrs. Helmer? [*Nora remains silent.*] It's also remarkable that the words '2 October' and the year are not in your father's handwriting, but in a handwriting I rather think I recognize.

Well, perhaps that could be explained. Your father might have forgotten to date his signature, and then somebody else might have made a guess at the date later, before the fact of your father's death was known. There is nothing wrong in that. What really matters is the signature. And *that* is of course genuine, Mrs. Helmer? It really was your father who wrote his name here?

Nora [*after a moment's silence, throws her head back and looks at him defiantly*]: No, it wasn't. It was me who signed father's name.

Krogstad: Listen to me. I suppose you realize that that is a very dangerous confession?

Nora: Why? You'll soon have all your money back.

Krogstad: Let me ask you a question: why didn't you send that document to your father?

Nora: It was impossible. Daddy was ill. If I'd asked him for his signature, I'd have to tell him what the money was for. Don't you see, when he was as ill as that I couldn't go and tell him that my husband's life was in danger. It was simply impossible.

Krogstad: It would have been better for you if you had abandoned the whole trip.

Nora: No, that was impossible. This was the thing that was to save my husband's life. I couldn't give it up.

Krogstad: But did it never strike you that this was fraudulent . . . ?

Nora: That wouldn't have meant anything to me. Why should I worry about you? I couldn't stand you, not when you insisted on going through with all those cold-blooded formalities, knowing all the time what a critical state my husband was in.

Krogstad: Mrs. Helmer, it's quite clear you still haven't the faintest idea what it is you've committed. But let me tell you, my own offence was no more and no worse than that, and it ruined my entire reputation.

Nora: You? Are you trying to tell me that you once risked everything to save your wife's life?

Krogstad: The law takes no account of motives.

Nora: Then they must be very bad laws.

Krogstad: Bad or not, if I produce this document in court, you'll be condemned according to them.

Nora: I don't believe it. Isn't a daughter entitled to try and save her father from worry and anxiety on his deathbed? Isn't a wife entitled to save her husband's life? I might not know very much about the law, but I feel sure of one thing: it must say somewhere that things like this are allowed. You mean to say you don't know that—you, when it's your job? You must be a rotten lawyer, Mr. Krogstad.

Krogstad: That may be. But when it comes to business transactions—like the sort between us two—perhaps you'll admit I know something about *them*? Good. Now you must please yourself. But I tell you this: if I'm pitched out a second time, you are going to keep me company.

[*He bows and goes out through the hall.*]

*Nora [stands thoughtfully for a moment, then tosses her head]:* Rubbish! He's just trying to scare me. I'm not such a fool as all that. *[Begins gathering up the children's clothes; after a moment she stops.]* Yet . . . ? No, it's impossible! I did it
for love, didn't I?

*The Children [in the doorway, left]:* Mummy, the gentleman's just gone out of the
gate.

*Nora:* Yes, I know. But you mustn't say anything to anybody about that gentleman. You hear? Not even to Daddy!

*The Children:* All right, Mummy. Are you going to play again?

*Nora:* No, not just now.

*The Children:* But Mummy, you promised!

*Nora:* Yes, but I can't just now. Off you go now, I have a lot to do. Off you go, my
darlings. *[She herds them carefully into the other room and shuts the door behind
them. She sits down on the sofa, picks up her embroidery and works a few stitches,
but soon stops.]* No! *[She flings her work down, stands up, goes to the hall door
and calls out.]* Helene! Fetch the tree in for me, please. *[She walks across to the
table, left, and opens the drawer; again pauses.]* No, really, it's quite impossible!

*Maid [with the Christmas tree]:* Where shall I put it, ma'am?

*Nora:* On the floor there, in the middle.

*Maid:* Anything else you want me to bring?

*Nora:* No, thank you. I've got what I want.

*[The maid has put the tree down and goes out.]*

*Nora [busy decorating the tree]:* Candles here . . . and flowers here—Revolting
man! It's all nonsense! There's nothing to worry about. We'll have a lovely
Christmas tree. And I'll do anything you want me to, Torvald; I'll sing for
you, dance for you. . . .

*[Helmer, with a bundle of documents under his arm, comes in by the hall door.]*

*Nora:* Ah, back again already?

*Helmer:* Yes. Anybody been?

*Nora:* Here? No.

*Helmer:* That's funny. I just saw Krogstad leave the house.

*Nora:* Oh? O yes, that's right. Krogstad was here a minute.

*Helmer:* Nora, I can tell by your face he's been asking you to put a good word in
for him.

*Nora:* Yes.

*Helmer:* And you were to pretend it was your own idea? You were to keep quiet
about his having been here. He asked you to do that as well, didn't he?

*Nora:* Yes, Torvald. But . . .

*Helmer:* Nora, Nora, what possessed you to do a thing like that? Talking to a person like him, making him promises? And then on top of everything, to tell
me a lie!

*Nora:* A lie . . . ?

*Helmer:* Didn't you say that nobody had been here? *[Wagging his finger at her.]* Never again must my little song-bird do a thing like that! Little song-birds must keep their pretty little beaks out of mischief; no chirruping out of tune! *[Puts his arm round her waist.]* Isn't that the way we want things to be? Yes, of course it is. *[Lets her go.]* So let's say no more about it. *[Sits down by the stove.]* Ah, nice and cosy here!

*[He glances through his papers.]*

*Nora [busy with the Christmas tree, after a short pause]:* Torvald!
*Helmer:* Yes.
*Nora:* I'm so looking forward to the fancy dress ball at the Stenborgs on Boxing Day.
*Helmer:* And I'm terribly curious to see what sort of surprise you've got for me.
*Nora:* Oh, it's too silly.
*Helmer:* Oh?
*Nora:* I just can't think of anything suitable. Everything seems so absurd, so pointless.
*Helmer:* Has my little Nora come to *that* conclusion?
*Nora [behind his chair, her arms on the chairback]:* Are you very busy, Torvald?
*Helmer:* Oh. . . .
*Nora:* What are all those papers?
*Helmer:* Bank matters.
*Nora:* Already?
*Helmer:* I have persuaded the retiring manager to give me authority to make any changes in organization or personnel I think necessary. I have to work on it over the Christmas week. I want everything straight by the New Year.
*Nora:* So that was why that poor Krogstad. . . .
*Helmer:* Hm!
*Nora [still leaning against the back of the chair, running her fingers through his hair]:* If you hadn't been so busy, Torvald, I'd have asked you to do me an awfully big favour.
*Helmer:* Let me hear it. What's it to be?
*Nora:* Nobody's got such good taste as you. And the thing is I do so want to look my best at the fancy dress ball. Torvald, couldn't you give me some advice and tell me what you think I ought to go as, and how I should arrange my costume?
*Helmer:* Aha! So my impulsive little woman is asking for somebody to come to her rescue, eh?
*Nora:* Please, Torvald, I never get anywhere without your help.
*Helmer:* Very well, I'll think about it. We'll find something.
*Nora:* That's sweet of you. *[She goes across to the tree again; pause.]* How pretty these red flowers look.—Tell me, was it really something terribly wrong this man Krogstad did?
*Helmer:* Forgery. Have you any idea what that means?
*Nora:* Perhaps circumstances left him no choice?

*Helmer:* Maybe. Or perhaps, like so many others, he just didn't think. I am not so heartless that I would necessarily want to condemn a man for a single mistake like that.

*Nora:* Oh no, Torvald, of course not!

*Helmer:* Many a man might be able to redeem himself, if he honestly confessed his guilt and took his punishment.

*Nora:* Punishment?

*Helmer:* But that wasn't the way Krogstad chose. He dodged what was due to him by a cunning trick. And that's what has been the cause of his corruption.

*Nora:* Do you think it would. . . ?

*Helmer:* Just think how a man with a thing like that on his conscience will always be having to lie and cheat and dissemble; he can never drop the mask, not even with his own wife and children. And the children—*that's* the most terrible part of it, Nora.

*Nora:* Why?

*Helmer:* A fog of lies like that in a household, and it spreads disease and infection to every part of it. Every breath the children take in that kind of house is reeking with evil germs.

*Nora [closer behind him]:* Are you sure of that?

*Helmer:* My dear Nora, as a lawyer I know what I'm talking about. Practically all juvenile delinquents come from homes where the mother is dishonest.

*Nora:* Why mothers particularly?

*Helmer:* It's generally traceable to the mothers, but of course fathers can have the same influence. Every lawyer knows that only too well. And yet there's Krogstad been poisoning his own children for years with lies and deceit. That's the reason I call him morally depraved. *[Holds out his hands to her.]* That's why my sweet little Nora must promise me not to try putting in any more good words for him. Shake hands on it. Well? What's this? Give me your hand. There now! That's settled. I assure you I would have found it impossible to work with him. I quite literally feel physically sick in the presence of such people.

*Nora [draws her hand away and walks over to the other side of the Christmas tree]:* How hot it is in here! And I still have such a lot to do.

*Helmer [stands up and collects his papers together]:* Yes, I'd better think of getting some of this read before dinner. I must also think about your costume. And I might even be able to lay my hands on something to wrap in gold paper and hang on the Christmas tree. *[He lays his hand on her head.]* My precious little singing bird.

*[He goes into his study and shuts the door behind him.]*

*Nora [quietly, after a pause]:* Nonsense! It can't be. It's impossible. It *must* be impossible.

*Maid [in the doorway, left]:* The children keep asking so nicely if they can come in and see Mummy.

*Nora:* No, no, don't let them in! You stay with them, Anne Marie.

*Maid:* Very well, ma'am.

*[She shuts the door.]*

*Nora [pale with terror]:* Corrupt my children . . . ! Poison my home? *[Short pause; she throws back her head.]* It's not true! It could never, never be true!

## ACT II

*The same room. In the corner beside the piano stands the Christmas tree, stripped, bedraggled and with its candles burnt out. Nora's outdoor things lie on the sofa. Nora, alone there, walks about restlessly; at last she stops by the sofa and picks up her coat.*

*Nora [putting her coat down again]:* Somebody's coming! *[Crosses to the door, listens.]* No, it's nobody. Nobody will come today, of course, Christmas Day— nor tomorrow, either. But perhaps. . . . *[She opens the door and looks out.]* No, nothing in the letter box; quite empty. *[Comes forward.]* Oh, nonsense! He didn't mean it seriously. Things like that *can't* happen. It's impossible. Why, I have three small children.

*[The Nursemaid comes from the room, left, carrying a big cardboard box.]*

*Nursemaid:* I finally found it, the box with the fancy dress costumes.

*Nora:* Thank you. Put it on the table, please.

*Nursemaid [does this]:* But I'm afraid they are in an awful mess.

*Nora:* Oh, if only I could rip them up into a thousand pieces!

*Nursemaid:* Good heavens, they can be mended all right, with a bit of patience.

*Nora:* Yes, I'll go over and get Mrs. Linde to help me.

*Nursemaid:* Out again? In this terrible weather? You'll catch your death of cold, Ma'am.

*Nora:* Oh, worse things might happen.—How are the children?

*Nursemaid:* Playing with their Christmas presents, poor little things, but . . .

*Nora:* Do they keep asking for me?

*Nursemaid:* They are so used to being with their Mummy.

*Nora:* Yes, Anne Marie, from now on I can't be with them as often as I was before.

*Nursemaid:* Ah well, children get used to anything in time.

*Nora:* Do you think so? Do you think they would forget their Mummy if she went away for good?

*Nursemaid:* Good gracious—for good?

*Nora:* Tell me, Anne Marie—I've often wondered—how on earth could you bear to hand your child over to strangers?

*Nursemaid:* Well, there was nothing else for it when I had to come and nurse my little Nora.

*Nora:* Yes but . . . how could you *bring* yourself to do it?

*Nursemaid:* When I had the chance of such a good place? When a poor girl's been in trouble she must make the best of things. Because *he* didn't help, the rotter.

*Nora:* But your daughter will have forgotten you.

*Nursemaid:* Oh no, she hasn't. She wrote to me when she got confirmed, and again when she got married.

*Nora [putting her arms round her neck]:* Dear old Anne Marie, you were a good mother to me when I was little.

*Nursemaid:* My poor little Nora never had any other mother but me.

*Nora:* And if my little ones only had you, I know you would. . . . Oh, what am I talking about! [*She opens the box.*] Go in to them. I must . . . Tomorrow I'll let you see how pretty I am going to look.

*Nursemaid:* Ah, there'll be nobody at the ball as pretty as my Nora.

[*She goes into the room, left.*]

*Nora [begins unpacking the box, but soon throws it down]:* Oh, if only I dare go out. If only I could be sure nobody would come. And that nothing would happen in the meantime here at home. Rubbish—nobody's going to come. I mustn't think about it. Brush this muff. Pretty gloves, pretty gloves! I'll put it right out of my mind. One, two, three, four, five, six. . . . [*Screams.*] Ah, they are coming. . . . [*She starts towards the door, but stops irresolute. Mrs. Linde comes from the hall, where she has taken off her things.*] Oh, it's you, Kristine. There's nobody else out there, is there? I'm so glad you've come.

*Mrs. Linde:* I heard you'd been over looking for me.

*Nora:* Yes, I was just passing. There's something you must help me with. Come and sit beside me on the sofa here. You see, the Stenborgs are having a fancy dress party upstairs tomorrow evening, and now Torvald wants me to go as a Neapolitan fisher lass and dance the tarantella. I learned it in Capri, you know.

*Mrs. Linde:* Well, well! So you are going to do a party piece?

*Nora:* Torvald says I should. Look, here's the costume, Torvald had it made for me down there. But it's got all torn and I simply don't know. . . .

*Mrs. Linde:* We'll soon have that put right. It's only the trimming come away here and there. Got a needle and thread? Ah, here's what we are after.

*Nora:* It's awfully kind of you.

*Mrs. Linde:* So you are going to be all dressed up tomorrow, Nora? Tell you what—I'll pop over for a minute to see you in all your finery. But I'm quite forgetting to thank you for the pleasant time we had last night.

*Nora [gets up and walks across the room]:* Somehow I didn't think yesterday was as nice as things generally are.—You should have come to town a little earlier, Kristine.—Yes, Torvald certainly knows how to make things pleasant about the place.

*Mrs. Linde:* You too, I should say. You are not your father's daughter for nothing. But tell me, is Dr. Rank always as depressed as he was last night?

*Nora:* No, last night it was rather obvious. He's got something seriously wrong with him, you know. Tuberculosis of the spine, poor fellow. His father was a horrible man, who used to have mistresses and things like that. That's why the son was always ailing, right from being a child.

*Mrs. Linde [lowering her sewing]:* But my dear Nora, how do you come to know about things like that?

*Nora [walking about the room]:* Huh! When you've got three children, you get these visits from ... women who have had a certain amount of medical training. And you hear all sorts of things from them.

*Mrs. Linde [begins sewing again; short silence]:* Does Dr. Rank call in every day?

*Nora:* Every single day. He was Torvald's best friend as a boy, and he's a good friend of *mine*, too. Dr. Rank is almost like one of the family.

*Mrs. Linde:* But tell me—is he really genuine? What I mean is: doesn't he sometimes rather turn on the charm?

*Nora:* No, on the contrary. What makes you think that?

*Mrs. Linde:* When you introduced me yesterday, he claimed he'd often heard my name in this house. But afterwards I noticed your husband hadn't the faintest idea who I was. Then how is it that Dr. Rank should. . . .

*Nora:* Oh yes, it was quite right what he said, Kristine. You see Torvald is so terribly in love with me that he says he wants me all to himself. When we were first married, it even used to make him sort of jealous if I only as much as mentioned any of my old friends from back home. So of course I stopped doing it. But I often talk to Dr. Rank about such things. He likes hearing about them.

*Mrs. Linde:* Listen, Nora! In lots of ways you are still a child. Now, I'm a good deal older than you, and a bit more experienced. I'll tell you something: I think you ought to give up all this business with Dr. Rank.

*Nora:* Give up what business?

*Mrs. Linde:* The whole thing, I should say. Weren't you saying yesterday something about a rich admirer who was to provide you with money. . . .

*Nora:* One who's never existed, I regret to say. But what of it?

*Mrs. Linde:* Has Dr. Rank money?

*Nora:* Yes, he has.

*Mrs. Linde:* And no dependents?

*Nora:* No, nobody. But. . . ?

*Mrs. Linde:* And he comes to the house every day?

*Nora:* Yes, I told you.

*Mrs. Linde:* But how can a man of his position want to pester you like this?

*Nora:* I simply don't understand.

*Mrs. Linde:* Don't pretend, Nora. Do you think I don't see now who you borrowed the twelve hundred from?

*Nora:* Are you out of your mind? Do you really think that? A friend of ours who comes here every day? The whole situation would have been absolutely intolerable.

*Mrs. Linde:* It *really* isn't him?

*Nora:* No, I give you my word. It would never have occurred to me for one moment. . . . Anyway, he didn't have the money to lend then. He didn't inherit it till later.

*Mrs. Linde:* Just as well for you, I'd say, my dear Nora.

*Nora:* No, it would never have occurred to me to ask Dr. Rank. . . . All the same I'm pretty certain if I were to ask him . . .

*Mrs. Linde:* But of course you won't.

*Nora:* No, of course not. I can't ever imagine it being necessary. But I'm quite certain if ever I were to mention it to Dr. Rank. . . .

*Mrs. Linde:* Behind your husband's back?

*Nora:* I have to get myself out of that other business. That's also behind his back. I *must* get myself out of that.

*Mrs. Linde:* Yes, that's what I said yesterday. But . . .

*Nora [walking up and down]:* A man's better at coping with these things than a woman. . . .

*Mrs. Linde:* Your own husband, yes.

*Nora:* Nonsense! *[Stops.]* When you've paid everything you owe, you do get your IOU back again, don't you?

*Mrs. Linde:* Of course.

*Nora:* And you can tear it up into a thousand pieces and burn it—the nasty, filthy thing!

*Mrs. Linde [looking fixedly at her, puts down her sewing and slowly rises]:* Nora, you are hiding something from me.

*Nora:* Is it so obvious?

*Mrs. Linde:* Something has happened to you since yesterday morning. Nora, what is it?

*Nora [going towards her]:* Kristine! *[Listens.]* Hush! There's Torvald back. Look, you go and sit in there beside the children for the time being. Torvald can't stand the sight of mending lying about. Get Anne Marie to help you.

*Mrs. Linde [gathering a lot of the things together]:* All right, but I'm not leaving until we have thrashed this thing out.

*[She goes into the room, left; at the same time Helmer comes in from the hall.]*

*Nora [goes to meet him]:* I've been longing for you to be back, Torvald, dear.

*Helmer:* Was that the dressmaker. . . ?

*Nora:* No, it was Kristine; she's helping me with my costume. I think it's going to look very nice . . .

*Helmer:* Wasn't that a good idea of mine, now?

*Nora:* Wonderful! But wasn't it also nice of me to let you have your way?

*Helmer [taking her under the chin]:* Nice of you—because you let your husband have his way? All right, you little rogue, I know you didn't mean it that way. But I don't want to disturb you. You'll be wanting to try the costume on, I suppose.

*Nora:* And I dare say you've got work to do?

*Helmer:* Yes. *[Shows her a bundle of papers.]* Look at this. I've been down at the Bank. . . .

*[He turns to go into his study.]*

*Nora:* Torvald!

*Helmer [stopping]:* Yes.

*Nora:* If a little squirrel were to ask ever so nicely . . . ?

*Helmer:* Well?

*Nora:* Would you do something for it?

*Helmer:* Naturally I would first have to know what it is.

*Nora:* Please, if only you would let it have its way, and do what it wants, it'd scamper about and do all sorts of marvellous tricks.

*Helmer:* What is it?

*Nora:* And the pretty little sky-lark would sing all day long. . . .

*Helmer:* Huh! It does that anyway.

*Nora:* I'd pretend I was an elfin child and dance a moonlight dance for you, Torvald.

*Helmer:* Nora—I hope it's not that business you started on this morning?

*Nora [coming closer]:* Yes, it is, Torvald. I implore you!

*Helmer:* You have the nerve to bring that up again?

*Nora:* Yes, yes, you *must* listen to me. You must let Krogstad keep his job at the Bank.

*Helmer:* My dear Nora, I'm giving his job to Mrs. Linde.

*Nora:* Yes, it's awfully sweet of you. But couldn't you get rid of somebody else in the office instead of Krogstad?

*Helmer:* This really is the most incredible obstinacy! Just because you go and make some thoughtless promise to put in a good word for him, you expect me. . .

*Nora:* It's not that, Torvald. It's for your own sake. That man writes in all the nastiest papers, you told me that yourself. He can do you no end of harm. He terrifies me to death. . . .

*Helmer:* Aha, now I see. It's your memories of what happened before that are frightening you.

*Nora:* What do you mean?

*Helmer:* It's your father you are thinking of.

*Nora:* Yes . . . yes, that's right. You remember all the nasty insinuations those wicked people put in the papers about Daddy? I honestly think they would have had him dismissed if the Ministry hadn't sent you down to investigate, and you hadn't been so kind and helpful.

*Helmer:* My dear little Nora, there is a considerable difference between your father and me. Your father's professional conduct was not entirely above suspicion. Mine is. And I hope it's going to stay that way as long as I hold this position.

*Nora:* But nobody knows what some of these evil people are capable of. Things could be so nice and pleasant for us here, in the peace and quiet of our home—you and me and the children, Torvald! That's why I implore you. . . .

*Helmer:* The more you plead for him, the more impossible you make it for me to keep him on. It's already known down at the Bank that I am going to give Krogstad his notice. If it ever got around that the new manager had been talked over by his wife. . . .

*Nora:* What of it?

*Helmer:* Oh, nothing! As long as the little woman gets her own stubborn way. . . ! Do you want me to make myself a laughing stock in the office? . . . Give people the idea that I am susceptible to any kind of outside pressure? You can imagine how soon I'd feel the consequences of that! Anyway, there's one other consideration that makes it impossible to have Krogstad in the Bank as long as I am manager.

*Nora:* What's that?

*Helmer:* At a pinch I might have overlooked his past lapses. . . .

*Nora:* Of course you could, Torvald!

*Helmer:* And I'm told he's not bad at his job, either. But we knew each other rather well when we were younger. It was one of those rather rash friendships that prove embarrassing in later life. There's no reason why you shouldn't know we were once on terms of some familiarity. And he, in his tactless way, makes no attempt to hide the fact, particularly when other people are present. On the contrary, he thinks he has every right to treat me as an equal, with his 'Torvald this' and 'Torvald that' every time he opens his mouth. I find it extremely irritating, I can tell you. He would make my position at the Bank absolutely intolerable.

*Nora:* Torvald, surely you aren't serious?

*Helmer:* Oh? Why not?

*Nora:* Well, it's all so petty.

*Helmer:* What's that you say? Petty? Do you think I'm petty?

*Nora:* No, not at all, Torvald dear! And that's why . . .

*Helmer:* Doesn't make any difference! . . . You call my motives petty; so I must be petty too. Petty! Indeed! Well, we'll put a stop to that, once and for all. *[He opens the hall door and calls.]* Helene!

*Nora:* What are you going to do?

*Helmer [searching among his papers]:* Settle things. *[The Maid comes in.]* See this letter? I want you to take it down at once. Get hold of a messenger and get him to deliver it. Quickly. The address is on the outside. There's the money.

*Maid:* Very good, sir.

*[She goes with the letter.]*

*Helmer [putting his papers together]:* There now, my stubborn little miss.

*Nora [breathless]:* Torvald . . . what was that letter?

*Helmer:* Krogstad's notice.

*Nora:* Get it back, Torvald! There's still time! Oh, Torvald, get it back! Please for my sake, for your sake, for the sake of the children! Listen, Torvald, please! You don't realize what it can do to us.

*Helmer:* Too late.

*Nora:* Yes, too late.

*Helmer:* My dear Nora, I forgive you this anxiety of yours, although it is actually a bit of an insult. Oh, but it is, I tell you! It's hardly flattering to suppose that anything this miserable pen-pusher wrote could frighten *me!* But I forgive you all the same, because it is rather a sweet way of showing how much you love me. *[He takes her in his arms.]* This is how things must be, my own darling Nora. When it comes to the point, I've enough strength and enough courage, believe me, for whatever happens. You'll find I'm man enough to take everything on myself.

*Nora [terrified]:* What do you mean?

*Helmer:* Everything, I said. . . .

*Nora [in command of herself]:* That is something you shall never, never do.

*Helmer:* All right, then we'll share it, Nora—as man and wife. That's what we'll do. *[Caressing her.]* Does that make you happy now? There, there, don't look at me with those eyes, like a little frightened dove. The whole thing is sheer imagination.—Why don't you run through the tarantella and try out the tambourine? I'll go into my study and shut both the doors, then I won't hear anything. You can make all the noise you want. *[Turns in the doorway.]* And when Rank comes, tell him where he can find me.

*[He nods to her, goes with his papers into his room, and shuts the door behind him.]*

*Nora [wild-eyed with terror, stands as though transfixed]:* He's quite capable of doing it! He would do it! No matter what, he'd do it.—No, never in this world! Anything but that! Help? Some way out . . . ? *[The door-bell rings in the hall.]* Dr. Rank . . . ! Anything but that, *anything!* *[She brushes her hands over her face, pulls herself together and opens the door into the hall. Dr. Rank is standing outside hanging up his fur coat. During what follows it begins to grow dark.]* Hello, Dr. Rank. I recognized your ring. Do you mind not going in to Torvald just yet, I think he's busy.

*Rank:* And you?

*[Dr. Rank comes into the room and she closes the door behind him.]*

*Nora:* Oh, you know very well I've always got time for you.

*Rank:* Thank you. A privilege I shall take advantage of as long as I am able.

*Nora:* What do you mean—as long as you are able?

*Rank:* Does that frighten you?

*Nora:* Well, it's just that it sounds so strange. Is anything likely to happen?

*Rank:* Only what I have long expected. But I didn't think it would come quite so soon.

*Nora [catching at his arm]:* What have you found out? Dr. Rank, you must tell me!

*Rank:* I'm slowly sinking. There's nothing to be done about it.

*Nora [with a sigh of relief]:* Oh, it's *you* you're. . . ?

*Rank:* Who else? No point in deceiving oneself. I am the most wretched of all my patients, Mrs. Helmer. These last few days I've made a careful analysis of my internal economy. Bankrupt! Within a month I shall probably be lying rotting up there in the churchyard.

*Nora:* Come now, what a ghastly thing to say!

*Rank:* The whole damned thing is ghastly. But the worst thing is all the ghastliness that has to be gone through first. I only have one more test to make; and when that's done I'll know pretty well when the final disintegration will start. There's something I want to ask you. Helmer is a sensitive soul; he loathes anything that's ugly. I don't want him visiting me. . . .

*Nora:* But Dr. Rank. . . .

*Rank:* On no account must he. I won't have it. I'll lock the door on him.—As soon as I'm absolutely certain of the worst, I'll send you my visiting card with a black cross on it. You'll know then the final horrible disintegration has begun.

*Nora:* Really, you are being quite absurd today. And here was I hoping you would be in a thoroughly good mood.

*Rank:* With death staring me in the face? Why should I suffer for another man's sins? What justice is there in that? Somewhere, somehow, every single family must be suffering some such cruel retribution. . . .

*Nora [stopping up her ears]:* Rubbish! Do cheer up!

*Rank:* Yes, really the whole thing's nothing but a huge joke. My poor innocent spine must do penance for my father's gay subaltern life.

*Nora [by the table, left]:* Wasn't he rather partial to asparagus and *pâté de foie gras?*

*Rank:* Yes, he was. And truffles.

*Nora:* Truffles, yes. And oysters, too, I believe?

*Rank:* Yes, oysters, oysters, of course.

*Nora:* And all the port and champagne that goes with them. It does seem a pity all these delicious things should attack the spine.

*Rank:* Especially when they attack a poor spine that never had any fun out of them.

*Nora:* Yes, that is an awful pity.

*Rank [looks at her sharply]:* Hm. . . .

*Nora [after a pause]:* Why did you smile?

*Rank:* No, it was you who laughed.

*Nora:* No, it was you who smiled, Dr. Rank!

*Rank [getting up]:* You are a bigger rascal than I thought you were.

*Nora:* I feel full of mischief today.

*Rank:* So it seems.

*Nora [putting her hands on his shoulders]:* Dear, dear Dr. Rank, you mustn't go and die on Torvald and me.

*Rank:* You wouldn't miss me for long. When you are gone, you are soon forgotten.

*Nora [looking at him anxiously]:* Do you think so?

*Rank:* People make new contacts, then . . .

*Nora:* Who make new contacts?

*Rank:* Both you and Helmer will, when I'm gone. You yourself are already well on the way, it seems to me. What was this Mrs. Linde doing here last night?

*Nora:* Surely you aren't jealous of poor Kristine?

*Rank:* Yes, I am. She'll be my successor in this house. When I'm done for, I can see this woman. . . .

*Nora:* Hush! Don't talk so loud, she's in there.

*Rank:* Today as well? There you are, you see!

*Nora:* Just to do some sewing on my dress. Good Lord, how absurd you are! *[She sits down on the sofa.]* Now Dr. Rank, cheer up. You'll see tomorrow how nicely I can dance. And you can pretend I'm doing it just for you—and for Torvald as well, of course. *[She takes various things out of the box.]* Come here, Dr. Rank. I want to show you something.

*Rank [sits]:* What is it?

*Nora:* Look!

*Rank:* Silk stockings.

*Nora:* Flesh-coloured! Aren't they lovely! Of course, it's dark here now, but tomorrow. . . . No, no, no, you can only look at the feet. Oh well, you might as well see a bit higher up, too.

*Rank:* Hm. . . .

*Nora:* Why are you looking so critical? Don't you think they'll fit?

*Rank:* I couldn't possibly offer any informed opinion about that.

*Nora [looks at him for a moment]:* Shame on you. *[Hits him lightly across the ear with the stockings.]* Take that! *[Folds them up again.]*

*Rank:* And what other delights am I to be allowed to see?

*Nora:* Not another thing. You are too naughty. *[She hums a little and searches among her things.]*

*Rank [after a short pause]:* Sitting here so intimately like this with you, I can't imagine . . . I simply cannot conceive what would have become of me if I had never come to this house.

*Nora [smiles]:* Yes, I rather think you do enjoy coming here.

*Rank [in a low voice, looking fixedly ahead]:* And the thought of having to leave it all . . .

*Nora:* Nonsense. You aren't leaving.

*Rank [in the same tone]:* . . . without being able to leave behind even the slightest token of gratitude, hardly a fleeting regret even . . . nothing but an empty place to be filled by the first person that comes along.

*Nora:* Supposing I were to ask you to . . . ? No . . .

*Rank:* What?

*Nora:* . . . to show me the extent of your friendship . . .

*Rank:* Yes?

*Nora:* I mean . . . to do me a tremendous favour. . . .

*Rank:* Would you really, for once, give me that pleasure?

*Nora:* You have no idea what it is.

*Rank:* All right, tell me.

*Nora:* No, really I can't, Dr. Rank. It's altogether too much to ask . . . because I need your advice and help as well. . . .

*Rank:* The more the better. I cannot imagine what you have in mind. But tell me anyway. You do trust me, don't you?

*Nora:* Yes, I trust you more than anybody I know. You are my best and my most faithful friend. I know that. So I will tell you. Well then, Dr. Rank, there is something you must help me to prevent. You know how deeply, how passionately Torvald is in love with me. He would never hesitate for a moment to sacrifice his life for my sake.

*Rank [bending towards her]:* Nora . . . do you think he's the only one who. . . ?

*Nora [stiffening slightly]:* Who. . . ?

*Rank:* Who wouldn't gladly give his life for your sake.

*Nora [sadly]:* Oh!

*Rank:* I swore to myself you would know before I went. I'll never have a better opportunity. Well, Nora! Now you know. And now you know too that you can confide in me as in nobody else.

*Nora [rises and speaks evenly and calmly]:* Let me past.

*Rank [makes way for her, but remains seated]:* Nora. . . .

*Nora [in the hall doorway]:* Helene, bring the lamp in, please. *[Walks over to the stove.]* Oh, my dear Dr. Rank, that really was rather horrid of you.

*Rank [getting up]:* That I have loved you every bit as much as anybody? Is *that* horrid?

*Nora:* No, but that you had to go and tell me. When it was all so unnecessary. . . .

*Rank:* What do you mean? Did you know. . . ?

*[The Maid comes in with the lamp, puts it on the table, and goes out again.]*

*Rank:* Nora . . . Mrs. Helmer . . . I'm asking you if you knew?

*Nora:* How can I tell whether I did or didn't. I simply can't tell you. . . . Oh, how could you be so clumsy, Dr. Rank! When everything was so nice.

*Rank:* Anyway, you know now that I'm at your service, body and soul. So you can speak out.

*Nora [looking at him]:* After this?

*Rank:* I beg you to tell me what it is.

*Nora:* I can tell you nothing now.

*Rank:* You must. You can't torment me like this. Give me a chance—I'll do anything that's humanly possible.

*Nora:* You can do nothing for me now. Actually, I don't really need any help. It's all just my imagination, really it is. Of course! *[She sits down in the rocking chair, looks at him and smiles.]* I must say, you are a nice one, Dr. Rank! Don't you feel ashamed of yourself, now the lamp's been brought in?

*Rank:* No, not exactly. But perhaps I ought to go—for good?

*Nora:* No, you mustn't do that. You must keep coming just as you've always done. You know very well Torvald would miss you terribly.

*Rank:* And *you?*

*Nora:* I always think it's tremendous fun having you.

*Rank:* That's exactly what gave me wrong ideas. I just can't puzzle you out. I often used to feel you'd just as soon be with me as with Helmer.

*Nora:* Well, you see, there are those people you love and those people you'd almost rather *be* with.

*Rank:* Yes, there's something in that.

*Nora:* When I was a girl at home, I loved Daddy best, of course. But I also thought it great fun if I could slip into the maids' room. For one thing they never preached at me. And they always talked about such exciting things.

*Rank:* Aha! So it's their role I've taken over!

*Nora [jumps up and crosses to him]:* Oh, my dear, kind Dr. Rank, I didn't mean that at all. But you can see how it's a bit with Torvald as it was with Daddy. . . .

*[The Maid comes in from the hall.]*

*Maid:* Please, ma'am . . . !

[*She whispers and hands her a card.*]

*Nora* [*glances at the card*]: Ah!

[*She puts it in her pocket.*]

*Rank:* Anything wrong?

*Nora:* No, no, not at all. It's just . . . it's my new costume. . . .

*Rank:* How is that? There's your costume in there.

*Nora:* That one, yes. But this is another one. I've ordered it. Torvald mustn't hear about it. . . .

*Rank:* Ah, so that's the big secret, is it!

*Nora:* Yes, that's right. Just go in and see him, will you? He's in the study. Keep him occupied for the time being. . . .

*Rank:* Don't worry. He shan't escape me.

[*He goes into Helmer's study.*]

*Nora* [*to the maid*]: Is he waiting in the kitchen?

*Maid:* Yes, he came up the back stairs. . . .

*Nora:* But didn't you tell him somebody was here?

*Maid:* Yes, but it was no good.

*Nora:* Won't he go?

*Maid:* No, he won't till he's seen you.

*Nora:* Let him in, then. But quietly. Helene, you mustn't tell anybody about this. It's a surprise for my husband.

*Maid:* I understand, ma'am. . . .

[*She goes out.*]

*Nora:* Here it comes! What I've been dreading! No, no, it can't happen, it *can't* happen.

[*She walks over and bolts Helmer's door. The maid opens the hall door for Krogstad and shuts it again behind him. He is wearing a fur coat, over-shoes, and a fur cap.*]

*Nora* [*goes towards him*]: Keep your voice down, my husband is at home.

*Krogstad:* What if he is?

*Nora:* What do you want with me?

*Krogstad:* To find out something.

*Nora:* Hurry, then. What is it?

*Krogstad:* You know I've been given notice.

*Nora:* I couldn't prevent it, Mr. Krogstad, I did my utmost for you, but it was no use.

*Krogstad:* Has your husband so little affection for you? He knows what I can do to you, yet he dares. . . .

*Nora:* You don't imagine he knows about it!

*Krogstad:* No, I didn't imagine he did. It didn't seem a bit like my good friend Torvald Helmer to show that much courage. . . .

*Nora:* Mr. Krogstad, I must ask you to show some respect for my husband.

*Krogstad:* Oh, sure! All due respect! But since you are so anxious to keep this business quiet, Mrs. Helmer, I take it you now have a rather clearer idea of just what it is you've done, than you had yesterday.

*Nora:* Clearer than *you* could ever have given me.

*Krogstad:* Yes, being as I am such a rotten lawyer. . . .

*Nora:* What do you want with me?

*Krogstad:* I just wanted to see how things stood, Mrs. Helmer. I've been thinking about you all day. Even a mere money-lender, a hack journalist, a—well, even somebody like me has a bit of what you might call feeling.

*Nora:* Show it then. Think of my little children.

*Krogstad:* Did you or your husband think of mine? But what does it matter now? There was just one thing I wanted to say: you needn't take this business too seriously. I shan't start any proceedings, for the present.

*Nora:* Ah, I knew you wouldn't.

*Krogstad:* The whole thing can be arranged quite amicably. Nobody need know. Just the three of us.

*Nora:* My husband must never know.

*Krogstad:* How can you prevent it? Can you pay off the balance?

*Nora:* No, not immediately.

*Krogstad:* Perhaps you've some way of getting hold of the money in the next few days.

*Nora:* None I want to make use of.

*Krogstad:* Well, it wouldn't have been very much help to you if you had. Even if you stood there with the cash in your hand and to spare, you still wouldn't get your IOU back from me now.

*Nora:* What are you going to do with it?

*Krogstad:* Just keep it—have it in my possession. Nobody who isn't implicated need know about it. So if you are thinking of trying any desperate remedies . . .

*Nora:* Which I am. . . .

*Krogstad:* . . . if you happen to be thinking of running away. . .

*Nora:* Which I am!

*Krogstad:* . . . or anything worse . . .

*Nora:* How did you know?

*Krogstad:* . . . forget it!

*Nora:* How did you know I was thinking of *that?*

*Krogstad:* Most of us think of *that,* to begin with. I did, too; but I didn't have the courage. . . .

*Nora [tonelessly]:* I haven't either.

*Krogstad [relieved]:* So you haven't the courage either, eh?

*Nora:* No, I haven't! I haven't!

*Krogstad:* It would also be very stupid. There'd only be the first domestic storm to get over. . . . I've got a letter to your husband in my pocket here. . . .

*Nora:* And it's all in there?

*Krogstad:* In as tactful a way as possible.

*Nora [quickly]:* He must never read that letter. Tear it up. I'll find the money somehow.

*Krogstad:* Excuse me, Mrs. Helmer, but I've just told you. . . .

*Nora:* I'm not talking about the money I owe you. I want to know how much you are demanding from my husband, and I'll get the money.

*Krogstad:* I want no money from your husband.

*Nora:* What do you want?

*Krogstad:* I'll tell you. I want to get on my feet again, Mrs. Helmer; I want to get to the top. And your husband is going to help me. For the last eighteen months I've gone straight; all that time it's been hard going; I was content to work my way up, step by step. Now I'm being kicked out, and I won't stand for being taken back again as an act of charity. I'm going to get to the top, I tell you. I'm going back into that Bank—with a better job. Your husband is going to create a new vacancy, just for me. . . .

*Nora:* He'll never do that!

*Krogstad:* He will do it. I know him. He'll do it without so much as a whimper. And once I'm in there with him, you'll see what's what. In less than a year I'll be his right-hand man. It'll be Nils Krogstad, not Torvald Helmer, who'll be running that Bank.

*Nora:* You'll never live to see that day!

*Krogstad:* You mean you . . . ?

*Nora:* Now I have the courage.

*Krogstad:* You can't frighten me! A precious pampered little thing like you. . . .

*Nora:* I'll show you! I'll show you!

*Krogstad:* Under the ice, maybe? Down in the cold, black water? Then being washed up in the spring, bloated, hairless, unrecognizable. . . .

*Nora:* You can't frighten me.

*Krogstad:* You can't frighten me, either. People don't do that sort of thing, Mrs. Helmer. There wouldn't be any point to it, anyway, I'd still have him right in my pocket.

*Nora:* Afterwards? When I'm no longer . . .

*Krogstad:* Aren't you forgetting that your reputation would then be entirely in my hands? *[Nora stands looking at him, speechless.]* Well, I've warned you. Don't do anything silly. When Helmer gets my letter, I expect to hear from him. And don't forget: it's him who is forcing me off the straight and narrow again, your own husband! That's something I'll never forgive him for. Goodbye, Mrs. Helmer.

*[He goes out through the hall. Nora crosses to the door, opens it slightly, and listens.]*

*Nora:* He's going. He hasn't left the letter. No, no, that would be impossible! *[Opens the door further and further.]* What's he doing? He's stopped outside. He's not going down the stairs. Has he changed his mind? Is he. . . ? [A letter falls into the letter-box. Then Krogstad's footsteps are heard receding as he walks

*downstairs. Nora gives a stifled cry, runs across the room to the sofa table; pause.]*
In the letter-box! *[She creeps stealthily across to the hall door.]* There it is!
Torvald, Torvald! It's hopeless now!

Mrs. Linde *[comes into the room, left, carrying the costume]:* There, I think that's
everything. Shall we try it on?

Nora *[in a low, hoarse voice]:* Kristine, come here.

Mrs. Linde *[throws the dress down on the sofa]:* What's wrong with you? You look
upset.

Nora: Come here. Do you see that letter? *There,* look! Through the glass in the
letter-box.

Mrs. Linde: Yes, yes, I can see it.

Nora: It's a letter from Krogstad.

Mrs. Linde: Nora! It was Krogstad who lent you the money!

Nora: Yes. And now Torvald will get to know everything.

Mrs. Linde: Believe me, Nora, it's best for you both.

Nora: But there's more to it than that. I forged a signature. . . .

Mrs. Linde: Heavens above!

Nora: Listen, I want to tell you something, Kristine, so you can be my witness.

Mrs. Linde: What do you mean 'witness'? What do you want me to. . . ?

Nora: If I should go mad . . . which might easily happen . . .

Mrs. Linde: Nora!

Nora: Or if anything happened to me . . . which meant I couldn't be here. . . .

Mrs. Linde: Nora, Nora! Are you out of your mind?

Nora: And if somebody else wanted to take it all upon himself, the whole blame,
you understand. . . .

Mrs. Linde: Yes, yes. But what makes you think. . . ?

Nora: Then you must testify that it isn't true, Kristine. I'm not out of my mind;
I'm quite sane now. And I tell you this: nobody else knew anything, I alone
was responsible for the whole thing. Remember that!

Mrs. Linde: I will. But I don't understand a word of it.

Nora: Why should you? You see something miraculous is going to happen.

Mrs. Linde: Something miraculous?

Nora: Yes, a miracle. But something so terrible as well, Kristine—oh, it must
*never* happen, not for anything.

Mrs. Linde: I'm going straight over to talk to Krogstad.

Nora: Don't go. He'll only do you harm.

Mrs. Linde: There was a time when he would have done anything for me.

Nora: Him!

Mrs. Linde: Where does he live?

Nora: How do I know. . . ? Wait a minute. *[She feels in her pocket.]* Here's his card.
But the letter, the letter. . . !

Helmer *[from his study, knocking on the door]:* Nora!

Nora *[cries out in terror]:* What's that? What do you want?

Helmer: Don't be frightened. We're not coming in. You've locked the door. Are
you trying on?

*Nora:* Yes, yes, I'm trying on. It looks so nice on me, Torvald.

*Mrs. Linde [who has read the card]:* He lives just round the corner.

*Nora:* It's no use. It's hopeless. The letter is there in the box.

*Mrs. Linde:* Your husband keeps the key?

*Nora:* Always.

*Mrs. Linde:* Krogstad must ask for his letter back unread, he must find some sort of excuse. . . .

*Nora:* But this is just the time that Torvald generally . . .

*Mrs. Linde:* Put him off! Go in and keep him busy. I'll be back as soon as I can.

[*She goes out hastily by the hall door. Nora walks over to Helmer's door, opens it and peeps in.*]

*Nora:* Torvald!

*Helmer [in the study]:* Well, can a man get into his own living-room again now? Come along, Rank, now we'll see . . . [*In the doorway.*] But what's this?

*Nora:* What, Torvald dear?

*Helmer:* Rank led me to expect some kind of marvellous transformation.

*Rank [in the doorway]:* That's what I thought too, but I must have been mistaken.

*Nora:* I'm not showing myself off to anybody before tomorrow.

*Helmer:* Nora dear, you look tired. You haven't been practising too hard?

*Nora:* No, I haven't practised at all yet.

*Helmer:* You'll have to, though.

*Nora:* Yes, I certainly must, Torvald. But I just can't get anywhere without your help: I've completely forgotten it.

*Helmer:* We'll soon polish it up.

*Nora:* Yes, do help me, Torvald. Promise? I'm so nervous. All those people. . . . You must devote yourself exclusively to me this evening. Pens away! Forget all about the office! Promise me, Torvald dear!

*Helmer:* I promise. This evening I am wholly and entirely at your service . . . helpless little thing that you are. Oh, but while I remember, I'll just look first . . .

[*He goes towards the hall door.*]

*Nora:* What do you want out there?

*Helmer:* Just want to see if there are any letters.

*Nora:* No, don't, Torvald!

*Helmer:* Why not?

*Nora:* Torvald, *please!* There aren't any.

*Helmer:* Just let me see.

[*He starts to go. Nora, at the piano, plays the opening bars of the tarantella.*]

*Helmer [at the door, stops]:* Aha!

*Nora:* I shan't be able to dance tomorrow if I don't rehearse it with you.

*Helmer [walks to her]:* Are you really so nervous, Nora dear?

*Nora:* Terribly nervous. Let me run through it now. There's still time before supper. Come and sit here and play for me, Torvald dear. Tell me what to do, keep me right—as you always do.

*Helmer:* Certainly, with pleasure, if that's what you want.

[*He sits at the piano. Nora snatches the tambourine out of the box, and also a long gaily-coloured shawl which she drapes round herself, then with a bound she leaps forward.*]

*Nora [shouts]:* Now play for me! Now I'll dance!

[*Helmer plays and Nora dances; Dr. Rank stands at the piano behind Helmer and looks on.*]

*Helmer [playing]:* Not so fast! Not so fast!

*Nora:* I can't help it.

*Helmer:* Not so wild, Nora!

*Nora:* This is how it has to be.

*Helmer [stops]:* No, no, that won't do at all.

*Nora [laughs and swings the tambourine]:* Didn't I tell you?

*Rank:* Let me play for her.

*Helmer [gets up]:* Yes, do. Then I'll be better able to tell her what to do.

[*Rank sits down at the piano and plays. Nora dances more and more wildly. Helmer stands by the stove giving her repeated directions as she dances; she does not seem to hear them. Her hair comes undone and falls about her shoulders; she pays no attention and goes on dancing. Mrs. Linde enters.*]

*Mrs. Linde [standing as though spellbound in the doorway]:* Ah . . . !

*Nora [dancing]:* See what fun we are having, Kristine.

*Helmer:* But my dear darling Nora, you are dancing as though your life depended on it.

*Nora:* It does.

*Helmer:* Stop, Rank! This is sheer madness. Stop, I say.

[*Rank stops playing and Nora comes to a sudden halt.*]

*Helmer [crosses to her]:* I would never have believed it. You have forgotten everything I ever taught you.

*Nora [throwing away the tambourine]:* There you are, you see.

*Helmer:* Well, some more instruction is certainly needed there.

*Nora:* Yes, you see how necessary it is. You must go on coaching me right up to the last minute. Promise me, Torvald?

*Helmer:* You can rely on me.

*Nora:* You mustn't think about anything else but me until after tomorrow . . . mustn't open any letters . . . mustn't touch the letter-box.

*Helmer:* Ah, you are still frightened of what that man might . . .

*Nora:* Yes, yes, I am.

*Helmer:* I can see from your face there's already a letter there from him.

*Nora:* I don't know. I think so. But you mustn't read anything like that now. We don't want anything horrid coming between us until all this is over.

*Rank [softly to Helmer]:* I shouldn't cross her.

*Helmer [puts his arm round her]:* The child must have her way. But tomorrow night, when your dance is done. . . .

*Nora:* Then you are free.

*Maid [in the doorway, right]:* Dinner is served, madam.

*Nora:* We'll have champagne, Helene.

*Maid:* Very good, madam.

[*She goes.*]

*Helmer:* Aha! It's to be quite a banquet, eh?

*Nora:* With champagne flowing until dawn. [*Shouts.*] And some macaroons, Helene . . . lots of them, for once in a while.

*Helmer [seizing her hands]:* Now, now, not so wild and excitable! Let me see you being my own little singing bird again.

*Nora:* Oh yes, I will. And if you'll just go in . . . you, too, Dr. Rank. Kristine, you must help me to do my hair.

*Rank [softly, as they leave]:* There isn't anything . . . anything as it were, impending, is there?

*Helmer:* No, not at all, my dear fellow. It's nothing but these childish fears I was telling you about.

[*They go out to the right.*]

*Nora:* Well?

*Mrs. Linde:* He's left town.

*Nora:* I saw it in your face.

*Mrs. Linde:* He's coming back tomorrow evening. I left a note for him.

*Nora:* You shouldn't have done that. You must let things take their course. Because really it's a case for rejoicing, waiting like this for the miracle.

*Mrs. Linde:* What is it you are waiting for?

*Nora:* Oh, you wouldn't understand. Go and join the other two. I'll be there in a minute.

[*Mrs. Linde goes into the dining-room. Nora stands for a moment as though to collect herself, then looks at her watch.*]

*Nora:* Five. Seven hours to midnight. Then twenty-four hours till the next midnight. Then the tarantella will be over. Twenty-four and seven? Thirty-one hours to live.

*Helmer [in the doorway, right]:* What's happened to our little sky-lark?

*Nora [running towards him with open arms]:* Here she is!

# Act III

*The same room. The round table has been moved to the centre of the room, and the chairs placed round it. A lamp is burning on the table. The door to the hall stands open. Dance music can be heard coming from the floor above. Mrs. Linde is sitting by the table, idly turning over the pages of a book; she tries to read, but does not seem able to concentrate. Once or twice she listens, tensely, for a sound at the front door.*

Mrs. Linde [*looking at her watch*]: Still not here. There isn't much time left. I only hope he hasn't . . . [*She listens again.*] Ah, there he is. [*She goes out into the hall, and cautiously opens the front door. Soft footsteps can be heard on the stairs. She whispers.*] Come in. There's nobody here.

Krogstad [*in the doorway*]: I found a note from you at home. What does it all mean?

Mrs. Linde: I had to talk to you.

Krogstad: Oh? And did it have to be here, in this house?

Mrs. Linde: It wasn't possible over at my place, it hasn't a separate entrance. Come in. We are quite alone. The maid's asleep and the Helmer's are at a party upstairs.

Krogstad [*comes into the room*]: Well, well! So the Helmers are out dancing tonight! Really?

Mrs. Linde: Yes, why not?

Krogstad: Why not indeed!

Mrs. Linde: Well then, Nils. Let's talk.

Krogstad: Have we two anything more to talk about?

Mrs. Linde: We have a great deal to talk about.

Krogstad: I shouldn't have thought so.

Mrs. Linde: That's because you never really understood me.

Krogstad: What else was there to understand, apart from the old, old story? A heartless woman throws a man over the moment something more profitable offers itself.

Mrs. Linde: Do you really think I'm so heartless? Do you think I found it easy to break it off.

Krogstad: Didn't you?

Mrs. Linde: You didn't really believe that?

Krogstad: If that wasn't the case, why did you write to me as you did?

Mrs. Linde: There was nothing else I could do. If I had to make the break, I felt in duty bound to destroy any feeling that you had for me.

Krogstad [*clenching his hands*]: So that's how it was. And all that . . . was for money!

Mrs. Linde: You mustn't forget I had a helpless mother and two young brothers. We couldn't wait for you, Nils. At that time you hadn't much immediate prospect of anything.

Krogstad: That may be. But you had no right to throw me over for somebody else.

Mrs. Linde: Well, I don't know. Many's the time I've asked myself whether I was justified.

*Krogstad [more quietly]:* When I lost you, it was just as if the ground had slipped away from under my feet. Look at me now: a broken man clinging to the wreck of his life.

*Mrs. Linde:* Help might be near.

*Krogstad:* It was near. Then you came along and got in the way.

*Mrs. Linde:* Quite without knowing, Nils. I only heard today it's you I'm supposed to be replacing at the Bank.

*Krogstad:* If you say so, I believe you. But now you do know, aren't you going to withdraw?

*Mrs. Linde:* No, that wouldn't benefit you in the slightest.

*Krogstad:* Benefit, benefit . . . ! I would do it just the same.

*Mrs. Linde:* I have learned to go carefully. Life and hard, bitter necessity have taught me that.

*Krogstad:* And life has taught me not to believe in pretty speeches.

*Mrs. Linde:* Then life has taught you a very sensible thing. But deeds are something you surely must believe in?

*Krogstad:* How do you mean?

*Mrs. Linde:* You said you were like a broken man clinging to the wreck of his life.

*Krogstad:* And I said it with good reason.

*Mrs. Linde:* And I am like a broken woman clinging to the wreck of her life. Nobody to care about, and nobody to care for.

*Krogstad:* It was your own choice.

*Mrs. Linde:* At the time there was no other choice.

*Krogstad:* Well, what of it?

*Mrs. Linde:* Nils, what about us two castaways joining forces.

*Krogstad:* What's that you say?

*Mrs. Linde:* Two of us on *one* wreck surely stand a better chance than each on his own.

*Krogstad:* Kristine!

*Mrs. Linde:* Why do you suppose I came to town?

*Krogstad:* You mean, you thought of me?

*Mrs. Linde:* Without work I couldn't live. All my life I have worked, for as long as I can remember; that has always been my one great joy. But now I'm completely alone in the world, and feeling horribly empty and forlorn. There's no pleasure in working only for yourself. Nils, give me somebody and something to work for.

*Krogstad:* I don't believe all this. It's only a woman's hysteria, wanting to be all magnanimous and self-sacrificing.

*Mrs. Linde:* Have you ever known me hysterical before?

*Krogstad:* Would you really do this? Tell me—do you know all about my past?

*Mrs. Linde:* Yes.

*Krogstad:* And you know what people think about me?

*Mrs. Linde:* Just now you hinted you thought you might have been a different person with me.

*Krogstad:* I'm convinced I would.

*Mrs. Linde:* Couldn't it still happen?

*Krogstad:* Kristine! You know what you are saying, don't you? Yes, you do. I can see you do. Have you really the courage . . . ?

*Mrs. Linde:* I need someone to mother, and your children need a mother. We two need each other. Nils, I have faith in what, deep down, you are. With you I can face anything.

*Krogstad [seizing her hands]:* Thank you, thank you, Kristine. And I'll soon have everybody looking up to me, or I'll know the reason why. Ah, but I was forgetting. . . .

*Mrs. Linde:* Hush! The tarantella! You must go!

*Krogstad:* Why? What is it?

*Mrs. Linde:* You hear that dance upstairs? When it's finished they'll be coming.

*Krogstad:* Yes, I'll go. It's too late to do anything. Of course, you know nothing about what steps I've taken against the Helmers.

*Mrs. Linde:* Yes, Nils, I do know.

*Krogstad:* Yet you still want to go on. . . .

*Mrs. Linde:* I know how far a man like you can be driven by despair.

*Krogstad:* Oh, if only I could undo what I've done!

*Mrs. Linde:* You still can. Your letter is still there in the box.

*Krogstad:* Are you sure?

*Mrs. Linde:* Quite sure. But . . .

*Krogstad [regards her searchingly]:* Is that how things are? You want to save your friend at any price? Tell me straight. Is that it?

*Mrs. Linde:* When you've sold yourself *once* for other people's sake, you don't do it again.

*Krogstad:* I shall demand my letter back.

*Mrs. Linde:* No, no.

*Krogstad:* Of course I will, I'll wait here till Helmer comes. I'll tell him he has to give me my letter back . . . that it's only about my notice . . . that he mustn't read it. . . .

*Mrs. Linde:* No, Nils, don't ask for it back.

*Krogstad:* But wasn't that the very reason you got me here?

*Mrs. Linde:* Yes, that was my first terrified reaction. But that was yesterday, and it's quite incredible the things I've witnessed in this house in the last twenty-four hours. Helmer must know everything. This unhappy secret must come out. Those two must have the whole thing out between them. All this secrecy and deception, it just can't go on.

*Krogstad:* Well, if you want to risk it. . . . But one thing I can do, and I'll do it at once. . . .

*Mrs. Linde [listening]:* Hurry! Go, go! The dance has stopped. We aren't safe a moment longer.

*Krogstad:* I'll wait for you downstairs.

*Mrs. Linde:* Yes, do. You must see me home.

*Krogstad:* I've never been so incredibly happy before.

*[He goes out by the front door. The door out into the hall remains standing open.]*

Mrs. Linde *[tidies the room a little and gets her hat and coat ready]*: How things change! How things change! Somebody to work for . . . to live for. A home to bring happiness into. Just let me get down to it. . . . I wish they'd come. . . . *[Listens.]* Ah, there they are. . . . Get my things.

*[She takes her coat and hat. The voices of Helmer and Nora are heard outside. A key is turned and Helmer pushes Nora almost forcibly into the hall. She is dressed in the Italian costume, with a big black shawl over it. He is in evening dress, and over it a black cloak, open.]*

Nora *[still in the doorway, reluctantly]*: No, no, not in here! I want to go back up again. I don't want to leave so early.

Helmer: But my dearest Nora . . .

Nora: Oh, please, Torvald, I beg you. . . . *Please*, just for another hour.

Helmer: Not another minute, Nora my sweet. You remember what we agreed. There now, come along in. You'll catch cold standing there.

*[He leads her, in spite of her resistance, gently but firmly into the room.]*

Mrs. Linde: Good evening.

Nora: Kristine!

Helmer: Why, Mrs. Linde. You here so late?

Mrs. Linde: Yes. You must forgive me but I did so want to see Nora all dressed up.

Nora: Have you been sitting here waiting for me?

Mrs. Linde: Yes, I'm afraid I wasn't in time to catch you before you went upstairs. And I felt I couldn't leave again without seeing you.

Helmer *[removing Nora's shawl]*: Well take a good look at her. I think I can say she's worth looking at. Isn't she lovely, Mrs. Linde?

Mrs. Linde: Yes, I must say. . . .

Helmer: Isn't she quite extraordinarily lovely? That's what everybody at the party thought, too. But she's dreadfully stubborn . . . the sweet little thing! And what shall we do about that? Would you believe it, I nearly had to use force to get her away.

Nora: Oh Torvald, you'll be sorry you didn't let me stay, even for half an hour.

Helmer: You hear that, Mrs. Linde? She dances her tarantella, there's wild applause—which was well deserved, although the performance was perhaps rather realistic . . . I mean, rather more so than was strictly necessary from the artistic point of view. But anyway! The main thing is she was a success, a tremendous success. Was I supposed to let her stay after that? Spoil the effect? No thank you! I took my lovely little Capri girl—my capricious little Capri girl, I might say—by the arm, whisked her once round the room, a curtsey all round, and then—as they say in novels—the beautiful vision vanished. An exit should always be effective, Mrs. Linde. But I just can't get Nora to see that. Phew! It's warm in here. *[He throws his cloak over a chair and opens the door to his study.]* What? It's dark. Oh yes, of course. Excuse me. . . .

*[He goes in and lights a few candles.]*

*Nora [quickly, in a breathless whisper]:* Well?

*Mrs. Linde [softly]:* I've spoken to him.

*Nora:* And. . . ?

*Mrs. Linde:* Nora . . . you must tell your husband everything.

*Nora [tonelessly]:* I knew it.

*Mrs. Linde:* You've got nothing to fear from Krogstad. But you must speak.

*Nora:* I won't.

*Mrs. Linde:* Then the letter will.

*Nora:* Thank you, Kristine. Now I know what's to be done. Hush . . . !

*Helmer [comes in again]:* Well, Mrs. Linde, have you finished admiring her?

*Mrs. Linde:* Yes. And now I must say good night.

*Helmer:* Oh, already? Is this yours, this knitting?

*Mrs. Linde [takes it]:* Yes, thank you. I nearly forgot it.

*Helmer:* So you knit, eh?

*Mrs. Linde:* Yes.

*Helmer:* You should embroider instead, you know.

*Mrs. Linde:* Oh? Why?

*Helmer:* So much prettier. Watch! You hold the embroidery like this in the left hand, and then you take the needle in the right hand, like this, and you describe a long, graceful curve. Isn't that right?

*Mrs. Linde:* Yes, I suppose so. . . .

*Helmer:* Whereas knitting on the other hand just can't help being ugly. Look! Arms pressed into the sides, the knitting needles going up and down— there's something Chinese about it. . . . Ah, that was marvellous champagne they served tonight.

*Mrs. Linde:* Well, good night, Nora! And stop being so stubborn.

*Helmer:* Well said, Mrs. Linde!

*Mrs. Linde:* Good night, Mr. Helmer.

*Helmer [accompanying her to the door]:* Good night, good night! You'll get home all right, I hope? I'd be only too pleased to . . . But you haven't far to walk. Good night, good night! *[She goes; he shuts the door behind her and comes in again.]* There we are, got rid of her at last. She's a frightful bore, that woman.

*Nora:* Aren't you very tired, Torvald?

*Helmer:* Not in the least.

*Nora:* Not sleepy?

*Helmer:* Not at all. On the contrary, I feel extremely lively. What about you? Yes, you look quite tired and sleepy.

*Nora:* Yes, I'm very tired. I just want to fall straight off to sleep.

*Helmer:* There you are, you see! Wasn't I right in thinking we shouldn't stay any longer.

*Nora:* Oh, everything you do is right.

*Helmer [kissing her forehead]:* There's my little sky-lark talking common sense. Did you notice how gay Rank was this evening?

*Nora:* Oh, was he? I didn't get a chance to talk to him.

*Helmer:* I hardly did either. But it's a long time since I saw him in such a good mood. *[Looks at Nora for a moment or two, then comes nearer her.]* Ah, it's wonderful to be back in our own home again, and quite alone with you. How irresistibly lovely you are, Nora!

*Nora:* Don't look at me like that, Torvald!

*Helmer:* Can't I look at my most treasured possession? At all this loveliness that's mine and mine alone, completely and utterly mine.

*Nora [walks round to the other side of the table]:* You mustn't talk to me like that tonight.

*Helmer [following her]:* You still have the tarantella in your blood, I see. And that makes you even more desirable. Listen! The guests are beginning to leave now. *[Softly.]* Nora . . . soon the whole house will be silent.

*Nora:* I should hope so.

*Helmer:* Of course you do, don't you, Nora my darling? You know, whenever I'm out at a party with you . . . do you know why I never talk to you very much, why I always stand away from you and only steal a quick glance at you now and then . . . do you know why I do that? It's because I'm pretending we are secretly in love, secretly engaged and nobody suspects there is anything between us.

*Nora:* Yes, yes. I know your thoughts are always with me, of course.

*Helmer:* And when it's time to go, and I lay your shawl round those shapely, young shoulders, round the exquisite curve of your neck . . . I pretend that you are my young bride, that we are just leaving our wedding, that I am taking you to our new home for the first time . . . to be alone with you for the first time . . . quite alone with your young and trembling loveliness! All evening I've been longing for you, and nothing else. And as I watched you darting and swaying in the tarantella, my blood was on fire . . . I couldn't bear it any longer . . . and that's why I brought you down here with me so early. . . .

*Nora:* Go away, Torvald! Please leave me alone. I won't have it.

*Helmer:* What's this? It's just your little game isn't it, my little Nora. Won't! Won't! Am I not your husband . . . ?

*[There is a knock on the front door.]*

*Nora [startled]:* Listen . . . !

*Helmer [going towards the hall]:* Who's there?

*Rank [outside]:* It's me. Can I come in for a minute?

*Helmer [in a low voice, annoyed]:* Oh, what does he want now? *[Aloud.]* Wait a moment. *[He walks across and opens the door.]* How nice of you to look in on your way out.

*Rank:* I fancied I heard your voice and I thought I would just look in. *[He takes a quick glance round.]* Ah yes, this dear, familiar old place! How cosy and comfortable you've got things here, you two.

*Helmer:* You seemed to be having a pretty good time upstairs yourself.

*Rank:* Capital! Why shouldn't I? Why not make the most of things in this world? At least as much as one can, and for as long as one can. The wine was excellent. . . .

*Helmer:* Especially the champagne.

*Rank:* You noticed that too, did you? It's incredible the amount I was able to put away.

*Nora:* Torvald also drank a lot of champagne this evening.

*Rank:* Oh?

*Nora:* Yes, and that always makes him quite merry.

*Rank:* Well, why shouldn't a man allow himself a jolly evening after a day well spent?

*Helmer:* Well spent? I'm afraid I can't exactly claim that.

*Rank [clapping him on the shoulder]:* But I can, you see!

*Nora:* Dr. Rank, am I right in thinking you carried out a certain laboratory test today?

*Rank:* Exactly.

*Helmer:* Look at our little Nora talking about laboratory tests!

*Nora:* And may I congratulate you on the result?

*Rank:* You may indeed.

*Nora:* So it was good?

*Rank:* The best possible, for both doctor and patient—certainty!

*Nora [quickly and searchingly]:* Certainty?

*Rank:* Absolute certainty. So why shouldn't I allow myself a jolly evening after that?

*Nora:* Quite right, Dr. Rank.

*Helmer:* I quite agree. As long as you don't suffer for it in the morning.

*Rank:* Well, you never get anything for nothing in this life.

*Nora:* Dr. Rank . . . you are very fond of masquerades, aren't you?

*Rank:* Yes, when there are plenty of amusing disguises. . . .

*Nora:* Tell me, what shall we two go as next time?

*Helmer:* There's frivolity for you . . . thinking about the next time already!

*Rank:* We two? I'll tell you. You must go as Lady Luck. . . .

*Helmer:* Yes, but how do you find a costume to suggest *that?*

*Rank:* Your wife could simply go in her everyday clothes. . . .

*Helmer:* That was nicely said. But don't you know what you would be?

*Rank:* Yes, my dear friend, I know exactly what I shall be.

*Helmer:* Well?

*Rank:* At the next masquerade, I shall be invisible.

*Helmer:* That's a funny idea!

*Rank:* There's a big black cloak . . . haven't you heard of the cloak of invisibility? That comes right down over you, and then nobody can see you.

*Helmer [suppressing a smile]:* Of course, that's right.

*Rank:* But I'm clean forgetting what I came for. Helmer, give me a cigar, one of the dark Havanas.

*Helmer:* With the greatest of pleasure.

[*He offers his case.*]

*Rank* [*takes one and cuts the end off*]: Thanks.

*Nora* [*strikes a match*]: Let me give you a light.

*Rank:* Thank you. [*She holds out the match and he lights his cigar.*] And now, goodbye!

*Helmer:* Goodbye, goodbye, my dear fellow!

*Nora:* Sleep well, Dr. Rank.

*Rank:* Thank you for that wish.

*Nora:* Wish me the same.

*Rank:* You? All right, if you want me to. . . . Sleep well. And thanks for the light.

[*He nods to them both, and goes.*]

*Helmer* [*subdued*]: He's had a lot to drink.

*Nora* [*absently*]: Very likely.

[*Helmer takes a bunch of keys out of his pocket and goes out into the hall.*]

*Nora:* Torvald . . . what do you want there?

*Helmer:* I must empty the letter-box, it's quite full. There'll be no room for the papers in the morning. . . .

*Nora:* Are you going to work tonight?

*Helmer:* You know very well I'm not. Hello, what's this? Somebody's been at the lock.

*Nora:* At the lock?

*Helmer:* Yes, I'm sure of it. Why should that be? I'd hardly have thought the maids. . . ? Here's a broken hair-pin. Nora, it's one of yours. . . .

*Nora* [*quickly*]: It must have been the children. . . .

*Helmer:* Then you'd better tell them not to. Ah . . . there . . . I've managed to get it open. [*He takes the things out and shouts into the kitchen.*] Helene! . . . Helene, put the light out in the hall. [*He comes into the room again with the letters in his hand and shuts the hall door.*] Look how it all mounts up. [*Runs through them.*] What's this?

*Nora:* The letter! Oh no, Torvald, no!

*Helmer:* Two visiting cards . . . from Dr. Rank.

*Nora:* From Dr. Rank?

*Helmer* [*looking at them*]: Dr. Rank, Medical Practitioner. They were on top. He must have put them in as he left.

*Nora:* Is there anything on them?

*Helmer:* There's a black cross above his name. Look. What an uncanny idea. It's just as if he were announcing his own death.

*Nora:* He is.

*Helmer:* What? What do you know about it? Has he said anything to you?

*Nora:* Yes. He said when these cards came, he would have taken his last leave of us. He was going to shut himself up and die.

*Helmer:* Poor fellow! Of course I knew we couldn't keep him with us very long. But so soon. . . . And hiding himself away like a wounded animal.

*Nora:* When it has to happen, it's best that it should happen without words. Don't you think so, Torvald?

*Helmer [walking up and down]:* He had grown so close to us. I don't think I can imagine him gone. His suffering and his loneliness seemed almost to provide a background of dark cloud to the sunshine of our lives. Well, perhaps it's all for the best. For him at any rate. *[Pauses.]* And maybe for us as well, Nora. Now there's just the two of us. *[Puts his arms round her.]* Oh, my darling wife, I can't hold you close enough. You know, Nora . . . many's the time I wish you were threatened by some terrible danger so I could risk everything, body and soul, for your sake.

*Nora [tears herself free and says firmly and decisively]:* Now you must read your letters, Torvald.

*Helmer:* No, no, not tonight. I want to be with you, my darling wife.

*Nora:* Knowing all the time your friend is dying. . . ?

*Helmer:* You are right. It's been a shock to both of us. This ugly thing has come between us . . . thoughts of death and decay. We must try to free ourselves from it. Until then . . . we shall go our separate ways.

*Nora [her arms round his neck]:* Torvald . . . good night! Good night!

*Helmer [kisses her forehead]:* Goodnight, my little singing bird. Sleep well, Nora, I'll just read through my letters.

*[He takes the letters into his room and shuts the door behind him.]*

*Nora [gropes around her, wild-eyed, seizes Helmer's cloak, wraps it round herself, and whispers quickly, hoarsely, spasmodically]:* Never see him again. Never, never, never. *[Throws her shawl over her head.]* And never see the children again either. Never, never. Oh, that black icy water. Oh, that bottomless . . . ! If only it were all over! He's got it now. Now he's reading it. Oh no, no! Not yet! Torvald, goodbye . . . and my children. . . .

*[She rushes out in the direction of the hall; at the same moment Helmer flings open his door and stands there with an open letter in his hand.]*

*Helmer:* Nora!

*Nora [shrieks]:* Ah!

*Helmer:* What is this? Do you know what is in this letter?

*Nora:* Yes, I know. Let me go! Let me out!

*Helmer [holds her back]:* Where are you going?

*Nora [trying to tear herself free]:* You mustn't try to save me, Torvald!

*Helmer [reels back]:* True! Is it true what he writes? How dreadful! No, no, it can't possibly be true.

*Nora:* It *is* true. I loved you more than anything else in the world.

*Helmer:* Don't come to me with a lot of paltry excuses!

*Nora [taking a step towards him]:* Torvald . . . !

*Helmer:* Miserable woman . . . what is this you have done?

*Nora:* Let me go. I won't have you taking the blame for me. You mustn't take it on yourself.

*Helmer:* Stop play-acting! *[Locks the front door.]* You are staying here to give an account of yourself. Do you understand what you have done? Answer me! Do you understand?

*Nora [looking fixedly at him, her face hardening]:* Yes, now I'm really beginning to understand.

*Helmer [walking up and down]:* Oh, what a terrible awakening this is. All these eight years . . . this woman who was my pride and joy . . . a hypocrite, a liar, worse than that, a criminal! Oh, how utterly squalid it all is! Ugh! Ugh! *[Nora remains silent and looks fixedly at him.]* I should have realized something like this would happen. I should have seen it coming. All your father's irresponsible ways. . . . Quiet! All your father's irresponsible ways are coming out in you. No religion, no morals, no sense of duty. . . . Oh, this is my punishment for turning a blind eye to him. It was for your sake I did it, and this is what I get for it.

*Nora:* Yes, this.

*Helmer:* Now you have ruined my entire happiness, jeopardized my whole future. It's terrible to think of. Here I am, at the mercy of a thoroughly unscrupulous person; he can do whatever he likes with me, demand anything he wants, order me about just as he chooses . . . and I daren't even whimper. I'm done for, a miserable failure, and it's all the fault of a feather-brained woman!

*Nora:* When I've left this world behind, you will be free.

*Helmer:* Oh, stop pretending! Your father was just the same, always ready with fine phrases. What good would it do me if you left this world behind, as you put it? Not the slightest bit of good. He can still let it all come out, if he likes; and if he does, people might even suspect me of being an accomplice in these criminal acts of yours. They might even think I was the one behind it all, that it was I who pushed you into it! And it's you I have to thank for this . . . and when I've taken such good care of you, all our married life. Now do you understand what you have done to me?

*Nora [coldly and calmly]:* Yes.

*Helmer:* I just can't understand it, it's so incredible. But we must see about putting things right. Take that shawl off. Take it off, I tell you! I must see if I can't find some way or other of appeasing him. The thing must be hushed up at all costs. And as far as you and I are concerned, things must appear to go on exactly as before. But only in the eyes of the world, of course. In other words you'll go on living here; that's understood. But you will not be allowed to bring up the children, I can't trust you with them. . . . Oh, that I should have to say this to the woman I loved so dearly, the woman I still. . . . Well, that must be all over and done with. From now on, there can be no question of happiness. All we can do is save the bits and pieces from the wreck, preserve appearances. . . . *[The front door-bell rings. Helmer gives a start.]* What's that? So late? How terrible, supposing. . . . If he should. . . ? Hide, Nora! Say you are not well.

*[Nora stands motionless. Helmer walks across and opens the door into the hall.]*

Maid *[half dressed, in the hall]*: It's a note for Mrs. Helmer.

Helmer: Give it to me. *[He snatches the note and shuts the door.]* Yes, it's from him. You can't have it. I want to read it myself.

Nora: You read it then.

Helmer *[by the lamp]*: I hardly dare. Perhaps this is the end, for both of us. Well, I must know. *[He opens the note hurriedly, reads a few lines, looks at another enclosed sheet, and gives a cry of joy.]* Nora! *[Nora looks at him inquiringly.]* Nora! I must read it again. Yes, yes, it's true! I am saved! Nora, I am saved!

Nora: And me?

Helmer: You too, of course, we are both saved, you as well as me. Look, he's sent your IOU back. He sends his regrets and apologies for what he has done. . . . His luck has changed. . . . Oh, what does it matter what he says. We are saved, Nora! Nobody can do anything to you now. Oh, Nora, Nora . . . but let's get rid of this disgusting thing first. Let me see. . . . *[He glances at the IOU.]* No, I don't want to see it. I don't want it to be anything but a dream. *[He tears up the IOU and both letters, throws all the pieces into the stove and watches them burn.]* Well, that's the end of that. He said in his note you'd known since Christmas Eve. . . . You must have had three terrible days of it, Nora.

Nora: These three days haven't been easy.

Helmer: The agonies you must have gone through! When the only way out seemed to be. . . . No, let's forget the whole ghastly thing. We can rejoice and say: It's all over! It's all over! Listen to me, Nora! You don't seem to understand: it's all over! Why this grim look on your face? Oh, poor little Nora, of course I understand. You can't bring yourself to believe I've forgiven you. But I have, Nora, I swear it. I forgive you everything. I know you did what you did because you loved me.

Nora: That's true.

Helmer: You loved me as a wife should love her husband. It was simply that you didn't have the experience to judge what was the best way of going about things. But do you think I love you any the less for that; just because you don't know how to act on your own responsibility? No, no, you just lean on me, I shall give you all the advice and guidance you need. I wouldn't be a proper man if I didn't find a woman doubly attractive for being so obviously helpless. You mustn't dwell on the harsh things I said in that first moment of horror, when I thought everything was going to come crashing down about my ears. I have forgiven you, Nora, I swear it! I have forgiven you!

Nora: Thank you for your forgiveness.

*[She goes out through the door, right.]*

Helmer: No, don't go! *[He looks through the doorway.]* What are you doing in the spare room?

Nora: Taking off this fancy dress.

*Helmer* [*standing at the open door*]: Yes, do. You try and get some rest, and set your mind at peace again, my frightened little song-bird. Have a good long sleep; you know you are safe and sound under my wing. [*Walks up and down near the door.*] What a nice, cosy little home we have here, Nora! Here you can find refuge. Here I shall hold you like a hunted dove I have rescued unscathed from the cruel talons of the hawk, and calm your poor beating heart. And that will come, gradually, Nora, believe me. Tomorrow you'll see everything quite differently. Soon everything will be just as it was before. You won't need me to keep on telling you I've forgiven you; you'll feel convinced of it in your own heart. You don't really imagine me ever thinking of turning you out, or even of reproaching you? Oh, a real man isn't made that way, you know, Nora. For a man, there's something indescribably moving and very satisfying in knowing that he has forgiven his wife—forgiven her, completely and genuinely, from the depths of his heart. It's as though it made her his property in a double sense: he has, as it were, given her a new life, and she becomes in a way both his wife and at the same time his child. That is how you will seem to me after today, helpless, perplexed little thing that you are. Don't you worry your pretty little head about anything, Nora. Just you be frank with me, and I'll take all the decisions for you. . . . What's this? Not in bed? You've changed your things?

*Nora* [*in her everyday dress*]: Yes, Torvald, I've changed.

*Helmer*: What for? It's late.

*Nora*: I shan't sleep tonight.

*Helmer*: But my dear Nora. . . .

*Nora* [*looks at her watch*]: It's not so terribly late. Sit down, Torvald. We two have a lot to talk about.

[*She sits down at one side of the table.*]

*Helmer*: Nora, what is all this? Why so grim?

*Nora*: Sit down. It'll take some time. I have a lot to say to you.

*Helmer* [*sits down at the table opposite her*]: You frighten me, Nora. I don't understand you.

*Nora*: Exactly. You don't understand me. And I have never understood you, either—until tonight. No, don't interrupt. I just want you to listen to what I have to say. We are going to have things out, Torvald.

*Helmer*: What do you mean?

*Nora*: Isn't there anything that strikes you about the way we two are sitting here?

*Helmer*: What's that?

*Nora*: We have now been married eight years. Hasn't it struck you this is the first time you and I, man and wife, have had a serious talk together?

*Helmer*: Depends what you mean by 'serious'.

*Nora*: Eight whole years—no, more, ever since we first knew each other—and never have we exchanged one serious word about serious things.

*Helmer*: What did you want me to do? Get you involved in worries that you couldn't possibly help me to bear?

*Nora:* I'm not talking about worries. I say we've never once sat down together and seriously tried to get to the bottom of anything.

*Helmer:* But, my dear Nora, would that have been a thing for you?

*Nora:* That's just it. You have never understood me . . . I've been greatly wronged, Torvald. First by my father, and then by you.

*Helmer:* What! Us two! The two people who loved you more than anybody?

*Nora [shakes her head]:* You two never loved me. You only thought now nice it was to be in love with me.

*Helmer:* But, Nora, what's this you are saying?

*Nora:* It's right, you know, Torvald. At home, Daddy used to tell me what he thought, then I thought the same. And if I thought differently, I kept quiet about it, because he wouldn't have liked it. He used to call me his baby doll, and he played with me as I used to play with my dolls. Then I came to live in your house. . . .

*Helmer:* What way is that to talk about our marriage?

*Nora [imperturbably]:* What I mean is: I passed out of Daddy's hands into yours. You arranged everything to your tastes, and I acquired the same tastes. Or I pretended to . . . I don't really know . . . I think it was a bit of both, some-times one thing and sometimes the other. When I look back, it seems to me I have been living here like a beggar, from hand to mouth. I lived by doing tricks for you, Torvald. But that's the way you wanted it. You and Daddy did me a great wrong. It's your fault that I've never made anything of my life.

*Helmer:* Nora, how unreasonable . . . how ungrateful you are! Haven't you been happy here?

*Nora:* No, never. I thought I was, but I wasn't really.

*Helmer:* Not . . . not happy!

*Nora:* No, just gay. And you've always been so kind to me. But our house has never been anything but a play-room. I have been your doll wife, just as at home I was Daddy's doll child. And the children in turn have been my dolls. I thought it was fun when you came and played with me, just as they thought it was fun when I went and played with them. That's been our marriage, Torvald.

*Helmer:* There is some truth in what you say, exaggerated and hysterical though it is. But from now on it will be different. Play-time is over; now comes the time for lessons.

*Nora:* Whose lessons? Mine or the children's?

*Helmer:* Both yours and the children's, my dear Nora.

*Nora:* Ah, Torvald, you are not the man to teach me to be a good wife for you.

*Helmer:* How can you say that?

*Nora:* And what sort of qualifications have I to teach the children?

*Helmer:* Nora!

*Nora:* Didn't you say yourself, a minute or two ago, that you couldn't trust me with that job.

*Helmer:* In the heat of the moment! You shouldn't pay any attention to that.

*Nora:* On the contrary, you were quite right. I'm not up to it. There's another problem needs solving first. I must take steps to educate myself. You are not the man to help me there. That's something I must do on my own. That's why I'm leaving you.

*Helmer [jumps up]*: What did you say?

*Nora*: If I'm ever to reach any understanding of myself and the things around me, I must learn to stand alone. That's why I can't stay here with you any longer.

*Helmer*: Nora! Nora!

*Nora*: I'm leaving here at once. I dare say Kristine will put me up for tonight. . . .

*Helmer*: You are out of your mind! I won't let you! I forbid you!

*Nora*: It's no use forbidding me anything now. I'm taking with me my own personal belongings. I don't want anything of yours, either now or later.

*Helmer*: This is madness!

*Nora*: Tomorrow I'm going home—to what used to be my home, I mean. It will be easier for me to find something to do there.

*Helmer*: Oh, you blind, inexperienced . . .

*Nora*: I must set about *getting* experience, Torvald.

*Helmer*: And leave your home, your husband and your children? Don't you care what people will say?

*Nora*: That's no concern of mine. All I know is that this is necessary for *me*.

*Helmer*: This is outrageous! You are betraying your most sacred duty.

*Nora*: And what do you consider to be my most sacred duty?

*Helmer*: Does it take me to tell you that? Isn't it your duty to your husband and your children?

*Nora*: I have another duty equally sacred.

*Helmer*: You have not. What duty might *that* be?

*Nora*: My duty to myself.

*Helmer*: First and foremost, you are a wife and mother.

*Nora*: That I don't believe any more. I believe that first and foremost I am an individual, just as much as you are—or at least I'm going to try to be. I know most people agree with you, Torvald, and that's also what it says in books. But I'm not content any more with what most people say, or with what it says in books. I have to think things out for myself, and get things clear.

*Helmer*: Surely you are clear about your position in your own home? Haven't you an infallible guide in questions like these? Haven't you your religion?

*Nora*: Oh, Torvald, I don't really know what religion is.

*Helmer*: What do you say!

*Nora*: All I know is what Pastor Hansen said when I was confirmed. He said religion was this, that and the other. When I'm away from all this and on my own, I'll go into that, too. I want to find out whether what Pastor Hansen told me was right—or at least whether it's right for *me*.

*Helmer*: This is incredible talk from a young woman! But if religion cannot keep you on the right path, let me at least stir your conscience. I suppose you do have some moral sense? Or tell me—perhaps you don't?

*Nora*: Well, Torvald, that's not easy to say. I simply don't know. I'm really very confused about such things. All I know is my ideas about such things are very different from yours. I've also learnt that the law is different from what I thought; but I simply can't get it into my head that that particular law is right. Apparently a woman has no right to spare her old father on his deathbed, or to save her husband's life, even. I just don't believe it.

*Helmer:* You are talking like a child. You understand nothing about the society you live in.

*Nora:* No, I don't. But I shall go into that too. I must try to discover who is right, society or me.

*Helmer:* You are ill, Nora. You are delirious. I'm half inclined to think you are out of your mind.

*Nora:* Never have I felt so calm and collected as I do tonight.

*Helmer:* Calm and collected enough to leave your husband and children?

*Nora:* Yes.

*Helmer:* Then only one explanation is possible.

*Nora:* And that is?

*Helmer:* You don't love me any more.

*Nora:* Exactly.

*Helmer:* Nora! Can you say that!

*Nora:* I'm desperately sorry, Torvald. Because you have always been so kind to me. But I can't help it. I don't love you any more.

*Helmer [struggling to keep his composure]:* Is that also a 'calm and collected' decision you've made?

*Nora:* Yes, absolutely calm and collected. That's why I don't want to stay here.

*Helmer:* And can you also account for how I forfeited your love?

*Nora:* Yes, very easily. It was tonight, when the miracle didn't happen. It was then I realized you weren't the man I thought you were.

*Helmer:* Explain yourself more clearly. I don't understand.

*Nora:* For eight years I have been patiently waiting. Because, heavens, I knew miracles didn't happen every day. Then this devastating business started, and I became absolutely convinced the miracle *would* happen. All the time Krogstad's letter lay there, it never so much as crossed my mind that you would ever submit to that man's conditions. I was absolutely convinced you would say to him: Tell the whole wide world if you like. And when that was done . . .

*Helmer:* Yes, then what? After I had exposed my own wife to dishonour and shame . . . !

*Nora:* When that was done, I was absolutely convinced you would come forward and take everything on yourself, and say: I am the guilty one.

*Helmer:* Nora!

*Nora:* You mean I'd never let you make such a sacrifice for my sake? Of course not. But what would my story have counted for against yours?—That was the miracle I went in hope and dread of. It was to prevent it that I was ready to end my life.

*Helmer:* I would gladly toil day and night for you, Nora, enduring all manner of sorrow and distress. But nobody sacrifices his *honour* for the one he loves.

*Nora:* Hundreds and thousands of women have.

*Helmer:* Oh, you think and talk like a stupid child.

*Nora:* All right. But you neither think nor talk like the man I would want to share my life with. When you had got over your fright—and you weren't concerned about me but only about what might happen to you—and when all danger was past, you acted as though nothing had happened. I was your little sky-lark again, your little doll, exactly as before; except you would have to protect it twice as carefully as before, now that it had shown itself to be so weak and fragile. *[Rises.]* Torvald, that was the moment I realised that for eight years I'd been living with a stranger, and had borne him three children. . . . Oh, I can't bear to think about it! I could tear myself to shreds.

*Helmer [sadly]:* I see. I see. There is a tremendous gulf dividing us. But, Nora, is there no way we might bridge it?

*Nora:* As I am now, I am no wife for you.

*Helmer:* I still have it in me to change.

*Nora:* Perhaps . . . if you have your doll taken away.

*Helmer:* And be separated from you! No, no, Nora, the very thought of it is inconceivable.

*Nora [goes into the room, right]:* All the more reason why it must be done.

*[She comes back with her outdoor things and a small travelling bag which she puts on the chair beside the table.]*

*Helmer:* Nora, Nora, not now! Wait till the morning.

*Nora [putting on her coat]:* I can't spend the night in a strange man's room.

*Helmer:* Couldn't we go on living here like brother and sister. . . ?

*Nora [tying on her hat]:* You know very well that wouldn't last. *[She draws the shawl round her.]* Goodbye, Torvald. I don't want to see the children. I know they are in better hands than mine. As I am now, I can never be anything to them.

*Helmer:* But some day, Nora, some day . . . ?

*Nora:* How should I know? I've no idea what I might turn out to be.

*Helmer:* But you are my wife, whatever you are.

*Nora:* Listen, Torvald, from what I've heard, when a wife leaves her husband's house as I am doing now, he is absolved by law of all responsibility for her. I can at any rate free you from all responsibility. You must not feel in any way bound, any more than I shall. There must be full freedom on both sides. Look, here's your ring back. Give me mine.

*Helmer:* That too?

*Nora:* That too.

*Helmer:* There it is.

*Nora:* Well, that's the end of that. I'll put the keys down here. The maids know where everything is in the house—better than I do, in fact. Kristine will come in the morning after I've left to pack up the few things I brought with me from home. I want them sent on.

*Helmer:* The end! Nora, will you never think of me?

*Nora:* I dare say I'll often think about you and the children and this house.

*Helmer:* May I write to you, Nora?

*Nora:* No, never. I won't let you.

*Helmer:* But surely I can send you . . .

*Nora:* Nothing, nothing.

*Helmer:* Can't I help you if ever you need it?

*Nora:* I said 'no'. I don't accept things from strangers.

*Helmer:* Nora, can I never be anything more to you than a stranger?

*Nora [takes her bag]:* Ah, Torvald, only by a miracle of miracles. . . .

*Helmer:* Name it, this miracle of miracles!

*Nora:* Both you and I would have to change to the point where . . . Oh, Torvald, I don't believe in miracles any more.

*Helmer:* But I *will* believe. Name it! Change to the point where. . . ?

*Nora:* Where we could make a real marriage of our lives together. Goodbye!

*[She goes out through the hall door.]*

*Helmer [sinks down on a chair near the door, and covers his face with his hands]:* Nora! Nora! *[He rises and looks round.]* Empty! She's gone! *[With sudden hope.]* The miracle of miracles. . . ?

*[The heavy sound of a door being slammed is heard from below.]*

QUESTIONS

ACT I

1. From the opening conversation between Helmer and Nora, what are your impressions of him? Of her? Of their marriage?
2. At what moment in the play do you understand why it is called *A Doll's House?*
3. In what ways does Mrs. Linde provide a contrast for Nora?
4. What in Krogstad's first appearance on stage, and in Dr. Rank's remarks about him, indicates that the bank clerk is a menace?
5. Of what illegal deed is Nora guilty? How does she justify it?
6. When the curtain falls on Act I, what problems now confront Nora?

ACT II

1. As Act II opens, what are your feelings on seeing the stripped, ragged Christmas tree? How is it suggestive?
2. What events that soon occur make Nora's situation even more difficult?
3. How does she try to save herself?
4. Why does Nora fling herself into the wild tarantella?

ACT III

1. For what possible reasons does Mrs. Linde pledge herself to Krogstad?
2. How does Dr. Rank's announcement of his impending death affect Nora and Helmer?
3. What is Helmer's reaction to learning the truth about Nora's misdeed? Why does he blame Nora's father? What is revealing (of Helmer's own character) in his remark, "From now on, there can be no question of happiness. All we can do is save the bits and pieces from the wreck, preserve appearances. . . ."?

4. When Helmer finds that Krogstad has sent back the note, what is his response? How do you feel toward him?
5. How does the character of Nora develop in this act?
6. How do you interpret her final slamming of the door?

## GENERAL QUESTIONS

1. In what ways do you find Nora a victim? In what ways at fault?
2. Try to state the theme of the play. Does it involve women's rights? Self-fulfillment?
3. What dramatic question does the play embody? At what moment can this question first be stated?
4. What is the crisis? In what way is this moment or event a "turning point"? (In what new direction does the action turn?)
5. Eric Bentley, in an essay titled "Ibsen, Pro and Con" (*In Search of Theater*, New York: Knopf, 1953), criticizes the character of Krogstad, calling him "a mere pawn of the plot." He then adds, "When convenient to Ibsen, he is a blackmailer. When inconvenient, he is converted." Do you agree or disagree?
6. Why is the play considered a work of realism? Is there anything in it that does not seem realistic?
7. In what respects does *A Doll's House* seem to apply to life today? Is it in any way dated? Could there be a Nora in North America in the 1990s?

## TRAGICOMEDY AND THE ABSURD

One of the more prominent developments in mid-twentieth-century drama has been the rise of **tragicomedies,** plays that stir us not only to pity and fear (echoing Aristotle's description of the effect of tragedy) but also to laughter. Although tragicomedy is a kind of drama we think distinctively modern, it is by no means a new invention. The term was used (although jokingly) by the Roman writer of comedy Plautus in about 185 B.C.

Since ancient times, playwrights have mingled laughter and tears, defying the neoclassical doctrine that required strict unity of action and tone (discussed on page 1081) and decreed that a play must be entirely comic or entirely tragic. Shakespeare is fond of tragicomic mingling: in *Hamlet,* the prince jokes with a grave digger; in *Antony and Cleopatra,* the queen commits suicide with a poisonous asp brought to her by a wise-cracking clown. Likewise, Shakespeare's darker comedies like *Measure for Measure* or *The Merchant of Venice* deal so forcefully with such stark themes (lust, greed, racism, revenge, and cruelty) that they often seem like tragedies until their happy endings. In the tragedies of Shakespeare and others, passages of clownish humor are sometimes called **comic relief,** meaning that the section of comedy introduces a sharp contrast in mood. But such passages can do more than provide relief. In *Othello* (III, iv, 1–22), the clown's banter with Desdemona for a moment makes the surrounding tragedy seem, by comparison, more poignant and intense.

No one doubts that *Othello* is a tragedy, but some twentieth-century plays leave us both bemused and confused: should we laugh or cry? One of the most talked-about plays since World War II, Samuel Beckett's *Waiting for Godot,* portrays two clownish tramps who mark time in a wasteland, wistfully looking for a savior who never arrives. Contemporary drama, by the way, has often featured such **antiheroes:** ordinary people, inglorious and inarticulate, who carry on not from bravery but from inertia. (The rise of the antihero in recent fiction is discussed briefly on page 69; those remarks could apply equally well to contemporary drama.) We cannot help laughing, in Beckett, at the tramps' painful situation; but, turning the idea around, we also feel deeply moved by their ridiculous plight. Perhaps a modern tragicomedy like *Godot* does not show us great souls suffering greatly—as Edith Hamilton has said we observe in a classical tragedy—but Beckett's play nonetheless touches mysteriously on the universal sorrows of human existence.

But perhaps the full effect of such a play takes time to sink in. Contemporary playwright Edward Albee suggests that sometimes the spectator's sense of relief after experiencing pity and fear (Aristotle calls it *katharsis*) may be a delayed reaction: "I don't feel that catharsis in a play necessarily takes place during the course of a play. Often it should take place afterwards."[1] If Albee is right, we may be amused while watching a tragicomedy, then go home and feel deeply stirred by it.

Straddling the fence between tragedy and comedy, the plays of some modern playwrights portray people whose suffering seems ridiculous. These plays belong to the **theater of the absurd:** a general name for a type of play first staged in Paris in the 1950s. "For the modern critical spirit, nothing can be taken entirely seriously, nor entirely lightly," says Eugène Ionesco, one of the movement's leading playwrights. Behind the literary conventions of the theater of the absurd stands a philosophical fear that human existence has no meaning. Every person, such playwrights assume, is a helpless waif alone in a universe full of ridiculous obstacles. In Ionesco's *Amédée* (1953), a couple share an apartment with a gigantic corpse that keeps swelling relentlessly; in his *Rhinoceros* (1958), the human race starts turning into rhinos, except for one man, who remains human and isolated. A favorite theme in the theater of the absurd is that communication between people is impossible. Language is therefore futile. Ionesco's *The Bald Soprano* (1948) accordingly pokes fun at polite social conversation in a scene whose dialogue consists entirely of illogical strings of catchphrases. In *Endgame* (1957), Samuel Beckett dramatizes his vision of mankind's present condition: the main character is blind and paralyzed, and his legless parents live inside two garbage cans. Oddly, the effect of the play isn't total gloom: we leave the theater both amused and bemused by it.[2]

Trends in drama change along with playwrights' convictions, and during the 1970s and 1980s the theater of the absurd no longer seemed the dominant influence on new drama in America. Along with other protests of the 1960s, experimental theater seemed to have spent its force. During the later period most of the critically celebrated new plays were neither absurd nor experimental. David

---

[1]"The Art of the Theater," interview in *The Paris Review*, No. 39, Fall 1966.
[2]For an excellent study of the theater of the absurd, see Martin Esslin, *The Theater of the Absurd*, revised edition (New York: Overlook, 1973).

Mamet's *American Buffalo* (1975) realistically portrayed three petty thieves in a junk shop as they plot to steal a coin collection. Albert Innaurato's *Gemini* (1977) took a realistic (and comic) view of family life and sexual awakening in one of Philadelphia's Italian neighborhoods. Beth Henley's 1979 Pulitzer Prize–winning play, *Crimes of the Heart* (the play appears on page 1598) presented an eccentric but still believable group of sisters in a small Southern town. The dialogue in all three plays showed high fidelity to ordinary speech. Meanwhile many of the most influential plays of **feminist theater,** which explores the lives, problems, and occasional triumphs of contemporary women, were also written in a realistic style. Notable success—with both critics and the ticket-buying public—greeted plays such as Marsha Norman's *'Night, Mother* (1983), Tina Howe's *Painting Churches* (1983), and Wendy Wasserstein's *The Heidi Chronicles* (1988).

Some leading critics, among them Richard Gilman, believed that the American theater had entered an era of **new naturalism.**[3] Indeed, many plays of this time subjected the lives of people, especially poor and unhappy people, to a realistic, searching light, showing the forces that shaped them. Sam Shepard in *Buried Child* (1978) explored violence and desperation in a family who dwelt on the edge of poverty; while August Wilson, in *Joe Turner's Come and Gone* (1988), convincingly portrayed life in a Pittsburgh ghetto lodging house. But if these newly established playwrights sometimes showed life as frankly as did the earlier naturalists, both of the plays just mentioned also contain rich and suggestive symbolism.

More recently, however, experimental drama, greatly influenced by the theater of the absurd, has made a comeback. David Hwang's work (see his one-act play, *The Sound of a Voice,* on page 1647) combines realistic elements with overtly symbolic devices. Caryl Churchill's *Top Girls* (1982) presents a dinner party in which a contemporary woman invites legendary women from history to a restaurant dinner party. Although Churchill's play examines serious political issues, her straightforward treatment of an impossible premise owes much to Ionesco and Albee. Tony Kushner's *Angels in America* (1992) also mixes realism and fantasy to dramatize the plight of AIDS. Shel Silverstein, popular author of children's poetry, wrote a raucous one-man play, *The Devil and Bill Markham* (1991), entirely in rhyme, about a series of fantastic adventures in hell featuring a hard-drinking gambler and the Prince of Darkness. Silverstein's play is simultaneously experimental in form but traditional in content with its homage to American ballads and tall tales.

The experimental theater continues to exert a strong influence, especially in the work of Edward Albee, whose idiosyncratic plays still seem fresh and provocative. His one-act play, *The Sandbox,* with its dark humor, overt but odd symbolism, and minimalist staging represents a uniquely American version of theater of the absurd.

---

[3]"Out Goes Absurdism—In Comes the New Naturalism," *The New York Times Book Review,* 19 March 1978.

# Edward Albee

*Edward Albee, born in 1928, was adopted by millionaire foster parents who gave him his name. As a boy, he was dismissed from Lawrenceville, a preparatory school, and Valley Forge, a military academy, before settling in at Choate School, where he began to write. He started college at Trinity in Hartford, Connecticut, but soon dropped out to become a writer of radio scripts. Living in Greenwich Village for ten years beginning in 1948, he held jobs as an office boy, a record salesman, a bartender, and a Western Union messenger. In 1958, in a three-week burst of energy, he wrote* The Zoo Story, *first performed in 1959 in West Berlin and in the following year (to critical acclaim) at the Provincetown Playhouse in*

Edward Albee

New York. Other plays followed, among them The Death of Bessie Smith, The Sandbox *(both in 1960),* The American Dream *(1961),* Who's Afraid of Virginia Woolf? *(1962; later a successful film);* Tiny Alice *(1964),* Malcolm *(which failed on Broadway after a five-day run; 1966), and* A Delicate Balance *(which received a Pulitzer Prize; 1966);* Seascape *(1975),* Listening *(1977), and* The Man Who Had Three Arms *(1983). In 1981 he adapted Vladimir Nabokov's* Lolita *for the stage. In 1994, Albee received his third Pulitzer for* Three Tall Women. *Albee currently divides his time between New York City and Long Island.*

A Brief Play, in Memory of My Grandmother (1876–1959)

Players

*The Young Man*, 25, a good-looking, well-built boy in a bathing suit
*Mommy*, 55, a well-dressed, imposing woman
*Daddy*, 60, a small man; gray, thin
*Grandma*, 86, a tiny, wizened woman with bright eyes
*The Musician*, no particular age, but young would be nice

Note. *When, in the course of the play, Mommy and Daddy call each other by these names, there should be no suggestion of regionalism. These names are of empty affection and point up the pre-senility and vacuity of their characters.*

Scene. *A bare stage, with only the following: Near the footlights, far stage right, two simple chairs set side by side, facing the audience; near the footlights, far stage left, a chair facing stage right with a music stand before it; farther back, and stage center,*

*slightly elevated and raked, a large child's sandbox with a toy pail and shovel; the back-*
*ground is the sky, which alters from brightest day to deepest night.*

*At the beginning, it is brightest day; the Young Man is alone on stage to the rear*
*of the sandbox, and to one side. He is doing calisthenics; he does calisthenics until quite*
*at the very end of the play. These calisthenics, employing the arms only, should suggest*
*the beating and fluttering of wings. The Young Man is, after all, the Angel of Death.*

*Mommy and Daddy enter from stage left, Mommy first.*

Mommy (*motioning to Daddy*): Well, here we are; this is the beach.

Daddy (*whining*): I'm cold.

Mommy (*dismissing him with a little laugh*): Don't be silly; it's as warm as toast.
Look at that nice young man over there: he doesn't think it's cold. (*Waves to
the Young Man*) Hello.

Young Man (*with an endearing smile*): Hi!

Mommy (*looking about*): This will do perfectly . . . don't you think so, Daddy?
There's sand there . . . and the water beyond. What do you think, Daddy?

Daddy (*vaguely*): Whatever you say, Mommy.

Mommy (*with the same little laugh*): Well, of course . . . whatever I say. Then, it's
settled, is it?

Daddy (*shrugs*): She's *your* mother, not mine.

Mommy: I know she's my mother. What do you take me for? (*A pause*) All right,
now; let's get on with it. (*She shouts into the wings, stage-left*) You! Out there!
You can come in now. (*The Musician enters, seats himself in the chair, stage-left,
places music on the music stand, is ready to play. Mommy nods approvingly.*)
Very nice; very nice. Are you ready, Daddy? Let's go get Grandma.

Daddy: Whatever you say, Mommy.

Mommy (*leading the way out, stage-left*): Of course, whatever I say. (*To the
Musician*) You can begin now. (*The Musician begins playing; Mommy and
Daddy exit; the Musician, all the while playing, nods to the Young Man.*)

Young Man (*with the same endearing smile*): Hi! (*After a moment, Mommy and
Daddy re-enter, carrying Grandma. She is borne in by their hands under her
armpits; she is quite rigid; her legs are drawn up; her feet do not touch the ground;
the expression on her ancient face is that of puzzlement and fear.*)

Daddy: Where do we put her?

Mommy (*the same little laugh*): Wherever I say, of course. Let me see . . . well . . .
all right, over there . . . in the sandbox. (*Pause*) Well, what are you waiting
for, Daddy? . . . The sandbox! (*Together they carry Grandma over to the sandbox and more or less dump her in.*)

Grandma (*righting herself to a sitting position; her voice a cross between a baby's laugh
and cry*): Ahhhhhh! Graaaaa!

Daddy (*dusting himself*): What do we do now?

Mommy (*to the Musician*): You can stop now. (*The Musician stops.*) (*Back to
Daddy*) What do you mean, what do we do now? We go over there and sit
down, of course. (*To the Young Man*) Hello there.

Young Man (*again smiling*): Hi! (*Mommy and Daddy move to the chairs, stage-right,
and sit down. A pause.*)

*Grandma* (*same as before*): Ahhhhhh! Ah-haaaaaa! Graaaaaa!

*Daddy*: Do you think . . . do you think she's . . . comfortable?

*Mommy* (*impatiently*): How would I know?

*Daddy* (*pause*): What do we do now?

*Mommy* (*as if remembering*): We . . . wait. We . . . sit here . . . and we wait . . . that's what we do.

*Daddy* (*after a pause*): Shall we talk to each other?

*Mommy* (*with that little laugh; picking something off her dress*): Well, *you* can talk, if you want to . . . if you can think of anything to say . . . if you can think of anything *new*.

*Daddy* (*thinks*): No . . . I suppose not.

*Mommy* (*with a triumphant laugh*): Of course not!

*Grandma* (*banging the toy shovel against the pail*): Haaaaaa! Ah-haaaaaa!

*Mommy* (*out over the audience*): Be quiet, Grandma . . . just be quiet, and wait. (*Grandma throws a shovelful of sand at Mommy.*) (*Still out over the audience*) She's throwing sand at me! You stop that, Grandma; you stop throwing sand at Mommy! (*To Daddy*) She's throwing sand at me. (*Daddy looks around at Grandma, who screams at him.*)

*Grandma*: GRAAAAAA!

*Mommy*: Don't look at her. Just . . . sit here . . . be very still . . . and wait. (*To the Musician*) You . . . uh . . . you go ahead and do whatever it is you do. (*The Musician plays. Mommy and Daddy are fixed, staring out beyond the audience. Grandma looks at them, looks at the Musician, looks at the sandbox, throws down the shovel.*)

*Grandma*: Ah-haaaaaa! Graaaaaa! (*Looks for reaction; gets none. Now . . . directly to the audience*) Honestly! What a way to treat an old woman! Drag her out of the house . . . stick her in a car . . . bring her out here from the city . . . dump her in a pile of sand . . . and leave her here to set. I'm eighty-six years old! I was married when I was seventeen. To a farmer. He died when I was thirty. (*To the Musician*) Will you stop that, please? (*The Musician stops playing.*) I'm a feeble old woman . . . how do you expect anybody to hear me over that peep! peep! peep! (*To herself*) There's no respect around here. (*To the Young Man*) There's no respect around here!

*Young Man* (*same smile*): Hi!

*Grandma* (*after a pause, a mild double-take, continues, to the audience*): My husband died when I was thirty (*indicates Mommy*), and I had to raise that big cow over there all by my lonesome. You can imagine what *that was like*. Lordy! (*To the Young Man*) Where'd they get *you*?

*Young Man*: Oh . . . I've been around for a while.

*Grandma*: I'll bet you have! Heh, heh, heh. Will you look at you!

*Young Man* (*flexing his muscles*): Isn't that something? (*Continues his calisthenics.*)

*Grandma*: Boy, oh boy; I'll say. Pretty good.

*Young Man* (*sweetly*): I'll say.

*Grandma*: Where ya from?

*Young Man*: Southern California.

Grandma (*nodding*): Figgers; figgers. What's your name, honey?

Young Man: I don't know . . .

Grandma (*to the audience*): Bright, too!

Young Man: I mean . . . I mean, they haven't given me one yet . . . the studio . . .

Grandma (*giving him the once-over*): You don't say . . . you don't say. Well . . . uh, I've got to talk some more . . . don't you go 'way.

Young Man: Oh, no.

Grandma (*turning her attention back to the audience*): Fine; fine. (*Then, once more, back to the Young Man*) You're . . . you're an actor, hunh?

Young Man (*beaming*): Yes. I am.

Grandma (*to the audience again; shrugs*): I'm smart that way. Anyhow, I had to raise . . . *that* over there all by my lonesome; and what's next to her there . . . that's what she married. Rich? I tell you . . . money, money, money. They took me off the *farm* . . . which was real decent of them . . . and they moved me into the big town house with *them* . . . fixed a nice place for me under the stove . . . gave me an army blanket . . . and my own dish . . . my very own dish! So, what have I got to complain about? Nothing, of course. I'm not complaining. (*She looks up at the sky, shouts to someone off stage*) Shouldn't it be getting dark now, dear? (*The lights dim; night comes on. The Musician begins to play; it becomes deepest night. There are spotlights on all the players, including the Young Man, who is, of course, continuing his calisthenics.*)

Daddy (*stirring*): It's nighttime.

Mommy: Shhhh. Be still . . . wait.

Daddy (*whining*): It's so hot.

Mommy: Shhhhhh. Be still . . . wait.

Grandma (*to herself*): That's better. Night. (*To the Musician*) Honey, do you play all through this part? (*The Musician nods.*) Well, keep it nice and soft; that's a good boy. (*The Musician nods again; plays softly.*) That's nice. (*There is an off-stage rumble.*)

Daddy (*starting*): What was that?

Mommy (*beginning to weep*): It was nothing.

Daddy: It was . . . it was . . . thunder . . . or a wave breaking . . . or something.

Mommy (*whispering, through her tears*): It was an off-stage rumble . . . and you know what *that* means . . .

Daddy: I forget . . .

Mommy (*barely able to talk*): It means the time has come for poor Grandma . . . and I can't bear it!

Daddy (*vacantly*): I . . . I suppose you've got to be brave.

Grandma (*mocking*): That's right, kid; be brave. You'll bear up; you'll get over it. (*Another off-stage rumble . . . louder.*)

Mommy: Ohhhhhhhhhh . . . poor Grandma . . . poor Grandma . . .

Grandma (*to Mommy*): I'm fine! I'm all right! It hasn't happened yet! (*A violent off-stage rumble. All the lights go out, save the spot on the Young Man; the Musician stops playing.*)

Mommy: Ohhhhhhhhhh . . . Ohhhhhhhhhh . . . (*Silence.*)

Grandma: Don't put the lights up yet . . . I'm not ready; I'm not quite ready. (*Silence*) All right, dear . . . I'm about done. (*The lights come up again, to brightest day; the Musician begins to play. Grandma is discovered, still in the sandbox, lying on her side, propped up on an elbow, half covered, busily shoveling sand over herself.*)

Grandma (*muttering*): I don't know how I'm supposed to do anything with this goddam toy shovel . . .

Daddy: Mommy! It's daylight!

Mommy (*brightly*): So it is! Well! Our long night is over. We must put away our tears, take off our mourning . . . and face the future. It's our duty.

Grandma (*still shoveling; mimicking*): . . . take off our mourning . . . face the future . . . Lordy! (*Mommy and Daddy rise, stretch. Mommy waves to the Young Man.*)

Young Man (*with that smile*): Hi! (*Grandma plays dead.*[!] *Mommy and Daddy go over to look at her; she is a little more than half buried in the sand; the toy shovel is in her hands, which are crossed on her breast.*)

Mommy (*before the sandbox; shaking her head*): Lovely! It's . . . it's hard to be sad . . . she looks . . . so happy. (*With pride and conviction*) It pays to do things well. (*To the Musician*) All right, you can stop now, if you want to. I mean, stay around for a swim, or something; it's all right with us. (*She sighs heavily*) Well, Daddy . . . off we go.

Daddy: Brave Mommy!

Mommy: Brave Daddy! (*They exit, stage-left.*)

Grandma (*after they leave; lying quite still*): It pays to do things well . . . Boy, oh boy! (*She tries to sit up*) . . . well, kids . . . (*but she finds she can't*) . . . I . . . I can't get up. I . . . I can't move . . . (*The Young Man stops his calisthenics, nods to the Musician, walks over to Grandma, kneels down by the sandbox.*)

Grandma: I . . . can't move . . .

Young Man: Shhhhh . . . be very still . . .

Grandma: I . . . I can't move . . .

Young Man: Uh . . . ma'am; I . . . I have a line here.

Grandma: Oh, I'm sorry, sweetie; you go right ahead.

Young Man: I am . . . uh . . .

Grandma: Take your time, dear.

Young Man (*prepares; delivers the line like a real amateur*): I am the Angel of Death. I am . . . uh . . . I am come for you.

Grandma: What . . . wha . . . (*then, with resignation*) . . . ohhhh . . . ohhhh, I see. (*The Young Man bends over, kisses Grandma gently on the forehead.*)

Grandma (*her eyes closed, her hands folded on her breast again, the shovel between her hands, a sweet smile on her face*): Well . . . that was very nice, dear. . .

Young Man (*still kneeling*): Shhhhh . . . be still . . .

Grandma: What I meant was . . . you did that very well, dear . . .

Young Man (*blushing*): . . . oh . . .

Grandma: No; I mean it. You've got that . . . you've got a quality.

Young Man (*with his endearing smile*): Oh . . . thank you; thank you very much . . . ma'am.

**Grandma** (*slowly; softly—as the Young Man puts his hands on top of Grandma's*):
You're . . . you're welcome . . . dear.

(*Tableau. The Musician continues to play as the curtain slowly comes down.*)

## QUESTIONS

1. What is unusual about the names of the characters in *The Sandbox?* How do the names affect our perceptions of the characters?
2. Where does the play take place? What does the presence of the sandbox suggest?
3. Does *The Sandbox* contain any traditional elements of plot structure? Does the play have a climax? If so, where?
4. Describe how Mommy and Daddy treat Grandma. How do they speak to her?
5. Albee tells the audience quite specifically that the Young Man is the Angel of Death. What other occupation does he have?
6. What purpose does the Musician serve in the play? Would *The Sandbox* have the same effect without this character?
7. In your own words, what do you think is the theme of *The Sandbox?* What parts of the play support your opinion?
8. What aspects of the play seem comic? What aspects appear unpleasant?

## SUGGESTIONS FOR WRITING

1. Demonstrate, in a paragraph or two, how Nora in *A Doll's House* resembles or differs from a feminist of today.
2. Placing yourself in the character of Ibsen's Torvald Helmer, write a defense of him and his attitudes as he himself might write it.
3. Choose the play in this chapter that in your opinion might best lend itself to television. Then tell your reader how you would go about adapting it. What changes or deletions, if any, would you make? What problems would you expect to meet in transferring it to a different medium?
4. Perform Albee's *The Sandbox* in your classroom. Assign all the roles, including the Musician (find a classmate who plays some instrument or, if worse comes to worst, has a portable tape deck). After you have performed or seen the play, write a short paper on what the experience revealed to you. Did seeing the play change your opinion of it—for better or worse? Did you understand it better, or did it seem more elusive than ever?

# 37 _Evaluating a Play_

To **evaluate** a play is to decide whether the play is any good or not; and if it is good, how good it is in relation to other plays of its kind. In the theater, evaluation is usually thought to be the task of the play reviewer (or, with nobler connotations, "drama critic"), ordinarily a person who sees a new play on its first night and who then tells us, in print or over the air, what the play is about, how well it is done, and whether or not we ought to go to see it. Enthroned in an excellent free seat, the drama critic apparently plies a glamorous trade. What fun it must be to whittle a nasty epigram: to be able to observe, as did a critic of a faltering production of _Uncle Tom's Cabin_, that "the Siberian wolf hound was weakly supported."

Unless you find a job on a large city newspaper or radio station, however, or write for a college paper, or broadcast on a campus FM station, the opportunities to be a drama critic today are probably few and strictly limited. Much more significant, for most of us, is the task of evaluation we undertake for our own satisfaction. We see a play, or a film, or a drama on television, and then we make up our minds about it; and we often have to decide whether to recommend it to anyone else.

To evaluate new drama isn't easy. (And in this discussion, let us define _drama_ broadly as including not only plays, but anything that actors perform in the movies or on television, for most of us see more movies and television programs than plays.) But at least a part of the process of evaluation has already been accomplished for us. To produce a new play, even in an amateur theater, or to produce a new drama for the movies or for television is complicated and involves large sums of money and the efforts of many people. Sifted from a mountain of submitted play scripts, already subjected to long scrutiny and evaluation, a new play or film, whether or not it is of deep interest, arrives with a built-in air of professional competence. It is probably seldom that a dull play written by the producer's relative or friend finds enough financial backers to reach the stage; only on the fictitious Broadway of Mel Brooks's film *The Producers* could there be a musical comedy as awful as *Springtime for Hitler*. Nor do most college and civic theaters afford us much opportunity to see thoroughly inept plays; usually they give us new productions of *Oedipus the King* or *Pygmalion;* or else (if they are less adventurous) new versions of whatever succeeded on Broadway in the recent past.

And so new plays—the few that we do see—are usually, like television drama, somebody's safe investment. More often than not, our powers of evaluation confront only slick, pleasant, and efficient mediocrity. We owe it to ourselves to discriminate. Here are a few suggestions designed to help you tell the difference between an ordinary, run-of-the-reel product and a work of drama that may offer high reward.

1. Discard any inexorable rules you may have collected that affirm what a drama ought to be. (One such rule states that a tragedy is innately superior to a comedy, no matter how deep a truth a comedy may strike.) Don't expect all plays to "observe the unities"—that is, unfold their events in one day and in one place, and keep tragedy and comedy strictly apart. (Shakespeare ignores such rules.) There is no sense in damning a play for lacking "realism" (what if it's an expressionist play, or a fantasy?).

2. Instead, watch the play (or read it) alertly, with your mind and your senses open wide. Recall that theaters, such as the classic Greek theater of Sophocles, impose conventions. Do not condemn *Oedipus the King* for the reason one spectator gave: "That damned chorus keeps sticking their noses in!" Do not complain that Hamlet utters soliloquies.

3. Ask yourself whether the characters are fully realized. Do their actions follow from the kinds of persons they are, or does the action seem to impose itself upon them, making the play seem falsely contrived? Does the resolution arrive (as in a satisfying play) because of the nature of the characters; or are the characters saved (or destroyed) merely by some *deus ex machina,* or nick-of-time arrival of the Marines?

4. Recognize drama that belongs to a family: a *farce,* say, or a *comedy of manners,* or a **melodrama**—a play in which suspense and physical action are the prime ingredients. Recognizing such a familiar type of drama may help make some things clear to you, and may save you from attacking a play for being what it is, in fact, supposed to be. After all, there can be satisfying melodramas, and excellent plays may have melodramatic elements. What is wrong with thrillers is not that they have suspense, but that suspense usually is all they have. Awhirl with furious action, they employ stick-figure characters.

5. If there are symbols, ask how well they belong to their surrounding worlds. Do they help to reveal meaning, or merely decorate? In Tennessee Williams's *The Glass Menagerie*, Laura's collection of figurines is much more than simply ornamental.

6. Test the play or film for **sentimentality,** the failure of a dramatist, actor, or director who expects from us a greater emotional response than we are

given reason to feel. (For further discussions of sentimentality, see pages 262 and 858.)

7. Decide what it is that you admire or dislike, and, for a play, whether it is the play that you admire or dislike, or the production. (It is useful to draw this distinction if you are evaluating the play and not the production.)

8. Ask yourself what the theme is. What does the drama reveal? How far and how deeply does its statement go; how readily can we apply it beyond the play to the human world outside? Be slow, of course, to attribute to the playwright the opinions of the characters.

Follow all these steps and you may find that evaluating plays, movies, and television plays is a richly meaningful activity. It may reveal wisdom and pleasure that had previously bypassed you. It may even help you decide what to watch in the future, how to choose those works of drama that help you to fulfill—not merely to spend—your waking life.

## Suggestions for Writing

1. Attend a performance of a play, and write a critical review of it. Consider both the play itself and its production. (For advice on reviewing and a sample review, see page 1785.)

2. Read two celebrated, still much performed plays of the same era, *Death of a Salesman* (1949) and *The Glass Menagerie* (1945), both in "Plays for Further Reading." Then, in an essay of 700 words or more, decide which you consider the finer play. Back up your evaluation by referring to both.

3. Read the printed text of a modern or contemporary play not included in this book. (If you can see the play on stage or videotape, so much the better.) Then, in an essay of 500 to 750 words, state your considered opinion of it. Among interesting plays to choose from are these:

> *The Zoo Story* by Edward Albee
> *Waiting for Godot* by Samuel Beckett
> '*Master Harold' and the Boys* by Athol Fugard
> *Hedda Gabler, The Master Builder,* or *Peer Gynt* by Henrik Ibsen
> *The Bald Soprano* or *The Chairs* by Eugène Ionesco
> *American Buffalo* by David Mamet
> '*Night, Mother* by Marsha Norman
> *Long Day's Journey into Night* by Eugene O'Neill
> *The Birthday Party* or *The Caretaker* by Harold Pinter
> *No Exit* by Jean-Paul Sartre
> *for colored girls who have considered suicide / when the rainbow is enuf* by Ntozake Shange
> *Major Barbara* or *Pygmalion* by Bernard Shaw
> *Buried Child* or *True West* by Sam Shepard
> *Rosencrantz and Guildenstern Are Dead* by Tom Stoppard
> *The Heidi Chronicles* by Wendy Wasserstein
> *Fences* or *The Piano Lesson* by August Wilson

# 38  Plays for Further Reading

All the world's a stage,
And all the men and women merely players:
They have their exits and their entrances,
And one man in his time plays many parts,
His acts being seven ages. At first, the infant
Mewling° and puking in the nurse's arms.                          *bawling*
Then the whining schoolboy with his satchel
And shining morning face, creeping like snail
Unwilling to school. And then the lover,
Sighing like furnace, with a woeful ballad
Made to his mistress' eyebrow. Then a soldier
Full of strange oaths and bearded like the pard°,              *leopard*
Jealous in honor, sudden and quick in quarrel,
Seeking the bubble reputation
Even in the cannon's mouth. And then the justice,
In fair round belly with good capon lined,
With eyes severe and beard of formal cut,
Full of wise saws°and modern instances°;              *sayings; examples*
And so he plays his part. The sixth age shifts
Into the lean and slippered pantaloon°,              *old man (from*
With spectacles on nose and pouch on side;              *Pantalone in*
His youthful hose well saved, a world too wide              *the commedia*
For his shrunk shank, and his big manly voice              *dell' arte)*
Turning again toward childish treble, pipes
And whistles in his sound. Last scene of all
That ends this strange eventful history
Is second childishness and mere oblivion,
Sans teeth, sans eyes, sans taste, sans everything.
                    —William Shakespeare, *As You Like It*, II, vii

## Sophocles

ANTIGONÊ                                                                    441 B.C.

*Translated by Dudley Fitts and Robert Fitzgerald*

*Sophocles (496?–406 B.C.), Athenian dramatist, is the subject of a biographical note on page 1105, preceding his play Oedipus the King. Antigonê was produced in 441 B.C.; Oedipus the King, not until fourteen or fifteen years later. Although written earlier than its companion play, Antigonê relates events supposed to have followed long after.*

Characters

*Antigonê*
*Ismenê*
*Eurydicê*
*Creon*
*Haimon*
*Teiresias*
*A Sentry*
*A Messenger*
*Chorus*

Scene. *Before the palace of Creon, King of Thebes. A central double door, and two lateral doors. A platform extends the length of the façade, and from this platform three steps lead down into the "orchestra," or chorus-ground.*

Time. *Dawn of the day after the repulse of the Argive army from the assault on Thebes.*

## PROLOGUE°

   *Antigonê and Ismenê enter from the central door of the palace.*

Antigonê: Ismenê, dear sister,
      You would think that we had already suffered enough
      For the curse on Oedipus°:

---

*Prologue:* Portion of the play containing the exposition, or explanation of what has gone before and what is now happening.
3 *the curse on Oedipus:* As Sophocles tells in *Oedipus the King*, the King of Thebes discovered that he had lived his life under a curse. Unknowingly, he had slain his father and married his mother. On realizing this terrible truth, Oedipus put out his own eyes and departed into exile. Now, years later, as *Antigonê* opens, Antigonê and Ismenê, daughters of Oedipus, are recalling how their two brothers died. After the abdication of their father, the brothers had ruled Thebes together. But they fell to quarreling. When Eteoclês expelled Polyneicês, the latter returned with an army and attacked the city. The two brothers killed each other in combat, leaving the throne to Creon. The new king of Thebes has buried Eteoclês with full honors, but, calling Polyneicês a traitor, has decreed that his body shall be left to the crows—an especially terrible decree, for a rotting corpse might offend Zeus, bring down plague, blight, and barrenness upon Thebes, and prevent the soul of a dead hero from entering the Elysian Fields, abode of those favored by the gods.

I cannot imagine any grief
That you and I have not gone through. And now— 5
Have they told you of the new decree of our King Creon?
*Ismenê:* I have heard nothing: I know
That two sisters lost two brothers, a double death
In a single hour; and I know that the Argive army
Fled in the night; but beyond this, nothing. 10
*Antigonê:* I thought so. And that is why I wanted you
To come out here with me. There is something we must do.
*Ismenê:* Why do you speak so strangely?
*Antigonê:* Listen, Ismenê:
Creon buried our brother Eteoclês 15
With military honors, gave him a soldier's funeral,
And it was right that he should; but Polyneicês,
Who fought as bravely and died as miserably,—
They say that Creon has sworn
No one shall bury him, no one mourn for him, 20
But his body must lie in the fields, a sweet treasure
For carrion birds to find as they search for food.
That is what they say, and our good Creon is coming here
To announce it publicly; and the penalty—
Stoning to death in the public square! 
There it is, 25
And now you can prove what you are:
A true sister, or a traitor to your family.
*Ismenê:* Antigonê, you are mad! What could I possibly do?
*Antigonê:* You must decide whether you will help me or not.
*Ismenê:* I do not understand you. Help you in what? 30
*Antigonê:* Ismenê, I am going to bury him. Will you come?
*Ismenê:* Bury him! You have just said the new law forbids it.
*Antigonê:* He is my brother. And he is your brother, too.
*Ismenê:* But think of the danger! Think what Creon will do!
*Antigonê:* Creon is not strong enough to stand in my way. 35
*Ismenê:* Ah sister!
Oedipus died, everyone hating him
For what his own search brought to light, his eyes
Ripped out by his own hand; and Iocastê died,
His mother and wife at once: she twisted the cords 40
That strangled her life; and our two brothers died,
Each killed by the other's sword. And we are left:
But oh, Antigonê,
Think how much more terrible than these
Our own death would be if we should go against Creon 45
And do what he has forbidden! We are only women,
We cannot fight with men, Antigonê!

The law is strong, we must give in to the law
In this thing, and in worse. I beg the Dead
To forgive me, but I am helpless: I must yield     50
To those in authority. And I think it is dangerous business
To be always meddling.

*Antigonê:*                    If that is what you think,
I should not want you, even if you asked to come.
You have made your choice, you can be what you want to be.
But I will bury him; and if I must die,     55
I say that this crime is holy: I shall lie down
With him in death, and I shall be as dear
To him as he to me.

                   It is the dead,
Not the living, who make the longest demands:
We die for ever . . .

                   You may do as you like,     60
Since apparently the laws of the gods mean nothing to you.

*Ismenê:* They mean a great deal to me; but I have no strength
To break laws that were made for the public good.

*Antigonê:* That must be your excuse, I suppose. But as for me,
I will bury the brother I love.

*Ismenê:*                    Antigonê,     65
I am so afraid for you!

*Antigonê:*          You need not be:
You have yourself to consider, after all.

*Ismenê:* But no one must hear of this, you must tell no one!
I will keep it a secret, I promise!

*Antigonê:*                    O tell it! Tell everyone!
Think how they'll hate you when it all comes out     70
If they learn that you knew about it all the time!

*Ismenê:* So fiery! You should be cold with fear.

*Antigonê:* Perhaps. But I am doing only what I must.

*Ismenê:* But you can do it? I say that you cannot.

*Antigonê:* Very well: when my strength gives out, I shall do no more.     75

*Ismenê:* Impossible things should not be tried at all.

*Antigonê:* Go away, Ismenê:
I shall be hating you soon, and the dead will too,
For your words are hateful. Leave me my foolish plan:
I am not afraid of the danger; if it means death,     80
It will not be the worst of deaths—death without honor.

*Ismenê:* Go then, if you feel that you must.
You are unwise,
But a loyal friend indeed to those who love you.

*Exit into the palace. Antigonê goes off, left. Enter the Chorus.*

# Párodos°

*Strophe°* 1

*Chorus:* Now the long blade of the sun, lying
    Level east to west, touches with glory
    Thebes of the Seven Gates. Open, unlidded
    Eye of golden day! O marching light
    Across the eddy and rush of Dircê's stream°,           5
    Striking the white shields of the enemy
    Thrown headlong backward from the blaze of morning!
*Choragos°:* Polyneicês their commander
    Roused them with windy phrases,
    He the wild eagle screaming           10
    Insults above our land,
    His wings their shields of snow,
    His crest their marshalled helms.

*Antistrophe°* 1

*Chorus:* Against our seven gates in a yawning ring
    The famished spears came onward in the night;           15
    But before his jaws were sated with our blood,
    Or pinefire took the garland of our towers,
    He was thrown back; and as he turned, great Thebes—
    No tender victim for his noisy power—
    Rose like a dragon behind him, shouting war.           20
*Choragos:* For God hates utterly
    The bray of bragging tongues;
    And when he beheld their smiling,
    Their swagger of golden helms,
    The frown of his thunder blasted           25
    Their first man from our walls.

*Strophe* 2

*Chorus:* We heard his shout of triumph high in the air
    Turn to a scream; far out in a flaming arc
    He fell with his windy torch, and the earth struck him.
    And others storming in fury no less than his           30
    Found shock of death in the dusty joy of battle.
*Choragos:* Seven captains at seven gates
    Yielded their clanging arms to the god

---

*Párodos:* a song sung by the chorus on first entering. Its *strophe* (according to scholarly theory) was sung while the chorus danced from stage right to stage left: its *antistrophe*, while they danced back again. Another párodos follows the prologue of *Oedipus the King.*    5 *Dircê's stream:* river near Thebes.    8 *Choragos:* leader of the Chorus and principal commentator on the play's action.

That bends the battle-line and breaks it.
These two only, brothers in blood, 35
Face to face in matchless rage,
Mirroring each the other's death,
Clashed in long combat.

*Antistrophe 2*

*Chorus:* But now in the beautiful morning of victory
  Let Thebes of the many chariots sing for joy! 40
  With hearts for dancing we'll take leave of war:
  Our temples shall be sweet with hymns of praise,
  And the long night shall echo with our chorus.

## SCENE I

*Choragos:* But now at last our new King is coming:
  Creon of Thebes, Menoikeus' son.
  In this auspicious dawn of his reign
  What are the new complexities
  That shifting Fate has woven for him? 5
  What is his counsel? Why has he summoned
  The old men to hear him?

  *Enter Creon from the palace, center. He addresses the Chorus from the top step.*

*Creon:* Gentlemen: I have the honor to inform you that our Ship of State, which
  recent storms have threatened to destroy, has come safely to harbor at last,
  guided by the merciful wisdom of Heaven. I have summoned you here this 10
  morning because I know that I can depend upon you: your devotion to King
  Laïos was absolute; you never hesitated in your duty to our late ruler
  Oedipus; and when Oedipus died, your loyalty was transferred to his children. Unfortunately, as you know, his two sons, the princes Eteoclês and
  Polyneicês, have killed each other in battle; and I, as the next in blood, have 15
  succeeded to the full power of the throne.
      I am aware, of course, that no Ruler can expect complete loyalty from
  his subjects until he has been tested in office. Nevertheless, I say to you at
  the very outset that I have nothing but contempt for the kind of Governor
  who is afraid, for whatever reason, to follow the course that he knows is best 20
  for the State; and as for the man who sets private friendship above the public
  welfare,—I have no use for him, either. I call God to witness that if I saw my
  country headed for ruin, I should not be afraid to speak out plainly; and I
  need hardly remind you that I would never have any dealings with an enemy
  of the people. No one values friendship more highly than I; but we must 25
  remember that friends made at the risk of wrecking our Ship are not real
  friends at all.

These are my principles, at any rate, and that is why I have made the
following decision concerning the sons of Oedipus: Eteoclês, who died as a
man should die, fighting for his country, is to be buried with full military    30
honors, with all the ceremony that is usual when the greatest heroes die; but
his brother Polyneicês, who broke his exile to come back with fire and sword
against his native city and the shrines of his fathers' gods, whose one idea
was to spill the blood of his blood and sell his own people into slavery—
Polyneicês, I say, is to have no burial: no man is to touch him or say the least    35
prayer for him; he shall lie on the plain, unburied; and the birds and the
scavenging dogs can do with him whatever they like.

This is my command, and you can see the wisdom behind it. As long as
I am King, no traitor is going to be honored with the loyal man. But whoever
shows by word and deed that he is on the side of the State,—he shall have    40
my respect while he is living, and my reverence when he is dead.

*Choragos:* If that is your will, Creon son of Menoikeus,
You have the right to enforce it: we are yours.

*Creon:* That is my will. Take care that you do your part.

*Choragos:* We are old men: let the younger ones carry it out.    45

*Creon:* I do not mean that: the sentries have been appointed.

*Choragos:* Then what is it that you would have us do?

*Creon:* You will give no support to whoever breaks this law.

*Choragos:* Only a crazy man is in love with death!

*Creon:* And death it is, yet money talks, and the wisest    50
Have sometimes been known to count a few coins too many.

*Enter Sentry from left.*

*Sentry:* I'll not say that I'm out of breath from running, King, because every time I
stopped to think about what I have to tell you, I felt like going back. And all
the time a voice kept saying, "You fool, don't you know you're walking
straight into trouble?"; and then another voice: "Yes, but if you let somebody    55
else get the news to Creon first, it will be even worse than that for you!" But
good sense won out, at least I hope it was good sense, and here I am with a
story that makes no sense at all; but I'll tell it anyhow, because, as they say,
what's going to happen's going to happen and—

*Creon:* Come to the point. What have you to say?    60

*Sentry:* I did not do it. I did not see who did it. You must not punish me for what
someone else has done.

*Creon:* A comprehensive defense! More effective, perhaps,
If I knew its purpose. Come: what is it?

*Sentry:* A dreadful thing . . . I don't know how to put it—    65

*Creon:* Out with it!

*Sentry:*                    Well, then;
The dead man—
                    Polyneicês—

*Pause. The Sentry is overcome, fumbles for words. Creon waits impassively.*

out there—

someone,—

New dust on the slimy flesh!

*Pause. No sign from Creon.*

Someone has given it burial that way, and
Gone . . .                                                                                     70

*Long pause. Creon finally speaks with deadly control.*

Creon: And the man who dared do this?
Sentry:                                                I swear I
Do not know! You must believe me!

Listen:

The ground was dry, not a sign of digging, no,
Not a wheeltrack in the dust, no trace of anyone.
It was when they relieved us this morning: and one of them,          75
The corporal, pointed to it.

There it was,

The strangest—

Look:

The body, just mounded over with light dust: you see?
Not buried really, but as if they'd covered it
Just enough for the ghost's peace. And no sign                       80
Of dogs or any wild animal that had been there.

And then what a scene there was! Every man of us
Accusing the other: we all proved the other man did it,
We all had proof that we could not have done it.
We were ready to take hot iron in our hands,                        85
Walk through fire, swear by all the gods,
*It was not I!*
*I do not know who it was, but it was not I!*

*Creon's rage has been mounting steadily, but the Sentry is too intent upon his story to notice it.*

And then, when this came to nothing, someone said
A thing that silenced us and made us stare                          90
Down at the ground: you had to be told the news,
And one of us had to do it! We threw the dice,
And the bad luck fell to me. So here I am,
No happier to be here than you are to have me:
Nobody likes the man who brings bad news.                           95
Choragos: I have been wondering, King: can it be that the gods have done this?

*Creon (furiously):* Stop!
    Must you doddering wrecks
    Go out of your heads entirely? "The gods"!
    Intolerable!                                             100
    The gods favor this corpse? Why? How had he served them?
    Tried to loot their temples, burn their images,
    Yes, and the whole State, and its laws with it!
    Is it your senile opinion that the gods love to honor bad men?
    A pious thought!—
                       No, from the very beginning        105
    There have been those who have whispered together,
    Stiff-necked anarchists, putting their heads together,
    Scheming against me in alleys. These are the men,
    And they have bribed my own guard to do this thing.

    *(Sententiously.)* Money!                              110
    There's nothing in the world so demoralizing as money.
    Down go your cities,
    Homes gone, men gone, honest hearts corrupted,
    Crookedness of all kinds, and all for money!
    *(To Sentry.)*                          But you—!
    I swear by God and by the throne of God,         115
    The man who has done this thing shall pay for it!
    Find that man, bring him here to me, or your death
    Will be the least of your problems: I'll string you up
    Alive, and there will be certain ways to make you
    Discover your employer before you die;         120
    And the process may teach you a lesson you seem to have missed:
    The dearest profit is sometimes all too dear:
    That depends on the source. Do you understand me?
    A fortune won is often misfortune.
*Sentry:* King, may I speak?
*Creon:*                  Your very voice distresses me.       125
*Sentry:* Are you sure that it is my voice, and not your conscience?
*Creon:* By God, he wants to analyze me now!
*Sentry:* It is not what I say, but what has been done, that hurts you.
*Creon:* You talk too much.
*Sentry:*               Maybe; but I've done nothing.
*Creon:* Sold your soul for some silver: that's all you've done.     130
*Sentry:* How dreadful it is when the right judge judges wrong!
*Creon:* Your figures of speech
    May entertain you now; but unless you bring me the man,
    You will get little profit from them in the end.

    *Exit Creon into the palace.*

*Sentry:* "Bring me the man"—!
    I'd like nothing better than bringing him the man!
    But bring him or not, you have seen the last of me here.
    At any rate, I am safe!

    *Exit Sentry.*

# ODE I°

*Strophe 1*

*Chorus:* Numberless are the world's wonders, but none
    More wonderful than man; the stormgray sea
    Yields to his prows, the huge crests bear him high;
    Earth, holy and inexhaustible, is graven
    With shining furrows where his plows have gone     5
    Year after year, the timeless labor of stallions.

*Antistrophe 1*

    The lightboned birds and beasts that cling to cover,
    The lithe fish lighting their reaches of dim water,
    All are taken, tamed in the net of his mind;
    The lion on the hill, the wild horse windy-maned,     10
    Resign to him; and his blunt yoke has broken
    The sultry shoulders of the mountain bull.

*Strophe 2*

    Words also, and thought as rapid as air,
    He fashions to his good use; statecraft is his,
    And his the skill that deflects the arrows of snow,     15
    The spears of winter rain: from every wind
    He has made himself secure—from all but one:
    In the late wind of death he cannot stand.

*Antistrophe 2*

    O clear intelligence, force beyond all measure!
    O fate of man, working both good and evil!     20
    When the laws are kept, how proudly his city stands!
    When the laws are broken, what of his city then?
    Never may the anárchic man find rest at my hearth,
    Never be it said that my thoughts are his thoughts.

---

Ode I: first song sung by the Chorus, who at the same time danced. Here again, as in the párodos, *strophe* and *antistrophe* probably divide the song into two movements of the dance: right-to-left, then left-to-right.

# Scene II

*Re-enter Sentry leading Antigonê.*

*Choragos:* What does this mean? Surely this captive woman
    Is the Princess, Antigonê. Why should she be taken?
*Sentry:* Here is the one who did it! We caught her
    In the very act of burying him.—Where is Creon?
*Choragos:* Just coming from the house.

    *Enter Creon, center.*

*Creon:*                             What has happened?     5
    Why have you come back so soon?
*Sentry (expansively):*                O King,
    A man should never be too sure of anything:
    I would have sworn
    That you'd not see me here again: your anger
    Frightened me so, and the things you threatened me with;     10
    But how could I tell then
    That I'd be able to solve the case so soon?

    No dice-throwing this time: I was only too glad to come!

    Here is this woman. She is the guilty one:
    We found her trying to bury him.     15
    Take her, then; question her; judge her as you will.
    I am through with the whole thing now, and glad of it.
*Creon:* But this is Antigonê! Why have you brought her here?
*Sentry:* She was burying him, I tell you!
*Creon (severely):*                  Is this the truth?
*Sentry:* I saw her with my own eyes. Can I say more?     20
*Creon:* The details: come, tell me quickly!
*Sentry:*                    It was like this:
    After those terrible threats of yours, King,
    We went back and brushed the dust away from the body.
    The flesh was soft by now, and stinking,
    So we sat on a hill to windward and kept guard.     25
    No napping this time! We kept each other awake.
    But nothing happened until the white round sun
    Whirled in the center of the round sky over us:
    Then, suddenly,
    A storm of dust roared up from the earth, and the sky     30
    Went out, the plain vanished with all its trees
    In the stinging dark. We closed our eyes and endured it.
    The whirlwind lasted a long time, but it passed;

And then we looked, and there was Antigonê!
I have seen                                                                          35
A mother bird come back to a stripped nest, heard
Her crying bitterly a broken note or two
For the young ones stolen. Just so, when this girl
Found the bare corpse, and all her love's work wasted,
She wept, and cried on heaven to damn the hands                                     40
That had done this thing.
                                  And then she brought more dust
And sprinkled wine three times for her brother's ghost.

We ran and took her at once. She was not afraid,
Not even when we charged her with what she had done.
She denied nothing.
                          And this was a comfort to me,                              45
And some uneasiness: for it is a good thing
To escape from death, but it is no great pleasure
To bring death to a friend.
                                  Yet I always say
There is nothing so comfortable as your own safe skin!
Creon (*slowly, dangerously*): And you, Antigonê,                                    50
    You with your head hanging,—do you confess this thing?
Antigonê: I do. I deny nothing.
Creon (*to Sentry*):                          You may go.

*Exit Sentry.*

(*To Antigonê.*) Tell me, tell me briefly:
Had you heard my proclamation touching this matter?
Antigonê: It was public. Could I help hearing it?                                    55
Creon: And yet you dared defy the law.
Antigonê:                                  I dared.
    It was not God's proclamation. That final Justice
That rules the world below makes no such laws.

Your edict, King, was strong,
But all your strength is weakness itself against                                    60
The immortal unrecorded laws of God.
They are not merely now: they were, and shall be,
Operative for ever, beyond man utterly.

I knew I must die, even without your decree:
I am only mortal. And if I must die                                                 65
Now, before it is my time to die,
Surely this is no hardship: can anyone
Living, as I live, with evil all about me,

Think Death less than a friend? This death of mine
Is of no importance; but if I had left my brother                    70
Lying in death unburied, I should have suffered.
Now I do not.
            You smile at me. Ah Creon,
Think me a fool, if you like; but it may well be
That a fool convicts me of folly.
*Choragos:* Like father, like daughter: both headstrong, deaf to reason!    75
    She has never learned to yield:
*Creon:*                     She has much to learn.
    The inflexible heart breaks first, the toughest iron
Cracks first, and the wildest horses bend their necks
At the pull of the smallest curb.
                    Pride? In a slave?
This girl is guilty of a double insolence,                           80
Breaking the given laws and boasting of it.
Who is the man here,
She or I, if this crime goes unpunished?
Sister's child, or more than sister's child,
Or closer yet in blood—she and her sister                           85
Win bitter death for this!
*(To Servants.)*         Go, some of you,
Arrest Ismenê. I accuse her equally.
Bring her: you will find her sniffling in the house there.

Her mind's a traitor: crimes kept in the dark
Cry for light, and the guardian brain shudders;                     90
But how much worse than this
Is brazen boasting of barefaced anarchy!
*Antigonê:* Creon, what more do you want than my death?
*Creon:*                       Nothing.
    That gives me everything.
*Antigonê:*           Then I beg you: kill me.
    This talking is a great weariness: your words                      95
Are distasteful to me, and I am sure that mine
Seem so to you. And yet they should not seem so:
I should have praise and honor for what I have done.
All these men here would praise me
Were their lips not frozen shut with fear of you.                   100
*(Bitterly.)*
Ah the good fortune of kings,
Licensed to say and do whatever they please!
*Creon:* You are alone here in that opinion.
*Antigonê:* No, they are with me. But they keep their tongues in leash.
*Creon:* Maybe. But you are guilty, and they are not.                105

*Antigonê:* There is no guilt in reverence for the dead.

*Creon:* But Eteoclês—was he not your brother too?

*Antigonê:* My brother too.

*Creon:*                        And you insult his memory?

*Antigonê (softly):* The dead man would not say that I insult it.

*Creon:* He would: for you honor a traitor as much as him.                    110

*Antigonê:* His own brother, traitor or not, and equal in blood.

*Creon:* He made war on his country. Eteoclês defended it.

*Antigonê:* Nevertheless, there are honors due all the dead.

*Creon:* But not the same for the wicked as for the just.

*Antigonê:* Ah Creon, Creon,                                                  115

   Which of us can say what the gods hold wicked?

*Creon:* An enemy is an enemy, even dead.

*Antigonê:* It is my nature to join in love, not hate.

*Creon (finally losing patience):*

   Go join them, then; if you must have your love,

   Find it in hell!                                                           120

*Choragos:* But see, Ismenê comes:

   *Enter Ismenê, guarded.*

   Those tears are sisterly, the cloud

   That shadows her eyes rains down gentle sorrow.

*Creon:* You too, Ismenê,

   Snake in my ordered house, sucking my blood                               125

   Stealthily—and all the time I never knew

   That these two sisters were aiming at my throne!

                                                         Ismenê,

   Do you confess your share in this crime, or deny it?

   Answer me.

*Ismenê:* Yes, if she will let me say so. I am guilty.                        130

*Antigonê (coldly):* No, Ismenê. You have no right to say so.

   You would not help me, and I will not have you help me.

*Ismenê:* But now I know what you meant; and I am here

   To join you, to take my share of punishment.

*Antigonê:* The dead man and the gods who rule the dead                       135

   Know whose act this was. Words are not friends.

*Ismenê:* Do you refuse me, Antigonê? I want to die with you:

   I too have a duty that I must discharge to the dead.

*Antigonê:* You shall not lessen my death by sharing it.

*Ismenê:* What do I care for life when you are dead?                          140

*Antigonê:* Ask Creon. You're always hanging on his opinions.

*Ismenê:* You are laughing at me. Why, Antigonê?

*Antigonê:* It's a joyless laughter, Ismenê.

*Ismenê:*                              But can I do nothing?

*Antigonê:* Yes. Save yourself. I shall not envy you.

   There are those who will praise you; I shall have honor, too.             145

*Ismenê:* But we are equally guilty!

Antigonê:                              No more, Ismenê.
    You are alive, but I belong to Death.
Creon (to the Chorus): Gentlemen, I beg you to observe these girls:
    One has just now lost her mind; the other,
    It seems, has never had a mind at all.                              150
Ismenê: Grief teaches the steadiest minds to waver, King.
Creon: Yours certainly did, when you assumed guilt with the guilty!
Ismenê: But how could I go on living without her?
Creon:                              You are.
    She is already dead.
Ismenê:              But your own son's bride!
Creon: There are places enough for him to push his plow.              155
    I want no wicked women for my sons!
Ismenê: O dearest Haimon, how your father wrongs you!
Creon: I've had enough of your childish talk of marriage!
Choragos: Do you really intend to steal this girl from your son?
Creon: No; Death will do that for me.
Choragos:                              Then she must die?              160
Creon (ironically): You dazzle me.
               —But enough of this talk!
    (To Guards.) You, there, take them away and guard them well:
    For they are but women, and even brave men run
    When they see Death coming.

    Exeunt Ismenê, Antigonê, and Guards.


# ODE II

Strophe 1

Chorus: Fortunate is the man who has never tasted God's vengeance!
    Where once the anger of heaven has struck, that house is shaken
    For ever: damnation rises behind each child
    Like a wave cresting out of the black northeast,
    When the long darkness under sea roars up                              5
    And bursts drumming death upon the windwhipped sand.

Antistrophe 1

    I have seen this gathering sorrow from time long past
    Loom upon Oedipus' children: generation from generation
    Takes the compulsive rage of the enemy god.
    So lately this last flower of Oedipus' line                              10
    Drank the sunlight! but now a passionate word
    And a handful of dust have closed up all its beauty.

Strophe 2

        What mortal arrogance
        Transcends the wrath of Zeus?

Sleep cannot lull him nor the effortless long months                                    15
Of the timeless gods: but he is young for ever,
And his house is the shining day of high Olympos.
      All that is and shall be,
      And all the past, is his.
No pride on earth is free of the curse of heaven.                                        20


Antistrophe 2

      The straying dreams of men
      May bring them ghosts of joy:
But as they drowse, the waking embers burn them;
Or they walk with fixed eyes, as blind men walk.
But the ancient wisdom speaks for our own time:                                         25
      *Fate works most for woe*
      *With Folly's fairest show.*
Man's little pleasure is the spring of sorrow.


## SCENE III

*Choragos:* But here is Haimon, King, the last of all your sons.
    Is it grief for Antigonê that brings him here,
    And bitterness at being robbed of his bride?

    *Enter Haimon.*

*Creon:* We shall soon see, and no need of diviners.
—Son,
    You have heard my final judgment on that girl:                                 5
    Have you come here hating me, or have you come
    With deference and with love, whatever I do?
*Haimon:* I am your son, father. You are my guide.
    You make things clear for me, and I obey you.
    No marriage means more to me than your continuing wisdom.                      10
*Creon:* Good. That is the way to behave: subordinate
    Everything else, my son, to your father's will.
    This is what a man prays for, that he may get
    Sons attentive and dutiful in his house,
    Each one hating his father's enemies,                                          15
    Honoring his father's friends. But if his sons
    Fail him, if they turn out unprofitably,
    What has he fathered but trouble for himself
    And amusement for the malicious?
So you are right
    Not to lose your head over this woman.                                         20
    Your pleasure with her would soon grow cold, Haimon,
    And then you'd have a hellcat in bed and elsewhere.

Let her find her husband in Hell!
Of all the people in this city, only she
Has had contempt for my law and broken it. 25

Do you want me to show myself weak before the people?
Or to break my sworn word? No, and I will not.
The woman dies.
I suppose she'll plead "family ties." Well, let her.
If I permit my own family to rebel, 30
How shall I earn the world's obedience?
Show me the man who keeps his house in hand,
He's fit for public authority.
                I'll have no dealings
With law-breakers, critics of the government:
Whoever is chosen to govern should be obeyed— 35
Must be obeyed, in all things, great and small,
Just and unjust! O Haimon,
The man who knows how to obey, and that man only,
Knows how to give commands when the time comes.
You can depend on him, no matter how fast 40
The spears come: he's a good soldier, he'll stick it out.

Anarchy, anarchy! Show me a greater evil!
This is why cities tumble and the great houses rain down,
This is what scatters armies!

No, no: good lives are made so by discipline. 45
We keep the laws then, and the lawmakers,
And no woman shall seduce us. If we must lose,
Let's lose to a man, at least! Is a woman stronger than we?
*Choragos:* Unless time has rusted my wits,
What you say, King, is said with point and dignity. 50
*Haimon (boyishly earnest):* Father:
Reason is God's crowning gift to man, and you are right
To warn me against losing mine. I cannot say—
I hope that I shall never want to say!—that you
Have reasoned badly. Yet there are other men 55
Who can reason, too; and their opinions might be helpful.
You are not in a position to know everything
That people say or do, or what they feel:
Your temper terrifies them—everyone
Will tell you only what you like to hear. 60
But I, at any rate, can listen; and I have heard them
Muttering and whispering in the dark about this girl.
They say no woman has ever, so unreasonably,
Died so shameful a death for a generous act:

"She covered her brother's body. Is this indecent?     65
She kept him from dogs and vultures. Is this a crime?
Death?—She should have all the honor that we can give her!"

This is the way they talk out there in the city.

You must believe me:
Nothing is closer to me than your happiness.     70
What could be closer? Must not any son
Value his father's fortune as his father does his?
I beg you, do not be unchangeable:
Do not believe that you alone can be right.
The man who thinks that,     75
The man who maintains that only he has the power
To reason correctly, the gift to speak, the soul—
A man like that, when you know him, turns out empty.

It is not reason never to yield to reason!

In flood time you can see how some trees bend,     80
And because they bend, even their twigs are safe,
While stubborn trees are torn up, roots and all.
And the same thing happens in sailing:
Make your sheet fast, never slacken,—and over you go,
Head over heels and under: and there's your voyage.     85
Forget you are angry! Let yourself be moved!
I know I am young; but please let me say this:
The ideal condition
Would be, I admit, that men should be right by instinct;
But since we are all too likely to go astray,     90
The reasonable thing is to learn from those who can teach.
*Choragos:* You will do well to listen to him, King,
If what he says is sensible. And you, Haimon,
Must listen to your father.—Both speak well.
*Creon:* You consider it right for a man of my years and experience     95
To go to school to a boy?
*Haimon:*                         It is not right,
If I am wrong. But if I am young, and right,
What does my age matter?
*Creon:* You think it right to stand up for an anarchist?
*Haimon:* Not at all. I pay no respect to criminals.     100
*Creon:* Then she is not a criminal?
*Haimon:* The City would deny it, to a man.
*Creon:* And the City proposes to teach me how to rule?
*Haimon:* Ah. Who is it that's talking like a boy now?
*Creon:* My voice is the one voice giving orders in this City!     105
*Haimon:* It is no City if it takes orders from one voice.

*Creon:* The State is the King!

*Haimon:*                  Yes, if the State is a desert.

    *Pause.*

*Creon:* This boy, it seems, has sold out to a woman.

*Haimon:* If you are a woman: my concern is only for you.

*Creon:* So? Your "concern"! In a public brawl with your father!        110

*Haimon:* How about you, in a public brawl with justice?

*Creon:* With justice, when all that I do is within my rights?

*Haimon:* You have no right to trample on God's right.

*Creon (completely out of control):* Fool, adolescent fool! Taken in by a woman!

*Haimon:* You'll never see me taken in by anything vile.             115

*Creon:* Every word you say is for her!

*Haimon (quietly, darkly):*           And for you.
    And for me. And for the gods under the earth.

*Creon:* You'll never marry her while she lives.

*Haimon:* Then she must die.—But her death will cause another.

*Creon:* Another?                                            120
    Have you lost your senses? Is this an open threat?

*Haimon:* There is no threat in speaking to emptiness.

*Creon:* I swear you'll regret this superior tone of yours!
    You are the empty one!

*Haimon:*               If you were not my father,
    I'd say you were perverse.                             125

*Creon:* You girl-struck fool, don't play at words with me!

*Haimon:* I am sorry. You prefer silence.

*Creon:*                      Now, by God—!
    I swear, by all the gods in heaven above us,
    You'll watch it, I swear you shall!
    *(To the Servants.)*            Bring her out!
    Bring the woman out! Let her die before his eyes!        130
    Here, this instant, with her bridegroom beside her!

*Haimon:* Not here, no; she will not die here, King.
    And you will never see my face again.
    Go on raving as long as you've a friend to endure you.

    *Exit Haimon.*

*Choragos:* Gone, gone.                                   135
    Creon, a young man in a rage is dangerous!

*Creon:* Let him do, or dream to do, more than a man can.
    He shall not save these girls from death.

*Choragos:*                    These girls?
    You have sentenced them both?

*Creon:*                 No, you are right.
    I will not kill the one whose hands are clean.           140

*Choragos:* But Antigonê?

Creon (*somberly*):     I will carry her far away
    Out there in the wilderness, and lock her
    Living in a vault of stone. She shall have food,
    As the custom is, to absolve the State of her death.
    And there let her pray to the gods of hell:                                    145
    They are her only gods:
    Perhaps they will show her an escape from death,
    Or she may learn,
                            though late,
    That piety shown the dead is pity in vain.

    *Exit Creon.*

## ODE III

*Strophe*

    *Chorus:* Love, unconquerable
    Waster of rich men, keeper
    Of warm lights and all-night vigil
    In the soft face of a girl:
    Sea-wanderer, forest-visitor!                                                  5
    Even the pure Immortals cannot escape you,
    And mortal man, in his one day's dusk,
    Trembles before your glory.

*Antistrophe*

    Surely you swerve upon ruin
    The just man's consenting heart,                                               10
    As here you have made bright anger
    Strike between father and son—
    And none has conquered but Love!
    A girl's glánce wórking the will of heaven:
    Pleasure to her alone who mocks us,                                            15
    Merciless Aphroditê°.

## SCENE IV

*Choragos (as Antigonê enters guarded):*

    But I can no longer stand in awe of this,
    Nor, seeing what I see, keep back my tears.
    Here is Antigonê, passing to that chamber
    Where all find sleep at last.

*Strophe 1*

    *Antigonê:* Look upon me, friends, and pity me                                 5
    Turning back at the night's edge to say

16 *Aphroditê:* Goddess of love and beauty.

Good-by to the sun that shines for me no longer;
Now sleepy Death
Summons me down to Acheron°, that cold shore:
There is no bridesong there, nor any music.                    10
*Chorus:* Yet not unpraised, not without a kind of honor,
You walk at last into the underworld;
Untouched by sickness, broken by no sword.
What woman has ever found your way to death?

*Antistrophe 1*

*Antigonê:* How often I have heard the story of Niobê°,         15
Tantalos' wretched daughter, how the stone
Clung fast about her, ivy-close: and they say
The rain falls endlessly
And sifting soft snow; her tears are never done.
I feel the loneliness of her death in mine.                    20
*Chorus:* But she was born of heaven, and you
Are woman, woman-born. If her death is yours,
A mortal woman's, is this not for you
Glory in our world and in the world beyond?

*Strophe 2*

*Antigonê:* You laugh at me. Ah, friends, friends,              25
Can you not wait until I am dead? O Thebes,
O men many-charioted, in love with Fortune,
Dear springs of Dircê, sacred Theban grove,
Be witnesses for me, denied all pity,
Unjustly judged! and think a word of love                      30
For her whose path turns
Under dark earth, where there are no more tears.
*Chorus:* You have passed beyond human daring and come at last
Into a place of stone where Justice sits.
I cannot tell                                                  35
What shape of your father's guilt appears in this.

*Antistrophe 2*

*Antigonê:* You have touched it at last: that bridal bed
Unspeakable, horror of son and mother mingling:
Their crime, infection of all our family!
O Oedipus, father and brother!                                 40
Your marriage strikes from the grave to murder mine.
I have been a stranger here in my own land:

9 *Acheron:* river in Hades, domain of the dead.     15 *story of Niobê:* in which this mother, when her
fourteen children were slain, wept so copiously that she was transformed to a stone on Mount
Sipylos. Her tears became the mountain's streams.

All my life
The blasphemy of my birth has followed me.
*Chorus:* Reverence is a virtue, but strength                                   45
    Lives in established law: that must prevail.
    You have made your choice,
    Your death is the doing of your conscious hand.

Epode°

*Antigonê:* Then let me go, since all your words are bitter,
    And the very light of the sun is cold to me.                         50
    Lead me to my vigil, where I must have
    Neither love nor lamentation; no song, but silence.

    *Creon interrupts impatiently.*

*Creon:* If dirges and planned lamentations could put off death,
    Men would be singing for ever.
    (*To the Servants.*)        Take her, go!
    You know your orders: take her to the vault                          55
    And leave her alone there. And if she lives or dies,
    That's her affair, not ours: our hands are clean.
*Antigonê:* O tomb, vaulted bride-bed in eternal rock,
    Soon I shall be with my own again
    Where Persephonê° welcomes the thin ghosts underground:              60
    And I shall see my father again, and you, mother,
    And dearest Polyneicês—
                 dearest indeed
    To me, since it was my hand
    That washed him clean and poured the ritual wine:
    And my reward is death before my time!                               65

    And yet, as men's hearts know, I have done no wrong,
    I have not sinned before God. Or if I have,
    I shall know the truth in death. But if the guilt
    Lies upon Creon who judged me, then, I pray,
    May his punishment equal my own.
*Choragos:*                O passionate heart,                          70
    Unyielding, tormented still by the same winds!
*Creon:* Her guards shall have good cause to regret their delaying.
*Antigonê:* Ah! That voice is like the voice of death!
*Creon:* I can give you no reason to think you are mistaken.
*Antigonê:* Thebes, and you my fathers' gods,                                  75
    And rulers of Thebes, you see me now, the last

---

48 *Epode:* the final section (after the strophe and antistrophe) of a lyric passage; whereas the earlier
sections are symmetrical, it takes a different metrical form.    60 *Persephonê:* whom Pluto, god of the
underworld, abducted to be his queen. (See D. H. Lawrence's poem "Bavarian Gentians," page 811.)

Unhappy daughter of a line of kings,
Your kings, led away to death. You will remember
What things I suffer, and at what men's hands,
Because I would not transgress the laws of heaven.                    80
(*To the Guards, simply.*) Come: let us wait no longer.

*Exit Antigonê, left, guarded.*

# ODE IV

*Strophe 1*

Chorus: All Danaê's beauty was locked away
    In a brazen cell where the sunlight could not come:
    A small room still as any grave, enclosed her.
    Yet she was a princess too,
    And Zeus in a rain of gold poured love upon her°.             5
    O child, child,
    No power in wealth or war
    Or tough sea-blackened ships
    Can prevail against untiring Destiny!

*Antistrophe 1*

And Dryas' son° also, that furious king,                              10
    Bore the god's prisoning anger for his pride:
    Sealed up by Dionysos in deaf stone,
    His madness died among echoes.
    So at the last he learned what dreadful power
    His tongue had mocked:                                       15
    For he had profaned the revels,
    And fired the wrath of the nine
    Implacable Sisters° that love the sound of the flute.

*Strophe 2*

And old men tell a half-remembered tale
    Of horror° where a dark ledge splits the sea                 20

---

1–5 *All Danaê's beauty . . . poured love upon her:* In legend, when an oracle told Acrisius, king of
Argos, that his daughter Danaê would bear a son who would grow up to slay him, he locked the
princess into a chamber made of bronze, lest any man impregnate her. But Zeus, father of the gods,
entered Danaê's prison in a shower of gold. The resultant child, the hero Perseus, was accidentally to
fulfill the prophecy by killing Acrisius with an ill-aimed discus throw.        10 *Dryas' son:* King
Lycurgus of Thrace, whom Dionysos, god of wine, caused to be stricken with madness.        18 *Sisters:*
the Muses, nine sister goddesses who presided over poetry and music, arts and sciences.        19–20 *a
half-remembered tale of horror:* As the Chorus recalls in the rest of this song, the point of this tale is
that being nobly born will not save one from disaster. King Phineas cast off his first wife Cleopatra
(not the later Egyptian queen, but the daughter of Boreas, god of the north wind) and imprisoned
her in a cave. Out of hatred for Cleopatra, the cruel Eidothea, second wife of the king, blinded her
stepsons.

And a double surf beats on the gráy shóres:
How a king's new woman, sick
With hatred for the queen he had imprisoned,
Ripped out his two sons' eyes with her bloody hands
While grinning Arês° watched the shuttle plunge                    25
Four times: four blind wounds crying for revenge,

Antistrophe 2

Crying, tears and blood mingled.—Piteously born,
Those sons whose mother was of heavenly birth!
Her father was the god of the North Wind
And she was cradled by gales,                                      30
She raced with young colts on the glittering hills
And walked untrammeled in the open light:
But in her marriage deathless Fate found means
To build a tomb like yours for all her joy.

## SCENE V

*Enter blind Teiresias, led by a boy. The opening speeches of Teiresias should be in
singsong contrast to the realistic lines of Creon.*

*Teiresias:* This is the way the blind man comes, Princes, Princes,
    Lockstep, two heads lit by the eyes of one.
*Creon:* What new thing have you to tell us, old Teiresias?
*Teiresias:* I have much to tell you: listen to the prophet, Creon.
*Creon:* I am not aware that I have ever failed to listen.                    5
*Teiresias:* Then you have done wisely, King, and ruled well.
*Creon:* I admit my debt to you. But what have you to say?
*Teiresias:* This, Creon: you stand once more on the edge of fate.
*Creon:* What do you mean? Your words are a kind of dread.
*Teiresias:* Listen, Creon:                                                   10
    I was sitting in my chair of augury, at the place
    Where the birds gather about me. They were all a-chatter,
    As is their habit, when suddenly I heard
    A strange note in their jangling, a scream, a
    Whirring fury; I knew that they were fighting,                    15
    Tearing each other, dying
    In a whirlwind of wings clashing. And I was afraid.
    I began the rites of burnt-offering at the altar,
    But Hephaistos° failed me: instead of bright flame,
    There was only the sputtering slime of the fat thigh-flesh        20
    Melting: the entrails dissolved in gray smoke,
    The bare bone burst from the welter. And no blaze!

25 *Arês:* god of war, said to gloat over bloodshed.    19 *Hephaistos:* god of fire.

This was a sign from heaven. My boy described it,
Seeing for me as I see for others.

I tell you, Creon, you yourself have brought                          25
This new calamity upon us. Our hearths and altars
Are stained with the corruption of dogs and carrion birds
That glut themselves on the corpse of Oedipus' son.
The gods are deaf when we pray to them, their fire
Recoils from our offering, their birds of omen                        30
Have no cry of comfort, for they are gorged
With the thick blood of the dead.
                                        O my son,
These are no trifles! Think: all men make mistakes,
But a good man yields when he knows his course is wrong,
And repairs the evil. The only crime is pride.                        35

Give in to the dead man, then: do not fight with a corpse—
What glory is it to kill a man who is dead?
Think, I beg you:
It is for your own good that I speak as I do.
You should be able to yield for your own good.                        40
*Creon:* It seems that prophets have made me their especial province.
All my life long
I have been a kind of butt for the dull arrows
Of doddering fortune-tellers!
                                No, Teiresias:
If your birds—if the great eagles of God himself                      45
Should carry him stinking bit by bit to heaven,
I would not yield. I am not afraid of pollution:
No man can defile the gods.
                                Do what you will,
Go into business, make money, speculate
In India gold or that synthetic gold from Sardis,                     50
Get rich otherwise than by my consent to bury him.
Teiresias, it is a sorry thing when a wise man
Sells his wisdom, lets out his words for hire!
*Teiresias:* Ah Creon! Is there no man left in the world—
*Creon:* To do what?—Come, let's have the aphorism!                   55
*Teiresias:* No man who knows that wisdom outweighs any wealth?
*Creon:* As surely as bribes are baser than any baseness.
*Teiresias:* You are sick, Creon! You are deathly sick!
*Creon:* As you say: it is not my place to challenge a prophet.
*Teiresias:* Yet you have said my prophecy is for sale.               60
*Creon:* The generation of prophets has always loved gold.
*Teiresias:* The generation of kings has always loved brass.
*Creon:* You forget yourself! You are speaking to your King.

*Teiresias:* I know it. You are a king because of me.
*Creon:* You have a certain skill; but you have sold out.                                    65
*Teiresias:* King, you will drive me to words that—
*Creon:*                                          Say them, say them!
    Only remember: I will not pay you for them.
*Teiresias:* No, you will find them too costly.
*Creon:*                                          No doubt. Speak:
    Whatever you say, you will not change my will.
*Teiresias:* Then take this, and take it to heart!                                           70
    The time is not far off when you shall pay back
    Corpse for corpse, flesh of your own flesh.
    You have thrust the child of this world into living night,
    You have kept from the gods below the child that is theirs:
    The one in a grave before her death, the other,                                    75
    Dead, denied the grave. This is your crime:
    And the Furies and the dark gods of Hell
    Are swift with terrible punishment for you.

    Do you want to buy me now, Creon?

                             Not many days,
    And your house will be full of men and women weeping,                              80
    And curses will be hurled at you from far
    Cities grieving for sons unburied, left to rot
    Before the walls of Thebes.

    These are my arrows, Creon: they are all for you.

    (*To Boy.*) But come, child: lead me home.                                         85
    Let him waste his fine anger upon younger men.
    Maybe he will learn at last
    To control a wiser tongue in a better head.

    *Exit Teiresias.*

*Choragos:* The old man has gone, King, but his words
    Remain to plague us. I am old, too,                                                90
    But I cannot remember that he was ever false.
*Creon:* That is true. . . . It troubles me.
    Oh it is hard to give in! but it is worse
    To risk everything for stubborn pride.
*Choragos:* Creon: take my advice.
*Creon:*                                          What shall I do?                           95
*Choragos:* Go quickly: free Antigonê from her vault
    And build a tomb for the body of Polyneicês.
*Creon:* You would have me do this!
*Choragos:*                                       Creon, yes!

And it must be done at once: God moves
Swiftly to cancel the folly of stubborn men.                                    100
Creon: It is hard to deny the heart! But I
    Will do it: I will not fight with destiny.
Choragos: You must go yourself, you cannot leave it to others.
Creon: I will go.
                    —Bring axes, servants:
    Come with me to the tomb. I buried her, I                                   105
    Will set her free.
                    Oh quickly!
    My mind misgives—
    The laws of the gods are mighty, and a man must serve them
    To the last day of his life!

*Exit Creon.*

# PAEAN°

Choragos: God of many names
Chorus:                                O Iacchos
                                    son
    of Kadmeian Sémelê
                    O born of the Thunder!
    Guardian of the West
                    Regent
    of Eleusis' plain
                    O Prince of maenad Thebes
    and the Dragon Field by rippling Ismenós°:                                   5

                                            *Antistrophe 1*

Choragos: God of many names
Chorus:                            the flame of torches
    flares on our hills
                    the nymphs of Iacchos
    dance at the spring of Castalia°:

*Paean:* a song of praise or prayer, here to Dionysos, god of wine.
1–5 *God of many names . . . Dragon Field by rippling Ismenós:* Dionysos was also called Iacchos (or, by
the Romans, Bacchus). He was the son of Zeus ("the Thunderer") and of Sémelê, daughter of Kadmos
(or Cadmus), legendary founder of Thebes. "Regent of Eleusis' plain" is another name for Dionysos,
honored in secret rites at Eleusis, a town northwest of Athens. "Prince of maenad Thebes" is yet
another: the Maenads were women of Thebes said to worship Dionysos with wild orgiastic rites.
Kadmos, so the story goes, sowed dragon's teeth in a field beside the river Ismenós. Up sprang a crop
of fierce warriors who fought among themselves until only five remained. These victors became the
first Thebans.        8 *Castalia:* a spring on Mount Parnassus, named for a maiden who drowned herself
in it to avoid rape by the god Apollo. She became a nymph, or nature spirit, dwelling in its waters. In
the temple of Delphi, at the mountain's foot, priestesses of Dionysos (the "nymphs of Iacchos") used
the spring's waters in rites of purification.

from the vine-close mountain
come ah come in ivy:
*Evohé evohé!*° sings through the streets of Thebes                              10

*Strophe 2*

Choragos: God of many names
Chorus:                              Iacchos of Thebes
heavenly Child
of Sémelê bride of the Thunderer!
The shadow of plague is upon us:
come
with clement feet
oh come from Parnasos
down the long slopes
across the lamenting water                              15

*Antistrophe 2*

Choragos: Iô° Fire! Chorister of the throbbing stars!
O purest among the voices of the night!
Thou son of God, blaze for us!
Chorus: Come with choric rapture of circling Maenads
Who cry Iô Iacche!
*God of many names!*                              20

## ÉXODOS°

*Enter Messenger from left.*

Messenger: Men of the line of Kadmos, you who live
Near Amphion's citadel°:
I cannot say
Of any condition of human life "This is fixed,
This is clearly good, or bad." Fate raises up,
And Fate casts down the happy and unhappy alike:
No man can foretell his Fate.
Take the case of Creon:
Creon was happy once, as I count happiness:
Victorious in battle, sole governor of the land,
Fortunate father of children nobly born.
And now it has all gone from him! Who can say
That a man is still alive when his life's joy fails?
He is a walking dead man. Grant him rich,

---

10 *Evohé evohé!*: cry of the Maenads in supplicating Dionysos: "Come forth, come forth!"      16 *Iô:*
"Hail" or "Praise be to. . . ." *Éxodos:* the final scene, containing the play's resolution.      2 *Amphion's
citadel:* a name for Thebes. Amphion, son of Zeus, had built a wall around the city by playing so beautifully on his lyre that the charmed stones leaped into their slots.

Let him live like a king in his great house:
If his pleasure is gone, I would not give
So much as the shadow of smoke for all he owns.                     15
*Choragos:* Your words hint at sorrow: what is your news for us?
*Messenger:* They are dead. The living are guilty of their death.
*Choragos:* Who is guilty? Who is dead? Speak!
*Messenger:*                                          Haimon.
Haimon is dead; and the hand that killed him
Is his own hand.
*Choragos:*                  His father's? or his own?                20
*Messenger:* His own, driven mad by the murder his father had done.
*Choragos:* Teiresias, Teiresias, how clearly you saw it all!
*Messenger:* This is my news: you must draw what conclusions you can from it.
*Choragos:* But look: Eurydicê, our Queen:
Has she overheard us?                                              25

*Enter Eurydicê from the palace, center.*

*Eurydicê:* I have heard something, friends:
As I was unlocking the gate of Pallas'° shrine,
For I needed her help today, I heard a voice
Telling of some new sorrow. And I fainted
There at the temple with all my maidens about me.                  30
But speak again: whatever it is, I can bear it:
Grief and I are no strangers.
*Messenger:*                              Dearest Lady.
I will tell you plainly all that I have seen.
I shall not try to comfort you: what is the use,
Since comfort could lie only in what is not true?                  35
The truth is always best.
                            I went with Creon
To the outer plain where Polyneicês was lying,
No friend to pity him, his body shredded by dogs.
We made our prayers in that place to Hecatê
And Pluto°, that they would be merciful. And we bathed             40
The corpse with holy water, and we brought
Fresh-broken branches to burn what was left of it,
And upon the urn we heaped up a towering barrow
Of the earth of his own land.
                            When we were done, we ran
To the vault where Antigonê lay on her couch of stone.             45
One of the servants had gone ahead,

---

27 *Pallas:* Pallas Athene, goddess of wisdom, and hence an excellent source of advice.
39–40 *Hecatê and Pluto:* two fearful divinities—the goddess of witchcraft and sorcery and the king of
Hades, underworld of the dead.

And while he was yet far off he heard a voice
Grieving within the chamber, and he came back
And told Creon. And as the King went closer,
The air was full of wailing, the words lost,                          50
And he begged us to make all haste. "Am I a prophet?"
He said, weeping, "And must I walk this road,
The saddest of all that I have gone before?
My son's voice calls me on. Oh quickly, quickly!
Look through the crevice there, and tell me                          55
If it is Haimon, or some deception of the gods!"

We obeyed; and in the cavern's farthest corner
We saw her lying:
She had made a noose of her fine linen veil
And hanged herself. Haimon lay beside her,                           60
His arms about her waist, lamenting her,
His love lost under ground, crying out
That his father had stolen her away from him.

When Creon saw him the tears rushed to his eyes
And he called to him: "What have you done, child? Speak to me.        65
What are you thinking that makes your eyes so strange?
O my son, my son, I come to you on my knees!"
But Haimon spat in his face. He said not a word,
Staring—
            And suddenly drew his sword
And lunged. Creon shrank back, the blade missed; and the boy,         70
Desperate against himself, drove it half its length
Into his own side, and fell. And as he died
He gathered Antigonê close in his arms again,
Choking, his blood bright red on her white cheek.
And now he lies dead with the dead, and she is his                    75
At last, his bride in the houses of the dead.

> *Exit Eurydicê into the palace.*

Choragos: She has left us without a word. What can this mean?
Messenger: It troubles me, too; yet she knows what is best,
        Her grief is too great for public lamentation,
        And doubtless she has gone to her chamber to weep              80
        For her dead son, leading her maidens in his dirge.
Choragos: It may be so: but I fear this deep silence.

> *Pause.*

Messenger: I will see what she is doing. I will go in.

> *Exit Messenger into the palace.*

*Enter Creon with attendants, bearing Haimon's body.*

Choragos: But here is the king himself: oh look at him,
    Bearing his own damnation in his arms.                    85
Creon: Nothing you say can touch me any more.
    My own blind heart has brought me
    From darkness to final darkness. Here you see
    The father murdering, the murdered son—
    And all my civic wisdom!                                  90

    Haimon my son, so young, so young to die,
    I was the fool, not you; and you died for me.
Choragos: That is the truth; but you were late in learning it.
Creon: This truth is hard to bear. Surely a god
    Has crushed me beneath the hugest weight of heaven,       95
    And driven me headlong a barbaric way
    To trample out the thing I held most dear.

    The pains that men will take to come to pain!

*Enter Messenger from the palace.*

Messenger: The burden you carry in your hands is heavy,
    But it is not all: you will find more in your house.      100
Creon: What burden worse than this shall I find there?
Messenger: The Queen is dead.
Creon: O port of death, deaf world,
    Is there no pity for me? And you, Angel of evil,
    I was dead, and your words are death again.               105
    Is it true, boy? Can it be true?
    Is my wife dead? Has death bred death?
Messenger: You can see for yourself.

*The doors are opened and the body of Eurydicê is disclosed within.*

Creon: Oh pity!
    All true, all true, and more than I can bear!             110
    O my wife, my son!
Messenger: She stood before the altar, and her heart
    Welcomed the knife her own hand guided,
    And a great cry burst from her lips for Megareus° dead,
    And for Haimon dead, her sons; and her last breath         115
    Was a curse for their father, the murderer of her sons.

---

114 *Megareus:* Son of Creon and brother of Haimon, Megareus was slain in the unsuccessful attack upon Thebes.

And she fell, and the dark flowed in through her closing eyes.

*Creon:* O God, I am sick with fear.

Are there no swords here? Has no one a blow for me?

*Messenger:* Her curse is upon you for the deaths of both.  120

*Creon:* It is right that it should be. I alone am guilty.

I know it, and I say it. Lead me in,

Quickly, friends.

I have neither life nor substance. Lead me in.

*Choragos:* You are right, if there can be right in so much wrong.  125

The briefest way is best in a world of sorrow.

*Creon:* Let it come,

Let death come quickly, and be kind to me.

I would not ever see the sun again.

*Choragos:* All that will come when it will; but we, meanwhile,  130

Have much to do. Leave the future to itself.

*Creon:* All my heart was in that prayer!

*Choragos:* Then do not pray any more: the sky is deaf.

*Creon:* Lead me away. I have been rash and foolish.

I have killed my son and my wife.  135

I look for comfort; my comfort lies here dead.

Whatever my hands have touched has come to nothing.

Fate has brought all my pride to a thought of dust.

*As Creon is being led into the house, the Choragos advances and speaks directly to the audience.*

*Choragos:* There is no happiness where there is no wisdom;

No wisdom but in submission to the gods.  140

Big words are always punished,

And proud men in old age learn to be wise.

# William Shakespeare

## THE TRAGEDY OF HAMLET, PRINCE OF DENMARK    AROUND 1600

*Edited by David Bevington*

*Kevin Kline as Hamlet*

*William Shakespeare (1564–1616), whose life is sketched in a note on page 1153, wrote* Hamlet *around 1600. The* Hamlet *story first appears in the Danish History of the twelfth-century writer Saxo Gramaticus. But the tale is probably even older than that. Saxo's version recounts the murder of the king of Denmark by his wicked brother, and the brother's marriage to the widowed queen; then Prince Amlethus, the dead king's son, feigns madness, escapes a plot on his life, and eventually gains revenge. There was an earlier English play (now lost)—in the 1580s—called* Hamlet, *which was probably written by Thomas Kyd. It is believed that Shakespeare based his own play on it. Although he borrowed his story (as he did the basic plot of* Othello*), Shakespeare made it entirely his own and populated it with some of the most memorable characters in English drama. It is usually assumed that* Hamlet *was the earliest of Shakespeare's four great mature tragedies (being written just before* Othello, King Lear, *and* Macbeth*). If this speculative dating is true,* Hamlet *represented something extraordinarily innovative in world drama, especially in respect to the title character—a deeply intelligent and reflective man compelled by justice and filial duty to avenge his father's murder but simultaneously riddled by self-doubt and moral conscience. In the brooding figure of Hamlet, Shakespeare presented both the prince's inner and exterior life with startling immediacy and mysterious depth. For centuries critics have considered* Hamlet *Shakespeare's most philosophical play, yet it does not lack action.* Hamlet *contains a vengeful ghost, two sorts of madness (one tragically genuine, the other comically feigned), a suicide, sword fights, poisonings, incest, and multiple murders. The play provides both the compelling entertainment beloved of Elizabethan audiences and a tragic meditation on human existence that has haunted readers of every subsequent age.*

*Glenn Close as Gertrude*

Dramatis Personae

*Ghost of Hamlet, the former King of Denmark*
*Claudius, King of Denmark, the former King's brother*
*Gertrude, Queen of Denmark, widow of the former King and now wife of Claudius*
*Hamlet, Prince of Denmark, son of the late King and of Gertrude*
*Polonius, councillor to the King*
*Laertes, his son*
*Ophelia, his daughter*
*Reynaldo, his servant*
*Horatio, Hamlet's friend and fellow student*
*Voltimand,*
*Cornelius,*
*Rosencrantz,*
*Guildenstern,* } *members of the Danish court*
*Osric,*
*A Gentleman,*
*A Lord,*
*Bernardo,*
*Francisco,* } *officers and soldiers on watch*
*Marcellus,*
*Fortinbras, Prince of Norway*
*Captain in his army*
*Three or Four Players, taking the roles of Prologue, Player King, Player Queen, and*
   *Lucianus*
*Two Messengers*
*First Sailor*
*Two Clowns, a gravedigger and his companion*
*Priest*
*First Ambassador from England*
*Lords, Soldiers, Attendants, Guards, other Players, Followers of Laertes, other Sailors,*
*another Ambassador or Ambassadors from England*

Scene: *Denmark*

# ACT I

### Scene I [Elsinore Castle. A Guard Platform.]

   *Enter Bernardo and Francisco, two sentinels, [meeting].*

*Bernardo:* Who's there?
*Francisco:* Nay, answer me. Stand and unfold yourself.

---

2 *me* (Francisco emphasizes that *he* is the sentry currently on watch.)   *unfold yourself* reveal your
identity

*Bernardo:* Long live the King!

*Francisco:* Bernardo?

*Bernardo:* He.                                                  5

*Francisco:* You come most carefully upon your hour.

*Bernardo:* 'Tis now struck twelve. Get thee to bed, Francisco.

*Francisco:* For this relief much thanks. 'Tis bitter cold,
    And I am sick at heart.

*Bernardo:* Have you had quiet guard?                       10

*Francisco:* Not a mouse stirring.

*Bernardo:* Well, good night.
    If you do meet Horatio and Marcellus,
    The rivals of my watch, bid them make haste.

    *Enter Horatio and Marcellus.*

*Francisco:* I think I hear them.—Stand, ho! Who is there?      15

*Horatio:* Friends to this ground.

*Marcellus:* And liegemen to the Dane.

*Francisco:* Give you good night.

*Marcellus:* O, farewell, honest soldier. Who hath relieved you?

*Francisco:* Bernardo hath my place. Give you good night.      20

                                  *Exit Francisco.*

*Marcellus:* Holla! Bernardo!

*Bernardo:* Say, what, is Horatio there?

*Horatio:* A piece of him.

*Bernardo:* Welcome, Horatio. Welcome, good Marcellus.

*Horatio:* What, has this thing appeared again tonight?        25

*Bernardo:* I have seen nothing.

*Marcellus:* Horatio says 'tis but our fantasy,
    And will not let belief take hold of him
    Touching this dreaded sight twice seen of us.
    Therefore I have entreated him along                   30
    With us to watch the minutes of this night,
    That if again this apparition come
    He may approve our eyes and speak to it.

*Horatio:* Tush, tush, 'twill not appear.

*Bernardo:*                         Sit down awhile,
    And let us once again assail your ears,                35
    That are so fortified against our story,
    What we have two nights seen.

---

14 *rivals* partners    16 *ground* country, land    17 *liegemen to the Dane* men sworn to serve the
Danish king    18 *Give* i.e., may God give    27 *fantasy* imagination    30 *along* to come along
31 *watch* keep watch during    33 *approve* corroborate    37 *What* with what

*Horatio:*                              Well, sit we down,
And let us hear Bernardo speak of this.
*Bernardo:* Last night of all,
When yond same star that's westward from the pole                    40
Had made his course t' illume that part of heaven
Where now it burns, Marcellus and myself,
The bell then beating one—

*Enter Ghost.*

*Marcellus:* Peace, break thee off! Look where it comes again!
*Bernardo:* In the same figure like the King that's dead.                   45
*Marcellus:* Thou art a scholar. Speak to it, Horatio.
*Bernardo:* Looks 'a not like the King? Mark it, Horatio.
*Horatio:* Most like. It harrows me with fear and wonder.
*Bernardo:* It would be spoke to.
*Marcellus:*                              Speak to it, Horatio.
*Horatio:* What are thou that usurp'st this time of night,                   50
Together with that fair and warlike form
In which the majesty of buried Denmark
Did sometime march? By heaven, I charge thee, speak!
*Marcellus:* It is offended.
*Bernardo:*                    See, it stalks away.
*Horatio:* Stay! Speak, speak! I charge thee, speak!          *Exit Ghost.*   55
*Marcellus:* 'Tis gone and will not answer.
*Bernardo:* How now, Horatio? You tremble and look pale.
Is not this something more than fantasy?
What think you on 't?
*Horatio:* Before my God, I might not this believe                          60
Without the sensible and true avouch
Of mine own eyes.
*Marcellus:*                    Is it not like the King?
*Horatio:* As thou art to thyself.
Such was the very armor he had on
When he the ambitious Norway combated.                                    65
So frowned he once when, in an angry parle,
He smote the sledded Polacks on the ice.
'Tis strange.

39 *Last . . . all* i.e., this *very* last night. (Emphatic.)     40 *pole* polestar, north star     41 *his* its.
*illume* illuminate     46 *scholar* one learned enough to know how to question a ghost properly     47
*'a* he     49 *It . . . to* (It was commonly believed that a ghost could not speak until spoken to.)
50 *usurp'st* wrongfully takes over     52 *buried Denmark* the buried King of Denmark     53 *sometime*
formerly     59 *on 't* of it     61 *sensible* confirmed by the senses.     *avouch* warrant, evidence
65 *Norway* King of Norway     66 *parle* parley     67 *sledded* traveling on sleds.     *Polacks* Poles

*Marcellus:* Thus twice before, and jump at this dead hour,
    With martial stalk hath he gone by our watch.        70
*Horatio:* In what particular thought to work I know not,
    But in the gross and scope of mine opinion
    This bodes some strange eruption to our state.
*Marcellus:* Good now, sit down, and tell me, he that knows,
    Why this same strict and most observant watch        75
    So nightly toils the subject of the land,
    And why such daily cast of brazen cannon
    And foreign mart for implements of war,
    Why such impress of shipwrights, whose sore task
    Does not divide the Sunday from the week.        80
    What might be toward, that this sweaty haste
    Doth make the night joint-laborer with the day?
    Who is 't that can inform me?
*Horatio:*                    That can I;
    At least, the whisper goes so. Our last king,
    Whose image even but now appeared to us,        85
    Was, as you know, by Fortinbras of Norway,
    Thereto pricked on by a most emulate pride,
    Dared to the combat; in which our valiant Hamlet—
    For so this side of our known world esteemed him—
    Did slay this Fortinbras; who by a sealed compact        90
    Well ratified by law and heraldry
    Did forfeit, with his life, all those his lands
    Which he stood seized of, to the conqueror;
    Against the which a moiety competent
    Was gagèd by our king, which had returned        95
    To the inheritance of Fortinbras
    Had he been vanquisher, as, by the same cov'nant
    And carriage of the article designed,
    His fell to Hamlet. Now, sir, young Fortinbras,
    Of unimprovèd mettle hot and full,        100
    Hath in the skirts of Norway here and there

69 *jump* exactly    70 *stalk* stride    71 *to work* i.e., to collect my thoughts and try to understand this    72 *gross and scope* general drift    74 *Good now* (An expression denoting entreaty or expostulation.)    76 *toils* causes to toil. *subject* subjects    77 *cast* casting    78 *mart* buying and selling    79 *impress* impressment, conscription    81 *toward* in preparation    87 *Thereto . . . pride* (Refers to old Fortinbras, not the Danish King.)    *pricked on* incited.    *emulate* emulous, ambitious    89 *this . . . world* i.e., all Europe, the Western world    90 *sealed* certified, confirmed    93 *seized* possessed    94 *Against the* in return for.    *moiety competent* corresponding portion    95 *gagèd* engaged, pledged.    *had returned* would have passed    96 *inheritance* possession    97 *cov'nant* i.e., the *sealed compact* of line 90    98 *carriage . . . designed* carrying out of the article or clause drawn up to cover the point    100 *unimprovèd mettle* untried, undisciplined spirits    101 *skirts* outlying regions, outskirts

Sharked up a list of lawless resolutes
For food and diet to some enterprise
That hath a stomach in 't, which is no other—
As it doth well appear unto our state—                              105
But to recover of us, by strong hand
And terms compulsatory, those foresaid lands
So by his father lost. And this, I take it,
Is the main motive of our preparations,
The source of this our watch, and the chief head                   110
Of this posthaste and rummage in the land.
*Bernardo:* I think it be no other but e'en so.
Well may it sort that this portentous figure
Comes armèd through our watch so like the King
That was and is the question of these wars.                        115
*Horatio:* A mote it is to trouble the mind's eye.
In the most high and palmy state of Rome,
A little ere the mightiest Julius fell,
The graves stood tenantless, and the sheeted dead
Did squeak and gibber in the Roman streets;                        120
As stars with trains of fire and dews of blood,
Disasters in the sun; and the moist star
Upon whose influence Neptune's empire stands
Was sick almost to doomsday with eclipse.
And even the like precurse of feared events,                       125
As harbingers preceding still the fates
And prologue to the omen coming on,
Have heaven and earth together demonstrated
Unto our climatures and countrymen.

*Enter Ghost.*

But soft, behold! Lo, where it comes again!                        130
I'll cross it, though it blast me. (*It spreads his arms.*) Stay, illusion!
If thou hast any sound or use of voice,

---

102 *Sharked up* gathered up, as a shark takes fish.     *list* i.e., troop.     *resolutes* desperadoes     103
*For food and diet* i.e., they are to serve as *food,* or "means," *to some enterprise;* also they serve in return
for the rations they get     104 *stomach* (1) a spirit of daring (2) an appetite that is fed by the *lawless
resolutes*     110 *head* source     111 *rummage* bustle, commotion     113 *sort* suit     115 *question*
focus of contention     116 *mote* speck of dust     117 *palmy* flourishing     119 *sheeted* shrouded
121 *As* (This abrupt transition suggests that matter is possibly omitted between lines 120 and 121.)
*trains* trails     122 *Disasters* unfavorable signs or aspects.     *moist star* i.e., moon, governing tides
123 *Neptune* god of the sea.     *stands* depends     124 *sick . . . doomsday* (See Matthew 24:29 and
Revelation 6:12.)     125 *precurse* heralding, foreshadowing     126 *harbingers* forerunners.     *still*
continually     127 *omen* calamitous event     129 *climatures* regions     130 *soft* i.e., enough,
break off     131 *cross* stand in its path, confront.     *blast* wither, strike with a curse.     *s.d. his* its

Speak to me!
If there be any good thing to be done
That may to thee do ease and grace to me, 135
Speak to me!
If thou art privy to thy country's fate,
Which, happily, foreknowing may avoid,
O, speak!
Or if thou hast uphoarded in thy life 140
Extorted treasure in the womb of earth,
For which, they say, you spirits oft walk in death,
Speak of it! (*The cock crows.*) Stay and speak!—Stop it, Marcellus.

*Marcellus:* Shall I strike at it with my partisan?

*Horatio:* Do, if it will not stand. [*They strike at it.*] 145

*Bernardo:* 'Tis here!

*Horatio:* 'Tis here! [*Exit Ghost.*]

*Marcellus:* 'Tis gone.
 We do it wrong, being so majestical,
 To offer it the show of violence, 150
 For it is as the air invulnerable,
 And our vain blows malicious mockery.

*Bernardo:* It was about to speak when the cock crew.

*Horatio:* And then it started like a guilty thing
 Upon a fearful summons. I have heard 155
 The cock, that is the trumpet to the morn,
 Doth with his lofty and shrill-sounding throat
 Awake the god of day, and at his warning,
 Whether in sea or fire, in earth or air,
 Th' extravagant and erring spirit hies 160
 To his confine; and of the truth herein
 This present object made probation.

*Marcellus:* It faded on the crowing of the cock.
 Some say that ever 'gainst that season comes
 Wherein our Savior's birth is celebrated, 165
 This bird of dawning singeth all night long,
 And then, they say, no spirit dare stir abroad;
 The nights are wholesome, then no planets strike,
 No fairy takes, nor witch hath power to charm,
 So hallowed and so gracious is that time. 170

---

137 *privy to* in on the secret of  138 *happily* haply, perchance  144 *partisan* long-handled spear
156 *trumpet* trumpeter  160 *extravagant and erring* wandering beyond bounds. (The words have
similar meaning.)  *hies* hastens  162 *probation* proof  164 *'gainst* just before  168 *strike*
destroy by evil influence  169 *takes* bewitches  170 *gracious* full of grace

*Horatio:* So have I heard and do in part believe it.
    But, look, the morn in russet mantle clad
    Walks o'er the dew of yon high eastward hill.
    Break we our watch up, and by my advice
    Let us impart what we have seen tonight                175
    Unto young Hamlet; for upon my life,
    This spirit, dumb to us, will speak to him.
    Do you consent we shall acquaint him with it,
    As needful in our loves, fitting our duty?
*Marcellus:* Let's do 't, I pray, and I this morning know      180
    Where we shall find him most conveniently.

                                  *Exeunt.*

### Scene II [The Castle.]

*Flourish. Enter Claudius, King of Denmark, Gertrude the Queen, [the] Council, as Polonius and his son Laertes, Hamlet, cum aliis [including Voltimand and Cornelius].*

*King:* Though yet of Hamlet our dear brother's death
    The memory be green, and that it us befitted
    To bear our hearts in grief and our whole kingdom
    To be contracted in one brow of woe,
    Yet so far hath discretion fought with nature           5
    That we with wisest sorrow think on him
    Together with remembrance of ourselves.
    Therefore our sometime sister, now our queen,
    Th' imperial jointress to this warlike state,
    Have we, as 'twere with a defeated joy—           10
    With an auspicious and a dropping eye,
    With mirth in funeral and with dirge in marriage,
    In equal scale weighing delight and dole—
    Taken to wife. Nor have we herein barred
    Your better wisdoms, which have freely gone       15
    With this affair along. For all, our thanks.
    Now follows that you know young Fortinbras,
    Holding a weak supposal of our worth,
    Or thinking by our late dear brother's death

---

*s.d. as* i.e., such as, including.     *cum aliis* with others     1 *our* my. (The royal "we"; also in the following lines.)     8 *sometime* former     9 *jointress* woman possessing property with her husband     11 *With . . . eye* with one eye smiling and the other weeping     13 *dole* grief     17 *that you know* what you know already, that; or, that you be informed as follows     18 *weak supposal* low estimate

Our state to be disjoint and out of frame,                               20
Co-leaguèd with this dream of his advantage,
He hath not failed to pester us with message
Importing the surrender of those lands
Lost by his father, with all bonds of law,
To our most valiant brother. So much for him.                            25
Now for ourself and for this time of meeting.
Thus much the business is: we have here writ
To Norway, uncle of young Fortinbras—
Who, impotent and bed-rid, scarcely hears
Of this his nephew's purpose—to suppress                                 30
His further gait herein, in that the levies,
The lists, and full proportions are all made
Out of his subject; and we here dispatch
You, good Cornelius, and you, Voltimand,
For bearers of this greeting to old Norway,                              35
Giving to you no further personal power
To business with the King more than the scope
Of these dilated articles allow.                       [*He gives a paper.*]
Farewell, and let your haste commend your duty.
*Cornelius, Voltimand:*
    In that, and all things, will we show our duty.                     40
*King:* We doubt it nothing. Heartily farewell.

                        [*Exeunt Voltimand and Cornelius.*]

And now, Laertes, what's the news with you?
You told us of some suit; what is 't, Laertes?
You cannot speak of reason to the Dane
And lose your voice. What wouldst thou beg, Laertes,                     45
That shall not be my offer, not thy asking?
The head is not more native to the heart,
The hand more instrumental to the mouth,
Than is the throne of Denmark to thy father.
What wouldst thou have, Laertes?
*Laertes:*                         My dread lord,                        50
    Your leave and favor to return to France,

---

21 *Co-leaguèd with* joined to, allied with.     *dream . . . advantage* illusory hope of having
the advantage. (His only ally is this hope.)     23 *Importing* pertaining to     24 *bonds*
contracts     29 *impotent* helpless     31 *His* i.e., Fortinbras'.     *gait* proceeding
31–33 *in that . . . subject* since the levying of troops and supplies is drawn entirely from the
King of Norway's own subjects     38 *dilated* set out at length     39 *let . . . duty* let your
swift obeying of orders, rather than mere words, express your dutifulness     41 *nothing* not
at all     44 *the Dane* the Danish king     45 *lose your voice* waste your speech
47 *native* closely connected, related     48 *instrumental* servicable     51 *leave and favor*
kind permission

From whence though willingly I came to Denmark
To show my duty in your coronation,
Yet now I must confess, that duty done,
My thoughts and wishes bend again toward France                    55
And bow them to your gracious leave and pardon.
*King:* Have you your father's leave? What says Polonius?
*Polonius:* H'ath, my lord, wrung from me my slow leave
By laborsome petition, and at last
Upon his will I sealed my hard consent.                            60
I do beseech you, give him leave to go.
*King:* Take thy fair hour, Laertes. Time be thine,
And thy best graces spend it at thy will!
But now, my cousin Hamlet, and my son—
*Hamlet:* A little more than kin, and less than kind.               65
*King:* How is it that the clouds still hang on you?
*Hamlet:* Not so, my lord. I am too much in the sun.
*Queen:* Good Hamlet, cast thy nighted color off,
And let thine eye look like a friend on Denmark.
Do not forever with thy vailèd lids                                70
Seek for thy noble father in the dust.
Thou know'st 'tis common, all that lives must die,
Passing through nature to eternity.
*Hamlet:* Ay, madam, it is common.
*Queen:*                                   If it be,
Why seems it so particular with thee?                             75
*Hamlet:* Seems, madam? Nay, it is. I know not "seems."
'Tis not alone my inky cloak, good Mother,
Nor customary suits of solemn black,
Nor windy suspiration of forced breath,
No, nor the fruitful river in the eye,                            80
Nor the dejected havior of the visage,
Together with all forms, moods, shapes of grief,
That can denote me truly. These indeed seem,

---

56 *bow . . . pardon* entreatingly make a deep bow, asking your permission to depart     58 *H'ath* he
has     60 *sealed* (as if sealing a legal document).     *hard* reluctant     62 *Take thy fair hour* enjoy
your time of youth     63 *And . . . will* and may your finest qualities guide the way you choose to
spend your time     64 *cousin* any kin not of the immediate family     65 *A little . . . kind* i.e., closer
than an ordinary nephew (since I am stepson), and yet more separated in natural feeling (with pun
on *kind* meaning "affectionate" and "natural," "lawful." This line is often read as an aside, but it need
not be. The King chooses perhaps not to respond to Hamlet's cryptic and bitter remark.)     67 *the
sun* i.e., the sunshine of the King's royal favor (with pun on *son*)     68 *nighted color* (1) mourning
garmets of black (2) dark melancholy     69 *Denmark* the King of Denmark     70 *vailèd lids* lowered eyes     72 *common* of universal occurrence. (But Hamlet plays on the sense of "vulgar" in line
74.)     75 *particular* personal     78 *customary* (1) socially conventional (2) habitual with me
79 *suspiration* sighing     80 *fruitful* abundant     81 *havior* expression     82 *moods* outward expression of feeling

For they are actions that a man might play.
But I have that within which passes show;                                          85
These but the trappings and the suits of woe.
King: 'Tis sweet and commendable in your nature, Hamlet,
To give these mourning duties to your father.
But you must know your father lost a father,
That father lost, lost his, and the survivor bound                                 90
In filial obligation for some term
To do obsequious sorrow. But to persever
In obstinate condolement is a course
Of impious stubbornness. 'Tis unmanly grief.
It shows a will most incorrect to heaven,                                          95
A heart unfortified, a mind impatient,
An understanding simple and unschooled.
For what we know must be and is as common
As any the most vulgar thing to sense,
Why should we in our peevish opposition                                           100
Take it to heart? Fie, 'tis a fault to heaven,
A fault against the dead, a fault to nature,
To reason most absurd, whose common theme
Is death of fathers, and who still hath cried,
From the first corpse till he that died today,                                    105
"This must be so." We pray you, throw to earth
This unprevailing woe and think of us
As of a father; for let the world take note,
You are the most immediate to our throne,
And with no less nobility of love                                                 110
Than that which dearest father bears his son
Do I impart toward you. For your intent
In going back to school in Wittenberg,
It is most retrograde to our desire,
And we beseech you bend you to remain                                            115
Here in the cheer and comfort of our eye,
Our chiefest courtier, cousin, and our son.
Queen: Let not thy mother lose her prayers, Hamlet.
I pray thee, stay with us, go not to Wittenberg.
Hamlet: I shall in all my best obey you, madam.                                   120

---

92 *obsequious* suited to obsequies or funerals.    *persever* persevere    93 *condolement* sorrowing
96 *unfortified* i.e., against adversity    97 *simple* ignorant    99 *As . . . sense* as the most ordinary
experience    104 *still* always    105 *the first corpse* (Abel's)    107 *unprevailing* unavailing, useless    109 *most immediate* next in succession    112 *impart toward* i.e., bestow my affection on.
*For* as for    113 *to school* i.e., to your studies.    *Wittenberg* famous German university founded in
1502    114 *retrograde* contrary    115 *bend you* incline yourself    120 *in all my best* to the best
of my ability

*King:* Why, 'tis a loving and a fair reply.
Be as ourself in Denmark. Madam, come.
This gentle and unforced accord of Hamlet
Sits smiling to my heart, in grace whereof
No jocund health that Denmark drinks today                    125
But the great cannon to the clouds shall tell,
And the King's rouse the heaven shall bruit again,
Respeaking earthly thunder. Come away.

                                    *Flourish. Exeunt all but Hamlet.*

*Hamlet:* O, that this too too sullied flesh would melt,
Thaw, and resolve itself into a dew!                          130
Or that the Everlasting had not fixed
His canon 'gainst self-slaughter! O God, God,
How weary, stale, flat, and unprofitable
Seem to me all the uses of this world!
Fie on 't, ah fie! 'Tis an unweeded garden                   135
That grows to seed. Things rank and gross in nature
Possess it merely. That it should come to this!
But two months dead—nay, not so much, not two.
So excellent a king, that was to this
Hyperion to a satyr, so loving to my mother                  140
That he might not beteem the winds of heaven
Visit her face too roughly. Heaven and earth,
Must I remember? Why, she would hang on him
As if increase of appetite had grown
By what it fed on, and yet within a month—                   145
Let me not think on 't; frailty, thy name is woman!—
A little month, or ere those shoes were old
With which she followed my poor father's body,
Like Niobe, all tears, why she, even she—
O God, a beast, that wants discourse of reason,              150
Would have mourned longer—married with my uncle,
My father's brother, but no more like my father
Than I to Hercules. Within a month,

124 *to* i.e., at.    *grace* thanksgiving    125 *jocund* merry    127 *rouse* drinking of a draft of liquor.
*bruit again* loudly echo    128 *thunder* i.e., of trumpet and kettledrum, sounded when the King
drinks; see 1.4.8–12    129 *sullied* defiled. (The early quartos read *sallied;* the Folio, *solid.*)    132
*canon* law    134 *all the uses* the whole routine    137 *merely* completely    139 *to* in comparison
to    140 *Hyperion* Titan sun-god, father of Helios.    *satyr* a lecherous creature of classical
mythology, half-human but with a goat's legs, tail, ears, and horns    141 *beteem* allow    147 *or
ere* even before    149 *Niobe* Tantalus' daughter, Queen of Thebes, who boasted that she had more
sons and daughters than Leto; for this, Apollo and Artemis, children of Leto, slew her fourteen children. She was turned by Zeus into a stone that continually dropped tears.    150 *wants . . . reason*
lacks the faculty of reason

Ere yet the salt of most unrighteous tears
Had left the flushing in her gallèd eyes,                                    155
She married. O, most wicked speed, to post
With such dexterity to incestuous sheets!
It is not, nor it cannot come to good.
But break, my heart, for I must hold my tongue.

*Enter Horatio, Marcellus, and Bernardo.*

*Horatio:* Hail to your lordship!
*Hamlet:*                              I am glad to see you well.          160
   Horatio!—or I do forget myself.
*Horatio:* The same, my lord, and your poor servant ever.
*Hamlet:* Sir, my good friend; I'll change that name with you.
   And what make you from Wittenberg, Horatio?
   Marcellus.                                                               165
*Marcellus:* My good lord.
*Hamlet:* I am very glad to see you. [*To Bernardo.*] Good even, sir.—
   But what in faith make you from Wittenberg?
*Horatio:* A truant disposition, good my lord.
*Hamlet:* I would not hear your enemy say so,                               170
   Nor shall you do my ear that violence
   To make it truster of your own report
   Against yourself. I know you are no truant.
   But what is your affair in Elsinore?
   We'll teach you to drink deep ere you depart.                           175
*Horatio:* My lord, I came to see your father's funeral.
*Hamlet:* I prithee, do not mock me, fellow student;
   I think it was to see my mother's wedding.
*Horatio:* Indeed, my lord, it followed hard upon.
*Hamlet:* Thrift, thrift, Horatio! The funeral baked meats                 180
   Did coldly furnish forth the marriage tables.
   Would I had met my dearest foe in heaven
   Or ever I had seen that day, Horatio!
   My father!—Methinks I see my father.
*Horatio:* Where, my lord?
*Hamlet:*                              In my mind's eye, Horatio.          185
*Horatio:* I saw him once. 'A was a goodly king.

155 *gallèd* irritated, inflamed     156 *post* hasten     157 *incestuous* (In Shakespeare's day, the marriage of a man like Claudius to his deceased brother's wife was considered incestuous.)     163 *change
that name* i.e., give and receive reciprocally the name of "friend" (rather than talk of "servant")
164 *make you from* are you doing away from     179 *hard* close     180 *baked meats* meat pies
181 *coldly* i.e., as cold leftovers     182 *dearest* closest (and therefore deadliest)     183 *Or ever*
before     186 *'A* he

Hamlet: 'A was a man. Take him for all in all,
    I shall not look upon his like again.
Horatio: My lord, I think I saw him yesternight.
Hamlet: Saw? Who?                                 190
Horatio: My lord, the King your father.
Hamlet: The King my father?
Horatio: Season your admiration for a while
    With an attent ear till I may deliver,
    Upon the witness of these gentlemen,             195
    This marvel to you.
Hamlet:               For God's love, let me hear!
Horatio: Two nights together had these gentlemen,
    Marcellus and Bernardo, on their watch,
    In the dead waste and middle of the night,
    Been thus encountered. A figure like your father,     200
    Armèd at point exactly, cap-à-pie,
    Appears before them, and with solemn march
    Goes slow and stately by them. Thrice he walked
    By their oppressed and fear-surprisèd eyes
    Within his truncheon's length, whilst they, distilled     205
    Almost to jelly with the act of fear,
    Stand dumb and speak not to him. This to me
    In dreadful secrecy impart they did,
    And I with them the third night kept the watch,
    Where, as they had delivered, both in time,           210
    Form of the thing, each word made true and good,
    The apparition comes. I knew your father;
    These hands are not more like.
Hamlet:                   But where was this?
Marcellus: My lord, upon the platform where we watch.
Hamlet: Did you not speak to it?
Horatio:                My lord, I did,           215
    But answer made it none. Yet once methought
    It lifted up its head and did address
    Itself to motion, like as it would speak;
    But even then the morning cock crew loud,
    And at the sound it shrunk in haste away          220
    And vanished from our sight.
Hamlet:                'Tis very strange.

---

193 *Season your admiration* restrain your astonishment     194 *attent* attentive     199 *dead waste*
desolate stillness     201 *at point* correctly in every detail.     *cap-à-pie* from head to foot     205
*truncheon* officer's staff.     *distilled* dissolved     206 *act* action, operation     208 *dreadful* full of
dread     217–218 *did . . . speak* began to move as though it were about to speak     219 *even then* at
that very instant

*Horatio:* As I do live, my honored lord, 'tis true,
And we did think it writ down in our duty
To let you know of it.

*Hamlet:* Indeed, indeed, sirs. But this troubles me. 225
Hold you the watch tonight?

*All:*                                        We do, my lord.

*Hamlet:* Armed, say you?

*All:* Armed, my lord.

*Hamlet:* From top to toe?

*All:* My lord, from head to foot. 230

*Hamlet:* Then saw you not his face?

*Horatio:* O, yes, my lord, he wore his beaver up.

*Hamlet:* What looked he, frowningly?

*Horatio:* A countenance more in sorrow than in anger.

*Hamlet:* Pale or red? 235

*Horatio:* Nay, very pale.

*Hamlet:* And fixed his eyes upon you?

*Horatio:* Most constantly.

*Hamlet:* I would I had been there.

*Horatio:* It would have much amazed you. 240

*Hamlet:* Very like, very like. Stayed it long?

*Horatio:* While one with moderate haste might tell a hundred.

*Marcellus, Bernardo:* Longer, longer.

*Horatio:* Not when I saw 't.

*Hamlet:* His beard was grizzled—no? 245

*Horatio:* It was, as I have seen it in his life,
A sable silvered.

*Hamlet:*                          I will watch tonight.
Perchance 'twill walk again.

*Horatio:*                                  I warrant it will.

*Hamlet:* If it assume my noble father's person,
I'll speak to it though hell itself should gape 250
And bid me hold my peace. I pray you all,
If you have hitherto concealed this sight,
Let it be tenable in your silence still,
And whatsoever else shall hap tonight,
Give it an understanding but no tongue. 255
I will requite your loves. So, fare you well.
Upon the platform twixt eleven and twelve
I'll visit you.

*All:*                          Our duty to your honor.

---

232 *beaver* visor on the helmet    233 *What* how    242 *tell* count    245 *grizzled* gray
247 *sable silvered* black mixed with white    248 *warrant* assure you    253 *tenable* held

*Hamlet:* Your loves, as mine to you. Farewell.

*Exeunt [all but Hamlet].*

My father's spirit in arms! All is not well.                                      260
I doubt some foul play. Would the night were come!
Till then sit still, my soul. Foul deeds will rise,
Though all the earth o'erwhelm them, to men's eyes.

*Exit.*


## Scene III [Polonius' Chambers.]

*Enter Laertes and Ophelia, his sister.*

*Laertes:* My necessaries are embarked. Farewell.
        And, sister, as the winds give benefit
        And convoy is assistant, do not sleep
        But let me hear from you.
*Ophelia:*                          Do you doubt that?
*Laertes:* For Hamlet, and the trifling of his favor,                              5
        Hold it a fashion and a toy in blood,
        A violet in the youth of primy nature,
        Forward, not permanent, sweet, not lasting,
        The perfume and suppliance of a minute—
        No more.
*Ophelia:*        No more but so?
*Laertes:*                          Think it no more.                              10
        For nature crescent does not grow alone
        In thews and bulk, but as this temple waxes
        The inward service of the mind and soul
        Grows wide withal. Perhaps he loves you now,
        And now no soil nor cautel doth besmirch                                   15
        The virtue of his will; but you must fear,
        His greatness weighed, his will is not his own.
        For he himself is subject to his birth.
        He may not, as unvalued persons do,
        Carve for himself, for on his choice depends                              20
        The safety and health of this whole state,
        And therefore must his choice be circumscribed

---

261 *doubt* suspect    3 *convoy is assistant* means of conveyance are available    6 *toy in blood* passing amorous fancy    7 *primy* in its prime, springtime    8 *Forward* precocious    9 *suppliance* supply, filler    11 *crescent* growing, waxing    12 *thews* bodily strength.    *temple* i.e., body    14
*Grows wide withal* grows along with it    15 *soil* blemish.    *cautel* deceit    16 *will* desire    17
*His greatness weighed* if you take into account his high position    20 *Carve* i.e., choose

Unto the voice and yielding of that body
Whereof he is the head. Then if he says he loves you,
It fits your wisdom so far to believe it                                25
As he in his particular act and place
May give his saying deed, which is no further
Than the main voice of Denmark goes withal.
Then weigh what loss your honor may sustain
If with too credent ear you list his songs,                             30
Or lose your heart, or your chaste treasure open
To his unmastered importunity.
Fear it, Ophelia, fear it, my dear sister,
And keep you in the rear of your affection,
Out of the shot and danger of desire.                                   35
The chariest maid is prodigal enough
If she unmask her beauty to the moon.
Virtue itself scapes not calumnious strokes.
The canker galls the infants of the spring
Too oft before their buttons be disclosed,                              40
And in the morn and liquid dew of youth
Contagious blastments are most imminent.
Be wary then; best safety lies in fear.
Youth to itself rebels, though none else near.

*Ophelia:* I shall the effect of this good lesson keep                  45
As watchman to my heart. But, good my brother,
Do not, as some ungracious pastors do,
Show me the steep and thorny way to heaven,
Whiles like a puffed and reckless libertine
Himself the primrose path of dalliance treads,                         50
And recks not his own rede.

*Enter Polonius.*

*Laertes:*                              O, fear me not.
I stay too long. But here my father comes.
A double blessing is a double grace;
Occasion smiles upon a second leave.

*Polonius:* Yet here, Laertes? Aboard, aboard, for shame!     55
　　The wind sits in the shoulder of your sail,
　　And you are stayed for. There—my blessing with thee!
　　And these few precepts in thy memory
　　Look thou character. Give thy thoughts no tongue,
　　Nor any unproportioned thought his act.     60
　　Be thou familiar, but by no means vulgar.──
　　Those friends thou hast, and their adoption tried,
　　Grapple them unto thy soul with hoops of steel,
　　But do not dull thy palm with entertainment
　　Of each new-hatched, unfledged courage. Beware     65
　　Of entrance to a quarrel, but being in,
　　Bear 't that th' opposèd may beware of thee.
　　Give every man thy ear, but few thy voice;
　　Take each man's censure, but reserve thy judgment.
　　Costly thy habit as thy purse can buy,     70
　　But not expressed in fancy; rich, not gaudy,
　　For the apparel oft proclaims the man,
　　And they in France of the best rank and station
　　Are of a most select and generous chief in that.
　　Neither a borrower nor a lender be,     75
　　For loan oft loses both itself and friend,
　　And borrowing dulleth edge of husbandry.
←──This above all: to thine own self be true,
　　And it must follow, as the night the day,
　　Thou canst not then be false to any man.     80
　　Farewell. My blessing season this in thee!
*Laertes:* Most humbly do I take my leave, my lord.
*Polonius:* The time invests you. Go, your servants tend.
*Laertes:* Farewell, Ophelia, and remember well
　　What I have said to you.     85
*Ophelia:* 'Tis in my memory locked,
　　And you yourself shall keep the key of it.
*Laertes:* Farewell.　　　　　　　　　　　　　　*Exit Laertes.*
*Polonius:* What is 't, Ophelia, he hath said to you?
*Ophelia:* So please you, something touching the Lord Hamlet.     90
*Polonius:* Marry, well bethought.

---

59 *Look* be sure that.　　*character* inscribe　　60 *unproportioned* badly calculated, intemperate. *his* its　　61 *familiar* sociable.　　*vulgar* common　　62 *and their adoption tried* and also their suitability for adoption as friends having been tested　　64 *dull thy palm* i.e., shake hands so often as to make the gesture meaningless　　65 *courage* young man of spirit　　67 *Bear 't that* manage it so that 69 *censure* opinion, judgment　　70 *habit* clothing　　71 *fancy* excessive ornament, decadent fashion　　74 *Are . . . that* are of a most refined and well-bred preeminence in choosing what to wear 77 *husbandry* thrift　　81 *season* mature　　83 *invests* besieges, presses upon.　　*tend* attend, wait 91 *Marry* i.e., by the Virgin Mary. (A mild oath.)

'Tis told me he hath very oft of late
Given private time to you, and you yourself
Have of your audience been most free and bounteous.
If it be so—as so 'tis put on me,                    95
And that in way of caution—I must tell you
You do not understand yourself so clearly
As it behooves my daughter and your honor.
What is between you? Give me up the truth.

_Ophelia:_ He hath, my lord, of late made many tenders    100
Of his affection to me.

_Polonius:_ Affection? Pooh! You speak like a green girl,
Unsifted in such perilous circumstance.
Do you believe his tenders, as you call them?—

_Ophelia:_ I do not know, my lord, what I should think.    105

_Polonius:_ Marry, I will teach you. Think yourself a baby
That you have ta'en these tenders for true pay
Which are not sterling. Tender yourself more dearly,
Or—not to crack the wind of the poor phrase,
Running it thus—you'll tender me a fool.              110

_Ophelia:_ My lord, he hath importuned me with love
In honorable fashion.

_Polonius:_ Ay, fashion you may call it. Go to, go to.

_Ophelia:_ And hath given countenance to his speech, my lord,
With almost all the holy vows of heaven.              115

_Polonius:_ Ay, springes to catch woodcocks. I do know,
When the blood burns, how prodigal the soul
Lends the tongue vows. These blazes, daughter,
Giving more light than heat, extinct in both
Even in their promise as it is a-making,              120
You must not take for fire. From this time
Be something scanter of your maiden presence.
Set your entreatments at a higher rate
Than a command to parle. For Lord Hamlet,
Believe so much in him that he is young,              125

95 _put on_ impressed on, told to    98 _behooves_ befits    100 _tenders_ offers    103 _Unsifted_ i.e.,
untried    108 _sterling_ legal currency.    _Tender_ hold, look after, offer    109 _crack the wind_ i.e.,
run it until it is broken-winded    110 _tender me a fool_ (1) show yourself to me as a fool (2) show me
up as a fool (3) present me with a grandchild. (_Fool_ was a term of endearment for a child.)    113
_fashion_ mere form, pretense.    _Go to_ (An expression of impatience.)    114 _countenance_ credit,
confirmation    116 _springes_ snares.    _woodcocks_ birds easily caught; here used to connote gullibil-
ity.    117 _prodigal_ prodigally    120 _it_ i.e., the promise    122 _something_ somewhat    123
_entreatments_ negotiations for surrender. (A military term.)    124 _parle_ discuss terms with the
enemy. (Polonius urges his daughter, in the metaphor of military language, not to meet with Hamlet
and consider giving in to him merely because he requests an interview.)    125 _so . . . him_ this
much concerning him

And with a larger tether may he walk
Than may be given you. In few, Ophelia,
Do not believe his vows, for they are brokers,
Not of that dye which their investments show,
But mere implorators of unholy suits,                                    130
Breathing like sanctified and pious bawds,
The better to beguile. This is for all:
I would not, in plain terms, from this time forth
Have you so slander any moment leisure
As to give words or talk with the Lord Hamlet.    *back to p. 1371*      135
Look to 't, I charge you. Come your ways.
*Ophelia:* I shall obey, my lord.                            *Exeunt.*

### Scene IV [*The Guard Platform.*]

*Enter Hamlet, Horatio, and Marcellus.*

*Hamlet:* The air bites shrewdly; it is very cold.
*Horatio:* It is a nipping and an eager air.
*Hamlet:* What hour now?
*Horatio:*                          I think it lacks of twelve.
*Marcellus:* No, it is struck.
*Horatio:*                          Indeed? I heard it not.
It then draws near the season                                              5
Wherein the spirit held his wont to walk.

*A flourish of trumpets, and two pieces go off [within].*

What does this mean, my lord?
*Hamlet:* The King doth wake tonight and takes his rouse,
Keeps wassail, and the swaggering upspring reels;
And as he drains his drafts of Rhenish down,                               10
The kettledrum and trumpet thus bray out
The triumph of his pledge.
*Horatio:*                          Is it a custom?
*Hamlet:* Ay, marry, is 't,
But to my mind, though I am native here
And to the manner born, it is a custom                                     15

---

127 *In few* briefly    128 *brokers* go-betweens, procurers    129 *dye* color or sort.    *investments* clothes. (The vows are not what they seem.)    130 *mere implorators* out and out solicitors    131 *Breathing* speaking    132 *for all* once for all, in sum    134 *slander* abuse, misuse.    *moment* moment's    136 *Come your ways* come along    1 *shrewdly* keenly, sharply    2 *eager* biting    3 *lacks of* is just short of    5 *season* time    6 *held his wont* was accustomed.    *s.d. pieces* i.e., of ordnance, cannon    8 *wake* stay awake and hold revel.    *takes his rouse* carouses    9 *wassail* carousal.    *upspring* wild German dance.    *reels* dances    10 *Rhenish* Rhine wine    12 *The triumph . . . pledge* i.e., his feat in draining the wine in a single draft    15 *manner* custom (of drinking)

More honored in the breach than the observance.
This heavy-headed revel east and west
Makes us traduced and taxed of other nations.
They clepe us drunkards, and with swinish phrase
Soil our addition; and indeed it takes                                    20
From our achievements, though performed at height,
The pith and marrow of our attribute.
So, oft it chances in particular men,
That for some vicious mole of nature in them,
As in their birth—wherein they are not guilty,                           25
Since nature cannot choose his origin—
By their o'ergrowth of some complexion,
Oft breaking down the pales and forts of reason,
Or by some habit that too much o'erleavens
The form of plausive manners, that these men,                            30
Carrying, I say, the stamp of one defect,
Being nature's livery or fortune's star,
His virtues else, be they as pure as grace,
As infinite as man may undergo,
Shall in the general censure take corruption                             35
From that particular fault. The dram of evil
Doth all the noble substance often dout
To his own scandal.

    *Enter Ghost.*

Horatio:                Look, my lord, it comes!
Hamlet: Angels and ministers of grace defend us!
Be thou a spirit of health or goblin damned,                             40
Bring with thee airs from heaven or blasts from hell,
Be thy intents wicked or charitable,
Thou com'st in such a questionable shape
That I will speak to thee. I'll call thee Hamlet,

16 *More . . . observance* better neglected than followed    17 *east and west* i.e., everywhere    18
*taxed of* censured by    19 *clepe* call.    *with swinish phrase* i.e., by calling us swine    20 *addition*
reputation    21 *at height* outstandingly    22 *The pith . . . attribute* the essence of the reputation
that others attribute to us    24 *for* on account of.    *mole of nature* natural blemish in one's con-
stitution    26 *his* its    27 *their o'ergrowth . . . complexion* the excessive growth in individuals of
some natural trait    28 *pales* palings, fences (as of a fortification)    29 *o'erleavens* induces a
change throughout (as yeast works in dough)    30 *plausive* pleasing    32 *nature's livery* sign of
one's servitude to nature.    *fortune's star* the destiny that chance brings    33 *His virtues else* i.e.,
the other qualities of *these men* (line 30)    34 *may undergo* can sustain    35 *general censure* general opinion that people have of him    36–38 *The dram . . . scandal* i.e., the small drop of evil blots
out or works against the noble substance of the whole and brings it into disrepute. To *dout* is to blot
out. (A famous crux.)    39 *ministers of grace* messengers of God    40 *Be thou* whether you are.
*spirit of health* good angel    41 *Bring* whether you bring    42 *Be thy intents* whether your intentions are    43 *questionable* inviting question

King, father, royal Dane. O, answer me!                            45
Let me not burst in ignorance, but tell
Why thy canonized bones, hearsèd in death,
Have burst their cerements; why the sepulcher
Wherein we saw thee quietly inurned
Hath oped his ponderous and marble jaws                            50
To cast thee up again. What may this mean,
That thou, dead corpse, again in complete steel,
Revisits thus the glimpses of the moon,
Making night hideous, and we fools of nature
So horridly to shake our disposition                               55
With thoughts beyond the reaches of our souls?
Say, why is this? Wherefore? What should we do?

                              *[The Ghost] beckons [Hamlet].*

*Horatio:* It beckons you to go away with it,
    As if it some impartment did desire
    To you alone.
*Marcellus:*       Look with what courteous action           60
    It wafts you to a more removèd ground.
    But do not go with it.
*Horatio:*          No, by no means.
*Hamlet:* It will not speak. Then I will follow it.
*Horatio:* Do not, my lord!
*Hamlet:*        Why, what should be the fear?
    I do not set my life at a pin's fee,                          65
    And for my soul, what can it do to that,
    Being a thing immortal as itself?
    It waves me forth again. I'll follow it.
*Horatio:* What if it tempt you toward the flood, my lord,
    Or to the dreadful summit of the cliff                        70
    That beetles o'er his base into the sea,
    And there assume some other horrible form
    Which might deprive your sovereignty of reason
    And draw you into madness? Think of it.
    The very place puts toys of desperation,                      75
    Without more motive, into every brain

---

47 *canonized* buried according to the canons of the church.    *hearsèd* coffined    48 *cerements* grave clothes    49 *inurned* entombed    52 *complete steel* full armor    53 *glimpses of the moon* pale and uncertain moonlight    54 *fools of nature* mere men, limited to natural knowledge and subject to nature    55 *So . . . disposition* to distress our mental composure so violently    59 *impartment* communication    65 *fee* value    69 *flood* sea    71 *beetles o'er* overhangs threateningly (like bushy eyebrows.)    *his* its    73 *deprive . . . reason* take away the rule of reason over your mind    75 *toys of desperation* fancies of desperate acts, i.e., suicide

That looks so many fathoms to the sea
And hears it roar beneath.
*Hamlet:* It wafts me still.—Go on, I'll follow thee.
*Marcellus:* You shall not go, my lord.                    [*They try to stop him.*]
*Hamlet:*                    Hold off your hands!                                    80
*Horatio:* Be ruled. You shall not go.
*Hamlet:*                    My fate cries out,
And makes each petty artery in this body
As hardy as the Nemean lion's nerve.
Still am I called. Unhand me, gentlemen.
By heaven, I'll make a ghost of him that lets me!                    85
I say, away!—Go on, I'll follow thee.

*Exeunt Ghost and Hamlet.*

*Horatio:* He waxes desperate with imagination.
*Marcellus:* Let's follow. 'Tis not fit thus to obey him.
*Horatio:* Have after. To what issue will this come?
*Marcellus:* Something is rotten in the state of Denmark.                    90
*Horatio:* Heaven will direct it.
*Marcellus:*                    Nay, let's follow him.                    *Exeunt.*

## Scene V [The Battlements of the Castle.]

*Enter Ghost and Hamlet.*

*Hamlet:* Whither wilt thou lead me? Speak. I'll go no further.
*Ghost:* Mark me.
*Hamlet:*                    I will.
*Ghost:*                    My hour is almost come,
When I to sulfurous and tormenting flames
Must render up myself.
*Hamlet:*                    Alas, poor ghost!
*Ghost:* Pity me not, but lend thy serious hearing                    5
To what I shall unfold.
*Hamlet:* Speak. I am bound to hear.
*Ghost:* So art thou to revenge, when thou shalt hear.
*Hamlet:* What?
*Ghost:* I am thy father's spirit,                    10
Doomed for a certain term to walk the night,

81 *My fate cries out* my destiny summons me    82 *petty* weak.    *artery* (through which the vital spirits were thought to have been conveyed)    83 *Nemean lion* one of the monsters slain by Hercules in his twelve labors.    *nerve* sinew    85 *lets* hinders    89 *Have after* let's go after him. *issue* outcome    91 *it* i.e., the outcome    7 *bound* (1) ready (2) obligated by duty and fate. (The Ghost, in line 8, answers in the second sense.)

And for the day confined to fast in fires,
Till the foul crimes done in my days of nature
Are burnt and purged away. But that I am forbid
To tell the secrets of my prison house,                                        15
I could a tale unfold whose lightest word
Would harrow up thy soul, freeze thy young blood,
Make thy two eyes like stars start from their spheres,
Thy knotted and combinèd locks to part,
And each particular hair to stand on end                                       20
Like quills upon the fretful porcupine.
But this eternal blazon must not be
To ears of flesh and blood. List, list, O, list!
If thou didst ever thy dear father love—
*Hamlet:* O God!                                                               25
*Ghost:* Revenge his foul and most unnatural murder.
*Hamlet:* Murder?
*Ghost:* Murder most foul, as in the best it is,
But this most foul, strange, and unnatural.
*Hamlet:* Haste me to know 't, that I, with wings as swift                     30
As meditation or the thoughts of love,
May sweep to my revenge.
*Ghost:*                                   I find thee apt;
And duller shouldst thou be than the fat weed
That roots itself in ease on Lethe wharf,
Wouldst thou not stir in this. Now, Hamlet, hear.                              35
'Tis given out that, sleeping in my orchard,
A serpent stung me. So the whole ear of Denmark
Is by a forgèd process of my death
Rankly abused. But know, thou noble youth,
The serpent that did sting thy father's life                                   40
Now wears his crown.
*Hamlet:* O, my prophetic soul! My uncle!
*Ghost:* Ay, that incestuous, that adulterate beast,
With witchcraft of his wit, with traitorous gifts—
O wicked wit and gifts, that have the power                                    45
So to seduce!—won to his shameful lust
The will of my most seeming-virtuous queen.

---

12 *fast* do penance by fasting    13 *crimes* sins.    *of nature* as a mortal    14 *But that* were it not
that    17 *harrow up* lacerate, tear    18 *spheres* i.e., eye-sockets, here compared to the orbits or
transparent revolving spheres in which, according to Ptolemaic astronomy, the heavenly bodies were
fixed    19 *knotted . . . locks* hair neatly arranged and confined    22 *eternal blazon* revelation of
the secrets of eternity    28 *in the best* even at best    33 *shouldst thou be* you would have to be.
*fat* torpid, lethargic    34 *Lethe* the river of forgetfulness in Hades    36 *orchard* garden    38
*forgèd process* falsified account    39 *abused* deceived    43 *adulterate* adulterous    44 *gifts* (1) talents (2) presents

O Hamlet, what a falling off was there!
From me, whose love was of that dignity
That it went hand in hand even with the vow                          50
I made to her in marriage, and to decline
Upon a wretch whose natural gifts were poor
To those of mine!
But virtue, as it never will be moved,
Though lewdness court it in a shape of heaven,                       55
So lust, though to a radiant angel linked,
Will sate itself in a celestial bed
And prey on garbage.
But soft, methinks I scent the morning air. ◄━
Brief let me be. Sleeping within my orchard,                         60
My custom always of the afternoon,
Upon my secure hour thy uncle stole,
With juice of cursèd hebona in a vial,
And in the porches of my ears did pour
The leprous distillment, whose effect                               65
Holds such an enmity with blood of man
That swift as quicksilver it courses through
The natural gates and alleys of the body,
And with a sudden vigor it doth posset
And curd, like eager droppings into milk,                           70
The thin and wholesome blood. So did it mine,
And a most instant tetter barked about,
Most lazar-like, with vile and loathsome crust,
All my smooth body.
Thus was I, sleeping, by a brother's hand  ◄━                        75
Of life, of crown, of queen at once dispatched,
Cut off even in the blossom of my sin,
Unhouseled, disappointed, unaneled,
No reckoning made, but sent to my account
With all my imperfections on my head.                               80
O, horrible! O, horrible, most horrible!
If thou hast nature in thee, bear it not.

50 *even with the vow* with the very vow    53 *To* compared to    54 *virtue, as it* as virtue    55
*shape of heaven* heavenly form    57 *sate . . . bed* cease to find sexual pleasure in a virtuously lawful
marriage    62 *secure* confident, unsuspicious    63 *hebona* a poison. (The word seems to be a form
of *ebony*, though it is thought perhaps to be related to *henbane*, a poison, or to *ebenus*, "yew.")    64
*porches of my ears* ears as a porch or entrance of the body    65 *leprous distillment* distillation causing
leprosylike disfigurement    69 *posset* coagulate, curdle    70 *eager* sour, acid    72 *tetter* eruption
of scabs.    *barked* covered with a rough covering, like bark on a tree    73 *lazar-like* leperlike
76 *dispatched* suddenly deprived    78 *Unhouseled* without having received the Sacrament.    *disappointed* unready (spiritually) for the last journey.    *unaneled* without having received extreme
unction    79 *reckoning* settling of accounts    82 *nature* i.e., the promptings of a son

Let not the royal bed of Denmark be
A couch for luxury and damnèd incest.
But, howsoever thou pursues this act,                                    85
Taint not thy mind nor let thy soul contrive
Against thy mother aught. Leave her to heaven
And to those thorns that in her bosom lodge,
To prick and sting her. Fare thee well at once.
The glowworm shows the matin to be near,                                 90
And 'gins to pale his uneffectual fire.
Adieu, adieu, adieu! Remember me.                           [*Exit.*]
*Hamlet:* O all you host of heaven! O earth! What else?
And shall I couple hell? O, fie! Hold, hold, my heart,
And you, my sinews, grow not instant old,                                95
But bear me stiffly up. Remember thee?
Ay, thou poor ghost, whiles memory holds a seat
In this distracted globe. Remember thee?
Yea, from the table of my memory
I'll wipe away all trivial fond records,                                 100
All saws of books, all forms, all pressures past
That youth and observation copied there,
And thy commandment all alone shall live
Within the book and volume of my brain,
Unmixed with baser matter. Yes, by heaven!                               105
O most pernicious woman!
O villain, villain, smiling, damnèd villain!
My tables—meet it is I set it down
That one may smile, and smile, and be a villain.
At least I am sure it may be so in Denmark.                              110

                                                      [*Writing.*]

So, uncle, there you are. Now to my word:
It is "Adieu, adieu! Remember me."
I have sworn 't.

*Enter Horatio and Marcellus.*

*Horatio:* My lord, my lord!
*Marcellus:* Lord Hamlet!                                                115
*Horatio:* Heavens secure him!
*Hamlet:* So be it.

84 *luxury* lechery    90 *matin* morning    91 *his* its    94 *couple* add.    *Hold* hold together
95 *instant* instantly    98 *globe* (1) head (2) world    99 *table* tablet, slate    100 *fond* foolish
101 *saws* wise sayings.    *forms* shapes or images copied onto the slate; general ideas.    *pressures*
impressions stamped    108 *tables* writing tablets.    *meet it is* it is fitting    111 *there you are* i.e.,
there, I've written that down against you    116 *secure him* keep him safe

*Marcellus:* Hilo, ho, ho, my lord!

*Hamlet:* Hillo, ho, ho, boy! Come, bird, come.

*Marcellus:* How is 't, my noble lord? 120

*Horatio:* What news, my lord?

*Hamlet:* O, wonderful!

*Horatio:* Good my lord, tell it.

*Hamlet:* No, you will reveal it.

*Horatio:* Not I, my lord, by heaven. 125

*Marcellus:* Nor I, my lord.

*Hamlet:* How say you, then, would heart of man once think it?
> But you'll be secret?

*Horatio, Marcellus:*     Ay, by heaven, my lord.

*Hamlet:* There's never a villain dwelling in all Denmark
> But he's an arrant knave. 130

*Horatio:* There needs no ghost, my lord, come from the grave
> To tell us this.

*Hamlet:*          Why, right, you are in the right.
> And so, without more circumstance at all,
> I hold it fit that we shake hands and part,
> You as your business and desire shall point you— 135
> For every man hath business and desire,
> Such as it is—and for my own poor part,
> Look you, I'll go pray.

*Horatio:* These are but wild and whirling words, my lord.

*Hamlet:* I am sorry they offend you, heartily; 140
> Yes, faith, heartily.

*Horatio:*                There's no offense, my lord.

*Hamlet:* Yes, by Saint Patrick, but there is, Horatio,
> And much offense too. Touching this vision here,
> It is an honest ghost, that let me tell you.
> For your desire to know what is between us, 145
> O'ermaster 't as you may. And now, good friends,
> As you are friends, scholars, and soldiers,
> Give me one poor request.

*Horatio:* What is 't, my lord? We will.

*Hamlet:* Never make known what you have seen tonight. 150

*Horatio, Marcellus:* My lord, we will not.

*Hamlet:* Nay, but swear 't.

---

119 *Hillo . . . come* (A falconer's call to a hawk in air. Hamlet mocks the hallooing as though it were a part of hawking.)     127 *once* ever     130 *arrant* thoroughgoing     133 *circumstance* ceremony, elaboration     142 *Saint Patrick* (The keeper of Purgatory and patron saint of all blunders and confusion.)     143 *offense* (Hamlet deliberately changes Horatio's "no offense taken" to "an offense against all decency.")     144 *an honest ghost* i.e., a real ghost and not an evil spirit

*Horatio:* In faith, my lord, not I.

*Marcellus:* Nor I, my lord, in faith.

*Hamlet:* Upon my sword. [*He holds out his sword.*] 155

*Marcellus:* We have sworn, my lord, already.

*Hamlet:* Indeed, upon my sword, indeed.

*Ghost* (*cries under the stage*): Swear.

*Hamlet:* Ha, ha, boy, sayst thou so? Art thou there, truepenny?
　　　Come on, you hear this fellow in the cellarage. 160
　　　Consent to swear.

*Horatio:*　　　　　Propose the oath, my lord.

*Hamlet:* Never to speak of this that you have seen,
　　　Swear by my sword.

*Ghost* [*beneath*]: Swear. [*They swear.*]

*Hamlet:* Hic et ubique? Then we'll shift our ground. 165

　　　　　　　　　　　　　[*He moves to another spot.*]

　　　Come hither, gentlemen,
　　　And lay your hands again upon my sword.
　　　Swear by my sword
　　　Never to speak of this that you have heard.

*Ghost* [*beneath*]: Swear by his sword. [*They swear.*] 170

*Hamlet:* Well said, old mole. Canst work i' th' earth so fast?
　　　A worthy pioner!—Once more remove, good friends.

　　　　　　　　　　　　　　[*He moves again.*]

*Horatio:* O day and night, but this is wondrous strange!

*Hamlet:* And therefore as a stranger give it welcome.
　　　There are more things in heaven and earth, Horatio, 175
　　　Than are dreamt of in your philosophy.
　　　But come;
　　　Here, as before, never, so help you mercy,
　　　How strange or odd soe'er I bear myself—
　　　As I perchance hereafter shall think meet 180
　　　To put an antic disposition on—
　　　That you, at such times seeing me, never shall,
　　　With arms encumbered thus, or this headshake,

---

153 *In faith . . . I* i.e., I swear not to tell what I have seen. (Horatio is not refusing to swear.)　155 *sword* i.e., the hilt in the form of a cross　156 *We . . . already* i.e., we swore *in faith*　159 *truepenny* honest old fellow　164 s.d. *They swear* (Seemingly they swear here, and at lines 170 and 190, as they lay their hands on Hamlet's sword. Triple oaths would have particular force; these three oaths deal with what they have seen, what they have heard, and what they promise about Hamlet's *antic disposition*.)　165 *Hic et ubique* here and everywhere. (Latin.)　172 *pioner* foot soldier assigned to dig tunnels and excavations　174 *as a stranger* i.e., needing your hospitality　176 *your philosophy* this subject called "natural philosophy" or "science" that people talk about　178 *so help you mercy* as you hope for God's mercy when you are judged　181 *antic* fantastic　183 *encumbered* folded

Or by pronouncing of some doubtful phrase
As "Well, we know," or "We could, an if we would,"                          185
Or "If we list to speak," or "There be, an if they might,"
Or such ambiguous giving out, to note
That you know aught of me—this do swear,
So grace and mercy at your most need help you.
*Ghost [beneath]:* Swear.                                    [*They swear.*]  190
*Hamlet:* Rest, rest, perturbèd spirit! So, gentlemen,
With all my love I do commend me to you;
And what so poor a man as Hamlet is
May do t' express his love and friending to you,
God willing, shall not lack. Let us go in together,                         195
And still your fingers on your lips, I pray.
The time is out of joint. O cursèd spite
That ever I was born to set it right!

                                        [*They wait for him to leave first.*]

Nay, come, let's go together.                                *Exeunt.*

# ACT II

### Scene I [*Polonius' Chambers.*]

*Enter Old Polonius With His Man [Reynaldo].*

*Polonius:* Give him this money and these notes, Reynaldo.

                                        [*He gives money and papers.*]

*Reynaldo:* I will, my lord.
*Polonius:* You shall do marvelous wisely, good Reynaldo,
Before you visit him, to make inquire
Of his behavior.
*Reynaldo:*          My lord, I did intend it.                               5
*Polonius:* Marry, well said, very well said. Look you, sir,
Inquire me first what Danskers are in Paris,
And how, and who, what means, and where they keep,
What company, at what expense; and finding
By this encompassment and drift of question                                 10

185 *an if* if     186 *list* wished.     *There . . . might* i.e., there are people here (we, in fact) who could tell news if we were at liberty to do so     187 *giving out* intimation.     *note* draw attention to the fact     188 *aught* i.e., something secret     192 *do . . . you* entrust myself to you     194 *friending* friendliness     195 *lack* be lacking     196 *still* always     197 *The time* the state of affairs.     *spite* i.e., the spite of Fortune     199 *let's go together* (Probably they wait for him to leave first, but he refuses this ceremoniousness.)     3 *marvelous* marvelously     4 *inquire* inquiry     7 *Danskers* Danes     8 *what means* what wealth (they have).     *keep* dwell     10 *encompassment* roundabout talking.     *drift* gradual approach or course

That they do know my son, come you more nearer
Than your particular demands will touch it.
Take you, as 'twere, some distant knowledge of him,
As thus, "I know his father and his friends,
And in part him." Do you mark this, Reynaldo?            15
*Reynaldo:* Ay, very well, my lord.
*Polonius:* "And in part him, but," you may say, "not well.
But if 't be he I mean, he's very wild,
Addicted so and so," and there put on him
What forgeries you please—marry, none so rank           20
As may dishonor him, take heed of that,
But, sir, such wanton, wild, and usual slips
As are companions noted and most known
To youth and liberty.
*Reynaldo:* As gaming, my lord.                          25
*Polonius:* Ay, or drinking, fencing, swearing,
Quarreling, drabbing—you may go so far.
*Reynaldo:* My lord, that would dishonor him.
*Polonius:* Faith, no, as you may season it in the charge.
You must not put another scandal on him                 30
That he is open to incontinency;
That's not my meaning. But breathe his faults so quaintly
That they may seem the taints of liberty,
The flash and outbreak of a fiery mind,
A savageness in unreclaimèd blood,                      35
Of general assault.
*Reynaldo:* But, my good lord—
*Polonius:* Wherefore should you do this?
*Reynaldo:* Ay, my lord, I would know that.
*Polonius:* Marry, sir, here's my drift,                40
And I believe it is a fetch of warrant.
You laying these slight sullies on my son,
As 'twere a thing a little soiled wi' the working,
Mark you,
Your party in converse, him you would sound,            45
Having ever seen in the prenominate crimes

---

11–12 *come . . . it* you will find out more this way than by asking pointed questions (*particular demands*)   13 *Take you* assume, pretend   19 *put on* impute to   20 *forgeries* invented tales. *rank* gross   22 *wanton* sportive, unrestrained   27 *drabbing* whoring   29 *season* temper, soften   31 *incontinency* habitual sexual excess   32 *quaintly* artfully, subtly   33 *taints of liberty* faults resulting from free living   35–36 *A savageness . . . assault* a wildness in untamed youth that assails all indiscriminately   41 *fetch of warrant* legitimate trick   43 *soiled wi' the working* soiled by handling while it is being made, i.e., by involvement in the ways of the world   45 *converse* conversation.   *sound* i.e., sound out   46 *Having ever* if he has ever.   *prenominate crimes* before-mentioned offenses

The youth you breathe of guilty, be assured
He closes with you in this consequence:
"Good sir," or so, or "friend," or "gentleman,"
According to the phrase or the addition                           50
Of man and country.
*Reynaldo:*                    Very good, my lord.
*Polonius:* And then, sir, does 'a this—'a does—
        what was I about to say? By the Mass, I was
        about to say something. Where did I leave?
*Reynaldo:* At "closes in the consequence."                       55
*Polonius:* At "closes in the consequence," ay, marry.
        He closes thus: "I know the gentleman,
        I saw him yesterday," or "th' other day,"
        Or then, or then, with such or such, "and as you say,
        There was 'a gaming," "there o'ertook in 's rouse,"       60
        "There falling out at tennis," or perchance
        "I saw him enter such a house of sale,"
        Videlicet a brothel, or so forth. See you now,
        Your bait of falsehood takes this carp of truth;
        And thus do we of wisdom and of reach,                    65
        With windlasses and with assays of bias,
        By indirections find directions out.
        So by my former lecture and advice
        Shall you my son. You have me, have you not?
*Reynaldo:* My lord, I have.
*Polonius:*                   God b' wi' ye; fare ye well.         70
*Reynaldo:* Good my lord.
*Polonius:* Observe his inclination in yourself.
*Reynaldo:* I shall, my lord.
*Polonius:* And let him ply his music.
*Reynaldo:* Well, my lord.                                        75
*Polonius:* Farewell.                                    *Exit Reynaldo.*

        *Enter Ophelia.*

        How now, Ophelia, what's the matter?
*Ophelia:* O my lord, my lord, I have been so affrighted!
*Polonius:* With what, i' the name of God?
*Ophelia:* My lord, as I was sewing in my closet,

---

47 *breathe* speak    48 *closes . . . consequence* takes you into his confidence in some fashion, as follows    50 *addition* title    60 *o'ertook in 's rouse* overcome by drink    61 *falling out* quarreling
63 *Videlicet* namely    64 *carp* a fish    65 *reach* capacity, ability    66 *windlasses* i.e., circuitous
paths. (Literally, circuits made to head off the game in hunting.)    *assays of bias* attempts through
indirection (like the curving path of the bowling ball, which is biased or weighted to one side)
67 *directions* i.e., the way things really are    69 *have* understand    70 *b' wi'* be with    72 *in
yourself* in your own person (as well as by asking questions)    79 *closet* private chamber

Lord Hamlet, with his doublet all unbraced,                                    80
No hat upon his head, his stockings fouled,
Ungartered, and down-gyvèd to his ankle,
Pale as his shirt, his knees knocking each other,
And with a look so piteous in purport
As if he had been loosèd out of hell                                          85
To speak of horrors—he comes before me.

*Polonius:* Mad for thy love?

*Ophelia:*                    My lord, I do not know,
    But truly I do fear it.

*Polonius:*                  What said he?

*Ophelia:* He took me by the wrist and held me hard.
    Then goes he to the length of all his arm,                                90
    And, with his other hand thus o'er his brow
    He falls to such perusal of my face
    As 'a would draw it. Long stayed he so.
    At last, a little shaking of mine arm
    And thrice his head thus waving up and down,                             95
    He raised a sigh so piteous and profound
    As it did seem to shatter all his bulk
    And end his being. That done, he lets me go,
    And with his head over his shoulder turned
    He seemed to find his way without his eyes,                              100
    For out o' doors he went without their helps,
    And to the last bended their light on me.

*Polonius:* Come, go with me. I will go seek the King.
    This is the very ecstasy of love,
    Whose violent property fordoes itself                                    105
    And leads the will to desperate undertakings
    As oft as any passion under heaven
    That does afflict our natures. I am sorry.
    What, have you given him any hard words of late?

*Ophelia:* No, my good lord, but as you did command                         110
    I did repel his letters and denied
    His access to me.

*Polonius:*                  That hath made him mad.
    I am sorry that with better heed and judgment
    I had not quoted him. I feared he did but trifle
    And meant to wrack thee. But beshrew my jealousy!                        115
    By heaven, it is as proper to our age

---

80 *doublet* close-fitting jacket.     *unbraced* unfastened     82 *down-gyvèd* fallen to the ankles (like
gyves or fetters)     84 *in purport* in what it expressed     93 *As* as if (also in line 97)     97 *bulk*
body     104 *ecstasy* madness     105 *property* nature.     *fordoes* destroys     114 *quoted* observed
115 *wrack* ruin, seduce.     *beshrew my jealousy* a plague upon my suspicious nature     116 *proper . .
. age* characteristic of us (old) men

To cast beyond ourselves in our opinions
As it is common for the younger sort
To lack discretion. Come, go we to the King.
This must be known, which, being kept close, might move           120
More grief to hide than hate to utter love.
Come.                                                                                    *Exeunt.*

## Scene II [The Castle.]

*Flourish. Enter King and Queen, Rosencrantz, and Guildenstern [with others].*

*King:* Welcome, dear Rosencrantz and Guildenstern.
Moreover that we much did long to see you,
The need we have to use you did provoke
Our hasty sending. Something have you heard
Of Hamlet's transformation—so call it,                                    5
Sith nor th' exterior nor the inward man
Resembles that it was. What it should be,
More than his father's death, that thus hath put him
So much from th' understanding of himself,
I cannot dream of. I entreat you both                                       10
That, being of so young days brought up with him,
And sith so neighbored to his youth and havior,
That you vouchsafe your rest here in our court
Some little time, so by your companies
To draw him on to pleasures, and to gather                             15
So much as from occasion you may glean,
Whether aught to us unknown afflicts him thus
That, opened, lies within our remedy.
*Queen:* Good gentlemen, he hath much talked of you,
And sure I am two men there is not living                               20
To whom he more adheres. If it will please you
To show us so much gentry and good will
As to expend your time with us awhile
For the supply and profit of our hope,
Your visitation shall receive such thanks                                25
As fits a king's remembrance.

---

117 *cast beyond* overshoot, miscalculate. (A metaphor from hunting.)      120 *known* made known
(to the King).      *close* secret      120–121 *might . . . love* i.e., might cause more grief (because of
what Hamlet might do) by hiding the knowledge of Hamlet's strange behavior to Ophelia than
unpleasantness by telling it      2 *Moreover that* besides the fact that      6 *Sith nor* since neither
7 *that* what      11 *of . . . days* from such early youth      12 *And sith so neighbored to* and since you are
(or, and since that time you are) intimately acquainted with.      *havior* demeanor      13 *vouchsafe
your rest* please to stay      16 *occasion* opportunity      18 *opened* being revealed      22 *gentry* courtesy      24 *supply . . . hope* aid and furtherance of what we hope for      26 *As fits . . . remembrance*
as would be a fitting gift of a king who rewards true service

*Rosencrantz:*                         Both Your Majesties
     Might, by the sovereign power you have of us,
     Put your dread pleasures more into command
     Than to entreaty.
*Guildenstern:*              But we both obey,
     And here give up ourselves in the full bent                                    30
     To lay our service freely at your feet,
     To be commanded.
*King:* Thanks, Rosencrantz and gentle Guildenstern.
*Queen:* Thanks, Guildenstern and gentle Rosencrantz.
     And I beseech you instantly to visit                                           35
     My too much changèd son. Go, some of you,
     And bring these gentlemen where Hamlet is.
*Guildenstern:* Heavens make our presence and our practices
     Pleasant and helpful to him!
*Queen:*                         Ay, amen!

                    *Exeunt Rosencrantz and Guildenstern [with some attendants].*

     *Enter Polonius.*

*Polonius:* Th' ambassadors from Norway, my good lord,                             40
     Are joyfully returned.
*King:* Thou still hast been the father of good news.
*Polonius:* Have I, my lord? I assure my good liege
     I hold my duty, as I hold my soul,
     Both to my God and to my gracious king;                                        45
     And I do think, or else this brain of mine
     Hunts not the trail of policy so sure
     As it hath used to do, that I have found
     The very cause of Hamlet's lunacy.
*King:* O, speak of that! That do I long to hear.                                   50
*Polonius:* Give first admittance to th' ambassadors.
     My news shall be the fruit to that great feast.
*King:* Thyself do grace to them and bring them in.

                                                         *[Exit Polonius.]*

     He tells me, my dear Gertrude, he hath found
     The head and source of all your son's distemper.                              55
*Queen:* I doubt it is no other but the main,
     His father's death and our o'erhasty marriage.

---

27 *of* over      28 *dread* inspiring awe      30 *in . . . bent* to the utmost degree of our capacity. (An archery metaphor.)      38 *practices* doings      42 *still* always      44 *hold* maintain.      *as* as firmly as      47 *policy* sagacity      52 *fruit* dessert      53 *grace* honor (punning on *grace* said before a *feast*, line 52)      56 *doubt* fear, suspect.      *main* chief point, principal concern

*Enter Ambassadors [Voltimand and Cornelius, with Polonius].*

*King:* Well, we shall sift him.—Welcome, my good friends!
    Say, Voltimand, what from our brother Norway?
*Voltimand:* Most fair return of greetings and desires.          60
    Upon our first, he sent out to suppress
    His nephew's levies, which to him appeared
    To be a preparation 'gainst the Polack,
    But, better looked into, he truly found
    It was against Your Highness. Whereat grieved        65
    That so his sickness, age, and impotence
    Was falsely borne in hand, sends out arrests
    On Fortinbras, which he, in brief, obeys,
    Receives rebuke from Norway, and in fine
    Makes vow before his uncle never more        70
    To give th' assay of arms against Your Majesty.
    Whereon old Norway, overcome with joy,
    Gives him three thousand crowns in annual fee
    And his commission to employ those soldiers,
    So levied as before, against the Polack,        75
    With an entreaty, herein further shown,

                                    *[giving a paper]*

    That it might please you to give quiet pass
    Through your dominions for this enterprise
    On such regards of safety and allowance
    As therein are set down.
*King:*                    It likes us well,        80
    And at our more considered time we'll read,
    Answer, and think upon this business.
    Meantime we thank you for your well-took labor.
    Go to your rest; at night we'll feast together.
    Most welcome home!            *Exeunt Ambassadors.*
*Polonius:*            This business is well ended.        85
    My liege, and madam, to expostulate
    What majesty should be, what duty is,
    Why day is day, night night, and time is time,
    Were nothing but to waste night, day, and time.
    Therefore, since brevity is the soul of wit,        90

And tediousness the limbs and outward flourishes,
I will be brief. Your noble son is mad.
Mad call I it, for, to define true madness,
What is 't but to be nothing else but mad?
But let that go.

Queen:              More matter, with less art.             95

Polonius: Madam, I swear I use no art at all.
That he's mad, 'tis true; 'tis true 'tis pity,
And pity 'tis 'tis true—a foolish figure,
But farewell it, for I will use no art.
Mad let us grant him, then, and now remains            100
That we find out the cause of this effect,
Or rather say, the cause of this defect,
For this effect defective comes by cause.
Thus it remains, and the remainder thus.
Perpend.                                     105
I have a daughter—have while she is mine—
Who, in her duty and obedience, mark,
Hath given me this. Now gather and surmise.
[He reads the letter.] "To the celestial and my soul's idol, the most beautified
Ophelia"—That's an ill phrase, a vile phrase; "beautified" is a vile phrase. 110
But you shall hear. Thus:                             [He reads.]
"In her excellent white bosom, these, etc."

Queen: Came this from Hamlet to her?

Polonius: Good madam, stay awhile, I will be faithful.

                                                [He reads.]

        "Doubt thou the stars are fire,                     115
            Doubt that the sun doth move,
        Doubt truth to be a liar,
            But never doubt I love.

O dear Ophelia, I am ill at these numbers. I have not art to reckon my
groans. But that I love thee best, O most best, believe it. Adieu.
Thine evermore, most dear lady, whilst this machine is to him, Hamlet."   120
This in obedience hath my daughter shown me,
And, more above, hath his solicitings,
As they fell out by time, by means, and place,
All given to mine ear.

---

98 *figure* figure of speech    103 *For . . . cause* i.e., for this defective behavior, this madness, has a
cause    105 *Perpend* consider    108 *gather and surmise* draw your own conclusions    112 *In . . .
bosom* (The letter is poetically addressed to her heart.)    *these* i.e., the letter    114 *stay* wait.
*faithful* i.e., in reading the letter accurately    115 *Doubt* suspect    119 *ill . . . numbers* unskilled at
writing verses    *reckon* (1) count (2) number metrically, scan    121 *machine* i.e., body    123
*more above* moreover    124 *fell out* occurred.    *by* according to    125 *given . . . ear* i.e., told
me about

*King*: But how hath she                            125
    Received his love?
*Polonius*:                 What do you think of me?
*King*: As of a man faithful and honorable.
*Polonius*: I would fain prove so. But what might you think,
    When I had seen this hot love on the wing—
    As I perceived it, I must tell you that,                 130
    Before my daughter told me—what might you,
    Or my dear Majesty your queen here, think,
    If I had played the desk or table book,
    Or given my heart a winking, mute and dumb,
    Or looked upon this love with idle sight?             135
    What might you think? No, I went round to work,
    And my young mistress thus I did bespeak:
    "Lord Hamlet is a prince out of thy star;
    This must not be." And then I prescripts gave her,
    That she should lock herself from his resort,           140
    Admit no messengers, receive no tokens.
    Which done, she took the fruits of my advice;
    And he, repellèd—a short tale to make—
  Fell into a sadness, then into a fast,
    Thence to a watch, thence into a weakness,          145
    Thence to a lightness, and by this declension
    Into the madness wherein now he raves,
    And all we mourn for.
*King [to the Queen]*:         Do you think 'tis this?
*Queen*: It may be, very like.
*Polonius*: Hath there been such a time—I would fain know that—     150
    That I have positively said " 'Tis so,"
    When it proved otherwise?
*King*:                 Not that I know.
*Polonius*: Take this from this, if this be otherwise.
    If circumstances lead me, I will find
    Where truth is hid, though it were hid indeed         155
    Within the center.
*King*:            How may we try it further?
*Polonius*: You know sometimes he walks four hours together
    Here in the lobby.

---

128 *fain* gladly     133 *played . . . table book* i.e., remained shut up, concealing the information
134 *given . . . winking* closed the eyes of my heart to this     135 *with idle sight* complacently or
incomprehendingly     136 *round* roundly, plainly     137 *bespeak* address     138 *out of thy star*
above your sphere, position     139 *prescripts* orders     140 *his resort* his visits     145 *watch* state of
sleeplessness     146 *lightness* lightheadedness.     *declension* decline, deterioration (with a pun on
the grammatical sense)     148 *all we* all of us, or, into everything that we     153 *Take this from this*
(The actor probably gestures, indicating that he means his head from his shoulders, or his staff of
office or chain from his hands or neck, or something similar.)     156 *center* middle point of the
earth (which is also the center of the Ptolemaic universe).     *try* test, judge

Queen: So he does indeed.

Polonius: At such a time I'll loose my daughter to him.

    Be you and I behind an arras then.                                160

    Mark the encounter. If he love her not

    And be not from his reason fall'n thereon,

    Let me be no assistant for a state,

    But keep a farm and carters.

King: We will try it.

*Enter Hamlet [reading on a book].*

Queen: But look where sadly the poor wretch comes reading.          165

Polonius: Away, I do beseech you both, away.

    I'll board him presently. O, give me leave.

*Exeunt King and Queen [with attendants].*

    How does my good Lord Hamlet?

Hamlet: Well, God-a-mercy.

Polonius: Do you know me, my lord?                                   170

Hamlet: Excellent well. You are a fishmonger.

Polonius: Not I, my lord.

Hamlet: Then I would you were so honest a man.

Polonius: Honest, my lord?

Hamlet: Ay, sir. To be honest, as this world goes, is to be one man picked out of  175
    ten thousand.

Polonius: That's very true, my lord.

Hamlet: For if the sun breed maggots in a dead dog, being a good kissing car-
    rion—Have you a daughter?

Polonius: I have, my lord.                                               180

Hamlet: Let her not walk i' the sun. Conception is a blessing, but as your daugh-
    ter may conceive, friend, look to 't.

Polonius [aside]: How say you by that? Still harping on my daughter. Yet he knew
    me not at first; 'a said I was a fishmonger. 'A is far gone. And truly in my
    youth I suffered much extremity for love, very near this. I'll speak to him  185
    again.—What do you read, my lord?

Hamlet: Words, words, words.

Polonius: What is the matter, my lord?

Hamlet: Between who?

Polonius: I mean, the matter that you read, my lord.                   190

---

159 *loose* (as one might release an animal that is being mated)    160 *arras* hanging, tapestry
162 *thereon* on that account    164 *carters* wagon drivers    165 *sadly* seriously    167 *board*
accost.    *presently* at once.    *give me leave* i.e., excuse me, leave me alone. (Said to those he hurries offstage, including the King and Queen.)    169 *God-a-mercy* God have mercy, i.e., thank you
171 *fishmonger* fish merchant    178–179 *a good kissing carrion* i.e., a good piece of flesh for kissing,
or for the sun to kiss    181 *i' the sun* in public (with additional implication of the sunshine of
princely favors).    *Conception* (1) understanding (2) pregnancy    184 *'a* he    188 *matter* substance. (But Hamlet plays on the sense of "basis for a dispute.")

*Hamlet:* Slanders, sir; for the satirical rogue says here that old men have gray beards, that their faces are wrinkled, their eyes purging thick amber and plum-tree gum, and that they have a plentiful lack of wit, together with most weak hams. All which, sir, though I most powerfully and potently believe, yet I hold it not honesty to have it thus set down, for yourself, sir, shall grow 195 old as I am, if like a crab you could go backward.

*Polonius [aside]:* Though this be madness, yet there is method in 't.—Will you walk out of the air, my lord?

*Hamlet:* Into my grave.

*Polonius:* Indeed, that's out of the air. [*Aside.*] How pregnant sometimes his 200 replies are! A happiness that often madness hits on, which reason and sanity could not so prosperously be delivered of. I will leave him and suddenly contrive the means of meeting between him and my daughter.—My honorable lord, I will most humbly take my leave of you.

*Hamlet:* You cannot, sir, take from me anything that I will more willingly part 205 withal—except my life, except my life, except my life.

*Enter Guildenstern and Rosencrantz.*

*Polonius:* Fare you well, my lord.

*Hamlet:* These tedious old fools!

*Polonius:* You go to seek the Lord Hamlet. There he is.

*Rosencrantz [to Polonius]:* God save you, sir! 210

[*Exit Polonius.*]

*Guildenstern:* My honored lord!

*Rosencrantz:* My most dear lord!

*Hamlet:* My excellent good friends! How dost thou, Guildenstern? Ah, Rosencrantz! Good lads, how do you both?

*Rosencrantz:* As the indifferent children of the earth. 215

*Guildenstern:* Happy in that we are not overhappy.
On Fortune's cap we are not the very button.

*Hamlet:* Nor the soles of her shoe?

*Rosencrantz:* Neither, my lord.

*Hamlet:* Then you live about her waist, or in the middle of her favors? 220

*Guildenstern:* Faith, her privates we.

*Hamlet:* In the secret parts of Fortune? O, most true, she is a strumpet. What news?

---

192 *purging* discharging.     *amber* i.e., resin, like the resinous *plum-tree gum*     193 *wit* understanding     195 *honesty* decency, decorum     196 *old* as old     198 *out of the air* (The open air was considered dangerous for sick people.)     200 *pregnant* quick-witted, full of meaning.     201 *happiness* felicity of expression     202 *prosperously* successfully     *suddenly* immediately     206 *withal* with     208 *old fools* i.e., old men like Polonius     215 *indifferent* ordinary, at neither extreme of fortune or misfortune     220 *favors* i.e., sexual favors     221 *her privates we* i.e., (1) we are sexually intimate with Fortune, the fickle goddess who bestows her favors indiscriminately (2) we are her private citizens     222 *strumpet* prostitute. (A common epithet for indiscriminate Fortune; see line 430.)

*Rosencrantz:* None, my lord, but the world's grown honest.

*Hamlet:* Then is doomsday near. But your news is not true. Let me question more  225
    in particular. What have you, my good friends, deserved at the hands of
    Fortune that she sends you to prison hither?

*Guildenstern:* Prison, my lord?

*Hamlet:* Denmark's a prison.

*Rosencrantz:* Then is the world one.  230

*Hamlet:* A goodly one, in which there are many confines, wards, and dungeons,
    Denmark being one o' the worst.

*Rosencrantz:* We think not so, my lord.

*Hamlet:* Why then 'tis none to you, for there is nothing either good or bad but
    thinking makes it so. To me it is a prison.  235

*Rosencrantz:* Why then, your ambition makes it one. 'Tis too narrow for your
    mind.

*Hamlet:* O God, I could be bounded in a nutshell and count myself a king of infi-
    nite space, were it not that I have bad dreams.

*Guildenstern:* Which dreams indeed are ambition, for the very substance of the  240
    ambitious is merely the shadow of a dream.

*Hamlet:* A dream itself is but a shadow.

*Rosencrantz:* Truly, and I hold ambition of so airy and light a quality that it is but
    a shadow's shadow.

*Hamlet:* Then are our beggars bodies, and our monarchs and outstretched heroes  245
    the beggars' shadows. Shall we to the court? For, by my fay, I cannot reason.

*Rosencrantz, Guildenstern:* We'll wait upon you.

*Hamlet:* No such matter. I will not sort you with the rest of my servants, for, to
    speak to you like an honest man, I am most dreadfully attended. But, in the
    beaten way of friendship, what make you at Elsinore?  250

*Rosencrantz:* To visit you, my lord, no other occasion.

*Hamlet:* Beggar that I am, I am even poor in thanks; but I thank you, and sure,
    dear friends, my thanks are too dear a halfpenny. Were you not sent for? Is it
    your own inclining? Is it a free visitation? Come, come, deal justly with me.
    Come, come. Nay, speak.  255

*Guildenstern:* What should we say, my lord?

*Hamlet:* Anything but to the purpose. You were sent for, and there is a kind of
    confession in your looks which your modesties have not craft enough to
    color. I know the good King and Queen have sent for you.

---

231 *confines* places of confinement    *wards* cells    240–241 *the very . . . ambitious* that seemingly
very substantial thing that the ambitious pursue    245 *bodies* i.e., solid substances rather than shadows (since beggars are not ambitious).    *outstretched* (1) far-reaching in their ambition (2) elongated as shadows    246 *fay* faith    247 *wait upon* accompany, attend. (But Hamlet uses the phrase
in the sense of providing menial service.)    248 *sort* class, categorize    249 *dreadfully attended*
waited upon in slovenly fashion    250 *beaten way* familiar path, tried-and-true course.    *make* do
253 *too dear a halfpenny* (1) too expensive at even a halfpenny, i.e., of little worth (2) too expensive
by a halfpenny in return for worthless kindness    254 *free* voluntary    257 *Anything but to the
purpose* anything except a straightforward answer. (Said ironically.)    258 *modesties* sense of shame.
259 *color* disguise

*Rosencrantz:* To what end, my lord?  260

*Hamlet:* That you must teach me. But let me conjure you, by the rights of our fellowship, by the consonancy of our youth, by the obligation of our ever-preserved love, and by what more dear a better prosper could charge you withal, be even and direct with me whether you were sent for or no.

*Rosencrantz [aside to Guildenstern]:* What say you?  265

*Hamlet [aside]:* Nay, then, I have an eye of you.—If you love me, hold not off.

*Guildenstern:* My lord, we were sent for.

*Hamlet:* I will tell you why; so shall my anticipation prevent your discovery, and your secrecy to the King and Queen molt no feather. I have of late—but wherefore I know not—lost all my mirth, forgone all custom of exercises; and  270 indeed it goes so heavily with my disposition that this goodly frame, the earth, seems to me a sterile promontory; this most excellent canopy, the air, look you, this brave o'erhanging firmament, this majestical roof fretted with golden fire, why, it appeareth nothing to me but a foul and pestilent congregation of vapors. What a piece of work is a man! How noble in reason, how  275 infinite in faculties, in form and moving how express and admirable, in action how like an angel, in apprehension how like a god! The beauty of the world, the paragon of animals! And yet, to me, what is this quintessence of dust? Man delights not me—no, nor woman neither, though by your smiling you seem to say so.  280

*Rosencrantz:* My lord, there was no such stuff in my thoughts.

*Hamlet:* Why did you laugh, then, when I said man delights not me?

*Rosencrantz:* To think, my lord, if you delight not in man, what Lenten entertainment the players shall receive from you. We coted them on the way, and hither are they coming to offer you service.  285

*Hamlet:* He that plays the king shall be welcome; His Majesty shall have tribute of me. The adventurous knight shall use his foil and target, the lover shall not sigh gratis, the humorous man shall end his part in peace, the clown shall make those laugh whose lungs are tickle o' the sear, and the lady shall say her mind freely, or the blank verse shall halt for 't. What players are  290 they?

*Rosencrantz:* Even those you were wont to take such delight in, the tragedians of the city.

261 *conjure* adjure, entreat    262 *the consonancy of our youth* our closeness in our younger days
263 *better* more skillful.    *charge* urge    264 *even* straight, honest    266 *of* on.    *hold not off*
don't hold back    268 *so . . . discovery* in that way my saying it first will spare you from revealing
the truth    269 *molt no feather* i.e., not diminish in the least    273 *brave* splendid.    *fretted*
adorned (with fretwork, as in a vaulted ceiling)    274–275 *congregation* mass.    275 *piece of work*
masterpiece    276 *express* well-framed, exact, expressive    277 *apprehension* power of comprehending    278 *quintessence* the fifth essence of ancient philosophy, beyond earth, water, air, and
fire, supposed to be the substance of the heavenly bodies and to be latent in all things    283 *Lenten
entertainment* meager reception (appropriate to Lent)    284 *coted* overtook and passed by    286
*tribute* (1) applause (2) homage paid in money.    287 *of* from    *foil and target* sword and shield
288 *gratis* for nothing.    *humorous man* eccentric character, dominated by one trait or "humor".
*in peace* i.e., with full license    289 *tickle o' the sear* easy on the trigger, ready to laugh easily. (A *sear*
is part of a gunlock.)    290 *halt* limp    292 *tragedians* actors

*Hamlet:* How chances it they travel? Their residence, both in reputation and profit, was better both ways. 295

*Rosencrantz:* I think their inhibition comes by the means of the late innovation.

*Hamlet:* Do they hold the same estimation they did when I was in the city? Are they so followed?

*Rosencrantz:* No, indeed are they not.

*Hamlet:* How comes it? Do they grow rusty? 300

*Rosencrantz:* Nay, their endeavor keeps in the wonted pace. But there is, sir, an aerie of children, little eyases, that cry out on the top of question and are most tyrannically clapped for 't. These are now the fashion, and so berattle the common stages—so they call them—that many wearing rapiers are afraid of goose quills and dare scarce come thither. 305

*Hamlet:* What, are they children? Who maintains 'em? How are they escoted? Will they pursue the quality no longer than they can sing? Will they not say afterwards, if they should grow themselves to common players—as it is most like, if their means are no better—their writers do them wrong to make them exclaim against their own succession? 310

*Rosencrantz:* Faith, there has been much to-do on both sides, and the nation holds it no sin to tar them to controversy. There was for a while no money bid for argument unless the poet and the player went to cuffs in the question.

*Hamlet:* Is 't possible?

*Guildenstern:* O, there has been much throwing about of brains. 315

*Hamlet:* Do the boys carry it away?

*Rosencrantz:* Ay, that they do, my lord—Hercules and his load too.

*Hamlet:* It is not very strange; for my uncle is King of Denmark, and those that would make mouths at him while my father lived give twenty, forty, fifty, a hundred ducats apiece for his picture in little. 'Sblood, there is something in 320 this more than natural, if philosophy could find it out.

*A flourish [of trumpets within].*

---

294 *residence* remaining in their usual place, i.e., in the city    296 *inhibition* formal prohibition (from acting plays in the city).    *late* recent.    *innovation* i.e., the new fashion in satirical plays performed by boy actors in the "private" theaters; or possibly a political uprising; or the strict limitations set on the theaters in London in 1600    300–317 *How . . . load too* (The passage, omitted from the early quartos, alludes to the so-called War of the Theaters, 1599–1602, the rivalry between the children's companies and the adult actors.)    301 *keeps* continues.    *wonted* usual    302 *aerie* nest.    *eyases* young hawks.    *cry . . . question* speak shrilly, dominating the controversy (in decrying the public theaters)    303 *tyrannically* outrageously.    *berattle* berate, clamor against. *common stages* public theaters    304 *many wearing rapiers* i.e., many men of fashion, afraid to patronize the common players for fear of being satirized by the poets writing for the boy actors.    *goose quills* i.e., pens of satirists    306 *escoted* maintained    307 *quality* (acting) profession.    *no longer . . . sing* i.e., only until their voices change    308 *common* regular, adult    309 *like* likely.    *if . . . better* if they find no better way to support themselves    310 *succession* i.e., future careers    311 *to-do* ado    312 *tar* set on (as dogs)    311–312 *There . . . question* i.e., for a while, no money was offered by the acting companies to playwrights for the plot to a play unless the satirical poets who wrote for the boys and the adult actors came to blows in the play itself    316 *carry it away* i.e., win the day    317 *Hercules . . . load* (Thought to be an allusion to the sign of the Globe Theatre, which was Hercules bearing the world on his shoulders.)    319 *mouths* faces    320 *ducats* gold coins. *in little* in miniature. *'Sblood* by God's (Christ's) blood    321 *philosophy* i.e., scientific inquiry

*Guildenstern:* There are the players.

*Hamlet [to Rosenkrantz and Guildenstern]:* Gentlemen, you are welcome to Elsinore. Your hands, come then. Th' appurtenance of welcome is fashion and ceremony. Let me comply with you in this garb, lest my extent to the  325 players, which, I tell you, must show fairly outwards, should more appear like entertainment than yours. You are welcome. But my uncle-father and aunt-mother are deceived.

*Guildenstern:* In what, my dear lord?

*Hamlet:* I am but mad north-north-west. When the wind is southerly I know a  330 hawk from a handsaw.

*Enter Polonius.*

*Polonius:* Well be with you, gentlemen!

*Hamlet:* Hark you, Guildenstern, and you too; at each ear a hearer. That great baby you see there is not yet out of his swaddling clouts.

*Rosencrantz:* Haply he is the second time come to them, for they say an old man  335 is twice a child.

*Hamlet:* I will prophesy he comes to tell me of the players. Mark it.—You say right, sir, o' Monday morning, 'twas then indeed.

*Polonius:* My lord, I have news to tell you.

*Hamlet:* My lord, I have news to tell you. When Roscius was an actor in Rome—  340

*Polonius:* The actors are come hither, my lord.

*Hamlet:* Buzz, buzz!

*Polonius:* Upon my honor—

*Hamlet:* Then came each actor on his ass.

*Polonius:* The best actors in the world, either for tragedy, comedy, history, pas-  345 toral, pastoral-comical, historical-pastoral, tragical-historical, tragical-comi-cal-historical-pastoral, scene individable, or poem unlimited. Seneca cannot be too heavy, nor Plautus too light. For the law of writ and the liberty, these are the only men.

*Hamlet:* O Jephthah, judge of Israel, what a treasure hadst thou!  350

324 *appurtenance* proper accompaniment.     325 *comply* observe the formalities of courtesy     *garb* i.e., manner.     *my extent* that which I extend, i.e., my polite behavior     326–327 *show fairly outwards* show every evidence of cordiality     327 *entertainment* a (warm) reception     330 *north-north-west* just off true north, only partly     331 *hawk, handsaw* i.e., two very different things, though also perhaps meaning a mattock (or *hack*) and a carpenter's cutting tool, respectively; also birds, with a play on *hernshaw*, or heron     334 *swaddling clouts* cloths in which to wrap a newborn baby     335 *Haply* perhaps     340 *Roscius* a famous Roman actor who died in 62 B.C.     342 *Buzz* (An interjection used to denote stale news.)     347 *scene individable* a play observing the unity of place; or perhaps one that is unclassifiable, or performed without intermission.     *poem unlimited* a play disregarding the unities of time and place; one that is all-inclusive.     *Seneca* writer of Latin tragedies     348 *Plautus* writer of Latin comedy.     *law . . . liberty* dramatic composition both according to the rules and disregarding the rules.     *these* i.e., the actors     350 *Jephthah . . . Israel* (Jephthah had to sacrifice his daughter; see Judges 11. Hamlet goes on to quote from a ballad on the theme.)

*Polonius:* What a treasure had he, my lord?

*Hamlet:* Why,

"One fair daughter, and no more,
The which he lovèd passing well."                                                    355

*Polonius [aside]:* Still on my daughter.

*Hamlet:* Am I not i' the right, old Jephthah?

*Polonius:* If you call me Jephthah, my lord, I have a daughter that I love passing well.

*Hamlet:* Nay, that follows not.

*Polonius:* What follows then, my lord?                                               360

*Hamlet:* Why,

"As by lot, God wot,"

and then, you know,

"It came to pass, as most like it was"—

the first row of the pious chanson will show you more, for look where my    365
abridgement comes.

*Enter the Players.*

You are welcome, masters; welcome, all. I am glad to see thee well.
Welcome, good friends. O, old friend! Why, thy face is valanced since I saw
thee last. Com'st thou to beard me in Denmark? What, my young lady and    370
mistress! By 'r Lady, your ladyship is nearer to heaven than when I saw you
last, by the altitude of a chopine. Pray God your voice, like a piece of uncurrent gold, be not cracked within the ring. Masters, you are all welcome.
We'll e'en to 't like French falconers, fly at anything we see. We'll have a
speech straight. Come, give us a taste of your quality. Come, a passionate    375
speech.

*First Player:* What speech, my good lord?

*Hamlet:* I heard thee speak me a speech once, but it was never acted, or if it was,
not above once, for the play, I remember, pleased not the million; 'twas
caviar to the general. But it was—as I received it, and others, whose judg-    380
ments in such matters cried in the top of mine—an excellent play, well
digested in the scenes, set down with as much modesty as cunning. I remember one said there were no sallets in the lines to make the matter savory, nor

---

354 *passing* surpassingly    362 *lot* chance.    *wot* knows    364 *like* likely, probable    365 *row*
stanza.    *chanson* ballad, song    366 *my abridgment* something that cuts short my conversation;
also, a diversion    368 *valanced* fringed (with a beard)    369 *beard* confront, challenge (with
obvious pun).    *young lady* i.e., boy playing women's parts    370 *By 'r Lady* by Our Lady    371
*chopine* thick-soled shoe of Italian fashion    371–372 *uncurrent* not passable as lawful coinage.
*cracked . . . ring* i.e., changed from adolescent to male voice, no longer suitable for women's roles.
(Coins featured rings enclosing the sovereign's head; if the coin was cracked within this ring, it was
unfit for currency.)    373 *e'en to 't* go at it    374 *straight* at once.    *quality* professional skill
379 *caviar to the general* caviar to the multitude, i.e., a choice dish too elegant for coarse tastes
380 *cried in the top of* i.e., spoke with greater authority than    381 *digested* arranged, ordered.
*modesty* moderation, restraint.    *cunning* skill    382 *sallets* i.e., something savory, spicy impropri-
eties    383 *indict* convict

no matter in the phrase that might indict the author of affectation, but
called it an honest method, as wholesome as sweet, and by very much more 385
handsome than fine. One speech in 't I chiefly loved: 'twas Aeneas' tale to
Dido, and there-about of it especially when he speaks of Priam's slaughter. If
it live in your memory, begin at this line: let me see, let me see—
"The rugged Pyrrhus, like th' Hyrcanian beast"—
'Tis not so. It begins with Pyrrhus:
"The rugged Pyrrhus, he whose sable arms, 390
Black as his purpose, did the night resemble
When he lay couchèd in the ominous horse,
Hath now this dread and black complexion smeared
With heraldry more dismal. Head to foot
Now is he total gules, horridly tricked 395
With blood of fathers, mothers, daughters, sons,
Baked and impasted with the parching streets,
That lend a tyrannous and a damnèd light
To their lord's murder. Roasted in wrath and fire,
And thus o'ersizèd with coagulate gore, 400
With eyes like carbuncles, the hellish Pyrrhus
Old grandsire Priam seeks."
So proceed you.
*Polonius*: 'Fore God, my lord, well spoken, with good accent and good discretion.
*First Player*:                         "Anon he finds him 405
Striking too short at Greeks. His antique sword,
Rebellious to his arm, lies where it falls,
Repugnant to command. Unequal matched,
Pyrrhus at Priam drives, in rage strikes wide,
But with the whiff and wind of his fell sword 410
Th' unnervèd father falls. Then senseless Ilium,
Seeming to feel this blow, with flaming top
Stoops to his base, and with a hideous crash

---

385 *handsome* well-proportioned.     *fine* elaborately ornamented, showy     386 *Priam's slaughter*
the slaying of the ruler of Troy, when the Greeks finally took the city     388 *Pyrrhus* a Greek hero
in the Trojan War, also known as Neoptolemus, son of Achilles—another avenging son.
*Hyrcanian beast* i.e., tiger. (On the death of Priam, see Virgil, *Aeneid*, 2.506 ff.; compare the whole
speech with Marlowe's *Dido Queen of Carthage*, 2.1.214 ff. On the *Hyrcanian* tiger, see *Aeneid*,
4.366–367. Hyrcania is on the Caspian Sea.)     390 *rugged* shaggy, savage.     *sable* black (for reasons of camouflage during the episode of the Trojan horse)     392 *couchèd* concealed.     *ominous*
*horse* fateful Trojan horse, by which the Greeks gained access to Troy     394 *dismal* ill-omened
395 *total gules* entirely red. (A heraldic term.)     *tricked* spotted and smeared. (Heraldic.)     397
*impasted* crusted, like a thick paste.     *with . . . streets* by the parching heat of the streets (because of
the fires everywhere)     398 *tyrannous* cruel     399 *their lord's* i.e., Priam's     400 *o'ersizèd* covered as with size or glue     401 *carbuncles* large fiery-red precious stones thought to emit their own
light     406 *antique* ancient, long-used     408 *Repugnant* disobedient, resistant     410 *fell* cruel
411 *unnervèd* strengthless.     *senseless Ilium* inanimate citadel of Troy     413 *his* its

Takes prisoner Pyrrhus' ear. For, lo! His sword,
Which was declining on the milky head 415
Of reverend Priam, seemed i' th' air to stick.
So as a painted tyrant Pyrrhus stood,
And, like a neutral to his will and matter,
Did nothing.
But as we often see against some storm 420
A silence in the heavens, the rack stand still,
The bold winds speechless, and the orb below
As hush as death, anon the dreadful thunder
Doth rend the region, so, after Pyrrhus' pause,
A rousèd vengeance sets him new a-work, 425
And never did the Cyclops' hammers fall
On Mars's armor forged for proof eterne
With less remorse than Pyrrhus' bleeding sword
Now falls on Priam.
Out, out, thou strumpet Fortune! All you gods 430
In general synod take away her power!
Break all the spokes and fellies from her wheel,
And bowl the round nave down the hill of heaven
As low as to the fiends!"
*Polonius:* This is too long. 435
*Hamlet:* It shall to the barber's with your beard.—Prithee, say on. He's for a jig or
a tale of bawdry, or he sleeps. Say on; come to Hecuba.
*First Player:* "But who, ah woe! had seen the moblèd queen"—
*Hamlet:* "The moblèd queen?"
*Polonius:* That's good. "Moblèd queen" is good. 440
*First Player:* "Run barefoot up and down, threat'ning the flames
With bisson rheum, a clout upon that head
Where late the diadem stood, and, for a robe,
About her lank and all o'erteemèd loins
A blanket, in the alarm of fear caught up— 445
Who this had seen, with tongue in venom steeped,
'Gainst Fortune's state would treason have pronounced.
But if the gods themselves did see her then
When she saw Pyrrhus make malicious sport

---

415 *declining* descending. *milky* white-haired 417 *painted* i.e., painted in a picture 418 *like
. . . matter* i.e., as though suspended between his intention and its fulfillment 420 *against* just
before 421 *rack* mass of clouds 422 *orb* globe, earth 424 *region* sky 426 *Cyclops* giant
armor makers in the smithy of Vulcan 427 *proof eterne* eternal resistance to assault 428
*remorse* pity 431 *synod* assembly 432 *fellies* pieces of wood forming the rim of a wheel 433
*nave* hub. *hill of heaven* Mount Olympus 436 *jig* comic song and dance often given at the end
of a play 437 *Hecuba* wife of Priam 438 *who . . . had* anyone who had (also in line 446).
*moblèd* muffled 441 *threat'ning the flames* i.e., weeping hard enough to dampen the flames 442
*bisson rheum* blinding tears. *clout* cloth 443 *late* lately 444 *all o'erteemèd* utterly worn out
with bearing children 447 *state* rule, managing. *pronounced* proclaimed

In mincing with his sword her husband's limbs,                                          450
The instant burst of clamor that she made,
Unless things mortal move them not at all,
Would have made milch the burning eyes of heaven,
And passion in the gods."

*Polonius:* Look whe'er he has not turned his color and has tears in 's eyes. Prithee,   455
no more.

*Hamlet:* 'Tis well; I'll have thee speak out the rest of this soon.—Good my lord,
will you see the players well bestowed? Do you hear, let them be well used,
for they are the abstract and brief chronicles of the time. After your death
you were better have a bad epitaph than their ill report while you live.        460

*Polonius:* My lord, I will use them according to their desert.

*Hamlet:* God's bodikin, man, much better. Use every man after his desert, and
who shall scape whipping? Use them after your own honor and dignity. The
less they deserve, the more merit is in your bounty. Take them in.

*Polonius:* Come, sirs.                                                    [*Exit.*]  465

*Hamlet:* Follow him, friends. We'll hear a play tomorrow. [*As they start to leave,
Hamlet detains the First Player.*] Dost thou hear me, old friend? Can you play
The Murder of Gonzago?

*First Player:* Ay, my lord.

*Hamlet:* We'll ha 't tomorrow night. You could, for a need, study a speech of some   470
dozen or sixteen lines which I would set down and insert in 't, could you not?

*First Player:* Ay, my lord.

*Hamlet:* Very well. Follow that lord, and look you mock him not. (*Exeunt Players.*)
My good friends, I'll leave you till night. You are welcome to Elsinore.

*Rosencrantz:* Good my lord!                                                   475

*Exeunt [Rosencrantz and Guildenstern].*

*Hamlet:* Ay, so, goodbye to you.—Now I am alone.
O, what a rogue and peasant slave am I!
Is it not monstrous that this player here,
But in a fiction, in a dream of passion,
Could force his soul so to his own conceit                                     480
That from her working all his visage wanned,
Tears in his eyes, distraction in his aspect,
A broken voice, and his whole function suiting
With forms to his conceit? And all for nothing!

453 *milch* milky, moist with tears.    *burning eyes of heaven* i.e., heavenly bodies    454 *passion*
overpowering emotion    455 *whe'er* whether    458 *bestowed* lodged    459 *abstract* summary
account    462 *God's bodikin* by God's (Christ's) little body, *bodykin*. (Not to be confused with *bodkin,* "dagger.").    *after* according to    470 *ha 't* have it.    *study* memorize    479 *But* merely
480 *force . . . conceit* bring his innermost being so entirely into accord with his conception (of the
role)    481 *from her working* as a result of, or in response to, his soul's activity.    *wanned* grew
pale    482 *aspect* look, glance    483–484 *his whole . . . conceit* all his bodily powers responding
with actions to suit his thought

For Hecuba!                                                                            485
What's Hecuba to him, or he to Hecuba,
That he should weep for her? What would he do
Had he the motive and the cue for passion
That I have? He would drown the stage with tears
And cleave the general ear with horrid speech,                                         490
Make mad the guilty and appall the free,
Confound the ignorant, and amaze indeed
The very faculties of eyes and ears. Yet I,
A dull and muddy-mettled rascal, peak
Like John-a-dreams, unpregnant of my cause,                                            495
And can say nothing—no, not for a king
Upon whose property and most dear life
A damned defeat was made. Am I a coward?
Who calls me villain? Breaks my pate across?
Plucks off my beard and blows it in my face?                                           500
Tweaks me by the nose? Gives me the lie i' the throat
As deep as to the lungs? Who does me this?
Ha, 'swounds, I should take it; for it cannot be
But I am pigeon-livered and lack gall
To make oppression bitter, or ere this                                                 505
I should ha' fatted all the region kites
With this slave's offal. Bloody, bawdy villain!
Remorseless, treacherous, lecherous, kindless villain!
O, vengeance!
Why, what an ass am I! This is most brave,                                             510
That I, the son of a dear father murdered,
Prompted to my revenge by heaven and hell,
Must like a whore unpack my heart with words
And fall a-cursing, like a very drab,
A scullion! Fie upon 't, foh! About, my brains!                                        515
Hum, I have heard
That guilty creatures sitting at a play
Have by the very cunning of the scene
Been struck so to the soul that presently

490 *the general ear* everyone's ear.    *horrid* horrible    491 *appall* (Literally, make pale.)    *free*
innocent    492 *Confound the ignorant* i.e., dumbfound those who know nothing of the crime that
has been committed.    *amaze* stun    494 *muddy-mettled* dull-spirited.    *peak* mope, pine
495 *John-a-dreams* a sleepy, dreaming idler.    *unpregnant of* not quickened by    497 *property* i.e.,
the crown; also character, quality    498 *damned defeat* damnable act of destruction    499 *pate*
head    501 *Gives . . . throat* calls me an out-and-out liar    503 *'swounds* by his (Christ's) wounds
504 *pigeon-livered* (The pigeon or dove was popularly supposed to be mild because it secreted no gall.)
505 *bitter* i.e., bitter to me    506 *region kites* kites (birds of prey) of the air    507 *offal* entrails
508 *Remorseless* pitiless.    *kindless* unnatural    510 *brave* fine, admirable. (Said ironically.)
514 *drab* whore    515 *scullion* menial kitchen servant (apt to be foul-mouthed).    *About* about it,
to work    518 *cunning* art, skill.    *scene* dramatic presentation    519 *presently* at once

They have proclaimed their malefactions; 520
For murder, though it have no tongue, will speak
With most miraculous organ. I'll have these players
Play something like the murder of my father
Before mine uncle. I'll observe his looks;
I'll tent him to the quick. If 'a do blench, 525
I know my course. The spirit that I have seen
May be the devil, and the devil hath power
T' assume a pleasing shape; yea, and perhaps,
Out of my weakness and my melancholy,
As he is very potent with such spirits, 530
Abuses me to damn me. I'll have grounds
More relative than this. The play's the thing
Wherein I'll catch the conscience of the King.          *Exit.*

# ACT III

### Scene I [The Castle.]

*Enter King, Queen, Polonius, Ophelia, Rosencrantz, Guildenstern, lords.*

*King:* And can you by no drift of conference
    Get from him why he puts on this confusion,
    Grating so harshly all his days of quiet
    With turbulent and dangerous lunacy?
*Rosencrantz:* He does confess he feels himself distracted, 5
    But from what cause 'a will by no means speak.
*Guildenstern:* Nor do we find him forward to be sounded,
    But with a crafty madness keeps aloof
    When we would bring him on to some confession
    Of his true state.
*Queen:*                Did he receive you well? 10
*Rosencrantz:* Most like a gentleman.
*Guildenstern:* But with much forcing of his disposition.
*Rosencrantz:* Niggard of question, but of our demands
    Most free in his reply.
*Queen:*                Did you assay him
    To any pastime? 15
*Rosencrantz:* Madam, it so fell out that certain players
    We o'erraught on the way. Of these we told him,

---

525 *tent* probe.    *the quick* the tender part of a wound, the core.    *blench* quail, flinch    530
*spirits* humors (of melancholy)    531 *Abuses* deludes    532 *relative* cogent, pertinent    1 *drift of*
*conference* directing of conversation    7 *forward* willing.    *sounded* questioned    12 *disposition*
inclination    13 *Niggard* stingy.    *question* conversation    14 *assay* try to win    17 *o'erraught*
overtook

And there did seem in him a kind of joy
To hear of it. They are here about the court,
And, as I think, they have already order                              20
This night to play before him.
Polonius:                             'Tis most true,
And he beseeched me to entreat Your Majesties
To hear and see the matter.
King: With all my heart, and it doth much content me
To hear him so inclined.                                              25
Good gentlemen, give him a further edge
And drive his purpose into these delights.
Rosencrantz: We shall, my lord.

                                    *Exeunt Rosencrantz and Guildenstern.*

King:                             Sweet Gertrude, leave us too,
For we have closely sent for Hamlet hither,
That he, as 'twere by accident, may here                              30
Affront Ophelia.
Her father and myself, lawful espials,
Will so bestow ourselves that seeing, unseen,
We may of their encounter frankly judge,
And gather by him, as he is behaved,                                  35
If 't be th' affliction of his love or no
That thus he suffers for.
Queen:                             I shall obey you.
And for your part, Ophelia, I do wish
That your good beauties be the happy cause
Of Hamlet's wildness. So shall I hope your virtues                    40
Will bring him to his wonted way again,
To both your honors.
Ophelia:                             Madam, I wish it may.

                                              *[Exit Queen.]*

Polonius: Ophelia, walk you here.—Gracious, so please you,
We will bestow ourselves. [*To Ophelia.*] Read on this book,   [*giving her a book*]
That show of such an exercise may color                               45
Your loneliness. We are oft to blame in this—
'Tis too much proved—that with devotion's visage
And pious action we do sugar o'er
The devil himself.

---

26 *edge* incitement    29 *closely* privately    31 *Affront* confront, meet    32 *espials* spies    41
*wonted* accustomed    43 *Gracious* Your Grace (i.e., the King)    44 *bestow* conceal    45 *exercise*
religious exercise. (The book she reads is one of devotion.)    *color* give a plausible appearance to
46 *loneliness* being alone    47 *too much proved* too often shown to be true, too often practiced

*King [aside]:* O, 'tis too true!                                                  50
How smart a lash that speech doth give my conscience!
The harlot's cheek, beautied with plastering art,
Is not more ugly to the thing that helps it
Than is my deed to my most painted word.
O heavy burden!                                                                    55
*Polonius:* I hear him coming. Let's withdraw, my lord.

*[The King and Polonius withdraw.]*

Enter Hamlet. *[Ophelia pretends to read a book.]*

*Hamlet:* To be, or not to be, that is the question:
Whether 'tis nobler in the mind to suffer
The slings and arrows of outrageous fortune,
Or to take arms against a sea of troubles                                          60
And by opposing end them. To die, to sleep—
No more—and by a sleep to say we end
The heartache and the thousand natural shocks
That flesh is heir to. 'Tis a consummation
Devoutly to be wished. To die, to sleep;                                           65
To sleep, perchance to dream. Ay, there's the rub,
For in that sleep of death what dreams may come,
When we have shuffled off this mortal coil,
Must give us pause. There's the respect
That makes calamity of so long life.                                               70
For who would bear the whips and scorns of time,
Th' oppressor's wrong, the proud man's contumely,
The pangs of disprized love, the law's delay,
The insolence of office, and the spurns
That patient merit of th' unworthy takes,                                          75
When he himself might his quietus make
With a bare bodkin? Who would fardels bear,
To grunt and sweat under a weary life,
But that the dread of something after death,
The undiscovered country from whose bourn                                          80
No traveler returns, puzzles the will,
And makes us rather bear those ills we have

---

53 *to* compared to.    *the thing* i.e., the cosmetic    56 s.d. *withdraw* (The King and Polonius may
retire behind an arras. The stage directions specify that they "enter" again near the end of the scene.)
59 *slings* missiles    66 *rub* (Literally, an obstacle in the game of bowls.)    68 *shuffled* sloughed,
cast.    *coil* turmoil    69 *respect* consideration    70 *of . . . life* so long-lived, something we willingly endure for so long (also suggesting that long life is itself a calamity)    72 *contumely* insolent
abuse    73 *disprized* unvalued    74 *office* officialdom.    *spurns* insults    75 *of . . . takes*
receives from unworthy persons    76 *quietus* acquitance; here, death    77 *a bare bodkin* a mere
dagger, unsheathed.    *fardels* burdens    80 *bourn* frontier, boundary

Than fly to others that we know not of?
Thus conscience does make cowards of us all;
And thus the native hue of resolution                                      85
Is sicklied o'er with the pale cast of thought,
And enterprises of great pitch and moment
With this regard their currents turn awry
And lose the name of action.—Soft you now,
The fair Ophelia. Nymph, in thy orisons                                     90
Be all my sins remembered.

*Ophelia*:                 Good my lord,
How does your honor for this many a day?

*Hamlet*: I humbly thank you; well, well, well.

*Ophelia*: My lord, I have remembrances of yours,
That I have longèd long to redeliver.                                       95
I pray you, now receive them.                        [*She offers tokens.*]

*Hamlet*: No, not I, I never gave you aught.

*Ophelia*: My honored lord, you know right well you did,
And with them words of so sweet breath composed
As made the things more rich. Their perfume lost,                          100
Take these again, for to the noble mind
Rich gifts wax poor when givers prove unkind.
There, my lord.                                       [*She gives tokens.*]

*Hamlet*: Ha, ha! Are you honest?

*Ophelia*: My lord?                                                        105

*Hamlet*: Are you fair?

*Ophelia*: What means your lordship?

*Hamlet*: That if you be honest and fair, your honesty should admit no discourse to
your beauty.

*Ophelia*: Could beauty, my lord, have better commerce than with honesty?     110

*Hamlet*: Ay, truly, for the power of beauty will sooner transform honesty from
what it is to a bawd than the force of honesty can translate beauty into his
likeness. This was sometime a paradox, but now the time gives it proof. I did
love you once.

*Ophelia*: Indeed, my lord, you made me believe so.                          115

*Hamlet*: You should not have believed me, for virtue cannot so inoculate our old
stock but we shall relish of it. I loved you not.

*Ophelia*: I was the more deceived.

---

85 *native hue* natural color, complexion     86 *cast* tinge, shade of color     87 *pitch* height (as of a
falcon's flight).     *moment* importance     88 *regard* respect, consideration.     *currents* courses
89 *Soft you* i.e., wait a minute, gently     90 *orisons* prayers     104 *honest* (1) truthful (2) chaste
106 *fair* (1) beautiful (2) just, honorable     108 *your honesty* your chastity     *discourse to* familiar
dealings with     110 *commerce* dealings, intercourse     112 *his* its     113 *sometime* formerly.     *a*
*paradox* a view opposite to commonly held opinion.     *the time* the present age     116 *inoculate*
graft, be engrafted to     117 *but . . . it* that we do not still have about us a taste of the old stock, i.e.,
retain our sinfulness

*Hamlet:* Get thee to a nunnery. Why wouldst thou be a breeder of sinners? I am myself indifferent honest, but yet I could accuse me of such things that it 120 were better my mother had not borne me: I am very proud, revengeful, ambitious, with more offenses at my beck than I have thoughts to put them in, imagination to give them shape, or time to act them in. What should such fellows as I do crawling between earth and heaven? We are arrant knaves all; believe none of us. Go thy ways to a nunnery. Where's your father? 125

*Ophelia:* At home, my lord.

*Hamlet:* Let the doors be shut upon him, that he may play the fool nowhere but in 's own house. Farewell.

*Ophelia:* O, help him, you sweet heavens!

*Hamlet:* If thou dost marry, I'll give thee this plague for thy dowry: be thou as 130 chaste as ice, as pure as snow, thou shalt not escape calumny. Get thee to a nunnery, farewell. Or, if thou wilt needs marry, marry a fool, for wise men know well enough what monsters you make of them. To a nunnery, go, and quickly too. Farewell.

*Ophelia:* Heavenly powers, restore him! 135

*Hamlet:* I have heard of your paintings too, well enough. God hath given you one face, and you make yourselves another. You jig, you amble, and you lisp, you nickname God's creatures, and make your wantonness your ignorance. Go to, I'll no more on 't; it hath made me mad. I say we will have no more marriage. Those that are married already—all but one—shall live. The rest shall 140 keep as they are. To a nunnery, go. *Exit.*

*Ophelia:* O, what a noble mind is here o'erthrown!
The courtier's, soldier's, scholar's, eye, tongue, sword,
Th' expectancy and rose of the fair state,
The glass of fashion and the mold of form, 145
Th' observed of all observers, quite, quite down!
And I, of ladies most deject and wretched,
That sucked the honey of his music vows,
Now see that noble and most sovereign reason
Like sweet bells jangled out of tune and harsh, 150
That unmatched form and feature of blown youth
Blasted with ecstasy. O, woe is me,
T' have seen what I have seen, see what I see!

---

122 *nunnery* convent (with possibly an awareness that the word was also used derisively to denote a brothel)　　120 *indifferent honest* reasonably virtuous　　121 *beck* command　　133 *monsters* (An illusion to the horns of a cuckold.)　　*you* i.e., you women　　137 *jig* dance.　　*amble* move coyly 137–138 *you nickname . . . creatures* i.e., you give trendy names to things in place of their God-given names　　138 *make . . . ignorance* i.e., excuse your affectation on the grounds of pretended ignorance　　139 *on 't* of it　　144 *expectancy* hope.　　*rose* ornament　　145 *The glass . . . form* the mirror of true self-fashioning and the pattern of courtly behavior　　146 *Th' observed . . . observers* i.e., the center of attention and honor in the court　　148 *music* musical, sweetly uttered　　151 *blown* blooming　　152 *Blasted* withered.　　*ecstasy* madness

*Enter King and Polonius.*

*King:* Love? His affections do not that way tend;
    Nor what he spake, though it lacked form a little,    155
    Was not like madness. There's something in his soul
    O'er which his melancholy sits on brood,
    And I do doubt the hatch and the disclose
    Will be some danger; which for to prevent,
    I have in quick determination    160
    Thus set it down: he shall with speed to England
    For the demand of our neglected tribute.
    Haply the seas and countries different
    With variable objects shall expel
    This something-settled matter in his heart,    165
    Whereon his brains still beating puts him thus
    From fashion of himself. What think you on 't?
*Polonius:* It shall do well. But yet do I believe
    The origin and commencement of his grief
    Sprung from neglected love.—How now, Ophelia?    170
    You need not tell us what Lord Hamlet said;
    We heard it all.—My lord, do as you please,
    But, if you hold it fit, after the play
    Let his queen-mother all alone entreat him
    To show his grief. Let her be round with him;    175
    And I'll be placed, so please you, in the ear
    Of all their conference. If she find him not,
    To England send him, or confine him where
    Your wisdom best shall think.
*King:*                                   It shall be so.
    Madness in great ones must not unwatched go.    180

                                        *Exeunt.*

## Scene II [The Castle.]

*Enter Hamlet and three of the Players.*

*Hamlet:* Speak the speech, I pray you, as I pronounced it to you, trippingly on the
    tongue. But if you mouth it, as many of our players do, I had as lief the town
    crier spoke my lines. Nor do not saw the air too much with your hand, thus,

---

154 *affections* emotions, feelings    157 *sits on brood* sits like a bird on a nest, about to *hatch* mischief
(line 158)    158 *doubt* fear.    *disclose* disclosure, hatching    161 *set it down* resolved    162
*For . . . of* to demand    164 *variable objects* various sights and surroundings to divert him    165
*This something . . . heart* the strange matter settled in his heart    166 *still* continually    167 *From
. . . himself* out of his natural manner    174 *queen-mother* queen and mother    175 *round* blunt
177 *find him not* fails to discover what is troubling him    2 *our players* players nowadays.    *I had as
lief* I would just as soon

but use all gently; for in the very torrent, tempest, and, as I may say, whirl-
wind of your passion, you must acquire and beget a temperance that may give       5
it smoothness. O, it offends me to the soul to hear a robustious periwig-pated
fellow tear a passion to tatters, to very rags, to split the ears of the
groundlings, who for the most part are capable of nothing but inexplicable
dumb shows and noise. I would have such a fellow whipped for o'erdoing
Termagant. It out-Herods Herod. Pray you, avoid it.                               10

*First Player:* I warrant your honor.

*Hamlet:* Be not too tame neither, but let your own discretion be your tutor. Suit
the action to the word, the word to the action, with this special observance,
that you o'erstep not the modesty of nature. For anything so o'erdone is from
the purpose of playing, whose end, both at the first and now, was and is to     15
hold as 't were the mirror up to nature, to show virtue her feature, scorn her
own image, and the very age and body of the time his form and pressure.
Now this overdone or come tardy off, though it makes the unskillful laugh,
cannot but make the judicious grieve, the censure of the which one must in
your allowance o'erweigh a whole theater of others. O, there be players that I   20
have seen play, and heard others praise, and that highly, not to speak it profanely, that, neither having th' accent of Christians nor the gait of Christian,
pagan, nor man, have so strutted and bellowed that I have thought some of
nature's journeymen had made men and not made them well, they imitated
humanity so abominably.                                                          25

*First Player:* I hope we have reformed that indifferently with us, sir.

*Hamlet:* O, reform it altogether. And let those that play your clowns speak no
more than is set down for them; for there be of them that will themselves
laugh, to set on some quantity of barren spectators to laugh too, though in
the meantime some necessary question of the play be then to be considered.      30
That's villainous, and shows a most pitiful ambition in the fool that uses it.
Go make you ready.                                                  [*Exeunt Players.*]

*Enter Polonius, Guildenstern, and Rosencrantz.*

How now, my lord, will the King hear this piece of work?

---

6 *robustious* violent, boisterous.     *periwig-pated* wearing a wig      8 *groundlings* spectators who paid
least and stood in the yard of the theater.     *capable of* able to understand      9 *dumb shows* mimed
performances, often used before Shakespeare's time to precede a play or each act      10 *Termagant* a
supposed deity of the Mohammedans, not found in any English medieval play but elsewhere portrayed as violent and blustering     *Herod* Herod of Jewry. (A character in *The Slaughter of the
Innocents* and other cycle plays. The part was played with great noise and fury.)      14 *modesty*
restraint, moderation     *from* contrary to      16 *scorn* i.e., something foolish and deserving of scorn
17 *the very . . . time* i.e., the present state of affairs.     *his* its.     *pressure* stamp, impressed character
18 *come tardy off* inadequately done.     *the unskillful* those lacking in judgment      19 *the censure
. . . one* the judgment of even one of whom.      20 *your allowance* your scale of values      21–22 *not
. . . profanely* (Hamlet anticipates his idea in lines 24–25 that some men were not made by God at
all.)      22 *Christians* i.e., ordinary decent folk      23 *nor man* i.e., nor any human being at all
24 *journeymen* laborers who are not yet masters in their trade      25 *abominably* (Shakespeare's usual
spelling, *abhominably*, suggests a literal though etymologically incorrect meaning, "removed from
human nature.")      26 *indifferently* tolerably      28 *of them* some among them      29 *barren* i.e., of
wit

*Polonius:* And the Queen too, and that presently.

*Hamlet:* Bid the players make haste.                              [*Exit Polonius.*]     35

    Will you two help to hasten them?

*Rosencrantz:* Ay, my lord.                                            *Exeunt they two.*

*Hamlet:*                                 What ho, Horatio!

    *Enter Horatio.*

*Horatio:* Here, sweet lord, at your service.

*Hamlet:* Horatio, thou art e'en as just a man

    As e'er my conversation coped withal.                                                                         40

*Horatio:* O, my dear lord—

*Hamlet:*                                 Nay, do not think I flatter,

    For what advancement may I hope from thee

    That no revenue hast but thy good spirits

    To feed and clothe thee? Why should the poor be flattered?

    No, let the candied tongue lick absurd pomp,                                                           45

    And crook the pregnant hinges of the knee

    Where thrift may follow fawning. Dost thou hear?

    Since my dear soul was mistress of her choice

    And could of men distinguish her election,

    Sh' hath sealed thee for herself, for thou hast been                                                50

    As one, in suffering all, that suffers nothing,

    A man that Fortune's buffets and rewards

    Hast ta'en with equal thanks; and blest are those

    Whose blood and judgment are so well commeddled

    That they are not a pipe for Fortune's finger                                                           55

    To sound what stop she please. Give me that man

    That is not passion's slave, and I will wear him

    In my heart's core, ay, in my heart of heart,

    As I do thee.—Something too much of this.—

    There is a play tonight before the King.                                                                   60

    One scene of it comes near the circumstance

    Which I have told thee of my father's death.

    I prithee, when thou seest that act afoot,

    Even with the very comment of thy soul

    Observe my uncle. If his occulted guilt                                                                    65

    Do not itself unkennel in one speech,

    It is a damnèd ghost that we have seen,

---

34 *presently* at once     40 *my . . . withal* my dealings encountered     45 *candied* sugared, flattering
46 *pregnant* compliant     47 *thrift* profit     49 *could . . . election* could make distinguishing choices
among persons     50 *sealed thee* (Literally, as one would seal a legal document to mark possession.)
54 *blood* passion.     *commeddled* commingled     56 *stop* hole in a wind instrument for controlling
the sound     64 *very . . . soul* your most penetrating observation and consideration     65 *occulted*
hidden     66 *unkennel* (As one would say of a fox driven from its lair.)     67 *damnèd* in league
with Satan

And my imaginations are as foul
As Vulcan's stithy. Give him heedful note,
For I mine eyes will rivet to his face,                                              70
And after we will both our judgments join
In censure of his seeming.
Horatio:                                    Well, my lord.
If 'a steal aught the whilst this play is playing
And scape detecting, I will pay the theft.

[*Flourish.*] *Enter trumpets and kettledrums, King,*

*Queen, Polonius, Ophelia, [Rosencrantz, Guildenstern, and other lords, with*
*guards carrying torches].*

Hamlet: They are coming to the play. I must be idle. Get you a place.        75
[*The King, Queen, and courtiers sit.*]
King: How fares our cousin Hamlet?
Hamlet: Excellent, i' faith, of the chameleon's dish: I eat the air, promise-
crammed. You cannot feed capons so.
King: I have nothing with this answer, Hamlet. These words are not mine.
Hamlet: No, nor mine now. [*To Polonius.*] My lord, you played once i' th' univer-   80
sity, you say?
Polonius: That did I, my lord, and was accounted a good actor.
Hamlet: What did you enact?
Polonius: I did enact Julius Caesar. I was killed i' the Capitol; Brutus killed me.
Hamlet: It was a brute part of him to kill so capital a calf there.—Be the players   85
ready?
Rosencrantz: Ay, my lord. They stay upon your patience.
Queen: Come hither, my dear Hamlet, sit by me.
Hamlet: No, good Mother, here's metal more attractive.
Polonius [*to the King*]: O, ho, do you mark that?                                    90
Hamlet: Lady, shall I lie in your lap?

                                                [*Lying down at Ophelia's feet.*]

Ophelia: No, my lord.
Hamlet: I mean, my head upon your lap?

---

69 *stithy* smithy, place of stiths (anvils)      72 *censure of his seeming* judgment of his appearance or
behavior      73 *If 'a steal aught* if he gets away with anything      75 *idle* (1) unoccupied (2) mad
76 *cousin* i.e., close relative      77 *chameleon's dish* (Chameleons were supposed to feed on air.
Hamlet deliberately misinterprets the King's *fares* as "feeds." By his phrase *eat the air* he also plays on
the idea of feeding himself with the promise of succession, of being the *heir*.)      78 *capons* roosters
castrated and *crammed* with feed to make them succulent      79 *have . . . with* make nothing of, or
gain nothing from.      *are not mine* do not respond to what I asked      80 *nor mine now* (Once spoken, words are proverbially no longer the speaker's own—and hence should be uttered warily.)
85 *brute* (The Latin meaning of *brutus*, "stupid," was often used punningly with the name Brutus.)
*part* (1) deed (2) role.      *calf* fool      87 *stay upon* await      89 *metal* substance that is *attractive*,
i.e., magnetic, but with suggestion also of *mettle*, "disposition"

*Ophelia:* Ay, my lord.

*Hamlet:* Do you think I meant country matters?                                               95

*Ophelia:* I think nothing, my lord.

*Hamlet:* That's a fair thought to lie between maids' legs.

*Ophelia:* What is, my lord?

*Hamlet:* Nothing.

*Ophelia:* You are merry, my lord.                                                          100

*Hamlet:* Who, I?

*Ophelia:* Ay, my lord.

*Hamlet:* O God, your only jig maker. What should a man do but be merry? For
   look you how cheerfully my mother looks, and my father died within 's two
   hours.                                                                                    105

*Ophelia:* Nay, 'tis twice two months, my lord.

*Hamlet:* So long? Nay then, let the devil wear black, for I'll have a suit of sables.
   O heavens! Die two months ago, and not forgotten yet? Then there's hope a
   great man's memory may outlive his life half a year. But, by'r Lady, 'a must
   build churches, then, or else shall 'a suffer not thinking on, with the hobby-         110
   horse, whose epitaph is "For O, for O, the hobbyhorse is forgot."

*The trumpets sound. Dumb show follows.*

*Enter a King and a Queen [very lovingly]; the Queen embracing him, and he her.
[She kneels, and makes show of protestation unto him.] He takes her up, and
declines his head upon her neck. He lies him down upon a bank of flowers. She,
seeing him asleep, leaves him. Anon comes in another man, takes off his crown,
kisses it, pours poison in the sleeper's ears, and leaves him. The Queen returns,
finds the King dead, makes passionate action. The Poisoner with some three or four
come in again, seem to condole with her. The dead body is carried away. The
Poisoner woos the Queen with gifts; she seems harsh awhile, but in the end accepts
love.*

*[Exeunt players.]*

*Ophelia:* What means this, my lord?

*Hamlet:* Marry, this' miching mallico; it means mischief.

*Ophelia:* Belike this show imports the argument of the play.

---

95 *country matters* sexual intercourse (making a bawdy pun on the first syllable of *country*)      99
*Nothing* the figure zero or naught, suggesting the female sexual anatomy. (*Thing* not infrequently has a
bawdy connotation of male or female anatomy, and the reference here could be male.)      103 *only*
*jig maker* very best composer of jigs, i.e., pointless merriment. (Hamlet replies sardonically to
Ophelia's observation that he is merry by saying, "If you're looking for someone who is really merry,
you've come to the right person.")      104 *within 's* within this (i.e., these)      107 *suit of sables* garments trimmed with the fur of the sable and hence suited for a wealthy person, not a mourner (but
with a pun on *sable*, "black," ironically suggesting mourning once again)      110 *suffer . . . on* undergo oblivion      111 *For . . . forgot* (Verse of a song occurring also in *Love's Labor's Lost,* 3.1.27–28.
The hobbyhorse was a character made up to resemble a horse and rider, appearing in the morris
dance and such May-game sports. This song laments the disappearance of such customs under pressure from the Puritans.)      113 *this' miching mallico* this is sneaking mischief      114 *Belike* probably.
*argument* plot

*Enter Prologue.*

*Hamlet:* We shall know by this fellow. The players cannot keep counsel; they'll 115
tell all.

*Ophelia:* Will 'a tell us what this show meant?

*Hamlet:* Ay, or any show that you will show him. Be not you ashamed to show,
he'll not shame to tell you what it means.

*Ophelia:* You are naught, you are naught. I'll mark the play. 120

*Prologue:* For us, and for our tragedy,
 Here stooping to your clemency,
 We beg your hearing patiently. [*Exit.*]

*Hamlet:* Is this a prologue, or the posy of a ring?

*Ophelia:* 'Tis brief, my lord. 125

*Hamlet:* As woman's love.

 *Enter [two Players as] King and Queen.*

*Player King:* Full thirty times hath Phoebus' cart gone round
 Neptune's salt wash and Tellus' orbèd ground,
 And thirty dozen moons with borrowed sheen
 About the world have times twelve thirties been, 130
 Since love our hearts and Hymen did our hands
 Unite commutual in most sacred bands.

*Player Queen:* So many journeys may the sun and moon
 Make us again count o'er ere love be done!
 But, woe is me, you are so sick of late, 135
 So far from cheer and from your former state,
 That I distrust you. Yet, though I distrust,
 Discomfort you, my lord, it nothing must.
 For women's fear and love hold quantity;
 In neither aught, or in extremity. 140
 Now, what my love is, proof hath made you know,
 And as my love is sized, my fear is so.
 Where love is great, the littlest doubts are fear;
 Where little fears grow great, great love grows there.

*Player King:* Faith, I must leave thee, love, and shortly too; 145
 My operant powers their functions leave to do.

---

115 *counsel* secret    118 *Be not you* provided you are not    120 *naught* indecent. (Ophelia is
reacting to Hamlet's pointed remarks about not being ashamed to show all.)    122 *stooping* bowing
124 *posy . . . ring* brief motto in verse inscribed in a ring    127 *Phoebus' cart* the sun-god's chariot,
making its yearly cycle    128 *salt wash* the sea.    *Tellus* goddess of the earth, of the *orbèd* ground
129 *borrowed* i.e., reflected    131 *Hymen* god of matrimony    132 *commutual* mutually.    *bands*
bonds    137 *distrust* am anxious about    138 *Discomfort* distress.    *nothing* not at all    139
*hold quantity* keep proportion with one another    140 *In . . . extremity* i.e., women fear and love
either too little or too much, but the two, fear and love, are equal in either case    141 *proof* experience    142 *sized* in size    146 *operant powers* vital functions.    *leave to do* cease to perform

And thou shalt live in this fair world behind,
Honored, beloved; and haply one as kind
For husband shalt thou—

*Player Queen:*     O, confound the rest!
Such love must needs be treason in my breast.     150
In second husband let me be accurst!
None wed the second but who killed the first.

*Hamlet:* Wormwood, wormwood.

*Player Queen:* The instances that second marriage move
Are base respects of thrift, but none of love.     155
A second time I kill my husband dead
When second husband kisses me in bed.

*Player King:* I do believe you think what now you speak,
But what we do determine oft we break.
Purpose is but the slave to memory,     160
Of violent birth, but poor validity,
Which now, like fruit unripe, sticks on the tree,
But fall unshaken when they mellow be.
Most necessary 'tis that we forget
To pay ourselves what to ourselves is debt.     165
What to ourselves in passion we purpose,
The passion ending, doth the purpose lose.
The violence of either grief or joy
Their own enactures with themselves destroy.
Where joy most revels, grief doth most lament;     170
Grief joys, joy grieves, on slender accident.
This world is not for aye, nor 'tis not strange
That even our loves should with our fortunes change;
For 'tis a question left us yet to prove,
Whether love lead fortune, or else fortune love.     175
The great man down, you mark his favorite flies;
The poor advanced makes friends of enemies.
And hitherto doth love on fortune tend;
For who not needs shall never lack a friend,
And who in want a hollow friend doth try     180

147 *behind* after I have gone 152 *None* i.e., let no woman. *but who* except the one who
153 *Wormwood* i.e., how bitter. (Literally, a bitter-tasting plant.) 154 *instances* motives. *move*
motivate 155 *base . . . thrift* ignoble considerations of material prosperity 160 *Purpose . . .
memory* our good intentions are subject to forgetfulness 161 *validity* strength, durability 162
*Which* i.e., purpose 164–165 *Most . . . debt* it's inevitable that in time we forget the obligations
we have imposed on ourselves 169 *enactures* fulfillments 170–171 *Where . . . accident* the
capacity for extreme joy and grief go together, and often one extreme is instantly changed into its
opposite on the slightest provocation 172 *aye* ever 176 *down* fallen in fortune 177 *The
poor . . . enemies* when one of humble station is promoted, you see his enemies suddenly becoming his
friends 178 *hitherto* up to this point in the argument, or, to this extent. *tend* attend 179
*who not needs* he who is not in need (of wealth) 180 *who in want* he who, being in need. *try*
test (his generosity)

Directly seasons him his enemy.
But, orderly to end where I begun,
Our wills and fates do so contrary run
That our devices still are overthrown;
Our thoughts are ours, their ends none of our own.                                    185
So think thou wilt no second husband wed,
But die thy thoughts when thy first lord is dead.
*Player Queen:* Nor earth to me give food, nor heaven light,
Sport and repose lock from me day and night,
To desperation turn my trust and hope,                                                  190
An anchor's cheer in prison be my scope!
Each opposite that blanks the face of joy
Meet what I would have well and it destroy!
Both here and hence pursue me lasting strife
If, once a widow, ever I be wife!                                                        195
*Hamlet:* If she should break it now!
*Player King:* 'Tis deeply sworn. Sweet, leave me here awhile;
My spirits grow dull, and fain I would beguile
The tedious day with sleep.
*Player Queen:*                                    Sleep rock thy brain,
And never come mischance between us twain!                                              200

                        *[He sleeps.] Exit [Player Queen].*

*Hamlet:* Madam, how like you this play?
*Queen:* The lady doth protest too much, methinks.
*Hamlet:* O, but she'll keep her word.
*King:* Have you heard the argument? Is there no offense in 't?
*Hamlet:* No, no, they do but jest, poison in jest. No offense i' the world.             205
*King:* What do you call the play?
*Hamlet:* *The Mousetrap.* Marry, how? Tropically. This play is the image of a mur-
    der done in Vienna. Gonzago is the Duke's name, his wife, Baptista. You
    shall see anon. 'Tis a knavish piece of work, but what of that? Your Majesty,
    and we that have free souls, it touches us not. Let the galled jade wince, our     210
    withers are unwrung.

181 *seasons him* ripens him into       183 *Our . . . run* what we want and what we get go so contrarily
184 *devices still* intentions continually       185 *ends* results       188 *Nor* let neither       189 *Sport . . .*
*night* may day deny me its pastimes and night its repose       191 *anchor's cheer* anchorite's or hermit's
fare.       *my scope* the extent of my happiness       192–193 *Each . . . destroy* may every adverse thing
that causes the face of joy to turn pale meet and destroy everything that I desire to see prosper.
*blanks* causes to blanch or grow pale       194 *hence* in the life hereafter       198 *spirits* vital spirits
202 *doth . . . much* makes too many promises and protestations       204 *argument* plot       204–205
*offense . . . offense* cause for objection . . . actual injury, crime       205 *jest* make believe       207
*Tropically* figuratively. (The First Quarto reading, *trapically*, suggests a pun on *trap* in *Mousetrap.*)
208 *Duke's* i.e., King's. (A slip that may be due to Shakespeare's possible source, the alleged murder
of the Duke of Urbino by Luigi Gonzaga in 1538.)       210 *free* guiltless.       *galled jade* horse whose
hide is rubbed by saddle or harness.       211 *withers* the part between the horse's shoulder blades
*unwrung* not rubbed sore

*Enter Lucianus.*

This is one Lucianus, nephew to the King.

*Ophelia:* You are as good as a chorus, my lord.

*Hamlet:* I could interpret between you and your love, if I could see the puppets
    dallying.         215

*Ophelia:* You are keen, my lord, you are keen.

*Hamlet:* It would cost you a groaning to take off mine edge.

*Ophelia:* Still better, and worse.

*Hamlet:* So you mis-take your husbands. Begin, murderer; leave thy damnable
    faces and begin. Come, the croaking raven doth bellow for revenge.     220

*Lucianus:* Thoughts black, hands apt, drugs fit, and time agreeing,
    Confederate season, else no creature seeing,
    Thou mixture rank, of midnight weeds collected,
    With Hecate's ban thrice blasted, thrice infected,
    Thy natural magic and dire property     225
    On wholesome life usurp immediately.

*[He pours the poison into the sleeper's ear.]*

*Hamlet:* 'A poison him i' the garden for his estate. His name's Gonzago. The story
    is extant, and written in very choice Italian. You shall see anon how the
    murderer gets the love of Gonzago's wife.

*[Claudius rises.]*

*Ophelia:* The King rises.     230

*Hamlet:* What, frighted with false fire?

*Queen:* How fares my lord?

*Polonius:* Give o'er the play.

*King:* Give me some light. Away!

*Polonius:* Lights, lights, lights!     235

*Exeunt all but Hamlet and Horatio.*

---

213 *chorus* (In many Elizabethan plays, the forthcoming action was explained by an actor known as
the "chorus"; at a puppet show, the actor who spoke the dialogue was known as an "interpreter," as
indicated by the lines following.)     214 *interpret* (1) ventriloquize the dialogue, as in puppet show
(2) act as pander     214–215 *puppets dallying* (With suggestion of sexual play, continued in *keen*,
"sexually aroused," *groaning*, "moaning in pregnancy," and *edge*, "sexual desire" or "impetuosity.")
216 *keen* sharp, bitter     218 *Still . . . worse* more keen, always *bettering* what other people say with
witty wordplay, but at the same time more offensive     219 *So even thus* (in marriage).     *mis-take*
take falseheartedly and cheat on. (The marriage vows say "for better, for worse.")     222 *Confederate
season* the time and occasion conspiring (to assist the murderer).     *else* otherwise.     *seeing* seeing
me     224 *Hecate's ban* the curse of Hecate, the goddess of witchcraft     225 *dire property* baleful
quality     227 *estate* i.e., the kingship.     *His* i.e., the King's     231 *false fire* the blank discharge
of a gun loaded with powder but no shot

*Hamlet:* "Why, let the strucken deer go weep,
     The hart ungallèd play.
     For some must watch, while some must sleep;
     Thus runs the world away."
Would not this, sir, and a forest of feathers—if the rest of my fortunes turn     240
Turk with me—with two Provincial roses on my razed shoes, get me a fel-
lowship in a cry of players?
*Horatio:* Half a share.
*Hamlet:* A whole one, I.
     "For thou dost know, O Damon dear,     245
     This realm dismantled was
     Of Jove himself, and now reigns here
     A very, very—pajock."
*Horatio:* You might have rhymed.
*Hamlet:* O good Horatio, I'll take the ghost's word for a thousand pound. Didst     250
perceive?
*Horatio:* Very well, my lord.
*Hamlet:* Upon the talk of the poisoning?
*Horatio:* I did very well note him.

     *Enter Rosencrantz and Guildenstern.*

*Hamlet:* Aha! Come, some music! Come, the recorders.     255
     "For if the King like not the comedy,
     Why then, belike, he likes it not, perdy."
     Come, some music.
*Guildenstern:* Good my lord, vouchsafe me a word with you.
*Hamlet:* Sir, a whole history.     260
*Guildenstern:* The King, sir—
*Hamlet:* Ay, sir, what of him?
*Guildenstern:* Is in his retirement marvelous distempered.
*Hamlet:* With drink, sir?
*Guildenstern:* No, my lord, with choler.     265

---

236–239 *Why . . . away* (Probably from an old ballad, with allusion to the popular belief that a wounded deer retires to weep and die; compare with *As You Like It,* Act II, Scene I, lines 33–66.) 237 *ungallèd* unafflicted     238 *watch* remain awake     239 *Thus . . . away* thus the world goes 240 *this* i.e., the play.     *feathers* (Allusion to the plumes that Elizabethan actors were fond of wearing.)     241 *turn Turk with* turn renegade against, go back on     241 *Provincial roses* rosettes of ribbon, named for roses grown in a part of France.     *razed* with ornamental slashing.     242 *fellowship . . . players* partnership in a theatrical company.     *cry* pack (of hounds)     245 *Damon* the friend of Pythias, as Horatio is friend of Hamlet; or, a traditional pastoral name     246–248 *This realm . . . pajock* i.e., Jove, representing divine authority and justice, has abandoned this realm to its own devices, leaving in his stead only a peacock or vain pretender to virtue (though the rhyme-word expected in place of *pajock* or "peacock" suggests that the realm is now ruled over by an "ass"). 246 *dismantled* stripped, divested     255 *recorders* wind instruments of the flute kind     257 *perdy* (A corruption of the French *par dieu,* "by God.")     263 *retirement* withdrawal to his chambers. *distempered* out of humor. (But Hamlet deliberately plays on the wider application to any illness of mind or body, especially to drunkenness.)

*Hamlet:* Your wisdom should show itself more richer to signify this to the doctor, for for me to put him to his purgation would perhaps plunge him into more choler.

*Guildenstern:* Good my lord, put your discourse into some frame and start not so wildly from my affair. 270

*Hamlet:* I am tame, sir. Pronounce.

*Guildenstern:* The Queen, your mother, in most great affliction of spirit, hath sent me to you.

*Hamlet:* You are welcome.

*Guildenstern:* Nay, good my lord, this courtesy is not of the right breed. If it shall 275 please you to make me a wholesome answer, I will do your mother's commandment; if not, your pardon and my return shall be the end of my business.

*Hamlet:* Sir, I cannot.

*Rosencrantz:* What, my lord? 280

*Hamlet:* Make you a wholesome answer; my wit's diseased. But, sir, such answer as I can make, you shall command, or rather, as you say, my mother. Therefore no more, but to the matter. My mother, you say—

*Rosencrantz:* Then thus she says: your behavior hath struck her into amazement and admiration. 285

*Hamlet:* O wonderful son, that can so stonish a mother! But is there no sequel at the heels of this mother's admiration? Impart.

*Rosencrantz:* She desires to speak with you in her closet ere you go to bed.

*Hamlet:* We shall obey, were she ten times our mother. Have you any further trade with us? 290

*Rosencrantz:* My lord, you once did love me.

*Hamlet:* And do still, by these pickers and stealers.

*Rosencrantz:* Good my lord, what is your cause of distemper? You do surely bar the door upon your own liberty if you deny your griefs to your friend.

*Hamlet:* Sir, I lack advancement. 295

*Rosencrantz:* How can that be, when you have the voice of the King himself for your succession in Denmark?

*Hamlet:* Ay, sir, but "While the grass grows"—the proverb is something musty.

*Enter the Players with recorders.*

---

267 *purgation* (Hamlet hints at something going beyond medical treatment to blood-letting and the extraction of confession.)    268 *choler* anger. (But Hamlet takes the word in its more basic humoral sense of "bilious disorder.")    269 *frame* order.    *start* shy or jump away (like a horse; the opposite of *tame* in line 271)    275 *breed* (1) kind (2) breeding, manners    277 *pardon* permission to depart    285 *admiration* bewilderment    288 *closet* private chamber    292 *pickers and stealers* i.e., hands. (So called from the catechism, "to keep my hands from picking and stealing.")    294 *liberty* i.e., being freed from *distemper*, line 293; but perhaps with a veiled threat as well.    *deny* refuse to share    298 *While . . . grows* (The rest of the proverb is "the silly horse starves"; Hamlet may not live long enough to succeed to the kingdom.)    *something* somewhat.    s.d. *Players* actors

O, the recorders. Let me see one. [*He takes a recorder*.] To withdraw with
you: why do you go about to recover the wind of me, as if you would drive 300
me into a toil?
*Guildenstern:* O, my lord, if my duty be too bold, my love is too unmannerly.
*Hamlet:* I do not well understand that. Will you play upon this pipe?
*Guildenstern:* My lord, I cannot.
*Hamlet:* I pray you. 305
*Guildenstern:* Believe me, I cannot.
*Hamlet:* I do beseech you.
*Guildenstern:* I know no touch of it, my lord.
*Hamlet:* It is as easy as lying. Govern these ventages with your fingers and thumb,
give it breath with your mouth, and it will discourse most eloquent music. 310
Look you, these are the stops.
*Guildenstern:* But these cannot I command to any utterance of harmony. I have
not the skill.
*Hamlet:* Why, look you now, how unworthy a thing you make of me! You would
play upon me, you would seem to know my stops, you would pluck out the 315
heart of my mystery, you would sound me from my lowest note to the top of
my compass, and there is much music, excellent voice, in this little organ,
yet cannot you make it speak. 'Sblood, do you think I am easier to be played
on than a pipe? Call me what instrument you will, though you can fret me,
you cannot play upon me. 320

*Enter Polonius.*

God bless you, sir!
*Polonius:* My lord, the Queen would speak with you, and presently.
*Hamlet:* Do you see yonder cloud that's almost in shape of a camel?
*Polonius:* By the Mass and 'tis, like a camel indeed.
*Hamlet:* Methinks it is like a weasel. 325
*Polonius:* It is backed like a weasel.
*Hamlet:* Or like a whale.
*Polonius:* Very like a whale
*Hamlet:* Then I will come to my mother by and by. [*Aside.*] They fool me to the
top of my bent.—I will come by and by. 330
*Polonius:* I will say so. [*Exit.*]

299 *withdraw* speak privately    300 *recover the wind* get to the windward side (thus driving the
game into the *toil*, or "net")    301 *toil* snare    302 *if . . . unmannerly* if I am using an unmannerly
boldness, it is my love that occasions it    303 *I . . . that* i.e., I don't understand how genuine love
can be unmannerly    309 *ventages* finger-holes or *stops* (line 315) of the recorder    316 *sound* (1)
fathom (2) produce sound in    317 *compass* range (of voice).    *organ* musical instrument
319 *fret* irritate (with a quibble on *fret*, meaning the piece of wood, gut, or metal that regulates the
fingering on an instrument)    322 *presently* at once    329 *by and by* quite soon.    *fool me* trifle
with me, humor my fooling.    330 *top of my bent* limit of my ability or endurance. (Literally, the
extent to which a bow may be bent.)

*Hamlet:* "By and by" is easily said. Leave me, friends.

*[Exeunt all but Hamlet.]*

'Tis now the very witching time of night,
When churchyards yawn and hell itself breathes out
Contagion to this world. Now could I drink hot blood                    335
And do such bitter business as the day
Would quake to look on. Soft, now to my mother.
O heart, lose not thy nature! Let not ever
The soul of Nero enter this firm bosom.
Let me be cruel, not unnatural;                                         340
I will speak daggers to her, but use none.
My tongue and soul in this be hypocrites:
How in my words soever she be shent,
To give them seals never my soul consent!                    *Exit.*

## Scene III *[The Castle.]*

*Enter King, Rosencrantz, and Guildenstern.*

*King:* I like him not, nor stands it safe with us
To let his madness range. Therefore prepare you.
I your commission will forthwith dispatch,
And he to England shall along with you.
The terms of our estate may not endure                                  5
Hazard so near 's as doth hourly grow
Out of his brows.
*Guildenstern:*          We will ourselves provide.
Most holy and religious fear it is
To keep those many many bodies safe
That live and feed upon Your Majesty.                                   10
*Rosencrantz:* The single and peculiar life is bound
With all the strength and armor of the mind
To keep itself from noyance, but much more
That spirit upon whose weal depends and rests
The lives of many. The cess of majesty                                  15
Dies not alone, but like a gulf doth draw
What's near it with it; or it is a massy wheel
Fixed on the summit of the highest mount,

---

333 *witching time* time when spells are cast and evil is abroad     338 *nature* natural feeling     339
*Nero* murderer of his mother, Agrippina     343 *How . . . soever* however much by my words.
*shent* rebuked     344 *give them seals* i.e., confirm them with deeds     1 *him* i.e., his behavior     3
*dispatch* prepare, cause to be drawn up     5 *terms of our estate* circumstances of my royal position
7 *Out of his brows* i.e., from his brain, in the form of plots and threats     8 *religious fear* sacred concern     11 *single and peculiar* individual and private     13 *noyance* harm     15 *cess* decrease, cessation     16 *gulf* whirlpool     17 *massy* massive

To whose huge spokes ten thousand lesser things
Are mortised and adjoined, which, when it falls,         20
Each small annexment, petty consequence,
Attends the boisterous ruin. Never alone
Did the King sigh, but with a general groan.

*King:* Arm you, I pray you, to this speedy voyage,
For we will fetters put about this fear,         25
Which now goes too free-footed.

*Rosencrantz:*               We will haste us.

*Exeunt gentlemen [Rosencrantz and Guildenstern].*

*Enter Polonius.*

*Polonius:* My lord, he's going to his mother's closet.
Behind the arras I'll convey myself
To hear the process. I'll warrant she'll tax him home,
And, as you said—and wisely was it said—
'Tis meet that some more audience than a mother,         30
Since nature makes them partial, should o'erhear
The speech, of vantage. Fare you well, my liege.
I'll call upon you ere you go to bed
And tell you what I know.

*King:*               Thanks, dear my lord.         35

*Exit [Polonius].*

O, my offense is rank! It smells to heaven.
It hath the primal eldest curse upon 't,
A brother's murder. Pray can I not,
Though inclination be as sharp as will;
My stronger guilt defeats my strong intent,         40
And like a man to double business bound
I stand in pause where I shall first begin,
And both neglect. What if this cursèd hand
Were thicker than itself with brother's blood,
Is there not rain enough in the sweet heavens         45
To wash it white as snow? Whereto serves mercy
But to confront the visage of offense?

---

20 *mortised* fastened (as with a fitted joint).   *when it falls* i.e., when it descends, like the wheel of
Fortune, bringing a king down with it   21 *Each . . . consequence* i.e., every hanger-on and unimportant person or thing connected with the King   22 *Attends* participates in   24 *Arm* prepare
28 *arras* screen of tapestry placed around the walls of household apartments. (On the Elizabethan stage,
the arras was presumably over a door or discovery space in the tiring-house facade.)   29 *process* proceedings.   *tax him home* reprove him severely   31 *meet* fitting   33 *of vantage* from an advantageous place, or, in addition   37 *the primal eldest curse* the curse of Cain, the first murderer; he killed
his brother Abel   39 *Though . . . will* though my desire is as strong as my determination   41
*bound* (1) destined (2) obliged. (The King wants to repent and still enjoy what he has gained.)
46–47 *Whereto . . . offense* what function does mercy serve other than to meet sin face to face?

And what's in prayer but this twofold force,
To be forestallèd ere we come to fall,
Or pardoned being down? Then I'll look up.                                        50
My fault is past. But O, what form of prayer
Can serve my turn? "Forgive me my foul murder"?
That cannot be, since I am still possessed
Of those effects for which I did the murder:
My crown, mine own ambition, and my queen.                                        55
May one be pardoned and retain th' offense?
In the corrupted currents of this world
Offense's gilded hand may shove by justice,
And oft 'tis seen the wicked prize itself
Buys out the law. But 'tis not so above.                                          60
There is no shuffling, there the action lies
In his true nature, and we ourselves compelled,
Even to the teeth and forehead of our faults,
To give in evidence. What then? What rests?
Try what repentance can. What can it not?                                         65
Yet what can it, when one cannot repent?
O wretched state, O bosom black as death,
O limèd soul that, struggling to be free,
Art more engaged! Help, angels! Make assay.
Bow, stubborn knees, and heart with strings of steel,                             70
Be soft as sinews of the newborn babe!
All may be well.                                                         [He kneels.]

Enter Hamlet.

Hamlet: Now might I do it pat, now 'a is a-praying;
And now I'll do 't. [He draws his sword.] And so 'a goes to heaven,
And so am I revenged. That would be scanned:                                      75
A villain kills my father, and for that,
I, his sole son, do this same villain send
To heaven.
Why, this is hire and salary, not revenge.
'A took my father grossly, full of bread,                                         80
With all his crimes broad blown, as flush as May;

---

49 *forestallèd* prevented (from sinning)    56 *th' offense* the thing for which one offended    57 *currents* courses    58 *gilded hand* hand offering gold as a bribe.    *shove by* thrust aside    59 *wicked prize* prize won by wickedness    61 *There* i.e., in heaven.    *shuffling* escape by trickery. *the action lies* the accusation is made manifest. (A legal metaphor.)    62 *his* its    63 *to the teeth and forehead* face to face, concealing nothing    64 *give in* provide.    *rests* remains    68 *limèd* caught as with birdlime, a sticky substance used to ensnare birds    69 *engaged* entangled.    *assay* trial. (Said to himself.)    73 *pat* opportunely    75 *would be scanned* needs to be looked into, or, would be interpreted as follows    80 *grossly, full of bread* i.e., enjoying his worldly pleasures rather than fasting. (See Ezekiel 16:49.)    81 *crimes broad blown* sins in full bloom.    *flush* vigorous

And how his audit stands who knows save heaven?
But in our circumstance and course of thought
'Tis heavy with him. And am I then revenged,
To take him in the purging of his soul,                                          85
When he is fit and seasoned for his passage?
No!
Up, sword, and know thou a more horrid hent.

                                              *[He puts up his sword.]*

When he is drunk asleep, or in his rage,
Or in th' incestuous pleasure of his bed,                                        90
At game, a-swearing, or about some act
That has no relish of salvation in 't—
Then trip him, that his heels may kick at heaven,
And that his soul may be as damned and black
As hell, whereto it goes. My mother stays.                                       95
This physic but prolongs thy sickly days.                             *Exit.*
*King:* My words fly up, my thoughts remain below.
Words without thoughts never to heaven go.                            *Exit.*

### Scene IV [*The Queen's Private Chamber.*]

*Enter [Queen] Gertrude and Polonius.*

*Polonius:* 'A will come straight. Look you lay home to him.
Tell him his pranks have been too broad to bear with,
And that Your Grace hath screened and stood between
Much heat and him. I'll shroud me even here.
Pray you, be round with him.                                                      5
*Hamlet (within):* Mother, Mother, Mother!
*Queen:* I'll warrant you, fear me not.
Withdraw, I hear him coming.

                                              *[Polonius hides behind the arras.]*

*Enter Hamlet.*

*Hamlet:* Now, Mother, what's the matter?

---

82 *audit* account.     *save* except for     83 *in . . . thought* as we see it from our mortal perspective
86 *seasoned* matured, readied     88 *know . . . hent* await to be grasped by me on a more horrid occasion.     *hent* act of seizing     89 *drunk . . . rage* dead drunk, or in a fit of sexual passion     91
*game* gambling     92 *relish* trace, savor     95 *stays* awaits (me)     96 *physic* purging (by prayer),
or, Hamlet's postponement of the killing     1 *lay home* thrust to the heart, reprove him soundly
2 *broad* unrestrained     4 *Much heat* i.e., the King's anger.     *shroud* conceal (with ironic fitness to
Polonius' imminent death. The word is only in the First Quarto; the Second Quarto and the Folio
read "silence.")     5 *round* blunt

*Queen:* Hamlet, thou hast thy father much offended. 10
*Hamlet:* Mother, you have my father much offended.
*Queen:* Come, come, you answer with an idle tongue.
*Hamlet:* Go, go, you question with a wicked tongue.
*Queen:* Why, how now, Hamlet?
*Hamlet:* What's the matter now?
*Queen:* Have you forgot me?
*Hamlet:* No, by the rood, not so: 15
    You are the Queen, your husband's brother's wife,
    And—would it were not so!—you are my mother.
*Queen:* Nay, then, I'll set those to you that can speak.
*Hamlet:* Come, come, and sit you down; you shall not budge.
    You go not till I set you up a glass 20
    Where you may see the inmost part of you.
*Queen:* What wilt thou do? Thou wilt not murder me?
    Help, ho!
*Polonius [behind the arras]:* What ho! Help!
*Hamlet [drawing]:* How now? A rat? Dead for a ducat, dead! 25

                  *[He thrusts his rapier through the arras.]*

*Polonius [behind the arras]:* O, I am slain!         *[He falls and dies.]*
*Queen:* O me, what has thou done?
*Hamlet:* Nay, I know not. Is it the King?
*Queen:* O, what a rash and bloody deed is this!
*Hamlet:* A bloody deed—almost as bad, good Mother,
    As kill a king, and marry with his brother. 30
*Queen:* As kill a king!
*Hamlet:* Ay, lady, it was my word.

            *[He parts the arras and discovers Polonius.]*

    Thou wretched, rash, intruding fool, farewell!
    I took thee for thy better. Take thy fortune.
    Thou find'st to be too busy is some danger.—
    Leave wringing of your hands. Peace, sit you down, 35
    And let me wring your heart, for so I shall,
    If it be made of penetrable stuff,
    If damnèd custom have not brazed it so
    That it be proof and bulwark against sense.
*Queen:* What have I done, that thou dar'st wag thy tongue 40
    In noise so rude against me?

10 *thy father* i.e., your stepfather, Claudius    12 *idle* foolish    15 *forgot me* i.e., forgotten that I am your mother.    *rood* cross of Christ    18 *speak* i.e., to someone so rude    25 *Dead for a ducat* i.e., I bet a ducat he's dead; or, a ducat is his life's fee    34 *busy* nosey    38 *damnèd custom* habitual wickedness.    *brazed* brazened, hardened    39 *proof* armor.    *sense* feeling

*Hamlet:*                          Such an act
   That blurs the grace and blush of modesty,
   Calls virtue hypocrite, takes off the rose
   From the fair forehead of an innocent love
   And sets a blister there, makes marriage vows        45
   As false as dicers' oaths. O, such a deed
   As from the body of contraction plucks
   The very soul, and sweet religion makes
   A rhapsody of words. Heaven's face does glow
   O'er this solidity and compound mass        50
   With tristful visage, as against the doom,
   Is thought-sick at the act.
*Queen:*                          Ay me, what act,
   That roars so loud and thunders in the index?
*Hamlet [showing her two likenesses]:* Look here upon this picture, and on this,
   The counterfeit presentment of two brothers.        55
   See what a grace was seated on this brow:
   Hyperion's curls, the front of Jove himself,
   An eye like Mars to threaten and command,
   A station like the herald Mercury
   New-lighted on a heaven-kissing hill—        60
   A combination and a form indeed
   Where every god did seem to set his seal
   To give the world assurance of a man.
   This was your husband. Look you now what follows:
   Here is your husband, like a mildewed ear,        65
   Blasting his wholesome brother. Have you eyes?
   Could you on this fair mountain leave to feed
   And batten on this moor? Ha, have you eyes?
   You cannot call it love, for at your age
   The heyday in the blood is tame, it's humble,        70
   And waits upon the judgment, and what judgment
   Would step from this to this? Sense, sure, you have,
   Else could you not have motion, but sure that sense

---

45 *sets a blister* i.e., brands as a harlot    47 *contraction* the marriage contract    48 *sweet religion makes* i.e., makes marriage vows    49 *rhapsody* senseless string    49–52 *Heaven's . . . act* heaven's face blushes at this solid world compounded of the various elements, with sorrowful face as though the day of doom were near, and is sick with horror at the deed (i.e., Gertrude's marriage)    53 *index* table of contents, prelude or preface    55 *counterfeit presentment* portrayed representation    57 *Hyperion's* the sun-god's.    *front* brow    58 *Mars* god of war    59 *station* manner of standing. *Mercury* winged messenger of the gods    60 *New-lighted* newly alighted    62 *set his seal* i.e., affix his approval    65 *ear* i.e., of grain    66 *Blasting* blighting    67 *leave* cease    68 *batten* gorge. *moor* barren or marshy ground (suggesting also "dark-skinned")    70 *heyday* state of excitement. *blood* passion    72 *Sense* perception through the five senses (the functions of the middle or sensible soul)

Is apoplexed, for madness would not err,
Nor sense to ecstasy was ne'er so thralled,                              75
But it reserved some quantity of choice
To serve in such a difference. What devil was 't
That thus hath cozened you at hoodman-blind?
Eyes without feeling, feeling without sight,
Ears without hands or eyes, smelling sans all,                           80
Or but a sickly part of one true sense
Could not so mope. O shame, where is thy blush?
Rebellious hell,
If thou canst mutine in a matron's bones,
To flaming youth let virtue be as wax                                    85
And melt in her own fire. Proclaim no shame
When the compulsive ardor gives the charge,
Since frost itself as actively doth burn,
And reason panders will.
Queen: O Hamlet, speak no more!                                          90
Thou turn'st mine eyes into my very soul,
And there I see such black and grainèd spots
As will not leave their tinct.
Hamlet:                              Nay, but to live
In the rank sweat of an enseamèd bed,
Stewed in corruption, honeying and making love                          95
Over the nasty sty!
Queen: O, speak to me no more!
These words like daggers enter in my ears.
No more, sweet Hamlet!
Hamlet:                              A murderer and a villain,
A slave that is not twentieth part the tithe                            100
Of your precedent lord, a vice of kings,
A cutpurse of the empire and the rule,

---

74 *apoplexed* paralyzed. (Hamlet goes on to explain that, without such a paralysis of will, mere madness would not so err, nor would the five senses so enthrall themselves to *ecstasy* or lunacy; even such deranged states of mind would be able to make the obvious choice between Hamlet Senior and Claudius.)   *err* so err     76 *But* but that     77 *To . . . difference* to help in making a choice between two such men     78 *cozened* cheated.     *hoodman-blind* blindman's buff. (In this game, says Hamlet, the devil must have pushed Claudius toward Gertrude while she was blindfolded.)   80 *sans* without     82 *mope* be dazed, act aimlessly     84 *mutine* incite mutiny     85–86 *be as wax . . . fire* melt like a candle or stick of sealing wax held over the candle flame     86–89 *Proclaim . . . will* call it no shameful business when the compelling ardor of youth delivers the attack, i.e., commits lechery, since the *frost* of advanced age burns with as active a fire of lust and reason perverts itself by fomenting lust rather than restraining it     92 *grainèd* dyed in grain, indelible     93 *leave their tinct* surrender their color     94 *enseamèd* saturated in the grease and filth of passionate lovemaking     95 *Stewed* soaked, bathed (with a suggestion of "stew," brothel)     100 *tithe* tenth part     101 *precedent lord* former husband.     *vice* buffoon. (A reference to the Vice of the morality plays.)

That from a shelf the precious diadem stole
And put it in his pocket!
*Queen:* No more! 105

*Enter Ghost.*

*Hamlet:* A king of shreds and patches—
Save me, and hover o'er me with your wings,
You heavenly guards! What would your gracious figure?
*Queen:* Alas, he's mad!
*Hamlet:* Do you not come your tardy son to chide, 110
That, lapsed in time and passion, lets go by
Th' important acting of your dread command?
O, say!
*Ghost:* Do not forget. This visitation
Is but to whet thy almost blunted purpose. 115
But look, amazement on thy mother sits.
O, step between her and her fighting soul!
Conceit in weakest bodies strongest works.
Speak to her, Hamlet.
*Hamlet:* How is it with you, lady?
*Queen:* Alas, how is 't with you, 120
That you do bend your eye on vacancy,
And with th' incorporal air do hold discourse?
Forth at your eyes your spirits wildly peep,
And, as the sleeping soldiers in th' alarm,
Your bedded hair, like life in excrements, 125
Start up and stand on end. O gentle son,
Upon the heat and flame of thy distemper
Sprinkle cool patience. Whereon do you look?
*Hamlet:* On him, on him! Look you how pale he glares!
His form and cause conjoined, preaching to stones, 130
Would make them capable.—Do not look upon me,
Lest with this piteous action you convert
My stern effects. Then what I have to do
Will want true color—tears perchance for blood.
*Queen:* To whom do you speak this? 135

---

106 *shreds and patches* i.e., motley, the traditional costume of the clown or fool    111 *lapsed* delaying    112 *important* importunate, urgent    116 *amazement* distraction    118 *Conceit* imagination    122 *incorporal* immaterial    124 *as . . . alarm* like soldiers called out of sleep by an alarm
125 *bedded* laid flat.    *like life in excrements* i.e., as though hair, an outgrowth of the body, had a life
of its own. (Hair was thought to be lifeless because it lacks sensation, and so its standing on end
would be unnatural and ominous.)    127 *distemper* disorder    130 *His . . . conjoined* his appearance joined to his cause for speaking    131 *capable* receptive    132–133 *convert . . . effects* divert
me from my stern duty    134 *want . . . blood* lack plausibility so that (with a play on the normal
sense of *color*) I shall shed colorless tears instead of blood

*Hamlet:* Do you see nothing there?
*Queen:* Nothing at all, yet all that is I see.
*Hamlet:* Nor did you nothing hear?
*Queen:* No, nothing but ourselves.
*Hamlet:* Why, look you there, look how it steals away!          140
    My father, in his habit as he lived!
    Look where he goes even now out at the portal!

                                                    *Exit Ghost.*

*Queen:* This is the very coinage of your brain.
    This bodiless creation ecstasy
    Is very cunning in.          145
*Hamlet:* Ecstasy?
    My pulse as yours doth temperately keep time,
    And makes as healthful music. It is not madness
    That I have uttered. Bring me to the test,
    And I the matter will reword, which madness          150
    Would gambol from. Mother, for love of grace,
    Lay not that flattering unction to your soul
    That not your trespass but my madness speaks.
    It will but skin and film the ulcerous place,
    Whiles rank corruption, mining all within,          155
    Infects unseen. Confess yourself to heaven,
    Repent what's past, avoid what is to come,
    And do not spread the compost on the weeds
    To make them ranker. Forgive me this my virtue;
    For in the fatness of these pursy times          160
    Virtue itself of vice must pardon beg,
    Yea, curb and woo for leave to do him good.
*Queen:* O Hamlet, thou hast cleft my heart in twain.
*Hamlet:* O, throw away the worser part of it,
    And live the purer with the other half.          165
    Good night. But go not to my uncle's bed;
    Assume a virtue, if you have it not.
    That monster, custom, who all sense doth eat,
    Of habits devil, is angel yet in this,
    That to the use of actions fair and good          170

---

141 *habit* clothes.    *as* as when    143 *very* mere    144–145 *This . . . in* madness is skillful in creating this kind of hallucination    150 *reword* repeat word for word    151 *gambol* skip away 152 *unction* ointment    154 *skin* grow a skin for    155 *mining* working under the surface    158 *compost* manure    159 *this my virtue* my virtuous talk in reproving you    160 *fatness* grossness. *pursy* flabby, out of shape    162 *curb* bow, bend the knee.    *leave* permission    168 *who . . . eat* which consumes all proper or natural feeling, all sensibility    169 *Of habits devil* devil-like in prompting evil habits

He likewise gives a frock or livery
That aptly is put on. Refrain tonight,
And that shall lend a kind of easiness
To the next abstinence; the next more easy;
For use almost can change the stamp of nature,                    175
And either . . . the devil, or throw him out
With wondrous potency. Once more, good night;
And when you are desirous to be blest,
I'll blessing beg of you. For this same lord,

                                         *[pointing to Polonius]*

I do repent; but heaven hath pleased it so                          180
To punish me with this, and this with me,
That I must be their scourge and minister.
I will bestow him, and will answer well
The death I gave him. So, again, good night.
I must be cruel only to be kind.                                    185
This bad begins, and worse remains behind.
One word more, good lady.
Queen:                              What shall I do?
Hamlet: Not this by no means that I bid you do:
    Let the bloat king tempt you again to bed,
    Pinch wanton on your cheek, call you his mouse,                 190
    And let him, for a pair of reechy kisses,
    Or paddling in your neck with his damned fingers,
    Make you to ravel all this matter out
    That I essentially am not in madness,
    But mad in craft. 'Twere good you let him know,                 195
    For who that's but a queen, fair, sober, wise,
    Would from a paddock, from a bat, a gib,
    Such dear concernings hide? Who would do so?
    No, in despite of sense and secrecy,

---

171 *livery* an outer appearance, a customary garb (and hence a predisposition easily assumed in time
of stress)    172 *aptly* readily    175 *use* habit.    *the stamp of nature* our inborn traits    176
*And either* (A defective line, usually emended by inserting the word *master* after *either,* following the
Fourth Quarto and early editors.)    178–179 *when . . . you* i.e., when you are ready to be penitent
and seek God's blessing, I will ask your blessing as a dutiful son should    182 *their scourge and minister* i.e., agent of heavenly retribution. (By *scourge,* Hamlet also suggests that he himself will eventually suffer punishment in the process of fulfilling heaven's will.)    183 *bestow* stow, dispose of.
*answer* account or pay for    186 *This* i.e., the killing of Polonius.    *behind* to come    189 *bloat*
bloated    190 *Pinch wanton* i.e., leave his love pinches on your cheeks, branding you as wanton
191 *reechy* dirty, filthy    192 *paddling* fingering amorously    193 *ravel . . . out* unravel, disclose
195 *in craft* by cunning.    *good* Said sarcastically (also the following eight lines.)    197 *paddock*
toad.    *gib* tomcat    198 *dear concernings* important affairs    199 *sense and secrecy* secrecy that
common sense requires

Unpeg the basket on the house's top,                                                    200
Let the birds fly, and like the famous ape,
To try conclusions, in the basket creep
And break your own neck down.
Queen: Be thou assured, if words be made of breath,
And breath of life, I have no life to breathe                                            205
What thou hast said to me.
Hamlet: I must to England. You know that?
Queen:                                            Alack,
I had forgot. 'Tis so concluded on.
Hamlet: There's letters sealed, and my two schoolfellows,
Whom I will trust as I will adders fanged,                                               210
They bear the mandate; they must sweep my way
And marshal me to knavery. Let it work.
For 'tis the sport to have the enginer
Hoist with his own petard, and 't shall go hard
But I will delve one yard below their mines                                              215
And blow them at the moon. O, 'tis most sweet
When in one line two crafts directly meet.
This man shall set me packing.
I'll lug the guts into the neighbor room.
Mother, good night indeed. This counselor                                               220
Is now most still, most secret, and most grave,
Who was in life a foolish prating knave.—
Come, sir, to draw toward an end with you.—
Good night, Mother.

*Exeunt [separately, Hamlet dragging in Polonius].*

200 *Unpeg the basket* open the cage, i.e., let out the secret     201 *famous ape* (In a story now lost.)
202 *try conclusions* test the outcome (in which the ape apparently enters a cage from which birds
have been released and then tries to fly out of the cage as they have done, falling to its death)
203 *down* in the fall: utterly     211–212 *sweep . . . knavery* sweep a path before me and conduct me
to some *knavery* or treachery prepared for me     212 *work* proceed     213 *enginer* maker of military
contrivances     214 *Hoist with* blown up by.     *petard* an explosive used to blow in a door or make
a breach     214–215 *'t shall . . . will* unless luck is against me, I will     215 *mines* tunnels used in
warfare to undermine the enemy's emplacements: Hamlet will countermine by going under their
mines     217 *in one line* i.e., mines and countermines on a collision course, or the countermines
directly below the mines.     *crafts* acts of guile, plots     218 *set me packing* set me to making
schemes, and set me to lugging (him), and, also, send me off in a hurry     223 *draw . . . end* finish
up (with a pun on *draw*, "pull")     s.d. *Enter . . . Queen* (Some editors argue that Gertrude never
exits in Act III, Scene IV, and that the scene is continuous here, as suggested in the Folio, but the
Second Quarto marks an entrance for her and at line 35 Claudius speaks of Gertrude's *closet* as
though it were elsewhere. A short time has elapsed, during which the King has become aware of her
highly wrought emotional state.)

# ACT IV

### Scene I [The Castle.]

*Enter King and Queen, with Rosencrantz and Guildenstern.*

King: There's matter in these sighs, these profound heaves.
    You must translate; 'tis fit we understand them.
    Where is your son?
Queen: Bestow this place on us a little while.

*[Exeunt Rosencrantz and Guildenstern.]*

    Ah, mine own lord, what have I seen tonight!       5
King: What, Gertrude? How does Hamlet?
Queen: Mad as the sea and wind when both contend
    Which is the mightier. In his lawless fit,
    Behind the arras hearing something stir,
    Whips out his rapier, cries, "A rat, a rat!"       10
    And in this brainish apprehension kills
    The unseen good old man.
King:                 O heavy deed!
    It had been so with us, had we been there.
    His liberty is full of threats to all—
    To you yourself, to us, to everyone.       15
    Alas, how shall this bloody deed be answered?
    It will be laid to us, whose providence
    Should have kept short, restrained, and out of haunt
    This mad young man. But so much was our love,
    We would not understand what was most fit,       20
    But, like the owner of a foul disease,
    To keep it from divulging, let it feed
    Even on the pith of life. Where is he gone?
Queen: To draw apart the body he hath killed,
    O'er whom his very madness, like some ore       25
    Among a mineral of metals base,
    Shows itself pure: 'a weeps for what is done.
King: O Gertrude, come away!
    The sun no sooner shall the mountains touch
    But we will ship him hence, and this vile deed       30
    We must with all our majesty and skill

---

1 *matter* significance.    *heaves* heavy sighs    11 *brainish apprehension* headstrong conception
12 *heavy* grievous    13 *us* i.e., me. (The royal "we"; also in line 15.)    16 *answered* explained
17 *providence* foresight    18 *short* i.e., on a short tether.    *out of haunt* secluded    22 *divulging*
becoming evident    25 *ore* vein of gold    26 *mineral* mine

Both countenance and excuse.—Ho, Guildenstern!

*Enter Rosencrantz and Guildenstern.*

Friends both, go join you with some further aid.
Hamlet in madness hath Polonius slain,
And from his mother's closet hath he dragged him.                    35
Go seek him out, speak fair, and bring the body
Into the chapel. I pray you, haste in this.

*[Exeunt Rosencrantz and Guildenstern.]*

Come, Gertrude, we'll call up our wisest friends
And let them know both what we mean to do
And what's untimely done . . . . . . . .                             40
Whose whisper o'er the world's diameter,
As level as the cannon to his blank,
Transports his poisoned shot, may miss our name
And hit the woundless air. O, come away!
My soul is full of discord and dismay.           *Exeunt.*   45

## Scene II [The Castle.]

*Enter Hamlet.*

*Hamlet:* Safely stowed.
*Rosencrantz, Guildenstern (within):* Hamlet! Lord Hamlet!
*Hamlet:* But soft, what noise? Who calls on Hamlet? O, here they come.

*Enter Rosencrantz and Guildenstern.*

*Rosencrantz:* What have you done, my lord, with the dead body?
*Hamlet:* Compounded it with dust, whereto 'tis kin.                   5
*Rosencrantz:* Tell us where 'tis, that we may take it thence
    And bear it to the chapel.
*Hamlet:* Do not believe it.
*Rosencrantz:* Believe what?
*Hamlet:* That I can keep your counsel and not mine own. Besides, to be demand-   10
    ed of a sponge, what replication should be made by the son of a king?
*Rosencrantz:* Take you me for a sponge, my lord?

---

32 *countenance* put the best face on     40 *And . . . done* (A defective line: conjectures as to the
missing words include *So, haply, slander* [Capell and others]; *For, haply, slander* [Theobald and others];
and *So envious slander* [Jenkins].)     41 *diameter* extent from side to side     42 *As level* with as
direct aim.     *his blank* its target at point-blank range     44 *woundless* invulnerable     10 *That
. . . own* i.e., that I can follow your advice (by telling where the body is) and still keep my own secret
10 *demanded of* questioned by     11 *replication* reply

*Hamlet:* Ay, sir, that soaks up the King's countenance, his rewards, his authorities. But such officers do the King best service in the end. He keeps them, like an ape, an apple, in the corner of his jaw, first mouthed to be last swallowed. When he needs what you have gleaned, it is but squeezing you, and, sponge, you shall be dry again. 15

*Rosencrantz:* I understand you not, my lord.

*Hamlet:* I am glad of it. A knavish speech sleeps in a foolish ear.

*Rosencrantz:* My lord, you must tell us where the body is and go with us to the 20 King.

*Hamlet:* The body is with the King, but the King is not with the body. The King is a thing—

*Guildenstern:* A thing, my lord?

*Hamlet:* Of nothing. Bring me to him. Hide fox, and all after! *Exeunt [running].* 25

## Scene III [The Castle.]

*Enter King, and two or three.*

*King:* I have sent to seek him, and to find the body.
How dangerous is it that this man goes loose!
Yet must not we put the strong law on him.
He's loved of the distracted multitude,
Who like not in their judgment, but their eyes, 5
And where 'tis so, th' offender's scourge is weighed,
But never the offense. To bear all smooth and even,
This sudden sending him away must seem
Deliberate pause. Diseases desperate grown
By desperate appliance are relieved, 10
Or not at all.

*Enter Rosencrantz, [Guildenstern,] and all the rest.*

          How now, what hath befall'n?

*Rosencrantz:* Where the dead body is bestowed, my lord,
We cannot get from him.

*King:*                   But where is he?

---

13 *countenance* favor. *authorities* delegated power, influence     19 *sleeps in* has no meaning to 22 *The . . . body* (Perhaps alludes to the legal commonplace of "the king's two bodies," which drew a distinction between the sacred office of kingship and the particular mortal who possessed it at any given time. Hence, although Claudius' body is necessarily a part of him, true kingship is not contained in it. Similarly, Claudius will have Polonius' body when it is found, but there is no kingship in this business either.)     25 *Of nothing* (1) of no account (2) lacking the essence of kingship, as in line 22 and note.     *Hide . . . after* (An old signal cry in the game of hide-and-seek, suggesting that Hamlet now runs away from them.)     4 *of* by.     *distracted* fickle, unstable     5 *Who . . . eyes* who choose not by judgment but by appearance     6 *scourge* punishment. (Literally, blow with a whip.)     *weighed* sympathetically considered     7 *To . . . even* to manage the business in an unprovocative way     9 *Deliberate pause* carefully considered action     10 *appliance* remedies

*Rosencrantz*: Without, my lord; guarded, to know your pleasure.

*King*: Bring him before us.

*Rosencrantz*: Ho! Bring in the lord. 15

    *They enter [with Hamlet].*

*King*: Now, Hamlet, where's Polonius?

*Hamlet*: At supper.

*King*: At supper? Where?

*Hamlet*: Not where he eats, but where 'a is eaten. A certain convocation of
    politic worms are e'en at him. Your worm is your only emperor for diet. We 20
    fat all creatures else to fat us, and we fat ourselves for maggots. Your fat king
    and your lean beggar is but variable service—two dishes, but to one table.
    That's the end.

*King*: Alas, alas!

*Hamlet*: A man may fish with the worm that hath eat of a king, and eat of the fish 25
    that hath fed of that worm.

*King*: What dost thou mean by this?

*Hamlet*: Nothing but to show you how a king may go a progress through the guts
    of a beggar.

*King*: Where is Polonius? 30

*Hamlet*: In heaven. Send thither to see. If your messenger find him not there,
    seek him i' th' other place yourself. But if indeed you find him not within
    this month, you shall nose him as you go up the stairs into the lobby.

*King [to some attendants]*: Go seek him there.

*Hamlet*: 'A will stay till you come.             *[Exeunt attendants.]* 35

*King*: Hamlet, this deed, for thine especial safety—
    Which we do tender, as we dearly grieve
    For that which thou hast done—must send thee hence
    With fiery quickness. Therefore prepare thyself.
    The bark is ready, and the wind at help, 40
    Th' associates tend, and everything is bent
    For England.

*Hamlet*: For England!

*King*: Ay, Hamlet.

*Hamlet*: Good. 45

*King*: So is it, if thou knew'st our purposes.

*Hamlet*: I see a cherub that sees them. But come, for England! Farewell, dear
    mother.

---

20 *politic worms* crafty worms (suited to a master spy like Polonius).   *e'en* even now.   *Your worm* your average worm (Compare *your fat king and your lean beggar* in lines 21-22)   *diet* food, eating (with a punning reference to the Diet of Worms, a famous *convocation* held in 1521)   22 *variable service* different courses of a single meal   25 *eat* eaten. (Pronounced *et*.)   28 *progress* royal journey of state   37 *tender* regard, hold dear.   *dearly* intensely   40 *bark* sailing vessel   41 *tend* wait.   *bent* in readiness   47 *cherub* (Cherubim are angels of knowledge. Hamlet hints that both he and heaven are onto Claudius' tricks.)

*King:* Thy loving father, Hamlet.

*Hamlet:* My mother. Father and mother is man and wife, man and wife is one    50
    flesh, and so, my mother. Come, for England!                 *Exit.*

*King:* Follow him at foot; tempt him with speed aboard.
    Delay it not. I'll have him hence tonight.
    Away! For everything is sealed and done
    That else leans on th' affair. Pray you, make haste.          55

                               *[Exeunt all but the King.]*

    And, England, if my love thou hold'st at aught—
    As my great power thereof may give thee sense,
    Since yet thy cicatrice looks raw and red
    After the Danish sword, and thy free awe
    Pays homage to us—thou mayst not coldly set          60
    Our sovereign process, which imports at full,
    By letters congruing to that effect,
    The present death of Hamlet. Do it, England,
    For like the hectic in my blood he rages,
    And thou must cure me. Till I know 'tis done,          65
    Howe'er my haps, my joys were ne'er begun.             *Exit.*

## Scene IV [The Coast of Denmark.]

    *Enter Fortinbras with his army over the stage.*

*Fortinbras:* Go, Captain, from me greet the Danish king.
    Tell him that by his license Fortinbras
    Craves the conveyance of a promised march
    Over his kingdom. You know the rendezvous.
    If that His Majesty would aught with us,             5
    We shall express our duty in his eye;
    And let him know so.

*Captain:* I will do 't, my lord.

*Fortinbras:* Go softly on.             *[Exeunt all but the Captain.]*

    *Enter Hamlet, Rosencrantz, [Guildenstern,] etc.*

*Hamlet:* Good sir, whose powers are these?           10

*Captain:* They are of Norway, sir.

---

52 *at foot* close behind, at heel    55 *leans on* bears upon, is related to    56 *England* i.e., King of England.   *at aught* at any value    57 *As . . . sense* for so my great power may give you a just appreciation of the importance of valuing my love    58 *cicatrice* scar    59 *free awe* voluntary show of respect    60 *coldly set* regard with indifference    61 *process* command.    *imports at full* conveys specific directions for    62 *congruing* agreeing    63 *present* immediate    64 *hectic* persistent fever    66 *haps* fortunes    2 *license* permission    3 *the conveyance of* escort during    6 *duty* respect.   *eye* presence    9 *softly* slowly, circumspectly    10 *powers* forces

*Hamlet:* How purposed, sir, I pray you?

*Captain:* Against some part of Poland.

*Hamlet:* Who commands them, sir?

*Captain:* The nephew to old Norway, Fortinbras. 15

*Hamlet:* Goes it against the main of Poland, sir,
　　Or for some frontier?

*Captain:* Truly to speak, and with no addition,
　　We go to gain a little patch of ground
　　That hath in it no profit but the name. 20
　　To pay five ducats, five, I would not farm it;
　　Nor will it yield to Norway or the Pole
　　A ranker rate, should it be sold in fee.

*Hamlet:* Why, then the Polack never will defend it.

*Captain:* Yes, it is already garrisoned. 25

*Hamlet:* Two thousand souls and twenty thousand ducats
　　Will not debate the question of this straw.
　　This is th' impostume of much wealth and peace,
　　That inward breaks, and shows no cause without
　　Why the man dies. I humbly thank you, sir. 30

*Captain:* God b' wi' you, sir. 　　　　　　　　　　　　　　*[Exit.]*

*Rosencrantz:* 　　　　　Will 't please you go, my lord?

*Hamlet:* I'll be with you straight. Go a little before.

　　　　　　　　　　　　　　　　　*[Exeunt all except Hamlet.]*

　　How all occasions do inform against me
　　And spur my dull revenge! What is a man,
　　If his chief good and market of his time 35
　　Be but to sleep and feed? A beast, no more.
　　Sure he that made us with such large discourse,
　　Looking before and after, gave us not
　　That capability and godlike reason
　　To fust in us unused. Now, whether it be 40
　　Bestial oblivion, or some craven scruple
　　Of thinking too precisely on th' event—
　　A thought which, quartered, hath but one part wisdom
　　And ever three parts coward—I do not know
　　Why yet I live to say "This thing's to do," 45
　　Sith I have cause, and will, and strength, and means
　　To do 't. Examples gross as earth exhort me:

16 *main* main part　　18 *addition* exaggeration　　21 *To pay* i.e., for a yearly rental of.　　*farm it* take a lease of it　　23 *ranker* higher.　*in fee* fee simple, outright　　27 *debate . . . straw* settle this trifling matter　　28 *impostume* abscess　　33 *inform against* denounce, betray: take shape against　　35 *market of* profit of, compensation for　　37 *discourse* power of reasoning　　38 *Looking before and after* able to review past events and anticipate the future　　40 *fust* grow moldy 41 *oblivion* forgetfulness.　*craven* cowardly　　42 *precisely* scrupulously.　*event* outcome　　46 *Sith* since　　47 *gross* obvious

Witness this army of such mass and charge,
Led by a delicate and tender prince,
Whose spirit with divine ambition puffed                                    50
Makes mouths at the invisible event,
Exposing what is mortal and unsure
To all that fortune, death, and danger dare,
Even for an eggshell. Rightly to be great
Is not to stir without great argument,                                      55
But greatly to find quarrel in a straw
When honor's at the stake. How stand I, then,
That have a father killed, a mother stained,
Excitements of my reason and my blood,
And let all sleep, while to my shame I see                                  60
The imminent death of twenty thousand men
That for a fantasy and trick of fame
Go to their graves like beds, fight for a plot
Whereon the numbers cannot try the cause,
Which is not tomb enough and continent                                     65
To hide the slain? O, from this time forth
My thoughts be bloody or be nothing worth!                    *Exit.*

## Scene V [The Castle.]

*Enter Horatio, [Queen] Gertrude, and a Gentleman.*

Queen: I will not speak with her.
Gentleman:                                    She is importunate,
      Indeed distract. Her mood will needs be pitied.
Queen: What would she have?
Gentleman: She speaks much of her father, says she hears
      There's tricks i' the world, and hems, and beats her heart,           5
      Spurns enviously at straws, speaks things in doubt
      That carry but half sense. Her speech is nothing,
      Yet the unshapèd use of it doth move
      The hearers to collection; they yawn at it,

---

48 *charge* expense      49 *delicate and tender* of fine and youthful qualities      51 *Makes mouths* makes
scornful faces.      *invisible event* unforeseeable outcome      53 *dare* could do (to him)      54–57
*Rightly . . . stake* true greatness does not normally consist of rushing into action over some trivial
provocation: however, when one's honor is involved, even a trifling insult requires that one respond
greatly (?)      *at the stake* (A metaphor from gambling or bear-baiting.)      59 *Excitements of*
promptings by      62 *fantasy* fanciful caprice, illusion.      *trick* trifle, deceit      63 *plot* plot of
ground      64 *Whereon . . . cause* on which there is insufficient room for the soldiers needed to
engage in a military contest      65 *continent* receptacle, container      2 *distract* distracted      5
*tricks* deceptions.      *hems* makes "hmm" sounds.      *heart* i.e., breast      6 *Spurns . . . straws* kicks
spitefully, takes offense at trifles.      *in doubt* obscurely      8 *unshapèd use* incoherent manner      9
*collection* inference, a guess at some sort of meaning.      *yawn* gape, wonder; grasp. (The Folio reading, *aim*, is possible.)

And botch the words up fit to their own thoughts, 10
Which, as her winks and nods and gestures yield them,
Indeed would make one think there might be thought,
Though nothing sure, yet much unhappily.
*Horatio:* 'Twere good she were spoken with, for she may strew
Dangerous conjectures in ill-breeding minds. 15
*Queen:* Let her come in. [*Exit Gentleman.*]
[*Aside.*] To my sick soul, as sin's true nature is,
Each toy seems prologue to some great amiss.
So full of artless jealousy is guilt,
It spills itself in fearing to be spilt. 20

*Enter Ophelia [distracted].*

*Ophelia:* Where is the beauteous majesty of Denmark?
*Queen:* How now, Ophelia?
*Ophelia* (*she sings*):
    "How should I your true love know
    From another one?
    By his cockle hat and staff, 25
    And his sandal shoon."
*Queen:* Alas, sweet lady, what imports this song?
*Ophelia:* Say you? Nay, pray you, mark.
    "He is dead and gone, lady, (*Song.*)
    He is dead and gone; 30
    At his head a grass-green turf,
    At his heels a stone."
    O, ho!
*Queen:* Nay, but Ophelia—
*Ophelia:* Pray you, mark. [*Sings.*] 35
    "White his shroud as the mountain snow"—

*Enter King*

*Queen:* Alas, look here, my lord.
*Ophelia:*
    "Larded with sweet flowers; (*Song.*)
    Which bewept to the ground did not go
    With true-love showers." 40
*King:* How do you, pretty lady?

---

10 *botch* patch      11 *Which* which words.      *yield* deliver, represent      12 *thought* intended      13 *unhappily* unpleasantly near the truth, shrewdly      15 *ill-breeding* prone to suspect the worst and to make mischief      18 *toy* trifle.      *amiss* calamity      19–20 *So . . . split* guilt is so full of suspicion that it unskillfully betrays itself in fearing betrayal      20 s.d *Enter Ophelia* (In the First Quarto, Ophelia enters, "playing on a lute, and her hair down, singing.")      25 *cockle hat* hat with cockle-shell stuck in it as a sign that the wearer had been a pilgrim to the shrine of Saint James of Compostella in Spain      26 *shoon* shoes      38 *Larded* decorated      40 *showers* i.e., tears

*Ophelia*: Well, God 'ild you! They say the owl was a baker's daughter. Lord, we
    know what we are, but know not what we may be. God be at your table!
*King*: Conceit upon her father.
*Ophelia*: Pray let's have no words of this; but when they ask you what it means,   45
    say you this:

        "Tomorrow is Saint Valentine's day,              (*Song*.)
        All in the morning betime,
        And I a maid at your window,
        To be your Valentine.                                  50
        Then up he rose, and donned his clothes,
        And dupped the chamber door,
        Let in the maid, that out a maid
        Never departed more.
*King*: Pretty Ophelia—                                    55
*Ophelia*: Indeed, la, without an oath, I'll make an end on 't:
        "By Gis and by Saint Charity,
        Alack, and he for shame!
        Young men will do 't, if they come to 't;
        By Cock, they are to blame.                         60
        Quoth she, 'Before you tumbled me,
        You promised me to wed.'"
    He answers:
        "So would I ha' done, by yonder sun,
        An thou hadst not come to my bed."                 65
*King*: How long hath she been thus?
*Ophelia*: I hope all will be well. We must be patient, but I cannot choose but
    weep to think they would lay him i' the cold ground. My brother shall know
    of it. And so I thank you for your good counsel. Come, my coach! Good
    night, ladies, good night, sweet ladies, good night, good night.       [*Exit*.]   70
*King* [*to Horatio*]: Follow her close. Give her good watch, I pray you.

                                    [*Exit Horatio*.]

    O, this is the poison of deep grief; it springs
    All from her father's death—and now behold!
    O Gertrude, Gertrude,
    When sorrows come, they come not single spies,                  75
    But in battalions. First, her father slain;
    Next, your son gone, and he most violent author

---

42 *God 'ild* God yield or reward.    *owl* (Refers to a legend about a baker's daughter who was turned
into an owl for being ungenerous when Jesus begged a loaf of bread.)    44 *Conceit* brooding    48
*betime* early    52 *dupped* did up, opened    57 *Gis* Jesus    60 *Cock* (A perversion of "God" in
oaths; here also with a quibble on the slang word for penis.)    65 *An* if    75 *spies* scouts sent in
advance of the main force

Of his own just remove; the people muddied,
Thick and unwholesome in their thoughts and whispers
For good Polonius' death—and we have done but greenly,                    80
In hugger-mugger to inter him; poor Ophelia
Divided from herself and her fair judgment,
Without the which we are pictures or mere beasts;
Last, and as much containing as all these,
Her brother is in secret come from France,                                85
Feeds on this wonder, keeps himself in clouds,
And wants not buzzers to infect his ear
With pestilent speeches of his father's death,
Wherein necessity, of matter beggared,
Will nothing stick our person to arraign                                   90
In ear and ear. O my dear Gertrude, this,
Like to a murdering piece, in many places
Gives me superfluous death.                                 *A noise within.*
Queen: Alack, what noise is this?
King: Attend!                                                              95
Where is my Switzers? Let them guard the door.

*Enter a Messenger.*

What is the matter?
Messenger:                    Save yourself, my lord!
The ocean, overpeering of his list,
Eats not the flats with more impetuous haste
Than young Laertes, in a riotous head,                                    100
O'erbears your officers. The rabble call him lord,
And, as the world were now but to begin,
Antiquity forgot, custom not known,
The ratifiers and props of every word,
They cry, "Choose we! Laertes shall be king!"                            105
Caps, hands, and tongues applaud it to the clouds,
"Laertes shall be king, Laertes king!"
Queen: How cheerfully on the false trail they cry!          *A noise within.*

78 *remove* removal.    *muddied* stirred up, confused    80 *greenly* in an inexperienced way, foolishly
81 *hugger-mugger* secret haste    84 *as much containing* as full of serious matter    86 *Feeds . . .*
*clouds* feeds his resentment or shocked grievance, holds himself inscrutable and aloof amid all this
rumor    87 *wants* lacks.    *buzzers* gossipers, informers    89 *necessity* i.e., the need to invent
some plausible explanation.    *of matter beggared* unprovided with facts    90–91 *Will . . . ear* will
not hesitate to accuse my (royal) person in everybody's ears    92 *murdering piece* cannon loaded so
as to scatter its shot    93 *Gives . . . death* kills me over and over    95 *Attend* i.e., guard me
96 *Switzers* Swiss guards, mercenaries    98 *overpeering of his list* overflowing its shore, boundary
99 *flats* i.e., flatlands near shore.    *impetuous* violent (perhaps also with the meaning of *impiteous*
[*impitious*, Q2], "pitiless")    100 *head* insurrection    102 *as if*    104 *The ratifiers . . . word*
i.e., *antiquity* (or tradition) and *custom* ought to confirm (*ratify*) and underprop our every word or
promise    106 *Caps* (The caps are thrown in the air.)

O, this is counter, you false Danish dogs!

*Enter Laertes with others.*

*King:* The doors are broke. 110
*Laertes:* Where is this King?—Sirs, stand you all without.
*All:* No, let's come in.
*Laertes:* I pray you, give me leave.
*All:* We will, we will.
*Laertes:* I thank you. Keep the door. [*Exeunt followers.*] O thou vile king, 115
    Give me my father!
*Queen [restraining him]:* Calmly, good Laertes.
*Laertes:* That drop of blood that's calm proclaims me bastard,
    Cries cuckold to my father, brands the harlot
    Even here, between the chaste unsmirchèd brow
    Of my true mother.
*King:*               What is the cause, Laertes, 120
    That thy rebellion looks so giantlike?
    Let him go, Gertrude. Do not fear our person.
    There's such divinity doth hedge a king
    That treason can but peep to what it would,
    Acts little of his will. Tell me, Laertes, 125
    Why thou art thus incensed. Let him go, Gertrude.
    Speak, man.
*Laertes:*         Where is my father?
*King:*                 Dead.
*Queen:* But not by him.
*King:*              Let him demand his fill.
*Laertes:* How came he dead? I'll not be juggled with.
    To hell, allegiance! Vows, to the blackest devil! 130
    Conscience and grace, to the profoundest pit!
    I dare damnation. To this point I stand,
    That both the worlds I give to negligence,
    Let come what comes, only I'll be revenged
    Most throughly for my father. 135
*King:* Who shall stay you?
*Laertes:* My will, not all the world's.

109 *counter* (A hunting term, meaning to follow the trail in a direction opposite to that which the game has taken.)    119 *between* in the middle of    122 *fear our* fear for my    123 *hedge* protect, as with a surrounding barrier    124 *can . . . would* can only peep furtively, as through a barrier at what it would intend    125 *Acts . . . will* (but) performs little of what it intends    129 *juggled with* cheated, deceived    132 *To . . . stand* I am resolved in this    133 *both . . . negligence* i.e., both this world and the next are of no consequence to me    135 *throughly* thoroughly    137 *My will . . . world's* I'll stop (*stay*) when my will is accomplished, not for anyone else's.

And for my means, I'll husband them so well
They shall go far with little.
King:                               Good Laertes,
If you desire to know the certainty                                    140
Of your dear father, is 't writ in your revenge
That, swoopstake, you will draw both friend and foe,
Winner and loser?
*Laertes:* None but his enemies.
*King:* Will you know them, then?                                       145
*Laertes:* To his good friends thus wide I'll ope my arms,
And like the kind life-rendering pelican
Repast them with my blood.
King:                               Why, now you speak
Like a good child and a true gentleman.
That I am guiltless of your father's death,                             150
And am most sensibly in grief for it,
It shall as level to your judgment 'pear
As day does to your eye.                              *A noise within.*
*Laertes:* How now, what noise is that?

*Enter Ophelia.*

*King:*                               Let her come in.
*Laertes:* O heat, dry up my brains! Tears seven times salt            155
Burn out the sense and virtue of mine eye!
By heaven, thy madness shall be paid with weight
Till our scale turn the beam. O rose of May!
Dear maid, kind sister, sweet Ophelia!
O heavens, is 't possible a young maid's wits                          160
Should be as mortal as an old man's life?
Nature is fine in love, and where 'tis fine
It sends some precious instance of itself
After the thing it loves.
*Ophelia:*
          "They bore him barefaced on the bier,          *(Song.)* 165
          Hey non nonny, nonny, hey nonny,
          And in his grave rained many a tear—"
          Fare you well, my dove!
*Laertes:* Hadst thou thy wits and didst persuade revenge,
It could not move thus.                                                 170

---

138 *for* as for    142 *swoopstake* i.e., indiscriminately. (Literally taking all stakes on the gambling table at once. *draw* is also a gambling term meaning "take from.")    147 *pelican* (Refers to the belief that the female pelican fed its young with its own blood.)    148 *Repast* feed    151 *sensibly* feelingly    152 *level* plain    156 *virtue* faculty, power    157 *paid with weight* repaid, avenged equally or more    158 *beam* crossbar of a balance    162 *fine in* refined by    163 *instance* token    164 *After . . . loves* i.e., into the grave, along with Polonius    169 *persuade* argue cogently for

*Ophelia:* You must sing "A-down a-down," and you "call him a-down-a." O, how
the wheel becomes it! It is the false steward that stole his master's daughter.

*Laertes:* This nothing's more than matter.

*Ophelia:* There's rosemary, that's for remembrance; pray you, love, remember.
And there is pansies; that's for thoughts.                                        175

*Laertes:* A document in madness, thoughts and remembrance fitted.

*Ophelia:* There's fennel for you, and columbines. There's rue for you, and here's
some for me; we may call it herb of grace o' Sundays. You must wear your rue
with a difference. There's a daisy. I would give you some violets, but they
withered all when my father died. They say 'a made a good end—                   180
[*Sings.*]     "For bonny sweet Robin is all my joy."

*Laertes:* Thought and affliction, passion, hell itself,
She turns to favor and to prettiness.

*Ophelia:* "And will 'a not come again?                              (*Song.*)
And will 'a not come again?                                                       185
No, no, he is dead.
Go to thy deathbed,
He never will come again.

"His beard was as white as snow,
All flaxen was his poll.                                                         190
He is gone, he is gone,
And we cast away moan.
God ha' mercy on his soul!"
And of all Christian souls, I pray God. God b' wi' you.

                                        [*Exit, followed by Gertrude.*]

*Laertes:* Do you see this, O God?                                               195

*King:* Laertes, I must commune with your grief,
Or you deny me right. Go but apart,
Make choice of whom your wisest friends you will,
And they shall hear and judge twixt you and me.
If by direct or by collateral hand                                               200

---

171 *You . . . a-down a* (Ophelia assigns the singing of refrains, like her own "Hey non nonny," to others present.)     172 *wheel* spinning wheel as accompaniment to the song, or refrain     *false steward* (The story is unknown.)     173 *This . . . matter* this seeming nonsense is more eloquent than sane utterance     174 *rosemary* (Used as a symbol of remembrance both at weddings and at funerals.) 175 *pansies* (Emblems of love and courtship; perhaps from French *pensées*, "thoughts.")     176 *document* instruction, lesson     177 *fennel* (Emblem of flattery.)     *columbines* (Emblems of unchastity or ingratitude.)     *rue* (Emblem of repentance—a signification that is evident in its popular name, *herb of grace*.)     179 *with a difference* (A device used in heraldry to distinguish one family from another on the coat of arms, here suggesting that Ophelia and the others have different causes of sorrow and repentance; perhaps with a play on *rue* in the sense of "ruth," "pity.")     *daisy* (Emblem of dissembling, faithlessness.)     *violets* (Emblems of faithfulness.)     182 *Thought* melancholy. *passion* suffering     183 *favor* grace, beauty     190 *poll* head     198 *whom* whichever of     200 *collateral hand* indirect agency

They find us touched, we will our kingdom give,
Our crown, our life, and all that we call ours
To you in satisfaction; but if not,
Be you content to lend your patience to us,
And we shall jointly labor with your soul                                          205
To give it due content.
*Laertes:*                              Let this be so.
His means of death, his obscure funeral—
No trophy, sword, nor hatchment o'er his bones,
No noble rite, nor formal ostentation—
Cry to be heard, as 'twere from heaven to earth,                                   210
That I must call 't in question.
*King:*                                        So you shall,
And where th' offense is, let the great ax fall.
I pray you, go with me.                                          *Exeunt.*

## Scene VI [The Castle.]

    *Enter Horatio and others.*

*Horatio:* What are they that would speak with me?
*Gentleman:* Seafaring men, sir. They say they have letters for you.
*Horatio:* Let them come in.                                [*Exit Gentleman.*]
I do not know from what part of the world
I should be greeted, if not from Lord Hamlet.                                       5

    *Enter Sailors.*

*First Sailor:* God bless you, sir.
*Horatio:* Let him bless thee too.
*First Sailor:* 'A shall, sir, an 't please him. There's a letter for you, sir—it came
from th' ambassador that was bound for England—if your name be Horatio,
as I am let to know it is.                                [*He gives a letter.*]   10
*Horatio* [*reads*]: "Horatio, when thou shalt have overlooked this, give these fellows some means to the King; they have letters for him. Ere we were two
days old at sea, a pirate of very warlike appointment gave us chase. Finding
ourselves too slow of sail, we put on a compelled valor, and in the grapple I
boarded them. On the instant they got clear of our ship, so I alone became      15
their prisoner. They have dealt with me like thieves of mercy, but they knew
what they did: I am to do a good turn for them. Let the King have the letters

---

201 *us touched* me implicated       208 *trophy* memorial.      *hatchment* tablet displaying the armorial
bearings of a deceased person       209 *ostentation* ceremony      211 *That* so that.      *call 't in question* demand an explanation       8 *an 't* if it      9 *th' ambassador* (Evidently Hamlet. The sailor is
being circumspect.)      11 *overlooked* looked over      12 *means* means of access      13 *appointment*
equipage      16 *thieves of mercy* merciful thieves

I have sent, and repair thou to me with as much speed as thou wouldest fly death. I have words to speak in thine ear will make thee dumb, yet are they much too light for the bore of the matter. These good fellows will bring thee where I am. Rosencrantz and Guildenstern hold their course for England. Of them I have much to tell thee. Farewell.

                                        He that thou knowest thine, Hamlet."
Come, I will give you way for these your letters,
And do 't the speedier that you may direct me                                    25
To him from whom you brought them.                              *Exeunt.*

## Scene VII [*The Castle.*]

*Enter King and Laertes.*

*King:* Now must your conscience my acquittance seal,
         And you must put me in your heart for friend,
         Sith you have heard, and with a knowing ear,
         That he which hath your noble father slain
         Pursued my life.
*Laertes:*              It well appears. But tell me                              5
         Why you proceeded not against these feats
         So crimeful and so capital in nature,
         As by your safety, greatness, wisdom, all things else,
         You mainly were stirred up.
*King:* O, for two special reasons,                                              10
         Which may to you perhaps seem much unsinewed,
         But yet to me they're strong. The Queen his mother
         Lives almost by his looks, and for myself—
         My virtue or my plague, be it either which—
         She is so conjunctive to my life and soul                               15
         That, as the star moves not but in his sphere,
         I could not but by her. The other motive
         Why to a public count I might not go
         Is the great love the general gender bear him,
         Who, dipping all his faults in their affection,                         20
         Work like the spring that turneth wood to stone,
         Convert his gyves to graces, so that my arrows,

---

18 *repair* come    20 *bore* caliber, i.e., importance    24 *way* means of access    1 *my acquittance seal* confirm or acknowledge my innocence    3 *Sith* since    6 *feats* acts    7 *capital* punishable by death    9 *mainly* greatly    11 *unsinewed* weak    15 *conjunctive* closely united. (An astronomical metaphor.)    16 *his* its    *sphere* one of the hollow spheres in which, according to Ptolemaic astronomy, the planets were supposed to move    18 *count* account, reckoning, indictment    19 *general gender* common people    21 *Work* operate, act.    *spring* i.e., a spring with such a concentration of lime that it coats a piece of wood with limestone, in effect gilding and petrifying it    22 *gyves* fetters (which, gilded by the people's praise, would look like badges of honor)

Too slightly timbered for so loud a wind,
Would have reverted to my bow again
But not where I had aimed them.                                    25
*Laertes:* And so have I a noble father lost,
A sister driven into desperate terms,
Whose worth, if praises may go back again,
Stood challenger on mount of all the age
For her perfections. But my revenge will come.                     30
*King:* Break not your sleeps for that. You must not think
That we are made of stuff so flat and dull
That we can let our beard be shook with danger
And think it pastime. You shortly shall hear more.
I loved your father, and we love ourself;                          35
And that, I hope, will teach you to imagine—

*Enter a Messenger with letters.*

How now? What news?
*Messenger:*                    Letters, my lord, from Hamlet:
This to Your Majesty, this to the Queen.

                                              *[He gives letters.]*

*King:* From Hamlet? Who brought them?
*Messenger:* Sailors, my lord, they say. I saw them not.          40
They were given me by Claudio. He received them
Of him that brought them.
*King:*                         Laertes, you shall hear them.—
Leave us.                                      *[Exit Messenger.]*
*[He reads.]* "High and mighty, you shall know I am set naked on your king-
dom. Tomorrow shall I beg leave to see your kingly eyes, when I shall, first  45
asking your pardon, thereunto recount the occasion of my sudden and more
strange return.    Hamlet."
What should this mean? Are all the rest come back?
Or is it some abuse, and no such thing?
*Laertes:* Know you the hand?
*King:*                           'Tis Hamlet's character. "Naked!"   50
And in a postscript here he says "alone."
Can you devise me?
*Laertes:* I am lost in it, my lord. But let him come.
It warms the very sickness in my heart
That I shall live and tell him to his teeth,                       55
"Thus didst thou."

---

23 *slightly timbered* light.     *loud* (suggesting public outcry on Hamlet's behalf)     24 *reverted*
returned     27 *terms* state, condition     28 *go back* i.e., recall what she was     29 *on mount* set up
on high     44 *naked* destitute, unarmed, without following     46 *pardon* permission     49 *abuse*
deceit.     *no such thing* not what it appears     50 *character* handwriting     52 *devise* explain to
56 *Thus didst thou* i.e., here's for what you did to my father

*King:*              If it be so, Laertes—
    As how should it be so? How otherwise?—
    Will you be ruled by me?
*Laertes:*                  Ay, my lord,
    So you will not o'errule me to a peace.
*King:* To thine own peace. If he be now returned,                    60
    As checking at his voyage, and that he means
    No more to undertake it, I will work him
    To an exploit, now ripe in my device,
    Under the which he shall not choose but fall;
    And for his death no wind of blame shall breathe,                  65
    But even his mother shall uncharge the practice
    And call it accident.
*Laertes:*                  My lord, I will be ruled,
    The rather if you could devise it so
    That I might be the organ.
*King:*                  It falls right.
    You have been talked of since your travel much,                   70
    And that in Hamlet's hearing, for a quality
    Wherein they say you shine. Your sum of parts
    Did not together pluck such envy from him
    As did that one, and that, in my regard,
    Of the unworthiest siege.                                          75
*Laertes:* What part is that, my lord?
*King:* A very ribbon in the cap of youth,
    Yet needful too, for youth no less becomes
    The light and careless livery that it wears
    Than settled age his sables and his weeds                          80
    Importing health and graveness. Two months since
    Here was a gentleman of Normandy.
    I have seen myself, and served against, the French,
    And they can well on horseback, but this gallant
    Had witchcraft in 't; he grew unto his seat,                       85
    And to such wondrous doing brought his horse
    As had he been incorpsed and demi-natured
    With the brave beast. So far he topped my thought

---

57 *As . . . otherwise* how can this (Hamlet's return) be true? Yet how otherwise than true (since we have the evidence of his letter)?     59 *So* provided that     61 *checking at* i.e., turning aside from (like a falcon leaving the quarry to fly at a chance bird).     *that* if     63 *device* devising, invention     66 *uncharge the practice* acquit the stratagem of being a plot     69 *organ* agent, instrument     72 *Your . . . parts* i.e., all your other virtues     75 *unworthiest siege* least important rank     78 *no less becomes* is no less suited by     80 *his sables* its rich robes furred with sable.     *weeds* garments     81 *Importing . . . graveness* signifying a concern for health and dignified prosperity; also, giving an impression of comfortable prosperity     84 *can well* are skilled     87 *As . . . demi-natured* as if he had been of one body and nearly of one nature (like the centaur)     88 *topped* surpassed

>           That I in forgery of shapes and tricks
>           Come short of what he did.

Laertes:                          A Norman was 't?                              90

King: A Norman.

Laertes: Upon my life, Lamord.

King:                          The very same.

Laertes: I know him well. He is the brooch indeed
>           And gem of all the nation.

King: He made confession of you.                                               95
>           And gave you such a masterly report
>           For art and exercise in your defense,
>           And for your rapier most especial,
>           That he cried out 'twould be a sight indeed
>           If one could match you. Th' escrimers of their nation,              100
>           He swore, had neither motion, guard, nor eye
>           If you opposed them. Sir, this report of his
>           Did Hamlet so envenom with his envy
>           That he could nothing do but wish and beg
>           Your sudden coming o'er, to play with you.                          105
>           Now, out of this—

Laertes:                          What out of this, my lord?

King: Laertes, was your father dear to you?
>           Or are you like the painting of a sorrow,
>           A face without a heart?

Laertes:                          Why ask you this?

King: Not that I think you did not love your father,                           110
>           But that I know love is begun by time,
>           And that I see, in passages of proof,
>           Time qualifies the spark and fire of it.
>           There lives within the very flame of love
>           A kind of wick or snuff that will abate it,                         115
>           And nothing is at a like goodness still,
>           For goodness, growing to a pleurisy,
>           Dies in his own too much. That we would do,
>           We should do when we would; for this "would" changes
>           And hath abatements and delays as many                             120

---

89 *forgery* imagining    93 *brooch* ornament    95 *confession* testimonial, admission of superiority
97 *For . . . defense* with respect to your skill and practice with your weapon    100 *escrimers* fencers
105 *sudden* immediate.    *play* fence    111 *begun by time* i.e., created by the right circumstance
and hence subject to change    112 *passages of proof* actual instances that prove it    113 *qualifies*
weakens, moderates    115 *snuff* the charred part of a candlewick    116 *nothing . . . still* nothing
remains at a constant level of perfection    117 *pleurisy* excess, plethora. (Literally, a chest inflam-
mation.)    118 *in . . . much* of its own excess.    *That* that which    120 *abatements* diminutions

As there are tongues, are hands, are accidents,
And then this "should" is like a spendthrift sigh,
That hurts by easing. But, to the quick o' th' ulcer:
Hamlet comes back. What would you undertake
To show yourself in deed your father's son                                    125
More than in words?
*Laertes:*                        To cut his throat i' the church.
*King:* No place, indeed, should murder sanctuarize;
Revenge should have no bounds. But good Laertes,
Will you do this, keep close within your chamber.
Hamlet returned shall know you are come home.                                  130
We'll put on those shall praise your excellence
And set a double varnish on the fame
The Frenchman gave you, bring you in fine together,
And wager on your heads. He, being remiss,
Most generous, and free from all contriving,                                   135
Will not peruse the foils, so that with ease,
Or with a little shuffling, you may choose
A sword unbated, and in a pass of practice
Requite him for your father.
*Laertes:*                        I will do 't,
And for that purpose I'll anoint my sword.                                     140
I bought an unction of a mountebank
So mortal that, but dip a knife in it,
Where it draws blood no cataplasm so rare,
Collected from all simples that have virtue
Under the moon, can save the thing from death                                  145
That is but scratched withal. I'll touch my point
With this contagion, that if I gall him slightly,
It may be death.
*King:*                        Let's further think of this,
Weigh what convenience both of time and means
May fit us to our shape. If this should fail,                                  150
And that our drift look through our bad performance,

---

121 *As . . . accidents* as there are tongues to dissuade, hands to prevent, and chance events to intervene        122 *spendthrift sigh* (An allusion to the belief that sighs draw blood from the heart.)        123
*hurts by easing* i.e., costs the heart blood and wastes precious opportunity even while it affords emotional relief        *quick o' th' ulcer* i.e., heart of the matter        127 *sanctuarize* protect from punishment. (Alludes to the right of sanctuary with which certain religious places were invested.)        129
*Will you do this* if you wish to do this        131 *put on those shall* arrange for some to        133 *in fine*
finally        134 *remiss* negligently unsuspicious        135 *generous* noble-minded        138 *unbated* not
blunted, having no button.        *pass of practice* treacherous thrust        141 *unction* ointment.
*mountebank* quack doctor        143 *cataplasm* plaster or poultice        144 *simples* herbs.        *virtue*
potency        145 *Under the moon* i.e., anywhere (with reference perhaps to the belief that herbs gathered at night had a special power)        147 *gall* graze, wound        150 *shape* part we propose to act
151 *drift . . . performance* intention should be made visible by our bungling

'Twere better not assayed. Therefore this project
Should have a back or second, that might hold
If this did blast in proof. Soft, let me see.
We'll make a solemn wager on your cunnings—          155
I ha 't!
When in your motion you are hot and dry—
As make your bouts more violent to that end—
And that he calls for drink, I'll have prepared him
A chalice for the nonce, whereon but sipping,          160
If he by chance escape your venomed stuck,
Our purpose may hold there. [*A cry within*.] But stay, what noise?

*Enter Queen.*

Queen: One woe doth tread upon another's heel,
    So fast they follow. Your sister's drowned, Laertes.
Laertes: Drowned! O, where?          165
Queen: There is a willow grows askant the brook,
    That shows his hoar leaves in the glassy stream;
    Therewith fantastic garlands did she make
    Of crowflowers, nettles, daisies, and long purples,
    That liberal shepherds give a grosser name,          170
    But our cold maids do dead men's fingers call them.
    There on the pendent boughs her crownet weeds
    Clamb'ring to hang, an envious sliver broke,
    When down her weedy trophies and herself
    Fell in the weeping brook. Her clothes spread wide,          175
    And mermaidlike awhile they bore her up,
    Which time she chanted snatches of old lauds,
    As one incapable of her own distress,
    Or like a creature native and endued
    Unto that element. But long it could not be          180
    Till that her garments, heavy with their drink,
    Pulled the poor wretch from her melodious lay
    To muddy death.
Laertes:            Alas, then she is drowned?
Queen: Drowned, drowned.
Laertes: Too much of water hast thou, poor Ophelia,          185
    And therefore I forbid my tears. But yet

---

154 *blast in proof* burst in the test (like a cannon)     155 *cunnings* respective skills     158 *As* i.e.,
and you should     160 *nonce* occasion     161 *stuck* thrust. (From *stoccado;* a fencing term.)
166 *askant* aslant     167 *hoar leaves* white or gray undersides of the leaves     169 *long purples* early
purple orchids     170 *liberal* free-spoken     *a grosser name* (The testicle-resembling tubers of the
orchid, which also in some cases resemble *dead men's fingers*, have earned various slang names like
"dogstones" and "cullions.")     171 *cold* chaste     172 *pendent* overhanging.     *crownet* made into
a chaplet or coronet     173 *envious sliver* malicious branch     174 *weedy* i.e., of plants     177
*lauds* hymns     178 *incapable of* lacking capacity to apprehend     179 *endued* adapted by nature

It is our trick; nature her custom holds.
Let shame say what it will. [*He weeps.*] When these are gone,
The woman will be out. Adieu, my lord.
I have a speech of fire that fain would blaze,                                    190
But that this folly douts it.                                          *Exit.*
*King*:                        Let's follow, Gertrude.
How much I had to do to calm his rage!
Now fear I this will give it start again;
Therefore let's follow.                                          *Exeunt.*

# ACT V

### Scene I [A Churchyard.]

*Enter two Clowns [with spades and mattocks].*

*First Clown:* Is she to be buried in Christian burial, when she willfully seeks her
    own salvation?
*Second Clown:* I tell thee she is; therefore make her grave straight. The crowner
    hath sat on her, and finds it Christian burial.
*First Clown:* How can that be, unless she drowned herself in her own defense?       5
*Second Clown:* Why, 'tis found so.
*First Clown:* It must be *se offendendo*, it cannot be else. For here lies the point: if I
    drown myself wittingly, it argues an act, and an act hath three branches—it
    is to act, to do, and to perform. Argal, she drowned herself wittingly.
*Second Clown:* Nay, but hear you, goodman delver—                                10
*First Clown:* Give me leave. Here lies the water; good. Here stands the man;
    good. If the man go to this water and drown himself, it is, will he, nill he, he
    goes, mark you that. But if the water come to him and drown him, he drowns
    not himself. Argal, he that is not guilty of his own death shortens not his
    own life.                                                                     15
*Second Clown:* But is this law?
*First Clown:* Ay, marry, is 't—crowner's quest law.
*Second Clown:* Will you ha' the truth on 't? If this had not been a gentlewoman,
    she should have been buried out o' Christian burial.
*First Clown:* Why, there thou sayst. And the more pity that great folk should       20
    have countenance in this world to drown or hang themselves, more than

187 *It is our trick* i.e., weeping is our natural way (when sad)       188–189 *When . . . out* when my
tears are all shed, the woman in me will be expended, satisfied       191 *douts* extinguishes. (The
Second Quarto reads "drowns.")       s.d. *Clowns* rustics       2 *salvation* (A blunder for "damnation,"
or perhaps a suggestion that Ophelia was taking her own shortcut to heaven.)       3 *straight* straightway, immediately. (But with a pun on *strait*, "narrow.")       *crowner* coroner.       4 *sat on her* conducted an inquest on her case       *finds it* gives his official verdict that her means of death was consistent with       6 *found so* determined so in the coroner's verdict       7 *se offendendo* (A comic mistake
for *se defendendo*, a term used in verdicts of justifiable homicide.)       9 *Argal* (Corruption of *ergo*,
"therefore.")       10 *goodman* (An honorific title often used with the name of a profession or craft.)
12 *will he, nill he* whether he will or no, willy-nilly       20 *there thou sayst*, i.e., that's right       21
*countenance* privilege

their even-Christian. Come, my spade. There is no ancient gentlemen but gardeners, ditchers, and grave makers. They hold up Adam's profession.

*Second Clown:* Was he a gentleman?

*First Clown:* 'A was the first that ever bore arms.                                                          25

*Second Clown:* Why, he had none.

*First Clown:* What, art a heathen? How dost thou understand the Scripture? The Scripture says Adam digged. Could he dig without arms? I'll put another question to thee. If thou answerest me not to the purpose, confess thyself—

*Second Clown:* Go to.                                                                                                   30

*First Clown:* What is he that builds stronger than either the mason, the shipwright, or the carpenter?

*Second Clown:* The gallows maker, for that frame outlives a thousand tenants.

*First Clown:* I like thy wit well, in good faith. The gallows does well. But how does it well? It does well to those that do ill. Now thou dost ill to say the gal-          35
lows is built stronger than the church. Argal, the gallows may do well to thee. To 't again, come.

*Second Clown:* "Who builds stronger than a mason, a shipwright, or a carpenter?"

*First Clown:* Ay, tell me that, and unyoke.

*Second Clown:* Marry, now I can tell.                                                                            40

*First Clown:* To 't.

*Second Clown:* Mass, I cannot tell.

*Enter Hamlet and Horatio [at a distance].*

*First Clown:* Cudgel thy brains no more about it, for your dull ass will not mend his pace with beating; and when you are asked this question next, say "a grave maker." The houses he makes lasts till doomsday. Go get thee in and          45
fetch me a stoup of liquor.

*[Exit Second Clown. First Clown digs.]*

*Song.*

"In youth, when I did love, did love,
Methought it was very sweet,
To contract—O—the time for—a—my behove,
O, methought there—a—was nothing—a—meet."                                                          50

---

*Hamlet:* Has this fellow no feeling of his business, 'a sings in grave-making?

*Horatio:* Custom hath made it in him a property of easiness.

*Hamlet:* 'Tis e'en so. The hand of little employment hath the daintier sense.

*First Clown:*                                                                                                       *Song.*

> "But age with his stealing steps
> Hath clawed me in his clutch,                                                                      55
> And hath shipped me into the land,
> As if I had never been such."

> *[He throws up a skull.]*

*Hamlet:* That skull had a tongue in it and could sing once. How the knave jowls
it to the ground, as if 'twere Cain's jawbone, that did the first murder! This
might be the pate of a politician, which this ass now o'erreaches, one that        60
would circumvent God, might it not?

*Horatio:* It might, my lord.

*Hamlet:* Or of a courtier, which could say, "Good morrow, sweet lord! How dost
thou, sweet lord?" This might be my Lord Such-a-one, that praised my Lord
Such-a-one's horse when 'a meant to beg it, might it not?                              65

*Horatio:* Ay, my lord.

*Hamlet:* Why, e'en so, and now my Lady Worm's, chapless, and knocked about
the mazard with a sexton's spade. Here's fine revolution, an we had the trick
to see 't. Did these bones cost no more the breeding but to play at loggets
with them? Mine ache to think on 't.                                                             70

*First Clown:*                                                                                                       *Song.*

> "A pickax and a spade, a spade,
> For and a shrouding sheet;
> O, a pit of clay for to be made
> For such a guest is meet."

> *[He throws up another skull.]*

*Hamlet:* There's another. Why may not that be the skull of a lawyer? Where be     75
his quiddities now, his quillities, his cases, his tenures, and his tricks? Why
does he suffer this mad knave now to knock him about the sconce with a
dirty shovel, and will not tell him of his action of battery? Hum, this fellow

---

51 *'a* that he       52 *property of easiness* something he can do easily and indifferently       53 *daintier
sense* more delicate sense of feeling       56 *into the land* i.e., toward my grave (?) (But note the lack of
rhyme in *steps, land.*)       58 *jowls* dashes (with a pun on *jowl,* "jawbone")       60 *politician* schemer,
plotter.       *o'erreaches* circumvents, gets the better of (with a quibble on the literal sense)       67
*chapless* having no lower jaw.       68 *mazard* i.e., head. (Literally, a drinking vessel.)       *revolution*
turn of Fortune's wheel, change.       *an* if       68–69 *trick to see* knack of seeing       69 *cost . . . but*
involve so little expense and care in upbringing that we may.       *loggets* a game in which pieces of
hard wood shaped like Indian clubs or bowling pins are thrown to lie as near as possible to a stake
72 *For* and and moreover       76 *quiddities* subtleties, quibbles. (From Latin *quid,* "a thing.").       *quillities* verbal niceties, subtle distinctions. (Variation of *quiddities.*).       *tenures* the holding of a piece of
property or office, or the conditions or period of such holding       77 *sconce* head       78 *action of battery* lawsuit about physical assault

might be in 's time a great buyer of land, with his statutes, his recognizances, his fines, his double vouchers, his recoveries. Is this the fine of his fines and 80 the recovery of his recoveries, to have his fine pate full of fine dirt? Will his vouchers vouch him no more of his purchases, and double ones too, than the length and breadth of a pair of indentures? The very conveyances of his lands will scarcely lie in this box, and must th' inheritor himself have no more, ha? 85

*Horatio:* Not a jot more, my lord.

*Hamlet:* Is not parchment made of sheepskins?

*Horatio:* Ay, my lord, and of calves' skins too.

*Hamlet:* They are sheep and calves which seek out assurance in that. I will speak to this fellow.—Whose grave's this, sirrah? 90

*First Clown:* Mine, sir. [*Sings.*]
    "O, pit of clay for to be made
    For such a guest is meet."

*Hamlet:* I think it be thine, indeed, for thou liest in 't.

*First Clown:* You lie out on 't, sir, and therefore 'tis not yours. For my part, I do 95 not lie in 't, yet it is mine.

*Hamlet:* Thou dost lie in 't, to be in 't and say it is thine. 'Tis for the dead, not for the quick; therefore thou liest.

*First Clown:* 'Tis a quick lie, sir; 'twill away again from me to you.

*Hamlet:* What man dost thou dig it for? 100

*First Clown:* For no man, sir.

*Hamlet:* What woman, then?

*First Clown:* For none, neither.

*Hamlet:* Who is to be buried in 't?

*First Clown:* One that was a woman, sir, but, rest her soul, she's dead. 105

*Hamlet:* How absolute the knave is! We must speak by the card, or equivocation will undo us. By the Lord, Horatio, this three years I have took note of it: the age is grown so picked that the toe of the peasant comes so near the heel of the courtier, he galls his kibe.—How long hast thou been grave maker?

*First Clown:* Of all the days i' the year, I came to 't that day that our last king 110 Hamlet overcame Fortinbras.

*Hamlet:* How long is that since?

---

79 *statutes, recognizances* legal documents guaranteeing a debt by attaching land and property    80 *fines, recoveries* ways of converting entailed estates into "fee simple" or freehold.    *double* signed by two signatories.    *vouchers* guarantees of the legality of a title to real estate    80–81 *fine of his fines . . . fine pate . . . fine dirt* end of his legal maneuvers . . . elegant head . . . minutely sifted dirt 83 *pair of indentures* legal document drawn up in duplicate on a single sheet and then cut apart on a zigzag line so that each pair was uniquely matched. (Hamlet may refer to two rows of teeth or dentures.)    *conveyances* deeds    84 *box* (1) deed box (2) coffin. ("Skull" has been suggested.) *inheritor* possessor, owner    89 *assurance in that* safety in legal parchments    90 *sirrah* (A term of address to inferiors.)    99 *quick* living    106 *absolute* strict, precise.    *by the card* i.e., with precision. (Literally, by the mariner's compass-card, on which the points of the compass were marked.) *equivocation* ambiguity in the use of terms    107 *took* taken    108 *picked* refined, fastidious 109 *galls his kibe* chafes the courtier's chilblain

*First Clown*: Cannot you tell that? Every fool can tell that. It was that very day that young Hamlet was born—he that is mad and sent into England.

*Hamlet*: Ay, marry, why was he sent into England?            115

*First Clown*: Why, because 'a was mad. 'A shall recover his wits there, or if 'a do not, 'tis no great matter there.

*Hamlet*: Why?

*First Clown*: 'Twill not be seen in him there. There the men are as mad as he.

*Hamlet*: How came he mad?            120

*First Clown*: Very strangely, they say.

*Hamlet*: How strangely?

*First Clown*: Faith, e'en with losing his wits.

*Hamlet*: Upon what ground?

*First Clown*: Why, here in Denmark. I have been sexton here, man and boy, thir-   125
ty years.

*Hamlet*: How long will a man lie i' th' earth ere he rot?

*First Clown*: Faith, if 'a be not rotten before 'a die—as we have many pocky corpses nowadays, that will scarce hold the laying in—'a will last you some eight year or nine year. A tanner will last you nine year.            130

*Hamlet*: Why he more than another?

*First Clown*: Why, sir, his hide is so tanned with his trade that 'a will keep out water a great while, and your water is a sore decaver of your whoreson dead body. [*He picks up a skull.*] Here's a skull now hath lien you i' th' earth three-and-twenty years.            135

*Hamlet*: Whose was it?

*First Clown*: A whoreson mad fellow's it was. Whose do you think it was?

*Hamlet*: Nay, I know not.

*First Clown*: A pestilence on him for a mad rogue! 'A poured a flagon of Rhenish on my head once. This same skull, sir, was, sir, Yorick's skull, the King's jester.   140

*Hamlet*: This?

*First Clown*: E'en that.

*Hamlet*: Let me see. [*He takes the skull.*] Alas, poor Yorick! I knew him, Horatio, a fellow of infinite jest, of most excellent fancy. He hath bore me on his back a thousand times, and now how abhorred in my imagination it is! My gorge   145
rises at it. Here hung those lips that I have kissed I know not how oft. Where be your gibes now? Your gambols, your songs, your flashes of merriment that were wont to set the table on a roar? Not one now, to mock your own grin-ning? Quite chopfallen? Now get you to my lady's chamber and tell her, let

---

124 *ground* cause. (But, in the next line, the gravedigger takes the word in the sense of "land," "coun-try.")    128 *pocky* rotten, diseased. (Literally, with the pox, or syphilis.)    129 *hold the laying in* hold together long enough to be interred.    *last you* last. (*You* is used colloquially here and in the following lines.)    133 *sore* i.e., terrible, great.    *whoreson* i.e., vile, scurvy    134 *lien you* lain. (See the note at line 129.)    139 *Rhenish* Rhine wine    144 *bore* borne    145 *My gorge rises* i.e., I feel nauseated    148 *were wont* used.    *mock your own grinning* mock at the way your skull seems to be grinning (just as you used to mock at yourself and those who grinned at you)    149 *chopfallen* (1) lacking the lower jaw (2) dejected

her paint an inch thick, to this favor she must come. Make her laugh at that.    150
Prithee, Horatio, tell me one thing.

*Horatio:* What's that, my lord?

*Hamlet:* Dost thou think Alexander looked o' this fashion i' th' earth?

*Horatio:* E'en so.

*Hamlet:* And smelt so? Pah! [*He throws down the skull.*]    155

*Horatio:* E'en so, my lord.

*Hamlet:* To what base uses we may return, Horatio! Why may not imagination
trace the noble dust of Alexander till 'a find it stopping a bunghole?

*Horatio:* 'Twere to consider too curiously to consider so.

*Hamlet:* No, faith, not a jot, but to follow him thither with modesty enough, and    160
likelihood to lead it. As thus: Alexander died, Alexander was buried,
Alexander returneth to dust, the dust is earth, of earth we make loam, and
why of that loam whereto he was converted might they not stop a beer barrel?
Imperious Caesar, dead and turned to clay,
Might stop a hole to keep the wind away.    165
O, that that earth which kept the world in awe
Should patch a wall t' expel the winter's flaw!

*Enter King, Queen, Laertes, and the corpse [of Ophelia, in procession, with Priest,
lords, etc.].*

But soft, but soft awhile! Here comes the King,
The Queen, the courtiers. Who is this they follow?
And with such maimèd rites? This doth betoken    170
The corpse they follow did with desperate hand
Fordo its own life. 'Twas of some estate.
Couch we awhile and mark.

    [*He and Horatio conceal themselves. Ophelia's body is taken to the grave.*]

*Laertes:* What ceremony else?

*Hamlet [to Horatio]:* That is Laertes, a very noble youth. Mark.    175

*Laertes:* What ceremony else?

*Priest:* Her obsequies have been as far enlarged
As we have warranty. Her death was doubtful,
And but that great command o'ersways the order
She should in ground unsanctified been lodged    180
Till the last trumpet. For charitable prayers,

---

150 *favor* aspect, appearance    158 *bunghole* hole for filling or emptying a cask    159 *curiously*
minutely    160 *modesty* plausible moderation    162 *loam* mortar consisting chiefly of moistened
clay and straw    164 *Imperious* imperial    167 *flaw* gust of wind    168 *soft* i.e., wait, be careful
170 *maimèd* mutilated, incomplete    172 *Fordo* destroy.    *estate* rank    173 *Couch we* let's
hide, lie low    178 *warranty* i.e., ecclesiastical authority    179 *great . . . order* orders from on
high overrule the prescribed procedures    180 *She should . . . lodged* she should have been buried in
unsanctified ground    181 *For* in place of

Shards, flints, and pebbles should be thrown on her.
Yet here she is allowed her virgin crants,
Her maiden strewments, and the bringing home
Of bell and burial.                                                                 185
*Laertes:* Must there no more be done?
*Priest:*                              No more be done.
We should profane the service of the dead
To sing a requiem and such rest to her
As to peace-parted souls.
*Laertes:*                              Lay her i' th' earth,
And from her fair and unpolluted flesh                                              190
May violets spring! I tell thee, churlish priest,
A ministering angel shall my sister be
When thou liest howling.
*Hamlet [to Horatio]:*              What, the fair Ophelia!
*Queen [scattering flowers]:* Sweets to the sweet! Farewell.
I hoped thou shouldst have been my Hamlet's wife.                                   195
I thought thy bride-bed to have decked, sweet maid,
And not t' have strewed thy grave.
*Laertes:*                              O, treble woe
Fall ten times treble on that cursèd head
Whose wicked deed thy most ingenious sense
Deprived thee of! Hold off the earth awhile,                                        200
Till I have caught her once more in mine arms.

                    *[He leaps into the grave and embraces Ophelia.]*

Now pile your dust upon the quick and dead,
Till of this flat a mountain you have made
T' o'ertop old Pelion or the skyish head
Of blue Olympus.
*Hamlet [coming forward]:* What is he whose grief                                   205
Bears such an emphasis, whose phrase of sorrow
Conjures the wandering stars and makes them stand
Like wonder-wounded hearers? This is I,
Hamlet the Dane.

---

182 *Shards* broken bits of pottery      183 *crants* garlands betokening maidenhood      184 *strewments*
flowers strewn on a coffin      184–185 *bringing . . . burial* laying the body to rest, to the sound of the
bell      188 *such rest* i.e., to pray for such rest      189 *peace-parted souls* those who have died at
peace with God      193 *howling* i.e., in hell      199 *ingenious sense* a mind that is quick, alert, of fine
qualities      204–205 *Pelion, Olympus* sacred mountains in the north of Thessaly      206 *emphasis*
i.e., rhetorical and florid emphasis. (*Phrase* has a similar rhetorical connotation.)      207 *wandering
stars* planets      208 *wonder-wounded* struck with amazement      209 *the Dane* (This title normally
signifies the King; see Act I, Scene I, line 17 and note.)

*Laertes [grappling with him]*: The devil take thy soul!                                    210
*Hamlet*: Thou pray'st not well.

> I prithee, take thy fingers from my throat,
> For though I am not splenitive and rash,
> Yet have I in me something dangerous,
> Which let thy wisdom fear. Hold off thy hand.                                             215

*King*: Pluck them asunder.
*Queen*: Hamlet, Hamlet!
*All*: Gentlemen!
*Horatio*: Good my lord, be quiet.

*[Hamlet and Laertes are parted.]*

*Hamlet*: Why, I will fight with him upon this theme                                        220

> Until my eyelids will no longer wag.

*Queen*: O my son, what theme?
*Hamlet*: I loved Ophelia. Forty thousand brothers

> Could not with all their quantity of love
> Make up my sum. What wilt thou do for her?                                               225

*King*: O, he is mad, Laertes.
*Queen*: For love of God, forbear him.
*Hamlet*: 'Swounds, show me what thou'lt do.

> Woo't weep? Woo't fight? Woo't fast? Woo't tear thyself?
> Woo't drink up eisel? Eat a crocodile?                                                   230
> I'll do 't. Dost come here to whine?
> To outface me with leaping in her grave?
> Be buried quick with her, and so will I.
> And if thou prate of mountains, let them throw
> Millions of acres on us, till our ground,                                                235
> Singeing his pate against the burning zone,
> Make Ossa like a wart! Nay, an thou'lt mouth,
> I'll rant as well as thou.

*Queen*:                                   This is mere madness,

> And thus awhile the fit will work on him;

---

210 s.d. *grappling with him* The testimony of the First Quarto that "*Hamlet leaps in after Laertes*" and the "Elegy on Burbage" ("Oft have I seen him leap into the grave") seem to indicate one way in which this fight was staged; however, the difficulty of fitting two contenders and Ophelia's body into a confined space (probably the trapdoor) suggests to many editors the alternative, that Laertes jumps out of the grave to attack Hamlet.)     213 *splenitive* quick-tempered     221 *wag* move. (A fluttering eyelid is a conventional sign that life has not yet gone.)     227 *forbear him* leave him alone 228 *'Swounds* by His (Christ's) wounds     229 *Woo't* wilt thou     230 *drink up* drink deeply. *eisel* vinegar.     *crocodile* (Crocodiles were tough and dangerous, and were supposed to shed hypocritical tears.)     233 *quick* alive     236 *his pate* its head, i.e., top.     *burning zone* zone in the celestial sphere containing the sun's orbit, between the tropics of Cancer and Capricorn     237 *Ossa* another mountain in Thessaly. (In their war against the Olympian gods, the giants attempted to heap Ossa on Pelion to scale Olympus.)     *an* if.     *mouth* i.e., rant     238 *mere* utter

Anon, as patient as the female dove                                                    240
When that her golden couplets are disclosed,
His silence will sit drooping.
Hamlet:                                          Hear you, sir.
What is the reason that you use me thus?
I loved you ever. But it is no matter.
Let Hercules himself do what he may,                                                   245
The cat will mew, and dog will have his day.

                                                              *Exit Hamlet.*

King: I pray thee, good Horatio, wait upon him.

                                                              *[Exit] Horatio.*

*[To Laertes.]* Strengthen your patience in our last night's speech;
We'll put the matter to the present push.—
Good Gertrude, set some watch over your son.—                                          250
This grave shall have a living monument.
An hour of quiet shortly shall we see;
Till then, in patience our proceeding be.                              *Exeunt.*

## Scene II [The Castle.]

*Enter Hamlet and Horatio.*

Hamlet: So much for this, sir; now shall you see the other.
You do remember all the circumstance?
Horatio: Remember it, my lord!
Hamlet: Sir, in my heart there was a kind of fighting
That would not let me sleep. Methought I lay                                            5
Worse than the mutines in the bilboes. Rashly,
And praised be rashness for it—let us know
Our indiscretion sometimes serves us well
When our deep plots do pall, and that should learn us
There's a divinity that shapes our ends,                                               10
Rough-hew them how we will—

---

241 *golden couplets* two baby pigeons, covered with yellow down.      *disclosed* hatched      245–246
*Let . . . day* i.e., (1) even Hercules couldn't stop Laertes' theatrical rant (2) I, too, will have my turn;
i.e., despite any blustering attempts at interference, every person will sooner or later do what he or
she must do      248 *in* i.e., by recalling      249 *present push* immediate test      251 *living* lasting.
(For Laertes' private understanding, Claudius also hints that Hamlet's death will serve as such a monument.)      252 *hour of quiet* time free of conflict      1 *see the other* hear the other news      6
*mutines* mutineers.      *bilboes* shackles.      *Rashly* on impulse. (This adverb goes with lines 12 ff.)
7 *know* acknowledge      8 *indiscretion* lack of foresight and judgment (not an indiscreet act)      9
*pall* fail, falter, go stale.      *learn* teach      11 *Rough-hew* shape roughly

*Horatio:*                                    That is most certain.
*Hamlet:* Up from my cabin,
    My sea-gown scarfed about me, in the dark
    Groped I to find out them, had my desire,
    Fingered their packet, and in fine withdrew                          15
    To mine own room again, making so bold,
    My fears forgetting manners, to unseal
    Their grand commission; where I found, Horatio—
    Ah, royal knavery!—an exact command,
    Larded with many several sorts of reasons                            20
    Importing Denmark's health and England's too,
    With, ho! such bugs and goblins in my life,
    That on the supervise, no leisure bated,
    No, not to stay the grinding of the ax,
    My head should be struck off.
*Horatio:*                               Is 't possible?                 25
*Hamlet [giving a document]:* Here's the commission. Read it at more leisure.
    But wilt thou hear now how I did proceed?
*Horatio:* I beseech you.
*Hamlet:* Being thus benetted round with villainies—
    Ere I could make a prologue to my brains,                            30
    They had begun the play—I sat me down,
    Devised a new commission, wrote it fair.
    I once did hold it, as our statists do,
    A baseness to write fair, and labored much
    How to forget that learning, but, sir, now                           35
    It did me yeoman's service. Wilt thou know
    Th' effect of what I wrote?
*Horatio:*                          Ay, good my lord.
*Hamlet:* An earnest conjuration from the King,
    As England was his faithful tributary,
    As love between them like the palm might flourish,                   40
    As peace should still her wheaten garland wear
    And stand a comma 'tween their amities,

---

13 *sea-gown* seaman's coat.     *scarfed* loosely wrapped     14 *them* i.e., Rosencrantz and
Guildenstern     15 *Fingered* pilfered, pinched.     *in fine* finally, in conclusion     20 *Larded* gar-
nished.     *several* different     21 *Importing* relating to     22 *bugs* bugbears, hobgoblins.     *in my
life* i.e., to be feared if I were allowed to live     23 *supervise* reading.     *leisure bated* delay allowed
24 *stay* await     30–31 *Ere . . . play* before I could consciously turn my brain to the matter, it had
started working on a plan     32 *fair* in a clear hand     33 *statists* statesmen     34 *baseness* i.e.,
lower-class trait     36 *yeoman's* i.e., substantial, faithful, loyal     37 *effect* purport     38 *conjuration* entreaty     40 *palm* (An image of health; see Psalm 92:12.)     41 *still* always.     *wheaten garland* (Symbolic of fruitful agriculture, of peace and plenty.)     42 *comma* (Indicating continuity,
link.)

And many suchlike "as"es of great charge,
That on the view and knowing of these contents,
Without debatement further more or less,                            45
He should those bearers put to sudden death,
Not shriving time allowed.
Horatio:                         How was this sealed?
Hamlet: Why, even in that was heaven ordinant.
    I had my father's signet in my purse,
    Which was the model of that Danish seal;                        50
    Folded the writ up in the form of th' other,
    Subscribed it, gave 't th' impression, placed it safely,
    The changeling never known. Now, the next day
    Was our sea fight, and what to this was sequent
    Thou knowest already.                                          55
Horatio: So Guildenstern and Rosencrantz go to 't.
Hamlet: Why, man, they did make love to this employment.
    They are not near my conscience. Their defeat
    Does by their own insinuation grow.
    'Tis dangerous when the baser nature comes                     60
    Between the pass and fell incensed points
    Of mighty opposites.
Horatio:                      Why, what a king is this!
Hamlet: Does it not, think thee, stand me now upon—
    He that hath killed my king and whored my mother.
    Popped in between th' election and my hopes,                   65
    Thrown out his angle for my proper life,
    And with such cozenage—is 't not perfect conscience
    To quit him with this arm? And is 't not to be damned
    To let this canker of our nature come
    In further evil?                                               70
Horatio: It must be shortly known to him from England
    What is the issue of the business there.
Hamlet: It will be short. The interim is mine.
    And a man's life's no more than to say "one."

43 "as"es (1) the "whereases" of a formal document (2) asses.    charge (1) import (2) burden
(appropriate to asses)    47 shriving time time for confession and absolution    48 ordinant directing    49 signet small seal    50 model replica    51 writ writing    52 Subscribed signed (with
forged signature).    impression i.e., with a wax seal    53 changeling i.e., substituted letter.
(Literally, a fairy child substituted for a human one.)    54 was sequent followed    58 defeat
destruction    59 insinuation intrusive intervention, sticking their noses in my business    60 baser
of lower social station    61 pass thrust.    fell fierce    62 opposites antagonists    63 stand me
now upon become incumbent on me now    65 election (The Danish monarch was "elected" by a
small number of high-ranking electors.)    66 angle fishhook.    proper very    67 cozenage trickery    68 quit requite, pay back    69 canker ulcer    69–70 come in grow into    74 a man's . . .
"one" one's whole life occupies such a short time, only as long as it takes to count to 1

But I am very sorry, good Horatio,                                    75
That to Laertes I forgot myself.
For by the image of my cause I see
The portraiture of his. I'll court his favors.
But, sure, the bravery of his grief did put me
Into a tow'ring passion.
*Horatio:*                        Peace, who comes here?          80

*Enter a Courtier [Osric].*

*Osric:* Your lordship is right welcome back to Denmark.
*Hamlet:* I humbly thank you, sir. [*To Horatio.*] Dost know this water fly?
*Horatio:* No, my good lord.
*Hamlet:* Thy state is the more gracious, for 'tis a vice to know him. He hath much
   land, and fertile. Let a beast be lord of beasts, and his crib shall stand at the   85
   King's mess. 'Tis a chuff, but, as I say, spacious in the possession of dirt.
*Osric:* Sweet lord, if your lordship were at leisure, I should impart a thing to you
   from His Majesty.
*Hamlet:* I will receive it, sir, with all diligence of spirit.
   Put your bonnet to his right use; 'tis for the head.                  90
*Osric:* I thank your lordship, it is very hot.
*Hamlet:* No, believe me, 'tis very cold. The wind is northerly.
*Osric:* It is indifferent cold, my lord, indeed.
*Hamlet:* But yet methinks it is very sultry and hot for my complexion.
*Osric:* Exceedingly, my lord. It is very sultry, as 'twere—I cannot tell how. My   95
   lord, His Majesty bade me signify to you that 'a has laid a great wager on your
   head. Sir, this is the matter—
*Hamlet:* I beseech you, remember.

                              *[Hamlet moves him to put on his hat.]*

*Osric:* Nay, good my lord; for my ease, in good faith. Sir, here is newly come to
   court Laertes—believe me, an absolute gentleman, full of most excellent dif-   100
   ferences, of very soft society and great showing. Indeed, to speak feelingly of
   him, he is the card or calendar of gentry, for you shall find in him the continent of what part a gentleman would see.

---

79 *bravery* bravado    85–86 *Let . . . mess* i.e., if a man, no matter how beastlike, is as rich in livestock and possessions as Osric, he may eat at the King's table    85 *crib* manger    86 *chuff* boor,
churl. (The Second Quarto spelling, *chough*, is a variant spelling that also suggests the meaning here
of "chattering jackdaw.")    90 *bonnet* any kind of cap or hat.    *his* its    93 *indifferent* somewhat
94 *complexion* temperament    99 *for my ease* (A conventional reply declining the invitation to put
his hat back on.)    100 *absolute* perfect    100–101 *differences* special qualities.    *soft society*
agreeable manners.    *great showing* distinguished appearance    101 *feelingly* with just perception
102 *card* chart, map.    *calendar* guide.    *gentry* good breeding    102–103 *the continent . . . see*
one who contains in him all the qualities a gentleman would like to see. (A *continent* is that which
contains.)

*Hamlet:* Sir, his definement suffers no perdition in you, though I know to divide him inventorially would dozy th' arithmetic of memory, and yet but yaw 105
neither in respect of his quick sail. But, in the verity of extolment, I take him to be a soul of great article, and his infusion of such dearth and rareness as, to make true diction of him, his semblable is his mirror and who else would trace him his umbrage, nothing more.

*Osric:* Your lordship speaks most infallibly of him. 110

*Hamlet:* The concernancy, sir? Why do we wrap the gentleman in our more rawer breath?

*Osric:* Sir?

*Horatio:* Is 't not possible to understand in another tongue? You will do 't, sir, really. 115

*Hamlet:* What imports the nomination of this gentleman?

*Osric:* Of Laertes?

*Horatio [to Hamlet]:* His purse is empty already; all 's golden words are spent.

*Hamlet:* Of him, sir.

*Osric:* I know you are not ignorant— 120

*Hamlet:* I would you did, sir. Yet in faith if you did, it would not much approve me. Well, sir?

*Osric:* You are not ignorant of what excellence Laertes is—

*Hamlet:* I dare not confess that, lest I should compare with him in excellence. But to know a man well were to know himself. 125

*Osric:* I mean, sir, for his weapon; but in the imputation laid on him by them, in his meed he's unfellowed.

*Hamlet:* What's his weapon?

*Osric:* Rapier and dagger.

*Hamlet:* That's two of his weapons—but well. 130

*Osric:* The King, sir, hath wagered with him six Barbary horses, against the which he has impawned, as I take it, six French rapiers and poniards, with their

104 *definement* definition. (Hamlet proceeds to mock Osric by throwing his lofty diction back at him.) *perdition* loss, diminution. *you* your description. *divide him inventorially* enumerate his graces 105 *dozy* dizzy. *yaw* swing unsteadily off course. (Said of a ship.) 106 *neither* for all that. *in respect of* in comparison with *in . . . extolment* in true praise (of him) 107 *of great article* one with many articles in his inventory. *infusion* essence, character infused into him by nature. *dearth and rareness* rarity 108 *make true diction* speak truly. *semblable* only true likeness. *who . . . trace* any other person who would wish to follow 109 *umbrage* shadow 111 *concernancy* import, relevance. *rawer breath* unrefined speech that can only come short in praising him 114 *to understand . . . tongue* i.e., for you, Osric, to understand when someone else speaks your language. (Horatio twits Osric for not being able to understand the kind of flowery speech he himself uses, when Hamlet speaks in such a vein. Alternatively, all this could be said to Hamlet.). *You will do 't* i.e., you can if you try, or, you may well have to try (to speak plainly) 121 *approve* commend 124–125 *I dare . . . himself* I dare not boast of knowing Laertes' excellence lest I seem to imply a comparable excellence in myself. Certainly to know another person well, one must know oneself 126 *for* i.e., with. *imputation . . . them* reputation given him by others 127 *meed* merit. *unfellowed* unmatched 130 *but well* but never mind 132 *he* i.e., Laertes. *impawned* staked, wagered. *poniards* daggers

assigns, as girdle, hangers, and so. Three of the carriages, in faith, are very dear to fancy, very responsive to the hilts, most delicate carriages, and of very liberal conceit. 135

Hamlet: What call you the carriages?

Horatio [to Hamlet]: I knew you must be edified by the margent ere you had done.

Osric: The carriages, sir, are the hangers.

Hamlet: The phrase would be more germane to the matter if we could carry a cannon by our sides; I would it might be hangers till then. But, on: six 140 Barbary horses against six French swords, their assigns, and three liberal-conceited carriages; that's the French bet against the Danish. Why is this impawned, as you call it?

Osric: The King, sir, hath laid, sir, that in a dozen passes between yourself and him, he shall not exceed you three hits. He hath laid on twelve for nine, and 145 it would come to immediate trial, if your lordship would vouchsafe the answer.

Hamlet: How if I answer no?

Osric: I mean, my lord, the opposition of your person in trial.

Hamlet: Sir, I will walk here in the hall. If it please His Majesty, it is the breath- 150 ing time of day with me. Let the foils be brought, the gentleman willing, and the King hold his purpose, I will win for him an I can; if not, I will gain nothing but my shame and the odd hits.

Osric: Shall I deliver you so?

Hamlet: To this effect, sir—after what flourish your 155
nature will.

Osric: I commend my duty to your lordship.

Hamlet: Yours, yours. [Exit Osric.] 'A does well to commend it himself; there are no tongues else for 's turn.

Horatio: This lapwing runs away with the shell on his head. 160

Hamlet: 'A did comply with his dug before 'a sucked it. Thus has he—and many more of the same breed that I know the drossy age dotes on—only got the

---

133 *assigns* appurtenances.  *hangers* straps on the sword belt (*girdle*), from which the sword hung. *and so and so on.  carriages* (An affected way of saying *hangers*; literally, gun carriages.)  134 *dear to fancy* delightful to the fancy.  *responsive* corresponding closely, matching or well adjusted. *delicate* (i.e., in workmanship)  135 *liberal conceit* elaborate design  137 *margent* margin of a book, place for explanatory notes  144 *laid* wagered  *passes* bouts. (The odds of the betting are hard to explain. Possibly the King bets that Hamlet will win at least five out of twelve, at which point Laertes raises the odds against himself by betting he will win nine.)  146 *vouchsafe the answer* be so good as to accept the challenge. (Hamlet deliberately takes the phrase in its literal sense of replying.)  150–151 *breathing time* exercise period.  *Let* i.e., if  154 *deliver you* report what you say  157 *commend* commit to your favor. (A conventional salutation, but Hamlet wryly uses a more literal meaning, "recommend," "praise," in line 158.)  159 *for 's turn* for his purposes, i.e., to do it for him  160 *lapwing* (A proverbial type of youthful forwardness. Also, a bird that draws intruders away from its nest and was thought to run about with its head in the shell when newly hatched; a seeming reference to Osric's hat.)  161 *comply . . . dug* observe ceremonious formality toward his nurse's or mother's teat  162 *drossy* laden with scum and impurities, frivolous

tune of the time and, out of an habit of encounter, a kind of yeasty collection, which carries them through and through the most fanned and winnowed opinions; and do but blow them to their trial, the bubbles are out. 165

*Enter a Lord.*

Lord: My lord, His Majesty commended him to you by young Osric, who brings back to him that you attend him in the hall. He sends to know if your pleasure hold to play with Laertes, or that you will take longer time.

Hamlet: I am constant to my purposes; they follow the King's pleasure. If his fitness speaks, mine is ready; now or whensoever, provided I be so able as now. 170

Lord: The King and Queen and all are coming down.

Hamlet: In happy time.

Lord: The Queen desires you to use some gentle entertainment to Laertes before you fall to play.

Hamlet: She well instructs me. [*Exit Lord.*] 175

Horatio: You will lose, my lord.

Hamlet: I do not think so. Since he went into France, I have been in continual practice; I shall win at the odds. But thou wouldst not think how ill all's here about my heart; but it is no matter.

Horatio: Nay, good my lord— 180

Hamlet: It is but foolery, but it is such a kind of gaingiving as would perhaps trouble a woman.

Horatio: If your mind dislike anything, obey it. I will forestall their repair hither and say you are not fit.

Hamlet: Not a whit, we defy augury. There is special providence in the fall of a 185 sparrow. If it be now, 'tis not to come; if it be not to come, it will be now; if it be not now; yet it will come. The readiness is all. Since no man of aught he leaves knows, what is 't to leave betimes? Let be.

*A table prepared. [Enter] trumpets, drums, and officers with cushions; King, Queen, [Osric,] and all the state; foils, daggers, [and wine borne in;] and Laertes.*

King: Come, Hamlet, come and take this hand from me.

*[The King puts Laertes' hand into Hamlet's.]*

---

163 *tune* temper, mood, manner of speech. *an habit of encounter* a demeanor in conversing (with courtiers of his own kind). *yeasty* frothy 163–164 *collection* i.e., of current phrases 164–165 *carries . . . opinions* sustains them right through the scrutiny of persons whose opinions are select and refined. (Literally, like grain separated from its chaff. Osric is both the chaff and the bubbly froth on the surface of the liquor that is soon blown away.) 165 *and do* yet do. *blow . . . out* test them by merely blowing on them, and their bubbles burst 169–170 *If . . . ready* if he declares his readiness, my convenience waits on his 172 *In happy time* (A phrase of courtesy indicating that the time is convenient.) 173 *entertainment* greeting 181 *gaingiving* misgiving 183 *repair* coming 187–188 *Since . . . Let be* since no one has knowledge of what he is leaving behind, what does an early death matter after all? Enough; don't struggle against it.

*Hamlet [to Laertes]*: Give me your pardon, sir. I have done you wrong,    190
    But pardon 't as you are a gentleman.
    This presence knows,
    And you must needs have heard, how I am punished
    With a sore distraction. What I have done
    That might your nature, honor, and exception    195
    Roughly awake, I here proclaim was madness.
    Was 't Hamlet wronged Laertes? Never Hamlet.
    If Hamlet from himself be ta'en away,
    And when he's not himself does wrong Laertes,
    Then Hamlet does it not, Hamlet denies it.    200
    Who does it, then? His madness. If 't be so,
    Hamlet is of the faction that is wronged;
    His madness is poor Hamlet's enemy.
    Sir, in this audience
    Let my disclaiming from a purposed evil    205
    Free me so far in your most generous thoughts
    That I have shot my arrow o'er the house
    And hurt my brother.
*Laertes*:                I am satisfied in nature,
    Whose motive in this case should stir me most
    To my revenge. But in my terms of honor    210
    I stand aloof, and will no reconcilement
    Till by some elder masters of known honor
    I have a voice and precedent of peace
    To keep my name ungored. But till that time
    I do receive your offered love like love,    215
    And will not wrong it.
*Hamlet*:              I embrace it freely,
    And will this brothers' wager frankly play.—
    Give us the foils. Come on.
*Laertes*:                Come, one for me.
*Hamlet*: I'll be your foil, Laertes. In mine ignorance
    Your skill shall, like a star i' the darkest night,    220
    Stick fiery off indeed.
*Laertes*:             You mock me, sir.
*Hamlet*: No, by this hand.

---

192 *presence* royal assembly    193 *punished* afflicted    195 *exception* disapproval    202 *faction* party    207 *That I have* as if I had    208 *in nature* i.e., as to my personal feelings    209 *motive* prompting    213 *voice* authoritative pronouncement.    *of peace* for reconciliation    214 *name ungored* reputation unwounded    217 *frankly* without ill feeling or the burden of rancor    219 *foil* thin metal background which sets a jewel off (with pun on the blunted rapier for fencing)    221 *Stick fiery off* stand out brilliantly

*King*: Give them the foils, young Osric. Cousin Hamlet,
    You know the wager?
*Hamlet*:               Very well, my lord.
    Your Grace has laid the odds o' the weaker side.        225
*King*: I do not fear it; I have seen you both.
    But since he is bettered, we have therefore odds.
*Laertes*: This is too heavy. Let me see another.

                    *[He exchanges his foil for another.]*

*Hamlet*: This likes me well. These foils have all a length?

                        *[They prepare to play.]*

*Osric*: Ay, my good lord.                         230
*King*: Set me the stoups of wine upon that table.
    If Hamlet give the first or second hit,
    Or quit in answer of the third exchange,
    Let all the battlements their ordnance fire.
    The King shall drink to Hamlet's better breath,      235
    And in the cup an union shall he throw
    Richer than that which four successive kings
    In Denmark's crown have worn. Give me the cups,
    And let the kettle to the trumpet speak,
    The trumpet to the cannoneer without,              240
    The cannons to the heavens, the heaven to earth,
    "Now the King drinks to Hamlet." Come, begin.

                      *Trumpets the while.*

    And you, the judges, bear a wary eye.
*Hamlet*: Come on, sir.
*Laertes*: Come, my lord. *[They play. Hamlet scores a hit.]*     245
*Hamlet*: One.
*Laertes*: No.
*Hamlet*: Judgment.
*Osric*:            A hit, a very palpable hit.

           *Drum, trumpets, and shot. Flourish.*
                  *A piece goes off.*

*Laertes*: Well, again.

---

225 *laid the odds o'* bet on, backed    227 *is bettered* has improved; is the odds-on favorite. (Laertes' handicap is the "three hits" specified in line 145.)    229 *likes me* pleases me    233 Or . . . *exchange* i.e., or requites Laertes in the third bout for having won the first two    235 *better breath* improved vigor    236 *union* pearl. (So called, according to Pliny's *Natural History*, 9, because pearls are *unique*, never identical.)    239 *kettle* kettledrum

*King*: Stay, give me drink. Hamlet, this pearl is thine.                    250

                    *[He drinks, and throws a pearl in Hamlet's cup.]*

    Here's to thy health. Give him the cup.
*Hamlet*: I'll play this bout first. Set it by awhile.
    Come. *[They play.]* Another hut; what say you?
*Laertes*: A touch, a touch, I do confess 't.
*King*: Our son shall win.
*Queen*:                    He's fat and scant of breath.                    255
    Here, Hamlet, take my napkin, rub thy brows.
    The Queen carouses to thy fortune, Hamlet.
*Hamlet*: Good madam!
*King*: Gertrude, do not drink.
*Queen*: I will, my lord, I pray you pardon me.                    *[She drinks.]*  260
*King [aside]*: It is the poisoned cup. It is too late.
*Hamlet*: I dare not drink yet, madam; by and by.
*Queen*: Come, let me wipe thy face.
*Laertes [to King]*: My lord, I'll hit him now.
*King*:                    I do not think 't.
*Laertes [aside]*: And yet it is almost against my conscience.             265
*Hamlet*: Come, for the third, Laertes. You do but dally.
    I pray you, pass with your best violence;
    I am afeard you make a wanton of me.
*Laertes*: Say you so? Come on.                    *[They play.]*
*Osric*: Nothing neither way.                    270
*Laertes*: Have at you now!

    *[Laertes wounds Hamlet; then, in scuffling, they change rapiers, and Hamlet*
                                 *wounds Laertes.]*

*King*:                    Part them! They are incensed.
*Hamlet*: Nay, come, again.                    *[The Queen falls.]*
*Osric*:                    Look to the Queen there, ho!
*Horatio*: They bleed on both sides. How is it, my lord?
*Osric*: How is 't, Laertes?
*Laertes*: Why, as a woodcock to mine own springe, Osric;                 275
    I am justly killed with mine own treachery.
*Hamlet*: How does the Queen?
*King*:                    She swoons to see them bleed.
*Queen*: No, no, the drink, the drink—O my dear Hamlet—
    The drink, the drink! I am poisoned.                    *[She dies.]*

---

255 *fat* not physically fit, out of training     256 *napkin* handkerchief     257 *carouses* drinks a toast
267 *pass* thrust     268 *make . . . me* i.e., treat me like a spoiled child, trifle with me     271 s.d. *in
scuffling, they change rapiers* (This stage direction occurs in the Folio. According to a widespread stage
tradition, Hamlet receives a scratch, realizes that Laertes' sword is unbated, and accordingly forces an
exchange.)     275 *woodcock* a bird, a type of stupidity or as a decoy.     *springe* trap, snare

*Hamlet:* O villainy! Ho, let the door be locked!                              280
　　Treachery! Seek it out.                    *[Laertes falls. Exit Osric.]*
*Laertes:* It is here, Hamlet. Hamlet, thou art slain.
　　No med'cine in the world can do thee good;
　　In thee there is not half an hour's life.
　　The treacherous instrument is in thy hand,               285
　　Unbated and envenomed. The foul practice
　　Hath turned itself on me. Lo, here I lie,
　　Never to rise again. Thy mother's poisoned.
　　I can no more. The King, the King's to blame.
*Hamlet:* The point envenomed too? Then, venom, to thy work.       290
　　　　　　　　　　　　　　　　　*[He stabs the King.]*

*All:* Treason! Treason!
*King:* O, yet defend me, friends! I am but hurt.
*Hamlet [forcing the King to drink]:*
　　Here, thou incestuous, murderous, damnèd Dane,
　　Drink off this potion. Is thy union here?
　　Follow my mother.                              *[The King dies.]*
*Laertes:*　　　　　　　He is justly served.                   295
　　It is a poison tempered by himself.
　　Exchange forgiveness with me, noble Hamlet.
　　Mine and my father's death come not upon thee,
　　Nor thine on me!                                 *[He dies.]*
*Hamlet:* Heaven make thee free of it! I follow thee.            300
　　I am dead, Horatio. Wretched Queen, adieu!
　　You that look pale and tremble at this chance,
　　That are but mutes or audience to this act,
　　Had I but time—as this fell sergeant, Death,
　　Is strict in his arrest—O, I could tell you—             305
　　But let it be. Horatio, I am dead;
　　Thou livest. Report me and my cause aright
　　To the unsatisfied.
*Horatio:*　　　　　　Never believe it.
　　I am more an antique Roman than a Dane.
　　Here's yet some liquor left.

　　*[He attempts to drink from the poisoned cup. Hamlet prevents him.]*

*Hamlet:*　　　　　　As thou'rt a man,                    310
　　Give me the cup! Let go! By heaven, I'll ha 't.

---

286 *Unbated* not blunted with a button.　　*practice* plot　　294 *union* pearl. (See line 236; with grim puns on the word's other meanings: marriage, shared death.)　　296 *tempered* mixed　　302 *chance* mischance　　303 *mutes* silent observers. (Literally, actors with nonspeaking parts.)　　304 *fell* cruel.　　*sergeant* sheriff's officer　　305 *strict* (1) severely just (2) unavoidable.　　*arrest* (1) taking into custody (2) stopping my speech　　309 *Roman* (Suicide was an honorable choice for many Romans as an alternative to a dishonorable life.)

O God, Horatio, what a wounded name,
Things standing thus unknown, shall I leave behind me!
If thou didst ever hold me in thy heart,
Absent thee from felicity awhile, 315
And in this harsh world draw thy breath in pain
To tell my story. *A march afar off [and a volley within].* What warlike noise is
 this?

*Enter Osric.*

*Osric:* Young Fortinbras, with conquest come from Poland,
 To th' ambassadors of England gives
 This warlike volley.
*Hamlet:*                    O, I die, Horatio! 320
 The potent poison quite o'ercrows my spirit.
 I cannot live to hear the news from England,
 But I do prophesy th' election lights
 On Fortinbras. He has my dying voice.
 So tell him, with th' occurrents more and less 325
 Which have solicited—the rest is silence.                    *[He dies.]*
*Horatio:* Now cracks a noble heart. Good night, sweet prince,
 And flights of angels sing thee to thy rest!

*[March within.]*

Why does the drum come hither?

*Enter Fortinbras, with the [English] Ambassadors [with drum, colors, and atten-
dants].*

*Fortinbras:* Where is this sight?
*Horatio:*                    What is it you would see? 330
 If aught of woe or wonder, cease your search.
*Fortinbras:* This quarry cries on havoc. O proud Death,
 What feast is toward in thine eternal cell,
 That thou so many princes at a shot
 So bloodily hast struck?
*First Ambassador:*                    The sight is dismal, 335
 And our affairs from England come too late.
 The ears are senseless that should give us hearing,
 To tell him his commandment is fulfilled,

---

321 *o'ercrows* triumphs over (like the winner in a cockfight)     324 *voice* vote     325 *occurrents*
events, incidents     326 *solicited* moved, urged. (Hamlet doesn't finish saying what the events have
prompted—presumably, his acts of vengeance, or his reporting of those events to Fortinbras.)
332 *quarry* heap of dead.     *cries on havoc* proclaims a general slaughter     333 *feast* i.e., Death
feasting on those who have fallen.     *toward* in preparation

That Rosencrantz and Guildenstern are dead.
Where should we have our thanks?
*Horatio:*                    Not from his mouth,         340
Had it th' ability of life to thank you.
He never gave commandment for their death.
But since, so jump upon this bloody question,
You from the Polack wars, and you from England,
Are here arrived, give order that these bodies         345
High on a stage be placèd to the view,
And let me speak to th' yet unknowing world
How these things came about. So shall you hear
Of carnal, bloody, and unnatural acts,
Of accidental judgments, casual slaughters,         350
Of deaths put on by cunning and forced cause,
And, in this upshot, purposes mistook
Fall'n on th' inventors' heads. All this can I
Truly deliver.
*Fortinbras:*         Let us haste to hear it,
And call the noblest to the audience.            355
For me, with sorrow I embrace my fortune.
I have some rights of memory in this kingdom,
Which now to claim my vantage doth invite me.
*Horatio:* Of that I shall have also cause to speak,
And from his mouth whose voice will draw on more.      360
But let this same be presently performed,
Even while men's minds are wild, lest more mischance
On plots and errors happen.
*Fortinbras:*               Let four captains
Bear Hamlet, like a soldier, to the stage,
For he was likely, had he been put on,          365
To have proved most royal; and for his passage,
The soldiers' music and the rite of war
Speak loudly for him.
Take up the bodies. Such a sight as this
Becomes the field, but here shows much amiss.        370
Go bid the soldiers shoot.

     *Exeunt [marching, bearing off the dead bodies; a peal of ordnance is shot off].*

---

340 *his* i.e., Claudius'     343 *jump* precisely, immediately.     *question* dispute, affair     346 *stage* platform     350 *judgments* retributions.     *casual* occurring by chance     351 *put on* instigated. *forced cause* contrivance     357 *of memory* traditional, remembered, unforgotten     358 *vantage* favorable opportunity     360 *voice . . . more* vote will influence still others     361 *presently* immediately     363 *On* on the basis of; on top of     365 *put on* i.e., invested in royal office and so put to the test     366 *passage* i.e., from life to death     368 *Speak* (let them) speak     370 *Becomes the field* suits the field of battle

## Arthur Miller

*Certain Private Conversations in Two Acts
and a Requiem*

Arthur Miller, born in 1915 into a lower-
income Jewish family in New York's
Harlem, grew up in Brooklyn. He studied
playwriting at the University of Michigan,
later wrote radio scripts, and in World War
II worked as a steamfitter. When the New
York Drama Critics named his All My
Sons best play of 1947, Miller told an
interviewer, "I don't see how you can write
anything decent without using as your basis
the question of right and wrong." (The play
is about a guilty manufacturer of defective
aircraft parts.) Death of a Salesman
(1949) made Miller famous. The
Crucible (1953), a dramatic indictment of

Arthur Miller

the Salem witch trials, gained him further attention at a time when Senator Joseph
McCarthy was conducting loyalty investigations. For a while (1956–1961), Miller
was the husband of actress Marilyn Monroe, whom the main character of his All That
Fall (1964) resembles. Among Miller's other plays are A View from the Bridge
(1955), The Price (1968), The Creation of the World and Other Businesses
(1972), Playing for Time (1980), written for television, and Broken Glass (1994).
He has written two novels, Focus (1945) and The Misfits (1960), which he made
into a screenplay featuring Monroe.

### Cast

| | | | |
|---|---|---|---|
| Willy Loman | Uncle Ben | Happy | Stanley |
| Linda | Howard Wagner | Bernard | Miss Forsythe |
| Biff | Jenny | The Woman | Letta |
| Charley | | | |

Scene: *The action takes place in Willy Loman's house and yard and in various
places he visits in the New York and Boston of today. Throughout the play, in the stage
directions, left and right mean stage left and stage right.*

## ACT I

*A melody is heard, played upon a flute. It is small and fine, telling of grass and
trees and the horizon. The curtain rises.*

*Before us is the Salesman's house. We are aware of towering, angular shapes behind
it, surrounding it on all sides. Only the blue light of the sky falls upon the house and*

*forestage; the surrounding area shows an angry glow of orange. As more light appears, we see a solid vault of apartment houses around the small, fragile-seeming home. An air of the dream clings to the place, a dream rising out of reality. The kitchen at center seems actual enough, for there is a kitchen table with three chairs, and a refrigerator. But no other fixtures are seen. At the back of the kitchen there is a draped entrance, which leads to the living room. To the right of the kitchen, on a level raised two feet, is a bedroom furnished only with a brass bedstead and a straight chair. On a shelf over the bed a silver athletic trophy stands. A window opens onto the apartment house at the side.*

*Behind the kitchen, on a level raised six and a half feet, is the boys' bedroom, at present barely visible. Two beds are dimly seen, and at the back of the room a dormer window. (This bedroom is above the unseen living room.) At the left a stairway curves up to it from the kitchen.*

*The entire setting is wholly or, in some places, partially transparent. The roof-line of the house is one-dimensional; under and over it we see the apartment buildings. Before the house lies an apron, curving beyond the forestage into the orchestra. This forward area serves as the backyard as well as the locale of all Willy's imaginings and of his city scenes. Whenever the action is in the present the actors observe the imaginary wall-lines, entering the house only through the door at the left. But in the scenes of the past these boundaries are broken, and characters enter or leave a room by stepping "through" a wall onto the forestage.*

*From the right, Willy Loman, the Salesman, enters, carrying two large sample cases. The flute plays on. He hears but is not aware of it. He is past sixty years of age, dressed quietly. Even as he crosses the stage to the doorway of the house, his exhaustion is apparent. He unlocks the door, comes into the kitchen, and thankfully lets his burden down, feeling the soreness of his palms. A word-sigh escapes his lips—it might be, "Oh, boy, oh, boy." He closes the door, then carries his cases out into the living room, through the draped kitchen doorway.*

*Linda, his wife, has stirred in her bed at the right. She gets out and puts on a robe, listening. Most often jovial, she has developed an iron repression of her exceptions to Willy's behavior—she more than loves him, she admires him, as though his mercurial nature, his temper, his massive dreams and little cruelties, served her only as sharp reminders of the turbulent longings within him, longings which she shares but lacks the temperament to utter and follow to their end.*

Linda (*hearing Willy outside the bedroom, calls with some trepidation*): Willy!
Willy: It's all right. I came back.
Linda: Why? What happened? (*Slight pause.*) Did something happen, Willy?
Willy: No, nothing happened.
Linda: You didn't smash the car, did you?
Willy (*with casual irritation*): I said nothing happened. Didn't you hear me?
Linda: Don't you feel well?
Willy: I am tired to the death. (*The flute has faded away. He sits on the bed beside her, a little numb.*) I couldn't make it. I just couldn't make it, Linda.
Linda (*very carefully, delicately*): Where were you all day? You look terrible.
Willy: I got as far as a little above Yonkers. I stopped for a cup of coffee. Maybe it was the coffee.

Linda: What?

Willy (after a pause): I suddenly couldn't drive any more. The car kept going onto the shoulder, y'know?

Linda (helpfully): Oh. Maybe it was the steering again. I don't think Angelo knows the Studebaker.

Willy: No, it's me, it's me. Suddenly I realize I'm goin' sixty miles an hour and I don't remember the last five minutes. I'm—I can't seem to—keep my mind to it.

Linda: Maybe it's your glasses. You never went for your new glasses.

Willy: No, I see everything. I came back ten miles an hour. It took me nearly four hours from Yonkers.

Linda (resigned): Well, you'll just have to take a rest. Willy, you can't continue this way.

Willy: I just got back from Florida.

Linda: But you didn't rest your mind. Your mind is overactive, and the mind is what counts, dear.

Willy: I'll start out in the morning. Maybe I'll feel better in the morning. (She is taking off his shoes.) These goddam arch supports are killing me.

Linda: Take an aspirin. Should I get you an aspirin? It'll soothe you.

Willy (with wonder): I was driving along, you understand? And I was fine. I was even observing the scenery. You can imagine, me looking at scenery, on the road every week of my life. But it's so beautiful up there, Linda, the trees are so thick, and the sun is warm. I opened the windshield and just let the warm air bathe over me. And then all of a sudden I'm goin' off the road! I'm tellin' ya, I absolutely forgot I was driving. If I'd've gone the other way over the white line I might've killed somebody. So I went on again—and five minutes later I'm dreamin' again, and I nearly—(He presses two fingers against his eyes.) I have such thoughts, I have such strange thoughts.

Linda: Willy, dear. Talk to them again. There's no reason why you can't work in New York.

Willy: They don't need me in New York. I'm the New England man. I'm vital in New England.

Linda: But you're sixty years old. They can't expect you to keep traveling every week.

Willy: I'll have to send a wire to Portland. I'm supposed to see Brown and Morrison tomorrow morning at ten o'clock to show the line. Goddammit, I could sell them! (He starts putting on his jacket.)

Linda (taking the jacket from him): Why don't you go down to the place tomorrow and tell Howard you've simply got to work in New York? You're too accommodating, dear.

Willy: If old man Wagner was alive I'd a been in charge of New York now! That man was a prince, he was a masterful man. But that boy of his, that Howard, he don't appreciate. When I went north the first time, the Wagner Company didn't know where New England was!

Linda: Why don't you tell those things to Howard, dear?

Willy (encouraged): I will, I definitely will. Is there any cheese?

*Linda*: I'll make you a sandwich.

*Willy*: No, go to sleep. I'll take some milk. I'll be up right away. The boys in?

*Linda*: They're sleeping. Happy took Biff on a date tonight.

*Willy* (*interested*): That so?

*Linda*: It was so nice to see them shaving together, one behind the other, in the bathroom. And going out together. You notice? The whole house smells of shaving lotion.

*Willy*: Figure it out. Work a lifetime to pay off a house. You finally own it, and there's nobody to live in it.

*Linda*: Well, dear, life is a casting off. It's always that way.

*Willy*: No, no, some people—some people accomplish something. Did Biff say anything after I went this morning?

*Linda*: You shouldn't have criticized him, Willy, especially after he just got off the train. You mustn't lose your temper with him.

*Willy*: When the hell did I lose my temper? I simply asked him if he was making any money. Is that a criticism?

*Linda*: But, dear, how could he make any money?

*Willy* (*worried and angered*): There's such an undercurrent in him. He became a moody man. Did he apologize when I left this morning?

*Linda*: He was crestfallen, Willy. You know how he admires you. I think if he finds himself, then you'll both be happier and not fight any more.

*Willy*: How can he find himself on a farm? Is that a life? A farmhand? In the beginning, when he was young, I thought, well, a young man, it's good for him to tramp around, take a lot of different jobs. But it's more than ten years now and he has yet to make thirty-five dollars a week!

*Linda*: He's finding himself, Willy.

*Willy*: Not finding yourself at the age of thirty-four is a disgrace!

*Linda*: Shh!

*Willy*: The trouble is he's lazy, goddammit!

*Linda*: Willy, please!

*Willy*: Biff is a lazy bum.

*Linda*: They're sleeping. Get something to eat. Go on down.

*Willy*: Why did he come home? I would like to know what brought him home.

*Linda*: I don't know. I think he's still lost, Willy. I think he's very lost.

*Willy*: Biff Loman is lost. In the greatest country in the world a young man with such—personal attractiveness, gets lost. And such a hard worker. There's one thing about Biff—he's not lazy.

*Linda*: Never.

*Willy* (*with pity and resolve*): I'll see him in the morning. I'll have a nice talk with him. I'll get him a job selling. He could be big in no time. My God! Remember how they used to follow him around in high school? When he smiled at one of them their faces lit up. When he walked down the street . . . (*He loses himself in reminiscences.*)

*Linda* (*trying to bring him out of it*): Willy, dear, I got a new kind of American-type cheese today. It's whipped.

*Willy*: Why do you get American when I like Swiss?

*Linda*: I just thought you'd like a change—

*Willy*: I don't want a change! I want Swiss cheese. Why am I always being contradicted?

*Linda* (*with a covering laugh*): I thought it would be a surprise.

*Willy*: Why don't you open a window in here, for God's sake?

*Linda* (*with infinite patience*): They're all open, dear.

*Willy*: The way they boxed us in here. Bricks and windows, windows and bricks.

*Linda*: We should've bought the land next door.

*Willy*: The street is lined with cars. There's not a breath of fresh air in the neighborhood. The grass don't grow any more, you can't raise a carrot in the back yard. They should've had a law against apartment houses. Remember those two beautiful elm trees out there? When I and Biff hung the swing between them?

*Linda*: Yeah, like being a million miles from the city.

*Willy*: They should've arrested the builder for cutting those down. They massacred the neighborhood. (*Lost.*) More and more I think of those days, Linda. This time of year it was lilac and wisteria. And then the peonies would come out, and the daffodils. What fragrance in this room!

*Linda*: Well, after all, people had to move somewhere.

*Willy*: No, there's more people now.

*Linda*: I don't think there's more people. I think—

*Willy*: There's more people! That's what's ruining this country! Population is getting out of control. The competition is maddening! Smell the stink from that apartment house! And another on the other side . . . How can they whip cheese?

*On Willy's last line, Biff and Happy raise themselves up in their beds, listening.*

*Linda*: Go down, try it. And be quiet.

*Willy* (*turning to Linda, guiltily*): You're not worried about me, are you, sweetheart?

*Biff*: What's the matter?

*Happy*: Listen!

*Linda*: You've got too much on the ball to worry about.

*Willy*: You're my foundation and my support, Linda.

*Linda*: Just try to relax, dear. You make mountains out of molehills.

*Willy*: I won't fight with him any more. If he wants to go back to Texas, let him go.

*Linda*: He'll find his way.

*Willy*: Sure. Certain men just don't get started till later in life. Like Thomas Edison, I think. Or B. F. Goodrich. One of them was deaf. (*He starts for the bedroom doorway.*) I'll put my money on Biff.

*Linda*: And Willy—if it's warm Sunday we'll drive in the country. And we'll open the windshield, and take lunch.

*Willy*: No, the windshields don't open on the new cars.

*Linda*: But you opened it today.

Willy: Me? I didn't. (*He stops.*) Now isn't that peculiar! Isn't that a remarkable—
(*He breaks off in amazement and fright as the flute is heard distantly.*)

Linda: What, darling?

Willy: That is the most remarkable thing.

Linda: What, dear?

Willy: I was thinking of the Chevvy. (*Slight pause.*) Nineteen twenty-eight . . .
when I had that red Chevvy—(*Breaks off.*) That funny? I coulda sworn I was
driving that Chevvy today.

Linda: Well, that's nothing. Something must've reminded you.

Willy: Remarkable. Ts. Remember those days? The way Biff used to simonize that
car? The dealer refused to believe there was eighty thousand miles on it. (*He
shakes his head.*) Heh! (*To Linda.*) Close your eyes, I'll be right up. (*He walks
out of the bedroom.*)

Happy (*to Biff*): Jesus, maybe he smashed up the car again!

Linda (*calling after Willy*): Be careful on the stairs, dear! The cheese is on the middle
shelf! (*She turns, goes over to the bed, takes his jacket, and goes out of the bedroom.*)

Light has risen on the boys' room. Unseen, Willy is heard talking to himself,
"Eighty thousand miles," and a little laugh. Biff gets out of bed, comes downstage a
bit, and stands attentively. Biff is two years older than his brother Happy, well
built, but in these days bears a worn air and seems less self-assured. He has succeeded less, and his dreams are stronger and less acceptable than Happy's. Happy
is tall, powerfully made. Sexuality is like a visible color on him, or a scent that
many women have discovered. He, like his brother, is lost, but in a different way,
for he has never allowed himself to turn his face toward defeat and is thus more
confused and hardskinned, although seemingly more content.

Happy (*getting out of bed*): He's going to get his license taken away if he keeps
that up. I'm getting nervous about him, y'know, Biff?

Biff: His eyes are going.

Happy: No, I've driven with him. He sees all right. He just doesn't keep his mind
on it. I drove into the city with him last week. He stops at a green light and
then it turns red and he goes. (*He laughs.*)

Biff: Maybe he's color-blind.

Happy: Pop? Why he's got the finest eye for color in the business. You know that.

Biff (*sitting down on his bed*): I'm going to sleep.

Happy: You're not still sour on Dad, are you, Biff?

Biff: He's all right, I guess.

Willy (*underneath them, in the living room*): Yes, sir, eighty thousand miles—
eighty-two thousand!

Biff: You smoking?

Happy (*holding out a pack of cigarettes*): Want one?

Biff (*taking a cigarette*): I can never sleep when I smell it.

Willy: What a simonizing job, heh!

Happy (*with deep sentiment*): Funny, Biff, y'know? Us sleeping in here again? The
old beds. (*He pats his bed affectionately.*) All the talk that went across those
two beds, huh? Our whole lives.

*Biff*: Yeah. Lotta dreams and plans.

*Happy* (*with a deep and masculine laugh*): About five hundred women would like to know what was said in this room.

*They share a soft laugh.*

*Biff*: Remember that big Betsy something—what the hell was her name—over on Bushwick Avenue?

*Happy* (*combing his hair*): With the collie dog!

*Biff*: That's the one. I got you in there, remember?

*Happy*: Yeah, that was my first time—I think. Boy, there was a pig! (*They laugh, almost crudely.*) You taught me everything I know about women. Don't forget that.

*Biff*: I bet you forgot how bashful you used to be. Especially with girls.

*Happy*: Oh, I still am, Biff.

*Biff*: Oh, go on.

*Happy*: I just control it, that's all. I think I got less bashful and you got more so. What happened, Biff? Where's the old humor, the old confidence? (*He shakes Biff's knee. Biff gets up and moves restlessly about the room.*) What's the matter?

*Biff*: Why does Dad mock me all the time?

*Happy*: He's not mocking you, he—

*Biff*: Everything I say there's a twist of mockery on his face. I can't get near him.

*Happy*: He just wants you to make good, that's all. I wanted to talk to you about Dad for a long time, Biff. Something's—happening to him. He—talks to himself.

*Biff*: I noticed that this morning. But he always mumbled.

*Happy*: But not so noticeable. It got so embarrassing I sent him to Florida. And you know something? Most of the time he's talking to you.

*Biff*: What's he say about me?

*Happy*: I can't make it out.

*Biff*: What's he say about me?

*Happy*: I think the fact that you're not settled, that you're still kind of up in the air . . .

*Biff*: There's one or two other things depressing him, Happy.

*Happy*: What do you mean?

*Biff*: Never mind. Just don't lay it all on me.

*Happy*: But I think if you just got started—I mean—is there any future for you out there?

*Biff*: I tell ya, Hap, I don't know what the future is. I don't know—what I'm supposed to want.

*Happy*: What do you mean?

*Biff*: Well, I spent six or seven years after high school trying to work myself up. Shipping clerk, salesman, business of one kind or another. And it's a measly manner of existence. To get on that subway on the hot mornings in summer. To devote your whole life to keeping stock, or making phone calls, or selling or buying. To suffer fifty weeks of the year for the sake of a two-week vacation, when all you really desire is to be outdoors, with your shirt off. And always to have to get ahead of the next fella. And still—that's how you build a future.

*Happy:* Well, you really enjoy it on a farm? Are you content out there?

*Biff (with rising agitation):* Hap, I've had twenty or thirty different kinds of jobs since I left home before the war, and it always turns out the same. I just realized it lately. In Nebraska when I herded cattle, and the Dakotas, and Arizona, and now in Texas. It's why I came home now, I guess, because I realized it. This farm I work on, it's spring there now, see? And they've got about fifteen new colts. There's nothing more inspiring or—beautiful than the sight of a mare and a new colt. And it's cool there now, see? Texas is cool now, and it's spring. And whenever spring comes to where I am, I suddenly get the feeling, my God, I'm not gettin' anywhere! What the hell am I doing, playing around with horses, twenty-eight dollars a week! I'm thirty-four years old, I oughta be makin' my future. That's when I come running home. And now, I get here, and I don't know what to do with myself. (*After a pause.*) I've always made a point of not wasting my life, and everytime I come back here I know that all I've done is to waste my life.

*Happy:* You're a poet, you know that, Biff? You're a—you're an idealist!

*Biff:* No, I'm mixed up very bad. Maybe I oughta get married. Maybe I oughta get stuck into something. Maybe that's my trouble. I'm like a boy. I'm not married, I'm not in business, I just—I'm like a boy. Are you content, Hap? You're a success, aren't you? Are you content?

*Happy:* Hell, no!

*Biff:* Why? You're making money, aren't you?

*Happy (moving about with energy, expressiveness):* All I can do now is wait for the merchandise manager to die. And suppose I get to be merchandise manager? He's a good friend of mine, and he just built a terrific estate on Long Island. And he lived there about two months and sold it, and now he's building another one. He can't enjoy it once it's finished. And I know that's just what I would do. I don't know what the hell I'm workin' for. Sometimes I sit in my apartment—all alone. And I think of the rent I'm paying. And it's crazy. But then, it's what I always wanted. My own apartment, a car, and plenty of women. And still, goddammit, I'm lonely.

*Biff (with enthusiasm):* Listen, why don't you come out West with me?

*Happy:* You and I, heh?

*Biff:* Sure, maybe we could buy a ranch. Raise cattle, use our muscles. Men built like we are should be working out in the open.

*Happy (avidly):* The Loman Brothers, heh?

*Biff (with vast affection):* Sure, we'd be known all over the counties!

*Happy (enthralled):* That's what I dream about, Biff. Sometimes I want to just rip my clothes off in the middle of the store and outbox that goddam merchandise manager. I mean I can outbox, outrun, and outlift anybody in that store, and I have to take orders from those common, petty sons-of-bitches till I can't stand it any more.

*Biff:* I'm tellin' you, kid, if you were with me I'd be happy out there.

*Happy (enthused):* See, Biff, everybody around me is so false that I'm constantly lowering my ideals . . .

*Biff:* Baby, together we'd stand up for one another, we'd have someone to trust.

*Happy:* If I were around you—

*Biff:* Hap, the trouble is we weren't brought up to grub for money. I don't know how to do it.

*Happy:* Neither can I!

*Biff:* Then let's go!

*Happy:* The only thing is—what can you make out there?

*Biff:* But look at your friend. Builds an estate and then hasn't the peace of mind to live in it.

*Happy:* Yeah, but when he walks into the store the waves part in front of him. That's fifty-two thousand dollars a year coming through the revolving door, and I got more in my pinky finger than he's got in his head.

*Biff:* Yeah, but you just said—

*Happy:* I gotta show some of those pompous, self-important executives over there that Hap Loman can make the grade. I want to walk into the store the way he walks in. Then I'll go with you, Biff. We'll be together yet, I swear. But take those two we had tonight. Now weren't they gorgeous creatures?

*Biff:* Yeah, yeah, most gorgeous I've had in years.

*Happy:* I get that any time I want, Biff. Whenever I feel disgusted. The only trouble is, it gets like bowling or something. I just keep knockin' them over and it doesn't mean anything. You still run around a lot?

*Biff:* Naa. I'd like to find a girl—steady, somebody with substance.

*Happy:* That's what I long for.

*Biff:* Go on! You'd never come home.

*Happy:* I would! Somebody with character, with resistance! Like Mom, y'know? You're gonna call me a bastard when I tell you this. That girl Charlotte I was with tonight is engaged to be married in five weeks. (*He tries on his new hat.*)

*Biff:* No kiddin'!

*Happy:* Sure, the guy's in line for the vice-presidency of the store. I don't know what gets into me, maybe I just have an overdeveloped sense of competition or something, but I went and ruined her, and furthermore I can't get rid of her. And he's the third executive I've done that to. Isn't that a crummy characteristic? And to top it all, I go to their weddings! (*Indignantly, but laughing.*) Like I'm not supposed to take bribes. Manufacturers offer me a hundred-dollar bill now and then to throw an order their way. You know how honest I am, but it's like this girl, see. I hate myself for it. Because I don't want the girl, and, still, I take it and—I love it!

*Biff:* Let's go to sleep.

*Happy:* I guess we didn't settle anything, heh?

*Biff:* I just got one idea that I think I'm going to try.

*Happy:* What's that?

*Biff:* Remember Bill Oliver?

*Happy:* Sure, Oliver is very big now. You want to work for him again?

*Biff:* No, but when I quit he said something to me. He put his arm on my shoulder, and he said, "Biff, if you ever need anything, come to me."

*Happy:* I remember that. That sounds good.

*Biff:* I think I'll go to see him. If I could get ten thousand or even seven or eight thousand dollars I could buy a beautiful ranch.

*Happy:* I bet he'd back you. 'Cause he thought highly of you, Biff. I mean, they all do. You're well liked, Biff. That's why I say to come back here, and we both have the apartment. And I'm tellin' you, Biff, any babe you want . . .

*Biff:* No, with a ranch I could do the work I like and still be something. I just wonder though. I wonder if Oliver still thinks I stole that carton of basketballs.

*Happy:* Oh, he probably forgot that long ago. It's almost ten years. You're too sensitive. Anyway, he didn't really fire you.

*Biff:* Well, I think he was going to. I think that's why I quit. I was never sure whether he knew or not. I know he thought the world of me, though. I was the only one he'd let lock up the place.

*Willy (below):* You gonna wash the engine, Biff?

*Happy:* Shh!

*Biff looks at Happy, who is gazing down, listening. Willy is mumbling in the parlor.*

*Happy:* You hear that?

*They listen. Willy laughs warmly.*

*Biff (growing angry):* Doesn't he know Mom can hear that?

*Willy:* Don't get your sweater dirty, Biff!

*A look of pain crosses Biff's face.*

*Happy:* Isn't that terrible? Don't leave again, will you? You'll find a job here. You gotta stick around. I don't know what to do about him, it's getting embarrassing.

*Willy:* What a simonizing job!

*Biff:* Mom's hearing that!

*Willy:* No kiddin', Biff, you got a date? Wonderful!

*Happy:* Go on to sleep. But talk to him in the morning, will you?

*Biff (reluctantly getting into bed):* With her in the house. Brother!

*Happy (getting into bed):* I wish you'd have a good talk with him.

*The light on their room begins to fade.*

*Biff (to himself in bed):* That selfish, stupid . . .

*Happy:* Sh . . . Sleep, Biff.

*Their light is out. Well before they have finished speaking, Willy's form is dimly seen below in the darkened kitchen. He opens the refrigerator, searches in there, and takes out a bottle of milk. The apartment houses are fading out, and the entire house and surroundings become covered with leaves. Music insinuates itself as the leaves appear.*

Willy: Just wanna be careful with those girls, Biff, that's all. Don't make any promises. No promises of any kind. Because a girl, y'know, they always believe what you tell 'em, and you're very young, Biff, you're too young to be talking seriously to girls.

*Light rises on the kitchen. Willy, talking, shuts the refrigerator door and comes downstage to the kitchen table. He pours milk into a glass. He is totally immersed in himself, smiling faintly.*

Willy: Too young entirely, Biff. You want to watch your schooling first. Then when you're all set, there'll be plenty of girls for a boy like you. (*He smiles broadly at a kitchen chair.*) That so? The girls pay for you? (*He laughs.*) Boy, you must really be makin' a hit.

*Willy is gradually addressing—physically—a point offstage, speaking through the wall of the kitchen, and his voice has been rising in volume to that of a normal conversation.*

Willy: I been wondering why you polish the car so careful. Ha! Don't leave the hubcaps, boys. Get the chamois to the hubcaps. Happy, use newspaper on the windows, it's the easiest thing. Show him how to do it, Biff! You see, Happy? Pad it up, use it like a pad. That's it, that's it, good work. You're doin' all right, Hap. (*He pauses, then nods in approbation for a few seconds, then looks upward.*) Biff, first thing we gotta do when we get time is clip that big branch over the house. Afraid it's gonna fall in a storm and hit the roof. Tell you what. We get a rope and sling her around, and then we climb up there with a couple of saws and take her down. Soon as you finish the car, boys, I wanna see ya. I got a surprise for you, boys.

Biff (*offstage*): Whatta ya got, Dad?

Willy: No, you finish first. Never leave a job till you're finished—remember that. (*Looking toward the "big trees."*) Biff, up in Albany I saw a beautiful hammock. I think I'll buy it next trip, and we'll hang it right between those two elms. Wouldn't that be something? Just swingin' there under those branches. Boy, that would be . . .

*Young Biff and Young Happy appear from the direction Willy was addressing. Happy carries rags and a pail of water. Biff, wearing a sweater with a block "S," carries a football.*

Biff (*pointing in the direction of the car offstage*): How's that, Pop, professional?

Willy: Terrific. Terrific job, boys. Good work, Biff.

Happy: Where's the surprise, Pop?

Willy: In the back seat of the car.

Happy: Boy! (*He runs off.*)

Biff: What is it, Dad? Tell me, what'd you buy?

Willy (*laughing, cuffs him*): Never mind, something I want you to have.

*Biff (turns and starts off):* What is it, Hap?

*Happy (offstage):* It's a punching bag!

*Biff:* Oh, Pop!

*Willy:* It's got Gene Tunney's signature on it.

*Happy runs onstage with a punching bag.*

*Biff:* Gee, how'd you know we wanted a punching bag?

*Willy:* Well, it's the finest thing for the timing.

*Happy (lies down on his back and pedals with his feet):* I'm losing weight, you notice, Pop?

*Willy (to Happy):* Jumping rope is good too.

*Biff:* Did you see the new football I got?

*Willy (examining the ball):* Where'd you get a new ball?

*Biff:* The coach told me to practice my passing.

*Willy:* That so? And he gave you the ball, heh?

*Biff:* Well, I borrowed it from the locker room. (*He laughs confidentially.*)

*Willy (laughing with him at the theft):* I want you to return that.

*Happy:* I told you he wouldn't like it!

*Biff (angrily):* Well, I'm bringing it back!

*Willy (stopping the incipient argument, to Happy):* Sure, he's gotta practice with a regulation ball, doesn't he? (*To Biff.*) Coach'll probably congratulate you on your initiative.

*Biff:* Oh, he keeps congratulating my initiative all the time, Pop.

*Willy:* That's because he likes you. If somebody else took that ball there'd be an uproar. So what's the report, boys, what's the report?

*Biff:* Where'd you go this time, Dad? Gee we were lonesome for you.

*Willy (pleased, puts an arm around each boy and they come down to the apron):* Lonesome, heh?

*Biff:* Missed you every minute.

*Willy:* Don't say? Tell you a secret, boys. Don't breathe it to a soul. Someday I'll have my own business, and I'll never have to leave home any more.

*Happy:* Like Uncle Charley, heh?

*Willy:* Bigger than Uncle Charley! Because Charley is not—liked. He's liked, but he's not—well liked.

*Biff:* Where'd you go this time, Dad?

*Willy:* Well, I got on the road, and I went north to Providence. Met the Mayor.

*Biff:* The Mayor of Providence!

*Willy:* He was sitting in the hotel lobby.

*Biff:* What'd he say?

*Willy:* He said, "Morning!" And I said, "You've got a fine city here, Mayor." And then he had coffee with me. And then I went to Waterbury. Waterbury is a fine city. Big clock city, the famous Waterbury clock. Sold a nice bill there. And then Boston—Boston is the cradle of the Revolution. A fine city. And a couple of other towns in Mass., and on to Portland and Bangor and straight home!

*Biff*: Gee, I'd love to go with you sometime, Dad.

*Willy*: Soon as summer comes.

*Happy*: Promise?

*Willy*: You and Hap and I, and I'll show you all the towns. America is full of beautiful towns and fine, upstanding people. And they know me, boys, they know me up and down New England. The finest people. And when I bring you fellas up, there'll be open sesame for all of us, 'cause one thing, boys: I have friends. I can park my car in any street in New England, and the cops protect it like their own. This summer, heh?

*Biff and Happy (together)*: Yeah! You bet!

*Willy*: We'll take our bathing suits.

*Happy*: We'll carry your bags, Pop!

*Willy*: Oh, won't that be something! Me comin' into the Boston stores with you boys carryin' my bags. What a sensation!

*Biff is prancing around, practicing passing the ball.*

*Willy*: You nervous, Biff, about the game?

*Biff*: Not if you're gonna be there.

*Willy*: What do they say about you in school, now that they made you captain?

*Happy*: There's a crowd of girls behind him everytime the classes change.

*Biff (taking Willy's hand)*: This Saturday, Pop, this Saturday—just for you, I'm going to break through for a touchdown.

*Happy*: You're supposed to pass.

*Biff*: I'm takin' one play for Pop. You watch me, Pop, and when I take off my helmet, that means I'm breakin' out. Then you watch me crash through that line!

*Willy (kisses Biff)*: Oh, wait'll I tell this in Boston!

*Bernard enters in knickers. He is younger than Biff, earnest and loyal, a worried boy.*

*Bernard*: Biff, where are you? You're supposed to study with me today.

*Willy*: Hey, looka Bernard. What're you lookin' so anemic about, Bernard?

*Bernard*: He's gotta study, Uncle Willy. He's got Regents next week.

*Happy (tauntingly, spinning Bernard around)*: Let's box, Bernard!

*Bernard*: Biff! (*He gets away from Happy.*) Listen, Biff, I heard Mr. Birnbaum say that if you don't start studyin' math he's gonna flunk you, and you won't graduate. I heard him!

*Willy*: You better study with him, Biff. Go ahead now.

*Bernard*: I heard him!

*Biff*: Oh, Pop, you didn't see my sneakers! (*He holds up a foot for Willy to look at.*)

*Willy*: Hey, that's a beautiful job of printing!

*Bernard (wiping his glasses)*: Just because he printed University of Virginia on his sneakers doesn't mean they've got to graduate him, Uncle Willy!

*Willy (angrily)*: What're you talking about? With scholarships to three universities they're gonna flunk him?

*Bernard*: But I heard Mr. Birnbaum say—

*Willy*: Don't be a pest, Bernard! (*To his boys.*) What an anemic!

*Bernard:* Okay, I'm waiting for you in my house, Biff.

*Bernard goes off. The Lomans laugh.*

*Willy:* Bernard is not well liked, is he?

*Biff:* He's liked, but he's not well liked.

*Happy:* That's right, Pop.

*Willy:* That's just what I mean. Bernard can get the best marks in school, y'understand, but when he gets out in the business world, y'understand, you are going to be five times ahead of him. That's why I thank Almighty God you're both built like Adonises. Because the man who makes an appearance in the business world, the man who creates personal interest, is the man who gets ahead. Be liked and you will never want. You take me, for instance. I never have to wait in line to see a buyer. "Willy Loman is here!" That's all they have to know, and I go right through.

*Biff:* Did you knock them dead, Pop?

*Willy:* Knocked 'em cold in Providence, slaughtered 'em in Boston.

*Happy (on his back, pedaling again):* I'm losing weight, you notice, Pop?

*Linda enters, as of old, a ribbon in her hair, carrying a basket of washing.*

*Linda (with youthful energy):* Hello, dear!

*Willy:* Sweetheart!

*Linda:* How'd the Chevvy run?

*Willy:* Chevrolet, Linda, is the greatest car every built. (*To the boys.*) Since when do you let your mother carry wash up the stairs?

*Biff:* Grab hold there, boy!

*Happy:* Where to, Mom?

*Linda:* Hang them up on the line. And you better go down to your friends, Biff. The cellar is full of boys. They don't know what to do with themselves.

*Biff:* Ah, when Pop comes home they can wait!

*Willy (laughs appreciatively):* You better go down and tell them what to do, Biff.

*Biff:* I think I'll have them sweep out the furnace room.

*Willy:* Good work, Biff.

*Biff (goes through wall-line of kitchen to doorway at back and calls down):* Fellas! Everybody sweep out the furnace room! I'll be right down!

*Voices:* All right! Okay, Biff.

*Biff:* George and Sam and Frank, come out back! We're hangin' up the wash! Come on, Hap, on the double! (*He and Happy carry out the basket.*)

*Linda:* The way they obey him!

*Willy:* Well, that's training, the training. I'm tellin' you, I was sellin' thousands and thousands, but I had to come home.

*Linda:* Oh, the whole block'll be at that game. Did you sell anything?

*Willy:* I did five hundred gross in Providence and seven hundred gross in Boston.

*Linda:* No! Wait a minute, I've got a pencil. (*She pulls pencil and paper out of her apron pocket.*) That makes your commission . . . Two hundred—my God! Two hundred and twelve dollars!

*Willy:* Well, I didn't figure it yet, but . . .

*Linda*: How much did you do?

*Willy*: Well, I—I did—about a hundred and eighty gross in Providence. Well, no—it came to—roughly two hundred gross on the whole trip.

*Linda (without hesitation)*: Two hundred gross. That's . . . (*She figures.*)

*Willy*: The trouble was that three of the stores were half closed for inventory in Boston. Otherwise I woulda broke records.

*Linda*: Well, it makes seventy dollars and some pennies. That's very good.

*Willy*: What do we owe?

*Linda*: Well, on the first there's sixteen dollars on the refrigerator—

*Willy*: Why sixteen?

*Linda*: Well, the fan belt broke, so it was a dollar eighty.

*Willy*: But it's brand new.

*Linda*: Well, the man said that's the way it is. Till they work themselves in, y'know.

*They move through the wall-line into the kitchen.*

*Willy*: I hope we didn't get stuck on that machine.

*Linda*: They got the biggest ads of any of them.

*Willy*: I know, it's a fine machine. What else?

*Linda*: Well, there's nine-sixty for the washing machine. And for the vacuum cleaner there's three and a half due on the fifteenth. Then the roof, you got twenty-one dollars remaining.

*Willy*: It don't leak, does it?

*Linda*: No, they did a wonderful job. Then you owe Frank for the carburetor.

*Willy*: I'm not going to pay that man! That goddam Chevrolet, they ought to prohibit the manufacture of that car!

*Linda*: Well, you owe him three and a half. And odds and ends, comes to around a hundred and twenty dollars by the fifteenth.

*Willy*: A hundred and twenty dollars! My God, if business don't pick up I don't know what I'm gonna do!

*Linda*: Well, next week you'll do better.

*Willy*: Oh, I'll knock 'em dead next week. I'll go to Hartford. I'm very well liked in Hartford. You know, the trouble is, Linda, people don't seem to take to me.

*They move on the forestage.*

*Linda*: Oh, don't be foolish.

*Willy*: I know it when I walk in. They seem to laugh at me.

*Linda*: Why? Why would they laugh at you? Don't talk that way, Willy.

*Willy moves to the edge of the stage. Linda goes into the kitchen and starts to darn stockings.*

*Willy*: I don't know the reason for it, but they just pass me by. I'm not noticed.

*Linda*: But you're doing wonderful, dear. You're making seventy to a hundred dollars a week.

*Willy:* But I gotta be at it ten, twelve hours a day. Other men—I don't know—
they do it easier. I don't know why—I can't stop myself—I talk too much. A
man oughta come in with a few words. One thing about Charley. He's a man
of few words, and they respect him.

*Linda:* You don't talk too much, you're just lively.

*Willy (smiling):* Well, I figure, what the hell, life is short, a couple of jokes. (*To
himself.*) I joke too much! (*The smile goes.*)

*Linda:* Why? You're—

*Willy:* I'm fat. I'm very—foolish to look at, Linda. I didn't tell you, but Christmas
time I happened to be calling on F. H. Stewarts, and a salesman I know, as I
was going in to see the buyer I heard him say something about—walrus. And
I—I cracked him right across the face. I won't take that. I simply will not
take that. But they do laugh at me. I know that.

*Linda:* Darling . . .

*Willy:* I gotta overcome it. I know I gotta overcome it. I'm not dressing to advantage, maybe.

*Linda:* Willy, darling, you're the handsomest man in the world—

*Willy:* Oh, no, Linda.

*Linda:* To me you are. (*Slight pause.*) The handsomest.

*From the darkness is heard the laughter of a woman. Willy doesn't turn to it, but it
continues through Linda's lines.*

*Linda:* And the boys, Willy. Few men are idolized by their children the way you
are.

*Music is heard as behind a scrim, to the left of the house, The Woman, dimly seen,
is dressing.*

*Willy (with great feeling):* You're the best there is, Linda, you're a pal, you know
that? On the road—on the road I want to grab you sometimes and just kiss
the life outa you.

*The laughter is loud now, and he moves into a brightening area at the left, where
The Woman has come from behind the scrim and is standing, putting on her hat,
looking into a "mirror" and laughing.*

*Willy:* 'Cause I get so lonely—especially when business is bad and there's nobody
to talk to. I get the feeling that I'll never sell anything again, that I won't
make a living for you, or a business, a business for the boys. (*He talks through
The Woman's subsiding laughter; The Woman primps at the "mirror."*) There's
so much I want to make for—

*The Woman:* Me? You didn't make me, Willy. I picked you.

*Willy (pleased):* You picked me?

*The Woman (who is quite proper-looking, Willy's age):* I did. I've been sitting at
that desk watching all the salesmen go by, day in, day out. But you've got
such a sense of humor, and we do have such a good time together, don't
we?

Willy: Sure, sure. (*He takes her in his arms.*) Why do you have to go now?

The Woman: It's two o'clock . . .

Willy: No, come on in! (*He pulls her.*)

The Woman: . . . my sisters'll be scandalized. When'll you be back?

Willy: Oh, two weeks about. Will you come up again?

The Woman: Sure thing. You do make me laugh. It's good for me. (*She squeezes his arm, kisses him.*) And I think you're a wonderful man.

Willy: You picked me, heh?

The Woman: Sure. Because you're so sweet. And such a kidder.

Willy: Well, I'll see you next time I'm in Boston.

The Woman: I'll put you right through to the buyers.

Willy (*slapping her bottom*): Right. Well, bottoms up!

The Woman (*slaps him gently and laughs*): You just kill me, Willy. (*He suddenly grabs her and kisses her roughly.*) You kill me. And thanks for the stockings. I love a lot of stockings. Well, good night.

Willy: Good night. And keep your pores open!

The Woman: Oh, Willy!

> The Woman bursts out laughing, and Linda's laughter blends in. The Woman disappears into the dark. Now the area at the kitchen table brightens. Linda is sitting where she was at the kitchen table, but now is mending a pair of silk stockings.

Linda: You are, Willy. The handsomest man. You've got no reason to feel that—

Willy (*coming out of The Woman's dimming area and going over to Linda*): I'll make it all up to you, Linda, I'll—

Linda: There's nothing to make up, dear. You're doing fine, better than—

Willy (*noticing her mending*): What's that?

Linda: Just mending my stockings. They're so expensive—

Willy (*angrily, taking them from her*): I won't have you mending stockings in this house! Now throw them out!

> Linda puts the stockings in her pocket.

Bernard (*entering on the run*): Where is he? If he doesn't study!

Willy (*moving to the forestage, with great agitation*): You'll give him the answers!

Bernard: I do, but I can't on a Regents! That's a state exam! They're liable to arrest me!

Willy: Where is he? I'll whip him, I'll whip him!

Linda: And he'd better give back that football, Willy, it's not nice.

Willy: Biff! Where is he? Why is he taking everything?

Linda: He's too rough with the girls, Willy. All the mothers are afraid of him!

Willy: I'll whip him!

Bernard: He's driving the car without a license!

> The Woman's laugh is heard.

Willy: Shut up!

Linda: All the mothers—

*Willy:* Shut up!

*Bernard (backing quietly away and out):* Mr. Birnbaum says he's stuck up.

*Willy:* Get outa here!

*Bernard:* If he doesn't buckle down he'll flunk math! *(He goes off.)*

*Linda:* He's right, Willy, you've gotta—

*Willy (exploding at her):* There's nothing the matter with him! You want him to be a worm like Bernard? He's got spirit, personality . . .

*As he speaks, Linda, almost in tears, exits into the living room. Willy is alone in the kitchen, wilting and staring. The leaves are gone. It is night again, and the apartment houses look down from behind.*

*Willy:* Loaded with it. Loaded! What is he stealing? He's giving it back, isn't he? Why is he stealing? What did I tell him? I never in my life told him anything but decent things.

*Happy in pajamas has come down the stairs; Willy suddenly becomes aware of Happy's presence.*

*Happy:* Let's go now, come on.

*Willy (sitting down at the kitchen table):* Huh! Why did she have to wax the floors herself? Everytime she waxes the floors she keels over. She knows that!

*Happy:* Shh! Take it easy. What brought you back tonight?

*Willy:* I got an awful scare. Nearly hit a kid in Yonkers. God! Why didn't I go to Alaska with my brother Ben that time! Ben! That man was a genius, that man was success incarnate! What a mistake! He begged me to go.

*Happy:* Well, there's no use in—

*Willy:* You guys! There was a man started with the clothes on his back and ended up with diamond mines!

*Happy:* Boy, someday I'd like to know how he did it.

*Willy:* What's the mystery? The man knew what he wanted and went out and got it! Walked into a jungle, and comes out, the age of twenty-one, and he's rich! The world is an oyster, but you don't crack it open on a mattress!

*Happy:* Pop, I told you I'm gonna retire you for life.

*Willy:* You'll retire me for life on seventy goddam dollars a week? And your women and your car and your apartment, and you'll retire me for life! Christ's sake, I couldn't get past Yonkers today! Where are you guys, where are you? The woods are burning! I can't drive a car!

*Charley has appeared in the doorway. He is a large man, slow of speech, laconic, immovable. In all he says, despite what he says, there is pity, and, now, trepidation. He has a robe over his pajamas, slippers on his feet. He enters the kitchen.*

*Charley:* Everything all right?

*Happy:* Yeah, Charley, everything's . . .

*Willy:* What's the matter?

*Charley:* I heard some noise. I thought something happened. Can't we do something about the walls? You sneeze in here, and in my house hats blow off.

*Happy*: Let's go to bed, Dad. Come on.

> *Charley signals to Happy to go.*

*Willy*: You go ahead, I'm not tired at the moment.
*Happy* (*to Willy*): Take it easy, huh? (*He exits.*)
*Willy*: What're you doin' up?
*Charley* (*sitting down at the kitchen table opposite Willy*): Couldn't sleep good. I had a heartburn.
*Willy*: Well, you don't know how to eat.
*Charley*: I eat with my mouth.
*Willy*: No, you're ignorant. You gotta know about vitamins and things like that.
*Charley*: Come on, let's shoot. Tire you out a little.
*Willy* (*hesitantly*): All right. You got cards?
*Charley* (*taking a deck from his pocket*): Yeah, I got them. Someplace. What is it with those vitamins?
*Willy* (*dealing*): They build up your bones. Chemistry.
*Charley*: Yeah, but there's no bones in a heartburn.
*Willy*: What are you talkin' about? Do you know the first thing about it?
*Charley*: Don't get insulted.
*Willy*: Don't talk about something you don't know anything about.

> *They are playing. Pause.*

*Charley*: What're you doin' home?
*Willy*: A little trouble with the car.
*Charley*: Oh. (*Pause.*) I'd like to take a trip to California.
*Willy*: Don't say.
*Charley*: You want a job?
*Willy*: I got a job, I told you that. (*After a slight pause.*) What the hell are you offering me a job for?
*Charley*: Don't get insulted.
*Willy*: Don't insult me.
*Charley*: I don't see no sense in it. You don't have to go on this way.
*Willy*: I got a good job. (*Slight pause.*) What do you keep comin' in here for?
*Charley*: You want me to go?
*Willy* (*after a pause, withering*): I can't understand it. He's going back to Texas again. What the hell is that?
*Charley*: Let him go.
*Willy*: I got nothin' to give him, Charley, I'm clean, I'm clean.
*Charley*: He won't starve. None a them starve. Forget about him.
*Willy*: Then what have I got to remember?
*Charley*: You take it too hard. To hell with it. When a deposit bottle is broken you don't get your nickel back.
*Willy*: That's easy enough for you to say.
*Charley*: That ain't easy for me to say.
*Willy*: Did you see the ceiling I put up in the living room?

*Charley:* Yeah, that's a piece of work. To put up a ceiling is a mystery to me. How do you do it?

*Willy:* What's the difference?

*Charley:* Well, talk about it.

*Willy:* You gonna put up a ceiling?

*Charley:* How could I put up a ceiling?

*Willy:* Then what the hell are you bothering me for?

*Charley:* You're insulted again.

*Willy:* A man who can't handle tools is not a man. You're disgusting.

*Charley:* Don't call me disgusting, Willy.

> *Uncle Ben, carrying a valise and an umbrella, enters the forestage from around the right corner of the house. He is a stolid man, in his sixties, with a mustache and an authoritative air. He is utterly certain of his destiny, and there is an aura of far places about him. He enters exactly as Willy speaks.*

*Willy:* I'm getting awfully tired, Ben.

> *Ben's music is heard. Ben looks around at everything.*

*Charley:* Good, keep playing; you'll sleep better. Did you call me Ben?

> *Ben looks at his watch.*

*Willy:* That's funny. For a second there you reminded me of my brother Ben.

*Ben:* I have only a few minutes. (*He strolls, inspecting the place. Willy and Charley continue playing.*)

*Charley:* You never heard from him again, heh? Since that time?

*Willy:* Didn't Linda tell you? Couple of weeks ago we got a letter from his wife in Africa. He died.

*Charley:* That so.

*Ben* (*chuckling*): So this is Brooklyn, eh?

*Charley:* Maybe you're in for some of his money.

*Willy:* Naa, he had seven sons. There's just one opportunity I had with that man . . .

*Ben:* I must make a train, William. There are several properties I'm looking at in Alaska.

*Willy:* Sure, sure! If I'd gone with him to Alaska that time, everything would've been totally different.

*Charley:* Go on, you'd froze to death up there.

*Willy:* What're you talking about?

*Ben:* Opportunity is tremendous in Alaska, William. Surprised you're not up there.

*Willy:* Sure, tremendous.

*Charley:* Heh?

*Willy:* There was the only man I ever met who knew the answers.

*Charley:* Who?

*Ben:* How are you all?

*Willy* (*taking a pot, smiling*): Fine, fine.

*Charley:* Pretty sharp tonight.

*Ben:* Is Mother living with you?

*Willy:* No, she died a long time ago.

*Charley:* Who?

*Ben:* That's too bad. Fine specimen of a lady, Mother.

*Willy* (*to Charley*): Heh?

*Ben:* I'd hoped to see the old girl.

*Charley:* Who died?

*Ben:* Heard anything from Father, have you?

*Willy* (*unnerved*): What do you mean, who died?

*Charley* (*taking a pot*): What're you talkin' about?

*Ben* (*looking at his watch*): William, it's half-past eight!

*Willy* (*as though to dispel his confusion he angrily stops Charley's hand*): That's my build!

*Charley:* I put the ace—

*Willy:* If you don't know how to play the game I'm not gonna throw my money away on you!

*Charley* (*rising*): It was my ace, for God's sake!

*Willy:* I'm through, I'm through!

*Ben:* When did Mother die?

*Willy:* Long ago. Since the beginning you never knew how to play cards.

*Charley* (*picks up the cards and goes to the door*): All right! Next time I'll bring a deck with five aces.

*Willy:* I don't play that kind of game!

*Charley* (*turning to him*): You ought to be ashamed of yourself!

*Willy:* Yeah?

*Charley:* Yeah! (*He goes out.*)

*Willy* (*slamming the door after him*): Ignoramus!

*Ben* (*as Willy comes toward him through the wall-line of the kitchen*): So you're William.

*Willy* (*shaking Ben's hand*): Ben! I've been waiting for you so long! What's the answer? How did you do it?

*Ben:* Oh, there's a story in that.

> *Linda enters the forestage, as of old, carrying the wash basket.*

*Linda:* Is this Ben?

*Ben* (*gallantly*): How do you do, my dear.

*Linda:* Where've you been all these years? Willy's always wondered why you—

*Willy* (*pulling Ben away from her impatiently*): Where is Dad? Didn't you follow him? How did you get started?

*Ben:* Well, I don't know how much you remember.

*Willy:* Well, I was just a baby, of course, only three or four years old—

*Ben:* Three years and eleven months.

*Willy:* What a memory, Ben!

*Ben:* I have many enterprises, William, and I have never kept books.

*Willy:* I remember I was sitting under the wagon in—was it Nebraska?

*Ben:* It was South Dakota, and I gave you a bunch of wild flowers.

*Willy:* I remember you walking away down some open road.

*Ben (laughing):* I was going to find Father in Alaska.

*Willy:* Where is he?

*Ben:* At that age I had a very faulty view of geography, William. I discovered after a few days that I was heading due south, so instead of Alaska, I ended up in Africa.

*Linda:* Africa!

*Willy:* The Gold Coast!

*Ben:* Principally, diamond mines.

*Linda:* Diamond mines!

*Ben:* Yes, my dear. But I've only a few minutes—

*Willy:* No! Boys! Boys! (*Young Biff and Happy appear.*) Listen to this. This is your Uncle Ben, a great man! Tell my boys, Ben!

*Ben:* Why, boys, when I was seventeen I walked into the jungle, and when I was twenty-one I walked out. (*He laughs.*) And by God I was rich.

*Willy (to the boys):* You see what I been talking about? The greatest things can happen!

*Ben (glancing at his watch):* I have an appointment in Ketchikan Tuesday week.

*Willy:* No, Ben! Please tell about Dad. I want my boys to hear. I want them to know the kind of stock they sprang from. All I remember is a man with a big beard, and I was in Mamma's lap, sitting around a fire, and some kind of high music.

*Ben:* His flute. He played the flute.

*Willy:* Sure, the flute, that's right!

*New music is heard, a high, rollicking tune.*

*Ben:* Father was a very great and a very wild-hearted man. We would start in Boston, and he'd toss the whole family into the wagon, and then he'd drive the team right across the country; through Ohio, and Indiana, Michigan, Illinois, and all the Western states. And we'd stop in the towns and sell the flutes that he'd made on the way. Great inventor, Father. With one gadget he made more in a week than a man like you could make in a lifetime.

*Willy:* That's just the way I'm bringing them up, Ben—rugged, well liked, all-around.

*Ben:* Yeah? (*To Biff.*) Hit that, boy—hard as you can. (*He pounds his stomach.*)

*Biff:* Oh, no, sir!

*Ben (taking boxing stance):* Come on, get to me! (*He laughs.*)

*Willy:* Go to it, Biff! Go ahead, show him!

*Biff:* Okay! (*He cocks his fist and starts in.*)

*Linda (to Willy):* Why must he fight, dear?

*Ben (sparring with Biff):* Good boy! Good boy!

*Willy:* How's that, Ben, heh?

*Happy:* Give him the left, Biff!

*Linda:* Why are you fighting?

*Ben:* Good boy! (*Suddenly comes in, trips Biff, and stands over him, the point of his umbrella poised over Biff's eye.*)

*Linda:* Look out, Biff!

*Biff:* Gee!

*Ben* (*patting Biff's knee*): Never fight fair with a stranger, boy. You'll never get out of the jungle that way. (*Taking Linda's hand and bowing.*) It was an honor and a pleasure to meet you, Linda.

*Linda* (*withdrawing her hand coldly, frightened*): Have a nice—trip.

*Ben* (*to Willy*): And good luck with your—what do you do?

*Willy:* Selling.

*Ben:* Yes. Well . . . (*He raises his hand in farewell to all.*)

*Willy:* No, Ben, I don't want you to think . . . (*He takes Ben's arm to show him.*) It's Brooklyn, I know, but we hunt too.

*Ben:* Really, now.

*Willy:* Oh, sure, there's snakes and rabbits and—that's why I moved out here. Why, Biff can fell any one of these trees in no time! Boys! Go right over to where they're building the apartment house and get some sand. We're gonna rebuild the entire front stoop right now! Watch this, Ben!

*Biff:* Yes, sir! On the double, Hap!

*Happy* (*as he and Biff run off*): I lost weight, Pop, you notice?

Charley enters in knickers, even before the boys are gone.

*Charley:* Listen, if they steal any more from that building the watchman'll put the cops on them!

*Linda* (*to Willy*): Don't let Biff . . .

Ben laughs lustily.

*Willy:* You shoulda seen the lumber they brought home last week. At least a dozen six-by-tens worth all kinds of money.

*Charley:* Listen, if that watchman—

*Willy:* I gave them hell, understand. But I got a couple of fearless characters there.

*Charley:* Willy, the jails are full of fearless characters.

*Ben* (*clapping Willy on the back, with a laugh at Charley*): And the stock exchange, friend!

*Willy* (*joining in Ben's laughter*): Where are the rest of your pants?

*Charley:* My wife bought them.

*Willy:* Now all you need is a golf club and you can go upstairs and go to sleep. (*To Ben.*) Great athlete! Between him and his son Bernard they can't hammer a nail!

*Bernard* (*rushing in*): The watchman's chasing Biff!

*Willy* (*angrily*): Shut up! He's not stealing anything!

*Linda* (*alarmed, hurrying off left*): Where is he? Biff, dear! (*She exits.*)

*Willy* (*moving toward the left, away from Ben*): There's nothing wrong. What's the matter with you?

*Ben:* Nervy boy. Good!

*Willy* (*laughing*): Oh, nerves of iron, that Biff!

*Charley:* Don't know what it is. My New England man comes back and he's bleedin', they murdered him up there.

*Willy:* It's contacts, Charley, I got important contacts!

*Charley* (*sarcastically*): Glad to hear it, Willy. Come in later, we'll shoot a little casino. I'll take some of your Portland money. (*He laughs at Willy and exits.*)

*Willy* (*turning to Ben*): Business is bad, it's murderous. But not for me, of course.

*Ben:* I'll stop by on my way back to Africa.

*Willy* (*longingly*): Can't you stay a few days? You're just what I need, Ben, because I— I have a fine position, but I—well, Dad left when I was such a baby and I never had a chance to talk to him and I still feel—kind of temporary about myself.

*Ben:* I'll be late for my train.

*They are at opposite ends of the stage.*

*Willy:* Ben, my boys—can't we talk? They'd go into the jaws of hell for me, see, but I—

*Ben:* William, you're being first-rate with your boys. Outstanding, manly chaps!

*Willy* (*hanging on to his words*): Oh, Ben, that's good to hear! Because sometimes I'm afraid that I'm not teaching them the right kind of—Ben, how should I teach them?

*Ben* (*giving great weight to each word, and with a certain vicious audacity*): William, when I walked into the jungle, I was seventeen. When I walked out I was twenty-one. And, by God, I was rich! (*He goes off into darkness around the right corner of the house.*)

*Willy:* . . . was rich! That's just the spirit I want to imbue them with! To walk into a jungle! I was right! I was right! I was right!

*Ben is gone, but Willy is still speaking to him as Linda, in nightgown and robe, enters the kitchen, glances around for Willy, then goes to the door of the house, looks out and sees him. Comes down to his left. He looks at her.*

*Linda:* Willy, dear? Willy?

*Willy:* I was right!

*Linda:* Did you have some cheese? (*He can't answer.*) It's very late, darling. Come to bed, heh?

*Willy* (*looking straight up*): Gotta break your neck to see a star in this yard.

*Linda:* You coming in?

*Willy:* What ever happened to that diamond watch fob? Remember? When Ben came from Africa that time? Didn't he give me a watch fob with a diamond in it?

*Linda:* You pawned it, dear. Twelve, thirteen years ago. For Biff's radio correspondence course.

*Willy:* Gee, that was a beautiful thing. I'll take a walk.

*Linda:* But you're in your slippers.

*Willy* (*starting to go around the house at the left*): I was right! I was! (*Half to Linda, as he goes, shaking his head.*) What a man! There was a man worth talking to. I was right!

*Linda* (*calling after Willy*): But in your slippers, Willy!

> *Willy is almost gone when Biff, in his pajamas, comes down the stairs and enters the kitchen.*

*Biff*: What is he doing out there?

*Linda*: Sh!

*Biff*: God Almighty, Mom, how long has he been doing this?

*Linda*: Don't, he'll hear you.

*Biff*: What the hell is the matter with him?

*Linda*: It'll pass by morning.

*Biff*: Shouldn't we do anything?

*Linda*: Oh, my dear, you should do a lot of things, but there's nothing to do, so go to sleep.

> *Happy comes down the stairs and sits on the steps.*

*Happy*: I never heard him so loud, Mom.

*Linda*: Well, come around more often; you'll hear him. (*She sits down at the table and mends the lining of Willy's jacket.*)

*Biff*: Why didn't you ever write me about this, Mom?

*Linda*: How would I write to you? For over three months you had no address.

*Biff*: I was on the move. But you know I thought of you all the time. You know that, don't you, pal?

*Linda*: I know, dear, I know. But he likes to have a letter. Just to know that there's still a possibility for better things.

*Biff*: He's not like this all the time, is he?

*Linda*: It's when you come home he's always the worst.

*Biff*: When I come home?

*Linda*: When you write you're coming, he's all smiles, and talks about the future, and—he's just wonderful. And then the closer you seem to come, the more shaky he gets, and then, by the time you get here, he's arguing, and he seems angry at you. I think it's just that maybe he can't bring himself to—to open up to you. Why are you so hateful to each other? Why is that?

*Biff* (*evasively*): I'm not hateful, Mom.

*Linda*: But you no sooner come in the door than you're fighting!

*Biff*: I don't know why. I mean to change. I'm tryin', Mom, you understand?

*Linda*: Are you home to stay now?

*Biff*: I don't know. I want to look around, see what's doin'.

*Linda*: Biff, you can't look around all your life, can you?

*Biff*: I just can't take hold, Mom. I can't take hold of some kind of a life.

*Linda*: Biff, a man is not a bird, to come and go with the springtime.

*Biff*: Your hair . . . (*He touches her hair.*) Your hair got so gray.

*Linda*: Oh, it's been gray since you were in high school. I just stopped dyeing it, that's all.

*Biff*: Dye it again, will ya? I don't want my pal looking old. (*He smiles.*)

*Linda:* You're such a boy! You think you can go away for a year and . . . You've got to get it into your head now that one day you'll knock on this door and there'll be strange people here—

*Biff:* What are you talking about? You're not even sixty, Mom.

*Linda:* But what about your father?

*Biff* (*lamely*): Well, I meant him too.

*Happy:* He admires Pop.

*Linda:* Biff, dear, if you don't have any feeling for him, then you can't have any feeling for me.

*Biff:* Sure I can, Mom.

*Linda:* No. You can't just come to see me, because I love him. (*With a threat, but only a threat, of tears.*) He's the dearest man in the world to me, and I won't have anyone making him feel unwanted and low and blue. You've got to make up your mind now, darling, there's no leeway any more. Either he's your father and you pay him that respect, or else you're not to come here. I know he's not easy to get along with—nobody knows that better than me—but . . .

*Willy* (*from the left, with a laugh*): Hey, hey, Biffo!

*Biff* (*starting to go out after Willy*): What the hell is the matter with him? (*Happy stops him.*)

*Linda:* Don't—don't go near him!

*Biff:* Stop making excuses for him! He always, always wiped the floor with you. Never had an ounce of respect for you.

*Happy:* He's always had respect for—

*Biff:* What the hell do you know about it?

*Happy* (*surlily*): Just don't call him crazy!

*Biff:* He's got no character—Charley wouldn't do this. Not in his own house—spewing out that vomit from his mind.

*Happy:* Charley never had to cope with what he's got to.

*Biff:* People are worse off than Willy Loman. Believe me, I've seen them!

*Linda:* Then make Charley your father, Biff. You can't do that, can you? I don't say he's a great man. Willy Loman never made a lot of money. His name was never in the paper. He's not the finest character that ever lived. But he's a human being, and a terrible thing is happening to him. So attention must be paid. He's not to be allowed to fall into his grave like an old dog. Attention, attention must be finally paid to such a person. You called him crazy—

*Biff:* I didn't mean—

*Linda:* No, a lot of people think he's lost his—balance. But you don't have to be very smart to know what his trouble is. The man is exhausted.

*Happy:* Sure!

*Linda:* A small man can be just as exhausted as a great man. He works for a company thirty-six years this March, opens up unheard-of territories to their trademark, and now in his old age they take his salary away.

*Happy* (*indignantly*): I didn't know that, Mom!

*Linda:* You never asked, my dear! Now that you get your spending money someplace else you don't trouble your mind with him.

*Happy:* But I gave you money last—

*Linda:* Christmas time, fifty dollars! To fix the hot water it cost ninety-seven fifty!
For five weeks he's been on straight commission, like a beginner, an unknown!

*Biff:* Those ungrateful bastards!

*Linda:* Are they any worse than his sons? When he brought them business, when
he was young, they were glad to see him. But now his old friends, the old
buyers that loved him so and always found some order to hand him in a
pinch—they're all dead, retired. He used to be able to make six, seven calls a
day in Boston. Now he takes his valises out of the car and puts them back
and takes them out again and he's exhausted. Instead of walking he talks
now. He drives seven hundred miles, and when he gets there no one knows
him any more, no one welcomes him. And what goes through a man's mind,
driving seven hundred miles home without having earned a cent? Why
shouldn't he talk to himself? Why? When he has to go to Charley and borrow fifty dollars a week and pretend to me that it's his pay? How long can
that go on? How long? You see what I'm sitting here and waiting for? And
you tell me he has no character? The man who never worked a day but for
your benefit? When does he get the medal for that? Is this his reward—to
turn around at the age of sixty-three and find his sons, who he loved better
than his life, one a philandering bum—

*Happy:* Mom!

*Linda:* That's all you are, my baby! (*To Biff.*) And you! What happened to the
love you had for him? You were such pals! How you used to talk to him on
the phone every night! How lonely he was till he could come home to you!

*Biff:* All right, Mom. I'll live here in my room, and I'll get a job. I'll keep away
from him, that's all.

*Linda:* No, Biff. You can't stay here and fight all the time.

*Biff:* He threw me out of this house, remember that.

*Linda:* Why did he do that? I never knew why.

*Biff:* Because I know he's a fake and he doesn't like anybody around who knows!

*Linda:* Why a fake? In what way? What do you mean?

*Biff:* Just don't lay it all at my feet. It's between me and him—that's all I have to
say. I'll chip in from now on. He'll settle for half my pay check. He'll be all
right. I'm going to bed. (*He starts for the stairs.*)

*Linda:* He won't be all right.

*Biff* (*turning on the stairs, furiously*): I hate this city and I'll stay here. Now what
do you want?

*Linda:* He's dying, Biff.

*Happy turns quickly to her, shocked.*

*Biff* (*after a pause*): Why is he dying?

*Linda:* He's been trying to kill himself.

*Biff* (*with great horror*): How?

*Linda*: I live from day to day.

*Biff*: What're you talking about?

*Linda*: Remember I wrote you that he smashed up the car again? In February?

*Biff*: Well?

*Linda*: The insurance inspector came. He said that they have evidence. That all these accidents in the last year—weren't—weren't—accidents.

*Happy*: How can they tell that? That's a lie.

*Linda*: It seems there's a woman . . . (*She takes a breath as—*)

*Biff* (*sharply but contained*): What woman?

*Linda* (*simultaneously*): . . . and this woman . . .

*Linda*: What?

*Biff*: Nothing. Go ahead.

*Linda*: What did you say?

*Biff*: Nothing. I just said what woman?

*Happy*: What about her?

*Linda*: Well, it seems she was walking down the road and saw his car. She says that he wasn't driving fast at all, and that he didn't skid. She says he came to that little bridge, and then deliberately smashed into the railing, and it was only the shallowness of the water that saved him.

*Biff*: Oh, no, he probably just fell asleep again.

*Linda*: I don't think he fell asleep.

*Biff*: Why not?

*Linda*: Last month . . . (*With great difficulty.*) Oh, boys, it's so hard to say a thing like this! He's just a big stupid man to you, but I tell you there's more good in him than in many other people. (*She chokes, wipes her eyes.*) I was looking for a fuse. The lights blew out, and I went down the cellar. And behind the fuse box—it happened to fall out—was a length of rubber pipe—just short.

*Happy*: No kidding?

*Linda*: There's a little attachment on the end of it. I knew right away. And sure enough, on the bottom of the water heater there's a new little nipple on the gas pipe.

*Happy* (*angrily*): That—jerk.

*Biff*: Did you have it taken off?

*Linda*: I'm—I'm ashamed to. How can I mention it to him? Every day I go down and take away that little rubber pipe. But, when he comes home, I put it back where it was. How can I insult him that way? I don't know what to do. I live from day to day, boys. I tell you, I know every thought in his mind. It sounds so old-fashioned and silly, but I tell you he put his whole life into you and you've turned your backs on him. (*She is bent over in the chair, weeping, her face in her hands.*) Biff, I swear to God! Biff, his life is in your hands!

*Happy* (*to Biff*): How do you like that damned fool!

*Biff* (*kissing her*): All right, pal, all right. It's all settled now. I've been remiss. I know that, Mom. But now I'll stay, and I swear to you, I'll apply myself. (*Kneeling in front of her, in a fever of self-reproach.*) It's just—you see, Mom, I don't fit in business. Not that I won't try. I'll try, and I'll make good.

*Happy*: Sure you will. The trouble with you in business was you never tried to please people.

*Biff*: I know, I—

*Happy*: Like when you worked for Harrison's. Bob Harrison said you were tops, and then you go and do some damn fool thing like whistling whole songs in the elevator like a comedian.

*Biff (against Happy)*: So what? I like to whistle sometimes.

*Happy*: You don't raise a guy to a responsible job who whistles in the elevator!

*Linda*: Well, don't argue about it now.

*Happy*: Like when you'd go off and swim in the middle of the day instead of taking the line around.

*Biff (his resentment rising)*: Well, don't you run off? You take off sometimes, don't you? On a nice summer day?

*Happy*: Yeah, but I cover myself!

*Linda*: Boys!

*Happy*: If I'm going to take a fade the boss can call any number where I'm supposed to be and they'll swear to him that I just left. I'll tell you something that I hate to say, Biff, but in the business world some of them think you're crazy.

*Biff (angered)*: Screw the business world!

*Happy*: All right, screw it! Great, but cover yourself!

*Linda*: Hap! Hap!

*Biff*: I don't care what they think! They've laughed at Dad for years, and you know why? Because we don't belong in this nut-house of a city! We should be mixing cement on some open plain, or—or carpenters. A carpenter is allowed to whistle!

*Willy walks in from the entrance of the house, at left.*

*Willy*: Even your grandfather was better than a carpenter. (*Pause. They watch him.*) You never grew up. Bernard does not whistle in the elevator, I assure you.

*Biff (as though to laugh Willy out of it)*: Yeah, but you do, Pop.

*Willy*: I never in my life whistled in an elevator! And who in the business world thinks I'm crazy?

*Biff*: I didn't mean it like that, Pop. Now don't make a whole thing out of it, will ya?

*Willy*: Go back to the West! Be a carpenter, a cowboy, enjoy yourself!

*Linda*: Willy, he was just saying—

*Willy*: I heard what he said!

*Happy (trying to quiet Willy)*: Hey, Pop, come on now . . .

*Willy (continuing over Happy's line)*: They laugh at me, heh? Go to Filene's, go to the Hub, go to Slattery's, Boston. Call out the name Willy Loman and see what happens! Big shot!

*Biff*: All right, Pop.

*Willy:* Big!

*Biff:* All right!

*Willy:* Why do you always insult me?

*Biff:* I didn't say a word. (*To Linda.*) Did I say a word?

*Linda:* He didn't say anything, Willy.

*Willy* (*going to the doorway of the living room*): All right, good night, good night.

*Linda:* Willy, dear, he just decided . . .

*Willy* (*to Biff*): If you get tired hanging around tomorrow, paint the ceiling I put up in the living room.

*Biff:* I'm leaving early tomorrow.

*Happy:* He's going to see Bill Oliver, Pop.

*Willy* (*interestedly*): Oliver? For what?

*Biff* (*with reserve, but trying, trying*): He always said he'd stake me. I'd like to go into business, so maybe I can take him up on it.

*Linda:* Isn't that wonderful?

*Willy:* Don't interrupt. What's wonderful about it? There's fifty men in the City of New York who'd stake him. (*To Biff.*) Sporting goods?

*Biff:* I guess so. I know something about it and—

*Willy:* He knows something about it! You know sporting goods better than Spalding, for God's sake! How much is he giving you?

*Biff:* I don't know, I didn't even see him yet, but—

*Willy:* Then what're you talkin' about?

*Biff* (*getting angry*): Well, all I said was I'm gonna see him, that's all!

*Willy* (*turning away*): Ah, you're counting your chickens again.

*Biff* (*starting left for the stairs*): Oh, Jesus, I'm going to sleep!

*Willy* (*calling after him*): Don't curse in this house!

*Biff* (*turning*): Since when did you get so clean!

*Happy* (*trying to stop them*): Wait a . . .

*Willy:* Don't use that language to me! I won't have it!

*Happy* (*grabbing Biff, shouts*): Wait a minute! I got an idea. I got a feasible idea. Come here, Biff, let's talk this over now, let's talk some sense here. When I was down in Florida last time, I thought of a great idea to sell sporting goods. It just came back to me. You and I, Biff—we have a line, the Loman Line. We train a couple of weeks, and put on a couple of exhibitions, see?

*Willy:* That's an idea!

*Happy:* Wait! We form two basketball teams, see? Two water-polo teams. We play each other. It's a million dollars' worth of publicity. Two brothers, see? The Loman Brothers. Displays in the Royal Palms—all the hotels. And banners over the ring and the basketball court: "Loman Brothers." Baby, we could sell sporting goods!

*Willy:* That is a one-million-dollar idea.

*Linda:* Marvelous!

*Biff:* I'm in great shape as far as that's concerned.

*Happy*: And the beauty of it is, Biff, it wouldn't be like a business. We'd be out playin' ball again . . .

*Biff* (*enthused*): Yeah, that's . . .

*Willy*: Million-dollar . . .

*Happy*: And you wouldn't get fed up with it, Biff. It'd be the family again. There'd be the old honor, and comradeship, and if you wanted to go off for a swim or somethin'—well, you'd do it! Without some smart cooky gettin' up ahead of you!

*Willy*: Lick the world! You guys together could absolutely lick the civilized world.

*Biff*: I'll see Oliver tomorrow. Hap, if we could work that out . . .

*Linda*: Maybe things are beginning to—

*Willy* (*widely enthused, to Linda*): Stop interrupting! (*To Biff.*) But don't wear sport jacket and slacks when you see Oliver.

*Biff*: No, I'll—

*Willy*: A business suit, and talk as little as possible, and don't crack any jokes.

*Biff*: He did like me. Always liked me.

*Linda*: He loved you!

*Willy* (*to Linda*): Will you stop! (*To Biff.*) Walk in very serious. You are not applying for a boy's job. Money is to pass. Be quiet, fine, and serious. Everybody likes a kidder, but nobody lends him money.

*Happy*: I'll try to get some myself, Biff. I'm sure I can.

*Willy*: I can see great things for you, kids, I think your troubles are over. But remember, start big and you'll end big. Ask for fifteen. How much you gonna ask for?

*Biff*: Gee, I don't know—

*Willy*: And don't say "Gee." "Gee" is a boy's word. A man walking in for fifteen thousand dollars does not say "Gee!"

*Biff*: Ten, I think, would be top though.

*Willy*: Don't be so modest. You always started too low. Walk in with a big laugh. Don't look worried. Start off with a couple of your good stories to lighten things up. It's not what you say, it's how you say it—because personality always wins the day.

*Linda*: Oliver always thought the highest of him—

*Willy*: Will you let me talk?

*Biff*: Don't yell at her, Pop, will ya?

*Willy* (*angrily*): I was talking, wasn't I?

*Biff*: I don't like you yelling at her all the time, and I'm tellin' you, that's all.

*Willy*: What're you, takin' over the house?

*Linda*: Willy—

*Willy* (*turning on her*): Don't take his side all the time, goddammit!

*Biff* (*furiously*): Stop yelling at her!

*Willy* (*suddenly pulling on his cheek, beaten down, guilt ridden*): Give my best to Bill Oliver—he may remember me. (*He exits through the living room doorway.*)

Linda (*her voice subdued*): What'd you have to start that for? (*Biff turns away.*) You see how sweet he was as soon as you talked hopefully? (*She goes over to Biff.*) Come up and say good night to him. Don't let him go to bed that way.

Happy: Come on, Biff, let's buck him up.

Linda: Please, dear. Just say good night. It takes so little to make him happy. Come. (*She goes through the living room doorway, calling upstairs from within the living room.*) Your pajamas are hanging in the bathroom. Willy!

Happy (*looking toward where Linda went out*): What a woman! They broke the mold when they made her. You know that, Biff?

Biff: He's off salary. My God, working on commission!

Happy: Well, let's face it: he's no hot-shot selling man. Except that sometimes, you have to admit, he's a sweet personality.

Biff (*deciding*): Lend me ten bucks, will ya? I want to buy some new ties.

Happy: I'll take you to a place I know. Beautiful stuff. Wear one of my striped shirts tomorrow.

Biff: She got gray. Mom got awful old. Gee, I'm gonna go in to Oliver tomorrow and knock him for a—

Happy: Come on up. Tell that to Dad. Let's give him a whirl. Come on.

Biff (*steamed up*): You know, with ten thousand bucks, boy!

Happy (*as they go into the living room*): That's the talk, Biff, that's the first time I've heard the old confidence out of you! (*From within the living room, fading off.*) You're gonna live with me, kid, and any babe you want you just say the word . . . (*The last lines are hardly heard. They are mounting the stairs to their parents' bedroom.*)

Linda (*entering her bedroom and addressing Willy, who is in the bathroom. She is straightening the bed for him*): Can you do anything about the shower? It drips.

Willy (*from the bathroom*): All of a sudden everything falls to pieces! Goddam plumbing, oughta be sued, those people. I hardly finished putting it in and the thing . . . (*His words rumble off.*)

Linda: I'm just wondering if Oliver will remember him. You think he might?

Willy (*coming out of the bathroom in his pajamas*): Remember him? What's the matter with you, you crazy? If he'd've stayed with Oliver he'd be on top by now! Wait'll Oliver gets a look at him. You don't know the average caliber any more. The average young man today—(*he is getting into bed*)—is got a caliber of zero. Greatest thing in the world for him was to bum around.

*Biff and Happy enter the bedroom. Slight pause.*

Willy (*stops short, looking at Biff*): Glad to hear it, boy.

Happy: He wanted to say good night to you, sport.

Willy (*to Biff*): Yeah. Knock him dead, boy. What'd you want to tell me?

Biff: Just take it easy, Pop. Good night. (*He turns to go.*)

Willy (*unable to resist*): And if anything falls off the desk while you're talking to him—like a package or something—don't you pick it up. They have office boys for that.

*Linda:* I'll make a big breakfast—

*Willy:* Will you let me finish? (*To Biff.*) Tell him you were in the business in the West. Not farm work.

*Biff:* All right, Dad.

*Linda:* I think everything—

*Willy* (*going right through her speech*): And don't undersell yourself. No less than fifteen thousand dollars.

*Biff* (*unable to bear him*): Okay. Good night, Mom. (*He starts moving.*)

*Willy:* Because you got a greatness in you, Biff, remember that. You got all kinds a greatness . . . (*He lies back, exhausted. Biff walks out.*)

*Linda* (*calling after Biff*): Sleep well, darling!

*Happy:* I'm gonna get married, Mom. I wanted to tell you.

*Linda:* Go to sleep, dear.

*Happy* (*going*): I just wanted to tell you.

*Willy:* Keep up the good work. (*Happy exits.*) God . . . remember that Ebbets Field game? The championship of the city?

*Linda:* Just rest. Should I sing to you?

*Willy:* Yeah. Sing to me. (*Linda hums a soft lullaby.*) When that team came out— he was the tallest, remember?

*Linda:* Oh, yes. And in gold.

> *Biff enters the darkened kitchen, takes a cigarette, and leaves the house. He comes downstage into a golden pool of light. He smokes, staring at the night.*

*Willy:* Like a young god. Hercules—something like that. And the sun, the sun all around him. Remember how he waved to me? Right up from the field, with the representatives of three colleges standing by? And the buyers I brought, and the cheers when he came out—Loman, Loman, Loman! God Almighty, he'll be great yet. A star like that, magnificent, can never really fade away!

> *The light on Willy is fading. The gas heater begins to glow through the kitchen wall, near the stairs, a blue flame beneath red coils.*

*Linda* (*timidly*): Willy, dear, what has he got against you?

*Willy:* I'm so tired. Don't talk any more.

> *Biff slowly returns to the kitchen. He stops, stares toward the heater.*

*Linda:* Will you ask Howard to let you work in New York?

*Willy:* First thing in the morning. Everything'll be all right.

> *Biff reaches behind the heater and draws out a length of rubber tubing. He is horrified and turns his head toward Willy's room, still dimly lit, from which the strains of Linda's desperate but monotonous humming rise.*

*Willy* (*staring through the window into the moonlight*): Gee, look at the moon moving between the buildings!

> *Biff wraps the tubing around his hand and quickly goes up the stairs. Curtain.*

# Act II

*Music is heard, gay and bright. The curtain rises as the music fades away. Willy, in shirt sleeves, is sitting at the kitchen table, sipping coffee, his hat in his lap. Linda is filling his cup when she can.*

Willy: Wonderful coffee. Meal in itself.

Linda: Can I make you some eggs?

Willy: No. Take a breath.

Linda: You look so rested, dear.

Willy: I slept like a dead one. First time in months. Imagine, sleeping till ten on a Tuesday morning. Boys left nice and early, heh?

Linda: They were out of here by eight o'clock.

Willy: Good work!

Linda: It was so thrilling to see them leaving together. I can't get over the shaving lotion in this house.

Willy (*smiling*): Mmm—

Linda: Biff was very changed this morning. His whole attitude seemed to be hopeful. He couldn't wait to get downtown to see Oliver.

Willy: He's heading for a change. There's no question, there simply are certain men that take longer to get—solidified. How did he dress?

Linda: His blue suit. He's so handsome in that suit. He could be a—anything in that suit!

*Willy gets up from the table. Linda holds his jacket for him.*

Willy: There's no question, no question at all. Gee, on the way home tonight I'd like to buy some seeds.

Linda (*laughing*): That'd be wonderful. But not enough sun gets back there. Nothing'll grow any more.

Willy: You wait, kid, before it's all over we're gonna get a little place out in the country, and I'll raise some vegetables, a couple of chickens . . .

Linda: You'll do it yet, dear.

*Willy walks out of his jacket. Linda follows him.*

Willy: And they'll get married, and come for a weekend. I'd build a little guest house. 'Cause I got so many fine tools, all I'd need would be a little lumber and some peace of mind.

Linda (*joyfully*): I sewed the lining . . .

Willy: I could build two guest houses, so they'd both come. Did he decide how much he's going to ask Oliver for?

Linda (*getting him into the jacket*): He didn't mention it, but I imagine ten or fifteen thousand. You going to talk to Howard today?

Willy: Yeah. I'll put it to him straight and simple. He'll just have to take me off the road.

*Linda*: And Willy, don't forget to ask for a little advance, because we've got the insurance premium. It's the grace period now.

*Willy*: That's a hundred. . . ?

*Linda*: A hundred and eight, sixty-eight. Because we're a little short again.

*Willy*: Why are we short?

*Linda*: Well, you had the motor job on the car . . .

*Willy*: That goddam Studebaker!

*Linda*: And you got one more payment on the refrigerator . . .

*Willy*: But it just broke again!

*Linda*: Well, it's old, dear.

*Willy*: I told you we should've bought a well-advertised machine. Charley bought a General Electric and it's twenty years old and it's still good, that son-of-a-bitch.

*Linda*: But, Willy—

*Willy*: Whoever heard of a Hastings refrigerator? Once in my life I would like to own something outright before it's broken! I'm always in a race with the junkyard! I just finished paying for the car and it's on its last legs. The refrigerator consumes belts like a goddam maniac. They time those things. They time them so when you finally paid for them, they're used up.

*Linda* (*buttoning up his jacket as he unbuttons it*): All told, about two hundred dollars would carry us, dear. But that includes the last payment on the mortgage. After this payment, Willy, the house belongs to us.

*Willy*: It's twenty-five years!

*Linda*: Biff was nine years old when we bought it.

*Willy*: Well, that's a great thing. To weather a twenty-five year mortgage is—

*Linda*: It's an accomplishment.

*Willy*: All the cement, the lumber, the reconstruction I put in this house! There ain't a crack to be found in it any more.

*Linda*: Well, it served its purpose.

*Willy*: What purpose? Some stranger'll come along, move in, and that's that. If only Biff would take this house, and raise a family . . . (*He starts to go.*) Good-by, I'm late.

*Linda* (*suddenly remembering*): Oh, I forgot! You're supposed to meet them for dinner.

*Willy*: Me?

*Linda*: At Frank's Chop House on Forty-eighth near Sixth Avenue.

*Willy*: Is that so! How about you?

*Linda*: No, just the three of you. They're gonna blow you to a big meal!

*Willy*: Don't say! Who thought of that?

*Linda*: Biff came to me this morning, Willy, and he said, "Tell Dad, we want to blow him to a big meal." Be there six o'clock. You and your two boys are going to have dinner.

*Willy*: Gee whiz! That's really somethin'. I'm gonna knock Howard for a loop, kid. I'll get an advance, and I'll come home with a New York job. Goddammit, now I'm gonna do it!

*Linda:* Oh, that's the spirit, Willy!

*Willy:* I will never get behind a wheel the rest of my life!

*Linda:* It's changing, Willy, I can feel it changing!

*Willy:* Beyond a question. G'by, I'm late. (*He starts to go again.*)

*Linda* (*calling after him as she runs to the kitchen table for a handkerchief*): You got your glasses?

*Willy* (*feels for them, then comes back in*): Yeah, yeah, got my glasses.

*Linda* (*giving him the handkerchief*): And a handkerchief.

*Willy:* Yeah, handkerchief.

*Linda:* And your saccharine?

*Willy:* Yeah, my saccharine.

*Linda:* Be careful on the subway stairs.

> *She kisses him, and a silk stocking is seen hanging from her hand. Willy notices it.*

*Willy:* Will you stop mending stockings? At least while I'm in the house. It gets me nervous. I can't tell you. Please.

> *Linda hides the stocking in her hand as she follows Willy across the forestage in front of the house.*

*Linda:* Remember, Frank's Chop House.

*Willy* (*passing the apron*): Maybe beets would grow out there.

*Linda* (*laughing*): But you tried so many times.

*Willy:* Yeah. Well, don't work hard today. (*He disappears around the right corner of the house.*)

*Linda:* Be careful!

> *As Willy vanishes, Linda waves to him. Suddenly the phone rings. She runs across the stage and into the kitchen and lifts it.*

*Linda:* Hello? Oh, Biff! I'm so glad you called, I just . . . Yes, sure, I just told him. Yes, he'll be there for dinner at six o'clock, I didn't forget. Listen, I was just dying to tell you. You know that little rubber pipe I told you about? That he connected to the gas heater? I finally decided to go down the cellar this morning and take it away and destroy it. But it's gone! Imagine? He took it away himself, it isn't there! (*She listens.*) When? Oh, then you took it. Oh— nothing, it's just that I'd hoped he'd taken it away himself. Oh, I'm not wor- ried, darling, because this morning he left in such high spirits, it was like the old days! I'm not afraid any more. Did Mr. Oliver see you? . . . Well, you wait there then. And make a nice impression on him, darling. Just don't perspire too much before you see him. And have a nice time with Dad. He may have big news too! . . . That's right, a New York job. And be sweet to him tonight, dear. Be loving to him. Because he's only a little boat looking for a harbor. (*She is trembling with sorrow and joy.*) Oh, that's wonderful, Biff, you'll save his life. Thanks, darling. Just put your arm around him when he comes into the restaurant. Give him a smile. That's the boy . . . Good-by, dear. . . . You got your comb? . . . That's fine. Good-by, Biff dear.

*In the middle of her speech, Howard Wagner, thirty-six, wheels in a small type-writer table on which is a wire-recording machine and proceeds to plug it in. This is on the left forestage. Light slowly fades on Linda as it rises on Howard. Howard is intent on threading the machine and only glances over his shoulder as Willy appears.*

Willy: Pst! Pst!

Howard: Hello, Willy, come in.

Willy: Like to have a little talk with you, Howard.

Howard: Sorry to keep you waiting. I'll be with you in a minute.

Willy: What's that, Howard?

Howard: Didn't you ever see one of these? Wire recorder.

Willy: Oh. Can we talk a minute?

Howard: Records things. Just got delivery yesterday. Been driving me crazy, the most terrific machine I ever saw in my life. I was up all night with it.

Willy: What do you do with it?

Howard: I bought it for dictation, but you can do anything with it. Listen to this. I had it home last night. Listen to what I picked up. The first one is my daughter. Get this. (*He flicks the switch and "Roll out the Barrel" is heard being whistled.*) Listen to that kid whistle.

Willy: That is lifelike, isn't it?

Howard: Seven years old. Get that tone.

Willy: Ts, ts. Like to ask a little favor if you . . .

*The whistling breaks off, and the voice of Howard's Daughter is heard.*

His Daughter: "Now you, Daddy."

Howard: She's crazy for me! (*Again the same song is whistled.*) That's me! Ha! (*He winks.*)

Willy: You're very good!

*The whistling breaks off again. The machine runs silent for a moment.*

Howard: Sh! Get this now, this is my son.

His Son: "The capital of Alabama is Montgomery; the capital of Arizona is Phoenix; the capital of Arkansas is Little Rock; the capital of California is Sacramento. . . " (*And on, and on.*)

Howard (*holding up five fingers*): Five years old, Willy!

Willy: He'll make an announcer some day!

His Son (*continuing*): "The capital. . . "

Howard: Get that—alphabetical order! (*The machine breaks off suddenly.*) Wait a minute. The maid kicked the plug out.

Willy: It certainly is a—

Howard: Sh, for God's sake!

His Son: "It's nine o'clock, Bulova watch time. So I have to go to sleep."

Willy: That really is—

Howard: Wait a minute! The next is my wife.

*They wait.*

*Howard's Voice:* "Go on, say something." (*Pause.*) "Well, you gonna talk?"

*His Wife:* "I can't think of anything."

*Howard's Voice:* "Well, talk—it's turning."

*His Wife* (*shyly, beaten*): "Hello." (*Silence.*) "Oh, Howard, I can't talk into this . . ."

*Howard* (*snapping the machine off*): That was my wife.

*Willy:* That is a wonderful machine. Can we—

*Howard:* I tell you, Willy, I'm gonna take my camera, and my bandsaw, and all my hobbies, and out they go. This is the most fascinating relaxation I ever found.

*Willy:* I think I'll get one myself.

*Howard:* Sure, they're only a hundred and a half. You can't do without it. Supposing you wanna hear Jack Benny, see? Bet you can't be at home at that hour. So you tell the maid to turn the radio on when Jack Benny comes on, and this automatically goes on with the radio . . .

*Willy:* And when you come home you . . .

*Howard:* You can come home twelve o'clock, one o'clock, any time you like, and you get yourself a Coke and sit yourself down, throw the switch, and there's Jack Benny's program in the middle of the night!

*Willy:* I'm definitely going to get one. Because lots of times I'm on the road, and I think to myself, what I must be missing on the radio!

*Howard:* Don't you have a radio in the car?

*Willy:* Well, yeah, but who ever thinks of turning it on?

*Howard:* Say, aren't you supposed to be in Boston?

*Willy:* That's what I want to talk to you about, Howard. You got a minute?

(*He draws a chair in from the wing.*)

*Howard:* What happened? What're you doing here?

*Willy:* Well . . .

*Howard:* You didn't crack up again, did you?

*Willy:* Oh, no. No . . .

*Howard:* Geez, you had me worried there for a minute. What's the trouble?

*Willy:* Well, to tell you the truth, Howard, I've come to the decision that I'd rather not travel any more.

*Howard:* Not travel! Well, what'll you do?

*Willy:* Remember, Christmas time, when you had the party here? You said you'd try to think of some spot for me here in town.

*Howard:* With us?

*Willy:* Well, sure.

*Howard:* Oh, yeah, yeah. I remember. Well, I couldn't think of anything for you, Willy.

*Willy:* I tell ya, Howard. The kids are all grown up, y'know. I don't need much any more. If I could take home—well, sixty-five dollars a week, I could swing it.

*Howard:* Yeah, but Willy, see I—

*Willy:* I tell ya why, Howard. Speaking frankly and between the two of us, y'know—I'm just a little tired.

*Howard:* Oh, I could understand that, Willy. But you're a road man, Willy, and we do a road business. We've only got a half-dozen salesmen on the floor here.

*Willy:* God knows, Howard, I never asked a favor of any man. But I was with the firm when your father used to carry you in here in his arms.

*Howard:* I know that, Willy, but—

*Willy:* Your father came to me the day you were born and asked me what I thought of the name of Howard, may he rest in peace.

*Howard:* I appreciate that, Willy, but there just is no spot here for you. If I had a spot I'd slam you right in, but I just don't have a single, solitary spot.

*He looks for his lighter. Willy has picked it up and gives it to him. Pause.*

*Willy (with increasing anger):* Howard, all I need to set my table is fifty dollars a week.

*Howard:* But where am I going to put you, kid?

*Willy:* Look, it isn't a question of whether I can sell merchandise, is it?

*Howard:* No, but it's a business, kid, and everybody's gotta pull his own weight.

*Willy (desperately):* Just let me tell you a story, Howard—

*Howard:* 'Cause you gotta admit, business is business.

*Willy (angrily):* Business is definitely business, but just listen for a minute. You don't understand this. When I was a boy—eighteen, nineteen—I was already on the road. And there was a question in my mind as to whether selling had a future for me. Because in those days I had a yearning to go to Alaska. See, there were three gold strikes in one month in Alaska, and I felt like going out. Just for the ride, you might say.

*Howard (barely interested):* Don't say.

*Willy:* Oh, yeah, my father lived many years in Alaska. He was an adventurous man. We've got quite a little streak of self-reliance in our family. I thought I'd go out with my older brother and try to locate him, and maybe settle in the North with the old man. And I was almost decided to go, when I met a salesman in the Parker House. His name was Dave Singleman. And he was eighty-four years old, and he'd drummed merchandise in thirty-one states. And old Dave, he'd go up to his room, y'understand, put on his green velvet slippers—I'll never forget—and pick up his phone and call the buyers, and without ever leaving his room, at the age of eighty-four, he made his living. And when I saw that, I realized that selling was the greatest career a man could want. 'Cause what could be more satisfying than to be able to go, at the age of eighty-four, into twenty or thirty different cities, and pick up a phone, and be remembered and loved and helped by so many different people? Do you know? When he died—and by the way he died the death of a salesman, in his green velvet slippers in the smoker of the New York, New Haven and Hartford, going into Boston—when he died, hundreds of salesmen and buyers were at his funeral. Things were sad on a lotta trains for months after that. (*He stands up. Howard has not looked at him.*) In those days there was personality in it, Howard. There was respect, and comradeship, and gratitude in it. Today, it's all cut and dried, and there's no chance for bringing friendship to bear—or personality. You see what I mean? They don't know me any more.

Howard (*moving away, to the right*): That's just the thing, Willy.

Willy: If I had forty dollars a week—that's all I'd need. Forty dollars, Howard.

Howard: Kid, I can't take blood from a stone, I—

Willy (*desperation is on him now*): Howard, the year Al Smith was nominated, your father came to me and—

Howard (*starting to go off*): I've got to see some people, kid.

Willy (*stopping him*): I'm talking about your father! There were promises made across this desk! You mustn't tell me you've got people to see—I put thirty-four years into this firm, Howard, and now I can't pay my insurance! You can't eat the orange and throw the peel away—a man is not a piece of fruit! (*After a pause.*) Now pay attention. Your father—in 1928 I had a big year. I averaged a hundred and seventy dollars a week in commissions.

Howard (*impatiently*): Now, Willy, you never averaged—

Willy (*banging his hand on the desk*): I averaged a hundred and seventy dollars a week in the year of 1928! And your father came to me—or rather, I was in the office here—it was right over this desk—and he put his hand on my shoulder—

Howard (*getting up*): You'll have to excuse me, Willy, I gotta see some people. Pull yourself together. (*Going out.*) I'll be back in a little while.

*On Howard's exit, the light on his chair grows very bright and strange.*

Willy: Pull yourself together! What the hell did I say to him? My God, I was yelling at him! How could I! (*Willy breaks off, staring at the light, which occupies the chair, animating it. He approaches this chair, standing across the desk from it.*) Frank, Frank, don't you remember what you told me that time? How you put your hand on my shoulder, and Frank . . . (*He leans on the desk and as he speaks the dead man's name he accidentally switches on the recorder, and instantly—*)

Howard's Son: ". . . of New York is Albany. The capital of Ohio is Cincinnati, the capital of Rhode Island is . . . " (*The recitation continues.*)

Willy (*leaping away with fright, shouting*): Ha! Howard! Howard! Howard!

Howard (*rushing in*): What happened?

Willy (*pointing at the machine, which continues nasally, childishly, with the capital cities*): Shut it off! Shut it off!

Howard (*pulling the plug out*): Look, Willy . . .

Willy (*pressing his hands to his eyes*): I gotta get myself some coffee. I'll get some coffee . . .

*Willy starts to walk out. Howard stops him.*

Howard (*rolling up the cord*): Willy, look . . .

Willy: I'll go to Boston.

Howard: Willy, you can't go to Boston for us.

*Willy:* Why can't I go?

*Howard:* I don't want you to represent us. I've been meaning to tell you for a long time now.

*Willy:* Howard, are you firing me?

*Howard:* I think you need a good long rest, Willy.

*Willy:* Howard—

*Howard:* And when you feel better, come back, and we'll see if we can work something out.

*Willy:* But I gotta earn money, Howard. I'm in no position—

*Howard:* Where are your sons? Why don't your sons give you a hand?

*Willy:* They're working on a very big deal.

*Howard:* This is no time for false pride, Willy. You go to your sons and tell them that you're tired. You've got two great boys, haven't you?

*Willy:* Oh, no question, no question, but in the meantime . . .

*Howard:* Then that's that, heh?

*Willy:* All right, I'll go to Boston tomorrow.

*Howard:* No, no.

*Willy:* I can't throw myself on my sons. I'm not a cripple!

*Howard:* Look, kid, I'm busy this morning.

*Willy (grasping Howard's arm):* Howard, you've got to let me go to Boston!

*Howard (hard, keeping himself under control):* I've got a line of people to see this morning. Sit down, take five minutes, and pull yourself together, and then go home, will ya? I need the office, Willy. (*He starts to go, turns, remembering the recorder, starts to push off the table holding the recorder.*) Oh, yeah. Whenever you can this week, stop by and drop off the samples. You'll feel better, Willy, and then come back and we'll talk. Pull yourself together, kid, there's people outside.

*Howard exits, pushing the table off left. Willy stares into space, exhausted. Now the music is heard—Ben's music—first distantly, then closer, closer. As Willy speaks, Ben enters from the right. He carries valise and umbrella.*

*Willy:* Oh, Ben, how did you do it? What is the answer? Did you wind up the Alaska deal already?

*Ben:* Doesn't take much time if you know what you're doing. Just a short business trip. Boarding ship in an hour. Wanted to say good-by.

*Willy:* Ben, I've got to talk to you.

*Ben (glancing at his watch):* Haven't the time, William.

*Willy (crossing the apron to Ben):* Ben, nothing's working out. I don't know what to do.

*Ben:* Now, look here, William. I've bought timberland in Alaska and I need a man to look after things for me.

*Willy:* God, timberland! Me and my boys in those grand outdoors!

*Ben:* You've a new continent at your doorstep, William. Get out of these cities, they're full of talk and time payments and courts of law. Screw on your fists and you can fight for a fortune up there.

*Willy:* Yes, yes! Linda! Linda!

*Linda enters as of old, with the wash.*

*Linda:* Oh, you're back?

*Ben:* I haven't much time.

*Willy:* No, wait! Linda, he's got a proposition for me in Alaska.

*Linda:* But you've got—(*To Ben.*) He's got a beautiful job here.

*Willy:* But in Alaska, kid, I could—

*Linda:* You're doing well enough, Willy!

*Ben* (*to Linda*): Enough for what, my dear?

*Linda* (*frightened of Ben and angry at him*): Don't say those things to him! Enough to be happy right here, right now. (*To Willy, while Ben laughs.*) Why must everybody conquer the world? You're well liked, and the boys love you, and someday—(*to Ben*)—why, old man Wagner told him just the other day that if he keeps it up he'll be a member of the firm, didn't he, Willy?

*Willy:* Sure, sure. I am building something with this firm, Ben, and if a man is building something he must be on the right track, mustn't he?

*Ben:* What are you building? Lay your hand on it. Where is it?

*Willy* (*hesitantly*): That's true, Linda, there's nothing.

*Linda:* Why? (*To Ben.*) There's a man eighty-four years old—

*Willy:* That's right, Ben, that's right. When I look at that man I say, what is there to worry about?

*Ben:* Bah!

*Willy:* It's true, Ben. All he has to do is go into any city, pick up the phone, and he's making his living and you know why?

*Ben* (*picking up his valise*): I've got to go.

*Willy* (*holding Ben back*): Look at this boy!

*Biff, in his high school sweater, enters carrying suitcase. Happy carries Biff's shoulder guards, gold helmet, and football pants.*

*Willy:* Without a penny to his name, three great universities are begging for him, and from there the sky's the limit, because it's not what you do, Ben. It's who you know and the smile on your face! It's contacts, Ben, contacts! The whole wealth of Alaska passes over the lunch table at the Commodore Hotel, and that's the wonder, the wonder of this country, that a man can end with diamonds here on the basis of being liked! (*He turns to Biff.*) And that's why when you get out on that field today it's important. Because thousands of people will be rooting for you and loving you. (*To Ben, who has again begun to leave.*) And Ben! when he walks into a business office his name will sound out like a bell and all the doors will open to him! I've seen it, Ben, I've seen it a thousand times! You can't feel it with your hand like timber, but it's there!

*Ben:* Good-by, William.

*Willy:* Ben, am I right? Don't you think I'm right? I value your advice.

*Ben:* There's a new continent at your doorstep, William. You could walk out rich. Rich. (*He is gone.*)

*Willy*: We'll do it here, Ben! You hear me? We're gonna do it here!

> *Young Bernard rushes in. The gay music of the boys is heard.*

*Bernard*: Oh, gee, I was afraid you left already!

*Willy*: Why? What time is it?

*Bernard*: It's half-past one!

*Willy*: Well, come on, everybody! Ebbets Field next stop! Where's the pennants? (*He rushes through the wall-line of the kitchen and out into the living room.*)

*Linda* (*to Biff*): Did you pack fresh underwear?

*Biff* (*who has been limbering up*): I want to go!

*Bernard*: Biff, I'm carrying your helmet, ain't I?

*Happy*: No, I'm carrying the helmet.

*Bernard*: Oh, Biff, you promised me.

*Happy*: I'm carrying the helmet.

*Bernard*: How am I going to get in the locker room?

*Linda*: Let him carry the shoulder guards. (*She puts her coat and hat on in the kitchen.*)

*Bernard*: Can I, Biff? 'Cause I told everybody I'm going to be in the locker room.

*Happy*: In Ebbets Field it's the clubhouse.

*Bernard*: I meant the clubhouse. Biff!

*Happy*: Biff!

*Biff* (*grandly, after a slight pause*): Let him carry the shoulder guards.

*Happy* (*as he gives Bernard the shoulder guards*): Stay close to us now.

> *Willy rushes in with the pennants.*

*Willy* (*handing them out*): Everybody wave when Biff comes out on the field. (*Happy and Bernard run off.*) You set now, boy?

> *The music has died away.*

*Biff*: Ready to go, Pop. Every muscle is ready.

*Willy* (*at the edge of the apron*): You realize what this means?

*Biff*: That's right, Pop.

*Willy* (*feeling Biff's muscles*): You're comin' home this afternoon captain of the All-Scholastic Championship Team of the City of New York.

*Biff*: I got it, Pop. And remember, pal, when I take off my helmet, that touchdown is for you.

*Willy*: Let's go! (*He is starting out, with his arm around Biff, when Charley enters, as of old, in knickers.*) I got no room for you, Charley.

*Charley*: Room? For what?

*Willy*: In the car.

*Charley*: You goin' for a ride? I wanted to shoot some casino.

*Willy* (*furiously*): Casino! (*Incredulously.*) Don't you realize what today is?

*Linda*: Oh, he knows, Willy. He's just kidding you.

*Willy*: That's nothing to kid about!

*Charley*: No, Linda, what's goin' on?

*Linda:* He's playing in Ebbets Field.

*Charley:* Baseball in this weather?

*Willy:* Don't talk to him. Come on, come on! (*He is pushing them out.*)

*Charley:* Wait a minute, didn't you hear the news?

*Willy:* What?

*Charley:* Don't you listen to the radio? Ebbets Field just blew up.

*Willy:* You go to hell! (*Charley laughs. Pushing them out.*) Come on, come on! We're late.

*Charley (as they go):* Knock a homer, Biff, knock a homer!

*Willy (the last to leave, turning to Charley):* I don't think that was funny, Charley. This is the greatest day of his life.

*Charley:* Willy, when are you going to grow up?

*Willy:* Yeah, heh? When this game is over, Charley, you'll be laughing out of the other side of your face. They'll be calling him another Red Grange. Twenty-five thousand a year.

*Charley (kidding):* Is that so?

*Willy:* Yeah, that's so.

*Charley:* Well, then, I'm sorry, Willy. But tell me something.

*Willy:* What?

*Charley:* Who is Red Grange?

*Willy:* Put up your hands. Goddam you, put up your hands!

> *Charley, chuckling, shakes his head and walks away, around the left corner of the stage. Willy follows him. The music rises to a mocking frenzy.*

*Willy:* Who the hell do you think you are, better than everybody else? You don't know everything, you big, ignorant, stupid . . . Put up your hands!

> *Light rises, on the right side of the forestage, on a small table in the reception room of Charley's office. Traffic sounds are heard. Bernard, now mature, sits whistling to himself. A pair of tennis rackets and an overnight bag are on the floor beside him.*

*Willy (offstage):* What are you walking away for? Don't walk away! If you're going to say something say it to my face! I know you laugh at me behind my back. You'll laugh out of the other side of your goddam face after this game. Touchdown! Touchdown! Eighty thousand people! Touchdown! Right between the goal posts.

> *Bernard is a quiet, earnest, but self-assured young man. Willy's voice is coming from right upstage now. Bernard lowers his feet off the table and listens. Jenny, his father's secretary, enters.*

*Jenny (distressed):* Say, Bernard, will you go out in the hall?

*Bernard:* What is that noise? Who is it?

*Jenny:* Mr. Loman. He just got off the elevator.

*Bernard (getting up):* Who's he arguing with?

*Jenny:* Nobody. There's nobody with him. I can't deal with him any more, and your father gets all upset everytime he comes. I've got a lot of typing to do, and your father's waiting to sign it. Will you see him?

*Willy* (*entering*): Touchdown! Touch—(*He sees Jenny.*) Jenny, Jenny, good to see you. How're ya? Workin'? Or still honest?

*Jenny:* Fine. How've you been feeling?

*Willy:* Not much any more, Jenny. Ha, ha! (*He is surprised to see the rackets.*)

*Bernard:* Hello, Uncle Willy.

*Willy* (*almost shocked*): Bernard! Well, look who's here! (*He comes quickly, guiltily, to Bernard and warmly shakes his hand.*)

*Bernard:* How are you? Good to see you.

*Willy:* What are you doing here?

*Bernard:* Oh, just stopped by to see Pop. Get off my feet till my train leaves. I'm going to Washington in a few minutes.

*Willy:* Is he in?

*Bernard:* Yes, he's in his office with the accountant. Sit down.

*Willy* (*sitting down*): What're you going to do in Washington?

*Bernard:* Oh, just a case I've got there, Willy.

*Willy:* That so? (*indicating the rackets.*) You going to play tennis there?

*Bernard:* I'm staying with a friend who's got a court.

*Willy:* Don't say. His own tennis court. Must be fine people, I bet.

*Bernard:* They are, very nice. Dad tells me Biff's in town.

*Willy* (*with a big smile*): Yeah, Biff's in. Working on a very big deal, Bernard.

*Bernard:* What's Biff doing?

*Willy:* Well, he's been doing very big things in the West. But he decided to establish himself here. Very big. We're having dinner. Did I hear your wife had a boy?

*Bernard:* That's right. Our second.

*Willy:* Two boys! What do you know!

*Bernard:* What kind of deal has Biff got?

*Willy:* Well, Bill Oliver—very big sporting-goods man—he wants Biff very badly. Called him in from the West. Long distance, carte blanche, special deliveries. Your friends have their own private tennis court?

*Bernard:* You still with the old firm, Willy?

*Willy* (*after a pause*): I'm—I'm overjoyed to see how you made the grade, Bernard, overjoyed. It's an encouraging thing to see a young man really—really— Looks very good for Biff—very—(*He breaks off, then.*) Bernard—(*He is so full of emotion, he breaks off again.*)

*Bernard:* What is it, Willy?

*Willy* (*small and alone*): What—what's the secret?

*Bernard:* What secret?

*Willy:* How—how did you? Why didn't he ever catch on?

*Bernard:* I wouldn't know that, Willy.

*Willy* (*confidentially, desperately*): You were his friend, his boyhood friend. There's something I don't understand about it. His life ended after that Ebbets Field game. From the age of seventeen nothing good ever happened to him.

*Bernard:* He never trained himself for anything.

*Willy:* But he did, he did. After high school he took so many correspondence courses. Radio mechanics; television; God knows what, and never made the slightest mark.

*Bernard* (*taking off his glasses*): Willy, do you want to talk candidly?

*Willy* (*rising, faces Bernard*): I regard you as a very brilliant man, Bernard. I value your advice.

*Bernard:* Oh, the hell with the advice, Willy. I couldn't advise you. There's just one thing I've always wanted to ask you. When he was supposed to graduate, and the math teacher flunked him—

*Willy:* Oh, that son-of-a-bitch ruined his life.

*Bernard:* Yeah, but, Willy, all he had to do was go to summer school and make up that subject.

*Willy:* That's right, that's right.

*Bernard:* Did you tell him not to go to summer school?

*Willy:* Me? I begged him to go. I ordered him to go!

*Bernard:* Then why wouldn't he go?

*Willy:* Why? Why! Bernard, that question has been trailing me like a ghost for the last fifteen years. He flunked the subject, and laid down and died like a hammer hit him!

*Bernard:* Take it easy, kid.

*Willy:* Let me talk to you—I got nobody to talk to. Bernard, Bernard, was it my fault? Y'see? It keeps going around in my mind, maybe I did something to him. I got nothing to give him.

*Bernard:* Don't take it so hard.

*Willy:* Why did he lay down? What is the story there? You were his friend!

*Bernard:* Willy, I remember, it was June, and our grades came out. And he'd flunked math.

*Willy:* That son-of-a-bitch!

*Bernard:* No, it wasn't right then. Biff just got very angry, I remember, and he was ready to enroll in summer school.

*Willy* (*surprised*): He was?

*Bernard:* He wasn't beaten by it at all. But then, Willy, he disappeared from the block for almost a month. And I got the idea that he'd gone up to New England to see you. Did he have a talk with you then?

*Willy stares in silence.*

*Bernard:* Willy?

*Willy* (*with a strong edge of resentment in his voice*): Yeah, he came to Boston. What about it?

*Bernard:* Well, just that when he came back—I'll never forget this, it always mystifies me. Because I'd thought so well of Biff, even though he'd always taken advantage of me. I loved him, Willy, y'know? And he came back after that month and took his sneakers—remember those sneakers with "University of Virginia" printed on them? He was so proud of those, wore them every day. And he took them down in the cellar, and burned them up in the furnace. We had a fist fight. It lasted at least half an hour. Just the two of us, punching each other down the cellar, and crying right through it. I've often thought of how strange it was that I knew he'd given up his life. What happened in Boston, Willy?

*Willy looks at him as at an intruder.*

**Bernard:** I just bring it up because you asked me.

**Willy** (*angrily*): Nothing. What do you mean, "What happened?" What's that got to do with anything?

**Bernard:** Well, don't get sore.

**Willy:** What are you trying to do, blame it on me? If a boy lays down is that my fault?

**Bernard:** Now, Willy, don't get—

**Willy:** Well, don't—don't talk to me that way! What does that mean, "What happened?"

*Charley enters. He is in his vest, and he carries a bottle of bourbon.*

**Charley:** Hey, you're going to miss that train. (*He waves the bottle.*)

**Bernard:** Yeah, I'm going. (*He takes the bottle.*) Thanks, Pop. (*He picks up his rackets and bag.*) Good-by, Willy, and don't worry about it. You know, "If at first you don't succeed . . ."

**Willy:** Yes, I believe in that.

**Bernard:** But sometimes, Willy, it's better for a man just to walk away.

**Willy:** Walk away?

**Bernard:** That's right.

**Willy:** But if you can't walk away?

**Bernard** (*after a slight pause*): I guess that's when it's tough. (*Extending his hand.*) Good-by, Willy.

**Willy** (*shaking Bernard's hand*): Good-by, boy.

**Charley** (*an arm on Bernard's shoulder*): How do you like this kid? Gonna argue a case in front of the Supreme Court.

**Bernard** (*protesting*): Pop!

**Willy** (*genuinely shocked, pained, and happy*): No! The Supreme Court!

**Bernard:** I gotta run. 'By, Dad!

**Charley:** Knock 'em dead, Bernard!

*Bernard goes off.*

**Willy** (*as Charley takes out his wallet*): The Supreme Court! And he didn't even mention it!

**Charley** (*counting out money on the desk*): He don't have to—he's gonna do it.

**Willy:** And you never told him what to do, did you? You never took any interest in him.

**Charley:** My salvation is that I never took any interest in anything. There's some money—fifty dollars. I got an accountant inside.

**Willy:** Charley, look . . . (*With difficulty.*) I got my insurance to pay. If you can manage it—I need a hundred and ten dollars.

*Charley doesn't reply for a moment; merely stops moving.*

**Willy:** I'd draw it from my bank but Linda would know, and I . . .

**Charley:** Sit down, Willy.

*Willy* (*moving toward the chair*): I'm keeping an account of everything, remember. I'll pay every penny back. (*He sits.*)

*Charley*: Now listen to me, Willy.

*Willy*: I want you to know I appreciate . . .

*Charley* (*sitting down on the table*): Willy, what're you doin'? What the hell is goin' on in your head?

*Willy*: Why? I'm simply . . .

*Charley*: I offered you a job. You can make fifty dollars a week. And I won't send you on the road.

*Willy*: I've got a job.

*Charley*: Without pay? What kind of a job is a job without pay? (*He rises.*) Now, look, kid, enough is enough. I'm no genius but I know when I'm being insulted.

*Willy*: Insulted!

*Charley*: Why don't you want to work for me?

*Willy*: What's the matter with you? I've got a job.

*Charley*: Then what're you walkin' in here every week for?

*Willy* (*getting up*): Well, if you don't want me to walk in here—

*Charley*: I am offering you a job.

*Willy*: I don't want your goddam job!

*Charley*: When the hell are you going to grow up?

*Willy* (*furiously*): You big ignoramus, if you say that to me again I'll rap you one! I don't care how big you are! (*He's ready to fight.*)

Pause.

*Charley* (*kindly, going to him*): How much do you need, Willy?

*Willy*: Charley, I'm strapped. I'm strapped. I don't know what to do. I was just fired.

*Charley*: Howard fired you?

*Willy*: That snotnose. Imagine that? I named him. I named him Howard.

*Charley*: Willy, when're you gonna realize that them things don't mean anything? You named him Howard, but you can't sell that. The only thing you got in this world is what you can sell. And the funny thing is that you're a salesman, and you don't know that.

*Willy*: I've always tried to think otherwise, I guess. I always felt that if a man was impressive, and well liked, that nothing—

*Charley*: Why must everybody like you? Who liked J. P. Morgan? Was he impressive? In a Turkish bath he'd look like a butcher. But with his pockets on he was very well liked. Now listen, Willy, I know you don't like me, and nobody can say I'm in love with you, but I'll give you a job because—just for the hell of it, put it that way. Now what do you say?

*Willy*: I—I just can't work for you, Charley.

*Charley*: What're you, jealous of me?

*Willy*: I can't work for you, that's all, don't ask me why.

*Charley* (*angered, takes out more bills*): You been jealous of me all your life, you damned fool! Here, pay your insurance. (*He puts the money in Willy's hand.*)

*Willy*: I'm keeping strict accounts.

*Charley*: I've got some work to do. Take care of yourself. And pay your insurance.

*Willy* (*moving to the right*): Funny, y'know? After all the highways, and the trains, and the appointments, and the years, you end up worth more dead than alive.

*Charley*: Willy, nobody's worth nothin' dead. (*After a slight pause.*) Did you hear what I said?

*Willy stands still, dreaming.*

*Charley*: Willy!

*Willy*: Apologize to Bernard for me when you see him. I didn't mean to argue with him. He's a fine boy. They're all fine boys, and they'll end up big—all of them. Someday they'll all play tennis together. Wish me luck, Charley. He saw Bill Oliver today.

*Charley*: Good luck.

*Willy* (*on the verge of tears*): Charley, you're the only friend I got. Isn't that a remarkable thing? (*He goes out.*)

*Charley*: Jesus!

*Charley stares after him a moment and follows. All light blacks out. Suddenly rau-cous music is heard, and a red glow rises behind the screen at right. Stanley, a young waiter, appears, carrying a table, followed by Happy, who is carrying two chairs.*

*Stanley* (*putting the table down*): That's all right, Mr. Loman, I can handle it myself. (*He turns and takes the chairs from Happy and places them at the table.*)

*Happy* (*glancing around*): Oh, this is better.

*Stanley*: Sure, in the front there you're in the middle of all kinds a noise. Whenever you got a party, Mr. Loman, you just tell me and I'll put you back here. Y'know, there's a lotta people they don't like it private, because when they go out they like to see a lotta action around them because they're sick and tired to stay in the house by theirself. But I know you, you ain't from Hackensack. You know what I mean?

*Happy* (*sitting down*): So how's it coming, Stanley?

*Stanley*: Ah, it's a dog's life. I only wish during the war they'd a took me in the Army. I coulda been dead by now.

*Happy*: My brother's back, Stanley.

*Stanley*: Oh, he come back, heh? From the Far West.

*Happy*: Yeah, big cattle man, my brother, so treat him right. And my father's coming too.

*Stanley*: Oh, your father too!

*Happy*: You got a couple of nice lobsters?

*Stanley*: Hundred per cent, big.

*Happy*: I want them with the claws.

*Stanley*: Don't worry, I don't give you no mice. (*Happy laughs.*) How about some wine? It'll put a head on the meal.

*Happy*: No. You remember, Stanley, that recipe I brought you from overseas? With the champagne in it?

*Stanley*: Oh, yeah, sure. I still got it tacked up yet in the kitchen. But that'll have to cost a buck apiece anyways.

*Happy*: That's all right.

*Stanley*: What'd you, hit a number or somethin'?

*Happy*: No, it's a little celebration. My brother is—I think he pulled off a big deal today. I think we're going into business together.

*Stanley*: Great! That's the best for you. Because a family business, you know what I mean?—that's the best.

*Happy*: That's what I think.

*Stanley*: 'Cause what's the difference? Somebody steals? It's in the family. Know what I mean? (*Sotto voce.*) Like this bartender here. The boss is goin' crazy what kinda leak he's got in the cash register. You put it in but it don't come out.

*Happy* (*raising his head*): Sh!

*Stanley*: What?

*Happy*: You notice I wasn't lookin' right or left, was I?

*Stanley*: No.

*Happy*: And my eyes are closed.

*Stanley*: So what's the—?

*Happy*: Strudel's comin'.

*Stanley* (*catching on, looks around*): Ah, no, there's no—

> He breaks off as a furred, lavishly dressed Girl enters and sits at the next table. Both follow her with their eyes.

*Stanley*: Geez, how'd ya know?

*Happy*: I got radar or something. (*Staring directly at her profile.*) Oooooooo . . . Stanley.

*Stanley*: I think that's for you, Mr. Loman.

*Happy*: Look at that mouth. Oh, God. And the binoculars.

*Stanley*: Geez, you got a life, Mr. Loman.

*Happy*: Wait on her.

*Stanley* (*going to The Girl's table*): Would you like a menu, ma'am?

*Girl*: I'm expecting someone, but I'd like a—

*Happy*: Why don't you bring her—excuse me, miss, do you mind? I sell champagne, and I'd like you to try my brand. Bring her a champagne, Stanley.

*Girl*: That's awfully nice of you.

*Happy*: Don't mention it. It's all company money. (*He laughs.*)

*Girl*: That's a charming product to be selling, isn't it?

*Happy*: Oh, gets to be like everything else. Selling is selling, y'know.

*Girl*: I suppose.

*Happy*: You don't happen to sell, do you?

*Girl*: No, I don't sell.

*Happy*: Would you object to a compliment from a stranger? You ought to be on a magazine cover.

*Girl* (*looking at him a little archly*): I have been.

    *Stanley comes in with a glass of champagne.*

*Happy*: What'd I say before, Stanley? You see? She's a cover girl.

*Stanley*: Oh, I could see, I could see.

*Happy* (*to The Girl*): What magazine?

*Girl*: Oh, a lot of them. (*She takes the drink.*) Thank you.

*Happy*: You know what they say in France, don't you? "Champagne is the drink of the complexion"—Hya, Biff!

    *Biff has entered and sits with Happy.*

*Biff*: Hello, kid. Sorry I'm late.

*Happy*: I just got here. Uh, Miss—?

*Girl*: Forsythe.

*Happy*: Miss Forsythe, this is my brother.

*Biff*: Is Dad here?

*Happy*: His name is Biff. You might've heard of him. Great football player.

*Girl*: Really? What team?

*Happy*: Are you familiar with football?

*Girl*: No, I'm afraid I'm not.

*Happy*: Biff is quarterback with the New York Giants.

*Girl*: Well, that is nice, isn't it? (*She drinks.*)

*Happy*: Good health.

*Girl*: I'm happy to meet you.

*Happy*: That's my name. Hap. It's really Harold, but at West Point they called me Happy.

*Girl* (*now really impressed*): Oh, I see. How do you do? (*She turns her profile.*)

*Biff*: Isn't Dad coming?

*Happy*: You want her?

*Biff*: Oh, I could never make that.

*Happy*: I remember the time that idea would never come into your head. Where's the old confidence, Biff?

*Biff*: I just saw Oliver—

*Happy*: Wait a minute. I've got to see that old confidence again. Do you want her? She's on call.

*Biff*: Oh, no. (*He turns to look at The Girl.*)

*Happy*: I'm telling you. Watch this. (*Turning to The Girl.*) Honey? (*She turns to him.*) Are you busy?

*Girl*: Well, I am . . . but I could make a phone call.

*Happy*: Do that, will you, honey? And see if you can get a friend. We'll be here for a while. Biff is one of the greatest football players in the country.

*Girl* (*standing up*): Well, I'm certainly happy to meet you.

*Happy*: Come back soon.

*Girl*: I'll try.

*Happy*: Don't try, honey, try hard.

*The Girl exits. Stanley follows, shaking his head in bewildered admiration.*

*Happy:* Isn't that a shame now? A beautiful girl like that? That's why I can't get married. There's not a good woman in a thousand. New York is loaded with them, kid!

*Biff:* Hap, look—

*Happy:* I told you she was on call!

*Biff (strangely unnerved):* Cut it out, will ya? I want to say something to you.

*Happy:* Did you see Oliver?

*Biff:* I saw him all right. Now look, I want to tell Dad a couple of things and I want you to help me.

*Happy:* What? Is he going to back you?

*Biff:* Are you crazy? You're out of your goddam head, you know that?

*Happy:* Why? What happened?

*Biff (breathlessly):* I did a terrible thing today, Hap. It's been the strangest day I ever went through. I'm all numb, I swear.

*Happy:* You mean he wouldn't see you?

*Biff:* Well, I waited six hours for him, see? All day. Kept sending my name in. Even tried to date his secretary so she'd get me to him, but no soap.

*Happy:* Because you're not showin' the old confidence, Biff. He remembered you, didn't he?

*Biff (stopping Happy with a gesture):* Finally, about five o'clock, he comes out. Didn't remember who I was or anything. I felt like such an idiot, Hap.

*Happy:* Did you tell him my Florida idea?

*Biff:* He walked away. I saw him for one minute. I got so mad I could've torn the walls down! How the hell did I ever get the idea I was a salesman there? I even believed myself that I'd been a salesman for him! And then he gave me one look and—I realized what a ridiculous lie my whole life has been! We've been talking in a dream for fifteen years. I was a shipping clerk.

*Happy:* What'd you do?

*Biff (with great tension and wonder):* Well, he left, see. And the secretary went out. I was all alone in the waiting-room. I don't know what came over me, Hap. The next thing I know I'm in his office—paneled walls, everything. I can't explain it. I—Hap, I took his fountain pen.

*Happy:* Geez, did he catch you?

*Biff:* I ran out. I ran down all eleven flights. I ran and ran and ran.

*Happy:* That was an awful dumb—what'd you do that for?

*Biff (agonized):* I don't know, I just—wanted to take something, I don't know. You gotta help me, Hap. I'm gonna tell Pop.

*Happy:* You crazy? What for?

*Biff:* Hap, he's got to understand that I'm not the man somebody lends that kind of money to. He thinks I've been spiting him all these years and it's eating him up.

*Happy:* That's just it. You tell him something nice.

*Biff:* I can't.

*Happy:* Say you got a lunch date with Oliver tomorrow.

*Biff:* So what do I do tomorrow?

*Happy:* You leave the house tomorrow and come back at night and say Oliver is thinking it over. And he thinks it over for a couple of weeks, and gradually it fades away and nobody's the worse.

*Biff:* But it'll go on forever!

*Happy:* Dad is never so happy as when he's looking forward to something!

> *Willy enters.*

*Happy:* Hello, scout!

*Willy:* Gee, I haven't been here in years!

> *Stanley has followed Willy in and sets a chair for him. Stanley starts off but Happy stops him.*

*Happy:* Stanley!

> *Stanley stands by, waiting for an order.*

*Biff (going to Willy with guilt, as to an invalid):* Sit down, Pop. You want a drink?

*Willy:* Sure, I don't mind.

*Biff:* Let's get a load on.

*Willy:* You look worried.

*Biff:* N-no. (*To Stanley.*) Scotch all around. Make it doubles.

*Stanley:* Doubles, right. (*He goes.*)

*Willy:* You had a couple already, didn't you?

*Biff:* Just a couple, yeah.

*Willy:* Well, what happened, boy? (*Nodding affirmatively, with a smile.*) Everything go all right?

*Biff (takes a breath, then reaches out and grasps Willy's hand):* Pal . . . (*He is smiling bravely, and Willy is smiling too.*) I had an experience today.

*Happy:* Terrific, Pop.

*Willy:* That so? What happened?

*Biff (high, slightly alcoholic, above the earth):* I'm going to tell you everything from first to last. It's been a strange day. (*Silence. He looks around, composes himself as best he can, but his breath keeps breaking the rhythm of his voice.*) I had to wait quite a while for him, and—

*Willy:* Oliver?

*Biff:* Yeah, Oliver. All day, as a matter of cold fact. And a lot of—instances—facts, Pop, facts about my life came back to me. Who was it, Pop? Who ever said I was a salesman with Oliver?

*Willy:* Well, you were.

*Biff:* No, Dad, I was a shipping clerk.

*Willy:* But you were practically—

*Biff (with determination):* Dad, I don't know who said it first, but I was never a salesman for Bill Oliver.

*Willy:* What're you talking about?

*Biff*: Let's hold on to the facts tonight, Pop. We're not going to get anywhere bullin' around. I was a shipping clerk.

*Willy* (*angrily*): All right, now listen to me—

*Biff*: Why don't you let me finish?

*Willy*: I'm not interested in stories about the past or any crap of that kind because the woods are burning, boys, you understand? There's a big blaze going on all around. I was fired today.

*Biff* (*shocked*): How could you be?

*Willy*: I was fired, and I'm looking for a little good news to tell your mother, because the woman has waited and the woman has suffered. The gist of it is that I haven't got a story left in my head, Biff. So don't give me a lecture about facts and aspects. I am not interested. Now what've you got to say to me?

*Stanley enters with three drinks. They wait until he leaves.*

*Willy*: Did you see Oliver?

*Biff*: Jesus, Dad!

*Willy*: You mean you didn't go up there?

*Happy*: Sure he went up there.

*Biff*: I did. I—saw him. How could they fire you?

*Willy* (*on the edge of his chair*): What kind of a welcome did he give you?

*Biff*: He won't even let you work on commission?

*Willy*: I'm out! (*Driving.*) So tell me, he gave you a warm welcome?

*Happy*: Sure, Pop, sure!

*Biff* (*driven*): Well, it was kind of—

*Willy*: I was wondering if he'd remember you. (*To Happy.*) Imagine, man doesn't see him for ten, twelve years and gives him that kind of welcome!

*Happy*: Damn right!

*Biff* (*trying to return to the offensive*): Pop, look—

*Willy*: You know why he remembered you, don't you? Because you impressed him in those days.

*Biff*: Let's talk quietly and get this down to the facts, huh?

*Willy* (*as though Biff had been interrupting*): Well, what happened? It's great news, Biff. Did he take you into his office or'd you talk in the waiting-room?

*Biff*: Well, he came in, see, and—

*Willy* (*with a big smile*): What'd he say? Betcha he threw his arm around you.

*Biff*: Well, he kinda—

*Willy*: He's a fine man. (*To Happy.*) Very hard man to see, y'know.

*Happy* (*agreeing*): Oh, I know.

*Willy* (*to Biff*): Is that where you had the drinks?

*Biff*: Yeah, he gave me a couple of—no, no!

*Happy* (*cutting in*): He told him my Florida idea.

*Willy*: Don't interrupt. (*To Biff.*) How'd he react to the Florida idea?

*Biff*: Dad, will you give me a minute to explain?

*Willy*: I've been waiting for you to explain since I sat down here! What happened? He took you into his office and what?

*Biff*: Well—I talked. And—and he listened, see.

*Willy*: Famous for the way he listens, y'know. What was his answer?

*Biff*: His answer was—(*He breaks off, suddenly angry.*) Dad, you're not letting me tell you what I want to tell you!

*Willy* (*accusing, angered*): You didn't see him, did you?

*Biff*: I did see him!

*Willy*: What'd you insult him or something? You insulted him, didn't you?

*Biff*: Listen, will you let me out of it, will you just let me out of it!

*Happy*: What the hell!

*Willy*: Tell me what happened!

*Biff* (*to Happy*): I can't talk to him!

> *A single trumpet note jars the ear. The light of green leaves stains the house, which holds the air of night and a dream. Young Bernard enters and knocks on the door of the house.*

*Young Bernard* (*frantically*): Mrs. Loman, Mrs. Loman!

*Happy*: Tell him what happened!

*Biff* (*to Happy*): Shut up and leave me alone!

*Willy*: No, no! You had to go and flunk math!

*Biff*: What math? What're you talking about?

*Young Bernard*: Mrs. Loman, Mrs. Loman!

> *Linda appears in the house, as of old.*

*Willy* (*wildly*): Math, math, math!

*Biff*: Take it easy, Pop.

*Young Bernard*: Mrs. Loman!

*Willy* (*furiously*): If you hadn't flunked you'd've been set by now!

*Biff*: Now, look, I'm gonna tell you what happened, and you're going to listen to me.

*Young Bernard*: Mrs. Loman!

*Biff*: I waited six hours—

*Happy*: What the hell are you saying?

*Biff*: I kept sending in my name but he wouldn't see me. So finally he . . . (*He continues unheard as light fades low on the restaurant.*)

*Young Bernard*: Biff flunked math!

*Linda*: No!

*Young Bernard*: Birnbaum flunked him! They won't graduate him!

*Linda*: But they have to. He's gotta go to the university. Where is he? Biff! Biff!

*Young Bernard*: No, he left. He went to Grand Central.

*Linda*: Grand—You mean he went to Boston?

*Young Bernard*: Is Uncle Willy in Boston?

*Linda*: Oh, maybe Willy can talk to the teacher. Oh, the poor, poor boy!

> *Light on house area snaps out.*

*Biff* (*at the table, now audible, holding up a gold fountain pen*): . . . so I'm washed up with Oliver, you understand? Are you listening to me?

*Willy* (*at a loss*): Yeah, sure. If you hadn't flunked—

*Biff*: Flunked what? What're you talking about?

*Willy*: Don't blame everything on me! I didn't flunk math—you did! What pen?

*Happy*: That was awful dumb, Biff, a pen like that is worth—

*Willy* (*seeing the pen for the first time*): You took Oliver's pen?

*Biff* (*weakening*): Dad, I just explained it to you.

*Willy*: You stole Bill Oliver's fountain pen!

*Biff*: I didn't exactly steal it! That's just what I've been explaining to you!

*Happy*: He had it in his hand and just then Oliver walked in, so he got nervous and stuck it in his pocket!

*Willy*: My God, Biff!

*Biff*: I never intended to do it, Dad!

*Operator's voice*: Standish Arms, good evening!

*Willy* (*shouting*): I'm not in my room!

*Biff* (*frightened*): Dad, what's the matter? (*He and Happy stand up.*)

*Operator*: Ringing Mr. Loman for you!

*Willy*: I'm not there, stop it!

*Biff* (*horrified, gets down on one knee before Willy*): Dad, I'll make good, I'll make good. (*Willy tries to get to his feet. Biff holds him down.*) Sit down now.

*Willy*: No, you're no good, you're no good for anything.

*Biff*: I am, Dad, I'll find something else, you understand? Now don't worry about anything. (*He holds up Willy's face.*) Talk to me, Dad.

*Operator*: Mr. Loman does not answer. Shall I page him?

*Willy* (*attempting to stand, as though to rush and silence the Operator*): No, no, no!

*Happy*: He'll strike something, Pop.

*Willy*: No, no . . .

*Biff* (*desperately, standing over Willy*): Pop, listen! Listen to me! I'm telling you something good. Oliver talked to his partner about the Florida idea. You listening? He—he talked to his partner, and he came to me . . . I'm to be all right, you hear? Dad, listen to me, he said it was just a question of the amount!

*Willy*: Then you . . . got it?

*Happy*: He's gonna be terrific, Pop!

*Willy* (*trying to stand*): Then you got it, haven't you? You got it! You got it!

*Biff* (*agonized, holds Willy down*): No, no. Look, Pop. I'm supposed to have lunch with them tomorrow. I'm just telling you this so you'll know that I can still make an impression, Pop. And I'll make good somewhere, but I can't go tomorrow, see?

*Willy*: Why not? You simply—

*Biff*: But the pen, Pop!

*Willy*: You give it to him and tell him it was an oversight!

*Happy*: Sure, have lunch tomorrow!

*Biff*: I can't say that—

*Willy*: You were doing a crossword puzzle and accidentally used his pen!

*Biff*: Listen, kid, I took those balls years ago, now I walk in with his fountain pen? That clinches it, don't you see? I can't face him like that! I'll try elsewhere.

*Page's voice*: Paging Mr. Loman!

*Willy*: Don't you want to be anything?

*Biff*: Pop, how can I go back?

*Willy*: You don't want to be anything, is that what's behind it?

*Biff* (*now angry at Willy for not crediting his sympathy*): Don't take it that way! You think it was easy walking into that office after what I'd done to him? A team of horses couldn't have dragged me back to Bill Oliver!

*Willy*: Then why'd you go?

*Biff*: Why did I go? Why did I go? Look at you! Look at what's become of you!

    *Off left, The Woman laughs.*

*Willy*: Biff, you're going to go to that lunch tomorrow, or—

*Biff*: I can't go. I've got no appointment!

*Happy*: Biff, for . . . !

*Willy*: Are you spiting me?

*Biff*: Don't take it that way! Goddammit!

*Willy* (*strikes Biff and falters away from the table*): You rotten little louse! Are you spiting me?

*The Woman*: Someone's at the door, Willy!

*Biff*: I'm no good, can't you see what I am?

*Happy* (*separating them*): Hey, you're in a restaurant! Now cut it out, both of you! (*The Girls enter.*) Hello, girls, sit down.

    *The Woman laughs, off left.*

*Miss Forsythe*: I guess we might as well. This is Letta.

*The Woman*: Willy, are you going to wake up?

*Biff* (*ignoring Willy*): How're ya, miss, sit down. What do you drink?

*Miss Forsythe*: Letta might not be able to stay long.

*Letta*: I gotta get up very early tomorrow. I got jury duty. I'm so excited! Were you fellows ever on a jury?

*Biff*: No, but I been in front of them! (*The Girls laugh.*) This is my father.

*Letta*: Isn't he cute? Sit down with us, Pop.

*Happy*: Sit him down, Biff!

*Biff* (*going to him*): Come on, slugger, drink us under the table. To hell with it! Come on, sit down, pal.

    *On Biff's last insistence, Willy is about to sit.*

*The Woman* (*now urgently*): Willy, are you going to answer the door!

    *The Woman's call pulls Willy back. He starts right, befuddled.*

*Biff*: Hey, where are you going?

*Willy*: Open the door.

*Biff*: The door?

*Willy*: The washroom . . . the door . . . where's the door?

*Biff* (*leading Willy to the left*): Just go straight down.

*Willy moves left.*

The Woman: Willy, Willy, are you going to get up, get up, get up, get up?

*Willy exits left.*

Letta: I think it's sweet you bring your daddy along.

Miss Forsythe: Oh, he isn't really your father!

Biff (*at left, turning to her resentfully*): Miss Forsythe, you've just seen a prince walk by. A fine, troubled prince. A hard-working, unappreciated prince. A pal, you understand? A good companion. Always for his boys.

Letta: That's so sweet.

Happy: Well, girls, what's the program? We're wasting time. Come on, Biff. Gather round. Where would you like to go?

Biff: Why don't you do something for him?

Happy: Me!

Biff: Don't you give a damn for him, Hap?

Happy: What're you talking about? I'm the one who—

Biff: I sense it, you don't give a good goddam about him. (*He takes the rolled-up hose from his pocket and puts it on the table in front of Happy.*) Look what I found in the cellar, for Christ's sake. How can you bear to let it go on?

Happy: Me? Who goes away? Who runs off and—

Biff: Yeah, but he doesn't mean anything to you. You could help him—I can't! Don't you understand what I'm talking about? He's going to kill himself, don't you know that?

Happy: Don't I know it! Me!

Biff: Hap, help him! Jesus . . . Help him . . . Help me, help me, I can't bear to look at his face! (*Ready to weep, he hurries out, up right.*)

Happy (*starting after him*): Where are you going?

Miss Forsythe: What's he so mad about?

Happy: Come on, girls, we'll catch up with him.

Miss Forsythe (*as Happy pushes her out*): Say, I don't like that temper of his!

Happy: He's just a little overstrung, he'll be all right!

Willy (*off left, as The Woman laughs*): Don't answer! Don't answer!

Letta: Don't you want to tell your father—

Happy: No, that's not my father. He's just a guy. Come on, we'll catch Biff, and, honey, we're going to paint this town! Stanley, where's the check? Hey, Stanley!

*They exit. Stanley looks toward left.*

Stanley (*calling to Happy indignantly*): Mr. Loman! Mr. Loman!

*Stanley picks up a chair and follows them off. Knocking is heard off left. The Woman enters, laughing. Willy follows her. She is in a black slip; he is buttoning his shirt. Raw, sensuous music accompanies their speech.*

Willy: Will you stop laughing? Will you stop?

The Woman: Aren't you going to answer the door? He'll wake the whole hotel.

*Willy:* I'm not expecting anybody.

*The Woman:* Whyn't you have another drink, honey, and stop being so damn self-centered?

*Willy:* I'm so lonely.

*The Woman:* You know you ruined me, Willy? From now on, whenever you come to the office, I'll see that you go right through to the buyers. No waiting at my desk any more, Willy. You ruined me.

*Willy:* That's nice of you to say that.

*The Woman:* Gee, you are self-centered! Why so sad? You are the saddest self-centeredest soul I ever did see-saw. (*She laughs. He kisses her.*) Come on inside, drummer boy. It's silly to be dressing in the middle of the night. (*As knocking is heard.*) Aren't you going to answer the door?

*Willy:* They're knocking on the wrong door.

*The Woman:* But I felt the knocking. And he heard us talking in here. Maybe the hotel's on fire!

*Willy* (*his terror rising*): It's a mistake.

*The Woman:* Then tell him to go away!

*Willy:* There's nobody there.

*The Woman:* It's getting on my nerves, Willy. There's somebody standing out there and it's getting on my nerves!

*Willy* (*pushing her away from him*): All right, stay in the bathroom here, and don't come out. I think there's a law in Massachusetts about it, so don't come out. It may be that new room clerk. He looked very mean. So don't come out. It's a mistake, there's no fire.

> *The knocking is heard again. He takes a few steps away from her, and she vanishes into the wing. The light follows him, and now he is facing Young Biff, who carries a suitcase. Biff steps toward him. The music is gone.*

*Biff:* Why didn't you answer?

*Willy:* Biff! What are you doing in Boston?

*Biff:* Why didn't you answer? I've been knocking for five minutes, I called you on the phone—

*Willy:* I just heard you. I was in the bathroom and had the door shut. Did anything happen at home?

*Biff:* Dad—I let you down.

*Willy:* What do you mean?

*Biff:* Dad . . .

*Willy:* Biffo, what's this about? (*Putting his arm around Biff.*) Come on, let's go downstairs and get you a malted.

*Biff:* Dad, I flunked math.

*Willy:* Not for the term?

*Biff:* The term. I haven't got enough credits to graduate.

*Willy:* You mean to say Bernard wouldn't give you the answers?

*Biff:* He did, he tried, but I only got a sixty-one.

*Willy:* And they wouldn't give you four points?

*Biff*: Birnbaum refused absolutely. I begged him, Pop, but he won't give me those points. You gotta talk to him before they close the school. Because if he saw the kind of man you are, and you just talked to him in your way, I'm sure he'd come through for me. The class came right before practice, see, and I didn't go enough. Would you talk to him? He'd like you, Pop. You know the way you could talk.

*Willy*: You're on. We'll drive right back.

*Biff*: Oh, Dad, good work! I'm sure he'll change it for you!

*Willy*: Go downstairs and tell the clerk I'm checkin' out. Go right down.

*Biff*: Yes, Sir! See, the reason he hates me, Pop—one day he was late for class so I got up at the blackboard and imitated him. I crossed my eyes and talked with a lithp.

*Willy* (*laughing*): You did? The kids like it?

*Biff*: They nearly died laughing!

*Willy*: Yeah? What'd you do?

*Biff*: The thquare root of thixthy twee is . . . (*Willy bursts out laughing; Biff joins him.*) And in the middle of it he walked in!

*Willy laughs and The Woman joins in offstage.*

*Willy* (*without hesitating*): Hurry downstairs and—

*Biff*: Somebody in there?

*Willy*: No, that was next door.

*The Woman laughs offstage.*

*Biff*: Somebody got in your bathroom!

*Willy*: No, it's the next room, there's a party—

*The Woman* (*enters, laughing. She lisps this*): Can I come in? There's something in the bathtub, Willy, and it's moving!

*Willy looks at Biff, who is staring open-mouthed and horrified at The Woman.*

*Willy*: Ah—you better go back to your room. They must be finished painting by now. They're painting her room so I let her take a shower here. Go back, go back . . . (*He pushes her.*)

*The Woman* (*resisting*): But I've got to get dressed, Willy, I can't—

*Willy*: Get out of here! Go back, go back . . . (*Suddenly striving for the ordinary.*) This is Miss Francis, Biff, she's a buyer. They're painting her room. Go back, Miss Francis, go back . . .

*The Woman*: But my clothes, I can't go out naked in the hall!

*Willy* (*pushing her offstage*): Get outa here! Go back, go back!

*Biff slowly sits down on his suitcase as the argument continues offstage.*

*The Woman*: Where's my stockings? You promised me stockings, Willy!

*Willy*: I have no stockings here!

*The Woman*: You had two boxes of size nine sheers for me, and I want them!

*Willy*: Here, for God's sake, will you get outa here!

*The Woman* (*enters holding a box of stockings*): I just hope there's nobody in the hall. That's all I hope. (*To Biff.*) Are you football or baseball?

*Biff*: Football.

*The Woman* (*angry, humiliated*): That's me too. G'night. (*She snatches her clothes from Willy, and walks out.*)

*Willy* (*after a pause*): Well, better get going. I want to get to the school first thing in the morning. Get my suits out of the closet. I'll get my valise. (*Biff doesn't move.*) What's the matter? (*Biff remains motionless, tears falling.*) She's a buyer. Buys for J. H. Simmons. She lives down the hall—they're painting. You don't imagine—(*He breaks off. After a pause.*) Now listen, pal, she's just a buyer. She sees merchandise in her room and they have to keep it looking just so . . . (*Pause. Assuming command.*) All right, get my suits. (*Biff doesn't move.*) Now stop crying and do as I say. I gave you an order. Biff, I gave you an order! Is that what you do when I give you an order? How dare you cry! (*Putting his arm around Biff.*) Now look, Biff, when you grow up you'll understand about these things. You mustn't—you mustn't overemphasize a thing like this. I'll see Birnbaum first thing in the morning.

*Biff*: Never mind.

*Willy* (*getting down beside Biff*): Never mind! He's going to give you those points. I'll see to it.

*Biff*: He wouldn't listen to you.

*Willy*: He certainly will listen to me. You need those points for the U. of Virginia.

*Biff*: I'm not going there.

*Willy*: Heh? If I can't get him to change that mark you'll make it up in summer school. You've got all summer to—

*Biff* (*his weeping breaking from him*): Dad . . .

*Willy* (*infected by it*): Oh, my boy . . .

*Biff*: Dad . . .

*Willy*: She's nothing to me, Biff. I was lonely, I was terribly lonely.

*Biff*: You—you gave her Mama's stockings! (*His tears break through and he rises to go.*)

*Willy* (*grabbing for Biff*): I gave you an order!

*Biff*: Don't touch me, you—liar!

*Willy*: Apologize for that!

*Biff*: You fake! You phony little fake! (*Overcome, he turns quickly and weeping fully goes out with his suitcase. Willy is left on the floor on his knees.*)

*Willy*: I gave you an order! Biff, come back here or I'll beat you! Come back here! I'll whip you!

*Stanley comes quickly in from the right and stands in front of Willy.*

*Willy* (*shouts at Stanley*): I gave you an order . . .

*Stanley*: Hey, let's pick it up, pick it up, Mr. Loman. (*He helps Willy to his feet.*) Your boys left with the chippies. They said they'll see you at home.

*A second waiter watches some distance away.*

*Willy:* But we were supposed to have dinner together.

*Music is heard, Willy's theme.*

*Stanley:* Can you make it?

*Willy:* I'll—sure, I can make it. (*Suddenly concerned about his clothes.*) Do I—I look all right?

*Stanley:* Sure, you look all right. (*He flicks a speck off Willy's lapel.*)

*Willy:* Here—here's a dollar.

*Stanley:* Oh, your son paid me. It's all right.

*Willy* (*putting it in Stanley's hand*): No, take it. You're a good boy.

*Stanley:* Oh, no, you don't have to . . .

*Willy:* Here—here's some more, I don't need it any more. (*After a slight pause.*) Tell me—is there a seed store in the neighborhood?

*Stanley:* Seeds? You mean like to plant?

*As Willy turns, Stanley slips the money back into his jacket pocket.*

*Willy:* Yes. Carrots, peas . . .

*Stanley:* Well, there's hardware stores on Sixth Avenue, but it may be too late now.

*Willy* (*anxiously*): Oh, I'd better hurry. I've got to get some seeds. (*He starts off to the right.*) I've got to get some seeds, right away. Nothing's planted. I don't have a thing in the ground.

*Willy hurries out as the light goes down. Stanley moves over to the right after him, watches him off. The other waiter has been staring at Willy.*

*Stanley* (*to the waiter*): Well, whatta you looking at?

*The waiter picks up the chairs and moves off right. Stanley takes the table and follows him. The light fades on this area. There is a long pause, the sound of the flute coming over. The light gradually rises on the kitchen, which is empty. Happy appears at the door of the house, followed by Biff. Happy is carrying a large bunch of long-stemmed roses. He enters the kitchen, looks around for Linda. Not seeing her, he turns to Biff, who is just outside the house door, and makes a gesture with his hands, indicating "Not here, I guess." He looks into the living room and freezes. Inside, Linda, unseen, is seated, Willy's coat on her lap. She rises ominously and quietly and moves toward Happy, who backs up into the kitchen, afraid.*

*Happy:* Hey, what're you doing up? (*Linda says nothing but moves toward him implacably.*) Where's Pop? (*He keeps backing to the right, and now Linda is in full view in the doorway to the living room.*) Is he sleeping?

*Linda:* Where were you?

*Happy* (*trying to laugh it off*): We met two girls, Mom, very fine types. Here, we brought you some flowers. (*Offering them to her.*) Put them in your room, Ma.

*She knocks them to the floor at Biff's feet. He has now come inside and closed the door behind him. She stares at Biff, silent.*

*Happy*: Now what'd you do that for? Mom, I want you to have some flowers—

*Linda (cutting Happy off, violently to Biff)*: Don't you care whether he lives or dies?

*Happy (going to the stairs)*: Come upstairs, Biff.

*Biff (with a flare of disgust, to Happy)*: Go away from me! (*To Linda.*) What do you mean, lives or dies? Nobody's dying around here, pal.

*Linda*: Get out of my sight! Get out of here!

*Biff*: I wanna see the boss.

*Linda*: You're not going near him!

*Biff*: Where is he? (*He moves into the living room and Linda follows.*)

*Linda (shouting after Biff)*: You invite him for dinner. He looks forward to it all day—(*Biff appears in his parents' bedroom, looks around, and exits*)—and then you desert him there. There's no stranger you'd do that to!

*Happy*: Why? He had a swell time with us. Listen, when I—(*Linda comes back into the kitchen*)—desert him I hope I don't outlive the day!

*Linda*: Get out of here!

*Happy*: Now look, Mom . . .

*Linda*: Did you have to go to women tonight? You and your lousy rotten whores!

> *Biff re-enters the kitchen.*

*Happy*: Mom, all we did was follow Biff around trying to cheer him up! (*To Biff.*) Boy, what a night you gave me!

*Linda*: Get out of here, both of you, and don't come back! I don't want you tormenting him anymore. Go on now, get your things together! (*To Biff.*) You can sleep in his apartment. (*She starts to pick up the flowers and stops herself.*) Pick up this stuff, I'm not your maid any more. Pick it up, you bum, you!

> *Happy turns his back to her in refusal. Biff slowly moves over and gets down on his knees, picking up the flowers.*

*Linda*: You're a pair of animals! Not one, not another living soul would have had the cruelty to walk out on that man in a restaurant!

*Biff (not looking at her)*: Is that what he said?

*Linda*: He didn't have to say anything. He was so humiliated he nearly limped when he came in.

*Happy*: But, Mom he had a great time with us—

*Biff (cutting him off violently)*: Shut up!

> *Without another word, Happy goes upstairs.*

*Linda*: You! You didn't even go in to see if he was all right!

*Biff (still on the floor in front of Linda, the flowers in his hand; with self-loathing)*: No. Didn't. Didn't do a damned thing. How do you like that, heh? Left him babbling in a toilet.

*Linda*: You louse. You . . .

*Biff*: Now you hit it on the nose! (*He gets up, throws the flowers in the wastebasket.*) The scum of the earth, and you're looking at him!

*Linda*: Get out of here!

*Biff:* I gotta talk to the boss, Mom. Where is he?

*Linda:* You're not going near him. Get out of this house!

*Biff (with absolute assurance, determination):* No. We're gonna have an abrupt conversation, him and me.

*Linda:* You're not talking to him!

*Hammering is heard from outside the house, off right. Biff turns toward the noise.*

*Linda (suddenly pleading):* Will you please leave him alone?

*Biff:* What's he doing out there?

*Linda:* He's planting the garden!

*Biff (quietly):* Now? Oh, my God!

*Biff moves outside, Linda following. The light dies down on them and comes up on the center of the apron as Willy walks into it. He is carrying a flashlight, a hoe and a handful of seed packets. He raps the top of the hoe sharply to fix it firmly, and then moves to the left, measuring off the distance with his foot. He holds the flashlight to look at the seed packets, reading off the instructions. He is in the blue of night.*

*Willy:* Carrots . . . quarter-inch apart. Rows . . . one-foot rows. (*He measures it off.*) One foot. (*He puts down a package and measures off.*) Beets. (*He puts down another package and measures again.*) Lettuce. (*He reads the package, puts it down.*) One foot—(*He breaks off as Ben appears at the right and moves slowly down to him.*) What a proposition, ts, ts. Terrific, terrific. 'Cause she's suffered, Ben, the woman has suffered. You understand me? A man can't go out the way he came in, Ben, a man has got to add up to something. You can't, you can't—(*Ben moves toward him as though to interrupt.*) You gotta consider, now. Don't answer so quick. Remember, it's a guaranteed twenty-thousand-dollar proposition. Now look, Ben, I want you to go through the ins and outs of this thing with me. I've got nobody to talk to, Ben, and the woman has suffered, you hear me?

*Ben (standing still, considering):* What's the proposition?

*Willy:* It's twenty thousand dollars on the barrelhead. Guaranteed, gilt-edged, you understand?

*Ben:* You don't want to make a fool of yourself. They might not honor the policy.

*Willy:* How can they dare refuse? Didn't I work like a coolie to meet every premium on the nose? And now they don't pay off? Impossible!

*Ben:* It's called a cowardly thing, William.

*Willy:* Why? Does it take more guts to stand here the rest of my life ringing up a zero?

*Ben (yielding):* That's a point, William. (*He moves, thinking, turns.*) And twenty thousand—that *is* something one can feel with the hand, it is there.

*Willy (now assured, with rising power):* Oh, Ben, that's the whole beauty of it! I see it like a diamond, shining in the dark, hard and rough, that I can pick up and touch in my hand. Not like—like an appointment! This would not be another damned-fool appointment, Ben, and it changes all the aspects.

Because he thinks I'm nothing, see, and so he spites me. But the funeral—(*Straightening up.*) Ben, that funeral will be massive! They'll come from Maine, Massachusetts, Vermont, New Hampshire! All the old-timers with the strange license plates—that boy will be thunder-struck, Ben, because he never realized—I am known! Rhode Island, New York, New Jersey—I am known, Ben, and he'll see it with his eyes once and for all. He'll see what I am, Ben! He's in for a shock, that boy!

*Ben* (*coming down to the edge of the garden*): He'll call you a coward.

*Willy* (*suddenly fearful*): No, that would be terrible.

*Ben*: Yes. And a damned fool.

*Willy*: No, no, he mustn't, I won't have that! (*He is broken and desperate.*)

*Ben*: He'll hate you, William.

*The gay music of the boys is heard.*

*Willy*: Oh, Ben, how do we get back to all the great times? Used to be so full of light, and comradeship, the sleigh-riding in winter, and the ruddiness on his cheeks. And always some kind of good news coming up, always something nice coming up ahead. And never even let me carry the valises in the house, and simonizing, simonizing that little red car! Why, why can't I give him something and not have him hate me?

*Ben*: Let me think about it. (*He glances at his watch.*) I still have a little time. Remarkable proposition, but you've got to be sure you're not making a fool of yourself.

*Ben drifts off upstage and goes out of sight. Biff comes down from the left.*

*Willy* (*suddenly conscious of Biff, turns and looks up at him, then begins picking up the packages of seeds in confusion*): Where the hell is that seed? (*Indignantly.*) You can't see nothing out here! They boxed in the whole goddam neighborhood!

*Biff*: There are people all around here. Don't you realize that?

*Willy*: I'm busy. Don't bother me.

*Biff* (*taking the hoe from Willy*): I'm saying good-by to you, Pop. (*Willy looks at him, silent, unable to move.*) I'm not coming back any more.

*Willy*: You're not going to see Oliver tomorrow?

*Biff*: I've got no appointment, Dad.

*Willy*: He put his arm around you, and you've got no appointment?

*Biff*: Pop, get this now, will you? Everytime I've left it's been a fight that sent me out of here. Today I realized something about myself and I tried to explain it to you and I—I think I'm just not smart enough to make any sense out of it for you. To hell with whose fault it is or anything like that. (*He takes Willy's arm.*) Let's just wrap it up, heh? Come on in, we'll tell Mom. (*He gently tries to pull Willy to the left.*)

*Willy* (*frozen, immobile, with guilt in his voice*): No, I don't want to see her.

*Biff*: Come on! (*He pulls again, and Willy tries to pull away.*)

*Willy* (*highly nervous*): No, no, I don't want to see her.

*Biff* (*tries to look into Willy's face, as if to find the answer there*): Why don't you want to see her?

*Willy* (*more harshly now*): Don't bother me, will you?

*Biff*: What do you mean, you don't want to see her? You don't want them calling you yellow, do you? This isn't your fault; it's me, I'm a bum. Now come inside! (*Willy strains to get away.*) Did you hear what I said to you?

*Willy pulls away and quickly goes by himself into the house. Biff follows.*

*Linda* (*to Willy*): Did you plant, dear?

*Biff* (*at the door, to Linda*): All right, we had it out. I'm going and I'm not writing any more.

*Linda* (*going to Willy in the kitchen*): I think that's the best way, dear. 'Cause there's no use drawing it out, you'll just never get along.

*Willy doesn't respond.*

*Biff*: People ask where I am and what I'm doing, you don't know, and you don't care. That way it'll be off your mind and you can start brightening up again. All right? That clears it, doesn't it? (*Willy is silent, and Biff goes to him.*) You gonna wish me luck, scout? (*He extends his hand.*) What do you say?

*Linda*: Shake his hand, Willy.

*Willy* (*turning to her, seething with hurt*): There's no necessity to mention the pen at all, y'know.

*Biff* (*gently*): I've got no appointment, Dad.

*Willy* (*erupting fiercely*): He put his arm around . . . ?

*Biff*: Dad, you're never going to see what I am, so what's the use of arguing? If I strike oil I'll send you a check. Meantime forget I'm alive.

*Willy* (*to Linda*): Spite, see?

*Biff*: Shake hands, Dad.

*Willy*: Not my hand.

*Biff*: I was hoping not to go this way.

*Willy*: Well, this is the way you're going. Good-by.

*Biff looks at him a moment, then turns sharply and goes to the stairs.*

*Willy* (*stops him with*): May you rot in hell if you leave this house!

*Biff* (*turning*): Exactly what is it that you want from me?

*Willy*: I want you to know, on the train, in the mountains, in the valleys, wherever you go, that you cut down your life for spite!

*Biff*: No, no.

*Willy*: Spite, spite, is the word of your undoing! And when you're down and out, remember what did it. When you're rotting somewhere beside the railroad tracks, remember, and don't you dare blame it on me!

*Biff*: I'm not blaming it on you!

*Willy*: I won't take the rap for this, you hear?

*Happy comes down the stairs and stands on the bottom step, watching.*

*Biff*: That's just what I'm telling you!

*Willy* (*sinking into a chair at the table, with full accusation*): You're trying to put a knife in me—don't think I don't know what you're doing!

*Biff*: All right, phony! Then let's lay it on the line. (*He whips the rubber tube out of his pocket and puts it on the table.*)

*Happy*: You crazy—

*Linda*: Biff! (*She moves to grab the hose, but Biff holds it down with his hand.*)

*Biff*: Leave it there! Don't move it!

*Willy* (*not looking at it*): What is that?

*Biff*: You know goddam well what that is.

*Willy* (*caged, wanting to escape*): I never saw that.

*Biff*: You saw it. The mice didn't bring it into the cellar! What is this supposed to do, make a hero out of you? This supposed to make me sorry for you?

*Willy*: Never heard of it.

*Biff*: There'll be no pity for you, you hear? No pity!

*Willy* (*to Linda*): You hear the spite!

*Biff*: No, you're going to hear the truth—what you are and what I am!

*Linda*: Stop it!

*Willy*: Spite!

*Happy* (*coming down toward Biff*): You cut it now!

*Biff* (*to Happy*): The man don't know who we are! The man is gonna know! (*To Willy.*) We never told the truth for ten minutes in this house!

*Happy*: We always told the truth!

*Biff* (*turning on him*): You big blow, are you the assistant buyer? You're one of the two assistants to the assistant, aren't you?

*Happy*: Well, I'm practically—

*Biff*: You're practically full of it! We all are! And I'm through with it. (*To Willy.*) Now hear this, Willy, this is me.

*Willy*: I know you!

*Biff*: You know why I had no address for three months? I stole a suit in Kansas City and I was in jail. (*To Linda, who is sobbing.*) Stop crying. I'm through with it.

*Linda turns away from them, her hands covering her face.*

*Willy*: I suppose that's my fault!

*Biff*: I stole myself out of every good job since high school!

*Willy*: And whose fault is that?

*Biff*: And I never got anywhere because you blew me so full of hot air I could never stand taking orders from anybody! That's whose fault it is!

*Willy*: I hear that!

*Linda*: Don't, Biff!

*Biff*: It's goddam time you heard that! I had to be boss big shot in two weeks, and I'm through with it!

*Willy*: Then hang yourself! For spite, hang yourself!

*Biff*: No! Nobody's hanging himself, Willy! I ran down eleven flights with a pen in my hand today. And suddenly I stopped, you hear me? And in the middle of that office building, do you hear this? I stopped in the middle of that building and I saw—the sky. I saw the things that I love in this world. The work and the food and time to sit and smoke. And I looked at the pen and said to myself, what the hell am I grabbing this for? Why am I trying to become what I don't want to be? What am I doing in an office, making a contemptuous, begging fool of myself, when all I want is out there, waiting for me the minute I say I know who I am! Why can't I say that, Willy? (*He tries to make Willy face him, but Willy pulls away and moves to the left.*)

Willy (*with hatred, threateningly*): The door of your life is wide open!

Biff: Pop! I'm a dime a dozen, and so are you!

Willy (*turning on him now in an uncontrolled outburst*): I am not a dime a dozen! I am Willy Loman, and you are Biff Loman!

*Biff starts for Willy, but is blocked by Happy. In his fury, Biff seems on the verge of attacking his father.*

Biff: I am not a leader of men, Willy, and neither are you. You were never anything but a hard-working drummer who landed in the ash can like all the rest of them! I'm one dollar an hour, Willy! I tried seven states and couldn't raise it. A buck an hour! Do you gather my meaning? I'm not bringing home any prizes any more, and you're going to stop waiting for me to bring them home!

Willy (*directly to Biff*): You vengeful, spiteful mutt!

*Biff breaks from Happy. Willy, in fright, starts up the stairs. Biff grabs him.*

Biff (*at the peak of his fury*): Pop, I'm nothing! I'm nothing, Pop. Can't you understand that? There's no spite in it any more. I'm just what I am, that's all.

*Biff's fury has spent itself, and he breaks down, sobbing, holding on to Willy, who dumbly fumbles for Biff's face.*

Willy (*astonished*): What're you doing? What're you doing? (*To Linda.*) Why is he crying?

Biff (*crying, broken*): Will you let me go, for Christ sake? Will you take that phony dream and burn it before something happens? (*Struggling to contain himself, he pulls away and moves to the stairs.*) I'll go in the morning. Put him—put him to bed. (*Exhausted, Biff moves up the stairs to his room.*)

Willy (*after a long pause, astonished, elevated*): Isn't that remarkable? Biff—he likes me!

Linda: He loves you, Willy!

Happy (*deeply moved*): Always did, Pop.

Willy: Oh, Biff! (*Staring wildly.*) He cried! Cried to me. (*He is choking with his love, and now cries out his promise.*) That boy—that boy is going to be magnificent!

*Ben appears in the light just outside the kitchen.*

Ben: Yes, outstanding, with twenty thousand behind him.

Linda (*sensing the racing of his mind, fearfully, carefully*): Now come to bed, Willy. It's all settled now.

*Willy* (*finding it difficult not to rush out of the house*): Yes, we'll sleep. Come on. Go to sleep, Hap.

*Ben:* And it does take a great kind of man to crack the jungle.

*In accents of dread, Ben's idyllic music starts up.*

*Happy* (*his arm around Linda*): I'm getting married, Pop, don't forget it. I'm changing everything. I'm gonna run that department before the year is up. You'll see, Mom. (*He kisses her.*)

*Ben:* The jungle is dark but full of diamonds, Willy.

*Willy turns, moves, listening to Ben.*

*Linda:* Be good. You're both good boys, just act that way, that's all.

*Happy:* 'Night, Pop. (*He goes upstairs.*)

*Linda* (*to Willy*): Come, dear.

*Ben* (*with greater force*): One must go in to fetch a diamond out.

*Willy* (*to Linda, as he moves slowly along the edge of the kitchen, toward the door*): I just want to get settled down, Linda. Let me sit alone for a little.

*Linda* (*almost uttering her fear*): I want you upstairs.

*Willy* (*taking her in his arms*): In a few minutes, Linda. I couldn't sleep right now. Go on, you look awful tired. (*He kisses her.*)

*Ben:* Not like an appointment at all. A diamond is rough and hard to the touch.

*Willy:* Go on now, I'll be right up.

*Linda:* I think this is the only way, Willy.

*Willy:* Sure, it's the best thing.

*Ben:* Best thing!

*Willy:* The only way. Everything is gonna be—go on, kid, get to bed. You look so tired.

*Linda:* Come right up.

*Willy:* Two minutes.

*Linda goes into the living room, then reappears in her bedroom. Willy moves just outside the kitchen door.*

*Willy:* Loves me. (*Wonderingly.*) Always loved me. Isn't that a remarkable thing? Ben, he'll worship me for it!

*Ben* (*with promise*): It's dark there, but full of diamonds.

*Willy:* Can you imagine that magnificence with twenty thousand dollars in his pocket?

*Linda* (*calling from her room*): Willy! Come up!

*Willy* (*calling from the kitchen*): Yes! Yes! Coming! It's very smart, you realize that, don't you, sweetheart? Even Ben sees it. I gotta go, baby. 'By! By! (*Going over to Ben, almost dancing.*) Imagine? When the mail comes he'll be ahead of Bernard again!

*Ben:* A perfect proposition all around.

*Willy:* Did you see how he cried to me? Oh, if I could kiss him, Ben!

*Ben:* Time, William, time!

*Willy*: Oh, Ben, I always knew one way or another we were gonna make it, Biff and I!

*Ben* (*looking at his watch*): The boat. We'll be late. (*He moves slowly off into the darkness.*)

*Willy* (*elegiacally, turning to the house*): Now when you kick off, boy, I want a seventy-yard boot, and get right down the field under the ball, and when you hit, hit low and hit hard, because it's important, boy. (*He swings around and faces the audience.*) There's all kinds of important people in the stands, and the first thing you know . . . (*Suddenly realizing he is alone.*) Ben! Ben, where do I . . . ? (*He makes a sudden movement of search.*) Ben, how do I . . . ?

*Linda* (*calling*): Willy, you coming up?

*Willy* (*uttering a gasp of fear, whirling about as if to quiet her*): Sh! (*He turns around as if to find his way; sounds, faces, voices, seem to be swarming in upon him and he flicks at them, crying.*) Sh! Sh! (*Suddenly music, faint and high, stops him. It rises in intensity, almost to an unbearable scream. He goes up and down on his toes, and rushes off around the house.*) Shhh!

*Linda*: Willy?

*There is no answer. Linda waits. Biff gets up off his bed. He is still in his clothes. Happy sits up. Biff stands listening.*

*Linda* (*with real fear*): Willy, answer me! Willy!

*There is the sound of a car starting and moving away at full speed.*

*Linda*: No!

*Biff* (*rushing down the stairs*): Pop!

*As the car speeds off, the music crashes down in a frenzy of sound, which becomes the soft pulsation of a single cello string. Biff slowly returns to his bedroom. He and Happy gravely don their jackets. Linda slowly walks out of her room. The music has developed into a dead march. The leaves of day are appearing over everything. Charley and Bernard, somberly dressed, appear and knock on the kitchen door. Biff and Happy slowly descend the stairs to the kitchen as Charley and Bernard enter. All stop a moment when Linda, in clothes of mourning, bearing a little bunch of roses, comes through the draped doorway into the kitchen. She goes to Charley and takes his arm. Now all move toward the audience, through the wall-line of the kitchen. At the limit of the apron, Linda lays down the flowers, kneels, and sits back on her heels. All stare down at the grave.*

## REQUIEM

*Charley*: It's getting dark, Linda.

*Linda doesn't react. She stares at the grave.*

*Biff*: How about it, Mom? Better get some rest, heh? They'll be closing the gate soon.

*Linda makes no move. Pause.*

*Happy* (*deeply angered*): He had no right to do that! There was no necessity for it. We would've helped him.

*Charley* (*grunting*): Hmmm.

*Biff*: Come along, Mom.

*Linda*: Why didn't anybody come?

*Charley*: It was a very nice funeral.

*Linda*: But where are all the people he knew? Maybe they blame him.

*Charley*: Naa. It's a rough world, Linda. They wouldn't blame him.

*Linda*: I can't understand it. At this time especially. First time in thirty-five years we were just about free and clear. He only needed a little salary. He was even finished with the dentist.

*Charley*: No man only needs a little salary.

*Linda*: I can't understand it.

*Biff*: There were a lot of nice days. When he'd come home from a trip; or on Sundays, making the stoop; finishing the cellar; putting on the new porch; when he built the extra bathroom; and put up the garage. You know something, Charley, there's more of him in that front stoop than in all the sales he ever made.

*Charley*: Yeah. He was a happy man with a batch of cement.

*Linda*: He was so wonderful with his hands.

*Biff*: He had the wrong dreams. All, all, wrong.

*Happy* (*almost ready to fight Biff*): Don't say that!

*Biff*: He never knew who he was.

*Charley* (*stopping Happy's movement and reply. To Biff.*): Nobody dast blame this man. You don't understand: Willy was a salesman. And for a salesman, there is no rock bottom to the life. He don't put a bolt to a nut, he don't tell you the law or give you medicine. He's a man out there in the blue, riding on a smile and a shoeshine. And when they start not smiling back—that's an earthquake. And then you get yourself a couple of spots on your hat, and you're finished. Nobody dast blame this man. A salesman is got to dream, boy. It comes with the territory.

*Biff*: Charley, the man didn't know who he was.

*Happy* (*infuriated*): Don't say that!

*Biff*: Why don't you come with me, Happy?

*Happy*: I'm not licked that easily. I'm staying right in this city, and I'm gonna beat this racket! (*He looks at Biff, his chin set.*) The Loman Brothers!

*Biff*: I know who I am, kid.

*Happy*: All right, boy. I'm gonna show you and everybody else that Willy Loman did not die in vain. He had a good dream. It's the only dream you can have—to come out number-one man. He fought it out here, and this is where I'm gonna win it for him.

*Biff* (*with a hopeless glance at Happy, bends toward his mother*): Let's go, Mom.

*Linda*: I'll be with you in a minute. Go on, Charley. (*He hesitates.*) I want to, just for a minute. I never had a chance to say good-by.

*Charley moves away, followed by Happy. Biff remains a slight distance up and left of Linda. She sits there, summoning herself. The flute begins, not far away, playing behind her speech.*

Linda: Forgive me, dear. I can't cry. I don't know what it is, but I can't cry. I don't understand it. Why did you ever do that? Help me, Willy, I can't cry. It seems to me that you're just on another trip. I keep expecting you. Willy, dear, I can't cry. Why did you do it? I search and search and search, and I can't understand it, Willy. I made the last payment on the house today. Today, dear. And there'll nobody home. (*A sob rises in her throat.*) We're free and clear. (*Sobbing more fully, released.*) We're free. (*Biff comes slowly toward her.*) We're free . . . We're free . . .

*Biff lifts her to her feet and moves out up right with her in his arms. Linda sobs quietly. Bernard and Charley come together and follow them, followed by Happy. Only the music of the flute is left on the darkening stage as over the house the hard towers of the apartment buildings rise into sharp focus, and—*

THE CURTAIN FALLS

Compare:

Death of a Salesman *and Arthur Miller's essay* "Tragedy and the Common Man" (page 1726).

## Tennessee Williams

*Tennessee Williams*

*Tennessee Williams (1914–1983) was born Thomas Lanier Williams in Columbus, Mississippi, went to high school in St. Louis, and was graduated from the University of Iowa. As an undergraduate, he saw a performance of Ibsen's Ghosts and determined to be a playwright himself. His family bore a close resemblance to the Wingfields in* The Glass Menagerie: *his mother came from a line of Southern blue-bloods (Tennessee pioneers); his sister Rose suffered from incapacitating shyness; and as a young man Williams himself, like Tom, worked at a job he disliked (in a shoe factory where his father worked), wrote poetry, sought refuge in moviegoing, and finally left home to wander and hold odd jobs. He worked as a bellhop in a New Orleans hotel, a teletype operator in Jacksonville, Florida, an usher and a waiter in New York. In 1945* The Glass Menagerie *scored a success on Broadway, winning a Drama Critics Circle award. Two years later Williams received a Pulitzer Prize for* A Streetcar Named Desire, *a grim, powerful study of a woman's illusions and frustrations, set in New Orleans. In 1955, another Pulitzer Prize went to* Cat on a Hot Tin Roof. *Besides other plays, including* Summer and Smoke *(1948),* Sweet Bird of Youth *(1959),* The Night of the Iguana *(1961),* Small Craft Warnings *(1973),* Clothes for a Summer Hotel *(1980), and* A House Not Meant to Stand *(1981), Williams wrote two novels, poetry, essays, short stories, and* Memoirs *(1975).*

> Nobody, not even the rain, has such small hands.
> E. E. Cummings

Characters

*Amanda Wingfield,* the mother. A little woman of great but confused vitality cling-ing frantically to another time and place. Her characterization must be carefully created, not copied from type. She is not paranoiac, but her life is paranoia. There is much to admire in Amanda, and as much to love and pity as there is to laugh at. Certainly she has endurance and a kind of heroism, and though her foolishness makes her unwittingly cruel at times, there is tenderness in her slight person.

*Laura Wingfield,* her daughter. Amanda, having failed to establish contact with reality, continues to live vitally in her illusions, but Laura's situation is even graver. A childhood illness has left her crippled, one leg slightly shorter than the other, and held in a brace. This defect need not be more than suggested on the stage. Stemming from this, Laura's separation increases till she is like a piece of her own glass collection, too exquisitely fragile to move from the shelf.

Tom Wingfield, her son. And the narrator of the play. A poet with a job in a warehouse. His nature is not remorseless, but to escape from a trap he has to act without pity.

Jim O'Connor, the gentleman caller. A nice, ordinary, young man.

Scene. An alley in St. Louis.

Part I. Preparation for a Gentleman Caller.
Part II. The Gentleman Calls.

Time. Now and the Past.

## Scene I

The Wingfield apartment is in the rear of the building, one of those vast hive-like conglomerations of cellular living-units that flower as warty growths in overcrowded urban centers of lower middle-class population and are symptomatic of the impulse of this largest and fundamentally enslaved section of American society to avoid fluidity and differentiation and to exist and function as one interfused mass of automatism.

The apartment faces an alley and is entered by a fire-escape, a structure whose name is a touch of accidental poetic truth, for all of these huge buildings are always burning with the slow and implacable fires of human desperation. The fire-escape is included in the set—that is, the landing of it and steps descending from it.

The scene is memory and is therefore unrealistic. Memory takes a lot of poetic license. It omits some details; others are exaggerated, according to the emotional value of the articles it touches, for memory is seated predominantly in the heart. The interior is therefore rather dim and poetic.

At the rise of the curtain, the audience is faced with the dark, grim rear wall of the Wingfield tenement. This building, which runs parallel to the footlights, is flanked on both sides by dark, narrow alleys which run into murky canyons of tangled clotheslines, garbage cans, and the sinister latticework of neighboring fire-escapes. It is up and down these side alleys that exterior entrances and exits are made, during the play. At the end of Tom's opening commentary, the dark tenement wall slowly reveals (by means of a transparency) the interior of the ground floor Wingfield apartment.

Downstage is the living room, which also serves as a sleeping room for Laura, the sofa unfolding to make her bed. Upstage, center, and divided by a wide arch or second proscenium with transparent faded portieres (or second curtain), is the dining room. In an old-fashioned what-not in the living room are seen scores of transparent glass animals. A blown-up photograph of the father hangs on the wall of the living room, facing *the audience, to the left of the archway. It is the face of a very handsome young man in a doughboy's First World War cap. He is gallantly smiling, ineluctably smiling, as if to say, "I will be smiling forever."*

*The audience hears and sees the opening scene in the dining room through both the transparent fourth wall of the building and the transparent gauze portieres of the dining-room arch. It is during this revealing scene that the fourth wall slowly ascends, out of sight. This transparent exterior wall is not brought down again until the very end of the play, during Tom's final speech.*

*The narrator is an undisguised convention of the play. He takes whatever license with dramatic convention as is convenient to his purposes.*

*Tom enters dressed as a merchant sailor from the alley, stage left, and strolls across the front of the stage to the fire-escape. There he stops and lights a cigarette. He addresses the audience.*

Tom: Yes, I have tricks in my pocket, I have things up my sleeve. But I am the opposite of a stage magician. He gives you illusion that has the appearance of truth. I give you truth in the pleasant disguise of illusion. To begin with, I turn back time. I reverse it to that quaint period, the thirties, when the huge middle class of America was matriculating in a school for the blind. Their eyes had failed them, or they had failed their eyes, and so they were having their fingers pressed forcibly down on the fiery Braille alphabet of a dissolving economy. In Spain there was revolution. Here there was only shouting and confusion. In Spain there was Guernica. Here there were disturbances of labor, sometimes pretty violent, in otherwise peaceful cities such as Chicago, Cleveland, St. Louis. . . . This is the social background of the play.

**(Music.)**

The play is memory. Being a memory play, it is dimly lighted, it is sentimental, it is not realistic. In memory everything seems to happen to music. That explains the fiddle in the wings. I am the narrator of the play, and also a character in it. The other characters are my mother, Amanda, my sister, Laura, and a gentleman caller who appears in the final scenes. He is the most realistic character in the play, being an emissary from a world of reality that we were somehow set apart from. But since I have a poet's weakness for symbols, I am using this character also as a symbol; he is the long delayed but always expected something that we live for. There is a fifth character in the play who doesn't appear except in this larger-than-life photograph over the mantel. This is our father who left us a long time ago. He was a telephone man who fell in love with long distances; he gave up his job with the telephone company and skipped the light fantastic out of town. . . . The last we heard of him was a picture post-card from Mazatlan, on the Pacific coast of Mexico, containing a message of two words—"Hello—Good-bye!" and an address. I think the rest of the play will explain itself. . . .

*Amanda's voice becomes audible through the portieres.*

**(Screen Legend: "Où Sont Les Neiges.")°**

*He divides the portieres and enters the upstage area.*

    *Amanda and Laura are seated at a drop-leaf table. Eating is indicated by gestures without food or utensils. Amanda faces the audience. Tom and Laura are seated in profile.*

    *The interior has lit up softly and through the scrim we see Amanda and Laura seated at the table in the upstage area.*

*Amanda* (*calling*): Tom?

*Tom:* Yes, Mother.

*Amanda:* We can't say grace until you come to the table!

*Tom:* Coming, Mother. (*He bows slightly and withdraws, reappearing a few moments later in his place at the table.*)

*Amanda* (*to her son*): Honey, don't push with your fingers. If you have to push with something, the thing to push with is a crust of bread. And chew—chew! Animals have sections in their stomachs which enable them to digest food without mastication, but human beings are supposed to chew their food before they swallow it down. Eat food leisurely, son, and really enjoy it. A well-cooked meal has lots of delicate flavors that have to be held in the mouth for appreciation. So chew your food and give your salivary glands a chance to function!

*Tom deliberately lays his imaginary fork down and pushes his chair back from the table.*

*Tom:* I haven't enjoyed one bite of this dinner because of your constant directions on how to eat it. It's you that makes me rush through meals with your hawk-like attention to every bite I take. Sickening—spoils my appetite—all this discussion of animals' secretion—salivary glands—mastication!

*Amanda* (*lightly*): Temperament like a Metropolitan star! (*He rises and crosses downstage.*) You're not excused from the table.

*Tom:* I am getting a cigarette.

*Amanda:* You smoke too much.

    *Laura rises.*

*Laura:* I'll bring in the blanc mange.

    *He remains standing with his cigarette by the portieres during the following.*

*Amanda* (*rising*): No, sister, no, sister—you be the lady this time and I'll be the darky.

*Laura:* I'm already up.

*Amanda:* Resume your seat, little sister—I want you to stay fresh and pretty—for gentlemen callers!

*Laura:* I'm not expecting any gentlemen callers.

---

(*Legend . . . Neiges.*"): "Where are the snows (of yesteryear)?" A slide bearing this line by the French poet François Villon is to be projected on a stage wall.

*Amanda* (*crossing out to kitchenette. Airily*): Sometimes they come when they are least expected! Why, I remember one Sunday afternoon in Blue Mountain— (*Enters kitchenette.*)

*Tom:* I know what's coming!

*Laura:* Yes. But let her tell it.

*Tom:* Again?

*Laura:* She loves to tell it.

*Amanda returns with bowl of dessert.*

*Amanda:* One Sunday afternoon in Blue Mountain—your mother received—*seventeen!*—gentlemen callers! Why, sometimes there weren't chairs enough to accommodate them all. We had to send the nigger over to bring in folding chairs from the parish house.

*Tom* (*remaining at portieres*): How did you entertain those gentlemen callers?

*Amanda:* I understood the art of conversation!

*Tom:* I bet you could talk.

*Amanda:* Girls in those days *knew* how to talk, I can tell you.

*Tom:* Yes?

**(Image: Amanda As A Girl On A Porch Greeting Callers.)**

*Amanda:* They knew how to entertain their gentlemen callers. It wasn't enough for a girl to be possessed of a pretty face and a graceful figure—although I wasn't slighted in either respect. She also needed to have a nimble wit and a tongue to meet all occasions.

*Tom:* What did you talk about?

*Amanda:* Things of importance going on in the world! Never anything coarse or common or vulgar. (*She addresses Tom as though he were seated in the vacant chair at the table though he remains by portieres. He plays this scene as though he held the book.*) My callers were gentlemen—all! Among my callers were some of the most prominent young planters of the Mississippi Delta—planters and sons of planters!

*Tom motions for music and a spot of light on Amanda. Her eyes lift, her face glows, her voice becomes rich and elegiac.*

**(Screen Legend: "Où Sont Les Neiges.")**

There was young Champ Laughlin who later became vice-president of the Delta Planters Bank. Hadley Stevenson who was drowned in Moon Lake and left his widow one hundred and fifty thousand in Government bonds. There were the Cutrere brothers, Wesley and Bates. Bates was one of my bright particular beaux! He got in a quarrel with that wild Wainright boy. They shot it out on the floor of Moon Lake Casino. Bates was shot through the stomach. Died in the ambulance on his way to Memphis. His widow was also well-provided for, came into eight or ten thousand acres, that's all. She married him on the rebound—never loved her—carried my picture on him the night he died! And there was that boy that every girl in the Delta had set her cap for! That beautiful, brilliant young Fitzhugh boy from Green County!

*Tom*: What did he leave his widow?

*Amanda*: He never married! Gracious, you talk as though all of my old admirers had turned up their toes to the daisies!

*Tom*: Isn't this the first you mentioned that still survives?

*Amanda*: That Fitzhugh boy went North and made a fortune—came to be known as the Wolf of Wall Street! He had the Midas touch, whatever he touched turned to gold! And I could have been Mrs. Duncan J. Fitzhugh, mind you! But—I picked your *father*!

*Laura* (*rising*): Mother, let me clear the table.

*Amanda*: No dear, you go in front and study your typewriter chart. Or practice your shorthand a little. Stay fresh and pretty!—It's almost time for our gentlemen callers to start arriving. (*She flounces girlishly toward the kitchenette.*) How many do you suppose we're going to entertain this afternoon?

*Tom throws down the paper and jumps up with a groan.*

*Laura* (*alone in the dining room*): I don't believe we're going to receive any, Mother.

*Amanda* (*reappearing, airily*): What? No one—not one? You must be joking! (*Laura nervously echoes her laugh. She slips in a fugitive manner through the half-open portieres and draws them gently behind her. A shaft of very clear light is thrown on her face against the jaded tapestry of the curtains.*) (**Music: "The Glass Menagerie" Under Faintly.**) (*Lightly.*) Not one gentleman caller? It can't be true! There must be a flood, there must have been a tornado!

*Laura*: It isn't a flood, it's not a tornado, Mother. I'm just not popular like you were in Blue Mountain. . . . (*Tom utters another groan. Laura glances at him with a faint, apologetic smile. Her voice catching a little.*) Mother's afraid I'm going to be an old maid.

**(The Scene Dims Out With "Glass Menagerie" Music.)**

## Scene II

*"Laura, Haven't You Ever Liked Some Boy?"*

*On the dark stage the screen is lighted with the image of blue roses.*

*Gradually Laura's figure becomes apparent and the screen goes out.*

*The music subsides.*

*Laura is seated in the delicate ivory chair at the small clawfoot table.*

*She wears a dress of soft violet material for a kimono—her hair tied back from her forehead with a ribbon.*

*She is washing and polishing her collection of glass.*

*Amanda appears on the fire-escape steps. At the sound of her ascent, Laura catches her breath, thrusts the bowl of ornaments away and seats herself stiffly before the* diagram of the typewriter keyboard as though it held her spellbound. Something has happened to Amanda. It is written in her face as she climbs to the landing: a look that is grim and hopeless and a little absurd.

She has on one of those cheap or imitation velvety-looking cloth coats with imitation fur collar. Her hat is five or six years old, one of those dreadful cloche hats that were worn in the late twenties, and she is clasping an enormous black patent-leather pocket-book with nickel clasp and initials. This is her full-dress outfit, the one she usually wears to the D.A.R.

Before entering she looks through the door.

She purses her lips, opens her eyes wide, rolls them upward and shakes her head.

Then she slowly lets herself in the door. Seeing her mother's expression Laura touches her lips with a nervous gesture.

Laura: Hello, Mother, I was—(She makes a nervous gesture toward the chart on the wall. Amanda leans against the shut door and stares at Laura with a martyred look.)

Amanda: Deception? Deception? (She slowly removes her hat and gloves, continuing the swift suffering stare. She lets the hat and gloves fall on the floor—a bit of acting.)

Laura (shakily): How was the D.A.R. meeting? (Amanda slowly opens her purse and removes a dainty white handkerchief which she shakes out delicately and delicately touches to her lips and nostrils.) Didn't you go to the D.A.R. meeting, Mother?

Amanda (faintly, almost inaudibly):—No.—No. (Then more forcibly.) I did not have the strength—to go to the D.A.R. In fact, I did not have the courage! I wanted to find a hole in the ground and hide myself in it forever! (She crosses slowly to the wall and removes the diagram of the typewriter keyboard. She holds it in front of her for a second, staring at it sweetly and sorrowfully—then bites her lips and tears it in two pieces.)

Laura (faintly): Why did you do that, Mother? (Amanda repeats the same procedure with the chart of the Gregg Alphabet.) Why are you—

Amanda: Why? Why? How old are you, Laura?

Laura: Mother, you know my age.

Amanda: I thought that you were an adult; it seems that I was mistaken. (She crosses slowly to the sofa and sinks down and stares at Laura.)

Laura: Please don't stare at me, Mother.

Amanda closes her eyes and lowers her head. Count ten.

Amanda: What are we going to do, what is going to become of us, what is the future?

Count ten.

Laura: Has something happened, Mother? (Amanda draws a long breath and takes out the handkerchief again. Dabbing process.) Mother, has—something happened?

Amanda: I'll be all right in a minute. I'm just bewildered—(count five)—by life. . .

Laura: Mother, I wish that you would tell me what's happened.

*Amanda:* As you know, I was supposed to be inducted into my office at the D.A.R. this afternoon. **(Image: A Swarm of Typewriters.)** But I stopped off at Rubicam's Business College to speak to your teachers about your having a cold and ask them what progress they thought you were making down there.

*Laura:* Oh . . .

*Amanda:* I went to the typing instructor and introduced myself as your mother. She didn't know who you were. Wingfield, she said. We don't have any such student enrolled at the school! I assured her she did, that you had been going to classes since early in January. "I wonder," she said, "if you could be talking about that terribly shy little girl who dropped out of school after only a few days' attendance?" "No," I said, "Laura, my daughter, has been going to school every day for the past six weeks!" "Excuse me," she said. She took the attendance book out and there was your name, unmistakably printed, and all the dates you were absent until they decided that you had dropped out of school. I still said, "No, there must have been some mistake! There must have been some mix-up in the records!" And she said, "No—I remember her perfectly now. Her hand shook so that she couldn't hit the right keys! The first time we gave a speed-test, she broke down completely—was sick at the stomach and almost had to be carried into the wash-room! After that morning she never showed up any more. We phoned the house but never got any answer"—while I was working at Famous and Barr, I suppose, demonstrating those—Oh! I felt so weak I could barely keep on my feet. I had to sit down while they got me a glass of water! Fifty dollars' tuition, all of our plans—my hopes and ambitions for you—just gone up the spout, just gone up the spout like that. (*Laura draws a long breath and gets awkwardly to her feet. She crosses to the victrola and winds it up.*) What are you doing?

*Laura:* Oh! (*She releases the handle and returns to her seat.*)

*Amanda:* Laura, where have you been going when you've gone out pretending that you were going to business college?

*Laura:* I've just been going out walking.

*Amanda:* That's not true.

*Laura:* It is. I just went walking.

*Amanda:* Walking? Walking? In winter? Deliberately courting pneumonia in that light coat? Where did you walk to, Laura?

*Laura:* It was the lesser of two evils, Mother. **(Image: Winter Scene In Park.)** I couldn't go back. I—threw up—on the floor!

*Amanda:* From half past seven till after five every day you mean to tell me you walked around in the park, because you wanted to make me think that you were still going to Rubicam's Business College?

*Laura:* It wasn't as bad as it sounds. I went inside places to get warmed up.

*Amanda:* Inside where?

*Laura:* I went in the art museum and the bird-houses at the Zoo. I visited the penguins every day! Sometimes I did without lunch and went to the movies.

Lately I've been spending most of my afternoons in the Jewel-box, that big glass house where they raise the tropical flowers.

*Amanda:* You did all this to deceive me, just for the deception? (*Laura looks down.*) Why?

*Laura:* Mother, when you're disappointed, you get that awful suffering look on your face, like the picture of Jesus' mother in the museum!

*Amanda:* Hush!

*Laura:* I couldn't face it.

*Pause. A whisper of strings.*

### (Legend: "The Crust Of Humility.")

*Amanda (hopelessly fingering the huge pocketbook):* So what are we going to do the rest of our lives? Stay home and watch the parades go by? Amuse ourselves with the glass menagerie, darling? Eternally play those worn-out phonograph records your father left as a painful reminder of him? We won't have a business career—we've given that up because it gave us nervous indigestion! (*Laughs wearily.*) What is there left but dependence all our lives? I know so well what becomes of unmarried women who aren't prepared to occupy a position. I've seen such pitiful cases in the South—barely tolerated spinsters living upon the grudging patronage of sister's husband or brother's wife!— stuck away in some little mouse-trap of a room—encouraged by one in-law to visit another—little birdlike women without any nest—eating the crust of humility all their life! Is that the future that we've mapped out for ourselves? I swear it's the only alternative I can think of! It isn't a very pleasant alternative, is it? Of course—some girls *do marry.* (*Laura twists her hands nervously.*) Haven't you ever liked some boy?

*Laura:* Yes I liked one once. (*Rises.*) I came across his picture a while ago.

*Amanda (with some interest):* He gave you his picture?

*Laura:* No, it's in the year-book.

*Amanda (disappointed):* Oh—a high-school boy.

### (Screen Image: Jim As A High-School Hero Bearing A Silver Cup.)

*Laura:* Yes. His name was Jim. (*Laura lifts the heavy annual from the clawfoot table.*) Here he is in *The Pirates of Penzance.*

*Amanda (absently):* The what?

*Laura:* The operetta the senior class put on. He had a wonderful voice and we sat across the aisle from each other Mondays, Wednesdays, and Fridays in the Aud. Here he is with the silver cup for debating! See his grin?

*Amanda (absently):* He must have had a jolly disposition.

*Laura:* He used to call me—Blue Roses.

### (Image: Blue Roses.)

*Amanda:* Why did he call you such a name as that?

*Laura*: When I had that attack of pleurosis—he asked me what was the matter
when I came back. I said pleurosis—he thought that I said Blue Roses! So
that's what he always called me after that. Whenever he saw me, he'd holler,
"Hello, Blue Roses!" I didn't care for the girl he went out with. Emily
Meisenbach. Emily was the best-dressed girl at Soldan. She never struck me,
though, as being sincere . . . It says in the Personal Section—they're
engaged. That's—six years ago! They must be married by now.
*Amanda*: Girls that aren't cut out for business careers usually wind up married to
some nice man. (*Gets up with a spark of revival.*) Sister, that's what you'll do!

*Laura utters a startled, doubtful laugh. She reaches quickly for a piece of glass.*

*Laura*: But, Mother—
*Amanda*: Yes? (*Crossing to phonograph.*)
*Laura* (*in a tone of frightened apology*): I'm—crippled!

**(Image: Screen.)**

*Amanda*: Nonsense! Laura, I've told you never, never to use that word. Why,
you're not crippled, you just have a little defect—hardly noticeable, even!
When people have some slight disadvantage like that, they cultivate other
things to make up for it—develop charm—and vivacity—and—*charm!*
That's all you have to do! (*She turns again to the phonograph.*) One thing your
father had *plenty of*—was *charm!*

*Tom motions to the fiddle in the wings.*

**(The Scene Fades Out With Music.)**

## Scene III

**(Legend On The Screen: "After The Fiasco—")**

*Tom speaks from the fire-escape landing.*

*Tom*: After the fiasco at Rubicam's Business College, the idea of getting a gentleman caller for Laura began to play a more important part in Mother's calculations. It became an obsession. Like some archetype of the universal unconscious, the image of the gentleman caller haunted our small apartment. . . .
**(Image: Young Man At Door With Flowers.)** An evening at home rarely
passed without some allusion to this image, this spectre, this hope. . . . Even
when he wasn't mentioned, his presence hung in Mother's preoccupied look
and in my sister's frightened, apologetic manner—hung like a sentence
passed upon the Wingfields! Mother was a women of action as well as words.
She began to take logical steps in the planned direction. Late that winter
and in the early spring—realizing that extra money would be needed to properly feather the nest and plume the bird—she conducted a vigorous cam-

paign on the telephone, roping in subscribers to one of those magazines for matrons called *The Home-maker's Companion*, the type of journal that features the serialized sublimations of ladies of letters who think in terms of delicate cup-like breasts, slim, tapering waists, rich, creamy thighs, eyes like wood-smoke in autumn, fingers that soothe and caress like strains of music, bodies as powerful as Etruscan sculpture.

**(Screen Image: Glamor Magazine Cover.)**

*Amanda enters with phone on long extension cord. She is spotted in the dim stage.*

*Amanda:* Ida Scott? This is Amanda Wingfield! We *missed* you at the D.A.R. last Monday! I said to myself: She's probably suffering with that sinus condition! How is that sinus condition? Horrors! Heaven have mercy!—You're a Christian martyr, yes, that's what you are, a Christian martyr! Well, I just now happened to notice that your subscription to the *Companion's* about to expire! Yes, it expires with the next issue, honey!—just when that wonderful new serial by Bessie Mae Hopper is getting off to such an exciting start. Oh, honey, it's something that you can't miss! You remember how *Gone With the Wind* took everybody by storm? You simply couldn't go out if you hadn't read it. All everybody *talked* was Scarlett O'Hara. Well, this is a book that critics already compare to *Gone With the Wind*. It's the *Gone With the Wind* of the post-World War generation!—What?—Burning?—Oh, honey, don't let them burn, go take a look in the oven and I'll hold the wire! Heavens—I think she's hung up!

**(Dim Out.)**

**(Legend On Screen: "You Think I'm In Love With Continental Shoemakers?")**

*Before the stage is lighted, the violent voices of Tom and Amanda are heard. They are quarreling behind the portieres. In front of them stands Laura with clenched hands and panicky expression.*

*A clear pool of light on her figure throughout this scene.*

*Tom:* What in Christ's name am I—
*Amanda (shrilly):* Don't you use that—
*Tom:* Supposed to do!
*Amanda:* Expression! Not in my—
*Tom:* Ohhh!
*Amanda:* Presence! Have you gone out of your senses?
*Tom:* I have, that's true, *driven* out!
*Amanda:* What is the matter with you, you—big—big—IDIOT!
*Tom:* Look—I've got *no thing*, no single thing—
*Amanda:* Lower your voice!

*Tom:* In my life here that I can call my OWN! Everything is—

*Amanda:* Stop that shouting!

*Tom:* Yesterday you confiscated my books! You had the nerve to—

*Amanda:* I took that horrible novel back to the library—yes! That hideous book by that insane Mr. Lawrence. (*Tom laughs wildly.*) I cannot control the output of diseased minds or people who cater to them—(*Tom laughs still more wildly.*) BUT I WON'T ALLOW SUCH FILTH BROUGHT INTO MY HOUSE! No, no, no, no, no!

*Tom:* House, house! Who pays rent on it, who makes a slave of himself to—

*Amanda* (*fairly screeching*): Don't you DARE to—

*Tom:* No, no, I mustn't say things! *I've* got to just—

*Amanda:* Let me tell you—

*Tom:* I don't want to hear any more! (*He tears the portieres open. The upstage area is lit with a turgid smoky red glow.*)

Amanda's hair is in metal curlers and she wears a very old bathrobe, much too large for her slight figure, a relic of the faithless Mr. Wingfield.
   An upright typewriter and a wild disarray of manuscripts are on the drop-leaf table. The quarrel was probably precipitated by Amanda's interruption of his creative labor. A chair lying overthrown on the floor.
   Their gesticulating shadows are cast on the ceiling by the fiery glow.

*Amanda:* You *will* hear more, you—

*Tom:* No, I won't hear more, I'm going out!

*Amanda:* You come right back in—

*Tom:* Out, out out! Because I'm—

*Amanda:* Come back here, Tom Wingfield! I'm not through talking to you!

*Tom:* Oh, go—

*Laura* (*desperately*): Tom!

*Amanda:* You're going to listen, and no more insolence from you! I'm at the end of my patience! (*He comes back toward her.*)

*Tom:* What do you think I'm at? Aren't I supposed to have any patience to reach the end of, Mother? I know, I know. It seems unimportant to you, what I'm *doing*—what I *want* to do—having a little *difference* between them! You don't think that—

*Amanda:* I think you've been doing things that you're ashamed of. That's why you act like this. I don't believe that you go every night to the movies. Nobody goes to the movies night after night. Nobody in their right minds goes to the movies as often as you pretend to. People don't go to the movies at nearly midnight, and movies don't let out at two A.M. Come in stumbling. Muttering to yourself like a maniac! You get three hours' sleep and then go to work. Oh, I can picture the way you're doing down there. Moping, doping, because you're in no condition.

*Tom* (*wildly*): No, I'm in no condition!

*Amanda*: What right have you got to jeopardize your job? Jeopardize the security of us all? How do you think we'd manage if you were—

*Tom*: Listen! You think I'm crazy *about* the *warehouse*? (*He bends fiercely toward her slight figure.*) You think I'm in love with the Continental Shoemakers? You think I want to spend fifty-five years down there in that—*celotex interior!* with—*fluorescent*—*tubes!* Look! I'd rather somebody picked up a crowbar and battered out my brains—than go back mornings! I *go!* Every time you come in yelling that God damn *"Rise and Shine!" "Rise and Shine!"* I say to myself "How *lucky dead* people are!" But I get up. I *go!* For sixty-five dollars a month I give up all that I dream of doing and being *ever!* And you say self—*self's* all I ever think of. Why, listen, if self is what I thought of, Mother, I'd be where he is—GONE! (*Pointing to father's picture.*) As far as the system of transportation reaches! (*He starts past her. She grabs his arm.*) Don't grab at me, Mother!

*Amanda*: Where are you going?

*Tom*: I'm going to the *movies!*

*Amanda*: I don't believe that lie!

*Tom* (*crouching toward her, overtowering her tiny figure. She backs away, gasping*): I'm going to opium dens! Yes, opium dens, dens of vice and criminals' hangouts, Mother. I've joined the Hogan gang, I'm a hired assassin, I carry a tommy-gun in a violin case! I run a string of cat-houses in the Valley! They call me Killer, Killer Wingfield, I'm leading a double-life, a simple, honest warehouse worker by day, by night a dynamic *czar* of the *underworld*, Mother. I go to gambling casinos, I spin away fortunes on the roulette table! I wear a patch over one eye and a false mustache, sometimes I put on green whiskers. On those occasions they call me—*El Diablo!* Oh, I could tell you things to make you sleepless! My enemies plan to dynamite this place. They're going to blow us all sky-high some night! I'll be glad, very happy, and so will you! You'll go up, up on a broomstick, over Blue Mountain with seventeen gentlemen callers! You ugly—babbling old—*witch*. . . . (*He goes through a series of violent, clumsy movements, seizing his overcoat, lunging to the door, pulling it fiercely open. The women watch him, aghast. His arm catches in the sleeve of the coat as he struggles to pull it on. For a moment he is pinioned by the bulky garment. With an outraged groan he tears the coat off again, splitting the shoulders of it, and hurls it across the room. It strikes against the shelf of Laura's glass collection, there is a tinkle of shattering glass. Laura cries out as if wounded.*)

**(Music Legend: "The Glass Menagerie.")**

*Laura* (*shrilly*): My glass!—menagerie. . . . (*She covers her face and turns away.*)

But Amanda is still stunned and stupefied by the "ugly witch" so that she barely notices this occurrence. Now she recovers her speech.

*Amanda* (*in an awful voice*): I won't speak to you—until you apologize! (*She crosses through portieres and draws them together behind her. Tom is left with Laura. Laura clings weakly to the mantel with her face averted. Tom stares at her stupidly for a moment. Then he crosses to shelf. Drops awkwardly to his knees to collect the fallen glass, glancing at Laura as if he would speak but couldn't.)*

**("The Glass Menagerie" steals in as the Scene Dims Out.)**

## Scene IV

*The interior is dark. Faint in the alley.*

*A deep-voiced bell in a church is tolling the hour of five as the scene commences.*

*Tom appears at the top of the alley. After each solemn boom of the bell in the tower, he shakes a little noise-maker or rattle as if to express the tiny spasm of man in contrast to the sustained power and dignity of the Almighty. This and the unsteadiness of his advance make it evident that he has been drinking.*

*As he climbs the few steps to the fire-escape landing light steals up inside. Laura appears in night-dress, observing Tom's empty bed in the front room.*

*Tom fishes in his pockets for the door-key, removing a motley assortment of articles in the search, including a perfect shower of movie-ticket stubs and an empty bottle. At last he finds the key, but just as he is about to insert it, it slips from his fingers. He strikes a match and crouches below the door.*

Tom (*bitterly*): One crack—and it falls through!

(*Laura opens the door.*)

Laura: Tom! Tom, what are you doing?
Tom: Looking for a door-key.
Laura: Where have you been all this time?
Tom: I have been to the movies.
Laura: All this time at the movies?
Tom: There was a very long program. There was a Garbo picture and a Mickey Mouse and a travelogue and a newsreel and a preview of coming attractions. And there was an organ solo and a collection for the milk-fund—simultane-ously—which ended up in a terrible fight between a fat lady and an usher!
Laura (*innocently*): Did you have to stay through everything?
Tom: Of course! And, oh, I forgot! There was a big stage show! The headliner on this stage show was Malvolio the Magician. He performed wonderful tricks, many of them, such as pouring water back and forth between pitchers. First it turned to wine and then it turned to beer and then it turned to whiskey. I know it was whiskey it finally turned into because he needed somebody to come up out of the audience to help him, and I came up—both shows! It was Kentucky Straight Bourbon. A very generous fellow, he gave souvenirs. (*He pulls from his back pocket a shimmering rainbow-colored scarf.*) He gave me this. This is his magic scarf. You can have it, Laura. You wave it over a canary cage and you get a bowl of gold-fish. You wave it over the gold-fish bowl and they fly away canaries. . . . But the wonderfullest trick of all was the coffin

trick. We nailed him into a coffin and he got out of the coffin without removing one nail. (*He has come inside.*) There is a trick that would come in handy for me—get me out of this 2 by 4 situation! (*Flops onto bed and starts removing shoes.*)

*Laura*: Tom—Shhh!

*Tom*: What're you shushing me for?

*Laura*: You'll wake up Mother.

*Tom*: Goody, goody! Pay'er back for all those "Rise an' Shines." (*Lies down, groaning.*) You know it don't take much intelligence to get yourself into a nailed-up coffin, Laura. But who in hell ever got himself out of one without removing one nail?

*As if in answer, the father's grinning photograph lights up.*

## (Scene Dims Out.)

*Immediately following: The church bell is heard striking six. At the sixth stroke the alarm clock goes off in Amanda's room, and after a few moments we hear her calling: "Rise and Shine! Rise and Shine! Laura, go tell your brother to rise and shine!"*

*Tom* (*sitting up slowly*): I'll rise—but I won't shine.

*The light increases.*

*Amanda*: Laura, tell your brother his coffee is ready.

*Laura slips into front room.*

*Laura*: Tom! it's nearly seven. Don't make Mother nervous. (*He stares at her stupidly. Beseechingly.*) Tom, speak to Mother this morning. Make up with her, apologize, speak to her!

*Tom*: She won't to me. It's her that started not speaking.

*Laura*: If you just say you're sorry she'll start speaking.

*Tom*: Her not speaking—is that such a tragedy?

*Laura*: Please—please!

*Amanda* (*calling from kitchenette*): Laura, are you going to do what I asked you to do, or do I have to get dressed and go out myself?

*Laura*: Going, going—soon as I get on my coat! (*She pulls on a shapeless felt hat with nervous, jerky movements, pleadingly glancing at Tom. Rushes awkwardly for coat. The coat is one of Amanda's inaccurately made-over, the sleeves too short for Laura.*) Butter and what else?

*Amanda* (*entering upstage*): Just butter. Tell them to charge it.

*Laura*: Mother, they make such faces when I do that.

*Amanda*: Sticks and stones may break my bones, but the expression on Mr. Garfinkel's face won't harm us! Tell your brother his coffee is getting cold.

*Laura* (*at door*): Do what I asked you, will you, will you, Tom?

*He looks sullenly away.*

Amanda: Laura, go now or just don't go at all!

Laura (rushing out): Going—going! (A second later she cries out. Tom springs up and crosses to the door. Amanda rushes anxiously in. Tom opens the door.)

Tom: Laura?

Laura: I'm all right. I slipped, but I'm all right.

Amanda (peering anxiously after her): If anyone breaks a leg on those fire-escape steps, the landlord ought to be sued for every cent he possesses! (She shuts door. Remembers she isn't speaking and returns to other room.)

As Tom enters listlessly for his coffee, she turns her back to him and stands rigidly facing the window on the gloomy gray vault of the areaway. Its light on her face with its aged but childish features is cruelly sharp, satirical as a Daumier print.

**(Music Under: "Ave Maria.")**

Tom glances sheepishly but sullenly at her averted figure and slumps at the table. The coffee is scalding hot; he sips it and gasps and spits it back in the cup. At his gasp, Amanda catches her breath and half turns. Then catches herself and turns back to window.

Tom blows on his coffee, glancing sidewise at his mother. She clears her throat. Tom clears his. He starts to rise. Sinks back down again, scratches his head, clears his throat again. Amanda coughs. Tom raises his cup in both hands to blow on it, his eyes staring over the rim of it at his mother for several moments. Then he slowly sets the cup down and awkwardly and hesitantly rises from the chair.

Tom (hoarsely): Mother. I—I apologize. Mother. (Amanda draws a quick, shuddering breath. Her face works grotesquely. She breaks into childlike tears.) I'm sorry for what I said, for everything that I said, I didn't mean it.

Amanda (sobbingly): My devotion has made me a witch and so I make myself hateful to my children!

Tom: No, you don't.

Amanda I worry so much, don't sleep, it makes me nervous!

Tom (gently): I understand that.

Amanda: I've had to put up a solitary battle all these years. But you're my right-hand bower! Don't fall down, don't fail!

Tom (gently): I try, Mother.

Amanda (with great enthusiasm): Try and you will SUCCEED! (The notion makes her breathless.) Why, you—you're just full of natural endowments! Both of my children—they're unusual children! Don't you think I know it? I'm so—proud! Happy and—feel I've—so much to be thankful for but—Promise me one thing, son!

Tom: What, Mother?

Amanda: Promise, son you'll—never be a drunkard!

Tom (turns to her grinning): I will never be a drunkard, Mother.

*Amanda*: That's what frightened me so, that you'd be drinking! Eat a bowl of Purina!

*Tom*: Just coffee, Mother.

*Amanda*: Shredded wheat biscuit?

*Tom*: No. No, Mother, just coffee.

*Amanda*: You can't put in a day's work on an empty stomach. You've got ten minutes—don't gulp! Drinking too-hot liquids makes cancer of the stomach. . . . Put cream in.

*Tom*: No, thank you.

*Amanda*: To cool it.

*Tom*: No! No, thank you, I want it black.

*Amanda*: I know, but it's not good for you. We have to do all that we can to build ourselves up. In these trying times we live in, all that we have to cling to is— each other. . . . That's why it's so important to—Tom, I—I sent out your sister so I could discuss something with you. If you hadn't spoken I would have spoken to you. (*Sits down*.)

*Tom* (*gently*): What is it, Mother, that you want to discuss?

*Amanda*: Laura!

*Tom puts his cup down slowly.*

### (Legend On Screen: "Laura.")

### (Music: "The Glass Menagerie.")

*Tom*: —Oh.—Laura . . .

*Amanda* (*touching his sleeve*): You know how Laura is. So quiet but—still water runs deep! She notices things and I think she—broods about them. (*Tom looks up*.) A few days ago I came in and she was crying.

*Tom*: What about?

*Amanda*: You.

*Tom*: Me?

*Amanda*: She has an idea that you're not happy here.

*Tom*: What gave her that idea?

*Amanda*: What gives her any idea? However, you do act strangely. I—I'm not criticizing, understand *that*! I know your ambitions do not lie in the warehouse, that like everybody in the whole wide world—you've had to—make sacrifices, but—Tom—Tom—life's not easy, it calls for—Spartan endurance! There's so many things in my heart that I cannot describe to you! I've never told you but I—*loved* your father. . . .

*Tom* (*gently*): I know that, Mother.

*Amanda*: And you—when I see you taking after his ways! Staying out late— and—well, you had been drinking the night you were in that—terrifying condition! Laura says that you hate the apartment and that you go out nights to get away from it! Is that true, Tom?

Tom: No. You say there's so much in your heart that you can't describe to me. That's true of me, too. There's so much in my heart that I can't describe to *you!* So let's respect each other's—

Amanda: But, why—*why*, Tom—are you always so *restless?* Where do you go to, nights?

Tom: I—go to the movies.

Amanda: Why do you go to the movies so much, Tom?

Tom: I go to the movies because—I like adventure. Adventure is something I don't have much of at work, so I go to the movies.

Amanda: But, Tom, you go to the movies *entirely* too *much!*

Tom: I like a lot of adventure.

*Amanda looks baffled, then hurt. As the familiar inquisition resumes he becomes hard and impatient again. Amanda slips back into her querulous attitude toward him.*

**(Image On Screen: Sailing Vessel With Jolly Roger.)**

Amanda: Most young men find adventure in their careers.

Tom: Then most young men are not employed in a warehouse.

Amanda: The world is full of young men employed in warehouses and offices and factories.

Tom: Do all of them find adventure in their careers?

Amanda: They do or they do without it! Not everybody has a craze for adventure.

Tom: Man is by instinct a lover, a hunter, a fighter, and none of those instincts are given much play at the warehouse!

Amanda: Man is by instinct! Don't quote instinct to me! Instinct is something that people have got away from! It belongs to animals! Christian adults don't want it!

Tom: What do Christian adults want, then, Mother?

Amanda: Superior things! Things of the mind and the spirit! Only animals have to satisfy instincts! Surely your aims are somewhat higher than theirs! Than monkeys—pigs—

Tom: I reckon they're not.

Amanda: You're joking. However, that isn't what I wanted to discuss.

Tom (*rising*): I haven't much time.

Amanda (*pushing his shoulder*): Sit down.

Tom: You want me to punch in red at the warehouse, Mother?

Amanda: You have five minutes. I want to talk about Laura.

**(Legend: "Plans And Provisions.")**

Tom: All right! What about Laura?

Amanda: We have to be making plans and provisions for her. She's older than you, two years, and nothing has happened. She just drifts along doing nothing. It frightens me terribly how she just drifts along.

*Tom:* I guess she's the type that people call home girls.

*Amanda:* There's no such type, and if there is, it's a pity! That is unless the home is hers, with a husband!

*Tom:* What?

*Amanda:* Oh, I can see the handwriting on the wall as plain as I see the nose in front of my face! It's terrifying! More and more you remind me of your father! He was out all hours without explanation—Then *left! Goodbye!* And me with the bag to hold. I saw that letter you got from the Merchant Marine. I know what you're dreaming of. I'm not standing here blindfolded. Very well, then. Then *do* it! But not till there's somebody to take your place.

*Tom:* What do you mean?

*Amanda:* I mean that as soon as Laura has got somebody to take care of her, married, a home of her own, independent—why, then you'll be free to go wherever you please, on land, on sea, whichever way the wind blows! But until that time you've got to look out for your sister. I don't say me because I'm old and don't matter! I say for your sister because she's young and dependent. I put her in business college—a dismal failure! Frightened her so it made her sick to her stomach. I took her over to the Young People's League at the church. Another fiasco. She spoke to nobody, nobody spoke to her. Now all she does is fool with those pieces of glass and play those worn-out records. What kind of a life is that for a girl to lead!

*Tom:* What can I do about it?

*Amanda:* Overcome selfishness! Self, self, self is all that you ever think of! (*Tom springs up and crosses to get his coat. It is ugly and bulky. He pulls on a cap with earmuffs.*) Where is your muffler? Put your wool muffler on! (*He snatches it angrily from the closet and tosses it around his neck and pulls both ends tight.*) Tom! I haven't said what I had in mind to ask you.

*Tom:* I'm too late to—

*Amanda* (*catching his arms—very importunately. Then shyly*): Down at the warehouse, aren't there some—nice young men?

*Tom:* No!

*Amanda:* There *must* be—some . . .

*Tom:* Mother—

    *Gesture.*

*Amanda:* Find one that's clean-living—doesn't drink and—ask him out for sister!

*Tom:* What?

*Amanda:* For *Sister!* To *meet!* Get *acquainted!*

*Tom* (*stamping to door*): Oh, my go-osh!

*Amanda:* Will you? (*He opens door. Imploringly.*) Will you? (*He starts down.*) Will you? *Will,* you, dear?

*Tom* (*calling back*): YES!

    *Amanda closes the door hesitantly and with a troubled but faintly hopeful expression.*

**(Screen Image: Glamor Magazine Cover.)**

*Spot Amanda at phone.*

*Amanda:* Ella Cartwright? This is Amanda Wingfield! How are you, honey? How is that kidney condition? (*Count five.*) Horrors! (*Count five.*) You're a Christian martyr, yes, honey, that's what you are, a Christian martyr! Well, I just happened to notice in my little red book that your subscription to the *Companion* has just run out! I knew that you wouldn't want to miss out on the wonderful serial starting in this new issue. It's by Bessie Mae Hopper, the first thing she's written since *Honeymoon for Three*. Wasn't that a strange and interesting story? Well, this one is even lovelier, I believe. It has a sophisticated society background. It's all about the horsey set on Long Island!

**(Fade Out.)**

## Scene V

**(Legend On Screen: "Annunciation.")** *Fade with music.*

*It is early dusk of a spring evening. Supper has just been finished in the Wingfield apartment. Amanda and Laura in light colored dresses are removing dishes from the table, in the upstage area, which is shadowy, their movements formalized almost as a dance or ritual, their moving forms as pale and silent as moths.*

*Tom, in white shirt and trousers, rises from the table and crosses toward the fire-escape.*

*Amanda* (*as he passes her*): Son, will you do me a favor?
*Tom:* What?
*Amanda:* Comb your hair! You look so pretty when your hair is combed! (*Tom slouches on sofa with evening paper. Enormous caption "Franco Triumphs."*) There is only one respect in which I would like you to emulate your father.
*Tom:* What respect is that?
*Amanda:* The care he always took of his appearance. He never allowed himself to look untidy. (*He throws down the paper and crosses to fire-escape.*) Where are you going?
*Tom:* I'm going out to smoke.
*Amanda:* You smoke too much. A pack a day at fifteen cents a pack. How much would that amount to in a month? Thirty times fifteen is how much, Tom? Figure it out and you will be astounded at what you could save. Enough to give you a night-school course in accounting at Washington U! Just think what a wonderful thing that would be for you, son!

*Tom is unmoved by the thought.*

*Tom:* I'd rather smoke. (*He steps out on landing, letting the screen door slam.*)

*Amanda* (*sharply*): I know! That's the tragedy of it. . . . (*Alone, she turns to look at her husband's picture.*)

**(Dance Music: "All The World Is Waiting For The Sunrise.")**

*Tom* (*to the audience*): Across the alley from us was the Paradise Dance Hall. On evenings in spring the windows and doors were open and the music came outdoors. Sometimes the lights were turned out except for a large glass sphere that hung from the ceiling. It would turn slowly about and filter the dusk with delicate rainbow colors. Then the orchestra played a waltz or a tango, something that had a slow and sensuous rhythm. Couples would come outside, to the relative privacy of the alley. You could see them kissing behind ash-pits and telephone poles. This was the compensation for lives that passed like mine, without any change or adventure. Adventure and change were imminent in this year. They were waiting around the corner for all these kids. Suspended in the mist over Berchtesgaden, caught in the folds of Chamberlain's umbrella—In Spain there was Guernica! But here there was only hot swing music and liquor, dance halls, bars, and movies, and sex that hung in the gloom like a chandelier and flooded the world with brief, deceptive rainbows. . . . All the world was waiting for bombardments!

*Amanda turns from the picture and comes outside.*

*Amanda* (*sighing*): A fire-escape landing's a poor excuse for a porch. (*She spreads a newspaper on a step and sits down, gracefully and demurely as if she were settling into a swing on a Mississippi veranda.*) What are you looking at?
*Tom:* The moon.
*Amanda:* Is there a moon this evening?
*Tom:* It's rising over Garfinkel's Delicatessen.
*Amanda:* So it is! A little silver slipper of a moon. Have you made a wish on it yet?
*Tom:* Um-hum.
*Amanda:* What did you wish for?
*Tom:* That's a secret.
*Amanda:* A secret, huh? Well, I won't tell mine either. I will be just as mysterious as you.
*Tom:* I bet I can guess what yours is.
*Amanda:* Is my head so transparent?
*Tom:* You're not a sphinx.
*Amanda:* No, I don't have secrets. I'll tell you what I wished for on the moon. Success and happiness for my precious children! I wish for that whenever there's a moon, and when there isn't a moon, I wish for it, too.
*Tom:* I thought perhaps you wished for a gentleman caller.
*Amanda:* Why do you say that?
*Tom:* Don't you remember asking me to fetch one?

*Amanda:* I remember suggesting that it would be nice for your sister if you brought home some nice young man from the warehouse. I think I've made that suggestion more than once.

*Tom:* Yes, you have made it repeatedly.

*Amanda:* Well?

*Tom:* We are going to have one.

*Amanda:* What?

*Tom:* A gentleman caller!

**(The Annunciation Is Celebrated With Music.)**

*Amanda rises.*

**(Image On Screen: Caller With Bouquet.)**

*Amanda:* You mean you have asked some nice young man to come over?

*Tom:* Yep. I've asked him to dinner.

*Amanda:* You really did?

*Tom:* I did!

*Amanda:* You did, and did he—*accept?*

*Tom:* He did!

*Amanda:* Well, well—well, well! That's—lovely!

*Tom:* I thought that you would be pleased.

*Amanda:* It's definite, then?

*Tom:* Very definite.

*Amanda:* Soon?

*Tom:* Very soon.

*Amanda:* For heaven's sake, stop putting on and tell me some things, will you?

*Tom:* What things do you want me to tell you?

*Amanda:* Naturally I would like to know when he's *coming!*

*Tom:* He's coming tomorrow.

*Amanda:* *Tomorrow?*

*Tom:* Yep. Tomorrow.

*Amanda:* But, Tom!

*Tom:* Yes, Mother?

*Amanda:* Tomorrow gives me no time!

*Tom:* Time for what?

*Amanda:* Preparations! Why didn't you phone me at once, as soon as you asked him, the minute that he accepted? Then, don't you see, I could have been getting ready!

*Tom:* You don't have to make any fuss.

*Amanda:* Oh, Tom, Tom, Tom, of course I have to make a fuss! I want things nice, not sloppy! Not thrown together. I'll certainly have to do some fast thinking, won't I?

*Tom:* I don't see why you have to think at all.

*Amanda*: You just don't know. We can't have a gentleman caller in a pig-sty! All
my wedding silver has to be polished, the monogrammed table linen ought
to be laundered! The windows have to be washed and fresh curtains put up.
And how about clothes? We have to *wear* something, don't we?

*Tom*: Mother, this boy is no one to make a fuss over!

*Amanda*: Do you realize he's the first young man we've introduced to your sister?
It's terrible, dreadful, disgraceful that poor little sister has never received a
single gentleman caller! Tom, come inside! (*She opens the screen door.*)

*Tom*: What for?

*Amanda*: I want to ask you some things.

*Tom*: If you're going to make such a fuss, I'll call it off, I'll tell him not to come.

*Amanda*: You certainly won't do anything of the kind. Nothing offends people
worse than broken engagements. It simply means I'll have to work like a
Turk! We won't be brilliant, but we'll pass inspection. Come on inside.
(*Tom follows, groaning.*) Sit down.

*Tom*: Any particular place you would like me to sit?

*Amanda*: Thank heavens I've got that new sofa! I'm also making payments on a
floor lamp I'll have sent out! And put the chintz covers on, they'll brighten
things up! Of course I'd hoped to have these walls re-papered.... What is
the young man's name?

*Tom*: His name is O'Connor.

*Amanda*: That, of course, means fish—tomorrow is Friday! I'll have that salmon
loaf—with Durkee's dressing! What does he do? He works at the warehouse?

*Tom*: Of course! How else would I—

*Amanda*: Tom, he—doesn't drink?

*Tom*: Why do you ask me that?

*Amanda*: Your father *did*!

*Tom*: Don't get started on that!

*Amanda*: He *does* drink, then?

*Tom*: Not that I know of!

*Amanda*: Make sure, be certain! The last thing I want for my daughter's a boy
who drinks!

*Tom*: Aren't you being a little premature? Mr. O'Connor has not yet appeared on
the scene!

*Amanda*: But will tomorrow. To meet your sister, and what do I know about his
character? Nothing! Old maids are better off than wives of drunkards!

*Tom*: Oh, my God!

*Amanda*: Be still!

*Tom* (*leaning forward to whisper*): Lots of fellows meet girls whom they don't
marry!

*Amanda*: Oh, talk sensibly, Tom—and don't be sarcastic! (*She has gotten a hair-brush.*)

*Tom*: What are you doing?

*Amanda*: I'm brushing that cow-lick down! What is this young man's position at
the warehouse?

*Tom* (*submitting grimly to the brush and the interrogation*): This young man's position is that of a shipping clerk, Mother.

*Amanda*: Sounds to me like a fairly responsible job, the sort of a job *you* would be in if you just had more *get-up*. What is his salary? Have you got any idea?

*Tom*: I would judge it to be approximately eighty-five dollars a month.

*Amanda*: Well—not princely, but—

*Tom*: Twenty more than I make.

*Amanda*: Yes, how well I know! But for a family man, eighty-five dollars a month is not much more than you can just get by on. . . .

*Tom*: Yes, but Mr. O'Connor is not a family man.

*Amanda*: He might be, mightn't he? Some time in the future?

*Tom*: I see. Plans and provisions.

*Amanda*: You are the only young man that I know of who ignores the fact that the future becomes the present, the present the past, and the past turns into everlasting regret if you don't plan for it!

*Tom*: I will think that over and see what I can make of it!

*Amanda*: Don't be supercilious with your mother! Tell me some more about this—what do you call him?

*Tom*: James D. O'Connor. The D. is for Delaney.

*Amanda*: Irish on *both* sides! *Gracious!* And doesn't drink?

*Tom*: Shall I call him up and ask him right this minute?

*Amanda*: The only way to find out about those things is to make discreet inquiries at the proper moment. When I was a girl in Blue Mountain and it was suspected that a young man drank, the girl whose attentions he had been receiving, if any girl *was*, would sometimes speak to the minister of his church, or rather her father would if her father was living, and sort of feel him out on the young man's character. That is the way such things are discreetly handled to keep a young woman from making a tragic mistake!

*Tom*: Then how did you happen to make a tragic mistake?

*Amanda*: That innocent look of your father's had everyone fooled! He *smiled*—the world was *enchanted!* No girl can do worse than put herself at the mercy of a handsome appearance! I hope that Mr. O'Connor is not too good-looking.

*Tom*: No, he's not too good-looking. He's covered with freckles and hasn't too much of a nose.

*Amanda*: He's not right-down homely, though?

*Tom*: Not right-down homely. Just medium homely, I'd say.

*Amanda*: Character's what to look for in a man.

*Tom*: That's what I've always said, Mother.

*Amanda*: You've never said anything of the kind and I suspect you would never give it a thought.

*Tom*: Don't be suspicious of me.

*Amanda*: At least I hope he's the type that's up and coming.

*Tom*: I think he really goes in for self-improvement.

*Amanda*: What reason have you to think so?

*Tom*: He goes to night school.

*Amanda* (*beaming*): Splendid! What does he do, I mean study?

*Tom*: Radio engineering and public speaking!

*Amanda*: Then he has visions of being advanced in the world! Any young man who studies public speaking is aiming to have an executive job some day! And radio engineering? A thing for the future! Both of these facts are very illuminating. Those are the sort of things that a mother should know concerning any young man who comes to call on her daughter. Seriously or—not.

*Tom*: One little warning. He doesn't know about Laura. I didn't let on that we had dark ulterior motives. I just said, why don't you come have dinner with us? He said okay and that was the whole conversation.

*Amanda*: I bet it was! You're eloquent as an oyster. However, he'll know about Laura when he gets here. When he sees how lovely and sweet and pretty she is, he'll thank his lucky stars he was asked to dinner.

*Tom*: Mother, you mustn't expect too much of Laura.

*Amanda*: What do you mean?

*Tom*: Laura seems all those things to you and me because she's ours and we love her. We don't even notice she's crippled any more.

*Amanda*: Don't say crippled! You know that I never allow that word to be used!

*Tom*: But face facts, Mother. She is and—that not's all—

*Amanda*: What do you mean "not all"?

*Tom*: Laura is very different from other girls.

*Amanda*: I think the difference is all to her advantage.

*Tom*: Not quite all—in the eyes of others—strangers—she's terribly shy and lives in a world of her own and those things make her seem a little peculiar to people outside the house.

*Amanda*: Don't say peculiar.

*Tom*: Face the facts. She is.

**(The Dance-Hall Music Changes To A Tango That Has A Minor And Somewhat Ominous Tone.)**

*Amanda*: In what way is she peculiar—may I ask?

*Tom* (*gently*): She lives in a world of her own—a world of—little glass ornaments, Mother. . . . (*Gets up. Amanda remains holding brush, looking at him, troubled.*) She plays old phonograph records and—that's about all—(*He glances at himself in the mirror and crosses to door.*)

*Amanda* (*sharply*): Where are you going?

*Tom*: I'm going to the movies. (*Out screen door.*)

*Amanda*: Not to the movies, every night to the movies! (*Follows quickly to screen door.*) I don't believe you always go to the movies! (*He is gone. Amanda looks worriedly after him for a moment. Then vitality and optimism return and she turns from the door. Crossing to portieres.*) Laura! Laura! (*Laura answers from kitchenette.*)

*Laura*: Yes, Mother.

*Amanda*: Let those dishes go and come in front! (*Laura appears with dish towel. Gaily.*) Laura, come here and make a wish on the moon!

*Laura* (*entering*): Moon—moon?

*Amanda*: A little silver slipper of a moon. Look over your left shoulder, Laura, and make a wish! (*Laura looks faintly puzzled as if called out of sleep. Amanda seizes her shoulders and turns her at an angle by the door.*) Now! Now, darling, wish!

*Laura*: What shall I wish for, Mother?

*Amanda* (*her voice trembling and her eyes suddenly filling with tears*): Happiness! Good Fortune!

*The violin rises and the stage dims out.*

## Scene VI

**(Image: High-School Hero.)**

*Tom*: And so the following evening I brought him home to dinner. I had known Jim slightly in high school. In high school Jim was a hero. He had tremendous Irish good nature and vitality with the scrubbed and polished look of white chinaware. He seemed to move in a continual spotlight. He was a star in basketball, captain of the debating club, president of the senior class and the glee club and he sang the male lead in the annual light operas. He was always running or bounding, never just walking. He seemed always at the point of defeating the law of gravity. He was shooting with such velocity through his adolescence that you would logically expect him to arrive at nothing short of the White House by the time he was thirty. But Jim apparently ran into more interference after his graduation from Soldan. His speed had definitely slowed. Six years after he left high school he was holding a job that wasn't much better than mine.

**(Image: Clerk.)**

He was the only one at the warehouse with whom I was on friendly terms. I was valuable to him as someone who could remember his former glory, who had seen him win basketball games and the silver cup in debating. He knew of my secret practice of retiring to a cabinet of the washroom to work on my poems when business was slack in the warehouse. He called me Shakespeare. And while the other boys in the warehouse regarded me with suspicious hostility, Jim took a humorous attitude toward me. Gradually his attitude affected the others, their hostility wore off and they also began to smile at me as people smile at an oddly fashioned dog who trots across their path at some distance.

I knew that Jim and Laura had known each other at Soldan, and I had heard Laura speak admiringly of his voice. I didn't know if Jim remembered her or not. In high school Laura had been as unobtrusive as Jim had been astonishing. If he did remember Laura, it was not as my sister, for when I asked him to dinner, he grinned and said, "You know, Shakespeare, I never thought of you as having folks!"

He was about to discover that I did. . . .

**(Light Up Stage.)**

**(Legend On Screen: "The Accent Of A Coming Foot.")**

*Friday evening. It is about five o'clock of a late spring evening which comes "scattering poems in the sky."*

*A delicate lemony light is in the Wingfield apartment.*

*Amanda has worked like a Turk in preparation for the gentleman caller. The results are astonishing. The new floor lamp with its rose-silk shade is in place, a colored paper lantern conceals the broken light fixture in the ceiling, new billowing white curtains are at the windows, chintz covers are on chairs and sofa, a pair of new sofa pillows make their initial appearance.*

*Open boxes and tissue paper are scattered on the floor.*

*Laura stands in the middle with lifted arms while Amanda crouches before her, adjusting the hem of the new dress, devout and ritualistic. The dress is colored and designed by memory. The arrangement of Laura's hair is changed; it is softer and more becoming. A fragile, unearthly prettiness has come out in Laura: she is like a piece of translucent glass touched by light, given a momentary radiance, not actual, not lasting.*

*Amanda (impatiently)*: Why are you trembling?

*Laura*: Mother, you've made me so nervous!

*Amanda*: How have I made you nervous?

*Laura*: By all this fuss! You make it seem so important!

*Amanda*: I don't understand you, Laura. You couldn't be satisfied with just sitting home, and yet whenever I try to arrange something for you, you seem to resist it. (*She gets up.*) Now take a look at yourself. No, wait! Wait just a moment—I have an idea!

*Laura*: What is it now?

*Amanda produces two powder puffs which she wraps in handkerchiefs and stuffs in Laura's bosom.*

*Laura*: Mother, what are you doing?

*Amanda*: They call them "Gay Deceivers"!

*Laura*: I won't wear them!

*Amanda*: You will!

*Laura*: Why should I?

*Amanda*: Because, to be painfully honest, your chest is flat.

*Laura*: You make it seem like we were setting a trap.

*Amanda*: All pretty girls are a trap, a pretty trap, and men expect them to be. **(Legend: "A Pretty Trap.")** Now look at yourself, young lady. This is the prettiest you will ever be! I've got to fix myself now! You're going to be surprised by your mother's appearance! (*She crosses through portieres, humming gaily.*)

Laura moves slowly to the long mirror and stares solemnly at herself.
    A wind blows the white curtains inward in a slow, graceful motion and with a faint, sorrowful sighing.

Amanda (*offstage*): It isn't dark enough yet. (*She turns slowly before the mirror with a troubled look.*)

**(Legend On Screen: "This Is My Sister: Celebrate Her With Strings!" Music.)**

Amanda (*laughing, off*): I'm going to show you something. I'm going to make a spectacular appearance!
Laura: What is it, Mother?
Amanda: Possess your soul in patience—you will see! Something I've resurrected from that old trunk! Styles haven't changed so terribly much after all. . . . (*She parts the portieres.*) Now just look at your mother! (*She wears a girlish frock of yellowed voile with a blue silk sash. She carries a bunch of jonquils—the legend of her youth is nearly revived. Feverishly.*) This is the dress in which I led the cotillion. Won the cakewalk twice at Sunset Hill, wore one spring to the Governor's ball in Jackson! See how I sashayed around the ballroom, Laura? (*She raises her skirt and does a mincing step around the room.*) I wore it on Sundays for my gentlemen callers! I had it on the day I met your father—I had malaria fever all that spring. The change of climate from East Tennessee to the Delta—weakened resistance—I had a little temperature all the time—not enough to be serious—just enough to make me restless and giddy! Invitations poured in—parties all over the Delta!—"Stay in bed," said Mother, "you have fever!"—but I just wouldn't.—I took quinine but kept on going, going!—Evenings, dances!—Afternoons, long, long rides! Picnics—lovely!—So lovely, that country in May.—All lacy with dogwood, literally flooded with jonquils!—That was the spring I had the craze for jonquils. Jonquils became an absolute obsession. Mother said, "Honey, there's no more room for jonquils." And still I kept bringing in more jonquils. Whenever, wherever I saw them, I'd say, "Stop! Stop! I see jonquils!" I made the young men help me gather the jonquils! It was a joke, Amanda and her jonquils! Finally there were no more vases to hold them, every available space was filled with jonquils. No vases to hold them? All right, I'll hold them myself! And then I—(*She stops in front of the picture.*) **(Music.)** met your father! Malaria fever and jonquils and then—this—boy. . . . (*She switches on the rose-colored lamp.*) I hope they get here before it starts to rain. (*She crosses upstage and places the jonquils in bowl on table.*) I gave your brother a little extra change so he and Mr. O'Connor could take the service car home.
Laura (*with altered look*): What did you say his name was?
Amanda: O'Connor.

*Laura:* What is his first name?
*Amanda:* I don't remember. Oh, yes, I do. It was—Jim!

> *Laura sways slightly and catches hold of a chair.*

### (Legend On Screen."'Not Jim!")

*Laura (faintly):* Not—Jim!
*Amanda:* Yes, that was it, it was Jim! I've never known a Jim that wasn't nice!

### (Music: Ominous.)

*Laura:* Are you sure his name is Jim O'Connor?
*Amanda:* Yes. Why?
*Laura:* Is he the one that Tom used to know in high school?
*Amanda:* He didn't say so. I think he just got to know him at the warehouse.
*Laura:* There was a Jim O'Connor we both knew in high school—(*Then, with effort.*) If that is the one that Tom is bringing to dinner—you'll have to excuse me, I won't come to the table.
*Amanda:* What sort of nonsense is this?
*Laura:* You asked me once if I'd ever like a boy. Don't you remember I showed you this boy's picture?
*Amanda:* You mean the boy you showed me in the year-book?
*Laura:* Yes, that boy.
*Amanda:* Laura, Laura, were you in love with that boy?
*Laura:* I don't know, Mother. All I know is I couldn't sit at the table if it was him!
*Amanda:* It won't be him! It isn't the least bit likely. But whether it is or not, you will come to the table. You will not be excused.
*Laura:* I'll have to be, Mother.
*Amanda:* I don't intend to humor your silliness, Laura. I've had too much from you and your brother, both! So just sit down and compose yourself till they come. Tom has forgotten his key so you'll have to let them in, when they arrive.
*Laura (panicky):* Oh, Mother—*you* answer the door!
*Amanda (lightly):* I'll be in the kitchen—busy!
*Laura:* Oh, Mother, please answer the door, don't make me do it!
*Amanda (crossing into kitchenette):* I've got to fix the dressing for the salmon. Fuss, fuss—silliness!—over a gentleman caller!

> *Door swings shut. Laura is left alone.*

### (Legend: "Terror!")

> *She utters a low moan and turns off the lamp—sits stiffly on the edge of the sofa, knotting her fingers together.*

### (Legend On Screen: "The Opening Of A Door!")

> *Tom and Jim appear on the fire-escape steps and climb to landing. Hearing their approach, Laura rises with a panicky gesture. She retreats to the portieres.*

*The doorbell. Laura catches her breath and touches her throat. Low drums.*

Amanda (*calling*): Laura, sweetheart! The door!

*Laura stares at it without moving.*

Jim: I think we just beat the rain.
Tom: Uh-huh. (*He rings again, nervously. Jim whistles and fishes for a cigarette.*)
Amanda (*very, very gaily*): Laura, that is your brother and Mr. O'Connor! Will you let them in, darling?

*Laura crosses toward kitchenette door.*

Laura (*breathlessly*): Mother—you go to the door!

*Amanda steps out of kitchenette and stares furiously at Laura. She points imperiously at the door.*

Laura: Please, please!
Amanda (*in a fierce whisper*): What is the matter with you, you silly thing?
Laura (*desperately*): Please, you answer it, *please!*
Amanda: I told you I wasn't going to humor you, Laura. Why have you chosen this moment to lose your mind?
Laura: Please, please, please, you go!
Amanda: You'll have to go to the door because I can't!
Laura (*despairingly*): I can't either!
Amanda: Why?
Laura: I'm *sick!*
Amanda: I'm sick, too—of your nonsense! Why can't you and your brother be normal people? Fantastic whims and behavior! (*Tom gives a long ring.*) Preposterous goings on! Can you give me one reason—(*Calls out lyrically.*) COMING! JUST ONE SECOND!—why should you be afraid to open a door? Now you answer it, Laura!
Laura: Oh, oh, oh . . . (*She returns through the portiers. Darts to the victrola and winds it frantically and turns it on.*)
Amanda: Laura Wingfield, you march right to that door!
Laura: Yes—yes, Mother!

*A faraway, scratchy rendition of "Dardanella" softens the air and gives her strength to move through it. She slips to the door and draws it cautiously open. Tom enters with the caller, Jim O'Connor.*

Tom: Laura, this is Jim. Jim, this is my sister, Laura.
Jim (*stepping inside*): I didn't know that Shakespeare had a sister!
Laura (*retreating stiff and trembling from the door*): How—how do you do?
Jim (*heartily extending his hand*): Okay!

*Laura touches it hesitantly with hers.*

Jim: Your hand's *cold*, Laura!
Laura: Yes, well—I've been playing the victrola. . . .

*Jim:* Must have been playing classical music on it! You ought to play a little hot swing music to warm you up!

*Laura:* Excuse me—I haven't finished playing the victrola. . . .

> *She turns awkwardly and hurries into the front room. She pauses a second by the victrola. Then catches her breath and darts through the portieres like a frightened deer.*

*Jim (grinning):* What was the matter?

*Tom:* Oh—with Laura? Laura is—terribly shy.

*Jim:* Shy, huh? It's unusual to meet a shy girl nowadays. I don't believe you ever mentioned you had a sister.

*Tom:* Well, now you know. I have one. Here is the *Post Dispatch.* You want a piece of it?

*Jim:* Uh-huh.

*Tom:* What piece? The comics?

*Jim:* Sports! *(Glances at it.)* Ole Dizzy Dean is on his bad behavior.

*Tom (disinterest):* Yeah? *(Lights cigarette and crosses back to fire-escape door.)*

*Jim:* Where are *you* going?

*Tom:* I'm going out on the terrace.

*Jim (goes after him):* You know, Shakespeare—I'm going to sell you a bill of goods!

*Tom:* What goods?

*Jim:* A course I'm taking.

*Tom:* Huh?

*Jim:* In public speaking! You and me, we're not the warehouse type.

*Tom:* Thanks—that's good news. But what has public speaking got to do with it?

*Jim:* It fits you for—executive positions!

*Tom:* Awww.

*Jim:* I tell you it's done a helluva lot for me.

**(Image: Executive At Desk.)**

*Tom:* In what respect?

*Jim:* In every! Ask yourself what is the difference between you an' me and men in the office down front? Brains?—No!—Ability?—No! Then what? Just one little thing—

*Tom:* What is that one little thing?

*Jim:* Primarily it amounts to—social poise! Being able to square up to people and hold your own on any social level!

*Amanda (offstage):* Tom?

*Tom:* Yes, Mother?

*Amanda:* Is that you and Mr. O'Connor?

*Tom:* Yes, Mother.

*Amanda:* Well, you just make yourselves comfortable in there.

*Tom:* Yes, Mother.

*Amanda:* Ask Mr. O'Connor if he would like to wash his hands.

*Jim:* Aw—no—thank you—I took care of that at the warehouse. Tom—

Tom: Yes?

Jim: Mr. Mendoza was speaking to me about you.

Tom: Favorably?

Jim: What do you think?

Tom: Well—

Jim: You're going to be out of a job if you don't wake up.

Tom: I am waking up—

Jim: You show no signs.

Tom: The signs are interior.

**(Image On Screen: The Sailing Vessel With Jolly Roger Again.)**

Tom: I'm planning to change. (*He leans over the rail speaking with quiet exhilaration. The incandescent marquees and signs of the first-run movie houses light his face from across the alley. He looks like a voyager.*) I'm right at the point of committing myself to a future that doesn't include the warehouse and Mr. Mendoza or even a night-school course in public speaking.

Jim: What are you gassing about?

Tom: I'm tired of the movies.

Jim: Movies!

Tom: Yes, movies! Look at them—(*A wave toward the marvels of Grand Avenue.*) All of those glamorous people—having adventures—hogging it all, gobbling the whole thing up! You know what happens? People go to the *movies* instead of *moving*! Hollywood characters are supposed to have all the adventures for everybody in America, while everybody in America sits in a dark room and watches them have them! Yes, until there's a war. That's when adventure becomes available to the masses! *Everyone's* dish, not only Gable's! Then the people in the dark room come out of the dark room to have some adventures themselves—Goody, goody—It's our turn now, to go to the South Sea Island—to make a safari—to be exotic, far-off—But I'm not patient. I don't want to wait till then. I'm tired of the *movies* and I am *about* to move!

Jim (*incredulously*): Move?

Tom: Yes!

Jim: When?

Tom: Soon!

Jim: Where? Where?

*Theme three music seems to answer the question, while Tom thinks it over. He searches among his pockets.*

Tom: I'm starting to boil inside. I know I seem dreamy, but inside—well, I'm boiling! Whenever I pick up a shoe, I shudder a little thinking how short life is and what I am doing!—Whatever that means. I know it doesn't mean shoes—except as something to wear on a traveler's feet! (*Finds paper.*) Look—

Jim: What?

*Tom*: I'm a member.

*Jim* (*reading*): The Union of Merchant Seamen.

*Tom*: I paid my dues this month, instead of the light bill.

*Jim*: You will regret it when they turn the lights off.

*Tom*: I won't be here.

*Jim*: How about your mother?

*Tom*: I'm like my father. The bastard son of a bastard! See how he grins? And he's been absent going on sixteen years!

*Jim*: You're just talking, you drip. How does your mother feel about it?

*Tom*: Shhh—Here comes Mother! Mother is not acquainted with my plans!

*Amanda* (*enters portieres*): Where are you all?

*Tom*: On the terrace, Mother.

> *They start inside. She advances to them. Tom is distinctly shocked at her appearance. Even Jim blinks a little. He is making his first contact with girlish Southern vivacity and in spite of the night-school course in public speaking is somewhat thrown off the beam by the unexpected outlay of social charm.*
>
> *Certain responses are attempted by Jim but are swept aside by Amanda's gay laughter and chatter. Tom is embarrassed but after the first shock Jim reacts very warmly. Grins and chuckles, is altogether won over.*

### (Image: Amanda As A Girl.)

*Amanda* (*coyly smiling, shaking her girlish ringlets*): Well, well, well, so this is Mr. O'Connor. Introductions entirely unnecessary. I've heard so much about you from my boy. I finally said to him, Tom—good gracious!—why don't you bring this paragon to supper? I'd like to meet this nice young man at the warehouse!—Instead of just hearing him sing your praises so much! I don't know why my son is so stand-offish—that's not Southern behavior! Let's sit down and—I think we could stand a little more air in here! Tom, leave the door open. I felt a nice fresh breeze a moment ago. Where has it gone? Mmm, so warm already! And not quite summer, even. We're going to burn up when summer really gets started. However, we're having—we're having a very light supper. I think light things are better fo' this time of year. The same as light clothes are. Light clothes an' light food are what warm weather calls fo'. You know our blood gets so thick during th' winter—it takes a while fo' us to *adjust* ou'selves!—when the season changes ... It's come so quick this year. I wasn't prepared. All of a sudden—heavens! Already summer!—I ran to the trunk an' pulled out this light dress—Terribly old! Historical almost! But feels so good—so good an' co-ol, y'know. . . .

*Tom*: Mother—

*Amanda*: Yes, honey?

*Tom*: How about—supper?

*Amanda*: Honey, you go ask Sister if supper is ready! You know that Sister is in full charge of supper! Tell her you hungry boys are waiting for it. (*To Jim.*) Have you met Laura?

Jim: She—

Amanda: Let you in? Oh, good, you've met already! It's rare for a girl as sweet an' pretty as Laura to be domestic! But Laura is, thank heavens, not only pretty but also very domestic. I'm not at all. I never was a bit. I never could make a thing but angel-food cake. Well, in the South we had so many servants. Gone, gone, gone. All vestiges of gracious living! Gone completely! I wasn't prepared for what the future brought me. All of my gentlemen callers were sons of planters and so of course I assumed that I would be married to one and raise my family on a large piece of land with plenty of servants. But man proposes—and woman accepts the proposal!—To vary that old, old saying a little bit—I married no planter! I married a man who worked for the telephone company!—that gallantly smiling gentleman over there! (*Points to the picture.*) A telephone man who—fell in love with long-distance!—Now he travels and I don't even know where!—But what am I going on for about my—tribulations? Tell me yours—I hope you don't have any! Tom?

Tom (*returning*): Yes, Mother?

Amanda: Is supper nearly ready?

Tom: It looks to me like supper is on the table.

Amanda: Let me look—(*She rises prettily and looks through portieres.*) Oh, lovely—But where is Sister?

Tom: Laura is not feeling well and she says that she thinks she'd better not come to the table.

Amanda: What?—Nonsense!—Laura? Oh, Laura!

Laura (*offstage, faintly*): Yes, Mother.

Amanda: You really must come to the table. We won't be seated until you come to the table! Come in, Mr. O'Connor. You sit over there and I'll—Laura? Laura Wingfield! You're keeping us waiting, honey! We can't say grace until you come to the table!

*The back door is pushed weakly open and Laura comes in. She is obviously quite faint, her lips trembling, her eyes wide and staring. She moves unsteadily toward the table.*

**(Legend: "Terror!")**

*Outside a summer storm is coming abruptly. The white curtains billow inward at the windows and there is a sorrowful murmur and deep blue dusk.*
  *Laura suddenly stumbles—She catches at a chair with a faint moan.*

Tom: Laura!

Amanda: Laura! (*There is a clap of thunder.*) **(Legend: "Ah!")** (*Despairingly.*) Why, Laura, you *are* sick, darling! Tom, help your sister into the living room, dear! Sit in the living room, Laura—rest on the sofa. Well! (*To the gentleman caller.*) Standing over the hot stove made her ill!—I told her that it was just too warm this evening, but—(*Tom comes back in. Laura is on the sofa.*) Is Laura all right now?

Tom: Yes.

Amanda: What *is* that? Rain? A nice cool rain has come up! (*She gives the gentleman caller a frightened look.*) I think we may—have grace—now ... (*Tom looks at her stupidly.*) Tom, honey—you say grace!

Tom: Oh ... "For these and all thy mercies—" (*They bow their heads, Amanda stealing a nervous glance at Jim. In the living room Laura, stretched on the sofa, clenches her hand to her lips, to hold back a shuddering sob.*) God's Holy Name be praised—

**(The Scene Dims Out.)**

## Scene VII

(*A Souvenir.*)

*Half an hour later. Dinner is just being finished in the upstage area which is concealed by the drawn portieres.*

    *As the curtain rises Laura is still huddled upon the sofa, her feet drawn under her, her head resting on a pale blue pillow, her eyes wide and mysteriously watchful. The new floor lamp with its shade of rose-colored silk gives a soft, becoming light to her face, bringing out the fragile, unearthly prettiness which usually escapes attention. There is a steady murmur of rain, but it is slackening and stops soon after the scene begins; the air outside becomes pale and luminous as the moon breaks out.*

    *A moment after the curtain rises, the lights in both rooms flicker and go out.*

Jim: Hey, there, Mr. Light Bulb!

*Amanda laughs nervously.*

**(Legend: "Suspension Of A Public Service.")**

Amanda: Where was Moses when the lights went out? Ha-ha. Do you know the answer to that one, Mr. O'Connor?

Jim: No, Ma'am, what's the answer?

Amanda: In the dark! (*Jim laughs appreciatively.*) Everybody sit still. I'll light the candles. Isn't it lucky we have them on the table? Where's a match? Which of you gentlemen can provide a match?

Jim: Here.

Amanda: Thank you, sir.

Jim: Not at all, Ma'am!

Amanda: I guess the fuse has burnt out. Mr. O'Connor, can you tell a burnt-out fuse? I know I can't and Tom is a total loss when it comes to mechanics. **(Sound: Getting Up: Voices Recede A Little To Kitchenette.)** Oh, be careful you don't bump into something. We don't want our gentleman caller to break his neck. Now wouldn't that be a fine howdy-do?

Jim: Ha-ha! Where is the fuse-box?

Amanda: Right here next to the stove. Can you see anything?

*Jim:* Just a minute.

*Amanda:* Isn't electricity a mysterious thing? Wasn't it Benjamin Franklin who tied a key to a kite? We live in such a mysterious universe, don't we? Some people say that science clears up all the mysteries for us. In my opinion it only creates more! Have you found it yet?

*Jim:* No, Ma'am. All these fuses look okay to me.

*Amanda:* Tom!

*Tom:* Yes, Mother?

*Amanda:* That light bill I gave you several days ago. The one I told you we got the notices about?

*Tom:* Oh.—Yeah.

**(Legend: "Ha!")**

*Amanda:* You didn't neglect to pay it by any chance?

*Tom:* Why, I—

*Amanda:* Didn't! I might have known it!

*Jim:* Shakespeare probably wrote a poem on that light bill, Mrs. Wingfield.

*Amanda:* I might have known better than to trust him with it! There's such a high price for negligence in this world!

*Jim:* Maybe the poem will win a ten-dollar prize.

*Amanda:* We'll just have to spend the remainder of the evening in the nineteenth century, before Mr. Edison made the Mazda lamp!

*Jim:* Candlelight is my favorite kind of light.

*Amanda:* That shows you're romantic! But that's no excuse for Tom. Well, we got through dinner. Very considerate of them to let us get through dinner before they plunged us into everlasting darkness, wasn't it, Mr. O'Connor?

*Jim:* Ha-ha!

*Amanda:* Tom, as a penalty for your carelessness you can help me with the dishes.

*Jim:* Let me give you a hand.

*Amanda:* Indeed you will not!

*Jim:* I ought to be good for something.

*Amanda:* Good for something? (*Her tone is rhapsodic.*) *You?* Why, Mr. O'Connor, nobody, *nobody's* given me this much entertainment in years—as you have!

*Jim:* Aw, now, Mrs. Wingfield!

*Amanda:* I'm not exaggerating, not one bit! But Sister is all by her lonesome. You go keep her company in the parlor! I'll give you this lovely old candelabrum that used to be on the altar at the church of the Heavenly Rest. It was melted a little out of shape when the church burnt down. Lightning struck it one spring. Gypsy Jones was holding a revival at the time and he intimated that the church was destroyed because the Episcopalians gave card parties.

*Jim:* Ha-ha.

*Amanda:* And how about coaxing Sister to drink a little wine? I think it would be good for her! Can you carry both at once?

*Jim:* Sure. I'm Superman!

*Amanda:* Now, Thomas, get into this apron!

*The door of kitchenette swings closed on Amanda's gay laughter; the flickering light approaches the portieres.*

*Laura sits up nervously as he enters. Her speech at first is low and breathless from the almost intolerable strain of being alone with a stranger.*

### (The Legend: "I Don't Suppose You Remember Me At All!")

*In her first speeches in this scene, before Jim's warmth overcomes her paralyzing shyness, Laura's voice is thin and breathless as though she has run up a steep flight of stairs.*

*Jim's attitude is gently humorous. In playing this scene it should be stressed that while the incident is apparently unimportant, it is to Laura the climax of her secret life.*

*Jim:* Hello, there, Laura.

*Laura (faintly):* Hello. (*She clears her throat.*)

*Jim:* How are you feeling now? Better?

*Laura:* Yes. Yes, thank you.

*Jim:* This is for you. A little dandelion wine. (*He extends it toward her with extravagant gallantry.*)

*Laura:* Thank you.

*Jim:* Drink it—but don't get drunk! (*He laughs heartily. Laura takes the glass uncertainly; laughs shyly.*) Where shall I set the candles?

*Laura:* Oh—oh, anywhere . . .

*Jim:* How about here on the floor? Any objections?

*Laura:* No.

*Jim:* I'll spread a newspaper under to catch the drippings. I like to sit on the floor. Mind if I do?

*Laura:* Oh, no.

*Jim:* Give me a pillow?

*Laura:* What?

*Jim:* A pillow!

*Laura:* Oh . . . (*Hands him one quickly.*)

*Jim:* How about you? Don't you like to sit on the floor?

*Laura:* Oh—yes.

*Jim:* Why don't you, then?

*Laura:* I—will.

*Jim:* Take a pillow! (*Laura does. Sits on the other side of the candelabrum. Jim crosses his legs and smiles engagingly at her.*) I can't hardly see you sitting way over there.

*Laura:* I can—see you.

*Jim:* I know, but that's not fair, I'm in the limelight. (*Laura moves her pillow closer.*) Good! Now I can see you! Comfortable?

*Laura:* Yes.

*Jim:* So am I. Comfortable as a cow. Will you have some gum?

*Laura:* No, thank you.

*Jim:* I think that I will indulge, with your permission. (*Musingly unwraps it and holds it up.*) Think of the fortune made by the guy that invented the first piece of chewing gum. Amazing, huh? The Wrigley Building is one of the sights of Chicago.—I saw it summer before last when I went up to the Century of Progress. Did you take in the Century of Progress?

*Laura:* No, I didn't.

*Jim:* Well, it was quite a wonderful exposition. What impressed me most was the Hall of Science. Gives you an idea of what the future will be in America, even more wonderful than the present time is! (*Pause. Smiling at her.*) Your brother tells me you're shy. Is that right, Laura?

*Laura:* I—don't know.

*Jim:* I judge you to be an old-fashioned type of girl. Well, I think that's pretty good type to be. Hope you don't think I'm being too personal—do you?

*Laura* (*hastily, out of embarrassment*): I believe I *will* take a piece of gum, if you— don't mind. (*Clearing her throat.*) Mr. O'Connor, have you—kept up with your singing?

*Jim:* Singing? Me?

*Laura:* Yes. I remember what a beautiful voice you had.

*Jim:* When did you hear me sing?

**(Voice Offstage In The Pause.)**

*Voice* (*offstage*):
O blow, ye winds, heigh-ho,
A-roving I will go!
I'm off to my love
With a boxing glove—
Ten thousand miles away!

*Jim:* You say you've heard me sing?

*Laura:* Oh, yes! Yes, very often . . . I—don't suppose you remember me—at all?

*Jim* (*smiling doubtfully*): You know I have an idea I've seen you before. I had that idea soon as you opened the door. It seemed almost like I was about to remember your name. But the name that I started to call you—wasn't a name! And so I stopped myself before I said it.

*Laura:* Wasn't it—Blue Roses?

*Jim* (*springs up, grinning*): Blue Roses! My gosh, yes—Blue Roses! That's what I had on my tongue when you opened the door! Isn't it funny what tricks your memory plays? I didn't connect you with the high school somehow or other. But that's where it was; it was high school. I didn't even know you were Shakespeare's sister! Gosh, I'm sorry.

*Laura:* I didn't expect you to. You—barely knew me!

*Jim:* But we did have a speaking acquaintance, huh?

*Laura:* Yes, we—spoke to each other.

*Jim:* When did you recognize me?

*Laura:* Oh, right away!

*Jim:* Soon as I came in the door?

*Laura:* When I heard your name I thought it was probably you. I knew that Tom used to know you a little in high school. So when you came in the door— Well, then I was—sure.

*Jim:* Why didn't you *say* something, then?

*Laura (breathlessly):* I didn't know what to say, I was—too surprised!

*Jim:* For goodness sakes! You know, this sure is funny!

*Laura:* Yes! Yes, isn't it, though . . .

*Jim:* Didn't we have a class in something together?

*Laura:* Yes, we did.

*Jim:* What class was that?

*Laura:* It was—singing—Chorus!

*Jim:* Aw!

*Laura:* I sat across the aisle from you in the Aud.

*Jim:* Aw.

*Laura:* Mondays, Wednesdays and Fridays.

*Jim:* Now I remember—you always came in late.

*Laura:* Yes, it was so hard for me, getting upstairs. I had that brace on my leg—it clumped so loud!

*Jim:* I never heard any clumping.

*Laura (wincing at the recollection):* To me it sounded like thunder!

*Jim:* Well, well, well. I never even noticed.

*Laura:* And everybody was seated before I came in. I had to walk in front of all those people. My seat was in the back row. I had to go clumping all the way up the aisle with everyone watching!

*Jim:* You shouldn't have been self-conscious.

*Laura:* I know, but I was. It was always such a relief when the singing started.

*Jim:* Aw, yes, I've placed you now! I used to call you Blue Roses. How was it that I got started calling you that?

*Laura:* I was out of school a little while with pleurosis. When I came back you asked me what was the matter. I said I had pleurosis—you thought I said Blue Roses. That's what you always called me after that!

*Jim:* I hope you didn't mind.

*Laura:* Oh, no—I liked it. You see, I wasn't acquainted with many—people. . . .

*Jim:* As I remember you sort of stuck by yourself.

*Laura:* I—I—never had much luck at—making friends.

*Jim:* I don't see why you wouldn't.

*Laura:* Well, I—started out badly.

*Jim:* You mean being—

*Laura:* Yes, it sort of—stood between me—

*Jim:* You shouldn't have let it!

*Laura:* I know, but it did, and—

*Jim:* You were shy with people!

*Laura:* I tried not to be but never could—

*Jim:* Overcome it?

*Laura:* No, I—I never could!

*Jim:* I guess being shy is something you have to work out of kind of gradually.

*Laura (sorrowfully):* Yes—I guess it—

*Jim:* Takes time!

*Laura:* Yes—

*Jim:* People are not so dreadful when you know them. That's what you have to remember! And everybody has problems, not just you, but practically everybody has got some problems. You think of yourself as having the only problems, as being the only one who is disappointed. But just look around you and you will see lots of people as disappointed as you are. For instance, I hoped when I was going to high school that I would be further along at this time, six years later, than I am now—You remember that wonderful write-up I had in *The Torch?*

*Laura:* Yes! (*She rises and crosses to table.*)

*Jim:* It said I was bound to succeed in anything I went into! (*Laura returns with the annual.*) Holy Jeez! *The Torch!* (*He accepts it reverently. They smile across it with mutual wonder. Laura crouches beside him and they begin to turn through it. Laura's shyness is dissolving in his warmth.*)

*Laura:* Here you are in *Pirates of Penzance!*

*Jim (wistfully):* I sang the baritone lead in that operetta.

*Laura (rapidly):* So—beautifully!

*Jim (protesting):* Aw—

*Laura:* Yes, yes—beautifully—beautifully!

*Jim:* You heard me?

*Laura:* All three times!

*Jim:* No!

*Laura:* Yes!

*Jim:* All three performances?

*Laura (looking down):* Yes.

*Jim:* Why?

*Laura:* I—wanted to ask you to—autograph my program.

*Jim:* Why didn't you ask me to?

*Laura:* You were always surrounded by your own friends so much that I never had a chance to.

*Jim:* You should have just—

*Laura:* Well, I—thought you might think I was—

*Jim:* Thought I might think you was—what?

*Laura:* Oh—

*Jim (with reflective relish):* I was beleaguered by females in those days.

*Laura:* You were terribly popular!

*Jim:* Yeah—

*Laura:* You had such a—friendly way—

*Jim:* I was spoiled in high school.

*Laura*: Everybody—liked you!

*Jim*: Including you?

*Laura*: I—yes, I—did, too—(*She gently closes the book in her lap.*)

*Jim*: Well, well, well!—Give me that program, Laura. (*She hands it to him. He signs it with a flourish.*) There you are—better late than never!

*Laura*: Oh, I—what a—surprise!

*Jim*: My signature isn't worth very much right now. But some day—maybe—it will increase in value! Being disappointed is one thing and being discouraged is something else. I am disappointed but I'm not discouraged. I'm twenty-three years old. How old are you?

*Laura*: I'll be twenty-four in June.

*Jim*: That's not old age!

*Laura*: No, but—

*Jim*: You finished high school?

*Laura* (*with difficulty*): I didn't go back.

*Jim*: You mean you dropped out?

*Laura*: I made bad grades in my final examinations. (*She rises and replaces the book and the program. Her voice strained.*) How is—Emily Meisenbach getting along?

*Jim*: Oh, that kraut-head!

*Laura*: Why do you call her that?

*Jim*: That's what she was.

*Laura*: You're not still—going with her?

*Jim*: I never see her.

*Laura*: It said in the Personal Section that you were—engaged!

*Jim*: I know, but I wasn't impressed by that—propaganda!

*Laura*: It wasn't—the truth?

*Jim*: Only in Emily's optimistic opinion!

*Laura*: Oh—

**(Legend: "What Have You Done Since High School?")**

*Jim lights a cigarette and leans indolently back on his elbows smiling at Laura with a warmth and charm which light her inwardly with altar candles. She remains by the table and turns in her hands a piece of glass to cover her tumult.*

*Jim* (*after several reflective puffs on a cigarette*): What have you done since high school? (*She seems not to hear him.*) Huh? (*Laura looks up.*) I said what have you done since high school, Laura?

*Laura*: Nothing much.

*Jim*: You must have been doing something these six long years.

*Laura*: Yes.

*Jim*: Well, then, such as what?

*Laura*: I took a business course at business college—

*Jim*: How did that work out?

*Laura*: Well, not very—well—I had to drop out, it gave me—indigestion—

    *Jim laughs gently.*

*Jim*: What are you doing now?

*Laura*: I don't do anything—much. Oh, please don't think I sit around doing nothing! My glass collection takes up a good deal of my time. Glass is something you have to take good care of.

*Jim*: What did you say—about glass?

*Laura*: Collection I said—I have one—(*She clears her throat and turns away again, acutely shy.*)

*Jim* (*abruptly*): You know what I judge to be the trouble with you? Inferiority complex! Know what that is? That's what they call it when someone low-rates himself! I understand it because I had it, too. Although my case was not so aggravated as yours seems to be. I had it until I took up public speaking, developed my voice, and learned that I had an aptitude for science. Before that time I never thought of myself as being outstanding in any way whatsoever! Now I've never made a regular study of it, but I have a friend who says I can analyze people better than doctors that make a profession of it. I don't claim that to be necessarily true, but I can sure guess a person's psychology, Laura! (*Takes out his gum.*) Excuse me, Laura. I always take it out when the flavor is gone. I'll use this scrap of paper to wrap it in. I know how it is to get it stuck on a shoe. Yep—that's what I judge to be your principal trouble. A lack of confidence in yourself as a person. You don't have the proper amount of faith in yourself. I'm basing that fact on a number of your remarks and also on certain observations I've made. For instance that clumping you thought was so awful in high school. You say that you even dreaded to walk into class. You see what you did? You dropped out of school, you gave up an education because of a clump, which as far as I know was practically non-existent! A little physical defect is what you have. Hardly noticeable even! Magnified thousands of times by imagination! You know what my strong advice to you is? Think of yourself as *superior* in some way!

*Laura*: In what way would I think?

*Jim*: Why, man alive, Laura! Just look about you a little. What do you see? A world full of common people! All of 'em born and all of 'em going to die! Which of them has one-tenth of your good points! Or mine! Or anyone else's, as far as that goes—Gosh! Everybody excels in some one thing. Some in many! (*Unconsciously glances at himself in the mirror.*) All you've got to do is discover in *what*! Take me, for instance. (*He adjusts his tie at the mirror.*) My interest happens to lie in electrodynamics. I'm taking a course in radio engineering at night school, Laura, on top of a fairly responsible job at the warehouse. I'm taking that course and studying public speaking.

*Laura*: Ohhhh.

*Jim*: Because I believe in the future of television! (*Turning back to her.*) I wish to be ready to go up right along with it. Therefore I'm planning to get in on the ground floor. In fact, I've already made the right connections and all that remains is for the industry itself to get under way! Full steam—(*His eyes are starry.*) Knowledge—Zzzzzp! Money—Zzzzzp!—Power! That's the cycle democracy is built on! (*His attitude is convincingly dynamic. Laura stares at him, even her shyness eclipsed in her absolute wonder. He suddenly grins.*) I guess you think I think a lot of myself!

*Laura:* No—o-o-o, I—

*Jim:* Now how about you? Isn't there something you take more interest in than anything else?

*Laura:* Well, I do—as I said—have my—glass collection—

*A peal of girlish laughter from the kitchen.*

*Jim:* I'm not right sure I know what you're talking about. What kind of glass is it?

*Laura:* Little articles of it, they're ornaments mostly! Most of them are little animals made out of glass, the tiniest little animals in the world. Mother calls them a glass menagerie! Here's an example of one, if you'd like to see it! This one is one of the oldest. It's nearly thirteen. (*He stretches out his hand.*) **(Music: "The Glass Menagerie.")** Oh, be careful—if you breathe, it breaks!

*Jim:* I'd better not take it. I'm pretty clumsy with things.

*Laura:* Go on, I trust you with him! (*Places it in his palm.*) There now—you're holding him gently! Hold him over the light, he loves the light! You see how the light shines through him?

*Jim:* It sure does shine!

*Laura:* I shouldn't be partial, but he is my favorite one.

*Jim:* What kind of a thing is this one supposed to be?

*Laura:* Haven't you noticed the single horn on his forehead?

*Jim:* A unicorn, huh?

*Laura:* Mmm-hmmm!

*Jim:* Unicorns, aren't they extinct in the modern world?

*Laura:* I know!

*Jim:* Poor little fellow, he must feel sort of lonesome.

*Laura (smiling):* Well, if he does he doesn't complain about it. He stays on a shelf with some horses that don't have horns and all of them seem to get along nicely together.

*Jim:* How do you know?

*Laura (lightly):* I haven't heard any arguments among them!

*Jim (grinning):* No arguments, huh? Well, that's a pretty good sign! Where shall I set him?

*Laura:* Put him on the table. They all like a change of scenery once in a while!

*Jim (stretching):* Well, well, well, well—Look how big my shadow is when I stretch!

*Laura:* Oh, oh, yes—it stretches across the ceiling!

*Jim (crossing to door):* I think it's stopped raining. (*Opens fire-escape door.*) Where does the music come from?

*Laura:* From the Paradise Dance Hall across the alley.

*Jim:* How about cutting the rug a little, Miss Wingfield?

*Laura:* Oh, I—

*Jim:* Or is your program filled up? Let me have a look at it. (*Grasps imaginary card.*) Why, every dance is taken! I'll just have to scratch some out. **(Waltz Music: "La Golondrina.")** Ahhh, a waltz! (*He executes some sweeping turns by himself, then holds his arms toward Laura.*)

*Laura* (*breathlessly*): I—can't dance!

*Jim:* There you go, that inferiority stuff!

*Laura:* I've never danced in my life!

*Jim:* Come on, try!

*Laura:* Oh, but I'd step on you!

*Jim:* I'm not made out of glass.

*Laura:* How—how—how do we start?

*Jim:* Just leave it to me. You hold your arms out a little.

*Laura:* Like this?

*Jim:* A little bit higher. Right. Now don't tighten up, that's the main thing about it—relax.

*Laura* (*laughing breathlessly*): It's hard not to.

*Jim:* Okay.

*Laura:* I'm afraid you can't budge me.

*Jim:* What do you bet I can't? (*He swings her into motion.*)

*Laura:* Goodness, yes, you can!

*Jim:* Let yourself go, now, Laura, just let yourself go.

*Laura:* I'm—

*Jim:* Come on!

*Laura:* Trying!

*Jim:* Not so stiff—Easy does it!

*Laura:* I know but I'm—

*Jim:* Loosen th' backbone! There now, that's a lot better.

*Laura:* Am I?

*Jim:* Lots, lots better! (*He moves her about the room in a clumsy waltz.*)

*Laura:* Oh, my!

*Jim:* Ha-ha!

*Laura:* Goodness, yes you can!

*Jim:* Ha-ha-ha! (*They suddenly bump into the table, Jim stops.*) What did we hit on?

*Laura:* Table.

*Jim:* Did something fall off it? I think—

*Laura:* Yes.

*Jim:* I hope that it wasn't the little glass horse with the horn!

*Laura:* Yes.

*Jim:* Aw, aw, aw. Is it broken?

*Laura:* Now it is just like all the other horses.

*Jim:* It's lost its—

*Laura:* Horn! It doesn't matter. Maybe it's a blessing in disguise.

*Jim:* You'll never forgive me. I bet that that was your favorite piece of glass.

*Laura*: I don't have favorites much. It's no tragedy, Freckles. Glass breaks so easily. No matter how careful you are. The traffic jars the shelves and things fall off them.

*Jim*: Still I'm awfully sorry that I was the cause.

*Laura (smiling)*: I'll just imagine he had an operation. The horn was removed to make him feel less—freakish! (*They both laugh.*) Now he will feel more at home with the other horses, the ones that don't have horns . . .

*Jim*: Ha-ha, that's very funny! (*Suddenly serious.*) I'm glad to see that you have a sense of humor. You know—you're—well—very different! Surprisingly different from anyone else I know! (*His voice becomes soft and hesitant with a genuine feeling.*) Do you mind me telling you that? (*Laura is abashed beyond speech.*) You make me feel sort of—I don't know how to put it! I'm usually pretty good at expressing things, but—This is something that I don't know how to say! (*Laura touches her throat and clears it—turns the broken unicorn in her hands.*) (*Even softer.*) Has anyone ever told you that you were pretty? **(Pause: Music.)** (*Laura looks up slowly, with wonder, and shakes her head.*) Well, you are! In a very different way from anyone else. And all the nicer because of the difference, too. (*His voice becomes low and husky. Laura turns away, nearly faint with the novelty of her emotions.*) I wish you were my sister. I'd teach you to have some confidence in yourself. The different people are not like other people, but being different is nothing to be ashamed of. Because other people are not such wonderful people. They're one hundred times one thousand. You're one times one! They walk all over the earth. You just stay here. They're common as—weeds, but—you—well, you're—*Blue Roses!*

**(Image On Screen: Blue Roses.)**

**(Music Changes.)**

*Laura*: But blue is wrong for—roses . . .

*Jim*: It's right for you—You're—pretty!

*Laura*: In what respect am I pretty?

*Jim*: In all respects—believe me! Your eyes—your hair—are pretty! Your hands are pretty! (*He catches hold of her hand.*) You think I'm making this up because I'm invited to dinner and have to be nice. Oh, I could do that! I could put on an act for you, Laura, and say lots of things without being very sincere. But this time I am. I'm talking to you sincerely. I happened to notice you had this inferiority complex that keeps you from feeling comfortable with people. Somebody needs to build your confidence up and make you proud instead of shy and turning away and—blushing—Somebody ought to—ought to—*kiss* you, Laura! (*His hand slips slowly up her arm to her shoulder.*) **(Music Swells Tumultuously.)** (*He suddenly turns her about and kisses her on the lips. When he releases her Laura sinks on the sofa with a bright, dazed look. Jim backs away and fishes in his pocket for a cigarette.*) **(Legend On Screen: "Souvenir.")** Stumble-john! (*He lights the cigarette, avoiding her* look. There is a peal of girlish laughter from Amanda in the kitchen. Laura slowly raises and opens her hand. It still contains the little broken glass animal. She looks at it with a tender, bewildered expression.) Stumble-john! I shouldn't have done that—That was way off the beam. You don't smoke, do you? (*She looks up, smiling, not hearing the question. He sits beside her a little gingerly. She looks at him speechlessly—waiting. He coughs decorously and moves a little farther aside as he considers the situation and senses her feelings, dimly, with perturbation. Gently.*) Would you—care for a—mint? (*She doesn't seem to hear him but her look grows brighter even.*) Peppermint—Life Saver? My pocket's a regular drug store—wherever I go . . . (*He pops a mint in his mouth. Then gulps and decides to make a clean breast of it. He speaks slowly and gingerly.*) Laura, you know, if I had a sister like you, I'd do the same thing as Tom, I'd bring out fellows— introduce her to them. The right type of boys of a type to—appreciate her. Only—well—he made a mistake about me. Maybe I've got no call to be say- ing this. That may not have been the idea in having me over. But what if it was? There's nothing wrong about that. The only trouble is that in my case—I'm not in a situation to—do the right thing. I can't take down your number and say I'll phone. I can't call up next week and—ask for a date. I thought I had better explain the situation in case you misunderstood it and—hurt your feelings. . . . (*Pause. Slowly, very slowly, Laura's look changes, her eyes returning slowly from his to the ornament in her palm.*)

*Amanda utters another gay laugh in the kitchen.*

Laura (*faintly*): You—won't—call again?
Jim: No, Laura, I can't. (*He rises from the sofa.*) As I was just explaining, I've—got strings on me, Laura, I've—been going steady! I go out all the time with a girl named Betty. She's a home-girl like you, and Catholic, and Irish, and in a great many ways we—get along fine. I met her last summer on a moonlight boat trip up the river to Alton, on the *Majestic*. Well—right away from the start it was—love! **(Legend: Love!)** (*Laura sways slightly forward and grips the arm of the sofa. He fails to notice, now enrapt in his own comfortable being.*) Being in love has made a new man of me! (*Leaning stiffly forward, clutching the arm of the sofa, Laura struggles visibly with her storm. But Jim is oblivious, she is a long way off.*) The power of love is really pretty tremendous! Love is something that—changes the whole world, Laura! (*The storm abates a little and Laura leans back. He notices her again.*) It happened that Betty's aunt took sick, she got a wire and had to go to Centralia. So Tom—when he asked me to dinner—I naturally just accepted the invitation, not knowing that you— that he—that I—(*He stops awkwardly.*) Huh—I'm a stumble-john! (*He flops back on the sofa. The holy candles in the altar of Laura's face have been snuffed out! There is a look of almost infinite desolation. Jim glances at her uneasily.*) I wish that you would—say something. (*She bites her lip which was trembling and then bravely smiles. She opens her hand again on the broken glass ornament. Then she gently takes his hand and raises it level with her own. She carefully places the unicorn in the palm of his hand, then pushes his fingers closed upon it.*) What are

you—doing that for? You want me to have him?—Laura? (*She nods.*) What for?

Laura: A—souvenir . . .

*She rises unsteadily and crouches beside the victrola to wind it up.*

**(Legend On Screen: "Things Have A Way Of Turning Out So Badly.")**

**(Or Image: "Gentleman Caller Waving Good-bye!—Gaily.")**

*At this moment Amanda rushes brightly back in the front room. She bears a pitcher of fruit punch in an old-fashioned cut-glass pitcher and a plate of macaroons. The plate has a gold border and poppies painted on it.*

Amanda: Well, well, well! Isn't the air delightful after the shower? I've made you children a little liquid refreshment. (*Turns gaily to the gentleman caller.*) Jim, do you know that song about lemonade?
  "Lemonade, lemonade
  Made in the shade and stirred with a spade—
  Good enough for any old maid!"

Jim (*uneasily*): Ha-ha! No—I never heard it.

Amanda: Why, Laura! You look so serious!

Jim: We were having a serious conversation.

Amanda: Good! Now you're better acquainted!

Jim (*uncertainly*): Ha-ha! Yes.

Amanda: You modern young people are much more serious-minded than my generation. I was so gay as a girl!

Jim: You haven't changed, Mrs. Wingfield.

Amanda: Tonight I'm rejuvenated! The gaiety of the occasion, Mr. O'Connor! (*She tosses her head with a peal of laughter. Spills lemonade.*) Oooo! I'm baptizing myself!

Jim: Here—let me—

Amanda (*setting the pitcher down*): There now. I discovered we had some maraschino cherries. I dumped them in, juice and all!

Jim: You shouldn't have gone to that trouble, Mrs. Wingfield.

Amanda: Trouble, trouble? Why it was loads of fun! Didn't you hear me cutting up in the kitchen? I bet your ears were burning! I told Tom how outdone with him I was for keeping you to himself so long a time! He should have brought you over much, much sooner! Well, now that you've found your way, I want you to be a very frequent caller! Not just occasional but all the time. Oh, we're going to have a lot of gay times together! I see them coming! Mmm, just breathe that air! So fresh, and the moon's so pretty! I'll skip back out—I know where my place is when young folks are having a—serious conversation!

Jim: Oh, don't go out, Mrs. Wingfield. The fact of the matter is I've got to be going.

Amanda: Going, now? You're joking! Why, it's only the shank of the evening, Mr. O'Connor!

Jim: Well, you know how it is.

Amanda: You mean you're a young workingman and have to keep workingmen's hours. We'll let you off early tonight. But only on the condition that next time you stay later. What's the best night for you? Isn't Saturday night the best night for you workingmen?

Jim: I have a couple of time-clocks to punch, Mrs. Wingfield. One at morning, another one at night!

Amanda: My, but you *are* ambitious! You work at night, too?

Jim: No, Ma'am, not work but—Betty! (*He crosses deliberately to pick up his hat. The band at the Paradise Dance Hall goes into a tender waltz.*)

Amanda: Betty? Betty? Who's—Betty? (*There is an ominous cracking sound in the sky.*)

Jim: Oh, just a girl. The girl I go steady with! (*He smiles charmingly. The sky falls.*)

**(Legend: "The Sky Falls.")**

Amanda (*a long-drawn exhalation*): Ohhhh . . . Is it a serious romance, Mr. O'Connor?

Jim: We're going to be married the second Sunday in June.

Amanda: Ohhhh—how nice! Tom didn't mention that you were engaged to be married.

Jim: The cat's not out of the bag at the warehouse yet. You know how they are. They call you Romeo and stuff like that. (*He stops at the oval mirror to put on his hat. He carefully shapes the brim and the crown to give a discreetly dashing effect.*) It's been a wonderful evening, Mrs. Wingfield. I guess this is what they mean by Southern hospitality.

Amanda: It really wasn't anything at all.

Jim: I hope it don't seem like I'm rushing off. But I promised Betty I'd pick her up at the Wabash depot, an' by the time I get my jalopy down there her train'll be in. Some women are pretty upset if you keep 'em waiting.

Amanda: Yes, I know—The tyranny of women! (*Extends her hand.*) Goodbye, Mr. O'Connor. I wish you luck—and happiness—and success! All three of them, and so does Laura!—Don't you, Laura?

Laura: Yes!

Jim (*taking her hand*): Goodbye, Laura. I'm certainly going to treasure that souvenir. And don't you forget the good advice I gave you. (*Raises his voice to a cheery shout.*) So long, Shakespeare! Thanks again, ladies—Good night!

*He grins and ducks jauntily out.*

*Still bravely grimacing, Amanda closes the door on the gentleman caller. Then she turns back to the room with a puzzled expression. She and Laura don't dare to face each other. Laura crouches beside the victrola to wind it.*

*Amanda* (*faintly*): Things have a way of turning out so badly. I don't believe that I would play the victrola. Well, well—well—Our gentleman caller was engaged to be married! Tom!

*Tom* (*from back*): Yes, Mother?

*Amanda*: Come in here a minute. I want to tell you something awfully funny.

*Tom* (*enters with macaroon and a glass of the lemonade*): Has the gentleman caller gotten away already?

*Amanda*: The gentleman caller has made an early departure. What a wonderful joke you played on us!

*Tom*: How do you mean?

*Amanda*: You didn't mention that he was engaged to be married.

*Tom*: Jim? Engaged?

*Amanda*: That's what he just informed us.

*Tom*: I'll be jiggered! I didn't know about that.

*Amanda*: That seems very peculiar.

*Tom*: What's peculiar about it?

*Amanda*: Didn't you call him your best friend down at the warehouse?

*Tom*: He is, but how did I know?

*Amanda*: It seems extremely peculiar that you wouldn't know your best friend was going to be married!

*Tom*: The warehouse is where I work, not where I know things about people!

*Amanda*: You don't know things anywhere! You live in a dream; you manufacture illusions! (*He crosses to door.*) Where are you going?

*Tom*: I'm going to the movies.

*Amanda*: That's right, now that you've had us make such fools of ourselves. The effort, the preparations, all the expense! The new floor lamp, the rug, the clothes for Laura! All for what? To entertain some other girl's fiancé! Go to the movies, go! Don't think about us, a mother deserted, an unmarried sister who's crippled and has no job! Don't let anything interfere with your selfish pleasure! Just go, go, go—to the movies!

*Tom*: All right, I will! The more you shout about my selfishness to me the quicker I'll go, and I won't go to the movies!

*Amanda*: Go, then! Then go to the moon—you selfish dreamer!

*Tom smashes his glass on the floor. He plunges out on the fire-escape, slamming the door. Laura screams—cut by door.*

*Dance-hall music up. Tom goes to the rail and grips it desperately, lifting his face in the chill white moonlight penetrating the narrow abyss of the alley.*

**(Legend On Screen: "And So Good-bye . . . ")**

*Tom's closing speech is timed with the interior pantomime. The interior scene is played as though viewed through sound-proof glass. Amanda appears to be making a comforting speech to Laura who is huddled upon the sofa. Now that we cannot hear the mother's speech, her silliness is gone and she has dignity and tragic beauty.*

*Laura's dark hair hides her face until at the end of the speech she lifts it to smile at her mother. Amanda's gestures are slow and graceful, almost dancelike, as she comforts the daughter. At the end of her speech she glances a moment at the father's picture—then withdraws through the portieres. At close of Tom's speech, Laura blows out the candles, ending the play.*

Tom: I didn't go to the movies, I went much further—for time is the longest distance between two places—Not long after that I was fired for writing a poem on the lid of a shoe-box. I left Saint Louis. I descended the steps of this fire-escape for a last time and followed, from then on, in my father's footsteps, attempting to find in motion what was lost in space—I traveled around a great deal. The cities swept about me like dead leaves, leaves that were brightly colored but torn away from the branches. I would have stopped, but was pursued by something. It always came upon me unawares, taking me altogether by surprise. Perhaps it was a familiar bit of music. Perhaps it was only a piece of transparent glass. Perhaps I am walking along a street at night, in some strange city, before I have found companions. I pass the lighted window of a shop where perfume is sold. The window is filled with pieces of colored glass, tiny transparent bottles in delicate colors, like bits of a shattered rainbow. Then all at once my sister touches my shoulder. I turn around and look into her eyes . . . Oh, Laura, Laura, I tried to leave you behind me, but I am more faithful than I intended to be! I reach for a cigarette, I cross the street, I run into the movies or a bar, I buy a drink, I speak to the nearest stranger—anything that can blow your candles out! (*Laura bends over the candles.*)—for nowadays the world is lit by lightning! Blow out your candles, Laura—and so good-bye. . . .

*She blows the candles out.*

**(The Scene Dissolves.)**

Compare:

The Glass Menagerie and Tennessee Williams's "How to Stage The Glass Menagerie" (page 1724).

> *The theater is one of the most useful and expressive instruments for a coun-
> try's edification, the barometer that registers its greatness or its decline.*

Federico García Lorca

## Beth Henley

CRIMES OF THE HEART                                                      1979

Beth Henley was born in Jackson, Mississippi, in 1952, daughter of an actress. As a
child she acted herself and even wrote her
first play in sixth grade. Henley attended
Southern Methodist University and studied
acting at the University of Illinois. In 1976,
she abandoned acting and moved to Los
Angeles to write plays and screenplays. Her
first full-length play, Crimes of the Heart
(1979), was produced first in Louisville
and then off-Broadway in New York. Not
until it won the Pulitzer Prize and The
New York Drama Critics Circle Award did
the play command a Broadway production.
Henley's later plays include The Miss
Firecracker Contest (1980) and The
Debutante Ball (1985). More recently,
Henley won an Academy Award nomina-

Beth Henley

tion for her 1986 screenplay for the popular film version of Crimes of the Heart, which
starred Jessica Lange, Diane Keaton, and Sissy Spacek as the three sisters, and actor-
playwright Sam Shepherd as Doc Porter.

For Len, C.C., and Kayo.

The Cast

Lenny MaGrath, 30, the oldest sister
Chick Boyle, 29, the sisters' first cousin
Doc Porter, 30, Meg's old boyfriend
Meg MaGrath, 27, the middle sister
Babe Botrelle, 24, the youngest sister
Barnette Lloyd, 26, Babe's lawyer

The Setting

*The setting of the entire play is the kitchen in the MaGrath sisters' house in Hazlehurst, Mississippi, a small southern town. The old-fashioned kitchen is unusually spacious, but there is a lived-in, cluttered look about it. There are four different entrances and exits to the kitchen: the back door; the door leading to the dining room and the front of the house; a door leading to the downstairs bedroom; and a staircase leading to the upstairs room. There is a table near the center of the room, and a cot has been set up in one of the corners.*

The Time

*In the fall; five years after Hurricane Camille*

# ACT I

*The lights go up on the empty kitchen. It is late afternoon. Lenny MaGrath, a thirty-year-old woman with a round figure and face, enters from the back door carrying a white suitcase, a saxophone case, and a brown paper sack. She sets the suitcase and the sax case down and takes the brown sack to the kitchen table. After glancing quickly at the door, she gets the cookie jar from the kitchen counter, a box of matches from the stove and then brings both objects back down to the kitchen table. Excitedly, she reaches into the brown sack and pulls out a package of birthday candles. She quickly opens the package and removes a candle. She tries to stick the candle into a cookie—it falls off. She sticks the candle in again but the cookie is too hard and it crumbles. Frantically, she gets a second cookie from the jar. She strikes a match, lights the candle and begins dripping wax onto the cookie. Just as she is beginning to smile we hear Chick's voice from offstage.*

Chick's voice: Lenny! Oh, Lenny! (*Lenny quickly blows out the candle and stuffs the cookie and candle into her dress pocket. Chick, 29, enters from the back door. She is a brightly dressed matron with yellow hair and shiny, red lips.*)
Chick: Hi! I saw your car pull up.
Lenny: Hi.
Chick: Well, did you see today's paper? (*Lenny nods.*) It's just too awful! It's just way too awful! How I'm gonna continue holding my head up high in this community, I do not know. Did you remember to pick up those pantyhose for me?

*Lenny:* They're in the sack.

*Chick:* Well, thank goodness, at least I'm not gonna have to go into town wearing holes in my stockings. (*Chick gets the package, tears it open and proceeds to take off one pair of stockings and put on another, throughout the following scene. There should be something slightly grotesque about this woman changing her stockings in the kitchen.*)

*Lenny:* Did Uncle Watson call?

*Chick:* Yes, Daddy has called me twice already. He said Babe's ready to come home. We've got to get right over and pick her up before they change their simple minds.

*Lenny* (*hesitantly*): Oh, I know, of course, it's just—

*Chick:* What?

*Lenny:* Well, I was hoping Meg would call.

*Chick:* Meg?

*Lenny:* Yes, I sent her a telegram: about Babe, and—

*Chick:* A telegram?! Couldn't you just phone her up?

*Lenny:* Well, no, 'cause her phone's . . . out of order.

*Chick:* Out of order?

*Lenny:* Disconnected. I don't know what.

*Chick:* Well, that sounds like Meg. My, these are snug. Are you sure you bought my right size?

*Lenny* (*looking at the box*): Size extra petite.

*Chick:* Well, they're skimping on the nylon material. (*Struggling to pull up the stockings.*) That's all there is to it. Skimping on the nylon. (*She finishes on one leg and starts on the other.*) Now, just what all did you say in this "telegram" to Meg?

*Lenny:* I don't recall exactly. I, well, I just told her to come on home.

*Chick:* To come on home! Why, Lenora Josephine, have you lost your only brain, or what?

*Lenny* (*nervously, as she begins to pick up the mess of dirty stockings and plastic wrappings*): But Babe wants Meg home. She asked me to call her.

*Chick:* I'm not talking about what Babe wants.

*Lenny:* Well, what then?

*Chick:* Listen, Lenora, I think it's pretty accurate to assume that after this morning's paper, Babe's gonna be incurring some mighty negative publicity around this town. And Meg's appearance isn't gonna help out a bit.

*Lenny:* What's wrong with Meg?

*Chick:* She had a loose reputation in high school.

*Lenny* (*weakly*): She was popular.

*Chick:* She was known all over Copiah County as cheap Christmas trash, and that was the least of it. There was that whole sordid affair with Doc Porter, leaving him a cripple.

*Lenny:* A cripple—he's got a limp. Just, kind of, barely a limp.

*Chick:* Well, his mother was going to keep *me* out of the Ladies' Social League because of it.

*Lenny:* What?

*Chick:* That's right. I never told you, but I had to go plead with that mean old woman and convinced her that I was just as appalled and upset with what Meg had done as she was, and that I was only a first cousin anyway and I could hardly be blamed for all the skeletons in the Magraths' closet. It was humiliating. I tell you, she even brought up your mother's death. And that poor cat.

*Lenny:* Oh! Oh! Oh, please, Chick! I'm sorry. But you're in the Ladies' League now.

*Chick:* Yes. That's true, I am. But frankly, if Mrs. Porter hadn't developed that tumor in her bladder, I wouldn't be in the club today, much less a committee head. (*As she brushes her hair.*) Anyway, you be a sweet potato and wait right here for Meg to call, so's you can convince her not to come back home. It would make things a whole lot easier on everybody. Don't you think it really would?

*Lenny:* Probably.

*Chick:* Good, then suit yourself. How's my hair?

*Lenny:* Fine.

*Chick:* Not pooching out in the back, is it?

*Lenny:* No.

*Chick* (*cleaning the hair from her brush*): All right then, I'm on my way. I've got Annie May over there keeping an eye on Peekay and Buck Jr., but I don't trust her with them for long periods of time. (*Dropping the ball of hair onto the floor.*) Her mind is like a loose sieve. Honestly it is. (*She puts the brush back into her purse.*) Oh! Oh! Oh! I almost forgot. Here's a present for you. Happy Birthday to Lenny, from the Buck Boyles! (*Chick takes a wrapped package from her bag and hands it to Lenny.*)

*Lenny:* Why, thank you, Chick. It's so nice to have you remember my birthday every year like you do.

*Chick* (*modestly*): Oh well, now, that's just the way I am, I suppose. That's just the way I was brought up to be. Well, why don't you go on and open up the present?

*Lenny:* All right. (*She starts to unwrap the gift.*)

*Chick:* It's a box of candy—assorted crèmes.

*Lenny:* Candy—that's always a nice gift.

*Chick:* And you have a sweet tooth, don't you?

*Lenny:* I guess.

*Chick:* Well, I'm glad you like it.

*Lenny:* I do.

*Chick:* Oh, speaking of which, remember that little polka-dot dress you got Peekay for her fifth birthday last month?

*Lenny:* The red-and-white one?

*Chick:* Yes; well, the first time I put it in the washing machine, I mean the very first time, it fell all to pieces. Those little polka dots just dropped right off in the water.

*Lenny (crushed):* Oh, no. Well, I'll get something else for her then—a little toy.

*Chick:* Oh, no, no, no, no, no! We wouldn't hear of it! I just wanted to let you know so you wouldn't go and waste any more of your hard-earned money on that make of dress. Those inexpensive brands just don't hold up. I'm sorry, but not in these modern washing machines.

*Doc Porter's voice:* Hello! Hello, Lenny!

*Chick (taking over):* Oh, look, it's Doc Porter! Come on in, Doc! Please come right on in! (*Doc Porter enters through the back door. He is carrying a large sack of pecans. Doc is an attractively worn man with a slight limp that adds rather than detracts from his quiet seductive quality. He is 30 years old, but appears slightly older.*) Well, how are you doing? How in the world are you doing?

*Doc:* Just fine, Chick.

*Chick:* And how are you liking it now that you're back in Hazlehurst?

*Doc:* Oh, I'm finding it somewhat enjoyable.

*Chick:* Somewhat! Only somewhat! Will you listen to him! What a silly, silly, silly man! Well, I'm on my way. I've got some people waiting on me. (*Whispering to Doc.*) It's Babe. I'm on my way to pick her up.

*Doc:* Oh.

*Chick:* Well, goodbye! Farewell and goodbye!

*Lenny:* 'Bye. (*Chick exits.*)

*Doc:* Hello.

*Lenny:* Hi. I guess you heard about the thing with Babe.

*Doc:* Yeah.

*Lenny:* It was in the newspaper.

*Doc:* Uh huh.

*Lenny:* What a mess.

*Doc:* Yeah.

*Lenny:* Well, come on and sit down. I'll heat us up some coffee.

*Doc:* That's okay. I can only stay a minute. I have to pick up Scott; he's at the dentist.

*Lenny:* Oh; well, I'll heat some up for myself. I'm kinda thirsty for a cup of hot coffee. (*Lenny puts the coffeepot on the burner.*)

*Doc:* Lenny—

*Lenny:* What?

*Doc (not able to go on):* Ah . . .

*Lenny:* Yes?

*Doc:* Here, some pecans for you. (*He hands her the sack.*)

*Lenny:* Why, thank you, Doc. I love pecans.

*Doc:* My wife and Scott picked them up around the yard.

*Lenny:* Well, I can use them to make a pie. A pecan pie.

*Doc:* Yeah. Look, Lenny, I've got some bad news for you.

*Lenny:* What?

*Doc:* Well, you know, you've been keeping Billy Boy out on our farm; he's been grazing out there.

*Lenny:* Yes—

*Doc*: Well, last night, Billy Boy died.

*Lenny*: He died?

*Doc*: Yeah. I'm sorry to tell you when you've got all this on you, but I thought you'd want to know.

*Lenny*: Well, yeah. I do. He died?

*Doc*: Uh huh. He was struck by lightning.

*Lenny*: Struck by lightning? In that storm yesterday?

*Doc*: That's what we think.

*Lenny*: Gosh, struck by lightning. I've had Billy Boy so long. You know. Ever since I was ten years old.

*Doc*: Yeah. He was a mighty old horse.

*Lenny* (*stung*): Mighty old.

*Doc*: Almost twenty years old.

*Lenny*: That's right, twenty years. 'Cause; ah, I'm thirty years old today. Did you know that?

*Doc*: No, Lenny, I didn't know. Happy Birthday.

*Lenny*: Thanks. (*She begins to cry.*)

*Doc*: Oh, come on now, Lenny. Come on. Hey, hey, now. You know I can't stand it when you Magrath women start to cry. You know it just gets me.

*Lenny*: Oh ho! Sure! You mean when Meg cries! Meg's the one you could never stand to watch cry! Not me! I could fill up a pig's trough!

*Doc*: Now, Lenny . . . stop it. Come on. Jesus!

*Lenny*: Okay! Okay! I don't know what's wrong with me. I don't mean to make a scene. I've been on this crying jag. (*She blows her nose.*) All this stuff with Babe, and old Granddaddy's gotten worse in the hospital and I can't get in touch with Meg.

*Doc*: You tried calling Meggy?

*Lenny*: Yes.

*Doc*: Is she coming home?

*Lenny*: Who knows. She hasn't called me. That's what I'm waiting here for— hoping she'll call.

*Doc*: She still living in California?

*Lenny*: Yes; in Hollywood.

*Doc*: Well, give me a call if she gets in. I'd like to see her.

*Lenny*: Oh, you would, huh?

*Doc*: Yeah, Lenny, sad to say, but I would.

*Lenny*: It is sad. It's very sad indeed. (*They stare at each other, then look away. There is a moment of tense silence.*)

*Doc*: Hey, Jell-O Face, your coffee's boiling.

*Lenny* (*going to check*): Oh, it is? Thanks. (*After she checks the pot.*) Look, you'd better go on and pick Scott up. You don't want him to have to wait for you.

*Doc*: Yeah, you're right. Poor kid. It's his first time at the dentist.

*Lenny*: Poor thing.

*Doc*: Well, 'bye. I'm sorry to have to tell you about your horse.

*Lenny*: Oh, I know. Tell Joan thanks for picking up the pecans.

Doc: I will. (*He starts to leave.*)

Lenny: Oh, how's the baby?

Doc: She's fine. Real pretty. She, ah, holds your finger in her hand; like this.

Lenny: Oh, that's cute.

Doc: Yeah. 'Bye, Lenny.

Lenny: 'Bye. (*Doc exits. Lenny stares after him for a moment, then goes and sits back down at the kitchen table. She reaches into her pocket and pulls out a somewhat crumbled cookie and a wax candle. She lights the candle again, lets the wax drip onto the cookie, then sticks the candle on top of the cookie. She begins to sing the "Happy Birthday" song to herself. At the end of the song she pauses, silently makes a wish, and blows out the candle. She waits a moment, then relights the candle, and repeats her actions, only this time making a different wish at the end of the song. She starts to repeat the procedure for the third time, as the phone begins to ring. She goes to answer it.*) Hello . . . oh, hello, Lucille, how's Zackery? . . . Oh, no! . . . Oh, I'm so sorry. Of course, it must be grueling for you . . . Yes, I understand. Your only brother . . . No, she's not here yet. Chick just went to pick her up . . . Oh, now, Lucille, she's still his wife, I'm sure she'll be interested . . . Well, you can just tell me the information and I'll relate it all to her . . . Uh hum, his liver's saved. Oh, that's good news! . . . Well, of course, when you look at it like that . . . Breathing stabilized . . . Damage to the spinal column, not yet determined . . . Okay . . . Yes, Lucille, I've got it all down . . . Uh huh, I'll give her that message. 'Bye, 'bye. (*Lenny drops the pencil and paper down. She sighs deeply, wipes her cheeks with the back of her hand, and goes to the stove to pour herself a cup of coffee. After a few moments, the front door is heard slamming. Lenny starts. A whistle is heard, then Meg's voice.*)

Meg's voice: I'm home! (*She whistles the family whistle.*) Anybody home?

Lenny: Meg? Meg! (*Meg, 27, enters from the dining room. She has sad, magic eyes and wears a hat. She carries a worn-out suitcase.*)

Meg (*dropping her suitcase, running to hug Lenny*): Lenny—

Lenny: Well, Meg! Why, Meg! Oh, Meggy! Why didn't you call? Did you fly in? You didn't take a cab, did you? Why didn't you give us a call?

Meg (*overlapping*): Oh, Lenny! Why, Lenny! Dear, Lenny! (*Then she looks at Lenny's face.*) My God, we're getting so old! Oh, I called for heaven's sake. Of course, I called!

Lenny: Well, I never talked to you—

Meg: Well, I know! I let the phone ring right off the hook!

Lenny: Well, as a matter of fact, I was out most of the morning seeing to Babe—

Meg: Now, just what's all this business about Babe? How could you send me such a telegram about Babe? And Zackery! You say somebody's shot Zackery?

Lenny: Yes, they have.

Meg: Well, good Lord! Is he dead?

Lenny: No. But he's in the hospital. He was shot in his stomach.

Meg: In his stomach! How awful! Do they know who shot him? (*Lenny nods.*) Well, who? Who was it? Who? Who?

*Lenny*: Babe! They're all saying Babe shot him! They took her to jail! And they're saying she shot him! They're all saying it! It's horrible! It's awful!

*Meg (overlapping)*: Jail! Good Lord, jail! Well, who? Who's saying it? Who?

*Lenny*: Everyone! The policemen, the sheriff, Zackery, even Babe's saying it! Even Babe herself!

*Meg*: Well, for God's sake. For God's sake.

*Lenny (overlapping as she falls apart)*: It's horrible! It's horrible! It's just horrible!

*Meg*: Now calm down, Lenny. Just calm down. Would you like a Coke? Here, I'll get you some Coke. (*Meg gets a Coke from the refrigerator. She opens it and downs a large swig.*) Why? Why would she shoot him? Why? (*Meg hands the Coke bottle to Lenny.*)

*Lenny*: I talked to her this morning and I asked her that very question. I said, "Babe, why would you shoot Zackery? He was your own husband. Why would you shoot him?" And do you know what she said? (*Meg shakes her head.*) She said, "'Cause I didn't like his looks. I just didn't like his looks."

*Meg (after a pause)*: Well, I don't like his looks.

*Lenny*: But you didn't shoot him! You wouldn't shoot a person 'cause you didn't like their looks! You wouldn't do that! Oh, I hate to say this—I do hate to say this—but I believe Babe is ill. I mean in-her-head ill.

*Meg*: Oh, now, Lenny, don't you say that! There's plenty of good sane reasons to shoot another person and I'm sure that Babe had one. Now what we've got to do is get her the best lawyer in town. Do you have any ideas on who's the best lawyer in town?

*Lenny*: Well, Zackery is, of course; but he's been shot!

*Meg*: Well, count him out! Just count him and his whole firm out!

*Lenny*: Anyway, you don't have to worry, she's already got her lawyer.

*Meg*: She does? Who?

*Lenny*: Barnette Lloyd. Annie Lloyd's boy. He just opened his office here in town. And Uncle Watson said we'd be doing Annie a favor by hiring him up.

*Meg*: Doing Annie a favor? Doing Annie a favor? Well, what about Babe? Have you thought about Babe? Do we want to do her a favor of thirty or forty years in jail? Have you thought about that?

*Lenny*: Now, don't snap at me! Just don't snap at me! I try to do what's right! All this responsibility keeps falling on my shoulders, and I try to do what's right!

*Meg*: Well, boo hoo, hoo, hoo! And how in the hell could you send me such a telegram about Babe!

*Lenny*: Well, if you had a phone, or if you didn't live way out there in Hollywood and not even come home for Christmas, maybe I wouldn't have to pay all that money to send you a telegram!

*Meg (overlapping)*: "Babe's in terrible trouble—Stop! Zackery's been shot—Stop! Come home immediately—Stop! Stop! Stop!"

*Lenny*: And what was that you said about how old we're getting? When you looked at my face, you said, "My God, we're getting so old!" But you didn't mean we—you meant me! Didn't you? I'm thirty years old today and my face is getting all pinched up and my hair is falling out in the comb.

*Meg:* Why, Lenny! It's your birthday, October 23. How could I forget. Happy Birthday!

*Lenny:* Well, it's not. I'm thirty years old and Billy Boy died last night. He was struck by lightning. He was struck dead.

*Meg (reaching for a cigarette):* Struck dead. Oh, what a mess. What a mess. Are you really thirty? Then I must be twenty-seven and Babe is twenty-four. My God, we're getting so old. (*They are silent for several moments as Meg drags off her cigarette and Lenny drinks her Coke.*) What's the cot doing in the kitchen?

*Lenny:* Well, I rolled it out when Old Granddaddy got sick. So I could be close and hear him at night if he needed something.

*Meg (glancing toward the door leading to the downstairs bedroom):* Is Old Granddaddy here?

*Lenny:* Why, no. Old Granddaddy's at the hospital.

*Meg:* Again?

*Lenny:* Meg!

*Meg:* What?

*Lenny:* I wrote you all about it. He's been in the hospital over three months straight.

*Meg:* He has?

*Lenny:* Don't you remember? I wrote you about all those blood vessels popping in his brain?

*Meg:* Popping—

*Lenny:* And how he was so anxious to hear from you and to find out about your singing career. I wrote it all to you. How they have to feed him through those tubes now. Didn't you get my letters?

*Meg:* Oh, I don't know, Lenny. I guess I did. To tell you the truth, sometimes I kinda don't read your letters.

*Lenny:* What?

*Meg:* I'm sorry. I used to read them. It's just, since Christmas reading them gives me these slicing pains right here in my chest.

*Lenny:* I see. I see. Is that why you didn't use that money Old Granddaddy sent you to come home Christmas; because you hate us so much? We never did all that much to make you hate us. We didn't!

*Meg:* Oh, Lenny! Do you think I'd be getting slicing pains in my chest if I didn't care about you? If I hated you? Honestly, now, do you think I would?

*Lenny:* No.

*Meg:* Okay, then. Let's drop it. I'm sorry I didn't read your letters. Okay?

*Lenny:* Okay.

*Meg:* Anyway, we've got this whole thing with Babe to deal with. The first thing is to get her a good lawyer and get her out of jail.

*Lenny:* Well, she's out of jail.

*Meg:* She is?

*Lenny:* That young lawyer, he's gotten her out.

*Meg:* Oh, he has?

*Lenny:* Yes, on bail. Uncle Watson's put it up. Chick's bringing her back right now—she's driving her home.

*Meg:* Oh; well, that's a relief.

*Lenny:* Yes, and they're due home any minute now; so we can just wait right here for 'em.

*Meg:* Well, good. That's good. *(As she leans against the counter.)* So, Babe shot Zackery Botrelle, the richest and most powerful man in all of Hazlehurst, slap in the gut. It's hard to believe.

*Lenny:* It certainly is. Little Babe—shooting off a gun.

*Meg:* Little Babe.

*Lenny:* She was always the prettiest and most perfect of the three of us. Old Granddaddy used to call her his Dancing Sugar Plum. Why, remember how proud and happy he was the day she married Zackery.

*Meg:* Yes, I remember. It was his finest hour.

*Lenny:* He remarked how Babe was gonna skyrocket right to the heights of Hazlehurst society. And how Zackery was just the right man for her whether she knew it now or not.

*Meg:* Oh, Lordy, Lordy. And what does Old Granddaddy say now?

*Lenny:* Well, I haven't had the courage to tell him all about this as yet. I thought maybe tonight we could go to visit him at the hospital, and you could talk to him and . . .

*Meg:* Yeah; well, we'll see. We'll see. Do we have anything to drink around here—to the tune of straight bourbon?

*Lenny:* No. There's no liquor.

*Meg:* Hell. *(Meg gets a Coke from the refrigerator and opens it.)*

*Lenny:* Then you *will* go with me to see Old Granddaddy at the hospital tonight?

*Meg:* Of course. *(Meg goes to her purse and gets out a bottle of Empirin Compound. She takes out a tablet and puts it on her tongue.)* Brother, I know he's gonna go on about my singing career. Just like he always does.

*Lenny:* Well, how is your career going?

*Meg:* It's not.

*Lenny:* Why, aren't you still singing at the club down on Malibu beach?

*Meg:* No. Not since Christmas.

*Lenny:* Well, then, are you singing someplace new?

*Meg:* No, I'm not singing. I'm not singing at all.

*Lenny:* Oh. Well, what do you do then?

*Meg:* What I do is I pay cold storage bills for a dog-food company. That's what I do.

*Lenny (trying to be helpful):* Gosh, don't you think it'd be a good idea to stay in the show business field?

*Meg:* Oh, maybe.

*Lenny:* Like Old Granddaddy says, "With your talent, all you need is exposure. Then you can make your own breaks!" Did you hear his suggestion about getting your foot put in one of those blocks of cement they've got out here? He thinks that's real important.

*Meg:* Yeh. I think I've heard that. And I'll probably hear it again when I go to visit him at the hospital tonight; so let's just drop it. Okay? (*She notices the sack of pecans.*) What's this? Pecans? Great, I love pecans! (*Meg takes out two pecans and tries to open them by cracking them together.*) Come on . . . Crack, you demons! Crack!

*Lenny:* We have a nutcracker!

*Meg* (*trying with her teeth*) Ah, where's the sport in a nutcracker? Where's the challenge?

*Lenny* (*getting up to get the nutcracker*): It's over here in the utensil drawer. (*As Lenny gets the nutcracker, Meg opens the pecan by stepping on it with her shoe.*)

*Meg:* There! Open! (*Meg picks up the crumbled pecan and eats it.*) Mmmm, delicious. Delicious. Where'd you get the fresh pecans?

*Lenny:* Oh . . . I don't know.

*Meg:* They sure are tasty.

*Lenny:* Doc Porter brought them over.

*Meg:* Doc. What's Doc doing here in town?

*Lenny:* Well, his father died a couple of months ago. Now he's back home seeing to his property.

*Meg:* Gosh, the last I heard of Doc, he was up in the East painting the walls of houses to earn a living. (*Amused.*) Heard he was living with some Yankee woman who made clay pots.

*Lenny:* Joan.

*Meg:* What?

*Lenny:* Her name's Joan. She came down here with him. That's one of her pots. Doc's married to her.

*Meg:* Married—

*Lenny:* Uh huh.

*Meg:* Doc married a Yankee?

*Lenny:* That's right; and they've got two kids.

*Meg:* Kids—

*Lenny:* A boy and a girl.

*Meg:* God. Then his kids must be half Yankee.

*Lenny:* I suppose.

*Meg:* God. That really gets me. I don't know why, but somehow that really gets me.

*Lenny:* I don't know why it should.

*Meg:* And what a stupid-looking pot! Who'd buy it anyway?

*Lenny:* Wait—I think that's them. Yeah, that's Chick's car! Oh, there's Babe! Hello, Babe! They're home, Meg! They're home. (*Meg hides.*)

*Babe's voice:* Lenny! I'm home! I'm free! (*Babe, 24, enters exuberantly. She has an angelic face and fierce, volatile eyes. She carries a pink pocketbook.*) I'm home! (*Meg jumps out of hiding.*) Oh, Meg—Look, it's Meg! (*Running to hug her.*) Meg! When did you get home?

*Meg:* Just now!

*Babe:* Well, it's so good to see you! I'm so glad you're home! I'm so relieved. (*Chick enters.*)

*Meg:* Why, Chick; hello.

*Chick:* Hello, Cousin Margaret. What brings you back to Hazlehurst?

*Meg:* Oh, I came on home . . . *(turning to Babe)* I came on home to see about Babe.

*Babe (running to hug Meg):* Oh, Meg—

*Meg:* How are things with you, Babe?

*Chick:* Well, they are dismal, if you want my opinion. She is refusing to cooperate with her lawyer, that nice-looking young Lloyd boy. She won't tell any of us why she committed this heinous crime, except to say that she didn't like Zackery's looks—

*Babe:* Oh, look, Lenny brought my suitcase from home! And my saxophone! Thank you! *(Babe runs over to the cot and gets out her saxophone.)*

*Chick:* Now, that young lawyer is coming over here this afternoon, and when he gets here he expects to get some concrete answers! That's what he expects! No more of this nonsense and stubborness from you, Rebecca MaGrath, or they'll put you in jail and throw away the key!

*Babe (overlapping to Meg):* Meg, come look at my new saxophone. I went to Jackson and bought it used. Feel it. It's so heavy.

*Meg: (overlapping to Chick):* It's beautiful. *(The room goes silent.)*

*Chick:* Isn't that right, won't they throw away the key?

*Lenny:* Well, honestly, I don't know about that—

*Chick:* They will! And leave you there to rot. So, Rebecca, what are you going to tell Mr. Lloyd about shooting Zackery when he gets here? What are your reasons going to be?

*Babe (glaring):* That I didn't like his looks! I just didn't like his stinking looks! And I don't like yours much either, Chick-the-Stick! So just leave me alone! I mean it! Leave me alone! Oooh! *(Babe exits up the stairs. There is a long moment of silence.)*

*Chick:* Well, I was only trying to warn her that she's going to have to help herself. It's just that she doesn't understand how serious the situation is. Does she? She doesn't have the vaguest idea. Does she now?

*Lenny:* Well, it's true, she does seem a little confused.

*Chick:* And that's putting it mildly, Lenny honey. That's putting it mighty mild. So, Margaret, how's your singing career going? We keep looking for your picture in the movie magazines. *(Meg moves to light a cigarette.)* You know, you shouldn't smoke. It causes cancer. Cancer of the lungs. They say each cigarette is just a little stick of cancer. A little death stick.

*Meg:* That's what I like about it, Chick—taking a drag off of death. *(Meg takes a long, deep drag.)* Mmm! Gives me a sense of controlling my own destiny. What power! What exhilaration! Want a drag?

*Lenny (trying to break the tension):* Ah, Zackery's liver's been saved! His sister called up and said his liver was saved. Isn't that good news?

*Meg:* Well, yes, that's fine news. Mighty fine news. Why, I've been told that the liver's a powerful important bodily organ. I believe it's used to absorb all our excess bile.

*Lenny:* Yes—well—it's been saved. (*The phone rings. Lenny gets it.*)

*Meg:* So! Did you hear all that good news about the liver, Little Chicken?

*Chick:* I heard it. And don't you call me Chicken! (*Meg clucks like a chicken.*) I've told you a hundred times if I've told you once not to call me Chicken. You cannot call me Chicken.

*Lenny:* . . . Oh, no! . . . Of course, we'll be right over! 'Bye! (*She hangs up the phone.*) That was Annie May—Peekay and Buck Jr. have eaten paint!

*Chick:* Oh, no! Are they all right? They're not sick? They're not sick, are they?

*Lenny:* I don't know. I don't know. Come on. We've got to run on next door.

*Chick (overlapping):* Oh, God! Oh, please! Please let them be all right! Don't let them die! Please, don't let them die!!

*Chick runs off howling with Lenny following after. Meg sits alone, finishing her cigarette. After a moment, Babe's voice is heard.*

*Babe's voice:* Pst—Psst!

*Meg looks around. Babe comes tiptoeing down the stairs.*

*Babe:* Has she gone?

*Meg:* She's gone. Peekay and Buck Jr. just ate their paints.

*Babe:* What idiots.

*Meg:* Yeah.

*Babe:* You know, Chick's hated us ever since we had to move here from Vicksburg to live with Old Grandmama and Old Granddaddy.

*Meg:* She's an idiot.

*Babe:* Yeah. Do you know what she told me this morning while I was still behind bars and couldn't get away?

*Meg:* What?

*Babe:* She told me how embarrassing it was for her all those years ago, you know, when Mama—

*Meg:* Yeah, down in the cellar.

*Babe:* She said our mama had shamed the entire family, and we were known notoriously all through Hazlehurst. (*About to cry.*) Then she went on to say how I would now be getting just as much bad publicity, and humiliating her and the family all over again.

*Meg:* Ah, forget it, Babe. Just forget it.

*Babe:* I told her, "Mama got national coverage! National!" And if Zackery wasn't a senator from Copiah County, I probably wouldn't even be getting statewide.

*Meg:* Of course you wouldn't.

*Babe (after a pause.):* Gosh, sometimes I wonder . . .

*Meg:* What?

*Babe:* Why she did it. Why Mama hung herself.

*Meg:* I don't know. She had a bad day. A real bad day. You know how it feels on a real bad day.

*Babe:* And that old yellow cat. It was sad about that old cat.

*Meg:* Yeah.

*Babe:* I bet if Daddy hadn't of left us, they'd still be alive.

*Meg:* Oh, I don't know.

*Babe:* 'Cause it was after he left that she started spending whole days just sitting there and smoking on the back porch steps. She'd sling her ashes down onto the different bugs and ants that'd be passing by.

*Meg:* Yeah. Well, I'm glad he left.

*Babe:* That old yellow cat'd stay back there with her. I thought if she felt something for anyone it woulda been that old cat. Guess I musta been mistaken.

*Meg:* God, he was a bastard. Really, with his white teeth, Daddy was such a bastard.

*Babe:* Was he? I don't remember. (*Meg blows out a mouthful of smoke. After a moment, uneasily.*) I think I'm gonna make some lemonade. You want some?

*Meg:* Sure. (*Babe cuts lemons, dumps sugar, stirs ice cubes, etc. throughout the following exchange.*) Babe. Why won't you talk? Why won't you tell anyone about shooting Zackery?

*Babe:* Oooh—

*Meg:* Why not? You must have had a good reason. Didn't you?

*Babe:* I guess I did.

*Meg:* Well, what was it?

*Babe:* I . . . I can't say.

*Meg:* Why not? (*Pause*) Babe, why not? You can tell me.

*Babe:* 'Cause . . . I'm sort of . . . protecting someone.

*Meg:* Protecting someone? Oh, Babe, then you really didn't shoot him? I knew you couldn't have done it! I knew it!

*Babe:* No, I shot him. I shot him all right. I meant to kill him. I was aiming for his heart, but I guess my hands were shaking and I—just got him in the stomach.

*Meg* (*collapsing*): I see.

*Babe* (*stirring the lemonade*): So I'm guilty. And I'm just gonna have to take my punishment and go on to jail.

*Meg:* Oh, Babe—

*Babe:* Don't worry, Meg, jail's gonna be a relief to me. I can learn to play my new saxophone. I won't have to live with Zackery anymore. And I won't have his snoopy old sister, Lucille, coming over and pushing me around. Jail will be a relief. Here's your lemonade.

*Meg:* Thanks.

*Babe:* It taste okay?

*Meg:* Perfect.

*Babe:* I like a lot of sugar in mine. I'm gonna add some more sugar. (*Babe goes to add more sugar to her lemonade, as Lenny bursts through the back door in a state of excitement and confusion.*)

*Lenny:* Well, it looks like the paint is primarily on their arms and faces, but Chick wants me to drive them all over to Doctor Winn's just to make sure. (*Lenny grabs her car keys off of the counter and as she does so, she notices the mess of lemons and sugar.*) Oh, now, Babe, try not to make a mess here; and be careful with this sharp knife. Honestly, all that sugar's gonna get you sick. Well, 'bye, 'bye. I'll be back as soon as I can.

*Meg:* 'Bye, Lenny.

*Babe:* 'Bye. (*Lenny exits.*) Boy, I don't know what's happening to Lenny.

*Meg:* What do you mean?

*Babe:* "Don't make a mess; don't make yourself sick; don't cut yourself with that sharp knife." She's turning into Old Grandmama.

*Meg:* You think so?

*Babe:* More and more. Do you know she's taken to wearing Old Grandmama's torn sunhat and her green garden gloves?

*Meg:* Those old lime-green ones?

*Babe:* Yeah; she works out in the garden wearing the lime-green gloves of a dead woman. Imagine wearing those gloves on your hands.

*Meg:* Poor Lenny. She needs some love in her life. All she does is work out at that brick yard and take care of Old Granddaddy.

*Babe:* Yeah. But she's so shy with men.

*Meg* (*biting into an apple*): Probably because of that *shrunken* ovary she has.

*Babe* (*slinging ice cubes*): Yeah, that *deformed* ovary.

*Meg:* Old Granddaddy's the one who's made her feel self-conscious about it. It's his fault. The old fool.

*Babe:* It's so sad.

*Meg:* God—you know what?

*Babe:* What?

*Meg:* I bet Lenny's never even slept with a man. Just think, thirty years old and never even had it once.

*Babe* (*slyly*): Oh I don't know. Maybe she's . . . had it once.

*Meg:* She has?

*Babe:* Maybe. I think so.

*Meg:* When? When?

*Babe:* Well . . . maybe I shouldn't say—

*Meg:* Babe!

*Babe* (*rapidly telling the story*): All right, then. It was after Old Granddaddy went back to the hospital this second time. Lenny was really in a state of deep depression, I could tell that she was. Then one day she calls me up and asks me to come over and to bring along my Polaroid camera. Well, when I arrive she's waiting for me out there in the sun parlor wearing her powder-blue Sunday dress and this old curled-up wig. She confided that she was gonna try sending in her picture to one of those lonely-hearts clubs.

*Meg:* Oh, my God.

*Babe:* Lonely Hearts of the South. She'd seen their ad in a magazine.

*Meg:* Jesus.

*Babe:* Anyway, I take some snapshots and she sends them on in to the club, and about two weeks later she receives in the mail this whole load of pictures of available men, most of 'em fairly odd-looking. But of course she doesn't call any of 'em up 'cause she's real shy. But one of 'em, this Charlie Hill from Memphis, Tennessee, he calls her.

*Meg:* He does?

*Babe:* Yeah. And time goes on and she says he's real funny on the phone, so they decide to get together to meet.

*Meg:* Yeah?

*Babe:* Well, he drives down here to Hazlehurst 'bout three or four different times and has supper with her; then one weekend she goes up to Memphis to visit him, and I think that is where it happened.

*Meg:* What makes you think so?

*Babe:* Well, when I went to pick her up from the bus depot, she ran off the bus and threw her arms around me and started crying and sobbing as though she'd like to never stop. I asked her, I said, "Lenny, what's the matter?" And she said, "I've done it, Babe! Honey, I've done it!"

*Meg (whispering):* And you think she meant that she'd done *it*?

*Babe (whispering back, slyly):* I think so.

*Meg:* Well, goddamn! *(They laugh with glee.)*

*Babe:* But she didn't say anything else about it. She just went on to tell me about the boot factory where Charlie worked and what a nice city Memphis was.

*Meg:* So, what happened to this Charlie?

*Babe:* Well, he came to Hazlehurst just one more time. Lenny took him over to meet Old Granddaddy at the hospital, and after that they broke it off.

*Meg:* 'Cause of Old Granddaddy?

*Babe:* Well, she said it was on account of her missing ovary. That Charlie didn't want to marry her on account of it.

*Meg:* Ah, how mean. How hateful.

*Babe:* Oh, it was. He seemed like such a nice man, too—kinda chubby with red hair and freckles, always telling these funny jokes.

*Meg:* Hmmm, that just doesn't seem right. Something about that doesn't seem exactly right. *(Meg paces about the kitchen and comes across the box of candy Lenny got for her birthday.)* Oh, God. "Happy Birthday to Lenny, from the Buck Boyles."

*Babe:* Oh, no! Today's Lenny's birthday!

*Meg:* That's right.

*Babe:* I forgot all about it!

*Meg:* I know. I did too.

*Babe:* Gosh, we'll have to order up a big cake for her. She always loves to make those wishes on her birthday cake.

*Meg:* Yeah, let's get her a big cake! A huge one! *(Suddenly noticing the plastic wrapper on the candy box.)* Oh, God, that Chick's so cheap!

*Babe:* What do you mean?

*Meg:* This plastic has poinsettias on it!

*Babe (running to see):* Oh, let me see—*(She looks at the package with disgust.)* Boy, oh, boy! I'm calling that bakery and ordering the very largest size cake they have! That Jumbo Deluxe!

*Meg:* Good!

*Babe:* Why, I imagine they can make one up to be about—*this* big. *(She demonstrates.)*

*Meg:* Oh, at least; at least that big. Why, maybe, it'll even be *this* big. (*She makes a very, very, very, large size cake.*)

*Babe:* You think it could be *that* big?

*Meg:* Sure!

*Babe (after a moment, getting the idea):* Or, or what if it were *this* big? (*She maps out a cake that covers the room.*) What if we get the cake and it's *this* big? (*She gulps down a fistful of cake.*) Gulp! Gulp! Gulp! Tasty treat!

*Meg:* Hmmm—I'll have me some more! Give me some more of that birthday cake!

*Suddenly there is a loud knock at the door.*

*Barnette's voice:* Hello . . . hello! May I come in?

*Babe (to Meg, in a whisper, as she takes cover):* Who's that?

*Meg:* I don't know.

*Barnette's voice (still knocking):* Hello! Hello, Mrs. Botrelle!

*Babe:* Oh, shoot! It's that lawyer. I don't want to see him.

*Meg:* Oh, Babe, come on. You've got to see him sometime.

*Babe:* No, I don't! (*She starts up the stairs.*) Just tell him I died. I'm going upstairs.

*Meg:* Oh, Babe! Will you come back here!

*Babe (as she exits):* You talk to him, please, Meg. Please! I just don't want to see him—

*Meg:* Babe—Babe! Oh, shit . . . Ah, come on in! Door's open!

*Barnette Lloyd, 26, enters carrying a briefcase. He is a slender, intelligent young man with an almost fanatical intensity that he subdues by sheer will.*

*Barnette:* How do you do? I'm Barnette Lloyd.

*Meg:* Pleased to meet you. I'm Meg MaGrath, Babe's older sister.

*Barnette:* Yes, I know. You're the singer.

*Meg:* Well, yes . . .

*Barnette:* I came to hear you five different times when you were singing at the club in Biloxi. Greeny's I believe was the name of it.

*Meg:* Yes, Greeny's.

*Barnette:* You were very good. There was something sad and moving about how you sang those songs. It was like you had some sort of vision. Some special sort of vision.

*Meg:* Well, thank you. You're very kind. Now . . . about Babe's case—

*Barnette:* Yes?

*Meg:* We've just got to win it.

*Barnette:* I intend to.

*Meg:* Of course. But, ah . . . (*She looks at him.*) Ah, you know, you're very young.

*Barnette:* Yes. I am. I'm young.

*Meg:* It's just, I'm concerned, Mr. Lloyd—

*Barnette:* Barnette. Please.

*Meg:* Barnette; that, ah, just maybe we need someone with, well, with more experience. Someone totally familiar with all the ins and outs and the this and thats of the legal dealings and such. As that.

*Barnette:* Ah, you have reservations.

*Meg (relieved):* Reservations. Yes, I have . . . reservations.

*Barnette:* Well, possibly it would help you to know that I graduated first in my class from Ole Miss Law School. I also spent three different summers taking advanced courses in criminal law at Harvard Law School. I made A's in all the given courses. I was fascinated!

*Meg:* I'm sure.

*Barnette:* And even now, I've just completed one year working with Jackson's top criminal law firm, Manchester and Wayne. I was invaluable to them. Indispensable. They offered to double my percentage if I'd stay on; but I refused. I wanted to return to Hazlehurst and open my own office. The reason being, and this is a key point, that I have a personal vendetta to settle with one Zackery F. Botrelle.

*Meg:* A personal vendetta?

*Barnette:* Yes, ma'am. You are correct. Indeed, I do.

*Meg:* Hmmm. A personal vendetta . . . I think I like that. So you have some sort of a personal vendetta to settle with Zackery?

*Barnette:* Precisely. Just between the two of us, I not only intend to keep that sorry s.o.b. from ever being re-elected to the state senate by exposing his shady, criminal dealings; but I also intend to decimate his personal credibility by exposing him as a bully, a brute, and a red-neck thug!

*Meg:* Well; I can see that you're—fanatical about this.

*Barnette:* Yes, I am. I'm sorry, if I seem outspoken. But for some reason, I feel I can talk to you . . . those songs you sang. Excuse me; I feel like a jackass.

*Meg:* It's all right. Relax. Relax, Barnette. Let me think this out a minute. *(She takes out a cigarette. He lights it for her.)* Now just exactly how do you intend to get Babe off? You know, keep her out of jail.

*Barnette:* It seems to me that we can get her off with a plea of self-defense, or possibly we could go with innocent by reason of temporary insanity. But basically, I intend to prove that Zackery Botrelle brutalized and tormented this poor woman to such an extent that she had no recourse but to defend herself in the only way she knew how!

*Meg:* I like that!

*Barnette:* Then, of course, I'm hoping this will break the ice and we'll be able to go on to prove that the man's a total criminal, as well as an abusive bully and contemptible slob!

*Meg:* That sounds good! To me that sounds very good!

*Barnette:* It's just our basic game plan.

*Meg:* But now, how are you going to prove all this about Babe being brutalized? We don't want anyone perjured. I mean to commit perjury.

*Barnette:* Perjury? According to my sources, there'll be no need for perjury.

*Meg:* You mean it's the truth?

*Barnette:* This is a small town, Miss MaGrath. The word gets out.

*Meg:* It's really the truth?

*Barnette (opening his briefcase):* Just look at this. It's a photostatic copy of Mrs. Botrelle's medical chart over the past four years. Take a good look at it, if you want your blood to boil!

*Meg (looking over the chart):* What! What! This is maddening. This is madness! Did he do this to her? I'll kill him; I will—I'll fry his blood!! Did he do this?

*Barnette (alarmed):* To tell you the truth, I can't say for certain what was accidental and what was not. That's why I need to talk with Mrs. Botrelle. That's why it's very important that I see her!

*Meg (her eyes are wild, as she shoves him toward the door):* Well, look, I've got to see her first. I've got to talk to her first. What I'll do is I'll give you a call. Maybe you can come back over later on—

*Barnette:* Well, then, here's my card—

*Meg:* Okay. Goodbye.

*Barnette:* 'Bye!

*Meg:* Oh, wait! Wait! There's one problem with you.

*Barnette:* What?

*Meg:* What if you get so fanatically obsessed with this vendetta thing that you forget about Babe? You forget about her and sell her down the river just to get at Zackery. What about that?

*Barnette:* I—wouldn't do that.

*Meg:* You wouldn't?

*Barnette:* No.

*Meg:* Why not?

*Barnette:* Because, I'm—I'm fond of her.

*Meg:* What do you mean you're fond of her?

*Barnette:* Well, she . . . she sold me a pound cake at a bazaar once. And I'm fond of her.

*Meg:* All right; I believe you. Goodbye.

*Barnette:* Goodbye. *(Barnette exits.)*

*Meg:* Babe! Babe, come down here! Babe!

*Babe comes hurrying down the stairs.*

*Babe:* What? What is it? I called about the cake—

*Meg:* What did Zackery do to you?

*Babe:* They can't have it for today.

*Meg:* Did he hurt you? Did he? Did he do that?

*Babe:* Oh, Meg, please—

*Meg:* Did he? Goddamnit, Babe—

*Babe:* Yes, he did.

*Meg:* Why? Why?

*Babe:* I don't know! He started hating me, 'cause I couldn't laugh at his jokes. I just started finding it impossible to laugh at his jokes the way I used to. And then the sound of his voice got to where it tired me out awful bad to hear it. I'd fall asleep just listening to him at the dinner table. He'd say, "Hand me some of that gravy!" Or, "This roast beef is too damn bloody." And suddenly I'd be out cold like a light.

*Meg:* Oh, Babe. Babe, this is very important. I want you to sit down here and tell me what all happened right before you shot Zackery. That's right, just sit down and tell me.

*Babe* (*after a pause*): I told you, I can't tell you on account of I'm protecting someone.

*Meg*: But, Babe, you've just got to talk to someone about all this. You just do.

*Babe*: Why?

*Meg*: Because it's a human need. To talk about our lives. It's an important human need.

*Babe*: Oh. Well, I do feel like I want to talk to someone. I do.

*Meg*: Then talk to me; please.

*Babe* (*making a decision*): All right. (*After thinking a minute.*) I don't know where to start.

*Meg*: Just start at the beginning. Just there at the beginning.

*Babe* (*after a moment*): Well, do you remember Willie Jay? (*Meg shakes her head.*) Cora's youngest boy?

*Meg*: Oh, yeah, that little kid we used to pay a nickel to, to run down to the drug-store and bring us back a cherry Coke.

*Babe*: Right. Well, Cora irons at my place on Wednesdays now, and she just happened to mention that Willie Jay'd picked up this old stray dog and that he'd gotten real fond of him. But now they couldn't afford to feed him anymore, so she was gonna have to tell Willie Jay to set him loose in the woods.

*Meg* (*trying to be patient*): Uh huh.

*Babe*: Well, I said I liked dogs, and if he wanted to bring the dog over here, I'd take care of him. You see, I was alone by myself most of the time 'cause the senate was in session and Zackery was up in Jackson.

*Meg*: Uh huh. (*Meg reaches for Lenny's box of birthday candy. She takes little nibbles out of each piece throughout the rest of the scene.*)

*Babe*: So the next day, Willie Jay brings over this skinny, old dog with these little crossed eyes. Well, I asked Willie Jay what his name was, and he said they called him Dog. Well, I liked the name; so I thought I'd keep it.

*Meg* (*getting up*): Uh huh. I'm listening. I'm just gonna get me a glass of cold water. Do you want one?

*Babe*: Okay.

*Meg*: So you kept the name—Dog.

*Babe*: Yeah. Anyway, when Willie Jay was leaving he gave Dog a hug and said, "Goodbye, Dog. You're a fine ole dog." Well, I felt something for him, so I told Willie Jay he could come back and visit with Dog any time he wanted, and his face just kinda lit right up.

*Meg* (*offering the candy*): Candy—

*Babe*: No thanks. Anyhow, time goes on and Willie Jay keeps coming over and over. And we talk about Dog and how fat he's getting, and then, well, you know, things start up.

*Meg*: No, I don't know. What things start up?

*Babe*: Well, things start up. Like sex. Like that.

*Meg*: Babe, wait a minute—Willie Jay's a boy. A small boy, about this tall. He's about this tall!

*Babe*: No! Oh, no! He's taller now! He's fifteen now. When you knew him he was only about seven or eight.

*Meg*: But even so—fifteen. And he's a black boy: a colored boy; a Negro.

*Babe (flustered):* Well, I realize that, Meg. Why do you think I'm so worried about his getting public exposure? I don't want to ruin his reputation!

*Meg:* I'm amazed, Babe. I'm really, completely amazed. I didn't even know you were a liberal.

*Babe:* Well, I'm not! I'm not a liberal! I'm a democratic! I was just lonely! I was so lonely. And he was good. Oh, he was so, so good. I'd never had it that good. We'd always go out into the garage and—

*Meg:* It's okay. I've got the picture; I've got the picture! Now, let's just get back to the story. To yesterday, when you shot Zackery.

*Babe:* All right, then. Let's see . . . Willie Jay was over. And it was after we'd—

*Meg:* Yeah! Yeah.

*Babe:* And we were just standing around on the back porch playing with Dog. Well, suddenly Zackery comes from around the side of the house. And he startled me 'cause he's supposed to be away at the office, and there he is coming from 'round the side of the house. Anyway, he says to Willie Jay, "Hey, boy, what are you doing back here?" And I said, "He's not doing anything. You just go on home. Willie Jay! You just run right on home." Well, before he can move, Zackery comes up and knocks him once right across the face and then shoves him down the porch steps, causing him to skin up his elbow real bad on that hard concrete. Then he says, "Don't you ever come around here again, or I'll have them cut out your gizzard!" Well, Willie Jay starts crying—these tears come streaming down his face—then he gets up real quick and runs away, with Dog following off after him. After that, I don't remember much too clearly; let's see . . . I went on into the living room, and I went right up to the davenport and opened the drawer where we keep the burglar gun . . . I took it out. Then I—I brought it up to my ear. That's right. I put it right inside my ear. Why, I was gonna shoot off my own head! That's what I was gonna do. Then I heard the back door slamming and suddenly, for some reason, I thought about Mama . . . how she'd hung herself. And here I was about ready to shoot myself. Then I realized—that's right, I realized how I didn't want to kill myself! And she—she probably didn't want to kill herself. She wanted to kill him, and I wanted to kill him, too. I wanted to kill Zackery, not myself. 'Cause I—I wanted to live! So I waited for him to come on into the living room. Then I held out the gun, and I pulled the trigger, aiming for his heart, but getting him in the stomach. *(After a pause.)* It's funny that I really did that.

*Meg:* It's a good thing that you did. It's a damn good thing that you did.

*Babe:* It was.

*Meg:* Please, Babe, talk to Barnette Lloyd. Just talk to him and see if he can help.

*Babe:* But how about Willie Jay?

*Meg (starting towards the phone):* Oh, he'll be all right. You just talk to that lawyer like you did to me. *(Looking at the number on the card, she begins dialing.)* See, 'cause he's gonna be on your side.

*Babe:* No! Stop, Meg, stop! Don't call him up! Please don't call him up! You can't! It's too awful. *(She runs over and jerks the bottom half of the phone away from Meg. Meg stands, holding the receiver.)*

Meg: Babe! (*Babe slams her half of the phone into the refrigerator.*)

Babe: I just can't tell some stranger all about my personal life. I just can't.

Meg: Well, hell, Babe; you're the one who said you wanted to live.

Babe: That's right. I did. (*She takes the phone out of the refrigerator and hands it to Meg.*) Here's the other part of the phone. (*Babe moves to sit at the kitchen table. Meg takes the phone back to the counter. Babe fishes a lemon out of her glass and begins sucking on it.*) Meg.

Meg: What?

Babe: I called the bakery. They're gonna have Lenny's cake ready first thing tomorrow morning. That's the earliest they can get it.

Meg: All right.

Babe: I told them to write on it, "Happy Birthday Lenny—A Day Late." That sound okay?

Meg (*at the phone*): It sounds nice.

Babe: I ordered up the very largest size cake they have. I told them chocolate cake with white icing and red trim. Think she'll like that?

Meg (*dialing on the phone*): Yeah, I'm sure she will. She'll like it.

Babe: I'm hoping.

CURTAIN

# ACT II

*The lights go up on the kitchen. It is later that evening on the same day. Meg's suitcase has been moved upstairs. Babe's saxophone has been taken out of the case and put together. Babe and Barnette are sitting at the kitchen table. Barnette is writing and rechecking notes with explosive intensity. Babe, who has changed into a casual shift, sits eating a bowl of oatmeal, slowly.*

Barnette (*to himself*): Mmm huh! Yes! I see, I see! Well, we can work on that! And of course, this is mere conjecture! Difficult, if not impossible, to prove. Ha! Yes. Yes, indeed. Indeed—

Babe: Sure you don't want any oatmeal?

Barnette: What? Oh, no. No, thank you. Let's see; ah, where were we?

Babe: I just shot Zackery.

Barnette (*looking at his notes*): Right. Correct. You've just pulled the trigger.

Babe: Tell me, do you think Willie Jay can stay out of all this?

Barnette: Believe me, it is in our interest to keep him as far out of this as possible.

Babe: Good.

Barnette (*throughout the following, Barnette stays glued to Babe's every word*): All right, you've just shot one Zackery Botrelle, as a result of his continual physical and mental abuse—what happens now?

Babe: Well, after I shot him, I put the gun down on the piano bench, and then I went out into the kitchen and made up a pitcher of lemonade.

Barnette: Lemonade?

*Babe:* Yes, I was dying of thirst. My mouth was just as dry as a bone.

*Barnette:* So in order to quench this raging thirst that was choking you dry and preventing any possibility of you uttering intelligible sounds or phrases, you went out to the kitchen and made up a pitcher of lemonade?

*Babe:* Right. I made it just the way I like it, with lots of sugar and lots of lemon—about ten lemons in all. Then I added two trays of ice and stirred it up with my wooden stirring spoon.

*Barnette:* Then what?

*Babe:* Then I drank three glasses, one right after the other. They were large glasses—about this tall. Then suddenly my stomach kind of swole all up. I guess what caused it was all that sour lemon.

*Barnette:* Could be.

*Babe:* Then what I did was . . . I wiped my mouth off with the back of my hand, like this . . . *(She demonstrates.)*

*Barnette:* Hmmm.

*Babe:* I did it to clear off all those little beads of water that had settled there.

*Barnette:* I see.

*Babe:* Then I called out to Zackery. I said, "Zackery, I've made some lemonade. Can you use a glass?"

*Barnette:* Did he answer? Did you hear an answer?

*Babe:* No. He didn't answer.

*Barnette:* So what'd you do?

*Babe:* I poured him a glass anyway and took it out to him.

*Barnette:* You took it out to the living room?

*Babe:* I did. And there he was, lying on the rug. He was looking up at me trying to speak words. I said, "What? . . . Lemonade? . . . You don't want it? Would you like a Coke instead?" Then I got the idea—he was telling me to call on the phone for medical help. So I got on the phone and called up the hospital. I gave my name and address and I told them my husband was shot and he was lying on the rug and there was plenty of blood. *(Babe pauses a minute, as Barnette works frantically on his notes.)* I guess that's gonna look kinda bad.

*Barnette:* What?

*Babe:* Me fixing that lemonade before I called the hospital.

*Barnette:* Well, not . . . necessarily.

*Babe:* I tell you, I think the reason I made up the lemonade, I mean besides the fact that my mouth was bone dry, was that I was afraid to call the authorities. I was afraid. I—I really think I was afraid they would see that I had tried to shoot Zackery, in fact, that I *had* shot him, and they would accuse me of possible murder and send me away to jail.

*Barnette:* Well, that's understandable.

*Babe:* I think so. I mean, in fact, that's what did happen. That's what is happening—'cause here I am just about ready to go right off to the Parchment Prison Farm. Yes, here I am just practically on the brink of utter doom. Why, I feel so all alone.

*Barnette:* Now, now, look—Why, there's no reason for you to get yourself so all upset and worried. Please don't. Please. (*They look at each other for a moment.*) You just keep filling in as much detailed information as you can about those incidents on the medical reports. That's all you need to think about. Don't you worry, Mrs. Botrelle, we're going to have a solid defense.

*Babe:* Please, don't call me Mrs. Botrelle.

*Barnette:* All right.

*Babe:* My name's Becky. People in the family call me Babe; but my real name's Becky.

*Barnette:* All right, Becky. (*Barnette and Babe stare at each other for a long moment.*)

*Babe:* Are you sure you didn't go to Hazlehurst High?

*Barnette:* No, I went away to a boarding school.

*Babe:* Gosh, you sure do look familiar. You sure do.

*Barnette:* Well, I—I doubt you'll remember, but I did meet you once.

*Babe:* You did? When?

*Barnette:* At the Christmas bazaar, year before last. You were selling cakes and cookies and . . . candy.

*Babe:* Oh, yes! You bought the orange pound cake!

*Barnette:* Right.

*Babe:* Of course, and then we talked for a while. We talked about the Christmas angel.

*Barnette:* You do remember.

*Babe:* I remember it very well. You were even thinner than you are now.

*Barnette:* Well, I'm surprised. I'm certainly . . . surprised. (*The phone begins to ring.*)

*Babe* (*as she goes to answer the phone*): This is quite a coincidence! Don't you think it is? Why, it's almost a fluke. (*She answers the phone.*) Hello . . . Oh, hello, Lucille . . . Oh, he is? . . . Oh, he does? . . . Okay. Oh, Lucille, wait! Has Dog come back to the house? . . . Oh, I see . . . Okay. Okay. (*After a brief pause.*) Hello, Zackery? How are you doing? . . . Uh huh . . . uh huh . . . Oh, I'm sorry . . . Please, don't scream . . . Uh huh . . . uh huh . . . You want what? . . . No, I can't come up there now . . . Well, for one thing, I don't even have the car. Lenny and Meg are up at the hospital right now, visiting with Old Granddaddy . . . What? . . . Oh, really? . . . Oh, really? . . . Well, I've got me a lawyer that's over here right now, and he's building me up a solid defense! . . . Wait just a minute. I'll see. (*To Barnette.*) He wants to talk to you. He says he's got some blackening evidence that's gonna convict me of attempting to murder him in the first degree!

*Barnette* (*disgustedly*): Oh, bluff! He's bluffing! Here, hand me the phone. (*He takes the phone and becomes suddenly cool and suave.*) Hello, this is Mr. Barnette Lloyd speaking. I'm Mrs. . . . ah, Becky's attorney . . . Why, certainly, Mr. Botrelle, I'd be more than glad to check out any pertinent information that you may have . . . Fine, then I'll be right over. Goodbye. (*He hangs up the phone.*)

*Babe:* What did he say?

*Barnette:* He wants me to come to see him at the hospital this evening. Says he's got some sort of evidence. Sounds highly suspect to me.

*Babe:* Oooh! Didn't you just hate his voice? Doesn't he have the most awful voice! I just hate it! I can't bear to hear it!

*Barnette:* Well, now—now, wait. Wait just a minute.

*Babe:* What?

*Barnette:* I have a solution. From now on, I'll handle all communications between you two. You can simply refuse to speak with him.

*Babe:* All right—I will. I'll do that.

*Barnette (starting to pack his briefcase):* Well, I'd better get over there and see just what he's got up his sleeve.

*Babe (after a pause):* Barnette.

*Barnette:* Yes?

*Babe:* What's the personal vendetta about? You know, the one you have to settle with Zackery.

*Barnette:* Oh, it's—it's complicated. It's a very complicated matter.

*Babe:* I see.

*Barnette:* The major thing he did was to ruin my father's life. He took away his job, his home, his health, his respectability. I don't like to talk about it.

*Babe:* I'm sorry. I just wanted to say—I hope you win it. I hope you win your vendetta.

*Barnette:* Thank you.

*Babe:* I think it's an important thing that a person could win a lifelong vendetta.

*Barnette:* Yes. Well, I'd better be going.

*Babe:* All right. Let me know what happens.

*Barnette:* I will. I'll get back to you right away.

*Babe:* Thanks.

*Barnette:* Goodbye, Becky.

*Babe:* Goodbye, Barnette. (*Barnette exits. Babe looks around the room for a moment, then goes over to her white suitcase and opens it up. She takes out her pink hair curlers and a brush. She begins brushing her hair.*) Goodbye, Becky. Goodbye, Barnette. Goodbye Becky. Oooh. (*Lenny enters. She is fuming. Babe is rolling her hair throughout most of the following scene.*) Lenny, hi!

*Lenny:* Hi.

*Babe:* Where's Meg?

*Lenny:* Oh, she had to go by the store and pick some things up. I don't know what.

*Babe:* Well, how's Old Granddaddy?

*Lenny (as she picks up Babe's bowl of oatmeal):* He's fine. Wonderful! Never been better!

*Babe:* Lenny, what's wrong? What's the matter?

*Lenny:* It's Meg! I could just wring her neck! I could just wring it!

*Babe:* Why? Wha'd she do?

*Lenny:* She lied! She sat in that hospital room and shamelessly lied to Old Granddaddy. She went on and on telling such untrue stories and lies.

*Babe:* Well, what? What did she say?

*Lenny:* Well, for one thing she said she was gonna have a RCA record coming out with her picture on the cover, eating pineapples under a palm tree.

*Babe:* Well, gosh, Lenny, maybe she is! Don't you think she really is?

*Lenny:* Babe, she sat here this very afternoon and told me how all that she's done this whole year is work as a clerk for a dog-food company.

*Babe:* Oh, shoot. I'm disappointed.

*Lenny:* And then she goes on to say that she'll be appearing on the Johnny Carson Show in two weeks' time. Two weeks' time! Why, Old Granddaddy's got a TV set right in his room. Imagine what a letdown it's gonna be.

*Babe:* Why, mercy me.

*Lenny (slamming the coffeepot on):* Oh, and she told him the reason she didn't use the money he sent her to come home Christmas was that she was right in the middle of making a huge multimillion-dollar motion picture and was just under too much pressure.

*Babe:* My word!

*Lenny:* The movie's coming out this spring. It's called, *Singing in a Shoe Factory*. But she only has a small leading role—not a large leading role.

*Babe (laughing):* For heaven's sake—

*Lenny:* I'm sizzling. Oh, I just can't help it! I'm sizzling!

*Babe:* Sometimes Meg does such strange things.

*Lenny (slowly, as she picks up the opened box of birthday candy):* Who ate this candy?

*Babe (hesitantly):* Meg.

*Lenny:* My one birthday present, and look what she does! Why, she's taken one little bite out of each piece and then just put it back in! Ooh! That's just like her! That is just like her!

*Babe:* Lenny, please—

*Lenny:* I can't help it! It gets me mad! It gets me upset! Why, Meg's always run wild—she started smoking and drinking when she was fourteen years old; she never made good grades—never made her own bed! But somehow she always seemed to get what she wanted. She's the one who got singing and dancing lessons, and a store-bought dress to wear to her senior prom. Why, do you remember how Meg always got to wear twelve jingle bells on her petticoats, while we were only allowed to wear three apiece? Why?! Why should Old Grandmama let her sew twelve golden jingle bells on her petticoats and us only three!

*Babe (who has heard all this before):* I don't know! Maybe she didn't jingle them as much!

*Lenny:* I can't help it! It gets me mad! I resent it. I do.

*Babe:* Oh, don't resent Meg. Things have been hard for Meg. After all, she was the one who found Mama.

*Lenny:* Oh, I know; she's the one who found Mama. But that's always been the excuse.

*Babe:* But, I tell you, Lenny, after it happened, Meg started doing all sorts of these strange things.

*Lenny:* She did? Like what?

*Babe:* Like things I never wanted to tell you about.

*Lenny:* What sort of things?

*Babe:* Well, for instance, back when we used to go over to the library, Meg would spend all her time reading and looking through this old, black book called *Diseases of the Skin*. It was full of the most sickening pictures you'd ever seen. Things like rotting-away noses and eyeballs drooping off down the sides of people's faces and scabs and sores and eaten-away places all over *all* parts of people's bodies.

*Lenny (trying to pour her coffee):* Babe, please! That's enough.

*Babe:* Anyway, she'd spend hours and hours just forcing herself to look through this book. Why, it was the same way she'd force herself to look at the poster of crippled children stuck up in the window at Dixieland Drugs. You know, that one where they want you to give a dime. Meg would stand there and stare at their eyes and look at the braces on their little crippled-up legs—then she'd purposely go and spend her dime on a double scoop ice cream cone and eat it all down. She'd say to me, "See, I can stand it. I can stand it. Just look how I'm gonna be able to stand it."

*Lenny:* That's awful.

*Babe:* She said she was afraid of being a weak person. I guess 'cause she cried in bed every night for such a long time.

*Lenny:* Goodness mercy. *(After a pause.)* Well, I suppose you'd have to be a pretty hard person to be able to do what she did to Doc Porter.

*Babe (exasperated):* Oh, shoot! It wasn't Meg's fault that hurricane wiped Biloxi away. I never understood why people were blaming all that on Meg—just because that roof fell in and crunched Doc's leg. It wasn't her fault.

*Lenny:* Well, it was Meg who refused to evacuate. Jim Craig and some of Doc's other friends were all down there and they kept trying to get everyone to evacuate. But Meg refused. She wanted to stay on because she thought a hurricane would be—oh, I don't know—a lot of fun. Then everyone says she baited Doc into staying with her. She said she'd marry him if he'd stay.

*Babe (taken aback by this new information):* Well, he has a mind of his own. He could have gone.

*Lenny:* But he didn't. 'Cause . . . 'cause he loved her. And then after the roof caved in and they got Doc to the high school gym, Meg just left. She just left him there to leave for California—'cause of her career, she says. I think it was a shameful thing to do. It took almost a year for his leg to heal and after that he gave up his medical career altogether. He said he was tired of hospitals. It's such a sad thing. Everyone always knew he was gonna be a doctor. We've called him Doc for years.

*Babe:* I don't know. I guess I don't have any room to talk; 'cause I just don't know. *(Pause.)* Gosh, you look so tired.

*Lenny:* I feel tired.

*Babe:* They say women need a lot of iron . . . so they won't feel tired.

*Lenny:* What's got iron in it? Liver?

*Babe:* Yeah, liver's got it. And vitamin pills.

*After a moment, Meg enters. She carries a bottle of bourbon that is already minus a few slugs, and a newspaper. She is wearing black boots, a dark dress, and a hat. The room goes silent.*

*Meg:* Hello.

*Babe (fooling with her hair):* Hi, Meg. *(Lenny quietly sips her coffee.)*

*Meg (handing the newspaper to Babe):* Here's your paper.

*Babe:* Thanks. *(She opens it.)* Oh, here it is, right on the front page. *(Meg lights a cigarette.)* Where's the scissors, Lenny?

*Lenny:* Look in there in the ribbon drawer.

*Babe:* Okay. *(Babe gets the scissors and glue out of the drawer and slowly begins cutting out the newspaper article.)*

*Meg (after a few moments, filled only with the snipping of scissors):* All right—I lied! I lied! I couldn't help it . . . these stories just came pouring out of my mouth! When I saw how tired and sick Old Granddaddy'd gotten—they just flew out! All I wanted was to see him smiling and happy. I just wasn't going to sit there and look at him all miserable and sick and sad! I just wasn't!

*Babe:* Oh, Meg, he is sick, isn't he—

*Meg:* Why, he's gotten all white and milky—he's almost evaporated!

*Lenny (gasping and turning to Meg):* But still you shouldn't have lied! It just was wrong for you to tell such lies—

*Meg:* Well, I know that! Don't you think I know that? I hate myself when I lie for that old man. I do. I feel so weak. And then I have to go and do at least three or four things that I know he'd despise just to get even with that miserable, old, bossy man!

*Lenny:* Oh, Meg, please, don't talk so about Old Granddaddy! It sounds so ungrateful. Why, he went out of his way to make a home for us, to treat us like we were his very own children. All he ever wanted was the best for us. That's all he ever wanted.

*Meg:* Well, I guess it was; but sometimes I wonder what we wanted.

*Babe (taking the newspaper article and glue over to her suitcase):* Well, one thing I wanted was a team of white horses to ride Mama's coffin to her grave. That's one thing I wanted. *(Lenny and Meg exchange looks.)* Lenny, did you remember to pack my photo album?

*Lenny:* It's down there at the bottom, under all that night stuff.

*Babe:* Oh, I found it.

*Lenny:* Really, Babe, I don't understand why you have to put in the articles that are about the unhappy things in your life. Why would you want to remember them?

*Babe (pasting the article in):* I don't know. I just like to keep an accurate record, I suppose. There. *(She begins flipping through the book.)* Look, here's a picture of me when I got married.

*Meg:* Let's see.

*Babe brings the photo album over to the table. They all look at it.*

*Lenny:* My word, you look about twelve years old.

*Babe:* I was just eighteen.

*Meg:* You're smiling, Babe. Were you happy then?

*Babe (laughing):* Well, I was drunk on champagne punch. I remember that! *(They turn the page.)*

*Lenny:* Oh, there's Meg singing at Greeny's!

*Babe:* Oooh, I wish you were still singing at Greeny's! I wish you were!

*Lenny:* You're so beautiful!

*Babe:* Yes, you are. You're beautiful.

*Meg:* Oh, stop! I'm not—

*Lenny:* Look, Meg's starting to cry.

*Babe:* Oh, Meg—

*Meg:* I'm not—

*Babe:* Quick, better turn the page; we don't want Meg crying—*(She flips the pages.)*

*Lenny:* Why, it's Daddy.

*Meg:* Where'd you get that picture, Babe? I thought she burned them all.

*Babe:* Ah, I just found it around.

*Lenny:* What does it say here? What's that inscription?

*Babe:* It says "Jimmy—clowning at the beach—1952."

*Lenny:* Well, will you look at that smile.

*Meg:* Jesus, those white teeth—turn the page, will you; we can't do any worse than this! *(They turn the page. The room goes silent.)*

*Babe:* It's Mama and the cat.

*Lenny:* Oh, turn the page—

*Babe:* That old yellow cat. You know, I bet if she hadn't of hung that old cat along with her, she wouldn't have gotten all that national coverage.

*Meg (after a moment, hopelessly):* Why are we talking about this?

*Lenny:* Meg's right. It was so sad. It was awfully sad. I remember how we all three just sat up on that bed the day of the service all dressed up in our black velveteen suits crying the whole morning long.

*Babe:* We used up one whole big box of Kleenexes.

*Meg:* And then Old Granddaddy came in and said he was gonna take us out to breakfast. Remember, he told us not to cry anymore 'cause he was gonna take us out to get banana splits for breakfast.

*Babe:* That's right—banana splits for breakfast!

*Meg:* Why, Lenny was fourteen years old, and he thought that would make it all better—

*Babe:* Oh, I remember he said for us to eat all we wanted. I think I ate about five! He kept shoving them down us!

*Meg:* God, we were so sick!

*Lenny:* Oh, we were!

*Meg* (*laughing*): Lenny's face turned green—

*Lenny:* I was just as sick as a dog!

*Babe:* Old Grandmama was furious!

*Lenny:* Oh, she was!

*Meg:* The thing about Old Granddaddy is, he keeps trying to make us happy, and we end up getting stomachaches and turning green and throwing up in the flower arrangements.

*Babe:* Oh, that was me! I threw up in the flowers! Oh, no! How embarrassing!

*Lenny* (*laughing*): Oh, Babe—

*Babe* (*hugging her sisters*): Oh, Lenny! Oh, Meg!

*Meg:* Oh, Babe! Oh, Lenny! It's so good to be home!

*Lenny:* Hey, I have an idea—

*Babe:* What?

*Lenny:* Let's play cards!!

*Babe:* Oh, let's do!

*Meg:* All right!

*Lenny:* Oh, good! It'll be just like when we used to sit around the table playing hearts all night long.

*Babe:* I know! (*getting up*) I'll fix us up some popcorn and hot chocolate—

*Meg* (*getting up*): Here, let me get out that old black popcorn pot.

*Lenny* (*getting up*): Oh, yes! Now, let's see, I think I have a deck of cards around here somewhere.

*Babe:* Gosh, I hope I remember all the rules—Are hearts good or bad?

*Meg:* Bad, I think. Aren't they, Lenny?

*Lenny:* That's right. Hearts are bad, but the Black Sister is the worst of all—

*Meg:* Oh, that's right! And the Black Sister is the Queen of Spades.

*Babe* (*figuring it out*): And spades are the black cards that aren't the puppy dog feet?

*Meg* (*thinking a moment*): Right. And she counts a lot of points.

*Babe:* And points are bad?

*Meg:* Right. Here, I'll get some paper so we can keep score.

*The phone begins to ring.*

*Lenny:* Oh, here they are!

*Meg:* I'll get it—

*Lenny:* Why, look at these cards! They're years old!

*Babe:* Oh, let me see!

*Meg:* Hello . . . No, this is Meg MaGrath . . . Doc. How are you? . . . Well, good . . . You're where? . . . Well, sure. Come on over . . . Sure I'm sure. Yeah, come right on over . . . All right. 'Bye. (*She hangs up.*) That was Doc Porter. He's down the street at Al's Grill. He's gonna come on over.

*Lenny:* He is?

*Meg:* He said he wanted to come see me.

*Lenny:* Oh. (*after a pause*) Well, do you still want to play?

*Meg:* No, I don't think so.

Lenny: All right. (*Lenny starts to shuffle the cards, as Meg brushes her hair*). You know, it's really not much fun playing hearts with only two people.

Meg: I'm sorry; maybe after Doc leaves, I'll join you.

Lenny: I know; maybe Doc'll want to play, then we can have a game of bridge.

Meg: I don't think so. Doc never liked cards. Maybe we'll just go out some-where.

Lenny (*putting down the cards; Babe picks them up*): Meg—

Meg: What?

Lenny: Well, Doc's married now.

Meg: I know. You told me.

Lenny: Oh. Well, as long as you know that. (*Pause*) As long as you know that.

Meg (*still primping*): Yes, I know. She made the pot.

Babe: How many cards do I deal out?

Lenny (*leaving the table*): Excuse me.

Babe: All of 'em, or what?

Lenny: Ah, Meg? Could I—could I ask you something? (*Babe proceeds to deal out all the cards*).

Meg: What?

Lenny: I just wanted to ask you—

Meg: What?

*Unable to go on with what she really wants to say, Lenny runs up and picks up the box of candy.*

Lenny: Well, just why did you take one little bite out of each piece of candy in this box and then just put it back in?

Meg: Oh. Well, I was looking for the ones with nuts.

Lenny: The ones with nuts.

Meg: Yeah.

Lenny: But there are none with nuts. It's a box of assorted crèmes—all it has in it are crèmes!

Meg: Oh.

Lenny: Why couldn't you just read the box? It says right here, "Assorted Crèmes," not nuts! Besides, this was a birthday present to me! My one and only birth-day present; my only one!

Meg: I'm sorry. I'll get you another box.

Lenny: I don't want another box. That's not the point!

Meg: What is the point?

Lenny: I don't know; it's—it's—You have no respect for other people's property! You just take whatever you want. You just take it! Why, remember how you had layers and layers of jingle bells sewed onto your petticoats while Babe and I only had three apiece?!

Meg: Oh, God! She's starting up about those stupid jingle bells!

Lenny: Well, it's an example! A specific example of how you always got what you wanted!

Meg: Oh, come on, Lenny, you're just upset because Doc called.

*Lenny:* Who said anything about Doc? Do you think I'm upset about Doc? Why, I've long since given up worrying about you and all your men.

*Meg (turning in anger):* Look, I know I've had too many men. Believe me, I've had way too many men. But it's not my fault you haven't had any—or maybe just that one from Memphis.

*Lenny (stopping):* What one from Memphis?

*Meg (slowly):* The one Babe told me about. From the—club.

*Lenny:* Babe!

*Babe:* Meg!

*Lenny:* How could you? I asked you not to tell anyone! I'm so ashamed! How could you? Who else have you told? Did you tell anyone else?

*Babe (overlapping, to Meg):* Why'd you have to open your big mouth?

*Meg (overlapping):* How am I supposed to know? You never said not to tell!

*Babe:* Can't you use your head just for once? (*Then to Lenny.*) No, I never told anyone else. Somehow it just slipped out to Meg. Really, it just flew out of my mouth—

*Lenny:* What do you two have—wings on your tongues?

*Babe:* I'm sorry, Lenny. Really sorry.

*Lenny:* I'll just never, never, never be able to trust you again—

*Meg (furiously, coming to Babe's defense):* Oh, for heaven's sake, Lenny, we were just worried about you! We wanted to find a way to make you happy!

*Lenny:* Happy! Happy! I'll never be happy!

*Meg:* Well, not if you keep living your life as Old Granddaddy's nursemaid—

*Babe:* Meg, shut up!

*Meg:* I can't help it! I just know that the reason you stopped seeing this man from Memphis was because of Old Granddaddy.

*Lenny:* What—Babe didn't tell you the rest of the story—

*Meg:* Oh, she said it was something about your shrunken ovary.

*Babe:* Meg!

*Lenny:* Babe!

*Babe:* I just mentioned it!

*Meg:* But I don't believe a word of that story!

*Lenny:* Oh, I don't care what you believe! It's so easy for you—you always have men falling in love with you! But I have this underdeveloped ovary and I can't have children and my hair is falling out in the comb—so what man can love me? What man's gonna love me?

*Meg:* A lot of men!

*Babe:* Yeah, a lot! A whole lot!

*Meg:* Old Granddaddy's the only one who seems to think otherwise.

*Lenny:* 'Cause he doesn't want to see me hurt! He doesn't want to see me rejected and humiliated.

*Meg:* Oh, come on now, Lenny, don't be so pathetic! God, you make me angry when you just stand there looking so pathetic! Just tell me, did you really ask the man from Memphis? Did you actually ask that man from Memphis all about it?

Lenny (*breaking apart*): No; I didn't. I didn't. Because I just didn't want him not to want me—

Meg: Lenny—

Lenny (*furious*): Don't talk to me anymore! Don't talk to me! I think I'm gonna vomit—I just hope all this doesn't cause me to vomit! (*Lenny exits up the stairs sobbing.*)

Meg: See! See! She didn't even ask him about her stupid ovary! She just broke it all off 'cause of Old Granddaddy! What a jackass fool!

Babe: Oh, Meg, shut up! Why do you have to make Lenny cry? I just hate it when you make Lenny cry! (*Babe runs up the stairs.*) Lenny! Oh, Lenny— (*Meg gives a long sigh and goes to get a cigarette and a drink.*)

Meg: I feel like hell. (*Meg sits in despair—smoking and drinking bourbon. There is a knock at the back door. Meg starts. She brushes her hair out of her face and goes to answer the door. It is Doc.*)

Doc: Hello, Meggy.

Meg: Well, Doc. Well, it's Doc.

Doc (*after a pause*): You're home, Meggy.

Meg: Yeah, I've come home. I've come on home to see about Babe.

Doc: And how's Babe?

Meg: Oh, fine. Well, fair. She's fair. (*Doc nods.*) Hey, do you want a drink?

Doc: Whatcha got?

Meg: Bourbon.

Doc: Oh, don't tell me Lenny's stocking bourbon.

Meg: Well, no. I've been to the store. (*Meg gets him a glass and pours them each a drink. They click glasses.*) So, how's your wife?

Doc: She's fine.

Meg: I hear ya got two kids.

Doc: Yeah. Yeah, I got two kids.

Meg: A boy and a girl.

Doc: That's right, Meggy, a boy and a girl.

Meg: That's what you always said you wanted, wasn't it? A boy and a girl.

Doc: Is that what I said?

Meg: I don't know. I thought it's what you said. (*They finish their drinks in silence.*)

Doc: Whose cot?

Meg: Lenny's. She's taken to sleeping in the kitchen.

Doc: Ah. Where is Lenny?

Meg: She's in the upstairs room. I made her cry. Babe's up there seeing to her.

Doc: How'd you make her cry?

Meg: I don't know. Eating her birthday candy; talking on about her boyfriend from Memphis. I don't know. I'm upset about it. She's got a lot on her. Why can't I keep my mouth shut?

Doc: I don't know, Meggy. Maybe it's because you don't want to.

Meg: Maybe. (*They smile at each other. Meg pours each of them another drink.*)

Doc: Well, it's been a long time.

*Meg:* It has been a long time.

*Doc:* Let's see—when was the last time we saw each other?

*Meg:* I can't quite recall.

*Doc:* Wasn't it in Biloxi?

*Meg:* Ah, Biloxi. I believe so.

*Doc:* And wasn't there a—a hurricane going on at the time?

*Meg:* Was there?

*Doc:* Yes, there was, one hell of a hurricane. Camille, I believe they called it. Hurricane Camille.

*Meg:* Yes, now I remember. It was a beautiful hurricane.

*Doc:* We had a time down there. We had quite a time. Drinking vodka, eating oysters on the half shell, dancing all night long. And the wind was blowing.

*Meg:* Oh, God, was it blowing.

*Doc:* Goddamn, was it blowing.

*Meg:* There never has been such a wind blowing.

*Doc:* Oh, God, Meggy. Oh, God.

*Meg:* I know, Doc. It was my fault to leave you. I was crazy. I thought I was choking. I felt choked!

*Doc:* I felt like a fool.

*Meg:* No.

*Doc:* I just kept on wondering why.

*Meg:* I don't know why . . . 'Cause I didn't want to care. I don't know. I did care though. I did.

*Doc (after a pause):* Ah, hell—(*He pours them both another drink.*) Are you still singing those sad songs?

*Meg:* No.

*Doc:* Why not?

*Meg:* I don't know, Doc. Things got worse for me. After a while, I just couldn't sing anymore. I tell you, I had one hell of a time over Christmas.

*Doc:* What do you mean?

*Meg:* I went nuts. I went insane. Ended up in L.A. County Hospital. Psychiatric ward.

*Doc:* Hell. Ah, hell, Meggy. What happened?

*Meg:* I don't really know. I couldn't sing anymore; so I lost my job. And I had a bad toothache. I had this incredibly painful toothache. For days I had it, but I wouldn't do anything about it. I just stayed inside my apartment. All I could do was sit around in chairs, chewing on my fingers. Then one afternoon I ran screaming out of the apartment with all my money and jewelry and valuables and tried to stuff it all into one of those March of Dimes collection boxes. That was when they nabbed me. Sad story. Meg goes mad. (*Doc stares at her for a long moment. He pours them both another drink.*)

*Doc (after quite a pause):* There's a moon out.

*Meg:* Is there?

*Doc:* Wanna go take a ride in my truck and look out at the moon?

*Meg:* I don't know, Doc. I don't wanna start up. It'll be too hard, if we start up.

*Doc:* Who says we're gonna start up? We're just gonna look at the moon. For one night just you and me are gonna go for a ride in the country and look out at the moon.

*Meg:* One night?

*Doc:* Right.

*Meg:* Look out at the moon?

*Doc:* You got it.

*Meg:* Well . . . all right. (*She gets up.*)

*Doc:* Better take your coat. (*He helps her into her coat.*) And the bottle—(*He takes the bottle. Meg picks up the glasses.*) Forget the glasses—

*Meg (laughing):* Yeah—forget the glasses. Forget the goddamn glasses.

*Meg shuts off the kitchen lights, leaving the kitchen lit by only a dim light over the kitchen sink. Meg and Doc leave. After a moment, Babe comes down the stairs in her slip.*

*Babe:* Meg—Meg?

*She stands for a moment in the moonlight wearing only a slip. She sees her saxophone then moves to pick it up. She plays a few shrieking notes. There is a loud knock on the back door.*

*Barnette's voice:* Becky! Becky, is that you? (*Babe puts down the saxophone.*)

*Babe:* Just a minute. I'm coming. (*She puts a raincoat on over her slip and goes to answer the door. It is Barnette.*) Hello, Barnette. Come on in. (*Barnette comes in. He is troubled but is making a great effort to hide the fact.*)

*Barnette:* Thank you.

*Babe:* What is it?

*Barnette:* I've, ah, I've just come from seeing Zackery at the hospital.

*Babe:* Oh?

*Barnette:* It seems . . . Well, it seems his sister, Lucille, was somewhat suspicious.

*Babe:* Suspicious?

*Barnette:* About you?

*Babe:* Me?

*Barnette:* She hired a private detective: he took these pictures. (*He hands Babe a small envelope containing several photographs. Babe opens the envelope and begins looking at the pictures in stunned silence.*) They were taken about two weeks ago. It seems she wasn't going to show them to Botrelle straight away. She, ah, wanted to wait till the time was right. (*The phone rings one and a half times. Barnette glances uneasily towards the phone.*) Becky? (*The phone stops ringing.*)

*Babe (looking up at Barnette, slowly):* These are pictures of Willie Jay and me . . . out in the garage.

*Barnette (looking away):* I know.

*Babe:* You looked at these pictures?

*Barnette:* Yes—I—well . . . professionally, I looked at them.

*Babe:* Oh, mercy. Oh, mercy! We can burn them, can't we? Quick, we can burn them—

*Barnette:* It won't do any good. They have the negatives.

*Babe (holding the pictures, as she bangs herself hopelessly into the stove, table, cabinets, etc.):* Oh, no; oh, no; oh, no! Oh, no—

*Barnette:* There—there, now—there—

*Lenny's voice:* Babe? Are you all right? Babe—

*Babe (hiding the pictures):* What? I'm all right. Go on back to bed. *(Lenny comes down the stairs. She is wearing a coat and wiping white night cream off of her face with a wash rag.)*

*Lenny:* What's the matter? What's going on down here?

*Babe:* Nothin! *(Then as she begins dancing ballet style around the room.)* We're— we're just dancing. We were just dancing around down here. *(Signaling to Barnette to dance.)*

*Lenny:* Well, you'd better get your shoes on, 'cause we've got—

*Babe:* All right, I will! That's a good idea! *(As she goes to get her shoes, she hides the pictures.)* Now, you go on back to bed. It's pretty late and—

*Lenny:* Babe, will you listen a minute—

*Babe (holding up her shoes):* I'm putting 'em on—

*Lenny:* That was the hospital that just called. We've got to get over there. Old Granddaddy's had himself another stroke.

*Babe:* Oh. All right. My shoes are on. *(She stands. They all look at each other as the lights black out.)*

CURTAIN

# ACT III

*The lights go up on the empty kitchen. It is the following morning. After a few moments, Babe enters from the back door. She is carrying her hair curlers in her hands. She goes and lies down on the cot. A few moments later, Lenny enters. She is tired and weary. Chick's voice is heard.*

*Chick's voice:* Lenny! Oh, Lenny! *(Lenny turns to the door. Chick enters energetically.)* Well . . . how is he?

*Lenny:* He's stabilized; they say for now his functions are all stabilized.

*Chick:* Well, is he still in the coma?

*Lenny:* Uh huh.

*Chick:* Hmmm. So do they think he's gonna be . . . passing on?

*Lenny:* He may be. He doesn't look so good. They said they'd phone us if there were any sudden changes.

*Chick:* Well, it seems to me we'd better get busy phoning on the phone ourselves. *(Removing a list from her pocket.)* Now I've made out this list of all the people we need to notify about Old Granddaddy's predicament. I'll phone half if you'll phone half.

*Lenny:* But—what would we say?

*Chick:* Just tell them the facts: that Old Granddaddy's got himself in a coma, and it could be he doesn't have long for this world.

*Lenny:* I—I don't know. I don't feel like phoning.

*Chick:* Why, Lenora, I'm surprised; how can you be this way? I went to all the trouble of making up the list. And I offered to phone half of the people on it, even though I'm only one-fourth of the granddaughters. I mean, I just get tired of doing more than my fair share, when people like Meg can suddenly just disappear to where they can't even be reached in case of emergency!

*Lenny:* All right; give me the list. I'll phone half.

*Chick:* Well, don't do it just to suit me.

*Lenny (she wearily tears the list into two halves):* I'll phone these here.

*Chick (taking her half of the list):* Fine then. Suit yourself. Oh, wait—let me call Sally Bell. I need to talk to her anyway.

*Lenny:* All right.

*Chick:* So you add Great-uncle Spark Dude to your list.

*Lenny:* Okay.

*Chick:* Fine. Well, I've got to get on back home and see to the kids. It is gonna be an uphill struggle till I can find someone to replace that good-for-nothing Annie May Jenkins. Well, you let me know if you hear anymore.

*Lenny:* All right.

*Chick:* Goodbye, Rebecca. I said goodbye. *(Babe blows her sax. Chick starts to exit in a flurry, then pauses to add:)* And you really ought to try to get that phoning done before twelve noon. *(Chick exits.)*

*Lenny (after a long pause):* Babe, I feel bad. I feel real bad.

*Babe:* Why, Lenny?

*Lenny:* Because yesterday I—I wished it.

*Babe:* You wished what?

*Lenny:* I wished that Old Granddaddy would be put out of his pain. I wished it on one of my birthday candles. I did. And now he's in this coma, and they say he's feeling no pain.

*Babe:* Well, when did you have a cake yesterday? I don't remember you having any cake.

*Lenny:* Well, I didn't . . . have a cake. But I just blew out the candles, anyway.

*Babe:* Oh. Well, those birthday wishes don't count, unless you have a cake.

*Lenny:* They don't?

*Babe:* No. A lot of times they don't even count when you do have a cake. It just depends.

*Lenny:* Depends on what?

*Babe:* On how deep your wish is, I suppose.

*Lenny:* Still, I just wish I hadn't of wished it. Gosh, I wonder when Meg's coming home.

*Babe:* Should be soon.

*Lenny:* I just wish we wouldn't fight all the time. I don't like it when we do.

*Babe:* Me, neither.

*Lenny:* I guess it hurts my feelings, a little, the way Old Granddaddy's always put so much stock in Meg and all her singing talent. I think I've been, well, envious of her 'cause I can't seem to do too much.

*Babe:* Why, sure you can.

*Lenny:* I can?

*Babe:* Sure. You just have to put your mind to it that's all. It's like how I went out and bought that saxophone, just hoping I'd be able to attend music school and start up my own career. I just went out and did it. Just on hope. Of course, now it looks like . . . Well, it just doesn't look like things are gonna work out for me. But I know they would for you.

*Lenny:* Well, they'll work out for you, too.

*Babe:* I doubt it.

*Lenny:* Listen, I heard up at the hospital that Zackery's already in fair condition. They say soon he'll probably be able to walk and everything.

*Babe:* Yeah. And life sure can be miserable.

*Lenny:* Well, I know, 'cause—day before yesterday, Billy Boy was struck down by lightning.

*Babe:* He was?

*Lenny (nearing sobs):* Yeah. He was struck dead.

*Babe (crushed):* Life sure can be miserable.

*(They sit together for several moments in morbid silence. Meg is heard singing a loud happy song. She suddenly enters through the dining room door. She is exuberant! Her hair is a mess and the heel of one shoe has broken off. She is laughing radiantly and limping as she sings into the broken heel.)*

*Meg (spotting her sisters):* Good morning! Good morning! Oh, it's a wonderful morning! I tell you, I am surprised I feel this good. I should feel like hell. By all accounts, I should feel like utter hell! *(She is looking for the glue.)* Where's that glue? This damn heel has broken off my shoe. La, la, la, la, la! Ah, here it is! Now let me just get these shoes off. Zip, zip, zip, zip, zip! Well, what's wrong with you two? My God, you look like doom! *(Babe and Lenny stare helplessly at Meg.)* Oh, I know, you're mad at me 'cause I stayed out all night long. Well, I did.

*Lenny:* No, we're—we're not mad at you. We're just . . . depressed. *(She starts to sob.)*

*Meg:* Oh, Lenny, listen to me, now; everything's all right with Doc. I mean, nothing happened. Well, actually a lot did happen, but it didn't come to anything. Not because of me, I'm afraid. *(Smearing glue on her heel.)* I mean, I was out there thinking, "What will I say when he begs me to run away with him? Will I have pity on his wife and those two half-Yankee children? I mean, can I sacrifice their happiness for mine? Yes! Oh, yes! Yes, I can!" But . . . he didn't ask me. He didn't even want to ask me. I could tell by this certain look in his eyes that he didn't even want to ask me. Why aren't I miserable! Why aren't I morbid! I should be humiliated! Devastated! Maybe these feelings are coming—I don't know. But for now it was . . . just such fun. I'm happy. I realized I could care about someone. I could want someone. And I sang! I sang all night long! I sang right up into the trees! But not for Old Granddaddy. None of it was to please Old Granddaddy! (*Lenny and Babe look at each other.*)

*Babe:* Ah, Meg—

*Meg:* What—

*Babe:* Well, it's just—It's . . .

*Lenny:* It's about Old Granddaddy—

*Meg:* Oh, I know; I know. I told him all those stupid lies. Well, I'm gonna go right over there this morning and tell him the truth. I mean every horrible thing. I don't care if he wants to hear it or not. He's just gonna have to take me like I am. And if he can't take it, if it sends him into a coma, that's just too damn bad!

*Babe and Lenny look at each other; Babe cracks a smile. Lenny cracks a smile.*

*Babe:* You're too late—Ha, ha, ha! (*They both break up laughing.*)

*Lenny:* Oh, stop! Please! Ha, ha, ha!

*Meg:* What is it? What's so funny?

*Babe (still laughing):* It's not—It's not funny!

*Lenny (still laughing):* No, it's not! It's not a bit funny!

*Meg:* Well, what is it, then? What?

*Babe (trying to calm down):* Well, it's just—it's just—

*Meg:* What?

*Babe:* Well, Old Granddaddy—he—he's in a coma! (*Babe and Lenny break up laughing.*)

*Meg:* He's what?

*Babe (shrieking):* In a coma!

*Meg:* My God! That's not funny!

*Babe (calming down):* I know. I know. For some reason, it just struck us as funny.

*Lenny:* I'm sorry. It's—it's not funny. It's sad. It's very sad. We've been up all night long.

*Babe:* We're really tired.

*Meg:* Well, my God. How is he? Is he gonna live?

(*Babe and Lenny look at each other.*)

*Babe:* They don't think so! (*They both break up again.*)

*Lenny:* Oh, I don't know why we're laughing like this. We're just sick! We're just awful!

*Babe:* We are—we're awful!

*Lenny (as she collects herself):* Oh, good; now I feel bad. Now, I feel like crying. I do; I feel like crying.

*Babe:* Me, too. Me, too.

*Meg:* Well, you've gotten me depressed!

*Lenny:* I'm sorry. I'm sorry. It, ah happened last night. He had another stroke. (*They laugh again.*)

*Meg:* I see.

*Lenny:* But he's stabilized now. (*She chokes up once more.*)

*Meg:* That's good. You two okay? (*Babe and Lenny nod.*) You look like you need some rest. (*Babe and Lenny nod again. Meg goes on, about her heel.*) I hope that'll stay. (*Meg puts the top on the glue. A realization—*) Oh, of course, now I won't be able to tell him the truth about all those lies I told. I mean, finally I get my wits about me, and he conks out. It's just like him. Babe, can I wear your slippers till this glue dries?

*Babe:* Sure.

*Lenny* (*after a pause*): Things sure are gonna be different around here . . . when Old Granddaddy dies. Well, not for you two really, but for me.

*Babe* (*depressed*): Yeah. It'll work out.

*Lenny:* I hope so. I'm afraid of being here all by myself. All alone.

*Meg:* Well, you don't have to be alone. Maybe Babe'll move back in here.

(*Lenny looks at Babe hopefully.*)

*Babe:* No, I don't think I'll be living here.

*Meg* (*realizing her mistake*): Well, anyway, you're your own woman. Invite some people over. Have some parties. Go out with strange men.

*Lenny:* I don't know any strange men.

*Meg:* Well . . . you know that Charlie.

*Lenny* (*shaking her head*): Not anymore.

*Meg:* Why not?

*Lenny* (*breaking down*): I told him we should never see each other again.

*Meg:* Well, if you told him, you can just untell him.

*Lenny:* Oh, no I couldn't. I'd feel like a fool.

*Meg:* Oh, that's not a good enough reason! All people in love feel like fools. Don't they, Babe?

*Babe:* Sure.

*Meg:* Look, why don't you give him a call right now? See how things stand.

*Lenny:* Oh, no! I'd be too scared—

*Meg:* But what harm could it possibly do? I mean, it's not gonna make things any worse than this never seeing him again, at all, forever.

*Lenny:* I suppose that's true—

*Meg:* Of course it is; so call him up! Take a chance, will you? Just take some sort of chance!

*Lenny:* You think I should?

*Meg:* Of course! You've got to try—You do! (*Lenny looks over at Babe.*)

*Babe:* You do, Lenny—I think you do.

*Lenny:* Really? Really, really?

*Meg:* Yes! Yes!

*Babe:* You should!

*Lenny:* All right. I will! I will!

*Meg:* Oh, good!

*Babe:* Good!

*Lenny:* I'll call him right now, while I've got my confidence up!

*Meg:* Have you got the number?

*Lenny:* Uh huh. But, ah, I think I wanna call him upstairs. It'll be more private.

*Meg:* Ah, good idea.

*Lenny:* I'm just gonna go on and call him up and see what happens—(*She has started up the stairs.*) Wish me good luck!

*Meg:* Good luck!

*Babe:* Good luck, Lenny!

*Lenny:* Thanks.

(*Lenny gets almost out of sight, when the phone begins to ring. She stops, Meg picks up the phone.*)

*Meg:* Hello? (*Then in a whisper.*) Oh, thank you very much . . . Yes, I will. 'Bye, 'bye.

*Lenny:* Who was it?

*Meg:* Wrong number. They wanted Weed's Body Shop.

*Lenny:* Oh. Well, I'll be right back down in a minute. (*Lenny exits.*)

*Meg* (*after a moment, whispering to Babe*): That was the bakery; Lenny's cake is ready!

*Babe* (*who has become increasingly depressed*): Oh.

*Meg:* I think I'll sneak on down to the corner and pick it up. (*She starts to leave.*)

*Babe:* Meg—

*Meg:* What?

*Babe:* Nothing.

*Meg:* You okay? (*Babe shakes her head.*) What is it?

*Babe:* It's just—

*Meg:* What?

(*Babe gets up and goes to her suitcase. She opens it and removes the envelope containing the photographs.*)

*Babe:* Here. Take a look.

*Meg* (*taking the envelope*): What is it?

*Babe:* It's some evidence Zackery's collected against me. Looks like my goose is cooked. (*Meg opens the envelope and looks at the photographs.*)

*Meg:* My God, it's—it's you and . . . is *that* Willie Jay?

*Babe:* Yeh.

*Meg:* Well, he certainly *has* grown. You were right about that. My, oh, my.

*Babe:* Please don't tell Lenny. She'd hate me.

*Meg:* I won't. I won't tell Lenny. (*Putting the pictures back into the envelope.*) What are you gonna do?

*Babe:* What can I do? (*There is a knock on the door. Babe grabs the envelope and hides it.*)

*Meg:* Who is it?

*Barnette's voice:* It's Barnette Lloyd.

*Meg:* Oh. Come on in, Barnette.

*(Barnette enters. His eyes are ablaze with excitement.)*

Barnette *(as he paces around the room)*: Well, good morning! *(Shaking Meg's hand.)* Good morning, Miss MaGrath. *(Touching Babe on the shoulder.)* Becky. *(Moving away.)* What I meant to say is . . . how are you doing this morning?

Meg: Ah—fine. Fine.

Barnette: Good. Good. I—I just had time to drop by for a minute.

Meg: Oh.

Barnette: So, ah, how's your Granddad doing?

Meg: Well, not very, ah—ah, he's in this coma. *(She breaks up laughing.)*

Barnette: I see . . . I see. *(To Babe.)* Actually, the primary reason I came by was to pick up that—envelope. I left it here last night in all the confusion. *(Pause.)* You, ah, still do have it? *(Babe hands him the envelope.)* Yes. *(Taking the envelope.)* That's the one. I'm sure it'll be much better off in my office safe. *(He puts the envelope into his coat pocket.)*

Meg: I'm sure it will.

Barnette: Beg your pardon?

Babe: It's all right. I showed her the pictures.

Barnette: Ah; I see.

Meg: So what's going to happen now, Barnette? What are those pictures gonna mean?

Barnette *(after pacing a moment)*: Hmmm. May I speak frankly and openly?

Babe: Uh huh.

Meg: Please do—

Barnette: Well, I tell you now, at first glance, I admit those pictures had me considerably perturbed and upset. Perturbed to the point that I spent most of last night going over certain suspect papers and reports that had fallen into my hands—rather recklessly.

Babe: What papers do you mean?

Barnette: Papers that, pending word from three varied and unbiased experts, could prove graft, fraud, forgery, as well as a history of unethical behavior.

Meg: You mean about Zackery?

Barnette: Exactly. You see, I now intend to make this matter just as sticky and gritty for one Z. Botrelle as it is for us. Why, with the amount of scandal I'll dig up, Botrelle will be forced to settle this affair on our own terms!

Meg: Oh, Babe! Did you hear that?

Babe: Yes! Oh, yes! So you've won it! You've won your lifelong vendetta!

Barnette: Well . . . well, now of course it's problematic in that, well, in that we won't be able to expose him openly in the courts. That was the original game plan.

Babe: But why not? Why?

Barnette: Well, it's only that if, well, if a jury were to—to get, say, a glance at these, ah, photographs, well . . . well possibly. . .

Babe: We could be sunk.

Barnette: In a sense. But! On the other hand, if a newspaper were to get a hold of our little item, Mr. Zackery Botrelle could find himself boiling in some awfully hot water. So what I'm looking for very simply, is—a deal.

*Babe:* A deal?

*Meg:* Thank you, Barnette. It's a sunny day, Babe. (*Realizing she is in the way.*) Ooh, where's that broken shoe? (*She grabs her boots and runs upstairs.*)

*Babe:* So, you're having to give up your vendetta?

*Barnette:* Well, in a way. For the time. It, ah, seems to me you shouldn't always let your life be ruled by such things as, ah, personal vendettas. (*Looking at Babe with meaning.*) Other things can be important.

*Babe:* I don't know, I don't exactly know. How 'bout Willie Jay? Will he be all right?

*Barnette:* Yes, it's all been taken care of. He'll be leaving incognito on the midnight bus—heading north.

*Babe:* North.

*Barnette:* I'm sorry, it seemed the only . . . way. (*Barnette moves to her—She moves away.*)

*Babe:* Look, you'd better be getting on back to your work.

*Barnette* (*awkwardly*): Right—'cause I—I've got those important calls out. (*Full of hope for her.*) They'll be pouring in directly. (*He starts to leave, then says to her with love.*) We'll talk.

*Meg* (*reappearing in her boots*): Oh, Barnette—

*Barnette:* Yes?

*Meg:* Could you give me a ride just down to the corner? I need to stop at Helen's Bakery.

*Barnette:* Be glad to.

*Meg:* Thanks. Listen, Babe, I'll be right back with the cake. We're gonna have the best celebration! Now, ah, if Lenny asks where I've gone, just say I'm . . . just say, I've gone out back to, ah, pick up some pawpaws! Okay?

*Babe:* Okay.

*Meg:* Fine; I'll be back in a bit. Goodbye.

*Babe:* 'Bye.

*Barnette:* Goodbye, Becky.

*Babe:* Goodbye, Barnette. Take care. (*Meg and Barnette exit. Babe sits staring ahead, in a state of deep despair.*) Goodbye, Becky. Goodbye, Barnette. Goodbye, Becky. (*She stops when Lenny comes down the stairs in a fluster.*)

*Lenny:* Oh! Oh! Oh! I'm so ashamed! I'm such a coward! I'm such a yellow-bellied chicken! I'm so ashamed! Where's Meg?

*Babe* (*suddenly bright*): She's, ah—gone out back—to pick up some pawpaws.

*Lenny:* Oh. Well, at least I don't have to face her! I just couldn't do it! I couldn't make the call! My heart was pounding like a hammer. Pound! Pound! Pound! Why, I looked down and I could actually see my blouse moving back and forth! Oh, Babe, you look so disappointed. Are you?

*Babe* (*despondently*): Uh huh.

*Lenny:* Oh, no! I've disappointed Babe! I can't stand it! I've gone and disappointed my little sister, Babe! Oh, no! I feel like howling like a dog!

*Chick's voice:* Oooh, Lenny! (*Chick enters dramatically; dripping with sympathy.*) Well, I just don't know what to say! I'm so sorry! I am so sorry for you! And for Little Babe, here, too. I mean to have such a sister as that!

*Lenny:* What do you mean?

*Chick:* Oh, you don't need to pretend with me. I saw it all from over there in my own backyard; I saw Meg stumbling out of Doc Porter's pickup truck, not 15 minutes ago. And her looking such a disgusting mess. You must be so ashamed! You must just want to die! Why, I always said that girl was nothing but cheap Christmas trash!

*Lenny:* Don't talk that way about Meg.

*Chick:* Oh, come on now, Lenny, honey, I know exactly how you feel about Meg. Why, Meg's a low-class tramp and you need not have one more blessed thing to do with her and her disgusting behavior.

*Lenny:* I said, don't you ever talk that way about my sister Meg again.

*Chick:* Well, my goodness gracious, Lenora, don't be such a noodle—it's the truth!

*Lenny:* I don't care if it's the Ten Commandments. I don't want to hear it in my home. Not ever again.

*Chick:* In your home?! Why, I never in all my life—This is my Grandfather's home! And you're just living here on his charity; so don't you get high-falutin' with me, Miss Lenora Josephine MaGrath!

*Lenny:* Get out of here—

*Chick:* Don't you tell me to get out! What makes you think you can order me around? Why, I've had just about my fill of you trashy MaGraths and your trashy ways: hanging yourselves in cellars; carrying on with married men; shooting your own husbands!

*Lenny:* Get out!

*Chick (to Babe):* And don't think she's not gonna end up at the state prison farm or in some—mental institution. Why, it's a clear-cut case of manslaughter with intent to kill!

*Lenny:* Out! Get out!

*Chick (running on):* That's what everyone's saying, deliberate intent to kill! And you'll pay for that! Do you hear me? You'll pay!

*Lenny (she picks up a broom and threatens Chick with it):* And I'm telling you to get out!

*Chick:* You—you put that down this minute—Are you a raving lunatic?

*Lenny (beating Chick with the broom):* I said for you to get out! That means out! And never, never, never come back!

*Chick (overlapping, as she runs around the room):* Oh! Oh! Oh! You're crazy! You're crazy!

*Lenny (chasing Chick out the door):* Do you hear me, Chick the Stick! This is my home! This is my house! Get out! Out!

*Chick (overlapping):* Oh! Oh! Police! Police! You're crazy! Help! Help! (*Lenny chases Chick out of the house. They are both screaming. The phone rings. Babe goes and picks it up.*)

*Babe:* Hello? . . . Oh, hello, Zackery! . . . Yes, he showed them to me! . . . You're what! . . . What do you mean? . . . What! . . . You can't put me out to Whitfield . . . 'Cause I'm not crazy . . . I'm not! I'm not! . . . She wasn't crazy, either . . . Don't you call my mother crazy! . . . No, you're not! You're not gonna. You're not! (*She slams the phone down and stares wildly ahead.*) He's not. He's not. (*As she walks over to the ribbon drawer.*) I'll do it. I will. And he won't . . . (*She opens the drawer; pulls out the rope; becomes terrified, throws the rope back in the drawer and slams it shut. Lenny enters from the back door swinging the broom and laughing.*)

Lenny: Oh, my! Oh, my! You should have seen us! Why, I chased Chick the Stick right up the mimosa tree. I did! I left her right up there screaming in the tree!

Babe (*laughing; she is insanely delighted*): Oh, you did!

Lenny: Yes, I did! And I feel so good! I do! I feel good! I feel good!

Babe (*overlapping*): Good! Good, Lenny! Good for you! (*They dance around the kitchen.*)

Lenny (*stopping*): You know what—

Babe: What?

Lenny: I'm gonna call Charlie! I'm gonna call him up right now!

Babe: You are?

Lenny: Yeah, I feel like I can really do it!

Babe: You do?

Lenny: My courage is up; my heart's in it; the time is right! No more beating around the bush! Let's strike while the iron is hot!

Babe: Right! Right! No more beating around the bush! Strike while the iron is hot! (*Lenny goes to the phone. Babe rushes over to the ribbon drawer. She begins tearing through it.*)

Lenny (*with the receiver in her hand*): I'm calling him up, Babe—I'm really gonna do it!

Babe (*still tearing through the drawer*): Good! Do it! Good!

Lenny (*as she dials*): Look. My hands aren't even shaking.

Babe (*pulling out a red cord of rope*): Don't we have any stronger rope than this?

Lenny: I guess not. All the rope we've got's in that drawer. (*About her hands.*) Now they're shaking a little. (*Babe takes the rope and goes up the stairs. Lenny finishes dialing the number. She waits for an answer.*) Hello? . . . Hello, Charlie. This is Lenny MaGrath . . . Well, I'm fine. I'm just fine. (*An awkward pause.*) I was, ah, just calling to see—how you're getting on . . . Well, good. Good . . . Yes, I know I said that. Now I wish I didn't say it . . . Well, the reason I said that before, about not seeing each other again, was 'cause of me, not you . . . Well, it's just I—I can't have any children. I—have this ovary problem . . . Why, Charlie, what a thing to say! . . . Well, they're not all little snot-nosed pigs! . . . You think they are! . . . Oh, Charlie, stop, stop! You're making me laugh . . . Yes, I guess I was. I can see now that I was . . . You are? . . . Well, I'm dying to see you, too . . . Well, I don't know when, Charlie . . . soon. How about, well, how about tonight? . . . You will? . . . Oh, you will! . . . All right, I'll be here. I'll be right here . . . Goodbye, then, Charlie. Goodbye for now. (*She hangs up the phone in a daze.*) Babe. Oh, Babe! He's coming. He's coming! Babe! Oh, Babe, where are you? Meg! Oh . . . out back—picking up pawpaws. (*As she exits through the back door.*) And those pawpaws are just ripe for picking up!

(*There is a moment of silence, then a loud, horrible thud is heard coming from upstairs. The telephone begins ringing immediately. It rings five times before Babe comes hurrying down the stairs with a broken piece of rope hanging around her neck. The phone continues to ring.*)

Babe (*to the phone*): Will you shut up! (*She is jerking the rope from around her neck. She grabs a knife to cut it off.*) Cheap! Miserable! I hate you! I hate you! (*She throws the rope violently around the room. The phone stops ringing.*) Thank God. (*She looks at the stove, goes over to it, and turns the gas on. The sound of gas escaping is heard. Babe sniffs at it.*) Come on. Come on . . . Hurry up . . . I beg of you—hurry up! (*Finally, Babe feels the oven is ready; she takes a deep breath and opens the oven door to stick her head into it. She spots the rack and furiously jerks it out. Taking another breath, she sticks her head into the oven. She stands for several moments tapping her fingers furiously on top of the stove. She speaks from inside the oven . . .*) Oh, please. Please. (*After a few moments, she reaches for the box of matches with her head still in the oven. She tries to strike a match. It doesn't catch.*) Oh, Mama, please! (*She throws the match away and is getting a second one.*) Mama . . . Mama . . . So that's why you done it!

(*In her excitement she starts to get up, bangs her head and falls back in the stove. Meg enters from the back door, carrying a birthday cake in a pink box.*)

Meg: Babe! (*Meg throws the box down and runs to pull Babe's head out of the oven.*) Oh, my God! What are you doing? What the hell are you doing?
Babe (*dizzily*): Nothing. I don't know. Nothing. (*Meg turns off the gas and moves Babe to a chair near the open door.*)
Meg: Sit down. Sit down! Will you sit down!
Babe: I'm okay. I'm okay.
Meg: Put your head between your knees and breathe deep!
Babe: Meg—
Meg: Just do it! I'll get you some water. (*Meg gets some water for Babe.*) Here.
Babe: Thanks.
Meg: Are you okay?
Babe: Uh huh.
Meg: Are you sure?
Babe: Yeah, I'm sure. I'm okay.
Meg (*getting a damp rag and putting it over her own face*): Well good. That's good.
Babe: Meg—
Meg: Yes?
Babe: I know why she did it.
Meg: What? Why who did what?
Babe (*with joy*): Mama. I know why she hung that cat along with her.
Meg: You do?
Babe (*with enlightenment*): It's 'cause she was afraid of dying all alone.

*Meg:* Was she?

*Babe:* She felt so unsure, you know, as to what was coming. It seems the best thing coming up would be a lot of angels and all of them singing. But I imagine they have high, scary voices and little gold pointed fingers that are as sharp as blades and you don't want to meet 'em all alone. You'd be afraid to meet 'em all alone. So it wasn't like what people were saying about her hating that cat. Fact is, she loved that cat. She needed him with her 'cause she felt so all alone.

*Meg:* Oh, Babe . . . Babe. Why, Babe? Why?

*Babe:* Why what?

*Meg:* Why did you stick your head into the oven?!

*Babe:* I don't know, Meg. I'm having a bad day. It's been a real bad day; those pictures, and Barnette giving up his vendetta; then Willie Jay heading north; and—Zackery called me up. (*Trembling with terror.*) He says he's gonna have me classified insane and send me on out to the Whitfield asylum.

*Meg:* What! Why, he could never do that!

*Babe:* Why not?

*Meg:* 'Cause you're not insane.

*Babe:* I'm not?

*Meg:* No! He's trying to bluff you. Don't you see it? Barnette's got him running scared.

*Babe:* Really?

*Meg:* Sure. He's scared to death—calling you insane. Ha! Why, you're just as perfectly sane as anyone walking the streets of Hazlehurst, Mississippi.

*Babe:* I am?

*Meg:* More so! A lot more so!

*Babe:* Good!

*Meg:* But, Babe, we've just got to learn how to get through these real bad days here. I mean, it's getting to be a thing in our family. (*Slight pause as she looks at Babe.*) Come on now. Look, we've got Lenny's cake right here. I mean don't you wanna be around to give her her cake, watch her blow out the candles?

*Babe* (*realizing how much she wants to be here*): Yeah, I do, I do. 'Cause she always loves to make her birthday wishes on those candles.

*Meg:* Well, then we'll give her her cake and maybe you won't be so miserable.

*Babe:* Okay.

*Meg:* Good. Go on and take it out of the box.

*Babe:* Okay. (*She takes the cake out of the box. It is a magical moment.*) Gosh, it's a pretty cake.

*Meg* (*handing her some matches*): Here now. You can go on and light up the candles.

*Babe:* All right. (*She starts to light the candles.*) I love to light up candles. And there are so many here. Thirty pink ones in all plus one green one to grow on.

*Meg* (*watching her light the candles*): They're pretty.

*Babe:* They are. (*She stops lighting the candles.*) And I'm not like Mama. I'm not so all alone.

*Meg:* You're not.

*Babe (as she goes back to lighting candles)*: Well, you'd better keep an eye out for Lenny. She's supposed to be surprised.

*Meg*: All right. Do you know where she's gone?

*Babe*: Well, she's not here inside—so she must have gone on outside.

*Meg*: Oh, well, then I'd better run and find her.

*Babe*: Okay; 'cause these candles are gonna melt down. *(Meg starts out the door.)*

*Meg*: Wait—there she is coming. Lenny! Oh, Lenny! Come on! Hurry up!

*Babe (overlapping and improvising as she finishes lighting candles)*: Oh, no! No! Well, yes—Yes! No, wait! Wait! Okay! Hurry up! *(Lenny enters. Meg covers Lenny's eyes with her hands.)*

*Lenny (terrified)*: What? What is it? What?

*Meg & Babe*: Surprise! Happy Birthday! Happy Birthday to Lenny!!

*Lenny*: Oh, no! Oh me! What a surprise! I could just cry! Oh, look: "Happy Birthday to Lenny—A Day Late!" How cute! My! Will you look at all those candles—it's absolutely frightening.

*Babe (spontaneous thought)*: Oh, no, Lenny, it's good! 'Cause—'cause the more candles you have on your cake, the stronger your wish is.

*Lenny*: Really?

*Babe*: Sure!

*Lenny*: Mercy. *(They start the song. Lenny, interrupting the song.)* Oh, but wait! I—can't think of my wish! My body's gone all nervous inside.

*Meg*: For God's sake, Lenny—Come on!

*Babe*: The wax is all melting!

*Lenny*: My mind is just a blank, a total blank!

*Meg*: Will you please just—

*Babe (overlapping)*: Lenny, hurry! Come on!

*Lenny*: Okay! Okay! Just go!! *(Meg and Babe burst into the "Happy Birthday" song. As it ends, Lenny blows out all of the candles on the cake. Meg and Babe applaud loudly.)*

*Meg*: Oh, you made it!

*Babe*: Hurray!

*Lenny*: Oh, me! Oh, me! I hope that wish comes true! I hope it does!

*Babe*: Why? What did you wish for?

*Lenny (as she removes the candles from the cake)*: Why, I can't tell you that.

*Babe*: Oh, sure you can—

*Lenny*: Oh, no! Then it won't come true.

*Babe*: Why, that's just superstition! Of course it will, if you made it deep enough.

*Meg*: Really? I didn't know that.

*Lenny*: Well, Babe's the regular expert on birthday wishes.

*Babe*: It's just I get these feelings. Now come on and tell us. What was it you wished for?

*Meg*: Yes, tell us. What was it?

*Lenny*: Well, I guess, it wasn't really a specific wish. This—this vision just sort of came into my mind.

*Babe*: A vision? What was it of?

Lenny: I don't know exactly. It was something about the three of us smiling and laughing together.

Babe: Well, when was it? Was it far away or near?

Lenny: I'm not sure, but it wasn't forever; it wasn't for every minute. Just this one moment and we were all laughing.

Babe: Then, what were we laughing about?

Lenny: I don't know. Just nothing, I guess.

Meg: Well, that's a nice wish to make. (*Lenny and Meg look at each other a moment.*) Here, now, I'll get a knife so we can go ahead and cut the cake in celebration of Lenny being born!

Babe: Oh, yes! And give each one of us a rose. A whole rose apiece!

Lenny (*cutting the cake nervously*): Well, I'll try—I'll try!

Meg (*licking the icing off a candle*): Mmmm—this icing is delicious! Here, try some!

Babe: Mmmm! It's wonderful! Here, Lenny!

Lenny (*laughing joyously as she licks icing from her fingers and cuts huge pieces of cake that her sisters bite into ravenously*): Oh, how I do love having birthday cake for breakfast! How I do! (*The sisters freeze for a moment laughing and eating cake; the lights change and frame them in a magical, golden, sparkling glimmer; saxophone music is heard. The lights dim to blackout, and the saxophone continues to play.*)

CURTAIN

## David Henry Hwang
THE SOUND OF A VOICE                                    1983

David Henry Hwang (b. 1957) grew up in San Gabriel, California, the son of first-generation Chinese immigrants. Hwang was born into a family of musicians: his mother was a concert pianist, his sister plays cello in a string quartet, and he studied the violin. As a senior at Stanford University, he directed his first play, F. O. B. (1979)—in a dormitory lounge. F. O. B. was later staged at the New York Shakespeare Festival Public Theater and won a 1981 Obie Award. The Sound of a Voice (1983) was also produced at the Public Theater (as part of a double bill with another Hwang one-act play, The House of Sleeping Beauties). Hwang enjoyed his greatest commercial and critical success with M. Butterfly (1988), which won the Tony Award for best play.

*David Henry Hwang*

While some of his plays are realistic in their approach, Hwang has been fascinated by the possibilities of symbolic drama. In The Sound of a Voice, Hwang creates a timeless, placeless scene in which two characters named Man and Woman act out a story reminiscent of a folk legend or a traditional Japanese Nō drama (a type of symbolic aristocratic drama developed in fourteenth-century Japan in which a ghost acts out the struggles of his or her life for a traveler). Hwang's interest in nonrealistic drama has recently led him into opera. He collaborated with composer Philip Glass on 1000 Airplanes on the Roof (1988), a science-fiction music drama, and The Voyage (1992), an allegorical grand opera that was commissioned by New York's Metropolitan Opera for the cinquecentenary of Christopher Columbus's arrival in America. Hwang currently lives in San Francisco.

Characters

Man, fifties, Japanese
Woman, fifties, Japanese

*Setting:* Woman's house, in a remote corner of the forest.

**Scene I.** Woman pours tea for Man. Man rubs himself, trying to get warm.

Man: You're very kind to take me in.
Woman: This is a remote corner of the world. Guests are rare.
Man: The tea—you pour it well.

Woman: No.

Man: The sound it makes—in the cup—very soothing.

Woman: That is the tea's skill, not mine. (*She hands the cup to him.*) May I get you something else? Rice, perhaps?

Man: No.

Woman: And some vegetables?

Man: No, thank you.

Woman: Fish? (*Pause.*) It is at least two days' walk to the nearest village. I saw no horse. You must be very hungry. You would do a great honor to dine with me. Guests are rare.

Man: Thank you.

Woman (*Woman gets up, leaves. Man holds the cup in his hands, using it to warm himself. He gets up, walks around the room. It is sparsely furnished, drab, except for one shelf on which stands a vase of brightly colored flowers. The flowers stand out in sharp contrast to the starkness of the room. Slowly, he reaches out towards them. He touches them. Quickly, he takes one of the flowers from the vase, hides it in his clothes. He returns to where he had sat previously. He waits. Woman re-enters. She carries a tray with food.*): Please. Eat. It will give me great pleasure.

Man: This—this is magnificent.

Woman: Eat.

Man: Thank you. (*He motions for Woman to join him.*)

Woman: No, thank you.

Man: This is wonderful. The best I've tasted.

Woman: You are reckless in your flattery. But anything you say, I will enjoy hearing. It's not even the words. It's the sound of a voice, the way it moves through the air.

Man: How long has it been since you last had a visitor? (*Pause.*)

Woman: I don't know.

Man: Oh?

Woman: I lose track. Perhaps five months ago, perhaps ten years, perhaps yesterday. I don't consider time when there is no voice in the air. It's pointless. Time begins with the entrance of a visitor, and ends with his exit.

Man: And in between? You don't keep track of the days? You can't help but notice—

Woman: Of course I notice.

Man: Oh.

Woman: I notice, but I don't keep track. (*Pause.*) May I bring out more?

Man: More? No. No. This was wonderful.

Woman: I have more.

Man: Really—the best I've had.

Woman: You must be tired. Did you sleep in the forest last night?

Man: Yes.

Woman: Or did you not sleep at all?

Man: I slept.

Woman: Where?

Man: By a waterfall. The sound of the water put me to sleep. It rumbled like the sounds of a city. You see, I can't sleep in too much silence. It scares me. It makes me feel that I have no control over what is about to happen.

Woman: I feel the same way.

Man: But you live here—alone?

Woman: Yes.

Man: It's so quiet here. How can you sleep?

Woman: Tonight, I'll sleep. I'll lie down in the next room, and hear your breathing through the wall, and fall asleep shamelessly. There will be no silence.

Man: You're very kind to let me stay here.

Woman: This is yours. (*She unrolls a mat; there is a beautiful design of a flower on the mat. The flower looks exactly like the flowers in the vase.*)

Man: Did you make it yourself?

Woman: Yes. There is a place to wash outside.

Man: Thank you.

Woman: Goodnight.

Man: Goodnight. (*Man starts to leave.*)

Woman: May I know your name?

Man: No. I mean, I would rather not say. If I gave you a name, it would only be made-up. Why should I deceive you? You are too kind for that.

Woman: Then what should I call you? Perhaps—"Man Who Fears Silence"?

Man: How about, "Man Who Fears Women"?

Woman: That name is much too common.

Man: And you?

Woman: Yokiko.

Man: That's your name?

Woman: It's what you may call me.

Man: Goodnight, Yokiko. You are very kind.

Woman: You are very smart. Goodnight. (*Man exits. Hanako° goes to the mat. She tidies it, brushes it off. She goes to the vase. She picks up the flowers, studies them. She carries them out of the room with her. Man re-enters. He takes off his outer clothing. He glimpses the spot where the vase used to sit. He reaches into his clothing, pulls out the stolen flower. He studies it. He puts it underneath his head as he lies down to sleep, like a pillow. He starts to fall asleep. Suddenly, a start. He picks up his head. He listens.*)

**Scene II.** Dawn. Man is getting dressed. Woman enters with food.

Woman: Good morning.

Man: Good morning, Yokiko.

Woman: You weren't planning to leave?

---

Hanako: The woman.

*Man:* I have quite a distance to travel today.

*Woman:* Please. (*She offers him food.*)

*Man:* Thank you.

*Woman:* May I ask where you're travelling to?

*Man:* It's far.

*Woman:* I know this region well.

*Man:* Oh? Do you leave the house often?

*Woman:* I used to. I used to travel a great deal. I know the region from those days.

*Man:* You probably wouldn't know the place I'm headed.

*Woman:* Why not?

*Man:* It's new. A new village. It didn't exist in "those days." (*Pause.*)

*Woman:* I thought you said you wouldn't deceive me.

*Man:* I didn't. You don't believe me, do you?

*Woman:* No.

*Man:* Then I didn't deceive you. I'm travelling. That much is true.

*Woman:* Are you in such a hurry?

*Man:* Travelling is a matter of timing. Catching the light. (*Woman exits; Man finishes eating, puts down his bowl. Woman re-enters with the vase of flowers.*) Where did you find those? They don't grow native around these parts, do they?

*Woman:* No; they've all been brought in. They were brought in by visitors. Such as yourself. They were left here. In my custody.

*Man:* But—they look so fresh, so alive.

*Woman:* I take care of them. They remind me of the people and places outside this house.

*Man:* May I touch them?

*Woman:* Certainly.

*Man:* These have just blossomed.

*Woman:* No; they were in bloom yesterday. If you'd noticed them before, you would know that.

*Man:* You must have received these very recently. I would guess—within five days.

*Woman:* I don't know. But I wouldn't trust your estimate. It's all in the amount of care you show to them. I create a world which is outside the realm of what you know.

*Man:* What do you do?

*Woman:* I can't explain. Words are too inefficient. It takes hundreds of words to describe a single act of caring. With hundreds of acts, words become irrelevant. (*Pause.*) But perhaps you can stay.

*Man:* How long?

*Woman:* As long as you'd like.

*Man:* Why?

*Woman:* To see how I care for them.

*Man:* I am tired.

*Woman:* Rest.

*Man:* The light?

*Woman:* It will return.

**Scene III.** *Man is carrying chopped wood. He is stripped to the waist. Woman enters.*

*Woman:* You're very kind to do that for me.

*Man:* I enjoy it, you know. Chopping wood. It's clean. No questions. You take your axe, you stand up the log, you aim—pow!—you either hit it or you don't. Success or failure.

*Woman:* You seem to have been very successful today.

*Man:* Why shouldn't I be? It's a beautiful day. I can see to those hills. The trees are cool. The sun is gentle. Ideal. If a man can't be successful on a day like this, he might as well kick the dust up into his own face. (*Man notices Woman staring at him. Man pats his belly, looks at her.*) Protection from falls.

*Woman:* What? (*Man pinches his belly, showing some fat.*) Oh. Don't be silly. (*Man begins slapping the fat on his belly to a rhythm.*)

*Man:* Listen—I can make music—see?—that wasn't always possible. But now—that I've developed this—whenever I need entertainment.

*Woman:* You shouldn't make fun of your body.

*Man:* Why not? I saw you. You were staring.

*Woman:* I wasn't making fun. (*Man inflates his cheeks.*) I was just—stop that!

*Man:* Then why were you staring?

*Woman:* I was—

*Man:* Laughing?

*Woman:* No.

*Man:* Well?

*Woman:* I was—Your body. It's . . . strong. (*Pause.*)

*Man:* People say that. But they don't know. I've heard that age brings wisdom. That's a laugh. The years don't accumulate here. They accumulate here. (*Pause; he pinches his belly.*) But today is a day to be happy, right? The woods. The sun. Blue. It's a happy day. I'm going to chop wood.

*Woman:* There's nothing left to chop. Look.

*Man:* Oh. I guess . . . that's it.

*Woman:* Sit. Here.

*Man:* But—

*Woman:* There's nothing left. (*Man sits; Woman stares at his belly.*) Learn to love it.

*Man:* Don't be ridiculous.

*Woman:* Touch it.

*Man:* It's flabby.

*Woman:* It's strong.

*Man:* It's weak.

*Woman:* And smooth.

*Man:* Do you mind if I put on my shirt?

*Woman:* Of course not. Shall I get it for you?

*Man:* No. No. Just sit there. (*Man starts to put on his shirt. He pauses, studies his body.*) You think it's cute, huh?

*Woman:* I think you should learn to love it. (*Man pats his belly, talks to it.*)

*Man (To belly):* You're okay, sir. You hang onto my body like a great horseman.

*Woman:* Not like that.

Man (*Ibid.*): You're also faithful. You'll never leave me for another man.
Woman: No.
Man: What do you want me to say? (*Woman walks over to Man. She touches his belly with her hand. They look at each other.*)

**Scene IV.** *Night. Man is alone. Flowers are gone from stand. Mat is unrolled. Man lies on it, sleeping. Suddenly, he starts. He lifts up his head. He listens. Silence. He goes back to sleep. Another start. He lifts up his head, strains to hear. Slowly, we begin to make out the strains of a single shakuhachi° playing a haunting line. It is very soft. He strains to hear it. The instrument slowly fades out. He waits for it to return, but it does not. He takes out the stolen flower. He stares into it.*

**Scene V.** *Day. Woman is cleaning, while Man relaxes. She is on her hands and knees, scrubbing. She is dressed in a simple outfit, for working. Her hair is tied back. Man is sweating. He has not, however, removed his shirt.*

Man: I heard your playing last night.
Woman: My playing?
Man: *Shakuhachi.*
Woman: Oh.
Man: You played very softly. I had to strain to hear it. Next time, don't be afraid.
    Play out. Fully. Clear. It must've been very beautiful, if only I could've heard
    it clearly. Why don't you play for me sometime?
Woman: I'm very shy about it.
Man: Why?
Woman: I play for my own satisfaction. That's all. It's something I developed on
    my own. I don't know if it's at all acceptable by outside standards.
Man: Play for me. I'll tell you.
Woman: No; I'm sure you're too knowledgeable in the arts.
Man: Who? Me?
Woman: You being from the city and all.
Man: I'm ignorant, believe me.
Woman: I'd play, and you'd probably bite your cheek.
Man: Ask me a question about music. Any question. I'll answer incorrectly. I
    guarantee it.
Woman: Look at this.
Man: What?
Woman: A stain.
Man: Where?
Woman: Here? See? I can't get it out.
Man: Oh. I hadn't noticed it before.
Woman: I notice it every time I clean.
Man: Here. Let me try.

---

*shakuhachi*: A Japanese bamboo flute.

Woman: Thank you.

Man: Ugh. It's tough.

Woman: I know.

Man: How did it get here?

Woman: It's been there as long as I've lived here.

Man: I hardly stand a chance. (*Pause.*) But I'll try. Uh—one—two—three—four! One—two—three—four! See, you set up . . . gotta set up . . . a rhythm— two—three—four. Like fighting! Like battle! One—two—three—four! Used to practice with a rhythm . . . beat . . . battle! Yes! (*The stain starts to fade away.*) Look—it's—yes!—whoo!—there it goes—got the sides—the edges— yes!—fading quick—fading away—ooo—here we come—towards the cen- ter—to the heart—two—three—four—slow—slow death—tough—dead! (*Man rolls over in triumphant laughter.*)

Woman: Dead.

Man: I got it! I got it! Whoo! A little rhythm! All it took! Four! Four!

Woman: Thank you.

Man: I didn't think I could do it—but there—it's gone—I did it!

Woman: Yes. You did.

Man: And you—you were great.

Woman: No—I was carried away.

Man: We were a team! You and me!

Woman: I only provided encouragement.

Man: You were great! You were! (*Man grabs Woman. Pause.*)

Woman: It's gone. Thank you. Would you like to hear me play *shakuhachi?*

Man: Yes I would.

Woman: I don't usually play for visitors. It's so . . . I'm not sure. I developed it— all by myself—in times when I was alone. I heard nothing—no human voice. So I learned to play *shakuhachi.* I tried to make these sounds resemble the human voice. The *shakuhachi* became my weapon. To ward off the air. It kept me from choking on many a silent evening.

Man: I'm here. You can hear my voice.

Woman: Speak again.

Man: I will.

**Scene VI.** *Night. Man is sleeping. Suddenly, a start. He lifts his head up. He listens. Silence. He strains to hear. The* shakuhachi *melody rises up once more. This time, however, it becomes louder and more clear than before. He gets up. He cannot tell from what direction the music is coming. He walks around the room, putting his ear to differ- ent places in the wall, but he cannot locate the sound. It seems to come from all direc- tions at once, as omnipresent as the air. Slowly, he moves towards the wall with the slid- ing panel through which the Woman enters and exits. He puts his ear against it, thinking the music may be coming from there. Slowly, he slides the door open just a crack, ever so carefully. He peeks through the crack. As he peeks through, the Upstage wall of the set becomes transparent, and through the scrim, we are able to see what he sees. Woman is Upstage of the scrim. She is tending a room filled with potted and vased flow-*

ers of all variety. The lushness and beauty of the room Upstage of the scrim stands out in stark contrast to the barrenness of the main set. She is also transformed. She is a young woman. She is beautiful. She wears a brightly colored kimono. Man observes this scene for a long time. He then slides the door shut. The scrim returns to opaque. The music continues. He returns to his mat. He picks up the stolen flower. It is brown and wilted, dead. He looks at it. The music slowly fades out.

**Scene VII.** Morning. Man is half-dressed. He is practicing sword maneuvers. He practices with the feel of a man whose spirit is willing, but the flesh is inept. He tries to execute deft movements, but is dissatisfied with his efforts. He curses himself, and returns to basic exercises. Suddenly, he feels something buzzing around his neck—a mosquito. He slaps his neck, but misses it. He sees it flying near him. He swipes at it with his sword. He keeps missing. Finally, he thinks he's hit it. He runs over, kneels down to recover the fallen insect. He picks up two halves of a mosquito on two different fingers. Woman enters the room. She looks as she normally does. She is carrying a vase of flowers, which she places on its shelf.

Man: Look.
Woman: I'm sorry?
Man: Look.
Woman: What? (He brings over the two halves of mosquito to show her.)
Man: See?
Woman: Oh.
Man: I hit it—chop!
Woman: These are new forms of target practice?
Man: Huh? Well—yes—in a way.
Woman: You seem to do well at it.
Man: Thank you. For last night. I heard your *shakuhachi*. It was very loud, strong—good tone.
Woman: Did you enjoy it? I wanted you to enjoy it. If you wish, I'll play it for you every night.
Man: Every night!
Woman: If you wish.
Man: No—I don't—I don't want you to treat me like a baby.
Woman: What? I'm not.
Man: Oh, yes. Like a baby. Who you must feed in the middle of the night or he cries. Waaah! Waaah!
Woman: Stop that!
Man: You need your sleep.
Woman: I don't mind getting up for you. (*Pause.*) I would enjoy playing for you. Every night. While you sleep. It will make me feel—like I'm shaping your dreams. I go through long stretches when there is no one in my dreams. It's terrible. During those times, I avoid my bed as much as possible. I paint. I weave. I play *shakuhachi*. I sit on mats and rub powder into my face. Anything to keep from facing a bed with no dreams. It is like sleeping on ice.

Man: What do you dream of now?

Woman: Last night—I dreamt of you. I don't remember what happened. But you were very funny. Not in a mocking way. I wasn't laughing at you. But you made me laugh. And you were very warm. I remember that. (*Pause.*) What do you remember about last night?

Man: Just your playing. That's all. I got up, listened to it, and went back to sleep. (*Man gets up, resumes practicing with his sword.*)

Woman: Another mosquito bothering you?

Man: Just practicing. Ah! Weak! Too weak! I tell you, it wasn't always like this. I'm telling you, there were days when I could chop the fruit from a tree without ever taking my eyes off the ground. (*He continues practicing.*) You ever use one of these?

Woman: I've had to pick one up, yes.

Man: Oh?

Woman: You forget—I live alone—out here—there is . . . not much to sustain me but what I manage to learn myself. It wasn't really a matter of choice.

Man: I used to be very good, you know. Perhaps I can give you some pointers.

Woman: I'd really rather not.

Man: C'mon—a woman like you—you're absolutely right. You need to know how to defend yourself.

Woman: As you wish.

Man: Do you have something to practice with?

Woman: Yes. Excuse me. (*She exits. He practices more. She re-enters with two wooden sticks. He takes one of them.*) Will these do?

Man: Nice. Now, show me what you can do.

Woman: I'm sorry?

Man: Run up and hit me.

Woman: Please.

Man: Go on—I'll block it.

Woman: I feel so . . . undignified.

Man: Go on. (*She hits him playfully with stick.*) Not like that!

Woman: I'll try to be gentle.

Man: What?

Woman: I don't want to hurt you.

Man: You won't—Hit me! (*Woman charges at Man, quickly, deftly. She scores a hit.*) Oh!

Woman: Did I hurt you?

Man: No—you were—let's try that again. (*They square off again. Woman rushes forward. She appears to attempt a strike. He blocks that apparent strike, which turns out to be a feint. She scores.*) Huh?

Woman: Did I hurt you? I'm sorry.

Man: No.

Woman: I hurt you.

Man: No.

Woman: Do you wish to hit me?

Man: No.

*Woman:* Do you want me to try again?

*Man:* No.

*Woman:* Thank you.

*Man:* Just practice there—by yourself—let me see you run through some maneuvers.

*Woman:* Must I?

*Man:* Yes! Go! (*She goes to an open area.*) My greatest strength was always as a teacher. (*Woman executes a series of deft movements. Her whole manner is transformed. Man watches with increasing amazement. Her movements end. She regains her submissive manner.*)

*Woman:* I'm so embarrassed. My skills—they're so—inappropriate. I look like a man.

*Man:* Where did you learn that?

*Woman:* There is much time to practice here.

*Man:* But you—the techniques.

*Woman:* I don't know what's fashionable in the outside world. (*Pause.*) Are you unhappy?

*Man:* No.

*Woman:* Really?

*Man:* I'm just . . . surprised.

*Woman:* You think it's unbecoming for a woman.

*Man:* No, no. Not at all.

*Woman:* You want to leave.

*Man:* No!

*Woman:* All visitors do. I know. I've met many. They say they'll stay. And they do. For a while. Until they see too much. Or they learn something new. There are boundaries outside of which visitors do not want to see me step. Only who knows what those boundaries are? Not I. They change with every visitor. You have to be careful not to cross them, but you never know where they are. And one day, inevitably, you step outside the lines. The visitor knows. You don't. You didn't know that you'd done anything different. You thought it was just another part of you. The visitor sneaks away. The next day, you learn that you had stepped outside his heart. I'm afraid you've seen too much.

*Man:* There are stories.

*Woman:* What?

*Man:* People talk.

*Woman:* Where? We're two days from the nearest village.

*Man:* Word travels.

*Woman:* What are you talking about?

*Man:* There are stories about you. I heard them. They say that your visitors never leave this house.

*Woman:* That's what you heard?

*Man:* They say you imprison them.

*Woman:* Then you were a fool to come here.

*Man:* Listen.

*Woman:* Me? Listen? You. Look! Where are these prisoners? Have you seen any?

*Man:* They told me you were very beautiful.

*Woman:* Then they are blind as well as ignorant.

*Man:* You are.

*Woman:* What?

*Man:* Beautiful.

*Woman:* Stop that! My skin feels like seaweed.

*Man:* I didn't realize it at first. I must confess—I didn't. But over these few days—your face has changed for me. The shape of it. The feel of it. The color. All changed. I look at you now, and I'm no longer sure you are the same woman who had poured tea for me just a week ago. And because of that I remembered—how little I know about a face that changes in the night. (*Pause.*) Have you heard those stories?

*Woman:* I don't listen to old wives' tales.

*Man:* But have you heard them?

*Woman:* Yes. I've heard them. From other visitors—young—hotblooded—or old—who came here because they were told great glory was to be had by killing the witch in the woods.

*Man:* I was told that no man could spend time in this house without falling in love.

*Woman:* Oh? So why did you come? Did you wager gold that you could come out untouched? The outside world is so flattering to me. And you—are you like the rest? Passion passing through your heart so powerfully that you can't hold onto it?

*Man:* No! I'm afraid!

*Woman:* Of what?

*Man:* Sometimes—when I look into the flowers, I think I hear a voice—from inside—a voice beneath the petals. A human voice.

*Woman:* What does it say? "Let me out"?

*Man:* No. Listen. It hums. It hums with the peacefulness of one who is completely imprisoned.

*Woman:* I understand that if you listen closely enough, you can hear the ocean.

*Man:* No. Wait. Look at it. See the layers? Each petal—hiding the next. Try and see where they end. You can't. Follow them down, further down, around—and as you come down—faster and faster—the breeze picks up. The breeze becomes a wail. And in that rush of air—in the silent midst of it—you can hear a voice.

*Woman* (*Woman grabs flower from Man.*): So, you believe I water and prune my lovers? How can you be so foolish? (*She snaps the flower in half, at the stem. She throws it to the ground.*) Do you come only to leave again? To take a chunk of my heart, then leave with your booty on your belt, like a prize? You say that I imprison hearts in these flowers? Well, bits of my heart are trapped with travellers across this land. I can't even keep track. So kill me. If you came here to destroy a witch, kill me now. I can't stand to have it happen again.

Man: I won't leave you.

Woman: I believe you. (*She looks at the flower that she has broken, bends to pick it up. He touches her. They embrace.*)

**Scene VIII.** *Day. Woman wears a simple undergarment, over which she is donning a brightly colored kimono, the same one we saw her wearing Upstage of the scrim. Man stands apart.*

Woman: I can't cry. I don't have the capacity. Right from birth, I didn't cry. My mother and father were shocked. They thought they'd given birth to a ghost, a demon. Sometimes I've thought myself that. When great sadness has welled up inside me, I've prayed for a means to release the pain from my body. But my prayers went unanswered. The grief remained inside me. It would sit like water, still. (*Pause; she models her kimono.*) Do you like it?

Man: Yes, it's beautiful.

Woman: I wanted to wear something special today.

Man: It's beautiful. Excuse me. I must practice.

Woman: Shall I get you something?

Man: No.

Woman: Some tea, maybe?

Man: No. (*Man resumes swordplay.*)

Woman: Perhaps later today—perhaps we can go out—just around here. We can look for flowers.

Man: All right.

Woman: We don't have to.

Man: No. Let's.

Woman: I just thought if—

Man: Fine. Where do you want to go?

Woman: There are very few recreational activities around here, I know.

Man: All right. We'll go this afternoon. (*Pause.*)

Woman: Can I get you something?

Man (*Turning around.*): What?

Woman: You might be—

Man: I'm not hungry or thirsty or cold or hot.

Woman: Then what are you?

Man: Practicing. (*Man resumes practicing; Woman exits. As soon as she exits, he rests. He sits down. He examines his sword. He runs his finger along the edge of it. He takes the tip, runs it against the soft skin under his chin. He places the sword on the ground with the tip pointed directly upwards. He keeps it from falling by placing the tip under his chin. He experiments with different degrees of pressure. Woman re-enters. She sees him in this precarious position. She jerks his head upward; the sword falls.*)

Woman: Don't do that!

Man: What?

Woman: You can hurt yourself!

Man: I was practicing!
Woman: You were playing!
Man: I was practicing!
Woman: It's dangerous.
Man: What do you take me for—a child?
Woman: Sometimes wise men do childish things.
Man: I knew what I was doing!
Woman: It scares me.
Man: Don't be ridiculous. (*He reaches for the sword again.*)
Woman: Don't! Don't do that!
Man: Get back! (*He places the sword back in its previous position, suspended between the floor and his chin, upright.*)
Woman: But—
Man: Sssssh!
Woman: I wish—
Man: Listen to me! The slightest shock, you know—the slightest shock—surprise—it might make me jerk or—something—and then . . . so you must be perfectly still and quiet.
Woman: But I—
Man: Sssssh! (*Silence.*) I learned this exercise from a friend—I can't even remember his name—good swordsman—many years ago. He called it his meditation position. He said, like this, he could feel the line between this world and the others because he rested on it. If he saw something in another world that he liked better, all he would have to do is let his head drop, and he'd be there. Simple. No fuss. One day, they found him with the tip of his sword run clean out the back of his neck. He was smiling. I guess he saw something he liked. Or else he'd fallen asleep.
Woman: Stop that.
Man: Stop what?
Woman: Tormenting me.
Man: I'm not.
Woman: Take it away!
Man: You don't have to watch, you know.
Woman: Do you want to die that way—an accident?
Man: I was doing this before you came in.
Woman: If you do, all you need to do is tell me.
Man: What?
Woman: I can walk right over. Lean on the back of your head.
Man: Don't try to threaten—
Woman: Or jerk your sword up.
Man: Or scare me. You can't threaten—
Woman: I'm not. But if that's what you want.
Man: You can't threaten me. You wouldn't do it.
Woman: Oh?
Man: Then I'd be gone. You wouldn't let me leave that easily.

*Woman:* Yes, I would.

*Man:* You'd be alone.

*Woman:* No. I'd follow you. Forever. (*Pause.*) Now, let's stop this nonsense.

*Man:* No! I can do what I want! Don't come any closer!

*Woman:* Then release your sword.

*Man:* Come any closer and I'll drop my head.

*Woman* (*Woman slowly approaches Man. She grabs the hilt of the sword. She looks into his eyes. She pulls it out from under his chin.*): There will be no more of this. (*She exits with the sword. He starts to follow her, then stops. He touches under his chin. On his finger, he finds a drop of blood.*)

**Scene IX.** *Night. Man is leaving the house. He is just about out, when he hears a shakuhachi playing. He looks around, trying to locate the sound. Woman appears in the doorway to the outside. Shakuhachi slowly fades out.*

*Woman:* It's time for you to go?

*Man:* Yes. I'm sorry.

*Woman:* You're just going to sneak out? A thief in the night? A frightened child?

*Man:* I care about you.

*Woman:* You express it strangely.

*Man:* I leave in shame because it is proper. (*Pause.*) I came seeking glory.

*Woman:* To kill me? You can say it. You'll be surprised at how little I blanche. As if you'd said, "I came for a bowl of rice," or "I came seeking love" or "I came to kill you."

*Man:* Weakness. All weakness. Too weak to kill you. Too weak to kill myself. Too weak to do anything but sneak away in shame. (*Woman brings out Man's sword.*)

*Woman:* Were you even planning to leave without this? (*He takes sword.*) Why not stay here?

*Man:* I can't live with someone who's defeated me.

*Woman:* I never thought of defeating you. I only wanted to take care of you. To make you happy. Because that made me happy and I was no longer alone.

*Man:* You defeated me.

*Woman:* Why do you think that way?

*Man:* I came here with a purpose. The world was clear. You changed the shape of your face, the shape of my heart—rearranged everything—created a world where I could do nothing.

*Woman:* I only tried to care for you.

*Man:* I guess that was all it took. (*Pause.*)

*Woman:* You still think I'm a witch. Just because old women gossip. You are so cruel. Once you arrived, there were only two possibilities: I would die or you would leave. (*Pause.*) If you believe I'm a witch, then kill me. Rid the province of one more evil.

*Man:* I can't—

*Woman:* Why not? If you believe that about me, then it's the right thing to do.

Man: You know I can't.

Woman: Then stay.

Man: Don't try and force me.

Woman: I won't force you to do anything. (*Pause.*) All I wanted was an escape—
for both of us. The sound of a human voice—the simplest thing to find, and
the hardest to hold onto. This house—my loneliness is etched into the walls.
Kill me, but don't leave. Even in death, my spirit would rest here and be
comforted by your presence.

Man: Force me to stay.

Woman: I won't. (*Man starts to leave.*) Beware.

Man: What?

Woman: The ground on which you walk is weak. It could give way at any
moment. The crevice beneath is dark.

Man: Are you talking about death? I'm ready to die.

Woman: Fear for what is worse than death.

Man: What?

Woman: Falling. Falling through the darkness. Waiting to hit the ground. Picking
up speed. Waiting for the ground. Falling faster. Falling alone. Waiting.
Falling. Waiting. Falling.

(*Woman wails and runs out through the door to her room. Man stands, confused, not
knowing what to do. He starts to follow her, then hesitates, and rushes out the door to
the outside. Silence. Slowly, he re-enters from the outside. He looks for her in the main
room. He goes slowly towards the panel to her room. He throws down his sword. He
opens the panel. He goes inside. He comes out. He unrolls his mat. He sits on it, cross-
legged. He looks out into space. He notices near him a shakuhachi. He picks it up. He
begins to blow into it. He tries to make sounds. He continues trying through the end of
the play. The Upstage scrim lights up. Upstage, we see the Woman. She is young. She
is hanging from a rope suspended from the roof. She has hung herself. Around her are
scores of vases with flowers in them whose blossoms have been blown off. Only the
stems remain in the vases. Around her swirl the thousands of petals from the flowers.
They fill the Upstage scrim area like a blizzard of color. Man continues to attempt to
play. Lights fade to black.*)

# Terrence McNally

*Terrence McNally was born in St. Peters-burg, Florida, in 1939, but he was raised mostly in Corpus Christi, Texas, where his Irish-Catholic father worked as a beer dis-tributor. After attending Columbia Univer-sity, McNally worked as a theatrical stage manager, magazine editor, and film critic while writing his first plays. A versatile dramatist, he has written plays, musicals, and screenplays. His screwball comedy* The Ritz *(1973) became a popular 1976 film, which McNally himself adapted for the screen. He also rewrote his romantic drama* Frankie and Johnny in the Claire de Lune *(1987) for Gary Marshall's film* Frankie and Johnny *(1991), starring Al Pacino and Michelle Pfeiffer. Other notable McNally plays include* The Lisbon

Terrence McNally

Traviata *(1985),* Lips Together, Teeth Apart *(1991), and* A Perfect Ganesh *(1993). His work for television includes an adaptation of John Cheever's "The 5:48" (1980). McNally's television version of* Andre's Mother *won an Emmy in 1990, but the original stage version—written as one brief and memorable scene—needs no video backup to communicate its troubling message of heartache and loss.*

Characters

Cal, a young man
Arthur, his father
Penny, his sister
Andre's Mother

Time: Now
Place: New York City, Central Park

*Four people—Cal, Arthur, Penny, and Andre's Mother—enter. They are nicely dressed and each carries a white helium-filled balloon on a string.*

Cal: You know what's really terrible? I can't think of anything terrific to say.
    Goodbye. I love you. I'll miss you. And I'm supposed to be so great with words!
Penny: What's that over there?
Arthur: Ask your brother.
Cal: It's a theatre. An outdoor theatre. They do plays there in the summer.
    Shakespeare's plays. (*To Andre's Mother.*) God, how much he wanted to play

Hamlet again. He would have gone to Timbuktu to have another go at that part. The summer he did it in Boston, he was so happy!

*Penny:* Cal, I don't think she . . . ! It's not the time. Later.

*Arthur:* Your son was a . . . the Jews have a word for it . . .

*Penny* (*quietly appalled*): Oh my God!

*Arthur:* Mensch, I believe it is, and I think I'm using it right. It means warm, solid, the real thing. Correct me if I'm wrong.

*Penny:* Fine, Dad, fine. Just quit while you're ahead.

*Arthur:* I won't say he was like a son to me. Even my son isn't always like a son to me. I mean. . . ! In my clumsy way, I'm trying to say how much I liked Andre. And how much he helped me to know my own boy. Cal was always two handsful but Andre and I could talk about anything under the sun. My wife was very fond of him, too.

*Penny:* Cal, I don't understand about the balloons.

*Cal:* They represent the soul. When you let go, it means you're letting his soul ascend to Heaven. That you're willing to let go. Breaking the last earthly ties.

*Penny:* Does the Pope know about this?

*Arthur:* Penny!

*Penny:* Andre loved my sense of humor. Listen, you can hear him laughing. (*She lets go of her white balloon.*) So long, you glorious, wonderful, I-know-what-Cal-means-about-words . . . *man!* God forgive me for wishing you were straight every time I laid eyes on you. But if any man was going to have you, I'm glad it was my brother! Look how fast it went up. I bet that means something. Something terrific.

*Arthur* (*lets his balloon go*): Goodbye. God speed.

*Penny:* Cal?

*Cal:* I'm not ready yet.

*Penny:* Okay. We'll be over there. Come on, Pop, you can buy your little girl a Good Humor.

*Arthur:* They still make Good Humor?

*Penny:* Only now they're called Dove Bars and they cost twelve dollars.

(*Penny takes Arthur off. Cal and Andre's Mother stand with their balloons.*)

*Cal:* I wish I knew what you were thinking. I think it would help me. You know almost nothing about me and I only know what Andre told me about you. I'd always had it in my mind that one day we would be friends, you and me. But if you didn't know about Andre and me . . . If this hadn't happened, I wonder if he would have ever told you. When he was sick, if I asked him once I asked him a thousand times, tell her. She's your mother. She won't mind. But he was so afraid of hurting you and of your disapproval. I don't know which was worse. (*No response. He sighs.*) God, how many of us live in this city because we don't want to hurt our mothers and live in mortal terror of their disapproval. We lose ourselves here. Our lives aren't furtive, just our feelings toward people like you are! A city of fugitives from our parents' scorn or heartbreak. Sometimes he'd seem a little down and I'd say, "What's the matter, babe?" and this funny sweet, sad smile would cross his face and he'd say, "Just a little homesick, Cal, just a little bit." I always accused him of being a country boy just playing at being a hotshot, sophisticated New Yorker. (*He sighs.*)

It's bullshit. It's all bullshit. (*Still no response.*)

Do you remember the comic strip *Little Lulu*? Her mother had no name, she was so remote, so formidable to all the children. She was just Lulu's mother. "Hello, Lulu's Mother," Lulu's friends would say. She was almost anonymous in her remoteness. You remind me of her. Andre's mother. Let me answer the questions you can't ask and then I'll leave you alone and you won't ever have to see me again. Andre died of AIDS. I don't know how he got it. I tested negative. He died bravely. You would have been proud of him. The only thing that frightened him was you. I'll have everything that was his sent to you. I'll pay for it. There isn't much. You should have come up the summer he played Hamlet. He was magnificent. Yes, I'm bitter. I'm bitter I've lost him. I'm bitter what's happening. I'm bitter even now, after all this, I can't reach you. I'm beginning to feel your disapproval and it's making me ill. (*He looks at his balloon.*) Sorry, old friend. I blew it. (*He lets go of the balloon.*)

Good night, sweet prince, and flights of angels sing thee to thy rest! (*Beat.*)

Goodbye, Andre's mother.

(*He goes. Andre's Mother stands alone holding her white balloon. Her lips tremble. She looks on the verge of breaking down. She is about to let go of the balloon when she pulls it down to her. She looks at it awhile before she gently kisses it. She lets go of the balloon. She follows it with her eyes as it rises and rises. The lights are beginning to fade. Andre's Mother's eyes are still on the balloon. The lights fade.*)

## August Wilson
### JOE TURNER'S COME AND GONE° 1988

*August Wilson was born (in 1945) and raised on The Hill, a Pittsburgh ghetto neighborhood. Although he quit school in the ninth grade when a teacher accused him of submitting a ghost-written paper, which in truth he had written himself, Wilson continued his education in local libraries, supporting himself by cooking and stock-clerking. In 1968 he co-founded a community troupe, the Black Horizons Theater, staging plays by LeRoi Jones and other militants; later he moved from Pittsburgh to Saint Paul, Minnesota, where at last he saw a play of his own performed. Jitney, his first effort, won him entry to a 1982 playwrights' conference at the Eugene O'Neill Theater Center. There, Lloyd*

*August Wilson*

*Richards, dean of Yale University School of Drama, took an interest in Wilson's work and offered to produce his plays at Yale. Ma Rainey's Black Bottom was the first to reach Broadway (in 1985), where it ran for ten months and received a prize from the New York Drama Critics Circle. In 1987 Fences, starring Mary Alice and James Paul Jones, won another Critics Circle award, besides a Tony award and the Pulitzer Prize for best American play of its year. It set a box office record for a Broadway nonmusical. Joe Turner's Come and Gone has also received high acclaim, and in 1990 his fourth major work, The Piano Lesson, won him a second Pulitzer Prize. A published poet, Wilson once told an interviewer, "After writing poetry for twenty-one years, I approach a play the same way. The mental process is poetic: you use metaphor and condense."*

## Characters

Seth Holly, owner of the boardinghouse
Bertha Holly, his wife
Bynum Walker, a rootworker°
Rutherford Selig, a peddler
Jeremy Furlow, a resident
Herald Loomis, a resident

Zonia Loomis, his daughter
Mattie Campbell, a resident
Reuben Scott, boy who lives next door
Molly Cunningham, a resident
Martha Pentecost, Herald Loomis's
   wife

---

*Joe Turner's Come and Gone:* In Tennessee around the turn of the century, Joe Turner became legendary: a professional bounty hunter, and one who claimed a reward for finding an escaped convict. To increase his profits, Turner impressed not only convicts into a chain gang but innocent men as well.

*rootworker:* a conjure man, or voodoo practitioner.

## Setting

*August, 1911. A boardinghouse in Pittsburgh. At right is a kitchen. Two doors open off the kitchen. One leads to the outhouse and Seth's workshop. The other to Seth's and Bertha's bedroom. At left is a parlor. The front door opens into the parlor, which gives access to the stairs leading to the upstairs rooms.*

*There is a small outside playing area.*

## The Play

*It is August in Pittsburgh, 1911. The sun falls out of heaven like a stone. The fires of the steel mill rage with a combined sense of industry and progress. Barges loaded with coal and iron ore trudge up the river to the mill towns that dot the Monongahela and return with fresh, hard, gleaming steel. The city flexes its muscles. Men throw countless bridges across the river, lay roads and carve tunnels through the hills sprouting with houses.*

*From the deep and the near South the sons and daughters of newly freed African slaves wander into the city. Isolated, cut off from memory, having forgotten the names of the gods and only guessing at their faces, they arrive dazed and stunned, their heart kicking in their chest with a song worth singing. They arrive carrying Bibles and guitars, their pockets lined with dust and fresh hope, marked men and women seeking to scrape from the narrow, crooked cobbles and the fiery blasts of the coke furnace a way of bludgeoning and shaping the malleable parts of themselves into a new identity as free men of definite and sincere worth.*

*Foreigners in a strange land, they carry as part and parcel of their baggage a long line of separation and dispersement which informs their sensibilities and marks their conduct as they search for ways to reconnect, to reassemble, to give clear and luminous meaning to the song which is both a wail and a whelp of joy.*

# ACT I

## Scene 1

*The lights come up on the kitchen. Bertha busies herself with breakfast preparations. Seth stands looking out the window at Bynum in the yard. Seth is in his early fifties. Born of Northern free parents, a skilled craftsman, and owner of the boardinghouse, he has a stability that none of the other characters have. Bertha is five years his junior. Married for over twenty-five years, she has learned how to negotiate around Seth's apparent orneriness.*

Seth (*at the window, laughing*): If that ain't the damndest thing I seen. Look here, Bertha.

Bertha: I done seen Bynum out there with them pigeons before.

Seth: Naw . . . naw . . . look at this. That pigeon flopped out of Bynum's hand and he about to have a fit.

*(Bertha crosses over to the window.)*

He down there on his hands and knees behind that bush looking all over for that pigeon and it on the other side of the yard. See it over there?

**Bertha:** Come on and get your breakfast and leave that man alone.

**Seth:** Look at him . . . he still looking. He ain't seen it yet. All that old mumbo jumbo nonsense. I don't know why I put up with it.

**Bertha:** You don't say nothing when he bless the house.

**Seth:** I just go along with that 'cause of you. You around here sprinkling salt all over the place . . . got pennies lined up across the threshold . . . all that hee-bie-jeebie stuff. I just put up with that 'cause of you. I don't pay that kind of stuff no mind. And you going down there to the church and wanna come home and sprinkle salt all over the place.

**Bertha:** It don't hurt none. I can't say if it help . . . but it don't hurt none.

**Seth:** Look at him. He done found that pigeon and now he's talking to it.

**Bertha:** These biscuits be ready in a minute.

**Seth:** He done drew a big circle with that stick and now he's dancing around. I know he'd better not . . .

*(Seth bolts from the window and rushes to the back door.)*

Hey, Bynum! Don't be hopping around stepping in my vegetables. Hey, Bynum . . . Watch where you stepping!

**Bertha:** Seth, leave that man alone.

**Seth** *(coming back into the house)*: I don't care how much he be dancing around . . . just don't be stepping in my vegetables. Man got my garden all messed up now . . . planting them weeds out there . . . burying them pigeons and whatnot.

**Bertha:** Bynum don't bother nobody. He ain't even thinking about your vegetables.

**Seth:** I know he ain't! That's why he out there stepping on them.

**Bertha:** What Mr. Johnson say down there?

**Seth:** I told him if I had the tools I could go out here and find me four or five fellows and open up my own shop instead of working for Mr. Olowski. Get me four or five fellows and teach them how to make pots and pans. One man making ten pots is five men making fifty. He told me he'd think about it.

**Bertha:** Well, maybe he'll come to see it your way.

**Seth:** He wanted me to sign over the house to him. You know what I thought of that idea.

**Bertha:** He'll come to see you're right.

**Seth:** I'm going up and talk to Sam Green. There's more than one way to skin a cat. I'm going up and talk to him. See if he got more sense than Mr. Johnson. I can't get nowhere working for Mr. Olowski and selling Selig five or six pots on the side. I'm going up and see Sam Green. See if he loan me the money.

*(Seth crosses back to the window.)*

Now he got that cup. He done killed that pigeon and now he's putting its blood in that little cup. I believe he drink that blood.

*Bertha*: Seth Holly, what is wrong with you this morning? Come on and get your breakfast so you can go to bed. You know Bynum don't be drinking no pigeon blood.

*Seth*: I don't know what he do.

*Bertha*: Well, watch him, then. He's gonna dig a little hole and bury that pigeon. Then he's gonna pray over that blood . . . pour it on top . . . mark out his circle and come on into the house.

*Seth*: That's what he doing . . . he pouring that blood on top.

*Bertha*: When they gonna put you back working daytime? Told me two months ago he was gonna put you back working daytime.

*Seth*: That's what Mr. Olowski told me. I got to wait till he say when. He tell me what to do. I don't tell him. Drive me crazy to speculate on the man's wishes when he don't know what he want to do himself.

*Bertha*: Well, I wish he go ahead and put you back working daytime. This working all hours of the night don't make no sense.

*Seth*: It don't make no sense for that boy to run out of here and get drunk so they lock him up either.

*Bertha*: Who? Who they got locked up for being drunk?

*Seth*: That boy that's staying upstairs . . . Jeremy. I stopped down there on Logan Street on my way home from work and one of the fellows told me about it. Say he seen it when they arrested him.

*Bertha*: I was wondering why I ain't seen him this morning.

*Seth*: You know I don't put up with that. I told him when he came . . .

(*Bynum enters from the yard carrying some plants. He is a short, round man in his early sixties. A conjure man, or rootworker, he gives the impression of always being in control of everything. Nothing ever bothers him. He seems to be lost in a world of his own making and to swallow any adversity or interference with his grand design.*)

What you doing bringing them weeds in my house? Out there stepping on my vegetables and now wanna carry them weeds in my house.

*Bynum*: Morning, Seth. Morning, Sister Bertha.

*Seth*: Messing up my garden growing them things out there. I ought to go out there and pull up all them weeds.

*Bertha*: Some gal was by here to see you this morning, Bynum. You was out there in the yard . . . I told her to come back later.

*Bynum (to Seth)*: You look sick. What's the matter, you ain't eating right?

*Seth*: What if I was sick? You ain't getting near me with none of that stuff.

(*Bertha sets a plate of biscuits on the table.*)

*Bynum*: My . . . my . . . Bertha, your biscuits getting fatter and fatter.

(*Bynum takes a biscuit and begins to eat.*)

Where Jeremy? I don't see him around this morning. He usually be around riffing and raffing on Saturday morning.

*Seth*: I know where he at. I know just where he at. They got him down there in the jail. Getting drunk and acting a fool. He down there where he belong with all that foolishness.

*Bynum*: Mr. Piney's boys got him, huh? They ain't gonna do nothing but hold on to him for a little while. He's gonna be back here hungrier than a mule directly.

*Seth*: I don't go for all that carrying on and such. This is a respectable house. I don't have no drunkards or fools around here.

*Bynum*: That boy got a lot of country in him. He ain't been up here but two weeks. It's gonna take a while before he can work that country out of him.

*Seth*: These niggers coming up here with that old backward country style of living. It's hard enough now without all that ignorant kind of acting. Ever since slavery got over with there ain't been nothing but foolish-acting niggers. Word get out they need men to work in the mill and put in these roads . . . and niggers drop everything and head North looking for freedom. They don't know the white fellows looking too. White fellows coming from all over the world. White fellow come over and in six months got more than what I got. But these niggers keep on coming. Walking . . . riding . . . carrying their Bibles. That boy done carried a guitar all the way from North Carolina. What he gonna find out? What he gonna do with that guitar? This the city.

*(There is a knock on the door.)*

Niggers coming up here from the backwoods . . . coming up here from the country carrying Bibles and guitars looking for freedom. They got a rude awakening.

*(Seth goes to answer the door. Rutherford Selig enters. About Seth's age, he is a thin white man with greasy hair. A peddler, he supplies Seth with the raw materials to make pots and pans which he then peddles door to door in the mill towns along the river. He keeps a list of his customers as they move about and is known in the various communities as the People Finder. He carries squares of sheet metal under his arm.)*

Ho! Forgot you was coming today. Come on in.

*Bynum*: If it ain't Rutherford Selig . . . the People Finder himself.

*Selig*: What say there, Bynum?

*Bynum*: I say about my shiny man. You got to tell me something. I done give you my dollar . . . I'm looking to get a report.

*Selig*: I got eight here, Seth.

*Seth* *(taking the sheet metal)*: What is this? What you giving me here? What I'm gonna do with this?

*Selig*: I need some dustpans. Everybody asking me about dustpans.

*Seth*: Gonna cost you fifteen cents apiece. And ten cents to put a handle on them.

*Selig*: I'll give you twenty cents apiece with the handles.

*Seth*: Alright. But I ain't gonna give you but fifteen cents for the sheet metal.

*Selig:* It's twenty-five cents apiece for the metal. That's what we agreed on.

*Seth:* This low-grade sheet metal. They ain't worth but a dime. I'm doing you a favor giving you fifteen cents. You know this metal ain't worth no twenty-five cents. Don't come talking that twenty-five cent stuff to me over no low-grade sheet metal.

*Selig:* Alright, fifteen cents apiece. Just make me some dustpans out of them.

*(Seth exits with the sheet metal out the back door.)*

*Bertha:* Sit on down there, Selig. Get you a cup of coffee and a biscuit.

*Bynum:* Where you coming from this time?

*Selig:* I been upriver. All along the Monongahela. Past Rankin and all up around Little Washington.

*Bynum:* Did you find anybody?

*Selig:* I found Sadie Jackson up in Braddock. Her mother's staying down there in Scotchbottom say she hadn't heard from her and she didn't know where she was at. I found her up in Braddock on Enoch Street. She bought a frying pan from me.

*Bynum:* You around here finding everybody how come you ain't found my shiny man?

*Selig:* The only shiny man I saw was the Nigras working on the road gang with the sweat glistening on them.

*Bynum:* Naw, you'd be able to tell this fellow. He shine like new money.

*Selig:* Well, I done told you I can't find nobody without a name.

*Bertha:* Here go one of these hot biscuits, Selig.

*Bynum:* This fellow don't have no name. I call him John 'cause it was up around Johnstown where I seen him. I ain't even so sure he's one special fellow. That shine could pass on to anybody. He could be anybody shining.

*Selig:* Well, what's he look like besides being shiny? There's lots of shiny Nigras.

*Bynum:* He's just a man I seen out on the road. He ain't had no special look. Just a man walking toward me on the road. He come up and asked me which way the road went. I told him everything I knew about the road, where it went and all, and he asked me did I have anything to eat 'cause he was hungry. Say he ain't had nothing to eat in three days. Well, I never be out there on the road without a piece of dried meat. Or an orange or an apple. So I give this fellow an orange. He take and eat that orange and told me to come and go along the road a little ways with him, that he had something he wanted to show me. He had a look about him made me wanna go with him, see what he gonna show me.

We walked on a bit and it's getting kind of far from where I met him when it come up on me all of a sudden, we wasn't going the way he had come from, we was going back my way. Since he said he ain't knew nothing about the road, I asked him about this. He say he had a voice inside him telling him which way to go and if I come and go along with him he was gonna show me the Secret of Life. Quite naturally I followed him. A fellow that's gonna show you the Secret of Life ain't to be taken lightly. We get near this bend in the road . . .

(*Seth enters with an assortment of pans.*)

Seth: I got six here, Selig.

Selig: Wait a minute, Seth. Bynum's telling me about the secret of life. Go ahead, Bynum. I wanna hear this.

(*Seth sets the pots down and exits out the back.*)

Bynum: We get near this bend in the road and he told me to hold out my hands. Then he rubbed them together with his and I looked down and see they got blood on them. Told me to take and rub it all over me . . . say that was a way of cleaning myself. Then we went around the bend in that road. Got around that bend and it seem like all of a sudden we ain't in the same place. Turn around that bend and everything look like it was twice as big as it was. The trees and everything bigger than life! Sparrows big as eagles! I turned around to look at this fellow and he had this light coming out of him. I had to cover up my eyes to keep from being blinded. He shining like new money with that light. He shined until all the light seemed like it seeped out of him and then he was gone and I was by myself in this strange place where everything was bigger than life.

I wandered around there looking for that road, trying to find my way back from this big place . . . and I looked over and seen my daddy standing there. He was the same size he always was, except for his hands and his mouth. He had a great big old mouth that look like it took up his whole face and his hands were as big as hams. Look like they was too big to carry around. My daddy called me to him. Said he had been thinking about me and it grieved him to see me in the world carrying other people's songs and not having one of my own. Told me he was gonna show me how to find my song. Then he carried me further into this big place until we come to this ocean. Then he showed me something I ain't got words to tell you. But if you stand to witness it, you done seen something there. I stayed in that place awhile and my daddy taught me the meaning of this thing that I had seen and showed me how to find my song. I asked him about the shiny man and he told me he was the One Who Goes Before and Shows the Way. Said there was lots of shiny men and if I ever saw one again before I died then I would know that my song had been accepted and worked its full power in the world and I could lay down and die a happy man. A man who done left his mark on life. On the way people cling to each other out of the truth they find in themselves. Then he showed me how to get back to the road. I came out where everything was its own size and I had my song. I had the Binding Song. I choose that song because that's what I seen most when I was traveling . . . people walking away and leaving one another. So I takes the power of my song and binds them together.

*(Seth enters from the yard carrying cabbages and tomatoes.)*

Been binding people ever since. That's why they call me Bynum. Just like glue I sticks people together.

Seth: Maybe they ain't supposed to be stuck sometimes. You ever think of that?

Bynum: Oh, I don't do it lightly. It cost me a piece of myself every time I do. I'm a Binder of What Clings. You got to find out if they cling first. You can't bind what don't cling.

Selig: Well, how is that the Secret of Life? I thought you said he was gonna show you the secret of life. That's what I'm waiting to find out.

Bynum: Oh, he showed me alright. But you still got to figure it out. Can't nobody figure it out for you. You got to come to it on your own. That's why I'm looking for the shiny man.

Selig: Well, I'll keep my eye out for him. What you got there, Seth?

Seth: Here go some cabbage and tomatoes. I got some green beans coming in real nice. I'm gonna take and start me a grapevine out there next year. Butera says he gonna give me a piece of his vine and I'm gonna start that out there.

Selig: How many of them pots you got?

Seth: I got six. That's six dollars minus eight on top of fifteen for the sheet metal come to a dollar twenty out the six dollars leave me four dollars and eighty cents.

Selig *(counting out the money)*: There's four dollars . . . and . . . eighty cents.

Seth: How many of them dustpans you want?

Selig: As many as you can make out them sheets.

Seth: You can use that many? I get to cutting on them sheets figuring how to make them dustpans . . . ain't no telling how many I'm liable to come up with.

Selig: I can use them and you can make me some more next time.

Seth: Alright, I'm gonna hold you to that, now.

Selig: Thanks for the biscuit, Bertha.

Bertha: You know you welcome anytime, Selig.

Seth: Which way you heading?

Selig: Going down to Wheeling. All through West Virginia there. I'll be back Saturday. They putting in new roads down that way. Makes traveling easier.

Seth: That's what I hear. All up around here too. Got a fellow staying here working on that road by the Brady Street Bridge.

Selig: Yeah, it's gonna make traveling real nice. Thanks for the cabbage, Seth. I'll see you on Saturday.

*(Selig exits.)*

Seth *(to Bynum)*: Why you wanna start all that nonsense talk with that man? All that shiny man nonsense.

Bynum: You know it ain't no nonsense. Bertha know it ain't no nonsense. I don't know if Selig know or not.

Bertha: Seth, when you get to making them dustpans make me a coffeepot.

Seth: What's the matter with your coffee? Ain't nothing wrong with your coffee. Don't she make some good coffee, Bynum?

Bynum: I ain't worried about the coffee. I know she makes some good biscuits.

Seth: I ain't studying no coffeepot, woman. You heard me tell the man I was gonna cut as many dustpans as them sheets will make . . . and all of a sudden you want a coffeepot.

Bertha: Man, hush up and go on and make me that coffeepot.

*(Jeremy enters the front door. About twenty-five, he gives the impression that he has the world in his hand, that he can meet life's challenges head on. He smiles a lot. He is a proficient guitar player, though his spirit has yet to be molded into song.)*

Bynum: I hear Mr. Piney's boys had you.

Jeremy: Fined me two dollars for nothing! Ain't done nothing.

Seth: I told you when you come on here everybody know my house. Know these is respectable quarters. I don't put up with no foolishness. Everybody know Seth Holly keep a good house. Was my daddy's house. This house been a decent house for a long time.

Jeremy: I ain't done nothing, Mr. Seth. I stopped by the Workmen's Club and got me a bottle. Me and Roper Lee from Alabama. Had us a half pint. We was fixing to cut that half in two when they came up on us. Asked us if we was working. We told them we was putting in the road over yonder and that it was our payday. They snatched hold of us to get that two dollars. Me and Roper Lee ain't even had a chance to take a drink when they grabbed us.

Seth: I don't go for all that kind of carrying on.

Bertha: Leave the boy alone, Seth. You know the police do that. Figure there's too many people out on the street they take some of them off. You know that.

Seth: I ain't gonna have folks talking.

Bertha: Ain't nobody talking nothing. That's all in your head. You want some grits and biscuits, Jeremy?

Jeremy: Thank you, Miss Bertha. They didn't give us a thing to eat last night. I'll take one of them big bowls if you don't mind.

*(There is a knock at the door. Seth goes to answer it. Enter Herald Loomis and his eleven-year-old daughter, Zonia. Herald Loomis is thirty-two years old. He is at times possessed. A man driven not by the hellhounds that seemingly bay at his heels, but by his search for a world that speaks to something about himself. He is unable to harmonize the forces that swirl around him, and seeks to recreate the world into one that contains his image. He wears a hat and a long wool coat.)*

Loomis: Me and my daughter looking for a place to stay, mister. You got a sign say you got rooms.

*(Seth stares at Loomis, sizing him up.)*

Mister, if you ain't got no rooms we can go somewhere else.

*Seth:* How long you plan on staying?

*Loomis:* Don't know. Two weeks or more maybe.

*Seth:* It's two dollars a week for the room. We serve meals twice a day. It's two dollars for room and board. Pay up in advance.

*(Loomis reaches into his pocket.)*

It's a dollar extra for the girl.

*Loomis:* The girl sleep in the same room.

*Seth:* Well, do she eat off the same plate? We serve meals twice a day. That's a dollar extra for food.

*Loomis:* Ain't got no extra dollar. I was planning on asking your missus if she could help out with the cooking and cleaning and whatnot.

*Seth:* Her helping out don't put no food on the table. I need that dollar to buy some food.

*Loomis:* I'll give you fifty cents extra. She don't eat much.

*Seth:* Okay . . . but fifty cents don't buy but half a portion.

*Bertha:* Seth, she can help me out. Let her help me out. I can use some help.

*Seth:* Well, that's two dollars for the week. Pay up in advance. Saturday to Saturday. You wanna stay on then it's two more come Saturday.

*(Loomis pays Seth the money.)*

*Bertha:* My name's Bertha. This my husband, Seth. You got Bynum and Jeremy over there.

*Loomis:* Ain't nobody else live here?

*Bertha:* They the only ones live here now. People come and go. They the only ones here now. You want a cup of coffee and a biscuit?

*Loomis:* We done ate this morning.

*Bynum:* Where you coming from, Mister . . . I didn't get your name.

*Loomis:* Name's Herald Loomis. This my daughter, Zonia.

*Bynum:* Where you coming from?

*Loomis:* Come from all over. Whicheverway the road take us that's the way we go.

*Jeremy:* If you looking for a job, I'm working putting in that road down there by the bridge. They can't get enough mens. Always looking to take somebody on.

*Loomis:* I'm looking for a woman named Martha Loomis. That's my wife. Got married legal with the papers and all.

*Seth:* I don't know nobody named Loomis. I know some Marthas but I don't know no Loomis.

*Bynum:* You got to see Rutherford Selig if you wanna find somebody. Selig's the People Finder. Rutherford Selig's a first-class People Finder.

*Jeremy:* What she look like? Maybe I seen her.

*Loomis:* She a brownskin woman. Got long pretty hair. About five feet from the ground.

*Jeremy:* I don't know. I might have seen her.

Bynum: You got to see Rutherford Selig. You give him one dollar to get her name on his list . . . and after she get her name on his list Rutherford Selig will go right on out there and find her. I got him looking for somebody for me.

Loomis: You say he find people. How you find him?

Bynum: You just missed him. He's gone downriver now. You got to wait till Saturday. He's gone downriver with his pots and pans. He come to see Seth on Saturdays. You got to wait till then.

Seth: Come on, I'll show you to your room.

(Seth, Loomis, and Zonia exit up the stairs.)

Jeremy: Miss Bertha, I'll take that biscuit you was gonna give that fellow, if you don't mind. Say, Mr. Bynum, they got somebody like that around here sure enough? Somebody that find people?

Bynum: Rutherford Selig. He go around selling pots and pans and every house he come to he write down the name and address of whoever lives there. So if you looking for somebody, quite naturally you go and see him . . . 'cause he's the only one who know where everybody live at.

Jeremy: I ought to have him look for this old gal I used to know. It be nice to see her again.

Bertha (giving Jeremy a biscuit): Jeremy, today's the day for you to pull them sheets off the bed and set them outside your door. I'll set you out some clean ones.

Bynum: Mr. Piney's boys done ruined your good time last night, Jeremy . . . what you planning for tonight?

Jeremy: They got me scared to go out, Mr. Bynum. They might grab me again.

Bynum: You ought to take your guitar and go down to Seefus. Seefus got a gambling place down there on Wylie Avenue. You ought to take your guitar and go down there. They got guitar contest down there.

Jeremy: I don't play no contest, Mr. Bynum. Had one of them white fellows cure me of that. I ain't been nowhere near a contest since.

Bynum: White fellow beat you playing guitar?

Jeremy: Naw, he ain't beat me. I was sitting at home just fixing to sit down and eat when somebody come up to my house and got me. Told me there's a white fellow say he was gonna give a prize to the best guitar player he could find. I take up my guitar and go down there and somebody had gone up and got Bobo Smith and brought him down there. Him and another fellow called Hooter. Old Hooter couldn't play no guitar, he do more hollering than playing, but Bobo could go at it awhile.

This fellow standing there say he the one that was gonna give the prize and me and Bobo started playing for him. Bobo play something and then I'd try to play something better than what he played. Old Hooter, he just holler and bang at the guitar. Man was the worst guitar player I ever seen. So me and Bobo played and after a while I seen where he was getting the attention of this white fellow. He'd play something and while he was playing it he be slapping on the side of the guitar, and that made it sound like he was playing more than he was. So I started doing it too. White fellow ain't knew no difference. He ain't knew as much about guitar playing as Hooter did. After we play awhile, the white fellow called us to him and said he couldn't make up his mind, say all three of us was the best guitar player and we'd have to split the prize between us. Then he give us twenty-five cents. That's eight cents apiece and a penny on the side. That cured me of playing contest to this day.

Bynum: Seefus ain't like that. Seefus give a whole dollar and a drink of whiskey.

Jeremy: What night they be down there?

Bynum: Be down there every night. Music don't know no certain night.

Bertha: You go down to Seefus with them people and you liable to end up in a raid and go to jail sure enough. I don't know why Bynum tell you that.

Bynum: That's where the music at. That's where the people at. The people down there making music and enjoying themselves. Some things is worth taking the chance going to jail about.

Bertha: Jeremy ain't got no business going down there.

Jeremy: They got some women down there, Mr. Bynum?

Bynum: Oh, they got women down there, sure. They got women everywhere. Women be where the men is so they can find each other.

Jeremy: Some of them old gals come out there where we be putting in that road. Hanging around there trying to snatch somebody.

Bynum: How come some of them ain't snatched hold of you?

Jeremy: I don't want them kind. Them desperate kind. Ain't nothing worse than a desperate woman. Tell them you gonna leave them and they get to crying and carrying on. That just make you want to get away quicker. They get to cutting up your clothes and things trying to keep you staying. Desperate women ain't nothing but trouble for a man.

(Seth enters from the stairs.)

Seth: Something ain't setting right with that fellow.

Bertha: What's wrong with him? What he say?

Seth: I take him up there and try to talk to him and he ain't for no talking. Say he been traveling . . . coming over from Ohio. Say he a deacon in the church. Say he looking for Martha Pentecost. Talking about that's his wife.

Bertha: How you know it's the same Martha? Could be talking about anybody. Lots of people named Martha.

Seth: You see that little girl? I didn't hook it up till he said it, but that little girl look just like her. Ask Bynum. (To Bynum.) Bynum. Don't that little girl look just like Martha Pentecost?

Bertha: I still say he could be talking about anybody.

Seth: The way he described her wasn't no doubt who he was talking about. Described her right down to her toes.

Bertha: What did you tell him?

Seth: I ain't told him nothing. The way that fellow look I wasn't gonna tell him nothing. I don't know what he looking for her for.

Bertha: What else he have to say?

*Seth:* I told you he wasn't for no talking. I told him where the outhouse was and to keep that gal off the front porch and out of my garden. He asked if you'd mind setting a hot tub for the gal and that was about the gist of it.

*Bertha:* Well, I wouldn't let it worry me if I was you. Come on get your sleep.

*Bynum:* He says he looking for Martha and he a deacon in the church.

*Seth:* That's what he say. Do he look like a deacon to you?

*Bertha:* He might be, you don't know. Bynum ain't got no special say on whether he a deacon or not.

*Seth:* Well, if he the deacon I'd sure like to see the preacher.

*Bertha:* Come on get your sleep. Jeremy, don't forget to set them sheets outside the door like I told you.

*(Bertha exits into the bedroom.)*

*Seth:* Something ain't setting right with that fellow, Bynum. He's one of them mean-looking niggers look like he done killed somebody gambling over a quarter.

*Bynum:* He ain't no gambler. Gamblers wear nice shoes. This fellow got on clod-hoppers. He been out there walking up and down them roads.

*(Zonia enters from the stairs and looks around.)*

*Bynum:* You looking for the back door, sugar? There it is. You can go out there and play. It's alright.

*Seth (showing her the door):* You can go out there and play. Just don't get in my garden. And don't go messing around in my workshed.

*(Seth exits into the bedroom. There is a knock on the door.)*

*Jeremy:* Somebody at the door.

*(Jeremy goes to answer the door. Enter Mattie Campbell. She is a young woman of twenty-six whose attractiveness is hidden under the weight and concerns of a dissatisfied life. She is a woman in an honest search for love and companionship. She has suffered many defeats in her search, and though not always uncompromising, still believes in the possibility of love.)*

*Mattie:* I'm looking for a man named Bynum. Lady told me to come back later.

*Jeremy:* Sure, he here. Mr. Bynum, somebody here to see you.

*Bynum:* Come to see me, huh?

*Mattie:* Are you the man they call Bynum? The man folks say can fix things?

*Bynum:* Depend on what need fixing. I can't make no promises. But I got a powerful song in some matters.

*Mattie:* Can you fix it so my man come back to me?

*Bynum:* Come on in . . . have a sit down.

*Mattie:* You got to help me. I don't know what else to do.

*Bynum:* Depend on how all the circumstances of the thing come together. How all the pieces fit.

*Mattie*: I done everything I knowed how to do. You got to make him come back to me.

*Bynum*: It ain't nothing to make somebody come back. I can fix it so he can't stand to be away from you. I got my roots and powders, I can fix it so wherever he's at this thing will come up on him and he won't be able to sleep for seeing your face. Won't be able to eat for thinking of you.

*Mattie*: That's what I want. Make him come back.

*Bynum*: The roots is a powerful thing. I can fix it so one day he'll walk out his front door . . . won't be thinking of nothing. He won't know what it is. All he knows is that a powerful dissatisfaction done set in his bones and can't nothing he do make him feel satisfied. He'll set his foot down on the road and the wind in the trees be talking to him and everywhere he step on the road, that road'll give back your name and something will pull him right up to your doorstep. Now, I can do that. I can take my roots and fix that easy. But maybe he ain't supposed to come back. And if he ain't supposed to come back . . . then he'll be in your bed one morning and it'll come up on him that he's in the wrong place. That he's lost outside of time from his place that he's supposed to be in. Then both of you be lost and trapped outside of life and ain't no way for you to get back into it. 'Cause you lost from yourselves and where the places come together, where you're supposed to be alive, your heart kicking in your chest with a song worth singing.

*Mattie*: Make him come back to me. Make his feet say my name on the road. I don't care what happens. Make him come back.

*Bynum*: What's your man's name?

*Mattie*: He go by Jack Carper. He was born in Alabama then he come to West Texas and find me and we come here. Been here three years before he left. Say I had a curse prayer on me and he started walking down the road and ain't never come back. Somebody told me, say you can fix things like that.

*Bynum*: He just got up day, set his feet on the road, and walked away?

*Mattie*: You got to make him come back, mister.

*Bynum*: Did he say goodbye?

*Mattie*: Ain't said nothing. Just started walking. I could see where he disappeared. Didn't look back. Just keep walking. Can't you fix it so he come back? I ain't got no curse prayer on me. I know I ain't.

*Bynum*: What made him say you had a curse prayer on you?

*Mattie*: 'Cause the babies died. Me and Jack had two babies. Two little babies that ain't lived two months before they died. He say it's because somebody cursed me not to have babies.

*Bynum*: He ain't bound to you if the babies died. Look like somebody trying to keep you from being bound up and he's gone on back to whoever it is 'cause he's already bound up to her. Ain't nothing to be done. Somebody else done got a powerful hand in it and ain't nothing to be done to break it. You got to let him go find where he's supposed to be in the world.

*Mattie*: Jack done gone off and you telling me to forget about him. All my life I been looking for somebody to stop and stay with me. I done already got too many things to forget about. I take Jack Carper's hand and it feel so rough and strong. Seem like he's the strongest man in the world the way he hold me. Like he's bigger than the whole world and can't nothing bad get to me. Even when he act mean sometimes he still make everything seem okay with the world. Like there's part of it that belongs just to you. Now you telling me to forget about him?

Bynum: Jack Carper gone off to where he belong. There's somebody searching for your doorstep right now. Ain't no need you fretting over Jack Carper. Right now he's a strong thought in your mind. But every time you catch yourself fretting over Jack Carper you push that thought away. You push it out your mind and that thought will get weaker and weaker till you wake up one morning and you won't even be able to call him up on your mind.

(*Bynum gives her a small cloth packet.*)

Take this and sleep with it under your pillow and it'll bring good luck to you. Draw it to you like a magnet. It won't be long before you forget all about Jack Carper.

Mattie: How much . . . do I owe you?

Bynum: Whatever you got there . . . that'll be alright.

(*Mattie hands Bynum two quarters. She crosses to the door.*)

You sleep with that under your pillow and you'll be alright.

(*Mattie opens the door to exit and Jeremy crosses over to her. Bynum overhears the first part of their conversation, then exits out the back.*)

Jeremy: I overheard what you told Mr. Bynum. Had me an old gal did that to me. Woke up one morning and she was gone. Just took off to parts unknown. I woke up that morning and the only thing I could do was look around for my shoes. I woke up and got out of there. Found my shoes and took off. That's the only thing I could think of to do.

Mattie: She ain't said nothing?

Jeremy: I just looked around for my shoes and got out of there.

Mattie: Jack ain't said nothing either. He just walked off.

Jeremy: Some mens do that. Womens too. I ain't gone off looking for her. I just let her go. Figure she had a time to come to herself. Wasn't no use of me standing in the way. Where you from?

Mattie: Texas. I was born in Georgia but I went to Texas with my mama. She dead now. Was picking peaches and fell dead away. I come up here with Jack Carper.

Jeremy: I'm from North Carolina. Down around Raleigh where they got all that tobacco. Been up here about two weeks. I likes it fine except I still got to find me a woman. You got a nice look to you. Look like you have mens standing in your door. Is you got mens standing in your door to get a look at you?

Mattie: I ain't got nobody since Jack left.

*Jeremy:* A woman like you need a man. Maybe you let me be your man. I got a
   nice way with the women. That's what they tell me.

*Mattie:* I don't know. Maybe Jack's coming back.

*Jeremy:* I'll be your man till he come. A woman can't be by her lonesome. Let me
   be your man till he come.

*Mattie:* I just can't go through life piecing myself out to different mens. I need a
   man who wants to stay with me.

*Jeremy:* I can't say what's gonna happen. Maybe I'll be the man. I don't know.
   You wanna go along the road a little ways with me?

*Mattie:* I don't know. Seem like life say it's gonna be one thing and end up being
   another. I'm tired of going from man to man.

*Jeremy:* Life is like you got to take a chance. Everybody got to take a chance.
   Can't nobody say what's gonna be. Come on . . . take a chance with me and
   see what the year bring. Maybe you let me come and see you. Where you
   staying?

*Mattie:* I got me a room up on Bedford. Me and Jack had a room together.

*Jeremy:* What's the address? I'll come by and get you tonight and we can go down
   to Seefus. I'm going down there and play my guitar.

*Mattie:* You play guitar?

*Jeremy:* I play guitar like I'm born to it.

*Mattie:* I live at 1727 Bedford Avenue. I'm gonna find out if you can play guitar
   like you say.

*Jeremy:* I plays it sugar, and that ain't all I do. I got a ten-pound hammer and I
   knows how to drive it down. Good god . . . you ought to hear my hammer
   ring!

*Mattie:* Go on with that kind of talk, now. If you gonna come by and get me I got
   to get home and straighten up for you.

*Jeremy:* I'll be by at eight o'clock. How's eight o'clock? I'm gonna make you forget
   all about Jack Carper.

*Mattie:* Go on, now. I got to get home and fix up for you.

*Jeremy:* Eight o'clock, sugar.

   (*The lights go down in the parlor and come up on the yard outside. Zonia is singing
   and playing a game.*)

*Zonia:*
   I went downtown
   To get my grip
   I came back home
   Just a pullin' the skiff

   I went upstairs
   To make my bed
   I made a mistake
   And I bumped my head
   Just a pullin' the skiff

I went downstairs
To milk the cow
I made a mistake
And I milked the sow
Just a pullin' the skiff

Tomorrow, tomorrow
Tomorrow never comes
The marrow the marrow
The marrow in the bone.

*(Reuben enters.)*

Reuben: Hi.
Zonia: Hi.
Reuben: What's your name?
Zonia: Zonia.
Reuben: What kind of name is that?
Zonia: It's what my daddy named me.
Reuben: My name's Reuben. You staying in Mr. Seth's house?
Zonia: Yeah.
Reuben: That your daddy I seen you with this morning?
Zonia: I don't know. Who you see me with?
Reuben: I saw you with some man had on a great big old coat. And you was walk-
   ing up to Mr. Seth's house. Had on a hat too.
Zonia: Yeah, that's my daddy.
Reuben: You like Mr. Seth?
Zonia: I ain't see him much.
Reuben: My grandpap say he a great big old windbag. How come you living in Mr.
   Seth's house? Don't you have no house?
Zonia: We going to find my mother.
Reuben: Where she at?
Zonia: I don't know. We got to find her. We just go all over.
Reuben: Why you got to find her? What happened to her?
Zonia: She ran away.
Reuben: Why she run away?
Zonia: I don't know. My daddy say some man named Joe Turner did something
   bad to him once and that made her run away.
Reuben: Maybe she coming back and you don't have to go looking for her.
Zonia: We ain't there no more.
Reuben: She could have come back when you wasn't there.
Zonia: My daddy said she ran off and left us so we going looking for her.
Reuben: What he gonna do when he find her?
Zonia: He didn't say. He just say he got to find her.
Reuben: Your daddy say how long you staying in Mr. Seth's house?

*Zonia:* He don't say much. But we never stay too long nowhere. He say we got to keep moving till we find her.

*Reuben:* Ain't no kids hardly live around here. I had me a friend but he died. He was the best friend I ever had. Me and Eugene used to keep secrets. I still got his pigeons. He told me to let them go when he died. He say, "Reuben, promise me when I die you'll let my pigeons go." But I keep them to remember him by. I ain't never gonna let them go. Even when I get to be grown up. I'm just always gonna have Eugene's pigeons.

*(Pause.)*

Mr. Bynum a conjure man. My grandpap scared of him. He don't like me to come over here too much. I'm scared of him too. My grandpap told me not to let him get close enough to where he can reach out his hand and touch me.

*Zonia:* He don't seem scary to me.

*Reuben:* He buys pigeons from me . . . and if you get up early in the morning you can see him out in the yard doing something with them pigeons. My grandpap say he kill them. I sold him one yesterday. I don't know what he do with it. I just hope he don't spook me up.

*Zonia:* Why you sell him pigeons if he's gonna spook you up?

*Reuben:* I just do like Eugene do. He used to sell Mr. Bynum pigeons. That's how he got to collecting them to sell to Mr. Bynum. Sometime he give me a nickel and sometime he give me a whole dime.

*(Loomis enters from the house.)*

*Loomis:* Zonia!

*Zonia:* Sir?

*Loomis:* What you doing?

*Zonia:* Nothing.

*Loomis:* You stay around this house, you hear? I don't want you wandering off nowhere.

*Zonia:* I ain't wandering off nowhere.

*Loomis:* Miss Bertha set that hot tub and you getting a good scrubbing. Get scrubbed up good. You ain't been scrubbing.

*Zonia:* I been scrubbing.

*Loomis:* Look at you. You growing too fast. Your bones getting bigger everyday. I don't want you getting grown on me. Don't you get grown on me too soon. We gonna find your mamma. She around here somewhere. I can smell her. You stay on around this house now. Don't you go nowhere.

*Zonia:* Yes, sir.

*(Loomis exits into the house.)*

*Reuben:* Wow, your daddy's scary!

*Zonia:* He is not! I don't know what you talking about.

*Reuben:* He got them mean-looking eyes!

*Zonia:* My daddy ain't got no mean-looking eyes!

*Reuben:* Aw, girl, I was just messing with you. You wanna go see Eugene's pigeons? Got a great big coop out the back of my house. Come on, I'll show you.

*(Reuben and Zonia exit as the lights go down.)*

## Scene 2

*It is Saturday morning, one week later. The lights come up on the kitchen. Bertha is at the stove preparing breakfast while Seth sits at the table.*

*Seth:* Something ain't right about that fellow. I been watching him all week. Something ain't right, I'm telling you.

*Bertha:* Seth Holly, why don't you hush up about that man this morning?

*Seth:* I don't like the way he stare at everybody. Don't look at you natural like. He just be staring at you. Like he trying to figure out something about you. Did you see him when he come back in here?

*Bertha:* That man ain't thinking about you.

*Seth:* He don't work nowhere. Just go out and come back. Go out and come back.

*Bertha:* As long as you get your boarding money it ain't your cause about what he do. He don't bother nobody.

*Seth:* Just go and come back. Going around asking everybody about Martha. Like Henry Allen seen him down at the church last night.

*Bertha:* The man's allowed to go to church if he want. He say he a deacon. Ain't nothing wrong about him going to church.

*Seth:* I ain't talking about him going to church. I'm talking about him hanging around *outside* the church.

*Bertha:* Henry Allen say that?

*Seth:* Say he be standing around outside the church. Like he be watching it.

*Bertha:* What on earth he wanna be watching the church for, I wonder?

*Seth:* That's what I'm trying to figure out. Looks like he fixing to rob it.

*Bertha:* Seth, now do he look like the kind that would rob the church?

*Seth:* I ain't saying that. I ain't saying how he look. It's how he do. Anybody liable to do anything as far as I'm concerned. I ain't never thought about how no church robbers look . . . but now that you mention it, I don't see where they look no different than how he look.

*Bertha:* Herald Loomis ain't the kind of man who would rob no church.

*Seth:* I ain't even so sure that's his name.

*Bertha:* Why the man got to lie about his name?

*Seth:* Anybody can tell anybody anything about what their name is. That's what you call him . . . Herald Loomis. His name is liable to be anything.

*Bertha:* Well, until he tell me different that's what I'm gonna call him. You just getting yourself all worked up about the man for nothing.

*Seth:* Talking about Loomis: Martha's name wasn't no Loomis nothing. Martha's name is Pentecost.

*Bertha:* How you so sure that's her right name? Maybe she changed it.

*Seth:* Martha's a good Christian woman. This fellow here look like he owe the devil a day's work and he's trying to figure out how he gonna pay him. Martha ain't had a speck of distrust about her the whole time she was living here. They moved the church out there to Rankin and I was sorry to see her go.

*Bertha:* That's why he be hanging around the church. He looking for her.

*Seth:* If he looking for her, why don't he go inside and ask? What he doing hanging around outside the church acting sneakly like?

*(Bynum enters from the yard.)*

*Bynum:* Morning, Seth. Morning, Sister Bertha.

*(Bynum continues through the kitchen and exits up the stairs.)*

*Bertha:* That's who you should be asking the questions. He been out there in that yard all morning. He was out there before the sun come up. He didn't even come in for breakfast. I don't know what he's doing. He had three of them pigeons line up out there. He dance around till he get tired. He sit down awhile then get up and dance some more. He come through here a little while ago looking like he was mad at the world.

*Seth:* I don't pay Bynum no mind. He don't spook me up with all that stuff.

*Bertha:* That's how Martha come to be living here. She come to see Bynum. She come to see him when she first left from down South.

*Seth:* Martha was living here before Bynum. She ain't come on here when she first left from down there. She come on here after she went back to get her little girl. That's when she come on here.

*Bertha:* Well, where was Bynum? He was here when she came.

*Seth:* Bynum ain't come till after her. That boy Hiram was staying up there in Bynum's room.

*Bertha:* Well, how long Bynum been here?

*Seth:* Bynum ain't been here no longer than three years. That's what I'm trying to tell you. Martha was staying up there and sewing and cleaning for Doc Goldblum when Bynum came. This the longest he ever been in one place.

*Bertha:* How you know how long the man been in one place?

*Seth:* I know Bynum. Bynum ain't no mystery to me. I done seen a hundred niggers like him. He's one of them fellows never could stay in one place. He was wandering all around the country till he got old and settled here. The only thing different about Bynum is he bring all this heebie-jeebie stuff with him.

*Bertha:* I still say he was staying here when she came. That's why she came . . . to see him.

*Seth:* You can say what you want. I know the facts of it. She come on here four years ago all heartbroken 'cause she couldn't find her little girl. And Bynum wasn't nowhere around. She got mixed up in that old heebie-jeebie nonsense with him after he came.

*Bertha:* Well, if she came on before Bynum I don't know where she stayed. 'Cause she stayed up there in Hiram's room. Hiram couldn't get along with Bynum and left out of here owing you two dollars. Now, I know you ain't forgot about that!

*Seth:* Sure did! You know Hiram ain't paid me that two dollars yet. So that's why he be ducking and hiding when he see me down on Logan Street. You right. Martha did come on after Bynum. I forgot that's why Hiram left.

*Bertha:* Him and Bynum never could see eye to eye. They always rubbed each other the wrong way. Hiram got to thinking that Bynum was trying to put a fix on him and he moved out. Martha came to see Bynum and ended up taking Hiram's room. Now, I know what I'm talking about. She stayed on here three years till they moved the church.

*Seth:* She out there in Rankin now. I know where she at. I know where they moved the church to. She right out there in Rankin in that place used to be shoe store. Used to be Wolf's shoe store. They moved to a bigger place and they put that church in there. I know where she at. I know just where she at.

*Bertha:* Why don't you tell the man? You see he looking for her.

*Seth:* I ain't gonna tell that man where that woman is! What I wanna do that for? I don't know nothing about that man. I don't know why he looking for her. He might wanna do her a harm. I ain't gonna carry that on my hands. He looking for her, he gonna have to find her for himself. I ain't gonna help him. Now, if he had come and presented himself as a gentleman—the way Martha Pentecost's husband would have done—then I would have told him. But I ain't gonna tell this old wild-eyed mean-looking nigger nothing!

*Bertha:* Well, why don't you get a ride with Selig and go up there and tell her where he is? See if she wanna see him. If that's her little girl . . . you say Martha was looking for her.

*Seth:* You know me, Bertha. I don't get mixed up in nobody's business.

*(Bynum enters from the stairs.)*

*Bynum:* Morning, Seth. Morning, Bertha. Can I still get some breakfast? Mr. Loomis been down here this morning?

*Seth:* He done gone out and come back. He up there now. Left out of here early this morning wearing that coat. Hot as it is, the man wanna walk around wearing a big old heavy coat. He come back in here paid me for another week, sat down there waiting on Selig. Got tired of waiting and went on back upstairs.

*Bynum:* Where's the little girl?

*Seth:* She out there in the front. Had to chase her and that Reuben off the front porch. She out there somewhere.

*Bynum:* Look like if Martha was around here he would have found her by now. My guess is she ain't in the city.

*Seth:* She ain't! I know where she at. I know just where she at. But I ain't gonna tell him. Not the way he look.

*Bertha*: Here go your coffee, Bynum.

*Bynum*: He says he gonna get Selig to find her for him.

*Seth*: Selig can't find her. He talk all that . . . but unless he get lucky and knock on her door he can't find her. That's the only way he find anybody. He got to get lucky. But I know just where she at.

*Bertha*: Here go some biscuits, Bynum.

*Bynum*: What else you got over there, Sister Bertha? You got some grits and gravy over there? I could go for some of that this morning.

*Bertha* (*sets a bowl on the table*): Seth, come on and help me turn this mattress over. Come on.

*Seth*: Something ain't right with that fellow, Bynum. I don't like the way he stare at everybody.

*Bynum*: Mr. Loomis alright, Seth. He just a man got something on his mind. He just got a straightforward mind, that's all.

*Seth*: What's that fellow that they had around here? Moses, that's Moses Houser. Man went crazy and jumped off the Brady Street Bridge. I told you when I seen him something wasn't right about him. And I'm telling you about this fellow now.

(*There is a knock on the door. Seth goes to answer it. Enter Rutherford Selig.*)

Ho! Come on in, Selig.

*Bynum*: If it ain't the People Finder himself.

*Selig*: Bynum, before you start . . . I ain't seen no shiny man now.

*Bynum*: Who said anything about that? I ain't said nothing about that. I just called you a first-class People Finder.

*Selig*: How many dustpans you get out of that sheet metal, Seth?

*Seth*: You walked by them on your way in. They sitting out there on the porch. Got twenty-eight. Got four out of each sheet and made Bertha a coffeepot out the other one. They a little small but they got nice handles.

*Selig*: That was twenty cents apiece, right? That's what we agreed on.

*Seth*: That's five dollars and sixty cents. Twenty on top of twenty-eight. How many sheets you bring me?

*Selig*: I got eight out there. That's a dollar twenty makes me owe you . . .

*Seth*: Four dollars and forty cents.

*Selig* (*paying him*): Go on and make me some dustpans. I can use all you can make.

(*Loomis enters from the stairs.*)

*Loomis*: I been watching for you. He say you find people.

*Bynum*: Mr. Loomis here wants you to find his wife.

*Loomis*: He say you find people. Find her for me.

*Selig*: Well, let see here . . . find somebody, is it?

(*Selig rummages through his pockets. He has several notebooks and he is searching for the right one.*)

Alright now . . . what's the name?

*Loomis:* Martha Loomis. She my wife. Got married legal with the paper and all.

*Selig (writing):* Martha . . . Loomis. How tall is she?

*Loomis:* She five feet from the ground.

*Selig:* Five feet . . . tall. Young or old?

*Loomis:* She a young woman. Got long pretty hair.

*Selig:* Young . . . long . . . pretty . . . hair. Where did you last see her?

*Loomis:* Tennessee. Nearby Memphis.

*Selig:* When was that?

*Loomis:* Nineteen hundred and one.

*Selig:* Nineteen . . . hundred and one. I'll tell you, mister . . . you better off without them. Now you take me . . . old Rutherford Selig could tell you a thing
or two about these women. I ain't met one yet I could understand. Now, you
take Sally out there. That's all a man needs is a good horse. I say giddup and
she go. Say whoa and she stop. I feed her some oats and she carry me wherever I want to go. Ain't had a speck of trouble out of her since I had her.
Now, I been married. A long time ago down in Kentucky. I got up one
morning and I saw this look on my wife's face. Like way down deep inside
her she was wishing I was dead. I walked around that morning and every
time I looked at her she had that look on her face. It seem like she knew I
could see it on her. Every time I looked at her I got smaller and smaller.
Well, I wasn't gonna stay around there and just shrink away. I walked out on
the porch and closed the door behind me. When I closed the door she
locked it. I went out and bought me a horse. And I ain't been without one
since! Martha Loomis, huh? Well, now I'll do the best I can do. That's one
dollar.

*Loomis (holding out dollar suspiciously):* How you find her?

*Selig:* Well now, it ain't no easy job like you think. You can't just go out there and
find them like that. There's a lot of little tricks to it. It's not an easy job
keeping up with you Nigras the way you move about so. Now you take this
woman you looking for . . . this Martha Loomis. She could be anywhere.
Time I find her, if you don't keep your eye on her, she'll be gone off someplace else. You'll be thinking she over here and she'll be over there. But like
I say there's lot of little tricks to it.

*Loomis:* You say you find her.

*Selig:* I can't promise anything but we been finders in my family for a long time.
Bringers and finders. My great-granddaddy used to bring Nigras across the
ocean on ships. That's wasn't no easy job either. Sometimes the winds would
blow so hard you'd think the hand of God was set against the sails. But it set
him well in pay and he settled in this new land and found him a wife of good
Christian charity with a mind for kids and the like and well . . . here I am,
Rutherford Selig. You're in good hands, mister. Me and my daddy have
found plenty Nigras. My daddy, rest his soul, used to find runaway slaves for
the plantation bosses. He was the best there was at it. Jonas B. Selig. Had
him a reputation stretched clean across the country. After Abraham Lincoln
give you all Nigras your freedom papers and with you all looking all over for

each other . . . we started finding Nigras for Nigras. Of course, it don't pay as much. But the People Finding business ain't so bad.

*Loomis* (*hands him the dollar*): Find her. Martha Loomis. Find her for me.

*Selig*: Like I say, I can't promise you anything. I'm going back upriver, and if she's around in them parts I'll find her for you. But I can't promise you anything.

*Loomis*: When you coming back?

*Selig*: I'll be back on Saturday. I come and see Seth to pick up my order on Saturday.

*Bynum*: You going upriver, huh? You going up around my way. I used to go all up through there. Blawknox . . . Clairton. Used to go up to Rankin and take that first righthand road. I wore many a pair of shoes out walking around that way. You'd have thought I was a missionary spreading the gospel the way I wandered all around them parts.

*Selig*: Okay, Bynum. See you on Saturday.

*Seth*: Here, let me walk out with you. Help you with them dustpans.

(*Seth and Selig exit out the back. Bertha enters from the stairs carrying a bundle of sheets.*)

*Bynum*: Herald Loomis got the People Finder looking for Martha.

*Bertha*: You can call him a People Finder if you want to. I know Rutherford Selig carries people away too. He done carried a whole bunch of them away from here. Folks plan on leaving plan by Selig's timing. They wait till he get ready to go, then they hitch a ride on his wagon. Then he charge folks a dollar to tell them where he took them. Now, that's the truth of Rutherford Selig. This old People Finding business is for the birds. He ain't never found nobody he ain't took away. Herald Loomis, you just wasted your dollar.

(*Bertha exits into the bedroom.*)

*Loomis*: He say he find her. He say he find her by Saturday. I'm gonna wait till Saturday.

(*The lights fade to black.*)


## Scene 3

*It is Sunday morning, the next day. The lights come up on the kitchen. Seth sits talking to Bynum. The breakfast dishes have been cleared away.*

*Seth*: They can't see that. Neither one of them can see that. Now, how much sense it take to see that? All you got to do is be able to count. One man making ten pots is five men making fifty pots. But they can't see that. Asked where I'm gonna get my five men. Hell, I can teach anybody how to make a pot. I can teach you. I can take you out there and get you started right now. Inside of two weeks you'd know how to make a pot. All you got to do is want to do it. I can get five men. I ain't worried about getting no five men.

*Bertha* (*calls from the bedroom*): Seth. Come on and get ready now. Reverend Gates ain't gonna be holding up his sermon 'cause you sitting out there talking.

*Seth*: Now, you take the boy, Jeremy. What he gonna do after he put in that road? He can't do nothing but go put in another one somewhere. Now, if he let me show him how to make some pots and pans . . . then he'd have something can't nobody take away from him. After a while he could get his own tools and go off somewhere and make his own pots and pans. Find him somebody to sell them to. Now, Selig can't make no pots and pans. He can sell them but he can't make them. I get me five men with some tools and we'd make him so many pots and pans he'd have to open up a store somewhere. But they can't see that. Neither Mr. Cohen nor Sam Green.

*Bertha* (*calls from the bedroom*): Seth . . . time be wasting. Best be getting on.

*Seth*: I'm coming, woman! (*To Bynum.*) Want me to sign over the house to borrow five hundred dollars. I ain't that big a fool. That's all I got. Sign it over to them and then I won't have nothing.

(*Jeremy enters waving a dollar and carrying his guitar.*)

*Jeremy*: Look here, Mr. Bynum . . . won me another dollar last night down at Seefus! Me and that Mattie Campbell went down there again and I played contest. Ain't no guitar players down there. Wasn't even no contest. Say, Mr. Seth, I asked Mattie Campbell if she wanna come by and have Sunday dinner with us. Get some fried chicken.

*Seth*: It's gonna cost you twenty-five cents.

*Jeremy*: That's alright. I got a whole dollar here. Say Mr. Seth . . . me and Mattie Campbell talked it over last night and she gonna move in with me. If that's alright with you.

*Seth*: Your business is your business . . . but it's gonna cost her a dollar a week for her board. I can't be feeding nobody for free.

*Jeremy*: Oh, she know that, Mr. Seth. That's what I told her, say she'd have to pay for her meals.

*Seth*: You say you got a whole dollar there . . . turn loose that twenty-five cents.

*Jeremy*: Suppose she move in today, then that make seventy-five cents more, so I'll give you the whole dollar for her now till she gets here.

(*Seth pockets the money and exits into the bedroom.*)

*Bynum*: So you and that Mattie Campbell gonna take up together?

*Jeremy*: I told her she don't need to be by her lonesome, Mr. Bynum. Don't make no sense for both of us to be by our lonesome. So she gonna move in with me.

*Bynum*: Sometimes you got to be where you supposed to be. Sometimes you can get all mixed up in life and come to the wrong place.

*Jeremy*: That's just what I told her, Mr. Bynum. It don't make no sense for her to be all mixed up and lonesome. May as well come here and be with me. She a fine woman too. Got them long legs. Knows how to treat a fellow too. Treat you like you wanna be treated.

*Bynum:* You just can't look at it like that. You got to look at the whole thing. Now, you take a fellow go out there, grab hold to a woman and think he got something 'cause she sweet and soft to the touch. Alright. Touching's part of life. It's in the world like everything else. Touching's nice. It feels good. But you can lay your hand upside a horse or a cat, and that feels good too. What's the difference? When you grab hold to a woman, you got something there. You got a whole world there. You got a way of life kicking up under your hand. That woman can take and make you feel like something. I ain't just talking about in the way of jumping off into bed together and rolling around with each other. Anybody can do that. When you grab hold to that woman and look at the whole thing and see what you got . . . why, she can take and make something out of you. Your mother was a woman. That's enough right there to show you what a woman is. Enough to show you what she can do. She made something out of you. Taught you converse, and all about how to take care of yourself, how to see where you at and where you going tomor-row, how to look out to see what's coming in the way of eating, and what to do with yourself when you get lonesome. That's a mighty thing she did. But you just can't look at a woman to jump off into bed with her. That's a foolish thing to ignore a woman like that.

*Jeremy:* Oh, I ain't ignoring her, Mr. Bynum. It's hard to ignore a woman got legs like she got.

*Bynum:* Alright. Let's try it this way. Now, you take a ship. Be out there on the water traveling about. You out there on that ship sailing to and from. And then you see some land. Just like you see a woman walking down the street. You see that land and it don't look like nothing but a line out there on the horizon. That's all it is when you first see it. A line that cross your path out there on the horizon. Now, a smart man know when he see that land, it ain't just a line setting out there. He know that if you get off the water to go take a good look . . . why, there's a whole world right there. A whole world with everything imaginable under the sun. Anything you can think of you can find on that land. Same with a woman. A woman is everything a man need. To a smart man she water and berries. And that's all a man need. That's all he need to live on. You give me some water and berries and if there ain't nothing else I can live a hundred years. See, you just like a man looking at the horizon from a ship. You just seeing a part of it. But it's a blessing when you learn to look at a woman and see in maybe just a few strands of her hair, the way her cheek curves . . . to see in that everything there is out of life to be gotten. It's a blessing to see that. You know you done right and proud by your mother to see that. But you got to learn it. My telling you ain't gonna mean nothing. You got to learn how to come to your own time and place with a woman.

*Jeremy:* What about your woman, Mr. Bynum? I know you done had some woman.

*Bynum:* Oh, I got them in memory time. That lasts longer than any of them ever stayed with me.

*Jeremy:* I had me an old gal one time . . .

*(There is a knock on the door, Jeremy goes to answer it. Enter Molly Cunningham. She is about twenty-six, the kind of woman that "could break in on a dollar anywhere she goes." She carries a small cardboard suitcase, and wears a colorful dress of the fashion of the day. Jeremy's heart jumps out of his chest when he sees her.)*

*Molly:* You got any rooms here? I'm looking for a room.

*Jeremy:* Yeah . . . Mr. Seth got rooms. Sure . . . wait till I get Mr. Seth. *(Calls.)* Mr. Seth! Somebody here to see you! *(To Molly.)* Yeah, Mr. Seth got some rooms. Got one right next to me. This is a nice place to stay, too. My name's Jeremy. What's yours?

*(Seth enters dressed in his Sunday clothes.)*

*Seth:* Ho!

*Jeremy:* This here woman looking for a place to stay. She say you got any rooms.

*Molly:* Mister, you got any rooms? I seen your sign say you got rooms.

*Seth:* How long you plan to staying?

*Molly:* I ain't gonna be here long. I ain't looking for no home or nothing. I'd be in Cincinnati if I hadn't missed my train.

*Seth:* Rooms cost two dollars a week.

*Molly:* Two dollars!

*Seth:* That includes meals. We serve two meals a day. That's breakfast and dinner.

*Molly:* I hope it ain't on the third floor.

*Seth:* That's the only one I got. Third floor to the left. That's pay up in advance week to week.

*Molly (going into her bosom):* I'm gonna pay you for one week. My name's Molly. Molly Cunningham.

*Seth:* I'm Seth Holly. My wife's name is Bertha. She do the cooking and take care of around here. She got sheets on the bed. Towels twenty-five cents a week extra if you ain't got none. You get breakfast and dinner. We got fried chicken on Sundays.

*Molly:* That sounds good. Here's two dollars and twenty-five cents. Look here, Mister . . . ?

*Seth:* Holly. Seth Holly.

*Molly:* Look here, Mr. Holly. I forgot to tell you. I likes me some company from time to time. I don't like being by myself.

*Seth:* Your business is your business. I don't meddle in nobody's business. But this is a respectable house. I don't have no riffraff around here. And I don't have no women hauling no men up to their rooms to be making their living. As long as we understand each other then we'll be alright with each other.

*Molly:* Where's the outhouse?

*Seth:* Straight through the door over yonder.

*Molly:* I get my own key to the front door?

*Seth:* Everybody get their own key. If you come in late just don't be making no whole lot of noise and carrying on. Don't allow no fussing and fighting around here.

*Molly:* You ain't got to worry about that, mister. Which way you say that out-house was again?

*Seth:* Straight through that door over yonder.

*(Molly exits out the back door. Jeremy crosses to watch her.)*

*Jeremy:* Mr. Bynum, you know what? I think I know what you was talking about now.

*(The lights go down on the scene.)*

## Scene 4

*The lights come up on the kitchen. It is later the same evening. Mattie and all the residents of the house, except Loomis, sit around the table. They have finished eating and most of the dishes have been cleared.*

*Molly:* That sure was some good chicken.

*Jeremy:* That's what I'm talking about. Miss Bertha, you sure can fry some chicken. I thought my mama could fry some chicken. But she can't do half as good as you.

*Seth:* I know it. That's why I married her. She don't know that, though. She think I married her for something else.

*Bertha:* I ain't studying you, Seth. Did you get your things moved in alright, Mattie?

*Mattie:* I ain't had that much. Jeremy helped me with what I did have.

*Bertha:* You'll get to know your way around here. If you have any questions about anything just ask me. You and Molly both. I get along with everybody. You'll find I ain't no trouble to get along with.

*Mattie:* You need some help with the dishes?

*Bertha:* I got me a helper. Ain't I, Zonia? Got me a good helper.

*Zonia:* Yes, ma'am.

*Seth:* Look at Bynum sitting over there with his belly all poked out. Ain't saying nothing. Sitting over there half asleep. Ho, Bynum!

*Bertha:* If Bynum ain't saying nothing what you wanna start him up for?

*Seth:* Ho, Bynum!

*Bynum:* What you hollering at me for? I ain't doing nothing.

*Seth:* Come on, we gonna Juba.

*Bynum:* You know me, I'm always ready to Juba.

*Seth:* Well, come on, then.

*(Seth pulls out a harmonica and blows a few notes.)*

Come on there, Jeremy. Where's your guitar? Go get your guitar. Bynum says he's ready to Juba.

*Jeremy:* Don't need no guitar to Juba. Ain't you never Juba without a guitar?

(*Jeremy begins to drum on the table.*)

*Seth:* It ain't that. I ain't never Juba with one! Figured to try it and see how it worked.

*Bynum* (*drumming on the table*): You don't need no guitar. Look at Molly sitting over there. She don't know we Juba on Sunday. We gonna show you something tonight. You and Mattie Campbell both. Ain't that right, Seth?

*Seth:* You said it! Come on, Bertha, leave them dishes be for a while. We gonna Juba.

*Bynum:* Alright. Let's Juba down!

(*The Juba is reminiscent of the Ring Shouts of the African slaves. It is a call and response dance. Bynum sits at the table and drums. He calls the dance as others clap hands, shuffle and stomp around the table. It should be as African as possible, with the performers working themselves up into a near frenzy. The words can be improvised, but should include some mention of the Holy Ghost. In the middle of the dance Herald Loomis enters.*)

*Loomis* (*in a rage*): Stop it! Stop!

(*They stop and turn to look at him.*)

You all sitting up here singing about the Holy Ghost. What's so holy about the Holy Ghost? You singing and singing. You think the Holy Ghost coming? You singing for the Holy Ghost to come? What he gonna do, huh? He gonna come with tongues of fire to burn up your woolly heads? You gonna tie onto the Holy Ghost and get burned up? What you got then? Why God got to be so big? Why he got to be bigger than me? How much big is there? How much big do you want?

(*Loomis starts to unzip his pants.*)

*Seth:* Nigger, you crazy!

*Loomis:* How much big you want?

*Seth:* You done plumb lost your mind!

(*Loomis begins to speak in tongues and dance around the kitchen. Seth starts after him.*)

*Bertha:* Leave him alone, Seth. He ain't in his right mind.

*Loomis* (*stops suddenly*): You all don't know nothing about me. You don't know what I done seen. Herald Loomis done seen some things he ain't got words to tell you.

(*Loomis starts to walk out the front door and is thrown back and collapses, terror-stricken by his vision. Bynum crawls to him.*)

*Bynum:* What you done seen, Herald Loomis?

*Loomis:* I done seen bones rise up out the water. Rise up and walk across the water. Bones walking on top of the water.

*Bynum:* Tell me about them bones, Herald Loomis. Tell me what you seen.

*Loomis:* I come to this place . . . to this water that was bigger than the whole world. And I looked out . . . and I seen these bones rise up out the water. Rise up and begin to walk on top of it.

*Bynum:* Wasn't nothing but bones and they walking on top of the water.

*Loomis:* Walking without sinking down. Walking on top of the water.

*Bynum:* Just marching in a line.

*Loomis:* A whole heap of them. They come up out the water and started marching.

*Bynum:* Wasn't nothing but bones and they walking on top of the water.

*Loomis:* One after the other. They just come up out the water and start to walking.

*Bynum:* They walking on the water without sinking down. They just walking and walking. And then . . . what happened, Herald Loomis?

*Loomis:* They just walking across the water.

*Bynum:* What happened, Herald Loomis? What happened to the bones?

*Loomis:* They just walking across the water . . . and then . . . they sunk down.

*Bynum:* The bones sunk into the water. They all sunk down.

*Loomis:* All at one time! They just all fell in the water at one time.

*Bynum:* Sunk down like anybody else.

*Loomis:* When they sink down they made a big splash and this here wave come up . . .

*Bynum:* A big wave, Herald Loomis. A big wave washed over the land.

*Loomis:* It washed them out of the water and up on the land. Only . . . only . . .

*Bynum:* Only they ain't bones no more.

*Loomis:* They got flesh on them! Just like you and me!

*Bynum:* Everywhere you look the waves is washing them up on the land right on top of one another.

*Loomis:* They black. Just like you and me. Ain't no difference.

*Bynum:* Then what happened, Herald Loomis?

*Loomis:* They ain't moved or nothing. They just laying there.

*Bynum:* You just laying there. What you waiting on, Herald Loomis?

*Loomis:* I'm laying there . . . waiting.

*Bynum:* What you waiting on, Herald Loomis?

*Loomis:* I'm waiting on the breath to get into my body.

*Bynum:* The breath coming into you, Herald Loomis. What you gonna do now?

*Loomis:* The wind's blowing the breath into my body. I can feel it. I'm starting to breathe again.

*Bynum:* What you gonna do, Herald Loomis?

*Loomis:* I'm gonna stand up. I got to stand up. I can't lay here no more. All the breath coming into my body and I got to stand up.

*Bynum:* Everybody's standing up at the same time.

*Loomis:* The ground's starting to shake. There's a great shaking. The world's busting half in two. The sky's splitting open. I got to stand up.

*(Loomis attempts to stand up.)*

My legs . . . my legs won't stand up!

Bynum: Everybody's standing and walking toward the road. What you gonna do, Herald Loomis?

Loomis: My legs won't stand up.

Bynum: They shaking hands and saying goodbye to each other and walking every whichaway down the road.

Loomis: I got to stand up!

Bynum: They walking around here now. Mens. Just like you and me. Come right up out the water.

Loomis: Got to stand up.

Bynum: They walking, Herald Loomis. They walking around here now.

Loomis: I got to stand up. Get up on the road.

Bynum: Come on, Herald Loomis.

(Loomis tries to stand up.)

Loomis: My legs won't stand up! My legs won't stand up!

(Loomis collapses on the floor as the lights go down to black.)


# Act II

### Scene 1

*The lights come up on the kitchen. Bertha busies herself with breakfast preparations. Seth sits at the table.*

Seth: I don't care what his problem is! He's leaving here!

Bertha: You can't put the man out and he got that little girl. Where they gonna go then?

Seth: I don't care where he go. Let him go back where he was before he come here. I ain't asked him to come here. I knew when I first looked at him something wasn't right with him. Dragging that little girl around with him. Looking like he be sleeping in the woods somewhere. I knew all along he wasn't right.

Bertha: A fellow get a little drunk he's liable to say or do anything. He ain't done no big harm.

Seth: I just don't have all that carrying on in my house. When he come down here I'm gonna tell him. He got to leave here. My daddy wouldn't stand for it and I ain't gonna stand for it either.

Bertha: Well, if you put him out you have to put Bynum out too. Bynum right there with him.

Seth: If it wasn't for Bynum ain't no telling what would have happened. Bynum talked to that fellow just as nice and calmed him down. If he wasn't here ain't no telling what would have happened. Bynum ain't done nothing but talk to him and kept him calm. Man acting all crazy with that foolishness. Naw, he's leaving here.

*Bertha*: What you gonna tell him? How you gonna tell him to leave?

*Seth*: I'm gonna tell him straight out. Keep it nice and simple. Mister, you got to leave here!

(*Molly enters from the stairs.*)

*Molly*: Morning.

*Bertha*: Did you sleep alright in that bed?

*Molly*: Tired as I was I could have slept anywhere. It's a real nice room, though. This is a nice place.

*Seth*: I'm sorry you had to put up with all that carrying on last night.

*Molly*: It don't bother me none. I done seen that kind of stuff before.

*Seth*: You won't have to see it around here no more.

(*Bynum is heard singing offstage.*)

I don't put up with all that stuff. When that fellow come down here I'm gonna tell him.

*Bynum* (*singing*):
Soon my work will all be done
Soon my work will all be done
Soon my work will all be done

I'm going to see the king.

*Bynum* (*enters*): Morning, Seth. Morning, Sister Bertha. I see we got Molly Cunningham down here at breakfast.

*Seth*: Bynum, I wanna thank you for talking to that fellow last night and calming him down. If you hadn't been here ain't no telling what might have happened.

*Bynum*: Mr. Loomis alright, Seth. He just got a little excited.

*Seth*: Well, he can get excited somewhere else 'cause he leaving here.

(*Mattie enters from the stairs.*)

*Bynum*: Well, there's Mattie Campbell.

*Mattie*: Good morning.

*Bertha*: Sit on down there, Mattie. I got some biscuits be ready in a minute. The coffee's hot.

*Mattie*: Jeremy gone already?

*Bynum*: Yeah, he leave out of here early. He got to be there when the sun come up. Most working men got to be there when the sun come up. Everybody but Seth. Seth work at night. Mr. Olowski so busy in his shop he got fellows working at night.

(*Loomis enters from the stairs.*)

*Seth*: Mr. Loomis, now . . . I don't want no trouble. I keeps me a respectable house here. I don't have no carrying on like what went on last night. This has been a respectable house for a long time. I'm gonna have to ask you to leave.

Loomis: You got my two dollars. That two dollars say we stay till Saturday.

(*Loomis and Seth glare at each other.*)

Seth: Alright. Fair enough. You stay till Saturday. But come Saturday you got to leave here.

Loomis (*continues to glare at Seth. He goes to the door and calls*): Zonia. You stay around this house, you hear? Don't you go anywhere.

(*Loomis exits out the front door.*)

Seth: I knew it when I first seen him. I knew something wasn't right with him.

Bertha: Seth, leave the people alone to eat their breakfast. They don't want to hear that. Go on out there and make some pots and pans. That's the only time you satisfied is when you out there. Go on out there and make some pots and pans and leave them people alone.

Seth: I ain't bothering anybody. I'm just stating the facts. I told you, Bynum.

(*Bertha shoos Seth out the back door and exits into the bedroom.*)

Molly (*to Bynum*): You one of them voo-doo people?

Bynum: I got a power to bind folks if that what you talking about.

Molly: I thought so. The way you talked to that man when he started all that spooky stuff. What you say you had the power to do to people? You ain't the cause of him acting like that, is you?

Bynum: I binds them together. Sometimes I help them find each other.

Molly: How do you do that?

Bynum: With a song. My daddy taught me how to do it.

Molly: That's what they say. Most folks be what they daddy is. I wouldn't want to be like my daddy. Nothing ever set right with him. He tried to make the world over. Carry it around with him everywhere he go. I don't want to be like that. I just take life as it come. I don't be trying to make it over.

(*Pause.*)

Your daddy used to do that too, huh? Make people stay together?

Bynum: My daddy used to heal people. He had the Healing Song. I got the Binding Song.

Molly: My mama used to believe in all that stuff. If she got sick she would have gone and saw your daddy. As long as he didn't make her drink nothing. She wouldn't drink nothing nobody give her. She was always afraid somebody was gonna poison her. How your daddy heal people?

Bynum: With a song. He healed people by singing over them. I seen him do it. He sung over this little white girl when she was sick. They made a big to-do about it. They carried the girl's bed out in the yard and had all her kinfolk standing around. The little girl laying up there in the bed. Doctors standing around can't do nothing to help her. And they had my daddy come up and sing his song. It didn't sound no different than any other song. It was just somebody singing. But the song was its own thing and it come out and took upon this little girl with its power and it healed her.

*Molly:* That's sure something else. I don't understand that kind of thing. I guess if the doctor couldn't make me well I'd try it. But otherwise I don't wanna be bothered with that kind of thing. It's too spooky.

*Bynum:* Well, let me get on out here and get to work.

*(Bynum gets up and heads out the back door.)*

*Molly:* I ain't meant to offend you or nothing. What's your name . . . Bynum? I ain't meant to say nothing to make you feel bad now.

*(Bynum exits out the back door.)*

*(To Mattie.)* I hope he don't feel bad. He's a nice man. I don't wanna hurt nobody's feelings or nothing.

*Mattie:* I got to go on up to Doc Goldblum's and finish this ironing.

*Molly:* Now, that's something I don't never wanna do. Iron no clothes. Especially somebody else's. That's what I believe killed my mama. Always ironing and working, doing somebody else's work. Not Molly Cunningham.

*Mattie:* It's the only job I got. I got to make it someway to fend for myself.

*Molly:* I thought Jeremy was your man. Ain't he working?

*Mattie:* We just be keeping company till maybe Jack come back.

*Molly:* I don't trust none of these men. Jack or nobody else. These men liable to do anything. They wait just until they get one woman tied and locked up with them . . . then they look around to see if they can get another one. Molly don't pay them no mind. One's just as good as the other if you ask me. I ain't never met one that meant nobody no good. You got any babies?

*Mattie:* I had two for my man, Jack Carper. But they both died.

*Molly:* That be the best. These men make all these babies, then run off and leave you to take care of them. Talking about they wanna see what's on the other side of the hill. I make sure I don't get no babies. My mama taught me how to do that.

*Mattie:* Don't make me no mind. That be nice to be a mother.

*Molly:* Yeah? Well, you go on, then. Molly Cunningham ain't gonna be tied down with no babies. Had me a man one time who I thought had some love in him. Come home one day and he was packing his trunk. Told me the time come when even the best of friends must part. Say he was gonna send me a Special Delivery some old day. I watched him out the window when he carried that trunk out and down to the train station. Said if he was gonna send me a Special Delivery I wasn't gonna be there to get it. I done found out the harder you try to hold onto them, the easier it is for some gal to pull them away. Molly done learned that. That's why I don't trust nobody but the good Lord above, and I don't love nobody but my mama.

*Mattie:* I got to get on. Doc Goldblum gonna be waiting.

*(Mattie exits out the front door. Seth enters from his workshop with his apron, gloves, goggles, etc. He carries a bucket and crosses to the sink for water.)*

*Seth:* Everybody gone but you, huh?

*Molly:* That little shack out there by the outhouse . . . that's where you make them pots and pans and stuff?

*Seth:* Yeah, that's my workshed. I go out there . . . take these hands and make something out of nothing. Take that metal and bend and twist it whatever way I want. My daddy taught me that. He used to make pots and pans. That's how I learned it.

*Molly:* I never knew nobody made no pots and pans. My uncle used to shoe horses.

*(Jeremy enters at the front door.)*

*Seth:* I thought you was working? Ain't you working today?

*Jeremy:* Naw, they fired me. White fellow come by told me to give him fifty cents if I wanted to keep working. Going around to all the colored making them give him fifty cents to keep hold to their jobs. Them other fellows, they was giving it to him. I kept hold to mine and they fired me.

*Seth:* Boy, what kind of sense that make? What kind of sense it make to get fired from a job where you making eight dollars a week and all it cost you is fifty cents. That's seven dollars and fifty cents profit! This way you ain't got nothing.

*Jeremy:* It didn't make no sense to me. I don't make but eight dollars. Why I got to give him fifty cents of it? He go around to all the colored and he got ten dollars extra. That's more than I make for a whole week.

*Seth:* I see you gonna learn the hard way. You just looking at the facts of it. See, right now, without the job, you ain't got nothing. What you gonna do when you can't keep a roof over your head? Right now, come Saturday, unless you come up with another two dollars, you gonna be out there in the streets. Down up under one of them bridges trying to put some food in your belly and wishing you had given that fellow that fifty cents.

*Jeremy:* Don't make me no difference. There's a big road out there. I can get my guitar and always find me another place to stay. I ain't planning on staying in one place for too long noway.

*Seth:* We gonna see if you feel like that come Saturday!

*(Seth exits out the back. Jeremy sees Molly.)*

*Jeremy:* Molly Cunningham. How you doing today, sugar?

*Molly:* You can go on back down there tomorrow and go back to work if you want. They won't even know who you is. Won't even know it's you. I had me a fellow did that one time. They just went ahead and signed him up like they never seen him before.

*Jeremy:* I'm tired of working anyway. I'm glad they fired me. You sure look pretty today.

*Molly:* Don't come telling me all that pretty stuff. Beauty wanna come in and sit down at your table asking to be fed. I ain't hardly got enough for me.

*Jeremy:* You know you pretty. Ain't no sense in you saying nothing about that. Why don't you come on and go away with me?

*Molly:* You tied up with that Mattie Campbell. Now you talking about running away with me.

*Jeremy:* I was just keeping her company 'cause she lonely. You ain't the lonely kind. You the kind that know what she want and how to get it. I need a woman like you to travel around with. Don't you wanna travel around and look at some places with Jeremy? With a woman like you beside him, a man can make it nice in the world.

*Molly:* Molly can make it nice by herself too. Molly don't need nobody leave her cold in hand. The world rough enough as it is.

*Jeremy:* We can make it better together. I got my guitar and I can play. Won me another dollar last night playing guitar. We can go around and I can play at the dances and we can just enjoy life. You can make it by yourself alright, I agrees with that. A woman like you can make it anywhere she go. But you can make it better if you got a man to protect you.

*Molly:* What places you wanna go around and look at?

*Jeremy:* All of them! I don't want to miss nothing. I wanna go everywhere and do everything there is to be got out of life. With a woman like you it's like having water and berries. A man got everything he need.

*Molly:* You got to be doing more than playing that guitar. A dollar a day ain't hardly what Molly got in mind.

*Jeremy:* I gambles real good. I got a hand for it.

*Molly:* Molly don't work. And Molly ain't up for sale.

*Jeremy:* Sure, baby. You ain't got to work with Jeremy.

*Molly:* There's one more thing.

*Jeremy:* What's that, sugar?

*Molly:* Molly ain't going South.

    *(The lights go down on the scene.)*


### Scene 2

*The lights come up on the parlor. Seth and Bynum sit playing a game of dominoes. Bynum sings to himself.*

*Bynum (singing):*
    They tell me Joe Turner's come and gone
    Ohhh Lordy
    They tell me Joe Turner's come and gone
    Ohhh Lordy
    Got my man and gone

    Come with forty links of chain
    Ohhh Lordy
    Come with forty links of chain
    Ohhh Lordy
    Got my man and gone

*Seth:* Come on and play if you gonna play.

*Bynum:* I'm gonna play. Soon as I figure out what to do.

*Seth:* You can't figure out if you wanna play or you wanna sing.

*Bynum:* Well sir, I'm gonna do a little bit of both.

(*Playing.*)

There. What you gonna do now?

(*Singing.*)

They tell me Joe Turner's come and gone
Ohhh Lordy
They tell me Joe Turner's come and gone
Ohhh Lordy

*Seth:* Why don't you hush up that noise.

*Bynum:* That's a song the women sing down around Memphis. The women down there made up that song. I picked it up down there about fifteen years ago.

(*Loomis enters from the front door.*)

*Bynum:* Evening, Mr. Loomis.

*Seth:* Today's Monday, Mr. Loomis. Come Saturday your time is up. We done ate already. My wife roasted up some yams. She got your plate sitting in there on the table. (*To Bynum.*) Whose play is it?

*Bynum:* Ain't you keeping up with the game? I thought you was a domino player. I just played so it got to be your turn.

(*Loomis goes into the kitchen, where a plate of yams is covered and set on the table. He sits down and begins to eat with his hands.*)

*Seth* (*plays*): Twenty! Give me twenty! You didn't know I had that ace five. You was trying to play around that. You didn't know I had that lying there for you.

*Bynum:* You ain't done nothing. I let you have that to get mine.

*Seth:* Come on and play. You ain't doing nothing but talking. I got a hundred and forty points to your eighty. You ain't doing nothing but talking. Come on and play.

*Bynum* (*singing*):

They tell me Joe Turner's come and gone
Ohhh Lordy
They tell me Joe Turner's come and gone
Ohhh Lordy
Got my man and gone

He come with forty links of chain
Ohhh Lordy

*Loomis*: Why you singing that song? Why you singing about Joe Turner?

*Bynum*: I'm just singing to entertain myself.

*Seth*: You trying to distract me. That's what you trying to do.

*Bynum* (*singing*):

> Come with forty links of chain
> Ohhh Lordy
> Come with forty links of chain
> Ohhh Lordy

*Loomis*: I don't like you singing that song, mister!

*Seth*: Now, I ain't gonna have no more disturbance around here, Herald Loomis. You start any more disturbance and you leavin' here, Saturday or no Saturday.

*Bynum*: The man ain't causing no disturbance, Seth. He just say he don't like the song.

*Seth*: Well, we all friendly folk. All neighborly like. Don't have no squabbling around here. Don't have no disturbance. You gonna have to take that someplace else.

*Bynum*: He just say he don't like the song. I done sung a whole lot of songs people don't like. I respect everybody. He here in the house too. If he don't like the song, I'll sing something else. I know lots of songs. You got "I Belong to the Band," "Don't You Leave Me Here." You got "Praying on the Old Campground," "Keep Your Lamp Trimmed and Burning" . . . I know lots of songs. (*Sings.*)

> Boys, I'll be so glad when payday come
> Captain, Captain, when payday comes
> Gonna catch that Illinois Central
> Going to Kankakee

*Seth*: Why don't you hush up that hollering and come on and play dominoes.

*Bynum*: You ever been to Johnstown, Herald Loomis? You look like a fellow I seen around there.

*Loomis*: I don't know no place with that name.

*Bynum*: That's around where I seen my shiny man. See, you looking for this woman. I'm looking for a shiny man. Seem like everybody looking for something.

*Seth*: I'm looking for you to come and play these dominoes. That's what I'm looking for.

*Bynum*: You a farming man, Herald Loomis? You look like you done some farming.

*Loomis*: Same as everybody. I done farmed some, yeah.

*Bynum*: I used to work at farming . . . picking cotton. I reckon everybody done picked some cotton.

*Seth*: I ain't! I ain't never picked no cotton. I was born up here in the North. My daddy was a freedman. I ain't never even seen no cotton!

*Bynum:* Mr. Loomis done picked some cotton. Ain't you, Herald Loomis? You done picked a bunch of cotton.

*Loomis:* How you know so much about me? How you know what I done? How much cotton I picked?

*Bynum:* I can tell from looking at you. My daddy taught me how to do that. Say when you look at a fellow, if you taught yourself to look for it, you can see his song written on him. Tell you what kind of man he is in the world. Now, I can look at you, Mr. Loomis, and see you a man who done forgot his song. Forgot how to sing it. A fellow forget that and he forget who he is. Forget how he's supposed to mark down life. Now, I used to travel all up and down this road and that . . . looking here and there. Searching. Just like you, Mr. Loomis. I didn't know what I was searching for. The only thing I knew was something was keeping me dissatisfied. Something wasn't making my heart smooth and easy. Then one day my daddy gave me a song. That song had a weight to it that was hard to handle. That song was hard to carry. I fought against it. Didn't want to accept that song. I tried to find my daddy to give him back the song. But I found out it wasn't his song. It was my song. It had come from way deep inside me. I looked long back in memory and gathered up pieces and snatches of things to make that song. I was making it up out of myself. And that song helped me on the road. Made it smooth to where my footsteps didn't bite back at me. All the time that song getting bigger and bigger. That song growing with each step of the road. It got so I used all of myself up in the making of that song. Then I was the song in search of itself. That song rattling in my throat and I'm looking for it. See, Mr. Loomis, when a man forgets his song he goes off in search of it . . . till he find out he's got it with him all the time. That's why I can tell you one of Joe Turner's niggers. 'Cause you forgot how to sing your song.

*Loomis:* You lie! How you see that? I got a mark on me? Joe Turner done marked me to where you can see it? You telling me I'm a marked man. What kind of mark you got on you?

*(Bynum begins singing.)*

*Bynum:*

> They tell me Joe Turner's come and gone
> Ohhh Lordy
> They tell me Joe Turner's come and gone
> Ohhh Lordy
> Got my man and gone

*Loomis:* Had a whole mess of men he catched. Just go out hunting regular like you go out hunting possum. He catch you and go home to his wife and family. Ain't thought about you going home to yours. Joe Turner catched me when my little girl was born. Wasn't nothing but a little baby sucking on her mama's titty when he catched me. Joe Turner catched me in nineteen hundred and one. Kept me seven years until nineteen hundred and eight. Kept everybody seven years. He'd go out hunting and bring back forty men at a time. And keep them seven years.

I was walking down this road in this little town outside of Memphis. Come up on these fellows gambling. I was a deacon in the Abundant Life Church. I stopped to preach to these fellows to see if maybe I could turn some of them from their sinning when Joe Turner, brother of the Governor of the great sovereign state of Tennessee, swooped down on us and grabbed everybody there. Kept us all seven years.

My wife Martha gone from me after Joe Turner catched me. Got out from under Joe Turner on his birthday. Me and forty other men put in our seven years and he let us go on his birthday. I made it back to Henry Thompson's place where me and Martha was sharecropping and Martha's gone. She taken my little girl and left her with her mama and took off North. We been looking for her ever since. That's been going on four years now we been looking. That's the only thing I know to do. I just wanna see her face so I can get me a starting place in the world. The world got to start somewhere. That's what I been looking for. I been wandering a long time in somebody else's world. When I find my wife that be the making of my own.

Bynum: Joe Turner tell why he caught you? You ever asked him that?

Loomis: I ain't never seen Joe Turner. Seen him to where I could touch him. I asked one of them fellows one time why he catch niggers. Asked him what I got he want? Why don't he keep on to himself? Why he got to catch me going down the road by my lonesome? He told me I was worthless. Worthless is something you throw away. Something you don't bother with. I ain't seen him throw me away. Wouldn't even let me stay away when I was by my lonesome. I ain't tried to catch him when he going down the road. So I must got something he want. What I got?

Seth: He just want you to do his work for him. That's all.

Loomis: I can look at him and see where he big and strong enough to do his own work. So it can't be that. He must want something he ain't got.

Bynum: That ain't hard to figure out. What he wanted was your song. He wanted to have that song to be his. He thought by catching you he could learn that song. Every nigger he catch he's looking for the one he can learn that song from. Now he's got you bound up to where you can't sing your own song. Couldn't sing it them seven years 'cause you was afraid he would snatch it from under you. But you still got it. You just forgot how to sing it.

Loomis (to Bynum): I know who you are. You one of them bones people.

(The lights go down to black.)

## Scene 3

The lights come up on the kitchen. It is the following morning. Mattie and Bynum sit at the table. Bertha busies herself at the stove.

*Bynum*: Good luck don't know no special time to come. You sleep with that up under your pillow and good luck can't help but come to you. Sometimes it come and go and you don't even know it's been there.

*Bertha*: Bynum, why don't you leave that gal alone? She don't wanna be hearing all that. Why don't you go on and get out the way and leave her alone?

*Bynum* (*getting up.*): Alright, alright. But you mark what I'm saying. It'll draw it to you just like a magnet.

(*Bynum exits up the stairs and Loomis enters.*)

*Bertha*: I got some grits here, Mr. Loomis.

(*Bertha sets a bowl on the table.*)

If I was you, Mattie, I wouldn't go getting all tied up with Bynum in that stuff. That kind of stuff, even if it do work for a while, it don't last. That just get people more mixed up than they is already. And I wouldn't waste my time fretting over Jeremy either. I seen it coming. I seen it when she first come here. She that kind of woman run off with the first man got a dollar to spend on her. Jeremy just young. He don't know what he getting into. That gal don't mean him no good. She's just using him to keep from being by herself. That's the worst use of a man you can have. You ought to be glad to wash him out of your hair. I done seen all kind of men. I done seen them come and go through here. Jeremy ain't had enough to him for you. You need a man who's got some understanding and who willing to work with that understanding to come to the best he can. You got your time coming. You just tries too hard and can't understand why it don't work for you. Trying to figure it out don't do nothing but give you a troubled mind. Don't no man want a woman with a troubled mind.

You get all that trouble off your mind and just when it look like you ain't never gonna find what you want . . . you look up and it's standing right there. That's how I met my Seth. You gonna look up one day and find everything you want standing right in front of you. Been twenty-seven years now since that happened to me. But life ain't no happy-go-lucky time where everything be just like you want it. You got your time coming. You watch what Bertha's saying.

(*Seth enters.*)

*Seth*: Ho!

*Bertha*: What you doing come in here so late?

*Seth*: I was standing down there on Logan Street talking with the fellows. Henry Allen tried to sell me that old piece of horse he got.

(*He sees Loomis.*)

Today's Tuesday, Mr. Loomis.

*Bertha* (*pulling him toward the bedroom*): Come on in here and leave that man alone to eat his breakfast.

*Seth:* I ain't bothering nobody. I'm just reminding him what day it is.

(*Seth and Bertha exit into the bedroom.*)

*Loomis:* That dress got a color to it.

*Mattie:* Did you really see them things like you said? Them people come up out the ocean?

*Loomis:* It happened just like that, yeah.

*Mattie:* I hope you find your wife. It be good for your little girl for you to find her.

*Loomis:* Got to find her for myself. Find my starting place in the world. Find me a world I can fit in.

*Mattie:* I ain't never found no place for me to fit. Seem like all I do is start over. It ain't nothing to find no starting place in the world. You just start from where you find yourself.

*Loomis:* Got to find my wife. That be my starting place.

*Mattie:* What if you don't find her? What you gonna do then if you don't find her?

*Loomis:* She out there somewhere. Ain't no such thing as not finding her.

*Mattie:* How she got lost from you? Jack just walked away from me.

*Loomis:* Joe Turner split us up. Joe Turner turned the world upside-down. He bound me on to him for seven years.

*Mattie:* I hope you find her. It be good for you to find her.

*Loomis:* I been watching you. I been watching you watch me.

*Mattie:* I was just trying to figure out if you seen things like you said.

*Loomis* (*getting up*): Come here and let me touch you. I been watching you. You a full woman. A man needs a full woman. Come on and be with me.

*Mattie:* I ain't got enough for you. You'd use me up too fast.

*Loomis:* Herald Loomis got a mind seem like you a part of it since I first seen you. It's been a long time since I seen a full woman. I can smell you from here. I know you got Herald Loomis on your mind, can't keep him apart from it. Come on and be with Herald Loomis.

(*Loomis has crossed to Mattie. He touches her awkwardly, gently, tenderly. Inside he howls like a lost wolf pup whose hunger is deep. He goes to touch her but finds he cannot.*)

I done forgot how to touch.

(*The lights fade to black.*)

### Scene 4

*It is early the next morning. The lights come up on Zonia and Reuben in the yard.*

*Reuben:* Something spooky going on around here. Last night Mr. Bynum was out in the yard singing and talking to the wind . . . and the wind it just be talking back to him. Did you hear it?

*Zonia:* I heard it. I was scared to get up and look. I thought it was a storm.

*Reuben:* That wasn't no storm. That was Mr. Bynum. First he say something . . . and the wind it say back to him.

*Zonia:* I heard it. Was you scared? I was scared.

*Reuben:* And then this morning . . . I seen Miss Mabel!

*Zonia:* Who Miss Mabel?

*Reuben:* Mr. Seth's mother. He got her picture hanging up in the house. She been dead.

*Zonia:* How you seen her if she been dead?

*Reuben:* Zonia . . . if I tell you something you promise you won't tell anybody?

*Zonia:* I promise.

*Reuben:* It was early this morning . . . I went out to the coop to feed the pigeons. I was down on the ground like this to open up the door to the coop . . . when all of a sudden I seen some feets in front of me. I looked up . . . and there was Miss Mabel standing there.

*Zonia:* Reuben, you better stop telling that! You ain't seen nobody!

*Reuben:* Naw, it's the truth. I swear! I seen her just like I see you. Look . . . you can see where she hit me with her cane.

*Zonia:* Hit you? What she hit you for?

*Reuben:* She says, "Didn't you promise Eugene something?" Then she hit me with her cane. She say, "Let them pigeons go." Then she hit me again. That's what made them marks.

*Zonia:* Jeez man . . . get away from me. You done see a haunt!

*Reuben:* Shhhh. You promised, Zonia!

*Zonia:* You sure it wasn't Miss Bertha come over there and hit you with her hoe?

*Reuben:* It wasn't no Miss Bertha. I told you it was Miss Mabel. She was standing right there by the coop. She had this light coming out of her and then she just melted away.

*Zonia:* What she had on?

*Reuben:* A white dress. Ain't even had no shoes or nothing. Just had on that white dress and them big hands . . . and that cane she hit me with.

*Zonia:* How you reckon she knew about the pigeons? You reckon Eugene told her?

*Reuben:* I don't know. I sure ain't asked her none. She say Eugene was waiting on them pigeons. Say he couldn't go back home till I let them go. I couldn't get the door to the coop open fast enough.

*Zonia:* Maybe she an angel? From the way you say she look with that white dress. Maybe she an angel.

*Reuben:* Mean as she was . . . how she gonna be an angel? She used to chase us out her yard and frown up and look evil all the time.

*Zonia:* That don't mean she can't be no angel 'cause of how she looked and 'cause she wouldn't let no kids play in her yard. It go by if you got any spots on your heart and if you pray and go to church.

*Reuben:* What about she hit me with her cane? An angel wouldn't hit me with her cane.

*Zonia:* I don't know. She might. I still say she was an angel.

*Reuben:* You reckon Eugene the one who sent old Miss Mabel?

*Zonia:* Why he send her? Why he don't come himself?

*Reuben:* Figured if he send her maybe that'll make me listen. 'Cause she old.

*Zonia:* What you think it feel like?

*Reuben:* What?

*Zonia:* Being dead.

*Reuben:* Like being sleep only you don't know nothing and can't move no more.

*Zonia:* If Miss Mabel can come back . . . then maybe Eugene can come back too.

*Reuben:* We can go down to the hideout like we used to! He could come back everyday! It be just like he ain't dead.

*Zonia:* Maybe that ain't right for him to come back. Feel kinda funny to be playing games with a haunt.

*Reuben:* Yeah . . . what if everybody came back? What if Miss Mabel came back just like she ain't dead? Where you and your daddy gonna sleep then?

*Zonia:* Maybe they go back at night and don't need no place to sleep.

*Reuben:* It still don't seem right. I'm sure gonna miss Eugene. He's the bestest friend anybody ever had.

*Zonia:* My daddy say if you miss somebody too much it can kill you. Say he missed me till it liked to killed him.

*Reuben:* What if your mama's already dead and all the time you looking for her?

*Zonia:* Naw, she ain't dead. My daddy say he can smell her.

*Reuben:* You can't smell nobody that ain't here. Maybe he smelling old Miss Bertha. Maybe Miss Bertha your mama?

*Zonia:* Naw, she ain't. My mama got long pretty hair and she five feet from the ground!

*Reuben:* Your daddy say when you leaving?

*(Zonia doesn't respond.)*

Maybe you gonna stay in Mr. Seth's house and don't go looking for your mama no more.

*Zonia:* He say we got to leave on Saturday.

*Reuben:* Dag! You just only been here for a little while. Don't seem like nothing ever stay the same.

*Zonia:* He say he got to find her. Find him a place in the world.

*Reuben:* He could find him a place in Mr. Seth's house.

*Zonia:* It don't look like we never gonna find her.

*Reuben:* Maybe he find her by Saturday then you don't have to go.

*Zonia:* I don't know.

*Reuben:* You look like a spider!

*Zonia:* I ain't no spider!

*Reuben:* Got them long skinny arms and legs. You look like one of them Black Widows.

*Zonia:* I ain't no Black Window nothing! My name is Zonia!

*Reuben:* That's what I'm gonna call you . . . Spider.

*Zonia:* You can call me that, but I don't have to answer.

*Reuben:* You know what? I think maybe I be your husband when I grow up.

*Zonia:* How you know?

*Reuben:* I ask my grandpap how you know and he say when the moon falls into a girl's eyes that how you know.

*Zonia:* Did it fall into my eyes?

*Reuben:* Not that I can tell. Maybe I ain't old enough. Maybe you ain't old enough.

*Zonia:* So there! I don't know why you telling me that lie!

*Reuben:* That don't mean nothing 'cause I can't see it. I know it's there. Just the way you look at me sometimes look like the moon might have been in your eyes.

*Zonia:* That don't mean nothing if you can't see it. You supposed to see it.

*Reuben:* Shucks, I see it good enough for me. You ever let anybody kiss you?

*Zonia:* Just my daddy. He kiss me on the cheek.

*Reuben:* It's better on the lips. Can I kiss you on the lips?

*Zonia:* I don't know. You ever kiss anybody before?

*Reuben:* I had a cousin let me kiss her on the lips one time. Can I kiss you?

*Zonia:* Okay.

*(Reuben kisses her and lays his head against her chest.)*

What you doing?

*Reuben:* Listening. Your heart singing?

*Zonia:* It is not.

*Reuben:* Just beating like a drum. Let's kiss again.

*(They kiss again.)*

Now you mine, Spider. You my girl, okay?

*Zonia:* Okay.

*Reuben:* When I get grown, I come looking for you.

*Zonia:* Okay.

*(The lights fade to black.)*


## Scene 5

*The lights come up on the kitchen. It is Saturday. Bynum, Loomis, and Zonia sit at the table. Bertha prepares breakfast. Zonia has on a white dress.*

*Bynum:* With all this rain we been having he might have ran into some washed-out roads. If that wagon got stuck in the mud he's liable to be still upriver somewhere. If he's upriver then he ain't coming until tomorrow.

*Loomis:* Today's Saturday. He say he be here on Saturday.

*Bertha:* Zonia, you gonna eat your breakfast this morning.

*Zonia:* Yes, ma'am.

*Bertha*: I don't know how you expect to get any bigger if you don't eat. I ain't never seen a child that didn't eat. You about as skinny as a bean pole.

*(Pause.)*

Mr. Loomis, there's a place down on Wylie. Zeke Mayweather got a house down there. You ought to see if he got any rooms.

*(Loomis doesn't respond.)*

Well, you're welcome to some breakfast before you move on.

*(Mattie enters from the stairs.)*

*Mattie*: Good morning.

*Bertha*: Morning, Mattie. Sit on down there and get you some breakfast.

*Bynum*: Well, Mattie Campbell, you been sleeping with that up under your pillow like I told you?

*Bertha*: Bynum, I done told you to leave that gal alone with all that stuff. You around here meddling in other people's lives. She don't want to hear all that. You ain't doing nothing but confusing her with that stuff.

*Mattie (to Loomis)*: You all fixing to move on?

*Loomis*: Today's Saturday. I'm paid up till Saturday.

*Mattie*: Where you going to?

*Loomis*: Gonna find my wife.

*Mattie*: You going off to another city?

*Loomis*: We gonna see where the road take us. Ain't no telling where we wind up.

*Mattie*: Eleven years is a long time. Your wife . . . she might have taken up with someone else. People do that when they get lost from each other.

*Loomis*: Zonia. Come on, we gonna find your mama.

*(Loomis and Zonia cross to the door.)*

*Mattie (to Zonia)*: Zonia, Mattie got a ribbon here match your dress. Want Mattie to fix your hair with her ribbon?

*(Zonia nods. Mattie ties the ribbon in her hair.)*

There . . . it got a color just like your dress. *(To Loomis.)* I hope you find her. I hope you be happy.

*Loomis*: A man looking for a woman be lucky to find you. You a good woman, Mattie. Keep a good heart.

*(Loomis and Zonia exit.)*

*Bertha*: I been watching that man for two weeks . . . and that's the closest I come to seeing him act civilized. I don't know what's between you all, Mattie . . . but the only thing that man needs is somebody to make him laugh. That's all you need in the world is love and laughter. That's all anybody needs. To have love in one hand and laughter in the other.

*(Bertha moves about the kitchen as though blessing it and chasing away the huge sadness that seems to envelop it. It is a dance and demonstration of her own magic,*

*her own remedy that is centuries old and to which she is connected by the muscles of her heart and the blood's memory.)*

You hear me, Mattie? I'm talking about laughing. The kind of laugh that comes from way deep inside. To just stand and laugh and let life flow right through you. Just laugh to let yourself know you're alive.

*(She begins to laugh. It is a near-hysterical laughter that is a celebration of life, both its pain and its blessing. Mattie and Bynum join in the laughter. Seth enters from the front door.)*

Seth: Well, I see you all having fun.

*(Seth begins to laugh with them.)*

That Loomis fellow standing up there on the corner watching the house. He standing right up there on Manila Street.

Bertha: Don't you get started on him. The man done left out of here and that's the last I wanna hear of it. You about to drive me crazy with that man.

Seth: I just say he standing up there on the corner. Acting sneaky like he always do. He can stand up there all he want. As long as he don't come back in here.

*(There is a knock on the door. Seth goes to answer it. Enter Martha Loomis [Pentecost]. She is a young woman about twenty-eight. She is dressed as befitting a member of an Evangelist church. Rutherford Selig follows.)*

Seth: Look here, Bertha. It's Martha Pentecost. Come on in, Martha. Who that with you? Oh . . . that's Selig. Come on in, Selig.

Bertha: Come on in, Martha. It's sure good to see you.

Bynum: Rutherford Selig, you a sure enough first-class People Finder!

Selig: She was right out there in Rankin. You take that first righthand road . . . right there at that church on Wooster Street. I started to go right-past and something told me to stop at the church and see if they needed any dustpans.

Seth: Don't she look good, Bertha.

Bertha: Look all nice and healthy.

Martha: Mr. Bynum . . . Selig told me my little girl was here.

Seth: There's some fellow around here say he your husband. Say his name is Loomis. Say you his wife.

Martha: Is my little girl with him?

Seth: Yeah, he got a little girl with him. I wasn't gonna tell him where you was. Not the way this fellow look. So he got Selig to find you.

Martha: Where they at? They upstairs?

Seth: He was standing right up there on Manila Street. I had to ask him to leave 'cause of how he was carrying on. He come in here one night—

*(The door opens and Loomis and Zonia enter. Martha and Loomis stare at each other.)*

Loomis: Hello, Martha.

Martha: Herald . . . Zonia?

*Loomis:* You ain't waited for me, Martha. I got out the place looking to see your face. Seven years I waited to see your face.

*Martha:* Herald, I been looking for you. I wasn't but two months behind you when you went to my mama's and got Zonia. I been looking for you ever since.

*Loomis:* Joe Turner let me loose and I felt all turned around inside. I just wanted to see your face to know that the world was still there. Make sure everything still in its place so I could reconnect myself together. I got there and you was gone, Martha.

*Martha:* Herald . . .

*Loomis:* Left my little girl motherless in the world.

*Martha:* I didn't leave her motherless, Herald. Reverend Tolliver wanted to move the church up North 'cause of all the trouble the colored folks was having down there. Nobody knew what was gonna happen traveling them roads. We didn't even know if we was gonna make it up here or not. I left her with my mama so she be safe. That was better than dragging her out on the road having to duck and hide from people. Wasn't no telling what was gonna happen to us. I didn't leave her motherless in the world. I been looking for you.

*Loomis:* I come up on Henry Thompson's place after seven years of living in hell, and all I'm looking to do is see your face.

*Martha:* Herald, I didn't know if you was ever coming back. They told me Joe Turner had you and my whole world split half in two. My whole life shattered. It was like I had poured it in a cracked jar and it all leaked out the bottom. When it go like that there ain't nothing you can do to put it back together. You talking about Henry Thompson's place like I'm still gonna be working the land by myself. How I'm gonna do that? You wasn't gone but two months and Henry Thompson kicked me off his land and I ain't had no place to go but to my mama's. I stayed and waited there for five years before I woke up one morning and decided that you was dead. Even if you weren't, you was dead to me. I wasn't gonna carry you with me no more. So I killed you in my heart. I buried you. I mourned you. And then I picked up what was left and went on to make life without you. I was a young woman with life at my beckon. I couldn't drag you behind me like a sack of cotton.

*Loomis:* I just been waiting to look on your face to say my goodbye. That goodbye got so big at times, seem like it was gonna swallow me up. Like Jonah in the whale's belly I sat up in that goodbye for three years. That goodbye kept me out on the road searching. Not looking on women in their houses. It kept me bound up to the road. All the time that goodbye swelling up in my chest till I'm about to bust. Now that I see your face I can say my goodbye and make my own world.

*(Loomis takes Zonia's hand and presents her to Martha.)*

Martha . . . here go your daughter. I tried to take care of her. See that she had something to eat. See that she was out of the elements. Whatever I know I tried to teach her. Now she need to learn from her mother whatever you got to teach her. That way she won't be no one-sided person.

(*Loomis stoops to Zonia.*)

Zonia, you go live with your mama. She a good woman. You go on with her and listen to her good. You my daughter and I love you like a daughter. I hope to see you again in the world somewhere. I'll never forget you.

Zonia (*throws her arms around Loomis in a panic*): I won't get no bigger! My bones won't get no bigger! They won't! I promise! Take me with you till we keep searching and never finding. I won't get no bigger! I promise!

Loomis: Go on and do what I told you now.

Martha (*goes to Zonia and comforts her*): It's alright, baby. Mama's here. Mama's here. Don't worry. Don't cry.

(*Martha turns to Bynum.*)

Mr. Bynum, I don't know how to thank you. God bless you.

Loomis: It was you! All the time it was you that bind me up! You bound me to the road!

Bynum: I ain't bind you, Herald Loomis. You can't bind what don't cling.

Loomis: Everywhere I go people wanna bind me up. Joe Turner wanna bind me up! Reverend Tolliver wanna bind me up. You wanna bind me up. Everybody wanna bind me up. Well, Joe Turner's come and gone and Herald Loomis ain't for no binding. I ain't gonna let nobody bind me up!

(*Loomis pulls out a knife.*)

Bynum: It wasn't you, Herald Loomis. I ain't bound you. I bound the little girl to her mother. That's who I bound. You binding yourself. You bound onto your song. All you got to do is stand up and sing it, Herald Loomis. It's right there kicking at your throat. All you got to do is sing it. Then you be free.

Martha: Herald . . . look at yourself! Standing there with a knife in your hand. You done gone over to the devil. Come on . . . put down the knife. You got to look to Jesus. Even if you done fell away from the church you can be saved again. The Bible say, "The Lord is my shepherd I shall not want. He maketh me to lie down in green pastures. He leads me beside the still water. He restoreth my soul. He leads me in the path of righteousness for His name's sake. Even though I walk through the shadow of death—"

Loomis: That's just where I be walking!

Martha: "I shall fear no evil. For Thou art with me. Thy rod and thy staff, they comfort me."

Loomis: You can't tell me nothing about no valleys. I done been all across the valleys and the hills and the mountains and the oceans.

Martha: "Thou preparest a table for me in the presence of my enemies."

Loomis: And all I seen was a bunch of niggers dazed out of their woolly heads. And Mr. Jesus Christ standing there in the middle of them, grinning.

*Martha:* "Thou anointest my head with oil, my cup runneth over."

*Loomis:* He grin that big old grin . . . and niggers wallowing at his feet.

*Martha:* "Surely goodness and mercy shall follow me all the days of my life, and I shall dwell in the house of the Lord forever."

*Loomis:* Great big old white man . . . your Mr. Jesus Christ. Standing there with a whip in one hand and tote board in another, and them niggers swimming in a sea of cotton. And he counting. He tallying up the cotton. "Well, Jeremiah . . . what's the matter, you ain't picked but two hundred pounds of cotton today? Got to put you on half rations." And Jeremiah go back and lay up there on his half rations and talk about what a nice man Mr. Jesus Christ is 'cause he give him salvation after he die. Something wrong here. Something don't fit right!

*Martha:* You got to open up your heart and have faith, Herald. This world is just a trial for the next. Jesus offers you salvation.

*Loomis:* I been wading in the water. I been walking all over the River Jordan. But what it get me, huh? I done been baptized with blood of the lamb and the fire of the Holy Ghost. But what I got, huh? I got salvation? My enemies all around me picking the flesh from my bones. I'm choking on my own blood and all you got to give me is salvation?

*Martha:* You got to be clean, Herald. You got to be washed with the blood of the lamb.

*Loomis:* Blood make you clean? You clean with blood?

*Martha:* Jesus bled for you. He's the Lamb of God who takest away the sins of the world.

*Loomis:* I don't need nobody to bleed for me! I can bleed for myself.

*Martha:* You got to be something, Herald. You just can't be alive. Life don't mean nothing unless it got a meaning.

*Loomis:* What kind of meaning you got? What kind of clean you got, woman? You want blood? Blood make you clean? You clean with blood?

*(Loomis slashes himself across the chest. He rubs the blood over his face and comes to a realization.)*

I'm standing! I'm standing. My legs stood up! I'm standing now!

*(Having found his song, the song of self-sufficiency, fully resurrected, cleansed and given breath, free from any encumbrance other than the workings of his own heart and the bonds of the flesh, having accepted the responsibility for his own presence in the world, he is free to soar above the environs that weighed and pushed his spirit into terrifying contractions.)*

Goodbye, Martha.

*(Loomis turns and exits, the knife still in his hands. Mattie looks about the room and rushes out after him.)*

*Bynum:* Herald Loomis, you shining! You shining like new money!

*The lights go down to BLACK.*

# 40  *Criticism: On Drama*

## Aristotle (384–322 B.C.)

TRAGEDY                                                      (about 330 B.C.)

Translated by L. J. Potts

Tragedy is an imitation of an action of high importance, complete and of some amplitude; in language enhanced by distinct and varying beauties; acted not narrated; by means of pity and fear effecting its purgation of these emotions. By the beauties enhancing the language I mean rhythm and melody; by "distinct and varying" I mean that some are produced by meter alone, and others at another time by melody. . . .

What will produce the tragic effect? Since, then, tragedy, to be at its finest, requires a complex, not a simple, structure, and its structure should also imitate fearful and pitiful events (for that is the peculiarity of this sort of imitation), it is clear: first, that decent people must not be shown passing from good fortune to misfortune (for that is not fearful or pitiful but disgusting); again, vicious people must not be shown passing from misfortune to good fortune (for that is the most untragic situation possible—it has none of the requisites, it is neither humane, nor pitiful, nor fearful); nor again should an utterly evil man fall from good fortune into misfortune (for though a plot of that kind would be humane, it would not induce pity or fear—pity is induced by undeserved misfortune, and fear by the misfortunes of normal people, so that this situation will be neither pitiful nor fearful). So we are left with the man between these extremes: that is to say, the kind of man who neither is distinguished for excellence and virtue, nor comes to grief on account of baseness and vice, but on account of some error; a man of great reputation and prosperity, like Oedipus and Thyestes and conspicuous people of such families as theirs. So, to be well formed, a fable must be single rather than (as some say) double—there must be no change from misfortune to good fortune, but only the opposite, from good fortune to misfortune; the cause must not be vice, but a great error; and the man must be either of the type specified or better, rather than worse. This is borne out by the practice of poets; at first they picked a fable at random and made an inventory of its contents, but now the finest tragedies are plotted, and concern a few families—for example, the tragedies about Alcmeon, Oedipus, Orestes, Meleager, Thyestes, Telephus, and any others whose lives were attended by terrible experiences or doings.

This is the plot that will produce the technically finest tragedy. Those critics are therefore wrong who censure Euripides on this very ground—because he does this in his tragedies, and many of them end in misfortune; for it is, as I have said, the right thing to do. This is clearly demonstrated on the stage in the competitions, where such plays, if they succeed, are the most tragic, and Euripides, even if he is inefficient in every other respect, still shows himself the most tragic of our poets. The next best plot, which is said by some people to be the best, is the tragedy with a double plot, like the *Odyssey,* ending in one way for the better people and in the opposite way for the worse. But it is the weakness of theatrical performances that gives priority to this kind; when poets write what the audience would like to happen, they are in leading strings.° This is not the pleasure proper to tragedy, but rather to comedy, where the greatest enemies in the fable, say Orestes and Aegisthus, make friends and go off at the end, and nobody is killed by anybody.

The pity and fear can be brought about by the *mise en scène*°; but they can also come from the mere plotting of the incidents, which is preferable, and better poetry. For, without seeing anything, the fable ought to have been so plotted that if one heard the bare facts, the chain of circumstances would make one shudder and pity. That would happen to any one who heard the fable of the *Oedipus.* To produce this effect by the *mise en scène* is less artistic and puts one at the mercy of the technician; and those who use it not to frighten but merely to startle have lost touch with tragedy altogether. We should not try to get all sorts of pleasure from tragedy, but the particular tragic pleasure. And clearly, since this pleasure coming from pity and fear has to be produced by imitation, it is by his handling of the incidents that the poet must create it.

. . . And in the characterization, as in the plotting of the incidents, the aim should always be either necessity or probability: so that they say or do such things as it is necessary or probable that they would, being what they are; and that for this to follow that is either necessary or probable. (Thus it is clear that the untying of the fable should follow on the circumstances of the fable itself, and not be done *ex machina,* as it is in the *Medea,* or in Book Two of the *Iliad.* But the *deus ex machina*° should be used for matters outside the drama—either things that

---

*in leading strings:* each is led, as by a string, wherever the audience wills.     *mise en scène:* arrangement of actors and scenery.     *deus ex machina:* "god out of the machine," or an arbitrary way of concluding a play. For a discussion of this term see page 1104.

happened before and that man could not know, or future events that need to be announced prophetically; for we allow the gods to see everything. As for extravagant incidents, there should be none in the story, or if there are they should be kept outside the tragedy, as is the one in the *Oedipus* of Sophocles.)

Since tragedy is an imitation of people above the normal, we must be like good portrait-painters, who follow the original model closely, but refine on it; in the same way the poet, in imitating people whose character is choleric or phlegmatic, and so forth, must keep them as they are and at the same time make them attractive. So Homer made Achilles noble, as well as a pattern of obstinacy.

—*Poetics*, VI, XIII–XV

## E. R. Dodds (1893–1979)

SOPHOCLES AND DIVINE JUSTICE                                                         1966

I take it, then, as reasonably certain that while Sophocles did not pretend that the gods are in any human sense just, he nevertheless held that they are entitled to our worship. Are those two opinions incompatible? Here once more we cannot hope to understand Greek literature if we persist in looking at it through Christian spectacles. To the Christian it is a necessary part of piety to believe that God is just. And so it was to Plato and to the Stoics. But the older world saw no such necessity. If you doubt this, take down the *Iliad* and read Achilles' opinion of what divine justice amounts to (xxiv. 525–33); or take down the Bible and read the Book of Job. Disbelief in divine justice as measured by human yardsticks can perfectly well be associated with deep religious feelings. "Men," said Heraclitus, "find some things unjust, other things just; but in the eyes of God all things are beautiful and good and just." I think that Sophocles would have agreed.

—On Misunderstanding the *Oedipus Rex*

## Thomas Rymer (1643?–1713)

THE FAULTS OF *OTHELLO*                                                              1692

Nothing is more odious in Nature than an improbable lie; and, certainly, never was any play fraught, like this of *Othello*, with improbabilities. . . . Othello is made a Venetian general. We see nothing done by him, nor related concerning him, that comports with the condition of a general, or indeed of a man, unless the killing himself, to avoid a death the law was about to inflict upon him. When his jealousy had wrought him up to a resolution of his taking revenge for the supposed injury, he sets Iago to the fighting part, to kill Cassio, and chooses himself to murder the silly woman his wife, that was like to make no resistance.

His love and his jealousy are no part of a soldier's character, unless for comedy. . . .

So much ado, so much stress, so much passion and repetition about an handkerchief! Why was this not called *The Tragedy of the Handkerchief?* Had it been Desdemona's garter, the sagacious Moor might have smelt a rat, but the handkerchief is so remote a trifle, no booby . . . could make any consequence from it. . . .

Desdemona dropped her handkerchief; therefore, she must be stifled. Othello, by law to be broken on the wheel, by the poet's cunning escapes with cutting his own throat. Cassio, for I know not what, comes off with a broken shin. Iago murders his benefactor Roderigo, as this were poetical gratitude. Iago is not yet killed, because there never yet was such a villian alive.

—*A Short View of Tragedy*

## W. H. Auden (1907–1973)

IAGO AS A TRIUMPHANT VILLAIN 1962

Any consideration of the Tragedy of Othello must be primarily occupied, not with its official hero but with its villain. I cannot think of any other play in which only one character performs personal actions—all the *deeds* are Iago's— and all the others without exception only exhibit behavior. In marrying each other, Othello and Desdemona have performed a deed, but this took place before the play begins. Nor can I think of another play in which the villain is so completely triumphant: everything Iago sets out to do, he accomplishes—(among his goals, I include his self-destruction). Even Cassio, who survives, is maimed for life.

If *Othello* is a tragedy—and one certainly cannot call it a comedy—it is tragic in a peculiar way. In most tragedies the fall of the hero from glory to misery and death is the work, either of the gods, or of his own freely chosen acts, or, more commonly, a mixture of both. But the fall of Othello is the work of another human being; nothing he says or does originates with himself. In consequence we feel pity for him but no respect; our aesthetic respect is reserved for Iago.

Iago is a wicked man. The wicked man, the stage villain, as a subject of serious dramatic interest does not, so far as I know, appear in the drama of western Europe before the Elizabethans. In the mystery plays, the wicked characters, like Satan or Herod, are treated comically, but the theme of the triumphant villain cannot be treated comically because the suffering he inflicts is real.

—"The Joker in the Pack"

Other dramatists can only gain attention by hyperbolical or aggravated characters, by fabulous and unexampled excellence or depravity, as the writers of barbarous romances invigorated the reader by a giant and a dwarf; and he that should form his expectations of human affairs from the play or from the tale would be equally deceived. Shakespeare has no heroes; his scenes are occupied only by men, who act and speak as the reader thinks that he should himself have spoken or acted on the same occasion; even where the agency is supernatural, the dialogue is level with life. Other writers disguise the most natural passions and most frequent incidents so that he who contemplates them in the book will not know them in the world: Shakespeare approximates the remote, and familiarizes the wonderful; the event which he represents will not happen, but, if it were possible, its effects would probably be such as he has assigned; and it may be said that he has not only shown human nature as it acts in real exigencies, but as it would be found in trials to which it cannot be exposed. . . .

Shakespeare's plays are not in the rigorous and critical sense either tragedies or comedies, but compositions of a distinct kind; exhibiting the real state of sublunary nature, which partakes of good and evil, joy and sorrow, mingled with endless variety of proportion and innumerable modes of combination; and expressing the course of the world, in which the loss of one is the gain of another; in which, at the same time, the reveler is hasting to his wine, and the mourner burying his friend; in which the malignity of one is sometimes defeated by the frolic of another; and many mischiefs and many benefits are done and hindered without design.

Out of this chaos of mingled purposes and casualties the ancient poets, according to the laws which custom had prescribed, selected some of the crimes of men, and some their absurdities; some the momentous vicissitudes of life, and some the lighter occurrences; some the terrors of distress, and some the gaieties of prosperity. Thus rose the two modes of imitation, known by the names of *tragedy* and *comedy*, compositions intended to promote different ends by contrary means, and considered as so little allied that I do not recollect among the Greeks or Romans a single writer who attempted both.

Shakespeare has united the powers of exciting laughter and sorrow not only in one mind, but in one composition. Almost all his plays are divided between serious and ludicrous characters, and, in the successive evolutions of the design, sometimes produce seriousness and sorrow, and sometimes levity and laughter.

That this is a practice contrary to the rules of criticism will be readily allowed; but there is always an appeal open from criticism to nature. The end of writing is to instruct; the end of poetry is to instruct by pleasing. That the mingled drama may convey all the instruction of tragedy or comedy cannot be denied, because it includes both in its alternations of exhibitions, and approaches nearer than either to the appearance of life, by showing how great machinations and slender designs may promote or obviate one another, and the high and the low co-operate in the general system by unavoidable concatenation.

—*Preface to Shakespeare*

AN ASIAN CULTURE LOOKS AT SHAKESPEARE                    1982

Is translation possible? I first found myself asking this question in the Far East, when I was given the task of translating T. S. Eliot's *The Waste Land* into Indonesian. The difficulties began with the first line: "April is the cruellest month . . . " This I rendered as "*Bulan Abril ia-lah bulan yang dzalim sa-kali . . .*" I had to take *dzalim* from Arabic, since Indonesian did not, at that time, seem to possess a word for *cruel*. The term was accepted, but not the notion that a month, as opposed to a person or institution, could be cruel. Moreover, even if a month could be cruel, how—in the tropics where all the months are the same and the concepts of spring and winter do not exist—can one month be crueller than another? When I came to *forgetful snow*—rendered as *thalji berlupa*—I had to borrow a highly poetical word from the Persian, acceptable as a useful descriptive device for the brown skin of the beloved but not known in terms of a climatic reality. And, again, how could this inanimate substance possess the faculty of forgetting? I gave up the task as hopeless. Evidently the imagery of *The Waste Land* does not relate to a universal experience but applies only to the northern hemisphere, with its temperate climate and tradition of spring and fertility rituals.

As a teacher in Malaysia, I had to consider with a mixed group of Malay, Chinese, Indian, and Eurasian students, seasoned with the odd Buginese, Achinese, and Japanese, a piece of representative postwar British fiction. Although the setting of the book is West Africa, I felt that its story was of universal import. It was a novel by Graham Greene called *The Heart of the Matter*—a tragic story about a police officer named Scobie who is a Catholic convert. He is in love with his wife but falls in love with another woman, discovers that he cannot repent of this adultery, makes a sacrilegious communion so that his very Catholic wife will not suspect that a love affair is in progress, then commits suicide in despair, trusting that God will thrust him into the outer darkness and be no longer agonized by the exploits of sinning Scobie. To us this is a tragic situation. To my Muslim students it was extremely funny. One girl said: "Why cannot this Mr. Scobie become a Muslim? Then he can have four wives and there is no problem."

The only author who seemed to have the quality of universal appeal in Malaysia was William Shakespeare. Despite the problems of translating him, there is always an intelligible residue. I remember seeing in a Borneo kampong the film of *Richard III* made by Laurence Olivier, and the illiterate tribe which surrounded me was most appreciative. They knew nothing here of literary history and nothing of the great world outside this jungle clearing. They took this film about mediaeval conspiracy and tyranny to be a kind of newsreel representation of contemporary England. They approved the mediaeval costumes because they resembled their own ceremonial dress. This story of the assassination of innocents, including children, Machiavellian massacre, and the eventual defeat of a tyrant was typical of their own history, even their contemporary experience, and they accepted Shakespeare as a great poet. Eliot would not have registered with them at all. Translation is not a matter of words only; it is a matter of making intelligible a whole culture. Evidently the Elizabethan culture was still primitive enough to survive transportation over much time and space.

—Spoken remarks on the "Importance of Translation"

## George Bernard Shaw (1856–1950)

IBSEN AND THE FAMILIAR SITUATION                                                    1913

Up to a certain point in the last act, A Doll's House is a play that might be turned into a very ordinary French drama by the excision of a few lines, and the substitution of a sentimental happy ending for the famous last scene: indeed the very first thing the theatrical wiseacres did with it was to effect exactly this transformation, with the result that the play thus pithed° had no success and attracted no notice worth mentioning. But at just that point in the last act, the heroine very unexpectedly (by the wiseacres) stops her emotional acting and says: "We must sit down and discuss all this that has been happening between us." And it was by this new technical feature: this addition of a new movement, as musicians would say, to the dramatic form, that A Doll's House conquered Europe and founded a new school of dramatic art. . . .

The drama was born of old from the union of two desires: the desire to have a dance and the desire to hear a story. The dance became a rant: the story became a situation. When Ibsen began to make plays, the art of the dramatist had shrunk into the art of contriving a situation. And it was held that the stranger the situation, the better the play. Ibsen saw that, on the contrary, the more familiar the situation, the more interesting the play. Shakespeare had put ourselves on the stage but not our situations. Our uncles seldom murder our fathers, and cannot legally marry our mothers; we do not meet witches; our kings are not as a rule stabbed and succeeded by their stabbers; and when we raise money by bills we do not promise to pay pounds of our flesh. Ibsen supplies the want left by Shakespeare. He gives us not only ourselves, but ourselves in our own situations. The things that happen to his stage figures are things that happen to us. One consequence is that his plays are much more important to us than Shakespeare's. Another is that they are capable both of hurting us cruelly and of filling us with excited hopes of escape from idealistic tyrannies, and with visions of intenser life in the future.

—The Quintessence of Ibsenism (second edition)

---

pithed: killed (to pith is to kill an animal by severing its spinal cord).

## Virginia Woolf (1882–1941)

### What If Shakespeare Had Had a Sister? 1929

Let me imagine, since facts are so hard to come by, what would have happened had Shakespeare had a wonderfully gifted sister, called Judith, let us say. Shakespeare himself went, very probably—his mother was an heiress—to the grammar school, where he may have learnt Latin—Ovid, Virgil and Horace—and the elements of grammar and logic. He was, it is well known, a wild boy who poached rabbits, perhaps shot a deer, and had, rather sooner than he should have done, to marry a woman in the neighborhood, who bore him a child rather quicker than was right. That escapade sent him to seek his fortune in London. He had, it seemed, a taste for the theater; he began by holding horses at the stage door. Very soon he got work in the theater, became a successful actor, and lived at the hub of the universe, meeting everybody, knowing everybody, practicing his art on the boards, exercising his wits in the streets, and even getting access to the palace of the queen. Meanwhile his extraordinarily gifted sister, let us suppose, remained at home. She was as adventurous, as imaginative, as agog to see the world as he was. But she was not sent to school. She had no chance of learning grammar and logic, let alone of reading Horace and Virgil. She picked up a book now and then, one of her brother's perhaps, and read a few pages. But then her parents came in and told her to mend the stockings or mind the stew and not moon about with books and papers. They would have spoken sharply but kindly, for they were substantial people who knew the conditions of life for a woman and loved their daughter—indeed, more likely than not she was the apple of her father's eye. Perhaps she scribbled some pages up in an apple loft on the sly, but was careful to hide them or set fire to them. Soon, however, before she was out of her teens, she was to be betrothed to the son of a neighboring wool-stapler. She cried out that marriage was hateful to her, and for that she was severely beaten by her father. Then he ceased to scold her. He begged her instead not to hurt him, not to shame him in this matter of her marriage. He would give her a chain of beads or a fine petticoat, he said; and there were tears in his eyes. How could she disobey him? How could she break his heart? The force of her own gift alone drove her to it. She made up a small parcel of her belongings, let herself down by a rope one summer's night and took the road to London. She was not seventeen. The birds that sang in the hedge were not more musical than she was. She had the quickest fancy, a gift like her brother's, for the tune of words. Like him, she had a taste for the theater. She stood at the stage door; she wanted to act, she said. Men laughed in her face. The manager—a fat, loose-lipped man—guffawed. He bellowed something about poodles dancing and women acting—no woman, he said, could possibly be an actress. He hinted—you can imagine what. She could get no training in her craft. Could she even seek her dinner in a tavern or roam the streets at midnight? Yet her genius was for fiction and lusted to feed abundantly upon the lives of men and women and the study of their ways. At last—for she was very young, oddly like Shakespeare the poet in her face, with the same grey eyes and rounded brows—at last Nick Greene the actor-manager took pity on her; she found herself with child by that gentleman and so—who shall measure the heat and violence of the poet's heart when caught and tangled in a woman's body?—killed herself one winter's night and lies buried at some cross-roads where the omnibuses now stop outside the Elephant and Castle.

That, more or less, is how the story would run, I think, if a woman in Shakespeare's day had had Shakespeare's genius. . . . Any woman born with a great gift in the sixteenth century would certainly have gone crazed, shot herself, or ended her days in some lonely cottage outside the village, half witch, half wizard, feared and mocked at. . . . To have lived a free life in London in the sixteenth century would have meant for a woman who was poet and playwright a nervous stress and dilemma which might well have killed her. Had she survived, whatever she had written would have been twisted and deformed, issuing from a strained and morbid imagination. And undoubtedly, I thought, looking at the shelf where there are no plays by women, her work would have gone unsigned.

—A Room of One's Own

## Edward Albee (b. 1928)

### THE THEATER OF THE ABSURD                                    1962

What of this theater in which, for example, a legless old couple live out their lives in twin ashcans, surfacing occasionally for food or conversation (Samuel Beckett's Endgame); in which a man is seduced, and rather easily, by a girl with three well-formed and functioning noses (Eugène Ionesco's Jack, or The Submission); in which, on the same stage, one group of Negro actors is playing at pretending to be Negro (Jean Genêt's The Blacks)?

What of this theater? Is it, as it has been accused of being, obscure, sordid, destructive, anti-theater, perverse, and absurd (in the sense of foolish)? Or is it merely, as I have so often heard it put, that, "This sort of stuff is too depressing, too . . . too mixed up; I go to the theater to relax and have a good time"?

I would submit that it is this latter attitude—that the theater is a place to relax and have a good time—in conflict with the purpose of The Theater of the Absurd—which is to make a man face up to the human condition as it really is—that has produced all the brouhaha and the dissent. I would submit that The Theater of the Absurd, in the sense that it is truly the contemporary theater, facing as it does man's condition as it is, is the Realistic theater of our time; and that the supposed Realistic theater—the term used here to mean most of what is done on Broadway—in the sense that it panders to the public need for self-congratulation and reassurance and presents a false picture of ourselves to ourselves, is, with an occasional very lovely exception, really and truly The Theater of the Absurd.

—"Which Theater Is the Absurd One?"

# Tennessee Williams (1914–1983)

## HOW TO STAGE THE GLASS MENAGERIE                                    1945

Being a "memory play," *The Glass Menagerie* can be presented with unusual freedom of convention. Because of its considerably delicate or tenuous material, atmospheric touches and subtleties of direction play a particularly important part. Expressionism and all other unconventional techniques in drama have only one valid aim, and that is a closer approach to truth. When a play employs unconventional techniques, it is not, or certainly shouldn't be, trying to escape its responsibility of dealing with reality, or interpreting experience, but is actually or should be attempting to find a closer approach, a more penetrating and vivid expression of things as they are. The straight realistic play with its genuine Frigidaire and authentic ice-cubes, its characters that speak exactly as its audience speaks, corresponds to the academic landscape and has the same virtue of a photographic likeness. Everyone should know nowadays the unimportance of the photographic in art: that truth, life, or reality is an organic thing which the poetic imagination can represent or suggest, in essence, only through transformation, through changing into other forms than those which were merely present in appearance.

These remarks are not meant as a preface only to this particular play. They have to do with a conception of a new, plastic theater which must take the place of the exhausted theater of realistic conventions if the theater is to resume vitality as a part of our culture.

THE SCREEN DEVICE. There is *only one important difference between the original and acting version of the play* and that is the *omission* in the latter of the device which I tentatively included in my *original* script. This device was the use of a screen on which were projected magic-lantern slides bearing images or titles. I do not regret the omission of this device from the present Broadway production. The extraordinary power of Miss Taylor's performance° made it suitable to have the utmost simplicity in the physical production. But I think it may be interesting to some readers to see how this device was conceived. So I am putting it into the published manuscript. These images and legends, projected from behind, were cast on a section of wall between the front-room and dining-room areas, which should be indistinguishable from the rest when not in use.

The purpose of this will probably be apparent. It is to give accent to certain values in each case. Each scene contains a particular point (or several) which is structurally the most important. In an episodic play, such as this, the basic structure or narrative line may be obscured from the audience; the effect may seem fragmentary rather than architectural. This may not be the fault of the play so much as a lack of attention in the audience. The legend or image upon the screen will strengthen the effect of what is merely allusion in the writing and allow the primary point to be made more simply and lightly than if the entire responsibility

---

*Miss Taylor's performance:* In the original Broadway production of the play in 1945, the role of Amanda Wingfield, the mother, was played by veteran actress Laurette Taylor.

were on the spoken lines. Aside from this structural value, I think the screen will have a definite emotional appeal, less definable but just as important. An imaginative producer or director may invent many other uses for this device than those indicated in the present script. In fact the possibilities of the device seem much larger to me than the instance of this play can possibly utilize.

THE MUSIC. Another extra-literary accent in this play is provided by the use of music. A single recurring tune, "The Glass Menagerie," is used to give emotional emphasis to suitable passages. This tune is like circus music, not when you are on the grounds or in the immediate vicinity of the parade, but when you are at some distance and very likely thinking of something else. It seems under those circumstances to continue almost interminably and it weaves in and out of your preoccupied consciousness; then it is the lightest, most delicate music in the world and perhaps the saddest. It expresses the surface vivacity of life with the underlying strain of immutable and inexpressible sorrow. When you look at a piece of delicately spun glass you think of two things: how beautiful it is and how easily it can be broken. Both of those ideas should be woven into the recurring tune, which dips in and out of the play as if it were carried on a wind that changes. It serves as a thread of connection and allusion between the narrator with his separate point in time and space and the subject of his story. Between each episode it returns as reference to the emotion, nostalgia, which is the first condition of the play. It is primarily Laura's music and therefore comes out most clearly when the play focuses upon her and the lovely fragility of glass which is her image.

THE LIGHTING. The lighting in the play is not realistic. In keeping with the atmosphere of memory, the stage is dim. Shafts of light are focused on selected areas or actors, sometimes in contradistinction to what is the apparent center. For instance, in the quarrel scene between Tom and Amanda, in which Laura has no active part, the clearest pool of light is on her figure. This is also true of the supper scene, when her silent figure on the sofa should remain the visual center. The light upon Laura should be distinct from the others, having a peculiar pristine clarity such as light used in early religious portraits of female saints or madonnas. A certain correspondence to light in religious paintings, such as El Greco's, where the figures are radiant in atmosphere that is relatively dusky, could be effectively used throughout the play. (It will also permit a more effective use of the screen.) A free, imaginative use of light can be of enormous value in giving a mobile, plastic quality to plays of a more or less static nature.

—The Author's Production Notes to *The Glass Menagerie*

## Arthur Miller (b. 1915)

### TRAGEDY AND THE COMMON MAN °                                    1949

In this age few tragedies are written. It has often been held that the lack is
due to a paucity of heroes among us, or else that modern man has had the blood
drawn out of his organs of belief by the skepticism of science, and the heroic
attack on life cannot feed on an attitude of reserve and circumspection. For one
reason or another, we are often held to be below tragedy—or tragedy above us.
The inevitable conclusion is, of course, that the tragic mode is archaic, fit only
for the very highly placed, the kings or the kingly, and where this admission is
not made in so many words it is most often implied.

I believe that the common man is as apt a subject for tragedy in its highest
sense as kings were. On the face of it this ought to be obvious in the light of modern psychiatry, which bases its analysis upon classific formulations, such as the
Oedipus and Orestes complexes, for instance, which were enacted by royal
beings, but which apply to everyone in similar emotional situations.

More simply, when the question of tragedy in art is not at issue, we never
hesitate to attribute to the well-placed and the exalted the very same mental
processes as the lowly. And finally, if the exaltation of tragic action were truly a
property of the high-bred character alone, it is inconceivable that the mass of
mankind should cherish tragedy above all other forms, let alone be capable of
understanding it.

As a general rule, to which there may be exceptions unknown to me, I think
the tragic feeling is evoked in us when we are in the presence of a character who
is ready to lay down his life, if need be, to secure one thing—his sense of personal
dignity. From Orestes to Hamlet, Medea to Macbeth, the underlying struggle is
that of the individual attempting to gain his "rightful" position in his society.

Sometimes he is one who has been displaced from it, sometimes one who
seeks to attain it for the first time, but the fateful wound from which the
inevitable events spiral is the wound of indignity, and its dominant force is indignation. Tragedy, then, is the consequence of a man's total compulsion to evaluate himself justly.

In the sense of having been initiated by the hero himself, the tale always
reveals what has been called his "tragic flaw," a failing that is not peculiar to
grand or elevated characters. Nor is it necessarily a weakness. The flaw, or crack
in the character, is really nothing—and need be nothing—but his inherent
unwillingness to remain passive in the face of what he conceives to be a challenge to his dignity, his image of his rightful status. Only the passive, only those
who accept their lot without active retaliation, are "flawless." Most of us are in
that category.

But there are among us today, as there always have been, those who act
against the scheme of things that degrades them, and in the process of action,

A complete essay, originally published in *The New York Times*.

everything we have accepted out of fear or insensitivity or ignorance is shaken before us and examined, and from this total onslaught by an individual against the seemingly stable cosmos surrounding us—from this total examination of the "unchangeable" environment—comes the terror and the fear that is classically associated with tragedy.

More important, from this total questioning of what has been previously unquestioned, we learn. And such a process is not beyond the common man. In revolutions around the world, these past thirty years, he has demonstrated again and again this inner dynamic of all tragedy.

Insistence upon the rank of the tragic hero, or the so-called nobility of his character, is really but a clinging to the outward forms of tragedy. If rank or nobility of character was indispensable, then it would follow that the problems of those with rank were the particular problems of tragedy. But surely the right of one monarch to capture the domain from another no longer raises our passions, nor are our concepts of justice what they were to the mind of an Elizabethan king.

The quality in such plays that does shake us, however, derives from the underlying fear of being displaced, the disaster inherent in being torn away from our chosen image of what and who we are in this world. Among us today this fear is as strong, and perhaps stronger, than it ever was. In fact, it is the common man who knows this fear best.

Now, if it is true that tragedy is the consequence of a man's total compulsion to evaluate himself justly, his destruction in the attempt posits a wrong or an evil in his environment. And this is precisely the morality of tragedy and its lesson. The discovery of the moral law, which is what the enlightenment of tragedy consists of, is not the discovery of some abstract or metaphysical quantity.

The tragic right is a condition of life, a condition in which the human personality is able to flower and realize itself. The wrong is the condition which suppresses man, perverts the flowing out of his love and creative instinct. Tragedy enlightens—and it must, in that it points the heroic finger at the enemy of man's freedom. The thrust for freedom is the quality in tragedy which exalts. The revolutionary questioning of the stable environment is what terrifies. In no way is the common man debarred from such thoughts or such actions.

Seen in this light, our lack of tragedy may be partially accounted for by the turn which modern literature has taken toward the purely psychiatric view of life, or the purely sociological. If all our miseries, our indignities, are born and bred within our minds, then all action, let alone the heroic action, is obviously impossible.

And if society alone is responsible for the cramping of our lives, then the protagonist must needs be so pure and faultless as to force us to deny his validity as a character. From neither of these views can tragedy derive, simply because neither represents a balanced concept of life. Above all else, tragedy requires the finest appreciation by the writer of cause and effect.

No tragedy can therefore come about when its author fears to question absolutely everything, when he regards any institution, habit or custom as being either everlasting, immutable or inevitable. In the tragic view the need of man to wholly realize himself is the only fixed star, and whatever it is that hedges his nature and lowers it is ripe for attack and examination. Which is not to say that tragedy must preach revolution.

The Greeks could probe the very heavenly origin of their ways and return to confirm the rightness of laws. And Job could face God in anger, demanding his right, and end in submission. But for a moment everything is in suspension, nothing is accepted, and in this stretching and tearing apart of the cosmos, in the very action of so doing, the character gains "size," the tragic stature which is spuriously attached to the royal or the high born in our minds. The commonest of men may take on that stature to the extent of his willingness to throw all he has into the contest, the battle to secure his rightful place in his world.

There is a misconception of tragedy with which I have been struck in review after review, and in many conversations with writers and readers alike. It is the idea that tragedy is of necessity allied to pessimism. Even the dictionary says nothing more about the word than that it means a story with a sad or unhappy ending. This impression is so firmly fixed that I almost hesitate to claim that in truth tragedy implies more optimism in its author than does comedy, and that its final result ought to be the reinforcement of the onlooker's brightest opinions of the human animal.

For, if it is true to say that in essence the tragic hero is intent upon claiming his whole due as a personality, and if this struggle must be total and without reservation, then it automatically demonstrates the indestructible will of man to achieve his humanity.

The possibility of victory must be there in tragedy. Where pathos rules, where pathos is finally derived, a character has fought a battle he could not possibly have won. The pathetic is achieved when the protagonist is, by virtue of his witlessness, his insensitivity, or the very air he gives off, incapable of grappling with a much superior force.

Pathos truly is the mode for the pessimist. But tragedy requires a nicer balance between what is possible and what is impossible. And it is curious, although edifying, that the plays we revere, century after century, are the tragedies. In them, and in them alone, lies the belief—optimistic, if you will—in the perfectibility of man.

It is time, I think, that we who are without kings took up this bright thread of our history and followed it to the only place it can possibly lead in our time— the heart and spirit of the average man.

## Maria Irene Fornes (b. 1930)

### CHARACTERS ARE NOT REAL PEOPLE                                    1988

I don't romanticize pain. In my work people are always trying to find a way out, rather than feeling a romantic attachment to their prison. Some people complain that my work doesn't offer the solution. But the reason for that is that I feel that characters don't have to get out, it's *you* who has to get out. Characters are not real people. If characters were real people, I would have opened the door for them at the top of it—there would be no play. The play is there as a lesson, because I feel that art ultimately is a teacher. You go to a museum to look at a painting and that painting teaches you something. You may not look at a Cézanne and say, "I know now what I have to do." But it gives you something, a charge of some understanding, some knowledge that you have in your heart. And if art doesn't do that, I am not interested in it.

—Interview with David Savran, *In Their Own Words*

## August Wilson (b. 1945)

### BLACK EXPERIENCE IN AMERICA                                       1989

INTERVIEWER: *Your plays are set in the past*—Joe Turner's Come and Gone *in 1911,* Ma Rainey's Black Bottom *in 1927,* Fences *in the 1950s. Do you ever consider writing about what's happening today?*

WILSON: I suspect eventually I will get to that. Right now I enjoy the benefit of the historical perspective. You can look back to a character in 1936, for instance, and you can see him going down a particular path that you know did not work out for that character. Part of what I'm trying to do is to see some of the choices that we as blacks in America have made. Maybe we have made some incorrect choices. By writing about that, you can illuminate the choices.

INTERVIEWER: *Give me an example of a choice that you think may have been the wrong one.*

WILSON: I think we should have stayed in the South. We attempted to plant what in essence was an emerging culture, a culture that had grown out of our experience of 200 years as slaves in the South. The cities of the urban North have not been hospitable. If we had stayed in the South, we could have strengthened the culture. . . .

INTERVIEWER: *One of your characters has said, "Everyone has to find his own song." How do these people find their song?*

WILSON: They have it. They just have to realize that, and then they have to learn how to sing it. In that particular case, in *Joe Turner,* the song was the African identity. It was connecting yourself to that and understanding that this is who you are. Then you can go out in the world and sing your song as an African. . . .

INTERVIEWER: *But if blacks keep looking for the African in them, if they keep returning spiritually or emotionally to their roots, can they ever come to terms with living in these two worlds? Aren't they always going to be held by the past in a way that is potentially destructive?*

WILSON: It's not potentially destructive at all. To say that I am an African, and I can participate in this society as an African, is to say that I don't have to adopt European values, European aesthetics, and European ways of doing things in order to live in the world. We would not be here had we not learned to adapt to American culture. Blacks know more about whites in the white culture and white life than whites know about blacks. We *have* to know because our survival depends on it. White people's survival does not depend on knowing blacks. . . .

\* \* \*

INTERVIEWER: *Don't you grow weary of thinking black, writing black, being asked questions about blacks?*

WILSON: How could one grow weary of that? Whites don't get tired of thinking white or being who they are. I'm just who I am. You never transcend who you are. Black is not limiting. There's no idea in the world that is not contained by black life. I could write forever about the black experience in America.

—"August Wilson's America," interview with Bill Moyers in *American Theatre*

## David Henry Hwang (b. 1957)

MULTICULTURAL THEATER                                               1989

INTERVIEWER: *How did you begin . . . exploring your [Chinese-American] heritage?*

HWANG: A lot of that happened in college. I was in college in the mid-to-late 1970s, and whereas most people seem to associate collegiate life in the seventies with [actor] John Travolta, there was at that time a third-world consciousness, a third-world power movement, in the universities, particularly among Hispanics and Asians. The blacks really started it in the late sixties and early seventies, and it took a while to trickle down into the other third-world communities. Asians probably picked it up last. . . . While I was never a very ardent Marxist, I studied the ideas and I was interested in the degree to which we all may have been affected by certain prejudices in the society without having realized it, and to what degree we had incorporated that into our persons by the time we'd reached our early twenties.

The other thing that I think fascinated me about exploring my Chineseness at that time was consistent with my interest in play-writing. I had become very interested in Sam Shepard, particularly in the way in which Shepard likes to create a sort of American mythology. In his case it's the cowboy mythology, but nonetheless it's something that is larger than simply our present-day, fast-food existence. In my context, creating a mythology, creating a past for myself, involved going into Chinese history and Chinese-American history. I think the combination of wanting to delve into those things for artistic reasons and being exposed to an active third-world-consciousness movement was what started to get me interested in my roots when I was college.

INTERVIEWER: *I wonder if there will come a time when the expression "ethnic theater" won't have any meaning.*

HWANG: I'm hopeful that there will be a time at some point, but I think it's going to be fifty years or so down the road. The whole idea of being ethnic only applies when it's clear what the dominant culture is. Once it becomes less clear and the culture is acknowledged to be more multicultural, then the idea of what's ethnic becomes irrelevant. I think even today we're starting to see that. The monoethnic theaters—that is, the Asian theaters, the black theaters, the Hispanic theaters—are really useful; they serve a purpose. But I think, if we do our jobs correctly, we will phase out our own need for existence, and the future of theaters will be in multicultural theaters, theaters that do a black play and a Jewish play and a classic and whatever . . .

There are so many people now who can't be labeled. I know a couple in which the man is Japanese and Jewish and the woman is Haitian and Filipino. They have a child, and sociologists have told them that a child of that stock probably hasn't existed before. When someone like that becomes a writer, what do we call him? Do we say he's an Asian writer, or what? As those distinctions become increasingly muddled, the whole notion of what is ethnic as opposed to what is mainstream is going to become more and more difficult to define.

—Interview in *Contemporary Authors*

# SUPPLEMENT: WRITING

# 1. *Writing about Literature*

All of us have some powers of reasoning and perception. And when we come to a story, a poem, or a play, we can do little other than to trust whatever powers we have, like one who enters a shadowy room, clutching a decent candle.

After all, in the study of literature, common sense (poet Gerard Manley Hopkins said) is never out of place. For most of a class hour, a renowned English professor rhapsodized about the arrangement of the contents of W. H. Auden's *Collected Poems*. Auden, he claimed, was a master of thematic continuity, who had brilliantly placed the poems in the best possible order, in which (to the ingenious mind) they complemented each other. Near the end of the hour, his theories were punctured—with a great inaudible pop—when a student, timidly raising a hand, pointed out that Auden had arranged the poems in the book not according to theme but in alphabetical order according to the first word of each poem. The professor's jaw dropped: "Why didn't you say that sooner?" The student was apologetic: "I—I was afraid I'd sound too *ordinary*."

Emerson makes a similar point in his essay, "The American Scholar": "Meek young men grow up in libraries, believing it their duty to accept the views which Cicero, which Locke, which Bacon have given; forgetful that Cicero, Locke, and Bacon were only young men in libraries when they wrote these books." Don't be afraid to state a conviction, though it seems obvious. Does it matter that you may be repeating something that, once upon a time or even just the other day, has been said before? There are excellent old ideas as well as new.

## BEGINNING

Offered a choice of literary works to write about, you probably will do best if, instead of choosing what you think will impress your instructor, you choose what appeals to you. And how to find out what appeals? Whether you plan to write a short paper that requires no research beyond the story or poem or play itself, or a long term paper that will take you to the library, the first stage of your project is reading—and note taking. To concentrate your attention, one time-honored method is to read with a pencil, marking (if the book is yours) passages that stand out in importance, jotting brief notes in a margin (*"Key symbol—this foreshadows the ending"*; *"Dramatic irony"*; *"IDIOT!!!"*; or other possibly useful remarks). In a long story or poem or play, some students asterisk passages that cry for comparison; for instance, all the places in which they find the same theme or symbol. Later, at a glance, they can review the highlights of a work and, when writing a paper about it, quickly refer to evidence. This method shoots holes in a book's resale value, but many find the sacrifice worthwhile. Patient souls who dislike butchering a book prefer to take notes on looseleaf notebook paper, holding one sheet beside a page in the book and giving it the book's page number. Later, in writing a paper, they can place book page and companion note page together again. This method has the advantage of affording a lot of room for note taking; it is a good one for short poems closely packed with complexities.

But by far the most popular method of taking notes (besides writing on the pages of books) is to write on index cards—the 3 × 5 kind, for brief notes and titles; 5 × 8 cards for longer notes. Write on one side only; notes on the back of the card usually get overlooked later. Cards are easy to shuffle and, in organizing your material, to deal. To save work, instead of copying out on a card the title and author of a book you're taking a note from, just keep a numbered list of the books you're using. Then, when making a note, you need write only the book's identifying number on the card in order to identify your source. (Later, when writing footnotes, you can translate the number into title, author, and other information.)

Now that coin-operated photocopy machines are to be found in all libraries, you no longer need to spend hours copying by hand whole poems and longer passages. If accuracy is essential (surely it is!) and if a poem or passage is long enough to be worth the small investment, you can lay photocopied material into place in your paper with transparent tape or rubber cement. The latest copyright law permits students and scholars to reproduce books and periodicals in this fashion; it does not, however, permit making a dozen or more copies for public sale.

Certain literary works, because they offer intriguing difficulties, have attracted professional critics by the score. On library shelves, great phalanxes of critical books now stand at the side of James Joyce's complex novels *Ulysses* and *Finnegans Wake*, and T. S. Eliot's allusive poem *The Waste Land*. The student who undertakes to study such works seriously is well advised to profit from the critics' labors. Chances are, too, that even in discussing a relatively uncomplicated work you will want to seek the aid of the finest critics. If you quote them, quote them exactly, in quotation marks, and give them credit. When employed in any but the most superlative student paper, a brilliant phrase (or even a not-so-brilliant sentence) from a renowned critic is likely to stand out like a golf ball in a garter snake's midriff, and most English instructors are likely to recognize it. If you rip off the critic's words, then go ahead and steal the whole essay, for good critics write in seamless unities. Then, when apprehended, you can exclaim—like the student whose term paper was found to be the work of a well-known scholar—"I've been robbed! That paper cost me twenty dollars!" But of course the worst rip-off is the one the student inflicted on himself, having got nothing for his money out of a college course but a little practice in touch typing. Giving proper acknowledgment to words and ideas not your own is both a moral and legal obligation. Take it seriously.

Taking notes on your readings, you will want to jot down the title of every book you might refer to in your paper, and the page number of any passage you might wish to quote. Even if you summarize a critic's idea in your own words, rather than quote, you have to give credit to your source. Nothing is cheaper to give than proper credit. Certainly it's easier to take notes while you read than to have to run back to the library during the final typing.

Choose a topic appropriate to the assigned length of your paper. How do you know the probable length of your discussion until you write it? When in doubt, you are better off to define your topic narrowly. Your paper will be stronger if you go deeper into your subject than if you choose some gigantic subject and then find yourself able to touch on it only superficially. A thorough explication of a short story is hardly possible in a paper of 250 words. There are, in truth, four-line poems whose surface 250 words might only begin to scratch. A profound topic ("The Character of Shakespeare's Hamlet") might overflow a book; but a topic more narrowly defined ("Hamlet's Views of Acting"; "Hamlet's Puns") might result in a more nearly manageable term paper. You can narrow and focus a large topic while you work your way into it. A general interest in "Hemingway's Heroes" might lead you, in reading, taking notes, and thinking further, to the narrower topic, "Jake Barnes: Spokesman for Hemingway's Views of War."

Many student writers find it helpful, in defining a topic, to state an emerging idea for a paper in a provisional **thesis sentence:** a summing-up of the one main idea or argument that the paper will embody. (A thesis sentence is for your own use; you don't have to implant it in your paper unless your instructor asks for it.) A good statement of a thesis is not just a disembodied subject; it comes with both subject and verb. ("The Downfall of Oedipus Rex" is not yet a complete idea for a paper; "What Caused the Downfall of Oedipus Rex?" is.) A thesis sentence may help you see for yourself what the author is *saying about* a subject. Not a full thesis, and not a sentence, "The Isolation of Laura in *The Glass Menagerie*" might be a decent title for a paper. But it isn't a useful thesis because it doesn't indicate what one might say about that isolation (nor what Tennessee Williams is saying about it). It may be obvious that isolation isn't desirable, but a clearer and more workable thesis sentence might be, "In *The Glass Menagerie*, the playwright shows how Laura's isolation leads her to take refuge in a world of dreams."

## DISCOVERING AND PLANNING

Writing is not likely to proceed in a straight line. Like thought, it often goes by fits and starts, by charges and retreats and mopping-up operations. All the while you take notes, you discover material to write about; all the while you tool over your topic in your mind, you plan. It is the nature of ideas, those headstrong things, to happen in any order they desire. While you continue to plan, while you write a draft, and while you revise, expect to keep discovering new thoughts— perhaps the best thoughts of all. If you do, be sure to let them in.

Topic in hand (which may get drastically changed as you continue), you begin to sort out your miscellaneous notes, thoughts, and impressions. If you can see that you haven't had enough ideas, you may wish to **brainstorm**—to set yourself, say, fifteen minutes in which to write down as fast as you can all the ideas on your topic that come into your head, without worrying whether they are going to be useful. (You can look over the results and decide that later.) Another method of discovery is to **freewrite:** to write rapidly and uncritically, letting your thoughts tumble onto paper as fast as your pen, typewriter, or word processor can capture them. Sometimes these methods will goad the unconscious into coming up with unexpectedly good ideas; at least, you will generate more potentially useful raw material.

To outline or not to outline? Unless your topic, by its nature, suggests some obvious way to organize your paper ("An Explication of a Wordsworth Sonnet" might mean simply working through the poem line by line), then some kind of outline will probably help. In high school or other prehistoric times, you perhaps learned how to construct a beautiful outline, laid out with Roman numerals, capital letters, Arabic numerals, and lower-case letters. It was a thing of beauty and symmetry, and possibly even had something to do with paper writing. But if now you are skeptical of the value of outlining, reflect: not every outline needs to be detailed and elaborate. Some students, of course, find it helpful to outline in detail—particularly if they are planning a long term paper involving several literary works, comparing and contrasting several aspects of them. For a 500-word analysis of a short story's figures of speech, though, all you might need is a simple list of points to make, scribbled down in the order in which you will make them. This order is probably not, of course, the order in which the points first occurred to you. Thoughts, when they first come to mind, can be a confused rabble.

While granting the need for order in a piece of writing, the present writer confesses that he is a reluctant outliner. His tendency (or curse) is to want to keep whatever random thoughts occur to him; to polish his prose right then and there; and finally to try to juggle his disconnected paragraphs into something like logical order. The usual result is that he has large blocks of illogical thought left over. This process is wasteful, and if you can learn to live with an outline, then you belong to the legion of the blessed, and will never know the pain of scrapping pages that cost you hours. On the other hand, you will never know the joy of meandering—of bursting into words and surprising yourself. As novelist E. M. Forster remarked, "How do I know what I think until I see what I say?"

An outline, if you use one, is not meant to stand as an achievement in itself. It should—as Ezra Pound said literary criticism ought to do—consume itself and disappear. Here is a once-valuable outline not worth keeping—a very informal one that enabled a student to organize the paper that appears on page 1751, "The Hearer of the Tell-Tale Heart." Before he wrote, the student jotted down the ideas that had occurred to him. Looking them over, he could see that certain ones predominated. Since the aim of his paper was to analyze Poe's story for its point of view, he began with some notes about the narrator of the story. His other leading ideas had emerged as questions: is the story supposed to be a ghost story or an account of a delusion? Can we read the whole thing as a nightmare, having no reality outside the narrator's mind? Having seen that his thoughts weren't a totally disconnected jumble, he drew connections. Going down his list, he numbered with the same numbers those ideas that belonged together.

1  Killer is mad—can listen in on Hell.

2  He is obsessed with the Evil Eye.

1  He thinks he is sane, we know he's mad.

Old man rich—a miser?

4 {  Is this a ghost story? NO! Natural explanations for
      the heartbeat:

      His mind is playing tricks.

      Hears his <u>own</u> heart (Hoffman's idea).

3  Maybe the whole story is only his dream?

Poe must have been crazy too.

The numbers now showed him the order in which he planned to take up each of his four chief ideas. Labeling with the number "1" his remarks about the narrator, he decided to open his paper with them and to declare at once that they indicated the story's point of view. As you can tell from his finished paper, he discarded two notions that didn't seem to relate to his purpose: the point about the old man's wealth and the speculation (which he realized he couldn't prove) that Poe himself was mad. Having completed this rough outline, he felt encouraged to return to Poe's story and on rereading it noticed a few additional points, which you will find in his paper. His outline didn't tell him exactly what to say at every moment, but it was clear and easy to follow.

## DRAFTING AND REVISING

Seated at last, or striking some other businesslike stance,[1] you prepare to write, only to find yourself besieged with petty distractions. All of a sudden you remember a friend you had promised to call, some dry cleaning you were supposed to pick up, a neglected Coke (in another room) growing warmer and flatter by the minute. If your paper is to be written, you have one course of action: to collar these thoughts and for the moment banish them.

[1] R. H. Super of the University of Michigan wrote a definitive biography of Walter Savage Landor while standing up, typing on a machine atop of a filing cabinet.

When first you draft your paper—that is, when you write it out in the rough—you will probably do best to write rapidly. At this early stage, you don't need to be fussy about spelling, grammar, and punctuation. To be sure, those picayune details matter, but you can worry about them later on, when you are **editing** (combing through your draft repairing grammar, cutting excess words, making small verbal improvements) and **proofreading** (going over your finished paper line by line, checking it for typographical or other mistakes). Right now, it is more important to get your thoughts down on paper in a steady flow than to keep taking time out to check spellings in the dictionary. Forge ahead, and don't be too nastily self-critical. Perhaps when you write your draft you won't even want to look at all those notes on your reading that you collected so industriously. When you come to a place where a note will fit, you might just insert a reminder to yourself, such as SEE CARD 19, or SEE ARISTOTLE ON COMEDY.

Let us admit that writing about literature is a fussier kind of writing than turning out a narrative essay called, "My Most Exciting Experience." You may need to draft some of your paper slowly and painstakingly. You'll find yourself coping with all sorts of small problems, many of them simple and mechanical. What, for instance, will you call the author whose work you are dealing with? Decide at the outset. Most critics favor the author's last name alone: "Dickinson implies. . . " ("Miss Dickinson" or "Ms. Dickinson" may sound fussily polite; "Emily," too chummy.) Will you include footnotes in your paper and, if so, do you know how they work? (Some pointers on handling the pesky things will come in a few pages.)

You will want to give credit to any critics who helped you out, and properly to do so is to be painstaking. To paraphrase a critic, you do more than just rearrange the critic's words and phrases; you translate them into language of your own. Say you wish to refer to an insight of Randall Jarrell's, who comments on the images of spider, flower, and moth in Robert Frost's poem "Design":

> Notice how the *heal-all*, because of its name, is the one flower in all the world picked to be the altar for this Devil's Mass; notice how holding up the moth brings something ritual and hieratic, a ghostly, ghastly formality to this priest and its sacrificial victim. . . .

It would be incorrect to say, without quotation marks:

```
Frost picks the heal-all as the one flower in all the
world to be the altar for this Devil's Mass. There is a
ghostly, ghastly formality to the spider holding up the
moth, like a priest holding a sacrificial victim.
```

That rewording, although not exactly in Jarrell's language, manages to steal his memorable phrases without giving him credit. Nor is it sufficient just to list Jarrell's essay in a bibliography at the end of your paper. If you do, you are still a crook; you merely point to the scene of your crime. What is needed, clearly, is to think through Jarrell's words to the point he is making; and if you want to keep any of his striking phrases (and why not?), put them in quotation marks:

> As Randall Jarrell points out, Frost portrays the spider
> as a kind of priest in a Mass, or Black Mass, elevating
> the moth like an object for sacrifice, with "a ghostly,
> ghastly formality."

To be scrupulous in your acknowledgment, tell where you found your quotation from Jarrell, citing the book and the page. (See "Documenting Your Sources," page 1743.) But unless your instructor expects you to write such a formal, documented paper, the passage as it now stands would make sufficiently clear your source, and your obligation.

One more word of Dutch-uncle warning. In this book you are offered a vocabulary with which to discuss literature: a flurry of terms such as *irony, symbol,* and *image,* printed in **boldface** when first introduced. In your writing you may decide to enlist a few of them. And yet, critical terminology—especially if unfamiliar—can tempt a beginning critic to sling it about. Nothing can be less sophisticated, or more misleading, than a technical term grandly misapplied: "The *myth-symbolism* of this *rime scheme* leaves one aghast." Far better to choose plain words you're already at ease with. Your instructor, no doubt, has met many a critical term and is not likely to be impressed by the mere sight of another one. Knowingly selected and placed, a critical term can help sharpen a thought and make it easier to handle. Clearly it is less cumbersome to refer to the *tone* of a story than to have to say, "the way the author makes you feel that she feels about what she is talking about." But the paper-writer who declares, "The tone of this poem is full of ironic imagery," fries words to a hash—mixed up and indigestible.

When you write your first draft, by the way, leave plenty of space between lines and enormous margins. Then, when later thoughts come to you, you can easily squeeze them in.

Does any writer write with perfection on the first try, and drop ideas with a single shot? Some writers have claimed to do so—among them the English novelist Anthony Trollope, who thought it "unmanly" not to write a thought right the first time. Jack Kerouac, leading novelist of the beat generation of the 1950s, believed in spontaneous prose. He used to write entire novels on uncut ribbons of teletype paper, thus saving himself the interruption of stopping at the bottom of each page. His specialty, though, was fiction of ecstasy and hallucination, not essays in explication, or comparison and contrast. For most of us, however, good writing is largely a matter of revising—of going back over our first thoughts word by word. Painstaking revision is more than a matter of tidying grammar and spelling: in the process of reconsidering our words, we sometimes discover fresher and sharper ideas. "Writing and rewriting," says John Updike, "are a constant search for what one is saying."

To achieve effective writing, you have to have the courage to be wild. Aware that no reader need see your rough drafts, you can treat them mercilessly—scissor them apart, rearrange their pieces, reassemble them into a stronger order, using staples or tape or glue. The art of revising calls for a textbook in itself, but here are a few simple suggestions:

1. Insofar as your deadline allows, be willing to revise as many times as need be.

2. Don't think of revision as the simple chore of fixing up spelling mistakes. That's proofreading, and it comes last. When you revise, be willing to cut and slash, to discover new insights, to move blocks of words around so that they follow in a stronger order. Stand ready to question your whole approach to a work of literature, to entertain the notion of throwing everything you have written into the wastebasket and starting over again.

3. At this stage, you may find it helpful to enlist outside advice—from your instructor, from your roommate or your mate, from any friend who will read your rough draft and give you a reaction. If you can enlist such a willing reader, ask: What isn't clear to you?

4. If you (or your willing reader) should find any places that aren't readily understandable, single them out for rewriting. After all, you don't need to revise a whole draft if only parts of it need work. Try rewriting any especially troublesome passage or paragraph.

5. Short, skimpy paragraphs of one or two sentences may indicate places that call for more thought, or more material. Can you supply them with more evidence, more explanation, more example and illustration?

6. A time-tested method of revising is to lay aside your manuscript for a while, forget about it, and then after a long interval (the Roman poet Horace recommended nine years, but obviously that won't do), go back to it for a fresh look. If you have time, take a nap or a walk, or at least a yawn and a stretch before you take yet another look.

7. When your paper is in a *last* draft—that's the time to edit it. Once you have your ideas in firm shape, you can check those uncertain spellings, look up the agreement of verbs in a grammar book or handbook, make your pronouns and numbers agree, cut needless words, pull out a weak word and send in a stronger one. Back when you were drafting, to get prematurely fussy about such small things might have frozen you up. But once you feel satisfied that you have made yourself clear, you can be as fussy as you like.

## THE FORM OF YOUR FINISHED PAPER

Now that you have smoothed your final draft as fleck-free as you can, your instructor may have specific advice for the form of your finished paper. If none is forthcoming, it is only reasonable

1. to choose standard letter-size ($8\frac{1}{2} \times 11$) paper;
2. to give your name at the top of your title page;

3. to leave an inch or more of margin on all four sides of each page, and a few inches of blank paper or an additional sheet after your conclusion, so that your instructor can offer comment;
4. to doublespace, or (if you handwrite) to use paper with widely spaced lines.

And what of titles of works discussed: when to put them in quotation marks, when to underline them? One rule of thumb is that titles of works shorter than book length rate quotation marks (poems, short stories, articles); but titles of books (including book-length poems: *The Odyssey*), plays, and periodicals take underlining. (In a manuscript to be set in type, an underline is a signal to the compositor to use *italics*.)

## DOCUMENTING YOUR SOURCES

When you quote from other writers, when you lift their information, when you summarize or paraphrase their ideas, make sure you give them their due. Document everything you take. Identify the writer by name; cite the very book, magazine, newspaper, pamphlet, letter, or other source you are using, and the page or pages you are indebted to.

By so doing, you invite your readers to go to your original source and check up on you. Most readers won't bother, of course, but at least your invitation enlists their confidence. Besides, the duty to document keeps you carefully looking at your sources—and so helps keep your writing accurate and responsible.

The latest and most efficient way for writers to document their sources is that recommended in the *MLA Handbook for Writers of Research Papers*, 3rd ed. (New York: Modern Language Association of America, 1988). In the long run, whether you write an immense term paper citing a hundred sources or a short paper citing only three or four, the MLA's advice will save you and your reader time and trouble.

These pointers cannot take the place of the *MLA Handbook* itself; but the gist of the method is this. Begin by listing your sources: all the works from which you're going to quote, summarize, paraphrase, or take information. Later on, when you type up your paper in finished form, you're going to *end* it with a neat copy of this list (once called a *bibliography*, now entitled "Works Cited"). But right now, in writing your paper, every time you refer to one of these works, you need give only enough information to help a reader locate it under "Works Cited." Usually, you can just give (in parentheses) an author's last name and a page citation. You incorporate this information right in the text of your paper, most often at the end of a sentence:

```
One recent investigation has suggested that few people
who submit poems to small literary magazines bother to
read those magazines; or indeed, bother to read poems by
anybody else (Horton 108-09).
```

Say you will want to cite *two* books or magazine articles by Horton—how to tell them apart? In your text, condense the title of each article into a word or two.

```
One recent investigation has shown that few people who
submit poems to small literary magazines bother to read
those magazines (Horton, "Magazines" 108-09).
```

If you have mentioned the name of the author in the body of your paper, you need give only the page number:

```
As a recent investigator, Louise Horton, has suggested,
few people who submit poems to small literary magazines
bother to read those magazines (108-09).
```

The beauty of this method is that you don't have to stop every two minutes to write a footnote identifying your source in full detail. At the end of your paper, in your list of works cited, your reader can find a fuller description of your source—in this case, a magazine article:

```
Horton, Louise. "Who Reads Small Literary Magazines and
    What Good Do They Do?" Texas Review Spring/Summer
    1984: 108-13.
```

It's imperative to keep citations in your text brief and snappy, lest they hinder the flow of your prose. You may wish to append a note supplying a passage of less important (yet possibly valuable) information or making careful qualifying statements ("On the other hand, not every expert agrees. John Binks finds that poets are often a little magazine's only cash customers; while Molly MacGuire maintains that . . ."). If you want to put in some such aside, and suspect that you couldn't give it in your text without interrupting your paper awkwardly, then cast it into a **footnote** (a note placed at the bottom of a page) or an **endnote** (a note placed at the end of a paper). Given a choice, most writers prefer endnotes. Far easier to collect all the notes at the end of a paper than to use footnotes—as any writer knows who has had to retype pages and pages again and again, to make the footnotes fit.[2]

How do you drop in such notes? The number of each consecutive note comes (following any punctuation) after the last word of a sentence. So that the number will stand out, you roll your typewriter carriage up a click (or order your word-processor to do a superscript), thus lifting the number slightly above the usual level of your prose.

```
as other observers have claimed.1
```

When you come to type the footnote or endnote itself, skip five spaces, elevate the number again, skip a space, and proceed.

---

[2] Nowadays, some word-processing programs make life easier for foonoters by helping to format each footnote and by automaticallly dropping it in at the bottom of its page.

Although now useful mainly for such slightly longwinded asides, footnotes and endnotes are time-honored ways to document *all* sources in a research paper. Indeed, some instructors still prefer them to the new MLA guidelines, and urge students to use such notes to indicate every writer cited. Though such notes take more work, they have the advantage of hiding dull data away from your reader's eyes, enabling you to end sentences with powerful bangs and inconspicuous note numbers instead of whimpering parentheses (Glutz-Finnegan, *Lesser Corollary* 1029-30). Besides, in a brief paper containing only one citation or two, to use footnotes or endnotes may be simpler and less showy than to compile a Works Cited list that has only two entries.

Large-mindedly, the MLA *Handbook* tolerates the continued use of footnotes and endnotes for documentation—indeed, offers advice for their preparation, which we will follow here. If you do use footnotes or endnotes to document all your sources, here is how to format them. A note identifying a magazine article looks like this:

16Louise Horton, "Who Reads Small Literary Magazines and What Good Do They Do?" <u>Texas Review</u> Spring/Summer 1984: 108-09.

Notice that, in notes, the author's first name comes first. (In a list of Works Cited, you work differently: you put last name first, so that you can readily arrange your list of authors in easy-to-consult alphabetical order.) A footnote or endnote for a reference to a book (and not a magazine article) looks like this:

17Elizabeth Frank, <u>Louise Bogan: A Portrait</u> (New York: Knopf, 1985) 59-60.

Should you return later to cite another place in Frank's book, you need not repeat all its information. Just write:

18Frank 192.

If in your paper you refer to *two* books by Elizabeth Frank, give the full title of each in the first note citing it. Then, if you cite it again, use a shortened form of its title:

19Frank, <u>Bogan</u> 192.

Your readers should not have to interrupt their reading of your essay to glance down at a note simply to find out whom you are quoting. It is poor form to write:

Dylan Thomas's poem "Fern Hill" is a memory of the poet's childhood: of his Aunt Ann Jones's farm, where he spent his holidays. "Time, which has an art to throw dust

on all things, broods over the poem."[1] The farm, indeed,
is a lost paradise—a personal garden of Eden.

---

[1]William York Tindall, _A Reader's Guide to Dylan Thomas_
(New York: Noonday, 1962) 268.

That is annoying, because the reader has to stop reading and look at the footnote to find out who made that resonant statement about Time brooding over the poem. A better way:

> "Time," as William York Tindall has observed, "which has
> an art to throw dust on all things, broods over the
> poem."[1]

Your footnote or endnote then cites Tindall's book:

---

[1]_A Reader's Guide to Dylan Thomas_ (New York: Noonday,
1962) 268.

What to do now but hand in your paper? "And good riddance," you may feel, after such an expenditure of thinking, time, and energy. But a good paper is not only worth submitting, it is worth keeping. If you return to it, after a while, you may find to your surprise that it will preserve and even renew what you have learned.

_Robert Wallace_ (b. 1932)

THE GIRL WRITING HER ENGLISH PAPER                                    1979

lies on one hip by the fire,
blond, in jeans.

The wreckage of her labor, elegant as Eden
or petals from a tree,
surrounds her—

a little farm, smoke rising from the ashtray,
book, notebooks, papers, fields;
a poem's furrows.

If the lights were to go out suddenly,
stars would be overhead,
the edge of the wood still and dark.

# 2. Writing about a Story

Like any coherent, forceful essay, a good discussion of fiction doesn't just toss forth a random lot of impressions. It makes some point about which the writer feels strongly. In order to write a meaningful paper, then, you need something you *want* to say—a meaningful topic. For suggestions on finding such a topic (also some pointers on organizing, writing, revising, and finishing your paper), please see "Writing about Literature," which begins on page 1735. The advice there may be applied to papers on fiction, poetry, and drama. Some methods especially useful for writing about stories are gathered in the present chapter.

Unlike a brief poem, or a painting you can take in with one long glance, a work of fiction—even a short story—may be too complicated to hold all at once in the mind's eye. Before you can write about it, you may need to give it two or more careful readings, and even then, as you begin to think further about it, you will probably have to thumb through it to reread passages. The first time through, perhaps it is best just to read attentively, open to whatever pleasure and wisdom the story may afford. On second look, you may find it useful to read with pencil in hand, either to mark your personal copy or to take notes to jog your memory. To see the design and meaning of a story need not be a boring chore—any more than it is to land a fighting fish and to study it with admiration.

In this chapter, all the discussions and examples refer to Edgar Allan Poe's short story "The Tell-Tale Heart" (page 61). If you haven't already read it, you can do so in only a few minutes, so that the rest of this chapter will make more sense to you.

## EXPLICATING

**Explication** is the patient unfolding of meanings in a work of literature. An explication—that is, an essay that follows this method—proceeds carefully through a story, poem, or play, usually interpreting it line by line—perhaps even word by word. A good explication dwells on details, as well as on larger things. It brings them to the attention of a reader who might have missed them (the reader probably hasn't read so closely as the writer of the explication). Alert and willing to take pains, the writer of such an essay notices anything meaningful that isn't obvious, whether it is a colossal theme suggested by a symbol or a little hint contained in a single word.

To write an honest explication of a story takes time and space, probably too much time and space to devote to a long and complex story unless you are writing a huge term paper, an honors thesis, or a dissertation. A thorough explication of Nathaniel Hawthorne's "Young Goodman Brown" would be likely to run much longer than the rich and intriguing short story itself. Ordinarily, the method of explication is best suited to a paper that deals only with a short passage or section of a story: a key scene, a crucial conversation, a statement of theme, an opening or closing paragraph. Storytellers who are especially fond of language invite closer attention to their words than others do. Edgar Allan Poe, for one, is a poet sensitive to the rhythms of his sentences and a symbolist whose stories abound in suggestions. Here is an explication, by a student, of a short but essential passage in "The Tell-Tale Heart." The passage occurs in the third paragraph of the story, and (to help us follow the explication) the student quotes it in full at the beginning of her paper.

### By Lantern Light: An Explication of a Passage in "The Tell-Tale Heart"

And every night, about midnight, I turned the latch of his door and opened it—oh, so gently! And then, when I had made an opening sufficient for my head, I put in a dark lantern, all closed, closed, so that no light shone out, and then I thrust in my head. Oh, you would have laughed to see how cunningly I thrust it in! I moved it slowly—very, very slowly, so that I might not disturb the old man's sleep. It took me an hour to place my whole head within the opening so far that I could see him as he lay upon his bed. Ha!—would a madman have been so wise as this? And then, when my head was well in the room, I undid the lantern cautiously—oh, so cautiously—cautiously (for the hinges creaked)—I undid it just so much that a single thin ray fell upon the vulture eye. And this I did for seven long nights—every night just at midnight—but I found the eye always closed; and so it was impossible to do the work; for it was not the old man who vexed me, but his Evil Eye.

Although Poe has suggested in the first lines of his story that the person who addresses us is insane, it is only when we come to the speaker's account of his preparations for murdering the old man that we find his madness fully revealed. Even more convincingly than his earlier words (for we might possibly think that someone who claims to hear things in heaven and hell is a religious mystic), these preparations reveal him to be mad. What strikes us is that they are so elaborate and meticulous. A significant detail is the exactness of his schedule for spying: "every night just at midnight." The words with which he describes his motions also convey the most extreme care (and I will indicate them with italics): "how wisely I proceeded—with what caution," "I turned the latch of his door and opened it—oh, so gently!" "how cunningly I thrust [my head] in! I moved it slowly, very slowly," "I undid the lantern cautiously—oh, so cautiously—cautiously." Taking a whole hour to intrude his head into the room, he asks, "Ha!—would a madman be as wise as this?" But of course the word wise is unconsciously ironic, for clearly it is not wisdom the speaker displays, but an absurd degree of care, an almost fiendish ingenuity. Such behavior, I understand, is typical of certain mental illnesses. All his careful preparations that he thinks prove him sane only convince us instead that he is mad.

Obviously his behavior is self-defeating. He wants to catch the "vulture eye" open, and yet he takes all these pains not to disturb the old man's sleep. If he behaved logically, he might go barging into the bedroom with his lantern ablaze, shouting at the top of his voice. And yet, if we can see things his way, there is a strange logic to his reasoning. He regards the eye as a creature in itself, quite apart from its possessor. "It was not," he says, "the old man who vexed me, but his Evil Eye." Apparently, to be inspired to do his deed, the madman needs to behold the eye—at least, this is my understanding of his remark, "I found the eye always closed; and so it was impossible to do the work." Poe's choice of the word work, by the way, is also revealing. Murder is made to seem a duty or a job; and anyone who so regards murder is either extremely cold-blooded, like a hired killer for a gangland assassination, or else deranged. Besides, the word suggests again the curious sense of detachment that the speaker feels toward the owner of the eye.

In still another of his assumptions, the speaker shows that he is madly logical, or operating on the logic of a dream. There seems a dreamlike relationship between his dark lantern "all closed, closed, so that no light shone out," and the sleeping victim. When the madman opens his lantern so that it emits a single ray, he is hoping that the eye in the old man's head will be open too, letting out its corresponding gleam. The latch that he turns so gently, too, seems like the eye, whose lid needs to be opened in order for the murderer to go ahead. It is as though the speaker is <u>trying</u> to get the eyelid to lift. By taking such great pains and by going through all this nightly ritual, he is practicing some kind of magic, whose rules are laid down not by our logic, but by the logic of dreams.

An unusually well-written paper, "By Lantern Light" cost the student two or three careful revisions. Rather than attempting to say something about *everything* in the passage from Poe, she selects only the details that strike her as most meaningful. In her very first sentence, she briefly shows us how the passage functions in the context of Poe's story: how it clinches our suspicions that the narrator is mad. In writing her paper, the student went by the following rough, simple outline—nothing more than a list of the points she wanted to express:

1. Speaker's extreme care and exactness—typical of some mental illnesses.
2. Speaker doesn't act by usual logic but by a crazy logic.
3. Dreamlike connection between latch & lantern and old man's eye.

As she wrote, she followed her brief list, setting forth her ideas one at a time, one idea to a paragraph. There is a different (and still easier) way to organize an explication: just work through the original passage line by line or sentence by sentence. The danger of this procedure is that you may find yourself falling into a boring singsong: "In the first sentence I noticed. . . ," "In the next sentence. . . ," "Now in the third sentence. . . ," "Finally, in the last paragraph. . . ." (If you choose to organize an explication in such a way, then boldly vary your transitions.) Notice that the student who wrote "By Lantern Light" doesn't inch through the passage sentence by sentence but freely takes up its details in whatever order she likes.

In a long critical essay in which we don't adhere to one method all the way through, the method of explication may appear from time to time—as when the critic, in discussing a story, stops to unravel a particularly knotty passage. But useful as it may be to know how to write an explication of fiction, it is probably still more useful (in most literature courses) to know how to write an analysis.

## ANALYZING

Assignment: "Write an **analysis** of a story or novel." What do you do? Following the method of analysis (from the Greek: "breaking up"), you separate a story or novel into its components, then (usually) select one part for close study. One likely topic for an analysis might be "The Character of James Thurber's Mr. Martin" (referring to "The Catbird Seat"), in which the writer would concentrate on showing us Martin's highly individual features and traits of personality. Other typical analyses might be written about, say, "Gothic Elements in a story by Joyce Carol Oates" (referring to "Where Are You Going, Where Have You Been?"), or "The Unidentified Narrator in 'A Rose for Emily.'"

To be sure, no element of a story dwells in isolation from the story's other elements. In "The Tell-Tale Heart," the madness of the leading character apparently makes it necessary to tell the story from a special point of view and probably helps determine the author's choice of theme, setting, symbolism, tone, style, and ironies. But it would be mind-boggling to try to study all those elements simultaneously. For this reason, when we write an analysis we generally study just one element, though we may suggest—probably at the start of the essay—its relation to the whole story. Indeed, analysis is the method used in this book, in which, chapter by chapter, we have separated fiction into its components of plot, point of view, character, tone and style, and so on. If you have read the discussion on the plot of "Godfather Death" (page 4), or the attempt to state the theme of Hemingway's "A Clean, Well-Lighted Place" (page 158), then you have already read some brief essays in analysis. Here is a student-written analysis of "The Tell-Tale Heart," dealing with just one element—the story's point of view.

### The Hearer of the Tell-Tale Heart

Although there are many things we do not know about the narrator of Edgar Allan Poe's story "The Tell-Tale Heart" — is he a son? a servant? a companion? — there is one thing we are sure of from the start. He is mad. In the opening paragraph, Poe makes the narrator's condition unmistakable, not only from his excited and worked-up speech (full of dashes and exclamation points), but also from his wild claims. He says it is merely some disease which has sharpened his senses that has made people call him crazy. Who but a madman, however, would say, "I heard all things in the heaven and in the earth," and brag how his ear is a kind of CB radio, listening in on Hell? Such a statement leaves no doubt that the point of view in the story is an ironic one.

Because the participating narrator is telling his story in the first person, some details in the story stand out more than others. When the narrator goes on to tell how he watches the old man sleeping, he rivets his attention on the old man's "vulture eye." When a ray from his lantern finds the Evil Eye open, he says, "I could see nothing else of the old man's face or person." Actually, the reader can see almost nothing else about the old man anywhere in the rest of the story. All we are told is that the old man treated the younger man well, and we gather that the old man was rich, because his house is full of treasures. We do not have a clear idea of what the old man looks like, though, nor do we know how he talks, for we are not given any of his words. Our knowledge of him is mainly confined to his eye and its effect on the narrator. This confinement gives that symbolic eye a lot of importance in the story. The narrator tells us all we know and directs our attention to parts of it.

This point of view raises an interesting question. Since we are dependent on the narrator for all our information, how do we know the whole story isn't just a nightmare in his demented mind? We have really no way to be sure it isn't, as far as I can see. I assume, however, that there really is a dark shuttered house and an old man and real policemen who start snooping around when screams are heard in the neighborhood, because it is a more memorable story if it is a crazy man's view of reality than if it is all just a terrible dream. But we can't take stock in the madman's interpretation of what happens. Poe keeps putting distances between what the narrator says and what we are supposed to think, apparently. For instance: the narrator has boasted that he is calm and clear in the head, but as soon as he starts (in the second paragraph) trying to explain why he killed the old man, we gather that he is confused, to say the least. "I think it was his eye!" the narrator exclaims, as if not quite sure. As he goes on to explain how he conducted the murder, we realize that he is a man with a fixed idea working with a patience that is certainly mad, almost diabolical.

Some readers might wonder if "The Tell-Tale Heart" is a story of the supernatural. Is the heartbeat that the narrator hears a ghost come back to haunt him? Here, I think, the point of view is our best guide to what to believe. The simple explanation for the heartbeat is this: it is all in the madman's mind. Perhaps he feels such guilt that he starts hearing things. Another explanation is possible, one suggested by Daniel Hoffman, a critic who has discussed the story: the killer hears the sound of his own heart.[1] Hoffman's explanation (which I don't like as well as mine) also is a natural one, and it fits the story as a whole. Back when the narrator first entered the old man's bedroom to kill him, the heartbeat sounded so loud to him that he was afraid the neighbors would hear it too. Evidently they didn't, and so Hoffman may be right in thinking that the sound was only that of his own heart pounding in his ears. Whichever explanation you take, it is a more down-to-earth and reasonable explanation than that (as the narrator believes) the heart is still alive, even though its owner has been cut to pieces. Then, too, the police keep chatting. If they heard the heartbeat too, wouldn't they leap to their feet, draw their guns, and look all around the room? As the author has kept showing us in the rest of the story, the narrator's view of things is untrustworthy. You don't kill someone just because you dislike the look in his eye. You don't think that such a murder is funny. For all its Gothic atmosphere of the old dark house with a secret hidden inside, "The Tell-Tale Heart" is not a ghost story. We have only to see its point of view to know it is a study in abnormal psychology.

---

[1]Poe Poe Poe Poe Poe Poe Poe (New York: Anchor, 1973), 227.

A temptation in writing an analysis is to include all sorts of insights that the writer proudly wishes to display, even though they aren't related to the main idea. In the preceding essay, the student resists this temptation admirably. In fairly plump and ample paragraphs, he works out his ideas, and he supports his contentions with specific references to Poe's story. Although his paper is not brilliantly written and contains no insight so fresh as the suggestion (by the writer of the first paper) that the madman's lantern is like the old man's head, still, it is a good brief analysis. By sticking faithfully to his purpose and by confronting the problems he raises ("how do we know the whole story isn't just a nightmare?"), the writer persuades us that he understands not only the story's point of view, but the story in its entirety.

Our analysis so far deals with one element in Poe's story: point of view. In another familiar writing assignment, the **card report,** one is asked to analyze a story into its *several* elements. Usually confined to the front and back of one 5 × 8-inch index card, such a report is just as challenging to write as an essay, if not more so. To do the job well, you have to see the story in its elements, then specify them succinctly and accurately. Here (on the following pages) is a typical card report listing and detailing the essentials of "The Tell-Tale Heart." In this assignment, the student was asked to include:

1. The title of the story and the date of its original publication.
2. The author's name and dates.
3. The name (if any) of the main character, together with a description of that character's dominant traits or features.

4. Other characters in the story, dealt with in the same fashion.
5. A short description of the setting.
6. The narrator of the story. (To identify him or her is, of course, to define the point of view from which the story is told.)

## Front of Card

(Student's name)          (Course and section)

<u>Story</u>: "The Tell-Tale Heart," 1850
<u>Author</u>: Edgar Allan Poe (1809–1849)

<u>Central character</u>: An unnamed younger man whom people call mad, who claims that a nervous disease has greatly sharpened his sense perceptions. He is proud of his own cleverness. <u>Other characters</u>: The old man, whose leading feature is one pale blue, filmed eye; said to be rich, kind, and lovable. Also three policemen, not individually described.

<u>Setting</u>: A shuttered house full of wind, mice, and treasures; pitch dark even in the afternoon.

<u>Narrator</u>: The madman himself.

<u>Events in summary</u>: (1) Dreading one vulturelike eye of the old man he shares a house with, a madman determines to kill its owner. (2) Each night he spies on the sleeping old man, but finding the eye shut, he stays his hand. (3) On the eighth night, finding the eye open, he suffocates its owner beneath the mattress and conceals the dismembered body under the floor of the bedchamber. (4) Entertaining some inquiring police officers in the very room where the body lies hidden, the killer again hears (or thinks he hears) the beat of his victim's heart. (5) Terrified, convinced that the police also hear the heartbeat growing louder, the killer confesses.

<u>Tone</u>: Horror at the events described, skepticism toward the narrator's claims to be sane, detachment from his gaiety and laughter.

7. A terse summary of the main events of the story, given in chronological order.
8. A description of the general tone of the story, as well as it can be sensed: the author's feelings toward the central character or the main events.

9. Some comments on the style in which the story is written. (Brief illustrative quotations are helpful, insofar as space permits.)
10. Whatever kinds of irony the story contains and what they contribute to the story.
11. In a sentence, the story's main theme.
12. Leading symbols (if the story has any), with an educated guess at whatever each symbol suggests.
13. Finally, an evaluation of the story as a whole, concisely setting forth the student's opinion of it. (Some instructors regard this as the most important part of the report, and most students find that, by the time they have so painstakingly separated the ingredients of the story, they have arrived at a definite opinion of it.)

### Back of Card

Style: Written as if told aloud by a deranged man eager to be believed, the story is punctuated by laughter, interjections ("Hearken!"), nervous halts, and fresh beginnings—indicated by dashes that grow more frequent as the story goes on and the narrator becomes more excited. Poe often relies on general adjectives ("mournful," "hideous," "hellish") to convey atmosphere; also on exact details: the lantern that emits "a single dim ray, like the thread of a spider."

Irony: The whole story is ironic in its point of view. Presumably the author is not mad, nor does he share the madman's self-admiration. Many of the narrator's statements therefore seem verbal ironies: his account of taking an hour to move his head through the bedroom door.

Theme: Possibly "Murder will out," but I really don't find any theme either stated or clearly implied.

Symbols: The vulture eye, called an Evil Eye (in superstition, one that can implant a curse), perhaps suggesting too the all-seeing eye of God the Father, from whom no guilt can be concealed. The ghostly heartbeat, sound of the victim coming back to be avenged (or the God who cannot be slain?). Death watches: beetles said to be death omens, whose ticking sound foreshadows the sound of the telltale heart "as a watch makes when enveloped in cotton."

Evaluation: Despite the overwrought style (to me slightly comicbookish), a powerful story, admirable for its concision and for its memorable portrait of a deranged killer. Poe knows how it is to be mad.

To fit so much on one card is, admittedly, somewhat like trying to engrave the Declaration of Independence on the head of a pin. The student who wrote this succinct report had to spoil a few trial cards before he was able to do it. Every word has to count, and making them count is a discipline worthwhile in almost any sort of expository writing. Some students enjoy the challenge. In doing such a report, though you may feel severely limited, you'll probably be surprised at how thoroughly you come to understand a story. Besides, if you care to keep the card for future reference, it won't take much storage room. A longer story, even a novel, may be analyzed in the same way; but insist on taking a second card if you are asked to analyze some especially hefty and complicated novel—say, Leo Tolstoi's panoramic, thousand-page *War and Peace*.

## COMPARING AND CONTRASTING

If you were to write on "The Humor of Frank O'Connor's 'First Confession' and Alice Munro's 'How I Met My Husband,' " you would probably employ one or two other methods. You might use **comparison,** placing the two stories side by side and pointing out their similarities; or you might use **contrast,** pointing out their differences. Most of the time, in dealing with a pair of stories, you will find them similar in some ways and different in others; and so you will be using both methods in writing your paper. No law requires you to devote equal space to each method. You might have to do more contrasting than comparing, or the other way around. If the stories are obviously similar but subtly different, you will probably compare them briefly, listing the similarities and then, at greater length, contrast them by calling attention to their important differences. If, however, the stories at first glance seem as different as peas and polecats yet are in fact closely related, you'll probably spend most of your time comparing them rather than contrasting them. (You might not just compare and contrast but also analyze, in that you might select one element of the stories for your investigation.) Other topics for papers involving two stories might be "The Experience of Coming of Age in James Joyce's 'Araby' and William Faulkner's 'Barn Burning'"; and "Mother and Daughter Relationships in Alice Walker's 'Everyday Use' and Tillie Olsen's 'I Stand Here Ironing.'"

Your paper, of course, will hang together better if you choose a pair of stories that apparently have much in common than if you choose two as unlike as cow and cantaloupe. Before you start writing, think: Do the two stories I've selected throw some light on each other? An essay that likened W. Somerset Maugham's terse, ironic fable "The Appointment in Samarra" with William Faulkner's rich, complex "Barn Burning" just might reveal unexpected similarities. More likely, it would seem strained and pointless.

You can also write an essay in comparison and contrast that deals with just one story. You might consider, say, the attitudes of the younger waiter and the older waiter in Hemingway's "A Clean, Well-Lighted Place." In Flannery

O'Connor's "Revelation," you might contrast Mrs. Turpin's smug view of herself with young Mary Grace's merciless view of her.

If your topic calls for both comparison and contrast and you are dealing with two stories, don't write the first half of your paper all about one story, then pivot and write the second half about the other, never permitting the two to mingle. The result probably would not be a unified essay in contrast and comparison but two separate commentaries yoked together. One workable way to organize such a paper is to make (before you begin) a brief list of points to look for in each story, then, as you write, to consider each point—first in one story and then in the other. Here is a simple outline for an essay bringing together William Faulkner's "A Rose for Emily" and Flannery O'Connor's "Revelation." The topic is "Two Would-be Aristocrats: The Characters of Emily Grierson and Mrs. Turpin."

1. Character's view of her own innate superiority

   a. Emily

   b. Mrs. Turpin

2. Author's evaluation of character's moral worth

   a. Emily

   b. Mrs. Turpin

3. Character's ability to change

   a. Emily

   b. Mrs. Turpin

It is best, however, not to follow such an outline in plodding, mechanical fashion ("Well, now it's time to whip over to Mrs. Turpin again"), lest your readers feel they are watching a back-and-forth tennis match. Some points are bound to interest you more than others, and, when they do, you will want to give them greater emphasis.

## SUGGESTIONS FOR WRITING

What kinds of topics are likely to result in papers that will reveal something about works of fiction? Here is a list of typical topics, suitable to papers of various lengths, offered in the hope of stimulating your own ideas. For other topics, see Suggestions for Writing at the end of every chapter. For specific advice on finding a topic of your own, see "Discovering and Planning," page 1737.

## TOPICS FOR BRIEF PAPERS (250–500 WORDS)

1. Consider a short story in which the central character has to make a decision or must take some decisive step that will alter the rest of his or her life. Faulkner's "Barn

Burning" is one such story; another is Updike's "A & P." As concisely and as thoroughly as you can, explain the nature of the character's decision, the reasons for it, and its probable consequences (as suggested by what the author tells us).

2. Write an informal (rather than a complete) explication of the opening paragraph or first few lines of a story. Show us how it prepares us for what will happen. (An alternate topic: take instead a closing paragraph and sum up whatever insight it leaves us with.) Don't feel obliged to deal with everything in the passage, as you would do in writing a more nearly complete explication. Within this suggested word length, limit your discussion to whatever strikes you as most essential.

3. Make a card report (see page 1753) on a short story in the Stories for Further Reading or one suggested by your instructor. Include all the elements in the report illustrated in this chapter (unless your instructor wishes you to emphasize some element or offers other advice).

4. Show how reading a specific short story caused you to change or modify an attitude or opinion you once had.

5. Just for fun, try writing a different ending to one of the short stories in this anthology. What does this exercise suggest about the wisdom of the author in ending things as done in the original? (Try to keep a sense of the author's style.)

6. Another wild idea: Write a sequel to one of your favorite short stories—or at least the beginning of a sequel, enough to give your reader a sense of it.

7. Argue from your own experience that a character in any story behaves (or doesn't behave) as people behave in life.


TOPICS FOR MORE EXTENDED PAPERS (600–1,000 WORDS)

1. Choose a short passage (one of, say, three or four sentences) in a story, a passage that interests you. Perhaps it will contain a decisive movement in a plot, a revealing comment on a character, or a statement of the story's major theme. Then write a reasonably thorough explication. Like the writer of the paper "By Lantern Light" (page 1748), go through the passage in some detail, noticing words that especially convey the author's meanings.

2. Write an analysis of a short story, singling out an element such as the author's voice (tone, style, irony), point of view, character, theme, symbolism, or Gothic elements (if the story has any). Try to show how this element functions in the story as a whole. For a typical paper in response to this assignment, see "The Hearer of the Tell-Tale Heart" (page 1751).

3. Analyze a story in which a character experiences some realization or revelation. How does the writer prepare us for the moment of enlightenment? What is the nature of each realization or revelation? How does it affect the character? Stories to consider might include "Miss Brill," "Gimpel the Fool," "Greasy Lake," "Araby," "The Chrysanthemums," "The Death of Ivan Ilych," "Revelation," and "Sonny's Blues."

4. Explore how humor functions in a story. What is funny? How is humor implied by the story's style or tone? Does humor help set forth a theme or reveal character? Any of the following stories deserves exploration: "A & P," "Gimpel the Fool," "Greasy Lake," "Where I'm Calling From," "Revelation," "First Confession," "The Conversion of the Jews," and "The Catbird Seat."

5. For anyone interested in a career in teaching: Explain how you would teach a story, either to an imaginary class or to the class you belong to now. Perhaps you might arrange with your instructor to write about a story your class hasn't read yet; and then, after writing your paper, actually to teach the story in class.

6. See if you can discover a new Stephen Crane—another journalist who brings literary skill to reporting (as Crane does in "The Open Boat"). In an essay, examine some news story, interview, or feature that you think reads like excellent fiction. Point out whatever elements of good storytelling you find in it. (Is there a plot? Lively dialogue? Suspense? Vivid style? Thought-provoking theme? Rounded characters, or at least memorable ones? Shrewd choice of a point of view?) For such a story, consult your daily newspaper or a weekly news magazine. Supply a clipping or copy of your discovery along with your finished paper.

7. If your daily newspaper lacks literary quality but you'd like to try that last topic, see any of the following books. Each contains some reporting that will show you storytelling art:

> Nora Ephron, *Crazy Salad: Some Things About Women* (New York: Knopf, 1975). Includes a portrait of the first woman umpire and a cutthroat national baking competition.

> Donald Hall, *Life Work* (Boston: Beacon Press 1993). An inspiring account of the pleasures of working at what one loves, especially good on the joys of writing.

> John Hersey, *Hiroshima* (New York: Knopf, 1946). The first atomic holocaust as seen by six survivors.

> Garrison Keillor, *Lake Wobegon Days* (New York: Viking, 1985). Gentle comic reports of a practically vanished small-town way of life.

> Tracy Kidder, *Among Schoolchildren* (Boston: Todd/Houghton Mifflin, 1989). Close observations of a year in the life of an elementary school teacher.

> Lillian Ross, *Reporting* (New York: Dodd, 1981). Seven classic essays in journalism, among them a profile of Ernest Hemingway.

> Hunter S. Thompson, *The Great Shark Hunt* (New York: Summit Books, 1979). Reports of politics, sports, and pleasure-seeking in the 1960s and 1970s.

> Tom Wolfe, *The Right Stuff* (New York: Farrar, 1979). The story of America's first astronauts.

## TOPICS FOR LONG PAPERS (*1,500 WORDS OR MORE*)

1. Selecting a short story from the Stories for Further Reading in this book, or taking one suggested by your instructor, write an informal essay setting forth (as thoroughly as you can) your understanding of it. Point out any difficulties you encountered in first reading the story, for the benefits of other students who might meet the same difficulties. If you find particularly complicated passages, briefly explicate them. An ample statement of the meaning of the story probably will not deal only with plot or only with theme but will also consider how the story is written and structured.

2. Dealing with a single element of fiction, write an analysis of Tolstoi's The Death of Ivan Ilych, Kafka's The Metamorphosis, or of some other long story that your instructor suggests.

3. Take a short story in which most of the events take place in the physical world (rather than inside some character's mind), and translate it into a one-act play, complete with stage directions. After you have done so, you might present a reading of it with the aid of other members of the class and then perhaps discuss what you had to do to the story to make a play of it.

4. Taking an author in this book whose work appeals to you, read at least three or four of his or her other stories. Then write an analysis of them, concentrating on an element of fiction that you find present in all.
5. Again going beyond this book if necessary, compare and contrast two writers' handling of a similar theme. Let your essay build to a conclusion in which you state your opinion: which author's expression of theme is deeper or more memorable?

# 3. *Writing about a Poem*

Assignment: write a paper about a poem. You can approach it as a grim duty, of course: any activity can look like a dull obligation. For Don Juan, in Spanish legend, even making love became a chore. But the act of writing, like the act of love, is easier if your feelings take part in it. Write about something you dislike and don't understand, and you not only set yourself the labors of Hercules, but you guarantee your reader discouragingly hard labor, too.

To write about a poem informatively, you need first to experience it. It helps to live with the poem for as long as possible: there is little point in trying to encompass the poem in a ten-minute tour of inspection on the night before the paper falls due. However challenging, writing about poetry has immediate rewards, and to mention just one, the poem you spend time writing about is going to mean much more to you than poems skimmed ever do.

Most of the problems you will meet in writing about a poem are the same ones you meet in writing about a play or a story: finding a topic, organizing your thoughts, writing, revising. For general advice on writing papers about any kind of literature, see "Writing about Literature" on page 1735. In a few ways, however, a poem requires a different approach. In this chapter we will deal briefly with some of them, and will offer a few illustrations of papers that students have written. These papers may not be works of immortal genius, but they are pretty good papers, the likes of which most students can write with a modest investment of time and care.

Briefer than most stories and plays, lyric poems look easier to write about. They call, however, for your keenest attention. You may find that, before you can discuss a short poem, you will have to read it slowly and painstakingly, with your mind (like your pencil) sharp and ready. Unlike a play or a short story, a lyric poem tends to have very little plot, and perhaps you will find little to say about what happens in it. In order to understand a poem, you'll need to notice elements other than narrative: the connotations or suggestions of its words, surely, and the rhythm of phrases and lines. The subtleties of language are so essential to a poem (and so elusive) that Robert Frost was moved to say, "Poetry is what gets lost in translation." Once in a while, of course, you'll read a story whose prose abounds in sounds, rhythms, figures of speech, imagery, and other elements you expect of poetry. Certain novels of Herman Melville and William Faulkner contain paragraphs that, if extracted, seem in themselves prose poems—so lively are they in their word-play, so rich in metaphor. But such writing is exceptional, and the main business of most fiction is to get a story told. An extreme case of a fiction writer who didn't want his prose to sound poetic is Georges Simenon, best known for his mystery novels, who said that whenever he noticed in his manuscript any word or phrase that called attention to itself, he struck it out. That method of writing would never do for a poet, who revels in words and phrases that fix themselves in memory. It is safe to say that, in order to write well about a poem, you have to read it carefully enough to remember at least part of it word for word.

Let's consider three commonly useful approaches to writing about poetry.

## EXPLICATING

In an **explication** (literally, "an unfolding") of a poem, a writer explains the entire poem in detail, unraveling any complexities to be found in it. This method is a valuable one in approaching a lyric poem, especially if the poem is rich in complexities (or in suggestions worth rendering explicit). Most poems that you'll ever be asked to explicate are short enough to discuss thoroughly within a limited time; fully to explicate a long and involved work, such as John Milton's epic *Paradise Lost,* might require a lifetime. (To explicate a short passage of Milton's long poem however, would be a practical and interesting course assignment.)

The writer of an explication tries to examine and unfold all the details in a poem that a sensitive reader might consider. These might include allusions, the denotations or connotations of words, the possible meanings of symbols, the effects of certain sounds and rhythms and formal elements (rime schemes, for instance), the sense of any statements that contain irony, and other particulars. Not intent on ripping a poem to pieces, the author of a useful explication instead tries to show how each part contributes to the whole.

An explication is easy to organize. You can start with the first line of the poem and keep working straight on through. An explication should not be confused with a paraphrase. A paraphrase simply puts the literal meaning of a poem into plain prose sense: it is a sort of translation that might prove helpful in clarifying a poem's main theme. Perhaps in writing an explication you wish to do some paraphrasing; but an explication (unlike a paraphrase) does not simply restate: it explains a poem, in great detail.

Here, for example, is a famous poem by Robert Frost, followed by a student's concise explication. (The assignment was to explain whatever in "Design" seemed most essential, in not more than 750 words.)

## Robert Frost (1874–1963)*

DESIGN                                                                    1936

I found a dimpled spider, fat and white,
On a white heal-all, holding up a moth
Like a white piece of rigid satin cloth—
Assorted characters of death and blight
Mixed ready to begin the morning right,                                    5
Like the ingredients of a witches' broth—
A snow-drop spider, a flower like a froth,
And dead wings carried like a paper kite.

What had that flower to do with being white,
The wayside blue and innocent heal-all?                                   10
What brought the kindred spider to that height,
Then steered the white moth thither in the night?
What but design of darkness to appall?—
If design govern in a thing so small.


An Unfolding of Robert Frost's "Design"

"I always wanted to be very observing," Robert Frost
once said, after reading his poem "Design" to an audience. Then he added, "But I have always been afraid of
my own observations" (Cook 126-27). What could Frost
have observed that could scare him? Let's observe the
poem in question and see what we discover.

Starting with the title, "Design," any reader of this
poem will find it full of meaning. As Webster's New
World Dictionary defines design, the word can denote
among other things a plan, or "purpose; intention; aim."
Some arguments for the existence of God (I remember from
Sunday School) are based on the "argument from design":

that because the world shows a systematic order, there must be a Designer who made it. But the word design can also mean "a secret or sinister scheme" — such as we attribute to a "designing person." As we shall see, Frost's poem incorporates all of these meanings. His poem raises the old philosophic question of whether there is a Designer, an evil Designer, or no Designer at all. Frost probably read William James on this question, as a critic has shown convincingly (Poirier 245-50).

Like many other sonnets, "Design" is divided into two parts. The first eight lines draw a picture centering on the spider, who at first seems almost jolly. It is dimpled and fat like a baby, or Santa Claus. It stands on a wild flower whose name, heal-all, seems ironic: a heal-all is supposed to cure any disease, but it certainly has no power to restore life to the dead moth. (Later, in line ten, we learn that the heal-all used to be blue. Presumably it has died and become bleached-looking.) In this second line we discover, too, that the spider has hold of another creature. Right away we might feel sorry for the moth, were it not for the simile applied to it in line three: "Like a white piece of rigid satin cloth." Suddenly the moth becomes not a creature but a piece of fabric — lifeless and dead — and yet satin has connotations of beauty. Satin is a luxurious material used in rich formal clothing, such as coronation gowns and brides' dresses. Additionally, there is great accuracy in the word: the smooth and slightly plush surface of satin is like the powder-smooth surface of moths' wings. But this "cloth," rigid and white, could be the lining to Dracula's coffin.

In the fifth line an invisible hand enters. The characters are "mixed" like ingredients in an evil potion.

Some force doing the mixing is behind the scene. The characters in themselves are innocent enough, but when brought together, their whiteness and look of rigor mortis are overwhelming. There is something diabolical in the spider's feast. The "morning right" echoes the word rite, a ritual — in this case apparently a Black Mass or a Witches' Sabbath. The simile in line seven ("a flower like a froth") is more ambiguous and harder to describe. A froth is white, foamy, and delicate — something found on a brook in the woods or on a beach after a wave recedes. However, in the natural world, froth also can be ugly: the foam on a polluted stream or a rabid dog's mouth. The dualism in nature — its beauty and its horror — is there in that one simile.

So far, the poem has portrayed a small, frozen scene, with the dimpled killer holding its victim as innocently as a boy holds a kite. Already, Frost has hinted that Nature may be, as Radcliffe Squires suggests, "nothing but an ash-white plain without love or faith or hope, where ignorant appetites cross by chance" (87). Now, in the last six lines of the sonnet, Frost comes out and directly states his theme. What else could bring these deathly pale, stiff things together "but design of darkness to appall?" The question is clearly rhetorical; we are meant to answer, "Yes, there does seem an evil design at work here!" I take the next-to-last line to mean, "What except a design so dark and sinister that we're appalled by it?" "Appall," by the way, is the second pun in the poem: it sounds like a pall or shroud. (The derivation of appall, according to Webster's, is from a Latin word meaning "to grow pale" — an interesting word choice for a poem full of white, pale images.) Steered carries the suggestion of a steering-wheel or rudder that some pilot had to control.

Like the word <u>brought</u>, it implies that some invisible
force charted the paths of spider, heal-all, and moth, so
that they arrived together.

Having suggested that the universe is in the hands of
that sinister force (an indifferent God? Fate? the
Devil?), Frost adds a note of doubt. The Bible tells us
that "His eye is on the sparrow," but at the moment the
poet doesn't seem sure. Maybe, he hints, when things in
the universe drop below a certain size, they pass completely out of the Designer's notice. When creatures are
that little, maybe God doesn't bother to govern them,
but just lets them run wild. And possibly the same mindless chance is all that governs human lives. And because
that is even more senseless than having an angry God
intent on punishing us, it is, Frost suggests, the worst
suspicion of all.

Works Cited

Cook, Reginald. <u>Robert Frost: A Living Voice</u>. Amherst: U of
Massachusetts P, 1974.

Poirier, Richard. <u>Robert Frost: The Work of Knowing</u>. New
York: Oxford UP, 1977.

Squires, Radcliffe. <u>The Major Themes of Robert Frost</u>. Ann
Arbor: U of Michigan P, 1963.

This excellent paper, while finding something worth unfolding in every line
in Frost's poem, does so without seeming mechanical. Notice that, although the
student proceeds through the poem from the title to the last line, she takes up
points when necessary, in any sequence. In paragraph two, the writer looks ahead
to the end of the poem and briefly states its main theme. (She does so in order to
relate this theme to the poem's title.) In the third paragraph, she deals with the
poem's *later* image of the heal-all, relating it to the first image. Along the way,
she comments on the form of the poem ("Like many other sonnets"), on its similes and puns, its denotations and connotations.

Incidentally, this paper demonstrates good use of manuscript form, following
the *MLA Handbook*, 3rd ed. Brief references (in parentheses) tell us where the
writer found Frost's remarks before an audience, name the critic (Poirier) who

showed that Frost had read the philosopher William James, and give page numbers for these sources and for another, a book by Radcliffe Squires. At the end of the paper, a list of these works cited uses abbreviations for *University* and *Press* that the *MLA Handbook* recommends (but doesn't insist upon).

It might seem that to work through a poem line by line is a mechanical task; and yet there can be genuine excitement in it. Randall Jarrell once wrote an explication of "Design" in which he managed to convey such excitement. In the following passage taken from it, see if you can sense the writer's joy in his work.

> Frost's details are so diabolically good that it seems criminal to leave some unremarked; but notice how *dimpled, fat,* and *white* (all but one; all but one;) come from our regular description of any baby; notice how the *heal-all,* because of its name, is the one flower in all the world picked to be the altar for this Devil's Mass; notice how *holding up* the moth brings something ritual and hieratic, a ghostly, ghastly formality, to this priest and its sacrificial victim; notice how terrible to the fingers, how full of the stilling rigor of death, that *white piece of rigid satin cloth* is. And *assorted characters of death and blight* is, like so many things in this poem, sharply ambiguous: a *mixed bunch of actors* or *diverse representative signs.* The tone of the phrase *assorted characters of death and blight* is beautifully developed in the ironic Breakfast-Club-calisthenics, Radio-Kitchen heartiness of *mixed ready to begin the morning right* (which assures us, so unreassuringly, that this isn't any sort of Strindberg *Spook Sonata,* but hard fact), and concludes in the *ingredients* of the witches' broth, giving the soup a sort of cuddly shimmer that the cauldron in *Macbeth* never had; the *broth,* even, is brought to life—we realize that witches' broth *is* broth, to be supped with a long spoon.[1]

Evidently, Jarrell's cultural interests are broad: ranging from August Strindberg's ground-breaking modern classic down to the Breakfast Club (a once-popular radio program that cheerfully exhorted its listeners to march around their tables). And yet breadth of knowledge, however much it deepens and enriches Jarrell's writing, isn't all that he brings to the reading of poetry. For him, an explication isn't a dull plod, but a voyage of discovery. His prose—full of figures of speech (*diabolically good, cuddly shimmer*)—conveys the apparent delight he takes in showing off his findings. Such a joy, of course, can't be acquired deliberately. But it can grow, the more you read and study poetry.

## ANALYZING

An **analysis** of a poem, like a news commentator's analysis of a crisis in the Middle East or a chemist's analysis of an unknown fluid, separates its subject into elements, as a means to understanding that subject—to see what composes it.

---

[1] From *Poetry and the Age* (New York: Knopf, 1953).

Usually, the writer of such an essay singles out one of those elements for attention: "Imagery of Light and Darkness in Frost's 'Design'"; "The Character of Satan in *Paradise Lost*."

Like explication, analysis can be particularly useful in dealing with a short poem. Unlike explication (which inches through a poem line by line), analysis often suits a long poem too, because it allows the writer to discuss just one manageable element in the poem. A good analysis casts intense light upon a poem from one direction. If you care enough about a poem, and about some perspective on it—its theme, say, or its symbolism, or its singability—writing an analysis can enlighten and give pleasure.

In this book you probably have met a few brief analyses: the discussion of connotations in John Masefield's "Cargoes" (page 651), for instance, or the examination of symbols in T.S. Eliot's "The *Boston Evening Transcript*" (page 797). In fact, most of the discussions in this book are analytic. Temporarily, we have separated the whole art of poetry into elements such as tone, irony, literal meaning, suggestions, imagery, figures of speech, sound, rhythm, and so on. No element of a poem, of course, exists apart from all the other elements. Still, by taking a closer look at particular elements, one at a time, we see them more clearly and more easily study them.

Long analyses of metrical feet, rime schemes, and indentations tend to make ponderous reading: such formal and technical elements are perhaps the hardest to discuss engagingly. And yet formal analysis (at least a little of it) can be interesting and illuminating: it can measure the very pulse beat of lines. If you do care about the technical side of poetry, then write about it, by all means. You will probably find it helpful to learn the terms for the various meters, stanzas, fixed forms, and other devices, so that you can summon them to your aid with confidence. Here is a short formal analysis of "Design" by a student who evidently cares for technicalities yet who manages not to be a bore in talking about them. Concentrating on the sonnet form of Frost's poem, the student actually casts light upon the poem in its entirety.

### The Design of "Design"

For "Design," the sonnet form has at least two advantages. First, as in most strict Italian sonnets, the argument of the poem falls into two parts. In the octave Frost draws a pale still-life of spider, flower, and moth; then in the sestet he contemplates the meaning of it. The sestet deals with a more general idea: the possible existence of a vindictive deity who causes the spider to catch the moth, and no doubt also causes other suffering. Frost weaves his own little web. The unwary reader is led into the poem by its opening story, and pretty soon is struggling with more than he expected. Even the rime scheme, by the way, has something to do with the poem's meaning. The word <u>white</u> ends the first line of the sestet. The same sound is echoed in the rimes that follow. All in all, half the lines in the poem end in an "ite." It seems as if Frost places great weight on the whiteness of his little scene, for the riming words both introduce the term <u>white</u> and keep reminding us of it.

A sonnet has a familiar design, and that is its second big advantage to this particular poem. In a way, writing "Design" as a sonnet almost seems a subtle joke. (I can just imagine Frost chuckling to himself, wondering if anyone will get it.) A sonnet, being a classical form, is an orderly world with certain laws in it. There is ready-made irony in its containing a meditation on whether there is any order in the universe at large. Obviously there's design in back of the poem, but is there any design to insect life, or human life? Whether or not the poet can answer this question (and it seems he can't), at least he discovers an order while writing the poem. Actually, that is just what Frost said a poet achieves: "a momentary stay against confusion."[1]

Although design clearly governs in this poem — in "this thing so small" — the design isn't entirely predictable. The poem starts out as an Italian sonnet, with just two riming sounds; then (unlike an Italian sonnet) it keeps the "ite" rimes going. It ends in a couplet, like a Shakespearean sonnet. From these unexpected departures from the pattern of the Italian sonnet announced in the opening lines, I get the impression that Frost's poem is somewhat like the larger universe. It looks perfectly orderly, until you notice the small details in it.

¹Robert Frost, "The Figure a Poem Makes," preface, <u>Complete Poems of Robert Frost</u> (New York: Holt, 1949) vi.

Unlike the student paper on pages 1763–1766, that documented its references (inside parentheses), "The Design of 'Design'" uses an endnote to cite its one outside source. (In so doing, it follows the form for such notes suggested in the *MLA Handbook,* 3rd ed.) To do so seems sensible here. This writer doesn't need a list of works cited, for such a list might have looked skimpy, like a one-car funeral. (In the endnote, by the way, *Holt* is a short, MLA-recommended contraction for the full name of the publisher: Holt, Rinehart, and Winston, Inc.)

## COMPARING AND CONTRASTING

To write a **comparison** of two poems, you place them side by side and point out their likenesses; to write a **contrast,** you point out their differences. If you wish, you can combine the two methods in the same paper. For example, even though you may emphasize similarities you may also call attention to significant differences, or vice versa.

Such a paper makes most sense if you pair two poems that have much in common. It would be possible to compare Wallace McRae's comic cowboy poem "Reincarnation" with John Milton's profoundly elegiac "Lycidas," but comparison would be difficult, perhaps futile. Though both poems are in English and both deal with the themes of death and transfiguration, the two seem hopelessly remote from each other—in diction, tone, complexity, and scope. Your first task, therefore, is to choose two poems that profit by being examined together.

Having found the right pair of poems that throw light on each other, you then go on in your paper to show further, unsuspected resemblances—not just the ones that are obvious ("'Design' and 'Wing-Spread' are both about bugs"). The interesting resemblances are ones that take thinking to discover. Similarly, you may want to show noteworthy differences—besides those your reader will see without any help.

In comparing two poems, you may be tempted to discuss one of them and be done with it, then spend the latter half of your paper discussing the other. This simple way of organizing an essay can be dangerous if it leads you to keep the two poems in total isolation from each other. The whole idea of such an assignment, of course, is to see what can be learned by comparing the two poems. There is nothing wrong in discussing all of poem A first, then discussing poem B—*if* in discussing B you keep looking back at A. Another procedure is to keep comparing the two poems all the way through your paper—dealing first, let's say, with their themes; then with their metaphors: and finally, with their respective merits.

More often than not, a comparison is a kind of analysis: a study of a theme common to two poems, for instance; or of two poets' similar fondness for the myth of Eden. But you also can evaluate poems by comparing and contrasting them: placing them side by side in order to decide which poet deserves the brighter laurels. Here, for example, is a paper that considers "Design" and "Wing-Spread," a poem of Abbie Huston Evans (first printed in 1938, two years after Frost's poem). By comparing and contrasting the two poems for (1) their language and (2) their themes, this student shows us reasons for his evaluation.

"Wing-Spread" Does a Dip

```
        The midge spins out to safety
        Through the spider's rope;
        But the moth, less lucky,
        Has to grope.
        Mired in glue-like cable                        5
        See him foundered swing
        By the gap he opened
        With his wing,

        Dusty web enlacing
        All that blue and beryl.                        10
        In a netted universe
        Wing-spread is peril.

                            —Abbie Huston Evans
```

"Wing-Spread," quoted above, is a good poem, but it is not in the same class with "Design." Both poets show us a murderous spider and an unlucky moth, but there are two reasons for Robert Frost's superiority. One is his more suggestive use of language, the other is his more memorable theme.

Let's start with language. "Design" is full of words and phrases rich in suggestions. "Wing-Spread," by comparison, contains few. To take just one example, Frost's "dimpled spider, fat and white" is certainly a more suggestive description. Actually, Evans doesn't describe her spider; she just says, "the spider's rope." (Evans does vividly show us the spider and moth in action. In Frost's view, they are dead and petrified — but I guess that is the impression he is after.) In "Design," the spider's dimples show that it is like a chubby little kid, who further turns out to be a kite-flier. This seems an odd, almost freaky way to look at a spider. I find it more refreshing than Evans's view (although I like her word cable, suggesting that the spider's web is a kind of high-tech food trap). Frost's word-choice — his harping on white — paints a more striking scene than Evans's slightly vague "All that blue and beryl." Except for her personification of the moth in her second stanza, Evans doesn't go in for any figures of speech, and even that one isn't a clear personification — she simply gives the moth a sex by referring to it as "him." Frost's striking metaphors, similes, and even puns (right, appall) show him, as usual, to be a master of figures of speech. He calls the moth's wings "satin cloth" and "a paper kite"; Evans just refers in line 8 to a moth's wing. As far as the language of the two poems goes, you might as well compare a vase brimming with flowers and a single flower stuck in a vase. (That is a poor metaphor, since Frost's poem contains only one flower, but I hope you will know what I mean.)

In fairness to Evans, I would say that she picks a pretty good solitary flower. And her poem has powerful sounds: short lines with the riming words coming at us again and again very frequently. In theme, however,

"Wing-Spread" seems much more narrow than "Design." The first time I read Evans's poem all I felt was: Ho hum, the moth's wings were too wide and got stuck. The second time I read it, I figured that she is saying something with a universal application. This message comes out in line 11, in "a netted universe." That is the most interesting phrase in her poem, one that you can think about. <u>Netted</u> makes me imagine the universe as being full of nets rigged by someone who is fishing for us. Maybe, like Frost, Evans sees an evil plan operating. She does not, though, investigate it. She says that the midge escapes because it is tiny. On the other hand, things with wide wing-spreads get stuck. Her theme as I read it is, "Be small and inconspicuous if you want to survive," or maybe, "Isn't it too bad that in this world the big beautiful types crack up and die, while the little puny punks keep sailing?" Now, that is a valuable idea. I have often thought that very same thing myself. But Frost's closing note ("If design govern in a thing so small") is really devastating, because it raises a huge uncertainty. "Wing-Spread" leaves us with not much besides a moth stuck in a web, and a moral. In both language and theme, "Design" climbs to a higher altitude.

## How to Quote a Poem

Preparing to discuss a short poem, it is a good idea to emulate the student who wrote on "Wing-Spread" and to quote the whole text of the poem at the beginning of your paper, with its lines numbered. Then you can refer to it with ease, and your instructor, without having to juggle a book, can follow you.

Quoted to illustrate some point, memorable lines can add interest to your paper, and good commentators on poetry tend to be apt quoters, helping their readers to experience a word, a phrase, a line, or a passage that otherwise might be neglected. However, to quote from poetry is slightly more awkward than to quote from prose. There are lines to think about—important and meaningful units whose shape you will need to preserve. If you are quoting more than a couple of lines, it is good policy to arrange your quotation just as its lines occur in the poem, white space and all:

```
At the outset, the poet tells us of his discovery of
            a dimpled spider, fat and white,
      On a white heal-all, holding up a moth
      Like a white piece of rigid satin cloth—
```

```
and implies that the small killer is both childlike and
sinister.
```

But if you are quoting less than two lines of verse, it would seem wasteful of paper to write:

```
The color white preoccupies Frost. The spider is
            fat and white,
      On a white heal-all
      and even the victim moth is pale, too.
```

In such a case, it saves space to transform Frost's line arrangement into prose:

```
The color white preoccupies Frost. The spider is "fat and
white,/On a white heal-all"—and even the victim moth is
pale, too.
```

Here, a diagonal (/) indicates the writer's respect for where the poet's lines begin and end. Some writers prefer to quote the passage from Frost as follows: "fat and white, / On a white heal-all. . . ." The ellipsis ( . . . ) in the last quotation indicates that words are omitted from the end of Frost's sentence; the fourth dot is a period. Some writers—meticulous souls—also stick in an ellipsis at the *beginning* of a quotation, if they're leaving out words from the beginning of a sentence in the original:

```
The color white preoccupies Frost in his description of
the spider ". . . fat and white,/ On a white heal-all. . . ."
```

Surely there's no need for an initial ellipsis, though, if you begin quoting at the beginning of a sentence. No need for a final ellipsis, either, if your quotation goes right to the end of a sentence in the original. If it is obvious that only a phrase is being quoted, no need for an ellipsis in any case:

```
The speaker says he "found a dimpled spider" and he goes
on to portray it as a kite-flying boy.
```

If you leave out whole lines, indicate the omission by an ellipsis all by itself on a line:

```
The midge spins out to safety

Through the spider's rope;

      . . .

In a netted universe

Wing-spread is peril.
```

## BEFORE YOU BEGIN

Ready at last to write, you will have spent considerable time in reading, thinking, and feeling. After having chosen your topic, you probably will have taken a further look at the poem or poems you have picked, letting further thoughts and feelings come to you. The quality of your paper will depend, above all, upon the quality of your readiness to write.

Exploring a poem, a sensitive writer handles it with care and affection as though it were a living animal, and, done with it, leaves it still alive. The unfeeling writer, on the other hand, disassembles the poem in a dull, mechanical way, like someone with a blunt ax filling an order for one horse-skeleton. Again, to write well is a matter of engaging your feelings. Writing to a deadline, on an assigned topic, you easily can sink into a drab, workaday style, especially if you regard the poet as some uninspired builder of chicken coops who hammers themes and images into place, and then slaps the whole thing with a coat of words. Certain expressions, if you lean on them habitually, may tempt you to think of the poet in that way. Here, for instance, is a discussion—by a plodding writer—of Robert Frost's poem.

```
    The symbols Frost uses in "Design" are very success-
ful. Frost makes the spider stand for Nature. He wants us
to see Nature as blind and cruel. He also employs good
sounds. He uses a lot of i's because he is trying to make
you think of falling rain.
```

(Underscored words are worth questioning.) What's wrong with that comment? While understandable, the words *uses* and *employs* seem to lead the writer to see Frost only as a conscious tool-manipulator. To be sure, Frost in a sense "uses" symbols, but did he grab hold of them and lay them into his poem? For all we know, perhaps the symbols arrived quite unbidden, and used the poet. To write a good poem, Frost maintained, a poet himself has to be surprised. (How, by the way, can we hope to know what a poet *wants* to do? And there isn't much point in saying that the poet is *trying* to do something. He has already done it, if he has written a good poem.) At least, it is likely that Frost didn't plan to fulfill a certain quota of *i*-sounds. Writing his poem, not by following a blueprint but probably by bringing it slowly to the surface of his mind (like Elizabeth Bishop's hooked fish), Frost no doubt had enough to do without trying to engineer the reactions of his possible audience. Like all true symbols, Frost's spider doesn't *stand for* anything. The writer would be closer to the truth to say that the spider *suggests* or *reminds us* of Nature, or of certain forces in the natural world. (Symbols just hint, they don't indicate.)

After the student discussed the paper in a conference, he rewrote the first two sentences like this:

```
    The symbols in Frost's "Design" are highly effective.
The spider, for instance, suggests the blindness and cru-
elty of Nature. Frost's word-sounds, too, are part of the
meaning of his poem, for the i's remind the reader of
falling rain.
```

Not every reader of "Design" will hear rain falling, but the student's revision probably comes closer to describing the experience of the poem most of us know.

In writing about poetry, an occasional note of self-doubt can be useful: now and then a *perhaps* or a *possibly*, an *it seems* or a modest *I suppose*. Such expressions may seem timid shilly-shallying, but at least they keep the writer from thinking, "I know all there is to know about this poem."

Facing the showdown with your empty sheaf of paper, however, you can't worry forever about your critical vocabulary. To do so is to risk the fate of the centipede in a bit of comic verse, who was running along efficiently until someone asked, "Pray, which leg comes after which?," whereupon "He lay distracted in a ditch/Considering how to run." It is a safe bet that your instructor is human. Your main task as a writer is to communicate to another human being your sensitive reading of a poem.

## SUGGESTIONS FOR WRITING

### TOPICS FOR BRIEF PAPERS (*250–500 WORDS*)

1. Write a concise explication of a short poem of your choice, or one suggested by your instructor. In a paper this brief, probably you won't have room to explain everything in the poem; explain what you think most needs explaining. (An illustration of one such explication appears on page 1763.)
2. Write an analysis of a short poem, first deciding which one of its elements to deal with. (An illustration of such an analysis appears on page 1768.) For examples, here are a few specific topics:

   "Kinds of Irony in Hardy's 'The Workbox'"

   "The Attitude of the Speaker in Marvell's 'To His Coy Mistress'"

   "The Theme of Pastan's 'Ethics.'"

"An Extended Metaphor in Yeats's 'Long-Legged Fly.'" (Explain the one main comparison that the poem makes and show how the whole poem makes it. Other likely possibilities for a paper on extended metaphor: Dickinson's "Because I could not stop for Death," Dove's "Daystar," Frost's "The Silken Tent," Lowell's "Skunk Hour," Rich's "Aunt Jennifer's Tigers," Stevenson's "The Victory.")

"The Rhythms of Plath's 'Daddy'"

(To locate any of these poems, see the Index of Authors and Titles, and Index of First Lines of Poetry at the back of this book.)

3. Select a poem in which the main speaker is a character who for any reason interests you. You might consider, for instance, Kees's "For My Daughter," Browning's "Soliloquy of the Spanish Cloister," Dove's "Daystar," or Eliot's "Love Song of J. Alfred Prufrock." Then write a brief profile of this character, drawing only on what the poem tells you (or reveals). What is the character's approximate age? Situation in life? Attitude toward self? Attitude toward others? General personality? Do you find this character admirable?

4. Although each of these poems tells a story, what happens in the poem isn't necessarily obvious: Cummings's "anyone lived in a pretty how town," Eliot's "Love Song of J. Alfred Prufrock," Stafford's "At the Klamath Berry Festival," Winters's "At the San Francisco Airport," James Wright's "A Blessing." Choose one of these poems and in a paragraph sum up what you think happens in it. Then in a second paragraph ask yourself: what, besides the element of story, did you consider in order to understand the poem?

5. Think of someone you know (or someone you can imagine) whose attitude toward poetry in general is dislike. Suggest a poem for that person to read—a poem that you like—and, addressing your skeptical reader, point out whatever you find to enjoy in it, that you think the skeptic just might enjoy too.

## TOPICS FOR MORE EXTENSIVE PAPERS (600–1,000 WORDS)

1. Write an explication of a poem short enough for you to work through line by line—for instance, Emily Dickinson's "My Life had stood–a loaded Gun" or MacLeish's "The End of the World." As if offering your reading experience to a friend who hadn't read the poem before, try to point out all the leading difficulties you encountered, and set forth in detail your understanding of any lines that contain such difficulties.

2. Write an explication of a longer poem—for instance, Eliot's "Love Song of J. Alfred Prufrock," Hardy's "Convergence of the Twain," or Plath's "Lady Lazarus." Although you will not be able to go through every line of the poem, explain what you think most needs explaining.

3. In this book, you will find four or more poems by each of these poets: Blake, Dickinson, Donne, Eliot, Frost, Hardy, Hopkins, Housman, Hughes, Keats, Shakespeare, Stevens, Tennyson, Whitman, Wilbur, William Carlos Williams, Wordsworth, and Yeats; and multiple selections for many more. (See Index to Authors and Titles, and Index of First Lines of Poetry.) After you read a few poems by a poet who interests you, write an analysis of more than one of the poet's poems. To do this, you will need to select just one characteristic theme (or other element) to deal with—something typical of the poet's work, not found only in a single poem. Here are a few specific topics for such an analysis:

"What Angers William Blake? A Look at Three Poems of Protest"

"How Emily Dickinson's Lyrics Resemble Hymns"

"The Humor of Robert Frost"

"Folk Elements in the Poetry of Langston Hughes"

"John Keats's Sensuous Imagery"

"The Vocabulary of Music in Poems of Wallace Stevens"

"Non-free Verse: Patterns of Sound in Three Poems of William Carlos Williams"

4. Compare and contrast two poems in order to evaluate them: which is more satisfying and effective poetry? To make a meaningful comparison, be sure to choose two poems that genuinely have much in common: perhaps a similar theme or subject. (For an illustration of such a paper, see the one given in this chapter. For suggestions of poems to compare, see Poems for Further Reading.)
5. Evaluate by the method of comparison two versions of a poem: early and late drafts, perhaps, or two translations from another language. For parallel versions to work on, see Chapter Twenty-seven, "Alternatives."
6. If the previous topic appeals to you, consider this. In 1912, twenty-four years before he printed "Design," Robert Frost sent a correspondent this early version:

IN WHITE

A dented spider like a snow drop white
On a white Heal-all, holding up a moth
Like a white piece of lifeless satin cloth—
Saw ever curious eye so strange a sight?—
Portent in little, assorted death and blight          5
Like ingredients of a witches' broth?—
The beady spider, the flower like a froth,
And the moth carried like a paper kite.

What had that flower to do with being white,
The blue prunella every child's delight.          10
What brought the kindred spider to that height?
(Make we no thesis of the miller's plight.)
What but design of darkness and of night?
Design, design! Do I use the word aright?

Compare "In White" with "Design." In what respects is the finished poem superior?

TOPICS FOR LONG PAPERS (1,500 WORDS OR MORE)

1. Write a line-by-line explication of a poem rich in matters to explain, or a longer poem that offers ample difficulty. While relatively short, Donne's "A Valediction: Forbidding Mourning" or Hopkins's "The Windhover" are poems that will take a good bit of time to explicate; but even a short, apparently simple poem such as Frost's "Stopping by Woods on a Snowy Evening" can provide more than enough to explicate thoughtfully in a longer paper.
2. Write an analysis of the work of one poet (as suggested above, in the third topic for more extensive papers) in which you go beyond this book to read an entire collection of that poet's work.
3. Write an analysis of a certain theme (or other element) that you find in the work of two or more poets. It is probable that in your conclusion you will want to set the poets' work side by side, comparing or contrasting it, and perhaps making some evaluation. Sample topics:

"Langston Hughes, Gwendolyn Brooks, and Dudley Randall as Prophets of Social Change."

"What It Is to Be a Woman: The Special Knowledge of Sylvia Plath, Anne Sexton, and Adrienne Rich."

"Popular Culture as Reflected in the Poetry of Wendy Cope, Edward Field, and Charles Martin."

4. Taking a passage from "Criticism: On Poetry," see what light it will cast on a poem that interests you. You might test Gray's "Elegy" by Poe's dictum that there is no such thing as a long poem. (Does the "Elegy" flag in intensity?) Or try reading several poems of Robert Frost, looking for the "sound of sense" (which Frost explains in his letter to John Bartlett on page 1030).

# 4. *Writing about a Play*

## METHODS

How is writing about a play any different from writing about a short story or a poem? Differences will quickly appear if you are writing about a play you have actually seen performed. Although, like a story or a poem, a play in print is usually the work of one person (and it is relatively fixed and changeless), a play on stage may be the joint effort of seventy or eighty people—actors, director, costumers, set designers, and technicians—and in its many details it may change from season to season, or even from night to night. Later on in this chapter, you will find some advice on reviewing a performance of a play, as you might do for a class assignment or for publication in, say, a campus newspaper. But in a literature course, for the most part, you will probably write about the plays you quietly read, and behold only in the theater of your mind. At least one advantage in writing about a printed play is that you can always go back and reread it, unlike the reviewer who, unless provided with a script, has nothing but memory to rely on.

Before you begin to write, it makes sense to read the *whole* play—not just the dialogue, but also everything in italics: descriptions of scenes, instructions to the actors, and other stage directions. This point may seem obvious, but the meaning of a scene, or even of an entire play, may depend on the tone of voice in which an actor is supposed to deliver a line. At the end of *A Doll's House*, we need to pay attention to what Ibsen tells the actor playing Helmer—"*A sudden hope leaps in him*"—if we are to understand that, when Nora departs, she ignores Helmer's last desperate hope for a reconciliation, and she slams the door emphatically. And of course there is a resounding meaning in the final stage direction, in "the sound of a door slamming shut."

Taking notes on passages you will want to quote or refer to in your paper, you can use a concise method for keeping track of them. Jot down the numbers of act, scene, and line—for instance: I, ii, 42. Later, when you write, this handy shorthand will save space, and you can use it both in footnotes and in the body of your essay. Even if you do without footnotes, you can still indicate the exact lines you are quoting, or referring to:

```
Iago's hypocrisy, apparent in his famous defense of
his good name (III, iii, 168-174), is aptly summed up
by Roderigo, who accuses him: "Your words and perfor-
mances are no kin together" (IV, ii, 190-191).
```

Any of the methods frequently applied in writing about fiction and poetry—explication, analysis, comparison and contrast—can serve in writing about a play. All three methods are discussed in "Writing about a Story," and again in "Writing about a Poem." (For student papers that illustrate explication, see pages 1748 and 1763; analysis, pages 1751 and 1768; comparison and contrast, page 1771.) For using these methods to write about plays in particular, here are a few suggestions.

A whole play is too much to cover in an ordinary **explication**—a detailed, line-by-line unfolding of meaning. An explication of *Othello* could take years; a more reasonable class assignment would be to explicate a single key speech or passage from a play: Iago's description of a "deserving woman" (*Othello*, II,i, 148–158); or the first chorus in *Oedipus the King*.

If you decide to write an essay by the method of **comparison and contrast** (two methods, actually, but they usually work together), you might set two plays side by side and point out their similarities and differences. Again, watch out: do not bite off more than you can chew. A profound topic—"The Self-deceptions of Othello and Oedipus"—might do for a three-hundred-page dissertation, but an essay of a mere thousand words could treat it only sketchily. Probably the dual methods of comparison and contrast are most useful for a long term paper on a large but finite topic: "Attitudes Toward Marriage in *A Doll's House* and *Trifles*." In a shorter paper, you might confine your comparing and contrasting to the same play: "Willy's Illusions and Biff's in *Death of a Salesman*."

For writing about drama, **analysis** (a separation into elements) is an especially useful method. You can consider just one element in a play, and so your topic tends to be humanly manageable—"Animal Imagery in Some Speeches from *Othello*," or "The Theme of Fragility in *The Glass Menagerie*." Not all plays, however, contain every element you might find in fiction and poetry. Unlike a short story or a novel, a play does not ordinarily have a narrator. In most plays, the point of view is that of the audience, who see the events not through some narrator's eyes, but through their own.[1] And though it is usual for a short story to be written in an all-pervading style, some plays seem written in as many styles as there are speaking characters. (But you might also argue that in Susan Glaspell's *Trifles* both main characters speak the same language.) Traditional poetic devices like rime schemes and metrical patterns are seldom found in contemporary plays, which tend to sound like ordinary conversation. To be sure, some plays *are* written in poetic forms: the blank verse of the greater portion of *Othello*. (If, by the way, you wish any advice to heed in quoting passages from a play in blank verse or in rime, see "How To Quote a Poem," on page 1773.) Despite whatever some plays may lack, most plays have more than enough elements for analysis, including characters, themes, tone, irony, imagery, figures of speech, symbols, myths, and conventions.

Ready to begin writing an analysis of a play, you might think at first that one element—the plot—ought to be particularly easy to detach from the rest, and write about. But beware. In a good play (as in a good novel or short story), plot and character and theme are likely to be one, not perfectly simple to tell apart. Besides, if in your essay you were to summarize the events in the play, and then stop, you wouldn't tell your readers much that they couldn't observe for themselves just by reading the play, or by seeing it. In a meaningful, informative analysis, the writer does not merely isolate an element, but also shows how it functions within its play and why it is necessary to the whole.

## WRITING A CARD REPORT

Instead of an essay, some instructors like to assign a **card report.** If asked to write a card report on a play, you will find yourself writing a kind of analysis. To do so, you first single out elements of a play, then you list them on 5 × 8-inch index cards as concisely as possible. Such an exercise is often assigned in a class studying fiction; and one student's card report on the Edgar Allan Poe story, "The Tell-Tale Heart," appears on page 1754. When you deal with a play, however, you will need to include some elements different from those in a short story. And because a full-length play may take more room to summarize than a short story, your instructor may suggest that, if necessary, you take two cards (four sides) for your report. Still, in order to write a good card report, you have to be both brief and specific. Before you start, sort out your impressions of the play, and try to decide which characters, scenes, and lines of dialogue are the most important and memorable. Reducing your scattered impressions to essentials, you will have to

[1] Point of view in drama is a study in itself; this mere mention grossly simplifies the matter. Some playwrights attempt to govern what the spectator sees, trying to make the stage become the mind of a character. An obvious example is the classic German film *The Cabinet of Dr. Caligari*, in which the scenery is distorted as though perceived by a lunatic. Some plays contain characters who act as narrators, directly addressing the audience in much the way that first-person narrators in fiction often address the reader. In Tennessee Williams's *The Glass Menagerie*, Tom Wingfield behaves like such a narrator, introducing scenes, commenting on the action. The Stage Manager in Thornton Wilder's *Our Town* (1938) actually addresses the audience directly. But such a character in a play does not alter our angle of vision, our physical point of view.

reexamine what you have read; and when you finish, you will know the play much more thoroughly.

Here is an example: a card report on Susan Glaspell's one-act play, *Trifles*. (For the play itself, see page 1066.) By including only the elements that seemed most important, the writer managed to analyze the brief play on the front and back of one card. Still, he managed to work in a few pertinent quotations to give a sense of the play's remarkable language. Although the report does not say everything about Glaspell's little masterpiece, an adequate criticism of the play could hardly be much briefer. For this report, the writer was assigned to include:

1. The playwright's name, nationality, and dates.
2. The title of the play and the date of its first performance.

## Front of Card

(Student's name)                   (Course and section)

Susan Glaspell, American, 1882–1948     <u>Trifles</u>, 1916

<u>Central characters</u>: Mrs. Peters, the sheriff's nervous wife, dutiful but independent, not "married to the law"—whose sorrows make her able to sympathize with a woman accused of murder. Mrs. Hale, who knows the accused; more decisive.

<u>Other characters</u>: The County Attorney, self-important but short-sighted. The Sheriff, a man of only middling intelligence, another sexist pig. Hale, a farmer, a cautious man. Not seen on stage, two others are central: Minnie (Foster) Wright, the accused, a music lover reduced to near despair by years of grim marriage and isolation; and John Wright, the victim, known for his cruelty.

<u>Scene</u>: The kitchen of a gloomy farmhouse in Nebraska after the arrest of a wife on suspicion of murder; little things left in disarray.

<u>Major dramatic question</u>: Why did Minnie Wright kill her husband? When this question is answered, a new major dramatic question is raised: Will Mrs. Peters and Mrs. Hale cover up incriminating evidence?

<u>Events</u>: In the exposition, Sheriff and C.A., investigating the death of Wright, hear Hale tell how he found the body and a distracted Mrs. Wright. Then (1) C.A. starts looking for a motive. (2) His jeering at Mrs. Wright (and all women) for their concern with "trifles" cause Mrs. Peters and Mrs. Hale to rally to the woman's defense.           [continued on back of card]

3. The central character or characters, with a brief description that includes leading traits.
4. Other characters, also described.
5. The scene or scenes and, if the play does not take place in the present, the time of its action.
6. The dramatic question. This question is whatever the play leads us to ask ourselves: some conflict whose outcome we wonder about, some uncertainty to whose resolution we look forward. (For a more detailed discussion of dramatic questions, see page 1079.)
7. A brief summary of the play's principal events, in the order in which the playwright presents them. If you are reporting on a play longer than *Trifles*, you may find it simplest to take each act, perhaps each scene, and sum up what happens in it.

## Back of Card

[Events, continued] (3) When the two women find evidence that Mrs. Wright had panicked (a patch of wild sewing in a quilt), Mrs. Hale destroys it. (4) Mrs. Peters finds more evidence: a wrecked birdcage. (5) The women find a canary with its neck wrung and realize that Minnie killed her husband in a similar way. (6) The women align themselves with Minnie when Mrs. Peters recalls her own sorrows, and Mrs. Hale decides her own failure to visit Minnie was "a crime." (7) The C.A. unwittingly provides Mrs. Peters with a means to smuggle out the canary. (8) The two women unite to seize the evidence.

Tone: Made clear in the women's dialogue: mingled horror and sadness at what has happened, compassion for a fellow woman, smoldering resentment toward men who crush women.

Language: The plain speech of farm people, with a dash of rural Midwestern slang (red-up for tidy; Hale's remark that the accused was "kind of done up"). Unschooled speech: Mrs. Hale says ain't— and yet her speech rises at moments to simple poetry: "She used to sing. He killed that too." Glaspell hints the self-importance of the County Attorney by his heavy reliance on the first person.

Central theme: Women, in their supposed concern for trifles, see more deeply than men do.

Symbols: The broken birdcage and the dead canary, both suggesting the music and the joy that John Wright stifled in Minnie.

Evaluation: A powerful, successful realistic play that conveys its theme with great economy—in its views, more than seventy years ahead of its time.

8. The tone of the play, as best you can detect it. Try to describe the play-wright's apparent feelings toward the characters or what happens to them.
9. The language spoken in the play: try to describe it. Does any character speak with a choice of words or with figures of speech that strike you as unusual, distinctive, poetic—or maybe dull and drab? Does language indicate a character's background or place of birth? Brief quotations, in what space you have, will be valuable.
10. In a sentence, try to sum up the play's central theme. If you find none, say so. But plays often contain more themes than one—which of them seems most clearly borne out by the main events?
11. Any symbols you notice, and believe to matter. Try to state in a few words what each suggests.
12. A concise evaluation of the play: what did you think of it? (For more suggestions on being a drama critic, see Chapter Thirty-seven, "Evaluating a Play.")

## REVIEWING A PLAY

Writing a **play review,** a brief critical account of an actual performance, involves making an evaluation. To do so, you first have to decide what to evaluate: the work of the playwright; the work of the actors, director, and production staff; or the work of both. If the play is some classic of Shakespeare or Ibsen, evidently the more urgent task for a reviewer is not to evaluate the playwright's work, but to evaluate the success of the actors, director, and production staff in interpreting it. To be sure, a reviewer's personal feelings toward a play (even a towering classic) may deserve mention. Writing of an Ibsen masterpiece, the critic H. L. Mencken made the memorable comment that, next to being struck down by a taxicab and having his hat smashed, he could think of no worse punishment than going to another production of *Rosmersholm.* But a newer, less well-known play is probably more in need of evaluation.

To judge a live performance is, in many ways, more of a challenge than to judge a play read in a book. Obviously there is much to consider besides the play-wright's script: acting, direction, costumes, sets, lighting, perhaps music, anything else that contributes to one's total experience in the theater. Still, many students find that to write a play review is more stimulating—and even more fun—than most writing assignments. And although the student with experience in acting or in stagecraft may be a more knowing reviewer than the student without such experience, the latter may prove just as capable in responding to a play and in judging it fairly and perceptively.

In the chapter "Evaluating a Play," we assumed that in order to judge a play one has to understand it, and be aware of its conventions. (For a list of things to consider in judging a play, whether staged or printed, see pages 1325–1326.) Some plays will evoke a strong positive or negative response in the reviewer, either at once or by the time the final curtain tumbles; others will need to be pondered. Incidentally, harsh evaluations sometimes tempt a reviewer to flashes of wit. One celebrated flash is Eugene Field's observation of an actor in a production of *Hamlet*, that "he played the king as though he were in constant fear that somebody else was going to play the ace." The comment isn't merely nasty; it implies that Field had closely watched the actor's performance and had discerned what was wrong with it. Readers, of course, have a right to expect that reviewers do not just sneer (or gush praise), but clearly set forth reasons for their feelings.

Reviewing plays seems an art with few fixed rules, but in general, an adequate play review usually gives us a small summary of the play—for the reader unacquainted with it—and perhaps also indicates what the play is about: its theme. If the play is familiar and often performed, some comment on the director's whole approach to it may be useful. Is the production exactly what you'd expect, or are there any fresh and apparently original innovations? And if the production is fresh, does it achieve its freshness by violating the play? (The director of one college production of *Othello*—a fresh, but not entirely successful, innovation—emphasized the play's being partly set in Venice by staging it in the campus swimming pool, with actors floating about on barges and a homemade gondola.) Does the play seem firmly directed, so that the actors neither lag nor hurry, and so that they speak and gesture not in an awkward, stylized manner, but naturally? Are they well cast? Usually, also, a reviewer pays attention to the performances of the leading actors, or principals; and to the costumes, sets, and lighting, if these are noteworthy. And if, all along, the reviewer has not been making clear an opinion of the play and its production, an opinion will probably come in the concluding paragraph.

For further pointers, read a few professional play reviews in magazines such as *The New Yorker, Time, Newsweek, The New Criterion, American Theatre*, and others; or on the entertainment pages of a metropolitan newspaper. Here is a good, concise review of an amateur production of *Trifles* as it might be written for a college newspaper, but similar to what your instructor might ask you to write for a course assignment.

<u>Trifles</u> Scores Mixed Success
in Monday Players' Production

Women have come a long way since 1916. At least, that impression was conveyed yesterday when the Monday Players presented Susan Glaspell's classic one-act play <u>Trifles</u> in Alpaugh Theater.

At first, in Glaspell's taut story of two subjugated farm women who figure out why a fellow farm woman strangled her husband, Lloyd Fox and Cal Federicci get to strut around. As a small-town sheriff and a county attorney, they lord it over the womenfolk, making sexist-pig remarks about women in general. Fox and Federicci obviously enjoy themselves as the pompous types that Glaspell means them to be.

But of course it is the women with their keen eyes for small details who prove the superior detectives. In the demanding roles of the two Nebraska Miss Marples, Kathy Betts and Ruth Fine cope as best they can with what is asked of them. Fine is especially convincing. As Mrs. Hale, a friend of the wife accused of the murder, she projects a growing sense of independence. Visibly smarting under the verbal lashes of the menfolk, she seems to straighten her spine inch by inch as the play goes on.

Unluckily for Betts, director Alvin Klein seems determined to view Mrs. Peters as a comedian. Though Glaspell's stage directions call the woman "nervous," I doubt she is supposed to be quite so fidgety as Betts makes her. Betts vibrates like a tuning fork every time a new clue turns up, and when obliged to smell a dead canary bird (another clue), you would think she was whiffing a dead hippopotamus. Mrs. Peters, whose sad past includes a lost baby and a kitten some maniac chopped up with a hatchet, is no figure of fun to my mind. Played for laughs, her character fails to grow visibly on stage, as Fine makes Mrs. Hale grow.

Klein, be it said in his favor, makes the quiet action proceed at a brisk pace. Feminists in the audience must have been a little embarrassed, though, by his having Betts and Fine deliver every speech defending women in an extra-loud voice. After all, Glaspell makes her points clear enough just by showing us what she shows. Not everything is overstated, however. As a farmer who found the murder victim, Cal Valdez acts his part with quiet authority.

Despite flaws in its direction, this powerful play still spellbinds an audience. Anna Winterbright's set, seen last week as a background for <u>Dracula</u> and just slightly touched up, provides appropriate gloom.

## SUGGESTIONS FOR WRITING

Finding a topic you care to write about is, of course, your most important step toward writing a valuable paper. (For some general advice on topic-finding, see pages 1737–1738.) The following list of suggestions is not meant to replace your own ideas but to stimulate them.

## TOPICS FOR BRIEF PAPERS (250–500 WORDS)

1.  When the curtain comes down on the conclusion of some plays, the audience is left to decide exactly what finally happened. In a short informal essay, state your interpretation of the conclusion of one of these plays: *The Sound of a Voice, Andre's Mother, The Glass Menagerie, Joe Turner's Come and Gone.* Don't just give a plot summary; tell what you think the conclusion means.

2.  Sum up the main suggestions you find in one of these meaningful objects (or actions): the handkerchief in *Othello*; the Christmas tree in *A Doll's House* (or Nora's doing a wild tarantella); Willy Loman's planting a garden in *Death of a Salesman*, Laura's collection of figurines in *The Glass Menagerie*.

3.  Here is an exercise in being terse. Write a card report on a short, one-scene play (other than *Trifles*) and confine your remarks to both sides of one 5 × 8-inch card. (For further instructions see page 1782.) Possible subjects: *Riders to the Sea, The Sound of a Voice, Andre's Mother.*

4.  Review a play you have seen within recent memory and have felt strongly about (for or against). Give your opinion of *either* the performance or the playwright's writing, with reasons for your evaluation.

5.  Write an essay entitled "Why I Prefer Plays to Films" (or vice versa). Cite some plays and films to support your argument. (If you have never seen any professional plays, pick some other topic.)

## TOPICS FOR MORE EXTENDED PAPERS (600–1,000 WORDS)

1.  From a play you have enjoyed, choose a passage that strikes you as difficult, worth reading closely. Try to pick a passage not longer than about 200 words, or twenty lines. Explicate it, working through it sentence by sentence or line by line. For instance, any of these passages might be considered memorable (and essential to their plays):

    Oedipus to Teiresias, speech beginning, "Wealth, power, craft of statesmanship" (*Oedipus the King*, scene 1, 163–186).

    Iago's soliloquy, "Thus do I ever make my fool my purse" (*Othello*, I, iii, 362–383).

    Tom Wingfield's opening speech, "Yes, I have tricks in my pocket," through "I think the rest of the play will explain itself. . . ." (*The Glass Menagerie*, Scene I).

2.  Take just a single line or sentence from a play—one that stands out for some reason as greatly important. Perhaps it states a theme, reveals a character, or serves as a crisis (or turning point). Write an essay demonstrating its importance: how it functions, why it is necessary. Some possible lines:

    Iago to Roderigo: "I am not what I am" (*Othello*, I, i, 67).

    Amanda to Tom: "You live in a dream; you manufacture illusions!" (*The Glass Menagerie*, VII).

    Charley to Biff: "A salesman is got to dream, boy. It comes with the territory" (*Death of a Salesman*, the closing Requiem).

3.  Write an essay in analysis, in which you single out an element of a play for examination—character, plot, setting, theme, dramatic irony, tone, language, symbolism, conventions, or any other element. Try to relate this element to the play as a whole. Sample topics: "The Function of Teiresias in *Oedipus the King*," "Imagery of Poison in *Othello* (or *A Doll's House*)," "Irony in *Antigone*," "Williams's Use of Magic-Lantern Slides in *The Glass Menagerie*," "The Theme of Success in *Death of a Salesman*," "Magic in *Joe Turner's Come and Gone*."

4.  Compare a character, situation, or theme in a play with a similar element in a short story. For instance: women's role in society as seen in *Trifles* and in Tillie Olsen's "I

Stand Here Ironing"; "The Ocean as an Opponent in *Riders to the Sea* and Stephen Crane's 'The Open Boat.'" or compare Garrison Keillor's comic version of "The Prodigal Son" with the original Gospel parable.

5. Imagine a completely different ending for a play you have read, one that especially interests you. Briefly summarize the new resolution you have in mind. Then, looking back over the play's earlier scenes, tell what would happen to the rest of the play if it were to acquire this new ending. What else would need to be changed? What, if anything, does this exercise reveal?

6. In an essay, consider how you would go about staging a play of Shakespeare, Sophocles, or some other classic, in modern dress, with sets representing the world of today. What problems would you face? Can such an attempt ever succeed?

## TOPICS FOR LONG PAPERS (1,500 WORDS OR MORE)

1. Choosing any of the four works in Chapter Thirty-eight, "Plays for Further Reading," or taking some other modern or contemporary play your instructor suggests, report any difficulties you encountered in reading and responding to it. Explicate any troublesome passages for the benefit of other readers.

2. Compare and contrast two plays—a play in this book and another play by the same author—with attention to one element. For instance: "The Theme of Woman's Independence in Ibsen's *A Doll's House* and *Hedda Gabler*"; "Antirealism in the Stagecraft of Tennessee Williams: *The Glass Menagerie* and *Camino Real*"; or "Christian Symbols and Allusions in Williams's *Menagerie* and *Night of the Iguana*."

3. Compare and contrast in *The Glass Menagerie* and *Death of a Salesman* the elements of dream-life and fantasy.

4. For at least a month, keep a journal of your experience in watching drama on stage, movie screen, or television. Make use of any skills you have learned from your reading and study of plays, and try to demonstrate how you have become a more critical and perceptive member of the viewing audience.

5. If you have ever acted or taken part in staging plays, consult with your instructor and see whether you both find that your experience could enable you to write a substantial paper. With the aid of specific recollections, perhaps, you might sum up what you have learned about the nature of drama or about what makes a play effective.

6. Watch a film version of a play, then read the original as produced on stage. What differences do you find, and how do you account for them? You might, for instance, compare one of the film versions of *Hamlet* with Shakespeare's original, or Beth Henley's *Crimes of the Heart* with the movie version for which Henley herself wrote the screenplay.

# 5. *Critical Approaches to Literature*

> The really competent critic must be an empiricist. He must conduct his exploration with whatever means lie within the bounds of his personal limitation. He must produce the effects with whatever tools will work. If pills fail, he gets out his saw. If the saw won't cut, he seizes a club.
>
> —H. L. Mencken

Literary criticism is not an abstract, intellectual exercise; it is a natural human response to literature. If a friend informs you she is reading a book you have just finished, it would be odd indeed if you did not begin swapping opinions. Literary criticism is nothing more than discourse—spoken or written—about literature. A student who sits quietly in a morning English class, intimidated by the notion of literary criticism, will spend an hour that evening talking animatedly about the meaning of R.E.M. lyrics or comparing the relative merits of the three *Star Trek* T.V. series. It is inevitable that people will ponder, discuss, and analyze the works of art that interest them.

The informal criticism of friends talking about literature tends to be casual, unorganized, and subjective. Since Aristotle, however, philosophers, scholars, and writers have tried to create more precise and disciplined ways of discussing literature. Literary critics have borrowed concepts from other disciplines, like linguistics, psychology, and anthropology, to analyze imaginative literature more perceptively. Some critics have found it useful to work in the abstract area of **literary theory,** criticism that tries to formulate general principles rather than discuss specific texts. Mass media critics, such as newspaper reviewers, usually spend their time evaluating works—telling us which books are worth reading, which plays not to bother seeing. But most serious literary criticism is not primarily evaluative; it assumes we know that *Othello* or *The Death of Ivan Ilych* are worth reading. Instead, it is analytical; it tries to help us better understand a literary work.

In the following pages you will find overviews of nine critical approaches to literature. While these nine methods do not exhaust the total possibilities of literary criticism, they represent the most widely used contemporary approaches. Although presented separately, the approaches are not necessarily mutually exclusive; many critics mix methods to suit their needs and interests. A historical critic may use formalist techniques to analyze a poem; a biographical critic will frequently use psychological theories to analyze an author. The summaries do not try to provide a history of each approach; nor do they try to present the latest trends in each school. Their purpose is to give you a practical introduction to each critical method and then provide one or more representative examples of criticism. If one of these critical methods interest you, why not try to write a class paper using the approach?

## FORMALIST CRITICISM

Formalist criticism regards literature as a unique form of human knowledge that needs to be examined on its own terms. "The natural and sensible starting point for work in literary scholarship," René Wellek and Austin Warren wrote in their influential *Theory of Literature*, "is the interpretation and analysis of the works of literature themselves." To a formalist, a poem or story is not primarily a social, historical, or biographical document; it is a literary work that can be understood only by reference to its intrinsic literary features—those elements, that is, found in the text itself. To analyze a poem or story, the formalist critic, therefore, focuses on the words of the text rather than facts about the author's life or the historical milieu in which it was written. The critic would pay special attention to the formal features of the text—the style, structure, imagery, tone, and genre. These features, however, are usually not examined in isolation, because formalist critics believe that what gives a literary text its special status as art is how all of its elements work together to create the reader's total experience. As Robert Penn Warren commented. "Poetry does not inhere in any particular element but depends upon the set of relationships, the structure, which we call the poem."

A key method that formalists use to explore the intense relationships within a poem is **close reading,** a careful step-by-step analysis and explication of a text. (For further discussion of explication, see page 1762). The purpose of close reading is to understand how various elements in a literary text work together to shape its effects on the reader. Since formalists believe that the various stylistic and thematic elements of literary work influence each other, these critics insist that form and content cannot be meaningfully separated. The complete interdependence of form and content is what makes a text literary. When we extract a work's theme or paraphrase its meaning, we destroy the aesthetic experience of the work.

When Robert Langbaum examines Robert Browning's "My Last Duchess" (the full poem is on page 594), he uses several techniques of formalist criticism.

First, he places the poem in relation to its literary form, the dramatic monologue (see page 593 for a discussion of this genre). Second, he discusses the dramatic structure of the poem—why the duke tells his story, whom he addresses, and the physical circumstances in which he speaks. Third, Langbaum analyzes how the duke tells his story—his tone, manner, even the order in which he makes his disclosures. Langbaum does not introduce facts about Browning's life into his analysis; nor does he try to relate the poem to the historical period or social conditions that produced it. He focuses on the text itself to explain how it produces a complex effect on the reader.

## Cleanth Brooks (1906–1994)

THE FORMALIST CRITIC                                                           1951

Here are some articles of faith I could subscribe to:

> That literary criticism is a description and an evaluation of its object.
>
> That the primary concern of criticism is with the problem of unity—the kind of whole which the literary work forms or fails to form, and the relation of the various parts to each other in building up this whole.
>
> That the formal relations in a work of literature may include, but certainly exceed, those of logic.
>
> That in a successful work, form and content cannot be separated.
>
> That form is meaning.
>
> That literature is ultimately metaphorical and symbolic.
>
> That the general and the universal are not seized upon by abstraction, but got at through the concrete and the particular.
>
> That literature is not a surrogate for religion.
>
> That, as Allen Tate says, "specific moral problems" are the subject matter of literature, but that the purpose of literature is not to point a moral.
>
> That the principles of criticism define the area relevant to literary criticism; they do not constitute a method for carrying out the criticism.

*       *       *       *

The formalist critic knows as well as anyone that poems and plays and novels are written by men—that they do not somehow happen—and that they are written as expressions of particular personalities and are written from all sorts of motives—for money, from a desire to express oneself, for the sake of a cause, etc. Moreover, the formalist critic knows as well as anyone that literary works are merely potential until they are read—that is, that they are recreated in the minds of actual readers, who vary enormously in their capabilities, their interests, their prejudices, their ideas. But the formalist critic is concerned primarily with the work itself. Speculation on the mental processes of the author takes the critic away from the work into biography and psychology. There is no reason, of course, why he should not turn away into biography and psychology. Such explorations are very much worth making. But they should not be confused with an account of the work. Such studies describe the process of composition, not the structure of the thing composed, and they may be performed quite as validly for the poor work as for the good one. They may be validly performed for any kind of expression—non-literary as well as literary.

"The Formalist Critic"

## Robert Langbaum (b. 1924)

On Robert Browning's "My Last Duchess"                    1957

When we have said all the objective things about Browning's "My Last Duchess," we will not have arrived at the meaning until we point out what can only be substantiated by an appeal to effect—that moral judgment does not figure importantly in our response to the duke, that we even identify ourselves with him. But how is such an effect produced in a poem about a cruel Italian duke of the Renaissance who out of unreasonable jealousy has had his last duchess put to death, and is now about to contract a second marriage for the sake of dowry? Certainly, no summary or paraphrase would indicate that condemnation is not our principal response. The difference must be laid to form, to that extra quantity which makes the difference in artistic discourse between content and meaning.

The objective fact that the poem is made up entirely of the duke's utterance has of course much to do with the final meaning, and it is important to say that the poem is in form a monologue. But much more remains to be said about the way in which the content is laid out, before we can come near accounting for the whole meaning. It is important that the duke tells the story of his kind and generous last duchess to, of all people, the envoy from his prospective duchess. It is important that he tells his story while showing off to the envoy the artistic merits of a portrait of the last duchess. It is above all important that the duke carries off his outrageous indiscretion, proceeding triumphantly in the end downstairs to conclude arrangements for the dowry. All this is important not only as content but also as form, because it establishes a relation between the duke on the one hand, and the portrait and the envoy on the other, which determines the reader's relation to the duke and therefore to the poem—which determines, in other words, the poem's meaning.

The utter outrageousness of the duke's behavior makes condemnation the least interesting response, certainly not the response that can account for the poem's success. What interests us more than the duke's wickedness is his immense attractiveness. His conviction of matchless superiority, his intelligence and bland amorality, his poise, his taste for art, his manners—high-handed aristocratic manners that break the ordinary rules and assert the duke's superiority when he is being most solicitous of the envoy, waiving their difference of rank

('Nay, we'll go / Together down, sir'); these qualities overwhelm the envoy, causing him apparently to suspend judgment of the duke, for he raises no demur. The reader is no less overwhelmed. We suspend moral judgment because we prefer to participate in the duke's power and freedom, in his hard core of character fiercely loyal to itself. Moral judgment is in fact important as the thing to be suspended, as a measure of the price we pay for the privilege of appreciating to the full this extraordinary man.

It is because the duke determines the arrangement and relative subordination of the parts that the poem means what it does. The duchess's goodness shines through the duke's utterance; he makes no attempt to conceal it, so preoccupied is he with his own standard of judgment and so oblivious of the world's. Thus the duchess's case is subordinated to the duke's, the novelty and complexity of which engages our attention. We are busy trying to understand the man who can combine the connoisseur's pride in the lady's beauty with a pride that caused him to murder the lady rather than tell her in what way she displeased him, for in that

> would be some stooping; and I choose
> Never to stoop.                                                        [lines 42–3]

The duke's paradoxical nature is fully revealed when, having boasted how at his command the duchess's life was extinguished, he turns back to the portrait to admire of all things its life-likeness:

> There she stands
> As if alive.                                                            [lines 46–7]

This occurs ten lines from the end, and we might suppose we have by now taken the duke's measure. But the next ten lines produce a series of shocks that outstrip each time our understanding of the duke, and keep us panting after revelation with no opportunity to consolidate our impression of him for moral judgment. For it is at this point that we learn to whom he has been talking; and he goes on to talk about dowry, even allowing himself to murmur the hypocritical assurance that the new bride's self and not the dowry is of course his object. It seems to me that one side of the duke's nature is here stretched as far as it will go; the dazzling figure threatens to decline into paltriness admitting moral judgment, when Browning retrieves it with two brilliant strokes. First, there is the lordly waiving of rank's privilege as the duke and the envoy are about to proceed downstairs, and then there is the perfect all-revealing gesture of the last two and a half lines when the duke stops to show off yet another object in his collection:

> Notice Neptune, though,
> Taming a sea-horse, thought a rarity,
> Which Claus of Innsbruck cast in bronze for me!                        [lines 54–6]

The lines bring all the parts of the poem into final combination, with just the relative values that constitute the poem's meaning. The nobleman does not hurry on his way to business, the connoisseur cannot resist showing off yet another precious object, the possessive egotist counts up his possessions even as he moves toward the acquirement of a new possession, a well-dowered bride; and most important, the last duchess is seen in final perspective. She takes her place as one of a line of objects in an art collection; her sad story becomes the *cicerone's* anecdote° lending piquancy to the portrait. The duke has taken from her what he wants, her beauty, and thrown the life away; and we watch with awe as he proceeds to take what he wants from the envoy and by implication from the new duchess. He carries all before him by sheer force of will so undeflected by ordinary compunctions as even, I think, to call into question—the question rushes into place behind the startling illumination of the last lines, and lingers as the poem's haunting afternote—the duke's sanity.

*The Poetry of Experience*

ON ROBERT BROWNING'S "MY LAST DUCHESS." *Cicerone's anecdote:* The Duke's tale. (In Italian, a *cicerone* is one who conducts guided tours for sightseers.)

# BIOGRAPHICAL CRITICISM

Biographical criticism begins with the simple but central insight that literature is written by actual people and that understanding an author's life can help readers more thoroughly comprehend the work. Anyone who reads the biography of a writer quickly sees how much an author's experience shapes—both directly and indirectly—what he or she creates. Reading that biography will also change (and usually deepen) our response to the work. Sometimes even knowing a single important fact illuminates our reading of a poem or story. Learning, for example, that Josephine Miles (see "Reason" on page 637) was confined to a wheelchair or that Weldon Kees (see "For My Daughter" on page 602) committed suicide at forty-one will certainly make us pay attention to certain aspects of their poems we might otherwise have missed or considered unimportant. A formalist critic might complain that we would also have noticed those things through careful textual analysis, but biographical information provided the practical assistance of underscoring subtle but important meanings in the poems. Though many literary theorists have assailed biographical criticism on philosophical grounds, the biographical approach to literature has never disappeared because of its obvious practical advantage in illuminating literary texts.

It may be helpful here to make a distinction between biography and biographical criticism. **Biography** is, strictly speaking, a branch of history; it provides a written account of a person's life. To establish and interpret the facts of a poet's life, for instance, a biographer would use all the available information—not just personal documents like letters and diaries, but also the poems for the possible light they might shed on the subject's life. A biographical *critic*, however, is not concerned with recreating the record of an author's life. Biographical criticism focuses on explicating the literary work by using the insight provided by knowledge of the author's life. Quite often biographical critics, like Brett C. Millier in her discussion of Elizabeth Bishop's "One Art," will examine the drafts of a poem or story to see both how the work came into being and how it might have been changed from its autobiographical origins.

A reader, however, must use biographical interpretations cautiously. Writers are notorious for revising the facts of their own lives; they often delete embarrassments and invent accomplishments while changing the details of real episodes to improve their literary impact. John Cheever, for example, frequently told reporters about his sunny, privileged youth; after the author's death, his biographer Scott Donaldson discovered a childhood scarred by a distant mother, a failed, alcoholic father, and nagging economic uncertainty. Likewise, Cheever's outwardly successful adulthood was plagued by alcoholism, sexual promiscuity, and family tension. The chilling facts of Cheever's life significantly changed the way critics read his stories. The danger in a famous writer's case—Sylvia Plath and F. Scott Fitzgerald are two modern examples—is that the life story can overwhelm and eventually distort the work. A savvy biographical critic always remembers to base an interpretation on what is in the text itself; biographical data should amplify the meaning of the text, not drown it out with irrelevant material.

## Leslie Fiedler (b. 1917)

### THE RELATIONSHIP OF POET AND POEM                                    1960

A central dogma of much recent criticism asserts that biographical information is irrelevant to the understanding and evaluation of poems, and that conversely, poems cannot legitimately be used as material for biography. This double contention is part of a larger position which holds that history is history and art is art, and that to talk about one in terms of the other is to court disaster. Insofar as this position rests upon the immortal platitude that it is good to know what one is talking about, it is unexceptionable; insofar as it is a reaction based upon the procedures of pre-Freudian critics, it is hopelessly outdated; and insofar as it depends upon the extreme nominalist definition of a work of art, held by many "formalists" quite unawares, it is metaphysically reprehensible. It has the further inconvenience of being quite unusable in the practical sphere (all of its proponents, in proportion as they are sensitive critics, immediately betray it when speaking of specific works, and particularly of large bodies of work); and, as if that were not enough, it is in blatant contradiction with the assumptions of most serious practicing writers.

That the antibiographical position was once "useful," whatever its truth, cannot be denied; it was even once, what is considerably rarer in the field of criticism, amusing; but for a long time now it has been threatening to turn into one of those annoying clichés of the intellectually middle-aged, proffered with all the air of a stimulating heresy. The position was born in dual protest against an excess of Romantic criticism and one of "scientific scholarship." Romantic aesthetics appeared bent on dissolving the formally realized "objective" elements in works of art into "expression of personality"; while the "scholars," in revolt against Romantic subjectivity, seemed set on casting out all the more shifty questions of value and *gestalt* as "subjective," and concentrating on the kind of "facts" amenable to scientific verification. Needless to say, it was not the newer psychological sciences that the "scholars" had in mind, but such purer disciplines as physics and biology. It was at this point that it became fashionable to talk about literary study as "research," and graphs and tables began to appear in analyses of works of art.

*     *     *     *

The poet's life is the focusing glass through which pass the determinants of the shape of his work: the tradition available to him, his understanding of "kinds," the impact of special experiences (travel, love, etc.). But the poet's life is more than a burning glass; with his work, it makes up his total meaning. I do not intend to say, of course, that some meanings of works of art, satisfactory and as far as they go sufficient, are not available in the single work itself (only a really *bad* work depends for all substantial meaning on a knowledge of the life-style of its author); but a whole body of work will contain larger meanings, and, where it is available, a sense of the life of the writer will raise that meaning to a still higher power. The latter two kinds of meaning fade into each other; for as soon as two works by a single author are considered side by side, one has begun to deal with biography—that is, with an interconnectedness fully explicable only in terms of a personality, inferred or discovered.

One of the essential functions of the poet is the assertion and creation of a personality, in a profounder sense than any nonartist can attain. We ask of the poet a definition of man, at once particular and abstract, stated and acted out. It is impossible to draw a line between the work the poet writes and the work he lives, between the life he lives and the life he writes. And the agile critic, therefore, must be prepared to move constantly back and forth between life and poem, not in a pointless circle, but in a meaningful spiraling toward the absolute point.

*No! in Thunder*

## Brett C. Millier (b. 1958)

ON ELIZABETH BISHOP'S "ONE ART"                                          1993

Elizabeth Bishop left seventeen drafts of the poem "One Art" among her papers. In the first draft, she lists all the things she's lost in her life—keys, pens, glasses, cities—and then she writes "One might think this would have prepared me / for losing one average-sized not exceptionally / beautiful or dazzlingly intelligent person . . . / But it doesn't seem to have at all. . . ." By the seventeenth draft, nearly every word has been transformed, but most importantly, Bishop discovered along the way that there might be a way to master this loss.

One way to read Bishop's modulation between the first and last drafts from "the loss of you is impossible to master" to something like "I am still the master of losing even though losing you looks like a disaster" is that in the writing of such a disciplined, demanding poem as this villanelle ("[*Write it!*]") lies the potential mastery of the loss. Working through each of her losses—from the bold, painful catalog of the first draft to the finely honed and privately meaningful final version—is the way to overcome them or, if not to overcome them, then to see the way in which she might possibly master herself in the face of loss. It is all, perhaps "one art"—writing elegy, mastering loss, mastering grief, self-mastery. Bishop had a precocious familiarity with loss. Her father died before her first birthday, and four years later her mother disappeared into a sanitarium, never to be seen by her daughter again. The losses in the poem are real: time in the form of the "hour badly spent" and, more tellingly for the orphaned Bishop "my mother's watch": the lost houses, in Key West, Petrópolis, and Ouro Prêto, Brazil. The city of Rio de Janeiro and the whole South American continent (where she had lived for nearly two decades) were lost to her with the suicide of her Brazilian companion. And currently, in the fall of 1975, she seemed to have lost her dearest friend and lover, who was trying to end their relationship. But each version of the poem distanced the pain a little more, depersonalized it, moved it away from the tawdry self-pity and "confession" that Bishop disliked in so many of her contemporaries.

Bishop's friends remained for a long time protective of her personal reputation, and unwilling to have her grouped among lesbian poets or even among the other great poets of her generation—Robert Lowell, John Berryman, Theodore Roethke—as they seemed to self-destruct before their readers' eyes. Bishop herself taught them this reticence by keeping her private life to herself, and by investing what "confession" there was in her poems deeply in objects and places, thus deflecting biographical inquiry. In the development of this poem, discretion is both a poetic method, and a part of a process of self-understanding, the seeing of a pattern in her own life.

Adapted by the author from<br>
*Elizabeth Bishop: Life and the Memory of It*

## HISTORICAL CRITICISM

Historical criticism seeks to understand a literary work by investigating the social, cultural, and intellectual context that produced it—a context that necessarily includes the artist's biography and milieu. Historical critics are less concerned with explaining a work's literary significance for today's readers than with helping us understand the work by recreating, as nearly as possible, the exact meaning and impact it had on its original audience. A historical reading of a literary work begins by exploring the possible ways in which the meaning of the text has changed over time. The analysis of William Blake's poem "London" (pages 652–654), for instance, carefully examines how certain words had different connotations for the poem's original readers than they do today. It also explores the probable associations an eighteenth-century English reader would have made with certain images and characters, like the poem's persona, the chimney-sweeper—a type of exploited child laborer who, fortunately, no longer exists in our society.

Reading ancient literature, no one doubts the value of historical criticism. There have been so many social, cultural, and linguistic changes that some older texts are incomprehensible without scholarly assistance. But historical criticism can even help us better understand modern texts. To return to Weldon Kees's "For My Daughter" (page 602), for example, we learn a great deal by considering two rudimentary historical facts—the year in which the poem was first published (1940) and the nationality of its author (American)—and then asking ourselves how this information has shaped the meaning of the poem. In 1940, war had already broken out in Europe and most Americans realized that their country, still recovering from the Depression, would soon be drawn into it; for a young man, like Kees, the future seemed bleak, uncertain, and personally dangerous. Even this simple historical analysis helps explain at least part of the bitter pessimism of Kees's poem, though a psychological critic would rightly insist that Kees's dark personality also played a crucial role. In writing a paper on a poem, you might explore how the time and place of its creation affected its meaning. For a splendid example of how to recreate the historical context of a poem's genesis, read the following account by Hugh Kenner of Ezra Pound's imagistic "In a Station of the Metro." (This poem is also discussed more briefly on pages 660–661.)

## Hugh Kenner (b. 1923)

IMAGISM                                                                 1971

For it was English post-Symbolist verse that Pound's Imagism set out to reform, by deleting its self-indulgences, intensifying its virtues, and elevating the glimpse into the vision. The most famous of all Imagist poems commenced, like any poem by Arthur Symons,° with an accidental glimpse. Ezra Pound, on a visit to Paris in 1911, got out of the Metro at La Concorde, and "saw suddenly a beautiful face, and then another and another, and then a beautiful child's face, and then another beautiful woman, and I tried all that day to find words for what they had meant to me, and I could not find any words that seemed to me worthy, or as lovely as that sudden emotion."

The oft-told story is worth one more retelling. This was just such an experience as Arthur Symons cultivated, bright unexpected glimpses in a dark setting, instantly to melt into the crowd's kaleidoscope. And a poem would not have given Symons any trouble. But Pound by 1911 was already unwilling to write a Symons poem.

He tells us that he first satisfied his mind when he hit on a wholly abstract vision of colors, splotches on darkness like some canvas of Kandinsky's (whose work he had not then seen). This is a most important fact. Satisfaction lay not in preserving the vision, but in devising with mental effort an abstract equivalent for it, reduced, intensified. He next wrote a 30-line poem and destroyed it; after six months he wrote a shorter poem, also destroyed; and after another year, with, as he tells us, the Japanese *hokku* in mind, he arrived at a poem which needs every one of its 20 words, including the six words of its title:

IN A STATION OF THE METRO

> The apparition of these faces in the crowd;
> Petals on a wet, black bough.

We need the title so that we can savor that vegetal contrast with the world of machines: this is not any crowd, moreover, but a crowd seen underground, as Odysseus and Orpheus and Koré saw crowds in Hades. And carrying forward the suggestion of wraiths, the word "apparition" detaches these faces from all the crowded faces, and presides over the image that conveys the quality of their separation:

> Petals on a wet, black bough.

Flowers, underground; flowers, out of the sun; flowers seen as if against a natural gleam, the bough's wetness gleaming on its darkness, in this place where wheels turn and nothing grows. The mind is touched, it may be, with a memory of Persephone, as we read of her in the 106th Canto,

> Dis' bride, Queen over Phlegethon,
> girls faint as mist about her.

—the faces of those girls likewise "apparitions."
What is achieved, though it works by way of the visible, is no picture of the thing glimpsed, in the manner of

> The light of our cigarettes
> Went and came in the gloom.

It is a simile with "like" suppressed: Pound called it an equation, meaning not a redundancy, *a* equals *a*, but a generalization of unexpected exactness. The statements of analytic geometry, he said, "are 'lords' over fact. They are the thrones and dominations that rule over form and recurrence. And in like manner are great works of art lords over fact, over race-long recurrent moods, and over tomorrow." So this tiny poem, drawing on Gauguin and on Japan, on ghosts and on Persephone, on the Underworld and on the Underground, the Metro of Mallarmé's capital and a phrase that names a station of the Metro as it might a station of the Cross, concentrates far more than it need ever specify, and indicates the means of delivering post-Symbolist poetry from its pictorialist impasse. "An 'Image' is that which presents an intellectual and emotional complex in an instant of time": that is the elusive Doctrine of the Image. And, just 20 months later, "The image . . . is a radiant node or cluster; it is what I can, and must perforce, call a VORTEX, from which, and through which, and into which, ideas are constantly rushing." And: "An *image* . . . is real because we know it directly."

The Pound Era

IMAGISM. *Arthur Symons:* Symons (1865–1945) was a British poet who helped introduce French symbolist verse into English. His own verse was often florid and impressionistic.

# Daryl Pinckney (b. 1953)

Fierce identification with the sorrows and pleasures of the poor black—"I myself belong to that class"—propelled Hughes toward the voice of the black Everyman. He made a distinction between his lyric and his social poetry, the private and the public. In the best of his social poetry he turned himself into a transmitter of messages and made the "I" a collective "I":

> I've known rivers:
> I've known rivers ancient as the world and older than the flow of
>      human blood in human veins.
>
> My soul has grown deep like the rivers.
>
> I bathed in the Euphrates when dawns were young.
> I built my hut near the Congo and it lulled me to sleep.
> I looked upon the Nile and raised the pyramids above it.
> I heard the singing of the Mississippi when Abe Lincoln went down
>      to New Orleans, and I've seen its muddy bosom turn all golden in
>      the sunset.
>
> ("The Negro Speaks of Rivers")

The medium conveys a singleness of intention: to make the black known. The straightforward, declarative style doesn't call attention to itself. Nothing distracts from forceful statement, as if the shadowy characters Sandburg wrote about in, say, "When Mammy Hums" had at last their chance to come forward and testify. Poems like "Aunt Sue's Stories" reflect the folk ideal of black women as repositories of racial lore. The story told in dramatic monologues like "The Negro Mother" or "Mother to Son" is one of survival life "ain't been no crystal stair." The emphasis is on the capacity of black people to endure, which is why Hughes's social poetry, though not strictly protest writing, indicts white America, even taunts it with the steady belief that blacks will overcome simply by "keeping on":

> I, too, sing America.
>
> I am the darker brother
> They send me to the kitchen
> When company comes,
> But I laugh,
> And eat well,
> And grow strong.
>
> ("Epilogue")

Whites were not the only ones who could be made uneasy by Hughes's attempts to boldly connect past and future. The use of "black" and the invocation of Africa were defiant gestures back in the days when many blacks described themselves as brown. When Hughes answered Sandburg's "Nigger" ("I am the nigger, / Singer of Songs . . . ") with "I am the Negro, / Black as the night is black,

/ Black like the depths of my Africa" ("Proem") he challenged the black middle
class with his absorption in slave heritage.

"Suitcase in Harlem"

## GENDER CRITICISM

Gender criticism examines how sexual identity influences the creation and reception of literary works. Gender studies began with the feminist movement and
were influenced by such works as Simone de Beauvoir's *The Second Sex* (1949)
and Kate Millett's *Sexual Politics* (1970) as well as sociology, psychology, and
anthropology. Feminist critics believe that culture has been so completely dominated by men that literature is full of unexamined "male-produced" assumptions.
They see their criticism correcting this imbalance by analyzing and combatting
patriarchal attitudes. Feminist criticism has explored how an author's gender
influences—consciously or unconsciously—his or her writing. While a formalist
critic like Allen Tate emphasized the universality of Emily Dickinson's poetry by
demonstrating how powerfully the language, imagery, and myth-making of her
poems combine to affect a generalized reader, Sandra M. Gilbert, a leading feminist critic, has identified attitudes and assumptions in Dickinson's poetry that she
believes are essentially female. Another important theme in feminist criticism is
analyzing how sexual identity influences the reader of a text. If Tate's hypothetical reader was deliberately sexless, Gilbert's reader sees a text through the eyes of
his or her sex. Finally, feminist critics carefully examine how the images of men
and women in imaginative literature reflect or reject the social forces that have
historically kept the sexes from achieving total equality.

Recently, gender criticism has expanded beyond its original feminist perspective. Critics have explored the impact of different sexual orientations on literary
creation and reception. A men's movement has also emerged in response to feminism. The men's movement does not seek to reject feminism but to rediscover
masculine identity in an authentic, contemporary way. Led by poet Robert Bly,
the men's movement has paid special attention to interpreting poetry and fables
as myths of psychic growth and sexual identity.

## Elaine Showalter (b. 1941)

TOWARD A FEMINIST POETICS                                              1979

Feminist criticism can be divided into two distinct varieties. The first type is concerned with *woman as reader*—with woman as the consumer of male-produced literature, and with the way in which the hypothesis of a female reader changes our
apprehension of a given text, awakening us to the significance of its sexual codes.
I shall call this kind of analysis the *feminist critique,* and like other kinds of critique it is a historically grounded inquiry which probes the ideological assumptions of literary phenomena. Its subjects include the images and stereotypes of
women in literature, the omissions of and misconceptions about women in criti-

cism, and the fissures in male-constructed literary history. It is also concerned with the exploitation and manipulation of the female audience, especially in popular culture and film; and with the analysis of woman-as-sign in semiotic systems. The second type of feminist criticism is concerned with *woman as writer*—with woman as the producer of textual meaning, with the history, themes, genres, and structures of literature by women. Its subjects include the psychodynamics of female creativity; linguistics and the problem of a female language; the trajectory of the individual or collective female literary career; literary history; and, of course, studies of particular writers and works. No term exists in English for such a specialized discourse, and so I have adapted the French term *la gynocritique*: "gynocritics" (although the significance of the male pseudonym in the history of women's writing also suggested the term "georgics").

The feminist critique is essentially political and polemical, with theoretical affiliations to Marxist sociology and aesthetics; gynocritics is more self-contained and experimental, with connections to other modes of new feminist research. In a dialogue between these two positions. Carolyn Heilbrun, the writer, and Catharine Stimpson, editor of the journal *Signs: Women in Culture and Society*, compare the feminist critique to the Old Testament, "looking for the sins and errors of the past," and gynocritics to the New Testament, seeking "the grace of imagination." Both kinds are necessary, they explain, for only the Jeremiahs of the feminist critique can lead us out of the "Egypt of female servitude" to the promised land of the feminist vision. That the discussion makes use of these Biblical metaphors points to the connections between feminist consciousness and conversion narratives which often appear in women's literature; Carolyn Heilbrun comments on her own text, "When I talk about feminist criticism, I am amazed at how high a moral tone I take."

"Toward a Feminist Poetics"


## Sandra M. Gilbert (b. 1936) and Susan Gubar (b. 1944)
### The Freedom of Emily Dickinson                     1985

[Emily Dickinson] defined herself as a *woman* writer, reading the works of female precursors with special care, attending to the implications of novels like Charlotte Brontë's *Jane Eyre*, Emily Brontë's *Wuthering Heights*, and George Eliot's *Middlemarch* with the same absorbed delight that characterized her devotion to Elizabeth Barrett Browning's *Aurora Leigh*. Finally, then, the key to her enigmatic identity as a "supposed person" who was called the "Myth of Amherst" may rest, not in investigations of her questionable romance, but in studies of her unquestionably serious reading as well as in analyses of her disquietingly powerful writing. Elliptically phrased, intensely compressed, her poems are more linguistically innovative than any other nineteenth-century verses, with the possible exception of some works by Walt Whitman and Gerard Manley Hopkins, her two most radical male contemporaries. Throughout her largely secret but always brilliant career, moreover, she confronted precisely the questions about the individual and society, time and death, flesh and spirit, that major precursors from Milton to Keats had faced. Dreaming of "Amplitude and Awe," she recorded sometimes vengeful, sometimes mystical visions of social and personal transformation in poems as inventively phrased and imaginatively constructed as any in the English language.

Clearly such accomplishments required not only extraordinary talent but also some measure of freedom. Yet because she was the unmarried daughter of conservative New Englanders, Dickinson was obliged to take on many household tasks; as a nineteenth-century New England wife, she would have had the same number of obligations, if not more. Some of these she performed with pleasure; in 1856, for instance, she was judge of a bread-baking contest, and in 1857 she won a prize in that contest. But as Higginson's "scholar," as a voracious reader and an ambitious writer, Dickinson had to win herself time for "Amplitude and Awe," and it is increasingly clear that she did so through a strategic withdrawal from her ordinary world. A story related by her niece Martha Dickinson Bianchi reveals that the poet herself knew from the first what both the price and the prize might be: on one occasion, said Mrs. Bianchi, Dickinson took her up to the room in which she regularly sequestered herself, and, mimicking locking herself in, "thumb and forefinger closed on an imaginary key," said "with a quick turn of her wrist, 'It's just a turn—and freedom, Matty!'"

In the freedom of her solitary, but not lonely, room, Dickinson may have become what her Amherst neighbors saw as a bewildering "myth." Yet there, too, she created myths of her own. Reading the Brontës and Barrett Browning, studying Transcendentalism and the Bible, she contrived a theology which is powerfully expressed in many of her poems. That it was at its most hopeful a female-centered theology is revealed in verses like those she wrote about the women artists she admired, as well as in more general works like her gravely pantheistic address to the "Sweet Mountains" who "tell me no lie," with its definition of the hills around Amherst as "strong Madonnas" and its description of the writer herself as "The Wayward Nun—beneath the Hill—/ Whose service is to You—." As Dickinson's admirer and descendant Adrienne Rich has accurately observed, this passionate poet consistently chose to confront her society—to "have it out"—"on her own premises."

Introduction to Emily Dickinson,
*The Norton Anthology of Literature by Women*

## PSYCHOLOGICAL CRITICISM

Modern psychology has had an immense effect on both literature and literary criticism. Sigmund Freud's psychoanalytic theories changed our notions of human behavior by exploring new or controversial areas like wish-fulfillment, sexuality, the unconscious, and repression. Freud also expanded our sense of how language and symbols operate by demonstrating their ability to reflect unconscious fears or desires. Freud admitted that he himself had learned a great deal about psychology from studying literature: Sophocles, Shakespeare, Goethe, and

Dostoevsky were as important to the development of his ideas as were his clinical studies. Some of Freud's most influential writing was, in a broad sense, literary criticism, such as his psychoanalytic examination of Sophocles' Oedipus.

This famous section of *The Interpretation of Dreams* (1900) often raises an important question for students: was Freud implying that Sophocles knew or shared Freud's theories? (Variations of this question can be asked for most critical approaches: does using a critical approach require that the author under scrutiny believed in it?) The answer is, of course, no; in analyzing Sophocles' Oedipus, Freud paid the classical Greek dramatist the considerable compliment that the playwright had such profound insight into human nature that his characters display the depth and complexity of real people. In focusing on literature, Freud and his disciples like Carl Jung, Ernest Jones, Marie Bonaparte, and Bruno Bettelheim endorse the belief that great literature truthfully reflects life.

Psychological criticism is a diverse category, but it often employs three approaches. First, it investigates the creative process of the artist: what is the nature of literary genius and how does it relate to normal mental functions? (Philosophers and poets have also wrestled with this question, as you can see in selections from Plato and Wordsworth in the "Criticism: On Poetry" section, beginning on page 1025.) The second major area for psychological criticism is the psychological study of a particular artist. Most modern literary biographies employ psychology to understand their subject's motivations and behavior. One recent book, Diane Middlebrook's controversial *Anne Sexton: A Biography*, actually used tapes of the poet's sessions with her psychiatrist as material for the study. The third common area of psychological criticism is the analysis of fictional characters. Freud's study of Oedipus is the prototype for this approach that tries to bring modern insights about human behavior into the study of how fictional people act.

## Sigmund Freud (1856–1939)

THE DESTINY OF OEDIPUS                                                          1900

*Translated by James Strachey. The lines from* Oedipus the King *are given in the version of David Grene.*

If *Oedipus the King* moves a modern audience no less than it did the contemporary Greek one, the explanation can only be that its effect does not lie in the contrast between destiny and human will, but is to be looked for in the particular nature of the material on which that contrast is exemplified. There must be something which makes a voice within us ready to recognize the compelling force of destiny in the *Oedipus*, while we can dismiss as merely arbitrary such dispositions as are laid down in *Die Ahnfrau*° or other modern tragedies of destiny. And a factor of this kind is in fact involved in the story of King Oedipus. His destiny moves us only because it might have been ours—because the oracle laid the same curse upon us before our birth as upon him. It is the fate of all of us, perhaps, to direct our first sexual impulse towards our mother and our first hatred and our first murderous wish against our father. Our dreams convince us that that is so. King Oedipus, who slew his father Laius and married his mother Jocasta, merely shows us the fulfillment of our own childhood wishes. But, more fortunate than he, we have meanwhile succeeded, insofar as we have not become psychoneurotics, in detaching our sexual impulses from our mothers and in forgetting our jealousy of our fathers. Here is one in whom these primeval wishes of our childhood have been fulfilled, and we shrink back from him with the whole force of the repression by which those wishes have since that time been held down within us. While the poet, as he unravels the past, brings to light the guilt of Oedipus, he is at the same time compelling us to recognize our own inner minds, in which those same impulses, though suppressed, are still to be found. The contrast with which the closing Chorus leaves us confronted—

> behold this Oedipus,—
> him who knew the famous riddles and was a man most masterful;
> not a citizen who did not look with envy on his lot—
> see him now and see the breakers of misfortune swallow him!

—strikes as a warning at ourselves and our pride, at us who since our childhood have grown so wise and so mighty in our own eyes. Like Oedipus, we live in ignorance of these wishes, repugnant to morality, which have been forced upon us by Nature, and after their revelation we may all of us well seek to close our eyes to the scenes of our childhood.

*The Interpretation of Dreams*

THE DESTINY OF OEDIPUS. *Die Ahnfrau:* "The Foremother," a verse play by Franz Grillparzer (1791–1872), Austrian dramatist and poet.


# Harold Bloom (b. 1930)

POETIC INFLUENCE                                                    1975

Let me reduce my argument to the hopelessly simplistic; poems, I am saying are neither about "subjects" nor about "themselves." They are necessarily about *other poems;* a poem is a response to a poem, as a poet is a response to a poet, or a person to his parent. Trying to write a poem takes the poet back to the origins of what a poem *first was* for him, and so takes the poet back beyond the pleasure principle to the decisive initial encounter and response that began him. We do not think of W. C. Williams as a Keatsian poet, yet he *began and ended as one,* and his late celebration of his Greeny Flower is another response to Keats's odes. *Only a poet challenges a poet as poet,* and so only a poet makes a poet. To the poet-in-a-poet, a poem is always *the other man,* the precursor, and so a poem is always a person, always the father of one's Second Birth. To live, the poet must *misinterpret* the father, by the crucial act of misprision, which is the rewriting of the father.

But who, what is the poetic father? The voice of the other, of the *daimon*, is always speaking in one; the voice that cannot die because already it has survived death—*the dead poet lives in one*. In the last phase of strong poets, they attempt to join the undying *by living in the dead poets* who are already alive in them. This late Return of the Dead recalls us, as readers, to a recognition of the original motive for the catastrophe of poetic incarnation. Vico, who identified the origins of poetry with the impulse towards divination (to foretell, but also to become a god by foretelling), implicitly understood (as did Emerson, and Wordsworth) that a poem is written to escape dying. Literally, poems are refusals of mortality. Every poem therefore has two makers: the precursor, and the ephebe's rejected mortality.

A poet, I argue in consequence, is not so much a man speaking to men as a man rebelling against being spoken to by a dead man (the precursor) outrageously more alive than himself.

*A Map of Misreading*

## SOCIOLOGICAL CRITICISM

Sociological criticism examines literature in the cultural, economic and political context in which it is written or received. "Art is not created in a vacuum," critic Wilbur Scott observed, "it is the work not simply of a person, but of an author fixed in time and space, answering a community of which he is an important, because articulate part." Sociological criticism explores the relationships between the artist and society. Sometimes it looks at the sociological status of the author to evaluate how the profession of the writer in a particular milieu affected what was written. Sociological criticism also analyzes the social content of literary works—what cultural, economic or political values a particular text implicitly or explicitly promotes. Finally, sociological criticism examines the role the audience has in shaping literature. A sociological view of Shakespeare, for example, might look at the economic position of Elizabethan playwrights and actors; it might also study the political ideas expressed in the plays or discuss how the nature of an Elizabethan theatrical audience (which was usually all male unless the play was produced at court) helped determine the subject, tone, and language of the plays.

An influential type of sociological criticism has been Marxist criticism, which focuses on the economic and political elements of art. Marxist criticism, like the work of the Hungarian philosopher Georg Lukacs, often explores the ideological content of literature. Whereas a formalist critic would maintain that form and content are inextricably blended, Lukacs believed that content determines form and that therefore, all art is political. Even if a work of art ignores political issues, it makes a political statement, Marxist critics believe, because it endorses the economic and political status quo. Consequently, Marxist criticism is frequently evaluative and judges some literary work better than others on an ideological basis; this tendency can lead to reductive judgment, as when Soviet critics rated Jack London a novelist superior to William Faulkner, Ernest Hemingway, Edith Wharton, and Henry James, because he illustrated the principles of class struggle more clearly. But, as an analytical tool, Marxist criticism, like other sociological methods, can illuminate political and economic dimensions of literature other approaches overlook.

## Georg Lukacs (1885–1971)

### Content Determines Form                                                          1962

What determines the style of a given work of art? How does the intention determine the form? (We are concerned here, of course, with the intention realized in the work; it need not coincide with the writer's conscious intention.) The distinctions that concern us are not those between stylistic "techniques" in the formalistic sense. It is the view of the world, the ideology or *Weltanschauung*° underlying a writer's work, that counts. And it is the writer's attempt to reproduce this view of the world which constitutes his "intention" and is the formative principle underlying the style of a given piece of writing. Looked at in this way, style ceases to be a formalistic category. Rather, it is rooted in content; it is the specific form of a specific content.

Content determines form. But there is no content of which Man himself is not the focal point. However various the *données*° of literature (a particular experience, a didactic purpose), the basic question is, and will remain: what is Man?

Here is a point of division: if we put the question in abstract, philosophical terms, leaving aside all formal considerations, we arrive—for the realist school—at the traditional Aristotelian dictum (which was also reached by other than purely aesthetic considerations): Man is *zoon politikon*,° a social animal. The Aristotelian dictum is applicable to all great realistic literature. Achilles and Werther, Oedipus and Tom Jones, Antigone and Anna Karenina: their individual existence—their *Sein an sich*,° in the Hegelian terminology; their "ontological being," as a more fashionable terminology has it—cannot be distinguished from their social and historical environment. Their human significance, their specific individuality cannot be separated from the context in which they were created.

*Realism in Our Time*

Content Determines Form. *Weltanschauung*: German for "worldview," an outlook on life.    *données*: French for "given"; it means the materials a writer uses to create his or her work or the subject or purpose of a literary work.    *zoon politikon*: Greek for "political animal."    *Sein an sich*: the German philosopher G. W. F. Hegel's term for "pure existence."

## Terry Eagleton (b. 1943)

### Art As Production                                                                1976

I have spoken so far of literature in terms of form, politics, ideology, consciousness. But all this overlooks a simple fact which is obvious to everyone, and not least to a Marxist. Literature may be an artefact, a product of social consciousness, a world vision; but it is also an *industry*. Books are not just structures of meaning, they are also commodities produced by publishers and sold on the market at a profit. Drama is not just a collection of literary texts; it is a capitalist business which employs certain men (authors, directors, actors, stagehands) to produce a commodity to be consumed by an audience at a profit. Critics are not just analysts of texts; they are also (usually) academics hired by the state to prepare students ideologically for their functions within capitalist society. Writers are not just transposers of trans-individual mental structures, they are also workers hired by publishing houses to produce commodities which will sell. "A writer," Marx comments in *Theories of Surplus Value*, "is a worker not in so far as he produces ideas, but in so far as he enriches the publisher, in so far as he is working for a wage."

It is a salutary reminder. Art may be, as Engels remarks, the most highly "mediated" of social products in its relation to the economic base, but in another sense it is also part of that economic base—one kind of economic practice, one type of commodity production, among many. It is easy enough for critics, even Marxist critics, to forget this fact, since literature deals with human consciousness and tempts those of us who are students of it to rest content within that realm. The Marxist critics I shall discuss . . . are those who have grasped the fact that art is a form of social production—grasped it not as an *external* fact about it to be delegated to the sociologist of literature, but as a fact which closely determines the nature of art itself. For these critics—I have in mind mainly Walter Benjamin and Bertolt Brecht—art is first of all a social practice rather than an object to be academically dissected. We may see literature as a *text*, but we may also see it as a social activity, a form of social and economic production which exists alongside, and interrelates with, other such forms.

*Marxism and Literary Criticism*

## MYTHOLOGICAL CRITICISM

Mythological critics look for the recurrent universal patterns underlying most literary works. (See Chapter 25, "Myth and Narrative," for a definition of myth and a discussion of its importance to the literary imagination.) Mythological criticism is an interdisciplinary approach that combines the insights of anthropology, psychology, history, and comparative religion. If psychological criticism examines the artist as an individual, mythological criticism explores the artist's common humanity by tracing how the individual imagination uses myths and symbols common to different cultures and epochs.

A central concept in mythological criticism is the **archetype,** a symbol, character, situation, or image that evokes a deep universal response. The idea of the archetype came into literary criticism from the Swiss psychologist Carl Jung, a lifetime student of myth and religion. Jung believed that all individuals share a "collective unconscious," a set of primal memories common to the human race, existing below each person's conscious mind. Archetypal images (which often relate to experiencing primordial phenomena like the sun, moon, fire, night, and blood), Jung believed, trigger the collective unconscious. We do not need to accept the literal truth of the collective unconscious, however, to endorse the archetype as a helpful critical concept. The late Northrop Frye defined the archetype in considerably less occult terms as "a symbol, usually an image, which recurs often enough in literature to be recognizable as an element of one's literary experience as a whole."

Identifying archetypal symbols and situations in literary works, mythological critics almost inevitably link the individual text under discussion to a broader context of works that share an underlying pattern. In discussing Shakespeare's *Hamlet*, for instance, a mythological critic might relate Shakespeare's Danish prince to other mythic sons avenging their father's deaths, like Orestes from Greek myth or Sigmund of Norse legend; or, in discussing *Othello*, relate the sinister figure of Iago to the devil in traditional Christian belief. Critic Joseph Campbell took such comparisons even further; his compendious study *The Hero with a Thousand Faces* demonstrates how similar mythic characters appear in virtually every culture on every continent.

## Northrop Frye (1912–1991)

MYTHIC ARCHETYPES                                                    1957

We begin our study of archetypes, then, with a world of myth, an abstract or purely literary world of fictional and thematic design, unaffected by canons of plausible adaptation to familiar experience. In terms of narrative, myth is the imitation of actions near or at the conceivable limits of desire. The gods enjoy beautiful women, fight one another with prodigious strength, comfort and assist man, or else watch his miseries from the height of their immortal freedom. The fact that myth operates at the top level of human desire does not mean that it necessarily presents its world as attained or attainable by human beings. . . .

Realism, or the art of verisimilitude, evokes the response "How like that is to what we know!" When what is written is *like* what is known, we have an art of extended or implied simile. And as realism is an art of implicit simile, myth is an art of implicit metaphorical identity. The word "sun-god," with a hyphen used instead of a predicate, is a pure ideogram, in Pound's terminology, or literal metaphor, in ours. In myth we see the structural principles of literature isolated; in realism we see the *same* structural principles (not similar ones) fitting into a context of plausibility. (Similarly in music, a piece by Purcell and a piece by Benjamin Britten may not be in the least *like* each other, but if they are both in D major their tonality will be the same.) The presence of a mythical structure in realistic fiction, however, poses certain technical problems for making it plausible, and the devices used in solving these problems may be given the general name of *displacement*.

Myth, then, is one extreme of literary design; naturalism is the other, and in between lies the whole area of romance, using that term to mean, not the historical mode of the first essay, but the tendency, noted later in the same essay, to displace myth in a human direction and yet, in contrast to "realism," to conventionalize content in an idealized direction. The central principle of displacement is that what can be metaphorically identified in a myth can only be linked in romance by some form of simile: analogy, significant association, incidental accompanying imagery, and the like. In a myth we can have a sun-god or a tree-god; in a romance we may have a person who is significantly associated with the sun or trees.

*Anatomy of Criticism*

## Maud Bodkin (1875–1967)

LUCIFER IN SHAKESPEARE'S *OTHELLO* 1934

If we attempt to define the devil in psychological terms, regarding him as an archetype, a persistent or recurrent mode of apprehension, we may say that the devil is our tendency to represent in personal form the forces within and without us that threaten our supreme values. When Othello finds those values of confident love, of honor, and pride in soldiership, that made up his purposeful life, falling into ruin, his sense of the devil in all around him becomes acute. Desdemona has become "a fair devil"; he feels "a young and sweating devil" in her hand. The cry "O devil" breaks out among his incoherent words of raving. When Iago's falsehoods are disclosed, and Othello at last, too late, wrenches himself free from the spell of Iago's power over him, his sense of the devil incarnate in Iago's shape before him becomes overwhelming. If those who tell of the devil have failed to describe Iago, they have lied:

> I look down towards his feet; but that's a fable.
> If that thou be'st a devil, I cannot kill thee.

We also, watching or reading the play, experience the archetype. Intellectually aware, as we reflect, of natural forces, within a man himself as well as in society around, that betray or shatter his ideals, we yet feel these forces aptly symbolized for the imagination by such a figure as Iago—a being though personal yet hardly human, concentrated wholly on the hunting to destruction of its destined prey, the proud figure of the hero.

*Archetypal Patterns in Poetry*

## READER-RESPONSE CRITICISM

Reader-response criticism attempts to describe what happens in the reader's mind while interpreting a text. If traditional criticism assumes that imaginative writing is a creative act, reader-response theory recognizes that reading is also a creative process. Reader-response critics believe that no text provides self-contained meaning; literary texts do not exist independently of readers' interpretations. A text, according to this critical school, is not finished until it is read and interpreted. The practical problem then arises that no two individuals necessarily read a text in exactly the same way. Rather than declare one interpretation correct and the other mistaken, reader-response criticism recognizes the inevitable plurality of readings. Instead of trying to ignore or reconcile the contradictions inherent in this situation, it explores them.

The easiest way to explain reader-response criticism is to relate it to the common experience of rereading a favorite book after many years. Rereading a novel as an adult, for example, that "changed your life" as an adolescent, is often a shocking experience. The book may seem substantially different. The character you remembered liking most now seems less admirable, and another character you disliked now seems more sympathetic. Has the book changed? Very unlikely, but *you* certainly have in the intervening years. Reader-response criticism explores how the different individuals (or classes of individuals) see the same text differently. It emphasizes how religious, cultural, and social values affect readings; it also overlaps with gender criticism in exploring how men and women read the same text with different assumptions.

While reader-response criticism rejects the notion that there can be a single correct reading for a literary text, it doesn't consider all readings permissible. Each text creates limits to its possible interpretations. As Stanley Fish admits in the following critical selection, we cannot arbitrarily place an Eskimo in William Faulkner's story "A Rose for Emily" (though Professor Fish does ingeniously imagine a hypothetical situation where this bizarre interpretation might actually be possible).

## Stanley Fish (b. 1938)

AN ESKIMO "A ROSE FOR EMILY"                                                        1980

The fact that it remains easy to think of a reading that most of us would dismiss out of hand does not mean that the text excludes it but that there is as yet no elaborated interpretive procedure for producing that text. . . . Norman Holland's analysis of Faulkner's "A Rose for Emily" is a case in point. Holland is arguing for a kind of psychoanalytic pluralism. The text, he declares, is "at most a matrix of psychological possibilities for its readers," but, he insists, "only some possibilities . . . truly fit the matrix": "One would not say, for example, that a reader of . . . 'A Rose for Emily' who thought the 'tableau' [of Emily and her father in the doorway] described an Eskimo was really responding to the story at all—only pursuing some mysterious inner exploration."

Holland is making two arguments: first, that anyone who proposes an Eskimo reading of "A Rose for Emily" will not find a hearing in the literary community. And that, I think, is right. ("We are right to rule out at least some readings.") His second argument is that the unacceptability of the Eskimo reading is a function of the text, of what he calls its "sharable promptuary," the public "store of structured language" that sets limits to the interpretations the words can accommodate. And that, I think, is wrong. The Eskimo reading is unacceptable because there is at present no interpretive strategy for producing it, no way of "looking" or reading (and remember, all acts of looking or reading are "ways") that would result in the emergence of obviously Eskimo meanings. This does not mean, however, that no such strategy could ever come into play, and it is not difficult to imagine the circumstances under which it would establish itself. One such circumstance would be the discovery of a letter in which Faulkner confides that he has always believed himself to be an Eskimo changeling. (The example is absurd only if one forgets Yeats's *Vision* or Blake's Swedenborgianism° or James Miller's recent elaboration of a homosexual reading of *The Waste Land*°.) Immediately the workers in the Faulkner industry would begin to reinterpret the canon in the light of this newly revealed "belief" and the work of reinterpretation would involve the elaboration of a symbolic or allusive system (not unlike mythological or typological criticism) whose application would immediately transform the text into one informed everywhere by Eskimo meanings. It might seem that I am admitting that there is a text to be transformed, but the object of transformation would be the text (or texts) given by whatever interpretive strategies the Eskimo strategy was in the process of dislodging or expanding. The result would be that whereas we now have a Freudian "A Rose for Emily," a mythological "A Rose for Emily," a Christological "A Rose for Emily," a regional "A Rose for Emily," a sociological "A Rose for Emily," a linguistic "A Rose for Emily," we would in addition have an Eskimo "A Rose for Emily," existing in some relation of compatibility or incompatibility with the others.

Again the point is that while there are always mechanisms for ruling out readings, their source is not the text but the presently recognized interpretive strategies for producing the text. It follows, then, that no reading, however outlandish it might appear, is inherently an impossible one.

*Is There a Text in This Class?*

AN ESKIMO "A ROSE FOR EMILY." *Yeats's* Vision *or Blake's* Swedenborgianism: Irish poet William Butler Yeats and Swedish mystical writer Emanuel Swedenborg both claimed to have received revelations from the spirit world; some of Swedenborg's ideas are embodied in the long poems of William Blake. *The Waste Land:* influential poem by T. S. Eliot.


## Robert Scholes (b. 1929)
### "HOW DO WE MAKE A POEM?"          1982

Let us begin with one of the shortest poetic texts in the English language, "Elegy" by W. S. Merwin:

Who would I show it to

One line, one sentence, unpunctuated, but proclaimed an interrogative by its grammar and syntax—what makes it a poem? Certainly without its title it would not be a poem; but neither would the title alone constitute a poetic text. Nor do the two together simply make a poem by themselves. Given the title and the text, the *reader* is encouraged to make a poem. He is not forced to do so, but there is not much else he can do with this material, and certainly nothing else so rewarding. (I will use the masculine pronoun here to refer to the reader, not because all readers are male but because I am, and my hypothetical reader is not a pure construct but an idealized version of myself.)

How do we make a poem out of this text? There are only two things to work on, the title and the question posed by the single, colloquial line. The line is not simply colloquial, it is prosaic; with no words of more than one syllable, concluded by a preposition, it is within the utterance range of every speaker of English. It is, in a sense, completely intelligible. But in another sense it is opaque, mysterious. Its three pronouns—who, I, it—pose problems of reference. Its conditional verb phrase—would . . . show to—poses a problem of situation. The context that would supply the information required to make that simple sentence meaningful as well as intelligible is not there. It must be supplied by the reader.

To make a poem of this text the reader must not only know English, he must know a poetic code as well: the code of the funeral elegy, as practiced in English from the Renaissance to the present time. The "words on the page" do not constitute a poetic "work," complete and self-sufficient, but a "text," a sketch or outline that must be completed by the active participation of a reader equipped with the right sort of information. In this case part of that information consists of an acquaintance with the elegiac tradition: its procedures, assumptions, devices, and values. One needs to know works like Milton's "Lycidas," Shelley's "Adonais," Tennyson's "In Memoriam," Whitman's "When Lilacs Last in the Dooryard Bloomed," Thomas's "Refusal to Mourn the Death by Fire of a Child in London," and so on, in order to "read" this simple poem properly. In fact, it could be argued that the more elegies one can bring to bear on a reading of this one, the better, richer poem this one becomes. I would go even further, suggesting that a knowledge of the critical tradition—of Dr. Johnson's objections to "Lycidas," for instance, or Wordsworth's critique of poetic diction—will also enhance one's reading of this poem. For the poem is, of course, an anti-elegy, a refusal not simply to mourn, but to write a sonorous, eloquent, mournful, but finally acquiescent, accepting—in a word, "elegiac"—poem at all.

Reading the poem involves, then, a special knowledge of its tradition. It also involves a special interpretive skill. The forms of the short, written poem as they have developed in English over the past few centuries can be usefully seen as compressed, truncated, or fragmented imitations of other verbal forms, especially the play, story, public oration, and personal essay. The reasons for this are too complicated for consideration here, but the fact will be apparent to all who reflect upon the matter. Our short poems are almost always elliptical versions of what can easily be conceived of as dramatic, narrative, oratorical, or meditative texts. Often, they are combinations of these and other modes of address. To take an obvious example, the dramatic monologue in the hands of Robert Browning is like a speech from a play (though usually more elongated than most such speeches). But to "read" such a monologue we must imagine the setting, the situation, the context, and so on. The dramatic monologue is "like" a play but gives us less information of certain sorts than a play would, requiring us to provide that information by decoding the clues in the monologue itself in the light of our understanding of the generic model. Most short poems work this way. They require both special knowledge and special skills to be "read."

To understand "Elegy" we must construct a situation out of the clues provided. The "it" in "Who would I show it to" is of course the elegy itself. The "I" is the potential writer of the elegy. The "Who" is the audience for the poem. But the verb phrase "would . . . show to" indicates a condition contrary to fact. Who would I show it to *if* I were to write it? This implies in turn that for the potential elegiac poet there is one person whose appreciation means more than that of all the rest of the potential audience for the poem he might write, and it further implies that the death of this particular person is the one imagined in the poem. If this person were dead, the poet suggests, so would his inspiration be dead. With no one to write for, no poem would be forthcoming. This poem is not only a "refusal to mourn," like that of Dylan Thomas, it is a refusal to elegize. The whole elegiac tradition, like its cousin the funeral oration, turns finally away from mourning toward acceptance, revival, renewal, a return to the concerns of life, symbolized by the very writing of the poem. Life goes on; there *is* an audience; and the mourned person will live through accomplishments, influence, descendants, and also (not least) in the elegiac poem itself. Merwin rejects all that. *If* I wrote an elegy for X, the person for whom I have always written, X would not be alive to read it; therefore, there is no reason to write an elegy for the one person in my life who most deserves one; therefore, there is no reason to write any elegy, anymore, ever. Finally, and of course, this poem called "Elegy" is not an elegy.

*Semiotics and Interpretation*

## DECONSTRUCTIONIST CRITICISM

Deconstructionist criticism rejects the traditional assumption that language can accurately represent reality. Language, according to deconstructionists, is a fundamentally unstable medium; consequently, literary texts, which are made up of words, have no fixed, single meaning. Deconstructionists insist, according to critic Paul de Man, on "the impossibility of making the actual expression coincide with what has to be expressed, of making the actual signs coincide with what is signified." Since they believe that literature cannot definitively express its subject matter, deconstructionists tend to shift their attention away from *what* is being said to *how* language is being used in a text.

Paradoxically, deconstructionist criticism often resembles formalist criticism; both methods usually involve close reading. But while a formalist usually tries to demonstrate how the diverse elements of a text cohere into meaning, the deconstructionist approach attempts to show how the text "deconstructs," that is, how it can be broken down—by a skeptical critic—into mutually irreconcilable positions. A biographical or historical critic might seek to establish the author's intention as a means to interpreting a literary work, but deconstructionists reject the notion that the critic should endorse the myth of authorial control over language. Deconstructionist critics like Roland Barthes and Michel Foucault have therefore called for "the death of the author," that is, the rejection of the assumption that the author, no matter how ingenious, can fully control the meaning of a text. They have also announced the death of literature as a special category of writing. In their view, poems and novels are merely words on a page that deserve no privileged status as art; all texts are created equal—equally untrustworthy, that is.

Deconstructionists focus on how language is used to achieve power. Since they believe, in the words of critic David Lehman, that "there are no truths, only rival interpretations," deconstructionists try to understand how some "interpretations" come to be regarded as truth. A major goal of deconstruction is to demonstrate how those supposed truths are at best provisional and at worst contradictory.

Deconstruction, as you may have inferred, calls for intellectual subtlety and skill, and isn't for a novice to leap into. If you pursue your literary studies beyond the introductory stage, you will want to become more familiar with its assumptions. Deconstruction may strike you as a negative, even destructive, critical approach, and yet its best practitioners are adept at exposing the inadequacy of much conventional criticism. By patient analysis, they can sometimes open up the most familiar text and find in it fresh and unexpected significance.

## Roland Barthes (1915–1980)

THE DEATH OF THE AUTHOR                                                     1968

Succeeding the Author, the scriptor no longer bears within him passions, humours, feelings, impressions, but rather this immense dictionary from which he draws a writing that can know no halt: life never does more than imitate the book, and the book itself is only a tissue of signs, an imitation that is lost, infinitely deferred.

Once the Author is removed, the claim to decipher a text becomes quite futile. To give a text an Author is to impose a limit on that text, to furnish it with a final signified, to close the writing. Such a conception suits criticism very well, the latter then allotting itself the important task of discovering the Author (or its hypostases: society, history, psyché, liberty) beneath the work: when the Author has been found, the text is "explained"—victory to the critic. Hence there is no surprise in the fact that, historically, the reign of the Author has also been that of the Critic, nor again in the fact that criticism (be it new) is today undermined along with the Author. In the multiplicity of writing, everything is to be *disentangled*, nothing *deciphered*; the structure can be followed, "run" (like the thread of a stocking) at every point and at every level, but there is nothing beneath: the space of writing is to be ranged over, not pierced; writing ceaselessly posits meaning ceaselessly to evaporate it, carrying out a systematic exemption of meaning. In precisely this way literature (it would be better from now on to say *writing*), by refusing to assign a "secret", an ultimate meaning, to the text (and to the world as text), liberates what may be called an anti-theological activity, an activity that is truly revolutionary since to refuse to fix meaning is, in the end, to refuse God and his hypostases—reason, science, law.

"The Death of the Author"
Translated by Stephen Heath

## Geoffrey Hartman (b. 1929)
### ON WORDSWORTH'S "A SLUMBER DID MY SPIRIT SEAL"      1987

Take Wordsworth's well-known lyric of eight lines, one of the "Lucy" poems, which has been explicated so many times without its meaning being fully determined:

> A slumber did my spirit seal;
>   I had no human fears:
> She seemed a thing that could not feel
>   The touch of earthly years.
>
> No motion has she now, no force;
>   She neither hears nor sees;
> Rolled round in earth's diurnal course,
>   With rocks, and stones, and trees.

It does not matter whether you interpret the second stanza (especially its last line) as tending toward affirmation, or resignation, or a grief verging on bitterness. The tonal assignment of one rather than another possible meaning, to repeat Susanne Langer° on musical form, is curiously open or beside the point. Yet the lyric does not quite support Langer's general position, that "Articulation is its life, but not assertion," because the poem is composed of a series of short and definitive statements, very like assertions. You could still claim that the poem's life is not in the assertions but somewhere else: but where then? What would articulation mean in that case? Articulation is not anti-assertive here; indeed the sense of closure is so strong that it thematizes itself in the very first line.

Nevertheless, is not the harmony or aesthetic effect of the poem greater than this local conciseness; is not the sense of closure broader and deeper than our admiration for a perfect technical construct? The poem is surely something else than a fine box, a well-wrought coffin.

That it is a kind of epitaph is relevant, of course. We recognize, even if genre is not insisted on, that Wordsworth's style is laconic, even lapidary. There may be a mimetic or formal motive related to the ideal of epitaphic poetry. But the motive may also be, in a precise way, meta-epitaphic. The poem, first of all, marks the closure of a life that has never opened up: Lucy is likened in other poems to a hidden flower or the evening star. Setting overshadows rising, and her mode of existence is inherently inward, westering. I will suppose then, that Wordsworth was at some level giving expression to the traditional epitaphic wish: Let the earth rest lightly on the deceased. If so, his conversion of this epitaphic formula is so complete that to trace the process of conversion might seem gratuitous. The formula, a trite if deeply grounded figure of speech, has been catalyzed out of existence. Here it is formula itself, or better, the adjusted words of the mourner that lie lightly on the girl and everyone who is a mourner.

I come back, then, to the "aesthetic" sense of a burden lifted, rather than denied. A heavy element is made lighter. One may still feel that the term "elation" is inappropriate in this context; yet elation is, as a mood, the very subject of the first stanza. For the mood described is love or desire when it *eternizes* the loved person, when it makes her a star-like being that "could not feel / The touch of earthly years." This *naive* elation, this spontaneous movement of the spirit upward, is reversed in the downturn or cata-strophe of the second stanza. Yet this stanza does not close out the illusion; it preserves it within the elegaic form. The illusion is elated, in our use of the word: *aufgehoben*° seems the proper term. For the girl is still, and all the more, what she seemed to be: beyond touch, like a star, if the earth in its daily motion is a planetary and erring rather than a fixed star, and if all on this star of earth must partake of its sublunar, mortal, temporal nature.

\*     \*     \*     \*

To sum up: In Wordsworth's lyric the specific gravity of words is weighed in the balance of each stanza; and this balance is as much a judgment on speech in the context of our mortality as it is a meaningful response to the individual death. At the limit of the medium of words, and close to silence, what has been purged is not concreteness, or the empirical sphere of the emotions—shock, disillusion, trauma, recognition, grief, atonement—what has been purged is a series of flashy schematisms and false or partial mediations: artificial plot, inflated consolatory rhetoric, the coercive absolutes of logic or faith.

"Elation in Hegel and Wordsworth"

ON WORDSWORTH'S "A SLUMBER DID MY SPIRIT SEAL." *Susanne Langer:* Langer (1895–1985) was an American philosopher who discussed the relationship between aesthetics and artistic form. *Aufgehoben:* German for "taken up" or "lifted up," but this term can also mean "canceled" or "nullified." Hartman uses the term for its double meaning.

# ACKNOWLEDGMENTS

## FICTION

James Baldwin. "Sonny's Blues," copyright © 1957 by James Baldwin, from *Going to Meet the Man* by James Baldwin. Used by permission of Doubleday, a division of Bantam Doubleday Dell Publishing Group, Inc.

Jorges Luis Borges. "The Gospel According to Mark" from *Doctor Brodie's Report* by Jorge Luis Borges. Copyright © 1970, 1971, 1972 by Emece Editores, S.A. and Norman Thomas di Giovanni. Used by permission of Dutton Signet, a division of Penguin Books USA Inc.

T. Coraghessan Boyle. "Greasy Lake." From *Greasy Lake and Other Stories* by T. Coraghessan Boyle. Copyright © 1982 by T. Coraghessan Boyle. Reprinted by permission of Viking Penguin, a division of Penguin Books USA Inc.

Raymond Carver. "Cathedral." From *Cathedral* by Raymond Carver. Copyright © 1981, 1982, 1983 by Raymond Carver. Reprinted by permission of Alfred A. Knopf, Inc. "Commonplace But Precise Language" excerpted from "A Storyteller's Shoptalk," *The New York Times* (Book Review), January 15, 1991. Copyright © 1981 by The New York Times Company. Reprinted by permission.

John Cheever. "The Five-Forty-Eight." From *The Stories of John Cheever* by John Cheever. Copyright 1954 by John Cheever. Reprinted by permission of Alfred A. Knopf, Inc.

Sandra Cisneros. "Barbie-Q." From *Woman Hollering Creek*. Copyright © by Sandra Cisneros 1991. Published by Random House, Inc., New York in 1991 and by Vintage books, a division of Random House, Inc. in 1992. Reprinted by permission of Susan Bergholz Literary Services, New York.

William Faulkner. "A Rose for Emily" (copyright 1930 and renewed © 1958 by William Faulkner) and "Barn Burning" (copyright 1950 by Random House, Inc. and copyright © 1977 by Jill Faulkner Summers) from *Collected Stories of William Faulkner* by William Faulkner. Reprinted by permission of Random House, Inc. "The Human Heart in Conflict with Itself" from William Faulkner's 1950 Nobel Prize for Literature acceptance speech. © The Nobel Foundation 1950. Reprinted by permission.

Gustave Flaubert. "The Labor of Style," translated by Francis Steegmuller. From *Madame Bovary* by Gustave Flaubert. Copyright © 1957 by Francis Steegmuller. Reprinted by permission of Random House, Inc.

Gabriel García Márquez. "The Woman Who Came at Six O'Clock" from *Innocent Erendira and Other Stories* by Gabriel García Márquez. English translation copyright © 1978 by Harper & Row, Publishers, Inc. Reprinted by permission of HarperCollins Publishers, Inc.

Nadine Gordimer. "The Defeated" from *The Soft Voice of the Serpent* by Nadine Gordimer. Reprinted by permission of Russell & Volkening as agents for the author. Copyright 1952, renewed © 1980 by Nadine Gordimer. "How the Short Story Differs from the Novel." Excerpted from "A Flash of Fireflies," first published as "South Africa" in *The Kenyon Review*—Original Series, Fall 1968, Col 30, No. 4. Copyright 1968 by Kenyon College. Reprinted by permission.

Jakob and Wilhelm Grimm, "Godfather Death" from *The Juniper Tree and Other Tales by the Brothers Grimm*, translated by Lore Segal and Randall Jarrell. Copyright © 1973 by Lore Segal. Reprinted by permission of Farrar, Straus and Giroux, Inc.

Ernest Hemingway. "A Clean, Well-Lighted Place." Reprinted with permission of Charles Scribner's Sons, an imprint of Macmillan Publishing Company, from *Winner Take Nothing* by Ernest Hemingway. Copyright 1933 by Charles Scribner's Sons. Copyright renewed © 1961 by Mary Hemingway.

Langston Hughes. "On the Road" from *Laughing to Keep from Crying* by Langston Hughes. Reprinted by permission of Harold Ober Associates Incorporated. Copyright 1952 by Langston Hughes. Copyright renewed 1980 by George Houston Bass.

Zora Neale Hurston. "Sweat" from *Spunk: Selected Short Stories* of Zora Neale Hurston. Copyright © 1985 by Turtle Island Foundation. Reprinted by permission of the author's estate.

Shirley Jackson. "The Lottery" from *The Lottery* by Shirley Jackson. Copyright 1948, 1949 by Shirley Jackson. Renewal copyright 1976, 1977 by Laurence Hyman, Barry Hyman, Mrs. Sarah Webster and Mrs. Joanne Schnurer. Reprinted by permission of Farrar, Straus and Giroux, Inc.

James Joyce. "Araby." From *Dubliners* by James Joyce. Copyright 1916 by B. W. Heubsch. Definitive text copyright © 1967 by the Estate of James Joyce. Reprinted by permission of Viking Penguin, a division of Penguin Books USA Inc.

Franz Kafka. "The Metamorphosis," translated by Willa and Edwin Muir. From *Franz Kafka: The Complete Stories* by Franz Kafka. Copyright © 1946, 1947, 1948, 1954, 1958, 1971 by Schocken Books, Pantheon Books, a division of Random House, Inc. Reprinted by permission of the publisher.

D. H. Lawrence. "The Rocking-Horse Winner." From *The Complete Short Stories of D. H. Lawrence*, Volume III. Copyright 1933 by the Estate of D. H. Lawrence. Copyright renewed © 1961 by Angelo Ravagli and C. M. Weekely, Executors of the Estate of Frieda Lawrence Ravagli. Reprinted by permission of Viking Penguin, a division of Penguin Books USA Inc.

Ursula K. Le Guin. "The Ones Who Walk Away from Omelas." Copyright © 1973 by Ursula K. Le Guin; first appeared in *New Dimensions* 3; reprinted by permission of the author and the author's agent, Virginia Kidd.

John Ashbery. "The Cathedral Is," from *As We Know* by John Ashbery. Copyright © 1979 by John Ashbery; "At North Farm," from *A Wave* by John Ashbery. Copyright © 1984 by John Ashbery. Originally appeared in *The New Yorker*. Both used by permission of Viking Penguin, a division of Penguin Books USA Inc.

Margaret Atwood. "you fit into me" from *Power Politics* by Margaret Atwood (House of Anansi Press Ltd.). Copyright © 1971 by Margaret Atwood. Reprinted by permission. "Siren Song," from *You Are Happy*, in *Selected Poems 1965-1975* (Copyright © 1967 by Margaret Atwood) and *Selected Poems 1966-1984* (Copyright © Margaret Atwood 1990). Reprinted by permission of Houghton Mifflin Company and Oxford University Press Canada. All rights reserved.

W. H. Auden. "James Watt" from "Academic Graffiti," "The Unknown Citizen," "As I Walked Out One Evening," and "Musée des Beaux Arts" from *W. H. Auden: Collected Poems*, edited by Edward Mendelson. Copyright 1940 and renewed 1968 by W. H. Auden. Reprinted by permission of Random House, Inc., and Faber and Faber Ltd.

David B. Axelrod. "Once in a While a Protest Poem" from *A Dream of Feet* by David Axelrod (1976). Reprinted by permission of the author and Cross Cultural Communications.

R. L. Barth. "The Insert" from *Forced Marching to the Styx: Vietnam War Poems* by R. L. Barth (1983). Reprinted by permission of Perivale Press; "Readers and listeners praise my books" from *Earthenware: XLIV Epigrams from Marital*, translated by R. L. Barth. Copyright © 1988 by R. L. Barth. Reprinted by permission.

Max Beerbohm. "On the imprint of the first English edition of *The Works of Max Beerbohm*." Final two lines inscribed by Max Beerbohm in a presentation copy of his book. Used by permission of Sir Geoffrey Keynes.

Hilaire Belloc. "The Hippopotamus" from *Cautionary Verses* by Hilaire Belloc. Reprinted by permission of Gerald Duckworth & Co. Ltd; "Fatigue" from *Complete Verse* by Hilaire Belloc (Pimlico). © Estate of Hilaire Belloc 1970. Reprinted by permission of the author.

Bruce Bennett. "Ironist" from *Not Wanting to Write Like Everyone Else* by Bruce Bennett (State Street Press, 1987); "The Lady Speaks Again" from *Taking Off* by Bruce Bennett (Orchises Press). Copyright © 1992 by Bruce Bennett. Reprinted by permission of the author.

Edmund Clerihew Bentley. "Sir Christopher Wren" from *Clerihews Complete* by E. C. Bentley, © E. C. Bentley. Reprinted by permission of Curtis Brown Ltd. on behalf of the Estate of E. C. Bentley.

John Betjeman. "In Westminster Abbey" from *Collected Poems* by John Betjeman, © John Betjeman 1958. Reprinted by permission of John Murray (Publishers) Ltd.

Elizabeth Bishop. "The Fish," "Sestina," "Filling Station," and "One Art" from *The Complete Poems 1927-1979* by Elizabeth Bishop. Copyright © 1940, 1946, 1952, 1953, 1955, 1956, 1960, 1961, 1962, 1964, 1965 by Elizabeth Bishop. Copyright © 1979, 1983 by Alice Helen Methfessel. Reprinted by permission of Farrar, Straus & Giroux, Inc.

Robert Bly. "Driving to Town Late to Mail a Letter" from *Silence in the Snowy Fields* by Robert Bly (Wesleyan University Press), copyright © 1959, 1960, 1961, 1962 by Robert Bly. Reprinted by permission of the author.

Louise Bogan. "The Dream" from *The Blue Estuaries* by Louise Bogan. Copyright 1938, © 1968 by Louise Bogan. Reprinted by permission of Farrar, Straus & Giroux, Inc.

Anne Bradstreet. "The Author to Her Book." Reprinted by permission of the publishers from *The Works of Anne Bradstreet* edited by Jeannine Hensley, Cambridge, Mass.: Harvard University Press, Copyright © 1967 by the President and Fellows of Harvard College.

Richard Brautigan. "Haiku Ambulance" from *The Pill Versus the Springhill Mine Disaster* by Richard Brautigan. Copyright © 1965 by Richard Brautigan. Reprinted by permission of Houghton Mifflin Company/Seymour Lawrence.

Van K. Brock. Lines from "Driving at Dawn" from *The Hard Essential Landscape* by Van K. Brock (University Presses of Florida, 1979). Copyright © 1979 by Van K. Brock. Reprinted by permission.

Gwendolyn Brooks, "The Bean Eaters," "We Real Cool," "Southeast Corner," and "The Rites for Cousin Vit" from *Blacks* by Gwendolyn Brooks, © 1991. Published by Third World Press, Chicago. Reprinted by permission of the author.

Taniguchi Buson. "The Piercing Chill I Feel." From *An Introduction to Haiku* by Harold G. Henderson. Copyright © 1958 by Harold G. Henderson. Used by permission of Doubleday, a division of Bantam Doubleday Dell Publishing Group, Inc.

Thomas Carper. "Facts" from *Fiddle Lane* (The Johns Hopkins University Press, 1991). Reprinted by permission of the publisher.

Hayden Carruth. "Let my snow-tracks lead" from *Collected Shorter Poems, 1946-1991*. Copyright © 1992 by Hayden Carruth. Used by permission Cooper Canyon Press, P.O. Box 271, Port Townsend, WA 98368.

Nina Cassian. "Like Gulliver" (translated by Peter Solomon) is reprinted from *Life Sentence, Selected Poems*, by Nina Cassian, edited by William Jay Smith, by permission of W. W. Norton & Company, Inc. Copyright © 1990 by Nina Cassian.

Fred Chappell. "Narcissus and Echo" reprinted by permission of Louisiana State University Press from *Source: Poems* by Fred Chappell. Copyright © 1985 by Fred Chappell.

John Ciardi. "In Place of a Curse" from *Selected Poems* by John Ciardi. Copyright © 1984 by John Ciardi. Reprinted by permission of the University of Arkansas Press.

Wlliam Cole. "On My Boat on Lake Cayuga" from "Some River Rhymes" in *Light Year '85* edited by Robert Wallace (Cleveland, Ohio: Bits Press). Copyright © 1983, 1984 by William Cole. Reprinted by permission of the author.

Wendy Cope. "Lonely Hearts" and lines from "From Strugnell's Rubaiyat" from *Making Cocoa for Kingsley Amis* by Wendy Cope. © Wendy Cope 1986. Reprinted by permission of Faber and Faber Ltd; "Variation on Belloc's 'Fatigue' " from *Serious Concerns* by Wendy Cope. © Wendy Cope, 1992. Reprinted by permission of Faber and Faber Inc. and Faber and Faber Ltd.

Cid Corman. Translation of the haiku by Issa from *One Man's Moon: Fifty Haiku* (Gnomon Press, 1984).

Reprinted by permission of the publisher and the author.

Frances Cornford. "The Watch" and "All Souls' Night" from *Collected Poems* by Frances Cornford © 1954 Cressett Press, Hutchinson Publishing Group. Reprinted by permission of Random Century Group Ltd. on behalf of the Estate of Frances Cornford.

Robert Creeley. "Oh No" from *Collected Poems of Robert Creeley, 1945-1975*. Copyright © 1983 The Regents of the University of California. Reprinted by permission of The Regents of the University of California and the University of California Press.

Countee Cullen. "For a Lady That I Know." Reprinted by permission of GRM Associates, Inc., Agents for the Estate of Ida M. Cullen. From the book *Color* by Countee Cullen. Copyright 1925 by Harper & Brothers; copyright renewed 1953 by Ida M. Cullen.

E. E. Cummings. "anyone lived in a pretty how town," "Buffalo Bill's," "in Just-," and "A politician is an arse upon" are reprinted from *Complete Poems, 1913-1962*, by E. E. Cummings, by permission of Liveright Publishing Corporation. Copyright © 1923, 1925, 1931, 1935, 1938, 1939, 1940, 1944, 1945, 1946, 1947, 1948, 1949, 1950, 1951, 1952, 1953, 1954, 1955, 1956, 1957, 1958, 1959, 1960, 1961, 1962 by the Trustees of the E. E. Cummings Trust. Copyright © 1961, 1963, 1968 by Marion Morehouse Cummings.

J. V. Cunningham, "Friend, on this scaffold Thomas More lies dead" and "This *Humanist* whom no beliefs constrained" from *The Exclusions of a Rhyme* by J. V. Cunningham (Ohio University Press). Copyright © 1971 by J. V. Cunningham . Reprinted by permission of Jessie C. Cunningham.

Dick Davis. Lines from *The Rubaiyat of Omar Khayyam*, translated by Dick Davis. © 1993 Dick Davis. Reprinted by permission of the translator.

Peter Davison. "The Last Word" (IV of "Four Love Poems") from *Pretending to Be Asleep* by Peter Davison. Reprinted by permission of Russell & Volkening as agents for the author. Copyright © 1970 by Peter Davison.

Walter de la Mare. "The Listeners" from *The Listeners and Other Poems* by Walter de la Mare (1912). Reprinted by permission of The Literary Trustees of Walter de la Mare and The Society of Authors as their representative.

Emily Dickinson. "I like to see it lap the Miles," "The Lightning is a Yellow Fork," "I heard a Fly buzz—when I died," "A dying Tiger—Moaned for Drink," "Because I could not stop for Death," " I started Early—Took my Dog," and "My Life had stood—a Loaded Gun." Reprinted by permission of the publishers and the Trustees of Amherst College from *The Poems of Emily Dickinson*, Thomas H. Johnson, ed., Cambridge, Mass.: The Belknap Press of Harvard University Press, Copyright © 1951, 1955, 1983 by the President and Fellows of Harvard College; Twenty-two lines from "My Life had stood—a Loaded Gun" from *The Complete Poems of Emily Dickinson*, edited by Thomas H. Johnson. Copyright 1929 by Martha Dickinson Bianchi, copyright © renewed 1957 by Mary L. Hampson. By permission of Little, Brown and Company in association with the Atlantic Monthly Press.

Emanuel di Pasquale. "Rain." Reprinted by permission of the author.

H. D. (Hilda Doolittle). "Heat" and "Helen" from *Collected Poems* by Hilda Doolittle. Copyright © 1982 by the Estate of Hilda Doolittle. Reprinted by permission of New Directions Publishing Corporation.

Rita Dove. "Daystar," reprinted from *Thomas and Beulah* by Rita Dove, by permission of Carnegie Mellon University Press. Copyright © 1986 by Rita Dove.

Richard Eberhardt. "The Fury of Aerial Bombardment." From *Collected Poems 1930-1986* by Richard Eberhardt. Copyright © 1988 by Richard Eberhardt. Reprinted by permission of Oxford University Press, Inc.

T. S. Eliot. "The Winter Evening Settles Down" from "Preludes," "The *Boston Evening Transcript*," and "The Love Song of J. Alfred Prufrock" from *Prufrock and Other Observations* by T. S. Eliot (1917). Reprinted by permission of the publisher, Faber and Faber Ltd.; "Virginia" and "Journey of the Magi" from *Collected Poems 1909-1962* by T. S. Eliot, copyright 1936 by Harcourt Brace & Company, copyright © 1964, 1963 by T. S. Eliot, reprinted by permission of the publishers, Harcourt Brace & Company and Faber and Faber Ltd.; "Emotion and Personality," excerpted from "Tradition and the Individual Talent" in *Selected Essays* by T. S. Eliot, copyright 1950 by Harcourt Brace & Company and renewed 1978 by Esme Valerie Eliot, reprinted by permission of the publishers, Harcourt Brace & Company and Faber and Faber Ltd. ; "Tradition and the Individual Talent" appeared in the September 1919 and November 1919 issues of *Egoist*.

Louise Erdrich. Lines from "Indian Boarding School: The Runaways" from *Jacklight* by Louise Erdrich. Copyright © 1984 by Louise Erdrich. Reprinted by permission of Henry Holt and Company, Inc.

Abbie Huston Evans. "Wing-Spread," reprinted from *Collected Poems* by Abbie Huston Evans, by permission of the University of Pittsburgh Press. Copyright 1950 by Abbie Huston Evans.

Edward Field. "Curse of the Cat Woman" Copyright © 1967 by Edward Field. Reprinted from Counting Myself Lucky: Selected Poems 1963-1992 with the permission of Black Sparrow Press.

Annie Finch. "Dickinson." Copyright 1992 by Annie Finch. Originally appeared in Osiris 34 (Summer 1992). Reprinted by permission of the author.

Carolyn Forché. "The Colonel" from The Country *Between Us* by Carolyn Forché. Copyright © 1980 by Carolyn Forché. Reprinted by permission of HarperCollins Publishers.

Robert Francis. "Catch" from The Orb Weaver, copyright 1960 by Robert Francis, Wesleyan University Press by permission of University Press of New England.

Robert Frost. "Out, Out—," "The Road Not Taken," "Birches," and "Mending Wall." Copyright 1916, © 1969 by Holt, Rinehart and Winston. Copyright 1944, © 1958 by Robert Frost. Copyright © 1962 by Leslie Frost Ballantine; "Fire and Ice," "The Silken Tent," "The Secret Sits," "Desert Places," " Never Again Would Birds' Song Be the Same," "Acquainted with the Night," "Nothing Gold Can Stay," "Stopping by Woods on a Snowy Evening," and "Design." Copyright 1923, 1928, © 1969 by Holt, Rinehart and Winston. Copyright 1936, 1942, 1951, © 1956 by Robert Frost. Copyright 1946, © 1970 by Leslie Frost Ballantine.

1926 by Alfred A. Knopf, Inc. and renewed 1954 by Langston Hughes) from *Selected Poems of Langston Hughes*. Reprinted by permission of Alfred A. Knopf, Inc.

Randall Jarrell. "The Death of the Ball Turret Gunner" from *The Complete Poems* by Randall Jarrell. Copyright 1945, renewed © 1973 by Mary von Schrader Jarrell. Reprinted by permission of Farrar, Straus & Giroux, Inc.

Robinson Jeffers. "Hands" (Copyright 1929 and renewed © 1957 by Robinson Jeffers) and "To the Stone-cutters" (Copyright 1924 and renewed 1952 by Robinson Jeffers) from *The Selected Poetry of Robinson Jeffers* by Robinson Jeffers. Reprinted by permission of Random House, Inc.

Elizabeth Jennings. "I Feel" from Growing Points (Carcanet Press, 1975). Reprinted by permission of David Higham Associates.

Donald Justice. "Men at Forty" from *Night Light*, copyright 1967 by Donald Justice, and "On the Death of Friends in Childhood" from *The Summer Anniversaries*, copyright 1981 by Donald Justice, Wesleyan University Press by permission of University Press of New England.

Greg Keeler. Lines from "There Ain't No Such Thing as a Montana Cowboy," *The Limberlost Review*, 1979. Reprinted by permission of the author.

Weldon Kees. "For My Daughter." Reprinted from *The Collected Poems of Weldon Kees*, Revised Edition, edited by Donald Justice, by permission of the University of Nebraska Press. Copyright 1943, 1947, 1954 by Weldon Kees. Copyright © 1960 by John A. Kees. Copyright © 1962, 1965 by the University of Nebraska Press.

Jane Kenyon. "The Suitor" form *From Room to Room*, © 1978 by Jane Kenyon. Reprinted courtesy of Alice James Books, 33 Richdale Avenue, Cambridge, MA 02138.

Hugh Kingsmill. "What, Still Alive at Twenty-Two?" from *The Best of Hugh Kingsmill*. Reprinted by permission of Victor Gollancz Ltd.

Bill Knott (Saint Geraud). "Poem" from *The Naomi Poems: Corpse and Beans* by Saint Geraud. Copyright © 1968 by William Knott. Reprinted by permission.

Yusef Komunyakaa. "Facing It" from *Dien Kai Dau*, copyright 1988 by Yusef Komunyakaa, Wesleyan University Press by permission of University Press of New England.

Ted Kooser. "A Child's Grave Marker" is reprinted from *One World at a Time*, by Ted Kooser, by permission of the University of Pittsburgh Press. © 1985 by Ted Kooser.

Philip Larkin. "Toads" and "Poetry of Departures" are reprinted from *The Less Deceived* by Philip Larkin by permission of The Marvell Press, England and Australia. Copyright © The Marvell Press 1955, 1960. "Aubade" from *Collected Poems* by Philip Larkin edited by Anthony Thwaite. Copyright © 1988, 1989 by the Estate of Philip Larkin; "Home Is So Sad" from *The Whitsun Weddings* by Philip Larkin. © 1964 by Philip Larkin. Both reprinted by permission of Farrar, Straus & Giroux, Inc., and Faber and Faber Ltd.

D. H. Lawrence. "Piano" and "Bavarian Gentians," from *The Complete Poems of D. H. Lawrence* by D. H. Lawrence. Copyright © 1964, 1971 by Angelo Ravagli and C. M. Weekley, Executors of the Estate of Frieda

Lawrence Ravagli. Used by permission of Viking Penguin, a division of Penguin Books USA inc.

Irving Layton, "The Bull Calf" from *A Red Carpet for the Sun* (McClelland & Stewart). Reprinted by permission of the author.

John Lennon and Paul McCartney. "Eleanor Rigby" by John Lennon and Paul McCartney. Copyright © 1966 *Northern Songs*. All Rights Controlled and Administered by MCA Music Publishing, A Division of MCA, Inc. under license from *Northern Songs*. Used by permission. International copyright secured. All rights reserved.

Denise Levertov. "Leaving Forever" and "Six Variations, iii" from *Poems 1960-1967* by Denise Levertov. Copyright © 1958, 1963, 1964, 1969 by Denise Levertov Goodman. "Leaving Forever" was first published in *Poetry*. Reprinted by permission of New Directions Publishing Corporation.

Philip Levine. "Animals Are Passing from Our Lives." Reprinted from *Not This Pig*, © 1968 by Philip Levine, Wesleyan University Press. By permission of University Press of New England.

Janet Lewis. "Girl Help" from *Poems Old and New, 1918-1978* by Janet Lewis (Ohio University Press/Swallow Press, 1981). Reprinted with the permission of The Ohio University Press/Swallow Press, Athens.

Shirley Geok-lin Lim. "To Li Po" from *Crossing the Peninsula & Other Poems*, Heinemann Education Books (Asia) Ltd. © Shirley Lim 1980. Reprinted by permission of the author.

Federico García Lorca, "La Guitarra" ("Guitar") from *Obras Completas* by Federico García Lorca. Copyright 1954 Aguilar S.A. de Ediciones. Reprinted by permission of New Directions Publishing Corporation. English translation by Keith Waldrop. Reprinted by permission.

Robert Lowell. "Skunk Hour" from *Life Studies* by Robert Lowell. Copyright © 1956, 1959 by Robert Lowell. Reprinted by permission of Farrar, Straus & Giroux, Inc.

Claude McKay. "America" from *Selected Poems of Claude McKay*, published by Harcourt Brace Jovanovich, 1981. By permission of The Archives of Claude McKay: Carl Cowl, Administrator.

Rod McKuen. "Thoughts on Capital Punishment" from *Stanyan Street and Other Sorrows* by Rod McKuen. Copyright 1954, © 1960, 1962, 1963, 1964, 1965, 1966 by Rod McKuen. Reprinted by permission of Random House, Inc.

Archibald MacLeish. "The End of the World" from *New and Collected Poems 1917–1982* by Archibald MacLeish. Copyright © 1985 by The Estate of Archibald MacLeish. Reprinted by permission of Houghton Mifflin Company. All rights reserved.

Wallace D. McRae, "Reincarnation" from *Cowboy Curmudgeon and Other Poems* (Gibbs Smith Publisher, P. O. Box 667, Layton, Utah 84041). Copyright © 1979, 1992 by Walllace D. McRae. Reprinted by permission of the author.

Charles Martin. "Taken Up" from *Room for Error* (University of Georgia Press, 1978). Reprinted by permission of the author.

John Masefield. "Cargoes" from *Poems* by John Masefield. Reprinted by permission of The Society of Authors as the literary representative of the Estate of

John Masefield.

David Mason "Disclosure" from *The Buried Houses* by David Mason. Copyright © 1991 by David Mason. Reprinted by permission of Story Line Press.

Samuel Menashe. "The Shrine Whose Shape I Am" from *Collected Poems* by Samuel Menashe. Copyright © 1986 by Samuel Menashe. Reprinted by permission of The National Poetry Foundation.

James Merrill. "Charles on Fire" from *Selected Poems 1946-1985* by James Merrill. Copyright © 1992 by James Merrill. Reprinted by permission of Alfred A. Knopf, Inc.

W. S. Merwin. "Song of Man Chipping an Arrowhead" from *Writing to an Unfinished Accompaniment* in *The Second Four Books of Poems* by W. S. Merwin (Copper Canyon Press). Copyright © 1973 by W. S. Merwin. Reprinted by permission of Georges Borchardt, Inc.

James Michie. Translation of Ode xi *The Odes of Horace*, Book i. Copyright © 1963 by James Michie. Reprinted by permission of Washington Square Press and Pocket books, divisions of Simon & Schuster, Inc.

Josephine Miles. "Reason" from *Poems 1930-1960* by Josephine Miles. Copyright © 1960 by Indiana University Press. Reprinted by permission.

Edna St. Vincent Millay. "Counting-Out Rhyme" and "Recuerdo" by Edna St. Vincent Millay. From *Collected Poems*, HarperCollins. Copyright 1922, 1928, 1950, © 1955 by Edna St. Vincent Millay and Norma Millay Ellis. Sonnet XLVII of *Fatal Interview* by Edna St. Vincent Millay. From *Collected Poems*, HarperCollins. Copyright 1931, © 1958 by Edna St. Vincent Millay and Norma Millay Ellis. All reprinted by permission of Elizabeth Barnett, literary executor.

N. Scott Momaday. "Simile" from *Angle of Geese* by N. Scott Momaday. Copyright © 1974 by N. Scott Momaday. Reprinted by permission of David R. Godine, Publisher.

Marianne Moore. "Silence" (Copyright 1935 by Marianne Moore, renewed 1963 by Marianne Moore and T. S. Eliot) and "The Mind Is an Enchanting Thing" (Copyright 1944, and renewed 1972, by Marianne Moore). Reprinted with permission of Macmillan Publishing Company from *Collected Poems of Marianne Moore*.

Frederick Morgan. "The Master" from Poems: New and Selected by Frederick Morgan. Copyright © 1982 by Frederick Morgan. Reprinted by permission of University of Illinois Press and the author.

Howard Moss. "The Pruned Tree" from *Finding Them Lost*. Copyright © 1963 by Howard Moss. "Shall I Compare Thee to a Summer's Day?" from *A Swim Off the Rocks*. Copyright © 1976 by Howard Moss. Reprinted by permission of Albert Stadler.

Howard Nemerov. "The Snow Globe" from *The Collected Poems of Howard Nemerov*. Copyright © 1977 by Howard Nemerov. Reprinted by permission of Margaret Nemerov.

Lorin Niedecker. "Popcorn-can Cover" and "Sorrow Moves in Wide Waves" from *From This Condensery: The Complete Writing of Lorine Niedecker*, edited by Robert J. Bertolf. Copyright © Cid Corman, Literary Executor of the Lorine Niedecker Estate. Reprinted by permission.

John Frederick Nims. "Horace Coping." Reprinted by permission of the University of Arkansas Press from *Sappho to Valery: Poems in Translation* by John Frederick Nims, copyright 1990. "Contemplation" from Of Flesh and Bone by John Frederick Nims. Copyright © 1967 by Rutgers University. Reprinted by permission of the author.

Sharon Olds. "Rites of Passage" from *The Dead and the Living* by Sharon Olds. Copyright © 1983 by Sharon Olds. Reprinted by permission of Alfred A. Knopf, Inc.

Charles Olson. "La Chute" from *The Collected Poems of Charles Olson*, edited by George F. Buttrick. Copyright © 1987 by the Estate of Charles Olson. Reprinted by permission of Richard H. Schimmelpfeng for the Estate of Charles Olson.

Wilfred Owen. "Dulce et Decorum Est," "Anthem for Doomed Youth," and lines from "Strange Meeting" from *Collected Poems* by Wilfred Owen. Copyright 1946, 1963 by Chatto & Windus Ltd. Reprinted by permission of New Directions Publishing Corporation.

José Emilio Pacheco. "High Treason" written in Spanish by José Emilio Pacheco and translated by Alastair Reid. From *Weathering* (E. P. Dutton). © 1977, 1978 by Alastair Reid. Reprinted by permission.

Dorothy Parker. "Resumé," copyright 1926, 1928, renewed 1954, © 1956 by Dorothy Parker, from *The Portable Dorothy Parker* by Dorothy Parker, Introduction by Bendan Gill. Used by permission of Viking Penguin, a division of Penguin Books USA Inc.

Linda Pastan. "Jump Cabling" from *Light Year '85* edited by Robert Wallace (Bits Press). Copyright © 1984 by Linda Pastan. Reprinted by permission of the author. "Ethics" is reprinted from *Waiting for My Life*, Poems by Linda Pastan, by permission of the author and W. W. Norton & Company, Inc. Copyright © 1981 by Linda Pastan.

Octavio Paz. "With Our Eyes Shut" from *The Collected Poems of Octavio Paz 1957-1987*. Copyright © 1986 by Octavio Paz and Eliot Weinberger. Reprinted by permission of New Directions Publishing Corporation. Translation reprinted by permission of John Felstiner. "European Languages and the Literature of the Americas." © 1990 The Nobel Foundation. Excerpted from the 1990 Nobel Prize Lecture by permission of The Nobel Foundation.

Robert Phillips. "Running on Empty" from *Personal Accounts: New and Selected Poems, 1966-1986* (Princeton: Ontario Review Press, 198). Copyright © 1981, 1986 by Robert Phillips. Reprinted by permission.

Sylvia Plath. "Metaphors" (Copyright © 1960 by Ted Hughes), "Lady Lazarus" (Copyright © 1963 by Ted Hughes), and "Daddy" (Copyright © 1963 by Ted Hughes) from *The Collected Poems of Sylvia Plath*, edited by Ted Hughes. Reprinted by permission of HarperCollins Publishers and Faber and Faber Ltd.

Ezra Pound. "In a Station of the Metro" and "The River-Merchant's Wife: a Letter," and "The Garret" from *Personae* by Ezra Pound. Copyright 1926 by Ezra Pound. Reprinted by permission of New Directions Publishing Corporation. Lines from "III Hiang Niao." Reprinted by permission of the publishers from *Shih-Ching: The Classic Anthology Defined by Confucius* translated by Ezra Pound, Cambridge, Mass.: Harvard University Press, Copyright 1954 by the President and Fellows of Harvard College.

Dudley Randall. "Ballad of Birmingham" from *Cities*

*Burning* by Dudley Randall (Broadside Press). Copyright © 1966 by Dudley Randall. Reprinted by permission. "Old Witherington" from A Litany of Friends: New and Selected Poems by Dudley Randall. Copyright © 1981 by Dudley Randall. Reprinted by permission.

John Crowe Ransom. "Bells for John Whiteside's Daughter" from *Selected Poems*, Third Edition, Revised and Enlarged, by John Crowe Ransom. Copyright 1924 by Alfred A. Knopf, Inc. and renewed 1952 by John Crowe Ransom. Reprinted by permission of Alfred A. Knopf, Inc.

Henry Reed, "Naming of Parts" from *A Map of Verona* by Henry Reed, © 1946 The Executor of the Estate of Henry Reed. Reprinted by permission of John Tydeman.

Alastair Reid. "Speaking a Foreign Language." From *Weathering* (E. P. Dutton). © 1960, 1988 by Alastair Reid. Originally in *The New Yorker*.

Adrienne Rich. "Women," "Aunt Jennifer's Tigers," "Peeling Onions," and "Power" are reprinted from *The Fact of a Doorframe*, Poems Selected and New, 1950-1984 by Adrienne Rich, by permission of W. W. Norton & Company, Inc. Copyright © 1984 by Adrienne Rich. Copyright © 1975, 1978 by W. W. Norton & Company, Inc. Copyright © 1981 by Adrienne Rich. "Feminist Re-Vision" is reprinted from *On Lies, Secrets, and Silences* Selected Prose 1966-1978, by Adrienne Rich, by permission of the author and W. W. Norton & Company, Inc.

John Ridland. "The Lazy Man's Haiku" and "Elegy for My Aunt" reprinted by permission of the author.

Alberto Ríos. "Spring in the Only Place Spring Was" from *Whispering to Fool the Wind* by Alberto Ríos (Sheep Meadow Press). Copyright © 1982 by Alberto Ríos. Reprinted by permission of the author.

Theodore Roethke. "My Papa's Waltz," copyright 1942 by Hearst Magazines, Inc., "Root Cellar," copyright 1943 by Modern Poetry Association, Inc., "I Knew a Woman, " copyright 1954 by Theodore Roethke, and "Elegy for Jane," copyright 1950 by Theodore Roethke, from *The Collected Poems of Theodore Roethke* by Theodore Roethke. Used by permission of Doubleday, a division of Bantam Doubleday Dell Publishing Group, Inc.

Raymond Roseliep. "campfire extinguished" from *Listen to Light Haiku* by Raymond Roseliep (Alembic Press, Ithaca, NY). Copyright © 1980 by Raymond Roseliep. Reprinted by permission.

Run D. M. C. Lines from "Peter Piper" (D. McDaniels/J. Simmons). © 1986 Protoons, Inc./Rush-Groove/ASCAP. Reprinted by permission.

Mary Jo Salter. "Welcome to Hiroshima" from *Henry Purcell in Japan* by Mary Jo Salter. Copyright © 1984 by Mary Jo Salter. Reprinted by permission of Alfred A. Knopf, Inc.,

Carl Sandburg. "Fog" from *Chicago Poems* by Carl Sandburg, reprinted by permission of Harcourt Brace & Company.

Carole Satyamurti. "I Shall Paint My Nails Red," © Carole Satyamurti 1990. Reprinted from *Changing the Subject* by Carole Satyamurti (1990) by permission of Oxford University Press.

Gjertrud Schnackenberg. "Signs" from *The Lamplite Answer*. Copyright © 1982, 1985 by Gjertud Schnakenberg. Reprinted by permission of Farrar,

Straus & Giroux, Inc.

Bertie Sellers. "In the Counselors's Waiting Room" from *Morning of the Red-Tailed Hawk* by Bertie Sellers (University Center, MI: GreenRiver Press, 1981). Reprinted by permission.

Anne Sexton. "Her Kind," from *To Bedlam and Part Way Back* by Anne Sexton. Copyright © 1960 by Anne Sexton. "Cinderella," from *Transformations* by Anne Sexton. Copyright © 1971 by Anne Sexton. Both reprinted by permission Houghton Mifflin Company. All rights reserved.

Karl Shapiro. "The Dirty Word" from *Selected Poems by Karl Shapiro*. Copyright 1947 by Karl Shapiro. Reprinted by permission of Wieser & Wieser Inc.

Stephen Shu-ning Liu. "My Father's Martial Art." Copyright © 1981 by The Antioch Review, Inc. First appeared in the *Antioch Review*, Vol. 39, No. 3 (Summer, 1981). Reprinted by permission of the Editors.

Charles Simic. "Butcher Shop" from *Dismantling the Silence* by Charles Simic. Copyright © 1971 by Charles Simic. Reprinted by permission of the publisher, George Braziller, Inc.

Paul Simon. Lyrics from "Richard Cory" by Paul Simon. Copyright © 1966 by Paul Simon. Reprinted by permission of Paul Simon Music.

L. E. Sissman. Lines from "In and Out: A Home Away from Home" from *Dying: An Introduction* by L. E. Sissman. Copyright © 1967 by L. E. Sissman. By permission of Little, Brown and Company in association with the Atlantic Monthly Press.

David R. Slavitt. "Titanic" reprinted by permission of Louisiana State University Press from *Big Nose: Poems* by David R. Slavitt. Copyright © 1983 by David R. Slavitt. Reprinted by permission of Louisiana State University Press.

Stevie Smith. "Not Waving but Drowning" and "This Englishwoman" from *The Collected Poems of Stevie Smith*. Copyright © 1972 by Stevie Smith. Reprinted by permission of New Directions Publishing Corporation.

William Jay Smith. "American Primitive." Reprinted by permission of Charles Scribner's Sons, an imprint of Macmillan Publishing Company, from *Collected Poems 1939-1989* by William Jay Smith. Copyright © 1957, 1990 by William Jay Smith.

W. D. Snodgrass. "Disposal," © 1970 by W. D. Snodgrass, reprinted from *Selected Poems 1957-1987* by W. D. Snodgrass courtesy of Soho Press, Inc.

Gary Snyder. "After weeks of watching the roof leak" from "Hitch Haiku" from *The Back Country*. Copyright © 1968 by Gary Snyder. Reprinted by permission of New Directions Publishing Corporation. "Mid-August at Sourdough Mountain Lookout" from *Riptrap* by Gary Snyder. Copyright © 1959 by Gary Snyder. Reprinted by permission of the author.

Richard Snyder. "Mongoloid Child Handling Shells on the Beach" from *Keeping in Touch* by Richard Snyder (Ashland Poetry Press, 1991). Reprinted by permission of the publisher.

William Stafford. "At the Un-National Monument Along the Canadian Border" (Copyright © 1977 by William Stafford), "Traveling Through the Dark" (Copyright © 1960 by William Stafford), and "At the Klamath Berry Festival" (Copyright © 1961 by William Stafford) from *Stories That Could Be True: New and*

Collected Poems (Harper & Row). Reprinted by permission of the author and the publisher.

Jon Stallworthy. "Sindhi Woman" is reprinted from The Aztec Sonata, New and Selected Poems, by Jon Stallworthy, by permission of W. W. Norton & Company, Inc. Copyright © 1986 by John Stallworthy.

George Starbuck. "Margaret Are You Drug" from "Translations from the English" from White Paper: Poems by George Starbuck. Copyright © 1965 by George Starbuck. First appeared in The Atlantic. By permission of Little, Brown and Company in association with the Atlantic Monthly Press.

Timothy Steele. "Epitaph." Reprinted by permission of Louisiana State University Press from Uncertainties and Rest by Timothy Steele, copyright © 1979. "summer" from Sapphics Against Anger and Other Poems by Timothy Steele (Random House, 1986). Copyright © 1986 by Timothy Steele. Reprinted by permission of the author.

James Stephens. "A Glass of Beer" (Copyright 1918 by Macmillan Publishing Company, renewed 1946 by James Stephens). Reprinted from Collected Poems by James Stephens by permission of The Society of Authors on behalf of the copyright owner, Mrs. Iris Wise.

Wallace Stevens. "Disillusionment of Ten O'Clock," "Thirteen Ways of Looking at a Blackbird," "Anecdote of the Jar," "The Emperor of Ice-Cream," and lines from "Sunday Morning." Copyright 1923 and renewed 1951 by Wallace Stevens. "Peter Quince at the Clavier." Copyright 1942 by Wallace Stevens. Reprinted from The Collected Poems of Wallace Stevens by permission of Alfred A. Knopf, Inc.

Anne Stevenson. "The Victory" and "Sous Entendu," © Anne Stevenson 1987. Reprinted from Selected Poems 1956-1986 by Anne Stevenson (1987) by permission of Oxford University Press.

Michael Stillman. "In Memoriam John Coltrane" from Occident, Fall 1971. Copyright © 1971 by Michael Stillman. "Lying in the field" from In an Eye of Minnows by Michael Stillman. Copyright © 1976 by Michael Stillman. Reprinted by permission of the author.

Ruth Stone. "Second Hand Coat" from The Iowa Review, Vol. 12: 2/3, Spring/Summer 1981. Reprinted by permission of the author.

Dabney Stuart. "Crib Death" from Don't Look Back, Poems by Dabney Stuart. Copyright © 1987 by Dabney Stuart. Reprinted by permission of Louisiana State University Press.

May Swenson. "Four-Word Lines" from The Love Poems of May Swenson. Copyright © 1991 by The Literary Estate of May Swenson. Reprinted by permission of Houghton Mifflin Company. All rights reserved.

Henry Taylor. "Riding a One-Eyed Horse" from An Afternoon of Pocket Billiards by Henry Taylor (Salt Lake City: University of Utah Press Poetry Series, 1975). Copyright © 1975 by Henry Taylor. Reprinted by permission of the publisher.

Cornelius J. Ter Maat. "Etienne de Silhouette" reprinted by permission of the author.

Dylan Thomas. "Do not go gentle into that good night" and "Fern Hill" from The Poems of Dylan Thomas. Copyright 1939, 1946 by New Directions Publishing Corporation, 1952 by Dylan Thomas. Reprinted by permission of New Directions Publishing

Corporation and David Higham Associates Ltd.

Jean Toomer. "Reapers" is reprinted from Cane by Jean Toomer, by permission of Liveright Publishing Corporation. Copyright © 1923 by Boni & Liveright. Copyright renewed 1951 by Jean Toomer.

John Updike. "Recital" from Telephone Poles and Other Poems by John Updike. Copyright © 1961 by John Updike. "Ex-Basketball Player" from The Carpentered Hen and Other Tame Creatures by John Updike. Copyright © 1957, 1982 by John Updike. Reprinted by permission of Alfred A. Knopf, Inc.

Amy Uyematsu. "Red Rooster, Yellow Sky" from 30 Miles from J-Town by Amy Uyematsu. Copyright © 1992 by Amy Uyematsu. Reprinted by permission of Story Line Press.

Mona Van Duyn. "Earth Tremors Felt in Missouri." From If It Be Not I by Mona Van Duyn. Copyright © 1964 by Mona Van Duyn. Reprinted by permission of Alfred A. Knopf, Inc.

Nicholas A. Virgilio, "on the cardboard box" from Selected Haiku, Second Edition, augmented by Nicholas A. Virgilio. Copyright © 1988 by Nicholas A. Virgilio. Reprinted by permission of Burnt Lake Press.

Derek Walcott. "The Virgins" from Sea Grapes by Derek Walcott. Copyright © 1976 by Derek Walcott. Reprinted by permission of Farrar, Straus & Giroux, Inc.

Keith Waldrop. "Proposition II" from The Garden of Effort (Burning Deck publishers, 1975). Reprinted by permission.

Robert Wallace. "The Girl Writing Her English Paper" from The Common Summer: New and Selected Poems by Robert Wallace. Copyright © 1989 by Robert Wallace. Copyright © 1989 by Robert Wallace. Reprinted by permission of Carnegie Mellon University Press.

Emma Lee Warrior. "How I Came to Have a Man's Name" from Harper's Anthology of 20th Century Native American Poetry, edited by Duane Niatum. Copyright © 1988 by Duane Niatum. Reprinted by permission of HarperCollins Publishers.

Ruth Whitman. "Castoff Skin" from The Passion of Lizzie Borden. Copyright © 1973 by Ruth Whitman. Reprinted by permission of October House.

Richard Wilbur. "In the Elegy Season" and "A Simile for Her Smile" from Ceremony and Other Poems, copyright 1950 and renewed 1978 by Richard Wilbur, reprinted by permission of Harcourt Brace & Company. "Transit" from New and Collected Poems, copyright © 1987 by Richard Wilbur, reprinted by permission of Harcourt Brace & Company. "The Writer" from The Mind Reader, copyright © 1971 by Richard Wilbur, reprinted by permission of Harcourt Brace & Company. "Sleepless at Crown Point" from The Mind Reader, copyright © 1973 by Richard Wilbur, reprinted by permission of Harcourt Brace & Company.

Hugo Williams. "Kites," © Hugo Williams 1979. Reprinted from Selected Poems by Hugo Williams (1989) by permission of Oxford University Press.

Miller Williams. "Thinking About Bill, Dead of AIDS" reprinted by permission of Louisiana State University Press from Living on the Surface: New and Selected Poems by Miller Williams. Copyright © 1989 by Miller Williams.

William Carlos Williams, "The Red Wheelbarrow,"

Miller. Reprinted by permission of Viking Penguin, a division of Penguin Books USA Inc.

William Shakespeare. Notes to *Hamlet* and *Othello* by David Bevington. From *The Complete Works of Shakespeare*, 4th ed. by David Bevington. Copyright © 1992 by HarperCollins Publishers. Reprinted by permission.

Bernard Shaw. "Ibsen and the Familiar Situation." Excerpt from *The Quintessence of Ibsenism* reprinted by permission of The Society of Authors on behalf of the Bernard Shaw Estate.

Sophocles. *The Antigone of Sophocles* from *Sophocles The Oedipus Cycle: An English Version* by Dudley Fitts and Robert Fitgerald, copyright 1939 by Harcourt Brace & Company and renewed 1967 by Dudley Fitts and Robert Fitzgerald, reprinted by permission of the publisher. CAUTION: All rights, including professional, amateur, motion picture, recitation, lecturing, performance, public reading, radio broadcasting, and television, are strictly reserved. Inquiries on all rights should be addressed to Harcourt Brace & Company, Permissions Department, Orlando, Florida 32887. *The Oedipus Rex of Sophocles* from *Sophocles The Oedipus Cycle: An English Version* by Dudley Fitts and Robert Fitzgerald, copyright 1949 by Harcourt Brace & Company and renewed 1977 by Cornelia Fitts and Robert Fitzgerald, reprinted by permission of the publisher. CAUTION: All rights, including professional, amateur, motion picture, recitation, lecturing, performance, public reading, radio broadcasting, and television, are strictly reserved. Inquiries on all rights should be addressed to Harcourt Brace & Company, Permissions Department, Orlando, Florida 32887.

Tennessee Williams. *The Glass Menagerie* and "How to Stage The Glass Menagerie." From *The Glass Menagerie* by Tennessee Williams. Copyright 1945 by Tennessee Williams and Edwina D. Williams and renewed 1973 by Tennessee Williams. Reprinted by permission of Random House, Inc.

August Wilson. *Joe Turner's Come and Gone*. Copyright © 1988 by August Wilson. Reprinted by arrangement with New American Library, a division of Penguin Books USA Inc., New York, NY. "Black Experience in America," excerpted from an interview with August Wilson. From *Bill Moyers: A World of Ideas* by Bill Moyers. Copyright © 1989 by Public Affairs Television, Inc. Used by permission of Doubleday, a division of Bantam Doubleday Dell Publishing Group, Inc.

Virginia Woolf. "What If Shakespeare Had a Sister?" Excerpt from "A Room of One's Own" from *A Room of One's Own* by Virginia Woolf, copyright © 1929 by Harcourt Brace & Company and renewed 1957 by Leonard Woolf, reprinted by permission of the publisher.

## CRITICAL APPROACHES TO LITERATURE

Roland Barthes. "The Death of the Author" from *Image/Music/Text* by Roland Barthes, translated by Stephen Heath. English translation ©1977 by Stephen Heath. Reprinted by permission of Farrar, Straus & Giroux, Inc.

Harold Bloom. "Poetic Influence" from *A Map of Misreading* by Harold Bloom. Copyright © 1975 by Oxford University Press, Inc. Reprinted by permission.

Cleanth Brooks. Excerpts from "The Formalist Critic." Copyright 1951 by Cleanth Brooks. Originally appeared in *The Kenyon Review*. Reprinted by the permission of the author.

Terry Eagleton. "Art as Production" from *Marxism and Literary Criticism* by Terry Eagleton. Copyright © 1976 by Terry Eagleton. Reprinted by permission of the University of California Press.

Leslie A. Fiedler. "The Relationship of Poet and Poem" from *No! in Thunder* by Leslie A. Fiedler. Copyright © 1960 by Leslie A. Fiedler. Reprinted by permission of Stein & Day, a division of Madison Books, Lanham, MD 20763.

Stanley Fish. "An Eskimo 'A Rose for Emily'." Reprinted by permission of the publishers from *Is There a Text in This Class?* by Stanley Fish, Cambridge, Mass: Harvard University Press, copyright © 1980 by the President and Fellows of Harvard College.

Sigmund Freud. "The Destiny of Oedipus" from *The Interpretation of Dreams*, by Sigmund Freud, translated and edited by James Strachey, published in the United States by Basic Books, Inc., New York by arrangement with George Allen & Unwin Ltd. and The Hogarth Press Ltd., London.

Northrop Frye. "Mythic Archetypes" from *Anatomy of Criticism*. Copyright © 1957, renewed 1985 by Princeton University Press. Reprinted by permission of Princeton University Press.

Sandra M. Gilbert and Susan Gubar. "The Freedom of Emily Dickinson" is reprinted from The Introduction to the poems of Emily Dickinson in *The Norton Anthology of Literature by Women: The Tradition in English*, Edited by Sandra M. Gilbert and Susan Gubar, by permission of W.W. Norton & Company, Inc. Copyright © 1985 by Sandra M. Gilbert and Susan Gubar.

Geoffrey Hartman. "On Wordsworth's 'A Slumber Did My Spirit Seal' " from "Elation in Hegel and Wordsworth" in *The Unremarkable Wordsworth* by Geoffrey Hartman. Copyright ©1987 by the University of Minnesota. Reprinted by permission of the University of Minnesota Press.

Hugh Kenner. "Imagism" from *The Pound Era* by Hugh Kenner. Copyright © 1971 by Hugh Kenner. Reprinted by permission of the University of California Press. "In a Station of the Metro" by Ezra Pound from *Personae* by Ezra Pound. Copyright 1926 by Ezra Pound. Reprinted by permission of New Directions Publishing Company.

Robert Langbaum. "On Robert Browning's 'My Last Duchess' " from *The Poetry of Experience* by Robert Langbaum. Copyright © 1957, 1986 by Robert Langbaum. Reprinted by permission of the publisher, the University of Chicago Press.

Georg Lukacs. "Content Determines Form" from *Realism in Our Time*. © 1962 Merlin Press Ltd., ©1964 George Steiner. Reprinted by permission.

Brett C. Millier. "On Elizabeth Bishop's 'One Art.' " Copyright © 1993 by Brett C. Millier. Used by permission of the author. A fuller treatment of the subject appears in *Elizabeth Bishop: Life and Memory of It* by Brett C. Millier (University of California Press, 1993).

Lines from the first draft of "One Art" are quoted by permission of the Special Collections of the Vassar College Libraries and Elizabeth Bishop's literary executor, Alice H. Methfessell.

Daryl Pinckney. "Langston Hughes" excerpted from "Suitcase in Harlem" by Daryl Pinckney, *The New York Review of Books*, 16 February 1989. Reprinted by permission from *The New York Review of Books*. Copyright © 1989 Nyrev, Inc. "The Negro Speaks of Rivers" and lines from "Epilogue" ("I, Too") from *Selected Poems* by Langston Hughes. Copyright 1926 by Alfred A. Knopf,

Inc. and renewed 1954 by Langston Hughes. Reprinted by permission of Alfred A. Knopf, Inc.

Robert Scholes. "How Do We Make a Poem?" from *Semiotics and Interpretation* by Robert Scholes. Copyright © 1982 by Yale University. Reprinted by permission of Yale University Press.

Elaine Showalter. Excerpt from "Toward a Feminist Criticism" (Copyright © 1979 by Elaine Showalter). From Elaine Showalter, ed., *Feminist Criticism: Essays on Women, Literature, and Theory* (Pantheon, 1985). Reprinted by permission of the author.

# PICTURE ACKNOWLEDGMENTS

*Unless otherwise acknowledged, all photographs are the property of Scott, Foresman and Company. Page abbreviations are as follows: (T) top, (C) center, (B)bottom.*

## FICTION

Page: 6 Brown Brothers 12 Bettmann 25 Bern Keating/Black Star 33 Courtesy Alfred A. Knopf, Inc. 37 The Dial Press. Photo by Mottke Weissman 61 Bettmann Archive 70 Jill Krementz 78 Bettmann 90 AP/Wide World 98 1982/Jerry Bauer 113 Missouri Historical Society 117 Bettmann Archive 129 1988 Pablo Campos 138 Courtesy, Putnam. 158 UPI/Bettmann 177 Berenice Abbott/Commerce Graphics Ltd., Inc. 183 UPI/Bettmann 211 Peabody Essex Museum, Salem 248 Erich Hartmann/Magnum Photos 255 Marian Wood 269 Bettmann Archive 311 AP/Wide World 347 AP/Wide World 392 Bettmann Archive 400 Willa Cather Pioneer Memorial Collection/Nebraska State Historical Society 415 Bettmann Archive 422 Robin Guzman 424 UPI/Bettmann 437 UPI/Bettmann 448 UPI/Bettmann 462 Bettmann Archive 474 UPI/Bettmann 481 AP/Wide World 490 Jerry Bauer 501 Published by Alfred A Knopf, Inc/Photo: Jerry Bauer 515 Jill Krementz 528 Elliott Erwitt/Magnum Photos 534 AP/Wide World 541 Elliott Erwitt/Magnum Photos 552 AP/Wide World 559 AP/Wide World 564 John D.Schiff, Courtesy New Directions 567 Harcourt Brace Jovanovich, Inc.

## POETRY

Page: 781 Kunsthistorisches Museum, Vienna 892 Doubleday & Co., Inc. 893 UPI/Bettmann 898 Farrar, Straus and Giroux, photo: Thomas Victor 908 Bettmann Archive 911 National Portrait Gallery, London and the Marquess of Lothian916 AP/Wide World 926 AP/Wide World 936 Bettmann Archive 939 Dorothy Alexander 944 UPI/Bettmann 949 National Portrait Gallery, London 951 Photo by Fay Godwin 969 AP/Wide World 971 North Point Photo 973 Courtesy Norton, Photo: George Murphy975 HarperCollinsPublishers979 Courtesy New Directions Publishing Corp., Photo: Boris De Rachewiltz 984 Colleen McKay 987 Imogene Cunningham 988 Jerry Bauer 990 National Portrait Gallery, London 1001 Bettmann Archive 1003 Bettmann Archive 1008 Chris Tachiki 1009 Reuters/Bettmann 1011 Pennsylvania Academy of the Fine Arts 1012 Rollie McKenna 1015 Courtesy New Directions, Photo: John D. Schiff 1017 National Portrait Gallery, London 1018 AP/Wide World 1020 Windsor Castle Copyright reserved to Her Majesty Photo: Pirie MacDonald

## DRAMA

Page: 1066 AP/Wide World 1083 Bettmann Archive 1095 AP/Wide World 1105 Bettmann Archive 1152 Martha Swope 1153 National Portrait Gallery, London 1359T Martha Swope 1359B PhotoFest 1476 Reuters/Bettmann 1548 Film Archives/Springer/Bettmann Archive 1647 Ted Thai/Sygma

# INDEX TO AUTHORS AND TITLES

Each page number immediately following a writer's name indicates a quotation from or reference to that writer. A number in **bold** refers you to the page on which you will find the author's biography.

# INDEX TO TERMS

NOTES

NOTES

NOTES

NOTES

NOTES

NOTES

NOTES

NOTES

# To the Student

As publishers, we realize that one way to improve education is to improve textbooks. We also realize that you, the student, very much determine the success or failure of textbooks. Although the instructor assigns them, the student buys and uses them. If enough of you don't like a book and do make your feelings known, the chances are your instructor will not assign it again.

Usually instructors but not students are asked about the quality of a textbook; their opinion alone is considered as revisions are planned or as new books are developed. Now, we would like to ask you about X. J. Kennedy and Dana Gioia's *Literature: An Introduction to Fiction, Poetry, and Drama, Sixth Edition*: how you liked or disliked it; why it was interesting or dull; if it taught you anything. Please fill in this form and return it to us: the English Literature Acquisitions Editor, HarperCollins College Publishers, 10 East 53rd Street, New York, NY 10022.

School: _____

Instructor's name: _____

Title of course: _____

1. Do you find this book too easy? _____ too difficult? _____

    about right? _____

2. Which chapters do you find most interesting? _____

3. Which chapters do you find least interesting? _____

    _____

4. Which stories do you like most? _____

    _____

5. Do you particularly dislike any of the stories? _____

    _____

6. Which statement comes closest to expressing your feelings about reading and studying literature? (Please check one, or supply your own statement.)

    _____ Love to read literature. It's my favorite subject.

    _____ Usually enjoy reading most literature.

    _____ Can take it or leave it.

_____ Usually find little of interest in most literature.

_____ Literature just is not for me.

Other: _____

7. Do you find this book helps you to enjoy fiction more than you did? _____

_____

8. Are the supplements "Writing about Literature," "Writing about a Story," "Writing about a Poem," and "Writing about a Play" very useful? _____ somewhat useful? _____ of no help? _____

9. In the sections about writing papers, do you prefer to see examples of writing by students? _____ or by professional critics? _____

10. Do you intend to keep this book for your personal library? Yes _____ No _____

11. Any other comments or suggestions: _____

_____

_____

_____

12. May we quote you in our efforts to promote this book? Yes _____ No _____

Date: _____

Signature (optional): _____

Address (optional): _____